TO THE MEMORY OF
Arthur Smith

AND TO
Frank Scott

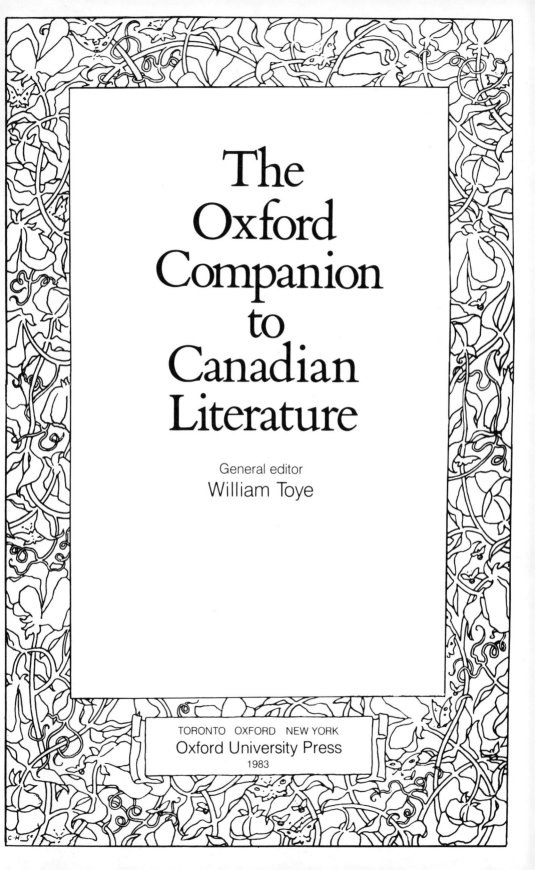

The Oxford Companion to Canadian Literature

General editor
William Toye

TORONTO OXFORD NEW YORK
Oxford University Press
1983

THE COST OF TRANSLATING ENTRIES
FROM THE FRENCH WAS ASSISTED BY
THE CANADA COUNCIL

CANADIAN CATALOGUING IN PUBLICATION DATA
The Oxford companion to Canadian literature
ISBN 0-19-540283-9
1. Canadian literature — Dictionaries.   2. Canadian literature — Bio-bibliography.
I. Toye, William
PS8015.093 1983   C810'.3'21   C83-098962-5
PR9180.2.093 1983

Introduction

This is the first volume in the famous series of Oxford Companions to be devoted solely to Canadian literature. Norah Story's *Oxford Companion to Canadian History and Literature* (1967), for which I was the publisher's editor, was, as the title indicates, devoted to two subjects. In the ten years since the *Supplement* to that work was published the development of literary criticism on all periods, an enormous outpouring of new and important creative writing in both English and French, reprints of countless little-known books, a great increase in translations from the French, and growing interest in Canadian writing abroad all pointed to the need for a *Companion* to Canadian literature alone. My own preference was for a work that would combine useful information *and* thoughtful and illuminating (though succinct) literary discussions by contributors who are authorities on their subjects. This *Companion* is the result.

Users will quickly realize that it encompasses two literatures. The inevitable emphasis on writing in English in this English-language reference book is complemented by a treatment of writing in French, and of French-Canadian writers, that is hardly less detailed. And rightly so. At least a few French-Canadian authors, and some of their works in translation, have been known to, and read by, generations of English-Canadian readers. In the past few decades the explosion of creative writing in English was paralleled by a development in French-Canadian writing that was just as strong, though different in nature. Numerous translations have reduced the gulf that once existed between the two literary cultures, so that today many French-language works in English are now part of the literary experience of English Canadians, for whom numerous entries will make more comprehensible the historical background, the range, and the most significant achievements in French-Canadian literature (though many of these works are still regrettably unknown to English-speaking readers).

The Canadian mosaic has introduced strains of other cultures into the overall literary picture. To represent some but by no means all of them, there are substantial entries on INDIAN LEGENDS, INDIAN LITERATURE, INUIT LITERATURE, UKRAINIAN WRITING, and YIDDISH LITERATURE. There are also entries on writers who settled in Canada in their maturity or, though not permanent residents, have strong Canadian ties.

The literary component of Norah Story's 1967 volume—its author entries and surveys of fiction, poetry, drama, biography, anthologies, literary magazines, and folklore—has been maintained. But the genre surveys have been greatly expanded, period by period. (To refer to only two of these overviews: NOVELS IN ENGLISH and NOVELS IN FRENCH are especially long because the sudden flowering of the genre after 1960, with the appearance of works by major novelists and many others, suggested the desirability of giving them a more extended critical treatment.) There are also numerous additions of entries, and some modifications of entry titles. I would draw the reader's attention to the following:

ACADIAN LITERATURE
CHILDREN'S LITERATURE
CHILDREN'S DRAMA
COLLECTIVE CREATIONS
CRITICISM
ESSAYS
EXPLORATION LITERATURE IN ENGLISH
FOREIGN WRITERS ON CANADA
HISTORICAL WRITING
HUMOUR AND SATIRE
JOUAL
MYSTERY AND CRIME
NATURE WRITING IN ENGLISH
NEW FRANCE, Writing in
NOVELS
PHILOSOPHY
PIONEER MEMOIRS
RELIGION AND THEOLOGY
SCIENCE FICTION AND FANTASY
SHORT STORIES
TRANSLATIONS
TRAVEL LITERATURE IN ENGLISH

Other departures from the Story *Companion* are biographical/critical entries on *dramatists, philosophers*, and a few *authors of children's books*; entries on a selection of famous *titles* that are notable for literary, historical, or other reasons, such as their popularity; separate entries on some *literary magazines* and *book publishers*; and six entries on *regional literature*: NEWFOUNDLAND, The MARITIMES, QUÉBEC (in English), ONTARIO, The PRAIRIES, and BRITISH COLUMBIA.

There is a heavy emphasis in this *Companion* on modern writing—on writers and their works of the last forty years. But early publications associated with Canada are also discussed, notably in two long and illuminating surveys: EXPLORATION LITERATURE and Writing in NEW FRANCE. And the creative writing of the nineteenth and early-twentieth centuries is strongly present in many entries. A number of obscure writers who published before the 1860s—whose works had a fleeting, sometimes local, renown, though a few had surprising literary qualities worth recording—have been given entries to throw a little light on the literary climate of the pre-Confederation era, which awaits a more detailed examination. Some of the critical work that is now being done on early popular fiction is reflected in the surveys of novels, and in numerous author entries (which would have been greater in number if space had allowed).

The very breadth of this *Companion* can easily lead to criticism for omissions of subjects or authors that might also seem to have deserved treatment. (Indeed, more than a few entries that had been originally planned for inclusion—surveys of popular fiction and historical fiction, among others—fell by the wayside for various reasons.) But the coverage is sufficiently detailed to provide in an accessible format the outlines of, and critical responses to, a rich literary culture in two languages—revealing at the same time new avenues of enjoyment for the general reader, and containing for the scholar silent reminders of subjects that remain to be studied, and absorbed into our comprehension of the Canadian literary past and present.

Readers might keep in mind that names, subjects, and book titles that appear in SMALL CAPITALS have entries of their own; and that of all the authors who do not have entries, only those who have received more than a passing mention in surveys have cross-references.

This *Companion* is organized as an alphabetical gathering of articles mainly on writers and genres. Embedded within it, however, is commentary that is not purely literary but belongs in other realms, such as history (see particularly HISTORICAL WRITING), sociology, and politics. A cursory look at its intricate network of cross-references and a brief examination of the various imaginative responses to experience that encompass several centuries of writing will make ludicrous the fear that used to haunt us: that Canada did not have a literary culture of any significance. For someone like myself, who has been involved with Canadian literature as an editor and reader for some thirty-five years—when, in the first half of that period, the question was sometimes asked, *Is* there a Canadian literature?—there was a strange irony in planning this reference book in 1980 to be confronted with a body of writing in two languages that was so immense and complex that space considerations produced real dilemmas about what to include, whom to give entries to. This perplexity became most severe in the coverage of the last fifteen years, when new writers worthy of attention have appeared in clusters from Newfoundland to Vancouver Island. While I have made every effort to be objective and balanced in preparing and editing this volume, I am aware that limitations of knowledge, and perhaps an unconscious indulgence of my own literary and historical interests, have produced weaknesses in the overall treatment. At this prepublication moment anomalies or omissions are not readily apparent; but where they do exist I take full responsibility for them. The relative lengths of entries may prompt the most immediate comment. While virtually all the most distinguished and prominent Canadian authors have appropriately long entries, often a long entry was brought about by a large output and necessary information about works published, and/or a complex biography, and implies historical or documentary rather than literary significance.

In spite of all weaknesses, however, there is offered here a wealth of detail and commentary, and many new critical insights, provided by 192 contributors. I am most grateful for their unstinting support, not only in accepting and writing their entries but in participating tactfully and patiently in the voluminous correspondence I brought about, or in responding helpfully to many phone calls. Above all I value their willingness to become involved in presenting a large subject of mutual interest as effectively as possible. Their respective contributions, which vary greatly in extent and substance (all are the result of far more time spent in research and writing than these condensed discussions might suggest), collectively represent an encyclopaedic offering of fact, learning, and perception that cannot be adequately appreciated without close study, or frequent consultation over a long period—which is what I hope this *Companion* will receive.

Many contributors gave me extra assistance, responding helpfully to my requests for advice, answering more than the usual number of tedious questions, or stepping in late to write entries that had been commissioned but had not materialized. I owe special thanks to Leslie Armour, Irene Aubrey, Donna Bennett, Russell Brown, John Robert Colombo, Jacques Cotnam, Frank Davey, Leonard Doucette, Sheila Egoff, Louise Forsyth, Michelle Gadpaille, Richard Giguère, Geoff Hancock, David M. Hayne, Elizabeth Hopkins, Alec Lucas, Mary Lu MacDonald, Cedric May, Bruce Meyer, James Noonan, Patrick O'Flaherty, James Polk, Zailig Pollock, David Staines, Tim Struthers, Elizabeth Trott, Tom Vincent, Miriam Waddington, Robert Weaver, and George Woodcock. Over a long period Sheila Latham, of the Metropolitan Toronto Library, efficiently answered questions.

Perhaps my happiest memory in editing this *Oxford Companion* was the immediate acceptance of virtually all the French-Canadian scholars I approached to contribute, and their full co-operation. Their entries on writings in French, and those of some of their English-Canadian colleagues, will I hope be as illuminating and interesting to users of this book as they have been to me. My adviser on French-Canadian literature was Professor Ben-Z. Shek, who also contributed nine entries. From the inception of this work to its completion he has been of the utmost assistance, first in directing me to appropriate writers of entries, and throughout the long editorial process in responding willingly to all requests for advice and information.

This *Companion* could not have been started or completed without the aid of several colleagues. I wish to thank Patricia Sillers, who has assisted me throughout the project, helping to edit entries and their revisions, ably translating some of them, and reading proofs. I am also grateful to my secretary Penny Moore, who dealt efficiently with the large flow of correspondence, entries, and revisions, and more-or-less simultaneously typed and retyped thousands of pages of letters and entries; to Phyllis Wilson, who oversaw the final stages of checking and compilation; and to Nancy Azzarello, who frequently interrupted her work to retype entries.

Finally I wish to thank Tilly Crawley, who first encouraged me to embark on this *Companion*; and Lorne Wilkinson, Managing Director of Oxford University Press Canada, who gave his blessing to this three-year project.

August 1983   WILLIAM TOYE

Contributors

Maroussia Ahmed
McMaster University

Jacques Allard
Université du Québec à Montréal

Leslie Armour
University of Ottawa

Ivor Arnold
University of Western Ontario

Irene Aubrey
National Library of Canada

Janet Baker
St Mary's University

Jars Balan

Douglas Barbour
University of Alberta

Caroline Bayard
McMaster University

Hélène Beauchamp

Donna Bennett

Katherine Berg
The Canada Council

Diane Bessai
University of Alberta

Joseph Bonenfant
Université de Sherbrooke

Nicole Bourbonnais
Université d'Ottawa

Russell Brown
University of Toronto

Peter Buitenhuis
Simon Fraser University

J.M. Bumsted
University of Manitoba

William Butt

Elspeth Cameron
University of Toronto

Robert Cockburn
University of New Brunswick

Joan Coldwell
McMaster University

Paulette Collet
University of Toronto

John Robert Colombo

Odette Condemine
Carleton University

L.W. Conolly
University of Guelph

Don Conway
University of New Brunswick

Dennis Cooley
University of Manitoba

Jacques Cotnam
York University

Terrence Craig
University of Western Ontario

Frank Davey
York University

Gwendolyn Davies
Mount Allison University

Patricia Demers
University of Alberta

The Rev. Lawrence Dewan, O.P.
Dominican College of Philosophy
and Theology

Lovat Dickson

Madeleine Dirschauer

Sandra Djwa
Simon Fraser University

Kerry Dodd
Provincial Archives of British Columbia

Joyce Doolittle
University of Calgary

Max Dorsinville
McGill University

Leonard Doucette
University of Toronto

James Doyle
Wilfrid Laurier University

Dennis Duffy
University of Toronto

Leon Edel

Mary Jane Edwards
Carleton University

Sheila Egoff
University of British Columbia

Doug Fetherling

Claude Filteau
Université de Sherbrooke

Sheila Fischman

David Flint

Louise Forsyth
University of Western Ontario

Edith Fowke
York University

Marian Fowler
York University

Wynne Francis
Concordia University

Michelle Gadpaille

Keith Garebian

Lise Gauvin
Université de Montréal

Gary Geddes
Concordia University

Carole Gerson
Simon Fraser University

Robert Gibbs
University of New Brunswick

Richard Giguère
Université de Sherbrooke

Susan Gingell
University of Saskatchewan

Barbara Godard
York University

Contributors

Jean-Cléo Godin
Université de Montréal

John Webster Grant
University of Toronto

Judith Skelton Grant
University of Guelph

Michael Greenstein
Université de Sherbrooke

Armand Guilmette
Université du Québec à Trois-Rivières

Bernadette Guilmette
Université du Québec à Trois-Rivières

Ralph Gustafson

Francess G. Halpenny

Kathryn Hamer
Mount Allison University

Geoff Hancock

Dick Harrison
University of Alberta

Jocelyn Harvey
The Canada Council

Ramon Hathorn
University of Guelph

David M. Hayne
University of Toronto

Annette Hayward
Queen's University

Jeffrey Heath
University of Toronto

Paul Hjartarson
University of Alberta

Anthony Hopkins
York University

Elizabeth Hopkins
York University

Chaviva Hošek
University of Toronto

David Jackel
University of Alberta

Susan Jackel
University of Alberta

J. Kieran Kealy
University of British Columbia

L.W. Keffer
Bishop's University

W.J. Keith
University of Toronto

David Ketterer
Concordia University

Joy Kuropatwa
University of Western Ontario

Eva Kushner
McGill University

Yvan Lamonde
McGill University

M. Travis Lane
University of New Brunswick

Louis Lasnier
C.E.G.E.P. de Saint-Laurent

David Latham
University of Lethbridge

Laurent Lavoie
University College of Cape Breton

Maurice Lebel
Université Laval

Alexander Leggatt
University of Toronto

Pierre H. Lemieux
Université d'Ottawa

John Lennox
York University

Douglas Lochhead
Mount Allison University

Robert Lovejoy
Carleton University

Alec Lucas
McGill University

Mary Lu MacDonald

S.R. MacGillivray
Lakehead University

Robin Gedalof McGrath

Louis K. MacKendrick
University of Windsor

Ken MacKinnon
St Mary's University

Carrie MacMillan
Mount Allison University

Lorraine McMullen
University of Ottawa

Laurent Mailhot
Université de Montréal

Marguerite Maillet
Université de Moncton

John Margeson
University of Toronto

Joyce Marshall

C.R.P. May
University of Birmingham

Bruce Meyer

Jacques Michon
Université de Sherbrooke

Guy Monette
Royal Military College of Canada

Ian Montagnes

Elaine Nardocchio
McMaster University

Pierre Nepveu
Université de Montréal

Gerald Noonan
Wilfrid Laurier University

James Noonan
Carleton University

John O'Connor
University of Toronto

Patrick O'Flaherty
Memorial University of Newfoundland

Jean O'Grady

David O'Rourke
Centennial College
of Applied Arts and Technology

F. Hilton Page
Dalhousie University

George L. Parker
Royal Military College of Canada

Michel Parmentier
Bishop's University

Jacques Pelletier
Université du Québec à Montréal

Michael Peterman
Trent University

Penny Petrone
Lakehead University

Richard Plant
Queen's University

A.I. Silver
University of Toronto

James Polk

Sherry Simon

Zailig Pollock
Trent University

Antoine Sirois
Université de Sherbrooke

Magdalene Redekop
University of Toronto

Patricia Smart
Carleton University

Keith Richardson

Cal Smiley
University of Toronto

Lucie Robert
Université Laval

Donald Smith
Carleton University

Ian Ross Robertson
University of Toronto

Paul Socken
University of Waterloo

Constance Rooke
University of Victoria

Alexander Sokalski
University of Saskatchewan

Marilyn Rose
Brock University

Sam Solecki
University of Toronto

Catherine Ross
University of Western Ontario

D.O. Spettigue
Queen's University

Malcolm Ross
Dalhousie University

David Staines
Smith College, Mass.

Mary Rubio
University of Guelph

Charles R. Steele
University of Calgary

Annette Saint-Pierre
Collège Universitaire de Saint-Boniface

Donald Stephens
University of British Columbia

Stephen Scobie
University of Victoria

Peter Stevens
University of Windsor

Andrew Seaman
St Mary's University

Philip Stratford
Université de Montréal

Phyllis Senese
University of Victoria

J.R. (Tim) Struthers

Vincent Sharman
Nipissing University College

Rosemary Sullivan
University of Toronto

Ben-Z. Shek
University of Toronto

Michael Tait
University of Toronto

Thomas E. Tausky
University of Western Ontario

Jules Tessier
Université d'Ottawa

Donald Theall
Trent University

Gerald Thomas
Memorial University of Newfoundland

Gillian Thomas
St Mary's University

William Toye

Elizabeth Trott

Claude Trottier

Claudette S. Trudeau

André Vanasse
Université du Québec à Montréal

Tom Vincent
Royal Military College of Canada

Miriam Waddington
York University

Anton Wagner
University of Toronto

Robert S. Wallace
York University

Germaine Warkentin
University of Toronto

Jack Warwick
York University

Elizabeth Waterston
University of Guelph

Robert Weaver

George Wicken
Centennial College
of Applied Arts and Technology

Ann Wilson

George Woodcock

Sally Zerker
York University

Francis Zichy
University of Saskatchewan

Cynthia Zimmerman
York University

Translators

I am grateful to Patricia Sillers for overseeing the translation of the entries that were submitted in French, and to the translators themselves:

Faith J. Cormier (ACADIAN LITERATURE; Nérée BEAUCHEMIN; TRANSLATIONS, ENGLISH TO FRENCH)

Sheila Fischman (COLLECTIVE CREATIONS IN QUÉBEC; Anne HÉBERT; KAMOURASKA; LITERARY MAGAZINES IN QUÉBEC)

David Lobdell (François CHARRON; Ronald DESPRÉS; Ubald PAQUIN; Jean-Guy PILON; Yves PRÉFONTAINE; André ROY)

Joyce Marshall (Jérôme DEMERS; Marcel DUGAS; ÉCOLE LITTÉRAIRE DE MONTRÉAL; Le NIGOG)

Larry Shouldice (NOVELS IN FRENCH 1920 TO 1940; 1960 TO 1981)

Patricia Sillers & Romana Perrot (Robert CHARBONNEAU; Jean CHARLEBOIS; Robert CHOQUETTE; Émile CODERRE; Alfred DESROCHERS; Rodolphe DUBÉ; Jean-Albert LORANGER; Clément MARCHAND; Émile NELLIGAN; Jean SIMARD)

Patricia Sillers (Jean BARBEAU; Gérard BESSETTE; Jacques BRAULT; Henri-Raymond CASGRAIN; William CHAPMAN; Pierre-Joseph-Olivier CHAUVEAU; DANS UN GANT DE FER; Pierre FALCON; Michel GARNEAU; Sylvain GARNEAU; Jean-Claude GERMAIN; L'INCUBATION; Michèle LALONDE; Jean LE MOYNE; LIBERTÉ; Antonine MAILLET; Joseph-Étienne-Eugène MARMETTE; Claire MARTIN; Paul MORIN; Jacques POULIN; La RELÈVE; La SAGOUINE; Eugène SEERS; Pierre TROTTIER; Pierre VADEBONCOEUR; VOIX ET IMAGES)

W.T.

The
Oxford
Companion
to
Canadian
Literature

A

Acadian literature. In 1958 Antonine MAILLET, not yet famous, published her first novel, *Pointe-aux-Coques*. Anselme Chiasson's first ethnological study, *Chéticamp: histoire et traditions acadiennes*, appeared three years later. Since then numerous other authors have been inspired by the anecdotal history, or tried to preserve the rich oral literature, of Acadia—the name given in the seventeenth century to French Atlantic-seaboard possessions in the New World. Student protests at the Université de Moncton in 1968 revealed, or gave birth to, a group of writers who both denounced the distressing conditions endured by the Acadians and exhorted them to break out of their fear and silence. These protesters, and the collectors of ancestral traditions and values, breathed new life into Acadian literature—or, as some would say, gave it birth. This entry will not linger over works published before 1960, especially since almost none are available in bookstores or even the best librairies. Extracts from the principal works published between 1609 and 1975 have been collected in *Anthologie de textes littéraires acadiens* (1979) edited by Marguerite Maillet.

1. THE BEGINNINGS. Marc Lescarbot created the myth of the Promised Land of Acadia in his account of the first permanent French settlement in North America. In the fourth volume of his *Histoire de la Nouvelle-France* (Paris, 1609) he lauded the many beauties and natural riches of Port-Royal in picturesque style and with biblical vision, emphasizing the enthusiasm and *joie de vivre* that existed there despite inevitable hardships. Until the middle of the eighteenth century French memorialists and essayists such as Pierre Biard, Nicolas Denys, N. Dièreville, and Louis Franquet echoed one or the other element of Marc Lescarbot's Edenic image of Acadia. (See also Writing in NEW FRANCE: 1.)

The deportation of the Acadians (1755-62) put a tragic end to the original enthusiasm of settlement, replacing it with a long century of suffering, confusion, and silence. There was no one, French or Acadian, to lament this Paradise Lost until 1847, when Henry Wadsworth Longfellow took up the theme and wrote EVANGELINE, which attracted the attention of America and Europe to the Aca-

dian people, whom he praised even as he mourned their disappearance. Evangeline, the image of faithfulness unto death, would represent a song of hope to the dispersed Acadians and inspire their rallying cry. Beginning in 1867 *Le moniteur acadien* (Shediac, N.B.) chronicled the birth and activities of an Acadian ruling class. Young, educated Acadians in New Brunswick and Nova Scotia—having become aware that their ancestors had been dispersed, disorganized, impoverished, and that they themselves had been made to feel inferior to their neighbours—held national conferences (1881, 1884, 1890), wrote in the newspapers, and gave lectures. Some (Pascal Poirier and Philéas Bourgeois) were conscious of giving birth to a truly Acadian literature. Orators and writers tried to convince their compatriots that their isolation had come to an end and that their inferior position was due entirely to the deportation. All reiterated the same thing: Acadia had had a glorious past before 1755; the deportees had been heroic; and as they themselves were no less valiant than their ancestors, their survival as a nation would be assured if they remained faithful to the traditions, language, and faith of their forefathers. During the 1930s, forties, and fifties this ideology of survival through keeping faith with the past was expressed in drama (J.-B. Jégo, J. Branch), fiction (Sabattis, A.-J. Léger, J.-A. Deveau), and poetry (F.-M. Lanteigne, N.-P. Landry). The unhappy phase of Acadian history was repeated over and over again and glorified, thus bringing the myth of Evangeline to its height.

2. 1958 TO THE PRESENT. The socio-political arena changed in 1960 when Acadian L.-J. Robichaud, who advocated 'an equal chance for all', was elected premier of New Brunswick. In literature the change in direction occurred in 1958 with the publication of Antonine MAILLET's *Pointe-aux-Coques* and Ronald DESPRÉS's *Silences à nourrir de sang*; and even more so with the foundation in 1972 of the first publishing house in Acadia, Les Éditions d'Acadie. Antonine Maillet dominates Acadian literature, as much by the number of books she has published as for the fame she achieved, nationally and internationally, even before receiving the Prix Goncourt. In *La* SAGOUINE (1972) she not

only universalized the complaints and demands of her people but expressed beautifully their *joie de vivre* and common sense: she forced attention onto Acadia. Her influence on Acadian literature is incontestable, both as to the content of her books (exploitation of the heritage and anecdotal history of Acadia) and as to their form (use of Acadian oral structures and the spoken word).

Ronald Després has been considered one of French Canada's good poets ever since *Silences à nourrir de sang* appeared in 1958; two other collections, *Les cloisons en vertige* (1962) and *Le balcon des dieux inachevés* (1968), confirm this judgement. His roman-sotie, or satirical farce, *Le scalpel ininterrompu* (1962), was also well received by critics; but Acadians are generally disturbed by these books, considering them to be overly bloody and obscure. Even so, Després's works, despite their purely esthetic and personal bent, are Acadian, if only because of his obsession with the sea. His anguish and his description of a dehumanizing society have found more than one echo in the literature of the 1970s—a decade during which young Acadian authors, beginning with the poets, resolutely committed themselves to the confrontation they felt was necessary to free their people.

2(a). *Poetry*. Raymond LeBlanc's *Cri de terre* (1973) was the first publication of Les Éditions d'Acadie. Torn between his refusal to live as a slave or colonial and his reluctance to become an exile, the poet tries to recapture the sacred flame in the very roots of his country, to re-invent his homeland through the magic of words. This collection cries out against the silence that permitted injustices and oppression and warns against the Anglicization of his people; at the same time it is a brotherly call to an awakening, and then a revolt, before the only hope left is in alliance between Acadia and Québec.

Following LeBlanc, Guy Arseneault, Herménégilde Chiasson, Calixte Duguay, and Ulysse Landry respectively showed the difficulty they had in identifying with their exploited, half-assimilated brothers—with those who had had all desire for revolt crushed out of them by fear. Since the Acadian's unacceptable position was perceived as being closely related to a problem of language, these poets—Calixte Duguay excepted—used different levels of language to better reach their people or better translate the reality they wished to denounce. This led them to question the possibility and the utility of poetry as a means of awakening

their society. Chiasson is the most avant-garde of this group, and possibly the most pessimistic. After the publication of his first collection, *Mourir à Scoudouc* (1974), a book of great poetic force and beauty, he remained torn between his determination to denounce firmly the aberrant, brutalizing realities in Acadia and his wish to give to the very language that was suppressing his people a poetic intensity that would load his words with promises (*Rapport sur l'état de mes illusions*, 1976). Duguay, who seemed the least committed, considered his people incapable of a collective revolt and offered them songs 'to make a summer out of the cold of our winters' and dreams of a land where solidarity and liberty would replace dispersion and subjugation. The magical Acadia of his *Les stigmates du silence* (1975) is only a dreamland in Léonard Forest's *Saisons antérieures* (1973), in which 'Bittersweet Lachigan' presents itself as 'castles of hope'. This poet, who uses such beautiful images and such a fresh style, received the Prix France-Acadie for his second collection, *Comme en Florence* (1979).

In the early eighties another generation of poets, one that had given up on commitment, published its first collections. Dyane Léger (*Graines de fées*, 1980), Clarence Comeau (*Entre amours et silences*, 1980), Gérald LeBlanc (*Comme un otage du quotidien*, 1981), Louis Comeau (*Moosejaw*, 1981), and Roméo Savoie (*Duo de démesure*, 1981) explore their own imaginations, searching their past as far back as their 'sad' childhood and 'tormented' youth. They uncover and try to understand the reasons behind so many smothered loves, dead ambitions, longings for flight, dreams that must continually be begun again. In the guise of a poetry that is formal or intimate or based on daily life, these poets demonstrate the same difficulty in existing and living in Acadia as their elders, who committed themselves and then became silent—though they are very conscious of being Comeau's 'children of a race/Which knocks/On Justice's door' (*Entre amours et silences*).

2(b). *Theatre*. The two recurring themes of the 1970s—protest and recovery—are both treated by the few dramatists whose works have been published. Antonine Maillet excepted, Laval Goupil has attracted the most attention from critics. His first play, *Tête d'eau* (1974), which is dream-like, surrealistic, fantastic, treats universal concerns: it supports all forms of creativity by showing the kind of madness that results when the imagination has been browbeaten. In contrast, *Le Djibou* (1975) is very realistic and is rooted in a specific Acadian socio-cultural milieu. The characters—whose language is violent, raw, and vulgar—try to trap and exorcise their past and present fears. The play ends when they begin to take steps to free themselves. In a relatively short text, *Les pêcheurs déportés* (1974), Germaine Comeau brings out several problems that hinder the development of Nova Scotia Acadians. But one theme is clear: the need to break down the barriers preventing people from speaking to, and understanding, each other.

Jules Boudreau wrote the book, and Ca-lixte Duguay the words and music, for the musical *Louis Mailloux* (created in 1978), which was so successful that the sound-track was recorded (Kapociré KC5304). Boudreau also used history as the source for his play *Cochu et le soleil* (1978): around 1783 the arrival of the Loyalists forces an Acadian family to uproot itself for the second time in less than thirty years. After watching some resist and the others submit, the younger daughter decides to give up this shameful existence and chooses life in a 'real' country, that of the English. The father, proud and stubborn, consoles himself for this disgrace as he sees his elder daughter continue the fight to maintain her culture and identity. In *Sacord-jeu* (1979) Claude Renaud brings back to life another moment in history, the revolt of the parishioners of Grand-Digue, N.B., in 1848. This play, never performed, denounces the sector of the clergy it judges to be hypocritical and allied with the colonizers and merchants to rob 'the poor'. *Cochu et le soleil* and *Sacordjeu* are not simply retellings of history—like, for instance, *Le Capitaine St-Simon*, one of Vincent Dumas's *Deux pièces acadiennes* (1979). Besides wishing to stimulate a renewal among their people, Boudreau and Renaud try to debunk the Longfellow myth of the submissive Aca-dian.

In addition to the few plays that have been published, a good number have been pro-duced, some—especially those of Herménégilde Chiasson and Raymond Le-Blanc—quite successfully.

2(c). *Legends, tales, stories, novels.* The publication of Anselme Chiasson's mono-graph, *Chéticamp: histoire et traditions aca-diennes* (1961), which featured popular cul-ture, along with Antonine Maillet's *Point-aux-Coques* (1958), marks the begin-ning of a movement that prompted several authors to turn towards the Acadian heri-tage, either to record it or to draw inspira-tion from it. This movement has grown; yet some, especially the poets, have protested or warned that another retreat into the past must not result in an unwillingness to de-nounce the current unacceptable situation. Even so, the vast majority of the works published recently in Acadia deal with anec-dotal history or oral literature.

Some authors transcribe and reproduce a few of the beautiful legends collected in New Brunswick and Nova Scotia (Francis Savoie, Anselme Chiasson, Catherine Joli-coeur), or publish fairy tales (Melvin Gal-lant, Gérald Aucoin); while others mix their own recollections with oral traditions, re-creating typical Acadians from the past (Félix-E. Thibodeau, Désiré d'Eon), or tell of their own life and that of the region (An-toinette Gallant, Lina Madore). This last cat-egory includes simply written accounts, by authors who not only are not professionals but are not especially concerned with creat-ing literary masterpieces. Louis Haché, who went from stories to novels, stands out clearly from this group. With his historical sketch of the little island of Miscou, *Char-mante Miscou* (1974), followed by his novel *Adieu P'tit Chipagan* (1978), and his short stories *Toubes jersiaises* (1980), the Acadian Peninsula seems to have found its historian-storyteller, and Acadia its bard of the sea.

In *La Mariecomo* (1974) Régis Brun tells the story of the witches of the south coast of New Brunswick during the second half of the nineteenth century. These people, with their strange tastes for gaiety and freedom, protested, by their very presence in an Aca-dian village, against a 'bourgeois' lifestyle dictated by clerical and national interests. Jacques Savoie's characters—in *Raconte-moi Massabielle* (1979)—are also on the fringes of society, but the author, instead of going back into the past, treats a very topical sub-ject, the expropriations at Kouchibouguac. *Raconte-moi* has a new tone: there are no lamentations, no violent denunciations, but instead humour, a pleasure in word-games, and above all a very modern form—it is not a book with a message. Claude LeBouthil-lier has published two novels set in the fu-ture: *L'Acadien reprend son pays* (1977) and *Isabelle-sur-mer* (1979). If in 1988 the Acadian has taken peaceful possession of his paradise, it is because he has lived through, and van-quished, his fear; and if the new country solves the world crisis in the year 2000, it is because Acadians have concentrated on the best of the old and new values: love of the arts, respect for nature, and fidelity to themselves and their roots. Such an optimistic vision of the future is exceptional among Acadian authors.

Two names stand out among those who published first novels in 1980 and 1981. Anne Levesque shows talent in her analysis of a difficult family situation (*Les jongleries*, 1980), and Laurier Melanson in *Zélica à Cochon Vert* (1981) has a great time depicting and giving voice to vivid characters who relegate the image of a suffering Acadia to the realm of legend once and for all. His verve and humour add a relaxed note to Acadian literature.

2(d). *Biography, memoirs, essays.* Biography was one of the first literary forms cultivated in Acadia; the foremost examples are *Le Père Lefebvre et l'Acadie* (1898) by Pascal Poirier and *Vie de l'abbé François-Xavier Lafrance* (1913) by Phileas Bourgeois. It subsequently attracted little interest until the publication of Camille-Antonio Doucet's *Une étoile s'est levée en Acadie: Marcel-François Richard* (1973), Alexandre Savoie's *Un demisiècle d'histoire: le Docteur A.-M. Sormany* (1976), and Eloi DeGrâce's *Mgr Stanislas Doucet* (1977). The goal is still the same: to honour the builders of Acadia. These three biographies are not necessarily more interesting than those published by Poirier and Bourgeois, but they are more complete and better documented. In the last few years, as Acadians have begun to tell their own story, their confidences or testimony have taken the form of poetry, diary, and fiction. Only Calixte Savoie has written his memoirs. Teacher, school principal, and superintendent, and then secretary and president of the Société l'Assomption (1926-62), he wrote his *Mémoires d'un nationaliste acadien* (1979) to tell the story of a life of struggle, and especially of the fight of a minority-nationalist whose compatriots obtained the most basic educational rights crumb by crumb. Whoever reads this book will better understand why some Acadian authors are so bitter and violent and also why some, like Michel Roy, see no future for Acadia except by joining with Québec. Roy has produced the most literary essay on Acadia in *L'Acadie perdue* (1978), whose fervour and passion leave no one unmoved. While the position he takes in most of this essay may inspire doubt or despair in some minds, there are pages in his book that can arouse positive speculation about Acadia's future.

MARGUERITE MAILLET

Acadian Magazine, The (Halifax, 1826-8). Published between July 1826 and Jan. 1828, *The Acadian Magazine; or Literary Mirror* was the most important literary journal in early-nineteenth-century Maritime Canada. It appeared monthly, printed by Jacob S. Cunnabel and edited by Beamish Murdock (1826 to mid-1827) and J. Scott Tremaine (mid-1827 to 1828). Nineteen numbers were issued; the average length of each was forty double-column pages. While it included reprints from British, American, and Upper Canadian sources, over three-quarters of the published material was locally written. Fiction and poetry were prominently featured, most of it original. There were pieces on local and North American history, a short series on travel in eastern Nova Scotia, and reviews of local literary productions. As well there were general essays on a wide variety of topics, and early issues included foreign and domestic news. During the life of the journal four handsome engravings by Halifax engraver Charles W. Torbett were published; one of them depicted the recently completed Province House (1819), seat of the legislative assembly of Nova Scotia.

Very little is known about the local contributors because most published anonymously. It is suspected that Thomas Chandler HALIBURTON wrote one of the longer poems, 'Western scenes'. John Templedon wrote several pieces of fiction, James Irving several literary essays, and Joseph Hart Clinch some poetry. There is clear evidence that the contributors were not concentrated in Halifax but came from the area: Saint John, Pictou, Truro, Cape Breton, Windsor, and Annapolis Royal.   TOM VINCENT

Achard, Eugène. See CHILDREN'S LITERATURE IN FRENCH: 2, 3.

Acorn, Milton (b. 1923). Born in Charlottetown, P.E.I., he served in the Second World War, suffering a serious head injury. On his return to P.E.I. he eventually became a carpenter, but gave up carpentry in 1956—after privately publishing his first collection of poems, *In love and anger*—to devote himself to poetry in Montreal, where he met Irving LAYTON, Al PURDY, and other poets. *The brain's the target* and a broadsheet, *Against a league of liars*, were published in 1960. In 1962 he married Gwendolyn MacEWEN in Toronto, and when the marriage failed the following year he moved to Vancouver. Fifty-eight of his poems were printed in a special issue of *The*

FIDDLEHEAD (Spring 1963) and in the same year *Jawbreakers* (1963) appeared. Throughout the sixties he became increasingly involved in political activities and many of his poems developed through public readings. At the end of the sixties he returned to Toronto. When *I've tasted my blood: poems 1956 to 1968* (1969), selected and introduced by Purdy, failed to win a Governor General's Award in 1970, a group of Toronto poets created the 'Canadian poetry award' for Acorn and named him 'The people's poet'. His next two collections were *I shout love and on shaving off his beard* (1971) and *More poems for people* (1972), which was dedicated to Dorothy LIVESAY and inspired by her *Poems for people* (1947). *The island means Minago* appeared in 1975 and won a Governor General's Award. *Jackpine sonnets* appeared in 1977, *Captain Neal MacDougal and the naked goddess* in 1982, and *Dig up my heart: selected poems of Milton Acorn 1952-1983* in 1983. He now lives in Charlottetown.

Acorn describes himself as a 'believer in Dialectics'. His Marxism is the most obvious manifestation of this belief, but it finds expression even in poems that seem totally unpolitical. Acorn's is a poetry of opposites, of delicacy and toughness, which come together in a single dialectical vision: the delicate beauty that Acorn celebrates in man and nature must be defended through toughminded unrelenting struggle and is the ultimate inspiration of even his most harshly aggressive works.

The poems of Acorn's early maturity, collected for the most part in the first half of *I've tasted my blood*, are generally brief and straightforward but have a subtlety of technique that gives them a surprisingly rich resonance. A sensitive ear for the nuances of North American speech rhythms and a gift for imagery, ranging from delicately precise notation to almost surrealistic evocativeness, are joined to a fine organizing intelligence. Acorn's best lyrics are miniature dramas in which conflict and resolution find expression through the subtle interplay of rhythm and imagery. Two outstanding examples are 'Poem for the astronauts' and the slightly later 'Words said sitting on a rock sitting on a saint', a statement of the artist's adversary role in modern society comparable in importance to A.M. KLEIN's 'Portrait of the poet as landscape'.

In the mid-sixties Acorn's poems tended to become longer and looser, the imagery less organic, speech rhythms yielding to the cruder rhythms of public exhortation and vituperation. Acorn's increasingly public stance in this period seemed to lead him away from the personal experience that nourished his best work. However, in many of the poems in *Jackpine sonnets*, and the sonnet sequence *Captain MacDougal and the naked goddess*, Acorn seems to have rediscovered the real source of his strength in the 'dialectical play of argument', which he defines as the essence of the sonnet ('Tirade by way of introduction', *Jackpine sonnets*). Though not as rich in sensuous appeal as the best early work, these sonnets and sonnet-like poems show a renewed control and vitality, and contain some of Acorn's most powerful expressions of his twin themes of love and anger.

See Dorothy Livesay, 'Search for a style: the poetry of Milton Acorn', CANADIAN LITERATURE 40 (Spring 1969).

See also POETRY IN ENGLISH 1950 TO 1982: 2.   ZAILIG POLLOCK

Adam, Graeme Mercer (1839-1912). Born in Loanhead, Midlothian, Scot., and educated in Edinburgh, Adam came to Toronto in 1858 as manager for the Canadian book-retailing enterprise of Cunningham Geikie. Two years later he assumed control of the business—which eventually became Adam, Stevenson and Company, publishers and booksellers. Adam was at times the publisher or editor of a series of important periodicals: *The British American Magazine* (1863-4), *The Canada Bookseller* (1869-72), *The Canadian Monthly and National Review* (1872-78), ROSE-BELFORD'S CANADIAN MONTHLY (1878-82), and *The Canadian Educational Monthly* (1883-8). At the same time he served as a literary assistant to Goldwin SMITH and as the business manager for Smith's *The Bystander* (1880-3). He eventually became a major contributor to *The WEEK* (1883-96), as well as to other periodicals and newspapers. Adam left Canada for the United States in 1892, apparently succumbing to the frustrations of literary life in Canada and to the financial attractions of the American publishing industry. He spent some time in Chicago and Akron, Ohio, but lived mostly in New York, where he died in 1912.

Through his own writings and his choice of contributors to the periodicals he edited, Adam promoted a literary life for Canada. He fought for a fair copyright law to protect Canadian publishers; he paid contributors to *The Canadian Monthly*; and he offered criticism and praise for the work of Canadian

Adam

authors. He also involved himself in the issues of the day, compiling the *Handbook of commercial union: a collection of papers read before the Commercial Union Club, Toronto, with speeches, letters and other documents in favour of unrestricted reciprocity with the United States* (Toronto, 1888); writing *The Canadian North-west: its history and its troubles from the early days of the fur-trade to the era of the railway and the settler; with incidents of travel in the region, and the narrative of three insurrections* (Toronto, 1885) in response to the Riel rebellion; and preparing *Toronto, old and new* (Toronto, 1891). He contributed an 'Outline of Canadian literature' to William Henry WITHROW's *History of Canada* (Toronto, 1876); compiled *Prominent men of Canada: a collection of persons distinguished in professional and political life, and the commerce and industry of Canada* (Toronto, 1892); and wrote a series of travel pieces, including *Canada from sea to sea, historical and descriptive* (Toronto, 1888), *Illustrated Quebec* (Montreal, 1891), *Illustrated Toronto* (Montreal, 1891), and *Muskoka illustrated* (Toronto, 1888). He revised Edmund Collins's *Canada's patriot statesman* (Toronto, 1891), a life of Sir John A. Macdonald; collaborated with George Dickson on the *History of Upper Canada College, 1829-1892* (Toronto, 1893); and wrote a *History of Toronto and county of York, Ontario* (Toronto, 1885). Adam also helped to produce a five-volume series of school readers, the *Royal Canadian readers* (Toronto, 1887), plus *The high school English word book: a manual of orthoepy, synonymy, and derivation* (Toronto, 1887), and the *Public school history of England and Canada* (Toronto, 1886).

Adam made one venture into fiction in a collaborative effort with the poet Agnes Ethelwyn WETHERALD—*An Algonquin maiden: a romance of the early days of Upper Canada* (Montreal, 1887). An unfocused look at aristocratic life in the Upper Canada of the 1820s, this novel sought to be no more than 'breezy, lofty, wholesome and bright'—Adam's own description of good fiction.

Adam nurtured Canadian literary life in the last quarter of the nineteenth century not with any artistic creativity but with his practical talents as an editor and publisher.

CAL SMILEY

Adams, Levi (1802-32). Probably born in the seigneury of Noyan, just east of the Richelieu R., he became an articled law clerk in the Montreal office of F.P. Bruneau in 1822 and was admitted to the bar in 1827.

He and his wife Elizabeth, whom he had married in 1830, both died in June 1832; they were among the first cholera victims of that epidemic year.

Adams' long poem *Jean Baptiste: a poetic olio, and II cantos* (1825) was published under his own name in Montreal. Adhering to the *ottava rima* verse-form of Byron's *Beppo* and *Don Juan*, often at the expense of logical speech patterns, it tells, in mock-heroic tones, how the bachelor politician of the title, rejected by his true love, comes eventually to marry the willing Rosalie. It is set in contemporary Montreal, and the central 'plot' is the occasion for 160 stanzas of discursive comment on the themes of mortality, love, marriage, literature, and the law. A few short poems, signed 'L.A.', were published in *The Montreal Herald* and *The Canadian Courant* in 1825 and 1826.

Adams also wrote two amateurish short stories—'The young lieutenant; a tale' and 'The wedding', both signed 'L.A.'—which appeared in *The Canadian Magazine and Literary Repository* (June 1825). Set in Canada, though they could have taken place anywhere in the world without changes in detail, they are narrated by an omniscient third person and written in a melancholic vein after the fashion of the day.

Like many other young men of his time, Adams seems to have ceased writing for publication once he entered his chosen profession. He is unusual in that he signed his own name to his major work in a period when gentlemen published their literary productions anonymously.

Because of similarities in form and subject between *Jean Baptiste* and an earlier volume, *The charivari*, Adams' name was linked for many years to this and other anonymous works subsequently proved to have been written by George LONGMORE. A modern edition of *Jean Baptiste*, with an introduction by C.F. KLINCK, was published by the Golden Dog Press, Ottawa, in 1978.

MARY LU MacDONALD

'Ahkoond of Swat, The: a threnody'. This humorous poem by George T. Lanigan (1846-86)—with its epigraph ' "The Ahkoond of Swat is dead"—Press dispatch'—was composed while Lanigan was working for the New York *World*. A.J.M. SMITH says in *The book of Canadian poetry* (1957) that Lanigan wrote the poem after receiving a cryptic message over the wires that the Ahkoond of Swat was dead, but J.D. Logan in *Highways of Canadian literature* (1924) quotes

L.J. Burpee as saying that 'one evening, after learning the fact from the English mail just received, Lanigan announced that the Ahkoond of Swat was dead and that he was writing a poem about him.'

Lanigan was born in St Charles, Lower Canada, became interested in journalism, and founded the Montreal *Star* with Hugh Graham (later Lord Atholstan) in 1869. Later he moved to the United States, where he pursued his career in journalism and wrote *Fables. Taken anywhere, anywhere out of the world, By G. Washington Aesop* (New York, 1878). He had previously published *National ballads of Canada. Imitated and trans. from the originals by Allid (pseud)* (Montreal, 1865). He died in Philadelphia.

VINCENT SHARMAN

Alianak, Hrant (b. 1950). Born in Khartoum, Sudan, he came to Canada in 1967 and studied economics at McGill University, Montreal, and English at York University, Toronto. He has worked as both playwright and director for stage, television, and film. The most important collection of his plays is *The return of the big five* (1975), which includes *Brandy, Christmas, Mathematics, Tantrums,* and *Western*. He is also the author of *Passion and sin* (1978) and of a number of so-far unpublished plays, including *Mousetown, The blues, Night, Lucky Strike,* and an adaptation of Shakespeare's *Titus Andronicus* as a Western. His work has been seen throughout Canada, and in the United States and England. In its surrealist quality, and its frequent allusions to film, it is characteristic of the experimental phase of Toronto underground theatre in the early 1970s. But it is also distinguished by a special inventiveness. In *Western* the characters act out conventional sex-and-power games in dialogue that consists mostly of one character's calling out the title of an old Western while another responds with the name of the star. *Mathematics* recounts a day in the life of a couple entirely in terms of properties thrown one by one onto the stage. Another wordless play, *Christmas,* traces the rhythm of the season through the brief career of a Christmas tree, played by an actor. These plays represent the best work of this occasionally undisciplined talent. Their strength lies not in a particular theme or vision but in the witty manipulation of the medium itself. Considering their essentially theatrical nature, their wit—embodied largely in stage directions—survives translation into print surprisingly well.   ALEXANDER LEGGATT

Allan, Peter John (1825-48). Born in York, Eng., he was brought to New Brunswick as a child and grew up in Fredericton. He briefly attended King's College (now the University of New Brunswick), but left to take up the study of law. In 1843 he began to publish verse in *The New Brunswick Reporter*, a Fredericton newspaper published by James Hogg, a sometime poet. Allan took his poetry seriously enough to plan a volume of verse and solicit subscriptions to underwrite the cost of publication, but he died suddenly in Frederiction. It was posthumously published under the title *The poetical remains of Peter John Allan* (London, 1853). Allan was influenced by the aesthetic principles of the Romantic movement, particularly with reference to perceiving ideal truths within the sensuality of nature. Not surprisingly, he was fascinated by the potential of human imagination and the range of perception it offered to human awareness. These aesthetic interests brought an intellectual toughness to his verse that prevented the overflow of emotion and controlled the sentimentality and banal moralizing that are so noticeable in the poetry of other local poets. In his nature poetry especially, a distinctive quality of tone and mood emerges from the interplay of intellectual perception and emotional sensitivity that looks forward to the early poetry of Charles G.D. ROBERTS and Bliss CARMAN.   TOM VINCENT

Allan, Ted (b. 1916). Born Allan Herman in Montreal, he left high school to supplement the family income, working first in the family gift store, then as a hardware clerk in Westmount. At eighteen, a dedicated Young Communist, he became Montreal correspondent for the *Toronto Daily Worker*. He served in the International Brigade in the Spanish Civil War and as political commissar in Dr Norman Bethune's blood-transfusion unit. In 1938 he married Kate Lenthier, by whom he had a son and a daughter; they divorced in 1957. Resident in London, Eng., for almost three decades, he now lives in Toronto and Los Angeles.

His best-known book is *The scalpel, the sword: the story of Doctor Norman Bethune* (1952, with Sydney Gordon; rev. 1971). A heroic biography (one million copies in print in nineteen languages), it is enthusiastically vivid about Bethune's personality, medical innovations, and revolutionary commitment. Acknowledging the flaws in his obsessive and mercurial temperament, it nevertheless occasionally sees Bethune's ear-

Allan

lier life—including its self-indulgent phases and his sad and stormy relationship with his wife Frances—as too prophetic of his later humanitarian dedication, in Spain and China, to fundamental political and social change.

Allan's novel of the Spanish Civil War, *This time a better earth* (1939), centres on Bob Curtis, a twenty-one-year-old Canadian volunteer in the International Brigade. Characters who are courageous, compassionate, and socialist, and compelling evocations of love, loyalty, and battle, are rendered sparely, without ideological sentimentality. Allan's science-fiction novel *Quest for Pajaro* (1970) was published under the pseudonym Edward Maxwell. A children's book, *Willie the squowse* (1977), with its half-squirrel, half-mouse hero, provides the opportunity for a parable about how two families wrongly value money and mistakenly equate financial success with happiness.

Allan's plays have been produced in Toronto, Paris, London, Rome, East Berlin, and Los Angeles. *Double image* (1957, with Roger MacDougall), which ran five years in Paris, is a murder mystery complicated by the hero's impersonating his twin—to the confusion of the police, his wife, and the audience. In *My sister's keeper* (1976) Allan establishes that Sarah, who desperately seeks emotional comfort from her brother Robert, suffers not insanity but an extreme sensitivity and a profound need for love. An authentic relationship between them is prevented by Robert's 'sanity'—his psychological refusal to risk genuine or generous emotion.

Though Allan has not been politically engaged for years, he retains in his writing an obvious left-wing orientation and a disgust with tyranny. But perhaps more significant thematically is his repeated exploration of the possibility of positive transformation through acceptance of another person or of a principle unconnected with the isolated ego.

Allan's short stories, which have not been collected, have appeared in many magazines, including *The New Yorker* and *Harper's*. He has also written several dozen radio and television dramas (and acted in many) for CBC, BBC, ITV, and films for major studios. He wrote the original screenplay for the film *Lies my father told me* (1976).   ANTHONY HOPKINS

Allen, Grant (1848-99). Although born on Wolfe Island near Kingston, Canada West (Ont.), Grant Allen owed little as a writer to his country of origin. Educated privately, and in France and England, he completed his formal education at Merton College, Oxford (1867-71). From 1873 to 1876 he taught at a newly founded school for Black students in Jamaica and when it failed he returned to England, where he wrote many unpublished articles on scientific subjects; published at his own expense *Physiological aesthetics* (London, 1877); and tried his hand at journalism in London. The book, which had no commercial success, did bring him to the attention of a few editors, including Leslie Stephen of the *Cornhill Magazine*, and Allen began to earn 'a modest—a very modest—and precarious income.' A second book, *The colour sense: its origin and development; an essay in comparative psychology* (London, 1879), attracted the notice of Alfred Wallace, Charles Darwin, and Herbert Spencer. But Allen had no success until 1880, when he began writing magazine fiction. His first collection was *Strange stories* (London, 1884); his first novel, *Philistia* (London, 1884), like many of the earlier magazine pieces, appeared under a pseudonym. From this time on, Allen's production of fiction was enormous: more than forty novels and collections of stories (along with thirty works of non-fiction). As a fiction writer Allen, who had the good journalist's sense of contemporary intellectual movements, presented advanced social ideas in an accessible form, such as questions of class and other social issues in *The British barbarians. A Hilltop novel* (London, 1895), and feminism and women's rights in *The woman who did. A Hilltop novel* (London, 1895). ('Hilltop' was Allen's house at Hindhead in Surrey, the highest spot in southeastern England.) Joseph Conrad equated Allen's popular fiction with that of Marie Corelli and Hall Caine, saying: 'There are no lasting qualities in their work.' In one small way, however, Allen assured himself of some lasting recognition: *An African millionaire: episodes in the life of the illustrious Colonel Clay* (London, 1897) introduces a character whom Frederic Dannay (half of 'Ellery Queen') describes as 'the first great thief of short mystery fiction,' anticipating by two years E.W. Hornung's much better-known A.J. Raffles.

Though Allen's work was known and discussed in Canada, and some of it appeared in *The Canadian Monthly and National Review*, it had no significant effect on Canadian literature and very little of it reflects his Canadian origins. Some titles have been reprinted, among them: *Physiological aesthetics* (New York, 1977), *The British barbarians* (New York, 1975), *Charles Darwin* (Philadelphia, 1973), *The evolution of the idea of God* (New York, 1977), and *An African millionaire* (New York, 1980), which has a useful introduction by Norman Donaldson that sketches Allen's career and comments on his place in the history of detective fiction.

DAVID JACKEL

Allen, Ralph (1913-66). Born in Winnipeg, Man., he was the son of a CPR railway agent, living in a succession of small railroad towns before his family settled in Oxbow, Sask. At sixteen he left Oxbow to become a sports writer for the Winnipeg *Tribune*, moving to the Toronto *Globe* in 1938. During the Second World War he served as a gunner in the Royal Canadian Artillery until 1943, when he became war correspondent for the Toronto *Globe and Mail*. Subsequently he was awarded the OBE for his coverage of the Allied landings in Sicily, Italy, and Normandy. In 1946 Allen moved to *Maclean's* as assistant editor, becoming editor in 1950. From 1960 to 1964, having resigned as editor, he spent half a year as contributing editor on *Maclean's* and the other half working on his own books. In 1964 he joined the Toronto *Star* as managing editor, a position he held when he died.

Allen wrote five novels, three of which deal with the ambivalence felt by men caught up in war. *Homemade banners* (1946) deals with Canadian soldiers who served overseas in the Second World War, emphasizing the fate of one man who joins the army in 1941, sees action, then returns to a broken home and comes to realize that he has risked life, home, and family for a cause that was not of his own choosing. *The high white forest* (1964), set during the Battle of the Bulge in Normandy, also portrays the experiences of soldiers, including two brothers in the Canadian Forestry Unit who have doubts about the war itself and particularly about the gratuitous execution of prisoners. *Ask the name of the lion* (1962), set in the Congo during the struggle for independence, portrays the conflicting opinions of a group of fugitives—including a UN troubleshooter, a Belgian colonial, and an idealistic Canadian doctor—who are forced to flee when an isolated hospital is attacked by a detachment of marauding Congolese soldiers. Allen also wrote *The chartered libertine*

(1954), a satire about the conflict between private-broadcast interests and the publicly owned CBC.

Allen's most successful novel (his personal favourite) is *Peace River country* (1958), the story of the journey from Saskatchewan of a mother—sporadically pursued by her alcoholic husband—and her two children to an assumed refuge in the unspoiled Northwest. In celebrating the faith and optimism of the mother, the novel becomes a bittersweet parable about the need for faith and determination in the pursuit of dreams. Its straightforward narrative style, sympathetic characters, and especially its exploration of the feelings of the sensitive adolescent son, have made the novel a favourite in Canadian schools.

Allen also wrote *Ordeal by fire: 1919-1945* (1961), a volume in the Doubleday Canadian History Series. A collection of Allen's newspaper and magazine articles, *The man from Oxbow: the best of Ralph Allen* (1967) was edited by Christina McCall-Newman.

MARILYN ROSE

Alline, Henry (1748-84). Born in Newport, Rhode Island, he received some formal schooling before his family immigrated in 1760 to Nova Scotia as part of the influx of New Englanders into the Annapolis Valley after the expulsion of the Acadians, taking up land in the future township of Falmouth. He remained on his father's farm until 1776, assisting in its operation and privately pursuing theological studies through the books that were available to him. His conversion came in Mar. 1775, and a year later, as political rebellion erupted in New England, Alline dedicated himself to raising the spiritual consciousness of Nova Scotia (which then included present-day New Brunswick) by preaching the gospel of Christ's salvation and the transcendence of God's grace. Preaching throughout the area until his death, Alline almost single-handedly precipitated a revival of faith that ultimately laid the foundation of the Baptist movement in the Maritimes. His followers were called the 'New Lights' and, although Alline himself avoided institutionalizing his faith, the 'New Lights' established themselves as 'churches' in various parts of Nova Scotia.

As part of his evangelical activities Alline sought to broaden his influence in the 1780s through the written word. He published three sermons and two theological treatises: *A sermon preached to a religious society of young men* (Halifax, 1782), *A sermon on a day of*

Alline

thanksgiving (Halifax, 1782), *A sermon preached at Fort Medway* (Halifax, 1783), *Two mites on some of the most important and much disputed points of divinity* (Halifax, 1781), and *The anti-traditionalist* (Halifax, 1783). The theological views presented in his sermons and treatises are not particularly original and not always logically coherent. Alline was influenced by the writings of the English theologian William Law, and found the pietistical bent of Law's theology, together with its mysticism and asceticism, particularly attractive. At the same time, however, he also asserted the need for enthusiastic evangelism, demanding a personal commitment to the active proclamation of the gospel of salvation. His view of God's love was Universalist and Arminian in nature: God's love was extended to all men, and those who had received this truth must actively participate in extending it to others. Alline was strongly attacked for his theological views, and his chief detractor was Jonathan Scott, a Calvinistic Congregationalist minister, who refuted Alline's theology in *A brief view of the religious tenets and sentiments . . . of Mr. Henry Alline* (Halifax, 1784).

In addition to his sermons and theological works, Alline published two volumes of hymns: *Hymns and spiritual songs* [I] (Halifax, 1782) and *Hymns and spiritual songs* [II] (Boston, 1786). These hymns, which generally follow the simple verse-forms established by Isaac Watts and other English hymnists of the late-seventeenth and early-eighteenth centuries, deal with aspects of Christian life, particularly with the glory of salvation and the agony of man's sinfulness. The 1786 edition, written during a lengthy illness just prior to Alline's death, may be viewed as a kind of spiritual autobiography describing the emotional ups and downs of his spiritual condition. Ironically, Alline was travelling to Boston to publish this work when he died at North Hampton, New Hampshire. His *Life and journals* (Boston, 1806) was published posthumously.

See M. Armstrong, 'The literature of the great awakening' in *The great awakening in Nova Scotia* (1948) and 'Henry Alline's "Hymns and spiritual songs" ', *Dalhousie Review* XXXIV (1955); J.M. Bumstead, *Henry Alline* (1971); and Thomas B. Vincent, 'Alline and Bailey', CANADIAN LITERATURE 68-69 (Spring/Summer 1976).

TOM VINCENT

Alphabet (1960-71). First published in Sept. 1960, this adventurous little magazine from London, Ont., was edited and distributed, and often typeset and printed, by its founder, James REANEY, whose interest in the theories of Northrop FRYE was given special prominence in the quotation that frequently headed the table of contents: 'There is such a thing as the iconography of the imagination.' Each issue was dedicated to an archetypal image or myth—for example, Narcissus (1), Icarus (4), and Horoscope (5). In content, viewpoint, and visual appearance, *Alphabet* changed impressively in the course of its nineteen issues. In the beginning it featured writers who were comfortable within traditional typographic conventions, and it contained few graphics. Later issues bristled with typographic collages, hand-drawn poems, and charts, as Reaney welcomed to *Alphabet* such unconventional writers as bill BISSETT, David W. Harris, bp NICHOL, and George BOWERING, as well as the London painters Jack Chambers and Greg Curnoe. It had an ever-expanding range of editorial curiosity: from myth and literature, it grew to include discussions of concrete poetry, popular music, Ojibwa art, cinema, sound poetry, and performance art. *Alphabet* became a place where the writing of the fifties could interact with that of the sixties, where early British Columbia concrete poets like bissett and Judith Copithorne could reach an eastern audience, and where the young Margaret ATWOOD could mature as both poet and reviewer. The nineteenth and final issue appeared in June 1971—seven issues short of Reaney's original hope of one issue for each letter of the alphabet.

FRANK DAVEY

Altham: a tale of the sea (London, 1849). Perhaps the most interesting early-Canadian novel because it is solidly and straightforwardly written, and because the plot is compelling enough to sustain interest, *Altham* was published in a two-volume edition in London, Eng., by Saunders and Otley. The first two-thirds of the work had appeared in BARKER'S CANADIAN MONTHLY MAGAZINE (Kingston) between Oct. 1846 and Apr. 1847, when *Barker's* ceased publication.

The author, John Swete Cummins, was born in Cork, Ire., in 1811. He immigrated to Canada as agent for Lord Mountcashel and lived on his employer's property near Delaware, Upper Canada, and at Amherst Island, near Kingston (Ont.). He was active in the militia in 1837, and in later years became a militia lieutenant-colonel, as well as chairman of the Midland District Council.

growing love between Angéline and Maurice, and share her joy in her adored father and her cherished fiancé. Suddenly, in a few pages of impersonal narrative, the situation changes: M. de Montbrun dies as a result of an accident while hunting; Angéline suffers a disfigurement (caused by a facial tumour in the early editions; by an operation, necessitated by a fall, in the later ones), and becomes convinced that Maurice's ardour has cooled. Proud and independent, Angéline returns his engagement ring and decides to live alone. The final section is made up of Angéline's diary, in which the entries recount her anguished solitude, and her determination to devote herself to the service of the humble inhabitants of the district.

For the novel's publication as a book, under the pseudonym 'Laure Conan', Abbé Henri-Raymond CASGRAIN wrote a preface, which contained biographical material about the author that Angers insisted must be deleted. In Casgrain's slightly altered 'study', he praised the novel as an edifying portrait of Christian resignation. Recent critics, however—particularly Sister Jean de l'Immaculée (Suzanne Blais), in her doctoral thesis submitted to the Université d'Ottawa, and Roger Le Moine in two articles published in the *Revue de l'Université d'Ottawa* in 1966—have shown that *Angéline de Montbrun* is really a transposed account of Laure Conan's disappointed love for the surveyor and Member of Parliament, Pierre-Alexis Tremblay. Others have noted the incestuous overtones in Angéline's excessive devotion to her father, even after the latter's death. Recent critics have also stressed the masochism of Angéline's isolation and self-chastisement, for it is by no means certain that Maurice has ceased to love her. Thus this century-old novel has become a focal-point of contemporary Québec criticism as scholars attempt to identify and unravel the psychological, autobiographical, and psychoanalytical elements in its composition—although all are united in praising its author's elegantly sober style.

An English translation, with a useful introduction, by Yves Brunelle appeared in 1974.　　　　　DAVID M. HAYNE

Angers, Marie-Louise-Félicité (1845-1924). Québec's first woman novelist, who used the pseudonym 'Laure Conan', was born at La Malbaie (Murray Bay), Qué. The daughter of a blacksmith, she was educated there and at the Ursuline Convent in Que-

bec City. She fell in love with a surveyor and politician, Pierre-Alexis Tremblay (1827-79), and this unrequited attachment, which lasted from 1862 to 1867, seems to have affected her whole existence, leading to a rather solitary life and furnishing a theme—frustrated love and the anguish attending it—that reappears in her fiction. Thereafter, except for the years 1893 to 1898 spent at the Monastery of the Precious Blood in St Hyacinthe, she lived most of her life in semi-retirement at La Malbaie, reading voraciously, particularly in pious works, and writing articles and books as a means of earning a living. She died at the Hôtel-Dieu in Quebec City.

Félicité Angers's first published work was a novelette entitled *Un amour vrai*; it was serialized in *La Revue de Montréal* in 1878-9 and later published, with an unauthorized change of title, as *Larmes d'amour* (Montreal, 1899). Thérèse Raynol is deeply in love with a young Scottish Protestant, Francis Douglas, but vows not to marry him until he becomes a Roman Catholic. Her death is eventually the instrument of his conversion. The author here introduces both the theme (an impossible love) and the narrative technique (a combination of epistolary and diary forms) that constitute the originality of Angers's early fiction. A similar frustrated love affair, again reminiscent of her own passion for P.-A. Tremblay, forms the basis of her best-known novel ANGÉLINE DE MONTBRUN (Québec, 1884). In her next novel, *A l'oeuvre et à l'épreuve* (Québec, 1891)—translated as *The master-motive: a tale of the days of Champlain* (1909)—Angers again treated aspects of her disappointed love affair, although with greater detachment. Drawing on the historical works of François-Xavier GARNEAU and Abbé Jean-Baptiste-Antoine Ferland, and utilizing the JESUIT RELATIONS for the years 1636 to 1649, she set about reconstructing the climate of mystical heroism that characterized the missionary period of New France, modelling her hero on the Jesuit martyr, Father Charles Garnier. Instead of fulfilling his parents' hope that he will marry Gisèle Méliande, an orphan girl they have raised, Garneau is ordained priest in 1635 and sent to the Canadian mission in Huronia, to die a martyr in the Iroquois onslaught of 1649. Gisèle lives on with the Garnier parents until their death, and then enters a Carmelite convent. As Angers had little information about Garnier's life, she concentrated on the mental and emotional states of her characters.

Angers

During her residence at the Monastery of the Precious Blood, Angers was greatly influenced by her friend Mother Catherine-Aurélie Caouette, founder of the Institute of the Precious Blood, who urged her to take a more positive view of her life; her subsequent fiction was therefore less autobiographical. In *L'oublié* (1900) she returned to the heroic days of New France to recount the life of Lambert Closse, garrison sergeant-major of Ville-Marie (Montreal), who was killed by marauding Iroquois in 1662. Closse had helped rescue some French prisoners taken by the Indians; among them was a young girl, Elisabeth Moyen, who, after saving Closse's life, became his bride. Once again the novelist concerned herself with the psychological motivation of her characters and the spiritual climate of the time, rather than with the chronicle of events, which she nevertheless recounted with a respect for historical accuracy. Awarded a small prize by the French Academy in 1903, *L'oublié* was unsuccessfully adapted by its author as a five-act play entitled *Aux jours de Maisonneuve* (1920).

During the last half-dozen years of her life the elderly Félicité Angers completed three less-important works of fiction. Her short novel *L'obscure souffrance* (1919)—which incorporated an early (1883) fragment, 'A travers les ronces'—is the imaginary journal of the daughter of an alcoholic father, whom she saves by her devotion. In *La vaine foi* (1921) a worldly and indifferent woman re-examines her faith when she is courted by a Protestant. *La sève immortelle* (1925)—Angers's third historical novel, written on her deathbed—is set in 1760: a French officer, Jean Le Gardeur de Tilly, decides to stay in Canada to help build a new French-Canadian society instead of returning to France with his French fiancée. Anger's last novel thus anticipates the transition from patriotic historical fiction to the nationalistic regional novels that would be dominant in Québec until the Second World War.

In addition to her fiction, Félicité Angers published numerous patriotic or moralizing works, such as her dialogue *Si les Canadiennes le voulaient* (Québec, 1886), in which she urged women to use their influence in the family to raise the standard of public life. She also wrote more than fifty articles on religious and moral subjects for the periodical *La Voix de Précieux Sang*, which she edited from 1894 to 1898, and published a widely read biography (1903) of Mother Elizabeth Seton (1774-1821), the founder in 1809 of the American branch of the Sisters of Charity.

Félicité Angers, whose work is distinguished by its psychological depth and its elegantly sober style, is one of nineteenth-century Québec's most original writers. The modern reader will find all her fiction conveniently presented and annotated in a three-volume edition prepared by Roger Le Moine and published by Fides in the 'Collection du Nénuphar' (1974-5).

DAVID M. HAYNE

Anne of Green Gables (1908). This enduring children's classic by Lucy Maud MONTGOMERY—perhaps the best-selling book by a Canadian author—was written in 1904-5 and rejected by five firms before it was published by L.C. Page of Boston in 1908; it has never been out of print since then. Montgomery called it a 'juvenilish story, ostensibly for girls', but it has proved very popular in several media with people of all ages, who have responded to Montgomery's wry humour, her deflating of stuffiness, her affectionate descriptions of the Prince Edward Island countryside, and her remarkably loquacious heroine. It is about the quest of the orphan Anne Shirley for acceptance both by the elderly brother and sister Matthew and Marilla, who adopt her, and by her community. Convinced that her red hair is a liability, Anne is consoled by her love of nature and her friendship with Diana; her rivalry with Gilbert Blythe ends with her winning a college scholarship, which she declines after Matthew's death in order to stay on the farm at Avonlea (Cavendish) with Marilla. One of the first portraits in Canadian fiction of the artist as a young girl, Anne's transformation from ugly duckling to comely maiden leads to a compromise between the private world of her imagination and the genteel, practical world around her. Mark Twain called Anne 'the dearest, and most lovable child in fiction since the immortal Alice', while generations of women have applauded Anne's determination to succeed on her own terms in a man's world and yet retain her identity.

The first Canadian edition was issued by the RYERSON PRESS in 1943. By 1980 *Anne*, and its seven sequels, had sold millions of copies in over fifteen languages. There were two film versions (1919 and 1939) and two different dramatic versions in 1937. An adaptation by Mavor Moore, Donald Harron, and Norman Campbell became the longest-running Canadian stage musical, with annual performances since 1965 at the

Charlottetown Summer Festival, P.E.I., and successful tours across Canada and to New York, London, and Japan. The novel was adapted for television in Britain and Japan. In 1974 Anne appeared on a Canadian stamp.   GEORGE L. PARKER

Anthologies in English: Poetry. Selections and retrospective surveys of Canadian poetry have played the predominant role in establishing a literary tradition. In the nineteenth century particularly they provided showcases for authors whose work was overshadowed in the mass-market publications that featured popular British and American writers. Edward Hartley DEWART addressed this problem when he compiled the first Canadian anthology, *Selections from Canadian poets with occasional critical and biographical notes and an introductory essay on Canadian poetry* (Montreal, 1864). Dewart knew the importance of a recognizable literary tradition, stating in his introduction that 'A national literature is an essential element in the formation of a national character.' His view of poetry as 'the medium by which the emotions of beauty, joy, admiration, reverence, harmony, or tenderness kindled in the poet-soul, in communion with Nature and God, is conveyed to the souls of others' was reflected in much of the conventional poetry of nineteenth-century Canada. Dewart singled out Charles SANGSTER, followed by Alexander McLACHLAN, as the best of a group of poets that included Charles HEAVYSEGE, William KIRBY, Thomas D'Arcy McGEE, and Susanna MOODIE.

The first major post-Confederation anthology is William Douw LIGHTHALL's *Songs of the great dominion: voices from the forests and waters, the settlements and cities of Canada* (London 1889). It demonstrates the spirit and flavour of Canadian life—the athletic virility of snowshoeing and moose-hunting, the joyous traditions of barn bees and winter carnivals, the romantic heritage of warriors and voyageurs, and the awesome geography of waterfalls and buffalo plains. Presenting a new generation of poets, Lighthall recognized a renaissance characterized by a tone of 'exultation and confidence' that superseded the 'apologetic and depressed' tone of the pre-Confederation poets. Here Charles G.D. ROBERTS replaces Sangster as the foremost poet, followed by Isabella Valancy CRAWFORD. The anthologist's foresight contrasts with the conventional notion of writers labouring long without recognition: shortly after their

first or second books were published, Sangster, Roberts, and Crawford were heralded as the best in the country.

Other early anthologies range from the superficial *Canadian birthday book, with selections for every day in the year from Canadian writers in English and French* (Toronto, 1887), edited by 'Seranus' (Susie Frances HARRISON) and limited to brief extracts from poems, to the overly moralizing *Treasury of Canadian verse: with brief biographical notes* (1900) edited by Theodore Harding Rand. While *Poems of wild life* (London, 1888), edited by Charles G.D. Roberts, includes only a few Canadian poems, *A Victorian Anthology: 1837-1885* (Boston, 1885), edited by E.C. Stedman, includes a large Canadian section of 140 pages. *Later Canadian poems* (Toronto, 1893), edited by J.E. Wetherell, is devoted to the young post-Confederation poets.

Edward S. Caswell's *Canadian singers and their songs* (1902; rev. 1919, 1925) introduced each poet's selection of verse with an autographed portrait. This popular format was emulated by John Garvin with his *Canadian poets and poetry* (1916; rev. 1926). The focus on poets as public figures gave way to two opposing trends: one was led by Lawrence Burpee, who compiled specialized anthologies showcasing a subject, a genre, or an ethnic group, as in *Flowers from a Canadian garden* (1909), *Songs of French Canada* (1909), *A century of Canadian sonnets* (1910), and *Humour of the North* (1912); and the other was represented by *The Oxford book of Canadian verse* (1913), edited by Wilfred CAMPBELL. Wishing to document both the origins and directions of the Canadian literary tradition, the manager of the Oxford University Press in Canada, S.B. Gundy, called in John D. Logan to help make the anthology more comprehensive.

War anthologies were too plentiful to be considered an extension of the interest in specialized anthologies. As is suggested in an early title, *Poems and songs on the South African War: an anthology from England, Africa, Australia, United States, but chiefly Canada* (edited by J.D. Barthwick in 1901), Canadians derived a greater proportion of their identity from foreign wars than did citizens of other countries. Other war anthologies are Carrie Ellen Holman (ed.), *In the day of battle: poems of the Great War* (1916); George Herbert Clarke (ed.), *A treasury of war poetry* (1917; rev. 1919); John Garvin (ed.), *Canadian poems of the Great War* (1918); and J.E. Wetherell (ed.), *The Great War in verse and*

Anthologies in English: Poetry

prose (1919)—recommended for use in schools.

In response to the nationalist pride that followed the war, anthologists during the 1920s demonstrate the confidence that Canadian literature should be studied in schools and performed on stage. Albert Durrant Watson and Lorne PIERCE edited *Our Canadian literature: representative prose and verse* (1922; rev. 1923), while Bliss CARMAN and Lorne Pierce edited *Our Canadian literature: representative verse, English and French* (1922; rev. by V.B. Rhodenizer and retitled *Canadian poetry in English,* 1954). Other anthologies of the twenties were E.K. and Eleanor Hammond Broadus (eds.), *A book of Canadian prose and verse* (1923; rev. 1934); A.M. Stephen (ed.), *The voice of Canada: a selection of prose and verse* (1926) and *The golden treasury of Canadian verse* (1928); John Murray Gibbon (ed.), *Canadian Folksongs (old and new)* (1927; rev. 1949); and W.R. Mackenzie (ed.), *Ballads and sea songs from Nova Scotia* (1928).

The anthologies of the 1930s showcase social verse by and about farmers, miners, and sealers. Examples include *An anthology of Y.C. verse: a volume of selections from the verse contributed by the Young Co-operators and published in the Western Producer from 1932 to 1936* (1937); *Rhymes of the miner: an anthology of Canadian mining verse* (1937), edited by Eugene Louis Chicanot; and *Songs sung by old time sealers of many years ago* (1935) edited by James Murphy. But in retrospect the anthology that dominates the populist decade is the élitist NEW PROVINCES: *poems of several authors* (1936), edited by A.J.M. SMITH and F.R. SCOTT as a self-conscious manifesto for a poetry reflecting the cosmopolitan modernism of 'contemporary English and American verse'. However, the impact of this anthology was not felt until the 1940s, when anthologists grew determined to establish a central historic tradition in Canadian literature. Ralph GUSTAFSON's modest *Penguin anthology of Canadian poetry* (1942) was followed by the decade's most important anthology: *A book of Canadian poetry: a critical and historical anthology* (1943; rev. 1948, 1957), an important work of scholarship edited by A.J.M. Smith in which he polarizes Canadian poetry, placing it in either a native or cosmopolitan tradition. The drift towards a continentalist mentality was further demonstrated by John SUTHERLAND's rebellious alternative anthology *Other Canadians: an anthology of the new poetry in Canada 1940-1946* (1947). Sutherland blamed Smith's omission of several young poets on the ideological argument over which cosmopolitan writers should be imitated. Sutherland preferred such American models as Williams and Moore to the British and American expatriates Auden and Eliot, whom Smith preferred.

Several of Sutherland's young poets emerged to dominate the literary scene of the 1950s. Louis DUDEK and Irving LAYTON edited *Canadian Poems 1850-1952* (1952) and Raymond SOUSTER edited *Poets '56: the younger English Canadians* (1956). *Cerberus* (1952) was an anthology that featured the poetry of all three. But the sudden prevalence of student anthologies in the fifties demonstrates the effort to cultivate still newer and younger voices. Earle BIRNEY edited *New Voices: Canadian university writing of 1956* (1956) and Anthony Frisch edited *First flowering: a selection of prose and poetry by the youth of Canada* (1956). John Robert COLOMBO began his career as an anthologist when still a student by editing *Rubato: new poems by young Canadian poets* (1958), *Jargon, 1958/59 by students of the University of Toronto* (1959), and *The Varsity chapbook* (1959); Leslie Kaye edited its companion *The McGill chapbook* (1959). Outside the trends of the decade are *Canadian anthology* (1955; rev. 1966, 1974), a teaching anthology edited by Carl KLINCK and R.E. Watters, and *The blasted pine: an anthology of satire, invective and disrespectful verse chiefly by Canadian writers* (1957; rev. 1967), edited by F.R. Scott and A.J.M. Smith.

The expansion of the universities and the revival of national pride during the 1960s are reflected in the number of anthologies designed for advanced studies. General surveys had to be supplemented with specialized surveys of historical periods. Malcolm Ross selected poetry by Roberts, Carman, Lampman, and D.C. Scott for his *Poets of the confederation* (1960) and Milton Wilson selected poetry by PRATT, F.R. Scott, Smith, LIVESAY, and KLEIN for his *Poets between the wars* (1967) and work by ten newer poets for his *Poetry of mid-century: 1940-1960* (1964). These New Canadian Library surveys of historical periods were completed with Eli MANDEL's *Poets of contemporary Canada, 1960-1970* (1972), featuring the work of ten young poets, and David Sinclair's *Nineteenth-century narrative poems* (1972), featuring one poem each by GOLDSMITH, HOWE, Sangster, Kirby, and McLachlan. Smith's *Oxford book of Canadian verse* (1960) is entirely unlike Campbell's 1913 predecessor, not only in the fact that it presents a chronological sampling of poets writing in both English and French. Smith's *Modern Canadian verse in English and French* (1967) is a modern supplement to his *Oxford book* and provides a wider range than Louis Dudek's *Modern Canadian poetry* (1965). *Fifteen Canadian poets* (1970; rev. as *15 + 5*, 1978) is a good textbook edited by Gary GEDDES and Phyllis Bruce, who supply critical introductions to the work of each poet. Another teaching anthology, but with virtually no apparatus, is John NEWLOVE's *Canadian poetry: the modern era* (1977). A discerning and colourfully presented selection for children is *The wind has wings: poems from Canada* (1968) edited by Mary Alice Downie and Barbara Robertson and beautifully illustrated by Elizabeth Cleaver.

Regional, ethnic, and experimental anthologies have dominated the literary scene since the 1970s. The national consciousness that emerged with the 1967 Centennial celebrations inevitably led to recognition of local distinctions, preservation of racial and cultural heritage, and explorations of alternatives to the newly identified traditions. From the east coast came *Voices underground: poems from Newfoundland* (1972) edited by Harold HORWOOD; *Baffles of wind and tide: a selection of Newfoundland writers* (1974), and *The blasty bough: a selection of Newfoundland writing* (1976), both edited by Clyde Rose. Robert Cockburn and Robert GIBBS edited *Ninety seasons: modern poems from the Maritimes* (1974) and Donald Cameron edited *Voices down east: a collection of new writing from the Atlantic provinces* (1974). To represent the English writers of Montreal, David Solway edited *Four Montreal poets* (1972) and André Farkas and Ken Norris edited *Montreal English poetry of the seventies* (1977). Laurence Ricou edited *Twelve prairie poets* (1976), Ken MITCHELL selected prose and poetry for *Horizon: writings of the Canadian prairie* (1977), and Dennis Cooley presents fifty-one poets for *Draft: an anthology of prairie poetry* (1981). John W. Chalmers edited *The Alberta Diamond Jubilee anthology: a collection from Alberta's best writers* (1980), J. Michael YATES edited *Contemporary poetry of British Columbia* (1970), and Gary Geddes edited *Skookum Wawa: writings of the Canadian Northwest* (1975).

The poetry of French Canada in translation (1970) was edited by John GLASSCO who, with F.R. Scott, contributed many of the translations. Scott translated all of the eleven poets presented in his beautifully printed *Poems of French Canada* (1977). Philip Strat-

ford edited *Voices from Quebec: an anthology of translations* (1977). The most active translator is Fred COGSWELL, who edited and translated three anthologies: *One hundred poems of modern Quebec* (1971), *A second hundred poems of modern Quebec* (1971), and *The poetry of modern Quebec* (1976). To commemorate Cogswell's work as a publisher of more than 300 Fiddlehead Poetry Books, Gregory Cook edited *Scroll* (1980), featuring fifty poets whom Cogswell had published.

The responsibility for reflecting Canada's multi-cultural heritage had long been left to one man: Watson KIRKCONNELL. Among his many volumes of translations, his *Canadian overtones: an anthology of Canadian poetry written originally in Icelandic, Swedish, Hungarian, Italian, Greek, and Ukrainian* (1935) best shows his own diversity as well as Canada's. The recent proliferation of editors and translators for ethnic anthologies reflects the widespread interest in preserving our heritage. J. Michael Yates edited *Volvox: poetry from the unofficial languages of Canada in English translation* (1971); Tomi Nishimura edited *Maple: poetry by Japanese-Canadians with English translations* (1975); Harold Head edited *Canada in us now: the first anthology of Black poetry and prose in Canada* (1976); Pier Giorgio DI CICCO edited *Roman candles: an anthology of poems by seventeen Italo-Canadian poets* (1978); and Harry Loewen edited *Mennonite images* (1980). William and Christine Mowat edited *Native peoples in Canadian literature* (1975), Marilyn BOWERING and David Day edited *Many voices: an anthology of contemporary Canadian Indian poetry* (1977), and John Robert Colombo edited *Poems of the Inuit* (1981).

With the central tradition and historical periods of Canadian literature now well established, anthologists have turned their attention to the trends of the future, to the experimental approaches of the avant-garde. *New Wave Canada: the new explosion in Canadian poetry* (1966) was an influential Canadian anthology of work inspired by the American Black Mountain school, whose followers lived on the west coast. Its editor, Raymond Souster, joined Douglas LOCHHEAD to edit the optimistic *Made in Canada: new poems for the seventies* (1970). Jack LUDWIG and Andy Wainwright introduce with equal optimism fourteen writers in *Soundings: new Canadian poets* (1970). John Robert Colombo's *New directions in Canadian poetry* (1971) includes some interesting critical commentary, and Al PURDY's *Storm Warning* (1971) includes self-conscious manifestos by thirty new poets; Purdy followed this by presenting a second group of new poets in *Storm Warning 2* (1976). A mature anthology of self-confident avant-garde writers is Eldon Garnet, ed., *Where? the other Canadian poetry* (1974). bp NICHOL edited the first Canadian anthology of concrete poetry, *The cosmic chef* (1970), a box containing the work of 52 poets ranging from Earl Birney and Margaret AVISON to Nichol and bill BISSETT. The best introduction to sound poetry is Steve McCaffery's and bp Nichol's *Sound poetry: a catalogue* (1978), which includes critical introductions to the texts of performances by the participants of the International Festival of Sound Poetry held in Toronto in 1978. In other genres Michael ONDAATJE edited *The long poem anthology* (1979) featuring experimental narratives by ten poets and Robert WEAVER edited *Poems for voices* (1970), a collection of six radio verse-dramas by Al Purdy, Margaret ATWOOD, John Newlove, Phyllis GOTLIEB, Tom MARSHALL, and Alden NOWLAN. New poets of the eighties are presented by Gary GEDDES in *The inner ear: an anthology of new poets* (1982).

Dorothy Livesay's *40 women poets of Canada* (1972) is the first of several anthologies devoted to what she called the 'female ghetto'. Her concern is among the several post-Centennial issues that are evident in *The New Oxford book of Canadian verse in English* (1982) edited by Margaret Atwood. In her introduction Atwood can speak with wit of cultural nationalism, regionalism, and feminism as no-longer controversial issues in a mature country. While she apologizes for ignoring the experiments of the concrete poets, she is as concerned about future trends as she is about the roots of our past. She is loyal to the cause of preserving the traditional favourites, cautious in her predictions of success for the most promising new talents, and determined in her concern that women poets receive a fair share in representing the Canadian literary tradition.

DAVID LATHAM

Short stories. I. HISTORICAL AND HISTORIC ANTHOLOGIES. The most fundamental and common principle of arranging short-story anthologies has been the historical basis introduced by Desmond PACEY in *A book of Canadian stories* (1947) and repeated in Robert WEAVER's *Canadian short stories* (1960), Giose Rimanelli's and Roberto Ruberto's *Modern Canadian stories* (1966), Alec Lucas's *Great Canadian short stories* (1971),

and Wayne Grady's *The Penguin book of Canadian short stories* (1980). Other anthologies—from Raymond KNISTER's superbly edited *Canadian short stories* (1928), the first anthology of its kind, to John METCALF's distinguished volume *Making it new: contemporary Canadian stories* (1982)—are historical in a different sense: they reflect Canadian short-story writing over a specific period.

Raymond Knister's *Canadian short stories* marked 'the outset of a new era'. It summed up the achievements made in the short-story form during the preceding four decades, and included work by Morley CALLAGHAN, Stephen LEACOCK, Thomas Murtha, Gilbert PARKER, Charles G.D. ROBERTS, Duncan Campbell SCOTT, Edward William THOMSON, and others. Knister's introduction, selections, and extensive critical apparatus continue to be of value. The history of short fiction in Canada during the period preceding Knister's is represented in two anthologies edited half a century later: David Arnason's *Nineteenth century Canadian stories* (1976) and Carole Gerson's and Kathy Mezei's *The prose of life: sketches from Victorian Canada* (1981). The decade immediately following that of Knister's anthology is represented in Donna Phillips' *Voices of discord: Canadian short stories from the 1930s* (1979). Robert Weaver's *Canadian short stories: second series* (1968) opens with stories by Morley Callaghan and Ethel WILSON, then concentrates on works from the 1950s and 1960s by the next generation of Canadian storytellers. John Metcalf's *The narrative voice: short stories and reflections by Canadian authors* (1972) gives evidence of the growing activity in the short-story form at the beginning of the 1970s; while Metcalf's *Making it new* takes stock of Canada's premier short-story writers at the outset of the 1980s.

In the approximately forty-year period between the publication of Knister's *Canadian short stories* and the celebration of Canada's Centennial, only a few short-story anthologies appeared. The most important was *A book of Canadian stories* (1947; rev. 1950, 1952, 1962), edited by Desmond Pacey, whose selections and lengthy critical introduction provided readers with a good sense of the historical development of the short-story form in Canada. Although his approach remained substantially the same from the first edition to the last, the final edition reflected the advancements made in Canadian short-story writing during the 1950s: Pacey narrowed his selections of earlier work and added stories by thirteen writers whose reputations were currently rising, such as Ethel Wilson, Ernest BUCKLER, Henry KREISEL, Alice MUNRO, and Alden NOWLAN. He also replaced Morley Callaghan's 'Father and son' with 'The blue kimono'. Other anthologies in this period were Robert Weaver's and Helen James's *Canadian short stories* (1952); William McConnell's *Klanak islands: a collection of short stories* (1959), which included work by Henry Kreisel, Robert HARLOW, Jane RULE, William McConnell, and four other writers; Robert Weaver's *Canadian short stories* (1960), first published in Oxford's World's Classics series, and his *Ten for Wednesday night* (1961), selected from stories read on CBC Radio; and Giose Rimanelli's and Roberto Ruberto's fine *Modern Canadian stories* (1966), a rare instance of an anthology arranged according to several principles, in that it adheres to a loosely historical structure overall, shifts thematically about midway from stories with an international outlook to ones with a stronger Canadian viewpoint, and concludes by acknowledging the recent emergence of more poetic conceptions of form and style in the short story.

Starting in 1968 (the publication year of Norman LEVINE's *Canadian winter's tales*, a collection of nine stories by Malcolm LOWRY, Brian MOORE, Morley Callaghan, Hugh HOOD, Margaret LAURENCE, Mavis GALLANT, Mordecai RICHLER, Levine, and Ethel Wilson) scores of short-story anthologies began to be published—a rapid development that paralleled exciting advances in all aspects of Canadian writing and publishing. Many of these anthologies appealed to the growing audiences for Canadian learning materials in high schools, colleges, and universities, audiences that energetic editors like Robert Weaver, John Metcalf, and Rudy WIEBE strove hard to cultivate. Among the very best anthologies were Metcalf's *The narrative voice: short stories and reflections by Canadian authors* (1972), BLAISE's and Metcalf's *Here & now: best Canadian stories* (1977), and Metcalf's *Making it new: contemporary Canadian stories* (1982). Fourteen exceptional writers are represented in Blaise's and Metcalf's *Here & now: best Canadian stories*: Norman Levine, Mavis Gallant, Margaret Laurence, Hugh Hood, Jane Rule, Alice Munro, Austin CLARKE, Leon ROOKE, Audrey THOMAS, Dave GODFREY, John Metcalf, Russell Banks, Clark Blaise, and Ray SMITH. However, works by only seven of these authors (Thomas, Munro,

Laurence, Godfrey, Hood, Levine, and Blaise) appear among the 24 selections in Ivon Owen's and Morris Wolfe's *The best modern Canadian short stories* (1978), and works by only three (Munro, Gallant, and Laurence) are included among the 26 selections in John Stevens' mistitled *Best Canadian short stories* (1981).

The narrative voice and *Making it new* are examples of the 'contemporary voices' type of anthology, a category that includes two more anthologies edited by Robert Weaver, *Canadian short stories: third series* (1978) and *Small wonders* (1982). This group also includes Tony Kilgallin's textbook, *The Canadian short story* (1971), Donald Stephens' *Contemporary voices: the short story in Canada* (1972), George BOWERING's *Fiction of contemporary Canada* (1980), Terence Byrnes's *Matinées daily* (1981), and the two strikingly different series begun in 1971 by OBERON PRESS and COACH HOUSE PRESS. The first volume in the essentially conservative or modernist Oberon Press series was David HELWIG's and Tom MARSHALL's wittily entitled *Fourteen stories high: best Canadian stories of 71* (1971). Successive volumes were edited by Helwig and Joan Harcourt under the titles *72: New Canadian stories, 73: New Canadian stories*, and so forth until 1977, when John Metcalf (having replaced Helwig as co-editor of the series the preceding year) felt that Canadian short-story writing had finally reached a height at which a Canadian anthology could dare to emulate *The best American short stories*: the new series title *Best Canadian stories* was introduced (though these volumes were shorter). The 1978, 1979, and 1980 Oberon anthologies were co-edited by Metcalf and Clark Blaise; the 1981 and 1982 instalments by Metcalf and Leon Rooke. At the end of 1982, when Metcalf and Rooke resigned to edit a new annual for General Publishing, *Best Canadian stories* continued under the editorship of David Helwig, again, and Sandra Martin. The most frequently anthologized writers in the Oberon series, as of 1982, were Alice Munro, Elizabeth SPENCER, and Kent THOMPSON—five times each in twelve volumes. The essentially experimental or postmodernist Coach House Press series originated with George Bowering's anthology *The story so far* (1971) and continued under a policy of rotating editorship with volumes edited by Matt COHEN (1973), David Young (1974), Steve McCaffery and bp NICHOL (1976), and Douglas BARBOUR (1978), and a bilingual selection of

Québécois fiction chosen by Nicole BROSSARD (1979). bp Nichol's fiction appeared in all five anglophone volumes of *The story so far*; while George Bowering, Matt Cohen, Daphne MARLATT, Steve McCaffery, and David Young were represented in three volumes apiece. Relatively few writers—Margaret ATWOOD, Clark Blaise, George Bowering, Matt Cohen, Jack HODGINS, Greg Hollingshead, W.P. KINSELLA, David McFADDEN, Alden Nowlan, Stephen SCOBIE, and Kent Thompson—have been anthologized in both the Oberon and the Coach House series.

2. REGIONAL AND COTERIE ANTHOLOGIES. Although PACEY's *A book of Canadian stories* contained a sizeable representation of stories from the Atlantic provinces, the regional anthology *per se* became popular only in the 1970s, beginning with Rudy WIEBE's *Stories from western Canada* (1972), Kent THOMPSON's *Stories from Atlantic Canada* (1973), Andreas SCHROEDER's and Rudy Wiebe's *Stories from Pacific and Arctic Canada* (1974), and Germaine Warkentin's *Stories from Ontario* (1974). The most interesting of these anthologies, rhetorically and imaginatively, is Warkentin's *Stories from Ontario*, which uses Stephen LEACOCK's 'The marine excursion of the Knights of Pythias' as a prologue to sections entitled 'In the clearings', ' "Is this the way to Sunshine?" ' (a line from Alice MUNRO's story 'Walker Brothers cowboy', included elsewhere in the anthology), 'Men and women', and 'Where the myth touches us' (the title of a Hugh HOOD story in this section), and concludes with Dave GODFREY's 'Out in Chinguacousy' as an epilogue. These anthologies were followed by Rudy Wiebe's and Aritha van Herk's *More stories from western Canada* (1980), Muriel Whitaker's *Stories from the Canadian North* (1980), and more specialized anthologies of stories from the western provinces—including David Carpenter's *Wild rose country: stories from Alberta* (1977), Robert KROETSCH's *Sundogs: stories from Saskatchewan* (1980), Joan Parr's *Manitoba stories* (1981), and Ron Smith's and Stephen Guppy's *Rainshadow: stories from Vancouver Island* (1982).

Francophone writing from Québec was recognized by Philip Stratford in his anthology of translations *Stories from Québec* (1974) and by *The Oxford book of French-Canadian short stories* (1983) edited by Richard Teleky. But anglophone writing from the same province went relatively unnoticed until Douglas Daymond's and Leslie Monkman's *Stories of Quebec* (1980) and Steve Luxton's *Saturday night at the Forum* (1981). Even more localized were anthologies of stories from a specific city, such as Joan Parr's *Winnipeg stories* (1974) and Morris Wolfe's and Douglas Daymond's *Toronto short stories* (1977).

The coterie anthology was represented by Rudy Wiebe's *Getting here* (1977), a collection of seven stories by seven women; by a number of small-press books; and by anthologies of stories reprinted from single magazines—such as *Stories to read again* (1965), selected by H. Gordon Green from the *Family Herald*, and *Fiddlehead greens: stories from The Fiddlehead* (1979), selected by Roger Ploude and Michael Taylor.

3. OTHER ANTHOLOGIES. A different type of anthology—for example, Michael ONDAATJE's *Personal fictions: stories by Munro, Wiebe, Thomas, & Blaise* (1977)—included several contributions by each writer, thereby providing some sense of the range of each author chosen. Clarke, Irwin's *New Canadian writing, 1968* and *New Canadian writing, 1969* offered selections of stories by three writers in each volume: David Lewis STEIN, Clark BLAISE, and Dave GODFREY in 1968; John METCALF, D.O. Spettigue, and C.J. Newman in 1969. OBERON's *First impressions* (1980), *Second impressions* (1981), and *Third impressions* (1982), which contained Metcalf's selections from the work of nine newer writers, were also anthologies of this kind.

Certain editors have used a few of the many unique sub-genres of short fiction as a principle of selection for individual anthologies. George BOWERING's *Great Canadian sports stories* (1979) is one such volume, as are Muriel Whitaker's *Great Canadian animal stories* (1978) and her *Great Canadian adventure stories* (1979) along with John Robert COLOMBO's and Michael Richardson's *Not to be taken at night: thirteen classic tales of mystery and the supernatural* (1981) and Michael Richardson's *Maddened by mystery: a casebook of Canadian detective fiction* (1982). Like Bowering's *The story so far* and his *Fiction of contemporary Canada*, as well as Geoff Hancock's *Magic realism* (1980), such anthologies rightly emphasize fiction's creative potential rather than its mimetic character. They provide a salutary alternative to the many historical and regional anthologies that have exerted the most influence up to the present time, and they might well represent the future of short-story anthologies in Canada.

J.R. (TIM) STRUTHERS

General. Probably the most significant anthologies of Canadian literature are the general anthologies of prose and poetry that seek to define the past and/or the present of the literature as a whole. The first group of these, appearing between the wars, included Albert Durrant Watson's and Lorne PIERCE's *Our Canadian literature: representative prose & verse* (1922; 2nd ed. 1923), Edmund Kemper Broadus's and Eleanor Hammond Broadus's *A book of Canadian prose and verse* (1923; 2nd ed. 1934), A.M. Stephen's *The voice of Canada: a selection of prose and verse* (1926), William K.F. Kendrick's *Canadian stories in verse and prose* (1932; 2nd ed. 1936), and Ralph GUSTAFSON's *Canadian accent: a collection of stories and poems by contemporary writers from Canada* (1944). More comprehensive and scholarly anthologies followed, beginning with Carl F. KLINCK's and Reginald E. Watters' pioneer teaching volume *Canadian anthology*, editions of which were published in 1955, 1966, and 1974. H. Gordon Green's and Guy Sylvestre's bilingual *A century of Canadian literature/Un siècle de littérature canadienne* was published in 1967, in honour of Canada's Centennial, and was succeeded by a flurry of major anthologies during the 1970s, most of them intended for classroom use: Mordecai RICHLER's *Canadian writing today* (1970), which was dedicated to Morley CALLAGHAN; Robert WEAVER's and William Toye's *The Oxford anthology of Canadian literature* (1973; 2nd ed. 1981); a four-volume series, under the general editorship of Mary Jane Edwards, entitled *The evolution of Canadian literature in English* (1973), to which was added Paul Denham's and Mary Jane Edwards' one-volume *Canadian literature in the 70's* (1980); Desmond PACEY's *Selections from major Canadian writers: poetry and creative prose in English* (1974); Catherine M. McLay's *Canadian literature: the beginnings to the 20th century* (1974); and Douglas Daymond's and Leslie Monkman's two-volume *Literature in Canada* (1978). The 1980s produced the first comprehensively annotated anthology, Russell Brown's and Donna Bennett's two-volume *An anthology of Canadian literature in English* (1982; 1983).

The impulse of Canadians to compile anthologies is closely tied to a desire to articulate the Canadian identity, or to establish a framework within which questions about it can be intelligently discussed. This tendency has found significant expression in a number of national anthologies consisting principally—and often exclusively—of prose: Malcolm Ross's *A book of Canadian essays* (1954), William Toye's *A book of Canada* (1962), Al Purdy's *The new Romans: candid Canadian opinions of the U.S.* (1968), Andy Wainwright's *Notes for a native land: a new encounter with Canada* (1969), Alan Dawe's *Profile of a nation: Canadian themes and styles* (1969), William Kilbourn's *Canada: a guide to the peaceable kingdom* (1970) and William H. New's *Modern Canadian essays* (1976). Two interesting anthologies, which offer unique portraits of Canada's imaginative and intellectual life, grew out of periodicals: Robert Weaver's *The first five years: a selection from The Tamarack Review* (1962) and J.L. Granatstein's and Peter STEVENS' *Forum: Canadian life and letters 1920-70: selections from The Canadian Forum* (1972).

The desire to articulate a specific part of the Canadian identity—a region or an ethnic group—produced numerous anthologies. The first major regional anthologies of prose and poetry were W.G. Hardy's *The Alberta Golden Jubilee anthology* (1955), Carlyle King's *Saskatchewan harvest: a Golden Jubilee selection of song and story* (1955), Reginald E. Watters' *British Columbia: a centennial anthology* (1958), Will R. BIRD's and Alec Lucas's *Atlantic anthology* (1959), and John Patrick Gillese's *Chinook arch: a centennial anthology of Alberta writing* (1967). Subsequent examples include Peter Neary's and Patrick O'Flaherty's *By great waters: a Newfoundland and Labrador anthology* (1974); Gary GEDDES's *Skookum wawa: writings of the Canadian Northwest* (1975); Jack HODGINS' *The frontier experience* (1975) and *The west coast experience* (1976); *East of Canada: an Atlantic anthology* (1976), edited by Raymond Fraser, Clyde Rose, and Jim Stewart; Ken MITCHELL's *Horizon: writings of the Canadian prairie* (1977); Philip Stratford's and Michael Thomas's *Voices from Québec: an anthology of translations* (1977); and John W. Chalmers' *The Alberta Diamond Jubilee anthology* (1980). Notable ethnic anthologies of prose and poetry are Harold Head's *Canada in us now: the first anthology of Black poetry and prose in Canada* (1976), Robin Gedalof's *Paper stays put: a collection of Inuit writing* (1980) and Gerri Sinclair's and Morris Wolfe's *The spice box: an anthology of Jewish Canadian writing* (1981). Alternatively, anthologies may be constructed according to an individual theme, as in the delightful *Peter Gzowski's spring tonic* (1979), or an individual image, as in Peter Carver's series *Air* (1977), *Earth* (1977), *Fire* (1978), and *Water* (1978).

At their best, what these anthologies

achieve is not so much a definition of part of, or the whole of, Canadian *life* as a representation of a verbal universe: Canadian *writing*. Indeed, certain anthologists follow this premise strictly and produce works selected entirely according to literary distinctions. A.J.M. SMITH's two-volume *The book of Canadian prose* (1965; 1973) showcases a wide range of addresses, letters, essays, sketches, portions of historical or autobiographical writing, excerpts from novels, and short stories. John Robert COLOMBO's *Other Canadas: an anthology of science fiction and fantasy* (1979) celebrates individual sub-genres that encompass both prose and poetry.

The general anthologies, then, possess much the same patterns as do anthologies of poetry or short fiction. An occasional anthology, such as Robert KROETSCH's *Creation: Robert Kroetsch; James Bacque; Pierre Gravel* (1970), is formally inventive. A few anthologies, such as Morris Wolfe's *Aurora: new Canadian writing 1978, Aurora: new Canadian writing 1979*, and *Aurora: new Canadian writing 1980*, reflect the leading edges of Canadian literature. But, on the whole, general anthologies are more conservative and traditional than various highly individual and innovative anthologies of poetry or short fiction.

J.R. (TIM) STRUTHERS.

Anthologies in French. 1. THE PIONEERS. The first great anthology was James Huston's *Le Répertoire national; ou, Receuil de littérature canadienne* (4 vols, 1848-50), for which he culled newspapers and periodicals published in Québec between 1777 and 1850, with the help of fellow members of the Institut Canadien. It contains mainly poems, short stories, and the texts of lectures. Huston's total exclusion of politics makes the selection somewhat bland and unrepresentative, but it is only now being superseded as a survey of literature before 1850. The anthology acknowledges Indian culture by including a war hymn in translation. Huston's substantial preface, the first and finest of Québec's many nineteenth-century literary manifestos, briefly surveys the difficult years after the Conquest and describes the enormous disincentives to the writer in French Canada (harsh criticism, lack of outlets, the oblivion of mainly newspaper publication); but he is heartened by signs of a growing enthusiasm for literature, by the appearance of libraries, and by signs that the literature is rising above its early obsession with politics, breaking its ties with

Europe, and achieving individuality.

Mgr Camille Roy (1870-1943) founded the academic study of Canadian literature and produced as teaching tools a manual of literary history and, to accompany it, *Morceaux choisis d'auteurs canadiens* (1934). He has been criticized for his benign paternalism and for praising indiscriminately, while imposing a conservative, patriotic pattern on Canadian writing; but his anthology is a substantial and judicious selection of texts, including 215 pieces by 82 authors, with poetry and history given greatest prominence. Notable are essays by the art historian Olivier Maurault, the criticism of Marcel DUGAS, and the early prose of Alain GRAND-BOIS. The 1948 edition includes ten pages of Roy's own definition of the 'terroiriste' vocation of Canadian literature: 'L'écrivain qui n'est pas fortement enraciné au sol de son pays, ou dans son histoire . . . court risque d'être un rêveur, un joueur de flûte, ou d'être inutile à sa patrie.'

2. POETRY. Jules Fournier's *Anthologie des poètes canadiens* (1920), which appeared two years after his death, was completed and prefaced by his friend and fellow journalist Olivar Asselin (1874-1937), who shared Fournier's view that there was no such thing as a national literature—that is, works of genuine literary merit—in French Canada. Asselin placed poetry higher than the other genres in French Canada and detected a considerable progress between 1800 and 1920. An anthology of poets, not of poems, it offers as wide a cross-section of writers as possible. A third edition, in which 26 poets had disappeared and 15 new ones added to give a total of 71, appeared in 1933, with the original preface. With laudably high standards, Asselin recognized in a handful of poets 'un souci de propreté' and acknowledged that French Canada came close to having great poets in Émile NELLIGAN, Paul MORIN, René CHOPIN, and Albert LOZEAU.

For years Guy Sylvestre's *Anthologie de la poésie canadienne française* (1942) fulfilled the need for a comprehensive selection. It appeared in five subsequent editions between 1958 and 1971 and was revised yet again as *Anthologie de la poésie québécoise* in 1974. No benign paternalism here either: Sylvestre is scrupulous in his insistence on intrinsic poetic worth, and half a dozen of the countless nineteenth-century poets find favour. Sylvestre's stylish, concise introduction, based on an intimate acquaintance with Canadian and French poetry, has lost none of its value as a brief general survey that covers more than a century of writing in Québec.

John Hare shows much more indulgence than Sylvestre in his treatment of early writers in his *Anthologie de la poésie Québécoise du XIXe siècle 1790-1890* (1979). This is a fine piece of scholarship—richly annotated—in an accessible form. Hare pays an indirect tribute to James Huston, time and again culling his examples from *Le répertoire national* and giving prominence to the poets of the 1830s—notably J.-G. Barthe—who were inspired by the liberal and patriotic spirit of those troubled years. Sadly, too few of the examples quoted can claim to be poetry.

Jeanne Paul-Crouzet compiled her *Poésie au Canada* (Paris, 1946) to present Canadians to the French in the post-war period of euphoria, following the Fournier/Asselin anthology very closely. Twenty-four poets represent a century of writing in four equal periods of roughly 25 years, and the principal poets are treated to a lengthy, meticulous literary analysis in the French manner. Her strictures on imitation appear harsh, but she notes tactfully that it can create 'une divergence entre l'instinct profond et la forme poétique dans une littérature naissante.' *Tradition du Québec/The Quebec tradition* (1946) is an anthology of poetry and prose selected by the painstaking chronicler of Canadian letters Séraphin Marion; French texts are accompanied by Watson KIRKCONNELL's translations.

A number of short anthologies prepared by poets have attempted the hazardous task of choosing the best from a year's production. Eli MANDEL and Jean-Guy PILON compiled *Poetry 62/Poésie 62* (1961) and Jacques GODBOUT and John Robert COLOMBO *Poetry 64/Poésie 64* (1964). Pilon offered to students— both as a textbook and a source of words and images—his *Poèmes 70* (1970), an attractive collection of verse (in French only) by thirty-three poets, selected from works published in 1969; it was followed by *Poèmes 71* (1972). This worthwhile tradition has been taken up more economically by journals—*La Nouvelle Barre du jour*, for example, publishing *Poésie 1980* (Issue 92-93) and *Poésie 1981* (Issue 100-101).

Like Pilon, Guy ROBERT saw his *Littérature du Québec: poésie actuelle* (1970), an augmented edition of a 1964 publication, as an inspiration to the young creative writers of the CEGEP generation, inviting them to draw from it breath for their demonstrations and meaning for their action. Robert's choice of poets is safe but astute. More than just an anthology, this book contains valuable comments by poets on their work and methods, particularly impressive being Paul CHAMBERLAND's powerful essays and an interview Robert acquired from Alain GRANDBOIS.

The most enjoyable anthologies of verse to handle and to use are A.J.M. SMITH's *Oxford book of Canadian verse: in English and French* (1960) and the equally attractive *Modern Canadian verse: in English and French* (1967), covering the previous forty years. Smith's experience as a teacher, his taste and accumulated wisdom as a critic, and his poet's flair make these two books richly authoritative. Jacques Cotnam's inexpensive, uncluttered *Poètes du Québec* (1969) offers a balanced and representative sample and does not put a foot wrong. Latest in this field of anthologies of poetry is that of Laurent Mailhot and Pierre Nepveu, discussed below in section seven.

3. DOCUMENTARY HISTORY. As well as serving to establish the literary corpus, anthologies are frequently used to give a community a sense of their roots. The pioneers in this field—Michel Brunet, Guy Frégault, and Marcel Trudel—published their two-volume *Histoire du Canada par les textes* (1963), which has done valuable service and has not been superseded. The selections are long and carefully chosen, each is prefaced by a lengthy historical comment, and sources and bibliographical notes together with the index make this work a mine of indispensable and reliable material. 'Classiques canadiens' includes a short volume entitled *Éloquence indienne* (1968). The books in this series—a kind of anthology in itself—make available, for the period of the French régime, selected texts by Cartier, Biard, Champlain, Lescarbot, Sagard, Brébeuf, Le Jeune, MARIE DE L'INCARNATION, Marguerite Bourgeoys, Talon, Frontenac, Charlevoix, and Elisabeth Bégon, whose names provide the titles for their respective volumes. (See also Writing in NEW FRANCE.) Cameron Nish's *Le Régime français 1534-1760* (1966) offers Canadians of all origins the opportunity to discover in the texts of the Jesuit missionaries and other founders of New France a common heritage. A somewhat similar volume, *La nouvelle France* (1976), was edited by a team led by Michel Allard. Both these anthologies—drawing on letter reports and official textes, and including many extracts that are rather brief—give a picture largely of public life; they fail to convey a sense of the day-to-day life of the population. *La civilisation de la Nouvelle-*

France d'après les témoins (1963) of Claude Francis and Sibylle Sinval, comprising first-hand accounts of the mission to New France, again from obvious sources, frequently distorts the texts by selecting passages that stress excessively the role played by the Church in founding New France; but it is attractively presented. Ostensibly just another anthology of historical documents, *Québec: hier et aujourd'hui* (1967), prepared by a McGill University team led by Laurier LaPierre, provides valuable materials for an intellectual history of Québec. Its three sections—each containing an introduction, bibliography, and questions for further study—cover intellectual and artistic life (32 authors), social and economic activity (28 authors), and politics (18 authors). This valuable collection is further enhanced with illustrations and a glossary. André Renaud's *Recueil de textes littéraires canadiens-français* (1968)—a companion volume to Roger Duhamel's *Manuel de littérature canadienne-française* (1967)—begins to have a dated appearance, but the section on nineteenth-century essayists is still most original and exciting. The second section, 'Une naissance laborieuse' (1840-1900), has extracts from Arthur Buies, Hector Fabre, Oscar Dunn, and the collector of short stories, Faucher de Saint-Maurice. Eighty-seven authors represent a century and a half of writing in this useful teaching text. Centennial year also saw the publication of an anthology of journalism, *Un siècle de reportage*, and Jacques Hébert's *Ah! mes aïeux! chronique de la vie sociale et politique des Canadiens français de 1867, tirée des journaux de l'époque*. Reine Malouin's *La poésie il y a cent ans* appeared in 1968. The voluminous and very diverse anthology of Gérard Boismenu, Laurent Mailhot, and Jacques Rouillard, *Le Québec en textes* (1980), subtitled a 'tour d'horizon de la réalité québécoise de 1940 à 1980', has space for extensive quotations from texts and the valuable advantage of drawing where possible on periodical and journalistic sources.

4. OTHER SPECIALIST ANTHOLOGIES. Adrien Thério's *L'humour au Canada français* (1968) shows some decidedly dubious examples (pastiches of Canadian authors, for example, a genre now totally out of fashion) but succeeds better with selections that draw on the resources of the music-hall and popular entertainment. Laurent Mailhot and Doris-Michel Montpetit co-edited an exceptionally valuable anthology, *Monologues québécois, 1890-1980* (1980), which brings belated recognition to many raconteurs who have delighted audiences in this mode of entertainment characteristic of Québec's oral and family culture. The difficulties of producing such an anthology led to the regretted omission of poets such as Claude GAUVREAU, Claude PÉLOQUIN and Raoul DUGUAY—showmen principally remembered for the public performance of their work, in what Péloquin used to call 'shows de la parole'—but this book illustrates nearly a century of Québec popular theatre, cabaret and music-hall, supplying valuable visual and biographical documentation. The texts constitute a priceless record of the evolution of the spoken language in Québec, allowing us to relive the profound shared emotion of theatre or music-hall when packed houses fell under the spell of Les Cyniques, Gratien GÉLINAS, Raymond Lévesque, Yvon Deschamps, Clémence Desrochers, and Marc Favreau ('Sol').

Gilles MARCOTTE's *Présence de la critique* (1966) serves both as a panorama of Québec criticism and as a very useful collection of literary essays and book reviews. Arranged chronologically by critic, with several examples from each, running from René Garneau to André BROCHU, it contains particularly valuable essays by René Garneau, Jean LE MOYNE, Jeanne Lapointe, a brief and incisive statement on Pierre Baillargeon from Maurice Blain, and the impressive early writing of Brochu. Four essays by Pierre de Grandpré are included, but a fuller selection from this fine critic is available in his own *Dix ans de vie littéraire au Canada français* (1966). Breaking new ground were Etienne-F. Duval's *Anthologie thématique du théâtre québécois au XIXe siècle* (1978), reflecting faithfully the nationalist and moralist aims of nineteenth-century Québec writing and of interest to the social historian as well as the student of literature; Guildo Rousseau's illuminating anthology of prefaces to novels, *Préfaces des romans québécois du XIXe siècle* (1970), witnessing to the artistic diffidence of almost all the novelists of the period; and Daniel Latouche and Diane Poliquin-Bourassa, *La manuel de la parole: manifestes québécois, t.1: 1760-1890* (1977), an indispensable guide to the growing national and political self-awareness and self-articulation of French Canada expressed in political, social, and literary manifestos. This last compilation should be read alongside a special number of *Études françaises* (16/3-4, 1980) that covers the whole development of a peculiarly Québécois form of pamphleteering. In addition to the Duval, Québec theatre has also been anthologized in Jan Doat's *Anthologie du théâtre québécois, 1606-1970* (1973), a collection of scenes from (mostly) contemporary plays (1945-70). Victor-Lévy BEAULIEU performed a curious but valuable service in recuperating many specimens of the ephemeral and often disturbingly unwholesome writing of the last century in his *Manuel de la petite littérature du Québec* (1974), which contains samples of temperance tracts, biographies of 'enfants martyrs', parish histories, and pulp literature and novelettes in which, he says, is to be found 'une imagerie fondamentale, un inconscient collectif qui cherchait à se libérer'. *Le Choc des langues au Québec, 1760-1970* (1972) compiled by G. Bouthillier and J. Meynaud, is a source-book, anthology, and crusading pamphlet; an introduction and chronology are followed by 700 dense pages culled from the record of two hundred years of impassioned debate on the French language in Québec. The sources are varied—speeches, parliamentary debates, travellers' journals—but much of the material is drawn from the press.

One-author anthologies are Gérard BESSETTE's *Albert Laberge* (1963); Adrien Thério's judicious selections from the work of Bishop Bourget in *Ignace Bourget, écrivain* (1975); and Laurent Mailhot's *Anthologie d'Arthur Buies* (1978), which follows a special number of *Études françaises* (VI, 3, 1970), presented by G.-A. Vachon, that contains a considerable biographical and critical apparatus on Buies (1840-1901), along with a selection from his writings. Mailhot includes copious extracts from Buies's journals; his social, historical, and political comment; his fascinating travel writing, particularly on the Saguenay and the Lower St Lawrence; and ends with an ingenious dictionary of observations and aphorisms. Buies dazzles by his boldness, wit, and intelligence, and gives us the first real and early apprehension of the vast strangeness of North America. This is anthologizing at its best.

The French presence outside Québec is only just beginning to receive attention in anthologies. Roger Motut produced in *Racines* (1979), a volume in the Alberta Heritage collection, an anthology of French writing on western Canada, much of it by immigrants or travellers, including Georges BUGNET, Marie LE FRANC and Maurice CONSTANTIN-WEYER. (See FOREIGN WRITERS ON CANADA IN FRENCH.) *Anthologie de textes littéraires acadiens, 1606-1975* appeared in Moncton in 1979. (See ACADIAN LITERA-

TURE.) Gaétan Vallières presents in *L'Ontario français par les documents* (1980) 250 texts—a good example of the valiant work being done on French Ontario at the Université d'Ottawa.

5. TRANSLATIONS. John Robert COLOMBO has followed his and Jacques GODBOUT's anthology of 1964 with *How do I love thee: sixty poets of Canada (and Quebec) select and introduce their own work* (1970), ten of the poets represented being French-Canadian. John GLASSCO's *The poetry of French Canada in translation* (1970), 47 poets translated by several hands, goes back even to pre-Conquest times. One must take issue with Glassco's contention, stated in his introduction, that Québec poets 'seem too often preoccupied by political and national ideas', as the reverse is, surprisingly, the case; but he is on safer ground when he deplores the effects of 'the dead hand of surrealism'. Fred COGSWELL continues to enhance his reputation as a translator with *One hundred poems of modern Quebec* (1970) and a second hundred in 1971. But the most outstanding endeavour in the translation of Canadian poetry remains the bilingual quarterly *Ellipse* (1969-). Short fiction and some non-fiction in translation from the French appear in the anthologies of William Kilbourn, Robert WEAVER, Mordecai RICHLER, and Wayne Grady described in ANTHOLOGIES IN ENGLISH. The most enjoyable of these is certainly William Kilbourn's *Canada: a guide to the peaceable kingdom* (1970), which contains a selection of some of the finest writing on Canada, including Kilbourn's own perceptive introduction on the 'alternative to insanity' Canada offers. The Québec writers represented are Pierre Trudeau, Pierre Trottier, Anne HÉBERT, Jean LE MOYNE, Claude Ryan, René Lévesque, Fernand DUMONT, André Laurendeau, and Jean ÉTHIER-BLAIS in a sensitive and moving personal portrait of Paul-Émile Borduas. A new historical anthology of short stories is *The Oxford book of French-Canadian short stories* (1983) edited by Richard Teleky.

6. SPREADING THE WORD. Anthologies produced outside Québec are growing proof of the wide interest in Canadian writing. Some of the anthologies already referred to fall into this category—those of Jeanne Paul-Crozet, A.J.M. SMITH, and Roger Motut. Laure Rièse published her *L'âme de la poésie canadienne-française* in Toronto in 1955. Gérard Tougas edited an attractive *Littérature canadienne-française contemporaine* (1969), giving separate sections to the novel, po-

etry, essays, and theatre; the 28 authors covered are represented by short but meaningful selections, each carefully and helpfully annotated. Alain Bosquet's *La poésie canadienne* (Paris, 1962) reappeared as *Poésie du Québec* (1968). The compiler has been criticized for his rather fulsome introduction, but his poet's flair in assembling the collection is undeniable. Serge Brindeau's ambitious compendium *Poésie contemporaine de langue française depuis 1945* (Paris, 1973), covering French poetry from Montreal to Beirut, from Martinique to Madagascar, gives nearly 100 pages and one of its five sections to Québec poetry, surveyed by Jacques Rancourt. He wisely chooses to give considerable space to a few poets—GAUVREAU, BROSSARD, PÉLOQUIN, DUGUAY, MIRON, GIGUÈRE, PILON, MORENCY, PARADIS, and OUELLETTE—and emphasizes vigorous prophetic utterance and neo-symbolist lyricism rather than arcane experiment. Other French anthologies are the *Littérature de langue française hors de France* (Paris, 1976), prepared by the Fédération internationale de professeurs de français, again covering the whole of the francophone world in what it calls an 'anthologie didactique'. A special number of *Les Lettres nouvelles* (Dec. 1966-Jan. 1967) presented Canadian writers of the sixties to the French public, 22 of the 30 authors included being French-Canadian, and the review *Europe* (1969) followed a survey of the arts in Québec with an anthology of recent prose and verse. Auguste Viatte, doyen of French studies, has followed his *Histoire littéraire de l'Amérique française* (Paris, 1954), and the best available general survey of the history and present extent of the influence of French language and culture in the world, *La francophonie* (Paris, 1969), with an *Anthologie littéraire de l'Amérique francophone* (1971). Eighty-seven Québécois authors, half of them poets, occupy half the book, the rest being given to writers from Louisiana and the Caribbean. The cut-off date of 1960, however, excludes the brilliant literary explosion that followed, so that theatre, the latecomer, is understandably the poor relation, represented only by Paul Toupin and Jacques LANGUIRAND. Ambitiously attempting 'un échantillonnage complet', this book is marked by scrupulous scholarship, but it reflects the natural preference of a foreign anthologist for local colour and the exciting theme of survival. An anthology compiled by Michel Le Bel and Jean-Marcel Paquette, *Le Québec par ses textes littéraires,*

1534-1976 (1979), is a Franco-Québécois production aimed particularly at a French readership—an attractive book, with photographs and some striking pen-and-ink sketches. The socio-historical approach is stressed, and historical documents and brief explanations culled from sociologists complement the literary selections. The weakness lies in the extreme brevity of the texts: lifted out of context, a 350-word passage from AQUIN's difficult and daring PROCHAIN ÉPISODE ceases to be part of a web of multiple reference and becomes a crude political statement. On the other hand, this anthology is the first to do justice to Québec's oral culture by including extracts from 11 dramatists and 14 singers and monologuists. In addition to anthologies in English translation, the following have appeared for other language groups: N.I. Vannilova, *Littérature canadienne de langue française, 1945-1965* (Moscow, 1969); Constantin Bida, *Poésie du Québec contemporain* (1968), a bilingual Ukrainian edition; Wolfram Burghardt, *Poésie/Québec, de Saint-Denys Garneau à nos jours* (1972), another bilingual French/Ukrainian collection; Eva Kushner, *Oda a szent löring folyóhoz Québec mai francia kilteszete* (Budapest, 1978) in Hungarian; and a collection of Québec short stories, *Storïau Québec*, has recently been prepared in Welsh by Paul Birt and is ready for publication.

7. THE CULMINATION OF THE ART. Alongside the best of the anthologies discussed here must be set two recent anthologies that represent the culmination of a long process of selection and reflection: a four-volume set from Gilles MARCOTTE and his team and a one-volume poetry anthology, again a collective venture, directed by the experienced anthologist Laurent Mailhot and the poet Pierre Nepveu. Marcotte's *Anthologie de la littérature québécoise* comes in four periods, each entrusted to a specialist or pair of specialists: Léopold Leblanc, *Écrits de la nouvelle France, 1534-1760* (1978); René Dionne, *La Patrie littéraire, 1760-1895* (1978); Gilles Marcotte and François Hébert, *Vaisseau d'or et croix du chemin, 1895-1935* (1979); and René Dionne and Gabrielle Poulin, *L'Âge de l'interrogation, 1937-1952* (1980). This priceless library fulfils all the functions of the anthology—didactic, celebratory, publicist, and evaluative. Over the whole reigns the benign presence of Marcotte, an urbane, gentle critic, at ease in his vast acquaintance with the literature of his people. His general introduction in the first volume

Aquin

is superb. The anthology starts with no pre-conceptions, adopts a liberal definition of literary writing, and avoids exclusive principles, though the first volume classifies texts under exploration, mission, description, and civilization. No genre is left out; sermon, poem, history, travel tale, literary criticism, novel, political speech, private diary, letters—all are here. Erudition and annotation, though not skimped, have been kept to a strict minimum: 'place aux textes' sums up the anthologists' policy. Generally the team deserves our gratitude for providing an anthology that, if it could be brought up to the present day, would not be superseded for years to come. The reader's enthusiasm is even more compellingly aroused by *La poésie québécoise des origines à nos jours* (1980) edited by Laurent Mailhot and Pierre Nepveu. Over 170 poets are featured and almost all are represented by their portraits—some by an illustration that evokes their imaginative world or by a reproduction of the title page of one of their books. There is an extensive bibliography, an authoritative and well-focused preface, and an uncluttered presentation of the texts on the page. The poets given the most space, in descending order, are P.-M. LAPOINTE, MIRON, Saint-Denys GARNEAU, NELLIGAN, BRAULT, CHAMBERLAND, HÉBERT, GIGUÈRE, GRAND-BOIS, LASNIER, GAUVREAU, OUELLETTE, HÉNAULT, LOZEAU, and BROSSARD; but it is refreshing to see two poets of the turn-of-the-century among them, and one poet representing the 1970s; the emphasis here is clearly on the automatistes—Lapointe, Miron, Giguère, Gauvreau, and Hénault in particular—but the selection is not otherwise tendentious. The compilers have made bold decisions about contemporary poets: almost the last third of all the texts are from poets still alive and active, and generous space is given to poets such as Roger des Roches, Nicole Brossard, and François CHARRON. If the prize goes to this anthology over all others, it is not because poetry ultimately anthologizes best of all the genres but because it is in its poetry that Québec has been most original and audacious, most truly itself; has come nearest to breaking the solitude that masks its authentic self and keeps it from us; and has found the voice that most faithfully articulates the song and the story of a people and a land. C.R.P. MAY

Short stories. Despite the large number of stories published in periodicals, there are relatively few anthologies of French-Canadian stories. The first is James Huston's *Légendes canadiennes* (Paris, 1853). This was followed by Abbé H.-R. CASGRAIN's popular manual of the same title (Québec, 1861) and at the turn of the century by Honoré BEAUGRAND's *La Chasse-galerie. Légendes canadiennes* (1900) and E.-Z. Massicotte's *Conteurs canadiens-français du XIXe siècle* (1902). More recent collections focusing on nineteenth-century material include Guy Boulizon's *Contes et récits d'autrefois* (1961) and John Hare's *Contes et nouvelles du Canada français, 1778-1859* (1971). Anthologies of more recent work are even rarer. Adrien Thério's *Conteurs canadiens-français* (1965, rev. 1970) includes work by 28 writers and in Gérard BESSETTE's *De Québec à Saint-Boniface* (1968) 16 authors are represented—the majority of them contemporaries. The issues of ÉCRITS DU CANADA FRANÇAIS (1954-) also provide a wealth of short stories. PHILIP STRATFORD

Appel de la race, L'. See Lionel-Adolphe GROULX.

Aquin, Hubert (1929-77). Born in Montreal's east end, near Parc Lafontaine, he did his pre-university studies at l'École Olier (the same elementary school attended by Émile NELLIGAN), l'Externat Saint-Croix, and Collège Sainte-Marie. In 1951 he completed a licentiate in philosophy at the Université de Montréal. After three years' study at the Institut d'Études politiques in Paris (1951-4), he returned to Montreal, where he worked as a producer at Radio-Canada (1955-9) and spent four years as a scriptwriter and film director for the National Film Board (1959-63). In 1960, while working as a stock-broker at the Montreal Stock Exchange, he joined the Rassemblement pour l'Indépendance nationale, in which he held executive positions from 1963 to 1968. In 1964 he disappeared for a time from public view, after stating in a press release that he was joining an underground terrorist movement; he was arrested in July 1964 while in possession of a stolen car and an automatic pistol and transferred from Montreal Prison to the Albert Prevost psychiatric institute, where he spent four months awaiting trial for illegal possession of a firearm. During this period he wrote his first and most famous novel, PROCHAIN ÉPISODE (1965). Acquitted in Dec. 1965, Aquin had become a literary sensation, described by establishment literary critic Jean-Éthier Blais

Aquin

as the 'great writer' Québec had been waiting for throughout its history.

The years following were characterized by a series of dramatic incidents that indicated Aquin's inability to compromise with any established structure, professional or political. In 1966 he was expelled from Switzerland, by his own account because of RCMP influence on the Swiss government. In 1968 he publicly broke with the RIN when it merged with René Lévesque's Mouvement Souveraineté-Association to form the Parti québécois, describing the merger as 'suicidal' for the Québec independence movement. In 1969 he became the first Québec writer to refuse the Governor General's Award (offered to him for *Trou de mémoire*) on political grounds. In 1971 he left the editorial board of LIBERTÉ magazine, accusing his co-directors of dependence on Canada Council support and of consequent silence in the face of the federal government's role in the 1970 October Crisis. In 1972 he was awarded the Prix David. In 1976, after eighteen months as literary director of *Éditions La Presse*, he resigned publicly, accusing the editor and director of *La Presse*, Roger LE-MELIN, of 'colonizing Québec from within'. His suicide on 15 Mar. 1977 was accompanied by a message to the public stating that his death was a free and positive choice: 'I have lived intensely, and now it is over.' He had consciously made his life a publicly acted-out myth that was meant to be seen as an incarnation of modern Québec's contradictions.

It is of course Aquin's writings—political articles and essays, television plays and films, as well as the novels—that account for his importance; and his inability to write after 1974 appears to be the only valid explanation of his suicide. Yet Aquin was constantly wary of being trapped as an artist in a role that would be a mere compensation for the economic and political power that he claimed history had denied him as a Québécois. The three novels he published after *Prochain épisode—Trou de mémoire* (1968), *L'antiphonaire* (1969; *The antiphonary*, 1973), and *Neige noire* (1974)—were attempts to make the novel into a 'total' artform, based on a process of co-creation shared by author and reader, that would integrate not only all the arts but the cognitive processes of modern science and the mythic and ritual dimensions of religious experience. The literary influences he most often mentioned were Joyce's *Ulysses* and the work of Vladimir Nabokov, as well as the detective novels he loved, whose 'whodunit' form suggests the often sadistic and teasing relationship his novels establish with the reader.

In *Trou de mémoire*, translated by Alan Brown as *Blackout* (1974), the main character is a revolutionary pharmacist-writer who, after murdering his English-Canadian lover, writes in a vain attempt to fill with words the absence created by her death—an absence that becomes a metaphor for Québec's tormented historical silence and its ambivalent relationship with English Canada. A series of doubles, mirror images, and contradictory narrative viewpoints develop an analogy between Québec and the colonized nations of the Third World. The other side of a historical 'rape' that goes back to the Conquest is shown as a need for violence that will seemingly explode the Québec male into manhood. The novel itself is presented as a historical 'event', a revolutionary and blasphemous act that will destroy the old order and permit the birth of a culture.

In *L'antiphonaire*, translated by Alan Brown as *The antiphonary* (1973), Aquin moved away from Québec history and politics to a broader canvas. The novel traces the decline of Christine Forestier, a medical student married to an epileptic, who attempts unsuccessfully to complete her thesis on sixteenth-century medicine and to take control of her life. It is constructed as an exchange of voices that establishes a contrapuntal relationship between twentieth-century Montreal and San Francisco and Europe in the sixteenth century, which is seen as the period of schism between religion and rationalism, science and culture; its central metaphor is an epileptic crisis. Christine's early identification with Paracelsus, whom she sees as a symbol of unity, gives way to a series of images in which the rape and violence in her own life reveal her as the double not of Paracelsus but of a fictional sixteenth-century victim of rape and violence. Her suicide, an escape into mystical passivity, appears now—like the suicides of the male protagonists of *Trou de mémoire*—as a literary foreshadowing of Aquin's own death.

In 1971 Aquin published *Point de fuite*, a collection of essays and letters preceded by a foreword in which he describes himself as isolated, aging, and out of tune with the new generation of Québec students and intellectuals. In 1974, however, he published *Neige noire* (translated by Sheila Fischman as *Hamlet's twin*, 1979), perhaps his greatest novel. An 'unfinishable' film scenario, and a modern reply to *Hamlet*, it attempts to integrate the temporal and the sacred in a philosophical meditation on time that counterpoints a violent and erotic detective-type plot. *Neige noire* is Aquin's final statement, his ultimate attempt to create the 'total novel': Aquin sees as the particular domain of literature an integration of the visual potency of film, the mobility of musical structure, and a mythical evocation. The novel was described by Joseph Bonenfant in *Lettres québécoises* (1974) as 'the most beautiful novel in our literature . . . a despairing book that makes one think of what the last book in human history might be like.'

Following *Neige noire*, Aquin intermittently worked on a novel with the working title *Obombre*, of which the very brief manuscript or outline appeared in *Liberté* (May-June 1981) and whose epigraph, taken from Schelling, reads: 'The beginning only appears as the beginning at the end.' In Mar. 1977 he took a pistol left to him in his father's will the preceding year, placed it to his temple, and shot himself.

Aquin's suicide, the final public gesture of a life always consciously linked with Québec's history, was, not surprisingly, experienced as a traumatic collective event. It has been followed by a number of works that attempt to 'demythify' Aquin—notably Jacques GODBOUT's NFB film *Deux épisodes dans la vie d'Hubert Aquin* and René Lapierre's literary study *L'imaginaire captif: Hubert Aquin*.

See Françoise Iqbal, *Hubert Aquin romancier* (1978); René Lapierre, *L'imaginaire captif: Hubert Aquin* (1981); and Patricia Smart, *Hubert Aquin agent double* (1973).

See also ESSAYS IN FRENCH: 7, and NOVELS IN FRENCH 1960 TO 1982:2.

PATRICIA SMART

Arcadian adventures with the idle rich (1914). Along with SUNSHINE SKETCHES OF A LITTLE TOWN, *Arcadian adventures* is one of Stephen LEACOCK's best and most popular books. It was published two years after *Sunshine sketches*, and, as numerous parallels between the two books in overall structure and detail indicate, it was intended as a companion-piece. It portrays the full flowering in a large American city (based in fact on Montreal) of the seeds of corrupt materialism already detected in smalltown Mariposa. In its bitter satire of the 'conspicuous consumption' of the 'idle rich', it shows the influence of *Theory of the leisure class* by Thorstein Veblen, Leacock's teacher at the University of Chicago. Unlike *Sunshine sketches, Arcadian adventures* shows sympathy not for those it satirizes but only for their hapless victims. There are few memorable characters; the inhabitants of Plutoria Street are presented primarily as hypocritical and dangerous embodiments of corrupt institutions or forces, such as the church, politics, finance, education. However, what the book lacks in charm and affection it makes up for in intensity; as it proceeds it becomes progressively darker until in its final chapter, 'The Great Fight', there is a foreshadowing of the tyranny and violence that were to grip the world in the twenties and thirties. It has been reprinted in the New Canadian Library (1969).

ZAILIG POLLOCK

As for me and my house (1941). This first novel by Sinclair ROSS, a classic of Canadian literature, is the story of Philip Bentley, a clergyman whose ministry brings him, with his wife, to a small town in Saskatchewan during the Depression. Narrated in diary form by Mrs Bentley, the novel portrays Philip as an ineffectual minister and frustrated artist whose term in Horizon represents his last chance to salvage the vocation for which he may never have been suited. Much of its tension arises from the ambiguity in the voice of Mrs Bentley. A woman who once dreamed of being a concert musician herself, and a wife temperamentally unsuited to the supportive public role required by Philip's work, she can easily be suspected of exaggerating Philip's artistic talent and drive, and his disaffection for the ministry, in order to rationalize and facilitate their permanent departure from the small-town life she finds so suffocating. Yet there is an authenticity and poignancy in her portrayal of Philip as an artist struggling against the stultifying conformity of the ironically named Horizon.

The novel is rich in both psychological subtlety and realistic detail. The wind, dust, meagre harvests, and the sense of profound physical isolation and spiritual aridity underscore the spiritual concerns at the heart of the novel. It explores concentric circles of isolation: just as Horizon sits alone on an empty expanse of prairie, the transient Bentley household is isolated from the rest of the town, and the Bentleys' marriage has disintegrated into two small circles of painful isolation, so that an abiding sense of alienation, symbolized by the diary form itself, pervades the novel—which is fundamentally a powerful and moving commentary on the

As for me and my house

human condition. *As for me and my house* was reissued in 1957 in the New Canadian Library, with an introduction by Roy DANIELLS.   MARILYN ROSE

Asselin, Olivar. See ANTHOLOGIES IN FRENCH: 2.

Assikinack, Francis. See INDIAN LITERATURE: 2.

'At the Mermaid Inn'. This column—conducted by the poets William Wilfred CAMPBELL, Archibald LAMPMAN, and Duncan Campbell SCOTT—appeared in the Toronto *Globe* every Saturday (with one exception) from 6 Feb. 1892 to 1 July 1893 and dealt with such wide-ranging concerns as literature, painting, history, politics, and religion. Each contributor was paid three dollars a week. The column argued vigorously for the promotion of Canadian literature: Campbell points to the need for an association of Canadian authors; Lampman calls for the establishment of 'a really good literary magazine'; Lampman and Scott bemoan the high tax on books and call for its removal; and Scott suggests the promotion of Canadian literature at the Chicago Exhibition of 1893. 'At the Mermaid Inn' also served as a forum for the development of the aesthetic values that were implicit in its contributors' poetry. Campbell, whose work approaches the decadent in 'How one winter came in the lake region' and 'The were-wolves', discusses the 'beauties and vastness of glory in the darkness.' Lampman, who had received considerable critical praise for such sonnets as 'The largest life' and 'The modern politician', writes extensively about the sonnet form. Scott, who explored Christian themes in 'The forsaken' and 'On the way to the mission', demands that poetry serve a moral purpose and calls nature 'a setting for man's life.'

The column was the object of controversy on 27 Feb. 1892 when Campbell observed that 'much of the earlier part of the Old Testament, such as the stories of Jonah, have all been proved to belong to the class of literature called mythic. The story of the cross itself is one of the most remarkable myths in the history of humanity . . .' The sensibilities of the *Globe*'s readers were offended by these observations and the following Monday the paper was obliged 'to condemn and repudiate' the poet's views and 'to express regret that the columns of the *Globe* should have been used to circulate them.'

Selections from the column, edited by Arthur S. BOURINOT, appear in *At the Mermaid Inn, conducted by A. Lampman, W.W. Campbell, and Duncan C. Scott* (1958). The entire run of the column has been reprinted, with an introduction by Barrie Davies, in *At the Mermaid Inn: Wilfred Campbell, Archibald Lampman, Duncan Campbell Scott in the Globe 1892-3* (1979).   GEORGE WICKEN

Atwood, Margaret (b. 1939). Margaret Eleanor Atwood was born in Ottawa and moved with her family to Sault Ste Marie in 1945 and to Toronto a year later. The daughter of an entomologist who specialized in forest insects, she came to know intimately the bush country of northern Ontario and Québec. She graduated from Victoria College, University of Toronto, in 1961 and received an A.M. degree from Radcliffe College, Harvard, in 1962. She has taught English in a number of Canadian universities; worked as an editor for the House of ANANSI, and was a member of the board, in the early seventies; and was president of the WRITERS' UNION OF CANADA in 1982-3. She was writer-in-residence at the University of Toronto in 1972-3. In 1961 she published a slim volume of poems, *Double Persephone*, and since 1966 has published steadily: her books include nine poetry collections, five novels, a collection of short stories and one of 'short fictions and prose poems', two works of criticism, an anthology, and two children's books. She has received the Governor General's Award (for *The circle game*, 1966), the Union Poetry Prize (*Poetry*, Chicago, 1969), the Bess Hopkins Prize (1974), the Molson Prize and a Guggenheim Fellowship Award (both in 1981), and honorary degrees from Trent (1973), Queen's (1974), and Concordia (1979) Universities, and from Smith College (1982). A writer of international prominence, she is almost as well known in the U.S., Europe, and Australia as she is in Canada.

Atwood's books are (POETRY) *The circle game* (1966), *The animals in that country* (1968), *The journals of Susanna Moodie* (1970), *Procedures for underground* (1970), *Power politics* (1973), *You are happy* (1974), *Selected poems* (1976), *Two-headed poems* (1978), *True stories* (1981); (NOVELS) *The edible woman* (1969), *Surfacing* (1972; rpr. 1983), *Lady oracle* (1976), *Life before man* (1979), *Bodily harm* (1981); (STORIES) *Dancing girls* (1977), *Murder in the dark* (1983); (CRITICISM) *Survival: a thematic guide to Canadian literature* (1972), *Second words: selected critical prose*

(1982); (HISTORY) *Days of the rebels: 1815-1840* (1977); (CHILDREN'S BOOKS) *Up in the tree* (1978) and *Anna's pet* (with Joyce Barkhouse, 1980). She is the editor of *The new Oxford book of Canadian verse in English* (1982).

In all her writing Atwood has demonstrated remarkable intellectual control of her material. Each book has a thematic unity and explores the central preoccupation of her work: the role of mythology, both personal and cultural, in the individual life. Like Northrop FRYE, whose influence on Atwood has been significant, she perceives the conventions that lie behind everyday reality—the mythological substructure of modern culture—with great acuity.

In her poetry Atwood continually startles the reader with her imagery, which she unfolds in a terse, elliptical style. The game of 'Ring-around-the-rosie', alluded to in the title of *The circle game*, is one of ritual exclusion in which the known is circumscribed by a garrison of bodies that keeps out the threatening unknown world. For Atwood the essential human impulse is to reduce an irrational and threatening environment to a closed circle of orthodoxy. Thus the writer's responsibility is to expose the conventions (psychological, linguistic, mythic) by which we invent convenient versions of ourselves. She sees modern man as being prey to continual invasions of fear and paranoia from the subliminal mind yet committed to an anachronistic belief in civilized order that is patently contradicted by the barbarism of this century. The rational mind must be integrated with the dark side of the psyche that has been repressed by humanistic ideas of order. To enter the wilderness of the self, then, is Atwood's major concern. In *The* JOURNALS OF SUSANNA MOODIE a nineteenth-century Canadian pioneer becomes the archetypal colonial entering the unknown wilderness of the New World. Imprisoned within the outmoded conventions of the Victorian world that she carries in her head, she retreats into her own circle game—projecting nostalgic Victorian preconceptions onto an alien landscape, while remaining ignorant of the challenges of her new environment. (For Atwood, as for Frye, such a garrison mentality has characterized the Canadian sensibility.) Moodie's last meditations are from underground. *Procedures from underground* explores the same themes in a different context. The title poem is indebted to West Coast Indian mythology for its motifs. Entering the mirror-world of

the psyche, the poet becomes a shaman whose visions are threatening to her tribe. From the 'underland' she sees the world as an ambiguous landscape of violence and death—the landscape we enter in many other poems in the book.

In the brief, aphoristic poems of *Power politics*, Atwood exposes, with the same scalpel-like precision, the sadistic deceptions implicit in the myth of romantic love. Lovers are predatory, even cannibalistic; relationships are a sophisticated form of consumption: love is power politics. Each individual seeks the security of role reinforcement from the other and remains trapped in an essential solipsism, committed only to his or her own needy appetite. *You are happy*, which represents an expansion of these themes, includes the brilliant sequence of 'Circe/Mud' poems in which the story of Odysseus arriving in Aiaia is retold from the perspective of Circe. Her experience represents the extortion of women, who must be entirely passive—malleable as clay to male desire. With these two books Atwood became a major voice in the feminist debate over personal relationships.

The themes of Atwood's recent poetry also include the world of modern politics and the domestic world of mother and child. In *Two-headed poems* she returns to a concern that first emerged in *Survival*: the complexities of being Canadian. The title poem is an elegy for a nation divided between two cultures: not only in the 'two-headed' national person—represented by a 'leader' who speaks duplicitously in two languages—but in the ensuing debate, which 'is not a debate/but a duet/with two deaf singers'. An antidote to this cynicism appears in poems that create potent myths for the child, offering a private magic, and in a treatment of nature that reveals its benevolence in the cyclical renewal of life. In *True stories* Atwood's political concerns are transferred to an international context. We live in a fragile security, cocooned from the global realities of famine, political terrorism, and war: our willed ignorance of such evils is a form of collusion. In a peculiarly Canadian way Atwood is a staunch moralist, essentially a writer of ideas—coldly, often brutally, insisting that modern man must reinvent himself. Her work challenges us to become human.

Perhaps needing a larger format for her exploration of social mythology, Atwood turned to fiction in the late 1960s. In each of her novels the main character is a woman living a professional life in a modern consumer society (a consumer research analyst, a commercial artist, a novelist, an anthropologist, a 'life-styles' journalist) who is forced to engage in a radical process of reassessment when the props supporting her carefully constructed version of herself are knocked out from under her. After experiencing a mental breakdown Marian, the narrator of *The edible woman*, exorcises the menace of a predatory sexist society by baking an 'edible woman' cake and ritualistically offering it to her man in place of herself. In *Lady Oracle* the narrator, Joan, lives her life as if it were a trashy and melodramatic script, one of the Costume Gothics she writes. When neurotic relationships and her invented personas (she has at least three identities) become too confusing, she decides to simulate her own death; but whether this escape into normalcy is successful is left ambiguous. *Life before man* is the story of a love triangle; but in an anaesthetized, plastic world—the puritanical world of WASP Toronto—the characters can't seem to transcend clichés of feeling. Renée discovers that her absconding husband is simply an opportunist who hopes to find through her a soggy mythic version of himself that he can love.

Atwood's best novels are *Surfacing* and *Bodily harm*. In *Surfacing* the unnamed narrator searches the wilderness of northern Québec for her father, a botanist, who has been reported missing. Trying to reestablish contact with her past, she must reevaluate all her cultural assumptions. In this retreat into the wilderness, which is both a literal and a psychological place, Atwood is challenging Western ways of seeing, particularly of relating to nature. The modern compulsion is to treat nature as raw material, to explain and master it in accordance with the technological myth of progress. By showing her protagonist moving through a ritual preparation that corresponds to the stages of shamanistic initiation, Atwood attempts to recover a primitive, mystical participation in nature, in which the heroine must recreate herself. In *Bodily harm* the heroine flees from a constricting consumer society and a broken relationship to another alien territory—the politically complex environment of a Caribbean island. Confronted with its stark realities, she comes to acknowledge her narcissistic entrapment in a culture where feelings are invented, packaged, and merchandised. *Bodily harm* employs a complex and unified narrative structure, unlike Atwood's other novels, which are made up of fragmented narratives and loosely connected observations that bring to mind the elliptical style of her poetry.

As a prose writer Atwood may be at her best in the short-story form, which allows for interesting technical experiments with point of view, dialogue, and epigrammatic style. In *Dancing girls* the characters—like the protagonists of her novels—are psychologically complex individuals trapped by paranoia and radical alienation. Two stories are representative. 'Polarities' is a study of madness, both inside and outside mental institutions, in which a clinically insane student proves to have a deeper understanding of the general psychosis of modern society than the so-called sane protagonist. 'The Grave of the Famous Poet' is perhaps Atwood's most compassionate study of the failure of relationships. With acerbic irony she penetrates beneath the level of clichéd passion to expose love as an addictive habit. *Murder in the dark: short fiction and prose poems* takes a new direction. The main subject is writing itself: what is the writer's plot against the reader? The title piece describes writing as a treacherous parlour game in which the writer is the murderer, the reader her victim, and, by the rules of the game, the writer must lie. The price the writer exacts from herself justifies her sinister assumption of authority: 'If you decide to enter the page, take a knife and some matches', because the journey is horrifying: 'You can become lost in the page forever.' The last section of the book explores the varieties of darkness beneath the page where the writer enters a limbo between sanity and madness. In these witty experimental pieces, as in all her work, Atwood has designs on our psyches—we are to be instructed through the underdarkness so that we can become saner and more resilient.

Atwood has published much informal literary criticism, beginning with SURVIVAL: A THEMATIC GUIDE TO CANADIAN LITERATURE, which argues that the literature is filled with negative portrayals of the victim. *The new Oxford book of Canadian verse in English*, for which she wrote a brilliant introductory overview of Canadian poetry, was published in the same year as *Second words: selected critical prose*. These book reviews, lectures, critical articles, and meditations on poetics represent Atwood's early interest in aesthetic questions of style and technique, in the importance of nationalism to the Canadian writer, and her growing involvement with human-rights' issues. While her style as a critic is witty and colloquial, Atwood is demanding when it comes to formal concerns.

Issue 41 of The MALAHAT REVIEW (Jan. 1977), edited by Linda Sandler, is entirely devoted to Atwood's work and career. See also Sherrill Grace, *Violent duality: a study of Margaret Atwood* (1980); *The art of Margaret Atwood: essays in criticism* (1981) edited by Arnold E. and Cathy N. Davidson; and Russell M. Brown, 'Atwood's sacred wells', *Essays on Canadian Writing* 17 (Spring 1981).

See also CRITICISM IN ENGLISH 5(d), NOVELS IN ENGLISH: 1960 TO 1982: 2, and POETRY IN ENGLISH 1950 TO 1982:2.

ROSEMARY SULLIVAN

Aubert de Gaspé, Philippe-Joseph (1786-1871). Born in Quebec City, he was the scion of an old and aristocratic French-Canadian family. His childhood was spent at the ancestral manor-house at Saint-Jean-Port-Joli on the south shore of the St Lawrence River, and in Quebec City. From 1798 to 1806 he completed his classical secondary course at the Petit Séminaire de Québec—latterly while living with a Church of England clergyman—and then studied law under the chief justice of Lower Canada, Jonathan Sewell. Admitted to the bar in Aug. 1811, he married later that year Susanne Allison (by whom he had thirteen children), and practised law in Quebec City. In 1816 he was named sheriff of the town; but, heavily in debt to the Crown, he was removed from office in 1822 and retired to Saint-Jean-Port-Joli. He was imprisoned for debt from 1838 to 1841 and released by a special act of parliament. In the meantime his journalist son Philippe-Ignace-François Aubert de Gaspé (1814-41) had written, with his father's help, the first French-Canadian novel, L'INFLUENCE D'UN LIVRE (Québec, 1837), and had died in Halifax.

After his release Aubert de Gaspé spent his summers on his estate and the winters in Quebec City, participating in the social and literary life of the capital. He belong to the 'Club des anciens' that met daily in Charles Hamel's shop, and he frequented Octave CRÉMAZIE's bookstore, which in the late 1850s became the meeting-place of the writers of the MOUVEMENT LITTÉRAIRE DE QUÉBEC. In 1862 Aubert de Gaspé, then in his mid-seventies, published in Les SOIRÉES CANADIENNES passages of a historical romance, Les ANCIENS CANADIENS. With the encouragement and assistance of Abbé Henri-Raymond CASGRAIN it became a novel that, when it was published in 1863, was an immediate success.

Three years later Aubert de Gaspé published his *Mémoires* (Québec, 1866), for which the seventy-nine-year-old author gathered hundreds of anecdotes and reminiscences that form a fascinating social history of Québec in the last years of the eighteenth century and the first quarter of the nineteenth. A further collection of posthumous fragments, *Divers*, appeared in 1893.

A few days after Aubert de Gaspé died in Quebec City on 29 Jan. 1871, Abbé Casgrain began publishing in *Le Courrier du Canada* an enthusiastic biography of his elderly friend. The modern reader will find the essential biographical information in an article by Luc Lacourcière in the DICTIONARY OF CANADIAN BIOGRAPHY, vol. X.

DAVID M. HAYNE

Aubin, Napoléon (1812-90). Aimé-Nicolas Aubin was born of Protestant parents near Geneva during its annexation to France; he adopted the name 'Napoléon' soon after immigrating first to New Orleans (1829), then to Lower Canada (Jan. 1835). Primarily a journalist, he wrote first for *La Minerve* in Montreal and *L'Ami du peuple* in Quebec City before founding his own newspaper, *Le Fantasque*, there in 1837. Most or all of each issue was written by Aubin himself, and his brilliant, humorous attacks on public figures and policies opposed to French-Canadian interests were widely influential. They led, however, to frequent difficulties with the authorities and, on one occasion (Jan.-Feb. 1839), to his imprisonment for sedition. Even before *Le Fantasque*'s demise in 1845 Aubin had founded *Le Castor* (1843). He subsequently founded *Le Canadien indépendant* (1849); the bilingual *Sentinelle du peuple* (1850); *La Tribune* (1863); and the political review *Les Veillées du père Bonsens* (two series, 1865 and 1873). He also edited, at various times, *Le Canadien* and *Le Pays*, and contributed to several other newspapers.

All of Aubin's non-journalistic literary production appeared between 1834 and 1839. This consisted of some 17 poems and 9 short stories. The poems express, in tones directly reminiscent of the French Romantic poet Pierre-Jean de Béranger, Aubin's firm patriotism ('Les Français aux Canadiens', 'L'amour de la patrie', 'Les Français en Canada') and the pervasive romanticism then current in France ('À Jenny', 'Quarante ans',

Aubin

'Tristesse', etc.). The personal and melancholy qualities of much of his lyric verse are directly modelled upon the works of Lamartine and Hugo, who were both practically unknown in Canada before Aubin. With his friend and early collaborator in journalism, Philippe Aubert de Gaspé *fils*, he was also a pioneer in introducing the short story to French-Canadian readers. Aubin's nine stories all appeared in newspapers, and they exhibit a remarkable variety of styles and themes. The longest, and generally considered the best of them, is 'Mon voyage à la lune', a satire on customs and conditions in Lower Canada. 'Une chanson—un songe— un baiser' skilfully exploits a Canadian voyageur legend, infusing it with romantic pathos. Still others, such as 'Une entrée dans le monde' and 'Monsieur Desnotes', are more conventional in subject and form.

Aubin's political stance, as evidenced in his journalism, was that of a *rouge*, turning more and more towards L.-J. Papineau after an initial period of distrust, and espousing the latter's arguments for annexation to the U.S. well after Confederation. His European education and wide interests gave him great advantage in his combative journalism, and are attested to in his pamphlets *La chimie agricole mise à la portée de tout le monde* (Québec, 1847), *Cours de chimie* (Québec, 1850), and *Manifeste adressé au peuple du Canada par le comité constitutionnel de la réforme et du progrès* (Québec, 1847); in his active membership in cultural and scientific organizations; in his public lectures; and finally in his establishment (1839) of an active theatrical group, 'Les amateurs typographes', whose influence would continue for a generation.

Aubin is the subject of an excellent monograph by J.-P. Tremblay, *À la recherche de Napoléon Aubin* (1969), in which Tremblay disproves the previously accepted attribution of the anonymous novel *Le rebelle* (1842) to Aubin.   LEONARD DOUCETTE

Avison, Margaret (b. 1918). Born in Galt, Ont., she graduated from Victoria College, University of Toronto, in 1940 and returned to do graduate work in English from 1964 to 1966. After attending schools of creative writing at the Universities of Indiana (1955) and Chicago (1956-7), she worked as a librarian, a lecturer at Scarborough College, University of Toronto, and a social worker for the Presbyterian Church Mission in Toronto. In 1973-4 she was writer-in-resi-

dence, University of Western Ontario.

Avison has published three collections of poetry. *Winter sun* (1960), which won a Governor General's Award, is intensely metaphysical, concerned with problems of belief and moral knowledge. The title refers to the soul's weather; the peculiarly beautiful but desolate light of a winter sun is a metaphor for the poet's state on the edge of imminent revelation: 'Light, the discovering light, is a beginning/where many stillnesses/ yearn' ('Prelude'). Stylistically difficult, sometimes excessively introspective, the poems are concerned with seeing. The controlling image is the 'optic heart' ('Snow'), which must venture in a quest for spiritual understanding. The American poet Cid Corman, in a commentary on *Winter sun*, spoke of the poet's protective coloration, as if Avison were hiding behind language ('Response', *Origin: featuring Margaret Avison*, 4, Jan. 1962). Avison's second collection, *The dumbfounding* (1966), is more direct; the language and imagery are less inward. The title poem records the experience of a religious vision that secured the poet in the Christian faith, which was to direct her future work: 'what before was *Possibility* is now *God*' ('Strong Yellow, for Reading Aloud'). These two collections have been published together in the Modern Canadian Poets series: *Winter sun/The dumbfounding: poems 1940-66* (1982).

Avison's third collection, *Sunblue* (1978), is the product of a profound religious conviction. Many of the poems are based on biblical myths and are increasingly orthodox in tone and vocabulary. However, Avison resists writing didactic poetry, and often tries to explore her Christian vision in poems about nature, where the natural world is used metaphorically to locate spiritual realities. Few Canadian poets can match Avison in the sophistication and beauty of her linguistic and imagistic gift, and even the reader who does not share her belief will find in her poetry a profound and imaginative perception of reality.

Avison has also translated poems from the Hungarian; see *The plough and the pen: writings from Hungary 1930-1956* (1963) edited by Ilona Duczyńska and Karl Polanyi.

For further reading on Avison, see Ernest Redekop, *Margaret Avison* (1970), in the Studies in Canadian Literature series, and Lawrence Jones, 'A core of brilliance', CANADIAN LITERATURE 38 (Autumn 1968). See also POETRY IN ENGLISH 1950 TO 1982: 2.   ROSEMARY SULLIVAN

Awful disclosures of Maria Monk (New York, 1836). In Oct. 1835 the *American Protestant Vindicator*, a New York newspaper supported by the Rev. W.C. Brownlee and the Rev. George Bourne, both of whom had recently published works of anti-Catholic propaganda, announced that a young woman was preparing the story of her life as a nun in the Hôtel Dieu Nunnery in Montreal; the story, *Awful disclosures of Maria Monk, as exhibited in a narrative of her sufferings during a residence of five years as a novice, and two years as a Black Nun, in the Hotel Dieu Nunnery at Montreal*, appeared in Jan. 1836. It describes the travails of Maria Monk, a young woman born a Protestant in St John's, Lower Canada (Qué.), who, after attending convent schools, converts to Roman Catholicism and becomes a nun of the Hôtel Dieu. She soon realizes her mistake, however: she learns, among other things, that nuns are forced to 'live in the practice of criminal intercourse with the priests' and that the offspring from these unions are killed after being baptized, their corpses thrown into lime-pits in the convent's cellar. Finding herself pregnant by 'Father Phelan', Maria escapes to the United States to save her child and rediscover her Protestant faith.

Awful disclosures caused a sensation. Thousands of copies were sold and it became a topic of discussion in newspapers in the United States and Canada. Although many believed its revelations, others—especially both Roman Catholics and Protestants in Montreal—denied their veracity. An affidavit, attributed to a woman said to be her mother, claimed that Maria Monk, subject to 'occasional mental derangement', had been taken advantage of by 'designing men' to make 'scandalous accusations against the priests and nuns of Montreal'. The 'designing men'—George Bourne; Theodore Dwight, to whom Maria was supposed to have dictated her story; William K. Hoyt[e], who allegedly brought her from Montreal; and the Rev. John J. Slocum, who became her legal guardian—were each said by contemporary sources to be the real author of *Awful disclosures*. The resemblances between it and other nuns' stories typical of the anti-conventual strain in Gothic fiction were noticed. A second edition (New York, 1836) contained as appendices 'Reception of the first editions'; 'Sequel of her narrative'; 'Review of the case'; a supplement 'Giving more particulars of the nunnery and grounds'; and 'Plan of the nunnery'. *Further disclosures by Maria Monk concerning the Hotel Dieu Nunnery of Montreal* (New York, 1837) included Slocum's *Reply to the priest's book*, his attempt to refute *Awful exposure of the atrocious plot formed by certain individuals, against the clergy and nuns of Lower Canada through the intervention of Maria Monk . . .* (New York, 1836).

By 1837, however, even Protestant believers in the 'Maria Monk affair' began to doubt. The Hôtel Dieu Nunnery was inspected and found to be unlike Maria's description of it. Her supporters quarrelled among themselves; finally, in May 1837, Maria and Slocum charged in a court case that Harper Brothers had 'wrongfully possessed' stereotyped plates of a work called 'The Hotel Dieu Nunnery Unveiled', 'pretended to take out another copyright of the work under the name 'Awful Disclosures' . . . in Massachusetts, . . . published a large number of impressions . . . and had large profits'. The judge dismissed the complaint, but advised Maria and Slocum to sue the Harpers for damages. Since there was no suit, and since no copy of *Awful disclosures* that names the Harpers as publishers apparently survives, their role in Maria's story remains unclear. After the court case Maria, possibly pregnant for a second time, left Slocum and disappeared. She is supposed to have died in prison in 1849, after being arrested as a pickpocket.

Her story, however, is interesting for several reasons. The motifs of subterranean passages, imprisoned nuns, and secret murders in *Awful disclosures* link it to the Gothic novel and show how suitable this type of fiction was for anti-Catholic literature. Its origin in New York City reveals how strong anti-Catholic feeling was among certain American Protestants in the 1830s and how easily it was projected onto what they perceived as the exotic, mysterious setting of French-Canadian, Roman Catholic Québec. The story's popularity in England suggests that it became part of the anti-Catholic literature and feeling there too. In *Lectures on the present position of Catholics in England* (1851), John Henry Newman analyses the role the 'very wicked, very mischievous' Maria Monk and her 'Awful Disclosures' played for English Protestants; he also notes that since 1836, 'from 200,000 to 250,000 copies' of 'the calumny' had been put into circulation in America and England. Finally, the new editions and translations that have appeared in the twentieth century emphasize the continued fascination of this sensational, but essentially sorry tale.

In *Maria Monk's daughter: an autobiography* (New York, 1874), Mrs L. St John Eckel (Lizzie Harper), claiming to be Maria's daughter, includes an extract from the court's judgment in the copyright case (pp. 171-3). A modern reprint of *Awful Disclosures* (Hamden, Conn.: Archon Books, 1962) contains an introduction by Ray Allan Billington—largely based on his essay 'Maria Monk and her influence', *Catholic Historical Review*, XXII (Oct. 1936)—in which he calls the book "the most influential single work of anti-Catholic propaganda in America's history'. See also Ralph Thompson, 'The Maria Monk affair', *The Colophon* 17, 6 (1934), and B. Dufèbvre (Emile Castonguay), 'Le "roman" de Maria Monk', *La Revue de l'Université Laval*, VIII (fév. 1954). The contemporary response to *Awful disclosures* is conveyed in such newspapers as the *New York Herald* (1836 ff.).

MARY JANE EDWARDS

B

Babiuk, Andrii. See UKRAINIAN WRITING.

Backwoods of Canada, The (London, 1836). Catharine Parr TRAILL's first 'Canadian' book, and her most famous one, it is composed of eighteen letters home to family and friends in Suffolk, Eng. Beginning with the departure of Thomas and Catharine Traill from Scotland in July 1832, they follow the Traills' progress through the spring of 1835, by which time, with the help of Mrs Traill's brother Samuel Strickland, they were comfortably settled in their own log house near the shore of Lake Katchewanook, just north of present-day Lakefield, Ont. The letters—probably edited in England by a sister, Agnes Strickland—were published by Charles Knight, in his popular series The Library of Entertaining Knowledge, as *The backwoods of Canada: being letters from the wife of an emigrant officer, illustrative of the domestic economy of British America*, a book that not only describes the Traills' adventures and adjustments as settlers but also provides useful information and practical advice for the womenfolk of British families contemplating 'a home amid our Canadian wilds'. The letters are of an optimistic and reassuring cast and draw deeply upon Mrs Traill's great fund of Christian patience and her faith in British character: throughout she is cheerful, uncomplaining, and practical. Unlike her sister Susanna MOODIE—who, in ROUGHING IT IN THE BUSH (1852), was given to emphasizing her emotional reactions and to dwelling upon her lost English home—Mrs Traill concentrates on what she finds in Upper Canada to stimulate her interest and curiosity. Having little aptitude for imaginative flights, and believing that in the backwoods 'Fancy would starve for lack of marvellous food', she attends instead to the settlers, the Indians, domestic details, and the *flora* and *fauna* around her. 'Habit reconciles us to many things that at first were distasteful,' she writes. Her adaptive attitude and objective eye contribute to one of the best-written records of settlement experience and British presence in Upper Canada. If her selective approach to nature is, as Northrop FRYE put it, 'reminiscent of Miss Muffet', it is but a part of the insistently positive outlook that was Mrs Traill's greatest resource as a pioneer and as a writer.

A 'selected edition', edited by Clara THOMAS, is in the New Canadian Library (1966).

MICHAEL PETERMAN

Bacque, James (b. 1929). Born in Toronto and educated at Upper Canada College and the University of Toronto, he worked as assistant editor on *Saturday Night*, as editor of *Canadian Packaging* and *Canadian Homes*, and as trade editor for the MACMILLAN COMPANY OF CANADA (1961-8). He was a co-founder of New Press, Toronto, in 1969. Of Bacque's three published novels, the first two deal with social upheaval as experienced by an outsider. In *The lonely ones* (1969) a painter becomes involved in the activities of a separatist cell in Québec in the sixties, and discovers that divisiveness and isolation threaten even this smallest of human units. In *A man of talent* (1972) a bright young man, who is dean of arts at a university, loses everything when he comes into conflict with both student radicals and the university administration, and simultaneously alienates his Indian lover and the native community that has accepted him through her. In the third novel, *The Queen comes to Minnicog* (1979)—the humorous tale of a fictional visit of the Queen of England to a small Georgian Bay town—the story relies for its humour on stock rural types and situations, and on dialogue heavily dependent on malapropisms. While carefully constructed and showing much attention to dialect, dialogue, and word-play, these three novels seem somewhat mechanical and uncompelling.

The anthology *Creation* (1970), edited by Robert KROETSCH, contains some of Bacque's fiction and poetry, as well as an interview.   MARILYN ROSE

Bailey, Alfred Goldsworthy (b. 1905). Born in Quebec City, he received his early schooling there, then completed a B.A. at the University of New Brunswick in 1927; he took his M.A. and Ph.D. at the University of Toronto (1934), combining studies in history, anthropology, archeology, and art. On a Royal Society fellowship he completed his formal education at the London School of Economics. In 1935 he became assistant director and associate curator of the New Brunswick Museum, and in 1937 professor of history at the University of New Brunswick, where he remained head of the department for more than thirty years. Now Professor Emeritus at UNB, he held there the positions of dean of arts (1946-64), honorary librarian (1946-70), and vice-president academic (1965-70). He was made a Fellow of the Royal Society of Canada in 1951 and an officer of the Order of Canada in 1978.

Bailey's career as a poet began with *Songs of the Saguenay* (1927) and *Tao* (1930), traditional verse in the style of the Canadian romantics. When he met such writers as Robert FINCH and Earle BIRNEY in Toronto, he began experimenting with new forms. As teacher and poet in Fredericton—where he helped to establish a poetry club and a magazine, *The* FIDDLEHEAD—he strongly influenced such younger writers as Elizabeth BREWSTER, Fred COGSWELL, and Robert GIBBS. His mature work appeared in *Border*

River (1952), *Thanks for a drowned island* (1973), and *Miramichi lightning: the collected poems of Alfred Bailey* (1981). Bailey's concerns in these books are personal, social, and intellectual, stemming from his background and his close involvement with the culture of his own community. His central themes are the impingement of one culture on another, the aspirations of explorers and settlers, and the difficulties of maintaining continuity and purpose. His style is compact and elliptical; sometimes playful, sometimes difficult.

Bailey's doctoral thesis, *The conflict of European and eastern Algonkian cultures, 1504-1700: a study in Canadian civilization* (1937; 2nd ed. 1969), is now recognized as seminal in its field. As an editor of *The literary history of Canada* (1965), he contributed the chapter 'Overture to Nationhood'. His *Culture and nationality: essays by A.G. Bailey* (1972) contains the important 'Creative moments in the culture of the Maritime Provinces'.
                    ROBERT GIBBS

Bailey, Jacob (1731-1808). Born in Rowley, Mass., he graduated from Harvard in 1755. After a brief career as a school teacher and Congregationalist minister, he converted to the Church of England. Ordained priest in 1760, and appointed to a frontier parish at Pawnalborough, Maine (then part of Massachusetts), he was resented by the largely Congregationalist community. As America slid towards open defiance of British authority, resentment of Bailey and the state-supported Church he represented sharpened. From 1774 on he was frequently harrassed and assaulted. In 1779 he was permitted to depart as a Loyalist refugee for Nova Scotia, where he served as parish priest at Cornwallis (1779-82) and at Annapolis Royal (1782-1808).

Bailey left a voluminous amount of correspondence, journals, sermons, moral commentaries, histories, expository prose 'descriptions', fiction, and poetry. W.S. Bartlet published selections from the journals and correspondence in *The frontier missionary* (Boston, 1853), but most of his work was never published. His most interesting works of non-fiction are his sermons—written in a clear, simple style, their tone amiable and intelligent—and his geographical 'descriptions', which are designed for the average intelligent reader: one is on Maine in the 1760s; the other describes Nova Scotia in the 1780s and employs a journey motif.

Bailey's fiction consists mainly of two incomplete novels—interesting attempts to integrate form and intention in the early North American novel. 'The flower of the wilderness' is a mixture of narrative, letter, and dialogue, set in frontier New England. A later and more coherent work structurally is 'Serena' (c. 1786-90), an epistolary novel about a Nova Scotian Loyalist girl who is captured and carried back to New England by rebel privateers.

Bailey's most sustained literary achievement lay in poetry. The best poem from his American period is 'Farewell to Kennebec' (1779), a valedictory lamenting his exile from Maine. The finest practitioner of Hudibrastic verse satire after Samuel Butler himself, Bailey produced a large number of verse satires. 'Character of a trimmer' (1779-80) attacks political fence-sitters as well as rebels, but much of its sharpness is lost in its dual focus. In 'America' (1780-4), an incomplete poem designed to present the Loyalist view of the causes of the Revolution, Bailey's satiric verse becomes a trenchant and incisive instrument for clarifying and articulating his fears, frustrations, and moral indignation. After the war Bailey turned his attention to social and political concerns pertinent to the emerging post-war society of Nova Scotia. His most ambitious poem, 'The adventures of Jack Ramble, the Methodist preacher' (c. 1785-late 1790s), incomplete in over 9200 lines, attacks evangelical itinerant preachers as purveyors of irrationality and immorality and as promoters of disrespect for all forms of order; it also deplores the increase of religious dissenters that undermined the strength of the Established Church, which together with government ensured the stability and order of society.

See T.B. Vincent, ed., *Narrative verse satire in Maritime Canada 1779-1814* (1978); R.P. Baker, 'The poetry of Jacob Bailey', *New England Quarterly* II (1929); Thomas B. Vincent, 'Alline and Bailey', CANADIAN LITERATURE 68-69 (Spring/Summer 1976), and 'The poetic development of Jacob Bailey', *Early American Literature* XIV (1979).

TOM VINCENT

Baillargeon, Pierre. See ESSAYS IN FRENCH: 5 and NOVELS IN FRENCH 1940 TO 1959: 2.

Baird, Irene (1901-81). Born in England, Irene Todd came with her parents to British Columbia in 1919 and pursued a career as a reporter for the Vancouver *Sun* and the *Daily Province*. She later married John Baird. In 1942 she joined the National Film Board and worked primarily in publicity and public relations. At her retirement from the federal civil service she was chief of information for the Department of Indian Affairs and Northern Development.

Baird's first novel, *John* (1937), restrained in style and precise in plotting, is a study of John Dorey, a Scot who has created a ten-acre haven for himself on Vancouver Island. Despite its love interest and a feud with a neighbour who is cruel to animals, the novel centres on the description and revelation of Dorey's character. *Waste heritage* (1939), her second novel, is an unacknowledged classic of Canadian literature. Initially received as a stylistically imperfect but powerful and honest portrayal of the predicament and rage of the chronically unemployed in the Depression, it later came to be admired only for its accurate documentation of events based on the trek to Victoria by 1,000 unemployed after the forcible expulsion of the 'sit-downers' from the Vancouver Post Office in 1938. These views neglect the thematic consistency through which Baird creates a vision of an entire society straining under tensions that can lead only to fruitless destruction. Both major and minor characters are repeatedly caught between a frustrated rage that demands radical economic and social reform and a desperate loyalty to the mythology of capitalist democracy. The inevitable conclusion is government betrayal of the men's attempt at mass action to gain jobs and dignity, the arrest of the twenty-three-year-old hero Matt Striker, and the death of his companion Eddy, whose ideal of economic and social security has narrowed to a simple-minded obsession—getting one new pair of shoes. In her third novel, *He rides the sky* (1941), Baird chronicles, through his letters home to Victoria, the emotions and experience of a young man who trains as a pilot with the RAF in 1938 and is lost in battle in 1940. Though the letters aim at creating a sense of spontaneity, their stylistic cohesiveness and painstaking detail render them artificial in tone and content. Also artificial is the persistently brash, enthusiastic naiveté of the hero, Peter O'Halloran. *Climate of power* (1971), Baird's last novel, is based on her experience of federal bureaucracy and her knowledge of the Arctic. Centring on the imminent retirement of George McKenna, it begins as an apparently mildly cynical examination of bureaucratic tactical politics and develops into a psychologically competent and carefully plotted study of the disintegration of McKenna's position and personality under the pressures of an unfaithful younger wife and an accidental opportunity for murder. Underlying the plot are government's sincere but muddled attempts to improve Inuit culture—though in fact they destroy it.

See Roger Leslie Hyman, 'Wasted heritage and *Waste heritage*: the critical disregard of an important Canadian novel', *Journal of Canadian Studies* 17, No. 4 (Winter 82/83).

ANTHONY HOPKINS

Ballantyne, R.M. (1825-94). Robert Michael Ballantyne was born in Edinburgh to a family of printers and publishers brought down in the financial ruin of Sir Walter Scott, and received only two years of formal schooling before joining the Hudson's Bay Company at the age of sixteen. He served as a clerk at Fort Garry, Norway House, and York Factory from 1841 to 1845, when he was transferred to the Lower St Lawrence district, taking charge of posts at Île-Jérémie and Sept-Îles and wintering at Tadoussac before sailing for home in May 1847.

His first book, *Hudson Bay; or Every-day life in the wilds of North America, during six years' residence in the territories of the Hon. Hudson Bay Company* (Edinburgh, 1848), was assembled from his journals and letters saved by his mother. With *Snowflakes and sunbeams; or, The young fur traders. A tale of the Far North* (London, 1856) and *Ungava; a tale of Exquimaux land* (London, 1858), he began a long and celebrated career as a writer of adventure stories for boys. While his most popular books included *The coral island* (London, 1858) and *Martin Rattler; or, A boy's adventures in the forests of Brazil* (London, 1858), Ballantyne continued to exploit his experiences in the Northwest, setting more than twenty of his 120 books in the New World. In addition to boys' books such as *Away in the wilderness* (London, 1863), *The buffalo runners: a tale of the Red River* (London, 1891), and *The giant of the North* (London, 1882), he wrote fiction for a general audience, such as *The Red Man's revenge; a tale of the Red River flood* (London, 1880).

In Ballantyne's tales the Northwest—interchangeable with the wilds of Brazil or the high seas—is a conveniently exotic wilderness to try the daring of the heroes. In spite of his first-hand experience, his New World settings never exhibit any vivid particularity, and whatever the company clerk must

have learned about the Indian people never emerges through the romancer's stereotyped noble savages and heathen devils. See Eric Quayle, *Ballantyne the brave* (1967), and *R.M. Ballantyne: a bibliography of first editions* (1968).   DICK HARRISON

Barbeau, Jean (b. 1945). Born in Saint-Romuald, near Quebec City, he studied at the Collège de Lévis and Université Laval. From 1966 to 1969 he experimented in various creative and collective forms of drama (all unpublished) that were put on in the Collège de Lévis, at the Estoc Theatre in Quebec City, and at Université Laval: *Caïn et Babel, La Geôle, Et caetera* (which reached the finals of the Dominion Drama Festival in 1968), *Les temps tranquilles*, and *Le frame all-dress*. 'To *write* drama is to limit it, to turn it away from its basic purpose,' Barbeau has said: he therefore sketches and improvises and refuses to be an 'author'. He became one in spite of himself, however, in *Le chemin de Lacroix* (1971), produced by the Théâtre quotidien de Québec (of which Barbeau was a founder and resident playwright) in 1970, which presents the 'stations' and 'passion' of a young unemployed workman at a police station. Lacroix is a victim of circumstances; nevertheless Barbeau refuses to allow him to fulfil the expectations of the audience by radicalizing him at the play's end. *Ben-Ur* (1971) presents another victim—Benoit-Urbain—who searches in comic strips for the ritual, the formulas, and the gestures of the hero. The two-character *Goglu* (1971) and the monologue *Solange* (1974) express in a simple manner intense and pathetic solitude.

0-71 is a kind of historical fresco; it is also a number (unlucky?) in Bingo and 1971, year zero, when everything in Québec was beginning all over again. *Le théâtre de la maintenance* and *Le chant du sink* (1973) still owe something to the revue and to the initiation ceremony (to both theatre and life—which to Barbeau are one and the same thing). In *0-71* and several other published pieces—*Tripez-vous, vous?, Lésés boys, Boursaille, L'herbe à puces*—Barbeau yields to situation comedy, or verbal comedy, that is a little facile, verbose, confusing. On the other hand *Manon Lastcall* and *Joualez-moi d'amour* (published together in 1972) are clearer and more lively. Manon is a waitress who has become a guide in the provincial museum, where she converts the curator to masterpieces of the flesh. In the second play the Parisian Julie and her Québec lover Jules are able to embrace only in JOUAL. Here, as in *Le chemin de Lacroix*, vulgarity is healthy and dramatically necessary; the author plays rapidly and effectively on the various levels of language and society.

Most of Barbeau's plays have had successful runs in Montreal and elsewhere in Québec, and in Toronto and Paris. Among the most recent, *Citrouille* (1974) places a normal, rather banal but sympathetic young man in a situation customarily reserved for women: he is held captive, violated, and humiliated by three young feminists. The sex-role reversal provides a highly dramatic situation and the play, written and performed with good humour, is an amusing and effective critique of phallocratism. In *Le jardin de la maison blanche* (1979) Barbeau attacks the values of contemporary North American society through five invalids who are stereotypical to the point of caricature: another phallocrat, a feminine woman, an unemployed worker, a Black, and a young girl so naive as to be almost a fool. All of them cling to life by means of electronic life-support systems and their ideological delusions. *Une marquise de Sade et un lézard nommé King Kong* (1979) centres on Hercule, a very minor civil servant, who prefers to dwell in a childish fantasy rather than confront reality. The other characters, also powerless socially and economically, are doubly alienated. For them, any form of art is merely one more illusion, an opaque veil, a prison that makes them restless and frantic. The 'moonshiner' in *Émile et une nuit* (1979) is more fortunate. Happily he is able to use literature, from *The thousand and one nights* (hence the title of the play) to the poems of Saint-Denys GARNEAU, to prevent a young man from committing suicide in the subway. For Émile, the wise man, 'words are the keys', just as music can be for the gypsy, Étienne. Though Jean Barbeau has abandoned *joual* for a more normal French, the problems that language and communication create remain at the core of his dramatic work.

Barbeau's language is more relaxed, less hard, broken, and tragic than that of Michel TREMBLAY. His themes, structure, and style approach rather those of the experimental companies Les P'tits Enfants Laliberté and Le Grand Cirque Ordinaire (whose *T'es pas tannée, Jeanne d'Arc?* influenced *Ben-Ur*). His characters are naive young provincials. Dispossessed, bittersweet, given to moods of violence or calm, they still love life, dreaming, and joking. Barbeau believes that 'all

the great québécois tragedies will be humorous ones because our greatest misfortune occurred in 1763 and nothing worse awaits us.'
LAURENT MAILHOT

Barbeau, Marius (1883-1969). Born at Sainte-Marie-de-la-Beauce, Qué., Charles-Marius Barbeau was the scion of a family whose beginnings in Canada can be traced to the 1660s, although his perfect bilingualism may have been influenced by an Irish paternal grandmother. Beginning formal studies in 1895, he completed his B.A. at the college of Saint-Anne-de-la-Pocatière in 1903. He studied law at Université Laval and he was admitted to the Bar in 1907. Concurrently he won a Rhodes Scholarship and in 1910 was awarded the B.SC. degree and diploma in anthropology by Oxford University for his thesis 'The totemic systems of the North Western tribes of North America'. During vacations in this period he also studied in Paris at the Sorbonne and the École d'Anthropologie. On his return to Canada in 1911 he was appointed as an anthropologist to the National Museum of Canada (then the Museum Branch of the Geological Survey of Canada), where he remained until his retirement in 1949, though he acted as a consultant for another fifteen years.

After meeting the influential American anthropologist Franz Boas in 1913, Barbeau added the traditional culture and folklore of French Canadians to his scholarly interests. He gave these interests tangible form in his role as associate editor of the *Journal of American Folklore*. From 1916 to 1950 he was responsible for ten Canadian issues, the contents of which remain the major body of published French-Canadian folklore *collectanea*; these include eight series of 'Contes populaires canadiens', many of which he had collected. He was president of the American Folklore Society in 1918. Barbeau's major interest was folksong, however, and his prolific field collections gave the National Museum a corpus of over 10,000 songs, including some 7,000 French-Canadian, 3,000 Indian, 1,500 English, and 195 Eskimo songs. He founded the Canadian Folk Music Society in 1956 as a branch of the International Folk Music Council, continuing as president until 1963 and as honorary president until his death.

Barbeau was made a member of the Royal Society of Canada in 1916, and was later awarded its Gold Medal. He was co-founder, with Lawrence J. Burpee, of the

Société historique du Canada, and won the Prix David in 1925, 1929, and 1945. He received honorary degrees from the universities of Laval, Oxford, and the Sorbonne; was made an honorary fellow of Oriel College, Oxford, in 1941; was awarded the Médaille Parizeau by the Association canadienne-française pour l'avancement des sciences in 1946; and in 1967 was one of the first Canadians to be named a Companion of the Order of Canada.

Barbeau was the founder of modern folklore studies in Canada. Apart from the pioneering work of Ernest Gagnon, whose *Chansons populaires du Canada* (1865) was long perceived as the definitive work on French-Canadian folksong, Barbeau was the first to undertake a methodical exploration of the traditions of French Canada. Early in his career he gathered about him a team of collectors, including E.-Z. Massicotte, Adélard Lambert, Frère Archange Godbout, and J.-Thomas Leblanc, whose materials formed the basis of the immense collections of the National Museum. Later he inspired a new generation of scholars: among them François Brassard, Madeleine Doyon, Carmen Roy, Félix-Antoine SAVARD, and Luc Lacourcière.

Barbeau's recognition of the need for a scholarly base for folklore studies was realized in 1944 with the creation of a chair of folklore at Université Laval occupied by Luc Lacourcière, whom Barbeau had introduced to the subject in the 1930s. Lacourcière, as director of the Archives de Folklore, was able to call upon Barbeau's immense experience both as a teacher (he was made a professor in the Faculté des Lettres at Laval in 1945) and as an editor of the prestigious series, *Les archives de folklore*. In 1947 Barbeau was honoured with the dedication of volume II of the series as a 'Hommage à Marius Barbeau'.

The range of Barbeau's research was vast. His insatiable curiosity led him to study the whole domain of the folklorist—clothing, foodways, housing, furniture, weapons, domestic utensils, games, formulas, customs and beliefs, folk art and imagery, tales, legends, anecdotes, song and music. He was a prolific, indeed compulsive, publisher of his research. He authored some 600 journal and newspaper articles, over 100 books and brochures, and collaborated on another sixty. Among his many scholarly publications on Indian culture, the most eminent include *Huron and Wyandot mythology with an appendix containing earlier published records*

(1915); *Totem poles on the Gitksan, Upper Skeena River, British Columbia* (1929); *Totem poles* (2 vols., 1950-1); *Haida myths illustrated in argillite carvings* (1953); *Haida carvers in argillite* (1957); and *Huron-Wyandot traditional narratives in translation and native texts* (1960). His scholarly writings on Indian lore are major documents of native ethnography. Barbeau used his knowledge of Indian culture in two novels: *The downfall of Temlaham* (1928) and *Mountain Cloud* (1944).

Barbeau's work on traditional French folksongs represents the single most important corpus of French-Canadian folksongs ever published: *Folk songs of French Canada* (1925, with Edward Sapir); *Chansons populaires du vieux Québec* (1935); *Le romancéro du Canada* (1937), his major scholarly contribution to Canadian folksong studies; *Alouette! Nouveau recueil de chansons populaires avec mélodies, choisies dans le Répertoire du Musée National du Canada* (1946); *Le rossignol y chante* (1962); and the series of 'Chants populaires du Canada', which he edited in collaboration with E.-Z. Massicotte (*Journal of American Folklore*, 1919).

Barbeau also edited several volumes of tales, legends, and other folklore studies aimed at the general public and scholars alike: *Au coeur de Québec* (1934), which includes legends, history, and artisans; *Grand'mère raconte* (1935), ten folktales; and *Quebec where ancient France lingers* (1936), with important studies on traditional artisans, and its French edition, *Québec ou survit l'ancienne France* (1937). *Maitres artisans de chez nous* (1942) also deals with folk artists and artisans. *L'arbre des rêves* (1948)—with its English edition, *The Tree of Dreams* (1955)—is a collection of legends presented in a somewhat literary manner; while the twelve volumes of *Les contes du grand'père sept-heures* (1950-3) were written for children; some of these stories were adapted by Michael Hornyansky and published in *The golden phoenix and other French-Canadian fairy tales* (1958).

Barbeau's love of art was not restricted to the traditional. He was instrumental in fostering appreciation of several Canadian artists in works such as *Cornelius Krieghoff, pioneer painter of North America* (1934) and *Painters of Quebec* (1946). He also wrote a number of short monographs on Krieghoff.

The 'Hommage à Marius Barbeau' (*Les Archives de Folklore*, vol. II, 1947) contains a 'Bio-bibliographie de Marius Barbeau' prepared by Clarisse Cardin, which is an indispensable guide to Barbeau's scholarly career;

an unpublished manuscript prepared by the National Museum in 1969 added well over 200 items to this bibliography.

GERALD THOMAS

Barbour, Douglas (b. 1940). Born in Winnipeg, he studied briefly at McGill University before completing his B.A. in English at Acadia University (1962) and his M.A. at Dalhousie (1964); he received a Ph.D. (1976) from Queen's University with a thesis on science-fiction literature. Since 1969 he has taught Canadian literature and creative writing at the University of Alberta. Barbour has served as editor of *Quarry* (1966-8), as a member of the editorial boards of *White Pelican* (1971-6) and *NeWest* (1980-), as poetry editor for *The* CANADIAN FORUM (1978-80), and as co-chairman (with Stephen SCOBIE) of the LEAGUE OF CANADIAN POETS (1972-4). In 1980 he co-founded Longspoon Press, Edmonton, with Stephen Scobie and Shirley Neuman.

In Barbour's first poetry collections—*A poem as long as the highway* (1971), *Landfall* (1971), and *White* (1973)—he uses a free-flowing lyrical style and vibrant images to capture the nuances of western landscapes, while at the same time introducing ideographic characters into some poems. This device he carried further in *Songbook* (1973) and *he & she &* (1974), which link Barbour with b p NICHOL and bill BISSET, for they show an interest in defying the confines of natural speech in order to accommodate a vast range of sound, tone, and spoken music. This interest is also demonstrated in Barbour's sound-poetry performances with Scobie, 'Re:Sounding', which they began in 1977. Barbour even employs sound poetry in the long narrative poem *Visions of my grandfather* (1976). It is less evident, however, in the recent *Shorelines* (1979), *Stargazing* (1980), and *The harbingers* (1983), a sequence of nineteen poems that explores the archetypal significance of the three white horses of death found in dreams, mythology, and folklore.

Barbour produces and writes the critical chapbook *Canadian poetry chronicle*. He edited *The story so far 5* (1978) and co-edited with Scobie the anthology of Canadian comic poetry *The maple laugh forever* (1981) and with Marni Stanley *Write right: poetry by Canadian women* (1982). Scobie and Barbour also collaborated on *The pirates of pen's chance* (1981), a homolinguistic (English into English) translation of well-known poems drawing on semantic and linguistic associations to create new and often comic works.

BRUCE MEYER

Barker's Canadian Monthly Magazine (May 1846-April 1847). Of the many pre-Confederation periodicals, this was the first whose contents were written entirely in Canada. The owner, editor, and publisher was Edward John Barker, born near London, Eng., in 1799. He had practised medicine in England before he immigrated to Canada in 1832, settling in Kingston (Ont.), where he edited newspapers owned by others before he began his own *British Whig* in 1834. The contents of *Barker's Magazine* varied in form, style, and quality. In addition to poetry and fiction, there were serious political articles and political satire, biographies of Canadian politicians, and reviews of books by Canadians or about Canada. Barker had announced that the magazine would be politically independent, and this seems to have been the case, since it was criticized by Tories for being Reform and by Reformers for being Tory. The two biographies—of John Beverly Robinson and Christopher Hageman—were certainly not hagiographic and, with one exception, the book reviews were savage. There was a great deal of competent poetry, though only the verse satire is interesting today, and some quite remarkable fiction: notably the first two-thirds of J.S. Cummins' novel ALTHAM and a series of 'Legends of the early settlements' by 'Cinna'. Many years later Henry Scadding identified 'Cinna' as W.B. Wells, a lawyer who was born in Augusta Twp, Upper Canada, in 1809. Since the attribution, made in Wells's lifetime, was not contradicted, and since what we know of 'Cinna' tallies with what we know of Wells, we can assume that he was the author of the two biographies, two articles, and several poems both long and short, as well as the following 'legends': 'Tula; or, the Ojibwa's leap', 'Maroon Hensey', and 'De Soulis; the runner of the woods'. They are somewhat romantic in tone, but the two articles, 'Deer stalking on the south branch' and 'A bear hunt', describe pioneer life with vigour and immediacy. Although Barker had hoped that the low price of 10 shillings per annum would bring him a thousand subscribers, there were only 400. Reluctantly he discontinued his magazine with vol. I, no. 12, at the end of the first year.

MARY LU MacDONALD

Barometer rising (1941). Hugh MacLEN-

NAN's first published novel was his first attempt to base his fiction securely on familiar and national ground. In an introduction to the New Canadian Library edition (1958), Hugo McPherson writes that it 'ushered in the most productive period in the nation's writing, and it introduced a novelist who was to lead his contemporaries in a most absorbing quest.' This quest was for a new relevance in fiction that would examine the Canadian consciousness.

The protagonist of this tightly structured novel—it takes place over eight days towards the end of 1917—is Neil Macrae. He returns incognito to Halifax from the First World War in the hope of clearing himself of a false accusation of insubordination, laid by Colonel Wain, a representative of the old colonial order who happens to be his hated uncle and father of his former sweetheart Penelope, who has another suitor, Angus Murray, though she remains faithful to Neil. (McPherson points to the outline of the Perseus legend visible in the novel; George WOODCOCK, in his essay 'A nation's odyssey', sees MacLennan using the Homeric epic as a source.) The tight, melodramatic plot unfolds against the compelling backdrop of wartime Halifax that permits frequent views of the harbour, Bedford Basin, the Narrows, and the shipping within. At the moment the *Imo* emerges from behind Richmond Bluff, all the characters seem to be inevitably arranged so that, after its fatal collision with the French munitions ship *Mont Blanc* and the frightful aftermath, all the threads of the plot explode in a dénouement. MacLennan shows superlative skill in conveying the effects of the ships' explosion, which were both researched and recollected (he witnessed them as a boy). The crisis (representing the death of the old Canada), and the response as his characters survive and attempt to bring about a kind of rebirth after the cataclysm, form a parable of Canadian self-realization that is firmly rooted in actual and vividly reconstructed historical events. MacLennan is less successful when he represents the unfolding of national consciousness by means of unconvincing reflections, by Neil and others, that relate panorama to felt nationalism. The overt didacticism of *Barometer rising*, however, is more than offset by its formal precision, imaginative power, and literary craftsmanship. With his first published novel MacLennan produced a minor classic of Canadian fiction.   D. O. SPETTIGUE

Barr, Robert (1850-1912). Born in Glasgow, Scot., he was taken by his family in 1854 to Wallacetown, Canada West (Ont.); after several moves the family settled in Windsor. Barr attended area schools and then obtained a temporary teaching certificate and taught until 1873, when he entered the Toronto Normal School to obtain a permanent licence. In 1875, after teaching in Wallaceburg and Walkerville, he became principal of Windsor Central School. In 1876 he married Eva Bennett and gave up teaching to become a reporter for the *Detroit Free Press*. Barr's success with the *Free Press*, evident from his quick rise to exchange editor by 1881, culminated with his move to London, Eng., to establish an English weekly edition. In 1892, with Jerome K. Jerome, he founded *The Idler*, an illustrated magazine for men, and became a well-known and well-travelled journalist and writer, counting among his friends and acquaintances Stephen Crane, George Gissing, Henry James, Joseph Conrad, and Arthur Conan Doyle. Well known on both sides of the Atlantic, Barr was featured in a number of magazine articles of the day, and in 1900 was awarded an honorary M.A. by the University of Michigan. He died at his home, 'Hillhead', in Woldingham, Surrey.

Barr's literary career began with his submissions in the form of ironic correspondence and humorous squibs—under the penname 'Luke Sharp'—to the Bothwell, Ont., *Advance*, and to the satiric Toronto periodical *Grip*. But he was not able to make much headway as a writer until he caught the attention of the editor of the *Detroit Free Press*, William E. Quinby, with his sketch 'A dangerous journey', and was invited to be a reporter. His first collection of sketches and short stories, *Strange happenings* (London, 1883), was followed by fourteen others, three of which were published posthumously. Probably the most notable of these collections is *The triumphs of Eugène Valmont* (1906), which, in catering to the contemporary vogue of the detective story, introduced the delightful Valmont, seen by recent critics as a precursor to, and possibly a model for, Agatha Christie's Hercule Poirot. Barr was at his best as a writer of short fiction, particularly the detective story. His ear for crisp, functional dialogue, his eye for social and national nuances, his ability to outline a situation, and his faculty for constructing, then quickly and credibly resolving a mystery, make these stories and sketches entertaining reading. The Eugène

Valmont stories are still included in anthologies. See the *Selected stories of Robert Barr* (1977) edited by John Parr.

Barr also wrote twenty novels that cover the literary range from historical romance to socio-political realism, but today only four are of interest: his first novel, *In the midst of alarms* (London, 1894; rpr. 1973), *The measure of the rule* (1907; rpr. 1973), *The mutable many* (New York, 1896), and *The victors* (1901). The first two make full and direct use of Barr's Canadian experience. *In the midst of alarms* is set in 1866 at the scene of the Battle of Ridgeway, a Fenian incursion into Canada. Barr well portrays the largely farcical battle and provides an accompanying message about the futility of war and a comic description of a revival meeting. Similarly *The measure of the rule*, making use of Barr's Toronto Normal School experiences in 1873, contains some trenchant material on the education of both students and teachers and on the social realities of Toronto boarding houses; there are also penetrating portraits of identifiable historical figures. But the latter part of the novel—treating the hero's career as a struggling artist in Paris and an eventual reunion with his beloved—is merely sentimental romance.

The lasting impression of a typical Barr novel is of individual portions that are in themselves well done but relate adventitiously to the whole. First and foremost a commercial writer who was more discerning than most, Barr exploited a popular formula for the writing of fiction. Arnold Bennett wrote in his *Journals* that Barr was 'an admirable specimen of the man of talent who makes of letters an honest trade', though he had not much, 'if any at all, feeling for literature.'

In addition, Barr completed *The O'Ruddy* (1903), a novel left unfinished by Stephen Crane at his death; collaborated with S. Lewis-Ransom to write a play, *The conspiracy* (London, n.d.); and wrote a travel book, *The unchanging east* (1900).

See Louis K. MacKendrick's introduction to the 1973 reprint of *The measure of the rule*, and John Parr, 'The measure of Robert Barr', *Journal of Canadian Fiction*, vol. III, no. 2 (1974).   S.R. MacGILLIVRAY

Barre du jour, La (1965-) Founded by Nicole BROSSARD, Marcel Saint-Pierre, Roger Soublière, and Jan Stafford, this Montreal periodical was initially committed to the development of a strong Québécois literature by documenting previously unpublished or unavailable texts from the nineteenth century—such as the correspondence of Albert LOZEAU (Feb. 1966), unpublished poems by Saint-Denys GARNEAU (Sept.-Oct. 1969), an inaccessible play, *L'anglomanie* (July-Dec. 1965), and a previously unpublished play, *Les républicains français* (Summer 1970), by Louis-Joseph QUESNEL; by publishing avant-garde literary modes and young authors who rejected the more conventional expectations of their contemporaries (Aug.-Sept. 1968); and by supporting the concept of literary transgression, its politics and stylistic consequences (Fall 1973). The magazine also noticed new methodological approaches to literature, such as the impact of structuralist theories on contemporary criticism (Spring-Summer 1973) and contemporary, as opposed to avant-garde, writers: the issue of May 1968 was devoted to Roland GIGUÈRE and that of Oct. 1970 to Gaston MIRON. In addition, para-literary and unconventional literary modes—such as cartoons, and their impact on literature—were featured in the issues of Winter and Spring 1975, and of Feb. 1977 and Feb. 1982.

After Nicole Brossard left *La Barre du jour* in 1975 to devote herself to the feminist monthly *Têtes de Pioche*, the magazine underwent a number of editorial changes and became in Sept. 1977 *La Nouvelle Barre du jour*. Brossard returned to it in that same year and gave it a feminist impulse, making it a highly visible focus for women's writings. *La Barre du jour*'s subsequent involvement with both avant-garde and feminist writings stemmed from a literary perception that was linked to major transformations in the image women have of themselves and to the role women have been given in the modern world.   CAROLINE BAYARD

Barrette, Jacquéline. See DRAMA IN FRENCH 1948 TO 1981: 4.

Barthe, Ulric. See NOVELS IN FRENCH 1900 TO 1920.

Basile, Jean (b. 1932). Jean Basile-Bezroudnoff was born in Paris of Russian parents and came to Québec as a young man. He has worked as a journalist on *Le Devoir* in Montreal since 1962—as editor of the weekly Arts and Letters section, as a critic of popular music (writing under the pseudonym Penelope), and now as the television critic. He left *Le Devoir* from 1969 to 1973 to collaborate on the underground monthly magazine *Mainmise*, which he co-founded—an exciting avant-garde expression of the Québec counterculture that enjoyed a remarkable commercial success. Since 1973 Basile has written on the media for various Québec magazines.

Basile's early work, his first novel *Lorenzo* (1963) and *Journal poétique* (1965), are restrained yet lyrical questionings of emotion. *Joli tambour* (1966), a historical play that explores the relationship between hangman and criminal in New France, has been performed only in English, in Toronto, as *The drummer-boy*.

With the trilogy initiated by *La jument des Mongols* (1964) Basile really found his voice as a writer of the sixties' generation in Québec. Despite their exotic titles, *La jument*, *Le Grand Khan* (1967), and *Les voyages d'Irkoutsk* (1970) are about Québec, and specifically about the personal and collective manifestations of underground culture in Montreal—presented as a city in North America. Each novel is narrated by one member of a trio—Jonathan, Jérémie, and Judith—and each narrative is a relentless flow of fantasy, humour, and reflection. Basile's writing becomes increasingly dazzling and dense as he enters the world of drug experimentation, and in *Les voyages* he weaves into the personal quests of his characters an overall view of the cultural turbulence of the time. *Les voyages* has by now acquired a serious documentary value, in addition to its interest as fiction.

SHERRY SIMON

Bates, Walter (1760-1842). Born in Stamford, Conn., he immigrated to Saint John, N.B., as a Loyalist with the Spring Fleet of 1783, settling at Kingston in King's County, where he was sheriff for many years. He wrote *The mysterious stranger* (New Haven, 1817), a popular account of 'Henry Moon' (Henry More Smith), a notorious horse thief who was incarcerated in Bates's prison for a time before being pardoned and then went to the United States where he continued his criminal activities. It was also published in England under the title *Companion for Caraboo: a narrative of the conduct and adventures of Henry Frederic Moon, alias Henry Frederic More Smith, alias William Newman . . . now under sentence of imprisonment, in Connecticut . . . containing an account of his unparalled artifices, impostures, mechanical ingenuity, &c. &c. displayed during and subsequently to his confinement in one of His Majesty's gaols in the province of New Brunswick . . . with an introductory description of New Brunswick; and a postscript,* *containing some account of Caraboo, the late female imposter, at Bristol* (London, 1817)—covering the 'dreadful doings' of Smith since the appearance of the first edition. (Many other editions followed.) Bates describes, not without some admiration, the exploits of his 'hero', but explains that his book was written 'to prevent future mischiefs'. Written in a quaint, unsophisticated style, *The mysterious stranger* is an intriguing oddity in early Canadian literature and provides an insight into the rough-and-ready conditions of prisons in the early nineteenth century. Bates also wrote a history of the church at Kingston, posthumously published by W.O. Raymond in *Kingston and the Loyalists of the 'Spring fleet' of A.D. 1783, with reminiscences of early days in Connecticut: a narrative. By Walter Bates, Esq., sometime high sheriff of the county of King's. To which is appended a diary written by Sarah Frost on her voyage to St. John, N.B., with the Loyalists of 1783* (Saint John, 1889). In this work he provides an authentic picture of the Connecticut Loyalists, their sufferings at the hands of the American revolutionists, and their subsequent hardships when they were forced to confront the Canadian wilderness.

DOUGLAS LOCHHEAD

Bauer, Walter (1904-76). Born in Merseburg, Germany, he graduated from the teacher's college there. He was a widely published author when the Nazis came to power and banned his books. Disillusioned with German attitudes, both during and after the Second World War, he immigrated in 1952 to Toronto, where he found work as a dishwasher. From 1954 to 1958 he attended the University of Toronto and taught there in the German department from 1958 until his retirement a few months before his death. He published more than seventy books in German—novels, story collections (one called *Fremd in Toronto:* A stranger in Toronto), biographies (of La Salle and Grey Owl, among others), poetry, essays, and children's books. In the last years of his life he wrote his poems in English.

Henry BEISSEL has translated two collections of Bauer's lyrical poetry, *The price of morning* (1968) and *A different sun* (1976). In his most striking poems in English, Bauer explored the experience of the immigrant. What the poet finds in the New World is ambivalence, expressed in the title poem of the second collection: 'A sun without depth, without shame, without guilt, without

45

shadows.' In 'Emigrant', from the first collection, the Old World has altered out of recognition: 'He lives now/On a huge new continent,/But he pines away/For a country that/No longer exists.' Experiencing Old World guilt and gratitude to the New, the poet merges the two into a maturity that is sometimes tinged with sentimentality.

Seven translations and eight poems written in English by Bauer are among the works collected by Beissel in his tribute to the poet in *The* TAMARACK REVIEW 77 & 78 (Summer 1979).   JOHN ROBERT COLOMBO

Beardsley, Charles E. See *The* VICTIMS OF TYRANNY.

Beauchemin, Nérée (1850-1931). Born at Yamachiche, Qué., he attended the Séminaire de Nicolet and studied medicine at the Université Laval, graduating in 1874. Early in life he showed his gift for poetry in work clearly influenced by the romanticism of that era. His first poem, 'Les petits pèlerins', was published in *L'Opinion publique* in 1871. He was the author of two poetry collections—*Les floraisons matutinales* (Trois-Rivières, 1897) and *Patrie intime* (1928)—and approximately 100 more poems appeared in magazines. Beauchemin also wrote close to 200 unpublished fragments of prose and correspondence, and over 600 variations of poems that he had chosen to publish. All are accounted for in the critical edition *Nérée Beauchemin, son oeuvre* (3 vols, 1973-4) edited by Armand Guilmette.

One of the most important regionalists in Québec's literary history, Beauchemin was above all a poet of transition between two great literary movements: the patriotic school of Québec and the literary school of Montreal. Like FRÉCHETTE and CRÉMAZIE, he was at first heavily influenced by Romanticism. He relied on the basic themes of his era—nature, homeland, religion—but thanks to a refined sensibility, and a more subtle artistry than that of his predecessors, his work gradually transcended the traditional flamboyant style. Though usually considered a poet of the nineteenth century, his best book appeared in the twentieth. He wrote for himself, secretly, in his country-doctor's office, tossing finished poems into a drawer with no thought of publication. Finally a friend persuaded him to publish *Patrie intime* and it was acclaimed by critics. It consists of short poems written in a spare style in which each word seems stamped with a special status. Beauchemin's poetic voice is muted and, despite Romantic accents, his poetry is subdued, showing delicate colours and many shades and modulations. He sought to create beauty out of the things around him: the simplicity of objects, a hand's skill, the patina of time—all are shown through homely things such as a cupboard, a chest, a glass-fronted cabinet, etc. Beauchemin said in his notes that he preferred slight, insignificant subjects so that the craftsmanship of execution would appear more striking. This attitude to art—a fierce desire to polish its form—helped to set him apart from the mainstream. The famous 'Cloche de Louisbourg' has been anthologized most frequently; yet other poems from *Les floraisons*—such as 'Hantise', 'Mirage', 'L'idylle dorée', and 'Rayons d'octobre'—are also important.

Besides the critical edition mentioned above, see also *Choix de poésies de Nérée Beauchemin* (1950) edited by Clément MARCHAND, who wrote *Nérée Beauchemin* (1957); and Armand Guilmette, 'Nérée Beauchemin, poète de la conciliation', *Cahiers de l'Acadamie canadienne-française*, vol. 14, 1972.   ARMAND GUILMETTE

Beauchemin, Yves (b. 1941). Born in Noranda, Qué., he attended elementary school in Clova, Abitibi, before moving to Joliette, where he completed his 'cours classique' at the Séminaire. In 1965 he obtained his License ès lettres from the Université de Montréal. After teaching for a while and working for the Bibliothèque générale of the Université de Montréal, he joined Holt, Rinehart and Winston in 1967. Then, in 1969, he went to Radio-Québec, where he has been working since.

Beauchemin published many articles in newspapers and magazines, such as *Sept Jours* and *Digest Éclair*, before writing his first novel, *L'enfirouapé* (1974). A satirical and imaginative blend of realism and fantasy that recalls the events of the October Crisis in 1970, it was well received by the critics. A naive young man who has been manoeuvred into prison by an unscrupulous politician seeks revenge for all the humiliations he has suffered in his life: he decides to organize the kidnapping of the politician, but he and those who join him must also kidnap an English-speaking businessman in order to compel the government to pay $500,000 ransom and to release thirteen political prisoners. An enraged would-be poet shoots the businessman for insulting his captors in English, and after a variety of episodes—

some hilarious—the terrorists decide to crash the plane taking them to sanctuary in Cuba on the crowd of policemen and politicians below. *Le matou* (1981) is a fast-paced story of fantasy and adventure. Florent Boisonneault, little thinking his action will disrupt his whole life, helps a man knocked senseless by a bronze quotation mark that has fallen from a sign. Soon, however, he receives a bizarre invitation from a witness to the accident—Egon Ratablavasky—who insists on meeting him. Later, little by little, Ratablavasky reveals his mysterious, diabolical plans. Warmly received in both Canada and France, this extraordinary novel was considered one of the best ever written in Québec and its author one of the most gifted storytellers to emerge in recent years in French-language literature.

See also NOVELS IN FRENCH 1960 TO 1982: 3.   JACQUES COTNAM

Beaugrand, Honoré (1848-1906). Born at Lanoraie, Qué., he spent four years at the Collège de Joliette before entering the Montreal Military School. At seventeen he enlisted in the Emperor Maximilian's army and served in the Mexican War (1865-7). After two years in France, where he was exposed to liberal, radical, and anticlerical philosophies, he moved to the United States in 1869 and pursued a career as a journalist and newspaper publisher in Fall River, Mass.; St Louis, Mo.; Boston; and Ottawa. In 1879 he founded *La Patrie*, a reformist newspaper, in Montreal; he was mayor of that city in 1885 and 1886, after which he abandoned politics. In 1887 he published the *Daily News*, which he soon left to travel in Europe and elsewhere. His 'Lettres de voyage' appeared often in the columns of *La Patrie*. Beaugrand retired at the age of forty-nine, after handing over *La Patrie* to J.-I. Tarte, and devoted himself until his death in Westmount to travel and folklore.

Beaugrand's novel *Jeanne-la-Fileuse: épisode de l'émigration franco-canadienne aux États-Unis* (Fall River, Mass., 1878, and Montreal, 1888) was as much a political pamphlet as a novel, aimed at justifying immigration to the United States at a period when many French Canadians associated this with a poverty-ridden and degenerate section of society.

Following his involvement with the first Canadian Folklore Society, a branch of the American Folklore Society, which was founded in Montreal in 1892, Beaugrand published, in 1900, *La chasse-galerie: légendes canadiennes* and *La chasse-galerie and other Canadian stories*. His *New studies of Canadian folk lore* (1904) includes an article on traditional French-Canadian beliefs; a translation of 'Macloune', a tale that had appeared earlier in *La chasse-galerie*; a lengthy study of Indian picture writing; and 'Legend of the North Pacific', in which Beaugrand suggests, somewhat romantically, that all the indigenous dwellers of America are descendants of the Japanese Ainus. As a folklorist Beaugrand's writing is very literary, but he remains nonetheless one of the pioneers of folklore studies in French Canada.

Beaugrand's travelogues, which he had contributed to *La Patrie*, were published in *Lettres de voyage—France—Italie—Sicile—Malte—Tunisie—Algérie—Espagne* (Montréal, 1889); in 1890, also in Montreal, he published a second volume, *Six mois dans les Montagnes Rocheuses—Colorado—Utah—Nouveau-Mexique*. Beaugrand had earlier published a highly appreciated book entitled *Le vieux Montréal, 1611-1803—Album historique, chronologique et topographique de la ville de Montréal depuis sa fondation* (Montréal, 1884).
                                                GERALD THOMAS

Beaulieu, Jocelyne. See DRAMA IN FRENCH 1948 TO 1981: 4.

Beaulieu, Michel (b. 1941). Born in Montreal, he was educated at the Collège Jean-de-Brébeuf and the Université de Montréal. There he edited the student newspaper, *Le Quartier Latin*, and directed the student press. He helped found Éditions Estérel in 1965, and the short-lived *Quoi* in 1967. In the seventies he was a member of the Centre d'essai des auteurs dramatiques; helped to found *Jeu*, the experimental theatre journal, in 1975; and was president of the association of literary translators. His sustained contribution at a high level of personal commitment and artistic integrity to the best of Québec's avant-garde was recognized by the award of the Prix de la revue *Études françaises* in 1973, the year that his first retrospective collection of poems, *Variables*, was published.

In poetry alone Beaulieu's listed titles number some thirty items, ranging from the 250 pages of *Desseins* (1980), collected poems from 1961 to 1966, to the literary spoof *Le 'Flying Dutchman'* (1976). *Desseins* and *Variables* are the principal sources of his lasting work, and contain extensive bibliographies of all poems published to date.

Beaulieu

Visages (1981) is an extensive collection of poems written in 1977 that is described as fifth and last in the cycle *Lettre des saisons*, another example of Beaulieu's desire to gather his production retrospectively into larger units. Several of his titles—*Desseins, Variables, Anecdotes* (1977), and *Visages*—point to the tension in his work between the fragment and the totality. Beaulieu writes series of brief poems, usually ten to twenty lines, though the links are not made explicit: any unity is a unity of voice—a quiet, private, personal voice, but one that strains insistently to be heard. His poetry is one of anguish, doubt, and shame patiently borne and painstakingly verbalized, though words are rarely his salvation: they provoke constant questionings and uncertainties. It is occasionally playful—he puns and makes recondite literary allusions and takes mischievous liberties with syntax—but it is never lighthearted. In the tight-knotted universe of Beaulieu ('*noeud*' is a key word in his writing), nothing is easy.

Beaulieu's novel *La représentation* (1972; new edn, 1980) is the monologue—constantly interrupted by asides in different type—of a timid, rather violent man coming to terms with the liberated woman and free love. It draws an analogy between the clumsiness, and scope for misunderstanding, of sexual communication with another person and the problems of self-expression in Québec.   C.R.P. MAY

Beaulieu, Victor-Lévy (b. 1945). Born in Saint-Jean-de-Dieu, near Rimouski, Qué., he is largely self-taught, and grateful to the classical-college teacher whose scorn for his prose drove him from school and saved him from university. To justify his lack of formal education he has written, in his own way, three theses: *Pour saluer Victor Hugo* (1971), *Jack Kerouac, essai-poulet* (1972)—translated by Sheila Fischman as *Jack Kerouac; a chicken essay* (1976)—and *Monsieur Melville* (3 vols, 1978). These writers and others whom he admires—such as James Joyce, Malcolm LOWRY, and Réjean DUCHARME—are polymaths like himself who, in their passionate search for the self, create a faithful picture of an age and a culture. Beaulieu's idiosyncratic scholarship closely resembles his highly personal fiction: *Monsieur Melville* was incorporated into one of his novel cycles. Directeur littéraire of Éditions du Jour, before helping to found Éditions de l'Aurore and then opening a bookshop and publishing from it his own

Éditions VLB, Beaulieu delights in being at the hub of the social and literary activity proliferating in Québec today: 'ce bouillonnement qui se cherche un sens'. He is the most prolific of the present generation of writers, having written thirteen novels in as many years, five plays, three essays, and more than 150 episodes of television serials, the latest of which, *Race de monde*, has had an unbroken three-year run. In recent years he has organized his early novels into two sequences. The first is the saga of les Beauchemin: *Race de monde* (1969); *La nuitte de Malcolm Hudd* (1970); *Jos Connaissant* (1970; rev., 1978), translated by Ray Chamberlain (1982); *Un rêve québécois* (1972), translated by Ray Chamberlain as *A Québécois dream* (1978); *Les grands-pères* (1972), translated by Marc Plourde as *The grandfathers* (1975); *Oh Miami, Miami, Miami* (1973); and *Don Quichotte de la démanche* (1974), winner of a Governor General's Award and translated by Sheila Fischman as *Don Quixote in Nighttown* (1978). The second sequence he calls *Voyageries: Blanche forcée* (1976), *N'évoque plus que le désenchantement de ta ténèbre, mon si pauvre Abel: lamentation* (1976), *Sagamo Job J* (1977), *Monsieur Melville*, and *Una* (1980), the latter written in France in six days. He is now embarked on a third cycle, *La grande tribu*.

Beaulieu's characters embody aspects of his own character and experience: he frankly explains their fantasies, hang-ups, phobias, madness, verbosity, and silence, and—beyond the ravages of everyday existence—man's quest for a truth to transcend the absurdity of modern urban life, for fulfilling relationships, and for a satisfying artistic form to express them. Beaulieu has evolved steadily, shedding the elaborate puns, quirky spellings, and some of the erotic fantasies of the early novels. His writing has gradually become less of a social fresco as it focuses, from *Don Quichotte* onwards, on the total personality of the writer engaged in the creative act, and on the constraints—social, political, domestic, psychological, literary, and professional—that he himself feels as a writer. 'Everything lives simultaneously in the author's head', says Beaulieu's writer-hero in *N'évoque plus*; but narrative convention and the linearity of language make the expression of this simultaneity difficult. Working on several levels at once, he sometimes introduces copious illustrations: photos, engravings, and the brooding, monster-ridden sketches and doodles of Victor Hugo; epigraphs and parentheses add further to these very personal palimpsests. A recurring theme is that of animal sexuality and fecundity, of abundant life contained in, or spewing from, belly-like tumescences—an obsessive metaphor for Beaulieu's disturbing fertility.

An admirer of Jacques FERRON, sharing his view (embodied in *Le ciel de Québec*, 1969) that Québec culture is alienated from reality, Beaulieu strives honestly and fiercely in his novels to bring it down to earth. He believes that despite the gains of the past twenty years, the Quiet Revolution broke with the past too hastily for the good of Québec's soul. His anthology, *Manuel de la petite littérature de Québec* (1975), saves from oblivion quaint lives of child martyrs, parish histories, temperance tracts, and other works of piety and naive spirituality.

Critics are divided over Beaulieu. Some find his work 'mal conçu, mal écrit, malsain'. Gérard BESSETTE (in *Trois romanciers québécois*, 1973) doubts that he is capable of profound psychological analysis. Since *Monsieur Melville*, however, critics have increasingly recognized Beaulieu's imaginative and verbal power and the ambitious scope of his vision.

The Bessette (above) contains the best critical writing on Beaulieu. See also Gabrielle Poulin, *Romans du paysage: 1968-1979* (1980), pp. 373-438; *Québec français* (45, 1982), VOIX ET IMAGES (III, 2, 1977); and *Études françaises* (1983/1).

See also NOVELS IN FRENCH1960 TO 1982: 3(a).   C.R.P. MAY

Beautiful Joe (Philadelphia, 1894). Subtitled *An autobiography* and narrated by a dog, this novel for children by Marshall SAUNDERS was designed to arouse for dogs the kind of sympathy stirred for horses by *Black Beauty* (1877; first American publication 1890). Joe's life story moves from puppy days, when his ears and tail were cruelly cropped by his first brutal owner, to happy times with kind Miss Laura and the Morris family. Joe prevents a burglary, takes a train-ride to a well-run farm, visits an ill-run one, and witnesses a fire in which the members of a performing troupe of animals perish. Readers of *Beautiful Joe* learn of the pleasures and responsibilities of raising dogs, cats, canaries, parrots, snakes, goldfish, and rabbits. They also see the life experiences of foxes, bears, sheep, cattle, and horses, all from a fellow-animal's point of view. This novel shared with the much finer contemporary animal stories of Charles G.D. ROBERTS and Ernest Thompson SETON a sympathy for animals and a recognition of cruel streaks in both animal and human life. *Beautiful Joe*, however, is unashamedly sentimental and didactic: Joe supports the views of Miss Laura and her friends on temperance, mannerliness, and worship, and exploits the reader's sympathy by indulging in sensitivities that seem inappropriate in an animal. In a revised version (1927) violence is softened and colloquialism reduced; but the quick succession of exciting incidents and the sense of a likeable voice still make this 'fine tale of an ugly dog' a world-wide best seller.

ELIZABETH WATERSTON

Beaven, James. See PHILOSOPHY IN CANADA: 3.

Beck, Lily Adams (d. 1931). The daughter of the British admiral John Moresby, she spent many years in the Orient, travelling in India, Ceylon, China, Java, Burma, Japan and Tibet, until 1919, when she came to Canada and settled in Victoria, B.C., where she became known as an eccentric proponent of Oriental customs and philosophy. Before 1925 Beck was known only as the author of a number of books and stories about Oriental philosophy and traditions. The revelation that she was more or less simultaneously writing popular historical romances, published under the name of E. Barrington, astounded contemporary readers. In addition Beck wrote three novels under the pseudonym Louis Moresby. Altogether she published almost thirty books. She died in Kyoto, Japan.

Lily Adams Beck was the author of *The ninth vibration and 8 other stories* (1922), *Dreams and delights* (1922), *The key of dreams* (1922), *The perfume of the rainbow* (1923), *The treasure of Ho* (1925), *The way of the stars* (1925), *The splendour of Asia* (1926), *The way of power* (1928), *The story of Oriental philosophy* (1928), *The garden of vision* (1929), and *The joyous story of Astrid* (1931).

As E. Barrington she wrote *The ladies* (1922), *The chaste Diana* (1923), *The gallants* (1924), *The divine lady* (1924), *Glorious Apollo* (1925), *The exquisite Perdita* (1926), *The house of fulfilment* (1927), *The thunderer* (1927), *The empress of hearts* (1928), *The laughing queen* (1929), *The duel of the queens* (1930), *The Irish beauties* (1931), *Anne Boleyn* (1932), and *The great romantic* (1933).

As Louis Moresby she wrote *The glory of Egypt* (1926), *Rubies* (1927), and *Captain Java* (1928).   MARILYN ROSE

Bégon

Bégon, Elisabeth. See Writing in NEW FRANCE: 4.

Beissel, Henry (b. 1929). Born in Germany, he studied philosophy at the University of Cologne and London and came to Canada in 1951. He attended the University of Toronto and is now professor of English at Concordia University, Montreal. Beissel's concern for human aspirations in the face of civilization's nihilistic march towards destruction first became apparent in his editorship of the controversial political and literary journal, *Edge*, which moved with him, from its beginnings in Edmonton in 1963, to its final year in Montreal in 1969. He was president of the LEAGUE OF CANADIAN POETS in 1980-1.

The necessity for artistic truth in the presence of modern civilization's betrayals and political machinations is a theme first sounded in Beissel's *New wings for Icarus* (1966), a poem in four parts that moves towards a statement of the poet's faith in man's idealistic aspirations, his ability to create, and his insistence on the value of human love. *Face on the dark* (1970) is his only book so far devoted to shorter poems, though even here the urge is towards the larger poetic statement, some selections being parts of longer uncompleted poems. *The salt I taste* (1975) is mainly devoted to the title poem, a sequence of meditations on the salty bitterness of life, with the image of the sea symbolizing life's continuance even as existence itself is continually eroded. Beissel is at present publishing in sections a book-length poem, *Cantos North*, sub-titled 'an epic poem about Canada in twelve cantos'.

Beissel's plays have often focused on Canadian themes and cultures, especially in his *Inook and the sun* (1974), a play for young people with an Inuit setting that was first performed at the Stratford Festival in 1973. His other plays include *Skinflint* (1969), a play for marionettes; *For crying out loud* (1975), a play for young people; *Under coyote's eye: a play about Ishi* (1980), about the last survivor of the doomed Yahi tribe; *Improvisations for Mr. X* (1979); and *Goya* (1978), which is less a historical play than a dramatic 'exploration of the creative imagination'. Beissel has also edited a collection of one-act plays, *Cues and entrances* (1977).

The wide range of Beissel's interest in a holistic cultural civilization is exemplified by his translations from many languages, particularly in his versions of the work of German-Canadian poet Walter BAUER: *The price of morning* (1968) and *A different sun* (1976).   PETER STEVENS

Belaney, Archibald Stansfeld (1888-1938). When Grey Owl—the famous trapper, writer, and lecturer—died suddenly in his fiftieth year in Saskatchewan, few were aware that he had no Indian blood but was in fact an Englishman named Archibald Stansfeld Belaney. Two elderly maiden ladies of extreme gentility and unquestionable veracity, living in Hastings, Eng., confirmed that Grey Owl was their nephew Archie, whom they had brought up, and who had gone to Canada as soon as he left school. The shock of this revelation at that time could be likened to an earthquake tremor. When the full story of his life became known, the character that surfaced was far more interesting than the Thoreau-like naturalist and writer who occasionally emerged from the Canadian woods to give lectures and assist in the promotion of his books.

Archie Belaney was born in Hastings, the son of George Belaney, a Victorian 'remittance man' who led a wandering life of adventure and dissipation in America. Brought up in a household of women, the boy created for himself an image of his missing father as a doughty fighter in the Wild West. He believed that his mother, who visited him briefly two or three times in his boyhood, was an Apache. The published history of Hastings Grammar School records that he read and dreamt of Indians; this is supported by the numerous drawings he made of Indians and animals in the margins of the books he left behind when he went to Canada.

Belaney immigrated to Canada in 1906, a young man of eighteen, and became a guide and packer in northern Ontario. Within a year he joined a band of Ojibwas who summered on Bear Island in Lake Temagami. In 1910 he married an Ojibwa girl, Angele Eguana, and quickly came under the influence of the band, which was then barely spoilt by any contact with civilization. Belaney lived and hunted with these Ojibwas and, by his own account, went through a ceremony of adoption and was given the name Grey Owl. But in 1912 he left the band and moved to Biscostasing, the headquarters of the Mississauga Reserve. He served in the First World War and was wounded. While recovering in England in 1917 he married Constance Holmes, a childhood sweetheart. The marriage was brief, for he soon returned to Canada, taking up again his life as trapper and guide in the Mississauga river country. Sickened by his war experiences, he turned again to the Indians. He resumed his Grey Owl identity, although he was still known to whites as Belaney.

His meeting in 1926 with Anahareo, an Iroquois girl with whom he had an eight-year passionate though stormy love affair, was the turning-point of his life. Anahareo's horror of his bloody trade as a trapper made him aware of what he was doing, and ultimately resulted in his fame. She persuaded him to save and bring into their cabin two baby beaver, whose mother had drowned in one of his traps. These infant creatures—pathetic relics of what then seemed, because of overtrapping, to be a vanishing species—adopted Grey Owl and Anahareo as their parents. Their affectionate behaviour and childlike ways made Grey Owl vow never to take the life of another beaver. He and Anahareo went to Cabano, in northern Québec, to find a sanctuary for the beavers and to found a colony for the preservation of the species. (Their heroic journey is unforgettably described in Grey Owl's best-known book, *Pilgrims of the wild*.) The couple and their charges were discovered by the Canadian Government in 1930. Grey Owl was appointed an Honorary Park Warden and a home was built for him and his beavers at Lake Ajawaan in Prince Albert National Park, Sask.

While at Cabano, Grey Owl had turned to writing to support his adopted 'family', as his sole income was a monthly war pension of fifteen dollars. His first published piece, 'The falls of silence', appeared under the name of A.S. Belaney in *Country Life*, the famous English sporting and social magazine. Its theme was the silence of the great north woods, 'the most silent country on the face of the globe, in which man moves observed only by animals whose senses are trained to hair-trigger delicacy'. With a further series of articles on animal lore, contributed to *Forest & Outdoors* in the next few years under the name of Grey Owl, he became well known in naturalist circles in Canada and the U.S.A.

In the eight years of his life remaining after the Canadian Government's discovery of him, Grey Owl wrote four books. In *Men of the last frontier* (1929) he recreated vividly and simply life as it was lived when he first came under the tutelage of the Ojibwa and

listened to their legends. *Pilgrims of the wild* (1935), which was published in England by Lovat Dickson Limited, established his fame as a writer. *The adventures of Sajo and her beaver people*, also published in 1935, was an attempt at fiction for children. Although this story of an Indian boy's attempt to find his lost beaver pet has a number of stock city characters that weaken its impact, it was enormously popular. *Tales of an empty cabin* (1936), which shows Grey Owl the writer at his best, is an impressive collection of sketches of men and animals in a forest world; it is full of humour and close, affectionate observation. All four books are a lament for a lost frontier.

In 1935-6 and 1937-8 Grey Owl made two highly successful lecture tours of the United States and Britain, ending with a lecture to the royal family at Buckingham Palace. Those who listened to him, and watched the half-dozen films a cameraman employed by the Canadian Government had made of him, saw something that would possibly never be seen again: man and animal living together in perfect harmony. Undeterred by the camera, the beavers came and went about their business, pushing open the door of Grey Owl's cabin and advancing with armfuls of sticks and mud to repair the structure of their house (built against an inner wall of the cabin but with an underwater outlet in the lake); or disporting themselves like so many water-nymphs around his canoe, inviting him to play. At the height of the Depression, Grey Owl's simple message touched something in the hearts of his audience. 'You are tired with years of civilization. I come to offer you what . . .? A single green leaf.' *The Times* of London called him 'A Canadian Thoreau'. Though known as a naturalist and environmentalist in his own time, Grey Owl was really an unsurpassed observer of animal behaviour and recorder of wilderness life.

His grave is beside his cabin on Lake Ajawaan in Prince Albert National Park. The cross that was first raised over it bore the name Archibald Stansfeld Belaney. A few years later the Canadian Government replaced this with a stone, bearing the name Grey Owl and the dates of his birth and death, and restored his cabin, which is frequently visited. After his death Angele Eguana, his Ojibwa wife, represented by John G. Diefenbaker, established that she had been truly married to him—she shrugged away his infidelity as 'he liked to go travel in the Indian way'. Although she had not seen him for many years, she was awarded the wife's share of his quite substantial estate.

Anahareo has written a revealing memoir of their life together: *Devil in deerskins* (1972). *The green leaf* (1938), edited by Lovat DICKSON, is an account of the controversy prompted by the revelation of Grey Owl's English origin. It includes some of Grey Owl's letters to his publisher, and a record of his last days. See also Lovat Dickson's biography, *Wilderness man* (1973).

LOVAT DICKSON

Belle Bête, La (1959). The first novel by Marie-Claire BLAIS, which was published to mingled astonishment and acclaim when she was only twenty—and was translated by Merloyd Lawrence as *Mad shadows* (1960, NCL 1971)—remains, despite some youthful crudities of structure, an important work, both as a brilliant introduction to the vision of a dazzling new writer and as a link between the social novelists of the 1940s and such later experimental Québec writers as Hubert AQUIN and Réjean DUCHARME. Striking in its macabre intensity, its denial of pure realism, and in the boldness of its imagery and sheer headlong force, the book presents characters less as individualized human beings than as raw essences—embodiments of evil, narcissism, jealousy, and greed. The setting is as stripped as the characters, almost featureless—a country house, a lake, a train, a faraway city. Against this background, which resembles a painted stage set more than any known landscape, the characters (all of them rootless and all obsessed—a frivolous mother, a beautiful imbecile boy, a jealous sister, a blind youth) move with the strict and inexorable fluidity of dance, enacting a nightmare ritual of envy, murder, betrayal, and disfigurement. The American critic Edmund Wilson, who pronounced Marie-Claire Blais a genius, called the book 'a tragic fairytale', but it is more precisely a hallucinatory moral fable—an examination of pure evil in a society torn from its roots.

JOYCE MARSHALL

Belles-soeurs, Les (1968). A major turning-point in the recent history of Québécois theatre, this play by Michel TREMBLAY was written in 1965 but turned down by many groups—including the Dominion Drama Festival in 1966—before being given a public reading by the Centre d'essai des auteurs dramatiques on 4 Mar. 1968. It was first performed by Montreal's Théâtre du Rideau-

vert, on 28 Aug. 1968. Many people were shocked by its use of JOUAL and by its frank depiction of an ugly reality; some critics thought it too peculiar—regional and parochial—to be exported beyond the linguistic boundaries of its setting. But success soon made it a 'classic'. It was performed in France; in Toronto, with an English premiere at the St Lawrence Centre on 31 Mar. 1973; in thirteen other Canadian cities; on CBC TV; and in the U.S.A. It was first published in 1968 (new edn 1974). The English translation, by Bill Glassco and John Van Burek, was published in 1974.

Les belles-soeurs is almost plotless. A poor woman, Germaine Lauzon, wins a million trading stamps and, realizing that 'it's gonna take forever to paste all those stamps', decides to give 'a stamp-pasting party' for fifteen women—neighbours, sisters, friends, but only one literal sister-in-law. The women, however, steal the stamps and the play ends in derision, with Germaine crying over her lost stamps and happiness and the other women standing at attention singing 'O Canada'. The stamp-pasting party is a vehicle for the women to voice their social and sexual deprivations; in so doing they realize how symbolic and short-lived their dreams of a better life are, how useless their revolt. Though it frequently provokes laughter, this pessimistic drama is justly perceived as a realistic depiction of the working-class in Montreal, or of the condition of women—figures of Québec's destiny—simmering in revolt.

A true (and perhaps necessary) metaphor for the national alienation, *Les belles soeurs* remains a landmark as a formally innovative play. The choruses and monologues that structure it express collective solitudes; and its diction, *joual*—which is used poetically, not realistically—is the language of visceral, spontaneous, and apparently disordered lamentation.

JEAN-CLÉO GODIN

Benoît, Jacques. See NOVELS IN FRENCH 1960 TO 1982: 3(e).

Beresford-Howe, Constance (b. 1922). Born in Montreal and educated at McGill University and Brown University, Rhode Island, she taught English literature at McGill and now teaches at the Ryerson Polytechnical Institute, Toronto. While living in Montreal she wrote four novels that explore the emotional lives of young women. The first three have contemporary settings: *The unreasoning heart* (1946) is the story of a homeless adolescent girl who wins a place in the family of a prosperous Montreal widow; *Of this day's journey* (1947) is about a young graduate of McGill and Radcliffe who comes to lecture at a college in a small American town; *The invisible gate* (1949) is set in Montreal just after the end of the Second World War, focusing on the romance of a high-spirited young woman whose suitor proves to be unworthy of her. The fourth novel, *My Lady Greensleeves* (1955), is a historical romance set in sixteenth-century England and based upon a documented Elizabethan lawsuit. With the exception of the last, where documentation and historical detail give the novel more substance, these early novels are slight and predictable in plot, though they are notable for the development of a fluid and natural prose style—a characteristic of all Beresford-Howe's novels.

After settling in Toronto in 1971, Beresford-Howe wrote the first of three critically acknowledged and popular novels that portray the day-to-day lives of contemporary women. *The book of Eve* (1973), the most successful, is a charming portrait of a spirited middle-class woman who suddenly, at the age of 65, decides to leave her ailing and demanding husband, trading comfort and social respectability for the freedom to be herself and live as she pleases. (*Eve* is a successful stage adaptation of this novel by Larry FINEBERG; starring Jessica Tandy, it premièred at the Stratford Festival in 1976.) In *A population of one* (1977), a thirty-year-old virgin leaves her sheltered family life in Toronto to take up a teaching position in Montreal, where she sets out to lose her virginity and learns that casual love affairs are neither as easy to come by nor as desirable as she had thought. *The marriage bed* (1981) describes a few weeks in the life of a 24-year-old woman who has two pre-school children, is eight months pregnant, and has been left by her lawyer husband, yet cheerfully continues to affirm the values, and indeed the pleasures, of domesticity and motherhood. These novels form a loose trilogy in that each deals with a phase in the life of a woman who at first seems conventional but eventually exercises her independence by rejecting one of the fashionable tenets of her day: the belief that a woman should dutifully stay with an ungrateful husband, that sexual promiscuity is fulfilling, or that women are bound to feel dissatisfied if they stay at home to raise children. The last two novels seem a little contrived, but all three

are ultimately moving in their portrayal of women who experience both social pressures and inner conflict, yet manage to face the world with wry humour and admirable resilience.

See also NOVELS IN ENGLISH 1960 TO 1982: OTHER TALENTS, OTHER WORKS: 5.

MARILYN ROSE

Berger, Carl. See HISTORICAL WRITING IN ENGLISH: 7.

Bernard, Harry (1898-1979). Born in London, Eng., he studied in Paris, then in St Alban's, Vermont, and from 1911 to 1918 at the Séminaire de Saint-Hyacinthe, Qué., where he received his B.A. After a short stay in Lowell, Mass., he registered in 1919 at the Université de Montréal, where he obtained his 'licence ès lettres'. Parliamentary correspondent for *Le Droit* in Ottawa from 1919 to 1923, he then became director of *Le Courrier de Saint-Hyacinthe* and was associated with that paper until 1970. In 1933-4 Bernard was also director of *L'Action nationale*. For over fifty years a contributor to many newspapers, he received the Prix David three times (1924, 1926, and 1932) and the Prix d'Action intellectuelle six times. In 1943 he was elected to the Royal Society of Canada and received its Silver Medal in 1959 and the Prix Olivar Asselin in 1961. He died in Saint-Hyacinthe.

Apart from numerous articles in newspapers (sometimes written under the pseudonym 'L'Illetré') and reviews, Bernard published more than a dozen books, but he is mainly remembered for his fiction, which gave him a place in the history of literary regionalism and the psychological novel in French Canada. In *L'homme tombé* (1924)—a rarity for the time in being set in a city (Saint-Hyacinthe)—Dr Étienne Normand marries, despite his mother's warnings, a working-class girl. He soon realizes his error as Alberte succumbs easily to the frivolous temptations of the city and begins to neglect her duties as wife and mother, but Normand is powerless to change her. The artificial characters in this didactic novel simply echo the ideologies of the day in Québec; élitism, suspicion of the city and its deceptive pleasures, the necessity for a wife to be submissive to her husband. (Jules-Ernest Larivière reworked the characters in a novel called *L'associée silencieuse* (1925), in which he tried to correct Bernard's portrait of Saint-Hyacinthe, showing that a working-class girl could very easily marry a man from a higher social class and be a worthy helpmate.) Bernard also used this theme of the city as the place of man's degradation in *La maison vide* (1925). The virtues of the land and the 'call of the race' were promoted in *La terre vivante* (1925) and *La ferme des pins* (1930). (In *La ferme*, unusually, it is an anglophone peasant from the Eastern Townships who feels the 'call of the race' and that his children are threatened with assimilation.) These novels, whose cardboard characters are simply mouthpieces for an agricultural ideology, were part of the flourishing Québec regional literature of the 1920s. *Juana, mon aimée* (1931) shows improvement in technique and in psychological verisimilitude. The narrator, Raymond Chatel, a journalist whose career in Ottawa and Montreal is interrupted when he is obliged to take a health cure in Saskatchewan, tells how he came to know and love Juana, and to lose her as a result of a misunderstanding. He likes the West, and says: 'If, instead of emigrating to the south, our excess population had moved immediately in the direction of the West, we would today be masters of the Prairies.' In *Dolorès* (1932), which is often reminiscent of *Juana mon aimée*, Bernard not only describes the pretty *paysage* of the Mont-Laurier region but gives an in-depth psychological analysis of his characters. His last novel, *Les jours sont longs* (1951), is similar in theme and technique to the previous two but is more successful and more convincing.

La dame blanche (1927) is a collection of fourteen stories, with an edifying tone, that were inspired by French-Canadian legends or historical events. The first nine, along with 'Montcalm se fâche', were published under that title in 1935. Bernard's *Essais littéraires* (1929)—which examines the work of Robert de ROQUEBRUNE, Émile CODERRE, Blanche Lamontagne, Jules Fournier, and Louis Dantin (Eugène SEERS)— was well received at the time but does not engage the present-day reader's attention.

For his doctoral thesis presented at the Université de Montréal, *Le roman regionaliste aux États-Unis, 1913-1940* (1949), Bernard drew up an inventory of some 3,000 American novels in which he sought to demonstrate the links between regionalism and literary nationalism. Bernard also wrote a children's book, *ABC du petit naturaliste canadien* (1935), and *Passages et routes d'eau en Haute Mauricie* (1953).   JACQUES COTNAM

Bernier, Hector. See NOVELS IN FRENCH 1900 TO 1920.

Bernier, Jovette-Alice (1900-81). Born in Saint-Fabien, Qué., she was educated at the École Normale des Ursulines, Rimouski, and taught from 1917 to 1923. Her first volume of poetry, *Roulades* (1924), drew little attention, but *Comme l'oiseau* (1926)—in which the poet dared to say 'Je' and to confess the deep deception of her love, her suffering, her remorse and nostalgia—was more successful. In *Tout n'est pas dit*—first published in 1928, then destroyed, and published again in an enlarged edition in 1929, with a preface by Louis Dantin (Eugène SEERS)—she used a variety of structures and metrical rhythms to convey her will to live fully and to taste the sensual pleasures of life, even though love is often deceptive and leaves painful memories. *Les masques déchirès* (1932), in which the poet, no longer able to endure hypocrisy and social convention, attempts to reveal her true self, acknowledges her happiness in having known love and in having suffered from it. The last section is composed of poems from *Roulades* and *Comme l'oiseau*. In *Mon deuil en rouge* (1945), which includes poems dating from 1933, Bernier continues to expose the wounds of love and to relate her sorrow and disillusion, while questioning, sometimes with irony, the human condition.

On vend le bonheur (1931), a collection of articles, tales, reflections on life, and memories of childhood, was not much appreciated by the critics. Bernier's first novel, *La chair décevante* (1931), however, was widely discussed and its morality questioned by critics who found its title too provocative. A melodrama, it tells the story of a young woman who had been abandoned by her lover and left with his child. This far-fetched tale, with its improbable episodes and clichés—mistaken identity, threat of incest, sudden death, a murder trial and acquittal, and the heroine's eventual madness—was considered daring and shocking in the Québec of the thirties. Although Bernier kept writing for newspapers, magazines, and radio broadcasts, she published no book between 1945 and 1969. The undoubtedly autobiographical *Non monsieur* (1969), which tells of an unfortunate love between a young schoolteacher and a Métis ladies' man named Noc, takes up again the theme of the difficulties of an independent girl in pursuit of happiness.   JACQUES COTNAM

Berton, Pierre (b. 1920). Pierre Francis de Marigny Berton was born in Dawson City, the Yukon, and was educated at the University of British Columbia. In 1942 he became city editor of the Vancouver *News-Herald*. He then served in the army, rising to captain/instructor at the Royal Military College. After the war he was a feature writer for the Vancouver *Sun*, joined *Maclean's* in 1947, and was its managing editor from 1952 to 1958, when he left to become a columnist and associate editor of the Toronto *Star*. In 1959 he was awarded the J.V. McAree Memorial Award for the best daily newspaper column in Canada. Devoting his time increasingly to radio and television work, Berton left the *Star* in 1962 to return to *Maclean's* for a year and to work for his own TV program, 'The Pierre Berton Show', which ran until 1973. For over 25 years a regular panelist on CBC's 'Front Page Challege', Berton is now host of two weekly television shows, 'The Great Debate' and 'My Country', and is heard daily on radio (CKEY, Toronto). He holds two ACTRA awards, one for integrity and outspokenness in broadcasting and a second for public-affairs broadcasting. He has been awarded several honorary degrees, is an officer of the Order of Canada, and chairman of the Heritage Canada Foundation.

The colour and excitement of Berton's spirited historical narratives and his passionate nationalism have done much to stir up interest in Canadian history. Berton received a Governor General's Award for *The mysterious North* (1956)—a graphic description of the Canadian North and an appraisal of its potentialities—and for *Klondike: the life and death of the last great goldrush* (1958; rev. 1972; U.S. title *Klondike fever*), considered by many to be Berton's finest work, in which he dramatically recreated the gaudy personalities who, from 1896 to 1903, were attracted to the Klondike by the lust for gold. Berton's Yukon background gave this book a notable degree of immediacy and enthusiasm. For young readers he wrote *The golden trail: the story of the Klondike rush* (1954), reprinted as *Stampede for gold* (1955). He also wrote and narrated the National Film Board documentary *City of gold*, winner of the Grand Prix (Cannes).

The history of the Canadian Pacific Railway is portrayed in two volumes: *The national dream, the great railway, 1871-1881* (1970) and *The last spike, the great railway, 1881-1885* (1971). *The national dream*, written as a heroic epic, and often criticized for being exaggerated and overly imaginative, describes the bitterness, intrigues, scandals, and personal animosities among politicians, surveyors, and railway contractors. While Berton's political interpretation identifies the good of the country with central-Canadian manufacturing and industrial interests, he provides new and captivating anecdotes and human-interest stories in describing the landscape and the politicians, financiers, eccentrics and ordinary people who struggled against handicaps of geography and economy to build the railway. The more subdued *The last spike* won Berton his third Governor General's Award. *The impossible railway* (1972) is a single-volume edition published for the American market; *The great railway illustrated* (1972) is another one-volume abridgement.

The invasion of Canada, 1812-1813 (1980) and *Flames across the border, 1813-1814* (1981) offer vivid descriptions of battle scenes and exact and extensive details of military history; many anecdotes reveal the ironies and tragedies of wartime. Berton is at his best depicting the experiences of rank-and-file soldiers and civilians who happen into the fighting—though his portrayal of soldiers, politicians, Indians, and frontiersmen is somewhat romantic. He believes that the most lasting impact of this 'absurd' war are the myths created by Canadians to justify their separateness from the United States.

Aware of the impact of mass media on the Canadian consciousness, Berton, in *Hollywood's Canada: the Americanization of our national image* (1975), expresses his outrage in an angry, often comical and entertaining diatribe against the American film industry's treatment of Canada as the American West transplanted. In *Why we act like Canadians: a personal exploration of our national character* (1982), a series of fictional letters to an American friend, Berton dispels American myths about Canada and explains that history, climate, and geography have given Canadians a unique lifestyle and sense of independence. *My country; the remarkable past* (1976) and *The wild frontier; more tales from the remarkable past* (1978) are, respectively, collections of eighteen and seven short biographies of bizarre Canadians and their exploits. In *The Dionne years: a thirties melodrama* (1977) Berton focuses on the public phenomenon surrounding the Dionne family, maintaining that the quintuplets were a symbol of hope in the Depression.

Berton's early writing was dominated by his journalistic interest in public opinion and his concern for contemporary social problems and issues. *The royal family; the story of the British monarchy from Victoria to Elizabeth* (1954) contains gossipy and often humorous character sketches. Five books are products of his entertaining *Star* newspaper columns: *Just add water and stir* (1959)—awarded the Leacock Medal for Humour; *Adventures of a columnist* (1960); *Fast fast fast relief* (1962); *The big sell: an introduction to the black art of door-to-door salesmanship and other techniques* (1963); and *My war with the 20th century* (1965), an adaptation of *The big sell* published for the American market. The Anglican Church commissioned the agonistic Berton to write *The comfortable pew* (1965), a critique of the church's public image that attacks the complacency of clergy and laity in the face of rapid social change. *The smug minority* (1968) somewhat tediously condemns the Canadian Establishment, identified by Berton as an inbred Liberal/Conservative, Protestant/capitalist minority that is reluctant to invest in education or the betterment of society.

The secret world of Og (1961; rpr. 1974) is an exuberant adventure fantasy for children. Berton is co-author, with his wife Janet, of the *Centennial food guide* (1966)—reissued in 1974 as the *Canadian food guide*—and editor of *Remember yesterday; a century of photographs* (1966), both of which are part of the Canadian Centennial Library series. He is author of *Historic headlines; a century of Canadian news drama* (1967), and *Drifting home* (1973)—a chronicle of the Berton family's holiday adventure on a northern river.

See also HISTORICAL WRITING IN ENGLISH: 6.   DAVID FLINT

Bessette, Arsène. See NOVELS IN FRENCH 1900 TO 1920.

Bessette, Gérard (b. 1920). Born on a farm in Sainte-Anne-de-Sabrevois, Qué., he spent his early childhood in the village of Saint-Alexandre before moving to Montreal in 1930. He was educated at the Sainte-Croix day school, the École Normale Jacques-Cartier, and the Université de Montréal, obtaining a master's degree in 1946 and a doctorate in 1950. He taught at the University of Saskatchewan (1946-9), Duquesne University in Pittsburgh (1951-8), the Royal Military College in Kingston (1958-60), and Queen's University (1960-79). In 1979 he began to devote his time entirely to writing. He has contributed to various periodicals and received several awards: the Prix du Concours Littéraire from the Province of Québec in 1947; two Governor General's Awards; and the Prix David in 1980. He became a member of the Royal Society of Canada in 1966.

Bessette began his career as a creative writer with the publication of *Poèmes temporels* (1954) and as a literary critic with *Les images en poésie canadienne-française* (1960). Later psychocritical studies of Émile NELLIGAN, Anne HÉBERT, Yves THÉRIAULT, and Gabrielle ROY in *Une littérature en ébullition* (1968), and of Victor-Lévy BEAULIEU, André LANGEVIN, and Roy in *Trois romanciers québécois* (1973), reveal a psychoanalytical approach to the study of literature that is Freudian in nature. Bessette has also compiled anthologies: *Anthologie d'Albert Laberge* (1962), which helped to introduce Québec's first naturalist writer (q.v.); *De Québec à Saint-Boniface (récits et nouvelles du Canada-français)* (1968); and *Histoire de la littérature canadienne-française* (1968) in collaboration with Lucien Geslin and Charles Parent.

During his father's fatal illness (1957-9) Bessette turned to novel-writing. *La bagarre* (1958) and *Les pédagogues* (1961) are realistic and traditional, his narrators objective and omniscient. *La bagarre* examines three aspects of French Canada and describes the problems that confront students—three types of student, three failures. Jules Lebeuf, who hopes to become a writer and goes out with a waitress who hardly interests him, eventually opts for trade-unionism; Sillery, a homosexual, chooses exile and the study of anthropology and colonialism; the American Weston plans the study of French Canadians for his thesis but abandons his project in favour of journalism. *La bagarre* was translated by Mark Lebel as *The brawl* (1976). *Les pédagogues* satirizes the narrow-minded atmosphere in a normal school whose director is a doctrinaire conformist: Sarto Pellerin can neither change his environment nor prevent the abuse inflicted by the clerical authorities. His failure is echoed in *Le libraire* (1960), a witty satire on book censorship in the Duplessis era. Hervé Jodoin, after losing his job as college proctor, becomes a cynical, depressed country librarian, but once again breaks the rules and loses his job for having sold a censored book to a student. This novel, which attacks the hypocrisy of a situation that could be saved only by a 'quiet revolution', was translated by Glen Shortliffe as *Not for every eye* (1962).

Le libraire prepared the ground for L'INCU-BATION (1965), in which the student-professor-bookseller of the first novels is a repressed librarian no longer belligerent but dismayed by the disintegration he sees in human relationships. The narrative, related by the librarian, takes the form of a long, unpunctuated stream of ideas and emotions. It won a Governor General's Award and was translated as *Incubation* (1967) by Glen Shortliffe.

La commensale (1975), which was written before *L'incubation* but not published until much later, pursues further the type of satire found in *La bagarre* and *Le libraire*. Directed at urban small business, it portrays harshly and ironically the manias of the autistic protagonist, Chayer, an accountant or book-keeper—a product of the repressive Duplessis era, like Jodoin the bookseller—who decides to oppose his boss. Formerly timid and compliant, these men come to life in a spirit of revolt—becoming devious, calculating, and sly—just as the Quiet Revolution dawns.

In 1954, in 'Les douze meilleurs romans français du XIXe siècle' (*Nouvelle revue canadienne,* III), Bessette revealed his principles as a novelist: the supremacy of persons; physical surroundings presented in human terms; believable characters; the development of passions outlined; individual feelings analysed; the interactions between social behaviour and inner response described; and the avoidance of bombast and excess. He seemed to dread the 'novel of the unconscious', the 'apparent break with tradition', the 'preference for the abnormal, the strange the unconscious', and the 'contempt for established critical methods, disparaged since the rise of Surrealism'. After Bessette wrote *La commensale,* however, his writing underwent a profound change: as he persisted with the introspective novel, while also trying to incorporate his understanding of psychology, his work evolved from a positivist rationalism into an exploration of the unconscious. He eliminated conventional punctuation, the better to convey a stream of consciousness, and invented new words, including composites made up of unexpected juxtapositions of nouns, adjectives, and verbs. To the simple parenthesis and hyphens that replace normal punctuation in *L'incubation,* Bessette adds double parentheses in *Le cycle* (1971) to indicate the emergence of a character's unconscious; hyphens frame physical observations and sensations; and single parentheses surround hallucinations or the preconscious. In *Le cycle* three generations of the same family—seven members presented through seven interior monologues—are reunited by the death of their relative, which offers an occasion for them to consider his life and ruminate on their own problems and ruling passions. *Le cycle* won a Governor General's Award.

Les anthropoïdes (1977) conducts the reader to the source of the interior monologue: to the birth of consciousness and speech, and to the beginnings of the individual and the species. A novel of origins, it is both an epic and a personal myth, and concerns the solitude of a young 'speaker'—an ancestor and son of heroes who is preparing for his test: to tell the history of the primitive horde. The book ends with a great battle among various opposing hordes, one horde winning with the help of another.

Le semestre (1979), an autobiographical novel, is about a university professor on the verge of retirement. He reflects on his youth, his career, his loves, his adventures with a young female student (much as Bernard Malamud does in *A new life*), and analyses the work of another author, Gilbert LAROQUE. A novel-essay, *Le semestre* is similar to *Mes romans et moi* (1979), in the first half of which Bessette recounts the first ten years of his life and in the second half analyses his novels. Both *Le semestre* and Bessette's second novel, *Les pédagogues,* have academic settings and criticize the educational system, the first dealing with a professor who looks forward to the end of his teaching life and the second with the failure of a young teacher at the start of his career.

La garden-party de Christophine (1980), a collection of all of Bessette's short stories, belongs to his 'assessment' period. One of these stories, 'Romance', is of particular interest for its subject matter and style; it uses a concise, biblical verse form and violent imagery in evoking the agony of an unemployed man who commits suicide after assessing his miserable life.

With their disregard for conventional punctuation, Bessette's narratives present different variations on the interior monologue—exploring the many levels of consciousness and the unconscious, and the link between the world of the emotions and the world of the senses. Together the novels compose a uniform picture of heroes who are in some way enclosed or trapped by circumstances—they observe, reflect, and question themselves from behind counters, desks, and windows, or within streetcars, automobiles, cubicles, caves, or labyrinthine basements. They struggle to break the barriers that surround them and escape to find their place in the outside world.

The novels of Bessette show not only the Québécois 'choirboy' in the process of becoming a Freudian, but that the ego can emerge in spite of a condition of orphanhood—the orphanhood of liberation. Bessette has made a major contribution to the exploration of the inner life of Québécois.

See Patricia Smart, 'Relire *l'Incubation', Études françaises*, VI, 2 (May 1970), and J.-J. Hamm, ed., *Lectures de Gérard Bessette* (1982), the proceedings of a symposium held at Queen's University in Nov. 1980.

See NOVELS IN FRENCH 1940 TO 1959:3; 1960 TO 1982: 1, 2, 3.   LOUIS LASNIER

Bidwell, Barnabas. See ESSAYS IN ENGLISH: 1.

Biography and memoirs in English. At their best, biography and autobiography are forms that encourage a high development of literary art; but they are also genres in which amateurs, with neither art nor craftsmanship, are most likely to indulge because they think their own experiences are worth recording, or because they believe the same of other people's careers. The result is that, though at least 2000 biographies, and autobiographies of various kinds (memoirs, journals, etc.) have been published in English by Canadians, a very high proportion tell of uninteresting lives (with perhaps here and there a sudden illumination for the social historian) in uninteresting ways. The account that follows—which excludes books discussed elsewhere under the headings EXPLORATION LITERATURE IN ENGLISH and PIONEER MEMOIRS—is inevitably selective.

1. COLLECTIONS AND SERIES. The most impressive works of Canadian biography in English before and after the turn of the century, when there were still relatively few full-scale biographies of well-known Canadians, appeared in biographical collections. Henry J. Morgan was a pioneer in this field with his *Bibliotheca canadensis* (Toronto, 1867), which contained short lives of pre-Confederation writers; he followed this, three decades later, with his *Canadian men and women of the time: a handbook of Canadian biography* (Toronto, 1898). The idea of a series of biographical volumes developed just after the turn of the century with the *Makers of Canada* series, published in Toronto by George Morang and edited by Duncan

Campbell SCOTT and Pelham Edgar. Its twenty volumes (1903-8) varied in quality; only a few, such as Scott's *John Graves Simcoe* (1905) and Adam Shortt's *Lord Sydenham* (1908), were well researched and written. Thirteen volumes in the 32-volume *Chronicles of Canada* series (1914-16) are centred on single historical figures, but the emphasis is on history rather than biography. After the First World War, Lorne PIERCE launched the *Makers of Canadian literature* series, of which eleven volumes were published between 1923 and 1926, with a twelfth (*Arthur Stringer: son of the North* by Victor Lauriston) appearing long afterwards, in 1941. They were only marginally biographical: a brief life of the writer was accompanied by a critical appraisal, a selection of his work, and a check-list of his writings. Biographical compilations, revealing an increasing degree of scholarly effort and accuracy, have continued to the present. W. Stewart Wallace's *Dictionary of Canadian biography* (1926) has been a standard work since its first appearance and has been revised several times, most recently in 1978 by W.A. McKay; this edition includes Canadians who died before 1976. All earlier biographical compilations are overshadowed by the DICTIONARY OF CANADIAN BIOGRAPHY, published under the auspices of the University of Toronto Press and the press of Université Laval. Between 1967 and the end of 1982, seven volumes have appeared in a series that has no equal in Canadian biographical scholarship for exactitude, concision, and clarity. Other reference books whose entries are wholly or largely biographical include *Canadian writers/Ecrivains canadiens: a biographical dictionary* (1964), edited by Guy Sylvestre, Brandon Conron, and Carl F. KLINCK, and Norah Story's *Oxford Companion to Canadian history and literature* (1967), with its *Supplement* (1973) edited by William Toye.

Two short-lived biographical series appeared in the early seventies. The first, established to supplement the *Dictionary of Canadian biography*, was composed of John L.H. Henderson's *John Strachan* (1969), Bruce Hodgins' *John Sandfield Macdonald* (1970), and J.M. Bumsted's *Henry Alline* (1971). The second, the Canadian Lives series of brief biographies launched by the Oxford University Press, combined good scholarship with clear writing and was directed to a general readership. It included Dorothy Blakey Smith's *James Douglas* (1971), Hartwell Bowsfield's *Louis Riel* (1971), David Flint's *William Lyon Macken-*

zie (1971), Donald Swainson's *John A. Macdonald* (1971), and George WOODCOCK's *Amor de Cosmos* (1975).

2. BIOGRAPHIES. Notable biographies of prominent figures in Canada's early history are such anglophone approaches to New France as W.D. LeSueur's *Count Frontenac* (1906) and W.J. Eccles' much richer *Frontenac, the courtier governor* (1959); E.B. Osler's *La Salle* (1967) and John Upton Terrell's *La Salle: the life and times of an explorer* (1968); and several books on Champlain, from Ralph Flenley's *Samuel Champlain: founder of New France* (1924) to Morris Bishop's *Champlain: the life of fortitude* (1963).

Aspects of Upper Canadian and Ontarian life and history are reflected in a non-scholarly manner in such biographies as Mary Agnes Fitzgibbon's *A veteran of 1812: the life of James Fitzgibbon* (1894); W.S. Wallace's sceptical *The story of Laura Secord: a study in historical evidence* (1932); W. Kaye Lamb's *The hero of Upper Canada* (1962), a life of Sir Isaac Brock; Jessie Beattie's *Black Moses: the real Uncle Tom* (1951), about Josiah Henson (1789-1883); Molly Gillen's account of the Duke of Kent's liaison with Mme St Laurent, *The prince and the lady* (1970); and Frederick C. Hamil's *Lake Erie baron: the story of Colonel Thomas Talbot* (1955).

A feature of recent western biography has been the appearance of well-documented lives of Indian leaders, such as William Fraser's *Big Bear, Indian patriot* (1966), Norman Sluman's *Poundmaker* (1967), and Hugh Dempsey's *Crowfoot, chief of the Blackfoot* (1972). The life of the fur traders—their travels and conflicts—has produced many good biographical or largely biographical works. Among the most valuable are John Morgan GRAY's *Lord Selkirk of Red River* (1963), Harold A. INNIS's *Peter Pond: fur trader and adventurer* (1930), A.S. Morton's *Sir George Simpson; overseas governor of the HBC* (1944), Marjorie Wilkins Campbell's *McGillivray: lord of the Northwest* (1962), J.G. MacGregor's *Peter Fidler: Canada's forgotten surveyor* (1966), *Cuthbert Grant of Grantown* (1963) by Margaret Arnett Macleod and W.L. MORTON, and Jean Murray Cole's *Exile in the wilderness* (1979), the life of Chief Factor Archibald Macdonald. One of the classic works on an architect of white settlement beyond the Rockies is Walter N. Sage's *Sir James Douglas and British Columbia* (1930); Derek Pethick's *James Douglas: servant of two empires* (1969) is well researched, if somewhat adulatory. Other aspects of far-

western life are represented in William Rodney's *Kootenai Brown, his life and times* (1969) and David R. Williams' '*The man for a new country': Sir Matthew Baillie Begbie* (1977).

The largest single group of Canadian biographies treats political leaders, though definitive lives of these people have in many cases not appeared until quite recently. Joseph Pope, John A. Macdonald's private secretary, wrote with insight on Canada's first prime minister in *Memoirs of the Right Honourable Sir John Alexander Macdonald* (1915), but his book is mainly of interest today for its documentary material. The first adequate biography—and the last to date—was D.G. CREIGHTON's *John A. Macdonald* (2 vols, 1952-5). Two substantial books on Wilfrid Laurier appeared during the 1920s: O.D. Skelton's *Life and letters of Sir Wilfrid Laurier* (1921) and John Stephen Willson's *Sir Wilfrid Laurier* (1926); but the most perceptive study of Laurier's personality is probably Joseph Schull's *Laurier: the first Canadian* (1965). Schull also produced the first complete biography of Laurier's predecessor as Liberal leader in his two-volume *Edward Blake* (1975-6).

Among Macdonald's associates, D'Arcy McGEE, doubtless because of the dramatic way he died, has received most biographical attention, beginning with Fenning Taylor's *The Hon. D'Arcy McGee: a sketch of his life and death* (1868), and continuing through Alexander Brady's *Thomas D'Arcy McGee* (1925), Josephine Phelan's *The ardent exile* (1951), and Thomas P. Slattery's *The assassination of D'Arcy McGee* (1968). Other notable biographies of nineteenth-century political figures include G.E. Fenety's *Life and times of the Hon. Joseph Howe: the great Nova Scotian and ex-lieutenant governor, with brief references to some of his contemporaries* (Saint John, 1896), Charles Biggar's *Sir Oliver Mowat* (1905), O.D. Skelton's *Life and times of Sir Alexander Tilloch Galt* (1920), William Kennedy's *Lord Elgin* (1926), Chester New's *Lord Durham, a biography* (1927), John Stephen Willison's *Sir George Parkin* (1929), George P. deT. Glazebrook's *Sir Charles Bagot in Canada* (1929), Ronald Stewart Longley's *Sir Francis Hincks* (1943), J.M.S. Careless's *Brown of the Globe* (2 vols, 1959, 1963), Dale Thompson's *Alexander Mackenzie: clear grit* (1960), and Alistair Sweeny's *George-Étienne Cartier* (1976).

Moving into the area of public affairs, one finds certain figures in the Canadian past who, because of the dramatic or enigmatic quality of their lives, have attracted more attention than others who were perhaps historically more important. A small literature has centred on William Lyon MACKENZIE, beginning with the two-volume *The life and times of William Lyon Mackenzie* (Toronto, 1863) by Charles Lindsey, a useful and conscientious presentation of incidents and documents, though not an unbiased biography, the author being Mackenzie's son-in-law. This literature continues through William Kilbourn's *The firebrand: William Lyon Mackenzie and the rebellion of Upper Canada* (1956) and William Dawson LeSueur's *William Lyon Mackenzie* (1979). This last is a biographical curiosity, for it was written half a century before it was published; suppressed at the insistence of Mackenzie's descendants, it became celebrated *in absentia*, and on publication turned out to be a very dull biography.

A third figure to attract attention in recent years has been Louis Riel. Among the biographies of him are E.B. Osler's rather superficial *The man who had to hang: Louis Riel* (1961), George F. Stanley's definitive *Louis Riel* (1963), and Thomas Flanagan's study of Riel's religious experiences, *Louis 'David' Riel: prophet of a new world* (1979). Riel's principal associate is the subject of George WOODCOCK's biography, *Gabriel Dumont* (1976).

Among twentieth-century politicians there is a similar disproportion, as in earlier generations, between the attention given to the more dramatic figures and that given to the dull and worthy. William Lyon Mackenzie King, who had a hand in the suppression of LeSueur's biography of his grandfather, had enough prime-ministerial eccentricities to make him the subject of far more books than any other Canadian political leader. These include Reginald Hardy's *Mackenzie King of Canada* (1949); Bruce HUTCHISON's *The incredible Canadian* (1952); *The age of Mackenzie King* (1955; 2nd edn 1976) by M.S. Ferns and Bernard Ostry; Robert MacGregor Dawson's *William Lyon Mackenzie King; a political biography* (1958)—a projected two-volume work whose second part, *Mackenzie King: the lonely heights* (1963), was written by M. Blair Neatby after Dawson's death; F.A. McGregor's *The rise and fall of Mackenzie King: 1911-1919* (1962); C.P. Stacey's bizarrely revelatory volume, *A very double life: the private world of Mackenzie King* (1976); J.L. Granatstein's *Mackenzie King: his life and world* (1977); and Joyce Esberey's psycho-biographical study, *Knight of the holy spirit* (1980). Already there

have been many books on Pierre Elliott Trudeau, the best by far being Richard Gwyn's *The northern magus* (1980). Gwyn had already written *Smallwood: the unlikely revolutionary* (1968). Still the best of the studies of John Diefenbaker is Peter C. NEWMAN's *Renegade in power: the Diefenbaker years* (1963). J.S. Woodsworth, the first leader of the CCF, has been the subject of two excellent books: by his daughter, Grace MacInnis, *J.S. Woodsworth; a man to remember* (1953), and by Kenneth McNaught, *A prophet in politics: a biography of J.S. Woodsworth* (1959). Other notable books on twentieth-century Canadian political figures include Margaret Prang's *N.W. Rowell: Ontario nationalist* (1976); Roger Graham's *Arthur Meighen* (3 vols, 1960-5); Dale Thompson's *Louis St. Laurent* (1967); Geoffrey Stevens' *Stanfield* (1973); Dennis Smith's *Gentle patriot: a political biography of Walter Gordon* (1973); John English's *Borden: his life and world* (1977); Robert Bothwell's *Pearson: his life and world* (1978); *C.D. Howe: a biography* (1979) by William Kilbourn and Roberth Bothwell; and Claude Bissell's *The young Vincent Massey* (1981).

Books on Canadian writers tend to fall into three categories, none of which is unadulterated literary biography. There are general studies, like those in the Canadian Writers and Studies in Canadian Literature series, launched in the later 1960s, which include biographical sections but are mainly concerned with critical discussion. Some of these books—for example George BOWERING's *Al Purdy* (1970) and Stephen SCOBIE's *Leonard Cohen* (1979)—offer especially interesting biographical insights that have a close bearing on the writers' works; but in general they fall outside the field of true biography, following a long-established Canadian tradition of combining the biographical and the critical. Early books of this kind are James Cappon's *Roberts and the influence of his time* (1905), Francis Blake Crofton's *Haliburton: the man and the writer* (1889), Theodore Arnold Haultain's *Goldwin Smith: his life and opinions* (1913), V.L.O. Chittick's *Thomas Chandler Haliburton: a study in provincial Toryism* (1924), Lorne PIERCE's *William Kirby: the portrait of a Tory loyalist* (1929), James Cappon's *Bliss Carman and the literary currents and influences of his time* (1930), Ralph L. Curry's *Stephen Leacock: humorist and humanist* (1959), and *Edwin J. Pratt: the man and his poetry* (1947) by Carl F. KLINCK and Henry C. Wells.

Another type of literary biography tends

to find reinforcement in areas outside the actual writing life of the subject. For example, William McCulloch's *Life of Thomas McCulloch* (1920) lays far more emphasis on the founding of the Pictou Academy than it does on McCULLOCH's earlier role as the pioneer of satirical fiction in Canada. Norman Shrive's excellent *Charles Mair: literary nationalist* (1965) has added interest because of MAIR's place in the history of Upper Canadian nationalism. Clara THOMAS's sensitive life of Anna Jameson, *Love and work enough* (1967), is mainly appealing as a study of a very intelligent woman, caught up in the difficulties of an unhappy Victorian marriage, who attempts to come to terms with a colonial society. W.H. Graham's *The tiger of Canada West* (1962) sees William Dunlop as an eccentric phenomenon of colonial society as much as it considers his intermittent literary career. And Lovat DICKSON's *Wilderness man: the strange story of Grey Owl* (1973; rpr. 1975) is a well-researched biography that corrects the gaps and errors in Dickson's earlier *Half-Breed: the story of Grey Owl* (1939), which was heavily influenced by the tales Archie BELANEY told of his past.

Literary biographies that centre on the relation between writers' lives and their work are few and of varying quality. Books like Elsie May Pomeroy's *Sir Charles G.D. Roberts: a biography* (1943) and C.F. Klinck's *Robert Service* (1976) tend to be informative but uncritical. Others, like Douglas Day's *Malcolm Lowry* (1973) and Elspeth Cameron's *Hugh MacLennan: a writer's life* (1981), tackle with insight the central problems of the sources of creativity.

Canadians have written biographies of a number of foreign writers. These include Phyllis Grosskurth's two fine works, *John Addington Symonds* (1964) and *Havelock Ellis* (1980), Doug Fetherling's *The five lives of Ben Hecht* (1978), Paul Delany's *D.H. Lawrence's nightmare* (1979), Lovat Dickson's *H.G. Wells: his turbulent life and times* (1969; rpr. 1971), and George Woodcock's *The crystal spirit: a study of George Orwell* (1966).

Moving into other specialized fields, books on artists tend to mingle sketchy biographical details with criticism or description in heavily illustrated volumes. However, a few good lives of painters have been written, including Donald Buchanan's *James Wilson Morrice* (1937), Moncrieff Williamson's *Robert Harris, 1849-1919* (1971), Maria Tippett's *Emily Carr* (1979), and Russell Harper's *Krieghoff* (1979). Terry Reksten's *Rattenbury* (1978) is a biography of the archi-

tect who put his stamp on Victoria, B.C., with his Parliament Buildings and Empress Hotel; but much of the book is devoted to his personal life, his murder in England, and its aftermath. The world of science in Canada is represented by Dora Hood's life of the discoverer of Peking Man, *Davidson Black* (1964), and Charles O. O'Brien's *Sir William Dawson: a life in science and religion* (1971). Medicine is covered in Lloyd Stevenson's *Sir Frederick Banting* (1946) and Iris Noble's *The doctor who dared: William Osler* (1959). Medicine and politics are both represented by two notable books on Norman Bethune: *The scalpel and the sword* (1952) by Ted Allan and Sydney Gordon and *Bethune* (1973) by Roderick Stewart; business by Michael Bliss's distinguished biography, *A Canadian millionaire: the life and business times of Sir Joseph Flavelle, Bart. 1858-1939* (1978); journalism by Murray Donnelly's *Dafoe of the Free Press* (1969); and education by Clara Thomas's *Ryerson of Upper Canada* (1969), which was preceded by C.B. Sisson's *Egerton Ryerson: his life and letters* (2 vols, 1937-47).

The life of crime found its way early into Canadian biography with a curious work by Walter BATES, *The mysterious stranger* (1817), a life of the horse thief Henry Moon. A good recent example of this genre is Thomas Patrick KELLEY's *The black Donnellys* (1954).

3. MEMOIRS. One of the earliest Canadian writers of autobiography was the novelist Major John RICHARDSON, who lived an eventful life and felt the urge to describe and justify it. The military experience of his teens led to *The War of 1812* (Brockville, 1842); his involvement in Upper Canadian politics to *Eight years in Canada* (Montreal, 1847). Both these books reflect Richardson's strong sense of having lived in the midst of stirring historic events. Memoirs of writers in the first half of the twentieth century featured a notable mediocrity that must be linked to the relative unoriginality of their other works. Goldwin SMITH's posthumously published *Reminiscences* (1910) has a special interest because of his position in Canadian public life. Laura Goodman SALVERSON's *Confessions of an immigrant's daughter* (1939) gives a clear picture of youth among Canadian Icelanders; and Federick NIVEN's *Coloured spectacles* (1938) is a sensitive evocation of a varied life. But imaginatively meagre are such autobiographies as Ernest Thompson SETON's *Trail of an artist naturalist* (1940), Nellie McCLUNG's *Clearing*

in the West (1935) and *The stream runs fast* (1945), Robert SERVICE's *Ploughman of the moon* (1945) and *Harper of heaven* (1948), and Mazo DE LA ROCHE's *Ringing the changes* (1957). Since the mid-1960s, however, Canadian writers have been inclined to write their autobiographies not as mere narratives of their lives but as creative works that extend the perimeters of their art. Often they have selected a comparatively short period, which for one reason or another seems to project the very essence of their lives, and this has enabled them to achieve a luminous concentration of insight. Such works include Margaret LAURENCE's *The prophet's camel bell* (1963), Morley CALLAGHAN's *That summer in Paris* (1963), John GLASSCO's *Memoirs of Montparnasse* (1970), and Dorothy LIVESAY's *Winnipeg childhood* (1973). Livesay experiments in another direction—producing a collage of documents and memories—in *Left hand right hand* (1977), her account of political involvement in the 1930s. Mordecai RICHLER's *The street* (1969)—perhaps his unacknowledged best book—a collection of half-fictional sketches and half-autobiographical stories, is on the verge between invention and recollection. James M. GRAY, in *The winter years* (1966) and *The boy from Winnipeg* (1970), sees his life against the background of prairie social events, and thus combines history and biography. Norman LEVINE in *Canada made me* (1958) used a journey home to tell his life story, and Earle BIRNEY's *Spreading time* (1980) tends to concentrate on the feuding politics of the Canadian literary world. More conventional accounts, in the sense that they are straightforwardly autobiographical, are Patrick ANDERSON's *Search me* (1957) and Hugh GARNER's characteristically irascible *One damn thing after another* (1973). Reminiscences of the writer as publisher are eloquently conveyed by Lovat DICKSON, who became a director of Macmillan of London, in *The ante-room* (1959 rpr. 1975) and *The house of woods* (1963, rpr. 1976), and by John Morgan GRAY, longtime head of MACMILLAN OF CANADA, in *Fun tomorrow: learning to be a publisher and much else* (1978).

All these memoirs have their share of imaginativeness, and perhaps here and there a touch of sheer invention, but in none has fact been so inextricably mingled with fiction as in Frederick Philip GROVE's *In search of myself* (1946), a novel masquerading as autobiography. The mysteries behind Grove's life have made him perhaps the most discussed of Canadian writers. Desmond

PACEY's *Frederick Philip Grove* (1945) was followed by books with the same title by Douglas Spettigue in 1969 and Margaret Stobie in 1973. It was Spettigue, in his *FPG: the European years* (1973), who showed, by splendid detective work, that Grove's account of his pre-Canadian years was almost wholly fictional, and that he was in fact a minor German writer, Felix Paul Greve, who had vanished from his own country after serving a term of imprisonment for fraud.

Other Canadian memoirs cover a wide field. Some of the most interesting autobiographical documents are journals or narratives snatched from the past long after the death of their writers. One of these is *The reminiscences of Doctor John Sebastian Helmcken* (1975) edited by Dorothy Blakey Smith. Helmcken (1824-1920) was a prominent early resident of Victoria, B.C.—the son-in-law of the 'Father of British Columbia', Sir James Douglas—who was not only a surgeon but a member of the legislative assembly of Vancouver Island and British Columbia. The most moving of these journals from the past is Edgar Christian's diary of starvation in the Arctic, originally published as *Unflinching: a diary of tragic adventure* (1937) and reissued as *Death in the barren ground* (1979), edited by George Whalley, who described the end of Christian and his cousin John Hornby in *The legend of John Hornby* (1962). There are reminiscences by scholars, like *My windows on the streets of the world* (1923) by James Mavor (1854-1925), a political scientist at the University of Toronto who had strong ties with Russia; John Kenneth Galbraith's *The Scotch* (1964), telling of his youth in Ontario's Glengarry County; and Kathleen Coburn's fascinating *In pursuit of Coleridge* (1977), which is both a biographical search and a personal memoir by a well-known (now retired) University of Toronto professor and Coleridge scholar. Some painters have produced lively autobiographies; for example, Charles Comfort's *Artists at work* (1956), A.Y. Jackson's *A painter's country* (1958), and Emily CARR's inimitable series: *Klee Wyck* (1941), *The book of Small* (1942), *The House of All Sorts* (1944), and *Growing pains* (1946), crowned by the posthumous publication of her journals, *Hundreds and thousands* (1966). Recollections by newspapermen almost always provide an interesting inside-outside look at public life. In this category are Bruce HUTCHISON's *The far side of the street* (1976), Wilfrid Eggleston's *While I still remember* (1969),

Grattan O'Leary's *Recollections of people, press and politics* (1977), and James F. Minifie's engagingly ironic *Expatriate* (1976). Many autobiographies by Canadian political leaders have been ghost-written by academics and are generally of scant literary merit—though not Joey Smallwood's *I chose Canada* (1973), the text of which bears the unmistakable stamp of his personality; it is perhaps the best memoir by a Canadian politician. There are illuminating and sophisticated accounts of observations and experience by several civil servants who had less prominent roles to play in Canadian public life. Among such books are the posthumously published *Public servant: the memoirs of Sir Joseph Pope* (1960), edited by his son Maurice Pope; Vincent Massey's *What's past is prologue* (1963); and Arnold Heeney's *The things that are Caesar's* (1972). But the classic memoir of a Canadian civil servant and diplomat has been presented in the three beautifully written volumes of Charles Ritchie's journals: *The siren years* (1974), *An appetite for life* (1977), and *Diplomatic passport* (1981). *The siren years*, which won a Governor General's Award, provided the first evidence that from the rich experience of a Canadian public servant, literature could be created.

GEORGE WOODCOCK

Biography and memoirs in French. BIOGRAPHIES 1. 1671 TO 1900. It was only in the 1850s that biographies began to appear with any frequency in French Canada and it is Father Étienne-Michel Faillon (1799-1870) who gave biographical writing its initial impetus. From 1852 to 1860 this French Sulpician—who visited the Canadian missions of his community in 1849, 1854, and 1857, staying in Montreal for five years on his last visit—wrote four biographies, totalling more than 2,500 pages, on Madame d'Youville (Ville-Marie, 1852), Marguerite Bourgeoys (Ville-Marie, 1853), Jeanne Mance (2 vols, Ville-Marie, 1854); and Jeanne Le Ber (Ville-Marie, 1860), which appeared in an abridged English translation the following year as *The Christian heroine of Canada; or Life of Miss Le Ber* (Montréal, 1861). These works are really hagiographies describing the many virtues of the great founders of the French-Canadian religious orders with a view to encouraging others to adopt a religious vocation and in order to promote in Rome the beatification of these heroines of New France, a necessary first step in their subsequent canonization. They were written in response to requests from the religious

communities themselves, who paid the printing costs and sold and distributed them with great zeal, for each religious order presumably wanted to be the first to have its founder recognized officially by the Pope. The biographies are generally well documented, but the supernatural world, and interventions from the Great Beyond play an important role.

The works of Father Faillon, as Serge Gagnon has shown in *Le Québec et ses historiens de 1840 à 1920* (Québec, 1978), are proof of the spectacular ascendancy of clericalism in French Canada during the second half of the nineteenth century. 'The historical story', he affirms, 'is the first step in the consecration of clerical power through recourse to history.' He elaborates: 'hagiography in the 19th century is an exceptional manifestation of the clergy's will to power.' Progressively assuming the national leadership from the 1840s on—that is, following the defeat of the Rebellion of 1837, which had put an end to the political aspirations of an often liberal-minded bourgeoisie—the clergy undertook the formulation of a collective memory. It was a conservative one, in keeping with its providentialist conception of history and inevitably reflecting its own concerns and values. To a conquered people anxious about its future, the clergy offered the refuge of a religion, preaching the supremacy of spiritual and moral values. At the same time, responding to the French Canadians' natural instinct for self-preservation, it laid the foundation of a nationalist ideology and maintained it by extolling a system of protective values centred on upholding traditions, the French language, and the Catholic religion, and respect for the Church and the family. In teaching people to distrust change, the clergy quite naturally overvalued the past—the period of New France in particular—vaunting the merits of agricultural and rural life to the detriment of industrial and urban life. In this context, history and literature were asked to take on a didactic function. Abbé CASGRAIN's *Histoire de la Mère Marie de l'Incarnation* (Québec, 1864) suggests that Canada was discovered in response to a plan of divine Providence—namely that of hastening the conversion of the native populations—and that MARIE DE L'INCARNATION participated in this plan: as a simple instrument in the hand of God, she made it her sacred duty to obey blindly His holy will. Endowed with a romantic temperament, Casgrain likes to evoke the marvellous and the supernatural; he speaks of the ecstasies and visions of Marie de l'Incarnation, even of the apparition of a deceased nun, as incontestable facts. His biography had a very great success.

A large number of edifying and patriotic biographies were published in the nineteenth century. With very few exceptions, most of the national heroes who were their subjects lived in the epic times of New France. Narcisse-Eutrope Dionne, who in his well-documented *Jacques Cartier* (Québec, 1889) had painted the discoverer of Canada as a devoted Christian more interested in giving new souls to God and new land to his king than in becoming rich, presented another great Catholic hero in his first volume of *Samuel de Champlain, fondateur de Québec et père de la Nouvelle-France: histoire de sa vie et de ses voyages* (2 vols, Québec, 1891, 1906). Even more virtuous than Cartier, Champlain had no personal ambition save that of converting as many Indians as possible to the only true religion. Casgrain, in his *Champlain, sa vie et son caractère* (Québec, 1898), also insisted on Champlain's strong faith in God and on his qualities as a missionary. Both H.J.J.B. Chouinard in his *Paul de Chomedey, sieur de Maisonneuve, fondateur de Montréal* (Québec, 1882) and Father P. Rousseau in his *Histoire de la vie de M. Paul de Chomedy, sieur de Maisonneuve, fondateur et premier gouverneur de Villemarie 1640-1676* (Montréal, 1886) recognized in their hero a man guided by the hand of God—like Mgr de Laval, whose exceptional qualities and numerous virtues, both as a priest and as an administrator, were praised by Abbé Auguste-Honoré Gosselin in his *Vie de Monseigneur de Laval, premier évêque de Québec et apôtre du Canada, 1622-1708* (2 vols, Québec, 1890). Indeed, this example of hagiography was intended to promote the case of Laval for canonization. Henri Lorin's *Le Comte de Frontenac; étude sur le Canada français à la fin du XVIIIe siècle* (Paris, 1895) was much more critical of the bishop's conduct and of his policies. While Father Félix Martin, a former missionary, was satisfied simply to relate Montcalm's glorious military career in his well-documented *De Montcalm; ou Les dernières années de la colonie française (1756-1760)* (Paris, 1867), Casgrain in his *Guerre du Canada, 1756-1760: Montcalm et Lévis* (2 vols, Québec, 1891; Tours, 1899), showing his bias against an impious France that had abandoned Canada and her children, was hostile to Montcalm; only Lévis appeared to be a bona fide hero.

Some families have been fortunate enough to generate heroes worthy of being remembered forever by their compatriots and descendants. A famous family, the Le Moynes of Longueuil, was the subject of *Les Macchabées de la Nouvelle France* (Québec, 1878) by Joseph MARMETTE, who portrayed the courage and patriotism of these men as a constant source of inspiration to French Canadians. Other edifying biographies of families are *Histoire des grandes familles françaises du Canada* (Montréal, 1867) by Abbé François Daniel; *Les Normands au Canada (1634-1668)* (Evreux, 1892) by Abbé Auguste-Honoré Gosselin; and *Nicolas Le Roy et ses descendants* (Québec, 1897) by Joseph-Edmond Roy. Not to be forgotten on the subject of pious and courageous ancestors are *Le premier colon de Lévis, Guillaume Couture* (Lévis, 1884) by Joseph-Edmond Roy; and Abbé Georges Dugas's *La première canadienne du Nord-Ouest; ou Biographie de Marie-Anne Gaboury* (Montréal, 1883), a portrait of the ideal French-Canadian wife of the time: obedient to her husband, entirely devoted to her children, pious, hard-working, and supportive of the priest in his mission.

By the last two decades of the century, ultramontane clergy and laymen had succeeded in imposing their reactionary views and conservative values on all spheres of French-Canadian society. Biographies of bishops, priests, missionaries, founders and members of religious communities were therefore very much in favour in French Canada. Such works, often on clerics who today rest in obscurity, are too numerous and undistinctive to mention here.

Many biographies paying tribute to politicians, educators, businessmen and men of the law were published in the last quarter of the nineteenth century. Quite flattering to their subjects in many cases, and supplying information that is sometimes inaccurate, they were often written by a friend or a devoted admirer. A very popular pattern for such books is first a sketchy physical description of the subject, then an enumeration of his many moral and intellectual qualities, followed by a discourse on his patriotism and sense of duty; finally, the biographer proposes his subject to the admiration of his compatriots. One could list here *Philemon Wright* (Montréal, 1871) by Joseph Tassé; *L'Honorable Sir G.E. Cartier, ministre de la milice* (Québec, 1873) by Louis-Philippe Turcotte; *Biographies canadiennes* (Québec, 1875) by Abbé Casgrain; *Biographies et por-*

traits (Montréal, 1876) by Laurent-Olivier David; *Les Canadiens de l'Ouest* (2 vols, Montréal, 1878) by Joseph Tassé; *La vie de Joseph-François Perrault, surnommé le père de l'éducation du peuple canadien* (Québec, 1878) by Philippe Baby Casgrain, a well-documented book; *Histoire de Joseph Montferrand* (Montréal, 1884; rev. 1889) by Benjamin Sulte; *L'Honorable Joseph-Adolphe Chapleau. Sa biographie, suivie de ses principaux discours* (Montréal, 1887) edited by A. de Bonneterre; *Biographie, discours, conférences, etc. de l'Honorable Honoré Mercier* (Montréal, 1890) by Joseph-Octave Pelland; *Mes contemporains* (Montréal, 1894) and *Les deux Papineau* (Montréal, 1896) by Laurent-Olivier David.

Biographies devoted to writers are fewer in number. Here the pattern is usually to provide brief biographical information, followed by a summary of the writer's main works and themes and a moral judgement on the quality and patriotic values of these works. Casgrain is the leading biographer in this category with his *François-Xavier Garneau* (Québec, 1866) and *Philippe Aubert de Gaspé* (Québec, 1871) and an 87-page 'Notice biographique' on Octave CRÉMAZIE preceding the poet's *Oeuvres complètes* (Montréal, 1886). In *Nos hommes de lettres* (Montréal, 1873) Louis-Michel Darveau gave fourteen short 'esquisses biographiques', while Pierre-Joseph-Oliver CHAUVEAU wrote the interesting *François-Xavier Garneau. Sa vie et ses oeuvres* (Montréal, 1883).

Albani (Québec, 1874), Napoléon Legendre's book on the famous French-Canadian opera singer Marie Louise Cécile Lajeunesse, better known as Emma Albani —written shortly after her Covent Garden début—is the only biography in its category.

2. 1900 TO 1920. Berthe Jetté's *Vie de la vénérable mère d'Youville, fondatrice des Soeurs de la Charité de Montréal, suivie d'un historique de son Institut* (1900), the first biography written by a woman, shows the tradition of hagiography being perpetuated into the twentieth century, and the supernatural and the number of miracles playing an even greater role than in the works of Father Faillon. Further evidence of that tradition can be found in *Une fleur mystique de la Nouvelle-France. Vie de la mère Marie-Catherine de Saint-Augustin, religieuse de l'Hôtel-Dieu de Précieux-Sang de Québec, 1632-1668* (1907) by Father Léonidas Hudon, and in *Le Frère Didace Pelletier, Récollet* (1910) by Abbé

Odoric-Marie Jouve—not to mention Narcisse-Eutrope Gagnon's biographies of several priests and nuns.

The history of New France remained much in favour. Jetté's and Hudon's heroines were from that period and so were the following historical figures: *Louis Jolliet, découvreur du Mississipi et du pays des Illinois* (1902, 1913, 1926) by Ernest Amédée Gagnon; *Frontenac et ses amis* (1902) by Ernest Myrand; *Jean Talon, intendant de la Nouvelle France, 1665-1672* (1904) by Thomas Chapais; and *Le Marquis de Montcalm (1712-1759)* (1911) by Thomas Chapais, a biased work in praise of Montcalm.

In *Laurier et son temps* (1905) Laurent-Olivier David testifies to his friendship with, and admiration for, the first French-Canadian prime minister, then at the height of his popularity. When Laurier died in 1919, David published *Laurier, sa vie, ses oeuvres* (1919), a revised and enlarged version of the earlier work. One year later, Alfred Duclos De Celles gave David's former title to a book of his own: *Laurier et son temps* (1920). This historian was already well known for having edited *Discours de Sir Wilfrid Laurier* (3 vols, 1909-20) and for writing a successful trilogy: *Papineau, 1786-1871* (1905; English trans., 1904; new trans., 1905), *Lafontaine et son temps* (1907), and *Cartier et son temps* (1907). These three books bear witness to French Canadians' growing interest in their political history and political leaders. In *Athlètes canadiens-français: recueil des exploits de force, d'endurance, d'agilité, des athlètes et des sportmen de notre race, depuis le XVIIIe siècle. Biographie, portraits, anecdotes, records* (1909), Edouard-Zotique Massicotte proposed more modest heroes for his compatriots to admire.

3. 1921 TO 1940. During these two decades New France remained an attraction and a field of scholarly interest for historians and biographers. Two new biographies of Jeanne Mance appeared in 1934, one by Pierre Benoit and the other by Marie-Claire Daveluy, whose book was honoured by the French Academy. While novelist Maurice CONSTANTIN-WEYER mixed fiction with reality in his *Champlain* (1931), Robert Rumilly's approach to the life of Marguerite Bourgeoys (1936) was that of a pious historian. Three years after *La grande aventure de Le Moyne d'Iberville* (1934) by Pierre Daviault, Father Louis-Marie Le Jeune published his well-documented *Le Chevalier Pierre Le Moyne, sieur d'Iberville* (1937). Le Jeune's reputation as a serious scholar had al-

ready been established by his *Dictionnaire général de biographie* (2 vols, 1931). There was an increased interest in the lives of explorers, pioneers, and adventurers. Besides the books written on d'Iberville, there were *Cavalier de La Salle* (1927) by Constantin-Weyer; *La Vérendrye, découvreur canadien* (1933) by Robert Rumilly; *Un pionnier canadien, Pierre Boucher* (1927) by Séraphin Marion; and *Pierre Radisson, roi des coureurs de bois* (1933) by Donatien Frémont.

As in the previous periods, religious figures were the subject of many biographies between 1920 and 1940, but for the most part the interpretation of historical facts and documents took precedence over the mere narration of virtues, miracles, visions, and supernatural interventions. Such biographies included *Le Curé Labelle. Sa vie et son oeuvre* (1930) by Abbé Elie-Joseph Auclair; *Mgr Taché et la naissance du Manitoba* (1930) by Donatien Frémont; *Mgr Provencher et son temps* (1935) by the same author; and *Mgr Laflèche et son temps* (1936) by Robert Rumilly. Only two hagiographies seem to have been published: *La vie de mère Marie-Rose* (1928) by Abbé Joseph-Marie Mélançon and *Kateri Tekakitha* (1934) by Robert Rumilly.

Bearing witness to the rise of French-Canadian nationalist fervour in the 1930s are the biographies of charismatic leaders: *Sir Wilfrid Laurier* (1931) and *Mercier* (1936) by Robert Rumilly; *Olivar Asselin* (1938) by Hermas Bastien; and *L'abbé Lionel Groulx* (1939) by André Laurendeau. Rumilly's *Chefs de file* (1934) treats a number of such figures.

Books on writers include *Louis Fréchette* (1924) by Henri d'Arles; *Antoine Gérin-Lajoie: la résurrection d'un patriote canadien* (1925) by Léon Gérin; *François-Xavier Garneau* (1926) by Gustave Lanctôt; *La vie aventureuse d'Arthur Buies* (1933) by Raymond Douville, a study of the prolific journalist; and a second book on Louis FRÉCHETTE: *Un romantique canadien* (1934) by Marcel DUGAS.

4. 1941 TO 1960. Biographies of heroes of New France and religious figures continued to predominate in this period. There were no less than three books on Marguerite Bourgeoys: by Albert Jammet (1942), Yvon Charron (1950), and Marie-Anne Goulthier-Landreville (1958). Thanks to Maurice CONSTANTIN-WEYER, Pierre Benoit, and Sister Allard, *La Vérendrye* (1941), *Maisonneuve* (1960), and *Jeanne Mance* (1960) remained in the limelight, while Esther Lefebvre and Father Léon Pouliot respectively made two other less-celebrated figures better known to historians and the public in general with *Marie Morin, premier historien de Ville-Marie* (1960) and *François-Xavier de Charlevoix* (1957).

Biographers were by now adopting a more critical and objective approach to their subjects, re-evaluating their predecessors' pious statements and conclusions and their patriotic bias in the light of a scientific and methodical analysis of facts and documents. Hence the undeniable value of the scholarly research undertaken by a new generation of historians, such as Guy Frégault, Marcel Trudel, Father Léon Pouliot, and Brother Philippe Sylvain. After *Iberville, le conquérant* (1944), Guy Frégault wrote *François Bigot, administrateur français* (2 vols, 1948) and *Le Grand Marquis, Pierre Rigaud de Vaudreuil et la Louisiane* (1952). In that book he attempted to rehabilitate Vaudreuil, who had previously often been decried by French-Canadian historians. Marcel Trudel, who would become a renowned historian of New France, published the well-documented *Chiniquy* (1955), on the scandal-ridden priest turned Presbyterian minister. That same year Father Pouliot produced the first volume of his monumental *Mgr Bourget et son temps* (5 vols, 1955–77), on the Bishop of Montreal (1799–1885), and Frère Philippe Sylvain published his *La vie et l'oeuvre de Henry de Courcy* (1955), on the historian. Many other books on priests (and missionaries) were published during these two decades by Fathers Antoine Bernard, Romain Légaré, and Gaston Carrière.

Albert Faucher introduced the world of finance and economics to French-Canadian biography with *Alphonse Desjardins, pionnier de la coopération d'épargne et de crédit en Amérique* (1950). Donatien Frémont wrote a book on *Les secrétaires de Riel: Louis Schmidt, Henry Jackson, Philippe Garnot* (1953). Raymond Tanghe, in *Laurier, artisan de l'unité canadienne* (1960), introduced a theme that was to be much debated in the years to come. The ever-productive Robert Rumilly wrote *Henri Bourassa. La vie publique d'un grand Canadien* (1953).

Rumilly's *Le Frère Marie Victorin et son temps* (1949) is a study of the writer and botanist (q.v.). Written at the eve of the Quiet Revolution, two other books on writers were devoted to well-known 'journalistes de combat': *Jules Fournier: journaliste de combat* (1955) by Adrien Thério and *Arthur Buies* (1957) by Léopold Lamontagne.

La vie et l'oeuvre du Frère Luc (1944) by Gérard Morrisset turned the attention of readers to the arts. La Bolduc (1959) by Pierre Benoit paid homage to a very popular French-Canadian singer.

5. 1961 TO 1981. For the most part biographies written in the last two decades reflect the new spirit of Québec, which calls into question traditional values. They are seldom written by clergy and many are by women.

Though biographers and historians continued to favour the times of New France, they certainly did not confine themselves to that period. Besides Dans le nid d'aiglons, la colombe. Vie de Jeanne Le Ber, la recluse (1963) and Paul de Chomedey, sieur de Maisonneuve (1967) by Léo-Paul DESROSIERS, and Les La Vérendrye et le poste de l'Ouest (1969) by Antoine Champagne, several books were written on people of lesser fame, such as La Gallissonnière et le Canada (1962) by Roland Lamontagne, Messire Pierre Boucher, seigneur de Boucherville (1967) by Estelle Mitchell, Claude-Thomas Dupuy, intendant de la Nouvelle-France (1969) by Jean-Claude Dubé, and François-Étienne Cugnet, entrepreneurs et entreprises en Nouvelle-France (1975) by Cameron Nish. Two books were written on the Marquis de Denonville by T. Falmagne (1965) and Jean Leclerc (1976).

In books on subsequent periods in the history of French Canada, attention continued to be focused on politicians and, to a lesser extent, on religious figures of the time: Camilien Houde, le p'tit gars de Ste-Marie (1961) by H. La Roque; La vie orageuse d'Olivar Asselin (1962) by Marcel-André Gagnon, who also published Olivar Asselin toujours vivant (1974); L'histoire bouleversante de Mgr Charbonneau (1962) by Renaude Lapointe; Lord Durham (1963) by Roger Viau; L'imprévisible Monsieur Houde (1964) by Charles Renaud; Henri Bourassa (1966) by Cameron Nish; Un bourgeois d'une époque révolue: Victor Morin, notaire (1967) by Renée Morin; Hector-Louis Langevin, un père de la Confédération canadienne (1969) by Andrée Désilets; Joseph-Charles Taché (1971) by Evelyne Bossé; Maurice Duplessis et son temps (2 vols, 1973) by Robert Rumilly; Étienne Parent (1975) by Jean-Charles Falardeau; Papineau et son temps (2 vols, 1977) by Robert Rumilly; Le curé Labelle: le colonisateur, le politicien, la légende (1979) by Robert Lévesque and Robert Miguier; Louis-François Laflèche, deuxième évêque de Trois-Rivières (1979) by Nive Voisine; Jean-Jacques Lartigue, premier évêque de Montréal (1980) by Gilles Chaussé;

La vie studieuse et obstinée de Denis-Benjamin Viger (1980) by Gérard Parizeau. Papineau: un être divisé (1960) and Julie Papineau, un cas de mélancolie et d'éducation janséniste (1961) by Fernand Ouellet are two socio-psychological studies of the well-known family.

Several books were devoted to Canadian politicians who won fame in the sixties and the seventies: Le vrai visage de Jean Drapeau (1962) by L. Patenaude; Les trois vies de Pearson (1968) by J.R. Beal and J.M. Poliquin; Le phénomène Trudeau (1972) by Jean Pellerin; René Lévesque, tel quel (1973) by François Aubin and René Lévesque, portrait d'un Québécois (1973) by Jean Provencher; and Daniel Johnson (1980) by Pierre Godin.

The large number of studies of Québec's writers published in the sixties and seventies shows the high degree of scholarly interest that had developed in French-Canadian literature. Few, if any, of these books could be classified as biographies, but most supply much useful information about the lives of the authors whose works they analyse and criticize—particularly those in the series 'Ecrivains canadiens d'aujourd'hui" (Éditions Fides) and 'Vie des lettres québécoises' (Les Presses de l'Université Laval). The former collection includes Germaine Guèvremont (1963) by Rita Gauthier-Leclerc; Anne Hébert (1965) by Pierre Pagé; Léo-Paul Desrosiers (1966) by Julia Richer; Émile Nelligan (1967) by Paul Wyzynski; Félix-Antoine Savard (1968) by André Major; Robert Élie (1968) by Marc Gagnon; Gabrielle Roy (1970) by François Ricard; Ringuet (1970) by Jean Panneton; Marcel Dubé (1970) by Maximilien Laroche; and Robert Charbonneau (1972) by Madeleine Ducrocq-Poirier. The more scholarly second collection includes Le ciel et l'enfer d'Arthur Buies (1965) by Marcel-A. Gagnon; Joseph Marmette (1844-1895): sa vie, son oeuvre (1968) by Roger Le Moine; and À la recherche de Napoléon Aubin (1969) by Jean-Paul Tremblay.

Other interesting biographies (all on writers who have entries in this Companion) are: Alain Grandbois (1968) by Jacques BRAULT; Jean-Charles Harvey et son oeuvre romanesque (1969) by Guildo Rousseau; Jean-Charles Harvey, précurseur de la Révolution tranquille (1970) by Marcel-Aimé Gagnon; Jacques Ferron malgré lui (1970) by Jean Marcel; Visages de Gabrielle Roy. L'oeuvre et l'écrivain (1973) by Marc Gagné; Marie Le Franc, deux patries, deux exils (1976) by Paulette Collet; Robert Choquette, romancier et dramaturge de la radio et de la T.V. (1977) by Renée Legris; Antoine Gérin-Lajoie, homme de lettres (1978) by René

Dionne; *Lionel Groulx* (1978) by Georges-Émile Giguère; *Claude Gauvreau, poète et mythocrate* (1979) by Jacques Marchand; and *Marie Le Franc. Au-delà du personnage* (1981) by Madeleine Ducrocq-Poirier. Of special interest are *Pour saluer Victor Hugo* (1971), *Jack Kerouac* (1972), and *Monsieur Melville* (1978) by Victor-Lévy BEAULIEU—biographical essays that tell as much, if not more, about the author than about his subjects.

Several books on French-Canadian artists published since the beginning of the sixties offer a mixture of biographical information and comments on their works: Guy ROBERT's *Pellan, sa vie et son oeuvre* (1963) and *Borduas* (1972); Hugues de Jouvancourt's *Suzor-Côté* (1967), *Marc-Aurèle Fortin* (1968), and *Clarence Gagnon* (1970); François-Marc Gagnon's *Paul-Émile Borduas* (1978); Jean ÉTHIER-BLAIS's *Autour de Borduas* (1979); and Jean-Pierre Duquette's *Fernand Leduc* (1980).

MEMOIRS 6: BEGINNINGS TO 1900. Philippe AUBERT DE GASPÉ's *Mémoires* (Ottawa, 1866) is the best-known work in this genre published in French Canada in the last century. These loosely structured recollections can be considered a by-product of his *Les ANCIENS CANADIENS* (1863), for they convey many anecdotes and legends that were to have appeared in that novel. With great charm, simplicity, and good nature Aubert de Gaspé tells about his life (1786-1871), people he met, and events he witnessed. A real storyteller, he wanders from one subject to another, letting one memory bring forth another and giving a nostalgic account of life in Québec at the beginning of the century.

Notes d'un condamné politique (Montréal, 1864), by François-Xavier Prieur, gives an interesting, though rather poorly written, account of the author's participation in the 1837 Rebellion and of his exile in Australia. It also describes the penitentiary system in New South Wales. Published the same year, *Mémoires sur les moeurs, coutumes et religions des sauvages de l'Amérique septentrionale* (Paris, 1864) by Nicolas Perrot (1643-1717) supplies still-useful information on Indian wars, habits, and ways of life. Perrot, a fur trader, also offers advice to Intendant Michel Bégon on the government of the colony. He draws attention to his personal contribution in establishing good relations between the French and the Indians, but regrets that his advice was not followed more often. Published more than a hundred years after the death of Louis Franquet (1697-1768), his

Voyages et mémoires sur le Canada (Québec, 1889) is a valuable source of information on life in New France in the years preceding the Conquest. A conscientious observer, Franquet, who was inspector of fortifications in New France in 1750-2, is considered most reliable by historians. Pierre de Sales Laterrière (1747-1815) intended to bring special moments of his eventful life to light in his private diary, *Mémoires de Pierre de Sales Laterrière et de ses traverses* (Québec, 1873), which Abbé Henri-Raymond CASGRAIN revealed in 1870, but the book seems to owe as much to fiction as to reality; he arrived in Canada in 1766 claiming to have studied medicine in France (he did some medical studies in Montreal), practised medicine for a time and then became manager of Forges de Saint-Maurice, was overtly pro-American against the British, and in 1779 was jailed for three years as a traitor.

In *Souvenirs d'un demi-siècle* (Montreal, 1885) Joseph-Guillaume Barthe (1818-93) recalls the years of his childhood and gives word-portraits of some of the political figures of his time, such as Vollières de Saint-Réal, Étienne Parent, Jacques Viger, and Louis-Joseph Papineau. *Cinquante ans dans l'Église de Rome* (Montreal, 1885) by Charles Chiniquy (1809-99) is probably the most successful book of memoirs to appear in French Canada in the nineteenth century. By 1898 it had been reprinted seventy times and had been translated into eight languages. It tells of the author's conversion to Protestantism after spending most of his life in the Catholic Church. Wishing to justify himself and to project his image as a saintly man, Chiniquy jumps at every opportunity to attack his former Church and to denounce not only the priests and their school system but also the sacrament of penance, the Eucharist, and the Virgin Mary. Needless to say, the book scandalized people. In *Le 38e fauteuil; ou Souvenirs parlementaires* (Montréal, 1891), Joseph Tassé (1848-1893), a member of the Conservative party and a deputy minister in Ottawa from 1878 to 1887, recalls some great moments of Canadian political life between 1867 and 1887 and makes lively comments on politicians he has known.

7. 1900 TO 1940. Louis FRÉCHETTE's *Mémoires*, which appeared for the most part in *Le Monde illustré* from May to Nov. 1900, were edited by George A. Klinck and published as a book in 1961. Mainly known as a poet, Fréchette obviously enjoys telling anecdotes about his youth and about his compatriots and their way of life; he proves him-

self to be a talented storyteller with a good sense of humour. Most memoirs published between 1900 and 1940 seem to have been written by politicians. In his *Souvenirs politiques* (2 vols, 1909), Charles Langelier tells of the beginning of the Liberal party in French Canada. Although his testimony is obviously far from impartial, it provides many anecdotes and very useful information on political life between 1878 and 1896. Other interesting political memoirs are Armand Lavergne's *Trente ans de vie nationale* (1934), which covers the period from 1880 to the eve of the First World War (a second volume was to have been written), and Philippe-Auguste Choquette's *Un demi-siècle de vie politique* (1936), on the years from 1880 to 1930. *Quatre-vingts ans de souvenirs* (1939), by Mme Frédéric-Liguori Beique, daughter of Louis-Antoine Dessaulles, also deals mainly with politics.

8. 1941 TO 1960. Edouard Montpetit's well-written *Souvenirs* (3 vols, 1944-55) tells of his career as a renowned professor of political science and a lecturer of international reputation, and is particularly interesting on the foundation of the Université de Montréal and the intellectual life in Québec in the author's day; it also gives personal views of some of the political issues of the time. In *Testament de mon enfance* (1952; *Testament of my childhood*, 1964), which mixes autobiography with fiction, Robert de ROQUEBRUNE describes the vanished world of his childhood in the family manor of Saint-Ours, at L'Assomption. This elegantly written book, often quoted from in anthologies, was acclaimed by most critics, in both France and Canada, and was awarded the Prix Duvernay. Two further memoirs followed: *Quartier Saint Louis* (1966) and *Cherchant mes souvenirs* (1968).

Father Émile Legault's *Confidences* (1955) is largely devoted to the establishment in 1937 and the history of Les Compagnons de Saint-Laurent, the theatre company of which he was the guiding spirit and that gave scope to French-language theatre in Québec until its dissolution in 1952. Mgr Olivier Maurault's *Confidences* (1959), which he first read on Radio-Canada, is disappointing in comparison, though Maurault, who was rector of the Université de Montréal from 1939 to 1955, had many anecdotes and memories worth telling. His *Confidences* often repeats commonplaces and is finally rather superficial.

9. 1960 TO 1980. Since 1960 politicians seem to have occupied the first place among

authors of memoirs in Québec—not surprisingly, considering the importance of politics in modern Québec society. Although tainted with political bias and a tendency towards self-justification, these memoirs supply first-hand information about behind-the-scenes events and tactics and bring to light the personalities of both important and lesser contemporary political figures. Worthy of mention are *Mémoires* (1960) by Télesphore-Damien Bouchard; *Mémoires* (1966) by Antonio Barrette; *Les mémoires du sénateur Raoul Dandurand* (1967); *Mémoires politiques* (1969) by René Chaloult; *Une femme chez les hommes* (1971) by Thérèse F. Casgrain (translated by Joyce MARSHALL as *A woman in a man's world: memoirs*, 1972); and *Mémoires, choses vues . . . entendues . . . vécues . . . en politique de 1906 à 1958* (1972) by Lionel Bertrand.

As priest, historian, teacher, lecturer, and prolific writer, Father Lionel GROULX played an influential role in the socio-cultural, intellectual, and political life of Québec; the four volumes of *Mes mémoires* (1970-4) are of great interest in giving a well-rounded picture of his personality, his work, and his times. Highlights are his description in Volume II of the Action française movement, the controversy that surrounded the publication of *L'appel de la race* (1922), and his portraits of Harry BERNARD and Léo-Paul DESROSIERS among others; the account in the third volume (1926 to 1939) of his stay in France and sketches of Armand Lavergne, Maurice Duplessis, and Jean-Charles HARVEY; and, in the last volume (1940-1967), Groulx's reflections on the Quiet Revolution and his advice to French Canadians on the years to come.

In *Sous le soleil de la pitié* (1965) by Jean-Paul Desbiens, the author of the famous *Insolences du Frère Untel* (1960) recalls the often difficult times of his first teaching experiences. In *Confidences* (1965), Ringuet (Philippe PANNETON) recounts a few of his memories through a series of well-chosen anecdotes, without any nostalgia for days gone by. With much humour he invites the romantic eulogists of the past to contemplate abandoning their modern comforts in favour of their grandparents' style of life.

In her remarkable DANS UN GANT DE FER (1965) and *La joue droite* (1966), Claire MARTIN remembers the traumatic years of her youth and offers a very critical judgement on the French-Canadian society of yesteryear and of its religious/moral values.

Journal et souvenirs (2 vols, 1973, 1975) by Félix-Antoine SAVARD gives us a good idea of the author's intellectual life between 1961 and 1964 and conveys his reflections on social and political changes in these first years of the Quiet Revolution.

Recent memoirs of interest are Albert Tessier's *Souvenirs en vrac* (1975); Alfred Laliberté's *Mes souvenirs*; Théodore Dupont's *Mes mémoires* (1980); *Une symphonie inachevée* (1972), by Québec's famous conductor Wilfrid Pelletier; *Une mémoire déchirée* (1978) by Thérèse Renaud, a member of the Automatiste movement and one of those who signed the REFUS GLOBAL in 1948; and *Mes romans et moi* (1979) by Gérard BESSETTE.

JACQUES COTNAM

are expressions of Bird's experiences in the First World War; *Thirteen years after: the story of the old front revisited* (1932) and *The communication trench* (1933) are compilations of his journalistic analyses of the war. *The two Jacks* (1954) deals with an episode from the Second World War, and *No retreating footsteps: the story of the North Nova Scotia Highlanders* (1954) and *The North Shore (New Brunswick) Regiment* (1963) are regimental histories. Two other histories, *A century at Chignecto: the key to old Acadia* (1928) and *Done at Grand Pré* (1955), treat Chignecto and Acadia before 1780. *This is Nova Scotia* (1950), *Off-trail in Nova Scotia* (1956), and *These are the Maritimes* (1959) are travel books.

KEN MacKINNON

Bird, Will R. (b. 1891). William Richard Bird was born in East Mapleton, N.S., and educated at Amherst Academy. After service overseas in the First World War, he became a freelance writer and subsequently an information officer for the Nova Scotia government. The author of 27 books, he is best known for his historical romances. Only three of his novels—*Maid of the marshes* (1935), *So much to record* (1951), and *The misadventures of Rufus Burdy* (1975)—have twentieth-century settings. His eight historical novels are all set in the raw atmosphere of eighteenth-century Nova Scotia. Portraying mainly humble folk, they require little psychological analysis but are attractive for their evocation of colourful incidents, characters, and settings. Bird's best work, *Here stays good Yorkshire* (1945), introduces the rough-hewn Crabtree family, settlers in the Chignecto region in the troubled times of the American Revolution. *Tristram's salvation* (1957) and *Despite the distance* (1961) make the Crabtree saga a trilogy. Two other novels are derived from Bird's Yorkshire-settlement heritage: *Judgment glen* (1947) and *The shy Yorkshireman* (1955). *The passionate pilgrim* (1949) is another Chignecto novel, set during the time of the Acadian expulsion. *To love and to cherish* (1953) portrays the founding of Shelburne by the Loyalists, and *An Earl must have a wife* (1969) is a lurid account of the life of a famous colonial administrator, J.F.W. DesBarres (1722-1824).

Bird's short stories have been collected in *Private Timothy Fergus Clancy* (1930), *Sunrise for Peter, and other stories* (1946), and *Angel Cove* (1972). As well, Bird edited *Atlantic anthology* (1959), a collection of writings by Maritime authors. Two memoirs, *And we go on* (1930) and *Ghosts have warm hands* (1968),

Birney, Earle (b. 1904). Alfred Earle Birney was born in Calgary, Alta, then part of the Northwest Territories, and spent his early life as an only child on an isolated farm near Lacombe. His family moved to Banff in 1911 and, following his father's service in the Great War, moved in 1916 to a fruit-farm near Creston, B.C. After high-school graduation Birney worked as a bank clerk, a farm labourer, and as a government labourer in the nearby national parks, before enrolling in chemistry at the University of British Columbia in 1922. During his second year he became interested in English literature and was appointed associate editor of the campus newspaper, *The Ubyssey*. He became editor-in-chief in 1925 and graduated in Honours English in 1926. After receiving his M.A. from the University of Toronto in 1927, he did further graduate work at the University of California at Berkeley, and accepted a lectureship at the University of Utah in 1930. In 1932-3 he completed doctoral coursework at the University of Toronto and became a party organizer for the Trotskyist branch of the Communist Party. After returning to Utah to teach for one more year, Birney received a fellowship to study in England, where he completed his dissertation, entitled 'Chaucer's Irony', worked for the Independent Labour Party, and travelled to Norway to interview Leon Trotsky.

On receiving his Ph.D. in 1938 Birney accepted a junior faculty position at the University of Toronto and undertook the literary editorship (1938-40) of The CANADIAN FORUM. He began writing poetry seriously at this time, and shortly after enlisting for officer training in the Canadian army published his first collection, *David* (1942), which won a Governor-General's Award. After serving overseas as a personnel selection officer, in 1946 he became supervisor of the International Service of the CBC. He published his second poetry collection, *Now is time*, in 1945. From Sept. 1946 to June 1948 he was editor of *The Canadian Poetry Magazine*. From 1948 to 1965 he was professor of medieval literature at the University of British Columbia, where he established Canada's first department of creative writing. In recent years he has served as writer-in-residence at several Canadian universities. He lives in Toronto.

Although he began writing poetry relatively late in life, Birney has been a marvellously resourceful and innovative writer. The Audenesque qualities of his first two collections, repeated in *Strait of Anian* (1948), were followed by the ingeniously varied styles of the verse-play *Trial of a city* (1952). In his next collection, *Ice cod bell and stone* (1962), Birney unveiled a precise new free verse, a colloquial first-person viewpoint, and a strong interest in visual or 'concrete' poetry; in its poems set in Latin America he presented the first of the world-travel poetry by which he would be widely known throughout the next two decades. *November walk near False Creek mouth* (1964), with its innovative, contrapuntally structured title poem, also contains impressively vivid travel meditations set in South America and the Far East. Throughout the 1960s and 1970s Birney's concern to expand the technical resources of his poetry was reflected in various kinds of hand-drawn poems, typewriter-concrete poems, and chant-poems that appeared in *Pnomes, jukollages & other stunzas* (1969), *Rag and bone shop* (1971), *What's so big about green* (1973), *The rugging and moving times* (1976), *Alphbeings and other seasyours* (1976), and *Fall by fury* (1978); and by the substitution of space for conventional punctuation marks that characterizes these books and the retrospective gatherings *Selected poems* (1966), *The poems of Earle Birney* (1969), *Collected poems* (1975), and *Ghost in the wheels: selected poems* (1977). In this later work Birney repudiates the humanistic themes of his first three books to envision a vast, indifferent cosmos in whose 'mammoth corridors' human energy is little more than a glorious absurdity. Overall, Birney's poetry is marked by extraordinary technical virtuosity, playfulness, and openness to experimentation. Most important of this work are his long poems 'David', 'The

damnation of Vancouver', and 'November walk near False Creek mouth', which reflect both his resourcefulness as a craftsman and his profound empathy with human limitation.

Birney's prose—of less interest than his poetry—includes the comic war novel *Turvey* (1949); the novel *Down the long table* (1955), which depicts the Trotskyist scene in which Birney worked in the 1930s; *Big bird in the bush* (1978), a collection of stories and sketches; and the semi-autobiographical non-fiction works *The creative writer* (1966), *The cow jumped over the moon* (1972), and *Spreading time: Book I, 1940-1949* (1980). International publication of Birney's work includes a pirated edition of *Turvey* called *The Kootenay Highlander* (London, 1960); three selections of his poems: *Memory no servant* (Trumansburg, N.Y., 1968), *The bear on the Delhi road* (London, 1973), and *The mammoth corridors* (Okemos, Mich., 1980); and his two editions of work by Malcolm LOWRY: *Selected poems* (San Francisco, 1962) and *Lunar caustic* (London, 1968). Birney has also edited the anthology *Twentieth-century Canadian poetry* (1953).

Considerable critical attention has been focused on Birney's writings. This includes monographs by Frank DAVEY (1971), Richard Robillard (1971), and Peter Aichinger (1978), and Bruce Nesbitt's collection of critical views (1974). *Turvey* (1963), *Down the long table* (1975), and *The poems of Earle Birney* (1969) are in the New Canadian Library.

See also POETRY IN ENGLISH 1900 TO 1950: 4; 1950 TO 1982:2.　　　FRANK DAVEY

bissett, bill (b. 1939). Although born in Halifax, N.S., bill bissett is associated with Vancouver and the west coast, where he has lived since the late 1950s and was important in the Vancouver cultural scene in the 1960s: he embodied the vision and idealism of the so-called 'hippy' movement. His open espousal of drug use has frequently led him into trouble with the police, and his books of poetry have been attacked by B.C. politicians on charges of obscenity, in the face of which he was able to rally impressive statements of support from the cultural community.

bissett's first book, *we sleep inside each other all* (1966), was followed by more than forty volumes of poetry, many published by his own BLEW OINTMENT Press, and in recent years by TALONBOOKS. Among his more important titles are *awake in the red des-*

ert (1968), *drifting into war* (1971), *pomes for yoshi* (1972, rpr. 1977), *pass th food release th spirit book* (1973), *living with the vishyun* (1974), MEDICINE *my mouths on fire* (1974), *plutonium missing* (1976), and *Sailor* (1978). There have been two volumes of selected poems: *nobody owns th earth* (1971), edited with Margaret ATWOOD and Dennis LEE, and *Selected poems: beyond even faithful legends* (1980). bissett's most recent work is *northern birds in color* (1981). He has also produced numerous paintings, drawings, and collages.

bissett has been a tireless experimenter in the forms of poetry, exploring visual and sound poems, chants, collages, short lyrics and extended narratives, and poems of vision and social satire. The most obvious and obtrusive aspect of his style has been his unconventional spelling and orthography: he believes that 'correct' spelling and grammar symbolize class oppression and are imaginatively restrictive. But one soon becomes accustomed to bissett's spelling, which quickly built up its own conventions. The importance of the orthography is mainly visual; bissett sees each poem as an arbitrary composition on the page—even line divisions are determined by visual rather than rhythmic criteria. The visual and oral elements of bissett's work are thus separate; but the oral is important, as his readings demonstrate—especially the chants, based on Indian chanting as much as on the tradition of sound poetry, which have a mesmeric, meditative effect that provides one of the foundations for his vision.

bissett's vision can be divided into the Blakean categories of 'innocence' and 'experience'. Although his frequent evocations of an ideal state of being—attained through communion with nature, drugs, sex, and the free expression of the personality unhampered by the social restraints of logic, law, or grammar—may be considered naive, simplistic, and unoriginal, they are expressed with a singular intensity and often transcend the banal images and the unsophisticated ideas. At his best, bissett writes with remarkable subtlety and quiet irony. In long narrative poems such as 'Killer whale' or 'Th emergency ward', the gentle humour and ironic distance show a fine control of nuance and tone. bissett's poetry comes together most convincingly in *Pomes for Yoshi*—which (along with *Sailor*) is his finest volume to date—in which a series of beautiful love lyrics is juxtaposed to an increasingly weird and nightmarish story of bissett's

troubles in the house he lives in; the long closing narrative, which ranks among his most brilliant accounts of the 'straight' world, ends with the simple humanistic assertion that 'its/beautiful/to feel so many/peopul around/me.'

bissett will be remembered less for individual poems than for the whole body of his work, and for the force he has exerted in west-coast culture.

See also POETRY IN ENGLISH 1950 TO 1982:2.   STEPHEN SCOBIE

Blais, Marie-Claire (b. 1939). Born in Quebec City, she left school at fifteen to work in a shoe factory. Later she took courses in French literature at Université Laval, where she was encouraged in her writing by Jeanne Lapointe and the Rev. Georges-Henri Lévesque. In 1962, after the publication when she was only twenty of her first novel *La belle bête*, and of *Tête blanche*, she was awarded a Guggenheim Fellowship (sponsored by Edmund Wilson). This enabled her to spend a year in France; she then spent some time in Cape Cod and Brittany. She now lives in Montreal.

Since the appearance in 1959 of *La* BELLE BÊTE—translated by Merloyd Lawrence as *Mad shadows* (1960, NCL 1971)—Blais has experimented in book after book with language, method, and form, using stream-of-consciousness, the crudest of street-talk, lyric symbolism, and various blends of the real and the surreal to depict her own particular world, in which evil exists as a monstrous force, relationships are doomed from the start or truncated, and children are destroyed by those around them or by the mere fact of growing up. Parents, except in some of the later works, are callous or depraved, nuns sadistic, priests venal or rascally or at least half mad. The featureless landscape of the early novels has become fuller, more recognizable, but always tinged with the phantasmagoric and with Blais's particular vision of rampant evil and of innocence betrayed. The style is always impelling—at times stripped and subtle, at other times lyrical, incantatory, rhapsodic, or brutally forceful.

Une saison dans la vie d'Emmanuel (1965)—translated by Derek Coltman as *A season in the life of Emmanuel* (1966)—ranks with *La belle bête* and the three Pauline Archange novels (see below) as her most significant and characteristic work. In this powerful and tragic novel, Blais makes a statement about the rural Québec society of the time by reducing it to its bleak and brutish essence. The sixteen children of an exhausted mother and an illiterate farmer-father live a life deprived of grace, beauty, and hope—even of such solaces as pictures and books. All their desires and strivings for something more are in succession stifled, brutalized, or corrupted by the rigidity of their society and the indifference or viciousness of those who should look after them. To one daughter life in a brothel seems a refuge, providing an ease and comfort she can never hope to find elsewhere; to the most gifted son, who had wanted to be a writer, death from tuberculosis comes as a welcome release from an existence that can offer him nothing. Over the series of frustrations, deprivations, and mutilations that mark the first months in the life of Emmanuel broods the figure of the grandmother, the one source of warmth for the children, to the youngest of whom she appears chiefly as a sturdy pair of feet that dominate the room. It is this strong if limited embodiment of the old virtues who offers at the end a sort of summation: 'You get used to everything, you'll see'—a message less of hope than of blind animal endurance. This novel was awarded the Prix France-Canada and the Prix Medicis of France.

In Blais's three semi-autobiographical novels about a girl growing up in Québec—*Les manuscrits de Pauline Archange* (1968), winner of a Governor General's Award; *Vivre! Vivre!* (1969); and *Les apparences* (1970)—the first two of which were translated by Derek Coltman and published in a single volume as *The manuscripts of Pauline Archange* (1969, NCL 1962) and the third by David Lobdell as *Dürer's angel* (1976)—a more robust central figure, the young Pauline, fights, often savagely, to maintain her integrity in a milieu in which parents, even though at times pitiable, are enemies and friendships are curtailed by death or become distorted. Even the priest who, if not as depraved as most of Blais's priests, is in his own words 'diseased with pity' and rendered powerless by the very force of his compassion. There is great vitality in these books in the character of Pauline Archange herself, in her determination to live as a free individual despite the flaws in her upbringing and education, and in the sense for the first time in Blais's work of a layered and complex society.

Three smaller novels—*Tête blanche* (1960), translated by Charles Fullman with the same title (1961, NCL 1974); *L'insoumise*

(1966), translated by David Lobdell as *The fugitive* (1978); and *David Sterne* (1967), translated by David Lobdell with the same title (1973)—deal with boys or young men who are all thwarted rebels, at odds with society and their own nature. *Le loup* (1972)—translated by Sheila Fischman as *The wolf* (1974)—uses a wider canvas to take a more profound and complicated look into human emotions. The homosexual youth who is the central character, though he is drawn again and again to relationships of the most mutually destructive sort—to 'souls', in his own words, 'who were only wounded but whom I left dying'—comes to feel finally that 'love given unstintingly, even if it is given very badly, is not wasted.' *Une liaison parisienne* (1975)—translated by Sheila Fischman as *A literary affair* (1970)—is a relatively slight novel satirizing Québécois romanticizing of the French literary scene: a young writer obtains a grant to work in Paris, where he is entranced and absorbed by, but finally escapes, a highly sophisticated, corrupt, and corrupting family of French intellectuals. *Un joualonais sa joualonie* (1973) is also satirical in intent; this time the target is those Québec writers who use JOUAL as a literary and political device. While the intellectuals debate the matter, two young members of the class they sentimentalize die wretched, almost disregarded deaths—one in a wild street demonstration (which Blais describes in a magnificent set-piece of surrealistic writing), the other despairingly, in a flophouse, of malnutrition. This novel was published in France as *À coeur joual* in 1974 and translated by Ralph Manheim—unfortunately with considerable misunderstanding of Québécois idiom, especially street idiom—as *St Lawrence blues* (1974). *Les nuits d'underground* (1978)—translated by Ray Ellenwood as *Nights in the underground* (1979)—is a study of the lesbian as outcast, combining vivid street-talk in both French and English with long, sinuous, looping sentences to trace the sometimes tragicomic, often tragic lives of a group that frequents a tawdry lesbian bar in Montreal. *Le sourd dans la ville* (1979)—which won a Governor General's Award and was translated by Carol Dunlop as *Deaf to the city* (1980)—returns to the underside of Montreal, this time a run-down hotel. As the life of petty corruption and small hopes goes on around them, two condemned people—a boy with a brain tumour who longs to live and a wealthy woman devastated by the desertion of her husband—contemplate one another, unable

Blais

to communicate, each hoping to read in the other's eyes some answer to their own and the world's pain. There is almost no dialogue, just a prolonged anguished contemplation described in lengthy twining sentences that shift from character to character, from present to past, often within a phrase. *Visions d'Anna* (1982) poses the same question—why should one live?—but provides for two of the characters at least a partial answer. Two young women who have withdrawn from a world of barbarism and indifference—one into petty crime, the other into complete nullity—become reconciled to their mothers and through this to the need to go on living. The style is a sort of third-person stream-of-consciousness, the sentences as long and dense as in Blais's two preceding novels, linking character and character, present and past, memory and hallucination, present despair and future dread.

Marie-Claire Blais has also published two collections of poetry, *Pays voilés* (1963) and *Existences* (1967), and three plays: *Exécution* (1968), translated by David Lobdell as *The execution* (1976); *Fièvre et autres textes dramatiques* (1974); and *Océan suivi de murmures* (1977). Two minor novellas—*Le jour est noir* (1962), a study of a group of children who see their parents' death as a betrayal, and *Les voyageurs sacrés* (1969), the story of a marital triangle in which disloyalty to a marriage is equated with disloyalty to childhood—have been translated by Derek Coltman and published in a single volume as *The day is dark and Three travelers* (1967).

Marie-Claire Blais's fiction is analysed by J. Raymond Brazeau in *An outline of contemporary French-Canadian literature* (1972) and, more philosophically, by Philip Stratford in a study in the Canadian Writers and Their Work series (1970). *Marie-Claire Blais: le monde perturbé des jeunes dans l'oeuvre* (1973), a critical study by Thérèse Fabi, includes 'Le fin d'un enfance', a brief autobiographical sketch by Blais, who contributed the preface to *Illustrations to two novels by Marie-Claire Blais* (1977), a collection of drawings by Mary Meigs illustrating *The manuscripts of Pauline Archange* and *St Lawrence Blues*.

JOYCE MARSHALL

Blaise, Clark (b. 1940). Born in Fargo, North Dakota, of a French-Canadian father and an English-Canadian mother, he grew up in various places, ranging from the American South to the Canadian Prairies. He was educated at Denison University and the University of Iowa's Writer's Workshop and has taught at various universities in Canada (Concordia in Montreal and York in Toronto) and the U.S. (Wisconsin, Iowa, and Skidmore College, Saratoga Springs, N.Y., where he teaches at present).

Blaise's fiction—the stories in *A North American education* (1973) and *Tribal justice* (1974), and the novel *Lunar attractions* (1979)—deals compassionately and unsentimentally with isolated, victimized people. His rich prose style firmly captures a sense of place as counterpoint to his displaced characters. The short stories are strongly linked to each other, a marked feature of *A North American education*, in which the skeleton of a novel lurks behind the tripartite sequence of stories. The contents of *Tribal justice*, which reflects the author's growing fascination with group movement and systems of control, are also divided into three sections. His novel *Lunar attractions* (winner of the *Books in Canada* award for a first novel) offers the moving first-person narrative of a confused adolescent whose self-absorption leads to bizarre violence. Blaise's fiction remains that of the outsider: the northerner in the South, the southerner on the Prairies or in Montreal. The outsider needn't always be a child—he may be an adult starting out with his displaced family in Montreal—but the essential theme of exploration and delicate adjustment, concluded often with a vision of loneliness, abides throughout his work. A new novel, *Lusts*—about a husband's examination of the reason for the suicide of his wife, a successful poet—will be published in the summer of 1983.

Days and nights in Calcutta (1977), written with the novelist Bharati Mukherjee, who is married to Blaise, offers an absorbing, penetrating account of a stay in India. Comprised of separate accounts (each with an epilogue) by the two authors, it presents an interesting and unusual vision as Blaise seeks to accommodate himself to conditions that his wife accepts more matter-of-factly but not uncritically.

DENNIS DUFFY

Blake, William Hume (1861-1924). Born in Toronto, the grandson of the Liberal politician Edward Blake, he was educated at the University of Toronto and admitted to the bar in 1885. He published two books of essays—*Brown waters and other sketches* (1915, rpr. 1925 with a preface by Vincent Massey) and *In a fishing country* (1922)—that are similar in structure, containing essays on fishing, camping, weather, the survival of legends and witchcraft, and portraits of *habitant* families. In both collections Blake expresses his love of the Laurentian wilderness and admiration for its Indian and French-Canadian inhabitants who lived close to nature. *A fisherman's creed* (1923) is an essay on the importance of the intellect in the elaboration of an individual religious faith. Blake's translations of Louis HÉMON's MARIA CHAPDELAINE (1921) and Adjutor Rivard's *Chez nous* (1924) brought to English-speaking readers two of the most traditional portraits of *habitant* life. Blake's essays and translations are clear evidence of his knowledge of French and of his sympathetic interest in French-Canadian rural life. They also provide an implicit indication of the image of French Canada—that of simple peasantry, traditional rural values, large families and unswerving religious faith—that was current in much of English Canada in Blake's time.   KATHRYN HAMER

Blewett, George. See PHILOSOPHY IN CANADA: 4.

Blew Ointment (1963-8). The first issue of this unconventionally political literary magazine, edited and published in Vancouver by bill BISSETT, appeared in Oct. 1963. The magazine was characterized by its editor's personal spelling conventions, and by his view of the artist as oppressed by state and corporate 'fascism'. Five volumes, with varying numbers per volume, were published until 1968. Subsequent issues were released as unnumbered 'specials': notably 'Fascist Court' (1970), 'Occupation Issue' (1970), 'Oil Slick Speshul' (1971), 'Open Picture Book nd th News' (1972), 'What isnt Tantrik Speshul' (1973), and 'End of the World Speshul Anthology' (1978). All issues were produced in crude mimeograph. Most were printed on variously sized and coloured paper and bound together with random newspaper clippings, and occasionally with one-of-a-kind drawings, so that individual issues differed considerably in appearance. The content made it both a community newsletter of the arts, documenting work-in-progress by Vancouver writers and graphic artists, and a national literary magazine. As Margaret ATWOOD reported in 1969: 'It can print poetry so awful you have to be high to appreciate it and poems so good they create their own high.' Contributors constituted a cross-section of Canadian poetry, and included Atwood, bissett, Mar-

garet AVISON, Colleen Thibaudeau, Gwendolyn MacEWEN, Earle BIRNEY, Michael ONDAATJE, George BOWERING, bp NICHOL, Al PURDY, Dennis LEE, John Robert COLOMBO, and John NEWLOVE.

Blew Ointment Press, founded by bissett in 1967, publishes books in a similarly unusual mimeographed format, but confines itself mostly to writers of the 1960s Vancouver counterculture.   FRANK DAVEY

Bliss, J.M. See HISTORICAL WRITING IN ENGLISH: 7.

Blodgett, E.D. See CRITICISM IN ENGLISH: 5(c), 5(h).

Blondal, Patricia. See NOVELS IN ENGLISH: 1940 TO 1960.

Boas, Franz. See INDIAN LEGENDS AND TALES: BIBLIOGRAPHY.

Boatman, The (1957). This collection by Jay MACPHERSON, one of the best-known works of poetry in Canadian literature, is an intricate sequence of epigrammatic poems that is a colloquial and familiar retelling of myths. Carefully constructed from biblical and classical allusions—their strict metres recalling ballads, nursery rhymes, and hymns—the poems are organized in six parts. (A model would be William Blake's *For the sexes: the gates of paradise* or *The crystal cabinet*.) While employing simple language, charming wit, and playful humour, they are richly metaphorical, recording the struggle from a fallen vision to an anagogic vision, where the imagination is resurrected by love. The first section, 'Poor child' (reminiscent of Blake), describes the archetypal human state as fallen: man longs to return to the security of the insatiate womb. The poet, symbolically orphaned, struggles wistfully to recover the third eye's fading vision. 'O earth return' (the title is from Blake's *Songs of experience*) describes the earth as a fallen woman (Northrop FRYE's fallen nature in female form): Eve, Sibylla, Sheba. In 'The ploughman in darkness' (also from Blake), man lives in an atrophied darkness, struggling against the failure of love. The fourth section, 'The sleepers', describes corresponding male figures: the shepherd (Endymion), Adonis, Adam—portraits of moral loves in the fallen garden of the world. Blake's theory that the human psyche must progress through three stages of vision, from innocence and experience to

Boatman

a higher innocence, provides an informing structure, implying that the world could be renewed if only the imagination could ignite the will. The fifth section, 'The boatman', reworks the motif of Noah and his ark. These poems—in which the ark speaks to Noah, as each poem speaks to its maker, or the creature to its creator—struggle towards a vision of man in his anagogic phase as creator. The sixth and final section is 'The fisherman: a book of riddles', and the last poem, 'The fisherman', is a portrait of man egotistically claiming the world as his idea until God intervenes and the creature realizes his 'creatureliness'. With the golden hook of love, fallen man catches the fish of wisdom.

The poet seems withdrawn into a mythological world that reflects the real world as in a glass globe, as though the mythological structures represented a delicate and poignant defence against a deeply personal anguish. What intrigues the reader is the voice of the poet trying to will her own renewal.

The boatman, which received a Governor General's Award, was reissued in 1968 with sixteen new poems, and this collection, along with Macpherson's second book, *Welcoming disaster* (1974), was republished in 1981 under the title *Poems twice told*, which includes decorations by the author.

ROSEMARY SULLIVAN

Bodsworth, Fred (b. 1918) Born and educated in Port Burwell, Ont., he worked as a reporter there and in St Thomas, Ont., before joining the *Toronto Star* in 1943. After the war his freelance journalism gained him a position with *Maclean's*, where he worked until 1955. As a journalist he has travelled widely and written on many subjects, but he is best known for his articles on nature. He has led birding tours to many parts of the world, and his ornithological expertise informs much of his periodical writing as well as his novels.

Bodsworth's first novel, *The last of the curlews* (1954; NCL 1963), portrays the extinction of the Eskimo curlew. Following in realistic detail a lonely male's seasonal migration and doomed search for a mate, the book expresses deep sorrow and pessimism about man's interference with nature. *The strange one* (1959), published in the United States as *The mating call*, tells a similar but much more optimistic story of two geese that is complemented by a parallel plot involving people. A Hebridean-born biologist's romance with a Cree woman in the James Bay area is set against the mating of a

Canada goose with a Hebridean barnacle goose that had been windswept across the Atlantic. Just as the barnacle goose resists his instincts in order to stay with his new mate, so the biologist takes a lesson from nature and remains with his lover. The plot is complicated by white racism, which drove the educated Cree woman back to her people and which the couple must combat together.

In *The atonement of Ashley Morden* (1964) an RCAF bombardier's sense of his war guilt drives him to become an altruistic scientist. Afraid that his research will be redirected into germ warfare by the Canadian military establishment, he tries to destroy his work and flees to the North to live with a German girl whose father had fled the Nazis. An anti-war book that is topical in its treatment of military distortion of medical research, it too employs birds to convey a didactic parallel with nature. *The sparrow's fall* (1967) explores nature's crueller side. A missionary's preaching is seen to have had a near-fatal influence on a young Ojibwa couple whose survival in the bush depends on the killing of animals: Christian concepts imported into the North seem out of place in the elemental struggles of people so close to the land. The two Ojibwas move towards a more practical philosophy based on the obvious lessons of nature.

Bodsworth's novels are sparely written and fast-paced, reflecting the care and authentic detail of an experienced journalist as well as his strong commitment to the preservation of nature, particularly in the Canadian North, and his belief that nature shows man the way to live. His interweaving of nature with human characters—exaggerated though some of them are—is done with much skill.

Bodsworth is also the author of *Pacific coast* (1970), a history of British Columbia, and a contributor to *Wilderness Canada* (1970).

TERRENCE CRAIG

Bolt, Carol (b. 1941). One of Canada's most prolific and successful playwrights, she was born in Winnipeg, grew up in British Columbia, and spent a year in Britain and Israel after graduating from the University of British Columbia in 1961. On her return to Canada, she and a few friends started a small theatre in Montreal, where she began writing children's plays. When it closed in the late sixties, she moved to Toronto, where she now works and lives with her husband, actor David Bolt, and their son.

In the late sixties and early seventies she developed her scripts through the COL-LECTIVE CREATION process with George Luscombe's Toronto Workshop Productions and Paul Thompson's Theatre Passe Muraille. Her early plays for adults—*Buffalo Jump* (1972), *Gabe* (1973), and *Red Emma* (1974), all developed collectively—offered a political re-interpretation of historical events, but Bolt rejects the 'documentary' label for them because of their theatricality. Essentially their dramatic strength lies in their colourful characters and their 'montage' of swiftly changing scenes, while idealism, heroism, and comic parody shade their historical actuality and political messages. While *Buffalo jump* explores the conflict between 'Red Evans' and R.B. Bennett during the 1935 unemployed workers' trek to Ottawa, and *Gabe* studies the relevance of Louis Riel and Gabriel Dumont to their modern descendants, *Red Emma* examines the nature of revolutionary commitment in the person of Emma Goldman, turn-of-the-century New York anarchist. Emma's belief in women's emancipation signals a change in Bolt's work at this time. Her next play, *Shelter* (1975), is a satirical rendition of the involvement of five Saskatchewan women with the contemporary political process. In this play her earlier emphasis on myth and heroism gives way to more naturalistic presentation and rounded character development.

Although her work since *Shelter* is still influenced by the unusual juxtapositions and comic characterization learned from Luscombe and the Theatre Passe Muraille, Bolt now prefers to write independently, concentrating on 'trying to make the form of a play more powerful.' (Wallace and Zimmerman, *The work: conversations with English-Canadian playwrights*, 1982.) Bolt's most successful play, *One night stand* (1977), started from the formal challenge of creating a thriller with a small cast. In it a casual encounter between boy and girl moves from situation comedy to a terrifying psychological exposé. Subtitled 'a comedy thriller', the play cuts through contemporary clichés to a bizarre conclusion that underscores the ominous relationship between social games and spontaneous reality. Bolt's adaptation of *One night stand* as a television film won three Canadian Film Awards in 1978. Her next play, *Escape entertainment* (1981), about making and reviewing Canadian films, pushes the absurdist juxtaposition of art and nature even further. Its exaggerated comic characters; its

multi-dimensional use of film, set, and soundstage; its stripping away of verbal clichés; and its pervasive conflict between romantic visions and real-life experiences—are all characteristics that summarize Bolt's work up to that point. Her most recent play is *Love or money*, which premièred at the Blythe Summer Festival in 1982 but is not yet published.

In addition to her plays for adults, Bolt has written several innovative children's scripts: *My best friend is twelve feet high* (1972), *Cyclone Jack* (1972), *Tangleflags* (1973), *Maurice* (1974), and *Finding Bumble* (1975). She has also written for radio and television and is an active promoter of Canadian theatre through Playwrights Canada, which first published most of her scripts.

ELIZABETH HOPKINS

Bonheur d'occasion (1945). This first novel by Gabrielle ROY was the first Canadian work to win a major French literary prize (the Prix Fémina) and has been translated into nine languages. In a flawed English translation by Hanna Josephson, *The tin flute* (1947), it won a Governor General's Award. A poetic, compassionate, and authentic portrayal of a Montreal slum family whose fortunes rise ironically—unique in French-language fiction for its sweep, its masterful characterization, and its creative unity—it has been seen as a progenitor of the protest literature that would explode in Québec in the 1960s.

When Roy returned from Europe in the spring of 1939 to settle in an area of Montreal where poverty and wealth rub shoulders, she was struck both by this tension and by the paradox that the war brought relative prosperity to the slum dwellers. *Bonheur d'occasion* deftly interweaves these thematic pulls and contradictions. It is set in Saint-Henri, criss-crossed by railway lines, bounded by the Lachine Canal and hemmed in by factories, with the elevated and prosperous Westmount to the north and the dump village of Pointe-Saint-Charles to the south. The action focuses on Florentine's search for security and love and on the trials of the Lacasse family. As in other Québec novels of the period, the family is in a state of disintegration: at the end, pregnant Florentine marries Emmanuel, who, like Florentine's father and brother, goes off to war; one brother gets a job in a munitions factory, one dies of leukemia, and a sister decides to become a nun. Deeply rooted in a historical period and sharply questioning the value of a social system that 'solves' its crises through war, the novel develops characterization and action with a minimum of authorial intervention. Roy captures, more extensively than Ringuet (Philippe PANNETON) had done earlier, several levels of popular speech, including JOUAL, thus anticipating the interest of many sixties' writers in this facet of Québec life.

The original Pascal edition of the novel, in two volumes, was succeeded in 1965 by the somewhat reworked text published by Beauchemin. (For a discussion of the changes, see R. Robidoux and A. Renaud, *Le roman canadien-français du vingtième siècle*, and B.-Z. Shek, *Social realism in the French-Canadian novel*.) *The tin flute* was reissued in the New Canadian Library in 1958; a new and not entirely successful English translation by Alan Brown, retaining the title, appeared in 1980 (NCL, 1981). A feature film, *The tin flute*, directed by Claude Fournier, was released in 1983.   BEN-Z. SHEK

Borduas, Paul-Émile. See ESSAYS IN FRENCH: 5 and REFUS GLOBAL.

Borson, Roo (b. 1952). Born in Berkeley, California, she received a B.A. in English from Goddard College, Vermont, where she came under the influence of the poet Louis Gluck and began submitting poems to little magazines. From the University of British Columbia she received an M.F.A. in creative writing, working initially under Pat LOWTHER and later under Robert Bringhurst, whom she considers the prime shaping force on her writing. Her first book, *Landfall* (1977), was followed by *In the smoky light of the fields* (1980), *Rain* (1980), and *A sad device* (1982), her strongest book. Her poetry is based on keen observation and often takes commonplace events and images to startling conclusions. Timothy FINDLEY has noted that her work 'creates a compelling atmosphere of wonder', while maintaining a 'sense of private distance which she shares with the reader.' Although Borson has retained her American citizenship, living in Canada as a landed immigrant, she has a strong attachment to the country for aesthetic and literary reasons. She is the youngest poet included in Margaret ATWOOD's *New Oxford book of Canadian verse* (1982).

See also POETRY IN ENGLISH 1950 TO 1982:3.   BRUCE MEYER

Bosco, Monique (b. 1927). Born in Vienna, she received her early education in France and came to Canada in 1948, receiving her M.A. from the Université de Montréal in 1951 and her Ph.D. in 1953 with a thesis on 'L'isolement dans le roman canadien-français'. She worked for many years as a freelance journalist until she became in 1963 a professor in the French department of the Université de Montréal.

Bosco's novels all treat basically the same themes—solitude and bitterness—but increase in intensity of rage from the lyrical *Un amour maladroit* (1961) and *Les infusoires* (1965) to *La femme de Loth* (1970), winner of a Governor General's Award and translated by John GLASSCO as *Lot's wife* (1975). This last novel is a strong and bitter jeremiad, the lament of a rejected woman who has not yet broken through her fascination with a mango. *New Medea* (1974) takes this rage to an even higher pitch, not quite succeeding in making convincing either Medea or her enormous act, but inspiring respect for the strength of her obsession. *Charles Lévy M.D.* (1977), despite the banality of its title and the familiarity of the situation it depicts (it is the monologue of a dying man), is a compassionate and subtle work, the confession of a weak man who is bound to his wife and convention through some fundamental lack of energy.

Jéricho (1971), a collection of verse, and *Schabbat 70-77* (1978), short prose-poems, share the same themes as well as the same forceful precision and grace of language as the novels.

See Gloria Escomel, 'Monique Bosco ou le miroir brisé', *La Nouvelle Barre du Jour 65* (1978).   SHERRY SIMON

Boucher, Denise. See DRAMA IN FRENCH 1948 TO 1981: 4.

Boucher, Pierre. See Writing in NEW FRANCE: 2.

Boucher, Yvon. See DRAMA IN FRENCH 1948 TO 1981: 3.

Bouchette, Robert-Errol. See NOVELS IN FRENCH 1900 TO 1920.

Boudreau, Jules. See ACADIAN LITERATURE 2(b).

Bourget, Elizabeth. See DRAMA IN FRENCH 1948 TO 1981: 4.

Bourinot, Arthur Stanley (1893-1969). Son of the historian Sir John Bourinot, he was born in Ottawa and educated at the University of Toronto. From 1915 to 1919 he served in the First World War, the last two years as a prisoner of war. He completed his legal training at Osgoode Hall, Toronto, and was called to the bar in 1920. He then practised law in Ottawa until his retirement in 1959.

With the encouragement of Sir Andrew MACPHAIL, Bourinot began to publish poems while still an undergraduate. His first books—*Laurentian lyrics and other poems* (1915), *Poems* (1921), *Lyrics from the hills* (1923), *Pattering feet: a book of childhood verses* (1925), *Ottawa lyrics and verses for children* (1929), and *Selected poems (1915-1935)* (1935)—are the work of a deft versifier enthralled with the beauty of nature, the major subject of both his poems and his paintings. More conservative than Duncan Campbell SCOTT, his close friend and mentor, Bourinot at first seldom engaged in formal experimentation. *Under the sun* (1939), which won a Governor General's Award, reveals a new versatility in its terse rhythms and free verse, and in its frank poems about the Depression and the coming war. The Second World War brought out Bourinot's ability as a war poet, displayed in *Canada at Dieppe* (1942) and *True harvest* (1945). After the publication of his *Collected poems* (1947) he produced more than a dozen books and chapbooks of poetry, the last being *Watcher of men: selected poems (1947-66)* (1966). His later work consisted largely of nature lyrics and contemplative poems; he was also a skilful narrative poet, often selecting themes from Canadian history.

An active member of the Canadian literary community, Bourinot edited the *Canadian Poetry Magazine* (1948-54 and 1966-8) and *Canadian Author and Bookman* (1953-4, associate editor 1957-60). His critical articles, in which he advocated simplicity, clarity, and 'reasonable experiment', were collected in *The quick and the dead: views and reviews on poetry* (1955). *Five Canadian poets* (1954, rev. 1956) contains essays on Duncan Campbell Scott, Archibald LAMPMAN, William E. Marshall, Charles SANGSTER, and George Frederick CAMERON. As well, Bourinot compiled and edited *Edward William Thomson (1849-1924): a bibliography, with notes and some letters* (1955); *Archibald Lampman's letters to Edward William Thomson (1890-98)* (1956); *The letters of Edward William Thomson to Archibald Lampman (1891-*

97) (1957); *At the mermaid inn, conducted by A. Lampman, W.W. Campbell, Duncan C. Scott* (1958), selections from the column (q.v.) in the *Globe; Some letters of Duncan Campbell Scott, Archibald Lampman and others* (1959); and *More letters of Duncan Campbell Scott (2nd series)* (1960). He collaborated with Marius BARBEAU in *Come a singing!* (1947), a collection of folk songs illustrated by Arthur Lismer.   CAROLE GERSON

Bourne, George. See FOREIGN WRITERS ON CANADA IN ENGLISH: 2.

Bouthillette, Jean. See ESSAYS IN FRENCH: 7.

Bowering, George (b. 1935). Born and raised in the Okanagan Valley of British Columbia, he was an RCAF aerial photographer after finishing high school (1954-7). He then enrolled at the University of British Columbia and received a B.A. in history (1960) and an M.A. in English (1963). At UBC, after an academic grounding in the English poets, he read William Carlos Williams and was electrified to discover that poetry could employ speech models and very simple words. Along with fellow students Frank DAVEY and Lionel KEARNS, he became influenced by the writing and theories of the American poets Robert Duncan, Robert Creeley, and Charles Olson—who were associated with Black Mountain College in North Carolina—particularly when Duncan visited Vancouver in 1961 and Creeley became a visiting professor (and his M.A. thesis adviser) at UBC. In 1961 Bowering—with Frank Davey, Fred WAH, and others—founded the controversial little magazine TISH. By 1963 he had acquired not only an M.A. but a sophisticated poetics. He then taught at the University of Calgary; did further graduate studies at the University of Western Ontario; taught at Sir George Williams (now Concordia) University; founded another little magazine, *Imago* (1964-74); and became contributing editor for Davey's OPEN LETTER. He now teaches at Simon Fraser University.

A prolific writer, Bowering has published almost 40 books since his first poetry collection, *Sticks and stones* (with a preface by Creeley), appeared in 1963 as a Tishbook. Among the books of poetry that followed were *Points on the grid* (1964); *The man in yellow boots* (1965); *The silver wire* (1966); *Baseball* (1967); *Two police poems* (1968); *Rocky*

Bowering

Mountain foot (1968) and *The gangs of Kosmos* (1969), which together won a Governor General's Award; *Sitting in Mexico* (1970); *Touch: selected poems 1960-1970* (1971); *Selected poems: particular accidents* (1980); and *Smoking mirror* (1982), which contains lyrics from the seventies. Since 1970 he has written long, book-length poems, including *George Vancouver* (1970) and *Autobiology* (1972), which were included in *The catch* (1976); his long poems have also been collected in *West window* (1982).

Bowering's prose fiction includes short stories—collected in *Flycatcher & other stories* (1974), *Protective footwear: stories and fables* (1978), and *A place to die* (1983); a novella, *Concentric circles* (1977); and two novels: *A mirror on the floor* (1967) and *Burning water* (1980; rpr. 1983), about George Vancouver's search for the Northwest Passage, which won a Governor General's Award.

Bowering prizes spare language and minute attention to phrasing in his poetry. The hesitations at the end of his (usually) short lines register the tensions between wanting to move on, restlessly, with the speed of the moment, and wanting to observe the moment so he will not betray, by sliding past it, the exact word he is on the verge of finding. He distrusts adjectives and metaphors and forms of premeditated writing, preferring to work as close as possible to the immediate and personal. The early poetry focuses on things, but—particularly when he took up the long poem in the late sixties—Bowering gradually concentrated on voicing his responses.

Bowering's prose has taken him in quite different directions. Wary of realism, he has composed his latest prose fictions (such as *A short sad book*, 1977) with an intense desire to invent and subvert. This writing, largely inspired by Gertrude Stein, displays his wit and his outrageous manipulations of the novel's conventions. Bowering has come more and more to think of writing as playing with the conventions of language and literature. In both his poetry and his prose fiction he observes the two chief features of post-modernism: he takes in his poetry a phenomenological position that attempts to respond to the flow of consciousness at the moment of occurrence, and in his prose fiction a semiotic position that goes out of its way to stress the artificial structures and practices of art.

Bowering's critical publications include a monograph on Al PURDY (1970), *A way with words* (1982), and *The mask in place: essays on fiction in North America* (1983). His criticism, though not always fair or judicious, is often shrewd. As Bowering chooses up sides he tends to overrate authors who share his views and to undervalue those who work from other assumptions. In his critical pieces the curiosity evident in his poetry sometimes gets lost in advocacy.

Two interesting interviews with Bowering are in Donald Cameron, *Conversations with Canadian novelists*, vol. 2 (1973) and Caroline Bayard and Jack David, *Outposts/Avant-postes* (1978). See also 'George Bowering' in Frank Davey, *From there to here* (1974); Ken Norris, 'The poetry of George Bowering' in Jack David, ed., *Brave new wave* (1978); Ellen Quigley, '*Tish*: Bowering's infield position', *Studies in Canadian Literature* (1980); Robin Blaser, 'George Bowering's plain song' in George Bowering, *Selected poems: particular accidents* (1980); and Frank Stewart, 'wonderfully conscious poetry', *Brick* 14 (Winter 1982).

See also CRITICISM IN ENGLISH: 5, NOVELS IN ENGLISH 1960 TO 1982: OTHER TALENTS, OTHER WORKS: 1, and POETRY IN ENGLISH 1950 TO 1982:2.   DENNIS COOLEY

Bowering, Marilyn (b. 1949). Born in Winnipeg and raised in Victoria, B.C., she attended the University of Victoria (B.A. 1971; M.A. 1973). She has made her living principally by teaching and editing; from 1978 to 1980 she was a lecturer (part-time and then full-time) in the Creative Writing Department of the University of Victoria. She has published five collections of poems: *The liberation of Newfoundland* (1973), *One who became lost* (1976), *The killing room* (1977), *Sleeping with lambs* (1980), which contains her best work to date, and *Giving back diamonds* (1982); two poetry pamphlets: *Third child/Zian* (1978) and *The book of glass* (1979); and a work of fiction, *The visitors have all returned* (1979). With David Day she co-edited *Many voices: contemporary Indian poetry* (1977).

Marilyn Bowering's poetry has certain obvious things in common with Susan MUSGRAVE's. Both poets make extensive use of west-coast (especially Indian) materials; both incline toward violent or gruesome natural imagery; and both employ a witch-like persona. The voice in Bowering's poetry is a kind of earth-spirit, hiding out—decidedly female, animal, and highly sexed. Her world is both violent and subtle, a world of myth that lies beneath the world of everyday and reveals itself in fragments. For some of Bowering's readers these revelations have seemed too cryptic, too precious. The peculiar screen that may seem to exist between her images and their actualization can disappear, however, when the reader adjusts his vision slightly and relaxes the insistence upon linear meaning: taken at the level of dream, the images can be very powerful. Bowering has a decided lyric gift; her poems are carefully and rhythmically made; and she is especially skilful at manipulating the short line.

The visitors have all returned might be described as fictional vignettes, prose poems, or a surrealist novel. It is a book made of shifting, overlapping realities, both within the consciousness of the heroine and in relation to the commonsensical standard carried by her mate. Touch-points dissolve, but the writing remains firm. *The visitors have all returned* is an intriguing, memorable work.

CONSTANCE ROOKE

Bowman, Louise Morey. See Writing in English in QUÉBEC: 2.

Braithwaite, Max. See HUMOUR AND SATIRE IN ENGLISH.

Brant, Joseph. See INDIAN LITERATURE: 1.

Brant-Sero, John. See INDIAN LITERATURE: 2.

Brault, Jacques (b. 1933). Born in Montreal, he studied philosophy there as well as in Paris and Poitiers. He teaches in the Institut des Sciences Médiévales and the Faculté des Lettres of the Université de Montréal.

In the poems collected in *Mémoire* (1965)—moving recollections of Brault's father and his brother Gilles, who died and was buried in Sicily—memory blends with eulogy, introspection, and learning. The poet faces the 'daily grape-shot' of the city streets; says 'Grief is the bread of my homeland.' He characterizes the land as having been 'born in the orphanage of the snow' and its people as 'half-rebels . . . the only Negroes to have beautiful white beliefs . . . savages in neckties', 'knees knocking and hands gnarled from crawling about in shame'. The same salutary mockery—which links Brault with Gaston MIRON—appears again in *La poésie ce matin* (1971). Here he speaks of 'we the sub-human, the valourless', but out of the 'long fatigue of the ages' arises forbearance. Fragmented, 'dazed' Québec is the only land to love; its

unrivalled poverty must be accepted. These first two collections—marked by an immediate, painful awareness of the state of things—were followed by two books that broke new ground. In *Poèmes des quatre côtés* (1975) Brault offers 'nontranslations' of the Nordic silence and solitude of the American poet John Haines; the 'spiral rhythms' of Gwendolyn MacEWEN; the ironic dread and chilly sensuality of Margaret ATWOOD; and the fascinating, pure lyricism of e.e. cummings. This work is more an 'exercise in self-criticism' than the development of a new theory. Rather than erecting false barriers between the different poets, Brault captures the spirit of a fraternity of craftsmen, of poets who reinvent language and who cannot be strangers because they are members of the same brotherhood.

In *L'en dessous l'admirable* (1975) Brault explores the world of the individual: 'I, thin skin of identity.' The peripatetic poet both contemplates and feels the 'suffering of the age', recreating it in the 'naked song of the inexpressible'. Brault's poetry entirely rejects formalism and sterile convention and thrives on simplicity and direct speech; it is concerned with what is seen and felt, dreamed and encountered. Free in both form and content, it expresses honestly his belief that 'Poetry and freedom are synonymous dreams.'

Brault has also written important prose, expressing himself as a poet in his criticism. In *Alain Grandbois* (Paris, 1968) he refers to the poet's 'unbridled delight in language', his insatiable desire to dwell in the world; in a 1966 article 'Mon ami Nelligan', included in *Chemin faisant*, he sees poetry that 'shelters us from sorrow' in the work of Nelligan; in Saint-Denys GARNEAU (whose *Oeuvres* Brault edited with Benoît Lacroix, 1971) he sees a poet whose language and everything else was taken from him, a fate 'we Québécois know well'. Brault writes most eloquently in *Miron le magnifique* (1969) of Gaston Miron's struggles, tenacity, love, and 'historic hope'. *Chemin faisant* (1975) is a collection of essays from various sources accompanied by reflective comments that trace the development of Brault's thought. A work of evaluation and intense scrutiny, without being pedantic, it is written in the style of Barthes, cultivating the pleasure of reading, writing, and reflection.

For the theatre Brault has written *Trois partitions* (1972), short plays that demonstrate his care in rendering the complexities of love, death, happiness, and sorrow in simple terms and situations. He has also published *Nouvelles* (1963), three stories that introduce characters—part real, part fictional—who are all striving for life's good fortune. His latest book, *Trois fois passera* (1981), employs both poetry and prose. The poet speaks, in short phrases and a concise style, of the hardships of life and of his joy in writing. He reflects on a profession that leaves him dissatisfied, wavering between the need to speak and the temptation to remain silent. However, the prose writer, 'lover of writing', always wins out. No poet better illustrates the indestructible link between living and writing, between writing and dying.

See Laurent Mailhot, 'Contre le temps et la mort: *Mémoire* de Jacques Brault', *Voix et images du pays III* (1970); Gabrielle Poulin, 'Des mémoires d'outre-neige (*L'en dessous l'admirable* de Jacques Brault)', *Relations* (July-Aug. 1976); and Michel Lemaire, 'Jacques Brault dans le matin', VOIX ET IMAGES, vol. 2, no. 2 (Dec. 1976).

JOSEPH BONENFANT

Brett, G.S. (1879-1944). George Sidney Brett was born in Wales of English parents, was head boy at Kingswood, Wesley's great school at Bath, Eng., and an Exhibitioner at Christ Church, Oxford, taking a first in 'Greats' in 1902. After teaching philosophy and English in India, where he published *Representative English poems* and *The philosophy of Gassendi*, he came in 1908 to Trinity College, Toronto, as lecturer in classics and librarian. From 1927 he was head of the department of philosophy at the University of Toronto. He was not only a trusted administrator but an outstanding teacher whose lectures were lightened by memorable phrases and quiet humour. A check-list of his writings contains 126 entries.

The philosophy of Gassendi (1908) is a tribute to a long-neglected French priest, humanist scholar, scientist, philosopher, and contemporary of Descartes. Later Brett was attracted to the similarly inclusive Santayana. In 'The achievement of Santayana' (*University of Toronto Quarterly*, IX, Oct. 1939) he applauds Santayana's assertion that science, philosophy, and literature have each a part to play in increasing 'the wealth of the world in its spiritual dimension'. In 'Parallel paths in philosophy and literature', a paper read before the English Association in 1929, Brett expressed his alarm at the commercialism of contemporary publishing that threatened the integrity of both philosophy and literature. *The government of man: an introduction to ethics and politics* (1919; 2nd ed. 1921) relates the historical development of moral and political ideas to the social and religious conditions that constitute their setting. Within its limits it foreshadows in miniature Brett's great contribution to scholarship: his three-volume *History of psychology* (1912-24). Since Brett's psychology was broader in range and more philosophical in content than today's, the title may now seem a misnomer. Its importance, however, is in giving full scope to Brett's vast learning; the result is a uniquely comprehensive portrayal of the diversities, development, and continuity of the human spirit.

Brett remains a continuing presence in Canadian literature. The novelist Phyllis Brett Young is his daughter. In Morley CALLAGHAN's *The Varsity story* (1948) Brett makes a brief appearance as 'a man with an orderly mind'. Hugh HOOD in *Reservoir ravine* (1979) relates an imaginary conversation between Brett and a newly appointed young lecturer in philosophy; while Ernest BUCKLER, in his essay 'The best place to be' (*Whirligig*, 1979), draws, from his own experience as a graduate student under Brett, a splendidly life-like sketch, a gracious and fitting tribute.

F. HILTON PAGE

Brewster, Elizabeth (b. 1922). Born at Chipman, N.B., she enjoyed a rural childhood in various parts of her native province. Between 1942 and 1946 she attended the University of New Brunswick, where she got to know a number of writers who eventually launched *The* FIDDLEHEAD; some of her poems appeared in early issues. After graduating with first-class honours in English and Greek, she studied at Radcliffe College (A.M. 1947), and at King's College, London. On returning to Canada she took a Bachelor of Library Science degree at the University of Toronto, and in 1962 obtained her Ph.D. from Indiana University. For many years she worked as a librarian and cataloguer in New Brunswick (where she was associate librarian of the Legislative Library) and in Ontario, Alberta, and British Columbia. She also lectured at the University of Victoria and taught creative writing at the University of Alberta. Since 1972 she has been on the English faculty of the University of Saskatchewan.

The subject of Brewster's doctoral dissertation, George Crabbe, has been a palpable influence on her poetry. One of her earlier descriptive poems, 'Lillooet: a Canadian village' (1954), reproduces her early memories in rhymed couplets that are looser than Crabbe's but share his interest in ordinary lives and maintain a similarly sharp, committed attitude to her subject. Many early poems interpret her rural upbringng and embody a curious tension between the intensely personal and the deliberately objective. They frequently draw upon biographical experience, discovering a form in memory and in the very process of writing. Old conventions are used in an original, revivifying way; and although nostaligia and reminiscence are frequently the inspiration behind her poetry, the poems themselves are remarkable for a tough honesty. Some of these early poems first appeared in small limited editions; the best of them were collected in *Passage of summer* (1969).

Later volumes include *Sunrise north* (1972), *In search of Eros* (1974), *Poems* (1977), *The way home*, and *Digging* (both 1982). Brewster's poems are generally short, and are written for the most part in so-called free verse, but with a careful control of rhythm and cadence. Certain themes recur—an undeveloped love affair, memories of dead parents and relatives, analysis of a doubtful faith—and there are frequent references to her work in libraries, her apartment overlooking a city, her frank reappraisals of an uneventful but satisfying life. Her poems are mainly about what she sees and feels in everyday situations, and she has a remarkable capacity to universalize her own modest experiences. Her unostentatious straightforwardness is not always suited to mythological subjects, which she treats in *In search of Eros*, but she can sometimes domesticate the great myths with acuteness and economy. Hers is the poetry of understatement, containing lines that rarely haunt the memory but impress during the process of reading by their sensitivity and delicate rightness. Her verse is valuable for its documentary accuracy as well as for its elegance and quiet grace.

Brewster has also published two novels. *The sisters* (1974) is concerned with a girl growing up in the Maritimes, living for a short time at Lillooet and attending the University of New Brunswick; it has the feel of autobiography and is structured by the reminiscences of the main characters. *Junction* (1983) is an intelligent and curiously absorbing romance about time-travel in early twentieth-century Canada. Brewster's short stories, collected in *It's easy to fall on the ice* (1977), are all about women who are mostly timid and lonely. Once again, situations recur—work in a library, attempted suicide, conversion to Catholicism. None is especially eventful; the ordinariness suggests autobiography rather than fictional 'making'. But these stories are finely crafted, and Brewster's intelligence and sensitivity are evident throughout. Although poetry is Brewster's chief means of expression, the thematic connections between her verse and prose give an impressive solidity to her work as a whole.

Studies of Brewster's poetry include Desmond PACEY's 'The poetry of Elizabeth Brewster' in *Ariel*, 4 (July 1973) and Robert GIBBS's 'From a different country' in CANADIAN LITERATURE 62 (Autumn 1974). Brewster's own useful account of her principles and practices as a poet, 'Chronology of summer', appeared in the *Humanities Association Bulletin* 21 (Winter 1970). See also POETRY IN ENGLISH 1950 TO 1982:1.   W.J. KEITH

Breyfogle, William Arthur. See NATURE WRITING IN ENGLISH: 4.

Bridle, Augustus. See NOVELS IN ENGLISH 1920 TO 1940.

Bringhurst, Robert. See POETRY IN ENGLISH 1950 TO 1982:3.

British Columbia, Writing in. Unless one counts the journals of exploration and discovery produced by Cook, Vancouver, Mackenzie, Thompson, and Fraser, the literature of British Columbia may be said to be barely a century old. The journals are important culturally and, along with travel writings such as Milton's and Cheadle's *The North-West Passage by land* . . . (London, 1865) and Morley Roberts' *Western avenues* (1887), provided a foretaste of what was to come when the educated imagination confronted an advanced primitive culture and an untamed and elemental terrain. Simon Fraser declared in 1808 that he had never seen anything like the country around Hell's Gate: 'It is so wild that I cannot find words to describe our situation at times.' David Thompson wrote in his journal in the Rockies that he felt 'a new world' was opening up before him.

The central struggle since that time has been to find the forms of expression that would make it possible to describe and interpret life in this intensely dramatic and infinitely various segment of the Canadian

British Columbia, Writing in

West. Emily CARR, who of course stands squarely in the centre of this search for appropriate artistic forms, said of her region: 'It is different. The spirit is different. Everyone knows that the moment we go from the Old Country to the New. . . . Misty landscapes and gentle cows do not express Western Canada, even the cows know that.' This difference is recorded not only in her remarkable paintings, but also in her writings, particularly *Klee Wyck* (1941). Roderick HAIG-BROWN, one of our finest essayists and nature authors, is another modern writer who has revealed much about British Columbia in such books as *A river never sleeps* (1946) and *Measure of the year* (1950), as has George WOODCOCK, whose many books in several genres include *Ravens and prophets: an account of journeys in British Columbia, Alberta and southern Alaska* (1952) and *People of the coast: the Indians of the Pacific Northwest* (1977).

The fiction of British Columbia begins just after the turn of the century, with works as diverse as Jack London's *The call of the wild* (1903), Morley Roberts' *The prey of the strongest* (1906), M. Allerdale GRAINGER's *Woodsmen of the west* (1908), Bertrand W. Sinclair's *Poor man's rock* (1920), and Frederick NIVEN's *Wild honey* (1927). As one might expect from such titles, these works celebrate the frontier virtues of courage and self-reliance in the face of severe hardships; they also make considerable use of the techniques of realism/naturalism to document the particulars of language, place, and social relations. Howard O'HAGAN's *Tay John* (1939) is the most important piece of fiction to come out of British Columbia before the Second World War. It is not only a brilliantly written and conceived mythic novel, which attempts to analyse the forces transforming the Canadian wilderness in the name of so-called progress, but also a work so self-reflexive, so overtly conscious of the limits of the fictive act, that it can be called Canada's first serious work of metafiction. O'Hagan's treatment of the collision of cultures during Construction lays the foundations for such future myth-makers as Sheila WATSON, Robert HARLOW, Rudy WIEBE, Robert KROETSCH, and Jack HODGINS.

If *Tay John* ushered British Columbia fiction into the modern period, the bulk of post-war fiction continued along more traditional lines, moving from popular romance to more sophisticated studies of character and society. Among the best works of this period are Ethel WILSON's *Hetty Dorval*

(1947), Hubert EVANS' *Mist on the river* (1954), and Earle BIRNEY's *Down the long table* (1955). Ethel Wilson went on to publish five more books before her death and to earn a high reputation as a stylist and exquisite ironist. Sheila Watson, however, dominates the post-war period of fiction, much as the mythical Coyote dominates the remote community of *The double hook* (1959). This novel, which is both moral fable and symbolist poem, represents a technical breakthrough of the calibre of *Tay John*. Although she owes a debt to French fiction and to Faulkner's *As I lay dying*, Watson does for prose what Ezra Pound did for poetry, paring it to the bone. Her spare, subtle, and evocative examination of the nature of human community is like nothing else in Canadian fiction. After *The double hook*, anything could happen in British Columbia fiction—and did.

The bountiful harvest of prose writers since 1960 includes such names as Jane RULE, Audrey THOMAS, George RYGA, Joy KOGAWA, Paul St Pierre, Richard WRIGHT, Robert Harlow, George BOWERING, Leon ROOKE, Dave GODFREY, J. Michael YATES, Gladys Hindmarch, W.D. VALGARDSON, John MILLS, John Peter, Alan Fry, Jan Drabek, and Jack Hodgins, some of whom are from abroad or elsewhere in Canada; following close on the heels of these gifted writers are lesser-known figures like Derk WYNAND, Beverley Mitchell, Ron Smith, Steve Guppy, Theresa Kishkan, and Sonia Birch-Jones, all of whom have published stories and may be expected to figure prominently in a few years.

If any one writer may be said to dominate the recent period, it is Jack Hodgins. In contrast to the spareness and economy of Watson, Hodgins has pushed fiction once more towards it epic beginnings with *The invention of the world* (1977). In this expansive novel, which draws inspiration and example from new fiction in Spanish from Central and South America, Hodgins follows in the myth-making tradition of O'Hagan and Watson, examining the tacky realities of life in British Columbia against a background of Utopian dreams. A witty and exuberant collage of lists, interviews, tall tales, improbable happenings, and epic desires, *The invention of the world* will be a permanent landmark in British Columbia fiction.

Not long after the war Roderick Haig-Brown published his best-known children's book, *Starbuck valley winter* (1946), and Catherine Anthony CLARK became Canada's first serious writer of fantasy for children. In *The golden pine cone* (1950) and other books set in British Columbia she made imaginative use of myths and legends of the Indian tribes. The possibilities of magic and enchantment in the B.C. forest were also seen by Ruth NICHOLS, who introduced herself as a remarkable fantasist with *A walk out of the world* (1969), written when she was only eighteen. It begins in an unidentified city resembling Vancouver and moves into the forest and thence into an 'Other World'. A third well-known writer for children from the west coast is Christie HARRIS, whose novel *Raven's cry* (1966) treats the white man's impact on the Haida. A notable use of Indian material by a native Indian author is *Son of raven, son of deer: fables of the Tseshaht* (1967) by George Clutesi.

Although the bulk of British Columbia poetry has been written since 1960, Earle BIRNEY, Dorothy LIVESAY, and P.K. PAGE may be said to have provided essential models for the new generation. Birney's narrative poem 'David' and his Pacific meditations clearly prepared the ground for the poets who would gather around the poetry newsletter TISH in the early sixties. On one level *Tish* functioned as a vehicle for 'killing' the literary forefathers by declaring new, and foreign, allegiances; on the other it unconsciously confirmed many of the lessons implicit in Birney's poetry, particularly what Frank DAVEY calls the *Tish* preference for 'localism of taste'. In fact poems such as Birney's 'Near False Creek Mouth' are deeply rooted in the particulars of language and place; and his verse drama, 'The damnation of Vancouver' (published in 1952 as 'Trial of a city'), though free-wheeling and mythic, reveals an obvious delight in both the history and the varieties of speech, particularly the vernacular, to be found in Vancouver. Among the poets of British Columbia who owe a debt to Birney, especially in his incarnations as philosopher and raconteur, are Patrick LANE, Peter Trower, Lionel KEARNS, Pat LOWTHER, Robin SKELTON, Florence McNeil, George Bowering, and Davey himself.

In the work of Dorothy Livesay the new poets found encouragement to explore both their emotional lives and their political condition. Livesay pioneered the documentation in poetry of private agony and public malaise. Her lyrics and narratives, such as 'The outrider' and 'Call my people home', about the evacuation of Japanese-Canadians from the West Coast during the Second

World War, anticipate the impassioned and socially committed work of Pat Lowther, Tom WAYMAN, and bill BISSETT, as well as the documentary concerns of Daphne MARLATT's *Steveston* (1975).

P.K. Page's poetry is characterized by wit, elegance, and impersonality. The finely wrought formal poems in *Cry Ararat!* (1967), which rely on surprising imagery and cross-fertilization of metaphor, tend more towards ambiguity and artifice than towards simplicity and directness of statement. This formalism, combined with a touch of mysticism, has made her example very extractive to a number of poets in British Columbia, including Daryl HINE, Phyllis WEBB, Robin Skelton, Susan MUSGRAVE and, to a lesser degree, Robert Bringhurst.

Of course homegrown influences never explain the full range and variety of what is happening at any given moment in the history of a nation's or a region's poetry. British Columbia poets were looking outward as well. The *Tish* group—which included Davey, Bowering, and Fred WAH—looked mainly towards the United States, to Charles Olson, Robert Creeley, and Robert Duncan, all of whom visited Vancouver in the early sixties at the invitation of Professor Warren Tallman of the University of British Columbia. The American poets emphasized the importance of biology, place, and history on the moment of creation—breath and speech rhythms, particularity, private and collective thought—elements that deepened our poetry in general but which, in the hands of many young poets, too often translated into an obsessive preoccupation with process.

The arrival of J. Michael YATES in Vancouver provided another pervasive influence: surrealism seen through an American filter. Yates started Sono Nis Press and published several of his own books, including *Great Bear Lake meditations* (1970). This surrealistic rendering of northern landscapes had something of the shock of Lawren Harris's Cubist paintings of the Arctic and did not fail to leave its mark on many young writers associated with the creative-writing program at UBC, including Derk Wynand, Andreas SCHROEDER, and George McWHIRTER.

Contemporary British Columbia poetry is too diverse to categorize accurately. Three of the strongest voices since 1960 are Phyllis Webb, whose *Selected poems* (1982) has recently appeared from Talonbooks; Pat Lowther, whose *Stone diary* (1975) appeared

British Columbia, Writing in

just after her tragic and untimely death; and Patrick Lane, whose work has progressed from the narrowly anecdotal to the grace and maturity of vision in *Old mother* (1982). These poets seem to stand beyond influences and to be perfecting forms that emphasize the inclusiveness of poetry as a medium of expression; they also reaffirm the great oral tradition of poetry. Other singular voices to celebrate are Robin Blaser, bill bissett, Alexander Hutchison, Helene Rosenthal, Robert Bringhurst, Jon Furberg, George WOODCOCK, Norbert Ruebsaat, Allan Safarik, Kevin Roberts, and Paul Belserene.

Anthologies give evidence of the large number of British Columbia poets. When I edited *Skookum Wawa: writings of the Canadian Northwest* (1975) more than forty poets were included. *New: West Coast* (1977), edited by Fred Candelaria, boasts seventy-two contemporary B.C. poets; and *Western windows* (1977) contains forty-four. Jim Brown and David Phillips had declared in their important early anthology *West Coast seen* (1969) that the poetry scene was 'essentially open, undefined', and the writers 'not provincial or limited by borders'. Perhaps the existence of such powerful natural and political boundaries as the Pacific Ocean, the Rockies, Alaska, and the 49th parallel has made B.C. poets both more parochial and more international than their counterparts elsewhere in Canada. Certainly the great influx of poets from beyond these boundaries results in a constantly changing literary mosaic.

Poetry and fiction in British Columbia have benefited by the stabilizing and energizing effects of indigenous magazines and publishing houses. No longer is it necessary to write pan-Canadian poems or stories in order to achieve acceptance or publication in Toronto. Outlets and audiences exist in B.C. for local writers, however regional or eclectic their work might be. In addition to TALONBOOKS, the important literary presses are Sono Nis, Oolichan, Pulp, Intermedia, Caledonia Writing Series, Blackfish, Harbour Publishing, and Blew Ointment. Among the vigorous literary magazines are *Capilano Review*, *Event*, *The* MALAHAT REVIEW, *Prism international*, *West Coast Review*, *BC Monthly*, *Island*, *Georgia Straight*, *Raincoast Chronicles*, and *NMFG*.

Until the sixties very little writing for the theatre appeared in B.C. Poets such as George Woodcock, Earle Birney, and Dorothy Livesay made occasional excursions into theatrical forms, writing scripts for CBC radio, some of which were produced on stage. But a new interest in theatre was generated by the appearance of George RYGA's one-act play *Indian* on CBC television in 1962. Ryga moved to Summerland, B.C., and continued playwriting, producing the controversial *The ecstasy of Rita Joe* (1971) and *Captives of a faceless drummer* (1971). His presence, along with encouragement for the arts in the form of government assistance, led to the establishment of new theatres and the emergence of a number of new writers. At the same time, TALONBOOKS began to publish playscripts, quickly becoming Canada's major publisher of new plays.

Today there is a tremendous amount of activity in drama, mostly centred in Vancouver. Herschel HARDIN has written several plays, the most interesting of which is *Esker Mike and his wife Agaluk* (1973); Cam Hubert (Anne Cameron) has done scripts for several media, including the successful 'Dreamspeaker'; Lawrence Russell, Margaret HOLLINGSWORTH, Paul Ledoux, Steve PETCH, and Sherman Snukal have made their presence known in theatre circles. Of the new generation of playwrights, the most important is Bryan WADE, who studied at the University of Victoria and in California and now lives in Toronto, where he has had more than a dozen plays, including *Blitzkrieg* (1974) and *This side of the rockies* (1977), produced or published.

New plays continue to emerge and find production or workshopping at the Arts Club Theatre, West Coast Theatre, Vancouver Playhouse, and Vancouver East Cultural Centre, where Tamanhous Theatre Company has provided guidance and inspiration to a new generation of playwrights.

GARY GEDDES

Brochu, André (b. 1942). Born in Saint-Eustache, Qué., he studied at the Université de Montréal and obtained his doctorate in Paris under Jean-Pierre Richard. He now teaches in the French department at the Université de Montréal. His *Privilèges de l'ombre* (1961) and *Délit contre délit* (1965) revealed him as an excellent young poet. With Jacques BRAULT and André MAJOR he published short stories in *Nouvelles* (1963). His only novel, *Adéodat I*, appeared in 1973. Brochu, however, is primarily a highly respected academic critic. He was one of the founders of PARTI PRIS, and his critical writings covering the 1960s—collected in *L'instance critique* (1974)—were directed against the moralistic approach of earlier Québec critics and devoted to a 'life-project' of representing the specificity of Québec literature through a systematic thematic study of the literary heritage. Brochu remains committed to thematic criticism, though he has abandoned both dogmatic nationalism and his vast project. Brochu's doctoral thesis on Victor Hugo, *Hugo—amour/crime/révolution* (1974), illustrates his stated conviction that Québécois critics must come to terms with the literature of France. In *La littérature et le reste* (1980), an engrossing epistolary exchange with critic Gilles MARCOTTE, Brochu shows his interest in the more formal approach of contemporary French critics, although he does not adopt their methods. Despite his attraction to theory, Brochu is above all a skilled, at times a brilliant, reader. He was one of the founders of the scholarly journal VOIX ET IMAGES.

SHERRY SIMON

Brooke, Frances (1723OS-89). The daughter of an Anglican clergyman in Claypole, Eng., Frances Moore was born there and grew up in rural Lincolnshire and in Peterborough. About 1748 she moved to London, where she became a distinguished woman of letters. In 1755-6, shortly after her marriage to the Rev. John Brooke, she used the pseudonym 'Mary Singleton, Spinster' to edit *The Old Maid*, a weekly periodical; although she wrote most of it herself, others—including John Boyle and the Earl of Cork and Orrery—contributed. In 1756, after David Garrick refused to produce her tragedy *Virginia* because there had already 'been two so lately on the same subject', it was published along with some 'Odes, Pastorals, and Translations', the last from the Italian of Battista Guarini. In 1760 she published her translation of Marie-Jeanne Riccoboni's extremely popular epistolary novel of 1759, *Letters from Juliet Lady Catesby, to her friend Lady Henrietta Campley*.

Mrs Brooke's own first epistolary novel, *The history of Lady Julia Mandeville* (London, 1763), a sentimental work ending with the death of the two chief characters, includes a plea for Great Britain's keeping the newly conquered French colony of Canada, 'an acquisition beyond our most sanguine hopes'. Shortly after it appeared, Mrs Brooke—seen off by Samuel Johnson, among others—left for 'this Canada'. Accompanied by her only son, she went to join her husband, who had been in Québec since 1760 as chaplain to the Garrison. The family returned permanently to England late in 1768.

Mrs Brooke's second epistolary novel, *The history of Emily Montague* (4 vols, London, 1769), is made up of 228 letters. Despite its English provenance and several features that make it an integral part of the tradition of late eighteenth-century European fiction, it is deservedly called the first Canadian novel, being set mostly in Canada in the 1760s. Ed. Rivers, the chief male character who eventually marries Emily Montague, arrives in Québec in June 1766, during the 'interregnum of government' between the departure of Gov. James Murray and the arrival of the next governor, Guy Carleton, to whom the novel is dedicated. Besides Rivers, a retired English army officer who plans to settle in Canada, the chief correspondent is Arabella Fermor, the clever 'coquet' who is Emily's best friend. The letters, which describe many aspects of Canada, are particularly detailed on the manners and customs of the Québécois and the Indians, and on the 'sublime' scenery of places like Montmorency Falls. They also deal with such subjects as taxation and freedom of worship in the Thirteen Colonies, and explore with sense and sensibility English-French relations in Canada. Partly because of this political content, Mrs Brooke worried that it would not be 'so popular a book by much' as *Lady Julia Mandeville*. In fact *Emily Montague* was well reviewed in the leading periodicals of the day and was reprinted several times during the eighteenth century in both London and Dublin. It was translated into Dutch and three times into French, and was imitated at least once by the anonymous author of *All's right at last* (1774), a novel sometimes wrongly attributed to Mrs Brooke.

Mrs Brooke continued to have an active writing career in England. Her translation of Nicholas-Étienne Framéry's epistolary novel *Mémoires de M. le Marquis de S. Forlaix* (1770) was published in 1770; her translation of Claude-François-Xavier Millot's *Elémens de l'historie d'Angleterre* (1769) in 1771. Her third and last novel, *The excursion* (1777), criticized David Garrick's management of the Drury Lane Theatre, particularly his refusal to get new works upon the stage. (Garrick by then had rejected not only *Virginia* but an opera by Mrs Brooke.) In the novel's second edition (1785) Mrs Brooke apologized for, and omitted, much of her criticism of the great actor-manager. She also wrote a preface for this 'new edition' in which she praised Samuel Richardson's 'divine writings' as an 'illustrious example' of her 'assertion' that the contemporary novel in England 'displayed the standard of moral truth, and breathed the spirit of purest virtue'. In the 1780s Mrs Brooke, having gained experience in the theatre through her involvement in the management of the King's Theatre, Haymarket, had three dramatic works staged and subsequently published: *The seige of Sinope: a tragedy* (1781) and two comic operas, *Rosina* (1783) and *Marian* (1788).

Frances Brooke died while visiting her son, a rural clergyman, and was buried in Sleaford, Lincolnshire. *The history of Charles Mandeville*, a sequel to *Lady Julia Mandeville*, appeared in 1790; but it too has been wrongly attributed to Mrs Brooke. Until the twentieth century her works—except for *Rosina*, which was still being produced and published late in the nineteenth century—were largely forgotten. Recently she has gained increasing recognition as the author of Canada's first novel and as an early feminist. A modern edition of *Emily Montague* is available in the New Canadian Library (1961), with an introduction by Carl KLINCK.

See the essay on Brooke by Lorraine McMullen in *Canadian writers and their work: fiction series: volume one* (1983) edited by Robert Lecker, Jack David, and Ellen Quigley.   MARY JANE EDWARDS

Brooker, Bertram (1888-1955). Born in Croydon, Eng., Bertram Richard Brooker came to Canada with his parents in 1905 and settled in Portage-la-Prairie, Man., where he and his father found work with the Grand Trunk Pacific Railway. He worked at various jobs there, and in Regina and Winnipeg, before moving to Toronto in 1921 and embarking on a career in advertising.

A man of many talents and boundless energy, Brooker gained recognition as a painter, illustrator, editor, columnist, novelist, poet, and musician. In all his activities he was an innovator and a catalyst who championed the avant-garde. Best known today as a pioneer of abstract painting in Canada—his most famous painting is probably the geometric *Sounds Assembling* (1928)—and as a charter member of the Canadian Group of Painters, he received nation-wide recognition as a novelist in 1937 when *Think of the earth* (1936) won the newly established Governor General's Award for fiction. A character study of an itinerant labourer who believes he is destined to commit an act of unmitigated evil that will ultimately lead to the salvation of mankind, this novel is perhaps best understood in the context of Brooker's vision of the spiritual, informed by both Lawren Harris's theosophical writings and Wassily Kandinsky's *Concerning the spiritual in art*. Brooker wrote two other novels, both of which explore spiritual concepts: *The tangled miracle* (1936), published under the pseudonum 'Huxley Herne', and *The robber; a tale of the time of the Herods* (1949), a study of Barrabas that was adapted for radio and broadcast by the CBC in 1950 and again in 1951.

The breadth of Brooker's interests is apparent in both 'The seven arts', a syndicated column he wrote for the Southam newspaper chain from 1928 to 1930, and in *The yearbook of the arts in Canada 1928-1929* (1929), which he designed, edited, and introduced, and for which he wrote an article on Canadian sculpture. Plans to make the yearbook an annual survey collapsed with the onset of the Depression, but Brooker managed a second volume, *Yearbook of the arts in Canada* (1936). Together the two volumes constitute a valuable resource for the study of Canadian culture in the twenties and thirties.

Brooker's achievement as a poet was recently recognized with the publication of *Sounds assembling: the poetry of Bertram Brooker* (1980), a selection edited by Birk Sproxton. This interesting collection of poems—most of which were unpublished in his lifetime—reveals not only Brooker's fascination with the spiritual and his ability to discover it in everyday life, but his willingness to experiment with form and line, his eye for detail, and his love of music. The volume also includes a number of Brooker's statements on poetry, painting, and the arts generally.

Under the pseudonym 'Richard Surrey', Brooker published three books on advertising: *Subconscious selling* (1923), *Layout technique in advertising* (1929), and *Copy technique in advertising* (1930).   PAUL HJARTARSON

Brossard, Nicole (b. 1943). Born in Montreal and educated at the Collège Marguerite Bourgeoys and at the Université de Montréal, she was an early participant in the avant-garde Québec poetry movements of the middle sixties as founder and editor of *La* BARRE DU JOUR. In her first book of poems, *Aube à la saison* (1965)—which stayed within the boundaries of traditional syntax and semantics—one can trace the formative influence of the preceding generation of poets; Brossard's metrical structures and use of metaphor are reminiscent of the work of Fernand OUELLETTE and Paul-Marie LAPOINTE in particular. But the irony and erotica of her subsquent collections—*Mordre en sa chair* (1966), *L'écho bouge beau* (1968), *Suite logique* (1970), *Le centre blanc* (1970)—reflect a steadfast determination to throw her readers off balance by challenging normal expectations about punctuation, spacing, and typography. She pursued these tendencies in her novels *Un livre* (1970), *Sold-out: étreinte/illustration* (1973), and *French kiss: étreinte/exploration* (1974), which followed the difficult and often tantalizing paths of the *nouveau roman*, both as a genre (delineated in France by Robbe-Grillet, Sarraute, and Butor) and as a challenge. In the Québec of the seventies writing became an act of sabotage or subversion aimed at overthrowing logic and mimetic modes; this included the blurring of grammatical constructions, the introduction of blanks, gaps, ruptures, and occasionally—as in *Sold-out*—the use of black frames to confuse the distinctions between text and comic strip, poem and film. Brossard's rejection of convention is also apparent in her preference for the term 'text'—meaning process and production—over 'poem' or 'novel'. In 1978 L'Hexagone produced a collection of her poetry, *Le Centre blanc: poèmes 1965–1975,* that includes—besides the original *Centre blanc*—all her other volumes plus a few new poems. In that same year Brossard won a Governor General's Award for a collection of new poetry, *Mécanique jongleuse suivi de masculin grammaticale* (1974).

From 1974 feminism gave a new dimension to Brossard's writings. Between 1976 and 1978 she worked on the editorial board of *Têtes de pioche,* a monthly feminist publication, and introduced feminist theory and writings into *La barre du jour.* Her participation in the collective play *La nef des sorcières* (1976) and the publication (1977) of *L'amèr ou le chapitre effrité* (subtitled *Theoretical fiction*) signalled both her realization of women's need to emerge from the silence imposed on them by the patriarchal society and her determination to give a voice to their repressed and censored desires. The poems of *Amantes* (1980) and *Le sens apparent* (1980) reflect the author's association of the writing/reading process with sexual pleasure. During the seventies and eighties many young Québec writers perceived meaning and the production of sense as sensual activities; but Brossard added a feminist and lesbian perspective: for her the production of meaning ceased to hinge on a relationship between a subject (writer/reader) and an object (text/interpretation) and became a participatory process between free-willed subjects. *Picture theory* (1982) continues and expands upon Brossard's earlier writings, being both a work of fiction (five women evolve within its pages) and a theoretical project (it deals with problems of representation and language and draws upon a vast conceptual apparatus that includes the ideas of Wittgenstein, Stein, Joyce, and others).

Brossard's interest in new and experimental approaches was also reflected in her editing of *Les stratégies du réel/The story so far* (1979), an anthology of avant-garde Québécois writings published by COACH HOUSE PRESS, Toronto. Coach House also published *A book* (1976)—a translation by Larry Shouldice of Brossard's *Un livre* (1970)—and *Turn of a pang,* a translation by Patricia Claxton of *Sold-out* (1973 and 1980).

Other translations of Brossard's work can be found in *Essays on Canadian Writing,* no. 7-8 (Fall 1977), which offered excerpts from *L'Amèr ou le chapitre effrité,* translated by Barbara Godard; and in *Clash of symbols,* (1979), a translation by Linda Gaborian of *La nef des sorcières.*

A bibliography of Brossard's work and a list of critical articles on her can be found in Issue 118-119 of *La Barre du jour* (nov. 1982), which includes papers read at a Nicole Brossard colloquium at the Université du Québec à Montréal in Oct. 1982.

See also NOVELS IN FRENCH 1960 TO 1982:3(g). CAROLINE BAYARD

Brown, Audrey Alexandra (b. 1904). Born and raised in Nanaimo, B.C., she is the last important representative of romantic poetry in Canada, deeply indebted to the English Romantic poets, especially Keats. Her five volumes of verse—*A dryad in Nanaimo* (1931; enlarged with eleven new poems 1934), *The tree of resurrection and other poems* (1937), *Challenge to time and death* (1943), *V-E day* (1946), and *All fools' day* (1948)—reveal little artistic development. Her finest poem, 'Laodamia', which appeared in her first volume, epitomizes her poetic world: her attraction to a legendary past, her love of colourful descriptions, her musical cadences, as well as a derivative dimension that leads to ornate and frequently undisciplined verse.

The log of a lame duck (1938) is Brown's prose diary of her ten-month treatment for rheumatic illness at Queen Alexandra Solarium on Malahat Beach. In *Poetry and Life* (1941), an address originally delivered to the CANADIAN AUTHORS' ASSOCIATION in Vancouver on 24 Aug. 1941, she defined her poetic creed: 'Poetry is to life what sunlight is to a stained-glass window. In poetry the mind of the poet strikes through life, revealing its pattern and colour . . . Poetry is life transfused and irradiated.' In 1944 Brown received the Royal Society's Lorne Pierce Medal 'for distinguished contributions to Canadian literature.'   DAVID STAINES

Brown, E.K. (1905-51). Edward Killoran Brown was born in Toronto and educated at the Universities of Toronto (B.A. 1926) and Paris, from which he received in 1935 a Docteur-ès-Lettres for a major thesis on Edith Wharton and a minor one on Matthew Arnold's prose. From 1929 to 1941 he taught English at the University of Toronto, except for two years when he served as chairman of the English department at the University of Manitoba (1935-7). He was chairman of English at Cornell University from 1941 to 1944, when he moved to the University of Chicago, where he remained until his death. The Royal Society of Canada awarded him its Lorne Pierce Medal posthumously.

Besides publishing many articles and reviews dealing with British and American writers (he wrote over 50 for the CANADIAN FORUM, of which he was an associate editor from 1930 to 1933), translations of Louis Cazamian's *Carlyle* (1932) and Balzac's *Père Goriot* (1946), editions of Arnold (*Representative essays*, 1936; *Four essays on life and letters,* 1947) and of Dickens' *David Copperfield* (1950), and an anthology (*Victorian poetry*, 1942), Brown was the author of *Matthew Arnold—a study in conflict* (1948); *Rhythm in the novel* (1950; rpr. 1978), the published version of the Alexander Lectures given at the University of Toronto in 1949 and a valuable study of technique in the novel, with special reference to E.M. Forster; and *Willa Cather: a critical biography* (1953; rpr. 1980), which was completed for publication by his friend and colleague Leon EDEL and has not been superseded.

Northrop FRYE has called Brown 'the first critic to bring Canadian literature into its proper context.' That context was one in which a national interest was not vitiated by the excesses of nationalism, and in which a cosmopolitan outlook never succumbed to the pressures of colonialism. From 1932 to 1941 Brown was one of the editors of the *University of Toronto Quarterly* and was instrumental in establishing its annual 'Letters in Canada' reviews. From 1936 to 1950 his judicious and perceptive articles on Canadian poetry exemplified his dedication to what he described as 'the raising of aesthetic and intellectual standards in Canada.' The early assessments—'The contemporary situation in Canadian literature' (1938) and 'The development of poetry in Canada, 1880-1940' (1941)—show Brown preparing himself for *On Canadian poetry* (1943; rpr. 1973), which incorporated the two articles and appeared in the same year as A.J.M. SMITH's *Book of Canadian poetry*. These two works established the standards of excellence and many of the subsequent directions of Canadian criticism.

As a 'critical essay', *On Canadian poetry*—which received a Governor General's Award and was reissued the following year in a revised and expanded version—was an advance on the tradition of mere historical enquiry. Brown's purpose in this lucid and cogently argued book was to show the difficulties of the Canadian writer in a colonial, materialistic, and puritanical society; to define the tradition of Canadian poetry by discovering what work 'remains alive and, in some degree at least, formative'; and to describe and assess the poetry of those who were in Brown's view the 'masters': LAMPMAN, D.C. SCOTT, and PRATT. Brown insisted that 'careful interpretation, conducted with insight and a measure of sympathy, must precede judgment'. In his revaluation of earlier writers he stressed the merits of Lampman and Scott and the limitations of ROBERTS and CARMAN. This revaluation was continued (with Scott's assistance) in Brown's edition of *At the Long Sault and other new poems by Archibald Lampman* (1943) and in the posthumously published *Selected poems of Duncan Campbell Scott* (1951), with a memoir by Brown.

Brown's emphasis on interpretation sometimes led him to be over-cautious in evaluating younger poets; his comments on the Canadian scene are occasionally too sweeping (perhaps betraying a central-Canadian perspective) to do justice to the diversity of the Canadian experience; his assertion that a great literature is produced by a 'mature and adequate society' but that it is 'not in the province of a student of letters to say how a society becomes mature and adequate' seems an abrogation of part of the critical function. Nevertheless Brown's stature as a major critic is assured. Had he not died so early, his authority would have been a valuable check on the narrow and wayward tendencies of much subsequent Canadian criticism.

In *Responses and evaluations: essays on Canada* (NCL, 1977) David Staines has gathered a valuable selection of Brown's essays, including his annual surveys for the *Quarterly*; Staines' introduction is the best commentary on Brown's achievement. See also Staines' indispensable bibliographical article in CANADIAN LITERATURE 83 (Winter 1979).

See also CRITICISM IN ENGLISH: 3.

DAVID JACKEL

Bruce, Charles (1906-71). Charles Tory Bruce was born of Scottish ancestry in Port Shoreham, N.S., and graduated from Mount Allison University in 1927. Joining the Canadian Press in Halifax, he became one of the original and most active members of the Song Fishermen, a group of regional poets that included Andrew Merkel, Robert NORWOOD, Kenneth LESLIE, Bliss CARMAN, and Charles G.D. ROBERTS. He later became a war correspondent and superintendent of the Canadian Press in London (England), and in 1945 was appointed general superintendent of the Canadian Press in Toronto.

Bruce's first collection of verse, *Wild apples* (1927), introduced the concrete images, musical rhythms, and fascination with the sea that are characteristic of his later work. It was followed by *Tomorrow's tide* (1932), a collection of personal and descriptive lyrics; *Personal note* (1941), 'a statement of belief' in the midst of war about the spirit 'of mankind at its best'; and *Grey ship moving* (1945), a series of poems affirming the values of kinship and regional identity, especially in wartime. In the narrative poem, *The flowing summer* (1947), an Ontario boy visiting Nova Scotian grandparents awakens to a sense of the land, the sea, and the traditions that are part of his heritage. These influences are further explored in *The Mulgrave Road* (1951), a collection that won a Governor General's Award for its finely crafted poems integrating landscape, mood, and a sense of the 'salt in the blood.'

A close relationship between environment, tradition, and community values in-

forms *The Channel Shore* (1954), Bruce's lyrical chronicle of three generations of family life in coastal Nova Scotia between 1919 and 1946. Similar in theme and in the skilful handling of time is *The township of time* (1959), a sequence of interrelated stories set along the Channel Shore between 1786 and 1950. Bruce's interest in family chronicles found further expression in *News and the Southams* (1968), a history of the Southam newspaper empire in Canada. However, it is the careful craftsmanship and vivid evocation of life in Bruce's creative writing that have continued to win for his work the respect of critics from William Arthur DEACON to John Moss.   GWENDOLYN DAVIES

Bruce, Harry. See ESSAYS IN ENGLISH: 4.

Brun, Régis. See ACADIAN LITERATURE: 2(c).

Brunet, Michel. See HISTORICAL WRITING IN FRENCH.

Bryce, George. See HISTORICAL WRITING IN ENGLISH: 4.

Buchan, John. See FOREIGN WRITERS ON CANADA IN ENGLISH: 1 and SCIENCE FICTION AND FANTASY IN ENGLISH AND FRENCH: 4.

Bucke, Richard Maurice (1837-1902). Born in Methwold, Eng., he was raised on a farm near London, Upper Canada (Ont.). Self-educated until he entered McGill University, he graduated in medicine in 1862 with the prize-winning dissertation. He studied abroad and practised in Sarnia and London (Ont.) before being appointed in 1877 superintendent of the Asylum for the Insane in London, a position he held until his death. Bucke pursued two different careers: he was a world-renowned alienist, professor of mental and nervous diseases at the future University of Western Ontario, and president of both the American Medico-Psychological Association and the Psychological Section of the British Medical Association; and, as a mystic and an idolator of Walt Whitman, he was the famous poet's editor, official biographer, and literary executor. Whitman visited Bucke in London twice, the first time in the summer of 1880 when he travelled to Montreal and Quebec City, a trip that was recorded in *Walt Whitman's diary in Canada with extracts from other of his diaries and literary note-books* (1904).

One night in the spring of 1872, after

Bucke

reading Whitman's poetry, Bucke experienced a mystical illumination—an epiphany in which he saw that the cosmos promises man fulfilment in happiness, love, and immortality. He elaborated on this Utopian vision in *Man's moral nature: an essay* (New York, 1879). The thesis of this book—that if the world is steadily improving, then the most advanced example of a superior moral nature must be embodied in a contemporary—was exemplified in his next work, *Walt Whitman* (Philadelphia, 1883), the first biographical study of the poet, whom Bucke saw as a paragon of moral nature. This *collecteana* of reminiscences, conversations, travels in Canada, bibliographical details, and a philosophical exegesis of the poetry incorporates revisions made by Whitman himself, some of which were directed at modifying Bucke's idolatrous tone.

Bucke wrote Whitman several letters—the last one written six days before the poet's death in 1892—about his theory of 'cosmic consciousness' (the omniscient, intuitional mind that transcends self-consciousness), seeking confirmation of nineteen points of cosmic consciousness that he suspected Whitman must have experienced. But on this subject Whitman never replied. Out of Bucke's theories grew his most ambitious and enduring work, *Cosmic consciousness: a study of the evolution of the human mind* (Philadelphia, 1901), a major contribution to the field of mysticism that remains in print. The book presents fourteen case-studies documenting evidence of mystical illuminations shared by Homer, Christ, Shakespeare, Blake, and Whitman, and concludes with a millennial vision of a world revolutionized by aerial navigation, of work revolutionized by socialism, and of souls revolutionized by cosmic consciousness. William James called it 'an addition to psychology of first-rate importance' and praised Bucke as 'a benefactor of us all'.

Bucke edited several posthumous volumes of Whitman's writings, including *The wound dresser. A series of letters written from the hospitals in Washington during the War of Rebellion by Walt Whitman* (Boston, 1898), and was one of the editors of the *Complete writings of Walt Whitman* (10 vols, 1902).

Artem Lozynsky's *Richard Maurice Bucke, medical mystic* (1977) is both a critical biography and an edition of Bucke's letters to Whitman and his friends. See also *Richard Maurice Bucke: a catalogue based upon the collections of the University of Western Ontario Libraries* (1978) edited by Mary Ann Jameson.

DAVID LATHAM

Buckler, Ernest (b. 1908). Born in Dalhousie West, N.S., he was educated at Dalhousie University and the University of Toronto. After a brief career in an actuarial office in Toronto, he returned to the family farm near Bridgetown, N.S., where he has lived in semi-retirement.

During the forties and fifties Buckler's short stories appeared in *Esquire, Saturday Night, Maclean's*, and *The Atlantic Advocate*. Many of them dramatize rural family relationships in an Annapolis Valley setting. Their characters and events are similar to those in *The mountain and the valley* (1952), Buckler's first novel and best-known publication. Described by Claude Bissell in the introduction to the New Canadian Library edition (1961) as 'a magnificent paean to the wonder and innocence of youth', it is a portrait of the potential artist. David Canaan, a precocious and over-sensitive child, is the gifted member of a family of sturdy, earthy, sensitive but largely inarticulate people. Their farm, the focus for David of all love, beauty, and security, is continually threatened by time and change. After achieving a momentary vision of the unity he has failed to recreate in his writing, he dies on the mountain that has symbolized his goal. The narrative—in six parts, each named for its controlling image—is framed by a Prologue and Epilogue that portray David, on the day of his death, standing at the farmhouse window, suggestively separated from a life in which 'everything was somewhere else'. Enclosed by his overprotective family, by the valley, and by his own supersensitive ego, David is another of the many portraits of the unfulfilled artist in Canada.

In Buckler's second novel, *The cruelest month* (1963), Paul Creed is a recluse who seasonally 'rents people'—renting out his rural retreat at Endlaw to city sophisticates and inviting his visitors to play dangerous intellectual parlour games in which they strip each others' personalities bare. The emotions released lead to unexpected rearrangements before, in the tradition of pastoral comedy, relations are re-established on a surer footing. Paul, too, needs rearranging; like David Canaan he is inwardly scarred. When a purifying forest fire helps the others to face themselves, and Paul—with Letty, his illiterate housekeeper—is brought close to death, he sees the error of his withdrawn life and symbolically embraces Letty. For most readers this is a somewhat arid book, but it confirms Buckler's sense of the primacy of the intuitive over the intellectual, and his concern with the nature of perception.

Ox bells and fireflies (1968) is Buckler's most genial book. In the tradition of the descriptive sketch and rural reminiscence, it recreates the country childhood (based partly on his own) of a simpler era. Its strength is in the affectionate details and whimsical anecdotes that one expects of the genre; but Buckler's intensity of descriptive simile—all phenomena are both exactly themselves and imaginatively something else—emphasizes the subjectivity of perception. The prose in *Ox bells*, and in *The mountain and the valley*, moves toward those moments of unity when, as Buckler says, inside and outside become one. In these passages his prose has a prelapsarian freshness that, if sometimes strained, still impresses with its emotional and visual accuracy.

In the sense that he looks to moments of unified being—where the conscious and unconscious selves are united with each other, with others, and with the external environment—as the essence of existence, Buckler is a romantic writer. He is also, however, a realist, aware of how rare, fleeting, and fragile such moments are. At its best his prose effects a unity between the rural setting and the individual attuned to it. In *Window on the sea* (1973) Buckler's descriptive commentary effectively complements photographs by Hans Weber. His fondness for word-play is shown not very happily in *Whirligig* (1977), a selection of light sketches, interspersed with comic and satiric verse, that did not enhance the author's reputation.

A selection of reviews and early Buckler criticism is contained in *Ernest Buckler* (1972) edited by Gregory Cook. The only sustained study of his work is contained in Robert Chambers, *Sinclair Ross and Ernest Buckler* (1978).   D.O. SPETTIGUE

Budd, Henry. See INDIAN LITERATURE: 2.

Buell, John (b. 1927). Born in Montreal, he was educated at the Université de Montreal, where he received a Ph.D. with a thesis on form and craft in Shakespeare. He is professor of communications at the Loyola campus of Concordia University. The author of four suspense novels of unusual skill, he is often misunderstood as a purely 'escapist' writer of thrillers and crime novels. He is really somewhere between Graham Greene and Raymond Chandler in his mode, for his central theme is the mystery of good and evil in a decaying world. In his first novel, *The pyx* (1959), filmed by Harvey Hart in 1973, the vulnerability and self-knowledge of Elizabeth Lucy, a high-class call-girl and drug addict, operate as counterpoints to the destructive Montreal underworld—especially the demonic setting of Keerson's Black Mass rituals. Although not entirely successful, this slim work skilfully blends Elizabeth's outer world of action and her inner world of dream, nightmare, and illusion. Elizabeth despairs of the 'huge nothingness of evil confronting her', and, without benediction, she falls victim to Keerson's criminal agents. In *Four days* (1962), ostensibly a chronicle of a young boy's fatal idealization of his criminal elder brother, reality is so perverted that life ultimately becomes an ambush. The tension in this book is far less contrived than that in *The pyx*, and the pacing is as expert as the probing of the young protagonist's innocence and paranoia.

Buell's most disciplined novels are *The Shrewsdale exit* (1972) and *Playground* (1976). In the first, the theme of unachieved retribution is worked out with relentless clarity as Joe Grant fails to obtain revenge against three motorcycle thugs who have murdered his wife and young daughter. *Playground* is an interior drama of a man trapped in a wilderness after a plane-crash. Buell tells this single-character story without mythicizing his protagonist or slipping into a philosophic essay on survival.

All of Buell's novels combine ordinariness, grim humour, and suspense. Life in them is a crucible for the protagonists who, nevertheless, come to learn something true about existence. This knowledge may be the characters' only spiritual grace, but it is a worthy one.

See Keith Garebian, 'The authority of the writer: an interview with John Buell', *Journal of Canadian Studies*, vol. 12, no. 2 (Spring 1977).   KEITH GAREBIAN

Bugnet, Georges (1879-1981). Born at Chalon-sur-Saône, Burgundy, Fr., he spent some time in a seminary; though he never became a priest, his deep faith reveals itself in his writing. After working briefly in France as a journalist, he immigrated to Canada in 1905 and settled north of Edmonton. For fifty years he worked on the land, writing to while away the winter hours and to supplement the meagre earnings farming brought him. He published his first two novels under the pseudonym 'Henry Doutremont'. *Le lys de sang* (1923) is a far-fetched adventure story set partly in Africa. In *Nipsya* (1924) a young Métisse has to make a choice between the white and Indian ways of life; she compromises by marrying a man who is half Indian and by becoming a Christian. This novel passed unnoticed in French, but in an excellent translation (1929) by Constance Davies-Woodrow it was acclaimed by English-speaking readers. In *La forêt* (1935), Bugnet's masterpiece, the Bourgoins, a young French immigrant couple, are doomed because instead of trying to live in harmony with nature, they struggle against it. Nature becomes a true protagonist and its pervading, awesome presence, which Bugnet conveys in powerful yet restrained language, accounts for the success of the book. It was translated by David Carpenter as *The forest* (1976). *Siraf: étranges révélations; ce qu'on pense de nous par-delà la lune* (1934) is a philosophical dialogue between two spirits who condemn modern man for his materialism and pride. *Les voix de la solitude* (1935) contains a fine short story, 'Le pin du maskeg', and philosophical poems in which the author celebrates the glory of night from which light is born. This poetry, interesting for the ideas rather than for the form, was re-edited in *Poêms* (1978), with an excellent introduction by Jean-Marcel Duciaume.

See Georges Bugnet, 'La forêt', *Le Canada français*, XXVII, 5 (jan. 1940) and 'Des valeurs littéraires', *Le Canada français*, XXVIII, 4 (déc. 1940); David C. Carpenter, 'Georges Bugnet: an introduction', *Journal of Canadian Fiction*, I, 4 (Fall 1972) and 'A Canadian Fête mobile*: interview with George Bugnet', *Journal of Canadian Fiction*, II, 2 (Spring 1973).

PAULETTE COLLET

Buies, Arthur. See ANTHOLOGIES IN FRENCH: 4 and ESSAYS IN FRENCH: 2.

Bullock, Michael (b. 1918). Michael Hale Bullock was born in London, Eng., and educated at the Hornsey College of Art. He came to Vancouver, B.C., in 1968 and is now a member of the Department of Creative Writing at the University of British Columbia.

As a poet, Bullock was greatly influenced by the London Surrealist Exhibition of 1936,when André Breton and others were invited to Britain. The English surreal groups generally disintegrated during the Second World War, but Bullock is one of the few writers in English who sustained their own particular approach to surrealism. In his first collection of poems, *Transmutations* (1938), which appeared under the pseudonym 'Michael Hale', he began his experiments with automatism, or freeflowing imagery. They expanded considerably in *Sunday is a day of incest* (1960), *Poems of solitude* (with Jerome Ch'en, 1961/70), *World without beginning amen* (1963/73), and *Zwei Stimmen in meinem Mund/Two voices in my mouth* (1967). After he arrived in Canada, Bullock—together with J. Michael YATES and Andreas SCHROEDER—was central in the development of the shortlived wave of 'West Coast surrealists' in B.C., which resulted in, among other things, the formation of two magazines: *Contemporary Literature in Translation* and CANADIAN FICTION MAGAZINE. He explored the possibilities of short fiction and prose-poetry in a series of brilliant short pieces collected in *A savage darkness* (1969), *Sixteen stories as they happened* (1969), and *Green beginning, black ending* (1971). The loose format of these collections became more developed and structured in *Randolph Cranstone and the pursuing river* (1975) and *Randolph Cranstone and the glass thimble* (1977). In these important works, dreamlike sequences unfold with their own fantastic logic, yet remain entirely convincing as the main character tries for aesthetic distance in his life, though he is forever chased by a torrent of words that causes everything about him to become transformed.

With *Black wings white dead* (1978), *Lines in the dark wood* (1981), and *Quadriga for Judy* (1982), Bullock returned to poetry, but the poems lack the concentrated force of his prose. Because surrealism has had only a minor impact in English Canada, Bullock's publishing is generally confined to small presses, but he has had a long association with *Canadian Fiction Magazine*, to which he has contributed essays on the prose-poem and on surrealism in fiction.

In addition to his own prolific output, Bullock has translated over 150 books and plays from German, French, and Italian. In 1978 he won the Canada Council Translation Prize for Michel TREMBLAY's *Stories for late night drinkers (Contes pour beuveurs attardés)*.

GEOFF HANCOCK

Burwell, Adam Hood (1790-1849). Probably the best lyric poet Canada produced in the early nineteenth century, he was born of

Loyalist parents near Fort Erie, Upper Canada. He was raised on the family farm in Welland County and moved to the Talbot Settlement about 1817. The details of his education have not been documented, but he was ordained deacon in 1827 and in 1828 priest of the Church of England. His first appointment was in Lennoxville, Lower Canada (Qué.), and while there he was married in Troy, N.Y., to a parishioner, Sarah Barnard. He served a joint pastorate at Nicolet, Trois-Rivières, and Rivière-du-Loup, and then moved to Hull as a missionary in 1832. By 1836 he had been expelled from the Anglican priesthood for doctrinal irregularity. He spent the remainder of his life in Kingston as a minister of the Catholic Apostalic Church ('Irvingite').

Burwell's earliest published poetry appeared in Upper Canadian newspapers from 1816, under the pseudonym 'Erieus'. A number of poems appeared in *The Scribbler* between 1821 and 1823 and in *The Canadian Review and Literary and Historical Journal* in 1825. For one year (Sept. 1830-Sept. 1831) Burwell edited a religious weekly, *The Christian Sentinel*, in which a number of his works, literary and theological, appeared both under his own name and under several pseudonyms. His Irvingite beliefs resulted in two tracts published in 1835, and a spate of tracts and long poems published just before his death, some of which appeared in *The* LITERARY GARLAND.

Much of Burwell's early poetry is inspired either by nature or by love. Using a variety of forms, he is at his best when he escapes from the jogging rhythms of end-stopped lines; sometimes he achieves an almost mystic intensity. Of greatest interest today are the poems that describe specific Canadian scenes and events, such as 'The Battle of Lundy's Lane', 'Talbot Road', 'Farewell to the shores of Erie', and 'Journal of a day's journey in Upper Canada'. The last poem in particular has several arresting scenes. Burwell's late poetry combines his life-long feeling for nature with his theological convictions—in it nature becomes a vehicle of revelation.

The poems of Adam Hood Burwell, pioneer poet of Upper Canada (1963), edited by C.F. KLINCK, is available from the University of Western Ontario Library. It excludes the poems that appeared in *The Christian Sentinel*.   MARY LU MacDONALD

Butler, Juan (1942-81). Born in London, Eng., the son of an English father and a Spanish mother, he came to Canada with his family in 1942 and grew up in Toronto. He dropped out of school after Grade 10, travelled extensively in Europe and Morocco, then returned to Canada at the end of the sixties to reside at various times in Toronto and Montreal. In 1981 he hanged himself in a Toronto psychiatric hospital.

Butler's three novels—*Cabbagetown diary: a documentary* (1970), *The garbageman* (1972), and *Canadian heating oil* (1974)—are impassioned indictments of a squalid world that robs man of dignity. Michael Armstrong Taylor, the young diarist of *Cabbagetown diary*, is an immigrant bartender whose callous eyes witness the stupidity and hypocrisy of his low-class associates and his high-class customers. Written from his slum apartment in downtown Toronto, the entries begin in July and end in October of one year—the length of an affair Michael abruptly ends when his girlfriend becomes pregnant: 'Somebody had to show her how to make out in this world.' The first-person narrator of *The garbageman* is an insane writer from Toronto. Incapable of love yet anxious for human contact, he commits murders in France and Spain. An inmate of the mental institution where his story ends summarizes the novel's theme: 'Life killing itself because of its lack of pride in itself.' The first-person narrator of *Canadian heating oil*, set in a timeless surrealistic universe, is 'I St. John, the Eagle, the evangelist whom Christ loved the most', who believes himself destined to bestow dignity on people through love. He falls in love with Miss Pat, who is a black woman, a Chinese woman, an Indian princess, and Joan of Arc. The narrator becomes Jean Brébeuf, achieving salvation in a martyrdom of love. The artist-as-martyr theme became a sad prophecy of Butler's final years, when his psychological suffering offered him no peace.

In 'The Happy Gang rides again' (*Northern Journey* 3, 1973) Butler attacks the Group of Seven and the London school of painters: 'A culture must be based on a feeling, not of geography, but of national community.'

DAVID STAINES

Butler, Samuel. See FOREIGN WRITERS ON CANADA IN ENGLISH: 1 and 'O GOD! O MONTREAL!'.

Butler, William Francis. See FOREIGN WRITERS ON CANADA IN ENGLISH: 1, PRAIRIE WRITING, and TRAVEL LITERATURE IN ENGLISH.

By Grand Central Station

By Grand Central Station I sat down and wept (1945). This novel by Elizabeth SMART was begun during the Second World War and completed in 1941 while the author was living alone in Pender Harbour, B.C., awaiting the birth of her first child. It was published by the 'little' magazine *Poetry* (London) in an edition of ten thousand copies. A mass-paperback edition came out in England in 1966 and the first North American edition in 1975. Since then it has been recognized as a classic. In her Foreword to the paperback edition Brigid Brophy calls it one of the 'half a dozen masterpieces of poetic prose in the world . . . *By Grand Central Station* is one of the most shelled, skinned, nerve-exposed books ever written.'

A love story written in the form of a rhapsodic prose-poem to the failure of love, it is quintessentially lyrical: sounding antiphonally throughout are rhythms, images, and refrains that echo the Song of Solomon. It takes its title from a play on the opening of Psalm 137 ('By the rivers of Bablyon, there we sat down, yea, we wept, when we remembered Zion.') Set in North America in the early years of the Second World War, it is a type of interior monologue where all attention is focused on the narrator's intense and obsessive passion for a married man. The other characters are shadowy archetypes: the wife, long-suffering but triumphant in her passivitiy; the lover, who taunts and resists two women and, finally, fails them both. There are few external events beyond a car journey through the United States, the narrator's ultimate return alone to the west coast of Canada to have her child, a reunion in New York, and the death of passion. No real place-names appear in the novel, only imagistic contexts for psychological states. The book is haunting because Smart moves the story into a mythological key in an effort to explore the intensity of romantic eroticism. She analyses the death-drive in romantic love, 'whoring after oblivion', seeing clearly the narcissistic root of her passion by identifying the myth of Narcissus as its controlling image.

ROSEMARY SULLIVAN

C

Cailloux, André. See CHILDREN'S DRAMA IN FRENCH.

Calef, George. See NATURE WRITING IN ENGLISH: 2.

Call, Frank Oliver. See POETRY IN ENGLISH 1900 TO 1950: 2 (b) and Writing in English in QUÉBEC: 2.

Callaghan, Barry (b. 1937). The son of Morley CALLAGHAN, he was born in Toronto and educated at St Michael's College, University of Toronto, where he received a B.A. in 1960 and an M.A. in 1962, and which he left in 1965 before completing his doctoral dissertation. He worked as a part-time reporter for CBC television news (1958-62) and gave weekly book reviews on the CBC radio program 'Audio' (1964-6). From Sept. 1966 to Mar. 1971 he was literary editor of the Toronto *Telegram*, for which he wrote essays and book reviews that were noted for their insight and controversial candour. After seven months as a host for the CBC TV program 'The Public Eye', he became host and documentary producer for the public affairs show 'Weekend' (Nov. 1969-Feb. 1972); in this capacity he made some 20 short films on political trouble-spots and taped interviews with international figures such as Golda Meir and King Hussein. He has also produced and directed a number of documentaries (he was imprisoned in South Africa in 1976 during the filming of *The white lager*). As a journalist Callaghan has received four national magazine awards, including the Gold Medal from the University of Western Ontario in 1979. Since 1965 he has taught contemporary literature at Atkinson College, York University, Toronto, where in 1972 he founded the literary magazine EXILE, and Exile Editions in 1975. He has since appeared weekly on the CTV morning show 'Canada A.M.', offering editorials in a frequently sardonic fashion.

Callaghan's *The Hogg poems and drawings* (1978) is a sequence detailing the protagonist's semi-religious quest to Jerusalem in order to liberate himself from the stifling conventions of Hogtown (Toronto). Finding passion, history, and even absurdity at the end of his pilgrimage, he makes a descent into the underworld of the Toronto subway, emerging with a new awareness of his identity and an acceptance of his roots. Although not all poems are of the same order, 'Judas Priest'—with its street wisdom, vernacular rhythm, and complex rhymes—is exceptionally fine. The sensuality, aloneness, and distrust for the 'thought-police' (any person or establishment that would identify the nonconformist with the criminal) that are apparent in the *Hogg poems* are also motifs in *The Black Queen stories* (1982), a collection of fourteen highly polished tales that range from vivid portraits of gamblers and gays to subtle explorations of their relationships. Callaghan's ear for the spoken word is most acute in 'The Cohen in Cowan' and 'Poodles John'. His use of symbolism is sophisticated—the outcome of a story is often foreshadowed in the opening paragraphs. Evident throughout is Callaghan's compassion for his characters; despite their idiosyncrasies and occasional outrageousness, they are shown to be people with the same joys and sorrows as anyone else. Eight of these stories have appeared in *Punch*, and two—'Crow Jane's blues' and 'A drawn blind'—were reprinted in *The Punch book of short stories* (1980 and 1981 respectively).

Callaghan is also a skilled memoirist in his introduction to *Shapes and sounds: poems of W.W.E. Ross* (1968) and in his recollections of Edmund Wilson in *Exile* I, no.2 (1972). His translations of the French poet Robert Marteau—*Atlante* (1979) and *Treatise on white and tincture* (1979)—are marked by sensitivity and intelligence. Two more translations—*Interlude* by Robert Marteau and *Singing at the whirlpool* by Miodrag Pavlovic—were published in 1982, and a second volume of Callaghan's poems, *Seven last words*, appeared in 1983.   DAVID O'ROURKE

Callaghan, Morley (b. 1903). Born in Toronto, where he has lived all his life, Morley Edward Callaghan was educated at St Michael's College, University of Toronto, from which he graduated in 1925, and at Osgoode Hall. He was called to the bar in 1928 but never practised law. As a student he had worked during summer vacations as a cub reporter on the Toronto *Daily Star* during Ernest Hemingway's short period there, and the American novelist had shown an interest in his stories, encouraging Callaghan to pursue writing instead of law. Hemingway demonstrated the solidity of his interest by taking some of Callaghan's stories to France, where they were published in expatriate literary magazines; while in the United States, stories that Callaghan himself had sent out were accepted by *American Caravan* and noticed by F. Scott Fitzgerald, who showed them to his New York publisher, Scribner's. In 1928 Scribner's published Callaghan's first novel, *Strange fugitive*, and a year later his first volume of short stories, *A native argosy*. In the same year, 1929, Callaghan went to Paris, where he encountered Hemingway again, became friendly with Joyce and Fitzgerald, and was ironically observed by the young John GLASSCO (see his *Memoirs of Montparnasse*). This Parisian interlude became the subject of one of Callaghan's most appealing books, *That summer in Paris* (1963).

Since then Callaghan has devoted most of his creative energy to fiction—both novels and short stories. For a brief period, in 1939, he turned to drama and wrote two plays, 'Turn home again' and 'Just ask for George', which was produced in New York in 1940; 'Turn home again', as 'Going home', was staged in 1949 in Toronto, where another play, 'To tell the truth', was performed the following year. The response to these productions, however, did not encourage Callaghan to continue as a playwright. During the Second World War, when he was writing comparatively little, Callaghan turned to radio as a means of livelihood, serving as chairman of the CBC Forum program 'Of things to come'; he has been intermittently involved in CBC programs since that time. He made a single foray into juvenile literature with *Luke Baldwin's vow* (1948); and in *The Varsity story* (1948) he described in a hybrid form, part fiction and part history, the growth of the University of Toronto.

Callaghan's career as a writer of fiction follows a strikingly uneven graph of productivity and silence. There is an early cluster of six novels written in the late 1920s and early-to-middle 1930s, from *Strange fugitive* (1928) to MORE JOY IN HEAVEN (1937). To this period also belong most of Callaghan's stories—collected in *A native argosy* (1929) and *Now that April's here* (1936), and brought together in *Morley Callaghan's stories* (1959)—and his Paris-printed novella, *No man's meat* (1931). There is a long interval from the end of the 1930s to the early 1950s before *The* LOVED AND THE LOST (1951), and after that almost a decade before the publication in fast succession of two other novels, *The many colored coat* (1960) and *A passion in Rome* (1961). There was a further long interval before Callaghan's late novels appeared—again in close succession: *A fine and private place* (1975) and *Close to the sun again* (1977). *A time for Judas* will be published in the fall of 1983.

Callaghan's three early novels—*Strange fugitive* (1928), *It's never over* (1930), and *A broken journey* (1932)—are gauche and tentative in manner, implausible and melodramatic in plot. They are novels of consequences, in which the characters' own acts shape their generally unhappy fates. *Strange fugitive* is a kind of Rake's Progress, whose central character graduates from a bullying lumberyard foreman into a bootlegger who dies under the sawed-off shotgun of his rivals. *It's never over* traces how the tangled emotions of the people close to a man about to be hanged for murder take them near to a second murder situation. *A broken journey* uses the rivalry between a mother and daughter to illuminate the problems of innocence and infidelity and the destructive aspects of love. In none of these novels did Callaghan really find himself as a writer: the influence of both Hemingway and Fitzgerald are intermittently evident. There is a quite striking contrast between the uncertain forms and feelings of these early novels and the laconic sureness of the early short stories in which, in the same period, Callaghan was so empathetically tracing the vagaries of human behaviour.

A sudden sureness of tone appeared in Callaghan's fourth novel, *Such is my beloved* (1934), and continued through *They shall inherit the earth* (1935) and *More joy in heaven* (1937), which have an economy of form and a lucidity of expression and feeling that make them the best of all Callaghan's works, and perhaps the best novels written in Canada during the 1930s. They were written after Callaghan had come under the influence of the French theologian, Jacques Maritain, then teaching in Toronto, and they show the way in which ideas can in fact influence form. For they are moralist novels that bear a generic resemblance to the *récits*

(or novellas) of French writers like Gide and Camus. Set in the Depression era, whose physical rigours their characters suffer, they avoid the political conclusions that so many novels of the era sought and offer the moral predicaments of their characters as routes to spiritual ends—which, however, they see only 'through a glass, darkly'.

Callaghan's next three novels—*The loved and the lost*, *The many colored coat*, and *A passion in Rome*—are all attempts to combine the moral searchings of the earlier novels with more ambitious formal structures, so that what emerges is an unhappy compromise between the simple economy of the moralistic novella and the more decorated complexity of the classic realist novel. What Callaghan once again shows, now in a negative rather than a positive way, is that, with his special talent for the shorter and more concise forms of fiction, he is not really equipped for the construction of larger fiction: in each of these three novels the attempt to adjust leads to a softening of style and a straining of credibility. The unity of conception and the force of moral passion that distinguished the novels of the 1930s are evident in neither *The loved and the lost* nor *A passion in Rome*; and *A many colored coat* is a moral tale that would have made an excellent novella but was laboured into an overlong and over-written full-length novel.

Of Callaghan's two most recent novels, *A fine and private place* may well be his least effective work, for it is the story of an unappreciated novelist that clearly has personal implications and is used to present a flattering self-analysis and a contemptuous dismissal of the characters who are blind to the worth of the novelist and clearly represent Callaghan's critics. Callaghan, however, redeemed his record with *Close to the sun again*, in which he returns successfully to the terse novella form of his best period, evading temptations of realism in favour of moral symbolism as he writes a strange story of how the will to power develops in men when their personal defeats dominate them and destroy their natural impulses.

Edmund Wilson once said (in *O Canada*, 1965) that Callaghan 'is perhaps the most unjustly neglected novelist in the English-speaking world.' The record of honours paid him does not now bear this out: the Governor General's Award for *The loved and the lost*; the Lorne PIERCE Medal of the Royal Society of Canada in 1960; the Canada Council Medal in 1966; the Molson Prize and the Royal Bank Award in 1970; and in

1982 his appointment as a Companion of the Order of Canada.

See *Morley Callaghan* by Brandon Conron (1966) and *Morley Callaghan* by Victor Hoar (1969).   GEORGE WOODCOCK

Cameron, George Frederick (1854-85). Born in New Glasgow, N.S., he moved with his family to Boston in 1869 and in 1872 entered Boston University to study law. Later he worked with a law firm there. His early interest was in the classics and he is said to have read most of Virgil and Cicero in the original before he was fourteen. While articling in law he contributed poems and essays to several Boston newspapers. In 1882 he entered Queen's University, Kingston, and was named the prize poet in 1883, when he was made editor of the Kingston *News*, a position he held until his death. In 1887 his brother, Charles L. Cameron, edited and published a selection of Cameron's poems under the title *Lyrics on freedom, love and death* (Kingston, 1887). Cameron's poetry was unlike other Canadian verse of the time: there is little effort to write about 'Canadian' subjects such as nature and patriotism. It reflects Cameron's strong interest in classical culture, and his wide political concerns in poems sympathetic to the independence of Cuba and in praise of the democratic aspirations of the United States. His poems are clouded, however, by a prevailing pessimism. Cameron also wrote the libretto for *Leo, the Royal cadet. An entirely new and original military opera in four acts* (Kingston, 1889), with music by Oscar F. Tegmann; it was performed in Kingston, Toronto, and elsewhere in Ontario in 1889.
                    DOUGLAS LOCHHEAD

Campbell, Paddy. See CHILDREN'S DRAMA IN ENGLISH.

Campbell, Wilfred (1858-1918). An Anglican clergyman's son, William Wilfred Campbell was born in Berlin, Canada West (now Kitchener, Ont.). Upon completing high school in Owen Sound, he taught for a year in a country school at Zion, near Wiarton, Ont. He enrolled at University College, University of Toronto, in 1880 but transferred to Wycliffe, the university's Anglican divinity school, in 1882. The following year he transferred again, this time to the Episcopal Theological School in Cambridge, Mass. Ordained in 1886, Campbell served parishes in West Claremont, N.H., St Stephen, N.B., and Southampton, Ont.,

before resigning from the ministry in 1891. For the rest of his life he worked in the Ottawa civil service, holding positions in such areas as the Department of Railways and Canals, the Department of the Secretary of State, the Department of Militia and Defence, the Privy Council Office, and the Public Archives. He died of pneumonia on 1 Jan. 1918.

In the late nineteenth century the encroachment of science upon religion and higher criticism of the Bible were subjects of considerable debate in Canadian intellectual circles. The poetry of Wilfred Campbell—who is sometimes included among the CONFEDERATION POETS—to a large extent is the chronicle of a sensitive man's struggle to find meaning in an age of shifting values. His first book, *Snowflakes and sunbeams* (St. Stephen, N.B., 1888; rpr. 1974) is concerned chiefly with nature, and the influence of the English Romantics is apparent in almost every poem. A Wordsworthian celebration of memory dominates 'Midwinter night's dream', and the beauty of nature is glorified in his best-known and most-anthologized poem, 'Indian summer'.

In *Lake lyrics and other poems* (Saint John, 1889) nature is perceived less as a manifestation of God's presence on earth than as a spiritual force in itself. 'Vapor and blue', 'On the ledge', and particularly 'To Thunder Cape' show the poet striving to touch the spirit in nature. In seeking to align his energy with that of nature, Campbell does not emulate the American transcendentalists but looks instead to the work of Bliss CARMAN. Carman's 'Low tide on Grand Pré', written in 1886, serves as a model of transcendental experience for Campbell in 'August evening on the beach, Lake Huron' (c. 1889). Campbell's most significant nature poetry is stark and horrifying in its imagery. In 'The winter lakes' (*Lake lyrics*) the poet casts off the conventional nineteenth-century pose of being transported by nature's beauty and probes instead a profound sense of doubt in the face of a landscape unrelieved by hope. Similarly, in 'How one winter came in the lake region' in *The dread voyage* (Toronto, 1898) he paints a bleak portrait of a world untouched by God's grace. Campbell's best dramatic poems arise, as well, from settings that are stark and threatening. In 'Lazarus' (*Lake lyrics*) the protagonist questions God's authority and embarks on a dangerous mission to wrest a suffering man from the horrors of hell; and in 'Unabsolved' (*The dread voyage*) a coward's unassuageable guilt is mirrored in the bleak, frozen vastness of the Arctic. In winter lakes and landscapes Campbell found a metaphor for his despair over the religious doubt of the age.

After the turn of the century Campbell, for whom the monarchy and empire provided a reassuring link between past and present, expressed his imperialist philosophy in verse. 'Victoria (Jubilee Ode, A.D. 1897)', which appears in *Beyond the hills of dream* (Boston, 1899), celebrates Victoria's diamond jubilee, and the elegiac 'Victoria', in *The poems of Wilfred Campbell*—also published under the title *The collected poems of Wilfred Campbell* (both 1905)—laments her death. Campbell's final book, *Sagas of vaster Britain: poems of the race, the Empire and the divinity of man* (1914), argues for the imperialist cause at a time when the Empire was going to war. His commitment to imperialism is also reflected in the two anthologies of poetry he edited: *The Oxford book of Canadian verse* (1913; rpr. 1976) and *Poems of loyalty by British and Canadian authors* (1913). Campbell saw in imperialism's idealism and continuity the potential for meaningful action in an age of uncertainty and flux.

A prolific writer, Campbell also wrote poetic drama, fiction, travel books, and newspaper columns. His poetic dramas, *Mordred and Hildebrand. A book of tragedies* (Ottawa, 1895) and *Poetical tragedies* (1908), offer somewhat convoluted plots and stilted Elizabethan dialogue. His two novels, *Ian of the Orcades; or The armourer of Girnigoe* (1906) and *A beautiful rebel: a romance of Upper Canada in 1812* (1909), are similarly exaggerated in plot and diction. *The beauty, history, romance and mystery of the Canadian lake region* (1910) is a travel book exploring the region where Campbell set many of his poems. Campbell provided the text for T. Mower Martin's collection of paintings, *Canada* (1907), and collaborated with George Bryce on the two-volume work *The Scotsman in Canada* (1911). As newspaper columnist, Campbell joined his fellow poets Archibald LAMPMAN and Duncan Campbell SCOTT to write the column 'AT THE MERMAID INN' for the Toronto *Globe* (1892-3). For the Ottawa *Evening Journal* Campbell wrote another column, 'Life and letters' (1903-5).

As a Romantic, a transcendentalist, and particularly as an imperialist, Wilfred Campbell was not held in high regard by the generation of Canadian poets who succeeded him, though his literary executor, W.J. Sykes, published *The poetical works of Wilfred Campbell* (1923) and Carl F. KLINCK wrote a fine biography of the poet, *Wilfred Campbell: a study in late provincial Victorianism* (1942; rpr. 1977). In some ways modernism defined itself in contrast to the very poetical and political values Campbell had come to represent, and his work remained virtually ignored until the 1970s, when there was a revival of critical interest in his poetry. Two selections have been published in recent years: *Selected poems* (1976) edited by Klinck and *Vapour and blue: Souster selects Campbell* (1978) edited by Raymond SOUSTER.

See George Wicken, 'William Wilfred Campbell (1858-1918): an annotated bibliography', *Essays on Canadian Writing* 9 (Winter 1977/78), and his critical study in *Canadian writers and their works: poetry series: volume 2* (1983) edited by Robert Lecker, Jack David, and Ellen Quigley.

GEORGE WICKEN

Canadian Authors' Association. It was founded in 1921 as a bi-national literary association by Stephen LEACOCK, Pelham Edgar, B.K. Sandwell, and John Murray Gibbon, who became its first president. Pilloried by F.R. SCOTT in his famous satirical poem 'The Canadian authors meet' (1927), the CAA, as it soon became known, worked to develop a sense of cultural and literary solidarity among writers throughout Canada. It was initially established to fight proposed copyright legislation that threatened to discriminate against Canadian writers and was composed of local branches across Canada that convened annually in the spring; it included a self-governing French Section that lasted until 1936, when planning for the Société des Ecrivains Canadiens (est. 1938) began. The CAA's membership grew quickly to 750 in its second year and sixty years later numbers 775 members. In the early twenties it lobbied successfully for changes in copyright legislation and kept its members informed in the pages of the *Canadian Bookman*, edited by Sandwell (1921-2), and successively in the *Authors' Bulletin* (1923-33), the *Canadian Author* (1933-40), and the *Canadian Author and Bookman* (1940-). In an attempt to make Canadians more aware of the writers and books of their country, the CAA sponsored the first Canada Book Week in Nov. 1921, which took place annually until 1957. Other literary initiatives came from the Association. The poetry chapbooks of the different branches, which had been privately printed in the late twenties and early thirties, culminated in the founding of the *Canadian Poetry Magazine* (1936), which eventually merged with the *Canadian Author and Bookman* in 1968. The CAA was also responsible for the establishment in 1937 of the GOVERNOR-GENERAL'S AWARDS, whose administration by the CAA under a specially appointed Awards Board (est. 1944) lasted until 1959, when it was assumed by the Canada Council. In 1946 the Awards Board was entrusted with the adjudication of the new Stephen Leacock Medal for Humour. In the same year the Association was also responsible for the preparation of a standard book contract and for securing from the federal government special income-tax provisions for writers. Since 1963 it has administered the Vicky Metcalf Award of $1000, given to a writer of children's books, and, since 1979, the Vicky Metcalf Short Story Award of $500. Since 1975 the CAA has awarded its Silver Medal and $1000 in each of four fields: prose fiction, prose non-fiction, poetry, and drama. See also WRITERS' UNION and LEAGUE OF CANADIAN POETS.   JOHN LENNOX

Canadian Fiction Magazine (1971-). Beginning as a student publication at the University of British Columbia, CFM has grown into an independent national journal. Since its first issue it has fostered a national and international awareness of contemporary Canadian fiction in both English and French, and in translation from the unofficial languages of Canada. Under the editorship of Geoff Hancock it has also published entire issues devoted to single authors (Robert HARLOW, Mavis GALLANT, Jane RULE, Leon ROOKE, Michel TREMBLAY); an ongoing series of interviews with fiction writers; and a 'Future of fiction' series that encourages discussion about the aesthetics of contemporary fiction.   GEOFF HANCOCK

Canadian Forum, The (1920-). This 'independent journal of opinion and the arts', as its masthead proclaims, sprang from *The Rebel*, a periodical that had been started at the University of Toronto by students and professors—one of whom, Barker FAIRLEY, became the first literary editor of the *Forum*. While it has generally been on the left side of the political spectrum—its writers on political and social matters have included F.H. Underhill, Eugene Forsey, and F.R. SCOTT—it has always been faithful to its title by allowing discussions of issues from all sides, while also devoting space to po-

etry, fiction, and book reviews. Because it published the first work of many Canadian poets, the monthly has been highly regarded by members of the Canadian literary community. In the early 1970s it started a policy of giving a double-page spread to new work by a different poet each month, a policy that has continued to the present. Among its editors, and literary editors, have been such writers and critics as Earle BIRNEY, Northrop FRYE, Milton Wilson, Abraham Rothstein, Peter STEVENS, and Tom MARSHALL.

See J.L. Granatstein and Peter Stevens (eds), *Forum: Canadian life and letters from 1920–70: selections from 'The Canadian Forum'* (1972).   PETER STEVENS

Canadian Literary Magazine, The (1833). An early cultural periodical, it was issued monthly between April and June 1833 in York (Toronto), Upper Canada. Its editor was John Kent, 'a gentleman recently arrived from England', its printer Thomas Dalton, and its publisher George Gurnett. Before the first number appeared on 6 Apr. 1833, Gurnett included in his newspaper, *The Courier of Upper Canada*, a prospectus and several advertisements about the 'Journal'. They announced its contents as articles on such subjects as the 'U.E. Loyalists' and 'News of the Literary World', invited contributions from 'provincial authors', and promised 64 pages and a 'lithograph engraving' in each number. The April issue had all these features; its 20 items included an introductory editorial, a description of Niagara Falls, three poems and a tale by Susanna MOODIE, a 'prize poem' by Henry Scadding, a review of a recently published sermon on the cholera epidemic of 1832 by Archdeacon George Jehoshaphat Mountain, and a sketch of the late Sir Walter Scott, accompanied by a lithograph 'engraved in Upper Canada . . . on Canadian Stone, and from thence, by means of a Canadian press, transferred to Canadian paper'. The succeeding two issues contained items by William 'Tiger' Dunlop and W.F. HAWLEY, and more poems by Susanna Moodie. The magazine, distributed in both Upper and Lower Canada, was well reviewed by newspapers in both provinces. Still, it ceased publication after the third issue—perhaps because its editor miscalculated the financial resources of the recently arrived well-educated English immigrants towards whom it was at least partly aimed. Nevertheless it was significant. As one of the first cultural periodicals in Upper Can-

Canadian Literary Magazine

ada it provided an early Canadian outlet for the works of its new settlers. For example, Susanna Moodie's 'Oh can you leave your native land: a Canadian song', which appeared in the April issue, was the first 'Canadian' poem she published. Furthermore, even though the magazine did not survive, its formula of mixing several types of articles on various subjects and encouraging local authors was similar to that used a few years later by the first really successful Canadian periodical, *The* LITERARY GARLAND.   MARY JANE EDWARDS

Canadian Literature (1959–). The first quarterly devoted entirely to the criticism and discussion of Canadian writing, it was founded in 1959 by George WOODCOCK and published at the University of British Columbia. The introductory editorial of the first issue declared that it 'will not adopt a narrowly academic approach, nor will it try to restrict its pages to any school of criticism or class of writers.' This policy led to a wide variety of critical approaches, and to contributions not only from the most distinguished Canadian critics but also from important writers in other fields, notably fiction and poetry. The same policy has been continued by W.H. New, who took over the editorship when Woodcock resigned in 1977.

Essays from the magazine have been collected in a number of anthologies. *A choice of critics: selections from 'Canadian Literature'* (1966) and *The sixties: Canadian writers and writing of the decade* (1969) are general selections. More specialized collections are *Malcolm Lowry: the man and his work* (1971), *Wyndham Lewis in Canada* (1971), *Poets and critics: essays from 'Canadian Literature' 1966–74* (1974), *Colony and Confederation* (1974), and *The Canadian novel in the twentieth century: essays from 'Canadian Literature'* (1975). All these volumes were edited by Woodcock, who wrote the introductions to them, except for *Colony and Confederation*, which was introduced by Roy DANIELLS. Other *Canadian Literature* anthologies are *Dramatists in Canada: selected essays* (1972), edited and introduced by W.H. New, and *Writers of the Prairies* (1973), edited and introduced by D.G. Stephens, who for a period was associate editor of the journal.
GEORGE WOODCOCK

Cape, Judith. Pseudonym of P.K. PAGE.

Cappon, James (1854-1939). Born in Dundee, Scot., and educated at the University of Glasgow, he taught literature for two years at Geneva and then at Glasgow, where he wrote his first critical study, *Victor Hugo* (1885). He became in 1888 professor of English language and literature at Queen's University, Kingston, and edited, and contributed articles frequently to, *Queen's Quarterly*. He was appointed the first dean of arts in 1906 and was elected to the Royal Society of Canada in 1917. His series of letters, collected as *Britain's title in South Africa* (1901), defends Britain's stand in the South African War.

Cappon's pamphlet *Charles G.D. Roberts and the influence of his times* (1905) was a milestone in Canadian literary criticism in placing a Canadian poet in his context. In it Cappon gives an overview of modern literary trends and traces in ROBERTS' work the Romantic influences of the early nature poetry through to the Pre-Raphaelite influences in the later poetry from the New York period, concluding with a carefully argued criticism of what he terms the lack of ethical centre that mars Roberts' work as a whole. This pamphlet was expanded to *Charles G.D. Roberts* (1925), a volume in the Makers of Canadian Literature series. Cappon wrote two other critical studies: *Bliss Carman and the literary currents and influences of his time* (1930) and *What classical education means* (n.d.). Cappon's critical writing is distinguished by its engagingly familiar yet scholarly style.

See also CRITICISM IN ENGLISH: 2.
JANET BAKER

Carman, Bliss (1861-1929). William Bliss Carman, a first cousin of Charles G.D. ROBERTS and a distant relation of Ralph Waldo Emerson, was born in Fredericton, N.B., and educated at the University of New Brunswick. He spent an unhappy year at Oxford and Edinburgh in 1882-3, and then tried various professions in Fredericton before attending Harvard in 1886-8, where he met Richard Hovey (1864-1900). He became a literary journalist in New York, first with a religious weekly, *The Independent*, and later in Boston, where he worked for *The Atlantic Monthly, The Chap-book*, and the Boston *Transcript*. On these and other periodicals, he helped Canadian writers into print. In 1896 he met Mary Perry King, who became his lifelong patron and companion, and after 1908 he settled near the Kings in Connecticut. In 1921, while recovering from a near-fatal illness, he undertook the first of several strenuous poetry-reading tours across Canada, and was acclaimed as an unofficial poet laureate. He was elected a corresponding member of the Royal Society of Canada in 1925 and received the Lorne PIERCE Medal for distinguished service to literature in 1928 and honorary degrees from the Universities of New Brunswick and McGill; he was awarded posthumously the medal of the Poetry Society of America. Carman died in New Canaan, Conn., following a reading tour, and his ashes were buried in Fredericton.

Carman wrote over fifty volumes of poetry. His work is uneven because he never learned to cut out repetitive passages and trite language; yet he showed great versatility with musical cadences, and with poetic forms ranging from lyrics and dramatic monologues to meditative verse. Carman was the first Canadian poet to transform the external landscape into an interior, psychic landscape that delineated his characteristic moods—yearning, loss of love, melancholy, grief, and, on occasion, rapture. However, his poems of lasting merit are limited to a handful of regional verses dealing with the Maritimes and New England. His particular sensibility was nurtured by Wordsworthian 'pantheism' and Emersonian transcendentalism, both of which emphasized man's oneness with the universe. He borrowed the Pre-Raphaelites' fondness for associating colours and emotions. He was attracted to contemporary *fin-de-siècle* Romanticism, which rejected the scientific rationalism of the age and sought reality in a visionary dream world whose symbols were drawn from art and nature. Having drifted from the Anglican faith, Carman recognized Nature as the source of his creative power and spiritual consolation. His poetry celebrates the 'kinship' he felt with all living things, and his work, particularly up to 1910, records his quest for a philosophical system to underpin his emotional experiences.

A mystical vision in 1886 sustained Carmen in his earliest volumes: *Low tide on Grand Pré: a book of lyrics* (New York, 1893), *Behind the arras: a book of the unseen* (Boston, Toronto, 1895), and *Ballads of lost haven: a book of the sea* (Boston, 1897). This experience is at the centre of his finest poem, 'Low tide on Grand Pré', in which the grieving speaker recaptures the timelessness and ecstasy of a past love affair. In these volumes Carman's voice, elegiac and gentle, observes the fragility of life, the passing of time, and the coming of death. In his collaboration

with Hovey on *Songs from Vagabondia* (Boston, 1895), Carman found another 'voice', that of the literary vagrant whose back-to-nature heartiness and optimism had wide appeal and helped to initiate a revolt against the genteel, dilettantish poetry of the time. Hovey helped Carman to see how exaltation of the physical could lead to spiritual insights. The sequels include *More songs from Vagabondia* (Boston, 1896) and *Last songs from Vagabondia* (1901); and Carman by himself wrote *Echoes from Vagabondia* (1912). Turning to classical themes in *Sappho: one hundred lyrics* (1904), Carman produced several flawless and timeless songs. The figure of Pan, the goat-god, traditionally associated with poetry and with the fusion of the earthly and the divine, becomes Carman's organizing symbol in the five volumes issued between 1902 and 1905 and reprinted as *The pipes of Pan: containing 'From the book of myths,' 'From the green book of the bards,' 'Songs of the sea children,' 'Songs from a northern garden,' 'From the book of valentines'* (1906). His intention was to trace the religious and philosophical evolution of man through Pan's music, but his Pan is too fleshless, the philosophy vague, and the volumes lack a sense of overall shape.

Carman's search for a more substantial philosophy was aided by Hovey's wife, who introduced him to François Delsarte's theories of education based on calisthenics; that is, the rhythmic arts of music, poetry, and dancing. Delsarte's complicated interrelationship between the human faculties and sensations was called Unitrinitarianism. Carman merged this philosophy with his own notions about personality—which he had drawn from the Greek concepts of Truth, Beauty, and the Good—into a system in which a balance was achieved between the physical, the emotional, and the mental. In collaboration with Mrs King, Carman expounded these theories in a book of essays, *The making of personality* (1908); and in two dramas, *Daughters of dawn: a lyrical pageant or series of historical scenes for presentation with music and dancing* (1913) and *Earth deities, and other rhythmic masques* (1914). Unfortunately his poems illustrating this theory are didactic and trite. His later poetry retains the same subjects and themes, but the mystical and visionary characteristics are less prominent, and his language and rhythms are closer to colloquial speech; too often the sound is more important than the sense. After 1914 Carman's popularity was due to semi-religious lyrics like the much-anthologized 'Vestigia'. His later volumes include *April airs* (1916); *Later poems* (1921); and *Ballads and lyrics* (1923); *Far horizons* (1925); *Wild garden* (1929; and *Sanctuary* (1929).

Carman's essays include *The kinship of nature* (1903); *The friendship of art* (1904); *The poetry of life: Longfellow, Emerson, Swinburne* (1905), reprinted by R. West in 1973; *Address to the graduating class 1911 of the Unitrinitarian school of personal harmonizing* (1911); *James Whitcomb Riley* (1917), reprinted by Folcraft in 1976; and *Talks on poetry and life; being a series of five lectures delivered before the University of Toronto, December 1925* (1926), transcribed by Blanche Hume. He edited *The world's best poetry* (10 vols, 1904), reprinted by Gordon Printing in 1975; *The Oxford book of American verse* (1927; rpr. 1976); and *Our Canadian literature; representative verse, English and French* (1922), edited with Lorne PIERCE, then revised by V.B. Rhodenizer as *Canadian poetry in English* (1954; rpr. 1976).

Carman's poetry in print includes a selection in *Poets of the Confederation* (NCL, 1960) edited and introduced by Malcolm Ross; and *Selected poems of Bliss Carman* (NCL, 1976) introduced by John Robert Sorfleet.

See H.D.C. Lee, *Bliss Carman: a study in Canadian poetry* (1912); Odell Shepard, *Bliss Carman* (1923); James CAPPON, *Bliss Carman and the literary currents and influences of his time* (1930); Malcolm Ross, 'A symbolic approach to Carman', *Canadian Bookman*, 14 (Dec. 1932); Desmond PACEY, 'Bliss Carman' in *Ten Canadian poets* (1958); Donald Stephens, *Bliss Carman* (1966); John Robert Sorfleet, 'Transcendentalist, mystic, evolutionary idealist: Bliss Carman 1886-1894', in *Colony and Confederation* (1974) edited by George WOODCOCK; Malcolm Ross, ' "A strange aesthetic ferment" ', CANADIAN LITERATURE 68-69 (Spring-Summer 1976); Robert GIBBS, 'Voice and persona in Carman and Roberts' in *Atlantic provinces literature colloquium papers* (1977) edited by Kenneth MacKinnon; D.M.R. Bentley, 'Pan and the Confederation Poets', *Canadian Literature* 81 (Summer 1979); *Letters of Bliss Carman* (1982) edited by H. Pearson Gundy; and the essay on Carman by Terry Whalen in *Canadian writers and their work: poetry series: volume two* (1983) edited by Robert Lecker, Jack David, and Ellen Quigley.

GEORGE L. PARKER

Caron, Louis (b. 1942). Born in Sorel, Qué., Caron worked at several occupations—broadcasting, public relations, and journalism—before publishing a selection of short stories and poems in 1973: *L'illusionniste suivi de Le guetteur*. A past president of the Union des Écrivains du Québec and the author of many radio and television plays for Radio-Canada, Caron in 1976 decided to devote his time completely to writing. He has since written four novels and is completing a fifth.

L'emmitouflé (Paris, 1977) won the French Prix Hermès and the Prix France-Canada. Certain changes made by the author appeared in the English translation by David Toby Homel (*The draft-dodger*, 1980); and a definitive French version soon followed (Seuil, 1982). Caron convincingly recreates the atmosphere of the 1917 conscription crisis and offers a point of view rarely heard or accepted in English Canada; namely, a sympathetic portrayal of a French Canadian refusing to fight a war he does not believe in. The juxtaposition of the elderly Nazaire's experiences with those of his nephew Jean-François, a Franco-American conscientious objector to the Vietnam war, provides an ideological continuity within the francophone community: the nephew's recollections of events in his grandfather's life enable the reader to understand Nazaire's flight from the law and his subsequent alienation. Caron's talents as a storyteller were confirmed in *Bonhomme sept-heures* (1978), whose title is the Québécois equivalent of 'the bogeyman'. The imaginary world of children contrasts with the horror of the 1955 flooding of Nicolet; on a symbolic level the author alludes to death itself and the death of childhood in all of us.

Le canard de bois (1981), the first volume of a trilogy entitled 'Les Fils de la liberté', won the Prix France-Québec. Once again a parallel storyline contrasts two different generations of the same family. Hyacinthe Bellerose, a humble villager from Port Saint-François, finds himself inexorably drawn into the Rebellion of 1837-8 and is ultimately exiled for his part in the uprising. On another level we meet 15-year-old Bruno Bellerose, who receives from his father's dying hands in 1935 a duck carved from wood by his ancestor, Hyacinthe. *La corne de brume* (1982) describes Hyacinthe's exile in Australia and his return to Sorel fifty years later. The main focus of the plot, however, is Tim Bellerose, the Irish orphan adopted by Hyacinthe and left behind in the care of a Métisse, Marie-Moitié. Now a grown man, Tim bridles at the injustices committed against the Métis in 1855, and his obsessive anger at the English lumber companies' economic exploitation of French-Canadian lumberjacks ultimately leads to his drowning.

Caron's storytelling skills recall both Jacques FERRON and Roch CARRIER, while his concern for the common man, swept along despite himself by historical events, reminds us of SAVARD's epic MENAUD, MAÎTRE-DRAVEUR (1937). In the tradition of DESROSIER's *Les engagés du grand portage* (1939), Caron's historical fresco in the three-volume saga of the Bellerose family brings to life colourful characters and milieu with vividness and authenticity. The trilogy is being adapted for television.

See also NOVELS IN FRENCH 1960 TO 1982:3(c).   RAMON HATHORN

Carr, Emily (1871-1945). Born in Victoria, B.C., she studied painting at the California School of Design in San Francisco (1891-3), in England (1899-1904), and Paris (1910-11); two of her paintings were hung in the prestigious Salon d'Automne in Paris in 1911. In the summer of 1898 she made the first of many trips to Indian villages, travelling by steamer up the west coast of Vancouver Island to Ucluelet. Here the seed of what was to be a lifelong interest in west-coast Indian peoples and culture germinated. In the summer of 1912 she made a highly productive trip to the remote Skeena River region and the Queen Charlotte Islands. In these Indian villages Carr gathered a wealth of images and impressions that would be a recurring focus of varying intensity throughout her career as a painter. The bold colours and aggressive brush strokes that characterized her work when she returned from Europe, and her 'new' way of looking at things, were not well received by local people, who were unprepared for any deviation from the English landscape tradition. After 1913 she painted less and turned to other means of supporting herself, including running an apartment house, called Hill House, on her father's property in Victoria; raising sheepdogs; and making pottery. A turning-point came in 1927 when Carr received an invitation to exhibit at the National Gallery in the Exhibition of Canadian West Coast Indian Art and travelled to Ottawa and Toronto, where she was greatly influenced by meeting with Lawren Harris and other Group of Seven artists. She revisited the Skeena River region and the Queen Charlottes in 1928, but a year later she abandoned her Indian themes and concentrated on the British Columbia

forests, which held a particular mystery for her.

From her many trips to Indian communities and the remote regions of British Columbia, Carr drew creative inspiration for powerful paintings of Indian culture—huge, pulsating skies bursting with light and energy and intense sculptural forests—and for the journals and notes that she later used for her published sketches and stories. She began keeping a journal in 1927, recording ideas, themes, or impressions that could be reworked in paint. Always a good storyteller, she enrolled in a short-story correspondence course in 1926 and in another course at Victoria College in the summer of 1934. Her first attempts at creative writing were aided by the constructive criticism of three 'literary' friends: Flora Burns, Ruth Humphrey, and Margaret Clay. After 1937, when Carr was often confined to bed as a result of several strokes and heart attacks, she turned seriously to writing. In 1940 some of her Indian stories were read on the CBC—first by Dr Garnet Sedgewick, head of English Department at the University of British Columbia, and then by Ira Dilworth, a regional director of the CBC in Vancouver. With Dilworth's encouragement and assistance, she completed her first book, *Klee Wyck* (1941)—the title, meaning 'laughing one' is the name the Nootka Indians gave her. This series of short stories, which won a Governor General's award, describes with perception, warmth, wit, and originality an aspect of British Columbian life, based on her visits to Indian villages. The next year *The book of Small* (1942) was published. Like all Carr's books, it is autobiographical: describing her family life and nineteenth-century Victoria from the point of view of Emily Carr the child (nicknamed 'Small'). Her writing style—simple, clear, direct, gently humorous, and carefully pruned of all but essential elements, like her painting—was now clearly established. A few months after the publication of *The House of All Sorts* (1944), which describes entertainingly her period as a landlady and raiser of bobtail sheepdogs, she died. Her autobiography, *Growing pains*—written between 1939 and 1944 and which, by her request, was to be published posthumously—appeared in 1946. This engaging account of her life highlights particularly her art-school days in San Francisco and London.

Other posthumous books followed. *Pause: a sketch book* (1953) centres on Carr's 15-month convalescence in the East Anglia

Sanatorium in Suffolk, Eng. (1903-4). These humorous and sometimes poignant reminiscences of the people and events in the sanatorium, written thirty years later, are supplemented by drawings and doggerel verse. *The heart of a peacock* (1953) is a selection of stories and previously unpublished prose sketches edited by Ira Dilworth, whom she had made her literary trustee. Selections from Carr's journals, composed between 1927 and 1941, were combined in *Hundreds and thousands: the journals of Emily Carr* (1966) which, in recording her joys, challenges, disappointments, and her constant search for the means to understand and express the world around her, is marked by the vivid descriptions and touching honesty of her very personal style. *An address* (1955), with an introduction by Ira Dilworth, contains a memorable speech Carr gave on 4 Mar. 1930 before the Victoria Women's Canadian Club, which was celebrating her first exhibition in her native city. See also *Fresh seeing: two addresses by Emily Carr* (1972), with a preface by Doris Shadbolt and an introduction to the 1930 speech by Ira Dilworth. *Klee Wyck*, *The book of Small*, *The House of All Sorts*, *Growing pains*, and *Hundreds and thousands* are all available in paperback.

Emily Carr's career as both a painter and writer are described in Maria Tippett, *Emily Carr: a biography* (1979); Doris Shadbolt, *The art of Emily Carr* (1979); and Edythe Hembroff-Schleicher, *Emily Carr: the untold story* (1978). See also *Emily Carr: a centennial exhibition celebrating the one hundredth anniversary of her birth, organized by the Vancouver Art Gallery* (1971); and *Emily Carr: her paintings and sketches* (1945), published for the National Gallery of Canada and the Art Gallery of Toronto by the Oxford University Press, with a biographical sketch by Ira Dilworth and an essay by Lawren Harris on Carr's paintings and drawings.

KERRY DODD

Carrier, Roch (b. 1937). Born in Sainte-Justine-de-Dorchester, a small village in the Beauce region of Québec, Carrier studied at the Université de Montréal and the Sorbonne, where he wrote a doctoral thesis on the poetry of Blaise Cendrars. He has been secretary-general of the Théâtre du Nouveau Monde in Montreal, and now combines teaching at the Collège Militaire St-Jean with writing. He is also a successful lecturer in both French and English; in the fall of 1982 he gave a series of lectures on Québec literature in six west-coast U.S. universities. He received the Prix de la Province du Québec in 1964 for *Jolis deuils* and the Grand Prix de la Ville de Montréal in 1981.

With Michel TREMBLAY, Carrier is one of the most widely read Québécois authors in English Canada as well as in Québec. Both authors express a humorous, ironic, sometimes sentimental view of Québec life (rural for Carrier, urban for Tremblay), often adopting the viewpoint of childhood. Though certain themes recur in Carrier's work (nostalgia for Québec's rural past, the reality of the dream world, a diffuse nationalism), it is much more varied, more ambitious, but less clearly unified in tone and style than Tremblay's. Carrier has moved through different narrative styles to develop his themes; some have been more successful than others.

Carrier's earliest publications were poems and short stories. His first book was *Jolis deuils* (1964), a collection of fantastic and allegorical tales. A series of three novels followed: *La guerre, yes sir!* (1968; trans. 1970); *Floralie, où es-tu?* (1969; *Floralie, where are you?* 1971) and *Il est par là le soleil* (1970; *Is it the sun, Philibert?*, 1972). *La guerre*, probably still Carrier's best-known and most popular work, is an account of the pressures put on both individuals and on village life in Québec at the start of the Second World War. Carrier combines extreme bitterness against les Anglais (who are uncomprehending and wooden British stereotypes) with the depiction of a warm and solid village life. A more dream-like *Floralie* goes back thirty years before this event to the wedding night of the parents of *La guerre*'s central character, combining a comic tale of religion and sex with nightmare. *Il est par là le soleil* is the dark story of a French-Canadian village boy confronting the horrors and corruption of work in Montreal.

Since 1972 Carrier has produced five more novels. Only *Le deux-millième étage* (1973; *They won't demolish me!*, 1974) has an urban setting. *Le jardin des délices* (1975; *The garden of delights*, 1978), one of his most successful works, is a free-wheeling and ironic story of the attempt by an unscrupulous profiteer to exploit the desires and credulity of a small town—but also a bitter exposé of the pettiness of those who would allow themselves to be exploited.

Il n'y a pas de pays sans grand-père (1979; *No country without grandfathers*, 1981) and *Les fleurs vivent-elles ailleurs que sur la terre* (1980) are both extended fables whose meaning finally refers to the activity of the writer. The first—which is more a statement of Carrier's literary and ideological affiliations than an original story—is a kind of twentieth-century rewrite of SAVARD's MENAUD, MAÎTRE-DRAVEUR. *Les fleurs* tells of how a very ordinary man's life was changed after his body was imprinted with rays from outer space: now he, like the writer, must 'tell and retell and retell' the story of his link with the beyond. *La dame qui avait des chaînes aux chevilles (1981)* is Carrier's most ambitious novel to date. A long, dense story of a woman's dream for revenge, it is harsh, bare, and intense. The strength of the novel, though, is severely prejudiced by the nature of the husband's unlikely crime—abandoning his baby in a snow-storm.

Les enfants du bonhomme dans la lune (1979) was translated as *The hockey sweater and other stories* (1979). The title story inspired *The Sweater*, an animated short subject by Sheldon Cohen produced by the National Film Board. Carrier has also published a children's book, *Les voyageurs de l'arc-en-ciel* (1980).

Carrier has made stage adaptations of *La guerre, yes sir!* (1970)—an English translation was successfully produced at the Stratford Festival in 1972—and *Floralie* (1973); and has written several other plays, including *La celeste bicyclette* (1980), which, as *The celestial bicycle*, was produced in English at the Tarragon Theatre, Toronto, in 1982. The English translations of Carrier's work have all been made by Sheila Fischman.

See Margot Northey, 'Sportive grotesque' in *Canadian Literature* 70 (Autumn 1976).

See also DRAMA IN FRENCH 1948 TO 1981:3 and NOVELS IN FRENCH 1960 TO 1982:3(b).   SHERRY SIMON

Cartier, Jacques. See Writing in NEW FRANCE: 1.

Casgrain, Henri-Raymond (1831-1904). Born at Rivière-Ouelle, Lower Canada (Qué.), he was educated in Quebec City and ordained a priest in 1856. With Hubert LaRUE, Antoine GÉRIN-LAJOIE, and Joseph-Charles TACHÉ he was actively involved in the renascence of French-Canadian letters as co-founder of the MOUVEMENT LITTÉRAIRE DE QUÉBEC and of the periodicals *Les SOIRÉES CANADIENNES* (1861) and *Le FOYER CANADIEN* (1863). He devoted his entire life to history and literature and was one of the

most prolific writers of the nineteenth century, sometimes using the pseudonyms 'Placide Lépine' and 'Eugène de Rives'. He benefited greatly from his lengthy visits to Paris, where his work at the Bibliothèque Nationale, and the associations he formed, helped to attract attention in the French intellectual community to Canada and its history. A founding member of the Royal Society of Canada (1882), he was its president in 1889.

Casgrain is best known as a historian, and he endeavoured to continue the work of F.-X. GARNEAU and J.B.A. Ferland. But he began his writing career with *Légendes canadiennes* (Québec, 1861), in which he retold French-Canadian folktales. He also wrote two books of poems, *A ma soeur Rosalie* (Québec, 1860) and *Les miettes: distractions poétiques* (Québec, 1869), of which fifty copies were printed; a work of literary criticism, *Chauveau* (Québec, 1872); *Silhouettes canadiennes* (Québec, 1872), a collection of literary profiles written in collaboration with J.-E.-E. MARMETTE and published under the pseudonym 'Placide Lépine'; and a series of eight biographies entitled *Biographies canadiennes* (Québec, 1875) on such figures as Champlain, Francis Parkman, his friend F.-X. Garneau, Gérin-Lajoie, and Philippe AUBERT DE GASPÉ. Casgrain's historical works are *Histoire de la Mère Marie de l'Incarnation* (Québec, 1864); *Histoire de l'Hôtel-Dieu de Québec* (Québec, 1878); *Une paroisse canadienne au XVIIᵉ siècle* (Québec, 1880); *Un pèlerinage au pays d'Evangeline* (Québec, 1887); *La Société des Filles du Coeur de Marie, d'après ses annales* (Paris, 1889); the two-volume *Montcalm et Lévis* (Québec, 1891); *Une seconde Acadie; l'Ile Saint-Jean—île du Prince Edward sous le régime français* (Québec, 1894); *L'Asile du Bon-Pasteur de Québec, d'après les annales de cet institut* (Québec, 1896); and *Les Sulpiciens et les Prêtres des Missions Etrangères en Acadie 1676–1762* (Québec, 1891). Casgrain also published the twelve-volume *Collection des manuscrits du maréchal de Lévis* (Québec and Montréal, 1889-95), in addition to leaving a massive correspondence with both foreign and Canadian authors. *Wolfe and Montcalm* (1905), a posthumous study written in English, is in the Chronicles of Canada series.

As a historian Casgrain was chiefly interested in heroic figures, striking portraits, and dramatic epochs. He preferred Lévis to Montcalm and considered *Montcalm et Lévis* to be his best work. Acadia fascinated him, as did the history of the early missionaries and clergy. Of an enthusiastic and romantic temperament, he nevertheless rid himself of the defects in style that had marred his early writings—an excessive use of figurative language, florid descriptions, and lack of taste—for his major works, which are marked by versatility, vigour, liveliness, controlled feeling, and fine composition—traits that contributed to Casgrain's gaining not only public acclaim but also the affection of the readers of his time.

Casgrain lived long enough to see publication of the three volumes of his *Oeuvres complètes* (Québec, 1873-5). He also collaborated on the publication of the *Oeuvres complètes* (1878-1882) of Octave CRÉMAZIE.

MAURICE LEBEL

Cather, Willa. See FOREIGN WRITERS ON CANADA IN ENGLISH: 2.

Chamberland, Paul (b. 1939). Born in Longueuil, Qué., he was educated at the Séminaire St-Croix and the Collège St-Laurent. Later he studied philosophy at the Université de Montréal and in 1963 was one of the founding members of PARTI PRIS. He also worked on a doctoral thesis at the Sorbonne under the supervision of Roland Barthes. In an act of revolutionary zeal during the turmoil of the 1968 student uprising in Paris, he deliberately destroyed the completed version of his thesis.

From his first collection of poems, *Génèses* (1962), to his most recent works, Chamberland has pursued specific themes. Fire—viewed not only as the supreme generator, an element that unites spirit and matter, but also as a man-made creation capable of producing a nuclear holocaust—is a central image and symbol. Since this work, which features the forge, hammer, and anvil of revolt, it is evident that both social and political explosions are at the core of his concerns. With *L'afficheur hurle* (1964)—a poem that is a cry, a howl, a shout of dereliction—and *L'inavouable* (1968), the poem becomes an angry, aggressive act of rupture, confirming Chamberland's statement that 'poetry is subversive or it is not poetry' (*parti pris*, Feb. 1966, p. 59). The subversion here is twofold: as a political statement the poem upholds the right of the Québécois people to self-determination and an egalitarian society; as a text it rejects aestheticism, formal perfection, and good taste. 'I am proud to write badly', he affirms in *L'afficheur hurle*. Yet for all of Chamberland's rejection of the canons of standard French, of

poetic humanism, he never really adopted JOUAL as a mode of expression.

The reading of Karl Marx and Frantz Fannon seem to have played a formative role in Chamberland's early years (1963-8). But in the 1980s his ideological trajectory has moved from a revolutionary Marxist viewpoint, centred on the necessity of armed struggle, to a more spiritual vision. Indeed, one notices in his writings of the seventies an element of social justice and balance that implies inner peace and personal change. Other changes—the shifts of focus from Québec to the planet Earth, and from nationalistic values to Utopian aspirations, appearing as early as 1972 in *Éclats de la pierre noire d'où jaillit ma vie*—were emphasized by his participation in the counter-culture magazine *Hobo Québec* during the seventies and were developed in *Demain les dieux naîtront* (1974), *Le Prince de Sexamour* (1976), *Extrême survivance, extrême poésie* (1978), *Terre souveraine* (1980), and *L'enfant doré* (1981). Love as the motivating force capable of generating global changes is first defined as a bond uniting man and woman; next it is viewed from a homosexual perspective; then it is expressed as love of children, of the fragile and the innocent, before being turned into a sentiment that encompasses all of humanity. Yet all these volumes anticipate an apocalypse, an unavoidable millenium, the imminence of man-made destruction as well as the promise of a new age.

Stylistically Chamberland's poems move from conventional typographic texts, organized in lines and stanzas, to montages of calligraphic poems strewn with newspaper clippings, photographs, quotations, rock-singers' lyrics, philosophers' thoughts, and news items. The attempt to fuse such diverse elements has been viewed as a reflection of their author's apocalyptic consciousness.

L'afficheur hurle is Chamberland's most frequently translated text. Malcolm Reid published a translation in *The shouting sign painters* (1972) and C.P. May translated extracts in *Ellipse* 8-9 (1971) under the title 'The poster-hanger howls'. Larry Shouldice has translated other poems in *Ellipse* 17 (1975). One of Chamberland's most famous critical essays, a political and critical commentary on the situation of Québec poetry in the fifties and sixties, was translated by Larry Shouldice as 'Founding the territory' and appeared in *Contemporary Quebec criticism* (1979). (See also ESSAYS IN FRENCH: 7.)

See Richard Giguère, 'Chamberland,

poète anthrope', *Lettres québécoises* 23 (Autumn 1981).   CAROLINE BAYARD

Champlain, Samuel de. See Writing in NEW FRANCE: 1.

Chapman, William (1850-1917). Born in Saint-François-de-la-Beauce, Canada East (Qué.), he studied at the Collège de Lévis and enrolled in the law school of Université Laval but never completed his courses. He became a businessman, an insurance broker, and then a journalist with *La Patrie* in 1883, and with *La Minerve* from 1884 to 1889; he also wrote for *La Vérité* and *Courrier du Canada*.

Chapman wrote six books of poetry: *Les Québecquoises* (Québec, 1876), *Les feuilles d'érable* (Montréal, 1890), *A propos de la guerre hispano-américaine* (Québec, 1898), *Les aspirations* (Paris, 1904), *Les rayons du nord* (Paris, 1910), and *Les fleurs de givre* (1912). A belated romantic of the Québec school, he was inspired both by his compatriots Octave CRÉMAZIE and Louis FRÉCHETTE and by Hugo, Gautier, Lamartine, François Coppée, and Longfellow—some of whose poems he translated. Preferring occasional verse to religious or love poetry, he never strove to perfect his craft: his thought lacks sustained elevation and his ponderous, wordy stanzas—chiefly alexandrines—are rarely lyrical or tender. He began with patriotic verses addressed to France, but gradually became fervently inspired by the landscapes of his native land: his best descriptions are of open spaces and of nature seen as violent and savage. Among his best poems are 'Janvier', 'La forêt vierge', 'Le lac dans les bois', 'Coucher de soleil', 'Le laboureur', 'La Beauce', 'L'Ile d'Orléans', 'Le Saguenay', and 'Le Saint-Laurent'.

Chapman's prose works, apart from his many magazine articles, include *Mines d'or de la Beauce* (Lévis, 1881); *Guide et souvenir de la St. Jean-Baptiste, Montréal* (Montréal, 1884); and two bitter attacks on the work of Louis Fréchette: *Le lauréat manqué—critique des oeuvres de M. Louis Fréchette* (Québec, 1894) and *Deux copains: réplique à Mm. Fréchette et Sauvalle* (Québec, 1894). Truculent, easily offended, irascible and violent, often narrow-minded and petty in his critical writing, Chapman was given to a polemical, flashy, and grandiloquent style that lacked taste and critical judgement.

MAURICE LEBEL

Charbonneau, Jean (1875-1960). Born in Montreal, the son of a carpenter, he was educated at the Collège Sainte-Marie and studied law at Université Laval. He later practised law and then pursued other activities. One of the founders of L'ÉCOLE LITTÉRAIRE DE MONTRÉAL, he is chiefly remembered for his poetry, but he was also the author of an important work on philosophy. The theatre was Charbonneau's first and persistent love and he wrote at least three (unpublished) plays: 'Zopyre' (1904), 'Les Emmurés' (1910), and 'La Mort de Tristan et d'Iseut' (n.d.). He published his first poem in *Le Samedi* under the pseudonym 'Delagny' (he later appeared as an actor under the same name). His first poetry collection, *Les blessures* (Paris, 1912), was attacked by the Catholic weekly *La Verité* as a threat to Christian belief, though its rather formal stanzas constitute chiefly a recall to classicism. The wounds of the title are ascribed in part to an 'unknown evil', but the main thrust of the often poignant stanzas is against the breach between past and present. *Les blessures* was followed by similar volumes: *L'âge de sang* (Paris, 1921), in which Charbonneau juxtaposes the hopes of civilization against the blood of the First World War, and *Les prédestinés* (1923), concerned with the idea and images of America and thought to be his best work. *L'ombre dans le miroir* (1925) speaks of the fountain of youth, and *La flamme ardente* (1928), perhaps his most metaphysical collection, is concerned with the discovery of the invisible world and the structure of visible nature. Charbonneau also published two other volumes of poems: *Tel qu'en sa solitude* (1940) and *Sur la borne pensive et L'ecrin de Pandore* (Paris, 1952). *Solitude*'s title suggests its theme, while *Pandore* is a long mythological poem that fills the second half of a volume whose other contents are varied. There are many unpublished poems in the archives at the University of Ottawa, as well as the manuscript of a novel, 'Tentative d'évasion', and a collection of prose writings, 'A l'ombre de l'oasis'.

Charbonneau's affiliations were strongly classical. In *L'École littéraire de Montréal* (1935) he recalls the literary movement as a revolt against the undisciplined romanticism that he and many of his friends thought to be widespread in both France and Québec. He sought a poetry less personal and more knowledgeable, and his inspiration was the Parnassian movement in France, which insisted on strict forms.

In *Des influences françaises au Canada* (3

vols, 1916-20)—for which he was made a laureate of the French Academy in 1922—Charbonneau deals at length with the state of philosophy in France and then with the situation in Canada, and attempts to associate philosophical tendencies and climates with social trends. He argues that there is a continuing tradition in Western civilization, which French thought had lost track of, that persists best, perhaps, in Québec. His philosophy has a Stoic tinge to it, though he appreciated Nietzsche and kept up with all the currents of European thought on visits to France.   LESLIE ARMOUR

Charbonneau, Robert (1911-67). Born in Montreal, he began his studies at the École Saint-Stanislas (1919-25) and continued at the Collège Sainte-Marie (1925-33), working during summer vacations as a labourer for the Canadian Pacific Railway. In 1933 he joined the Young Canada Movement. After a year of studies at the Université de Montréal, he received a diploma in journalism (1934). With Paul Beaulieu he founded La RELÈVE (1934-40), a literary review influenced by Jacques Maritain's neo-Thomism and E. Mounier's Personalism. During this period of the Depression the review proposed a humanistic transformation of the individual rather than social revolution.

To earn a living Charbonneau first worked as a journalist on *La Patrie* (1934-7), *Le Droit* (1937-8), and *Le Canada* (1938-42). In 1940 he founded, with Claude Hurtubise, Les Éditions de l'Arbre, which republished literary works that had been prohibited in France and young French-Canadian writers such as Roger LEMELIN, Jean-Jules RICHARD, and Yves THÉRIAULT. An affiliation with *La Relève* produced *La Nouvelle Relève* (1941-8). From here on Charbonneau divided his time between working as an editor and a writer. While convalescing from pleurisy in 1936 he had begun work on his first novel, *Ils posséderont la terre* (1941), for which he was awarded the Prix David. This work launched a series of psychological novels that were popular with the intellectuals of the forties and fifties. In an essay entitled *Connaissance du personnage* (1944), Charbonneau made known his aesthetic and philosophical positions, explaining that a novel's role was not to reflect an era or a society but to emphasize man's spiritual quest, his search for identity. He developed this theme in such novels as *Fontile* (1945) and *Les désirs et les jours* (1948), which describe interior

conflicts and the personal dramas of characters in search of an authenticity that eludes them. Their refusal to make a choice, their fear of action, their paralysis of will—making existence impossible—are typical concerns of the psychological novel about *la vie intérieure*, whose passive, forever inward-looking heroes cannot respond to worldly conventions.

Apart from his activities as editor and well-known writer (he received the Prix Duvernay for *Fontile* in 1945), Charbonneau helped found and direct the Académie canadienne-française (1944). As president of the Société des éditeurs (1945-8) he was a staunch supporter of French-Canadian literature, which he defended in a series of articles—later published in *La France et nous* (1947)—that placed him in opposition to certain French intellectuals. He also published a poetry collection, *Petits poèmes retrouvés* (1945).

Les Éditions de l'Arbre and *La Nouvelle Relève* were forced to terminate in 1948. After fourteen years of intense activity Charbonneau suddenly saw himself cut off from his usual literary functions. In 1949 he returned to his former post as journalist at *La Presse*, and from 1950 he performed numerous editorial and managerial functions for Radio-Canada. For many years his writing was confined to radio scripts: a drama entitled 'Précieuse Elizabeth' in 1949; adaptations of his last two novels in 1951; and eighteen radio talks or lectures on French-Canadian novelists, published in 1972. He returned to fiction with the short story 'Aucun chemin n'est sûr' (1959) and a novel, *Aucune créature* (1961), which reintroduced the romantic universe of the troubled hero. In *Chronique de l'âge amer* (1967) Charbonneau abandoned the psychological novel in favour of a thinly veiled semi-autobiographical narrative that recreated the literary generation between 1934 and 1936. Unfortunately he could not follow up on these disguised memoirs. In the midst of full activity, after having been named president of the Société des écrivains (1966), Charbonneau was fatally stricken by a heart attack.

See Jean-Charles Falardeau, *Notre société et son roman* (1972), and Madeleine Durocq-Poirier, *Robert Charbonneau* (1972).

See also NOVELS IN FRENCH 1940 TO 1959:2.   JACQUES MICHON

Charlebois, Jean (b. 1945). Born in Quebec City, he studied literature at the Université de Montréal. He now works as an editor, translator, proofreader, and researcher. In the last ten years he has produced six collections of poetry, all published by Les Éditions du Noroît of St Lambert, Qué.

Popèmes absolument circonstances incontrôlables (1972), *Tête de bouc* (1973), and *Tendresses* (1975) represent Charlebois's first phase and are marked by humour and whimsy, puns and buffoonery, a bantering and provocative tone. Nevertheless the author's sensitivity and a tender quality emerge, giving the love theme—inspired primarily by Paul Éluard—an important place in his work. *Hanches neige* (1977) is a pivotal book, composed of a script, a photoromance, a lampoon, a fictional interview with the author, and theatre dialogues, whose appearance on the page—a skilful assembly of quotations, photographs, advertising slogans, proverbs, and distortions of famous poems—is remarkably original. Here Charlebois's sense of parody and raillery is at its peak. In *Conduite intérieure* (1978) and *Plaine lune suivi de Corps fou* (1980) the sensuality in the language of love is accompanied by reflections on death, and the lighthearted tone of the first collections is replaced by a serious, pensive voice, increasingly aware of the uncertainties of life and love. Youthful bragging gives way to sober, adult reflection. The engaging tone and liveliness of the first collections endure, however, making Charlebois one of the foremost exponents of the new lyricism in Québec poetry.   RICHARD GIGUÈRE

Charlevoix, Pierre-François-Xavier de. See Writing in NEW FRANCE: 1.

Charron, François (b. 1952). Born in Longueuil, Qué., he began writing poetry in his teens; in 1975 he became interested in painting and has had several exhibitions. A member of the editorial board of *Chroniques*, he was also a co-founder of *Stratégies* and a contributor to *Dérives* and *La* BARRE DU JOUR. His closest literary ties, however, have been with the modernist writers associated with the publishing house and periodical *Les Herbes rouges*. He was awarded the Prix Nelligan for his poetry collection *Blessures* (1978). A prolific writer (over 15 published works since 1972), Charron is a leader of the Québec literary avant-garde. From a Marxist-Leninist approach, much influenced by PARTI PRIS and the first writings of Paul CHAMBERLAND, he has developed towards the more intimate one of *Toute parole m'éblouira* (1982), in which the couple

supersedes the collectivity as the new hope for survival. Charron manifests his desire to subvert any norm or 'doxa' in writing that is constantly renewed by means of breaking down language and submitting it to multiple experiments—a 'theoretical fiction' that removes all boundaries that separate theory of art and literature, poetry, history, ideology, subjectivism, political slogans, JOUAL, parody, and lyricism.

Charron's collections—*Dix-huit assauts* (1972), *Au 'sujet' de la poésie* (1972), *Projet d'écriture pour l'été 76* (1973), *Littérature/obscénités* (1974), and *Pirouette par hasard poésie* (1975)—either disparage traditional writings or make parodic assaults on earlier conventional writers; while *Enthousiasme* (1976) and *Propagande* (1977) call for both textual and political subversion. But *La traversée/le regard* (1973), *Persister et se maintenir dans les vertiges de la terre qui demeurent sans fin* (1974), *Du commencement à la fin* (1977), and *Feu* (1978) contain a lyricism that celebrates physical interaction in the loves and life of an artist who pictures himself as a 'sexed subject' and moves through an everchanging historical reality that can neither be annexed by any institution (such as the family or the nation) nor mythicized. The more recent collections—*Le temps échappé des yeux* (1979), *D'où viennent les tableaux?* (1980), and *1980* (1981)—explore poetically art theory, painters, and poets, seeking openness, extremism, and intensity. An intertextual dialogue (with Borduas's manifesto REFUS GLOBAL) launches *Peinture automatiste* précédé de *Qui parle dans la théorie?* (1979), in which Charron rediscovers both the relevance of the historical dimension of artistic creation and its autonomy *vis-à-vis* any norm or creed—automatism being the very expression of the artist's freedom.

The dialectic of creation and ideology inherent in *Refus global* is essential to Charron and reappears in *La passion d'autonomie: littérature et nationalisme* (1982), in which he attacks the nationalistic writings of his predecessors. His later work—particularly in *Blessures* (1980) and *Mystère* (1981)—shows a new feminine dimension that perceives the act of writing as a possible substitute for the Mother as opposed to the 'Law of the Father'.

Charron's entire work reflects an obsession with unity. Again and again it reconsiders the interaction between the creating subject and his place in history, using a diversity of expression that continually evolves against all norms and constraints.

See Philippe Haeck, 'Toute l'angoisse' and 'Soulèvement' in *Naissance de l'écriture québécoise* (1979), and Pierre Nepveu, 'François Charron, l'urgence de l'écriture' in *Lettres québécoises* 18 (Summer 1980).

MAROUSSIA AHMED

Châtillon, Pierre. See NOVELS IN FRENCH 1960 TO 1982: 3(f).

Chauveau, Pierre-Joseph-Olivier (1820-90). The precocious son of a Quebec City merchant, he attended the Petit Séminaire de Québec and at seventeen began to study law under Judge Hamel; he opened his own law office, after being admitted to the Bar, at twenty-one and received the degree of doctor of laws from McGill University in 1857. At twenty-four he was elected to the Québec House of Assembly. He was solicitor general in the Hincks-Morin ministry (1851), provincial secretary and QC (1853), minister of education (1866-7), and the first prime minister of the new province of Québec (1867-73). In 1873 he resigned to join the Senate, where he was made speaker. He resigned four years later and was named sheriff of Montreal district (1877-90). Chauvin founded in 1857 the Écoles normales in Montreal and Quebec, along with the *Journal de l'instruction publique* and its English counterpart, the *Journal of Education*. He was dean of the law faculty at Université Laval, Montreal, from 1884 to 1890. In 1848 he married Marie Louise Flore Masse and they had eight children.

Lawyer, administrator, politician, lecturer and orator, university professor, poet, novelist, biographer, historian, and bibliophile (his personal library was extensive), Chauveau was deeply involved in the intellectual life of his time. His most interesting publication is *Charles Guérin: roman des moeurs canadiennes* (Montréal, 1853), the fifth novel to appear in French Canada and one of the best novels of the nineteenth century. Plainly showing the influence of Chateaubriand, Balzac, and Hugo, it is a slight love story that unfolds over three years (1830-3) and ends unexpectedly and inexplicably, in the epilogue, at the Battle of Saint-Eustache in Dec. 1837. The novel has many defects, among them an insipid style that was fashionable at the time and much holding-forth on philosophy, politics, and socio-economics (though some of these observations still have force today). It is impressive, however, for its rich and precise vocabulary, for its use in dialogue of popular speech (employed here for the first time in French-Canadian fiction), and for its portrayal of the society of the day and its customs, with the occasional introduction of lively characters. Among Chauveau's other books are *Souvenirs et légendes* (Québec, 1877), a collection of poetry, and *François-Xavier Garneau: sa vie et ses oeuvres* (Montréal, 1883). MAURICE LEBEL

Chevalier, Henri-Émile (1828-79). Born at Châtillon-sur-Seine, France, he was imprisoned as the result of an article in which he attacked the government of Napoleon III. When freed, the republican journalist went to New York and for a year worked for the *Courrier des États-Unis*. In 1852 he arrived in Montreal, where he contributed articles to *Le Pays* and *La Patrie* and took an active part in the intellectual life of the city. He was one of the founders of *La Ruche littéraire*, a monthly periodical in which he published as serials his first novels: *La Huronne des Lorettes* (1854) and *L'Île de Sable* (1854), later published in Paris as *39 hommes pour une femme, épisode de la colonisation du Canada* (1862) and translated as *Legends of the sea: 39 men for one woman* (New York, 1862). Here the heroine, disguised as a man, is left on Sable Island with thirty-nine men, most of them mutineers; is kidnapped by a deaf mute, none other than her own father; and after five years of horrendous experiences is reunited with her love only to die in childbirth shortly afterwards. In 1860 Chevalier returned to France, where he wrote for various newspapers and continued to work on a series of novels—some thirty of them—that have the general title 'Drames de l'Amérique du Nord'. Though he was a great admirer of François-Xavier GARNEAU, Chevalier wrote books about Canada that have little to do with history but are adventure stories. The plot of *L'Île de sable* is no more melodramatic than those of his other books, and such titles as *Les mystères de Montréal* (Montréal, 1855), *Le pirate du Saint-Laurent* (Montréal, 1859), and *Le chasseur noir* (Paris, 1877) indicate his subject matter. Professor David Hayne considers Chevalier 'le roi du roman feuilleton au Canada'.

Beatrice Corrigan's article, 'Henri-Émile Chevalier and his novels of North America' (*Romantic Review*, XXXV, 3, 1944) contains a complete bibliography of Chevalier's Canadian works. PAULETTE COLLET

Chiasson, Herménégilde. See ACADIAN LITERATURE: 2(a).

Children's drama in English

Child, Philip (1898-1978). Born in Hamilton, Ont., the son of a major figure in that city's steel industry, Philip Albert Child attended schools in Germany and Switzerland. A student at Trinity College, University of Toronto, in 1917, he enlisted in the army and served as an artillery officer during the Great War. He returned to Trinity in 1919, taking a B.A. in 1921 and winning one of the first Moss Scholarships. He also won an affiliated B.A. at Christ's College, Cambridge, in 1921, and took an M.A. at Harvard in 1923. A lecturer in English at Trinity from then until 1926, he married Gertrude Potts, and they had two children. Work on his Harvard Ph.D. began in 1926 and was completed in 1928. He then worked for a time as a journalist and settlement worker in New York; in 1928 he taught for a year at the University of British Columbia before returning to Harvard, where he tutored and pursued his second occupation as a creative writer. In 1942 he returned to Toronto and was on the staff of Trinity College for the rest of his teaching career, latterly as Chancellor's Professor of English. He was president of the CANADIAN AUTHORS' ASSOCIATION in 1946.

Child's fiction is characterized by a surface realism that yields to a preoccupation with the visionary, the dreamlike and nightmarish, and the fabular. His first and most successful work, *Village of souls* (1933), a historical novel set in seventeenth-century New France, is less an examination of that society than a depiction of a modernist 'wasteland' through which a troubled hero passes in his search for some ground of being. Torn between two women (Lys, from France, and Anne, the half-Europeanized Indian who symbolizes the new Canadian environment), the *voyageur* Jornay ultimately assumes a passive role, since it is Lys's death, while nursing the inhabitants of an Indian village afflicted with smallpox, that throws him into permanent union with Anne. The disease-filled community offers a stark parody of the peaceful village of souls depicted in the Indian legend of life after death. At the high point of the novel, Lys appears to Jornay in a vision while he lies near death in a blizzard.

Its bleak setting marks *Village of souls* as post-war fiction. The grim experiences of war stamped themselves on Child's writing, especially on his second novel *God's sparrows* (1937, NCL 1978), and on a long poem on the war, *The wood of the nightingale* (1965), his last complete work. *God's sparrows* is a com-

bination of family saga and war novel and at its conclusion the hero, David Thatcher, is shattered by his combat experiences. Though he comes to terms in a dream with his steely *alter ego*, his cousin Quentin, the final image is one of battlefield desolation. *The wood of the nightingale* narrates in blank verse a variation on the story of *God's sparrows*. Dealing with the theme of doubling, and with a personal struggle against a universe of death, it concludes with a noble testament of humility and compassion—a passage that was read aloud at the author's funeral.

Stress, pain, and shock are familiar experiences in Child's subsequent novels. *Blow wind, come rack* (1945)—published under the pseudonym 'John Wentworth'—is a spy thriller in which an academic gets sucked into the violent world of counter-espionage. *Day of wrath* (1945) offers a grim account of a German Jew under Hitler. *Mr. Ames against time* (1949) concerns a father's efforts to save his son from a frame-up on a murder charge. A mystery novel written with compassion for its hero, an old man whose strongest enemy is time itself, it won the Ryerson Fiction Award and a Governor General's Award.

Child's most integrated narrative poem, *The Victorian house* (1951), funnels the break-up of the Anglo-Canadian cultural values of tradition and piety through the narrator's recollections of a family dwelling he finally refuses to sell.

In *Village of souls*, with its concern for European adaptation to the Canadian environment, and *The Victorian house*, with its concern for the loss of coherent social structures, Child reflected the cultural preoccupations of Upper Canada.

DENNIS DUFFY

Children's drama in English. Since the founding in 1953 of the first professional company performing for young people, Holiday Theatre of Vancouver, hundreds of scripts have been created or commissioned by many other such groups across Canada; they began to be published, however, only in 1972. While some writers have created plays of great power and joy that transcend severe limitations of place, time, and human resources, often a perceptive producer has been required to realize the stage potential of seemingly prosaic material. Most scripts have been written for specific theatre companies or occasions and are one-act plays, about 45 minutes long, tailored to fit between two bells in a school schedule. Weekend, holiday, or subscription-series presentations featured full-length plays such as *Anne of Green Gables* (1972), a musical by Norman Campbell adapted by Donald Harron from the novel by L.M. MONTGOMERY, which opened the Charlottetown Festival in 1965; or the Stratford Festival's first play for young people, *Inook and the sun* (1974) by Henry BEISSEL, produced in 1973, which borrows from both Japanese Bunraku puppet tradition and Inuit culture to create a strong poetic evocation of a young boy's quest for adulthood.

Frequently producers and artistic directors of young people's companies have invited writers well known in other media to contribute plays to their seasons. For Holiday Theatre Eric NICOL wrote *The clam made a face* (1972), a charming short participation play based on the potlatch and storytelling traditions of West Coast Indians, and *Beware the quickly who* (1973), written for Canada's Centenary, about a boy's and a nation's search for identity. Betty Lambert, who had written for radio, contributed *The riddle machine* (1974) to Holiday's centennial cross-Canada tour. Set in a space ship, it is about inner as well as outer space. *The dandy lion* (1972) and *The popcorn man* (1973)—sprightly musicals that have been repeatedly revived—were commissioned by Susan Rubes for the Young People's Theatre, Toronto, from radio writers Dodi Robb and Pat Patterson. Two other accomplished radio writers who have written plays for children are Len PETERSON, whose *Almighty voice* (1974) dramatizes one Indian's poignant struggle against the white man's code, and W.O. MITCHELL, whose *The devil's instrument* (1973) is the powerful story of a young man's revolt against the repressive rules of his Mennonite community.

Of the many scripts developed for a specific company with close collaboration between a director and a writer, one was James REANEY's *Names and nicknames* (1973), directed by John Hirsch and Robert Sherrin and produced at the Manitoba Theatre Centre in 1963. Using choral speech, improvisation, and mime, and creating its only 'scenery' with bodies and voices alone, it deploys an eclectic and unconventional array of lists, objects, rituals, rites of passage—characteristic of Reaney's theatre-pieces in general—and a list of names taken from the old speller of Reaney's father. The poet's craft evokes the clear conflict between good and evil and the deep feelings associated with names. Reaney's 'Listener Workshops' in London, Ont., resulted in three more plays by him for young people: *Apple butter*, a marionette play; *Geography match*; and *Ignoramus*. These three plays, along with *Names*, were published in one volume by Talonbooks in 1973 as *Apple butter and other plays for children*; all four were reprinted separately in 1979.

Some playwrights for children's theatre, learning their craft through the rapid creation of short scripts, have since written successful full-length plays for adult audiences. Rex Deverell has written shows for both children and adults for Regina's Globe Theatre, which was founded in 1966 by Ken and Sue Kramer to produce and tour the plays—containing elements of audience participation—of British producer and playwright Brian Way. Deverell used participation in *Shortshrift* (1974), whose political overtones were evident in the children's efforts to help the actors 'rebuild' the town hall in opposition to an impersonal government bureaucracy, while his *Sarah's play* (1975) uses a 'computer' into which the audience feeds data by whispering words from their seats in a circle on the floor. Deverell's plays, frequently set in Saskatchewan but successfully performed elsewhere, also include *The Copetown City kite crisis* (1974), *The Shinbone General Store caper* (1977), *The uphill revival* (1977), and *Superwheel* (1979), a satirical musical with songs by Geoffrey Ursell about man and the motor car. Paddy Campbell, an actress in the first Globe Theatre touring company, copied the style of Brian Way in her first play *Chinook* (1973), which uses the Indian concept of personifying the seasons as Ice Woman and Fire Woman and is about loyalty, bravery, and respect for tradition, while also explaining how the chinook wind got its name. Another participation play by Campbell, *Too many kings* (1978), was written for the Arts Centre Company, Calgary, and directed by Douglas Riske. Riske, Lucille Wagner, and Paddy Campbell founded Alberta Theatre Projects in 1972 to produce plays for children based on Alberta's history and to be presented in the historic Canmore Opera House in Calgary's Heritage Park. Campbell wrote many of the company's early scripts, including *Under the arch* (1976), which uses a nineteenth-century music-hall format, with music by William Skolnik, to dramatize the history of western Canada. Carol BOLT is another playwright who has written many plays for young people. Her scripts for the Young People's Theatre, Toronto, include *Cyclone Jack* (1972), *My best friend is twelve feet high* (1972), *Tangleflags* (1974), and *Maurice* (1974).

The Green Thumb Theatre for Young People, of Vancouver, B.C., was founded in 1972 by Dennis Foon and Jane H. Baker to develop and produce new scripts for children. Their plan was to offer a variety of theatrical styles and to present plays about contemporary problems that confront young people. This led to a rich mix in repertoire, including Foon's *Heracles* (1978), a verse-drama about the ambiguities of heroism and man's relationship to his gods; *Raft baby* (1978), which tells the story (possibly apocryphal) of a baby found on a raft by a trapper in British Columbia in 1890, using songs and story to evoke the life of towns and trappers, and underlines the dependency of children on the integrity of adults; and *The Windigo* (1978), based on an old Ojibwa belief about the spirit of hunger that visits the empty stomach and can induce unsuccessful hunters to kill their loved ones. Also for Green Thumb, Campbell Smith worked with teenagers to create, write, and direct *Juve* (1979), a rock musical with monologues, songs, and scenes based on autobiographical material. Irene Watts, whose *A chain of words* (1978) uses Japanese folk tales and elements of Kabuki theatre traditions, was commissioned by Green Thumb to write *Tomorrow will be better* (1980), composed of stories, thoughts, and poems created by British Columbia children; both plays exemplify a growing trend to involve young people more directly in the creation of works intended for them.

Ottawa's Great Canadian Children's Theatre Company specializes in plays based on local history. Three scripts developed for its troupe were published in the anthology *Playmakers: adventures in Canadian drama* (1980): *The secret of the golden fiddle* by Robin Mathews; *The curse of the Viking grave*, Mathews' adaptation of Farley MOWAT's novel; and *Shantymen of Cache Creek* by Arthur Milner. For Edmonton's Citadel-on-Wheels, Isabelle Foord wrote *Shaman* (1973), *A dream of sky people* (1973), *Junkyard* (1973), and *Say Hi to Owsley* (1975). Jan Truss wrote *A very small rebellion* (1978) and *The judgement of Clifford Sifton* (1979) for Alberta Theatre Projects, and *Oomeraghi oh!* (1978) for the Department of Drama at the University of Calgary. Other plays written for specific companies were Betty Jane Wylie's *Kingsayer* (1978) for the Manitoba

Theatre Centre and *The old woman and the pedlar* (1978) for the Young People's Theatre of Toronto; and Bonnie LeMay's *Boy who has a horse* (1974) and Gloria Sawai's *Neighbor* (1982) for Alberta Theatre Projects.

Although a play of consequence is seldom published without first being professionally produced, some excellent plays have been performed but not published. Evelyn Garbury, founding director of the Mermaid Theatre of Wolfville, N.S., has written numerous plays that especially fit the company's resources for which the founding designer, Tom Miller, created masks and giant puppets that were so integral to Mermaid's style that these plays would seldom suit another company. The team of Sheldon ROSEN, director Yurek Bogajewicz, and actors Stuart Mentin, Menlo Skye MacFarland, David McLean, and Patricia Best created *Shadowdance* for Green Thumb in 1977, a play that was widely admired, but for which no agreement was reached among its creators on royalty rights or credits. Also unpublished are many historical plays written by David MacKenzie for the Carousel Theatre of St Catherines, Ont., as well as the innovative and colourful scripts by Rick McNair written for Stage-Coach Players (the touring arm of Theatre Calgary), and the evocative creations of Elizabeth Gorrie, artistic director of Kaleidoscope Theatre, Victoria B.C.   JOYCE DOOLITTLE

Children's drama in French. Theatre for young people is a very recent development in Québec. In the 1950s and early sixties adult theatre companies in Montreal—such as Les Compagnons de Saint-Laurent, Le Théâtre-Club, Les Apprentis-Sorciers, and Les Saltimbanques—took special pains to produce plays that would delight young audiences. Actors and producers, however, were faced with a serious problem: the lack of scripts for such productions. Theatre companies, therefore, tried to interest authors of children's literature in writing for the theatre.

In 1960 Le Théâtre-Club of Montreal succeeded in acquiring and producing a play by Luan Asslani, *Les trois désirs de Coquelicot* (1973). Inspired by the popularity in children's theatre of fairy tales—especially those of Charles Perrault—Asslani created, in *Les trois désirs*, a young hero whose battles with elves and fairies teach him to have a sense of generosity towards others. The first company to devote itself entirely to productions for young audiences was Le Théâtre pour

Children's drama in French

Enfants de Québec (1965-70) of Quebec City. Ably directed by Pauline Geoffrion, it resolutely adopted a policy favouring the creation of original plays for children, and produced works by Monique Corriveau, Roland Lepage, Patrick Mainville, and Pierre MORENCY—the only one of these authors to publish his plays for children. Morency's *Tournebire et le malin Frigo* (1978) is typical of this company's productions, which encouraged audience participation in games featuring robots, or heroes of 'soft' science-fiction adventures that usually occurred in mysterious laboratories inhabited by absent-minded professors.

Between 1970 and 1980 the number of children's plays written both by collectives and by individual authors increased greatly, though not many have been published. When André Cailloux—whose plays are published by Éditions Leméac—assumed the artistic direction of the youth section of Montreal's Théâtre du Rideau Vert, 'Manteau d'Arlequin 5-15', in 1970, he elected to produce his own plays. *Frizelis et Gros Guillaume* (1973) and *Frizelis et la Fée Doduche* (1973) both take place in a land called Milieu, the realm of Frizelis, king of elves. This kingdom, in which the woodcutter, Gros Guillaume, and his wife Charlotte continually become mired or lost, is coveted by the greedy Fée Doduche. Magic objects appear and disappear; characters become instantly and mysteriously transformed; voyages are made into space and time; and all these activities are punctuated by the verbal participation of the children in the audience. Magic is also featured in Cailloux's *François et l'oiseau du Brésil; ou La comédie des erreurs* (1977), in which identity-changes and tricks of illusion play a central part. Although these three plays are light and highly entertaining, they tend to confuse credulous youngsters who cannot always distinguish—especially in the theatre—between the real and the imaginary. Cailloux turned to educational subjects—pollution, respect for the past, astronomy, geography—for two more plays: *L'Île-au-Sorcier* (1974), a folkloric tale in which the young hero is led by the fabulous Raccoon and Renaak to discover a magic bracelet that controls the weather; and *Tombé des étoiles* (1977), which—less felicitously—adopts the situations and style of the 'police-thriller'. In these two plays the author attempts, with only partial success, to combine an exciting plot with serious content.

Treatment of serious themes is characteristic of the development of young people's drama from 1973 to the present. Contemporary playwrights strive consciously to write plays that will establish links between the spectacle on the stage and the experience of the children in the audience. Marie-Francine Hébert, long associated with Montreal's Le Théâtre de la Marmaille, has written *Cé tellement 'cute' des enfants* (1980), a pioneering play in which children playing in back-alleys on a school holiday fail to conform wholly to their elders' idealized view of them: using a language so frank and realistic that it amounts to a social document and a political statement, the children set up an infernal racket of disputes and misunderstandings. Altogether different from Hébert's previous play—the poetic and gently amusing *Une ligne blanche au jambon* (1974)—*Cé tellement 'cute'* is a landmark of the 'new children's theatre' which, since 1975, has concentrated on reflecting the realities that children and adolescents know and recognize: this is real theatre for real audiences. *Un jeu d'enfants* (1980), created by Montreal's Le Théâtre de Quartier, is about a group of children who are unhappy because they have no playground, and portrays their reactions to having their schoolyard turned into a parking lot. The child-characters in *On est capable* (1981), by Louis-Dominique Lavigne, manoeuvre bravely through a world of fears and taboos; written in a poetico-realist style, the play encourages youngsters to recognize their own talents and strengths and urges them to dare, to hope, and to have confidence. *On n'est pas des enfants d'école* (to be published), by Gilles Gauthier in collaboration with Le Théâtre de la Marmaille, stresses the fact that school is not the only place to learn, and that it can be a centre of sharing and belonging. *Histoire de Julie qui avait une ombre de garçon* (1982), by Denis Chouinard and Nicole-Marie Rhéault, tells of a touching encounter in the park between Julie, a tomboy, and the clownish but gentle François, who are both the butts of their uncomprehending parents.

Regarde pour voir (1981), a creation of Montreal's Le Théâtre de l'Oeil, is a puppet play designed to make this mode of expression accessible to children: within the framework of preparations being made by Lise and Jocelyn for their own neighbourhood puppet-show, it describes the history of puppetry, shows how puppets can be made from second-hand materials, and presents sketches showing examples of what can be achieved. Puppets are also used in *La couleur chante un pays* (1981), by Diane Bouchard *et. al.*, which introduces the audience to the history of Québec painting. Characters created by Québec artists are brought to life through puppets and masks that are faithful to the period and style of each artist represented.

For very young children—ages three to six—Suzanne Lebeau has written a very fine poetic piece that uses sound and rhythm to great advantage: *Une lune entre deux maisons* (1980) employs a flashback method to show the gradual shedding of fears and growth of friendship between two very dissimilar persons, Plume and Taciturne.

Since 1950 authors have left behind the conventions of the fairy tale and television and built new themes and structures, styles and forms, suited to young audiences. Children's drama in Québec has evolved into a specific genre, worthy of appreciation and analysis.

See the *Répertoire des textes* (1981) of Le Centre d'Essai des Auteurs dramatiques; Hélène Beauchamp, *L'histoire et les conditions du théâtre pour enfants au Québec 1950-1980* (Université de Sherbrooke thesis, 1982); Hélène Beauchamp, *Le théâtre à la p'tite école* (1980), a study for the Ministry of Cultural Affairs for Québec.   HÉLÈNE BEAUCHAMP

Children's literature in English. 1. THE EARLY YEARS. The growing awakening in early Victorian England to the imaginative and intellectual possibilities of literature for children was slow to develop in Canadian writing. This is not surprising in a country whose scattered population was essentially non-literate and composed mainly of recent immigrants and exiles, explorers and visitors. Among the earliest publications for children was *The* SNOW DROP; *or, Juvenile magazine* (Montreal, 1847-53), which could have been published in London, with its moral and religious tales, indifferent verse, and historical and natural-history anecdotes that pointed a lesson—though its six-year duration suggests that it was well received. Catharine Parr TRAILL's *The Canadian Crusoes: a tale of the Rice Lake Plains* (London, 1852)—reprinted as *Lost in the backwoods: a tale of the Canadian forest* (London, 1882)—reveals two characteristics that were to become constants in our best literature for children: a love of the vast though dangerous land and of its animal inhabitants, and (Margaret ATWOOD's survival theory notwithstanding) a determination to come to terms with the land, exuberantly and suc-

cessfully—not only in forest, but on plain, sea, tundra, and ice. Traill's account of three young people lost in the Ontario wilderness, north of what in now Cobourg, Ont., is not the work of a genuine storyteller—her Christian moralizing takes over what plot there is—but *Canadian Crusoes*, like its English predecessor, was based on a true event and can now be seen to have a genuinely Canadian sensibility in its portrayal of the Canadian landscape and of children's participation in it.

It was left to a temporary resident, R.M. BALLANTYNE, to see, and use successfully, the possibilities of Canadian subject-matter in strengthening the fairly new British tradition of adventure stories for boys. His gift for creating strong plots and spirited protagonists, for gripping narrative and lively descriptive detail—beginning with *The young fur traders* (London, 1856)—would make him one of the leading practitioners of the genre in the nineteenth century. Ballantyne's interest in only the external features of character and incident was shared by countless other writers of outdoor adventures who followed him, including James DE MILLE, the author of numerous children's books, including *B.O.W.C.; a book for boys* (Boston, 1869), and other books about the B.O.W.C. ('Brothers of the White Cross'). Surprisingly for its time in Canada, this is a school story; but most of the action takes place outside the school, sailing and adventuring on the Bay of Fundy in Nova Scotia. The boys have stereotyped companions, such as the hearty but obtuse ship's captain and an equally obtuse but good-natured 'darky'. That Canadian writers of boys' books in this period were not interested in individualizing their characters is also apparent in the works of James MacDonald OXLEY, the author of twenty books for boys, including *Up among the ice floes* (Philadelphia, 1890), *Fife and drum at Louisbourg* (Boston, 1899), and *L'Hasa at last* (London, 1902), an unusual tale about an expedition to the Forbidden City. The Rev. Egerton Ryerson YOUNG was a direct heir of Catharine Parr Traill in his frank use of the outdoor adventure story to inculcate Christian precepts in *Three boys in the Wild North Land, Summer* (Toronto, 1896), and its sequel *Winter adventures of three boys in the Great Lone Land* (London, 1899). His son and namesake, Egerton Ryerson Young (1869-1962), also wrote books for boys—including *Duck Lake* (1905), *Just dogs* (1926), and *Three Arrows: the young buffalo-hunter* (1932), which are almost carbon-copies of his father's works. Norman DUNCAN carried outdoor adventure to the sea, writing in *The adventures of Billy Topsail* (1906) a popular story about young Billy's travails and adventures in and on the waters off Newfoundland, and his acceptance by the crew of a deep-sea fishing vessel. Billy's adventures were included in school readers until the 1930s. Ernest Thompson SETON's TWO LITTLE SAVAGES: *being the adventures of two boys who lived as Indians and what they learned* (1906)—set in the bush country around Lindsay, Ont.—is the most enduring and the finest of these outdoor adventure stories, bringing together Seton's knowledge as a naturalist, his competence as a writer for the young, and his skill as an artist (his marginal drawings are an integral part of the book).

Books about animals have been a Canadian specialty, and in this period one such book became a bestseller and is still read today. BEAUTIFUL JOE: *an autobiography* (Philadelphia, 1894) by Marshall SAUNDERS resembles in form and purpose Anna Sewell's *Black Beauty* (1877), but it is about a homely dog (rather than a handsome horse) whose powers of speech are frequently devoted to moralizing. A new and comparatively realistic trend in fictionalizing animal behaviour was initiated by two other Canadian writers. Ernest Thompson Seton showed true originality in his WILD ANIMALS I HAVE KNOWN (New York, 1898), in which he created a new genre, the animal biography—a genuine native product that eventually influenced the animal story around the world. Charles G.D. ROBERTS—who had previously published *Earth's enigmas: a book of animal and nature life* (Boston, 1896)—used the same approach in his *The kindred of the wild* (1902). The stories in the Seton and Roberts books are of course fictional; but, unlike previous animal stories, they are so closely based on knowledge and observation of wild animals in their own environments as to be almost documentaries. Seton's stories are written in the matter-of-fact style of a professional naturalist, while Roberts' stories—based on his boyhood experiences in the woods of New Brunswick—are the somewhat romantic tales of a literary artist. Both authors used the form of the animal biography to relate the thoughts and emotions of their subjects, as well as their instincts (and both have been criticized for the anthropomorphism in their stories). Their fascinating detailed descriptions, and their ability to arouse emotions in their readers, have kept *Wild animals* and *Kindred of the Wild* very much alive as children's books. Seton and Roberts followed these early publications with many others in the same vein. In between these two books came W.A. FRASER's now almost unknown *Mooswa and others of the boundaries* (1900), a story that has many echoes of Kipling's *Jungle books* but also reflects a deep knowledge of animal life as Fraser observed it in the Athabasca region of Alberta. Despite its convention of employing animals that converse intelligently and colloquially, it is a novel of lasting appeal—and unique of its kind in Canadian literature for its lack of sentimentality, its humour, emotion, and mystical bonding of animals and humans.

In the turn-of-the-century period, two Canadian authors had great success with domestic fiction that was both sentimental and informed with Christian uplift (like some English books in the Edwardian period). GLENGARRY SCHOOLDAYS (1902) by Ralph Connor (Charles William GORDON) was written for adults, but its youthful characters, schoolhouse scenes, and descriptions of pioneer activities in which children were involved quickly captured the interest of the young. Connor's sentimental look backwards to pioneer days in Glengarry Country, Ont., gave him ample opportunity for some gentle proselytizing, but this never quite detracts from the force of his narrative skill or his ability to arouse emotion. *Glengarry schooldays* remains in print and can still be read with pleasure. This cannot be said of Nellie McCLUNG's *Sowing seeds in Danny* (1908), whose herione, twelve-year-old Pearlie Watson, is closely related to the pious and sacrificial Elsie Dinsmore. Yet McClung shared with Connor an ability to write vividly about a particular setting, in this case the small-town and farm life of Manitoba.

L.M. MONTGOMERY wrote the most famous of all Canadian children's books, ANNE OF GREEN GABLES (1908). Montgomery certainly belongs to the 'sweetness and light' school of Saunders, Connor, and McClung, but in the whole stream of Edwardian books for children—filled with the unbearable goodness of Lord Fauntleroy, Elsie Dinsmore, Pollyanna, and others—Anne sounded an original and refreshing note. Owing to pressures exerted by her publisher, Montgomery turned out many books of sticky sweetness that are best forgotten; but even these contain effective lyrical passages on the natural beauty of Prince

Edward Island, and cast a humorous look at adult behaviour. Her Emily books—*Emily of New Moon* (1923), *Emily climbs* (1925), and *Emily's quest* (1927)—which appear to be largely autobiographical, are outstanding examples of realistic domestic novels for the young that are surprising for the period in not ignoring such manifestations of the adult world as the broken family, closet skeletons, family feuds, tensions, and the rigid standards of period and place. Montgomery had a sharp ear for dialogue; and though her books are not strongly plotted, she manages to keep reader interest to the very end. True to her period, and to the canons of children's literature of the time, Montgomery was a moralist; but unlike most of her contemporaries, she was not doctrinaire.

In many ways the early period summarized above represents a high plateau of Canadian children's literature that in terms of originality, popularity, and lasting appeal has rarely been attained since. Very few titles by new authors were published between the early part of the century and the 1940s. The only memorable book in this period was *Sajo and her beaver people* (1935) by Grey Owl (George Stansfeld BELANEY). Another strongly plotted animal story, it differs from its Canadian predecessors in showing a highly emotional link between children and wild animals, as well as in using entirely naturalistic descriptions of the behaviour and habitat of beavers.

The leading titles of the modern period, to the present, will be discussed below by genre.

2. THE OUTDOOR ADVENTURE STORY. The outdoor adventure story (with male protagonists) has continued to attract major writers. Roderick L. HAIG-BROWN's *Starbuck Valley winter* (1943), with its expert woodlore and affectionate descriptions of the wild terrain of British Columbia, would seem at first glance to be in the direct, extrovert tradition of BALLANTYNE. But when Haig-Brown had his protagonist sacrifice his whole winter's catch on the traplines to speed his injured friend to medical help on a long and dangerous canoe trip, he added a moral dimension to the outdoor tale. And in showing that the young man's path to heroism was a process of development rather than a melodramatic change of heart, he also brought Canadian children's literature into the modern age. While *Starbuck Valley winter*, and its sequel *Saltwater summer* (1948), are filled with information—from

skinning a buck to seining—Haig-Brown's convincing style never veers into pedagogy.

The same solid substance and feeling for the land underlies the works of Farley MOWAT. At his peak in writing for children—with *Lost in the Barrens* (1956), *The dog who wouldn't be* (1957), *Owls in the family* (1961), and *The black joke* (1962)—he well deserved to be called the 'Mr Canada' of children's literature. In addition to his knowledge and skills as a naturalist and conservationist, Mowat's contributions to the adventure story were tight plots, a page-turning pace, and a larger-than-life quality that are the marks of the genuine storyteller. *Owls in the family* and *The dog who wouldn't be* brought a welcome note of humour to children's fiction, along with gentle irony and satire. Mowat's absence from the children's literary scene for the last twenty years is regrettable, although many children quickly move on to his adult books, such as *Never cry Wolf*. For a short time David WALKER, in *Dragon Hill* (1963) and *Pirate Rock* (1969), appeared to be taking the adventure story down a wider path: both books combine outdoor activities with penetrating scenes of domestic life; they have unusual, highly climactic plots, introspective protagonists, and are written in a sharper, more cinematic style than was customary at the time. However, like Mowat, David Walker seems to have abandoned writing for the young.

The modern exponent of the environmental adventure story is James HOUSTON who, beginning with *Tikta'Liktak* (1965), has produced a substantial body of work rooted in Inuit life. *Tikta'Liktak* represents the essence of the frozen Arctic, as the desert-island story represents the exotic southern seas. From floating ice-pan to barren island, a young Inuit uses all the skills he has—and a bit more—to live and to return to his mainland home. Although the story is based on an actual adventure, Houston has clothed it in the dignified and impersonal language of legend to make a classic tale. His *The white archer* (1967) is about another young Inuit who finally gives up his planned revenge upon an Indian tribe who slaughtered his family and abducted his sister. The most memorable of all Houston's books, it deals, in a simple yet moving style, with the achievement of inner power and discipline. Its concentration on character development makes it seem more modern than his later book, *Frozen fire* (1977), which has the old-hat ploy of two boys of differing backgrounds learning from one another as they fight for survival, and the equally unoriginal major theme of a culture clash between Inuit and white man.

3. THE REALISTIC ANIMAL STORY. Canadian children's literature is filled with animal lore, but the true animal biography, as realized by SETON and ROBERTS, has not attracted many modern writers, although its natural appeal to the young and its timeless quality give it almost in-built success. Roderick L. HAIG-BROWN in *Silver: the life of an Atlantic salmon* (1931) produced a tour-de-force in making the life-cycle of a salmon interesting; but it now appears that the presence of the 'Good Fisherman', with his adult philosophies on sportsmanship, has less interest for the young. Haig-Brown's *Ki-Yu: a story of panthers* (1934; also published as *Panther*), about a duel between hunter and animal, is more reportage than literary craft. In 1960 the sentimentality and popularity of Marshall SAUNDERS' *Beautiful Joe* (although not its didacticism) resurfaced in Sheila Burnford's *The incredible journey* (1960), which arouses more emotion than credulity. The true heir of Seton and Roberts is Cameron Langford, whose *The winter of the fisher* (1972) is a distinguished full-length animal biography in which a one-year-old fisher eludes both the impersonal dangers of the wilderness and the calculated pursuit of the trapper.

4. FANTASY. The best fantasies for children have been bred in Great Britain—the land of romantic and bloody history and of myth, legend, and poetry. Apart from its Indian and Inuit legends, Canadian literature lacks most of the components that make up the stuff of fantasy, which is fundamentally a literature of place—there has to be a place to go to, or even to come from. Our few fantasists have wisely used the Canadian terrain for their 'other worlds', and have even managed to make a virtue of its vastness and anonymity.

Catherine Anthony CLARK set her six fantasies in, on, and around the towns, mountains, valleys, lakes, and rivers of British Columbia. In her first book, *The golden pine cone* (1951), her children are at home in their natural environment, but are able to step lightly into a quasi-magical world of Lake Snakes, Rock Pucks, Ice Maidens, and Indian spirits. Sometimes, as in *The one-winged dragon* (1955), Clark introduces the fabulous, such as a Chinese dragon; but in so doing she only shows Canada as the multi-ethnic land that it is. She is a storyteller in the traditional manner, using an easy-flowing style to create exciting quest plots that move to a climax and end with a satisfying resolution.

Ruth NICHOLS, who has written two fantasies for children—*A walk out of the world* (1969) and *The marrow of the world* (1972)—is steeped in the tradition of C.S. Lewis and J.R.R. Tolkien. These influences put her books in the realm of epic fantasy rather than in that of lighter magic espoused by Catherine Anthony Clark. Nichols' heroines face genuine evil—its outer manifestations in *A walk out of the world*, and its inner destructiveness in *The marrow of the world*. But as in the works of Clark, Nichols' landscapes appear to participate in the action and the mood. In tune with the plot, her settings move from the light woods of Vancouver, across waters, mountains, and grasslands (*A walk out of the world*), to the rugged lake country around Georgian Bay, Ont. (*The marrow of the world*). Her settings are distinctly and distinctively Canadian, but her other-world characters are borrowed from English folklore and fantasy—though they fit well into their New-World setting. Nichols' style is more mannered and formal than Clark's, but it suits her greater sophistication in the construct of fantasy. Our latest fantasy, Janet Lunn's *The root cellar* (1980), is more in the tradition of Clark than of Nichols in that the fantasy is secondary to realistic events—in the case of Lunn's book, the American Civil War. While it is an interesting experiment, it lacks that essential component of fantasy that is present in her first book, *Double spell* (1968) (also published as *Twin spell*)—the knife-edge of terror.

5. INDIAN AND INUIT LEGENDS. The 1960s, which brought so many changes to children's literature, especially some emanating from the United States, was marked in Canada by the flowering of an indigenous tradition: the Indian and Inuit legend. Early Indian collections were few in number, the most important and memorable being Pauline JOHNSON's *Legends of Vancouver* (1911) and Cyrus Macmillan's *Canadian wonder tales* (1918) and *Canadian fairy tales* (1922), the two latter titles being reprinted in 1974 as *Canadian wonder tales*. In retrospect it can be seen that the question of how indigenous tales were to be retold, especially for children, was not to be easily answered. Although Pauline Johnson was herself half Mohawk, *Legends of Vancouver* is still a book in translation, since she recorded the legends

from the halting English of a West Coast chief. Cyrus Macmillan cast his tales in the style of the romantic European fairy tale, with the result that almost all come across as good stories, which certainly made them more appealing to the young; but their polished narratives are more European in flavour than Canadian. Retellers of the 1960s were a group of non-natives who in various books, and within a specific Indian group, undertook to give meaning, brevity, and coherence to what appeared (to the non-native) to be a large, unwieldy, fragmented, rough-hewn body of anecdotal material. These books were Frances Fraser's *The bear who stole the Chinook* (1959, Blackfoot), Robert Ayre's *Sketco the raven* (1961, West Coast), Christie HARRIS's *Once upon a totem* (1963, West Coast), Kathleen Hill's *Glooscap and his magic: legends of the Wabanaki Indians* (1963), and Dorothy Reid's *Tales of Nanabozho* (1963, Ojibway). This trend has continued to the present with Christie Harris's *Mouse woman and the vanished princesses* (1976) and its sequels, and Gail Robinson's *Raven the trickster* (1981).

Leaving aside the problems of translation, authenticity, and whether or not such tales can really be interpreted by people outside the native culture, these works have made some of the finest and most important of the legends—such as 'The mountain goats of Temlaham' and 'How raven brought fire to the people'—available to a wide audience. Furthermore, the natives—both Indian and Inuit—have now begun recalling and collecting their own tales. The results can be seen in such works as *Tales from the longhouse* (1973), told by Indian children in British Columbia, and Pitseolak's mythic *Pictures out of my life* (1971), in which an elderly Inuit artist tells of life 'before there were many white men'.

The most notable and pleasurable collection, in terms of appeal to children, has been *Son of Raven, son of Deer: fables of the Tse-shaht people* (1967) by the West Coast Indian, George Clutesi. His stories often seem closer to Aesop's fables than to the main body of Indian legend, but they serve the chief purpose of the oral tradition: to transmit the manners and mores of a society to the next generation.

The late 1960s and 1970s brought a welcome innovation in this genre: the single illustrated legend. Conspicuous here both for simple and direct retelling, and brilliant collage illustrations, is the team of William Toye and the illustrator Elizabeth Cleaver in

The mountain goats of Temlaham (1969), *How summer came to Canada* (1969), *The loon's necklace* (1977), and *The fire stealer* (1979). Some Inuit legends were simply and dramatically retold by Ronald Melzak in *The day Tuk became a hunter & other Eskimo stories* (1967) and *Raven, creator of the world* (1970), while the first Inuit-legend picture-book, *Kiviok's magic journey: an Eskimo legend*, was retold and illustrated by James HOUSTON, in 1973.

6. HISTORICAL FICTION. Canadian writers know, and have written about, their history—almost to a dreary extent—but few writers of historical fiction have understood the *art* of fiction. One problem may be that Canada's history is so well documented that writers have seen little need to invent; frequently plot and character are mere adjuncts to historical events, with little life or colour of their own. This approach is seen most clearly in the works of the prolific John Hayes in such books as *Flaming prairie* (1965), on the Northwest Rebellion of 1885, and *The steel ribbon* (1967), on the building of the CPR. Our two finest historical novels, Edith Lambert Sharp's *Nkwala* (1958) and Roderick L. HAIG-BROWN's *The whale people* (1962), are set in a time before recorded history. Both describe West Coast Indian life and are concerned with the theme of responsibility, that of a boy towards his tribe. Both writers are steeped in anthropological research, but they manage to show what early Indian societies were like as a natural part of the story, while also evoking strong associations with boys who succeed in 'finding' themselves, and their place in the world around them.

Most of our writers of historical fiction have simply involved young men or teenagers in the large events of Canadian history. A few, however, have injected a note of freshness into the genre by focusing on the characters themselves rather than on the historical setting. Mary Alice and John Downie in *Honor bound* (1971), while using a typical background—the flight of Loyalists after the American War of Independence and their settling in Ontario—create a believable family, two very natural children, a bit of mystery, and a pair of interesting villains. Bill Freeman in *The shantymen of Cache Lake* (1975) describes an unusual piece of social history as a group of Ontario lumbermen attempt to form a trade union in the 1920s; the plot is enlivened by two spirited children, and the illustrations, which are contemporary photographs of lumber camps, give the story the feel of a documentary. Other unusual and more recent contributions to the genre are Barbara Smucker's *Underground to Canada* (1977) and *Days of terror* (1980). The main thrust of each story is outside of Canada, although both books describe journeys to Canada. *Underground to Canada*, as its title suggests, concerns the escape from Southern slavery of two young black girls via the route that came to be known as the 'underground railway'. *Days of terror* is set in Russia during the Revolution when the Mennonites were terrorized into immigrating to Canada and the United States. These books—a triumph of the holding power of actual events—are a model of their kind in their skilful use of selective detail and their appealing young characters, who are the victims of history but survive its outrages.

7. HISTORY AND BIOGRAPHY. Few outstanding Canadian works of history and biography are available to children, a rather strange (and unfortunate) situation in a country that has produced many eminent historians and biographers in the adult field. One notable example—providing almost a groundplan for authentic and dramatically presented history—is William Toye's *The St Lawrence* (1959), which has the added advantage of being visually attractive, with bold, stylized drawings and maps and many halftone illustrations. In the late 1950s and early 1960s a large slice of the Canadian past and its colourful figures was served up in over thirty books of the 'Great Stories of Canada' series. Inevitably, because of their didactic purpose, these books tended to make all people and all events sound alike. However, there were a few examples of authentic and lively historical writing. Pierre Berton in *The Golden Trail: the story of the Klondike* (1954) and Marjorie Wilkins Campbell in *The Nor'Westers: the fight for the fur trade* (1961) rose above the series obstacle of presenting history to young people because they are professional writers and experts on their periods. The series idea continued in the 1970s with 'Canadian Lives', chiefly political biographies on such figures as John A. Macdonald, Louis Riel, Lester Pearson, *et al.*; both accurate and readable, they were intended for an older age group than the 'Great Stories of Canada', which frequently indulged in fictional conversations in order to entice readers. History for young children is best represented by William Toye's *Cartier discovers the St Lawrence* (1971), which is a successful attempt to recount an important

event in our history as well as to lavish the utmost visual attractiveness on it with large picture-book illustrations by Laszlo Gal. A strong graphic appeal is also the hallmark of some autobiographies and glimpses of social history for younger children. In *A child in prison camp* (1971) Shizuye Takshima illustrated and recounted, in a restrained style that tends to heighten emotion, her memories of her life as a child internee in British Columbia during the Second World War. The noted Ukrainian-Canadian painter William Kurelek both wrote and illustrated *A prairie boy's winter* (1973) and *A prairie boy's summer* (1975), which are nostalgic childhood scenes of farm and school life, work and play, against the Manitoba skies. Other strongly pictorial reminiscences are Ethel Vineberg's *Grandmother came from Dworitz* (1969) and *Pitseolak: pictures out of my life* (1971). The visual aspects of all these books attract young readers especially, but in their quiet look at their respective ethnic backgrounds they are valuable and memorable reflections of our multi-cultural society that are of interest to everyone.

8. OTHER GENRES. Since the 1960s the major thrust in writing and publishing for children, particularly in the United States, has been in the area of realistic fiction—that is, books of contemporary urban life and the problems of the young 'growing up old' in a rapidly shifting society. Considering the fact that at least 75.5% of Canadians live in an urban environment, it is surprising that our children's literature hardly reflects Canadian children as they are today. The few novels with city backgrounds have virtually no Canadian flavour—with two exceptions. Frances Duncan's *Kap-Sung Ferris* (1977), set in a highly recognizable Vancouver, is a moving story of a Korean orphan who finally comes to terms with her adoption and her heritage. Kevin Major's *Hold fast* (1978) is much more in the American mould, with its wrenching family problems and explicit language; however, it makes fine use of a regional setting as the young protagonist is forced from the freedom of his outport home to face the constraints and hostility of Newfoundland urban life. A few books in this small group are set in the recent past. Jean LITTLE's *From Anna* (1972), and its sequel *Listen for the singing* (1977), are set in Toronto just before and during the Second World War; tension is provided by the fact that Anna is both disabled and German. The family in Myra Paperny's *The wooden people* (1976) moves from the coast of British Co-

lumbia in the early 1920s to a small northern prairie town; the engaging children (tired of moving) disobey their strict father and create for themselves a world of puppetry.

Only in modern times has Canadian verse had any impact on children's reading: it is probably safe to say that virtually every English-speaking child in Canada knows Dennis LEE's poem 'Alligator Pie'. Lee is a well-known Canadian poet, but to Canadian children he represents their own brand of Mother Goose. He gives them a sense of their particular time and space—something that obviously cannot be accomplished in writing from other countries, no matter how excellent it is—and wins them with his sense of the incongruous and his internal rhyme and strong beat, much as in the English nursery rhymes themselves. His best-known books—*Alligator pie* (1974), *Nicholas Knock* (1974), *Garbage delight* (1977), and *The ordinary bath* (1979)—are most attractively illustrated (by Frank Newfeld) and produced, as is Edith Fowke's *Sally go round the sun* (1969), a collection of songs, rhymes, and games of Canadian children. Canadian poems of interest to children have been imaginatively selected by Mary Alice Downie and Barbara Robertson in *The wind has wings: poems from Canada* (1968).

In the realm of science fiction, a popular genre with many children and a flourishing aspect of writing and publishing in the United States and England, we have only one important writer: Monica HUGHES, who has produced a substantial body of work, including *The tomorrow city* (1978), *Beyond the dark river* (1979), *Keeper of the Isis light* (1980), and *The guardian of Isis* (1981). Her science fiction is lively, more than competently written, and, like so much futuristic writing, is predicated on future disasters; but her dénouements are more optimistic than those of most other writers in this field. She has developed as a writer since her first book, *Crisis on Conshelf Ten* (1977).

The high-adventure story—that is, larger-than-life adventure in the tradition of *Treasure Island*—is not a strong part of modern Canadian children's literature: most writers these days are intent upon a message of some sort or another. However, two books set in the past, Bill Freeman's *The last voyage of the Scotian* (1976) and Joan Clark's *The hand of Robin Squires* (1977), are strongly plotted page-turning adventures whose style and believable events (at least while one is engrossed in them), and lively characterization, lend credence to Emily Dickinson's

lines: 'There is no frigate like a book/To take us lands away.'

Canadian children's fiction began with a sturdy base, the outdoor adventure story, which continues to be our forte. It also began with writers—SETON, ROBERTS, DE MILLE, OXLEY, MONTGOMERY—who published many books. Today we do not have serious professional writers who have produced a large body of work (like many English, American, and Australian authors). In modern times Canadian children's literature is filled with one- or two-book authors, such as James REANEY, author of *The boy with an R in his hand* (1965), William Stevenson, author of *The bush babies* (1965), and Myra Paperny, author of *The wooden people*, among others—whose books are excellent. It is safe to say that they—along with Farley MOWAT, David WALKER, and Ruth NICHOLS, who have not published a children's book for many years—ran out of encouragement rather than talent. With the massive competition from other English-speaking countries—mostly the United States, for American books are preferred and widely read in Canada—our individualistic and solid Canadian books require more assiduous promotion and recognition from those who are involved in the publishing and purchasing of books for children. However, good they are, however current their subject-matter, non-Canadian books do not tell us about ourselves.

See Sheila Egoff, *The republic of childhood: a critical guide to Canadian children's literature in English* (2nd ed., 1975) and Irma McDonough, *Canadian books for young people* (1980).

See also CHILDREN'S DRAMA IN ENGLISH.

SHEILA EGOFF

Children's literature in French. 1. THE NINETEENTH CENTURY. Canadian children's literature in French does not have a long tradition. Nineteenth-century examples include mostly books that were read by children though not especially written for them—Claude Potvin's enlarged edition of *Le Canada français et sa littérature de jeunesse* (1982) mentions the 16-page *William, ou l'imprudent corrigé; petite histoire dédiée à l'enfance, suivi de La mendiante* (Québec, 1840), author unknown, containing two didactic stories of which one teaches a lesson in obedience and the other a lesson in generosity. One early book that was popular because of its subject matter was *L'enfant perdu et retrouvé; ou Pierre Cholet* (Montréal, 1887; rpr.

1978), by Jean-Baptiste Proulx, an adventure story about three kidnapped children who are sold as cabin-boys to a sea captain; only the eldest survives to tell of his adventures, which eventually bring him back to Canada.

Several books were devoted to tales and legends rooted in the past and were enjoyed by children because of the familiar background and speech patterns (more easily understood than such books imported from France as the translation of Frederick Marryat's *The settlers in Canada, Les colons du Canada* (Paris, 1852; rpr. 1869): *Contes populaires* (Ottawa, 1867; rpr. 1912) by Paul Stevens, *Légendes canadiennes* (Québec, 1861; rpr. 1876) by Henri-Raymond CASGRAIN, *Le tomahawk et l'épée* (Québec, 1877) by Joseph MARMETTE, *La terre paternelle* (Montréal, 1871; rpr. 1924) by Patrice LACOMBE, and *Une de perdue, deux de trouvées* (2 vols, Montréal, 1874; rpr. 1956) by Pierre-Georges Boucher de Boucherville. These books were often distributed as school prizes by the Départment de l'Instruction Publique (Québec). The policy of circulating books in the schools began in 1876 and continued through the early part of the twentieth century in the hope that a sound basis for the development of children's literature could be established.

2. 1900 TO 1939. *À l'oeuvre et à l'épreuve* (Québec, 1891) by Laure Conan (Félicité ANGERS), the romanticized story of the Jesuit martyr, Charles Garnier, was widely read by young people well into the 1940s; but another book of hers was even more popular with children and young people, *L'oublié* (1900, rpr. 1964), a novel about Lambert Closse, who participated in the founding of Ville-Marie. Over the years Félicité Angers wrote articles on Canadian personalities and collected several of them in *Silhouettes canadiennes* (1917; rpr. 1922), which she dedicated to the French-speaking school children of Ontario.

The preface of *Contes et légendes* (1915), by Adèle Bourgeoys Lacerte, states that it represents 'a completely new genre in Canada, where no one, until now, had made the effort to write particularly for children'. Four years later, *Récits laurentiens* (1919; rpr. 1964) by Frère MARIE-VICTORIN (Conrad Kirouac) was dedicated to 'la vaillante jeunesse du pays d'érable'. It was translated as *The chopping bee and other stories* (1925).

One of the important events in the first stages of the development of French-Canadian literature for children took place in 1920, when Arthur Saint-Pierre, managing editor of the magazine *L'Oiseau bleu* (published by the Société St-Jean-Baptiste), asked Marie-Claire Daveluy to contribute a pioneer story in which the principal characters were children. Her story, about two French orphans who settle in New France, was serialized in *L'Oiseau bleu*; published in book form as *Les aventures de Perrine et de Charlot* (1923), it received the Prix David and was reprinted several times. Although Daveluy also wrote modern fairy tales, she is best known for her series of historical novels on the early French settlers. Other budding writers of the period, like Marie-Louise d'Auteuil (*Mémoires d'une souris canadienne*, 1932; rpr. 1945), contributed to the output and success of *L'Oiseau bleu*, which ceased publication in 1940.

Three other well-known authors who began to write in the 1920s were Maxine, Eugène Achard, and Claude Melançon. Maxine—the pseudonym of Marie-Caroline Alexandra Taschereau-Fortier—was a prolific author of rather fanciful historical novels and short biographies of well-known figures (*Le marin de Saint-Malo, Jacques Cartier*, 1946). She is best, and fondly, remembered for her novel *Le petit page de Frontenac* (1930; rpr. 1963). Eugène Achard, who emigrated from France, had a writing career that extended over forty years, beginning in 1921 with *Aux quatre coins des routes canadiennes* and ending with *Sur les sentiers de la Côte Nord* (1960). He wrote some seventy books, including retellings of traditional tales (*L'oiseau vert et la princesse fortunée*, 1956) and biographies (*Les grands noms de l'histoire canadienne*, 1940), but mostly fiction (*Sous les plis du drapeau blanc*, 1935) and collections of modern fairy tales with a Canadian or Québec setting (*Les contes de la claire fontaine*, 1943). During this period there were several books on the natural sciences, fostered by the creation of the Cercle des jeunes naturalistes and nurtured by one of its founders, Frère Marie-Victorin: *ABC du petit naturaliste canadien* (9 vols, 1936) by Harry BERNARD, *A travers les champs et les bois* (1931) by Louis-Jean Gagnon, *Les confidences de la nature* (1936) by Adolphe Brassard, *Nos animaux domestiques* (1933) by Odette Oligny, and *Oiseaux de mon pays* (1939; rpr. 1970) by Alice Duchesnay. The trend was continued in the 1940s by Marcelle Gauvreau, who wrote *Plantes curieuses de mon pays* (1943), and by Claude Melançon, who wrote several books, including one on the birds of Québec (*Char-*

mants voisins, 1940; rpr. 1964) and one on Canadian animals (*Mon alphabet des animaux* 1944). Claude Melançon's books are something of a landmark in French children's-book publishing in Canada. Besides the two books cited above, he wrote his popular *Légendes Indiennes du Canada* (1967) and several other informational books on a variety of subjects; for example, *Mon alphabet des villes du Québec* (1944) and *Les poissons de nos eaux* (1936). His first publication, *Par terre et par eau* (1928), an adventure story of two kidnapped children, is overwhelmed by a geography lesson on Québec. Although informative, it is tedious, and children today would find it difficult to read and to identify themselves with the hero and heroine, who act beyond their years. In many books the child was pictured as a model child—obviously a reflection of the feeling that adults entertained about children. There were few novels portraying children in the home or in their daily lives, but two books that show how children were taught to behave are *Autour de la maison* (1916) and *La plus belle chose du monde* (1937; rpr. 1961) by Michelle Le Normand (pseudonym of Marie-Antoinette Desrosiers).

3. 1940 TO 1970. During the Second World War few French children's books were available in Québec and publishers attempted to fill the gap. The ever-popular genre of fairy tales and legends was represented by Achard's *Les deux bossus de l'Île d'Orléans et autres contes* (1944); two collections by Marius BARBEAU, *Les contes du grand-père sept-heures* (1950-3) in twelve paperback volumes—some of these stories were adapted and translated by Michael Hornyansky in *The golden phoenix and other fairy tales of French Canada* (1958; rpr. 1980)—and *Les rêves des chasseurs* (1942); and Félix LECLERC's successful trilogy of fables and poems *Adagio* (1943; rpr. 1976), *Allegro* (1944; rpr. 1976), and *Andante* (1944; rpr. 1975). Guy Boulizon (who emigrated from France) and Ambroise Lafortune wrote adventure stories in which some of the principal characters were Boy Scouts. A typical book by Lafortune, who was himself a Scout leader, is *Le secret de la rivière perdue* (1946). Boulizon's *Prisonniers des cavernes* (1950) was rewritten and published in 1979 as *Alexandre et les prisonniers des cavernes*. A few other notable books of this period were Claude Aubry's *La vengeance des hommes de bonne volonté* (1944), reprinted twice under the title *Le loup de Noel*, and Andrée MAILLET's picturebook *Ristontac* (1945), illus-

trated by Robert Lapalme, and *Le marquiset têtu et le mulot réprobateur* (1944).

It was evident at this time that public interest in children's books was on the wane. There was good reason for this: the themes and treatment of the historical novels and the many books of folk and fairy tales, history and biography, had a certain sameness, and the literary quality was marked by mediocrity. French-Canadian children's literature had now reached a stage in its development where changes were necessary in order to reflect new societal attitudes and to provide children with a greater number of books that responded to their needs and interests. Fortunately in the late fifties four writers began to bring some distinction to the field: Paule DAVELUY, Yves THÉRIAULT, Claudine Vallerand, and Monique Corriveau—Daveluy with *L'été enchanté* (1958—translated as *Summer in Ville-Marie*, 1962), Thériault with *Alerte au camp 29* (1959), Vallerand (under the pseudonym 'Maman Fonfon') with *Chante et joue* (1957), and Corriveau with *Le secret de Vanille* (1959; rpr. 1981) and *Le Wapiti* (1964; *The Wapiti*, 1968), a captivating romance of seventeenth-century New France that offers not only a marvellous adventure story but genuine insight into the lives of both the Indians and the French in Canada's earliest days. Corriveau's main characteristic is her ability to develop atmosphere that becomes an essential component of the story, as in *Les saisons de la mer* (1975), about an Irish family in Newfoundland in the 1920s. Another interesting writer who began to be published in this period is Suzanne Martel, whose *Quatre Montréalais en l'an 3000* (1963)—reprinted under the title *Surréal 3000* (1980) and translated as *The city underground* (1982)—shows her lively ability to introduce humour even in her inventive science-fiction novels, of which *Nos amis robots* (1981) is the most recent. Claude Aubry's *Agouhanna* (1974; rpr. 1981), written in a simple, even poetic manner, is another novel of the period that has worn well. Informational books on a variety of subjects—*Le chevalier du roi; vie de saint Ignace de Loyola* by Beatrice Clément (1956)—were not as appealing to young readers as were the mystery and adventure stories.

Between 1965 and 1970 a slump occurred in children's literature: books were no longer given as school prizes, and French and Belgian imports increased. Retail trade declined, while textbook publishing increased to keep up with the demands brought about by the changes in the newly laicized educational system. Between 1965 and 1968 only about 80 trade titles appeared, and in 1969 and 1970 fewer than 10—a mere trifle compared to the 1,000 children's books that were published annually in France.

4. 1971 TO THE PRESENT. The founding of Communication-Jeunesse in Québec in 1971 inspired authors, illustrators, publishers, booksellers, librarians, and teachers to work together, and this organization became a key factor in the promotion of children's-book publishing in the province. Working within the whole socio-cultural and political context of 1976, the year the Parti Québécois came to power, Communication-Jeunesse is now developing the need for a specifically Québec children's literature.

Several writers responded to this need. Bertrand Gauthier writes very inventive, droll stories filled with puns. *Hébert Luée* (1980), in which the two main characters search for a circus in Montreal, offers a critical view of contemporary society without being preachy; it was illustrated with colourful, often outlandish pictures by Marie-Louise Gay, who has also written and illustrated a counting book, *De zéro à minuit* (1981). Ginette Anfousse has written and illustrated a series of books about a little girl and her toy ant-eater, all of which have been translated into English and published by NC Press. The first two—*La cachette* (English title, *Hide and seek*) and *Mon ami Pichou* (English title, *My friend Pichou*) were published in 1976; all the titles in the series have been reprinted and may well become classics. Tibo (Gilles Thibault) created the colour pictures for *Le tour de l'île* by Félix LECLERC (1980) and excellent black-and-white drawings for *Je te laisse une caresse* (1976) and *Mon petit lutin s'endort* (1976), two small books of verse by André Cailloux (1976). *Une fenêtre dans ma tête* (2 vols, 1979) by Raymond Plante, which describes a young child's fantasy world, was illustrated with lively and colourful drawings by Roger Paré. A charming fantasy, in which three children go on a search for time, is *Le voyage à la recherche du temps* (1981) by Lucie Ledoux, illustrated in black and white by Philippe Béha.

In 1974 Fides inaugurated its series 'Du Goéland', whose titles include *Le garçon au cerf-volant* (1974) by Monique Corriveau; *Le ru d'Ikoué* (1963; rpr. 1977) by Yves THÉRIAULT; *Le chat de l'Oratoire* (1978) by Bernadette Renaud; and *Chansons pour un or-*

dinateur (1980) by Francine Loranger. Les Éditions Héritage, which publishes the magazine *Hibou* (an adaptation of the English-language magazine *Owl*), launched several series of children's books, among them 'Pour lire avec toi', designed for young readers in the post-picturebook transitional phase. Fantasy and reality intermingle in three books belonging to this series: *Fend-le-vent et le visiteur mystérieux* (1980) by Serge Wilson, *Emilie la baignoire à pattes* (1976) by Bernadette Renaud, and *Alfred dans le métro* (1980), written and illustrated by Cécile Gagnon. *La révolte de la courtepointe* (1979) by Bernadette Renaud also combines the real and the fantastic. The Héritage series, 'Katimavik', includes Suzanne Martel's *Pi-Oui* (1974)—which was translated into English as *Peewee*—and *Contes de mon pays* (1980) by Germain Lemieux. The series 'Jeunesse Pop', published by Les Éditions Paulines, includes Louis Landry's *Glausgab créateur du monde* (1981) and *Glausgab le protecteur* (1981), two novels that create a new mythological hero, an Algonquin Indian who lands in France in the late fifteenth century and is invited by the French court to tell his story. The joint title of the two books is *La véritable histoire du Grand Manitou Algonquin*.

Young francophone readers have been introduced to good texts from English Canada by a series called 'Deux solitudes—jeunesse', published by Les Éditions Pierre Tisseyre. Among its titles are stories about growing up—*La promesse de Luke Baldwin* (1980) by Morley CALLAGHAN, translated by Michelle Tisseyre *(Luke Baldwin's vow)* and *Je t'attends à Peggy's Cove* (1982) by Brian Doyle, translated by Claude Aubry *(You can pick me up at Peggy's Cove)*; about handicapped children—*Écoute l'oiseau chantera* (1980) by Jean LITTLE, translated by Paule DAVELUY *(Listen for the singing)*; about animals—*Deux grands ducs dans la famille* (1980) by Farley MOWAT, translated by Paule Daveluy *(Owls in the family)*; about the Mennonites in Russia who eventually settled in Manitoba—*Jours de terreur* (1981) by Barbara Smucker, translated by Paule Daveluy *(Days of terror)*; and about the North—*L'archer blanc* (1978) by James HOUSTON *(The white archer)*.

Several recent books offered children a chance to discover authors appreciated by their elders: *Les quatre saisons de Piquot* (1979) and *Quelques pas dans l'univers d'Eva* (1981) by Gilles VIGNEAULT; *Les voyageurs de l'arc-en-ciel* (1980) by Roch CARRIER, in which a boy and girl who live in the country go searching for frogs and learn the meaning of sharing; and *Les contes du sommet bleu* (1980), written and illustrated by Claude JASMIN, a collection of stories, set in the Laurentians, in which the author involves himself.

For older readers Suzanne Martel has written several novels with historical settings, such as *Jeanne, fille du roy* (1974), set in the seventeenth century. Martel's other books in the series 'Les Montcorbier' (*L'apprentissage d'Arahé*, 1979, and *Premières armes*, 1979) and 'Menfou Carcajou' (*Ville-Marie*, 1980, and *La baie du Nord*, 1980) are written for adults, although they would appeal to mature young readers. The heroes in 'Les Montcorbier' are Arnaud and Paul Montcorbier and the action takes place in a fictitious country at the beginning of the twentieth century. In 'Menfou Carcajou' Xavier Cormier de Villefoy is the young, colourful hero whose exploits take place in the seventeenth century. Another book for older readers is *La planète guenille* (1980) by Gilles Rivard and Jean Clouâtre. It is a farcical and fanciful—almost surreal—story of a boy—living on a strange planet surrounded by mushrooms, grapes, a bee, and a few rags—who is continually searching for love. A series called 'Légendes du Québec' has been published by Ovale, although the stories are not necessarily authentic. It includes *La grange aux lutins* (1980) adapted by Robert Piette; *La chasse-galerie* (1980) adapted by Madeleine Chénard; and *Les feux follets* (1981) adapted by Johanne Bussières. The illustrations in the series are original and extremely colourful—one of the best-illustrated books is *La chasse-galerie*—but too often the pictures, busy with detail, tend to dwarf the text. A mystery set in Montreal's Museum of Fine Arts (*Le visiteur du soir*, 1980, by Robert Soulières) and another set in a manor house at the start of the colonial period (*L'épée arhapal*, 1981, by Daniel Sernine) are among popular longer works.

Fantasy, humour, and word-play have become increasingly prevalent, with such works as *Un jour d'été à Fleurdepeau* (1981) by Bertrand Gauthier; *Crapauds et autres animaux* (1981), a book of original verse by Yvan Adam in collaboration with several other authors; *Monsieur Genou* (1981) by Raymond Plante, a novel in which the main character, Monsieur Genou, is preoccupied with becoming a character in a book; and *Une journée dans la vie de Craquelin 1er, roi de soupe-au-lait* (1981) by Jean-Marie Poupart. Of the last two novels, *Monsieur Genou* has

the more satisfying story line; *Une journée* is rambling and farcical.

In other regions of Canada where francophone communities exist, efforts are being made to publish children's books in French. Les Éditions d'Acadie in New Brunswick have embarked on a new venture to publish picture books (one example is *Caprice à la campagne*, 1982, by Melvin Gallant); Les Éditions des Plaines in Manitoba published an excellent story for middle readers about a dinosaur in Alberta (*Le petit dinosaure d'Alberta*, 1980, by Nadine MacKenzie); and Les Éditions Prise de Parole in Ontario have published a beautiful modern version of the Ojibwa legend of Nanabozho in the Thunder Bay region: *Nanna Bijou, le géant endormi* by Jocelyne Villeneuve (English title, *Nana Bijou the sleeping giant*, Penumbra Press, 1981). Other publishers, like Scholastic-TAB in Ontario, are publishing French translations of Canadian or foreign titles; for example, *La princesse à la robe de papier* (1981) by Robert Munsch, translated by Françoise Marois (English title, *The paper bag princess*, Annick Press, 1980), and *Jérôme Lafeuille part à la rescousse* (1982) by Mike Wilkins and translated by Québec author/illustrator Christiane Duchesne (English title, *Harold Greenhouse to the rescue*, 1982).

The momentum engendered at the beginning of the 1970s by Communication-Jeunesse has not abated and has wrought certain changes, especially in the growing number and quality of books published each year in the areas of the picturebook, the beginning reader, and translations. Illustrators are exploring new techniques and are now making a more effective use of design. Whether the pictures are in black and white (as in *Des animaux pour rire* (1982) by Jacques Pasquet, illustrated by Jean-Christian Knaff) or in colour (as in *Seul au monde* (1982) by Robert Soulières, illustrated by Philippe Béha), they are becoming more and more an integral part of the text as a whole.

French-Canadian children's books still do not cover all interests and tastes. Good non-fiction and more novels with contemporary settings, for instance, are desperately needed to provide Canadian children with themes close to home. But the fine work of such authors as Ginette Anfousse, Claude Aubry, Suzanne Martel, Bertrand Gauthier, and Henriette Major—known outside Québec and, in some cases, outside Canada—suggests that a strong literature for francophone Canadian children is at last developing.

Children's literature in French 4

See Claude Potvin, *Le Canada français et sa littérature de jeunesse* (1982), and Louise Lemieux, *Pleins feux sur la littérature de jeunesse au Canada français* (1972).

IRENE E. AUBREY

Chiniquy, Charles. See BIOGRAPHY AND MEMOIRS IN FRENCH: 6.

Chittick, V.L.O. See CRITICISM IN ENGLISH: 2.

Chopin, René. See POETRY IN FRENCH: 4.

Choquette, Ernest (1862-1941). Born at Beloeil, Canada East (Qué.), he took his classical secondary course at the Collège de Saint-Hyacinthe and studied medicine in Montreal. He received his medical degree in 1886, and practised in Saint-Hilaire for the rest of his life. He was elected mayor of the village several times and in 1910 was appointed to the Québec legislative council. He died in Montreal.

Choquette is the author of three novels, a collection of short stories, and two plays adapted from his fiction. *Les Ribaud: une idylle de 37* (Montréal, 1898) reflects renewed popular interest in the Rebellion of 1837 after the publication in the 1880s of two conflicting accounts, Charles-Auguste-Maximilien Globensky's *La Rébellion de 1837 à Saint-Eustache* and Laurent-Olivier David's *Les Patriotes de 1837-1838*. In Choquette's novel a sexagenarian *patriote*, Dr Ribaud, whose father died fighting the English at Waterloo and whose son has been killed in a duel with an English officer, is furious when his daughter Madeleine falls in love with an English captain, Percival Smith. Despite the doctor's machinations, Percival's high-mindedness during the Rebellion, Madeleine's innocent passion, and the parish priest's wise counsel combine to ensure the triumph of love over bigoted nationalism—an unusual outcome for the period. With the assistance of a French critic, Charles ab der Halden, the novel was adapted as a play and performed in Jan. 1903 at the Théâtre National in Montreal under the title *Madeleine*, enjoying considerable success.

Choquette's second novel, *Claude Paysan* (Montréal, 1899), was first published as a serial in *La Patrie*; an abridged version later appeared in France. It recounts the silent love of the *habitant* Claude Drioux for a summer visitor from the city, Fernande Tissot, and his lonely wait each winter for her return. When she dies of tuberculosis, Claude disappears, and his body is later recovered from the river. Here again Choquette's primary theme is love, although the original edition also contains substantial descriptions of rural life.

The following year Choquette brought out, under the title *Carabinades* (Montréal, 1900), a lively collection of twenty-six anecdotes and stories drawn from his years as a medical student (*carabin*) and general practitioner. His last novel, *La terre* (1916), composed some years before its publication, is a didactic work setting forth the thesis that the French-Canadian population can hope to survive only by remaining agricultural and avoiding competition with English-speaking Canadians. Old Beaumont has two sons, Lucas and Yves: the former takes over the family farm, the latter becomes a skilled chemist but finds his career constantly blocked by English rivals. Discouraged, Yves goes off to fight in the Transvaal, while his older brother falls into alcoholism, neglects his land, and even commits a murder. When Yves returns from South Africa he takes charge of the farm, having learned from the Boers to value agriculture and to resist assimilation. *La Terre*, adapted for the stage in 1927 under the title *La Bouée*, thus fitted into the regionalist pattern that was dominant in Québec fiction in the early years of this century—although it assumed a hereditary incapacity for commerce and industry among French Canadians, a view not usually expressed in such fiction.

Choquette is a secondary Québec novelist, but his books show some thematic originality, and his fictional technique improved steadily over the dozen years during which he wrote his novels and stories.

The only recent articles devoted to Choquette's novels are those found in the *Dictionnaire des oeuvres littéraires du Québec*, vols I and II (1978, 1980).

DAVID M. HAYNE

Choquette, Robert (b. 1905). Born in Manchester, N.H., of parents who had emigrated from Québec, he spent his early youth in Lewiston, Maine. Following his mother's death in 1913, he returned with his family to Montreal, where his father opened a medical practice. He studied at the Collège Notre-Dame, the Collège Saint-Laurent, and Loyola College. After a short period as a reporter with the *Gazette*, he became secretary and librarian at the École des Beaux-Arts in Montreal (1928-31), at the same time becoming literary editor of *La Revue moderne*. In the early thirties he began his long career as a writer for radio and, later, television.

Choquette's first poetry was written at Loyola College where, influenced by the English and French Romantics, he composed some fifty poems that were published under the title *A travers les vents* (1925). Conventional for the most part, they reveal a gift for epic and a feeling for the sweep and grandeur of North America that won for the young poet the Prix David in 1926. A lyric-epic poem, *Metropolitan Museum* (1931), astonished critics by its breadth of vision: a panorama of the history of art, from ancient to modern times, that evokes the realities of science, mechanization, and urban life in the great American cities. In 1932 Choquette was again awarded the Prix David, both for this work and for the manuscript of a poetry collection, *Poésies nouvelles* (1933), that recalls the themes and style of his previous books. *Suite marine* (1953), a long poem in twelve cantos begun in 1934, marked the summit of both his poetic art and the lyric-epic vein. It won the Prix de l'Académie française in 1954 and the Prix David in 1956. *Oeuvres poétiques* (1956), assembled by the author, includes revisions of the first three collections, a reprinting of *Suite marine*, and 'Vers inédits'. A French edition of *Metropolitan Museum*, containing a preface by André Maurois, was published in 1963.

Choquette also wrote *La pension Leblanc* (1927; rpr. 1976), a novel that attempts to portray village life in the realistic manner of Flaubert. *Les Velder* (1941) and *Elise Velder* (1958; rpr. 1973) are adaptations of scripts written for radio. *Le curé de village* (1936) is composed of extracts from Québec's first radio serial (CKAC, 1935-8); related to the regionalist novels of the thirties, it became a model for many later serials. Other works by Choquette include *Le fabuliste La Fontaine à Montréal* (1935), a series of fifteen fables originally presented in the form of radio plays; a play, *Sous le règne d'Augusta* (1974); *Le sorcier d'Anticosti et autres légendes* (1975); and *Moi, Petruchka* (1980).

During his long career Choquette has written innumerable scripts for radio and television (sketches and dramatic serials, plays, cultural programs), only a few of which have been published. The best-known of the radio and television plays, *La pension Velder* (1938-42 and 1957-61) and *Métropole* (1943-56), use satire and caricature to create an amusing social protrait of Montreal. After leaving the airwaves at the start of the sixties, Choquette lived in Paris in 1962-3, and visited Italy and Greece, returning to Ottawa to accept the post of associate commissioner of the Centennial Commission (1963-4). His diplomatic career began when he was Canadian consul-general in Bordeaux, France, from 1964 to 1968. He next served as Canadain ambassador to Argentina, Uruguay, and Paraguay from 1968 to 1970 and was director-general of Information Canada in Québec (1971-3). He has since held various honorary posts and continued his work as writer. He was named Companion of the Order of Canada in 1969.

Representative selections of Choquette's poetry and prose can be found in *Robert Choquette* (1959) edited by André Melançon; *Poèmes choisis* (1970); and *Le choix de Robert Choquette* (1981). For critical studies of his work, see *Robert Choquette, romancier et dramaturge de la télévision* (1977) by Renée Legris; *Le comique et l'humour à la radio québécoise, 1930-1970* (1976) by Pierre Pagé and Renée Legris; *Paragraphes* (1931) by Alfred DESROCHERS; and *Poètes de l'Amérique française* (1934) by Louis Dantin (Eugène SEERS).   RICHARD GIGUÈRE

Chouinard, Ernest. See NOVELS IN FRENCH: 1900 TO 1920.

Christie, Robert. See HISTORICAL WRITING IN ENGLISH: 2.

Chronicles of Canada. See BIOGRAPHY AND MEMOIRS IN ENGLISH: 1.

Cité libre. See LITERARY MAGAZINES IN QUÉBEC: 3.

***CIV/n* (**1953-5). A Montreal little magazine nominally edited by Aileen Collins, it was heavily influenced by the editorial ideas of Louis DUDEK and Irving LAYTON, in whose home editorial meetings were held. The name was contributed by Dudek from a line about civilization in an Ezra Pound letter: 'CIV/n not a one man job.' The seven issues carried both poems and reviews, the latter nearly all by Dudek and Layton. Poets who contributed were mostly Canadian and included, as well as Dudek and Layton, Anne WILKINSON, Phyllis WEBB, Miriam WADDINGTON, Raymond SOUSTER, A.J.M. SMITH, Eli MANDEL, D.G. JONES, and Robert Currie.

The seven issues have been reprinted in *CIV/n: a literary magazine of the 50's* (1983)

edited by Aileen Collins, with the assistance of Simon Dardick.   FRANK DAVEY

Clark, Catherine Anthony (1892-1977). Born in London, Eng., Catherine Smith immigrated to Canada in 1914. In 1919 she married Leonard Clark and settled in the Kootenay Mountains of British Columbia, where she raised her family and wrote part time, not publishing her first book until she was 58. *The golden pine cone* (1950) chronicles the adventures of two children who abandon the security of their families and journey to the mysterious world of fantasy (what Clark calls the 'inner world') to rescue their dog and to return a magical pine cone to its rightful owner. This plot reappears in various guises in all of Clark's subsequent fantasies: *The sun horse* (1950), *The one-winged dragon* (1955), *The silver man* (1959), *The diamond feather* (1962), and *The hunter and the medicine man* (1966) are all quests set within the Kootenay wilderness so familiar to Clark.

But it is not Clark's plots that define her importance in Canadian children's literature; it is the uniqueness of her fantasy world and the moral values that it embodies. Her 'inner world' is not the never-never-land of traditional fantasies but the quasi-magical world of Indian lore; a world inhabited not by giants and ogres but by the Glass-Witch, the Flame-lighter Woman, and other figures drawn from Indian legends. Here the natural and supernatural merge; there is no rigorous distinction between the real and the unreal.

Similarly, Indian legends influence Clark's presentation of moral values. Her fantasies present no absolute goodness or evil; rather, individuals are judged as either selfish or selfless. The true hero is judged not for his courage but for his ability to give to others; his identity is defined in terms of the community. All Clark's fantasies preach a common doctrine: man survives by acting, by confronting chaos, and by caring for his fellow man. Her heroes do not discover magical treasures; rather, they find their place in society.

Clark's tales are clearly both formulaic and predictable and her prose, at best, is uneven. In addition, her approach to fantasy does not allow the imaginative flourishes so often associated with the genre. For this reason, perhaps, Clark is not widely read today. But what she does provide is a unique approach to fantasy, a merging of the traditional elements of fantasy with Indian folklore. Thus, Canada's first major

fantasist also provides the prototype for a distinctly Canadian fantasy.

See two essays in CANADIAN LITERATURE: Joan Selby, 'The creation of fantasy: the fiction of Catherine Anthony Clark' (Issue 11, Winter 1962), and J. Kieran Kealy, 'The flamelighter woman: Catherine Anthony Clark's fantasies' (Issue 78, Autumn 1978).

J. KIERAN KEALY

Clark, Joan. See CHILDREN'S LITERATURE IN ENGLISH: 8.

Clarke, Austin (b. 1932). Born in Barbados, Austin Chesterfield Clarke was educated, and became a schoolteacher, there before moving to Canada in 1955 to study at the University of Toronto. In 1959-60 he worked as a reporter in Timmins and Kirkland Lake, Ont., before joining the CBC and eventually becoming a freelance broadcaster. Between 1968 and 1974 he taught creative writing and was writer-in-residence at Yale, Brandeis, Williams, and Duke Universities and at the University of Texas. In 1974-5 he was appointed cultural attaché to the Barbadian embassy in Washington, followed by a year as general manager of the Caribbean Broadcasting Corporation and adviser to the prime minister of Barbados. Returning to Canada, he served as writer-in-residence at Concordia University, Montreal, in 1976-7. An acknowledged spokesman for the black community in Toronto, Clarke served on the Metro Toronto Library Board from 1973 to 1976. He won the Cuban literary prize, the Casa de las Americas, in 1980.

Clarke's first two works of fiction deal with life in Barbados. *Survivors of the crossing* (1964) and *Amongst thistles and thorns* (1965)—the latter a collection of short stories—present Barbados as economically bleak and impoverished, full of desperate people struggling for survival. For the ambitious individual escape to North America is the only chance for prosperity. *The meeting point* (1967), the first novel in Clarke's trilogy about the lives of Caribbean immigrants in Toronto, explores what that chance means in human terms. Introducing a group of West Indian immigrants, it presents the underside of wealthy Toronto by revealing the racist exploitation of Blacks. *Storm of fortune* (1971) and *The bigger light* (1975) chart their slow and eventful adaptation to Canadian social values and conventions. These novels are filled with bitterness and sadness, lightened by the indomitable humour and spirit of Clarke's characters, the most successful of whom renounces his hard-earned material success in Canada to investigate Black Power pride in the United States—a move that seems to imply the impossibility of his finding a meaningful life in Canada. While exposing racial hypocrisy in Canada, Clarke describes both white and black sides with fairness and perspicuity. These novels—which say as much about Canada in general as about the concerns of Blacks in Toronto and Barbados in particular—are enriched by Clarke's mastery of dialogue, realism, and psychologically subtle characterizations. His second collection of short stories, *When he was free and young and he used to wear silks* (1971), further elaborates the theme of Blacks struggling to make good in Canada. *The prime minister* (1977), an exposé of political corruption in a developing nation that grew out of Clarke's experiences as a civil servant in Barbados, expresses his cynical view of the upper class there, even though this novel is deliberately vague in its tropical setting.

The first volume of Clarke's autobiography, *Growing up stupid under the Union Jack* (1980), continues this trend toward universality. Although Clarke concentrates on his own childhood, allusions to the larger framework of British colonialism expand his topic as he demonstrates what the British Empire meant to its non-white population. The autobiography continues with *Colonial innocency* (1982).   TERRENCE CRAIG

Cloutier, Cécile (b. 1930). Born in Québec City (Lower Town), she studied literature and esthetics at Université Laval, where she obtained a Licence-ès-lettres and a Diplôme d'études supérieures, and then at the Sorbonne, where she obtained a Doctorat de l'Université (1962). Keenly interested in languages, she has also studied—in addition to French and English—Greek, Latin, Spanish, German, Polish, Sanskrit, Inooktituk, and Chinese. In the early sixties she taught French and Québec literature and esthetics in Quebec City and at the Université d' Ottawa. Since 1966 she has been professor of French at the University of Toronto. She is married to Jerzy Wojciechowska and has two daughters.

The history and traditions of Québec society influenced Cloutier deeply, although she rarely refers to them explicitly in her writing. The nature of her vision and creative practice has not changed through her five volumes of poetry: *Mains de sable* (1960);

Cuivre et soies (1964); *Cannelles et craies* (1969); *Paupières* (1970) and *Câblogrammes* (1972), which contain almost exactly the same pieces, although ordered differently; and *Chaleuils* (1978), which was translated by Alexandre Amprimoz as *Springtime of spoken words* (1979). Cloutier's first theoretical formulation on poetry was given in an address in 1958, which was first published in 1959 as 'Propos sur la poésie' and republished under the title 'Cum' in *Paupières*. Her maturation as a poet has been typified by a heightened intensity and a growing effectiveness of language and imagery.

Since the mid-sixties Cloutier's poetry has emerged out of the vital tensions that exist for her among sensation, spiritual revelation, and poetic creation. Cloutier—who perceives the world as animated by great energy, proffering signs to those who would listen to, and hear, its infinite silence—sees the poem as a window, a fleeting vision of what is usually hidden in the universe. Her short, elliptical poems are a search for the essential word, a return to the origin of things when they can be named for the first time. Her images—without embellishment, and frequently emerging out of stark contradiction and opposition—are carefully chosen to pass beyond deceptive appearances, so that the things of this world can be seen in their essential nature.

Cloutier's one-act play 'Utinam', which has been produced in Montreal and Quebec City, was published in *La* BARRE DU JOUR (mai-août 1977) and translated by Josée M. LeBlond in *Room of one's own* (1978). Cloutier is the author of a number of articles on the poets of her generation.

See *Livres et auteurs québécois* (1964, 1970, 1971, 1979).   LOUISE FORSYTH

Clutesi, George. See CHILDREN'S LITERATURE IN ENGLISH: 5 and INDIAN LEGENDS AND TALES: BIBLIOGRAPHY.

Coach House Press. Synonomous with fine-crafted books and adventurous editorial policies, this publishing house was founded in Toronto in 1965 by Stan Bevington, with the editorial assistance of Wayne Clifford. Clifford was succeeded as editor in 1966 by Victor COLEMAN, who by 1973 had built Coach House into one of the three largest publishers in Canada of new literary titles. Since 1974 Coach House has been edited by a collective consisting of Bevington; writers bp NICHOL, Michael ONDAATJE, Frank DAVEY, and David Young; graphic artist

Coach House Press

Rick/Simon (who resigned in 1979); and lawyer Linda Davey. In recent years they have been joined by playwright Martin KINCH, art-historian Dennis Reid, freelance editor Val Frith, and in-house editors Clifford James and Sarah Sheard. Its early years, under Coleman's editorship, were characterized by hand-set type, multi-coloured offset printing, fortuitous collaborations between author and designer, and titles by open-form writers from both the U.S. and Canada. These included Ondaatje, Bowering, Bill Hutton, Nichol, David Rosenburg, David McFADDEN, Joe ROSENBLATT, Daphne MARLATT, Matt COHEN, Allen Ginsberg and Robert Creeley. In many ways Coach House represented a continuation of Contact Press, extending Contact's welcome to new poets and supporting most of the writers of the Contact Press anthology *New wave Canada: the new explosion in Canadian poetry* (1966). More recently it has also published work by Stan Dragland, D.G. JONES, Phyllis WEBB, Louis DUDEK, Eli MANDEL, Sheila WATSON, and Robert KROETSCH; numerous first books; and a Québec translation series that has included titles by Victor-Lévy BEAULIEU, Jacques FERRON, Nicole BROSSARD, and Claude GAUVREAU. Art and photography books have also been a specialty since its founding. In recent years Coach House has been a leader in computer applications to literary publishing. All typesetting operations were computerized in 1974; design and page layout have been computer-assisted since 1978. In 1980 facilities were introduced to receive text files by telephone from both mainframe and personal computers.

FRANK DAVEY

Coburn, Kathleen. See BIOGRAPHY AND MEMOIRS IN ENGLISH: 3.

Coderre, Émile (1893-1970). Coderre, who wrote under the pseudonym 'Jean Narrache', was born in Montreal and orphaned at an early age. He was educated at the Séminaire de Nicolet (1904-12) and received his licentiate's degree in pharmacology from the Université de Montréal in 1919. He assumed the management of a pharmacy in one of Montreal's poorer districts where he came to know the most impoverished victims of the Depression. He was editor-in-chief of the *Pharmacien* (1939-42), secretary of the Collège des pharmaciens (1945-60), and professor of pharmaceutical legislation at the Université de Montréal (1953-61).

A brief association with the ÉCOLE LITTÉRAIRE DE MONTRÉAL in 1912-13 awakened Coderre's serious interest in literature, and between 1922 and 1963 he published five books of poetry and two of prose. *Les signes sur le sable* (1922) is a collection of poetry largely inspired by the Romantics and Symbolists; the only poems that stand out from the others are those of the vagabond-poet reminiscent of Villon, Jean Richepin, or Jehan Rictus (for example, 'La chanson des gueux'). Stirred by the Depression, Coderre published *Quand j'parl' tout seul* (1933) and *J'parl' pour parler. . .* (1939) under the pseudonym 'Jean Narrache' (*'j'en arrache'*: I have a hard time making ends meet). Conveying the same sense of humour, and suggesting the same sad smile of many a 'Jean Narrache' during the Depression and after, these books were an instant success and gained Coderre a large following in the press and on radio. The two collections are based on acute observation of the habits and conditions of the poor, while at the same time analysing the bourgeois class, often most harshly. Here the poet of the destitute found a suitable formula: a sincere tone mixed generously with grinding humour, irony, and even sarcasm, in a language later to be known as JOUAL. *Bonjour, les gars!* (1948) is composed mainly of 'revamped verses' taken from the preceding collections, offering only eight new pieces. However, it is enriched by an interesting biographical introduction. *J'parle tout seul quand Jean Narrache* (1961) is a collection of previously published and unpublished verse. *Histoires du Canada. . .* (1937) recounts in prose some 'revamped lives' (Columbus, Cartier, Maisonneuve, Laviolette, La Vérendrye). In treating the history of Canada and alluding to both historical and contemporary events and politicians, it contains a strong dose of social criticism. *Jean Narrache chez le diable* (1963) presents a series of dialogues with the devil, examining such topics as politics and separatism, journalism and radio, art and literature. None of the books of prose, however, possess the humour, the critical scope, or the sting of the poetry of the thirties.

In 1932 Coderre began writing humorous sketches, dramatic series, plays, and short stories for radio and theatre, most of which are unpublished. Starting in the 1940s, he produced his best-known works where, in monologue form, he gave both recollections and commentaries on current events: 'Rêveries de Jean Narrache' (1940-41, 1946, 1947-8), 'Jean Narracheries' (1944), 'Le vag-

Cohen

abond qui chante' (1941-5, 1947-8), 'Les souvenirs de Jean Narrache' (1947), and 'Zigzags à travers mes souvenirs' (1956). The humour of these radio scripts lies in a distinctive mixture of wisdom, melancholy, and lightheartedness which, for the author, are the only attitudes that resist the ravages of time.

For discussions of Coderre's work, see Jacques Blais, *De l'ordre et de l'aventure: la poésie au Québec de 1934 à 1944* (1975); Richard Giguère, 'Quand j'parl' tout seul' and 'J'parl' pour parler . . .' in *Dictionnaire des oeuvres littéraires du Québec* (1980); and Pierre Pagé and Renée Legris, *Le comique et l'humour à la radio québécois, 1930-1970* (1979).

RICHARD GIGUÈRE

Cody, Hiram Alfred (1872-1948). Born in Cody's, N.B., on the Canaan River north of Saint John, and educated at the Saint John Grammar School and King's College, Windsor, N.S., he was ordained in 1898 as an Anglican clergyman. During his career as a priest he served a number of parishes in his native New Brunswick—he became rector of St James Church, Saint John, in 1910—and as far afield as the Yukon. Cody's first book was a biography of Bishop Bompas, *An apostle of the North* (1908). He went on to write twenty-three novels, published between 1910 and 1937, among them *The frontiersman: a tale of the Yukon* (1910), *The fourth watch* (1911), *The long patrol; a tale of the Mounted Police* (1912), *The king's arrow: a tale of United Empire Loyalists* (1922), and *The trail of the Golden Horn* (1923).

Although Cody's fiction owes much to the boy's-adventure-tale tradition of R.M. BALLANTYNE and Marryat, it attempted to reach beyond an all-male readership by providing both a 'romantic interest' and a Christian message. His novels are imbued with the 'muscular Christianity' that emerged in the latter part of the nineteenth century and flourished sporadically until the 1930s. In *The unknown wrestler* (1918), for example, the accomplished fighter who wins the respect of a tough rural community eventually reveals himself as their new Anglican minister. Cody's fiction typically owes more to his literary ancestors than to his own immediate observations and experiences. Despite his familiarity with the North, his Yukon tales never really go beyond well-worn stereotypical scenes and events.

GILLIAN THOMAS

Cogswell, Fred (b. 1917). Frederick Wil-liam Cogswell was born in East Centreville, N.B., where he grew up. After serving in the Canadian Army (1940-5), he completed a B.A. at the University of New Brunswick in 1949 and an M.A. in 1950. After earning a Ph.D. from Edinburgh University in 1952, he returned to the University of New Brunswick to teach in the department of English, where he has remained. Editor of *The* FIDDLEHEAD from 1952 to 1967, he inaugurated Fiddlehead Books, a publishing enterprise involving more than 300 titles that he continued until 1981.

Cogswell's poems—characterized by compression, wit, the use of a wide variety of both traditional and modern forms, and a gentle, ironic view of the world—appear in thirteen volumes: *The stunted strong* (1954), *The haloed tree* (1956), *Descent from Eden* (1959), *Lost dimension* (1960), *Star-People* (1968), *Immortal plowman* (1969), *In praise of chastity* (1970), *The chains of Liliput* (1971), *The house without a door* (1973), *Light bird of life: selected poems* (1974), *Against perspective* (1977), *A long apprenticeship: collected poems* (1980), *Selected poems* (1983), edited with a preface by Antonio D'Alfonso, and *Pearls* (1983). Cogswell's strengths as a craftsman are evident in his five books of translations: *The testament of Cresseid* (1957), *One hundred poems of modern Quebec* (1970), *A second hundred poems of modern Quebec* (1971), *Confrontations* by Gatien LAPOINTE, *The poetry of modern Quebec* (1976), and *The complete poems of Émile Nelligan* (1983). Cogswell's criticism includes four articles in *The literary history of Canada* (1965; 2nd ed. 1976): 'Newfoundland (1715-1880)', 'The Maritime Provinces (1720-1815)', 'Haliburton', 'Literary activity in the Maritime Provinces (1815-1880)', and a monograph on Sir Charles G.D. ROBERTS (1983).

As critic, editor, publisher, and poet, Cogswell has maintained a broadly tolerant and humane stance, a disregard of fashion, and a wide eclecticism of taste. He has been particularly encouraging to young and unknown writers. In 1980 the Writers' Federation of Nova Scotia honoured him with *Scroll*, a collection of poems in tribute by forty-nine Canadian poets. He was made a member of the Order of Canada in 1981.

ROBERT GIBBS

Cohen, Leonard (b. 1934). Born in Montreal, he grew up in its affluent Westmount district and attended McGill University. Shortly after graduating he published his first book of poetry, *Let us compare mytholo-*

Cohen

gies (1956). In the next few years he attempted graduate study at Columbia University, worked in his family's clothing business, and wrote an unpublished novel, 'Ballet of lepers'. After publishing a second book of poetry, *The spice box of earth* (1961), and spending some time in England, he published a novel, *The favorite game* (1963). Since then he has lived intermittently on the Greek island of Hydra, in California, New York, and Montreal. In the 1960s he published the poetry collections *Flowers for Hitler* (1964); *Parasites of heaven* (1966); a second novel, *Beautiful losers* (1966); *Selected poems* (1968), for which he declined a Governor General's Award; and began a successful career as a popular composer-singer. His most recent books of poetry are *The energy of slaves* (1972) and *Death of a lady's man* (1978). His song albums are *Songs of Leonard Cohen* (1968), *Songs from a room* (1969), *Songs of love and hate* (1971), *Live songs* (1973), *New skins for the old ceremony* (1974), *The best of Leonard Cohen* (1975), and *Death of a lady's man* (1977).

Throughout the sixties Cohen's poetry and fiction were extremely popular, particularly with high-school and college readers. The appeal of his poetry was based chiefly on a traditional and recognizably 'poetic' prosody, suggestive imagery that the subjective reader could easily project himself into, and a theme of moral non-responsibility. George WOODCOCK has argued that Cohen has usually been conservative in poetic craft and escapist in theme. The poetry of his first two books draws heavily on Greek and Hassidic mythologies—not to reveal them as alive in the present but to convert the present into the sepulchral figures of mythology. Cohen's language here is highly decorative, reminiscent of the early Yeats. While the poems of his third book, *Flowers for Hitler*, adventure into both satire and experimental verse forms, those of the fourth, *Parasites of heaven*, return to the conventional and dispassionate measures of the earlier volumes.

A consistent theme in these books—the importance of reducing life to ceremony, of escaping from life by transmuting its slippery actualities into the reliable simplicities of myth and art—is developed most clearly in Cohen's novels. It is the lesson by which Breavman 'comes of age' in *The favorite game*. In *Beautiful losers* it is the lesson 'I' must learn from 'F', and includes not only the transmuting of object and event but the self-reduction of personal identity into the

anonymity of sainthood. The loser triumphs by escaping the desire to win. A clear extension of this belief appears in *The energy of slaves*, a collection of fragments, failed poems, and anti-poems. On the surface its directness and self-deprecating cynicism appear to mark a repudiation of the earlier poetry; in fact it represents a logical step in the saintly self-abnegation Cohen has always advocated: master becomes slave, poetic craftsman becomes his own beautiful loser—in his words, 'only a scribbler'. Once again Cohen is working towards a kind of martyrdom. This opposition between decadent craftsman and beautiful loser reappears in *Death of a lady's man*, which juxtaposes texts exemplifying a quest for beauty and sardonic commentaries. Here Cohen manages, simultaneously and with equal weight, to affirm his visions of ceremony and to deconstruct them. Thus the book becomes both his most traditional and most postmodern work.

There have been two critical studies of Leonard Cohen's writings: by Michael ONDAATJE (1971) and Stephen SCOBIE (1978). A collection of critical views of Cohen has been edited by Michael Gnarowski (1976).

See also POETRY IN ENGLISH 1950 TO 1982: 1.

FRANK DAVEY

Cohen, Matt (b. 1942). Born in Kingston, Ont., he moved with his family to Ottawa, where he attended grade school and high school, from which he graduated in 1960. Though his parents were Jewish, he has recorded that his upbringing was not religious. He went on to the University of Toronto, where he graduated in 1964. His post-graduate degree was an M.A. in political theory, for which he prepared a thesis on Albert Camus. In 1967 he was appointed lecturer in the department of religion at McMaster University, where he taught the sociology of religion. The following year he abandoned his teaching career to take up full-time writing, though at intervals since then he has returned to the academic ambience. In 1975-6 he was writer-in-residence at the University of Alberta; in 1979-80 he was visiting professor of creative writing at the University of Victoria; and in 1981-2 he was writer-in-residence at the University of Western Ontario.

Since giving up his post at McMaster, Cohen has lived partly in Toronto and partly on a farm—170 acres of rocky land—he owns at Verona, in the country north of Kingston, that has been the setting of much of his fiction. He has also lived for a short period in the Queen Charlotte Islands, which gave him the background for his novel *Wooden hunters*.

Matt Cohen has worked in a variety of literary genres. For a period he was fiction editor for the COACH HOUSE PRESS, and prepared the second volume of that house's *The story so far* (1972). He has written book reviews and articles; a radio play and two television plays; fiction that verges on ironic poetry in *Peach Melba* (1974); and a book for children, *Leaves of Louise* (1977). But it is as a writer of novels and short stories that he has found his real literary vocation.

Korsoniloff (1969) was followed shortly afterwards by a fantasy novella, *Johnny Crackle sings* (1971). These are both tales of inner alienation, of divisions within the consciousness that can end only in permanent loss and that hold the characters on a wavering edge of madness. In *Korsoniloff* a schizoid teacher of philosophy tells the separate but inter-intrusive lives of the cold and analytical 'I' and the ineffectually passionate and amoral Korsoniloff, who seeks the truths that would destroy him. *Johnny Crackle sings*—a freer fantasy that lacks the clinical verisimilitude of his first novel—is the tale of a country boy ruined by an ambition to become a bigtime folk-singer, which he does not possess the talent to sustain. In its exploration of drug-created states of mind it moves constantly on the edge of surrealism and has the kind of self-consciousness that shows a writer still searching for his appropriate form. While this novel was being written, Cohen was already working on the stories included in *Columbus and the fat lady* (1972), which established the territory he would occupy in his later novels. *Night flights* (1978) includes some stories from *Columbus* and offers the same mixture of rural fantasy in stories that prefigure the larger novels and somewhat symbolic tales that explore the verges of psychological breakdown in a similar way to Cohen's earlier, smaller novels. *The expatriate* (1982) is a complete collection of his stories to date.

The five novels published between 1974 and 1981—*The disinherited* (1974), *Wooden hunters* (1975), *The colours of war* (1977), *The sweet second summer of Kitty Malone* (1979), and *Flowers of darkness* (1981)—are at first glance more conventional than Cohen's earlier books, but they can be linked with the more obviously experimental novels because they work less by linear chronology than by a constant interpenetration of past

and present. There is a disturbing sense of the provisional in the lives of all their characters, and ominous transitions that do not always turn out to be disastrous. All these novels—except for *Wooden hunters*, which takes place among deprived Indians and washed-up whites on an island resembling one of the Queen Charlottes—are set, or end, in the fictional Salem, in a southern Ontario countryside where the once-prosperous farming economy established by Loyalists and British immigrants is fast disintegrating. *The disinherited* is a chronicle novel that develops the theme of agrarian decline through the changes in the lives of a pioneering family. *The colours of war* seems at first to be a futurist novel as it describes a journey across a Canada riven by civil war; but the hero's journey through the future, and his destination in the heart of the Ontario countryside that Cohen has made his special terrain, represent a flight into the protective past. *The sweet second summer of Kitty Malone* centres on two drunken, ugly, life-worn people and their eventual happiness, and gains its effect by inverting the pattern of the customary romance. *Flowers of darkness*, which shows the destruction by the consequences of his own hypocrisy of a demonic preacher, reads in many ways like a genial parody of William Faulkner, to whose Yoknapatawpha County Cohen's creation of his own country of the imagination has been compared.

See John Kertzer, 'Time and its victims: the writing life of Matt Cohen', *Essays on Canadian Writing* 17 (Spring 1980); and John Moss, *Sex and violence in the Canadian novel* (1977), pp. 185-98.   GEORGE WOODCOCK

Cohen, Nathan (1923-71). Born in Sydney, N.S., he attended Mount Allison University from 1939 to 1942, acting and directing for the Mount Allison Players and writing for the *Argosy Weekly*. His columns in the *Argosy* (which he edited in 1942) already revealed Cohen's self-confident and often controversial views on politics, theatre, and the arts. After obtaining his B.A. in English, he wrote for and edited the labour *Glace Bay Gazette* in Nova Scotia from 1943 to 1945. In Toronto, he began to attract attention with his theatre reviews for the *Canadian Jewish Weekly* and *Wochenblatt* in 1946. He was the CBC's Toronto drama critic from 1948 to 1958, gaining national exposure on the programs 'Across the Footlights' and 'CJBC Views the Shows'. Besides editing his own publication, *The Critic*, from 1950 to 1953, and working as a CBC Television story editor from 1956 to 1958, Cohen chaired the CBC TV series 'Fighting Words (also aired on CBC Radio) from 1953 to 1962, and appeared as theatre critic on the radio series 'Critically Speaking'. His weekly theatre column appeared in the Toronto *Telegram* in 1957-8. From 1959 until his death he was the drama critic of the Toronto *Star*.

In his twenty-five years as a Toronto and national theatre critic, Cohen helped to guide the transformation of indigenous Canadian theatre from an amateur activity to fully professional status, and in his often controversial Toronto *Star* columns he made Canadian theatre a matter of national interest. Cohen saw the critic as the conscience of the theatre and demanded the highest standards of play production and dramatic writing, often infuriating actors and directors with his devastating reviews. He insisted that theatre be a vital art form and not merely a social diversion. 'What I expect from a play, from any play, is that passion and human concern that makes the stage unique.' Cohen repeatedly called for the writing and production of Canadian plays, while demanding that Canadian theatres meet international professional production standards—an attitude that frequently caused unprecedented animosity in the theatre community. Philip Stratford, in the CANADIAN FORUM (Feb. 1960), declared that 'the Cohen mystique consists in bringing ultra-Broadway standards to bear on a sub-Broadway product, and the result is always dispiriting, often ludicrous.' Cohen, however, defended his high critical standards by asserting that 'I don't think it's my duty to tell half-competent actors or playwrights that they're competent or brilliant. I don't think it's my job to lie. I seek perfection in the theatre.'

Cohen's life and critical work are surveyed in Wayne E. Edmonstone's *Nathan Cohen: the making of a critic* (1977). His colourful personality and impact on Canadian theatre and culture were dramatized in Rick SALUTIN's *Nathan Cohen: a review*, which was produced by Theatre Passe Muraille, Toronto, and published by the *Canadian Theatre Review* in 1981.   ANTON WAGNER

Coleman, Victor (b. 1944). Born in Toronto, he grew up there and in Montreal and was a high-school drop-out. Living on Toronto's Ward's Island in 1965, he founded the magazine *Island* and Island Press, which helped to shift the avant-garde poetry centre from Vancouver to Toronto. He entered book publishing as a production assistant for the Oxford University Press, Toronto (1966-7), and in 1967 joined COACH HOUSE PRESS, where for nearly a decade he served as the major Coach House editor: his catholic tastes were reflected in the work of the new Canadian writers and the American poets published by Coach House. After discontinuing *Island* and Island Press, he founded the Coach House literary magazine *Is*. For two years Coleman was director of the Nightingale Arts Council, operating in Toronto as A Space, which sponsored literary readings and performance art. He has also worked as editor and writer for the Association of Non-Profit Artist-Run Centres and published *Retrospective 4: documents of artist-run centres in Canada* (1981). At present he is director of the National Film Theatre, Kingston, Ont.

An important figure in Canadian avant-garde or post-modernist verse, Coleman believes poetic form to be the natural extension of content. Though influenced by many American poets—including Jack Spicer, Charles Olson, and Robert Creeley—he has developed his own distinctive voice. His poems are usually short reflections that eschew any formal structure. His early volumes—*From Erik Satie's notes to the music* (1965), *One/eye/love* (1967), *Light verse* (1969), *Old friends' ghosts: poems 1963-68* (1970), *Back east* (1971), and *Some plays: on words* (1971)—are filled with idiosyncratic verses condensed almost to the point of impenetrability. Yet the poems are always playful and challenging: intoxicated with the limitless possibilities of imagery and thought existing as inseparable entities, they demand to be seen as moments of intuition or discovery. More recent volumes— *America* (1972), *Parking lots* (1972), *Strange love* (1974), *Speech sucks* (1974), and *Traffic at both ends* (1978)—continue, sometimes at greater length, his experiments to shape language to its maximum force. Letting sound and movement create the form of poetry, Coleman rarely uses any tense other than the present, preferring to have all subjects exist simultaneously in the ear and the mind. Though some poems suffer from his tendency to play linguistic games for their own sake, more often his rejection of formal structures makes his verse a linguistic exploration and an intellectual discovery.

DAVID STAINES

Collective creations in English. A collective creation is the product of a cohesive theatre group's exploration of a given topic through research and the improvisation of scenes and characters. These improvisations are criticized and reworked until a basic shape for a full-length play emerges under the guidance of a director. However, as Paul Thompson, the major proponent of collective theatre in English Canada, emphasizes: 'the actor is more than a puppet . . . He's got his observations and he's quite as capable as anybody else of making a statement.' (Bob Wallace, 'Paul Thompson at Theatre Passe Muraille: bits and pieces', OPEN LETTER, series 2, no. 7, Winter 1974.) Although a rough script might record the main shape of the play for stage-management purposes, most collective creations do not exist in written form at all. Only the most successful productions might be scripted for publication: for example, Rick SALUTIN's *1837: the farmers' revolt* (1976), Ted Johns' *The farm show* (1976), and Linda Griffiths' and Paul Thompson's *Maggie and Pierre* (1979)—all Theatre Passe Muraille productions.

Often associated with words like 'alternate', 'documentary', 'agit-prop', and 'populist', collective creation began in France in the early sixties with Roger Planchon and came to Canada via Paul Thompson, who started a small collective theatre group (to become Theatre Passe Muraille) at Toronto's Rochdale College in the late sixties. Since then the collective method has had an important and widespread influence on Canadian theatre. Collective companies have sprung up from Newfoundland to British Columbia and, in the post-1967 years, created plays with national and regional Canadian subjects where none had existed. The number of collective companies declined, but the subjects of collective plays have broadened, and the rather loose 'collage' format of early collective creations has developed into a more coherent narrative structure. The great appeal of a collective creation lies in the actors' sense of commitment and immediacy, while its main weakness is a tendency to be predictable in attitudes and theatrical devices.

A quite different, but equally important, way in which collective creation has influenced Canadian drama is in its workshop development of a playwright's new work. Here the initial script is improvised upon by actors, sometimes vetted by an audience, before the playwright tackles the final version of the play, incorporating what he or she has learned from the collective workshop. Many successful plays have grown out of this process: Carol BOLT's *Buffalo jump* (1976) was collectively workshopped with Theatre Passe Muraille in 1972; Ken GASS's *Hurray for Johnny Canuck* (1978) was the result of Toronto's Factory Theatre Lab's treatment in 1974; and Rex Deverell's *Medicare* (1981) was a collaboration with Regina's Globe Theatre in 1979.

Toronto's Theatre Passe Muraille is undoubtedly the major theatre collective in Canada, with over thirty collective creations to its credit, including *Doukhobours* (prod. 1971), *I love you, Baby Blue* (prod. 1974), *The west show* (prod. 1976), and *Les maudits anglais* (prod. 1978). It has directly and indirectly influenced most of the collectives in Canada throughout the 1970s. The Mummers Troupe of Newfoundland with *They club seals, don't they?* (prod. 1976), Saskatoon's 25th Street House with *Paper wheat* (prod. 1977), Edmonton's Theatre Network with *Hard hats and stolen hearts* (prod. 1977) and its Catalyst Theatre's *Stand up for your rights* (prod. 1980) all follow the Passe Muraille pattern of critical examination of social issues in an episodic framework. However, Passe Muraille's political and social emphasis has been less influential on west-coast collectives like Vancouver's Tamahnous Theatre. Founded in 1971 to explore the psycho-dramatic theories of Grotowski and Artaud, it is a tightly knit collective headed by Larry Lillo. However, when shaping its collective creations, it makes majority decisions rather than deferring to a director as Passe Muraille does; and it has been more interested in exploring man's internal, rather than his social, nature in over twenty collective creations, including *The shaman's cure* (prod. 1975), *Deep Thought* (prod. 1977), and *Vertical dreams* (prod. 1979).

See Alan Filewood, 'Collective creation: process, politics and poetics', *Canadian Theatre Review* 34 (Spring 1980); and Robert Wallace and Cynthia Zimmerman, *The work: conversations with English-Canadian playwrights* (1982).   ELIZABETH HOPKINS

Collective creations in Québec. In the strict sense of a form of dramatic writing truly shared by all the actors, collective creation has been one of the main currents in Québec theatre since 1965. Fernand Villemure, who counted '415 collective creations produced in Québec between 1965 and 1974', cites as the first a work entitled

Collective creations in Québec

L'homme approximatif, performed at the Séminaire Saint-Antoine de Trois-Rivières in 1965. Le Théâtre universitaire de Université Laval ('Les Treize') was one of the first groups to devote itself to collective creation, beginning in 1968. Villemure's figures show a clear increase in this trend, beginning in 1970: 'There were 35 different creations in 1970, then 60 in 1971, 92 in 1972, and 112 in 1973.' Since 1975, however, the movement has slowed down, though it is still important.

Two companies in particular left their mark on the 1970s: Le Grand Cirque Ordinaire and Le Théâtre Euh!. Founded in 1969, the first of these had a remarkable success with *T'es pas tannée, Jeanne d'Arc?*, which played in Montreal and on tour from 1969 to 1973, and contributed more than any other show to the development of collective creation. *La famille transparente* (1970, *T'en rappelles-tu, Pibrac?* (1971), *L'opéra des pauvres* (1973), and *La tragédie américaine de l'enfant prodigue* ('rock opera' 1975) also made Le Grand Cirque Ordinaire the most influential and most-imitated group, until its dissolution in 1977. Théâtre Euh!, which defined itself as an 'agit-prop' group, performed mainly in Quebec City between 1970 and 1975. It gave 436 shows in all, generally in the street, or in cafeterias or other public places. Since 1971 the mode of operation of Théâtre de l'Eskabel in Montreal has been that production is a joint effort, but the script is generally signed. This model may be compared with the activity of the playwright Michel GARNEAU who, for several years, defined himself as a 'one-man collective'—an author who based his writing on suggestions from an actors' collective. Between 1969 and 1971 Jean-Claude GERMAIN worked in a similar way, presenting *Les enfants de Chenier dans un autre grand spectacle d'adieu* (1969), *Si Aurore m'était contée deux fois* (1970), and *Mise à mort d'la Miss des Miss* (1970), among other plays.

Since 1974 Le Théâtre Parminou in Victoriaville has become unquestionably the most active group in the area, putting on shows with Marxist-Leninist ideological leanings related to those of Théâtre Euh!. Other groups marked by their social commitment are Les Gens d'en bas in Rimouski, Le Théâtre de Quartier and Le Théâtre à l'ouvrage in Montreal, and Le Théâtre de Carton in Longueuil. Since 1973 several children's theatre companies have devoted themselves (though not exclusively) to collective creation: La Marmaille, La Grosse Valise, Le Théâtre de l'Oeil, and Le Théâtre de Carton, etc.

Although several companies are still producing collective creations, the latest trend seems to emphasize shared ideology and the collective operation of the group rather than joint writing. Thus there are now several 'women's collectives', although the best known of these, Le Théâtre expérimental des Femmes, has recently performed two 'signed' works, after having presented several collective creations. The Théâtre expérimental de Montréal, also dedicated to collective creation, has become the Nouveau Théâtre expérimental de Montréal after the formation of the Théâtre expérimental des Femmes as a distinct group. It created the Ligue nationale d'Improvisation in 1978, and since 1980 has devoted most of its time to Jean-Pierre Ronfard's cycle of plays, *Le roi boiteux*; *Perus*, a new collective creation, was staged in Nov. 1982. In Sherbrooke and elsewhere there is a new emphasis on theatrical animation, which may be seen as another form of collective creation that appeals to the spectator as well as the actor. With the return to dramaturgy, this trend is the most recent—perhaps the last—stage in the development of collective creation in Québec.

See Michel Vaïs, 'Auteur/création collective: mythe et réalité', *Jeu 4*; Fernand Villemure, 'Aspects de la création collective au Québec' *Jeu 4*; and articles by Gérald Sigouin in *Jeu 3* and *Jeu 4*.   JEAN-CLÉO GODIN

Collin, W.E. See *The* WHITE SAVANNAHS.

Colombo, John Robert (b. 1936). Born in Kitchener, Ont., he studied at the University of Toronto and while there he organized poetry readings at The Bohemian Embassy and edited *The Varsity Chapbook* (1959). In the near quarter-century since his graduation—as in-house editor for various publishers, managing editor of *The* TAMARACK REVIEW, teacher of creative writing, essayist and book-reviewer, editor and anthologist, translator and poet—he has become a national figure: John Robert Colombo, Man of Letters.

In the mid-sixties Colombo co-edited *Poetry 64/Poésie 64* (1963) with Jacques GODBOUT, an anthology of some of the most important new poets of his generation, and published his first book of 'found poetry', or what he also terms 'redeemed prose', *The Mackenzie poems* (1966). He has never looked back but become more and more the 'Master Gatherer' Robin SKELTON named him in an early review. And, although he earns artistic and critical recognition as a poet, he has gained mass popularity by becoming the pack-rat of Canadian culture and history.

Probably Canada's best-known maker of 'found poetry', Colombo creates in *The Mackenzie poems, John Toronto: new poems by Dr. Strachan* (1969), *The great wall of China* (1966), and *The great San Francisco earthquake and fire* (1971) pure examples of the genre. His first major collection, *Abracadabra* (1967), reveals a writer of larger ambitions, one who seeks to encounter the poem where previous texts and life collide. *Neo poems* (1970) is a paradigmatic example of his generous and open poetic. Hardly any of its poems contain clearly found prose, yet all of them insist that almost everything we know or imagine depends upon some previous 'text'. A richly ironic, devious, and witty book, it is dedicated to the great Dada collagist, Kurt Schwitters. In 'A Found Introduction' to the 'Found Poetry' section of *Open poetry* (1973) edited by Ronald Gross, Colombo says found poetry can teach us to 'respond aesthetically to the universe around us, not just to those separate parts of the world called works of art. It is possible to act as if the universe itself were an immense piece of art, a collage perhaps.' The slight found poems of *Praise poems* (1972) name figures Colombo wishes to honour through an acrostic use of other names. In *The sad truths* (1974) he mixes found texts with various kinds of commentary on privileged sub-texts to reveal the traces of previous writing on our lives. One of Colombo's most provocative books, *The great cities of antiquity* (1979), is a collection of found poems in a dizzying variety of modes, based on entries in the famous Eleventh Edition of the *Encyclopaedia Britannica*. Written in 1969, it is possibly Colombo's most extreme collage, a veritable textbook on the many formal experiments of modern and post-modern poetry. Colombo's mastery of his chosen art is clearly demonstrated in *Selected poems* (1982).

Collage, of course, is the great art of juxtaposition, and Colombo is a master of the witty juxtaposition, as the whole of *Translations from the English: found poems* (1974) demonstrates. Basically the same impulse that led to the notes and commentaries of that book led to that vast collection, *Colombo's Canadian quotations* (1974), his first mass-market book. A critic can fit this reference work into Colombo's creative *oeuvre*

with no trouble, for although Colombo has not 'redeemed' its prose, he has organized it so that the whole emerges as a massive *trouvé* designed to show us what has been said of and in Canada throughout its history. His other reference works, *Colombo's Canadian references* (1976) and *Colombo's names and nicknames* (1979), while not quite so audaciously successful, are manifestations of the same impulse to gather and collate various leaves of the world's book.

Colombo's book of Canada (1978) is 'a primer of basic Canadiana and a reader of unusual Canadian writing.' Other compilations—such as *Colombo's little book of Canadian proverbs, graffitti, limericks & other vital matters* (1975), *Colombo's Hollywood* (1979), and *222 Canadian jokes* (1981)—are slapstick-comedy versions of the more serious reference books, but they spring from the same impulse to collect the texts of ordinary life and frame them aesthetically. One of Colombo's most delightful books, *Mostly monsters* (1977), is both comic compilation and witty found poetry. It is a collage of the pop mythology of the past century in which pulp fiction, films, radio shows, comic strips, and much else are ransacked to create a vision of our dreams of good, nightmares of evil, and of our ambiguous awareness that real power lies somewhere between and cannot easily be identified or found on the 'right' side.

Displaying as an editor the same wide-ranging curiosity that activates his poetry, Colombo has edited several anthologies of verse, including *How do I love thee: sixty poets of Canada (and Québec) select and introduce their favorite poems from their work* (1970), *Rhymes and reasons: nine Canadian poets discuss their work* (1971), and *The poets of Canada* (1978); a number of anthologies dedicated to the fantastic, beginning with *Other Canadas: an anthology of science fiction and fantasy* (1979), and including *Years of light* (1982) and *Windigo* (1982); and some anthologies of translations, including *Under the eaves of a forgotten village* (with Nikola Roussanoff, 1975), *The Balkan range: a Bulgarian reader* (with Nikola Roussanoff, 1976), *Poems of the Inuit* (1981) and, in its way, his *Selected translations* (1982).

If the impression left by all these titles is one of indefatigable energy and unstoppable enthusiasm, that is in fact what Colombo's poetic is all about. Doug Fetherling's 'The literary politics of John Robert Colombo' (*Saturday Night*, May 1974) and Jean Mallinson's 'John Robert Colombo: a documen-

Colombo

tary poet as visionary' (*Essays on Canadian Writing*, Fall 1976) offer further insights into this protean literary force.

DOUGLAS BARBOUR

Combustion (1957-60). Raymond SOUSTER's fourth little magazine (following *Direction*, 1943-6; *Enterprise*, 1948; and CONTACT, 1952-4), *Combustion* was probably begun to help replace the U.S. magazine *Origin*, recently suspended by its editor, Souster's friend Cid Corman, who wrote weekly to Souster during the *Combustion* years suggesting subscribers and contributors and offering manuscripts that might otherwise have been published in *Origin*.

Combustion was mimeographed in editions of 100 to 125 copies. Initially its content was balanced between Canadian and international material; but in the later issues international work predominated, including generous selections by American writers previously published in *Origin*: Robert Creeley, Gary Snyder, Robert Duncan, Fielding Dawson, and Louis Zukofsky. *Combustion* made a significant contribution to U.S. literature, and a modest one to Canadian writing by keeping it informed of international accomplishments. Souster published fourteen issues, the last appearing in Aug. 1960, eight months before Corman's launching of the second series of *Origin*.

FRANK DAVEY

Conan, Laure. Pseudonym of Marie-Louise-Félicité ANGERS.

Cone, Tom. See DRAMA IN ENGLISH 1953 TO 1981.

Coney, Michael G. See SCIENCE FICTION AND FANTASY: 3.

Confederation poets. Since the publication of Malcolm Ross's influential anthology *Poets of the Confederation* (1960)—with selections from the poetry of Charles G.D. ROBERTS, Bliss CARMAN, Archibald LAMPMAN, and Duncan Campbell SCOTT—the term 'Confederation poets' has been generally taken to refer to these four writers, although others, such as William Wilfred CAMPBELL, George Frederick CAMERON, or Isabella Valancy CRAWFORD, are sometimes included in this designation. (See Roy Daniells, 'Crawford, Carman and D.C. Scott', in the *Literary History of Canada*.)

Publishing their first volumes of verse in the 1880s and 1890s, Roberts, Lampman, Carman, and Scott were pre-eminent among the first really good poets writing in the recently formed Dominion. There are other good reasons, both biographical and literary, for grouping them. All were close contemporaries born in the early 1860s; Roberts and Carman were cousins; Roberts briefly edited *The* WEEK, in which Carman published his first poem; Lampman was encouraged in his poetic efforts by his reading of Roberts' *Orion and other poems* (Philadelphia, 1880). Lampman and Scott were close friends; with Wilfred Campbell they began the 'AT THE MERMAID INN' column in the Toronto *Globe*, in 1892; after Lampman died, Scott published a memorial edition of his poems in 1900. All four poets drew much of their inspiration from Canadian nature, but they were also trained in the classics and cosmopolitan in their literary interests. All were serious craftsmen who assimilated their borrowings from English and American writing in a personal mode of expression, treating—frequently in a Canadian setting—universal themes and subjects. W.J. Keith has aptly called them the first distinctly Canadian school of writers in 'Archibald Lampman', *Profiles in Canadian literature* (1980), edited by Jeffrey M. Heath.

FRANCIS ZICHY

Connor, Ralph. Pseudonym of Charles William GORDON.

Constantin-Weyer, Maurice (1881-1961). Born in Bourbonnne-les-Bains, France, he had to interrupt his science studies at the Sorbonne for lack of funds. He immigrated to Canada in 1903 and settled in Saint-Claude, Man., where he raised cattle and became a jack-of-all-trades. In 1914, after an unsuccessful marriage to a Métisse, he returned to France to fight in the war and was gravely wounded. Contrary to what was long believed, he never returned to Canada. He spent the rest of his long life, mostly in Paris and Vichy, working as a newspaper editor, writing numerous articles, and about fifty books: novels, biographies, essays on a variety of subjects, translations, and even a play about Shakespeare, *Le grand Will* (Paris, 1945). In 1932 he received the Legion of Honour.

Some fifteen books by Constantin-Weyer have Canadian content and are grouped under the title 'L'épopée canadienne'. In his first novel, *Vers l'ouest* (Paris, 1921), translated as *Towards the West* (1931)—the love story of two Métis set against the back-

140

ground of the war between the Sioux and the Métis—Louis Riel's father plays a minor role. *La bourrasque* (Paris, 1926)—the translation of which was called *The half-breed* (1930) in the U.S. and *A martyr's folly* (1930) in Canada—is a highly fictionalized treatment of Louis Riel's stormy career. Both works are marred by the extravagant liberties the author takes with history, especially in *La bourrasque*, where Riel becomes a grotesque figure. Constantin-Weyer was attacked by some writers for caricaturing the Métis (see Donatien Frémont, *Sur le ranch de Constantin-Weyer*, 1932), yet he was not devoid of sympathy for them, as *Napoléon* (Paris, 1931), the story of a Métis, shows. His best-known work, *Un homme se penche sur son passé* (Paris, 1928)—translated by Slater-Brown as *A man scans his past* (1929)—won him the Prix Goncourt and fame. The plot, partly autobiographical, is a variation on the love triangle, and the characters are rather superficial; but the critics praised 'the atmosphere of the Prairies and the Forests, of the Great North and Cold (. . .) in this poem of Action' (Robert Garric). Also well received were his essay *Manitoba* (Paris, 1924); *Cinq éclats de silex* (Paris, 1927), which is subtitled 'novel' but is rather a collection of five separate stories; and *Clairière: récits du Canada* (Paris, 1929), another essay about Manitoba—translated by Conrad Elphinstone as *Forest wild* (London, 1932)—in which Constantin-Weyer, a keen observer of fauna and flora, poignantly depicts what he calls the 'rhythm of Life and Death'. His admiration for physical strength and moral courage is evident in his biographies of great men: *Cavalier de la Salle* (Paris, 1927)—translated as *The French adventurer: the life and exploits of La Salle* (1931); *Champlain* (Paris, 1931); *La Vérendrye* (Paris, 1941); and *Autour de l'épopée canadienne* (Paris, 1941), a series of sketches of the builders of New France. *Une corde sur l'abîme* (Paris, 1937), *Un sourire dans la tempête* (Paris, 1934), and *Telle qu'elle était en son vivant* (Paris, 1936)—which was reissued under the title *La loi de Nord* (Paris, 1947) and made into a successful film, *La piste du Nord*, by Jacques Feyder—show men pitched against the North and against each other. Even in the novels of Constantin-Weyer that take place in France, memories of Canada are often present. Of the francophones who have written novels about western Canada, he is certainly the most prolific, and Roger Motut considers him to be the best painter of the western landscape.

See Marguerite Constantin-Fortin, *Une femme se penche sur son passé* (Paris, 1939) and Roger Motut, *Maurice Constantin-Weyer, écrivain de l'Ouest et du Grand Nord* (1982).

PAULETTE COLLET

Contact (1952-4). The third little magazine founded by Raymond SOUSTER, following *Direction* (1943-6) and *Enterprise* (1948), it was begun in Jan. 1952 in open discontent with the policies of John SUTHERLAND's NORTHERN REVIEW. Souster's two principal advisers in this project were Louis DUDEK, who hoped it could be a 'workshop' for young Canadians, and the American poet and editor Cid Corman, who advocated high standards, even to the exclusion of Canadian contributors. For the most part Souster steered a middle course, although publishing many more American and international writers than Dudek liked. *Contact* was thus the first Canadian magazine to publish U.S. poets of the Black Mountain school—among them Charles Olson, Robert Creeley, Paul Blackburn, Denise Levertov, and Vincent Ferrini. It led eventually to Souster's arranging public readings for both Olson and Creeley in Toronto, in his Contact Poetry Readings of 1959-62. Published in mimeograph format, *Contact* continued for ten issues until Mar. 1954. Despite its U.S. and European contributors (among the latter were Octavio Paz, Jean Cocteau, Hugh McDiarmid, Jacques Prévert, and George Seferis), it never attracted more than fifty subscribers.

See Ken Norris, 'The significance of *Contact* and *CIV/n*' in *CIV/n: a literary magazine of the 50's* edited by Aileen Collins, with the assistance of Simon Dardick. FRANK DAVEY

Contact Press. See Louis DUDEK.

Contemporary Verse (1940-52). One of the leading Canadian poetry magazines of the 1940s and early 1950s, it was founded by Alan Crawley; at various times he was assisted by Dorothy LIVESAY, Anne MARRIOTT, Doris Ferne, and Floris Clarke McLaren. The first issue was published from North Vancouver in Sept. 1940; later the journal was edited from Victoria. *Contemporary Verse* played an important role at a time when there were few literary magazines in Canada. Crawley sought to maintain a high standard of writing, while keeping his pages open to poets of many inclinations. The criteria he announced in one of his editorials were that the work he

Contemporary Verse

published must be 'serious in thought and expression and contemporary in theme, treatment, and technique'. The more than 120 poets that appeared included virtually every important name in that vital era in the development of a Canadian poetic tradition, as well as new talents; a number of our best contemporary poets were first published in his magazine. Thirty-nine issues had appeared by the time Crawley felt he had completed his task and ceased publication at the end of 1952.

See *Alan Crawley and 'Contemporary Verse'* (1976) edited by Joan McCullagh, with a reminiscent introduction by Dorothy Livesay. GEORGE WOODCOCK

Contes du pays incertain (1962). The most important work of Jacques FERRON and winner of a Governor General's Award, it is a collection of legends, fables, and tales that illustrate the *indépendentiste* notion that the 'uncertain' country' has become an essential political and literary myth in Québec, opposing and contradicting the 'two-solitudes' myth created by Hugh MacLENNAN. Ferron shows that French Canada will remain an uncertain and absurd country as long as its territorial imagination extends from St John's to Victoria, from 'one pond to another'. *Contes du pays incertain* established Ferron as the most gifted 'conteur' of Québec. His imagination excels in the use of fable, irony, and allegory.

These tales were inspired by Ferron's contact with storytellers in the Gaspé. Their themes identify the problems of an 'uncertain people': the breaking down of the myth that the land and the *revanche des berceaux* are means of survival; the slavery of the city-dweller victimized by capitalism; the corruption of politicians; the complicity of the Church with the politically powerful and the wealthy; the hypocrisy of French writers like Saint-Denys GARNEAU who describe their personal anguish instead of helping to construct a national literature; the desirability of the Indian nations and the Québécois to work together towards common goals of territorial and cultural recognition. In 'Mélie et le boeuf', the most striking tale, a depressed and sickly mother of thirteen (the typical mother of Québécois 'anti-terroir' literature) becomes emotionally close to her favourite calf, which eventually becomes an English-speaking bull that excites all the cows in the country. In 'Le paysagiste' Ferron explores one of his most positive recurring themes: the need to be close to nature in

order to achieve personal and collective awareness.

Contes du pays incertain was republished in 1968 with *Contes anglais et autres* and *Contes inédits*. A selection of these stories, many of them from the first collection, was translated by Betty Bednarski and published in English under the title *Tales from an uncertain country* (1972).

See Gérard BESSETTE, ' "Mélie et le boeuf" de Jacques Ferron', *Modern Fiction Studies*, vol. XXII, 3 (1976); and Jean-Pierre Boucher, *Les contes de Jacques Ferron* (1974). DONALD SMITH

Cook, Michael (b.1933). Born in London, Eng., Cook attended various schools until he was fifteen. In 1949 he joined the British Army, serving for the next twelve years in Europe and the Far East and rising to the rank of sergeant. Some of his time was spent devising theatrical entertainment for the troops. After leaving the army, he worked briefly in a ball-bearing factory and in 1962 he entered Nottingham University, where he trained as a teacher. In the mid-1960s he arrived in Newfoundland and soon afterwards was employed as a drama specialist in Memorial University's Extension Service. Subsequently he joined the university's English department and in 1979 was promoted to associate professor. He has been active in Newfoundland as a promoter of theatre, a critic, director, actor, and, after 1970, as a playwright. He has recently taken extended leaves from teaching to devote himself to writing.

Cook's first published play was *Colour the flesh the colour of dust* (1972), a historical drama set in St John's in 1762. It is strongly influenced by Brecht, and Cook later described it, somewhat too harshly, as 'a lousily structured play'. The 1973 radio drama *Tiln* (1976) perhaps showed too plainly the influence of Beckett. *The head, guts and sound bone dance* (1974) is an effort to evoke the antiquated attitudes of oldtime Newfoundlanders as a bizarre contrast to the contemporary life-style on the island. It features—for perhaps the first time in Canadian theatre—the splitting and gutting of codfish on stage. *Jacob's wake* (1975) is an ambitious and occasionally powerful depiction of the disintegration of a Newfoundland outport family. *Quiller* (1975) and *Terese's creed*, which is included in *Tiln & other plays* (1976), are one-act plays, the latter a monologue in which Cook explores the inner life of outport characters. *Quiller* is probably

Cook's finest play to date. *On the rim of the curve* (1977) is an attempt to dramatize the final days on earth of the Beothuk Indians, Newfoundland's aboriginal people. *The Gayden chronicles* (1979) is a three-act play exploring the life of a rebel in the British navy who was hanged in St John's in 1812. The Newfoundland setting here is of no importance, which suggests that Cook may have been trying to give his work more general appeal. In 1980, however, he published the first chapter of a novel set in a Newfoundland outport (in *Aurora: new Canadian writing*, edited by Morris Wolfe): thus his fascination with Newfoundland continues.

Cook's plays celebrate the elemental and instinctive; they are harangues—assaults upon the audience's sense of decorum, and even upon intellect. Cook has written: 'I've always had a deep distrust in my own head of intellectual responses.' One critic has suggested that he is one of the 'rebarbarizers of civilized culture'. His plays achieve few subtle effects, yet they are daring, passionate, and full of movement.

Cook's plays have been collected in *Tiln & other plays* and *Three plays* (1977). He has discussed his own life and work in *Canadian Theatre Review*, I (1974) and XVI (1977); in *Canadian Drama*, II (1976); and in Geraldine Anthony, ed., *Stage voices* (1978). There is a comment by Donald R. Bartlett on Cook's work in *The Newfoundland Quarterly*, vol. LXXVIII, no. 3 (1982). PATRICK O'FLAHERTY

Cook, Ramsay. See HISTORICAL WRITING IN ENGLISH: 5.

Copway, George. See INDIAN LITERATURE: 2.

Corriveau, Monique. Pseudonym of Monique Chouinard. See CHILDREN'S LITERATURE IN FRENCH: 3 and SCIENCE FICTION AND FANTASY: 3.

Costain, Thomas B (1885-1965). Thomas Bertram Costain was born in Brantford, Ont., and educated there. He began his journalistic career as a reporter for the Brantford *Expositor* and then worked in Guelph and for the Maclean-Hunter publications in Toronto. He became editor of *Maclean's* in 1914 and held that post until 1920, when he immigrated to the United States (he later became an American citizen) to be an associate editor of *The Saturday Evening Post*. In 1934 he became eastern story editor for Twentieth-Century Fox, and from 1939 to 1946 was advisory editor for Doubleday in New York. In this period he began to write historical fiction, and his first novel, *For my great folly* (1942), was a bestseller. This was followed by *Ride with me* (1944). In 1946 he began to devote his full time to writing fiction.

Costain's novels remain entertaining specimens of the historical-romance/adventure mode of popular fiction, and range in subject-matter from the Cathay of Kubla Khan, to Napoleon's Europe, to New France. Fast-paced, exciting, stocked with easily understood characters, both fictional and historical, and employing complex, coincidence-packed plots, his works sold in the millions. *The black rose* (1945), for example, topped the two-million mark in all editions and was made into a Hollywood spectacle film. Other novels include *The moneyman* (1947), *The silver chalice* (1952), *The tontine* (1955), *Below the salt* (1955), and *The darkness and the dawn* (1959). Costain's novels with Canadian settings are *High towers* (1949), a treatment of the Le Moyne family of New France that ranges from Hudson Bay to New Orleans; and *Son of a hundred kings* (1950), the rags-to-riches story of an orphaned immigrant boy in a Canadian small town in the 1890s. Costain also wrote a popular history of New France: *The white and the gold: the French régime in Canada* (1954).

Costain's career follows in some respects a pattern set by Gilbert PARKER and others, in which small-town Canadians made their way in the great metropolitan centres on the strength of their gifts as writers of popular fiction and romance. His books sold nearly 12 million copies. His success as a popular writer was recognized by academe when he was given an honorary doctorate by the University of Western Ontario.

DENNIS DUFFY

Coulter, John (1888-1980). Born in Belfast, he attended the School of Art and School of Technology there and then won a scholarship to the University of Manchester. He returned to Ireland in 1912 and taught textile design at the School of Technology, Belfast, for one year, then art and English at the Coleraine Academical Institution, Ulster, for two years, and at Wesley College, Dublin, until 1919. He moved to Dublin chiefly to be close to the leaders of the Irish literary renaissance and to the Abbey Theatre. While there he began to write for the theatre, before returning to Belfast in the hope or organizing a theatre company. But the conflict over Irish independence was at its height and made this venture impossible. He moved to London to write and do freelance work for the BBC, for which he worked until 1936. During those years he edited the *Ulster Review* in 1924, and wrote for John Middleton Murry's *The Adelphi*, becoming managing editor (1927-30) when Murry reorganized it and renamed it *The New Adelphi* in 1927. There Coulter met Olive Clare Primrose, a Canadian writer whom he married in 1936 after settling in Toronto. They intended to return to England, but her poor health and the approach of war kept them in Canada. Coulter published the story of their courtship in *Prologue to a marriage: letters and diaries of John Coulter and Olive Clare Primrose* (1979), a tribute to their happy life together until her death in 1971. They had two daughters: Primrose, a writer, and Clare, a well-known actress.

Besides writing for journals, magazines, and radio in both Canada and Britain, and working for three years (1938-41) in New York for CBS radio, Coulter published plays, librettos, poetry, a novel, a biography, and his memoirs. His early plays, reflecting his Irish background in setting and theme, are noteworthy for their local colour and careful construction; but their lack of an element of surprise or dramatic reversal detracts from their overall effect. *The house in the quiet glen* (1937), which won several prizes at the Dominion Drama Festival in 1937, is a one-act comedy about an Irish girl whose parents arrange to marry her to a widower, not knowing she has designs on the widower's son. *The family portrait* (1937) is a full-length comedy, written for the Abbey Theatre, about the reactions of a Belfast family to its playwrighting son and his successful play, which mirrors their own lives. It was not produced at the Abbey because of Coulter's inability to rewrite the final scenes to the satisfaction of Lennox Robinson, who nevertheless used the first act as a text for his acting classes there. *The drums are out* (1971) treats a more solemn theme: the effect of the Irish civil war on Protestants and Catholics alike. Set in Belfast in the early 1920s, it focuses on a family whose father is a policeman and whose daughter is secretly married to a member of the Irish Republican Army. It was premiered at the Abbey Theatre on 12 July 1948. The inclusion in the published text of both the revised and the original versions of the third act is a concrete indication of Coulter's difficulty in providing a totally satisfying ending for his plays.

Coulter became fascinated with the Métis leader Louis Riel and wrote three plays about him. In 1949 he completed *Riel* (1962; 1972; rev. 1975), a wide-ranging dramatization of events in Riel's life between the Red River Rebellion of 1870 and his hanging in 1885. According to the author's note, it was 'designed for presentation in the Elizabethan manner'—a farsighted step to take four years before the construction of Stratford's revolutionary thrust stage. In 1975 *Riel* received a production worthy of that design at the National Arts Centre, directed by Jean Gascon, with Albert Millaire as Riel. *The trial of Louis Riel* (1968), a courtroom drama and a much more limited play, uses transcripts from the trial and includes some French dialogue, with English translation supplied by an interpreter. Since its first production in Regina, where Riel was hanged, this play has become an annual attraction there. *The crime of Louis Riel* (1975)—the most readable play in the trilogy, combining the expansiveness of *Riel* with the intensity of *The trial of Louis Riel*—won the Dominion Drama Festival's regional prize for best Canadian play of 1967.

Coulter wrote three opera librettos, all for the Canadian composer Healey Willan. *Transit through fire* (1942), a short verse-drama, concentrates on the bitter reflections of a young soldier on leave, and of his wife, about the society before the Second World War that gave its youth great hopes and then sent it to war. This, and *Deirdre of the sorrows* (1944)—a retelling in verse and prose of the ancient Irish story of the foundling girl whose lovers are fated to die—were the first two Canadian operas commissioned and broadcast by the CBC. Coulter's first published play, *Conochar* (1917), is about the same legend. *Deirdre* (1966), a slightly revised version of the 1944 work, was first staged in 1965 at the Macmillan Theatre, Toronto, and was also the first Canadian opera to be produced, in 1967, by the Canadian Opera Company, at Toronto's O'Keefe Centre.

Coulter's *The blossoming thorn* (1946)—a collection of light, lyrical, romantic, elegiac, and sometimes humorous poems that are superior to the verse in his three librettos—is his alternative to what he considered to be the over-intellectual and unemotional qualities in modern verse. His one novel, *Turf smoke: a fable of two countries* (1945)—an adaptation of an unpublished play, *Holy Manhattan*—tells of an Irish immigrant in New York who is unable to adapt to the American way of life but finally realizes he cannot return to Ireland either. While little attempt is made to explore character or situation, it is notable for its descriptive passages in which the immigrant recalls his native land. Coulter also wrote *Churchill* (1945), which he called a 'dramatic biography'—a short journalistic account based on the sources he used for an unpublished 'living-newspaper' play, *Mr Churchill of England*.

In later life Coulter continued to write and revise plays for the stage and for radio. One of these, *François Bigot: a rediscovery in dramatic form of the fall of Quebec* (1978), was revised from a version broadcast on CBC radio in 1970. In the form of a 'Man Alive' series of interviews, it explores the character and deviousness of the last Intendant of New France. Two unpublished radio presentations further indicate Coulter's interest in, and sympathy for, French Canada: *A tale of old Québec* and *Québec in 1670*, broadcast on BBC radio in 1935 and on CBS in 1940. Other unpublished scripts are *Oblomov*, adapted from the Russian novel of Goncharov, which has been translated into several languages and was produced on CBC television in 1962; *Sleep, my pretty one*, a verse-play about a woman who cannot accept her stepmother, produced at Toronto's Centre Stage in 1961; *A capful of pennies* (also titled *This glittering dust*), about the off-stage life of the famous British actor Edmund Kean, produced in Toronto on stage and on CBC radio in 1967; and *God's Ulsterman*, a sequence of two plays (*Dark days of ancient hate* and *Red hand*) about the injustice committed by Cromwell in Ireland and its legacy in strife-torn Belfast, both produced on CBC radio in 1974.

Coulter spent his last years writing his memoirs, *In my day* (1980), a long account of his life, career, and of people he knew in Canada and abroad. It was published the year he died in a signed limited edition of 93 copies—one for each year of the author's life. He had also been editing his wife's journals and had written two new plays that he had given to Theatre Passe Muraille for production.

Coulter was active in the cultural life of Canada in other ways. In 1944 he was among the artists who presented a brief to the Turgeon Committee of the House of Commons, which was responsible for the formation of the Massey Commission, and thus the Canada Council; and in 1952 he persuaded his friend Tyrone Guthrie to come to Canada to direct the first production of the Stratford Festival. Coulter was also a founder of the Canadian Arts Council, now the Canadian Conference of the Arts. Near the end of his life he received an honorary doctorate from York University and an honorary life membership in the Association for Canadian Theatre History. For both his eightieth and ninetieth birthdays the CBC produced special radio and television tributes to him.

Coulter was perhaps never totally at home in Canada. His preference for non-Canadian subjects, and in his Canadian plays for historical topics and formal dialogue rather than contemporary settings and a Canadian idiom, suggests that he was not completely in touch with Canadian life. At the age of ninety he remarked: 'I don't think anyone can emigrate successfully after their mid-20s. I never did feel truly Canadian and I don't now.' Nevertheless he showed younger writers that they must write from their own roots and that Canadian history could be interesting on stage.

The Mills Memorial Library of McMaster University has a collection of Coulter's literary essays and plays; many of his out-of-print and unpublished works can be found in the Metropolitan Toronto Library. Coulter wrote a short account of his writing career in an introduction to *The drums are out*, and in a chapter of *Stage voices* (1978), edited by Geraldine Anthony, who has also written the only book on Coulter for the Twayne World Authors Series (1976).

JAMES NOONAN

Crath, Paul. See UKRAINIAN WRITING.

Crawford, Isabella Valancy (1850-87). Born in Dublin of an educated and cultured family, she came to Canada in 1858, living first in Paisley, Canada West (Ont.), where her father, Dr Stephen Dennis Crawford, was the first doctor. She moved with her family to Lakefield, staying initially in the house of Robert Strickland, nephew of Mrs MOODIE and Mrs TRAILL; then to Peterborough, where Dr Crawford died in 1875 and Isabella's only surviving sister died in 1876; and finally to Toronto, remaining there with her mother in poverty until her death from heart failure. The Crawford family history is a record of hardships that included the childhood deaths of all of the twelve or thirteen Crawford children except Isabella Valancy, Emma Naomi, and Stephen Walter; the family's frequent moves and progressive impoverishment; and the disgrace of Dr Crawford's trial and conviction for misappropriation fo public funds while he was township treasurer in Paisley. This event—accounts of which Eric Parker has recently uncovered in the *Paisley Advocate* (1865, 1866, and 1867)—provides a hitherto unsuspected explanation for the Crawford family's later reputation for being proud and keeping to themselves.

Although Isabella Valancy Crawford wrote a great many short stories and novelettes, largely for the American magazine market, her literary reputation is based on her poems, particularly her narrative poems. She published only one book in her lifetime, *Old Spookses' Pass, Malcolm's Katie, and other poems* (Toronto, 1884), 1,000 copies of which James Bain & Son produced at the author's expense. Despite generally favourable reviews in the English and Canadian publications to which she sent this 224-page volume, only fifty copies were sold. No definitive and complete edition of her poetry exists—many poems that appeared in newspapers have been uncollected—though it has been published in four volumes: *Old Spookses' Pass* (1884), which was reissued in 1886 and 1898, and which Crawford herself declared was as 'decorated with press errors as a Zulu chief is laden with beads'; John Garvin's cavalierly edited *The collected poems of Isabella Valancy Crawford* (1905), with an introduction by Ethelwyn WETHERALD, reprinted in facsimile edition along with a new introduction by James REANEY (1972); Katherine Hale's selected anthology *Isabella Valancy Crawford* (1923), reproducing the editorial 'improvements' of her husband John Garvin that he made for the 1905 edition; and *Hugh and Ion* (1977), Glenn Clever's edition of the incomplete but nonetheless powerful narrative poem found by Dorothy LIVESAY buried among the four boxes of Crawford manuscripts and materials in the Lorne Pierce Collection of the Douglas Library at Queen's University.

Crawford's prose, generally considered to be the bread-and-butter writing by which she earned her precarious living, is even less accessible. Much of it is in manuscript form in the Lorne Pierce Collection, and probably much more is still hidden in unindexed nineteenth-century magazines. Some, however, has recently been published: *Selected stories of Isabella Valancy Crawford* (1975) and *Fairy*

tales of Isabella Valancy Crawford (1977), both edited by Penny Petrone, and *The Halton boys: a story for boys* (1979) edited by Frank M. Tierney. The fiction displays a skilful and energetic use of literary conventions made popular by Dickens, such as twins and doubles, mysterious childhood disappearances, stony-hearted fathers, sacrificial daughters, wills and lost inheritances, recognition scenes, and, to quote one of her titles, 'A kingly restitution'.

With her own life filled with tribulation, Crawford chose to make the dialogue of hope and despair and the purgatorial role of suffering the central themes of much of her work, including the narrative poems 'Malcolm's Katie' and *Hugh and Ion*. Written in blank verse interspersed with lyrics of various metrical forms, they are early milestones in Canada's tradition of narrative poetry. In 'Malcolm's Katie' Crawford adapted to the setting of pioneer Canada the domestic idyll as she learned it from Tennyson. Striking and new, however, is Crawford's location of Max and Katie's conventional love story within a context of Indian legends—Indian Summer and the battle of the North and South Winds. In *Hugh and Ion*, an incomplete poem written near the end of Crawford's life, two friends who have fled the noxious city—probably contemporary Toronto—for purification in the primal wilderness, carry on a sustained dialogue, Hugh arguing for hope, light, and redemption and Ion pointing out despair, darkness, and intractable human perversity. 'Old Spookses' Pass' is a dialect poem, set in the Rocky Mountains, concerning a dream vision of a midnight cattle stampede toward a black abyss that is stilled by a whirling lariat; 'The helot' makes use of the Spartans' practice of intoxicating their helots in order to teach their own children not to drink, as the starting-point for a highly incantory and hypnotic poem that ends in Bacchic possession and death; and 'Gisli the Chieftain' fuses mythic elements such as the Russian spring goddess Lada and the Icelandic Brynhild into a narrative of love, betrayal, murder, and reconciliation. These poems follow a pattern of depicting the world as a battleground of opposites—light and dark, good and evil—reconciled by sacrificial love.

Recognition of Isabella Valancy Crawford's extraordinary mythopoeic power and her structural use of images came first in James Reaney's lecture 'Isabella Valancy Crawford ' in *Our living tradition* (series 3,

1959). *The Isabella Valancy Crawford symposium* (1979), a collection of papers delivered at the University of Ottawa in 1977, presents a good cross-section of the new research being done on editing Crawford, tracking down her elusive biography, and evaluating her work. See also Lynne Suo's 'Annotated bibliography on Isabella Valancy Crawford' in *Essays in Canadian Writing* 11 (Spring 1977).   CATHERINE ROSS

Crawley, Alan. See CONTEMPORARY VERSE.

Creighton, D.G. (1902-79). Donald Grant Creighton was born in Toronto and educated at the University of Toronto. He never lived for long away from his birthplace and its vicinity, except for a brief period at Oxford University, from which he returned in 1927 to teach in the department of history at Toronto. He remained there, acting as chairman from 1954 to 1959; he was made University Professor of History in 1968 and when he died he was a Fellow of Massey College.

Though Creighton was a natural writer to a degree few historians attain, his literary inclinations never diminished his zest for teaching, and in other respects he was a dedicated participant in the academic community, active in the Royal Society of Canada, to which he was elected in 1946 and whose Tyrrell Medal he won in 1951, and in the Canadian Historical Association, of which he was president in 1956-7. He twice won the Governor General's Award, in 1952 and 1955, for the two volumes of his biography of Sir John A. Macdonald; he was one of the first winners of the Molson Prize (in 1964); and in 1967 he became a Companion of the Order of Canada. He was advisory editor for the eighteen volumes of histories in the Canadian Centenary Series.

Creighton was never merely an academic historian, for he placed a high value on literary style, writing in a craftsmanly prose and deliberately making his books accessible to a large public outside the universities. He wrote with great strength of opinion, so that his historical narratives are coloured by his conservative and nationalistic political attitudes. He always remained at heart an Upper Canadian, distrustful of the aspirations of Québec and unwilling to give importance to the regional differences between central and western Canada. He disputed freely with the liberal historians who, in his younger days, represented the dominant

trend in his own discipline in Canada. But his controversial stance had its positive aspects, for he thought daringly, designed his books on a dramatic scale, and created some enduring Canadian myths. Like the Greeks, who assigned history its own muse—Clio—Creighton regarded his discipline as a creative art.

Perhaps the most important formative influence on Creighton was that of Harold INNIS, who wrote as an economist but contributed much to our understanding of Canadian history through books like *The fur trade in Canada* (1930) and *The cod fisheries* (1940), in which he showed that Canada had an economic history before it had a political one. Creighton adopted and considerably adapted Innis's ideas, expressing them, in their changed forms, in an attractively fluent prose that contrasted with the gnarled and obscure manner in which his mentor wrote. (Later Creighton paid his intellectual debt by writing a tribute, *Harold Adams Innis: portrait of a scholar*, 1957.) Creighton's first book, *The commercial empire of the St. Lawrence: 1760-1850* (1937)—reprinted in 1956 as *The empire of the St. Lawrence*—showed how the fur-trading system of the St Lawrence and the Great Lakes created an east-west pattern of transport, occupation, and development that became an enduring historical factor, countering the geographical lines of the continent that run from north to south. *British North America in Confederation* (1939), a more specialized and limited book, was concerned with the balance of financial and economic powers in 1867, the year of Confederation.

In his third book, *Dominion of the North: a history of Canada* (1944), Creighton developed on a much larger time-scale the insights projected in *The empire of the St. Lawrence*. Since he saw the process of early Canadian development as dependent on a single urge—that of fur-trading and consequent exploration—lasting almost a century to the eve of Confederation, he tended to have a highly unified view of the history of Canada. He was not a regionalist, impressed by the historical differences between the various parts of Canada; nor was he a continentalist, impressed by the geographical urge that pointed towards a coalescence between Canada and the United States. *Dominion of the North* shows that he was an early Canadian nationalist, and he remained one to the end of his life. It demonstrated Creighton's conviction that Canada had its own manifest destiny, defined by the old trade routes that went east to west from Montreal to the Pacific, the routes that railways and highways would later follow. *Dominion of the North* is at once brilliantly polemical and impeccably researched; the combination of information and imagination resulted in a grand mythic view of Canadian history that the rest of Creighton's works developed.

A myth requires a hero. The idea of Canada as a nation emerged in the movement towards Confederation that followed the decline of the fur traders, and Creighton saw the personification of that idea in Sir John A. Macdonald, the Dominion's founding prime minister, whose first adequate biography he wrote. The first volume, *The young politician* (1952), takes Macdonald's career to the high point of Confederation; the second and final volume, *The old chieftain* (1955), deals with the years of power and decline. Most political biographies submerge the man in the events, but in these two books Creighton sustained the biographical intent and produced a vital—if perhaps excessively heroic—portrait of Macdonald.

After the rather pedestrian *Story of Canada* (1959), Creighton's next book showed him still deeply involved in Macdonald's period. *The road to Confederation: the emergence of Canada, 1863-67* (1964) is an account of how British North Americans, from Nova Scotia to Upper Canada, recognized that unity was the best way to solve their common economic problems and perhaps the only way to protect themselves from the political danger posed by an America resurgent at the end of the Civil War.

Nationalistic myths, like any other, are subject to erosion by events, and by 1970, when Creighton published *Canada's first century, 1867-1967*, he was considerably less confident about Canada's destiny than in his earlier books. He recognized that the north-south pull was stronger than he had thought, and that Canada's historic east-west ties were strained by the cultural and economic invasion from the United States. He also saw the trend to provincial autonomy and the rise of Québec separatism as elements weakening the Canadian political structure. He was unable to admit that stronger regions might build a new kind of confederalism, and as a result he felt a weakening confidence regarding the future of his country.

This pessimistic mood was further developed in his last major work, *The forked road: Canada 1939-1957* (1976), in which Macken-

zie King is cast—in contrast to John A. Macdonald—as the betrayer of Canada's future, the politician who sold the past to continentalism. The element of gloom does not lessen the power of these later and less hopeful books. Indeed, it provides the element of shadow that is perhaps necessary for a great myth.

Among Creighton's lesser works are *Towards the discovery of Canada* (1972), a collection of memoirs, essays, and speeches; *Canada: the heroic beginnings* (1974), a pictorial history that revives some of his earlier confidence in Canada's destiny; and *Takeover* (1978), his only adventure into imaginative writing—a highly ambiguous novel about Canadian-American relations that reinforces one's feeling that Creighton in the end saw his early vision of Canada ending, like so many myths of great adventure, in negation.

No account of Creighton is complete without reference to the obliquity of his influence. He has rarely been popular among other historians. But to imaginative writers—poets and novelists—he has offered a pattern within which they could shape their intuitions about Canadian life. On writers whose deep sense of history was modified by their awareness of place—like Hugh MacLENNAN, Margaret LAURENCE, Margaret ATWOOD, and Al PURDY—his glancing effect is evident.

See George WOODCOCK, 'Literary echoes', in *Books in Canada* (Mar. 1980); and J.M.S. Careless, 'Donald Creighton and Canadian history: some reflections' in J.S. Moir, ed., *Character and circumstance: essays in honour of Donald Grant Creighton* (1970).

See also HISTORICAL WRITING IN ENGLISH: 7.   GEORGE WOODCOCK

Crémazie, Octave (1827-79). Claude-Joseph-Olivier Crémazie, called Octave by his mother, was born in Quebec City and studied at the Petit Séminaire from 1836 to 1843. In Jan. 1884 he opened a bookstore in Québec that sold, along with books, a variety of imported goods and became within a decade an important business establishment. Crémazie was an active member of the Institut canadien de Québec, founded in 1847 to promote French cultural activities and to ensure the preservation of the French language. His first verse was published in 1849; by 1858 he was being called the national bard. When his bookstore became bankrupt in Nov. 1862, owing to some questionable financial transactions, he left for France, changed his name to 'Jules Fontaine', and for sixteen years lived mostly in Paris, subsisting on a small allowance sent by his brothers. He died in Le Havre.

Two patriotic poems brought fame to Crémazie: 'Le vieux soldat canadien' (1855), celebrating the arrival in 1855 of *La Capricieuse*, the first French naval ship to visit Québec in almost a century, and 'Le Drapeau de Carillon' (1858), marking the centenary of Montcalm's victory at Fort Carillon (Fort Ticonderoga). Québécois were deeply moved by Crémazie's stanzas expressing their undying attachment to the land, the language, and the traditions of their ancestors. Both poems include a song in the manner of Béranger; set to music, their popularity lasted for many years.

Following a visit to Paris in 1856, Crémazie began to explore traditional themes in a series of lyric poems: death and faith in 'Les Morts'; tragedy striking at humble folk in 'La fiancée du marin'; the exotic lure of Spain, Italy, and the Orient in 'Mille-Îles'; and the courage of the Canadian logger in 'Le Chant des voyageurs'. Attracted later by the concept and realism of Gautier's 'La comédie de la mort', and seeking to give leadership to the emerging literary movement, Crémazie conceived a lengthy narrative poem in three parts, 'Promenade de trois morts', of which only Part I was completed.

Crémazie ceased to write verse when he went into exile at the age of thirty-five. From France he corresponded regularly with his family and occasionally with friends. Of special interest are his letters to abbé Henri-Raymond CASGRAIN, in which the poet presents his views on many questions relating to literature. During the Franco-Prussian war, Crémazie wrote a diary that gives, besides an account of life in Paris during the siege, a further insight into the opinions and character of the writer.

Most of Crémazie's poems were first published in *Le Journal de Québec*; 'Promenade de trois morts' appeared in Les SOIRÉES CANADIENNES (1862). *La Littérature canadienne de 1850 à 1860* (vol. II, 1864) reprinted 25 of Crémazie's poems. The *Oeuvres complètes* (Montréal, 1882) presented 24 poems, the 'Journal du siège de Paris', and 46 letters. The modern critical edition of Crémazie's complete works is in two volumes: *Oeuvres I—poésies* (1972) and *Oeuvres II—prose* (1976).

Some biographical and critical writings dealing with Crémazie are: H.-R. Casgrain's 'Notice biographique' in the 1882 *Oeuvres complètes*; O. Condemine's introductions to *Oeuvres I—poésies* and *Oeuvres II—prose*; S. Marion, 'Octave Crémazie', in *Les lettres canadiennes d'autrefois*, V (1946); and several studies in *Crémazie et Nelligan, recueil d'études* (1981), edited by Réjean Robidoux and Paul Wyczynski.   ODETTE CONDEMINE

Criticism in English. 1. THE NINETEENTH CENTURY. Written chiefly in the form of the instructive essay, early criticism tends to be corrective in function, addressing writers as much as readers about the need for a practical literature that would further the establishment of the Canadian community while maintaining the values, standards, and aesthetics of nineteenth-century Britain. Most critics were predisposed to admire or call for a literature of an idealized reality portraying Canadian experience and affirming Protestant morality. The inhibiting or distorting effect of American and British dominance of the culture, and of its publishing industry, are the subject of recurring commentary, beginning with Susanna MOODIE's introduction to *Mark Hurdlestone* (London, 1853). Sir Daniel Wilson, in his review article in *The Canadian Journal of Industry, Science and Art* (Jan. 1858), comments on the difficulties that arise for writers who see the settler's Canada either in terms of European myths or indigenous Indian lore. Edward H. DEWART compiled *Selections from Canadian poets* (Montreal, 1864; rpr. 1973), the first anthology of Canadian poetry, in the belief that 'A national literature is an essential element in the formation of national character.' In his introductory essay, he writes unequivocally that 'the growth of an indigenous literature' had been stunted by 'our colonial position'. While admitting the 'crudity and imperfection' of Canadian poetry of the time, he nevertheless finds much 'true poetry'—in the work of SANGSTER, McLACHLAN and others. The twenty-five years that elapsed between this pioneer work and William Douw LIGHTHALL's *Songs of the great Dominion* (London, 1889; rpr. 1971) saw many changes: a political identity for Canada; a spirit not only of patriotism but of enthusiasm and hopefulness; and a great increase in the number of what Dewart would have called 'true poets'. In his introduction to *Songs of the great Dominion* (compiled mainly for a British readership), Lighthall points to the contrast between the 'apologetic and depressed' verse of Dewart's anthology and the new poetry in his collection, which was not only 'more confident, but far better.' His book's organization ('The new nationality', 'The Indian', 'Settlement life', 'The spirit of Canadian history', 'Places', 'Seasons' etc.) is an early attempt to offer unifying myths and themes that grew out of a vision of a unified culture in which the individual is entirely subordinate. This viewpoint shaped and coloured the critical approach to Canadian literature for many decades.

Archibald LAMPMAN's 'Two Canadian Poets: A Lecture' (on ROBERTS and CAMERON), delivered in 1891 (*University of Toronto Quarterly* 13, no. 4, July 1944), expresses the view that the character of Canada is to be found in a literature based upon local experience. Although the idea of the 'local' was by Lampman's time associated more with a regional than with a national milieu (as opposed to the earlier colonial/imperial distinction), Lampman sees another important geographical opposition: the rural versus the urban. Since English-Canadian poetry treated the former exclusively (the latter, according to Lampman, was the realm of fiction), he saw poetry as offering most promise for a strongly Canadian literature. In the late nineteenth century, however, the older vision of Canadian writing—as a shadowy imitation of British, or occasionally of American, literature—largely continued, particularly among writers and critics whose viewpoint was imperial or continental. John G. Bourinot, in *Our intellectual strength and weakness* (Montreal, 1893; rpr. 1973), expands on earlier ideas about Canadian literature mentioned in his *Intellectual development of the Canadian people* (Toronto, 1881), seeing English-Canadian writing as inferior to both French-Canadian and American—principally because it lacked a strong national identity, which he thought should be developed by creating an imperialistic and bicultural literature.

Most Canadian criticism written between 1820 and 1920 did not appear in book form, or appeared only as hard-to-find contributions to books, and is not readily available today. A selection of early critical pieces can be found in *The search for English-Canadian literature* (1975) edited by Carl Ballstadt. See also the journalism of Wilfred CAMPBELL, Lampman, and Duncan Campbell SCOTT that appeared in 'AT THE MERMAID INN' (the Toronto *Globe*, 1892-3), reprinted in *At the Mermaid Inn* (1979) edited by Barrie Davies; and the essays of Charles G.D. ROBERTS collected in *Selected poetry and critical prose*

(1974) edited by W.J. Keith.

2. THE EARLY TWENTIETH CENTURY. The first extended critical study in Canadian letters is James CAPPON's *Roberts and the influences of his time* (1905; later expanded as a book in the Makers of Canadian Literature series, *Charles G.D. Roberts*, 1925). Cappon faults Roberts for creating a pale aesthetic pastoralism instead of focusing on everyday rural life, realistically centred on man and his community, that would by its familiarity produce a national poetry. Cappon was the first critic to identify a characteristically Canadian poetic form—a nature poetry of detailed description that he contrasts with the then-popular neoclassical idyll. He also gives voice to the growing populist movement by calling for a more democratic, less aristocratic, literature; yet he wants one that, unlike the 'erotic' aestheticism in contemporary American and British poetry, retains an ethical centre. Although his *Bliss Carman* (1930) is less impressive, Cappon's use of texts was exceptional for his period in Canadian studies: he looked at lines not just for their metrics but for their thematic and tonal aspects. Even though Cappon seems to have rejected modernist literature, his analyses anticipate those of the 'New Critics' who emerged following the imagist movement.

During the next fifteen years criticism appeared in the form of surveys, as well as in prefatory statements in several anthologies: Archibald MacMurchy's *Handbook of Canadian literature* (1906); Lawrence Burpee's *A Little book of Canadian essays* (1909), which consists of individual appreciations of several authors; T.G. Marquis' *English-Canadian literature* (1914)—originally published as vol. 12 of *Canada and its provinces* (1914; rpr. 1973); John Garvin's *Canadian poets and poetry* (1916; rpr. 1926), an anthology in which selections from appreciative reviews precede each writer's work; and Pelham Edgar's chapter on 'English-Canadian literature' in *The Cambridge history of English literature* (1916). Most of these discussions are little more than lists, with biographies and plot summaries attached, affirming the existence of Canadian literature. (An important exception is Arthur STRINGER's preface to his own book of poetry, *Open water*, 1914, which contains a very early—and striking—statement on modernism.) Only Edgar's introductory essay, written for a British audience, is evaluative, albeit apologetic; in it he notes again the problems of a colonial literature—the product of 'a young country born into the old age of the world'—and the need to view such literature tolerantly because of its youth. He also sees Canada's literature as principally British in origin and sensibilities.

In contrast, Ray Palmer Baker's *A history of English Canadian literature to the Confederation: its relation to the literature of Great Britain and the United States* (1920), written for an American readership, considers the literature to be more American in its antecedents than British, and assumes that it is old enough to merit serious book-length examination. However, like Edgar, Baker concluded that Canadian literature was an extension of the literature of another country and that its real identity was yet to emerge. Duncan Campbell SCOTT, in his essay 'Poetry and progress' (1922; rpr. in S.L. Dragland, ed., *Duncan Campbell Scott: a book of criticism*, 1974), also emphasizes this sense of evolutionary process, seeing Canadian literature as maintaining a fixed ethical viewpoint while changing in technique and topic. Also in 1922, Albert Watson and Lorne PIERCE brought out the anthology *Our Canadian literature*, in which they perceive a search for identity to be the overriding preoccupation in Canadian writing. They see Canadian literature, at its best, as having universal appeal, a moral tone, and such national characteristics as a sense of historical and political continuity, a communitarian spirit, and an awareness of the 'vastness of our spaces'.

Odell Shepard's *Bliss Carman* (1923) exemplifies the hostility towards modernism that was prevalent in Canadian criticism at the time. (Compare Roberts' 'A note on modernism', *Open house*, 1931.) Neither a cultural biography nor a detailed analysis of Carman's life or work, it is a good example of impressionistic criticism. In contrast are V.L.O. Chittick's and John Logan's studies of Thomas Chandler HALIBURTON, both of which appeared in 1924; no less Victorian in approach, these works grew out of the tradition of historical criticism. Chittick's biography—written for an American audience and the more scholarly of the two—discusses the contradictory sides of Haliburton's philosophy, aiming to give insights into the man. Logan, more interested in the literature, seeks to establish both Haliburton's cultural heritage and the contemporary contexts. This book is an early example of thesis criticism—in this case that Haliburton presented throughout his fiction a systematic argument for economic and cultural unity among all peoples of British origin.

Logan also wrote, with Daniel French, *Highways of Canadian literature* (1924), in which origins, backgrounds, and influences not only form the substance of analyses of individual writers, but also of the discussions of literary movements and genres in Canadian writing. Taking a progressive and idealistic view, Logan and French concluded that Canadian literature was still in its adolescence. *Highways* also attempts to assess Canadian critics up to 1924—particularly Archibald MacMECHAN, whose *Headwaters of Canadian literature* came out in the same year (NCL, 1974). Logan and French disliked MacMechan's approach (although, in its historical orientation, it was not unlike their own): MacMechan judged Canadian writing by external standards and found it prosaic and imitative, lacking inventiveness and realism, outmoded in content, and too popular in its aims. MacMechan was also an extreme nationalist in his designation of 'Canadian' authors: MOODIE and CRAWFORD were among the writers excluded from his consideration.

Lionel Stevenson's *Appraisals of Canadian literature* (1926) is an important watershed in Canadian criticism. Stevenson, who later became known for his cultural criticism documenting the impact of Darwinism and other new modes of thought on late-Victorian English writers, attempted not only to confirm the existence of Canadian literature (as had many critics before him), but also to define it in a more systematic way. In this seminal work he discusses the mythopoeic quality of Canadian writing ('In Canada the modern mind is placed in circumstances approximating those of the primitive mythmakers'), and suggests that Canadians' 'sympathy with nature is practically an inbred trait', leading them to respond 'to those features of religion, myth, or philosophy that retain some meaning as interpretations of Ancient Earth and man's relationship to her.' Like Northrop FRYE after him, Stevenson thought that Canadians, remaining attached to the European sources of their civilization, attempted to shut out the New World wilderness. He was the first critic to detect a central cultural pattern in Canadian literature.

In *The poetry of Archibald Lampman* (1927) Norman Guthrie sees Canadian poetry, exemplified by the work of Lampman, as meditative, not lyric—a poetry in which the poet merges with the landscape, and human values and relationships become abstract. Published in the same year, O.J. Stevenson's

Criticism in English 2

A people's best (1927) is of interest today as an example of a blending of criticism with the popular Canadian form of the sketch, while Lorne PIERCE's *An outline of Canadian literature* (1927) continues his critical assessment of Canadian literature that extended over a number of books and into his editorial influences at the RYERSON PRESS. Similar in viewpoint to his *Our Canadian literature*, the new book is more overtly nationalistic, calling for protection against assimilation. It also depicts Canada as searching not just for identity but for a yet-to-be-realized destiny. Canada's literature, Pierce thought, was generally dependent on surface realism and moral epigram.

A.J.M. SMITH, in 'Wanted—Canadian criticism' (CANADIAN FORUM, April 1928), calls for a modern criticism to guide Canadian writers into twentieth-century art. He sees Canadian critics as using moral, not aesthetic, criteria and supporting writers who used clichéd themes and trite Canadian images to produce a false, romantic ideal of Canada. Smith believed that Canada's adolescence was over and that its 'adult' writing should therefore be realistic, and should not exclude irony, cynicism, and a liberal viewpoint. This article was the formal declaration of a split between those critics who supported modernist sensibilities and those who adhered to nationalistic goals.

3. TOWARDS MODERNISM. By the end of the twenties the notion of 'realism' had changed in Canada from an earlier 'idealized realism' to that of social realism, a depiction of everyday life that pointed to the problems of society, if not to solutions. Frederick Philip GROVE, in *It needs to be said* (1929), a collection of essays on literature, provides a good statement of Canadian social realism in calling for a literature that, while adopting universal concerns, focuses on regional actualities. In the decade to follow, historians, writers, and literary critics alike tended to seek a new vision of Canada by looking at small details (the mundane specifics of fur trading, the everyday life of farm and factory, the particulars of individual texts) in order to discover the larger patterns of Canadian culture that had been ignored by their predecessors. These writers were responding to a need in the Depression for a revision of previous concepts of Canadian identity. V.B. Rhodenizer's survey, *A handbook of Canadian literature* (1930), calls for more realism and supports a regionalism that is tempered with a national consciousness. E.K. BROWN, in his first extended ar-

ticle on Canadian writing, 'The immediate present in Canadian literature' (*Sewanee Review* 41, 1933), is in accord with A.J.M. SMITH about the lack of a vital Canadian criticism. Brown specifically attacks the jingoism that had become popular following the Great War; he also enunciates the Canadian writer's economic difficulties and lack of a perceptive Canadian audience, and sees the necessary role of the writer in such a culture as being that of rebel.

W.E. Collin, in *The* WHITE SAVANNAHS (1936; rpr. 1975), the first book of modernist criticism in Canada, discusses the work of LAMPMAN, PICKTHALL, PRATT, LIVESAY, F.R. SCOTT, KLEIN, Smith, and KENNEDY. Explicating texts rather than discussing influences and contexts, Collin found a central image in the work of each writer and argued that Canadian literature as a whole was evolving into a literature of redemption. His central Canadian images—landscape, dream, the garden in the wilderness and the accompanying Eden myth, epic heroism of real men, stoic puritanism, exile, martyrdom, faith, and redemption—are ones that writers and critics have continued to use and discuss. Doctrinaire in many ways, and stronger on contemporary writers than on earlier ones, *The white savannahs* extends an important concept in Canadian criticism: the notion of mythic renewal.

E.K. Brown's *On Canadian poetry* (1943; rev. 1944; rpr. 1973) is the second modern book-length study of Canadian literature. Although it is a historical survey, it utilizes close textual readings to present assessments of individual poets (Lampman, D.C. SCOTT, and Pratt) and of Canadian poetry in general, and also provides a social and cultural commentary on Canada. To Brown the isolation of the individual was a condition both of the nineteenth-century poet cut off from his cultural roots and the literary mainstream, and of the young post-war poet at odds with his own society and an outsider to any other. Brown related the old complaints of a lack of audience, publishers, and critics in Canada to the psychological restrictions on the Canadian writer—the result of a colonial spirit, the lack of a national crisis, practical frontier attitudes, puritanism (by which Brown meant a Calvinistic materialism), and regionalism. These points were reiterated in his other essays on Canadian literature (collected in *Responses and evaluations*, 1977, edited by David Staines). Brown's type of cultural criticism, in which society and writing are viewed as inseparable, has remained the single most-used approach to literary analysis in Canada.

A.J.M. SMITH's essays of the 1940s, included in *Toward a view of Canadian letters: selected critical essays 1928-1971* (1973) and in *On poetry and poets* (NCL 1977), were written from the activist perspective that Brown had prescribed. In 'Canadian anthologies, new and old' (1942), Smith condemns critical and literary writing that is unthinkingly nationalistic, romantic, or complacent, and supports work that is intense, intellectual, and universal in theme and concern. Smith's introduction to the first edition of his influential *The book of Canadian poetry* (1943) was not only his most extensive statement of his view of Canadian literature, but the source of a lengthy critical debate between John SUTHERLAND and himself, in which Northrop FRYE and Milton Wilson, among others, played intermittent roles, and which marked the two major directions modernist writing took in Canada following the Great War. In that essay Smith divides Canadian poetry into two groups that cut across period, movement, and location. The first, a 'cosmopolitan' poetry in which emotions universal elements of life and on world-wide advances, utilizes man-centred perspectives, and deals with 'the civilizing culture of ideas'; its opposite, 'native' poetry, which is emotional and unintellectual, is concerned with individual awareness, with unique and specific events or locales, and with providing a realistic description of environment. Smith saw the cosmopolitan stream as superior to that of native poetry, which he viewed as subject to nationalistic rhetoric or romantic sentimentalism. Underlying this evaluative aspect of Smith's categories is another critical assumption: he believed that the search for identity that preoccupied Canadian critics and writers was not only fruitless but trivial. Nationalism and a national sense of self were unimportant in the modern, global environment—in which Smith saw Canadian writers helping to define not so much Canada but Canada's place in a new international age. Northrop Frye, in a contemporary review of Smith's anthology ('Canada and its poetry', reprinted in *The bush garden*, 1971), avoids dealing directly with Smith's categories (though he later suggested that every Canadian writer struggles with both the cosmopolitan and native urges). Frye states that there are definable characteristics of Canadian poetry and that a *national* writing is preferable to the 'creative schizophrenia' of a colonial one,

which includes both a large imperial vision and a cramped provincial or regional perspective. In this review Frye notes for the first time that what he finds central in Canadian poetry is 'the evocation of stark terror' in the face of the 'frightening loneliness of the huge land', sometimes combined with a tenacious 'refusal to be bullied by space and time, [and] an affirmation of the supremacy of intelligence and humanity over stupid power.' (In the frequent references made to this observation by later critics, the notion of terror tends to be cited without Frye's qualifications about the conquering abilities of the mind and heart.) Like E.K. Brown, Frye finds in Canadian literature the image of an isolated man; but for Frye the picture of man in epic struggle against a native reality rivals any mere cosmopolitan vision.

Another important response to Smith's divisions was John Sutherland's defence of the second stream of modernism that developed in Canada: militant realism. In his introduction to *Other Canadians* (1947)—an anthology edited by Sutherland to focus attention on those writers he felt Smith had overlooked—he identifies socially aware poets with Smith's 'native' tradition, and—like Brown and several other observers of early modern culture—links 'native' with nationalistic; for him 'cosmopolitan' concealed a colonial attitude that was inappropriate to the indigenous Canadian experience. The conflict that developed between Smith and Sutherland over this issue is of some importance in the development of Canadian literature and its criticism: Smith enunciated the neoclassical aspect of modernism, with its accompanying standards and judicial criticism, while Sutherland favoured an egalitarian modernism, colloquial in style and diction and concerned more with social revolution than with literary innovation. However, the two viewpoints were not entirely dissimilar. While the 'realists' engaged in substantial social activism and (in the statements of Dorothy Livesay, Sutherland, and Louis DUDEK) developed the beginnings of a Marxist criticism, they never supported for long the extremes of social and literary change advocated by such groups in other English-speaking cultures; with the possible exception of Livesay, their proletarianism often resembled middle-class liberalism or humanitarianism. Smith, while resisting the perennial call to describe a coherent national literature, strove like his predecessors to give the populace a literature and criticism that Canadian readers could identify as their own. See also Smith's introductions to *The Oxford book of Canadian verse* (1960) and his anthologies of Canadian criticism: *Masks of fiction* (1961) and *Masks of poetry* (1962); as well as *John Sutherland: essays, controversies, and poems* (1973) edited by Miriam WADDINGTON, and *The making of modern poetry in Canada* (1967) edited by Louis Dudek and Michael Gnarowski, a useful anthology that features critical articles from the forties.

4. POST-WAR CRITICISM. Another important critic to establish himself in the forties was Desmond PACEY. In *Frederick Philip Grove* (1945) Pacey makes biographical consideration secondary to critical evaluation; he judges GROVE by standards similar to the Aristotelian ones Grove himself articulated, though he also delineates Grove's cultural, historical, and literary contexts. In discussing Grove as a failed but worthy novelist—the best that Canada had yet offered—and a better essayist than fiction writer, Pacey established his own standards for Canadian fiction. He thought writing should be both regional and universal, but should originate in real experience. PRATT and Grove came nearest to fulfilling his ideal, for they depicted real Canadian ways of life, dealt with significant social issues, portrayed man's true humanity in crises, and saw the special relationship Canadians have with nature. Pacey's survey, *Creative writing in Canada* (1952; rev. 1961), became a standard text on Canadian literature. *Ten Canadian poets* (1958), also an influential book, is a particularly good example of Pacey's critical technique. Although he agreed with the New Critics about the value of close textual reading, his own analyses often tend to develop from his overview rather than from the dynamics of the texts themselves. His articles were collected in *Essays in Canadian criticism: 1938-1968* (1969).

Edwin J. Pratt: the man and his poetry (1947) expressed the general feeling among literary critics of the forties that Pratt was the father of modernism in Canada and the country's most exemplary poet; but it is unusual for combining a historical-biographical essay on Pratt by Carl KLINCK with a comparative study by Henry Wells of nine poems as parallelled to nine works from world literature. Condemning the sentimental romanticism of early twentieth-century Canadian poetry, Klinck sees Pratt as shifting the focus in Canadian poetry from nature to man and thereby discovering new content, new myths, and new structures for Canadian writing. Wells employs comparative criticism to distinguish those features of Pratt's writing that are unique to him or to Canada from those that are universal. Both Klinck and Wells attempt objective criticism, but W.P. Percival's subjective biographical survey of the following year, *Leading Canadian poets* (1948), once again takes up the task of discovering the qualities of 'good poetry' in Canadian writing.

Though the ideal of scientific, unbiased literary analysis had influenced American and British criticism since the nineteenth century, it played a relatively small role in Canadian criticism prior to the fifties. Before then, most criticism developed out of a kind of romantic idealism and had a messianic or missionary nature, designed to convert the ignorant and restore misguided believers to the right path. By the end of the Second World War few critics valued criticism written before 1936; many rejected the perspectives, values, and techniques of even the best writing prior to the late twenties. This sense of being distinct from, and discontinuous with, writing and criticism of the nineteenth and early twentieth centuries led critics to reassess the past; they tended either to reshape it in order to find the hidden origins of the modern movements that had previously been misperceived as typical of Canadian romanticism, or to approach early texts as sources from which to develop social or historical theses on given periods. Edward McCOURT's *The Canadian West in fiction* (1949, rev. 1970) was the first book to construct a regional literary history in order to discover the origins of modern western literature. Although he uses literary standards of judgement, McCourt does not limit himself to works of literature, but develops an overview of western writing that traces its characteristic factual, unornamental, succinct style to accounts by fur traders, explorers, missionaries, and Mounties, and its romance formulas to preconceived notions from the east, found in the dime novel. McCourt approaches writers as diverse as Ralph Connor (Charles William GORDON), Nellie McCLUNG, Sinclair ROSS, and Margaret LAURENCE from a socio-historical viewpoint, seeing in their work the evolution of a western culture and values based on mobility that retards tradition.

The most important criticism of the fifties was done by critics who had established themselves in the previous decade: Desmond Pacey, who published both books and essays, and A.J.M. SMITH and Northrop

FRYE, who published articles and reviews. (Frye's contribution was particularly felt after 1950, when he took over from E.K. BROWN the summary reviews of the year's poetry for *The University of Toronto Quarterly*'s annual 'Letters in Canada'.) Of the critical books published in this decade a number were collections, frequently of essays that had originally been created for oral presentation—lectures, broadcast scripts, or papers from conferences. Books such as *Canadian writers* (1951) by Arthur Phelps—a series of lectures on individual English- and French-Canadian authors—reflect the often casual and simplified nature of their original oral presentation. *Writing in Canada* (1956), edited by George Whalley, consists of speeches and discussions from the Canadian Writers' Conference at Queen's University in July 1955, the first meeting of its kind in Canada, which brought together creative writers, critics, and publishers. It is essentially a declaration that Canadian writers need no longer be isolated from one another. *Our living tradition* (1957), edited by Claude Bissell, was the first of a series of five volumes (published until 1965; subsequent volumes were edited by Robert L. McDougall) made up from lectures given at the Institute of Canadian Studies, Carleton University. Reflecting the Institute's program of interdisciplinary cultural history, the lectures generally were conservative in technique and in their goal of establishing the real continuities we share with our cultural past. Of particular interest in the series are Smith's essay on D.C. SCOTT, Earle BIRNEY's on E.J. Pratt and his critics, both in Volume II, and James REANEY's on Isabella Valancy CRAWFORD in Volume III. *The culture of contemporary Canada* (1957), edited by Julian Park, is a collection of essays directed at Americans. In it Millar MacLure's 'Literary scholarship' argues that Canadian literary history tends to be chauvinistic and that Canadian criticism is influenced by the British tradition of impressionistic interpretations and comprehensive commentaries rather than by the bibliographic and annotative criticism that had prevailed in Europe and America. *Our sense of identity* (1954), edited by Malcolm Ross, is a collection of literary and other essays, and prose selections, which Ross hoped would clarify some of the confusion about the Canadian identity. In his introduction he sees Canada as a nation characterized not by compromise but by irony, and Canadians as a 'bifocal people' who perceive themselves as being 'at once inside and outside', with 'no simple reconciliation'—a situation that produced a strong need to orient oneself in space and time. By bringing together the shared perspectives of literary and social critics, historians, and creative writers, Ross suggests that the goals of cultural definition will be best served by an interdisciplinary approach that has continued to influence criticism in Canada. Wilfrid Eggleston's *The frontier and Canadian letters* (1957), a history of Canadian writing from its pre-Confederation beginnings (not, as is often mistakenly assumed, a study of western-Canadian literature), is the most extensive application to Canadian writing of the widely disseminated 'frontier thesis' formulated by American historian Frederick Turner, who saw in America's developments a progressive and evolutionary movement from frontier culture to an established native one. R.E. Rashley's *Poetry in Canada: the first three steps* (1958), while dependent on some of the assumptions about assimilation popularized by this thesis, points to a literary evolution in Canada marked by a break with aristocratic British values. This book has been seen as the first piece of Canadian Marxist criticism.

In *The arts in Canada* (1958), another anthology of essays edited by Malcolm Ross, Claude Bissell, writing on the novel, points out that contemporary Canadian fiction began with the 'contemplative realism' of Grove and CALLAGHAN, which examined man in his social environment and illuminated rather than resolved his problems. He says that this type of fiction dominated the Canadian novel until the fifties, when formal experiments finally started with Ethel WILSON's fiction, and when a comic vision began to appear in the novels of Earle Birney and Robertson DAVIES. In a discussion of poetry, Northrop Frye returns to Smith's dichotomy, arguing that the cosmopolitan and native urges do not constitute a true division between writers but are 'centrifugal' and 'centripetal' impulses to be found within each poet. He distinguishes between contemporary Canadian poets who seek to unify man and nature by finding a central myth (the academic mythopoeic poets) and writers for whom the depiction of reality is more important (F.R. SCOTT, SOUSTER, DUDEK, and LAYTON).

The recurrent concern over whether or not there is an evolving Canadian literature that shows marked improvement over its precursors—given new prominence after the

Smith-Sutherland debate—continued to play an important role in fifties' criticism. Milton Wilson in 'Other Canadians and After' (TAMARACK REVIEW 9, Autumn 1958), instead of finding a progressive development of a native Canadian literature, sees a tradition of a colonial or 'permanent tourist' (the phrase is borrowed from a P.K. PAGE poem) mentality. Thus neither Smith's nor Sutherland's use of the terms 'cosmopolitan', 'native', and 'colonial' have much value for Wilson. Since Canadian poets had always borrowed forms from other cultures, he thinks that, instead of bemoaning the British colonialism of the PREVIEW group or the American colonialism of the FIRST STATEMENT writers, critics need to respect a traditional native literature that draws its substance from its own culture and only its structures from abroad. Wilson locates Canada's uniqueness in its ahistorical condition, in which its sense of time is foreshortened and its sense of space made discontinuous (resulting in a transcontinental 'hopping regionalism')—a state of flux that brings to Canadian writing a tradition of 'the inclusive, the self-sustaining, even the encyclopaedic'.

Louis Dudek, whose work as an editor has had a wide influence, published a number of his short critical pieces in the fifties. The most important of these on Canadian literature may be found in his *Selected essays and criticism* (1978). (A second collection of his essays is in a special issue of OPEN LETTER, 4th series, nos. 8-9, 1981.) Although often a polemicist and social commentator as much as a literary critic, Dudek sees the chief critical act as that of relating the text to reality, to the experience of the external world, not to theory or ideology. He identifies two large schools of Canadian criticism: the historical or social realists, and the mytho-symbological critics, who do not realize that symbols should correspond directly to experience.

James REANEY's article, 'The Canadian poet's predicament' (*University of Toronto Quarterly* 26, April 1957), expresses a growing sense among Canadian writers and critics of the fifties that they must remain in Canada, no longer choosing expatriation or extended periods of education abroad but absorbing and transforming the wealth of culture from both outside and inside Canada. In 'The Canadian imagination', a succinct statement in a special Canadian issue of *Poetry*, Chicago (94, June 1959), Reaney sees the early poets as using the 'wilderness and frontier not as facts but as symbols of something undeveloped in the human imagination—as a rich but brooding hostile monster'. In the work of Pratt and the writers who followed him, the environment remains seductively evil, but it is now one that man can humanize through myth-making. The two most influential figures for contemporary Canadian writers, according to Reaney, are Pratt, because he introduced the image of man capable of struggling against the landscape and what it symbolizes, and Frye, because his first two books gave Canadian poets a handbook of 'maps' and designs for poems, as well as an example of precision and organization.

John SUTHERLAND became one of the first critics to identify a major shift affecting Canadian literature and criticism in 'The past decade in Canadian poetry' (NORTHERN REVIEW, Dec.-Jan. 1950-1), where he argued that the activist poetry of the forties, based on the notion of class oppression, was being replaced by a religious sort of poetry grounded in the universal guilt of each individual. In a 1954 essay, 'Refining fire: the meaning and use of poetry', A.J.M. SMITH similarly assigns a spiritualizing function to literature. Rejecting the ephemeral goal of objective realism as a literary method and that of social amelioration as an end, he opts for a poet who will be an 'uncoverer of the hidden secrets', revealing the decay caused by mechanization and secularization and—through the recovery of myth and spiritual responsibility—'restoring the individual . . . to grace or society to civilization'. (Smith elsewhere suggested—in 1955, and again in 1960—that Canadians were particularly well suited to producing this kind of literature because they possessed an 'eclectic detachment' that enabled them to utilize a variety of forms and ideas from other cultures. This concept, picked up by Milton Wilson and others, may also be seen as underlying Frye's theories of education and Marshall McLUHAN's notion of the global village.) This represents the growing sense of a sacred dimension to literature in which the writer, sometimes in the role of seer, sometimes of sacrificial victim, produced gnostic writing that required critics to play the part of priests who would initiate the reader into the literary mysteries. The emergence of Northrop FRYE as a critic of world reputation—following the publication in 1957 of his theoretical magnum opus, *Anatomy of criticism*, with its account of literature as descending from sacred texts such as myth and the Bible—may be seen as part of this new vision.

Among Frye's ideas on the nature of Canadian literature and society is his suggestion that Canada has a dualistic culture, in which the pull towards the primitive and the mysterious is always countered by a pull towards civilization and objective knowledge. He also suggests that in an environment like that of Canada—a railway-created 'nation of stops', with an east-west orientation and a people divided by language and virtually surrounded by wilderness—narrative, not lyric, is the more natural poetic form. (See in particular 'The narrative tradition in English-Canadian poetry', 1946, and 'Preface to an uncollected anthology', 1956, in *The bush garden*.) Frye's most extended piece of Canadian criticism, the Conclusion to the *Literary history of Canada* (1965), contains some of his best-known statements, including his view of Canadian culture as having been shaped by a garrison mentality that arose from the settlers' tendency to shut out the wilderness while attempting to maintain the ways of the old world, and his idea of Canada's having an 'imaginative continuum' that Canadian writers can draw on as they face new threats to their identity.

Frye's idea that literature develops from cultural milieu, and national identity from literature, was formulated during a period of great cultural stress and change for Canada. Most of the criticism of the fifties was in effect a catalogue of national literary traits and often took the form of manifesto. The 1951 *Report* of the Massey Commission—in itself a piece of literary and cultural criticism—had profound effects, both direct and indirect, on literary studies. It concluded that national identity and unique ways of life were strongly affected by the cultural environment and that, following the Second World War, Canada was more endangered by American mass culture than by any political or economic takeover. Harold INNIS's investigations into the nature of communications and mass media, and Marshall McLuhan's declaration of the end of distinct nations and the emergence of a global village provided, like Frye's theories, large patterns of social structure and spoke to the fears and sense of loss felt by many Canadians. Historians and other social commentators lamented the encroachment of populist taste, specialized technological education, and mass cultural forms on Canada's more classical, more general forms of learning and on

its conservatism in the arts and in society. Literary critics and writers, however, found themselves in a more complicated position: because Canadian literature had, since the twenties, been in rebellion against its old order, defining genuine Canadian literary values did not involve affirming a traditional standard but choosing one of several recently emergent modern standards. In a 1961 article, 'Canadian literature in the fifties', Desmond Pacey outlined three modern traditions he saw developing: that of the mythopoeic writers, whose work he often disliked because he saw it as literature on literature; that of the urban realists, whose vision he tended to affirm; and that of the rural or regional poets, whose work he also valued.

5. THE SIXTIES TO THE EIGHTIES. (a). The volume of Canadian literary criticism has increased substantially in the last twenty-five years, partly because Canadian literature became a recognized field of academic study in the late sixties. Several reprint series (especially McCLELLAND AND STEWART's New Canadian Library, under the general editorship of Malcolm Ross) made accessible previously unavailable works, many of them bearing introductions that are important contributions to criticism. With the founding by George WOODCOCK in 1959 of CANADIAN LITERATURE at the University of British Columbia, the outlet for critical essays on Canadian writing increased dramatically. This was followed in the seventies by other critical journals, including *The Journal of Canadian Fiction* (1972-), *Essays on Canadian Writing* (1974-), *Studies in Canadian Literature* (1976-), *Canadian Poetry: Studies, Documents and Reviews* (1977-), and *The Journal of Canadian Poetry* (1978-). (See LITERARY MAGAZINES IN ENGLISH: 3, 4.) A number of magazines have produced special issues on the work of some of the leading writers (e.g. *Journal of Canadian Studies* on Hugh MacLENNAN; *Canadian Drama* on Robertson DAVIES; *Essays on Canadian Writing* on HOOD, BIRNEY, and REANEY; DESCANT on LEE; *Journal of Canadian Fiction* on LAURENCE; OPEN LETTER on KROETSCH), and several of these have been republished as books. Three series of small-format critical studies—chiefly aimed at student readers seeking introductions to individual writers—were founded in 1969: Canadian Writers, under the general editorship of Dave GODFREY; Canadian Writers and Their Work, under the general editorship of William FRENCH; and Studies in Canadian Literature, under the editorship

of Gary GEDDES and Hugo McPherson. Books in the Canadian Writers series are very short (around 15,000 words each) and, for that reason, often superficial; but as part of the New Canadian Library they were widely distributed and some of them (such as ONDAATJE on Leonard COHEN, Davies on LEACOCK, and Milton Wilson on PRATT) provide commentaries of lasting interest. Canadian Writers and Their Work produced only a few studies of English-Canadian writers, but their format is less rigid and their space less constricted; of particular interest is Eli MANDEL's introductory study of LAYTON. The Studies in Canadian Literature series, which aims at more sophisticated readers and has frequently broken new ground, first appeared as small paperbacks of 35,000 words and up, but has since shifted to full-sized book format. Among its most notable studies are *Frederick Philip Grove* by Douglas Spettigue; *Hugh MacLennan* by George Woodcock; *Sinclair Ross & Ernest Buckler* by Robert Chambers; *E.J. Pratt: the evolutionary vision* by Sandra Djwa; and *Louis Dudek & Raymond Souster* by Frank DAVEY. Two recent series are *Profiles in Canadian literature* (vols 1 and 2, 1980; vols 3 and 4, 1982), edited by Jeffrey Heath, and *Canadian writers and their works* (vol. 1 of the fiction series and vol. 2 of the poetry series were published in 1983), edited by Jack David, Robert Lecker, and Ellen Quigley. The extensive American-based Twayne World Authors' series has been including full-length studies of Canadian authors, usually by Canadian critics, since its inception in 1966. Two somewhat different series are Critical Views on Canadian Writers (begun in 1969 under the general editorship of Michael Gnarowski; no new volumes since 1976), collections of reviews and critical essays on individual writers; and Reappraisals, which publishes the proceedings of conferences on established Canadian writers held at the University of Ottawa, including important volumes on CRAWFORD, D.C. SCOTT, GROVE, Pratt, LAMPMAN, and KLEIN.

5(b). Other occasional monographs (such as Glenn Clever's *On E.J. Pratt*, 1977, and Grazia Merler's *Mavis Gallant: narrative patterns and devices*, 1978), and several full-scale critical books dealing with single authors, have appeared in the last two decades. Margaret ATWOOD has had the most—and often the most critically sophisticated—attention devoted to her; in addition to Sherrill Grace's study, *Violent duality* (1980), and

Frank Davey's *Margaret Atwood: feminist poetics* (1983), there have been two collections of previously unpublished critical essays: *The art of Margaret Atwood: essays in criticism* (1981), edited by Arnold and Cathy Davidson, and *Margaret Atwood: language, text and system* (1983), edited by Sherill Grace and Lorraine Weir, as well as a special Atwood issue of MALAHAT REVIEW (no. 41, 1977). Clara THOMAS—who has been a prolific critic, producing handbooks such as *Canadian novelists, 1920-1945* (1946) and *Our nature—our voices* (1972)—expanded her Canadian Writers study of Margaret Laurence into *The Manawaka world of Margaret Laurence* (1976), while Patricia Morley, another critic who has published widely, paired authors in two studies, *The immoral moralists: Hugh MacLennan and Leonard Cohen* (1972) and *The comedians: Hugh Hood and Rudy Wiebe* (1977). W.J. Keith wrote a full-length study of Rudy WIEBE's novels, *Epic fiction* (1981), and edited a collection of essays on the author, *A voice in the land* (1981). Karen Mulhallen, Donna Bennett, and Russell Brown edited *Tasks of passion* (1982), an innovative collection of work about and by Dennis Lee. More specialized approaches to authors include Gretl Fischer's *In search of Jerusalem: religion and ethics in the writings of A.M. Klein* (1975) and Patricia Monk's *The smaller infinity: the Jungian self in the novels of Robertson Davies* (1982). (Davies' work was also the subject of a collection of essays by various hands: *Studies in Robertson Davies' Deptford Trilogy*, 1980, edited by Robert Lawrence and Samuel Macey.)

Among the literary biographies of the last two decades are Norman Shrive's *Charles Mair: literary nationalist* (1965), a revisionist work written to balance the conflict between old admiring literary values and critical-historical ones, and to portray the effects of post-Confederation nationalism on literary writing; two biographies on Stephen Leacock—by Ralph Curry (1959) and David Legate (1970); Clara Thomas's *Love and work enough: the life of Anna Jameson* (1967); and Marian Fowler's *Redney: a life of Sara Jeannette Duncan* (1983). Of special note are three works: *F.P.G.: the European years* (1973), in which D.O. Spettigue, who had begun his research on Grove for his Studies in Canadian Literature monograph, reveals Grove's true identity and background; *Like one that dreamed: a portrait of A.M. Klein* (1982) by Usher Caplan, which sheds new light on Klein's breakdown and lapse into silence; and Elspeth Cameron's *Hugh Mac-Lennan: a writer's life* (1982), a thorough treatment of MacLennan's career. *The embroidered tent: five gentlewomen in early Canada* (1982) by Marian Fowler gives short but valuable critical biographies of Catharine Parr TRAILL, Susanna MOODIE, and Anna Jameson among others.

Two of the most important literary studies of this period were reference books: the *Literary history of Canada* (1965; expanded and revised 1976), edited by Carl F. KLINCK and others, and Norah Story's *The Oxford companion to Canadian history and literature* (1967). These two books gave Canadians new and easily available access to Canadian literature and to the events and individuals who had shaped it. The *Literary history* deals not just with literature proper, but with Canadian writing in general, discussed by scholars in separate essays organized by period, place, and genre. While many of its chapters tend to be more annotated bibliography than essay, several are useful for the non-specialist, particularly those on specific genres—and Northrop FRYE's Conclusion. Story's book is especially valuable for its dictionary-style format, giving easy access to information about both writers and their work and about Canadian history. (A *Supplement*, edited by William Toye, appeared in 1973.)

5(c). By the late fifties international or comparative criticism became important in Canada. Canadian comparative critics saw in their literature qualities that were not only distinct from those of Britain and the United States but were similar to those of other countries that opposed being absorbed into a 'superstate' yet were not actively able to fend off cultural assaults from the increasingly American-dominated media. R.E. Watters, for example, in an essay that influenced later critics, 'A quest for national identity' (*Proceedings of the IIIrd Congress of the International Comparative Literature Association*, 1962), outlined this vision of Canadian literature by describing differences in plot structures of British, American, and Canadian fiction. He sees British fiction as often dealing with an individual's rebellion against the class structure, which tends to be resolved by his assimilation, according to merit, into a ranking class; the American form, on the other hand, deals with the encroachment upon an individual's liberty of 'an entangling net of circumstances' from which he can only flee and begin a new life. In contrast to both, the Canadian narrative features an individual who neither rebels nor flees but, through an ability to 'absorb and transform' infringements upon the sense of self, is able 'to maintain his own separate identity *within* the social complex'. This essay marks the beginning of discussions not of literary traits, but of patterns of action. John P. Matthews' *Tradition in exile* (1962), which compares Australian and Canadian poetry, also expressed this new spirit of internationalism.

Ronald SUTHERLAND, in his two collections of essays—*Second image* (1971) and *The new hero* (1977)—compares, by content analysis alone, the literatures of Québec and English Canada. Sutherland finds 'no fundamental differences between the two major ethnic groups of Canada' as he traces, through their literatures, parallels in the relationship of English- and French-Canadians to the land and to their conception of 'Divine Order'; he believes their writings have been strongly affected by differing forms of puritanism, but that both cultures have now achieved a healthier, guilt-free vision that shows up in the more positive depictions of heroes and events in recent works.

Among those critics who have sought to locate English-Canadian literature in larger or alternate English-language traditions, W.H. New in *Among worlds: an introduction to modern Commonwealth and South African fiction* (1975) treats it as one facet of Commonwealth literature. (A similar treatment occurs in the periodicals *Journal of Commonwealth Literature* and *World Literature Written in English*.) In addition, there has been renewed interest in what is now often referred to as 'Canadian-American relations'. Marcia Kline in *Beyond the land itself: views of nature in Canada and the United States* (1970) contrasts attitudes to nature in nineteenth-century Canadian and American literature; although this monograph is somewhat superficial, especially in its acceptance of the frontier thesis as descriptive of Canadian settlement, it offers sound observations about differing attitudes in the two cultures and pairs works interestingly for comparison. The proceedings of two conferences on western literature—*The westering experience in American literature* (1977) edited by Merrill Lewis and L.L. Lee, and *Crossing frontiers* (1979), edited by Dick Harrison—contain several papers that make connections between Canadian and American responses to the West. The former deals chiefly with American works, but contains several essays on Canadian or comparative topics, including 'Problems in comparing Canadian and American western fiction' by Harrison. The latter volume, in which comparative questions are central, contains essays by Kroetsch, Mandel, and the American critic Leslie Fiedler, plus responses and summations by Sandra Djwa, Rosemary Sullivan, Henry KREISEL, and others. There is also a special issue of *Essays on Canadian Writing* (No. 22, 1981) on 'Canadian-American literary relations'.

This new interest in comparative work resulted both in a special issue of *Mosaic* (vol. 14, no. 2 1982), 'Beyond nationalism: the Canadian literary scene in global perspective', and in the wide-ranging and critically sophisticated essays by E.D. Blodgett collected in *Configuration: essays on the Canadian literatures* (1982). Blodgett makes comparisons between Canadian writers and those from world literature, and between English-speaking and other Canadian writers (from both French and other ethnic groups). His 'The Canadian literatures as a literary problem' provides a history and evaluation of the studies done in comparative criticism. Another valuable overview is David M. Hayne's 'Comparative Canadian literature: past history, present state, future needs' in the journal *Canadian Review of Comparative Literature* 3 (1976).

5(d). Canadian criticism—unlike that of the United States, Britain, and Europe—lends itself to classification by goals rather than by methodology. Although it has assimilated a number of critical techniques and values—such as modernist aesthetics, formalist analysis, and comparativist procedures—these innovations have remained secondary to a larger, usually cultural, orientation. Since 1960, however, several writers influenced by FRYE's criticism have been grouped together as 'thematic' critics because their criticism is based on the idea that literature has controlling archetypes or myths. Their critical writings have been variously attacked as non-literary, in that they emphasize content over style and form; as too literary, in that they treat works as if they exist hermetically, outside historical contexts; or simply as too generalizing and reductive. Of these critics, Eli MANDEL is the most literary and wide-ranging. In *Criticism: the silent-speaking words* (1966), he is the first Canadian critic to suggest that the advent of new literary forms (what is now called post-modern literature) necessitates corresponding innovations in critical methodology. He rejects American 'New Criticism' and traditional Canadian criticism, which he sees as chiefly concerned with environmental determinism. He calls instead for a 'savage criticism'—a type of 'phenomenological criticism' that would enable the critic to 'participate' in the work, rather than evaluate or explain it. Mandel's own criticism, however, as well as being phenomenological, is also archetypal. He also shows an interest in language and silence, and in the relationship of the dream to the text. His best essays (collected in *Another time*, 1977) are more meditations than analyses and are valuable not for the answers they supply but for the questions they ask.

The other major 'thematicists'—D.G. Jones, Margaret Atwood, and John Moss—are more interested in developing a thesis about national identity than in participating in literary analysis. (Atwood's early critical writings are also strongly nationalistic.) Their criticism blends Frye's mythic or archetypal analysis with his concept of a 'thematic' criticism. Historically oriented, Jones, Atwood, and Moss seek to discover a central vision that is the common mode of perception in Canadian writers, and, by extension, in the Canadian people; and they tend to read a body of texts as one would a medieval allegory or a difficult modernist lyric—uncovering controlling 'myths' or conceptual frameworks expressed in narrative form.

JONES' highly prescriptive book, *Butterfly on rock: a study of themes and images in Canadian literature* (1970), which developed from his 1965 *Canadian Literature* essay, 'The sleeping giant', tries to amend the notion that Canadians live with 'a sense of exile, of being estranged from the land and divided within', by finding, along with numerous images supporting this idea, others suggesting that this alienation is not permanent—that Canadians can recreate a 'vital community'. Jones detects in early Canadian literature a recurrent Adam archetype, with Adam more imprisoned by the garden than protected from the wilderness beyond. (In the course of his argument, he recasts this archetype into the sleeping giant, Noah, and Job—all of whom he collectively calls the 'major man'.) Like W.E. Collin before him, Jones uncovers in Canadian literature a progress towards redemption, finding in recent Canadian writing an Adam who escapes from his self-imposed garrison and comes to terms with the wilderness. *Butterfly on rock* has many of the strengths and weaknesses of thesis criticism. Its first chapters are particularly dazzling, summoning an array of images to support the presence of the Adam archetype. But Jones so fragments the texts he uses that some critics reject the study on principle, and the general reader may be wary of unseen distortions. Such free movement among texts (necessary to Jones' type of criticism, and also characteristic of the work of Frye, Mandel, and Atwood) requires a reader's absolute faith in the critic's judgement, especially when it leads to cultural generalizations. Jones' essay, 'Myth, Frye and the Canadian writer' (*Canadian Literature* 55, Winter 1973), serves as a conclusion to *Butterfly on rock*.

The brevity and casual style of Margaret ATWOOD's SURVIVAL: A THEMATIC GUIDE TO CANADIAN LITERATURE (1972)—originally conceived as a manual for secondary-school teachers, and eventually becoming a handbook for the general reader—gave it a currency that made it the most influential work of Canadian criticism in the last decade. While dominated by an evaluative, nationalistic argument, it has an underlying conceptual model that echoes Frye's garrison thesis: for Atwood, Canadians are not only alienated from their environment but—having long existed in a colonial relationship, first to England and then to America—have become obsessed with an image of themselves as victims. Beneath *Survival's* insistent attempt to prove that Canadians are implicated in their own victimization (a concept not really new or startling) lies a witty guide to the themes and images in Canadian literature. (Despite its deliberately selective range of material, *Survival* examines the same subjects that LIGHTHALL and those who followed him considered typical of Canadian writing: Indians, explorers, Calvinists, settlers, immigrants, wilderness, nature, and death.) Though its notions seem to have been absorbed into the popular consciousness, critical reaction was not simply mixed but polarized, with the majority of academic critics rejecting it, finding its argument more rhetorical than cogent.

Atwood's significant contribution lies in her notion that the important images, archetypes, and genres in Canadian literature are tied to concepts of monsters, ghosts, and the Gothic. (Mandel, in his essays 'Atwood Gothic' and 'Criticism as ghost story', was the first to notice the pervasive link between Atwood and the Gothic; he suggested that *Survival* should be read as a ghost story.) In *Second words* (1982), a collection of her short critical pieces, Atwood reprints her 1977 lec-

ture, 'Canadian monsters: some aspects of the supernatural in Canadian fiction', which (like *Survival*) tends to become a catalogue—in this case, of supernatural elements in Canadian fiction. The assumptions that underlie the Gothic and its sister genres, the mystery and the horror story, are indeed the real sources of Atwood's conceptual framework: given a seemingly frightening setting filled with threatening father-figures, the protagonist (whether a fictional character or a real writer, a woman, or simply a Canadian) must find some flaw in the environment through which a true reality can be penetrated where he/she will become part of the environment, at one with it, and able to control it. In other words, Atwood too has a redemptive vision—or at least a redemptive hope. (The topic of the Gothic in Canadian literature has been further developed by Margot Northey in *The haunted wilderness: Gothic and grotesque in Canadian fiction*, 1976, which, while lacking a well-defined concept of Gothic literature, is the first study of Canadian writing to focus on genre.)

John Moss, the most prolific of the thematic critics, began his work with *Patterns of isolation* (1974), another book built around the image of the Canadian as exiled individual. Moss's study—which distinguishes four types of cultural exile: garrison, frontier, colonial, and immigrant—is primarily an attempt to apply to the concept of isolation the stages of the American 'frontier thesis'. Here Moss looks not so much for literary images or themes as for underlying discussions of the 'Canadian experience', concluding that novels are an index of the developing national identity, and then devotes over two-thirds of the remainder of his study to discussing fiction that will not fit into his categories. This contradiction, and Moss's equivocations, stem, on the one hand, from his attempt at a 'thematic' criticism, that quickly becomes social commentary (reading literature in order to read a culture), and on the other from his honesty, which forces him to include works that argue against his thesis. Although repudiating thematic criticism in the introduction to his *Sex and violence in the Canadian novel* (1977), Moss proceeds to examine the literature thematically, in a not very persuasive counterpart to Leslie Fiedler's *Love and death in the American novel*. Moss's strength in his first two books—and in his later handbook, *A reader's guide to the Canadian novel* (1981)—lies in his encyclopaedic knowledge of Canadian fiction, and in his ability to give the general reader critical access to the problems and content of the books he discusses.

Warren Tallman's collection of essays, gathered in OPEN LETTER, 3rd series, no. 6 (1977), reprints three important essays on Canadian literature, including 'Wolf in the snow' (1960), which has been seen as one of the earliest examples of 'thematic' criticism. Tallman, like Frye, finds in several Canadian novels an individual isolated because of landscape, but views this as a North American condition. Anticipating Jones, Tallman discerns images of a new relationship forming between man and his environment, in which 'the gods come back—snow gods, wind gods, wolf gods—but life gods too.'

Under the methods of the thematic critics lie four rather divergent goals: to indulge in nationalistic polemic; to continue to formulate theories about national identity; to show that literature is regionally or locally defined; and to see writing in literary rather than in sociological terms. The debate about thematics has obscured the fact that the issues raised by these types of criticism—nationalistic, national, regional, and formalist—have generally been the most important in Canada in the last two decades.

5(e). Prominent in the 1960s and 1970s was nationalistic criticism that called for social action, or for a change in the way one perceived Canadian literature and experience. Dennis LEE's important essay, 'Cadence, country, silence: writing in a colonial space' (*Open Letter* 2, no. 6, Fall 1973, and elsewhere), states that because American and British influences shaped the language in Canada and thereby determined conceptualization, he was deprived of both a culture and a truly native language to call his own. Writing in Canada, which had always been concerned with the colonial condition, had hitherto been forced to take an external perspective. Therefore to establish a 'Canadian' language, and thus a literature and national identity, he felt he had to fall silent for a time, until he could define words in terms of Canadian experience; only then could he reject the alien values inherent in the old definitions. Lee believes there is a 'press of meaning'—a culturally indigenous energy that he calls 'cadence'—whose local nature gives actuality to one's words. In *Savage fields: an essay in literature and cosmology* (1977), and in his article written in response to reviews, 'Reading *Savage fields*' (*Canadian Journal of Political and Social Theory* 3, no. 2, Spring-Summer 1979), he continued to discuss the difficulties of writing in a colonized state. Although over three-quarters of *Savage fields* discusses two works by Canadian authors (ONDAATJE's *Billy the kid* and COHEN's *Beautiful losers*), in this book Lee moved beyond his nationalistic position, extending his concerns to the problems of creating literature in a complex environment. He finds their source in a modern value system that treats the concepts of nature and civilization as dualities—in which nature and the efforts of man are pitted against each other. Lee does not suggest that this 'liberal' dualism comes only from outside the Canadian tradition, or that it should be replaced by any conceptual unity, but opts for a different duality: 'earth' (or energy) and 'world' (or consciousness), which exist not as separate entities but as contraries that are in dynamic tension and offer new ways of seeing the same things. While Lee's ideas are abstract and sometimes obscure, his sense that Canadians must redefine their world is shared by a number of contemporary Canadian critics.

A different kind of nationalistic stand is taken by Robin Mathews in *Canadian literature: surrender or revolution* (1978) and elsewhere. Seen by some commentators as more Marxist-reactionary than nationalist, Mathews—like Lee—struggles against modernity, which he sees as embodied in American 'liberal anarchist individualism'. He divides English Canada into two social groups: the exploiters, who prefer foreign dominance; and the community builders, who uphold the values of 'communal, responsible Christian conservation'. What is important in Mathews' criticism is his attempt to begin an analysis of the relation of class structure to literature, a form of Marxist-influenced criticism little seen in Canada. Unfortunately Mathews too often tends to look at writers simply for evidence of their right-mindedness on certain key issues, examining works from different periods primarily for support of what he considers necessary attitudes and beliefs today, and equating good writing with moral righteousness. Mathews' criticism is basically concerned with identifying those writers who ought to be excluded from the real 'Canadian literary tradition'; among the many he rejects are Frye, Atwood, Lee, and Mandel.

Mathews' ideas on 'revolution' are more clearly stated in 'Developing a language of struggle: Canadian literature and literary criticism', in Paul Cappon's collection of essays calling for a Marxist literature and criticism in Canada: *In our own house: social perspectives on Canadian literature* (1978). In this article Mathews proposes a class analysis of past literature that would expose 'the forces of exploitation, of oppression' that have governed Canada, and calls for an anti-establishment literature that would see 'ordinary' Canadians as heroic. Cappon and his contributors think of literary criticism as a form of sociology that should make a prescriptive analysis based on the standards of an extreme social realism and a set of approved social beliefs. An example of the problems arising from this type of criticism of Canadian literature can be seen in the Mathews-influenced book by Keith Richardson, *Poetry and the colonized mind: Tish* (1976). Although Richardson limits himself to what is essentially a regional examination, he ignores the fact that Canadian regions have a natural affinity for north-south rather than east-west alliances. Condemning this west-coast school of poets and critics as betraying the 'Canadian tradition'—which, for Richardson, is apparently that of Ontario—he fails to deal with the complexities of east-west, north-south dynamics.

5(f). Of the writers who continued to search for a national identity, George WOODCOCK, in his essays and review articles (in various journals, particularly *Canadian Literature*), has contributed more to our notions of what constitutes Canada and Canadian writing than most writers of organized book-length theses. His discussions of Canadian writers and their work have been collected in *Odysseus ever returning: essays on Canadian writers and their writings* (NCL, 1970) and *The world of Canadian writing: critiques & recollections* (1980). Although Woodcock sometimes links writers to large myths and believes that certain myths, such as the story of Odysseus, are particularly appropriate to Canadian writing, he generally uses them as devices to structure his essays rather than as keys to an underlying unity in the Canadian imagination. Writing in the belletristic tradition, he rarely focuses on a single work; instead he tends to examine a writer's corpus—fitting the author into the Canadian tradition and explaining the work in terms of the larger contexts of European and British writing. His essays provide both particular insights and general evaluations, and his personal sympathy lies first with the writer and then with the general reader—never with the academic specialist.

Some of the essays of W.H. New, who is Woodcock's successor as editor of *Canadian Literature*, have been collected in *Articulating West: essays on purpose and form in modern Canadian literature* (1972). In his introduction, New argues that avoiding definitive statements, or the 'sentencing' of one's new environment out of existence, is characteristic of Canadian writing and a result of a Canadian duality that he describes as the ordering 'east' and the undefined frontier 'west'. Canada has a shifting 'west' that is vulnerable to its inhabitants' need to find a new language to describe their experience. But once the 'west' is articulated, it becomes another 'east' and loses its essence. The frontiersman's choice is paradoxical: he may either remain invisible in his new surroundings by refusing to speak or, finding words, he may lose his new-found land. The essays and review-articles in *Articulating West*, which tend to look at a single book and trace a particular image or pattern in relation to the writer's larger work, deal with the problems of ordering reality through language.

One of the most important anthologies of Canadian criticism is Eli MANDEL's *Contexts of Canadian criticism* (1971). Mandel brings together the disciplines of history, philosophy, and literary theory in essays by E.K. BROWN, W.L. MORTON, H.A. INNIS, William Kilbourn, F.H. Underhill, and George GRANT, and of such theoreticians as Northrop FRYE, Marshall McLUHAN, and Francis SPARSHOTT. There are also important critical articles, including overviews by Frye and Milton Wilson; two 1960 essays, 'Ethos and epic: aspects of contemporary Canadian poetry' by Paul West, and 'Wolf in the snow' by Warren Tallman; and three essays on special topics: 'The Dodo and the Cruising auk', Robert L. McDougall's 1963 article on class in Canadian literature; Henry KREISEL's discussion of regional psychology, 'The prairie: a state of mind' (1968); and Dorothy LIVESAY's attempt to define a native Canadian literary form, 'The documentary poem: a Canadian genre' (1969). This collection places Canadian literary criticism within the larger context of post-war cultural criticism in Canada.

There are two more recent collections of essays on Canadian literature and its place in the national identity. *The Canadian imagination: dimensions of a literary culture* (1977), edited by David Staines, is another attempt to define Canada to an American audience and includes essays by Margaret Atwood, Peter Buitenhuis, Douglas Bush, Frye, McLuhan, and Woodcock. *The arts in Canada: the last fifty years* (1980), edited by W.J.

Criticism in English 5(f)

Keith and B.-Z. Shek—originally the fiftieth-anniversary issue of *The University of Toronto Quarterly*—includes agreeably personal essays by Frye, Hugh MacLENNAN, Robertson DAVIES, Ralph GUSTAFSON, and Woodcock.

Another attempt to define a Canadian tradition can be found in Tom MARSHALL's *Harsh and lovely land: the major Canadian poets & the making of a Canadian tradition* (1979). While Marshall's rather derivative book is composed of brief essays (mostly appreciations of individual poets) that identify some characteristic features of each writer's work (Ondaatje's 'violence', MacEWEN's 'arcane knowledge'), its striking neglect of western writing, such as that of the *Tish* group and the prairie poets, leads to a distorted view of Canadian poetry as a progressive evolution that culminates in the work of central-Canadian poets of the sixties and after.

Two recent books that continue the tradition of evaluative criticism in Canada are D.J. Dooley, *Moral vision in the Canadian novel* (1979), and Wilfred Cude, *A due sense of differences: an evaluative approach to Canadian literature* (1980). Dooley invokes evaluative standards that derive from late-nineteenth- and early-twentieth-century realism as well as from the long-standing Canadian critical tradition of desiring a literature that is moral, pragmatic, and realistic. Cude, asserting that he will restore evaluation to a criticism now dominated by a search for patterns and contexts, suggests that critical consensus is the main criterion for establishing that a book is a classic; he examines *As for me and my house*, *Fifth business*, *Lady Oracle*, and *St. Urbain's Horseman* as 'classics'. (The issue of what constitutes a 'classic' was central to the 1978 Calgary conference on the Canadian novel, the proceedings of which were published in *Taking stock* (1982), edited by Charles Steele; the conclusions of the conference—especially its lists of 'classic' books—have since been the subject of debate.)

5(g). Edward McCOURT's ground-breaking 1949 study of regional literature, *The Canadian West in fiction*, had no immediate successors; however, by the time of its revised publication in 1970, regionalism had become an important critical topic. Since then there have been several regional studies, with the Prairie West receiving the most attention. Henry KREISEL's 1968 essay, 'The prairie: a state of mind', in which he discusses 'the impact of the landscape upon the mind', gave new impetus to consideration of the West as a literary region, as did a series of multi-disciplinary conferences on the Prairies. Since the late sixties four critics—Laurence Ricou, Dick Harrison, Eli MANDEL, and Robert KROETSCH—have made extensive statements about the nature of western, or prairie, literature and two full-length studies have appeared: Ricou's *Vertical man/horizontal world: man and landscape in Canadian prairie fiction* (1973) and Harrison's *Unnamed country: the struggle for a Canadian prairie fiction* (1977), both of which are concerned with the relationship between environment and literature. Ricou views the prairie landscape as 'obsessing' its writers and producing a psychology in which man sees himself as 'vertical' or objective, devoted to life and industry, in relation to the 'horizontal' land, associated with meaninglessness and death. In this psychological reading of literature in the West, in which anxiety about individual identity is strongly affected by a growing knowledge of what the prairie is, Ricou emphasizes the importance of the experience of place but does not ignore the fact that individual temperament ultimately controls a writer's vision. Harrison, like McCourt, treats the entire spectrum of western writing in his attempt to show how writers have adapted to their environment—throwing off inherited cultural structures and old ways of seeing for new and appropriate indigenous ones—and created, in the last generation, not only a true prairie literature but one that is moving away from a social to a psychological realism. In many ways Harrison's book provides a conclusion to McCourt's, for McCourt announced that there was a nascent western literature and Harrison has declared its maturity.

Both Eli Mandel and Robert Kroetsch have developed theories about the West's relation to the literary imagination. In *Another Time* Mandel includes three important essays on the meaning of the West as a literary region: 'Images of prairie man', 'Romance and realism in western-Canadian fiction', and 'Writing west'. In them he suggests—following Frye—that environment is the literary construct of the mind, as opposed to the more common thesis of regional critics that environment shapes literature. Thus to Mandel, unlike Harrison, the notion of 'prairie' is nothing more than 'a mental construct, a region of the human mind, a myth'. Mandel believes that the central prairie myth is one in which an innocent sees the world anew and names his surroundings. The critical ideas of Robert Kroetsch—expressed in essays collected in OPEN LETTER (5th series, no. 4, 1973), and in lectures and published interviews—have been very influential since the early seventies. Kroetsch originally felt that prairie writers in what is still a newly settled environment had to name the as-yet-undefined features of their experience and find myths to give life meaning in the vast and empty prairie landscape. In his 1974 essay 'Unhiding the hidden', Kroetsch modifies his earlier views, suggesting that, before naming, Canadian writers must 'un-name' their environment. Like Lee in 'Cadence, country, silence', Kroetsch believes languages contain concealed alien experiences; because of this, writers should subvert or demythologize 'the systems that threaten to define them'. Kroetsch's later criticism uses a structuralist framework. In 'The fear of women in prairie fiction: an erotics of space' (1979), Kroetsch attempts to establish a grammar of western experience by describing opposing pairs—horse/house, man/woman, movement/stability—that define the narrative structures of the region.

Other regional literatures have been the subject of less extensive study. Patrick O'Flaherty's The rock observed: studies in the literature of Newfoundland (1979) emphasizes Newfoundland history as well as the 'relentless pressures of geography' that produced 'a race apart'. Like McCourt and Harrison, O'Flaherty provides useful examinations of early non-literary writing, finding in it the origins of the imaginative consciousness that eventually resulted in the work of E.J. PRATT and Margaret DULEY, and in the emerging writers of the province. In Gardens, covenants, exiles: loyalism in the literature of Upper Canada/Ontario (1982) Dennis Duffy writes a regional account that emphasizes history rather than landscape. Like Jones, Duffy also sees 'the garden' as the primary Canadian myth: because of their experience, Canadians developed a sense of Canada as the lost garden and its inhabitants as fallen exiled Adams. Duffy, however, does not make any pleas for changing or coming to terms with the condition he describes. Lorraine McMullen edited Twentieth-century essays on Confederation literature (1976), a collection that is largely regional (Upper Canada/Ontario) as well as historical, and one that contains important articles by critics such as D.C. SCOTT, Smith, Pelham Edgar, F.W. Watt, Elizabeth Waterston, and James Polk.

While there has been a general feeling among Canadian critics that British Columbia has a separate regional character, there have been no critical or historical studies of the literature of the province, though there have been several anthologies of B.C. writing, some of which contain statements about its regional nature. However, a fair amount of commentary exists on the TISH movement. C.H. Gervais collected a number of essays and interviews in The writing life: historical and critical views of the Tish movement (1978); and there was the earlier Poetry and the colonized mind: Tish by Keith Richardson. Several of the Tish writers are themselves critics, and their criticism is distinctive enough to qualify as a west-coast school, especially in the essays of its leading practitioners, George BOWERING and Frank DAVEY. This criticism is implicitly regional in that these critics have a distinctive aesthetic and set of critical concerns and tend to give their sympathetic attention most often to west-coast authors and other writers who have responded to similar post-modern and phenomenological strains in poetry and criticism. Both Bowering and Davey have been prolific essayists and reviewers. Like those of Tallman, Bowering's critical essays in A way with words (1982) and The mask in place: essays on fiction in North America (1982) utilize poetic techniques—word-play, associative leaps, dramatizations of the movements of the mind, a juxtaposition of subjective and objective responses—that are the consequence of assuming that the essence of the poem or novel is not easily expressed in discursive prose and must therefore be approached indirectly in an evocative fashion. Though Bowering's arguments are occasionally oblique and his style and tone unorthodox, several of his essays—such as 'The poems of Fred WAH' and 'That fool of a fear: notes on A jest of God'—succeed in conveying the spirit of contemporary writing better than more traditional approaches. Davey's From there to here: a guide to English-Canadian literature since 1960 (1974) deliberately resists generalizations (especially of the 'thematic' kind) by providing sixty separate discussions of the writers covered. In Surviving the paraphrase and other essays (1983), Davey attempts to break free of the linear argument featured in the traditional critical essay. In his book Margaret Atwood: feminist poetics (1983) he deals with another emerging strain of critical theory—feminist criticism—by discussing Atwood's work in terms of two grids, language and pattern, and discovers in her writing an ongoing quarrel with patriarchal inheritance and its formalist rules. Davey's essay 'Surviving the paraphrase', originally published in *Canadian Literature* 70 (Autumn, 1976), is important because it calls for an end to 'thematic' discussions. It suggests that it is time Canadian critics set aside questions of nationality or identity and began to emulate the close reading of the formalist or New Critical school, and to approach literature through generic criticism, phenomenological criticism (by which he seems to mean the 'criticism of consciousness' that derives from the work of Georges Poulet), and 'archetypal' criticism (an application of Frye's theory of modes from *The anatomy of criticism*). In 'Critic, culture, text: beyond thematics' (*Essays on Canadian Writing* 11, 1978), Russell Brown analyses Davey's essay and other recent Canadian criticism, and suggests some of the implications of the advent of structuralist criticism. He argues that 'thematics' can still be useful when combined with newer critical theories.

5(h). So far only a few critics in Canada—mostly in the West—have been influenced by recent critical methodologies (mostly emerging from France) that have strongly affected American and English critical dialogues of late. Three recent books suggest some of the new directions in Canadian criticism. In *On the line: readings in the short fiction of Clark Blaise, John Metcalf, and Hugh Hood* (1982), Robert Lecker seeks to capture the 'unnameable, elusive quality' of the literature he treats—partly by working in the meditative or phenomenological tradition of Mandel and Bowering, though he adds a very close textual reading in order to convey the 'feel' of an individual story. In *Configuration: essays on the Canadian literatures* (1982), E.D. Blodgett uses post-structuralist methods to discuss Grove, MacLennan, Alice MUNRO, and others. As one of the founding editors of *Boundary 2: A Journal of Postmodern Literature* (1973-), Robert KROETSCH has supported innovative critical theory. In *Labyrinths of voice* (1982)— an extended interview with Shirley Neuman and Robert Wilson—he discusses his and other Canadian writing in the light of such European and American theorists as Roland Barthes, Julia Kristeva, Harold Bloom, Jacques Derrida *et al*.

Canadian criticism has long had the political function of first proving that Canadian literature existed and then that it was worth reading. In the last decade critics have assumed that a vital literature exists and have sought to establish an equally stimulating criticism.   DONNA BENNETT

Criticism in French. The beginning of genuine French literary criticism in Canada coincides with the dawn of the twentieth century. It took more than a hundred years of patient development for French-Canadian society to acquire a fledgling literary establishment, complete with its first critic, Camille Roy (1870-1943). Roy's many publications constitute the inaugural manifestations of a genre that we understand today as literary criticism.

1. THE NINETEENTH CENTURY. Clerical criticism—a non-critical criticism, a kind of historical impressionism, at once serious but often too kind, always polite and ceremonious and, while concerned about the collective future, more anxious to set incorrect terms and texts straight than to consider drab or threadbare expression—dominated almost the entire century, leaving not much room for current aesthetic preoccupations. This was the period when Québécois called themselves *Canadiens*, when the Church loomed all-powerful, and when *Canadiens* were busy reinstating (after the English Conquest of 1760) history and reality.

Camille Roy was preceded by several sporadic chroniclers such as Valentin Jautard (?-1785?), who was known as the 'spectateur tranquille' of *La Gazette de Montréal* (1778); by gifted dilettantes, of whom André-Romuald Cherrier (1821-63) is an example; and by talented promoters, such as Henri-Raymond CASGRAIN. The latter, a Catholic priest and a polymath by taste and interest, was the great animator of the MOUVEMENT LITTÉRAIRE DE QUÉBEC around 1860, and one of the founding fathers of the francophone literary establishment. At his instigation criticism, along with other productions, blossomed following the discovery of a collective destiny that had been forged in the crucible of a feverishly active press (mainly periodical and retrospective). Casgrain set the tone right up to the ultramontane excesses at the close of the century: literature was to be Catholic, conservative, and 'clericaliste'. Accordingly criticism was a kind of national service, obliging in tone and content. Objective criticism was no more possible then than were realistic and naturalistic works of fiction. Other typical and historical consequences of this context—criticism's lack of continuity, its superficial nature, and its mosaic quality—

were all due to the medium used: chronicles are not syntheses. Above all, criticism's development depended upon the growth and spread of fiction.

Against this background it is not surprising that Monseigneur Camille Roy emerged as the 'father of French-Canadian criticism'. A doctor of philosophy and former student at the Sorbonne and the Institut Catholique de Paris, he was very prolific, producing some twenty works, one being dedicated to his forerunner, Casgrain. Roy's *Manuel d'histoire de la littérature canadienne-française* (1918) remained unchallenged long after his death. In this charitable, painstakingly dedicated work, Roy relayed the best of Casgrain, practising a style of critical discourse that rarely strayed from mere compilation. Nevertheless Roy did not forget his French masters Brunetière, Faguet, and Lanson, as is readily apparent in his collected lectures, *La critique littéraire au XIXe siècle, de Mme de Stael à Emile Faguet* (1918).

2. 1934 TO 1962. The heritage of clerical criticism continued to define the horizon into the 1930s—until the inevitable economic crisis that followed industrialization and urbanization gave birth to a new and modern attitude. Signs of change, however, were already visible in the twenties; and even prior to that (1914) in the writing of the defrocked Louis Dantin (Eugène SEERS) in his Boston refuge, and Marcel DUGAS in Paris, leader of the 'exotistes' (historical enemies of the regionalists)—both defenders of aesthetic values who were thus seen as undermining the clericalist message and its chauvinistic reduction.

But especially important to the new look of the thirties was the group of young intellectuals self-acclaimed as 'La Relève' (literally 'the relief crew'); *La* RELÈVE was also the name of their monthly periodical dedicated to philosophy, religion, and literature. This journal began publishing in 1934, the same year that saw publication of the famous novel *Les demi-civilisés* by Jean-Charles HARVEY, who is also remembered as an essayist and critic (*Pages de critique*, 1926). Among *La Relève's* founders were Robert CHARBONNEAU, who later became director of the 'Service des textes' for Radio-Canada; and Jean LE MOYNE, later chief editor of the literary section of *Le Canada*. Other important critics were Guy Sylvestre (b. 1918), founder of the periodical *Les Gants du ciel* (1943-6), who went on to become national librarian; and Roger Duhamel (b. 1916), Queen's Printer from 1960 to 1969. Many of these writers, whether from *La Relève* or other periodicals, were formed by the famous 'ratio studiorum' of the Collèges Jean-de-Brébeuf and Sainte-Marie in Montreal: as students of the Jesuits they did not exactly follow Camille Roy, but instead were influenced by Emmanuel Mounier (1905-50) and his Parisian review *Esprit* (1932)—and by Maritain, Péguy, Mauriac, and Bernanos. This background helps to explain the group's critical distance and uncompromising attitude: as if from a tower, they had a point of view that foreshortened the regionalist scene below, where so many of their elders—and even some contemporary writers—still roamed, combatweary. They rose above the fighting by means of the attention they gave to the individual quest apparent in the new writers and their works. *La Relève's* gifted poet of free verse, Hector de Saint-Denys GARNEAU, was an exemplary figure for the group in that his poetry reflected the Catholic, metaphysical, Bernanosian, and Mauriacian restlessness that tends to inflect traditional clerical discourse. But above all this group dedicated itself to studies of modern forms of writing. And even though the first issue of *La Relève* appeared on 15 Mar. 1934—Annunciation Day—the work of the journal secularized theology. All these characteristics left an imprint on their works of imagination, as well as on their criticism of contemporary literature, which in their view was mainly French. Some of these writers went beyond reviews and published essays, such as Charbonneau with *Connaissance du personnage* (1944) and the posthumous *Romanciers canadiens* (1972). *La Relève*—rebaptized *La Nouvelle Relève* in 1941—lasted until 1948, by which time the people involved with it were so firmly established in the various media (they were influential for twenty years to come) that the journal was no longer needed.

After being founded in 1950, *Cité libre*—obviously conserving *La Relève's* main reference points but shedding its literary pretensions—carried on the task of renewal. Its humanist and universalist writers attacked both nationalism and clericalism and set their sights on the political arena, as is shown in the careers of two members of its editorial board: former minister Gérard Pelletier and Pierre-Elliot Trudeau, now Prime Minister. More important still were those who were fervent enemies of ecclesiastical power—the automatiste painters and poets who signed the REFUS GLOBAL (1948) of

Criticism in French 2

Paul-Émile Borduas (1905-60). The *Relève* group quickly engaged in a dialogue with these surrealist writers, asking for an 'ordre nouveau'—while keeping their faith and despising anarchy. But the automatistes' influence was long-lasting, especially among some writers published by Gaston MIRON's Les Éditions de l'Hexagone (1953-), and among the founders of LIBERTÉ.

Meanwhile academic circles kept their distance from reviews and journals. Camille Roy, founder of Quebec studies ('Études canadiennes') at Université Laval, had no important disciples. In the forties important studies on nineteenth- and twentieth-century writing were carried out at the Université d'Ottawa, where Séraphin Marion (b. 1896) produced *Les lettres canadiennes d'autrefois* (9 vols, 1939-58) and David Hayne (b. 1921) *The historical novel and French Canada* (doctoral thesis, 1945). Serious research continued with Auguste Viatte's *Histoire de la littérature française des origines à 1950* (1954); Samuel Baillargeon's *Littérature canadienne-française* (1957); and Gérard BESSETTE's *Les images en poésie canadienne-française* (1960).

As the sixties were ushered in, literary criticism progressively addressed modern concerns, particularly aesthetic ones, though it was still somewhat dependent on religious and primalistic traditions, and still trying to come to terms with forties' novels of social realism by such writers as Ringuet (Philippe PANNETON), Gabrielle ROY, and Roger LEMELIN. Periodical criticism, so often confined to biographical or moral considerations, was directed towards sociological analysis, necessary to the understanding of realistic fiction. Notable among these sociological 'amateurs' was Guy Sylvestre, author of *Panorama des lettres canadiennes-françaises* (1964). The young (25-year-old) friend of *La Relève*'s elders, Gilles MARCOTTE, began writing for *Le Devoir* in 1950, giving precise attention to the literary text, its narrative structure, and its social aim or value. Like the contributions of Pierre de Grandpré (b. 1920), such criticism was not highly specialized: the writer shows through, and the scope is bounded mainly by writing elsewhere.

At this time, when television was being introduced in Canada (1952), Québec criticism was refined and about to mature: while still maintaining its clerical connection (though casting aside the consecrating or polemical tone), it was becoming secularized, more demanding, modern. This period, however, produced no definitive synthesis or thorough work: critics were still questioning the mere fact of Québec literature, as had been the practice since the nineteenth century. They were somewhat awed by the emergence of Québec's 'parole' and by the media structure. Riveted to the moment in Québec, and only slightly moved by theory, they were nevertheless well informed on current events in France and elsewhere.

3. 1962 TO 1982. In considering the current phase, several social and historical facts should be recalled: the atmosphere of the sixties in particular; widespread political reforms; left-wing nationalism; the rise of unions; changing moral values; and finally the new liberalism of a society that invests more in the state than in the Church—which was gradually being abandoned by great masses of the population and by so many of its own priests. In these years of 'quiet revolution', the well-worn path of clerical and traditional discourse fades from view. This period is described in the title of Gérard Bessette's *Une littérature en ébullition* (1968), containing essays on Claude-Henri GRIGNON, Anne HÉBERT, Émile NELLIGAN, Gabrielle ROY, and Yves THÉRIAULT.

The predominant 'amateurs' decided to give the critical edifice a thorough housecleaning, sorting out their articles and preserving only the best. Jean LE MOYNE's *Convergences* (1961) was a true flower of *La RELÈVE*'s philosophical, religious, and literary ideas. Other important critical works of the period were Pierre de Grandpré's *Dix ans de vie littéraire au Canada français* (1966); Maurice Blain's *Approximations* (1967); Gilles MARCOTTE's *Une littérature qui se fait* (1962); and Jean ÉTHIER-BLAIS's *Signets* (vols 1 and 2, 1967; vol. 3, 1973). A few critics remained true to tradition, despite the excitement, as Roger Duhamel illustrates in *Aux sources du romantisme français* (1964); but in general the cry is 'Let's take stock!' MARCOTTE's *Présence de la critique* (1966), an anthology of representative articles from 1941 to 1965, gives the last word to André BROCHU: Marcotte appoints him the new generation's spokesman. Brochu's *La littérature par elle-même* (1962) is unquestionably a reliable guide for the era, with its autarkical title so like that of Marcotte (*Une littérature qui se fait*). In his introduction, Brochu makes an appeal to history and to a 'devenir concret', opposing Marx and Sartre on the one hand and St Thomas Aquinas on the other. This young critic also called for coherence and commitment to end the reign of 'amateurs'. His appeal bore fruit in 1963, with the appearance of PARTI PRIS, a literary and political periodical that set the tone for an entire new generation of writers and critics. 'Laïcité', 'indépendance', and 'socialisme' were the word-wedges that broke up old roads and routines and pointed the way towards another REFUS GLOBAL instead of another *Relève*. When *parti pris* expired in 1968, most of its literary contributors were integrated into the academic structure, where they frequently followed the new French criticism. As critical works by 'amateurs' declined, university criticism came into being.

Obviously academics had been preparing the ground beforehand. A group of scholars, working under the guidance of Paul Wyczynski, had been busy at 'Le Centre de recherche en civilisation canadienne-française' at the Université d'Ottawa, from whence came many basic studies, among them the series *Archive des lettres canadiennes* (4 vols: 1961, 1963, 1965, 1975), which provided new and pertinent data on literary history. Those who remained unsure about the existence of Québec literature found many of their doubts removed by the depth and quality of these studies. In addition, works coming out of Université Laval were proving to be fundamental: for example, a special issue ('Littérature et société canadienne-française') of Jean-Charles Falardeau's and Fernand Dumont's journal, *Recherches sociographiques* (1964), constituted what can now be viewed as a cultural event. Meanwhile at the Université de Montréal, Ernest Gagnon (1905-78), author of *L'homme d'ici* (1952), Albert Le Grand (1916-76), and younger professors such as Laurent Mailhot (b. 1931), Réginald Hamel (b. 1931), André BROCHU, and others continue to define Québec studies.

Another example of the scholarly vitality of the sixties is to be found in the rise of basic journals: *Livres et auteurs canadiens* (changed to 'québécois' in 1969) founded in 1961; *Études françaises* (Université de Montréal) in 1963; VOIX ET IMAGES (Université de Québec à Montréal) in 1967; and *Études littéraires* (Laval) in 1968. Finally, manuals and literary histories became numerous: *Histoire de la littérature canadienne-française* (1960) by Gérard Tougas; *Manuel de littérature canadienne-française* (1967) by Roger Duhamel; *Histoire de la littérature canadienne-française par les textes* (1968) by Gérard BESSETTE, Lucien Gélin, and Charles Parent,

and Pierre de Grandpré's *Histoire de la littérature française du Québec* (4 vols. 1967-9), which is still very useful. One should also mention the many essays and monographs appearing during this period. Their number is proportional to the widespread social evolution that characterized Québec society, and to the increased subsidies granted by the Canada Council after 1957. The number of critical essays doubled from 1961 to 1965, tripled from then to 1970, and hovered near fifty or so in 1980—an expansion that reflects the giant strides made in the production of works of the Québec imagination: Québec songs increased tenfold, becoming a veritable repertoire of popular poetry; works by novelists doubled in number—and so on.

Literary criticism in the sixties, contained within a French-oriented range, thus appears diversified: hermeneutical and structuralist tools were being widely used in the reading of Québec's nationalistic representation—the only remaining thread of a time-honoured tradition. Such approaches were generally maintained during the seventies— a decade that saw, however, the gradual attenuation of the nationalist point of view. The *parti pris* generation laid claim to French literature, publishing many essays on French authors: *Henri Bosco: une poétique du mystère* (1968) by Jean-Cléo Godin; *Albert Camus ou l'imagination du désert* (1968) by Laurent Mailhot; *Flaubert ou l'architecture du vide* (1972) by Jean-Pierre Duquette; *Hugo, amour, crime, révolution* (1974) by André Brochu; *Mallarmé, grammaire générative des contes indiens* (1975) by Guy Leflèche; and *Zola, le chiffre du texte* (1978) by Jacques Allard. These works obviously raise several questions. What were these critics, also read for their studies in Québec literature, out to prove? Were they simply asserting their claim to 'universal' literature? Were they seeking a larger audience? Were they dissatisfied with the confines of a 'village voice'? Were they staking their claim on literature of the 'motherland'? Or, more ambitious still, were they giving form and substance to a Québec discourse on 'other' literature? Such questions remain pertinent to the ongoing development of literary criticism in Québec today.

Another remarkable feature of recent years is to be found in the publication of anthologies and many useful reference works, including those of the 'companion' sort: *Dictionnaire des oeuvres littéraires du Québec* (3 vols: 1979, 1980, 1982; vol. 4 in preparation) by Maurice Lemire; *Dictionnaire pratique des auteurs québécois* (1967, with a new edition being prepared) by Réginald Hamel, John Hare, and Paul Wyczynski; *Anthologie de la littérature du Québec* (4 vols, 1978-80) by Gilles Marcotte *et al.*; *Théâtre québécois* (2 vols, 1970, 1980) by Jean-Cléo Godin and Laurent Mailhot; *La littérature québécoise* (1974) by Laurent Mailhot; *La poésie québécoise des origines à nos jours* (1980) by Mailhot and Pierre Nepveu; and the new periodical *Histoire littéraire du Québec et du Canada français* edited by René Dionne.

Important general studies on poetry include *Les mots à l'écoute* (1979) by Pierre Nepveu, on Fernand OUELLETTE, Gaston MIRON, and Paul-Marie LaPOINTE, and *Poésie des frontières—études comparées des poésies canadienne et québécoise* (1979) by Clément Moisan. Similar work is appearing on the novel, such as *Le roman à l'imparfait* (1976) by Gilles Marcotte and *Le romancier fictif* (1980) by André Belleau. Publications of criticism have now become almost too numerous. In 1978—an exceptional year— there appeared a hundred essays of diverse kinds. On criticism itself, the most important is *La littérature et le reste* (1980) by André Brochu and Gilles Marcotte, an epistolary volume by two authors who are representative of a historical shift in Québec criticism from a rather journalistic level to its present scholarly standing, in which the historical, sociological, psychoanalytical (pioneered by Gérard Bessette), and semiotic fields predominate.

4. BIBLIOGRAPHY. The titles that follow are a selection of important critical writings not mentioned above: Jacques Allard, 'Les lettres québécoises depuis 1930', *University of Toronto Quarterly*, vol. 50, no. 1 (1980); Gérard Bessette, *Trois romanciers québécois* (1973) containing studies of Victor-Lévy BEAULIEU, André LANGEVIN, and Gabrielle ROY; André Brochu, *L'instance critique 1961-1973* (1974); Jean-Charles Falardeau, *Notre société et son roman* (1967), and *Imaginaire social et littérature* (1974); D.M. Hayne, *Bibliographie analytique de la critique littéraire au Québec* (1981); and Ben-Zion Shek, *Social realism in the French-Canadian novel* (1977). See also *Contemporary Quebec criticism* (1979) edited and translated by Larry Shouldice.

JACQUES ALLARD

Cummins, John Swete. See ALTHAM: A TALE OF THE SEA.

Curwood, James Oliver. See FOREIGN WRITERS ON CANADA IN ENGLISH: 2.

D

Daigle, Jean. See DRAMA IN FRENCH 1948 TO 1981: 4.

Daniells, Roy (1902-79). Born in London, Eng., he came with his family in 1910 to Victoria, B.C., where he went to school After trying various farming jobs he became a school teacher, went on to the University of British Columbia, and then to the University of Toronto for graduate studies. He taught English at Victoria College, Toronto, from 1935 to 1937; at the University of Manitoba; and at UBC, where he became head of the English department in 1948. He retired in 1974 and was Professor Emeritus from 1977 until his death. As a scholar he was chiefly interested in seventeenth-century English poetry: he edited Thomas Traherne's 'A serious and pathetical contemplation of the mercies of God' in 1941, and published his major work, *Milton, mannerism and baroque*, in 1963. Throughout his career he wrote critical articles and reviews of Canadian literature that showed his continuing concern for the development of an authentic Canadian voice. Most important were 'Poetry and the novel' in *The Culture of contemporary Canada* (1957) edited by Julian Park, and several chapters on the CONFEDERATION POETS in the *Literary history of Canada*. He received the Lorne Pierce Gold Medal in 1970 and was made a Companion of the Order of Canada in 1971.

As a poet Daniells used traditional forms, particularly sonnet sequences linked by a common persona or an underlying theme, such as the sense of a quest or journey. Always evident are his technical skill, scrupulous phrasing, and a highly accomplished arrangement of effects, including dislocation and surprise. Clearly attracted by the new 'metaphysical' poets of the 1920s and 1930s, Daniells drew upon symbol and myth for ironic and witty counterpoint to images from contemporary life. His scholarly work on seventeenth-century poets influenced his technique, as well as his religious and philosophical thought. Two sonnet sequences make up the major part of *Deeper into the forest* (1948). The 'Anthony' sequence centres upon an ironic character, at the time of the Spanish Civil War, whose skepticism, rash impulses, and desire for action reflect that period's longing for belief and a sure cause. The tone is that of witty yet casual conversation and reminiscence, though beneath the surface lurk the symbols of both despair and faith. The twenty-one sonnets of the 'Forest' sequence—linked by the image of an emblematic forest drawn from folklore and legend, both frightening and enchanted—are concerned especially with the confrontations with death that the modern world forced upon the poet's generation. A few poems at the end of the volume, notably 'Farewell to Winnipeg', are markedly different in tone and subject. *The chequered shade* (1963) is also chiefly a collection of sonnets, arranged in three series. The first represents a pilgrimage across Europe by a travelling poet-humanist who is both vitally alive to landscape and works of art and aware of the cruelties and triumphs of the past; the second group is a rewriting of Bible stories, psalms (some reminiscent of A.M. KLEIN's psalms of Abraham and David), and parables in which contemporary images and colloquial speech reflect the doubts and tensions of an individual seeking a lost faith. The last series, bringing the seeker back to Canada, asks insistently: what must the artist, the poet, do in this land and in this age?

Daniells also wrote *Alexander Mackenzie and the North West* (1969), a well-crafted biography for young people.

A brief autobiographical piece of unusual interest, 'Plymouth brother', was published posthumously in CANADIAN LITERATURE 90 (Autumn, 1981).   JOHN MARGESON

Dans un gant de fer (1965). This first of two books of memoirs by Claire MARTIN is both the record of a wretched childhood and a clear and devastating account of a society too long oppressed by the prohibitions and taboos of a crushing monolithism. The entire account is dominated by the menacing presence of the all-powerful father, who establishes a reign of terror and a complete lack of freedom in a home that is a microcosm of the oppressive climate of Québec between the wars. The narrative moves from the ill-treatment and deprivations suffered at home to the injustices and insults endured in a convent; but hovering over everything is the spectre of the tyrannical father, or in other words the Law descending from a coercive religion. Those few nuns who manage to show kindness or real competence are swiftly undermined by ignorance and stupidity; at home it is the gentle mother who is completely dominated. The only oasis of tenderness in this arid desert of meanness is provided by visits to the maternal grandparents, whose kindness and warmth are in striking contrast to the general atmosphere of hatred and denial, and help the reader to understand the author's opening declaration: 'I have forgiven everything.' This unvarnished autobiographical account of an unhappy childhood filled with abuse and humiliations has the structure, objectivity, and saving humour of a fine novel. Remarkably it is without bitterness or recriminations.

Dans un gant de fer, and its sequel *La joue droite* (1966), were translated by Philip Stratford as *In an iron glove* (1973) and *The right cheek* (1975).   NICOLE BOURBONNAIS

Dantin, Louis. Pseudonym of Eugène SEERS.

Daveluy, Paule (b. 1919). Paule Cloutier was born in Ville-Marie in northwestern Québec. She received her formal education with the Commission des écoles catholiques de Montréal and the Pensionnat Mont-Royal and pursued further studies in social work at the Institut Notre-Dame-du-Bon-Conseil and in creative writing at the Université de Montréal. She married André Daveluy in 1944 and is the mother of six children. One of the few Québec authors who write successful fiction for young people, Daveluy has long been active not only as a writer of children's books but also in promoting children's literature and related cultural material. She was one of the founders of Communication-Jeunesse (1970) and the Association canadienne pour l'avance-

Daveluy

ment de la littérature de jeunesse (1977), and is presently employed with the publishing firm Éditions Pierre Tisseyre as a translator and director of a series in translation, Deux Solitudes—Jeunesse. She successfully co-ordinated, and presided over, a symposium on children's book publishing in Québec and, with Guy Boulizon, collated the texts in *Création culturelle pour la jeunesse et identité québécoise; textes de la rencontre de 1972, Communication-Jeunesse* (1973).

Among Daveluy's themes are first love and its joys and sorrows, friendship, family life, and the relevance of natural beauty in our daily lives. Daveluy reflects sensitivity, humour, a zest for life, and a sound understanding of young people's behaviour. Her books contain colourful descriptions of the regions that she knows and loves—for example, Montreal and its environs, Témiscamingue, and the Gaspé. Her first novel *L'été enchanté; roman* (1958)—translated by Munroe Stearns as *Summer in Ville-Marie* (1962)—takes place in the 1930s and revolves around a sixteen-year-old girl, Rosanne Fontaine, and her experience with first love. With the success of this novel, which won two awards, Daveluy undertook to write a quartet in which she would describe her heroine in each of the four seasons. *L'été enchanté* was followed by *Drôle d'automne; roman pour adolescentes* (1961) and *Cet hiver-là; roman* (1967). Then Éditions Fides published, in two volumes, a revised condensed version of the three novels, plus the unpublished text of a fourth, *Cher printemps*, under the title *Une année du tonnerre* (1977). The heroine's personality undergoes positive changes as she develops new friendships and becomes more aware of her responsibilities at home and at work. She gains in inner strength and knowledge of herself and, in the end, finds true love.

Daveluy has also written, in diary form, two novels about Sylvette Forest, who learns to share in family life and accept her father's remarriage: *Sylvette et les adultes; roman pour adolescentes* (1962) and its sequel, *Sylvette sous la tente bleue; roman* (1964). Although well structured and accurately portraying tourist life in the Gaspé area, these two novels were not as popular as the earlier books about Rosanne Fontaine. *Cinq filles compliquées; nouvelles* (1965, 1980) is composed of five short stories that are rich in details of human behaviour as they describe five girls and their attempts to overcome their problems. *Pas encore seize ans . . .* (1982) is another collection of short stories

that faithfully depict young people learning to cope with the pressures and challenges of today's society. Daveluy is also the author of two novels for adult readers: *Chérie Martin; roman* (1957) and *Les Guinois; chroniques de la maison heureuse* (1957), both of which met with limited success.

Daveluy has translated several well-known English-language books: Barbara Smucker's *Underground to Canada* (*Les chemin secrets de la liberté*, 1978) and *Days of terror* (*Jours de terreur*, 1981), Farley MOWAT's *Owls in the family* (*Deux grands ducs dans la famille*, 1980), and Jean LITTLE's *Listen for the singing* (*Écoute, l'oiseau chantera*, 1980). In 1980 she was chosen children's author of the year by the Association des littératures canadienne et québécoise at the annual meeting of the Congrès des sociétés savantes.

IRENE E. AUBREY

Davey, Frank (b. 1940). Born in Vancouver and brought up in Abbotsford, B.C., he attended, in the early 1960s, the University of British Columbia, where he was one of the founders, and the editor, of the influential (and, in some circles, notorious) poetry newsletter TISH, whose first nineteen issues he later brought together in one volume (1975). After doing graduate work at the University of Southern California (Ph.D. 1968, with a thesis on Black Mountain poetics), Davey taught at Sir George Williams University (Concordia) before settling in Toronto, where he has taught at York University since 1970.

Davey's early books of poetry include *D-Day and after* (1963), *City of the gulls and sea* (1964), *Bridge force* (1965), and *The scarred hull* (1966); work from this period was collected in *L'an trentiesme: selected poems 1961-1970* (1972). A second major period of Davey's writing occurred in the early 1970s: the poems in *Four myths for Sam Perry* (1970), *Weeds* (1970), *King of swords* (1972), *Griffon* (1972), *Arcana* (1973), and *The Clallam* (1974) formed the basis for a second selection, *Selected poems: the arches* (1980). His recent work includes a 'manuscript edition' of *War poems* (1979), *Capitalistic affection!* (1982), and the as-yet-unpublished sequence of poems, 'Edward and Patricia'.

Davey's poetry has been balanced between public and private themes, the public poems dealing with Canadian history, especially shipwrecks, and the private poems with sexual relationships, particularly the break-up of his first marriage. bp NICHOL suggests that 'notions of responsibility &

duty within a context of trust, & of how that trust is realized or betrayed' form a link between the two. Stylistically Davey has been concerned with expanding Charles Olson's poetic into the Canadian context, and with what he himself has called 'the validity of fact': a strong distrust of metaphor is evident in both his poetry and his criticism.

The historical poems *(Griffon, Clallam)* reject the idea that the 'documentary' can confine itself to objective facts; rather, these facts fuel the poet's intense anger at the incompetence and arrogance of ships' captains, and at the imperialist habit of mind they represent. The more personal poems analyse the sterility of relationships based on the false ideals of chivalric or imperialist culture. *King of swords* and *Arcana* subject the material of the Arthurian legends to a ruthlessly contemporary criticism: 'the death of Arthur continues' in Belfast and in the suburbs of Vancouver.

Davey's recent work approaches 'the validity of fact' in the form of long, factual, seemingly prosaic anecdotes. His poetry, however, has always been characterized by tightness of form and control of language; and the apparently rambling lines of *War poems* create a complex mood that counters the innocent tone of the child persona with the ironic reticence of the mature poet. Davey has never received widespread recognition in Canada; he has been seen as a 'poet's poet', employing his precise craftsmanship and theoretical intelligence within an esoteric set of intellectual concerns defined by *Tish* and OPEN LETTER (see below). But his work is by no means inaccessible, and its emotional force could well speak to a much wider audience.

Since 1965 Davey has edited *Open Letter*, a magazine that has consistently been the most interesting and provocative forum in Canada for theoretical and critical explorations of contemporary and experimental writing. His critical writings include *Five readings of Olson's 'Maximus'* (1970), *Earle Birney* (1971), *From there to here: a guide to English-Canadian literature since 1960* (1974), *Louis Dudek and Raymond Souster* (1982), and a chapbook, *The contemporary Canadian long poem* (1983). His numerous articles include important commentaries on the work of E.J. PRATT and a seminal attack on the prevalence of thematic criticism in Canada, 'Surviving the paraphrase' in CANADIAN LITERATURE 70 (Autumn 1976); this is the title essay in *Surviving the paraphrase: eleven essays on Canadian literature* (1983).

The finest criticism of Davey's own work is to be found in bp Nichol's Introduction to *The arches*; there is also an excellent article by Douglas BARBOUR, 'Finding a voice to say what must be said', in *The Lakehead University Review* (1974). An indispensable guide to Davey's career is the 92-page interview with George BOWERING, 'Starting at our skins', in *Open Letter* (1979).

See also CRITICISM IN ENGLISH: 5(g) and POETRY IN ENGLISH 1950 TO 1982: 2.						STEPHEN SCOBIE

Davies, Robertson (b. 1913). William Robertson Davies was born in Thamesville, Ont. (the Deptford of three of his novels), where he lived for five years. The newspaper interests of his father W. Rupert Davies, later Senator, took the family to Renfrew, where Davies attended a country schoolhouse, and then to Kingston (the Salterton of his first three novels). He attended Upper Canada College in Toronto, Queen's University in Kingston, and Balliol College, Oxford, where he took his B. Litt. in 1938. He then acted briefly with a provincial acting company before joining the Old Vic Company for two seasons of acting bit parts, teaching theatre history in its school, and doing literary work for the director. In 1940 he married Brenda Mathews, who had been a stage manager with the Old Vic. Rejected for military service, he returned to Canada. He was literary editor of *Saturday Night* in Toronto until 1942, when he joined the editorial staff of the Peterborough *Examiner* (a paper his father owned), becoming editor and owner (with his two brothers) in 1946. For ten years after the war he threw his considerable energies into theatre, writing, and directing plays for the 'Little Theatre' and for several professional companies. He sat on the board of the Stratford Festival from 1953 to 1971. When he moved to Toronto in 1963 as Master of Massey College, University of Toronto, he ceased to edit the *Examiner*, though he maintained an active interest in the paper until it was sold in 1968. At the university he taught in the English department and in the newly established Drama Centre until he retired in 1981. He was awarded the Lorne Pierce Medal for his outstanding contribution to Canadian literature in 1961 and was made FRSC in 1967, a Companion of the Order of Canada in 1972, and in 1980 an honorary member of the American Academy and Institute of Arts and Letters (the first Canadian to be so honoured).

Davies had a distinctive and productive career as a journalist. He made the *Examiner* one of the most frequently quoted papers in Canada. His weekly Saturday column of urbane and witty comment on the Canadian scene, written under the pseudonym 'Samuel Marchbanks' in the *Examiner* and several other papers between 1943 and 1953, yielded three books. *The diary of Samuel Marchbanks* (1947) and *The table talk of Samuel Marchbanks* (1949) both capture Davies' early voice, since the selections from the column are largely unchanged. *Marchbanks' almanack* (1967), which includes the exuberant 1949-50 letters when the column was called 'The correspondence of Samuel Marchbanks', and the more conventional single-paragraph entries from the column's final two years, also incorporates almanac data and amusing drawings created in the sixties. *A voice from the attic* (1960) includes a dozen or so of the regular review articles Davies wrote for *Saturday Night* during his second stint as its literary editor from 1953 to 1959, but the bulk of the book is fresh material. This volume (with its handy index) offers an invaluable introduction to his indiosyncratic cast of mind, since the books and ideas discussed are favourites. In *A voice*, Davies appears in the role of educator, arguing that Canada needs intelligent, literate, general (as opposed to professional) readers as a stimulus to writers and as the basis of civilized life. The same urge towards education, stimulation, and liberation appears in his fiction, from *A mixture of frailties* (1958) on, in the many characters who broaden the horizons of hero, heroine, and reader, and in the general air of intellectual playfulness. *The enthusiasms of Robertson Davies* (1979)—reprinting samples of Davies' journalism from the *Saturday Night* period in the forties, through his *Toronto Star* column, 'A writer's diary' (1959-62), and his many freelance articles—gives a good sense of the quality and range of his journalism. *The well-tempered critic: one man's view of theatre and letters in Canada* (1981) gathers Davies' astute commentary on two aspects of Canadian culture (1940-80). Both compilations were edited by Judith Skelton Grant.

Davies has played an important part in the development of Canadian drama. His first theatrical publications had an unusual focus that continued to interest him. His fine Oxford thesis, published as *Shakespeare's boy actors* (1939), involved a thoughtful investigation of the capacities of boys and what they might be trained to do. Drawing on this knowledge, he selected appropriate scenes and gave useful advice on acting and scenery in the frequently reprinted *Shakespeare for young players: a junior course* (1942). Later he wrote *A masque of Aesop* (1952) and *A masque for Mr Punch* (1963) for the boys of the Preparatory School of Upper Canada College.

More influential than the masques were his lively topical plays for adults, which made Davies Canada's most important playwright in the late forties and early fifties. Like his fiction, the plays are handsomely crafted. They are witty, balanced, urbane, reaching poetically just dénouements at the conclusion of carefully controlled actions replete with dramatic twists, mystery, eccentric characters, ritual, and occasional violence. Indeed his plays (and his fiction) share many of the characteristics of melodrama and stories of suspense. A recurrent theme in his early plays is Canada's failure to see art as essential to its development into a civilized nation. Of his five one-act plays, *Overlaid* (1948) and *Hope deferred*— which appeared in *Eros at breakfast and other plays* (1949) with the title play, *The voice of the people*, and *At the gates of the righteous*— are particularly fine. In *Overlaid*, his most frequently acted play, the life-enhancing force of art meets temporary defeat at the hands of a death-centred religion of respectability as 'Pop' relinquishes a cultural spree in New York to his daughter's yearning for a solid granite family tombstone. In the historical play *Hope deferred*, emissaries from the Catholic Church successfully oppose the playing of Molière's *Tartuffe* in the New France of Count Frontenac. The full-length plays *Fortune, my foe* (1949) and *At my heart's core* (1950), while similar in their thematic concerns, reveal Davies effectively manipulating his broader theatrical resources. *Fortune, my foe* makes lively use of jokes and wit to underscore its thematic points, and in *At my heart's core* the Rebellion of 1837 patterns and deepens the action centring on the personal rebellions of the characters Susanna MOODIE, Catharine Parr TRAILL, and Frances Stewart. *Four favourite plays* (1968) reprints *Eros at breakfast*, *The voice of the people*, *At the gates of the righteous*, and *Fortune, my foe*.

During the fifties Davies wrote three plays for the Crest Theatre, Toronto: *A jig for the gypsy* (1954), *Hunting Stuart* (written in 1955), and *General confession* (written in 1956 but published with *Hunting Stuart* and an earlier play, *King Phoenix*, in *Hunting*

Stuart and other plays in 1972). In these plays art, magic, imagination, and love triumph. All three reveal Davies in command of his art but, curiously, the never-produced *General confession* is the strongest. In this highly theatrical piece the aged Casanova summons the spirits of Voltaire, the Ideal Beloved, and Cagliostro from three bookcases of forbidden books. Representing Casanova's Intellect, his Ideal Beloved, and his Contrary Destiny, these three spirits and Casanova act out charades dealing with key incidents in Casanova's life, scenes that result in his gaining self-knowledge. The play ends with a trial in which the spirits accuse, defend, and try Casanova and through which he gains self-acceptance. Full of unexpected twists, it is as wise as it is witty in its depiction of the human condition.

The emergence of a number of talented Canadian playwrights in the late fifties and sixties, and his own growing reputation as a novelist, have obscured Davies' more recent plays. The adaptation of his novel *Leaven of malice*—titled *Love and libel* when it was produced in 1960 and renamed *Leaven of malice* for its revivals in 1973 at the Hart House Theatre and in 1975 at the Shaw Festival—has finally been published in *Canadian drama* 7, no. 2 (1981). The 1974 television play *Brothers in the black art*, inspired by tales Davies' father told about his early experience as a printer, has also been published recently (1981), but only in a limited edition put out by the Alcuin Society of Vancouver. *Question time* (1975), on the other hand—a Jungian play in which Canada's prime minister undergoes an identity crisis that has national implications—appeared in print soon after it was produced. *Pontiac and the Green Man*, written for the University of Toronto's sesquicentennial in 1977, has not been published.

Neither his journalism nor his drama is as important as the fiction that in the seventies won Davies a preëminent place among writers in Canada, and international recognition. In the fifties he wrote *Tempest-tost* (1951), *Leaven of malice* (1954), and *A mixture of frailties* (1958), three novels linked by their setting in the university town of Salterton and by the recurrence of some characters. They have been called satiric romances and there is some truth in the term, for their plots are romantic and their omniscient narrator observes the foibles of small-town Ontario sharply. But these witty and urbane novels are also comedies of manners. All three are elegantly constructed and their action is

neatly framed. *Tempest-tost*, the slightest of the three, pursues the various stages of the local Little Theatre's production of *The tempest*, which offers a standard against which contemporary character and action are measured. A central strand of the action focuses on Hector Mackilwraith, a middle-aged mathematics teacher who, stirred and troubled by Shakespeare's play, falls in love with the beautiful young Griselda Webster and, despairing, tries to commit suicide on the play's first night. In *Leaven of malice* a false engagement notice in Salterton's *Evening Bellman* initiates a series of reactions culminating in the unmasking of the malicious prankster and the publication of a genuine engagement notice. Focusing on the distorting power of malice and the role of truth in public and private life, the book begins and ends in the *Bellman*'s editorial office, where Gloster Ridley strives to make his paper accurate and responsible, while in the heart of the story Ridley and the two young people linked by the false engagement notice confront and share private truths. In *A mixture of frailties*, the most powerful book of the trilogy, Mrs Bridgetower's will requires that her estate be used to train a young Salterton woman in the arts until Solly Bridgetower has male issue. As the story continues we see the effects of this will for Solly and for Monica Gall, a singer. The erudite lore Davies lodges with Monica's teachers is a real strength, expanding and deepening one of the book's central themes: the nature of art. But the book's balance is askew. We are led to expect parallel treatment of Solly and Monica, though only Monica's experience is fully dramatized.

The Deptford trilogy—FIFTH BUSINESS (1970), *The manticore* (1972), and *World of wonders* (1975)—completes the move begun in *A mixture of frailties* away from the 'novel' proper, with its roots in the comedy of manners, to fictional autobiography or 'confession', one of the four categories of prose fiction Northrop FRYE defines in his 'Theory of genres' (the Fourth Essay in his *Anatomy of criticism*). This is a particularly happy shift for Davies, since theoretical and intellectual interests (always an aspect of his writing) are as central to the confession as presentation of character. The trilogy's three first-person narrators (each handled differently) tell the intertwined stories of the lives shaped by the throwing of a stone-laden snowball and introduce fascinatingly diverse lore appropriate to each narrator's situation. In *Fifth business*, the master-work of the trilogy,

Dunstan Ramsay tells the story of his life as a memoir to be read only after his death. He can thus speak frankly about himself and others as he tells how ducking the fateful snowball resulted in his lifelong fascination with saints and his eventual brush with the devil. In *The manticore* the story of Boy Staunton, thrower of the snowball, is revealed indirectly as his son, the eminent lawyer David Staunton, undergoes analysis. David tells his (and his father's) story, first in his record of his initial impressions and conversations at the Jungian Institute in Zurich; then in a notebook in which he examines his life chronologically and records his analyst's reactions; and finally in diary entries spanning the week when he encounters Dunstan, Magnus Eisengrim, and Liesl Naegli, all of whom have special insights into his father's death. In *World of wonders* Davies supplies yet another context for his first-person narrative. As historian, creating a 'document' on a great man, Dunstan provides a verbatim record of Magnus recounting, over a series of lunches and dinners, the surprising life that began prematurely as a result of his mother's being hit by the snowball. Magnus reveals himself deeply knowledgeable about carnivals, vaudeville, travelling theatre companies, mechanical toys, and the nineteenth-century illusions of Robert Houdin. Like *The manticore*, however, *World of wonders* is not as satisfying as *Fifth business*. There the lore about saints was creatively linked to the gradual revelation of Dunstan's character. But in *The manticore* the Jungian interpretative material remains too separate from David Staunton's life story; and in *World of wonders* parts of the information about carnivals and the theatre company take on a life of their own apart from the story of Magnus's development.

In *The rebel angels* (1981) Davies has again shifted his fictional mode, this time towards what Frye calls 'Menippean satire' or 'anatomy'. Some of the characters thus appear not as fully rounded people but as mental attitudes, and even more emphasis is placed on ideas and theories. The short form of the anatomy—the dialogue or colloquy—is present in the Senior Common Room Guest Nights at Ploughwright College (Massey College), and the exuberance of the anatomist appears in the piling up of erudite lore in catalogues, like the list of medieval terms for faeces of animals. Narrated alternately by a gifted graduate student, Maria Magdalene Theotoky, and a middle-aged professor

of New Testament Greek, Father Darcourt, *The rebel angels* takes as its chief intellectual interest the nature of a university, presenting it as an institution rooted in the middle ages, dedicated to the pursuit of learning and wisdom both secular and divine, but also prone to petty and gross betrayals of its professed standards. Davies' highly coloured story (it encompasses research into human excrement, gypsy lore, fortune-telling, and a bizarre murder) is enriched by a stream of references to Rabelais, Paracelsus, and Aubrey, reminding readers that philosophy, science, and biography, like the university itself, have long roots.

Davies has written, or collaborated in the writing of, several other books. He wrote most of the three volumes commemorating the Stratford Festival's crucial first three years: *Renown at Stratford: a record of the Stratford Shakespeare Festival in Canada, 1953* (1953, with Tyrone Guthrie and Grant Macdonald), *Twice have the trumpets sounded: a record of the Stratford Shakespeare Festival in Canada, 1954* (1954, with Tyrone Guthrie and Grant Macdonald), and *Thrice the brinded cat hath mew'd: a record of the Stratford Shakespeare Festival in Canada, 1955* (1955, with Tyrone Guthrie, Boyd Neel, and Tanya Moiseiwitsch). He wrote a short critical study, *Stephen Leacock* (1970), and edited *Feast of Stephen: an anthology of the less familiar writings of Stephen Leacock* (1970) and *The Penguin Stephen Leacock* (1981). With Michael R. Booth, Richard Southern, Frederick Marker, and Lise-Lone Marker he prepared *The Revels history of drama in English. Volume VI: 1750-1880* (1975). One half of *Robertson Davies: provocative pronouncements on a wide range of topics* (1977), a selection of speeches and stories originally read aloud, includes 'Jung and the theatre' and four lectures called 'Masks of evil'—all five valuable for the light they shed on ideas in the Deptford trilogy. *High spirits* (1982) collects the eighteen ghost stories read at Massey College's Christmas celebration, called Gaudy Night, from 1963 to 1980.

Three short critical books have appeared on Davies' writing. Elspeth Buitenhuis's study appeared in the series Canadian Writers & Their Works (1972), Patricia Morley's (on the plays only) in Profiles in Canadian Drama (1977), and Judith Skelton Grant's in the Canadian Writers Series of the New Canadian Library (1978). Patricia Monk's *The smaller infinity: the Jungian self in the novels of Robertson Davies* (1982) tackles an aspect of Davies' writing that has long intrigued readers. There are also three collections of articles on Davies' work. A special Robertson Davies number of the *Journal of Canadian Studies* (12, no. 1, Feb. 1977) includes Gordon Roper's 'A Davies log', a useful biblio- and biographical list. *Studies in Robertson Davies' Deptford trilogy* (1980), edited by Robert G. Lawrence and Samuel L. Macey, encompasses ten articles and an introduction in which Davies reveals the seminal notes for *Fifth business*. The eight articles in the Robertson Davies issue of *Canadian Drama* 7, no. 2 (1981) provide critical perspectives on the long-neglected plays. Volume 3 of *The annotated bibliography of Canada's major authors* (1982) includes a comprehensive bibliography of writings on and by Davies to the end of 1980.

Tempest-tost, Leaven of malice, A mixture of frailties, Fifth business, The manticore, World of wonders, and *One half of Robertson Davies* are available in Penguin; *Tempest-tost, Leaven of malice,* and *At my heart's core & Overlaid* are Clarke Irwin paperbacks. *A voice from the attic* and *Samuel Marchbanks' almanack* are in the New Canadian library and *Stephen Leacock* in the accompanying Canadian Writers series.

See also NOVELS IN ENGLISH 1960 TO 1982: 2.   JUDITH SKELTON GRANT

Davin, Nicholas Flood (1840-1901). Born Nicholas Francis Davin in Kilfinane, Ire., he spent six years of his youth as an ironmonger's apprentice before going to London in 1865 to read law at the Middle Temple, supporting himself through shorthand reporting in the House of Commons press gallery. Called to the bar in 1868, he continued an active career in journalism, serving as correspondent to London and Dublin papers during the Franco-Prussian war, and then becoming editor of the *Belfast Times*. In 1872 he brought his combined talents in law and journalism to Toronto, where he joined the editorial staff of George Brown's *Globe*; he later switched to the opposition *Mail*, which accorded more closely with his Conservative sympathies. Davin won public acclaim as a lecturer, and his celebrated address, *British versus American civilization* (Toronto, 1873), was published as the second in a series of pamphlets put out by the Canada First group. In 1874 he was called to the Canadian bar and made his legal reputation in Canada by his defence of the man accused of murdering George Brown in 1880.

After rendering valuable services to the Conservative cause in politics, Davin moved in 1883 to Regina, the capital of the Northwest Territories, to establish the *Regina Leader*. His coverage of the Riel rebellion and trial once again brought Davin's name into national prominence, restoring his hopes for a political career. From 1887 to 1900 he sat in the House of Commons as Conservative member for Assiniboia. His increasing identification with regional aspirations and the interests of the Territories complicated his political life, however, and prevented him from acceding to government measures with the unquestioning loyalty that might have brought him the cabinet post he ardently desired.

Davin's pamphlet and periodical production was considerable. It included long articles on John Stuart Mill, Disraeli, 'Ireland and the Empire', 'Culture and practical power', and many others on political and cultural topics, as well as an edited pamphlet promoting immigration to the Northwest, *Homes for millions* (Toronto, 1891). A play, *The fair grit; or, The advantages of coalition* (Toronto, 1876), is a political satire. *The Irishman in Canada* (Toronto, 1877) is a 700-page study cataloguing the contributions of Irish immigrants to Canadian political, economic, and cultural life.

Declaring 'the cultivation of taste and imagination as important as the raising of grain', Davin published three slim volumes of verse as 'a step towards the creation of a Canadian literature'. *Album verses and other poems* (Ottawa, 1882) was published privately; an enlarged and revised version appeared as *Eos: a prairie dream and other poems* (Ottawa, 1884). Enlarged and revised once more, *Eos: an epic of the dawn and other poems* (Regina, 1889) was offered to the public as 'the first purely literary work printed and published in the North-West Territories'. Notoriously ambitious in his other endeavours, Davin was uncharacteristically (but realistically) modest about his poetic powers. In the long title poem Eos, goddess of the dawn, takes the narrator on an aerial trip across the Old World to the New, enabling Davin to combine descriptive passages with commentary on new versus old forms of civic life. American-style democracy he deplores, but the 'young Dominion . . . /gives large promise of the mightier day'. 'The critics' in the same volume is an engaging mixture of satire and honest self-appraisal.

Davin's powers as critic and supporter of literature led him to urge Parliament in 1890 to enlarge its library's appropriations for literary publications, citing Archibald LAMP-MAN's work as that of 'a genuine poet'. In 1893, during a tariff debate, Davin argued successfully for the removal of duty on university texts. Won over to the cause of women's independence by his long association with the poet, story-writer, and journalist Kate Simpson Hayes ('Mary Markwell'), by whom he had two children, Davin moved in Parliament on 8 May 1895 that women be given the vote, a measure that was not granted federally until 1918.

G.B. Koester has written a full and reliable biography in *Mr. Davin, M.P.* (1980), while Davin's life in western Canada has been made the subject of a play by Ken MITCHELL: *Davin: the politician* (1979).

SUSAN JACKEL

Day, Frank Parker (1881-1950). Born in Shubenacadie, N.S., and educated at Pictou Academy and Mount Allison University, he attended Oxford University as New Brunswick's second Rhodes Scholar and later studied at the University of Berlin. From 1909 to 1912 he was a professor of English at the University of New Brunswick. He then moved to the United States and taught English at the Institute of Technology, Swarthmore, and from 1929 to 1933 was president of Union College, Schenectady, N.Y. In the First World War he served in the Canadian army and was instrumental in recruiting and training the 185th Infantry Battalion, the Cape Breton Highlanders; he was promoted to the rank of colonel at Amiens and was commanding officer of the 25th Overseas Battalion.

In middle life Day became a writer, the author of three novels and a work of non-fiction. *River of strangers* (1926) is an imaginative account of life on the Churchill River. There is no evidence, however, that he ever visited the North. In his best-known novel, *Rockbound* (1928; rpr. 1973)—a realistic account of life in a primitive south-shore fishing community of Nova Scotia in the decade preceding the Great War—the passions of ambition, greed, and jealousy are exposed. Day depicts the narrow, harsh, and primitive life of the Rockbound Island fishermen and their families against the hostile and often violent background of the Atlantic. In *John Paul's Rock* (1932) the central character is a Micmac Indian who has run from the white man's law to live in isolation among the many lakes and barrens of inland Nova Scotia. In his solitude John Paul attempts to come to terms with God through the folk-lore of Glooscap, the God of the Indians, and the morality of his Micmac background. For Day, God was 'the sum total of all human idealism, aesthetic and moral desires, and the craving for perfection'. In his *Autobiography of a fisherman* (1927) he demonstrates his deep knowledge of inland fishing and his close familiarity with nature: 'Nature always wins or takes her revenge because we refuse to face the fact that we are animals—fine animals to be sure—in a world of nature.' DOUGLAS LOCHHEAD

Deacon, William Arthur (1890-1977). Born in Pembroke, Ont., he was raised in Stanstead, Qué., where he lived until he was seventeen. He was educated at Stanstead College and Victoria College, University of Toronto, which he left at the end of his second year. In 1918 he earned the degree of LL.B at the University of Manitoba and later joined the Pitblado law firm in Winnipeg. Meanwhile he had developed an intense enthusiasm for literature and undergone years of rigorous self-training in writing, publishing essays and reviews in Canadian and American periodicals. His conversion to Theosophy in 1917, his appointment in 1921 as assistant literary editor of the *Manitoba Free Press*, and his charter membership the same year in the Winnipeg Branch of the CANADIAN AUTHORS' ASSOCIATION were crucial in confirming his conviction of his literary vocation. In 1922 he left Winnipeg and went to Toronto where, on the recommendation of B.K. Sandwell, he was hired as literary editor of *Saturday Night*.

Deacon's six years with *Saturday Night* (1922-8)—which coincided with, and reflected, a period of buoyant Canadian nationalism—were stimulated by his enthusiastic commitment to the encouragement of Canadian writers and to the building of a reading public for their work. His plain, direct style as a reviewer (he was most at ease with fiction, biography, and history) and his special literary sections speedily attracted and held a community of readers, while his column 'Saved from the wastebasket', containing book news and writers' gossip, served as an informal literary forum.

During these years Deacon's essays and reviews continued to appear in several publications, including H.L. Mencken's *American Mercury*, The *Saturday Review of Literature*, and The *International Book Review*. Encouraged by Lorne PIERCE of the RYERSON PRESS, he published two essay collections: *Pens and pirates* (1923), composed of humorous and whimsical pieces on a wide range of topics, and *Poteen* (1926), containing essays on national themes and a lengthy critical discussion of Canadian literature. Deacon also wrote an appreciative monograph, *Peter McArthur* (1924), for Pierce's Makers of Canadian Literature series and The FOUR JAMESES (1927), a comic celebration of four of Canada's best bad poets and the work for which he is best remembered. All of his writing in this decade was marked by a commitment to Canadian cultural nationalism and a considerable wit.

Dismissed from *Saturday Night* in April 1928 after a series of disagreements over Hector Charlesworth's rigorous editorializing policies, Deacon began syndicating book reviews in newspapers across Canada. But within a few months he was working almost exclusively for Toronto's *Mail and Empire*. With Wilfred Reeves he edited *Open house* (1931), a collection of essays by members of the Toronto Writers' Club that addressed controversial political and social subjects. Under the stresses of the thirties, Deacon's interests and his journalistic capacities broadened remarkably into the fields of national and world affairs. He became active in the Couchiching Conferences on International Affairs, instituted in 1932. The intensity of his concerns for world peace and for Canada's future was articulated in the impassioned rhetoric of *My vision of Canada* (1933), in which Deacon imagined a romantic, Utopian national destiny for Canada. *The literary map of Canada* (1936) was a handsome four-colour poster featuring writers and places significant to Canadian literature. His pamphlet attacking censorship, *Sh-h-h . . . here comes the censor* (1940), was his last independent publication. When the *Mail and the Empire* was sold to the *Globe* in 1936, Deacon became literary editor of the new *Globe and Mail*, a position he held until 1960.

Always active in the Toronto Branch of the Canadian Authors' Association, and for some time its president, Deacon became national president of the CAA in 1946. He formed committees that produced a standard book contract; secured from the federal government special income-tax provisions for Canadian writers; and engaged Earle BIRNEY as editor of the *Canadian Poetry Magazine*. He had been active in establishing the GOVERNOR-GENERAL'S AWARDS under the aegis of the CAA in 1937 and served as chairman of the Awards Board from 1944 to

1949. However, his hope that in the immediate post-war years the CAA would be completely rebuilt by the strength and energies of young upcoming writers proved elusive. The old constituency was resistant to change and the young were impatient. By the 1950s Deacon was himself experiencing the fatigue of more than thirty years of full-time reviewing. Inevitably attention shifted to younger critics.

Throughout his career Deacon was engaged in a voluminous correspondence with Canadian writers, such as E.J. PRATT, Raymond KNISTER, and Grey Owl (George Stansfeld BELANEY) in the twenties and thirties; Hugh MacLENNAN, Roger LEMELIN, and Gabrielle ROY in the forties; and Thomas RADDALL, Peter NEWMAN, and June Callwood in the fifties and sixties. Deacon's papers—some 18,000 items now housed in the Thomas Fisher Rare Book Library of the University of Toronto—bear eloquent testimony to four decades of commitment to the encouragement of Canadian writers and to their eager and grateful response.

Deacon retired from *The Globe and Mail* in Jan. 1961 but continued his news and gossip column, 'The fly leaf', until 1963. Four publishers—McCLELLAND AND STEWART, Ryerson, MACMILLAN, and Doubleday—negotiated with him about a history of his life and times in Canadian literature. He finally contracted with George Nelson of Doubleday for two volumes, but age and infirmity prevented him from completing his work.

Deacon's essay, 'The Canadian novel turns the corner' (1960), has recently been reprinted in *Canadian novelists and the novel* (1981) edited by Douglas Daymond and Leslie Monkman. Clara THOMAS and John Lennox discuss the first decade of Deacon's reviewing career in 'William Arthur Deacon and *Saturday Night*, 1922-1928' (*Essays on Canadian Writing*, 11 (Summer, 1978)). They are also co-authors of his biography: *William Arthur Deacon: a Canadian literary life* (1982).

JOHN LENNOX

De Grandmont, Éloi (1921-70). Born in Baie du Febvre, Qué., he attended classical college in Nicolet and studied art at L'École des Beaux Arts de Montréal, the Sorbonne, and L'École du Louvre. He worked as a journalist and theatre critic for several Montreal papers, including *Notre Temps*, which he founded in 1954. He also wrote numerous short stories and radio dramas for

De Grandmont

Radio-Canada, and hosted a series of variety and talk shows on radio. Between 1951 and 1954 he served as secretary general of the Théâtre du Nouveau Monde. Shortly before his death be became a professor at the Université de Montréal's École de Traduction.

De Grandmont wrote the first play by a Canadian to be presented by the Théâtre du Nouveau Monde: *La fontaine de Paris* (1953), a one-act farce of little consequence that was produced as a radio play in 1952 and 1953 and was the basis for a ballet televised by Radio-Canada in 1954. His three-act drama *Un fils à tuer* (1950) was not particularly well received when it was first performed in Montreal in 1949, but it has since obtained some critical recognition for its elegant style, classical structure, and socio-political connotations. The action takes place in New France and revolves around a bitter father-son conflict of wills—between a stern, intolerant, and unsympathetic man who believes strongly in his patriotic duty to the land and a young idealist who would seek adventure in France but is killed as a deserter by his father. It is typical of a number of plays written and produced in Québec after the Second World War in that it vehemently defends the notion of individual freedom of thought and action and sanctions the concept of a pluralistic society. Unusual, however, is the hero's longing to seek his fortune in France and not, as others would, in North America.

A macabre one-act drama, *Le temps des fêtes* (1952), was published with *La fontaine de Paris*, as well as in the collection of his plays, *Théâtre I* (1968).

Of De Grandmont's several translations and adaptations, his 1968 French version of *Pygmalion* was the most popular and controversial: his Professor Higgins attempts to teach standard French to a young woman who speaks JOUAL. De Grandmont's collaborative works include a lively and successful musical comedy, *Doux temps des amours*, written with Louis-Georges Carrier and produced in 1964, and a pictorial history of the Théâtre du Nouveau Monde, *Dix ans de Théâtre au Nouveau Monde* (1961).

Although De Grandmont is now considered to be of minor importance as a poet, his poetry was well received when first published in the collections *Le voyage d'Arlequin* (1946), *La jeune fille constellée* (1948), *Premiers secrets* (1951), *Plaisirs* (1953), *Chardon à Foulon* (1963), and *Une saison en chanson* (1963).

De Grandmont was a man of letters whose numerous publications include discussions of Émile NELLIGAN in (*Poèmes choisis*, 1966) and Alfred Pellan (*Cinquante dessins d'Alfred Pellan*, 1946), and three books on his travels in Europe: *Voyageurs ou touristes* (1970), *Je n'aurais jamais cru* (1971), and *Vernousser* (1971).

See Laurent Mailhot, 'Deux saisons dans le vie de la Nouvelle France: un fils (ou un père) à tuer' in Jean-Cléo Godin and Laurent Mailhot (eds), *Théâtre québécois* (1970) pp. 45-58.   ELAINE NARDOCCHIO

de Grandpré, Pierre. See ANTHOLOGIES IN FRENCH: 4.

De Koninck, Charles (1906-65). Born and educated in Belgium, his doctoral dissertation, presented to the University of Louvain in 1934, was entitled *La philosophie de Sir Arthur Eddington*. From 1934 until his death he was professor of natural philosophy at Université Laval, Quebec City, serving as dean of the faculty of philosophy from 1939 to 1956, and again from 1964. He lectured widely, and from 1957 to 1963 was visiting professor at the University of Notre Dame, Indiana. He died in Rome while accompanying Maurice Cardinal Roy of Québec to the Second Vatican Council in the role of theological expert to the Cardinal—the only layman who held such a position on that occasion.

De Koninck published extensively on philosophical and theological topics, writing in both English and French with admirable lucidity. A primary feature of his scholarly interest was an insistence on the unity of the philosophical spirit, whether manifesting itself in the heights of metaphysics or on such questions as why dogs run in a certain way. He deplored the divorce of philosophy and science as resulting in the impoverishment of both. He also sought to distinguish the doctrines of perennial validity—particularly those contained in Aristotle's *Physics* (for example, on the nature of time)—from what is no longer tenable. In *The hollow universe* (1960), De Koninck's Whidden lectures given at McMaster University in 1959, he moved progressively through considerations of mathematics, physics, and biology in order to bring to light the distinction (in all these domains) between the work of the calculative mind and the contemplative mind.

De Koninck was anything but an ivory-tower thinker. Highly adept at communicating his philosophical seriousness, he attracted as dean at Laval students from all over North America who became disciples in the best sense. That seriousness showed itself, in a rather polemical setting, after the publication of his *De la primauté du bien commun contre les personnalistes; Le principe de l'ordre nouveau* (1943). This book contains two quite distinct essays. 'Le principe de l'ordre nouveau' is an ironic reference to Marxism, radicalism, and nihilism. It was the other essay that provoked injured outcries. De Koninck was troubled by the teachings of certain Thomist philosophers (he names Mortimer Adler and Walter Farrell) who, in their opposition to totalitarianism, tended to set up an either/or situation as between 'person' and 'society'. He sought to reshape the discussion. Instead of asking, Is the person better than society? he asked, Is the proper good of the person better than his common good? De Koninck affirmed the primacy of the common good (cf. his later 'In defence of Saint Thomas', *Laval Théologique et philosophique*, vol. I, no. 2, 1945). Father I. Th. Eschmann, O.P., of the Pontifical Institute of Mediaeval Studies, Toronto, took this essay to be an attack on Jacques Maritain (it can hardly be denied that Maritain was seen, even by De Koninck, as to some extent open to its criticism). Eschmann's 'In defence of Jacques Maritain' accused De Koninck of proposing a new and entirely unacceptable interpretation of St Thomas by means of quite amateurish methods of interpretation. Eschmann's paper had at least the effect of provoking De Koninck into a fuller presentation of his (as it seems to us) quite invulnerable position with 'In defence of Saint Thomas', the tone of which is at times harsh, though its philosophizing is painstaking.

De Koninck was quite vocal in the controversies of the early 1960s in Québec concerning public schools with no religious affiliation ('non-confessional' schools). In *Tout homme est mon prochain* (1964)—reprints of letters to editors, etc.—we read his beautifully clear defences of freedom of conscience for non-believers as well as believers: he knew how to express the grounds of tolerance. This is public controversy at its best.

A bibliography of De Koninck's writings can be found in *Mélanges à la mémoire de Charles De Koninck* (1968) published by Les presse de l'Université Laval.

LAWRENCE DEWAN, O.P.

De Lamirande, Claire. See NOVELS IN FRENCH 1960 TO 1982: 3(g).

Delaney, Marshall. Pseudonym of Robert FULFORD.

De la Roche, Mazo (1879-1961). Born in Toronto of lower-middle-class parents who moved frequently in search of betterment, she was educated there and in Galt, Ont., and studied art briefly in Toronto. She and her family later lived for a time on a fruit and stock farm near Bronte, Ont. Her years in a cottage on a gentleman-farmer's estate near Clarkson, Ont., supplemented by earlier experiences, gave her a picture of rural gentry that she would idealize in her fiction. De la Roche spent the greater part of her life with her beloved cousin and companion, Carolyn Clement, and adopted two children, a brother and sister. The family lived in England, visiting Toronto from time to time. The outbreak of the Second World War sent them to Toronto, where 'Windrush Hill' in York Mills became their permanent residence.

De la Roche's first short story appeared in the *Atlantic Monthly* in 1915, and her life was more than half over before her first lengthy work appeared: *Explorers of the dawn* (1922), a collection of sticky short stories that are set in a never-never land of cosy late-Victorian domesticity fitfully translated to Ontario. *Possession* (1923) takes place in a somewhat idealized rural Ontario resembling Bronte, where De la Roche passed some of her late adolescence; yet the opening idyllic atmosphere yields to grim realism, concluding with a forced marriage and the prospect of financial ruin. In *Delight* (1926; NCL, 1961) she created her first protagonist, an immigrant girl, marked by instinctive and passionate responses to life. This novel, like her later *Growth of a man* (1938), vigorously conveys the constrictions of life within a rural slum.

A course that might have earned De la Roche a place alongside a rural realist and romanticist like Martha OSTENSO was shunted aside by the remarkable success of JALNA (1927)—about the Whiteoaks family, whose existence was centred on the house called 'Jalna' in present-day Clarkson, Ont.—which was followed not only by popular accolades and literary dinners but by a demand for more such novels. De la Roche hadn't planned a serial fiction—her temporal sequences in *Jalna* were too precise and limiting for that—but she responded by producing fifteen sequels that moved forward or backward in time. (Her construction of *Jalna* was not loose enough to permit

De la Roche

a lateral exploration of the lives of her characters.) In vain she attempted to escape the series through writing other works, but only the Jalna books allowed her to exercise the unique strengths of her imagination, and only they could support her comfortable lifestyle. The series deals first of all with a house, a property, and an estate whose tone is set by Adeline Whiteoak (Gran), a vital, energetic, high-tempered Ontario version of Victoria Regina. She and her grandson Renny, an adolescent dream of a strong, tempestuous yet loving man (an Ontario Heathcliff), do not so much govern Jalna as energize it. Adeline's and/or Renny's appearance generally brings about a heightening of emotions. Credibility, however, forced De la Roche to allow Gran to die; and the need for new material shifted the focus of subsequent episodes to a younger generation. In the set of amiable fictions she classified as her autobiography (*Ringing the changes*, 1957), De la Roche took some care to emphasize her United Empire Loyalist ancestry, and at Jalna English Canada remains firmly British. Renny serves out the Second World War in a British regiment; the younger generation passes its most idyllic moments in an essentially Edwardian Great Britain; most trips to New York end in disaster; and Renny's American wife proves a constant source of tension within the household. The burgeoning modernism, American in origin, that threatens Jalna with highways and subdivisions is greeted by Renny in the brusque manner of a gentleman-officer putting upstart rebels in their place. Profoundly unintellectual in tone, discourse in Jalna rests on a bedrock of familial and imperial certainties that only the attractions of television appear to threaten seriously at the end of the series.

The fifteen novels that followed *Jalna* are *Whiteoaks of Jalna* (1929), *Finch's fortune* (1931), *The master of Jalna* (1933), *Young Renny* (1935; 1978), *Whiteoak harvest* (1936), *Whiteoak heritage* (1940; 1978), *Wakefield's course* (1941), *The building of Jalna* (1944; 1978), *Return to Jalna* (1946), *Mary Wakefield* (1949; 1978), *Renny's daughter* (1951), *Whiteoak brothers* (1953; 1978), *Variable winds at Jalna* (1954), *Centenary at Jalna* (1958), and *Morning at Jalna* (1960). If there exists an Upper Canadian dream, it is found in the pages of these chronicles. Soap-opera they may be, yet any body of fiction with sufficient world-wide popularity to have sold 11 million copies (9 million of them in hardcover) by 1966, and to remain in print still,

deserves considered attention. For millions of European readers the Ontario landscape portrayed in these books remains *the* Canadian landscape, however displaced it may appear to Canadians. De la Roche had a genius for producing undemanding yet titillating narratives that grew out of an adolescent daydream, one that endures because it intersects, however quirkily, at crucial points with a society's sense of itself. She wrote her Jalna books—before, during, and after a world war—in a Canada that was dominated by an aggressive entrepreneurial system waxing fat on banks, insurance companies, transportation combines, mercantile networks, and the exploitation of nonrenewable resources. It is not surprising, therefore, that her myth of a humane, harmless gentry—living in the Canadian Great Good Place, largely through farming and horse-trading, and never allowing their quarrelsomeness to overcome their mutual loyalties—appealed to so many.

Other works by De la Roche include children's and animal stories (*Beside a Norman tower*, 1934; *The very house*, 1937; *Portrait of a dog*, 1930; *The sacred bullock and other stories of animals*, 1939; *The song of Lambert*, 1955; and *Bill and Coo*, 1958); novels dealing with the tensions between individuals and their social environment (*The two saplings*, 1942, and *A boy in the house*, 1952); *Lark ascending* (1932), a romance set in Sicily; and *Québec: historic seaport*, a sustained meditation upon the romantic personalities of the Old Régime and the early years of the Conquest. Three of De la Roche's one-act plays—*Low life* (1925), *Come true* (1927), and *The return of the emigrant* (1929)—were performed at Hart House Theatre, University of Toronto; they are included in *Low life and other plays* (1929). Some of her short fiction has been collected in *Selected stories of Mazo de la Roche* (1979) edited by Douglas Daymond.

See Ronald Hambelton, *Mazo de la Roche of Jalna* (1956); George Hendrick, *Mazo de la Roche* (1970); and Dennis Duffy, *Gardens, covenants, exiles: Loyalism in the literature of Upper Canada/Ontario* (1982). DENNIS DUFFY

Delisle, Jeanne-Mance. See DRAMA IN FRENCH 1948 TO 1981: 4.

Delta (1957-66). Edited, printed, and published by Louis DUDEK in 26 issues between Oct. 1957 and Oct. 1966, *Delta* offered not only poems, mostly by younger Canadian writers, but quotations from Dudek's personal readings in politics, science, and soci-

De Mille

ology, and occasionally poems, essays, and reviews by Dudek himself. Overall it reflected Dudek's conviction that poetry was an essential part of man's intellectual life, inseparable from the chief issues of its time. Although clearly a vehicle for his personal views of literature, *Delta* was used generously by Dudek to assist younger writers and to welcome new developments. Issue 16 (Nov. 1961) published 'Njarit,' an early typewriter-concrete poem by Earle BIRNEY; Issue 19 (Oct. 1962) was devoted to Vancouver poetry, largely from the TISH group, and included examples of Lionel KEARNS' 'stacked verse'.　　　　FRANK DAVEY

Demers, Jérôme (1774-1853). Born at Saint-Nicholas, near Quebec City, he was educated at the Séminaire de Québec, where philosophy had been taught since 1665, and the Collège des Sulpiciens, Montreal. Ordained a priest in 1798, he became in 1800, and remained until 1842, a professor of philosophy and science at the Séminaire de Québec. Demers was the author of the first work of philosophy published in Canada, *Compendium philosophicae ad usum studiosae juventutis* (Québec, 1835). This work, the greater part of it in Latin, was actually his philosophy courses, which he had been improving constantly since the beginning of the century. Marked by the philosophical controversy that had just ended when the book appeared, it covers the three traditional areas of philosophy—logic, metaphysics, and ethics—with the addition of several pages in French on proofs of revealed religion. Eclectic in nature, it clearly reflects the difficulty experienced at the time by those who sought to find a 'Catholic' philosophy to oppose Descartes and the ideas of the Enlightenment. Demers could not follow Descartes on the question of the origin of ideas or on the criteria of certainty; he could not support knowledge on the authority of evidence (Descartes) or on the evidence of authority (common sense and traditionalism). In refuting the ideas of the Enlightenment and the French Revolution, which asserted the sovereign power of the people, the *Compendium* opposes the divine origin of political power and counters 'systems' of atheism with lengthy proofs of the existence of God.

Though Demers left many manuscripts and much correspondence, he published only the *Compendium*, which was used by several generations of students in the five classical colleges in Lower Canada.

See also PHILOSOPHY IN CANADA: 1.
　　　　　　　　　　YVAN LAMONDE

Demi-civilisés, Les. See Jean-Charles HARVEY.

De Mille, James (1833-80). Born in Saint John, N.B., he was educated at Horton Academy and Acadia College in Wolfville. In 1850-1 he and his brother Elisha toured Britain and Europe; Italy made a lasting impression on James. After obtaining his M.A. from Brown University, Providence, R.I., he spent a year in Cincinatti, Ohio, and returned to Saint John for a brief, unsuccessful attempt at bookselling. In 1859 he married Elizabeth Ann Pryor, the daughter of the first president of Acadia; he taught classics at Acadia from 1860 to 1865. He then taught history, rhetoric, and literature at Dalhousie College, Halifax, until his death.

De Mille was one of North America's most popular novelists in the last quarter of the nineteenth century. His intricate plots, his deft handling of comedy and suspense, and his gift for dialogue—the raciest and slangiest since T.C. HALIBURTON's Clockmaker stories—contributed to this popularity. In his haste to publish—possibly to pay off debts—De Mille padded excessively; yet his books reflected his own delight in linguistic puzzles and puns and his hatred of sham and humbug. Indeed, his 'potboilers' (as he called them) were often parodies of the fictional conventions of his day. He wrote historical romances, 'international' novels of manners and adventure, and sensational novels of mystery and ratiocination. His archetypal situation is a voyage, for pleasure or escape, by a group of men and women. Before the dénouement the protagonist becomes increasingly obsessed, even temporarily insane, and each novel centres on one or more poetic scenes evoking terror.

De Mille's first two novels reveal his interest in early Christianity: *The martyr of the catacombs; a tale of ancient Rome* (New York, 1865), a children's story, and *Helena's household; a tale of Rome in the first century* (New York, 1867). His first hit, *The dodge club; or, Italy in MDCCCLIX* (New York, 1869; rpr. 1980), a series of comic sketches about American tourists in war-torn Italy, spoofs national traits and flatters De Mille's American readers with the first of his gallery of sharp-witted Yankees. The same setting reappears in *The American baron; a novel* (New York, 1872) and in *The babes in the*

De Mille

wood; a tragic comedy; a tale of the Italian Revolution of 1848 (New York, 1875). The lady of the ice; a novel (New York, 1870; rpr. 1973), a first-person narrative about the foibles of two British garrison officers at Québec, contains a satiric explanation of the Fenian takeover of the United States and an Irish parody of Homer's Iliad. A comedy of terrors (New York, 1872) has a spectacular balloon escape from Paris during the Franco-Prussian war. De Mille's imitations of the mysteries popularized by Poe, Dickens, and Wilkie Collins—Cord and creese; a novel (New York, 1869), The cryptogram; a novel (New York, 1871; rpr. 1973), and The living link; a novel (New York, 1874)—are exciting, carefully convoluted stories of secret codes and assumed identities. The simpler plot of The lily and the cross; a tale of Acadia (Boston, 1874) deals with the rescue of a French lady from Louisbourg by an American-raised Frenchman; as De Mille's only historical romance with a Maritime setting, it anticipates Charles G.D. ROBERTS' treatment of similar themes.

A strange manuscript found in a copper cylinder (New York, 1888; NCL 1969) is the most complex and philosophical nineteenth-century Canadian novel. Possibly written in the 1860s, it was published posthumously to cash in on the fashion for fantasy travels to imaginary societies—and anonymously, to protect its copyright. Adam More, a practical British seaman, narrates his experiences among the Kosekin of Antarctica, and his story is framed by the commentary of several gentlemen on a pleasure cruise who discover the manuscript. In the tradition of Thomas More's Utopia, Swift's Gulliver's travels, and Poe's Narrative of Arthur Gordon Pym, De Mille organizes his double-edged satire around the Kosekin's worship of poverty, darkness, and death to present a mirror reflection of European values; but what first appears as superior to them is ultimately revealed as far worse.

One of the first Canadians to write for boys, De Mille avoided the overt didacticism commonly found in children's literature. The Brethren of the White Cross series, drawing on the author's boyhood pranks around the Minas Basin, includes The 'B.O.W.C.' (Boston, 1869), The boys of Grand Pré school (Boston, 1870), Lost in the fog (Boston, 1870), Fire in the woods (Boston, 1872), Picked up adrift (Boston, 1872), and The treasure of the seas (Boston, 1873). The Young Dodge Club series includes Among the brigands (Boston, 1871), The seven hills

(Boston, 1873), and The winged lion; or, stories of Venice (New York, 1877). Other works by De Mille include the famous comic poem 'Sweet maiden of Passamaquoddy'; a religious monograph, The early English church (Halifax, 1877); a textbook containing a defence of 'humorous' and 'pathetic' literature, The elements of rhetoric (New York, 1877); and the posthumously published threnody, Beyond the veil; a poem (Halifax, 1893) edited by Archibald MacMECHAN, which deals with a mystic quest for a lost love and culminates in the discovery of divine love.

See Douglas E. MacLeod, A critical biography of James De Mille (M.A. thesis, Dalhousie university, 1968); Minerva Tracy, 'James De Mille', DICTIONARY OF CANADIAN BIOGRAPHY, vol. 10 (1972); Crawford Kilian, 'The cheerful inferno of James De Mille', Journal of Canadian Fiction 2 (Summer 1973); W.R. Kime, 'The American antecedents of James De Mille's A strange manuscript found in a copper cylinder', Dalhousie Review 55 (Summer 1975); M.G. Parks, 'Strange to strangers only', CANADIAN LITERATURE 70 (Autumn 1976); Patricia Monk, 'James De Mille as mystic: a reconsideration of Beyond the veil', Canadian Poetry 3 (1978); George WOODCOCK, 'De Mille and the Utopian vision', and Kenneth J. Hughes, 'A strange manuscript: sources, satire, a positive Utopia', both in The Canadian novel, vol. II: beginnings (1980) edited by John Moss; 'Kosekin country' in Dictionary of imaginary places (1980) edited by Alberto Manguel and Gianni Guadelupi; and the essay on De Mille by Carole Gerson in Canadian writers and their work: fiction series: volume one (1983) edited by Robert Lecker, Jack David, and Ellen Quigley.   GEORGE L. PARKER

de Montigny, Louvigny. See DRAMA IN FRENCH: 1900 TO 1948.

Denison, Merrill (1893-1975). Playwright, journalist, raconteur, broadcaster, historian, summer-resort owner (at Bon Echo, Ont.), conservationist, and man of many other interests and abilities, Denison was born in Detroit of a Canadian mother and American father. His early training was in architecture at the Universities of Toronto and Pennsylvania, but he soon turned to writing as his profession. Denison's output in many literary forms was prodigious; its quality, however, ranged from the first-rate to the embarrassing.

Denison's major contribution to Canadian letters was as a playwright. Throughout the 1920s he was at the forefront of Canada's Little Theatre movement as designer, actor, and playwright for Toronto's Hart House Theatre. Denison published some of his best work, in which he established himself as a kind of backwoods Sean O'Casey, in *The unheroic North: four Canadian plays* (1932), containing 'Brothers in arms', 'The weather breeder', 'From their own place', and 'Marsh hay'. Set in the backwoods of northern Ontario, the plays gently satirize the eccentricities and pretensions of backwoods people, astutely capturing their environment and the ironies of their various predicaments. Only 'Marsh hay', a full-length play, takes on a sombre note, aiming to illuminate what Denison sees as the tragic futility of his characters' lives. In all four plays Denison is in full command of structure and dialogue. *The prize winner* (1928) is an effective one-act comedy dealing with a down-at-heel carnival road show; and *Balm*, published in *Canadian plays from Hart House*, vol. 1 (1926), is a perfectly constructed and perceptive short piece on the foibles of old age. *On Christmas night* (1934) is a predictable and wholly unoriginal nativity play.

Denison made a significant contribution to radio drama (then in its infancy), though his achievement in this medium is less memorable than his stage plays. *Henry Hudson and other plays* (1931) contains six romantic historical radio dramas: 'Henry Hudson', 'Pierre Radisson', 'Montcalm', 'Seven Oaks', 'Laura Secord', and 'Alexander Mackenzie'. All were broadcast on CNRM, Montreal, in 1931, directed by Tyrone Guthrie. *An American father talks to his son* (1939)—broadcast on CBS radio and sponsored by the Council Against Intolerance in America—is a well-intentioned but trite apology for the principles of American democracy. *Haven of the spirit* (1939) and *The U.S. vs. Susan B. Anthony* (1941) openly espouse the same principles but artistically are much more satisfying because they begin to recognize the complexities of their subject: religious and political prejudice.

As a historian of Canadian commerce, Denison wrote *Harvest triumphant: the story of Massey-Harris, a footnote to Canadian history* (1948), *The barley and the stream: the Molson story* (1955), and *Canada's first bank: a history of the Bank of Montreal* (2 vols, 1966, 1967). Based on original documents in company archives and engagingly written, these studies suffer from a lack of rigorous objectivity (the books invariably being commissioned by the company concerned) and scholarly discipline, a jaunty style often taking precedence over historical substance.

In addition to his histories and plays, Denison wrote *Boobs in the woods; sixteen sketches by one of them* (1927), a collection of more-or-less satirical essays dealing mostly with his experience as a resort owner at Bon Echo; *Canada, our Dominion neighbour* (1944), a pamphlet intended for uninformed American readers; and *Klondike Mike: an Alaskan odyssey* (1945), a bestseller about the Canadian folk hero Michael 'Mike' Mahoney. Denison also wrote some witty sketches of prominent Canadian figures to accompany Jack McLaren's caricatures in *Twelve caricatures cut in linoleum* (1932), for which E.J. PRATT wrote the foreword.

Denison's first wife, Muriel, was the author of the successful 'Susannah' series of children's books. *Mugwump Canadian: the Merrill Denison story* (1973) by Dick MacDonald is a skimpy biography padded by lengthy excerpts from Denison's books.

L.W. CONOLLY

de Pasquale, Dominique. See DRAMA IN FRENCH 1948 TO 1981: 3.

Derome, Gilles. See DRAMA IN FRENCH 1948 TO 1981: 2.

Desbiens, Jean-Paul. See JOUAL.

Descant (1970-) began as a literary supplement to the newsletter of the Graduate English Association, University of Toronto. In 1974, under the present editor Karen Mulhallen, it left the university, becoming an independent journal for poetry, short fiction, articles, interviews, and the visual arts. Following a recent trend among Canadian literary magazines, *Descant* has expanded its range of content to include international authors. It has also produced a special critical issue on Dennis LEE (no. 39, 1982), which was simultaneously released as a hard-cover book, *Tasks of passion: Dennis Lee at mid career*, under the imprint of Descant Editions.

BRUCE MEYER

Desmarchais, Rex (1908-74). Born in Montreal and educated at Mont Saint-Louis and the Collège Sainte-Marie, he first worked for Albert Lévesque at the Librairie d'Action française. He then began to contribute to newspapers such as *L'Ordre*, *Le Devoir* and *Le Canada*. Later, while employed by the Montreal Catholic School

Board, he wrote for *L'Ecole canadienne*. In 1948 he became editor-in-chief of that journal and in 1955 its director. He published many articles in various magazines, reviews, and newspapers under more than a dozen pseudonyms.

In 1932 Desmarchais published 'Altitudes', a short story, in *Almanach de la langue française*, and *L'initiatrice*, a psychological novel, said to be largely autobiographical, that was much influenced by Maurice Barrès. It is a melodrama about a man's love for the rather stand-offish Violaine. After her death at the age of 22 he learns that she was illegitimate and wished to sacrifice her love in atonement for her mother's sin; her death teaches him the true value of life. *Le feu intérieur* (1933), the story of a mismatched couple, also deals with an unfortunate love. *Tentatives*, published in *Les oeuvres d'aujourd'hui* (1937), is a collection of five essays that harshly criticize contemporary French-Canadian society and values. Desmarchais encourages young people to put aside political and religious verbiage and to discover their own values and the taste of an authentic intellectual life. *Pour la vie française au Canada* (1938) and *La France immortelle* (1941) are also critical of his milieu, but Desmarchais's ideas regarding change are vague.

Bête de proie (1942), a philosophical novella, was followed by *La Chesnaie* (1942), a novel that is less interesting as literature than for going against the literary current of the time by publicly expressing not only a nationalist viewpoint but a right-wing ideology. By means of a rather incredible plot and characters that are little more than puppets, it tells the story of Hugues Larocque, whose ambition is to become the French-Canadian Salazar, believing that only a dictator can put Québec back on the road to its destiny as an independent, French-speaking, Catholic country in North America. Democracy would be restored only after an educated élite were in a position to govern in accordance with Larocque's ideas for an 'integral nationalism', which borders on fascism. Larocque urges his compatriots to capture control of their economy (now in the hands of English-speaking people) by developing its agriculture, arts, and crafts. This novel shocked many readers for its revolutionary ideas and for advocating the use of violence to overthrow the government. Perhaps it is no coincidence that it was reissued in 1971.   JACQUES COTNAM

Després, Ronald (b. 1935). Born in Moncton, N.B., he studied at King George School and at St Joseph, L'Assomption, and Ste Anne Colleges. Between the ages of seven and twenty he gave piano recitals on radio and television and during a brief stay in Paris, while writing sketches for the Moncton paper *Évangéline*, he studied music and philosophy. On his return to Canada he spent a year as a journalist and then became a translator in the House of Commons, Ottawa, where he inaugurated a new system of translation and interpretation and assisted in a training program for translators.

Després's first collection of poems, *Silences à nourrir de sang* (1958), was published by Éditions d'Orphée at the author's expense. Though the themes are conventional—love, the sea, rain, dreams—the poems are profoundly moving for their lyricism and delicate melodiousness, reminiscent of Verlaine and Éluard. Quite different is *Les cloisons en vertige* (1962), which depicts a cloistered, impenetrable world from which the poet struggles to break free; anguish reigns here, and only the sea is capable of bringing a furtive hope as fragile as shifting sand. The compound words, alliteration, and assonance of these poems recall the style of Laforgue. *Le scalpel ininterrompu* (1962), modelled on a medieval farce, uses a sadism similar to that of Poe to attack modern science for being the ruination of mankind and to cry out against the misery of living in a cold, impassive, masochistic, and mechanistic world. *Le balcon des dieux inachevés* (1969), a compact collection of delicate lyrical poems celebrating human individuality and the power of imagination, deals with love, work, the macabre, youth, and spring. In *Paysages en contrebande* (1974) Després returns to his Acadian background, recalling memories of his youth and visiting various corners and landscapes of his birthplace; but the poems render everything vague, distant, and foreign.

LAURENT LAVOIE

DesRochers, Alfred (1901-78). Born in Saint-Élie d'Orford, near Sherbrooke, Qué., he studied at the Collège Séraphique de Trois-Rivières (1918-1921) and joined the staff of *La Tribune*, Sherbrooke, in 1925. Except for the interruptions of founding and managing the weekly *L'Étoile de l'Est* (1927-8) in Coaticook, Qué., military service in the Canadian army (1942-4), and work as a parliamentary translator in Ottawa (1944-5), DesRochers was employed by the Sherbrooke weekly until 1950 as translator, sports editor, and advertising director. From 1953 to 1956 he worked for the Canadian Press as a translator. He went into semi-retirement after the death of his wife in 1964.

While working on *La Tribune*, DesRochers became known as a poet. He met other young writers (Jovette BERNIER and Éva Senécal, among others) and founded the Société des Écrivains de l'Est, a literary movement that flourished in the late twenties and early thirties. The interests of this Sherbrooke group went beyond the Eastern Townships region, since DesRochers organized meetings that attracted writers from Montreal, Trois-Rivières, Quebec City, and even from New England. His reputation as a poet grew with the publication of *L'offrande aux vierges folles* (1928), a collection that shows the influence of the Romantics, Baudelaire, and the Parnassians. The poet's own voice became evident in *À l'ombre de l'Orford* (1929), which included the famous prefatory 'Je suis un fils déchu'; two parts of the 'Cycle des bois et des champs', sonnets inspired by life in lumber camps and on farms; and three long poems, notably 'Hymne au vent du nord'. This collection confirmed DesRocher's technical excellence and his pre-eminent place as a poet of the rural scene and of the call of the North, of freedom and adventure. *À l'ombre de l'Orford* won the Prix David of the Province of Quebec in 1932.

During the forties and fifties DesRocher's only published collection was the third edition of *À l'ombre de l'Orford* (1948), which included the thirteen sonnets of the 'Cycle du village' and the poem 'Ma patrie'. In the sixties he produced two collections: *Le retour de Titus* (1963), fifty 'stances royales' inspired by the love of the Roman emperor Titus for Bérénice, composed during the thirties, and *Élégies pour l'épouse en-allée* (1967), a series of forty-nine elegiac sonnets written after the death of his wife. In 1977, with the poet's co-operation, Romain Legaré gathered together the previously published collections and the unfinished thematic series of the thirties and forties under the collective title *Oeuvres poétiques* (2 vols, 1977). While not including the entire corpus of DesRochers's poetry, the two volumes contain some 6,000 verses written over a 45-year period (1922-67).

DesRochers's critical writings were overlooked until well into the sixties. And yet *Paragraphes. Interviews littéraires* (1931)—thirteen articles in the form of imaginary interviews with books (not their authors), and criticisms of writers of the thirties like Jovette Bernier, J.-C. HARVEY, Alice Lemieux, Robert CHOQUETTE, Simone ROUTIER, and Éva Senécal—was well received. In this work, as well as in other articles and essays that appeared in various publications, DesRochers revealed himself as a critic of the highest order. He had an innovative perception of both old and contemporary Québec writers, doubling as theoretician and relentless defender of traditional verse.

Towards the end of his life DesRochers receives awards and distinctions that recognized the quality of his writing and his position as one of the major Québec literary figures between the wars: the Prix Duvernay in 1964, a doctorate *honoris causa* from the Université de Sherbrooke in 1976, and the medal of the Order of Canada in 1978.

See Richard Giguère, 'Alfred Des-Rochers, *Oeuvres poétiques I et II*', *Livres et auteurs québécois 1977* (1978); Jacques Pelletier, 'Alfred DesRochers, critique', VOIX ET IMAGES *du pays* VII (1973); and Jack Warwick, 'Alfred DesRochers: reluctant regionalist', *Queen's Quarterly* (Winter 1965).

RICHARD GIGUÈRE

Desrosiers, Léo-Paul (1896-1967). Born in Berthier-en-Haut, Qué., he studied law at the Université de Montréal and was associated with *L'Action française*. He worked as Ottawa parliamentary correspondent for *Le Devoir* before abandoning journalism to devote himself more fully to writing. He was employed as French editor of the *Proceedings and orders of the House of Commons* from 1928 until 1941, when he became librarian of the Montreal Municipal Library, from which he retired in 1953.

Desrosiers's first work, *Ames et paysages* (1922), a volume of conventional anecdotal tales, early displayed his mastery of language and description. *Nord-Sud* (1931), a novel for which Desrosiers was honoured by the Académie française, records the exodus in the 1840s of young Québécois from a birthplace no longer able to nurture all its sons, and the ensuing tragedies when gold fever and the hope of a better life lures many—including the main character, Vincent Douaire—to California. A loosely knit, often rambling plot serves mainly to provide a framework for vivid evocations of the Québec rural experience and the traditional occupations of farmer, *voyageur*, lumberman, and *colon*. In his most important historical novel, *Les engagés du Grand Portage* (1939)—winner of the Prix David and translated by Christina van Oordt as *The making of Nicolas Montour* (1978)—an earlier, more colourful era of Canadian history is dramatically captured as Nicolas Montour, an unscrupulous *voyageur*, climbs to the upper echelons of the North West Company in the highly competitive fur trade of the early 1800s. The harsh environment forms a backdrop to the realities of bitter personal rivalries. Narrated in an epic present tense, this novel is enhanced by a descriptive power that Desrosiers was to consolidate in later work. He shifted towards a more idyllic portrayal of the strengths of his province's 'grassroots' with *Les opiniâtres* (1941), a tale of the trials of day-to-day living in New France under the threat of Indian marauders, and with *Sources* (1942), in which Nicole de Rencontre stout-heartedly renounces twentieth-century urban comforts for the solitary and often emotionally crushing world of the land. *L'ampoule d'or* (1951)—whose theme is the inevitability of suffering and the harsh consolations of Holy Scripture—is the tale of a passionate young woman twice denied human love and saved from despair by a sense of the indestructibility of a love for God. Theme, plot, and setting (a Gaspé village) are overshadowed by a text that is intensely poetic both in feeling and imagery. Continuous narrative, verging on 'stream-of-consciousness', enables Desrosiers to capture the inner thoughts and emotions of his troubled heroine. Achieving a psychological impact that is typical of much French and French-Canadian fiction of the 1960s and 1970s, *L'ampoule d'or* is regarded as a modest masterpiece. Desrosiers chose not to develop the admirable technique it displays but to pursue its underlying spiritual philosophy in a more ambitious trilogy (1958-1960): *Vous qui passez (Vous qui passez; Les angoisses et les tourments; Rafales sur les cimes)*. Centered on the tribulations of Romain Heurfils, a Québec engineer, it evokes the *mores* of contemporary middle-class society but collapses by the middle of the second volume under the weight of excessive metaphysical discussion.

Desrosiers published a second collection of stories, *Le livre des mystères* (1936). His historical bent was expressed in several works of non-fiction: *L'accalmie* (1937), a portrait of Lord Durham; *Commencements* (1939), a preliminary for a major work on the role of the Iroquois in French-Canadian

history, *Iroquoisie 1534-1646* (1947); and two religious biographies: of Marguerite de Bourgeoys in *Les dialogues de Marthe et de Marie* (1957), and of Jeanne le Ber in *Dans le nid d'aiglons, la colombe: vie de Jeanne le Ber, la recluse* (1963).

See Julia Richer, *Léo-Paul Desrosiers* (1966), and Michelle Gélinas, *Léo-Paul Desrosiers ou le récit ambigu* (1973).

IVOR ARNOLD

Deverell, Rex. See CHILDREN'S DRAMA IN ENGLISH.

Dewart, Edward Hartley (1828-1903). Born in Stradone, Co. Cavan, Ire., Dewart was six years old when his parents settled in Dummer Township, Upper Canada (Ont.). He attended local schools and the provincial Normal School, entered the Methodist ministry in 1851, and was ordained in 1855. In 1879 he received a D.D. from Victoria University, Toronto. He held various posts in Canada East and West until 1869, when he became editor of the *Christian Guardian*, Toronto, remaining in that position until 1894. Dewart compiled the first and last collection of Canadian poetry prior to Confederation, *Selections from Canadian poets; with occasional critical and biographical notes, and an introductory essay on Canadian poetry* (Montreal, 1864). He attempted to preserve poetry that he feared would be lost. In his introductory essay he attributed the lack of acceptance for Canadian poetry to a general preference among the educated for poems inspired by the romantic past of the countries in which they were born and argued for the role of poetry in building a national spirit. Dewart marked out 'a future bright with promise' as the alternative inspiration for Canadian poets.

Dewart also published a book of original verse, *Songs of life* (Toronto, 1869); a collection of essays and verse, *Essays for the times: studies of eminent men and important living questions* (Toronto, 1898); and numerous pamphlets on religious subjects. CAL SMILEY

Dewdney, Christopher. See POETRY IN ENGLISH 1950 TO 1982: 3.

Di Cicco, Pier Giorgio (b. 1949). Born in Arezzo, Italy, he was brought by his parents to Montreal in 1952 and lived briefly in Toronto before his family moved to Baltimore, where Di Cicco received his early education. He returned to Canada in 1968 to attend high school and then the University of Toronto, where he studied creative writing under F.W. Watt and received a B.A. in English and a B. Ed. He worked as an assistant editor for *Books in Canada* and became involved with several literary journals, including *Waves, Poetry Toronto,* DESCANT, Argomenti Canadesi (Rome), and *Italia-America* (San Francisco). His first collection of poetry, *We are the light turning*, was published in 1975; but his writing did not come to public attention until it was anthologized in Al PURDY's *Storm warning II* (1976). Thereafter his poems appeared in a great many literary magazines in Canada and abroad. Writing with originality and honesty about a wide range of interests—from the Italo-Canadian experience to neo-surrealism—and employing a variety of forms, including surrealism and 'deep images' (images in which the vehicle tends to be both archetypal and subconscious), Di Cicco has published nine other collections in five years: *The sad facts* (1977), *The circular dark* (1977), *Dancing in the house of cards* (1978), *A burning patience* (1978), *Dolce-amaro* (1979), *The tough romance* (1979), *Dark to light: reasons for humanness* (1981), *A straw hat for everything* (1981), and *Flying deeper into the century* (1982). He has also edited an anthology of Italian-Canadian verse, *Roman candles* (1978).   BRUCE MEYER

Dickson, Gordon R. See SCIENCE FICTION AND FANTASY IN ENGLISH AND FRENCH: 2.

Dickson, Lovat (b. 1902). Horatio (Rache) Lovat Dickson was born in New South Wales, Australia, the son of a mining engineer, and was taken to South Africa at the age of seven. He attended school in England from 1913 to 1917 and then came to Canada to join his father in Ottawa. He worked at various jobs, travelling widely, and founded and edited a weekly newspaper at the Blue Diamond Mine in Alberta. In 1923 he enrolled at the University of Alberta, where he was encouraged and influenced by the head of the English department, E.K. Broadus. He graduated with distinction in 1927, winning the Governor-General's Gold Medal, and stayed on to lecture for a year. He then accepted the offer of a wealthy Canadian, who had bought the *Fortnightly Review*, to edit that periodical and thus entered the London publishing world, in which he remained for much of his adult life. (He also edited *The Review of Reviews* from 1931 to 1934.) In 1932 he started his own publishing firm, Lovat Dickson Limited, and in 1933 launched *Lovat Dickson's Magazine* to establish his imprint in the literary world. One of his first publishing successes was *Pilgrims of the Wild* (1935); he made its author, Grey Owl (Archibald Stansfeld BELANEY), a celebrity in England by arranging two highly successful lecture tours for him in 1936-7 and 1937-8. In 1938 Dickson sold his publishing list to Peter Davies and joined the Macmillan Company as assistant editor of general books, working under the editor, Harold Macmillan. He became chief editor, and then a director of the firm in 1941; when he retired in 1967 he moved with his wife Marguerite to Toronto. He is currently writing a history of the Royal Ontario Museum, at the invitation of that institution.

Dickson's lifelong devotion to writing and writers, which led him into publishing, sustained another career as a biographer. Unlike many editors, Dickson is a born writer, with the literary skill to master a variety of subjects and present them in a graceful narrative. The subject with whom he is most identified as a biographer is Grey Owl, who became his friend. In 1938, shortly after Grey Owl's death, Dickson published *A green leaf: a tribute to Grey Owl*, which includes an affectionate account of Grey Owl's two visits to England as a celebrated author, press commentaries, and Grey Owl's letters. This was followed by *Half-breed: the story of Grey Owl* (1939), a somewhat romantic portrait, with lyrical descriptions of Grey Owl's Canadian wilderness; based partly on anecdotes told by Grey Owl to the author, it is coloured by the desire to defend him against the charge of being an impostor. It was superseded after Dickson's retirement by the definitive *Wilderness man: the strange story of Grey Owl* (1973; rpr. 1975), the product of assiduous research and greater objectivity, in which a complex and well-rounded Grey Owl emerges. Dickson's other biographies are *Richard Hillary* (1950), about the author of a classic war memoir, *The last enemy*, who was disfigured in the Second World War and was later killed in action at 23; *H.G. Wells: his turbulent life and times* (1969; rpr. 1971), a study of the author, with an emphasis on his works, that was written with the permission of two of Wells's sons and the encouragement of another Macmillan author, Rebecca West; and *Radclyffe Hall and the well of loneliness: a Sapphic chronicle* (1975), a biography of the lesbian novelist that Dickson was asked to write by her companion, Una Troubridge.

All Dickson's biographies—which are informed by his own involvement in the world of letters—have to do with writers, and quite apart from their biographical excellence they make a valuable contribution to the lore of books and publishing. This theme, and Dickson's flair for relating the influential events and atmosphere of a life (in this case his own), come together most successfully in two volumes of memoirs: *The ante room* (1959; rpr. 1975), and *The house of words* (1963; rpr. 1976), which takes him into his early years with Macmillan's. The autobiography of an unusual Canadian who forged a distinguished career in London as editor, publisher, and writer, it is the record of an eventful life, filled with friendships, lived and recounted with evident enjoyment.

Dickson is also the author of a romantic novel, *Out of the west land* (1944), written during the war out of nostalgia for Canada and based in part on his arrival there as a youth and on his life as a student in Alberta. WILLIAM TOYE

Dictionary of Canadian biography/Dictionnaire biographique du Canada. The largest sustained historical research project ever undertaken in Canada and one of the country's most important reference works, the *DCB/DBC* has been planned chronologically, according to the death dates of the persons included. Thus the current series of volumes I to XII, to be completed about 1988, will present individuals who died between the years 1001 and 1900. Volume I (1000-1700) was published in 1966. By 1983 eight volumes had been published : I to V and IX to XI, as well as an index to volumes I-IV. The decision to arrange volumes chronologically has meant that persons related in their lives, or living through much the same events, are also associated in print; the volumes therefore make a substantial contribution to the social history of a developing Canada as well as to biography. The 500-to-600 biographies in each volume, arranged alphabetically, are based as far as possible on documentary sources and are prepared by hundreds of contributors in Canada, the United States, Great Britain, France, and Australia. The *DCB/DBC* has a staff of professional editors, with graduate training usually in history, who are based at the University of Toronto and Université Laval and who work under the direction of a general editor (from 1969, Francess G. Halpenny) and a directeur général adjoint (from

1973, Jean Hamelin). Each volume appears in two editions published simultaneously, one in English (published by the University of Toronto Press) and one in French (published by Les Presses de l'Université Laval). There is a specially bound Laurentian Edition containing illustrations.

The project came into being as a result of a bequest by a Toronto businessman, James Nicholson (1861-1952), which made provision for the use of the income from the residue and bulk of his estate by the University of Toronto to create a dictionary of national biography for Canada, modelled on the *Dictionary of national biography* of Great Britain. The bequest became available in 1959, the University having meanwhile entrusted the publication to the UNIVERSITY OF TORONTO PRESS. Dr George W. Brown was the first general editor, and before he died in 1963 he established the tradition of wide discussion with the scholarly community and with research institutions such as libraries and archives, which has been a notable aspect of the *DCB/DBC*. In Mar. 1961 arrangements were completed with Université Laval and its Press for a French edition. The *DCB/DBC* quickly became a bilingual, bicultural project in which there is full and daily collaboration between its two offices in all aspects of planning, writing, and editing, and in maintaining a high level of translation as contributions, written in either English or French, are translated into the other language. The second general editor, Dr David Hayne (1965-9), was particularly concerned with the methodologies of translation and bibliography to be followed. Marcel Trudel was directeur général adjoint of the *DCB/DBC* in its founding years (1961-5) and was succeeded for 1965-71 by André Vachon.

By 1972 the financial needs of the project had gone well beyond the capacities of the Nicholson bequest and special subventions from the Canada Council, the Centennial Commission, and Québec's Ministère des Affaires culturelles. In 1973 and 1974 the *DCB/DBC*, with an enlarged staff, received increased funds from the Canada Council, and for 1975-80 and 1980-5 it has had large grants from the Social Sciences and Humanities Research Council, with further help from various government bodies.

The *DCB/DBC* is in several senses a 'public' project. Maintained by public funds, it is public in the visibility of its activities; in its reliance on numerous consultants, contributors, and institutions; in reaching out to general readers as well as scholars; and in its very subject: the people of Canada from east to west, from south to north.   FRANCESS G. HALPENNY

di Michele, Mary. See POETRY IN ENGLISH 1950 TO 1982: 3.

Dobbs, Kildare (b. 1923). Born at Merrut, India, Kildare Robert Eric Dobbs was educated at St Columba's College, Rathfarnum, Ireland, and Jesus College, Cambridge, where he graduated in 1947. Following a family tradition of imperial service, he was a colonial officer in Tanganyika from 1948 to 1952. In the latter year he immigrated to Canada and from 1953 to 1961 worked as editor for the MACMILLAN COMPANY OF CANADA. In 1956 he was among the group that founded *The* TAMARACK REVIEW; from 1965 to 1967 he served as managing editor of *Saturday Night*; and in 1968 he became a literary columnist and later book editor of the *Toronto Star*. In recent years Dobbs has been working as a freelance journalist, particularly as a travel writer.

Dobbs' first book, *Running to paradise* (1962), which won a Governor General's Award, is a work of embroidered autobiography, a series of sketches from his life in India, Ireland, Africa, and Canada. These pieces set the tone of urbanity, broken by wayward Celtic wit, that has distinguished Dobbs from the laboured Leacockian tradition of Canadian humour. (In 1974 it was reissued in paperback with two new pieces.) With the photographer Peter Varley, Dobbs next wrote a somewhat lyrical travel book on his adopted country, *Canada* (1964: rev. 1969). In *Reading the time* (1968) he collected a series of idiosyncratic literary essays. His sense of the incongruous, which tends to make or mar emphatically whatever he writes, reaches a level of fantasy near to surrealism in *The great fur opera* (1970), a comic and punning history of the Hudson's Bay Company, written in collaboration with the British caricaturist Ronald Searle, and one of the few good recent examples of humorous writing in Canada. *Pride and fall* (1981), in which Dobbs steps over the borderline from fanciful autobiography to avowed fiction, contains a novella, which gives the book its title, and six stories. All the stories take place in settings taken from Dobbs' past: Ireland; a naval ship; and, for five out of the seven items, Africa in the colonial age. They are essentially stories of manners, recreating past imperial ways of living and evoking, in a style somewhat reminiscent of the early Evelyn Waugh, the less heroic traits of the colonizers and the colonized. The irony with which Dobbs observes his exiled white men and his sometimes excessively comic black men saves this book from being an exercise in fashionable nostalgia, though the nostalgia is still there. Clearly Dobbs has found it impossible to shed his pre-Canadian past.

See also ESSAYS IN ENGLISH: 4.
                    GEORGE WOODCOCK

Donnell, David. See POETRY IN ENGLISH 1950 TO 1982: 3.

Dooley, D. See CRITICISM IN ENGLISH: 5(f).

Double hook, The. See Sheila WATSON.

Doucet, Louis-Joseph. See POETRY IN FRENCH: 3.

Dougall, Lily (1858-1923). Born in Montreal and educated in New York, and at the University of Edinburgh and St Andrew's University in Scotland, she lived in Montreal from 1897 to 1903, when she moved to Cumnor, Eng., becoming the centre of a group dedicated to religious thought. She wrote twelve novels before 1908, four with Canadian settings. *What necessity knows* (London, 1893) deals with religious conflict in Québec's Matapedia Valley, and focuses on an obsessed religious leader. In *The madonna of a day: a study* (London, 1895) the heroine wanders into a mining camp in B.C., where her attitudes and values are challenged. *The mermaid: a love tale* (New York, 1895), set on Prince Edward Island and the Magdalens, is about a doctor who is profoundly affected by the murder of a child that he had witnessed in his youth. *The Zeitgeist* (London, 1895) is the story of a young man's movement towards pantheism. In all her fiction Dougall tends to use the framework of the popular mystery novel of her day: such melodramatic conventions as coincidence, disguise, hidden identity, and thwarted love abound. Her novels' chief interest today lies less in their literary merit than in Dougall's thinly veiled exploration of religious and philosophical themes and her thorough research into contemporary religious sects.

Dougall was the first editor of *The World Wide* (Montreal), a journal of contemporary thought. After 1908 she turned to writing religious tracts, the first of which, published anonymously, was the essay *Pro Christo and ecclesia* (1910). MARILYN ROSE

Downie, Mary Alice and John. See CHILDREN'S LITERATURE IN ENGLISH: 6.

Doyle, Mike (b. 1938), who has also written under the name of Charles Doyle, was born in England of Irish parents. He lived in New Zealand from 1951 to 1966 and was educated there. After a year at Yale University he settled in Canada and has been teaching at the University of Victoria since 1968. From 1969 to 1974 he edited *Tuatara*, a poetry magazine distributed from Victoria.

Owing to his varied background of travel and residence, Doyle's poetry has always shown a concern with place, at times taking on the focus of locality that is at the centre of the poetry of William Carlos Williams, whom Doyle has always been interested in. He edited *William Carlos Williams: the critical heritage* (1980), and has completed a soon-to-be-published critical work on Williams's poetry. Doyle's *Earth meditations: one to five* (1971) is concerned with time and place in a series of five loosely connected poems; while recognizing that 'a newcomer cannot feel/ chords a place plays/ on those who have cultivated/ that ground for a century', the poet firmly suggests that the newcomer 'brings his own song'. Doyle's own song has gone through some variation since his arrival in Canada, from the sparse imagistic notations about love in *Preparing for the ark* (1973), to the more formally constructed poems in *Stonedancer* (1976), which includes poems from the small 1973 collection as well as some from his New Zealand period. This volume best illustrates Doyle's principal themes: concern with time and place; the relation of art to life, with poems using other artists' work, especially paintings, as springboards for his own thoughts; and human relationships, particularly within the context of family. No longer speaking with the slightly rambling colloquial flow of *Earth meditations*, Doyle's poetic voice retains a clear-eyed sense of irony and a deft satirical touch.

Doyle has written books on two New Zealand authors: H.A.K. Mason (1970) and James Baxter (1976, as well as a critical survey, *Aspects of New Zealand poetry* (1967).
PETER STEVENS

Dragland, Stan. See NOVELS IN ENGLISH 1960 TO 1982: OTHER TALENTS, OTHER WORKS: 4.

Drama in English. The beginnings to 1953. 1. EIGHTEENTH AND NINETEENTH CENTURIES. Although several garrison and amateur groups were performing plays in the Maritimes in the late eighteenth century, no Canadian drama emerged, well-known English plays being the standard repertoire. Two dull verse dramas—George Cockings' *The conquest of Canada; or, The siege of Quebec* (London, 1766), and Robert Rogers' *Ponteach; or, The savages of America* (London, 1766)—are Canadian only by virtue of their subject matter and their authors' brief sojourns in Canada. In the nineteenth century the situation began to change rapidly. An indigenous dramatic literature developed despite the domination of Canadian theatre by foreign touring stars and companies throughout the century. A prominent genre was verse drama, most of which lacks theatrical vitality and literary originality. Eliza Lanesford Cushing published poetic plays on historical and biblical themes in the LITERARY GARLAND in the late 1830s and early 1840s. Charles HEAVYSEGE's *Saul* (Montreal, 1857), although admired by Hawthorne and Longfellow, is turgid, as is his later *Count Filippo; or, The unequal marriage* (Montreal, 1860). *The enamorado* (Summerside, P.E.I., 1879) and *De Roberval* (Saint John, 1888) by John HUNTER-DUVAR are undistinguished blank-verse history plays. Charles MAIR's ponderous *Tecumseh* (Toronto, 1886) was widely acclaimed in its time; but, like Sarah Ann Curzon's *Laura Secord; or, The heroine of 1812* (Toronto, 1887), it is marked more by patriotic excess than by literary or theatrical quality. Two historical verse dramas by Wilfred CAMPBELL were published in one volume as *Mordred and Hildebrand* (Ottawa, 1895), appearing again, with *Daulac* and *Morning* (Ottawa, 1897), in *Poetical tragedies of Wilfred Campbell* (Toronto, 1908). Political and social satire was a livelier and far more stageworthy dramatic genre than verse drama. Many satires were published anonymously in such periodicals as *Grip* and the *Canadian Illustrated News*; others appeared as independent publications, though still sometimes anonymously, as was the case with *The female consistory of Brockville* (Brockville, 1856) by 'Caroli Candidus', an imperfect but sharp attack on hypocrisy in the Presbyterian Church, and two interesting political sketches by 'Sam Scribble': *Dolorsolatio* (Montreal, 1865) and *The king of the beavers* (Montreal, 1865). Nicholas Flood DAVIN's *The fair Grit; or, The advantages of* *coalition* (Toronto, 1876) is one of the best nineteenth-century political satires, but it did not meet with the stage success of William Henry Fuller's *H.M.S. Parliament; or, The lady who loved a government clerk* (Ottawa, 1880), an attack on Sir John A. Macdonald and his National Policy that was performed in many Canadian cities in 1880. Sarah Anne Curzon ridiculed sexual discrimination in *The sweet girl graduate* (first published in *Grip-Sack*, volume 1, 1882). *Ptarmigan; or, A Canadian carnival* (Hamilton, 1895), by Jean Newton McIlwraith, is a less adroit satire on the annexation issue. Parodies and burlesques were other lively and popular nineteenth-century genres. John Wilson Bengough's *Bunthorne abroad; or, The lass that loved a pirate* (Toronto, 1883) is a parody of Gilbert and Sullivan operettas; and two burlesques by George Broughall, *The 90th on active service; or, Campaigning in the North West* (Winnipeg, 1885) and *The tearful and tragical tale of the tricky troubadour; or, The truant tracked* (Winnipeg, 1886) were performed at Winnipeg's Princess Opera House in 1885 and 1886. The masques, comic operettas, fantasies, and burlesques of Frederick Dixon were well received as private theatricals in Government House, Ottawa, in the 1870s.

2. THE TWENTIETH CENTURY. The first half of the twentieth century, like the nineteenth, produced a wide variety of dramatic forms. *A runaway couple* (1910), *The man who went* (1918), and other romantic comedies and melodramas by W.A. Tremayne, were popular in both Canada and the United States and are wholly conventional. Equally conventional are the morality plays of Ida Potter, such as *Wanted—a chauffeur* (1928), a temperance play performed at the Manitoba Provincial Temperance Convention in May 1928. Many plays written for children (see CHILDREN'S DRAMA) betray similar moral and didactic purposes. Didacticism is the hallmark too of workers' plays of the 1930s, some of which are printed in *'Eight men speak' and other plays from the Canadian workers' theatre* (1976), edited by Richard Wright and Robin Endres. There is a raw dramatic force in these political plays; however, they suffer inevitably from plot predictability and unsubtle language and characterization. Greater skills are evident in radio drama, a genre that attracted many playwrights (and listeners) in the 1930s and 1940s. Merrill DENISON's *Henry Hudson and other plays* (1931) contains six unsophisticated examples of radio drama; more mature

are the plays of Lister Sinclair in *'A play on words' and other radio plays* (1948). Hundreds of radio playscripts are now housed in a unique archive at Montreal's Concordia University.

The development of stage plays in the early years of the twentieth century was encouraged by several related factors: the decline in foreign touring companies because of increased costs and the popularity of movies; the establishment of competitions, like the Earl Grey Musical and Dramatic Competition (1907-11) and the Dominion Drama Festival (1932-70); and the rise of the Little Theatre movement, led by groups such as the Arts and Letters Players of Toronto, formed in 1905. Also important was the work of theatre critics and essayists. Essays like Fred Jacob's 'Waiting for a dramatist' (*Canadian Magazine*, vol. 43, 1914), Vincent Massey's 'The prospects of a Canadian drama' (*Queen's Quarterly*, vol. 30, 1922), Merrill Denison's 'Nationalism and drama' (*Yearbook of the arts in Canada 1928-1929*, ed. Bertram BROOKER, 1929), and Herman VOADEN's introduction to *Six Canadian plays* (1930)—though differing in arguments and conclusions—provided an intelligent critical context for playwrights and prospective playwrights. Other writers—among them B.K. Sandwell, Arthur Phelps, John COULTER, and Hector Charlesworth—contributed to the critical discussion of Canadian drama. Charlesworth's theatre reminiscences are collected in two of his books: *Candid chronicles: leaves from the note book of a Canadian journalist* (1925) and *More candid chronicles: further leaves from the note book of a Canadian journalist* (1928). Some essayists were also important playwrights: Denison, Voaden, and Coulter, for example. Other notable playwrights of the period are Gwen Pharis RINGWOOD, Elsie Park Gowan, and Mazo DE LA ROCHE. De la Roche's *'Low Life' and other plays* (1929) contains three one-act plays—*Low life, Come true*, and *The return of the emigrant*—each well constructed and showing a keen sense of comedy and irony. *Whiteoaks* (1936) is a full-length dramatization of her novel *Whiteoaks of Jalna* (1929). Elsie Park Gowan wrote radio plays, children's plays, and one-act comedies.

The one-act play was, in fact, the major form of early-twentieth-century Canadian drama—scores being published and many more performed in amateur community theatres throughout the country. One-act plays dominate the several drama anthologies published in Canada from the 1920s to the 1950s. Collectively these anthologies reveal the strengths and weaknesses of Canadian drama during this period. Fred Jacob's *One third of a bill* (1925) contains five one-acts: *Autumn blooming, The clever one, And they meet again, Man's world*, and *The basket*, all performed in Ontario in the 1920s. With the exception of *The basket*, they are lightly satirical and witty middle-class comedies, reminiscent of the plays of Noel Coward, but lacking their elegance and substance. *The basket* is a rather heavy-handed mystery drama. Volume one of *Canadian plays from Hart House* (1926), edited by Vincent Massey, includes Merrill Denison's *Brothers in arms, The weather breeder*, and *Balm*, as well as five other plays produced at Hart House: Duncan Campbell SCOTT's *Pierre*, a domestic melodrama set in a Québec village; Marian Osborne's *The point of view*, an amusing domestic comedy owing something to Shaw's *Heartbreak House*; Henry Borsook's black comedy *Three weddings of a hunchback*; Isabel MacKay's psychological drama *The second lie*; and Britton Cooke's melodrama, *The translation of John Snaith*. Other short plays by Scott are published in *The poems of Duncan Campbell Scott* (1926). Isabel MacKay wrote two well-constructed three-act plays: *Two too many* (1927) and *Goblin gold* (1933). Volume two of *Canadian plays from Hart House theatre* (1927) contains three full-length plays: Carroll Aikins' *The god of gods*, a refreshingly unsentimental view of Indian customs; L.A. MacKay's *The freedom of Jean Guichet*, a tragi-comedy ruined by a melodramatic ending; and Leslie Reid's toothless comedy about the chauvinism of an English M.P., *Trespassers*. There are nineteen plays in *One-act plays by Canadian authors* (1926), none showing much genuine dramatic imagination. *Six Canadian plays* (1930), edited by Herman Voaden, contains the best plays submitted to a competition organized by Voaden at Toronto's Central High School of Commerce in 1929-30. Two are worthy of note: T.M. Morrow's *Manitou portage*, for its interesting central character, an arrogant and bullying lumberjack, and its partly expressionistic form; and Jessie Middleton's adroitly handled domestic drama *Lake Doré*. Nathaniel Benson's *Three plays for patriots* (1930) has two simplistic history plays: *The paths of glory* (in praise of General Brock) and *The patriot* (in praise of William Lyon Mackenzie), and a more interesting work, *The leather medal*, a bitter attack on political patronage. There

are eight forgettable plays in Hilda Mary Hooke's *One-act plays from Canadian history* (1942), and another undistinguished history play, *General Wolfe*, by Raymond Card, in *Curtain rising: seven one-act plays* (1958) edited by W.S. Milne. Milne's volume also includes five comedies (by Merrill Denison, Milne, Virginia Knight, Elsie Park Gowan, and Robertson DAVIES) and a serious drama about the clash of western and traditional cultures in Japan, *Protest*, by Norman Williams.

Catering mainly for audiences of middle-class tastes and expectations, and having to rely almost exclusively on amateur companies for production of their plays, Canadian playwrights in the first half of the twentieth century, with only isolated exceptions, opted for traditional forms and unprovocative subject matter. Many achieved technical competence; many wrote stageworthy plays. Missing, however, was the incentive to surpass the ordinary. Eventually some measure of that incentive was provided by the spread of professional theatre in Canada, spurred by the founding of the Stratford Festival in 1953, and government's acceptance of a responsibility to fund the arts, ratified by the formation of the Canada Council in 1957.   L.W. CONOLLY

1953 to 1981. The present vitality of English-language drama in Canada gained its initial impetus from a group of at least a dozen professionally oriented theatre companies that grew out of the post-war ferment in the arts. Their impact on Canadian drama is difficult to measure, but among them was Dora Mavor Moore's New Play Society, Toronto, which produced 47 new Canadian scripts between 1946 and 1956. Other theatre companies included the Montreal Repertory Theatre, the Canadian Repertory Theatre in Ottawa, Kingston's International Players, Calgary's Workshop 47, and Sidney Risk's Everyman Theatre in the West. This movement to found professional theatres and standards had its culmination in the early fifties with the establishment of the Jupiter Theatre, Toronto, in 1951; the touring Canadian Players in 1953; the Stratford Shakespearean Festival in 1953; and the Crest Theatre, Toronto, in 1954. The changing theatrical climate meant that the current works of the period's leading playwright, Robertson DAVIES—*A jig for the gypsy* (1954) and *Hunting Stuart* (1955; pub. 1972)—were performed by Toronto's professional Crest Theatre instead of by one of several local Little Theatres. Yet, making a living as a playwright was not easy at the time, as Davies often remarked. His biting, satirical view of a philistine Canada was hardly endearing, despite the Shavian wit and eloquence with which it was expressed.

Before and during this period the main outlet for Canadian playwrights was provided by radio drama, produced by the Canadian Broadcasting Corporation. The most prolific radio dramatist, Lister Sinclair (b. 1921), had a notable stage success in the 1950s with *The blood is strong* (1956; CBC radio, 1957; Jupiter Theatre)—about a nine-teenth-century Scots immigrant family in Cape Breton, N.S. W.O. MITCHELL was another writer who made stage adaptations of his radio dramas, none of which has been as critically successful as his novel, WHO HAS SEEN THE WIND. In *The devil's instrument* (broadcast in 1949) he allowed an excellent idea—the revolt of a Hutterite youth against his religion—to remain underdeveloped; he displayed merely a light dry humour in *The black bonspiel of Wullie MacCrimmon* (broadcast in 1951), in which Wullie competes against the devil, an avid curler. (These are among the five plays in *Dramatic W.O. Mitchell*, 1982.) The poet Earle BIRNEY turned his gifts to radio drama in the verse play *Trial of a city* (1952), a witty indictment of Vancouver for despoiling Buttle Creek; it was later adapted for the stage under its original title *The damnation of Vancouver* (1966). A more popular radio drama of the period was Patricia Joudry's *Teach me how to cry* (1955), a sentimental and psychologically naive play about small-town prejudice. Broadcast in 1953 and staged by the Crest Theatre in 1955, it won a Dominion Drama Festival Award but was not a success when produced in New York and London; it became a film, *The restless years*. John Reeves, owing a debt to Dylan Thomas's *Under Milkwood*, wrote *A beach of strangers: an excursion* (1961), a lyrical prose drama for radio that was critical of Canadian puritanism. John COULTER, whose Irish plays were popular in amateur theatre, also wrote for radio, but gained his greatest success with *Riel* (1962), an emotionally charged portrait of the martyred Riel, which drew attention to the use of a Canadian as a heroic figure. (Coulter followed this with two other plays about Riel: *The trial of Louis Riel,* 1968, and *The crime of Louis Riel,* 1976.) Also in 1962 Len PETERSON's Inuit tragedy, *The great hunger* (1967), which had been staged in 1960 by the Arts Theatre, Toronto, was aired on the CBC. Almost two decades earlier Peterson had begun writing for the radio with the slightly avant-garde *Burlap bags* (1972; CBC 1946), which pictured an alienated post-war world—the title comes from characters wearing bags to shield them from reality. These two modestly successful plays represent the highest achievement of this prolific author.

The sixties witnessed the appearance of what has come to be loosely termed 're-gional theatres': the Vancouver Playhouse (1962); the Neptune Theatre, Halifax (1963); the Citadel Theatre, Edmonton (1966); the Globe Theatre, Regina (1966); The National Arts Centre, Ottawa (1967); Theatre New Brunswick, Fredericton (1968); Theatre Calgary (1968); Centaur Theatre, Montreal (1969); Toronto Arts Productions/St. Lawrence Centre, Toronto (1970); and Theatre London (1971). Based to a degree on the model established by the Manitoba Theatre Centre, Winnipeg (1958), these theatres offered audience-development programs in each locale, provided high production standards, and employed artists from across the country. The regional movement added to the momentum engendered by a decade of public funding of the arts and combined with the nationalism surrounding the Canadian Centennial to help create an unprecedented increase in the quantity and quality of drama in the late sixties—an increase that continued through the seventies.

Centennial year, 1967, saw the production of three plays that remain important. John HERBERT's *Fortune and men's eyes* (1967; 2nd edn 1974) graphically depicted the violent, homosexually exploitative world of Canadian prisons, implying that the outside world of the time was little better. Although given a workshop production at the Stratford Festival in 1965, this controversial play did not receive a full commercial staging until Feb. 1967 in New York; it was filmed in Montreal in 1971. George RYGA captured national attention with *The ecstasy of Rita Joe* (1971), a provocative dramatization of an Indian woman's destruction by an urban white society. The play's use of music, and an episodic structure that demanded a lyrical, non-realistic staging, suggested new possibilities for Canadian dramatists. Ryga's concern for social and political issues shaped his next plays, at least two of which—the 'hippie' *Grass and wild strawberries* (contained in *The ecstasy of Rita Joe and other plays*, 1971) and *Captives of a faceless drummer* (1971), about anarchists kidnapping a Canadian diplomat—became embroiled in heated controversy. The third Centennial-year title was *Colours in the dark* (1969), staged by the Stratford Festival and the first of James REANEY's innovative dramas to receive a major professional performance. In previous amateur productions of his early sixties' plays—*The Easter egg* (1962), *The killdeer* (1962; rev. 1972) and *Listen to the wind* (1972)—Reaney evolved an improvisational drama based on fragmented, often melodramatic plots and with mythopoeic echoes resonating between a dialogue rich in imagery and the physical presence of characters, actions, or objects. In the seventies Reaney vaulted into pre-eminence among English-Canadian playwrights with the Donnelly trilogy—*Sticks and stones* (1976), *The St. Nicholas Hotel* (1976), and *Handcuffs* (1977)—which transformed Ontario history into universal myth.

Also in 1967, but of more local notice, Ann Henry's *Lulu Street* (1972), about the 1919 Winnipeg strike, was performed at the Manitoba Theatre Centre. Two years later, British Columbia's Beverly SIMONS wrote *Crabdance* (1969) in which she used absurdist techniques to depict the stresses of modern life on her middle-aged heroine, Sadie Goldman. In the same year a transplanted British Columbian, Herschel HARDIN saw his Inuit drama *Esker Mike and his wife, Agiluk* published in the *Drama Review* (14, no. 1, 1969); it was published in book form in 1973.

The late sixties and early seventies witnessed the growth of many small professional theatres that were dedicated to Canadian plays. There was a concentration of them in Toronto: Theatre Passe Muraille (1968), Factory Theatre Lab (1969), Toronto Free Theatre (1970), Tarragon Theatre (1971). Scattered across the rest of the country were others, such as the Mummers Troupe (1972) and Codco (1973?) in St. John's, Nfld; Twenty Fifth Street Theatre (1973) in Saskatoon; Alberta Theatre Projects (1972) in Calgary; Theatre Network (1975) in Edmonton; and Tamahnous (1971) in Vancouver. One might also mention Festival Lennoxville, founded in 1972 as a summer theatre for the production of Canadian plays. The seventies also saw the establishment in Toronto of Playwrights' Co-op (1972)—now Playwrights Canada—the main source for scripts in Canada, and of its west-coast equivalent, the New Play Centre (1970), which not only published scripts but produced them. (TALONBOOKS, founded in 1967, maintains a vigorous program of publishing leading Canadian plays in handsome editions.)

Some of the new theatres produced 'documentary dramas' evolved from a COLLECTIVE CREATION process in which acting companies improvised around an idea or historical event. Toronto Workshop Productions introduced a related and influential style of performance when the theatre was founded by George Luscombe, a disciple of England's Joan Littlewood, in 1958. Actors playing multiple roles, rapid changes of time and place, and a vignette structure are characteristics of a form that finds its strength in topicality, polemicism, and an inventive presentational acting style rather than deep probing of a subject. Among the best of such productions were *The farm show* (1976) by Theatre Passe Muraille and *Paper wheat* (*Canadian Theatre Review* 17, 1978) by Saskatoon's Twenty-Fifty Street Theatre. The collective process sometimes involved a playwright: Rudy WIEBE's *Far as the eye can see* (1977) and Rick SALUTIN's *1837: the farmer's revolt* (1976) were both scripted with Theatre Passe Muraille. Salutin's very popular *Les Canadiens* (1977) also showed characteristics of documentary drama and collective creation, but offered a more thorough analysis of its subject: Québec history.

Conventional realism was another major form chosen by playwrights throughout the seventies. David FREEMAN began his association with the Tarragon Theatre with a successful production of *Creeps* (1972)—set in the washroom of a sheltered workshop for the cerebral palsied—which is a lacerating comedy revealing the metaphorical 'lower depths' that trap the physically or psychologically handicapped. His next play, *Battering ram* (1972), showed the multi-leveled interdependence among a crippled youth, a young woman, and her mother; but his third play, *You're gonna be alright, Jamie Boy* (1974), rarely rose above a TV sitcom level. David FRENCH entered the seventies with as much force as Freeman, and has shown more staying power. *Leaving home* (1972), and its sequel *Of the fields, lately* (1973), detail the psychological tensions in a Newfoundland family forced to move to Toronto. A realistic poolroom drama, *One crack out* (Toronto 1975), followed these emotionally powerful plays; but recently French has developed the humorous bent that gave so much life to his early work. *Jitters* (1980), about the opening of a new Canadian play, is a clever comedy of manners satirizing Canadian theatre in particular and Canadian foibles in general. William Fruet's *Wedding in white* (1973) and Tom WALMSLEY's drug-culture sex and violence in *The workingman* (1976), *The Jones boy* (1978), and *Something red* (1978) were also part of seventies' realism. On the Prairies, Joanna GLASS used a realistic mode for her slightly clichéd portrayal of a ménage-à-trois in *Artichoke* (1979), as did Rex Deverell for *Boiler room suite* (1978)—first produced at the Globe, Regina—in which an old wino couple find joy in each other's company. The Centaur Theatre, Montreal, has been the theatrical home of David FENNARIO, who followed the success of his *On the job* (1976) and *Nothing to lose* (1977)—short, realistic plays about the plight of exploited workers—with his award-winning *Balconville* (1980). In *Balconville*, as in the two earlier works, Fennario lightened what might otherwise have been a sombre, even didactic play about the oppressed poor of Montreal with generous amounts of comedy, much of it derived from the clash of languages and attitudes among French- and English-speaking tenement dwellers. Using a less realistic mode, Carol BOLT attracted attention for her documentary satire *Buffalo jump* (1972), about farm and labour unrest on the Prairies in the 1930s, and for her episodic portrait of the feminist/anarchist Emma Goldman in *Red Emma* (1974). However, *One night stand* (1977), a psychological thriller with a melodramatic ending, and the shallow satire *Escape entertainment* (1981), raised the possibility that Bolt had compromised her talent. Among five major works by Sharon POLLOCK, *Generations* (1982), in which different generations of a prairie family clash over a homestead inheritance, was the only play in a realistic convention. The other four depend on an imaginative rearranging of historical reality that forces one to concentrate on issues around the events portrayed. *Walsh* (1972), first produced by Theatre Calgary, uses an episodic structure to present the famous general's anguish over the injustice that duty made him commit against Sitting Bull. In *The Komagata Maru incident* (1978) Pollock indicted Canada's racist handling of a 1914 shipload of Sikh immigrants by giving the action a side-show atmosphere. *One tiger to a hill* (1981) dramatizes the complex tensions in a prison hostage-taking. In *Blood relations* (1981) Pollock skilfully employed a play-within-a-play device and juxtaposed different time-frames to create a tantalizing ambiguity about Lizzie Borden's guilt in the famous murders, allowing us to see a range of forces controlling her destiny. It won the first Governor General's Award for published drama.

The muted but powerful feminism of *Blood relations* points to a theme that has grown in importance over the past three decades, coinciding with the heightened presence of women in society. As Pollock's work so richly testifies, women playwrights have contributed significantly to contemporary drama. While there are many lesser playwrights who might be termed 'feminist', such labelling would diminish the scope of major women dramatists who have embedded feminist themes among others in their works. In addition to Pollock and Bolt, the perceptive, witty Erica RITTER has demonstrated a feminist concern. But it is only one of the themes in *Automatic pilot* (Toronto 1980), an adroitly written comedy that is her most important play to date. While we see the central character, a stand-up comedienne/writer, exploited by the masculine world around her, we are aware of broader psychological and identity problems that she and the male characters all must face. Margaret HOLLINGSWORTH, too, explored psychological relationships in addition to strictly feminist ones in plays like *Alli, Alli oh* (1977), *Mother country* (1980), and *Everloving* (1980).

In addition to the boundaries crossed by feminist writers, by James Reaney's idiosyncratic genius, and by the innovations of documentary drama and the collective-creation method, the national preference for traditional modes was disturbed by a group of 'experimental' playwrights. To some extent conventional English-Canadian drama was challenged by Québécois works staged in translation, notably by Michel TREMBLAY's multi-layered and forceful plays throughout the seventies. Among English-Canadian works, Michael HOLLINGSWORTH's *Clear light* (1973) and *Strawberry fields* (1973) were mildly bizarre. Lawrence Russell used surrealism in his short plays *Penetration* (1972) and *The mystery of the pig killers' daughter* (1975). Nor can one ignore Michael ONDAATJE's very successful adaptation of his *Collected works of Billy the kid*, which remains unpublished as a play-script although it has been produced numerous times since its first staging in 1971. The anti-fascist *Hurray for Johnny Canuck!* (Toronto 1975) by Ken GASS maintained a cartoon-like quality derived from the Johnny Canuck comic books. Gass's controversial *Winter offensive* (1978) dramatizes a kinky sex party for Nazi officers hosted by Mrs Adolf Eichmann. Bryan WADE also showed a fascination with Nazi dreams of sex and power in his Hitler/Eva Braun play, *Blitzkreig* (1974). Many of Wade's short plays—*Lifeguard* (prod. 1973), for instance, *Alias* (1974), and *Aliens* (prod. 1975)—display imaginative qualities reminiscent of early Sam Shepard, but they have not been followed by anything substantial. Hrant ALIANAK experimented with a range of satirical, non-realistic modes, and there were hints of unconventionality in the early works of Larry FINEBERG. But Fineberg's later plays have been sufficiently mainstream to receive Stratford Festival productions: his adaptation of a novel by Constance BERESFORD-HOWE, *Eve* (1977), is undistinguished, but allows an actress a star turn; his treatment of Euripides' *Medea* (1978) merely limits the scope of the original. George WALKER's 'cartoon' *Bagdad saloon* (1973), *Zastrozzi* (1977), and *Theatre of the film noir* (1981) are possessed of entertaining theatricality spoofing traditional dramatic and film conventions. But they express no more than a perceived modern-day chaos and decay and a longing for a better world. One of the most inventive plays in recent years was Richard Krizanc's *Tamara*, which allowed audience members to follow individual actors throughout the old mansion where it was staged in Toronto in 1981—'spying', as it were, on the political and amorous intrigues unfolding simultaneously in the many rooms. A form of 'environmental drama', hence difficult to capture in a traditional script, *Tamara* requires an analytical method as unconventional as the performance itself.

As John Coulter's *Riel* foretold, Canadian individuals and events became a focus after the late sixties in a body of history plays. In Newfoundland, Michael COOK used early Canadian history in a somewhat Brechtian way to comment on present-day social and political injustices. In his major plays *Colour the flesh the colour of dust* (1972), *The Gayden chronicles* (*CTR* 13, 1977), and *On the rim of the curve* (1977), for all their richness in themes and language, dramatic effectiveness is muted by a diffused focus. Cook's less historical plays, which included *The head, guts and sound bone dance* (1974), *Quiller* (1975) and *Tiln* (1976), among others, comment philosophically on present-day Newfoundland life. Other Canadian history plays worth mentioning include John Thomas McDonough's *Charbonneau and le Chef* (1968), James Nichol's *Sainte-Marie*

among the Hurons (1977), Ron Chudley's *After Abraham* (1978), and Alden NOWLAN's and Walter Learning's *The dollar woman* (1981). At the same time the lure of foreign history drew Canadian writers: Munro Scott to a Chinese folk tale in the engaging *Wu-feng* (1971); Stewart Boston to Queen Elizabeth I in *Councillor extraordinary* (1972); and Michael Bawtree to aristocratic Russia for his dull *Last of the Tsars* (1973).

In addition to the fact that Canadian playwrights tended towards short plays, one of the notable characteristics of the past thirty years was that very few dramatists had more than one or two considerable titles to their credit. The well-known novelist Timothy FINDLEY wrote *Can you see me yet?* (1977), a philosophical anti-war play set in an insane asylum. Jim Garrard, one of the founders of Theatre Passe Muraille, wrote the often-produced *Cold comfort* (1982), an obliquely humorous Gothic tale that speaks metaphorically of spiritual starvation and sexual sterility in Canada. American-born Sheldon ROSEN in *Ned and Jack* (1978) brought together the flamboyant Jack Barrymore and a quiet Ned Sheldon to discover themselves as they dealt with Ned's imminent death. In *Memoir* (1978) John MURRELL created a dramatically uncompelling yet theatrical vehicle for an actress playing the aged Sarah Bernhardt dictating her memoirs to her secretary, and in *Waiting for the parade* (1980) he evoked nostalgia to link vignettes from the lives of five women in a Canadian city during the Second World War.

Canadian dramatists have fallen prey to recent economic cut-backs in the theatre, which encouraged small-cast plays. One-person shows, like the immensely popular and often perceptive *Billy Bishop goes to war* (1981) by John GRAY, have become prevalent. *Billy Bishop* exemplified a trend in recent Canadian theatre towards musical drama: here the script is punctuated with songs and piano accompaniment. Other popular works in this genre are Gray's *18 wheels* (unpublished) and *Rock and roll* (*CTR* 35, Summer 1982) and Ken MITCHELL's *Cruel tears* (1977), a trucker's *Othello*. Mitchell has been an active playwright with *Davin: the politician* (1979) and *The shipbuilder* (*CTR* 21, Winter 1979) among his two-dozen titles. *Herringbone (Three plays by Tom Cone,* 1976) is a one-man show by American-born Tom Cone in which an old vaudevillean soft-shoes through the story of his life. Cone's *Star-gazing* (1978) received a Stratford Festival Third Stage production in 1978 but is a weak script that takes us on a familiar journey where characters discover commonplace truths about themselves. Paul Thompson and Linda Griffiths, in the very popular *Maggie and Pierre* (1980), utilized the topicality of Pierre Trudeau's notorious marriage and the novelty of Griffiths' playing all three roles in the cast to hide a very thin script. Such concessions to the commercial viability of theatres undoubtedly will continue to influence Canadian drama. Already situation comedies, such as the inferior *Westmount* (1981) by Richard Ouzounian, have begun to proliferate. Fortunately one effect of this is that playwrights with more serious intentions—such as Allan Stratton, author of the subtle, insightful *Rexy* (1981) about Mackenzie King—can earn a living from the commercial success of frothy, entertaining pieces like *Nurse Jane goes to Hawaii*, also by Stratton.

Overall the current scene has the advantage of a group of experienced, relatively young playwrights who in the next few years should move towards their most mature work. These dramatists are backed by another group of younger writers whose early plays show promise, among them Anne Chislett, Larry Jeffrey, Frank Moher, Gordon Pengilly, Charles Tidler, and Geoffrey Ursell. Without the prophet's eye one cannot tell if this promise will be fulfilled, but one can hope.   RICHARD PLANT

Bibliography. The extensive compiling of bibliographic tools for the study of Canadian drama in English is a recent occurrence. The following titles will provide essential references: Anton Wagner (ed.), *The Brock bibliography of published Canadian plays in English 1766-1978* (1980); Patrick B. O'Neill, 'A checklist of Canadian dramatic materials to 1967' in *Canadian Drama/l'Art dramatique Canadien* (vol 8, no 2, 1982), and his *Canadian plays—a supplementary checklist to 1945* (1978), which complement the *Brock* and include unpublished copyright plays; and John Ball and Richard Plant (eds), *A bibliography of Canadian theatre history 1583-1975* (1976) and the *Supplement 1975-76 to A bibliography of Canadian theatre history 1583-1976*.

The eight titles listed hereafter represent important sources for critical commentary on Canadian drama. Geraldine Anthony (ed.), *Stage voices* (1978), and Robert Wallace and Cynthia Zimmerman, *The work: conversations with English-Canadian playwrights*

(1982), are collections of interviews with major playwrights. Don Rubin and Alison Cranmer-Byng (eds.), *Canada's playwrights: a biographical guide* offers brief biographical sketches of 70 playwrights and bibliographies of their work. Murray D. Edwards, *A stage in our past: English-language theatre in Eastern Canada from the 1790's to 1914* (1967) is a pioneer history of the subject but marred by numerous errors, many of which are now being corrected in post-graduate theses (see the Ball-Plant bibliographies) and by other published scholarship. Articles on Canadian drama and its history are published in *The Canadian Theatre Review* (1974-); *Canadian Drama/L'Art dramatique Canadien* (1975-); and *Theatre History in Canada/Histoire du théâtre au Canada* (1980). William H. New (ed.), *Dramatists in Canada* (1972), is a collection of essays on a range of authors and drama.

In addition to the titles cited in the preceding drama entries, as well as individual published scripts and collections of plays by various authors, Canadian drama is printed in the following notable anthologies: Alive Theatre Workshop, *Dialogue and dialectic: a Canadian anthology of short plays* (1972); Henry Beissel (ed.), *Cues and entrances: ten Canadian one-act plays* (1977); Eugene Benson (ed.), *Encounter: Canadian drama in four media* (1973); Diane Bessai (ed.), *Prairie performance: an anthology of short plays* (1980); Diane Bessai and Don Kerr (eds), *Showing West: three prairie docu-dramas* (1982); Constance Brissenden (ed.), *West Coast plays* (1975); Canadian Authors' Association (Montreal Branch), *One-act plays by Canadian authors* (1926); Neil Carson (ed.), *New Canadian drama I* (1980); Rolf Kalman (ed.), *A collection of Canadian Plays* (5 vols, 1972-8); Vincent Massey (ed.), *Canadian plays from Hart House Theatre* (2 vols, 1926-7); W.S. Milne (ed.), *Curtain rising: seven one-act plays* (1958); Patrick B. O'Neill (ed.), *New Canadian drama II* (1981); Edward Peck (ed.), *Transitions I: short plays* (1978); Playwrights Co-op, *Five Canadian plays* (1975); Joseph L. Shaver (ed.), *Contemporary Canadian drama* (1974); John Stevens (ed.), *Ten Canadian short plays* (1975); Madeline Thompson (ed.), *Women write for the theatre* (4 vols, 1976); Herman VOADEN (ed.), *Six Canadian plays* (1930); Anton Wagner and Richard Plant (eds), *Canada's lost plays, volume I: the nineteenth century* (1978); Anton Wagner (ed.), *Canada's lost plays, volume two: women pioneers* (1979); Anton Wagner (ed.), *Canada's lost plays, volume three: the de-*

Drama in English: bibliography

veloping mosaic (1980); Anton Wagner (ed.), *Canada's Lost Plays, volume four: colonial Québec: French-Canadian drama, 1606-1966* (1982); Marian M. Wilson (ed.), *Popular performance plays of Canada* (2 vols, 1976, 1981); Richard Wright and Robin Endres (eds), *Eight men speak and other plays* (1976).

RICHARD PLANT, L.W. CONOLLY

Drama in English: collective creations. See COLLECTIVE CREATIONS IN ENGLISH.

Drama in French. The beginnings to 1900. The first play written in French in North America was Marc Lescarbot's fanciful *Théâtre de Neptune en la Nouvelle-France*, performed at Port Royal in Nov. 1606 to celebrate the return of the colony's leaders from an expedition. Published in his *Muses de la Nouvelle-France* (Paris, 1609), the short text belongs more validly to French than Canadian literature, yet it contains a serious attempt to reproduce a New World setting, with its four 'Indian' roles and its scattering of words from native languages. The play is of the type known as a *réception*, long practised in France, composed to celebrate the visit or return of an important personage. This is the only genre to have taken root in New France, and two other surviving dramatic texts belong to it: the anonymous *Réception de monseigneur le vicomte d'Argenson* (Québec, 1890), performed in 1658, which is remarkable for its use of Amerindian languages; and a *Réception de monseigneur de Saint-Vallier* published in *Mgr de Saint-Vallier et l'Hôpital Général de Québec* (Québec, 1882), written in verse by the Jesuit P.-J. de La Chasse and performed in Québec in 1727.

By 1650 there had also developed a tradition of staging, at least sporadically, plays by major French authors, in particular those of Pierre Corneille. But all such 'profane' performances ceased as a result of the conflict in 1694 between Governor Frontenac and Bishop Saint-Vallier over the former's intention to present Molière's controversial *Tartuffe*. The Bishop bought off Frontenac on this occasion, and succeeded in prohibiting all public theatre thereafter. Rare are the references to dramatic performances for the rest of the French régime.

Soon after the Treaty of Paris (1763) occasional performances are again reported. The British garrison often took the lead in presenting plays in French, favouring Molière's works. Theatre returned to the schools as

well, and a manuscript text from 1780, entitled *L'éducation négligée*, suggests a nascent native dramaturgy. By the end of the decade, French-born Joseph QUESNEL, a resident of Montreal since 1779, had written *Colas et Colinette; ou Le bailli dupé*, the first operetta composed in the New World; performed in 1790, it was published in Québec in 1808. But to the Catholic Church public theatre was suspect, so that any attempts at establishing a permanent stage were discouraged. This period has been studied in admirable detail by B. Burger in *L'activité théâtrale au Québec, 1765-1825* (1974).

From the nineteenth century some 150 plays by 75 known authors survive, the vast majority of them composed after 1875. Apart from a series of anonymous political satires in dramatic form, never intended for performance and generally referred to as 'Les comédies du statu quo', written in 1834 and re-edited by N.-E. Dionne in *Les trois comédies du statu quo* (Québec, 1909), the first play published by a native French Canadian was *Griphon; ou La vengeance d'un valet* (Québec, 1837) by Pierre PETITCLAIR. The 1830s also saw the performance and publication of plays by French immigrants, notably *Valentine; ou La Nina canadienne* (Montréal, 1836) by H.-P. LEBLANC DE MARCONNAY. But Lord Durham's observation that French Canada seemed, in 1839, incapable of maintaining a national stage was indeed valid. And despite the number of plays written before the 1890s, no real native dramatic tradition arose. In 1842 a second play by Petitclair, *La donation*, was performed with some success and revived several times before its publication in 1848. A. GÉRIN-LAJOIE, while still a student, wrote and had performed, in 1844, the patriotic tragedy *Le jeune Latour*, which was successful enough to be published four times that same year. His formula, apart from its verse form, was to prove the most popular one for generations: historical drama with strong nationalistic appeal, such as L.-H. FRÉCHETTE's *Félix Poutré* (Montréal, 1871), which was performed with great success in 1862, and his *Papineau* (1880), both of which attempted to rehabilitate the heroes of 1837-8. Extracts from many of these nationalistic plays have been included by E.-F. Duval in his *Anthologie thématique du théâtre québécois au xixe siècle* (1978). New France was the setting for a dozen historical plays, from the immensely popular adaptations of P.-J. AUBERT DE GASPÉ's *Les* ANCIENS CANADIENS (Québec, 1863) (the first of which, by Camille Caisse and Pierre-Arcade Laporte, was performed in Montreal in 1865 and published in 1894), to J.-L. Archambault's *Jacques Cartier; ou Canada vengé* (Montréal, 1879) and J. MARMETTE's *L'intendant Bigot* (Montréal, 1872). Patriotic sentiment with more immediate application was the theme of *Si les Canadiennes le voulaient* (Québec, 1886) by Laure Conan (Félicité ANGERS), P. LEMAY's *Rouge et bleu* (Québec, 1891), and of two works occasioned by the Métis rebellions: *Riel* by C. Bayer and E. Parage, and another play of the same title by E. Paquin, both published in Montreal in 1886. At the same time the increasingly frequent tours by professional companies from Paris, so long and so bitterly contested by the Church (see *L'église et le théâtre au Québec*, 1979, by J. Laflamme and R. Tourangeau), began to influence playwrights after 1870. Evidence of this influence can be seen in the polished light theatre of F.-G. MARCHAND, whose *Les faux brillants* (Montréal, 1885) was revived with modest success in 1977; in the situation comedies of the prolific Régis Roy—*Consultations gratuites* (Montréal, 1896) and *Nous divorçons* (Montréal, 1897); and the 30-odd adaptations of foreign works by the lawyer J.G.W. McGown (1847-1914). Soon the clergy took to composing or adapting plays for purposes of propaganda, such as the anonymous *Soirées de village* (Montréal, 1860) and *Stanislas de Kostka* (Montréal, 1878) by H.-A. Verreau for campaigns against drunkenness, as in *L'hôte à Valiquet; ou Le fricot sinistre* (Montréal, 1881) by J.-B. Proulx; or in favour of colonization, as in *Les pionniers du lac Nominingue; ou Les avantages de la colonisation* (Montréal, 1883), also by Proulx.

In the 1890s the first professional troupes were established in Montreal, playing a mixture of adaptations and indigenous plays—influenced by the light-comedy tradition of boulevard theatre in France—in the first permanent theatres for francophones. That decade represents the most active period in the history of French-Canadian theatre before the twentieth century.

See Jean Béraud, *350 ans de théâtre au Canada français* (1958). This period is also the subject of a monograph by J.-M. Larrue, *Le théâtre à Montréal à la fin du xixᵉ siècle* (1981). That flowering proved to be brief, but for a moment, before the advent of cinema, it appeared that Durham's remarks would finally lose their truth. (*Theatre in French Canada, 1606-1867*, by Leonard Doucette, will be published in 1984.) LEONARD DOUCETTE

1900 to 1948. By the turn of the century theatrical activity in French had been established not only in Québec but also in Manitoba, Ontario, and New Brunswick, and over the next fifty years it expanded and evolved considerably. If foreign influences were strong, the terrain was being prepared so that, after the Second World War, Canadian drama—particularly in Québec—was able to develop and flourish: theatres were built; public taste for theatre developed; a great number of amateur and professional actors, actresses, directors, and technicians were trained; and, thanks to the emergence of radio, dramatists were able to earn a living with their writing. While no great works of dramatic literature were produced in the first half of the century, E.-F. Duval estimates in his *Le jeu de l'histoire et de la société dans le théâtre québécois, 1900-1950* (1981) that 193 Quebec authors wrote more than 813 plays. This anthology demonstrates that almost all the plays written during this period, many of which have remained unpublished, were on historical subjects reflecting the dominant theme of nationalism. Most dramatists of the period showed little originality in subject, style, or dramatic technique. Many of these playwrights and plays were first catalogued by Édouard G. Rinfret in the four-volume *Le théâtre canadien d'expression française* (1975, 1976, 1977, 1978).

In the early twentieth century, theatrical activity outside Québec, and in most cases outside Montreal, was usually produced by students for educational purposes in colleges and convents, frequently to mark a special event. A strict segregation of the sexes in these college productions, and in most amateur productions, was observed until the 1930s. Many amateur groups were active throughout the first half of the century and were so widespread that when the Dominion Drama Festival was founded in 1933, Little Theatre companies throughout Canada were able to offer performances in French of very high quality. Particularly noteworthy was Le Cercle Molière, founded in 1925 in St Boniface, which is still the centre of theatrical activity in francophone Manitoba. (See Annette Saint-Pierre's *Le rideau se lève au Manitoba* (1980), which provides considerable documentation on college and amateur productions and original drama in Manitoba.)

Until the last decade of the nineteenth century all theatres in Montreal had English owners and most of their productions were

Drama in French 1900 to 1948

in English; by 1899 touring American shows and local productions consistently provided them with an intensely active and varied theatre season. Touring French theatre and opera companies, however, bringing many stage stars to Canada, made a significant contribution to the emergence of taste for French theatre after 1880, the date of Sarah Bernhardt's first North American tour. In 1894, when the first French theatre, the Monument National, was constructed under the auspices of the Société Saint-Jean-Baptiste, French theatre in Canada had a home, in real and symbolic terms. The inauguration, with the sanction of the Church, at the Monument National of an amateur theatre company, Les Soirées de famille (1898-1901), marked the beginning of regular theatrical activity in French in Montreal. Les Soirées presented a new play each week drawn from the repertory of popular French theatre and melodrama. For the first time on the public stage in Québec, men and women played together.

The first permanent professional company, Le Théâtre National (1900-17), performed comedies, melodramas, operettas, and vaudeville. Other companies followed, such as Les Nouveautés (1902-8), which tried to appeal to an élite audience by presenting the latest Paris hits. More than 20 professional companies followed during the pre-war period. At the National the aim was necessarily on commercial success, but considerable effort was also made to encourage Canadian playwrights by organizing contests and producing original plays. Of the thousands of plays produced there, about fifty were by Québec writers: W.A. Baker, Jean CHARBONNEAU, Ernest CHOQUETTE, Rodolphe GIRARD, Louis Guyon, Madeleine Huguenin, and Régis Roy. The most gifted dramatist of the period, Louvigny de Montigny, whose Les boules de neige was presented at the Monument National in 1903, has written eloquently of the almost insurmountable difficulties encountered by Canadian dramatists in the early twentieth century. The subject matter of de Montigny's plays is drawn from Québec legend and contemporary society. Les boules des neiges, for example, is a scathing satire of hypocrisy in the Montreal bourgeosie. Information on this first period of professional theatre in Montreal is found in Palmieri (Joseph Archambault), Mes souvenirs de théâtre (1944); Robert Prévost, Que sont-ils devenus? (1939); and Geo. Robert, L'annuaire théâtral (1909). During the same period there was awareness

of the need for training in language and acting skills, and the Conservatoire d'art dramatique, which still exists, was founded in 1907.

The popular taste for film, which came to Québec in 1902, and commercial theatre of all kinds, led to renewed opposition to commercial public entertainment from the Church around 1907, a situation discussed in Jean Laflamme and Rémi Tourangeau, L'église et le théâtre au Québec (1979). Burlesque dominated the Québec stage between 1930 and 1950. Nevertheless, as Chantal Hébert shows in Le burlesque au Québec, un divertissement populaire (1981), the many Québec burlesque players, who began by imitating American routines in English, soon created a body of highly original material in French.

In the area of popular drama was the unique phenomenon of Léon Petitjean's and Henri Rollin's Aurore l'enfant martyre, which was published for the first time, with lengthy explanatory material by Alonzo Le Blanc, in 1982. Taking its story from the sensational trial of a stepmother who brutalized and finally killed her child, Aurore enjoyed great success as a touring show from 1921 to 1951, when a film was made of it. It is difficult today to understand public acceptance of this scandalous and horrifying show; but the company of Petitjean and Rollin consistently attracted sell-out crowds to this 'comedy', later modified into a melodrama.

College theatre entered an important new phase in Québec during the thirties. Gustave Lamarche, a professor at the Collège de Joliette, sought to recapture the spirit of medieval religious drama in his grandiose poetic spectacles. He is the author of over 50 plays, the best known of which is Jonathas (1935). Lamarche and his students toured the province with their productions until 1947. The two shows for which he is best known—La défaite de l'enfer (1938) and Notre-Dame-de-la-Couronne (1947)—were staged in Montreal in the open air with casts of hundreds and spectators numbering perhaps over 100,000. A similar spectacle, Mystère de la messe, was staged on the Plains of Abraham in Quebec City in 1938 by Émile Legault, who taught at the Collège de Saint-Laurent, and Les Compagnons de Saint-Laurent. Legault's inspiration in founding his soon-to-be famous Compagnons in 1937 was, like that of Lamarche, strongly religious. However, unlike Lamarche, Legault quickly moved away from grandiose spectacle towards a complete renewal of theatrical technique following the example of French director Jacques Copeau. It would be impossible to overestimate the importance of Legault and the Compagnons in the development of drama in Québec. For the first time in college theatre, men and women performed together under his direction, a fact that considerably expanded the range of dramatic possibilities. Legault took the quality of theatrical performance, rather than quick commercial success or an uplifting moral message, very seriously. He introduced an international repertory to Québec audiences; he encouraged a new generation of young Québec dramatists, such as Félix LECLERC; and above all he trained as people of the theatre a new generation of men and women, many of whom have remained on the professional stage in Québec or have established its most famous companies, including the Théâtre du nouveau monde (1951) founded by Jean Gascon and Jean-Louis Roux.

During the thirties a minor revival of commercial repertory theatre occurred, particularly at Le Stella (1930-5), under Fred Barry. One of the most popular dramatic forms was that of the revue, containing original comic sketches as found in *Monologues québécois, 1890-1980* (1980), edited by Laurent Mailhot and Doris-Michel Montpetit. This genre quickly became popular in the new medium of radio, where many of Québec's best-known writers discovered, for the first time in Québec, the possibility of earning a living through their creative gifts. In addition to humorous sketches, these writers produced dramatizations of Québec works; for example, Henri Letondal, *La famille Gauthier* (1935); Robert CHOQUETTE, *Le curé de village* (1935); Henry Deyglun, *Vie de famille* (1938); and Claude-Henri GRIGNON, *Un homme et son péché* (1939). Many young writers—such as Pierre Dagenais, Félix Leclerc, Léo-Paul DESROSIERS, and Robert CHARBONNEAU—produced a great quantity and variety of original plays. CBC Radio's drama productions allowed writers to learn their trade and to reach a larger audience than ever before. One of the most famous radio sketches was Gratien GÉLINAS's 'Fridolinons', with its subject-matter and language drawn from the lives of ordinary Québec people—which was first broadcast by CKAC in 1937 and ran until 1941. In 1938 Gélinas also turned his humorous radio sketches into a live revue, *Fridolinades*, which was staged annually until

1946. One of the 1946 sketches, 'Le retour du conscrit', was the starting-point for Gélinas's famous TIT-COQ (1950), the play that marks the beginning of contemporary drama in Québec.

For further information on theatre and drama in French during the 1900-50 period, see Georges Bellerive, *Nos auteurs dramatiques, anciens et contemporains. Répertoire analytique* (1933); Jean Béraud, *350 ans de théâtre au Canada français* (1958); Jean Hamelin, *Le renouveau du théâtre au Canada français* (1962); and *Le théâtre canadien-français. Archives des lettres canadiennes*, vol. V (1976).

LOUISE FORSYTH

1948 to 1981. 1. 1948-59: THE BEGINNINGS OF A POPULAR FRENCH-CANADIAN DRAMA: GÉLINAS TO DUBÉ. The contemporary drama of Québec may be dated from the first performance of Gratien GÉLINAS's play TIT-COQ (1950) at the Théâtre Monument National in Montreal in 1948. Presenting a genuine French-Canadian hero, the 'little rooster' of the title who searches in vain for love and a family, and written in the popular spoken French of the day, it showed Québécois that someone close to their own experience could be portrayed convincingly on the stage. In spite of the enormous influence on French-Canadian theatre of Père Émile Legault's Les Compagnons de Saint-Laurent, this company performed only one Canadian play during its entire career (1937-52): Félix LECLERC's *Maluron* (unpublished) in 1947. With the arrival of Gélinas and Leclerc, the emphasis on classical and religious drama in Québec theatre was gradually broadened to include plays about ordinary Québécois.

Gélinas did not produce another play of his own until 1959, *Bousille et les justes* (1960), which was followed by *Hier les enfants dansaient* (1968) in 1966. His influence was principally as a man of the theatre rather than as a playwright, especially with his founding of the Comédie Canadienne in 1958 for the production of Canadian plays. Leclerc, on the other hand, continued to write for the stage such works as *Dialogues d'hommes et de bêtes* (1949), *Théâtre de village* (1951), *Le p'tit bonheur* (1959; rpr. 1966), and *Sonnez les matines* (1964). They evoke the world of working-class rural Québec in moving and often ironic tones, but the possibilities of the situations described are rarely developed beyond the level of sketches ('saynettes', Leclerc calls them).

Many playwrights who were published in

the 1950s had made careers in fields other than drama, and some did not develop this craft sufficiently to leave a lasting mark on French-Canadian theatre. Prominent among them was Paul Toupin, primarily an essayist and academic, who published three plays—*Le choix* (1950), *Brutus* (1952), and *Chacun son amour* (1953)—and then a volume of collected plays, *Théâtre* (1961). Though carefully structured and written in a precise, almost classical, style, none of them relates specifically to the people of Québec. The best is *Brutus*, which treats in a psychologically probing and carefully structured manner the relationship between Brutus and Caesar and the former's remorse after betraying his friend. Jacques FERRON—a medical doctor who also writes novels, short stories, and essays—published several plays with a variety of themes and moods, from *L'ogre* (1950), a clever and lighthearted farce on the struggle for survival, to a historical and nationalist drama, *Les grands soleils* (1958), on the French-Canadian *Patriotes* (led by Jean-Olivier Chenier) in the Rebellion of 1837-8. Ferron later published several of his plays in two volumes, *Théâtre I* (1968) and *Théâtre II* (1975). Éloi DE GRANDMONT, better known as a poet and art critic, wrote one notable play, *Un fils à tuer* (1950), set in Québec in the seventeenth century, which deals in a somewhat stark and elemental way with the struggle between the forces of order and freedom as represented by a harsh father and the determined son whom he kills. This and two other plays, *La fontaine de Paris* and *Le temps des fêtes* (1955), were published in his *Théâtre I* (1968). Robert ÉLIE, better known as a novelist and critic, published one of several plays, *L'étrangère*, in the first issue of ÉCRITS DU CANADA FRANÇAIS in 1954, a periodical that for many years was one of the few publishers of plays in Québec and continues to publish French-Canadian plays regularly. A sombre treatment of the solitude of the individual, *L'étrangère* was too discursive and intellectual to win Élie popularity as a dramatist, although it was produced on television by Radio-Canada in 1964. Jacques LANGUIRAND's best-known play, *Les grands départs* (1958), was published during this period. Other plays by him produced in the 1950s but published later—*Les insolites* (which won the Barry Jackson award as the best Canadian play in the Dominion Drama Festival in 1957), *Le gibet* (1960), *Les violons de l'automne* (1962)—established his reputation as an experimental dramatist who used techniques of the

Theatre of the Absurd to express his ironic but basically optimistic view of man's fate. Both *Les grands départs* and *Klondyke* (1971)—a fantasy with music by Gabriel Charpentier—are symbolic treatments of the situation of Québécois—the one showing the difficulty, the other showing the need for a spirit of adventure and determination, in affirming their identity. *Les grands départs* was translated by Albert Bermel as *The departures* and published in *Gambit* 5(1966).

Anne HÉBERT also wrote plays in the 1950s before establishing her reputation as a novelist. One of these, *La mercière assassinée*, was published in *Écrits du Canada français* (vol. 4, 1958); it is a police drama enriched by her poetic imagination and sense of humour. But her poetry was not able to rescue *Le temps sauvage* (1963) and *Les invités au procès* (both published with *La mercière assassinée* under the title *Le temps sauvage* in 1967)—allegorical plays that are weighed down by complicated plots and excessive symbolism. André LANGEVIN wrote a political satire on Québec politics, *L'oeil du peuple* (1958), which won first prize in a contest sponsored by the Théâtre du Nouveau Monde, where it was produced in 1957. Though very funny in parts, the satire is too obvious and extreme and the play was not well received by Montreal audiences. André Laurendeau, who was more at home in journalism and politics, made a contribution to the theatre with *La vertu des chattes*, published in *Écrits du Canada français* (vol. 5, 1959), and two other plays in the same periodical: *Deux femmes terribles* (vol. 11, 1961) and *Marie-Emma* (vol. 15, 1963); the three were republished in *Théâtre* (1970). Realistic, humorous, and literate, Laurendeau's plays deal seriously with human relationships, but they lack theatrical immediacy and are overly discursive.

The most important dramatist to emerge in these years was Marcel DUBÉ, who was to dominate the Montreal stage in the 1960s and remains the most published and accomplished French-Canadian dramatist even today. In the 1950s he began to make his mark as a dramatist with three plays (among his most popular) set in the east end of Montreal: *Zone* (1955), about a group of young smugglers; *Un simple soldat* (1958), which portrays a ne'er-do-well who cannot adjust to civilian life after the Second World War; and *Le temps des lilas* (1958), a Chekhov-inspired play about lonely, disillusioned people in a Montreal boarding-house.

2. 1960-8: THE AGE OF DUBÉ. This second phase is marked by the predominance of Marcel DUBÉ's plays on stage, on television, and in print. With the exception of Françoise LORANGER, no other dramatist wrote a large body of work in these years, although several had one or two significant plays published. In keeping with the higher standard of living of many Québécois, Dubé's plays now reflected the plight of middle-class characters and their difficult relationships in *Florence* (1960), *Octobre* (1964), *Virginie* (1968), *Bilan* (1968), *Les beaux dimanches* (1968), *Pauvre amour* (1969), and what many consider his masterpiece, *Au retour des oies blanches* (1969), which resembles *Oedipus the king* in plot and structure but has a distinctively Québec setting. Like many of his plays in this period, *Au retour* is an attempt to create a tragedy out of contemporary Québec experience. Though all these plays are marred at times by melodrama, their humanist vision and poetic prose have made several of them classics of French-Canadian drama. In the 1970s Dubé published some plays that were written and produced in the fifties and sixties and that show the same destruction of human relationships in a world of so-called progress: *Le naufragé* (1971), *Un matin comme les autres* (1971), *Entre midi et soir* (1971), *Paradis perdu* (1972), *La cellule* (1973), and *Manuel* (1973). In the mid-1970s a more mellow mood permeates such plays as *L'été s'appelle Julie* (1975) and the comedies *L'impromptu du Québec; ou Le testament* (1974) and *Dites-le avec fleurs* (1976). Dubé then returned to his tragic view of life in a somewhat static treatment of recent developments in Québec, *Le reformiste; ou L'honneur des hommes* (1977).

If Dubé can be compared to Chekhov, Loranger is more akin to Strindberg. She shows the same preoccupation with family relationships as Dubé, but at a more elemental and violent level. Her treatment of the family is seen in her early plays: *Une maison . . . un jour* (1965), which probes the relationships of three generations of a family; *Encore 5 minutes* (1967), which deals with unhappy love and marriage; and the television play *Un cri qui vient de loin* (1967), which shows a happy resolution to marital problems after considerable pain. At the end of this period Loranger turned to political and social problems and adopted a different style—a more Brechtian one that sometimes involved the audience. *Double jeu* (1969) attempts to adapt the 'living theatre' to the Québec stage and invites audience participa-

tion; *Le chemin du roy* (1969), anticipating Rick SALUTIN's *Les Canadiens*, depicts the struggle between Québec and Ottawa in the form of a hockey game presided over by President de Gaulle on his famous visit to Canada in 1967. An even more nationalist play is *Médium saignant* (1970), which pits the two sides in the struggle for language rights in Québec against one another at a municipal meeting. The heated reaction of supporters of both positions at the initial production at the Comédie Canadienne in 1970 was repeated when a revised version was presented at Montreal's Place des Arts in 1976; it opened there eleven days before the Parti Québécois's victory brought René Lévesque to power.

One dramatist who broke even earlier from realism in the theatre was Gilles Derome, who combines somewhat uneasily elements of both Pirandello and Brecht in his two published plays: *Qui est Dupressin?* (*Écrits du Canada français*, vol. 14, 1972), a farce about a search for identity set in a mental hospital, and *La maison des oiseaux* (1973), a tragedy about the difficulty of living with oneself and with others. In the same volume of *Écrits du Canada français*, Eugène Cloutier's *Le dernier beatnik* explored rather verbosely the tensions and rivalries in a contemporary love triangle. The novelist Marie-Claire BLAIS wrote a macabre work, *L'éxécution* (1968), about boys in a residential school who murder one of their fellow students. While demonstrating the author's deftness in examining the evil and distortions of life, the play too often substitutes discussion for dramatic action.

Few French-Canadian dramatists in these years looked to the past for their material. One who did was novelist and folklorist Félix-Antoine SAVARD. His *La folle* (1960), written in free verse, is based on an Acadian legend of loss and recovery, and *La dalle-des-morts* (1965), set on the island of Montreal in 1830, glorifies the exploits of the *coureurs-de-bois* who went to their deaths while keeping alive the spirit of adventure that Savard considers necessary for the survival of French Canadians. Though his style is poetic and elegant and filled with noble sentiments, too many of his characters are one-dimensional. Also elegantly written, though less patriotic, is Jean BASILE's *Joli tambour* (1966). Set in mid-eighteenth-century Québec, it is the story of a young man appointed public executioner to avoid punishment for a crime of which he was unjustly convicted. (As *The drummer boy* it was produced in Toronto in

1968.) Jean-Louis Roux, better known as an actor and director than a playwright, wrote a historical drama, *Bois-brûlés* (1968), which he labelled an epic documentary on the rise and fall of Louis Riel, but little attention is given to the portrayal or development of character. It includes music by Gabriel Charpentier.

The beginnings of a truly avant-garde theatre in Québec were seen in Jean Morin's *Vive l'empereur* (1966), Jacques Duchesne's *Le quadrillé* (1968), and Roger Dumas's *Les millionaires* (1967) and *Les comédiens* (1969). Often absurdist in style and showing the theatre reflecting consciously on itself, these plays were not widely produced in Québec but they helped prepare the way for writers who would take this style for granted in the 1970s. Morin's play and those of Dumas were also important because they appeared in the first issues of a series called 'Théâtre vivant' published by Holt, Rinehart and Winston, which was a serious attempt to publish more French-Canadian drama. It was soon taken over by the Montreal publishing firm Leméac whose two collections, 'Théâtre Canadien' (later changed to 'Théâtre Leméac') in 1968 and 'Répertoire Québécois' in 1969, marked a new era in Québec drama. One of the last plays in the 'Théâtre vivant' series was *Les* BELLES-SOEURS (1968), the first published play by Michel TREMBLAY, who soon became the dominant figure in what might be called the coming of age of Québécois drama.

3. 1969-76: MICHEL TREMBLAY AND THE USE OF 'JOUAL'. Michel TREMBLAY was the single most important dramatist in Québec in the 1970s. His plays led the way to acceptance in the theatre of JOUAL, the vernacular used by many urbanized Québécois today. *Les* BELLES-SOEURS—whose production in Montreal in 1968 began the assault of *joual* on the theatre and the heated debate about its validity—is about lower-class women living in the east end of Montreal who speak the fractured, vital language that may be heard on the streets there. It reveals not only Tremblay's ability to present convincingly Québécois women, but also his sense of rhythmic dialogue and musical structure: the women speak both as individuals and as a chorus. *Les belles-soeurs* became the first of a series of eleven plays based on the lives of characters living for the most part in the same section of Montreal, many of whom appear in several plays. These plays were all published by Leméac as follows: *En pièces détachées* and *La Duchesse de Langeais* (pub-

lished together in 1970), *A toi pour toujours, ta Marie-Lou* (1971), *Demain matin, Montréal m'attend* (1972), *Hosanna* (1973), *Bonjour, là, bonjour* (1974), *Les héros de mon enfance* (1976), *Sainte-Carmen de la Main* (1976), *Damnée Manon, Sacrée Sandra* and *Surprise! Surprise!* (published together in 1977). *À toi pour toujours, ta Marie-Lou* (1973), perhaps Tremblay's finest play to date, offers a harrowing picture of a Québec family whose two daughters, Carmen and Manon, ten years after the violent death of their parents, reflect on the quality of life in their home and the lasting effects it has had on them. The role of musical structure in Tremblay's work is seen to advantage here as the girls' conversation is intertwined with the bickering of their parents in the past. The two plays that bear the names of Carmen and Manon involve transvestitism. Here, and in two plays about homosexuality, *La Duchesse de Langeais* and *Hosanna*, the central figures and their fate become symbolic of the Québécois themselves, whom Tremblay sees as having been forced to betray their true identity and to put on a disguise that is foreign to them.

After the Parti Québécois victory in 1976, Tremblay felt that much of the political message of his plays had been heard; he even allowed his plays to be produced in English in Québec. The direction of his drama changed, as is shown in *L'impromptu d'Outremont* (1980), which takes as its subject the concerns of middle-class women, and in *Les anciennes odeurs* (1981), in which he explores a homosexual relationship more directly and psychologically than in *Hosanna* and *La Duchesse de Langeais* and without their political overtones. Most of Tremblay's plays are available in English translation and have been produced in English, in and outside Québec.

Robert GURIK—who came to prominence about the same time as Tremblay, although some of his plays were published earlier—combines a Brechtian style of propagandist theatre with social concerns that are both indépendantiste and international. While ingenious and clever, the satire in his plays is often too obvious and heavy-handed. Thus his *Hamlet, prince du Québec* (1968) uses Shakespeare's play as a model to depict the struggle between federalists and separatists. *Les tas de sièges* (1971) is a series of three one-act plays, each concerned with issues raised during the October Crisis of 1970. *Le procès de Jean-Baptiste M.* (1972) is about one man's fruitless protest against the conformity demanded by a consumer society that prevails both in Québec and throughout the Western world. Gurik's wider concern is evident also in *Le pendu* (1967), a somewhat bitter comment on how a society treats those who would be its saviours; in *À coeur ouvert* (1969), a depiction of an Orwellian world in which man's inhumanity to man is shown by the allegory of a heart bank that is manipulated by whatever group is in power; in *Api 2967* (1971), a futurist play that shows the fruitless efforts of Adam and Eve characters to restore humanity to a world dominated by technology; and in *La palissade* (1971), a more hopeful play about the possibility of love and humanity. In Gurik's later plays, specific people or events are used to throw light on injustice in various parts of the world: *Lénine* (1975) is on the failure of workers in today's world to achieve the goals of the Russian leader, *Le champion* (1977) is on the failure of the boxer Mohammed Ali to gain respect for his people, and *La baie des Jacques* (1978) is on the emptiness of workers' lives that are exploited for the benefit of their employers. Many of his plays finish inconclusively and open-endedly, presumably so that the audience will be moved to action by the scenes they have witnessed.

An even more aggressive political stance is taken by Dominique de Pasquale in his *On n'est pas sorti du bois* (1972), a fast-paced musical that depicts Québécois as primitives who refuse to submit to the annihilation of their race, chanting, 'We will not go to our burial . . .' and inviting the audience to join in. A similar stridency characterizes de Pasquale's *Oui chef!* and *L'arme au poing ou larme à l'oeil* which were published in one volume in 1973.

The most imaginative and satirical *joual* dramatist is Jean-Claude GERMAIN, who combines seriousness and good humour in his treatment of Québec's past and present. As a founder in 1969 of Le Théâtre du Même Nom and of a theatre group that performed there—Les Enfants de Chenier and then (in 1971) Les P'tits Enfants Laliberté—he had a base from which to produce his plays. *Diguidi, diguidi, ha! ha! ha!* (1972) is a biting commentary on the conflicts and oppressions that have existed in Québec family life, while his later satire *Mamours et conjugats* (1979), a history of marital relations in *la belle province*, is subtitled 'Scènes de la vie amoureuse québécoise'. *Si les Sansoucis s'en soucient, ces Sancoucis-ci s'en soucierent-ils? Bien parler c'est se respecter!* (1972) is a farce on

the serious theme of the complicity of Québécois with their English oppressors. *Le roi des mises à bas prix* (1972) takes up the fate of one member of the Sansoucis family who has accepted unquestioningly the worst aspects of North American culture. Germain's later plays include what he called a trilogy on the theatre, which becomes another metaphor for Québec life and history: *Les hauts et les bas dla vie d'une diva: Sarah Ménard par eux-mêmes* (1976) looks at Québec through the character of a would-be opera singer; *Un pays dont la devise est je m'oublie* (1976), whose title changes Québec's motto from 'Je me souviens', uses two travelling actors to re-enact with comic flair unpleasant and decisive moments in Québec's history; and *L'école des rêves* (1979) focuses on the joys and sorrows of itinerant actors in Québec, in the forties and fifties, who become symbols of the Québécois themselves. (*Un pays* . . . was performed with great success in French in Toronto in 1982.) In *Les faux brillants de Félix-Gabriel Marchand* (1977) Germain revised a comedy first published in 1885 by Marchand, who became the premier of Québec in 1897.

One of the most inventive *joual* dramatists is Jean BARBEAU, whose characters express great alienation and disenchantment with society. Two short plays, *Goglu* (1971) and *Solange* (1974), show this poignantly, as does *Ben-Ur* (1971), whose title is a 'pop' version of the anti-hero's name, Joseph Benoît Urbain Théberge, and a nickname that labels him for life. Like Barbeau's later *Le jardin de la maison blanche* (1979), the play is an indictment of the superficiality of many aspects of North American society. The main character in *Le Chemin de Lacrois* (1971), besides undergoing his own 'passion' of injustice in scenes announced like the Catholic Stations of the Cross, is mocked by a friend from France who corrects his *joual* and urges him to speak proper French. A lighter but still satirical approach to *joual* is taken in two plays published together in 1972: *Manon Lastcall*, which presents a seductive museum guide who describes paintings in *joual*, and *Joualez-moi d'amour*, in which a couple can make love only if they speak *joual*. With less emphasis on *joual* in his later plays, Barbeau continued to look at the alienated in *Citrouille* (1974), a somewhat violent treatment of women who take out their anger by violating a man; in *Une brosse* (1975), in which two unemployed Québec workers turn to drinking, violence, and murder; in *Une marquise de Sade et un lézard nommé King Kong*, (1979), in which the characters are alienated from both life and art; and in the more hopeful *Émile et une nuit* (1979), in which literature and music give meaning to the lives of two alienated characters.

An outspoken theoretician for *joual* in the theatre is Victor-Lévy BEAULIEU, who said in an interview in 1974: 'The true counter-culture in Québec at the level of language is created in *joual*.' A case for this is made in *En attendant Trudot* (1974), in which the central character, Ti-Bé, a symbol of the repressed Québécois, revolts against the emptiness of his life and realizes he must create his own identity. The same is found in *Ma Corriveau* (1976), a retelling of a Québec legend, which insists on the necessity of Québécois's having their own legends and a language in which to tell them. *Cérémonial pour l'assassinat d'un ministre* (1978), subtitled 'oratorio' and written in poetic prose, makes a case for the use of violence by the would-be liberators of a society, and includes obvious reference to the murderers of Pierre Laporte.

One of the most talented and popular of Québécois dramatists to emerge in this period is Michel GARNEAU, who excels in both poetic language and musical structure. He has written light comedy in *Sur le matelas* (1974); a symphonic statement on the plight of Québécois women of different generations in *Quatre à quatre* (1974)—translated as *Four to four* (1978) by Christian Bédard and Keith Turnbull and published in *A collection of Canadian plays, Volume 5* (1978), edited by Rolf Kalman; a memory play, *Strauss et Pesant (et Rosa)* (1974), portraying moral, religious, and political corruption in the days of Duplessis; and an impressionistic poetic drama on the life of Emily Dickinson in a Québec setting, *Émilie ne sera plus jamais cueillie par l'anémone* (1981). He also wrote two successful adaptations for the stage: *Gilgamesh* (1976), and *Macbeth* (1978).

During this prolific period some established writers were able to have plays published that had been written or produced some years earlier. Yves THÉRIAULT, who had written radio and television plays for Radio-Canada, went beyond the immediate concerns of many French-Canadian playwrights to deal with the elemental forces of life in a family or a community in plays whose settings are often indefinite: *Le marcheur* (1968) takes place 'in a country kitchen', *Frédange* (1970) 'somewhere in the world', *Les terres neuves* (1970) 'in the mountains'. *Le marcheur* shows how the oppression of a tyrannical father stifles his children's need to develop and grow until they finally rebel. *Frédange* is filled with foreboding as a husband returns to his wife after abandoning her for six years, only to submit to the command of his paralysed mother that he, and not the shepherd his wife has taken, must leave. *Les terres neuves* shows a poor and unhappy people from a miserable village on their way to a new village; as they approach this 'promised land' they meet its inhabitants leaving for the place they have deserted.

Guy Dufresne—another dramatist who has written much for radio and television—deals with the French-Canadian experience more directly than Thériault and looks at it from a broader perspective than many of the *joual* dramatists. *Le cri de l'engoulevent* (1969)—translated by Philip London and Laurence Berard as *The cry of the whippoorwill* (1972)—is a realistic drama in which a strong-minded Québec farmer refuses to make a deal to sell his land to an American, and as a result loses both his money and his daughter to the American. First produced in 1960, it can be seen as underlining both the necessity for Québec to accept the ways of the new and open industrial society and also the difficulties and dangers this entails. Dufresne's *Les traitants* (1969), based on an inquest in New France into the sale of intoxicating beverages to Indians in 1665, is overburdened by research and depicts rather statically a shameful episode in Canadian history. Sections of two of Dufresne's popular TV series have been published: *Cap-aux-Sorciers* (1969), a legend about a navy captain, his daughter, and three granddaughters, and *Ce maudit Lardier* (1975), a drama of conflict between shipbuilders and fur traders in New France in 1737 taken from the first season of his téléroman, 'Les forges de Saint-Maurice'. Dufresne's ability to write in *joual* is evident in *Docile* (1972), a slight comedy about a palmist who reads people's fortunes in their toes and thighs.

The plays of Claude JASMIN deal with pressing social and political problems in realistic settings and situations, but they are sometimes melodramatic. The hero is often a young man seeking to save himself or his society. An early television play, *Blues pour un homme averti* (1964), presents a young man searching for his father as he tries to make up for a wasted life in the underworld of a big city. *Tuez le veau gras* (1970), also written for TV, dramatizes the story of a young intellectual who compromises himself by failing to set up a union for workers in a town's biggest plant. The irony suggested by the title ('Kill the fatted calf') is most evident in the final scene when he leaves, discouraged and physically beaten, to take up a teaching post at a small college: the contrast between his reception and that of the prodigal son in the Bible becomes clear. In a similar style, and in the discouraging mood suggested by the title, *C'est toujours la même histoire* (1970) deals with the failure and eventual suicide of a young American who plans to set up a youth centre in the Laurentians but meets opposition from the townspeople and his girlfriend's father. *Le veau dort* (1979)—written in a more impersonal, Brechtian style in ten tableaux—is a sweeping condemnation of injustices throughout the course of history; the title refers to the golden calf that men have too often worshipped. It won the Dominion Drama Festival award for the best Canadian play in 1965.

Two popular Québec dramatists who are out of the mainstream of the *joual* writers were published during this period: Roch CARRIER and Roland Lepage. Primarily a novelist and storyteller who is concerned with recreating aspects of Québec's recent past or 'Dark Ages', Carrier has adapted some of his fiction for the stage. His best-known play, *La guerre, yes sir!* (1970), based on his novel of the same title (1968), takes place in a rural Québec community in 1942 and shows the misunderstanding and violence that arise when the body of a French-Canadian killed in the war is accompanied to his home by a group of non-French-speaking English-Canadian soldiers. In 1972 it became the first Québec play to be produced (in translation) at the Stratford Festival in Ontario. *Floralie* (1974), an adaptation of Carrier's novel *Floralie, où es-tu?* (1969), treats a rural Québec community some thirty years earlier and explores the religious and cultural traditions that shaped the French-Canadian characters of *La guerre, yes sir!* The action takes place immediately before and after the wedding of Floralie and Anthyme, the parents of the boy whose body was brought home in the earlier play, and includes an elaborate fantasy, not always successful, in which the Seven Deadly Sins are personified. Carrier's first work for the stage alone is *La céleste bicyclette* (1981), a monologue written for the gifted actor and director Albert Millaire. A richly poetic play, it is set in the psychiatric ward of a hospital where an actor, confined with

his bicycle, imagines himself cycling in the skies and philosophizes on many aspects of life to show how unlimited is the human spirit. As *The celestial bicycle* it was performed in English by Millaire at the Tarragon Theatre, Toronto, in 1982. Roland Lepage's best-known play, *Le temps d'une vie* (1974)—translated by Sheila Fischman as *In a lifetime* (1978)—is set in Québec's Abitibi region. Using several characters to portray the life of a long-suffering woman from the turn of the century until her death in the 1970s, it is an effective, if at times tedious, evocation of the lot of many Québécois women. Besides playing in many parts of Québec, it toured France and Belgium and won the Chalmers Award for its production in English at Toronto's Tarragon Theatre in 1978. *La complainte des hivers rouges* (1974) is yet another Québec play about the Patriotes of 1837-8, written after the Liberal Party's victory in Québec in 1973 to remind Québécois of the need to work for independence; although it contains much elevated and heroic language, it suffers at times from a certain heaviness and melodrama. *La pétaudière* (1974), a musical satire on Québec's language law, Bill 22, is lighter in tone. Lepage has also written *Icare* (1979), a mythological fantasy for children.

Antonine MAILLET's plays are remarkable for their use of a language that is a survival of sixteenth-century French brought to Acadia from central France, somewhat coarsened but still spoken in some regions of New Brunswick among the poor—Maillet's heroines and heroes. *Les crasseux* (1968) is a comedy that contrasts their lives with those of the rich in a small village and shows how, after years of subservience, the poor manage by determination and shrewdness to take over their wealthy neighbours' land. *La SAGOUINE* (1971) makes a central character out of a charwoman who appeared in *Les crasseux* as a spy for the poor. Maillet continued her saga of Acadian characters. In *Gapi et Sullivan* (1973), expanded and republished as *Gapi* (1976), the husband of La Sagouine, who is now dead, becomes the central figure. *Évangéline deusse* (1975) transplants a modern EVANGELINE figure of eighty to a park in Montreal, where she displays the same indomitability of spirit as her namesake. Maillet has adapted several of her novels for the stage: *Emmanuel à Joseph à Dâvit* (1975), not yet published in dramatic form; *Les cordes-de-bois* (1977), dramatized as *La veuve enragée* (1977); and *Mariaagelas* (1973), dramatized as *La contrabandière*

(1981). *La joyeuse criée*, monologues spoken by characters from the world of *La Sagouine*, starred Viola Léger and premièred in Moncton and Montreal in 1982; it was performed in Toronto by Léger in Mar. 1983. *Le bourgeois gentleman* (1978) is a witty but obvious adaptation of the Molière play to a Montreal setting, where a *nouveau-riche* Québécois wants to move from Rosemount to Westmount.

Three dramatists stand out among the avant-garde writers for the stage in this period: Yves Sauvageau, Yvon Boucher, and Claude GAUVREAU. Sauvageau's *Wouf wouf!* (1970) is completely non-linear in its conception of time, and a violent rejection of the realistic theatre. Much of the dialogue is incomprehensible on the rational level; by the end, several characters are reduced to adding the words 'wouf-wouf' to anything they say. An absurdist reaction to the frustrations of the human spirit in a dehumanized world, the play is at times confusing and repetitive, but its lively theatricality made it very popular with Montreal audiences and influenced writers and theatre groups in the 1970s. Boucher's *L'ouroboros* (1973), also reacting against the realistic tradition, is a more abstract work, reflecting self-consciously on the relation between theatre and reality. The characters, who meet outside a theatre to discuss the play they have just seen, are identified only by numbers and engage in a sometimes brilliant critique of the *raison d'être* of theatre itself. Boucher prefaces the text with an attack on, and letters from, Québec publishers who rejected the play because they couldn't categorize it. Gauvreau—who, like Sauvageau, took his own life—extended the boundaries of theatre by two plays in particular: *La charge de l'orignal épormyable*, a sympathetic portrayal of a patient in a mental hospital, and *Les oranges sont vertes*, in which language is often forced into new forms to suggest a breaking of the bonds that limit body and spirit. Both plays, after important presentations at the Théâtre du Nouveau Monde in 1972 and 1974 respectively, were published posthumously with other plays in the 1500-page *Oeuvres créatrices complètes* (1977) of Gauvreau.

English readers can discover the work of some of the younger playwrights of this period in a translation of seven Québécois plays included in *A collection of Canadian plays, Volume 5* (1978), edited by Rolf Kalman, which shows how dramatic technique has become even more innovative in

Québec since the early Tremblay plays so that a more open, non-realistic, at times musically structured type of drama has become the norm. Besides Michel Garneau's choric *Quatre à quatre*, already mentioned, one of the most moving plays in the volume is *Encore un peu* (1974) by Serge Mercier (translated by Allan van Meer as *A little bit left*), a tender story of an elderly married couple waiting for their days to end. Two of the plays have been published only in English—Rénald Tremblay's *La céleste Greta* (translated by Allan van Meer as *Greta the divine*), a sprawling panoramic look at unpleasant aspects of French Canada's history up to 1760, and Serge Sirois's *Dodo, l'enfant do* (translated by John van Burek as *Dodo*), which shows the breakdown of a modern working-class Québécois family. Claude Roussin's *Une job* (1975) (translated by Allan van Meer as *Looking for a job*) is a comic fantasy on the political situation in Québec shortly before and after the War Measures Act that paints a bleak picture of Québec's will to self-determination; while André Simard's *En attendant Gaudreault* (1976), translated by Henry BEISSEL and Arlette Francière as *Waiting for Gaudreault*, is a more realistic and compact treatment of the plight of workers whose jobs are at the mercy of a heartless foreman. Finally, Louis-Dominique Lavigne's *As-tu peur des voleurs?* (1977), translated by Henry Beissel as *Are you afraid of thieves?*, is a highly orchestrated comedy about three couples that comes close to sound poetry and music and emphasizes how far theatrical invention has progressed since Tremblay. The strong comic element in this Québécois volume of Kalman's anthology, even when serious themes are being treated, anticipates the final section of this survey.

4. 1977–81: WIDER PERSPECTIVES AND WOMEN WRITERS. From the late seventies on in the work of Québécois playwrights there was a shift in mood and subject beyond the political situation in Québec, and an emphasis on comedy for its own sake—perhaps owing to the satisfaction many dramatists felt at the election of the Parti Québécois in Nov. 1976. Michel TREMBLAY typified the reactions of several of these playwrights when he said that this event realized much of what he had been writing about regarding a Québécois identity; as a result he allowed his plays to be performed in English in Québec. (They had already been performed in English in other parts of Canada.) Besides a shift in Tremblay's own work, as seen in *L'im-*

promptu d'Outremont (1980), the change was epitomized by Louis Saia, who spoke of his collaborations with Claude Meunier: 'Ours is a *"théâtre social"* about Québécois who are not identified with Québécois problems. We are not concerned, as writers, with a Québec identity.' Their play, *Appelez-moi Stéphane* (1981), involves middle-class characters who are amateur actors in a drama class that brings out both comic and poignant aspects of their lives as individuals. Saia, with Louise Roy, wrote the comedy *Une amie d'enfance* (1980) and the one-woman show *Bachelor* (1981). Saia and Meunier, along with five other writers, wrote sketches for *Broue* (as yet unpublished), a hilarious comedy with three male actors playing multiple roles as they depict a day in the life of a Montreal tavern. *Broue* has travelled throughout Québec since it opened in 1979 and, after sold-out performances in English as *Brew* at Montreal's Centaur Theatre in 1982, began a tour of English Canada; it has become of the most-performed plays in Canadian theatre history. This lighter mood is seen in other collaborations, such as André Boulanger's and Sylvie Prégent's *Eh! qu'mon chum est platte!* (1979).

A shift from the preoccupation with Québec's problems is also evident among those writing serious drama, even when Québec's past is the setting. Jean Daigle's *Le débâcle* (1979) is set in a farm kitchen near Quebec City in 1931, though this sometimes melodramatic play is basically the Phaedra story carefully adapted to its new environment. In Daigle's *Le jugement dernier* (1979) an old man, Alphonse, reviews incidents in his life from 1923 to 1979; the décor is described as 'the skull of Alphonse at the moment of death'. Like *Le débâcle*, this is a personal and pessimistic story with universal rather than local significance.

The most ambitious work to be produced and published in Québec in recent years is the six-play epic by Jean-Pierre Ronfard, *Vie et mort du roi boiteux* (2 vols, 1981). Director, playwright, actor, and drama teacher, Ronfard brought to Canada a wide theatrical experience gained in Algeria, Greece, Portugal, and Austria when he became the first director of the French section of the National Theatre School in 1960. After directing many plays in Montreal, he wrote *Vie et mort du roi boiteux* with and for his own Nouveau Théâtre Expérimental de Montréal, where it was performed in 1981 and 1982 before playing in Lennoxville, Ottawa, and Hull. Written as six interconnected plays, it involves 25 actors playing 150 roles in a production that lasts fifteen hours, including intermissions for lunch and dinner. Subtitled 'a gory and grotesque epic', the play embodies a world of its own that reaches from Montreal to the fictitious land of Azerbaijan; juxtaposes past and present, cultured French and *joual*; presents a conflict over centuries between two warring families—the Roberges and the Ragones; includes such diverse figures as God, Moses, Aristotle, Joan of Arc, Brecht, Mata-Hari, Einstein, and comic-book characters; and draws on the cultures of both East and West, including the Bible and Shakespeare.

Another important development in recent French-Canadian theatre has been the emergence of women playwrights, supported by Montreal-based women's theatre groups such as Le Théâtre des Cuisines, formed in 1974, and Le Théâtre Expérimental des Femmes, established in 1979, and by women's publishing companies such as Les Éditions du Remue-Ménage (the word means 'stirring up') and Les Éditions de la Pleine Lune. Some of their plays are propagandist statements for women's rights or grievances; others present women's problems without calling for action, or give a woman's perspective on life itself. (A number of them are COLLECTIVE CREATIONS.) Because of their authors' determination to be heard, the plays were often produced quickly and roughly, and while they have an evident sincerity and a sense of urgency, they sometimes suffer from a lack of structure and dramatic form. Such is the case of *La nef des sorcières* (1976). Seen by many as the beginning of a truly feminine force in the theatre, it is a collage of six monologues written and performed by different women, the best-known writer being Marie-Claire BLAIS. There is little attempt to tie together these individual statements about the modern woman and the work can hardly be described as a play. *Môman travaille pas, a trop d'ouvrage* (1976), a collective work by the Théâtre des Cuisines, is a strong propaganda piece that insists on the right of women working in the home to a salary. More unified than *La nef des sorcières*, it is written in a documentary style that appeals directly to the audience in song and argument. Denise Boucher's *Les fées ont soif* (1978) became a *succès de scandale* because of the attack it made on the ideal image of womanhood fostered by the cult of the Virgin Mary. The play was picketed in Montreal by religious groups and an injunction was brought against the distribution of the book for alleged blasphemy and profanity. A strong affirmation that women in Québec have been repressed politically and sexually by this religious image, the play suffers from being somewhat simplistic and too blatantly iconoclastic.

Jovette MARCHESSAULT's *La saga des poules mouillées* (1981) is a statement of the need for a women's culture written in the form of a mythic meeting of four famous French-Canadian women writers of the nineteenth and twentieth centuries: Laure Conan (Félicité ANGERS), Germaine GUÈVREMONT, Anne HÉBERT, and Gabrielle ROY. Translated by Linda Gaboriau as *The saga of wet hens*, the play was presented in English at Toronto's Tarragon Theatre in 1982. Jocelyne Beaulieu's *J'ai beaucoup changé depuis . . .* (1981) combines realism and fantasy to make a moving statement about a woman's right to her own identity. The heroine, called simply 'F'—F as in *folle* and *femme*, the author says in the subtitle—is aided by a sympathetic woman psychiatrist who uses the approach of R.D. Laing to help her recover her sanity, overcome her past, and begin a new life.

Jacqueline Barrette anticipated those recent women dramatists who explore the problems not only of women but of women in relationships, often in a family setting and in society. Her *Ça-dit-qu'essa-à-dire* (1972), like *La nef des sorcières*, is a series of monologues on many topics illustrating the routine and often wearisome life of the Québécois. Sometimes poetic and poignant, the work is interspersed with music, but is not shaped into a drama. *Bonne fête papa* (1973) is an effective and disturbing treatment of the tensions and sexual frustrations in a middle-class Montreal family. Elizabeth Bourget examines the relationships of two young unmarried couples in *Bernadette et Juliette; ou La vie c'est comme la vaisselle, c'est toujours à recommencer* (1979). The promise shown in this first play was more fully realized in *Bonne fête, maman* (1982), a popular comedy about the problems of a middle-aged woman who decides that life with her taxi-driver husband is not enough after her children have left home. Louisette Dussault's one-woman show, *Moman* (1981), is also a serio-comic play about the problems of a mother; in this case the bus journey of a mother with her three-year-old twin daughters from Montreal to Nicolet becomes the occasion, filled with humour and tenderness, for a rejection of the mother's tradi-

tional role as a policewoman. France Vézina, who has also published poetry, wrote a fanciful poetic drama, *L'hippocanthrope* (1979), about the stifling nature of family relationships in which the free form and imaginative dialogue become a paradigm for the freedom the characters seek.

Two women playwrights have explored dark aspects of life in rural Québec. Jeanne-Mance Delisle's *Un réel, ben beau, ben triste* (1980) is a tragic study of incest in a small Abitibi village in the 1960s. Marie Laberge's *C'était avant la guerre à l'Anse à Gilles* (1981), set in 1936 in the village of the title, also concerns the exploitation of women; at the end of the play the heroine, explicitly rejecting the example of Maria Chapdelaine, decides to leave the limiting world of her native village and the man who loves her to seek her fortune in the city. A more ambitious work is Laberge's *Ils étaient venus pour . . .* (1981), a Brechtian play on the rise and fall (from 1902 to 1927) of the village of Van-Jolbert, which dies when the mill-owner closes down its only industry; though fragmented and not specific enough, it reflects sensitivity for the workers and their families and throws light on the human dimension of social problems.

Two other women playwrights celebrate life without emphasizing a particular problem. Louise MAHEUX-FORCIER is a prize-winning novelist who has recently published several plays. Her television play *Neige et palmiers* (1974) is a lyric memory play about a woman who rejoices that she has kept the child she had planned to abort, while *Un arbre chargé d'oiseaux* (1976)—which has appeared on television in France, Switzerland, and Belgium, as well as Canada—combines mystery, romance, and fantasy in the tale of a woman real-estate agent who learns of life, love, and death from an old lady whose home is for sale. *Un parc en automne* (1982), Maheux-Forcier's first stage play, is filled with poetry and nostalgia as two former lovers find each other in a retirement home. Finally, Jocelyne Goyette's *Ma p'tite vache a mal aux pattes* (1981) exemplifies several features of recent Québec drama: comedy, theatricality, the one-person play, a woman's perspective, assured use of a distinctively Québécois French, and attention to daily life as opposed to social or political concerns. As in other recent plays, there is a certain roughness here that comes from lack of experience in dramatizing this story of a day in the life of a young mother-lover-actress.

CONCLUSION. New and established French-Canadian playwrights continue to be produced and published in Québec and elsewhere in Canada. Leméac's several series of French-Canadian plays now number over 150 titles and continue to grow, and many other publishers of plays have recently emerged. Indeed, the rapidity and frequency with which French-language playwrights now get published suggests that too many plays are published without sufficient care to separate the very good from the ordinary. The plays and playwrights examined above, however, attest to the dynamism of a period when a truly Québécois drama and theatre-going public came into being. Whatever direction Québécois society and culture take in the future, there is no doubt that its playwrights will mirror and criticize them with passion, humour, and inventiveness.

Bibliography. In English, articles and book reviews on French-Canadian drama may be found in *Dramatists in Canada: selected essays* (1972), edited by W.H. New; in *Stage voices* (1978), edited by Geraldine Anthony; and in the periodicals *Canadian Drama/L'Art dramatique canadien*, *Canadian Theatre Review*, *Theatre History in Canada*, CANADIAN LITERATURE, *Queen's Quarterly*, and the *University of Toronto Quarterly*. Mavor Moore's introduction to Gratien GÉLINAS in *Four Canadian playwrights* (1973) has a brief overview, as does *Marcel Dubé and French-Canadian drama* (1970) by Edwin C. Hamblet. Studies in English on individual dramatists are *Gratien Gélinas* (1974) and *Michel Tremblay* (1982), both by Renate Usmiani.

Useful studies in French on contemporary Québec theatre are *350 ans de théâtre au Canada français* (1958) by Jean Béraud; *Le renouveau du théâtre au Canada français* (1961) and *Le théâtre au Canada français* (1964) by Jean Hamelin; *Le théâtre québécois (I): introduction à dix dramaturges contemporains* (1970) and *Le théâtre québécois II: nouveau auteurs, autres spectacles* (1980) by Jean-Cléo Godin and Laurent Mailhot; *Dictionnaire critique du théâtre québécois* (1972) by Alain Pontaut; *Le renouveau du théâtre québécois* (1973) by Michel Belair; *Un théâtre en effervescence: critiques et chroniques 1965-72* (1975) by Martial Dassylva; *Le théâtre canadien d'expression française: répertoire analytique des origines à nos jours* (4 vols, 1976, 1977, 1978) by Edouard-G. Rinfret; *Le théâtre canadien français* (1976), vol. 5 in the series 'Archives des lettres canadiennes', a large work by many authors that includes a good bibliography and dates

of first productions of plays by John Hare; *Le théâtre québécois; instrument de contestation sociale et politique* (1976) by Jacques Cotnam; *Le fou et ses doubles: figures de la dramaturgie québécoise* (1978) by Pierre Gobin; *L'église et le théâtre au Québec* (1979) by Jean Laflamme and Rémi Tourangeau; and *Le théâtre et l'état au Québec: essai* (1981) by Adrien Gruslin. The annual *Livres et auteurs canadiens* (1960-8), which became *Livres et auteurs québécois* (1969-), has a bibliography and reviews of published plays. *Nord* 4-5 (1973) is a special issue entitled 'Le théâtre au Québec 1950-1972', which includes 'Bibliographie du théâtre québécois de 1935 à nos jours' by Jean Du Berger. See also *Jeu* (1976-), a periodical devoted to the theatre.

The anthology *Monologues québécois, 1890-1980* (1980), co-edited by Laurent Mailhot and Doris-Michel Montpetit, illustrates nearly a century of Québec theatre, cabaret, and music-hall, and provides a valuable record of the evolution of the spoken language of Québec.   JAMES NOONAN

Drama in French: collective creations. See COLLECTIVE CREATIONS IN QUÉBEC.

Drew, Wayland. See NOVELS IN ENGLISH 1960 TO 1982: 4.

Drummond, William Henry (1854-1907). Born at Currawn House, near Mohill, County Leitrim, Ireland, he immigrated with his parents to Montreal at the age of ten. He attended Montreal High School, McGill University (in 1878), and Bishop's University, Lennoxville, where he received an M.D. degree in 1884. He practised medicine in Montreal and died of a stroke in Cobalt, Ont., after going there to help control a smallpox outbreak at a mine owned by his brothers. He is buried in Mount Royal Cemetery, Montreal.

Drummond's distinctive dialect verse, most of it amusing and most of it dealing with French-Canadian *habitant* life, was Canada's most popular poetry at the turn of the century. (His non-dialect verse never achieved great popularity.) His wife, May Isobel Harvey, helped collate scattered poems from correspondence and newspaper columns for Drummond's first collection, *The habitant and other French-Canadian poems* (New York, 1897), with an introduction by Louis FRÉCHETTE. Its popularity led to the publication of five other collections: two

Drummond

narrative poems in one volume, *Phil-o-Rum's canoe and Madeleine de Verchères* (New York and London, 1898); *Johnnie Courteau and other poems* (1901); *The voyageur and other poems* (1905); *The great fight* (1908), a posthumous collection containing a biographical sketch of Drummond by his wife; and *The poetical works of William Henry Drummond* (1912), again with an introduction by Fréchette. A selection of poems was published in 1926 by McClelland and Stewart and reprinted in 1959 in the New Canadian library with an introduction by Arthur L. Phelps.

Although Drummond professed to let his rustic Québécois 'tell their own stories in their own way' (Preface to *The habitant*), he deliberately shaped his own mixture of French and English to provide animation, sentiment, and humour. Many English-speaking readers in Canada, the United States, and England delighted in what they felt was a realistic insight into the voice and attitudes of the *habitant*. Nonetheless, as the *Montreal Star* (whose editor had been a friend of the poet) noted at the time of his death, Drummond's medical practice had been mostly in Montreal and his country experience 'was not among the French-Canadians but among the Highland Scotch'. Drummond actually modelled the mischievous five-year-old in 'Leetle Bateese' and the wan mystic child in 'The last portage' on his own sons; and the title place of 'Little Lac Grenier' was his own favourite fishing spot. His exposure to the variety of broken English used by French-Canadian woodsmen and farmers occurred at Bord-à-Plouffe, where Drummond worked for six summers, from the age of fifteen, as a telegrapher. In his later poetry, however, the distinctive language of his *habitant* characters is more accurate as a measure of Drummond's artistic achievement than of Québécois utterance. Fréchette's introductory comments, though they express a general approval of Drummond's 'daring experiment', focus admiration in part upon the poet's personal cultivation of his material 'with tools and means of his own invention'. That point is made more strongly in some observations at the time by the French-language press: 'This very special language is confined to a particular group in our population' and 'cet idiôme bâtard . . . has the attraction of the comedy of travesty' (translated from *La Patrie*, 15 Dec. 1901). *Le Journal de Françoise* referred to 'the bizarre language that he had created initially' (2 Nov. 1907, in transla-

tion). Critics agreed with Fréchette, however, in concluding that Drummond's *habitant* poems expressed a friendly spirit.

The autobiographical base of Drummond's work is documented by the poet's wife in an unpublished biography in the Osler Library, McGill University. Drummond's distinctive use of language is discussed most fully by R.E. Rashley in 'W.H. Drummond and the dilemma of style', *Dalhousie Review* (vol. xxviii, no. 4, Jan. 1949). Rashley credits Drummond with 'a freshened, renewed language, a genuine discovery' and implies what a later critic, Louis DUDEK, stated more strongly when he said that Drummond unconsciously 'loosened the straitjacket of literary puritanism and made it possible for free language for the expression of real life and human character' ('Literature in English', *Selected essays and criticism*, 1978).   GERALD NOONAN

Dubé, Marcel (b. 1930). Born in Montreal, he attended the Jesuit Collège Saint-Marie and the Université de Montréal, which he left after one year of graduate studies in the Faculté des Lettres to pursue a career of writing for the theatre. He also spent six months in the Canadian army, and in 1953-4 attended theatre schools in Paris. Primarily a playwright for stage and television, Dubé has also written poetry, short stories, a novel, radio scripts, adaptations and translations of plays written in English, and topical articles for such journals as *Perspectives, Le Magazine Maclean*, and *Cité libre*.

The most published and successful dramatist in Québec, Dubé is possibly the best Canadian dramatist writing in English or French. This pre-eminence results from a highly poetic prose style, acute sensitivity to the nuances of feeling and emotion, a classic sense of dramatic structure, and a tragic vision of life applied to contemporary situations in Québec society. Yet his work is not pessimistic. As he explained in an important letter to *Le Devoir* in 1958: 'I write because I believe in the future; tragedy appeals to me because I believe.' His stage and television plays are concerned with man's search for an invariably fleeting or unattainable happiness; the fragility of human relationships; and the emptiness of modern urban life. However, his work is often marred by sentimentality and melodrama (presumably both are demanded on television). Dubé has been influenced by Jean Anouilh and by the realists of the modern American theatre, especially Arthur Miller, whose *Death of a sales-*

man he adapted for French television. He uses the distinctive speech of French Canadians, but unlike many other contemporary Québec dramatists, he rarely attempts to reproduce JOUAL.

Some thirty of Dubé's plays have been published to date. They may be divided into three groups: those in the first, written for the most part between 1951 and 1959, deal with the lower classes, often in the east end of Montreal where Dubé grew up; the second group consists of plays (1959-72) about the emptiness and disillusionment of Québec middle-class life; and the last shows Dubé's departure into comedy, musical comedy, ballet, satire, and a return to tragedy.

Though Dubé's first stage play, the one-act *Le bal triste* (unpublished), was produced in 1950, he came to prominence with the successful production of *Zone* (1955; 1968), judged the best Canadian play at the 1953 Dominion Drama Festival. It is a realistic if sometimes sentimental story of a teenage gang of smugglers whose lives are restricted by the area or 'zone' in which they live. *Le naufragé* (1971) and *De l'autre côté du mur* (1973) have many resemblances to *Zone* in theme and style. The latter was published with five other short plays written between 1959 and 1972 (*Rendez-vous du lendemain, Le visiteur, L'aiguillage, Le père idéal*, and *Les frères enemis*). *Un simple soldat* (1958; 1967) depicts the dissolute and disheartening life of Joseph Latour, who, unable after the Second World War to adjust to civilian life and the demands of his father and stepmother, returns to the army to serve in the Korean War, in which he is killed. Its theme and popularity recall GÉLINAS's TIT-COQ. *Le temps des lilas* (1958; 1969; 1973), a sad and moving play about a group of people in a Montreal boarding-house, is reminiscent of Chekhov (Dubé's favourite playwright) in its sensitive portrayal of the disillusionment of the characters and the final quiet resignation of an old couple. Other plays in this first group are *Paradis perdu*, published with *L'échéance du vendredi* (1972), *La cellule* (1973), and *Medée* (1973).

Florence (1960; 1970), a transitional work, shows Dubé's shift in interest to middle-class characters. Portraying the frustrations of a young secretary attempting to break away from her traditional family to live a more exciting life, it heralds the mature work of his second period, which includes *Bilan* (1968)—the title means 'balance sheet'—about the human cost of financial success; *Les beaux dimanches* (1968), about the desperate efforts of four wealthy and unhappy couples to divert themselves in the course of one Sunday; and *Un matin comme les autres* (1971), about the infidelities of two couples. *Au retour des oies blanches* (1969), translated by Jean Remple as *The white geese* (1972) and considered by many to be Dubé's finest play, portrays an upper-class family in Quebec City and their gradual discovery of the truth about their relationships. The climax occurs when the central character, Geneviève, reveals that she conceived a child by Thomas, thought to be her uncle but discovered to be her father. Its plot, structure, and emotional impact, which resemble those of *Oedipus the King*, make it Dubé's closest approach to classical tragedy. Lesser plays from this same period are *Pauvre amour* (1969), *Le coup de l'étrier* and *Avant de t'en aller* (1970), *Octobre* (1964; 1977), *Virginie* (1968; 1974), *Entre midi et soir* (1971), and *Manuel* (1973). In an introduction to *Manuel*, Dubé makes explicit his increasing bitterness towards society: 'Each of us bears within himself the seeds of survival and hope, but we are marching towards total and meaningless extinction under the pretext that we are involved in social progress.'

Though Dubé was not prolific during the 1970s, partly because of poor health and frequent hospitalization, the third category of his writing, mostly of this period, seems to offer relief from an unrelenting tragic vision. Some of these plays—such as *Hold-up!* (1969), a 'photo-roman'—were written in collaboration with Louis-Georges Carrier, who directed many of Dubé's dramas. *Jérémie* (1973) is a brief scenario for a ballet presented in 1973 by Les Ballets Jazz Contemporains at Sir George Williams University, Montreal; the published version contains an English translation by Jean Remple. *Dites-le avec fleurs* (1976), a comedy with songs, written in collaboration with the playwright Jean BARBEAU, is a satire on communal marriage and on the unsatisfactory quality of life in a commune. *L'impromptu de Québec; ou Le testament* (1974) was Dubé's first full-fledged comedy—written, as were several of his more recent plays, for the Théâtre de Marjolaine in Eastman, Qué., a summer playhouse near Dubé's residence at Cherry River in the Eastern Townships. Based on the play *Le légataire universel* by the seventeenth-century French writer Jean-François Regnard, it has an underlying serious note: the fraudulent inheritor loses his fortune in the market collapse of 1929. The mellow play *L'été s'appelle Julie* (1975) suggests that in his later work Dubé offers, as a bulwark against an unstable and dehumanizing world, integration within the individual of the forces of beauty and nature—symbolized by Julie. Dubé's most recent published play, *Le reformiste; ou L'honneur des hommes* (1977), comments on facets of modern Québec life: the revised educational system, the decline of family life, unionism, corrupt work practices, political power, and loss of faith. Rather than abandon humanism and tradition in education, the hero—Régis, an ex-Jesuit—flawed by his pride and stubbornness, takes his own life. Though interesting to read, the play is verbose and relatively static on stage. Its tragic intensity suggests that Dubé may be using the more serious vision of his middle period to focus on immediate social problems.

Dubé has written two major television series, 'La côte de sable' and 'De 9 à 5'. From the latter series on the life of white-collar workers in Montreal a number of dramas were developed and brought together on Radio-Canada under the title 'Le monde de Marcel Dubé'. The Montreal firm Leméac—directed by Marcel's brother Yves—which publishes more plays than any other Québec publisher, has published most of Dubé's plays and a volume of his poetry, *Poèmes de sable* (1974), which recalls the themes of many of his plays: loneliness, suffering, beauty, nature, love, and death. Simple, direct, and lyrical, the poems are not innovative in style or technique. Dubé has also published two volumes of non-dramatic prose—essays on literary figures, speeches, and letters—under the titles *Textes et documents* (1968) and *La tragédie est un acte de foi* (1973).

See Edwin C. Hamblet, *Marcel Dubé and French-Canadian drama* (1970), which places Dubé and his work in the context of the contemporary theatre in Québec. Maximilien Laroche, *Marcel Dubé* (1970), and Jean-Cléo Godin's chapter on Dubé in *Le théâtre québécois* (1970), by Godin and Laurent Mailhot, are both useful studies in French.

JAMES NOONAN

Dubé, Rodolphe (b. 1905). The poet, novelist, essayist, and philosopher who wrote under the pseudonym 'François Hertel' was born in Rivière-Ouelle, Qué. He was a student at Sainte-Anne-de-la-Pocatière and at the Séminaire de Trois-Rivières before entering the Jesuit Order at the age of twenty.

A licentiate in theology and philosophy, he received a doctorate from Rome and was ordained priest in 1938. He taught subsequently at the Collège Jean-de-Brébeuf, Montreal, and at the Collège de Sudbury (Ont.), where he founded the newspaper *L'Ami du peuple*. Becoming a secular priest in 1943, he wrote for various Montreal periodicals and was editor for two years of the review *Amérique française*. In 1946, when he was shaken by a crisis of faith, he left the Jesuit Order; at his request he was permitted a gradual return to secular life. While he was admired by young people as an intellectual, a spiritual guide, and a daring innovator, the ex-Jesuit was considered dangerous by a certain élite. Stifled by orthodox religion and Québec's cultural stagnation, he left Montreal for Paris in 1947 and remained in France after 1949. He founded and edited the art review *Rythmes et couleurs*; a review of the occult, *Radiesthésie Magazine*; and ran the publishing house 'La Diaspora française', which published most of his books. He still lives in France.

A dozen collections published between 1934 and 1967 have given Hertel's poetry a respectable place in anthologies of Québec literature. His poems are both sweet and bitter, lyrical, ironic, vindictive, and at times choleric. *Poèmes d'hier et d'aujourd'hui* (1967) represents all these veins in about a hundred poems; both descriptive and philosophical, they are always speculative. This selection retains the meditative and romantic texts of the first collections, as well as of the religious poems of the forties: the traditional verse of *Les voix de mon rêve* (1934), as well as the free verse and lyrical prose-poems of *Axe et parallaxes* (1941) and *Strophes et catastrophes* (1943). These collections must be considered within the context of the spiritual preoccupations of poetry during the war. However, while certain poets like Alain GRANDBOIS and Simone ROUTIER returned from Europe, and others increasingly favoured taking root in Québec, Hertel went into exile. So did his poetry: it became either philosophical or religious and metaphysical. The poems written after the war, and in the fifties and sixties—collected in *Cosmos* (1945), *Quatorze* (1948), *Mes naufrages* (1951), *Jeux de mer et de soleil* (1951), *Poèmes européens* (1964), and *Poèmes perdus et retrouvés* (1966)—return to a classical verse style and a more intimate voice. All anthologies of Québec poetry cite the poems of *Mes naufrages* as the most painful and personal of the poet's work.

Hertel the philosopher surfaces throughout his work, but most particularly in five or six books in which he developed his key ideas. In *Pour un ordre personnaliste* (1942) he confronted the major movements of his era: the atheistic existentialism of Sartre, the Christian existentialism of Gabriel Marcel, and the 'personnalisme' of Emmanuel Mounier. To Hertel, philosophy represented the spirit of seeking rather than a system, and he rejected all dogmatism. *Journal philosophique et littéraire* (1961), *Méditation théologique* (1964), and *Vers une sagesse* (1966) show a thinker in quest of an original explanation of the universe, of matter, spirit, and time. Although theology may appear subordinate to his philosophy, it nevertheless constitutes its epistemological basis. Even after the crisis of 1946, the central figure of God is omnipresent in his poetry, novels, and essays. From the *Journal d'Anatole Laplante* (1947) to *Mystère cosmique et condition humaine* (1975), the apostate progressively erases the idea of a personal God; but the abstract conception remains.

Hertel's essays are concerned with social and political matters as well as with aesthetics and the philosophy of language: he never hesitated to become involved in contemporary issues. In *Leur inquiétude* (1936) he was preoccupied with the restlessness of youth in the thirties and, following in the footsteps of Jacques Maritain, denounced mechanization, the death of the individual, and the myth of rationalism. Hertel faced squarely the problems of that critical period: bilingualism and the economic handicap of French Canadians. Anti-capitalist, he upheld social corporatism and a form of 'personnalisme' (a moral and social philosophy) anchored in Québec society. Taking a stand based on the nationalistic ideology of Lionel GROULX, he was in favour of a Laurentian state, independent from the rest of Canada. And yet he did not accept Québec society as it was (see the virulent poem 'Au pays du Québec' of 1939). He continued to defend the nationalist position in *Nous ferons l'avenir* (1945), *Du séparatisme québécois* (1963), and *Cent ans d'injustice* (1967). In *Du métalangage* (1968) the hierarchy of spiritual values is taken up again—both objectively and symbolically—as the essayist expresses his allegiance to a spiritual vision of the world and to a culture that is essentially humanistic.

Hertel's novels—*Le beau risque* (1939), *Anatole Laplante, curieux homme* (1944), *Journal d'Anatole Laplante* (1947), and *Louis Préfontaine, apostat* (1967)—are almost forgotten today. Meditation and dialogue are doubtless more important to Hertel than refined novelistic structures. Still, the portraits and characterizations in these novels are rich and varied, and Hertel's satires slash out at the intellectual and bourgeois milieux of the times. The short-story collections—*Six femmes, un homme* (1949) and *Jérémie et Barrabas* (1959)—reveal a storyteller whose technique is better in short narratives than in novels. Occasionally working in the genres of theatre, travel, and personal accounts of his adventures, Hertel also wrote *Un canadien errant* (1953), *Afrique* (1955), *Claudine et les écueils suivi de La folle* (1953), *La morte* (1965), *Souvenirs, historiettes, réflexions* (1972), and *Nouveaux souvenirs, nouvelles réflexions* (1973).

Writing of Hertel in 1973, a critic asserted that it was time to 'break the silence that threatens to obscure a body of work of great value to us.' And yet this silence still remains to be broken. Beyond friends and old disciples who are still living, and a few critics and literary historians, not many know the work of François Hertel, who has received little recognition of any kind in Québec.

See Jean ÉTHIER-BLAIS, 'François Hertel—le train sifflera deux fois' in *Signets II* (1967); Robert Giroux, 'François Hertel, le surhomme noyé', in *Présence francophone* (no. 6, Spring 1973); Jean Tétreau, 'François Hertel, une pensée, un style, un art de vivre' in *Livres et auteurs canadiens 1966* (1967); and Gilles Thérien, 'François Hertel, curieux homme' in VOIX ET IMAGES, vol. 2, no. 1 (Sept. 1976).   RICHARD GIGUÈRE

Ducharme, Réjean (b. 1942). Biographical information about Réjean Ducharme is minimal. Born in Saint Félix de Valois, Qué. (near Sorel), he attended classical college in Joliette, but dropped out before completing Grade 12. He spent six months at the École Polytechnique de Montréal and a few weeks in the Canadian Air Force. He now lives in or near Montreal. Ducharme has neither been seen in public nor interviewed since Sept. 1966, at which time he stated in a brief interview with Gérald GODIN in *Le Magazine Maclean*: 'I don't want my face to be known, I don't want people to link me and my novel . . . My novel is public, but I'm not.'

Ducharme's novels have been described by critic Gilles MARCOTTE as 'both the apotheosis and the negation of the novel.' The author practises a kind of literary terrorism, building elaborate word-plays that simultaneously provoke interpretation and confound meaning. His protagonists are fiercely individualistic adolescents, determined to survive on their own terms in a world they find hypocritical. Their quests for infinite knowledge and love, which are tragically defeated by the limits of reality, are marvellously poetic, semantically evocative, and farcical in tone—Ducharme assaults the Western cultural heritage with humour or 'niaiserie' (silliness). His inventory of languages (biblical, mythological, literary, scientific, Marxist, nationalist, countercultural) declares all language both false and impotent to capture the complexity of reality: 'There are tons of words. But nothing to say. There are tons of things. But nothing to do.' In spite of this pessimism, the joy of his language expands and explodes in all directions.

Ducharme's first novel, *L'avalée des avalés* (1966)—which won a Governor General's Award and was translated by Barbara Bray as *The swallower swallowed* (1968)—is one of the high points of modern French-Canadian fiction. Its half-Jewish, half-Catholic heroine, Bérénice Einberg, who transfers her love for the neglectful mother she adores to her brother, becomes manipulative (like her quarrelling parents) and callous to protect herself, choosing to hate whatever she cannot fully possess: she decides to 'swallow' the world in order not to be swallowed up by it. Her pain is brilliantly portrayed in farcical/comic terms as she rejects all traditional values and invents an anti-social and incomprehensible language, 'le bérénicien', to replace normal language that for her is based on illusion.

Le nez qui voque (1967) is the journal of a sixteen-year old boy who has made a suicide pact with his fourteen-year old girlfriend rather than allow the compromises of adult life and sexuality to separate them. As the pun in the title suggests, this novel is about equivocation and ambiguity; it is also about the pleasure and hypocrisy of growing up, and about the tragedy of attempting to cling to absolute purity and truth. It was awarded the Prix littéraire de la Province de Québec. *L'océantume* (published in 1968 but written before *L'avalée des avalés*) is the most lyrical and least cynical of Ducharme's novels. In it two young girls, who reject the adult world, journey together to the sea, but find disillusionment instead of the ideal. *La fille de Christophe Colomb* (1969), a mock epic written in determinedly ridiculous verse, is Du-

charme's most radical attack on traditional literary structure and meaning. The wandering around the world of Columbus's modern daughter Colombe in a vain search for friendship is the pretext for a condemnation of civilization and of literature's pretense of transmitting meaning. In *L'hiver de force* (1973) and *Les enfantômes* (1976), Ducharme's protagonists are somewhat older and more sophisticated but no less uncompromising than their predecessors. In *L'hiver de force* André Ferron and his sister Nicole make their living as proof-readers but are 'drop-outs' from society, determined to do literally nothing. The novel has the same vitality and poetry as Ducharme's earlier works, but is more realistic in its satire of the political and cultural milieu of 1970s Montreal. It was regarded by many as a *roman à clef*. *Les enfantômes*, the story of Vincent Falardeau, his wife Alberta and his sister Fériée, is—like the other novels—a baroque journey evoking the dreams, joys, and anguish of insatiable child-adults united against the world.

Ducharme's four dramatic works—*Inès Pérée et Inat Tendue* (1976), *Le cid maghané*, *Le marquis qui perdit*, as yet unpublished, and *HA ha!* (1982), which won a Governor General's Award—treat the same themes as the novels, and like them display a savage joy in the possibility of deconstructing language. In recent years the author has turned to film and has collaborated with Francis Manckiewicz on the very successful *Les bons débarras* (1979) and *Les beaux souvenirs* (1981), whose innocently cruel young heroines are familiar figures to readers of the novels.

See Gérald Godin, 'Gallimard publie un Québécois de 24 ans, inconnu' (the only existing interview with Ducharme) in *Le Magazine Maclean* (Sept. 1966), and Michel Van Schendel, 'Ducharme l'inquiétant' in *Littérature canadienne-française* (conférences J.-A. de Sève 1-10, 1969). See also a special issue, entitled 'Avez-vous relu Ducharme?', of *Études françaises*, vol. 11, nos 3 and 4 (Oct. 1975).

See also NOVELS IN FRENCH 1960 TO 1982: 2, 3, 3(f).   PATRICIA SMART

Dudek, Louis (b. 1918). Born in the east end of Montreal, of Polish immigrant parents, he attended McGill University and after graduating in 1940 worked as an advertising copywriter and freelance journalist. In 1943 he moved to New York and began graduate studies in journalism and history at Columbia University; shortly afterwards he changed his major from journalism to literature. On completion of his doctoral course work, he accepted an English appointment at City College, New York; he became acquainted with writers Paul Blackburn, Cid Corman, and Herbert Gold, and began a correspondence with Ezra Pound. In 1951 Dudek returned to Montreal, where he lectured at McGill in modern poetry, Canadian literature, the art of poetry, and European literature, until his retirement in 1982.

Dudek began his career as a poet in the 1936-40 period, publishing social-protest verse in the *McGill Daily*. In 1943 he joined John SUTHERLAND and Irving LAYTON in editing FIRST STATEMENT, which Sutherland had founded in 1942, and throughout his New York years Dudek contributed to it and to its successor, NORTHERN REVIEW. On his return to Canada he became immediately a major force in Canadian small-press publishing and influenced the development of Canadian poetry. Instructed by the editorial activities of Americans such as Pound and Corman, he was convinced of the necessity for poets to take their means of publication out of the hands of commercial publishers and into their own. In 1952-4 he was instrumental in shaping the editorial direction of Raymond SOUSTER's little magazine CONTACT. In 1952, together with Souster and Layton, he founded Contact Press, which, between 1952 and 1967, published early books by most of the major poets of the sixties and early seventies. In 1956 he began another publishing venture, the McGill Poetry Series, in which he published first poetry books by McGill students, beginning with Leonard COHEN's *Let us compare mythologies* (1956). Despite its name, the series was mostly financed and edited by Dudek. In 1957 he began *Delta*, a personal literary magazine in which he attempted to promote further the urbane, realistic kind of writing his earlier editorial activities had encouraged. He terminated *Delta* in 1966; but the next year he co-founded, with Glen Siebrasse and Michael Gnarowski, the small press Delta Canada. On its dissolution in 1970 he co-founded, with Aileen Collins, yet another small press, D.C. Books, which is still active.

Dudek's poetry collections are *East of the city* (1946), *Twenty-four poems* (1952), *The searching image* (1952), *Europe* (1955), *The transparent sea* (1956), *En Mexico* (1958), *Laughing stalks* (1958), *Atlantis* (1967), *Collected poetry* (1971), *Selected poems* (1979), *Poems from Atlantis* (1980), *Cross-section* (1980), and *Continuation* (1981). His early poems are mostly short lyrics that proceed from incidental observation and description towards a concluding insight or philosophical statement. Employing few metaphors or elaborate images, the descriptions are direct and realistic. Although many of the scenes are from ghetto and working-class life, and many of the sentiments are Marxist, a definite pessimism about human accomplishment pervades these poems. Optimism is usually reserved for nature's powers—'the soon-rampant seed', 'the great orchestrating principle of gravity'.

With the publication of *Europe* and *En Mexico*, Dudek moved from short, incidentally related lyrics to book-length meditations with prose-like rhythms and a didactic tone. Unlike the lyrics, they interweave the general and particular so that their relationship is obscured; some passages seem to be illustrated sermons, while others offer flashes of inspiration gained from particulars. Dudek has remarked in his one book of literary theory (*The first person in literature*, 1967) that, because of our 'anarchically subjective' age, the egoist as writer must become a 'great moralist'. In *Europe, En Mexico*, and *Atlantis* Dudek attempts to be the morally responsible egoist, to make his self universal, to come to terms with 'the dichotomy of the self and the not-self, the I-myself and the mankind-to-which-I-belong'; but he is still pessimistic about mankind's ability to reform and save itself. Joy, beauty, and eternity are certain residents only of nature. At the end of *Atlantis*, when the poet finally gains a vision of the lost continent, its 'palaces, and domes' are a North Atlantic iceberg—'a piece of eternity', 'a carved silent coffin', that promises only 'darkness' and 'infinite night'.

Dudek is also the author of *Epigrams* (1975) and *Literature and the press* (1960), a revision of his Ph.D. thesis, which is a history of printing, printed media, and their relation to literature. In collaboration with Irving Layton he compiled *Canadian poems: 1850-1952* (1952), and in collaboration with Michael Gnarowski *The making of modern poetry in Canada* (1967), an extremely useful anthology of documents relating to the development of Canadian poetry since 1910. Dudek is also the editor of *Poetry of our time* (1965), an introduction to twentieth-century poetry, including Canadian poetry. Most of his essays on Canadian literature were included in *Selected essays and criticism* (1978), which was followed by two further prose collections: *Technology and culture* (1979) and *Texts and essays* (1981), a special issue of the magazine OPEN LETTER, which also contains photostats of manuscript pages from *Europe* and *Atlantis*. Dudek's correspondence during the 1950s with Ezra Pound was published as *D/k: some letters of Ezra Pound* (1974).

The one major study of Dudek's work is Frank DAVEY, *Louis Dudek and Raymond Souster* (1981).

See also POETRY IN ENGLISH 1950 TO 1982:1.   FRANK DAVEY

Dufresne, Guy. See DRAMA IN FRENCH 1948 TO 1981: 3.

Dugas, Marcel (1883-1947). Born at St-Jacques de Lachigan, Qué., he studied law at the Université Laval in Montreal and worked as a journalist, chiefly covering the theatre. From 1910 to 1914 he lived in Paris, studying literature at the Sorbonne. The war forced him to leave Europe, but he returned in 1920 and remained in Paris—working for the Canadian Archives and frequenting the cafés and literary salons—until his final departure in 1940. *Pots de fer* (1941) offers a moving account of his last days in occupied France. Dugas was associated, over the years, with three artistic and literary movements in Montreal—Le Soc (1910), La Tribu des Casoars, which amalgamated with L'Arche (1916-17), and Le NIGOG (1918)— and, in Ottawa, with Le Groupe des Sept (1943-6).

Dugas's writing is eminently poetic, although he published only one poetry collection, *Salve alma parens* (1941). Reviews that he wrote for *Le Nationaliste* were published under the pseudonym 'Marcel Henry' in *Le théâtre de Montréal, propos d'un Huron canadien* (1911). His prose falls into two categories: critical essays and poetic essays. He worshipped Verlaine, Péguy, and Le Cardonnel, enthusiastically praising all three authors in *Feux de Bengale à Verlaine glorieux* (1915) and *Versions. Louis Cardonnel. Charles Péguy* (1917). A frequent reviewer of his compatriots' works, he usually selected those of his friends; thus, Léo-Pol Morin, Alain GRAND-BOIS, François Hertel (Rodolphe DUBÉ), Saint-Denys GARNEAU, and Simone ROUTIER-DROUIN were 'approached with affection and a desire to understand them, to mark their passage and pay tribute to their qualities' (*Approches*, 1942). Friends from the early days had received similar kindhearted attention in *Apologies: M. Albert Lozeau, M. Paul Morin, M. Guy Delahaye, M. Robert La Roque de Roquebrune, M. René Chopin* (1919). These five studies were reprinted in *Littérature canadienne: aperçus* (1929), along with essays on the work of Jean-Aubert LORANGER, Jean Nolin, Robert CHOQUETTE, and Pierre Dupuy. Dugas's criticism, which is sometimes quite biased, is often more beautifully written and more skilful than the works under study. However, in *Un romantique canadien: Louis Fréchette, 1839-1908* (Paris, 1934; Montréal, 1946), he was a bit hard on poor Louis FRÉCHETTE, calling him 'this bourgeois playing at being a revolutionary' and a mere artisan, 'the brutality of whose sentiments is only rarely saved by his expression'. Only with effort could he begin to like the author of *La légende d'un peuple*, whose tastes and ideas were so remote from his own. But when studying his friends' texts he searched his soul; while speaking of them he was concerned with himself. In his poetic essays Dugas cultivated emotion with a growing obsession, sharing his troubled or disturbed inner states. He venerated in *Phèdre* 'the sad renewal of hearts that recover the illusion of loving' (*Psyché au cinéma*, 1916), because Phèdre tried to submit to fate instead of running from it, and, though a skeptic, to bring about a return to 'benevolent illusion' (*Cordes anciennes*, 1933). Other works by Dugas are *Confins* (1921) and *Nocturnes* (1936), both published under pseudonyms— although *Confins* was later published under his own name as *Flacons à la mer. Proses* (1923).

As esthete infatuated with ornate language and long, unbroken, harmonious sentences, Dugas bridged in a unique manner the gap between his fragile universe and the outside world. With him one truly enters into what Barthes calls 'the pleasure of the text', and willingly subscribes to the judgement of Philippe PANNETON that Dugas is 'the greatest of our prose writers for the richness of his language'.

BERNADETTE GUILMETTE

Duguay, Calixte. See ACADIAN LITERATURE: 2(a).

Duguay, Raoul (b. 1939). Born in Val d'Or, Qué., he was the seventh of eleven children. When his fiddler father Armand Duguay died, Raoul was only five and was sent first to an orphanage, then to his Acadian grandparents, who raised him in New

Brunswick. As a teenager he was sent to the seminary at Amos, Qué., where he developed an interest in music. At nineteen he left the seminary and studied philosophy at the Université de Montréal, while teaching esthetics at Collège Sainte-Croix and media techniques at the Université de Québec in Montreal.

In the early and middle sixties Duguay began to publish poems in LIBERTÉ, *Passepartout*, and *Les Écrits du Canada français*; he also became involved with the young Marxist and separatist ideologues who gravitated around PARTI-PRIS. In a number of articles published in *parti-pris*, Duguay articulated indépendentist and Marxist positions—from which he stood aloof in the early seventies. His articles on a sound theory, phonetics, and the physical and spiritual properties of the spoken word, published in *Quoi* in 1967, demonstrate a strong commitment to the politics of sound as distinct from the politics of countries and territorial boundaries. From this point on, the aural properties of speech appear to be a central concern: how to use sound vibrations, how to turn the mantric qualities of words to a specific purpose, and how to reach a wide public.

Duguay's first collections of poetry, *Ruts* (1966; 2nd edn 1974) and *Or le cycle du sang dure donc* (1967; 2nd edn 1975) won him more lasting attention. As erotic writings they celebrate a lover's body and sexual pleasure, but they also reveal a penchant for syncopated rhythms, linguistic break-ups, and non-semantic sound patterns. From 1968 to 1971 Duguay dedicated himself to the performance of his own poetic and musical shows. He founded the Infonie group, realizing what he called 'a harmony between music and poetry, a synthesis of the two'; creating something for both the ear and the eye; and exploring the physical dimension of a poem in the context of an audience's presence and response. With the Infonie group Duguay travelled across Canada; he also performed alone on the Bobino stage in Paris. During this time he became acquainted with the German composer Stockhausen and studied his musical theories. The early seventies saw the culminating point of Duguay's creative energies: out of his performing experiments with L'Infonie came *Le manifeste de l'Infonie* (1970) and *Lapokalipsô* (1971). Both volumes exemplify Duguay's theory of sound, as well as the multimedia aspects of his performances. All poems are phonetically written: some call for 99 typewriters, others for a variety of instruments and sounds—wind, waterfalls, and various languages.

Duguay—who also likes to use the reverse spelling of his name, Luoar Yaugud—dedicated himself, after 1972, almost entirely to the performing arts and the recording of his music. Performing for him did not imply moving away from writing (though it did mean publishing less), but aimed at 'bringing what had previously been looked upon as mysterious and esoteric to a wide audience. My voice is my most natural instrument and I want to give it to everybody *(toulmonde)*. I shall sing my poems as some eat an apple.'

See Christiane L'Heureux, *Raoul Duguay ou Le poète à la voix d'or* (1979); chapter VII of Clément Moisan, *Poésie des frontières* (1979); and an interview with Duguay in Caroline Bayard and Jack David, *Out-posts/Avantpostes* (1978).   CAROLINE BAYARD

Duley, Margaret (1894-1968). Born in St John's, Nfld., the daughter of a well-to-do jeweller, she was educated at the local Methodist College and in 1913 enrolled in the London Academy of Music and Dramatic Art in London, Eng. From 1918 until she began serious writing in the 1930s her life was occupied with travel, reading, partying with the St John's élite, and local feminist agitation. She never married. In the Depression years her father's business declined and Duley began writing fiction, apparently to make money. During the Second World War she helped to run a hostel for allied servicemen in St John's; and for a brief period afterwards she did public-relations work with the Newfoundland division of the Canadian Red Cross. In her late years she suffered from Parkinson's disease.

Duley grew up amid the snobbery and comforts of the St John's East merchant class. She knew the Newfoundland outports only from a distance, from the perspective of an occasional summer visitor; yet it was to the outports that she turned for inspiration for her first novel, *The eyes of the gull* (1936), where outharbour existence is depicted as unremittingly stifling, condemning the heroine, Isabel Pyke, to a deprived and horrid round of loveless days. Real love is seen as something attainable only in the world of culture and sophistication outside Newfoundland. This is Duley's most superficial and snobbish novel. Yet it is more carefully plotted than the later books. *Cold pastoral* (1939) takes a similar outport heroine out of her native cove, now evoked in all its squalour and coarseness, and brings her to the greater world of St John's and, ultimately, London. Urban values are espoused until the end of the book, when she feels a sudden twinge of affection for her own 'bit of earth' in Newfoundland. This is the beginning of a reconciliation that is the theme of *Highway to valour* (1941), Duley's third and final novel with a Newfoundland setting. Her new heroine, after living through a number of grim episodes in a country that terrifies and dominates her, at length turns her face in acceptance 'towards the cold sea that was her heritage.' These books show a progressive deepening in the author's understanding of the nature of life in Newfoundland; they appear to be stages in an odyssey of discovery and acceptance. As Duley developed as a novelist, she saw Newfoundland with an increasing intensity and clarity, but never fully overcame a distaste for the jagged landscapes and stormy seas of her uncomfortable home. Nevertheless she portrayed Newfoundland with rare truthfulness and vividness.

These three books dramatize encounters between a heroine and the inappropriate 'masculine' environment in which she had to function. The theme—women in pursuit of love—takes the novelist perilously close to sentimental excess. Yet after *The eyes of the gull* there is an effort to move beyond storybook romancing. If we consider all four of Duley's novels, adding *Novelty on earth* (1942)—published in England as *Green afternoon* (1944) and in Sweden as *Så stred Sara* (1946)—in which the Newfoundland setting is jettisoned, we can see a theme emerging in her work that engrosses her even more than her connection with her homeland: she is struggling to define a feminist sensibility. Duley's independent womanhood is reflected in all her books. She appears to have been torn between her desire to comment on the external world and her wish to explore the nature of her feminine sensitivity towards it, and towards men. In *Novelty on earth* the setting is unimportant as Duley minutely, and perhaps tediously, chronicles a love affair between a twice-widowed woman and a married man. At the end her heroine rejects her lover because she 'couldn't be a squaw-woman and give him what he wanted.' We have a free modern woman before us. Duley thus transcended her provincial concerns to make a larger statement.

Duley also wrote *The caribou hut; the story of a Newfoundland hostel* (1949), a little book

with much astute commentary on Newfoundland. She contributed a foreword to R.B. Job's *John Job's family* (1953). Her mother, Mrs. T.J. Duley, published a pamphlet, *A pair of grey socks; facts and fancies* (c. 1916), that contains 'Verses' by Margaret Duley.

There is an article by Duley in the *Atlantic Guardian* (July 1956) in which she discusses her novels in the context of Newfoundland writing. Margot Duley Morrow has written a biographical sketch of her in a reprint of *Highway to valour* (1977).

PATRICK O'FLAHERTY

Dumont, Fernand (b. 1927). Born in Montmorency, near Quebec City, he studied at Université Laval—where he is now director of the Institute supérieur des sciences humaines, and co-director of the journal *Recherches sociographiques*—and at the Université de Paris. Dumont is currently president (1979-84) of the Institut québécois de recherche sur la culture, which sponsors and co-ordinates research projects aimed at safeguarding the national heritage.

Dumont's attitude as a writer and teacher through the years of rapid change in Québec has been described by the epithet 'conscience vigilante', prompted by the title of his collection of essays, *La vigile du Québec* (1971). Dumont is, for Québec, what his fellow sociologists call 'un définisseur de la situation'; he exhibits a serene lucidity as he confidently grapples with the problems thrown up by the contemporary cultural revolution.

The desire to 'define the situation' and to see clearly the process by which a society elaborates its culture—its 'mental tools'— can be traced in Dumont's teaching, and in three colloquia organized by the review *Recherches sociographiques*, the proceedings of which appear in *Situation de la recherche sur le Canada frabçais* (1962), *Littérature et société canadiennes-français* (1964), and *Le pouvoir dans la société canadienne-française* (1966).

Chantiers (1973), a further volume of essays all previously published (1958-70), contains powerful theoretical studies chiefly on the role of ideology in the elaboration of cultural identity. Typical of Dumont's mode of scholarly examination is an early essay, 'L'étude systématique d'une société globale', which surveys previous attempts at a structural analysis of Québec society (by Trudeau, Brunet, et al.) and points to the need for a new analytical approach that takes into account Québec's distinctive development. *Les idéologies*, a powerful single essay that proposes an analysis of the concept and function of ideology in the social sciences, was published in Paris in 1974. His first sociological work, a study (written with Yves Martin) of the region of Saint-Jérôme just north of Montreal, *L'analyse des structures sociales régionales* (1963), examines the effect on traditional life in this town of the opening of the Laurentian autoroute, which both bypassed it and gave its inhabitants rapid access to the city. Leaving field-work behind in his later essays—*Pour la conversion de la pensée chrétienne* (1964), *Le lieu de l'homme* (1967), and *La dialectique de l'objet économique* (Paris, 1970)—Dumont looks at the ways in which culture conceptualizes experience, allowing members of a society to stand away from it and recognize the unfamiliar. He sees conformism as the sclerosis of the symbolical framework with which experience is processed. The portrait that emerges, of a society ill-equipped to adapt, suggests Québec—though the essays proceed with a minimum of reference to concrete situations and are fed by the widest, most eclectic erudition. Dumont's thoughts on the transformation of the anachronistic concept of a Christian culture in Québec are reflected in the report of the Commission d'étude sur les laïcs et l'Église, which he headed: *Pour la conversion de la pensée chrétienne* (1971). Dumont's latest work, *L'anthropologie en l'absence de l'homme* (Paris, 1981), attempts an ambitious synthesis of the social sciences and seeks to revitalize anthropology.

Dumont's definition of an ideology as 'la *justification* d'une définition de la situation d'un groupe en vue de l'action' allows him to see both the sociologist and the writer as concerned with the same collective vision. Through his limpid, orderly poetry—*L'ange du matin* (1952) and *Parler de septembre* (1970)—Dumont fits his own definition of both the sociologist and the writer: 'Un homme [qui], en pensant aux autres, ose tenter de définir son univers d'existence.'

C.R.P. MAY

Duncan, Frances. See CHILDREN'S LITERATURE IN ENGLISH: 8.

Duncan, Norman (1871-1916). Born in North Norwich Township, Oxford County, Ont., Norman McLean Duncan also spent parts of his boyhood in other Ontario towns. Between 1891 and 1894 he attended the University of Toronto, where he knew W.L. Mackenzie King, but did not graduate. Soon afterwards he began a career as a journalist in the United States. In the summer of 1900 he went to Newfoundland to write articles for *McClure's Magazine*, a journal that specialized in geographical adventure. He returned to Newfoundland for other summer visits between 1901 and 1906, and again in 1910, forming a strong attachment to the Manuel family of Exploits Island in Notre Dame Bay. In an appreciation of Duncan, Wilfred GRENFELL noted that he had been 'a guest aboard our little hospital vessel' along the Labrador coast. Duncan also travelled farther afield, to the Near East and to Australasia. From 1902 to 1908 he taught English and rhetoric at Washington and Jefferson College in Washington, Pa., and at the University of Kansas. During his last years drinking became a serious problem to him. He died suddenly, on a golf course, in Fredonia, N.Y.

Duncan was a prolific and popular author. His writings have been neglected by recent critics, perhaps because his defects—sentimentality, a flowery, rhetorical style, and a liking for melodrama—are so apparent, and his subject matter is often so remote from ordinary North American experience. Like his contemporary, Jack London, Duncan went for literary inspiration to northern frontiers and to the lives of forgotten people. His spirit was democratic, his writings affirmations of the imaginative possibilities inherent in common life. His first book was *The soul of the street: correlated stories of the New York Syrian quarter* (1900), a collection revealing his familiarity with the legends and lives of Syrian immigrants and showing his compassion and his interest in out-of-the-way modes of life. His experiences in Newfoundland stirred him deeply and provided material for ten works of fiction, much of it written for a juvenile audience: *The way of the sea* (1903; rpr. 1970, 1982), *Doctor Luke of the Labrador* (1904), *The adventures of Billy Topsail: a story for boys* (1906), *The cruise of the Shining Light* (1907), *Every man for himself* (1908), *Billy Topsail & company: a story for boys* (1910), *The best of a bad job: a hearty tale of the sea* (1912), *Billy Topsail, M.D.: a tale of adventure with Doctor Luke of the Labrador* (1916), *Battles royal down north* (1918), and *Harbor tales down north* (1918). His collection of essays on Newfoundland, *Dr. Grenfell's parish: the deep sea fishermen* (1905), expresses his admiration for Grenfell, who was undoubtedly the model for Dr Luke in his most popular novel. Of these works the most important is

The way of the sea, a book of stories that explore the outharbour life of Newfoundland with profound understanding and sympathy. His response to the ocean is striking. Andrew MACPHAIL said in an unpublished essay that Duncan wrote of the sea 'as one might write of the sky and the land, who had looked upon the heavens and the earth for the first time with his bodily eyes.'

Nothing else Duncan experienced seems to have fired his imagination so strongly as Newfoundland. Yet he wrote eight other books. *The mother* (1905) is a touching novel that probably expresses his grief over the death of his own mother in 1904. A similar domestic novel, *The suitable child* (1909), describes a boy's rejection by his family. *Going down from Jerusalem; the narrative of a sentimental traveller* (1909) is an account of his travels in Palestine, Syria, and Egypt that aims at conjuring up the lives of camel drivers rather than describing monuments. *Finding his soul* (1913) is a fictional representation of this journey. *Higgins; a man's Christian* (1909) is an account of Francis Edmund Higgins' missionary work among Minnesota lumberjacks, a subject that Duncan again treated in the novel *The measure of a man; a tale of the big woods* (1911). *The bird-store man; an old-fashioned story* (1914) is another book for children. *Australian byways: the narrative of a sentimental traveler* (1915) describes travels in Australasia in 1912-13.

Although his style often seems laboured, Duncan was capable of sustained passages of exquisite, resonant prose. Writing about Newfoundland—the 'frayed edge' of North America where he found obscure inhabitants of a hidden world of adventure—he created an unwitting epic of outport life in stories showing the stamp of genius.

PATRICK O'FLAHERTY

Duncan, Sara Jeannette (1861-1922). The daughter of a Scottish father and an Ulster Protestant mother, she was born and raised in Brantford, Canada West (Ont.). She attended the Toronto Normal School, but soon abandoned teaching for journalism. A high-spirited trip to the 1884 New Orleans Cotton Exposition as a freelance correspondent was followed by such substantial jobs as editorial writer and book reviewer for the Washington *Post* (1885-6), columnist for the Toronto *Globe* (1886-7), and finally columnist for the *Montreal Star* (1887-8). She also wrote extensively during this period for *The* WEEK. In Sept. 1888 she set off with a fellow journalist, Lily Lewis, on an ambitious round-the-world tour. In Calcutta she met Everard Cotes, a museum official and subsequently a journalist. She married him in Dec. 1890 and lived with him in Calcutta and Simla (then the summer administrative capital of India) for most of the next three decades, though she spent large stretches of time alone in London. In the mid-1890s she wrote editorials for the *Indian Daily News*, a newspaper her husband edited. Early personal and professional fulfilment appear to have been followed by unhappiness in India and a nostalgic affection for Canada. The last few years of her life were spent in England, where she died.

Duncan's journalism comments with intelligence, vigour, and wit on an astonishing variety of Canadian social, political, and cultural questions. Her remarks on literary issues display a shrewd understanding of contemporary controversies. Throughout her career Duncan was keenly aware of developments in fiction—she even sought out personal contact with Howells, Forster, and James. (She knew Howells in Washington and Paris and entertained Forster in India; she sent James her novel *His honour and a lady*, which he acknowledged tardily and with elaborate, distancing graciousness, describing it as 'extraordinarily keen and delicate and able' before criticizing it gently but astutely.) Her first book, *A social departure: how Orthodocia and I went round the world by ourselves* (London and New York, 1890), is an edited version of her globe-trotting newspaper articles, unified by the invention of a naive young Englishwoman as the narrator's companion. It has many lively episodes (particularly those dealing with Japan, a country Duncan found delightful), but is overlong and uneven. The more inventive and polished *An American girl in London* (London and New York, 1891)—like its predecessor a collection of light sketches, which are here presented as a novel—concerns the adventures of a Chicago baking-powder heiress who is eagerly sought after by predatory Englishmen. Both books were very favourably reviewed and appear to represent the height of Duncan's commercial success. In *A voyage of consolation* (London and New York, 1898) the heroine of *An American girl* ventures onto the Continent, and the recently discovered *Two girls on a barge* (London and New York, 1891) chronicles the self-conscious exploits of another unconventional heroine.

Duncan takes her emancipated female protagonist much more seriously in *A daughter of to-day* (London and New York, 1894), a novel that ends with the heroine's suicide. This ambitious work, set in the artist quarters of Paris and London, has admirable scenes but suffers from pretentiousness and an ultimate plunge into melodrama. Duncan's first outstanding literary achievement is *The simple adventures of a memsahib* (London and New York, 1893), an account of a conventional young Englishwoman's entry into Anglo-Indian society as narrated by a sophisticated veteran 'memsahib'. A subtle tragi-comedy, it reveals that in the years since Duncan's first sight of India she had immeasurably deepened her understanding of the Anglo-Indian character. Two very slight works—*Vernon's aunt* (London, 1894; New York, 1895), and a juvenile, *The story of Sonny Sahib* (London, 1894; New York 1895)—were followed by *His Honour, and a lady* (London and New York, 1896), her first serious study of Indian politics. In this very impressive work Duncan interweaves the fates of two women: the emancipated protagonist she so often portrayed and a more conventional heroine. Her considerable powers of social observation are at their best in this novel, which also has a stylistic lightness and grace she was never quite able to recapture. *The path of a star* (American title, *Hilda: a story of Calcutta*; London and New York, 1899), like *A daughter of to-day*, has an artist protagonist—an actress this time—and strongly melodramatic elements. It widens the focus of Duncan's study of Calcutta society, taking in the religious, theatrical, and commercial communities as well as the civil servants; but it is flawed by a ponderous pseudo-Jamesian prose style.

It was not until 1902 that Duncan made North America a major setting for her fiction, in *Those delightful Americans* (1902), a light but entertaining story about a young English matron's discovery of American high society. Duncan's most Canadian novels—*The imperialist* (1904; rpr. 1961) and *Cousin Cinderella; or, A Canadian girl in London* (1908, rpr. 1971)—are also her best. She wrote in a letter that, for patriotic reasons, she was 'trying very hard to make [*The imperialist*] my best book.' It is a witty though balanced and sympathetic portrait of Brantford (called Elgin), a community in which 'nothing compared with religion but politics, and nothing compared with politics but religion' as sources of interest, and where a certain leading citizen was 'no more disposed to an extravagant opinion than to wear one side whisker longer than the other.' Advena Murchison, the novel's passionate, independent, and intellectual heroine, is the finest example of an autobiographical character type Duncan had depicted in several previous novels; the elder Murchisons are affectionate portraits of Duncan's own parents. The narrative ingeniously alternates parallel plots involving severe challenges to idealistic impulses in politics and love. Though Duncan insisted that 'my book offers only a picture of life and opinion, and attempts no argument', the title character's struggle to convert his stubbornly pragmatic fellow-townsmen to the imperialist faith is presented sympathetically. *The imperialist* has been reprinted in the New Canadian Library with an introduction by Claude Bissell. *Cousin Cinderella*, an account of the efforts made by a Canadian brother and sister to gain social recognition for themselves and their country in London, is Duncan's most subtle and accomplished version of the international theme. Like *The imperialist*, it centres on an emerging sense of national consciousness and a struggle against lingering colonialism. As the narrator remarks in *The imperialist*, 'We are here at the making of a nation.'

Duncan's final two Indian novels, *Set in authority* (1906) and *The burnt offering* (1909, rpr. 1979), deal with Imperialism on another front: the challenge to British rule created by the rise of militant Indian nationalism. Both books show increased sympathy towards the Indian character, and venture upon daring interracial subjects, though melodrama prevails in the end. *The consort* (1912, rpr. 1979), about British politics, is far less penetrating than its Canadian and Indian counterparts. Duncan's final novels—*His royal happiness* (1914), *Title clear* (1922), and *The gold cure* (1924)—rework the international theme in uninspired ways. In her final decade Duncan made dogged but sadly unimpressive efforts to become a successful playwright.

Duncan also wrote two autobiographical works. *On the other side of the latch* (American title, *The crow's nest*; 1901) describes, with some evasion but also some sincere emotion, a bout with tuberculosis after Duncan and her husband moved to Simla; it also contains perceptive, often acid, analyses of Simla's social conventions. In a lighter vein the recently discovered *Two in a flat* (1908) contains interesting information about Duncan's sojourns in Kensington. Simla is the setting for 'An impossible ideal', the most impressive work in Duncan's short-story collection, *The pool in the desert* (1903, rpr. 1979). The story's theme is the stultifying effect of a conformist society on the development of an artist.

Among the best articles on *The imperialist* are two in the *Journal of Canadian Studies*: by Michael Peterman (vol. XI, no. 2, 1976) and Clara THOMAS (vol. XII, no. 2, 1977) respectively. Thomas E. Tausky has written the first full-length critical study, *Sara Jeannette Duncan: novelist of empire* (1980), and edited a selection of Duncan's journalism (1978). Marian Fowler's biography, *Redney* (1983), contains important new information and a lively portrait of the author.

THOMAS E. TAUSKY

Dunlop, William 'Tiger'. See NATURE WRITING IN ENGLISH: 1 and Writing in ONTARIO: 1.

Duplessis, Marie-Andrée Regnard. See Writing in NEW FRANCE: 2.

Durkin, Douglas Leader (1884-1968). Raised on a farm in Ontario, he left with his family to homestead in the Swan River area of Manitoba, travelling beyond the railway with a 'prairie schooner' drawn by oxen. After studying philosophy and English at the University of Manitoba (B.A., 1908), he was a high-school principal in Carman, Man., then taught for four years at Brandon College. He was with the English department of the University of Manitoba (1915-22), though on leave of absence from 1920 to 1922, before leaving Canada, probably in 1921, for New York, where Martha OSTENSO joined him. For three years he gave a course on 'The technique of the novel' at Columbia University. It is now thought that the novels published under Ostenso's name were co-authored by Durkin, although *Wild geese* is considered to be primarily Ostenso's work. In 1931 Durkin and Ostenso moved to Gull Lake, Minnesota; they married in 1945 and moved to Seattle in 1963. Writing both under his own name and under the pseudonym Conrad North, Durkin published poetry, novels, short stories,

and serial novels, and co-authored a screenplay.

His novel *The magpie* (1923, rpr. 1974), which can be associated with the tradition of prairie realism, is set in Winnipeg and environs: it opens in July 1919, the year of the Winnipeg General Strike. Its hero, nicknamed 'The magpie', has just returned from fighting in the First World War and has resumed working at the grain exchange, where his honesty is seen as something of an amusing quirk. Characters differ as to whether post-war society should re-establish pre-war conditions or look to new aims. The hero's initial desire for reform abates and then reasserts itself; he is finally driven temporarily to madness when his work and his marriage both fail. Regarded as a valuable depiction of post-First-World-War conditions, *The magpie* contributed to the movement towards realism, particularly urban realism, in Canadian fiction.

Durkin's other novels are *The heart of Cherry McBain* (1919), a sentimental romance set in the Swan River area, and *The Lobstick Trail: a romance of Northern Manitoba* (1921), set in The Pas and environs, in which characters appreciate the land primarily as either a home or for the exploitation of its resources. *Mr. Gumble sits up* (1930) is a novel of black humour in which Mr Gumble awakens to find himself in his coffin and discovers that his fellow villagers, having mistaken him for dead, have settled his accounts and are no longer willing to acknowledge him. He leaves his village, meets a series of weird characters, and has inordinately strange adventures. Durkin also published *The fighting men of Canada* (1918), a collection of poems in which war is seen as marking the threshold of a new era.

For further discussion of *The magpie*, see Peter E. Rider's introduction to the 1974 reprint in the Social History of Canada series, and David Arnason's unpublished Ph.D. thesis, 'The development of prairie realism' (University of New Brunswick, 1980).

JOY KUROPATWA

Dussault, Louisette. See DRAMA IN FRENCH 1948 TO 1981: 4.

E

Eaton, Arthur Wentworth Hamilton (1849-1937). Born in Kentville, N.S., he attended Acadia College, Wolfville, before completing his studies in Massachusetts at Newton Theological Seminary and Harvard University. He was ordained in the Protestant Episcopal Church in 1885 and served a year in parish work in Boston. He then moved to New York, where he was head of the English department at the Cutler School until 1907. After his retirement from teaching, Eaton lived in Boston as a clergyman and littérateur while researching and writing historical accounts of his native province.

Eaton's poetry, with its evocative glimpses of the French and Indian era in Acadian history, first appeared in *Acadian legends and lyrics* (London, 1889) and was reviewed as belonging to a Longfellow tradition. Apart from the historic glamour and musical emphasis of Eaton's verse, it is an independent, not a derivative, creation. The lyrics are simple, sensuous, and frankly nostalgic rather than passionate. A few poems from this first volume reappear in *Acadian ballads and DeSoto's last dream* (1905). The 'ballads' masterfully evoke a full pageant of history, from the earliest times of the French régime to the coming of the Planters, the refugee fleet of John Howe, and the Loyalists; however, they tend to deal with the pictorial surface of powdered wigs and dress swords rather than with how the immigrants felt. Eaton's *Poems of the Christian year* (1905) contains sturdy religious verses remarkable for their restrained yet hopeful feeling, if not for novelty of expression. *The lotus of the Nile and other poems* (1907) completes the early cycle of poetry books and *Acadian ballads and lyrics in many moods* (1930) brought together his best work.

Eaton co-authored with C.L. Betts *Tales of a garrison town* (New York, 1892), a volume of moral and satirical sketches of Halifax society. His best literary effort in later life was his biography, *The famous Mather Byles, the noted Boston Tory preacher, poet and wit, 1707-1788* (1914), a memorable portrait of the elder Byles portrayed against the anxious literary and intellectual background of Revolutionary Boston; it is supplemented with an account of the lives of Byles' children, including Mather Byles the younger, a Loyalist cleric who lived in Halifax and Saint John.

Eaton's *History of King's County, Nova Scotia* (1910) was his most impressive single historical work. It was followed by other studies of eighteenth-century Nova Scotia and the New England origins of its settlers that appeared in periodicals, notably *Americana*, between 1913 and 1915.

KEN MacKINNON

Eccles, W.J. See HISTORICAL WRITING IN ENGLISH: 7.

École littéraire de Montréal. This was a literary society founded in 1895 by Jean CHARBONNEAU and a few young friends who met regularly in each others' homes to read poetry and to discuss their work. They reacted against the patriotic literary fashion in Québec and were inspired by the Parnassian and decadent verse of France and Belgium, examples of which appeared in the 1890s in Montreal journals such as *Le Monde illustré* and *Le Samedi*. Four public meetings were held in the winter of 1898-9, the last two at the Château de Ramezay. The group honoured the sixty-year-old Louis FRÉCHETTE and, also in 1899, public readings by Émile NELLIGAN were acclaimed with wild enthusiasm. Never truly a literary school, the group was split by rivalry after 1900, but survived fitfully until 1925 and even beyond. The École produced a collective publication in 1900, *Les soirées du Château de Ramezay*; a similar volume in 1925; and a periodical, *Le Terroir* (ten numbers in twelve months in 1909-10), which marked a switch to more traditional patriotic themes. The names associated with the second period of activity (1907-12) are those of Jean Charbonneau, who later wrote a history of the École (1935), Albert LABERGE, Charles GILL, and Albert LOZEAU. In the 1920s, when the group's fortunes again revived, Ringuet (Philippe PANNETON), C.-H. GRIGNON, and J.-A. LORANGER appeared as occasional members, testifying to the diversity of this coterie. The discussions, largely literary, occasionally concerned education and science and other more general matters. Although activity was spasmodic and often the École was kept going by as few as three or four members, it did much

École littéraire de Montréal

to stimulate literary activity, to heighten public awareness of literature and, in particular, to promote the poetry of Québec.

C.R.P. MAY

Écrits du Canada français, Les (1954-). Founded in Montreal by a group of writers and intellectuals—including Jean-Louis Gagnon (the acknowledged founder), Claude Hurtubise, Robert ÉLIE, Gilles MARCOTTE, Gerard Pelletier, Paul Toupin, and Pierre Elliott Trudeau—this journal began with a statement of intent specifying that it would be a 'collection d'oeuvres libres', meaning that no particular thematic or critical point of view was sought and that it would encourage the propagation of French-Canadian literature of all genres. It has since published many of the leading novelists, poets, playwrights, and historians of Québec—with occasional reproductions of 'textes anciens' by Louis Riel, Marc Lescarbot, and others. The *Écrits* began as an annual publication; but since 1960 the rate of publication has varied from one to three issues per year (with no publications in the years 1956, 1975, and 1977). Notwithstanding its apparent conservative thrust, it has built a solid intellectual reputation and is the most long-lived journal of its kind in French Canada.

CLAUDETTE S. TRUDEAU

Edel, Leon (b. 1907). The son of immigrant parents, he was born in Pittsburgh, Pennsylvania, and raised in Yorkton, Sask. He attended McGill University where, with A.J.M. SMITH and F.R. SCOTT, he became a founding member of the *McGill Fortnightly Review* (1925-7). He graduated with a B.A. in 1927 and an M.A. in 1928; his thesis, an early study of the experimental novel, discussed the work of Joyce, Woolf, and Henry James, whose unpublished plays were the subject of his D.Litt. thesis at the Sorbonne (1932). In France, Edel sent back to Montreal sparkling 'Montparnasse letters'—redolent of modern music, the new art, and Paris in the spring—that were published in the *Canadian Mercury* (1927-9). During the Depression he worked as a journalist, and from 1936 to 1938, under a Guggenheim Fellowship, edited James's plays in Paris, returning to journalism in New York. Following service overseas in the Psychological Warfare Branch of the American Army, Edel wrote *James Joyce: the last journey* (1947) and, after the death of E.K. BROWN, the second half of Brown's *Willa Cather: a critical biography* (1953). In 1953 he was appointed associate professor at New York University and in 1966 Henry James Professor of English and American Literature. Following his retirement in 1971 he became Citizens' Professor of English at the University of Hawaii. A member of the American Academy of Arts and Letters and a Fellow of the Royal Society of England, Edel has received numerous awards, including the Pulitzer Prize for biography and the National Book Award for non-fiction in 1963.

Edel began his career as Henry James's biographer by editing the primary works: *The complete plays* (1949), *The ghostly tales* (1949), *Selected fiction* (1953), *Selected letters* (1955), *The American essays* (1956), *The complete tales* (1962-5), *The diary of Alice James* (1964) and *The diary of Henry James* (1965). As he edited and introduced the early fiction, separate volumes of his majestic five-volume life of Henry James—described by A.L. Rowse as 'the greatest literary biography of our time'—appeared at intervals: *The untried years* (1953), *The conquest of London* (1962), *The middle years* (1962), *The treacherous years* (1969), and *The master* (1972). Critics were unanimous in their praise of Edel's artistry, his narrative tact and sense of character, and his unobtrusive scholarship. In his use of a fluid time sequence, which attempted to render James's own perception of experience, and in his application of contemporary psychology to the realm of biography, Edel's achievement parallels Joyce's experiments with language and form in the novel: Edel is a major contributor to the reshaping of twentieth century biography. Among his other publications are a pioneer study, *The psychological novel 1900-50* (1955); *Literary biography* (1957), first given as the Alexander Lectures at the University of Toronto (1955-6); *Bloomsbury: a house of lions* (1979); and *Stuff of sleep and dreams: experiments in literary psychology* (1982), which applies psychoanalytic theory to the writings of Thoreau, Joyce, Eliot, and Woolf. In the sixties Edel edited the complete tales of Henry James and the ten-volume Bodley Head Henry James; and in the seventies he edited the selected James letters and the Edmund Wilson papers.

Edel has written a series of occasional essays on members of the Montreal Group of poets (Scott, Smith, Leo KENNEDY, et al.). He wrote a warmly nostalgic introduction to the recollections of a fellow expatriate in the twenties, *Memoirs of Montparnasse* (1970) by John GLASSCO. After Glassco's death, Edel published 'John Glassco (1909-

1981) and his erotic muse' in CANADIAN LIT-ERATURE 93 (Summer 1962). He also wrote an introduction to the reissue of Kennedy's *The shrouding* (1933; rpr. 1975) and contributed papers to conferences honouring A.M. KLEIN (*The Klein symposium*, 1974), Smith ('The worldly muse of A.J.M. Smith', *University of Toronto Quarterly*, Spring 1978), Morley CALLAGHAN (*The Callaghan symposium, 1980*), and Scott (*F.R. Scott: Canadian*, 1983). Following Smith's death, Edel's memorial address, 'Arthur and Jeannie: in memoriam'—read at Michigan State University on 11 Apr. 1981—was published in *The* TAMARACK REVIEW 83/84 (Winter, 1982). Edel is now preparing a book of his Canadian writings.

SANDRA DJWA

Élie, Robert (1915-73). Born in Pointe Saint-Charles, a working-class neighbourhood in Montreal, he was educated at the Collège Saint-Marie and spent one year at the Université de Montréal and at McGill respectively. With Robert CHARBONNEAU, Jean LE MOYNE, and Saint-Denys GARNEAU among others, he was one of the founders in 1934 of the cultural magazine La RELÈVE, writing art criticism for it from 1935 to 1940 and for its successor *La Nouvelle Relève*. He wrote art and drama criticism for Le Canada in 1940-1, and for *La Presse*, then did public-relations work for the CBC before becoming director of L'École des Beaux-Arts in 1958. In the sixties he occupied various government positions related to the arts in both Québec and Ottawa, and was the first cultural attaché for the Delegation générale du Québec in Paris.

Essayist, novelist, and dramatist, Élie has been called 'one of the first complete intellectuals' in Québec letters. As a critic he is best known for his numerous articles on the painter Paul-Émile Borduas and on Saint-Denys Garneau. With Jean Le Moyne he edited both Garneau's *Poésies complète* (1949) and his *Journal* (1954), and wrote the preface to the first.

Élie's best-known novel, *La fin des songes* (1950)—awarded the Prix David and translated into English by Irene Coffin as *Farewell my dreams* (1954)—is a patient examination of solitude and a devoted search for values. It is the story of two school companions, Marcel and Bernard, who in their thirties come to question the authenticity of their values and emotions. The first commits suicide; the second, more combative, draws from the failure of his friend the strength to commit himself to life. The writing is graceful and sensual in conveying the nuances of despair. Still Élie's most popular work, this novel was well received when it appeared. *Il suffit d'un jour* (1957) treats a larger canvas—a village in the process of moving from traditional to modern life, and the pettiness and self-interest that inform people's lives. Elisabeth, the moral centre of the story, is an adolescent who has discovered the need to break with hypocrisy and move courageously towards life. This novel is not as intense as the first and not as carefully dedicated to the analysis of emotion.

Élie's *Oeuvres* (1979) contains two previously unpublished novels, *Les naufragés* and *Elisabeth*, as well as five short stories. Containing also his collected essays and plays, the *Oeuvres* is a valuable document in the history of an important generation in Québec letters.

SHERRY SIMON

Elliot, George. See NOVELS IN ENGLISH 1960 TO 1982: 4.

Emblem Books. Publication of this short-lived series of poetry booklets was begun in Toronto by Jay MACPHERSON in 1954 with her own collection *O earth return* and Daryl HINE's *Five poems* (1955). Although Macpherson's intention had been to publish only these two brief works for private circulation by their authors, she agreed in the spring of 1955 to publish a further booklet by Dorothy LIVESAY. The press's name was inspired by the emblems (originally linocuts by Macpherson, but redrawn for publication by Laurence Hyde) that appeared on the covers of the first two booklets. The Livesay selection, *New poems* (1955), bore a similar design drawn by Hyde and was edited by Milton Wilson.

Although still not interested in becoming a publisher, Macpherson undertook as *ad hoc* projects three more titles in the next few years: Heather Spears' *Asylum poems* (1958), Violet Anderson's *The ledge* (1958), and Dorothy Roberts' *In star and stalk* (1959). Like the earlier titles, each was professionally mimeographed, then hand-assembled by Macpherson. These would have been the final publications in the series had not Macpherson made contact in 1960 with Robert Rosewarne of Ottawa, who owned a manual letterpress and wished to attempt fine literary printing. A brief collaboration resulted in Emblem's two most attractive titles, each containing colour graphics by Rosewarne: Alden NOWLAN's *Wind in a rocky country*

Emblem Books

(1960 [1961]) and Al PURDY's *The blur in between* (1962 [1963]).　　FRANK DAVEY

Emily Montague, The history of. See Frances BROOKE.

Engel, Howard. See MYSTERY AND CRIME.

Engel, Marian (b. 1933). Marian Passmore was born in Toronto but grew up in other Ontario towns—Galt, Sarnia, and Hamilton. She was educated at McMaster and McGill Universities and in 1960 received a Rotary Foundation Scholarship that enabled her to study French literature at Aix-en-Provence, France. She lived for several years in France and in the Levant, where she taught for a while in Cyprus. She returned to Canada in 1964, married Howard Engel, from whom she was later divorced, and has made Toronto her home. She has been very active in the movement to give Canadian writers a collective voice in their relations with publishers and governments and was elected the first chairperson of the WRITERS' UNION.

Of Engel's ten works of fiction, *Adventure at Moon Bay Towers* (1974) and *My name is not Odessa Yarker* (1977) are children's books. *Inside the easter egg* (1975) is a collection of short stories. The remaining seven fictions are novels: *No clouds of glory* (1968), which was reissued in 1974 as *Sara Bastard's notebook; The Honeyman festival* (1970); *Monodromos* (1973), which in 1975 was reissued as *One way street; Joanne* (1975); *Bear* (1976; rpr. 1983) *The glassy sea* (1978); and *Lunatic villas* (1981), published in England as *The year of the child*.

Engel's novels are strongly concerned with the situation of women in society, yet they are not feminist so much as novels reflecting on the human condition from the point of view of women, with a woman in each case as the central character, and often as the narrator. They are simply formed, deftly patterned, and clearly written, and with one exception they are short books. In these respects they resemble much modern French fiction, and there seems no doubt that Engel's studies of French literature have considerably influenced the form of her writing. The economy of structure of which Engel is capable appears at its best in her second novel, *The Honeyman festival*, a brief work of 131 pages in which the unities of time and place are strictly followed, since it

takes place in a single house on a single night; yet through incident and memory it presents the tapestry of the heroine's whole life.

Engel's novels can be seen as a gallery of feminine roles in contemporary Western society. *No clouds of glory*—her most irascible book—presents the woman as academic, challenging men in the career world, but also challenging women who take a more traditionally feminine role. *The Honeyman festival* presents a kind of quintessential earth-mother who has passed through a romantic period as actress and film director's lover to enter—loaded with her memories—maternity and marriage. *Monodromos* is Engel's most elaborate novel in a structural sense, heavily decorated with background detail of life in Cyprus that satisfies one's sociological curiosity rather than one's aesthetic feelings; for this reason it is perhaps the least sharply drawn of all her works. Here the woman is a divorced wife suddenly caught in a spin of insecurity and moving back, through a surrogate sisterhood with her former husband, towards a renewed individuality. *Joanne* is a novel of less substance than the others; originally written in diary form to be read over CBC radio, it concerns the woman as wife and mother finding her way to stability through the ruins of a failing marriage. There are no successful marriages in Engel's world.

Bear, which won a Governor General's Award and gained as well something of a *succès de scandale* for its daring plot of a woman enamoured of a pet bear, is really a fable rather than a novel in the ordinary sense, and presents the woman as a personification of humanity recognizing and uniting with its animal nature. *The glassy sea* presents the woman as nun, re-entering the world and returning with new experience to the life of religious observance and service. If *Bear* shows humanity's need to recognize oneness with the natural world, *The glassy sea* shows how the spiritual life can give meaning to the brutal chaos of existence. It is perhaps Engel's best novel, beautifully concise and exemplary in the way every word tells and adds. The compassion, the lyricism, the resonance of prose that characterize all her novels are here brought together in their most powerful expression. *Lunatic villas* can best be described, in the sense Graham Greene used the word, as an 'entertainment' rather than a novel. The story of the adventures of a haphazardly united family led by a single parent, it is a vacation into farce, whereas Engel's talent is for *la comédie humaine*.

Though Engel has an unusual gift for imaginative and truthful characterization, her prose style, with its excellent simplicity and perfect pitch, may well be her prime virtue as a writer.

See also NOVELS IN ENGLISH 1960 TO 1982: 3.
GEORGE WOODCOCK

Epps, Bernard. See Writing in English in QUÉBEC: 3 and NOVELS IN ENGLISH: OTHER TALENTS, OTHER WORKS: 6(c).

Eskimo literature. See INUIT LITERATURE.

Essays in English. In Canadian literature the informal essay (as opposed to literary CRITICISM and other technical essays) is not merely one of those odds-and-ends of writing that defy categorization elsewhere; it is a genre in its own right that holds a central place. Essayists are to be found in every region of Canada; and since almost all of them began by writing for local newspapers and journals, their works provide an index to the tastes, attitudes, and values of the educated élite in Canada, which they helped to form for their time.

1. In the nineteenth century the informal essay continued the tradition that was already well established in England by such works as the *Table talk* and *Round table essays* of William Hazlitt. The common association of the informal essay with conversation is significant, because its best examples display the same skills as those of the gifted conversationalist: allusions drawn from a mind well furnished with the best that has been thought and said; illustration by anecdote (usually humorous or moral); an acute eye for contemporary events (whether social, political, or economic); and a penchant for recollecting past events and for strong opinions—all expressed with a personal flair that depends largely on spontaneity. Indeed, a number of Canadian essays were speeches that were later committed to print, like Joseph HOWE's *Poems and essays* (Halifax, 1874) edited by Sydenham Howe (rpr. 1973 with an introduction by M.G. Parks).

Because of the genre's highly idiosyncratic nature examples differ widely, depending on the particular interest and emphasis of the writer. Early essayists range from newspaper economists (Barnabas Bidwell, *The prompter*, Kingston, 1821), to Montreal military officers (John H. Willis, *Scraps and sketches; or The album of a literary lounger*, Montreal, 1831), to Newfoundland Anglican ministers (Philip TOCQUE, *Wandering thoughts; or Solitary hours*, London, 1845; and *Kaleidoscope echoes; being historical, philosophical, scientific and theological sketches, from the miscellaneous writing of Philip Tocque, edited by his daughter, Annie S.W. Tocque*, Toronto, 1895). Some, like Tocque and Bidwell, were serious and didactic and paid little attention to literary embellishment. They sought the moral improvement of Canadian society (both men passionately espoused temperance, for example). More typically, others aimed to edify the reader subtly by describing what Willis called 'those occurrences which sometimes jut out from the commonplace . . . One of those luminous specks in the monotonous gloom of existence . . . that shed a brightened glow of sublimity on the purer attributes of our existence.' Willis's prose is highly florid and his romanticism extremely sentimental, yet he maintained that his was 'the romance of reality'. His reflections and melodramatic anecdotes are usually stimulated by a 'ramble' through nature. In Canada, however, this well-established pastime of the Victorian English gentleman began, almost from the outset, to take on new meaning. Not only were local social and historical patterns (*voyageurs*, Canadian military battles and monuments) unlike those of England, but the climate struck such impressive extremes that reflections on Nature began to alter. Not surprisingly, many essays took a specific season (especially winter) as their point of departure, and some collections were arranged so that they concluded at a dramatic point in the yearly cycle. Thus John Fraser in *Canadian pen and ink sketches* (Montreal, 1890) offers among his more patriotic historical reminiscences a series of six 'Summer morning walks' around Montreal; and Alexander Rae Garvie in *Thistledown: miscellanies in prose and verse* (Toronto, 1875) concludes his series of essays with 'Autumnal tints'. Some collections, like Robert Jackson MacGeorge's *Tales, sketches and lyrics* (Toronto, 1895), mixed informal essays with poetry and short stories.

By the end of the nineteenth century two main types of informal essay had emerged, both of which can be traced right back to the contradictory impulses found in Catharine Parr TRAILL's collection of letters, *The BACKWOODS OF CANADA* (London, 1836). One was a conservative inclination to preserve the cultural accomplishments of an educated élite; the other was a gradual and increasingly sympathetic exploration of the natural environment encountered by the immigrants. The first impulse found expression in the 'sketch', characteristic of the British gentry of the time, in which Nature produced sublime moods and elevated thoughts. Essayists such as Fraser and MacGeorge attempted to accomplish in words what the artist conveyed in sketching: a brief, personal impression, conventionally but creatively executed. The structure of these essays tended to reflect the 'disorder' of conversation—like the authors on their walks, they rambled—but they were written by educated men who interspersed lines of poetry, or quoted from Shakespeare, the Bible, or the English Romantic poets where appropriate. The second type of essay was more down to earth, offering what Bidwell called 'the philosophy of common life': proverbial sayings, moral poetry, and homespun wisdom garnered more from experience than from books. Here Nature was a source of information to those who studied her. Plainly didactic, such essays arranged material logically rather than through spontaneous association. Anecdotes tended to be humorous accounts of the doings of ordinary folk, as in Bruce Munro's *Groans and grins of one who survived* (Toronto, 1889).

2. Right up to the middle of the twentieth century the highly civilized 'sketch' continued—the work of men (never women) who gloried in a classical education and were confident that most of the problems of the present could be resolved by applying moral lessons from history and humanist values from literature. Some were decidedly intellectual in approach, following in the tradition set by Howe. The essays in Sir Andrew MACPHAIL's *Essays in Puritanism* (1905), *Essays in politics* (1909), and *Essays in fallacy* (1910), many of which were first published in his UNIVERSITY MAGAZINE, were outstanding examples of the well-informed mind reflecting deeply on such issues as puritanism, the arts, Canada's national duty to England, religion, and women's role in society. With more urbanity, Toronto classics professor Maurice Hutton applied Greek thought to modern life in *Many minds* (1927), *All the rivers run into the sea* (1928), and *The sisters Jest and Earnest* (1930). John Charles Robertson (with *Mixed company*, 1939) and Gilbert Norwood (with *Spoken in jest*, 1938), also classics professors, followed suit. In a lesser way Martin Burrell in *Betwixt heaven and Charing Cross* (1928) and

Crumbs are also bread (1934) extolled the pleasure and virtue of reading; Edmund Broadus in *Saturday and Sunday* (1935) shared Burwell's erudite idealism; and Herbert Leslie Stewart in *From a library window: reflections of a radio commentator* (1940) offered social, historical, political, and philosophical observations.

Perhaps because of his deep attachment to the England he knew as a child, Cecil Francis Lloyd—in *Sunlight and shadow* (1928) and *Malvern essays* (1930)—wrote in a more sentimental and Victorian manner than any of his contemporaries. Others sought to awaken the reader's soul to the eternal verities through descriptive rhapsodies aimed at an elaborate re-creation of mood. A minor essayist in this vein was Arthur John Lockhart, a Canadian expatriate living in Maine, who wrote *The papers of Pastor Felix* (1903). But he was greatly overshadowed by two Maritimers: Archibald MacMECHAN, professor of literature at Dalhousie University, Halifax, and the poet Bliss CARMAN. Both were idealists, and as a result of common assumptions in their classical education they took for granted a coherent world view. MacMechan espoused the absolute values of Christian idealism and negated those of liberal empiricism. He proclaimed his ideas through edifying romantic fantasy in *The porter of Bagdad and other fantasies* (1901), and in reflections on the 'decency principle' of Victorian morality in his miscellaneous collection of essays *The life of the little college* (1914), drawing his ideals from the ethical concerns expressed in mid-Victorian poetry and prose. Carman, however, found no difficulty in accepting liberal empiricism, while finding in Nature a source of inspiration and in Emerson's theory of transcendentalism a compelling version of idealism. His continual search for a philosophic basis for his emotional experiences led him to apply François Delsarte's theories of calisthenics to spiritual ends. It was this odd use of theoretical principles to harmonize the physical and emotional aspects of life, and thereby to achieve mystical heights, that led Stephen LEACOCK to comment: 'The vague and hysterical desire to "uplift" one's self merely for exaltation's sake is about as effective an engine of moral progress as the effort to lift one's self in the air by a terrific hitching up of the breeches' ('The devil and the deep sea: a discussion of modern morality', 1910, in *The social criticism of Stephen Leacock*, 1973, edited by Alan Bowker). Carman presented his theories in numerous books of essays:

The kinship of Nature (1904), *The friendship of art* (1904), *The poetry of life* (1905), *The making of personality* (1908), and *Talks on poetry and life: being a series of lectures delivered before the University of Toronto in December XXV* (1926). Neither MacMechan nor Carman was less idealistic than their intellectual contemporaries; but they considered that the direct Wordsworthian experience of Nature would imprint the soul with the best values. For literary allusions they turned more often to romantic poetry, with its rhythmic mysticism, than to the edifying prose works favoured by other intellectual idealists.

It was inevitable that the mores of a postindustrial society should undermine such a coherent world view, especially since Canada was situated next to the United States, where a utilitarian and materialistic ethic was finding expression in the rising social sciences. Several essayists with a keen eye for contemporary events noted the threat to Victorian idealism and treated it in a variety of ways. One of the first was Goldwin SMITH's secretary, Arnold Haultain (1857-1941), who noted in his *Two country walks in Canada* (1903)—later reprinted as *Of walks and walking tours* (1914)—'The race for success in life is now a scramble. Once the ignoble [uneducated] were handicapped; now all are scratched.' Working for the great continentalist, Haultain was well situated to observe and record, often in detailed statistics, the real state of economic affairs. Nonetheless, Haultain 'in ruminations . . . as rambling as my walk', and with liberal quotations from poetry, sought a ' "Tête-à-tête" with the Infinite', and argued that more reverence should be shown for classical tongues.

Many essayists downplayed these social and economic changes because their experience was rooted directly in nature or in small rural communities. Their essays touched little upon the effects of urban industrialization. Rather they combined the 'jubilee of the soul', found in the florid romantic essayists of the nineteenth century, with observations on 'rural economy' that were also influenced by their predecessors. Outstanding in this early twentieth-century group is William Hume BLAKE, who in *Brown waters* (1915) combined vigorous descriptive passages with homespun philosophy about outdoor life among the *habitants* of the Laurentides. Blake, like Isaak Walton, found in fishing a perfect paradigm for the contemplative man: reverence for created nature, practical wisdom obtained after long and careful observation of it, and a tendency for thought to arise from deep within, like the salmon to the hook. The effect is 'Edenic', as in Frederick Philip's GROVE's mystical encounters with snow in *Over prairie trails* (1922), which describes a sparkling fairyland. But Grove—whose descriptions of the trips he made between Falmouth and Gladstone, Man., are rooted in precise observations—encompassed both rhapsodic and grim experiences of the prairie. In this he was not unlike Blake, for whom nature was no idealized Eden of the nineteenth century. As his title suggests, Blake loved the muddy 'brown waters' more than the shimmering blue. Or, as this preference was expressed by a prolific and popular essayist from the Ontario village of Ekfrid, Peter McARTHUR (author of *In pastures green*, 1915; *The red cow and her friends*, 1919; *The affable stranger*, 1920; *Around home*, 1925; *Familiar fields*, 1925; and *Friendly acres*, 1927): 'I like to keep my feet on the earth—in good Canadian mud—even when indulging the wildest flights of imagination.' McArthur was the first to use the animal anecdote as a vehicle for his 'philosophy of common life'. His essays offer more social observation than Blake's and more humour, and indeed are almost perfectly balanced in their mix of classical allusion, quotations from poetry (some from Canadian poets), and the use of history in recollecting and honouring the efforts of Canadian pioneers. The essays of Newton McTavish are in a similar vein, though somewhat more whimsical and charming: *Thrown in* (1923); later expanded into *Newton McTavish's Canada: selected essays of Newton McTavish* (1963) edited by Ellen Stafford. Two women essayists of this period tended to handle the informal essay personally, emphasizing literary style. For both Nina Jamieson in *The cattle in the stall* (1932) and Emily CARR in *Klee Wyck* (1941), and the collections of sketches that followed, reverence for life and recollections of childhood were central. At the other extreme, in the tradition of earlier historical and political writers like John Fraser, some informal essayists sought primarily to preserve the past through personal recollections of public rather than domestic events. Hector Charlesworth in *Candid chronicles* (1925) and *More candid chronicles* (1928) wrote in a manner that resembled what he called 'vivacious conversation' about politicians and other public figures, deriving his information from recollections of men he knew.

3. The mid-twentieth century marked the

high point of the informal essay. Two world wars and Canada's developing autonomy stimulated a sense of national identity that transcended the regional associations of earlier essayists. Journals that enjoyed national circulation found a wider and roughly homogeneous audience, united at least by their hopes for Canada. This new perspective was anticipated as early as the mid-twenties by William Arthur DEACON in *Pens and pirates* (1923) and *Poteen* (1926), and by B.K. Sandwell (1876-1954) in *The privacity agent and other modest proposals* (1928) and *The diversions of Duchesstown and other essays* (published posthumously, 1955). Both men had found an outlet for their informal essays in *Saturday Night*, Toronto, where Deacon was editor from 1922 to 1928 and Sandwell from 1932 to 1951. Although they occasionally wrote skittishly, like Leacock, their pieces were informed by the seriousness of defining Canada's identity, assessing the nation's cultural achievements, and stimulating national prowess. On the whole such essays tended to look back nostalgically on 'the good old days', preferring the way things were—when intimate small communities rather than large metropolitan centres were dominant—to the way things are. Sandwell pinpointed this as a recurring strain when he wrote that *'laudator temporis acti'*. 'Things are not what they were' was an enduring aspect of the informal essay. A similar nostalgia informs *Leaves from Lantern Lane* (1936) and *More leaves from Lantern Lane* (1937) by the liberal Christian feminist Nellie McCLUNG. These collections contain the best of her syndicated newspaper pieces: anecdotes, sketches, and reflections—often humorous and usually moral—on a wide range of topics drawn from ordinary life in the tradition of Bruce Munro (see 1 above).

Four essayists who brought out their first collections near the end of the 1950s, and continued to publish for several years afterwards, wrote in the best tradition of the informal essay. Two of them, Robertson DAVIES and Hugh MacLENNAN, practised their craft as intellectuals and humanists. The other two, Roderick HAIG-BROWN and Kenneth McNeil WELLS, continued the more rural tradition through social observation and the cultivation of a close relationship to nature. For his columns in the *Peterborough Examiner* Davies developed a curmudgeonly narrator, Samuel Marchbanks, whose social observations reflected a concern for the arts, a distaste for the bourgeois predilections of Canadians, a belief in

humanist ideals, and an insatiable interest in eclectic literacy and philosophical works. Davies collected the best of these humorous columns in *The diary of Samuel Marchbanks* (1947), *The table talk of Samuel Marchbanks* (1949), and *Marchbanks' almanac* (1967). On a more serious level Davies addressed his essays in *A voice from the attic* (1961) to the 'clerisy', by which he meant those who enjoy reading books.

Hugh MacLennan, in a wide range of essays collected from the many journalistic pieces he wrote for American and Canadian publications, chiefly *The Montrealer*, drew on his classical education for standards and attitudes that echoed those of earlier classicists like MacMechan and Hutton. But despite his idealism, MacLennan was no ivory-tower theorist. Political and social observation on a national scale were combined with a wry wit and a deep appreciation of nature to produce essays that 'rambled' towards philosophical, aesthetic, or nationalistic conclusions in *Cross-country* (1949), *Thirty and three* (1954)—both winners of a Governor General's Award—*Scotchman's return* (1961), and *The other side of Hugh MacLennan* (1978). Whereas Davies followed in the path of Leacock and Sandwell, MacLennan amplified and refined the approach of Deacon. Both essayists espoused humanist values in what they observed to be an increasingly materialistic world, and defended traditional modes of education as a means of perpetuating sound values. Similarly, the Scottish immigrant J.B. McGeachy, in *A touch of McGeachy* (1962), combined classical humanism with independent social and political observation in essays for the *The Financial Post*, and William T. Allison amused himself in his time off from teaching by writing human-interest editorials for the *Winnipeg Herald Tribune*, where he was literary editor for more than twenty years. His essays were collected in *This for remembrance* (published posthumously, 1949).

Roderick Haig-Brown—a naturalist who settled a farm at Campbell River, Vancouver Island, B.C., and later became a magistrate and judge of the juvenile court there—developed the 'Edenic' tradition of Blake. For Haig-Brown, too, fishing was a passion that transcended its practical purpose in *Fisherman's spring* (1951) and *Fisherman's summer* (1959). His first collection of essays, *The measure of the year* (1950), has as its goal the close observation of the seasonal cycle to 'take the measure of each year' and thereby acquire a deeper wisdom than that of any city-dweller. His profound rapport with nature, however, did not induce him to reject books, for reading as a pastime, once the days' chores are done, enhances man's grasp of life's purpose and meaning. But it is nature's patterns that most inform man, and Haig-Brown, like McArthur, uses animal anecdotes to illustrate the supremacy of instinct over mere book-learning.

The animal anecdote and the down-to-earth philosophy of common life is best illustrated by Kenneth Wells' popular Medonte essays: *The owl pen* (1947), *By Moonstone Creek* (1949), *Up Mendonte way* (1951), and *By Jumping Cat Bridge* (1956). His often-humorous accounts of 'pioneering' in an explicitly 'Edenic' setting extol folk wisdom at the expense of modern science. Wells undercuts the potential sentimentality of his anecdotes and descriptions with a sharp eye for realistic detail.

4. Shifts in political, social, and moral values, as well as developments away from the traditional classical education that had nurtured earlier essayists, spawned a new breed of informal essayist in the 1960s. Kildare DOBBS, in the preface to his second collection *Reading the time* (1968), expresses this intellectual and cultural shift. Culture, he maintains, is no longer a 'fixed body of experience passed on from generation to generation'; hence there can be no fixed point of view. The common body of knowledge has become so vast that no one mind can encompass it. In addition, contemporary man is a 'nomad' moving literally or figuratively through a world he can never comprehensively interpret. 'I am like a man running for a trolley-car,' Dobbs says, trying to make a pattern out of the blur of sense impressions that bombard him. Hence the essayist is qualified to 'read the time' not by his well-stocked mind, but by his admission of ignorance. The resulting tone is deeply ironic. Dobbs' earlier collection, *Running to paradise* (1962), which received a Governor General's Award, consists of reminiscences of an uprooted, alienated, and cosmopolitan life.

The political and cultural observations in Robert FULFORD's *Crisis at the Victory Burlesk* (1968) reflect an equally ironic view of the modern world. Fulford experiments technically, using a notebook style or fractured sentences to reflect his sense that the decorum of the gentlemanly essay must somehow adjust to mirror the disintegration of a coherent world view. Pithy and insightful, his pieces include much material that would earlier have been thought inappropriate for this genre: for example, Pop art, strippers, and moonshots as viewed on television. In fact, like the classical humanists and the 'Edenic' essayists who preceded him, Fulford expresses deep misgivings about the advancements of technology and science. Like Deacon and MacLennan, he turns to a nurturing of the indigenous arts as an antidote. The fracturing of one view into many is actually dramatized by the minor essayist Harry Bruce (b. 1934), whose Hyde-like persona, Max MacPherson, contemplates Toronto in a sequence of 'walks' (*The short, happy walks of Max MacPherson*, 1968) that seem like parodies of the 'rambles' of the nineteenth century essayists.

That superlative ironist Mordecai RICHLER wrote his informal essays (*Hunting tigers under glass*, 1968; *Shovelling trouble*, 1972; *Notes on an endangered species and others*, 1974; and *The great comic book heroes and other essays*, 1978) to goad his fellow-Canadians out of materialistic complacency and into thoughtful, creative living. Like Fulford, he included studies of the sub-culture (comic books, movies, and James Bond thrillers) as worthy of philosophical reflection. The essays of Naim KATTAN in *Reality and theatre* (1972), translated by Alan Brown, are cosmopolitan like Richler's, but uniquely so. The sense of alienation that results in irony for Dobbs, Fulford, Bruce, and Richler is exaggerated in Kattan because of an extraordinary cosmopolitan upbringing—part Arab, part Jewish—that allows him to express profound irony through personal reflection. Like the more intellectual essayists who preceded him, Kattan draws on an impressive background of reading and tries to place himself not simply in nature but in more than one perception of Nature.

The appeal of, and the readership for, the informal essay—especially the rural 'Edenic' type—has been greatly reduced by increasing materialism, urbanization, mobility, and pluralism. The essayist needs the sense of an audience with a background and ideas like his own. Nonetheless the predominant characteristics of the genre—its flexibility, and the freedom it offers for idiosyncratic expression—may very well ensure its continuance.

See also HISTORICAL WRITING IN ENGLISH: 5.

ELSPETH CAMERON

Essays in French. At each stage in its history French-Canadian writing has produced spokesmen who have attempted to characterize the spirit of the nation. Priests from CASGRAIN to GROULX, historians from F.-X. GARNEAU to Michel Brunet, politicians from Papineau to René Lévesque, poets from FRÉCHETTE to CHAMBERLAND, journalists from Parent to Laurendeau, literary critics from James Huston to Jacques GODBOUT, have sought to articulate the experience of being French in North America. Each in his own way, and through his own specialism, has expressed a Québécois vision of the world—inevitably coloured by personality, and by religious and political persuasion. Alongside this tradition occasional sharp-shooters have sniped at the consensus: Arthur Buies, Olivar Asselin, François Hertel (Rodolphe DUBÉ), Paul-Émile Borduas, Gilles LeClerc, Jean-Paul Desbiens, Pierre Vallières, and Jacques FERRON. Yet another spirit has permitted rare individuals to adopt a detached, serene viewpoint, giving us the powerful reflections of Abraham-Edmond de Nevers, Félix-Antoine SAVARD, Ernest Gagnon, Fernand DUMONT, Pierre VADEBONCOEUR, Jacques BRAULT, Fernand OUELLETTE, and Jean Bouthillette.

1. SALVAGING THE PAST. James Huston (1820-54), in the preface to his *Répertoire national* (1848), wrote the first essay on the nature and function of literature in Québec, sympathizing eloquently with those who sought to publish poetry or essays in the teeth of only a scattering of critical comment, a total lack of outlets for creative writing, and many discouragements. Henri-Raymond CASGRAIN stamped Québec culture with the patriotic, messianic character it would conserve for a century; but he was the first to give his essays and travelogues a personal voice and an individual ring. See his *Oeuvres complètes* (4 vols, 3rd ed, 1895-6).

2. THE PRESS AS NATIONAL VOICE. In his short-lived anti-clerical journal *La Lanterne* (1868-9), Arthur Buies (1840-1901) inveighed against censorship and obscurantism in Québec in limpid, caustic prose that he had learned as a journalist in Paris. His later essays were collected in *Chroniques: humeurs et caprices* (Québec, 1873), reprinted as *Chroniques: voyages etc* (Québec, 1875); *Petites chroniques pour 1877* (Québec, 1878); and *Chroniques canadiennes: humeurs et caprices* (Québec, 1884)—in which Buies sang his ardent love of science and literature and described Canada with poetry and precision. His writing is informed by a vision of freedom and intelligence, a model of humanity that he never tired of propounding. Nine-

teenth-century prose is made impersonal and, with the exception of the writings of Buies, is short on specifics because of its didacticism, euphemization, and moralizing. This is true of the essays and sermons of Bishop Ignance Bourget (1799-1885), published in *Fioretti viscovili* (Montréal, 1872); of Bishop Louis-François Laflèche (1818-98), anthologized in the *Classiques canadiens* series (1970); and of Jules-Paul Tardivel (1851-1905), the Kentucky-born author of POUR LA PATRIE and an ardent convert to Québec patriotism. His writings are anthologized in *Classiques canadiens* (1969). Grandiose rhetoric and moral abstractions prevented these writers from ever indulging in confidences or entertaining doubts. Though Abraham-Edmond de Nevers (Edmond Boisvert) left Québec for Paris, he made in his *L'avenir du peuple canadien-français* (Paris, 1896) a plea for the arts, the sciences, and a modern industrial economy.

At the beginning of the twentieth century good journalism set the pace. Henri Bourassa (1868-1952) in *Le Devoir*, Olivar Asselin (1874-1937) with *Le Nationaliste*, and Jules Fournier (1884-1918), who founded *L'Action* in 1911, set new standards and engaged in impassioned polemical exchanges. Bourassa orchestrated an anti-Empire, nationalist opposition to Wilfrid Laurier, while Asselin took a balanced view of the conscription crisis of 1917. Fournier, who died of Spanish influenza at thirty-four, was described by Asselin as 'one of the sharpest minds and the noblest hearts French Canada has ever known.' His essays were collected in *Mon encrier* (2 vols, 1922; rpr. 1965), but he also left his acerbic *Souvenirs de prison* (*Écrits du Canada français*, VII), written after a spell in jail for libelling Lomer Gouin.

3. THE AGE OF DEBATE. While writers like Adjutor Rivard (1868-1945), in slightly syrupy sketches of country life—*Chez nous* (1914) and *Chez nos gens* (1918), combined in *Chez nous* (1919)—were perpetuating Canada's regionalist tradition, a spirited national debate was proceeding on the French language in Canada and on the nature and existence of French-Canadian literature. (Fournier and Asselin had found few signs of a true French-Canadian culture worthy of the name.) Louis Dantin (Eugène SEERS) argued convincingly, and with admirable objectivity, the prodigious talent of his tragic young friend Émile NELLIGAN in the edition he edited of Nelligan's poems. Marcel DUGAS wrote equally judicious literary criticism—notably in *Un romantique canadien:*

Louis Fréchette, 1839-1908 (Paris, 1934; Montreal, 1946). Dugas also wrote brief, delicate prose-poems—exquisite essays to which he gave the title *Flacons à la mer* (1923). The language debate was carried on by Henri Bourassa, Jules-Paul Tardivel, Adjutor Rivard, and Lionel GROULX, while Albert Pelletier and Victor Barbeau, in essays of great force and perception that bring the two themes of language and literature together, lift the discussion to a high plane. The debate can be followed in *Le choc des langues au Québec, 1760-1970* (1972), compiled by G. Bouthillier and J. Meynaud, where the principal texts are anthologized.

The intellectual life of French Canada was also enormously enhanced by the progress made in the 1920s by men of science. Frère MARIE-VICTORIN, a botanist and member of the Teaching Brothers, wrote charming vignettes of life in the Laurentians in his *Croquis laurentiens* (1920), translated by James Ferrer as *The chopping bee and other Laurentian stories* (1925). Filled with minute observation and prodigious knowledge, they are suffused with Christian mysticism. In 1920 the Université de Montréal became autonomous, and the first secretary and director of its Social Science School, Edouard Montpetit (1881-1955), has left *Souvenirs* (1944), which encapsulates his philosophy of life. Inspired by Barrès, he celebrates the value to the nation of village and river 'poeticized by toil'. He defends the French language, linchpin of French-Canadian resistance and a bulwark for all Canadians against a certain mindless Americanization.

Having basically humanist intentions, all these writers deserve to be mentioned here because they contributed to the refinement of the definition of the Québécois identity, 'a human type incarnate' (Groulx) in the face of the challenge from Ottawa or from the rest of North American culture.

4. THE ANXIOUS THIRTIES. An upsurge of nationalist feeling in the 1930s responded to the growing encroachment of American capital in Canada. François Hertel (Rodolphe DUBÉ) summed up the mood of the time in *Leur inquiétude* (1936)—inspired by *Notre inquiétude* of Daniel-Rops—which with heavy erudition traces the history of philosophical anxiety. Hertel sees Barrès, Mauriac, and Gide as the recent analysts of this state of mind and lists compassionately the causes of mental disarray among young Catholics in French Canada: the dehumanizing influence of the machine age; Americanization, particularly through the growing importance of money; the economic inferiority of Québec within Confederation; the fears of the francophone minorities outside Québec; the arid ritualistic character of Québec Catholicism; and the anguish peculiar to young French Canadians politically alienated within their own province. He looks to a renewed Catholic spirituality, along the lines advocated by Jacques Maritain, to counter the demoralization of young French Canadians. Jean LE MOYNE, friend of the poet Saint-Denys GARNEAU, shares his heightened spirituality while also mirroring the climate of the time in the memorable essays collected in *Convergences* (1961). Another notable writer of the 1930s, Félix-Antoine SAVARD, published his reflections in *Journal et souvenirs* (2 vols, 1973, 1975) and *Carnet du soir intérieur* (2 vols, 1978, 1979). His political testament (*Le Devoir*, 6, 1, 1978, p. 5) reads very much like the writing of Hertel over forty years earlier: this essay has the same mixture of anxiety and hope, though Savard comes down firmly in favour of reconciliation within a federal framework.

5. CUTTING THE CORD. Pierre VADEBONCOEUR—in his vital essay on independence of mind in Québec, *La ligne du risque* (1963)—saw no evidence of real originality in Québec, no real 'sages inquiétants'. The one exception he admits to is Paul-Émile Borduas (1905-1960). REFUS GLOBAL (1948), largely the work of Borduas, is a pitiless history of the fear, anguish, and servility that maintained the spiritual and intellectual blockade of Québec; it called for the release of psychic energy through a new openness to the transcendent forces of modern art. In his other writings—edited by Guy ROBERT in *Borduas* (1972)—Borduas describes his teaching methods and the gradual ostracism that his originality cost him. Pierre Baillargeon (1916-67) shares Borduas's ruthless independence of thought in *Le scandale est nécéssaire* (1962), which is spiced with wicked humour. Believing that the scandal of Québec was that Québécois had been damned for non-use of their intelligence, he looked to the prestigious culture of France for salvation. Gilles Leclerc swears by Pascal and Spengler in his brilliant and massive critique of Québécois obscurantism entitled *Journal d'un inquisiteur* (1960; 1974). If these twelve chapters—written in an abstract, highly metaphorical, and aphoristic prose— were more concise and more analytical, and had clearer emphases, they would comprise the most impressive series of essays written

in Québec. The *Journal* is a painful critique of the oppression by a hierarchical power, with a monopoly on thought and expression, of a conquered people who have never seen any other solution than patience. The argument is punctuated with refrains that epitomize Leclerc's thought, such as 'la société québécoise manque de contradicteurs'. Leclerc would not give much for the chances of Socrates, Jesus, or Dante had they been born in his province. Other sardonic moralists, who are not common in Québec, are Félix LECLERC, author of *Le Calepin d'un flâneur* (1961), and Jean SIMARD, whose *Répertoire* (1961) and *Nouveau répertoire* (1965) draw on European moralists, on Simard's experience of small-town parochialism, and on his life as an art teacher.

In an issue of *Études littéraires*—vol. 5, no. 1 (1972) devoted to the essay—Robert Vigneault traces what he calls 'la naissance d'une pensée' in the Québec essay in recent years. Drawing on the writings of men like Jean LE MOYNE, Ernest Gagnon, Pierre TROTTIER, and Pierre Vadeboncoeur, he illustrates the way in which Québec thought, and particularly the French-Canadian's reflections on his own personality expressed in his culture, has gradually freed itself from the grips of stifling orthodoxy. The effort this liberation called for can, incidentally, be felt as it betrays itself in the tetchiness and bitter humour of men like Jean Simard and Jean Le Moyne. This emancipation can be traced back to the intellectual vandalism of the 'école automatiste' and the breath of fresh air introduced by the writings of Borduas.

In *L'homme d'ici* (1963), containing influential essays of the 1950s, Father Ernest Gagnon (1905-78) combined insights derived from the teaching of the Church and his experience as an anthropologist. Pierre-Elliott Trudeau's collection of essays, *Le fédéralisme et la société canadienne-française* (1967)—published in English as *Federalism and the French Canadians* (1968)—shows him and his fellow contributors to *Cité libre* taking up the struggle of intellectual emancipation in the 1950s. Pierre Vadeboncoeur, one of the team that founded *Cité libre* in 1950, shares the independence of mind and the passionate objectivity of his fellow writers. The path he followed, of radical socialist thought and militant trade unionism, from the days of opposition to Maurice Duplessis to public support for the principles and objectives of the Parti Québécois, can be clearly traced in his collections of essays: *La

ligne du risque* (1963; 1969), *L'autorité du peuple* (1965), *Lettres et colères* (1969), *La dernière heure et la première* (1970), *Indépendances* (1972), *Un génocide en douce* (1976), *Chaque jour, l'indépendance* (1978) and—the most eloquent of all—*Les deux royaumes* (1978), which contemplates with the clear vision of a child and the sombre realism of advancing years the prospect of a despiritualized world.

6. BROADENING THE MIND. Other writers of the 1960s who made an important contribution to the essay were Fernand DUMONT, Jacques Grand'maison, Pierre TROTTIER, André Laurendeau, and Gaston MIRON. Dumont offers us calm and lucid reflections on rapid cultural change in his native province in impressive essays contained in *Le lieu de l'homme* (1968) and *La vigile du Québec* (1971). *Une foi ensouchée dans ce pays* (1979), the latest work of Jacques Grand'maison, is the meditation of a priest on Christian commitment to direct political action—as a parliamentary candidate. It is a complete reversal of the author's previous position and a departure from his more specifically theological writing. Pierre Trottier, a career diplomat who spent many years in posts abroad, presents himself as an Oedipus returned from exile in *Mon Babel* (1963) and *Un pays baroque* (1979). With elegant clarity and playful detachment he explores, through the medium of universal myth, Québec's spiritual odyssey and his own. One of French Canada's chief spokesmen and intellectual leaders was André Laurendeau (1912-68), whose life of action as editor of *L'Action nationale* in the 1930s, leader of the 'bloc populaire' in the 1940s, editor of *Le Devoir* in the 1950s, and co-chairman of the Royal Commission on Bilingualism and Biculturalism, gave his writings a sense of urgency and realism. All his moods—from biting sarcasm and polemical anger to serene meditation—can be caught in *Ces choses qui nous arrivent: chronique des années 1961-1966* (1970)—a selection, prefaced by Fernand Dumont, of the editorials Laurendeau wrote for *Le Magazine Maclean*. Gaston Miron's *L'homme rapaillé* (1970) contains essays of 1957 to 1965—eloquent statements of his commitment to poetry as social therapy and a sharp analysis of Québec's triple alienation: economic, political, and psychological.

Naim KATTAN's reflections on art, politics, language, and religion in *Le réel et le théâtral* (1970)—translated by Alan Brown as *Reality and theatre* (1972)—contrast his native

Iraq with Western civilization and values. Jean ÉTHIER-BLAIS—principally a literary critic and university teacher who has published poetry, short stories, and a novel—contributed for many years a regular personal essay to *Le Devoir* and produced a *Dictionnaire de moi-même* (1976), a series of intimate moral reflections in the pure *belles-lettres* tradition—reflections provoked by words such as *amour, bonheur, désir*, and *exil*. Louis-Marcel Raymond gave us, just before his death, his much-admired *Géographies* (1971), containing memories of youth and portraits of friends mingled with descriptive writing. Gérard Robitaille, an expatriate painter living in Paris, describes his quest for self in *Un Huron à la recherche de l'art* (1967); it contains an enthusiastic preface by Henry Miller, to whom he once acted as secretary. A few months spent in France in 1962 were decisive in the development of Pierre Vallières, author of *Nègres blancs d'Amérique* (1968)—translated by Joan Pinkham as *White niggers of America* (1971). Half autobiography and half political pamphlet, this influential book offers glowing portraits of Vallière's friends Jacques FERRON, Gaston Miron, and Charles Gagnon; a graphic description of 'la petite misère' in Québec; and develops the 'colonial' explanation of Québec's underdevelopment. Vallières's later essay, *L'urgence de choisir* (1971)—translated by Penelope Williams as *Choose!* (1972)—shows the former extremist re-evaluating political violence and opting for the democratic process and the program of the Parti Québécois.

7. THE ANGUISH OF LUCIDITY. The Québec essay finds its culmination in writing of fearsome intelligence and clarity published since 1968. Almost without exception the essayists of the 1970s-80s write out of an 'indicible malaise' (Bouthillette), 'silence and anguish' (Brault), 'a sense of shame, servitude and danger' (Chamberland). To write in our time, says Fernand Ouellette, means: 'ne pas détourner la tête d'un temps invivable'. *Point de fuite* (1971) and *Blocs erratiques* (1977) are collections of texts broadcast by Hubert AQUIN or published in journals, principally *Quartier latin* and LIBERTÉ. *Blocs erratiques*, overshadowed by Aquin's suicide, underlines the sense of headlong flight, or vertigo, of a taste for nothingness. The Aquin who is familiar from his novels—brilliant, witty, enigmatic, the most frighteningly clever of Québec's writers—appears in 'Essai crucimorphe': Montreal's Place Ville-Marie, a 42-storey com-

mercial complex with a cruciform plan, becomes a symbol of the ambiguities, the humiliating palliatives, the non-being of Québec's colonial status. Aquin's most important essay in *Blocs érratiques*, however, is his long reply to Pierre Trudeau: 'La fatigue culturelle du Canada français', a reasoned defence of a tenable nationalist stance.

Disturbingly lucid too is Jean Bouthillette's concise, incisive *Le Canadien français et son double* (1972). French Canadians, he finds, are at every turn on the losing side in the history of Canadian duality; though he concludes by pointing to the French-Canadian instinct for freedom. Bouthillette's essay is a triptych: the first two phases are profoundly negative—demonstrating how prolonged denial of identity destroys the personality and leads to the destruction of self-respect, the internalizing of shame and self-disgust; but the third phase demonstrates the eventual desperate affirmation of hope and freedom.

Jacques BRAULT's collected essays are reprinted with valuable marginal comments in *Chemin faisant* (1975), in which studies of his favourite poets (for example his excellent 'MIRON le magnifique'), essays on criticism, poetry, politics, literature, and language in Québec, and on 'le délire innommable' of Oct. 1970, appear between short personal statements expressing his open-ended commitment to the process of writing and rewriting himself. *Le réformiste* (1975) is a collection of essays by Jacques GODBOUT, who expresses his commitment to peaceful change, to the power of literature and the democratic process to transform society, while also warning that the euphoria in Québec in the 1960s, and the Québécois's sense of 'Notre libération' (the best of the essays), may be nothing more than pipe-dreams. Jacques FERRON is one of the father-figures and 'maîtres à penser' of contemporary Québec. Tirelessly—in book reviews, letters to the press, and newspaper articles—he continues to make his benign and original presence felt. *Du fond de mon arrière-cuisine* (1973) and *Escarmouches* (2 vols, 1975) contain the best of Ferron's ephemera. His genial erudition, his memory for the fine detail of recent history (his and other people's), his eye for the significance of the apparently trivial, give his texts their specificity; their tone is princely, full of spice and mischief. Ferron tries to put the record straight in the fields of medicine, culture, and public affairs, and we excuse him his injustices, so charmed are we by the way he thinks as well as by the way he writes.

The last two essayists are poets whose prose is charged with mystery and grandeur. Paul CHAMBERLAND identifies with 'Terre Québec'—with its anger, despair and bitterness, its determination and its hope— though few of his newspaper essays have been republished. In *Terre souveraine* (1980) he develops the 1960s notion of 'appartenance' (belonging) and asks how the Québec community can be given reality. Though Chamberland is under no illusions about the precariousness of Québec's future, nor about the size of the opposition, seen chiefly as a capitalist conspiracy and the power of the trans-nationals, he believes in the possibility of a Utopia—a revitalized democracy, a parish without priests—in which the soul-power of the individual can be mobilized to realize the community's true potential. Chamberland's Utopianism is all the more admirable when one considers the traumas he suffered, chronicled in *Éclats de la pierre noire d'où jaillit ma vie* (1972).

Fernand OUELLETTE relates a similar oscillation between despair and Utopia—or between ecstasy and gloom—in *Les actes retrouvés* (1970). Here, with an impressive blend of self-awareness and intuition, he retraces the steps by which he discovered himself through poetry, and in the process revealed his compatriots to themselves. This collection of essays contains the oft-quoted 'La dualité des langues', in which Ouellette describes the painful discovery of his linguistic impoverishment caused by his belonging to a bilingual culture. Three other such volumes followed: *Depuis Novalis* (1973), *Journal dénoué* (Prix de la revue *Études françaises*, 1974), and *Écrire en notre temps* (1979). The latter contains 'Divagations sur l'essaie', a groping definition of the essayist as 'un être de la divagation et de l'espace ludique' in which the freedom of the essay makes accessible surprising and luminous insights.

The modern Québec essay is creative, serious, and exploratory—though frequently dogmatic and ideological. Often abstract and highly conceptual, impassioned and lyrical, it is also frequently exciting, offering, at its best, words of destiny.

C.R.P. MAY

Estuaire. See LITERARY MAGAZINES IN QUÉBEC: 4.

Éthier-Blais, Jean (b. 1925). Born in Sudbury, Ont., he studied literature at the Un-

iversité de Montréal from 1946 to 1948. He then took courses at the École normale supérieure and the École pratique des hautes études in Paris. After receving an Adenauer scholarship, he spent a year in Munich. From 1953 to1960 he held a post at the Canadian embassy in Paris and then in Warsaw. In 1960 he was appointed professor of French literature at Carleton University. Two years later he went to McGill University, where he still teaches.

Since 1961 Éthier-Blais has regularly contributed articles to the literary section of *Le Devoir*. Many of his elegantly styled and interesting chronicles, in which he freely expresses his views on both French and French-Canadian literature, on the arts and humanities in general, and on politics, have been reprinted in three volumes entitled *Signets* (2 vols 1967; 1 vol. 1973). On 7 April 1965 he gave an important lecture on the works of Paul MORIN, Marcel DUGAS and François Hertel (Rodolphe DUBÉ) that was published in 1969 as *Exils*. It is informative not only about those writers but also about Éthier-Blais himself, who has much in common with them. *Dictionnaire de moi-même* (1976) tells more about himself and his tastes and dislikes. He became a member of the French-Canadian Academy in 1971. In his inaugural address, published in 1973 with Olivar Asselin's *L'oeuvre de l'abbé Groulx*, he paid a moving tribute to Father Lionel GROULX, whose disciple he was proud to be. Keenly interested in Paul-Émile Borduas, the subject of his Ph.D. thesis (Laval, 1971), he has written on Borduas and his group in *Ozias Leduc et Paul-Émile Borduas* (with François Gagnon and Georges-André Vachon, 1973) and *Autour de Borduas* (1977).

Éthier-Blais has written two novels: *Mater Europa* (1968) and *Les pays étrangers* (1982), which recreates the life of certain Montreal intellectual circles in 1947-8. *Le manteau de Ruben Dario* (1974) is made up of three graceful short stories. His collections of poems are *Asies* (1969) and *Petits poèmes presque en prose* (1978), in which the dominant themes are departure, memories, and times past.

Éthier-Blais is one of Quebec's most cultured and well-read *hommes de lettres*. Literature is his life, and his knowledge encompasses the world. His roots seem to be mostly in France, however, and in that respect he bears witness sometimes to a search for identity that has been experienced by many of Québec's writers and intellectuals.

Though his style may seem slightly affected and even pedantic to some readers, he is nevertheless one of the best francophone writers outside France. Whether one agrees or disagrees with his views and judgements, they leave no one indifferent.

JACQUES COTNAM

Evangeline: a tale of Acadie (1847). This lengthy narrative poem by Henry Wadsworth Longfellow is based on a tale of hearsay (which the poet heard from a friend of Hawthorne, who had it from an Acadian woman), told against the historical background of the British expulsion in 1755 of the French-speaking Acadians from their lands along the shores of the Bay of Fundy—*le grand dérangement* (as the Acadians still call it), which had to do with the end of a 150-year struggle between France and England for possession of what is now Nova Scotia. *Evangeline* tells the story of an Acadian girl who is separated from her betrothed at the time of the expulsion and wanders in search of him throughout the American Midwest and the Atlantic states, only to find him years later on his deathbed. After he dies in her arms, Evangeline too dies, released from a life of exile and steadfast loyalty that has received no reward on earth. For background Longfellow drew on the work of the French historian and encyclopedist, the Abbé Raynal, and on Thomas Chandler HALIBURTON's *An historical and statistical account of Nova Scotia* (Halifax, 1829). In his choice of hexameters, and in the characterization of his heroine, Longfellow was influenced by Goethe's *Hermann und Dorothea* (1797), a heartfelt depiction of a young woman's expulsion from her native soil. One of the most famous works in the English language, *Evangeline* appeared in some 270 editions and 130 translations between 1847 and 1947, including a notable translation into French by Pamphile LEMAY (Québec, 1865). FRANCIS ZICHY

Evanturel, Eudore. See POETRY IN FRENCH: 2.

Evans, Allen Roy (1885-1965) Born in Napanee, Ont., he grew up on a Manitoba farm, received a B.A. from the University of Manitoba and an M.A. from the University of Chicago, and did further graduate work at Columbia. Evans taught English in British Columbia high schools and by 1937 had organized an advisory and marketing service for writers in Vancouver. In addition to writing short stories for Canadian, American, and British magazines, he published one slim volume of poetry and four novels.

Bitter-sweet (1933) is a series of prosaic narrative and expository poems about commonplace misfortunes, revealing Evans as a competent versifier with a bitter but sentimental concern for the wronged and underprivileged. *Reindeer trek* (1935), a fictionalized account of the drive (1929-34) of 3,000 Russian reindeer from Alaska to the Mackenzie delta, effectively sustains the suspense of a journey into the unknown, though characterization is slight and incidents often implausible. It enjoyed wide popularity both in England as *Meat: a tale of the reindeer trek (1929-1935)* (1935) and when translated into several European languages. *All in a twilight* (1944) is a psychological novel of pioneering narrated from the points of view of a prairie farmer and his wife, an eastern school teacher. In presenting the human costs of pioneer success, Evans carries on the realism of Frederick Philip GROVE, but without the same depth or intensity. In *Northward Ho!* (1947) a young delinquent is brought painfully but swiftly to maturity by the hardships of helping to build the Alaska Highway. The novel is weakened by the contrived resolution of obvious moral conflicts and by the author's evident lack of familiarity with his setting. *Dream out of dust: a tale of the Canadian Prairies* (1956) is a clear, cold account of a twenty-seven-year domestic war between a tyrannical prairie farmer and his young wife, who longs for something more. DICK HARRISON

Evans, Hubert (b. 1892). Hubert Reginald Evans was born in Vankleek Hill, Ont., and grew up in Galt. By 1910 he was a journalist in Toronto; he also worked for a time in British Columbia. In 1915 he joined the Canadian army and was wounded at Ypres in 1916. After the war Evans moved to British Columbia, finally settling on the coast. Married in 1920, he supported himself and his family not only as a freelance writer but also as a fisherman, fisheries officer, logger, and beachcomber—activities that greatly influenced his literary subjects and brought him into contact with local Indians for whom he expresses a strong sympathy in his writing. Evans has written magazine serials; radio plays; short fiction, some of which was collected in *Forest friends* (1926) and *The silent call* (1930); and three novels. *The new front line* (1927) addresses the basic choices facing a soldier after the First World War;

Mist on the river (1954; NCL 1973), his best-known book, illustrates analogous choices facing the Indian peoples in their attempts to balance their heritage against an encroaching white society. Evans gives his Indian characters strong, frequently anguished voices to express their often conflicting ideals of freedom and responsibility. *O time in your flight* (1979), an autobiographical novel, recounts the poignant, sometimes comic, clash between a young Ontario boy and his parents that finally confirms his belief that his freedom and future lie in far-off British Columbia.

Evans has also published four novels for young readers: *Derry, airedale of the frontier* (1928), *Derry's partner* (1929), *Derry of Totem Creek* (1930), *Mountain dog* (1956) [*Son of the Salmon People* (1981)]; and a biography of explorer David Thompson, *North to the unknown river* (1949). In late life Evans published two books of poetry, *Whittlings* (1976), which includes most of the pamphlet *Bits and pieces* (1974), and *Endings* (1981). He is currently preparing a memoir of his early years in British Columbia.

KEITH RICHARDSON

Everson, R.G. (b. 1903). Born in Oshawa, Ont., Ronald Gilmour Everson attended Victoria College, University of Toronto, and Osgoode Hall Law School. After practising law for several years, he took up public-relations work until his retirement in 1963. Everson started writing poetry in the late twenties, publishing then, and during the thirties and forties, in magazines in Canada and the United States. His first book, *Three dozen poems* (1957), initiated a series of volumes of carefully crafted descriptive and reflective verse: *A lattice for Momos* (1958), *Blind man's holiday* (1963), *Four poems* (1963), *Wrestle with an angel* (1965), *Incident on Côte des Neiges and other poems* (1966), *Raby Head* (1967), *The dark is not so dark* (1969), *Selected poems 1920/1970* (1970), *Indian summer* (1976), and *Carnival* (1978).

Rooted in the Ontario and Québec landscapes he knows, Everson's poetry has remained fundamentally the same throughout his career: short and gentle delineations of a horizon, a human being, or a limited action. His vision of life is direct and uncomplicated, his tone matter-of-fact and understanding. Everson is a patient and loving observer of the human condition. Especially in his two most recent volumes he sometimes shows personal discomfort with the contemporary world; more often he is simply content to depict, to find a sudden analogy that captures a person or an incident. Though they abound in allusions to literary and historical personages, the poems seek to calm the reader by establishing a natural affinity and bond between the observing poet and the reader, who comes to see the scenes through the poet's understanding eyes.

DAVID STAINES

Exile. A literary quarterly founded by Barry CALLAGHAN and first published in June 1972 by Atkinson College, York University, Toronto, it continues under these auspices, although Callaghan has been sole publisher since vol. 1, no. 4 (1974), in addition to being editor. International in flavour and substantial in extent (up to 160 pages an issue and up to 260 pages a double issue), it specializes in adventurous poetry, short stories, and artwork of high calibre. *Exile* features styles ranging from the naturalistic to the surreal and has published such writers as Jerzy Kosinski, Joyce Carol Oates, and Leonard COHEN. Exile Editions, founded by Callaghan in 1975, began with the publication of *Drawings* by the Canadian artist Claire Weisman Wilks. By late 1982 it will have released thirty-five titles, including works by Marie-Claire BLAIS and Jacques FERRON.

DAVID O'ROURKE

Exploration literature in English. 1 IN-TRODUCTION. The early English-speaking explorers of Canada were assiduous writers. From the beginning their superiors—whether mercantile or military—required detailed reports on the new land, and many of the explorers' letters and documents describe their attempts to preserve these precious records while they travelled, and to continue to write them despite great deprivation and physical suffering. To 'write down every occurrence', to describe 'everything as it is', was a duty that eighteenth-century rationalism not only applauded but considered a serious philosophical task. Yet the explorers of Canada—men of the factual world, with a great deal to attend to and little time for the imaginative life—felt they had literary skills sufficient only for 'a plain unvarnished tale and adorned language; all matter of fact', in the words of John McDonald of Garth. Nevertheless the texts that record their experiences—fur-trade journals, diaries, letters, scientific reports, autobiographies, and treatises—form the earliest record in English-Canadian culture of the confrontation between the rationalist component of the European imagination and a vast and sensuous network of river valleys, lakes, and heights of land that invited far more in the way of interpretation than a strictly descriptive account.

The most interesting and imaginative literary phase of such writing is intimately associated with the exploration of the West and North, after they had been penetrated by the French (see Writing in NEW FRANCE), and with the great period of the fur trade. Its typical published expression has been the personal journal, mingling adventurous narrative and scientific description. The European audience for such writings was a large and well-informed one: readers abroad were as likely to have perused Hearne and Mackenzie and Henry on Canada as they were to have read their fellow explorers on other unknown lands. Many of these writings—for example, those recording purely maritime exploration and the search for a Northwest Passage—are hard to associate with our imaginative literature because they really belong to the colonial history of England. In this entry 'exploration literature' will be defined as those texts produced by an observer who is describing and interpreting for the first time Canadian regions unknown to his own culture and that he experiences as a sojourner rather than a settler. These interpretations, which naturally reflect the bias of the writer's culture, became a part of the accumulating body of explanation that entered into, and shaped, the emerging consciousness of the new English-Canadian culture and assumed an imaginative role in our literary heritage.

Exploration writing is often classed with 'quest' literature; but quests tend to have a mythic shape and a predetermined goal. In exploration writing such a goal is usually announced and may even be achieved (the crossing of the Barrens, the mapping of the Northwest, even the 'ruining' of a trading territory), but the shape of the adventure itself is not predetermined; literally anything may befall the observer, and his obligation is less to mould the account of it according to narrative conventions (though that of course sometimes happens, as in Alexander Henry's famous account of the massacre at Fort Michilimackinac) than to observe and record exactly what occurred, usually on a day-to-day basis. Thus there is a definite displacement of the mythic values of the quest into a scientific and mercantile ethos that insists on the primary value of the strictly factual account. There is a firm rejec-

tion of everything 'poetic'; all subjective, metaphorical, and visionary perspectives are treated with embarrassment or brisk skepticism; and familiar literary devices such as structural patterning, irony, and verbal play are almost entirely absent. (Paradoxically many Hudson's Bay Company men came to Canada as 'writers', which in the terminology of the fur trade meant 'accountant'.) In a country without a genuine native idiom, this evasion of the intimidating example of polished literary models produced a genuinely new form of discourse. While saturated with empirical values both scientific and historical, it was closely linked with autobiography and the first-person narrative and indirectly produced some myth-making elements of a new literature. The chronicle form, and the factual language and open-ended vision of these early writers, contributed to what Northrop FRYE calls the 'documentary tradition' in English-Canadian literature.

The explorer is uniquely a man of one book; the record of his experiences thus becomes a kind of heroic testimony, and was so perceived by his fellows. The man in the field—whether fur trader or scientific explorer—kept a daily log: a chronicle of events, natural observations, and astronomical measurements. This log he wrote up as often as he could into a journal which, if he were a fur trader, constituted his report to his masters. This might be copied out for him by a clerk before it was sent 'home'; and, indeed, by the early nineteenth century such records formed an important means of communication in the emerging culture of the fur trade and among scientific men in London. At the end of his posting he looked forward to consulting his journals (as Samuel Hearne did) and turning them into a narrative that might gain him literary renown.

2. THE EXPLORER-WRITERS. Canadian exploration writing in English emerges late in the seventeenth century from contexts provided both by the personal narratives in Hakluyt's *Voyages* and the elements of folktale and legend in the popular 'traveller's tale'. It is immediately and definitively transformed, however, by the more everyday structure of the ship's log. The journals kept by Henry Kelsey (c. 1667-1724), during his years with the newly founded Hudson's Bay Company, clearly illustrate both these influences. *The Kelsey papers* (1929), edited by A.G. Doughty and Chester Martin, includes his journal of a youthful jour-

ney (1690-2) into the interior, with a prologue by Kelsey in doggerel verse clearly
shaped by popular narrative traditions:

Now Reader Read for I am well assur'd
Thou dost not know the hardships I endur'd
In this same desert where Ever yt I have been
Nor will thou believe without yt thou had
seen
The emynent Dangers that did often me
attend . . .

This tale in verse is a skilfully told story of
which the skeptical and audacious teller is
the hero, and its time-honoured form contrasts awesomely with the novelty of the experience; for this youthful Englishman, solitary except for his Indian companions, was
the first white man to see the Prairies. In the
prose journals Kelsey does not lose his feeling for the shape of experience, as we see
when he notes 'ye end of a Tedious winter
and tragical journal' in 1697; but the practical need for a day-by-day record displaces
the desire to tell a tale of adventure.

Throughout the early eighteenth century
the Hudson's Bay Company hugged the
coast, reluctant to send men to the interior
as long as the Indians could be persuaded to
bring their furs to the Bayside posts. But
Company factors kept post journals, and
James Isham (c. 1716-61) of Churchill went
beyond this kind of record to compile in
1743 his *Observations on Hudson's Bay . . .*
(1949), edited by E.E. Rich, in which we see
at close quarters life in this 'disconsolate part
of the world', and, more important, hear the
very voice of an eighteenth-century fur
trader. Writing in the leisure of a sickbed,
Isham describes Indian life and customs, assembles facts of natural history, and editori-
alizes mildly on Company policy. He elsewhere says of a later piece of writing, 'as
such is wrote but in a bad Style, I hope itt
will be Excusable'; but Isham's prose style is
the meat of his *Observations*, for he writes as
an unselfconscious monologist. The 'dialogues' Isham included to illustrate the Indian language have the same vividness:
'Freind come I want to trade,' says the Indian; 'Presently i am Eating,' responds the
trader. 'Make haste its flood I want to be
gone,' pleads the Indian; 'Presently presently,' says the trader. Andrew Graham
(c. 1734-1815) strove over many years to
compile a systematic account of the Bay
area, its fauna, and the life and trading habits
of white men, Eskimos, and Indians. Ill-
educated and no scientist, Graham nevertheless collected data, from about 1770 onward,
with an eye to the needs of the Royal Soci-

ety, and systematized his findings, with the
elegance and comprehensiveness of an Enlightenment intellectual addressing his
peers, in the ten manuscript volumes published as *Observations on Hudson's Bay 1767-
91* (1969) edited by Glyndwr Williams. The
same desire to synthesize appears in Edward
Umfreville's *The present state of Hudson's Bay
. . .* (London, 1770; W. Stewart Wallace ed.,
1954), but Umfreville (b. 1755, *fl.* 1771-89)
was bitterly angry at the Company, his former employers. Despite Umfreville's insistence that his style is plain and his tale a true
one, the objective goal of the treatise is persistently distorted by the passionate language of polemic. The book's real vindication comes from such chilling passages as
Umfreville's terse and melancholy account
of the wilderness ordeal of John Farrant,
James Tomson, and James Ross during the
winter of 1772.

It was Anthony Henday's journey to the
interior in 1754-5 and Matthew Cocking's
of 1772-3 that produced the model on which
most exploration writing about the land itself was to be developed: the daily journal
written in the field, with its emphasis on
landscape description and ethnography.
Both men wrote brief and inexpressive
chronicles of the events that befell them, yet
even here the individuality of the observer
makes itself felt. Travelling on horseback,
Anthony Henday (*fl.* 1750-62) notes without much comment a considerable range of
natural and human detail; he is at ease with
his Indian companions and always mentions
their dancing and drumming appreciatively.
And he confirms his masters' suspicions that
the interior is already occupied by the
'French pedlars'. Henday's journal is noteworthy for its account of his meeting with
the distant Blackfoot Indians, to which
'Equestrian Natives' he, and later Cocking,
give the respect due real nobility. By the
time Matthew Cocking (1743-99) travelled
inland, Québec was in the hands of the English, and Scots traders were soon to command the interior. Cocking's journal suggests a better picture than Henday's of the
domestic life of an exploring group. 'A Male
child born. Hungry times,' he notes briefly,
reminding us of the groups of women and
children who were an important part of exploration culture and, by Daniel Harmon's
time, posed a major responsibility for the
great trading companies.

Of these shorter narratives, the most outstanding is that of the 22-year-old Peter
Fidler (1769-1822), who went to live alone

with the Chipewyan Indians in 1791-2 in order to learn their language (he ended up dreaming in it). Lonely, hungry, and for a time without trousers, he drifted with the Indians, recording his adventures, the habits of his hosts, and the usual scientific observations in a stream-of-consciousness narrative that is both uninhibited and succinct. Despite the remarkable adversity he suffered, he concludes: 'Upon the whole this has been rather an agreeable winter than otherwise. . . .' Fidler's journal recounts one winter in the life of a young man. Peter Pond's vivid, phonetically spelled narrative, of which only a portion now exists, was begun about 1800, and attempts to sum up an entire adventurous life, of which the major achievement was the discovery in 1778 of Methy Portage, a feat that unlocked the Athabasca region to the fur trade. Pond (1740-c. 1807) left behind him in the West a legacy of controversy—David Thompson was to describe him scathingly as 'of a violent temper and unprincipled character'— but his narrative (written after a careful study of the travel writings of Baron Lahontan and Jonathan Carver) is full of shrewd humour and rich in human observation. His knowledge of the genre in which he was writing gave Pond a skeptical perspective on the obligation of verisimilitude. As he writes pungently: 'It would Sound two much Like a travelers Storey to Say What I Realey Beleve from What I have Sean.' But in his narrative we see an early attempt at turning the explorer's chronicle of his journey to a larger task: the explanation of a life.

Five notable narratives of notable explorations—by Hearne, Henry, Mackenzie, Thompson, and Franklin—share this desire for a more general reading of nature and human experience. These volumes are linked as well by their portrayal of a common world that, though still unexplored at its periphery, by now had evolved its own society, customs, and history. (Captain John Franklin in 1819 encountered Chipewyan Indians who claimed that as children they had 'travelled with Mr. Hearne'.) Each volume had its origin in a chronicle of daily events made by a man constantly on the move, and in a detailed record of natural and astronomical observations, and each transformed the log-book—a difficult task for an unreflective man like Mackenzie, one of whose letters depicts the writer's block he developed as he tried to turn observed fact into explanatory account.

Samuel Hearne (1745-92) was a Hudson's Bay Company man with naval training who, in 1770-2, on the instructions of his masters, travelled on foot from Fort Prince of Wales to the mouth of the Coppermine River on the Arctic Ocean. Alone except for a constantly changing band of Indian companions directed by the Cree leader Matonabbee, Hearne drifted as the Indians' hunting habits determined. His goal was to find the sea and certain legendary deposits of copper; theirs was to conduct a massacre of their hereditary enemies, the Eskimo. Hearne's *Journey from Prince of Wales's Fort in Hudson's Bay to the Northern Ocean . . .* (London, 1795; Richard Glover ed., 1958) is the first great classic of Canadian exploration, in which Hearne transcended the limitations of Henday and Cocking to produce the archetype of such travel journals. A straightforward account of events as they transpired, the *Journey* nevertheless rises constantly to the challenge of generalization, as Hearne attempts both to report on, and to interpret, the meaning of the changing landscape and the Indian life he experienced with such intimacy. Hearne's scientific exploration of this utterly unknown territory (he himself did not yet know its relationship to the Western Sea) was subject to criticism in its day and to ceaseless revision since; but it remains of the first importance. Equally interesting is his picture of human life in the Barrens. Hearne's persona is that of the ideal travelling companion: unassertive, resourceful, capable of great endurance, a comprehensive observer not easily repelled by the unexpected. His richly detailed account of Cree and Chipewyan life is nevertheless a rationalist one, drawn in the eighteenth-century conviction that 'the proper study of mankind is man', as the portrayal of Matonabbee in the character of 'noble savage' suggests. Hearne is urbane, judicious, and often deeply concerned; but he never sees the Indian from the inside because of his conviction that his companions, however fascinating, are essentially 'void of common understanding'. This duality leads to an unusual juxtaposition in Hearne's anguished account of the massacre at Bloody Fall, where the rigorously exact description of the empirical observer is coupled with the personal response of a man whose only language of feeling is that of the Age of Sensibility.

Alexander Henry the Elder (1739-1824) represents the entrepreneurial spirit of the Scots and Americans who flooded the

Exploration literature in English 2

Northwest after the fall of Québec. His *Travels and adventures in Canada and the Indian territories . . .* (New York, 1809) covers fifteen years of trading and exploration around the Sault and on the Prairies from 1760 to 1776, and it too focuses on a famous massacre, which Henry barely escaped, at Fort Michilimackinac in 1763. It relates in the first part a classic captivity narrative, the centrepiece of which is a brilliant recounting of the massacre, coloured by Henry's own point of view. Here the characteristic first-person stance of exploration narrative is even more dramatically restricted by Henry's stress on the helpless narrator's limited knowledge of his situation. The result is a Gothic atmosphere of tension and mystery. In Part Two, Henry is no longer the victim but the genial master of his situation ('despair is not made for man,' he observes at one moment of considerable adversity), and he reverts to pure chronicle in describing his penetration north to Cumberland House and west towards the buffalo-hunting Plains Indians. Henry's book is of greater ethnographic than geographical value, and it is his very interest in Indian life that reveals why, as a work of literature, his *Travels and adventures* divides itself so sharply between the conventions of Gothic and chronicle. When his Indian 'brother' warns him in Chippewa (a tongue he speaks) of the impending massacre, Henry misunderstands because the Indian's language is so 'extravagantly figurative'. To Henry, the 'occasions of speech' for a white man are 'the records of history, the pursuits of science, the disquisitions of philosophy'. Thus for him language cannot lead beyond the data of experience to the intensity of metaphor, which suggests why he took convenient refuge in the Gothic mode to shape the tense experience of captivity and calmly dropped it to revert to chronicle in describing his travels in the West.

Like Henry, Sir Alexander Mackenzie (1763-1820) of the North West Company was an entrepreneur, but one on a heroic scale. Grasping at once the nature of the interior as a mercantile problem, he made two brief, hard-driving journeys of immense importance. The first, in 1789, was down the river bearing his name to the Arctic Ocean; the second—an expedition of great daring and rapidity—took him from Fort Chipewyan and across the Rockies to Bella Coola on the Pacific coast in 1793. He was thus the first white man to cross the continent of North America. His *Voyages . . .*

through the continent of North America (London, 1801) gained him immediate fame, and a knighthood. Mackenzie, clearly recognizing that his *Voyages* could constitute an interpretation, a 'reading' of the vast territory he had crossed, prefaced the daily chronicle of his two journeys with an invaluable systematic history of the fur trade (probably from the hand of his cousin, Roderick McKenzie). The *Voyages* concludes with a 'short geographical view' in which Mackenzie attempts an organized account of the whole of British North America, seen as a geographical and economic entity. He thus built, on the foundation of the field journal, an empirical basis for the first cohesive image of the Canada that exists today. The magnitude of this vision contrasts poignantly with the severe repression in Mackenzie's writing of every level of language beyond the factual. The *Voyages* was revised by the hand of an infamous English literary hack, William Combe. A comparison of the manuscript of Mackenzie's Arctic narrative with Combe's doctored version shows that behind the latter's imperial polish and near-Augustan prose lies a much more terse, unemotive, and often rough turn of phrase. Mackenzie's genius as an explorer in the field lay in the fact that he never stopped to reflect. His narrative (whether in his own rough words, as in the journey to the Arctic, or in Combe's more polished working-up of the crossing of the Rockies) is characterized by an acute tension between the drama of real events surrounding him and his men, and the compression and terseness with which he reports what transpired. Though Mackenzie is a painstaking observer of externals, his trader's eye always measuring and counting, the heroic scale of his exploration clearly depended on the ruthless elimination of other kinds of insight. Against this severe restriction of emotional range is balanced his attempt to portray a single economic significance for territories whose extreme boundaries were still unknown—a visionary insight, given the power in later Canadian culture of economic themes and mercantile values.

It was the imagination and aggressiveness of such Nor'Westers that drew to their ranks David Thompson (1770-1857), who in 1797 left the Hudson's Bay Company, where he had been an apprentice and trader since 1784, to become astronomer and surveyor for its rival—and 'the greatest practical land geographer who ever lived', according to J.B. Tyrrell. In a series of journeys between

1798 and 1812, sometimes accompanied by his wife and young family, he mapped an area of the West stretching from Fort William to the interior of what is now British Columbia. *David Thompson's narrative of his explorations in western North America 1784-1812* (1916; Richard Glover ed., 1962) was compiled in his old age (1845-50) from nearly four-dozen manuscript volumes of field journals, and reveals the remarkable powers of synthesis that made possible his great systematization of these landforms. Thompson's aim from the beginning seems to have been to impose an autobiographical scheme on the chronicle form of the log, yet make the result a vehicle for wide-ranging though subtle analysis. Thus his rugged but expressive narrative takes us from his youth at York Factory to the moment when at last he 'goes down' to Montreal, with a family to educate and his precious researches in hand. In the course of this chronicle he draws his experiences into large-scale patterns, interpreting phenomena that can be understood only in juxtaposition: the world of the Nahathaway and Piegan Indians, the geographical coherence of the Prairies, the challenges and conflicts of exploration on the edge of a fur-trade war. His vision is diametrically opposed to Mackenzie's: Thompson exemplifies the organic and mythopoeic preoccupations of nineteenth-century Romanticism as clearly as Mackenzie represents those of Utilitarianism. Thompson describes himself at one point as 'a solitary traveller unknown to the world'; and reading him we are in the company of an intensely private sensibility that is also very open to the impress of experience. Less aware than Thoreau of the metaphoric complexity in the image of the journal, Thompson nevertheless resembles him in his willingness to unfold almost endlessly the imaginative richness of observed fact, whether in describing the bedevilling northern mosquito, the implications of a river system, or the mythopoeic significance of the exploitation of the beaver.

Finally there is the *Narrative of a journey to the shores of the Polar Sea . . .* (London, 1823) in which Captain John Franklin (1786-1847) described the adventures of the British naval expedition under his command, which in 1819-22 returned so disastrously and with such drama to the Barrens that Hearne had visited fifty years earlier. Franklin's *Narrative* strives for an entirely objective effect, yet it is the most intensely dramatic of all these books. Inadequately prepared, ill-advised, surrounded by suspicious and quarrelling traders, this British naval officer found himself in command of a group often at odds with itself, on a journey that escaped complete tragedy almost by accident. These tensions are vividly expressed in Franklin's need to justify the decisions he took, which leads to an anxious emphasis on the stance of the voracious chronicler; he incorporates into his text long excerpts from the detailed journals of the three other officers of his expedition, men of widely varying temperament and perspectives. The result is not the customary single first-person narrative but a corporate journal replete with unstated ironies that reveal themselves when, with the aid of other documents, we learn of the sexual jealousies, murder, cannibalism, and internal dissention that dogged the group's nonetheless heroic endeavours. Franklin portrays the fur-trade culture with absolute courtesy, yet growing hostility. The conflicts of Hudson's Bay men and Nor'Westers, soon to be resolved in the 1821 union of the two companies, are as disastrous for his enterprise as the dissent among his own men; but even more important is his despair at what he terms the superstition, apprehensiveness, and irresponsibility of *voyageur* customs, and at the larger mystery of Indian life, which he must master in order to retain his command. There is a terrible irony in the moment at Fort Enterprise when the filthy, ragged, and starving officers are at last fed, cleansed, and clothed by the rescuing Chipewyan, and the face of the Northwest discloses itself unasked: 'The Indians set about every thing with an activity that amazed us. Indeed, contrasted with our emaciated figures and extreme debility, their frames appeared to us gigantic, and their strength supernatural.' Franklin's death on another Arctic expedition thirty years later resulted in a mystery that gripped the European imagination for two decades. Of that tragic undertaking there is no narrative—only fragments of evidence to be pieced together slowly by others.

These great explorations by Hearne, Henry, Mackenzie, Thompson, and Franklin were matched in grandeur by the brief but epic journey in 1808 down the near-impassable Fraser Canyon by Simon Fraser (1776-1862). But Fraser has a different significance: he sought both to surpass Sir Alexander Mackenzie as an explorer and to write a journal that would bring him equal fame. The latter he could not do (lacking either Mackenzie's doggedness or the aid of a William Combe), but his extant log—a detailed, factual, and gripping record of one of the most hazardous and, ironically, least profitable of all expeditions of discovery—is perhaps that more interesting for its simplicity. Fraser marks a turning-point in our account because he was strongly aware of his participation in a great tradition of exploration that had ideals of achievement and a conventional form of expression. Furthermore, he was among the first of the explorers to attempt self-consciously to ensure the continuance of a wilderness world that, although thinly populated, had densely wrought links of culture and custom in which Cree and Chipewyan, Scots entrepreneur and Orkney boatman, Métis voyageur and Loyalist soldier, lived together. The kinds of settlement envisioned in this world did not extend much past the trading-posts Fraser sought to establish; but as Mackenzie had already surmised, the trading-post was one way of imposing order on territories it seemed inconceivable to manage by any other system.

The intellectual life of the explorers and fur traders was not barren. Some were scientists (albeit self-educated) who eagerly purchased new books in their fields and often read more widely. In 1799 Peter Fidler ordered from England Mrs Radcliffe's *The mysteries of Udolpho* and John Gay's *Fables*, as well as Buffon's *Natural history*. About the same time David Thompson sent for *Paradise lost* and Johnson's *The rambler*, and John Bird was reading Lucan, Tasso, Pope, and Akenside. The North West Company in particular provided books for its men; F.-W. Wentzel was eventually to describe its Athabaska post as 'formerly the delight and school of the North'. The journal of Daniel Harmon (1778-1843)—published in *Sixteen years in the Indian country: the journal of Daniel William Harmon 1800-1816* (1957) edited by W. Kaye Lamb—is not a travel journal (he explored very little) but a true diary that reflects this intellectual atmosphere. It reveals the inner life of a devout and decorous man of modest culture, living on the borderline between unexplored frontier and nascent community. Harmon was a devoted family man, a passionate gardener, and an assiduous correspondent with gentlemen of the company living at nearby posts. He had a genius for friendship, and the many evenings he spent smoking and talking with fellow traders, who made difficult journeys to join him, remind us of the deepening and solidifying texture of life on the frontier as old kinds of exploration began to give way

to new. The heroic scale of the solitary ordeal, however, persisted. Even farther west, Peter Skene Ogden (1794-1854) was to make the rapacious forays below the forty-ninth parallel that briefly linked the learned science of discovery with the scorched-earth policy pursued here in the 'Snake Country' by the Hudson's Bay Company in its intensive rivalry with American interests. Ogden's *Snake-Country journals* (1950, 1961, 1971) have some of the terseness of Mackenzie's and Fraser's writings; but their range and detail make them a valuable, if disturbing, portrait of a man of relentless drive, superior organizing ability, and great cunning.

For all these men, great and small, the journal was the primary, the essential, form of utterance, as is pathetically demonstrated by the story of Benjamin Frobisher (1782-1819), a Nor' Wester whose conflicts with certain Hudson's Bay men led to his injury and jailing at York Factory in 1819. Though deprived of pen and ink by his captors, Frobisher attempted to keep a journal throughout his ordeal. Escaping with two companions, he set out across a thousand miles of wilderness to reach safety, though he was starving, half clothed, and often raving from the effects of concussion. He persisted in writing his account of their suffering; when his half-burned body was recovered not far from a trading-post, the pencilled fragments of his journal were at his side.

By the second quarter of the nineteenth century, however, the narrative journal is increasingly displaced by purely scientific description and anecdotal history, though sometimes light was cast on the imaginative life of exploration, as in the *Character book* (1832) of Hudson's Bay Governor Sir George Simpson (1792-1860), which contains superlatively venomous portrayals of individuals and types from trading-post life. The explorer as such was giving way to travellers like J.J. Bigsby (1792-1881), author of *The shoe and canoe* (London, 1850), and exploration was producing its own historiography in three works by Alexander Ross (1783-1856), in which he described the life of the fur trade, and exploration, during the first half of the nineteenth century.

In 1859 the expeditions of John Palliser (1817-87) and Henry Youle Hind (1823-1908) were crisscrossing the West—in the words of Hind 'to ascertain the practicability of establishing an emigrant route between Lake Superior and Selkirk settlement.' The hegemony of the Hudson's Bay Company

Exploration literature in English: bibliography

was soon to be broken and the trader to give way to what Palliser called 'the agriculturist'. Hind's *Narrative of the Canadian Red River exploring expedition of 1857 . . .* (London, 1860) reflects this moment of transition very sharply: the detailed physiographic and ethnographic reportage of the age of exploration mingles with interviews with the pioneer farmers of the Selkirk Settlement and repeated analyses of the settlement potential of the land; and both are fused in the sanguine voice of a professorial, didactic narrator.

3. THE INFLUENCE OF THESE WRITINGS. The imaginative role of exploration literature in Canadian writing is still not fully understood, though these texts hold the same place in our literary heritage as theological treatises and captivity narravites do in early American literature. Initially a subject for historical study, the explorers have emerged as writers in their own right with the proliferation of scholarly editions of their journals in the twentieth century. Poets like John NEWLOVE and Don GUTTERIDGE have treated the men themselves as mythic figures; or, like George BOWERING, have used them to query the very notion of myth. But almost none of the exploration narratives, save Hearne's, is securely situated in the evolving canon of Canadian literature. Yet with the emergence of the character of the literature—deeply committed to close observation, to local and individual circumstance, and to an ambiguous borderline between 'document' and 'literary work'—we increasingly see links between the imaginations of the explorers and of our contemporary writers, links that suggest how much both are the product of the practical, mercantile, and scientific culture of middle-class men in the Romantic age. Twentieth-century Canadian writing reflects some of the same deep inhibitions about language and metaphor, and shows the same abiding trust in the primacy of the document. The image of the log book or journal abounds, if not as a direct inheritance from the explorers, then as the result of a similar habit of mind that is reflected also in literary analysis, which often employs the image of 'map-making' as a term of critical discourse. This habit of mind reappears in the enthusiasm for autobiographical first-person novels and stories, in the poet's fascination with the image of the 'field note' or scientific observation (Robert KROETSCH, Christopher Dewdney), or in the way novelist Timothy FINDLEY's narrators struggle to unearth from some infinitely detailed but somehow unyielding documentary account the real significance of 'everything as it is'. Most importantly, perhaps, it appears in the persistence with which English-Canadian writers adopt the metaphor of exploration to describe the very act of writing itself, a persistence that underlines the perceptiveness of Don Gutteridge when he calls the explorers 'our first philosophers'.

Bibliography. Titles and sources of works not cited above follow: Matthew Cocking, *Journal 1772-73* edited by Lawrence J. Burpee in *Transactions of the Royal Society of Canada* (hereafter *TRSC*), Sec. II, 1908; Peter Fidler, *Journal of a journey with the Chepawyans or Northern Indians, to the Slave Lake, & to the east & west of the Slave River, in 1791 & 2* in *Journals of Samuel Hearne and Philip Turnor* (1934) edited by J.B. Tyrrell; Simon Fraser, *Letters and journals 1806-1808* (1960) edited by W. Kaye Lamb; Benjamin Frobisher: Samuel Hull Wilcocke, *The Death of Benjamin Frobisher* (1819) in L.R. Masson ed., *Les bourgeois de la compagnie du Nord-ouest*, II (1889-90); Anthony Henday, *Journal 1754-55*, edited by Lawrence J. Burpee, in *TRSC*, Sec. II, 1907; Sir Alexander Mackenzie, *Journals and letters* (1970) edited by W. Kaye Lamb; John McDonald of Garth, 'Autobiographical notes, 1791-1816' (in Masson, vol. II; see Frobisher above); John Palliser, *The papers of the Palliser expedition 1857-1860* (1968) edited by Irene Spry; Peter Pond, *Narrative* in Charles M. Gates ed., *Five fur traders of the Northwest* (1933); Alexander Ross, *Adventures of the first settlers on the Oregon or Columbia River* (London, 1849), *The fur hunters of the Far West* (1855; Kenneth A. Spaulding ed., 1956), *The Red River Settlement: its rise, progress, and present state* (1856; intro. W.E. MORTON, 1972); Sir George Simpson, *The 'character book' of Governor George Simpson, 1832* in Glyndwr Williams ed., *Hudson's Bay miscellany 1670-1870* (1975); and Willard-Ferdinand Wentzel, *Letters to the Hon. Roderic McKenzie 1807-1824* (in Masson, vol. I; see Frobisher above).

GERMAINE WARKENTIN

F

Faessler, Shirley (b.?) Born in Toronto, she writes mainly short stories about first- and second-generation Jewish immigrants living in the Kensington Market area of Toronto in the 1930s. They feature robust characters and wry humour in portraying family life within this particular Jewish community prior to the Second World War. Her stories have appeared in *The Atlantic Monthly* and *The* TAMARACK REVIEW; 'A basket of apples' and 'Henye' were included in the anthologies *Sixteen by twelve* (1970) and *The narrative voice* (1972) respectively, both edited by John METCALF.

Faessler's one novel, *Everything in the window* (1979), employs the same setting and relates the disintegration of the marriage between Sophie Glicksman, the daughter of an immigrant Romanian Jew, and Billy James, a WASP swimming instructor. Although the novel is weak in character development over its lengthy time-span and in the handling of time and plot transitions, it is successful in exploring the cultural gap between gentiles and Jews, in portraying the damaging preconceptions and mutual suspicion that can so easily sabotage relationships between them, and (as in Faessler's short stories) in its rich portrayal of minor characters and its evocative sense of place.   MARILYN ROSE

Faillon, Étienne-Michel. See BIOGRAPHIES AND MEMOIRS IN FRENCH: 1.

Fairley, Barker (b. 1887). Scholar, painter, poet, and teacher, Barker Fairley was born in Barnsley, Yorkshire, the second son of the headmaster of an elementary school. He won a county scholarship to Leeds University, graduating in 1907 with first-class honours in modern languages, with distinction in German. This led to his appointment the same year as Lektor in English literature at the ancient German university of Jena, where he obtained his Ph.D. An accidental meeting in his boarding house at Jena with a Canadian professor, who was scouting Europe for academic staff for the newly founded University of Alberta, resulted in his being offered a lectureship in German there. Five years later, in 1915, he was appointed associate professor of German at the University of Toronto.

In Toronto the painter J.E.H. MacDonald recognized in this shy, remote young man of his own age an intellectual restlessness and dissatisfaction with the oppressive traditions of late Victorianism and introduced him to the little group of artists—A.Y. Jackson, Arthur Lismer, Fred Varley, and others—who a few years later were to form the Group of Seven. Fairley became a close friend of the Group, and an early collector and champion of their paintings. (His collection may be seen in the Barker Fairley Lounge of the Faculty Club, University of Toronto.) At the same time he came under the influence of a lively figure on campus, Professor Sam Hooke of Victoria College, the editor of an undergraduate paper, *The Rebel*, whose views were very much those Fairley had inherited: a dissatisfaction with the social order and a conviction that it could be remedied. In 1914 Fairley had married Margaret Keeling, the daughter of the headmaster of Yorkshire's leading grammar school. She shared and reinforced his radical sympathies, and in Toronto *The Rebel* provided an opportunity to express their opinions. Fairley contributed poems, critical articles, and reviews to it, gradually assuming an influential position in shaping its policy. It was he who suggested that *The Rebel* should 'go to the country' with a new title: *The* CANADIAN FORUM. This was in 1920, the year the Group of Seven was officially formed. Fairley links the two events.

His scholarly and literary work is chiefly associated with Goethe, though his first published book was a biography of C.M. Doughty (1927), author of *Travels in Arabia deserta*. In 1932 Fairley accepted the Simon Professorship of German Language and Literature at Manchester University. He knew at once that he had made a mistake. The familiar company of friends and artists had vanished and he was face-to-face with blighted industrial England in the depth of the Great Depression. In 1936 he returned thankfully to the University of Toronto as head of the German department and set to work on the books that were to win him wide recognition as a German scholar. The first of these, *A study of Goethe* (1947), elicited an enthusiastic letter from Thomas Mann, and drew favourable notices in England. *Heine: an interpretation* followed in

1959 and *William Raabe: an introduction to his novels* in 1961. Fairley's authoritative translation of Goethe's *Faust* (1970) and his *Goethe as revealed in his poetry* completed his canon on Goethe. In 1972 came surprisingly a collection of verse, *Poems of 1922, or soon after*—ruminative soliloquies notable for the epigrammatic quality of many of the poems and for the glimpses they provide of a very private man under stress.

Painting had always been his passion and his consolation. After his retirement from teaching in 1956, Fairley turned for a time mostly to landscapes, but he also did many portraits, quickly executed, generally in a single sitting. In the seventies the demand for his work accelerated sharply—exhibitions were sold out at high prices even before they opened—and towards the end of a long life devoted to scholarly work, fame and comparative wealth came to Fairley as a painter. (See *Barker Fairley portraits* (1981) edited by Gary Michael Dault.)

Margaret Fairley—who edited *The selected writings of William Lyon Mackenzie* (1960)—died in 1968. Barker Fairley married in 1978 Nan Purdy, who is the subject of some of his best late paintings.   LOVAT DICKSON

Falcon, Pierre (1783-1876). Born at Elbow Fort (Man.), the son of Pierre Falcon, a Québécois employed by the North West Company, and a Cree, he was baptized in 1798 at L'Acadie (Qué.), where he lived with relatives and learned to read and write. In 1806 he returned to Red River to work for the North West Company and in 1812 he married Marie, the sister of Cuthbert Grant Jr, a Métis clerk in the Company; they had seven children. After the union in 1821 of the North West Company and the Hudson's Bay Company, Falcon remained in service until 1825. With other Métis he joined Grant, founder of Grantown (Saint-François-Xavier), and became a farmer and buffalo hunter; he was made a justice-of-the-peace in 1855 and died there.

Falcon's literary significance is as a folk poet who interpreted local incidents in lively, mocking songs for which, in two cases, he also composed melodies. He was present at Seven Oaks (1816) when Grant led some Métis and Indians in a skirmish in which Governor Robert Semple and twenty other people of the Red River Settlement (established by the Hudson's Bay Company) were killed. His 'La chanson de la Grenouillère' ('Chant de verité'), describing the confrontation at Seven Oaks, is a rous-

ing song composed to celebrate the Métis 'victory' and ends with a stanza saying that it had been composed by 'Pierre Falcon, poète du canton'. It marked the birth of popular writing in French-speaking Manitoba. A related song, 'Le Lord Selkirk au Fort William' or 'La danse des Bois-Brûlés', parodies the ball held at Fort William by Selkirk after he had taken the Nor'Westers' headquarters in retaliation for Seven Oaks. The vigorous tempi of both songs must have set the toes tapping or the oars swinging of all who were associated with the Pays d'en haut.

Another famous ballad, 'Le Général Dickson', is a sardonic acount of the departure from Grantown in 1837 of an American adventurer who styled himself 'Liberator of the Indian Nations'. Falcon composed 'Les tribulations d'un roi malheureux' in his old age, during the Red River Rebellion of 1870, after a party of Métis, sent by Louis Riel, prevented Governor William McDougall from reaching Red River and his 'kingdom', the Northwest Territories. 'Le dieu du Libéral' expresses the bitter feelings of the Métis when Dr. J.C. Schultz, who had opposed Riel in 1869 and been imprisoned by him, ran for Liberal member of Parliament in 1871. These three songs are very different in composition and style from the first two, even allowing for the fact that they used borrowed melodies ('Dans tous les cantons', 'Un Canadien errant', and 'Cadet Rousselle' respectively): it is thought that the pastor of Saint-François-Xavier, Father Émile Dugas, may have had a hand in polishing them.

'The buffalo hunter's song'—known only in English translations that are presumed to be based on verses by Falcon—raises to six the number of songs by 'Pierre le rimeur', the Bard of the Plains ('Le barde des plaines'). He doubtless composed other songs but they have been lost, or entered the realm of oral literature.

Lake Falcon in Manitoba was probably named after this popular poet of Red River.

See Margaret Complin, 'Pierre Falcon's "Chanson de la grenouillère" ', *Transactions of the Royal Canadian Society* (Sec. III, 1929, p. 39); Margaret Arnette McLeod, 'Songs of the Insurrection', *The Beaver: a magazine of the North* (Spring 1957); McLeod, 'Dickson, the liberator', *The Beaver* (Summer 1956); McLeod, *Songs of old Manitoba* (1960); and Annette Saint-Pierre, *Au pays des Bois-Brûlés* (1977), published by the Collège universitaire de Saint-Boniface, Saint-Boniface, Man.   ANNETTE SAINT-PIERRE

Faludy

Faludy, George (b. 1910). Born in Budapest, Hungary, he was educated at universities in Berlin, Vienna, Graz, and Paris. He served in the Hungarian army, 1933-4, and was charged with anti-Nazi activities. In 1938 he immigrated to Paris, then to Morocco, where he was among those European intellectuals invited by President Roosevelt to enter the United States, which he did in 1941. He served as honorary secretary of the Free Hungary Movement and enlisted in the U.S. army, serving in the South Pacific. Invited to return to Hungary in 1945, he settled in Budapest and worked as a journalist for five years until his arrest as a conspirator and American spy. He was imprisoned for six months in the cellar of the secret-police headquarters in Budapest, then served three years of a twenty-five-year sentence at the forced-labour camp at Recsk (1950-3). During the 1956 Revolution he escaped from Hungary and settled in London, Eng., where he served as editor-in-chief of the *Hungarian Literary Gazette* (1957-61) and honorary secretary of PEN's Centre for Writers in Exile (1959-64). He joined friends in Toronto in 1967 and became a Canadian citizen in 1976. An occasional lecturer at North American universities, he was awarded a Doctor of Letters (*honoris causa*) by the University of Toronto in 1978.

Arthur Koestler once wrote: 'There is no doubt in my mind that Faludy belongs to the handful of contemporary Hungarian poets of international stature; and that among that handful he is *primus inter pares.*' Faludy rocketed to fame with *Villon balladái* (Ballads of Villon, Budapest, 1937), which is, despite its title, a collection of original poems written in the manner of the French troubadour. Their disdain for authority and intense musicality, coupled with technical invention, captivated a generation of readers. But not everyone was charmed: the Nazis burnt the eleventh edition in 1943 and the Communists confiscated the fifteenth edition in 1947, the last year a book of Faludy's poetry appeared in Hungary.

Faludy published a dozen books in Hungarian between 1937 and 1980, the year his *Összegyüjtött versei* (Collected poems) was published in New York. He has published four books in English: *My happy days in hell* (London, 1962; New York, 1963), a meticulously observed and harrowing account of his three years at Recsk; *Karton* (London, 1966; a.k.a. *City of splintered gods*, New York, 1966), a historical novel set in Roman

times; *Erasmus of Rotterdam* (London, 1970; New York, 1971), a sympathetic biography and a study of humanism in action; and *East and west* (Toronto, 1978), a selected poems in English translations by various hands, with a memoir by Barbara Amiel and a bibliography. Unfortunately the music of the originals does not come through in these translations. Offsetting this loss are such strong features as the sense of locale (Budapest, Morocco, London, Philadelphia, Toronto, etc.); the feeling that love, though deep, is doomed; the belief that art ennobles and endures; the conviction that Eastern Europe is sadistic and the Western world masochistic; and the abhorrence of autocratic authority—this may take the form of invective (as in 'Ode to Stalin on his seventieth birthday') or extreme playfulness (like the last lines of 'Characteristics of G.F.', in which the poet explains: 'He bowed down too soon, rose up too late./ Yet he had neither fears nor inhibitions/ when attacking a Monster State.').

Faludy's position as a leading *émigré* writer is the subject of a series of letters to the editor of *The Times Literary Supplement*—sparked by George Mikes's review of the collected poems (27 Mar. 1981)—which concluded on 15 May 1982.

JOHN ROBERT COLOMBO

Fennario, David (b. 1947). Born David Wiper, he assumed the name 'Fennario', which a girlfriend gave him from a Bob Dylan song. He was raised in Pointe-Saint-Charles, Verdun, a working-class district of Montreal, where most of his plays are set and where he still lives with his wife Elizabeth and one child. He left school at sixteen, worked at odd jobs, and was part of the hippie generation of the late sixties, spending time in Montreal, Toronto, and New York. After being laid off in 1969 from the shipping department of Simpson's, he attended Dawson College, Montreal, as a mature student. While there he read widely and became a convinced Marxist; he is now a member of the Socialist Labour Party. He submitted a journal he had kept, as an assignment, to one of his English teachers, who helped him to publish it through the college under the title *Without a parachute*. Later published commercially (1974), it is an honest, straightforward, somewhat rambling record of his life and reflections from Dec. 1969 to May 1971. It caught the interest of Maurice Podbrey, artistic director of Montreal's Centaur Theatre, who asked

Fennario to write a play for Centaur; later Fennario became, and remains, playwright-in-residence at the theatre.

Fennario's career as a playwright was launched at the Centaur in 1975 with a production of *On the job* (1976), a one-act play about workers on Christmas eve in the shipping-room of a Montreal dress factory. Realistic, earthy, honest, and humorous, it depicts the plight of workers performing mindless jobs and finally rebelling against their employers. This same concern for the worker is shown in a longer one-act play. *Nothing to lose* (1977), produced in 1976 at the Centaur, whose setting is a tavern in Pointe-Saint-Charles, where workers discuss their maltreatment at the hands of a company foreman and finally decide to stage a sitdown strike, since they have 'nothing to lose'. Here Fennario introduces a character who plays himself. Jerry Nines, who has rejoined his worker friends after publishing a journal and having his first play successfully produced, is not a convincing character and represents a self-indulgent tendency in Fennario's work that detracts from his often powerful dramatic statements. This tendency is also evident in his next play *Toronto*—produced in Montreal in 1978 but unpublished—in which Jerry Nines is casting for the Toronto production of a play called *Nothing to lose*—and in two unpublished stage adaptations based on his journal: *Without a parachute*, performed in 1978; and *Changes*, performed in 1980.

Balconville (1980), Fennario's most successful and accomplished play to date, had its première at the Centaur in 1979. Set among the balconies of the tenement houses of Point-Saint-Charles where eight characters, English and French, live out the hot days of one summer, it is considered the first bilingual Canadian play and shows a genuine understanding and concern for the working poor who struggle to survive and fight for their dignity, often humorously, in a depressing social situation; it also shows that their suffering goes deeper than the English-French conflict. The play has toured Canada, was performed at the Old Vic Theatre in London, and in 1979 received the Chalmers Award for the best Canadian play produced in the Toronto area that year.   JAMES NOONAN

Ferron, Jacques (b. 1921). Born in Louiseville, Qué., he was educated at College Brébeuf, Trois-Rivières, and at Université Laval, where he graduated in medicine. Di-

sheartened, while studying at Brébeuf, by the élitism of the French-Canadian upper class, he found himself turning more and more towards socialism. At the same time, discussions with Franco-Ontarians and Franco-Manitobans led him to realize that Québécois alone have the opportunity to survive as a strong French-speaking nation in North America. While completing his medical studies he married Madeleine Therien, a Communist who provided a new approach to class problems. Divorced and remarried, he spent one year in the army, where it became increasingly apparent to him that Canada and Québec were incompatible solitudes, two nations that should be independent from each other. He first practised medicine on the Gaspé Peninsula, where he met several storytellers who have since become some of his most cherished characters. After eleven years as a general practitioner in working-class Montreal, he specialized briefly in caring for the mentally retarded before moving to Longueuil, where he is a family doctor. Ferron is well known for his political and social activities. In 1949 he was arrested for participating in a demonstration against the North Atlantic Pact. In 1954 he was elected president of the Canadian Peace Congress. The following year he ran unsuccessfully as a candidate for the 'Parti social démocratique', claiming that Québec socialism was controlled by English Canadians. In 1963 he founded the Rhinoceros Party, a nonsense federalist party whose motto is 'From one pond to another'. After the murder of Pierre Laporte during the 1970 October Crisis, the FLQ requested that Ferron be the government negotiator. The Bourassa government accepted, and Ferron played a key role in the surrender of the Rose brothers and François Simard.

Ferron's first literary works were primarily plays concerned with metaphysical and social problems in which Québec is almost never referred to directly. Reminiscent of Molière, Marivaux, and Labiche, they lack originality and are regarded as a minor part of his works. *Le licou* (1947) satirizes the classical notion of romantic and eternal love. *L'ogre* (1948) denounces the corruption of politics and religion. *Le dodu; ou Le prix du bonheur* (1956), *Tante Élise; ou Le prix de l'amour* (1958), *Le cheval de Don Juan* (1957), and *Cazou; ou le prix de la virginité* (1963) all ridicule the rituals and conventions of love: seductions, fashion, marriages based on convenience and money.

Ferron

In his next two plays Ferron's unique talents as a writer appear for the first time; his style is entertaining, ironical and symbolic. His imaginative, whimsical, and humorous approach is reminiscent of the magic of a 'conteur'. *L'Américaine; ou Le triomphe de l'amitié* (1958) is a social allegory in which an educated and uneducated Québécois become friends and symbolically steal the purse of the all-American beauty, Biouti Rose. *Les grands soleils* (1958), Ferron's most important play, replaces the established political and religious myths of Dollard des Ormeaux and Saint-Jean Baptiste by the memory of the Patriotes. *Le tête du roi* (1963) juxtaposes two historical events: the decapitation, by the FLQ in 1963, of the statue of General Wolfe on the Plains of Abraham and the Métis uprisings of 1870 and 1885.

Ferron's first novel, *La barbe de François Hertel* (1951), is an ironical and imaginative work that mocks the philosophical and sophistic mind of François Hertel (Rodolphe DUBÉ). In 1962 Ferron published his first major work, CONTES DU PAYS INCERTAIN, which won a Governor General's Award. Using legends, fables, and tales to illustrate Québec's uncertain future, Ferron portrays the land, formerly seen as a haven for survival, as being in an advanced state of decay; life in the city, however, does not offer a viable alternative, for the tillers of the land find slavery as members of the exploited working class in the city. *Contes du pays incertain* was republished in 1968 with *Contes anglais et autres* and *Contes inédits*. A selection of these stories, many of them from the first collection, was translated by Betty Bednarski and published in English under the title *Tales from the uncertain country* (1972). *Cotnoir* (1962), a novel that stylistically resembles a tale, presents one of Ferron's favourite themes: the necessity for a doctor to be both close to the people and a champion of freedom—which, in Québec, implies political independence. It has been translated by Pierre Cloutier as *Doctor Cotnoir* (1973). *La nuit* (1965) tells the story of François Ménard, a materialistic and bourgeois Québécois who, having lost contact with his heritage, gradually discovers a social order based on equality and historical awareness. It was translated by Ray Ellenwood as *Quince jam* (1977). *Papa Boss* (1966; republished with minor changes in 1972) describes the possession of an anonymous working-class woman by a capitalist angel, Papa Boss. *La charrette* (1968) depicts a doctor who, like François Ménard, liberates himself from social 'deconditioning' (unawareness) and endeavours to help the 'cart-people' (workers) victimized by the diabolical boss, Bélial. It has been translated by Ray Ellenswood as *The cart* (1981). The young narrator of *L'amélanchier* (1970) is initiated by her father into the 'good side of things': family and national history as indispensable tools for growing up, and the pressing need for the preservation of the flora, fauna, and historical landmarks of Québec. It was translated by Raymond Chamberlain as *The juneberry tree* (1975). *Le salut de l'Irlande* (1970), which demonstrates that the salvation of Québec and Ireland are closely linked, also tells the story of a young person who comes to realize that colonial and liberal ideologies, along with urban speculation, represent the real danger for Québécois eager to preserve their identity in a healthy environment. In *Les roses sauvages* (1972)—translated by Betty Bednarski as *Wild roses* (1976)—the businessman Baron learns the message of 'salvation' too late and joins the socially insane described in the short text, *Lettre d'amour*, which follows *Les roses sauvages*. Baron's daughter, however, will not be destroyed by ambition. Like Tinamer in *L'amélanchier* and Connie in *Le salut de l'Irlande*, she has understood the tale of survival; she will become a psychiatrist in order to help people like Rosaire Gélineau (*Rosaire*, 1981), whose mental illness is brought about by a society that discourages small craftsmen and thrives on assembly lines and seasonal unemployment. These Montreal novels are works of awareness and apprenticeship, quite obvious products of the sixties, when Québec was seen by most writers as a 'stupid and defenceless' suburb *(L'amélanchier)* of the USA, and when the FLQ warned that the homeland must be redeemed. For Ferron, violence is at once a threat, a warning, and a temptation.

Le ciel de Québec (1969)—Ferron's longest, most complex, and perhaps only true novel—cleverly intertwines four main stories centred in Quebec City in 1937-8 (the centennial of the Patriote rebellion): representatives of the Church involve themselves in politics, politicians display their skill in the use of patronage, Québécois reveal their feelings of exile in the West, the Métis are torn between staying on the Prairies and living in Québec. Several digressions develop other themes: 1837; the English in Québec; the role of Québécois writers in the elaboration of Quebec nationalism and identity. In *Le Saint-Elias* (1972), another historical novel, the launching of a ship in 1896 parallels the launching, by Dr Fauteux, of the ideals of the Patriotes. A decisive battle ensues between the supporters of the zealous monarchist Monseigneur Laflèche and the devoted and patriotic Doctor Fauteux. It was translated by Pierre Cloutier as *The Saint Elias* (1975). In *La chaise du maréchal ferrant* (1972) Ferron returns to the Gaspé and through legend and folklore shows the devastating effects of ambition and money on an old Québec family torn apart by the 'capitalist devil' and an amazing flying machine, the blacksmith's chair. The tale is humorously linked to the treachery of the 'federalist villain', Mackenzie King, and the 'provincial villain', Duplessis. Ferron's imaginative approach to history, inspired by Anthony Hamilton and Tallemant des Réaux and central to most of his works, is best illustrated in *Historiettes* (1969), a collection of tales or anecdotes in which historical and political figures are freely transformed into literary characters.

Most of Ferron's later novels display the same characteristics as *Contes du pays incertain*: condensed plot; legend; parable; imaginative and fabulous atmosphere; animation of the animal and plant worlds; a surrealistic and fantastic vision; fantasy as seen through the eyes of a child; irony, satire, and wordplay. His tales, novels, and plays evoke both Lewis Carroll *(L'amélanchier* is a witty transposition of *Alice in Wonderland)* and *The thousand and one nights*. Ferron's father, who was a lawyer and political organizer, is a key antagonist in many of his novels. Ferron even claimed that he wanted to be a writer in order to denounce his conservative, élitist, and corrupt father; not surprisingly, biographical references are scattered throughout his works. There are also obvious links between Ferron's education and his writing. The tyranny and prejudices of religious communities encountered in his school life constitutes one of his major themes.

Les confitures de coings (1972) is composed of new versions (all with minor changes) of the novels *Papa Boss, La nuit* (given the new title 'Les confitures de coings'), as well as 'La créance', an autobiographical tale dealing with social injustices in Louiseville, and 'Appendice aux *Confitures de coings* ou Le congédiement de Frank Archibald Campbell', an imaginative interpretation of *Les confitures de coings* combined with autobiographical insights and revelations. *Gaspé-Mattempa* (1980) is another tale that recreates Ferron's sojourn in the Gaspé.

Ferron's social and political ideas have had considerable influence on modern Québec society. His thirty-odd works form a coherent system in which their predominant themes—justice; social concepts of love; the physical and psychological effects of capitalism; the doctor's role in society; religious excesses; the creation of new myths related to Québec history and politics; Québec and foreign writers in relation to Ferron's view of the world—are articulated in an original and esthetically pleasing setting. Ferron is in fact several writers in one: a 'conteur', a fabulist, a symbolist, and creator of myths. A literary geographer, historian, botanist, and folklorist of the 'uncertain country', he, more than any other Québec writer, has turned real people and real situations into literary beings and fictional places.

Du fond de mon arrière-cuisine (1973) and *Escarmouches, la longue passe* (1975) give an excellent sampling of Ferron's innumerable articles dealing with history, medicine, literature, and politics that originally appeared in various journals and newspapers. Several books have been written on Ferron: Jean-Pierre Boucher, *Jacques Ferron au pays des amélanchiers* (1973) and *Les 'Contes' de Jacques Ferron* (1974); Jacques De Roussan, *Jacques Ferron* (1971); Jean Marcel, *Jacques Ferron malgré lui* (1970); Yves Taschereau, *La médecine dans l'oeuvre de Jacques Ferron* (1975); and Pierre L'Hérault, *Jacques Ferron, cartographe de l'imaginaire* (1980). Special issues of *Études françaises* (1976) and VOIX ET IMAGES (1982) are devoted to Ferron.

See also ESSAYS IN FRENCH: 7 and NOVELS IN FRENCH 1960 TO 1982:2.

DONALD SMITH

Fiamengo, Marya (b. 1926). Born in Vancouver, where she still lives, she was educated at the University of British Columbia and received an M.A. in creative writing, under thesis director Earle BIRNEY, for her book of poems *The ikon: measured work* (1961). She now teaches in the English department at UBC. Her other poetry collections—*Quality of halves* (1958), *Overheard at the oracle* (1969), *Silt of iron* (1971), and *In praise of old women* (1976), some poems from which were reprinted in *North of the cold star* (1978)—are reflective, intellectual, humorous, and passionate. In addition to writing about political oppression and social injustice, she is especially effective in dealing with the oppression of women by themselves. Her poem 'In praise of old women' criticizes aging North American women who attend beauty salons in order to remain attractive to men. Her ironic wit keeps her matter-of-fact imagery—which often draws upon her Slavic origins—from becoming forced and her poems from becoming mere tracts or polemics. Her later poems continue her interest in Canadian ancestry, especially the strengths of immigrant women, and include meditations on nature, Norman Bethune, the RCMP, and a favourite target: American academics in Canadian unversities, against whom she wages a constant guerilla action.   GEOFF HANCOCK

Fiddlehead, The. A literary magazine published continuously at the University of New Brunswick since 1945. Founded as a poetry magazine by Alfred BAILEY and a group of student writers, and modelled on PREVIEW and FIRST STATEMENT, it served until 1953 as a purely local magazine. Fred COGSWELL, who became editor in that year and held the job until 1967, expanded it to include writers from across and outside Canada and to print stories and reviews as well as poems. The magazine has followed a widely eclectic policy, which allowed it to publish many young and relatively unknown writers. A number of these—such as Al PURDY, Milton ACORN, Jay MACPHERSON, Alden NOWLAN, and Elizabeth BREWSTER—have become well established. Kent THOMPSON, Robert GIBBS, and Roger Ploude were the magazine's editors from 1967 to 1981, when Peter Thomas assumed the editorship.   ROBERT GIBBS

Fidler, Peter. See EXPLORATION LITERATURE IN ENGLISH: 2.

Fifth business (1970). The first novel in the Deptford trilogy by Robertson DAVIES, it established him as one of Canada's leading writers of fiction. The story has a double focus. As the 'autobiography' of the schoolmaster Dunstan Ramsay it narrates key events in his life: his ducking of a fateful snowball, his boyhood love for the saintly Mary Dempster, his experiences in the First World War, his researches as a hagiographer, and his encounters with the business magnate Boy Staunton, the magician Magnus Eisengrim, and the fantastically ugly Liesl Naegli. While Ramsay figures as hero, he plays quite a different part in the lives of Mary Dempster, her son Paul, Leola Cruikshank, and Boy Staunton: he is 'fifth business', playing a subsidiary but essential role in the drama of their lives and bringing the action to an appropriate conclusion.

Gordon Roper's 'Fifth business and "That old fantastical duke of dark corners, C.G. Jung" ' in the Journal of Canadian Fiction 1, No. 1 (Winter 1972) first drew critical attention to Davies' rich use of Jung's ideas. Ramsay's gradual achievement of self-knowledge can be compared to Jung's 'individuation', and the characters encountered along the way to Jungian archetypes. For Jung, coming to terms with oneself involves retrieving and facing the contents of the unconscious—which contains significant character models or archetypes to which he gave appropriate names. He called a man's unconscious notion of woman the Anima; those elements rejected from the conscious personality the Shadow; the characters inherited in the collective unconscious memory, shared by all people, the Magus or Magician, the Devil, the Wise Old Man, and so on. One achieves self-mastery by recognizing that the unconscious may distort one's view of other people and by reclaiming the archetype that has been unconsciously projected on another person. In Fifth business the archetypes are not only projections that must be recognized and recovered but elements in a story that has a fairy-tale or mythic quality. At one level we are persuaded to accept a romantic world where figures like a saint (Mary Dempster), and Magus (Magnus Eisengrim), and a Wise Old Man (Padré Blazon) act out their archetypal roles unrestrained by prosaic reality.

Fifth business was published simultaneously in Canada, the United States, and England, and has been translated into Polish, Norwegian, French, Swedish, and Chinese. It is available as a Penguin paperback.   JUDITH SKELTON GRANT

Finch, Robert (b. 1900). Robert Duer Claydon Finch was born at Freeport, Long Island, N.Y. He studied at University College, University of Toronto, and at the Sorbonne in Paris, and in 1928 joined the staff of the Department of French, University College, Toronto, where he was a full professor from 1952 until his retirement in 1968. Finch has also been a well-known poet, and a painter and harpsichordist of considerable reputation. His masque, 'A century has roots', was presented for the centenary of University College in 1953. His distinguished career as a scholar, particularly of seventeenth- and eighteenth-century French poetry, came to fruition in The sixth sense: individualism in French poetry 1686-1760 (1966) and in an anthology, French individualist poetry (1971), which he edited with E. Joliat. He received the Lorne Pierce Gold Medal in 1968, and was elected to the Royal Society of Canada in 1963.

Finch was one of six poets included in the anthology NEW PROVINCES (1936). From the beginning he was primarily a lyric poet. In *Poems* (1946), which received a Governor General's Award, his skill with language and form gave his wit full scope in epigrams and satiric portraits. Like other poets reacting against the confessional poetry of the Romantic era, Finch treated emotional experience with reticence and allusiveness. *The strength of the hills* (1948) contains many emblematic and allegorical poems, and features a sonnet sequence on mountains that develops moral and religious themes. Other poems include exact and vivid re-creations of places and seasons, and a series on the transforming power of snow that uses images of beauty rather than the stereotyped symbol of a hostile force.

Although two volumes published in 1961, *Acis in Oxford* (first privately printed in 1959) and *Dover Beach revisited*, contain a number of brief lyrics in Finch's characteristic voice, they revealed new interests and a considerable extension of range. *Acis in Oxford* (winner of a Governor General's Award) includes three poems linked by associations with an Oxford college, its gardens, a public park, and the river, that also draw easily on long traditions of myth and culture. The problem of faith is central to *Dover Beach revisited*, which begins with a reconsideration of Arnold's famous poem by eleven speakers who, though loosely associated with the poem's provenance, are themselves timeless. A second section, 'The place revisited', consists of nine vigorous blank-verse poems about 'Operation Dynamo', the battle of Dunkirk.

Silverthorn bush (1966) has greater variety of form, subject, and image than any previous volume. Finch ranges widely through Chinese calligraphy, ancient and modern Tibet, early Canadian history, and the Western literary tradition; but, wearing his learning lightly, he also records the small experiences of ordinary life on a road, in a train, in a shop. *Variations and theme* (1980) consists of reflections on the nature of poetry, evocative miniatures of particular times and places, witty epigrams, hints of the experience of old age and memory. The title poem

'Variations and Theme'—fourteen variations, with a final section in rhyming couplets—concerns the moments of illumination offered by the senses and the imagination: past experience enters the present, but each experience also opens towards the future, towards an infinity beyond guessing.

The seven parts of *Has and is and other poems* (1981) reflect Finch's characteristic diversity. Urbane, elegant, and vigorous, the poems evince ease of manner and control of tone throughout. The last poem, 'The arbiter', brings together art, poetry, and life as a single entity, a unified conception. His latest collections are *Twelve for Christmas* (1982), twelve rondeaux on poets, and *The Grand Duke of Moscow's favourite solo* (1983).

JOHN MARGESON

Findley, Timothy (b. 1930). Born in Toronto and educated at secondary schools there and elsewhere in Ontario, he travelled widely in his first career as an actor. He worked for the Stratford Shakespearean Festival in its first season (1953) before moving to London to study at the Central School of Speech and Drama. He toured England, Europe, and the United States as a contract player with H.M. Tennant between 1953 and 1956, and during this period began to write fiction, with the encouragement of Thornton Wilder, in whose play *The matchmaker* he performed in London and New York. After his return to Canada he worked in radio, television, and the theatre before turning to writing as a full-time career in 1962. He has continued his involvement with radio and television, writing plays and documentaries, many of the latter in collaboration with William Whitehead, with whom he lives in Cannington, Ont. Among their award-winning scripts are the CBC drama series *The national dream* (1974) and *Dieppe 1942* (1979). Findley also wrote five of the scripts for *The Whiteoaks of Jalna* (CBC, 1971-2), and two of the plays for the CBC series *The newcomers* (1978-9). Story versions of the latter, entitled 'Island' and 'A long hard walk', are included in the book based on the series, *The newcomers* (1979). His plays for TV and radio include *The journey* (1971), winner of the Armstrong Award for radio drama.

Greatly affected as a child by newsreels of the Second World War, Findley continues to be haunted by images of a civilization gone mad. His fiction uses metaphors derived from film and structural devices resembling camerawork to project the nightmares that have actually happened. Madness, violence, and power—especially as epitomized by Fascism and the Nazi dream of racial perfection—form some part of each of his novels. In an insane world an act of violence may be the only sane response: an act of love. This paradox is at the heart of Findley's first novel, *The last of the crazy people* (1967). Here a southern-Ontario family in the 1960s, to whom inherited wealth has brought nothing but dessication and spiritual emptiness, is the microcosm of a doomed civilization. Through the course of one hot, rainless summer (heat is a recurrent image in Findley's work, suggesting a living hell and the build-up of unbearable tension before the cataclysmic storm), the family is observed in claustrophobic detail through the eyes of an eleven-year-old son who is desperate for the love and attention he can find only in the Negro maid and his much-tended cats. (Animals, and minority groups accustomed to persecution, are elsewhere in Findley's work seen as potential survivors of the apocalypse.) The novel ends with an 'insane' act of mercy-killing, arrived at through a child's logic, intuition, and love.

In *The butterfly plague* (1969) Findley's exploration of morality penetrates the very heart of the film world. The action centres on a Hollywood family threatened by inherited disease, and parallels historical events unfolding in Nazi Germany in the 1930s, some of which the daughter, a champion swimmer, had witnessed. California—with its disastrous canyon fires, adulation of glamorous appearance, quest for physical perfection, and its position at the edge of a 'pacific' ocean—offers a rich lode of symbolism and analogy that Findley tends to overwork. One is almost suffocated by significance, as if by a plague of monarch butterflies that are beautiful and fragile individually, but in their masses bring destruction.

The wars (1977), winner of a Governor General's Award, is Findley's most successful novel to date. It has been translated into nine languages (the Québec title is *Guerres*, 1980, translated by Eric Diacon), and is the basis of a film (completed 1982) directed by Robin Phillips. Reduced to its essentials, it is a story of the First World War: an officer, Ross, reacts to the horror of the trenches, graphically depicted, with an act of treason that could also be interpreted as a self-affirming deed of heroism and love. The novel's unique vision is given through the device of a narrator who, working from photographs, clippings, letters, and interviews, tries to understand the kind of man Ross was; as an intermediary between Ross and the reader he narrows the gap between past and present and forces awareness of all 'wars' against the human spirit.

Within a seemingly conventional framework—a thrilling spy chase across Europe at the end of the Second World War—*Famous last words* (1981) blends a variety of narrative devices and points of view. It is the fictional story of Hugh Selwyn Mauberley, adopted from Ezra Pound's poem of that name. Pound himself figures in the novel, as do other historical characters, such as the Duke and Duchess of Windsor, von Ribbentrop, and Sir Harry Oakes. The main narrative, inscribed by Mauberley on the walls of a deserted grand hotel—like the cavepaintings of Altamira whose symbols it incorporates—records the last days of what seemed, under the spread of Fascism, to be the end of a civilization. Interweaving factual and fictional material with paraphrases of Pound's work, the book is a disturbing study of the relationship between aestheticism and fascism. Elitism and the search for perfection are presented—more successfully here than in *The butterfly plague*—through brilliant evocations of high society and a subtle incorporation of the movie world.

The play *Can you see me yet?* (1977), performed at the National Arts Centre, Ottawa, in 1976, incorporates Findley's favourite themes and metaphors. Set in an asylum for the insane in 1938, it raises again the question of who is mad, who sane, and of where sanctuary is to be found in a world on fire. Cassandra, the significantly named heroine, comes from a loveless, stultifying family like that in *The last of the crazy people*. Her fellow-patients assume the roles of figures from her past and in so doing subtly alter her perceptions of her family and herself. The ironic implications of the title—a question Cassandra repeatedly addresses to God—suggest a spark of hope in the midst of near-despair.

The moral vision informing Findley's work is discussed in two interviews: with Donald Cameron in *Conversations with Canadian novelists* (1973), and with Graeme GIBSON in *Eleven Canadian novelists* (1973). There is also an interview with Johan Aitken in *Journal of Canadian Fiction* 33 (1982). Eva-Marie Kroller has an article entitled 'The exploding frame: uses of photography in Timothy Findley's *The Wars*' in *Journal of*

Canadian Studies (Autumn/Winter 1981), and CANADIAN LITERATURE 91 (Winter 1981) is mainly devoted to 'Timothy Findley and the war novel'.

See also NOVELS IN ENGLISH 1960 TO 1982: 3.   JOAN COLDWELL

Fineberg, Larry (b. 1945). Born in Montreal and educated at McGill University and Emerson College, Massachusetts, he began his theatrical career as an assistant director in New York and London. His published plays include *Death* (1972), *Hope* (1972), *Stonehenge trilogy* (1972), *Waterfall* (1974), *Eve* (1977; winner of the Chalmers Award for Best Canadian Play), *Human remains* (1978), *Medea* (1978), a revised version of *Stonehenge trilogy*: *Stonehenge* (1978) and *Montreal* (1982). *Death, Hope, Human remains*, and *Stonehenge* have been collected in *Four plays by Larry Fineberg* (1978). Other dramas, produced but not yet published, include *All the ghosts, Life on Mars*, and the musical *Fresh disasters*. Though most of Fineberg's important work has been seen first in Toronto underground theatres, he is also one of a relatively small number of Canadian playwrights to have been closely associated with the Stratford Festival. *Eve* (an adaptation of Constance BERESFORD-HOWE's *The book of Eve*) was produced there in 1976, as was *Medea* (based on Euripides) in 1978. *Devotion*, scheduled for production in 1978, was cancelled following the illness of the director.

Fineberg's work presents a fundamentally bleak view of humanity: his characters, seemingly uninterested in each other or even in themselves, lead lives empty of affection; when suggestions of love, or at least concern, do appear, they are usually given oblique expression. Perhaps his most powerful play is the one-act *Death*, which in a series of short scenes, full of sternly economical dialogue, shows the despair of a dying old man and the emptiness of the lives that surround him. The play's austerity of manner produces a tight fusion of form and content.

Elsewhere Fineberg's style is more eclectic, not always to the advantage of his work. *Hope*, with acknowledgments to Edward Gorey, explores a vein of macabre fantasy (in a typical moment an exploding croquet mallet severs its victim's hand and blows it through the air till it lands, fingers down, in a mousse). The children's musical *Waterfall* also experiments with fantasy, but in a more gentle, even soft-centred way. *Stonehenge* and *Human remains* combine surface realism with fantasy in a slightly unstable mixture, though the former—scenes in the life of a middle-class Jewish community—also contains some grimly witty social satire.

ALEXANDER LEGGATT

Finnigan, Joan (b. 1925). Born in Ottawa, Joan Finnigan studied at Carleton University, Ottawa, and Queen's University, Kingston. She lives in Renfrew, Ont. Her early poetry in *Through a glass darkly* (1957), *A dream of lilies* (1965), and *It was warm and sunny when we set out* (1970) concentrates on personal relationships and is sometimes confessional in tone, with an elegiac note of loss. *Entrance to the green-house* (1968) is a series of almost haiku-like lyrics, linking her feelings to the sudden upsurge of life in nature. The large page-size of *In the brown cottage on Loughborough Lake* (1970), describing her 'limbo all summer long' as she reflects on the death of love, allows for a visually appealing marriage between her poems and photographs by Erik Christensen.

Finnigan wrote the script for a National Film Board movie, *The best damn fiddler from Calabogie to Kaladar* (1969), and since that film her writing has reflected a strong interest in localities and people who live in them. *Living together* (1976) contains sequences about the Ottawa Valley, the regions around Kitchener and Kingston and in northern Ontario. Her fascination with communities is also apparent in *A reminder of familiar faces* (1978). *This series has been discontinued* (1980) was chosen as one of the last poetry collections to be published by Fiddlehead Books under the direction of Fred COGSWELL.

Finnigan's tapes of stories and histories of people living in the Ottawa Valley have been used for radio programs and books, including *I come from the valley* (1976), *Canadian colonial cooking* (1976), *Some of the stories I told you were true* (1981), and *Giants of Canada's Ottawa Valley* (1981). She has also written a local history: *Kingston: celebrate this city* (1976).   PETER STEVENS

First Statement (1942-5). Founded in Montreal in Sept. 1942 by John SUTHERLAND and his sister Betty, Robert Simpson, Keith MacLellan, and Audrey Aikman, *First Statement* was Sutherland's response to a rejection of his creative writing by the recently founded PREVIEW. Intended as a fortnightly, but appearing irregularly, the magazine averaged 8-to-10 mimeographed pages for its first 15 issues, with a core circulation of

First Statement

75. In Issue 5 it incorporated *The Western Free-lance* and its Vancouver editor, Geoffrey Ashe, and made claims to being national. By 1943 Simpson and MacLellan had dropped from the board, and were replaced by Irving LAYTON and Louis DUDEK, with Sutherland still editor-in-chief; a shift from eclecticism to a poetry that articulated the local and everyday experience in plain language and from a North American perspective now became more pronounced. Unlike its frequent editorial target, *Preview*—known for the wit, technical sophistication, and cosmopolitan concerns of its slightly older and more established contributors—*First Statement* disavowed any poetry that seemed 'colonial', favouring work that was influenced by American models, such as Ezra Pound and William Carlos Williams, over what was considered to be *Preview*'s British influences: W.H. Auden, T.S. Eliot, and Dylan Thomas. With the acquisition of a printing press, *First Statement* improved in appearance with vol. 2, no. 1 (Aug. 1943). It became an irregular monthly with more than double the number of pages and—in addition to the usual poetry, short stories, and criticism—offered book reviews. Because of financial constraints it became a bi-monthly in Oct.-Nov. 1944 and averaged 35 pages per issue.

In 1945 First Statement Press launched the important New Writers chapbook series with Layton's first collection, *Here and now*, which was followed later in the year by Patrick ANDERSON's *A tent for April* and Miriam WADDINGTON's *Green world*. In late 1945, after 33 issues, *First Statement* merged with *Preview* to become NORTHERN REVIEW with Sutherland as managing editor. He maintained control of First Statement Press, publishing Raymond SOUSTER's *When we are young* (1946); *Other Canadians: an anthology of the new poetry in Canada, 1940-46* (1947), compiled in reaction to A.J.M. SMITH's first anthology, *The book of Canadian poetry* (1943); Layton's *Now is the place* (1948); Anne WILKINSON's *Counterpoint to sleep* (1951); and Kay Smith's *Footnote to the Lord's Prayer* (1951).

See Neil H. Fisher, *'First Statement': an assessment and an index* (1974).

DAVID O'ROURKE

Fleming, May Agnes (1840-80). Born in Portland, near Saint John, N.B., May Agnes Early published her first story—'The last of the Montjoys; or, Tale of the days of Queen Elizabeth'—in the New York *Mer-* *cury* while she was still attending the Convent of the Sacred Heart in Saint John. She went on to become one of the first Canadians to pursue a highly successful career as a writer of popular fiction. In the 1860s, first as 'Cousin May Carleton', and then after her marriage in 1865, as May Agnes Fleming, she sold short stories and serialized novels to such newspapers as the Boston *Pilot*, the New York *Mercury* and *Metropolitan Record*, the Philadelphia *Saturday Night*, and the Saint John *Western Recorder and Weekly Herald*. After their first appearance in these periodicals, her works were usually republished, often with a different title, in volume form; sometimes they were dramatized. In the early 1870s Mrs Fleming was offered an arrangement whereby her stories would appear simultaneously in the New York *Weekly* and the London *Journal* and then be republished in book form by G.W. Carleton in New York. The *Weekly* paid $100 per instalment and the *Journal* £12; she received a 15-per-cent royalty from Carleton. Since her annual output was at least one novel that ran to about 30 instalments, she became wealthy enough by the mid-1870s to leave her alcoholic husband and move with her four children to Brooklyn, where she died from Bright's disease at thirty-nine. Her popularity was such that her stories were published even after her death, and other stories not by her, some apparently written by a man, continued to appear under her name.

In her novels Mrs Fleming was able to achieve a balance between the domestic and the exotic that accounts chiefly for their appeal to her largely urban, middle-class, married women readers. Much of the action of her later stories was set in New York City; but her settings also included London and Paris, large estates in the U.S. and Great Britain, and—because French Canada provided an exotic locale for American readers—Montreal and the villages of Québec. Her protagonists were often relatively poor working women such as seamstresses and teachers, and her plots usually centred on marrying them to apparently good, prosperous men, preferably with connections to the British aristocracy. Complications arose from the greed and inexperience of the women, who often chose weak husbands, and the evil nature of the men. Mrs Fleming's books allowed her readers not only to live out in fantasy their most romantic dreams and bizarre impulses, but to reassure themselves that, however humble and humdrum their lives might seem, true nobility lay not in external appearances but in internal reality and eternal truths.

Among the novels by Mrs Fleming that were published in her lifetime were *La Masque; or, The midnight queen* (New York, 1863); *A mad marriage* (New York, 1875); *Kate Danton; or, Captain Danton's daughters* (New York, 1876); and *The heir of Charlton* (New York, 1878).

See the entry on Mrs Fleming by Fred COGSWELL in the *Dictionary of Canadian biography*, vol. 10 (1972), and the section on her in John Moss, *A reader's guide to the Canadian novel* (1981)—though Moss seems to have consulted a much-reduced version of *Kate Danton*. MARY JANE EDWARDS

Folklore in English. The term 'folklore' refers both to the material handed on in tradition, whether by word of mouth or by custom and practice, and to the study of that material. Until recently most Canadian publications have emphasized the material rather than its study. Of primary concern to folklorists are books that present folklore as it actually circulated among the folk, rather than those that present it in a more literary form, as interpreted by the author.

For this *Companion* it is appropriate to emphasize the oral aspects of folklore: what may be termed oral literature or the verbal arts, of which the most important are folksongs and folktales. Folklore's customs and beliefs, however, were the first of its aspects to be reported in the writings of the early missionaries, explorers, and travellers. The journals of Henry Kelsey, David Thompson, Paul KANE, and John Franklin all included information on the beliefs and customs of the Indians and Inuit. More relevant to folklore in English were such memoirs by travellers and settlers as Anna Jameson's *Winter studies and summer rambles in Canada* (London, 1838), Catherine Parr TRAILL's *The backwoods of Canada* (London, 1836), John C. Geikie's *George Stanley; or, Life in the woods* (London, 1844), and Susanna MOODIE's *Roughing it in the bush; or, Life in Canada* (London, 1852), which provided early accounts of pioneer customs. However, the first direct collecting of Anglo-Canadian folklore did not occur until the present century, and until recently most collectors have looked for songs rather than for other genres.

The first major collector of folksongs was W. Roy Mackenzie, who tracked down traditional singers in his native Nova Scotia

and gave a fascinating account of them in *The quest of the ballad* (1919). His later *Ballads and sea songs from Nova Scotia* (1928) is an important and still highly regarded collection, both for its early texts and for Mackenzie's careful documenting of each song's background.

Mackenzie's successor, Helen Creighton, began her collecting in 1929 and over the next half-century published a series of books: *Songs and ballads from Nova Scotia* (1932); *Traditional songs from Nova Scotia* (1950) with Doreen Senior; *Gaelic songs in Nova Scotia* (1964) with Calum MacLeod; *Maritime folk songs* (1962); and *Folksongs from southern New Brunswick* (1971).

Another important Nova Scotia collection was that of Carrie Grover, who spent her childhood in Canada, later moved to the States, and there recorded the songs of her mother and father in an undated manuscript entitled *A heritage of songs*, which was published in 1973.

When Newfoundland entered Confederation, it enriched Canada's folklore enormously. The earliest published collection of the island's songs appears to be James Murphy's *Songs and ballads of Newfoundland, ancient and modern* (1902). Later Murphy published several other booklets, as did other local bards like John Burke; and Gerald S. Doyle, a St John's merchant and folksong enthusiast, popularized many of the island's native songs through his series of pamphlets: *The old-time songs and poetry of Newfoundland* (1927, 1940, 1955, 1966, 1978). The first systematic collecting started in 1920, when Elisabeth Bristol Greenleaf began noting the songs around Sally's Cove, where she was serving as a Grenfell mission teacher. Nine years later she and a musician, Grace Yarrow Mansfield, returned to spend a fruitful summer as the Vassar College Folklore Expedition; this resulted in the first major Newfoundland collection, *Ballads and sea songs of Newfoundland* (1933). The Vassar girls included songs of both British and North American origin; but when Maud Karpeles, of the English Folk Dance and Song Society, visited the island in the summers of 1929 and 1930, she concentrated on the old British songs. Some of these she published with piano accompaniments in 1934, and the bulk of her collection in 1971 as *Folk songs from Newfoundland*.

Between 1951 and 1961 Kenneth Peacock made six summer field-trips to the island for the National Museum, and the result was his massive three-volume *Songs of the New-*

Folklore in English

foundland outports (1965). The same year MacEdward Leach, of the University of Pennsylvania, published the findings of a summer trip, sponsored by the National Museum, in *Folk ballads and songs of the lower Labrador Coast.*

Those books all included more old British songs than native Newfoundland ones, but two recent songbooks return to the pattern of the early pamphleteers by concentrating on local songs: *The ballads of Johnny Burke: a short anthology* (1974), assembled by Paul Mercer, and *Hauling rope & gaff: songs and poetry in the history of the Newfoundland seal fishery* (1978), compiled by Shannon Ryan and Larry Small. The students of Memorial University, St John's, also published two useful song references: *A regional discography of Newfoundland and Labrador 1904-1972* (1975) by Michael Taft, and *Newfoundland songs and ballads in print 1942-1974: a title and first-line index* (1979) by Paul Mercer.

New England scholars were the first to collect in New Brunswick. Phillips Barry, Fannie H. Eckstorm, and Mary W. Smyth included forty Canadian songs in *British ballads from Maine* (1929). Local interest developed in 1947 when Lord Beaverbrook asked Louise Manny to collect the songs of his native Miramichi. Some twenty years later Manny and her music editor, James Reginald Wilson, produced *Songs of Miramichi* (1968).

Another New England folklorist, Edward D. Ives of the University of Maine, has worked extensively in the Canadian Maritimes. He published 'Twenty-one folksongs from Prince Edward Island" in *Northeast Folklore* (vol. 5, 1963) and pioneered the detailed study of local songwriters with three important volumes: *Larry Gorman: the man who made the songs* (1964), *Lawrence Doyle: the farmer-poet of Prince Edward Island* (1971), and *Joe Scott: the woodsman-songmaker* (1978).

Some smaller Maritime publications include *Folk songs of Prince Edward Island* (1973) by Christopher Gledhill, *Folksongs from Prince Edward Island* (1973) by Randall and Dorothy Dibblee, and *Songs & stories from Deep Cove Cape Breton as remembered by Amby Thomas* (1979) edited by Ron MacEachern.

Little was known of Ontario songs until the 1950s, when Edith Fowke began her search in the Peterborough region and later extended it to the Ottawa Valley and Glengarry County. She was fortunate in discovering many fine traditional singers, and pub-

lished some of their songs in two volumes: *Traditional singers and songs from Ontario* (1965), which emphasized old Irish and British ballads, and *Lumbering songs from the northern woods* (1969), which was the first Canadian book to concentrate on the songs of a particular occupation.

West of Ontario very few Anglo-Canadian songs have been reported. Margaret Arnett McLeod published *Songs of old Manitoba* (1960), which is notable for its interesting Métis ballads, including some by the famous songwriter Pierre FALCON; and Barbara Cass-Beggs produced two small pamphlets: *Eight songs of Saskatchewan* (1963) and *Seven Métis songs of Saskatchewan* (1967). So far no book has recorded Alberta songs, but in British Columbia, Philip Thomas published *Songs of the Pacific Northwest* (1979), compiled partly from archives and partly from his own collecting. It emphasizes songs that illustrate aspects of British Columbia's history, and Thomas has provided extensive background notes.

Supplementary to those regional collections, Edith Fowke and Richard Johnston published two general anthologies with piano accompaniments as *Folk songs of Canada* (1954) and *More folk songs of Canada* (1967); Edith Fowke and Alan Mills brought out *Canada's story in song* (1960), stressing the relationship between songs and history; and Edith Fowke also published another anthology, *The Penguin book of Canadian folk songs* (1973).

While songs dominated the field until recently, some general folklore books appeared in the first half of this century. In 1931 two scholars pursuing graduate degrees published collections covering Nova Scotia tales, customs, and superstitions: for his Masters degree at the University of Pennsylvania, Arthur Huff Fauset reported on the Black community in *Folklore from Nova Scotia*, while Mary L. Fraser, a Catholic nun, published her doctoral dissertation as *Folklore of Nova Scotia*. Twenty years later two more general collections appeared—this time, coincidentally, both devoted to areas originally settled by Germans: Helen Creighton's *Folklore of Lunenburg County, Nova Scotia* (1950) and W.J. Wintemberg's *Folklore of Waterloo County, Ontario* (1950).

In contrast to the many folksong collections, very few Anglo-Canadian folktales have appeared. Both Mary Fraser and Arthur Fauset included some tales in their theses; Herbert Halpert published 'Tall tales and other yarns from Calgary, Alberta' in the *California Folklore Quarterly* (vol. 4:1, 1945); and Helen Creighton and Edward D. Ives presented 'Eight folktales from Miramichi as told by Wilmot MacDonald' in *Northeast Folklore* (vol. 4, 1962). More recently C.I.N. MacLeod published *Stories from Nova Scotia* (1974), translations of Gaelic tales he had collected in Cape Breton, and Carol Spray brought out *Will o the wisp: folktales and legends of New Brunswick* (1979).

More numerous are various books based partly on folktales but adapted by the authors: for example, the Maritime series by Archibald M. MacMECHAN, beginning with *Old province tales* (1924), and by William C. Borrett, beginning with *Tales told under the old town clock* (1942). There were also two undated volumes: *The treasury of Newfoundland stories* by L.W. Janes and *Newfoundland wit, humour, and folklore* by H.N. Reader; and F.H. MacArthur told *Tales of Prince Edward Island* (1966). John D. Robins retold the tales he had heard in northern Ontario as *Logging with Paul Bunyan* (1957), and Robert E. Gard produced a prairie collection, *Johnny Chinook: tall tales and true from the Canadian West* (1967), based on material collected by the Alberta Folklore and Local History Project.

The French-Canadian heritage of folktales has been much richer than the Anglo-Canadian, and several authors have published their versions of these tales in English. Early samples appeared in Philippe-Joseph AUBERT DE GASPÉ's *Les ANCIENS CANADIENS* of 1864 (translated by Sir Charles G.D. ROBERTS as *The Canadians of old* 1890), W.L. Greenough's *Canadian folklife and folk lore* (New York, 1897), J.M. LeMoine's *The legends of the St. Lawrence* (Québec, 1898), and Honoré BEAUGRAND's *La chasse galerie and other Canadian stories* (Montréal, 1900). These were followed by Paul A.W. Wallace's *Baptiste Larocque: legends of French Canada* (1923), Edward C. Woodley's *Legends of French Canada* (1931), Natalie S. Carlson's *The talking cat and other stories of French Canada* (1952), Hazel Boswell's *Legends of Québec from the land of the golden dog* (1966), Claude Aubry's *The magic fiddler and other legends of French Canada* (1968) translated by Alice Kane, and Mary Alice Downie's *The witch of the North: folktales of French Canada* (1975). Perhaps most interesting in this group are two by Marius BARBEAU: *The tree of dreams* (1955) and *The golden phoenix and other French-Canadian fairy tales* (1958), the latter retold by Michael Hornyansky. Nearly all these books are based on tradi-

tional material, but it has been adapted by the authors. In *Folktales of French Canada* (1980) Edith Fowke gives more literal translations in an attempt to come closer to the style of the original French narrators.

The folklife and customs depicted in various nineteenth-century narratives continue to form an important part of the multitudinous volumes of local history and personal reminiscences pouring from our presses. There are far too many to survey here, but among the best are John McDougall's *Rural life in Canada* (1913), Edwin C. Guillet's *Early life in Upper Canada* (1933), Charles W. Dunn's *Highland settler: a portrait of the Scottish Gael in Nova Scotia* (1953), John Kenneth Galbraith's *The Scotch* (1964), and Barry Broadfoot's *The pioneer years, 1893-1914: memories of pioneers who opened the West* (1976). Similarly, some books describing Canada's occupations contain valuable folklore, for example George S. Thomson's *Up to date; or, The life of a lumberman* (Peterborough, 1895), George Allan England's *Vikings of the ice: being the log of a tenderfoot on the great Newfoundland seal hunt* (1924), J.W. Grant MacEwan's *Blazing the old cattle trail* (1962), and Victor Butler's *The little Nord Easter: reminiscences of a Placentia bayman* (1975) edited by Wilfred W. Wareham.

In the second part of this century the more varied types of folklore began to receive greater attention. Helen Creighton supplemented her folksong collections with two interesting books: *Bluenose ghosts* (1957), dealing with poltergeists, forerunners, buried treasure, haunted houses, and phantom ships; and *Bluenose magic: popular beliefs and superstitions in Nova Scotia* (1968). Richard S. Lambert assembled the same kind of material from a wider area in *Exploring the supernatural: the weird in Canadian folklore* (1955); and Sterling Ramsay produced a smaller book dealing with the supernatural in *Folklore Prince Edward Island* (1976).

Children's lore is still relatively undocumented. Some early reports appeared in a Canadian issue of the *Journal of American Folklore* (vol. 31:1, 1918), and half a century later Edith Fowke published *Sally go round the sun: 300 songs, rhymes, and games of Canadian children* (1969) and *Ring around the moon: 200 songs, tongue twisters, riddles and rhymes of Canadian children* (1977). The first detailed study of one type of children's lore is Robert C. Cosbey's *All in together, girls: skipping songs from Regina, Saskatchewan* (1980).

Of increasing interest to folklorists is the very broad genre of folk art and material

Folklore in English

culture. Much of the relevant material to date appears in books that are general rather than specifically folkloristic. As with folklife and customs, books containing some information are pracically unlimited, but a list of a few important publications in this field will indicate its range: *'Keep me warm one night': early handweaving in eastern Canada* (1975) by Harold B. and Dorothy K. Burnham; *Quilts & other bed coverings in the Canadian tradition* (1979) by Ruth McKendry; *'Twas ever thus: a selection of eastern Canadian folk art* (1979) by Ralph Price; *Contextual studies of material culture* (1978) edited by David Zimmerly; *The ancestral roof: domestic architecture of Upper Canada* (1963) by Marion MacRae and Anthony Adamson; and *The heritage of Upper Canadian furniture* (1978) by Howard Pain.

As folklore gained recognition as an academic discipline, the emphasis shifted from collecting to studying folk materials to see what they revealed about the people from whom they came. The development of a folklore department at Memorial University, St John's, prompted a number of scholarly publications, of which one of the most important was *Christmas mumming in Newfoundland: essays in anthropology, folklore, and history* (1969), edited by Herbert Halpert and G.M. Story. It studied the mumming tradition in widely scattered areas of the island and Labrador and provided insights into the rural communities and their folk customs. Another unusual sociological study was John D.A. Widdowson's *If you don't be good: verbal social control in Newfoundland* (1977).

In the 1970s an increasing body of scholars produced numerous papers, some of which were incorporated in books such as *Folklore and oral history: papers from the second annual meeting of the Canadian aural/oral history association at St. John's, Newfoundland, October 3-5, 1975* (1978) edited by Neil V. Rosenberg, and *Canadian folklore perspectives* (1978) edited by Kenneth S. Goldstein. Goldstein and Rosenberg also edited *Folklore studies in honour of Herbert Halpert: a festschrift* (1980), which contained half-a-dozen articles on Canadian topics. Other studies appeared in three fairly recent Canadian folklore periodicals: *Canadian Folk Music Journal* (1973-), *Culture & Tradition* (1976-), and *Canadian Folklore Canadien* (1979-), as well as in various American and British journals.

Postgraduate students from Memorial University have begun to publish their research on a wide variety of topics. A whole series of books came out in 1979: *On sloping ground: reminiscences of outport life in Notre Dame Bay, Newfoundland* by Audrey M. Tizzard; *More than 50%: women's life in a Newfoundland outport 1900-1950* by Hilda C. Murray; *Textile traditions of eastern Newfoundland* by Gerald L. Pocius; *Skill and status: traditional expertise within a rural Canadian family* by Laurel Doucette; *'Bloody decks and a bumper crop': the rhetoric of sealing counter-protest* by Cynthia Lamson; and *Folk music in a Newfoundland outport* by Gordon S.A. Cox.

While Newfoundland scholars were turning out these many specialized publications, two Toronto folklorists produced three more general books. Edith Fowke's *Folklore of Canada* (1976) was the first anthology to give a cross-section of the nation's varied oral traditions drawn from authentic sources. Carole Henderson Carpenter's *Many voices: a study of folklore activities in Canada and their role in Canadian culture* (1979) gave the first comprehensive account of the history and development of Canadian folklore studies. More recently Fowke and Carpenter published *A bibliography of Canadian folklore in English* (1981), the first attempt to compile a comprehensive listing of books, articles, periodicals, films, and records dealing with all the different genres of Canadian folklore.   EDITH FOWKE

Folklore in French. There are two distinct groups of French-speaking Canadians: Québécois and Acadians. The former settled originally in the valley of the St Lawrence, while the latter occupied what is today Nova Scotia. While both colonies were founded early in the seventeenth century, historical factors made Québec the only province with a francophone majority; the dispersal of the Acadians in 1755 led to the creation of many little 'Acadies', with the chief concentration today in New Brunswick and with smaller groups scattered throughout Nova Scotia, Prince Edward Island, on the Gaspé peninsula and the Magdalen Islands, and in western Newfoundland. Following the cession to England of Acadia (1713) and Québec (1763), when English was used to impose British rule (there were few French schools), oral tradition was the major binding force that helped French-speaking Canadians maintain their identity.

Awareness of the value of tradition became evident in Québec in the 1860s with the publication of Joseph-Charles TACHÉ's *Forestiers et voyageurs, étude de moeurs*

(Québec, 1863) and Philippe AUBERT DE GASPÉ's Les ANCIENS CANADIENS (Québec, 1864). Although these writers were of a literary rather than a folkloristic bent, they depicted with considerable understanding and sensitivity the life and legends of the lumbermen and seigneurial and peasant ways respectively. The first genuine folklore work to appear in Canada was Ernest Gagnon's Chansons populaires du Canada (Montréal, 1865), in which Gagnon noted the melodies of 100 songs and provided data on his sources. There was very little activity in the field for the rest of the century, although a number of literary figures published material that made use of folklore in Les SOIRÉES CANADIENNES (5 vols, Québec, 1861-5), Le FOYER CANADIEN (8 vols, Québec, 1863-6), and Les nouvelles soirées canadiennes (7 vols, Montréal, 1882-6).

It was not until Marius BARBEAU became interested in French folklore after 1914 that significant strides were made in the field. Supported by the National Museum of Canada, Barbeau collected extensively in many parts of Québec, and attracted others—such as E.Z. Massicotte; an especially fine collector of folksongs, Evelyn Bolduc; Gustave Lanctôt; and Adélard Lambert—all of whom collected traditional songs and narratives. Much that they collected was published in eight French numbers of the Journal of American Folklore (between 1916 and 1950), where it represents one of the most substantial bodies of Canadian French folklore yet published. It should be added that although the major sections of the French numbers of the JAF covered narratives and songs, two issues (vol. 33: 4, 1920, and vol. 32: 1, 1919) dealt with children's folklore and traditional beliefs respectively, both of which are due to Massicotte. The publication of such material was, in Canada, innovative.

Barbeau's contributions are listed elsewhere, but mention should be made of his Romancéro du Canada (1937). He drew to him another group of followers in the late 1930s. One of these, Joseph-Thomas Leblanc, collected some 1,200 Acadian folksongs through the medium of his newspaper, L'Évangéline (Moncton, N.B.); François Brassard made a large collection of songs in the Saguenay region and in northern Ontario. But by far the most important recruit to Canadian folklore studies made by Barbeau was Luc Lacourcière, who in 1944 began teaching folklore at Université Laval and organized the Archives de Folklore

there. Almost at once he began publishing a series of works under the imprint of the Archives. The first four volumes (1946, 1947, 1948, 1950) were collections of articles and studies on a broad range of folklore topics, and constituted the first elements of what remains the major scholarly folklore series in Canada, French or English. Many subsequent publications in the series have been dissertations, and volumes 5 and 6, Soeur Marie-Ursule's La civilisation traditionnelle des Lavalois (1951), is a model of the precise ethnographic documentation undertaken by Lacourcière's students.

Volume 7 of the Archives de Folklore series was Russell Scott Young's Vieilles chansons de Nouvelle-France (1956); this was followed by Nora Dawson's study of the material culture of a Québec community, La vie traditionnelle à Saint-Pierre (Ile d'Orléans) (1960). Volume 9 of the series, James E. La Follette's Étude linguistique de quatre contes folkloriques du Canada français (1969), underlined the interest folklore can offer to other disciplines; and volume 10, Germain Lemieux's Placide-Eustache. Sources et parallèles du conte-type 938 (1970), was the first scholarly study devoted to the folk-narrative tradition. Reflecting Lacourcière's interest in the comparative study of folktales are three superb analyses of the distribution and variation of Canadian versions of international folktale types and legends: Catherine Jolicoeur's La vaisseau fantôme. Légende étiologique (vol. 11, 1970), Hélène Bernier's La fille aux mains coupées (conte-type 706) (vol. 12, 1971), and Nancy Schmitz's La mensongère (conte-type 710) (vol. 14, 1972). In a somewhat different vein Antonine MAILLET earned her doctorate with Rabelais et les traditions populaires en Acadie (vol. 13, 1971), an illuminating study of the similarities between the folklore of Maillet's native Acadie and the traditional content of the famous Renaissance author's works. Volume 15 in the series was Georges Gauthier-Larouche's Évolution de la maison rurale traditionnelle dans la région de Québec (1974), while volume 16 presented an important collection of Acadian folksongs collected by Dominique Gauthier, Chansons de Shippagan (1975). The major works to appear in the Archives series to date (1981) are devoted to the classification and analysis of French folksongs from all over the world, prepared by Conrad Laforte, Lacourcière's long-time collaborator. The first tome, Poétiques de la chanson traditionnelle française (vol. 17, 1976), describes the rationale and methodology adopted by

Folklore in French

Laforte. It was followed by *Le catalogue de la chanson folklorique française: I, Chansons en laisse* (vol. 18, 1977), *IV, Chansons énumératives* (vol. 19, 1979), and *II, Chansons strophiques* (vol. 20, 1981); a subsequent volume(s) shortly conclude the *Catalogue*.

Germain Lemieux, a student of Lacourcière, has devoted much of his life to the collection and study of Franco-Ontarian folklore. Much of his collection has been published in *Les vieux m'ont conté*, a series, beginning in 1973, that was introduced by the useful and informative *Les jongleurs du billochet* (1973), which examined the story-telling contexts and some of the storytellers themselves; the seventeenth volume appeared in late 1981. Lemieux has also included both Franco-Manitoban and Québec tales in his publications.

Mélanges en l'honneur de Luc Lacourcière: folklore français d'Amérique (1978), edited by Jean-Claude Dupont, contains numerous articles and tributes to Lacourcière from former students, colleagues, and friends, as well as a bibliography and list of theses and dissertations directed by him. Lacourcière's major contribution to folklore scholarship in Canada, the as-yet unpublished *Catalogue raisonné du conte populaire français en Amérique du nord*, is eagerly awaited by folktale scholars all over the world.

Among the contributors to Lacourcière's *Mélanges* are Carmen Roy, who took over folklore studies at the National Museum from Marius Barbeau, and whose *Littérature orale en Gaspésie* (1955, 1962) is one of the best folklore works to appear under the imprint of the National Museum; and Frère Anselme Chiasson, a pioneer collector of Acadian and especially Cape Breton folklore, whose four series of *Chansons d'Acadie* (1942, 1945, 1948, and 1972), with Frère Daniel Boudreau, were followed by *Chéticamp: histoire et traditions acadiennes* (1961) and *Les légendes des Îles de la Madeleine* (1969). Chiasson was also the driving force in establishing folklore at the Centre d'études acadiennes, Université de Moncton, where considerable research has been undertaken in recent years.

Jean-Claude Dupont, current director of Université Laval's Centre d'études sur la langue, les arts et les traditions populaires des francophones en Amérique du nord (CELAT, which now includes the Archives de Folklore), while a specialist in material culture and folk art and artisans, has published a number of works of popular and scholarly appeal on 'contes', such as *Le*

légendaire de la Beauce (1974) and *Contes de bûcherons* (1976); he has also collected in Acadia, as his *Héritage d'Acadie* (1977) and *Histoire populaire de l'Acadie* (1979) attest. Other works on Acadian folklore that show the influence of Lacourcière's training include Lauraine Léger's innovative *Les sanctions populaires en Acadie* (1978) and Catherine Jolicoeur's *Les plus belles légendes acadiennes* (1981), a work of popular appeal that stems from her vast research into Acadian legends and her preparation of a classification system of legends.

Two recent noteworthy additions to Acadian folklore include Marielle Boudreau's and Melvin Gallant's *La cuisine traditionnelle en Acadie* (1975), a valuable description of Acadian foodways in an area of folklore studies that has received relatively little attention; and Georges Arsenault's *Complaintes acadiennes de l'Île-du-Prince-Edouard* (1980), an important study of the tradition of locally composed songs, and the first scholarly study of the French folklore of Prince Edward Island.

West of Ontario one of the few important folklore studies of French traditions is Marcien Ferland's *Chansons à répondre du Manitoba* (1979). Perhaps the smallest French minority in Canada is that of Newfoundland. Confined to the Port-au-Port peninsula-Bay St George area and including both Acadian and metropolitan French settlers, it has been researched by Gerald Thomas, who founded the Centre d'Études Franco-Terreneuviennes at Memorial University in 1975, with the encouragement of Luc Lacourcière. The Centre has a large archive of recordings and studies of Franco-Newfoundland folklore; and articles by Thomas, Geraldine Barter, and Gary Butler have appeared in *Culture & Tradition*, a joint publication of folklore students at Memorial and Laval Universities, and *Canadian Folklore Canadien*, published by the Folklore Studies Association of Canada. A study by Thomas of folktales told by French Newfoundlanders, *Les deux traditions: le conte populaire chez les Franco-Terreneuviens*, is awaiting publication.

Although he is a specialist in Québécois folklife, Robert-Lionel Séguin has also published works on a wide variety of folklore topics. Founder of the Centre documentaire en civilisation traditionnelle at the Université de Québec at Trois-Rivières, his most significant book, *L'injure en Nouvelle-France* (1976), has received little scholarly attention from Canadian folklorists. Lately there has been considerable publication in folklore that emphasizes popular appeal, while making use of scholarly input, as in a series published by Les Éditions Quinze, Montreal, edited by Laval-trained Jean-Pierre Pichette. Conrad Laforte's *Menteries drôles et merveilleuses. Contes traditionnels du Saguenay* (1978), Clément Legaré's *La bête à sept têtes et autres contes de la Mauricie* (1980), and Gérald E. Aucoin's *L'oiseau de la vérité et autres contes des pêcheurs acadiens de l'île du Cap-Breton* (1980) all attempt, in different ways, to add to the straightforward presentation of tales.

GERALD THOMAS

Ford, R.A.D. (b. 1915). Robert Arthur Douglas Ford was born in Ottawa and educated at the University of Western Ontario, London, where he studied English literature and history. He did graduate work in history at Cornell University and this led to a brief appointment in the history department there (1938-40). He then joined the Department of External Affairs and pursued a diplomatic career, during which he has held various posts at the ambassadorial level. Since 1968 he has been Canadian ambassador to the USSR; in 1971 he was made dean of the diplomatic corps in Moscow.

Ford's first volume of poetry, *A window on the North* (1956), won a Governor General's Award. As the title suggests, much of this collection focuses on northernness, the climatic extremes often becoming metaphors for the violent extremes in contemporary life. The poems generally offer a cold and bleak attitude to life, though this atmosphere is tempered by love poems and some meditative reminiscences of warmer times and places. This volume also includes translations of the work of modern Russian poets. Ford has had a continual interest in translation; however, he has suggested that his versions are more like 'imitations' than literal translations. Other translated renderings appear in *The solitary city* (1969), though in this collection he included not only Russian poems but translations from Brazilian, Serbo-Croat, and French works. Ford's own poems here still have a distanced bleakness, even though the details of scenes and landscapes are taken from his sojourns in South America and the Middle East. The studied objectivity and control of languge are emphasized by his frequent use of formal metrical structures. Conservative forms reappear in *Holes in space* (1979). The somewhat arid and objective tones remain, though there is a simplification of the

poems' metaphorical thrust. Ford's vision of general repression and cruelty, loss and betrayal, is consistent throughout his poetry. The only obvious change in this latter work is a stripping down of both language and form.

PETER STEVENS

Foreign writers on Canada in English. This article is a survey of literary works—mostly fiction—that have Canada as a setting and are by British and American writers whose involvement with Canada was brief or vicarious. On the whole, British authors have had an interest in Canada as a frontier setting for adventure fiction. Americans, finding sufficient inspiration in their own western frontier, have been more interested in the exotic elements of early Canadian history and contemporary French Canada. Though few of these foreign writers rose higher than romance or adventure in writing about the country, a chronicle of their 'Canadian' books is of historical interest in revealing both the ways in which Canada has appealed to creative writers outside the country, and the image of it that their books—some of which were very widely read—propagated. (See also Writing in NEW FRANCE, EXPLORATION LITERATURE, TRAVEL LITERATURE, FOREIGN WRITERS ON CANADA IN FRENCH.)

1. BRITISH WRITERS. The earliest published British literary responses to Canada were in verse. *Englands honour revived* (1628) by Martin Parker (d. 1656?) is a crudely written broadside ballad celebrating the temporary capture of Québec from the French in 1628. The same year saw the publication of *Quodlibets, lately come over from New Britaniola, old Newfound-land* (London, 1628) by Robert HAYMAN, a former governor of the Bristol merchants' plantation at Conception Bay. This miscellaneous collection of 'epigrams . . . both morall and divine' also contains 'bad unripe Rimes' in praise of Newfoundland—the work of a sincere propagandist who had no pretensions as a poet. ('You feare the *Winters* cold, sharp, piercing ayre./They love it best, that have once wintered there.') *Liberty asserted* (London, 1704) by John Denis (1657-1734) introduced Canada by name, if nothing else, to the London stage. Set in New France in the seventeenth century and described as 'a Satyr upon the government of the French', it has to do with the struggle between the French under Frontenac, and their allies the Hurons, and the English and their allies the Iroquois, and involves a noble savage, the

Foreign writers on Canada in English 1

Iroquois Ulamor who loves the same Indian girl as General Beaufort. (It turns out that Ulamor is the son of Frontenac by a Huron princess.) The play provides an interesting glimpse of British pre-Conquest hostility to the French in 'a vast Tract Land in Northern America, on the Back of New England and New York'.

The British conquest of Québec inspired a number of literary tributes. Thomas Paine (1737-1809) was still a loyal Englishman when he wrote 'The death of General Wolfe' (1759), a brief poetic celebration of patriotism and heroism. *Québec: a poetical essay in imitation of the Miltonic stile* (1760) by 'J. Patrick', was a more ambitious exploitation of the Conquest, complete with explanatory footnotes possibly reflecting a firsthand knowledge of the setting. In James Belsham's Latin ode *Canadia* (London, 1760), Montcalm is magnanimously saluted as a valiant foe, but the poem as a whole is a stilted celebration of English military glory. This is the main interest also of a long poem by George Cockings (d. 1802), a British colonial official who lived until 1776 in Boston, where he wrote *War: an heroic poem, from the taking of Minorca, by the French; to the reduction of the Havannah, by the Earle of Albermarle* (Boston, 1762), a bombastic Miltonic imitation that includes detailed accounts of the captures of Louisbourg and Quebec. Cockings gives more concentrated attention to the New World in *The conquest of Canada; or, The siege of Québec. An historical tragedy of five acts* (Albany, 1773). The most ambitious poetic celebration of the British victory in Canada is Henry Murphy's *The conquest of Quebec* (Dublin, 1790), an eight-book epic modelled on *Paradise lost*, which includes episodes in heaven confirming the justice of the victory and a climactic hand-to-hand duel between Wolfe and Montcalm.

With the defeat of the French in the New World, the beginnings of English settlement, and the economic development of Canada, a less bellicose image of the colonies began to appear, catering to the eighteenth-century fondness for 'prospect' poetry and fiction. The earliest and the most artistically significant of the post-Conquest literary travelogues on Canada is Frances BROOKE's epistolary romance, *The history of Emily Montague* (London, 1769). Other early literary responses to post-Conquest Canada are George Cartwright's *Labrador: a poetical epistle* (London, 1792), which makes the grim and barren northland appear like a Scottish tourist resort; J. Mackay's *Quebec hill; or Canadian scenery* (London, 1797); and Cornwall Bayley's *Canada: a descriptive poem* (Quebec, 1806)—the last two conventional neo-classical prospect poems. The popular Irish poet Thomas Moore (1779-1852) visited Canada in 1804 and wrote his famous 'Canadian boat song', along with a few other occasional pieces reflecting his meditative responses to Canadian scenery.

By the third decade of the nineteenth century the novel was rapidly gaining its ascendancy in English literature and a few fiction writers turned their attention to Canada. Most of them expressed their conceptions of the country in either the immigrant novel or the wilderness adventure novel. The most distinguished fictional representation of the immigrant experience is *Bogle Corbet* (London, 1831) by John GALT. A lively adventure novel of about the same time is the anonymous *The Canadian girl; or The pirate of the lakes* (London, 1838), set in 'one of the sublime wildernesses of Upper Canada' and involving mysterious encounters, fervent love scenes, languishing beauties, noble savages, and startling revelations. The earliest and best-known example that combines adventure and immigration propaganda is *The settlers in Canada* (London, 1844), by Captain Frederick Marryat (1792-1848), who visited Canada in 1838. In this novel episodes of hunting and Indian fighting are interspersed in a chronicle of house building and land cultivation in the Bay of Quinte region of Canada West (Ontario) as the author strives to assert the virtues of a genteel English society transplanted to North America.

Like Captain Marryat, the prolific Mayne Reid (1818-83), whose prime source of fiction material was the American West, addressed his one Canadian novel, *The young voyageurs; or The boy hunters in the North* (London, 1854), to juvenile readers. Another author of adventure stories for young people was R.M. BALLANTYNE, some of whose works extol the heroic qualities of Britain's empire in North America and the men who created and sustained it through the fur trade and exploration. William Henry Giles Kingston (1814-80), the secretary of a colonization society, wrote novels glorifying the Empire and promoting immigration that were set in Canada as well as in Australia and New Zealand. His Canadian novels are *The log house: a tale of Canada* (London [1864]), possibly inspired by *Bogle Corbet* (to which one of the characters admiringly refers); *Snow-shoes and canoes; or,*

The early days of a fur-trader in the Hudson's Bay territory (London, 1876), which includes an idealized representation of the Red River Settlement; and The frontier fort; or, Stirring times in the North-west Territory (London, 1879).

Sir William Francis Butler (1838-1910), explorer, adventurer, and author of many books of travel—including the classic The great lone land: a narrative of travel and adventure in the Northwest of America (London, 1872)—wrote one novel set in Canada, Red Cloud, the solitary Sioux (London, 1882). Written for English boys, it provides many vivid scenes of travel, hunting, and fighting on the Canadian Prairies incorporated into an episodic tale about the tragic but stoical title character. Another literary exploitation of the northern frontier, noteworthy for the identity of its authors if not for its artistic achievement, is The frozen deep (1857), a three-act melodrama written for amateur performance by Charles Dickens and Wilkie Collins. Based on the Franklin expedition and set in England, the high Arctic, and Newfoundland, the play is a rather artificial and bombastic tribute to heroism and self-sacrifice.

Unlike writers of travel narratives, who were frequently attracted to Montreal and Quebec, with their exotic Francophone culture, British novelists and poets of the nineteenth century confined their attention largely to contemporary and historical narratives of pioneering and adventure in the wilderness. But one writer who treated contemporary Canadian city life was Samuel Butler (1835-1902), author of Erewhon and many other works, who spent parts of 1874 and 1875 in Canada in a futile attempt to retrieve money he had invested in speculative companies. His 28-line free-verse poem, 'A psalm of Montreal' (1878), with its well-known refrain 'O GOD! O MONTREAL!', denounces the aesthetic insensitivity of colonial society and reflects Butler's general feelings of disgust with Canada.

Nineteenth-century British writers were surprisingly indifferent to the epic conflict between France and England that ended in British supremacy in North America. Among noteworthy exceptions is G.A. Henty (1832-1902), the prolific romancer and exponent of imperialism for British schoolboys, whose With Wolfe in Canada; or, The winning of a continent (London [1887]) is an account of the Seven Years' War as seen through the eyes of a young British soldier. (The historical background is drawn from Parkman.) Sir Arthur Conan Doyle (1859-1930) in The refugees: a tale of two continents (London, 1893) adapted formulas from Dumas and Cooper to recount a tale of Huguenot refugees exiled to Canada after the revocation of the Edict of Nantes in 1685. The many romantic novels of Sir Arthur Quiller-Couch (1863-1944) include the brief Fort Amity: a story of French Canadian life in the time of Wolfe and Montcalm (London [1906]), which celebrates the strenuous life in the wilderness and the virtues of masculine loyalty and honour. Neither of these novels was based on first-hand acquaintance with Canada: Doyle did not visit North American until 1894, and Quiller-Couch never did make the trip.

Another noteworthy historical novel of the late nineteenth century, dealing with a different region and period, is Under the great seal (London [1893]) by Joseph Hatton (1841-1907). Set in Newfoundland 'in the youngest days of the oldest British colony', this is a melodramatic but gripping fictionalization of a little-known episode of maritime history when the British fishing fleet, under royal orders, attempted to abolish year-round settlements on the Newfoundland coast. The character, individual and social, of the rural Maritimes in the mid-nineteenth century provides the point of departure for The master (1895) by the English novelist and playwright Israel Zangwill (1864-1926). In this long ironic Bildungsroman, a young would-be painter flees his Nova Scotia backwoods home to find social and economic conflict, and eventually a barren artistic success, in England.

By the early twentieth century the most popular form of literary exploitation of Canada by British writers was the outdoor romance of adventure and love set in the Arctic, the northwestern Prairies, or the forest wilderness. Heavily influenced by the conventions of the American western romance and by the popular Kondike tales of Jack London, these stories also celebrated the glories of the British Empire and idealized the resourceful, self-reliant colonial adventurer, as opposed to his effete stay-at-home countryman. Many of the writers of these northwest romances were themselves adventurers in the outposts of empire. They include Roger Pocock (1865-1941), who worked on the Lake Superior section of the Canadian Pacific Railway in 1883, served in the Northwest Mounted Police (1884-6), and was the author of Tales of western life, Lake Superior, and the Canadian Prairies (Ottawa, 1888) and an autobiographical work, *The frontiersman* (1903). Among the Canadian novels of Ridgewell Cullum (1867-1943) are *The hound from the North* (1904) and *The triumph of John Kars* (1917), set in Manitoba and the Yukon; and *The rising of the red man: a romance of the Louis Riel rebellion* (1905) by John Mackie (1862-1939). The most prolific writer of this kind of fiction was Harold Bindloss (1866-1946), whose output included at least thirty novels set in Canada, beginning with *Alton of Somasco* (1906), through *Lorimer of the Northwest* (1909), and *Vane of the timberlands* (1911).

In 1897 Rudyard Kipling paid tribute to Canada's aspirations for sovereignty within imperial federation in his brief poem 'Our lady of the snows'; after visiting Canada in 1907, he included a series of impressionistic, allusive lyrics inspired by his experiences of the Prairies and northern forests in his *Letters to the family (notes on a recent trip to Canada* (Toronto, 1908). The Gothic novelist Algernon Blackwood (1869-1951) spent ten years wandering through Canada and the United States and used Canadian settings in a number of short stories, including 'A haunted island' (1906), 'Skeleton Lake' (1906), 'The wendigo' (1910), and several pieces in *The wolves of God and other fey stories* (1921). Blackwood's suspenseful tales of loneliness, madness, terror, and death make effective use of the northern forest and of French-Canadian and Indian folklore.

Mrs Humphry Ward (1851-1920) turned her attention to the Dominion in *Canadian born* (1910), a leisurely fictionalization of her trip across Canada by rail, which contains some provocative comments on Canadian-British relations and Canada's prospects in the twentieth century; but the light atmosphere is marred by an irrelevant and predictable melodramatic plot.

Melodrama is also a weakness of *Sick Heart River* (1941), one of the two posthumously published works of fiction by the famous Scottish novelist John Buchan (1875-1940), who as Lord Tweedsmuir was governor-general of Canada from 1935 until his death. In the story of a dying man who seeks a climax to his life of action and duty in the northern wilderness, Buchan tries to develop a moral theme of Christian salvation and a psychological theme of the search for the self; but the plot elements involving mysterious disappearance and insanity are too conventional to sustain the author's philosophical interests.

The novel of northwest adventure has been carried on by Hammond Innes in *Campbell's kingdom* (1952), a melodrama of love, oil drilling, and intrigue in the Canadian Rockies, and in *The land God gave to Cain: a novel of the Labrador* (1958), about the search for truth—and gold—in the Arctic. The same sort of formula was adapted by Nicholas Monsarrat in *The time before this* (1963), a pretentious mystery set in the Québec Arctic, and by Alistair Maclean in *Athabaska* (1980), a thriller set in Alaska and Alberta.

An important variation on the northern adventure novel is the science-fiction or futuristic fantasy narrative, in which the remote and mysterious Arctic becomes associated with a hypothetical post-atomic holocaust era, or with extra-terrestrial visitors. *The Chrysalids* (1955), by the distinguished novelist John Wyndham, is set in a post-holocaust Labrador, depicted as a land of forests, farms, and villages where intellectually superior mutants struggle to escape a reactionary, repressive society.

In the past thirty years a few British writers have produced novels about modern Canadian urban life. Margaret Bullard, wife of an eminent physicist who was a visiting professor at the University of Toronto in the late 1940s, wrote *Wedlock's the devil* (1951), an acerbic satire of the academic community in 'New Glasgow' (Toronto) and the social environment of the Wychwood Park district of the city, where the Bullards lived. A more critical but more imaginative response to Canada was expressed by the painter and writer Wyndham Lewis in *Self condemned* (1954), in which a British exile during the Second World War finds reflections of his own and the world's cultural disorientation and spiritual despair in the cheerless streets of 'Momaco' (an amalgam of Montreal and Toronto). Simon Gray, who studied at Dalhousie University, Halifax, before returning to his native England to pursue a career as a playwright, wrote *Colmain* (1963), a satirical novel about the lieutenant-governor of a fictitious Canadian province (obviously Nova Scotia), where the narrowness of society is reflected in petty political conflicts and dull social routine. Another of Gray's novels, *Simple people* (1965), aims its satire in two directions, with the story of a naive Canadian student at Cambridge who is exploited by decadent British acquaintances.

The most ambitious recent British literary use of Canada is Malcolm Macdonald's novel *Goldeneye* (1981), which portrays it as a pioneering country in a story about forty years in the life of a Scottish woman who immigrates to Saskatchewan. Macdonald, a historical novelist who has specialized in works set in Victorian England, apparently researched his topic well; but *Goldeneye*, on the whole, is more soap opera than epic.

2. AMERICAN WRITERS. The earliest imaginative exploitation of Canada by republican American writers is probably a work by Hugh Henry Brackenridge (1748-1816), *The death of General Montgomery in the storming of the city of Quebec* (Philadelphia 1777), a pompous closet tragedy in verse that glorifies the life and death of the American leader and casts distasteful glances at the snowbound setting and untrustworthy inhabitants of Canada. The failure of the American campaign of 1775-6, together with Protestant hostility to French Roman Catholicism, persistent national recollections of French and Indian depredations throughout the eighteenth century, and republican antagonism to British imperialism, all contributed to a longstanding antipathy that is reflected in much of the imaginative use of Canada by Americans. At the same time, however, many American writers recognized Canadians, both French and English, as pioneers like themselves, engaged in the struggle for survival against the wilderness. This ambivalence between hostility and sympathy is reflected in *The history of Maria Kittle* (Hartford, 1797) by Ann Eliza Bleecker (1752-83), a novel that recreates the terror of a French and Indian attack on an American settlement and the winter march into captivity in Canada, while presenting the people of Montreal as reasonably kind and civilized.

From the earliest years of literary activity in the United States, the imaginative response to Canada was in the form of the historical romance, particularly as the genre was developed by James Fenimore Cooper. Harriet Vaughn Cheney, a Boston novelist who lived briefly in Montreal, wrote *The rivals of Acadia; an old story of the New World* (Boston, 1827), which recounts the legendary conflict between two feudal chieftains, Charles d'Aulnay and Charles de La Tour. John Greenleaf Whittier used Canadian settings and historical incidents in several poems, including 'St. John' (1841), a retelling of the D'Aulnay-La Tour rivalry; 'The ranger' (1856), about the French and Indian wars; and 'The bay of Seven Islands' (1856), a melodrama of tragic love. The New York poetaster Alfred B. Street (1811-81) wrote a

long jingling narrative poem, *Frontenac* (London, 1849), in which the governor of New France is mixed up in a complex plot of miscegenation and revenge.

Most of these historical fictions reflect the widespread nineteenth-century American suspicion of French Roman Catholicism. Fanatical anti-Catholicism is the main element in a novel by George Bourne (1780-1845), who lived in Quebec in 1825-8: *Lorette. The history of Louise, daughter of a Canadian nun. Exhibiting the interior of female convents* (New York, 1833), a conglomeration of hackneyed Gothic devices such as lecherous priests, mad nuns, and mysterious dungeons. The same formula is exploited in the notorious AWFUL DISCLOSURES OF MARIA MONK . . . (New York, 1836). The Gothic image of French Canada appears at an even more debased level in Benjamin Barker's *Cecilia; or, The white nun of the wilderness: a romance of love and intrigue* (Boston, 1845), and in Justin Jones's *Jessie Manton; or The novice of Sacre-Coeur. A tale of the Canadian invasion* (Boston, 1848).

These calumnies against the Church in French Canada promoted Maryland Catholic novelist James McSherry (1819-69) to write *Père Jean; or, The Jesuit missionary: a tale of the North American Indians* (Baltimore, 1847), which uses Cooper-style formulas to idealize the story of the seventeenth-century priest Isaac Jogues. Mary Anne Sadlier (1820-1903), an Irish-born American who lived for some years in Montreal, included among her many pro-Catholic novels *Elinor Preston; or, Scenes at home and abroad* (New York, 1861), which sentimentalizes the contemporary life of Irish and French Catholics in Canada.

Further antidotes to the anti-French, anti-Catholic romance tradition are provided by American writings dealing with the Acadian expulsion. Catherine A. Williams (1781-1872), of Rhode Island, expressed her sympathy for the Acadians in *The neutral French; or, The Acadians of Nova Scotia* (Providence, 1841), a novel in which a group of exiles gradually become defiant revolutionaries in the American mould. Nathaniel Hawthorne (1804-64) presented a briefer and more moderate version of the expulsion in 'The Acadian exiles', part of his collection of historical fictionalizations for children, *The whole history of Grandfather's chair* (Boston, 1841). But the most famous version of the Acadian story is Henry Wadsworth Longfellow's narrative poem EVANGELINE: *a tale of Acadie* (1847). Although marred by an awkward verse form and by saccharine sentimentality, it is a suggestive myth of Northern American history that dramatizes the obliteration of a primeval Edenic imaginative ideal by the ruthless realities of progress.

Nineteenth-century American authors did not neglect English Canada. Jesse Walker (1810-52) wrote *Fort Niagara* and *Queenston* (both published in Buffalo, 1845; both subtitled 'a tale of the Niagara frontier'), two didactic fictionalized tourist guides that portray, through a series of dialogues, the border region of Canada West (Ontario). Owen Duffy's *Walter Warren; or, The adventurer of the northern wilds* (New York, 1854) is also set in Canada West, where the young American hero struggles through adversity to fortune, first in Hamilton and subsequently in the Lake Superior region. John B. Coppinger's *The renegade: a tale of real life* (New York, 1855) is a melodramatic story of two young Americans who pursue truth among the Indians north of Lake Ontario. P. Hamilton Myers (1812-78) made an ambitious attempt to present the complex issues of the Rebellion of 1837-8 in a Cooper-influenced narrative, *The prisoner of the border: a tale of 1838* (New York, 1857).

Other regions of British North America were occasionally exploited by early nineteenth-century American writers. Robert Traill Spence Lowell (1816-91), the brother of James Russell Lowell (and grandfather of the twentieth-century poet Robert Lowell), served for a time as an Episcopalian priest in Newfoundland and wrote *The new priest in Conception Bay* (Boston, 1858), in which he convincingly represented the dialect and customs of outport fishermen; but the novel is marred by a lurid plot and by the author's fanatical anti-Catholicism. Mary L. Savage wrote *Miramichi* (Boston, 1865), another partisan religious novel, in which New England Methodists attempt to bring the 'New Light' to the New Brunswick backwoods.

After the Civil War, American literary exploitations of Canada began to reflect various new theories and influences that grew out of the changing cultural atmosphere of the United States. William Dean Howells (1837-1920), chief theorist of the realist movement, wrote *Their wedding journey* (Boston, 1872), a travelogue novel that uses the popular tourist regions of the St Lawrence as background for the leisurely experiences and reflections of two middle-class American tourists. *A chance acquaintance* (Boston, 1873) involves one of Howells' favourite themes, the contrast between New England and the West, as personified by two tourists in Quebec City whose respective reactions to Canada reveal their personal and regional prejudices. Howells also uses Canadian settings in *The quality of mercy* (New York, 1892), involving a defaulting American businessman who flees to Canada and finds in the hostile winter landscape of the Saguenay a reflection of his own moral and spiritual disintegration.

Another important literary traveller of this period was the poet Walt Whitman (1819-92), whose *Diary in Canada* (written in 1880 but not published until 1904) is an impressionistic and often lyrical evocation of the pastoral landscape and picturesque inhabitants of southwestern Ontario and the St Lawrence country.

Various 'local-colour' authors of the late nineteenth century wrote tourist fiction set in Canada. The midwestern novelist Alice French (1850-1934), who wrote as 'Octave Thanet', used a Saguenay setting for a long story included in her *Knitters in the sun* (Boston, 1887): 'The ogre of Ha-Ha Bay', which presents the sordid lives of a group of French-Canadian villagers as seen through the disillusioned eyes of two American tourists. Robert Grant (1852-1940), a Boston jurist and author of many novels of social criticism, began his writing career with *Jack in the bush; or, A summer on a salmon river* (Boston, 1888), a book for boys that celebrates Americanism and the manly life through an episodic narrative of fishing adventures in the Restigouche (Québec-New Brunswick) region. S. Weir Mitchell (1829-1914), a Philadelphia physician, wrote a more mature 'fishing romance' set in the same region, *When all the woods are green* (New York, 1894), a tale of leisurely outdoor amusement and conversation involving a group of American tourists. *The lady of the flag-flowers* (Chicago, 1899), by the minor poet Florence Wilkinson, is an ambitious but melodramatic novel involving a young American who comes to Canada under the influence of Tolstoy's idealism, and whose intrusion into the primitive world of the Québec backwoods results in the moral ruin and murder of a half-breed girl. The clergyman Henry Van Dyke (1852-1933) wrote many local-colour tales based on his vacations in the Québec backwoods, focusing on a stereotyped image of the cheerful and primitive French Canadian; they were collected in *The ruling passion: tales of nature and human nature* (New York, 1901) and other volumes.

Historical novels about early Canada continued to be popular through the late nineteenth century and were revitalized by the magnificent multi-volume history of New France by the Boston historian Francis Parkman (1823-91): *France and England in North America*, which appeared between 1865 and 1892. Charles Hall's *Twice taken: an historical romance of the maritime British province* (Boston, 1867) uses the battle for Louisbourg as background for a lurid tale involving a sinister Jesuit priest. Edward P. Tenney (1835-1916) wrote *Constance of Acadia* (Boston, 1886), a retelling of the d'Aulnay-La Tour rivalry. W.H.H. Murray (1840-1904) was the author of *Mamelons and Ungava: a legend of the Saguenay* (Boston, 1890), a pretentiously poetic adventure novel inspired by Cooper's Leatherstocking tales. Mary Hartwell Catherwood (1847-1902), an Ohio-born writer, adapted information from Parkman to a series of romances that exalted American-style individualism and feminism in *The romance of Dollard* (New York, 1889), *The story of Tonty* (Chicago, 1890), and *The lady of Fort St. John* (Boston, 1892).

After 1900 the most prominent American image of Canada in American literature was that of the northern frontier; it was inspired by American involvement in the Klondike gold rush and was notably expounded by California writer Jack London. In many short stories—collected in *The son of the wolf* (1900), *Children of the frost* (1902), and other volumes, as well as in his famous novels, *The call of the wild* (1903), *White Fang* (1906), etc.—London used his experiences of the Klondike to develop his naturalist theories about the universal struggle for survival and the need for altruism in the efforts to establish human society above the animalistic level. Unfortunately London's suggestive image of the North was soon debased into mechanical formulas by other writers, beginning with Michigan-born James Oliver Curwood (1878-1927). In novels such as *The danger trail* (1910), *God's country—and the woman* (1915), *The country beyond* (1922), and others too numerous to mention, Curwood glorified adventure, romantic love, and simplistic notions of courage and endurance, in what he called 'God's country', roughly identifiable with the northern prairie provinces and southern portions of the Northwest Territories.

The immense popularity of the northern forest romances of Curwood and his imitators prompted Sinclair Lewis to one of his cynical satires in *Mantrap* (1926), involving a Babbit-type American businessman who goes on vacation to northern Manitoba in search of the primitive life in the great outdoors and encounters mosquitoes, fatigue, picayune quarrels with his companions, and, at the end of the trail, a village settlement no different from the 'main-street' society he left behind.

Oliver Curwood also applied his formulas to early Canadian history in a series of romances set in New France, including *The black hunter* (1926), *The Plains of Abraham* (1928), and *The crippled lady of Pembonka* (1929). New France continued to be a popular subject for American historical romancers throughout the twentieth century. (Only a few representative works will be mentioned here.) Benedict Fitzpatrick's *Donjon of demons* (1931) is the story of Father Brébeuf, as seen by a Catholic writer; Grace Stone's *The cold journey* (1934) is a retelling of the seventeenth-century French and Indian attack on Deerfield, Mass., and the subsequent forced march to Canada. Muriel Elwood, an English-born American, wrote a series of novels about early French Canada, including *Heritage of the river: an historical novel of early Montreal* (1945) and *Deeper the heritage* (1946), which devote more attention to the fictionalized family of Canadian settlers than to the panoramic background of New France's struggle for survival. But there is one distinguished modern American romance of New France: Willa Cather's *Shadows on the rock* (1931). In this sombre but optimistic novel of Quebec between 1689 and 1698, the city on the rock becomes, like the mesas of the author's native Southwest, a symbol of primeval isolation where Old World immigrants attempt to create a new social and cultural order based on an ideal vision of the traditions and institutions of Europe.

A few twentieth-century American novelists have found material in modern Québec. William E. Barrett, author of several popular novels involving Catholic themes, set *The empty shrine* (1958) in a fictionalized Île d'Orléans, where an American writer learns about reverence and imaginative experience while investigating an alleged miraculous vision. Grace Metalious (of *Peyton Place* fame) set the early scenes of *No Adam in Eden* (1963) in Québec, then traced the sex-pervaded life of her French-Canadian heroine through twenty years in New Hampshire. Similarly Michael Rubin begins his novel *In a cold country* (1971) on the Québec side of the St Lawrence River and then focuses his narrative on the search for identity in the United States of a half-Italian, half-French-Canadian drifter for whom Canada becomes associated with grotesque and violent childhood memories.

In the last forty years American literary exploitations of various Canadian regions and character types have been wide-ranging and numerous. Film-maker Robert Flaherty's *The captain's chair* (1938), a suggestive quest novel reminiscent of Joseph Conrad's *Heart of darkness*, follows the Arctic experiences of a romantic young adventurer in his search for an enigmatic sea captain. Flaherty's *The white master* (1939), involving the Hudson's Bay Company in Labrador, is a study of the effects of the North on the white man. Walter O'Meara's *The grand portage* (1951) is about British and French fur traders in the country north of Lake Superior in the early nineteenth century, with much emphasis on the crudity and violence of frontier life. The same historical period, and a similar emphasis on primitivism, are featured in Vardis Fisher's *Pemmican* (1956), a long episodic story unified by a brutish trader's romantic pursuit of a white girl raised by Indians.

Iowa-born novelist Wallace Stegner spent a few childhood years in Saskatchewan. (His *Wolf willow* (1963) is a nostalgic memoir of growing up in a pioneer Saskatchewan community.) He wrote *On a darkling plain* (1940), a novel about an invalid veteran of the Great War who seeks isolation on a Saskatchewan homestead, but eventually learns the value of human community during the 1917-18 influenza epidemic. Stegner's *The big rock candy mountain* (1943) is more ambitious, tracing the life of an itinerant American whose restless pursuit of the American dream takes him all over the Middle West and eventually into Saskatchewan, where he finds his illusive visions reduced to dirt farming and whisky smuggling. Frederick G. Walsh, a Massachusetts-born professor of drama, wrote *The trial of Louis Riel* (1965), a two-act play originally presented by the North Dakota Institute for Regional Studies. Riel's religious fanaticism and his conflict with the Canadian authorities are articulately presented, but the emphasis on his iconoclasm and the oversimplification of the Canadian political situation reflect the playwright's interest in making Riel a frontier hero on the American model.

Margaret Craven, a California writer, achieved rather inexplicable popular success with *I heard the owl call my name* (1967), a saccharine novel about a fatally ill Anglican priest working among Indians on the northwest coast of British Columbia. John Porter's *Winterkill* (1967), about an American family who established a resort hotel in northern Ontario during the Depression, presents an oversimplified view of Canada through the egocentric eyes of the American characters.

Born in Massachusetts of Canadian parents, the poet Elizabeth Bishop spent a few childhood years and many summers in Nova Scotia. Her memories of early experiences, as well as her fascination with the rough contours of the northeast coast, are reflected in a few of her poems, including 'The map', 'Large bad picture' (describing a painting by a great-uncle of 'some northerly harbor of Labrador'), 'Cape Breton', and 'First death in Nova Scotia' (all included in her *Complete poems*, 1969).

Detroit artist and poet Gerald Dumas pays tribute to his German-Canadian grandparents, and expresses his nostalgia for boyhood summers spent in southwestern Ontario, in a long elegaic poem, *An afternoon in Waterloo Park* (1972). Young New Jersey novelist John Birmingham recounts the drugtaking, hitchhiking, party-crashing adventures of two American youths in British Columbia at the height of the so-called 'hippie' phenomenon in *The Vancouver split* (1973), an exuberant but morally conscientious novel probably influenced by the works of J.D. Salinger and Jack Kerouac. California writer Ishmael Reed, whose specialty has been the fictionalization of Black history and culture, looks at the fugitive slave tradition in *Flight to Canada* (1976), a wildly unpredictable comic novel in which nineteenth- and twentieth-century history is deliberately confused, and in which Canada emerges as the disillusioning anti-climax to the misguided American quest for freedom through geographical movement.

3. COMMONWEALTH WRITERS. English-speaking writers of present and former Commonwealth countries, apart from a few who have immigrated to Canada, have tended to be indifferent to this country. Three exceptions, however, might be noted. The Australian poet Douglas Sladen (1856-1947) travelled across Canada in 1889 and, besides producing an autobiographical account of his experiences, wrote *Lester the Loyalist: a romance of the founding of Canada* (Tokyo, 1890), a book-length narrative poem written in the hexameters of EVANGE-LINE that attempts to show the Anglo-

American refugees of the Revolution in the same tragic light as Longfellow's Acadians. Another Australian poet, Francis Webb, includes in his *Leichhardt in theatre* (1952) a lengthy but apparently unfinished poem, 'A view of Montreal', in which the nineteenth-century explorer of Australia, Ludwig Leichhardt, is implicitly compared to Jacques Cartier. The poem focuses on images of human suffering and elemental conflict associated with primitive landscapes and modern city scenes. Arthur Nortje (1942-70), a talented white South African poet, spent two years in Canada before his early death in England. His one published book, *Dead roots* (1971), includes about twenty brief lyrics inspired by Canada, emphasizing the paradoxical feelings of strangeness and familiarity experienced by the Commonwealth immigrant, the blight of industrialism in the midst of fertile landscapes, and the shoddy atmosphere of Toronto inner-city life.   JAMES DOYLE

Foreign writers on Canada in French. Before Haitian immigrants began recently to publish in Québec, all foreign francophones who wrote in Canada or about Canada originally came from France. After 1760 communications between Paris and the former French colony were restricted. Joseph QUESNEL, the first Frenchman who wrote in Canada, came to this country by chance in 1779; he married and settled in Montreal, where he took an active part in theatrical life. In 1789 he composed *Colas et Colinette; ou Le bailli dupé* (Québec, 1808), the first comic opera ever to be performed in North America, and he also wrote poetry and plays. Joseph Mermet (1775-1828) came to Canada with a Swiss regiment to fight the Americans and was stationed in Kingston from 1813 to 1816. His epic poems, of which 'La victoire de Châteauguay' is the best known, relate the events of 1812. But Canada, both east and west, was to be a source of inspiration to novelists rather than poets. Baron Philippe Régis de Trobriand (1816-97), who became an officer in the U.S. army, spent a few weeks in Canada in 1841 and wrote the second work of fiction ever to be published in Quebec, *La rebelle* (1842; first published in *Le Courrier des États-Unis*, 1841), a melodramatic short story set against the background of the Rebellion of 1837-8. The prolific Henri-Émile CHEVALIER spent nine active years in Montreal, where some of his numerous adventure novels with a Canadian setting were published in *La Ruche littéraire*, of which he was a founder. Xavier Marmier (1802-92), an erudite and indefatigable globe-trotter, came to Canada in 1849. He wrote one epistolary novel as a result of his trip, *Gazida* (Paris, 1860), but with its summary characters and preposterous plot it is interesting only as a repertory of Indian customs and legends. Canada is frequently mentioned in the books and articles Marmier wrote about his travels in North America (see Jean Ménard, *Xavier Marmier et le Canada*, 1967).

Jules Verne (1828-1905), the greatest French writer of science fiction, spent '192 hours' on the North American continent in 1867. Apart from Niagara Falls, he saw little of Canada. What he knew of the country and its history he found in books. *Le pays des fourrures* (Paris, 1873), translated by N. D'Anvers as *The fur country; twenty degrees latitude north* (New York, 1873), is the preposterous adventure of a Hudson's Bay Company agent who establishes a new trading post on what he believes to be an island, but that is really an iceberg. *Famille-sans-nom* (Paris, 1889), Verne's only historical novel, has as a background the Rebellion of 1837-8, the author's sympathy being wholly with the Patriotes; but the work is marred by its melodramatic style and situations. Léon de Tinseau (1844-1921) came to Canada several times, and on his first trip in 1890 crossed the country from east to west. Canadians and Canada play a part in several of his sentimental and rather melodramatic novels, which were once very popular but have now sunk into oblivion. *Faut-il aimer* (Paris, 1892) is a love story set in the West. *Sur les deux rives* (Paris, 1909) tells of the hardships suffered by a family of ruined French aristocrats who attempt to settle in northern Québec: only the young son is able to adjust. 'Eugène Diraison-Seylor' (pseudonym of Eugène Diraison, 1873-1916) was forced to resign from the French army because of the scandal caused by *Maritimes* (Paris, 1900) in which he denigrated some identifiable officials. He thought of settling in Canada and in 1907 came to Montreal, but did not find the freedom he expected and soon returned to France. He contributed articles to *La Patrie* and wrote one vitriolic novel, *Le pays des petites filles* (Paris, 1909), in which he depicts Montreal women as coquettes and the Church as an obstacle to progress. Georges Lechartier (1868-1955) came to Canada several times on lecture tours and wrote *L'irréductible force* (1905), a Corneillian story of sacrifice in which a

Foreign writers on Canada in French

Montrealer renounces her love for a Frenchman to remain faithful to her alcoholic husband. André Siegfried (1875-1959), an economist who travelled round the world after completing his studies in Paris, wrote one of the most enlightened books about the problems facing Canada because of the different attitudes of francophones and anglophones. *Le Canada, les deux races: problèmes politiques contemporains* (Paris, 1906) translated as *The race question in Canada* (1907; ed. Frank H. Underhill, 1966) is a masterpiece from the point of view of both content and form. Marie LE FRANC, who was to become one of the most prolific French authors to find inspiration in Canada, arrived in Montreal in 1906. No other writer has been able to capture the atmosphere and beauty of the Laurentians with as much sensitivity. *Grand-Louis l'innocent* (1925), set partly in Canada, partly in her native Brittany, won her the Prix Fémina. Louis HÉMON wrote the most widely read of Québec land novels, the world-famous MARIA CHAPDELAINE (1916; first published in *Le Temps*, 1914).

At the turn of the century a few French writers were attracted to the West by government brochures promising rapid wealth to new settlers. None of these immigrant authors became rich, but if it were not for them the West would cut a poor figure in the Canadian francophone novel. 'Georges Forestier' (the pseudonym of Georges Schaeffer, 1874-1915) spent about seven years in Manitoba. His novel *La Pointe-aux-Rats* (Paris, 1907), which aims at discouraging immigration, and the posthumous *Dans l'ouest canadien* (Paris, 1915), a volume of short stories both humorous and moving, have the West as a background. Joseph-Émile Poirier (1875-1935), a Breton poet, was inspired by the Métis rebellion in Saskatchewan. Though he never set foot in Canada, *Les arpents de neige* (Paris, 1909)—later reissued under the title *Tempête sur le fleuve* (Paris, 1931)—was better received than Constantin-Weyer's *La bourrasque* on the same subject. Poirier's work rings true and the battle scenes are particularly convincing. Maurice CONSTANTIN-WEYER, one of the greatest and certainly the most prolific of the French writers who came to Canada, spent ten years in the West. Some fifteen of his fifty books are set in Canada. Among these, his most famous novel, *Un homme se penche sur son passé* (Paris, 1928) won him the Prix Goncourt. Georges BUGNET came to the West in 1905 and, unlike Forestier and Constantin-Weyer, stayed and farmed for fifty years in Alberta. He spent his few leisure hours writing, his most successful novels being *Nipsya* (1924) and *La forêt* (1935). Louis-Frédéric ROUQUETTE describes man's fight against the mercilessness of nature, and of his fellow men, in three novels about the Northwest. Victor Forbin (1869-1947), an ardent globe-trotter, wrote *La fée des neiges* (Paris, 1926), the only Inuit novel by a Frenchman. The half-Inuit heroine attempts to join her mother's tribe but finds its ways incompatible with her philosophy of life. *Rose Beaulieu, canadienne* (Paris, 1931) is a somewhat moralistic novel about a French-Canadian woman from the West who resists the temptations of fame and adulterous love to lead a life of abnegation. Forbin also wrote three essays about Canada: *17000 km de film au Canada* (Paris, 1928), which describes his trip from the Atlantic to the Pacific; *Les justiciers du pôle* (Paris, 1933), about police work in the Arctic; and *La grande passion d'un petit peuple* (Paris, 1935), the story of the Acadians. Maurice Genevoix (1890-1980), a member of the French Academy, spent four months in Canada in 1939, travelling from east to west. In *Canada* (Paris, 1944) he vividly described his journey and the people he met. His two novels—*Laframboise et Bellehumeur* (Paris, 1944), the story of two Québec trappers who curse their life in the forest and yet cannot resist its call when autumn returns, and *Eva Charlebois* (Paris, 1944), whose heroine, exiled in the West, longs for her native Québec—are two of the best Canadian novels written by Frenchmen, thanks to Genevoix's feeling for nature. Pierre Hamp (1876-1962), whose novels about manual work are grouped under the title 'La peine des hommes', spent one year teaching at the École d'Hôtellerie of Saint-Paul-l'Ermite in 1947. In *Hormisdas le canadien* (Paris, 1952) he describes the tragic changes brought to a Québec farming community when, in 1944, a munitions factory is built in the village.

Canada has been a source of inspiration for several French novelists in recent times, no doubt owing to more frequent cultural exchanges between Québec and France and to the renewed interest France is now taking in her former colony. Bernard Clavel (b. 1923), a Prix Goncourt winner and one of France's most popular authors, who has visited Quebec several times (staying two years in 1977), wrote *Les compagnons du Nouveau Monde* (Paris, 1981), a novel of the seventeenth century. His hero, the carpenter Bisontin-la-Vertu, and the young woman he loves, attempt to start a new life in Québec. But Bisontin soon discovers that New France, ruled by the iron-fisted Jesuits for whom he works, is no place for non-conformists. Instead of a new life, Bisontin and Jarnigoine, returning home to France, find death in a shipwreck (masterfully described). *Harricana* (Paris, 1982) recounts the heroic struggle of a family that settles in northern Temiscamingue, where a new railway line is being built, at the turn of the century. Clavel has also written two novellas: *La bourrelle* (Paris, 1980), set in seventeenth-century Québec, and *L'Iroquoise* (Paris, 1979), which takes place partly in Canada and partly in the United States in the 1940s. Anne Golon (b. 1925) and Serge Golon (1903-72) are the joint authors of the immensely popular Angélique series of adventure novels with a seventeenth-century background. Since *Angélique et le Nouveau Monde* (Paris, 1967)—translated as *The Countess Angélique* by Marguerite Barnett—the action has been taking place in the American colonies, with frequent incursions into New France. The most recent volume is *Angélique à Québec* (Paris, 1980). Though Michel Desgranges (b. 1942), a Parisian journalist, never visited Canada, he suggests quite successfully the atmosphere of the Prairies in his novel *Manitoba* (Paris, 1981). Originally inspired by Riel and the Métis rebellion, the work is nonetheless a product of the author's imagination and should not be regarded as a historical novel. 'Eve Combroux', the pseudonym of Geneviève de Montcombroux (b. 1939), who now lives in western Canada, is the author of *Fugue dans le Grand Nord* (Paris, 1981), a romance that has some vivid chapters set in the Far North, with which she is familiar.

Since the late sixties a number of Haitian immigrants have been writing in French, or in Franco-Haitian, in Québec, and publishing sometimes in Canada, sometimes in France or occasionally in Port-au-Prince. Their main themes are the plight of Haiti under the Duvaliers and the hardships of exile. Among the best known and most prolific are Anthony Phelps (b. 1928), whose political novel, *Mémoire en colin-maillard* (1976), and a book of poems, *Points cardinaux* (1966), were published in Montreal; and Gérard Étienne (b. 1936), whose works include the novels *Le nègre crucifié* (1974), *Un ambassadeur macoute à Montréal* (1979), and two books of poems: *Lettre à Montréal* (1966) and *Dialogue avec mon ombre* (1972).

PAULETTE COLLET

'Forsaken, The'. See Duncan Campbell SCOTT.

Four Horsemen, The. This sound-poetry performance group began in 1970 when, after a joint reading by bp NICHOL and Steven McCaffery, Rafael Barreto-Rivera proposed that they should get together, with Paul Dutton, and 'jam'. They have been performing together ever since, learning to understand and trust each other instinctively and moving beyond unstructured improvisations to develop notational systems that permit a more precise interaction of the four voices. Each member, however, has pursued an individual career and has published separately.

The Four Horsemen work within the traditions of sound poetry established by such early-twentieth-century pioneers as Hugo Ball and Kurt Schwitters and continue to perform regularly at international festivals. They stress the *sound* of language as the primary means and material of their work, using such techniques as chant, repetition, and the counterpoint of up to four voices speaking simultaneously, to emphasize the physical nature of their medium rather than its meaning. Sometimes the effect is one of emphasizing the meaning in new ways, but often the work tends towards a diminution or 'abstraction' of the semantic content, a celebration of pure vocal sound. They set a standard of inventiveness, energy, and exuberant concern for language that challenges all poets, whether or not they are working at the same edge of experimentation.

The Four Horsemen have made several recordings, including *CaNADAda* (1973), *Live in the West* (1977), and *Bootleg* (1981), a cassette. (However, these recordings are no substitute for live performance.) In book form the group has produced *Horse d'oeuvres* (1975), mostly made up of individual rather than collective compositions; *A little nastiness* (1980); *Schedule for another place* (1981); and *The prose tattoo* (1982). STEPHEN SCOBIE

Four Jameses, The (1927). This famous literary satire by William Arthur DEACON consists of biographical and critical appreciations of four real-life but mercifully obscure Canadian poetasters whose only connection was their common Christian name, their lack of talent, and the mock-admiration they aroused in Deacon, a prominent literary journalist of the day. Of the four, three wrote their doggerel about rural Ontario: James Gay (who called himself the

Four Jameses

poet laureate of Canada), James McIntyre (author of the dreadful 'Ode on the mammoth cheese'), and James MacRae (less inherently offensive than the others, but still a poet whose rhymes make the fillings in one's teeth ache). The fourth James was James Gillis of Cape Breton, who was ambidextrous, being equally ungifted in prose. *The Four Jameses*, which appeared in a revised edition in 1953 and was reprinted again in 1974, is distinguished both by Deacon's use of quotation to enhance the reputations of his subjects, and by the straightness of his face while doing so.

DOUG FETHERLING

Fournier, Jules. See ESSAYS IN FRENCH: 2.

Fournier, Roger. See NOVELS IN FRENCH 1960 TO 1982: 3(b).

Foyer canadien, Le. A monthly literary magazine published in Quebec City from 1863 to 1866, it owed its origin to a disagreement in Oct. 1862 among the editors of its predecessor, *Les* SOIRÉES CANADIENNES (1861-5). As a result, three editors—Abbé Henri-Raymond CASGRAIN, Dr Hubert La Rue, and Antoine GÉRIN-LAJOIE—withdrew from the *Soirées*; together with three new colleagues—Abbé Jean-Baptiste-Antoine Ferland, Louis-Joseph-Cyprien Fiset, and Joseph-Octave CRÉMAZIE—they founded *Le Foyer canadien*. (Although Crémazie signed the prospectus, he left Québec a few days later for a bankrupt's exile in France.) The intention of the new periodical was to encourage the publication of original French-Canadian writing, but some French material was also included.

At first the magazine enjoyed great success, having more than 2,000 subscribers. It published biographies, fiction, poems, travel accounts, and folklore, and its contributors included several members of the MOUVEMENT LITTÉRAIRE DE QUÉBEC: Philippe AUBERT DE GASPÉ, Pierre-Joseph-Olivier CHAUVEAU, Alfred GARNEAU, Pamphile LEMAY, and Adolphe-Basile Routhier. During its first three years *Le Foyer* published several long works that extended over many issues. To meet competition from the continuing *Soirées canadiennes*, and from the new Montreal monthly *La Revue canadienne* (1864-1922), the magazine was reorganized in 1866 to include more current features. Nevertheless the death in Jan. 1865 of the senior editor, Abbé Ferland, coupled with the departure later that year for the new capital, Ottawa, of both Gérin-Lajoie and the *Foyer's* printer, Georges Desbarats, doomed the magazine. Its final issue appeared in Dec. 1866; its disappearance, followed in Feb. 1867 by the belated publication of the last 1865 issue of *Les Soirées canadiennes*, marked the break-up of the Mouvement littéraire de Québec.

Le Foyer canadien gave a powerful impetus to French-Canadian literature in the 1860s, both by the number and importance of its contributors and by the volume of publication it achieved: in addition to receiving the monthly 32-page numbers, subscribers were entitled to bonus volumes offered at reduced prices or gratis. For the first time French-Canadian writing became available to a wider audience at reasonable prices.

See Réjean Robidoux, 'Les Soirées canadiennes et Le Foyer canadien dans le mouvement littéraire québécois de 1860', *Revue de l'Université d'Ottawa*, XXVIII, no. 4 (Oct.-Dec. 1958). DAVID M. HAYNE

Franklin, John. See EXPLORATION LITERATURE IN ENGLISH: 2.

Franquet, Louis. See BIOGRAPHY AND MEMOIRS IN FRENCH: 6 and Writing in NEW FRANCE: 1.

Fraser, Simon. See EXPLORATION LITERATURE IN ENGLISH: 2.

Fraser, Sylvia. See NOVELS IN ENGLISH 1960 TO 1982: OTHER TALENTS, OTHER WORKS: 4.

Fraser, William Alexander (1857-1933). Born in River John, N.S., he was educated in New York and Boston. After many years as an engineer in the oil districts of western Ontario, Burma, India, and western Canada, he began his writing career with stories published in *The Detroit Free Press*. Most of his writing life was spent in Georgetown, Ont., and Toronto, where he died. Fraser made a substantial reputation as a writer of popular fiction, using the various locales in which he had lived in short stories and novels: the Far East in story collections such as *The eye of the god and other tales of the East and West* (New York, 1899) and *The Sa'zada tales* (1905); the Canadian West in *Mooswa and others of the boundaries* (New York, 1900) and *The blood lilies* (1903); Ontario in *The lone furrow* (1907); and New York State in

Thoroughbreds (1902), about horse-racing, a favourite subject. He created a literary curiosity (recalling Kipling's *Jungle Book*) in *Mooswa*, which employs a large cast of animals who converse intelligently, have their own laws, and discipline each other; but the western forest setting and animal characteristics are carefully observed. Fraser, who also treated such issues as drug-taking and drug-trafficking in his fiction (*The lone furrow, Bulldog Carney*, 1909), wrote with a strong air of moral didacticism, though he was not always supportive of formal law-enforcement agencies, such as the RCMP, which he satirized in *Bulldog Carney*. *The lone furrow* is perhaps his best novel. Set in western Ontario and Montreal, it uses intrigues and motifs of murder fiction, and demonstrates a not-entirely conventional concern with moral and religious issues.

CHARLES R. STEELE

Fréchette, Louis (1839-1908). Born at Hadlow Cove near Lévis, Qué., a seventh-generation Canadian, he was educated under self-employed schoolmasters, at the college of the Brothers of the Christian Schools in Lévis, and at three different classical secondary colleges, from two of which he was expelled, presumably for neglecting his studies. Graduating from the college of Nicolet in 1859, he began to study law at the newly established (1852) Université Laval the following year.

While a law student Fréchette composed his first play, *Félix Poutré*, in 1862. The next year he published, at his own expense, a collection of his verse, *Mes loisirs*, the first volume of lyric poetry to appear in Québec. The influence of the French Romantics Lamartine and Hugo was apparent in Fréchette's choice of amorous and nostalgic themes and in his experimentation with some forty different stanza forms.

In 1864 Fréchette opened an unsuccessful law office in Lévis, where he and his brother Edmond founded two short-lived Liberal newspapers. In June 1866, discouraged by these experiences and by the prospect of a Conservative Confederation, he moved to Chicago—where another brother, Achille, had a law practice—and remained there until 1871, working for the Illinois Central Railroad, founding more newspapers, visiting New Orleans, and writing poetry and plays, most of which were destroyed in the Chicago fire of 1871. The only major work to survive from this period was a violent verse attack on George-Étienne Cartier and

the authors of the 1867 Confederation, published in Québec newspapers in 1867-8 under the title *La voix d'un exilé*; two pamphlet editions were published in Chicago in 1868 (18 pages) and 1869 (46 pages).

Returning to Lévis in 1871, Fréchette was soon embroiled in an exchange of articles with a former friend, Adolphe-Basile Routhier, who in his *Causeries du dimanche* (Montréal, 1871) had criticized Fréchette's poetry and politics. Fréchette ran unsuccessfully in the provincial election of 1871 and in the federal election of 1872; but from 1874 to 1878 he sat in the House of Commons as a Liberal member for Lévis. Although he was not re-elected, his economic future was assured by his marriage in 1876 to Emma Beaudry, the daughter of a Montreal financier.

Fréchette's third book of poetry, *Pêle-mêle* (Montréal, 1877), was well received: its 64 poems included ten reprinted from *Mes loisirs* and seventeen sonnets, a form that was becoming popular in Québec in the 1870s. Two years later, at the suggestion of a correspondent in France, Fréchette hurriedly assembled a new volume of verse under the double title *Les fleurs boréales. Les oiseaux de neige* (Québec, 1879) and entered it in the annual competition of the French Academy. On 5 Aug. 1880, at the annual public session of the Academy in Paris, Fréchette received a Prix Montyon of 2,500 francs. On his return to Canada he was fêted at a huge public banquet on 17 Nov. and was henceforth considered the unofficial poet laureate of French Canada. In the summer of 1880 he had also brought out two plays, *Papineau* and *Le retour de l'exilé*; the latter was later shown to be largely borrowed from a French novel, *La bastide rouge* (Paris, 1853) by Élie Berthet. Furthermore Fréchette was soon the centre of controversy again over his publication of an anti-monarchical brochure entitled *Petite histoire des rois de France* (Montréal, 1883) and other provocative articles in the Montreal Liberal newspaper *La Patrie*.

During the 1880s Fréchette composed a number of long historical poems for his major work, *La légende d'un peuple* (Paris, 1887), which he completed during a summer spent in Britanny in 1887. Modelled on Victor Hugo's *La légende des siècles*, this was a collection of 47 tableaux arranged in three chronological sequences covering the seventeenth, eighteenth, and nineteenth centuries of Québec's history. Despite its lack of unity and the unevenness of its execution, this was

Fréchette

Fréchette's greatest achievement; its grandiose conception and its stirring passages make it the most important volume of poetry published in nineteenth-century Québec.

Three years later Fréchette issued his last verse collection, *Feuilles volantes* (Québec, 1890), and thereafter wrote chiefly in prose. He published in rapid succession an amusing collection of portraits of eccentric Québec characters (*Originaux et détraqués: douze types québécois*, Montréal, 1892); a series of letters criticizing classical secondary education (*A propos d'éducation*, Montréal, 1893); an exchange of articles (1894) on the subject of his supposed plagiarisms, with his former disciple William CHAPMAN; a collection of *Mémoires intimes* that appeared serially in *Le Monde illustré* (May-Nov. 1900); a volume of romantic short stories published in both English and French under the titles *Christmas in French Canada* (Toronto, 1899) and *La Noël au Canada* (Toronto, 1900); and an introduction for William Henry DRUMMOND's *The habitant and other French-Canadian poems* (New York, 1897). The sexagenarian poet was now laden with honours: he was a Chevalier de la Légion d'honneur, a Companion of the Order of St Michael and St George, an honorary doctor of four universities, President of the Royal Society of Canada, and Honorary President of the ÉCOLE LITTÉRAIRE DE MONTRÉAL. Since 1889 he had also held the largely honorary appointment as Clerk of the Legislative Council of Québec.

In declining health, Fréchette set about a definitive three-volume edition of his works, which would include his unpublished verse play 'Veronica' (1903), another example of 'collaboration' with a French author, Maurice de Pradel. The collected edition, under the title *Poésies choisies*, appeared a few months after Fréchette's death from a stroke on 31 May 1908. The modest attendance at his funeral demonstrated the transience of public favour: the intellectual climate had changed since 1890, and the once-revered Romantic poet had become a distant echo of a forgotten literary school.

More detailed information about individual works by Fréchette will be found in the appropriate articles of the *Dictionnaire des oeuvres littéraires du Québec, I: des origines à 1900* (1978). A short study of his poetry by David M. Hayne is included in Robert L. McDougall (ed.), *Canada's past and present: a dialogue* (*Our living tradition*, fifth series, 1965).   DAVID M. HAYNE

Freeman, Bill. See CHILDREN'S LITERATURE IN ENGLISH: 6, 8.

Freeman, David (b. 1947). Born in Toronto, he is a victim of cerebral palsy caused by brain damage at birth. He attended Toronto's Sunnyview School for the Handicapped until he was seventeen and began writing short stories and poetry there. In 1962 he attended the Interfraternity Adult Cerebral Palsy Workshop in Toronto for six months to learn a trade, then left to do more satisfying work on his own, especially writing. One of his articles, 'The world of can't'—an indictment of sheltered workshops like the one Freeman had attended—was published in *Maclean's* in 1964. The CBC commissioned him to write a play based on the article and he did; but the producer, who thought Freeman's script would make unpleasant viewing on the national network, turned it down. In 1966 Freeman enrolled at McMaster University and graduated with a B.A. in political science. By that time he had shown his script to Bill Glassco, who encouraged him to rewrite it. Glassco directed *Creeps* (1972), a long one-act play, at the Factory Theatre Lab in Toronto early in 1971 and it was an instant success. Set in the men's washroom of a workshop for CP victims, *Creeps* dramatizes, not without humour, the anger and inner rebellion these victims feel towards a society that looks down on them and will not let them forget that they are different. Later in 1971 Glassco made *Creeps* the opening play at his new Tarragon Theatre in Toronto. It won the first Chalmers Award for the outstanding Canadian play produced in the Toronto area, and a New York production won Freeman a New York Critics Drama Desk Award for the outstanding new playwright of the 1973-4 season. In 1981 it made a successful seven-week tour of Britain.

With the help of a Canada Council grant Freeman travelled to England in 1972 to visit theatres and get more background for his writing. The first evidence of his wider experience was *Battering ram* (1974), a longer and more complexly structured work than *Creeps*. The central character, Virgil, is a cripple who is taken into the home of a middle-aged woman and her nubile daughter. In portraying the mutual exploitation of the emotions and sexual needs of all three characters, it shows Freeman's ability to go beyond the concerns of the handicapped to explore explosive situations between the sexes.

With *You're gonna be alright Jamie boy* (1974) Freeman moved away from the world of the physically handicapped, though he used a short period he had spent at the Clarke Institute of Psychiatry in Toronto in 1972 as the background of the main character, Jamie Dinsdale, who returns home from the Clarke to realize painfully how his family—father, mother, daughter, and son-in-law—are addicted to television and derive their life values from it. Structured as a situation comedy, it reflects the dehumanizing qualities of TV-centred lives. In 1975 Freeman moved to Montreal to live with his friend Francine, also a CP victim. His next play was *Flytrap* (1980), produced at Montreal's Saidye Bronfman Centre in 1976; it is about a husband and wife, with a floundering marriage, who invite a young man to live with them. The result is a poor cross between Albee's *Who's afraid of Virginia Woolf?* and Pinter's *The birthday party* in which Freeman attempted a more sophisticated humour than in his previous plays. *Flytrap* is often merely shallow, however, its situational possibilities undeveloped, and its easy resolution unconvincing.

Freeman has written an interesting account of his career as a playwright in *Stage voices* (1978), edited with an introduction and bibliography by Geraldine Anthony.

JAMES NOONAN

Frégault, Guy. See HISTORICAL WRITING IN FRENCH.

French, David (b. 1939). Born in Coley's Point, Nfld, he moved with his family to Toronto in 1945. At home there were few books, the two principal ones being the *Bible* and *The book of common prayer*; both were to influence his imagery and concerns when he turned to playwrighting. French was an indifferent student, whose life was changed when a teacher in grade eight told him—as a disciplinary measure—to read a book. On completing that book—*Tom Sawyer*—he decided to become a writer. He began with short stories and poems, many of which were published in the United Church magazine, *The Canadian Boy*. After graduating from Toronto's Oakwood Collegiate in 1958 he studied acting, first in Toronto and then at the Pasadena Playhouse in California. In 1960 he returned to Toronto and worked as an actor in CBC television drama. Two years later he sold a one-act play, *Beckons the dark river* (unpublished), to the CBC for the network series Shoestring

Theatre. About this time he gave up acting and wrote several radio and television scripts for the CBC, and some short stories. In 1971 he took a job in the post office so that he could have time to write a novel, *A company of strangers* (unpublished). He then wrote *Leaving home*, whose success started him on a career as a playwright. Married to the dance and movement teacher Leslie Grey, French lives in Toronto but spends the summers writing at his cottage on the north shore of Prince Edward Island.

Leaving home (1977) was produced at the Tarragon Theatre, Toronto, in 1972 under the direction of Bill Glassco, who has directed the first production of all French's plays at the same theatre. The subject came from French's own experience: the breakup of a Newfoundland family that has settled in Toronto. The main protagonists are Jacob Mercer, the carpenter father, and Ben, the elder son. When the younger son, Billy, is about to marry and leave home, Ben's decision to leave too precipitates a family crisis as the father is forced to face his insecurities and his need for his children. The play's mixture of pathos and comedy, its convincing and lovable characters and distinctively Canadian flavour, made it one of the most popular and widely produced Canadian plays. A sequel, *Of the fields, lately* (1975)—which had a similar success—resumes the story of the Mercer family. Ben returns from Saskatchewan on the occasion of his aunt's death, hoping for a reconciliation with his father. Once again, finding that the hostilities between them cannot be resolved and that his presence causes renewed friction between the mother and father, he leaves. A memory device (similar to that of Tennessee Williams in *The glass menagerie*) frames the main action. This play is more low-key than *Leaving home*; death and separation, and the difficulty and pain of human relationships, are treated more subtly, at times poetically. It won the Chalmers Award for 1973 and, along with *Leaving home*, made French one of the few Canadian playwrights able to support himself by playwrighting alone. Both plays have been produced on CBC television.

In *One crack out* (1976), produced in 1975, French explores the world of gamblers, pool sharks, pimps, prostitutes, and strippers, capturing their distinctive, often brutal jargon and the precarious nature of their lives. Unfortunately the main character—Charlie Evans, a pool player who is losing confidence and his wife's respect—is not fully drawn, and at times the dialogue is sentimental. Though there are some genuinely comic and satiric scenes, they are not always well integrated with the main action.

Jitters (1980) is set in a Canadian theatre like the Tarragon and portrays a group—author, director, actors, stage people—before, during, and after the opening night of a new play. As they await a prospective New York producer (who fails to arrive) the play becomes a perceptive commentary on the hopes and insecurities of the Canadian theatre community. It is at once satiric, sad, sophisticated, and even farcical—the French work that is most pervaded by comedy.

The riddle of the world (unpublished), which premièred in 1981, was a disappointment. Ron, whose girl leaves him to join an ashram in India, tries many things—psychotherapy, casual sex, and finally mysticism—to cope with his new situation. The play deals with the struggle between the flesh and the spirit—in him and in an ex-priest friend, Steve, whose wife is divorcing him. Containing fast-paced comedy that is at odds with its serious situations, *Riddle* also suffers from the playwright's lack of familiarity with his subject.

French worked closely with Donna Orwin, a scholar of Russian literature, in successfully preparing a translation of Chekhov's *The seagull* (1978), which was produced at Tarragon. His first three plays have all been produced off-Broadway and *Of the fields, lately* had a brief run on Broadway. *Jitters* was scheduled for a Broadway opening on 14 April 1981, but this was cancelled. (See James Noonan, 'The comedy of David French and the rocky road to Broadway' in *Thalia: studies in literary humor*, vol. 3, no. 2, 1980-81.)

French gives an account of his background and the process of composing *Leaving home* in Geraldine Anthony ed., *Stage voices* (1978), which also contains an introduction and bibliography. JAMES NOONAN

French, William (b. 1926). Born in London, Ont., he graduated from the University of Western Ontario in 1948, when he joined the Toronto *Globe and Mail* as a general reporter. In 1954 he held a Nieman Fellowship to Harvard and in 1960, with the retirement of William Arthur DEACON, he became the *Globe*'s literary editor. Since 1971 he has written an intelligent and often witty literary column in the *Globe* devoted to serious book reviews and occasionally to publishing news. He has won the President's Medal of the University of Western Ontario for the best general-magazine article (1965) and National Newspaper Awards for critical writing (1978, 1979). Since 1955 he has been an instructor in journalism at Ryerson Polytechnical Institute and a CBC radio journalist. He is the author of *A most unlikely village: a history of Forest Hill* (1964).
GEOFF HANCOCK

Frobisher, Benjamin. See EXPLORATION LITERATURE IN ENGLISH: 2.

Fry, Alan: See NOVELS IN ENGLISH 1960 TO 1982: OTHER TALENTS, OTHER WORKS: 2.

Frye, Northrop (b. 1912). Herman Northrop Frye was born in Sherbrooke, Qué. He began his education at home, where his mother taught him to read and play the piano by the age of three, and continued it in primary and high schools in Moncton, N.B., where, after leaving school, he took a course in a business college. In 1929 he enrolled in Victoria College, University of Toronto, from which he graduated in 1933, standing first in the Honours course in Philosophy and English. Then he went on to study theology at Emmanuel College, Toronto, and in 1936 was ordained to the ministry of the United Church. He served briefly as a preacher in Saskatchewan; but by this time he had realized that his real vocation lay in the academic twilight world that embraced both teaching and writing, and shortly afterwards he went to Merton College, Oxford, receiving his M.A. there in 1940. Already, in 1939, he had started teaching as a lecturer in English at Victoria College; he became a professor in 1947, chairman of the English department in 1952, and principal of Victoria College in 1959. He retired from that rank at the end of 1966, and early in 1967 became the first University Professor of English at the University of Toronto. In 1978 he was appointed chancellor of Victoria University, Toronto.

Apart from the books that will be discussed below, Frye's extra-academic activities have included editorship of the CANADIAN FORUM (1948-52) and membership on the Canadian Radio-Television and Tele-Communications Commission (1968-77). He is supervisory editor of the textbook series, *Uses of the imagination*, published by Harcourt, Brace, Jovanovitch, New York.

Frye's achievements as teacher, scholar, and writer have earned him many honours, including thirty honorary doctorates from universities in Canada and the United States. He became a Fellow of the Royal Society in 1951, Companion of the Order of Canada in 1972, and president of the Modern Language Association in 1976. He received the Royal Society's Lorne Pierce Medal in 1958, the Molson Prize in 1971, and the Royal Bank Award in 1978.

Frye's interests have led him to combine several roles in a single career. He is the loyal academic, seeking to sustain a scholarly community that will play an active role in the national intellectual life. His activities as a university teacher and administrator, as well as many of his essays and lectures, have been devoted to that end; and though from childhood he cherished the ambition to be a writer, he has never even considered leaving the university to pursue an independent literary career. His books, however broad their influence and repute, have always been written within a framework of academic preoccupations.

Yet Frye has played his part in the development of a Canadian tradition of public as well as academic criticism. As early as 1936 he began to contribute critical articles to the *Canadian Forum*, and when he was editor of that journal he encouraged the new poets who began to emerge in Canada during the later 1960s by publishing their works. He also began in 1950 to write each year the section on Canadian poetry in English for the *University of Toronto Quarterly*'s annual critical roundup, 'Letters in Canada'. His surveys of current verse continued from 1950 to 1960, and in writing them Frye contributed more than any other critic to establishing the criteria by which Canadian writing might be judged.

Frye's chronicles in 'Letters in Canada' form the core of *The bush garden: essays on the Canadian imagination* (1971), in which he collected what he had written, over a quarter of a century, on Canadian literature and its creators. With its penetrating but endlessly patient judgements on individual writers, and its development of seminal attitudes to the function of a writer in a society emerging from colonialism, *The bush garden* helps to explain the influence Frye has wielded, not only on academic and public critics alike but also, in a much more direct way, on Canadian poets. Among other items, *The bush garden* includes the 'Conclusion' that Frye wrote for the first edition of the *Literary history of Canada* (1965), in which he traced the liberation of Canadian culture from the 'gar-

rison mentality' of colonial days. Frye was one of the editors of the *Literary history*, and to its second edition (1976) he wrote a further 'Conclusion', reflecting on the more recent richness of Canadian literary production and commenting that, despite the accompanying 'misery, injustice and savagery' in the world, what may 'matter more, eventually, is what man can create in the face of the chaos he also creates'. *Divisions on a ground: essays on Canadian culture* (1982) is his latest collection of writings and addresses on subjects of particular Canadian interest.

Frye has been one of Canada's most significant critics, for not only has he been the pioneer of systematic criticism in Canada, but his writings have a scope that extends far beyond the purviews of a national literature. His work can—apart from the critiques of Canadian writing—be divided into two distinct categories. On one side, in his books of general relevance, he proceeds from an awareness of the essential universality of intellectual pursuits to develop theories of the function of criticism, of the character of literary genres, and of the nature of the myths that inspire the culture of Western man. The earliest of his works of major stature is *Fearful symmetry: a study of William Blake* (1947), his first book, which goes far beyond studying Blake himself to examine in depth the role of myth and symbol in the various literary genres. In *Anatomy of criticism* (1957) Frye analyses the principles and techniques of criticism, isolating its various modes: the historical, the ethical, the archetypal or mythopoeic, and the rhetorical or classificatory. It is an impressive structure of prose and thought that often seems to stand in splendid independence of the literature that is its nominal reason for existence, and to develop in practice Oscar Wilde's concept of criticism as a creative art. *The great code* (1982) is the first volume of the two-part work, *Literature and the Bible*, which brings together all that Frye has learnt—not only from literature, but also from his study of the unorthodox anthropologist James Fraser, the maverick psychologist Carl Jung, and the King James Bible—to consider how much the Bible itself may be considered a work of literature and how far it has been the source of Western literature as we know it. Since Frye plays somewhat cavalierly with the role of earlier mythological traditions, from the Homeric to the Ovidian, the two volumes of *Literature and the Bible*, which he clearly regards as the destination of his career, will likely be in effect as controversial as they may be seminal. (See also RELIGION AND THEOLOGY.)

These three works are without doubt Frye's masterpieces, monumentally self-contained and self-consistent in their systematization of literary and cultural history. His other books reflect the essential division between Frye the writer and Frye the teacher, since they are mainly collections of lectures and articles, gathered in such ways as to illuminate rather unevenly certain common themes. Four volumes are concerned with great English poets: *T.S. Eliot* (1963); *The return of Eden; five essays on Milton's epics* (1965); *A natural perspective: the development of Shakespearean comedy and romance* (1965); and *Fools of time: studies in Shakespearean tragedy* (1967). *A study of English romanticism* (1968) returns to the period, and to many concerns, of *Fearful symmetry*. The other more miscellaneous collections, published over the past quarter-of-a-century, include *Culture and the national will* (1957), *By liberal things* (1960), *The well-tempered critic* (1963), *The educated imagination* (1963), *Fables of identity: studies in poetic mythology* (1963), *The modern century* (1967), *The stubborn structure: essays on criticism and society* (1970), *The critical path: an essay on the social context of literary criticism* (1971), *The secular scripture: a study of the structure of romance* (1976), *Spiritus mundi: essays on literature, myth and society* (1976), and *Creation and recreation* (1980).

Apart from articles in periodicals, the significant studies of Frye are *Northrop Frye in modern criticism: selected papers from the English Institute* (1966) edited by Murray Krieger; *Northrop Frye* (1972) by Ronald Bates in the Canadian Writers Series; and *Northrop Frye: an enumerative bibliography* (1974) edited by Robert Denham.

See also CRITICISM IN ENGLISH: 2, 3, and 4.   GEORGE WOODCOCK

Fulford, Robert (b. 1932). Born in Ottawa, he is descended from several generations of Canadian newspapermen and began his journalistic career as a teenager with the Toronto *Globe and Mail*. Later he moved to the Toronto *Star* where—except for one two-year period—he has written a daily or weekly column on cultural questions since 1960. He has also been on the staffs of several Canadian magazines, including *Maclean's*, but is most thoroughly identified with *Saturday Night*, which he has edited since 1968. Although mainly a periodical writer, he has also published books reflecting the liberalism that lies at the heart of his work and his transition from reporter to literary observer to social critic. *This was Expo* (1968), a work of almost instant reporting, nonetheless betrays a deep concern with the role of ideas in the national spectacle. *Crisis at the Victory Burlesk: culture, politics, and other diversions,* published the same year, is mainly a collection of representative *Star* columns about popular culture in the broadest sense. Fulford's immersion in that subject—he has long been considered almost its only serious exponent in Canada—found its fullest expression in *Marshall Delaney at the movies: the contemporary world as seen on film* (1974), in which he publicly revealed the identity behind the 'Marshall Delaney' pseudonym he uses for cinema reviews in *Saturday Night*. Although he has continued to range widely over cultural matters—*An introduction to the arts in Canada* (1977) is an overview for students and New Canadians—he has become since 1970 more concerned with the place of traditional liberal ideology in society generally, as evidenced in *The Fulford file* (1980), an olio of his *Saturday Night* editorials. The transition, which followed his embrace of a more nationalistic viewpoint, also suggests a reversion to the natural concerns of a writer shaped by the cultural environment of the 1950s—with its agonized debate on psychoanalysis, Communism, sexual repression, and the application of those topics to virtually every other subject. Fulford has more or less abandoned several of his early public interests, particularly fine art and jazz, gaining a new reputation as a cogent political commentator, public scold, and wit.

See also ESSAYS IN ENGLISH: 4.
                                                DOUG FETHERLING

G

Gagnon, Ernest. See ESSAYS IN FRENCH: 5.

Gallant, Mavis (b. 1922). Born Mavis de Trafford Young in Montreal, she attended seventeen different schools there and in the eastern United States. She left Canada for Europe in 1950, after a short period working for the National Film Board and as a writer for the *Montreal Standard*, and after a brief marriage to John Gallant. Since then, living in Paris, she has been remarkably dedicated to imaginative writing, maintaining a long connection with *The New Yorker*; most of her short stories have appeared there, the first in the issue of 1 Sept. 1951. She was made an Officer of the Order of Canada in 1981. In Nov. 1982 she visited Toronto for the première of her first play, *What is to be done?*, at the Tarragon Theatre. For 1983-4 she has accepted a position as writer-in-residence at the University of Toronto.

Gallant has published two novels: *Green water, green sky* (1959) and *A fairly good time* (1970); and six collections of shorter fiction: *The other Paris* (1956); *My heart is broken* (1964; rpr. 1982; Eng. title *An unmarried man's summer*, 1964); *The Pegnitz Junction: a novella and five short stories* (1973; rpr. 1982); *The end of the world and other stories* (NCL 1973), selected and edited by Robert WEAVER; *From the Fifteenth District: a novella and eight short stories* (1979); and *Home truths: selected Canadian stories* (1981), which won a Governor General's Award.

Gallant's talents have always been best deployed in shorter fiction. The first of her two novels, *Green water, green sky*, is no longer than many novellas, and this story of the moral destruction of a girl by her foolish, protective mother is so episodic in structure that it reads rather like a cycle of related short stories. The second novel, *A fairly good time*, is longer and much more closely knit, using with great skill a variety of devices—journals, letters, interior monologues, recollective flashbacks—to illuminate the central story of the failure of a marriage between a Canadian girl and a member of a stuffy French family.

The difficulty of entering an alien culture is a theme that runs through many of Gallant's stories. Frequently they are about Anglo-Saxons—British as well as Canadians—leading empty and often spiteful lives in France or Italy. One collection, *The Pegnitz Junction*, deals with the alienation of a whole people, the post-1945 Germans, not from their native land but from the past they seek desperately to forget. Even in *Home truths*, a collection of her Canadian stories, Canadians are shown as 'foreigners' not merely when they are abroad. Perhaps the most impressive cycle in that collection, the Linnet Muir stories, concerns the failure of a young returning Montrealer to find her bearings even in the city where she was born and spent her childhood. It is perilous to generalize about well over 100 stories that show a great variety of situation, characterization, and approach; but most concern people who have built up a protection from the world, and who in the end have been made to realize how precarious such defences are and how hiding from life has only increased their vulnerability. Gallant's stories are witty and often humorous in their manner of expression yet pathetic in their ultimate effect; detached in viewpoint—at times to the seeming verge of callousness—they are nevertheless so involving that the final emotion is always nearer compassion than contempt. At times Gallant's writing seems satirical, but she is not a true satirist, for the satirist writes in the hope that mankind can be reformed. Gallant seems to conclude, sadly, that the people she writes of cannot be changed.

Many of Gallant's stories have highly complex structures, involving the interplay of varying points of view. Some of them, like the novella 'The Pegnitz Junction', move beyond ordinary mental connections into psychic areas where conversation and even recollections are replaced by strange telepathic awarenesses. Here, and in 'The four seasons', which opens *From the Fifteenth District*, the handling of incident, and the way the visible and audible outer world cuts away from the inner world and back again, reminds one of Gallant's early training in the cutting-room of the NFB. But if the handling of impressions in such stories has a cinematic quality, there is a distinctly dramatic feeling in the juxtaposition of scenes and in the strength of dialogue (whether spoken or understood). Gallant writes a clear, supple prose, and the verbal texture of her writing is impeccable—never a wrongly chosen word. She has such a fine eye for detail—settings, appearances, mannerisms, ways of speaking—and such a sense of the appropriate interrelationships of those details, that her stories always have a remarkably visual quality that makes the words seem like a translucent veil. Thus in many of her stories she achieves an extraordinary double effect. The scene is clearly observed, as concrete as a painting, and yet one is always moving through it into the characters' states of mind, which are so convincing because they are related constantly to the physical here-and-now.

Gallant's non-fiction writings have been scanty and uncollected, but some of them are memorable. They include her account of experiences and observations during the abortive revolutionary situation in France during 1968, 'The events in May: a Paris notebook' (*New Yorker*, 14 Sept., 21 Sept., 1968), in which she gives a rare personal assessment of the country she has so long inhabited; her long introduction to *The affair of Gabrielle Russier* (1971), an account of the ordeal of a thirty-year-old French schoolteacher who had a love affair with an adolescent student; and her extensive review article in *The New York Times Book Review* (6 Oct. 1974) of Michael Corfino's *Daughter of a revolutionary*, a book centring on Alexander Herzen's daughter Natalie. For some years Gallant has been working on a study, now approaching publication, of that perennial spring of French national anger and guilt, the Dreyfus case.

Because of her self-created exile and her custom of publishing her stories mainly in a single American magazine, Gallant's excellence was recognized slowly in her native country. In the first edition of the *Literary history of Canada* (1965) even the titles of her books were unmentioned; not until the early 1970s did Canadian publishers become interested in issuing her works under their imprints. Canadian critics were equally slow in recognizing Gallant: Peter STEVENS' 1973 essay, 'Perils of compassion' (CANADIAN LITERATURE 56), was an almost isolated study until, in 1978, CANADIAN FICTION MAGAZINE devoted the whole of its Issue 28 to a symposium on Gallant. See also *Mavis Gallant: narrative patterns and devices* (1978) by Grazia Merler.

See also NOVELS IN ENGLISH 1960 TO 1982: 2.   GEORGE WOODCOCK

Galt, John (1779-1839). Born in Irvine, Ayrshire, Scot., he combined business and literary careers before coming to Canada. By 1820 he had travelled through Europe and had worked as a political lobbyist, first for the promoters of a Glasgow-Edinburgh Canal and then for the United Empire Loyalists who sought redress for losses during the War of 1812. In 1820 Galt suggested a way to satisfy UEL claimants: the Canada Company, organized to raise funds by purchasing Crown lands and selling them to immigrants, hired him as secretary and sent him to Upper Canada (Ont.) in 1825. Meantime he was adding to his work as biographer, dramatist, and historian a series of novels that rivalled Walter Scott's in popularity, writing eleven between 1820 and 1825.

Galt's *Autobiography* (London, 1833), and to a lesser extent his *Literary life and miscellanies* (London, 1834), present vivid details of his Canadian experiences: dashing travels with 'Tiger' Dunlop, political clashes with Bishop Strachan and Governor Maitland, the ritualistic founding of Guelph, explorations from York to Penetanguishene, then to Goderich by boat. There are also sharp speculations about the future of the colony. (Galt, now Cambridge, was named after him.) Traces of these ideas and experiences appear also in fictional form in *Lawrie Todd; or, The settlers in the woods* (London, 1830), a novel set partly in upstate New York, and in the third volume of *Bogle Corbet; or, The emigrants* (London, 1831); both novels were published during the period of reversal and imprisonment that followed Galt's return to Britain in 1829.

Bogle Corbet and *Lawrie Todd* are rightly seen as a pair—not so much because they deal with the same experience (immigration) at the same time (around 1825), and in roughly the same place (north and south of Lake Ontario), as because they discriminate carefully between group settlement and independent settlement. The Scot-turned-Canadian, Bogle Corbet, is more genteel, more inhibited and dour, and more rigid in opinions than is Lawrie Todd, the revolutionary Scot turned successful American. Of the two books *Lawrie Todd* was more popular, partly because of its more varied descriptions of bush and river, roads and settlements. But *Bogle Corbet*, with its unheroic protagonist, his shrewish wife, inefficient co-workers, burdensome dependants, bad luck, and uninspiring setting, opens an important line of Canadian fiction: that of counter-romance, made palatable by the play of pawky humour and by subtlety and staunch honesty of reportage.

Journal articles by Galt generalized on New World themes and scenes: five items in *Blackwood's*, 1829-30, and three in *Fraser's*, 1832. Longer treatments included *The Canadas* (Edinburgh, 1832), a collaboration with Andrew Picken, and *Forty years in America* (London, 1833), Galt's edition of the autobiography of Grant Thorburn, the real-life prototype of Lawrie Todd. By the time Galt died, his three sons—John, Thomas, and Alexander Tilloch Galt—had returned to Canada, where they would contribute to political, judicial, and financial development.

Many of Galt's Scottish novels have been reissued, and the Canadian section of *Bogle Corbet* was republished in a New Canadian Library edition (1977) edited by Elizabeth Waterston. The standard biography is Ian Gordon's *John Galt: the life of a writer* (1972); critical studies appear in all histories of Scottish literature, most recently in F.R. Hart's *The Scottish novel* (1978). See also the collection of essays, *John Galt, 1779-1979* (1979), edited by C.A. Whatley.

ELIZABETH WATERSTON

Garber, Lawrence (b. 1937). Born in Toronto, he was educated at Vaughan Road Collegiate and the University of Toronto (M.A. 1962, Ph.D. 1973). He has lived in France, Spain, Italy, and England, but since 1967 has lived in London, Ont., where he is associate professor of English at the University of Western Ontario.

Garber's tales from the Quarter (1969), critically regarded as one of the most successful experimental novels of the sixties, contains a series of witty and bawdy tales about the Latin Quarter in Paris that form a demonic parody of the novel. The protagonist, named Larry Garber, controls the action of several characters, each of whom believes he is in a novel written by one of the others (each character is given a distinctive prose style). In *Sirens and Graces* (1983), a nostalgic return to Europe in the 1960s, the narrator, whose name changes with each chapter, recollects adventure and romantic dalliance in several cities, recalls wistfully many of the characters from the first novel, and concludes his odyssey in suburban Toronto as an unhappy, bored student adviser. While the novel contains witty passages and parodic reviews, it lacks the verve and excess of Garber's earlier works, particularly *Circuit*

(1970). In this trilogy of experimental stories, which twists and subverts the conventions of movie-star fiction, the horror story, and the spy thriller, rich detail and comic scenes intertwine madly in a hallucinatory rush. Garber's inventiveness, however, makes these stories hard to follow, and any statement they may contain is lost in the dense imagery.

See Kenneth Gibson, *Canadian Forum*, XLIX, no. 590 (1970) and LI, nos. 606-7 (1971); and Stephen SCOBIE, *Canadian Literature* 52 (1972).   GEOFF HANCOCK

Garneau, Alfred. See POETRY IN FRENCH: 2.

Garneau, François-Xavier (1809-66). Born at Quebec, the eldest in a relatively poor family, he showed considerable intellectual promise as a child but received little formal education beyond age fourteeen. While training as a notary, Garneau benefited from the generosity and encouragement of his employers and patrons, Joseph-François Perrault and Archibald Campbell, whose private libraries and tutoring helped him to become well- but self-taught in the French, English, and Latin classics and in history. The limitations of self-tuition would mark many of his works.

Having trained as a notary, Garneau rarely practised his profession. In 1828 he travelled in the northeastern United States and Upper Canada, and in 1831 set sail for England for a brief stay. He remained, however, in London until 1833 as secretary to Denis-Benjamin Viger, the House of Assembly delegate to the Colonial Office. Garneau's nationalist leanings were intensified during the years abroad. In London he met leading British liberals and through them met many European nationalist refugees resident in London. On two trips to France he experienced at first hand the heady liberalism of the July Monarchy. (See his *Voyage en Angleterre et en France dans les années 1831, 1832, et 1833*, Québec, 1855; rpr. 1968.) It is not surprising that, on his return to Québec, he became actively involved in the Patriote cause and formed close, lasting friendships with the movement's leading members. Garneau was increasingly drawn to journalism in the 1830s but, having married in 1835, was unable to support a family with his writing. From 1837 to 1842 he worked as a bank clerk and performed only a few notarial duties. Through the influence of

Garneau

Étienne Parent, Garneau became the French translator to the Legislative Assembly of the Province of Canada, and in 1844 he was made clerk of the City of Quebec, a position he held until ill health forced him to resign just before his death.

Garneau's literary reputation rests largely on the monumental and influential *Histoire du Canada depuis sa découverte jusqu'à nos jours* (3 vols, Québec, 1845-8; 9 vols, Montréal, 1944-6), which he began writing in 1840. Taking the story to 1791, this masterwork established Garneau as the *historien national* of French Canada and until the 1940s was not surpassed. Written from an essentially secular, liberal, and nationalist viewpoint, the *Histoire* drew a hostile clerical reaction until revised in 1859, but inspired succeeding generations of poets, novelists, historians, journalists, and politicians by its vivid images and heroic account of a small nation struggling against all odds to survive and prosper.

Garneau's poetry—at once original and imitative, conventional and unique—barely survived his lifetime. While many of his poems were modelled on the metaphors and images of eighteenth-century French classicism—poems such as 'Les oiseaux blancs', 'L'hiver', 'Le dernier Huron', 'Le vieux chêne'—many more were inspired by the Romanticism of the 1830s. The strength of his poetry lies in its appeal to the glories of a heroic French-Canadian past, and in its call for a national struggle to survive, which Garneau effects through emotional evocations of the landscape and by explicitly linking the aspirations of his people with those of the great nationalist struggles in the Europe of his day. The secular liberal sentiments that suffuse his poetry explain why most of it was virtually ignored until the 1960s, with the resurgence of nationalism in Québec and the celebrations of the centennial of Garneau's death.

None of Garneau's writing is remembered for its mastery of style, form, or phrase. As vibrant examples of an important current in the intellectual life of Québec in the 1830s and 1840s, however, the poetry and the *Histoire du Canada* are now receiving the attention they deserve. Garneau the *historien national* survived; Garneau the poet is being rediscovered. His stature as a major nineteenth-century French-Canadian nationalist has never been greater.

See 'François-Xavier Garneau' in the DICTIONARY OF CANADIAN BIOGRAPHY, vol. IX (1976) and a series of articles in *Archives de lettres canadiennes* vol. 4: *La poésie canadienne-française* (1969).

See also HISTORICAL WRITING IN FRENCH.

PHYLLIS SENESE

Garneau, Hector de Saint-Denys (1912-43). Born in Montreal, he spent his early childhood at the family's manor in Sainte-Catherine-de-Fossambault and from 1923 lived in Montreal's middle-class Westmount district, under the shadow of the Depression. His studies at Collège Saint-Marie were interrupted by an illness that left him with a 'cardiac lesion'. With friends such as André Laurendeau, Robert ÉLIE, Paul Beaulieu, and Jean LE MOYNE, he founded a small journal, *La* RELÈVE, which sought to reconcile fearless in-depth intellectual inquiry with the demands of the Catholic faith. In 1937 he underwent a spiritual crisis that filled him with self-doubt and loneliness. Reported to have once been joyous, even dynamic, he gradually withdrew from contact with others and in 1941 moved to Sainte-Catherine-de-Fossambault, where he died.

Considered to be the founder of modern 'liberated' poetry in Québec, Garneau published only one book of poems during his lifetime, *Regards et jeux dans l'espace* (1937), a highly symbolic title for a book that holds a promise of conquering space through poetic vision. Later poems were published posthumously by Robert Élie under the title 'Solitudes'—a title he thought appropriate—as part of *Poésies complètes—Regards et jeux dans l'espace, Les solitudes* (1949). Some poems were translated by F.R. SCOTT in *Saint-Denys Garneau and Anne Hébert: translations/traductions* (1962). Garneau's diary of 1935-39, entitled *Journal* (1954) with a preface by Gilles MARCOTTE, was edited by Élie and Le Moyne. An English translation by John GLASSCO was published in 1962. The *Journal* discusses many facets of life, art, and literature; gradually, however, especially towards the end, it turns to painful self-analysis. A similar evolution can be noted in the correspondence, much of which was first presented in *Lettres à ses amis* (1961) by Robert Élie, Claude Hurtubise, and Jean Le Moyne. The letters reveal Garneau's involvement with the group of culturally and politically aware young intellectuals who were his friends, his determination to contribute to Québec culture through poetry and painting, as well as his liveliness and sense of humour. These letters, too, end in 'complete despair' (Nov. 1938). In 1971

Benoît Lacroix and Jacques BRAULT published a major critical edition of the complete *Oeuvres*, including not only all his poetry but his autobiographical and fictional writings, as well as his correspondence.

Influenced perhaps by his experience as a painter and by the Platonic tinge of his philosophical and religious thinking, Garneau searches in his poetry for a transforming poetic vision—one that is inaccessible to the materialists who dominate society. This vision, however, is threatened from within and without and leads to progressive alienation. The poetry conveys not only the anguish of Garneau's personal experience but also his striving for a non-traditional form of expression, its themes and symbols often suggesting isolation from others, even from God, and distrust of himself. The structure of *Regards et jeux dans l'espace* traces a decline from tentative hope to despair. In the poem 'Esquisses en plein air' the poet becomes intoxicated with the light that streams from the trees, while in 'Spectacle de la danse' all movement and vision are blocked; the sequence 'Deux paysages' portrays two hills, their light and their sombre slopes marking a division between life and death, so that the water-lilies in all their splendour become funeral flowers. A series of quasi-mythical visions ensues in which the theme of death becomes all-consuming and space undergoes extreme contraction: the poet sees himself reduced to the dimensions of his rib-cage, inhabited by a bird that will devour his heart. Whether this alienation was caused by the moralizing attitudes to sex of Garneau's educators; the social, economic, and cultural dispossession experienced by young Québécois intellectuals in the thirties; the pressure of capitalistic English Canada upon Québécois nationhood; or a painful Oedipus complex—Saint-Denys Garneau the poet is viewed by his successors as a vanquished hero whose violence was directed towards himself rather than towards the injustices of the world. His use of deceptively simple language to create metaphors for the total adventure of the poetic self and its relations with the world ushered in the era of 'liberated verse' in Québec.

See Jacques Blais, *De Saint-Denys Garneau* (1971) in the Dossiers de documentation sur la littérature canadienne-française, no. 7; Roland Bourneuf, *Saint-Denys Garneau et ses lectures européennes* (1969); Eva Kushner, *Saint-Denys Garneau* (1967); and Robert Vigneault, *Saint-Denys Garneau* (1973).

EVA KUSHNER

Garneau, Jacques. See NOVELS IN FRENCH 1960 TO 1982: 3(f).

Garneau, Michel (b. 1939). Radio announcer, poet, singer, and writer-celebrity—at one and the same time romantic, popular, and modern—he is a 'jack-of-all-arts', a one-man-band and a one-man-show. After writing historical fantasies such as *Who's afraid of General Wolfe* (unpublished), he turned to producing slim volumes of poetry—*Langage, Moments*, and *Elégie au génocide des Nasopodes* (1974)—and then, in 1977, he published a collection of major poems, *Les petits chevals amoureux*. His 'Cousine des écureuils' is a warm and thoughtful tribute to the American poet Emily Dickinson, like his play *Émilie ne sera plus jamais cueillie par l'anémone* (1981).

Garneau's dramatic works are as improbable as they are arresting. From *La chanson d'amour de cul* (1974) to *L'usage du coeur dans le domaine réel*, a mind and body seem to be searching for each other. The language of these plays, which is elaborate—occasionally archaic and scholarly—appears natural because it is extremely precise. Other plays—even *Les célébrations suivi de Adidou Adidouce* (1977), which won a Governor General's Award, declined by Garneau—are too talkative and a little bit loose. *Quatre à quartre* (1974), about a generation of women, and *Strauss et Pesant (et Rosa)* (1974), about the clerico-constabulary and misogynistic Duplessisism, are Garneau's strongest plays, along with his magnificent adaptations of *Macbeth* (1978) and *The tempest* (1982), rendered in Québec French. Garneau is well known in both Canada and France, especially for *Quatre à quatre*.

LAURENT MAILHOT

Garneau, Sylvain (1930-53). Born in Montreal, he spent his childhood near Rivière-des-Prairies, Qué., and attended the Collège Stanislas. When he was sixteen he began to publish his first poems in *Le Jour, Notre Temps*, and *Amérique française*. In 1948 he joined the Merchant Marine and travelled briefly through Denmark, Poland, Italy, Spain, and Portugal. After his return to Montreal, Garneau worked on construction and then as a journlist for *La Presse* and as a broadcaster for CKVM and Radio-Canada. He died accidentally in a hotel room after wounding himself fatally with his own rifle.

His first poetry collection, *Objets trouvés* (1951), contained a preface by Alain GRAND-

Garneau

BOIS and appeared in an edition of 500 copies paid for by his parents. A second collection, *Les trouble-fête* (1952)—also 500 copies—was illustrated by Pierre Garneau. It was fitting that Grandbois should write the preface to the first collection of a young poet whose work was animated by a spirit of freedom and a yearning for wide open spaces. Grandbois detected in this work a certain 'lack of substance'—surely a gentle reproach—that was undoubtedly attributable to immaturity rather than to flightiness or superficiality. The complete works were collected in *Objets retrouvés* (1965), edited with an introduction and notes by Guy ROBERT, which includes a long narrative poem, 'La bleue', that is filled with memories of childhood, of outdoor games and pastimes, and with Garneau's love of nature, play, fantasy, and fun. Garneau's prose, which is rhythmical and precise and has exceptional clarity and soothing fluidity, also shows his gift for 'suggestive wizardry' (Beaudelaire), especially in 'Le serpent et la pêche' and 'Les vacances de Sébastien'.

Sylvain Garneau was unique among Québecois writers in writing with apparently effortless spontaneity and unselfconsciousness. He had a skilful command of traditional verse forms and was equally at home in dealing with fear, despair, and delight. Above all he is Québec's poet of childhood, which he represents in the image of the castle: 'O châteaux lumineux! la fête à chaque étage/Les enfants dans la chambre, et la bûche au foyer'. He shows the lyricism of adolescent wanderlust, of escape; and in the multiplicity of his sudden flights and returns, his lightning changes, he resembles Rimbaud. He was always fascinated by the unknown, an obsession that seemed to foreshadow his unexpected and tragic end.

Garneau's verse was swept into oblivion by the surge of nationalist poetry, with its themes of homeland and alienation, that began to dominate the field after his death, until this gave way to the revolutionary poetry of the late sixties and the formalist seventies. It does not belong to this historical scuffle but to its own post-war era, well before the end of the Duplessis régime. His poetry is neither militant before its time, nor does it reflect the Québécois alienation that was so darkly portrayed by NELLIGAN and Saint-Denys GARNEAU. Since 1953 no one else has attempted to write in a similar style.

Amérique française (1954) includes interesting studies of Garneau's work by Marcel DUBÉ and Angèle Dupuis. An innovative and important analysis by Jean-Cléo Godin, 'La voix retrouvée de Sylvain Garneau', appeared in VOIX ET IMAGES *du pays II* (1969).

JOSEPH BONENFANT

Garner, Hugh (1913-79). In his autobiography *One damn thing after another* (1974) Garner described his birthplace—Batley in the West Riding, Yorkshire—as 'a typical English industrial-town working-class house of the type I recognized in D.H. Lawrence's *Sons and lovers* and later saw in such movies as *Room at the top* and *Saturday night and sunday morning*.' In 1919 his father, who had worked briefly in Ontario before the First World War, moved his family to Toronto, settling in Cabbagetown, an east-central downtown area that Garner later described as 'a sociological phenomenon, the largest Anglo-Saxon slum in North America.' The father deserted his family, and Hugh Garner, a brother, and two stepsisters were brought up by their hardworking mother. Garner attended public school and a technical high school, and after graduation was briefly a copy boy on the Toronto *Star*. In 1933, one of the worst years of the Depression, he went on the road, stooking wheat in Saskatchewan, working for 20¢ a day in a relief camp in Kamloops, B.C., jailed as a vagrant in West Virginia. This itinerant life came to an end when he enlisted in the Abraham Lincoln Brigade to fight for the Loyalists in the Spanish Civil War. During the Second World War he served on a corvette in the Canadian navy.

After the war Garner set out to make his living as a writer. His first published novel, *Storm below* (1949), which drew on his wartime naval experience for its background, has been described by the critic Hugo McPherson as 'an unheroic but oddly warming record of an encounter of nature, fate and man during six days at sea in 1943.' In 1950 a butchered version of Garner's earlier novel *Cabbagetown* appeared in paperback. When the complete text was finally published in 1968, this story of the painful and sometimes melodramatic coming-of-age of Ken Tilling and his friends, with its description of working-class life in Toronto in the 1930s, was seen to be one of the major social novels written by a Canadian. Garner's other novels include *The silence on the shore* (1962), a multi-character study set in a Toronto rooming house; *A nice place to visit* (1970), in which an aging writer-journalist investigates a sensational criminal case in a small town not far from Toronto; and a novel that began as a television play (never shown) for the CBC, *The intruders* (1976), about trendy members of the middle class who have moved into the former Cabbagetown slum area. In the 1970s Garner wrote three police novels, all set in Toronto, about Inspector Walter McDumont: *The sin sniper* (1970), *Death in Don Mills* (1975), and *Murder has your number* (1978).

As a working writer with a family to support, Garner found it necessary to turn his hand to a great many literary and quasi-literary activities. He wrote journalism for newspapers and magazines; appeared frequently on radio and television panel shows; and had a genius for discovering the maximum number of markets for his short stories, including radio and television dramatizations. He took pride in some of his novels (he thought that *The silence on the shore* had been unjustly neglected) and particularly in the best of his short stories, of which he published more than fifty in his lifetime; he won a Governor General's Award for *Hugh Garner's best stories* (1963). In his most successful fiction he was 'the loser's advocate . . . Garner's people are life's outsiders, and this is consistent because he himself is an outsider . . .' (Robert FULFORD). To the end of his life Garner's spirit never really left Toronto's Cabbagetown, and it seems fitting that in 1982 the Hugh Garner Co-operative, a housing development, was built on Cabbagetown's Ontario Street, a few blocks north of the place where the Garners first lived in Toronto. *Cabbagetown* is available in a paperback edition, and a critical study, *Hugh Garner* by Doug Fetherling, was published in 1972.

See also NOVELS IN ENGLISH 1960 TO 1982: OTHER TALENTS, OTHER WORKS: 6a.

ROBERT WEAVER

Gass, Ken (b. 1945). Born and raised in Abbotsford, B.C., he studied creative writing and theatre at the University of British Columbia, completing a B.A. and M.A. before moving to Toronto in 1968. After a brief period teaching English at Parkdale Collegiate, and freelance directing at John HERBERT's Garret Theatre and Theatre Passe Muraille, he founded in 1970 the Factory Theatre Lab, where he remained as artistic director until 1979, when he resigned to devote more time to script-writing. While at the Factory he spearheaded an unprecedented wave of Canadian playwriting, producing and directing new work by George

F. WALKER, John PALMER, Larry FINEBERG, David FREEMAN, and Bryan WADE, to mention a few of the playwrights attracted to the Factory's all-Canadian production policy. In 1970 Gass also helped organize Toronto's Festival of Underground Theatre (F.U.T.), which included productions of four of his experimental plays under the collective title *Light* (1979) and is regarded by many as the origin of the so-called 'alternate' theatre movement in Toronto that saw small, nationalistically inclined theatres develop in reaction to the policies of their larger, more solvent regional and commercial counterparts.

Gass's career at the Factory informs both the subject and style of his best play, *The boy bishop* (published in *The Canadian Theatre Review* 12, Fall 1976). Extending and developing the 'cartoon' techniques of his first published play, *Hooray for Johnny Canuck* (1975)—a two-act satire in 18 scenes in which the popular war-time comic-book superhero, Johnny Canuck, deals a devastating blow to the Nazi war machine—*The boy bishop* cloaks contemporary issues in the historical dress of a 'fantasy' set in New France. The Boy of the title is a precocious street urchin who blackmails his way into the position of Bishop-for-a-day, only to refuse to relinquish the robes of power, and turning what was to have been a glorious day of freedom for the peasants into a reign of debauchery and disorder. The process of self-discovery that the Boy unwittingly begins parallels his education in the psychology of the colonial mind as he comes to view his peasant compatriots as dependent victims of a will to mediocrity. His insanity and death at the end of the play suggest the degree to which the play rises above comic caricature to become a brutal satire filled with ironic despair. Suggestive of Gass's own meteoric rise to a position of influence and responsibility at the Factory, the Boy's predicament in the play was interpreted at the time as symbolic of Gass's frustration with the conservative nature of the Canadian theatre audience and the cautious funding policies of governmental arts councils. His seeming contempt was given much fuller, though less effective expression in *Winter offensive* (1978), another full-length 'historical fantasy' in which a group of assorted Germans—including Goebbels, Rommel, and Hitler—are entertained by Mrs Eichman on Christmas Eve 1944 at an elegant dinner party that quickly deteriorates into an orgy of depravity and death. Intended as an indictment of the violence that Gass locates at the centre of Western civilization, *Winter offensive* uses explicit sexuality and deliberate shock techniques that were criticized by the Toronto reviewers as symptomatic of, rather than antidotal to, contemporary decadence. Their reviews prompted a useful debate in the daily press over the nature of obscenity and the possible justifications for censorship and moved Gass to write that 'it is the theatre's job to outrage.' His unpublished COLLECTIVE CREATIONS, *Revolutionary project* and *Tea-cup entertainments*, as well as his radio play *Terror*, suggest that his desire to unsettle and inflame an audience is consistent throughout his career from the time of his first full-length play *Red revolutionary* (unpublished), an adaptation of Charles MAIR's *Tecumseh*, to his present work in television and film.

Gass has been an outspoken critic of the forces that he considers inhibiting to the development of a prestigious repertoire of Canadian plays. In the Wallace/Zimmerman collaboration *The work: conversations with English-Canadian playwrights* (1982) he gives a useful summary of his views on his own work and on the state of Canadian theatre.

ROBERT S. WALLACE

Gatenby, Greg (b. 1950). Born in Toronto and educated at Glendon College, York University, he has acted since 1975 as co-ordinator of the Reading Series at Harbourfront, the Toronto cultural complex. He is the founder and organizer of its annual International Festival of Authors, which was first held in 1980. Two books of his poems, *Rondeaus for Erica* and *Adrienne's blessing*, appeared in 1976. Two notable subsequent collections are *The salmon country* (1978) and *Growing still* (1981), in which there is evidence of an uneasy truce between the hard-nosed poems that satirize cultural and national concerns and melodious lyric poems about life and love. He edited *Whale sound* (1977), an anthology of Canadian poems and art inspired by whales and dolphins, and a world anthology of poetry, prose, art, and music about these sea mammals, *Whales: a celebration* (1983). JOHN ROBERT COLOMBO

Gauvreau, Claude (1925-71). Born in Montreal, he attended the Collège Ste-Marie, then studied philosophy at the Université de Montréal. He made his literary début at the age of thirteen, when he wrote and produced a play, *Ma vocation*. During the forties he became friendly with the painter Paul-Émile Borduas, through whom he acquainted himself with Dadaism, Surrealism, Automatism, and the artists, journalists, and essayists who gravitated towards this important figure of the Montreal artistic community. These associations were to have a lasting effect on Gauvreau's aesthetic choices and his personal growth as a writer. He not only co-signed Borduas's famous manifesto, REFUS GLOBAL, but also articulated the theoretical aspects of automatism for the general public. A constant defender of modern art after 1948, he never hesitated to engage in polemics, against both conservative art critics and ecclesiastical authorities (who looked upon non-figurative painting as an attack against the traditional virtues upheld by the Church and good Christian families).

From 1944 on Gauvreau wrote poetry that was not published until much later. A series of poems, 'Entrailles', did not appear until 1956 in *Sur fil métamorphose*. *Étal mixte* (1968) was composed in 1950. *Brochuges*, however, which he worked on during the summer of 1954, was published in 1956. These poems subvert average expectations: their word order is irretrievably broken; syntactical structures appear in disarray; phonic sounds, free of semantic charge, ultimately turn a shattered textual fabric into oneiric screams and howls.

While continuing to compose poems, Gauvreau also wrote numerous plays and had a few of them produced in various Montreal theatres: *Bien-être* in 1947, and *La jeune fille et la lune* and *Les grappes lucides* in 1959. His plays were never popular with audiences, and a number of directors commented bitterly on the insurmountable difficulties they posed. Jean Gascon, after reading Gauvreau's first long play *L'asile de la pureté*, written in 1953, declared that it was 'unproduceable'—a comment possibly inspired by its strong surrealist and automatist leanings. Yet three decades later this play can be seen to summarize Gauvreau's preoccupation with suicide, unrequited love, and polemical fights; and offers surprising glimpses of his view of himself and his contemporaries. The premature obituary of the hero by one of his foes appears to fit both Gauvreau's destiny and self-image: 'He was a polemicist, lover, pornographer, man of letters, prophet, journalist, anarchist, wrestler, libertine, epic author.' Gauvreau also wrote plays for radio: *Le coureur de Marathon*, composed in the early fifties, which won him the Canadian Radio Award in

1957; *Magruhilne et la vie*, written in 1952 and produced in 1969 at Studio d'Essai; and *L'oreille de Van Gogh*, which displays Gauvreau's obsessions, as well as those of the painter, by repeatedly using images associated with Van Gogh's anguish: mutilations, ear, mirror, knife, and bat.

Gauvreau's dramatic works, as well as his poetry, represent a search for new meanings as well as new forms. Often conveniently and superficially dismissed as esoteric or hermetic, they nevertheless paved the way for later poetic developments, such as those of Raoul DUGUAY, Claude PÉLOQUIN, and Denis Vanier in the late sixties, and the experiments of the young writers who were associated with La BARRE DU JOUR in the seventies. All of his texts reveal a need to peel off the various linguistic layers held tight by grammar, syntax, and semantics.

Prone to intense fits of depression, for which he underwent psychiatric internments, Gauvreau committed suicide in 1971. Then, ironically, he captured public attention. In 1972 the Théâtre du Nouveau Monde produced *Les oranges sont vertes* and two years later *La charge de l'orignal épormyable*. Large audiences finally discovered Gauvreau's theatre and his violent, masochistic, surreal metaphors. *Les oranges sont vertes*, written between 1958 and 1970, has been regarded by many as his testament and the cornerstone of his aesthetic convictions. Its main character, Yvirnig, a young writer and art critic who sinks slowly into madness after the suicide of his lover, is kicked to death by other jealous artists. Hallucinations, automatic word-assocations, erotic digressions, hymns to free love, and tirades against censorship lead towards the writer's inevitable destruction.

The entrails (1981) contains translations of some of Gauvreau's early poems by Ray Ellenwood, who also translated a surrealist play, 'The good life', and three brief surrealistic dramatic sketches in EXILE—vol. 1, no. 2 (1972) and vol. 3, no. 2 (1976) respectively. Gauvreau's *Oeuvres créatrices complètes* (1971; 2nd ed. 1977) was published by Éditions Parti Pris. Janous St-Denis, a friend of Gauvreau's, wrote a memoir, *Claude Gauvreau, le cygne* (1978). Jacques Marchand's *Claude Gauvreau, poète et mythocrate* (1979) provides readers with a detailed critical and scholarly examination of the texts, along with the most complete bibliography. André Bourassa has offered useful insights into Gauvreau's aesthetic objectives in 'Claude Gauvreau', *Surréalisme et littérature*

Québécoise (1977) and 'Gauvreau et le critique baroque', VOIX ET IMAGES, III, no 1 (Sept. 1977).   CAROLINE BAYARD

Geddes, Gary (b. 1940). Born in Vancouver, he was raised on the Prairies and the west coast. He attended the University of British Columbia and the University of Toronto, where he obtained a Ph.D. He has taught at the University of Victoria and is now a member of the English department at Concordia University, Montreal. He lives on a farm in southeastern Ontario, where he runs Quadrant Editions, and commutes to Montreal to teach.

Geddes's early collections of verse—*Poems* (1971), *Rivers inlet* (1971), *Snakeroot* (1973), and *Letter of the master of horse* (1973)—reveal a sharp eye for physical detail, a keen and uncompromising intellect, and a poetic sensibility that balances subjectivity and objectivity, the personal and the impersonal, and criticism and compassion. The lyric sequence of *Rivers inlet* moves from external descriptions to internal parallels, the British Columbia coastal landscape becoming a map of the poet's ancestry that explains the relationship of the past to the present. Another long suite of poems, *War measures and other poems* (1976), marks a new development in Geddes's writing. Paul Joseph Chartier died on 18 May 1966 in the men's washroom of the House of Commons when a bomb he was carrying accidentally exploded. Through the mind of Chartier the poetic sequence mirrors the society that resorts to violence and destruction, so that *War measures* becomes a scathing portrait and an impassioned indictment, a fable of contemporary Canada. Its violence and insanity surface again in *The acid test* (1981), though the setting expands to include the entire world: political tyranny, the arms race, and environmental ravage are but a few of its themes that reflect the absurd inhumanity of man. As controlled and disciplined as Geddes's earliest verse, *The acid test* has a passionate power that derives from the intensity of his commitment and intelligence. This volume, which also contains a revised version of *Letter of the master of horse* , won the national poetry prize given by the Canadian Authors' Association.

Geddes has edited two important college anthologies: *Twentieth-century poetry and poetics* (1969: 2nd ed. 1973) and *15 Canadian poets* (with Phyllis Bruce, 1971; rev. and enlarged as *15 Canadian poets plus 5*, 1978); *Skookum wawa: writings of the Canadian*

Northwest (1975); and *Divided we stand* (1977), reflections from distinguished Canadians on their country after the victory of the Parti Québécois. With Hugo McPherson he was general editor of Copp Clark's 'Studies in Canadian literature' series. His critical study, *Conrad's later novels* (1980), is based on his Ph.D. dissertation. In collaboration with Theatre Passe Muraille, Toronto, Geddes wrote *Les maudits anglais*, a bilingual political farce about French-English relations in Canada. It was produced in 1978 and published in 1983.

DAVID STAINES

Gedge, Pauline. See NOVELS IN ENGLISH 1960 TO 1982: OTHER TALENTS, OTHER WORKS: 7.

Gélinas, Gratien (b. 1909). Born in Saint-Tite-de-Champlain, near Trois-Rivières, Qué., he moved with his family shortly afterwards to Montreal. He was educated at the juniorate of the Blessed Sacrament Fathers in Terrebonne, and the Collège de Montréal, where he completed the program in classical studies and was active in the school's dramatic society. Forced to leave school in 1929 because of the Depression, he worked in a Montreal department store and then as an accountant with an insurance firm, taking evening courses at the Écoles des Hautes Études Commerciales. But he continued his involvement in theatre by founding the Troupe des Anciens du Collège de Montréal and by acting with the Montreal Repertory Theatre in both English and French and on radio. In 1935 he married Simone Lalonde; they have six children.

The first important figure in the modern Québec theatre, Gélinas acted in 1934 in the first Radio-Canada serial, *Le curé de village* (1936), by Robert CHOQUETTE. The following year he showed his talent as a monologist in a series of sketches he performed in a satirical revue entitled *Télévise-moi-ça*. These shows prepared him for a radio series of his own in which he played a simple, sensitive, Chaplinesque character named Fridolin, a role he played on radio from 1937 to 1941. It was at this time that he decided to become a full-time writer and actor. In 1938 he began an annual stage revue, *Fridolinons*, based on the same character, at the Théâtre Monument National. It played annually until 1946, with a final retrospective revue in 1956. Two of these skits and monologues, *Le départ du conscrit* and *Le retour du conscrit*, became the basis of his first full-length play, TIT-COQ (1980). The opening night of *Tit-Coq* at the Monument National on 22 May 1948 was a landmark in the history of popular theatre in Québec. The play ran for over 500 performances and made Gélinas the best-known and best-loved actor and playwright in the province.

Though his next play, *Bousille et les justes* (1960), was not produced until 1959, Gélinas was busy in other theatrical activities. In 1954 he wrote and starred in a weekly comedy on Radio-Canada television, *Les quat'fers en l'air*. In 1956 he played leading roles in Stratford, Ont., productions of *Henry V* and *The merry wives of Windsor*, and was named vice-president of the Greater Montreal Arts Council, a post he held until 1963. In 1958 he founded the Comédie canadienne in Montreal, a theatrical company, and a theatre of the same name. (This theatre was later taken over by, and named after, another important Montreal acting company, Le Théâtre du Nouveau Monde.) That same year Gélinas was elected president of the Canadian Theatre Centre, and in 1960 he was one of the founders of the National Theatre School in Montreal. In 1964 he wrote and performed in a satirical revue at the Comédie canadienne called *Le diable à quatre* (unpublished).

Gélinas played the leading role in *Bousille et les justes*, portraying a simple-minded and honest man victimized by the intrigues of relatives wanting to avoid a family scandal. When it is discovered that Bousille, a cousin, is the only witness of a murder committed by a member of the Gravel family, they force him to perjure himself; but his remorse is such that he hangs himself, forcing the family to face the consequences of their actions as an inquest is called into Bousille's death. A straightforward, tightly structured play, *Bousille* raises the issue of moral honesty versus family pride, and satirizes some traditional religious practices in Québec and their failure to sensitize people to moral concerns. A type of modern morality play, it has been performed in many parts of Canada. An English translation by Kenneth Johnstone and Joffre Miville-Dechêne, *Bousille and the just*, was published in 1961.

Gélinas's third play, *Hier les enfants dansaient* (1968), which was published in an English translation by Mavor Moore as *Yesterday the children were dancing* (1967), is about a family divided by the issues of federalism and separatism in Québec. Just as the father, Pierre Gravel, is being offered a safe seat in Parliament and a position as justice minister in the federal cabinet, he discovers that his sons are involved in separatist bombings in Montreal and relinquishes his ambitions. However topical the play—it was first produced in 1966 at the Comédie canadienne and in 1967 in English at the Charlottetown Festival—Gélinas insists, 'This isn't a political manifesto, it's a love story.' Yet it is a powerful presentation of the political issues that divide Québécois; but the family drama is at times sentimental. Both *Yesterday* and *Bousille* have been presented on CBC television.

Gélinas expanded his involvement in the cultural life of Canada when he assumed chairmanship of the Canadian Film Development Corporation in 1969—a crucial time for the film industry in Canada. Under Gélinas's direction this agency supported several important Canadian feature films, such as *The apprenticeship of Duddy Kravitz*, *Outrageous*, *Why shoot the teacher?*, and *Who has seen the wind*. Though he took the post originally for one or two years, he stayed on until 1977. He now lives in the village of Oka, near Montreal.

Gélinas has received honorary doctorates from six universities—Montreal, Toronto, Saskatchewan, McGill, New Brunswick, and Trent—as well as the Grand Prize of the Society of Dramatic Authors, the Victor Morin theatre award from the Société Saint-Jean Baptiste, and the Toronto Drama Bench Award for his distinguished contribution to Canadian theatre; he is also an officer of the Order of Canada. For his theatre activities over forty years and his dramatic works—which prepared the way for later playwrights in giving an authentic and memorable picture of Québec life—Gélinas remains an influential figure in the cultural life of Québec and the whole of Canada.

Gélinas has begun publishing the *Fridolinons* revues: *Les fridolinades 1945 et 1946* (1980) and *Les fridolinades 1943 et 1944* (1981), with useful introductory material by Laurent Mailhot. There will be two succeeding volumes.

See Renate Usmiani, *Gratien Gélinas* (1977), in the Profiles in Canadian Drama series; an appendix contains a translation of Gélinas's 1949 address, 'A national and popular theatre'. His 'Credo of the Comédie-canadienne' is in *Queen's Quarterly*, LXVI (Spring 1959). Mavor Moore has written a short introduction to Gélinas and Québec theatre in *Four Canadian playwrights* (1973).

JAMES NOONAN

Generals die in bed. See Charles Yale HARRISON.

Gérin-Lajoie, Antoine (1824-82). Born in Yamachiche, Lower Canada (Qué.), into a large farming family, he attended local schools before entering the Collège de Nicolet in 1837. By the time he graduated from Nicolet he had already acquired a certain reputation, writing the well-known folksong, 'Un Canadien errant' (1847), dedicated to the exiled leaders of the Rebellion of 1837-8, and a verse play in three acts, *Le jeune Latour* (Montréal, 1844), the first tragedy written and published in Canada. In this play, which relies heavily on the since-disproved account in Michel Bibaud's *Histoire du Canada sous la domination française* (Montréal, 1837, 1843), Claude La Tour seeks possession for England in 1629 of the fort at Cape Sable, last outpost of the French in Canada after the successful raids by the Kirke brothers. His son 'Roger' is commander of the fort, and is resolved to retain it for France. Despite its static character and immature psychological analysis, and obvious reliance upon Corneille for its style and tone, the warm patriotism of this work struck a responsive chord in contemporary Québec: witness its publication in full in three Canadian newspapers (1844). It was subsequently reprinted in both editions of Huston's *Répertoire national* (1848-50, 1893), and most recently (in 1969) by Réédition-Québec.

After studying law, Gérin-Lajoie went on to a varied career as a civil servant, copyist, translator, and eventaully as parliamentary librarian in Toronto, Québec and, after 1865, in Ottawa. Despite these occupations, his lively interest in literature, politics, and journalism continued. He is the author of a *Résumé impartial de la discussion Papineau-Nelson sur les événements de Saint-Denis en 1837* (Montréal, 1848); of a handbook to the Canadian political system of the time, *Catéchisme politique; ou Les éléments du droit public et constitutionnel du Canada, mis à la portée du peuple* (Montréal, 1851); and of a useful constitutional history, *Dix ans au Canada, de 1840 à 1850: histoire de l'établissement du gouvernement responsable* (Québec, 1891), published posthumously, as were his *Mémoires*, which were edited by H.-R. CASGRAIN and published in the second volume of Casgrain's own *Oeuvres complètes* (Montréal, 1885) and separately the following year.

Gérin-Lajoie was among the founders of

the two most important literary reviews of the period, *Les* SOIRÉES CANADIENNES (1861-5) and *Le* FOYER CANADIEN (1863-6), to both of which he contributed frequently, and in which his most important literary works, the two JEAN RIVARD novels, were first published: *Jean Rivard; le défricheur* in *Les Soirées canadiennes* (vol II, 1862), and its sequel *Jean Rivard, économiste* in *Le Foyer canadien* (vol. II, 1864).

Gérin-Lajoie maintained close contact with most of the intellectuals and writers of his time, helping to found the Institute canadien in 1844, becoming president of its Montreal branch the following year, and at the same time serving as secretary to the fledgeling Société Saint-Jean-Baptiste. A pioneer in theatre, in the novel, and in political history, he was one of the most influential French-Canadian authors of his age. His son, Léon Gérin, wrote the first biography of him: *Antoine Gérin-Lajoie: la résurrection d'un patriote canadien* (1925), an unrevealing work. He is the subject, however, of an excellent modern study by René Dionne, *Antoine Gérin-Lajoie, homme de lettres* (1978).

LEONARD DOUCETTE

Germain, Jean-Claude (b. 1939). Primarily a journalist and drama critic, he founded in Montreal, in 1969, Le Théâtre du Même Nom, or TMN, an anagram mocking the very formal and heavily subsidized Théâtre du Nouveau Monde (TNM). Originally acting as secretary for TMN, which set out to produce collaborative works, Germain increasingly became involved in scriptwriting. He worked at first with theatrical clichés and myths and then proceeded from *Si Aurore m'était contée deux fois*, which is anti-melodrama and against the 'boulevard' style associated with Guitry, and to the sham western *Rodéo et Juliette*, and *Don Quickshot*—all unpublished plays. Rather than ignoring or repudiating theatrical tradition, Germain subverted it—though not without a certain affection. Frequently carried away by his own verbal agility and eloquence and his Rabelaisian wit, he occasionally seems more of a raconteur than a performer or playwright.

Germain's most successful works are the still unpublished *Dédé Mesure*, about a fashion designer, the women's 'boss'; *Les hauts et les bas dla vie d'une diva: Sarah Ménard par eux-mêmes* (1976), about an opera singer who briefly believes herself to be Sarah Bernhardt; and *Un pays dont la devise est je m'oublie* (1976), about the history of French

Canada in the form of a reply to Lord Durham. Germain has also found it equally interesting and amusing to revive, with great vivacity, *Les faux brillants* (1971), a comedy by Félix-Gabriel Marchand, Liberal premier of Québec at the end of the nineteenth century.

See also DRAMA IN FRENCH 1948 TO 1981: 3.

LAURENT MAILHOT

Gibbs, Robert (b. 1930). Born in Saint John, N.B., he was educated at the University of New Brunswick and at Cambridge University; in 1970 he received his Ph.D. from UNB, where he teaches English. He has long been associated with *The* FIDDLEHEAD and the Maritime Writers' Workshop. His books of poetry are *The road from here* (1968), *Earth charms heard so early* (1970), *A dog in a dream* (1971), *A kind of wakefulness* (1973), and *All this night long* (1978). *A space to play in* (1981) is a selection of his poems published in pamphlet form by the League of Canadian Poets. His poems contain sensual and witty descriptions of human and non-human landscapes (as in 'The road from here' and the sequence 'Verse journal'), subtle insights into relationships (as in 'Earth charms heard so early' and 'The contenders'), and a sophisticated understanding of the workings of the mind, of the mutterings of dream, of the interrelationships of conscience and the subconscious (as in the short sequence 'Morning songs' and the longer sequence 'A dog in a dream'). The titles of Gibbs' books reflect these pervading concerns. Although his poetry has been admired ever since it was introduced by Fred COGSWELL in his collection *Five New Brunswick poets* (1962), it has not received the critical attention it deserves.

Gibbs also writes highly effective short stories, which have been collected in *I've always felt sorry for decimals* (1978). Other notable stories are 'I always knew there was a Lord' in *Stories from Atlantic Canada* (1972) and 'Oh think of the home over there' in *Journal of Canadian Fiction*, IV, i (1975). All his stories recreate, through the mind of the same observant and imaginative child, a provincial society just now fading into history—New Brunswick in the late 1930s and early 1940s. Gibbs' child narrator combines the role of author/creator with that of the innocent rememberer of things past, a 'petit Marcel' of a purer, simpler era. In both his poetry and prose, Gibbs shows a delicate ear for the nuances of Maritime speech and decorum.

Gibbs has written numerous articles and review articles, notably on E.J. PRATT, and has edited two anthologies, *Ninety seasons: modern poems from the Maritimes* (1974, with Robert Cockburn) and *Reflections on a hill behind a town* (1980).

Reviews or appreciations of Gibbs' work can be found in M. Travis Lane, 'Roads round about here: the poetry of Robert Gibbs', the *Humanities Association Bulletin* (Fall 1972); in Edna Barker's review of *I've always felt sorry for decimals* in the *Canadian Book Review Annual* (1978); in Marian ENGEL, 'Be grateful for Pompman and Hutchie; in the *Globe and Mail* (7 Oct. 1978); and in Alden NOWLAN, 'Gibbs' magic spell conjures up childhood' in the Saint John *Telegraph Journal* (2 Dec. 1978). M. TRAVIS LANE

Gibson, Graeme (b. 1934). Born in London, Ont., he studied at the University of Western Ontario and has taught at the Ryerson Polytechnical Institute, Toronto. He has been an important figure in cultural politics since the early 1970s and has served as chairman of the WRITERS' UNION and of the Writers' Development Trust. He has travelled widely and now lives in Toronto with Margaret ATWOOD and their daughter Jess.

Gibson's first novel, *Five legs* (1969), was also the first novel published by the House of ANANSI. In both style and content seeming to announce an iconoclastic new force in Canadian letters, *Five legs* concerns a professor, Lucas Cracknell, and two of his students, one of whom has just died in a hit-and-run accident as a symbolic expression of his capitulation to the same repressive, conventional forces that have determined Cracknell's life. The other student, Felix Oswald, wants to escape such deforming and deadening forces; he turns to nature, but cannot progress beyond an identification with animal victims. Gibson's version of the stream-of-consciousness is only a partial success. Literary echoes (Joyce, LOWRY, Eliot, and others) are too pronounced, and the text is plagued by obscurity and overwriting. Also, the theme and character deployment are overdone: like Prufrock ('balding skull wet comb-disguised, he comes down the stairs'), all the male characters are victims of guilt and conformity, and yearn for the freedom of a writer's life, while all the women are either frigid, stultifying, marrying types or sensual and free.

Communion (1971) continues the story of Felix, whose flight from conformity provided an ambiguously hopeful close for *Five legs*. It confirms, however, the darkness of Gibson's first novel. Like Felix who tries to save him, and like the hit-and-run victim of *Five legs*, the sick husky in *Communion* chooses to be a victim—and is run down by Felix's car. Thus a flight to the wilds is aborted; and Felix's subsequent flight to America ends with his being set afire by nightmarish urban children, so that the self-directed violence of Canada is turned inside-out. Again Gibson has structured his novel around parallel characters, establishing through their sexual fantasies a remoteness from authentic life. Gibson's experiments with style and structure are generally more successful in *Communion* than in *Five legs*. Both novels were reprinted in one volume in 1983.

Perpetual motion (1982), Gibson's best and most accessible novel to date, returns to rural Ontario and the nineteenth century in order to study the sources of our culture's alienation from nature. Robert Fraser, the obsessed entrepreneurial hero, attempts to create a perpetual-motion machine, and by that and other means to harness nature's energy for his own dynastic purposes. Again, animal victims carry great symbolic weight—including the mastodon unearthed (and turned into a carnival freak) by the protagonist, and the pigeons he helps the Americans to slaughter. But a new vibrancy at work in Gibson's fiction, something more ample and inventive, makes *Perpetual motion* seem a celebration of life.

See also NOVELS IN ENGLISH 1960 TO 1982: OTHER TALENTS, OTHER WORKS: 1.

CONSTANCE ROOKE

Gibson, Margaret (b. 1948). Born and raised in Toronto, her formal education ending with grade ten, she has suffered from mental illness for most of her life and is still undergoing intensive therapy. She was hospitalized for the first time at fifteen and for several years thereafter was a voluntary mute. Perhaps the most important friendship of her life has been with Craig Russell, the talented female impersonator who played a leading role in the Canadian film *Outrageous* (adapted from Gibson's story 'Making it'). In 1971 she made an unfortunate marriage that ended in divorce in 1974. Also in 1974 her story 'Ada' appeared in the annual Oberon anthology, *New Canadian stories*; it was later produced by CBC-TV, from a script written by Gibson and Claude Jutra. Her first collection of stories, *The butterfly ward* (1976), whose first edition bore the name Gilboord (her married name), was an outstanding critical success and a recipient of the City of Toronto Award. Gibson's second collection, *Considering her condition* (1978), was somewhat less successful; its title is that of a story in *The butterfly ward*. She now lives in Toronto with her son Aaron.

Madness is Gibson's central theme. Often her protagonists are shown 'functioning' outside of institutions, disguising themselves, walking 'the fine line between reality and fantasy'; but reality—which cannot simply be equated with normalcy or its opposite—is the hideousness of the world, from which the narrator tries to avert her gaze, as well as those rare moments of innocence when delight takes over. Although in both perceptions of reality Gibson's beautiful losers are more 'real' than her normal people, madness is no escape. 'Sometimes it can be beautiful inside this space', but more often it feels like being damned. Violence is everywhere—much of it directed against women. But there is also tenderness, especially for small children and for others who suffer alongside Gibson's protagonists. And there is sometimes a lovely gallantry in all the pain.

Gibson's style has a fine authenticity, lapsing very occasionally into cliché. She uses run-on sentences as well as unconventional punctuation, and her stories are often interestingly structured. Among the best are 'Ada', 'Making it', 'Considering her condition', 'Brian Tattoo', and 'Still life'.

CONSTANCE ROOKE

Giguère, Roland (b. 1929). Born in Montreal, he trained as a printer at the Écoles des Arts Graphiques there and at the École Éstienne in Paris. In 1949 he founded Éditions Erta in Montreal, which has been publishing books of poems and prints by Québécois writers and artists ever since. During his stays in France, from 1954 till 1963, he participated in the activities of the Phases group and associated with the Surrealists and André Breton. Giguère's production as a printer has been uninterrupted, and his work is frequently exhibited in Canada and abroad.

Forever inspired by the purest spirit of surrealism, from which it never deviated, Giguère's poetry exemplifies a centred yet constantly evolving mode of writing. His care for form and structure as a poet, reminiscent of his discipline as a printer, is at the service of an ever-springing flow of dream-like imagery whose power derives from an authentic inner exploration of the individual and collective unconscious. His first collections of poems—*Faire naître* (1949), *Trois pas* (1950), *Les nuits abat-jour* (1950), *Images apprivoisées* (1953), *Les armes blanches* (1954), and *Le défaut des ruines est d'avoir des habitants* (1957)—display an acute sense of the prevalent political and cultural oppression under the Duplessis régime. Giguère's is one of the strongest voices of rebellion; but for him revolt and the search for freedom are not simply a reaction against historically limited circumstances but more fundamentally a continuous struggle against the very roots of oppression in civilization. Reconciliation occurs in his poetry, as in *Adorable femme des neiges* (1959), but only by virtue of a momentary and precarious balance. All the books cited, as well as *Pouvoir du noir* (1966) and *Naturellement* (1968), were collected first in *L'âge de la parole: poèmes 1949-1960* (1965) and in *La main au feu, 1949-1968* (1973). His more recent works—*Abécédaire* (1975), *J'imagine* (1976), and *Forêt vierge folle* (1978)—carry on the same devotion to the essence of Surrealism: an unflinching faith in the subversive power of the imagination, the only weapon upon which man can rely, provided he does not give up his struggle.

Giguère won the Prix France-Canada and the Grand Prix Littéraire de la ville de Montréal in 1966. *La main au feu* won a Governor General's Award, which Giguère declined. A special issue of *La* BARRE DU JOUR 11-12-13 (Dec. 1967-May 1968) was devoted to his work. A book-length collection of some of his poems translated by Sheila Fischman, *Mirror and letters to an escapee*, was published in 1977.   MICHEL PARMENTIER

Gill, Charles-Ignace-Adélard (1871-1918). Born in Sorel, Qué., Charles Gill was educated at the Collège de Nicolet and the Collège de Saint-Laurent. He then studied painting in Montreal and Paris, where he lived intermittently in the early nineties. On his return to Montreal he taught drawing at the École Normale Jacques-Cartier. Gill was the most active and prominent member of the ÉCOLE LITTÉRAIRE DE MONTRÉAL. A collection of his short, largely dedicatory poems, and a long extract from his incomplete epic 'Le Cap Éternité', appeared posthumously under the title *Le Cap Éternité: poème suivi des Étoiles filantes* (1919). The preface, by his close friend Albert LOZEAU, remains the best introduction to this belated Romantic. He sees Gill as 'la figure la plus caractéristique de la littérature canadienne-française contemporaine' because of his admiration for Hugo and Lamartine and his misty idealism and escapism. Gill ponders on the destiny of the 'peuple agonisant', the North American Indians, and this inspires his patriotic laments for his own 'peuple abandonné'. The fragment of 'Le Cap Éternité', set on the Saguenay River, is the most ambitious of the early attempts to match in verse the scale, the mystery, and the grandeur of the Canadian landscape, and it achieves a genuine impressive elegiac nobility. Gill was married to Gaétane de Montreuil (1867-1951), the prolific pioneer of women's journalism in Québec.

Gill's *Correspondance* (1969) was edited by Réginald Hamel. Besides a few letters to his mother, it consists largely of his lively and scurrilous correspondence, from 1910 to 1918, with Louis-Joseph Doucet. Full of valuable biographical detail, it provides a vivid portrait of the eccentric Gill.

C.R.P. MAY

Girard, Rodolphe (1879-1956). Joseph-Octave-Louis-Rodolphe Girard was born in Trois-Rivières, Qué., and attended the École Sainte-Ursule there until the family moved to Montreal in 1891. He then studied at the Académie Commerciale Catholique de Montréal (1891-4) and the Collège de Montréal (1894-8). While still a student, he composed his first novel, *Florence* (1900), which was inspired by the Rebellion of 1837-8. Having become a reporter for *La Patrie* in 1899 and for *La Presse* the following year, Girard married Regina Lefaivre in 1901. The next year he published *Mosaique*, a collection of short stories and plays: five of his plays would be performed in Montreal between 1902 and 1912, and two others at a later date. When his best-known novel, MARIE CALUMET (1904), was published and denounced by the Archbishop of Montreal, he was dismissed by *La Presse* and joined the staff of Ottawa's *Le Temps*. In 1905 he became a junior clerk in the Secretary of State's office and three years later was appointed a translator for the House of Commons. His third novel, *Rédemption* (1906), which includes the saving of a 'fallen woman', gives a true account of the life of the fishermen of Paspébiac around 1892. This was followed by *L'Algonquine* (1912), about the love of a Frenchman for an Algonquin girl in seventeenth-century New France and containing detailed descriptions of Algonquin life. In the meantime Girard had been elected presi-

dent of the Institut canadien-français in Ottawa (1907) and had founded the Ottawa branch of the world-wide Alliance française (1908). After his wife died in 1911, he married Cécile Archambault the following year. During the First World War Girard served in the Canadian Forestry Corps, becoming a lieutenant-colonel and being twice decorated. He was a prolific contributor to newspapers and magazines, publishing over 400 short stories and reminiscences until long after his retirement in 1941. He is remembered today chiefly for the irreverent *Marie Calumet*; but in his time he was recognized as a leading promoter of French cultural organizations, a popular dramatist, a military figure, and as a gifted public speaker.

See André Vanasse, *'Marie Calumet'*, *Dictionnaire des oeuvres littéraires du Québec*, II (1980). MADELEINE DIRSCHAUER

Giroux, André. See NOVELS IN FRENCH 1940 TO 1959: 2.

Glass, Joanna (b. 1936). Joanna McClelland was born in Saskatoon, Sask. She wrote advertising copy at a Saskatoon radio station for a year after graduating from high school in 1955, then moved to Calgary for similar work in television. While an acting student of Betty Mitchell at Calgary's Workshop 14, her portrayal of Anne Boleyn in *Anne of the thousand days*, entered in the 1957 Dominion Drama Festival, led to an Alberta Arts Council Scholarship to study acting at the Pasadena Playhouse, Calif. She was briefly a contract player at Warner Brothers. Since her marriage to physicist Alexander Glass in 1959, she has remained in the United States and lives in Guilford, Conn.

Glass's best qualities as a writer—in her plays and one novel—lie in her capacity to explore with wit and perception the nuances of relationships among the walking wounded of contemporary society. Her earliest plays—*Satacqua*, and two one-acters, *Jewish strawberries* and *Trying*—were given workshop productions. Her skills as a playwright were first widely recognized with *Canadian Gothic* and *American modern* (1977). Set in a small prairie town and a New York suburb respectively, these companion pieces are powerfully contrasting studies of modern domestic despair. They were premièred at the Manhattan Theatre Club, N.Y., in 1972 and first performed in Canada at Pleiades Theatre, Calgary, in 1973. *Canadian Gothic* appeared in *Best short plays of 1978*

Glass

(1980) and in *Prairie performance* (1980), edited by Diane Bessai. Glass's full-length play *Artichoke* (1979), a comedy with a Saskatchewan farm setting, was premièred at the Long Wharf Theatre, New Haven, Conn., in 1975, starring Colleen Dewhurst; Bill Glassco mounted the first Canadian production at Tarragon Theatre, Toronto, in 1976. Glass's witty dialogue and sharp-eyed view of western-Canadian rural society enliven this play about a middle-aged wife who astonishes her family by deciding to take a lover for the summer. Glass developed a similar theme in her only published novel, *Reflections on a mountain summer* (1974). Set alternately in the Canadian Rockies and Gross Point, Mich., it combines the author's perceptions of Canadian and American personality and her response to the traumas of modern living. It was serialized as a 10-part program for the BBC in 1975.

The Manitoba Theatre Centre commissioned *The last chalice* in 1977. Set in Saskatoon, it provides both a grim and comic study of an alcoholic home; the play is derived from a short story 'At the King Edward Hotel', written in 1975 and published in *Winter's tales 22* (1976). Glass was awarded a Guggenheim Fellowship in 1981 for a revision of this work. Her most recent drama, *To Grandmother's house we go* (1981), starred Eva Le Gallienne in its première at the Biltmore Theatre, New York, in Jan. 1981. Another 'serious' comedy, it is set in an old family home in Hartford, Conn., where three generations meet on a Thanksgiving weekend to sort out their lives in a mix of traditional and modern modes of self-expression.

Detailed performance information about Glass's plays is available in *Canada's playwrights: a biographical guide* edited by Don Rubin and Alison Cranmer-Byng; see also Hetty Clews' critical study, 'Kindred points: the twin world of Joanna M. Glass', *Atlantis* (Autumn 1978).   DIANE BESSAI

Glassco, John (1909-81). Born in Montreal of a merchant family, John Glassco, known to his friends as Buffy, was educated at Selwyn House, Bishop's College School, and Lower Canada College. He entered McGill in 1925 but left in 1928 without graduating. Defying his father's displeasure, he preferred to complete his education in sensibility in Paris. He stayed in France for three years, frequenting expatriate and artistic circles, living often in deep poverty, and finally contracting tuberculosis, which forced him to return to Montreal for treatment. His account of this interlude, *Memoirs of Montparnasse* (1970), was immediately recognized as one of the finest Canadian autobiographies when it was published forty years later. (He says in a prefatory note that he wrote all but the first three chapters while in hospital before and after a critical operation. Patricia Whitney, in doing research for a literary biography of Glassco, discovered in the Public Archives the text of all but the first chapter, which had been published in *This Quarter* in 1929, handwritten with a ballpoint pen in six scribblers dated 1964.) It is a remarkably vivid account of what it was like to be young in the Paris of the late Third Republic, still recognizably the city of Verlaine and Baudelaire, even the city of Balzac. Glassco profited by the opportunity to meet, and had the sharp eye and clear memory to characterize, such writers as George Moore (whose *Confessions*, he said, were a model for the *Memoirs*), James Joyce, Ford Madox Ford, André Breton, Robert McAlmon, Gertrude Stein ('a rhomboidal woman'), and a score of others. All is recorded with a glittering freshness of prose that gives the book a sense of complete contemporaneity with the scene and its inhabitants; in addition, the controlled ordering of happenings, and the vitality of the dialogue, lend the flavour of fiction to the narrative.

In 1935, having survived the removal of a lung, Glassco retired to Foster, in the Eastern Townships of Québec, and immersed himself in the local life, running the rural mail route, founding the Foster Horse Show in 1951, and acting as mayor of Foster from 1952 to 1954. During his later decades he divided his time between Montreal and Foster.

Glassco once remarked that he was 'as much a novelist, anthologist, translator and pornographer' as he was a poet or a fine memoirist. His earliest publication, a surrealist poem called 'Conan's Fig', appeared in *transition* in 1928, and he first became widely known to Canadians as a poet through *The deficit made flesh* (1958). His later books of verse are *A point of sky* (1964); *Selected poems* (1971), which won a Governor-General's Award; and the long satiric-parodic poem, *Montreal* (1973). His prose works, besides *Memoirs of Montparnasse*, are the three novellas in *The fatal woman* (1974) or appeared under a variety of noms-de-plume. 'A season in limbo' by 'Silas M. Gooch', a fictional treatment of a later stay in hospital, appeared in *The* TAMARACK REVIEW 23 (1962). Other pseudonymous works are largely exercises in mannered pornography: *Contes en crinoline* (1930) by 'Jean de Saint-Luc'; *The English governess* by 'Miles Underwood'; *The temple of pederasty* (1970); 'after Ihara Saikaku'; and *Fetish girl* (1972) by 'Sylvia Beyer'. *The English governess* was eventually published under Glassco's name as *Harriet Marwood, governess* (1976). 'I came'—he wrote in *Memoirs*—'under the renewed influence of Huysmans, Pater, Villiers, Barbey D'Aurevilly and others of the so-called Decadents, and decided to write books utterly divorced from reality, stories where nothing happened.' This meant, as Edmund Wilson said in *Axel's Castle*, 'cultivating one's fantasies, encouraging one's private manias, ultimately preferring one's absurdest chimeras to the most astonishing contemporary realities'. Following this direction, Glassco wrote not only the pseudonymous novels and novellas listed above, but also completed *Under the hill* (1959), Aubrey Beardsley's unfinished romance.

As a poet John Glassco stands in the classic tradition; his combination of the bucolic and elegiac modes links him to the Augustans as well as to the decadent writers of the 1890s, while also owing much to his familiarity with the poetry of both France and Québec. Indeed, his excellent translations of the poems of Saint-Denys GARNEAU, and other Québec writers, should be considered a part of his poetic *oeuvre*, for he achieved the rare feat of writing fine English poetry while translating from the French. His translations can be found in *The poetry of French Canada in translation* (1970), which he edited, and in the *Complete poems of Hector de Saint-Denys-Garneau* (1962), whose *Journal* he also translated (1962).

Glassco's poems—unlike his prose—are largely concerned with the simple actualities of life in the Eastern Townships ('no way of living but a mode of life', as he described it). His rural poems are full of images of derelict farmhouses and decaying roads that peter out in the bush; but reflections on the human condition are never far away from the descriptions of the countryside, so that the life of the land and the lives of people are woven together. In such poems, whose sensitivity towards the natural world strangely balances the deliberate artificiality of his fiction, Glassco combines a true joy in beauty with a sense of the pathetic in human existence—a sense of loss stirred by his reading of history and literature and of his experi-

ence of a rural Québec that time had passed over and left neglected. But not all of Glassco's poems are bucolic. Some provide a link with his prose by moving into the mythology of literature and history: 'The death of Don Quixote' and 'Brummel at Calais' show Glassco as a master of echoes, and of parody and pastiche in the best sense; they evoke the philosophy of the nineteenth-century dandy and decadent (Brummel, Baudelaire, Wilde) that is also evident in his prose writings.

Glassco compiled the anthology *English poetry in Quebec* (1963), which grew out of a poetry conference held at Foster in 1963. In addition to translating poetry, he also translated three novels from French Canada: *Lot's wife* (*La femme de Loth*, 1975) by Monique BOSCO, *Creature of the chase* (*Un dieu chasseur*, 1979) by Jean-Yves Soucy, and *Fear's folly* (*Les demi-civilisés*, 1982) by Jean-Charles HARVEY.

See two articles in CANADIAN LITERATURE—Charles Murdoch, 'Essential Glassco' (Issue 65, Summer 1975), and Leon EDEL, 'John Glassco (1909-1981) and his erotic muse' (Issue 93, Summer 1982)—and *Ellipse* 14/15 (1974), which is devoted to Glassco and Alain GRANDBOIS.

GEORGE WOODCOCK

Glengarry school days (1902). A collection of loosely interrelated sketches by Charles William GORDON, who used the pseudonym 'Ralph Connor', *Glengarry school days: a story of early days in Glengarry* is memorable for its depiction of typical one-room-schoolhouse events—the spelling bee, the annual examination, the game of shinny—drawn from Gordon's childhood memories of Glengarry, the easternmost county in Ontario, in the 1860s. About the teaching of self-mastery, the story begins as Archie Munro's days as teacher at the 'Twentieth' school draw to a close. His commanding example of self-control is succeeded first by brute force, next by weakness, and finally by cynicism. The last teacher, John Craven, gradually becomes a worthy successor to Archie Munro under the influence of the book's most powerful inculcator of moral values, the Presbyterian minister's wife, Mrs Murray. Her example, and that of Mrs Finch, gently civilize and inspire boys and men alike.

Since Connor's earlier books had been pirated, this one was serialized in Canadian, American, and British periodicals to ensure complete international copyright coverage.

Glengarry school days

Glengarry school days has been reprinted frequently over the years, in both Canada and the United States, and is currently available in paperback in the New Canadian Library (1975) with an introduction by S. Ross Beharriell.　　　　JUDITH SKELTON GRANT

Godbout, Jacques (b. 1933) Born in Montreal, he studied under the Jesuits at Collêge Brébeuf. After obtaining an M.A. in French literature from the Université de Montréal in 1954 (with a thesis on Arthur Rimbaud), he taught from 1954 to 1957 at the University College of Addis Ababa in Ethiopia, returning to Montreal to work as film director and script writer for the National Film Board, where he has remained. In 1960 he was one of the founders of LIBERTÉ, a literary review that he edited for a time. He was also a founder of the Mouvement laïque de langue française in 1962, and in 1977 of the Québec writers' union of which he was the first president.

Godbout's three volumes of poetry—*Carton-pâte* (1956), *Les pavés secs* (1958), and *C'est la chaude loi des hommes* (1960)—introduce the reader to an ironic world where global anxiety in the age of the atomic bomb makes love difficult. The tension between the private and public domains and the use of irony and intellectual pyrotechnics to control and mask emotion are characteristics of both his poetry and his fiction. As Godbout himself has often stated, the evolution of his novels, from *L'aquarium* (1962) to *Les têtes à Papineau* (1981), consciously parallels the evolution of Québec society on the level of language, ideology and myth. He has been a perceptive reader of the tensions and directions of Québec over the last twenty years, from 'Americanity' through JOUAL and feminism to the post-Referendum split in the Québec psyche.

with no precise location in time or space, but with a clearly allegorical motif. It records the perceptions of a group of passive foreigners in a Third World country on the brink of revolution. Clearly inspired by the author's African experience, it can also be seen as a symbolic interpretation of Québec on the verge of the Quiet Revolution. It was awarded the Prix France-Canada. *Le couteau sur la table* (1965)—translated by Penny Williams as *Knife on the table* (1968)—continues the allegory of *L'aquarium*, recounting the outer and inner journeys through Canada and the United States of a nameless Québécois narrator as he seeks to link his identity with the garish artificiality of

Disneyland décors and the repressed puritanical atmosphere of the CPR towns of western Canada. These journeys lead finally to a break with his English-Canadian mistress Patricia and a suggestion that Québec's identity may perhaps be achieved only through violence. Godbout has claimed that the novel was conceived as a love story, but changed direction when the FLQ bombings began in 1963. SALUT GALARNEAU! (1967)—translated by Alan Brown as *Hail Galarneau!* (1970)—is Godbout's most successful novel, largely because of the irrepressible humour and humanity of its central character, who provides a satiric and immensely funny view of Québec's economic and language problems and its domination by an America that it loves. It received a Governor General's Award. *D'Amour, P.Q.* (1972), which is much more mannered, looks at the then-controversial question of *joual* and its relation to classical French. The novel consists of three versions of a novel written by Thomas D'Amour, a priggish intellectual whose language and themes bear little relation to Québec reality. He takes his manuscript to two secretaries, who speak a literary and a vulgar version of Québec working-class French. Feminism was clearly on the author's mind in this novel, for the secretaries succeed in transforming D'Amour's novel, in dominating his life, and in getting him into bed, where the final version of the novel is produced. In *L'île au dragon* (1976) the central images are of global pollution and destruction that threaten the mind as well as the planet, and of a Québec that is slowly succumbing to the vulgarities of the American way of life. Michel Beauparlant, a writer and a modern version of Saint Michael the Archangel, confronts his dragon in the form of an American capitalist who has bought the island Beauparlant lives on in order to use it as a site for atomic waste.

After a silence of five years, during which he claimed that the election of the Parti Québécois and the 'static' of the Referendum period were interfering with his ability to write, Godbout returned to the literary scene in late 1981 with *Les têtes à Papineau*, a short and breezy analysis of Québec's cultural duality that tells the story of a two-headed monster, Charles-François Papineau. Like Louis-Joseph Papineau—who, after leading the 1837 Rebellion, chose exile in the U.S. and finally became an elected member of the Parliament of the United Canadas—Charles-François (read Canadien-français) is an incarnation of Québec's divided soul. Charles is conservative, anglophile, and somewhat melancholy; François is a man of action, French in his tastes, and full of *joie de vivre*. Tired of their conflicting personalities, the two agree to an operation by an English-Canadian surgeon, who plans to join the left lobe of Charles's brain to the right lobe of François's, thus producing a new one-headed Québécois. Unfortunately the doctor's computers fail to locate the French-speaking ability in the left side of François's brain and the operation produces an English-speaker who signs himself as Charles F. Papineau and works at a computer-science centre at English Bay in Vancouver. Although it is one of the funniest Québec novels of recent years, as a comment on the struggle between René Lévesque and Pierre Trudeau for Québec's allegiance it is extremely pessimistic.

While Godbout's novels are always clever and socially relevant, his work since *Salut Galarneau!* has lacked depth. In some ways his irony and mastery of paradox make him a better essayist than novelist; his collected essays were published in 1976 under the title *Le réformiste*.

See André Smith, *L'univers romanesque de Jacques Godbout* (1976).

See also NOVELS IN FRENCH 1960 TO 1982: 1, 3.   PATRICIA SMART

Godfrey, Dave (b. 1938). Born in Winnipeg, Man., he spent most of his early years in rural Ontario. After brief attendance at the University of Toronto, he did undergraduate and graduate work in the U.S., receiving a B.A. from the University of Iowa in 1960, an M.A. from Stanford in 1961, an M.F.A. in creative writing from Iowa in 1963, and a Ph.D. in English from Iowa in 1967. Under the auspices of the Canadian University Service Overseas (CUSO), Godfrey served as acting head of the English department of Adisadel College, Cape Coast, Ghana, from 1963 to 1965. On returning to Canada from Iowa in 1966 he taught English at Trinity College, University of Toronto; was writer-in-residence at Erindale College (1973-4); joined the creative-writing program of York University in 1977; and in 1978 was named chairman of the creative-writing department of the University of Victoria, where he currently teaches.

Godfrey has been a major force in Canadian publishing and a strong advocate of nationalist policies. With Dennis LEE he co-founded the important literary press, House of ANANSI, in 1966. In 1967, hoping that a broad spectrum of Canadian titles might have a larger cultural impact than the purely literary, he joined with James BACQUE and Roy McSkimming to found another Toronto publishing house, New Press. He worked as general editor of McCLELLAND & STEWART's 'Canadian Writers' series from 1968 to 1972; joined the advisory panel of the Canada Council in 1971; and was fiction editor of the CANADIAN FORUM in 1971-2. In 1972 he joined the editorial board of the *Journal of Canadian Fiction*, became founding director of the Association for the Export of Canadian Books, and, having separated himself from both House of Anansi and New Press, founded Press Porcépic, a literary press that he and his wife Ellen continue to operate. He co-edited with the nationalist economist Mel Watkins *Gordon to Watkins to you: a documentary of the battle for control of the Canadian economy* (1970) and with Robert FULFORD and Abraham Rotstein co-edited *Read Canadian; a book about Canadian books* (1972), a polemical appeal for more action to promote Canadian book publication. In recent years he has devoted himself to the cultural implications of micro-computer technology, and has argued that the decentralization of data-banks and computer communications is essential for both the regional and national well-being of Canadian art and literature. With Douglas Parkhill he co-edited *Gutenberg Two* (1979), a pioneering investigation of the social and political meaning of new electronic technologies; and with Ernest Chang he co-authored *The Telidon book* (1981), a guide to the technological requirements and social implications of videotex and electronic publishing.

As significant and valuable as his teaching and publishing activities have been, Godfrey's fiction—first published in Issue 19 of *The* TAMARACK REVIEW (1961): 'River Two Blind Jacks'—has been an even greater accomplishment. *Death goes better with Coca-Cola* (1967), his first collection of stories, is noteworthy for its subtle techniques of juxtaposed narratives and symbolic use of the kitsch of U.S. popular culture to depict the greed and latent violence of twentieth-century man. His only novel, *The new ancestors* (1970), which won a Governor-General's Award, juxtaposes four different temporal perspectives of the same events to create an Einsteinian vision of relative values. Although this novel is set in Ghana, its principal content is its depiction of human experience as relative, non-linear, and atemporal.

Godfrey has moved even further from conventional realism in *I Ching Kanada* (1976) and *Dark must yield* (1978), a collection of fifteen stories. *I Ching Kanada*—a prose meditation that takes the hexagrams of the traditional *I Ching* as its starting-point—is composed in images, often merely noun phrases: each meditation focuses on culture, showing how culture, born of mother and hearth, grows to become country. *Dark must yield* offers stories that blend different voices and blur expected distinctions between story and essay, story and autobiography. Their effect resides not in narrative or characterization but in the inferences a reader can draw from the juxtapositions and contrasts of voice; these stories insist that the ultimate ground of political sovereignty lies in the individual consciousness.

See also NOVELS IN ENGLISH 1960 TO 1982: 3.　　　　　　　　　　FRANK DAVEY

Godfrey, Ellen. See MYSTERY AND CRIME.

Godin, Gérald (b. 1938). Born in Trois-Rivières, Qué., he dropped out of school to work as a proof-reader for the newspaper *Le Nouvelliste*. Later he was employed as a reporter for *Le Nouveau Journal* in Montreal and as a researcher for the Radio-Canada daily news-commentary program, *Aujourd'hui*. An early contributor to PARTI PRIS, he was for a time editor of the magazine and director of Les Éditions Parti Pris. In the PQ sweep of 1976 he was elected to the Québec National Assembly in Robert Bourassa's old riding of Mercier. Re-elected in 1981, he is now Minister of Cultural Communities and Immigration with responsibility for all aspects, except education, of Bill 101, Québec's language law.

As well as satirical short stories and polemical articles contributed to *parti pris*, Godin has published five volumes of poetry: *Chansons très naïves* (1960), *Poèmes et cantos* (1962), *Nouveaux poèmes* (1963), *Les cantouques* (1967), and *Libertés surveillées* (1975). Like other writers of the *parti pris* group, he has made considerable use of JOUAL, calling this 'a sort of literary sit-in'—a way of using what he saw as the degradation of the French language in Canada as an instrument of revolution. Most of his poetry, however, is personal rather than political in the narrow sense. There are ironic or wrily tender love poems, mocking glances at some of his fellow-revolutionaries and at the contradictions in his own mental processes, much gaiety and exuberance, and a sheer delight in words; his rage on behalf of such victims of social injustice as lumberjacks and city slum-dwellers is never brutal. A true poet with a marvellous sense of language and its possibilities, Godin is unique among younger French-Canadian writers for his balance and good humour.

English translations of some of Godin's poems were published in *Ellipse* I and in John GLASSCO's *The poetry of French Canada in translation* (1970). Malcolm Reid's discussion of Godin as poet and political thinker in *The shouting signpainters* (1972) includes English renderings of two poems.

JOYCE MARSHALL

Golden Dog, The (1877). This famous historical romance of Quebec in 1748, by William KIRBY, was first published in the United States (Rouses Point, N.Y., 1877) and not copyrighted; it was pirated by a New York publisher the next year. In a later 'authorized edition', with corrections and other changes by Kirby and some cutting by the publisher, its full title was given as *The Golden Dog (Le Chien d'or): a romance of the days of Louis Quinze in Quebec* (Boston, 1896); this edition was reprinted many times.

At the centre of the story are two beauties: the scheming, ruthless Angélique who, though loving and being loved by an army officer, Le Gardeur de Repentigny, is determined to seduce the Intendant, François Bigot, and become the most powerful woman in New France; and Le Gardeur's sister, the equally passionate though virtuous Amélie, who loves Pierre Philibert, son of the honest proprietor of the trading house called 'The Golden Dog'. Shaped in the mould set by Sir Walter Scott and Alexandre Dumas, *The Golden Dog* is a tale of ambition, greed, deception, passion, and murder, embroidered with Gothic details. It portrays a Québec that suggests Europe rather than North America, just as the Gothic conventions of the story—aristocratic villains, a witch, and a mysterious woman hidden in the vault of a château—suggest the Old World rather than the New. But in spite of its romanticized setting and hyperbolical style (overheated dialogue and soliloquies, inflated sentiments, melodramatic plot devices), in the modern abridgement read today it holds the interest as a sweeping, emotional tale of human perversity.

Kirby began to work on the novel after a visit to Quebec City in the summer of 1865 and took great pains to research the period. He leaned heavily on information and legends imparted by James Le Moine in his *Maple leaves* (7 vols, 1863-1906), and based his main characters on real people, altered to suit his purposes. Angélique was suggested by Angélique Péan, wife of the adjutant at Quebec and mistress of the corrupt Intendant Bigot (who did not actually arrive at Quebec until Aug. 1748). La Corriveau, who entered the legends of New France after she was hanged in 1763 for murdering her husband, appears as a professional poisoner. Philibert *père* and Le Gardeur de Repentigny were based on men of the same name, the former having been murdered by the latter in 1748 (as in the novel). This historical incident is connected with 'The Golden Dog'. On the front of the house of Nicolas Jacquin *dit* Philibert, at the corner of Côte de la Montagne and rue Buade, was a bas-relief of a dog with a bone between its paws and an inscription in French, translated by Kirby as: 'I am a dog that gnaws his bone,/I couch and gnaw it all alone—/A time will come, which is not yet,/When I'll bite him by whom I'm bit.' The stone is thought to have been made in the seventeenth century by the previous owner of the house, Timothée Roussel, as a copy of one dated 1561 that was found at Pezenas, near Roussel's home town of Montpellier, France. It can be seen today on the front of the post office that was built on the site of Philibert's house.

However hackneyed the novel may now appear, it offers a treasure-house of English-Canadian attitudes toward the fact of French Canada. A descendant of United Empire Loyalists, Kirby presented in this novel an account of how the two Canadas—despite their historical differences—formed in fact a single national entity, the basis of which resided in what the author viewed as the principal characteristic of French Canada: loyalty. Betrayed by her old imperial masters (villainy and virtue in the novel often reveal themselves in terms of Old World corruption versus New World innocence), French Canada remained loyal to her new masters during the American Revolution and the War of 1812. Thus a moral foundation underlay both societies, legitimizing the hegemony of English Canada.

The 624-page edition of 1896 was abridged by Derek Crawley for the New Canadian Library (1969). DENNIS DUFFY

THE FRENCH TRANSLATION. On its publication in 1877 *The Golden Dog* was enthusiastically reviewed in French-Canadian newspapers and magazines, and Kirby was repeatedly urged to have the novel translated into French. After some hesitation he signed a contract in May 1884 with Senator François-Xavier-Anselme Trudel, founding editor of the Montreal newspaper *L'Étendard*, to have a translation prepared by the poet Léon-Pamphile LEMAY, who in 1865 had translated Longfellow's EVANGELINE. Lemay's very free translation of Kirby's novel appeared serially in *L'Étendard*, under the title *Le Chien d'or*, from Aug. 1884 to Feb. 1885. (The author's remuneration for this serial publication was the copyright to the French version—the only copyright protection Kirby ever received for his novel.) It was then published as a book, in two volumes, for which Kirby received a ten-per-cent royalty. Thirty years later Lemay revised his translation, which appeared after his death in a second edition (1926) that included a posthumous introduction and notes by a lifelong friend of Kirby's, the Quebec journalist and historian Benjamin Sulte (1841-1923). A facsimile reprint of the 1926 edition was published in 1971.

The correspondence connected with the translation is preserved in the Ontario Public Archives. DAVID M. HAYNE

Goldsmith, Oliver (1794-1861). Born in Saint Andrews, N.B., he grew up in the Annapolis Valley and subsequently worked for the commissariat of the British army in Halifax (1810-33), Saint John (1833-44), Hong Kong (1844-8), and Newfoundland (1848-53). He retired to England and died at his sister's home in Liverpool.

Goldsmith's literary career was brief and limited: his narrative poem, *The rising village*, was published in London in 1825 and reprinted in Saint John in 1834 with some revisions and a few additional short lyrics; an *Autobiography*, found in family papers, was edited by W.E. Myatt and published in 1943. The narrative of *The rising village* describes the stages of growth in frontier life: the first building, the coming of other settlers, the addition of communal institutions and occupations that shape village life, and the emotional conflicts that come with social interaction and that form the folk history of the settlement.

Goldsmith has been acclaimed as the first native-born poet to publish a volume of verse, but a biographical curiosity has attracted more attention than the poem: the fact that he was the grandnephew of the popular British novelist, dramatist, and poet Oliver Goldsmith, author of *The vicar of Wakefield* (1766) and *The deserted village* (1770). The obsession of commentators with this relationship, which the author himself promoted, has tended to deflect critical attention from the poem itself. Contemporary British reviewers were generally disappointed with *The rising village* in comparison with *The deserted village*; Canadian reviewers, flattered and delighted by the connection, tended to be over-complimentary to the younger Goldsmith. In both cases the shadow of the elder Goldsmith distorted appreciation of the inherent intention and value of the Canadian poem. Recent critical readings have also been plagued by the Goldsmith connection, but have generally interpreted the meaning of the poem in terms of its apparent relationship to the social and political development of colonial Nova Scotia in the 1820s and 1830s. This approach, however, tends to exaggerate the intellectual complexity of the poem by implicitly giving an allegorical or ironic intention to what is ostensibly a straightforward expository narrative. Such readings do not take into account the fact that the poem, originally published in London, was designed for a British audience for whom veiled allegorical or ironic subtleties would mean nothing. Both British and colonial readers would have grasped that the central subject of the poem was the settlement and civilizing of a wilderness area, that the heart of this experience lay in nurturing right human values (virtue) in a physical environment that was ill-suited and even hostile to their sustenance, and that the virtue invested in communal life was always vulnerable to corruption, not only from external circumstances but from internal weakness as well. Striving for civilized life while recognizing its essential vulnerability was elemental to appreciating the drama of colonial experience and is, not surprisingly, a deep-rooted theme in colonial Canadian literature.

Michael Gnarowski has edited a modern reprint of *The rising village* (1968). See also K.J. Hughes, 'Oliver Goldsmith's "The rising village" ', *Canadian Poetry* 1 (1977); W.J. Keith, 'The Rising Village again', *Canadian Poetry* 3 (1978); and G. Lynch, 'Oliver Goldsmith's *The Rising Village*: controlling nature', *Canadian Poetry* 6 (1980).

TOM VINCENT

Gordon, Charles William (1860-1937). Canada's first best-selling author, who published under the pseudonym 'Ralph Connor', was born in Glengarry County, Canada West (Ont.), the son of the Presbyterian minister Daniel Gordon and Mary Robertson. In 1883 he completed a B.A. in classics and English at the University of Toronto. After graduating from Knox College in 1887, he spent a year at Edinburgh University, was ordained in the Presbyterian ministry in 1890, and became Doctor of Divinity in 1906. At a loss after his mother's death in 1890, he found his feet during three years as a missionary to the miners, lumbermen, and ranchers around Banff, Alta., and spent another year in Edinburgh raising money for the missions in western Canada. In 1894 he accepted a call from St Stephen's, a mission church on the outskirts of Winnipeg and his charge for the rest of his life. In 1899 he married Helen Skinner King, daughter of the Rev. John M. King; they had one son and six daughters. As president of the Social Service Council of Manitoba, he was a prominent advocate of temperance in the years before the Great War. He accompanied the 43rd Highlanders to war in 1915 as their chaplain (some 350 of them were from his own congregation); he then became senior Protestant chaplain to the Canadian forces. In 1917 he was sent on a lecture tour to present the Allied view of the war to Americans. From 1920, until it had completed its work in 1924, he chaired the highly successful Manitoba Council of Industry, which mediated labour disputes after the Winnipeg General Strike of 1919. Generously unsectarian in his views, as moderator of the Presbyterian Church in 1921-2 he helped move his church towards union with the Methodists: this was realized in 1924 by the creation of the United Church of Canada.

The western missions turned Charles William Gordon, minister, into Ralph Connor, author. Seeking support for this work Gordon, drawing on his missionary experience, wrote several fictional sketches for the Presbyterian magazine *The Westminster*. They so delighted editor and readers that he was asked for more, and again more. The series was collected as *Black Rock: a tale of the Selkirks* (Toronto, 1898); its immediate success in Canada and the United States established him as an author. The pattern thus set—a serial run in *The Westminster*, followed by a book for the Christmas market—persisted through the publication in 1912 of *Corporal*

Cameron of the North West Mounted Police: a tale of the Macleod Trail. Often this rhythm meant that the book appeared before the serial run was complete. Gordon's pseudonym, 'Connor', resulted when a wireless operator changed the first vowel of the middle syllables of Brit. *Can. Nor.* West Mission to an 'o'.

In Ralph Connor's stories Christian principle always wins through in the end. His action-packed plots allow ample opportunity for the display of the physical courage that is as much a part of a Connor hero as the more-important moral courage. Like many earlier Victorian writers, Connor deliberately stirred his readers' softer emotions with scenes of pathos; like them, he appeared to find such feeling morally valuable. Tapping a broad audience that read gospel fiction like Charles M. Sheldon's popular *In his steps: 'What would Jesus do?'* (1897), Connor wrote for the many readers who liked their fiction to combine adventure, lively characterization, and Christian uplift.

Gordon's career peaked early. His publishers sold five million copies of his first three books—*Black Rock, The sky pilot: a tale of the foothills* (Toronto, 1899), and *The man from Glengarry: a tale of the Ottawa* (1901); while the quarter-million first edition of his minor classic, GLENGARRY SCHOOL DAYS: *a story of early days in Glengarry* (1902), was followed by immediate reprintings in Canada, the United States, and Britain. *Gwen's canyon* (Toronto, 1899: chapters 11 to 13 of *The sky pilot*) and *Gwen: an idyll of the canyon* (New York, 1899 and 1904: chapters 9 to 13) were also popular. Though his later novels sold well, their sales never achieved the heady heights of those early volumes. Few of his books are still in print. Since his characters now seem one-sided, his plots melodramatic, and his Christianity oversimplified, only *The man from Glengarry* and *Glengarry school days* (both available in paperback) are widely read today for their authentic depiction of scenes and characters of pioneer Ontario and the early West.

In *Black Rock* and *The sky pilot* Gordon discovered the subject that focused his energies as a novelist until the Great War (and in two later books): the frontier. This provided colourful figures—cowboys, ranchers, shantymen, who were involved in drinking, gambling, and fighting. He typically confronts such characters with a civilizing agent like a minister (a 'sky pilot'), a doctor, schoolmaster, policeman, or good woman in plots that bring the licentious figures back within the structures and controls of civilization. The anarchy that is brought within bounds is both within and without, and the goal of each story is both self-mastery and the creation of a stable, caring community. The battle between evil and good is bodied forth at least once in each story in a game, contest, or match demanding skill, courage and principle. The description of the football game between Varsity and McGill in *The prospector: a tale of the Crow's Nest Pass* (1904) is a fine example of the vigour of Gordon's handling of such physical action. During this period Gordon also wrote *The life of James Robertson: missionary superintendent in Western Canada* (1908), a biography (almost a hagiography) of the man who sent him to the western mission field. The superintendent hovers in the background of a number of Gordon's books, including *The doctor: a tale of the Rockies* (1906). Of the remaining western books—*The pilot at Swan Creek and other stories* (1905), *The foreigner: a tale of Saskatchewan* (1909), *Corporal Cameron*, its lacklustre sequel *The patrol of the Sun Dance Trail* (1914), and *The Gaspards of Pine Croft: a romance of the Windermere* (1923)—only *The foreigner* is a work of distinction. It presents a powerful portrait of the sordid boarding-house life of Slavic immigrants on the outskirts of Winnipeg in the 1880s and then follows a lad to a farm in Saskatchewan, where he gradually learns a Canadian rather than an Old World ideal of manhood.

The remaining three frontier books are set in the East and draw on Gordon's own experience as a young boy in Glengarry, the easternmost county in Ontario, and on his parents' earlier experience ministering to pioneers. *The man from Glengarry*, one of Gordon's best-known books, traces the development of Ranald Macdonald into a man of self-control and principle whose energies are ultimately thrown into the struggle to civilize the West and to make it part of Canada. It captures such pioneering rituals as a sugaring-off, a wake, and a logging bee; like Gordon's other frontier stories, it makes lively use of dialect for French Canadian, Irish, and Scots characters. *Glengarry school days* is about the teaching of self-mastery, while the later and slighter *Torches through the bush* (1934) focuses on a Presbyterian revival of the early 1860s. Gordon's mother figures in all three Glengarry books, disguised as the saintly Mrs Murray; and judging by his portrait of her in *Postscript to adventure: the autobiography of Ralph Connor*

Gordon

(1938; revised and introduced by Gordon's son, J. King Gordon), she is the informing spirit behind many other idealized women in the early books.

The Great War redirected Gordon's energies. Appalled at the apathetic attitude to the war effort he found at home when on leave, he wrote *The major* (1917) to stimulate afresh the enthusiasm that carried men overseas to fight for empire and freedom in 1914. (The second chapter of *The major* appeared separately as *A fight for freedom* in 1917.) His most powerful war book emotionally, however, is *The sky pilot in no man's land* (1919). It begins with a vivid depiction of masculine beauty and friendship as the novel's young padré, Barry Dunbar, dives nude from a rock during a camping trip with his father. The meaning of this scene becomes clear during the book's keynote sermon, in which Barry tells a batallion of soldiers that their role is to offer clean, fit bodies as a sacrifice to God. The overplotted *Treading the wine press* (1925), concerning Canadian naval action in the war, is much less effective.

Several novels sprang from Gordon's involvement in industrial disputes and from his fascination with the stock market crash in 1929. *To him that hath: a novel of the West today* (1921) articulates both labour and management positions during a strike, then brushes aside the tougher aspects of labour's position in its solution. Three novels that tackle the stock market, either alone or in combination with labour problems—*The arm of gold* (1932), *The girl from Glengarry* (1933), and *The gay crusader* (1936)—combine oversimplified economics with potboiler romance.

Historical novels were likewise not Gordon's strength. Though more interesting than his industrial or economic novels, they sink under the weight of historical explanation and detail. *The runner: a romance of the Niagaras* (1929) examines crosscurrents in the American, Indian, and Canadian scene before and during the War of 1812 as they affect Upper Canada, with Tecumseh and General Brock as central figures. Brock reappears in *The rock and the river: a romance of Quebec* (1931), which explores attitudes and events in Lower Canada in the same period, while *The rebel Loyalist* (1935) is concerned with Loyalist activities during the American War of Independence.

Gordon also published several books and stories amplifying incidents in Christ's life. These are *The angel and the star* (1908), *The dawn by Galilee: a story of the Christ* (1909),

The recall of love (1910), *The friendly four and other stories* (1926), and *He dwelt among us* (1936). *Christian hope* (n.d.) is a sermon on that subject, while the pamphlet *The Colporteur* (n.d.) is noteworthy for its critical attitude towards the Catholic Church in Québec—a surprising departure from Gordon's generally liberal position towards churches other than his own.

Gordon has attracted critical interest not for the intrinsic merit of his writing (he made no claim to be a writer and no effort to achieve a style), but for its revelation of views and opinion about such subjects as imperialism, women, labour, and Indians. In the most substantial of these recent evaluations ('Blessed are the peacemakers: the labour question in Canadian social gospel fiction', *Journal of Canadian Studies* 10, No. 3, Aug. 1975), M. Vipond provides a useful historical perspective on *To him that hath*. Atypical of this recent critical trend is 'Ralph Connor and the Canadian identity' by J. Lee Thompson and John H. Thompson in *Queen's Quarterly* 79 (1972). In their view Connor's work as a whole, in its capacity to define English-Canadian identity, rises above the 'sentimentality and triteness' that mar individual novels.

The man from Glengarry (1960) and *Glengarry school days* (1975) are both available in paperback in the New Canadian Library, with introductions by S. Ross Beharriell. *Postscript to adventure* is a McClelland and Stewart paperback, with an introduction by Clara THOMAS (1975). Hardback editions of several novels are in print in the United States. The University Press of Kentucky reprinted *The sky pilot* (1970), with an introduction by Robin W. Winks; and Lightyear Press added *Black Rock, The doctor, The major, The man from Glengarry, The sky pilot,* and *The sky pilot in no man's land* to its list in 1976.   JUDITH SKELTON GRANT

Gotlieb, Phyllis (b. 1926). Born in Toronto, Phyllis Fay Gotlieb (née Bloom) was educated at Victoria and University Colleges, University of Toronto. Her poetry, verse-dramas, short stories, and novels (mostly science fiction) share a pervasive interest in family relations, historical roots, and the specific details and possible implications of biology ethically and imaginatively considered. Her pamphlet of poems, *Who knows one* (1961), was followed by *Within the zodiac* (1964), which reprinted some of the earlier poems and announced Gotlieb's developed style: musicality, colloquialism, re-lish for names, numbers, domestic details, art, and literature, and use of her own family and Jewish heritage. *Ordinary, moving* (1969) is similarly excellent. The title sequence is constructed from folk verse, game songs, and jump-rope ditties; its locale is the school play-yard of all time, all villages, all galaxies; its subject humanity, primitive or sophisticated, suffering or fortunate; it ends, as does the children's game, with '*begin again*'. Louis Martz ('New books in review', *The Yale Review*, LIX, 4 June 1970) calls it 'a celebration and lament for all the world's children, ourselves.'

Doctor Umlaut's earthly kingdom (1974) includes not only shorter poems (of which the elegy 'Jennie Gotlieb Bardikoff' is perhaps the most touching), but also most of the verse-drama commissioned by the CBC: 'Doctor Umlaut's earthly kingdom' (published by the CBC in *Poems for voices* in 1969), 'Silent movie days' (1971), and 'Garden varieties' (1972), a miracle play from Creation through Noah's flood with nuances of the music hall, don marquis, and Thornton Wilder. Another verse-drama, 'The contract', is included in *The works* (1978), which does not, however, include a later verse-drama, also commissioned by the CBC, 'God on trial before Rabbi Ovadia' (1976). The best articles on Gotlieb's poetry so far are probably the Martz essay mentioned above and Douglas BARBOUR's 'A cornucopia of poems' in *The* TAMARACK REVIEW 76 (1979).

Gotlieb has been publishing short science-fiction stories in magazines since 1959, and her first SF novel *Sunburst* (1964) was an immediate success and has been published internationally and translated into several languages. It deals with the problems for family and community of handling juvenile delinquents and psychopaths genetically cursed with telekinetic and telepathic powers. *Why should I have all the grief?* (1969) shows an Auschwitz survivor coping with a painful return to the contingencies and inter-relationships of the family situation while recalling and re-understanding his own father. (Best reviews: Janis Rapoport, 'The grief is shared', *The Tamarack Review* 54, (1970), and Anne Montagnes, 'Gotlieb's misery', *Saturday Night* 84 (May 1969).) In Gotlieb's third novel, *O master Caliban!* (1976)—which has also been published internationally and translated into several languages—the protagonists cope with semi-human machines, father-and-son relationships, adolescence, and the possible

problems of genetic mutation. *A judgment of dragons* (1980) follows a pair of cat Candides as they become educated in the ways of the world, past as well as present. (In one episode they return to the ancestral village of the characters of *Why should I have all the grief?*) A fifth novel, *Emperor, swords, pentacles* (1982), is a successor to *A judgment of dragons*. Gotlieb has published numerous SF stories in magazines, among which are 'Gingerbread boy' (*If*, Jan. 1961), 'Valedictory' (*Amazing*, Aug. 1964), and 'The military hospital' (included in *Fourteen stories high* (1971), a short-story collection published by OBERON PRESS). (See also SCIENCE FICTION AND FANTASY: 3.)

Gotlieb's novels are an extension of her poetic interest in personal history, psychology, and biology. They retain her poetry's vigorous language and colourful imagery. Her heroes and heroines—the white, avuncular, Montaigne-quoting goat and the huge, affectionate, crimson cats in *A judgment of dragons*; the floating genius-infant and the boy with four arms in *O master Caliban!*—have the magical charm of illustrations by Chagall or Tchelitchew. Her poetry distinguishes itself by a melodic but vivacious rhythm uncommon among her peers, and by ethical concerns and a joy in the created universe.

Gotlieb contributed a paper, 'Hasidic influences in the work of A.M. KLEIN', for *The A.M. Klein Symposium* (1974) edited by Seymour MAYNE; future students may write on Hasidic influences in the work of Gotlieb, not as it views God, but as it views the natural universe.

See also POETRY IN ENGLISH 1950 TO 1982: 2.   M. TRAVIS LANE

Goupil, Laval. See ACADIAN LITERATURE: 2(b).

Governor General's Literary Awards. With the approval of the then Governor General, Lord Tweedsmuir (the novelist John Buchan), the Governor General's Awards were launched in 1937 by the CANADIAN AUTHORS' ASSOCIATION. Initially prizes were awarded for the best books of fiction, non-fiction, poetry, or drama published by a Canadian writer in the previous year; only books in English (or translated from French into English) were eligible. The CAA's National Executive took on the judging themselves; but in 1944 a standing committee of judges was set up, known as the Awards Board. The awards were usually

Governor General's Literary Awards

presented as the finale of the CAA annual convention, which was held in various cities across the country. Initially the prize consisted of a bronze medal; but in 1942 silver medals began to be awarded. In 1951 the Association of Canadian Magazine Publishers donated $250 to accompany each medal. During the initial period, three changes were made in the award categories. In 1942 the drama category was dropped, and non-fiction was split into two categories: creative and academic. In 1949 an award for juveniles was added. The Awards Board was always free to recommend that no award be given, if in its opinion no work of sufficient quality had been published, and it exercised this right on a few occasions.

In 1959 the Canada Council agreed to administer the awards and to provide at least six prizes of $1,000 each for awards in both French and English in poetry or drama, fiction or drama, and non-fiction. It also agreed to pay the costs of the medals, the annual dinner, and travel fares for winners attending the presentation ceremony. The Governor General's reception was followed by a dinner hosted by the Council for the winners. In 1971 the Council took on the entire responsibility for appointing the juries. At the same time it reorganized the board and expanded its membership to eighteen: two nine-person juries (one for French works, one for English) divided into three sub-committees—one each for fiction, non-fiction, and poetry and drama. Juries were composed of experienced writers, professors of literature, and literary critics. The amount of the prizes was increased in 1966 to $2,500, and in 1975 to $5,000. Since 1964 the winners have received specially bound copies of their award-winning books. In 1980, with the agreement of Governor General Edward Schreyer, the Council decided to move the presentation of the awards outside Government House and to hold ceremonies in different cities across the country; and, the better to publicize the awards and the work of Canadian writers, to publish the names of finalists in all categories about a month before releasing the names of the winners. In 1981 a separate category for drama was inaugurated to recognize the best published play of the year.

JOCELYN HARVEY, KATHERINE BERG

A list of winners to 1983 follows:

1936
Bertram BROOKER. *Think of the earth.* Fiction.

T.B. Robertson. *T.B.R.*—newspaper pieces. Non-fiction.

1937
Laura G. SALVERSON. *The dark weaver.* Fiction.
E.J. PRATT. *The fables of the goats.* Poetry.
Stephen LEACOCK. *My discovery of the West.* Non-fiction.

1938
Gwethalyn GRAHAM. *Swiss sonata.* Fiction.
Kenneth LESLIE. *By stubborn stars.* Poetry.
John Murray Gibbon. *Canadian mosaic.* Non-fiction.

1939
Franklin Davey McDowell. *The Champlain Road.* Fiction.
Arthur S. BOURINOT. *Under the sun.* Poetry.
Laura G. SALVERSON. *Confessions of an immigrant's daughter.* Non-fiction.

1940
Ringuet (Philippe PANNETON). *Thirty acres.* Fiction.
E.J. PRATT. *Brébeuf and his brethren.* Poetry.
J.F.C. Wright. *Slava Bohu.* Non-fiction.

1941
Alan SULLIVAN. *Three came to Ville Marie.* Fiction.
Anne MARRIOTT. *Calling adventures.* Poetry.
Emily CARR. *Klee Wyck.* Non-fiction.

1942
G. Herbert Sallans. *Little man.* Fiction.
Earle BIRNEY. *David and other poems.* Poetry.
Bruce HUTCHISON. *The unknown country.* Non-fiction.
Edgar McInnes. *The unguarded frontier.* Non-fiction.

1943
Thomas H. RADDALL. *The pied piper of Dipper Creek.* Fiction.
A.J.M. SMITH. *News of the phoenix.* Poetry.
John D. Robins. *The incomplete anglers.* Non-fiction.
E.K. BROWN. *On Canadian poetry.* Non-fiction.

1944
Gwethalyn GRAHAM. *Earth and high heaven.* Fiction.
Dorothy LIVESAY. *Day and night.* Poetry.

Dorothy Duncan. *Partner in three worlds.* Non-fiction.

Edgar McInnes. *The war: fourth year.* Non-fiction.

1945

Hugh MacLENNAN. TWO SOLITUDES. Fiction.

Early BIRNEY. *Now is time.* Poetry.

Evelyn M. Richardson. *We keep a light.* Non-fiction.

Ross Munro. *Gauntlet to Overlord.* Non-fiction.

1946

Winifred Bambrick. *Continental revue.* Fiction.

Robert FINCH. *Poems.* Poetry.

Frederick Philip GROVE. *In search of myself.* Non-fiction.

A.R.M. Lower. *Colony to nation.* Non-fiction.

1947

Gabrielle ROY. *The tin flute.* Fiction.

Dorothy LIVESAY. *Poems for people.* Poetry.

William Sclater. *Haida.* Non-fiction.

R. MacGregor Dawson. *The Government of Canada.* Non-fiction.

1948

Hugh MacLENNAN. *The precipice.* Fiction.

A.M. KLEIN. *The rocking chair and other poems.* Poetry.

Thomas H. RADDALL. *Halifax: warden of the north.* Non-fiction.

C.P. Stacey. *The Canadian Army, 1939-1945.* Non-fiction.

1949

Philip CHILD. *Mr Ames against time.* Fiction.

James REANEY. *The red heart.* Poetry.

Hugh MacLENNAN. *Cross-country.* Non-fiction.

R. MacGregor Dawson. *Democratic government in Canada.* Non-fiction.

R.S. Lambert. *Franklin of the Arctic.* Juvenile.

1950

Germaine GUÈVREMONT. *The outlander.* Fiction.

James Wreford Watson. *Of time and the lover.* Poetry.

Marjorie Wilkins Campbell. *The Saskatchewan.* Non-fiction.

W.L. MORTON. *The Progressive Party in Canada.* Non-fiction.

Donalda Dickie. *The great adventure.* Juvenile.

1951

Morley CALLAGHAN. *The* LOVED AND THE LOST. Fiction.

Charles BRUCE. *The Mulgrave Road.* Poetry.

Josephine Phelan. *The ardent exile.* Non-fiction.

Frank MacKinnon. *The Government of Prince Edward Island.* Non-fiction.

John F. Hayes. *A land divided.* Juvenile.

1952

David WALKER. *The pillar.* Fiction.

E.J. PRATT. *Towards the last spike.* Poetry.

Bruce HUTCHISON. *The incredible Canadian.* Non-fiction.

Donald G. CREIGHTON. *John A. Macdonald: the young politician.* Non-fiction.

Marie McPhedran. *Cargoes on the Great Lakes.* Juvenile.

1953

David WALKER. *Digby.* Fiction.

Douglas LePAN. *The net and the sword.* Poetry.

N.J. Berrill. *Sex and the nature of things.* Non-fiction.

J.M.S. Careless. *Canada: a story of challenge.* Non-fiction.

John F. Hayes. *Rebels ride at night.* Juvenile.

1954

Igor Gouzenko. *The fall of a titan.* Fiction.

P.K. PAGE. *The metal and the flower.* Poetry.

Hugh MacLENNAN. *Thirty and three.* Non-fiction.

A.R.M. Lower. *This most famous stream.* Non-fiction.

Marjorie Wilkins Campbell. *The Nor'westers.* Juvenile.

1955

Lionel Shapiro. *The sixth of June.* Fiction.

Wilfred WATSON. *Friday's child.* Poetry.

N.J. Berrill. *Man's emerging mind.* Non-fiction.

Donald G. CREIGHTON. *John A. Macdonald: the old chieftain.* Non-fiction.

Kerry Wood. *The map-maker.* Juvenile.

1956

Adele WISEMAN. *The sacrifice.* Fiction.

Robert A.D. FORD. *A window on the north.* Poetry.

Pierre BERTON. *The mysterious North.* Non-fiction.

Joseph Lister Rutledge. *Century of conflict.* Non-fiction.

Farley MOWAT. *Lost in the barrens.* Juvenile.

Governor General's Literary Awards

1957

Gabrielle ROY. *Street of riches*. Fiction.
Jay MACPHERSON. *The BOATMAN*. Poetry.
Bruce HUTCHISON. *Canada: tomorrow's giant*. Non-fiction.
Thomas H. RADDALL. *The path of destiny*. Non-fiction.
Kerry Wood. *The great chief*. Juvenile.

1958

Colin McDougall. *Execution*. Fiction.
James REANEY. *A suit of nettles*. Poetry.
Pierre BERTON. *Klondike*. Non-fiction.
Joyce Hemlow. *The history of Fanny Burney*. Non-fiction.
Edith L. Sharp. *Nkwala*. Juvenile.

1959

Hugh MacLENNAN. *The watch that ends the night*. Fiction.
Irving LAYTON. *A red carpet for the sun*. Poetry.
André Giroux. *Malgré tout, la joie*. Fiction.
Félix-Antoine SAVARD. *Le barachois*. Non-fiction.

1960

Brian MOORE. *The luck of Ginger Coffey*. Fiction.
Frank Underhill. *In search of Canadian liberalism*. Non-fiction.
Margaret AVISON. *Winter sun*. Poetry.
Paul Toupin. *Souvenirs pour demain*. Non-fiction.
Anne HÉBERT. *Poèmes*. Poetry.

1961

Malcolm LOWRY. *Hear us oh Lord from heaven thy dwelling place*. Fiction.
T.A. Goudge. *The ascent of life*. Non-fiction.
Robert FINCH. *Acis in Oxford*. Poetry.
Yves THÉRIAULT. *Ashini*. Fiction.
Jean LE MOYNE. *Convergences*. Non-fiction.

1962

Kildare DOBBS. *Running to paradise*. Fiction and autobiographical writing.
Marshall McLUHAN. *The Gutenberg galaxy*. Non-fiction.
James REANEY. *Twelve letters to a small town* and *The killdeer and other plays*. Poetry and drama.
Jacques FERRON. *CONTES DU PAYS INCERTAIN*. Fiction.
Gilles MARCOTTE. *Une littérature qui se fait*. Non-fiction.
Jacques LANGUIRAND. *Les insolites et les violons de l'automne*. Drama.

1963

Hugh GARNER. *Hugh Garner's best stories*. Fiction.
J.M.S. Careless. *Brown of The Globe*. Non-fiction.
Gatien LAPOINTE. *Ode au Saint-Laurent*. Poetry.
Gustave Lanctot. *Histoire du Canada*. Non-fiction.

1964

Douglas LePAN. *The deserter*. Fiction.
Phyllis Grosskurth. *John Addington Symonds*. Non-fiction.
Raymond SOUSTER. *The colour of the times*. Poetry.
Jean-Paul Pinsonneault. *Les terres sèches*. Fiction.
Réjean Robidoux. *Roger Martin du Gard et la religion*. Non-fiction.
Pierre PERRAULT. *Au coeur de la rose*. Poetry.

1965

Alfred PURDY. *The cariboo horses*. Poetry.
James Eayrs. *In defence of Canada*. Non-fiction.
Gilles VIGNEAULT. *Quand les bateaux s'en vont*. Poetry.
Gérard BESSETTE. *L'incubation*. Fiction.
André-S. Vachon. *Le temps et l'espace dans l'oeuvre de Paul Claudel*. Non-fiction.

1966

Margaret LAURENCE. *A jest of God*. Fiction.
George WOODCOCK. *The crystal spirit: a study of George Orwell*. Non-fiction.
Margaret ATWOOD. *The circle game*. Poetry.
Claire MARTIN. *Le joue droite*. Fiction.
Marcel Trudel. *Histoire de la Nouvelle-France: vol. II., Le comptoir, 1604-1627*. Non-fiction.
Réjean DUCHARME. *L'avalée des avalés*. Poetry and theatre.

1967

Eli MANDEL. *An idiot joy*. Poetry.
Alden A. NOWLAN. *Bread, wine and salt*. Poetry.
Norah Story. *The Oxford companion to Canadian history and literature*. Non-fiction.
Jacques GODBOUT. *SALUT GALARNEAU!* Fiction.
Robert-Lionel Séguin. *La civilisation traditionelle de 'l'habitant' aux XVIIe et XVIIIe siècles*. Non-fiction.
Françoise LORANGER. *Encore cinq minutes*. Drama.

1968

Alice MUNRO. *Dance of the happy shades*. Fiction.

Mordecai RICHLER. *Cocksure* and *Hunting tigers under glass*. Fiction and essays.

Leonard COHEN. *Selected Poems 1956-68* (declined).

Hubert AQUIN. *Trou de mémoire*. Fiction (declined).

Marie-Claire BLAIS. *Les manuscrits de Pauline Archange*. Fiction.

Fernand DUMONT. *Le lieu de l'homme*. Non-fiction.

1969

Robert KROETSCH. *The studhorse man*. Fiction.

George BOWERING. *Rocky Mountain foot* and *The gangs of Kosmos*. Poetry.

Gwendolyn MacEWEN. *The shadow-maker*. Poetry.

Louise MAHEUX-FORCIER. *Une forêt pour Zoé*. Fiction.

Jean-Guy PILON. *Comme eau retenue*. Poetry.

Michel Brunet. *Les Canadiens après la conquête*. Non-fiction.

1970

Dave GODFREY. *The new ancestors*. Fiction.

Michael ONDAATJE. *The collected works of Billy the Kid*. Prose and Poetry.

bp NICHOL. *Still water, The true eventual story of Billy the Kid, Beach head, The cosmic chef: an evening of concrete*. Poetry.

Monique BOSCO. *La femme de Loth*. Fiction.

Jacques BRAULT. *Quand nous serons heureux*. Drama.

Fernand OUELLETTE. *Les actes retrouvés*. Non-fiction (declined).

1971

Mordecai RICHLER. *St Urbain's horseman*. Fiction.

John GLASSCO. *Selected poems*. Poetry.

Pierre BERTON. *The last spike*. Non-fiction.

Gérard BESSETTE. *Le cycle*. Fiction.

Paul-Marie LAPOINTE. *Le réel absolu*. Poetry.

Gérald Fortin. *La fin d'un règne*. Non-fiction.

1972

Robertson DAVIES. *The manticore*. Fiction.

Dennis LEE. *Civil elegies*. Poetry.

John NEWLOVE. *Lies*. Poetry.

Antonine MAILLET. *Don l'Orignal*. Fiction.

Gilles HÉNAULT. *Signaux pour les voyants*. Poetry.

Jean Hamelin and Yves Roby. *Histoire économique du Québec 1851-1896*. Non-fiction.

1973

Rudy WIEBE. *The temptations of Big Bear*. Fiction.

Miriam Mandel. *Lions at her face*. Poetry.

Michael Bell. *Painters in a new land*. Non-fiction.

Réjean DUCHARME. *L'hiver de force*. Fiction.

Albert Faucher. *Québec en Amérique au dix-neuvième siècle*. Non-fiction.

Roland GIGUÈRE. *La main au feu*. Special Award (declined).

1974

Margaret LAURENCE. *The diviners*. Fiction.

Ralph GUSTAFSON. *Fire on stone: a collection of poetry*. Poetry.

Charles Ritchie. *The siren years*. Non-fiction.

Victor-Lévy BEAULIEU. *Don Quichotte de la démanche*. Fiction.

Nicole BROSSARD. *Mécanique jongleuse suivi de Masculin grammaticale*. Poetry.

Louise Déchêne. *Habitants et marchands de Montréal au dix-septième siècle*. Non-fiction.

1975

Brian MOORE. *The great Victorian collection*. Fiction.

Milton ACORN. *The island means Minago*. Poetry.

Anthony Adamson, Marion MacRae. *Hallowed walls*. Non-fiction.

Anne HÉBERT. *Les enfants du sabbat*. Fiction.

Pierre PERRAULT. *Chouennes*. Poetry.

Louis-Edmond Hamelin. *Nordicité canadienne*. Non-fiction.

1976

Marian ENGEL. *Bear*. Fiction.

Joe ROSENBLATT. *Top soil*. Poetry.

Carl Berger. *The writing of Canadian history*. Non-fiction.

André MAJOR. *Les rescapés*. Fiction.

Alphonse Piché. *Poèmes 1946-68*. Poetry.

Fernand OUELLET. *Le Bas Canada 1791-1840 changements structureux et crise*. Non-fiction.

1977

Timothy FINDLEY. *The wars*. Fiction.

D.G. JONES. *Under the thunder the flowers light up the earth*. Poetry and drama.

Frank SCOTT. *Essays on the Constitution*. Non-fiction.

Governor General's Literary Awards

Gabrielle ROY. *Ces enfants de ma vie*. Fiction.

Michel GARNEAU. *Les Célébrations suivie de Adidou Adidouce*. Poetry and drama.

Denis Monière. *Le developpement des idéologies au Québec des origines à nos jours*. Nonfiction.

1978

Alice MUNRO. *Who do you think you are?* Fiction.

Patrick LANE. *Poems new and selected*. Poetry.

Roger Caron. *Go boy*. Non-fiction.

Jacques POULIN. *Les grandes marées*. Fiction.

Gilbert LANGEVIN. *Mon refuge est un volcan*. Poetry.

F.M. Gagnon. *Paul-Émile Borduas*. Nonfiction.

1979

Jack HODGINS. *The resurrection of Joseph Bourne*. Fiction.

Michael ONDAATJE. *There's a trick with a knife I'm learning to do*. Poetry.

Maria Tippett. *Emily Carr*. Non-fiction.

Marie-Claire BLAIS. *Le sourd dans la ville*. Fiction.

Robert Melançon. *Peinture eveugle*. Poetry.

D. Clift & S. McLeod Arnopoulos. *Le fait anglais au Québec*. Non-fiction.

1980

George BOWERING. *Burning water*. Fiction.

Stephen SCOBIE. *McAlmon's Chinese Opera*. Poetry.

Jeffrey Simpson. *Discipline of power*. Nonfiction.

Pierre Turgeon. *La première personne*. Fiction.

Michel Van Schendel. *De l'oeil et de l'écoute*. Poetry.

Maurice Champagne-Gilbert. *La famille et l'homme à délivrer du pouvoir*. Non-fiction.

1981

Mavis GALLANT. *Home truths*. Fiction.

F.R. SCOTT. *The collected poems of F.R. Scott*. Poetry.

George Calef. *Caribou and the barren-lands*. Non-fiction.

Sharon POLLOCK. *Blood relations and other plays*. Drama.

Denys Chabot. *La province lunaire*. Fiction.

Michel BEAULIEU. *Visages*. Poetry.

Madeleine Ouellette-Michalska. *L'échappée des discours de l'oeil*. Non-fiction.

Marie Laberge. *C'était avant la guerre à l'Anse à Gilles*. Drama.

1982

Guy VANDERHAEGHE. *Man descending*. Fiction.

Phyllis WEBB. *The vision tree: selected poems*. Poetry.

Christopher Moore. *Louisbourg portraits: life in an eighteenth-century garrison town*. Non-fiction.

John GRAY. *Billy Bishop goes to war, a play by John Gray with Eric Peterson*. Drama.

Roger Fournier. *Le cercle des arènes*. Fiction.

Michel Savard. *Forages*. Poetry.

Maurice Lagueux. *Le Marxisme des années soixante: une saison dans l'histoire de la pensée critique*. Non-fiction.

Réjean DUCHARME. *HA ha!. . .* Drama.

Goyette, Jocelyne. See DRAMA IN FRENCH 1948 TO 1981: 4.

Graham, Andrew. See EXPLORATION LITERATURE IN ENGLISH: 2.

Graham, Gwethalyn (1913-65). Gwethalyn McNaught Erichsen-Brown was born in Toronto. She attended Rosedale Public School and Havergal College there; the Pensionnat des Allières in Switzerland; and Smith College, Mass. A novelist and journalist, her writing most often deals with the need for justice, tolerance, and international understanding. Her first novel, *Swiss sonata* (1938), which won a Governor General's Award, explores the interwoven stories of more than twenty residents at a Swiss boarding school on the eve of the Second World War. Although somewhat awkward because of its large cast of characters and lack of a clear focus, it is an effective and timely appeal for international understanding in the face of the gathering fascist momentum in Europe. Her second and much stronger novel, *Earth and high heaven* (1944; NCL 1960), also won a Governor General's Award. Set in Montreal during the Second World War, it is the story of Erica Drake, an independent young journalist from an affluent Westmount family, who falls in love with a Jewish lawyer. The novel focuses on the blatant anti-Semitism of her socially prominent family, especially her father, and is an unsparing and compelling portrait of a kind of upper-class anti-Semitism that is all the more insidious because it is covert. An overnight sensation in Canada, the novel was both a popular and critical success and was translated into ten languages. The plan to film it was cancelled when *Gentleman's agreement* was released in 1948.

As a journalist Graham was a frequent contributor to *Maclean's* and *Saturday Night*, and while living in Montreal she was actively involved in political issues related to the preservation of civil liberty and artistic freedom. *Dear enemy* (1963), which Graham wrote in collaboration with Solange Chaput-Rolland, is an exchange of letters exploring the conflicts between English and French Canadians during a period of escalating separatist ferment in Québec.

MARILYN ROSE

Grainger, Martin Allerdale (1874-1941). Born in London, Eng., he spent most of his childhood in Australia where his father, Henry Allerdale Grainger, was agent general for South Australia. In 1893 he won a scholarship to Cambridge, where he excelled in mathematics. Upon graduating in 1896 he spent several adventurous years in northern British Columbia, then fought in the Boer War; he returned to British Columbia, trying his hand at placer mining, logging, and some journalism. In 1908, while in England, he wrote *Woodsmen of the West* (1908) to raise enough money on which to marry. In 1910 he began his career in the British Columbia forest industry, first as secretary of the Royal Commission on Forestry (writing most of the report that led to the establishment of the B.C. Forest Service) and rose to the position of chief forester in 1917. From 1920 until his death he devoted his energies to his private lumbering businesses.

Woodsmen of the West—reprinted in the New Canadian Library (1964) with an introduction by Rupert Schieder—was based on Grainger's letters to his future wife. Less a novel than a sequence of realistic, dramatized personal observations, it is recounted by a first-person narrator who retains the author's name and identity. Enthralled by the challenge of a frontier environment and intrigued by the individualism and initiative of the western logger, Mart recounts incidents illustrating the character type he most frequently encountered: men who were enterprising yet foolhardy, pragmatically shrewd yet financially naive, physically fearless yet emotionally undisciplined. The rather spare plot centres on Mart's conflicts with his boss, Carter, who personifies the raw spirit of free enterprise. Despite his personal distaste for the man, Mart remains in his employ, held by his fascination with Carter's ruthless and single-minded exploitation of both the land and his men. Carter emerges as a villain in his relations with human beings, but as a hero in his determination to conquer both an inhospitable environment and the vagaries of the anonymous world of big business. Grainger's detailed descriptions of the unromantic life of the west-coast handlogger, and of the climate and terrain of northern British Columbia, make *Woodsmen of the West* one of the best examples of early-Canadian literary realism.

CAROLE GERSON

Grainger, Tom (b. 1921). Born in Lancashire, Eng., he left school at fourteen to work in a cotton mill and held other menial jobs, finally serving in the Royal Air Force before immigrating to Canada in 1956. In 1965 he was awarded a fellowship to study at the Yale School of Drama and in 1970 moved to Vancouver, where he now lives with his family.

Grainger's plays, which he admits have been influenced by Sean O'Casey and Tennessee Williams, bear similarities to those of Harold Pinter, having impoverished characters (including tramps) and such settings as a room seen as a refuge, whose safety is shattered by the arrival of an intruder. In all of his plays—from *Daft dream adyin* (1969), his first play, which won the National Playwriting Seminar Award in 1964, to *The injured* (1976)—Grainger, like Pinter, draws masterful portraits of society's marginal people, who strive in their powerlessness to affect their destinies.

In *The helper* (1975) the tramp Nimrod ('Just one more victim of the system') is offered work by Tiggy in a printing shop that covers a counterfeiting operation sponsored by a league dedicated to the destruction of capitalism. The two agents who arrive to collect the counterfeit money reveal to Nimrod that the league has collapsed and that they are pocketing the profits. They try to kill him (offstage) but he kills them instead and proceeds to appropriate their lucrative fraud. In *The last death of Abraham Schurmann* (1971) the intruder is Schurmann's younger son, who comes to take the ailing old man from his room in a boarding house, thus forcing Schurmann to recognize the true condition of old age.

In *The injured*, which won the first annual Clifford E. Lee Playwriting Award, the pattern of the intruder destroying the safety of the refuge is modified. The intruder, Miss Rogers, discovers the terrible truth at the centre of the Slaters' marriage when she comes to board with them: it was Judd

Slater who raped and murdered their daughter and then allowed a tramp to be convicted. To protect their secret, Mrs Slater murders Miss Rogers. Suddenly the home is not a refuge but a trap holding the Slaters as partners in deceit and murder. Loston, the setting of both *The injured* and *Daft dream adyin*, is a symbol of their alienation and the metaphorical home of all of Grainger's characters.   ANN WILSON

Grandbois, Alain (1900-75). Born in Saint-Casimir de Portneuf, Qué., he studied law at Université Laval and, though admitted to the bar in 1925, never practised. A considerable inheritance allowed him to travel abroad almost continuously between 1918 and 1938. Based in Paris—where he met fellow-expatriates Hemingway, Cendrars, and Supervielle—he travelled extensively in Europe, Africa, India, Russia, China, and Japan. After his return to Canada he wrote steadily, earning his living by giving many radio talks on his travels on the CBC, lecturing, and writing articles, as well as working as bibliographer at the Bibliothèque Saint-Sulpice. In 1944 he was co-founder, with Victor Barbeau, of L'Académie canadienne-française, a group he never lost touch with. (In this period he translated Merrill DENISON's *The barley and the stream: the Molson story*, 1955, under the title *Au pied du courant*, 1955.) Grandbois went back to France in 1955, and in 1956 took up residence in Mont Rolland, north of Montreal. In 1960-1 he travelled in France and Italy on a Canada Council fellowship and then settled in Quebec City, where he worked for the Musée de la Province de Québec. He was three times awarded the Prix David; he also received the Prix Duvernay, the Lorne Pierce Medal, and an honorary doctorate from Université Laval.

Grandbois was justly renowned as a poet. A casual acquaintance published seven of his poems in Hankow (China) in 1934. These, with minor variants, were included in *Les îles de la nuit* (1944); this was followed by *Rivages de l'homme* (1948) and *L'étoile pourpre* (1957). His poems are admired for the sonorous harmonies and exotic colours of their language and for their impelling, incantatory rhetoric. The poet writes as a solitary figure in a harsh and implacable universe. His themes are love, the fleeting years, the mortality of man. *Rivages de l'homme* bears as an epigraph a statement from Tolstoy: 'If man has learned to think, it is of little importance what he thinks about; always at the back of his mind there is the thought of his own death.' Still, faced with the reality of death, the poet finds comfort in obstinately refusing to accept it, repeating frequently the words 'et pourtant'.

Grandbois's prose writings, close in theme to his poetry, reflect his love of travel. They include biographies of explorers who, on their journeys in search of earth's 'éblouissants secrets', courted danger and death; *Né à Québec: Louis Jolliet* (Paris, 1933; Montreal, 1949, 1969), which was published in an English translation by Evelyn Brown as *Born in Quebec* (1964); and *Les voyages de Marco Polo* (1942). *Avant le chaos* (1945), a collection of short stories (republished in 1964 with four additional tales), recalls the cosmopolitan world from Paris to Djibouti, Canton to Cannes—a world irrevocably destroyed by the 'chaos' of the Second World War. In a tone of elegant detachment and suppressed passion, Grandbois describes the sights, sounds, and ambience of exotic milieux, conveying the ugliness and violence lurking behind scenes of spectacular beauty, and the alienation and loss, exile and displacement, passion and regret that underlie charm and graciousness. His astringent evocations of human emotion are subtle and resonant. Personal reflections by Grandbois on the interwar years, written for the CBC in 1951, have been published in *Visages du monde: images et souvenirs de l'entre-deux guerres* (1971), presented by Léopold Leblanc.

An anthology of Grandbois's verse and prose, *Alain Grandbois* (Paris, 1968), ably presented by Jacques Brault, contains three poems previously unpublished. A bilingual collection of his poetry, *Selected poems* (1965), contains translations by Peter Miller with the French originals. Grandbois's influence on post-war poetry in French Canada has been acknowledged by the poets of the fifties and sixties: by Jean-Guy PILON and Gaston MIRON in the review *Amérique française in* 1954; in a special number of LIBERTÉ (1960); and by the publication of Grandbois's collected *Poèmes* (1963), a new edition (1979) of which includes fourteen additional poems—confirming Grandbois's astonishing consistency of theme, vocabulary, and tone—that had been presented by Jacques Blais in his *Présence d'Alain Grandbois* (1975). Blais's essay is a tasteful and detailed biography of the poet's early years, merging into a study of his work and a brief survey of critical responses to it, and a full bibliography. Blais has also acknowledged, and skilfully demonstrated, Grandbois's role in the modernization of poetry in Québec in *De l'ordre et de l'aventure* (1975). More unpublished poems appeared in *Délivrance du jour et autres inédits* (1980), the main title referring to a collection of poems planned as early as 1948.

See also S. Dallard, *L'univers poétique d'Alain Grandbois* (1975); M. Greffard, *Alain Grandbois* (1975); and *Ellipse* 14/15 (1974), devoted to Grandbois and John GLASSCO.

C.R.P. MAY, WILLIAM TOYE

Grand'maison, Jacques. See ESSAYS IN FRENCH: 6.

Grant, George (b. 1918). George Parkin Grant was born in Toronto and educated at Upper Canada College; Queen's University, Kingston; and Oxford University, where he was a Rhodes Scholar. His paternal grandfather, George Monro Grant (author of OCEAN TO OCEAN), had been a principal of Queen's, and his maternal grandfather, Sir George Parkin—who, like his father, had been a principal of Upper Canada College—had headed the Rhodes Trust. From 1947 to 1960 George Grant taught philosophy at Dalhousie University, Halifax, becoming head of the department; he was then chairman of the department of religion at McMaster University, Hamilton, Ont., until 1980, when he returned to Dalhousie as Killam Professor.

Grant's writings have occupied a major place in Canadian intellectual life since the appearance of *Philosophy in the mass age* (1959). His influence has been significant in literature, political theory, and religious thinking, though he has remained outside the bounds of most professional philosophers. Christianity has always been central to his thought. He was influenced for a time by Hegel; but his strongest philosophical inclinations have generally been Platonic, and both Simone Weil and Martin Heidegger have influenced his later thought. *Philosophy in the mass age* (following a small work, *The Empire, yes or no?*, 1945) sought to establish the importance of the Judaeo-Christian tradition as a major element in the understanding of man's freedom and the transcendence of nature, while seeking to retain the relevance of the classical notion of a natural order that sets limits to human behaviour. *Lament for a nation: the defeat of Canadian nationalism* (1965; 2nd ed., with a new introduction by the author, 1970) exercised a wide influence on proponents of Canadian economic nationalism with its thesis that Canada had been destroyed as a viable nation by the ideology of American liberalism backed by technology and corporate capitalism. Grant's nostalgia for the values expounded by John G. Diefenbaker (Conservative prime minister of Canada from 1957 to 1963) suggests a strong conservative strand in his thought. Grant describes his break with the New Democratic Party, which occurred when the party supported the official (Liberal) Opposition in a vote critical of Diefenbaker's position on the stationing of American nuclear missiles in Canada. Grant's conservatism is of the sort that figures in Canadian politics as 'red Toryism', having little to do with the support of 'free enterprise' but emphasizing social responsibility, the duties of the strong to the weak, and the sense of continuing community. The theses in *Lament for a Nation* were extended somewhat in *Technology and empire* (1969), essays that clearly associated Grant's thought with that of Leo Strauss and Jacques Ellul.

Grant's writings emphasize tradition and imply a severe critique of the notion that the primary meaning of human life is to be found in history that exemplifies continuous progress. His CBC Massey Lectures, published as *Time as history* (1969) and focusing on an examination of Nietzsche, insist that there are eternal values, and that basic Christian notions soundly limit what can be done to and with human beings. In *English-speaking justice* (1974) Grant returned to criticizing liberal ideology with a cutting analysis of the philosophy of John Rawls, and of other recent forms of the social-contract theory. While Grant's philosophical interests have changed and developed considerably over the years, the centre of his political thought continues to reflect clearly his original Platonism, with its insistence on stability rather than change, eternal values rather than temporal pleasures, and community rather than individuality.

LESLIE ARMOUR, ELIZABETH TROTT

Grant, George Monro. See OCEAN TO OCEAN.

Gray, James H. (b. 1906). He grew up and was educated in Winnipeg during its boom years. After a succession of jobs at the Winnipeg Grain Exchange and with stockbrokers, he was forced to go on relief during the Depression. He took to writing articles, and as a result was engaged in 1935 as a re-

Gray

porter on the *Winnipeg Free Press*; he became an editorial writer in 1941 and Ottawa correspondent in 1946. From 1947 to 1955 he edited the *Farm and Ranch Review*, and from 1955 to 1958 the *Western Oil Examiner*; he then worked for the Home Oil Company promoting a pipeline to Montreal.

After his early retirement in 1963, Gray embarked on a series of vivid, unconventional social histories of the Prairies. Three books are chiefly autobiographical: *The boy from Winnipeg* (1970) captures the atmosphere of childhood; *The winter years* (1966) describes how the Prairies survived the Depression with such expedients as food vouchers and 'boondoggling' work projects; and *Troublemaker!* (1978) tells of Gray's career as a journalist and the causes that engaged him, such as the threat of American domination in oil exploration, the shortcomings of the grain market, and the plight of the prairie farmers. Other works investigate aspects of prairie life that had received scant documentation. *Men against the desert* (1967) celebrates the success of the Dominion Experimental Farms and the Prairie Farm Rehabilitation Administration in helping farmers to combat the drought, dust, and insect infestations of the thirties. *Red lights on the Prairies* (1971) is the history of prostitution in prairie towns before the Depression, showing the growth of segregated red-light areas, the periodic morality crusades, and the ambivalent attitudes of the police. *Booze* (1972) documents the tradition of heavy drinking on the Prairies and chronicles the temperance and prohibition movements until about 1925. Gray returned to the subject with *Bacchanalia revisited: western Canada's boozy skid to social disaster* (1982), which deals with the modern era. *The roar of the twenties* (1975) describes everyday prairie life in an era of gambling, oil exploration, wheat pools, co-operatives, and church union. *Boomtime* (1979) is a lavishly illustrated record of the stream of immigrants to the Prairies prior to the First World War.

Gray's works, which have won several awards, are based on extensive research in newspapers and published reports and numerous personal interviews, as well as on the author's own experience. Lively, perceptive, and humane, they give a vivid sense of life on the Prairies and of the geographical and historical forces that have shaped a unique culture.   JEAN O'GRADY

Gray, John (b. 1946). Born in Ottawa, Gray was raised in Truro, N.S. After graduating from Mount Allison University, he studied at the University of British Columbia, where he received an M.A. in theatre. As a playwright, composer, and director he has sustained an association with the theatre community of Vancouver both as the founder of Tamahnous Theatre and through his current affiliation with the Vancouver East Cultural Centre. In 1975 he came to Toronto to compose music for productions at Theatre Passe Muraille. Gray has since written *18 wheels* (prod. 1977), *Billy Bishop goes to war* (1981), which won a Governor General's Award, and *Rock and roll* (*Canadian Theatre Review*, 1982).

Gray's best-known work, written in collaboration with Eric Peterson, is *Billy Bishop goes to war*. With Gray providing musical accompaniment as the Piano Player, Peterson played Billy Bishop who, speaking directly to the audience, recreates incidents and personalities central to Bishop's rise as the ace pilot of the First World War. *Billy Bishop* is the story of a young man forced by war to come of age. 'War is exactly like life, only faster. If you survive, you'll get to see your friends die,' Gray said in an interview with Robert Wallace. When it was redesigned for American audiences, and again for BBC television, the eloquence of the original simplicity was lost in the attempt to make it more elaborate theatrically.

The coming-of-age theme recurs in *Rock and roll*, in which the characters tell stories of youthful glory that are now only memories (as in *Billy Bishop*). The question at the end of *Billy Bishop* could be asked at the end of *Rock and roll*: 'Makes you wonder what it was all for?' Bishop's assessment is equally appropriate to both plays: 'I would have to say, it was a hell of a time!'   ANN WILSON

Gray, John Morgan (1907-78). Born in Toronto, publisher and author John Gray was educated at Lakefield College and Upper Canada College and the University of Toronto, where he did not take his degree. Following a year as an assistant master at Lakefield, an introduction to Hugh Eayrs, the unpredictable but brilliant president of the MACMILLAN COMPANY OF CANADA—whose exasperating qualities and mannerisms are drawn with a novelist's skill in Gray's memoirs, *Fun tomorrow*—procured him a job as an educational representative. The years of crossing and recrossing the continent in the Depression gave Gray a knowledge of book publishing, and of people in hard times. This was to serve him well when, after four years' active service in Europe—during which he rose to become GSO(2) in the Intelligence Corps of the First Canadian Army in Holland—he returned somewhat reluctantly to publishing.

Hugh Eayrs died in 1940, and the appointment of a successor had been postponed by Macmillan of London until the war ended. Gray was appointed in 1946, first as manager and within a year as president, with full powers of acquisition and of forming company policy. His boisterous sense of fun and gift for caricature and for puncturing pomposity—qualities that had hampered his early career—hid, as it turned out, executive abilities that put him among the leaders of post-war Canadian publishing. This was a propitious time to take charge of a Canadian publishing company. The long servitude of the industry to its British and American overlords, which had made many publishers no more than importing agencies, was about to be transformed. Given full powers and resources, limited only by British Exchange Control restrictions, Gray was provided with an opportunity to become not only a leader but, by virtue of his partnership in a world-wide publishing organization, a spokesman for the trade. Gray was one of several young veterans—like Jack McCLELLAND of McCLELLAND AND STEWART and Marsh JEANNERET, later to join the UNIVERSITY OF TORONTO PRESS—who had returned to civilian life with new ideas and boundless energy that would serve the Canadian publishing industry. Established and influential figures, like Lorne PIERCE of the RYERSON PRESS who had worked with Gray on joint educational enterprises, were supportive. Youthful successors were now at the helm of a number of houses. With the Massey Report (1951) pointing the way, and one of its recommendations, the Canada Council (1957), providing both publishers and authors with the backing they needed, the Canadian publishing industry was about to mature.

Gray's part in this period of growth in Canadian publishing can be traced in the numerous papers he gave at publishing conferences and in public addresses. The experience and achievements of the fifties and sixties are summed up in an article he contributed to CANADIAN LITERATURE 33 (Spring 1967). Master of a simple, unadorned style with humorous undertones, he had always wanted to be a writer. His chief interest was in Canadian history, and his *Lord Selkirk of Red River* (1962), which was awarded the University of British Columbia medal for the best biography of the year, shows what Canadian writing lost to Canadian publishing when he opted for a career as a publisher.

Gray had the gift of subordinating his own ambition to the problems of his writers. Many leading Canadian authors joined the Macmillan list, and the evidence of how well Gray served them as editor is preserved in the correspondence in the Macmillan archives, now at McMaster University.

Fun tomorrow (1978), published a few weeks after Gray's death from cancer, was to have been the first volume of a two-volume memoir. A delightful and amusing impression of a Canadian upbringing, and of his first faltering steps in publishing, the book ends at the point where he took over command of the Macmillan Company of Canada.

Gray married in 1932 Antoinette Lalonde, the heroine of *Fun tomorrow*. He was appointed an Officer of the Order of Canada in 1975. The recipient of many honorary degrees from Canadian universities, he was a (founding) member of the Board of Governors of York University from 1960 to 1970.   LOVAT DICKSON

Gregory, Claudius Jabez. See NOVELS IN ENGLISH 1920 TO 1940: 1.

Grenfell, Wilfred Thomason (1865-1940). Born at Parkgate, Cheshire, Eng., he attended Marlborough College in Wiltshire. In 1883 he entered medical school in the London Hospital, and in 1888 was entered as a member of the Royal College of Surgeons and the Royal College of Physicians. While a medical student he wandered one evening into a meeting conducted by the American preacher D.L. Moody and came away 'feeling that I had crossed the Rubicon.' Determining on a life of service, in 1888 he started work with the medical section of the National Mission to Deep Sea Fishermen, serving in the North Atlantic from Iceland to the Bay of Biscay and becoming an expert sailor. In 1892 he travelled to Newfoundland to assess the need for medical services in the northern regions of the colony. He returned the following year with two doctors and two nurses and established at Battle Harbour the first hospital of what would be called the Labrador Medical Mission. His life thereafter was devoted to the advancement of his medical work in Newfoundland and Labrador. In 1912 the International

Grenfell

Grenfell Association was formed to co-ordinate and promote Grenfell's activities. Grenfell also experimented with ways to improve the Newfoundland economy, emphasizing self-help, home industries, co-operatives, and a diversified approach to the development of resources. He was the recipient of many honours, including an honorary M.D. from Oxford University in 1907; he was knighted in 1927.

Grenfell was a brilliant publicist, and his numerous speeches, magazine articles, and books were part of his favourite activity of promoting and financing his mission. His books are somewhat repetitive and opinionated, but they are not without a certain liveliness and power, and their number reflects his popularity as a writer and the fame that came to surround him. His cocksure, dominant personality, and the sheer drama of his life on a perilous, bleak coastline, hold our interest. The books fall into three main categories. First, there are his factual, scientific, and promotional accounts of Labrador: *Vikings of to-day; or, Life and medical work among the fishermen of Labrador* (London, 1895); *Labrador: the country and the people* (1909), a symposium to which he contributed ten of sixteen chapters; *Labrador's fight for economic freedom* (1929); and *The romance of Labrador* (1934), an eloquent statement of his love for his adopted homeland.

The second kind of book by Grenfell is the Labrador storybook—true tales of the people and of his experiences among them. The best is *Adrift on an ice-pan* (1909)—first published as *A voyage on a pan of ice* (1908)— a hair-raising account of a brush with death that first brought Grenfell's name to the attention of the world. It can still be read with genuine pleasure, for Grenfell had real gifts as a storyteller. Other books in this category are *The harvest of the sea: a tale of both sides of the Atlantic* (1905), *Off the rocks: stories of the deep-sea fisherfolk of Labrador* (1906), *Down to the sea: yarns from the Labrador* (1910), *Down north on the Labrador* (1911), *Tales of the Labrador* (1916), *Labrador days: tales of the sea toilers* (1919), *Northern neighbours: stories of the Labrador people* (1923), *That Christmas in Peace Haven and Three Eyes* (1923), and *Deeds of daring* (1934).

A third group of books by Grenfell comprises his religious and autobiographical works. Though born an Anglican, Grenfell had been brought to something close to an evangelical conversion by Moody, and his religion was an untroubled, wholehearted commitment to a life of Christian action. He wrote many books displaying an unshakeable and simple faith: *A man's faith* (1908); *A man's helpers* (1910); *What life means to me* (1910); *What will you do with Jesus Christ* (1910); *What the church means to me: a frank confession and a friendly estimate by an insider* (1911); *Shall a man live again? A vital assurance of faith in immortality* (1912); *What can Jesus Christ do with me* (1912); *The adventure of life: being the William Belden Noble Lectures for 1911* (1912); *On immortality* (1912); *The attractive way* (1913); *The prize of life* (1914); *A Labrador doctor: the autobiography of Wilfred Thomason Grenfell* (1919), expanded in 1932 under a new title, *Forty years for Labrador; Yourself and your body* (1924); *Religion in everyday life* (1926); *What Christ means to me* (1926); *Labrador looks at the Orient: notes of travel in the Near and the Far East* (1928); *The fishermen's saint* (1930); and *A Labrador logbook* (1938).

Labrador looks at the Orient and *A Labrador logbook* are in some ways his most engaging books, revealing Grenfell's idiosyncratic opinions and the extent of his miscellaneous reading.

Grenfell's life and work have yet to be fully appraised. The closest we have to a critical biography is J. Lennox Kerr's *Wilfred Grenfell: his life and work* (1959). Pierre BERTON has a fine chapter on Grenfell in *The wild frontier* (1978).   PATRICK O'FLAHERTY

Grey, Francis William (1860-1939). Born in England, he was the son of the Hon. Jane Stuart and Admiral the Hon. George Grey, grandson of Charles, the second Earl Grey, prime minister of England when the Reform Bill of 1831 was passed, and first cousin of the fourth Earl Grey, governor-general of Canada from 1904 to 1911. It is not known when he came to North America, but he was teaching at Manhattan College, New York, in 1885 when he married Jessie, daughter of Jessie Chisolm and Charles Octave Rolland, seigneur of Ste Marie de Monnoir in the Richelieu district; at this time he had probably converted to Roman Catholicism. From 1903 to 1904 he taught English literature and elocution at the University of Ottawa, from which he received in 1908 the degree of Doctor of Letters for his 'many literary productions . . . in both prose and verse.' In 1905 he joined the Dominion Archives in a clerical position that was made permanent in 1908, and in 1912 he was appointed translator. He resigned in 1913 on a pension of $500 a year. In later years Grey lived in Edinburgh, where he died. His wife predeceased him in 1928. At the time of his death Grey was heir presumptive to the fifth Earl Grey. In 1963 his great-grandson succeeded to the title.

Grey is best remembered for his novel, *The curé of St. Philippe: a story of French-Canadian politics* (London, 1899), a realistic and entertaining portrait of a small Québec community, based on the Rolland seigneury, at the end of the nineteenth century. Wide-ranging in theme and characterization in the tradition of the nineteenth-century English novel, it incorporates the religious and political interests evident in Grey's later plays and essays. The establishment of a new parish in the Richelieu district, and events surrounding the 1896 federal election—in which, for the first time in Québec, the Rouges (Liberals) overcome the Bleus (Conservatives)—provide the central issues. English-speaking and French-speaking Catholics and Protestants, clergymen, landowners, and local politicians all become involved. Religion, romance, and business intrigues are interwoven with English-French relations, the clergy's role in the community, and political corruption. An intrusive narrator—citing numerous literary figures (of whom Carlyle is the favourite) and maintaining a low-key and lightly humorous tone—fills in the background and comments on the issues. This light, ironic tone, along with the novel's accurate portrayal of the intricacies of the political and religious issues of late nineteenth-century Québec, recommend the novel to us today.

Grey's plays are historical and religious. *Sixty-nine: a series of historical tableaux* (1904) concerns intrigues against Frontenac, newly appointed governor of Canada. Grey later published *Four plays* (1931), containing *Bishop and king*, which deals with the execution of Blessed Oliver Plunkett by Charles II as a result of wrongful accusation; *The bridegroom cometh*, a one-act play about the parable of the wise and foolish virgins; *The valiant woman*, demonstrating the truth of Isaiah's prophecy, 'Every age shall shew/a valiant woman'; and *Love's pilgrimage*, which tells of a pilgrim in the time of Christ. All are didactic, none memorable.

Grey also published a collection of poetry, *Love crucified and other sacred verse* (Ottawa, 1902). His poetry and essays—dealing with religious, literary, historical, and educational topics—appeared in a variety of Canadian, American, and British publications, including the UNIVERSITY MAGAZINE, *Fortnightly Review*, *Westminster Review*, *American Catholic Quarterly*, and the *University of Ottawa Review*.

See Rupert Schieder's introduction to the New Canadian Library edition (1970) of *The curé of St. Philippe*.   LORRAINE McMULLEN

Grey Owl. See George Stansfeld BELANEY.

Grier, Eldon (b. 1917). Born in London, Eng., of Canadian parents (his father was a captain in the Canadian army), he was raised in Montreal and began his professional career as a painter. In 1945 he went to Mexico to study fresco painting with Alfredo Zalce, and was later apprenticed to Diego Rivera as a plasterer. On his return to Montreal he became a teacher under Arthur Lismer at the Montreal Museum of Fine Arts.

In his middle thirties Grier developed tuberculosis, recovered, married his second wife (painter Sylvia Tait), and began to write poetry. Between 1955 and 1965 he travelled extensively in Europe—he began to write poetry while living in Spain—and spent a number of winters in Mexico. His poetry collections include *A morning from scraps* (1955), *Poems* (1956), *The ring of ice* (1957), *Manzanillo & other poems* (1958), *A friction of lights* (1963), *Pictures on the skin* (1967), *Selected poems* (1971), and *The assassination of colours* (1978).

Like much writing begun in maturity, his early collections contain no false starts or stumblings: Grier seemed to find his voice immediately. His poems are the product of critical intelligence and a highly visual imagination. He writes in the tradition of Modernism, displaying a remarkable linguistic virtuosity. Pleasure in language is the centre of his aesthetic experience—'Is there a single word which doesn't respond/like a servant torn from sleep?'—and his reflective poems are infused with the colloquial. He is fascinated by formal control and his poems play with line shifts, rhyme, and complicated stanzaic shapes. Some poems are surreal collages of images that push through bizarre juxtapositions to new insights. With a temperament that is urbane yet energetic, Grier earned his urbanity through a lifetime of visiting foreign parts. He has written many travel poems, of which those on Mexico are exceptionally powerful. The enormous impact of painting on his work is evident, not only in the numerous poems to painters and sculptors (Morandi, Marini, Picasso, Modigliani, Morrice, Giacometti) but in the frequency with which he approaches a poem like a still life: a 'ceramic' of images, light and colour. Many of Grier's poems are anecdotal, focusing on an emotionally fraught moment in which a character is deftly portrayed in a phrase or two, although he shares a modern cynicism—we have 'survived the relevance of our survival'—and acknowledges the 'tragic angularity' of the world. Grier in his poetry is committed to a belief in the will's capacity to reassert human values: tenderness, simplicity, beauty. Reading his work one encounters a sensibility of deep generosity and compassion; a writer committed to new explorations of creativity as an antidote to the modern temptation to nostalgia: 'we must die with conviction of regret'. He is a fine poet who deserves to be much better known.   ROSEMARY SULLIVAN

Grignon, Claude-Henri (1894-1976), who used the pseudonym 'Valdombre', was born in Sainte-Adèle, Qué. After being educated partly at the Collège Saint-Laurent, Montreal, and partly at home, he moved to Montreal and became a civil servant. From 1916 to 1939 he wrote articles for various newspapers, but returned to the Laurentians in 1936 and started a second career as a radio writer. He was elected mayor of Sainte-Adèle (1941-51) and became prefect of Terrebonne county. A member of the ÉCOLE LITTÉRAIRE DE MONTRÉAL since 1928, he received the Prix David in 1935 and was elected to the Royal Society of Canada in 1961.

As a journalist Grignon was a well-known polemicist and an earnest nationalist, having worked with such prominent figures as Olivar Asselin. He collected some of his numerous book reviews and critical articles on literature in *Ombres et clameurs: regards sur la littérature canadienne* (1933). From 1936 to 1943 he singlehandedly published a notorious and widely read periodical, *Les pamphlets de Valdombre*, which discloses his rather conservative political and literary ideas and conveys the ideal of a French-Canadian literature based on regionalism.

Grignon's first novel, *Le secret de Lindbergh* (1928), celebrates Colonel Charles Lindbergh's successful flight over the Atlantic in 1927. It conveys the writer's enthusiasm, especially in many epic and lyrical descriptions, but contains an undue amount of moralizing. This was followed by the important novel *Un homme et son péché* (1933), which has been reprinted many times, is still in print, and was translated by Yves Brunelle as *The woman and the miser* (1978). Its

plot was the basis of a highly successful radio series (1939-65), a well-known television serial (1956-70), and two motion pictures, shot in 1948 and 1950. *Un homme et son péché* represents, within a sociological perspective, the consequences of the economic crisis of the thirties, symbolized by the selfish miser, Séraphin Poudrier, and male domination of women, symbolized by the cruel treatment and ensuing death of Séraphin's wife. Its strength lies in its realistic style and in the portrayal of the sadomasochistic relationship of the lustful husband and the submissive wife. The dramatized series expanded the novel into a larger picture of rural life in Québec. Grignon's *Précisions sur 'Un homme et son péché'* (1936)—a bitter reply to his detractors, who saw only the sordid aspects of his novel—explains how his book was based on actual events and real characters and scolds his contemporaries for their lack of imagination and their failure to write good 'regional' novels.

Le déserteur et autres récits de la terre (1934; rpr. 1976) is a collection of six short stories that reveals Grignon's knack for creating interesting characters and for depicting popular customs; but the book is weakened by constant attempts to demonstrate the advantages of rural over city life.

Grignon's polemical writings are the subject of Jean-Pierre Bonneville's *De Valdombre à André Gide* (1948). More recently, a number of review articles have been published: 'Séraphin ou la dépossession' by Pierre Desjardins (PARTI PRIS, Jan.-Feb. 1967); 'Concupiscence et avarice chez Séraphin Poudrier' by Claude-Marie Gagnon (VOIX ET IMAGES, Dec. 1975); and five analyses of his works by Renée Legris, Alonzo LeBlanc, Gilles Dorion, and Maurice Lemire in the *Dictionnaire des oeuvres littéraires du Québec*, t. II (1980).   LUCIE ROBERT

Groulx, Lionel-Adolphe (1878-1967). Born in Vaudreuil, Qué., Groulx was ordained a priest in 1903 and completed a doctorate in theology in Rome five years later. His appointment in 1915 to the chair of Canadian history at Université Laval (Montreal) launched him on a lifetime career of writing, speaking and lecturing, during the course of which he became a major intellectual figure in Québec. Topics such as the linguistic rights of French-Canadian minorities, their role within Confederation, the importance to them of a 'homeland', and the essential differences between the two 'races' of Canada caused Groulx to be praised by some, denounced by others (including Louis Saint-Laurent and *Time*), and to be widely read. When he died, the Québec government proclaimed a day of national mourning and honoured him with a state funeral.

Groulx's efforts to promote a 'national consciousness' among his compatriots led to controversy: at the height of the Conscription Crisis of 1917, his course on the origins of Confederation, which harshly criticized the founding fathers, brought demands from the university administration for an oath of loyalty to the Crown. As editor from 1921 to 1928 of a monthly review, *L'Action française* (still being published under the title *L'Action nationale*), Groulx the polemicist remained in the vanguard of French-Canadian nationalism. Each year a particular theme was treated in depth, his 1925 attack on bilingualism and his 1927 re-evaluation of Confederation on its sixtieth anniversary being the most provocative.

As a historian Groulx was intensely interested in the French presence in North America and the lessons it could draw from the past in order to survive as a culturally autonomous group within the Canadian political reality. The following book titles reflect this facet of his interpretation of history: *La confédération canadienne, ses origines* (1918), *La naissance d'une race* (1919), *Notre maître le passé* (three series: 1924, 1936, 1944), *Histoire du Canada français depuis la découverte* (4 vols, 1950-2), *Notre grande aventure* (1958), and *Chemins de l'avenir* (1958). At age 68 Groulx founded the Institut d'histoire de l'Amérique française, and one year later, in 1947, a scholarly journal, the *Revue d'histoire de l'Amérique française*, which still appears regularly and is highly respected. Even after his retirement, Groulx continued to write prolifically; his *Constantes de vie* (1967), urging his compatriots to continue, like their forefathers before them, to nurture their North American and French heritage, appeared on the very day of his death, at age 89. The four-volume *Mes mémoires* (1970-4), edited by his niece Mme Juliette Rémillard, was published posthumously.

Groulx's reputation as an essayist and pamphleteer is widely acknowledged, but Groulx the fiction-writer is relatively unknown in English Canada. In *Les rapaillages* (1916) he evokes memories of childhood and the countryside in a series of *contes* written in a bucolic vein. In the expanded 1935 edition one sketch, 'Comment j'ai quitté la politique', stands out: describing a village school

election between the *rouges* and the *bleus* in 1890, Groulx demonstrates a surprising skill as storyteller and a whimsical sense of humour that remind us of Stephen LEACOCK and Roch CARRIER.

Groulx also wrote two novels under the pseudonym Alonié de Lestres (because of his clerical status): *L'appel de la race* (1922; 1957), which became a *cause célèbre* upon publication, and *Au Cap Blomidon* (1932). One of the rare Québécois novels to be set in Ontario, *L'appel de la race* (titled *Le coin de fer* before publication) reflects the tensions aroused in the French-Canadian community by Ontario's Regulation Seventeen (1912), which limited French instruction in francophone schools to one hour per day. The protagonist, Jules de Lantagnac, is an Ottawa lawyer who has become anglicized by his McGill education, his marriage to an anglophone, and the social demands of his profession. His wife, Maud Fletcher—an Anglican who converted to Catholicism in order to marry him and is 'dominated by ethnic pride' and staunchly British in sentiment and loyalty—reflects the Anglo-Saxon stereotype popular in French Canada around the First World War. As the Regulation is being hotly debated, Lantagnac undergoes a psychological crisis that leads him, despite consequent social ostracism, to become a spokesman in the House of Commons for his Franco-Ontarian compatriots. Maud, who is innately anti-French, decides to separate from him, and the family is split irrevocably—two teenaged children siding with the mother and two with the father. For its apparently racist arguments and vocabulary *L'appel de la race* seems shocking, but its language and rhetoric are quite restrained compared to the bitter and frequently specious arguments for eliminating French as the language of instruction in Franco-Ontarian schools that appeared in the Ontario press of the period. The novel portrays Parliament as an 'arena where two races and two civilizations confront and oppose each other' and the bonds of intermarriage as strained by 'two warring souls or spirits', each seeking constantly to dominate. The long and bitter debate within the French-Canadian community over the author's rejection of 'interracial marriage' is well documented in Bruno Lafleur's introduction to the 1957 edition.

Groulx's second novel, *Au Cap Blomidon* (1932), aroused little controversy and much praise. Jean Bérubé, a young Laurentian farmer of Acadian descent, inherits his uncle's fortune on condition that he try to regain ownership of the ancestral homestead in Nova Scotia. Working as farm manager for a Scot (Hugh Finlay, the present owner of the Bérubé property), Jean eventually gains title to the land, fulfilling Groulx's dream of Acadian re-settlement by the scattered descendants of the eighteenth-century deportees. (*La ferme des pins*, 1930, by Harry BERNARD, which described the repossession of the Eastern Townships through francophone colonization, may have been a model for the plot.)

See Susan Mann Trofimenkoff's *Variations on a nationalist theme* (1973), which offers a broad selection of excerpts from Groulx's writings in English translation; Georges-Émile Giguère's biography *Lionel Groulx* (1978); Pierre Gaboury, *Le nationalisme de Lionel Groulx: aspects idéologiques* (1970); and Susan Mann Trofimenkoff, *Action française: French Canadian nationalism in the twenties* (1975).

See also NOVELS IN FRENCH 1920 TO 1940: 3 and HISTORICAL WRITING IN FRENCH.

RAMON HATHORN

Grove, Frederick Philip (1879-1948). Born Felix Paul Greve in Radomno, Prussia, he was raised in Hamburg where his parents, Carl Edward and Bertha (Reichentrog) Greve, settled in 1881. He attended the Lutheran parish school at St Pauli, and later the classical Gymnasium in preparation for university. Family life apparently was not happy; his parents divorced.

Early in Felix's first university year, at Bonn, his mother died and his life became unsettled. He lived extravagantly, borrowing large sums on various pretexts, mostly from a well-to-do fellow student named Herman Kilian. Greve left Bonn without graduating and spent a *Wanderjahr* in Italy. In 1902 he resumed his studies, this time at Munich, but again failed to complete his degree. That same year his first two books were privately published—*Wanderungen* (poems) and *Helena and Damon* (a verse-drama)—and he was associated briefly with the Stefan George group of young neo-Romantic poets. To earn a precarious living, he began translating English authors into German, and he wrote some impressionistic criticism, mostly on Oscar Wilde. Moving to Berlin, Greve formed a liaison with Elsa Ploetz, wife of an architect; the two spent the winter of 1902-3 in Italy and Sicily, again largely on money borrowed from Kilian under false pretences. On his return to Germany in 1903 Felix was charged by Kilian with fraud and spent a year in prison. Immediately on his release in June 1904 he travelled to Paris to meet André Gide, whom he had previously written to and whose works he was then translating. Gide's record of this first meeting—published as 'Conversation avec un Allemand' in his *Oeuvres complètes* (1935)—portrays an elegant young man who, while confessing to compulsive mendacity (he was frank about his imprisonment), seemed at the same time to be soliciting some sort of encouragement from Gide. For the next five years—living with Elsa, first on the French coast at Étaples and later in Berlin—Greve worked feverishly to pay off his debts translating, from English into German, Wilde, Pater, Dowson, Browning, Wells, Meredith, Swift, and the Junius letters; and Gide, Murger, Flaubert, Balzac, and LeSage from the French. His translations of Cervantes, supposedly from the Spanish, apparently used English models, as did his major project, a translation of the *Thousand and one nights*, which remained popular in Germany for half a century. Greve's original works from this period included at least one play, some pamphlets and articles on Oscar Wilde, a few poems and reviews, and two novels: *Fanny Essler* (1905) and *Maurermeister Ihles Haus* (1906).

Despite this great productivity, Greve's effort to free himself from debt and make a living by his pen failed. The competition was too keen, the rewards too small, the pressures overwhelming. Greve was in financial, and perhaps again in legal, difficulties when, late in 1909, he faked a suicide and fled to North America. He probably spent the next three years as an itinerant labourer in the U.S. and Canada, a life graphically described in *A search for America*. Under the name Fred Grove he then became a schoolteacher in Manitoba, initially at Haskett and Winkler in German-speaking Mennonite districts. In 1914 he married Catherine Wiens (1892-1972). Their only daughter, born in 1915, died in 1927. A son, Leonard Grove, born in 1930, lives in Toronto. After teaching in several Manitoba communities, Grove retired in 1923 to devote himself to writing.

Grove had begun writing again by 1915, at first long philosophical poems and then, in 1919, prose. His first book in English, *Over prairie trails* (1922), grew directly out of his weekend commutings in 1917, when he had taught at Gladstone, Man., and Catherine had a small school in the bush some 35 miles north. Though not entirely free of Grove's rather pendantic amateur scientific observations, *Over prairie trails* is for many readers his most engaging and confident book. Along with *The turn of the year* (1923), it attracted critical attention for its loving descriptions of nature sustained by the narrative of his almost epic weekend struggles through fog and winter storms to reach home and the longed-for 'domestic island'.

This initial success confirmed Grove's commitment to writing and to Canada: his application for citizenship virtually coincided with the acceptance of *Over prairie trails* by McCLELLAND AND STEWART in 1920. His first Canadian novel, *Settlers of the marsh* (1925)—begun in German but completed in English—was considered too frank for public taste in the 1920s and did not sell well. It has gradually won recognition, however, as one of the first works of prairie realism. A measure of financial success came with publication of the partly autobiographical *A search for America* (1927)—one of the most compelling of many North American quasi-novels that record the suffering and disillusionment, as well as the idealism, of the immigrant—and of the naturalistic novel *Our daily bread* (1928). Three cross-country tours under Canadian Club auspices in 1928 and 1929 brought Grove to prominence, and at the end of 1929 he moved to Ottawa as president of Ariston Press, a subsidiary of Graphic Publishers. Selected addresses were published as *It needs to be said* (1929).

The Graphic venture was not successful. Grove believed that the true circumstances of the company, and the fact that he had no real control, had been concealed from him. (The experience was to bear fruit in *The master of the mill*, in which Sam Clark makes a similar discovery.) Grove left Ottawa after a year, bought a farm near Simcoe, Ont., and tried raising dairy cattle. In the deepening economic depression of the thirties the attempt failed. Forced to sell most of his land, Grove lived in near-poverty for a decade, supported by his wife's private teaching. After *The yoke of life* (1930) and *Fruits of the earth* (1933) there were no books published until *Two generations* (1939). Sub-titled *A story of present-day Ontario*, this novel drew on Grove's dairying experience, but the triumph of Phil and Alice Patterson revealed a new buoyancy.

Grove's last years brought belated recognition and the publication of his most thoughtful works: *The master of the mill* (1944), Grove's second Ontario novel, which records the growth of monopoly capitalism in the story of the Clark dynasty; *In search of myself* (1946), a fictionalized autobiography; and *Consider her ways* (1947), a sometimes pedantic, often humorous, surprisingly human, satire in which a colony of ants undertakes a study of mankind.

Grove had been awarded the Lorne Pierce Medal in 1934; in 1941 he was elected FRSC. *Frederick Philip Grove*, a study of his life and work by Desmond PACEY, was published in 1945. In 1947 Grove received a Governor General's Award for *In search of myself*. He died the following year.

Following Pacey, early critics tended to read Grove in the light of the supposed autobiography that describes a luxurious Swedish childhood and has him frequenting artistic circles and leading a dilettante life in Europe before being overtaken by unexpected poverty, wandering in America for twenty years, and re-emerging in Canada as a teacher, cosmopolitan author, and near-prophet. Some readers almost revered him: in Phelps's words, 'He was *the* man.' Others were offended by Grove's superior tone, and pointed to his stilted language and occasional woodenness. For still others these qualities were appropriate to the level of high tragedy on which Grove wrote: his novels of prairie pioneering drew such epithets as 'tragedy' and 'stark realism'— aspects of Grove's writing that hold the attention of readers, particularly in high schools and universities, today.

Grove's novels, particularly the German ones, abound in detail that is often maddeningly trivial but cumulatively effective in creating a sense of character in relation to milieu. It is this characteristic, rather than their larger purposes—what he calls 'the tragic interpretation of life'—that led critics to label Grove a 'naturalist' or 'realist'. Most of the novels portray dynamic, creative, but limited pioneer figures whose possessions turn to ashes with the alienation of family and community. In the two set in the Big Grassy Marsh district near Lake Manitoba, the young Swede Niels Lindstedt in *Settlers of the marsh* becomes a successful pioneer only to be ruined by a disastrous marriage, while *The yoke of life* records the early idealism, disillusionment, and suicide of Len Sterner (it was once described as 'a Canadian *Jude the obscure*'). In Grove's two prairie novels the patriarch John Elliot of *Our daily bread* escapes being cared for by his unsympathetic children by returning to the abandoned homestead to die; *Fruits of the earth* chronicles Abe Spalding's rise to power and the resultant alienation of his family. Though in Grove's German novels the protagonists are young women, many of the Canadian protagonists—John Elliot, Abe Spalding, Sam Clark, Ralph Patterson, and the narrator of *In search of myself*—are older men whose failures may be predetermined but who nevertheless are driven to try to understand. In their recurrent phrase, 'I am I', character is seen as fate: these men are what they are, and at their best they are heroic and universal. Facing death, or watching their achievements slip away from them, they challenge the illusion of human progress, question the values of society, and ask where mankind has failed. Projecting himself in them, Grove transcends his own failures. In the emotional confrontations of *Settlers of the marsh* and *The yoke of life*, in the balanced complexities of *The master of the mill*, even in the allegorical *Consider her ways*, Grove wrestled with manifestations of his own psyche that may account for much in his work that earlier critics found unconvincing—such as the unexpectedly romantic elements that sometimes appear, like the unicorn Len Sterner fancies he sees in the Manitoba bush.

No extended critical work has been done on Grove's poetry or short stories. The *Wanderungen* poems are in process of translation. There are a few unpublished lyrics and fragments in German; most of the poetry in English remains in typescript. Excerpts from the memorial 'Ode' for his daughter were published in the CANADIAN FORUM (1930, 1932). Many of the short stories were first published in a series in the Winnipeg *Tribune* (1926-7). Some of these were closely related to, or excerpted from, the material of the western novels. While a few deserve attention—and 'Snow', first published in *Queen's Quarterly* (Spring, 1932), has been much anthologized—Grove was seldom happy in the shorter form.

Ronald SUTHERLAND's *Frederick Philip Grove* (NCL, 1969) attempted to place Grove's work in the international context of literary naturalism. In the same year D.O. Spettigue's *Frederick Philip Grove* deflected Grove criticism towards biography. Scrutinizing Grove's past in order to date the Grove canon, Spettigue could find no foundation for either the European childhood or the American years as Grove had described them, and this insight led to a period of research and the publication of *FPG: the European years* (1973), which revealed Grove as

Greve, and Grove's autobiography *In search of myself* as a curious blend of fiction and distorted fact. In 1973 also Margaret Stobie's *Frederick Philip Grove* examined critically the teacher/author as he had appeared to his Manitoba contemporaries. Despite gaps, these books—together with the *Letters* (1976) edited by Pacey (which includes the German correspondence)—made it possible at last to relate Grove/Greve the man to the writings, both late and early. This advantage, combined with advances in literary criticism in Canada, has led to more psychologically oriented studies that have viewed the characters of Grove's Canadian novels as aspects of the author's personality, and the protagonists of Greve's German novels as precursors. A feminist interest is apparent in both the German and Canadian novels. In *Fanny Essler*—deplored by one contemporary as a *roman à clef* and reviewed by another as a 'search for the self' that was divided uncertainly between literary naturalism and the psychological school—the battle of the sexes and of the generations is prominent, as it is in the Canadian books.

Grove's contribution to the literature of his adopted country—as an early realist and something of a feminist, as a perceptive social critic and a cosmopolitan, if idiosyncratic, literary critic—was considerable; though as he never wrote down to his readers, and never was a 'popular' writer, his critical influence was largely exemplary and indirect. Apart from Pacey's 1945 study and the support of such discerning friends as A.L. Phelps, Watson KIRKCONNELL, Barker FAIRLEY, and W.J. Alexander, recognition of his achievement had to await the expansion of Canadian literary studies in the 1960s. Beginning with *Over prairie trails* in 1957, seven of his books were reprinted in the New Canadian Library series. In 1963 the Grove papers were purchased from his widow by the University of Manitoba. The Grove canon was expanded in 1971 with the publication of a selection of the short stories, *Tales from the margin* (1971), and the *Letters*, both edited by Desmond Pacey. In 1976 the first of his German works was published in English: *The master mason's house*, translated by Paul Gubbins and edited by A.W. Riley and D.O. Spettigue. A translation of *Fanny Essler* is in progress. Unpublished manuscripts remain in the Grove Collection. An annotated bibliography, compiled by Paul Hjartarson and D.O. Spettigue, will be published by ECW Press. Issue 27-28 (1982) of *Canadian Children's Literature* is a special

Grove issue containing the first authentic publication of a novel he wrote for boys, *The adventure of Leonard Broadus*, in 1939, and articles on it by Mary Rubio.

See also CRITICISM IN ENGLISH: 3.

D.O. SPETTIGUE

Guèvremont, Germaine (1893-1968). Germaine Grignon, a cousin of Claude-Henri GRIGNON, was born in Saint-Jérôme, Qué., and educated there and in Lachine and Toronto. She married Hyacinthe Guèvremont in 1916 and moved to Sorel, Qué., where she started her career as a journalist on the staff of *Le Courrier de Sorel* (1928-35); after she moved to Montreal in 1935 she worked for the Montreal *Gazette*. A member of the Société des Écrivains canadiens, she was elected to the Académie canadienne-française (1949) and to the Royal Society of Canada (1961). For her first novel, *Le survenant*, she received the Prix Duvernay (1945), the Prix David (1947), and the Prix Olivier-de-Serres, Paris (1947). She won a Governor General's Award for *The outlanders*, an English translation of *Le survenant* and *Marie-Didace*.

Her first book, *En pleine terre* (1942)—a collection of three short stories and fourteen rural sketches (an extra story was added in the 1955 edition)—deals with life in the Sorel islands, in what is called the Chenal du Moine. Featuring the colourful language of the region's inhabitants and both realistic and impressionistic descriptions to record the simple life of a rural family, it received only mild attention. With the publication of *Le survenant* in Québec (1945) and Paris (1947), Guèvremont became well known. In 1947 she wrote a second novel, *Marie-Didace*, which was to form part of a trilogy. (The third segment was never completed, though one chapter, 'Le plomb dans l'aile', was published in the *Cahiers de l'Académie canadienne-française* in 1959.) Both novels concern the Beauchemin family and depict the disintegrating rural world in a spare, highly realistic manner. *Le survenant* recounts the sudden intrusion of a stranger into a tight family circle and the consequences upon the social organization of the community. *Marie-Didace* deals with the extinction of the male line of the family by the birth of Marie-Didace. (In what we know of the third part, Marie-Didace is about to leave the Chenal du Moine during the economic crisis of the thirties to look for work in Sorel.) Both novels were translated into English and published together as *The out-*landers (Toronto, 1950) and *Monk's reach* (London, 1950). The story of the Beauchemin family also had great success when it was dramatized as a radio series (1952-4) and serialized for television (1954-60).

The most important studies of Germaine Guèvremont's work are by Rita Leclerc, *Germaine Guèvremont* (1963), and by Jean-Pierre Duquette, *Germaine Guèvremont, une route, une maison* (1973).

See also NOVELS IN FRENCH 1940 TO 1959: 4.

LUCIE ROBERT

Gunn, Donald. See HISTORICAL WRITING IN ENGLISH: 3.

Gunnars, Kristjanna. See POETRY IN ENGLISH 1950 TO 1982: 3.

Gurik, Robert (b. 1932). Born in Paris of Hungarian parents, he came to Canada in 1950, and in 1957 received his professional engineer's certification from the Institut Polytechnique de Montréal. While working as an engineer in and around Montreal, he had his first plays—*Le chant du poète* (1963), *Les portes* (1965), and *Api or not Api* (1966)—produced by little theatres and in regional competitions of the Dominion Drama Festival. In 1967 *Le pendu* (1967) was judged the best play and the best Canadian play at the Dominion Drama Festival finals held in Newfoundland. A co-founder of the Centre d'essai des auteurs dramatiques, Gurik had four more plays produced in Montreal—*Les louis d'or* (1967), *Api 2967* (1967), *Hamlet, prince du Québec* (1968), and *A coeur ouvert* (1969)—and a public reading in 1965 of *Hello police*, written in collaboration with Jean-Pierre Morin and later published as *Allo . . . police!* (1974), before leaving engineering work in 1972 to devote himself to the theatre. He has since written and produced radio and TV dramas and several full-length plays, including *Le procès de Jean-Baptiste M.* (1972), *Le tabernacle à trois étages* (1973), and *La baie des Jacques* (1978). Some of his one-act plays have been collected in *Les tas de sièges* (1971) and *Sept courtes pièces* (1974).

Api 2967, Le pendu, and *Le procès de Jean-Baptiste M.* have been particularly popular both in Québec and abroad and were translated into English: *Api 2967* (1974) by Marc F. Gélinas; *The hanged man* (1972) by Philip London and Laurence Bérard; and *The trial of Jean-Baptiste M* (1974) by Alan Van Meer. These three plays illustrate Gurik's preoccupation with runaway technology and consu-

Gurik

merism, authoritarian régimes, the hardships of the poor, and the naïvety of those who either refuse to accept the status quo or actively try to change it. *Api 2967* is a clever and amusing play set in a futuristic world of test-tube babies, food in capsule form, long but sterile and perfectly controlled life, television monitors watching everyone, and dictionaries from which words describing such outmoded concepts as love and passion have been removed. Only the two main characters, the professor and his female research assistant, resist the system and discover and enjoy some hitherto unknown and forbidden pleasures before they perish. The hero of *Le pendu*, Yonel, is a poor young beggar and former miner who is apparently, but not really, blind. With his father's help he devises a money-making scheme: he will pretend to plan to hang himself and then try to sell a piece of 'hangman's rope'—a popular, if somewhat macabre, good-luck charm. At first he makes money and seems to help several luckless members of his entourage; but when they learn that the hanging is not to occur and that he means to establish organizations to help the world's poor, they force him to hang himself. The play ends with a chorus, sung by a group of children playing in the background, telling how nothing has improved in the village since Yonel's death.

Gurik's plays not only criticize those who would impose their will on society; they also offer little hope for those who conform to, and profit from, the consumer society, as in *Le procès de Jean-Baptiste M.*: the name, which evokes 'Monsieur tout le monde' and Québec's patron saint, John the Baptist, suggests a Québécois Everyman, in this case hoping to get and keep a steady job. Though handicapped by lack of education and an unwarranted prison record, he is finally hired by a big industrial firm in Montreal, but his efficiency and inventiveness create unrest and jealousies and he is eventually fired. Frustrated by the injustice, he shoots and kills several of his former bosses. The events leading up to the shooting alternate with scenes of Jean-Baptiste's grotesque trial in which witness, judge, and jury are played by the same group of unfeeling and hysterical individuals. In the end Jean-Baptiste is convicted of both the murder and the more serious crime, in the jury's eyes, of disobeying society's laws, thereby interfering with orderly production and consumption.

Many of Gurik's plays point to the socio-political situation in Québec: in *Hamlet, prince du Québec* Shakespeare's characters wear the masks of institutions and of people who have been involved in the modern Québec nationalist movement; *J'écoute* and *Face à face* (*Les tas de sièges*) and *Le trou* (*Sept courtes pièces*) allude to the October Crisis of 1970; in *Le tabernacle à trois étages* and *Playball* (*Sept courtes pièces*) the playing of the Canadian national anthem lends a special nationalistic flavour to the action; *La baie des Jacques* is coloured by two songs about the road to independence and the need for change; and *Le champion* (1977) contains references to a Quiet Revolution slogan, 'Maîtres chez nous'. But Québec society is not Gurik's only target. *La baie des Jacques* also attacks Palestine and Bengal, and *La palissade* (1971—with *Api 2967*) shows filmed scenes of violence and unrest in the U.S., France, Germany, Yugoslavia, and South America. The socio-political aspects of Gurik's theatre are as obvious as his use of such Brechtian devices as slogans, songs, news bulletins, suspended animation, and grotesque make-up. Though some critics praise his determination to criticize society and his efforts to force the audience to make judgements, perhaps even to initiate change, others decry the didactic elements of his work, his thin plots, superficial characters, and use of language that is too clever to make any lasting effect on Québec dramaturgy. Nevertheless Gurik was one of the most prolific and most produced Québec playwrights in the sixties and seventies. He will no doubt continue to be applauded for reminding his audience of the threat posed to individual and collective freedom by modern technology, giant corporations, powerful institutions, and of the importance of defending the concept of a pluralistic and humanitarian society.

Gurik has published two novels: *Spirales* (1966), a stream-of-consciousness description of one man's feelings of isolation and eventual nervous breakdown; and *Jeune délinquant* (1980), about the struggles of a group of juvenile delinquents, some of whom reform. Based on a script Gurik wrote as a five-part TV series for Radio-Canada, *Jeune délinquant* is less like a novel than a dialogue interspersed with extensive stage directions.

See Jean-Cléo Godin and Laurent Mailhot, 'Le procès de (Jean-Baptiste) Gurik, ingénieur' in *Théâtre Québécois*, II (1980).

ELAINE NARDOCCHIO

Gustafson, Ralph (b. 1909). Ralph Barker

Gustafson was born in Lime Ridge, Qué., of Anglo-Scandinavian ancestry. He was educated at Bishop's University, Lennoxville, Qué. (B.A. and M.A. 1929, 1930) and then at Oxford University (B.A. 1933). He returned to Canada and taught briefly at St Alban's, Brockville, Ont., then went to live in England from 1934 to 1938. His long and prolific career as a poet can be divided into three phases. During his early English phase he was essentially a romantic writing conventional verse: *The golden chalice* (1935), which won the Prix David of the Province of Québec, and the verse-play, *King Alfred* (1937). After leaving England in 1938 and spending a brief period in Canada, he settled in New York, where his exposure to American poetry and New York musical and literary life inaugurated his second phase. The war thrust him from romance into reality. In 1942 he went to work for the British Information Services in Manhattan, one of his tasks being the reading of the American press to furnish summaries on U.S. attitudes towards Britain. His poetry now began to show qualities of irony and bitterness and a sardonic lyricism; his constant exposure to headlines may have led to his later topical poems of indignation at the world's tyrannies and terrors. Two privately printed volumes were harbingers of change: *Epithalamium in time of war* (1941) and *Lyrics unromantic* (1942).

In New York Gustafson met other Canadian expatriates, including Leon EDEL and A.J.M. SMITH, both of whom had been in the Montreal literary movement of the 1920s. Smith exercised on Gustafson the particular influence he had had on other Canadian poets: a combination of modernism, tradition, and wit wedded to precise diction and economy of form. *Flight into darkness* (1944) reflected Gustafson's war melancholy, but showed he had opened himself up to greater colloquialism and a freer style.

A sophisticated and handsome man, Gustafson lived in a small flat off Central Park, surrounded by his books and papers. In addition to publishing much verse, he wrote short stories that were later collected in the anthologies *The brazen tower* (1974) and *The vivid air* (1980). Beginning during the war years, Gustafson edited three anthologies for Penguin: *Anthology of Canadian poetry (English)* (1942); *Canadian accent* (1944), a collection of stories and poems; and *The Penguin book of Canadian verse* (1958; rev. 1967). Other anthologies of the forties were *Voices* (1943) and *A little anthology of Canadian poets* (1943).

Gustafson's third phase began with his return to Canada in 1960 and his becoming poet-in-residence at his *alma mater*, Bishop's University, where he was also professor of English. Shortly before his repatriation he had undertaken extensive travels. These yielded *Rocky mountain poems* (1960) and *Rivers among rocks* (1960) and announced a new style, that of the quasi-confessional travelogue. His travel verse, vivid and visual, suggests that he is most comfortable when he can feed on externals rather than plough his inner world. He is sharp and ironic, and adept at the poetry of indignation, as in his multi-media script on the world's violence, *Themes and variations for sounding brass* (1972). But he also shows tenderness and delicacy, particularly in such travel miniatures as 'Old lady seen briefly at Patras' or 'On the road to Vicenza'. His best travel poems, representing four years of voyaging, appear in *Sift in an hourglass* (1966) and *Ixion's wheel* (1969). Book succeeded book: *Selected poems* (1972), *Fire on stone* (1974), *Corners in glass* (1977), *Soviet poems* (1978), *Sequences* (1979), *Landscape without rain* (1980), *Conflicts of spring* (1981), and *Gradations of grandeur* (1982). For some years a music critic for the CBC, Gustafson has constantly used musical references in his verse, arguing that 'thought in music is sensuous' and that the quest of poetry is to arrive at the condition of music. If, in his topical poetry, he confuses anger with intensity, he compensates for this in his other work by his concreteness and visuality and his concision in the abstracting of intellectual experience.

Gustafson has received many honours, including the Governor General's Award for *Fire on stone*.

In addition to various articles in literary journals on Gustafson's work, there exists a full-length critique in Wendy Keitner, *Ralph Gustafson* (1977). L.M. Allison and Wendy Keitner are compiling a bibliography.

LEON EDEL

Guthrie, Norman. See CRITICISM IN ENGLISH: 2.

Gutteridge, Don (b. 1937). Donald George Gutteridge was born in the village of Point Edward, Lambton Co., Ont., and graduated in English from the University of Western Ontario, where he was a teaching fellow in 1962-3. After teaching high school for seven years, he joined the department of English at Western, where he is now a professor in the Faculty of Education. He has written many articles on educational methodology and a textbook, *Language and expression: a modern approach* (1970).

Gutteridge won the President's Medal of the University of Western Ontario for *Death at Quebec* (1971), a poetry collection of monologues by historical figures (including the Jesuits in Huronia) and village poems. This work came between *The village within: poems towards a biography* (1970) and *Saying grace: an elegy* (1972), both of which show his inclination to stitch together his own life with that of his village and country. His talent for mythologizing history—for fusing his poetic spirit with the spirit of historical figures, somewhat in the manners of ATWOOD, PURDY, and ONDAATJE—shows best in *Riel: a poem for voices* (1968), the beginning of a tetralogy about Indians and explorers entitled *Dreams and visions; the land*. Much of *Riel* is a documentary collage in which letters, newspaper and diary entries, political proclamations, and posters are mixed with long-lined monologues and welded into a single metaphor. In *Coppermine: the quest for North* (1973) Samuel Hearne's journals are the source for a horrific, sometimes surreal, Canadian version of the El Dorado myth. *Borderlands* (1975) uses violence, irony, and a skilful interplay of voices to re-create John Jewitt's two-year enslavement by the Nootka Indians. More

political is *Tecumseh* (1976), with its theme of genocide, but Gutteridge does not capture fully his main character's personality.

Gutteridge passed to personal themes in his second tetralogy, *Time is the metaphor*, written in a demotic style and beginning with the comic and sometimes poignant novel *Bus-ride* (1974), set in a small Ontario town in Mar. 1939, which focuses on a Junior B hockey player bewildered by the process of growing up. In *The true history of Lambton County* (1977), a long poem with multiple voices, the poet assembles an album of his own history and childhood memories that are droll, romantic, and tragic. *All in good time* (1981), a small-scale comic novel, takes up some of the characters from *Bus-ride* at a later period, and, using sports, politics, and sex, tells a touching and ironic story of a people on the edge of winter and war. *God's geography* (1982), a collection of poems that juxtapose village memories and childhood with later experience and world events, shows that the tetralogy forms a narrative of the past from which the poet evolved.

See 'Don Gutteridge's mythic tetralogy' by Keith Garebian, CANADIAN LITERATURE 87 (Winter 1980); 'Riel: historic man or literary symbol' by Don Gutteridge, *Bulletin de l'association des humanités* (Autumn 1970); and 'Teaching the Canadian mythology: a poet's view' by Don Gutteridge, *Journal of Canadian Studies* (Feb. 1973).

KEITH GAREBIAN

H

Haas, Maara. See UKRAINIAN WRITING.

Haché, Louis. See ACADIAN LITERATURE: 2(c).

Haig-Brown, Roderick (1908-1976). Born in Lansing, Sussex, Eng., Roderick Langmore Haig-Brown was educated at Charterhouse, where his grandfather had been headmaster. He left school at 17 and immigrated to Washington state in 1926. In 1927 he moved to British Columbia, where

he worked as a cougar hunter, boxer, tourist guide, and fisherman. He went to England in 1929 and wrote his first novel there; but, homesick for B.C., he returned in 1931. In 1934 he married Ann Elmore of Seattle and they raised four children. Appointed magistrate in the village of Campbell River on Vancouver Island in 1942, he served as a provincial court judge for thirty-three years until his death. During the Second World War he was a captain and a major in the Canadian army, and was briefly on loan to the RCMP. Haig-Brown was director of the National and Provincial Parks Association of Canada, a member of the International Pacific Salmon Commission, served on a federal electoral boundaries commission, and was chancellor of the University of Victoria. He also fought publicly, and often with little support, against hydro and industrial development in B.C. for harming the natural environment. His home, 'Above Tide', on a twenty-acre farm near Campbell River, is now a residence for conservationists and writers.

Haig-Brown wrote twenty-five books—including adult novels, short stories, and children's books—but he is best known as a nature writer, specializing in fishing and natural history. An outdoorsman who was also one of the finest prose stylists in Canada, he was skilled at observing creatures in natural settings, especially 'the strangeness and beauty of the fish, their often visible remoteness, their ease in another world, the mystery of their movements and habits and whims.' He wrote the first item in the first issue of CANADIAN LITERATURE about the writer in isolation.

His first publications were *Silver: the life story of an Atlantic salmon* (1931), written when he was 23; *Pool and rapid: the story of a river* (1932); *Panther* (1934; American title, *Ki-yu: story of a panther*); *The western angler* (1939), which describes the Pacific salmon and western trout and established Haig-Brown as a fishing authority; and *Timber* (1942), a novel about unionizing a lumber camp (Eng. ed.; *The tall trees fall*, 1943). *Return to the river* (1941) is about the chinook salmon run in B.C. rivers. These were followed by some of his best books: *A river never sleeps* (1946); *Starbuck Valley winter* (1946), which won the Canadian Library Association Award for best juvenile fiction; its sequel, *Saltwater summer* (1948), winner of a Governor General's Award for best juvenile fiction; and *Measure of the year* (1950), an evocative book of essays describing the cycle of Haig-Brown's year as writer, magistrate, fisherman, and community leader. He then began his best-known work, a tetralogy: *Fisherman's spring* (1951), *Fisherman's winter* (1954), *Fisherman's summer* (1959), and *Fisherman's fall* (1964). *Winter* is perhaps the best, combining satisfying descriptive writing with practical information for anglers. It also describes a brief fishing trip to Chile and Argentina in 1950. *Summer*, a collection of angling adventures, stresses conservation. *Spring*, which is about the es-

sence of sport angling and the fisherman's relationship to the fish, the river, and the natural world, best captures the quiet philosophy of Walton's *Compleat angler*. *Fall*, Haig-Brown's favourite angling season, gives an excellent account of the migratory cycles of the Pacific salmon and steelhead trout. In the remarkable final chapter he takes to scuba diving in his river and identifies himself too strongly with the fish to catch and kill. This is probably his last important book.

Other works include *Mounted Police patrol* (1954), a juvenile; *On the highest hill* (1955), a novel; *Captain of the Discovery* (1959), a biography of Captain George Vancouver; *The farthest shores* (1960), a history of B.C. that began as a series of radio dramatizations; *The living land* (1961), an account of the natural resources of B.C.; *The whale people* (1962), a children's book portraying the life and hunting methods of the Nootka Indians who went out in canoes to hunt whales; *Fur and gold* (1962), a history of Sir James Douglas and the Hudson's Bay Company in B.C.; and *A primer of fly fishing* (1964). His last works include two uninspired monographs for Fisheries and Oceans Canada: *Canada's Pacific salmon* (1967) and *The salmon* (1974). *Bright waters, bright fish* (1980), published posthumously, is an examination of sport fishing as a social and economic resource. Haig-Brown's daughter Valerie edited a three-volume collection, *The world of Haig-Brown*, made up of *Woods and river tales* (1980), mostly unpublished short stories dating from the 1930s and 1950s; *The master and his fish* (1981); and *Writings and reflections* (1982), drawing on Haig-Brown's papers in the archives of the University of British Columbia.

See also CHILDREN'S LITERATURE IN ENGLISH: 2, 3, 6.   GEOFF HANCOCK

Hailey, Arthur. See NOVELS IN ENGLISH 1960 TO 1982: OTHER TALENTS, OTHER WORKS: 7.

Haliburton, T.C. (1796-1865). Born in Windsor, N.S., of New England stock—his father's family were Rhode Islanders and his mother's were Loyalists from Connecticut—Thomas Chandler Haliburton was educated at King's College and was called to the bar in 1820. He practised law in Annapolis Royal, representing that constituency in the provincial assembly from 1826 to 1829, when he was appointed a judge of the Inferior Court of Common Pleas. He was promoted to the Supreme Court of Nova Scotia in 1841. In 1856 he retired and went to live in England, where he held a seat in the House of Commons from 1859 until just before his death in Isleworth, Middlesex.

During his life Haliburton's reputation was characterized by two contradictions: his apparent transformation from a political moderate to an inflexible Tory and his love-hate for Nova Scotia. A conservative from the first, he saw Nova Scotia as a society in which public life was directed by the Crown, the established church, and an educated élite, and believed that the colony would prosper within the empire. However, in the 1820s he advocated the removal of legal disabilities against Roman Catholics; a provincial grant to Pictou Academy, Pictou, N.S., which had been founded by the Presbyterian minister, the Rev. Thomas McCULLOCH; and a system of common schools—all of which his party regarded as radical and progressive measures. When Haliburton was elevated to the bench in 1829, a political maverick was removed from the assembly (it was widely believed that he had sacrificed his views for the sake of advancement). In the 1840s, when his fellow Nova Scotians rejected government by the Loyalist, Anglican 'family compact' in favour of a more democratic system of responsible government, Haliburton could hardly contain his contempt for them behind good-humoured satire. His disappointment undoubtedly contributed to his decision to forsake Nova Scotia and go 'home' to England to pursue his literary and political ambitions. Yet the tensions created by his praise and criticism of Nova Scotia resulted in his most enduring work.

His first literary effort, the historical pamphlet *A general description of Nova Scotia, illustrated by a new and correct map* (Halifax, 1823), appeared anonymously. Encouraged by the interest in local history, and hoping to raise the status of Nova Scotia in the eyes of the world, Haliburton enlarged it into *An historical and statistical account of Nova-Scotia* (2 vols, Halifax, 1829). From the emphasis in this account on romantic highlights like the expulsion of the Acadians, Henry Wadsworth Longfellow drew his inspiration for EVANGELINE (1847). Although Haliburton's access to documents was limited, his history, which ends in 1763, was one of the major pieces of historical writing in nineteenth-century Canada. (See also HISTORICAL WRITING IN ENGLISH: 1.)

This book, which brought him little acclaim, did not allow him to criticize contemporary events, so Haliburton turned to satiric sketches, contributing—with his friend, the reformer Joseph HOWE, and others—to 'The Club Papers (1828-31) in *The Novascotian*. In 1835-6 he wrote 21 sketches entitled 'Recollections of Nova Scotia' for that newspaper, and they proved so popular that Haliburton enlarged them into *The clockmaker; or The sayings and doings of Samuel Slick, of Slickville* (Halifax, 1836). His satiric purpose was to show that actions, not complaints, were the only way to improve local conditions, and each sketch—composed mainly of dialogue—begins with an entertaining incident and ends with a pithy moral observation. He drew on his own experiences as a judge to send his fictional squire around Nova Scotia in company with Sam Slick, the brash Yankee clock pedlar whose aggressive salesmanship is a compound of 'soft sawder' and 'human natur'. Although Slick is not a rounded personality, his contradictions perfectly catch Haliburton's own ambivalent attitudes towards Maritimers, Americans, and, in later books, towards the British. Slick praises American commercial know-how and attacks Nova Scotian apathy, yet he is suspicious of American demagoguery and praises Nova Scotia's natural resources and its hardy inhabitants. But the message was almost lost, because Slick's energetic high spirits and his Yankee dialect—an unceasing flow of homely aphorisms and epigrams—charmed audiences everywhere: Slick, the archetypal swaggering and sharp American trader, became one of the most popular comic figures of the century and turned *The Clockmaker* [first series] into the first Canadian bestseller. This book was directed at a Nova Scotia audience. Haliburton next addressed British readers in two sequels: *The clockmaker; or, The sayings and doings of Samuel Slick, of Slickville, second series* (London, 1838) and *The clockmaker; or, The sayings and doings of Samuel Slick, of Slickville, third series* (London, 1840). He now believed that Nova Scotia's economic and political troubles could not be solved by the province but by changes in Colonial Office policy, and he introduced scenes in which North Americans and British personages clashed.

Haliburton pursued the contrasts between North America and England in later books. Exploiting the new transatlantic steamship services, he wrote *The letterbag of the Great Western; or, Life in a steamer* (London, Halifax, 1840), a series of letters from Canadian,

American, and English travellers to their friends at home in which Haliburton poked fun at national characteristics. Slick reappears in *The attaché; or, Sam Slick in England: First series* (2 vols, London, 1843) and *Second series* (2 vols, London, 1844) as a member of the American legation at the Court of St James's, to point out the follies and stupidities of the English; but the satire is less effective here because of Haliburton's ignorance of English life.

Haliburton's finest picture of Nova Scotia, *The old judge; or, Life in a colony* (2 vols, London, 1849), is a sympathetic, rich canvas delineating vice-regal rituals, country picnics, and village court-trials. It is the first literary collection of folklore, legends, and ghost tales, of which 'The Witch of Inky Dell' is one of the most evocative stories in nineteenth-century Canada. Haliburton uses three narrators to give coherence to the loosely structured sketches and stories: the British traveller who opens the story; the Windsor judge, Barclay, who guides the visitor and explains the details of colonial life to him; and Stephen Richardson, a vigorous and enterprising farmer who acts as master of ceremonies at an inn where a group of friends entertain each other with stories.

In *Sam Slick's wise saws and modern instances; or, What he said, did, or invented* (2 vols, London, 1853), Slick returns to Nova Scotia as an agent sent by the President to study the fisheries. The Sam Slick series ends with its sequel, *Nature and human nature* (2 vols, London, 1855). Haliburton edited two anthologies of American humour: *Traits of American humour, by native authors* (3 vols, London, 1852) and *The Americans at home; or, Byeways, backwoods and prairies* (3 vols, London, 1855). His final book of prose sketches, *The season-ticket* (London, 1860), employs a railway setting for dialogues between the British narrator and his fellow British and American travellers. A principal topic is the need for improved communications for Britain's colonial empire.

Haliburton is recognized as one of the founders of American humour. He is rightly regarded as the last in the Loyalist Tory satiric tradition, but he was also the first fiction writer to exploit regional dialects; the first to use dialogue that is colloquial and racy; and the first to define the Maritime (and, by extension, the Canadian) character in terms of dual allegiances to American and British roots. Most of his fictions involve a journey into a new country and a first-person narrator (a mouthpiece for Haliburton), who investigates the new society. At times he uses several narrators in order to milk humour from the clash of perspectives between his characters, the author, and the reader. The literary influences on his humour have been attributed to Thomas McCulloch's 'Letters of Mephibosheth Stepsure' in *The Acadian Recorder* (Halifax) in 1821-3 and to Seba Smith's *Life and writings of Major Jack Downing; of Downingville, away down east in the state of Maine* (Boston, 1833).

After the 1837 Rebellion in the Canadas, Haliburton's hardening Tory attitudes caused a rift with Howe and frequently marred the artistry of his books. His savage attacks on Lord Durham's *Report* (1838) in *The bubbles of Canada* (London, 1839), and in a series of letters to the London *Times*—reprinted as *A reply to the report of the Earl of Durham* (London, 1840)—arose from Haliburton's anger at the British abandonment of British North America. He was opposed to a union of the Maritime Provinces and the Canadas because he believed it would lead to independence and even annexation to the United States, and he attacked responsible government because he thought it would lead to mob rule and party factions. Even after the British North American provinces had achieved responsible government, Haliburton argued against it in *The English in America* (2 vols, London, 1851; reprinted 1975), which was republished as *Rule and misrule of the English in America* (2 vols, New York, 1851). However, in *An address on the present condition, resources and prospects of British North America* (London, 1857), he grudgingly accepted the notion of a colonial federation, although he preferred an imperial federation in which the colonies would be represented at Westminster.

Recent editions of Haliburton's works include *Sam Slick* (1923, rpr. 1981) edited by Ray Palmer Baker; the New Canadian Library edition of *The clockmaker*, 1st series (1958), with an introduction by R.L. McDougall; *The old judge* (1968), edited by R.E. Watters; *The Sam Slick anthology* (1969), selected and introduced by R.E. Watters, with 'A note on the speech of Sam Slick' by W.S. Avis; *The letter bag of the Great Western; or, Life in a steamer* (1973); *The season ticket* (1973); *A reply to the report of the Earl of Durham* (1976), introduced by A.G. Bailey; and *The old judge; or, Life in a colony* (1978), edited by M.G. Parks.

Haliburton

See Ray Palmer Baker, 'Haliburton and the Loyalist tradition in the development of American humour', in *A history of English-Canadian literature to the confederation* (1920); V.L.O. Chittick, *Thomas Chandler Haliburton: a study in provincial toryism* (1924); R.L. McDougall, 'Thomas Chandler Haliburton', in *Our living tradition* (2nd and 3rd series, 1959); Fred COGSWELL, 'Haliburton', in the *Literary history of Canada* (1965; second edition, 1976); and R.A. Davies, ed., *On Thomas Chandler Haliburton: selected criticism* (1979).   GEORGE L. PARKER

Hambleton, Ronald. See POETRY IN ENGLISH 1900 TO 1950: 5.

Hardin, Herschel (b. 1936). Born and raised in Vegreville, Alta, he graduated in philosophy from Queen's University, Kingston, in 1958 and travelled in Europe for two years before settling in Vancouver, where he still lives. Impressed with the plays of Shakespeare, George Büchner, and Bertolt Brecht, he reveals in his own plays a consistent concern with the exploitation of indigenous culture and the oppression of native peoples by utilizing episodic structures reminiscent of the chronicle and epic forms of his mentors. Although his first play, *The great wave of civilization* (1976), was written in 1962, it was not produced until after his third play, *Esker Mike and his wife, Agiluk* (1973), was first produced by Toronto's Factory Theatre Lab in 1971. Both his second and fourth plays—a full-length adaptation of Brecht's *Threepenny opera* entitled *School for swindle* and *William Lyon MacKenzie, Part 1*—remain unpublished and unproduced.

Hardin's published plays are notable both for the scope of their subjects and the rich variety of language they employ. A dramatization of the effect of the liquor trade on the Blackfoot Indians, *The great wave of civilization* is the less successful of the two, mixing songs, poetry, and dialogue in ten scenes that trace the reduction of a proud culture to poverty and despair. Although the elevation of the Indians' language to poetic heights is appropriate to the 'endistanced' style of the play, in which summaries of the action precede each scene so as to preclude suspense and focus attention on the social significance of the narrative, it reduces the Indian characters to the status of symbols, and forgoes the emotional authenticity that would make their decline a compelling political statement. *Esker Mike* is more effective in depicting the economic destruction of the North because of its consistently metaphoric language and simple 'presentational' style. Centring the play on Agiluk, an Eskimo woman who refuses to sleep with her common-law husband until he accepts the responsibility of providing for their children, Hardin creates an austere yet impassioned portrait of a village culture doomed to extinction by southern society's duplicity and misunderstanding. Agiluk's act of infanticide that precipitates the play's despairing conclusion adheres to a sense of justice that is totally vulnerable to the white man's laws.

Overlooked and underproduced, Hardin stopped writing for the stage in 1974 to become a freelance broadcaster and economic analyst. He is the author of a study of Canadian economics, *A nation unaware* (1974).
                                    ROBERT S. WALLACE

Hardy, W.G. See NOVELS IN ENGLISH 1920 TO 1940: 2.

Harlow, Robert (b. 1923). Born in Prince Rupert, B.C., he moved with his family to Prince George in 1926, where his father was a roadmaster with the CNR. After graduating from high school in 1941, Harlow joined the RCAF and was discharged Flying Officer, DFC, in 1945. He earned a B.A. from the University of British Columbia (1945-8), where he was a member of one of Earle BIRNEY's first creative-writing workshops, and was the first Canadian to attend Paul Engle's Writers' Workshop at the University of Iowa, where he received an MFA in 1950. Harlow joined the CBC as a public-affairs producer and in 1953, with Robert WEAVER, was instrumental in planning and inaugurating the literary program 'Anthology'. His story 'The sound of the horn' appeared in the collection *Klanak Islands* (1959). In 1959 he joined with Birney and others to found the literary magazine *Prism International*. He was appointed director of radio, B.C. region, for the CBC in 1955. In 1965 he was appointed founding head of the Department of Creative Writing at UBC, a position he held until 1977. He continues to teach at UBC.

Harlow's first three novels—*Royal Murdoch* (1962), *A gift of echoes* (1965), and *Scann* (1972)—form a trilogy about the fictional town of Linden, B.C., modelled on Prince George. Connected by the maturing of relationships between generations, they feature grotesque characters, lavish metaphors, and sudden bursts of violence. *Royal Murdoch*, the most traditional, tells the story of an old man, Royal Murdoch, who gathers his friends and family about him to witness his final days. The plot draws on his reflections on past personalities and antagonisms, especially the tension between his wife and an Indian mistress, who represent civilized and natural woman. *A gift of echoes* concentrates more on commentary than on plot as the protagonist, John Grandy, contemplates the passage of time and sees that 'the structure of his history was dismembered'. The metaphysical aspect of the novel, which at times makes it seem aimless, is offset by melodramatic action: bouts with alcohol, accidents, fights, and the destruction of a lumber mill by fire. *Scann*, Harlow's major novel, interlocks five novellas about Amory Scann, editor of the Linden newspaper. Supposedly writing a special issue about the fiftieth anniversary of the town, he actually writes about his faltering marriage, his Second World War experiences, an epidemic, and chronicles the saga of trapper Linden and settler Thrain, two men central to the history of the town. Their epic struggle in the wilderness against a wolverine (partially modelled on O'HAGEN's *Wilderness men*) is one of the great set-pieces in western-Canadian fiction. The novel concludes with Scann's burning of the manuscript he has written, which constitutes the novel itself. A complex and richly orchestrated work, its clarity is achieved by an omniscient narrator who comments on the various stories and whose voice unifies them.

Making arrangements (1977), a comic novel about horseracing, portrays a group of hangers-on in a cheap Vancouver hotel attempting to raise enough money for a once-in-a-lifetime bet on a horse race. Another complex work that is composed of several novellas, it involves drugs, the kidnapping of an industrialist, and Pay-TV sex. Less philosophical than *Scann*, it includes among its characters a legless narrator, a detective with prostate trouble, a cab driver, and a prostitute; racetrack and off-track betting slang in its dialogue; and concludes with a new reading of the chariot race in the *Iliad* as described by modern track-wise punters. A new novel, *Paul Nolan*, is scheduled for 1983 publication.

Harlow's critical essays appear in *Margaret Laurence* (1977) edited by W.H. New, *Ernest Buckler* (1972) edited by G. Cook, and *Critical essays on Wallace Stegner* (1982) edited by Anthony Arthur.

Issue 19 of CANADIAN FICTION MAGAZINE

(Autumn 1975) is devoted to Harlow and contains an interview, and issue 30/31 (Summer 1979) includes his essay on the novel, novella, and short story.

See also NOVELS IN ENGLISH 1960 TO 1982: OTHER TALENTS, OTHER WORKS: 1, 6(b).

GEOFF HANCOCK

Harmon, Daniel. See EXPLORATION LITERATURE IN ENGLISH: 2.

Harris, Christie (b. 1907). She was born in New Jersey and moved as a small child to British Columbia. Married to an immigration officer and the mother of five children, she lives in Vancouver and in the sixties established a reputation as a writer of children's books. Her early works—*Cariboo trail* (1957), *West with the white chiefs* (1965), and *Forbidden frontier* (1968)—though carefully researched, are dramatically effective only in isolated sections. Three realistic novels—*You have to draw the line somewhere* (1964), *Confessions of a toe-hanger* (1967), and *Let X be excitement* (1969)—are based on experiences with her children; but while containing effective moments, they are without a strong spirit of imagination.

Harris's major contribution is her presentation, in fantasies and other stories, of Northwest Coast Indian material and her retellings of Indian legends and folktales, beginning with *Once upon a totem* (1963). She has written historical fiction in *Raven's cry* (1966), a well-researched but weakly fictionalized account of the tragic treatment of the Haida by traders, missionaries, and government officials; a crime novel in *Mystery at the edge of two worlds* (1978), about the theft of Indian artifacts; fantasies, based partly upon Indian folk material, in *Secret in the Stlalakum wild* (1972) and *Sky man on the totem pole?* (1975), which borders on science fiction; and retellings of Indian folktales and legends in *Once more upon a totem* (1963), *Mouse woman and the vanished princesses* (1976), *Mouse woman and the mischief-makers* (1977), *Mouse woman and the muddleheads* (1979), *The trouble with princesses* (1980), and *The trouble with adventuring* (1982). Harris's stories create a link with another culture and age and ask us to see ourselves in a significantly 'other' way. Her creative powers are most fully realized in attempting to provide the reader with the Indian world-view, for Harris goes beyond simply retelling legends and tales to reinvent them so that readers are encouraged to examine their own culture in an entirely different context.

Harris

See Harris's autobiographical remarks, 'In tune with tomorrow', in CANADIAN LITERATURE 78) (Fall 1978).   ROBERT LOVEJOY

Harris, John Norman. See MYSTERY AND CRIME.

Harrison, Charles Yale (1898-1954). Born in Philadelphia, he left school in grade four—over a dispute, it is said, with a teacher about *The merchant of Venice*—and at sixteen was working for the *Montreal Star*. Soon after the outset of the First World War he enlisted in the Royal Montreal Regiment and was a machine-gunner in Belgium and France; he was wounded at Amiens in 1918. He returned to Montreal and worked as a theatre manager, a real-estate salesman, and newspaper reporter before moving to New York, where he worked as a public-relations consultant, a radio commentator, and a writer.

Harrison's contribution to Canadian literature was a powerful war novel based on his experiences with his Canadian regiment: *Generals die in bed*, which was published in England in 1930 and reprinted in 1975 with an introduction by Robert F. Nielsen. Parts appeared in magazines—some German—by 1928, the year before publication of Erich Maria Remarque's *All quiet on the Western Front*, Ernest Hemingway's *A farewell to arms*, and Robert Graves' *Goodbye to all that*. (Neilsen suggests that Remarque may have been influenced by these extracts while writing his novel.) Ford Madox Ford praised *Generals* and it was translated into Spanish, French, and Russian. Beginning in Montreal, the setting quickly changes to Europe and trench warfare, moving briefly (and terrifyingly) to no-man's land, behind the trenches, and to London. The narrator, an eighteen-year-old Canadian soldier, relates his experiences in a deceptively simple style, describing explicitly and objectively the relentless horrors of trench warfare. Fighting is not romanticized, compassion for the soldier's plight is not restricted by nationality, and war is depicted as a brutalizing process. The narrator concludes that the enemies are 'the lice, some of our officers and Death'. Neilsen compares the memorable scene in which the narrator kills a soldier at close range and has difficulty in removing the bayonet from the body to a similar scene in Remarque's novel. *Generals die in bed* is characterized by its strength and simplicity of diction, unifying motifs, cutting irony, and black humour.

Harrison's other novels are *A child is born* (1931), about impoverished lives in the waterfront district of Red Hook, New York; *There are victories* (1933), partly set in Montreal; *Meet me on the barricades* (1938), about a musician who is drawn into the Spanish Civil War, which combines a realistic prose narrative with a surreal play-like sequence; and *Nobody's fool* (1948), about a hoodwinking scheme that is recounted by a New York public-relations executive. Harrison also wrote the pamphlet *Next please!* (1927), the forward to which is signed by John Dos Passos, among others, about a case similar to that of Saccho and Vanzetti; *Clarence Darrow* (1931), the first book-length biography of the famous lawyer; and *Thank God for my heart attack* (1949), a reassuring account of his cardiac problem.

For further discussion of *Generals die in bed*, see Robert F. Nielsen's unpublished thesis, 'A barely perceptible limp: the First World War in Canadian fiction' (University of Guelph, 1971); see also John Moss, *A reader's guide to the Canadian novel* (1981).

JOY KUROPATWA

Harrison, Dick. See CRITICISM IN ENGLISH: 5(g).

Harrison, Susie Frances (1859-1935). Susie Frances Riley, who often used the pseudonym 'Seranus', was born in Toronto and educated there at a private school for girls, and for two years in Montreal. While living in the province of Québec she developed a keen interest in French-Canadian culture that would become evident in her writing. In 1879 she married John W.F. Harrison, a professional musician; they had two children. After living in Ottawa until 1887, she made Toronto her permanent home. There she became well known as a professional pianist and vocalist, an authority on French-Canadian folksongs, and was principal of the Rosedale Branch of the Toronto Conservatory of Music for twenty years. Beginning to write when she was sixteen, she contributed literary and musical reviews (some of these appearing under the name 'Gilbert King'), articles, essays, short stories, and poetry to Canadian, British, and American newspapers and literary magazines. She was a regular correspondent for the Detroit *Free Press* and the Toronto *Globe*, and was editor of *The* WEEK for nine months.

Her first book, *Crowded out and other sketches* (Ottawa, 1886), is a collection of stories, most of which attempt to capture particular characteristics of Canadians. The title story depicts, with psychological intensity, the frustrations of a Canadian writer who tries in London, Eng., to publish works with Canadian content. There are several stories whose haunted, disturbed characters, first-person narrative, and weird events show the influence of Edgar Allan Poe. Many of the stories contain French-Canadian characters and settings, which were the specialty of 'Seranus'. Harrison wrote two novels: *The forest of Bourg-Marie* (London, 1898), a mythic study of the disintegration of French-Canadian society as the younger generation leave their native land and tradition for the wealth of the United States, and *Ringfield* (1914), a melodrama in which an idealistic Methodist minister is corrupted by a bohemian French-Canadian actress and her English poet-lover. While the French-Canadian setting is used effectively in the early novel to heighten its mythic qualities, it is a mere backdrop for the romantic plot in the later work.

Harrison was best known in her day as a poet. Her most ambitious poetry collection is *Pine, rose, and fleur de lis* (Toronto, 1891), a collection of lyrical verse organized in sections that include a long travel sequence, 'Down the River', consisting mostly of villanelles, a form appropriate to its subject matter, which is a fancy-free boat ride through French Canada; a monody on Isabella Valancy CRAWFORD, several poems on England ('From the pine to the rose'); and a miscellany of nature and love poetry. (Several of the poems appear with accompanying music.) Conventional in language and form, and lacking emotional intensity, these poems are of interest mainly for their subject matter: the celebration of the people and landscape of Canada and the point of view of Canadians. Her other poetry collections—most of them privately published—are short (twenty pages maximum): *Song of welcome in honor of His Excellency, the Marquis of Lansdowne, Governor-General of Canada* (Ottawa, 1883), *In northern skies, and other poems* (1912?), *Songs of love and labour* (1925?), *Later poems and new villanelles* (1928), *Penelope and other poems* (n.d.), and *Four ballads and a play* (1933). The play in the last collection, *A phantom born of song*, is a one-act melodrama set in a northern mining camp. Harrison also published *The Canadian birthday book* (Toronto, 1887), a blank diary whose right-hand pages contain excerpts from English- and French-Canadian poetry.

In the late nineteenth century Harrison enjoyed a favourable critical reception in Canada and her work was reviewed not only in Canada but in England and the United States—in *The Week*, the *Canadian Magazine, Literary World, London Spectator, Saturday Review*, and *Critic*—where she was praised for her knowledge of French Canada, her 'new world conceits', and her gift of song. She is significant as a minor poet and novelist who, as a member of the Confederation generation, attempted to identify and express a distinct Canadian voice and character.   CARRIE MacMILLAN

Hart, Julia Catherine (1796-1867), *née* Beckwith. Born in Fredericton, N.B., of New England and French ancestry, she gathered many stories and travel impressions on her childhood visits to relatives in Québec and Nova Scotia. A number of these were incorporated into her first novel, ST. URSULA'S CONVENT; *or, The nun of Canada* (Kingston, 1824), the first novel published in British North America written by a native-born author. In 1820 she moved from Fredericton to Kingston, Upper Canada, where she lived with her aunt, the mother of Québec historian Abbé Ferland. Between 1822 and 1824 she married George Henry Hart; conducted a girls' boarding school in Kingston; and moved to the United States with her husband. In 1831 the Harts settled in Fredericton, where George Hart held a position in the Crown Lands office. Mrs Hart remained in her native city for the rest of her life, contributing short fiction to the *New Brunswick Reporter and Fredericton Advertiser* and working on an unpublished two-volume novel, *Edith; or, The doom*. In all her writing she revealed a heightened romantic sensibility and a strict adherence to the conventions of popular fiction. *St. Ursula's Convent* is therefore typical in introducing shipwrecks, kidnappers, exchanged babies, and a false priest into a sentimental story of Québec seigneurial and convent life. A less sensational novel is *Tonnewonte; or The adopted son of America* (Watertown, N.Y., 1824-5), a two-volume romance published in three different editions in the United States after the Harts had moved there in 1824. Set in France and in upper-state New York, *Tonnewonte* appealed to American patriotic feelings by contrasting the democratic opportunities and naturalness of American life with the chaos and class-consciousness of France during the Napoleonic era. Like *St. Ursula's Convent*, it also reflected Mrs Hart's interest in incorporating North American history and landscape into her fiction. This interest was extended into her writing of *Edith; or The doom*, which focuses on a family curse and its expiation during the time of the American Revolution. In her preface to *St. Ursula's Convent* Mrs Hart noted that the 'dawn of literary illumination' had not yet come to British North America. For the rest of her life she saw her fiction as part of a process of literary awakening, and as an encouragement to 'others of real and intrinsic merit' to write.

GWENDOLYN DAVIES

Harvey, Jean-Charles (1891-1967). Born at La Malbaie (Murray Bay), Qué., Harvey took the traditional 'cours classique' at the Petit Séminaire de Chicoutimi (1905-8), then spent several years as a Jesuit scholastic (1908-15). A reporter with *La Presse* (1915) and *La Patrie* (1916-18), he was subsequently hired by La Machine agricole nationale in Montmagny to handle the firm's public relations. In 1922 he moved to *Le Soleil* in Quebec City, acting as editor-in-chief from 1927 until Apr. 1934, when he was relieved of this position the day after the Archbishop of Québec condemned his novel *Les demi-civilisés*. Premier Taschereau appointed Harvey director of the Office of Statistics for Québec, but after Maurice Duplessis's election in Aug. 1936 he was fired a second time. For nine years Harvey published his own weekly newspaper, *Le Jour* (1937-46). After the war he lectured widely, worked as a radio commentator (with CBC International and CKAC), and edited two papers, *Le Petit Journal* and *Le Photo Journal* (1953-66). Interested for a time in Marxist theory, he had become a staunch anti-Communist by the late 1940s. Later, during the unsettled 1960s, Harvey defended both federalism and bilingualism and spoke out against separatism, warning his anglophone friends, however, that Québécois would need constitutional changes guaranteeing the survival of their language and culture if they were to realize their full potential as North American francophones within a federalist state.

Harvey's career as writer paralleled that of journalist and public commentator. Author of the three novels—*Marcel Faure* (1922), *Les demi-civilisés* (1934; 2nd edn 1962), and *Le paradis de sable* (1953)—he also wrote three collections of short stories: *L'homme qui va* (1926), *Sébastien Pierre* (1935), and *Des bois . . . des champs . . . des bêtes* (1965), as well as a volume of poetry, *La fille du silence* (1958).

Among his six volumes of essays are *Pages de critique* (1926), *Art et combat* (1937), *Les grenouilles demandent un roi* (1942; Eng. trans. *The eternal struggle*, 1943), and *Pourquois je suis anti-séparatiste* (1962). He was awarded the medal of the Officier de l'Académie française in 1928 and the Prix David in 1929.

In *Marcel Faure* Harvey criticized the conservatism of Québec's business and clerical élite and denounced the widespread exploitation of the working class. By introducing a radically new, technically oriented education for his workers, Faure sets up a steel company owned and operated by French Canadians that competes successfully with Anglo-American businesses and transforms a tiny village on the St Lawrence into a thriving community.

Harvey's best-known novel, *Les demi-civilisés*, marks a turning-point in the liberation of Québec fiction from unrealistic and socially irrelevant depictions of life and morality. Here he condemns the control of Québec's economy by the English community and, more significantly, scathingly denounces the power of the Québec clergy in all spheres, attacking in particular their betrayal of the spirit of the Gospel message. Through the sexual liaison of Max Hubert and Dorothée Meunier and the free-thinking ideas of their revolutionary magazine, Harvey criticizes the lack of intellectual and moral freedom in Québec during the 1920s. His anti-clericalism is harshly expressed through Hermann Lillois, who wonders what Christ would think of 'the triple alliance of capital, civil power and the Church' that keeps his people in fear and 'servile silence'. This attack on the political, economic, and religious *status quo* brought a swift public condemnation of the book by Cardinal Villeneuve. As a result of writing this novel Harvey was for many years a pariah, but he is now recognized in Québec as a defender of intellectual, moral, and artistic freedom. *Les demi-civilisés* was first translated as *Sackcloth for banner* (1938). A recent and far-superior translation, *Fear's folly* (1982), was made by John GLASSCO.

Two major studies of Harvey's works are Guildo Rousseau's *Jean-Charles Harvey et son oeuvre romanesque* (1969) and Marcel-Aimé Gagnon's *Jean-Charles Harvey, précurseur de la révolution tranquille* (1970). See also John O'Connor's long introduction to *Fear's folly*.

RAMON HATHORN

Harvey, Moses (1820-1901). An Irishman

of Scottish descent, Harvey was born in Armagh and educated at Belfast, where he was ordained as a minister in the Presbyterian church in 1844. In 1852 he became pastor of St Andrew's Free Presbyterian Church in St John's, Nfld, and was soon prominent as a lecturer on biblical and scientific subjects. In 1878 he retired from the active ministry, apparently because his voice failed him, and dedicated himself to the profession of letters. In 1891 he was awarded an honorary LL.D. by McGill University. He committed suicide in St John's.

Harvey was a writer of wide interests, great industry and enthusiasm, and impressive ability. A Victorian polymath and optimist, he ranged in subject matter over history, science, poetry, religion, and contemporary society. A belief in progress was his *idée fixe*. He declared his faith that 'We are now on the topmost billow of this mighty tide of progress' in his early publication, *The characteristic features of the present age, and the prospects of the coming era: a lecture delivered to the Mechanics' Institutions of Workington and Maryport* (1849). His literary life was preoccupied with reiterating this theme. There is little that is lighthearted or imaginative in his writing, although it should be noted that his 'Chronicles of Punch Bowl' in the *Maritime Monthly* of 1873 and 1874 are an early attempt to fictionalize a Newfoundland outport. But he is usually a serious propounder of some beneficial notion, a supplier of information, an educator, or propagandist. His earnestness is displayed in his first book of general interest, *Lectures, literary and biographical* (Edinburgh, 1864), a miscellany of rambling essays on literature and science that showed his grasp of current ideas. One of the papers in the book, 'Human progress—Is it real?', was later expanded into a work portentously entitled *Where are we and whither tending? Three lectures on the reality and worth of human progress* (Boston, 1886).

In the late 1860s Harvey started applying his principles to his adopted country and began what might be described as a massive publicity campaign on behalf of the colony. In periodical articles, newspaper columns, speeches, encyclopaedia entries, and books, he indefatigably brought the potential of Newfoundland to the attention of outsiders. The most relentless, and possibly the most gifted, of a generation of literary boosters of Newfoundland, he wrote: *This Newfoundland of ours: a lecture* (St John's, 1878); *Across Newfoundland with the governor; a visit to our mining region; and This Newfoundland of ours. Being a series of papers on the natural resources and future prospects of the colony* (St John's, 1879); *Newfoundland; the oldest British colony, its history, its present condition, and its prospects in the future* (London, 1883); *Hand-book of Newfoundland: containing an account of its agricultural and mineral lands, its forests, and other natural resources* (Boston, 1886); *Newfoundland as it is in 1894: a hand-book and tourist's guide* (St John's and London, 1894); *Newfoundland in 1897; being Queen Victoria's diamond jubilee year and the four hundredth anniversary of the discovery of the island by John Cabot* (London, 1897); and *Newfoundland in 1900; a treatise of the geography, natural resources and history of the island, embracing an account of recent and present large material movements* (New York and St John's, 1900). This last book was reissued in 1902 as *Newfoundland at the beginning of the 20th century, a treatise of history and development* (it was characteristic of Harvey to recycle material under different titles). The most important of these works was *Newfoundland; the oldest British colony*, which was written in collaboration with the English novelist and journalist Joseph Hatton (1841-1907). There was an American edition (1883) and two years later it appeared in an abridged version for Newfoundland schools. Harvey's numerous publications, with their burning message about the country's resources, possibly had incalculable effects upon generations of Newfoundland writers.

In addition to the works listed, Harvey wrote four theological tracts: *Thoughts on the poetry and literature of the Bible* (St John's, 1853); *The testimony of Nineveh to the veracity of the Bible* (St John's, 1854); *Lectures on the harmony of science and Revelation* (Halifax and St John's, 1856); and *Lectures on Egypt and its monuments, as illustrative of Scripture* (St John's, 1857). He also published an edition of W.E. Cormack's *Narrative of a journey across the island of Newfoundland* (St John's, 1873).   PATRICK O'FLAHERTY

Hatton, Joseph. See FOREIGN WRITERS ON CANADA IN ENGLISH: 1.

Haultain, Arnold. See ESSAYS IN ENGLISH: 2.

Hawley, William Fitz (1804?-55). Born in Lacolle, Lower Canada (Qué.), he lived at various times in both Quebec and Montreal. At his death in Laprairie he was registrar of No. 1 Division of the County of Huntingdon. He began to publish poetry in Canadian newspapers and periodicals in 1826, and his continuing appearances therein made him well known and admired as a native Canadian writer. Some of his early verse was collected in *Quebec, the harp, and other poems* (Montreal, 1829). The long poem 'Quebec' describes the grandeur of the city's site and history; 'The harp', which won a prize from the Quebec Society for the Encouragement of the Arts and Sciences, displays a thorough knowledge of classical mythology; 'The triumph of envy' is a thinly veiled account of the effects of slander in an unnamed garrison city; other shorter poems deal with familiar human scenes and emotions.

Hawley also published *The unknown; or the lays of the forest* (Montreal, 1831), a short novel interspersed with narrative poems. The first English-Canadian fiction to be set in New France—in this case Trois-Rivières in 1633—it is about the rescue of a French maiden captured by Indians, and has enough suspense to make the reader impatient of the tedious but competent interpolations: four long poems with Greek, Persian, and Roman settings, the supposed work of the novel's hero. The preface points out that this structure derives from Thomas Moore's *Lalla Rookh* (1817), a prose story in which the hero narrates four oriental tales in verse. Hawley's hero, 'the Unknown', whose real name is never given, is a young Frenchman who attempts to win the Indians to a more settled life by adopting their ways and gaining their confidence. The Indians, however, are too wise to agree to his plan and he settles, in the end, for marriage to the maiden in whose rescue he has been instrumental. Both 'the Unknown' and the girl's father, M. de Lauzon, are instructed in New World survival by Piscaret, an Algonquin chief—a 'noble savage' for whose character Hawley owes much to Chateaubriand. The three female protagonists are one-dimensional, but the males, both European and Indian, are somewhat complex. Both scenery and action are realistically described.

Two other books, *The legend of Niagara* and *History of the Canadas*, were announced in 1830 and 1837 respectively but never appeared. Hawley collected a great number of five-shilling subscriptions for the latter; in 1840, when the subscribers began to demand either the book or a refund, he was still promising that it would be published shortly.　　　　MARY LU MacDONALD

Hayes, John. See CHILDREN'S LITERATURE IN ENGLISH: 6.

Hayman, Robert (1575-1629). Reared in Devon, Eng., he was a graduate of Exeter College, Oxford, and a student at Lincoln's Inn, London. During his stay at Lincoln's Inn, 'his geny being well known to be poetical', he became acquainted with Michael Drayton, Ben Jonson, George Withers, and other poets. Around 1618 he became governor of the Bristol merchants' plantation at Bristol's Hope in Conception Bay, Nfld. His initial visit to the colony was for fifteen months; he returned in successive summers until around 1628. In an address to Charles I in 1628 Hayman admitted that the commodities so far retrieved from Newfoundland 'are in their particulars base, and meane'; yet, he added, 'they honestly imploye many people'. He proposed that Charles rename the island Britaniola. Hayman died while on an expedition up the Oyapock River in South America.

Hayman was the author of *Qvodlibets, lately come over from New Britaniola, old Newfound-land. Epigrams and other small parcels, both morall and diuine. The first foure bookes being the authors owne: the rest translated out of that excellent epigrammatist, Mr. Iohn Owen, and other rare authors: With two epistles of that excellently wittie doctor, Francis Rablais: translated out of his French at large. All of them composed and done at Harbor-Grace in Britaniola, anciently called Newfound-Land* (London, 1628). The first book of English poetry to be written in what is now Canada, it contains much uncritical praise of the climate and resources of Newfoundland. In this respect Hayman is to be linked with such propagandists for settlement in Newfoundland as Richard Whitbourne and William Vaughan. As poetry, *Quodlibets* (i.e. 'What you will') is rough, homely verse, with here and there a touch of irony or a compelling phrase. Hayman knew his book consisted of 'bad unripe Rimes', but he apparently published it to make a point about the literary potential of the new colony: 'For if I now growne dull and aged, could doe somewhat, what will not sharper, younger, freer inventions performe there?' He was thus a conscious pioneer—not just as a colonist, but also as a poet.　　　　PATRICK O'FLAHERTY

Hearne, Samuel. See EXPLORATION LITERATURE IN ENGLISH: 2.

Heavysege, Charles (1816-76). His birthplace has been given as Huddersfield, Eng., but in letters to the London critic Charles Lanman, Heavysege claims only that his 'ancestors on the paternal side' were from Yorkshire and that Bayard Taylor's article in the *Atlantic Monthly* (Oct. 1865), which gave Liverpool as his birthplace, was 'generally correct.' He immigrated to Canada in 1853 and settled in Montreal, where he was employed as a woodcarver in a cabinet works. He later became a journalist on the staff of the *Transcript* and the *Daily Witness*.

There are two versions of Heavysege's first dramatic poem, *The revolt of Tartarus*, a six-book epic in blank verse. The first version, bearing his name, was published in London and Liverpool in 1852; the second, considerably edited, appeared anonymously in Montreal in 1855. His successive poems and dramas draw from the Bible, Shakespeare, Byron's *Cain* and 'Hebrew melodies', and the popular dramas *Saul* and *Filippo* by Vittorio Alfieri.

In *Saul: a drama in three parts* (Montreal, 1857) Saul's character is developed to show a growing hubris that ultimately becomes satanic. Coventry Patmore, in an unsigned review in *The British North American*, praised it as 'indubitably the best poem ever written out of Great Britain.' Much of Heavysege's subsequent literary effort was dedicated to the rewriting of *Saul,* his best work: a second edition was published in London and Montreal in 1859, a third in Boston in 1859. This third edition was reprinted by John Lovell in 1876; in 1967 it was reprinted in *Saul and selected poems*, with a critical introduction by Sandra Djwa.

The verbal wit and sustained eroticism of the tragicomedy *Count Filippo; or The unequal marriage* (Montreal, 1860; rpr. 1973) made the drama unpalatable to Victorian Canada. In *Jephthah's daughter* (Montreal, London, 1865) Heavysege turns to the Bible for its saga of the great but rash Israelite leader who must sacrifice his daughter to keep his vow to God. Heavysege's protagonists are typically romantic rebels ruled by a dominant passion: Saul is proud and Jephthah rash. Paradoxically, however, each is placed within the old Shakespearian world of order and universal degree where spiritual revolt must be punished.

Heavysege wrote a number of shorter poems, many of which are now unavailable. Copies of his *Sonnets* (Montreal, 1856), 'The owl', a poem of twenty-five stanzas, and the 'Ode' read at the Shakespeare Tercentenary in Montreal on 23 Apr. 1864, have not been found. He included some sonnets in *Jephthah's daughter*, four of which are in *Saul and selected poems*. An undistinguished excerpt from the 'Ode' was published in the *New Dominion Monthly* of 1876. 'The dark huntsman' was published in the *Canadian Monthly and National Review* (Aug. 1876) with the mistaken assertion that the poem was written just before his death; an earlier version had been published by the Witness press of Montreal in 1864. 'Jezebel'—a poem that appeared in the *New Dominion Monthly* (Jan. 1868) and was reprinted by Golden Dog Press, Ottawa, in 1972—contains a description of the death of Jezebel, her bones licked by dogs, that has a macabre vitality. Heavysege also published a novel, *The advocate* (Montreal, 1865; rpr. 1973). A potboiler of unassimilated Gothic elements, it marshals an improbably euphuistic style under chapter headings culled from Shakespeare.

Overvalued during his lifetime by critics wishing to assert the existence of a Canadian literature, Heavysege has been undervalued since his death, largely because of the wave of revisionist criticism in the 1920s that dismissed him as British rather than Canadian, partly because the bulk of closet drama and the connotations of his name encourage easy satire. Robertson DAVIES in *Leaven of Malice* puns on the 'heavy' aspects of *Saul* and wittily dubs his fictional critic, Solly Bridgetower, as the Heavysege man in 'Amcan'. Yet Heavysege was an examplar to the early poets Charles SANGSTER, Charles G.D. ROBERTS, and W.D. LIGHTHALL, and was admired by the moderns W.W.E. ROSS and A.J.M. SMITH. It is his presentation of nature—the backdrop to the sacrifice of Jephthah's daughter—on which Northrop FRYE leans heavily in his highly influential critical thesis of the existence of cruel nature in English Canadian poetry. (This interpretation is doubtful, however, as Heaveysege borrows his description from Tennyson's *Morte d'Arthur*.) To the modern reader Heavysege offers passages of genuine poetic vigour and psychological insight. Handicapped by limitations in his literary background and by the lack of a supportive Canadian culture, his considerable achievements in his best works, *Saul* and *Jephthah's daughter*, are all the more impressive. He is the major figure in the Canadian literary world up to 1870.   SANDRA DJWA

Hébert, Anne (b. 1916). Born at Sainte-Catherine-de-Fossambault, Qué., she spent her childhood and adolescence in Quebec

City and since the mid-1950s has been living in Paris, making frequent visits to Canada. For her distinguished poetry and fiction she was awarded the Molson Prize in 1967, and in 1982 she won the Prix Fémina for her novel *Les fous de Bassan*.

Anne Hébert's father, Maurice Hébert, who was a provincial civil servant and an exacting literary critic, encouraged his daughter to write and had a distinct influence on the rigour of her style. Another considerable influence, this time on the content of her writing, was that of her cousin, Hector de Saint-Denys GARNEAU. A privileged witness to the development of his poetry, Hébert assimilated some of his major symbols (hand, heart, bone, the word, etc.), while modifying them considerably. His death in 1943 shattered all Hébert's tranquil notions, and her own writing would henceforth be marked by revolt. Beginning with the short story 'Le torrent' (written in 1945), her characters would be rebellious, in open revolt against their fate as Québécois.

Hébert's first collection of relatively traditional poems, *Les songes en équilibre* (1942), which won the Prix David, depicts a mournful existence steeped in dream. However, overly cautious publishers would delay until 1950 the appearance of her collection of short stories *Le torrent*; the title story, about repression, has a powerful explosive charge that was, for informed readers, a symbolic depiction of the French Canadian's inner deprivation. (*Le torrent* was reissued with four new stories in 1963.)

Meanwhile Hébert was working on a collection of poems, *Le tombeau des rois* (1953), in which harsh revolt is given a highly personal expression and an ultimately liberating outcome. The title poem, a classic of modern Québécois literature, is an exploration of the unconscious filled with symbols: a bird (the poet), kings (the voices of the past), jewels and flowers (the allurements of the dead), water (dread), closed chambers (tombs), bones (death), and light (an awakening). Here liberation is as much psychological as poetic and consists in mentally expelling the figures of dead kings—those master-images, with civil as well as religious significance, that had for so long dominated the colonized, clericalized minds of the Québécois.

A similar liberation appeared in the rather static novel *Les chambres de bois* (1958). Catherine marries Michel, whose life is dominated by dreams. He forces his young wife to live shut away in their Parisian rooms, then leads her to the gates of death. Catherine revolts, and in the last part of the novel we see her in a situation of light and love.

In 1954 Hébert began a new cycle of poems inspired by light, the sun, the world, and the word: *Mystère de la parole*, which was published in Paris in 1960, along with a new edition of *Le tombeau des rois*, under the title *Poèmes* (winner of a Governor General's Award). Thus Hébert's poetic trajectory was complete: from writing about solitary, anguished dreams, she had arrived at a form of expression that was both opulent and committed to the real world.

Anne Hébert's plays—*Le temps sauvage*, *La mercière assassinée*, and *Les invités au procès*, published in a single volume under the title *Le temps sauvage* in 1967—transpose into dramatic terms her progression from dream to language. In *Le temps sauvage*, her major play, she describes the progress of Québec from rural and silent to urban and dynamic. The central character, Agnès, would like to keep her children 'outside of time', in her own silent, maternal night; the children grow impatient, force destiny, and in the end Agnès agrees to live in a world of speech and communication.

Hébert next started to work on a four-novel cycle that begins in the nineteenth century and gradually moves into recent times. KAMOURASKA (1970), her most important and best-known novel, was based on an actual murder committed in nineteenth-century Québec. *Les enfants du sabbat* (1975), set in the 1930s and 1940s, is a story of sorcery based on rigorous research into ancient and local witchcraft. The central character, Julie, and her brother Joseph, are the children of parents who live on the fringes of society and engage in secret practices in the countryside outside Quebec City. Hébert uses the technique of flashback, but with a twist; Sister Julie of the Trinity, who is gifted with vision into the past, mentally leaves her convent and is literally transported to her birthplace in her parents' shanty. The main action is set in the convent, where the nuns and church authorities are increasingly scandalized by the peculiar behaviour of Sister Julie, the daughter of a sorcerer, who is dedicated to sorcery through an initiatory rape by her father. She is submitted to divine exorcism, without result. Even worse, she finds herself mysteriously pregnant and gives birth to a baby that the authorities leave to die in the snow. However, the rebellious Julie runs away from the convent to join a waiting lover.

The third novel in this cycle, *Héloïse* (1980), is no less astonishing. Here the action is set in modern Paris and the author uses the devices of fantasy and somnambulism to show how a young man, Bernard, succumbs to the lure of death and the past as embodied in a dead woman who has become a vampire named Héloïse and wanders day and night through the Paris Métro sucking people's blood. In her latest novel, *Les fous de Bassan* (1982), Hébert skilfully blends the voices of the wind, the sea, and the birds (les fous de Bassan) with those of six narrators who try to reconstruct the dark events that occurred one August night in 1936 in the little English-speaking village of Griffin Creek in the Gaspé, when two lovely young girls, Nora and Olivia, were raped and murdered on the beach.

The astonishing violence of her plots, the rigour of her vocabulary, the sureness of her craft, and her intense dramatic sense have brought Anne Hébert an enviable reputation as a novelist that extends beyond her native Québec to reach both France and English Canada.

Hébert's fiction has been translated as *Kamouraska* (Norman Shapiro, 1974), *The silent rooms* (Kathy Mezei, 1975), *Children of the Black Sabbath* (Carol Dunlop-Hébert, 1978), and *Héloise* (Sheila Fischman, 1982). *The torrent* (1967) was translated by Gwendolyn Moore. Hébert's poems have been translated into English by Alan Brown (*Poems*, 1975), F.R. SCOTT, Peter Miller, and John GLASSCO. *Dialogues sur la traduction à propos du 'Tombeau des rois'* (1970), with a preface by Northrop FRYE, is an exchange of letters between Hébert and Scott about his translation of her important poem that first appeared in *The* TAMARACK REVIEW 23 (Summer 1962).

See two articles on Hébert's poetry in CANADIAN LITERATURE: Patricia Purcell, 'The agonizing solitude', in Issue 10 (Autumn 1961) and Kathy Mezei, 'Ann Hébert: a pattern repeated' in Issue 72 (Spring 1977). See also Pierre Pagé, *Anne Hébert* (1965); René Lacôte, *Anne Hébert* (1969); and Pierre H. Lemieux, *Entre songe et parole: structure du Tombeau des rois d'Anne Hébert* (1978).

See also NOVELS IN FRENCH 1940 TO 1959: 5; 1960 TO 1982: 3(e).   PIERRE H. LEMIEUX

Hébert, Marie-Francine. See CHILDREN'S DRAMA IN FRENCH.

Helwig, David (b. 1938). Born in Toronto, he lived there, in Hamilton, Ont., and on Niagara-on-the-Lake before attending the University of Toronto and doing graduate work at the University of Liverpool (1960-2). He then taught at Queen's University, Kingston. He has also worked as a story editor for CBC-TV, but has now returned to teaching at Queen's.

Helwig's lucid and direct poems were first collected in *Figures in a landscape* (1967); here they tend to focus on ordinary domestic events, but there are also poems on Edward Hicks, Canaletto, Matisse, Gordon Craig, and John Bunyan that grow out of Helwig's wide cultural interests, as well as two short plays, 'The dreambook' and 'The dancers of Colbek', and a two-act play, 'A time of winter'. Many of the poems in this volume were included in *The sign of the gunman* (1969), of which the title sequence indicates the movement his work has taken towards darker and more violent themes. In *The best name of silence* (1972) the poems attempt to extract meaning and security from life while wrestling with rapacity and greed; many are narratives or dramatic monologues whose characters struggle with spiritual crises in situations full of risk and danger. The narrative poems in *Atlantic crossing* (1974) focus on four travellers—a follower of St Brendan, a slave trader, Christopher Columbus, and a Norse woman—though some arise from old legends and fairy tales seen in terms of paradoxes in human behaviour, the stress of evil and violence against the urge to decency. Sometimes the polarities are moral calm and intelligence versus creative inventiveness or even madness. Such conflict is one of the principal themes established in the opening poem of *A book of the hours* (1979) concerning the scholar Thomas Bullfinch and his ward, though this volume also includes some of Helwig's lyrical contemplations of ordinary life.

Helwig's fiction is often thematically parallel to his poetry. *The streets of summer* (1969), a collection of short stories, emphasizes ordinary situations described in a sober, realistic mode. The grittier and shadowy aspects of life appear first in *A book about Billie* (1972), created from taperecorded interviews with a habitual criminal and revealing a fascination with criminal cleverness and cunning. *The day before tomorrow* (1971), about a diplomat turned spy, describes terror and violence in calm and measured prose. *The king's evil* (1981) juxtaposes contemporary existence with legendary and historical events.

Helwig

Helwig's most ambitious work in fiction is a tetralogy set in Kingston: *The glass knight* (1976), *Jennifer* (1979), *It is always summer* (1982), and *A sound like laughter* (1983). Robert Mallen, his wife Jennifer, or his lover Elizabeth Ross play major roles in all except *A sound like laughter*, which is the third novel in the sequence, although it was published a year later than *It is always summer*. In these novels Helwig skilfully conveys the complexity of ordinary lives as he describes with perceptive clarity the somewhat messy human relationships, the desires and disillusionments, of unexceptional people who, though often disagreeable or unattractive, are made sympathetic and even interesting.

Helwig has co-edited a series of short-story anthologies for OBERON PRESS (1970-5) and has edited several books of readings in the area of the social and political concerns of culture, including *The human elements* (1978; Second series, 1981) and *Love and money: the politics of culture* (1980).

See also NOVELS IN ENGLISH 1960 TO 1982: OTHER TALENTS, OTHER WORKS: 1.

PETER STEVENS

Hémon, Louis (1880-1913). Born in Brest, France, he moved to Paris with his family when he was still young. His father, Félix Hémon, was a university instructor and France's inspector-general of public education. Louis took courses in oriental languages at the Sorbonne and received a law degree. After finishing his military service at Chartres (1901-2), he set off for England (1903) and made London his home for eight years. In England, he honed his writing skills as correspondent for a French sports magazine (*Le Vélo*, later renamed *L'Auto*); he also won that magazine's literary contest in 1904 and 1906. During that period he married Lydia O'Kelly, with whom he had a daughter, Lydia Kathleen. Leaving both wife and daughter with her family in England, he set sail for Canada in 1911.

Hémon spent short periods in Quebec City and Montreal—he worked briefly as a bilingual stenographer for a Montreal insurance company—and then went north, living at Péribonka in the Lac Saint-Jean area, working on the farm of Samuel Bédard. It was there that he wrote his now-famous MARIA CHAPDELAINE: *récit du Canada français*. After sending the manuscript to France, he set out for western Canada but was killed in a train mishap at Chapleau, Ont., at the age of thirty-three.

Maria Chapdelaine appeared in serial form in *Le Temps* (Jan.-Feb. 1914) but was not published in book form in Canada until 1916. Criticized by some French Canadians for the unromantic view it presented of life among the *habitants*, it was nevertheless quickly recognized as an important work of fiction and has achieved the status of a classic. An English translation by William Hume BLAKE, with the subtitle *A tale of the Lake St. John country*, was published in 1921 and remains the standard one.

Hémon wrote other novels (*Battling Mallone, Colin-Maillard*, and *Monsieur Ripois et la Némésis*), as well as a collection of short stories (*La Belle que voilà*). All his works were published posthumously. A new edition of *Maria Chapdelaine* (Boréal Express, 1980), edited by Nicole Deschamps, is faithful to the original manuscript submitted by Hémon, and eliminates the many stylistic changes that had been effected by previous editors.

Louis Hémon's fascinating life and death have been the subject of much speculation. Since the seventies Hémon has been presented to the public as a rebel. Jacques Ferron, in his introduction to *Colin-Maillard*, (1972), sees him rejecting the values of an oppressively colonial France, seeking new vistas in England and Canada, and finally taking his own life at Chapleau. In *Le mythe de Maria Chapdelaine* (1980) Nicole Deschamps portrays Hémon as a social reformer whose novel seeks, not to glorify colonized Québécois, but to awaken in them a sense of their own plight. Deschamps previously edited *Louis Hémon, lettres à sa famille* (1968).

Alfred Ayotte and Victor Tremblay point out in *L'aventure Louis Hémon* (1974) that Hémon's birthdate, Oct. 12, is the anniversary of Columbus's discovery of America, which is presumably a reference to Hémon's 'discovery' of a North American culture virtually unknown to Europeans of the period. All that may be said with certainty about this extraordinary man is that his life and his work provoked French Canadians to scrutinize their own culture in a way they had never done before. For this reason alone, if for no other, Canadians may claim Hémon as their own.

PAUL SOCKEN

Hénault, Gilles (b. 1920). Born at St Majorique, Qué., and educated in Montreal, he quit school early owing to financial circumstances and subsequently educated himself through voracious reading. He trained as a

344

journalist with *Le Jour* (1939), *Le Canada* (1940-2), and *La Presse* (1942-4). He then worked with the news service of Radio-Canada (1945-6) and the radio-station CKAC (1946-7). A union organizer and publicist in Montreal and Sudbury from 1949 to 1956, he resumed his journalistic career in 1957, working as a freelance writer for Radio-Canada till 1959, when he became head of the arts and letters section at *Le Devoir*; in 1961 he was a commentator on international affairs at *Le Nouveau Journal*. In 1962-3 he worked as a writer for the Royal Commission on Bilingualism and Biculturalism. He taught improvisation at the École Nationale de Théâtre in 1964 and was an interviewer for Radio-Canada in 1965. Appointed director of the Museum of Contemporary Art in Montreal in 1966, he held that position until 1971, when he became an adviser on museum affairs with the Department of Cultural Affairs of Québec. Since 1973 he has worked as a freelance writer and translated several books; he was writer-in-residence at the Université d'Ottawa in 1974-5 and conducted writing workshops at the Université du Québec à Montréal in 1976 and 1977.

Hénault was co-founder with Éloi DE GRANDMONT, in 1946, of Les Cahiers de la file indienne, a series in which his first collection of poems, *Théâtre en plein air*, was published that very year. He was already preparing the way for a new era in Québec poetry that explored a cosmic dimension, that searched for an elemental centre from which liberation could spring forth, trusting in the power of words to re-create the world, and employing surrealistic images— all of which were to be essential preoccupations of the new generation of poets. However, despite his association with the Montreal writers and painters known as Les Automatistes, and the influence exerted by surrealism at the time, Hénault resisted the 'automatic' mode of writing: his poetry preserved a clarity and intelligibility that it was never to lose. Indeed, reason and irony remained his chosen weapons against oppression. Although actively involved in social issues, he did not write overtly militant poetry; rather he believed that poetry and life are, and should be kept in, a dialectical, complementary relationship. He expressed this view in 'La poésie et la vie', his contribution to *La poésie et nous* (1958), a collection of essays by Michael Van Schendel, Jacques BRAULT, Wilfred Lemoine, Yves PRÉFONTAINE, and Hénault. His second volume of poems, *Totems* (1953), revives a mythical In-

dian presence, images of a wild virgin land to be reclaimed. The imagery embodies the theme of a call for new beginnings that was taken up by most subsequent Québec writing. It is, however, in his preoccupation with the autonomy of words that Hénault is the precursor of modernity in Québec poetry: his poems attempt to create a world of language rather than to use language to describe any particular perception of the world. This preoccupation, already present in his first books, is amplified in *Voyages au pays de mémoire* (1959) and *Sémaphore* (1962); the latter was awarded the Prix du Grand Jury des Lettres and the second prize in the Concours littéraire du Québec. Hénault's poetry reveals a constant struggle with language: the need to express truly the self and its environment drives him to fight linguistic and literary conventions to the point of wishing to produce a 'naked scream'; simultaneously he is tempted by a purely self-referential use of language. These conflicting forces are nevertheless subordinated to the pervasive desire to create a poetry that is a 'signal'—a rallying point for potential seekers of a new reality. This is suggested by the title of his latest book, *Signaux pour les voyants* (1972), in which his previous work was collected; it also contains 'L'invention de la roue' (1941), four 'Allégories' (1941), and 'Dix poèmes de dissidence'. *Signaux* won a Governor General's Award, a timely recognition of Hénault's work as a significant turning-point.

English translations of Hénault's poems are available in *Hénault—seven poems, from Le Théâtre en plein air and Totems* (1955); in *The poetry of French Canada in translation* (1970) edited by John GLASSCO; and in *Ellipse* 18 (1976).

See H. Corriveau, *Gilles Hénault: lecture de Sémaphore* (1978).   MICHEL PARMENTIER

Henday, Anthony. See EXPLORATION LITERATURE IN ENGLISH: 2.

Hendry, Tom (b. 1929). When Tom Hendry started his practice as a chartered accountant in Winnipeg in 1955, he was also writing short stories for the CBC, acting in television and amateur productions, and playing the part of Buddy Jackson in the radio serial *The Jacksons and their neighbours*. His first play, *Do you remember?*, originally produced by CBC Winnipeg in 1954, was directed by John Hirsch for the Rainbow Stage in the summer of 1957. That same year Hirsch and Hendry co-founded Theatre

77, which later became the Manitoba Theatre Centre. After giving up accounting in 1960 to work in the theatre full time, Hendry was the producer of Winnipeg's Rainbow Stage for several years, and then returned to the Manitoba Theatre Centre, which produced his plays *Trapped* (1961) and *All about us* (1964), a musical revue that toured the country. From 1964 to 1969 he was the secretary-general of the Canadian Theatre Centre and in 1967 was awarded the Centennial Medal for his service to Canadian theatre. Since then he has served as literary manager for the Stratford Festival for one year, co-founded Playwrights Co-op and Toronto Free Theatre, and in 1974 helped create the Banff Playwrights Colony (which workshopped a number of his unpublished plays) and directed its program for two years. His three-year association with the CBC as a writer for *King of Kensington* ended in 1969. He is currently treasurer of Playwrights Canada and president of Toronto Free Theatre.

Hendry's *Fifteen miles of broken glass*, produced by CBC-TV in 1966 and adapted for the stage in 1969, won the 1970 Lieutenant-Governor's Medal. The central character, Alec McNabb, a passionately committed air-force cadet, despairs when the Second World War ends three months before he comes of age. Some people were outraged by Hendry's musical *Gravediggers of 1942* (1973)—with music by Steven Jack—which contrasts the facts of the Dieppe disaster with the youthful enthusiasm of a group of kids trying to raise money for war bonds. But this play, like *Fifteen miles*, points out how naively courageous Canadians were and how much they wanted to be a part of things. In both plays the idealistic and romantic yearning to participate in a great conflict is set against the harsh realities the young characters must later face.

Satyricon (1969)—called by the author a 'disposable opera'—was the first big-budget Canadian play performed at the Avon Theatre, Stratford. It is a satire on middle-class values and vulgarity based on the satirical romance by Nero's resident arbiter of elegance, Petronius. The songs by Stanley Silverman became the basis for Richard Foreman's off-Broadway production *Doctor Selavy's magic theatre* (1972), the United Artists recording of which is now a collector's album. Hendry's next major work, *How are things with the walking wounded?* (1972), set in Montreal during Expo 67, opens with Willy, an affluent English-Canadian busi-

nessman, hosting a party for his young French-Canadian lover, René, in celebration of their homosexual marriage. Much to his dismay Willy discovers that his fortune is not enough to keep René, and he is left to re-arrange his alliances.

Hendry's more recent *Byron*, with music by Steven Jack (1976), and *Hogtown: Toronto the Good* (1981), with music by Paul Hoffert, both present imagined meetings and struggles between historic figures. In *Byron* Harriet Beecher Stowe, a friend of Lady Byron's, visits Lord Byron in Italy and, with puritanical zeal, rails against his aristocratic humanitarian stance. She demands from him heroic action. The central characters in *Hogtown* are taken from local history: Toronto mayor William Howland and the madam of a brothel, Belle Howard. In spite of a structurally complex script and the ambitious attempt to mount a full-scale musical, *Hogtown* was poorly produced and closed early. Although *Hogtown* presented its material lightheartedly, at its core was an important issue: the legislation of civic morality. The use of serious subject matter, plus the inclusion of a musical score that is intended to widen the work's popular appeal, are characteristic of Hendry's plays. Hendry's most recent work is an adaptation of *The merchant of Venice*, which was produced at the Toronto Free Theatre in the spring of 1982.

See Robert Wallace and Cynthia Zimmerman, *The work: conversations with English-Canadian playwrights* (1982).

CYNTHIA ZIMMERMAN

Hennepin, Louis. See Writing in NEW FRANCE: 1.

Henry, Alexander, the Elder. See EXPLORATION LITERATURE IN ENGLISH: 2.

Henry, George. See INDIAN LITERATURE: 2.

Henry, Walter (1791-1860). Born in Donegal, Ire., he became a surgeon in the British army. In 1827 he was posted to Canada with the 66th Regiment and remained here until his death. He was well known in the medical world of his time; internationally because he had been an observer at Napoleon's autopsy, and in Canada because of his advanced views on hygiene and the treatment of cholera. He held the important post of Inspector-General of Military Hospitals before he retired in 1855 to Belleville, Canada West (Ont.).

Henry was also a well-known literary figure in Canada. His two-volume memoirs *Trifles from my port-folio; or Recollections of scenes and small adventures during twenty-nine years' military service in the Peninsular War and invasion of France, the East Indies, campaign in Nepaul, St Helena during the detention and until the death of Napoleon, and Upper and Lower Canada*, printed by William Neilson at Quebec in 1839, sold three times as many copies as John RICHARDSON's *Canadian brothers* when it appeared the following year. The memoirs were widely reviewed and praised. In 1843, revised and considerably extended, and retitled *Events of a military life*, the work was published in London by William Pickering, again receiving extensive laudatory notices. Henry was an associate member of the Quebec Literary and Historical Society when he did not reside in that city, and one of its active officers when his regiment was stationed there. He wrote frequently for the New York *Albion*, using the pseudonyms 'Miles' and 'Piscator'. As 'Miles' he wrote commentaries on British North American politics, and as 'Piscator' he described his fishing adventures—fishing being his lifetime hobby.

Trifles from my port-folio includes ten very mediocre poems, and *Events of a military life* ends with a conventional short story set in New France about 1640, recounting the love of a noble young Frenchman for a beautiful Indian maiden whom he finally marries. But the value of these volumes is in the autobiography: the maturing of a very young officer through the peninsular campaigns, where the savagery of war is mixed with amorous adventures; the campaigns in India, a country he disliked intensely; the intrigues at St Helena; a depressing return to his native Ireland; and the final posting to Canada. From his account of Canadian events in the decade before the Rebellion of 1837-8, he does not appear to have been sympathetic to either Papineau or Mackenzie or their cause.

Henry's memoirs are solidly rooted in the custom of his age, which saw many army officers publish autobiographical accounts of their adventures. They are more interesting and better written than many of the genre. His fellow citizens were proud of his attainments and frequently referred to the honour he brought to Canada by residing here.   MARY LU MacDONALD

Herbert, John (b. 1926). Born John Herbert Brundage, he was educated in Toronto until age seventeen, when he went to work, first in the advertising department of Eaton's. Following a six-month sentence in the Guelph reformatory in 1946—the outcome of being harassed by local toughs and accused by them of homosexuality at a time when it was illegal—he worked at a variety of jobs. In 1955 he began to study ballet and theatre in Toronto, and during the 1960s he served successively as artistic director for three Toronto theatre companies, including his own Garret Theatre. Dancer, playwright, director, designer, stage manager and novelist, he has also held appointments in theatre at universities and the editorship of an arts newspaper, *Onion*.

Of Herbert's published dramas, the most famous is *Fortune and men's eyes* (1967; 2nd edn 1974). Set in a Canadian reformatory, it explicitly derives from, but does not duplicate, his own crucial experience of incarceration. The hero, Smitty, an inexperienced seventeen-year-old—through psychological pressure, physical abuse, and homosexual harassment—changes from a person of innocent decency into an aggressive, domineering, violent homosexual predator. Violent also in language and powerfully frank in its delineation of homosexual personality and conflict throughout, the play is particularly moving in its penultimate episode in which Jan, normally passive and pliant, refuses Smitty's physical advances, stressing the strength and redeeming power of genuine affection. *Fortune and men's eyes* was given a workshop at the Stratford Festival in 1965 and received its first commercial production at the Actors' Playhouse, in New York, in Feb. 1967; the film adaptation (1971) was directed by Harvey Hart.

Omphale and the hero (1974) is reminiscent of, but does not imitate, the style and technique of Tennessee Williams. Realistic in situation and dialogue, it calls for expressionism in its set design and in the characters' personalities; but it is also implicitly allegorical, offering the audience an opportunity to equate the characters and their predicaments with cultural, political, economic, and moral circumstances in Canada. In a town on the border between two French- and English-speaking provinces, a drifter, Mac, and a prostitute, Antoinette, become lovers out of loneliness and a need for comfort. Partly because of greed, partly under pressure from the mayor and policeman, Mac deserts Antoinette for a rich Italian widow.

Herbert

Four short plays published together as *Some angry summer songs* (1976)—*Peace divers*, *Beer room*, *Close friends* and *The dinosaurs*—also deal with varieties of relationship and betrayal, further exploring the frequent emphasis in Herbert's work on the desperate need people have for human contact, the desperate measures they will take to achieve it, and the even more despairing retreats they will often ultimately choose in favour of personal security and safety.

ANTHONY HOPKINS

Herbert, Sarah (1824-46) and **Mary Eliza** (1829-72). Sarah and Mary Eliza Herbert were half-sisters born in Ireland and Halifax, N.S., respectively. Raised and educated in a staunch temperance and Methodist environment, both women devoted much of their energy to Sabbath School, Temperance Society, and Benevolent Society activities in Halifax.

Sarah Herbert conducted a school in 1843-4 and from 1844 to 1845 acted as editor of a temperance newspaper, *The Olive Branch*. Between 1840 and 1846 her religious and domestic poetry appeared in regional publications under the pseudonym 'Sarah'. Appealing to pious and conventional tastes, her verse established her literary reputation in the Maritimes and created an audience for her two fictional works. *Agnes Maitland* (Halifax, 1843), a fluently written but didactic tale, won a temperance award from *The Olive Branch* for its dramatization of a self-indulgent woman's descent into alcoholism. Its serialized successor, *The history of a Halifax belle* (*The Olive Branch*, 1844), was even more relentless in denouncing 'the serpent coils of the pernicious habit', and reinforced the impression that Sarah's interest in fiction lay in its utilitarian rather than its aesthetic possibilities. Her early death from tuberculosis captured the public imagination, and for many years afterward her sister Mary Eliza's literary reputation was overshadowed by the memory of 'the gifted authoress' Miss Herbert.

By 1851, however, Mary Eliza Herbert had established her name by publishing occasional verse and by founding a women's literary periodical, *The Mayflower; or, Ladies' Acadian Newspaper*. Always supportive of regional writing, this journal became an outlet for Mary Eliza's poetry and prose, written in a romantic and commemorative vein. It also published her first long fiction, *Emily Linwood; or The bow of promise* (1851) and *Ambrose Mandeville* (1852), two novellas

about the devout woman of educated heart who was to be a convention in all Mary Eliza's narratives. After the collapse of *The Mayflower* in 1852 because of poor economic conditions and competition from American journals, Mary Eliza contributed poems and prose-sketches to *The Novascotian*, *The Provincial Wesleyan*, and the Halifax *Morning Sun*, and published some of her poems and occasional pieces in *The Aeolian harp; or Miscellaneous poems* (Halifax, 1857) and *Flowers by the wayside: a miscellany of prose and verse* (Halifax, 1865). *The Aeolian harp*, containing poetry by the deceased Sarah as well as by Mary Eliza, became a popular gift book in the Maritimes and did much to enhance the reputation of the sisters as writers of genteel verse.

Of Mary Eliza's three fictions published after the demise of *The Mayflower*, *Belinda Dalton; or Scenes in the life of a Halifax belle* (Halifax, 1859) best illustrates the author's potential for developing lively confrontation, local colour, and domestic detail. While less emphatic in its treatment of the marriage theme than *Lucy Cameron*, her unpublished novel, *Belinda Dalton* reveals Mary Eliza's insight into the financial vulnerability of women in Victorian society. Unfortunately she tended to sacrifice social analysis and in-depth characterization to the conventions of popular moral fiction, and *Woman as she should be; or Agnes Wiltshire* (Halifax, 1861) and *The young men's choice* (Halifax, 1869) suffered from the same didacticism and sentimentality found in her earlier novels. In the last years of her life, Mary Eliza occasionally published excerpts from a manuscript entitled *A woman's thoughts on passages of scripture* and continued to make regular contributions in prose and verse to regional publications. Much respected locally for her lyric poetry and sentimental fiction, she represented the last of a coterie of Nova Scotian Methodists who, between the 1840s and the 1870s, made Halifax and *The Provincial Wesleyan* centres of church literary activity.

GWENDOLYN DAVIES

Here and Now. See LITERARY MAGAZINES IN ENGLISH: 3.

Herron, Shaun. See MYSTERY AND CRIME.

Hertel, François. Pseudonymn of Rodolphe DUBÉ.

Hexagone, Les Éditions de 1'. See Gaston MIRON and POETRY IN FRENCH: 5.

Hickman, Albert (1877-1957). Born in Dorchester, N.B., into a shipbuilding family, William Albert Hickman grew up in Pictou, N.S., and graduated in 1899 from Harvard University, where he was a noted sculler. Working out of Saint John as New Brunswick Commissioner, he prepared *A handbook of New Brunswick* (1900). Experiments conducted at Pictou led Hickman after 1906 to become preoccupied with the development and promotion of advanced speedboat technology. His success as a marine engineer prompted him, after the First World War, to relocate his engineering firm in New England.

Hickman was also a writer of fiction, including the novel *The sacrifice of the Shannon* (1903), a highly readable blend of adventure, humour, and romance. The story is narrated in a breezy and slightly ingenuous vein by an Englishman of rank and cosmopolitan experience whose background is gradually linked with the milieu of his Pictou shipowning employers. The novelist successfully combines sporting sketches of the Nova Scotia yachting élite with epic tales of ice-breakers in the dangerous pack-ice of the Gulf of St Lawrence.

Hickman contributed stories and marine-sport articles to *The Century*, *The American Magazine*, and other U.S. publications. *An unofficial love story* (1909), a novelette of manners set in Saint John, N.B., again casts the well-to-do Englishman in Canada as something of an innocent abroad. In 1909 and 1910 Hickman published, as a series in *The Century* rather than as a single volume, two other novelettes: 'The A-flat major Polonaise' and 'Compensated', which share a Pictou setting, a number of characters, and similar combinations of humour, sport, and adventure. All three novelettes, together with four short stories, were collected in his *Canadian nights* (1914).   KEN MacKINNON

Hiebert, Paul. See SARAH BINKS.

Hill-Tout, Charles. See INDIAN LEGENDS AND TALES: BIBLIOGRAPHY.

Hind, Henry Youle. See EXPLORATION LITERATURE IN ENGLISH: 2.

Hine, Daryl (b. 1936). Born in Vancouver, B.C., he studied classics and philosophy at McGill University, Montreal. In 1958 he received a Canada Council (Rockefeller) Award for poetry and travelled to Europe, living in France until 1962. Between 1963 and 1967 he completed his M.A. and Ph.D. degrees in comparative literature at the University of Chicago; the subject of his dissertation was the Latin poetry of the sixteenth-century Scottish humanist George Buchanan. In 1967 he joined the English department at Chicago, where he currently teaches writing and comparative literature. From 1968 to 1978 he edited the prestigious magazine *Poetry*.

Hine is the author of ten books of poetry: *Five poems* (1954), published by EMBLEM BOOKS; *The carnal and the crane* (1957); *Heroics* (1961); *The devil's picture book* (1961); *The wooden horse* (1965); *Minutes* (1968); *In and out* (1975); *Resident alien* (1975); *Daylight saving* (1978); and *Selected poems* (1980). Though his most recent collection was published in both Toronto (Oxford) and New York (Atheneum), most of his books have originated in the U.S., where Hine has a high critical reputation.

The *Selected poems* presents a carefully chosen cross-section of themes and styles. From the beginning Hine's signature as a poet has been his formal control. His poetry is complex, intellectual, and technically sophisticated. He delights in traditional forms, experimenting with villanelles, satires, sestinas, and metrical patterns such as iambic pentameter with complicated rhyme schemes. The traditional forms might seem archaic, except that Hine's tone and themes are modern, his voice is intensely personal, and he creates startling colloquial metaphors. The tension between his extraordinary technical mastery and an anguished exploration of the chaos of personal life—as in 'Aftermath'—lends some of his poetry considerable power.

Hine's training as a classical scholar has provided him with his major themes: a repeated strategy in his poetry is to reinterpret classical mythology in the light of contemporary experience. Committed to a dualistic vision of human nature as split by the antithetical claims of mind and body, he resorts to the myth of Eros and Psyche to provide an imagery that can be seen to operate throughout his work. His enduring obsession is the ambiguity of desire: 'to please self and then the soul / Is difficult and terrible.' The self is a 'Double-Goer' caught in time and space, vascillating between affection and hatred, and always seeking an illusory peace through the *other*, who is both vehicle and victim in a quest for escape from the self. Occasionally the baroque language seems to be a defence, and the poems fall into preciousness and a debilitating over-refinement: the poet's control seems almost a neurotic strategy against an unidentified potential chaos. Most of Hine's poetry, however, is remarkable for the wit, candour, and intelligence with which he explores the range of emotions from lust to love.

Hine has also written a novel, *The Prince of Darkness and Co.* (1961), constructed as an elaborate parody of mythology. Its hero, British poet Philip Sparrow, author of *A guide to witchcraft*, lives on an island called Xanadu. The climax of the book occurs on Midsummer Night in an adolescent orgy of sacrifice. Hine's purpose is to contrast those who play intellectually with the 'powers of darkness' and those for whom such forces are real. Hine also wrote a travelogue, *Polish subtitles: impressions from a journey* (1962)—after living briefly in Warsaw to edit English sub-titles for a Polish film—and has published translations from the Greek: *The Homeric hymns and the Battle of the Frogs and the Mice* (1972). ROSEMARY SULLIVAN

Historical writing in English. Virtually all historians who have written about Canada could agree that history is a branch of literature. Historians in the past, however, were in some senses far more willing to pay at least lip service to the literary conventions of their time than are those of the present generation, many of whom would maintain that the critical canons of historical writing are not necessarily identical with those of literature. In recent years, as social-science conceptualization and methodology have become increasingly prevalent in history studies—especially in the academy—one of the basic if often unspoken questions revolves around the extent to which historical writing needs to be bound by older and essentially literary assumptions about style, structure, and scope. Mountains of evidence and clarity of exposition—rather than the portrayal of settings, situations, and personalities and the skilful handling of elaborate descriptive detail—have become the commonly acceptable stylistic goals of contemporary Canadian historians. Analysis, rather than the elaboration of the passage of time through narrative, has become the norm, and limited topics exhaustively investigated in the archives have replaced sweeping ones more aesthetically considered. In short, to

comment today that a historian 'writes well' no longer implies that he seeks to emulate the author of imaginative literature. Indeed, many academic historians would regard the telling of a rousing story as extraneous to their function—little more than an attempt to cater to the public's limited capacities for absorbing the facts and meanings of history. If the criteria for literary merit are the traditional and internationally acceptable ones of substantial sweep, clear narrative voice, and an eye for picturesque detail and descriptive setting, historians of Canada have produced few outstanding works. Nevertheless the record is not a total wasteland. Historians of Canada, particularly outside the academy, have produced more writings deserving of consideration (and reading) as literature than is usually recognized. Moreover, not all of the historical genres in which they have worked have been equally conducive to literary pretensions, and some have been positively antagonistic to them.

1. PROMOTIONAL HISTORY. The first historical writings about Canada were, understandably, not deliberately intended as history at all, but utilized accounts of the past as part of a larger purpose of publicizing the merits and progress of infant settlements abroad, often publicizing the author in the process. In such works the historical material was typically interspersed with information about geography, climate, flora, and fauna. The tone was enthusiastic, and the emphasis was on both past progress and future promise, since the object was to impress and persuade the audience. Naturally enough, literary merit was not a principal concern of these authors, although the best and most successful of them appreciated that a work well constructed and well written was more likely to be read than one that lacked these qualities. But the focus on the presentation of information often detracted from the flow of the historical narrative, and these promotional works were usually ill-organized and digressive, depending on the personal knowledge and particular intention of the author. Perhaps the two most stylish of these early histories are John Stewart's *An account of Prince Edward Island* (London, 1806), and Thomas Chandler HALIBURTON's *An historical and statistical account of Nova Scotia* (2 vols, Halifax, 1829). Stewart (1758?-1834), a Scots-born office-holder resident many years on the island, produced his account 'to make the Colony better known among those who are interested in its prosperity; or on whose judgment and determi-

nations its future prospects depend.' Like most colonial publicists, Stewart had an axe to grind, but in his case his principal point was that the history of settlement and the administration of the island since its allocation to proprietors in 1767 had a consistency, for 'any disappointment which has been experienced in regard to its colonization and settlement, is fairly to be charged to the neglect of those into whose hands, the property of the lands unfortunately fell, and not to any defect in the climate or soil.' He did not note that he acted as spokesman for the other group to whom lack of progress might fairly be attributed. In any event the result was a coherent narrative of early development, told by one who had participated in many of the key events. Stewart's perspective and consistent interpretation kept the narrative flowing; he had a story to present and he told it well. Indeed, Stewart's account was so persuasive that it provided the basic foundations of subsequent interpretations of the early British period on the island until very recently.

Haliburton's *History of Nova Scotia* was a later and more ambitious production than Stewart's. The research and writing occupied Haliburton's spare time for many years, and its publication was intended both to gain applause for its author and to demonstrate to the world how far the province had progressed. Unfortunately, here as elsewhere in Haliburton's historical output—he wrote several later histories on North American topics—there is less evidence of the literary stylist than of the antiquarian compiler. Haliburton stayed too close to his limited sources to free his pen, and the narrative sweep (especially in the second volume) is much impeded by statistical information. Nevertheless, Haliburton intended his history in part as a contribution to literary culture, and there are flashes of the literary skills he later revealed in fictional works that often deal amusingly with historical incidents.

2. THE COMPILING TRADITION. If the promotional aspects of early writing on Canadian history did not positively discourage literary standards and pretensions, the tendency towards compilation certainly did. The problems facing the historians of a newly settled wilderness were many. None had any training, most wrote their histories in moments snatched from a busy life, and all faced substantial problems of documentation. Many of the pioneer historians spent long hours collecting documents, and al-

most without exception they were not certain how best to employ them. Moreover, the collection of documents was seen as essential chiefly because there were so few secondary writings upon which to rely. Equally significantly, there were problems of voice and point-of-view. Unlike later generations of professional scholars emulating the Germanic tradition, however, the early historians did not consider objectivity based on the historical record as a positive ideal; rather they often hid behind the documents out of a sense of insecurity. This latter strategy was certainly true for William Smith, Jr. (1769-1847), whose two-volume *History of Canada* appeared in 1826, eleven years after it had been printed in Quebec 'for the author'. (It took many years to convince him to publish, so afraid was he of offending someone.) Smith was able to employ French secondary sources to deal with the history of French Canada before the Conquest, and his volume dealing with New France, while scarcely original or insightful, had considerable charm. But as he got beyond the French literature and was forced to come to terms with the recent historical record and the part played in it by his father, who had been chief justice of Québec (1786-93), he attempted to head off criticism by paraphrasing and eventually merely reprinting the documents he had collected. Many other historians adopted a similar approach, especially to the more recent past, and such multi-volume works of men like William Kingsford (1819-98) and Robert Christie (1788-1856) are little more than undigested compilations: Kingsford's *The history of Canada* (10 vols, London, 1887-98) and Christie's *A history of the late province of Lower Canada* . . . (vols 1-5, Quebec, 1848-54; vol. 6, Montreal, 1855) were compiled almost verbatim from secondary material and the documentary record. This scissors-and-paste approach stood very much in the way of literary standards, either in terms of narrative voice or of writing style. History based almost exclusively on the official record is bound to be both dull in content and lacking in graceful exposition.

3. THE PARTICIPANT HISTORIANS. While the documentary record often got in the way of the pioneer historians, it was possible to be both well informed and possessed of a narrative voice. Most of the colonies of British North America were young, and many men had witnessed their development, even participated in the central events as perceived at the time. Almost every colony had its participant historians, who re-

lied less on the documents than on their own memories, writing less as historians than as memoirists. Such writers could offer a narrative viewpoint, and their recollections often extended beyond the administrative and political details of the official record. From a literary standpoint early participant histories are by far the most attractive and successful of Canadian historical productions. Perhaps the most readable and satisfying of them is *The Red River Settlement: its rise, progress and present state* (London, 1856) by the fur trader Alexander Ross (1783-1856). Ross's work was—as its title suggests—partly promotional. Unlike John Stewart, however, Ross had some literary models culled from a lifetime of reading. This book was not his first effort, but rather the third volume of an informal trilogy that began with *Adventures of the first settlers on the Oregon or Columbia River* (London, 1849) and *The fur hunters of the Far West* (2 vols, London, 1855). Ross had all the ingredients for a major literary achievement at his disposal, and he did not waste them. Not only did the early West provide a topic with both chronological and geographical sweep, but the major theme of *The Red River Settlement*—the conflict and tension between the indigenous cultures of the West and of European civilization—lent itself to literary development. Moreover, the early West provided both picturesque settings and fascinating personalities, which the author was fully prepared to exploit. Although he denied in his Preface a 'claim either to the ornaments of diction, or to the embellishments of imagination', the reader soon discovers that the text belies the author's diffidence. Ross faced consciously one of the major structural problems of the historian: that of keeping the narrative moving while providing analysis of topics that extended beyond the chronological bounds of the story. He resolved this difficulty by constructing a narrative framework that allowed occasional disgressions to discuss key topics in detail. *The Red River Settlement*, Ross's masterpiece, has been unjustly neglected, largely because on the surface it deals with an isolated colony that—despite his best efforts—had retained an image of being essentially barbaric. But his thematic emphasis on the conflict between 'savagery' and civilization, his eye for the telling detail of character and circumstance, the propelling narrative told in plain style, all make it a major literary achievement—perhaps the most successful historical work produced by

a Canadian on a Canadian theme before the twentieth century.

The participant historian has always enjoyed a major literary advantage over the archival specialist, in that his involvement in the events he chronicles leads him away from undue reliance on the documentary record while providing a strong narrative voice. Other participant historians include John Reeves (ca. 1752-1829), whose *History of the government of the Island of Newfoundland* (London, 1793) set the terms for the standard interpretation of the early development of the island, and Donald Gunn (1797-1878), whose *History of Manitoba from the earliest times* (Ottawa, 1880) was marked by its author's personal hostility to Lord Selkirk and the Hudson's Bay Company.

The participant tradition has not died, of course, and of modern practioners none has been more successful than James H. GRAY. In a series of works, beginning with *The winter years* (1966), Gray has employed his own history to explore larger themes in Canada's past. *The winter years* deals with the Depression period on the Prairies, and Gray's personal experiences as an unemployed relief recipient play a central role in his account of one of the most devastating eras in Canadian history. Gray reaches an audience desperate for an accessible past, which his narrative voice provides.

4. THE SKILLED AMATEUR. By the later years of the nineteenth century, historical study in Canada was changing in nature, particularly in terms of an increasing awareness that it required a discipline beyond the occasional dabblings of those interested in the subject. Not until 1892, however, when G.M. Wrong became a lecturer at the University of Toronto, was anyone appointed to a university post in Canada specifically as a historian, and the growth of Canadian history in the academy was a slow and gradual process. But even before Wrong's appointment, a new sophistication had been emerging. The Rev. George Bryce (1844-1931), founder of Manitoba College, was responsible for organizing the Manitoba Historical Society (1875) and the Manitoba Historical and Scientific Society (1879), both of which were devoted to the more systematic study of the past. In a sense his *Manitoba: its infancy, growth, and present condition* (London, 1882), though it concentrated on the period before 1820, was written in the tradition of promotional history; but in other ways it was quite different. Bryce obtained access to the extensive family papers of the Selkirks in

Scotland, and whatever his original intention, the book turned into a careful and sympathetic biography of Lord Selkirk, the creator of Manitoba. The events Bryce treated lent themselves to stirring narrative, and underlying his writing was the old theme of the conflict between barbarianism and civilization, updated by use of new documentary evidence. Bryce never allowed himself to be overwhelmed by his research, however, and the result is a book that can still be enjoyed. In his later studies of the early settlers of Manitoba, as well as in his pioneering *A short history of the Canadian people* (London, 1887; rev. 1914), Bryce attempted to get beyond political and constitutional development to understand Canadian society and its dynamics.

Further east, Goldwin SMITH was a major influence on historical study in Canada. Having served as Regius Professor of History at Oxford from 1858 to 1866, he settled in Toronto in 1871 and spent the remainder of his long life there. Despite his professorial background, Smith in Canada operated mainly as a publicist and journalist. Nevertheless he published late in life full-length histories of the United States and the United Kingdom, and one major volume on a Canadian topic, *Canada and the Canadian question* (London, 1891). In this book Smith undertook to survey the history of Canada as the 'presentation of a case and of a problem'. The use of evidence was plainly selective, but the work has a certain sweep and a clear perspective, as well as an abundance of the snide remarks for which Smith is now usually remembered. In his opening chapter he set the tone, noting the problems of providing unity to so complex a topic as the historical development of a federal Canada and opining that 'to impart anything like liveliness to a discussion of the British North America Act one must have the touch of Voltaire.' Smith was no Voltaire, but he offered a lively presentation of the Dominion's past, designed to demonstrate that Confederation was an artificial political solution that ran contrary to geography, race, language, and commercial interest. However much Smith's polemic ran against the main current of Canadian historical writing, it was a brilliant personal exposition of a version of Canadian development.

Unlike Goldwin Smith, the civil servant William Dawson LeSueur (1840-1917) lacked any formal credentials as a historian. Nevertheless he adhered far more closely than Smith to the developing Germanic

canons of scholarship, which emphasized accuracy based upon exhaustive research in the contemporary record. In common with Smith, however, LeSueur took issue with the standard interpretations of Canadian history of his time (and later), particularly in his study of William Lyon MACKENZIE, which, though completed in 1908, remained unpublished until recently because of successful efforts of the subject's family (notably Mackenzie King) to suppress its appearance in print. It was eventually published in the Carleton Library as *William Lyon Mackenzie: a reinterpretation* (1979), edited and with an introduction by A.B. McKillop. LeSueur wrote well; he had a splendid topic, a consistent narrative perspective, and his study—both of Mackenzie and of his times—was iconoclastic. It disputed vigorously the common view of Mackenzie as heroic popular reformer and of his enemies, the Family Compact, as hopeless oligarchs who governed despite public opinion. Apart from its historiographical importance, LeSueur's book stands out mainly for its literary merits. The prose is always lucid, often clever, and the author never lost touch with his plot or his purpose. Probably only the absence of contemporary publication has kept the work from becoming accepted as one of Canada's major contributions to historical literature.

One final author in the transitional period from amateur to professional history may be mentioned. Sir Andrew MACPHAIL, a native of Prince Edward Island, used his skills as a journalist to finance a medical education. A professor of the history of medicine at McGill for thirty years, he is usually remembered today as a journal editor, critic, and literary doyen who turned his dynamic prose style to history on several occasions. His study, *The medical services* (1925), the inaugural volume of the series *The official history of the Canadian Forces in the Great War*, remains a classic analysis of the non-combative aspects of modern war, written in Macphail's usual clear and assertive style. In *The Master's wife*, published posthumously in 1939, Macphail produced a historical work that is *sui generis*, combining personal memoir, biography, historical detail, and novelistic techniques in a brilliant evocation of life in his native province. Because the book satisfies neither conventional literary nor historical conventions, it has never been fully appreciated as the substantial achievement it represents. Macphail also produced one long historical essay, an account of Prince Edward Island for Shortt and Doughty's series *Canada and its provinces* (23 vols, 1913-17). It bears all the hallmarks of his style, and remains—however buried in obscurity—one of the best-written pieces of provincial history ever produced.

5. THE ESSAY. This is a greatly neglected and undervalued genre within Canadian historical writing. Differing substantially from the monographic article, which represents the vast bulk of the scholarly production of academics, the essay seeks to involve the wider public in historical questions, combining erudition with a lively style and a lucid argument. Most good historical essays have sought less to advance new research than to discuss existing research in a larger and more general context. Both Goldwin SMITH and Andrew MACPHAIL wrote superb essays on historical topics as part of their literary activities, and many other historians have occasionally turned to the genre. The two most successful practitioners of the art of the historical essay in Canada, however, have been Frank Underhill and Ramsay Cook.

Frank H. Underhill (1889-1971) was professor of history at the University of Toronto from 1927 to 1955. A founder of the CCF in the 1930s who moved to the Liberal party in later years, he was for most of his lifetime the gadfly of the historical profession in Canada. He has often been taken to task for the extent of his involvement in affairs of the day and for his tendency to devote himself to relating history to contemporary affairs rather than concentrating on pure scholarship in monographs and books. Much of his best work appeared as essays and reviews in *The* CANADIAN FORUM, a journal with which he was intimately associated for many years. Underhill's essays, most readily accessible in a collected volume, *In search of Canadian liberalism* (1960), are characterized by their iconoclasm and trenchant wit often bordering on sarcasm. He greatly admired the 'graceful style, the lightness of touch, . . . the subtle irony' of the *Manchester Guardian*, but recognized that 'the secret of a good style is to have something to say.' Underhill always did, although often his impatience to deliver his message detracted from the grace of his performance. Underhill's essays often now seem dated (the risk one runs in remaining too close to the editorial page), but are still models worth emulating by the commited historian.

Ramsay Cook (b. 1931), professor of his-

tory at York University, Toronto, whose writings are more conventionally within the academic tradition than Underhill's, has also enjoyed remarkable success as an essayist. Cook's central themes are the politics of contemporary Canada placed in historical perspective, and especially the presentation of French-Canadian culture to the Anglophone audience. He has undoubtedly been an important interpreter of the aspirations of modern Québec to those outside that province. Cook's essays tend to be more consciously erudite than Underhill's, studded with references drawn from wide reading, and his best work often deals with exposition and criticism of the writings of other historians. But while historiographic issues are not the easiest ones to present to the lay audience, such essays demonstrate Cook's real skill at placing historical writing in the largest context of social, intellectual, cultural, and political developments within the Canadian community. Cook occasionally oversimplifies, but he never condescends. His style is lucid, his tone reasonable, his arguments sensible. The essays in his *Canada and the French-Canadian question* (1966) show him at his best.

6. POPULAR HISTORY. Since accessibility for the general audience has become a constantly decreasing factor in most Canadian historical writing, particularly within the academy, the mantle of readability has fallen on those whose work is designed not to impress peers on tenure and promotion committees but readers in bookstores. The emphasis among academic historians on critical analysis and revision of previous interpretations has usually come at the expense of sequential narrative. Moreover, the focus on abstract historical forces—such as class—rather than on the interaction of personalities as the basis of development has further altered the academic approach. Few scholars have attempted to combine abstract analysis with a strong narrative voice concentrating on personality conflict, and such a goal may indeed by virtually impossible. But the price has been high in terms of interest from the lay public.

Many Canadian literary figures have turned their hand to historical writing as part of their literary activity, and a few authors have actually specialized in historical writing. Among the occasional figures, the most significant work has been done by Thomas Raddall and Farley Mowat. Among the specialists Pierre Berton stands alone.

Thomas RADDALL had always been fascinated by the past of the Maritimes region, and his first three novels were all given historical settings based on substantial research. After the Second World War, Raddall became far more consciously involved in historical writing, beginning with an account of the activities of the West Nova Scotia Regiment from 1939 to 1945 (*West Novas*, 1948) and a study of Halifax (*Halifax: warden of the North*, 1948). He subsequently produced *The path of destiny* (1957) in a series edited by Thomas B. COSTAIN intended to survey Canadian history for the North American audience. While *West Novas* did not sell well and has been virtually forgotten, it offered Raddall an opportunity to apprentice in the field, and undoubtedly helped contribute to the success of the Halifax book. Raddall's strength had always been in forceful narrative and accurate setting, rather than in characterization, and in the history of Halifax he had a focus that he brilliantly exploited. *The path of destiny* is usually regarded as less successful, the author himself acknowledging that the task of dealing with the broad sweep of Canadian events from the Conquest to 1850 was an impossible one, particularly given his inclination to emphasize military history. Nevertheless, Raddall's fascination with the warfare of the American Revolution and the War of 1812—'I could not write my way around the wars, dismissing them in a few pages as a wretched waste of blood and treasure', he wrote in his autobiography—does suggest one of the major differences between the scholar and the writer, for the essential ingredients of military history are colourful events that can be understood only in a narrative framework. It is no accident that a disproportionate number of the most familiar and readable histories, from those of Francis Parkman to those of Pierre Berton, have exploited military themes.

Like Raddall, Farley MOWAT has always been fascinated with the past. His major venture into historical writing has been *The Regiment* (1955), an account of the Hastings and Prince Edward Regiment of Ontario during the Second World War. Mowat, like Raddall, clearly recognized the dramatic possibilities of regimental history. Investing the unit with a life of its own—'a thing possessed of special animation'—Mowat combined the traditional narrative overview with the novelistic techniques of montage to produce a highly readable book. The paragraphs are short, and his punchy prose, bordering on the journalistic, drives on relentlessly through the various European campaigns. Little attempt at individual characterization is attempted: the Regiment itself is the protagonist.

Undoubtedly the most successful of the modern-day popular historians is Pierre BERTON. His first historical writings were about the Canadian North, a region in which he had grown up. In one sense these works are participant history, Berton himself confessing: 'My whole life has been conditioned by the Klondike; it hangs behind me like a theatrical backdrop, it haunts my dreams and my memories.' *The golden trail* (1955) was followed by *The mysterious North* (1956) and *Klondike* (1958), a book many still regard as Berton's major literary achievement. The topic is a romantic and exciting one, lending itself to narrative and to description of setting and personality. Berton was not afraid to introduce dialogue at critical points in the story for dramatic effect, although his style is largely conventional. Despite his claim to tell 'the unvarnished story of the Klondike phenomenon', the book tends to highlight the colourful and play down the prosaic, a principal criticism of most of Berton's historical writing.

Berton returned to large-canvas history in 1970 with the first volume of his study of the Canadian Pacific Railway, *The national dream: the great railway, 1871-1881* (1970). While the construction of railroads does not seem at first glance a subject of wide interest, Canadians have long retained a peculiar fascination for the railroad as an instrument of national unity, and the story of the CPR involves a large cast of characters that can be set against a dramatic backdrop in Parliament and in boardrooms. Berton employed a conventional narrative technique, but introduced a plethora of picturesque detail. *The national dream* ended with the parliamentary passage of the Pacific Railway Bill of 1881. Characteristically the author interwove into the political account a lengthy description of the Ottawa social season in the winter of 1881, and concluded with a passage that asserted 'there was not a single man, woman, or child in the nation who would not in some way be affected, often drastically, by the tortured decision made in Ottawa that night.' The second volume, *The last spike: the great railway, 1881-1885* (1971) brought the tale through the completion of construction and the employment of the railroad in the second Riel uprising of 1885. Throughout these books Berton judiciously employed novelistic techniques of description and dialogue. Having found his métier, Berton's mext major project was the War of 1812, a subject that had already attracted writers like Thomas Raddall. Again there were two large volumes, a size that gave the topic room to breathe and Berton an opportunity to develop further his unerring eye for the little-known dramatic incident and the telling piece of descriptive detail. Some have protested that *The invasion of Canada 1812-1813* (1980) and *Flames across the border: the invasion of Canada 1813-1814* (1981) are overwritten, but the book-buying public obviously appreciates its history that way.

7. ACADEMIC HISTORY. While there have been many well-written books produced by university-based historians over the past century, few if any can be seriously regarded as literary achievements. Among the first generation of academics, George Wrong (1860-1948) in his *A Canadian manòr and its seigneurs* (1908) and *The rise and fall of New France* (2 vols, 1928) did attempt to meet literary criteria, his models being the great nineteenth-century historians of Britain and the United States. The principal modern Canadian historian with a conscious commitment to history as literature has been Donald CREIGHTON. In *The commercial empire of the St. Lawrence* (1937; rpr. 1956 as *The empire of the St. Lawrence*), Creighton demonstrated what could be achieved within the realm of Canadian political and economic history when it was presented with artistry. As has often been pointed out, this work was designed as a three-act drama, with the St Lawrence River as the major protagonist. Here, as elsewhere in his writing, Creighton presented the river as something possessed of special animation around which men and events revolved. The years 1783, 1821, and 1849 separated each of the acts, and the 1849 conclusion of the 'entire drama' saw the parliament buildings in flames and Canadian businessmen seeking links with the United States.

Although Creighton claimed that he wrote his books instinctively and 'not in conscious accordance with any literary principles', he was obviously steeped in fiction (especially the realist and naturalist schools of the later nineteenth and earlier twentieth centuries) and sought to translate its forms into historical terms. In his two-volume biography of John A. Macdonald—*John A. Macdonald: the young politician* (1951) and *John A. Macdonald: the old chieftan* (1955)—Creighton attempted with considerable suc-

cess to recreate an age through the eyes of his protagonist, describing in vivid detail such matters as weather conditions and other personalities based on a complete command of the historical evidence and the author's total indentification with the perspectives of his protagonist. For Creighton, personalities often became characters exemplifying ideas or forces, and setting was painted in loving detail as more than background.

For many other academic historians besides Creighton, biography has been a way to reconcile the contradictory demands of modern scholarship and the literary aesthetic. Good biography requires both considerable literary craftsmanship and sound historical research. Personalities are to the fore, the subject's life has a built-in sequential quality that encourages narrative and even permits a narrative voice, and the genre by its very nature eschews abstract forces. (At the same time, many modern scholars would argue that biography ought not properly to be regarded as history, and the concentration upon it by many of Canada's leading historians has in some quarters been seen as evidence of the backward and provincial quality of the historical study of Canada.) Conspicuous for their literary qualities among recent biographies are William Kilbourn's *The firebrand: William Lyon Mackenzie and the rebellion in Upper Canada* (1956), John Morgan GRAY's *Lord Selkirk of Red River* (1963), W.J. Eccles' *Frontenac, the courtier governor* (1959), and J.M. Bliss's *A Canadian millionaire: The life and business times of Sir Joseph Flavelle, bart. 1858-1939* (1978). (See BIOGRAPHY AND MEMOIRS IN ENGLISH.)

A useful study of the modern academic tradition among Canadian historians, good on the literary styles of its subjects and itself gracefully written, is Carl Berger's *The writing of Canadian history: aspects of English-Canadian historical writing: 1900 to 1970* (1976). J.M. BUMSTED

Historical writing in French. It was only after the Conquest that the first printing press came to Canada. In Québec, newspapers soon appeared that could both create and satisfy a demand for home-grown literary production in the form of verse, essays, reminiscences, and historical sketches. The latter stimulated an effort to find and preserve historical documents, and notable collections were made by the poet-editoressayist Jacques Viger (1787-1858), as well as by the Literary and Historical Society of Quebec, founded in 1824. Out of this literary and historical interest emerged the *Histoire du Canada* of Michel Bibaud (1782-1837), which was published in three volumes with the subtitles *Sous la domination française* (Montréal, 1837; rev. 1843) and *Sous la domination anglaise* (2 vols, Montréal, 1844, 1878). A pioneering work, especially in its treatment of the post-Conquest period, Bibaud's history did not win popularity because, in a time of militant French-Canadian nationalism, he wrote from a conservative and loyalist point of view.

Better able to express the aspirations of the time was François-Xavier GARNEAU, whose *Histoire du Canada depuis sa découverte jusqu'à nos jours* (3 vol., 1845-8) is still considered the first great masterpiece of French-Canadian literature. Journalist, clerk, notary, essayist, and poet, Garneau had been associated with the Lower Canadian reform movement during the 1830s, and his work expressed its nationalism as well as much of its ambivalence about reform and religion. While he made some criticisms of the clergy of New France, he considered Catholicism an essential element of French-Canadian nationality; and while he praised the idea of liberty, his goal was essentially to promote a conservative nationalism: 'the conservation of our religion, our language, and our laws.'

Garneau wrote shortly after the failure of the 1837-8 rebellions, after the publication of Lord Durham's remark that French Canadians had 'no history, and no literature', and after the imposition of a political régime that threatened the whole national future of French Canada. Garneau's work was a rallying call and a vindication of the demands of French Canadians that their nationality be respected. Though he made a careful study of available documents, Garneau was inspired by his 'profound and heartfelt sympathy' with the national cause. His history, therefore, is full of heroic deeds by which 'a people of farmers, hunters, and soldiers' opened up the greater part of a vast continent, pushing back its frontiers and marking it with the character of French civilization. His quintessential Canadians are military heroes like Iberville, or adventurous explorers and empire-builders like La Vérendrye: such men had forged a past to which French Canadians must still be true. Led now by political spokesmen rather than by soldiers, they must yet adhere to the traditions bequeathed by their history. 'Our traditions are a source of strength for us; let us not turn away from them.'

For a French Canada asserting its nationalism, Garneau's romantic portrayal of history was profoundly inspiring. But in mid-nineteenth-century Québec, clerical influence was becoming more and more powerful, and it was necessary to go beyond Garneau to emphasize the historical role of Catholicism. This was done by the Abbé Jean-Baptiste-Antoine Ferland, in his *Cours d'histoire du Canada* (2 vols, 1861-5). Ferland wrote, as he said in his introduction, as a 'French Canadian by birth and a Catholic above all'. His history of New France tells especially of the progress of religion; his heroes are Christians first and foremost, his quintessential Canadians the Jesuit martyrs. Ferland had worked long in the French archives—and his history was solidly researched—but he wrote with a good deal of creative imagination, like the other historians of his century. These were men of broad literary interests, often writers of essays, poetry, novels, or even plays, as well as history. While they went to the sources for their 'facts', they exerted their literary talents to weave them into a living narrative and to give them general sense or significance. For a century after Garneau, that sense was nationalist and Catholic. History and religious nationalism, in fact, were scarcely separable in the late nineteenth century. 'O Canada', exclaimed A.B. Routhier (1839-1920), in a poem that would be set to music and become the national anthem, 'your arm . . . holds high the cross, your history is an epic of the most brilliant exploits' (*Les échos*, Québec, 1882). History taught French Canadians their national duties, their God-given mission to live out the life of a Catholic people—an agricultural life close to nature and its Creator. With minor variations, these basic convictions inspired most French-Canadian historical writing till the Second World War. Given that so much history was written by clerics—who wrote almost half the articles in the leading historical journal as late as 1950—this was hardly surprising.

Clerical historians were particularly prominent outside Québec. Prairie settlement, for instance, had involved a tremendous effort by colonizing missionaries, some of whom wrote significant western histories to justify and maintain a French-Catholic presence in the region. Thus, Adrien-Gabriel Morice (1859-1938) stressed the efforts of the western clergy to promote

Historical writing in French

French-Canadian settlement and secure French-Catholic rights—not only in his *Histoire de l'Église catholique dans l'Ouest canadien, du lac Supérieur au Pacifique* (3 vols, 1912); *History of the Catholic Church in Western Canada, from Lake Superior to the Pacific* (2 vols, 1910)—but even in his general western histories. French Canadians, he wrote in *Aux sources de l'histoire manitobaine* (1907), must remain true to a past whose very meaning was the expansion of conservative and clerical values. 'The parish spire must, in the West as everywhere else, be the rallying point for all those who would remain faithful to the past of our race.'

This sort of history seemed appropriate in a period when most French Canadians lived on farms, close to the parish church and under the guidance of lay and clerical notables. But turn-of-the century industrialization soon changed that: by 1920 the majority of Quebeckers lived in towns and cities, and a history that taught them they had an agricultural vocation seemed increasingly inconsistent with the world around them. A literature that assumed the leadership of the traditional élite would soon become embattled as social and political influence passed from French-Canadian lawyers, priests, notaries and even MPs to English-speaking factory-owners, bankers, and managers.

The many publications of the Abbé (later Canon) Lionel GROULX expressed the anxieties of French-Canadian nationalism in the first half of the twentieth century as powerfully as Garneau had expressed its young aspirations in the 1840s. Groulx aimed to inspire French Canadians at a time when industry was transforming their province, turning the long-settled *habitant* into a poor, urban worker, rootless and insecure, his language tainted with anglicisms. Groulx also responded to the imposition of conscription in wartime, to the abolition of French in Manitoba and Ontario schools, and to a massive immigration that threatened to drown French Canada in a sea of aliens. No wonder he saw demoralization all around in his compatriots!

History, he felt, could inspire French Canadians with a will to resist, with pride, and with a determination to assert themselves. 'To be proud,' he wrote in his 1937 collection of essays, *Notre maître le passé*, 'our young people need only to know who they are. The sons of those great Frenchmen who created the masterpiece which was New France need not search elsewhere than in their own past to find reason for self-respect.' True, there was tragedy as well as glory in the past—particularly in the Conquest, which subjected French Canada to foreign domination that was perpetuated by Confederation, as well as by the anglophone grip on Québec's economic life. Still, those who were true to the greatness of their history would strive for their nation's emancipation. Great steps had already been taken: religious freedom, political liberties, and even provincial autonomy had already been won, thanks largely to the efforts of great men, heroes who expressed and even embodied the aspirations of their race. Without such men, Groulx wrote in his *Histoire du Canada français depuis la découverte* (4 vols, 1950-2), 'nothing great is accomplished in history.' That was why Groulx celebrated the heroes of the past, both as historian and as nationalist organizer and pamphleteer, and looked for a modern hero to lead French Canada into the future.

Groulx himself helped lead French-Canadian history into the future, not only by his work in inspiring later generations of nationalist historians but more importantly, perhaps, by his promotion of scholarly research through the founding of the Institut d'histoire de l'Amérique française in 1946, by his work between 1947 and 1967 as editor of the *Revue d'Histoire de l'Amérique française* (which, under him, became French Canada's leading forum for historical research), and by his help in establishing a professional history department at the Université de Montréal. Indeed, it was only after the Second World War that French-Canadian universities established regular history departments; men who had obtained their Ph.D.s abroad returned to run them, bringing new scholarly values and interests.

The new professional historians, armed with their secular training and accustomed to living in big cities, were no longer satisfied with the old rural and religious ideals. If Groulx had seen the modern world of business, commerce, and industry as something alien to French Canada and her traditions, his successors at Montreal looked on it as a normal part of any society's development. They began, therefore, to look for a business class in French Canada's past. Following up on an idea first suggested by his colleague Maurice Séguin (b. 1918), Guy Frégault (1918-77) began to portray a New France that was commercially oriented and business-directed. If French Canadians had not followed through from such beginnings, it was because the Conquest had ruined their business class by forcing it to operate within the alien structures of British mercantilism, a context in which British merchants had an unbeatable advantage. Developed by Frégault in his 1955 masterpiece *La guerre de la conquête* (translated in 1969 as *Canada: the War of the Conquest*), this interpretation was pursued and its long-term consequences for French-Canadian history were explored by another Université de Montréal professor, Michel Brunet (b. 1917), first in some remarkably influential essays contained in his collection *La présence anglaise et les Canadiens* (1958), and later in *Les Canadiens après la conquête* (1969; GGA).

An analytical concern about social classes and economic history had thus entered Québec's literature. At first it coexisted with older concerns. Frégault and Brunet, for example, were both much influenced by Groulx's nationalism. Again, while both believed in 'scientific' history, in a very rigorous and critical examination of documents, and in the importance of economics, they did not abandon all literary values. Frégault in particular was much admired for his fine narrative style. Personalities, great figures, played an important part in much of his work, from *Iberville le conquérant* (1944) on, and Frégault, especially in his early career, was able to derive a Groulx-like inspiration from national history. 'Oh history of ours!' he exclaimed in one rapturous outburst. 'It is through our history that French Canada has best expressed itself, best explained itself, best affirmed itself. . . . History remains our great strength.'

Such preoccupations were foreign to Marcel Trudel (b. 1917), who came to Université Laval in 1947—like Brunet and Frégault with an American Ph.D. Trudel specifically repudiated the idea that present-day or ideological preoccupations might concern the historian. 'I'm content,' he said, 'to find the past.' Nor was the past to be found in great intuitive interpretations presented in colourful and poetic style. History had for too long been 'comfortably ensconced in the chair of rhetoric.' It must confine itself more to a minute analysis of documents and facts. Trudel's own *Histoire de la Nouvelle-France*, which covers the period down to 1663 in three volumes—*Les vaines tentatives, 1524-1603* (1963), *Le comptoir, 1604-1627* (1966; GGA), and *La seigneurie des Cent-Associés, 1627-1663*, part 1 (1979)—is a remarkable example of this rigorous and painstaking approach to history.

As the age of the professional historian advanced, history seemed less and less concerned with the literary, more and more with the 'scientific'. The great books of the last two decades have provoked excitement not by rhetoric so much as by the originality of their research techniques and the new problems they have explored. Thus the appearance in 1966 of the *Histoire économique et sociale du Québec, 1760-1850* (*Economic and social history of Québec: 1760-1850*, Carleton Library, 1980), by Fernand Ouellet (b. 1926), shook the whole Canadian historical community because of the tools of analysis (particularly quantitative) that it employed, the new types of evidence it considered, and the extraordinarily comprehensive way in which it examined and related the economic, social, ideological, and political elements of history. French-Canadian nationalism itself, which had inspired historians from Garneau to Frégault and Brunet, was seen by Ouellet as merely the product of certain economic and social circumstances present in early nineteenth-century Québec.

But if Ouellet's work was exciting in its scope, approach, methods, and conclusions it was not the sort of colourful narrative that one could easily read. The price-curve of wheat at Quebec, the volume of timber exported, crop yields and population density—these now assumed more importance than the character and heroic deeds of great men. Was history, then, no longer part of literature? Were numbers, graphs, population movements and notarial inventories to replace colour, personality, and style? Were *structures* and *conjonctures* to push aside character and circumstance?

Certainly non-literary elements had permanently entered historical writing. Economic preoccupations would now be central, and with them an increased use of quantification, or other complex and highly technical methods. As nationality ceased to be the only criterion by which historians identified human groups, social class drew more and more attention. Marxian analysis appeared, and with it, too often, a sort of socio-economic jargon that added nothing to the clarity of scholars' expositions. In modern Québec working-class life and union organization were given particular attention for the first time—but farmers, settlers, and lumbermen were also studied, as investigators exercized their ingenuity to find new sorts of evidence about the daily life and culture of the nameless ordinary people. Cultural phenomena at all levels were analysed as functions of social and economic structures, ideologies and intellectual currents as expressions of class interest and outlook. In all this, the character and actions of outstanding individuals had little significance. In the monumental *Habitants et marchands de Montréal au XVIIᵉ siècle* (1974; GGA) by Louise Dechêne (b. 1932) population, landholding, business structures, social classes, property, religion are all carefully counted, defined, calculated, and put together to form a whole society; but narrative—the account of individual actions—is not part of the edifice.

Yet history-as-literature still flourishes. Outside the university the Martinique-born Robert Rumilly (1897-1983) produced an immense body of published work. His 41-volume *Histoire de la province de Québec* (1940-63), his lives and times of great personalities, his *Compagnie du Nord-Ouest* (1980), and many other publications—are written with epic verve, a passionate style, a love for men who are larger than life and for great deeds and human drama. Thus Rumilly carried on the old historical tradition.

Academic historians have not entirely departed from this tradition. Biographies are still written—of businessmen and labour leaders, churchmen and politicians. Moreover, once the economic, social, and ideological structures had been identified, it was still necessary to come back to events. In *Le Bas-Canada, 1791-1840* (1976; GGA)—of which a badly abridged English version, *Lower Canada, 1791-1840*, appeared in 1980—Fernand Ouellet, while adding to his earlier quantitative demonstration, focuses as well on individual politicians, churchmen, and administrators, showing how their personalities acted together with economic and social pressures to produce those actions that traditionalists would have recognized as 'history'.

Books that weave the various strands of history into coherent and meaningful accounts—general syntheses—will always be wanted. The great success of the *Histoire du Québec contemporain: De la Confédération à la crise, 1867-1929* (1979; Eng. trans. 1983), by Paul-André Linteau, René Durocher, and Jean-Claude Robert, illustrates this point, as does Robert's briefer and more general *Du Canada français au Québec libre* (1975), which was written for a French readership to explain the historical background of current developments in Québec. Both interpret, and put into the context of a coherent and readable synthesis, the results of recent specialized research. However, the *Histoire*—fuller, more detailed, and richer from the scholarly point of view—raises a final consideration. It integrates so much material that its authors could not use a unified narrative, but resorted to both a thematic and chronological structure. The collaborative nature of the work also deprived it, in some measure, of the unity and personality that are usually associated with works of literature. As so many types and levels of experience are now being studied (only one of them having to do with individual action), it seems that it will no longer be possible to integrate them as a single narrative, marked by the mind of a single author, except in the briefest of surveys. If this is the case, history as literature may refer in future to nothing more than a certain clarity, perhaps elegance, of style.

See also *Quebec and its historians* (1983) by Serge Gagnon, translated by Yves Brunelle.

A.I. SILVER

Hodgins, Jack (b. 1938). He grew up in the logging and farming settlement of Merville on Vancouver Island and studied creative writing under Earle BIRNEY at the University of British Columbia, from which he received a B.Ed. in 1961. On graduation he returned to Vancouver Island to teach high school in Nanaimo. In the seventies he travelled to Ireland and Japan and served as writer-in-residence at Simon Fraser University (1977) and at the University of Ottawa (1979-80). He lives in Ottawa, where he is visiting professor and writer-in-residence at the University of Ottawa.

Northern Vancouver Island, particularly the Comox Valley where Jack Hodgins was born, has been the setting for all four of his immensely good-humoured works of fiction. His first major work was the short-story collection *Spit Delaney's island* (1976), which introduced the recurrent theme that imagination can redeem or transcend the physical. The stories focus either on unhappy characters, limited by their belief that they can 'know' only what they see, or on dreamers, like Spit Delaney himself, who are notable for their shocking, unconventional behaviour. Structurally unremarkable, the stories feature eccentric characterizations and a pervasive fusion of realism and parable.

Hodgins has also published two novels, *The invention of the world* (1977) and *The res-*

urrection of Joseph Bourne (1980), which won a Governor-General's Award, and a collection of stories published during the seventies, *The Barclay family theatre* (1981). Central to all these books are the seven daughters of the Barclay family, together with their husbands and children, who first appeared in *Spit Delaney's island* ('Other people's troubles'). Because of inconsistent characterization, however, the interconnections between the books occur more in mood, setting, and theme than in the family's history.

Both *The invention of the world* and *The resurrection of Joseph Bourne* are much more satisfying than the story collections because the novel form allows for a structural adventurousness and energy of language that can replicate the dauntless energies of the major characters: Maggie Kyle (daughter of Christina Barclay) and the poet Joseph Bourne. In *The invention of the world* larger-than-life characters—an evangelist who has beguiled an entire Irish village to come to Vancouver Island to serve him at his personal colony, an old woman who has spent her life combing the island with donkey and manure-spreader in an unsuccessful search for her birthplace, loggers whose Bunyanesque loves and brawls culminate in an epic wedding that is both feast and battle—are presented in a style that moves easily from fable to interior monologue to epic list.

In *The resurrection of Joseph Bourne* Hodgins' contention that the human spirit can 'invent' the world is manifested in the surprising changes brought about in Port Annie, an isolated Vancouver Island community, by a tidal wave that bears both a Peruvian ship and an ostensibly magical young woman of quintessential grace and beauty. Consciously defying the tradition of 'modern novels' in which 'believers were always made to look like fools', Hodgins creates an extravagant, life-affirming book that encompasses parody, romance, mystery, biblical allegory, and backwoods humour.

The Barclay family theatre illuminates the background of his Barclay characters, but even though several of the stories make impressive use of discontinuous narrative—notably the long 'More than conquerors'—the collection is inferior to the novels. Hodgins' expansive, extravagant talent is at its best with space to invent and play.

Hodgins has edited three school anthologies: *Voice and vision* (1971) with W.H.

New, *The frontier experience* (1975), and *The west coast experience* (1976).

See also NOVELS IN ENGLISH 1960 TO 1982: 2.
FRANK DAVEY

Hollingsworth, Margaret (b. 1940). Born in London, Eng., and trained as a librarian at Loughborough College, she completed her education in Canada, with a B.A. in psychology from Lakehead University (1972) and an MFA in theatre and creative writing from the University of British Columbia (1974). She has been a librarian, an editor, a freelance journalist, and a teacher of English in Italy and Japan. She now lives in Vancouver.

Hollingsworth won a national drama competition at the age of eighteen and had plays performed on BBC-TV and by semi-professional companies in London before immigrating to Canada in 1968. Since 1972 her radio plays, and adaptations of her stage plays, have been broadcast in Canada, Britain, Australia, New Zealand, and West Germany. (Radio plays available in CBC archives (from 1973) are *Prairie drive, As I was saying to Mr Dideron, Wayley's children, War games, Webster's revenge*, and *The apple in the eye*.)

Hollingsworth's one-act stage plays excel at conveying the gist of a lifetime in a brief episode of the present. *Bushed* (1972) is set in a laundromat, used as shelter and meeting-place by two retired workers; the relentless turning of the machines and the mimed sheet-folding are emblematic of a world of action from which these men are excluded except in fantasy and memory. *Alli Alli Oh* (1977) is virtually the monologue of a woman retreating to insanity from two contrasting lifestyles, neither of whose demands she is willing or able to fulfil. A more complex one-act play is *Operators* (1974; rev. 1981), which deals with the friendship of two women, night-workers in a northern-Ontario factory, who have used dreams and games to ward off boredom, frustration, and the dangers of self-knowledge. The action becomes melodramatic when an intruder threatens their relationship; but this episode leads to new awareness and a positive conclusion. The original version of *Operators* (whose conclusion was less hopeful) employed techniques of simultaneous action, flashback, and 'freezing' that are revived in *Ever loving* (1980), a multi-scene play that uses popular songs of the period and tells the stories of three war brides of the

Hollingsworth

1940s—English, Scottish, and Italian—and their difficulties in adapting to Canada and to their husbands' lives. Hollingsworth's most effective play, the two-act *Mother country* (1980), is set on an island off the west coast and captures the eccentricities of Canadians who are more English than the English. Through three adult daughters it comically portrays the attempt to break ties both with England and with the mother, who embodies qualities traditionally associated with England.

Many of Hollingsworth's characters use speech as a weapon against silence and emptiness, or against other people. Hollingsworth, who speaks several languages, has an impeccable ear for the nuances of English, especially the variations brought to it by Canadian speakers of different national origins, and often exploits the comic potential of words imperfectly understood. In *Mother country* and *Alli Alli Oh* she sets conversations at tangents to one another, or on parallel lines, thus creating a slightly surreal effect. Such dialogue is well suited to radio drama and is expertly used in *The apple in the eye*, where a woman's 'thought voice' develops an elaborate and revealing fantasy in counterpoint to the banal Sunday-afternoon activities described by her own and her husband's 'present' voice. This play is in *Branching out*, IV, 5 (Dec., 1977); George WOODCOCK comments on it in 'Voices set free', CANADIAN LITERATURE 85 (Summer 1980).

JOAN COLDWELL

Hollingsworth, Michael (b. 1950). Born in Swansea, Wales, he immigrated to Canada with his parents in 1956 and now lives in Toronto. He is a playwright and musician, primarily interested in integrating rock music, video, and live theatre. Since his first play, *Strawberry fields* (1973), premièred at Toronto's Factory Theatre Lab in 1973, his work has become exceedingly complex. With the Hummer Sisters in 1978 he formed the Video Cabaret Theatre of Science which became Video Cabaret International—the only group in North America, and one of the pioneering theatre groups in the world, experimenting with video production: pretaped sequences interact with live video, live actors, the audience, and the theatrical aspects of rock music. Hollingsworth was a founding member of the punk rock group, The Government.

Hollingsworth's published plays include *Clear light* (1973), based on transcripts of the Watergate trials and bad LSD experiences.

The Metropolitan Toronto Police Morality squad closed the production for alleged obscenity in film sequences featuring pornographic clips. His play *Strawberry fields* was inspired by John Lennon's lyrics and focuses on the aftermath of a rock concert. He has also published *Transworld* (1979), which—like all his plays—deals with psychotics, madness, drug abuse, or political oppression that represent the collective psychosis of society.

Hollingsworth's other productions include *Punc rok* (1977), *Cheap thrills* (1977), and *White noise* (1977), based on the life of rock singer Janis Joplin. The poor critical reception of these plays led to the founding of Videocabaret and to *Electric eye* (1978), a multimedia study of urban depravity based on the Son of Sam murders in New York and the murder of a shoe-shine boy in Toronto. Hollingsworth then moved to video adaptations of George Orwell's *Nineteen eighty-four* (1978) and Aldous Huxley's *Brave new world* (1981). A ceaseless experimenter, he frequently revises his plays. *Nineteen eighty-four*, for example, appeared in productions ranging from four hours to eighty minutes, and in taverns as well as theatrical settings. Hollingsworth is currently working on a video play based on the Shah of Iran, which includes twenty live actors on stage and over 100 on video.

Influenced by Peter Brook, who considers theatre a 'hot' experience, and Artaud's Theatre of Cruelty concepts—in which the audience is assaulted by the play until it achieves catharsis—Hollingsworth sees the visual image as more natural than the word image to an audience raised on television, and feels that the results of his experimentation will lead to a redefinition of drama.

Hollingsworth discusses his theatrical concepts with Robert Wallace and Cynthia Zimmerman in *The work: conversations with English-Canadian playwrights* (1982).

GEOFF HANCOCK

Homme et son péché, Un. See Claude-Henri GRIGNON.

Hood, Hugh (b. 1928). Born in Toronto, Hugh John Hood was educated in Roman Catholic schools there and graduated from the University of Toronto, from which he received his Ph.D. in 1955. His dissertation, 'Theories of imagination in English thinkers 1650-1790', examines the psychology that the English Romantics inherited (Hood's fiction deals frequently with visionary experiences of recall that echo Wordsworth). Until 1961 he taught English at St Joseph's College, Hartford, Connecticut. He then joined the English department at the Université de Montréal, where he has remained. The son of an English-Canadian banker and a French-Canadian mother, he teaches comfortably within a bilingual system.

Three salient characteristics mark Hood's fiction: 1. An undramatic, 'knowing' acquaintance with the working lives of his subjects: technical aspects of jobs and intimate knowledge of the inner workings of bureaucratic, commercial, artistic, and political systems appear frequently in his expositions of characters. 2. An unobtrusive but easily discernible Roman Catholic view of experience, in which earthly doings bear the symbolic weight of supernatural patterns of blessing and redemption. 3. The ability to view Canada's history (and national peculiarities), as well as social and technological processes, in local terms that relate to larger patterns within the western world. These characteristics of his fiction are present in his collection of social and personal essays and superior journalism, *The Governor's Bridge is closed* (1973)—the title piece of which is a memorable reminiscence of Toronto centred on the Rosedale Ravine—and are strongly evident in his ongoing series of novels, *The New Age*.

First recognized, and still most highly esteemed by some, as a writer of short fiction, Hood has thus far published five volumes of stories, in addition to *Selected stories* (1978). *Flying a red kite* (1962) has for its title story a delicate handling of the process by which the enactment of love can lift one out of the depression caused by routine disillusionment and banality. Two stories in this collection—'Flying a red kite' and 'Recollections of the Works Department', based on a summer job experience in Toronto—are the most widely anthologized of his stories. *Around the mountain: scenes from Montreal life* (1967) masks an elaborate calendrical and seasonal scheme behind a series of twelve urban sketches. Light in texture and profound in meaning, the cycle concludes with the evocation of a visionary moment of peace and engagement with life's deeper rhythms in 'The river behind things'. *The fruit man, the meat man and the manager* (1971), Hood's finest single collection to date, marked a new level of complexity and resonance in his stories. At least three of them— the title story, 'Getting to Williamstown', and 'Brother André'—are among the finest

stories this author, or any Canadian, has written. *Dark glasses* (1976), as the title indicates, denotes a heightening of the writer's sense of tragedy and evil. The patterns beneath the surface of these stories reveal peril and terror—elements that are also present in *None genuine without this signature* (1980), a collection that reveals a heightened preoccupation with philosophical and moral issues.

The novels *White figure, white ground* (1964) and *The camera always lies* (1967) are about a painter and an actress respectively; the details of their careers are, as usual, convincingly described. Both blend concern with betrayal and deception with an investigation into the nature of perception, moral and physical, and conclude with affirmations of love that do not overlook the tentative nature of the two ventures. *A game of touch* (1970) takes a brash young cartoonist through a Montreal scene involving both politics and the arts. It is typical of Hood's willingness to risk handling 'unfictional' material that this novel contains a lengthy discussion of taxation practices by its noblest figure: the process of taxation is viewed as the most abstract expression of the social contract that Jake, the hero, must learn. *You can't get there from here* (1972), a highly allegorized but somewhat ponderous satire of multi-national corporations and global philanthropists let loose on Third World countries, depicts the downfall of a decent man who attempts to channel the aspirations of two warring peoples shoved together by geography.

The first of the projected twelve novels in Hood's *New Age* series was *The swing in the garden* (1975), of which Hood has said: '. . . it is supposed to be about becoming aware that one is a human being in Toronto in the thirties. In a sense, then, it's Toronto in the thirties, and Canadian society too.' *A new Athens* (1977) and *Reservoir ravine* (1979) take the series up to the late 1970s, with plenty of gaps made available for narratives of earlier decades. *Black and white keys* (1982) deals with the period of the Second World War, contrasting the Europe of the death camps with the innocence of Toronto at that time; visions of death and resurrection alternate with convincing evocations of the era's popular culture. The chief narrator of the series is Matthew Goderich, whose ancestral memories stretch back to the 1880s; subsequent volumes will include narratives by other figures. *The New Age*, which will conclude about the year 2000 with science-fiction projections of the world to come, is the most demanding prospectus ever issued by a writer of Canadian fiction. Hood has said that he is imitating *Remembrance of things past*, specifically Proust's 'narrative technique, the appeal to the philosophy of time, certain subtleties in the handling of the narrator'. He has set out to express 'historical mythology, the articulation of the past, the articulation of the meaning of our society in terms of the way we live our lives'. So ambitious a project, so bravely expressed, must have its detractors. Their objections include the insipidity of the narrator; the relentless optimism with which events are sometimes viewed; and the frequent discursive essay-like disquisitions on politics, the arts, fashion, religion, and so forth. Defenders of the project admire the sheer bravado of attempting such a work; the depth, richness, and vividness of its many moments of visionary recollection of the past; and the skill with which Hood shuttles back and forth between vast shifts in Western experience and the accommodation to them on the part of his Canadian characters, historical and fictional. Whatever their ultimate judgement, readers will find in his work an inexhaustible cornucopia of the life of his time.

Hood's career as a writer of both short and lengthy fiction has moved towards a deeper concern with the philosophical and moral. Future readers will judge whether that evolution has been in fact a devolution, but no one can deny Hood's enterprise in pursuing a philosophic course at a time when matters of epistemology and morality are not usually explored so directly in fiction.

References to sports occur often in Hood's fiction; *A game of touch* offers the most obvious example of this. The author of an excellent sports biography, *Strength down centre: the Jean Beliveau story* (1970), Hood has also written the text for Seymour Segal's *Scoring: the art of hockey* (1979).

Criticism, a bibliography, and an important interview can be found in J.R. (Tim) Struthers, ed., *Before the flood: Hugh Hood's work in progress*, in Issue 13/14 of *Essays in Canadian Writing* (1979). The interview therein, and one with Robert FULFORD in Issue 66 of *The* TAMARACK REVIEW (1975), from which the above quotations have been taken, illuminate Hood's intentions in writing *The New Age*.

See also NOVELS IN ENGLISH 1960 TO 1982: 3.   DENNIS DUFFY

Horwood, Harold (b. 1923). Harold An-

drew Horwood was born in St John's, Nfld., and received his formal education at Prince of Wales College there. In 1945, with his brother Charles, he founded *Protocol*, a journal that published experimental writing. Another contributor to *Protocol* was Irving Fogwill, who, Horwood stated many years later, 'introduced me to contemporary writing.' From 1949 to 1951 Horwood was a Liberal member of the Newfoundland legislature. His important column in the St John's *Evening Telegram*—'Political notebook' (1952-8)—was at first conciliatory in its attitude towards the administration of J.R. Smallwood but eventually became harshly critical of its policies. Horwood thus provided a voice of dissent in a decade of political domination by the Liberal party in Newfoundland. In 1958 he turned to freelance writing, a move that appears to have coincided with a growing radicalism in political outlook. In the sixties and seventies he became an apologist for the 'counter-culture' and adopted, to some extent, the hippie life-style. He was writer-in-residence at the University of Western Ontario in 1976-7 and later served in the same capacity at the University of Waterloo. A founding member of the WRITERS' UNION OF CANADA, he was its chairman in 1980-1. He now lives in Nova Scotia.

Horwood's books show him to be a well-read man of wide-ranging intellectual interests, with a tendency to parade his knowledge before the reader and to seize upon ideas with the enthusiasm of a literary novice. He is perhaps at his best as a writer when he simply observes the natural environment and displays his sensitivity to the normally unnoticed world of flora and fauna. Yet he is rarely content to do just that. His characteristic posture is that of a harbinger of new modes of life and thought. Typically he wishes to promote what he regards as enlightened notions, while jettisoning and denouncing the old; he is less an onlooker than a kind of teacher, or even (though the word may seem odd when applied to Horwood) a preacher. Few authors of fiction so persistently editorialize about their material as Horwood. His first novel, *Tomorrow will be Sunday* (1966), is a beautifully written book spoiled for many readers by humourless sermonizing. The setting is an isolated Newfoundland outport, 'Caplin Bight', and the theme is the intellectual and physical coming-of-age of one of its inhabitants, Eli Pallisher. The outport is richly portrayed, and there are passages of lyrical and dramatic power; but the adversary role that is adopted by the author towards religion and traditional institutions is so strident that it becomes tiresome. Moreover, the alternative views Horwood supports (for example, the idea expressed by the character Christopher Simms that sex is 'something to be enjoyed with a carefree heart, like a picnic, or a swim in the ocean') are quickly perceived as shallow. The book is, at bottom, a restatement of the stock romantic themes of the inherent goodness of the human heart and the superiority of youthful instinct and passion over conventional values and restraints.

Horwood's second book, *The foxes of Beachy Cove* (1967), is a work of meditation and observation that invites comparison with Thoreau's *Walden*. Horwood takes us on walks through the Newfoundland countryside and on canoe trips up its rivers, impressing us with the thoroughness of his knowledge of external nature and making us see what we had not before learned to look for, with little hectoring of the reader. This is Horwood at his best, but it is a genre that he did not attempt again. Instead, in his second novel. *White Eskimo; a novel of Labrador* (1973), we find him plunging once more into romantic excess. This time his subject is the Inuit of Labrador, who are seen as noble savages exploited by the 'white racist' Moravians and the meddling Dr GRENFELL (disguised as 'Dr. Tocsin'). It is hard to accept such extreme judgements, even from a novelist. Horwood in this book appears to have utterly rejected what he calls 'the sickness of Western society'. Indeed, as late as 1977 he announced in public that he remained 'deeply opposed to the way our society is organized.' Even with advancing years, Horwood has not ceased to issue his jeremiads.

White Eskimo, Tomorrow will be Sunday, and *Foxes of Beachy Cove* have proved to be his most important books to date and all three have been reprinted in PaperJacks, the first in 1972, the other two in 1975. In 1979, however, Horwood stated that the two novels were in 'a style and method that I was finished with before 1970.' His collection of short stories, *Only the gods speak* (1979), formed, in his description, 'a kind of watershed' between these books and 'the fiction I hope to go on writing the rest of my life.' In fact the seventeen stories in this volume do not strike the reader as very different from the earlier books, except in superficial matters of technique. They are all, Horwood

says, 'about people seeking salvation', and they convey some of his 'deepest concerns, from the need for closer communion between people to the fear that white civilization has shot its bolt.' Such themes are not new in Horwood's work, though they are expressed more forcefully in the hippie propagandizing of some of these later stories.

Horwood has produced a number of less-ambitious yet sometimes valuable books. *Newfoundland* (1969) is a collection of impressionistic essays about the province, reprinted from magazine articles and broadcasts. He collaborated with Stephen Taylor to produce a coffee-table book on Newfoundland's Great Northern Peninsula entitled *Beyond the road: portraits & visions of Newfoundlanders* (1976). He has also written a fine biography of Captain Bob Bartlett, *Bartlett: the great Canadian explorer* (1977), and is the author of the second volume in the Canada's Illustrated History series, *The colonial dream 1497/1760* (1978). In addition he edited *Voices underground* (1972), an anthology containing poems by Des Walsh, Michael Wade, Drew, and Eric Hoyles, and *Tales of the Labrador Indians* (1981). The phrase 'With Harold Horwood' appears on the title-page of Cassie Brown's *Death on the ice: the great Newfoundland sealing disaster of 1914* (1972).

There is a revealing interview with Horwood in *Quill & Quire* (Aug. 1972).

PATRICK O'FLAHERTY

Houston, James (b. 1921) Born in Toronto, he attended the Ontario College of Art. After serving with the Toronto Scottish Regiment during the Second World War he went north to Baffin Island, where for nine of his twelve years there he was the region's first civil administrator. He is generally credited with the initial development of Eskimo art in Canada. Houston has travelled extensively and studied art in France, Japan, and the United States. He is currently a director of Steuben Glass in New York.

Best known as a writer of juvenile fiction, Houston has three times won the Book-of-the-Year Award of the Canadian Association of Children's Librarians. Beginning with *Tikta' liktak: an Eskimo legend* (1965), he has written and illustrated eleven books for children and young adults, all full of factual information about native customs that he has woven into the action of the stories. *The white archer: an Eskimo legend* (1967) and *Akavak: an Eskimo journey* (1968) both centre upon journeys in which physical courage parallels moral development. *Wolf run: a Caribou Eskimo tale* (1971) followed. Houston's plotting is generally very loose, his emphasis being on events rather than character development; the protagonist is most often a child or young adult who, through a series of crises, grows to maturity. *Kiviok's magic journey: an Eskimo legend* (1973), which is for very young children, is the only Eskimo legend that Houston did not change substantially. The writer claimed that of 100 traditional Inuit stories, perhaps only three would work for a non-Inuit writer in their present form because of differences in the literary tradition. In *Frozen fire: a tale of courage* (1977) and *River runners: a tale of hardship and bravery* (1979) Houston moved away from traditional themes and began dealing with problems in the modern Inuit world. In *Long claws: an Arctic adventure* (1981) he makes good use of the bear as a visible sign of terror. Houston considers a bear-attack a staple of Canadian children's literature about the North and says: 'The weather isn't quite enough to express the danger that is present in the Arctic, whereas a bear can symbolize that in a wonderful wây. He's white and he's big; he's like a terrible storm; he's an allegorical kind of thing sometimes. And I think I've often used bears in an allegorical way.' His most recent children's book is *Black diamonds: a search for Arctic treasure* (1982). Houston, who spends considerable time living in a cabin in the Queen Charlotte Islands, also wrote *Eagle mask: a West Coast Indian tale* (1966) and *Ghost paddle: a Northwest Coast Indian tale* (1972).

Houston's adult novels, like many of his children's books, draw on true stories of native contact with Europeans. *The white dawn: an Eskimo saga* (1971) was based on an incident in 1896 when three New England whalers were first rescued and then killed by Eskimos. Houston heard of these men from Inuit friends on Baffin Island and was later able to confirm parts of the story from the ship's log of the *Abby Bradford*. *Ghost fox* (1977), about the abduction of a New England farm girl by Abnaki Indians in the 1750s, contains the historical and anthropological accuracy of his other works. *Spirit wrestler* (1980) is a fictional examination of the spirituality and chicanery of shamanism. For *Eagle song* (1983) Houston consulted the journal of John R. Jewitt, of the American brig *Boston*, who was captured by the Nootka chief Maquinna in 1803. The story is told by Maquinna's brother-in-law.

Houston's non-fiction works include *Canadian Eskimo art* (1955), *Eskimo graphic art* (1960), *Eskimo prints* (1967), the introduction to *The private journal of Captain G.F. Lyon* (1970), and *Ojibway summer* (1972). Houston frequently uses authentic Inuit and Indian poetry in his novels, an interest that resulted in *Songs of the dream people: chants and images from the Indians and Eskimos of North America* (1972). He has also written several screenplays, beginning with one for a film based on *The white dawn*, which was released in 1974. Houston was made an officer of the Order of Canada for his work as an administrator, artist, and writer.

See also CHILDREN'S LITERATURE IN ENGLISH: 2.   ROBIN GEDALOF McGRATH

Howe, Joseph (1804-73). Born in Halifax, N.S., he received some formal schooling but at the age of thirteen was taken as an apprentice into the family printing and newspaper business, the same office that had earlier published the first literary journal, the NOVA-SCOTIA MAGAZINE. He went on to a brilliant career as an author and journalist, establishing his newspaper the *Novascotian* as the leading journal in nineteenth-century Halifax; but he is best remembered as the pre-eminent politician of nineteenth-century Nova Scotia. He was elected to the legislative assembly in 1836 and for the next twelve years fought for responsible government. He reached the peak of his provincial political career as premier from 1860 to 1863. In the Confederation debate of the mid-1860s Howe led the opposition forces in Nova Scotia and ran as an Opposition candidate in the first federal election in 1867. He won, but by 1869 became convinced that opposing Confederation was futile. He accepted an appointment to the federal cabinet as secretary of state for the provinces, and served as minister until appointed lieutenant-governor of Nova Scotia in Apr. 1873, two months before his death at Government House, Halifax.

In the 1820s and 1830s Howe wrote a substantial amount of verse, most of which was published in local newspapers. It was later collected and posthumously published in *Poems and essays* (Montreal, 1874), in which there are two poems of more than passing interest: 'Melville Island', which was first published in 1825, and 'Acadia'. In the first Howe uses a description of a former military prison near Halifax as a point of departure for philosophic observations on human experience. His intention is to suggest that life in Nova Scotia should not be considered remote or isolated from the mainstream of human civilization. In 'Acadia' (probably written in the early 1830s) the frame of reference against which past and present experiences are viewed is a rather vague vision of a bright social, political, and economic future for the people of Nova Scotia. Howe's intention is not made clear; he was better equipped to pursue his vision in the world of partisan politics and through the manipulation of political power.

Howe's formal prose works, while competently written, reflect the limitations and topicality of his concerns. *The speeches and public letters of the honorable Joseph Howe* (London & Boston, 1858; Halifax, 1909) is of some historical interest, but his addresses on non-political subjects are too general and simplistic to merit much attention. Some of his early journalistic pieces, however, have a vivacity and sharpness of observation that make them a continuing delight to read. Of particular note are his 'Western rambles' and 'Eastern rambles'—which ran serially in the *Novascotian* between 1828 and 1831—where he describes two journeys in Nova Scotia employing anecdotes, commentary, and observation, in the manner of William Cobbett's 'Rural rides'. At the same time Howe contributed to 'The Club Papers', a series of satiric and witty dialogue discussions of people and events by an ostensibly fictitious group of Halifax gentlemen; the articles are not unlike the 'Noctes Ambrosianae' series in *Blackwood's Magazine*.

Howe's greatest contribution as a cultural figure, however, lay in his life-long belief in the necessity of developing a local literature and in the encouragement he gave to those around him to write and publish. After purchasing the *Novascotian* (1824-1926) from George Renny Young in Jan. 1828, he (together with John Sparrow THOMPSON) turned the paper into a cultural and intellectual vehicle in the community, opening its weekly columns to local essayists, fiction writers, and poets. During Howe's proprietorship (and even after he sold it in 1840), the *Novascotian* actively promoted local literary activity, and counted among its contributors George Renny Young, Thomas Chandler HALIBURTON, Angus Gidney, Andrew SHIELS, Mary Jane KATZMANN, and John McPHERSON. Howe himself, through the 'Rambles' and 'The Club Papers' in the 1820s and 1830s, helped to set the literary tone of the times and to nurture the confidence that Nova Scotian writers developed

in themselves and in the cultural potential of colonial society.

M.G. Parks has edited and written introductions to a modern edition of *Poems and essays* (1973) and to *Western and eastern rambles: travel sketches of Nova Scotia* (1973). See also *The heart of Howe: selections from the letters and speeches of Joseph Howe* (1939) edited by D.C. Harvey and *Joseph Howe: conservative reformer, 1804-1848*, vol. 1 (1983) by J. Murray Beck.   TOM VINCENT

Hughes, Monica (b. 1925). Born in Liverpool, Eng., Hughes had lived in Egypt, England, Scotland, and Zimbabwe, before coming to Canada in 1952. She is now married and lives in Edmonton. Hughes speaks of the shock she felt upon entering the Canadian landscape, of the fear and loneliness created by the Laurentian Shield and the Prairies. This sense of alienation inherent in the setting recurs in her novels, especially *Earthdark* (1977), the Isis trilogy (*Guardian of Isis*, 1981; *Keeper of the Isis light*, 1982; *The Isis pedlar*, 1982), and *Beyond the dark river* (1979). One of the most important and talented writers for adolescents of the present day, Hughes has produced historical fiction (*The gold-fever trail*, 1974; *The treasure of the Long Sault*, 1982), and realistic novels (*Ghost dance caper*, 1978; *Hunter in the dark*, 1982); but she is best known for her science fiction (the Isis trilogy, *Crisis on Conshelf Ten*, 1975; *The tomorrow city*, 1978). The teen-age heroes/heroines in Hughes' novels become isolated by circumstances, which force them to make choices that define their character and identity. They face the universal adolescent difficulties of parental shortsightedness, the fear and hostility aroused by being 'different', the loneliness of isolation, and the need for close friendships. Hughes insists upon a character's search for truth and humanistic values. Presented as a saving remnant against the dehumanization of modern or future mass cultures, and usually caught in a web of intolerance and power, her main characters undergo a struggle that is of importance to the survival of their civilization.

Two major themes permeate Hughes' fiction: the conflict of cultures and respect for the power and beauty of nature. These very Canadian themes are most forcefully handled in the Isis trilogy, and in *Hunter in the dark* and *Beyond the dark river*. In the conflict of cultures, those who survive do so because of their deep fidelity to the traditional humanistic values of courage, tolerance, and individual choice. Cultures that violate these values carry self-destruction within them. Culture, however, is never isolated from place and landscape—one must either adapt through knowledge to the power of Nature or succumb to it. As in most important children's literature, the value of revering nature is closely associated with development of self and respect for others.

Known both in North America and in Europe, Hughes received the Canada Council Children's Literature Prize in 1982. See 'The writer's quest', *Canadian Children's Literature* 26 (1982) for Hughes' comments on her methods and intentions in writing, and also in that magazine (no. 17, 1980), 'Monica Hughes: an overview' by Gerald Rubio.

See also CHILDREN'S LITERATURE IN ENGLISH: 8.   ROBERT LOVEJOY

Hull, Edna Mayne. See SCIENCE FICTION AND FANTASY IN ENGLISH AND FRENCH: 2.

Humour and satire in English. Because satire has long been a mainstay of Canadian literature, it is fair to say that an important part of the Canadian literary imagination is critical, ironic, and mockingly humorous. Among our most widely read writers are two accomplished satirists from the past, T.C. Haliburton and Stephen Leacock; while the satirical fiction of Mordecai Richler and Robertson Davies, and the satirical poetry of Earle Birney and F.R. Scott, are much enjoyed and admired today. Nonsatiric humour tends to be restrained, stressing irony, but occasionally rising to the fullness of comedy, as in other novels by Richler and those of Robert Kroetsch.

The satires of Thomas McCULLOCH and T.C. HALIBURTON are largely, but certainly not exclusively, topical. To modern readers the effects of humour in their work are weakened by ponderous prose, moralizing, and verbosity; but Haliburton has survived more successfully than McCulloch because Sam Slick, the central character of much of Haliburton's writing, sometimes transcends his own limitations and becomes an engaging humorist, though the humorous effects of his dialect, witty aphorisms, and figures of speech are often weighed down by repetition and archaic Tory philosophy. McCulloch's Mephibosheth Stepsure, the lame Presbyterian minister, lacks Sam Slick's verbal power, and his humour at the expense of his profligate neighbours seems condescending and self-righteous—even for a satirist. One of McCulloch's best satires points out

that poetic diction and classical allusion are inappropriate to North American writing, and in a mock dream-vision Stepsure journeys up Parnassus to hear Apollo's wisdom and finds a bouquet of Parnassian flowers stuck in a pad of cow dung. Although *The letters of Mephibosheth Stepsure* (published in book form in 1862, but appearing as letters in the *Acadian Recorder* in 1821) is McCulloch's only publication in this genre, Haliburton wrote, besides four Sam Slick collections, several other satirical-humorous books.

Stephen LEACOCK's writings are often slight, their humour depending on the tedious device of nonsense created by irrelevance, puns, and ambiguity. His books, however, contain many successful sketches, and an air of near-fantasy can strengthen Leacock's best work, such as his minor masterpiece SUNSHINE SKETCHES OF A LITTLE TOWN (1912), in which ruinous nonsense is held in check and a subtle and carefully designed mock-heroic form dominates. The pretensions of small-town Canada (Mariposa in the satire) are contrasted with the satiric norms of New York, London, King Edward VII, Rockefeller, and Carnegie. Mariposans are seen by Leacock's unrelentingly critical eye as gullible, vain, stupid, incompetent, and self-interested. ARCADIAN ADVENTURES OF THE IDLE RICH (1914) satirizes city life in sketches on social, financial, educational, religious, and political affairs. Cameo characterizations help to give unity to this work: President Boomer of the University, the Rev. Fareforth Furlong and the Rev. Uttermost Dumfarthing of the Episcopalian and Presbyterian churches, the Overend brothers, the financiers Fysshe and Rasselyer-Brown, and the Rev. McTeague, who finally reconciles Hegel and St Paul when he realizes that life is a paradox and the seemingly important things are unimportant. When he becomes concerned for ordinary people, and spends time in friendly discourse with people he meets on the street, he is thought to have gone mad.

Leacock's influence can be seen in the work of Paul Hiebert, author of SARAH BINKS (1947), a fictional biography of the Sweet Songstress of Saskatchewan whose marvellously banal 'poetry' is analysed with suitable academic over-kill. The theme of Canadian provincialism is carried on from Haliburton and Leacock, but whereas Sam Slick and Leacock's persona in *Sunshine sketches* are both worldly, Sarah's biographer is as naive as she is. Hiebert contributes the name Willows, Sask., to Canadian fictional place names in *Sarah Binks*, but his *Willows revisited* (1967) is less successful than its predecessor in giving humorous life to a rural area.

Salterton, Ont., is the small city of Robertson DAVIES' *Tempest-tost* (1951) and *Leaven of malice* (1954). The third work in this trilogy of often forced humour, *A mixture of frailties* (1958), is less satiric than the other two, but all three attack the provincialism of Salterton, an old university town. Davies' situation humour—sometimes Leacockian in its extravagance—and characterizations of university professors, the local little-theatre group, and the town's social élite, are at times farcical. Davies also attacks Canadian cultural stagnation in *The diary of Samuel Marchbanks* (1947) and *The table talk of Samuel Marchbanks* (1949)—sketches of biting humour, most of which appeared in the Peterborough *Examiner* when Davies was editor.

Perhaps the most successful Canadian writer of humour in prose satire is Mordecai RICHLER, in *The incomparable Atuk* (1963) and *Cocksure* (1968). *Atuk*, a formal satire bound only superficially by the conventions of realism, ranges from witty analogies between Jews and Eskimos to low and grotesque imagery in the activities of the Gentile-hating Panofsky, in the sex lives of the various characters, and in Atuk's murder of his brother. It is one of Canada's most complete works in its use of the conventions of humorous satire. *Cocksure*, on the other hand, uses these conventions in realistic novel form and is somewhat diffuse, although its black humour is chillingly effective. There is also a Leacockian exaggeration in incidents that satirize the avant-garde in the arts and liberalism in education and other areas: Star Maker, Hollywood producer—the ultimate narcissist—possesses a surgically developed androgyneity that enables him to impregnate himself and become pregnant.

Early BIRNEY's *Turvey: a military picaresque* (1949) has an analogue in Hasek's *The good soldier Schweik*. Its picaresque adventures celebrate the 'naturally loving and obstinately life-preserving' forces (present in the simple and earthy Private Turvey and his friend Mac) over the 'mechanical and life-destroying' (the Army, its tests, regulations, and courts-martial). Birney, however, is also a poet, and his humorous satirical poems flay society's ignorant, arrogant, and bigoted in such poems as 'Appeal to a

woman with a diaper', 'Billboards build for freedom', and 'Anglosaxon Street'. 'Twenty-third flight' and 'The way to the West' take aim at powerful business, the Kaiser Corporation, and International Nickel. Birney is also sometimes satirical in his delightful experiments with language and verse forms in the collection *Rag and bone shop* (1971).

F.R. SCOTT is another poet who writes effective satire, attacking with sharp and unsparing wit the Canadian Authors' Association ('The Canadian authors meet'), capitalism ('Efficiency'), the dehumanization in a technological society ('Mural'), Prime Ministers R.B. Bennett and Mackenzie King, and other subjects. Irving LAYTON's satiric humour, on the other hand, which is frequently aphoristic, is all too often pursued with the self-indulgence of a carping iconoclast. Scott and A.J.M. Smith edited *The blasted pine: an anthology of satire, invective and disrespectful verse* (1957; rev. 1967), which contains poems by colonial writers (for example, Alex Glendinning, Alexander McLACHLAN, and Standish O'GRADY, who damn the British, the Americans, and even the climate of Lower Canada); by LAMPMAN of the CONFEDERATION POETS, a most unhumorous group; by L.A. MacKay; the McGill group (especially Smith and Scott); and by contemporary poets Margaret ATWOOD, Birney, Layton, Al PURDY, and Raymond SOUSTER. A recent humorous anthology is *The maple laugh forever: an anthology of Canadian comic poetry* (1981) edited by Douglas BARBOUR and Stephen SCOBIE.

In 1958 James REANEY made an ambitious attempt to use humour in his long satire *A suite of nettles* (1958; 2nd edn 1975), based on Edmund Spenser's *Shepheardes calender*. Essentially a beast fable in twelve eclogues, Reaney's work is often pedantically obscure, and the humour of geese discoursing on human affairs often suffers accordingly.

Contributions to non-satiric humour in poetry have been made by W.H. DRUMMOND and Robert SERVICE. Drummond, writing at the turn of the century, employed for comic purposes his own version of the broken English used by Québec *habitants* in narrative poems about their courting, marriage, family occasions, and about individuals who have stirred local interest: Jean Bateese, who goes to the United States, becomes rich, but returns gratefully to Québec after he loses his money; Madame

Humour and satire in English

Albani, world-famous singer, who is still just 'de Chambly girl'; and Louis Desjardin who outwits the Devil, driving him off by enveloping himself in a cloud of smoke from the pungent local tobacco. Robert Service also sets much of his poetry in a specific locale—the Yukon, at the time of the Gold Rush and after. His few humorous poems—with their simple characters, engaging rhythms, and imagery from the difficult northern life—include two classics, 'The cremation of Sam McGee' and 'The shooting of Dan McGrew', among others that are less well known.

Nearly all our good poets include some humour in their work but excepting that of Service and Drummond it usually tends to be ironic—Atwood's 'They eat out', Purdy's 'Linear B', or Souster's 'The girl at the corner of Elizabeth and Dundas'. Leonard COHEN's personae frequently have a touch of ironic humour in their attitudes, and in *Death of a lady's man* (1977) the informality of the critical commentator's audacity sometimes contrasts wittily with the seriousness of the poem under discussion. Many of George JOHNSTON's poems in *The cruising auk* (1959) have an innocent humour that is ironically reminiscent of children's verse. The contemporary poet whose non-satirical poems are most pervasively humorous is Irving Layton. His witty phrases, colloquialisms, bawdy diction, and violent images often give his love poems an ironic, earthy perspective.

In non-satirical humorous prose works the image of the small town or rural community is frequent. These works can be idyllic, such as Robert Fontaine's delightful, nostalgic *The happy time* (1945); L.M. MONTGOMERY's *Anne* books, which centre on that high-spirited, intelligent, sensitive girl and young woman; and W.O. MITCHELL's *Who has seen the wind* (1973), whose Brian O'Connal, his friends, and family give imaginative definition to a small prairie town, just as Anne does to Prince Edward Island. Mitchell's *The kite* (1962), also set in a small town, uses the convention of friendship between an independent old man and a young boy. The old man's speech and confusions are often humorous, but episodes sometimes approach the tall tale, which in a realistic novel strains credibility.

Max Braithwaite's humorous novels are set in rural and small-town Saskatchewan. Although in general they lack serious thematic interest, *The Commodore's barge is alongside* (1979) and *The night we stole the Mountie's car* (1975) are two simple, unpretentious, and thoroughly funny novels.

Also giving a strong sense of place to the Prairies are some of the novels of Robert KROETSCH, particularly *The words of my roaring* (1977), *The studhorse man* (1977), and *Gone Indian* (1981). Bawdy and full of ingenious, humorous incidents, they are permeated with a sense of the ridiculous. His central characters, who occupy heroically imaginative worlds surrounded by banality, are classical gods and goddesses or Odyssean wanderers embodying a vision of life that is serious, but vigorous and earthy, hilarious, but ironic and sad.

Along with Kroetsch, Mordecai Richler raises humour to its highest development in Canadian prose in *St. Urbain's horseman* (1978), *The apprenticeship of Duddy Kravitz* (1969), and *Joshua then and now* (1980). Duddy Kravitz is often humorous in his frankness, in his witticisms, and in his naiveté as he struggles to develop some sophistication. He seeks identity through owning land, while guilt-ridden Jake Hersh, in *St. Urbain's horseman*, searches vainly for a hero to worship. This novel—a superb compendium of life in the 1950s and sixties—makes effective use of verbal irony, comedy, colourful characterizations, low language, Jewish-gentile cultural confusions, and unconventional material such as newspaper clippings and a Mensa test.

Other novels touched with the comic spirit are Sara Jeannette DUNCAN's *The imperialist* (1904), Brian MOORE's *The luck of Ginger Coffey* (1977), Cohen's *Beautiful losers* (1981), ENGEL's *Lunatic villas* (1981), Morley Torgov's *The outside chance of Maximilian Glick* (1982; Leacock Medal for Humour), and Atwood's *Lady oracle* (1976), in which the overweight heroine describes others caustically ('the indistinct wives' of businessmen) and herself ironically ('I stood in front of the mirror . . . and examined myself much as a real estate agent might examine a swamp, with an eye to future development'). Leo SIMPSON's *Arkwright* (1971) develops a kind of surrealism, whose effect is weakened by wordiness and extravagant conceits. Characters tend to be stereotypes, as they are in his comedy of manners, *Kowalski's last chance* (1980), which uses the 'dumb cop' convention. Though its farce is sometimes effective, this novel is too often silly rather than funny. Simpson's *The Peacock papers* (1973) mixes satirical and non-satirical humour in a work that is, at times, close to fantasy. Of particular note is the mock-heroic Battle of the Bradfarrow Library, as the technocrats attempt to take over and put the contents of the books on electronic devices. John METCALF's *Goin' down slow* (1975), a more successful blend of satire and comedy, portrays the vicissitudes of a sardonic young English immigrant teaching in Montreal, but his *General Ludd* (1980), more ironic than satiric, has only a few touches of humour. Jack MacLeod's hilarious *Zinger and me* (1979), an epistolary novel that deals with some of the vagaries of academic life, covers a broad spectrum of deftly handled techniques, from intellectual wit to the low humour of body functions. His *Going grand* (1982) is less humorous and fails to resolve problems created by mixing comedy and pathos.

Short stories are an important part of Canadian writing and humour has a significant place in them. W.O. Mitchell's stories in *Jake and the kid*, though sometimes sentimental, have humorous moments in their depiction of the affairs of the hired man and the little boy. Ethel WILSON's *Mrs. Golightly and other Stories* (1961) reveals her deft style and gentle humour, particularly in the estimable 'A drink with Adolphus'. Frederick Philip GROVE skilfully uses understated humour in 'The midwife'. Some of Margaret Atwood's stories can be said to be humorous, but her *forte* is the pointed, mocking phrase. Mavis GALLANT's exquisite stories are often touched with light irony; Shirley FAESSLER and Jack LUDWIG contribute to the body of Canadian humorous Jewish literature, for example with 'A basket of apples' and 'A woman of her age' respectively. John Metcalf's 'Private parts: a memoir' is an excellent, funny fictional reminiscence.

W.P. KINSELLA's *Born Indian* (1981) is often touching; but at times the humorous stories tease credibility in their exaggerated simplicity, and their farcical humour may lose force through predictability. This collection uses, however, an effective native Indian author-persona who finds inspiration for his stories in the inhabitants of the Ermineskin Reservation, in Alberta. H.T. Schwartz also turns to Canadian natives for his collection of interesting and funny erotic Indian stories, *Tales from the smokehouse* (1974).

Humorous reminiscences, sketches, and journalism, some of it fictional, abound in Canadian writing. Of these rather ephemeral forms, perhaps Don Harron and Farley MOWAT are two of the most important practitioners, with Eric NICOL, Peter McARTHUR, Gregory Clark, and R.T. Allen also making significant contributions. In Harron's series by 'Charlie Farquarson', the Parry Sound (Ont.) farmer gives us his *Jogfree of Canada, the whirld and other places* (1976), *The histry of Canada* (1972), plus his own version of the Old Testament, and his *K-O-R-N filled allmynack*. The humour in these works depends on distortion of fact, misspellings, dialect, prurience, puns, and malapropisms.

For *The boat who wouldn't float* (1969), Farley Mowat won the 1970 Stephen Leacock Memorial Medal, which is offered annually for the best work of humour by a Canadian. His entertaining reminiscences of sailing a run-down schooner from Newfoundland to (eventually) Montreal have aspects of a comic epic, including the apparent intervention by spiritual forces in the running of the ship's engine. These adventures are never sentimental or affected; the realism of the situation never falters in its accommodation of the humour.

Though occasionally serious and entertaining, books of newspaper humour are often sexist, condescending, moralistic, and sentimental. Eric Nicol writes 'A drag down mammary lane'; to Greg Clark, the rich are nearly always bores. R.T. Allen's wife is apparently without a sense of humour; he feels that today's children are likely to think the world of his youth stupid and funless, and he writes *We gave you the electric toothbrush* (1971) to argue his point. One exception to these writers is Peter McARTHUR, whose ironic, light-hearted view of life is expressed by an easy-going, very human persona. The intellectual level of his sketches—which are often bucolic and may deal with art, poetry, and nature—is higher than that of other examples in this genre.

There is humour of a relatively sophisticated kind in John GLASSCO's autobiographical *Memoirs of Montparnasse* (1970), about a delightfully honest and indolent young man's experiences in Paris in the late 1920s, including a soirée at Gertrude Stein's where 'the atmosphere was almost ecclesiastical'. Emily CARR's frequently amusing autobiographical writings in *The book of Small* (1942) and *The House of All Sorts* (1944) tell of her life in Victoria, B.C., the former of her childhood and the latter of her years as the landlady of her apartment house. *Running to paradise* (1962), a book of Kildare DOBBS' essays, begins with his childhood in Ireland, moves through his experiences as a sailor in the British navy and as an administrator in Africa, and ends with his immigration to Canada. However, these slight but often elegant and entertaining pieces are on occasion marred by racially patronizing attitudes. Dobbs also wrote one of the finest modern humorous books: *The great fur opera* (1970), a comic history of the Hudson's Bay Company with illustrations by Ronald Searle.

Humour fares less well in Canadian drama than in other forms. Of *Three plays by Eric Nicol* (1975) two are comedies: *Like father like son* and *The fourth monkey*. The first is marred by clichés about preparing a young man for his initiation into sex; the second has a fairly witty use of language, but is dated and trite in its references to the USSR. Merrill DENISON's plays have humorous episodes: *The weather breeder* and *Balm*, from Volume I of *Canadian plays from Hart House Theatre* (1926), for example, and *Brothers in arms* (1923).

Critics have noted James Reaney's penchant for playfulness in *his* dramas but too often the deliberate obfuscation of meaning in dialogue, and the use of word games, detract from the humour. *The killdeer* (1962, rev. 1972), however, shows some effective contrast between the humorous and the dark or grotesque, *The easter egg* (1972), a comedy of manners, has Shavian repartee at times, and *One-man masque* (1962) some good verbal humour and effective stage business.

Robertson Davies' best plays are sometimes satirical (*Overlaid*, *Hope deferred*, and *A masque for Mr. Punch*), and there are others, such as those in *Eros at breakfast and other plays* (1949) and in *Four favourite plays* (1968), which are humorous if rather slight.

A collection of Canadian plays (3 vols, 1972-8), edited by Rolf Kalman, contains some impressive comedies: Sheldon ROSEN's *Myer's room* (1972), a fast-moving absurdist play in which humour is created by misunderstandings and confusions of meanings; Donald Jack's *Exit muttering* (1972), a sex-oriented farce of bawdy and situation humour; and Mavor Moore's witty *The pile*, based on amusing semantic and logical arguments, and *The store*, a very funny play in which a woman badgers the store manager with her complaints until he goes mad and stabs her (*The pile; The store; Inside out*, 1973).

Three other examples of successful comedies are David FRENCH's *Jitters* (1980), which deals with the anxieties of the professional production of a play—the practical difficulties as well as those of interpersonal relationships; David FENNARIO's bilingual *Balconville* (1980), which is set in a working-class part of Montreal where, in the summer heat, problems of life are dealt with on the balconies, and in the street below, by earthy English- and French-Canadian characters; and Erika RITTER's *Automatic pilot* (1980), which deals, through themes of alcoholism, love, and homosexuality, with a comedienne's fear of success. The humour of the play, very successful at times, comes both from repartee among characters and from the frantic nightclub routines that reveal, while trying to hide, the comedienne's private agonies.

Two interesting articles on the theory of Canadian literary humour are R.E. Watters's 'A special tang' (CANADIAN LITERATURE, Summer 1960) and Margaret Atwood's 'What's so funny? Notes on Canadian Humour' (*Second words: selected critical prose*, 1982). Watters proposes that the Canadian hero, as best exemplified by characters in Leacock's works, is self-aware, diffident, and self-confident. Atwood, on the other hand, finds that our humour is often structured on the contrast of our cosmopolitan values' being undercut by a certain 'irrevocable' provincialism.

In the body of Canadian writing many works of humour are interesting documents in the development of a culture, rather than significant pieces of literature. With only a few exceptions, however, the highlights are modern. But when one considers the frequency of humour in the literature of the last ten decades, and the stature of those writers who handle it well (Richler, Kroetsch, Birney, *et al.*), one can conclude that humour is a major element in Canadian literature and perhaps its most impressive single achievement. VINCENT SHARMAN

Humour and satire in French. Humour and satire have been essential elements of the oral tradition in French Canada, being found in varying degrees in the traditional folksongs and numerous stories passed on from generation to generation. In the novels, poetry, and plays of the nineteenth century, however, these elements are almost entirely absent—though some early novels, dealing frequently with historical topics or preaching moral or 'patriotic' messages, sometimes incorporate rudimentary attempts to provide the reader with reason to laugh. In historical fiction set at the time of the Conquest, for example, anglophone characters, such as the haughty British officer, are invariably treated mockingly. Joseph MARMETTE adds a new twist in his *François de Bienville* (Québec, 1980) by consistently using a 'vendu'—a French Canadian sympathetic to the British troops—as his comic relief.

Negative and satirical reactions to the Anglo-Saxon 'conqueror' are found as early as 1767 when, in a poem published for New Year's Day in *La Gazette de Québec*, rhyming couplets praise the new governor with discreet, tongue-in-cheek irony. Joseph QUESNEL's one-act play *L'Anglomanie; ou Le dîner à l'angloise*, composed around 1803, pokes fun at the French-Canadian élite who only too eagerly ape British ways and customs. *Épîtres, satires, chansons, épigrammes et autres pièces de vers* (Montréal, 1830) by Michel Bibaud (1782-1857) reflects the influence of the seventeenth-century French writer of epistles and satires, Boileau. Louis FRÉCHETTE's bitterness at the proposed Confederation of 1867 is apparent in his poem 'La voix d'un exilé' (1866), published during his voluntary political exile in Chicago. Praising the rebellious Patriotes of 1837, Fréchette satirizes the 'sordid band' of Cartier and Macdonald as they cynically get drunk on truffles and champagne now that they have succeeded in imposing Confederation on his French-speaking compatriots. A light-hearted tone characterizes Marmette's unpublished 'comédie de salon', *Il ne faut désespérer de rien* (Québec, 1880).

In the twentieth century, humour and satire are markedly absent from the writing of Québec poets. One notable exception is Émile CODERRE, whose poetry of social criticism derives from his sympathy for the exploited poor during the Depression. Using the pseudonym 'Jean Narrache' and the colourful language of the working class, he prefigures the 'joualisants' of the 1960s (those intellectuals preferring to write in JOUAL rather than in a European French). In *Quand j'parl' tout seul* (1933)—a sequence of poems in the form of tragi-comic monologues by the unemployed 'Jean Narrache'—puns and word-play abound, though the essentially tragic tenor of the social criticism, ranging from the bittersweet to the vitriolic, is underscored by abrasive humour, irony, and sarcasm. One particular incident illustrates Coderre's sense of humour and recalls at the same time Roch Carrier's short story 'The hockey sweater'. Praising the politics of a member of the Saint Jean-Baptiste Society, Jean Narrache

becomes violently angry that these 'patriotic' flag-wavers on behalf of Québec's independence buy their flags from Eaton's in Toronto. A parallel to Coderre in the evolution of Québec song was provided by La Bolduc (Mary Travers), a popular singer during the 1930s who described scenes similar to those of Jean Narrache, singing in the language of the poor and using humour and satire to make her critical point. Jacques GODBOUT's ironic humour is tentatively present in an early volume of poetry, *Les pavés secs* (1958), and would come to fruition in his novels.

Edmond Grignon published a light-hearted collection of short stories dealing with human foibles, *Quarante ans sur le bout du blanc* (1932), in which wit, maliciousness, and burlesque parody issue forth from the mouth of a narrator-judge sitting on his bench in the remote Laurentians. Abbé Lionel GROULX reveals a warm sense of gentle humour in 'Comment j'ai quitté la politique', a chapter of *Les rapaillages* (1935), which describes his childhood and the village milieu. Groulx humorously recalls his first foray into politics at the age of twelve when, in a school election between the 'Rouges' and 'Bleus', he, the chief speaker for the 'Bleu' party, suffered ignominious defeat through the 'shameless, corrupt means' of the Liberal opposition.

When discussing the history of theatre in Québec, one thinks automatically of historical dramas or biblically inspired pageants, but alongside the formal 'play' existed the popular monologue of 'improvisateurs'—storytellers presenting dramatic monologues in the local accent to an eager and often unsophisticated audience. From the oral literature of New France springs the long and popular tradition of the 'revue' or the 'sketch', which in the sixties and seventies was used by dramatist, poet and chansonnier alike and has now found its full expression in the recent 'monologuiste' movement. (See *Monologues québécois 1890-1980*, 1980, by Laurent Mailhot and Doris-Michel Montpetit.) Régis Roy's satirical description of Federal politics as described by the candidate for election, Baptiste Tranchemontagne (cf. *On demande un acteur*, 1896), is typical of these presentations, which were usually topical in nature. Jean Narrache, smoking his pipe in front of the fire, became the modern prototype of these monologuists. The most important writer of monologues, however, was Paul Coutlee, who provides the link between his amateurish

Humour and satire in French

predecessors and the more polished performances of Yvon Deschamps and Viola Léger. Coutlee's comic rendering in 1920 of 'Le recensement' (The census), in which the father of a large family cannot remember whether he has nine or twelve children, would be radically adapted by Antonine Maillet in La SAGOUINE. Both Maillet, the author of La Sagouine's monologues, and Deschamps, creator of his own, represent the flowering of a long tradition of humour that uses popular speech, puns, invented words, and curious syntax blended with pessimistic irony and biting satire bordering on 'black humour'. Contemporary realities are perceived and interpreted by alienated and marginal characters. Clémence Desrochers and Marc Favreau (the actor Sol) follow in the same tradition. In the realm of formal theatre, Gratien GÉLINAS's annual series of amusing sketches in the 1940s, Les Fridolinades, and to a lesser extent his TIT-COQ (1950), as well as the plays of Michel TREMBLAY, with their black humour and choral monologues, come from this same tradition. So does Jean-Claude GERMAIN's witty use of 'popular' French, though much of his humour derives from buffoonery, mockery, sarcasm, irony, and vulgarity as he unflinchingly parodies sacred cows of Québec ideological mythology in such plays as Un pays dont la devise est je m'oublie (1976) and Mamours et conjugat (1979).

Humour and satire in Québec fiction until after the Second World War appear only occasionally. Rodolphe GIRARD injected some earthy humour and light anti-clerical comment into MARIE CALUMET (1904), through references by the parish priest's housekeeper to the visiting bishop's 'holy piss' and the accidental baring of her buttocks to the 'curé' as his parishioners looked on. Girard's experiment in humour, however, brought swift public condemnation by Monseigneur Bruchési, the bishop of Montreal, and Girard's firing as director of La Presse. Abbé Groulx's controversial and best-selling novel, L'appel de la race (1922), illustrated the dangers of cultural assimilation through marriage between English and French Canadians. Debate about Regulation 17, depriving Franco-Ontarians of an education in French, provided Groulx with grist for satiric comment: the Union Jack in his novel becomes the 'flag of the conqueror' flying haughtily over the country's capital, and Parliament itself a 'battlefield where since Sainte-Foy two races and two civilizations

confront and oppose each other'. Outspoken anti-clericalism and a scathingly satiric portrayal of the Québec establishment by Jean-Charles HARVEY in Les demi-civilisés (1934) earned him the same fate as Girard: public clerical condemnation and loss of his job as editor of Le Soleil.

The widespread acceptance of Roger LEMELIN's realistic depiction of Quebec City's Lower Town in Les PLOUFFE (1948) not only confirmed the changing nature of Québec society—Lemelin's satiric verve and his comic personalities enabled Québécois to laugh at themselves—but it is the first Québec novel to be suffused with humour from beginning to end (while also retaining a critical purpose). This successful venture into social realism with a comic vein was later taken up by three major writers: Jacques Ferron, Jacques Godbout, and Roch Carrier. FERRON, in debunking traditional myths within Québec, invented new ones based on his re-interpretation of historical fact. Good-natured humour is used in La nuit (1965) and Le ciel de Québec (1969) to poke fun at Scots and at Anglican archbishops whose ancestors have lived in Québec since the Conquest. Anti-clerical humour, traditionally negative and biting, takes an amusing turn in Le Saint-Elias (1972) as the newly ordained priest, arriving in a country parish, is soon seduced by an admiring parishioner he was trying to convert and must be rapidly transferred to avoid scandal. In L'amélanchier (1970), however, the good-natured Dr Ferron heaps vitriolic scorn on the medical profession for their callous treatment of the mentally ill. Roch CARRIER, like Ferron, has his intellectual roots in the oral tradition. In his short stories and novels he excels in the use of situation comedy; he is known particularly for his disquieting 'black humour', with its subversive undertones (La guerre, yes sir!, 1968) and humorously bawdy dialogue (Le jardin des délices, 1975).

Gérard BESSETTE and Jacques GODBOUT have honed the art of satire to a fine degree in their numerous novels. Malicious irony seems to be Bessett's forte, whether he is dissecting religious hypocrisy in Le libraire (1960) or mocking Orange-Loyalist families in L'incubation (1965) and academic colleagues in Le semestre (1979). In Le couteau sur la table (1965) Godbout prefers heavyhanded satire in sketching 'racial' (i.e. anglophone and francophone) stereotypes and expressing anti-clerical sentiments. Irony and laughter are skilfully intertwined in SALUT GALARNEAU! (1967) and D'amour P.Q.

(1972). The whimsical nature of *L'isle au dragon* (1976), with its light-hearted punishment of the American industrialist, Shaheen, for dumping atomic wastes into the St Lawrence, represents a masterful use of humour that does not lessen the seriousness of the problems posed by multinational companies.

In recent years women writers have made significant use of humour and satire. In Antonine MAILLET's novels and plays, which contain amusing dialogue and situations, the humorous weaknesses of her colourful rural characters arouse sympathetic laughter; there is none of the bitterness found in Lemelin and Carrier. Three overtly feminist writers exhibit judicious and effective use of humour as a vehicle for social criticism. In *L'euguélionne* (1976) Louky Bersianik invents an extra-terrestrial feminine version of Candide who comes from outer space to comment on the curious hierarchical relationship existing between the two sexes on the planet Earth. Iconoclastic at the ideological level, Bersianik excels in illustrating with wit and irony the absurd sexism of the French language. (As she points out, in the sentence 'Three hundred women and one cat walked down the street', the masculine cat takes grammatical precedence over the 300 females.) Tragi-comic relationships between couples illustrate feminist themes in Elisabeth Bourget's *Bernadette et Juliette* (1980) while, in *La saga des poules mouillées* (1981), Jovette MARCHESSAULT amuses her theatre audiences by putting swear words in the mouth of Laure Conan (Félicité ANGERS) and four-letter ones into Gabrielle ROY's. Incidentally, while humour is not primarily associated with the fiction of Roy, her vision of life and character is often mellowed by gentle irony.

Claude JASMIN's most recent novel, *Maman-Paris, Maman-la-France* (1982), treats humorously a topic touched on by both novelists and playwrights: the amusing differences between the people and language of France and Québec. Most refreshing and innovative is the underlying mischievous current of humour in Yves BEAUCHEMIN's *Le matou* (1981), with its voraciously hungry little boy, Monsieur Émile, who gets drunk regularly by siphoning the cook's cognac and feeds his equally hungry tomcat, Déjeuner, black pudding and sardines indiscriminately.   RAMON HATHORN

Hunter Duvar, John (1821-99). John Hunter was born in Newburgh, Scot., and became a reporter and agent in England for the old Associated Press of New York. In 1857 he and his wife Anne Carter—who, according to a note scribbled on her husband's will, was an illegitimate first cousin of Queen Victoria—immigrated to Prince Edward Island. In 1861 he legally changed his surname to Hunter Duvar. He served as a militia officer and a justice of the peace, edited the Summerside *Progress* (1875-9), and was Dominion inspector of fisheries (1879-89). At his Hernewood estate he led the life of a gentleman and scholar, joined several literary societies, and corresponded with many public figures. He died at Alberton, P.E.I.

As a poet, Hunter Duvar was equally at ease with short and long poems and developed two distinct voices: one of them a realistic and colloquial contemporary style, often satiric, and the other a rich, bilingual, allusive, medieval style. Both frequently avoided the cloying sentimentality of much Victorian verse. Usually ignoring Canadian subjects, he set his poems in Renaissance France and Spain, or in a fanciful 'fairyland', reflecting the Victorian fondness for medieval subjects. Yet his poems have parallels to his own life, for his protagonists are lonely travellers into new and alien lands; when they fail, they are sustained by the faith of their ladies and by their own poetic vision. *The enamorado; a drama* (Summerside, 1879), dedicated to Swinburne and based on an event in the life of the historical fifteenth-century Mazias of Gallicia, tells of the *Othello*-like betrayal of its soldier-poet hero and is written in the style of Jacobean and Restoration heroic tragedies. The title piece of *De Roberval, a drama; also The emigration of the fairies, and The triumph of constancy, a romaunt* (Saint John, 1888), with its echoes of Shakespearean tragedy, describes how the austere, aloof French nobleman's vision of a harmonious New World society is destroyed by Old World corruption. This publication includes two poems of contrasting style and subject. *The triumph of constancy* successfully recreates the language and flavour of a Chaucerian-style folk-tale in which a questing knight finds salvation in constancy after savouring the pleasures of promiscuity. The other is Hunter Duvar's most anthologized poem, the humorous *The emigration of the fairies*, which may have been written as a private joke about the discovery by him and Anne (the fairies) of Hernewood. In it the world of imagination—with its ancient affinities for the woods and the sea—is transported from old England to Prince Edward Island, the Edenic New World. In all these stories of knights, explorers, and fairy folk, the saving grace is their imaginative vision.

Hunter Duvar also published *John a' Var; gentilhomme et troubadour. His lays* (1874?) and *Fin de siècle; a comedy* (n.d.), which are very rare; a satiric prose work, *Annals of the court of Oberon; extracted from the records* (London, 1895); and an archaeological study of science, folklore, and legend, *The Stone Bronze and Iron Ages* (London, 1892).

See *Hernewood. The personal diary of Col. John Hunter Duvar June 6 to September 17 1857. The story of Anne of Hernewood a fascinating lady and The emigration of the fairies* (1979) edited by L. George Dewar, and Stephen Campbell's *John Hunter-Duvar; a biographical introduction, check-list of his works and selected bibliography*, an M.A. thesis submitted in 1966 to the University of New Brunswick and available on microfilm from the National Library.   GEORGE L. PARKER

Huston, James. See ANTHOLOGIES IN FRENCH: 1, ESSAYS IN FRENCH: 1, and POETRY IN FRENCH: 2.

Hutchison, Bruce (b. 1901). Born in Ontario, he was taken to British Columbia as an infant and grew up in Victoria. He became a high-school journalist for the Victoria *Times* in 1918 and a political reporter in Ottawa in 1925; he returned to the *Times*, also reporting on the provincial legislature for the Vancouver *Province*. He was an editorial writer and columnist on the Vancouver *Sun* (1938), assistant editor of the Winnipeg *Free Press* (1944), and then returned to the Victoria *Times*, where he served as editor from 1950 to 1963, establishing his reputation as a leading political journalist and commentator. In 1963 he became editorial director of the Vancouver *Sun* and in 1979 editor emeritus. In addition to his newspaper work, Hutchison wrote dozens of pulp stories in the 1920s, a novel, and even a film script, 'Park Avenue Logger', which was produced in Hollywood. He has won three National Newspaper Awards, three Governor General's Awards, the Royal Society of Arts Award for Journalism, and the Bowater Prize.

In sixty years of political reporting, Hutchison developed friendships with such political personalities as Lester Pearson and Louis St Laurent. His writings on Canada and some of its political figures is characterized by the confidential vignette, but he has been criticized for partisan loyalty to the Liberal party—a charge he has always denied. His best-known book, *The unknown country: Canada and her people* (1943)—which won a Governor General's Award, and is still in print after several revised editions—is a delightful panorama of Canada, containing vivid descriptions of place and personality, with short lyrical vignettes between chapters. Hutchison also deals successfully with the larger movements of politics and economics. His novel *The hollow men* (1944), the story of a newspaper correspondent disillusioned by world war, combines subtle political satire with sympathy for wilderness life.

His other titles include *The Fraser* (1950) in the 'Rivers of America' series; *The incredible Canadian: a candid portrait of Mackenzie King, his works, his times, and his nation* (1952; GGA); *Canada's lonely neighbour* (1954); *The struggle for a border* (1955); *Canada: tomorrow's giant* (1957; GGA); and *Mr. Prime Minister: 1867-1964* (1964), which was condensed as *MacDonald to Pearson: the prime ministers of Canada* (1967). Hutchison also wrote a short literary study of Canada, *Western windows* (1967), as well as the text for *Canada: the years of the land* (1967), the lavish picture book on Canada produced by the National Film Board. At the age of eighty Hutchison published *Uncle Percy's wonderful town* (1981), a dozen fictional and nostalgic accounts of life in 'Emerald Vale, B.C.', a town with the features of Merrit, Cranbrook, and Nelson in British Columbia. While short on emotional range, these stories—narrated by a fourteen-year-old boy—combined historical and fictional persons in a manner that evokes a vanished time and place. Hutchison's autobiography, *The far side of the street* (1976), which expresses a highly personal view of the growth of his generation, reaffirmed his vision of a modern and responsible Canada.

                    GEOFF HANCOCK

Huyghue, Douglas Smith (1816-91). Samuel Douglas Smith Huyghue was born in Charlottetown, P.E.I., while his father was stationed there with the military, and was educated in Saint John, N.B. In 1840-1 he was living in Halifax and contributing poetry to *The Halifax Morning Post* under his pseudonym 'Eugene'. A year later he was again resident in Saint John and had become a regular contributor of poetry, fiction, and prose to the literary periodical *The*

Amaranth. His activities between 1841 and 1844 included co-hosting an exhibition of Indian artifacts in Saint John with New Brunswick's Indian commissioner, Moses Perley, and working with the Boundary Commission settling the border between Maine and New Brunswick after the Aroostook War. His novel *Argimou: A legend of the Micmac* (Halifax, 1847) first appeared as a serial in *The Amaranth* in 1842. Two years later he left the Maritimes and moved to London, England, where he contributed descriptive sketches to *Bentley's Miscellany* and published a second novel, *The nomades of the West; or Ellen Clayton* (London, 1850). In 1852 Huyghue immigrated to Australia and in 1854 witnessed the Eureka uprising while working as a government clerk in the goldfields at Ballarat. His impressions of the experience were recorded in a watercolour now housed in the Ballarat Fine Art Gallery and in an unpublished memoir, 'The Ballarat Riots'. Huyghue held various govern-ment posts in Australia until his retirement in 1878. He died in Melbourne in 1891.

Huyghue's poems and stories reflected his life-long interest in the culture and society of native peoples. Although *Argimou* purports to be a romance set in Acadia in 1755, it is in reality an impassioned novel of conscience exploring the disintegration of Micmac culture under the influence of European settlement. One of the first Canadian novels to describe the expulsion of the Acadians, *Argimou* was popular enough to be re-serialized in Saint John as late as 1860. Its successor, *Nomades of the West*, never achieved the same reputation, although it too reflected the author's intimate understanding of native people 'before their ranks were thinned, or their spirit broken by aggression.' Perhaps discouraged by the novel's failure in Britain, Huyghue wrote only periodical and private pieces after 1850, and in Australia seemed to favour his art work rather than his writing.

GWENDOLYN DAVIES

I

Incubation, L' (1965). This novel by Gérard BESSETTE is important in modern Québec fiction for its exploration of the depths of the human psyche—symbolized by the labyrinthine basements of the library where the narrator, Legarde, works—and for its innovative, frequently imitated, style: the text is an implosive and introspective first-person narration in one long paragraph. Legarde strives to stay afloat in a world that continually threatens to drown him, and expresses passive despair at the degeneration of the relationships that surround him. Long, unpunctuated sentences record the stream of his ideas and emotions (in the spirit of Claude Simon's 'nouveau roman'). He accompanies his dissolute friend Gordon to Montreal where Gordon meets his former lover, Néa, after twenty years. They are both guilt-ridden for having wished the death of Néa's husband—a wish that was fulfilled. Néa longs for some 'overwhelming confrontation', a 'catastrophic event to restore her equilibrium and moral tran-quility'. Because of Néa, Gordon's wife leaves him, but Néa, realizing that Gordon no longer cares for her, commits suicide. Néa is the novel's only passionate character: the men (including the repressed narrator) are rendered helpless by acute neurosis.

In *Mes romans et moi* (1979) Bessette suggested that serious emotional crises preceded the writing of this novel: 'With a great many distortions and changes, *L'incubation* recounts a drama that I have experienced, both in reality and in fantasy.' It won a Governor General's Award and was translated into English as *Incubation* (1967) by Glen Shortliffe.

LOUIS LASNIER

Indian legends and tales. Legends and tales are part of the oral traditions inherited by Canadian Indians from their forefathers and preserved through countless recitations. Because they are not a homogeneous people, because they speak a number of languages, practise many diverse customs, and

Indian legends and tales

hold many distinctive beliefs, their mythology is varied and vast.

From the beginning of the seventeenth century, when early missionaries first recorded a number of Huron and Algonkin tales in their JESUIT RELATIONS, Indian stories have been gathered piecemeal by such interested laymen as traders, explorers, travellers, clergymen and Indian agents. Towards the end of the nineteenth century the 'doomed-culture theory'—the belief that the Indians would soon be extinct—prompted a more systematic effort to preserve their oral heritage. Expeditions of anthropologists, ethnologists, folklorists—and, much later, sociologists—went to live and work in specific regions among particular tribes. These trained specialists recorded the tales verbatim, transcribing them into literal translations, in simple English, with little or no attempt at literary style, in order to preserve their integrity. In many instances their publications offered the narratives in the original, with an interlinear literal English translation, thus adhering as closely as possible to the forms in which the tales were told. In their concern for scientific accuracy these specialists invariably commented on their methods of obtaining texts and translations, often even citing the names and backgrounds of their native informants and their interpreters. Interpreting and evaluating their materials from the point of view of their academic disciplines, they produced numerous valuable scholarly studies. And, in an effort to systematize Indian lore, they applied a European system of categories and classifications. To prove their pet hypotheses they exaggerated similarities to Scandinavian, Greek, and Hindu mythologies and found Jewish and Christian analogies; they also studied resemblances among the tales themselves. Though many modern scholars have deemed such comparative studies futile speculation, recurrent patterns and motifs do exist in Indian legends and tales and they transcend geographical and linguistic barriers: otherworld journeys, heroic encounters with supernatural powers, animal wives and husbands, animal divinities, powerful magicians, guardian spirit quests; the ritual observance of animal corpses; belief in the significance of dreams, in the indwelling spirit of every created thing, inanimate and animate, in the coupling of all animate and inanimate things or beings (even colours and words), and in the magical power of numbers (4—Ojibways; 5—Athabascans). Metamorphosis and anthropomorphism are essential and significant features. And plots may offer ancient tribal rituals (those of the shaking tent, sweat lodge, bearwalk, Sun, rain and ghost dances, potlatch), purification and expiation ceremonies, as well as initiation, puberty, and mortuary rites. The vision quest—requiring fasting, prayer, deprivation, and ceremonial purity—holds a prominent place in Indian legends and tales.

The culture hero or trickster-transformer figure, who brings about the origins of life as a series of transformations, is the central character in the majority of Canadian Indian myths. Human or animal, he is known to the different tribes under various names. Raven, of the Pacific coast tribes, accounts for the existence of all things—the sun, moon, stars, fire, water, even the alternation of tides; for the Cree and Saulteaux, Wisakedjak (there are many phonetically similar versions of his name) is responsible for shaping the existing world; while the Micmacs' Glooscap and the Ojibwa's Hare made the world ready for man; Manabozho, son of the West Wind and great grandson of the Moon, gave the Central Chippewa the necessities of life; and for the Plains Indians, Coyote or 'old man', who existed on earth before mankind, when humans and animals were not really distinct, is credited with putting the world in order.

At times the hero-trickster is presented in antithetical roles: as an actual creator or as a helper who might either co-operate with or thwart the creator; as a beneficent culture hero and helper of mankind or a malevolent being; as an all-wise, powerful shaman or a credulous fool; as a crafty trickster able to change himself into animal and human shapes or the butt of ridicule; as a joker or a scapegoat who often falls victim to his own and others' wiles. His adventures, whether mischievous or not, always lie in well-known localities within the territory of the band among which the story is told. The trickster performs his altruistic services first to satisfy his own ends and only incidentally for men. A variety of animals—wolverine, badger, raccoon, mink, crow, fisher—might also be selected as trickster-transformer.

For a reader preoccupied with exact chronology and factual details, native chronicles based on oral traditions are disappointing. The constant evocation of a confusing assemblage of mythological figures, and the frequent introduction of supernatural causes and interventions, have created a hodgepodge of details concerning historical origins. Countless variations of a single tale, even within the same tribe or band, are confusing: the treatment of a story may be altered by the taste, gender, or life-circumstances of the narrator, as well as by the place and time of the telling, and even the particular audience. West Coast families have handed down their own versions of stories that often contradict the traditions of their neighbours; there is no interest in reconciling such differences. Although the Iroquois form of government inspired the praise and emulation of the American founding fathers, and their traditions are among the most systematic and coherent, their chronicles lack historical data. For example, details concerning Deganahwidah—the chief who carried out such important constitutional change as the formation of the League of the Iroquois—are often obscure and casual. The famous Ojibwa interpreter and author, Peter Jones (1802-56), stated that the Indians' 'notions as to their origins are little better than a mass of confusion'. Many traditions, he claimed, were founded on dreams, 'which will account for the numerous absurd stories current amongst them'.

Because of their many wanderings and because the history of European-Indian relations has obscured many original Indian values and attitudes, much legendary lore has been debased and distorted by later generations or has entirely disappeared and been forgotten by the living. During the last 300 years elements of European thought and missionary teaching (Bible stories had a strange fascination for Indians) have been so assimilated into an acculturated tradition that it is difficult to separate the European accretions from authentic Indian lore. The *Jesuit Relations* state that the notion of the Great Manitou in its personal sense was introduced by the Jesuits themselves; that the concepts of one incorporeal god, the devil as prince of darkness, the distinction between good and evil gods and the pitting of one against the other, and the belief in future punishment or in an abode of evil spirits, were all foreign to the Algonkin tribes. In modern times some tribes (with only a handful of elderly Indians remembering) tend to emphasize what is most recent in their collective memory, relating stories of events that took place since the advent of whites.

Indian folklore, as it is commonly recorded by scholars, presents other difficulties. Language manipulation is a problem in the translation process. Since collectors have depended chiefly on the broken English of (mostly ageing) native informants or of half-breed interpreters, both of whom were unable or unwilling to translate or explain the full implications of the words or episodes, mistranslations and misconceptions have undoubtedly arisen. And the more literary the English texts, the more apt they are to misinterpret the originals. The Euro-Canadian mind—with its different conceptions of time, the supernatural, material possessions, the phenomena of nature, and humour—finds it difficult to comprehend and appreciate Indian mythology. Foreign to western sensibilities are totemism, metamorphosis, and animism; a moral code that, while it prescribes right conduct, glorifies the ingenious rogue whose cleverness seems to deserve success (fools deserve to be duped); and the realistic and imaginative depictions of erotic love, procreation, and excretory processes, which are considered obscene. When compared with the more developed mythologies, Canadian Indian mythology appears to offer a puerile and an oversimplified view of reality.

Viewed in the context of English literary standards—rather than as a non-literate people, who have developed in a different cultural framework, might perceive them—Indian myths offer little or no narrative appeal. They lack dramatic emphasis and highlights, subtlety, characterization, and plot motivation. Anecdotal and episodic, they tend to be a pot-pourri of unrelated and incomplete fragments, often very brief and almost incoherent; some are merely summaries of reports or events. To people schooled in the English literary tradition (including many Indians who understand little of the language of their ancestors), the rambling conversational manner and exaggerated action of Indian myths can be tedious, their arcane subject matter and hermetic meanings frustrating.

According to Indians themselves, much of the dramatic power and fun of their mythology and folklore emerges only when their stories are told in performance in the native language. Many Indian tales (some of which were sung) comprise the dramatic portions of ritual, festival, and ceremony—elements considered more important than plot and characterization. In print—particularly in English—they lose their dramatic force; but the native linguistic context brings to life their pungent wit and rich vein

Indian legends and tales

of comic pleasantry, metaphorical skill, imagination, and psychological insight. Their humour—sometimes considered obscene by non-Indians—provides comic relief in a violent world; the variations and incongruities, which detractors find chaotic, mirror the rich diversity the Indians saw in nature. Indeed, there are scholars today whose knowledge of Indian languages and traditions has led them to recognize an appropriateness and coherence in Indian myths and folklore—in the context of the Indian way of life—that had not previously been understood.

Countless Indian tales have been interpreted by non-Indians. Partly because of the demands of the market-place, much reshaping and editing has been affected: references to sex, procreation, and excretory matters expunged or minimized; difficult allegories and allusions either ignored or simplified; repetitions, digressions, asides, and obscurities omitted; missing links provided; loose structure tightened; a 'childishness' concealed; and poor syntax and faulty grammar corrected. To be fair, these editorial revisions have often been carried out with every attempt to recreate the spirit of the Indian originals, but the well-intentioned desire to extract English storytelling elements from them has sometimes led to total misrepresentations. Generally speaking, non-Indian storytellers, unable to fathom the Indian mind, have failed to master Indian material.

Up until now Canadian Indian myths and tales have been most successfully interpreted in the form of children's stories, by authors—assiduously drawing on the numerous rough plots and incidents—who have not sacrificed their unique character. The rich quarry of Indian imagery and metaphor has also been mined by Canadian poets—such as Isabella Valancy CRAWFORD and, more recently, John NEWLOVE—who have attempted to come to imaginative grips with the Canadian wilderness and the Canadian identity.

Bibliography. There is a staggering collection of Indian folklore, more from some tribes than from others. Much of it lies buried in journals of learned societies like the American Folklore Society, the Royal Society of Canada, the Canadian Institute, and the British Association Committee; in reports and bulletins of government agencies, such as the Geological Survey of Canada and the National Museum of Canada; and in monographs not readily available, as well as in manuscripts in archival and personal collections. Much of this voluminous material, however, has been gathered more in the interests of scientific data than for literary reasons.

The first professional collector to record Indian myths in English was the American ethnologist Henry Rowe Schoolcraft (1793-1864), who worked among the Ojibwa of the Great Lakes and was probably most responsible for popularizing the Indians' oral literature. His *Algic researches, comprising inquiries respecting the mental characteristics of the North American Indians* (2 vols, New York, 1839) provided the earliest source material for compilers and editors. In 1956 Mentor L. Williams brought together Schoolcraft's tales in a single volume entitled *Schoolcraft's Indian legends from Algic researches, The myth of Hiawatha, Oneóta, The red race in America, and Historical and statistical information respecting . . . the Indian tribes of the United States.*

Dr Franz Boas (1858-1942), considered to be the first professional anthropologist to do field work in Canada, and other anthropologists associated with him, collecting and analysing masses of texts and tales, made significant scholarly contributions, many of which were published by American agencies such as the Smithsonian Institution, Bureau of American Ethnology: *Tsimshian texts* (Bulletin 27, 1902); *Tsimshian mythology based on texts recorded by Henry W. Tate* (1916, rpr. 1970); *Kutenai tales* (Bulletin 59, 1918), with texts collected by Alexander Chamberlain; and by Columbia University in its Contributions to Anthropology: *Kwakiutl tales* (1910, rpr 1969), text in Kwakiutl and English; *Bella Bella Texts* (1928, rpr. 1969; *The religion of the Kwakiutl Indians* (2 vols, 1930), Part 1, Texts; Part 2, Translations. Texts collected by the Tlingit George Hunt, are in *Kwakiutl tales* (New Series, 2 vols, 1935), Part 1, Translations; Part 2, Texts. Tales recorded by Hunt of Fort Rupert are in *Contributions to the ethnology of the Kwakiutl* (1969), in which Kwakiutl texts and English translation are on opposite pages. *Ojibwa texts* (2 vols, 1917), collected by William Jones, edited by Trueman Michaelson, is a publication of the American Ethnology Society. Published by the American Museum of Natural History, Publications of the Jesup North Pacific Expedition, Hunt recording, Boas editing, are *Kwakiutl texts* (Memoirs, vol. 5, 1905); *Kwakiutl texts* (Second Series, Memoirs, vol. 14, part 1, 1906); and *The Kwakiutl of Vancouver Island* (Memoirs, vol. 8, part 2, 1909). Also published for the Museum are Leonard Bloomfield, *Plains Cree texts* (1934), and John R. Swanton, *Haida texts—Masset dialect* (1908). For the American Folklore Society, Boas compiled *Bella Bella tales* (Memoirs, vol. 25, 1932) and edited *Folk-tales of Salishan and Sahaptin tribes* (Memoirs, vol. 11, 1917).

The Society also published Alexander Chamberlaine, *Tales of the Mississaugas* (vol. 2, 1889); Edward Jack, *Maliseet legends* (vol. 8, 1895); Stansbury Hagar, *Weather and the seasons in Micmac mythology* (vol. 10, 1897); James A. Teit, *Traditions of the Thompson River Indians of British Columbia* (Memoirs, vol. 6, 1898), in which Coyote is the principal character, and *Tahltan Tales* (vol. 32, 1919); W.H. Mechling, *Maliseet tales* (vol. 26, 1913); William Jones, *Ojibwa tales from the north shore of Lake Superior* (vol. 29, 1916); Frank G. Speck, *Montagnais and Naskapi: tales from the Labrador Peninsula* (vol. 38, 1925); and Douglas Leechman, *Loucheux tales* (vol. 63, 1950).

Many collections were published under the auspices of the new (1910) anthropology division of the Geological Survey of Canada. In *Some myths and tales of the Ojibwa of southeastern Ontario* (Memoir 48, no. 2, 1914) Paul Radin (1883-1959) offers fifty-five tales in English, in many of which Nenebojo (Nanabozho) plays the role of trickster. In his essay *Literary aspects of North American mythology* (Bulletin no. 16, series no. 6, 1915), Radin characterizes North American mythology as a distinctive literature and explains the variability in versions of one myth. Other Geological Survey texts are W.H. Mechling, *Malecite tales* (Memoir 49, no. 4, 1914); Frank G. Speck, *Myths and folk-lore of the Timiskaming, Algonquin and Timagami Ojibwa* (Memoir 71, no. 9, 1915); and Marius BARBEAU, *Huron and Wyandot mythology with an appendix containing earlier published records* (Memoir 80, no. 11, 1915), in which he treats such subjects as literary style, themes, and diffusion in the Introduction. Much that has been recorded here shows the influence of European tales, riddles, and fables. Names and descriptions, as well as photographs of the native informants, are included; English translations only are given. Published by the Canadian Institute are Father A.G. Morice, *Three Carrier myths* (Toronto, 1895), and James Cleland Hamilton, *Famous Algonquins: Algic legends* (Toronto, 1898); by the Royal Society of Canada, Charles Hill-Tout (1858-1944), *The origin of the totemism of the aborigines of British Columbia* (Ottawa, Section II, 1901); and by the National Museum of Canada,

Leonard Bloomfield, *Sacred stories of the Sweet Grass Cree* (Bulletin no. 60, Anthropological Series, No. 11, 1930), which includes both the original Cree and English translations; and Barbeau's *Huron-Wyandot traditional narratives in translations and native texts* (Bulletin no. 165, Anthropological Series no. 47, 1960). Since Huron-Wyandot, an Iroquoian dialect, is now extinct, the forty texts presented by Barbeau, 'chiefly for linguistic purposes', are extremely valuable. Free translations of texts appear in the first part, with original texts and English literal transcriptions in parallel columns in the second part; the Appendix contains texts with French interlinear translations taken from the JESUIT RELATIONS. Barbeau's *Indian days on the western Prairies* (National Museum, Bulletin no. 163, Anthropological Series no. 46, 1960) contains narratives from the Stoney Indians of the Morley Reserve in Alberta. William Benyon of Port Simpson, B.C., Barbeau's native assistant from 1915 to 1960, recorded *Tsimsyan myths* (National Museum, Bulletin no. 174, Anthropological Series no. 51, 1961), which includes only English translations, and Barbeau himself wrote *Haida myths; illustrated in argillite carvings* (Bulletin 127, Anthropological Series no. 32, 1953). Diamond Jenness (1886-1969), chief anthropologist of the National Museum of Canada (1926-48), was the author of a number of valuable scientific reports on the Indian tribes of Canada, notably *The corn goddess and other tales from Indian Canada* (Bulletin no. 141, no. 39, 1956), for which he selected 'such tales as appear to possess literary merit'.

Pioneer collectors of Northeast Woodland lore are Silas T. Rand (1810-89), missionary and philologist, and Charles Leland. They produced the earliest and the two most frequently cited authentic sources: *Legends of the Micmacs* (New York and London, 1894), in which Rand offers stories of Glooscap, the central figure of northeastern Algonkin mythology; and *The Algonkin legends of New England; or myths and folklore of the Micmac, Passamaquoddy, and Penobscot tribes* (Boston, 1884), in which Leland makes detailed comparisons with the Norse eddas and sagas.

Other early regional presentations of Indian tales include Sir James David Edgar, *The white stone canoe: a legend of the Ottawas* (Toronto, 1885); Egerton Ryerson YOUNG, *Algonquin Indian tales* (1903); George E. Laidlaw, *Ojibway myths and tales* (1915); and Alfred Carmichael, *Indian legends of Vancouver Island* (1922). In Charles Clay,

Indian legends and tales: bibliography

Swampy Cree legends; being twenty folk tales from the annals of a primitive, mysterious, fast-disappearing Canadian race, as told to Charles Clay . . . by Kuskapatchees, the Smoky One (1938), Wesukechak, the trickster hero, appears as the principal figure. (Clay notes the influence of biblical prose, the only type of literature to which the North Manitoba Swampy Cree had been exposed.) See also Alice Ravenhill, *Folklore of the Far West* (1953); James F. Sanderson, *Indian Tales of the Canadian Prairies* (1965); and Ella Elizabeth Clark, *Indian Legends from the northern Rockies* (1966). Frances Fraser's *The wind along the river* (1968) contains seventeen Blackfoot tales that include several ancient Creation myths of Old Man or Nape. *Once upon an Indian tale: authentic folk tales* (1968) by Norman H. Lerman and Helen S. Carkin is a collection of nine folktales told by Indian women of the British Columbia coast and Fraser River valley. *Legends of the river people* (1976) by Norman Lerman and Betty Keller is a collection of thirty legends told by the Chilliwack Indians of British Columbia. See also Herbert T. Schwartz, *Windigo and other tales of the Ojibway* (1969); Marion Robertson, *Red earth; tales of the Micmac* (Nova Scotia Museum, 1969); George Bauer, *Tales from the Cree* (1973); Peter Desbarats, *What they used to tell about Indian legends from Labrador* (1969); James Stevens, *Sacred legends of the Sandy Lake Cree* (1971); Patricia Mason, *Indian tales of the Northwest* (1976), a collection of twenty-three tales from British Columbia, with an accompanying Teacher's Guide; Harold HORWOOD, *Tales of the Labrador Indians* (1981); and Howard Norman, who gathered and translated Cree Windigo tales in *Where the chill came from* (1982). Ralph Maud provides a fresh approach to a new field of study in *A guide to B.C. Indian myth and legend* (1982), which contains brief biographies of the myth collectors and their native informants (Boas, Teit, Hill-Tout, Barbeau, Swanton, Jenness, and Sapir), as well as evaluations of their work.

The trickster figure, in relation to Greek mythology and to psychology, is the subject of Paul Radin in *The trickster: a study in American Indian mythology* (1956; rpr. 1972). Radin bases his important study on the texts of the Winnebago trickster cycle, but he also includes summaries of the Assiniboine and Tlingit trickster myths.

Useful compilations of a general nature are Margaret Bemister, *Thirty Indian legends of Canada* (1917, rpr. 1973); Katherine Judson, *Myths and legends of British North America* (1917); Mabel Burkholder, *Before the white man came* (1923); Marius Barbeau and Grace Melvin, *The Indian speaks* (1943); Hilda Mary Hooke, *Thunder in the mountains: legends of Canada* (1947); Douglas Leechman, *Indian Summer* (1949); Cyrus Macmillan, *Glooskap's country, and other Indian tales* (1956) a selection from Macmillan's *Canadian wonder tales* (1918) and *Canadian fairy tales* (1922)—which are combined in *Canadian wonder tales* (1974), illustrated by Elizabeth Cleaver; Ella Elizabeth Clark, *Indian legends of Canada* (1960); Olive M. Fisher and Clara L. Tyner, *Totem, tipi and tumpline: stories of Canadian Indians* (1962); John S. Morgan, *When the morning stars sang together* (1974), draws parallels between the ancient Greek and Indian stories; and Herbert S. Schwartz, *Tales from the smokehouse* (1974), which includes little-known erotic tales from the Ojibwa, Mohawk, Naskapi, and other tribes.

Of the many collections that have been published in French, see *Traditions indiennes du Canada nord-ouest* (Paris, 1886; rev. ed. 1887) by Émile Petitot, which offers the Indian dialect and French translation in parallel columns; *Carcajou et le sens du monde récits Montagnais Naskapi* (1971) by Rémi Savard; *Légendes indiennes du Canada* (1967) by Claude Mélançon; *Anish-Nah-Be: contes adultes du pays Algonquin* (1971) by Bernard Assiniwi; and *Atanúkana: legendes montagnaises* (1971), collected and translated by Marie-Jeanne Basile and Gérard E. McNulty.

Scholars have presented versions of one myth and analysed them. In *Tshakabesh: récits Montagnais—Naskapi* (1971), Madeleine Lefebvre examines the versions of a Montagnais-Naskapi myth provided by four different narrators. Catherine McClellan studies eleven versions of the girl who married a bear in *The girl who married the bear: a masterpiece of oral tradition* (National Museum of Canada, 1970).

Legends recounted by Indians have been published in native and non-native newspapers and collected in numerous books, including: *The life and traditions of the red man* (Bangor, Maine, 1893; rpr. 1979) by Joseph Nicolar; *Legends of Vancouver* (1911, new ed. 1961) by the famous Mohawk poet Pauline JOHNSON, who adapted the legends of the Squamish tribe told to her by Chief Joseph Capilano; *Abenaki Indian legends; grammar and place names* (1932) by Henry Lorne Masta; *Tales of the Kitimat* (1956) by William Gordon Robinson; *Men of Medeek* (2nd edn.,

1962), as told in 1935-6 to Will Robinson by Walter Wright, a Tsimshian chief of the Kitselas Band of the Middle Skeena River—this material concerns the legendary city of Tum-L-Hanna and the migration westward to Kitselas Canyon in British Columbia; *Legends of my people: the great Ojibway* (1965) by the prominent Ojibwa artist, Norval Morriseau; *Son of Raven, Son of Deer* (1967), a collection of twelve tales of the Tse-Shaht people by Goerge Clutesi, who also wrote an apologia for his people's potlatch ceremony in *Potlatch* (1969). *Tales of Nokomis* (1970) by Patronella Johnston presents Ojibwa legend and custom within the narrative framework of children visiting their grandmother. In *Voice of the Plains Cree* (1973) Ruth M. Buck edited legends collected by the Rev. Edward Ahenakew (1885-1961). *Squamish legends* (1966) was edited by Oliver N. Wells from tape-recorded interviews with Chief August Jack Khahtsahlano and Domanic Charlie. *Visitors who never left: the origins of the people of Damelahamid* (1974)—translated by Chief Kenneth B. Harris, a Tsimshian chief, in collaboration with Francis M.D. Robinson—is a collection of eight myths dealing with the origin and history of the Indians from the regions of the Skeena and Nass Rivers in northern British Columbia. In *Wild drums* (1972) Alex Grisdale relates tales and legends of the Plains Indians to Nan Shipley. See also *Tales of the Mohawks* (1975) by Alma Greene (Forbidden Voice); *Ojibway heritage* (1976), which offers ceremonies, rituals, songs, dances, prayers, and legends of the Ojibwa by Basil H. Johnston, who also published *Tales the Elders told: Ojibway legends* (1981); *The adventures of Nanabush: Ojibway Indian stories* (1979) told by Sam Snake, Chief Elijah Yellowhead, Alder York, David Simcoe, Annie King, compiled by Emerson Coatsworth and David Coatsworth; *Kwakiutl legends* (1981) as told to Pamela Whitaker by Chief James Wallas; and *Tagish Tlaagu Tagish stories* (1982), told in English by Angela Sidney.

See also CHILDREN'S LITERATURE IN ENGLISH: 5.   PENNY PETRONE

Indian literature. 1. THE HISTORICAL BACKGROUND. The literature of the Indians of Canada had its origins in an oral tradition that was rooted in, and transmitted through, the social contexts of storytelling and ceremony. Storytelling included all types of myths, legends, tales, and folklore, while compositional elements of ceremony offered a wide range of songs, ritual chants, drama, poems, prayers, and orations. This spoken literature first became printed when scattered specimens were translated into French and recorded in the JESUIT RELATIONS. The missionaries expressed amazement at the Indians' literary faculties, Father Paul Le Jeune observing that 'metaphor is largely in use among these Peoples' (1636). Because Indians associate an idea with an object, with visual memory, they invariably make use of metaphors and analogies, and because they pay more attention to the implications or suggested meanings of their words—the connotative as opposed to the specific or denotative meaning—their metaphors embody an emotional force. It is this power of arousing emotion by making apt comparisons that constitutes one of the great strengths of their oratory. Oratorical skill was held in the highest esteem. Le Jeune stated that an Indian leader was obeyed in proportion to his use of eloquence because his followers had no other law than his word. In his *Relation* of 1633 Le Jeune commended a Montagnais chief for a 'keenness and delicacy of rhetoric that might have come out of the schools of Aristotle or Cicero.' In his *Relation* of 1645 Father Jérôme Lalemant quotes a speech given by an Iroquois spokesman to Governor Montmagny at Quebec that illustrates the Indian orator's style: 'Onontio, thou hast dispersed the clouds; the air is serene; the Sky shows clearly, the Sun is bright. I see no more trouble. Peace has made everything calm: my heart is at rest. I go away very happy.' Sentences are short and straightforward. Language is clear and simple. A nature image dramatizes the speaker's feelings. A poetic quality and a certain grace permeate the entire speech, while courtesy as well as a sense of dignity and a laconic reserve dominate. However, if the occasion warranted a long speech, the Indian had appropriate metaphors and vocabulary, a syntax that allowed him to formulate complex relationships between ideas, as well as a vivid imagination and literary inventiveness.

In time numerous samples of Indian eloquence in translation, from different tribal cultures across Canada, appeared in the writings of white explorers, traders, travellers, adopted Indian captives, missionaries, and settlers. Admired chiefly for their literary value rather than for their content, they were recorded to illustrate certain stylistic qualities: the Indian's 'pathos', 'caustic wit', or 'genial pleasantry'.

Translation into French and English presented many difficulties. The Indian predilection for figurative and symbolic language, for allegorical meanings and allusions, contributed in no small measure to the problems of exact translation. The eighteenth-century English fur-trader, Alexander Henry, recognized this dilemma when he explained that 'The Indian manner of speech is so extravagantly figurative, that it is only for a very perfect master to follow and comprehend it entirely.' The speeches of two outstanding eighteenth-century warrior-orators—the Ottawa war-chief, Pontiac (1720-69) and the Iroquois Thayendanegea, better known as Joseph Brant (1742-1807)—exemplify Indian eloquence at its best. Pontiac could not write, but his recorded speeches in council outlining his vision of a separate, independent Indian confederacy allied to the French inspired the revolt in 1763-4 of nearly all the tribes around Lake Superior, and as far south as the lower Mississippi. His dictated letters to British and French officials are also impressive, demonstrating the cunning either of an astute warrior or of a brilliant diplomat or a wily politician as the need arose. The great orator Joseph Brant was a spokesman for the Mohawk Loyalists who moved to the Grand River (Ont.) in 1784. Besides his speeches, his extant writings consist mainly of letters to British and American military and civil authorities, and to royalty, many of them expressing his idealistic vision of an independent Indian confederacy that would be a sovereign ally to the British. Written in lucid, direct, highly persuasive English, and notable for their patrician tone, they can be read in W.L. Stone's *Life of Joseph Brant* (2 vols, New York, 1838) and Charles M. Johnston's *The valley of the Six Nations* (1964). The celebrated Shawnee Chief, Tecumseh (1768-1813), renowned for his military genius, also used his remarkable oratorical talents not only in his attempts to unite the Indians into a western confederacy but also in support of the British cause in the War of 1812. Tecumseh's famous speeches in council reveal his adroit reasoning powers as well as his keen political sense, at times combining dry sarcasm with rich metaphor.

The many treaties that emerged out of the complexities of Indian-white relations over the span of three centuries also represent recorded Indian literature. During treaty-making sessions, which resembled ancient councils in their drama and ceremonial formality, Indian orators delivered highly rhetorical speeches using the ancient formulaic metaphors of chain, fire, sun, tree, road, hatchet, and pipe, and made traditional analogies to the natural world while they poured forth their embittered eloquence in defense of home and hunting ground. Western orators of the late nineteenth century—like Crowfoot, Poundmaker, Big Bear, Sweet Grass, and Misto-wa-sis—kept alive the tradition of their forefathers to persuade and lead by means of the oratory of exhortation, which contained inherited images and a strong element of didacticism and aphoristic, dignified language; their speeches can be read in Morris's *The treaties of Canada with the Indians* . . . (1880; rpr. 1971).

2. THE NINETEENTH CENTURY. The first signs of literary creativity in English among the Indians appeared as a result of organized missionary efforts to convert them. Christianized Indians, who themselves became missionaries (mostly Methodist), were encouraged to write for an international audience in order to create interest in, and possibly raise money for, the Indian people. Since they wrote for an international audience of Christian philanthropists, they had a deliberate aim: to encourage compassion and support for the 'poor Indian', who required patience and understanding in the process of being assimilated into the blessings and benefits of European civilization. Their mainly autobiographical works present a wealth of proudly recounted historical information about tribal beliefs, ceremonies, customs, and folklore; ironically, for the modern reader, they are pervaded by deep Christian piety and biblical cadences, the Bible being the predominant literary influence in these Indians' lives. Their books comprise the first body of Canadian Indian literature in English; they also offer the first written evidence of the ideas, responses, and feelings of individual Indians as opposed to the collective expressions contained in myths and legends.

The first Canadian Indian to publish a book in English was George Copway (1818-69), Kah-ge-ga-gah-bowh (He who stands forever), who was born near the mouth of the Trent River in Upper Canada and lived for a time in the Rice Lake area before moving to the U.S. An Ojibwa (Mississauga) Methodist minister who later converted to Roman Catholicism, lecturer, orator, Indian-rights leader, and herbal doctor, Copway wrote *The life, history, and travels of Kah-ge-ga-gah-bowh (George Copway), a young Indian chief of the Ojibwa nation, a con-*

vert to the Christian faith, and a missionary to his people for twelve years: with a sketch of the present state of the Ojibwa nation, in regard to Christianity and their future prospects. Also an appeal; with all the names of the chiefs, now living, who have been Christianized, and the missionaries now labouring among them, written by himself (Albany, 1847). An instant success, it was reprinted six times by the end of the year and republished in London under the main title *Recollections of a forest life . . .* (1850). What is probably Copway's most famous work, described by himself as 'the first volume of Indian history written by an Indian', is *The traditional history and characteristic sketches of the Ojibwa nation* (London, 1850). Written to 'awaken in the American heart a deeper feeling for the race of red men, and induce the pale-face to use greater effort to effect an improvement in their social and political relations', this book was later reprinted in the U.S.A. under the title *Indian life and Indian history by an Indian author . . .* (Boston, 1860). A modern edition appeared in 1978 and a facsimile edition of the 1850 original was published by Coles in 1972.) Copway wrote a compelling and vigorous prose. One contemporary newspaper praised his 'biting satire', 'pungent anecdote', 'strokes of wit and humour', 'touches of pathos', and 'most poetical descriptions of nature'. His success as a writer brought him international recognition and he toured Europe as a celebrity, writing of his experiences in *Running sketches of men and places in England, France, Germany, Belgium and Scotland* (New York, 1851).

Another remarkable Indian author was the Rev. Peter Jones (1802-56), Kahkewaquowaby (Sacred Waving Feathers), the son of a white surveyor and a Mississauga woman, who was born at Burlington Heights (present-day Hamilton, Ont.). Interpreter, translator, author, Indian-rights leader, preacher, and the first native Methodist minister in Canada, Jones was a prolific and indefatigable writer who played a vigorous role in the religious and secular life of his time. His autobiography, *Life and journals of Kah-Ke-Wa-Quo-Na-By (Rev. Peter Jones) Wesleyan minister* (Toronto, 1860), was published posthumously, as was his *History of the Ojibway Indians; with especial reference to their conversion to Christianity* (London, 1861; rpr. 1970). Jones was a gifted writer whose prose in English is highly personal and literate, and occasionally amusing and anecdotal. He also translated several books of the Bible and many

hymns. His hymn translations appear in *A collection of Ojebway and English hymns for the use of the native Indians. Translated by the late Rev. Peter Jones Wesleyan Indian missionary. To which are added a few hymns translated by the Rev. James Evans and George Henry* (Toronto, 1877). The writings of two other ministers reveal the lucid, correct style that many of these men attained. *Journal of the Reverend Peter Jacobs, Indian Wesleyan missionary from Rice Lake to the Hudson's Bay Territory, and returning. Commencing May, 1852. With a brief account of his life, and a short history of the Wesleyan Mission in that country* (Toronto, 1854) is a straightforward factual record of the three-month journey from Toronto to York Factory of Peter Jacobs (1805-90), who was a keen observer; his diary entries are written with precision and clarity. *The diary of the Reverend Henry Budd 1870-1875* (1974), edited by Katherine Pettipas for the Manitoba Record Society Publications, offers the personal record of a former Hudson's Bay Company clerk who was a farmer, a teacher, and for thirty-five years a missionary in the remote diocese of Rupert's Land. He was the first ordained Indian Anglican minister in North America (1858).

Besides the native missionaries, a number of other educated Indians also wrote and published. George Henry (born in 1810), a translator and interpreter, was chief of a group of Ojibwa dancers who made a very successful tour of Europe (1844-8) and the author of two pamphlets: *Remarks concerning the Ojibway Indians, by one of themselves, called Maungwudaus, who has been travelling in England, France, Belgium, Ireland, and Scotland* (Leeds, 1847); and *An account of the Chippewa Indians, who have been travelling among the whites, in the United States, England, Ireland, Scotland, France and Belgium* (Boston, 1848), which, along with Peter Jones's reactions, offers the earliest known detailed impressions of Europeans from the native perspective.

Francis Assikinack (1824-63)—a young Roman Catholic interpreter and school teacher on Manitoulin Island who had studied at Upper Canada College, Toronto—wrote three informative essays for the *Canadian Journal* in 1858: 'Legends and traditions of the Odahwah Indians'; 'The Odahwah Indian language'; and 'Social and warlike customs of the Odahwah Indians'. Assickinak was a competent writer—controlled and dignified, though at times stiffly pedantic.

The last half of the nineteenth century did not have the flood of literary publications that characterized the first half. However, a few missionary-sponsored journals encouraged such literary activities as story-writing, memoirs, conversion anecdotes, various expressions of ethnic pride, and letter-writing: *Petaubun (Peep of Day)*, published in Sarnia (Ont.) in 1861-2; the *Algoma Missionary News and Shingwauk Journal* (Sault Ste Marie, 1877-84); and *Na-Na-kwa; or Dawn on the northwest coast* (Kitimaat, B.C., 1898-1903). Peter Edmund Jones, son of the Rev. Peter Jones, published *The Indian* (Hagersville, Ont., 1885-6); though short-lived, this is of interest because it was the first Canadian periodical edited by an Indian for Indians. The last three decades of the century produced only two books of any significance by Indians, both histories. Peter Dooyentate Clark wrote *Origin and traditional history of the Wyandotts, and sketches of other Indian tribes of North America: true traditional stories of Tecumseh and his league, in the years 1811 and 1812* (Toronto, 1870), an attempt to present historical personages and events through a series of vividly dramatized tableaux. Louis Jackson was the author of a booklet, *Our Caughnawagas in Egypt: a narrative of what was seen and accomplished by the contingent of North American voyageurs who led the British boat expedition for the relief of Khartoum up the cataracts of the Nile* (Montreal, 1885), which gives a first-hand account, both factual and observant, of the famous Nile expedition to the Sudan in 1884-5.

The best-known native writer before and after the turn of the century was a poet, Emily Pauline JOHNSON, Tekahionwake, author of *The white wampum* (London 1895), *Canadian born* (1903), and *Flint and feather* (1912; rev. 1914; paperback 1972), her collected poems. She also wrote short fiction, notably *The moccasin maker* (1913).

Probably the most interesting native author of the fist decade of the twentieth century was John Brant-Sero (1867-?), Ojijatekha, interpreter, poet, and dramatist of Hamilton, Ont. He saw himself as the historian of the Six Nations Indians, dedicated to make known his 'hitherto untold lore', and gave public concerts and lectures in Great Britain and North America. He translated 'God Save the King' into Mohawk and was the author of six articles: 'Some descendants of Joseph Brant', *Ontario Historical Society papers and records*, I (1899), 'The Six Nations Indians in the Province of Ontario, Canada', *Wentworth Historical Society, Transactions*, II (1899), 'Dekanawideh: the law-giver of the Caniengahakas', *Man* (1901); 'Indian Rights Association after government scalp', *Wilshire's Magazine* (Oct. 1903); 'View of a Mohawk Indian', *Journal of American Folklore* 58 (1905); and 'O-no-dah-', *Journal of American Folklore* XXIV (1911). Brant-Sero combined a sense of the enduring past with the realities of the present; but his writing, though straightforward, is flat.

3. THE MODERN PERIOD. In the 1960s more and more Indian newspapers and periodicals sprang up across Canada to provide a forum for growing, politically conscious Indian organizations. Native speakers emerged and Indian oratory once again became a vigorous literary form. Idiomatic and rhetorical speeches were recorded in native and non-native newspapers and journals alike. Journalistic prose, in the form of reports and essays, also became popular as native activists began to attack and criticize the dominant society. Whether in speech or essay, they have reacted politically to Indian problems in a frank and often angry and bitter manner, and in languge that is sometimes flamboyant but always direct and forceful. Concerned with what they perceived to be the wrongs inflicted on their people, they have been more interested in content than in literary style. Native-authored books—frequently written with the aid of a collaborator or amanuensis—reveal five trends: (1) a pan-Indian approach that plays down tribal affiliation and focuses on a common native identity, while sometimes shifting from emphasis on the shared experiences of the group to the single experiences of the individual; (2) a greater diversification of literary *genres*; (3) inspirational writing intended to provide a sense of historical continuity and making use of what is perceived to be ancient beliefs and values; and (4 and 5) two militant approaches: one that advocates separation from the dominant society, and another that seeks an as-yet-undefined revisionist presence in society.

The statement of the Government of Canada on Indian policy (1969), the controversial 'White Paper' that recommended the abolition of special rights for native peoples, sparked a burst of literary activity. An immediate and angry reaction to the government proposals came from the Alberta Cree, Harold Cardinal, in *The unjust society: the tragedy of Canada's Indians* (1971). He argued shrilly for the retention of special rights within the strengthened contexts of treaty and Indian Act and his book, which gained national prominence, has become a classic on the Indian situation in Canada. Arguing a minority point of view, William Wuttunee, a Calgary Cree lawyer originally from Saskatchewan, opposes special status as a barrier to progress and in his controversial *Ruffled feathers: Indians in Canadian society* (1971) advocated instead integration, individual development, and a radical change in the Indian psyche itself. *Bulletin 201* (1970), edited and published by the Anglican Church of Canada, is a collection of the responses to the White Paper by such native writers as Dave Courchene, the Rev. Ernest Willie, Walter Currie, Harold Sappier, and the Rev. Adam Cuthand, who wrote the Preface.

The growing self-consciousness of Indians in recent years has produced more protest literature, some of it written by militant patriots and couched in strident, sloganistic language. Examples of such books are *Prison of grass: Canada from the native point of view* (1975) by Harold Adams; Harold Cardinal's *The rebirth of Canada's Indians* (1977); *Half-breed* (1973) by Maria Campbell; and *We are Métis* (1980) by Duke Redbird.

Antitheses of such angry presentations are a number of recent popular histories focusing on personal experience as well as family and tribal traditions. In *The feathered U.E.L.'s* (1973), Enos T. Monture recreates some memorable occasions in the lives of the first Indian United Empire Loyalists and their descendants. He combines fully dramatized scenes with dialogue and folksy entertaining anecdotes. In *A social history of the Manitoba Métis* (1974) Émile Pelletier tries to prove—in an affirmative and optimistic text, with maps and statistical tables and quotations from primary sources—that the demand for aboriginal rights of the Métis has a strong moral and legal basis. *My tribe the Crees* (1979) by Joseph F. Dion, a treaty Cree descendant of Big Bear, traces the history of the Crees before the arrival of the white man and provides insights, from an Indian perspective, into the Northwest Rebellion of 1885. This was edited by Hugh A. Dempsey, who also edited *My people the Bloods* (1979), drawn from a book-length manuscript entitled 'Indians of the Western Plains', completed in 1936 by Mike Mountain Horse (1888-1964). It is well written and of historical interest. *The ways of my grandmothers* (1980) by Beverly Hungry Wolf records the ancient ways of the Blood women as well as some personal and tribal

history. Two historical books have a strong quality of prophecy and vision: *The fourth world: Indian reality* (1974) by George Manuel and Michael Posluns, in which the background of Manuel as a Shuswap from British Columbia is used to trace the Canadian Indian's struggle for recognition and Manuel offers his vision of a fourth world where the values of special-status people are integrated with those of all peoples; and *These mountains are our sacred places* (1977) by Chief John Snow, of the Wesley band of Stoney Indians, who records the past of his people in a moving and sometimes lyrical prose.

Biography, and its allied forms, is a favourite genre of Indian writers. At their best such books—which are sometimes the result of taped interviews, collaborations, or translation—have a good-humoured, warm, flowing narrative style. *Recollections of an Assiniboine chief* (1972) by the highly articulate Dan Kennedy (1877-1973), Ochankugahe, an Assiniboine Saskatchewan Indian, brings together his writings of the twenties, thirties, and forties and offers primary data about his tribe's history and culture in an engaging and informative style. *Great leader of the Ojibway: Mis-quona-queb* (1972) by James Redsky (edited by James R. Stevens), the last of the Midewin holy men in the Lake of the Woods area, traces the history of the last Ojibwa war leader, Misquonaqueb. More documentary than literary, this book includes a section devoted to the Midewin Society and another containing explanations of Ojibwa customs such as the Shaking Tent. *Guests never leave hungry: the autobiography of James Sewid, a Kwakiutl Indian* (1969) describes Sewid's successful adjustment to the culture change in British Columbia. Anahareo, who had lived with the famous Englishman turned Ojibwa, Grey Owl (Archibald Stansfeld BELANEY), and author of *Devil in deerskins: my life with Grey Owl* (1940, rpr. 1980), published a more recent memoir, *Grey Owl and I: a new autobiography* (1972). *First among the Hurons* by Max Gros-Louis in collaboration with Marcel Bellier, translated from the French by Sheila Fischman, is the autobiography of a Québec chief who played a vital role in the James Bay project. *No foreign land: the biography of a North American Indian* by Wilfred Pelletier (edited by Ted Poole) tells, in a straightforward manner, of Pelletier's life in two worlds—both on and off the reservation. *Buffalo days and nights* (1976), containing the memoirs of Peter Erasmus (1833-1931), the last surviving member of the Palliser Expedition of 1857-60, as told to Henry Thompson in 1920, was published by the Glenbow-Alberta Institute. It includes an introduction by Dr Irene Spry, copious footnotes, a bibliography, and an index that make it by far the most scholarly of these memoirs.

I am an Indian (1969) edited by the non-Indian, Kent Gooderham, was the first anthology of Indian literature to be published in Canada. It offers a wide assortment of literary forms from legends, essays, and stories to poems by such well-known Indian writers as Duke Redbird, Chief Dan George, Howard Adams, Alma Greene, Ethel Brant Monture, and George Clutesi. *The only good Indian: essays by Canadian Indians* (1970) edited by Waubageshig (Harvey McCue) deals with aboriginal rights, red power, Indian education and identity, and contains a few protest poems by Duke Redbird, a short play by Nona Benedict, as well as the well-known essay by Chief Dan George, 'My very good dear friends . . .', and an extract from 'Citizens plus', often called 'The red paper', prepared by the Indian Chiefs of Alberta. Two collections of essays were published by the Neewin Publishing Company Limited of The Nishnawbe Institute in Toronto, an Indian educational, cultural, and research centre: *For every North American Indian who begins to disappear, I also begin to disappear* (1971) and *Who is chairman of this meeting?* (1972).

Although poetry and song constituted an integral part of the Indians' literary heritage—special occasions in life were celebrated with song—recent attempts have lagged behind prose. However, in 1963 there appeared the interesting Sepass poems: *The songs of Y-Ail-Mihth* (1963), a cycle of fifteen sacred songs of the Chilliwack people recited by Chief Kholserten Sepass, translated by her mother, Mrs. Sophia Street. The 1970s was a decade of productive activity in which young poets experimented with loose, irregular verse forms. The obsessive outrage against the dominant society, so evident in the social-protest poetry of the angry young Duke Redbird, among others, was balanced by an output that expressed a new affirmative spirit and often featured wit and irony. In fact *Loveshine and red wine* (1981), the collected verse of Duke Redbird, reflects both these attitudes: a mellow loving, mature Redbird appears, as well as the angry young man. Chief Dan George's lyrical responses to life are enjoyable and his vision of the divine in living things is mirrored in his prose poem 'My heart soars' (1974). In

1977 the Highway Bookshop published two collections of verse: *Wisdom of Indian poetry* and *Okanagan Indian*, by the West Coast Indian, Ben Abel, who writes gentle lyrical verse and is most compelling when he deals with his own experiences. George Kenny, an Ontario Indian, is the author of *Indians don't cry* (1977), in which the best poems are permeated with a sense of the abiding ironies of Indian life. *Poems of Rita Joe* (1978) is an autobiographical sequence by a Micmac woman, Rita Joe, detailing the experiences and values that have helped her define the Indian perception of life. The texts of a few of the poems offer both Micmac and English in parallel columns.

Many voices (1977) is an anthology of contemporary Canadian Indian poetry edited by two non-natives, David Day and Marilyn BOWERING. Over thirty Indian poets from across Canada are represented in this volume, which is marked by variety of thought, tone, topic, and treatment.

Indian stage plays based chiefly on tribal ritual, legend, and ancient custom also appeared in the 1970s. *Wasawkachak* (1974) by the versatile Duke Redbird used traditional and contemporary song and dance in dramatizing the creation of man. *October stranger* by George Kenny was performed in Monaco at the sixth International Theatre Festival in 1977. *Ayash* by Jim Morris, a stage adaptation of an ancient Ojibwa legend, had its première in Sioux Lookout, Ont., on 18 Feb. 1983.

The best Indian short-story writer is the gifted Basil Johnston. His entertaining *Moose meat & wild rice* (1979) uses gentle irony and satire to poke fun at the pretensions and prejudices of Indian and non-Indian alike.

See also INDIAN LEGENDS AND TALES.

PENNY PETRONE

'In Flanders fields'. See John McCRAE.

Influence d'un livre, L' (Québec, 1837), the first French-Canadian novel, was written by Philippe-Ignace-François Aubert de Gaspé, son of Philippe-Joseph AUBERT DE GASPÉ. Born in Quebec City on 8 Apr. 1814, Aubert de Gaspé Jr. took part of his classical secondary course at the Séminaire de Nicolet before becoming a stenographer and journalist. Imprisoned for a month in 1835 following an altercation with a member of parliament, he avenged himself by planting a stinkpot in the vestibule of the legislative assembly. He was then obliged to take refuge in the family manor-house at Saint-Jean-Port-Joli, where he amused himself by reading fiction and composing a novel of his own, which was published by subscription in Sept. 1837. The young Aubert de Gaspé subsequently worked as a journalist in Halifax, where he died in his twenties on 7 Mar. 1841.

L'influence d'un livre: roman historique is a pre-Romantic novel of mystery, adventure, and love. The title refers to a popular manual of superstitious recipes that encouraged Charles Amand, an eccentric amateur alchemist living on the shores of the St Lawrence River, to seek the philosopher's stone. One of his macabre experiments requires the use of a black hen stolen at the full moon; another involves a *main de gloire*, the dried arm of a hanged man, which Amand removes from the dissection room after the execution of a murderer. Duped by practical jokers and shipwrecked off Anticosti Island, Amand suffers one disappointment after another until, after five years' absence, he finds a modest treasure of five hundred dollars. The lover in the tale is an elegant young student, Saint-Céran, who becomes a doctor and wins the hand of Amand's daughter Amélie. At least one chapter of the novel (the legend of Rose Latulippe in Chapter V) appears to have been written by Aubert de Gaspé's father, who later composed *Les* ANCIENS CANADIENS.

Published just as the Rebellion of 1837 was beginning, *L'influence d'un livre* received little attention, although one 'letter to the editor' criticized its lack of realism. Aubert de Gaspé retorted that Amand was modelled on a person he had known, and historians have since shown that certain of the events and characters are based on reality: the murder actually took place at Saint-Jean-Port-Joli in Aug. 1829, and some of the secondary characters (the giant Capistrau, la mère Nolet) are drawn from persons known in the district.

Long after its author's death the novel was reprinted in 1864 in one of the bonus volumes offered with *Le* FOYER CANADIEN, and was later distributed as a prize in schools. But Abbé Henri-Raymond CASGRAIN, considering it too daring for the conservative tastes of that period, had expurgated the text with the approval of Aubert de Gaspé's aged father: he changed the title to *Le chercheur de trésors*, removed references to 'dangerous' European authors, and bowdlerized the love passages. Reprinted in 1968 in a facsimile of this edition, Québec's first novel is thus chiefly known in a version very different from that composed by its young author.

The best recent studies of Aubert de Gaspé Jr. and his novel are by Luc Lacourcière, 'Aubert de Gaspé, fils, 1814-1841', *Les Cahiers des Dix* (no. 40, 1975), and Maurice Lemire, '*L'influence d'un livre*' in *Dictionnaire des oeuvres littéraires du Québec, I: des origines à 1900* (1978).

DAVID M. HAYNE

Innis, Harold Adams (1894-1952). Born on a farm near Otterville, Ont., he was educated in Otterville and Woodstock and was a scholarship student in political science at McMaster University, Hamilton. Upon graduating in 1916 he enlisted in the army, took part in the attack on Vimy Ridge in Apr. 1917, and was wounded in the leg a few months later. He received an M.A. from McMaster and a Ph.D. from the University of Chicago with a thesis that was published as *A history of the Canadian Pacific Railway* (1923). In Chicago he met and married Mary Quayle, who later became a writer and economic historian; they had four children. In 1920 he was appointed to the department of political economy in the University of Toronto, where he remained for the rest of his life.

Simultaneously involved in research, teaching, compilation, travel, and publication, Innis became the driving force behind the intellectual development of political economy specifically, and of social science generally, in the university and throughout Canada. He devised 'a philosophy of economic history applicable to new countries' that for Canada has come to be known as the 'staple approach': an analytical method that stresses the dominance of a succession of export commodities—or staples—in Canadian development; the subordination of other activities to the production of staples; the vulnerability of an economy that grows around staples in a dependent relation with centres of Western civilization; and the political repercussions that were a consequence of that vulnerability. *The fur trade in Canada: an introduction to Canadian economic history* (1930) is his best-known publication using this methodology, but he pursued this approach in numerous papers, essays, and editing tasks, and with a major study of Canada's earliest staple, *The cod fisheries: the history of an international economy* (1940).

Innis's disillusionment with the rising irrationality expressed in world events of the 1930s and 1940s, and with the inadequate approach for understanding such complexities, led him to consider the study of empires. Aware that the severest difficulty with this undertaking was the scholar's problem with bias, he proceeded to address 'bias' by focusing on various empirical communications systems and analysing their impact on the nature and structure of society. Two important books emerged from this field of study: *Empire and communications* (1946) and *The bias of communication* (1951).

Though Innis was not a talented writer—he often overwhelms or confuses his readers with a sometimes cryptic prose that tends to be swamped with unnecessary detail—he was one of Canada's most prolific and influential authors. He transformed Canadians' awareness of the source and basis of their nationhood, and contributed—as no other Canadian scholar has—to the discussion of important philosophical questions dealing with the human condition and survival. His creative ideas have influenced a succession of Canadian scholars (including Donald CREIGHTON) and a variety of disciplines in the social sciences.

After Innis's death Mary Quayle Innis edited his *Essays in Canadian economic history* (1956). See also Jane Ward, 'The published works of H.A. Innis', *Canadian Journal of Economics and Political Science* (May 1953) for a list of Innis's extensive publications; D.G. Creighton, *Harold Adams Innis: portrait of a scholar* (1956, 2nd edn 1978); the chapter on Innis in Carl Berger, *The writing of Canadian history: aspects of Canadian historical writing: 1900-1970* (1976); and Graeme Patterson, 'Harold Innis and the writing of history', CANADIAN LITERATURE 83 (Winter 1979).

SALLY ZERKER

Inuit literature. 'Eskimo' or Inuktitut as a written language did not develop in the Arctic but was introduced with Christianity in the early eighteenth century. Moravian missionaries in London were publishing the gospels in the Labrador dialect by 1813, and as Christianity spread, both the Old and New Testaments, hymnals, and the Book of Common Prayer were translated and published. A demand for non-religious literature quickly developed, and abridged classics such as *The Odyssey* and *Pilgrim's Progress* were published in Inuktitut, the Inuit language. The writing systems for Inuktitut vary across Canada, from modified Roman orthographies in Labrador and in the Mackenzie district in the West to a system of shorthand called syllabics that is in use throughout the Central Arctic. In recent years most Inuit literature has been written by Inuit authors and published in both Inuktitut and English. Dozens of English/Inuktitut periodicals such as *Inuktitut, Inuit Today*, and *Igalaaq* have flourished, and hundreds of books have been produced by commercial publishers as well as by religious, governmental, and cultural agencies.

There are two major sources of traditional Inuit poetry: Knud Rasmussen's ten-volume report *The fifth Thule expedition—the Danish ethnographical expedition to Arctic North America, 1921-24* (1928-45, 1976), and Helen Roberts' and Diamond Jenness's *Songs of the Copper Eskimos: report of the Canadian Arctic expedition 1913-18, Vol XIV* (1925). Some of the songs in these reports have been reprinted in several collections: *Anerca* (1959) edited by Edmund Carpenter; *Beyond the high hills: a book of Eskimo poems* (1961) edited by Guy-Marie Rousselière; James HOUSTON's *Songs of the dream people: chants and images from the Indians and Eskimos of North America* (1972); and Charles Hofmann's *Drum dance: legends, ceremonies, dances and songs of the Eskimos* (1974). All are reliable and varied treatments of these old Eskimo poems. John Robert COLOMBO's *Poems of the Inuit* (1981) arranges and assesses the traditional poems in a format that is both accessible to popular taste and academically sound. Colombo's introduction provides a cultural context for the songs, and his notes give specific information on the works of Aua, Orpingalik, and other leading Inuit poets.

Until relatively recently Inuit legends appeared only in academic and scientific publications such as the reports of Rasmussen and Jenness. Traditional stories were thought to be too bloody, too bawdy, and, curiously, too boring in their original form to interest the general reader. This attitude changed considerably with the development of the soapstone-carving industry in the North. Zebedee Nungak's and Eugene Arima's *Stories from Povungnituk, Québec* (1969), an English/Inuktitut collection, was the first book of genuine Inuit legends aimed at this new market. *Tales from the Igloo* (1972), translated and edited by the Rev. Maurice Metayer, was followed by *How kabloonat became and other Inuit legends* (1974) by the Inuk newspaper editor Mark Kalluak, and by *Stories from Pangnirtung* (1976), illustrated by Germaine Arnaktauyok. She also illustrated *Inuit legends* (1977), which contained further stories collected by Father Metayer and edited after his death by Leoni Kappi.

Diaries and autobiographies constitute an important element of Inuit literature today. Since Lydia Campbell's *Sketches of Labrador life* (1980) was first published in the St John's, Nfld., *Evening Telegram* in 1894, Inuit have produced numerous reminiscences and excerpts from diaries for magazines and newspapers. *The autobiography of John Ayaruaq* (1969) is available only in a syllabic edition, but life in the old days in the Western Arctic is described in *I,Nuligak* (1966), translated and edited by Maurice Metayer. *People from our side* (1975), by Dorothy Eber and Peter Pitseolak, documents the more recent contact culture through the very personal and humorous memoirs of one of Cape Dorset's legendary leaders. Alice French describes her education in a boarding school in Aklavik in *My name is Masak* (1977) and Minnie Aodla Freeman's *Life among the Quallunaat* (1978) reveals the pain and loneliness such experiences brought to Inuit children. Anthony Apakark Thrasher, whose father was a contemporary of Nuligak, gives a much grimmer picture of modern Inuit life in *Thrasher: skid row Eskimo* (1976). Thrasher's view of life from a Prince Albert jail is counterbalanced by the lyrical and humorous *Shadows* (1975) by the Rev. Armand Tagoona. Dorthy Eber's *Pitseolak: pictures out of my life* (1971) is an oral biography of the famous Eskimo printmaker Pitseolak Ashoona. Many more oral biographies can be found in recent catalogues from printmaking centres such as Cape Dorset, Holman Island, and Baker Lake.

Traditional Inuit did not distinguish between children's and adults' literature, believing that any good story or song had something for everyone. With the introduction of formalized schooling in the Arctic, however, numerous books in both English and Inuktitut were produced for Eskimo children. Though most of these books are not easily available in southern Canada, Markoosie's *Harpoon of the hunter* (1970), the first Eskimo novel, has been published in a dozen languages; and two lavishly illustrated memoirs—*Peter Pitseolak's escape from death* (1977), edited by Dorothy Eber, and Norman Ekoomiak's *An Arctic childhood* (1980)—give some idea of what is being written for Inuit children today.

Most Inuit publications now appear in bilingual or trilingual editions, have a high proportion of illustration, and include both transcribed oral material and texts from original manuscripts. Books such as *The northerners* (1974), edited by Josepi Padlayat, and *We don't live in snow houses now* (1976), edited by Susan Cowan, respond to the requirements of the literature by printing texts in English, Roman orthography, Inuktitut, syllabics, and sometimes French, all within one cover. *Paper stays put: a collection of Inuit writing* (1980), edited by Robin Gedalof, includes examples of both traditional and contemporary literature from most of the major Inuit publications of the 1960s and 1970s. More Eskimo literature can be found listed in Gedalof's *An annotated bibliography of Canadian Inuit literature* (1979).

The emendation of government policies on native language rights, the development of a standard Roman orthography, the modification of the syllabic system, and technological developments affecting the typing and printing of Inuktitut, have all ensured that Eskimo-language publications will continue. At the same time the interest of publishers and readers in southern Canada suggests that Inuit literature in English will also flourish in the future. It would seem that the movement from an oral to a written literature in northern Canada does not destroy but rather helps to preserve and develop a tradition.   ROBIN GEDALOF McGRATH

Irchan, Myroslaw. Pseudonym of Andrii Babiuk. See UKRAINIAN WRITING.

Isham, James. See EXPLORATION LITERATURE IN ENGLISH: 2.

Iwaniuk, Wacław (b. 1915). Born in Chełm lubelski, Poland, he studied at the Free University in Warsaw, contributing prose and poetry to avant-garde literary periodicals, and during the Second World War served with the Polish Mountain Brigade. He then studied at Cambridge University and in 1948 immigrated to Canada, becoming a citizen in 1953 and working in Toronto as a court-room translator until his retirement in 1978. His poems, essays, reviews, and short fiction have been published in leading Polish-language *émigré* periodicals.

Between 1936 and 1978 eleven collections of Iwaniuk's poems appeared in Polish, only the first two being published in Poland; the rest were issued by Western *émigré* houses in London, Brussels, and Paris. *Dark Times: selected poems of Wacław Iwaniuk* (1979) is a volume of English-language translations (largely the work of the Polish-born Vancouver-based writer Jagna Boraks); *Evenings on Lake Ontario* (1981) consists of poems written in English. Iwaniuk's aesthetic is expressed in intellectual imagery, economy of language, measured emotion, ironic comment, and free verse. In the deracinated nature of Eastern and Central European society, Iwaniuk has found a conning tower from which to oversee the condition of man in the contemporary Western world; he shares with others from Central and Eastern Europe the need to contrast pre-war and post-war living conditions. While in his homeland 'All that was mine/was burned/broken/silenced', in the West he sees dehumanization ('All that fills my sight ap-

pears anonymous'). But despair is tempered with lyricism; to the question posed in 'As a bone bare', 'Is there still room/for a credible word?', he gives an affirmative answer. The English-language poems of *Evenings on Lake Ontario* document the acceptance of a new homeland to replace an old one that may never be revisited.

Podróg do Europy (Travels to Europe, 1982), a Polish-language selection of Iwaniuk's short fiction, was issued in London. With John Robert COLOMBO, Iwaniuk has translated into English poems by the contemporary Cracow poet Ewa Lipska: *Such times* (1981).   JOHN ROBERT COLOMBO

J

Jacob, Fred. See NOVELS IN ENGLISH 1920 TO 1940: 3.

Jacobs, Peter. See INDIAN LITERATURE: 2.

Jalna (1927). When the manuscript of this novel by Mazo DE LA ROCHE was submitted for the $10,000 *Atlantic Monthly* prize and won it, the publisher, Little Brown, ordered an initial printing of 45,000 copies in Oct.; by Christmas sales were approaching 100,000. Its sequels would also become international bestsellers, while portions of the saga of the Whiteoaks family of Jalna would be adapted as a play (*Whiteoaks,* 1936), a film (*Jalna,* 1935), and an abortive TV series produced by the CBC (*Jalna,* 1972). It was the first of sixteen book-length episodes of the Whiteoak family story featuring Jalna, the Ontario house (located at present-day Clarkson, Ont.) named after the Indian Hill station where the soldier Philip Whiteoak and his bride Adeline spent their first married years; Adeline (Gran), a matriarch who is both authoritarian and sensuous; Renny, the headstrong grandson fated to rule Jalna after her death at the age of 100; Adeline's various progeny, down to her greatgrandson, who populate the house; and a parrot that swears in Hindi. A series of sexual intrigues forms the action of *Jalna.* Renny falls

in love with the American bride of his brother Eden. Another brother, Piers, elopes with a neighbour's illegitimate daughter, with whom Eden has an affair. The formula—a strong undercurrent of sex, family outbursts, and devotion to property—would be repeated in the many novels that followed, in all of which the house is central: enduring, expandable, accommodating. However limited the social vision of the series, it is very real: that of a structure embodying family values and assured social position that cannot be destroyed by either individual misconduct or social tremors. Old World graciousness, New World informality and drive, the timeless tensions of family existence—all these forces reconcile themselves through the magic of Jalna.

DENNIS DUFFY

Jameson, Anna. See Writing in ONTARIO: 1 and TRAVEL LITERATURE IN ENGLISH.

Janes, Percy (b. 1922). Born in St John's, Nfld., Percy Maxwell Janes moved in 1929 with his family to Corner Brook—where his father, Eli Janes, a blacksmith, had found work in the new pulp-and-paper mill—and passed his formative years in this frontier boom town. From 1938 to 1940 he attended Memorial University College, St John's, but at eighteen he left for Montreal and enlisted in the Canadian navy, serving for nearly four years in the medical corps. He then enrolled in Victoria College, University of Toronto, and became acquainted with modern literature. Graduating in 1949, he worked as a tutor, principally at Grove School in Lakefield, Ont., and as a carpenter. From the early 1960s his life has been dedicated to writing. He has travelled widely, living for many years in England, and now lives and writes in Newfoundland.

Janes's first book was *So young and beautiful* (1958), a novel set in small-town Ontario. Though largely undistinguished, we can see in it the stirrings of a real talent and the germs of ideas and characters that would emerge fully in *House of hate*; one character, Newfie, is of particular interest as a prefiguring of Saul Stone in the later novel. In the mid-1960s, following the death of his father, Janes decided to write about the life of his family in Corner Brook, and the result was *House of hate* (1970), a brilliant, obsessive, bleak novel about the corrosive effects of a cantankerous father, Saul Stone, upon his wife and children. Janes takes us into the lives of Saul's children to show how each in turn was twisted and coarsened by the atmosphere of recrimination, suspicion, and violence that Saul created in his home. There is considerable artfulness in the way Janes avoids the monotonous repetition that seems inherent in such a structure. He rivets our attention upon domestic scenes of frightening rawness; analyses with brutal frankness, yet with much compassion, the motives of the central character; and accurately conveys Newfoundland habits of speech. We feel that we are on the boundary between autobiography and fiction and are witnessing the rare phenomenon of a man telling the whole truth about himself, his family, and his society. The novel was reprinted in the New Canadian Library in 1976, with an introduction by Margaret LAURENCE.

Janes has continued to write both fiction and poetry. *Light and dark: poems* (1980) contains poems on Newfoundland themes that reveal an alert, ironic sensibility affectionately bemused by what is happening in his native province, and more personal pieces in which he broods over his craft and middle age. His latest works of fiction show a growing attachment to Newfoundland. *Newfoundlanders: short stories* (1981) is often lighthearted and whimsical, while the novel

Eastmall (1982), a far less impressive work than *House of hate*, focuses on local concern over large-scale municipal development in St John's. He has edited, with Harry Cuff, *Twelve Newfoundland short stories* (1982).

PATRICK O'FLAHERTY

Jarvis, William Henry Pope (1876-1944). Born in Summerside, P.E.I., he was a journalist in western and central Canada and died in Canton, Ont. His three volumes of fiction are of interest mainly for their recreations of local colour. *Letters of a remittance man to his mother* (1908), set in Winnipeg and on Manitoba farms, sketches with comic hyperbole the practical education of a supercilious young Englishman. *Trails and tales in Cobalt* (1908) is a collection of anecdotes from western and northern mining camps drawn loosely together within the framework of a prospecting adventure in northern Ontario. *The great Gold Rush* (1913) follows a group of Klondike stampeders through the hardships of the wilderness and of dealing with corrupt officials and noble but inflexible Mounted Policemen. In the preface to *Trails and tales in Cobalt* Jarvis claims to have known the mining regions of B.C. and to have spent five years prospecting and mining in Alaska and the Yukon. His tales are heavy with particulars of scene and with exhaustive explanations of the principles and processes of prospecting, mining, and wilderness living that continually overcome his uncertain grasp of fictional form and technique. DICK HARRISON

Jasmin, Claude (b. 1930). Born in Montreal, he studied at the Collège Grasset and the École des Arts appliqués. He has been a ceramist, actor, art teacher and critic, a television designer at Radio-Canada, and director of the literary and art pages of the *Journal de Montréal*.

Jasmin has published ten novels, three plays, a collection of short stories, three *récits*, and a short book about his reactions to criticism of his work, *Jasmin-uiusvf* (1970). The novels—most of which are first-person narrations—reflect social hatred for the well-to-do and shame for the heroes' low social rank, as well as a strong degree of disgust for shallow intellectualism and pretension. Revolt and violence, some of it politically motivated, and revulsion against the absence or weakness of the father-figure, are other recurring features.

His first novel, *Et puis tout est silence . . .* (1965), written in 1959, is based on his experiences as an *animateur de théâtre* for the Montreal Parks Department and contains reminiscences of the neighbourhood where he grew up—the multi-ethnic working-class area of north-east Montreal that reappears in nearly every novel. *La corde au cou* (1960), which won the Prix du Cercle du Livre de France, is a violent novel about a schizophrenic who kills in order to achieve temporary liberation from a life of cultural and economic alienation. *Délivrez-nous du mal* (1961) deals with a homosexual relationship between the wealthy André Dastous and Georges Langis, a translator of modest origins. Jasmin's best-known, and perhaps most successful, novel is *Ethel et le terroriste* (1964)—translated by David Walker as *Ethel and the terrorist* (1965)—based on the first fatal FLQ incident in Apr. 1963. *Pleure pas Germaine!* (1965), also partly concerned with terrorist activity, is a JOUAL novel in which the narrator and his family try to retrace their origins on a long auto trip through Québec to the mother's native Gaspé.

After nine years in which Jasmin wrote no fiction, he published *Revoir Ethel* (1976), *Le loup de Brunswick City* (1976), and *La sablière* (1979), the latter winning the Prix France-Canada. The first novel—a kind of sequel to *Ethel et le terroriste*—concerns Germain (formerly Paul), an art critic and broadcaster still interested in radical politics after having served a four-year sentence for terrorism. Though he now rejects urban guerilla warfare, he is drawn against his will into a plot to explode a bomb over Montreal's Olympic Stadium. This is a largely unbelievable story, awkwardly narrated by an impersonal, omniscient 'on', in contrast to the palpable first-person narration of *Ethel et le terroriste*. Similarly handicapped and even less credible is *Le loup* . . . . Allegedly based on a true incident, this short work relates the adventures of Louis Laberge, lost at the age of two by his parents and captured while living with a group of marauding wolves at thirteen. *La sablière* is a fine, often very moving novel. The narrator, Clovis Jhie (assonant with 'Claude J.' in French), is an imaginative sixteen-year-old whose fabulous playacting with his younger, slightly retarded brother, Mario, has cured the boy's stammer. The stammer returns, however, when the father decides to send Mario to an orphanage. Clovis manages his brother's escape from the institution—to which the child has set fire—and a kindly Cistercian monk invites Mario to live and work on the Order's communal farm. In spite of some weaknesses, the novel deftly weds pathos and poetry.

In 1982 Jasmin published two novels that are interesting, but not among his best. *L'armoire de Pantagruel* is reminiscent of *La corde au cou* and *Ethel et le terroriste* in its treatment of violent crime resulting from sordid social conditions, and in its anti-intellectual tone. There is some successful play of rhythm and poetic prose and a multi-faceted use of the symbol of the title's *armoire* (the balcony cupboard of the hero's childhood, where he was locked for bad behaviour, his jail cell, the beer refrigerator of the Pantagruel bar, the container of the church's sacred vessels). But this melodramatic tale of multiple murders stretches credibility. *Maman-Paris, Maman-la-France* is about Clément Jobin (cf. Clovis Jhie), a ceramics designer, and his wife Rachel, a publicist and amateur photographer, who take their first trip to France, where she participates in the finals of a contest for the best picture-album in the francophone world. In diary entries Jobin waxes lyrical—but not without a certain amount of irony and satire—on the richness of continental French speech and clarity and on the ancient civilization of the 'mother' country.

Most of the ten stories in the collection *Les coeurs empaillés* (1967) are about women who hope for affection, happiness, gratitude, or social involvement and are cruelly and sadly disappointed. The stories feature surprise endings (often of gratuitous violence or suicide), the tactile presence of Montreal and its popular speech, and satire of the media, intellectual artificiality, and bourgeois 'charity'. Told by an ironic narrator, often using the *'style indirect libre'*, the stories are of uneven quality.

Three of Jasmin's plays for radio, television, and the stage have been published. *Blues pour un homme averti* (1965) portrays a sordid alcoholic, raised in an orphanage, who has never ceased to search for his father. Caught in a web of crime, he mistakes a police-inspector, pursuing him for murder, for his father. The naturalism of the settings—a cheap restaurant, tavern, cabaret dressing-room, rundown apartment block, and alleyway—is modulated throughout by the presence of a jazz band. *Tuez le veau gras* (1970), whose theme is moral surrender in a labour setting, is set in a small lumbering town in the Duplessis era. The father-son conflict is again central, but the play is melodramatic, with weak characterization and artificial dialogue. Similar problems beset

C'est toujours la même histoire (1971), which deals with a drug-free youth centre in the Laurentians organized by David Kauffman, a U.S. draft resister.

One of Jasmin's most convincing pieces of writing is *Rimbaud mon beau salaud!* (1969), an imaginary dialogue between Jasmin and the French poet, which offers striking childhood reminiscences and evocations of the past, present, and future of Québec and its people that are marked by an optimistic view of self-determination. *L'Outaragasipi* (1971), a saga of the settlers of the Portage-Assomption area of Québec, is a thin work that fails to achieve its aim of linking history with actuality.

The title of the first of a three-part series of autobiographical sketches, *La petite patrie* (1972)—referring to Jasmin's early childhood in the Villeray district of north-east Montreal—became a catch-phrase in Québec, as well as the title of a 75-part TV series begun in 1974; this book had seven reprintings in seven years. The second volume, *Pointe-Calumet boogie-woogie* (1973), concerns the years 1940-6; the third, *Sainte-Adèle-la-vaisselle* (1974), leaps into 1951 and relates the events of a ten-month period. The three works develop the stages of the youth's adolescence. More recently Jasmin has published two collections of non-fiction commentaries. *Feu à volonté* (1976), composed of columns written for Montreal periodicals, reveals aspects of the author's involvement in reform politics in Montreal. The best pieces are useful documents of Québec's recent socio-cultural history, though Jasmin is sometimes a simplistic and irrational polemicist. *Feu sur la télévision* (1977) advocates quality broadcasting, more public recognition for Québec's creative writers, and increased telecasting of Québec drama.

In 1981 Jasmin received the Prix Duvernay for the corpus of his work.

For a critical evaluation of Jasmin's novels, see Gilles MARCOTTE's 'L'aventure romanesque de Claude Jasmin' in *Littérature canadienne-française, conférences J.-A. de Sève* (1969). A socio-critical evaluation is given in B.-Z. Shek's *Social realism in the French-Canadian novel* (1977), and a psychoanalytical one in Jacques Cotnam's *Violence in the Canadian novel since 1960* (1981), edited by V. Marger-Grinling and Terry Goldie. See also Mireille Trudeau, *Dossiers de documentation sur la littérature canadienne-française, 9: Claude Jasmin* (1973).

See also DRAMA IN FRENCH 1948 TO 1981: 3 and NOVELS IN FRENCH 1960 TO 1982: 1, 3.   BEN-Z. SHEK

Javor, Pavel. See George SKVOR.

Jeanneret, Marsh (b. 1917). Born in Toronto, he graduated from the University of Toronto in 1938 and entered publishing as a traveller in textbooks for Copp Clark Co. Ltd, rising to a senior position before joining the UNIVERSITY OF TORONTO PRESS in 1953 as its director. During the next 24 years, until his retirement from that position, he built the Press from modest stature to its present status as one of the largest and most respected university presses in North America. Jeanneret was the first Canadian elected president of the Association of American University Presses (1970) and was founding president of both the bilingual Association of Canadian University Presses (1972) and the International Association of Scholarly Publishers (1976). His impact on Canadian publishing extended well beyond the academic field. He served as president of the Canadian Copyright Institute (1965-7) and of the Canadian Book Publishers' Council (1968), bringing to these offices characteristic concentration, energy, and imagination. In 1970 he was appointed one of three members (and the only publisher) of the Ontario Royal Commission on Book Publishing, and was the principal author of its final report, *Canadian publishers and Canadian publishing* (1973), which offered broad recommendations to encourage Canadian publishing in its English-language centre. Jeanneret is the author of three high-school history texts—*Story of Canada* (1947), *Notre histoire* (1949), and *Canada in North America* (1961)—as well as of numerous articles on publishing and education. He was appointed an Officer of the Order of Canada in 1978.

As head of the University of Toronto Press, Jeanneret stressed the importance of international distribution and international standards in this country's scholarly publishing, and under his leadership the Press pioneered Canadian participation at the Frankfurt International Book Fair and opened its own offices in Buffalo, N.Y., and London, Eng. He also frequently stressed the importance of university publishing to Canadian self-understanding. It was impossible, he argued, to depend on commercial houses or foreign university presses alone to publish the growing number of studies by Canadian scholars in Canadian literature, history, and social sciences. To this end he encouraged the development of university presses, publishing in both official languages, on campuses other than his own.

IAN MONTAGNES

Jean Rivard. Antoine GÉRIN-LAJOIE's *Jean Rivard: le défricheur* (Montréal, 1874), together with its sequel *Jean Rivard: économiste* (Montréal, 1876), comprise one of the foremost novels of nineteenth-century French Canada. The critical consensus on that point is not due to the work's innate literary merits but rather to the thematic influence it almost immediately exerted on socio-economic policy, and on the prose fiction that espoused that policy for two generations after its author's death. *Jean Rivard* was Gérin-Lajoie's first and only excursion into the novel, for he was primarily a social historian by background and inclination. It was conceived as a means of arresting and redirecting the immigration of rural Québécois to the U.S. Excluded from their traditional life, as land in the established parishes was all allotted, they were drawn there increasingly by the possibility of jobs in American industry. The two novels advocate, in exemplary fashion, a rural rebirth of the nation based on the land-based economics of the previous century in France.

In *Jean Rivard: le défricheur* the twenty-year-old hero, still in college, is faced with a crucial decision on his father's sudden death: should he continue his studies, entering one of the three careers to which they then led—medicine, the Church, or the law—or should he attempt to work one of the small overcrowded farms in the old parishes, shrunken now by years of subdivision? He decides against both, opting instead for the rude life of the pioneering farmer in an unsettled area of the province. Despite discouragements, taunts, and fearful challenges, he creates fertile land and bounteous harvests from the wilderness, building his own home in which his childhood sweetheart will join him. Two years later, in *Jean Rivard: économiste*, the untamed forest has become a prosperous village known as 'Rivardville', of which he is elected mayor. Rivard's pioneering zeal is now turned towards its welfare, and he constructs for it a social policy based upon the simpler views of the previous century, according to which only the farmer is considered truly productive, a creator of wealth: all others are, in effect, parasites and must therefore be subordinate to the agricultural class. Jean Rivard's signal success in putting this theory into operation attracts

much attention and he is elected to the legislature. But Rivard soon resigns—to return, as the principles of the novel demand, to the simple farming life that alone is healthy, productive, and godlike. One's garden must be cultivated with reverence, for that is the most natural and liberating task man can perform.

The text of both novels is homespun, unembellished, and at times arid, exhibiting some of the worst qualities of the *roman à thèse* in its didacticism, its moralizing tone, its simplification of character and plot, and in the utter predictability of its hero's success in all his undertakings. But Gérin-Lajoie had no illusions about their literary worth, insisting from the beginning that he was not setting out to create a novel in any traditional sense but to portray in realistic terms what could be done to improve social conditions for his countrymen. These novels, however, had a far-reaching effect on French-Canadian literature, for the rural novel that would dominate it for so long owed much of its proselytizing zeal to *Jean Rivard*.

See M. Lemire's unpublished thesis, '*Jean Rivard* d'Antoine Gérin-Lajoie: un plan de conquête économique' (Laval, 1962), the principal points of which are reproduced in *Dictionnaire des oeuvres littéraire du Québec*, vol. I (1978). The novel is also discussed in every standard critical work on the literature of French Canada, especially in *Le roman de la terre au Québec* (1974) by M. M. Servais-Maquoi.

LEONARD DOUCETTE

Jenness, Diamond. See INDIAN LEGENDS AND TALES: BIBLIOGRAPHY.

Jesuit Relations. This is the collective name given to a series of reports sent from Québec to the Provincial Father of the Society of Jesus in Paris and signed by the Québec Superior. The first collective edition (Québec, 1858) was superseded by the scholarly work of Reuben Gold Thwaites, who added to these *Relations* a mass of personal letters, memoirs, journals, and other documents. His monumental edition, the 73 volumes of *The Jesuit Relations and allied documents; travels and exploration of the Jesuit missionaries, in New France 1610-1791*, heavily annotated and with page-for-page translation, was published in Cleveland from 1896 to 1901 in an edition of 750 sets. Combining a wealth of minutiae about life in New France, and the customs of the native population, with dramatic narratives of travel, exploration, and adventure, and written by educated Europeans, these materials have provided rich source material for historians, geographers, philologists, and ethnologists—as well as for writers of creative literature. The Thwaites edition can be broken down into four fairly distinct categories:

I. The main series of *Relations* begun in 1632 by Paul Le Jeune and uniformly published in Paris by Sébastien Cramoisy and family until 1673. Notable topics here are the development of the Huron missions, and Iroquois warfare on the St Lawrence and in Huronia.

II. Earlier letters and reports by Pierre Biard from Port-Royal, and by Charles Lalemant from Kebec, dated between 1611 and 1629; some of these were published by *Mercure françois*.

III. Journals, letters, draft reports (not only in French but also in Latin and Italian), and personal and business correspondence extending as far as 1791. This category includes the *Journal des Jésuites* (the Quebec Superior's daily record of noteworthy events, management of Jesuit affairs, and observations on the colony and its public figures, 1645 to 1668). The *Journal* and the reports sent to Quebec were used in preparation of the annual *Relations*, so there is considerable duplication of material.

IV. Letters from more widespread posts in North America, giving accounts of priests, travels, mission activities, and the native population to 1763, when the Society of Jesus was suppressed.

Assignment of authorship can seldom be definitive. The Quebec Superiors who signed the *Relations* usually had only the last hand on the copy before it went to Paris. Even when signatures appear on sections sent in to these author-editors, the exact degree of authorship is not self-evident: any of the 320 Jesuit missionaries who went to New France and Louisiana (listed in Thwaites, vol. 71) could have contributed at some time.

The best sustained passages of the *Relations* are in the central early reports (Thwaites, vols 5 to 35), from Paul Le Jeune in 1632 to Paul Ragueneau in 1650. Le Jeune lands at Quebec on 5 July, and after two months of domestic administration records a curious decision: the major victories for God are to take place elsewhere. While all 'savages' are eager to be rescued from their misery, the stable Huron population in a fertile area east of Georgian Bay (southern Ontario) offers the best chance of conversion.

Hereafter the Huron missions occupy an increasing portion of the annual Relations until, in 1650, Ragueneau writes of the destruction in 1649 of Saint-Marie (near Midland, Ont.), where he had been Superior for four years, struggling against odds and witnessing the martyrdom of his brethren. From Le Jeune to Ragueneau—via Fathers Brébeuf, Jérôme Lalemant, Garnier, Vimont, Chaumont, Lemercier, and Dablon, among others—the heroic rhetoric of conversion is mixed with the determined application of spiritual exercises. One modern critic has described this series of the *Relations*, with its exotic characters, grotesque details, and miraculous events, as a baroque drama with paradox and inversion of values at its centre.

The *Relations* can also be read as a record of day-to-day happenings, ranging from minute episodes to personal accounts of major events in the colony, all narrated with elegance and charm. One remembers Le Jeune's visit to a Montaignais cabin; his description of *sagamité*, the staple food; the ceremonial arrivals at Quebec of the colony's chief officers; the gatherings of Indian councils for peace negotiations; the numerous accounts of religious institutions at Quebec, such as the hospital and the Ursuline seminary; the daily routines and spiritual discipline of the Jesuits themselves; and the many accounts of Indian life, with emphasis on an edifying and exaggerated portrayal of the Indians' response to the Christian message.

Among many other memorable episodes in the *Relations* are Father Biard's account of Acadia (vol. 3), which is logically organized in chapters dealing with different aspects of the land, Indian life, disputes in the embryonic colony, travel, and policy recommendations; although a personal touch is maintained and some striking characters, such as Membertou, are introduced, the aim is more scientific than conversational. Other authors of special interest are Fathers Lamberville and Cauchetière, who wrote about Kateri Tekakwitha (vol. 42); Father Jacques Marquette, who descended the Mississippi with Louis Jolliet in 1673 (vol. 59); and Father Joseph-François Lafitau (vol. 47), whose contribution to the myth of the 'bon sauvage' is one of the major works of New France.

'Relation de voyage' is a standard phrase in French and is found in other writings on New France. What makes the *Jesuit Relations* original is their sustained and relatively standardized serial character. Each annual 'Relation de ce qui s'est passé en la Nouvelle France' in the main series addresses the reader in a personal manner and gives an agreeable, often humorous account of matters great and small in a curious, distant land. An official optimism sustains even the most discouraging accounts, as if to encourage the admiration and support of sponsors in France and maintain the good social tone of letters that might be read aloud in company.

The Thwaites edition is available in a 1959 reprint (New York: Pageant Book Co.); it should be supplemented by *Thwaites' Jesuit Relations: errata and addenda* by Joseph P. Donnelly (Chicago, Loyola University Press, 1967). *The Jesuit Relations and allied documents* is also the title of abridged and selected editions by Edna Kenton (1954) and S.R. Mealing (Carleton Library, 1963). Edna Kenton also published selections under the titles *Indians of North America* (1927) and *Black gown and Redskin* (1954). The DICTIONARY OF CANADIAN BIOGRAPHY contains authoritative articles on many of the writers in the series.

See also INDIAN LITERATURE: I.

JACK WARWICK

Johnson, Pauline (1861-1913). Born on the Six Nations Reserve near Brantford, Canada West (Ont.), she was the daughter of a Mohawk father and an English mother, Emily Susanna Howells (a relative of William Dean Howells). Her education was for the most part informal, but she very early became familiar with the poetry of Byron, Scott, Longfellow, Tennyson, and Keats. Her Indian background was less influential than popular tradition would have it, although she knew the history of her father's family and listened as a child to tales and legends told by her grandfather.

Her poems first appeared in the New York magazine *Gems of Poetry* in 1884, and thereafter in several British and North American magazines, including The WEEK. Two of her poems were included by W.D. LIGHTHALL in his anthology *Songs of the Great Dominion* (London, 1889), and they were praised by Theodore Watts-Dunton in his review of the book, creating Johnson's reputation as an authentic 'Indian' voice in poetry. This reputation was firmly established by her public readings, particularly after she adopted Indian dress (which she wore when she recited Indian poems; otherwise she wore evening dress). From 1892, until her retirement to Vancouver in 1909,

Johnson was an extremely popular and compelling performer, touring not only Canada but parts of the United States; she also visited London, attracting favourable public attention there in 1894, and again in 1906. Johnson's abilities as a performer gave her poetry much of the high reputation it enjoyed during her lifetime.

Johnson's first volume of poems, *The white wampum* (London, 1895), was published by the Bodley Head. Other volumes were *Canadian born* (1903) and *Flint and feather* (1912), misleadingly described as 'the complete poems'. After her retirement she produced *Legends of Vancouver* (1911), a collection of short pieces inspired by the tales and legends she heard from her friend Joe Capilano, a Squamish chief. *The Shaggan-appi* (1913) and *The moccasin maker* (1913) appeared posthumously; both are primarily collections of short sentimental and didactic fiction, including some previously published boys' adventure stories. *The moccasin maker* contains 'My mother', Johnson's fictionalized and romantic account of her parents' courtship and her own early years.

Today the bulk of Johnson's poetry appears derivative and shallow, echoing the styles and themes of Romantic and Victorian writers, and of such Canadian poets as Charles G.D. ROBERTS and Bliss CARMAN. The Indian qualities of the verse were exaggerated, because Johnson used native materials that for the most part lent themselves to conventional poetic expression. At times, however, she did speak for the Indians—in 'A cry from an Indian wife', 'The corn husker', and 'Silhouette'—and she was influential in her use of native legends. Johnson's attitude to her Indian heritage was ambiguous. She insisted with pride and conviction on its importance—in 1886 she adopted the name 'Tekahionwake' (although not legally entitled to it), and she knew and resented the bigoted treatment Indians often endured—yet she also wrote poems and stories that celebrated European culture, and often presented the Indian in picturesque and conventional terms. Feeling the claims of both cultures, she never resolved them—a tension that occasionally found poetic expression, as in 'The idlers' and 'Re-voyage'.

Most books about Pauline Johnson deal with the legend rather than the woman. Walter McRaye's *Pauline Johnson and her friends* (1947) is in this category, but it offers insight into Johnson's career as an entertainer from a man who was for many years her performing partner. Of major importance are Norman Shrive's 'What happened to Pauline?' CANADIAN LITERATURE 13 (Summer 1962) and Pauline Loosely's 'Pauline Johnson' in *The clear spirit* (1966), edited by Mary Quayle Innis. Betty Keller's *Pauline* (1981) follows similar lines of interpretation in greater detail and with more documentation; her biography is also valuable for its inclusion of some of the uncollected and unpublished poems. Johnson's poetry is most readily accessible in the Paperjacks edition of *Flint and feather* (1972).

DAVID JACKEL

Johnston, George (b. 1913). George Benson Johnston was born in Hamilton, Ont., and educated at the University of Toronto. After several years as a freelance writer in England, he joined the RCAF at the outbreak of the Second World War and served as a reconnaissance pilot in Africa. He returned to the University of Toronto for graduate studies and taught at Mount Allison University, Sackville, N.B., from 1947 to 1949. He then joined the staff of Carleton College (later University) in Ottawa, where he became a popular teacher of Anglo-Saxon and Old Norse and an internationally known scholar of the Icelandic sagas. He retired as professor of English in 1980. His work as scholar, teacher, and poet has been recognized by honorary degrees from several universities.

All of Johnston's poetry is informed by his intelligence, warm personality, sense of absurdity, and compassion, from the serious light verse of his early poems to the plain speech, austere forms, and sometimes complex rhythms of his later work. Although many of the poems in his first collection, *The cruising auk* (1959), were first published in journals, they seem to belong to a complete and self-sufficient world that unifies the book: a small city like Ottawa that has not yet acquired the anonymity of a huge metropolis is viewed as if through reflecting mirrors that distort and change perspectives. The central portion of the book depicts a dream world, a surrealistic landscape, with its own set of characters who are observed with affection and ironic amusement. The poems combine fantasy with direct simplicity, in the manner of James REANEY's rural fables, and comment upon the desires and illusions of ordinary humanity. Their wit and satiric edge are sharpened by the apparently simple stanzaic forms, playful metres, and rhyme.

Home free (1966) includes several poems involving the same characters and displaying similar qualities of lively wit and fluent movement; but other poems—more directly colloquial in speech—experiment with varied rhythms and touch upon personal experience or turn to social and political satire. Two long poems have public themes. 'Under the tree' is a passionate poem about the effects of capital punishment upon the hangman, the hanging judge, and the whole community involved in an execution. 'Love in high places', a narrative and reflective poem, concerns the transformation over two generations of love into an obsession with worldly success. Sharp in observation, often witty in expression, it has seemed to some readers to lack a central focus and a unifying emotional force.

Happy enough: poems 1935-1972 (1972) contains the two earlier collections and a number of new poems that show Johnston's delight in what language can do, even in its barest and simplest forms. Johnston adapts the rhythms and stress patterns of colloquial speech to verse in ways that show the influence of Anglo-Saxon and Norse modes. The new poems—lyrics or brief narratives about farm, sea, or rock-bound coast—move away from the urban atmosphere of his earlier work towards the elemental and primitive. However, many poems celebrate personal affection or reflect wryly and humorously on domestic occasions.

The new poems in *Happy enough* led naturally to *Taking a grip* (1979), which shows many of the same characteristics of style and subject. Johnston has a gift for universalizing a small incident from everyday life. 'Taking a grip' suggests the need for maintaining some kind of order—in things as basic as drains and cess-pit or in the whole threatened world—in the face of possible chaos. His feeling for the tragic and heroic elements in sagas and ballads has made Johnston sensitive to the heroic qualities of ordinary life in the modern world. In several poems there is an elegiac quality, but Johnston's wit and humour are still evident, and there are festive celebrations of the coming together of family and friends.

In 1981 Johnston published *Auk redivivus: selected poems*, a personal selection and arrangement of forty-three poems from his previous volumes, which shows the range and variety of his poetic output and suggests, by title and substance, that the old auk is far from dead.

Johnston's translations from Old Norse

include *The saga of Gisli* (1963), with its interpolated poems in complex patterns, *The Faroe Islanders' saga* (1975), and *The Greenlanders' saga* (1976). In 1981 Johnston published an admirable verse translation of the work of modern Faroese poets, *Rocky shores: an anthology of Faroese poetry*.

Two valuable articles about Johnston's poetry appeared in CANADIAN LITERATURE: by George Whalley (35, Winter 1968) and D.G. JONES (59, Winter 1974).

JOHN MARGESON

Jonas, George (b. 1935). Born in Budapest, Hungary, he came to Canada in 1956. Since that time he has written poetry, fiction, and non-fiction; and produced and directed for radio and television in Toronto, where he is a producer with the CBC.

Jonas's three volumes of poetry—*The absolute smile* (1967), *The happy hungry man* (1970), and *Cities* (1973)—reveal him as a student of modern man's bleak and lonely existence. An ironic wit offers the only relief to the monotonous vacuum depicted in his sparse and spare verse. In the first volume the protagonist leads an empty life in poems of unhappiness and alienation. Little levity or optimism appears in *The happy hungry man*, where the narrator's cynicism distances himself and his reader from the human scene. *Cities* is a suite of poems that journeys from contemporary Toronto, the poet's adopted city, back through his urban haunts of New York, London, and Vienna to his Hungarian birthplace, Budapest. The autobiographical dimension underlies the prevailing self-absorption, which evokes not the world's great cities but the poet himself and his interests.

The undecorated style of Jonas's verse often borders on the prosaic, and it is no coincidence that in recent years Jonas has turned almost completely to prose. He contributes articles and reviews to many Canadian and American magazines and writes regular columns for *Toronto Life* and *Canadian Lawyer*. With Barbara Amiel he wrote *By persons unknown: the strange death of Christine Demeter* (1977), an exhaustive prose account of the murder of a Toronto woman and the conviction of her wealthy Hungarian-born developer husband. Behind the facts is the authors' analysis of the social and ethnic backgrounds of the main characters and a scathing dissection of the complex legal processes involved in the trial. This work won the Edgar Allan Poe Award for Best Fact Crime Book. In *Final decree* (1982),

Jonas's first novel, a Hungarian-born carpenter who lives in Toronto arrives home one day to find his wife and two children gone as his wife begins her search for personal fulfilment. Costly and inhumane legal machinations unfold once she files for divorce. The novel's compelling structure, weaving back and forth in time through the carpenter's mind, propels the plot relentlessly and naturally to a violent climax in which the hero, now the victim of a seemingly inexorable legal network, takes the law into his own hands.

Jonas has also written the librettos to two operas by Tibor Polgar: *The European lover* (1966) and *The glove* (1973). His play *Pushkin*, a dramatization in three acts of Pushkin's life and the conflict between romanticism and idealism, was commissioned by Theatre Plus, Toronto and produced in May, 1978.

DAVID STAINES

Jones, Alice (1853-1933). The daughter of Lieutenant-Governor Alfred Gilpin Jones of Nova Scotia, she was born and educated in Halifax. In the 1880s and 1890s she studied languages while living in France and Italy and contributed short fiction to the Halifax *Critic*, *Frank Leslie's Monthly*, and *The* WEEK. Her visits to Algeria, Brittany, Venice, London, and various European centres led to a series of travel essays in *The Week* in the 1890s and later informed her short stories and novels with an intimate understanding of continental settings, customs, and social expectations.

After her return to Canada, Alice Jones turned to novel writing while continuing to contribute short fiction to journals like *The Canadian Magazine*. *The Night-Hawk: a romance of the 60's* (1901) appeared in New York under her sometime pseudonym 'Alix John' and is set in Paris, Halifax, and the Confederacy during the American Civil War. Incorporating a thinly disguised version of the famed 'Tallahassee' episode into its tale of blockade-running, it introduced the strong female figure common to all Jone's fiction. *Bubbles we buy* (1903)—reprinted in England as *Isobel Broderick* (1904)—developed a plot of international intrigue against a backdrop of Europe's fashionable society and Nova Scotia's age of sail. Successful in Britain as well as in North America, it resembled three subsequent novels—*Gabriel Praed's castle* (1904), *Marcus Holbeach's daughter* (1912), and *Flame of frost* (1914)—in counterpointing the shallowness of the international set against the vitality of

Canada's less tradition-bound society. Like *Gabriel Praed's castle*, *Bubbles we buy* is also a story of young North American artists struggling to achieve recognition at the Salon in Paris. While both novels introduced strong 'new woman' figures into this environment, *Gabriel Praed's castle* expanded the international theme by exploring the vulnerability of a forthright Canadian businessman when confronted with European decadence and corruption.

In 1905 Jones moved to Menton, France, remaining there until her death. She continued to write on Canadian themes, developing, in the rugged Gaspé and wilderness settings of *Marcus Holbeach's daughter* and *Flame of frost* respectively, the strong relationship between environment and character that had entered her earlier work. Considered by *The Canadian Magazine* in 1903 to be potentially 'the leading woman novelist in Canada', she invites comparison with Sara Jeannette DUNCAN in her emphasis on strong woman characters and in her treatment of international themes. GWENDOLYN DAVIES

Jones, D.G. (b. 1929). Douglas Gordon Jones was born in Bancroft, Ont., and educated at the Grove School in Lakefield, at McGill University, from which he graduated in 1952, and at Queen's University, where he received his M.A. in 1954. After teaching English literature in Ontario at the Royal Military College in Kingston and the Ontario Agricultural College in Guelph, he moved to Québec and taught at Bishop's University before moving to the Université de Sherbrooke. In 1969 he founded *Ellipse*, the only Canadian magazine in which poetry in English and French are reciprocally translated. As an anglophone teaching in a French-language university, and as an editor of a bilingual journal, he and his writings reflect an openness to both the Canadian cultures. His translations of poems by Paul-Marie LAPOINTE, *The terror of the snows*, appeared in 1976.

Jones first became known as a poet of unusual, if rather unfashionable, lyrical clarity and philosophic intensity. His first volume, *Frost on the sun* (1957), was followed by *The sun is axeman* (1961), *Phrases from Orpheus* (1967), *Under the thunder the flowers light up the earth* (1977), which won a Governor-General's Award, and *A throw of particles: the new and selected poetry of D.G. Jones* (1983). As the title *Phrases from Orpheus* suggests, Jones has tended to see his larger, more embracing forms in mythological terms,

though he has been saved from the amorphous vagueness of much mythopoeic poetry (for example that of Charles G.D. ROBERTS) by an aesthetic precision, an economy of language, and a neo-imagistic sharpness of outline. The neo-imagism is perhaps most apparent in *Under the thunder the flowers light up the earth*, but the empathies of this book range more widely than those of the earlier volumes. The myths have not departed from the poet's vision, but they have changed their forms. The gods come this time in other guises, and often as painters, for two of the five sections of the book are devoted to poems inspired by David Milne and Alex Colville. Jones matches an appreciation of the lyrical qualities of these painters with a strong visual and 'painterly' element in his own verse. *Under the thunder* reflects the biculturalism of other aspects of the poet's life by including, along with the expected poems in English, others that are partly or wholly in French and one poem at least that is in a Caribbean patois.

A concern for the guiding myths of literature found a place not only in Jones's poems but in his single work of criticism, *Butterfly on rock: a study of themes and images in Canadian literature* (1970), in which he sees the dominant themes and images in the literature of Canada as emanations of the mythical and moral structure of our society when, at a critical changing point, it ceases to be the garrison society described by Northrop FRYE and enters into a dialogue with the natural world it had formerly rejected in fear. It has become a classic of critical writing in Canada.

See two essays on Jones in CANADIAN LITERATURE: E.D. Blodgett, 'The masks of D.G. Jones' (Issue 60, Spring 1974), and George BOWERING, 'Coming home to the world' (Issue 65, Summer 1975).

See also CRITICISM IN ENGLISH: 5(d).
GEORGE WOODCOCK

Jones, Peter. See INDIAN LITERATURE: 2.

Joual. Literary *joual* came into prominence in Québec in 1964 and was of major interest for about ten years. Before 1964 the word 'joual' had been used as a pejorative: its existence as a dialect pronunciation of 'cheval' is well attested in rural Québec, Normandy, and other parts of France. Claude-Henri GRIGNON and André Laurendeau had referred to it to denote not only a corrupt speech but the deprived culture that went with it. Émile CODERRE ('Jean Narrache') had developed in his poetry an orthographic and lexical style to record the resentment and frustration of the down-and-out Montrealer of the Depression years, admitting a certain sympathy and even sentimentality. Popular idioms peculiar to Canadian French had been used in other literary works but kept remote from the authorial voice. Jean-Paul Desbiens drew widespread attention to the use of *joual*, particularly in the lower-class districts of Montreal, in his *Les insolences du Frère Untel* (1960; translated by Miriam Chapin as *The impertinences of Brother Anonymous*, 1962), in which he regarded it as a disease like malnutrition. Gérald GODIN first applauded Desbiens's call for educational reform, but later criticized himself, and 'Frère Untel', for this haughty attitude (PARTIS PRIS II, 5 Jan. 1963). Desbiens also changed his position in later writing.

1964 saw the publication of *Le cassé*, a novella by Jacques RENAUD, and in the following year a short novel, *Pleure pas, Germaine*, by Claude JASMIN; in 1968 Michel TREMBLAY's *Les* BELLES SOEURS (1968) was performed. For all three works the authors chose a literary form that could fully exploit the novelty of making uneducated speech the main medium of expression and standard French a marginal, usually comic, intrusion. The popularity of these works in *joual* had a major impact on Québec letters. Marie-Claire BLAIS's *Un joualonais, sa joualonie* (1974) mocked the literary affectation of proletarian language, which by that time had become repetitive. Her bitter parody marked the beginning of the end of the literary use of *joual*, but its influence remains in a less intensive cult of oral style.

We can distinguish certain common features of *joual* in literature, though their proportions differ considerably from one author to another: anglicisms and barely assimilated English words (frequent in Jasmin's novels, rare in the works of Tremblay); obscenities and picturesque blasphemies (intense in Renaud's novella), and non-standard syntax and orthography that often imply an erosion of basic grammar. The thematic correlatives are violence and alienation; murder, rape, abortion, perversion, and prostitution; the boredom of factory work and the hopelessness of the unemployed; unsupportive relations with family, friends, and sexual partners; lack of direction or positive awareness of social goals; and resentment, vituperation, and an inability to communicate—all are found, in different mixes, in *joual* works.

JACK WARWICK

Journals of Susanna Moodie, The (1970). One of the most important efforts in literature to create a Canadian myth of the wilderness, this sequence of poems by Margaret ATWOOD is based on the life of Susanna MOODIE, an English gentlewoman who immigrated in 1832 to Upper Canada (Ont.). It is divided into three sections. Journal I describes Moodie's arrival in Canada, her voyage up the St Lawrence past cities 'rotting with cholera', and her experiences during seven years of settlement in the Ontario bush. Her efforts as a pioneer failed, and Journal II records her escape to Belleville, Ont., where her husband had been made sheriff. Journal III describes Moodie as an old woman living in estrangement from the artificial civility of a Canadian Victorian town. In the last poems of the cycle she is resurrected as a spirit haunting the twentieth-century Canadian mind with accusations of its betrayal of its historical traditions. From the first poem ('Disembarking at Québec'), through 'The wereman', a poem about Moodie's husband, 'Departure from the bush', 'Death of a young son by drowning', the 'Dream' poems (which include 'The bush garden' and 'Brian the still-hunter'), and 'Thoughts from underground', this collection is perhaps the most memorable literary evocation of immigrant experience in modern Canadian literature.

Susanna Moodie provides Atwood with a Canadian archetype that enables her to explore her enduring obsession with the moral and psychological problems of colonialism. As Atwood explains in her 'Afterword': 'We are all immigrants to this place even if we were born here: the country is too big for anyone to inhabit completely, and in the parts unknown to us we move in fear, exiles and invaders.' The Canadian psyche, Atwood feels, is schizophrenic, split by a deep ambivalence: while we preach ardent affection for Canada, we remain detached and critical observers. Through Moodie, Atwood reveals how this mentality was established in the process of colonization. With a fine perceptive irony she records the pathetically incongruous conjunction of a Victorian sensibility, and its world of porcelain civility, with a mysterious and hostile wilderness that makes no accommodation to the human. In these poems Moodie becomes a heroic figure struggling to 'unlearn' old European codes of behaviour in order to speak a new language. At the end of the cycle she is the spirit of the land, accusing Canadians of erecting a garrison mentality: alienated in a world of concrete and glass, they remain ignorant of the wilderness that surrounds them.

See also SURVIVAL: A THEMATIC GUIDE TO CANADIAN LITERATURE.

ROSEMARY SULLIVAN

Juchereau de La Ferté, Jeanne-Françoise. See Writing in NEW FRANCE: 2.

K

Kalm, Peter. See TRAVEL LITERATURE IN ENGLISH.

Kamouraska (1970). Anne HÉBERT's most successful novel, *Kamouraska* skilfully combines two plots. The first—based on an actual murder-case in nineteenth-century Québec—takes place during the Rebellion of the Patriotes in Lower Canada: in 1839 a young woman, Elisabeth, induces her American lover, Doctor Nelson, to kill her husband, a violent man who is seigneur of Kamouraska. Nelson accomplishes the dreadful deed, then flees to the United States. Elisabeth is arrested, imprisoned, and finally released. She assumes the obligatory mask of bourgeois respectability, marrying a Quebec City notary named Rolland. The second plot, which reinterprets the first, is set some twenty years later. Elisabeth's second husband, gravely ill, is about to die. She will soon be free again, but what will she do with that freedom? Remain faithful to her honourable role of widow and mother, or try to rejoin her American lover? As she contemplates these choices she sees again, in the course of a single night of terrifying lucidity, all her violent past. Arriving at a dreadful realization of her sealed fate, she decides to cling to her false respectability. This devastating portrait of a woman in anguish, consumed by passion, is written in broken, telegraphic sentences that give the novel a breathlessly romantic style. It is also studded with details about the manners, dress, and customs of nineteenth-century Québec.

A visually beautiful film directed by Claude Jutra, *Kamouraska* (1973), captures the dramatic subtleties of the novel.

For historical background to the novel, see Françoise Dufresne, 'Le drame de Kamouraska' in *Québec-Histoire*, vol. 1, nos. 5-6 (June-Aug., 1972). For a good discussion of the novel, see Grazia Merler, 'La réalité dans la prose d'Anne Hébert' in *Écrits du Canada français*, vol. 33 (1971).

PIERRE H. LEMIEUX

Kane, Paul (1810-71). Born in Ireland, he came to York (Toronto) about 1819 (subsequently he claimed to have been born in York). He studied portrait painting as a young man, and lived and worked in Toronto, Cobourg, Detroit, and Mobile, Alabama. He toured Europe in 1841-2 and spent time in London in 1842-3, where he became a friend of George Catlin, who had lived and painted among forty-eight Indian tribes in the United States. Kane left London in 1843 determined to paint the Indians of Canada. His three-year western journey began from Toronto on 17 June 1845, and took him to Georgian Bay and thence, by way of a number of Hudson's Bay Company posts, to Fort Vancouver. From there he made sketching trips to Oregon, to the north-west region then known as New Caledonia, and to the southern part of Vancouver Island. Kane's best-known works are the 100 canvases he painted largely from sketches made during his travels; several hundred surviving sketches are important not only for their documentary value but also for their freshness and immediacy. Both sketches and canvases are an impressive artistic record of a way of life that was soon to disappear. Kane is also known as the author of *Wanderings of an artist among the Indians of North America . . .* (London, 1859), a classic of Canadian travel literature. Based on his diary—expanded with extracts from field logs, stories, and legends about the Indians he encountered—it provides extensive and careful information and description in a narrative that is free of the heavy embellishment that was characteristic of other Victorian writing. It was illustrated with reproductions of a number of Kane's sketches and paintings. The English-language edition sold out; French, Danish, and German editions appeared between 1860 and 1863; and a second English edition appeared in 1925.

See *Paul Kane's frontier: including 'Wanderings of an artist among the Indians of North America' by Paul Kane* (1971), edited with a catalogue raisonné by J. Russell Harper—a large, lavishly illustrated volume that contains a definitive biographical study by Dr. Harper.   KATHRYN HAMER

Kattan, Naim (b. 1928). Born in Bagdad, Iraq, of Jewish parents, he attended a Hebrew school, where he learned Arabic, French, and English in preparation for his studies in the law faculty of the University of Bagdad. Because of the unfavourable political climate he left Iraq at the end of the Second World War for Paris, where he studied literature at the Sorbonne before coming to Montreal in 1954. In Canada he has edited and written essays for a variety of political and literary journals and is at present the head of the literary section of the Canada Council.

The three worlds Kattan has lived in—the Middle East, Europe, and North America—and the cultures he has immersed himself in—Jewish, Arabic, French, and North American—inform his essays, novels, and short stories with an unusually wide range of perceptions, which he conveys with remarkable clarity. His first book of essays, *Le réel et le théâtral* (1970)—which won the Prix France-Canada in 1971 and was translated by Alan Brown as *Reality and theatre* (1972)—combines informal autobiography with formal speculation on the cultural, religious, and linguistic differences between the occidental and oriental ways of perceiving reality: the latter confronts reality directly, while the former resorts to theatrical mediation. In the tradition of the French structuralists, Kattan operates through a series of binary oppositions—the image and the unseen, object and shadow, groups and communities, actors and dictators, word and place. He repeats this method in his second volume of essays, *La mémoire et la promesse* (1978), as he continues to explore such dichotomies as occident and orient, Arabic and French, Jew and Arab, male and female, particular and universal, and memory and promise.

Some of these preoccupations find their way into Kattan's fiction, beginning with his first autobiographical novel *Adieu, Babylone* (1975), which appeared in an English translation by Sheila Fischman as *Farewell, Babylon* (1976). The nameless narrator recounts his childhood experiences in Bagdad during the Second World War, describing his family's fear of the Germans and the *Farhoud*, a pogrom-like attack by the bedouins against the Jewish population. The narrator's sexual and literary apprenticeship is described with very little dialogue to interfere with the discursive narration. In Kattan's second novel, *Les fruits arrachés* (1977)—*Paris interlude* (1979) in its English-translation by Sheila Fischman—the protagonist Méir has a much smaller narrative role as Kattan shifts to a more dramatic form where dialogue predominates. Having left Iraq, Méir studies literature at the Sorbonne at a time when France is recovering from the trauma of the Second World War. His alternating love affairs with a French, a Polish, and a Dutch lover symbolize the instability of post-war Europe. As in the first novel, the second ends with a departure, this time for North America, where the third novel of Kattan's trilogy will be set.

If the first novel displayed Kattan the essayist and the second Kattan the dramatist, Kattan the short-story writer emerges with the proper balance of dialogue and narration in his four collections of stories: *Dans le désert* (1974), *La traversée* (1976), *Le rivage* (1979), and *Le sable de l'île* (1981). Many of these stories focus on incomplete love affairs in which one of the lovers discovers the weakness of the other and must choose, by the end of the story, whether to depart or to renew the relationship. Many stories are set in bars, hotels, or airports, reflecting the transience of these liaisons, the fragility leading to departure. The short story seems to be the appropriate genre for examining these short-lived affairs, departures, or endings, and the need for self-renewal. Some of Kattan's short stories have been translated into English by Judith Madley and Patricia Claxton and collected in *The neighbour and other stories* (NCL, 1982).

Kattan's short plays have been collected in *La discrétion, la neige, le trajet, les protagonistes* (1974). He has edited three volumes of literary criticism, *Écrivains des Amériques* (1976), covering contemporary fiction of the United States, English Canada, and South America. He has also supervised the publications of Le Cercle juif de langue française, Montreal, editing and contributing to the two volumes of its Cahiers: I. *Les juifs et la communauté française* (1965) and II. *Juifs et Canadiens* (1976).   MICHAEL GREENSTEIN

Katzmann, Mary Jane (1828-90). Born in Preston, N.S., she showed exceptional intelligence at an early age, but because she was female she was not given the benefit of a formal education. In 1845 her poetry came to the attention of Joseph HOWE, who praised it in 'Nights with the muses', a series of articles on Nova Scotia writers in the *Novascotian*. In 1852, at the age of twenty-four, she became editor of a new literary magazine, the PROVINCIAL (Jan. 1852-Dec. 1853). As the foremost female editor of her time, she encouraged other women writers to project a humanistic vision of society through writing. She married William Lawson in 1869 and died of cancer in Halifax.

From 1848 to 1851 Katzmann published a large amount of verse in *The Guardian* (Halifax), and in the late fifties and sixties her verse appeared frequently in local newspapers. A collection, *Frankincense and myrrh* (Halifax, 1893), was published posthumously, as was her *History of the townships of Dartmouth, Preston, and Lawrencetown* (Halifax, 1893). As a poet Katzmann was prone to generalities, melodramatic effects, and dull religious and moral didacticism—characteristics that mark the verse of contemporary 'female poets' in Britain and the United States upon whom she patterned herself—but she was always technically competent, at her best when writing descriptive verse or charming song-like lyrics.
                                    TOM VINCENT

Kearns, Lionel (b. 1937). Lionel John Kearns was born in Nelson, B.C., and grew up in the Kootenay region of British Columbia. He played amateur hockey throughout his teens, and spent one year playing semi-professional hockey in Mexico City before enrolling in English at the University of British Columbia in 1958. While at UBC he became a close friend of George BOWERING, Frank DAVEY, and Fred WAH and contributed significantly to the development of their magazine TISH. There also he worked out his proposal for 'stacked verse'—a system of poetry notation that indicates the most heavily stressed syllable in

each phrase of a poem—and illustrated this in his collection of poems 'Songs of circumstance', which he presented as his master's thesis in 1963.

On graduation Kearns accepted the teaching post at Simon Fraser University that he still holds. *Songs of circumstance* (1963) was published in a limited edition by Tishbooks and republished, minus the stacked-verse notation, under the title *Pointing* (1967) by the RYERSON PRESS. These well-crafted poems, marked by irony and understated humour, were followed by *Listen, George* (1965), a long-line verse-letter recalling Kearns's youth and his days as a hockey player, and expressing disillusionment with the apparent restrictedness of his present life. Here, and in the poems of *By the light of the silvery McLune* (1969), Kearns used the long line, prose measure, and coarse humour as symbols of rebellion against both literary form and excessive systematization in society. *About time* (1974) and *Practicing up to be human* (1978), however, marked a return to the rhythmically crafted, intellectually intense poems of his first book. Kearns' most recent work, 'Convergences', is a massive verse-history of the collapse of Haida Indian culture and has to date been published only in excerpts. His considerable technical skills are here well used in a collage of three distinct voices and documentary materials.   FRANK DAVEY

Keith, Marian. Pseudonym used by Mary Esther MacGREGOR.

Kelley, Thomas P. (1905-82). Born at Campbellford, Ont., he travelled as a youngster with his father's medicine show, then boxed professionally in the United States. His career as a pulp writer began in 1937, when he sold the first of three fantasy-adventure serials ('The last pharaoh', 'I found Cleopatra', and 'A million years in the future') to *Weird tales*. Employing a variety of pseudonyms, he filled many an issue of *Uncanny Tales*, the leading Canadian pulp magazine of the Second-World-War period. Thereafter he turned out some two-dozen pocket-books, largely of the true-crime variety. *The Black Donnellys* (1954) and *Vengeance of the Black Donnellys* (1969)—his lurid accounts of the nineteenth-century Irish blood feud and its aftermath, which took place in Lucan, Ont., in the 1880s—have sold hundreds of thousands of copies. *The fabulous Kelley* (1968; rev. 1974) is a surprisingly sensitive evocation of the life and times of his father, who was known as 'Doc Kelley, Canada's King of the Medicine Men'. Thomas Kelley, who claimed that he was 'king of the Canadian pulp writers' and 'the fastest author in the East', encouraged stories about himself, though he became reclusive in later years. He died in Toronto, leaving an unpublished fantasy-adventure novel set in A.D. 7109.

JOHN ROBERT COLOMBO

Kelsey, Henry. See EXPLORATION LITERATURE IN ENGLISH: 2.

Kennedy, Leo (b. 1907). Born in Liverpool, Eng., he moved with his family to Montreal in 1912. He graduated in 1929 from the University of Montreal, where he studied business, and became closely associated with F.R. SCOTT and A.J.M. SMITH of the *McGill Fortnightly Review* (1925-7) after they discovered Kennedy as the pseudonymous 'Helen Laurence' in the lonely-hearts columns of the Montreal *Star*. In 1928, with Scott, he founded and edited the short-lived *Canadian Mercury*. In 1933 his only collection of poetry, *The shrouding*, was published by Macmillan at the urging of E.J. PRATT.

Kennedy was a modernist who sought to replace the sentimental romanticism of the 'Maple Leaf school' with objective craftsmanship. Under the influence of the metaphysical and mythic sensibilities of T.S. Eliot and Sir James Frazer, he wrote poems that seek salvation from the winter wasteland of death and oblivion by fusing Christian faith in the resurrection with the myth of renewal found in the order of nature: buried bones are like crocus bulbs awaiting the spring to sprout heavenward. By 1936, when his poems were included in the modernist anthology *New provinces*, he was already turning his back on much of what he dismissed as surrealist literary exercises. He began writing committed criticism of social realities for radical periodicals like *New Frontier*. Paradoxically, during this socialist phase he moved to New Canaan, Conn., to write copy for a New York advertising firm. In 1978 he returned to Montreal, where he is now working on his memoirs.

The shrouding was reprinted in 1975 with an introduction by Leon EDEL, who describes Kennedy as the sprightly leader of Canada's 'graveyard school' of metaphysical poetry. For a selection of criticism by and about Kennedy, see *The McGill movement:*

A.J.M. Smith, F.R. Scott and Leo Kennedy (1969) edited by Peter STEVENS.

DAVID LATHAM

Kidd, Adam (1802-31). Of the many early Canadian writers who produced a single volume of poetry, Adam Kidd has received more attention from modern critics than the quality of his work merits. Many others wrote equally well, on similar themes, but Kidd's flamboyant personality, and the tragedy of his early death, combine to make him a sympathetic subject for study.

Born in Ireland, he settled in Quebec with his family while in his teens. Sometime in the mid-1820s he was considered as a candidate for the Church of England priesthood, but having displeased Bishop Mountain for an undocumented reason he was rejected as unsuitable. He travelled in Upper Canada in 1828, but late in that year was living in Montreal and publishing poetry in the local radical newspaper, *The Irish Vindicator*, as well as in *The Irish Shield* (Philadelphia), both under his own name and under the pseudonym 'Slievegallin'. After his collection of poems, *The Huron chief* (1830), appeared, he set off on a journey through Upper Canada, publicizing his book and gathering material and subscriptions for a new one, also on an Indian theme. He seems to have spent the winter of 1830-1 with friends in Kingston. Aware that he was dying—he published a farewell poem, 'Impromptu', in the *Kingston Chronicle* (12 Mar. 1831)—he returned to Quebec. He died there in July.

Another Montreal poet, W.F. HAWLEY, had also published many poems in the *Vindicator*. When Hawley's book *Quebec, the harp, and other poems* appeared in 1829, several courteous mentions in that newspaper were followed by a savage review, which one suspects was written by Kidd. *The Huron chief's* publication in Montreal a little later provided occasion for critical revenge. The book was mockingly dissected in the *Gazette* and spiritedly defended by the author in the *Vindicator*. The *Gazette* correspondent also told of Kidd's selling subscriptions for his book from door to door. If Kidd did indeed sell 1,500 copies of *The Huron chief* as he claimed, that number is more than double the recorded sales of any other pre-Confederation literary work.

Criticism of *The Huron chief* was not confined to the pages of local newspapers. Taking exception to a footnote that attacked Mr Buchanan, the British Consul in New York, for policies he advocated with regard to the navigation of the St Lawrence, Buchanan's sons and a 'friend' attacked Kidd on a Montreal street and subjected him to a public thrashing. There are two versions of the story: one by Kidd in which he emerges triumphant; the other by the 'friend', which portrays the poet as beneath the notice of a gentleman. It appears that only Kidd's dignity was hurt, but the incident is a striking indication of the status of poets in early Canadian society.

The Huron chief demonstrates the nobility of the Indian in his natural state and the perfidy of the whites who attempt to convert him while seizing his land. The central figure is the chief Skenandow, a wise and peaceful man, ultimately murdered by whites whose release from captivity he has effected. Kidd, as narrator, spends much time recording details of the Indian way of life and describing the scenery of the Great Lakes area. A number of shorter poems complete the volume, many of them addressed to young ladies.

An article on Kidd and his work by C.F. KLINCK appeared in *Queen's Quarterly* (Autumn 1958).   MARY LU MacDONALD

Kilbourn, William. See HISTORICAL WRITING IN ENGLISH: 7.

Kinch, Martin (b. 1943). Born in London, Eng., Martin Robert Newman Kinch immigrated with his parents in 1948 to Toronto; from there he moved to London, Ont., in 1956 to complete his high-school and university education. His work as a director and actor at the University of Western Ontario, from which he received an Honours B.A. in English in 1966, led to a grant from the Ontario Department of Education to apprentice at the Birmingham Repertory Theatre as an assistant director in 1967-8. Returning to Canada, he worked as a project director for the Central Ontario Drama League before founding with John PALMER in 1969 the Canadian Place Theatre at Stratford, Ont., which, although short-lived, was one of the first Canadian theatres to have an all-Canadian production policy. After two seasons as an assistant director at the Stratford Shakespeare Festival and assuming numerous directorial jobs in Toronto's burgeoning 'alternate' theatres, he co-founded with Palmer and Tom HENDRY in 1971 the Toronto Free Theatre. He remained as artistic director until 1978, when he resigned to devote greater time to playwriting. He now works for CBC Television in Toronto.

Of Kinch's four stage plays, *Me?* (1975) has achieved the most success. *Separate cell* and *Vampyr*, two early unpublished works, are historically significant in that the former was produced in 1970 at the Festival of Underground Theatre (F.U.T.), a benchmark in the development of Toronto theatre, and the latter contributed to the early notoriety of Toronto's Theatre Passe Muraille, where it was produced in 1971. *Me?*, first directed by Palmer at Toronto Free Theatre in 1973, is a much tighter, more naturalistic work than the earlier plays, which relied on ritual and shock techniques. Although *Me?* was staged in a somewhat surrealistic set that became even more exaggeratedly environmental when it was revived in 1977 (again at Toronto Free Theatre, with Palmer directing), it is essentially a five-character domestic drama involving a young and egocentric writer's attempts to resolve conflicts with the people closest to him—his wife, mistress, best friend, and brother. Intended as a castigation of the self-absorption of the 'me generation', it offers carefully etched portraits of characters typical of Toronto's artistic community of the time. (In his Introduction to the printed text William Lane asserts that 'every one of the four major characters of the play were in the audience' on opening night.) The play transcends its coterie aspects, however, to become an authentic and perceptive study of an artist struggling with questions about communication and commitment that trouble people of many circumstances. In that regard it is similar to Kinch's fourth play, *April 29, 1975* (unpublished), which explores the after-effects of violence and the trauma that the exigencies of survival effect on vulnerable characters and relationships. Set on the day the United States withdrew from Viet Nam, the play has a broader scope than *Me?* that results from a wider range of character types. Although none are as fully realized as Terry, the central character of *Me?*, each contributes a well-defined aspect to a tensely realistic study of the aftermath of a car crash between American and Canadian cars. The cultural differences revealed by the characters' response to violence is the real focus of the play and what led the Toronto Drama Bench to nominate it for the Chalmers Award for best new Canadian play of 1975, an honour also awarded to *Me?* in 1973.

Kinch's television and film scripts include his adaptation of *Me?*, which won the Best

Foreign Film award at the 1974 Toulon Film Festival. His cogent analysis of Toronto theatre in the mid-seventies, 'Canadian theatre in for the long haul', is included in *Debates and controversies* (1979), edited by Daniel Drache. ROBERT S. WALLACE

King, Basil (1859-1928). Born in Charlottetown, P.E.I., William Benjamin Basil King was educated locally and at King's College, Windsor, N.S. He was ordained an Anglican priest and served St Luke's Pro-cathedral, Halifax, as rector from 1884. He became rector of Christ Church, Cambridge, Mass., in 1892. Failing eyesight forced him to resign his charge in 1900 and he devoted the rest of his life to travel and writing.

From his first novel, *Griselda* (1900), King worked within the conventions of popular moral fiction. Disparagement of divorce is evident in his second title, *Let not man put asunder* (1901). *In the garden of Charity* (1903), his only digression from Boston-New York settings and from the portrayal of the international world of wealthy Americans, is set among Nova Scotia fisherfolk. Its themes of love, betrayal, and marital fidelity are worked out with compelling vigour. In *The steps of honour* (1904) a Harvard professor plagiarizes scholarship in a vain attempt to win a Cambridge bluestocking. *The giant's strength* (1907) shows the richest man in America learning moral sensitivity through his daughter's suffering. King's early novels did not, however, reach a wide audience until they were reprinted after two successive bestsellers made him famous. These were *The inner shrine* (1909), a trite exercise in the Howells-James international mould, and *The wild olive* (1910), a more interesting drama of moral crisis.

King, who used his fiction to promote understanding across class, sex, and international barriers, over-exploited in his later work popular themes about the crossing of class boundaries, especially through marriage, but was adept at portraying capable women and was eager to explain the social background of the many Canadian characters who appear in about half of his 22 novels. British and American social viewpoints are contrasted convincingly in *The street called Straight* (1912). *The way home* (1913), set partly in the Canadian Northwest, but mainly filtering its social Christian issues through a New York Episcopal rectory, received high praise from W.D. Howells. Two diffuse, didactic marriage novels, *The letter of the contract* (1914) and

The side of the angels (1916), illustrate how King's clever plots were declining into mere formulae until his response to First World War conditions gave him a renewed social conviction and a counterweight to his tedious pandering to popular morality.

The Canadian heroine-narrator of *The high heart* (1917) marries a rich American but differs strongly in her opinions of the war from both British and U.S. characters. *The lifted veil* (1917) and *The city of comrades* (1919) also portray Canadians in the U.S.A. against a wartime background. Class, and to some extent race, are the main postwar concerns in *The thread of flame* (1920). These themes recur in *The empty sack* (1921) and *The dust flower* (1922), where upwardly mobile Canadians are contrasted with other immigrants, and with wealthy establishment New Yorkers. *The happy isles* (1923), *The high forfeit* (1925), *Pluck* (1928), *Satan as lightning* (1929), and *The break of day* (1930) are, like King's other novels, parables of waywardness and redemption, but add nothing to his reputation. *The spreading dawn* (1927) is a collection of stories that gathers some of his short fiction from magazines. In the 1920s King became a kind of popular sage, issuing *The abolishing of death* (1919), an account of spiritualism; *The conquest of fear* (1921), popular philosophy; *The discovery of God* (1923) and *The Bible and common sense*, biblical commentaries; *Faith and success* (1925) and *Adventures in religion* (1929), popular theology; and *The seven torches of character* (1929). 30,000 copies of his best-known religious-philosophical work, *The conquest of fear*, were sold in 1930 alone. KEN MacKINNON

Kingsford, William. See HISTORICAL WRITING IN ENGLISH: 2.

Kinsella, W.P. (b. 1935). William Patrick Kinsella was born in Edmonton, Alta., and spent nearly two decades in business before earning a B.A. in creative writing at the University of Victoria (1974) and an M.F.A. at the University of Iowa (1978), where he was enrolled in the Writer's Workshop. A teacher of creative writing and modern literature at the University of Calgary since 1978, he now has to his credit four volumes of short fiction, two novels, and numerous uncollected pieces. Kinsella's fiction is marked by spontaneity, sentiment, compassion, and a euphoric anti-authoritarianism. The Indian stories in *Dance me outside* (1977), *Scars* (1978), *Born Indian* (1981), and *The* *moccasin telegraph* (1983) incline towards satire, pathos, and rich human significance, while the short fantasies in *Shoeless Joe Jackson comes to Iowa* (1980) display imaginative power and manic verve. In the Indian stories, as in the fantasies, Kinsella attacks vice, prejudice, dullness, and rampant absurdity, his constant touchstone being a good heart endowed with the ability to dream.

In the Indian stories Kinsella stations himself 'inside the skin of an 18 year-old Indian boy and imagine[s] how he might react' to the situations he observes. Silas Ermineskin's spare but vivid idiom deftly expresses his mingled naiveté and shrewdness. Seen through his eyes, the white world is repressive, humourless, moralistic, theoretical, and legalistic; its excessive rationalism and materialism have left it loveless and sterile. By contrast the Indian world is frankly sexual, pragmatic, and spontaneous, drawing its strength from the joyous and resilient anarchy embodied most notably in wise Mad Etta, the 400-lb medicine woman. Recurring motifs and familiar characters knit these stories together into a unified fictional world. Using the empathetic Silas as a narrative lens and listening post, Kinsella likes to reverse clichés: in 'Illiana comes home' a white suitor is brought home to an Indian mother and in 'Canadian culture' a white government official agrees to be raped by an Indian.

In the title story of *Shoeless Joe Jackson comes to Iowa*, a high-spirited blend of 'fact and fantasy, magic and reality', a Kinsella-like narrator obeys a mysterious voice that bids him construct a backyard left field as a shrine to his father's hero, Shoeless Joe Jackson, unjustly disgraced in the 1919 White Sox scandal. This touching and liberating fantasy about love, innocence, the land, and the mystique of baseball later became the novel *Shoeless Joe* (1982), in which Joe redeems himself, and the narrator 'kidnaps J.D. Salinger and takes him to a baseball game at Fenway Park in Boston.' Another story, 'The Grecian urn', tells of a man with special powers who inhabits works of art and drives his rival into an insane asylum.

Shoeless Joe won the Houghton Mifflin Literary Fellowship in 1982 and the *Books in Canada* Award for First Novels in 1983.

JEFFREY HEATH

Kirby, William (1817-1906). Despite his apotheosis as the voice of United Empire Loyalism in his day, Kirby was born in Kingston-upon-Hull, Eng., the son of a Yorkshire tanner. His parents immigrated to the United States in 1832 and he arrived in Upper Canada in 1839. After visiting briefly in Toronto, Quebec City, and Montreal, he took up a lifelong residence in Niagara-on-the-Lake, where his house still stands. The grandson of a United Empire Loyalist, Kirby carried on his trade as a tanner until marrying Eliza Madaline Whitmore, herself part of the extensive Servos family of Niagara-region UELs. Editor of the *Niagara Mail*, from 1871 to 1895 collector of customs, and a charter member of the Royal Society of Canada in 1882, Kirby delivered the principal address at the 1884 UEL Centennial celebrations.

Kirby's historical importance rests chiefly on his authorship of *The* GOLDEN DOG (Rouses Point, N.Y., 1877), which gained him considerable fame in his own day. Set in Quebec in 1748, with characters based on historical figures, it is imbued with conventions of the European Gothic novel that make it highly romantic and unrealistic, though one can admire its emotional complexity and ambitious conception. It has been reprinted many times and can be read today in an edition abridged by Derek Crawley for the New Canadian Library (1969).

Kirby's lesser works demonstrate the contours of an Upper Canadian Tory imagination. *The U.E.: a tale of Upper Canada* (Niagara, 1859) is an epic poem in twelve cantos, with a heroic-couplet stanzaic form. While having slight aesthetic interest, it presents several keystones of the Upper-Canadian Loyalist mythology that has remained influential in the culture of Ontario. Some of the tenets of that interpretation of history, found in Kirby's poem, are the melding of the 1837 Rebellion into the cycle of Loyalist conflicts of 1776 and 1812; the vision of Upper Canada as an Edenic garden under constant threat from outside marauders and inside traitors; and the stretching of the concept of Loyalism (held by those exiled from their country as a result of the American Revolution) beyond its historical boundaries to include anyone with the disposition to defend Canadian institutions and territory. Ethwald, the martyred hero, described as a Loyalist, springs from a father who did not arrive in Canada until after 1812. The actual Loyalist in the poem, Ranger John, forms the link between the various wars, for he has been slaking his bloodthirstiness against the Americans since 1776. It is he who warns the English immigrants of the struggles they may have to wage against American invaders and Canadian traitors, though in the Rebellion of 1837 his son Hugh traitorously fights for the 'Americans' (Mackenzie's rebels are not considered Canadian). Most of the poem presents a conventional pastoral view of Upper Canada, of happy rustics and fertile fields, as a local bard retells the myth of Daphne and Apollo in Amerindian terms. The forest does not loom in the manner of the savage wilderness of John RICHARDSON; instead it denotes Upper Canada's distance from urban corruption. Indeed, the forest meets its highest purpose when it furnishes masts for British warships. Arcadia must be defended, and the Ranger's sons—one loyal, one a rebel—die in a skirmish, as does Ethwald. The poem concludes with a scene in which Ethwald's father and the Ranger declaim about loyalty and patriotism.

Under the pseudonym 'Britannicus', Kirby had written a *Counter manifesto to the Canadian annexationists* (Niagara, 1849), and various poems and historical pieces flowed from his pen before and after publication of *The Golden Dog*. In that historical romance he had extended the concept of loyalty so that it became the principal moral attribute of French as well as English Canada.

Canadian idylls (Welland, Ont., 1894), a collection of poems that had seen periodical publication, deals with patriotic and historical themes, including local legends. 'Spina Christi' presents a jocular/grisly anecdote about the digging-up and scattering of rebel and 'sympathizer' skeletons that lay buried in Niagara's soil. *Annals of Niagara* (Welland, 1846) is a shapeless historical narrative dwelling on the repression and expulsion of the disaffected and seditious, as well as on barbarities, in the desultory frontier warfare along the Niagara border after the Battle of Queenston Heights. The reader of these grim works easily accepts the account of Kirby's biographer, Lorne PIERCE, of how Kirby relished the souvenir his son sent him from Regina—a piece of the rope that had hanged Riel.

The writings and career of Kirby reveal the extent to which the virtue of loyalty contracted in his time to a concept of Loyalty; how what had originally been a historical designation changed into a rhetorical label expressing conservative approbation.

See W.R. Riddell, *William Kirby* (1925) and Lorne Pierce, *William Kirby: the portrait of a Tory loyalist* (1929). See also L.R. Early, 'Myth and prejudice in Kirby, Richardson, and Parker', CANADIAN LITERATURE 81 (Summer 1979). DENNIS DUFFY

Kiriak, Illia. See UKRAINIAN WRITING.

Kirkconnell, Watson (1895-1977). Born in Port Hope, Ont., he was educated at Queen's University, the Toronto Conservatory of Music, and Oxford University. From 1922 to 1940 he taught English, and later classics, at Wesley College, Winnipeg. From 1940 to 1948 he was head of the English department at McMaster University, and from 1948, until his retirement in 1964, he was president of Acadia University. In 1966 he came out of retirement for two years as head of Acadia's English department. A founding member of the CANADIAN AUTHORS' ASSOCIATION, he served two terms as national president (1942-4, 1956-8), and was appointed honorary president in 1968. During the Second World War he chaired the Writers' War Committee and was active in the creation of the Humanities Research Council, which led to the writing, with A.S.P. Woodhouse, of *The humanities in Canada* (1947). He was elected to the Royal Society of Canada in 1936. In addition to numerous European literary awards, he received the Lorne PIERCE Medal in 1942.

Kirkconnell was doubtless Canada's most prolific and industrious scholar, with more than 150 books and booklets and over 1000 published articles. A tireless linguist, he translated poetry from over 50 languages. His chief works of translation are: *European elegies: one hundred poems chosen and translated from European literature in fifty languages* (1928); *The North American book of Icelandic verse* (1930); *The Magyar muse: an anthology of Hungarian poetry, 1400-1932* (1933); *Canadian overtones: an anthology of Canadian poetry written originally in Icelandic, Swedish, Hungarian, Italian, Greek, and Ukrainian* (1935); *Arany's 'The death of King Buda'* (1936); *A little treasury of Hungarian verse* (1947); *Prince Ihor's raid against the Polovisti* (1947); Mickiewicz's *Pan Tadeusz; or the last foray in Lithuania* (1962); in collaboration with Séraphin Marion, *Tradition du Québec/The Québec tradition* (1946); and in collaboration with C.H. Andrusyshen, *The Ukrainian poets, 1189-1962* (1963) and *The poetical works of Taras Shevchenko* (1964).

Providing a trilogy of valuable critical aids to Milton's poetry, Kirkconnell wrote *The celestial cycle: the theme of Paradise Lost in world literature, with translations of the major analogues* (1952); *That invincible Samson: the theme of Samson Agonistes in world literature with translations of the major analogues* (1964); and *Awake the courteous echo: the themes of Comus, Lycidas, and Paradise Regained in world literature with translations of the major analogues* (1973).

Kirkconnell's major contribution to Canadian scholarship was his annual comprehensive review of Canadian writing in languages other than English and French for the 'Letters in Canada' survey in the *University of Toronto Quarterly*. Between 1938 and 1965 he supplied 28 such annual reviews, which evaluated specific works and commented upon trends and themes peculiar to the ethnic press. Characterized by a strong religious and anti-Communist bias, these reviews as a whole provide a record of Canadian literary accomplishment accessible to few. Kirkconnell's promotion of the literature of immigrant groups within their Old World traditions, as well as his massive translations of European poetry, and his constant championing of immigrants in the face of prejudice, were warmly appreciated by many groups. Examples of his role as an intermediary presenting European culture to Canadians include *An outline of European literature* (1927) and *The European heritage: a synopsis of European cultural achievement* (1930). To assure Canadians of the loyalty of these immigrants in wartime, he also produced *Canadians all: a primer of national unity* (1940).

Kirkconnell's own poetry incongruously mixed classical forms with modern themes, as in *The tide of life* (1930) and *The eternal quest* (1934). *The flying bull and other tales* (1940) forces a series of western 'tall tales' into the form of the *Canterbury tales*. More poems were collected in *Manitoba symphony* (1937); *Lycra sacra: four occasional hymns* (1939); *Western idyll* (1940); *The flavour of Nova Scotia* (1976); and lastly *The coronary muse* (1977), written in hospital. *Centennial tales and selected poems* (1965) contains narrative poems on historical themes. *Titus the toad* (1939) is a children's book. A short light opera, *The mod at Grand Pré*, was published in 1955.

Kirkconnell's publications cover an astonishingly wide field, ranging from economics to natural history, pedagogy, political theory, and multiculturalism. His autobiography, *A slice of Canada* (1967), links many of his varied concerns to reveal the intellectual integrity, Christian faith, and wide knowledge of world literature that informed them. It contains a selective bibliography in its appendix. A fuller, yet still selective, bibliography is in *The Acadia Bulletin* (Jan. 1961). TERRENCE CRAIG

Kirouac, Conrad. See MARIE-VICTORIN.

Klein, A.M. (1909-72). Abraham Moses Klein was born in Ratno in the Ukraine and in 1910 his family moved to Montreal, where he spent the rest of his life. His background was orthodox and he received a solid Jewish education in Hebrew, the Bible, and the Talmud (his poem 'Sophist' offers an affectionately ironic portrait of his Talmud teacher, Rabbi Simcha Garber). Although Klein's teachers encouraged him to enter the rabbinate, by his high-school years he had abandoned strict religious orthodoxy, acquiring in its stead his lifelong commitment to Zionism. In 1926 he entered McGill University, where he met the *McGill Fortnightly Review* group: Leon EDEL, Leo KENNEDY, F.R. SCOTT, and A.J.M. SMITH. Klein never published in the *Review*; his one submission was rejected because he refused to change the word 'soul', which the editors considered insufficiently modern. However, at about this time he began to publish in Canadian and American periodicals, both Jewish and non-Jewish: *Menorah Journal* in 1927; *Poetry* in 1928; *The* CANADIAN FORUM and *Canadian Mercury* in 1929. (Klein continued this practice throughout his career, publishing in *The Canadian Jewish Chronicle, The Canadian Zionist, The Jewish Standard, Opinion,* CONTEMPORARY VERSE, FIRST STATEMENT, PREVIEW, NORTHERN REVIEW, and *New Directions*.) Also at about this time he first read James Joyce's *Ulysses*, which was to influence his poetry and prose throughout his career. In 1930 he graduated from McGill and enrolled as a law student in the Université de Montréal, graduating in 1933 to practise law, a profession he never found very satisfying or remunerative. In 1935 he married his childhood sweetheart, Bessie Kozlov, and they eventually had three children. In 1936 a highly laudatory account of his work appeared in W.E. Collin's pioneering study of Canadian literature, *The* WHITE SAVANNAHS, and in the same year two of his poems, 'Out of the pulver and the polished lens' and 'Soirée of Velvel Kleinburger', were included in the anthology NEW PROVINCES. In 1938, to supplement his salary as a lawyer, Klein took on the editorship of *The Canadian Jewish chronicle* and in 1939 he became speechwriter and public relations adviser to Samuel Bronfman. He published

Klein

Hath not a Jew . . . in 1940. In the early forties Klein came in contact with a number of younger writers involved in *Preview* and *First Statement* who encouraged his interest in modern poetry: Patrick ANDERSON, P.K. PAGE, Louis DUDEK, John SUTHERLAND, and Irving LAYTON (whom he had known for some years). In 1944 he published *Poems* and *The Hitleriad* and in 1948 *The rocking chair and other poems*, which won a Governor General's Award. From 1945 to 1948 he was a lecturer in the English Department of McGill. The following year he ran for the CCF in the federal riding of Cartier, where he suffered a personally devastating defeat. Soon after this he was sent by the Canadian Jewish Congress on a fact-finding trip to Israel and to Jewish refugee camps in Europe and North Africa. *The second scroll* (1951) is a novel inspired by that trip. Not long after its publication he began to show signs of psychological distress, leading to several suicide attempts in 1954. After a partial recovery he became increasingly reclusive, giving up his law practice and his editorship of the *Chronicle*, avoiding contact with anyone but his immediate family, and ceasing to write altogether. He never recovered.

In his preface to *Hath not a Jew . . .* Ludwig Lewisohn described Klein as 'the first contributor of authentic Jewish poetry to the English language.' Although Klein's best poetry, in *The rocking chair*, leaves explicitly Jewish themes behind, this aspect of Klein's achievement is crucial. Klein formed an important link to the vital Yiddish culture of Montreal, especially the poems of Y.Y. SEGAL, and his translations of Segal and a number of other Yiddish and Hebrew writers make up a substantial and often impressive body of work. Even more important, Klein's distinctly Jewish perspective provided a stimulus to many younger Jewish writers in Montreal such as Layton, Leonard COHEN, Seymour MAYNE, and Mordecai RICHLER (whose *St. Urbain's horseman* owes much in conception to *The second scroll*).

Hath not a Jew . . ., consisting almost entirely of poems from the late twenties and early thirties, most fully explores Klein's relationship to his Jewish heritage, whose rich diversity is the keynote of the volume (see the manifesto poem, 'Ave atque vale'). His celebration of the unity underlying this diversity, of the One in the many, is the theme of the volume's finest poem, 'Out of the pulver and the polished lens', and has many parallels in Klein's later works. Stylistically most of these poems are skilful but immature, often substituting a quaint charm for genuine intensity. They are clearly influenced by Keats, Tennyson, Browning, and, to a certain extent, the imagists, and contain many echoes of the Elizabethans and the King James Version.

The essentially celebratory and optimistic vision of *Hath not a Jew . . .* did not survive the thirties. The Depression, the rise of Nazism, and Klein's own difficult personal circumstances seemed to overwhelm him and he wrote relatively little in this period— a few satirical poems and short stories of a vaguely Marxist tendency in which he gropes for a tenable point of view. It was only with the outbreak of the Second World War that Klein returned to serious sustained creative writing. *The Hitleriad*, an attack on Hitler that reflected Klein's interest in eighteenth-century satire, especially Pope's *Dunciad*, falls flat as a whole despite some witty passages. Klein the satirist is at his best when he can recognize in the object of his satire genuine human qualities, however distorted. Understandably he cannot achieve this perspective on Hitler and as a result is often reduced to bombast and trivial abuse. Much more impressive are the anguished, prophetic psalms that were gathered together, along with some earlier works, to form 'The psalter of Avram Haktani', the most important section of *Poems*. A note of forced rhetoric mars several of them, but in the past the immediacy of Klein's confrontation with evil gives rise to a sense of pathos and intensity that is missing in most of the earlier work.

Klein's later poetry, beginning with the psalms, is distinguished by a new-found interest in dialectical modes of thought that came to dominate his later work. The negative aspects of experience, which he had been forced to acknowledge in the thirties and which had nearly silenced him as a poet, now gave rise to a dialectical vision in which negation, in the form of social and spiritual fragmentation, is seen to lead inevitably to the eventual achievement of a higher unity (see 'Sestina on the dialectic'). The most moving statement of this vision occurs in the final poem of *The rocking chair*, 'Portrait of the poet as landscape', in which the poet's isolation from his community comes to be seen as a temporary stage in a process of self-transformation ('he makes of his status as zero a rich garland'); the Québécois poems in *The rocking chair* are a profoundly dialectical study of the power of community for both good and evil (see especially 'The rocking chair' and 'Political meeting)'). This is Klein's finest collection. Stimulated by modern poets such as Eliot, Auden, Dylan Thomas, and Karl Shapiro, as well as by the Metaphysicals and Hopkins and, above all, by Joyce, Klein developed a striking idiom of his own, by turns highly allusive and startlingly direct, coolly ironical and warmly sympathetic, and marked by great flexibility and subtlety of rhythm. Although there are striking differences between early and late Klein, certain features are constant: a kaleidoscopic profusion of metaphors; puns, often multilingual; richly varied vocabulary making substantial use of foreign loanwords, archaisms, and, especially in the later Klein, Joycean neologisms; and non-linear structures that work through a mosaic-like accumulation of varied perspectives. These aspects of Klein's poetic technique seem most closely related to his central vision of a unity achieved through the greatest possible diversity.

The second scroll is Klein's most complex and ambitious work, both formally and conceptually, and the most important expression of his Zionism. It is a celebration of the basic human capacity for self-renewal, especially through language, even in the face of the apparently overwhelming evil of the Holocaust. While writing it Klein was deeply involved in a massive, never-to-be-completed commentary on Joyce's *Ulysses*, and Joyce's influence is everywhere apparent: the structural principle of parallels between the five chapters (and glosses) of the novel and the five books of the Pentateuch recalls Joyce's extensive use of Homeric parallels, and Klein's highly wrought polyphonic prose (see especially 'Gloss Gimel') owes much to Joyce's example. Another important influence was Klein's growing fascination with Kabbalistic creation myths stressing the interdependence of evil and good, exile and redemption. Uncle Melech, the object of the narrator's search throughout the novel, embodies the Messianic yearning of the exiled many for the ideal One; but, as Melech's story and the history of his people illustrate, it is only through the dialectical process of affirmation through negation, summed up by the Kabbalistic phrase 'Aught from Naught', that this ideal is achieved.

Although Klein's dialectical vision led to most of his greatest work, he eventually found it impossible to maintain. Much of the poetry and prose of the late forties and early fifties attests to a growing sense of despair, with an increasing emphasis on isolation, futility, and self-disgust (see, for example, 'Meditation upon survival', 'Les vespasiennes', and the unfinished novel, 'The inverted tree'). Klein wrote little poetry after *The rocking chair* but some of his late prose is among his finest work. Two late short stories stand out in particular from Klein's large but mostly ephemeral body of works in this genre. 'Letter from afar' and 'The bells of Sobor Spasitula' are impressive treatments of the impact of totalitarianism on the human spirit, and signal Klein's final rejection of the dialectical vision as a destructive self-delusion. Even more impressive are the two completed chapters of a projected novel on the theme of the golem; their ironic exploration of the nature of creativity and the limits of art, which grew out of Klein's personal agony and self-doubt, foreshadows central concerns of much of the postmodernism of recent years.

Most of Klein's published poems are included in *The collected poems of A.M. Klein* (1974) edited by Miriam WADDINGTON. Unfortunately Waddington's texts are frequently unreliable (see Z. Pollock, 'Errors in *The collected poems of A.M. Klein*', *Canadian Poetry* 10, 1982). *The second scroll* is available in the New Canadian Library with an introduction by M.W. Steinberg (1951). Two volumes of Klein's collected works, published by the UNIVERSITY OF TORONTO PRESS, have so far appeared: *Beyond Sambation: selected essays and editorials 1928-1955* (1982) edited by M.W. Steinberg and Usher Caplan, and *A.M. Klein: short stories* (1983) edited by M.W. Steinberg. This series will make extensive use of Klein's papers deposited in the Public Archives of Canada in 1973.

Like one that dreamed: a portrait of A.M. Klein (1982) by Usher Caplan is an excellent biography with many photographs of Klein and his milieu and excerpts from his work, many previously unpublished. Miriam Waddington's *A.M. Klein* (1970) is a stimulating short study that emphasizes Klein's secular humanist side. *In search of Jerusalem: religion and ethics in the writings of A.M. Klein* (1975) by G.K. Fischer explores Klein's roots in Jewish traditions. Two useful collections of studies are *A.M. Klein* (1970) edited by Tom MARSHALL and *The A.M. Klein symposium* (1975) edited by Seymour MAYNE.   ZAILIG POLLOCK

Klinck, Carl F. (b. 1908). Born in Elmira, Ont., he holds a B.A. from Waterloo College (1927), Waterloo, Ont., and an M.A. (1929) and Ph.D. (1943) from Columbia University. From 1928 to 1947 he taught at Waterloo where he became Dean of Arts. In 1947 he began a distinguished career at the University of Western Ontario, London, where he became head of the English department (1948), professor of Canadian literature (1955), and at his retirement in 1973 Professor Emeritus. His honours have included the Order of Canada (1973) and a D. Litt. from the University of Western Ontario (1974).

Klinck began to be a scholar-adventurer in the field of Canadian literature—as an editor, biographer, critic, and bibliographer—long before this discipline had any academic stature. His personal bibliography is substantial. He has edited books on or by Samuel Strickland, Abraham Homes, Tecumseh, John Norton, Adam Hood BURWELL, 'Tiger' Dunlop, and John RICHARDSON. Subjects of his many articles include John GALT, Archibald LAMPMAN, Adam KIDD, Levi ADAMS, and the relationship between early Canadian and American literatures. He has edited and introduced the New Canadian Library editions of Susanna MOODIE's ROUGHING IT IN THE BUSH (1962), Frances BROOKE's The history of Emily Montague (1961), Richardson's WACOUSTA (1967), and Rosanna LEPROHON's Antoinette de Mirecourt (1973). He co-edited the college text Canadian anthology (with R.E. Watters, 1955; 2nd edn. 1966), and the biographical reference work Canadian writers/Écrivains canadiens (with Guy Sylvestre and Brandon Conron, 1964), and has published biographical and critical studies of E.J. PRATT (with Henry W. Wells, 1947), Wilfred CAMPBELL (his dissertation, 1943), and Robert SERVICE (1976). From 1959 to 1972 Klinck compiled 'These in preparation' for CANADIAN LITERATURE's annual bibliography. He is best known, however, as general editor of the Literary history of Canada (1956; 2nd edn. 1976), to which he contributed two chapters on literary activity in the Canadas from 1812 to 1880. His longtime importance as a senior statesman of Canadian letters cannot be overestimated: it rests on his making accessible much early writing long before it was regarded as important to the national literary consciousness. Approaching this literature and its authors from the beginning in a spirit of modest proselytizing and thorough scholarship, Klinck made contributions to the advancement, breadth, and maturity of Canadian studies that are an enduring and major academic achievement.

See also CRITICISM IN ENGLISH: 4.

LOUIS K. MacKENDRICK

Knister, Raymond (1899-1932). John Raymond Knister was born in Ruscomb, near Stoney Point, Essex County, Ont., and attended Victoria College, University of Toronto, and Iowa State University. He worked on his father's farm near Blenheim, Ont., from 1920 to 1923, when he moved to Iowa City to become associate editor of an avant-garde literary magazine, The Midland. In 1924 he lived in Chicago briefly before returning to Canada in the autumn. In 1925 his poem 'A row of horse stalls' and his stories 'Elaine' and 'The fate of Mrs. Lucier' appeared in This Quarter. In 1926 he moved to Toronto, where he freelanced; his work appeared in the Toronto Star Weekly and Saturday Night. The next year Knister married Myrtle Gamble and for the summer they moved to Hanlan's Point, Toronto Island, where Knister completed his first published novel, White narcissus. He was commissioned by Macmillan to edit the anthology Canadian short stories (1928), considered to be the first anthology of its kind; his introduction to it is still of critical interest. In 1929 the Knisters moved to a farmhouse near Port Dover, Ont., where Knister wrote My star predominant (1934); a daughter, Imogen, was born in 1930. Frederick Philip GROVE encouraged Knister to submit My star predominant to Graphic Publishers' Canadian Novel Contest, and in 1931 it won the $2,500 first prize. In 1931-2 he lived in and near Montreal, returning to Ontario after Lorne PIERCE had offered him a job on the editorial staff of the RYERSON PRESS that would allow him time to write. While swimming off Stoney Point, Lake St. Clair, in Aug. 1932, Knister drowned. At the time of his death a number of Knister's stories and poems and two novels were unpublished; a good deal of this material has been published in the last decade.

White narcissus (1929, NCL 1962) was published in Toronto, London and New York. Set in rural southwestern Ontario, it concerns a writer, Richard Milne, who returns home in order to make a final attempt to convince his childhood sweetheart, Ada Lethen, to marry him. Ada feels it is her duty to stay at home because for years, as a consequence of a quarrel, her parents have communicated only through her. The white narcissus of the title becomes a symbol of obsession, a subject given serial exploration in the course of the novel. Knister depicts his characters in relation to social and physical environments, and there are powerful evocations of farm life and nature. While the novel is usually and justly considered a work of realism, it has also been suggested that it contains elements of romanticism and that the lyricism of some passages approaches prose-poetry. *My star predominant*, posthumously published in both London and Toronto, is a well-researched novel based on the last years of the life of John Keats, in which the poet's social milieu is vividly conveyed. The unpublished novels *Soil in smoke* and *Turning loam*—both set in rural southwestern Ontario—have more of the atmosphere of the twenties than *White narcissus*.

Of Knister's many short stories probably the best known is 'Mist-green oats', about a young man's break with his life on the family farm. His stories recurrently focus on some form of psychological initiation. Knister also wrote novellas. In 'Innocent man' the story of a man's wedding frames the tale of his false arrest and wedding-night spent in a Chicago jail. During the night each prisoner tells the story not of his guilt but of his innocence; the tension between black and white prisoners, and between inmates and guards, threatens to explode in violence. 'Peaches, peaches' is set on a fruit farm; as an overabundant crop of peaches ripens, a young man first encounters sexual politics. A strength of these two novellas—both of which are included in *The first day of spring: stories and other prose* (1976) edited by Peter STEVENS—is the power with which atmosphere is evoked. Other stories, as well as essays, appear in *Raymond Knister: poems, stories, and essays* (1975) edited by David Arnason, and six stories are included in *Selected stories of Raymond Knister* (1972) edited by Michael Gnarowski.

Knister is now considered one of the first modern poets in Canada. His poetry, which contains powerful descriptions of nature, is usually associated with the imagist school, although Knister also employed the forms of the prose-poem ('Poisons'), the serial poem ('A row of horse stalls'), and the longer poem ('Corn husking'). Dorothy LIVESAY edited the *Collected poems* (1949), which is actually a selection: more poems are found in *Raymond Knister: poems, stories and essays*.

Helpful to an understanding of Knister's work is his defence of literary realism, 'Dissecting the T.B.M.' (*Saturday Night*, 6 Sept. 1930).

See Dorothy Livesay's memoir in the *Collected poems* and 'Raymond Knister—man or myth?' in *Essays on Canadian Writing* 16 (1979-80) by Imogen Givens, Knister's daughter, which includes a diary account by her mother of the day of Knister's drowning. See also Marcus Waddington's essay 'Biographical note' in *Raymond Knister: poems, stories, and essays*, the preface to which, by David Arnason, discusses Knister in terms of his cultural era; and, concerning Knister's poetry, see David Arnason's 'Canadian poetry: the interregnum', *CVII*, Vol. 1, No. 1 (Spring 1975). For locating work by and about Knister, see Anne Burke, *Raymond Knister: an annotated bibliography* (1981).   JOY KUROPATWA

Knowles, R.E. (1868-1946). Robert Edward Knowles was born in Maxwell, Ont., the son of an Irish Presbyterian minister. Educated at Galt Collegiate, Queen's University, and Manitoba College, he was ordained in 1891 and served as pastor of Stewarton Presbyterian Church, Ottawa. In 1896 he married Emma Jones of North Carolina, and they had a son and a daughter. In 1898 he settled in Galt, Ont., as minister of Knox Presbyterian Church.

Between 1905 and 1911 Knowles wrote seven novels, published by Fleming H. Revell in New York and Toronto, and reissued in Edinburgh and London by Oliphant and Co. They gained considerable popularity—Ontario sales of *The attic guest* in 1909 rivalled those of works by Ralph Connor (C.W. GORDON) and L.M. MONTGOMERY. The religious themes and style of these novels owe much to pulpit oratory and to biblical rhythms and phraseology. Interest centres on the moral choice and religious experience of the characters; the plots, often relying heavily on coincidence, echo the parable of the Prodigal Son or illustrate the biblical admonition, 'your sin will find you out', while deathbed scenes and the sacramental union of parent and child point frequently to an extra-temporal world. At the same time, however, the novels provide a realistic glimpse of life in the villages and towns of Ontario.

In *St. Cutherbert's* (1905), published in Britain as *St. Cuthbert's of the West*, the minister-narrator frequently diverges from his plot to give loving, humorous vignettes of the rugged Scots Presbyterians who settled in New Jedboro a generation before. *The undertow* (1906), psychologically more complex, portrays a young minister torn between his ambitions in a wealthy Hamilton parish and the simpler rural values of his father, and includes his experiences in Britain, where he falls in love with a Salvation Army girl. *The dawn at Shanty Bay* (1907) is more an extended parable than a novel, using such symbols as the snowy Ontario landscape, the dawn, and the Christmas season to portray the conversion of a proud, unforgiving Scotsman. The complex plot of *The web of time* (1908) centres on Harvey Simmons' struggle against alcoholism when he leaves home to attend college and to work in the big city. *The attic guest* (1909) effectively uses a new narrator—a southern girl who marries Gordon, a visiting minister—and includes a dramatic scene in which Gordon tries to stop a lynching. The chief theme, however, is Gordon's struggle with the Higher Criticism and religious doubt. In *The handicap* (1910) the growth of a pioneer settlement over two generations is the background to the romance of two 'handicapped' lovers, a pub-keeper's daughter and an illegitimate youth. The least church-centred of Knowles' novels, it culminates in the arrival of Sir John A. Macdonald, wise in the ways of the human heart, who brings the lovers together. *The singer of the Kootenay* (1911) is less remarkable for its hero, a young singer, than for its portrait of Armitage, the dry, formalistic minister who journeys to British Columbia, where he leads pitifully unsuccessful revival meetings but eventually finds his own regeneration.

Ill-health put an end to Knowles' career as a novelist and forced him to retire from the ministry in 1914. In the twenties, while recuperating, he turned to journalism; as a special writer for the Toronto *Star* he travelled widely to interview such celebrities as Albert Einstein and Ramsay MacDonald, and provided many short, thoughtful columns. He was in great demand as a lecturer and after-dinner speaker. Knowles was remarried in 1923, to Georgia Hogg, and joined the United Church after its formation in 1924. He died in Galt.   JEAN O'GRADY

Kogawa, Joy (b. 1935). Born in Vancouver, she moved with her family to the interior of British Columbia in the evacuation of the Japanese from the West Coast during the Second World War. Since then she has lived in Saskatoon and Ottawa, where she worked as a writer in the Prime Minister's office (1974-6) and was writer-in-residence at the University of Ottawa (1978). She now lives in Toronto.

Kogawa's first volume of poems, *The splintered moon* (1968), established her direct, often understated voice in short-lined pieces relying mainly on an epigrammatic tightness. It is possible to see some of her Japanese heritage in these short poems, as they express a moment's experience without comment; yet they do not, as in *haiku*, summarize the transitory quality of the experience by focusing on an image, but rather state the experience directly in pared-down phrasing. Her subsequent writings have increasingly focused on her oriental background. The first half of *A choice of dreams* (1974) is devoted to poems detailing a visit to Japan. But even here they often shift away from orientalism, combining a clear-eyed, ironically undramatic sensibility and a Canadian no-nonsense approach. A more personal poetry, with a dense emotional thrust, appears at the end of the book. The tones and moods of this collection are also evident in two *Jericho Road* (1978), although these poems develop through more strongly metaphorical language.

Kogawa's novel *Obasan* (1981), which was selected for the Literary Guild Book Club and the Book of the Month Club of Canada, has its source in her experience of the wartime evacuation of the Japanese from the West Coast. It gains much of its strength from its measured and sober prose, which rigorously avoids any expression of bitterness or resentment.   PETER STEVENS

Korn, Rahel (Rachel) (1898-1982). A major poet of the modern Yiddish literature that flourished in eastern Europe before the Holocaust, she was born and educated in Galicia (part of the Austrian Empire annexed by Poland in 1919). When the Germans invaded Poland in 1939, Korn fled to the Soviet Union where she spent the war years making her way from the refugee camps in Tashkent and Uzbekistan to Moscow. There she was welcomed and assisted by the Yiddish writers' community that included Shlomo Mihoels, Peretz Markish, and David Bergelson. After the war she returned to Poland and resumed her literary activities in Lodz, where she was elected to the executive of the Yiddish Writers Union. Subsequently she represented them at a PEN Congress in Stockholm, and from there, without returning to Poland, she immigrated to Canada. She settled in Montreal in 1949 and lived there until her death.

Korn is the author of nine books of poetry and two collections of short stories, as well as numerous critical essays. Two of her manuscripts, which were to be published in Kiev, were destroyed when the Nazis laid waste the city and liquidated the Yiddish publishing house and all its staff. Her first book of poems, *Dorf* (Country, 1928), received universal critical acclaim when it appeared in Vilnius, the literary and cultural centre of Yiddish life before the advent of Hitler. Her subsequent books were published in Tel Aviv and Montreal and she remained, throughout her life, a frequent and influential contributor of essays, poems, and stories to every prestigious Yiddish journal in America, Israel, and Europe. As well, she was awarded nearly all the existing literary prizes for Yiddish literature: the Laevik prize, the Lamed prize, the Manger prize, and the SEGAL prize among others.

Her poems are beloved and celebrated for their lyrical vision and realistic depiction of country life and landscape, and her stories are famous for their profound psychological penetration and dense, complex, and unsentimental style. Her themes of art and language, exile, human suffering, and endurance are reflected in the titles of her books: *Erd* (Earth 1935); *Roiter Mon* (Red poppies 1937); *Shnitt* (Harvest, 1941—destroyed by the Nazis); *Haym un Haymlozikeit* (Home and homelessness, 1948); *Bashertkeit* (Fatedness, 1949); *9 Erzehlungen* (9 Stories, 1958); *Fun Yener Zeit Lied* (From beyond poetry, 1962); *Shirim V'odomeh* (Songs of the homeland, with facing Hebrew translation by Shimshon Melzer, 1966); *Die Gnod fun Vort* (The grace of words, 1968); *Oif der Sharf vun a Rega* (In the flash of an instant, 1972); and *Farbittene Vor* (Transformed reality, 1977). Her work has been translated into Hebrew, Polish, Russian, French, and German, and a volume of her selected poems has appeared in English translation: *Generations* (1982), edited by Seymour MAYNE.

MIRIAM WADDINGTON

Kostash, Myrna. See UKRAINIAN WRITING.

Kreisel, Henry (b. 1922). Born in Vienna, he left Austria for England in 1938 after the Nazi take-over. Sent to Canada by the British authorities in 1940, he was interned for eighteen months. He then attended Jarvis Collegiate, Toronto, and the University of Toronto. There he was introduced to the work of A.M. KLEIN, which showed him that 'it was possible and in fact quite all right for me to use my own background and tra-

ditions and yet still integrate myself with the country where I had decided I wanted to settle.' Kreisel received his B.A. (1946) and M.A. (1947) from the University of Toronto, and his Ph.D. from the University of London (1954). He began teaching at the University of Alberta in 1947, and has had a distinguished career there, serving as head of the English department (1961-7) and vice-president, academic (1970-5). In 1975 he was named University Professor.

Kreisel has described himself as being 'one of the first people probably to bring to modern Canadian literature the experience of the immigrant.' Both of his novels have as protagonists men who find it difficult to come to terms with the contrast between the 'hell' of Austria in the 1930s and the bland, but more secure, character of Canadian life. In *The rich man* (1948), Jacob Grossman, a presser in a Toronto clothing factory, returns to Europe after more than three decades in North America. His seemingly innocent decision to 'throw money around like a rich man' becomes a trap when his Viennese relatives, in the anti-Semitic and repressive climate of 1935, turn to him for financial help he cannot provide. Grossman's growing awareness of the moral blunder into which vanity and lack of self-knowledge have led him is very effectively presented, as is the tension created within a family of strong-minded individuals who are sometimes bound together and sometimes thrown apart by adverse circumstances. The novel was reissued in the New Canadian Library (1961) with an introduction by John Stedmond.

The betrayal (1964), described by Kreisel as a 'morality tale', deals with moral irresponsibility in a more dramatic, less atmospheric, way. Theodore Stappler, a young Austrian seeking with his mother to escape the Nazis, is ignobly paralysed by fear when he realizes that both of them have been betrayed by a fellow Jew. Stappler survives, ultimately to confront his enemy in Edmonton. The troubled consciences of both Stappler and his betrayer, who has plausible self-justifications to offer, are powerfully rendered. The less forceful characterization of Mark Lerner, the Jewish-Canadian professor who narrates the story, has sometimes been regarded as a weakness; but his increasing, though often ambivalent, sense of involvement with Stappler is a convincing study of North American naiveté attempting to comprehend the dark European heritage.

The almost meeting and other stories (1981) brings together stories with both European and western Canadian settings that Kreisel has written over a period of more than two decades. In the latter category is the much-admired and widely reprinted 'The broken globe', and the charmingly wry 'The travelling nude'. Kreisel's essay, 'The prairie: a state of mind' (1968), is a seminal study of the literary implications of the prairie sensibility and has been reprinted several times (see Donna Bennett and Russell Brown, eds, *An anthology of Canadian literature in English: volume II*, 1983). Kreisel also edited *Aphrodite and other poems* (1959) by John Heath.

An interesting interview with Kreisel by Felix Cherniavsky appears in *The sphinx*, II, no. 3 (1977). The best criticism of Kreisel is by Sidney Warhaft in his introduction to the New Canadian Library reprint of *The betrayal* (1971).   THOMAS E. TAUSKY

Kroetsch, Robert (b. 1927). Born and raised in Heisler, Alta, he attended the University of Alberta (B.A. 1948), then spent the next six years working in various parts of the Canadian North as a labourer and as a civilian information officer for the U.S. Air Force in Labrador. In 1954 he attended McGill for a year to study under Hugh MacLENNAN, and in 1956 he completed an M.A. at Middlebury College, Vermont. He later attended the Writers' Workshop at the University of Iowa, earning a Ph.D. in 1961. For the next fourteen years he remained in the U.S., teaching English at the State University of New York at Binghamton. Since 1975 he has been writer-in-residence at the Universities of Lethbridge, Calgary, and Manitoba; he is now a professor of English at Manitoba.

In 1965 Kroetsch published his first novel, *But we are exiles*. (The title comes from a line in the poem known as 'The lone shieling', or 'Canadian boat song', that appeared in *Blackwood's Edinburgh Magazine* in 1829.) Based on Kroetsch's experiences while working on Mackenzie River riverboats, it is written largely in the realistic tradition. Even in this first book, however, Kroetsch's interest in finding mythic and literary parallels to the events of a narrative is evident: in particular, the epigraph from Ovid that originally appeared on the title page calls attention to resemblances between the protagonist's story and the Greek myth of Narcissus.

In the three interrelated novels that followed—*The words of my roaring* (1966), and,

more especially, *The studhorse man* (1969) and *Gone Indian* (1973)—Kroetsch moved away from realism: by using an exuberantly comic treatment, surreal and fabulous events, and actions in which the mythic level dominates the literal, he shifted his fiction towards fable. In the latter two novels he also uses metafictional and self-reflexive techniques that cast doubt on the events described, thereby removing this fiction still further from realism and indicating his growing interest in the post-modern literary movement. (In 1972 Kroetsch was one of two founders of the influential critical journal *Boundary 2: A Journal of Post-Modern Literature*.) These three novels form the 'Out West' trilogy (Kroetsch refers to them as a triptych). Set in small-town Alberta in the thirties, forties, and seventies, they represent Kroetsch's commitment to creating the 'story' of his place. (He once remarked to Margaret LAURENCE that '. . . we haven't got any identity until somebody tells our story. The fiction makes us real'. *Creation*, 1970.) The trilogy, which uses comic parallels between the modern world of the Canadian West and Western civilization as a whole, suggests that each is at the end of an old era—and at the beginning of a new. The novels have a mythic structure that Kroetsch sees as appropriate to three crucial decades of twentieth-century history. In *The words of my roaring* he playfully adapts the myth of Hades' abduction of Persephone to the tale of J.J. Backstrom, an undertaker in the Depression who, inspired by a politician named Applecart (modeled on 'Bible Bill' Aberhart), runs for office on the whimsical promise of bringing rain to the drought-stricken countryside. (Backstrom, who is mentioned in *The studhorse man* and reappears in *Gone Indian*, serves as the chief unifying element of the trilogy.) *The studhorse man*, which won a Governor General's Award, both parallels and parodies the Odyssey: in it Hazard LePage wanders the Prairies looking for the perfect mare in order to continue his breed of horses, not recognizing that, after the Second World War, the day of the horse on the Prairies is over. This novel, and the works that came after it, are shaped not only by European myths but by Kroetsch's reading of North American Indian mythology; Kroetsch has been especially attracted to the Indian trickster myth (which he first encountered in Sheila WATSON's *The double hook*). *Gone Indian* concludes the trilogy with a tale of an American graduate student who, fascinated by Grey

Owl (George Stansfeld BELANEY), comes to Canada seeking the vanished American frontier and finds himself in a dream-like series of adventures centring on a winter-carnival celebration. The novel contains allusions to several Indian myths, as well as to the Funeral Games section of Virgil's *Aeneid*, to Dante's *La vita nuova*, and to the Norse myth of Ragnarok.

In Kroetsch's next novel, *Badlands* (1975), one of the characters remarks, 'There are no truths, only correspondences'—a line that suggests much about Kroetsch's technique of allusion and parallels, as well as about why post-modernism has such an appeal for him. *Badlands* is the story of William Dawe, a paleontologist who, with other members of his expedition, river-rafts through the Alberta Badlands in search of dinosaur bones. It is narrated in the form of an account of Dawe's daughter of information left her in her father's field notes. (Kroetsch's Anna Dawe represents his only attempt to portray a woman in some depth.) The situation is a deliberate inversion of Twain's *Huckleberry Finn*, while the action—patterned on a descent into the underworld—has some resemblances to Margaret ATWOOD's *Surfacing*.

In the novel that followed, *What the crow said* (1978), Kroetsch continued his investigation of myth (the seduction of a young woman by a swarm of bees in the opening chapter has several mythic sources) and his ironic reconsideration of the literary tradition he inherits; however, more than in any previous work, Kroetsch here locates events in the realm of the fantastic (in a way that suggests the influence of contemporary South American writers), while reducing his story to an elemental and episodic tall tale. He has described the book as an attempt to 'deconstruct' the novel. *The crow journals* (1980), an account of his writing this novel, provides insights into Kroetsch's methods of composition. In 1983 Kroetsch published *Alibi*, a story of a search for a perfect spa. (Water and wasteland imagery recur in all his fiction.) While retaining the mythic quality that characterizes his novels, *Alibi* returns to the stronger narrative line of his earlier work.

During the seventies Kroetsch turned increasingly to poetry. *The stone hammer poems* (1975) collects most of his shorter work. Since that time he has been engaged in writing a long poem, sections of which were published as *The ledger* (1975), *Seed catalogue* (1977), and *The sad Phoenician* (1979). *Field notes* (1981)—which assembles these, along with other sections, into an eight-part work that Kroetsch regards as still in progress— thus becomes a long poem made up of long poems; it does not use narrative structures but is unified through juxtaposition, repetition, permutation, and voice.

Kroetsch has also been important as a critic. His essays—characterized by an informal voice that is at once playful and oracular—are collected in a special issue of OPEN LETTER, 5th Series, no. 4 (1983). Of particular interest are 'For play and entrance: the contemporary Canadian long poem', 'The fear of women in prairie fiction: an erotics of space', and 'Unhiding the hidden: recent Canadian fiction' (an important statement on the contemporary Canadian writer's relationship to tradition). In a book-length interview with Shirley Neuman and Robert Wilson, *Labyrinths of voice* (1981), he discusses theoretical questions and contemporary criticism as it relates to him as a writer, and draws heavily on his reading of recent post-structuralistic critics. Kroetsch edited *Creation* (1970), containing miscellaneous writings by himself and a conversation with Margaret Laurence (along with writings by, and interviews with, James Bacque and Pierre Gravel).

See Peter Thomas, *Robert Kroetsch* (1980); Rosemary Sullivan, 'The fascinating place between: the fiction of Robert Kroetsch', *Mosaic* 11, no. 3 (1978); Ann Mandel, 'On Kroetsch's uninventing structures: cultural criticism and the novels of Robert Kroetsch', *Open Letter*, 3d Series, no. 8 (1978); and Russell Brown, *Robert Kroetsch* (1981) in the *Profiles in Canadian literature* series.

See also CRITICISM IN ENGLISH: 5(g), 5(h), NOVELS IN ENGLISH 1960 TO 1982: 3, and POETRY IN ENGLISH 1950 TO 1982: 2.

RUSSELL BROWN

L

Laberge, Albert (1877-1960) is best known for his novel *La Scouine*, but he was also the author of thirteen published volumes of stories and sketches and an unpublished novel, as well as of poems and literary articles published in periodicals. Some of his journalism appears under the pseudonym 'Adrien Clamer'. He was born in Beauharnois, Qué., where his family had occupied the same land since 1659. While attending the Collège Sainte-Marie in Montreal, apparently expecting to prepare for the priesthood after his *cours classique*, he occasionally visited the library of an uncle who was a doctor and avidly read the French Naturalists. A confession of this 'sin' led to his expulsion from the Collège and, so far as we can judge from his story 'La vocation manquée', to his lifelong anti-clericalism. For four difficult years Laberge held odd jobs and studied law—feeling an aversion, one presumes, to returning to the family farm. In 1896 he began to work for *La Presse*, where he continued for thirty-six years, mainly as sports writer but also as art critic. In 1932 he retired to Châteauguay, where he was able to give more time to writing.

His literary talent showed early. In 1895 Laberge won a prize offered by the newspaper *Le Samedi* for a realistic story; shortly afterwards he became a frequent visitor to the ÉCOLE LITTÉRAIRE DE MONTRÉAL. A dedication to realism and a high regard for writing as an art became permanent obsessions. *La* SCOUINE (*Bitter bread*, 1977)—considered to be the first realistic novel in Canada—was published in 1918 in an edition of sixty copies because it was too offensive for its time in Canada. (Rodolphe GIRARD, after a much milder show of disrespect for the clergy, was being persecuted by loss of employment and ostracism.) All Laberge's other works were published after his retirement. But it has been argued that he could not develop fully in spare-time writing. All his books, including his novel, consist of short pieces that were much worked over and show the constraints of the author's negativism. His stories were collected in *Visages de la vie et de la mort* (1936), *La fin du voyage* (1942), *Scènes de chaque jour* (1942), *Le destin des hommes* (1950), *Fin de roman* (1951), *Images de la vie* (1952), and *Le dernier souper*

(1953). He also published two volumes of sketches and prose poems: *Quand chantait la cigale* (1936) and *Hymnes à la terre* (1955); and three volumes of memoirs and criticism: *Peintures et écrivains d'hier et d'aujourd'hui* (1938), *Journalistes, ecrivains et artistes* (1945), and *Propos sur nos écrivains* (1954). Thirteen of his stories and extracts from his other works are included in *Anthologie d'Albert Laberge* (1963), which has a valuable introduction by Gérard BESSETTE.

Most of Laberge's works treat village or farm life. He wrote many urban sketches too; but, unusually for his time, he dealt with city and country life in much the same way: there is no opposition of wicked city to edifying country. Indeed, his sketches of the country are characterized by grim realism, though he avoids all but the slightest rare hint of didacticism. His characters are determined by their narrow milieu and seem incapable of learning; often they live in a complete moral void. Laberge excels in the sharp detail—such as a set of false teeth left among wedding keepsakes in 'Le notaire'—to epitomize the grotesque incongruity between reality and our conventional images of life.

A thorough bibliography is contained in Jacques Brunet, *Albert Laberge sa vie et son oeuvre* (1969). JACK WARWICK

Laberge, Marie. See DRAMA IN FRENCH 1948 TO 1981: 4.

Lacerte, Alcide. See NOVELS IN FRENCH: 1900 TO 1920.

Lachance, Louis (1899-1963). Born in Saint-Joachim de Montmorency, Qué., he studied at the Petit Séminaire de Québec and, after graduating in 1920, joined the Dominican Order at St-Hyacinthe, the traditional stronghold of Québec Thomism, which sent him to study at its philosophical college in Ottawa. He remained there as a teacher until 1936, apart from the years (1929-31) when he studied in Rome. His *Nationalisme et religion* (1936), which sets out to show how nationalist convictions could be reconciled with a religion that was international in scope, provided the foundation for a nationalism based on reason, as distinct from the nationalism of Abbé Lionel GROULX, which was founded chiefly on tradition and feeling. Lachance's basic notion—which was to become influential among French-speaking intellectuals in Canada and would help turn Roman Catholic scholars towards a friendly posture on nationalism—was that the modern nation is the most effective way of achieving the necessary collective response to modern problems, and that the nation provides a vehicle for moral action. Lachance generally expressed himself as a cautious federalist, but in Québec his concerns about culture and language endeared him to both separatists and federalists. His thoughts on moral practice appear in *Où vont nos vies* (1934).

In 1936 Lachance was called to teach philosophy in Rome at the Angelicum University. On the outbreak of war he returned to Canada, where he served as a priest in the diocese of Sherbrooke and took part in the founding of the Séminaire Saint-Apôtres. In 1943 he moved to the Université de Montréal, first as professor, and later as dean, in the faculty of philosophy. His pioneering *Philosophie du langage* (1944) substantially predates the popularity of 'linguistic philosophy' and raises many basic questions. While in Montreal he produced *Le droit et les droits de l'homme* (1959), which develops the theory that human rights are meaningless if seen merely in the context of the individual subject and his desires: they depend upon the community, and so must be related to the common good and to basic social responsibilities. In its emphasis on community and responsibility, Lachance's theory has affinities with the work of Simone Weil, and resembles in important respects the theory of rights put forward in English Canada by John WATSON. Lachance also wrote a historical legal study, *Le concept de droit selon Aristote et St. Thomas* (1948); a metaphysical study, *L'être et ses propriétés* (1950); and a religious study, *La lumière de l'âme* (1955).

Though Lachance read widely, wrote originally, and built upon various philosophical traditions, St Thomas always held a central place in his work. At the end of his life he returned to a revision of his *L'humanisme politique de St. Thomas d'Aquin* (2 vols, 1939), but did not live to finish this work; a partly revised second edition was published in 1964.   LESLIE ARMOUR

Lacombe, Patrice (1807-63). Born at Lac-des-Deux-Montagnes, Qué., he studied first at Oka, then at the Collège de Montréal, becoming a notary in 1930 and working as an accountant for the Séminaire de Montréal until his death. His short novel, *La terre paternelle* (Montréal, 1846), the prototype of the 'roman paysan' in Québec, began a literary tradition that was to last over 100 years and spawn some sixty variations. (First appearing, unsigned, in the *Album littéraire et musical de la Revue canadienne*, it had ten printings from 1871 to 1924; the most recent edition, 1972, contains a study by André Vanasse.) Having deeded the Chauvin family's land to his eldest son, the father is compelled by the son's mismanagement to repossess it; attracted, however, by the prestige of the merchant class, he then rents out the farm and settles in the village; eventually his business there fails, he loses the farm to Anglo-Saxons, and the family is forced to move to a slum in the Montreal suburbs where father and son eke out a living as carters of water. The farm is restored to the family name only when a wayward son, who has spent years with the Northwest Company, returns and buys it back. Basically a defence of the traditional ideological preference for the agricultural rather than the urban life, the novel also portrays peasant avarice; this element, and the tension that develops between father and son after the deeding of the land, are at odds with the attempt to idealize agricultural life. Lacombe sprinkles his work with many realistic touches and with popular speech—though, like other nineteenth-century authors, he sets it off in italics and adds standard equivalents.   BEN-Z. SHEK

La Corne, Luc de (known as La Corne Saint-Luc). See Writing in NEW FRANCE: 1.

Ladoo, Harold Sonny (1945-73). Born in Couva, Trinidad, he came to Toronto in 1968 and received a B.A. in English from Erindale College, University of Toronto. He died in Trinidad under mysterious circumstances and was presumably murdered. Ladoo's talent as a novelist was recognized and encouraged by Peter SUCH and Dennis LEE, but Ladoo found no popular acceptance as a writer while he lived. Before he left Toronto for the last time he was working as a dishwasher in a restaurant. Lee's long poem, 'On the death of Harold Ladoo', is a meditation on a talent destroyed prematurely.

Although Ladoo's estate includes fragments from nine uncompleted novels, only two have been published: *No pain like this body* (1972) and *Yesterdays* (1974), published posthumously. Ladoo intended these works to form part of a Faulknerian cycle of up to 100 novels encompassing the history of the West Indies, his own biography, a history of Canada in the Caribbean, and slavery. *No pain like this body* is a plotless novel about a family of East-Indian rice-growers in 1905, on the imaginary Carib Island. Written in dialect, and incorporating poetic imagery as if perceived from the point-of-view of a child terrified by a rainstorm, the novel treats with an engaging lyricism brutality, death, insanity, and sickness. *Yesterdays* is about a Hindu in Trinidad in 1955 who wants to come to Canada and convert Canadians to Hinduism, in the same way Canadian missionaries went to Trinidad to convert the people there. Under a simple plot lies a fine comic sense, often bawdy or scatological, and beneath that is a bitter indictment of colonialism, poverty, and enforced religion.

See also NOVELS IN ENGLISH 1960 TO 1982: OTHER TALENTS, OTHER WORKS: 2.

GEOFF HANCOCK

Lafitau, Joseph-François. See Writing in NEW FRANCE: 1

Lahaise, Guillaume. See POETRY IN FRENCH: 4.

Lahontan, Louis-Armand de Lom d'Arce de. See Writing in NEW FRANCE: 1.

Lalonde, Michèle (b. 1937). Poet, essayist, dramatist, and writer for radio, she began writing and publishing while still a student at the Université de Montréal. After receiving a degree in philosophy in 1959 she did research at Harvard in 1960, at Baltimore (1962-3), and London (1963-4). She wrote a series of programs on philosophers and intellectuals for Radio-Canada in 1964 and in 1965 began work at the Université de Montréal on a doctorate she never completed.

Lalonde's first book of poetry, *Songe de la fiancée détruite* (1958), a poem written for radio (produced by Jean-Guy PILON, Radio-Canada, 1958), is based on the themes of solitude and the inability of people to communicate. *Geôles* (1959) presents a 'climat cauchemardesque' (nightmare)—voids and abysses, hatred, cries, anger, violence, and destruction—and shows the influence of Saint-Denys GARNEAU and Anne HÉBERT in

particular. At about this time Lalonde became involved in editing, and writing essays for, intellectual reviews, first as a member of the editorial staff of *Situations* (1959) and then by contributing regularly to LIBERTÉ. She became a member of the editorial board (1963-4) of *Liberté* with Pilon, Jacques GODBOUT, and Fernand OUELLETTE, writing news stories and articles. Ten years later, as one of the editorial team of *Maintenant* (1973-4), she wrote a series of essays on Québec nationalism and the linguistic debate.

A profound change occurred in Lalonde's poetic concepts in the mid-sixties. Formerly esoteric, her poems became 'committed': no longer addressed to a limited readership, they sought a wider audience and adherence to the socio-political concerns of the people. In addition, the borders between poetry and the essay began to disappear for her, 'commitment' becoming the major concern in her work. This was evident in the poem she wrote for the symphonic fresco *Terre des hommes* (music by André Prévost) that inaugurated Expo 67 in Montreal; in the celebrated poem 'Speak white' (1968) recited at the 'Nuit de la poésie' in Mar. 1970; and in her lectures, essays, manifestos, and statements on politics, the role of writers and intellectuals, and the status of women in Québec.

In recent years the impact of Lalonde's work has continued to spread in Québec and abroad. She has collaborated with writers, intellectuals, painters, and musicians to develop new means of expression, giving her a closer contact with the public. In 1977 she experimented with a historical play entitled *Dernier recours de Baptiste à Catherine* (having had her first play, *Ankrania ou Celui qui crie*, produced in 1957). She edited an important selection of texts, *Défense et illustration de la langue québécoise suivie de proses et poèmes* (1979), and was awarded the Prix Duvernay in 1980 for the body of her work. She is currently preparing a retrospective collection of her poetry.

See Jean-Pierre Faye, 'La défense de Michèle Lalonde ou le goût de POTLAID MICKEY' in *Liberté*, no. 129, May-June 1980; François Hébert, 'Des dazibaos à Outremont' in *Liberté*, no. 127, Jan.-Feb. 1980; and D.G. JONES, 'An interview with Michèle Lalonde' in *Ellipse*, no. 3 (Spring 1970).

RICHARD GIGUÈRE

Lambert, Betty. See CHILDREN'S DRAMA IN ENGLISH.

Lampman, Archibald (1861-99). He was born in Morpeth, Canada West (Ont.), where his father was an Anglican clergyman. His family moved to Parrytown in 1866 and the next year to Gore's Landing in the Rice Lake district, where Lampman came to know the Strickland sisters, Susanna MOODIE and Catharine Parr TRAILL. In 1868 he contracted rheumatic fever, which probably contributed to his early death. In 1874 his family moved to Cobourg and from 1876 to 1879 he attended Trinity College School, Port Hope, and then Trinity College, Toronto, where he contributed literary essays and poems to *Rouge et noir*, the college magazine. In the spring of 1880 he read, 'in a state of wildest excitement', a new book of poems, *Orion* (1880), by Charles G.D. ROBERTS, whom he would later know. In 1883, after a brief and unsuccessful attempt at teaching in Orangeville High School, he became a clerk in the Post Office Department, Ottawa, a position he held for the rest of his life. From Ottawa he made walking tours of the surrounding countryside—which he loved, and loved to describe in verse—and with his friend Duncan Campbell SCOTT (also a government employee) canoeing expeditions into the wilderness. From 1883 until the last year of his life Lampman's poems appeared frequently in Canadian, American, and British periodicals, notably *The* WEEK and the Toronto *Globe* and, in the United States, *Harper's, Scribner's*, and *Youth's Companion*, a Boston magazine edited by his friend E.W. THOMSON. In 1887 Lampman married Maud Playter, and with the help of a small legacy she provided he published privately *Among the millet and other poems* (Ottawa, 1888). A daughter, Natalie, was born in 1892. From 6 Feb. 1892 to 1 July 1893 he joined Scott and Wilfred CAMPBELL in writing 'AT THE MERMAID INN', a weekly column of literary and social comment that appeared in the *Globe*. In 1894 his wife bore him a son, Arnold, who died at four months. Lampman was elected to the Royal Society of Canada in 1895 and that same year *Lyrics of earth* was published by Copeland and Day, Boston. A second son, Archibald Otto, was born in 1898.

In 1889 Lampman fell in love with Katherine Waddell, a fellow clerk. The exact nature of their relationship is still unclear, but they may have lived together for a time. This attachment was a source of great distress for Lampman in his last years. He was at work on the proofs of *Alcyone*, which he

intended to have published in Edinburgh, when he died. Scott, as Lampman's literary executor, ordered a printing of twelve copies (Ottawa, 1899). This was the first of several editions of Lampman's poems edited by Scott, who endeavoured, all his life, to keep his friend's reputation alive. Scott also edited *The poems of Archibald Lampman* (1900), for which he provided a memoir; *Lyrics of earth: songs and ballads* (1925); *At the Long Sault and other new poems* (1943, with E.K. BROWN); and *Selected poems of Archibald Lampman* (1947).

At present no definitive account of Lampman's work is possible because of the lack of a comprehensive study of his papers held in archives, an adequate biography, or an edition of complete poems. A substantial number of Lampman's poems in manuscript remains unpublished; and, although the most important work has been collected in *The poems* of 1900 and *At the Long Sault*, these editions are not reliable. On the basis of material available in print and in manuscript, however, the essential nature of Lampman's achievement seems fairly clear. His reputation as the finest of the CONFEDERATION POETS is largely based on a small body of nature poetry written, for the most part, relatively early in his brief career. In recent years, however, critical emphasis has shifted from Lampman as gently melancholic heir of the Romantics and Victorians to Lampman as alienated precursor of modernism, leading to a new interest in Lampman's more obviously troubled later works and to new ways of looking at many of the justly admired nature poems.

Like Keats and Tennyson, the two greatest influences on his diction, Lampman was a master of sonority with few, if any, rivals in Canadian literature. Rhythmically he is sometimes fluent to the point of monotony, but he is capable of creating, through slight rhythmic variation, the impression of an immediate notation of moment-to-moment sensation. Lampman's later poetry was often experimental in its rhythms. The classical Greek metric scheme of 'Sapphics', the seven-foot anapestic line of 'The woodcutter's hut', the complex stanzaic form of 'An ode to the hills', all suggest a deliberate effort by Lampman to submit to the discipline of unusual and challenging metres. Other poems, such as 'Alcyone' or 'Personality', display a new rhythmic freedom. 'At the Long Sault' reflects both tendencies: the striking contrast between the very free iambs of the main narrative and the much more regular anapests of the lyrical ending is one of the finest rhythmic effects in Canadian poetry.

At least as important as the music of Lampman's verse is its pictorial quality. Lampman's nature poems abound in vivid pictures of the Canadian landscape that are both objective in their precise descriptiveness and subjective in their evocation of the intensely felt essence of the scene. Lampman's ability to express his vision with great immediacy through the accumulation and arrangement of musical and pictorial effects is at its best in his sonnets (e.g. 'In November', 'Solitude', 'Among the orchards', 'Sunset at Les Eboulements', 'Winter uplands'). The restraint and discipline of the sonnet form discouraged the shapelessness and discursiveness that mar much of his verse.

Lampman's vision owes much to Wordsworth in particular and the Romantics in general. Man, spiritually exhausted by his unhealthy existence in the city, must renew himself through a solitary communion with nature that in its exalted state is usually described by Lampman as a 'dream', the most charged word in his vocabulary. In this dream-state man's energies are no longer at odds with one another, and the self-destructive 'strife' and 'change' of the city are replaced by an exquisite balance in which opposites are taken up into a larger whole. (Lampman's account of the 'dream' is clearly influenced by Keats; another probable influence is the German lyric poet Eduard Mörike. In this and other respects Mörike's poetry bears striking resemblances to that of Lampman, who was of partly German extraction and studied and wrote about German literature.) However, the Romantic influence on Lampman, important though it is, is undercut by other elements, to the ultimate enrichment of the poetry. Wordsworth's 'wise passiveness' ('Expostulation and reply') was difficult to maintain in the face of either the apparently intractable problems of late-nineteenth-century society or the harsh Canadian environment. In many of Lampman's finest poems (e.g. 'April', 'Heat', 'In November', 'Winter uplands') the celebration of nature is touched by unease, even fear. In particular the passivity involved in communion with nature comes to be seen as threatening, with its final end not a higher vision but death ('Death', 'A summer evening', 'The frost elves').

If Lampman's nature poetry at its best transforms the conventions he inherited into something personal and vivid, the same cannot be said about most of the rest of his verse. In his philosophical poems, very much influenced by Matthew Arnold, Lampman turns for consolation to idealized abstractions ('Beauty', 'Virtue'), to poetry ('What do poets want with gold?'), or to hope in the future ('The clearer self', 'The largest life'). These poems tend to be conventional and characterless in thought and diction. The narrative poems (apart from 'At the Long Sault', which is in a mixed lyric-narrative mode) are even less successful. Lampman, with his meditative cast of mind, shows little skill in the creation of plot or character, and his gift for capturing immediate sensations finds no scope in these poems, with their heightened rhetoric and bookishly exotic settings. One partial exception is 'A story of an affinity', his only narrative set in nineteenth-century Canada, which seems to reflect Lampman's painful relationship with Katherine Waddell. His earlier love poems, little more than sentimental literary exercises, are less interesting than the poems inspired by Waddell, published posthumously in At the Long Sault and other new poems ('A portrait in six sonnets') and, more recently, in Lampman's Kate: late love poems of Archibald Lampman (1975) edited by Margaret Coulby Whitridge. Lampman's strong-minded 'friend', as he calls her, is a more convincing and challenging presence than the shadowy beloved of the earlier lyrics. Even these poems, however, lack passion or sensuality, for Lampman shared the prudery of his age with regard to 'uninnocent emotion' (see his essay, 'The modern school of poetry in England'). The most intense note in the late love lyrics is of frustration and despair, as in 'Man', one of his finest and most painful poems.

The darkness of Lampman's late love lyrics typifies much of the poetry of his last years where passive acceptance of nature's healing power is rejected as Lampman becomes increasingly concerned with the value of decisive action. This development is probably a response to his growing sense of helplessness in the face of unrewarding work at the post office, his agonizing relationship with Katherine Waddell, the deaths of his son and father, and his own failing health. His espousal of socialism in these years (see 'The Land of Pallas', or the untitled essay on socialism) seems diametrically opposed to his earlier praise of the solitary dream of nature far from the world of men: there is nothing dreamy about the powerful and sometimes strident invective in much of the later verse ('To a millionaire', 'The modern politician', 'Liberty'). In most of this poetry, with the exception of some excellent sonnets, the freshness of the earlier work tends to be sacrificed for larger, more abstract effects. But Lampman's new directions lead to successes that could never have been predicted on the basis of his earlier work. One of the most impressive of these is 'The city of the end of things', a visionary poem in which industrial society is presented in nightmarish terms; the 'grim idiot at the gate', with which the poem ends, is Lampman's most powerful evocation of the deathlike passivity to which his society threatened to reduce man's creative powers. The finest of the late poems is undoubtedly 'At the Long Sault: May 1660', describing the successful but suicidal attempt of Adam Dollard (called Daulac) and his company to save Ville-Marie against an Iroquois attack. Lampman did not fully revise it before his death, but even in its imperfect state it is outstanding, not only for its formal boldness but also for its breadth of vision. Nature here is a source of both good and evil; man must choose to make of the world what he can. 'Dream' is once more a key word, but there is nothing passive about the dreaming of Daulac and his men. The lyric at the close, in which a harmony between man and nature has been achieved through active struggle and sacrifice, is a touching statement of the vision towards which Lampman had been moving in his later years.

Much of Lampman's previously inaccessible prose has recently been published. The *Selected prose* (1975), edited by Barrie Davies, contains a number of pieces that throw important light on the poetry. 'Hans Fingerhut's frog lesson', an allegorical fairy tale, explores the poet's relationship to nature and society; the essay 'On happiness' expresses faith in 'creative activity' as a means of overcoming the frustrations of existence; an untitled essay on socialism provides useful insights into Lampman's later poems of social criticism. His most intrinsically valuable prose is to be found in his letters to Edward Thomson edited by Arthur Bourinot (1956) and, in more complete form, by Helen Lynn (1980), and in his contributions to 'At the Mermaid Inn' (see *At the Mermaid Inn . . .*, 1979, with an introduction by Barrie Davies). The Lampman of these writings is more varied and attractive than we might suspect from his poetry. His range of interests is surprisingly great and he shows himself capable of an irony—sometimes gently humorous, sometimes bitter—that the poems altogether lack.

As Lampman's prose suggests, much of what was most vital in him never found expression in his poetry. This anomaly was no doubt partly owing to his difficult personal circumstances and early death, but it also reflects the state of contemporary Canadian culture. In a more critically mature milieu Lampman might not have devoted so much of his time and energy to stillborn imitations of dated Romantic and Victorian models; even his best nature poetry often falls into clichés of sentiment and morality that suggest a certain immaturity of culture. And the Canadian culture of his day could provide little support or guidance for the poetry of radical social criticism he was beginning to write in his later works. Whether he would have succeeded along these bold new lines must remain a matter of conjecture; had he done so, the development of Canadian poetry would almost certainly have been very different.

Lyrics of earth and the Scott edition of *The poems* are available in recent reprints: the first edited by D.M.R. Bentley (1978) and the second, including 'At the Long Sault', with an introduction by Margaret Coulby Whitridge (1974), who also edited *Lampman's sonnets, 1884-1899* (1976). See also *Comfort of the fields: the best-known poems of Archibald Lampman* (1979), a selection by Raymond SOUSTER, and *Selected poetry of Archibald Lampman* (1980) edited by Michael Gnarowski.

Carl Y. Connor, *Archibald Lampman: Canadian poet of nature* (1929), is a good biography but is out of date. Two useful collections of essays are Michael Gnarowski, *Archibald Lampman* (1970), and Lorraine McMullen, *The Lampman symposium* (1976). For an excellent brief overview see Sandra Djwa, 'Lampman's fleeting vision', CANADIAN LITERATURE 55 (1973). The manuscript material relating to Lampman is summarized in George Wicken, *Archibald Lampman: an annotated bibliography* (1980), which also includes Lampman's contributions to periodicals, works on the poet, and selected reviews. See also the recent essay on Lampman by L.R. Early in *Canadian writers and their work: poetry series: volume two* (1983), edited by Robert Lecker, Jack David, and Ellen Quigley.

See also POETRY IN ENGLISH TO 1900: 6.

ZAILIG POLLOCK

Lane

Lane, M. Travis. See Writing in the MARI-TIMES: 6.

Lane, Pat (b. 1939). Born in Nelson, B.C., and educated at the University of British Columbia, Lane has lived mostly in the West and on the west coast, supporting himself by various jobs including logging, fishing, mining, trucking, and teaching. He has been writer-in-residence at the Universities of Ottawa, Manitoba, and Alberta. With bill BISSETT and Seymour MAYNE, he established the small press Very Stone House in the early 1960s. His poetry collections include *Letters from a savage mind* (1966); *Separations* (1969); *Mountain oysters* (1972); *The sun has begun to eat the mountains* (1972); *Passing into stone* (1973); *Beware the months of fire* (1973); *Unborn things* (1975), illustrated with Lane's own drawings; *Albino pheasants* (1977); *Poems new and selected* (1979), which won a Governor General's Award; *The measure* (1980); and *Old Mother* (1982). In 1969 he published a collection with Lorna Uher, called *No longer two people*. He has also edited the work of his brother (q.v.), who died in 1964: *The collected poems of Red Lane* (1968). He lives in Regina.

The locus of much of Lane's early poetry—particularly in *Mountain oysters* and *The sun has begun to eat the mountains*—is the West Coast and the Prairies as he writes of logging camps and forests, native people, hunting and bush farming. The poems are toughminded and anecdotal, full of narratives about working-class people; they show a remarkable and moving empathy for lives that are hard, painful, and vulnerable. Lane has a fine gift for image and writes of the tragic not histrionically but in understatement, often deflecting attention in a poem to some small detail that is made to carry the full horror of a situation. His genuine understanding of violence—the woman who aborts herself in a dingy hotel ('There was a woman bending'); the pregnant cat dipped in gasoline and set alight ('Last night in darkness')—challenges the reader's complacency. In later books—like *Unborn things* and *Albino pheasants*—Lane's language and imagery developed in subtlety and there is a more reflective voice, with a broader historical and literary reference. The locus of the poems also broadened to include Europe and Latin America. *Poems new and selected* demonstrates the evolution of his work from a poetry that relied on narrative impact for its effects to one that expresses a pain-fully achieved personal vision in passages of lyrical beauty. In *Old Mother*, his most recent and best collection to date, sombre, elegiac poems grieve for the violations of history and human disorder. Life is a brutal pantomime of sexual conquest and deadly combat. In allegories of slaughter and bestial rapacity, such as 'The young man' and 'All my pretty ones', Lane explores the grotesque monsters that live 'below the mind' and concludes that the atavistic root of the psyche is the lust for death. Birds, especially predators and wild fowl, are a recurring motif. Many poems, like 'Old mother' and 'The mother', undertake a generic quest for shelter, but Lane finds the archetypal mother a predator: 'your talon deep in my heart'. Yet the most moving poem in the book, 'A red bird bearing on his back an empty cup', provides a talisman that seems a source of patience. In the image of the bird, Lane finds love of a kind, a source of commiseration in pain and emptiness.

There is an interesting essay by Lane in which he describes his poetics: 'To the outlaw' in *New: American and Canadian poetry* 15 (1971).   ROSEMARY SULLIVAN

Lane, Red (1936-64). Richard Stanley 'Red' Lane, the elder brother of Patrick LANE, was born in Nelson, B.C., and died in Vancouver of a cerebral haemorrhage. During his short life he lived in various parts of western Canada and worked at jobs that accommodated the 'maverick' wanderings recorded in his poems. Although most of his work appeared posthumously, Lane's poems were published in little magazines in the early sixties. The Toronto journal *Ganglia* devoted its second issue to his book *1962: poems of Red Lane*, which brought him to the attention of poets such as Milton ACORN, who later lamented Lane's untimely death in the elegiac poem 'Words said sitting on a rock sitting on a saint'. In 1968 Seymour MAYNE and Patrick Lane (who cites his brother as an important influence on his decision to write) published *Collected poems of Red Lane* under their imprint, Very Stone House. (It was reprinted in 1978 by Black Moss Press.) The poems in the first section, 'The surprise sandwich', were written for children and are statements of feelings, experiences, and observations that conclude with questions involving the reader in a game of self-reflection and response. The core of the book, however, lies in the later sections, which chronicle Lane's experiences in a manner that, although not yet fully developed, is crisp and visually powerful and sometimes experimental. The book concludes with a haunting poem, 'Death of a poet (for Milton Acorn, ultimately)', that eerily foreshadows Lane's sudden death at twenty-eight. Like Acorn, Lane views the world from a populist standpoint: his poems portray incidents—on street-corners, in beer parlours and cheap hotels—in detailed observations that grow out of the poet's participation in these events. *War-Cry* (1973) is a long anti-war poem dedicated to Lane's father and edited from manuscripts by his brother Patrick. Much of Red Lane's poetry bears marks of the uneasiness and lack of polish of the developing poet; but his work is significant for its controlled use of colloquial speech and its strong and direct treatment of unadorned reality.   BRUCE MEYER

Langevin, André (b. 1927). Born in Montreal, he had lost both his father and mother by the age of seven. His next five years were spent in an institution that he later described as 'asylum-like', a 'locked-in world', worse than the Saint-Vincent-de-Paul penitentiary: the child was dehumanized, reduced to a mere number. He later enrolled in the Collège de Montréal, pursuing his studies to the level of Belles-Lettres. After working at a series of odd jobs, his first regular employment was in 1945 as a messenger for *Le Devoir* where, six months later, he was made responsible for the paper's literary section. He remained in that position for three years, reading voraciously and 're-educating' himself: he was influenced by the writings of Camus and Sartre, and particularly by Gabrielle ROY's BONHEUR D'OCCASION. He published a great many articles, mostly on literary or artistic subjects, in *Le Devoir* and *Notre Temps*, as well as literary criticism for the CBC. In 1948 he joined the information staff of Radio-Canada, becoming a producer there, a position he still holds. Langevin was awarded a Guggenheim fellowship in 1955. A frequent contributor of articles on subjects of political or social interest to periodicals, he was awarded the 1967 Prix Liberté for his articles in *Le Magazine Maclean*. In 1978 he was voted 'Grand Montréalais' of the preceding two decades in the field of literature. Married to the daughter of a long-established doctor in Thetford Mines (the town that was the model for Macklin in *Poussière sur la ville*), he now lives in Frelighsburg in the Eastern Townships.

Langevin has written five novels that have established him as an important contemporary Québec writer. *Évadé de la nuit* (1951), which won him his first Prix du Cercle du Livre de France, revealed a powerful imagination that at the time outstripped his craftsmanship. Though it lacks unity, is forced in tone, and flawed by such excesses as ten deaths—including two suicides—it is nonetheless a compelling drama of human incommunicability. Twenty-year-old Jean Cherteffe—who never knew his mother, was abandoned by his alcoholic father, and raised amid the terrors and sordidness of an orphanage—unsuccessfully attempts to rehabilitate Roger Benoît, a drunken poet he once admired and whom he gradually identifies with his father. The last two chapters relate the growing love between Jean and Micheline, the death of Micheline in childbirth, and Jean's suicide in the snow.

In POUSSIÈRE SUR LA VILLE (1953) Langevin relates the tragedy of Alain Dubois, a young doctor in the mining town of Macklin, and his unfaithful wife Madeleine. This short novel, which has all the elements of classical tragedy and is written in a beautifully simple style, was translated by John Latrobe and Robert Gottlieb as *Dust over the city* (1955).

Pity for his fellow men is the chief characteristic of Pierre Dupas in Langevin's third novel, *Le temps des hommes* (1956), whose title refers directly to Job, 10:5. Set in the forests of northern Québec five years after the end of the Second World War, it portrays the fate of Dupas, a defrocked priest, who lost his faith ten years earlier when, unable to perform an expected miracle, he was obliged to watch a twelve-year-old boy die of meningitis. The action takes place at the Rivière Verte hotel near the mill town of Scottsville, and in an isolated lumber camp on the frozen shores of the Grand Lac Désert. Framing the revelations of Dupas's personal tragedy is the conflict between Laurier and Gros Louis, foreman of the logging crew and lover of Laurier's frustrated twenty-eight-year-old wife of five years, Yolande. Spurred by his blind, jealous love for Yolande, Laurier sows death and destruction; his actions lead to the spiritual collapse and physical mutilation of Dupas, who neither saves Laurier's soul nor redeems his own. This novel, in which all the characters seem to be the hapless playthings of a cruel and unfathomable fate, fails to integrate the themes associated with Dupas into the plot of violence, jealousy, and revenge.

Sixteen years later Langevin published the

Langevin

quite different *L'élan d'Amérique* (1972), which is infinitely complex and full of symbolic imagery, and constantly shifts back and forth between dream and reality. Heralded as a significant literary event, it was awarded in Mar. 1973 the Grand Prix Littéraire of the city of Montreal. Here Langevin presents Claire Smith, an American with roots in Québec on her mother's side, who is married to Stephen Peabody, the wealthy vice-president of the United States Pulp and Paper Company. Amoral, liberated, but spiritually lost and empty, she searches in vain for the male who will dominate her. Through Antoine, a guide working for an American logging company who has left his wife and children to live in the forest, she acquires dignity and strength. A tremendous moose appears in the forest—'l'élan d'Amérique'—symbolizing the perfection of creation and of man, the male, the master of the universe. The first instinctive reaction of Claire is to slaughter him; Antoine's is to protect him. But in the end the moose is killed and Antoine brings back to Claire its head and antlers. He then flees from a world full of ugliness and disorder, seeking refuge in the woods, and Claire, after shoving the moosehead out of the Cessna that was flying her back to civilization, commits suicide by jumping after it. In this book Langevin has written pages full of rare violence denouncing some of the conditions that enslave the people of Québec: existential alienation, exploitation, dispossession, and assimilation by the North American whole.

In Langevin's fifth novel, *Une chaîne dans le parc* (1974), many of the themes of *Évadé de la nuit* are dealt with in such a way as to give the impression that it was preceded by *Une chaîne*, which portrays with extraordinary vividness the violence or indifference of adults in their dealings with young children, as experienced by eight-year-old Pierrot whose father has abandoned him after his mother died of tuberculosis. He has spent the last four years with 400 other orphans, defenceless victims of the viciousness and perversity of several nuns. Arranged in twenty-seven unnumbered chapters, the novel recounts Pierrot's experiences with his legal guardian, Uncle Napoléon, and his three old-maid aunts in the working-class district of east-end Montreal during the eight-day period between 6 June 1944 and the following Tuesday, when he is shipped off to learn a trade in another institution. In the first orphanage Pierrot, intelligent and

precocious, compensated for his unhappiness by inventing a fantasy world. This imaginary universe collides with his experience of the outside world, where he must come to terms with an astounding array of human misery, venery, and brutality, as well as with some humanity, generosity, and tenderness.

The thematic continuity in four of Langevin's five novels is striking: orphaned, deserted, and dead or dying children are recurring figures. In the world they portray there are no winners: his orphans and outsiders despair at their inability to communicate or to escape from the resulting solitude. A compassionate yet bitter tribute to these losers, the novels are inspired by profound pity for their helplessness and unhappiness in a hostile world.

Langevin has written two stage plays. *Une nuit d'amour* (1954) was the first play by a Québécois author to be produced by the Théâtre du Nouveau Monde. The action takes place in Acadia after the Conquest. *L'oeil du peuple* (1958), a satire on municipal political corruption and leagues for moral decency, won first prize in the Théâtre du Nouveau Monde drama competition.

Langevin has also written several television dramas, which have been produced by Radio-Canada, and short stories: 'L'homme qui ne savait plus jouer' (*Écrits du Canada français*, vol. 1, 1954); 'Noce' (*Chatelaine*, vol. 2, no. 3, Mar. 1961); and 'Un parfum de rose bleue' (LIBERTÉ, no. 62, Mar.-Apr. 1969).

See Gabrielle Pascal, *La quête de l'identité chez André Langevin* (1976), and David J. Bond, *The temptation of despair: a study of the Quebec novelist André Langevin* (1982).

See also NOVELS IN FRENCH 1940 TO 1959: 2; 1960 TO 1982: 3(e).   L.W. KEFFER

Langevin, Gilbert (b. 1938). Born in La Dorée, Qué., in the Haut-Saguenay, where he received his early schooling, he arrived in Montreal in 1958 for further studies but did not complete them. In 1959 he founded Éditions Atys, which he directed until 1965. From this period date his encounters with other poets (Gaston MIRON, Gilles Leclerc) as well as his involvement—after a brief flirtation with the Parti Communiste—in the Mouvement fraternaliste. Around 1960 Langevin began organizing poetry recitals throughout Québec, but particularly in Montreal at the Bar des Arts and the Perchoir d'Haïti. Later he became active in the Atelier d'expression multidisciplinaire. He has worked at the Bibliothèque Saint-Sulpice, the press of the Université de Montréal, and Radio-Canada.

Langevin was awarded the Du Maurier Prize in 1966 for *Un peu plus d'ombre au dos de la falaise* and more recently the Governor-General's Award for *Mon refuge est un volcan* (1978). To date, besides sixteen books of poetry—including three 'hors-commerce': *Le vertige de sourire* (1960), *Poèmes-effigies* (1960), and *Au milieu de la nuit* (1977)—he has to his credit three series of 'écrits', mixtures of prose and poetry, that share the same themes, characters, and style attributed to 'Zéro Legal', one of his eight 'hétéronymes': *Les écrits de Zéro Legel* (1972), *La douche ou la seringue* (1973), and *L'avion rose* (1976). He has also written numerous songs that he describes as 'much rougher and more compact' than his poems, and some of which have been recorded by Pauline Julien and the group Offenbach. They have been published in two collections: *Chansons et poèmes* (1973) and *Chansons et poèmes 2* (1974). Langevin himself is featured on a Radio-Canada long-play record, *Où mes racines parlent d'elles-mêmes* (1981).

Langevin's other poetry collections include: *A la gueule du jour* (1959); *Symptômes* (1963); *Noctuaire* (1967); *Pour une aube* (1967)—collected, together with the poems in *Un peu plus d'ombre*, in *Origines 1959-1967* (1971); *Stress* (1971); *Ouvrir le feu* (1971); *Novembre* followed by *La vue du sang* (1973); *Griefs* (1975); *Le fou solidaire* (1980); and *Issue de secours* (1981). His poems, which constitute a sort of inner autobiography, are distinguished by their extreme conciseness, verbal inventiveness, imagery of decay, and tragic tonality.

See Raoul DUGUAY, Littérature québécoise, in PARTI-PRIS 4, no. 1 (Sept.-Oct. 1966), and Pierre Nepveu, 'La poétique de Gilbert Langevin', *Livres et auteurs québécois (1973)*. ALEXANDER SOKALSKI

Langford, Cameron. See CHILDREN'S LITERATURE IN ENGLISH: 3.

Languirand, Jacques (b. 1931). Born and raised in Montreal, he obtained a classical education at the Collèges Saint-Laurent and Sainte-Croix before spending a few years (1949-53) studying theatre in Paris with Charles Dullin and Michel Vitold. Shortly after his return to Montreal he hosted a popular talk show on Radio-Canada, 'Le Dictionnaire insolite', and began writing radio dramas. In 1956 he entered the Dominion Drama Festival with his bizarre piece, *Les insolites* (1962), which won first prize for the best Canadian play; its month-long run in Montreal established Languirand as the leader of avante-garde theatre in Québec. He held this position throughout the late fifties and early sixties, for his first absurdist play was followed in quick succession by other stage and TV productions. *Le roi ivre* (1970), produced in 1956 at Languirand's own experimental but short-lived Théâtre de Dix Heures; *Les grands départs* (1958), televised in 1957; *Diogène* (1965) and *Le gibet* (1962), produced in 1958; and *Les violons de l'automne* (1962), produced in 1961. Since 1962, when Languirand received the Governor General's Award for *Les insolites* and *Les violons de l'automne*, he has become increasingly involved with radio and television. His musical comedy *Klondyke* (1970) was well received in Montreal and at the Commonwealth Arts Festival in 1965; but his last piece for theatre—an elaborate, multi-media work, *L'age de Pierre*—has never been performed in French and failed to capture any critical or popular acclaim when it was produced in English in 1970 as *Man Inc.* at Toronto's St Lawrence Centre.

Languirand's biggest concern, in all his plays, is the lack of communication between individuals and the social and psychological forces that keep them apart. Influenced by Artaud, Beckett, Ionesco, Brecht, and the existentialists, Languirand continually experimented with new ideas and forms of expression. In *Les insolites*, the result of an experiment with automatic writing, his disorienting style creates an atmosphere of riotous folly. The action takes place in a bar where, among the people brought together by chance, an old woman is shot dead in the dark, and an innocent but agitated bartender is arrested for murder. The absurd ending is consistent with Languirand's strange world where injustice reigns, death is senseless, and communication impossible. In *Le roi ivre* a cruel tyrant irrationally abuses and exploits his subjects, his servants, and his queen, who are all too weak or too cowardly to resist. The question of individuals who do little to change their lives is taken up again in *Les grands départs*, in which an unsuccessful writer and the disgruntled members of his family day-dream about building a new life for themselves while waiting for the movers to take them to more squalid living-quarters. (It was translated by Albert Bermel as *The departures* and published in *Gambit* 5, 1966.) In *Le gibet* Languirand focuses on the vulnerability of a hopelessly idealistic character who is trying to break the world flagpole-sitting record. Alone and aloft, he observes but fails to understand the malevolence and infidelity of his friends and family. The suffering and humiliation of the old are at the centre of *Les violons de l'automne*, a cynical love story that depicts the futile efforts of an aged couple to consummate their marriage. In this absurdist poetic drama the characters are called simply 'He', 'She', and 'The Other Man'.

Though these plays make no direct reference to Québec, they convey harsh criticism of individuals who refuse to fight the dishonesty, exploitation, and injustice of régimes similar to that of Duplessis. Languirand also deplores the moral and intellectual paralysis of those who reject innovation in the name of reason and tradition, and effectively shows that attitudes must change and communication channels must be opened if one is to thrive in the modern world. In *Klondyke* Languirand's message is more overtly topical. Set in the Yukon of the Gold Rush, the plot is loosely centred on the adventures of two prospectors who eventually leave the Klondyke penniless. Although obviously interested in the American dream, Languirand was clearly warning his audience of the dangers of crass materialism at a time when Québec was in the middle of a modernization program.

Languirand has also published a travel book, *J'ai découvert le Tahiti* (1961); a humorous dictionary, *Le dictionnaire insolite* (1961); a psychological novel, *Tout compte fait* (1963); and a futurist essay, *De McLuhan à Pythagore* (1972).

See Jean-Cléo Godin, 'Révolution dans le langage: Languirand insolite', in Jean-Cléo Godin and Laurent Mailhot, *Théâtre québécois* (1970).   ELAINE NARDOCCHIO

Lanigan, George T. See 'AHKOOND OF SWAT, The'.

Lapointe, Gatien (1931-83). Born in Sainte-Justine-de-Dorchester, Qué., he was educated at the Petit Séminaire in Quebec City and continued his studies for a year at the École des Arts Graphiques, then in the Faculté des Lettres of the Université de Montréal. Between 1956 and 1962 he travelled extensively in Europe and completed a doctoral thesis on Paul Éluard at the Sorbonne in Paris. After returning to Québec he taught at the Collège Militaire Royal, St

Jean, before accepting a position at the Université du Québec, Trois-Rivières, where he remained. While devoting a great deal of his energies to writing and teaching, Lapointe also founded in 1971 a small publishing house, Les Écrits des Forges, which publishes young and unknown poets.

Lapointe's first collection of poems, *Jour malaisé* (1953), reflects his early artistic training and his interest in lay-out and typography, while its title testifies to his *mal de vivre*. It also reveals the emotional climate of Québec in the fifties: Lapointe once referred to *Jour malaisé* as the muffled but liberating shout of a poet inhabiting the oppressive desert of the Duplessis era. Ironically, it was with *Le temps premier, suivi de Lumière du monde* (1962), which he wrote in France—an alien space—that he found his 'terra nova', his own universe and origins. It is a powerful book, one that is looked upon retrospectively as a 'founding text'—part of a ground-swelling surge of poetry that proceeded to name Québec's trees, land, rivers, and faces because only by doing this could its inhabitants find and claim their territory: Lapointe's poems were very much part of this collective and spontaneous impulse. *L'ode au St. Laurent, précédée de J'appartiens à la terre* (1963)—which won a Governor General's Award—proceeds from the same instinctual needs: 'Je suis la première enfance du monde/je crée mot à mot le bonheur de l'homme/et pas à pas j'efface la souffrance.' It deciphers a primordial morning and celebrates the many joys of its coming. *Le premier mot, précédé de Le pari de ne pas mourir* (1967) shows a much more sombre and anguished mood: the certitude that writing does not allay suffering, does not relieve human loneliness or political injustices, does not even ultimately bring any satisfactory answers. But it stands as a wager against death, an attempt at holding it at bay to survive a few moments longer. With *Arbre-radar* (1980), and especially *Corps et graphies* (1981), Lapointe moves into a different territory. Barthes, Blanchot, Deleuze, and the searchings of a younger generation of poets who gravitated around the magazine *La nouvelle* BARRE DU JOUR and the avant-garde publisher Les Herbes Rouges, give his concerns a different textual fabric. *Corps et graphies* takes us into a much more fragmented and broken-up syntax: Lapointe viewed these poems as an attempt to let the human body dance upon the white stage of pure pleasure, with no rhyme or reason and no rational finality. *Barbare inoui* (1981) and

Corps-transistor (1981) appear to have evolved out of the same need.

There is an interview with Gatien Lapointe by Donald Smith, 'Le corps est aussi un absolu', in *Les lettres québécoises* 24 (Winter 1981-2). See also Jean-Cléo Godin, ' "Le premier mot" et "Le pari de ne pas mourir",' *Études françaises*, vol. III, no. 4 (Nov. 1967), and Maximilien Laroche, 'L'Américanité ou l'ambiguité du "je",' *Études littéraires*, vol. 8, no. 1 (Apr. 1975).

CAROLINE BAYARD

Lapointe, Paul-Marie (b. 1929). Born in Saint-Félicien, Qué., he studied at Collége St Laurent and the École des Beaux-Arts in Montreal before becoming a journalist with *L'Événement-Journal* (1950-4) and *La Presse* (1954-60) and co-founding, with Jean-Louis Gagnon, *Le Nouveau Journal* (1961). A freelance writer and journalist for Radio-Canada in 1962-3, and editor-in-chief of *Le Magazine Maclean* (1964-8), in 1968 he joined Radio-Canada, where he is now radio-program director in the French Services division.

Although as yet unaware of Les Automatistes, Lapointe had read the French poet Paul Éluard, and his first collection of poems, written over a three-month period in 1947, was produced in the true spirit of automatic writing. Claude GAUVREAU, to whom the manuscript was submitted, helped to publish it under the title *Le vierge incendié* in 1948. That same year Lapointe wrote a series of poems entitled 'Nuit du 15 au 26 novembre 1948', which did not appear until 1969, when it was published in a special issue of La BARRE DU JOUR devoted to Les Automatistes. Whereas the first collection displayed an absolute faith in poetry and the regenerating power of revolt, 'Nuit' marked a recognition of the limits of language: the proliferation of meaningless neologisms and the gradual disintegration of syntax led to static repetition. The threat of silence that was present in these poems was real: Lapointe did not publish again until 1960. That year *Choix de poèmes—arbres* appeared; it was followed in 1964 by *Pour les âmes*. Both these collections—which showed a movement away from pure revolt towards reintegration—are characterized by an improvisation modelled on jazz. The poem 'Arbres', a magnificent litany, expressed a 're-appropriation', the will to retrieve one's heritage, that coincided with the new socio-political climate of Québec in the sixties: this, along with its literary merit, made it Lapointe's best-known work. All the works cited were gathered in *Le réel absolu: poèmes, 1948-1965* (1971), a book that had a tremendous influence on the new generation of poets of the seventies. In particular the reappearance of *Le vierge incendié*, which had until then been little read, was enthusiastically received: the exemplary freedom of the images, the glorification of revolt, the theme of the purification of dead flesh on the altar of love, the provocative mixture of the sacred and profane, all combined to make Lapointe a pioneering figure in the eyes of the new generation. *Le réel absolu* won the Prix David and a Governor General's Award.

Lapointe's writing took a new turn again with *Tableaux de l'amoureuse suivi de Une unique; Art égyptien; Voyage; Huit autres poèmes* (1974) and *Bouche rouge* (1976), both illustrated by Gisèle Verreault. In the first volume the poet took his inspiration from the work of the artist; the second was a joint creation, the result of a continuing exchange between poet and artist, and is a celebration of woman through the ages. Lapointe's monumental *Écritures* (1979)—more than a thousand pages—stems from yet another creative mode: writing as a purposefully gratuitous act, devoid of meaning or coherence and designed to resist all interpretations. It is a demanding work that requires the reader to experience the presence, the materiality, of words themselves as they are actually set on paper, empty of intended reference or even expression. *Tombeau de René Crevel* (1979), with illustrations by Betty Goodwin, was written as a homage to the French surrealist who had a seminal influence on Lapointe. The text consists entirely of material extracted from Crevel's works—the process of selection being based on an arbitrarily pre-defined set of rules devised by Lapointe—and recombined into new patterns.

Lapointe's writing, consistent yet constantly renewing itself, has been a leading example for the new poetry of Québec. In 1976 Lapointe received the prize of the International Poetry Forum in the United States and the *La Presse* prize in 1980.

English translations of his work appear in *The Poetry of French Canada in translation* (1970), edited by John GLASSCO, and in *Ellipse*, 11 (1972). A selection of his poems translated by D.G. JONES was published in *The terror of the snows* (1976). *Le vierge incendié* is explored in an original study by Jean Fisette, *Le texte automatique* (1977), as well as in *La nuit incendiée* (1978) by Jean-Louis Major. *Études françaises* 16/2 (1980) is a special issue devoted to his work.

MICHEL PARMENTIER

LaRocque, Gilbert (b. 1941). Born in Montreal, the son of a blacksmith, he completed five years of an eight-year *collège classique* program and dropped out to become a clerk for the city of Montréal-Nord for eight years, spending his leisure time writing his first two novels. With the publication of *Le nombril* (1970), his life changed and he became involved in Montreal's most important publishing ventures, working for Éditions du Jour under Jacques Hébert; for Éditions de l'Homme as editor-in-chief; and for L'Aurore as literary director under Victor-Lévy BEAULIEU. After L'Aurore failed, LaRocque helped to establish the VLB publishing company, before going on to create Éditions Québec/Amérique (where he is working now), which has become one of the most important and viable of Québec's publishing houses. Writing all the time, he waited patiently for recognition, which came with the Prix France-Canada for his fifth novel *Les masques* (1980).

His novels are rather tough on the reader. With terrible insistence LaRocque plunges us into a universe of pettiness generated by characters trapped in futile family or marriage problems. He is well known for his penchant for shocking descriptions (oozing garbage, rot, excrement, odours, the world of sickness etc.), and for such scenes as the one in which Gaby, the heroine of *Après la boue*, provokes her abortion (with a knitting needle) in a bathtub in which she literally swims in blood. The fact that the *dégoûtant* in LaRocque's novels demonstrates his mastery of eloquent prose does not make these passages any easier to take.

With the first cycle of novels—*Le nombril, Corridors* (1971), and *Après la boue* (1972)—readers feared that LaRocque's talent was dwindling into mere repetition. But with the publication of *Serge d'entre les morts* (1976), there was a definite break with the past in a new quality of tenderness that raised his prose to the sublime. In this novel—about an incestuons relationship between Serge (an orphan) and his cousin Colette, which ends suddenly with Colette's marriage to another man—the world becomes wondrous, fantastic. This quality was further expressed in *Les masques*, which relates in hallucinatory prose the anguish of a narrator-hero whose son drowns while on

a weekend visit with him. *Le refuge* (1979), LaRocque's only dramatic work, which was televised by Radio-Canada, sets this drowning tragedy against the background of *Le nombril*, which is about the rebellion of an office clerk.

Gérard BESSETTE, who was among the first to notice this shift in his writing, based his novel *Le semestre* on *Les masques*, using LaRocque's novel as the object of a literary analysis, which is cleverly worked out by Bessette's hero, Omer Marin.

See also NOVELS IN FRENCH 1960 TO 1982: 3(a).

ANDRÉ VANASSE

La Roque de Roquebrune, Robert. See Robert Laroque de ROQUEBRUNE.

La Rue, François-Alexis-Hubert (1833-81). Born in Saint-Jean (Île d'Orléans), his brilliant studies at the Séminaire de Québec attracted the attention of that institution's superiors, who in 1855 persuaded him to undertake studies at Louvain and Paris with a view to teaching medicine at the newly founded Université Laval on his return. This he did, remaining professor of medicine there from 1859 until his death. He was very active in literary, cultural, and scientific circles, helping to found the influential reviews *Les* SOIRÉES CANADIENNES (1861-5) and *Le* FOYER CANADIEN (1863-6).

LaRue's many publications fall into three main categories, the first and largest comprising those of scientific, pedagogic, and social interest, such as *Éléments de chimie et de physique agricole* (Québec, 1868). Next are two historical works: *Histoire populaire du Canada; ou Entretiens de madame Genest à ses petits-enfants* (Québec, 1875 and 1913) and *Petite histoire des États-Unis très élémentaire; ou Entretiens de madame Genest avec ses petits-enfants* (Québec, 1880). The third category is more literary and includes contributions to periodicals, notably a 'Voyage autour de l'île d'Orléans' in *Les soirées canadiennes*, Vol. I (1861), and a useful study, 'Les chansons populaires et historiques du Canada' in *Le foyer canadien*, Vols I (1863) and IV (1865); two characteristically mixed volumes, *Mélanges historiques, littéraires et d'économie politique* (Québec, 1870 and 1881); a play, *Le défricheur de langue* (Québec, 1859); and a collection of essays, *Voyage sentimental sur la rue Saint-Jean: départ en 1860, retour en 1880* (Québec, 1879).

Le défricheur de langue, written in collaboration with Dr J.-C. TACHÉ and published under the pseudonym 'Isidore Méplats', is a three-act satire (LaRue called it a 'tragédie-bouffe') directed against the immigrant French editor of the review *La Ruche littéraire*, H.-E. CHEVALIER, whose turgid style and simplistic pseudo-scientific views on the evolution of French in North America are brilliantly parodied in this fanciful closet-drama. Ever a conservative, La Rue despised the liberal, anti-clerical views espoused by Chevalier and his friends. *Voyage sentimental* is a whimsical trip in time and space along Quebec's main street, mingling the author's personal recollections, history, and popular legend in twenty short essays.

See Charles Angers ('Jean du Sol'), *Le docteur Hubert LaRue et l'idée canadienne-française* (1912). Useful also is the short thesis of A. Talbot, 'Dr Hubert LaRue, médecin et écrivain' (Université de Montréal, 1943).

LEONARD DOUCETTE

Lasnier, Rina (b. 1915). Born in Saint Grégoire d'Iberville, Qué., she studied in Montreal and in England. She has worked as a journalist and now lives in Joliette, Qué.

Lasnier is widely recognized as one of the most accomplished poets in Québec. Though her religious themes mark her work as marginal to contemporary Québécois poetry, her skills as a poet make her nevertheless a highly respected literary figure. She has pursued a vigorously independent course, evolving within the parameters of her personal universe rather than within the often destructive values of modernism. Her poems combine classical control with a great semantic and rhythmical density; and much of their power is drawn from the tension between their theme (the conflicting pull of this world and the other) and the great sensuality of their language. The complexity of her poetry has been compared to that of Margaret AVISON. The list of Lasnier's publications is long. *Images et proses* (1941) is largely religious in inspiration; *Madones canadiennes* (1944) is a series of lyrics written to illuminate pictures chosen by Marius BARBEAU to illustrate the art of Québec as exemplified in statues of the madonna; *Le chant de la montée* (1947) is a series of chants inspired by the story of Jacob and Rachel. The major works of her maturity are *Présence de l'absence* (1956), *Mémoire sans jours* (1960), *Miroirs: proses* (1960), *Les gisants* (1963), and *L'arbre blanc* (1966).

La salle des rêves (1971) won the first A.J.M. SMITH prize for Canadian poetry. It was followed by *L'invisible* (1971); *Le rêve du quart jour* (conte) (1973); *Amour* (1975); *L'échelle des anges* (proses, 1975); *Les signes* (1976); *Matins d'oiseaux* (vol. I, 1978); *Paliers de paroles* (vol. II, 1978); *Entendre l'ombre* (vol. I., 1981); and *Voir la nuit* (vol. II, 1981). Some of Lasnier's collections have been republished in *Poèmes I* (1972) and *Poèms II* (1972).

Lasnier has also written several plays inspired by the religious history of Québec. *Féerie indienne: Kateri Tekakwitha* (1939) is based on the life of the celebrated Mohawk girl (1656-80?), an Indian convert recently beatified; *Le jeu de la voyagère* (1941) on the career of Marguerite Bourgeoys; and *Les fiançailles d'Anne de Noüe* (1943) on the work of a Jesuit missionary. *Notre-Dame du pain* (1947) was written for the Eucharistic Congress held in Ottawa. *La mère de nos mères* (1943) is a biographical essay on Marguerite Bourgeoys.

Lasnier has received many awards for her work, including the Prix David (in 1943 and 1974), the Prix Duvernay (1957), the Molson Prize (1971), the Prix France-Canada (1973-4), and an honorary doctorate from the Université de Montréal (1977).

One issue of LIBERTÉ (no. 108, vol. 18) is devoted entirely to Lasnier and contains an important bibliography, including her poems, journalism, and translations of poems by A.J.M. Smith (see also CANADIAN LITERATURE 39, Winter 1969). A special issue of the French magazine *Les Pharaons* (no. 20, Autumn 1974) is also devoted to Lasnier, as is *Ellipse* 22 (1978), containing poems by Lasnier in translation and a long interview.

See Sylvie Sicotte, *L'arbre dans la poésie de Rina Lasnier* (1977), and Eva Kushner, *Rina Lasnier* (1964)—the latter more apology than criticism. Selections of her work are found in *Rina Lasnier: textes choisis* (1961), edited by Jean Marcel, and in *La part du feu* (1970), an anthology of her poetry that has a critical introduction by Guy ROBERT.

SHERRY SIMON

Last of the Eries, The (1849). By 'H.H.B.'. As interesting and as competently written as better-known Canadian novels of the period, it was printed at the newspaper office in Simcoe, Canada West, and advertised for sale throughout the province. Despite the attempt to tell a story about Canada to Canadians, it does not seem to have been widely noticed at the time, and only two copies—in the libraries of the University of

Last of the Eries

Western Ontario and Acadia University—are reported as surviving today.

Set in the 1750s, the novel is one of the very early English-Canadian attempts to use New France as a romantic background for fiction. The plot owes much to French-Canadian legends, beginning with 'L'Iroquoise', that revolve around the love of a young, nobly born French soldier for a beautiful Indian maiden. The Erie tribe of the title has been virtually exterminated by the Six Nations. The survivors are still pursued by the villainous Iroquois Coswenago, who abducts Pale Lily, the half-white daughter of their chief. The French soldier Pierre, a friend of the Eries and sympathetic to their way of life, rescues her. Most of the action takes place in an unnamed area of the Canadian interior in 1756, some of it at Fort Frontenac and the remainder at Québec in 1760, where all but seven of the remaining Eries die fighting on the French side. Pale Lily, the only convert to Christianity, marries Pierre and they settle in Lower Canada. There is little, except her forest background, to distinguish Pale Lily from a standard white heroine, and among the male characters neither villainy nor heroism is exclusive to Indians or Europeans.

The narrative device is that of a tale within a tale. One of a group of friends in present time reads on successive nights the story of the extermination a century earlier of the Erie tribe. The ensuing discussions, augmented by authorial asides, tell much about Indian customs and comment on such diverse subjects as the relations of the French to the Indians, the role of the French at Culloden, theology, and the vast improvement made by England in the civilization of North America. The narrative focuses on action rather than description, and suspense about the outcome of various crises and the fate of various individuals carries the reader rapidly forward.   MARY LU MacDONALD

Laterrière, Pierre de Sales. See BIOGRAPHY AND MEMOIRS IN FRENCH: 6.

Laurence, Margaret (b. 1926). Canada's most successful novelist was born Jean Margaret Wemys in the prairie town of Neepawa, Man., which inspired her fictional 'Manawaka'. Her parents, of Scots and Irish descent, died when she was young and she was brought up by an aunt who had become her stepmother. Having decided as a child on a career as a writer, she contributed to school and college magazines and as early as 1939 used the invented name 'Manawaka' in a story for a *Winnipeg Free Press* contest. After graduating in Honours English from United College, Winnipeg, in 1947 she worked as a reporter for the *Winnipeg Citizen*. In 1947 she married Jack Laurence, a civil engineer, and in 1949 moved with him to England. From 1950 to 1957 they lived in Africa, for the first two years in the British Protectorate of Somaliland (now Somalia), then in Ghana just before its independence. Laurence's experience of these countries led to a variety of writings on African subjects over a period of some sixteen years: the first of these was *A tree for poverty* (1954), an essay on and collection of Somali poetry and prose, which she completed while in Somaliland. Two children, Jocelyn and David, were born to the Laurences before their return to Canada in 1957. While living in Vancouver from 1957 to 1962 Laurence saw the appearance in Canadian journals of her African short stories, later collected in *The tomorrow-tamer* (1963), and the publication of her African novel, *This side Jordan* (1960). At the same time she was writing a first draft of a novel set in Canada, which would eventually be rewritten and published as *The stone angel* (1964). After separating from her husband in 1962 (the Laurences were divorced in 1969), she moved with her children to England, where she lived for ten years. In this prolific decade she published a memoir of her life in Somaliland, *The prophet's camel bell* (1963); three of the four Manawaka novels: *The stone angel* (1961), *A jest of God* (1966), *The fire-dwellers* (1969); a collection of linked stories, also set in Manawaka, *A bird in the house* (1970); a children's book, *Jason's quest* (1970); and *Long drums and cannons* (1968), a critical study of Nigerian writing in English during a fifteen-year period of cultural renaissance that was to be ended by the tribal warfare of the mid-sixties. The period also saw the publication of several magazine articles, which were later collected to form *Heart of a stranger* (1976). Between 1969 and 1974 Laurence was writer-in-residence at three Ontario universities and since 1974 has made her home in Lakefield, Ont., spending summers at her cottage on the Otonabee River, near Peterborough, where most of the fourth Manawaka novel, *The diviners* (1974), was written. She has written three more children's books: *Six darn cows* (1979); *The olden days coat* (1979), which was made into an award-winning television drama in 1981; and *The Christmas birthday story* (1980).

Since 1961, when her story 'A gourdful of glory' was awarded the President's Medal, University of Western Ontario, and her novel *This side Jordan* earned the Beta Sigma Phi First Novel Award, Margaret Laurence has earned numerous prizes, honorary degrees, and awards. She received a Governor General's Award for *A jest of God* and again for *The diviners*. She was made a Companion of the Order of Canada in 1971 and received a Molson Prize in 1975. She has served as chancellor of Trent University since 1980.

Laurence's work has been published in several languages and in a variety of paperback editions. In their English and American editions some of the books are differently titled: *The prophet's camel bell* appeared in New York as *New wind in a dry land* (1964); the English paperback of *A jest of God* was entitled *Now I lay me down* (1968), and the Warner Brothers film of this novel was called *Rachel, Rachel* (1968). In addition to radio, television, and stage adaptations of her writings, there is a National Film Board documentary on her life and work, *Margaret Laurence, first lady of Manawaka* (1979).

Laurence's African writings introduce the themes of survival, freedom, and individual dignity that dominate her major novels. In the deserts of Somaliland, she translated and paraphrased the oral poems and stories of the Somali nomads, to form the first collection in English of this material. Her introduction to *A tree for poverty* tells of the harsh, drought-ridden lives and compensatory culture of the nomads; she later wrote essays on two poets who particularly fascinated her, the warrior 'Mad Mullah' and the love-poet Elmi Bonderii, and these are included in *Heart of a stranger*. The best of Laurence's African books, *The prophet's camel bell*, was written a decade after she left Somaliland and is a recollection of her experience there. A travelogue based on her diaries, it creates a vivid picture of landscape and people, including some of the most sympathetic portraits of European colonizers to be found in her work. As a personal document, it records the author's spiritual journey from naive enthusiasm and hasty judgement to a respect for the privacy and dignity of others. The two books dealing with Ghana, the novel *This side Jordan* and *The tomorrow tamer*, are more overtly political; set in the period when the country faced its independence, they give full rein to Laurence's anti-

imperialist, anti-colonial views. *This side Jordan* suffers from a rigid structure and contrived ending because it endeavours to give equal weight to two points of view: those of the white imperialists facing expulsion and of the black African caught between the old world of his ancestors and the new world of Christianity and urban technology. Laurence sometimes attempts to see through African eyes, but is less successful in this novel than in the semi-allegorical story 'Godman's master', which appears in *The tomorrow-tamer*. Stories in this collection examine closely, and often ironically, the nature of freedom, and show special sympathy for those, both African and European, who no longer belong anywhere. The title story illustrates the book's main concern, the conflict between old and new ways.

Laurence's greatest achievement to date lies in the four Canadian novels dominated by the town of Manawaka, which is not simply a fictional version of Neepawa, though similar in many details, but an amalgam of all prairie small towns infused with the spirit of their Scots-Presbyterian founders. In this respect it is like the small-town settings of Sinclair ROSS and W.O. MITCHELL that were an early influence on Laurence. Although only *A jest of God* is set entirely in Manawaka, the town—with its paralysing, often hypocritical, respectability and harsh social divisions—represents in each novel a constricting force to be overcome by the main characters. Insofar as it shapes each protagonist, Manawaka is an aspect of her own being that must be confronted from within; at another level the town is an emblem of life itself. Laurence's chief concern as novelist is the depiction of character, and at the centre of each novel is a powerfully realized woman. Ninety-year old Hagar in *The* STONE ANGEL tries to stave off physical disintegration and death with all the dignity she can. She acquires a measure of grace in acknowledging the pride which, though it has been her strength, has shackled her emotions and stopped her from loving freely. Unlike Hagar, who has a rich and humorous zest for life, Rachel, the unmarried schoolteacher in *A jest of God*, endures a sterile, introverted living death. She is finally able to break away from Manawaka after a sexual affair and its traumatic consequences bring her a liberating self-knowledge. Rachel's sister Stacey, the protagonist of *The fire-dwellers*, is a spiritually isolated housewife and mother threatened by domestic and social chaos, which she fears both as personal hell-fire and nuclear holocaust. Experience of real tragedies and near-disasters, together with the help of a stranger (as in Hagar's case), results in a hopeful conclusion that offers the possibility of communication with others. Morag in *The diviners* faces the dilemma of trying to live her own life as a writer, while coping with the emotional and physical demands of being wife and mother. Unlike the three previous heroines, she was not brought up in a middle-class family but in the haphazard environment of the garbage-collector's unconventional home. She thus understands social ostracism, so familiar to the Métis, who are powerfully represented here, as elsewhere in the cycle, by the Tonnerre family. Morag's liaison with Jules Tonnerre produces a daughter whose consciousness of her mixed heritage, painful though it is, holds promise of a better future. Of the four novels, *The diviners* deals most richly with their shared themes of ancestral heritage and the relation of past to present. Time sequence is differently handled in each novel: *The stone angel* alternates present and past episodes; *A jest of God* is a monologue in the present tense; *The fire-dwellers* tries to capture the multiple, simultaneous workings of consciousness by rendering Stacey's inner voice, outer dialogues, dreams and fantasies through changes of type-face and manipulation of space on the page. Time, memory, and understanding are most thoroughly explored in *The diviners*, where the narrative method is varied by such devices as 'Memory bank movies' and the use of present tense for past events, of past tense for present.

Laurence has a rich ear for nuances of speech, ranging from everyday slang to the colourful, oracular poetry of chanted myth. There is much humour in her work and a strong sense of irony. Depth is given to the prose by a wide range of metaphorical and symbolic allusion, most notably to the Bible and to the natural world; names are used in full consciousness of their derivations or associations. Each of the Manawaka novels is dominated with imagery associated with one of the four elements; and this, together with numerous cross-references and the unifying presence of the town itself, justifies the reading of the four works as a unit, a tetralogy expressing Laurence's view of the human condition where grace, symbolized by water, may ultimately be offered to those who endure.

A bird in the house (1970), also set in Man-awaka, stands slightly apart from the four novels in that it is, as Laurence has said, 'semi-autobiographical'. The short stories about the girlhood of Vanessa MacLeod re-create some of the experiences of the young Margaret Laurence, especially in facing the death of a parent and coming to terms with the autocratic spirit of a stern grandfather. The narrator is the adult Vanessa, but her voice belongs simultaneously to the young Vanessa who, as an apprentice writer, makes a point of listening and observing and so has much to report. Through her we encounter the tensions and consolations of family life and, in the later stories, social issues with the particular flavour of small-town and rural life during the Depression.

Laurence has been generous in granting interviews, which are listed, together with critical articles on her work, in *Margaret Laurence, an annotated bibliography* (1979) by Susan J. Warwick. There is a biography, which sometimes points to the facts behind fictional details, in Joan Hind-Smith's *Three voices* (1975), and a detailed chronology, compiled by Susan J. Warwick, in *Journal of Canadian Studies*, vol. 13, No. 3 (Fall, 1978), which is a special issue devoted to Margaret Laurence. Of other periodical numbers devoted to Laurence, the most notable is *Journal of Canadian Fiction*, 27 (Summer, 1980), which includes four early Laurence stories not previously reprinted. There is a collection of reviews and articles reprinted from a variety of sources in William New's *Margaret Laurence, the writer and her critics* (1977). For book-length critical studies, see Clara THOMAS's *The Manawaka world of Margaret Laurence* (1975) and, in the Twayne World Authors series, Patricia Morley's *Margaret Laurence* (1981).

See also NOVELS IN ENGLISH 1960 TO 1982: 2.   JOAN COLDWELL

Laurendeau, André. See ESSAYS IN FRENCH: 6.

Lavigne, Louis-Dominique. See DRAMA IN FRENCH 1948 TO 1981: 3.

Layton, Irving (b. 1912). Born in Romania, he came to Montreal with his parents (Lazarovitch) at the age of one, and was educated at Baron Byng High School and Macdonald College, where he earned a B.Sc. in agriculture. After brief service in the Canadian Army (1942-3), he did postgraduate work in economics and political science at McGill University, obtaining an M.A. in

1946. He taught English at a parochial school in Montreal, while also teaching part-time at Sir George Williams College (now Concordia University). He was appointed writer-in-residence at Sir George in 1965, and to a similar post at the University of Guelph in the winter of 1969. That year he was appointed professor of English at York University, Toronto, from which post he retired in 1978. He was awarded a Doctor of Civil Laws by Bishop's University in 1970.

Layton was a member of the active group of young poets in Montreal who contributed to FIRST STATEMENT, founded by John SUTHERLAND in 1942. With Louis DUDEK in 1943 he joined Sutherland in editing the magazine and remained an editor until it merged with PREVIEW in 1945 to become NORTHERN REVIEW. He resigned in the 1950s when a change in editorial policy was adopted by Sutherland. In 1952 he was associated with Dudek and Raymond SOUSTER in founding Contact Press, a co-operative venture to publish the work of Canadian poets. Together with Dudek, he was instrumental in shaping the editorial policy of Aileen Collins' magazine *CIV/n* (1953-4). In 1955 he declined an invitation by Charles Olson to join the faculty of Black Mountain College in North Carolina and the editorial board of the *Black Mountain Review*. However, he was in close contact with the American poets Robert Creeley, Cid Corman, and Jonathan Williams throughout the 1950s, and in 1956 edited a Canadian issue of Corman's magazine *Origin*.

Layton's poetry has dazzled, puzzled, angered, and astonished its readers since its first publication. He has vigorously opposed the aestheticist concept of the poem as a paradigm of the beautiful. To Layton the poem must convey truth, which can reside in the most ignoble and 'unpoetic' subjects and be expressed in blatantly non-poetic forms. The craft of poetry lies in finding the words, however unconventional, to manifest the vision of truth. The poet must simultaneously be as resourceful as a master criminal and as imaginative as the universe.

Many of Layton's collections of poetry are prefaced by attacks on alleged restricters of the freedom of the poet's imagination—professors, critics, clergymen, rationalist poets, puritan editors—who are all abetted by the female in attempting to confine the poet's Apollonian spirit to a world of comfort, convention, and predictability. Layton defiantly breaks what is to him a puritan embargo on image, magic, and sexuality, and made the irrational an accepted part of Canadian poetry for the first time since LAMPMAN and CARMAN. His vitality and ironic vulgarity, moreover, create an irrational that is vivid and brutal where before it had been sentimental and vague. In rehabilitating the irrational he invariably includes himself among the liars, hypocrites, Yahoos, and philistines of whom he writes. His voice thus comes from inside the primal energy and vileness of our world, as an honest testimony to its dangers and powers. The most impressive of Layton's poems capture the poet's own extravagance, as 'The day Aviva came to Paris', 'Shakespeare', and 'Keine Lazarovitch', and reveal a wit that can astonish with both appropriateness and reach. Layton's voice in such poems is confident, bawdy, and at times hyperbolic, yet capable of discerning self-perception.

Layton began publishing in *First Statement* in 1943; between 1943 and 1952 he wrote relatively little, publishing three books, two of which reprint significant portions of the first, and contributing a small number of poems to *Cerberus* (1952), a collection he shared with Dudek and Souster. From 1953 onward he has been extraordinarily prolific, publishing an average of one book a year. Layton's publication in the first two decades of his career—*Here and now* (1945); *Now is the place* (1948); *The black huntsman* (1951); *Love the conqueror worm* (1953); *In the midst of my fever* (published in Mallorca by Robert Creeley, 1954); *The long pea-shooter* (1954); *The cold green element* (1955); *The blue propeller* (1955); *The bull calf and other poems* (1956); *The improved binoculars* (published in North Carolina by Jonathan Williams and with an introduction by William Carlos Williams, 1956); *Music on a kazoo* (1956); *A laughter in the mind* (also published by Jonathan Williams, 1958); and *A red carpet for the sun* (1959, Governor General's Award)—establish the underlying dichotomies of his vision: poet v. society, poetry v. literature, the individual v. the state, passion v. reason, creativity v. order, sacrifice v. rationalization, rudeness v. decorum, imperfection v. perfection, life v. art. The later poems continually expand the amount of the ostensibly horrific, trivial, or crude that this life-affirming vision must necessarily and paradoxically include. His later collections—*The swinging flesh* (1961), *Balls for a one-armed juggler* (1963), *The laughing rooster* (1964), *Collected poems* (1965), *Periods of the moon*

(1967), *The shattered plinths* (1968), *The whole bloody bird: obs, alphs, and poems* (1969), *Nail polish* (1971), and *Lovers and lesser men* (1973)—are increasingly angry and strident in tone, possibly because the poet fears that growing critical acceptance is likely to confer literary respectability that will 'emasculate' his poems. In recent collections— *The pole vaulter* (1974), *For my brother Jesus* (1976), *The covenant* (1977), *The tightrope dancer* (1978), *Droppings from heaven* (1979), *For my neighbours in hell* (1980), and *Europe and other bad news* (1981)—Layton has given renewed emphasis to anti-Christian themes and to his Jewishness, using the latter as a symbol of passion, dignity, and truth. His poetry can be examined in depth in *The collected poems of Irving Layton* (1971), in two volumes of selected poems: *The darkening fire 1945-68* (1975) and *The unwavering eye 1969-75* (1975); and in *A wild peculiar joy, 1945-1982* (1982).

Layton edited *Pa-nic: a selection of contemporary Canadian poems* (1958) and *Love where the nights are long: Canadian love poems* (1962). He collaborated with Louis Dudek in editing *Canadian poems: 1850-1952* (1952). In 1972 he published *Engagements: the prose of Irving Layton*, a collection of ten short stories, articles, prefaces, and reviews, and in 1977 *Taking sides: the collected social and political writings*. Recent international publication of Layton's work has included *Selected poems* (London, 1974), *The poems of Irving Layton* (New York, 1977), *Seventy-five Greek poems* (Athens, 1974), *Il freddo verde elemento* (Torino, 1974), and *Il puma ammansito* (Milan, 1979). Other books are *Uncollected poems 1935-59* (1976); a collection of letters *An unlikely affair* (1980, with Dorothy Rath); and the anthologies *Poems for 27 Cents* (1961), *Anvil Blood* (1966), and *Shark tank* (1977), the latter two being work by his students.

Eli MANDEL has written a critical study of Layton's poetry (1969; rev. 1981), and Seymour MAYNE has edited a collection of critical views of Layton (1978).

See also POETRY IN ENGLISH 1950 TO 1982: 1.   FRANK DAVEY

Leacock, Stephen (1869-1944). Stephen Butler Leacock was born in Swanmore, Eng. His father, after failing at farming in South Africa and Kansas, took his family in 1876 to Canada, where they settled on a farm in the Lake Simcoe district of Ontario. It was never a success and Leacock's father eventually abandoned his wife, leaving her

to raise the family of eleven children (of whom Stephen was the third). Leacock was educated locally and then at Upper Canada College. After a year at the University of Toronto he became an unenthusiastic schoolteacher in 1888, and from 1889 to 1899 taught at Upper Canada College, finding time to complete a degree in modern languages at the University of Toronto in 1891. In 1899, inspired by Thorstein Veblen's *Theory of the leisure class*, he enrolled at the University of Chicago, where he did graduate work in political economy under Veblen. He married Beatrix Hamilton in 1900, and upon receiving his Ph.D. in 1903 was appointed lecturer in the Department of Economics and Political Science at McGill University. In 1906 he published his first and most profitable book: *Elements of political science* (rev. 1921), a college textbook. In 1907-8 he went on a lecture tour of the British Empire to promote Imperial Federation, and when he returned to McGill he became head of his department, helped found the University Club, and built a summer home on Lake Couchiching near Orillia, Ont. McGill, the University Club, and the home in Orillia became the focal points of his existence. In 1910 the first of Leacock's many books of humour, *Literary lapses* (NCL), appeared. Elected to the Royal Society of Canada in 1919, he became a charter member of the CANADIAN AUTHORS' ASSOCIATION in 1921, and that year went on a lecture tour of England. He remained chairman of his department until his enforced retirement in 1936, after which he made a triumphant lecture tour of western Canada that resulted in *My discovery of the West: a discussion of east and west in Canada* (1937), winner of a Governor-General's Award. In 1937 he received the Lorne Pierce Medal of the Royal Society of Canada. He continued to write prolifically until his final illness.

Leacock's humorous books usually gathered together, in time for the Christmas trade, miscellaneous pieces that had appeared previously in various magazines. As a result, most of them have little or no overall unifying structure. The mix in *Literary lapses* is typical: funny stories, some little more than anecdotes, others more extended; monologues and dialogues; parodies ranging from fashionable romantic novels to Euclid; humorous reflections and essays on a wide variety of topics. Much of Leacock's humour, in this book and others, is exuberant nonsense that, like Lewis Carroll's, sometimes breaks out into a violence that would be disturbing if it were not so obviously in fun. More modern parallels might be the Marx Brothers or *Monty Python's flying circus*. Leacock's parodies (see especially *Nonsense novels*, 1911; *Frenzied fiction*, 1918; and *Winsome Winnie, and other nonsense novels*, 1920), which are undervalued today, offered him an excellent opportunity to give vent to this strain of irresponsible anarchy. Lord Ronald in 'Gertrude the governess; or Simple seventeen', who 'flung himself upon his horse and rode madly off in all directions', is the most famous example of this strain of Leacock's humour. Other parodies—such as 'Guido the gimlet of Ghent: a romance of chivalry' and 'Sorrows of a super soul; or, The memoirs of Marie Mushenough'—provide examples of almost equally inspired absurdity. Often, however, a more serious note mingles with the humour, and some of Leacock's funniest pieces—such as 'My financial career', 'Hoodoo McFiggin's Christmas', or any of the sketches from ARCADIAN ADVENTURES WITH THE IDLE RICH (1914)—show genuine sympathy for decent but ineffectual victims of a coldly indifferent or actively hostile world. It is clear from pieces such as these why Leacock considered Mr Pickwick and Huckleberry Finn to be the two greatest creations of comic literature, and why he was approached to write a screenplay for Charlie Chaplin.

The most striking aspect of Leacock's style is the illusion of a speaking voice, which is so strong in all his works. Like his masters, Dickens and Mark Twain, Leacock was a great lecturer and raconteur, and many of his pieces must be read aloud or recited for their full effect. North American humour has always been rooted in the oral tradition, from Thomas Chandler HALIBURTON (whom Leacock did not admire but with whom he had much in common) through Artemus Ward, Mark Twain, and many others, including Robert Benchley and James Thurber, who were both influenced by Leacock. Leacock's idiom, though, has none of the frontier raciness we associate with Sam Slick and his numerous progeny. Much of the humour of his best pieces comes from their modesty of tone. They seem to be recounted, as simply and straightforwardly as possible, by someone who is not intending to amuse us and would probably find our amusement puzzling. Leacock's finest achievement in this respect is the naively self-revealing narrator of SUNSHINE SKETCHES OF A LITTLE TOWN (1912).

Another aspect of Leacock's humour that may also owe something to the oral tradition is the way in which he elaborates a single idea, capping one ingenuity with another until he reaches an inevitable but absurd climax (the final irrational act of the narrator that follows a crescendo of humiliations in 'My financial career') or collapses into an equally inevitable but absurd anticlimax (as in the apparent tragedy turned farce of 'The marine excursion of the Knights of Pythias' or 'The Mariposa bank mystery' in *Sunshine sketches*).

Leacock's two best books are *Sunshine sketches* and *Arcadian adventures*. The first is a regional idyll portraying the essentially good-natured follies of Mariposa, a small Ontario town based on Orillia. The second, set in an American city, is much harsher in its criticism of a hypocritical and destructive plutocracy. These two books stand apart from the rest of Leacock's humorous writings in their artistic unity and seriousness of purpose. Apart from the works already mentioned, Leacock's thirty-odd books of humour include *Behind the beyond, and other contributions to human knowledge* (1913, NCL), *Moonbeams from the larger lunacy* (1915, NCL), *Further foolishness: sketches and satires on the follies of the day* (1916, NCL), *The Hohenzollerns in America: with the Bolsheviks in Berlin and other impossibilities* (1919), *Over the footlights* (1923), *Winnowed wisdom: a new book of humour* (1925, NCL), *Short circuits* (1928, NCL), *The iron man & the tin woman, with other such futurities: a book of little sketches of today and to-morrow* (1929), *The dry Pickwick and other incongruities* (1932), *Funny pieces: a book of random sketches* (1936), *Model memoirs and other sketches from simple to serious* (1938), *My remarkable uncle, and other sketches* (1942, NCL), and *Last leaves* (1945, NCL).

After the appearance of *Literary lapses* in 1910 Leacock published, on the average, one book of humour a year; but he found time to produce many non-humorous works as well—numerous articles, and some twenty-seven books, most of which are of little lasting interest. Two exceptions are *My discovery of England* (1922, NCL) and *The boy I left behind me* (1946). The first is based on Leacock's 1921 lecture tour of England and contains two of his best pieces: ' "We have with us to-night" ', a hilarious account of the tribulations of a public lecturer, and 'Oxford as I see it', a powerful defence of the ideal of education as a humane experience. *The boy I left behind me* consists of the opening chapters of an autobiography that was interrupted by Leacock's death. It is shrewd and unsentimental but evocative, and even in its truncated form is one of Leacock's finest sustained pieces of writing. Leacock's other non-humorous books, while skilful and sometimes genuinely eloquent, are lacking in originality, seldom rising much above the level of competent popularizations. However, many of these works provide important insights into the issues that concerned Leacock all his life and that underlie much of his best humour.

Leacock's most dearly held belief, which links him to the Victorian Age in which he spent his formative years, was in progress, which he saw as culminating in the achievements of Anglo-Saxon civilization. This belief underlies his many works of history, political science, and economics, such as *Baldwin, Lafontaine, Hincks: responsible government* (1907), *Economic prosperity in the British Empire* (1930), *Canada: the foundations of its future* (1941), and *Montreal: seaport and city* (1942), among many others. For Leacock the essence of progress was an ever-increasing capacity for human kindness, which found its highest artistic expression in Anglo-Saxon humour, especially as it is reflected in the works of Mark Twain and Dickens. He argued this thesis most notably in *Mark Twain* (1932), *Charles Dickens, his life and work* (1933), *Humor: its theory and technique* (1935), and *Humor and humanity* (1937). Leacock's belief in progress may appear complacent, but it was not lightly held. Throughout his life there was a tension between his proclaimed optimism about the continuing progress of mankind and his feeling of unease (expressed most forcefully in *The unsolved riddle of social justice*, 1920) about the triumph of materialism, with its exaltation of laissez-faire individualism and its undermining of traditional social ties. Leacock's hostility to the chaotic forces that he saw threatening human progress often came out in unpleasant ways, as in his suspicion of higher education for women or in his unyielding opposition to non-Anglo-Saxon immigration to Canada; but whatever the forms his world view sometimes took, it was deeply rooted in a genuine concern that the gradual progress of mankind not be brought to a halt.

Most readers of Leacock agree that his writing career shows little sign of development, either intellectual or artistic. He did, however, continue to produce excellent pieces intermittently throughout his career, such as 'Eddie the bartender' (1929), 'My

Victorian girlhood by Lady Nearleigh Slopover' (1939), and 'My remarkable uncle' (1942); and in his last years he wrote some very fine essays, essentially serious but leavened with humour, among the best of which are the final chapter of *Humor: its theory and technique*, with its vision of the universe as a great cosmic joke, and two meditations on old age: 'When men retire' (1939), and 'Three score and ten—the business of growing old' (1942). Nonetheless there remains a sense of disappointment, of unfulfilled potential, in his career. It has been argued that, perhaps because of his impoverished and unstable childhood, Leacock craved the reassurance that fame and money brought, and that this led him to fall back uncritically on successful formulas. This is undoubtedly true; but another deeper reason may be that the kindly view of an ever-progressing world that Leacock wished to maintain was at odds with his gift. Leacock's insistence that humour should be kindly is clearly wrongheaded when tested against the world's great humour, including his own, especially *Sunshine sketches* and *Arcadian adventures* with their critique—implicit in the former and bitterly explicit in the latter—of 'money-getting in the city'. It is hard to see how Leacock could have continued in the far-from kindly direction that seemed to lie ahead of him after *Arcadian adventures* if he were to maintain his faith in progress. His emphasis on the need for kindliness in humour seems, then, a rationalization for his pulling back from the fullest implications of his essentially pessimistic vision of man in the modern industrial age. Ironically it may have been Leacock's need to maintain his faith in the progress of humanity that thwarted his own progress as an artist and the fullest development of the gifts with which he was so generously endowed.

See *Feast of Stephen: a Leacock anthology* (1974) edited by Robertson DAVIES; Ralph L. Curry, *Stephen Leacock: humorist and humanist* (1959); D.A. Cameron, *Faces of Leacock, an appreciation* (1967); Robertson Davies, *Stephen Leacock* (1970); and Carl Berger, 'The other Mr. Leacock', CANADIAN LITERATURE 55 (Winter 1973.)

ZAILIG POLLOCK

League of Canadian Poets, The. Founded in 1966 by Raymond SOUSTER, with the help of Earle BIRNEY, John Robert COLOMBO, Louis DUDEK, and Al PURDY, it had as its original goal 'the advancement of poetry in Canada and the promotion of interests of Canadian poets.' Membership was intended as a mark of 'recognition of achievement among peers' on the Canadian poetry scene. (The League also sponsors associate memberships for emerging poets.) It organizes tours for its full members, offers contract advice, and maintains an active lobby for poetry-related causes in Canada. Chairpersons have been Raymond Souster (1967-71), Douglas BARBOUR and Stephen SCOBIE (1972-4); Pat LOWTHER (1974-5); Marya FIAMENGO (1975-6); Shirley Gibson and Brian Thackeray (1976-8). In 1977 the office of chairperson was replaced by that of president: Francis SPARSHOTT (1977-9); Sid Stephen (1979-80); Henry BEISSEL (1980-1); Elizabeth Woods (1981-2); and David Donnell (1982-3). The League has also produced several publications, including the members' catalogue *The League of Canadian Poets* (1980) and *When is a poem: creative ideas for teaching poetry collected from Canadian poets* (1980). It is located at 24 Ryerson Ave., Toronto M5T 2P3.   BRUCE MEYER

LeBlanc, Raymond. See ACADIAN LITERATURE: 2(a).

Leblanc de Marconnay, Hyacinthe-Poirier (1794-1868). Born in Paris into an old aristocratic family, he immigrated to Montreal in 1834, apparently because of his involvement in suspect political activity in France. He remained in Canada until 1841 and was active in Montreal, from the moment of his arrival, in journalism, politics, freemasonry, and the theatre. He edited in turn the newspapers *La Minerve, L'Ami du peuple, Le Populaire*, and *L'Aurore des Canadas*, adopting at first a political stance strongly favouring francophone rights and the Patriote party. This is apparent in the work he wrote a few months after his arrival, *Relation historique des événements de l'élection du comté du Lac des Deux-Montagnes en 1834* (Montréal, 1835). But as the possibility of armed conflict grew more real, he withdrew his support of the Patriotes in his editorials and in his stinging attack on the group surrounding L.-H. Lafontaine in *La petite clique dévoilée; ou Quelques explications sur les manoeuvres dirigées contre la minorité patriote qui prit part au vote des subsides dans la session de 1835 à 1836* (Rome, N.Y., 1836). His last political work published in Canada, *Réfutation de l'écrit de Louis-Joseph Papineau, ex-orateur de la Chambre d'assemblée du Bas-Canada, intitulé 'Histoire de l'insurrection du Canada'* (Montréal, 1839), shows how far the author's loyalties had evolved by then, for it is patently hostile to the rebels and their leaders.

Before leaving France, Leblanc de Marconnay had collaborated on a one-act comic opera, *L'hôtel des princes*, which was staged with some success in Paris in 1831 and published there the same year. In Canada his interest in theatre remained, as he signed his name to two plays that were published and performed in Montreal in 1836, the year he was elected president of the short-lived 'Société dramatique des auteurs français'. The first of these, *Le soldat* (which may have been written in collaboration with Napoléon AUBIN), described as an 'Intermède en 2 parties, mêlé de chants', comprises only eight pages and one role: that of a chauvinistic French soldier who, in Part I, extols the glories of a military career and in Part II, wounded and dying, reads a long, bathetic letter to his beloved, asking her to take care of his poor old mother . . . and his dog. The second play, *Valentine; ou La Nina canadienne*, is much better developed and represents an important step in the evolution of theatre in French Canada. Its author has been falsely accused of plagiarizing his subject from the eighteenth-century French author B.-J. Marsollier des Vivetières, whose operetta, *Nina; ou La folle par amour* (Paris, 1786), had enjoyed considerable success. In fact the indebtedness is minimal and sufficiently acknowledged in Leblanc de Marconnay's title. Acquainted with stage techniques in France, he has constructed an entirely new and different play, solidly Canadian in setting, reflecting local speech patterns and with references to Canadian history and politics, along with skilful use of French-Canadian folk-songs. *Valentine*, like *Le soldat*, was performed at least twice at the Théâtre Royal in Montreal.

After his return to France in 1841, Leblanc de Marconnay resumed the intense masonic activity that characterized his early years there (he had reached the 32nd degree by 1828). Although he had indicated, in his correspondence with Governor Sir Charles Bagot, his willingness to return to Canada, he never did.

See Claude Galarneau's article in *The* DICTIONARY OF CANADIAN BIOGRAPHY, vol. IX; J.-N. Fauteux, 'Débuts du journalisme au Canada français', in *Le journaliste canadien-français* I (1955); and E.-Z. Massicotte, 'Leblanc de Marconnay', in the *Bulletin de la revue d'historique* XXVI (1920).

LEONARD DOUCETTE

LeBouthillier

LeBouthillier, Claude. See ACADIAN LIT-
ERATURE: 2(c).

Leclerc, Félix (b. 1914). Born at La Tuque,
Qué., he was educated there, at a secondary
school in Ottawa, and at the Université
d'Ottawa, which he attended for two years.
From 1934 to 1942 he was employed as a
radio announcer in Quebec City and Trois-
Rivières and by Radio-Canada. He became a
popular performer, reading his stories and
poems and singing his own songs on the
radio, and from 1942 to 1945 acting with the
Compagnons de Saint-Laurent. A precursor
of the French-Canadian *chansonniers* who
have become internationally popular, from
1951 to 1953 he lived in Paris; he toured
Europe and the Near East and was known as
'Le Canadien'. He received Le Grand Prix
du Disque in 1951 for his recording of *Moi,
mes souliers*, and twice again. In 1966 he went
to Europe, where he has remained popular.
A militant nationalist, he lives on the Île
d'Orléans.

Leclerc is a troubador whose 'songs are on
all lips', a writer who is simple without
being naive. His books of stories, fables,
songs, poems, plays, and reminiscences reflect his love of nature and folklore, his
lighthearted attitude to life, his humour, and
a fresh and spontaneous style of writing. His
popularity in Québec is revealed by the fact
that all his books have been reissued several
times, and by the cover blurb of one of his
novels—*Carcajou; ou Le diable des bois*
(1973)—which says merely: 'Félix Leclerc
n'a pas besoin d'être présenté. Il est *lui*.
Beaucoup plus qu'un célèbre, un grand
Québécois.' His first publications were *Adagio* (1943; rpr. 1976), stories; *Allegro* (1944;
rpr. 1976), fables; and *Andante* (1944; rpr.
1975), poems. (*Le hamac dans les voiles*, 1952,
is a selection from these three books.) He
has written two memoirs: *Pieds nus dans
l'aube* (1946), about his happy childhood in
La Tuque, and *Moi, mes souliers: journal d'un
lièvre à deux pattes* (Paris, 1955), about his careers as writer, actor, playwright, singer,
etc. Other books are *Dialogues d'hommes et de
bêtes* (1949), thirteen tales; *Le fou de l'île*
(Paris, 1958)—translated by Philip Stratford
as *The madman, the kite and the island* (1976;
1983); and *Le calepin d'un flâneur* (1961), reflections. His plays are *Théâtre de village*
(1951), *L'auberge des morts subites* (1964), *Sonnez les matines* (1964), and *Le p'tit bonheur*
(1959; rpr. 1966), 12 short plays that were
widely performed as a group.

See Jean-Claude LePennec, *L'univers

poétique de Félix Leclerc (1967), and Jean-
Noel Samson, *Félix Leclerc* (1967), in the series Dossiers de documentation sur la littérature canadienne-française.   WILLIAM TOYE

Leclerc, Gilles. See ESSAYS IN FRENCH: 5.

Lee, Dennis (b. 1939). Born in Toronto, he
attended the University of Toronto Schools
and Victoria College, University of
Toronto (B.A., 1962; M.A., 1965), where he
taught for several years. He was a founder of
the experimental Rochdale College,
Toronto, and co-founder (with Dave GOD-
FREY) of the House of ANANSI Press. After
his association with Anansi ended, he was
consulting editor for the MACMILLAN COM-
PANY OF CANADA from 1974 to 1979. He has
been writer-in-residence at the University of
Toronto (1978-9) and a Scottish-Canadian
Exchange Fellow at the University of Edinburgh (1980-1). He is now literary adviser to
McCLELLAND & STEWART.

Poet, editor, and critic, Lee regards these
trinitarian roles as a calling. A central concern in his critical work *Savage fields: an essay
on literature and cosmology* (1977), and in his
essay 'Cadence, country, silence' (OPEN LET-
TER 2, no. 6, Fall 1973), has been to define
both the creative and critical acts as fundamentally religious in nature. In his first book
of poems, *Kingdom of absence* (1967), he explores 'a cosmos gone askew' in a sequence
of sonnets that abound in images of alienation, absence, loss, and disinheritance. He
comes armed in his next book, *Civil elegies*
(1968)—and in the revised and enlarged
Civil elegies and other poems (1972), which
won a Governor General's Award—with
the pessimism of George GRANT's *Lament for
a nation*, and with his own sense of disappointment and complicity in charting his
country's 'failures of nerve and its sellouts'.
These elegies, which are at times too abstract to engage the reader's senses, expand
beyond themselves and their Canadian focus
to encompass the history of material interests, imperialism, and war.

Lee's dialogue of self and soul continues
through his next two works: *The death of
Harold Ladoo* (1976), an elegy in which the
poet examines the cultural and spiritual currents surrounding the death of his friend and
fellow writer (q.v.) and declares that the notion of art as an absolute brings only 'redemptive lunacy' or 'bush league paranoia';
and *The gods* (1978), a meditation upon life
in the uncivil, technological space we inhabit, where, despite the absence of values

442

and signposts, we should 'honour the gods in their former selves,/albeit obscurely, at a distance, unable/to speak the older tongue; and to wait/till their fury is spent and they call on us again/for passionate awe in our lives, and a clean high style.' These two long poems, and the earlier *Not abstract harmonies but* (1974), were revised and published together in *The gods* (1979).

Perhaps in response to the absence of a listening God, Lee is obsessed with the idea of voice. He has achieved considerable success in presenting poetically 'the texture of our being here', the 'grunt of prose', and the 'grainy sense of life'; and, although his meditations lack the drama and dynamic of narrative, he has provided a moving testament of his search for authentic speech in the age of information explosion and spiritual deafness—and in a country that continues to earn the description *colonial*.

Lee has a talent for writing zany poems for children, collected in *Wiggle to the laundromat* (1970), and in the very popular *Alligator pie* (1974), *Nicholas Knock and other people* (1974), *Garbage delight* (1977), and *The ordinary bath* (1979). In 1983 he began writing song lyrics for the children's TV program *Fraggle Rock*.

Lee edited (with Roberta Charlesworth) two textbooks for high schools, *An anthology of verse* (1964) and *The second century anthology of verse: book 2* (1967). Tributes to his talent as an editor of other people's books, and essays on his writing, are contained in *Task of Passion: Dennis Lee at mid-career* (1982).

See also CHILDREN'S LITERATURE IN ENGLISH: 8, CRITICISM IN ENGLISH: 5(e), and POETRY IN ENGLISH 1950 TO 1982:2.

GARY GEDDES

Le Franc, Marie (1879-1964). Born in Banastère-en-Sarzeau, a hamlet in Brittany, she spent most of her childhood by the sea—one of the main themes in her books. After completing the École Normale in Vannes she became a teacher, but dreamed of travels in exotic lands. In 1906 she came to Montreal to marry Arsène Bessette, a journalist with whom she had corresponded. The wedding did not take place, but she remained in Montreal, where she taught privately and in a girl's school in Westmount. The first few years were hard, but she later acknowledged that they moulded her character. After twenty years in Montreal she returned to Brittany and for the rest of her life divided her time and allegiance between France and Canada. She died in Saint-Germain-en-Laye.

Marie Le Franc's first works were two volumes of conventional poetry, *Les voix du coeur et de l'âme* (1920) and *Les voix de misère et d'allégresse* (Paris, 1923), whose main themes are her love for Canada, her nostalgia for Brittany, and the memory of her two brothers killed in the war. *Grand-Louis l'innocent* (1925)—translated by George and Hilda Shiveley as *The whisper of a name* (1928)—was unnoticed when published in Canada, but when it came out in Paris (1927) it won the Prix Fémina. The success of this novel was due mainly to the poetic and sensuous descriptions of the Breton and Canadian landscapes, which vie with each other in the heroine's mind just as her two loves—for an English-Canadian businessman and for Grand-Louis, an amnesiac fisherman she has met in Brittany—vie in her heart. In several of Le Franc's books human beings become mere personifications of landscape, among them Grand-Louis, Hélier in *Hélier fils des bois* (Paris, 1930), and Antonin in *Le fils de la forêt* (Paris, 1952), which is a kind of remake of *Hélier*. In *La randonnée passionnée* (Paris, 1930) the thin plot is an excuse for describing the landscape of Saint-Maurice. Le Franc is at her best when depicting scenery, and no other francophone writer has captured the spirit of the Laurentian forest as she has. Some of her novels were written with a social message. In *La rivière solitaire* (Paris, 1934) she describes with deep human warmth the hardships endured by a group of unemployed workers from Hull and Montreal sent to clear land in Temiskaming, and *Pêcheurs de Gaspésie* (Paris, 1938) draws attention to the plight of the Gaspé fishermen. *Au pays canadien-français* (Paris, 1932) is a book of essays, with a powerful prose-poem, 'Chant canadien', in which she affirms her love for Canada. *Visages de Montréal* (1934) is a series of sketches of Montrealers she has known. Not all Le Franc's books have a Canadian setting: *Le poste sur la dune* (Paris, 1928), *Dans l'île, roman d'Ouessant* (Paris, 1932), and *Pêcheurs du Morbihan* (Paris, 1946) all take place in Brittany. Several works have both France and Canada as background: *Grand-Louis le revenant* (Paris, 1930), a poor sequel to *Grand-Louis l'innocent*; two books of short stories: *Dans la tourmente* (Issy-les-Moulineaux, 1944) and *O Canada! terre de nos aïeux* (Issy-les-Moulineaux, 1947); and *Inventaire* (Paris, 1930), a strange, introspective work so teeming with images that it sometimes

Le Franc

becomes obscure. Le Franc also wrote a large number of essays and short stories that appeared in French and Canadian periodicals.

Her last publication, the charming *Enfance marine* (1959), about her childhood in Brittany, came out in Montreal, and several of her books were reissued there. Though she never became naturalized, Canadian critics have claimed Le Franc as a Canadian. W.E. Collin included a study of Le Franc's fiction in *The* WHITE SAVANNAHS. France gave her the Légion d'honneur, and Canada named a lake in the Mont Tremblant district after her.

See Paulette Collet, *Marie Le Franc: deux patries, deux exils* (1976), and Madeleine Ducrocq-Poirier, *Marie Le Franc. Au-delà du personnage* (1981).   PAULETTE COLLET

Lefrançois, Alexis (b. 1943). The mystery that surrounds his birthplace is in itself emblematic of his personality and of his place among the contemporary poets of Québec. Lefrançois is a 'nowhere man', a perpetual traveller of the real and the imaginary world. Probably born somewhere in Europe, he lived and studied in Germany between 1955 and 1961. He then moved to Belgium and Greece, the latter being a kind of spiritual homeland to which he returns from time to time and whose presence can be felt in some of his poetry. Since the end of the sixties Lefrançois has divided his time between Québec and various parts of the world—in particular Senegal, where he was a teacher from 1971 to 1973, and Western Europe and the Caribbean.

In spite of a presence in Québec that is both infrequent and discreet, Lefrançois has established himself as an important French-Canadian poet of his generation, ranking with such poets as Michel BEAULIEU, Marcel Bélanger, and Pierre MORENCY. As a poet he has defied any easy definition and has shown a total indifference to the mainstream and the trends of modern Québec poetry. His first two books, *Calcaires* (1971) and *36 petites choses sur la 51* (1971), seem to have been written by two different men. The former contains sharp images and a tense syntax to express anguish, passion, and irrationality: it is remote from any realistic or descriptive concern, almost classic in its economy. The latter is much lighter in tone, close to the tradition of such French poets as Queneau, Prévert, and Vian. Anxiety and sorrow, though very much present, are overwhelmed by a wry humour and by an irony that makes use of the elements of daily life, in particular streets and scenes of cosmopolitan Montreal. Language is made fun of by means of phonetic spellings.

Since 1971 Lefrançois's poems have kept alive these two orientations. After producing *Mais en d'autres fontières déjà . . .* (1976) in a limited edition, he returned the next year with two books that are complementary to his first two: *Rémanences* (1977), a lyric suite that is a search for light and transparency, and *La belle été suivi de la tête* (1977), a playful collection with nursery-rhyme overtones. More recently Lefrançois has published in Paris a book of poems, *Quand je serai grand* (1978), and a tale for children, *Eglantine et Mélancolie* (1979), while continuing to contribute poetry and prose of a more classical tone to Québec literary magazines. It is apparent that childhood is one of the keys to the unity of Lefrançois's work, to its central affirmation that life is deeply irrational but promises somewhere light, clarity, a form of rebirth. Childhood is not for him merely another form of nostalgia: it is a reality that he reaches through language and song and is an answer to the tragedy of life and death.

See Pierre Nepveu, 'Alexis Lefrançois, les mots éblouis de silence', *Lettres québécoises* 4 (Oct. 1977).   PIERRE NEPVEU

Lemay, Pamphile (1837-1918). Léon-Pamphile Lemay, son of a merchant-farmer, was born in Lotbinière, Lower Canada (Qué). After attending the Séminaire de Québec, where he studied law, he travelled to the U.S. and tried many jobs, eventually deciding to enter the priesthood. He enrolled at the seminary of the Université d'Ottawa, but illness obliged him to leave the priesthood and resume the study of law in 1860. Although called to the bar in 1865, Lemay worked as a civil servant, first as a parliamentary translator in Ottawa, then as parliamentary librarian at Quebec, where he compiled the *Catalogue de la bibliothèque de la Législature de Québec* (Lévis, 1873). During the evenings he read his poems at CRÉMAZIE's bookstore, where he met with other members of the ÉCOLE LITTÉRAIRE DE QUÉBEC. A founding member of the Royal Society of Canada, Lemay was a much-honoured poet, winning prizes and an honorary doctorate from Université Laval and the rosette of an Officier de l'Instruction Publique of France.

Lemay's first collection of poems, *Essais poétiques* (Québec, 1865), lacked both originality and technical skill. Admitting his ignorance of the rules of French versification, Lemay set about correcting this, revising most of his poems through subsequent editions. His translation of Longfellow's EVANGELINE, first published in this collection, was re-edited with revisions as *Evangéline* (1870), and again in *Evangéline et autres poèmes de Longfellow* (1912). He had considerable success with the popular epic mode in his *La découverte du Canada* (1869), a 21-stanza narrative of the war against the Indians, and the patriotic *Hymne pour la fête nationale des Canadiens français* (1869), both of which won a Laval poetry contest and were published in *Deux poèmes couronnés par Laval University* (Québec, 1870). In *Les vengeances: poème canadien* (Québec, 1875), a heroic poem ranging from the tragic episodes of 1837 to the picturesque manners of Québec life, Indian vengeance—the kidnapping of a child—is contrasted with the Christian miracle that brings the evil Tonkourou to repentence. Lemay adapted it for the stage (Québec, 1876) and prepared two revisions: *Tonkourou* (Québec, 1888) and *Les vengeances* (Montréal, 1930). *La chaine d'or* (Québec, 1879), sold in aid of the St Vincent de Paul Society, is the true story in rhyme of a man fallen on hard times who is helped by a friend's charity. Equally didactic is *Fables canadiennes* (Québec, 1882), an immensely popular but weak imitation of La Fontaine. After twenty years of working in other genres, Lemay produced his masterpiece, *Les gouttelettes* (Montréal, 1904), a collection of sonnets, characterized by restraint and simplicity, following the Parnassian trend of the decade and featuring religious or rustic scenes transfused with emotion; these finely drawn miniatures are not unlike the work of the CONFEDERATION POETS. Lemay continued polishing and condensing in his last year, bringing out two more revisions and rearrangements of his earlier poems: *Les épis* (1914) and *Reflets d'antan* (1916).

Today there is more interest in Lemay's fiction than in his poetry. Generally condemned in the nineteenth century for heaviness of style, his novels show subtle humour, though they have melodramatic plots, filled with endless peripeteia and complicated subplots, and improbable coincidences that rework the basic themes of the narrative poems. Although written as a pair, *Le pélérin de Sainte-Anne* (Québec, 1877) and *Picounoc le maudit* (Montréal, 1878; rpr. 1972), are connected by plot, not style. The first tells the story of Jos, an orphan involved with the gang of the villain Picounoc

the elder, and his difficulties in marrying his beloved. The sequel develops an *Othello* plot in which the son, Picounoc the damned, plays Iago to his friend Jos. In both books hypocrisy is unmasked, vice punished, and good rewarded. Undaunted by their poor critical reception, Lemay went on to write *L'affaire Sougraine* (Québec, 1884)—a pioneer detective fiction in Québec based on an actual murder committed in the forests of Lotbinière by an Indian, Sougraine—which retains a certain historical interest for its satirical depiction of life in Quebec City. In the same year Lemay's translation of William KIRBY's *The* GOLDEN DOG, *Le Chien d'or* (Québec, 1884), did much to popularize the historical novel in Québec.

After a lengthy silence, Lemay published his major work of prose, *Contes vrais* (Québec, 1899; rev. 1907; first edn. rpr. 1975). His tendency to digress is here accommodated within the form, tale being embedded in tale as narrators exchange stories. Though these legends contain marvellous and supernatural elements, Lemay demystifies the fantastic by placing them in real places and within real historical events. Their variety, and the vivacity of Lemay's style, have made this book a favourite nineteenth-century work.

Fêtes et corvées (Lévis, 1898) is a collection of essays that describe the calendar of rural labours and celebrations in Québec, and includes songs, dances, and stories. Lemay also wrote three comedies that were collected in *Rouge et bleu, comédies* (Québec, 1891), and a one-act vaudeville, produced for the Royal Society, *Entendons-nous* (1911).

See Anne Gagnon's introduction to *Picounoc le maudit* (1972); Romain Legaré's introduction to *Contes vrais* (1973); and the entries on Lemay's works in the *Dictionnaire des oeuvres littéraires du Québec* (1978). For an interesting comparative study linking Lemay with his contemporaries, the Confederation Poets, see Lucille Begley, 'Harmonies canadiennes: Pamphile Le May, Archibald Lampman', *Lectures*, 6 (June 1960).

BARBARA GODARD

Lemelin, Roger (b. 1919). Born in a working-class district of Quebec City, he was the eldest of ten children. He left school in eighth grade during the Depression, beginning to work at fourteen and reading and studying independently. Since 1961 he has been a full-time businessman, first in Quebec City, where he managed advertising, food-processing, and lumber firms, then in Montreal, where he is publisher and president of *La Presse*. His first novel, *Au pied de la pente douce* (1944), translated by Samuel Putnam as *The town below* (1948; NCL 1961), was a pioneer novel of the urban working-class in Québec; its widely read translation provided English-speaking readers with their first insight into that milieu. It won the Prix David and a prize from the Académie française. Lemelin's second novel, *Les* PLOUFFE (1948), translated by Mary Finch as *The Plouffe family* (1950; NCL 1975), became the basis for a popular TV series on the French and English networks of the CBC, beginning in 1952, the year in which Lemelin published *Pierre le magnifique*, translated by Harry Binsse as *In quest of splendour* (1955). In 1946 Lemelin was awarded a Guggenheim fellowship; in 1953 a Rockefeller Foundation grant; and in 1954 the Prix de l'Académie des Arts et des Lettres of Paris. He was made a corresponding member of the Académie Goncourt in 1974.

Lemelin's three novels, all set in Quebec City, are linked thematically and chronologically. The dominant theme is the stifling of ambition in the most gifted young people from the poor sections of the city who are frustrated in their desire to rise above their milieu (the passage upward is represented symbolically in the first two novels by the staircases and roads leading from Lower to Upper Town) and to secure a place in the prosperous secular world. The first novel treats the last years of the Depression; the second starts from that point and continues until the spring of 1945; and the third takes place between the summer of 1949 and the spring of 1950. From the crowded working-class parish in the first novel (centred on two families), the focus shifts in *Les Plouffe* to a single family in a more secular setting that includes various parts of Quebec City (though the United States and the battlefields of Europe are evoked by secondary characters), where family and parish are in a state of disintegration. In the third novel, *Pierre le magnifique*, the parish becomes ill-defined, the action taking place mostly in Upper Town, with some important events occuring at the provincial Parliament Buildings, the Petit and the Grand Séminaire, and Université Laval.

Denis Boucher (who appears in lesser roles in the other two novels) and Jean Colin in *Au pied de la pente douce* are Lemelin's most successful characters, among a group of largely one-dimensional caricatures. In Lemelin's novels the working-class family is dominated by the mother. The father—when he exists—is in the background, timid, crushed, passive, but often breaking out into fits of anger to compensate for his lack of authority. The 'couple'—as a sharing, consultative unit—is often the mother and the priest. A keen observer of French-Canadian life, Lemelin portrays strains and conflicts between the poor and those who are somewhat better off, and sometimes between the poor and the wealthy. The suffering of the poor—who must work for well-to-do '*étrangers*', or depend economically upon non-French Canadians—is sometimes increased by their sense of cultural alienation, symbolized in *Au pied de la pente douce* and *Les Plouffe* by allusions to a people without a flag. Political alienation is suggested in the latter work by French-Canadian recruits faced with hostile English-speaking officers and the Québec masses confronted with ecclesiastical support for conscription.

A critic of the *ancien régime* and of the right-wing nationalism that held sway for so long in Québec, Lemelin castigates—particularly through Denis Boucher—the narrowness and backwardness of the traditional rural parish transplanted into the city, and its spiritual leaders, the clergy. His social satire not only reflects the growing Americanization of Québec and the abrupt end of its isolationism with the advent of the Second World War, but announces the modern, secular, liberal era that was to come to fruition with the Quiet Revolution in the sixties. These three novels display verve, spontaneity, humour, and satire (sometimes diminished by Lemelin's penchant for melodrama). With them Lemelin became, along with Ringuet (Philippe PANNETON) and Gabrielle ROY, an initiator of social realism in French-Canadian fiction.

Lemelin wrote the scripts for the TV version of *Les Plouffe* and for the film (1980) directed by Gilles Carle. He has also published *Fantaisies sur les péchés capitaux* (1940), seven short stories that deal, rather superficially, with physical illness, obsession with sin, adultery, murder, and suicide. The best story, a satire on the clergy of Quebec City, is the much-anthologized 'Le chemin de la croix'. (An English translation by Mary Finch, 'The stations of the Cross', is included in *Canadian short stories* (1960; rpr. 1966) edited by Robert WEAVER. It reappeared in Lemelin's *La culotte en or* (1980), somewhat incongruously stuck in the midst of various reminiscences, particularly of his formative years in Lower Town. The title refers to the gold-coloured shorts—made from the plush seat of a dismembered 1920 Cadillac—that Lemelin's indigent mother forced him to wear. Lemelin also tells, in five episodes, of his acquaintance with the jeweller Albert Guay, who had his wife and 22 other passengers blown up in a DC-3 in north-eastern Québec in Sept. 1949. A somewhat transposed version of this tragedy appears in *Le crime d'Ovide Plouffe* (1982), a sequel to *Les Plouffe*. The fumbling Ovide is given some of the attributes of Guay (minus the criminality) in a very long melodrama that mixes fictional and historical characters (e.g. Trudeau, Jean Marchand), as well as literary genres (satire, social realism, farce). The verve of the earlier novels is present only occasionally in *Le crime* and is overwhelmed by authorial intervention, lengthy explanations (even notes), and stiff dialogue. In June 1983 shooting began on a film and TV version, directed by Gilles Carle and Denys Arcand.

See also NOVELS IN FRENCH 1940 TO 1959: 1.   BEN-Z. SHEK

LeMoine, Sir James MacPherson. See Writing in English in QUÉBEC: 1.

Le Moyne, Jean (b. 1913). Born in Montreal, he almost completed a classical education under the Jesuits at Collège Saint-Marie, but the onset of deafness obliged him to interrupt his studies. With the encouragement of his father, a physician, who fostered in him an interest in Greek culture and the Bible, Le Moyne undertook to educate himself. In this endeavour he was influenced by such diverse figures as Spinoza and Maritain; by French, English, Spanish, Russian, and American literature; the music of Bach, Beethoven, and Mozart; the great religious mystics; and Teilhard de Chardin. With the international perspective thus acquired, he was not affected by the nationalism of his era. He learned from Henry James, however, to identify himself as a North American without forgetting his European heritage. In *Convergences* he wrote: 'I want to keep my French heritage, but it is just as important for me to keep my English chattels and to go to the limit of my American gift of invention.'

In 1929 Le Moyne became associated with a group of dynamic young intellectuals who were to influence the literary and intellectual life of Québec: Robert CHARBONNEAU, Claude Hurtibise, Paul Beaulieu, and the man responsible for directing the evolution of French-Canadian poetry towards modernism, Hector de Saint-Denys GARNEAU. With them, and with Robert ÉLIE, he was active in founding, in 1934, the periodical *La RELÈVE*. The articles by this group—and contributions by the French writers Jacques Maritain, Daniel-Rops, and Emmanuel Mounier—helped to free Québec from its clerical restraints and to open it up to the outside world. Le Moyne published many pieces in *La Relève*; however, while his associates became increasingly interested in literature and social and political problems, he became more preoccupied with religious questions, though not to the exclusion of poetry and music.

Le Moyne began a journalistic career in 1941, working for *La Presse* and transferring in 1943 to *Le Canada*. He joined the CBC in 1951 and was managing editor of *La Revue moderne* from 1953 until 1959, when he became a writer and researcher for the National Film Board. In 1969 he joined the prime minister's staff in Ottawa, where he remained until his retirement in 1978. With Robert Élie he edited Saint-Denys Garneau's *Poésies complètes* (1949), *Journal* (1954), and *Lettres à ses amis* (1967).

Le Moyne's *Convergences* (1961), a collection of articles that first appeared between 1941 and 1961, is one of the notable French-Canadian publications of its time. It is remarkable not only for being a masterpiece of essay writing but also for its brilliant insights into French-Canadian life and literature, which are coloured by an unflinching heterodoxy. These writings were the contribution to the Quiet Revolution of a unique French Canadian: a penetrating thinker and polished literary stylist whose intellectual roots were international rather than provincial. The topics discussed include the author's early intellectual development, theology (a subject that permeates his writing), Saint-Denys Garneau, Teilhard de Chardin, Rabelais, Pickwick, Henry James, and some great composers. But it is his aphoristic essays on aspects of French Canada—focusing on the role of religion and of women—that make the strongest impression. 'Our education', he writes, 'was a long soak in the high water of clericalism.' Ecclesiastical authority, 'having once saved us from the peril of extinction . . . kept up the habit but thereafter tended to save us from life.' A major preoccupation of Le Moyne is the problem of dualism—the relation between the spirit and the flesh—which implies 'a defective attitude toward matter and toward the flesh', engendering guilt, fear, alienation, and accounting for a morbid, neurotic strain in French Canada. 'Two signs suffice to identify this dualism: it ignores Easter and it hates women.' In the French-Canadian society of which he writes, women were relegated to fulfilling the myth of the French-Canadian mother. 'We multiplied greatly though rejecting the flesh . . . we deceived ourselves by entering into a union in which the wife was the mother.' These neuroses had two main effects on French-Canadian fiction over a long period, from Laure Conan (Félicité ANGERS) to Marie-Claire BLAIS, sister-novelists who 'share the same psychological heredity': true women were absent from it, and it had a common subtext: 'It is forbidden to love and be happy because—guess why—because it is a sin.'

Such ideas, which ran counter to the current ideology, were those of a deeply religious man who criticized the Church from within; of a committed French Canadian who, dismissing nationalism as 'a kind of folklore', aspired to be a total man, while seeing for French Canada a destiny and culture of its own. Le Moyne's gifts as a writer and thinker were recognized by several awards: *Convergences* won a Governor General's Award, the Prix France-Canada, and the first prize of the Concours littéraires de la Province de Québec; and in 1968 Le Moyne received the Molson Prize for his unique contribution to Canadian arts and letters. With some essays deleted and replaced by others, an English translation by Philip Stratford, *Convergence: essays from Québec*, was published in 1966. All the above extracts are quoted from that edition.

ANTOINE SIROIS

LePage, John (1812-86). Born at Pownal, P.E.I., he spent most of his life as a school teacher at Malpeque and Charlottetown, where he died. He was best known to the public as an 'occasional' poet, frequently publishing verse in local newspapers under the initials P.L.I. or P.L.J. He also published several pamphlets of verse and a number of broadsheets, but his most ambitious works were *The Island minstrel: a collection of the poetical writings of John LePage* (Charlottetown, 1860) and *The Island minstrel . . . volume II* (Charlottetown, 1867). He wrote public verse for events and occasions: odes, eulogies, elegies, songs, satires. Of these, the most interesting are his satires on social and political events in the life of the Island. Here

he could employ doggerel rhythms and verse forms with devastating effect, puncturing pomposity, stupidity, and greed whenever he saw it. A good example is *An authentic history of the land commission and stirring events in Prince Edward Island* (Charlottetown, 1862)—a satire on the ineffectual efforts of a Royal Commission set up to solve the province's land-tenure problem—in which he balances indignation and a wry sense of irony.   TOM VINCENT

Lepage, Roland. See DRAMA IN FRENCH 1948 TO 1981: 3.

LePan, Douglas (b. 1914). Douglas Valentine LePan was born in Toronto. After obtaining degrees from the Universities of Toronto and Oxford, he served as instructor and tutor in English literature at Harvard University (1938-41), leaving to become personal adviser on army education to General McNaughton. From 1943 to 1945 he served as a gunner with the First Canadian Field Regiment in Italy. At the end of the war he entered the diplomatic service as first secretary on the staff of the High Commissioner's Office in London. It was during these years that he completed and published his first volume of poems *The wounded prince* (1948). LePan remained with the Department of External Affairs until 1959, holding various appointments, including that of special assistant to the secretary of state, counsellor and later minister counsellor at the Canadian Embassy in Washington (1951-5), secretary and director of research of the Royal Commission on Canada's Economic Prospects (1955-8), and assistant under-secretary of state for external affairs (1958-9). After five years as professor of English at Queen's University (1959-64), LePan served as principal of University College, University of Toronto (1964-70), and as University Professor (1970-9). He was appointed senior fellow of Massey College in 1970. In 1976 he was awarded the Lorne Pierce Medal of the Royal Society of Canada for distinguished contributions to Canadian literature.

LePan's poetry, from *The wounded prince* to his recent work, is notable for its formal purity and its immaculate ordering of sight, sound, and sense. A learned poet who can see his own time and his own place from afar as well as from deep within, LePan negotiates his northern rivers with the expectant eye of the coureur-de-bois and the visionary second-sight of the myth-maker. In poems like 'A country without a mythology' and 'Canoe-trip' (*The wounded prince*), he makes us see our own land as an outsider might see it, and for the first time. But the insider with second-sight hints at the riddle of a hidden landscape of the mind, and we come to know our land as no outsider ever could. In much later poems, like 'The green man' and 'Rough sweet land', the myth-making faculty goes beyond hints into realized and original symbol.

LePan's second volume of poetry, *The net and the sword* (1953), which won a Governor-General's Award, expresses the experience of transplanted Canadian men in the Old World—a world of war and desolation in which young Canadian soldiers, homesick for their own distant landscape, aliens in a world they cannot fully comprehend, live and die, brave in their fears and with compassion in their bones. There are reflective and elegiac poems here, like 'Tuscan villa' and 'Elegy in the Romagna', in which LePan contemplates the fury of the moment in the long perspective of history. As no other Canadian has done, LePan in this book has given us in a mighty paradox the utter meaninglessness of war and the indestructible meaning of the intrinsically human.

His novel *The deserter* (1964), which also won a Governor-General's Award, is a quest for a sustaining faith among the broken shards of values at war's end. Pursued by the military police and by gangs of criminals, haunted by the memory of a perfect moment of love (a paradise not to be regained), the protagonist Rusty is 'away without leave' and seemingly without hope. In this nightmare underworld of pursuit and flight, evidences of simple human courage and sacrifice bring Rusty at last to the realization, in a kind of epiphany, that the rock upon which he must build his faith and rest his hope is not made from a dream of the perfect but instead, as D.G. JONES puts it (in *Butterfly on rock*), from 'the love of persons' and 'of a perishing imperfect world'.

In his most recent collection, *Something still to find* (1982), LePan continues his quest for meaning and order. There are poems of savage irony—like 'Hideout' and 'Crack-up'—in which a world 'at peace' seems more terrible than the world at war in *The net and the sword*. There are sensitive, personal poems of loss and dissolution, like 'Hysterica passio' ('O my lost kingdom'). There are poems of the land like 'The green man', which gives to this country its mythology and its meaning. And there are prayer-like poems, like 'Say in October'.

Bright glass of memory (1979) is LePan's recollection of some of the central moments in his career as a public servant. The novelist is at work here in vivid sketches of General McNaughton, Lord Keynes, and Vincent Massey; and we are aware of the poet in the insets and miniatures, and in the reflective moments of self-scrutiny set down in quiet between the fusillades of the politicians. In this book, which gives us a fresh insight into some of the most significant moments in recent Canadian history, we see the man of letters and the man of affairs as one man, single and indivisible.

See S.C. Hamilton, 'European emblem and Canadian image: a study of Douglas LePan's poetry', *Mosaic*, vol. 3, no. 2 (Winter 1970); Donald F. Priestman, 'Man in the maze', CANADIAN LITERATURE 64 (Spring 1975); and F.W. Watt, 'Letters in Canada' (*The deserter*), *University of Toronto Quarterly*, vol. 34 (July 1965). There are discussion of LePan's work in Tom MARSHALL, *Harsh and lovely land* (1979), and D.G. Jones, *Butterfly on rock* (1970).   MALCOLM ROSS

Leprohon, Rosanna (1829-79). Rosanna Eleanora Mullins was born in Montreal, where her Irish-born father was a prosperous merchant. She attended the Convent of the Congregation of Notre Dame and, encouraged to write by the nuns who educated her, she began publishing in The LITERARY GARLAND: under the initials R.E.M. two poems appeared in Nov. 1846, and a story, 'The Stepmother', was serialized in the spring of 1847. Her contributions to this periodical were soon noticed by such people as Susanna MOODIE. (In *The Victoria Magazine*, June 1848, Mrs Moodie praised R.E.M.'s 'Ida Beresford' as a 'story written with great power and vigor'.) As Rosanna Mullins she continued to contribute to the *Garland* until it ceased publication in 1851. In that year she married Jean-Lucien Leprohon, a medical doctor whose ancestors had come to New France in the eighteenth century. They lived in Montreal, except for a few years after their marriage, when they lived in Saint-Charles, Qué.; they had thirteen children.

Three of Rosanna Leprohon's most significant novels appeared in the 1860s: 'The manor house of De Villerai: a tale of Canada under the French dominion', which was serialized in *The Family Herald* from 16 Nov. 1859 to 8 Feb. 1860; *Antoinette de Mirecourt; or Secret marrying and secret sorrowing. A Canadian tale* (Montreal, 1864); and *Armand Durand; or, A promise fulfilled* (Montreal,

1868). Using conventional patterns of nine-teenth-century fiction, each story focuses on aspects of French-Canadian society, with French Canadians as the chief characters. 'The manor house of De Villerai' is set in Canada in the years immediately preceding the Conquest, and *Antoinette de Mirecourt* in Canada shortly 'after the royal standard of England had replaced the fleurs-de-lys of France'. Both novels explore such themes as the psychological problems facing the 'old French' who stayed in 'their country' after 'it had passed under a foreign rule', and love between people of different national, religious, and social backgrounds. Using as her main plot the French Roman Catholic Antoinette's 'secret marriage' to a Protestant English army officer, Mrs Leprohon developed these themes with some complexity in what she called this 'essentially Canadian' tale. *Armand Durand*, set in the nineteenth century, traces what in many ways is a typical French-Canadian career: that of a bright young farmer's son who becomes a lawyer and then a politician. These works were well reviewed at the time of their first publication in both the English- and French-Canadian press, and a French translation of each was published. *Le Manoir de Villerai* (Montréal, 1884) and a French translation of *Armand Durand* were still being published in the mid-1920s.

Mrs Leprohon continued to write for Canadian periodicals until shortly before her death. 'Clive Weston's wedding anniversary', a story dealing with the early years of a Montreal businessman's marriage, was serialized in *The Canadian Monthly and National Review* in 1872. *The Canadian Illustrated News* serialized several stories, including 'Ada Dunmore: an autobiography' (1869-70) and her last published work, 'A school-girl friendship' (1877). Edward Hartley DEWART included in his *Selections from Canadian poets* (1864) five of her poems—one, 'Given and taken', is an elegy on the death of her 'first-born'; another, 'Winter in Canada', celebrates the beauties of winter 'spite of ice and snow'. But it was only after her death that John Lovell published *The poetical works of Mrs. Leprohon (Miss R.E. Mullins)* (Montreal, 1881), compiled and introduced by John Reade.

Mrs Leprohon has never been entirely forgotten, but since the 1970s there has been renewed interest in her life and works. *Antoinette de Mirecourt* has been republished in both the New Canadian Library (1973), with an introduction by Carl KLINCK, and in the Literature of Canada reprint series (1973). Her poems and short stories are included in several recent anthologies of Canadian literature; 'Clive Weston's wedding anniversary', for example, was reprinted in *The evolution of Canadian literature in English*, vol. 1 (1973). Critics have pointed to her gifts as a storyteller, her realistic portrayal of French-Canadian life and French-English relations, and her conservative but nevertheless feminist views on the education of women and on marriage as a partnership. She has been recognized as one of the first English-Canadian writers to depict French Canada in a way that earned the praise of, and resulted in her novels' being read by, both French- and English-Canadians.

See *The* DICTIONARY OF CANADIAN BIOGRAPHY, vol. 10 (1972); the *Dictionnaire des oeuvres littéraires du Québec*, vol. 1(1978); and the essay on Leprohon by Carole Gerson in *Canadian writers and their work: fiction series: volume one* (1983) edited by Robert Lecker, Jack David, and Ellen Quigley.

MARY JANE EDWARDS

Lescarbot, Marc. See DRAMA IN FRENCH: TO 1900 and Writing in NEW FRANCE: 1.

Leslie, Kenneth (1892-1974). Born in Pictou, N.S., he was educated at Dalhousie (B.A. 1912), Nebraska (M.A. 1914), and Harvard, where he continued graduate studies in philosophy and mysticism. His marriage to Elizabeth Moir, daughter of the wealthy Halifax candy merchant, enabled him to pursue such literary interests as the Song Fishermen—a Nova Scotia literary group he formed with Charles G.D. ROBERTS, Bliss CARMAN, Charles BRUCE, and Robert NORWOOD. This period of his life culminated in his best collection of poetry, *By stubborn stars and other poems* (1938), for which he won a Governor General's award.

Leslie then moved to New York, where he edited the radical *Protestant Digest* (later called *Protestant*) from 1938 to 1949. After Senator Joseph McCarthy and Bishop Fulton Sheen implicated him as a Communist (*Life* magazine included him with Charlie Chaplin, Albert Einstein, and Thomas Mann in a group of fifty suspected 'fellow travellers'), he returned to Halifax, where he continued to edit *Protestant* until 1953. As the editor of *Man* and *New man* from 1957 to 1972, he was subjected to RCMP surveillance. Leslie once cited Christ and the First Baptist Church as the sources for his commitment to social reform; such poems as 'O'Malley to the Reds' (inspired by Father Moses Coady of the co-operative self-help Antigonish Movement) suggest his preference for Christian socialism motivated by love, over Marxist violence motivated by rhetoric.

After *Windward rock* (1934), *Lowlands low* (1935), *Such a din!* (1936), and *By stubborn stars*, Leslie turned to political verse that was occasionally relieved by Vachel Lindsay-like African rhythms, as in 'Remember Lamumba'. His best poems, however, are steeped in the imagery of the sea. In 'Cape Breton lullaby', for which he wrote a haunting melody, the lost lambs in a shepherd's pasture remind a mother of her husband spending the night at sea. 'Halibut cove harvest' is a lament for the heroic toil of fishermen who have been replaced by sea-raping trawlers. In 'By stubborn stars', a sonnet-sequence like George Meredith's 'Modern love', Leslie charts the course of a tempest-tost love affair. After a defiant vow to go his own way—'I sail by stubborn stars, let rocks take heed,/and should I sink . . . then sinking be my creed'—he grows to realize that he will find consolation only through song, by which he recognizes his personal experience as archetypal. Sean Haldane's curiously edited selection *The poems of Kenneth Leslie* (1971) led Leslie to make his own selection: *O'Malley to the Reds and other poems* (1972).

Burris Devanney has published an introductory biography and preliminary bibliography in *Canadian Poetry* 5 (1979). See also Susan Perly's memoir, 'We bury our poets; Kenneth Leslie: a homesick Bluenoser', in *The* CANADIAN FORUM (June 1975) and Milton ACORN's tribute in his *Jackpine sonnets* (1977).   DAVID LATHAM

Lesperance, John (1835-91). An American whose family was probably French in origin, he immigrated to Canada from his native Missouri in the late 1860s, settling in St Johns (Saint-Jean), Qué., where he married and worked on *The News and Frontier Advocate*. Later he continued his career as a journalist in Montreal. From 1873 to 1880 he edited *The Canadian Illustrated News* and for several years in the 1880s, using the pseudonym 'Laclède', he contributed a weekly Saturday column to *The Gazette*. In 1888, after a stint as a provincial immigration officer, he became the first editor of *The Dominion Illustrated News*. The articles that were published about Lesperance when he died used information about his early life that he seems to have disseminated, several details of which—including an education in Paris and Heidelberg, and service as a Confederate soldier in the American Civil War—now appear to be false. According to Jesuit records, after studying at St Louis University (1845-51) Lesperance entered the novitiate of St Stanislas at Florissant, Missouri. Although he never completed his training, he studied and taught at Jesuit institutions in Missouri, Kentucky, and New York, and in Namur, Belgium, until 1865—when, owing to illness, he was 'dispensed from his vows by lawful ecclesiastical authority'.

Lesperance made a not-unimportant contribution to late nineteenth-century Canadian culture as an editor and critic. He had an eye for literary talent and regularly published works of poetry and fiction by such writers as Rosanna LEPROHON and Charles MAIR. In a letter to George Taylor Denison in 1889 he reminisced about his 'friend Mair, for whom [he] published, for the first time, his "Last Bison" and "Kanata" in the [*Dominion*] *Illustrated*'. Elected a founding member of the Royal Society of Canada in 1882, Lesperance read at its annual meetings papers on such subjects as 'The literature of French Canada' (1883) and 'The poets of Canada' (1884); in the latter he asked the Society to 'send a word of greeting' to Charles G.D. ROBERTS—whose *Orion* had been published four years before—and to 'encourage him to go on cultivating a talent which must inevitably lead him to fame.'

Lesperance achieved some fame himself for the fiction and poetry he wrote after he came to Canada. Although he never forgot his Missouri background—his story 'My Creoles', a fictionalized autobiographical memoir of the Mississippi Valley, was serialized in the St Louis *Republican* in 1878, over a year before it appeared in *The Canadian Illustrated News*—most of his creative writing had a strong Canadian content. 'Rosalba; or Faithful to two loves. An episode of the Rebellion of 1837-38' (*Canadian Illustrated News*, 1870), published under the pseudonym 'Arthur Faverel', explores English-French relations by dealing with the marriage of a French-Canadian girl first to a Patriote and then to an English-Canadian loyalist. His most popular work, *The Bastonnais: tale of the American invasion of Canada 1775-76* (Toronto, 1877), focuses mainly on events in Québec and on a complicated series of romantic entanglements featuring English and American—or, as the French-Canadians called them, *Bastonnais*—officers and French-Canadian women. Gothic motifs and legends are used to build suspense and mystery in this novel, which appeared originally as a serial in *The Canadian Illustrated News* (1876-7). *One hundred years ago* (Montreal, 1876), a drama set during the American Revolution and dealing with themes similar to those of *The Bastonnais*, is attributed to Lesperance, although it was published anonymously. French translations of 'Rosalba', *The Bastonnais*, and the drama were also published.

Among Lesperance's other works was *Tuque bleue; a Christmas snowshoe sketch* (Montreal, 1882), which uses the courtship of two young couples to describe the activities of the 'Old Montreal' and other snowshoe clubs during the winter of 1872-3. Lesperance also prepared a collection of verse, apparently called 'The book of honour', but it does not seem to have been printed. William Douw LIGHTHALL included three poems by him in *Songs of the great Dominion* (London, 1889).

See William B. Faherty, S.J., *Better the dream: St Louis University and community, 1818-1968* (1968); Mary Jane Edwards, 'Essentially Canadian', CANADIAN LITERATURE 52 (1972); and the articles on the French translations in the *Dictionnaire des oeuvres littéraires du Québec*, vol. I(1978).

MARY JANE EDWARDS

LeSueur, William Dawson. See BIOGRAPHY AND MEMOIRS IN ENGLISH: 2 and HISTORICAL WRITING IN ENGLISH: 4

Levesque, Anne. See ACADIAN LITERATURE: 2(c).

Levi, Helen. See NOVELS IN ENGLISH 1960 TO 1982: OTHER TALENTS, OTHER WORKS: 5.

Levine, Norman (b. 1923). Born and brought up in Ottawa, he served in the RCAF during the Second World War and afterwards studied at McGill University. He went to England in the late 1940s and lived there—for most of the time in St Ives, Cornwall—until his return to Canada in 1980. He is now living in Toronto. He has been a fulltime writer for most of his adult life.

Levine's first book, *The tight-rope walker* (1950)—a collection of poetry, much of it about the physical presence of St Ives—was followed by a war novel, *The angled road* (1952), which was quite unlike the naturalistic and panoramic war novels of such American writers as Norman Mailer and James

Jones. Small in size and scope, sensitive and personal, it is the story of the coming-of-age of David Wrixon, who is commissioned in the RCAF and has two youthful love affairs in England; the dramatic events of life in wartime usually take place offstage.

In the tradition of Henry Miller (mentioned in the Author's Note) and George Orwell, the autobiographical *Canada made me* (1958) sets out to examine Canadian society from the underside as Levine observes life in Canada in the 1950s from a consistent, if unfashionable, point of view. 'I like the lower towns,' he writes, 'the place across the tracks, the poorer streets not far from the river. They represent failure, and for me failure here has a strong appeal.' Setting out on his journey of rediscovery with very little money, he lived in cheap hotels and rooming houses, waiting anxiously for small cheques to reach him, eating in greasy spoons and drinking beer in barren beverage rooms. By the time his journey ends in Quebec City, both the book and its author seem to have been nearly overcome by exhaustion. Levine's portrait of the optimistic and often complacent society of Canada in the 1950s offended some Canadians. Though both English and American editions of *Canada made me* were published in 1958, only a few copies of the English edition were distributed in Canada. While it began to have an underground reputation here, its first Canadian edition didn't appear until 1979, when his own country, in which profound changes had taken place, finally caught up with Levine.

In his fiction Levine has been preoccupied with the precarious existence of the writer (his Grub Street being a resort town in Cornwall), the abrasions and the loving closeness of marriage and family life, and the need to come to terms with the past. He writes autobiographical fiction in the modern manner—examining the details and the repetitions of daily life in an often deliberately fragmentary prose. These preoccupations are the subject of the novel *From a seaside town* (1970) and of such frequently reprinted short stories as 'By a frozen river', 'We all begin in a little magazine', 'Champagne barn', 'To Blisland', 'By the Richelieu', 'I don't want to know anyone too well', and 'Thin ice'—collected in *One-way ticket* (1961), *I don't want to know anyone too well* (1972), *Selected stories* (1975), and *Thin ice* (1979). Levine's short stories have appeared in both popular and small-circulation literary magazines in England and Canada;

many of them have been broadcast by the CBC and BBC; and his work has been widely translated in Europe, particularly in Holland, Switzerland, and East and West Germany.

I walk by the harbour (1976) is a second collection of his poetry, mostly written in St Ives in 1949. Levine edited the anthology *Canadian winter's tales* (1968).

See Frederick Sweet, *Norman Levine* (1983), in Profiles in Canadian Literature, vol. 4.   ROBERT WEAVER

Lewis, Wyndham. See FOREIGN WRITERS ON CANADA IN ENGLISH: 1.

Liberté. Founded in 1959 by such Montreal writers and intellectuals as André Belleau, Jacques GODBOUT, Gilles HÉNAULT, and Fernand OUELLETTE, the magazine was headed by Jean-Guy PILON and Michel van Schendel. Still appearing every two months, it originally set out to become a 'national magazine', featuring contributions by writers—both French- and English-speaking—from across Canada, that would establish a 'forum for the discussion of cultural matters, hoping to attract worthwhile ideas and to promote dialogue'. Very soon, however, with the advent of the Quiet Revolution in the sixties, the magazine ceased to be apolitical and, counting among its contributors some of the founders of the Rassemblement pour l'Indépendance National (R.I.N.), became neo-nationalist and secular; along the lines of the magazine *Cité libre*, it began to advocate the democratization of Québec's political institutions, reform of the educational system, and greater state intervention in the economy. When the Parti Québécois came to power in the seventies, *Liberté* became less reformist and nationalist and gradually reverted to its origins as a cultural and literary magazine. Since the mid-seventies it has featured the work of such writers as François Hébert, René Lapierre, Robert Melançon, François Ricard, and Yvon Rivard. *Liberté*, and especially André Belleau, are responsible for the establishment in the sixties of international writers' conferences.

See also LITERARY MAGAZINES IN QUÉBEC: 3.   JACQUES PELLETIER

Lighthall, William Douw (1857-1954). Although he was born in Hamilton, Ont., Lighthall's career was closely associated with Montreal and the province of Québec. Educated at the Montreal High School and McGill University (B.A., 1879; B.C.L., 1881;

M.A., 1885), he practised law in that city until 1944 and held offices in local historical and literary societies and on municipal commissions and military bodies. Mayor of Westmount from 1900 to 1903, he helped to found the Union of Canadian Municipalities. He wrote three historical sketches of Montreal: *A new Hochelagan burying-ground discovered at Westmount on the western spur of Mount Royal, Montreal, July-September 1898* (Montreal, 1898); *Montreal after 250 years* (Montreal, 1892); and *Sights and shrines of Montreal: a guide book for strangers and a handbook for all lovers of historic spots and incidents* (1907). Lighthall was elected to the Royal Society of Canada in 1905 and became its president in 1918.

The underpinning for Lighthall's literary career was a rather abstract philosophy of idealism, which he described in *Superpersonalism. The outer consciousness, a biological entity: reflections on the independence of instinct and its characteristics in evolution* (1926). In the earliest phase of his writing career he mixed this idealism with a strong dose of Canadian nationalism to produce a novel, *The young seigneur; or, Nation making* (Montreal, 1888)—written under the thin pseudonym 'Wilfrid Châteauclair'—in which a young French-Canadian politician describes to his colleague from Ontario his spiritual growth towards an ideal of national service. The ideal is frustrated, for the young man falls victim to corrupt political practices; but his accidental death rescues the situation by removing him to a plane beyond this world so that he may become an inspiration to all. Death also saves the situation in Lighthall's second novel, *The false chevalier; or, The lifeguard of Marie Antoinette* (Montreal, 1898). A young French Canadian with a prosperous merchant father finds himself in France just prior to the Revolution and succeeds in introducing himself into society as a noble. Brought to trial by the revolutionaries, he chooses to maintain his personal integrity by withholding the truth about himself and accepting execution. Lighthall's idealism found a more remote expression in *The master of life: a romance of the Five Nations and prehistoric Montreal* (1908). Here Lighthall turned the story of Hiawatha, and the founding of the Iroquois confederacy in the sixteenth century, into an object lesson in the power of pure ideals to influence history. The hero's true significance, as in the other novels, comes as much from his death as his deeds.

Lighthall's occasional verse, collected in

Old measures: collected verse (1922), ranges over similar ground—from inspirational pieces on Canada, the Empire, and the war to expressions of man's unity in a greater Spirit and a struggle to rise above the commonality of everyday life.

Lighthall is usually remembered today as editor of the second major anthology of Canadian poetry (the first being that by Edward Hartley DEWART)—*Songs of the great Dominion: voices from the forests and waters, the settlements and cities of Canada* (London, 1889; rpr. 1971). In his introductory essay Lighthall highlighted the new tone of national confidence, while he lamented the editorial limitations that prevented him from including subjective pieces in addition to those descriptive of Canadian life. Nevertheless, the anthology—which includes the poets of the time who are still respected, and many others now forgotten—enjoyed some success and was reissued in a reduced form in 'The Canterbury poets' as *Canadian poems and lays: selections of native verse, reflecting the seasons, legends, and life of the Dominion* (London and New York, 1893).

Lighthall affirmed many of the national and humanistic ideals of late-nineteenth-century Canada and he saw literature as the active promoter of such values—not as the means to explore the reality he experienced in his legal and political careers. CAL SMILEY

Lillard, Charles (b. 1944). Born in Long Beach, California, he was educated at the University of Alaska and the University of British Columbia. He has lived in dozens of locations in Alaska and B.C., working in the bush and on the water. His poems are attempts to understand what he calls the last frontier of the Pacific Northwest. Lillard writes out of a strong sense of place, but his combination of regionalism and Indian mythology has a link with European classicism. He is therefore not a typical bush poet who celebrates the lonely life of man in the wilderness: his poems are neither romantic nor understated. In the last frontier of the Canadian wilderness he finds a frontier of the human spirit.

Since his first collection, *Cultus Coulee* (1971), Lillard has incorporated west-coast Indian mythology in his poems. But in his more disciplined and mature collections, *Drunk on wood* (1973) and *Voice, my shaman* (1976), he finds a balance between Indian mythology and the poetic lessons learned from classical European literature. His major long poem, *Jabble* (1976)—privately

printed and now out of print—was followed by another privately printed collection, *Poems (Mythistoria-I)*, 1979. The imagery of his poems—which are often evocations of rugged landscape—includes rivers, logging trucks, ravens, and totems. Myths intersect with reality as he writes about the wildness of landscape, the wildness within men and women, and the wildness of mythology. As the poet, who was 'born with a landscape', meditates on the power of nature without, he finds spiritual strength within.

Lillard elaborated on his attitude towards the west coast of Canada as guest editor of Issues 45, 50, and 60 of *The MALAHAT REVIEW*. He also co-edited (with J. Michael YATES) *Volvex* (1971), the first collection of poetry in translation from the unofficial languages of Canada; and (with Geoff Hancock) the first collection of fiction in translation from the unofficial languages of Canada in CANADIAN FICTION MAGAZINE (1976).

GEOFF HANCOCK

Literary Garland, The (1838-51). This monthly magazine was begun in Dec. 1838 by Montreal publisher John Lovell—an Irishman who came to Canada in 1820 and later made a reputation as a publisher of directories, school texts, and gazetteers—and his brother-in-law John Gibson, who served initially as editor and after 1842 as co-publisher. For its time the *Garland* had the longest lifespan and was the leading literary journal in British North America. Taking seriously James Holmes's assertion that 'the literature of a country is the *measure* of its progress towards refinement' (Aug. 1840), it set about providing, in the early numbers, a mix of poetry, book reviews, essays, prose fiction, news of the arts, jokes, anecdotes, helpful household hints ('make your own catsup'), and music scores designed to appeal to a wide range of readers. Eventually the *Garland's* pages were filled with essays on linguistics, dramatic sketches (often with a biblical setting), poems of Victorian gift-book calibre, and a plethora of formulaic romantic-historic fiction—material that appealed only to a small coterie of readers and contributors who saw themselves as upholders and promoters of a genteel tradition. Parts of John RICHARDSON's *The Canadian brothers* appeared in the *Garland* (1839); Rosanna Mullins (LEPROHON) contributed poetry and prose from an early age; and Charles SANGSTER contributed poems. But apparently few Canadian writers could produce what the *Garland* thought to be worthy of publication: too rarely did such material as Susanna MOODIE's six sketches—published in 1847 (Jan., Mar., May, June, Aug., Oct.), and later to reappear in ROUGHING IT IN THE BUSH—find its way there. Many of its writers, not surprisingly, had cultural allegiances and values that were located elsewhere, and they were not interested in making the *Garland* a vehicle of Canadian literary expression, which was one of its aims. There was, finally, little to distinguish the *Garland* from its American competitors. With John Gibson's death in 1850 it lost its chief moving force. There were simply not enough subscribers who shared, and were willing to pay for, the cultural values evidenced by the *Garland's* principal contributors, and the financial problems became too daunting. With no. 12 of vol. IX (Dec. 1851) it succumbed to the indifference of those for whom it was to have been a voice, and to foreign competition—a pattern that would be repeated again and again in Canadian periodical publishing.

See Carl F. KLINCK, ed., *Literary history of Canada* (2nd edn, 1976), vol. I, pp. 159-61, 195-6.   S.R. MacGILLIVRAY

Literary magazines in English: 1. THE EIGHTEENTH AND NINETEENTH CENTURIES. The first British North American periodical in English was *The* NOVA SCOTIA MAGAZINE (1789-92). Claiming to be 'a comprehensive review of literature, politics and news', this monthly consisted chiefly of reprinted articles and extracts, both domestic and foreign. *The Quebec Magazine* (1792-4), also a monthly, was our first bilingual magazine. Also depending mostly on reprints, it was described as a 'useful and entertaining repository of science, morals, history, politics, etc., adapted for use in British America'.

After a dry period of two decades the literary community was enlivened by *The Scribbler* (1821-7), 'a series of weekly essays on literary, critical, satirical, moral, and local subjects, interspersed with pieces of poetry', emanating from Montreal. Its colourful editor, 'Samuel Wilcocke', enjoyed gossiping in print about Montreal businessmen and was also notorious for his political lampoons. On the other hand he kept a close watch on the literary scene and reviewed every Canadian book he could find. He claimed, with some justification, to be 'the first that regularly assumed the critic's chair in Canada'. *The Canadian Literary Miscellany* (1822-3) also appeared in Montreal but survived for only six issues. Wilcocke was scornful of the *Miscellany*, claiming it was 'too much occupied with newspaper controversy, and newspaper criticism, both objects that are, in most cases, beneath the dignity of an essayist.'

Other magazines of the 1820s with some literary dimension include *The Christian Examiner* (1819-20) from Kingston; *The Enquirer* (1821-2) from Quebec; and *The* ACADIAN MAGAZINE; *or Literary Mirror* (1826-8), published by Joseph Howe in Halifax. *The Christian Guardian*, founded in York (Toronto) in 1829, is chiefly interesting as the origin of the Methodist Book and Publishing House, later known as the RYERSON PRESS. The two most ambitious magazines of the 1820s were *The Canadian Magazine and Literary Repository* (1823-5), a monthly, and its rival *The Canadian Review and Literary and Historical Journal* (1824-6), a quarterly that was renamed *The Canadian Review and Magazine*. Both of these Montreal periodicals aimed to 'equal' the great British reviews such as *Blackwood's, The Edinburgh Review*, and *The Quarterly*. The first was devoted 'to all that tends to improve the mind, and develope [sic] the moral and physical history of this colony . . .', and 'the diffusion of useful knowledge throughout this country.' The second made a more determined effort to attract Canadian writers. Its literary policy was quite clear: '. . . we prefer the substantial realities of a virtuous education . . . and useful learning, to the evanescent and fanciful colouration of *modern* polite literature.'

The conservatism of these early Canadian magazines may be explained by the fact that the editors themselves were most often immigrants whose tastes had been formed abroad. Their antipathy to Romantic literature, for example, was a reflection of that expressed in the prestigious (and conservative) British quarterlies they sought to emulate. The conditions of the colony simply strengthened such prejudices and confirmed the need for practical counsel, moral firmness, and sobriety of tone. Fiction, for example, especially of the Gothic kind, was firmly discouraged as tending to distract the mind from 'more useful pursuits'. Poetry was welcomed, providing it was 'decorous', or 'graceful', and morally refined. (Poets were urged to avoid high flights of fancy, to ground their verses in their colonial experience, and to lend their talents to the description and celebration of the true beauties and resources of this fair land.) Most of the material of these early magazines, however, was expository, and aside from those pieces written by the editors themselves, much of it was not native, or 'original'. It would be another decade before any editor attempted to rely solely on 'domestic' talent.

In the 1830s five new magazines appeared, none lasting more than three years. From the Maritimes came *The Halifax Monthly Magazine* (1830-3); *The Bee* (1835-8), 'a Weekly Journal devoted to News, Politics, Literature, Agriculture, Etc.'; and *The Colonial* (or *Halifax*) *Pearl* (1837-40). Two other monthlies, emanating from York in 1833, expired within the year: *The Canadian Magazine* and *The* CANADIAN LITERARY MAGAZINE. The latter is of interest for its intention to publish only 'fine Canadian writing'.

The only successful magazine of the pre-Confederation period was *The* LITERARY GARLAND (1838-51), a monthly from Montreal. Patterned after British popular journals like *Godey's Lady's Book*, the *Garland* provided original tales, sketches, and sentimental romances in fiction and verse. Its chief value lay in the encouragement it offered to Canadian writers such as Susanna MOODIE and Catharine Parr TRAILL.

Except for the short-lived *Amaranth* (1841-2), from New Brunswick, the *Garland* was the only literary magazine extant between 1840 and 1845. In 1846 BARKER'S CANADIAN MONTHLY MAGAZINE was founded in Kingston. This, claimed Mrs Moodie, was 'decidedly the best magazine that had appeared in the Upper Province'. However, *Barker's* ceased publication within the year. In 1847 Mrs Moodie and her husband launched *The Victoria Magazine* from Belleville, with the hope of 'inducing a taste for polite literature among the working classes.' It too lasted but one year. (When this magazine was reprinted in 1968 George WOODCOCK described it as representing 'the dregs of early Victorian genteel writing'.) *The Magic Lantern* (1848), though it lasted only six months, is perhaps worth noting for its opposition to the romanticism and sentimentality of the young ladies publishing in such magazines. One other magazine to appear in the 1840s was *The Canadian Gem and Family Visitor* (1848-50), notable chiefly as an indication of a trend towards the popular magazine.

When, mainly because of financial difficulties, the *Garland* folded in 1851, its editor expressed 'the hope that the day will yet come, when Canada will be able to support, not one, but several periodicals, although at present the abundance and cheapness of foreign publications, render it difficult.'

The number of literary magazines did increase in the next quarter of the century. As one might expect, during the decades before and after Confederation their thrust was strongly political. Several were launched and edited by newspapermen; brilliant political journalists like D'Arcy McGEE and Goldwin SMITH were frequent contributors. Their main concern was to foster an independent Canadian literature, which they considered to be essential to the growth of a national consciousness, the necessary correlative of political independence. Hence many pages of their magazines were devoted to problems of the publishing trade, the state of libraries, the encouragement of literary societies and the need for copyright laws and for legislation to protect Canadians against the flood of British and American books and periodicals. These magazines also published reviews of Canadian books and as much creative material by Canadians as space allowed. Clearly their importance is that they attracted talented writers and intellectuals and helped to prepare a climate for the 'first flowering' of Canadian literature in the eighties and nineties.

A selection follows of the more important magazines launched between 1850 and 1875. Their very titles are often an indication of the various concepts of nationalism current at the time: *The* PROVINCIAL: *or Halifax Monthly Magazine* (1852-3); *The Canadian Journal* (1852-78); *The British Colonial Magazine* (1852-3), a weekly from Toronto; *The Anglo-American Magazine* (1852-5), a Toronto monthly; *The British Canadian Review* (1862-3), a Quebec monthly devoted exclusively to Canadian literature; *The British American Magazine* (1863-4), a Toronto monthly; *The British American Review* (1865-7), Toronto; *The Canadian Quarterly Review and Family Magazine* (1864-6), Hamilton; STEWART'S LITERARY QUARTERLY (1867-72), Saint John, N.B.; *The New Dominion Monthly* (1867-79), Montreal; *The Family Herald and Weekly Star* (1869-1968), Montreal; *The Canadian Illustrated News* (1869-83), 'Canada's First National Magazine', a Montreal weekly; *The Canadian Literary Journal* (1870-1), 'devoted to select original literature and the interest of Canadian Literary Societies', Toronto; *The Canadian Literary Magazine* (1871-2), and *The Maritime Monthly* (1873-5), a journal of 'light' literature, science, and art.

Certain trends may be observed among

the publications of this period. One is the growth of the popular family magazine and the mass-circulation illustrated periodical. Both favoured news, human-interest stories, and the literature of entertainment over the more serious intellectual fare provided by the reviews. A second trend is towards diversification. Special areas of interest—such as history, religion, and science—were beginning to generate their own journals. Politics also had its own magazines, such as *The Nation* and *The Bystander*. The prototype of the academic journal also emerged at this time. *The Canadian Journal* (1852-78) is an example. Subtitled 'A Repertory of Industry, Science and Art', this periodical was dominated by academics, notably from the University of Toronto. It did not include creative work. Its broad range of topics was balanced by scholarly depth; and it was directed to the intelligent reader who had not succumbed to the 'invidious habit' of reading for pleasure.

Such diversification clarified (and narrowed) the role of the literary periodical, leaving it to concentrate on the cultivation of polite letters and the dissemination of informed opinion on social, political, and cultural issues. *The Canadian Monthly and National Review* (1872-8), which was continued as ROSE-BELFORD'S CANADIAN MONTHLY (1878-82), was founded 'to deal with Canadian questions and to call forth Canadian talent'. This review provided a forum for the best minds of the decade, including a core of artists and writers involved with the 'Canada First' movement.

In the last quarter of the century only two magazines of comparable stature emerged. *The* WEEK (1883-96), which inherited contributors and subscribers from *The Canadian Monthly*, saw itself as a bastion against the erosion of literary standards, refined taste, and informed opinion. For thirteen years it was the main vehicle for the work of the major poets and essayists of the Confederation period. During the 1890s this central function of the literary periodical was maintained by *The Canadian Magazine* (1893-1939), though it gradually assumed the character of a popular magazine. (During the 1930s it reached a circulation of 90,000.)

Other magazines that flourished in the 1890s followed a similar course. *The Dominion Illustrated Monthly* (1888-95) deliberately broke with the genteel tradition, emphasized a 'masculine' journalism, and unabashedly encouraged fiction as entertainment. *Saturday Night* (1887-) was from the begin-

ning a 'Busy Man's Magazine'; during various periods in its subsequent history, however, it has played a significant literary role. *Maclean's* (1896-) and *Westminster* (1897-1916) had few literary pretensions but they did provide outlets for popular fiction during the early years of the new century. No new review comparable to *The Week* appeared in the next two decades. A very small intellectual minority was served, however, by the new academic quarterlies, which preserved the broad concept of literature as 'letters', providing erudite articles on topics drawn mostly from the humanities. *Queen's Quarterly*, founded in 1893 as an alumni journal, did not become a significant literary periodical until 1920. Since then it has functioned both as an academic review and as an outlet for new Canadian poetry and fiction. *The University of Toronto Quarterly* (1895-) has retained its scholarly character and still does not accept creative material; however, since the 1930s it has performed a valuable service by devoting most of one issue annually to a survey of letters in Canada. *The McGill University Magazine* (1901-6), a semi-annual that lasted for ten issues, was succeeded by the UNIVERSITY MAGAZINE (1907-20), a quarterly edited by Andrew MACPHAIL that set out to provide 'lengthy treatments of subjects of general interest in literature and science'. It took over the *McGill Magazine*'s subscription list and numbered its issues consecutively, beginning with vol. VI. *The Dalhousie Review* (1920-) has been faithful to its chosen role as 'A Canadian Journal of Literature and Opinion'. For several years it carried, in addition to academic essays, a column devoted to 'Topics of the Day', and another devoted to 'Current Magazines'. It reserved several pages too for reviews of current Canadian books.

2. THE TWENTIES AND THIRTIES. No new literary magazines of note appeared in the first two decades of this century. Canada was still culturally insecure, its literary development still dependent on the growth of a national consciousness. Moreover, a lingering taste for late-Victorian romanticism, a persistent pragmatic bent, and a puritanical distrust of the arts combined to favour conservative writing and to delay the acceptance of Modernism in this country. Two magazines emerged in response to these conditions. *The Canadian Bookman*, 'a quarterly devoted to Literature, The Library and The Printed Book', was established in 1919. Its aim was to encourage and protect Canadian

writers by attending to such practical matters as marketing, distribution, and copyright; it also promised to provide much-needed criticism, but this aim was not realized. In 1921 it became the organ of the CANADIAN AUTHORS' ASSOCIATION, which it had helped to found. Thereafter the policy of the magazine was adapted to the needs of that essentially conservative and professionally oriented organization, resorting in the twenties to a noisy boosterism that favoured quantity over quality and patriotism over literary worth. Deservedly or not, the reputation of both the Association and its house-organs has suffered from this stigma ever since. The *Bookman* became *The Canadian Author and Bookman* in 1943. Another CAA publication, *The Canadian Poetry Magazine*, founded in 1936 (the first all-poetry magazine in Canada), was absorbed by the *CA&B* in 1969.

The CANADIAN FORUM (1920-) was founded as an élitist magazine resembling *The* WEEK in format and was equally proud of its minority position. Though openly nationalistic, it maintained a critical stance politically and was strongly opposed to literary boosterism and the mediocrity that policy had encouraged. Its most notable service to Canadian literature in the twenties was its encouragement of rigorous criticism and its openness to the work of the first generation of Canadian Modernists. The *Forum* has remained consistent in policy and format, resisting the trend towards specialization and especially deploring the divorce of literature from the broader (social and political) cultural context.

In the late twenties two other élitist magazines emerged, both from Montreal. During their brief lives neither the *McGill Fortnightly Review* (1925-7), founded by A.J.M. SMITH and F.R. SCOTT, nor *The Canadian Mercury* (1928-9), founded by Scott and Leo KENNEDY, had the breadth of influence of the *Forum*; but in retrospect they are significant as having been the prime vehicles for the early work of the Montreal Modernists headed by Smith and Scott. Because of their aggressive defence of Modernism, these two magazines are sometimes regarded as precursors of the 'littles' of the forties. However, both in appearance and in breadth of content they were much closer to the *Forum* and to such foreign models as *The Nation* or *The New Republic*.

During the thirties, aside from *The Canadian Poetry Magazine*, only two new literary journals were launched. *The Masses* (1932-4)

was primarily political. *The New Frontier* (1936-7), which mixed politics with socially oriented poetry and criticism of a more radical cast than that to be found in the *Forum*, is notable for having published such writers as A.M. KLEIN, Dorothy LIVESAY, and Leo Kennedy. *Quill & Quire*, a journal geared to the needs of booksellers and librarians, was founded in 1935; in 1969 it expanded its format to interest publishers and writers as well and in 1972 introduced formal book reviews.

3. THE FORTIES TO THE SIXTIES. In the forties a new trend became evident. Within the decade about a dozen mimeographed poetry-centred 'little' magazines were founded to challenge the conservatism of the literary establishment. They were distinguished from the traditional minority review by their modest format, their narrower literary focus, and their emphasis on Modern poetry. Not all of these 'littles' were militantly avant-garde, but all were of service in providing much-needed outlets for Canada's second wave of Modernists such as Raymond SOUSTER, Louis DUDEK, Irving LAYTON, Patrick ANDERSON, P.K. PAGE, and Miriam WADDINGTON. CONTEMPORARY VERSE (1941-52), and *The* FIDDLEHEAD (1945-), both eclectic from the start, proved to be the most durable, the latter eventually becoming a full-fledged review that is still very much alive. PREVIEW (1942-5) and FIRST STATEMENT (1942-5), both more aggressively Modern, were short-lived. By the time these two merged to become NORTHERN REVIEW (1945-56), the forties' movement had begun to flag. *Northern Review* became increasingly conservative, thus losing its character as a 'little' and evolving, in the fifties, into something more closely resembling the traditional minority review. *Here and Now* (1947-9), designed and edited by Paul Arthur in Toronto, was distinguished for its large, handsome format, typographic flair, and interesting contents, which included stories, poems, and articles. It lasted for only three issues.

During the fifties over a dozen new magazines appeared. Among the more durable, *Quarry*, founded as a student periodical at Queen's in 1952, later acquired status as an eclectic review. *The* TAMARACK REVIEW (1956-82), an independent quarterly, existed for twenty-five years as one of the prime outlets for 'cosmopolitan' Canadian writing. *Prism* (1959-) began as an independent magazine of contemporary writing and later became associated with the creative-writing program at the University of British Columbia. CANADIAN LITERATURE emerged from the same university in 1959.

Among several new littles, CONTACT (1952-4) and COMBUSTION (1957-60) from Toronto favoured international (mainly American) new writing. CIV/N (1954-6) and *Yes* (1954-70) focused on Montreal poets and the eastern-Canadian tradition of social realism. DELTA (1957-66) was unique. Its editor, Louis Dudek, encouraged the search for new techniques that would serve to extend the tradition of Modernism in Canada without sacrificing ideational content and social relevance. Unlike most other 'littles', *Delta* sought to maintain a broad cultural context for the new poetry.

In the sixties Canadians experienced a new surge of nationalism—encouraged, no doubt, by preparations for the celebration of the Centenary in 1967. The new nationalism coincided with a period of affluence and with a bulge in the numbers of college-age young people. In various combinations these factors account for the sudden growth in quantity, size, and quality of literary magazines. For example, the unprecedented increase in the student population required the expansion of colleges and universities throughout the country; and the new nationalism favoured the introduction of Canadian studies and Canadian literature into the curriculum. In response to the market thus engendered, commercial publishers engaged in a spate of activity to make new and out-of-print Canadian texts available. Scholars now turned their attention more zealously to the provision of histories, bibliographies, and criticism of Canadian writing. And, most importantly, a new generation of talented writers joined their seniors in an enthusiastic exploration of Canadian themes.

The sixties thus witnessed both a burgeoning of scholarship and creativity and the enlargement of a reading public eager to discover its 'Canadian identity' and predisposed towards any writing that explored the 'Canadian imagination' or fostered 'Canadian unity'. Magazines were divided (as they had been from the beginning of Canadian literary history) on the question of how the development of literature in Canada might best be served—whether by deliberate fostering of 'native' talent or by exposure to international 'cosmopolitan' standards.

During this decade *Canadian Literature* had a singular importance. It was the first critical journal exclusively devoted to Canadian literature. With a policy that avoided both chauvinism and academicism, *CL* helped to shape as well as to reflect the new literary nationalism. *Edge* (1963-9) was an independent journal of opinion and the arts. Its policy (and mission) was to confront those elements of the Canadian psyche that had so far inhibited the creative imagination: namely, conservatism, conformity, and puritanism. *The University of Windsor Review* (1965-) combined the function of an academic journal with that of a magazine of new Canadian writing. *The Journal of Canadian Studies* (1966-) from Trent University reserved some pages for topics related to Canadian literature. *Wascana Review* (1966-) addressed itself 'not to residents of Saskatchewan only, or of Canada, or of North America, but to whatever general audience our particular human voice will reach'. *West Coast Review* (1966-), from Simon Fraser University, was devoted to 'contemporary North American' writers. *Mosaic* (1967-) was founded at the University of Manitoba as a scholarly quarterly for the comparative study of literature. *Contemporary Literature in Translation* (1968) from the University of British Columbia provided a wide sampling of foreign writers. (*Prism*, too, founded in 1959 and becoming *Prism International* in 1969, offered many translations along with indigenous writing.) *Ellipse* (1969-), from the University of Sherbrooke, was the first journal to be devoted to the translation of French- and English-Canadian work. *The* MALAHAT REVIEW, from the University of Victoria—founded in 1967 to celebrate 'the coming of age' of our country—was subtitled 'An International Quarterly of Art and Life' and soon gained an international reputation for cosmopolitan excellence.

Three other magazines of this decade deserve special mention. *Evidence* (1960-7), a lively independent review from Toronto, was designed to offer 'evidence' of vigorous new writing in Canada and at the same time give serious attention to the state of cultural institutions in this country. It was eclectic, hoping to provide a bridge between older and younger writers, between the east- and west-coast orientations, and between tradition and contemporary developments. It took a strong stand, however, against experimental writing as an end in itself and expressly declined the role of an avant-garde magazine.

ALPHABET (1960-71), from the University of Western Ontario, was dedicated to the 'iconography of the imagination'. Each issue juxtaposed a particular myth with illustrative documents chosen from local history. Each theme was then reflected in a selection of contemporary verse and prose by Canadian authors. Far from being an academic journal, *Alphabet* played an important role in the ferment of creativity in all the arts in London, Ont., and the surrounding region—an early example of what editor James REANEY has called 'the regional liberation front'. Reaney's fascination with the magical and incantatory powers of language made him more receptive to forms of experimental writing than were the more conservative reviews. Frank DAVEY's OPEN LETTER (1965-9, 1971-) is staid in appearance; but its contents are intellectually most challenging. Subtitled 'A journal of writing and sources', it explores the philosophical assumptions and the theoretical and critical implications of Postmodernism, as well as the more esoteric reaches of the language revolution, and is one of the most advanced journals of its kind anywhere in the world.

Though these magazines existed on the fringe of the establishment, they were known, or at least accessible, to the literary community. By contrast, an extraordinary number of other magazines of the decade remained virtually unknown and inaccessible to the general reading public. These were the new littles—ephemeral, mostly mimeographed, poetry-centred, often 'unperiodical' publications that, taken singly, seem to have small importance but collectively proved very significant. Numbering at least sixty (closer to ninety if we include those that published fewer than four issues) and appearing sporadically throughout the country, they constituted an informal network of little magazines and presses that before the decade was over would redirect the course of poetry in this country. Generally speaking these new littles were indifferent, if not antipathetic, to both nationalism and tradition, whether cosmopolitan, native, or any other. Rather they were linked in spirit with literally thousands of similar underground publications in various languages, and in other countries throughout the world—publications that were not only anti-establishment and anti-academic but also anti-literary. Refusing to be bound by traditional literary forms, categories, conventions, proprieties, and standards, and disdaining the usual criteria of 'successful' publishing, such as regularity of appearance and format, consistent editorial policy, professional production, and financial stability,

the 'little mags', here and abroad, were an affront to the literary establishment. They did not, in fact, address themselves to the literary community but to each other. Their young writers, editors, and publishers were intent upon developing not simply new writing but writing that would reflect a whole new vision of reality, cosmic in its reach, and profoundly challenging to existing values. It would be too much to assume that every little-mag editor entertained such an awesome vision, but it is certainly true that most of them were deliberately (and sometimes gleefully) playing a subversive role. They were an integral part of that international revolutionary subculture that served so effectively during the sixties to disseminate the values of the so-called new consciousness. The new titles reflected a radical and irreverent attitude (*Bust, Weed, Luv, Gronk, Laid Bare, Mainline, Up the Tube with One I Open*), and were often cryptic (BLEW OINTMENT, *Elfin Plot, Tish, Is, Imago*). The writers who published in such magazines represented the first wave of Postmodernism; and their most influential poet-editors—Frank Davey, George BOWERING, Victor COLEMAN, bill BISSETT, and bp NICHOL—were to continue to be in the vanguard of that movement throughout the seventies.

The established literary community of the sixties—absorbed in the definition, defence, and cultivation of 'Canadian Literature'—took little notice of the underground movement. Only one 'little mag' drew serious attention. TISH, founded in 1961, was seen to be most flagrantly under the influence of the 'new poetry' from the United States, loosely identified as 'Black Mountain'. Fear of American imperialism made *Tish* the centre of a controversy that was to be echoed in numerous magazines (and books!) well into the seventies. But the issue was spurious, and the notoriety it engendered served mainly to obscure the broader implications of the little-magazine/small-press movement of the sixties.

The aesthetic to which both the *Tish* poets and their American mentors subscribed simply reflected a multi-faceted movement operating in all the arts and in most countries of the Western world. Its values called for a total transformation of Western consciousness—an ideal that transcends all nationalism and all languages. Proof of this lay very close to home: nationalists from English Canada who attacked the Vancouver poets overlooked the fact that the young avant-garde Québécois writers and editors of the early sixties—spokesmen for the Quiet Revolution—were deeply imbued with the 'new zeitgeist' (as one of them called it), yet their writing owed nothing to *Tish*, nor to any North American influence. Even more significant was the commitment of several of the most conspicuously avant-garde writers in both English Canada and Québec to the 'language revolution', a radically experimental movement that was more advanced in South America and Europe than in the United States. In fact, of the many new poetries to emerge during the decade—sound, found, visual, kinetic, typographic, video, etc.—the *Tish*/Black Mountain variety was the most conservative and, perhaps because of its sense of place, proved to be the most adaptable to a 'Canadian' regionalist orientation.

By the end of the sixties the subculture had surfaced. The underground, as such, no longer had a function and the guerilla fighters (the little mags typical of the decade) died with it.   WYNNE FRANCIS

4. THE SEVENTIES will be remembered as a period of intense literary activity in Canada: there were more active writers than at any other time in Canadian history, and there were more magazines available to publish their work than ever before. In this decade the experimental and fledgling voices of the sixties joined a relatively strong literary community that spoke not only to the Canadian audience but to an international readership. Literary magazines during the seventies—surmounting the challenge of limited financial resources with craft, elegance, and determination—fell into three distinct groups: university-sponsored journals, student magazines, and independent reviews. Physically the magazines took many shapes, ranging from 'perfect-bound' book formats of up to 400 pages to small saddle-stitched (stapled) pamphlets of under twenty pages. As the forum where new authors tested their skills and ideas, and where established authors broke in new work for public viewing, they had a significant influence on Canadian literature.

Long the mainstay of the Canadian literary-magazine community, university magazines continued to maintain their presence, offering not only scholarly criticism but poetry, fiction, and reviews. Journals such as *The* FIDDLEHEAD and *Dalhousie Review* in the Maritimes were joined by *The Antigonish Review* (1971-) from St Francis Xavier Uni-

versity, which extended its Canadian content by introducing many overseas authors to Canadian readers.

Along with the bilingual journal *Ellipse* (1969-), *Le Chien d'Or/Golden Dog* (1972-5) and *Outset* (1973-4) from Sir George Williams University, and *Matrix* (1975-) from Champlain College, also helped to maintain the presence in Québec of creative writing in English.

In Ontario established literary/scholarly journals such as *The University of Toronto Quarterly* and *Queen's Quarterly* continued their leadership in a field that expanded to include *Arc* (1979-) at Carleton University; *Waves* (1972-), which began at York and later became a front-running independent quarterly; *The University of Windsor Review* (1966-), which publishes both criticism and creative writing; *Lakehead University Review* (1968-77); and *The New Quarterly* (1980-) from Waterloo University.

In the West, *Ariel: A Review of International English Literature* (1970-), from the University of Calgary, took a commanding position on the merit of its literary contributions and the quality of its criticism. The University of Manitoba was the centre for three significant periodicals: *The Far Point* (1968-73), *Northern Light* (1975-7; 1981-), and *CV/II* (1975-)—a revival of its influential namesake, CONTEMPORARY VERSE.

Magazines published from such institutions as the University of British Columbia and the University of Victoria present a stunning portrait of the wide variety of writing produced on the west coast during the decade. While *Prism* (1959-) and CANADIAN LITERATURE (1959-) at UBC maintained their importance, new magazines such as *event* (1971-) at Douglas College, the *West Coast* Review at Simon Fraser University, *The* MALAHAT REVIEW (1967-) at the University of Victoria, *Capilano Review* (1972-) at Capilano College, and *Writing* (1979-) at David Thompson University published not only west-coast writing but serious work from the other provinces and abroad.

Scholarship in Canadian literature, particularly in poetry, was noteworthy during the seventies because of the efforts of such journals as *Canadian Poetry: Studies, Documents and Reviews* (1977-) from the University of Western Ontario and *Studies in Canadian Literature* (1976-) and the *Journal of Canadian Poetry* (1978-) from the University of New Brunswick. An important journal of Canadian literary criticism, *Essays on Canadian Writing* (1974-), is published at York University, and ECW Press has evolved from it. Also published at York is *CTR: Canadian Theatre Review* (1974-). Two other important magazines in the same field are *Theatre History in Canada/Histoire du Théâtre au Canada* (1980-) and *Canadian Drama/L'Art dramatique canadien* (1972-).

The student population of Canadian universities also became more active in the publication of literary journals during the seventies. Magazines such as Canada's oldest literary publication *Acta Victoriana* (1878-) at Victoria College, University of Toronto, provided a model for other student periodicals by offering opportunities for young writers and editors to test and polish their skills. Many were well produced and proved that new ideas and energies could be infused into the Canadian literary scene from this quarter. Ontario universities were probably the most lively centres for student publications during the decade, with a large number issuing from the University of Toronto. From 1975 to 1980 no less than seven reputable journals were produced by students at U of T colleges. *The University of Toronto Review* (1975-), founded as a focus for creative writing on the campus, joined a pantheon of others that included *The Grammateion* (1974-) and *Rune* (1974-) from St Michael's College; *The University College Review* (1971-); *Laomedon Review* (1972-9) and later the *Erindale Review* (1981-); *Writ* (1970-) from Innis College; and *Scarborough Fair* (1974-). Ryerson Polytechnical Institute's undergraduates published the finely crafted *White Wall Review* (1973-) and students at the University of Western Ontario produced *The Pom Seed* (1974-). Other Ontario journals included *Portico* (1975-82) at Sheridan College, *Poetry WLU* (1981-) at Wilfrid Laurier University, and *Direction* and *Skatwin*, both published at York University. Noteworthy Maritimes publications included *Sift* (1974-80) at St Mary's University; *Alpha* (1976-9), which succeeded *Either/Or* at Acadia University; *Skylight* (1976-8) at Dalhousie; and *First Encounter* (1969-) at Mount Allison. In Québec *Los* (1975-82) from Loyola College was contemporary with the McGill publications *Cyan Line* (1975-6), *Scrivener* (1981-), and *Atropos. Ion* (1976-8) and *From an Island* (1980-) were produced at the University of Victoria.

Assistance from arts councils, both national and regional, coupled with a new public awakening to the virtues and importance of Canadian writing, plus the demand for opportunities to present new authors, sparked numerous enterprises by individuals who believed that they could create journals that had something unique and important to say. In the Maritimes *Germination* (1974-) from River Hebert, N.S., *Pottersfield Portfolio* (1980-), also from Nova Scotia, and *Iconomatrix* (1975-) from Fredericton became significant forums for poetry, fiction, and reviews on the east coast. In Québec, journals such as *Cross Country* (1975-), *Athanor* (1978-82), and *The Alchemist* (1974-) brought renewed energy to the Montreal scene, while *The Moosehead Review* (1977-), a lively journal of poetry and fiction, appeared from Waterville, Qué.

Ontario cities—Toronto, Hamilton, and London, in particular—became centres for a large number of independent magazines, partly because of the number of editors there who were able to devote their time to such publications and the abundance of writers who could contribute to them, and partly because of the readership that was at hand. Of the Toronto periodicals, DESCANT (1970-) emerged from its origins as a graduate-student magazine at the University of Toronto to become one of Canada's leading magazines for poetry and fiction. CANADIAN FICTION MAGAZINE (1971-), also based in Toronto, took the lead in the publication of short stories and fiction-related articles. *Poetry Canada Review* (1979-) appeared quarterly in tabloid format and featured new writing by both established and younger poets, as well as articles on poetry activities from across the country. *Cross Canada Writers Quarterly* (1979-) published a newsstand magazine that offered articles, creative writing, and reviews, as well as the first cross-country workshop by mail. *Poetry Toronto* (1975-) served as a vital instrument for poets and writers by providing monthly market information and listings of literary activities. EXILE (1972-), although Toronto based, expanded its horizons to the international sphere and published outstanding works of major authors, as did *Intrinsic* (1975-9). The Haiku interests on the Toronto scene were served by *Cicada* (1976-81) and later *Inkstone* (1982-). Doubleday Company Limited, based in Toronto, published the annual anthology *Aurora* (1977-80), which was considered by many to be the finest bridge between book-style literary magazines and actual books. *The Canadian Literary Review* (1982-), published in Toronto, was designed as a national literary review with editorial input from across the country. Other

Toronto magazines included the feminist journal *Fireweed* (1975-), *Harvest* (1977-82), *Nimbus* (1979-82), *Another Poetry Magazine* (1970-71), and *Acanthus* (1978-80), all of which featured poetry and short fiction in saddle-stitched formats. Having been founded in Victoria (1965), OPEN LETTER began to be published in Toronto in 1971. The most recent magazine to appear (out of Toronto) is *Ethos* (1983-), devoted to literature and the arts, with an international perspective. Hamilton and London boasted several small but lively journals during the seventies and early eighties. In Hamilton *Wee Giant* (1977-82) and *Origins* (1967-83) published poetry in quarterly formats, while the London literary scene featured several journals: *Stuffed Crocodile* (1972-8); *Jubilee* (1973-5); *SWOP* (1977-80), which also featured information on markets and short reviews; *Applegarth's Folly* (1973-9); *Brick* (1978-), a fine journal of reviews and literary articles; *Other Voices* (1965-75); *Twelfth Key* (1975-8); and *Watchwords* (1982-). Northern Ontario was represented by the visually beautiful *Northward Journal* (1975-) from Moonbeam; by *Copperfield* (1969-76), which, like the *Journal*, focused on northern themes and issues; and by the North Bay magazine *Nebula* (1974-). Ottawa was the centre for several magazines that included *Manna* (1972-4), *Northern Journey* (1971-7), *Review Ottawa* (1977-8), and its successor *Anthos* (1978-). *Canadian Children's Literature* (1975-), published in Guelph, is a journal of criticism and review.

Manitoba, Saskatchewan, and Alberta were also part of the literary explosion of the seventies. Of the magazines that appeared from the West during the decade, *Grain* (1973-), published in Saskatoon, evolved as the leader in western writing and featured some of the most important prairie authors. Also significant were *Imago* (1965-73), which began in Calgary and later moved between Montreal and Vancouver; *Dandelion* (1975-), published in Calgary; *Poetic License* (1977-80) from Edmonton; *White Pelican* (1971-8), also from Edmonton: *Salt* (1972-80) from Moose Jaw; *The Camrose Review* (1981-) from Camrose, Alta; *Wordloom* (1981-) from Winnipeg; and *The Alberta Poetry Yearbook* (1927-), an annual publication of the CANADIAN AUTHORS' ASSOCIATION.

On the west coast the feminist magazine *Room of One's Own* (1974-), published in Vancouver, consistently offers fine writing and editing. Other notable independent west-coast literary magazines from the seventies and early eighties include *WOT* (1979-81), *Karaki* (1976-9), *Periodics* (1977-80), *Tuatara* (1969-72)—all from Victoria—and *Blackfish* (1971-5) from Burnaby and *Air* (1971-5) from Vancouver.

By 1980 Canada has as many literary magazines per capita as the United States—a fact that is a testament to the energies of those involved in their publication and to the productivity of Canadian writers. The most startling characteristic of these magazines is their range of content. The sudden rise in the number of journals stimulated the pursuit of excellence.   BRUCE MEYER

Literary magazines in Québec. Periodicals have always been instrumental in the dissemination, and even in the creation, of Québec literature. In the nineteenth century book publishers were reluctant to produce works of fiction. To compensate several newspapers brought out serially either complete novels or shorter pieces, such as stories and poems. When specifically literary magazines began to appear, they functioned as organs for various groups that pointed to important moments in Québec literature.

1. THE NINETEENTH CENTURY. The first goal of one of the earliest periodicals, *La Ruche littéraire illustrée* (1853-9), was to bring together Canadian literary works, but it soon began to include works translated from other languages as well; and in fact it specialized in stories with a romantic tinge by writers newly arrived from France, of whom the best known was Henri-Émile CHEVALIER. Three publications that first appeared in the mid-nineteenth century, at the time of the MOUVEMENT LITTÉRAIRE DE QUÉBEC, made the first real attempts to become established. Les SOIRÉES CANADIENNES (1861-5), subtitled 'a compendium of national literature', had as an epigraph Nodier's celebrated remark: 'Let us make haste to recount the charming stories of the people before they are forgotten.' Its goal was 'to rescue our fine Canadian legends from the oblivion which now threatens them more than ever, thereby maintaining those memories that have been preserved by our old storytellers and making popular certain little-known episodes in the history of our country.' The first issue contained 'Trois légendes de mon pays' by Joseph-Charles TACHÉ and 'La Jongleuse' by Abbé CASGRAIN; among the other contributors and editors were Hubert LARUE and Antoine GÉRIN-LAJOIE. *Les Soirées canadiennes* sought to promote a literature based on folklore and

banished from its pages any political discussion. Founded as a result of dissent within the group at *Les Soirées*, Le FOYER CANADIEN (1862-6) was a literary and historical compendium with the same objectives, while it also aimed to publish 'any Canadian work distinguished by originality in point of view, thought, or style'—one of which was Antoine Gérin-Lajoie's JEAN RIVARD, *économiste*. These two periodicals were succeeded by *Les Nouvelles Soirées canadiennes* (1882-8), which sought to encourage original literary works with the aim of 'strengthening our institutions and our language', even stating that it would 'be first and always Canadian and Catholic, or, in other words, essentially national.' Expressing a concept of literature that was basically moral and nationalist, it promoted a sense of rootedness and articulated a Canadian specificity that was most often evoked through folkloric themes. In a general way these leanings were shared by *L'Opinion publique* (1870-83), a political and literary magazine, *L'Album universel* (1884-1902), and *La Revue canadienne* (1864-1922), which was more open to the overall intellectual life of French Canada.

2. THE EARLY TWENTIETH CENTURY. The question of a national literature was being examined in terms of the regional, as opposed to the universal, option when in 1909 a group of writers founded *Le Terroir*, which set out to give prominence to 'the French-Canadian soul', as well as to make possible 'the exaltation of our native soil' and the 'bringing together of Canadian literary youth'. Under the direction of members of the ÉCOLE LITTÉRAIRE DE MONTRÉAL, including Charles GILL and Albert Ferland, the contents of the magazine were very eclectic and it lasted only one year. Some ten years later an equally short-lived publication, *Le NIGOG* (1918), echoed *Le Terroir* by opting for a certain universalism and declaring the need to relate to modern times and contemporary literature. The debates stirred up by these magazines were to be continued in the work of such essayists and pamphleteers as Victor Barbeau and Claude-Henri GRIGNON in the 1930s and centred on the question of the kind of French to be used for writing.

At this time other periodicals were integrating literature into a broader perspective. *Les Idées* (1935-9), edited by Albert Pelletier, attacked the 'lack of a life of the mind' and spoke of an intellectual life that was getting soft as it moved 'gradually into the limbo of instinct'. *La RELÈVE* (1934-41), the most important cultural magazine of the first part of

the twentieth century, was put out by Robert CHARBONNEAU, Paul Beaulieu, Hector de Saint-Denys GARNEAU, and Robert ÉLIE. It aimed at a spiritual and humanistic renewal to which art would be a privileged witness: 'In the great revolution that is taking shape and that should signify humanity's return to spiritual concerns', wrote Saint-Denys Garneau, 'it is essential that art—that crown of man, the supreme expression of his soul and of his will—rediscover its lost meaning and become the splendid expression of that upward striving.' The literary works of this group were far removed from folklore: they focused on the expression of the ego, the inner life, and those spiritual problems that affected modern civilization. *Amérique française* (1941-64) would pursue these themes, while posing the problem of twin loyalties, both French and American.

3. THE MID-TWENTIETH CENTURY. As they were moving progressively away from a narrow notion of a 'national literature', later twentieth-century periodicals continued to bear the mark of a certain sort of Catholicism. Even *Cité libre* (1950-66) did not escape. This magazine—founded in the midst of the Duplessis period by Pierre Elliott Trudeau, Jean Marchand, and Gérard Pelletier, who are better known today for their subsequent political careers—opposed the conservative ideology that had dominated Québec for more than a century, advocating a form of internationalism at the expense of the concept of 'nation'. More political than literary, *Cité libre* nonetheless left a mark on Québec's cultural history by declaring—two years after the publication of REFUS GLOBAL (1948)—the right to speak and to dissent. The group would soon become the favourite target of the editors of PARTI PRIS (1963-8), a political and cultural periodical with a threefold objective: an independent, socialist, and secular Québec. Most of its editorial committee was composed of writers: Paul CHAMBERLAND, Jacques RENAUD, André MAJOR, *et al*. The *parti pris* group differed from earlier movements, first of all because they moved the national question to the left, considering the case for Québec without confining it to a hidebound nationalism. Important as well for articulating the relations between literature and politics—and for challenging both—*parti pris* was concerned with both the literary *fact* (that is, literature as an institution) and the *making* of literature, bringing together the practice of fiction and a theory to explain this practice. Among the questions fre-

quently taken up in its pages were the status of the writer, the situation of culture and literature in a colonial context, and the sort of French to be used. *parti pris* is particularly well known for having briefly, and for political reasons, espoused JOUAL; its writers sought as well to take up Sartre's great themes—namely, 'For whom and for what do we write?'—in the practice of a literature that would be known henceforth as Québécois.

Between the founding of *Cité libre* and *parti pris* another periodical appeared, which today is still one of the most prestigious literary magazines in Québec. LIBERTÉ, founded in 1959, described itself first as 'a centre for the discussion of cultural problems, which intends to welcome all valid ways of thinking as well as to encourage dialogue.' Far from being 'the organ of a closed group', it intended to be 'open to everyone with something to say'. *Liberté*—whose editors specified at the outset that it would not be associated with any political position—was a meeting-place and crossroads for various literary and cultural currents. An issue from 1961 does, however, contain a sort of manifesto: 'We are for: total, universal, immediate disarmament; love, liberty, friendship; jazz; those who have the youth of Varèse, Russell, Henry Miller, Abel Gance; a Department of Public Education; respect for consciences; cultural democracy; secular universities; the refined use of sex.' In its early years *Liberté* strove to denounce the problems of 'culture fatigue'. In 1963 it published the first writings of the *parti pris* group, and titled one of its issues 'Québec and the language struggle'. Among more recent special issues, the Acts of the various meetings organized by the editorial board each year are important documents. Although *Liberté* publishes works from such countries as Israel, the United States, France, and Romania, it still reserves a select spot for young local writers. After several years in transition, the editorship of the magazine passed from Jean-Guy PILON to François Ricard; the editorial committee was reorganized and the magazine got its second wind. In 1981 a highly valued issue appeared on 'The Québec literary institution'.

4. THE MODERNIST PERIOD. The average life-span of a literary generation, particularly in Québec, is about ten years. Thus, while PARTI PRIS rebelled against *Cité libre* and took a position to the left of LIBERTÉ, *La BARRE DU JOUR* (1965-76), founded by Nicole BROSSARD and Roger Soublières,

broke with a certain social concept of literature, claiming that the writer was no longer a seismograph to measure society's pain but was concerned with his or her own urges. After a few years and a change in editorial committee, *La Barre du jour* became *La Nouvelle Barre du jour* (1977-), and the writing expresses a modernism midway between theory and fiction; theory, considered a form of fiction, even becomes fiction—hence its inevitable step into formalism that led to charges of mandarinism and class-specific writing. To such criticisms the new writers reply that reading habits inculcated by bourgeois culture must be changed. For more easily located and recognizable codes they substitute the notion of the text; over linear, absolutist writing, they prefer the fragment. Successive editorial teams have become involved in a series of renewals, violations, and reversals of language. Nothing is self-evident: in the beginning is the 'game', which leads to the 'fabrication' of fables and tales written 'literally', to the 'page/image' and to 'diasynchronic chronicles'. The challenge is considerable. Each text must reinvent itself, under penalty of falling into the comfortable purr of the familiar. Inevitably the challenge is not always successful.

Alongside *La Barre du jour*, *Les Herbes rouges* (1968-), under Marcel and François Hébert, devotes each issue, in the form of a small volume, to work by a single writer. Addressing the central questions of modernism, it offers no programmatic utterances: practice is enough. Concerning this practice, Roger DesRoches, like the editors of *La Barre du jour*, talks of the materiality of the text as a place for questioning and for play, of the intention to 'illustrate the particularities of pleasure and desire, of the body as the seat of thought, thinking of its fine deaths', and also of 'differences in all manner of madness'. The contents of *Les Herbes rouges* are usually more provocative than those of *La Barre du jour*; more subversive and more playful too; more counter-cultural and mythic. Everything is raw material for texts, for poetry—from advertising to comic strips, from social discourse to political awareness.

Estuaire (1976-), the product of a group that calls itself 'poètes sur paroles', is essentially a poetry magazine, publishing work based on the oral tradition, on proclamation and sharing. Pierre MORENCY, one of its guiding lights, once rented a billboard in the heart of Quebec City and had his poems printed on it. Other members of the group have constructed picture-poems and poster-poems. *Estuaire* reserves a special place for poetry for the eye and the voice, and for a mode of speech that has deep roots in the heart of the land and the landscape. It is no coincidence that the magazine has published interviews with Gaston MIRON, Hélias and Pierre PERRAULT—all craftsmen of the word who were moulded initially by the heritage of folklore. This initial orientation, how-ever, seems to be gradually giving way as *Estuaire* turns to a more modern poetry that nonetheless remains to some extent accessi-ble to the reader.

5. RECENT CROSS-CULTURAL VENTURES. Between 1960 and 1980 other magazines were born, only to live somewhat ephe-meral lives. *Maintenant* (1962-75) attempted to reconcile the national question and left-wing Catholicism. *Mainmise* (1970-8) made itself the organ for an American-style counter-culture attempting to take root in Québec, while *Presqu'Amérique* (1970-3) sought to define new kinds of local identifi-cation. *Brèches* (1973-7) examined literature and culture in the wake of Parisian critical currents. Both *Chroniques* (1975-8) and *Stratégie* (1972-7) analysed the literary object and its surrounding critical discourses from a Marxist perspective. *Les Têtes de pioche* (1976-9) brought together the most radical elements of the women's movement, then in full bloom. *Les Écrits du Canada français* (1954-) and *Les Cahiers des dix* (1940-), if they still exist, appear so irregularly that their impact is negligible.

Informational literary periodicals are *Livres et auteurs québécois* (1961), an annual collection of critical writing on Québec lit-erary production; *Lettres québécoises* (1976), a systematic review of current publications; and *Spirale* (1979), in which literary criti-cism runs counter to clichés and conven-tional wisdom. In the field of theatre the ex-cellent *Jeu* (1976) makes the link between theory and practice, keeps a close watch on theatrical productions, interviews troupes, and provides an account of what is at stake in theatrical activity in Québec.

Various scholarly periodicals put out by the universities are generally devoted to the study of one theme, one writer, or one ques-tion. This is the case for *Études littéraires* (Laval) and *Études françaises* (Université de Montréal). VOIX ET IMAGES, published by Les Presses de l'Université du Québec and born out of *Voix et images du pays*, the only publication devoted entirely to Québec,

allots part of each issue to one writer. *Ellipse* (Université de Sherbrooke) is of singular importance in presenting literary works, generally poetry, in both French and Eng-lish, with the original versions on facing pages. *Présence francophone* provides an ac-count of literary activity in French-language countries. In Ottawa *Incidences* and *La Revue de l'Université d'Ottawa* open their pages to literary questions.

A number of new publications have ap-peared since 1975: *Dérives* (1975), *Possibles* (1976), *Intervention* (1978), *Le Temps fou* (1978), *Focus* (1978). Reflecting a spirit of anti-dogmatism, they share a desire to tear down the walls dividing various fields of cultural activity. Although *Intervention* is primarily concerned with various artistic ac-tivities, it also deals with such related mat-ters as distribution, galleries, publishing, etc., as well as with current sociological issues and government policies. *Dérives* is an interdisciplinary publication that attempts to establish a dialogue between Québec and the Third World and publishes articles by very diverse contributors. *Possibles*, which brings together sociologists and literary writers, has since its inception been musing over Québec, its political future, and the self-management practices that are becoming es-tablished there; literary and artistic creation is viewed as an essential component of the societal imagination, a kind of preferred meeting-ground for both individual and joint 'possibilities'. *Le Temps fou*, the only one of these periodicals to appear monthly, systematically detects what is innovative in different areas of culture and society, while *Focus* provides an account of activities in the Saguenay-Lac Saint-Jean area. In these inter-disciplinary times new periodicals are inte-grating literary creation in a global social project. And in this time of decentralization a brand new literary periodical has appeared in Acadia, called *Héloise* (1981). In keeping with the widespread interest in the extrater-restrial, two publications are devoted to science fiction: *Solaris* (formerly *Requiem*, 1975) and *Imagine* (1979).

An analysis of cultural periodicals shows that several trends co-exist, survive, and struggle for symbolic recognition, whereas the literary history of Québec had accus-tomed us to seeing a single dominant group arise in any one period. These many facets make generalization difficult, but several conclusions may be drawn. Between 1960 and 1980 the writer generally shed his bad conscience and moved away from the national 'wailing wall'; writing became a matter of craft, with roots in a social and political context, in which it is easier to say *I* than *we*; and where groups are concerned, ruptures are less violent than at the time of REFUS GLOBAL and PARTI PRIS. Nowadays opposition has given way to transposition and transgression.   LISE GAUVIN

Little, Jean. (b. 1932). Born in Taiwan to parents who were medical missionaries for the United Church of Canada, she came to Canada shortly before the Second World War. Almost blind since birth, she was educated in Guelph, where she still lives, and at Victoria College, University of Toronto, receiving an Honours B.A. in English (1955). After training as a 'Special Education' teacher in the U.S.A., she combined teaching and writing until royalties from her children's books supported her entirely. She has travelled extensively, living for two years in Japan, and has made numerous lecture tours in the U.S. and Canada. She periodically teaches courses in children's literature at the University of Guelph.

Jean Little has published ten novels to date: *Mine for keeps* (1962), *Home from far* (1965), *Spring begins in March* (1966), *Take wing* (1968), *One to grow on* (1969), *Look through my window* (1970), *Kate* (1971), *From Anna* (1972), *Stand in the wind* (1975), and *Listen for the singing* (1977). Her own childhood memories, her eleven nieces and nephews, and the children she meets provide stimulus for her imagination. Her themes—such as a child's need for friendship and acceptance—are universal ones that she ties to a contemporary time and place. She occasionally depicts disabled children, but always goes beyond the handicap to examine the universalities it engenders: feelings of self-pity, loneliness, inadequacy, jealousy. Her psychological realism explores various external manifestations of inner tensions in children, and shows the child working towards greater self-understanding after a crisis. Jean Little has received several awards, including the Canada Council Children's Book Award (1977) and the Youth Literature Prize from Germany (1981), and her books have been translated into French, German, Danish, Dutch, Japanese, and Braille.

See also CHILDREN'S LITERATURE IN ENGLISH: 8.   MARY RUBIO

Livesay, Dorothy (b. 1909). Born in Winnipeg, she came to Toronto in 1920 when her father became manager of the Canadian Press. She attended Glen Mawr private school for girls, where she met women teachers who—together with her father—encouraged her to consider questions of atheism and socialism. Influenced by Shaw, Ibsen, and Emma Goldman, whose lecture series in Toronto she attended early in 1926, she enrolled in the fall of that year in French and Italian at Trinity College, University of Toronto, where her evolving ideas about socialism and women's rights led her to the private study of Emily Dickinson, H.D., Katharine Mansfield, and the sociological writings of Friedrich Engels. She published her first poetry collection, *Green pitcher* (1928), when only eighteen. Although these were well-crafted poems that not only showed skilled use of the imagist technique but prefigured Margaret ATWOOD's condemnations of exploitative and fearful attitudes to the Canadian landscape, the book disappointed Livesay by its failure to deal openly with social issues. She spent 1929-30, her junior year of university study, in the south of France, and on graduation in 1931 went to Paris to study at the Sorbonne. Deeply moved by the poverty and violence created by the Depression, she returned in 1932 to the University of Toronto, where she entered the School of Social Work and shortly after joined the Communist Party. Her second book, *Signpost* (1932), however, reflected few of these interests; rather it showed the increasing sophistication of her imagist skills, as in 'Green rain', and an original sense of feminine sexuality.

As is now well documented in her retrospective collection of essays, poems, letters, and reminiscences, *Right hand left hand* (1977), Livesay spent the thirties organizing for the Party; employed as a social worker in Montreal, Englewood, N.J., and Vancouver; writing for the Marxist news magazine *New Frontier*; and learning from Auden, Spender, and Day Lewis how to marry political ideas to poetic craftsmanship. Although Livesay's powerful poems from this period, focusing on Depression conditions and the Spanish Civil War, did not see book publication until *Selected poems* (1956) and *Collected poems: the two seasons* (1972), they appeared throughout the thirties in periodicals such as *New Frontier*, The CANADIAN FORUM, and *Canadian Poetry Magazine*.

In the 1940s Livesay continued to publish overtly political poetry: *Day and night* (1944, Governor General's Award), concerning workers' contributions to wartime industry;

Poems for people (1947, Governor General's Award); and *Call my people home* (1950), a verse-play for radio dramatizing the persecution of Japanese-Canadians during the Second World War. Most of this work was marred by unconvincing dramatic voices and simplistic political diction.

After an extended residence in Vancouver, where she married and raised two children, Livesay travelled to Zambia, where she taught English for UNESCO from 1960 to 1963. In the mid-1960s, stimulated by the rapidly evolving Vancouver poetry scene and by her study of linguistics while earning an M.Ed. from the University of British Columbia (1963-4), Livesay began writing a new kind of poetry, concrete and phenomenological in style, and in content centring on womanhood and physical love. These changes resulted in her two finest books: *The unquiet bed* (1967) and *Plainsongs* (1969). A new concern to give voice to vigorous old age appeared in *Ice age* (1975) and *The woman I am* (1977). Overall, Livesay's career has had a remarkable range, spanning—as she notes herself in *Right hand left hand*—the imagist lyric of *Green pitcher*, political polemic in the poems of the 1930s, documentary realism in *Day and night* and *Call my people home*, and the lyric confessional in her most recent work. Livesay's other publications include the long-poem collection *The documentaries* (1968), *Plainsongs extended* (1971), *Nine poems of farewell* (1973), *The raw edges: voices from our time* (1981), and *Beginnings: a Winnipeg childhood* (1973), fictionalized reminiscences. She also edited the anthology *Forty women poets of Canada* (1972).

Livesay has been writer-in-residence and professor of English at several Canadian universities. She divides her time between a cottage in Winnipeg in the summer and an island south of Vancouver in the winter. In 1975 Livesay founded the important magazine of poetry and poetry criticism *CV/II*, the title of which is a tribute to Alan Crawley's CONTEMPORARY VERSE (1942-53).

A special issue of *A Room of One's Own*, vol. 5, no. 1/2 (1979) is devoted to Livesay. See also Susan Zimmerman, 'Livesay's houses', CANADIAN LITERATURE 61 (Summer 1974).   FRANK DAVEY

Lochhead, Douglas (b. 1922). Born in Guelph, Ont., Douglas Grant Lochhead grew up in Fredericton, N.B., and Ottawa. He was educated at McGill and the University of Toronto and served overseas as a Canadian army officer in the Second World War. Before becoming professor of English at University College, University of Toronto (and librarian of Massey College there), he taught at the University of Victoria, and at Cornell, Dalhousie, and York Universities. He is currently Davidson Professor of Canadian Studies and director of the Centre for Canadian Studies at Mount Allison University, Sackville, N.B.

The short lyrics that make up Lochhead's first collection of poems, *The heart is fire* (1959)—in which he responds to his experience of war and the primal forces of nature—exhibit his preference for conversational rhythms, impressionistic but sharply observed detail, and forceful imagery that is muted by irony, wit, and balance. The collections that followed in this period are similar in their dependence on the concreteness associated with the forces of wind, sea, stone, and sky. These works include *It is all around* (1960), *Poems in folio, #1, #2* (1959 and 1963), and *Poet talking* (1964).

Lochhead's second phase begins with *A & B & C &: an alphabet* (1969) and develops with *Millwood Road: poems* (1970), which are suburban, domestic, nostalgic but also restless in tone. A mundane Toronto world is transformed by sprinklings of wit, irony, beauty, pathos, and Scots whimsy. There is as well a keen awareness of nature's power over our supposedly urbanized souls. *Prayers in a field* (1974)—ten poems presented in a fine limited edition, with five drawings by Paulette Dennis—is a celebratory and expiatory chant to accompany the scattering of the body's ashes, a record of spiritual resolution, and signals Lochhead's move towards a more unconventional style. *The full furnace: collected poems* (1975) reprints the best work from the poet's earlier volumes and has a final section, 'Poems roughly divided, 1961-74', that sums up his Toronto period. The variety of short pieces here makes it clear that he is no mere outdoor or regional poet but an intensely personal one with a broad range of thematic interests. His poetic sequence 'October diary' anticipates the verse written on his return to the Maritimes.

Lochhead's New Brunswick work is best represented by *High Marsh Road* (1980), possibly his most notable achievement. This long poem or sequence of poems is subtitled 'Lines for a diary' and evokes, with a full awareness of Charles G.D. ROBERTS and John THOMPSON as poetic precedents, the complexity of the historical and natural environment of the Tantramar, utilizing its autumnal marsh moods to communicate a personal search for meaning. *A & E* (1980) is a representation of the wily conjectures of 'a couple lying in bed talking, in the intervals, about life', omitting nothing from their 'double mirror' because love in maturity has come to mean 'admitting, comparing, debating.' Like *A & E*, a third New Brunswick book, *Battle sequence* (1980), was issued as a limited edition. Both works are conceived within the diary format and epigrammatic poetic structure that objectify the highly personal feeling of Lochhead's later poetry.

In the field of scholarship Lochhead has edited Thomas McCULLOCH's *The Stepsure letters* with Northrop FRYE and John Irving (1960), A.G. Gilbert's *From Montreal to the Maritime Provinces and back* (1967), *Made in Canada: new poems of the seventies* (1970) with Raymond SOUSTER, *Bibliography of Canadian bibliographies* (2nd edn, 1972), *100 poems of nineteenth-century Canada* (1974) with Souster, and *Specimen of printing types and ornaments . . . Lovell and Gibson, Montreal, 1846* (1976). He is general editor of the University of Toronto Press series Literature of Canada: Poetry and Prose in Reprint (21 vols) and of the Toronto Reprint Library of Canadian Prose and Poetry (25 vols).

KEN MacKINNON

Lodge, Rupert C. (1886-1961). Born in Manchester, Eng. (a nephew of Sir Oliver Lodge, the physicist and spiritualist), Rupert Clendon Lodge came to North America in 1914 and taught at the University of Minnesota and then at the University of Alberta, before moving in 1920 to the University of Manitoba, where he remained (apart from a year as visiting professor at Harvard, and other occasional absences) until he retired in 1947. Later he taught at Queen's University, Kingston, Ont., and at Long Island University. He died in St Petersburg, Florida.

Probably the most widely read philosopher to work in Canada, Lodge played an important role in the development of pluralist ideas, in bringing philosophy to the Canadian West, and in the development of the 'philosophical federalism' that characterized Canadian thought in the inter-war years. His *Introduction to modern logic* (1920) shows the influence of the British idealists. Thereafter he pursued his own ideas, maintaining that philosophy was irreducibly pluralistic and that every philosophical question could be answered from the viewpoint of a realist, an idealist, and a pragmatist: one

may view the world either as a collection of objects that is simply 'there', as a system of experiences, or as something whose nature cannot be objectively defined but can be used in the furtherance of one's goals. His books—beginning with *The questioning mind* (1937) and *The philosophy of education* (1937)—develop this theme across a wide range of philosophical issues. *The philosophy of business* (1945) applies this trichotomy to practical life and to the theory of business, and *Applying philosophy* (1951) extends the thesis to other workaday domains. Lodge wrote with great clarity and simplicity and conveyed ideas to a wide audience; his books achieved a popularity that is rare in modern books in philosophy. *The philosophy of education* was widely consulted in colleges and faculties of education, especially in the United States. *The great thinkers* (1949), in which he discussed the major philosophers from the past in an easy-going style almost wholly without technical jargon (though with a good deal of scholarly acumen), continues to be widely read. It illustrates Lodge's thesis that philosophy is a continuing enterprise whose past actively influences its present. This belief was widely criticized (especially by G.S. BRETT), but Lodge defended it with skill and persistence.

Lodge is also remembered for his *Plato's theory of education* (1947), *Plato's theory of art* (1953), and *The philosophy of Plato* (1956).

LESLIE ARMOUR, ELIZABETH TROTT

Logan, John. See CRITICISM IN ENGLISH: 2.

London, Jack. See FOREIGN WRITERS ON CANADA IN ENGLISH: 2.

Longfellow, Henry Wadsworth: See EVANGELINE: A TALE OF ACADIE and FOREIGN WRITERS ON CANADA IN ENGLISH: 2.

Longmore, George (1793-1867). Born in Quebec City, the son of a British army doctor stationed there, he spent part of his youth in Québec before he was commissioned ensign in the Royal Staff Corps, a military engineering unit, at Hythe, Eng., in 1809. He served in the Peninsular War and in 1820 was posted to Montreal, where he may have been engaged in surveying possible canal sites. He returned to England in 1824. Longmore never again resided in his native land, although he did seek an appointment here in the late 1840s, and a younger brother settled, and both his parents died, in Canada. Before going on half-pay with the rank of major in 1832, he had been acting surveyor-general of Mauritius for three years. In 1834 he received an appointment in Cape Colony, where he served successively as stipendiary magistrate, as aide-de-camp to two governors, and finally as librarian and sergeant-at-arms to the legislative assembly of the colony. He published seven volumes of poetry in Cape Town between 1837 and 1860.

In the early 1820s, while he was in Montreal, Longmore published anonymously *The charivari; or Canadian poetics: a tale after the manner of Beppo* (Montreal, 1824), by 'Launcelot Longstaff'. A humorous poem in 179 *ottava rima* stanzas, it is modelled on Byron's *Beppo* (1818) and tells of the courtship and marriage-day of an old bachelor, Baptisto, and the young widow of his choice, Annette. The protagonists were said, at the time, to be well-known Montreal residents, and the work itself comments satirically on many aspects of Montreal life. A charivari—in its earliest form the noisy serenading of a newly married couple on their wedding night—had become in Montreal the means by which mobs, not always good-humoured, extorted funds for drink or charity from well-to-do bridegrooms. During a riotous charivari in 1823 a passerby had been shot, a house destroyed, and participants on both sides forced to flee the country. There were public demands that charivaris be outlawed. Longmore's portrayal of a charivari with a happy ending was intended to suggest that the custom was an innocent one that did not necessarily lead to riot and destruction. Before Longmore's identity as the author of *The charivari* was established, an attribution of the work to Levi ADAMS had long been accepted.

Another work of Canadian interest by Longmore is 'Tecumthé', a poem as long as *The charivari*, which appeared in *The Canadian Review and Literary and Historical Journal* (Dec. 1824). An account of the great chief's life and death, and of the early years of the War of 1812, 'Tecumthé' focuses principally on its hero and his life, unlike John RICHARDSON's *Tecumseh*, published four years later, in which the events of the war have as much prominence as the life of Tecumseh. It was included in the anonymous *Tales of chivalry and romance* (Edinburgh and London, 1826), along with other long and short poems, many of which had been published in Montreal periodicals.

Longmore also published, under his own name, a 250-page verse account of the Peninsular War, *The war of the isles* (Edinburgh and London, 1826), and a play, *Mathilde; or the Crusaders* (Edinburgh and London, 1827).

In verse form, and in their romantic subject matter, all Longmore's works owe much to the influence of Byron and Scott. At his best when writing about people, places, and events of which he had firsthand knowledge—and showing flashes of wit in his early works that seem to have disappeared in his later publications—Longmore was an amateur versifier, but an unusually competent one: rough metre or awkward rhymes are rare in his poetry.

See M.L. MacDonald, 'George Longmore: a new literary ancestor', *Dalhousie Review* (Summer 1979). There is an excellent analysis of *The charivari* in '*The charivari* and Levi Adams' by C.F. KLINCK, *Dalhousie Review* (Spring 1960). An edition of *The charivari*, with an introduction by Mary Lu MacDonald, was published by the Golden Dog Press, Ottawa, in 1977.

MARY LU MacDONALD

Loranger, Françoise (b. 1913). Born in Saint-Hilaire, Qué., she studied literature and science in Montreal and then began working in 1939 as a writer for the CBC in Montreal. She now lives in Quebec City. Her early radio dramas (*L'école des parents, Ceux qu'on aime, La vie commence demain*) showed her gifts for authentic dialogue and psychological penetration. Her first published work, *Mathieu* (1949), is a well-written novel that describes the anguish of a young man in revolt against the repressive atmosphere of Duplessis Québec. Critics have praised its free-flowing style and the refined psychological observation of Mathieu. Loranger's career moved quite naturally towards the spoken word and she became a key figure in French-Canadian television drama. In the fifties, sixties, and early seventies her television plays (*Madame la présidente, Jour après jour, Georges . . . oh! Georges, Un cri qui vient de loin, Un bel automne*), and serials (*A moitié sage, Sous le signe du lion*) helped her to perfect her skills as a playwright. In a province where the family was seen to be eternal and untouchable, she is regarded today as having been prophetic in her descriptions of family break-ups and strife.

Loranger became known internationally in 1965 when the Théâtre du Rideau Vert performed *Une maison . . . un jour* in Montreal, France, and Russia. In this very successful play, centred on the theme of departure—departure from one's parents and ultimately departure from life itself—the dialogues are poetic and lyrical and the various episodes comment on the decaying morals and values of bourgeois Québécois. *Encore cinq minutes* (1967), which won a Governor General's Award, is another psychological play (with feminist overtones) that describes a family break-up symbolized by the cracking walls of the house. A critical and box-office success, it is perhaps Loranger's best traditional play.

Le chemin du roi (1968), which Loranger wrote with Claude Levac, represents a turning-point in her career as a playwright: it shows a change of themes (anti-bourgeois theatre giving way to political theatre) and of technique (towards participatory theatre). Lester B. Pearson, John Diefenbaker, Jean Marchand, and Judy LaMarsh play a hockey game against Daniel Johnson, Jean Lesage, and René Lévesque, while General de Gaulle acts as a kind of referee. Fast-paced and elaborately staged, and requiring the actors to change roles continually, *Le chemin du roi* (the King's Highway, on which de Gaulle travelled from Quebec to Montreal in 1967) shows the influence of Brecht, Artaud, Pirandello, Grotowski, the Living Theatre, and the Open Theatre, though it develops an original approach to the relationship between actors and audience, exploiting identification and physical participation to the utmost. It was first produced at the Théâtre du Gésu, Montreal, in 1968 and was a commercial success.

In *Double jeu* (1969), performed by La Comédie canadienne, Loranger attempts to create a 'happening' (audience participation) and a psychodrama (therapeutic acting-out of a situation to allow the spectators to learn more about themselves). Unfortunately the story of impossible romantic love that the audience is supposed to enact is too mystical and abstract to permit effective and spontaneous participation. *Médium saignant* (1970), 'a patriotic play' about the 'good-guys' who favour French unilingualism and the 'bad-guys' who believe in freedom of choice for the language of education, is too simplistic and stereotyped to endure. It had a brief success that was related to the emotional Bill 63 debate and to audience participation, but it lacks the nuanced ideology and effective caricature used in *Le chemin du roi*.

See Jean-Pierre Crête, *Françoise Loranger, à*

la recherche d'une identité (1974), and Jean-Pierre Ryngaert, 'Françoise Loranger: à la recherche d'un nouveau théâtre', *Livres et auteurs québécois* (1972).   DONALD SMITH

Loranger, Jean-Aubert (1896-1942). Born in Montreal into a well-known family of writers and jurists, he received a private education. After a few brief jobs he began a career as a journalist that led him successively from *La Patrie* (1923-7) to *La Presse* (1927-30) and—after a two-year interruption as private secretary to the minister of Marine in Ottawa—to Jean-Charles HARVEY's weekly, *Le Jour* (1938-9), then back to *La Patrie* (1939-42). He became news-editor of *Montréal-Matin* just before his sudden death.

At the end of the First World War Loranger's cousin, Robert Laroque de ROQUEBRUNE, introduced him to the Montreal literary milieu through a group of intellectuals that met in Fernand Préfontaine's Westmount literary salon. In 1918 this group founded *Le* NIGOG, an avant-garde review that extolled freedom of inspiration and expression in the arts. An avid reader of *La Nouvelle Revue Française* and of contemporary French writers (Apollinaire, Proust, Saint-John Perse), Loranger was influenced for a time by the *unanimiste* doctrine of such writers as Charles Vildrac and Jules Romains, and published in quick succession *Les atmosphères, le passeur, poëmes et autre proses* (1920) and *Poëmes* (1922). The critics were nonplussed by these collections. Their themes, however, were not so astonishing: obsession with departures for foreign shores; disillusionment and despair in the face of unfulfilled longing; loneliness; marking time; old age and the pangs of death. Loranger's modernity was rather a matter of form: a foreshortened elliptical quality; succinct, incisive imagery; bold metaphors; and simple anti-declamatory syntax.

Besides poetry, Loranger published between 1918 and 1942 many stories. They were first collected in *Le village: contes et nouvelles du terroir* (1925), and then many more appeared in the review *Les Idées*, in the weekly *Le Jour*, and in the daily *La Patrie*. In these stories the experimental poet, surprisingly, is a traditional storyteller 'in search of a certain regionalism'. Loranger's tales of local customs and anecdotes make use of traditional themes and characters, local colour, and the rich lexicon of colloquial language.

In the seventies critics granted Loranger a place between NELLIGAN and Saint-Denys GARNEAU in modern Québec poetry, noting the reconciliation he had attempted between the regional and the exotic in literature between the wars. Gilles MARCOTTE wrote a preface to a new edition of Loranger's poems, *Les atmosphères, suivi de Poëmes* (1970)—though this does not include the remaining fragments of a lost manuscript, 'Terra nova'—and Bernadette Guilmette edited and introduced a complete edition of the *Contes* (1978). *Ellipse*, no. 20 (1977) contains poems and prose by Loranger (with translations) followed by a study of his work.

See Marcel DUGAS, *Littérature canadienne, aperçus* (1929); Robert Giroux, 'Patterns in Jean-Aubert Loranger' in *Ellipse*, no. 20 (1977); Gilles MARCOTTE, 'Jean-Aubert Loranger' in *Écrits du Canada français*, no. 35 (1972); and Bernadette Guilmette, 'Jean-Aubert Loranger, du *Nigog* à l'École littéraire de Montréal', in *L'École littéraire de Montréal* (1972).   RICHARD GIGUÈRE

Loved and the lost, The (1951). One of Morley CALLAGHAN's most successful novels, *The loved and the lost* is set in downtown Montreal: the Ritz Carlton Hotel, the Montreal Forum where the *Canadiens* play, the night clubs and restaurants of the inner city, and the grand residences of upper Westmount. Jim McAlpine, an ambitious former university professor who is hoping to become a political columnist on the Montreal *Sun*, has come to the city at the invitation of the newspaper's publisher Joseph Carver. He is attracted to Carver's wealth and power and by his daughter Catherine. But he also becomes involved with another woman, Peggy Sanderson, who has dropped out of middle-class society (long before that became a life style) and spends much of her time in the city's small Negro community. Trying at one point to explain herself to McAlpine, Peggy says that 'all kinds of people walk in on me.' Finally the wrong person walks in and she is brutally murdered. McAlpine's involvement with her destroys his prospects at the *Sun*, but he has already been destroyed by her death, and by his conviction that he has betrayed her by not being constant. Admired and enjoyed for its elements of an urban thriller, for its affecting love story and the subtle exploration of Peggy Sanderson, *The loved and the lost* won a Governor General's Award, and a paperback edition sold half a million copies in Canada and the United States. It was in large part because of reading this book that the American critic Edmund Wilson de-

scribed Callaghan in *The New Yorker* as 'perhaps the most unjustly neglected novelist in the English-speaking world . . . a writer whose work may be mentioned without absurdity in association with Chekhov's and Turgenev's . . .'   ROBERT WEAVER

Lowell, Robert Traill Spence. See FOREIGN WRITERS ON CANADA IN ENGLISH: 2 and Writing in NEWFOUNDLAND.

Lowry, Malcolm (1909-57). Clarence Malcolm Lowry—who also went by the name of Malcolm Boden Lowry—was born in Birkenhead, Eng., a Cheshire dormitory-town to Liverpool, where his father was a wealthy cotton-broker with Methodist affiliations. Educated in upper-middle-class schools, Lowry early displayed—especially in an enthusiasm for jazz, which led him in his teens to attempt a career as a song-writer—an inclination to break away from the business life his family assumed he would follow and that his brothers accepted. This inclination to escape was first expressed actively when, in 1928, he signed on as a cabin-boy on a freighter bound for the China coast, an experience whose more harrowing aspects found a place in his first novel, *Ultramarine*; however, it did not prevent him from sailing two years later as deckhand on a ship bound for Oslo, where he sought the Norwegian novelist Nordahl Grieg, whose novel *The ship sails on* (1927) greatly influenced Lowry's early work. Already Lowry's growing enthusiasm for literature had led him into a correspondence with the American poet and novelist Conrad Aiken, who took him as a paying guest in the summer of 1929 and whose *Blue voyage* (1927) impressed Lowry and finds an echo in *Ultramarine*. In the autumn of 1929 Lowry entered St Catherine's College, Cambridge, graduating in 1932; but his encounters with Aiken, Grieg, and with younger writers he met at Cambridge contributed far more to his literary persona than did his academic studies.

At Cambridge, Lowry began seriously to write. *Ultramarine* was completed in 1932; rewritten after the manuscript had been stolen from the car of a publisher's reader, it finally appeared in 1933. This was the unusual beginning of a strange literary career that was marked by intense industry and little apparent production. Lowry published only two books during his lifetime: *Ultramarine* (which he later rejected as immature) and *Under the volcano* (1947). Another of his novels, *In ballast to the white sea*, was lost, this time irretrievably—burnt in 1945 when a fire destroyed the shack Lowry inhabited at Dollarton, B.C. But his scanty publication was due mainly to an obsessional inability to complete to his own satisfaction any work longer than a short story. During the years following the completion of *Under the volcano* in 1945, he worked on a whole cycle of novels, of which it would form part: this was to be entitled *The voyage that never ends*.

Two of the novels intended for inclusion in this cycle—*Dark as the grave wherein my friend is laid* and *October ferry to Gabriola*—were published posthumously, in 1968 and 1970 respectively; but in neither case was the final form Lowry's own, for the editors (Margerie Lowry, his wife, and Douglas Day in the first case and Margerie Lowry in the second) had to deal with chaotic manuscripts offering alternative versions of many passages. Other works by Lowry published after his death are *Lunar caustic* (1963), a novella; *Hear us O Lord from heaven Thy dwelling place* (1961), a collection of short stories; *Selected poems* (1962), edited by Lowry's friend Earle BIRNEY; *Selected letters* (1965), edited by Harvey Breit and Margerie Lowry; and *Psalms and songs* (1975), edited by Margerie Lowry, a miscellany bringing together some early and late stories, most of them previously uncollected, with a few recollections by friends and acquaintances.

In these works one can trace Lowry's physical journey through life, shadowed by alcoholism and paranoia, and an inner journey marked by spiritual hopes and terrors. His life, between leaving Cambridge and his death twenty-five years later, falls into three periods. First was the time of wandering, in Spain and France, Mexico, and the United States. During this period he married his first wife, Jan Gabrial, in 1933; went to Hollywood in 1935; and in 1936 proceeded to Mexico, which made a profound and morbid impression on him and inspired *Under the volcano*, the first version of which he completed in 1937. In 1938—his first marriage having foundered—he left Mexico for the United States and in 1937 reached Canada, where he married Margerie Bonner in 1940 and lived until 1954, mainly in a beach shack at Dollarton. The profound impression his Canadian years made on him is shown not only in the stories contained in *Hear us O Lord* but also in *October ferry to Gabriola*. There were interludes spent in Oakville and Niagara-on-the-Lake, Ont., and again in Mexico (a disastrous second jour-

ney during which Lowry found his way into prison) and in Haiti, before he left Canada in 1954 to wander in Europe and to die—apparently of a combined overdose of alcohol and barbiturates—at Ripe, Sussex, in the summer of 1957. The coroner's verdict was 'Death by misadventure'.

Under the volcano has often been treated as Lowry's only successful work; it is without doubt his best. In this story of the murder of an alcoholic British consul, the human drama is integrated in a closely knit formal and metaphorical structure, and the sinister aspects of Mexico are used admirably to symbolize the metaphysical overtones; the strong autobiographical element is admirably subsumed in the fictional. In none of the other novels is the structural integration so complete. The facts and preoccupations of Lowry's life are insistently obvious in all, though *October ferry to Gabriola* presents a deeply moving, if imperfect, counterpart to *Under the volcano* and represents Lowry's Paradiso as compared with his Inferno.

In recent years Lowry has attracted a great deal of attention and become the object of a minor literary cult. The most important general studies of him are *Malcolm Lowry* (1971) by W.H. New, *Malcolm Lowry* (1972) by Richard Hauer Costa, *Malcolm Lowry: a biography* (1973) by Douglas Day, *Lowry* (1973) by Tony Kilgallin, and *Malcolm Lowry* (1974) by M.C. Bradbrook. Collections of essays exploring various aspects of Lowry's work are *Malcolm Lowry: the man and his work* (1971) edited by George WOODCOCK, and *The art of Malcolm Lowry* (1978) edited by Anne Smith. *The private labyrinth of Malcolm Lowry* (1969) by Perle Epstein is a controversial study of the cabbalistic symbolism of *Under the volcano*.

GEORGE WOODCOCK

Lowther, Pat (1935-75). Born in Vancouver, Patricia Tinmuth came from a working-class background. Her mother was a dancer and her father was a sheet-metal worker who suffered spinal meningitis shortly before her birth. She left school at sixteen and took office jobs to support her writing. At eighteen she married Bill Domphousse, a fellow worker at the North Vancouver Shipbuilding Company, with whom she had two children. They were divorced and in 1963 she married Roy Lowther, a public-school teacher who was eventually dismissed for his radical politics; the family often survived on welfare. Before her untimely death, Pat Lowther had been elected president of The LEAGUE OF CANADIAN POETS and was teaching creative writing at the University of British Columbia. In 1977 her husband was convicted of her murder.

Pat Lowther published three books of poetry in her lifetime: *This difficult flowring* (1968), *The age of the bird* (1972), and *Milk stone* (1974). *A stone diary* (1977) was accepted for publication by Oxford before she died and was published posthumously. A last collection, *Pat Lowther: final instructions: early and uncollected poems*, edited by Dona Sturmanis and Fred Candelaria, was published as an issue of *West Coast Review* in 1980.

This difficult flowring, illustrated by S. Slutsky and published by Very Stone House, is a vindication of the small publishing house: drawings and poems work in a fine balance. Lowther began tentatively as a poet with a variety of technical experiments in image and form (chants, poems for voices, compositions by field in the style of the American Black Mountain school of poetry). The poems in this book take as their subject female experience and include some of the more convincing poems about motherhood—the body occupied by new life as the mind is by the poem. They try to make sense out of the pain, and normalcy, of private domestic life. Deeply influenced by the Chilean poet Pablo Neruda, Lowther had a political motive: the poems search for a new attitude to the body, an organism, to oppose the chameleon-like conformity that defines modern social life. Their directive cry is 'Be human'.

In her later books Lowther discovered the enduring obsession that was to become a focus in her poetry: life juxtaposed with the natural cycle; atavistic relations between man and woman as primitive giants trapped in the 'Janus-pain' of love. West-coast Indian mythology provides metaphors for her themes. Animals become spirit symbols of an elemental liberty that is destroyed by domestic rituals. *A stone diary* contains Lowther's best work. Here the poems have the directness and authority of an assured and sophisticated voice; they are simpler in style and more anecdotal and personal. Their controlling metaphor is the quest for a symbiotic relationship with the landscape, where psyche and landscape engage in a fluid interchange as the poet aligns herself with nature's resistance to the encroachments of technology and mechanism. A sequence dedicated to the memory of Pablo Neruda identifies Lowther's need to assert

the poet's political voice. The poems are also preoccupied with pain and violence, and inevitably have a prophetic, elegiac tone: 'Love is an intersection/where I have chosen/unwittingly to die.' Although silenced prematurely, Lowther achieved in this book a range and depth that will give her work a permanent place in Canadian poetry.

See Sean Ryan, 'Florence McNeill and Pat Lowther', CANADIAN LITERATURE 74 (Autumn 1977).   ROSEMARY SULLIVAN

Lozeau, Albert (1878-1924). Born in Montreal, he contracted Potts disease at age 13 and was paralysed and bedridden from 1896. Charles GILL introduced him to members of the ÉCOLE LITTÉRAIRE DE MONTRÉAL, with whom he corresponded and who helped him complete his literary education. His poetry is that of *L'âme solitaire* (1907), the title of his first collection, and typifies quite strikingly the intimate strain in Québec poetry that sees life framed and muted by a pane of glass: 'Je regarde ma vitre avec un plaisir calme.' Bearing his sufferings with good grace, Lozeau was saved by his incapacity from indulging in a patriotic treatment of the theme of the land, and his short life was enriched by a platonic love affair, a 'sereine et chaste ivresse', which inspired a rather improbable 'volupté de vivre'. In *Le miroir des jours* (1912) he reflects on the theme of time and the melancholy of the seasons, though he braces himself against the 'dangerous charm', the 'sweet poison', and the dust and ashes of autumn. One of the first Québec poets to give original expression to genuine feelings and a private vision—'Sur ma profonde nuit mes yeux se sont ouverts'—Lozeau was made a member of the Royal Society of Canada in 1911 and honoured by the French government in 1912. His *Poésies complètes* (3 vols, 1925-6), which includes *Lauriers et feuilles d'érable* (1916), appeared shortly after his death. An anthology of his work, *Albert Lozeau* (1958) edited by Yves de Margerie, is available in the 'Classiques canadiens' series. C.R.P. MAY

Ludwig, Jack (b. 1922). A native of Winnipeg, Ludwig graduated from the University of Manitoba in 1944 and moved to California to pursue a career as a writer. He later took a Ph.D. in English at UCLA (1953), and has taught at Williams College (Mass.), Bard College (N.Y.), and the University of Minnesota. (While at Bard he co-founded, with colleagues Saul Bellow and Keith Botsford, the little magazine *The Noble Savage*.)

Ludwig currently makes his home in Toronto and commutes to Long Island, where he has been teaching at the State University of New York (Stony Brook) since 1962.

Ludwig is the author of three novels that bring a ribald tall-tale style to the mordant, self-mocking type of social satire found in the work of such Jewish novelists as Mordecai RICHLER and Philip Roth. *Confusions* (1967) is both a comedy of manners and an academic satire that details the confusions and cultural schizophrenia of an American Jew who tries to master the 'Ivy League mythology' of Harvard, only to wind up on the faculty of a California university for which neither his working-class Jewish background nor his Harvard-acquired credentials and style have prepared him. *Above ground* (1968), another story of confusion and constant change, is the semi-autobiographical account of a boy who, undaunted after a childhood injury hospitalizes him for an extended period and leaves him permanently lame, pursues 'the bait of life' and grows into a man who falls in love with one woman after another. As in *Confusions*, the montage of episodes in *Above ground* forms the comic monologue of a man trying to sort out the dark and consuming reality that he sees lurking behind life's everyday appearance. But the novel is not simply patterned on a descent beneath the surfaces of that life: its protagonist struggles to emerge into a daylight world 'above ground' (the title responds to Dostoyevsky's 'Notes from underground'). In an early critical monograph, *Recent American novelists* (1962) Ludwig wrote that the novelists of his generation were 'turning from the Kafkaesque "Underground Man"' towards an '"Aboveground Man"', the hero who breaks out of his real, or symbolic, sealed-off room to re-enter the world of action and history.' The central character of *A woman of her age* (1973) makes just such a re-entry in her 85th year. An expansion of a short story first published in *The* TAMARACK REVIEW 12 (Summer 1959) and revised for *The Quarterly Review of Literature*, it offers an affecting portrait of Doba Goffman, an old woman living in the Montreal Jewish community, and deftly drawn sketches of the characters who array themselves around her. The 'confusions' of Ludwig's earlier novels reappear, chiefly in Doba, who has experienced the perplexing metamorphosis from youthful radical to wealthy matron, and young Franklin, who represents both

destructive and constructive change. The search for vitalizing change, which recurs throughout Ludwig's fiction, is embodied here in the Jewish conception of *t'shuvoh*—a word that suggests turning or returning to the correct path, repentance, and finding an answer to a question. With its powerful conclusion, this is Ludwig's most effective novel.

Around the time he wrote *A woman of her age*, Ludwig turned to writing literate, sensitive, and intelligent sports journalism, publishing *Hockey night in Moscow* (1972), which was expanded and published in the U.S. as *The great hockey thaw, or the Russians are here* (1974), and *Games of fear and winning* (1976), a collection of essays originally published in *Maclean's* and *The Canadian*. In 1976 Ludwig also published *The five-ring circus*, about the Montreal Olympics, and *The great American spectaculars*, which chronicles a year of 'big events' in America—such as the Kentucky Derby, the Indianapolis 500, the political conventions, the Rosebowl football game. Ludwig's stories, which have won prizes and been reprinted in collections of O. Henry Prize stories and in *Best American short stories*, will be published in a collection in 1984. Critical pieces on Ludwig include Lila Stonehewer, 'Anatomy of confusion: Jack Ludwig's evolution', CANADIAN LITERATURE 29 (Summer 1966); E. James, 'Ludwig's confusions', *Canadian Literature* 40 (Spring 1969); Russell Brown, 'The Canadian Eve', *Journal of Canadian Fiction* 3, no. 1 (1974); and Margaret LAURENCE's introduction to the New Canadian Library edition of *Above ground* (1974).   RUSSELL BROWN

Lunn, Janet. See CHILDREN'S LITERATURE IN ENGLISH: 4.

Lyall, William (1811-90). Born in Paisley, Scot., and educated at the Universities of Glasgow and Edinburgh, he was ordained into the Church of Scotland and took the part of the Free Church in the Great Disruption of 1843. He came to Toronto as a tutor at Knox College in 1848. In 1850 he moved to Halifax and remained there for the rest of his life, apart from three years in Truro, N.S. After a decade at the Free Church College, he taught philosophy at Dalhousie University until his death.

Lyall's major work, *Intellect, the emotions and the moral life* (Edinburgh, 1855)—which was widely read and used in colleges of the Maritime Provinces for half a century—set out to bridge the gap between the intellect and the emotions that had played a central role in philosophy since Plato. Weaving a complex synthesis of common-sense realism and Augustinian neo-Platonism, Lyall argued that the emotions in general, and love in particular, were crucial sources of knowledge and formed an essential basis for action. In Lyall's theory the direct object of an emotion (the source of joy or anger, or the object or person loved or hated) affects the indirect object—the state of mind and character of the person who has that emotion. With the education of the emotions and the imagination, the individual may become aware of more appropriate direct objects; sexual love, for instance, may develop into love of God. (The wide diffusion of Lyall's ideas helps to explain the 'moralistic' trend in Maritimes fiction described by Fred COGSWELL in the *Literary history of Canada*, vol. I, 2nd edn, 1976.) Lyall's Augustinian

political thesis—that the state, though necessary to human beings in their fallen condition, is to be regarded with a measure of suspicion—contrasts sharply with that of his predecessor at Dalhousie, Thomas McCULLOCH, who sought a political order based on a natural relation between man and his physical environment. Lyall saw fallen man as needing an elaborate political organization and saw the isolated communities of the Maritimes in the context of a larger world. His ideas thus mark a passage in political thought in the Maritime Provinces towards the era of compromise and negotiation that led to Confederation.

One copy of Lyall's *Sermons* (Edinburgh, 1848) is in the British Museum.

LESLIE ARMOUR, ELIZABETH TROTT

Lysenko, Vera. See UKRAINIAN WRITING.

M

McArthur, Peter (1866-1924). Peter Gilchrist McArthur was born in Ekfrid Township, Middlesex County, Canada West (in a log house now standing at Doon, Ont.), and attended local schools; in 1887 he received a teacher's certificate at the Strathroy Model School. In 1888, after teaching for six months, he entered the University of Toronto—to make ends meet he contributed jokes to *Grip*—but in 1890 he left university to become a reporter for the Toronto *Mail*. From 1890 to 1895 he freelanced in New York, largely as a jokesmith for *Judge, Life,* and *Town Topics,* and then became editor of *Truth* (1895-7). After another period of freelancing in New York he went to England (1902), where he wrote for *Punch* and worked on Stead's *Review of Reviews* and *Daily Paper.* He returned to New York (1904) and opened an advertising agency. It failed, and in 1909, without work or funds, he had to take refuge on the Ekfrid homestead.

While in New York McArthur had written short stories for *Truth;* a book, *The prodigal and other poems* (1907); and articles for

Ainslie's Magazine and *The Atlantic Monthly;* in England he had published a satire on Canadian-British relations, *To be taken with salt; being an essay on teaching one's grandmother to suck eggs* (1903). McArthur made his name at Ekfrid, however, with his articles for the Toronto *Globe* (1909-24) and *The Farmer's Advocate* (1910-22). From these were drawn *In pastures green* (1915), *The red cow and her friends* (1919), *Around home* (1925), *Familiar fields* (1925), and *Friendly acres* (1927). Centring on pioneers and the simple life, farm activities and farm animals (which he treats mainly as comic characters), the delights of nature and an almost Messianic 'back-to-the land' message, these essays made him the leading Canadian writer in the rural tradition. They also disclosed his gift for humour, which gave him special insight for his critical study *Stephen Leacock* (1923).

McArthur also wrote many essays about politics and economics. These subjects were central, too, to *Ourselves* (1910-12), his farm magazine for 'Cheerful Canadians'; his eulogistic *Sir Wilfrid Laurier* (1919); and his commentary on American society, *The affable stranger* (1921). In addition he wrote five pamphlets, *The last law—brotherhood* (1921), and a poem, 'A chant of Mammonism' (1922), extolling life insurance. By ignoring the pamphlets and misdating the poem (1908), however, F.W. Watt in 'Peter McArthur and the agrarian myth' (*Queen's Quarterly*, Summer 1960) misrepresents McArthur. His attacks on big business notwithstanding, he was always devising schemes—even one for Henry Ford—to make money and in 1922 became a trust-company executive. Inconsistent as this may seem, McArthur considered insurance to be the people's capitalism, protecting farmers and thereby rural independence; it was his favourite among financial organizations. Despite questionable arguments (and heavy-handed satire), McArthur's discussions of farm politics and economics add much to the comprehensiveness of a vital and imaginative treatment of old-time rural life.

ALEC LUCAS

McClelland and Stewart Limited. Founded in 1906 by John McClelland, formerly manager of the library department of the Methodist Book Room (later the RYERSON PRESS), in partnership with Frederick Goodchild from the same company, it began as a library supply house selling books secured from foreign publishers. The imprint 'McClelland and Goodchild' was initiated three years later. In 1910 the new company's first Canadian book, L.M. MONTGOMERY's *Kilmeny of the orchard*, appeared. Three years after it was incorporated in 1911, George Stewart, a Bible salesman from the Methodist Book Room, joined the firm. In 1918 Goodchild formed his own company (Frederick D. Goodchild) and the firm became McClelland and Stewart Limited.

Prior to the First World War, M&S expanded its activities as agents for British and American firms by starting to build a list of Canadian publications. In 1917 it became the publisher of Ralph Connor (Charles William GORDON); its other Canadian authors at that time included Bliss CARMAN, Marjorie PICKTHALL, Marshall SAUNDERS, Duncan Campbell SCOTT, Isabel Ecclestone MacKay, and Marian Keith (Mary Esther MacGREGOR). Between the wars, books by Stephen LEACOCK, Arthur STRINGER, Frederick Philip GROVE, Laura Goodman SALVERSON, and Thomas H. RADDALL were added to its list.

After the Second World War—under the direction of John (Jack) Gordon McCLELLAND, who joined his father's firm in 1946 and became president in 1952—M&S began its steady shift away from handling agencies to concentrate on its Canadian publishing. Three celebrated Québec novels were published in translation: Gabrielle ROY's *The tin flute* (BONHEUR D'OCCASION), which appeared in 1947, and Roger LEMELIN's *The town below (Au pied de la pente douce)* and *The Plouffe family (Les PLOUFFE)*, which appeared in 1948 and 1951 respectively. In the late forties, also, the beautifully designed Indian File Series of poetry books—including collections by James REANEY, Robert FINCH, and Phyllis WEBB—began the strong commitment of M&S to poetry publishing that continues to this day. By 1954 forty per cent of the firm's revenues came from Canadian publications. In 1958 the famous New Canadian Library reprint series of major Canadian works was started, and the following year M&S published Irving LAYTON's *A red carpet for the sun*, Mordecai RICHLER's *The apprenticeship of Duddy Kravitz*, and Sheila WATSON's *The double hook*. By 1962 it had dropped most of its foreign agencies, a decision that seemed well justified by the commercial success of books by Pierre BERTON, Farley MOWAT, of Peter NEWMAN's *Renegade in power* (1963), Margaret LAURENCE's *The STONE ANGEL* (1964), and, in the years that followed, of subsequent works by these authors and books by Margaret ATWOOD, Earle BIRNEY, Marie-Claire BLAIS, and Leonard COHEN, among other well-known writers. In the area of scholarship, M&S published in 1963 the first two volumes in its 18-volume history of Canada, The Canadian Centenary Series, under the editorship of W.L. MORTON and Donald CREIGHTON. Despite severe financial difficulties (government grants had been successfully sought in 1970 and 1978 to keep the company from folding), there is now hardly an area of literature, and of Canadian life, that is not represented by M&S publications, which include not only fiction and poetry and a wide range of non-fiction, but children's literature, and school and college textbooks.

In 1982 McClelland appointed his vice-president of publishing, Linda McKnight, president of the firm and became chairman of the board. He is also president of Seal Books, a collaborative paperback venture between M&S and Bantam Books.

ELSPETH CAMERON

McClelland

McClelland, Jack (b. 1922). John Gordon McClelland was born in Toronto, the only son of John McClelland, who owned and ran the publishing firm McCLELLAND AND STEWART LIMITED. After attending the University of Toronto Schools and St Andrew's College, he enrolled in maths and physics at the University of Toronto in 1940 and the next year enlisted as a commissioned officer in the Royal Canadian Navy and volunteered for active duty on torpedo boats in the English Channel. In 1945 he completed a B.A. at Trinity College, University of Toronto, and married Elizabeth Matchett; they have four daughters and one son.

Jack McClelland joined his father's firm in 1946. Early on he pressed his father to rely less on the distribution of British and American books and to work towards establishing a solid list of Canadian authors. In 1952, when he had become familiar with all aspects of the business, he became president. His intuitive sense of what makes a good manuscript, his formidable energy, and his genius for friendship enabled him to enlist many of the best Canadian authors of his time: Irving LAYTON, Earle BIRNEY, Gabrielle ROY, Leonard COHEN, Sheila WATSON, Roger LEMELIN, Mordecai RICHLER, and Margaret LAURENCE, to name but a few. With some authors, such as Pierre BERTON and Farley MOWAT, he formed enduring friendships. His motto has been 'McClelland and Stewart publish authors, not books.'

A colourful maverick, McClelland is known for the flamboyant gimmicks he has used in promotion. His 1982 Molson Prize, however, attests to the enormous contribution he has made not only to Canadian publishing but to Canadian culture in producing a large and diverse list of books that collectively represent the cornerstone of Canadian literature.

In 1982 McClelland appointed his former vice-president of publishing, Linda McKnight, president of the firm. He is now chairman of the board and president of Seal Books, a collaborative paperback venture between McClelland and Stewart and Bantam Books. ELSPETH CAMERON

McClung, Nellie L. (1873-1951). Helen Letitia Mooney was born on a farm near Chatsworth, Grey Co., Ont., the youngest of six children of Methodist Scotch-Irish parentage. The family moved to Manitoba in 1880 and took up homestead land on the Souris River. Attending school for the first time at age ten, Nellie was enrolled in Winnipeg's Normal School within six years. She taught at rural schools in Manitoba, returning to Winnipeg in 1893-5 to complete high school at the Collegiate Institute. In 1896, having picked out her mother-in-law several years before, she married pharmacist Wesley McClung.

An avid reader of fiction, with a lively imagination and easily stirred sympathies for the voiceless, downtrodden, and unfortunate, Nellie was caught up by the novels of Charles Dickens and the serials in the weekly *Family Herald*. Early ambitions to write stories about the Manitoba countrypeople she lived among were sidetracked by the responsibilities of her growing family and by her widening activism in temperance and suffrage organizations. She achieved commercial success as a writer with her first book: *Sowing seeds in Danny* (1908; rpr. 1965), which sold over 100,000 copies and helped pave the way for her rise soon afterwards to political prominence. Her political achievements were numerous: she was a prominent member of Winnipeg's Political Equality League, Women's Press Club, Women's Christian Temperance Union, and the CANADIAN AUTHORS' ASSOCIATION, and was a front-line campaigner in the Manitoba elections of 1914 and 1915 that led to the enfranchisement of the province's women in 1916. She gave equally effective leadership in the Alberta suffrage cause after the McClung family's removal to Edmonton (1914), and unrelenting platform service in the campaign for prohibition; was elected to the Alberta legislature as a Liberal in 1921 (she was defeated in 1925); and was one of the 'famous five' who pursued the Persons Case to its successful conclusion in 1930. On Wes's retirement in 1935 the McClungs moved from Calgary, where they had lived since 1923, to Gordonhead, near Victoria, B.C. Here Nellie combined gardening, writing, and continued public service. In 1936 she began a six-year term on the newly formed CBC's Board of Governors, and in 1938 was named a Canadian delegate to the League of Nations conference in Geneva.

McClung published sixteen books and numerous uncollected stories and articles for newspapers and magazines. Her dramatic flair, charisma, and wit reached large audiences across Canada and the U.S. through her public readings from *Sowing seeds in Danny*, a loosely knit novel about Danny's sister, the dauntless twelve-year-old Pearlie Watson, and her irrepressible Irish family.

Two later novels, *The second chance* (1910) and *Purple Springs* (1921), take Pearlie—whose temperament, philosophy, and adventures closely matched those of McClung's—through an independent young womanhood as a teacher and a campaigner for temperance and suffrage, ending with her marriage to an idealistic, progressive doctor. *Painted fires* (1925), McClung's last full-scale novel, showed her lifelong concern for immigrant groups in Canada through the trials of Helmi, a young Finnish girl. McClung's other fiction includes two novellas, *The Black Creek stopping-house and other stories* (1912) and *When Christmas crossed 'The Peace'* (1923), as well as short sketches mixed with personal essays in volumes like *The next of kin* (1917) and *All we like sheep* (1926). *Three times and out* (1918) was Nellie's rendition of an escaped prisoner-of-war's experiences in the First World War.

Although McClung's penchant for pathos and moral uplift dates her fiction, the humour and sprightliness of her stories and characters can still offer amusement. McClung could effectively puncture stuffiness and pretension, and she had an ear for the colloquial rhythms and usages of turn-of-the-century westerners. Epigrammatic wit enlivens her novels, stories, sketches, and polemical writing alike, and it is clear that neither McClung nor her early readers cared much for the distinctions of prose forms. She was also adept at sentimental and satiric verse.

Present-day readers will find abundant evidence of McClung's common sense and vivacity in her four collections of newspaper sketches and stories: *Be good to yourself* (1930), *Flowers for the living* (1931), *Leaves from Lantern Lane* (1936), and *More leaves from Lantern Lane* (1937). Of more enduring value, however, are her two fine volumes of autobiography, *Clearing in the West* (1936; rpr. 1976) and *The stream runs fast* (1945; rpr. 1965). *In times like these* (1915), a classic statement of Canadian feminism, was reprinted in 1972 by the University of Toronto Press, with an introduction by V. Strong-Boag.

In *Our Nell: a scrapbook biography of Nellie L. McClung* (1979) Candace Savage has brought together excerpts from McClung's writings, excellent illustrations, and a good bibliography. Mary Lile Bentham's *Nellie McClung* (1975) is a reliable booklet for schools.   SUSAN JACKEL

McCourt, Edward (1907-72). Edward

Alexander McCourt was born in Mullinger, Ire., and brought to Canada in 1909; he grew up on a farm outside Kitscoty, Alta. After taking his high-school education by correspondence, he studied English literature at the University of Alberta and, as a Rhodes Scholar, at Oxford University, from which he received his M.A. in 1937. On returning to Canada he taught English at Ridley College and Upper Canada College in Ontario, at the University of New Brunswick, and Queen's University, before accepting a position at the University of Saskatchewan in Saskatoon, where he taught from 1944 until his death.

McCourt's novels are character studies that explore the boundary between illusion and reality, faith and despair. 'The life of everyman', Dr Fotheringham declares in *The wooden sword*, 'is no more than a succession of disillusionments. Each disillusionment constitutes a crisis. And a man's happiness—a relative term only—depends on the success or otherwise with which he meets each crisis.' McCourt's first and best-known novel, *Music at the close* (1947), traces the progressive disillusion of Neil Fraser, an orphan given to romantic dreams, from his arrival on his great-uncle's prairie farm at the age of twelve until his death in the Second World War. A winner of the Ryerson All-Canada Fiction Award, it has been reprinted in the New Canadian Library (1966) with an introduction by Allan Bevan, and in the Alberta Heritage Series (1979). *Home is the stranger* (1950) focuses on Norah Armstrong, a hypersensitive Irish war bride struggling to make a new life for herself in a small prairie farming community; disillusioned by her failure as a wife and mother, she attempts suicide. A prairie university is the setting of *The wooden sword* (1956), a psychological case-study of Stephen Veneer, a professor of English whose adolescent dreams of heroism have been shattered by his war experiences, and whose unwillingness to come to terms with those experiences has driven him to the verge of mental breakdown. It has been reprinted in the New Canadian Library (1975) with an introduction by Winnifred M. Bogaards. *Walk through the valley* (1958) focuses on fourteen-year-old Michael Troy, whose faith in his father, Dermot, and in the romantic tales of adventure with which his father regales him, are all but destroyed when the police close in on Dermot's whisky-running operation. In *Fasting friar* (1963), published in England as *The Ettinger affair*, the process of disillusionment is reversed: Walter Ackroyd—an aging, fastidious, and ascetic professor of English at a prairie university—finds new hope and courage when he falls in love with Marion Ettinger, wife of a colleague dismissed for writing a racy novel.

McCourt is best known as a literary critic for *The Canadian West in fiction* (1949), a study of prairie writers that focuses on Ralph Connor (Charles W. GORDON), Frederick NIVEN, and Frederick Philip GROVE; a revised edition appeared in 1970. He also wrote *Remember Butler: The story of Sir William Butler* (1967), a biography of the author of *The great lone land* (see FOREIGN WRITERS ON CANADA IN ENGLISH: 1).

The North West Rebellion of 1885 is the subject of three books McCourt wrote for young people. *The flaming hour* (1947) is a tale of cattle-rustling, gun-running, and romance set in the Cypress Hills at the outbreak of fighting. The other two are volumes in the Great Stories of Canada series: *Buckskin brigadier: the story of the Alberta Field Force* (1955) concerns the role played by General Tom Strange's expeditionary force in the suppression of the rebellion; *Revolt in the west: the story of the Riel Rebellion* (1958) recounts the events of that rebellion.

McCourt is also the author of three travel books. *The road across Canada* (1965) is an account of the McCourts' trip across Canada on the newly opened Trans Canada Highway. Both *Saskatchewan* (1968) and *The Yukon and the Northwest* (1969) are volumes in the Traveller's Canada series, and combine local history and travelogue in a celebration of place.

See also CRITICISM IN ENGLISH: 4, 5(g).

PAUL HJARTARSON

McCrae, John (1872-1918). Born in Guelph, Ont., he grew up under the influence of his military-minded father, and as an adolescent belonged to the Guelph Highland Cadets. His poems began to appear in periodicals as early as 1894. Graduating in medicine from the University of Toronto in 1898, he worked during that year at the Toronto General Hospital, and spent part of 1899 at John Hopkins. After serving in South Africa (1899-1900), McCrae became a pathologist at McGill University; he was later associated with the Montreal General Hospital, the Alexandra Hospital, and the Royal Victoria Hospital. (He also published several medical publications.) In Sept. 1914 he embarked as a medical officer for the European theatre of war. His best-known

poem, 'In Flanders fields', was written during the second battle of Ypres in the spring of 1915 and first appeared in *Punch*, in Dec. 1915. In June 1915 McCrae left the Front for the military General Hospital in Boulogne, where he died of pneumonia on 27 Jan. 1918. Sir Andrew MACPHAIL published twenty-nine of McCrae's poems, which had appeared in periodicals during 1894-1917, as *In Flanders fields and other poems* (1919). They demonstrate McCrae's careful attention to poetic craft, his commitment to fruitful labour, and his profound concern for the fellowship of the dead, whom he portrays as wakeful and anxious lest their labours have been in vain. In his later poems these labours specifically include British Imperial military service. Only rarely, as in 'Flanders fields', does McCrae fuse his craft and concern for worthwhile service into an evocative statement on sacrifice for a higher principle. *In Flanders fields and other poems* concludes with a memorial tract by Macphail, 'An essay in character', appropriately dated 4 Nov. 1918, which includes biographical information as well as extracts from McCrae's journal and letters.

KEITH RICHARDSON

McCulloch, Thomas (1776-1843). Born in Ferenze, Renfrewshire, Scot., he was educated at the University of Glasgow and at Divinity Hall, Whitburn. A member of the secession branch of the Presbyterian Church, he was ordained in 1799 and in 1803 was sent to Prince Edward Island. He was unable to reach his destination and stopped in Pictou, N.S. After a year, despite entreaties to move to P.E.I., McCulloch accepted a call to remain there. A frail man, but with incredible energy, McCulloch soon became involved in many activities outside his ministry. He founded Pictou Academy (incorporated 1816) and became caught up in the Anglican Church's endeavours to dominate education in the province: he was unable to obtain funds for the academy or the power to grant degrees. McCulloch was a natural reformer, and under his leadership Pictou became a centre of protest against the Establishment. *The Colonial Patriot*, founded there in 1827, was edited anonymously by one of McCulloch's former pupils and financial supporters, Jotham Blanchard. McCulloch's skill as a teacher and public speaker was widely recognized. In 1838 he became the first president of Dalhousie University, a non-sectarian institution of higher learning in Halifax, and remained in this post until his death. He founded a theological seminary at West River, Pictou County, which was moved after his death to Truro in 1858 and two years later joined with the Free Church Seminary to form the Halifax Presbyterian College. In 1925 this institution amalgamated with the Mount Allison Faculty of Theology to form Pine Hill Divinity Hall of the United Church of Canada. McCulloch's influence is even felt in the newly founded Atlantic School of Theology (1970). McCulloch was also a naturalist in the nineteenth-century tradition. His collection of bird specimens attracted the attention of John James Audubon, who visited him in 1833.

McCulloch was a prodigious letter-writer and pamphleteer on a wide range of subjects who managed also to write books of general as well as of educational and theological interest, often driving himself to the point of exhaustion. As a writer he is best known for his *Letters of Mephibosheth Stepsure*, which first appeared in serial form in the *Acadian Recorder* between 22 Dec. 1821 and 11 May 1822 and in Jan. and Mar. 1823. The letters were reprinted in 1862 and, as *The Stepsure letters*, in the New Canadian Library in 1960. McCulloch's satiric and humorous account of the rural life of Pictou County in the 1820s created a furore in the newspaper columns of the time. Northrop FRYE, in his introduction to the 1960 edition, describes McCulloch as 'the founder of genuine Canadian humour; that is, of the humour which is based on a vision of society and is not merely a series of wisecracks on a single theme.' *The Stepsure letters* had a strong influence on HALIBURTON's Sam Slick sketches, and it can be stated that McCulloch wrote in the tradition that had its flowering in LEACOCK. In 1824 he published in *The Novascotian* the moral tale 'William', depicting the fortunes of an emigrant and the difficulties awaiting those who were not prepared to work hard in the New World. 'William' was joined with a similar work and reprinted as *Colonial gleanings: William and Melville* (Edinburgh, 1826).

McCulloch also wrote in the fields of education and religion. He was a strong proponent of liberal education and published his ideas in *The nature and uses of a liberal education* (Halifax, 1819). While advancing the cause of Presbyterianism and public education, he ran afoul of Bishop Edmond Burke, the Roman Catholic Bishop. In two major works, amounting to over 800 pages—*Popery condemned by scripture and the Fathers*

(Edinburgh, 1808) and *Popery condemned again* (Edinburgh, 1810)—McCulloch outthought and out-wrote his Catholic opponents in an astonishing display of theological argument. Posthumously published was *Calvinism: the doctrine of the scriptures* (Glasgow, 1849). In this 270-page work he outlined his own faith in his typically vigorous and authoritative style. McCulloch's correspondence was wide and varied. He maintained his connections in Scotland and contributed letters on political, economic, and social subjects to *The Pictou Herald* and *The Acadian Recorder*. Lucid and well conceived, his correspondence (now being collected) provides a wide and penetrating view of nineteenth-century life in the Maritimes, and of McCulloch's central role.

The only book-length biographical study is *Life of Thomas McCulloch, D.D. Pictou* (1920) by his son William McCulloch D.D.; it was unfortunately heavily edited by his granddaughters.   DOUGLAS LOCHHEAD

Macdonald, John. See PHILOSOPHY IN CANADA: 6.

Macdonald, Malcolm. See FOREIGN WRITERS ON CANADA IN ENGLISH: 1.

MacDonald, Wilson (1880-1967). Wilson Pugsley MacDonald was born in Cheapside, Ont., and educated at Woodstock College and McMaster University. In *The song of the undertow* (1935), he wrote: 'I have been, in my varied career, a view agent, seaman, cabin-boy, bartender (one night), schoolteacher, actor, inventor, producer, playwright, composer, advertizement writer, newspaper reporter, editorial writer, columnist, banker, and poet. When my poetry would not sell, circumstances forced these other tasks upon me.' He died in Toronto.

A minor poet who satisfied the public taste with his 'romantic sensibility' and came into prominence just after the First World War, MacDonald had a strongly religious and Anglo-oriented background that influenced much of his early work. Today he appears as the last Canadian writer of a brand of romantic verse that was rooted in the nineteenth century, its most obvious characteristics being its abundance of colour and its musical quality. The poems are invariably well balanced because of his musical interest; parts of stanzas are repeated for emphasis and direction—as major melodies in music would be—with other lines juxtaposed to heighten the emotional effect. For

MacDonald, civilization eventually was an evil; man had made a mockery of life in art, religion, and education and must return to the soil if he was not to be destroyed by his own vanity. *Comber cove* (1937) reflects his disappointment in society and the people who corrupt it. While his contemporaries were invoking universal love and compassion, MacDonald drew upon his Christian beliefs to expose hypocrisy and smugness—the marks, in his view, of twentieth-century man. Towards the end of his life he became known as a satirist, but much of what he wrote was petulant and bitter; he held strong, frequently unpopular, opinions, and did not care what others thought of him. His collections of verse are: *Song of the prairie land, and other poems* (1918); *The miracle songs of Jesus* (1921); *Out of the wilderness* (1926); *A flagon of beauty* (1931); *Quintrains of 'Callander' and other poems* (1935); *The song of the undertow and other poems* (1935); *Comber cove* (1937); *Greater poems of the Bible: metrical versions, biblical forms, and original poems* (1943); and *The lyric year, poems and pen-work* (1952).

MacDonald attained a popular following in Canada and abroad, but received little critical acclaim from those, in the 1930s, who preferred F.R. SCOTT, A.J.M. SMITH, and Dorothy LIVESAY. Beginning in the early twenties, he went across the country reading his poetry to audiences in large cities and small towns. His personal shyness disappeared on stage, where he became dynamic; humming, chanting, and singing, he synchronized his whole performance to make poems come alive for his audience. On one of his tours he kept a note-book record of his journey, embellished with illuminations and drawings that showed his versatility in the arts. It is described by Stan Dragland in *Wilson MacDonald's western tour, 1923-24* (1976).   DONALD STEPHENS

McDougall, Colin. See NOVELS IN ENGLISH: 1940 TO 1960.

McDougall, E. Jean (pseudonym, Jane Rolyat). See NOVELS IN ENGLISH 1920 TO 1940: 2.

McDougall, John (1842-1917). Born in Owen Sound, Canada West (Ont.), John Chantler McDougall grew up on the Methodist mission stations conducted by his father, the Rev. George Millward McDougall, among the Ojibwa Indians of the Great Lakes. His formal education was limited to backwoods schools and two terms at Victoria College, Cobourg. The eldest of eight children, he left college at sixteen to accompany the mission family to Norway House on Lake Winnipeg. There he served as schoolteacher to the native children, becoming fluent in Swampy Cree.

Beginning in 1862 McDougall worked for ten years as translator, provisioner, and apprentice missionary in the McDougall mission network, now moved inland to stations on the North Saskatchewan River. Whitefish, Victoria (Pakan), Edmonton, and Pigeon Lake were his homes, but he led a life of constant travel, following the Indian camps as they in turn followed the buffalo. In 1865 he married Abigail Steinhauer, daughter of the Ojibwa missionary Henry Bird Steinhauer and his Cree wife, and they had three daughters. Abigail died in Apr. 1871 and McDougall remarried in 1872, shortly after his ordination as a Methodist minister.

McDougall's familiarity with northwest travel routes and methods, as well as his position of trust among the Cree and Stoney Indians, involved him in government commissions, treaty negotiations, and a complex array of educational, social, and religious measures affecting the region's Indian and mixed-blood inhabitants. An accomplished linguist, especially in the several dialects of Cree, he and a colleague, the Rev. E.B. Glass, published a *Primer and language lessons* and a revised Cree *Hymn book*, both in 1908. However, John McDougall is primarily known for six other books that made him a favourite with the turn-of-the-century Canadian reading public. A biography of his father, *George Millward McDougall: pioneer, patriot and missionary* (Toronto, 1888), was followed by five books of memoirs detailing his own adventurous life on the frontier among the Indians. The entire series is marked by surprising consistency of tone and freshness of recall. *Forest, lake and prairie: twenty years of frontier life in western Canada, 1842-62* (Toronto, 1895) describes his boyhood and youth; *Saddle, sled and snowshoe: pioneering on the Saskatchewan in the sixties* (Toronto, 1896) covers the years from 1862 to McDougall's first marriage in 1865. *Pathfinding on plain and prairie: stirring scenes of life in the Canadian North-west* (Toronto, 1898; rpr. 1971), which recounts events from 1865 to 1868, went into several printings and was given a facsimile reprint. The most consciously structured and most satisfying of the series, *In the days of the Red River rebellion: life and adventure in the far west of Canada (1862-1872)* (1903), tells of the mounting strains on the interior region's residents during the period of unrest and up-rising at Fort Garry. *On western trails in the early seventies: frontier life in the Canadian North-west* (1911) carries the story to 1875. J.E. Nix edited a sixth volume of memoirs, *Opening the great West* (1970), which had been left in manuscript at McDougall's death. It describes the events of 1876, chief among which was George McDougall's death on the plains near Calgary.

The little-known *Wa-pee Moos-tooch; or, White Buffalo, the hero of a hundred battles: a tale of Canada's great west during the early days of the last century* (1908)—privately printed by the author in Calgary—is an episodic narrative of a young chief's education and testing, remarkable for being both ethno-logically sound and competent as a work of historical fiction. The occasional idiomatic aberration in the prose style can be explained by McDougall's imaginative engagement with his young Cree hero, whose thoughts and speech reflect the customs and phrasing of the woods-and-plain Cree.

The only full-scale biography, *McDougall of Alberta: a life of Rev. John McDougall, D.D., pathfinder of empire and prophet of the plains* (1927) by his co-religionist John Maclean, needs updating. A useful brief book on the historical place of the two McDougalls, George and John, is J.E. Nix's *Mission among the buffalo* (1960).

SUSAN JACKEL

McDowell, Franklin Davy. See NOVELS IN ENGLISH 1920 TO 1940: 2.

MacEwen, Gwendolyn (b. 1941). Born in Toronto, she attended schools there and in Winnipeg. She published her first poem in *The* CANADIAN FORUM when she was seven-teen and left school at eighteen to pursue a literary career, which has included the writ-ing of half-a-dozen plays and dramatic doc-umentaries—so far unpublished—for CBC radio, and numerous works of poetry and fiction. She was married for six years to the Greek singer Nikos Tsingos and in 1972 they operated The Trojan Horse, a Toronto coffee house. Her links with Greece led her to write a volume of travel recollections, *Mermaids and ikons: a Greek summer* (1978), and to translate with Tsingos two long poems of the contemporary Greek writer Yannis Ritsos. These were published in *Tro-jan women* (1981), which also contains

MacEwen's new version of Euripedes' *The Trojan women*.

MacEwen has published two novels, *Ju-lian the magician* (1963) and *King of Egypt, king of dreams* (1971), as well as a collection of short stories, *Noman* (1972), and two chil-dren's books, *The chocolate moose* (1979) and *The honey drum* (1983). Her verse includes two early privately published pamphlets, *Selah* (1961) and *The drunken clock* (1961), and eight larger volumes: *The rising fire* (1963), *A breakfast for barbarians* (1966), *The shadow-maker* (1969)—winner of a Governor General's Award—*The armies of the moon* (1972), *Magic animals* (1975), *The fire eaters* (1976), *The T.E. Lawrence poems* (1982), and *Earthlight* (1982). *Magic animals* and *Earth-light* are selections, though the first also con-tains some new poems.

In approaching MacEwen's verse and prose alike the reader is tempted, as Mar-garet ATWOOD has said, 'to become preoc-cupied with the brilliant and original verbal surfaces she creates.' But this bright enamel of words and images, which woos the reader's initial pleasure, overlies profundi-ties of thought and feeling. The extraordin-ary feat of empathy represented by *The T.E. Lawrence poems*—the voice seems to be Lawrence's own—suggests the oracular seriousness in her verse, and a growing in-clination to move away from the elusive feyness of the first poems. This develop-ment can be seen by comparing the selec-tions included in *Magic animals* with those in *Earthlight*, published seven years later. The poems in the latter volume have a greater solidity of texture and concreteness of imag-ery, a sharper visualness; they reveal a preoccupation with time and its multiple meanings, with the ambivalences of exis-tence, with the archetypal patterns that emerge and re-emerge from ancient times to now, but also with the actual human lives that carry on in their mundane way within such patterns. There are few Canadian poets with a grasp as broad as MacEwen's of the poetic dimensions of history—the realm of the muse Clio—and of its necessarily Zoroastrian duality, expressed in the last line of her most recent book: as T.E. Lawrence dies, his mind exclaims, 'Night comes and the stars are out. Salaam.' Light lives in darkness; darkness nurtures light.

Such concerns, recurring throughout her poetry, take personified form in MacEwen's novels that blend fantasy with history: *Julian the magician*, with its early-renaissance preoccupation with hermetic quasi-philosophies and their ambiguous relationship to Christianity; *King of Egypt, king of dreams*, with its imaginative reconstruction of the gallant and eventually futile life of the heterodox pharoah, Akhnaton. The stories in *Noman* are united by the central enigmatic character who names the book, and here the protean quality of MacEwen's talent takes full flight as her vision of 'Kanada' whirls in a mythological carousel whose turning unites us with every temporal past and every spatial present.

See Margaret ATWOOD, 'MacEwen's muse', CANADIAN LITERATURE 45 (Summer 1970), reprinted in Atwood, *Second words* (1982), which contains a further discussion of MacEwen's work in 'Canadian monsters'; Frank DAVEY, 'Gwendolyn MacEwen: the secret of alchemy', OPEN LETTER (Spring 1973); and Gary GEDDES, 'Now you see it . . .', *Books in Canada* (July 1976).

See also POETRY IN ENGLISH 1950 TO 1982: 2 and SCIENCE FICTION AND FANTASY IN ENGLISH AND FRENCH: 4.

GEORGE WOODCOCK

McFadden, David (b. 1940). Noted for his poetry of pop-art image and ironic ingenuousness, he lived his first thirty-nine years in Hamilton, Ont. In 1962 he joined the staff of the *Hamilton Spectator* as a proofreader, became a reporter for the paper in 1970, and resigned in 1976 to take up freelance writing and editing. He was appointed writer-in-residence at Simon Fraser University in 1978, and since 1979 has lived in Nelson, B.C., where he teaches creative writing at the David Thompson University Centre. McFadden's poetry appeared first in TISH, *Is, Evidence, Weed, Talon*, and McFadden's own mimeographed magazine *Mountain* (1962).

The poems of McFadden's first major collections—*Letters from the earth to the earth* (1968), *Poems worth knowing* (1971), and *Intense pleasure* (1972)—use his family life with his wife and two daughters as their central symbol. Details about cooking meals or repairing toys are affirmed as important, despite the larger twentieth-century context of brutality and commercial exploitation. McFadden personified this conflict between family life and North American media advertising in his characterization of Ricky Wayne, the protagonist of his first novel, *The great canadian sonnet* (1970).

In the seventies McFadden's writing shifted its focus from the family home to the family's exploration of the outside world. The major poems of *A knight in dried plums* (1975) are the marvellously comic tourist poems 'Somewhere south of Springhill' and 'A typical Canadian family visits Disneyworld', in which an ostensibly naïve narrator satirizes both the conventional expectations of the tourist and the outside world's eager fulfilment of these expectations. *On the road again* (1978) continued this exploration, although without the family as a central image.

McFadden followed these books with two comic novels, *A trip around Lake Erie* (1980) and *A trip around Lake Huron* (1980). In exceedingly brief, discontinuous chapters these two picaresque works illustrate the struggle of the small man to make sense of an increasingly surreal and commercialized century. *Animal spirits: stories to live by* (1983) is a retrospective collection of McFadden's short stories.

Other books by McFadden are *The poem poem* (1967); *The Saladmaker* (1968); *The ova yogas* (1972); *The poet's progress* (1977); *I don't know* (1978); *A new romance* (1979); *My body was eaten by dogs* (1981), a selected poems edited and introduced by George BOWERING; *Country of the open heart* (1982), a book-length poem; *Three stories and ten poems* (1982); and *A pair of baby lambs* (1983), which contains two long, charming, funny poems, 'The cow that swam Lake Ontario' and 'Stormy January'.   FRANK DAVEY

McFarlane, Leslie (1903-77). Born at Carleton Place, Ont., and raised in Haileybury, he worked as a reporter on the Cobalt *Nugget* and on other newspapers before writing for the pulp magazines under such pseudonyms as 'Roy Rockwood' (for juveniles), 'James Cody Ferris' (westerns), and 'Bert Standish' (general articles). In 1926, responding to an advertisement ('Experienced Fiction Writer Wanted to Work from Publisher's Outlines') in an American trade paper placed by the Stratemeyer Syndicate, he commenced two decades of ghost-writing. He explained in his lively autobiography, *Ghost of the Hardy Boys* (1976), how he wrote the Hardy Boy books under the house name Franklin W. Dixon. Beginning with *The tower treasure*, he completed twenty in all, and was the first writer to use the name Carolyn Keene, the byline later identified with the Nancy Drew books. Under his own name he wrote and published *Streets of shadow* (1930), a romantic novel, and *McGonigle scores!* (1966), a hockey juvenile. Having lived in the United

States for many years, he returned to Canada, residing in Ottawa and Toronto, and settling finally in Whitby, Ont. He scripted a number of documentary films for the National Film Board and contributed dramatic scripts to CBC-TV, serving as the corporation's chief drama editor in 1958-60. His son, the sports announcer Brian McFarlane, is the author of the Peter Puck hockey books for youngsters.   JOHN ROBERT COLOMBO

McGee, Thomas D'Arcy (1825-1868). Born in Carlingford, Ire., he immigrated in 1842 to the United States, where he worked for the Boston *Pilot*, and began his professional life as a spokesman for, and interpreter of, Ireland in New England. After three years he returned to Ireland as a political journalist, became involved in the Young Ireland movement, and when sought by the British as one of the leaders in the abortive 1848 revolution, escaped back to the United States. He continued his activities as a political journalist in New York and Buffalo until 1857, when he left for Canada, after having earlier offended the Roman Catholic bishop of New York by attacking the Irish clergy for discouraging rebellion, and then progressively alienating Americans by criticizing their anti-Roman Catholicism, their anti-foreign bias, and the corruption and bullying of American ward politics.

Though McGee has sometimes been accused of subordinating political and cultural ideals to considerations of personal advantage, he had been consistent in his efforts on behalf of the disadvantaged Irish, as he saw them, and continued to further their cause upon his arrival in Montreal in 1857, when he founded *The New Era*. Elected to the House of Assembly in 1858 as an independent representing the Irish and Roman Catholics of his Montreal constituency, he first favoured the reformers and achieved initial success through their patronage, serving as president of council in 1862. He subsequently aligned himself with the conservatives and enjoyed even greater success, serving as minister of agriculture in 1864. He was an influential participant in the Charlottetown and Quebec conferences that laid the groundwork for Confederation, achieving fame as an oratorical proponent of Confederaton in the years immediately preceding its establishment in 1867. He was elected to the first Canadian parliament in 1867. In the cause of advocating full Irish support for Confederation, McGee had joined battle against the North American Fenian movement and was assassinated by one of its adherents, Patrick James Whelan, on 7 Apr. 1868.

Many of his publications were directly related to his political activities, and to his attempts to further Irish knowledge of, and pride in, Irish culture, in whatever nation Irishmen lived. Such works include *Eva MacDonald; a tale of the united Irishman* (Boston, 1844), *The Irish writers of the seventeenth century* (Dublin, 1846), *A history of the Irish settlers in North America . . .* (Boston, 1851; 2nd edn 1852), and *A popular history of Ireland . . .* (2 vols, New York, 1863). The second most prolific subject of McGee's publications in prose was Canada: *Two speeches on the union of the provinces* (pamphlet, Quebec, 1865); *Speeches and addresses, chiefly on the subject of British American union* (London and Montreal, 1865), translated by L.G. Gladu (St Hyacinthe, 1865); and *The mental outfit of the new Dominion* (pamphlet, Montreal, 1867).

McGee also enjoyed, and still bears, a reputation as a poet, but during his life he published only one collection of verse, *Canadian ballads and occasional verses* (Montreal, 1858). Few of these poems are actually on Canadian subjects; many express his love for Ireland and for things Irish; some articulate a rather conventional religious faith. The strongest are his most personal—evocations of his love for his wife. After his death his poems were assembled by Mary Anne Sadlier in *The poems of D'Arcy McGee* (New York, 1869).

McGee's life and significance have received occasional scholarly comment over the years, most extensively in the centenary works of Alexander Brady, *Thomas D'Arcy McGee* (1925), and Isabel Skelton, *The Life of Thomas D'Arcy McGee* (1925), and in the more recent *The ardent exile: the life and times of Thomas D'Arcy McGee* (Toronto, 1951), by Josephine Phelan.   CHARLES R. STEELE

McGill Poetry Series, The. See Louis DUDEK.

MacGregor, Mary Esther (1876-1961), née Miller, was born in Rugby, Ont., and educated in Orillia and at the Toronto Normal School. She married a Presbyterian minister, the Rev. Donald MacGregor, and—using the pseudonym 'Marian Keith'—was a prolific writer of popular fiction reflective of this background. Most of her stories depict rural life, particularly in predominantly Scottish settlements in Ontario in the 1880s, and many deal with church and manse. *Duncan Polite: the watchman of Glenoro* (1905) is about a minister whose desire to install an organ in the church causes a furore. *Little Miss Melody* (1921) is the story of a minister's daughter. *Lilacs in the dooryard* (1952) tells of a wounded clergyman recuperating in rural Ontario. Other novels, such as *The silver maple: a tale of Upper Canada* (1906), focus on the necessity for brotherhood, in this case a community's need to overcome rivalries between settlers of different national origin. In all MacGregor wrote fourteen novels—the last, *A grand lady*, being published a year before her death. Although overly didactic and sentimental by modern standards, and sharing the character and plot weaknesses of much formula fiction, they retain some value as regional idylls—in their local colour, and particularly in their inclusion of interesting details about everyday life in small Ontario communities before the turn of the century.

MacGregor also wrote short stories, religious biography, such as *Glad days in Galilee* (1935), and a travel book, *Under the grey olives* (1927), about a visit to the Holy Land. She contributed to *Courageous women* (1934), a collection of biographical sketches by prominent women writers of the time and designed for use in schools. MARILYN ROSE

Machar, Agnes Maule (1837-1927), who sometimes used the pen-name 'Fidelis', was born in Kingston, Upper Canada (Ont.), and spent her life there. Her father, the Rev. Dr John Machar, was minister of St Andrew's Presbyterian Church for over thirty-five years (1827-63) and principal of Queen's University (1846-53). Learning, Christian piety, and social service were the cornerstones of her upbringing. As a writer of poetry, fiction (both juvenile and adult), verse-drama, biography, history, and essays for American, British, and Canadian journals on such issues as public education, the co-education of women, social justice for the poor, and Christian belief, she revealed a lively intellect, wide reading, and a commitment to non-sectarian Christian humanism.

Agnes Machar wrote eight novels, of which five—*Katie Johnson's cross, a Canadian tale* (Toronto, 1870), *Lucy Raymond; or The children's watchword* (Toronto, 1871), *For king and country; a story of 1812* (Toronto, 1874), *Lost and won; a story of Canadian life* (issued serially in *The Canadian Monthly*, Jan. to Dec. 1875) and *Marjorie's Canadian*

winter; a story of the Northern Lights (Boston, 1892)—were for children. Of the other three—*Roland Graeme, knight: a novel of our time* (Montreal, 1892), *Down the river to the sea* (New York, 1894), and *The heir of Fairmount Grange* (Toronto, 1895)—only the first is of interest today. *Roland Graeme* is a serious attempt to deal with socio-economic issues, especially as revealed in the activities of the Knights of Labor movement. A travelogue posing as a novel, *River to the sea* celebrates, in a manner reminiscent of Charles SANGSTER's 'The St. Lawrence and the Saguenay', the beauties of the Canadian landscape from Niagara to the Gaspé. *The heir of Fairmount Grange* is a forgettable society novel of the sort so popular late in the nineteenth century. Machar's fiction uses stereotyped characterization, faint plot lines, and the familiar Victorian mixture of Protestant piety and commitment to social justice.

A representative selection of her poems, *Lays of the true north and other Canadian poems* (1892)—which appeared in an enlarged edition that includes her verse-drama *The winged victory* (1902)—reveals a competent, if typically minor, Victorian poetry that celebrates British-Canadian nationalism and the joy, peace, and wonder to be found in nature.

Machar also wrote, or co-authored, two biographies: *Faithful unto death; a memorial of John Anderson* (Kingston, 1859); and, with her mother, *The memorials of the life and ministry of the Reverend John Machar, D.D.* (Kingston 1873); histories for young readers, *Stories of New France* (Boston, 1890), and *Stories of the British Empire for young folks and busy folks* (1913); and a still-valuable account of the early history of her home city, *The story of Old Kingston* (1908). At the age of 82 she published *Young soldier hearts of France* (1919), a series of letters from two young French soldiers to their families during the First World War.

Always ready (with her pen or through good works) to advance causes in which she believed, Machar was the first Canadian to be named a life member of the International Council of Women. After her death funds from her estate were used to establish a home for indigent elderly widows.

See F.L. MacCallum, 'Agnes Maule Machar', *Canadian Magazine* 62 (Mar. 1942); Henry Morgan, *Canadian men and women of the time* (1912); and Rosa L. Shaw, *Proud heritage* (1957). S.R. MacGILLIVRAY

McIlwraith, Jean Newton (1859-1938). Born in Hamilton, Canada West (Ont.), the daughter of Thomas McIlwraith, a well-known ornithologist, she was educated at the Ladies' College in Hamilton and through the correspondence program in modern literature offered by Queen Margaret College, Glasgow University. From 1902 to 1919 she worked as a publisher's reader in New York while establishing herself as a versatile and respected writer of literary criticism, biography, and fiction. She returned to Canada in 1922 and died in Burlington, Ont.

In 1890 McIlwraith began to contribute short stories to such American magazines as *Harper's Magazine*, *Harper's Bazaar*, *The Cornhill*, and *Atlantic Monthly*. She is best known, however, for her historical romances. *The curious career of Roderick Campbell* (1901) is about three close-knit Scottish families after they immigrated to Canada. *A Diana of Quebec* (1912) is set in Québec during the American Revolution, while *Kinsmen at war* (1927), a sentimental and less successful tale, is about conflicting loyalties during the War of 1812. McIlwraith also collaborated with William McLENNAN on *The span o'life: a tale of Louisbourg and Quebec* (1899), which first appeared in serial form in *Harper's Magazine*. Her novels are well documented and rich in historical detail and texture, though dated by the form and conventions of the post-Confederation popular historical romance.

McIlwraith also wrote a well-regarded biography, *Sir Frederick Haldimand* (1904), for the Makers of Canada series. She was the author of several books for young people, including *A book about Shakespeare* (1898), *A book about Longfellow* (1900), and the prize-winning *The little admiral* (1924), set in the period of the fall of Quebec.

MARILYN ROSE

MacInnes, Tom (1867-1951). Thomas Robert Edward MacInnes, who changed the spelling of his name from McInnes, was a son of Thomas McInnes, a lieutenant-governor of British Columbia (1897-1902). Born in Dresden, Ont., he went with his family to New Westminster, B.C., in 1881, was educated at the University of Toronto, and was called to the bar in 1893. He was secretary to the Bering Sea Commission (1896-7) and helped supervise the importation of goods to Skagway (1897) for members of the Klondike Gold Rush. He practised law in Vancouver and was in-

volved with the drafting of immigration laws in 1910, and with import regulations and the control of narcotics. From 1916 to 1927 MacInnes spent long periods in China, where he had business interests. As a result he developed a sympathy for the treatment of Orientals living in B.C.; his views of British Columbia prejudice appeared in the pamphlet *Oriental occupation of British Columbia* (1927). MacInnes's autobiographical *Chinook days* (1926) contains his impressions of people, places, and events in British Columbia history. He died in Vancouver.

MacInnes's narrative poems—concerned with adventure or dramatic situations in strange environments (his attitude is bohemian), and expressing his enjoyment of life—were highly popular in his lifetime. He wrote light, easy verse that dismissed smugness and respectability with unconcerned humour, as Stephen LEACOCK did in his short anecdotes. Even when MacInnes is sometimes serious, an amused detachment underlies his work, as though poetry were merely one form of expression, as good as any other. He felt that any subject was appropriate for poetry and was especially interested in examining man within a natural landscape, on the fringes of society. Though uninterested in poetic subtleties—his rhythms are often forced and pedantic, his rhyme-schemes careless and rough—he was intrigued with elaborate poetic forms, such as the villanelle, and with a five-line stanza of his own he called the 'mirelle'. His belief that joy and delight, rather than the prevalent melancholic outpourings of the soul, were essential to poetry was expressed in one of his later and best-known poems, 'The tiger of desire', which fits an allusion to the past (Blake) and to contemporary concerns (a type of Darwin-mysticism) into his usual structure, the villanelle. His collections are *A romance of the lost* (1908), reprinted with other poems in *Lonesome bar, A romance of the lost, and other poems* (1909); *In amber lands* (1910); *Rhymes of a rounder; a fool of joy* (1918); *Roundabout rhymes* (with a Foreword by Charles G.D. ROBERTS, 1923); *Complete poems of Tom MacInnis* (1923); *High low along: a didactic poem* (1934); and *In the old of my age* (1947).   DONALD STEPHENS

MacKay, L.A. See POETRY IN ENGLISH 1900 TO 1950: 3.

Mackenzie, Sir Alexander. See EXPLORATION LITERATURE IN ENGLISH: 2.

Mackenzie

Mackenzie, William Lyon (1795-1861). Born in Scotland, where both his grandfathers had fought for the rebel cause at Culloden, Mackenzie immigrated to Upper Canada in 1820. He founded *The Colonial Advocate* (Queenston, 1824; York, 1824-34) and a succession of other newspapers, which he edited, published, and wrote much of the copy for: *The Correspondent and Advocate* (Toronto, 1834-6); *The Welland Canal* (Toronto, Dec. 1835); *The Constitution* (Toronto, 1836-Nov. 1837); *Mackenzie's Gazette* (New York, 1838-9; Rochester, 1839-40); *The Volunteer* (Rochester, 1841-2); *The New York Examiner* (New York, 1843); *Mackenzie's Weekly Message* (Toronto, 1852-6); and *The Toronto Weekly Message* (1856-60). In his simultaneous career as a radical politician and agitator, Mackenzie was elected to—and expelled from—the Upper Canada house of assembly several times and was the first mayor of Toronto for nine months in 1834-5. A leader in the 1837 Rebellion, which collapsed following two skirmishes with government forces near and in Toronto on Dec. 7, Mackenzie escaped to the United States. He returned to Canada under the Amnesty Act of 1849, was re-elected to the assembly in 1851, and resigned in 1858.

Mackenzie's interests were encyclopaedic, as even the titles of these essay collections and almanacs suggest: *Essay on canals and inland navigation* (Queenston, 1824); *Catechism of education* (York, 1830); *Sketches of Canada and the United States* (London, 1833); *Poor Richard; or the Yorkshire Almanac . . . by Patrick Swift* (York, 1831?). All of his work was in large part polemical and the following titles indicate the prevailing tone: *The legislative black list of Upper Canada; or, Official corruption and hypocrisy unmasked* (York, 1828); *Celebrated letter of Joseph Hume, esq., M.P., to William Lyon Mackenzie* (Toronto, 1834); *The seventh report from the select committee of the house of assembly of Upper Canada on grievances* (Toronto, 1835). Mackenzie's fondness was for the farmers of Upper Canada; he was at heart an agrarian Utopian, and this yearning places him firmly in that Canadian pastoral tradition expressed in such contemporary works as Thomas McCULLOCH's *Stepsure letters* or parts of Oliver GOLDSMITH's *The rising village*. While his life and publications may be interpreted as a quest to make of his nation a genuinely charitable community, he possessed an irrepressible assertiveness of personality that was a main cause of the controversies, the love *and* hate, that surrounded him.

Mackenzie was also a raconteur, a teller of tales of war and intrigue (*Head's flag of truce*, Toronto, 1853?); of frontier rowdiness (*The history of the destruction of the 'Colonial Advocate' press*, York, 1826); of escape and adventure (*Mackenzie's own narrative of the late rebellion*, Toronto, 1838). He wrote memorable character sketches of some of his Canadian and European contemporaries, of Andrew Jackson (*Life and opinions of Andrew Jackson*, York, 1829), and *The sons of the Emerald Isle; or Lives of one thousand remarkable Irishmen* (New York, 1845). He also wrote of Upper and Lower Canada, its scenes and people, in an organized, concrete, and observant fashion that earns him a place among significant Canadian travel writers. He was an articulate satirist, a puritan moralizer, a chronic denouncer of the 'family compact' of Upper Canada and of several Americans (*The life and times of Martin Van Buren*, Boston, 1846; *The lives and opinions of Benjamin Franklin Butler, United States district attorney, and Jesse Hoyt, counsellor at law, formerly collector of customs for the port of New York*, Boston, 1845). His exposés mix shrill invective with a prophet's holy wrath and millennial visions.

Mackenzie's writing is quite as eclectic in style as in subject. His expository and polemical pieces, at their best, proceed via methodical arguments buttressed with fact, example, and illustration. Long sentences with skilfully sustained parallelisms and subordinations build in rhythm and sound toward conclusions that are as climactic in cadence as in meaning. He uses such techniques as irony; rhetorical questions, catalogues, and lists; and the punch of the brief sharp sentence. His wide reading and literary flare enabled him to mix homely tales and similes from Scottish folklore, rustic frontier anecdotes, and biblical analogies with paragraphs devoted to elevated declarations of principle. Often his rhetoric is oral in effect, irresistibly invoking for the reader images of Mackenzie the vivid orator. Some of his work has the quality of poetry: see John Robert COLOMBO's selection of 'redeemed prose', *The Mackenzie poems* (1960), and the 'found poem' from Mackenzie's 1837 Navy Island proclamation in Raymond SOUSTER's *Hanging in* (1979).

Finally, mention should be made of Mackenzie's appearance as a character in Canadian literature—in, for example, Rick SALUTIN's drama *1837* (1976); in James REANEY's children's novel *The boy with an R in his hand* (1965); or in William Kilbourn's *The firebrand* (1956), a biography that, like the writings of its subject, often achieves literary stature. A study of Mackenzie as a maker not only of history but of literature cannot but enhance the reputation of a man who, however controversial, will always be with us and who, as Dennis LEE writes (in *Nicholas Knock and other people*, 1974), will always be needed as every nation needs its millennialists.

See *The selected writings of William Lyon Mackenzie: 1824-1837 (1960)* edited by Margaret Fairley, and the passages by Mackenzie in A.J.M. SMITH's *The book of Canadian prose, vol. I: early beginnings to Confederation* (1965). WILLIAM BUTT

M'Kinnon, William Charles (1828-62). Born near North Sydney, Cape Breton (N.S.), into a military family of Loyalist and Scottish background, he was educated in a rural Cape Breton schoolhouse. Between 1846 and 1850 he founded and edited three partisan Liberal newspapers: *The Cape-Breton Spectator* (North Sydney), *The Times* (North Sydney), and *The Commercial Herald* (Sydney). Following the demise of the *Herald* he tried unsuccessfully to establish a literary career in Boston, Halifax, and Sydney, at one point editing the Halifax *New Era* while continuing to write fiction and poetry. After entering the Methodist ministry in 1853, he abandoned creative writing and channelled his literary energies into works of a theological and geological nature. He died of tuberculosis at the age of thirty-four while serving the Methodist circuit of Shelburne, N.S.

M'Kinnon's first literary publication was a collection of poems, *The Battle of the Nile* (Sydney, 1844), which revealed a precocious and sophisticated understanding of poetic convention for a youth of sixteen. He next published two historical novellas—*Castine: a legend of Cape Breton* and *The midnight murder: a legend of Cape-Breton*—in *The Commercial Herald*, and then in *The Waverley Magazine* of Boston (1850). *Castine* was also serialized in *The Eastern Chronicle* of Pictou in 1850 and published in book form as *St. Castine* (Sydney, 1850). Set in Louisbourg at the time of the 1758 siege, *St. Castine* is typical of M'Kinnon's narratives in weaving melodrama, disguise, intrigue, and romance into a fabric of actual events and characters. *The midnight murder*, based on Sydney's 1833 Flahaven murder, illustrates the author's penchant for lecherous villains and exotic background characters and introduces a Yankee sailor, a Gaelic backlander, and thinly disguised local figures into a busy plot of blood, betrayal, and vindication. Probably the first fictional interpretation of contemporary Cape Breton, it enjoyed a readership of 13,000 in Boston alone. On returning to Nova Scotia from Boston in 1851, M'Kinnon wrote *Francis; or Pirate Cove, a legend of Cape-Breton* (Halifax, 1851), a somewhat melodramatic historical romance about the activities of Jordan the Pirate off Cape Breton and New England in the eighteenth century. His most ambitious effort, however, was *St. George; or The Canadian league: a tale of the outbreak* (Halifax, 1852), a two-volume work about a secret society in Lower Canada during the Rebellion of 1837. Although M'Kinnon introduced historical figures like Papineau and Mackenzie into the novel, and defended the historical accuracy of his tale in a lengthy introduction, he could not make the hypnotic powers and villainy of his central character seem credible. His entry into the ministry, and disappointment over the book's reception, resulted in his eschewing romances and destroying his published novels. These works had emerged from his avowed interest in Sir Walter Scott and Bulwer-Lytton and provide yet another illustration of the influence of the Scott tradition on the popular literature of nineteenth-century Canada. GWENDOLYN DAVIES

McLachlan, Alexander (1818-96). Born in Johnstone, Scot., he worked in a cotton factory until he was apprenticed to a tailor in Glasgow. In 1840 he immigrated to Caledon, Upper Canada, to take possession of the farm of his father, who had died. He sold it the next year and cleared land for three other farms before moving in 1850 to Erin Twp, where he worked as a tailor to support his family of eleven children; achieving a reputation as a speaker, he also gave lectures for the Mechanics' Institute. Through his friendship with D'Arcy McGEE, he was made immigration agent for Canada in Scotland in 1862. In 1877 he moved to a farm in Amaranth Twp, Ont., where he remained until he retired to a house in nearby Orangeville in 1895.

For his idylls about log houses, 'hosses', and oxen in the bush, McLachlan is the poet of the backwoods pioneers; in his time he was known as 'the Burns of Canada' for his celebration of the democratic spirit of brotherhood and the toil of the common man. He

McLachlan

is at his best in light lyrics that document the customs of country life, as in 'Sparking' (the pioneers' slang for courtship). Like Burns, he complements his reverence for the common man with kindly humour, satirizing skinflints and mistreaters of oxen. Occasionally, as in 'We live in a rickety house', he rises to the ironic pitch of a Blakean nursery song in condemning the naivety of pious charity workers who fail to recognize the church's responsibility for the ignorance and crime that exist among the poor. Of his five volumes of verse—*The spirit of love and other poems* (Toronto 1846), *Poems* (Toronto 1856), *Lyrics* (Toronto 1858), *The emigrant and other poems* (Toronto, 1861), and *Poems and songs* (Toronto 1874)—the 1874 volume is his best collection, while 'The emigrant' is his most ambitious single poem, an unfinished epic in narrative couplets and songs telling of the Scottish immigrants who voyaged across the ocean to clear land for a home in the backwoods of Upper Canada. McLachlan wrote many poems about Scotland: the elegaic song, 'The halls of Holyrood', won *The British Workman*'s prize for the best poem about Queen Mary's palace; other Scottish poems, like the rousing 'Curling song', are in dialect.

McLachlan, like Burns, was interested in the delineation of character, but his gift for characterization was that of the mimic. The probing of character achieved no more depth than the glimpse at the faith that sustains a long-suffering widow in 'Old Hannah'. As E.H. DEWART noted in his introduction to the posthumous collection *The poetical works of Alexander McLachlan* (Toronto, 1900), McLachlan 'was too often satisfied with putting the passing thoughts that occupied his mind into easy, homely rimes.'

A 1974 reprint of *The poetical works of Alexander McLachlan* includes an introduction by E. Margaret Fulton and Dewart's 'Introductory Essay and Biographical Sketch' from the original edition. Her appendix of eight poems regrettably omits 'We live in a rickety house'. DAVID LATHAM

McLaren, Floris Clarke. See POETRY IN ENGLISH 1900 TO 1950: 2(a).

MacLennan, Hugh (b. 1907). Born in Glace Bay, N.S., the son of a medical doctor, he grew up in Halifax, was educated at Dalhousie University and, as a Rhodes Scholar, at Oxford, and travelled in Europe before taking his doctoral degree in classical studies at Princeton. His dissertation, published as *Oxyrhynchus: an economic and social study* (1935; rpr. 1968), showed a leftist bias that was later cured by MacLennan's visit to Russia in 1937; but some critics point to the relevance for his fiction of its analysis of the decay of a Roman colony cut off from its roots in the parent civilization. While at Princeton, MacLennan also began writing fiction but, out of economic necessity, turned to the teaching of Latin and history at Lower Canada College, Montreal, in 1935. Originally encouraged to write by the American writer Dorothy Duncan, whom he married in 1936, he made two abortive attempts at novels with international settings. According to MacLennan, Dorothy directed him to the national theme and setting that he knew, and the result was BAROMETER RISING (1941), which drew on his boyhood experience of the Halifax explosion of 1917. On the strength of its *succès d'estime* he spent a year in New York on a Guggenheim Fellowship. He returned reluctantly to Lower Canada College, but when TWO SOLITUDES (1945) became a commercial success and won a Governor General's Award he decided to turn to freelance journalism and broadcasting. *The precipice* (1948) also won a Governor General's Award, as did his first volume of essays, *Cross country* (1949). MacLennan was now a celebrity, writing regularly for *Maclean's* and other national magazines; in 1952 he received the Lorne Pierce Medal and in 1953 he was elected to the Royal Society of Canada. His second volume of essays, *Thirty and three* (1954), brought him a fourth Governor General's Award; but by this time financial pressure and Dorothy's chronic illness obliged him to seek academic security and he began lecturing part-time in the English Department of McGill University. The impact on MacLennan of Dorothy's death is apparent in the emotional intensity of *The watch that ends the night* (1959), the novel—for many readers his best—that brought him a record fifth Governor General's Award. He followed it the next year with a third volume of essays: *Scotchman's return and other essays* (1960). In 1967 he became a Companion of the Order of Canada; in 1968 he was made a full professor at McGill and received his seventh honorary degree. He retired as professor emeritus in 1979 and lives with his second wife, Frances Walker, at North Hatley, Qué.

Though MacLennan's public honours have been closely associated with his reputation as a nationalist, his larger subject is Graeco-Roman civilization and its long decline to the present. This Spenglerian view—in which the key to survival and to more fulfilling lives may be found in learning the lessons of history and the wisdom taught by both classical and Judaeo-Christian writers—accounts for MacLennan's vision, in the early novels, of Canada, heir of European culture, as a mediator between the crude, vital New World and an Old World informed by classical ideals; and it justifies his use of classical models, particularly Homeric epic. George WOODCOCK and others have pointed to the prominence in MacLennan's fiction of the Odyssean archetype—a figure that is often not simply a homeseeker but an emissary of civilization to an increasingly indifferent world.

Though a self-conscious nationalism has always been an element in our literature, MacLennan's deliberate choice of Canadian concerns for his subjects, and his early view of Canada as mediating between an inherited culture and North American obsessive materialism, have earned him a too-facile reputation as a crusading nationalist. Of course he is a nationalist. Neil Macrae of *Barometer rising* could have no identity until the colonial past, engendered in violence, had been violently destroyed. As Neil's identity is acknowledged, so is that of the nation: it has earned the right to be itself. In *Two solitudes* Paul Tallard and Heather Methuen combine artistic creativity with a symbolic marriage of the two founding peoples, and Paul determines to write a novel about Canada. In *Each man's son*, which features the Cape Breton of MacLennan's childhood, Alan MacNeil is saved from the crippling life of the mines and taught the privilege of belonging to civilization, especially in Canada, respected honest broker of the post-war world, where the past can meet the energy of the future. However, the optimism inherent in MacLennan's early nationalism soon soured. In *The precipice* there is already a sense of dismay at the destructive power of American industry and less confidence in Canada's ability to meliorate it. The small Ontario town in which the action begins has only potential; not even the Second World War can arouse it until American energy, in the person of Stephen Lassiter, invades it. In *The watch that ends the night* it is openly acknowledged that scientific, military, economic, and even political power ultimately reside outside Canada; salvation is not national but an individual and personal dream.

Jerome Martel—doctor, saviour, man of violence—returns, almost from the grave, to threaten the happiness of timid, bourgeois George Stewart and his sick wife Catherine, who was once married to Jerome. But through him, George and Catherine—who represents what is gracious and civilized in a declining world—learn to accept her death.

The tone of MacLennan's two latest novels is much darker. *Return of the Sphinx* (1967) deals with the nation's failure to heal the rift between French- and English-speaking Canadians, and with the perpetuation in the New World not of the values but of the hatreds of the Old. With this novel MacLennan concedes that Canada's future, like its politics and economics, is beyond our control: everything the protagonist, Alan, has stood for seems lost, the only hope being represented by a rural French-Canadian wedding and Alan's awareness of love for his children. *Voices in time* (1980), set in Montreal fifty years after it was destroyed by a nuclear holocaust, portrays a world like that of Orwell's *Nineteen eighty four* as John Wellfleet, like Orwell's Winston, finds and puzzles over the evidence of his family past and a former civilization: decline and fall are here complete. MacLennan moves back and forth in time and space to repeat his major theme: that the failures to learn the lessons of the past and to guarantee civilized values made the destruction of the West—like the destruction of the classical world—inevitable.

MacLennan has endowed his writing with a strong element of regionalism, in the conviction that place too has its personality; this finds its most sustained expression in *The rivers of Canada* (1974) but pervades the fiction as well. Included in the regional 'personalities' of his novels is the local manifestation of general attitudes, particularly the puritanism that MacLennan, perhaps naively at first, thought of as Canadian and tended to associate with the Scots and the Presbyterian church. All his protagonists are prone to puritanical self-examination, and *The precipice* and *Each man's son* are explicit analyses of inherent guilt in the individual and the community. The early MacLennan seemed to see the joylessness of Calvinism as inimical both to the arts and to individual expression. Usually his puritans are men; his female protagonists embody life-giving joy, creativity, sensuousness, and love.

MacLennan's novels have been criticized for their didacticism, the tendency to tell us rather than show us. Too often the author

MacLennan

stops to reflect on national and historical issues or to explain in laboured dialogue or monologue what his characters are supposed to mean. Though he can be sensitive, he sometimes becomes embarrassed and rhetorical in intimate scenes, especially sexual ones. Generally well within the realistic mode, his protagonists (notably Jerome Martell) sometimes seem more romantic than real. Some of them, however—George Stewart, Athanase Tallard—are memorable as well as representative, and each of the novels does address a technical as well as a thematic problem. The Halifax explosion in *Barometer rising*, Jerome's recollection of his escape from the lumber camp in *The watch*, and Archie MacNeil's decline in *Each man's son* show MacLennan's gift for fast-paced, exciting narrative. With *The precipice* the characterization becomes more overtly psychological, and in all the novels a sustained structure of imagery reinforces character and theme.

MacLennan's essays, most of which are journalistic and occasional pieces dealing with politics, contemporary personalities, and comparative Canadian-American attitudes, have tended to date rather quickly. Those concerned with his own writing and with literature (e.g. 'My first novel'), those narratives that suggest MacLennan's potential in the short story (e.g. 'An orange from Portugal' and 'The lost love of Tommy Waterfield'), and the later social vignettes and commentary, such as 'Have you had many Wimbledons?' and 'The curtain falls on the grand style', are often whimsical, humorous, and urbane. One understands some critics' preference for MacLennan as essayist, where he is often more professional than he is in the novels, but the unity of purpose the essays share with the novels should not be overlooked; they too champion civilized values in a philistine world, and though less intense than the novels, they also express a lament for civilization. Related to the three volumes of essays are the texts for *The colour of Canada* (1967); *McGill: the story of a university* (1961); and *The rivers of Canada*, which is a much-revised version of *Seven rivers of Canada* (1961). Its introductory essay, 'Thinking like a river', acknowledges the 'watershed of the '60s' that changed the writer's, and our, world: MacLennan's realization that for Canada and the Western world a cycle of civilization, or order and human values, was ending, to be replaced by the violent era of the 'rough beast'. This realization informs the fiction and the non-

fiction alike and gives unity to MacLennan's work. His essays on the rivers, like those on Canadian cities, effectively personify characteristics of the landscape he loves. *The other side of Hugh MacLennan* (1978), essays edited by Elspeth Cameron, selects the best of the non-fiction and testifies to MacLennan's skill in the shorter form.

MacLennan has enjoyed more critical attention than most of his Canadian contemporaries. Significantly the first full-length study, by Paul Goetsch, appeared in Germany (1961); Goetsch subsequently edited the MacLennan volume (1973) in the McGraw-Hill Ryerson Critical Views series. George Woodcock's *Hugh MacLennan* (1969) first demonstrated the Odyssean parallel; Alec Lucas's *Hugh MacLennan* (1970) draws on the relevance of *Oxyrhynchus*; Peter Buitenhuis's *Hugh MacLennan* (1971) relates the essays to the fiction; Robert Cockburn's *The novels of Hugh MacLennan* (1971) has useful critical analyses; Patricia Morley's *The immoral moralists* (1972) is a helpful summary of characteristics of puritanism but links MacLennan and Leonard COHEN unconvincingly. Elspeth Cameron's *Hugh MacLennan: a writer's life* (1981) provides a wealth of personal data and anecdotes with careful documentation. *Hugh MacLennan: 1982*, edited by Elspeth Cameron, makes available the papers and personal reminiscences from the MacLennan Conference at the University of Toronto.

See also ESSAYS IN ENGLISH: 3 and NOVELS IN ENGLISH 1960 TO 1982: 1.

D. O. SPETTIGUE

McLennan, William (1856-1904). Born in Montreal, McLennan was educated at the Montreal High School and at McGill University (BCL, 1880). He was a senior partner in a firm of notaries until 1900, when ill-health forced him to move to Italy. He died there, and is buried in the English cemetery at Florence.

Elected a fellow of the Royal Society of Canada in 1899, McLennan was considered one of Canada's finest writers of historical fiction. He saw himself preserving the folk tales, songs, and myths of French Canada in his translations, short stories, and longer fiction. His translations of French-Canadian songs were collected in *Songs of Old Canada* (Montreal, 1886). He made his greatest impact on the public, however, with a series of short stories about French-Canadian life that appeared in *Harper's Magazine* in 1891-2. Based on personal research into the traditions of his native province, they were combined with other stories set in revolutionary France and collected in *In Old France and New* (Toronto, 1900).

Two of McLennan's finest stories are 'The indescretion of Grosse Boule', a comic tale in the *fabliaux* tradition, and 'Le coureur-de-neiges', an interesting blend of history and the supernatural. In his stories historical research supported but did not dominate the romantic legends. This was not true of *Spanish John* (New York, 1898), a crude reworking of the memoirs of Captain John McDonnell, which were originally published in *The Canadian Magazine* (1825). The novel lacks any effective literary design and the critics were quick to point out the absence of a love plot, considered mandatory in a historical novel. In apparent response to this criticism, McLennan collaborated with Jean McILWRAITH on his next novel, *The span o' life: a tale of Louisbourg and Quebec* (New York, 1899). He found his character and setting in the autobiography of Chevalier Johnstone, a Scotsman who fought in the Old World and the New in support of the Jacobite cause. McLennan provided the historical setting and McIlwraith the love story, but their united efforts produced a sprawling work that adheres to the formula for historical fiction without achieving a satisfactory resolution of its elements.

Although today he is forgotten, the praise and recognition that McLennan received in his lifetime—justifiably so for his short stories—are captured in Duncan Campbell SCOTT's poem, 'At William Maclennan's grave' (*The poems of Duncan Campbell Scott*, 1926).   CAL SMILEY

MacLeod, Alistair (b. 1936). Born in North Battleford, Sask., he lived on the Prairies until his parents moved back to the family farm in Cape Breton, where he attended high school. After obtaining his Teacher's Certificate from Nova Scotia Teacher's College in Truro, N.S., he attended St Francis Xavier University, Antigonish, for his B.A. and B.Ed. He then did graduate work at the Universities of New Brunswick (M.A., 1961) and Notre Dame (Ph.D., 1968). He taught at the University of Indiana for three years (1966-9) before moving to the University of Windsor, where he now teaches English and creative writing; he is also fiction editor of *The University of Windsor Review*.

MacLeod's short fiction has appeared in Canadian and American journals since the mid-fifties, but his only book is *The lost salt gift of blood* (1976; NCL 1981). Of the seven stories in this collection, two had already been included in the annual collection, *Best American short stories*—'The boat' in 1969, and the title story in 1975. MacLeod displays the regional writer's preoccupation with the categories of exile, here available equally to those returning to Cape Breton and to those who leave for the mainland. MacLeod's first-person narrators are self-consciously elegiac and lyrical as they explore the ties of family and memory that bind them to the various 'livings' of Cape Breton: the sea and its boats in 'The boat' and 'The lost salt gift of blood', the coal-mines in 'The vastness of the dark' and 'The return', and the land in 'The road to Rankin's Point'. These livings provide the young narrators—all of whom have either left their island home or have left only to return—with that divided inheritance of loss and belonging suggested by the title.

MacLeod's stories have continued to appear in respected fiction journals, notably 'The closing down of summer' in FIDDLEHEAD (Fall 1976), and 'Second spring' in CANADIAN FICTION MAGAZINE (no. 34/35, 1980).   MICHELLE GADPAILLE

MacLeod, Jack. See HUMOUR AND SATIRE IN ENGLISH and NOVELS IN ENGLISH 1960 TO 1982: OTHER TALENTS, OTHER WORKS: 3.

McLuhan, Marshall (1911-80). Herbert Marshall McLuhan was born in Edmonton, Alta, and spent his youth in Winnipeg. He attended the University of Manitoba and received a doctorate in English Literature from Cambridge University. After teaching English in various U.S. universities, he returned to Canada in 1944 to teach at Assumption College (now Windsor University). From 1946 until shortly before his death he taught English at St Michael's College, University of Toronto, where he became interested in media of communication, culture, and technology, organizing an interdisciplinary seminar in 1954 under the sponsorship of the Ford Foundation. Outgrowths of this project included the publication *Explorations*, which he co-edited with E.S. Carpenter from 1953 to 1959, and the Centre of Culture and Technology at the University of Toronto (1963-81), of which he was founding director. One of the first scholars to occupy the Albert Schweitzer Chair at Fordham University in 1967, he was elected FRSC in 1964 and was named a

McLuhan

Companion of the Order of Canada in 1970.

Although usually described as a communication scholar, McLuhan made major contributions to literary studies, cultural theory, and the understanding of the role of media and technology in society. His first major work, *The mechanical bride: folklore of industrial man* (1951), applied the strategies of a satirically focused critical interpretation to the products of popular culture and the media industries. His international reputation was established by two works bridging historical and theoretical problems of communications, culture, and technology. *The Gutenberg galaxy: the making of typographic man* (1962, GGA) analyses the pre-print, oral/aural culture and the results of Gutenberg's invention of movable type and the mass-production of books; it introduced one of McLuhan's most famous phrases in stating that the world had become a 'global village' in its electronic interdependence. *Understanding media: the extension of man* (1964) examines the radical changes in man's responses caused by electronic communications, and contains another of his celebrated statements: ' "The Medium is the Message" because it is the medium that shapes and controls the scale and form of human association and action.' After publication of this book, McLuhan's name became a word in itself, such as *mcluhanisme* in France. His work paralleled the interests of other Canadian scholars, particularly H.A. INNIS—who has often been described, erroneously, as his mentor. (McLuhan, however, shared with Innis a realization of the importance of technology in shaping human cultural development.) While McLuhan was interested, like Northrop FRYE, in problems of interpretation and symbolism, he had a broader scope, seeking a total cultural criticism; he emphasized the way polysemy in language (e.g. puns, ambiguity, metaphor) reveals the continuum between all orders of cultural expression.

Adapting the work of avant-garde writers such as Wyndham Lewis and James Joyce, McLuhan created a series of *essais concrètes* combining photography, layout, advertising techniques, headlines, typography, and visual arrangement, such as *The medium is the massage* (1967) and *Peace and war in the global village* (1968). Other books by McLuhan include *The literary criticism of Marshall McLuhan 1943-62* (1969), *Counterblast* (1969), *Culture is our business* (1970), *Take today: the executive as dropout* (with Barrington Nevitt, 1972), *The city as classroom* (1977), and *Verbi-voco-visual explorations* (1967), which was originally issue 8 of *Explorations*. He co-authored (with Wilfred WATSON) *From cliché to archetype* (1970) and (with Harley Parker) *Through the vanishing point* (1968), a study of the contemporary revolution by media and the avant-garde against the assumptions of Renaissance perspective and print culture. In addition to *Explorations*, McLuhan edited an important information letter for those involved in government, business, and academia, *The Dew Line*, of which his son was also an editor. *The interior landscape: the literary criticism of Marshall McLuhan 1943-62* (1969) was edited by Eugene McNAMARA.

McLuhan conceived of himself as a 'poet manqué' who produced do-it-yourself creativity kits. Despite obvious weaknesses in his writings (such as a tendency towards technological determinism), their perceptions, theoretical suggestivity, and paradoxes are distinctive, inventive, and very much a product of his having pursued his career in Canada. Possessing a typical Canadian sensitivity to the ways in which U.S. technology, cultural products, and media affect the quality of life, McLuhan was first to recognize that technology had become one of the major factors in human evolution and in the changing shape of modern culture. As his literary criticism and concern with history suggest, his thought was rooted in humanism and in an avant-garde version of Thomism that grew out of his conversion to Catholicism.

McLuhan's theoretical contributions to the interface between rapidly evolving technology and human culture were recognized in the Teleguide-McLuhan Prize awarded through UNESCO.

The primary writings on McLuhan's work are Dennis Duffy, *Marshall McLuhan* (1969), Jonathan Miller, *McLuhan* (1971), and Donald Theall, *The medium is the rear view mirror: understanding McLuhan* (1971). Two excellent collections of essays are *McLuhan: pro and con* (1968) edited by Raymond Rosenthal and *McLuhan hot and cool* (1967) edited by Gerald E. Stearn.

DONALD THEALL

MacMechan, Archibald (1862-1933). Born in Berlin (Kitchener), Ont., Archibald McKellar MacMechan was educated at the University of Toronto and Johns Hopkins University and was professor of English at Dalhousie University, Halifax, from 1889 until two years before his death. He was made a Fellow of the Royal Society of Canada in 1926 and was awarded the Lorne PIERCE medal for distinguished service to Canadian literature in 1931.

MacMechan is principally known for his engaging familiar essays. Three early collections are *The porter of Bagdad and other fantasies* (1901), a small volume of typically late-Victorian whimsical essays; *The life of a little college* (1914), the title essay of which deals with MacMechan's affectionate ties with Dalhousie University; and *The book of Ultima Thule* (1928), essays concerned mostly with the author's personal response to Nova Scotia geography and history. His familiarity with the sea, and the local history relating to it, is central to three historically based collections that represent the writing he considered to be of most lasting value: *Sagas of the sea* (1923), *Old Province tales* (1924), and *There go the ships* (1928). *Tales of the sea* (1948), edited by Thomas RADDALL, is a posthumous collection of essays drawn from these books. MacMechan's critical survey of the principal works of English- and French-Canadian authors, *Headwaters of Canadian literature* (1924; NCL 1974), sets forth his strongly held views concerning the need for a native literature worthy of international recognition. His adherence to idiosyncratic standards and his recognition of the dual national culture make this book an important contribution to early Canadian literary criticism. On local history MacMechan also wrote *Red snow on Grand Pré* (1921) and *The Halifax explosion* (unpublished); and on political history, *The winning of popular government* (1916) in the Chronicles of Canada series. His published verse includes *Three sea songs* (1919) and the posthumous *Late harvest* (1934). As a scholar of non-Canadian literature he published his doctoral dissertation, *The relation of Hans Sachs to the Decameron as shown in an examination of the thirteen Shrovetide plays from that source* (1889); and edited editions of two works by Thomas Carlyle, *Sartor resartus* (1896) and *Heroes and hero worship* (1901), the *Select poems of Lord Tennyson* (1907), and the Thoreau chapter in the *Cambridge history of American literature* (1916). From 1907 until his death MacMechan was a weekly book reviewer for *The Montreal Standard*, writing under the non-de-plume 'The Dean'.

See also CRITICISM IN ENGLISH: 2 and ESSAYS IN ENGLISH: 2.   JANET BAKER

Macmillan, Cyrus. See CHILDREN'S LITER-ATURE IN ENGLISH: 5 and INDIAN LEGENDS AND TALES: BIBLIOGRAPHY.

Macmillan Company of Canada, The. Like a number of other Canadian branches of English publishing companies, the Macmillan Company of Canada owes its existence to the absence of copyright protection in the United States for foreigners in the nineteenth century. Alexander Macmillan visited the U.S. at the end of the Civil War to look into the prospects for setting up a North American establishment to stock and sell his books, and so discourage 'pirates' from producing unlicensed editions. He found the right man to head such a business in George Edward Brett, who was succeeded by his son, and then by his grandson. The New York firm worked Canadian territory, but when it rose to the front rank of American publishers it became necessary to have a house in Canada that would incidentally enable Macmillan's to obtain imperial copyright, an ironic reversal of the purpose that had brought it into existence. The Canadian Macmillan Company was incorporated in 1905, as one of a chain of branches and depots then being established around the Empire. The New York company, because of its size, was permitted to hold an interest in it.

Macmillan of Canada took off well, and within two years had put up a building at 70 Bond Street, Toronto, where the company was to remain until 1980. During the Great War the management under Frank Wise had become slack. In 1917 a young Yorkshireman, Hugh Eayrs (1894-1940), who had been in Canada for five years with Maclean-Hunter, joined Macmillan, and in 1921 he succeeded Wise as president. The elderly London partners were deriving a good profit from the great American business they had founded, which was now entirely self-managing but still subject to London's control. Eayrs impressed them with his youthful vigour, his brilliant, though sometimes impractical, plans, and his evangelistic belief in the future of Canada. Within two years he had published W.H. BLAKE's translation of Louis HÉMON's MARIA CHAPDELAINE, which became a great success in Britain and the U.S., as well as in Canada. Encouragement of their aggressive young Canadian manager must have seemed to the London partners a way of keeping the American Bretts—who appeared to be growing too big for their boots—in order. Eayrs was allowed his head, acquiring the

Macmillan Company of Canada

agency for Cambridge Bibles and prayer-books as well as for a whole group of British medical publishers, and even for one or two of Brett's American rivals.

When, in 1950, the London partners decided to sell The Macmillan Company, New York—now a giant bigger than themselves and impossible to control—they bought back, as part of the deal, the interest the American company had been allowed to have in the Canadian company. Eayrs had died during the war and was succeeded in 1946 by John GRAY. From that point on, until Gray's retirement in 1973, Macmillan Canada, riding the crest of the wave of Canada's post-war publishing expansion under Gray's expert leadership, became one of the largest and most successful publishing companies in Canada. Its list of Canadian authors included Mazo DE LA ROCHE, Morley CALLAGHAN, Hugh MacLENNAN, Robertson DAVIES, and Donald CREIGHTON.

Difficulty in finding a suitable successor to John Gray caused the London partners to sell Macmillan Canada to Maclean-Hunter in 1973. In 1980 Macmillan of Canada was taken over by Gage Publishing Limited, who retained the imprint but made the trade publishing activities of Macmillan a division of its largely educational business.

LOVAT DICKSON

McNamara, Eugene (b. 1930). Born in Oak Park, Illinois, and educated in the Chicago area, he came to Canada in 1959 to teach English at the University of Windsor (then Assumption University), where he was instrumental in starting the Creative Writing Program and has continued to be its director since 1967. He has long been associated with the academic and cultural life of Windsor, editing *The University of Windsor Review* since 1965 and co-founding Sesame Press in 1973; he has also been connected with various Windsor little magazines, including *Mainline* and *Connexion*.

The dominant mood of McNamara's poetry in *For the mean time* (1965), *Passages* (1972), *Hard words* (1972), and *In transit* (1975) is one of gently brooding melancholy about the passage of time. It also features epiphanies discovered through external reality, both on and below the surface, often centring on the joys and pains of family and human love, as other titles suggest: *Outerings* (1970), *Love scenes* (1970), *Diving for the body* (1974), and *Forcing the field* (1981). For many years McNamara has been a movie critic, writing a weekly column for the

Windsor Star and reviewing movies for CBC radio; he sees movies as mirrors of our world, creating myths about it. *Screens* (1977) and *Dillinger poems* (1971) show both a fondness for the movie vision and a thorough perception of film's romantic sentiments and falsifications: the movie is a way into life as well as a kind of barrier to reality. The poems themselves, with their clean and direct images, have a filmic sharpness, and in *Dillinger* take on a documentary realism that somehow still retains some of the aura of movie glamour.

McNamara's fiction, collected in two volumes—*Salt: short stories* (1975) and *The search for Sarah Grace and other stories* (1977)—has the same clarity, though an obliqueness of approach suggests mysterious resonances in the atmosphere and unfathomable depths in his characters.

McNamara has published critical articles in a variety of academic journals, his main interest being in modern literature, particularly American. He edited *The interior landscape: selected literary criticism of Marshall McLuhan* (1969)   PETER STEVENS

McNeil, Florence. See POETRY IN ENGLISH 1950 TO 1982: 3.

Macphail, Sir Andrew (1864-1938). He was born John Andrew McPhail at Orwell, P.E.I. Following grammar school he won an entrance scholarship to Prince of Wales College, Charlottetown. The excellent teaching and classical ideals he encountered in his two years there influenced him permanently. After three years as a teacher in rural Prince Edward Island, he proceeded to McGill University, where he received a B.A. (1888) and an M.D. (1891). He married Georgina Burland of Montreal in 1893, and practised medicine for about ten years, while also teaching in the medical faculty of the University of Bishop's College, Montreal, from 1893 to 1905. In 1907 he was appointed McGill's first professor of the history of medicine, a chair he held for thirty years. He had become editor of the monthly *Montreal Medical Journal* in 1903; when it merged with another medical periodical eight years later to establish the *Canadian Medical Association Journal*, Macphail was made editor of the new monthly. Serving overseas in the Canadian army medical services (1915-19), he attained the rank of major. He was knighted in 1918.

After the death of his wife in 1902, Macphail began to take a serious interest in literature, publishing more than ten books and scores of shorter pieces. His novel *The vine of Sibmah; a relation of the Puritans* (1906), set in the Restoration period and related in the first person, abounds in deeds of gallantry, miraculous escapes, incredible coincidences, tangential encounters with the great, romantic and seemingly hopeless love, and has a happy ending. In 1921 he published the first translation of Louis HÉMON's classic MARIA CHAPDELAINE, which he described as 'the book that has interested me most in all my lifetime'—a fondness that reflected his deep commitment to a rural and traditional way of life and his sentimental admiration for French Canada. (Macphail had attempted to collaborate with W.H. BLAKE on a translation, but they were unable to agree on stylistic matters and each did his own. Macphail's translation preceded Blake's by a matter of months, but Blake's has become the standard one.) Macphail's only other serious attempt at fiction was a lengthy didactic drama set in contemporary Montreal: *The land: a play of character, in one act with five scenes* (1914), in which most of the protagonists, unhappy and materially oriented, secretly long to renew contact with the soil. It was apparently never produced.

A prolific and forceful writer and an accomplished stylist, Macphail was the best Canadian personification of the nineteenth-century ideal of the non-specialist man-of-letters who wrote in a confident tone on a wide range of subjects. His favourite and most successful medium was the essay. *Essays in Puritanism* (1905) is a series of biographical studies of literary and religious figures; *Essays in politics* (1909) is about contemporary political issues, particularly the nature, real and ideal, of the imperial connection between Canada and Great Britain; *Essays in fallacy* (1910) offers lengthy polemical critiques of feminism, modern education, and modern theological trends; and *Three persons* (1929) is made up of extended reviews of memoirs by three figures of the Great War, including T.E. Lawrence. Most of the essays in the second and third collections had already appeared, in whole or in part, in *The UNIVERSITY MAGAZINE*, a quarterly Macphail edited from 1907 to 1920, with the exception of the time he spent overseas. In many respects this magazine was his most remarkable achievement as a man-of-letters.

The book to which Macphail devoted most care, and which he considered his best, was published posthumously: *The master's wife* (1939; NCL 1977). An autobiographical reminiscence of Prince Edward Island, it focuses particularly on his father, who was a school inspector ('the master' of the title), on his mother, and on Orwell. The Island never lost its importance for Macphail, and following the death of his father in 1905 he spent his summers there. The characters in the book are real: as well as his parents and local people, they include literary and academic figures like Edward William THOMSON (disguised as 'the Old Gentleman'), who spent two or three summer holidays in P.E.I. as the guest of Macphail, and James Mavor. For Macphail, his native province represented a way of life—emphasizing stability and traditional ties and a relative lack of materialism—that provided the basis for the romantic anti-industrial sensibility that formed the core of his social criticism.

Macphail also published *The book of sorrow* (1916), an anthology of poetry that he had initially compiled after the death of his wife and that includes two Petrarchan sonnets by himself; *In Flanders fields and other poems* (1919), a collection of John McCRAE's verse, with a 95-page essay on the poet; the *Official history of the Canadian forces in the Great War, 1914-1919: the medical services* (1925); and *The Bible in Scotland* (1931).

See Ian Ross Robertson, 'Sir Andrew Macphail as a social critic' (unpublished Ph.D. thesis, University of Toronto, 1974), which contains a complete bibliography of Macphail's published and unpublished works.

See also ESSAYS IN ENGLISH: 2.

IAN ROSS ROBERTSON

Macpherson, Jay (b. 1931). Born in England, she came to Newfoundland with her mother and brother at the age of nine, and in 1944 the family settled in Ottawa. She studied at Carleton College (1951-2), McGill University (1953), and the University of Toronto (M.A. 1955; Ph.D. 1964), where she is professor of English at Victoria College. Her first poetry collection, *Nineteen poems* (1952), was published by Robert Graves' Seizen Press. *O earth return* (later to become section two of *The boatman*) came out in 1954 under the imprint of her own small press, EMBLEM BOOKS. Macpherson has not published a great deal of poetry, yet her reputation as an important Canadian poet was firmly established with her first commercially published book, *The BOAT-MAN* (1957), which won a Governor General's Award. In this collection she was revealed as a poet of wit and erudition who—influenced by Northrop FRYE's theory of mythic displacement—rewrote mythological themes in colloquial style. *The boatman* was reissued in 1968 with sixteen new poems. Her next book, *Welcoming disaster* (1974), was privately published. Both volumes—including the 'new poems' in the second edition of *The boatman*—were reissued in 1981 under the title *Poems twice told*, with decorations by the author. *Four ages of man: the classical myths* (1962) is Macpherson's retelling of Greek myths for young people.

The poems in *The boatman*, and some of Macpherson's later poems, have the resonance of archetypal experience in the manner of William Blake's more epigrammatic pieces. In *Welcoming disaster*, a complex and difficult work, the poems record a psychological struggle against poetic silence in a personal wasteland. They follow an archetypal pattern: the way up and the way down are the same. The sequence begins in a dark night of the soul, with the poet metaphorically orphaned. The controlling symbol, a child's teddy-bear called Tedward, functions as a substitute for Him not there (father, lover, God), an embodiment of a childish need in the adult psyche and of a metaphysical longing. The struggle towards 'Recognition' (Section IV) is realized when the child's bear is transformed into the constellation Ursa Major. The poet recognizes that direction can be found only when the dark impulses in the self are acknowledged and explored.

The best discussions of Macpherson's poetry are James REANEY's 'The Third Eye', CANADIAN LITERATURE 3 (Winter 1960) and Northrop Frye's review of *The boatman* reprinted in *The bush garden: essays on the Canadian imagination* (1971).

See also POETRY IN ENGLISH 1950 TO 1982: 1.   ROSEMARY SULLIVAN

McPherson, John (1817-45). Born in Liverpool, N.S., he received his early schooling there. At about the age of seven, following the death of his parents, he went to live with his uncle at North Brookfield, a farming area inland from Liverpool, and there he met Angus M. Gidney, a young school teacher and poet, who recognized his gift for verse. In the late 1830s Gidney went on to become an editor of several newspapers in Halifax and was instrumental in introducing McPherson to other literary-minded people whenever he visited the city.

Encouraged by this attention, McPherson decided to dedicate himself to writing poetry. Neither through this nor through a variety of jobs could he support himself, however, and in 1841 he returned to North Brookfield, settled on schoolteaching, married, and fathered a daughter. He soon found his work onerous, his income insufficient, and his health (always delicate) failing, though he managed to sustain a high level of poetic activity, frequently publishing verse in Halifax newspapers and a prize poem, *In praise of water* (Halifax, 1843). In 1843, when poverty and sickness made his situation desperate, friends in Halifax raised a small sum to help him build a cottage near North Brookfield, but by the time he and his family moved in (Dec. 1844), his health was broken and the place was found to be unfit for winter habitation. In May 1845 McPherson was carried to his uncle's home and finally died there on 26 July. His poems were collected and edited by John Sparrow THOMPSON and ultimately published under the title *Poems, descriptive and moral by John McPherson* (Halifax, 1862).

As with Grizelda TONGE, much of McPherson's local fame rested on the tragic circumstances of his life. But there is more to McPherson than myth: he left a substantial body of verse. Apart from a large number of conventional poems on moral and religious subjects (especially temperance), there is a group that can be loosely classified as nature poems in which an intense awareness of mortality introduces elements of nostalgia and melancholy into the tone and mood. The poems are sentimental in character, but in the best of them the sentiment is counterbalanced by an intellectual appreciation of ideal harmony between man and nature.   TOM VINCENT

McWhirter, George (b. 1939). Born in Belfast, Northern Ireland, he was educated at Queen's University, Belfast—where he taught high school—and at the University of British Columbia, where he is now an associate professor of creative writing. His poems and stories, which are included in several antholgies *(Stories from Pacific and Arctic Canada, Volvox,* and *Illusion)*, contain such Latin American influences as surrealism, strongly textured detail, and alien or grotesque creatures. His first book, *The Catalan poems* (1971), was deeply immersed in Spain, where McWhirter was an English instructor in Barcelona. The sharp imagery, language strong in physical detail, and the precise style of these poems continued in his autobiographical book-length cycle of 52 poems, *Queen of the sea* (1976), in which the technology of the shipbuilding trades in McWhirter's native Belfast provides extended metaphors. Pagan and Christian motifs are intercut with a young shipbuilder's rejection of his Irish heritage and with his subsequent spiritual growth. *Twenty-five* (1978) is a small collection of poems on the central theme of village life in Mexico. *The island man* (1981) is a poem cycle set on Vancouver Island in the 1930s and based on motifs derived from *The Odyssey*. McWhirter has also published a small chapbook, *Bloodlight for Malachi McNair* (1974).

In style and structure, McWhirter's short stories are among the most innovative and experimental in Canada. The nineteen poetic stories in *Bodyworks* (1974), about a character named Hermione who lives in a mythological country, Srane, are enriched by water imagery, an Irish comic vision, heroic gods, and humour (scatalogical and sexual). *Counterparts* is the overall title of a two-volume collection. *God's eye* (1981) contains eleven stories about Mexico that stress the universal values of humility, shame, rebellion, and the erosion of these values by invading tourists in the lives of children, professors, and the elderly. *Coming to grips with Lucy* (1982) is a series of reminiscences about the perils of growing up in Ireland and growing old in B.C. The Irish stories are poetic, textured, and use intercut story lines, while the B.C. stories are often hard-edged and brutal, with an emotional undercurrent suggested by animal imagery.

McWhirter was co-editor (with J. Michael YATES) of *Contemporary poetry of British Columbia* (1970) and edited *Words from Inside* (1974, 1975), a magazine of prison writings. He is an advisory editor of the literary magazine *Prism International*.   GEOFF HANCOCK

Maheux-Forcier, Louise (b. 1929). Born in Montreal, she studied at the École supérieure Sainte-Croix and at the Conservatoire de musique et d'art dramatique de Québec, and spent two years studying music in Paris on a Québec government scholarship (1952-4). After courses in art history at the Université de Montréal, and another brief period in Europe in 1959, she abandoned music for writing. One of the finest novelists of contemporary Québec, she has received inadequate critical attention, perhaps because while the artistic

agenda was focusing on the national question, she was developing a private vision that is both feminine and feminist. Her novels, often musical in their themes and structures, affirm sensual and esthetic values in opposition to the patriarchal world of the Catholic bourgeois family. Themes of metamorphosis and movement are played out against an obsessive search for a female double associated with childhood, art, and an esthetic past that embraces all of the European cultural heritage.

Maheux-Forcier's three novels of the 1960s—*Amadou* (1963), *L'île joyeuse* (1965), and *Une forêt pour Zoé* (1969), which won a Governor General's Award—form a triptych evoking a gradual move from paralysis and violence to the discovery of a sacred woman-centred world. The opening line of *Amadou*—in which the narrator, symbolically isolated in a house in the Québec countryside, announces she has killed her husband—signifies a violent rejection of the traditional patriarchal value system and inaugurates a process of birth that will continue throughout the triptych. Although the nostalgia for a childhood paradise, symbolized by the sandy island of *L'île joyeuse*, remains a constant in Maheux-Forcier's work, the succession of goddess figures in *Une forêt pour Zoé* marks a reconciliation with time and process and an ever-more-joyous rejection of traditional societal structures. In the 1970s Maheux-Forcier became more explicitly concerned with her own art and its relation to life. In *Paroles et musiques* (1973) a woman writer facing death attempts to evaluate her life and finds its meaning in her loves, her refusal to compromise, and above all in her writing. In *Appassionata* (1978) the author plays ironically on the relation between autobiography and fiction. The novel opens with a letter from Maheux-Forcier to her publisher in which she reflects on her literary career and presents the novel as the manuscript of a friend who has committed suicide and who had lived in the shadow of Maheux-Forcier's own success. Again the theme of the feminine couple ('Siamese twins in the heart of the womb') captures the nostalgia for a unity that transcends time, and the rich sensuality of Maheux-Forcier's evocations contradicts the tragic destinies of her characters. *Appassionata* introduces humour in Maheux-Forcier's work. This quality is further developed in *En toutes lettres* (1980), a collection of wry, anecdotal, elegant short stories—whose titles follow the letters of the alphabet—that treat different facets, and different relationships, in the lives of women; it has been translated by David Lobdell as *Letter by letter* (1983). Maheux-Forcier is also the author of two television plays, *Neige et palmiers* (1974) and *Un arbre chargé d'oiseaux* (1976), and of a stage play, *Un parc en automne* (1982).

See Jean-Guy Blondin, 'Aux sources de la rêverie poétique chez Louise Maheux-Forcier' in *Livres et auteurs québécois 1971.*

See also DRAMA IN FRENCH 1948 TO 1981: 4.   PATRICIA SMART

Mailhot, Michèle. See NOVELS IN FRENCH 1960 TO 1982: 3(g).

Maillet, Andrée (b. 1921). Born in Montreal, she has been a journalist and lecturer as well as the author of poetry, novels, short stories, and plays for theatre, television, and radio. Her writing has appeared in numerous journals. After several years' residence in France, she became a member of L'Association de presse anglo-américaine in Paris following publication of her series of articles written on the Russian army of occupation in Germany. From 1952 to 1960 Maillet was editor of *Amérique française*. In 1972 she was elected to the Académie canadienne-française. She now lives in Montreal.

Andrée Maillet's first two novels, *Profil de l'orignal* (1953) and *Les remparts du Québec* (1965), were both re-issued by Éditions de l'Hexagone, the first with a preface by Gilles MARCOTTE (1974), the second with a preface by François Ricard (1977). *Profil de l'orignal* is Maillet's most original work, a complex, symbolic novel of quest in which, in a series of completely independent sketches, the hero, Paul Bar, moves from one identity to another—from hunter to professor to urbane literary critic. It is at once mystical, fantastic, and satirical. *Les remparts du Québec* is a penetrating portrait of a young girl, rendered in a prose of great pathos and beauty. Indeed, it is Maillet's language—speaking forcefully in her poetry and in some of her novels and stories (her production is quite uneven)—that creates the interest of her best work. Subsequent novels are *Le bois-pourri* (1971); *Le doux mal* (1972); *A la mémoire d'un héros* (1975); *Lettres au surhomme* (vol. I, 1976); and *Miroir de Salomé* (*Lettres au surhomme*, vol. II, 1977).

Maillet's other works are: (POETRY) *Elémentaires* (1964), *Le paradigme de l'idole* (1964), *Le chant de l'Iroquoise* (1967), and *Ski nocturne dans les Laurentides* (1976); (SHORT STORIES) *Le chêne des tempêtes suivi d'autres contes* (1965); *Ristontac* (1945); *Les Montréalaises* (1963); *Le lendemain n'est pas sans amour* (1963); *Nouvelles Montréalaises* (1966); *Les bois de renards* (1967); (PLAYS) *Le meurtre d'Igouille* (1965); *La Montréalaise* (1968); *Souvenirs en accords brisés* (1969); and *La dépendance* (1973); (CHILDREN'S BOOKS) *Le marquiset têtu et le mulot réprobateur* (1944, rpr. 1965); *Le chêne des tempêtes* (1944; tr. by F.C.L. Muller as *Storm oak*, 1972). Excerpts from Maillet's 'Journal intime' were recently read in a series on Radio-Canada, and several of her works have been adapted for television and radio.   SHERRY SIMON

Maillet, Antonine (b. 1929). Born in Bouctouche, N.B., she was educated at schools in Memramcook and Moncton, N.B., and at the Université de Montréal and Laval, where she received a Doctorat ès Lettres in 1970. She teaches literature and folklore at Laval and is a Companion of the Order of Canada.

Antonine Maillet is the leading writer of Acadia. She has revealed to a large public—through her books, and particularly through many performances (in both French and English) by Viola Léger of *La* SAGOUINE—the striking character of Acadian oral culture and language, which is a version of the sixteenth-century French of her ancestors, somewhat 'distorted by the climate and sharpened by the sea; by the salty air in the larynx and the obsessive beating of the waves in the ears.' The success of *La Sagouine* (1971) aroused interest in all her novels. *Pointe-aux-Coques* (1972), a village chronicle, was unnoticed when it first appeared in 1958, but was reissued by the publisher Leméac. *On a mangé la dune* (1962), tales about children, and *Par derrière chez mon père* (1972), a collection of picturesque, boisterous sketches and lively portraits (e.g. 'Soldat Bidoche'), are in the same humorous, touching, folkloric vein. Maillet's *L'Acadie pour quasiment rien* (1973) is a very personal travel guide. Her thesis *Rabelais et les traditions populaires en Acadie* (1972) collects for the first time more than 500 archaisms (from Touraine and Berry) still used in the francophone ghettoes of the Atlantic provinces.

Maillet, who was an observant storytelling child, learned her craft as an adult storyteller from her pioneer relatives, from rural folklore, village entertainers, and at election meetings and social gatherings. At once direct, spicy, and learned, Maillet's writings are meant to be narrated, performed. Her language is not *chiac* (from Shediac, the small fishing port near Moncton)—the equivalent of the most anglicized urban *joual*—but an old domestic French, coloured (and somewhat gratingly roughened, coarsened) by her personal touch and a special local intonation and accent. *La Sagouine* (freely translated as The Slattern) is a series of sixteen monologues that offer the reminiscences, grievances, anecdotes, and homilies of a seventy-two-year-old charwoman, a former prostitute, the wife of an Acadian fisherman. (An English edition, translated by Luis de Céspedes, was published in 1979.) *Les Crasseux* (1968), a dialectal drama, and the fantasy *Don l'Orignal* (1972; *The tale of Don l'Orignal*, 1978)—which won a Governor General's Award—treat similar themes and have recurring types. The 'gens d'En-bas' (those who live on the other side of the tracks) fight with the big-shots, the powerful, who are named for their occupations—the Mayoress, the Barber, the Milliner, the Playboy—while Noume, Citrouille, General Michel-Archange, La Sainte, La Cruche, and other 'Sagouins' are given surnames. These actor-storytellers appear in one work after another—indestructible, welcomed, having echoes of Homer, Rabelais, Balzac, and of characters in a picaresque novel, while remaining Acadians, a minority within a minority. *Gapi et Sullivan* (1973), reprinted under the title *Gapi* (1976), portrays two contrasting characters: the settled Acadian, a former fisherman who is now a light-house keeper, and the wandering Irishman, a sailor with exotic memories and imagination. In the novel *Mariaagélas* (1973), and in the play *Evangéline Deusse* (1977), Maillet again creates indomitable, marginal women, who remain upright and haughty despite their illegal traffic in alcohol and flesh. They sell, but they never truly sell themselves. Their plain language, their faces, and their demeanour evoke scenes from the Flemish school of painting.

After completing several quick and easy projects, one of which was *Bourgeois gentleman* (a most un-Molière-like play), Maillet undertook the ambitious task of chronicling the return of the Acadians—French settlers of what is now Nova Scotia who were expelled by British troops in the 1750s and scattered through British colonies in America and the West Indies. *Pélagie-la Charrette* (1979) recounts the odyssey and tribulations of one woman and a small group of outcasts who, picking up scores of other displaced Acadians, make their way over a period of ten years from the southern United States towards their ancestral homeland. It won the 1979 Prix Goncourt (the first time this prize had been awarded to an author who is not a native of France), became a bestseller, and was translated by Philip Stratford as *Pélagie: the return to a homeland* (1982). *Cent ans dans les bois* (1981), a title reminiscent of Marquez, is another epic and picaresque novel, whose action occurs in 1880, near the New Brunswick border. Its use of folklore sometimes enhances and sometimes obscures the narrative.

See also ACADIAN LITERATURE: 2, DRAMA IN FRENCH 1948 TO 1981: 3, and NOVELS IN FRENCH 1960 TO 1982: 3(c).

LAURENT MAILHOT

Mair, Charles (1838-1927). Born in Lanark, Upper Canada (Ont.), a timber town in the Ottawa Valley, Mair began medical studies in 1856 at Queen's University, Kingston, but left in 1857 to work for ten years in his family's timber business. In 1868, after another year at Queen's, he went to Ottawa, where he became one of the founders of the Canada First movement. He then accepted a job as paymaster to a government road party at the Red River Settlement (present-day Winnipeg). His vividly descriptive letters to his brother, who forwarded them to the Toronto *Globe*, praised the Northwest but insulted the halfbreeds, particularly the women, and caused a furore in the Settlement. In Dec. 1870, during the Red River Rebellion, Mair was imprisoned and sentenced to death by Louis Riel. Escaping from Fort Garry, he later made his way back east, to Toronto, where he roused Ontario's Orangemen over Riel's execution of Thomas Scott. Angry over Riel's confiscation of his poems, Mair returned to the West to join the suppression of Riel's North West Rebellion of 1885. Back in Toronto, he received a medal of honour and was proclaimed the 'warrior bard'.

Dreamland and other poems (Montreal, 1868), written before Mair joined Canada First, reveals a conventional imitator of Keats. Its preface, asking for guidance through candid criticism, is the first indication of Mair's method of composing poetry—creativity through consensus. R.G. Haliburton urged Mair to Canadianize his subject matter, to look to the Prairie buffalo rather than to Milton's 'Comus' for inspiration. Leaving the Northwest, where he had been a storekeeper in Portage la Prairie and Prince Albert, Mair moved to Windsor in 1882 to do research for *Tecumseh: a drama* (Toronto, 1886), a verse-play based on a central event for nineteenth-century writers, the War of 1812. This work (which benefitted from the advice of George Denison, Goldwin SMITH, Daniel Wilson, Charles G.D. ROBERTS, and even Matthew Arnold) contrasts what Mair saw as the Canadian tradition of co-operative self-sacrifice with the American tradition of divisive self-interest. He identifies both Tecumseh and Isaac Brock as exemplars of self-sacrifice—'the spirit and springs of action which have made Canada what she is.' A Shakespearean model is effective in Mair's description of the Northwest as being vast as an ocean, with its shoreless prairies and roaring waves of earth-rumbling bison, and as he depicts low Yankee ruffians using slang mimicked from T.C. HALIBURTON's Yankee pedlar. The play's central metaphors are the axe as both tool and weapon, and water as both redemptive stream and drowning flood. Its occasional flaws now look quaint and comical: one Byronic character enters 'carrying his rifle, and examining a knot of wild flowers'.

All of Mair's other poems repeat the flaws rather than the epic strengths of *Tecumseh*. The revisions recorded in *Tecumseh: a drama, and Canadian poems* (Toronto, 1901) reveal Mair's effort to Canadianize his earliest poems by replacing medieval knights with the warriors and heroines of 1812. 'The last bison' presents a hermaphrodite bison singing a conservationist song before it dies. Mair supported the concern of this poem with an essay, 'The American bison', that led to the federal government's establishment of a sanctuary for the world's last bison herd. Another prose work was *Through the Mackenzie Basin; a narrative of the Athabaska and Peace River Treaty Expedition of 1899* (1908)—Mair was secretary of the commission that was sent to negotiate land transfers with the Indians there. Appointed in 1898 to the federal immigration service in the West, he retired in 1921 to Victoria, B.C.

Shortly before Mair's death, John Garvin published his collected poetry and prose: *Tecumseh: a drama, and Canadian poems; Dreamland and poems; The American bison; Through the Mackenzie basin; Memoirs and reminiscences* (Toronto, 1926). In his introduction, Robert Norwood wildly proclaims that 'Mair is our greatest Canadian poet'. For a well-balanced view of the warrior bard, see Norman Shrive's biography *Charles Mair: literary nationalist* (1965) and Shrive's introduction to *Dreamland and other poems/Tecumseh: a drama* (1974) in the series Literature of Canada: Poetry and Prose in Reprint. DAVID LATHAM

Major, André (b. 1942). Born in Montreal, he early became interested in separatist politics and was expelled from the Collège des Eudistes for his writings in leftist student publications. He was a contributor to PARTI PRIS, but broke with the group in 1965, after an ideological quarrel, to become editor of the literary section of *L'Action nationale*, the organ of the older Catholic nationalists of the right. He has been an arts editor of the weekly tabloid *Le Petit Journal*, a publisher's reader, a theatre and book critic for *Le Devoir*, and a radio producer.

A precocious poet, Major had his first collection, *Le froid se meurt*, published in 1961. This was followed by *Holocauste à 2 voix* (1962) and *Poèmes pour durer* (1969), his own selection from his earlier work, with new poetry. He writes of winter and coldness, usually as metaphors for Québec and its people, of the everyday life of city streets, and of love and the flight of time. Some of his poems are personal, others political. All are marked by great energy and simplicity, hard, clear images, and an assured use of language.

Major's early short stories, most of which deal with Montreal slum life, were published—along with those of Jacques BRAULT and André BROCHU—in *Nouvelles* (1963), and in his own first collection *La chair de poule* (1965). A story from the latter group, 'La semaine dernière pas loin du pont', was made into a short film; another, 'Mental test pour tout le gang', is a thinly disguised account of the arrest of Hubert AQUIN. A more recent collection, *La folle d'Elvis* (1982), is less political, with wry, often slight stories about possible encounters that fail to take place, or when they do take place are merely tentative or disillusioning. His novel *Le cabochon* (1964), written while he was still a member of the *parti pris* group, is the ideological and personal history of a young Montreal slum-dweller's progress towards revolutionary politics. *Le vent du diable* (1968), a love-triangle with a rural setting, may be read symbolically, the two young women involved representing two aspects of the hero's love for his 'native land' of Québec. In his most mature and ambitious work, a trilogy subtitled *Histoires des déserteurs*, Major makes nominal and somewhat eccentric use of the classic police-chase form to make a sociological and psychological statement about rural Québec life. In these three novels—*L'épouvantail* (1974), *L'épidémie* (1975), and *Les rescapés* (1976), which received a Governor General's Award—he weaves a tale of lust, murder, suicide, and violence of every sort to depict a society severed from its roots and yet still obsessed by a past that is at once too distant and too close. *L'épouvantail* has been translated by Sheila Fischman as *The scarecrows of Saint-Emmanuel* (1977) and *L'épidémie* by Mark Czarnecki as *Inspector Therrien* (1980). Major has also published a stage play, *Une soirée en Octobre* (1975), and two radio plays, *Le désir suivi de Le perdant* (1973), the latter with a preface by François Ricard.

Major's *Félix-Antoine Savard* (1968), in the collection Écrivains canadiens d'aujourd'hui, is a critical biography of the late nationalist writer (q.v.), to whom Major feels deeply indebted.

Major was one of the six young French-Canadian poets included by Jacques GOD-BOUT and John Robert COLOMBO in the bilingual anthology *Poésie/Poetry* (1964). Translations of some of his poems have also been published in *The poetry of French Canada in translation* (1970) edited by John GLASSCO. An account of his ideological shift, with translations of extracts from his poetry and prose, can be found in *The shouting signpainters* (1972), Malcolm Reid's study of the *parti pris* writers.

See also NOVELS IN FRENCH 1960 TO 1982: 3(a).   JOYCE MARSHALL

Major, Kevin. See CHILDREN'S LITERATURE IN ENGLISH: 8.

Makers of Canada. See BIOGRAPHY AND MEMOIRS IN ENGLISH: 1.

Malahat Review, The. Conceived in 1965 by Robin SKELTON and John Peter as an international quarterly of life and letters, the first issue—published under the auspices of the University of Victoria—appeared in 1967. The title suggests the regional basis that complements the *Review*'s cosmopolitan ambitions; the Malahat is a mountain near Victoria over whose slopes the main road runs northward up Vancouver Island. Skelton and Peter shared the editorship until 1971, when Skelton became editor (assisted at times by Derk WYNAND, Charles LILLARD, and William David Thomas). Skelton

was succeeded by Constance Rooke in 1982.

What has made *The Malahat Review* exceptional, and important among Canadian magazines, has been its policy of printing the best of Canadian writing alongside the best writing that could be obtained internationally. Equally important have been the publication of English versions of foreign works never before translated, and of special booklength issues relating to specific authors or areas of literature. These include the *Herbert Read memorial symposium* (no. 9, 1969, reprinted as a book, 1970); the *Friedrich Nietzsche symposium* (no. 24, 1972); the *Gathering in celebration of the 80th birthday of Robert Graves* (no. 35, 1975); *Austrian writing today* (no. 37, 1976); and the *Margaret Atwood symposium* (no. 41, 1977). Perhaps the most ambitious of these special projects has been a group of three issues devoted to *The West Coast renaissance* (1978, 1979, 1981). The magazine has also published articles on the visual arts and reproductions of the works of notable modern artists, with a strong emphasis on those of international importance.

GEORGE WOODCOCK

Mandel, Eli (b. 1922). Elias Wolf Mandel was born in Estevan, Sask.—'a small town', he tells us, that 'bears the mark of Cain'. He left the University of Saskatchewan to serve in the Army Medical Corps during the Second World War. He then studied at the universities of Saskatchewan and Toronto, and taught English at the Collège Militaire Royal de St Jean and the University of Alberta. In 1963 he was appointed to Glendon College, Toronto, but returned to Edmonton a year later. In 1967 he took up an appointment at York University, Toronto, where he is now professor of English and humanities. Since living in Toronto he has spent summers in Vancouver, Banff, Estevan, South America, and Europe; travelled in India; spent sabbatical years in Europe, principally in Spain (1971-2), and in Saskatchewan (1978-9) as writer-in-residence for the City of Regina; and held a visiting professorship (1979-80) at the University of Victoria.

Mandel began publishing poetry in the early 1950s in magazines such as CIV/n and CONTACT; his first significant collection, 'Minotaur poems', appeared (together with poems by Phyllis WEBB and Gael Turnbull) in the Contact Press anthology *Trio* (1954). His first book was *Fuseli poems* (1960); this was followed by *Black and secret man* (1964);

Mandel

An idiot joy (1967), which won a Governor General's Award; *Stony plain* (1973); *Crusoe* (1973), a selected poems; *Out of place* (1977); *Life sentence* (1981); and *Dreaming backwards: selected poems* (1981). Mandel has also been extremely active as an editor and critic. *Criticism: the silent-speaking words* (1966), a collection of eight essays—previously presented as radio talks on the CBC—called for an emotionally engaged criticism that recognizes that poetry is 'beyond system'. In 1969 he published a monograph on his fellow poet and colleague at York, Irving LAYTON (rev. 1981), and in 1977 a provocative collection of critical essays, *Another time*, that assert the fictive nature of literary reality. Mandel's editing has been instrumental in shaping the canon of Canadian poetry. His first anthology, *Poetry 62/Poésie 62* (1961), which he co-edited with Jean-Guy PILON, brought to public attention a number of the neglected newcomers of the 1950s—Al PURDY, Milton ACORN, D.G. JONES, Alden NOWLAN, Leonard COHEN, and John Robert COLOMBO. A later anthology, *Poets of contemporary Canada: 1960-1970* (1972), in the New Canadian Library, gave Joe ROSENBLATT and bill BISSETT their first significant publication. Mandel's other anthologies include *Five modern Canadian poets* (1970), *Eight more Canadian poets* (1972), and *English poems of the twentieth century* (1971), which he co-edited with D.E.S. Maxwell. He also edited *Contexts of Canadian criticism* (1971) in the University of Chicago Press series Patterns of Literary Criticism.

The Second World War, and the horrors of the Jewish concentration camps in particular, appear to have profoundly affected Mandel's poetry. Although specific references to the war do not occur until 1973 and *Stony plain*, all of his work is characterized by macabre images of suffering and destruction, and by a pervasive pessimism. The 'Minotaur poems' of *Trio* concern themselves with the brutality of the western Canadian landscape, a land of 'sharp rocks . . . /cold air where birds fell like rocks/and screams, hawks, kites and cranes.' *Fuseli poems* is titled in honour of the eighteenth-century Swiss-born English painter Henry Fuseli, whose work frequently depicted tragic subjects fantastically contorted by desperation and isolated in wildly Gothic backgrounds. The poems here speak of horrifying violence, despair, self-accusation, 'fables of indifferent rape/and children slain indifferently/and daily blood'. The succeeding volumes—*Black and secret man, An idiot joy, Stony plain*—suggest little change in this bleak outlook. His two most recent books of new poetry—*Out of place*, a long meditative poem that focuses on failed Jewish settlements in Saskatchewan, and *Life sentence*, a collection of travel poems and journal entries largely set in India, Peru, and Ecuador—while less dramatic in their presentation of human misfortune, sustain a quietly pessimistic vision. For Mandel the world is static, an arena of eternal and meaningless persecution. In Germany there is Auschwitz; in Estevan, Sask., a sun that kills 'cattle and rabbis . . . in the poisoned slow air.'

In style, Mandel is intellectual and contemplative—an ironic poet rather than an angry one. A central feature of his work is a deliberate lack of emotion, which amplifies the stark hopelessness of his outlook. His early work, exceedingly complex in syntax, formal in prosody, and literary in references, appears written for a scholarly rather than a public audience. Here, as in most of his poetry, Mandel sees ancient myths and literary stories as being alive in contemporary actuality, but obscuring the actual and personal. Because the poems lack a strong sense of the actual events that brought the particular myths to the poet's attention, many of the myths seem arbitrarily applied. However, beginning with the poetry of *Black and secret man*, Mandel enriched his work by introducing open verse-forms, spare but colloquial language, simplified syntax, and reportorial detail. While the meditative style remains, a resourceful, witty tone replaces the earlier sombreness. Mandel's recent poetry has been increasingly experimental: prose poems, concrete poems, and found poems can be seen in both *An idiot joy* and *Stony plain*; lists and found materials punctuate the intentionally flat tones of *Out of place*. Mandel maintains his black and mythological vision of the present, but the mythology is now rooted in anecdotal actuality.

See Peter Stevens, 'Poet as critic as prairie poet', *Essays on Canadian Writing* 18/19 (Summer/Fall 1980) and an interview in the same issue.

See also CRITICISM IN ENGLISH 5(d), 5(f), 5(g), and POETRY IN ENGLISH 1950 TO 1982: 2.

FRANK DAVEY

Manning, Laurence E. See SCIENCE FICTION AND FANTASY IN ENGLISH AND FRENCH: 2.

Marchand, Clément (b. 1912). Born in

Sainte-Geneviève de Batiscan, Qué., he has been a poet, journalist, publisher, and an editor of two magazines and one newspaper. In 1933, after completing his studies at the Séminaire de Trois-Rivières, he joined the editorial staff of the regional weekly newspaper *Le Bien Public*. He became its co-owner with Raymond Douville, and at the same time managed the printing plant as well as Les Éditions du Bien Public. He wrote poems, news items, articles, and short stories that were published either in his weekly, in the review *Le Mauricien* (founded in 1937, it became *Horizons* in 1940), or in book form. In forty years Les Éditions du Bien Public published more than 300 titles, from history to the work of young poets, making Marchand one of the chief promoters of literature and culture. His reputation extended beyond his region after he became a member of the Royal Society of Canada in 1947, and later president of the Comité consultatif du livre. In 1959 Marchand became the sole owner of *Le Bien Public*; he sold the newspaper and printing plant in 1978, remaining head of Les Éditions du Bien Public.

Bas-reliefs (1932), a collection of poetry and prose written by three authors for the tricentenary of Trois-Rivières, contains a series of twelve sonnets by Marchand entitled 'Le Geste de la croix'. Recounting the story of the erection of a cross by the captain of the *Émérillon* on Cartier's expedition of 1534-5, the series is an epic with strong religious and patriotic overtones whose alexandrines attest to the young poet's mastery of verse techniques. In 1939 Marchand was awarded the Prix David for the manuscript of *Les soirs rouges* which, though written in the thirties, was not published until 1947. Describing the 'factory nights', the 'nights reddened by the high flames of the iron works' during the Depression, the poet cries out in revolt, in the name of the displaced peasant become labourer in a city that exploits him. The collection was a first for Québec literature in expressing interest in urban labourers and in openly taking the side of the proletariat. *Courriers des villages* (1940) is a collection of news items, articles, and short stories by Marchand that had first appeared in *Le Bien Public*, describing the habits and psychological make-up of rural characters. It was awarded the Prix David and was reprinted several times during the forties.

Marchand demonstrated his admiration for the regionalist poetry of Nérée BEAU-

CHEMIN by editing a collection of his works: *Nérée Beauchemin: textes choisis* (1957).

See Jacques Blais, *De l'ordre et de l'aventure. La poésie au Québec de 1934 à 1944* (1975), and Claude-Henri GRIGNON, 'Clément Marchand, peintre de la campagne' in *Les pamphlets de Valdombre*, series 4, no. 6-7 (Nov.-Dec. 1940).

RICHARD GIGUÈRE

Marchand, Félix-Gabriel (1832-1900). Born in Saint-Jean d'Iberville, Qué., he was educated at local schools and at the Séminaire de Saint-Hyacinthe. He became a qualified notary, but found that profession less attractive than politics, journalism, and the theatre. His political career spanned thirty-three years, from 1867 to his death, during which time he occupied various cabinet posts before becoming, in 1892, leader of the provincial Liberal party and, in 1897, premier of Québec.

Marchand helped found the newspaper *Le Franco-Canadien* in 1860, and became editor of Montreal's *Le Temps* in 1883. In literature he is best remembered for his five plays: the one-act comedy *Fatenville* (Montreal, 1869); the vaudeville *Erreur n'est pas compte; ou Les inconvénients d'une ressemblance* (Montréal, 1872); two verse comedies, *Un bonheur en attire un autre* (Montréal, 1883) and *Les faux brillants* (Montréal, 1885); and a comic operetta, also in verse, *Le lauréat* (Montréal, 1899). All of these were republished in his *Mélanges poétiques et littéraires* (Montréal, 1899), along with various occasional poems—some satirical ('Les travers du siècle', 'Nos ridicules'), some patriotic ('Hymne aux martyrs de 1837', etc.)—and essays on political and social topics. His theatre shows the influence of the popular Parisian stage and is characterized by its lightness of touch and the distance it establishes, especially in his verse plays, between itself and its public's everyday preoccupations. His best-known work is the three-act *Les faux brillants*, reminiscent of Molière's *Tartuffe* with its theme of an intriguing schemer who insinuates himself into a wealthy bourgeois family and attempts to subvert its resources to his own ends. The play was revived in an adapted version by Jean-Claude GERMAIN in Montreal in 1977.

See Bernard Chevrier, 'Le ministère de Félix-Gabriel Marchand', in *Revue d'histoire de l'Amérique française*, vol. 22, no. 1 (1968-9); and the unpublished theses by Berthe Deland, 'Bio-bibliographie de M. Félix-Gabriel Marchand' (Université de Montréal,

1946) and Helen-Anna Gaubert, 'Notes bio-bibliographiques sur Félix-Gabriel Marchand, dramaturge' (Université de Montréal, 1949).   LEONARD DOUCETTE

Marchbanks, Samuel. See Robertson DAVIES.

Marchessault, Jovette (b. 1938). Born in Montreal, she was obliged to leave school at thirteen and go to work in a textile factory. She is a radical lesbian feminist, proud of her Amerindian heritage, who is both a visual artist (the first exhibition of her paintings, sculptures, and masks took place in 1970 at the Maison des Arts La Sauvegarde, Montreal) and a novelist and playwright whose work is highly original in its development of a creative universe in which all divine and human power is female. Her first autobiographical novel, *Comme une enfant de la terre /1. Le Crachat solaire* (1975), which received the Prix France-Québec, relates the odyssey of the narrator—an extra-terrestrial being linked to the sun and cosmic forces, who manifests a 'solar spittle'—through the events of her own life and her family's past (particularly the painful destruction of Amerindian society) towards her goal of reclaiming a lost paradise. *La mère des herbes* (1980), the second volume of a proposed trilogy, combines the poetic qualities of the mystic quest with explicit social commentary. 'Chronique lesbienne du moyen-âge québécois', in *Tryptique lesbien* (1980), is structured around a genealogy of generations of women; it celebrates women's power and vehemently denounces the destructive forces in male-dominated society. Two other prose texts in *Tryptique lesbien* are 'Les vaches de nuit' and 'Les faiseuses d'anges'. 'Les vaches', an extended metaphor associating the narrator and her mother with milk cows, has been performed as a dramatic text in French and English by Pol Pelletier in Montreal, New York, Paris, Toronto, and Vancouver. The theme of 'Les faiseuses' is abortion: the narrator's mother is an abortionist, or 'angel-maker', who expresses her creative energy in knitting as well as in using her needles to abort foetuses. Through an original use of extended paradox, Marchessault argues poetically in favour of women's right to choose. Marchessault has published two full-length plays: *La saga des poules mouillées* (1981) and *La terre est trop courte, Violette Leduc* (1982). In *La saga*, which had a successful run at Montreal's Théâtre du Nou-veau Monde and, in a translation by Linda Gaboriau, at Toronto's Tarragon Theatre (1981), four of Québec's best-known women writers of the nineteenth and twentieth centuries—Laure Conan (Félicité ANGERS), Germaine GUÈVREMONT, Gabrielle ROY, and Anne HÉBERT—meet in a mythic space where each assumes a poetically established totemic identity. The play offers an imaginative reading of their works and a reinterpretation, from a feminist perspective, of their creative experience. *La terre*, which also reinterprets women's cultural history, dramatizes the tragic events in Violette Leduc's life. It was performed at Montreal's Théâtre Expérimental des Femmes (1981).

Lettre de Californie (1982) is a short work that pays homage to radical American feminist Meridel Le Sueur (b. 1900) and contains a poem inspired by her and ten brief portraits of heroic and creative women of the past.

Several of Marchessault's books include texts and critical commentary by women with whom she has worked: of particular interest are those by Gloria Feman Orenstein in *La Mère des herbes*, *Tryptique lesbien*, and *La saga des poules mouillées*, as well as those by Michelle Rossignol in *La saga*.

LOUISE FORSYTH

Marcotte, Gilles (b. 1925). Born in Sherbrooke, Qué., he was educated there and at the Université de Montréal. Literary critic for *Le Devoir* for seven years, then literary editor of *La Presse*, he has taught in the French department of the Université de Montréal since 1966. Marcotte, one of the most prominent literary critics in Québec today, is probably the most prolific. The bibliography included in the special dossier on him in VOIX ET IMAGES (vol. VI, no. 1, automne 1980) lists some 300 titles produced between 1955 and 1979.

Marcotte's first work of criticism, *Une littérature qui se fait* (1962; rev. 1968), was an important beginning in the construction of Québécois criticism. Along with his *Le roman à l'imparfait* (1976), essays on the contemporary Québec novel, it is considered the most important of his books. Other critical works are *Présence de la critique* (1966), an anthology of critical texts that he edited; *Le temps des poètes* (1970), a survey of modern Québec poetry that won the City of Montreal Prize for Literature; and *Les bonnes rencontres* (1971), a collection of Marcotte's literary journalism. Marcotte was the over-all editor for the massive four-volume *Anthologie de la littérature québécoise* (1978). As a critic, Marcotte is highly respected for the acuity of his judgement and the wide range of his knowledge. He has maintained a basically socio-critical approach, although he has been tempted—but only marginally—by a more modish formalist approach (in *Le roman à l'imparfait*). In general Marcotte is not anguished by the exigencies of theory, opting for the 'universal' values of international humanism and remaining committed to thematic concerns. *La littérature et le reste* (1981), an epistolary exchange with critic André BROCHU, is an occasionally prolix but generally interesting and serious examination of the activity and role of the Québec critic. Marcotte shows himself to be master on his own territory but never afraid to admit the limits of this ground. He is a receptive, generous, and incisive critic—at home both in scholarly criticism and in journalism. Marcotte's 'The poetry of exile' appears in English translation in Larry Shouldice's *Contemporary Quebec criticism* (1979).

Marcotte has also written three novels. *Le poids de Dieu* (1962) describes the crisis of Claude Savoie, a young priest from a middle-class family who is confronted with the problems of a working-class parish. It was translated into Spanish by Jesus Lopez Pacheco as *El peso de Dios* (Barcelona, 1963) and into English by Elizabeth Abbott as *The burden of God* (New York, 1964). In *Retour à Coolbrook* (1965) the protagonist, Marcel Parenteau, is destroyed by his attempt to cut himself off emotionally. *Un voyage* (1973) tells of the possibility of transcendance in the mediocre life of a Québec civil servant.

SHERRY SIMON

Maria Chapdelaine (1916). A widely read classic of world literature, this novel by Louis HÉMON was published first in France in serial form in 1914, then in Montreal as a book in 1916. It is set in the Lac Saint-Jean region of Québec and portrays the farmers' attempts to tame the harsh land. On the death of the man she loves, and to whom she was betrothed, Maria is faced with the choice of marrying Lorenzo Surprenant, who would take her to a much easier life in the United States, or Eutrope Gagnon, who can offer her mothing better than the same difficult life she and her family have always known. In rejecting the opportunity to flee, she sacrifices herself in order that the values of her family and her community may be safeguarded. This devotion symbolizes

Québec's determined struggle to secure a foothold for rural, Catholic, French society away from the onslaught of modern, urban, English-dominated life. Although Hémon had been living in Canada for less than three years when he began to write the novel, he succeeded in capturing the essence of Québec's cultural ideal as it was promoted at the beginning of the twentieth century.

Maria Chapdelaine: récit du Canada français is a masterpiece that belongs solidly within the tradition of the *roman de la terre* or 'agricultural novel', and may even be said to represent its perfected form. Among its many literary qualities are its range of styles, from the lyrical prose describing springtime and Maria's exchange of vows, to the muscular, spare accounts of the harsh winter and the death it brings; its sharply drawn characters; and its convincingly rendered scenes. The novel has been transformed into a political football, its literary merits virtually ignored, first by ideologues anxious to celebrate the characters' fidelity and to propose this as an ideal worthy of emulation, and more recently by critics intent on proving that the characters' submissiveness only enslaved them. The novel may indeed crystallize, as Nicole Deschamps has suggested, 'a moment in the collective history of French Canada and thereby have become inseparable from the debate on that history.' What has been sacrificed during the heated 'political' debate about *Maria Chapdelaine* is an appreciation of it as a work of art, an aspect that one presumes has not eluded its readers in more than twenty languages.

An English translation (1921) by William Hume BLAKE, with the subtitle *A tale of the Lake St. John country*, remains the standard one; it is available in the Laurentian Library. *Marie Chapdelaine* has been filmed three times: in 1939 (with Madeleine Renaud and Jean Gabin; Julien Duvivier dir.), in 1949 (with Michèle Morgan and Phillipe Lemair; Marc Allegret dir.) and in 1983 (with Carole Laure and Nick Mancuso; Gilles Carle dir.).

See also NOVELS IN FRENCH: 1900 TO 1920.   PAUL SOCKEN

Marie Calumet (1904). This satirical novel by Rodolphe GIRARD is set in the Québec countryside of 1860. Father Lefranc, the parish priest of St-Apollinaire, visits his neighbour, Father Flavel, the pastor of St-Ildefonse, whose rectory is in chaos. Lefranc sends him Marie Calumet, a still-comely forty-year-old woman who is a remarkable

Marie Calumet

housekeeper. She soon has the presbytery running like clockwork, while unwittingly attracting the romantic interest of Narcisse, the hired man, and Zéphirin, the verger. Narcisse wins her hand and Zéphirin avenges himself by pouring a laxative into one of the dishes of the wedding feast. Most of the characters are naive, but sensitive and warmhearted. Marie has an exaggerated admiration for all things connected with the Church and its priests. During the bishop's pastoral visit, after pondering whether to save it, she asks where to put Monsignor's 'holy piss'; and wearing a crinoline and no underwear at the harvest feast, she trips on a walnut-tree root and scandalizes the pastor, who threatens excommunication. Another scandalous episode occurs when the pastor's teenage niece reads the most sensual verses (taking up 13 pages in the novel) from J.F. Ostervald's version of the 'Song of Songs', which had been forbidden to the masses. These and other scenes are described by Girard both satirically and humorously.

When *Marie Calumet* was published in 1904, 1000 copies were sold almost immediately; but it was condemned by the Church as 'gross, immoral and impious'. For the 1946 edition Girard, in addition to making many stylistic improvements, modified many irreverent religious references and omitted the final chapter, with its scatalogical description of the consequences produced by the laxative. Even in the revised version, however, the novel conveys a realistic depiction of the customs, language, and morality of Québec around 1860. *Marie Calumet* is the first major French-Canadian novel to treat the Church and clergy in a humorous way. The expurgated edition, translated by Irène Currie, appeared in 1976.

See also NOVELS IN FRENCH: 1900 TO 1920.   MADELEINE DIRSCHAUER

Marie de l'Incarnation (1599-1672). Born Marie Guyart in Tours, Fr., she was married at eighteen and widowed two years later. In 1633 she entered the Ursuline monastery of Tours and in 1639 sailed for Québec, with three other Ursulines and Madame de la Peltrie, to found a 'seminary' for Indian children and a boarding school for French girls. For more than thirty years, while she alternated as head of the monastery, she wrote thousands of letters to her son, Claude Martin, a Benedictine priest, and to various benefactors in France. Though a cloistered nun, Marie de l'Incarnation was in touch with everyone in the colony—the Jesuits, the gover-

nors and other notables, the Indian converts and common people. Her letters rank with the JESUIT RELATIONS as source material for the period. Because not intended for publication, they are more personal and informal and cover not only the triumphs and tragedies of the Jesuit mission but such mundane matters as the earthquake of 1663, the weather, the crops, the coming of the king's girls, and the fire that destroyed the Ursuline monastery in 1650. The style is lively, at times hasty and even breathless, shrewd and often tart in its observations, by turns practical and high-minded. Marie de l'Incarnation was the first social historian of Canada, and the breadth and vividness of the picture provided is remarkable in view of the fact that she frequently wrote of events she had not personally witnessed.

After Marie de l'Incarnation's death Claude Martin published 228 of her letters in *Lettres de la vénérable mère Marie de l'Incarnation . . .* (Paris, 1681). These were re-issued by P.F. Richaudeau in two volumes: *Lettres de la révérende Mère Marie de l'Incarnation . . .* (Tournai, 1876). Albert Jamet's more scholarly four-volume edition—*Marie de l'Incarnation, fondatrice des Ursulines de la Nouvelle France* (1923-39)—adds four more letters and some devotional writing but covers only the period 1639-1652. *Word from New France: the selected letters of Marie de l'Incarnation* (1967), Joyce MARSHALL's translation of 66 letters, includes a complete biography and historical introduction.

Other source material includes Claude Martin's life of his mother, *La vie de la vénérable Mère Marie de l'Incarnation* (Paris, 1677), and *The autobiography of the Venerable Marie of the Incarnation* (1964), John J. Sullivan's translation of her 'spiritual autobiography'.   JOYCE MARSHALL

Marie-Victorin (1885-1944). Born Conrad Kirouac at Kingsey Falls in the Eastern Townships, Qué., he moved to Quebec City as a child and was educated first at the parish school of Saint-Sauveur and later at the Académie commerciale. In 1901 he entered the Order of the Brothers of the Christian Schools and took the name (in religion) of Marie-Victorin. In the following years he taught at Saint-Jérôme, Westmount, and Longueuil. After becoming interested in botany, he was appointed professor of botany at the Université de Montréal in 1920 and in 1922 received his Ph.D. in sciences from that university, where he would teach for the rest of his life. In 1923 he founded

ACFAS (Association canadienne-française pour l'avancement des sciences) and was elected to the Royal Society of Canada the following year. In 1939 he founded the Botanical Gardens of Montréal. He received the Prix David twice (1923, 1931) and several provincial, national, and international distinctions for his scientific contributions.

Récits laurentiens (1919), translated by James Ferres as *The chopping bee and other Laurentian stories* (1925), is a collection of nine short stories in which Marie-Victorin often recalls the years of his childhood in developing themes of the then-popular *terroir* school. *Croquis laurentiens* (1920) is a collection of picturesque sketches that describe with a remarkable mixture of poetic images and precise terminology the Laurentian landscape and the land that had been settled by French Canadians for centuries. *Peuple sans histoire* (1925), an adaptation for the stage of a short story included in *Récits laurentiens*, and first performed on 31 Jan. 1918, portrays Lord Durham as a man who was not an enemy of the French-Canadian people but was rather ignorant of their history. *Charles Le Moyne* (1925) is a patriotic historical drama that was performed at the Collège de Longueuil, 13 and 14 May 1910. Marie-Victorin's most important book is *Flore laurentienne, illustrée de 22 cartes et de 1800 dessins* (1935; rpr. 1947; rev. 1964), an inventory of 1,917 plants found in Québec that describes these plants with a rare mixture of scientific precision and poetry and reveals the richness of the French-Canadian vocabulary for naming plants. Other works include *Itinéraires botaniques dans l'île de Cuba* (1942), *Les filicinées de Québec* (1923), *Études floristiques sur la région du Lac Saint-Jean* (1925), *Les équisétinées du Québec* (1927), *Le dynamisme dans le flore de Québec* (1929), and *Histoire de l'Institut botanique de l'Université de Montréal* (1941). *Confidences et combat* (1969) is a selection of Marie-Victorin's letters written between 1924 and 1944, annotated by Gilles Beaudet.

See Robert Rumilly, *Le Frère Marie-Victorin et son temps* (1949); L.-P. Audet, *Le Frère Marie-Victorin* (1942); and M. Gauvreau, *Le Président de l'ACFAS* (1938).

JACQUES COTNAM

Maritimes, Writing in the. 1. 1751 TO 1812. The imaginative articulation of experience in the early journals, essays, adventure narratives, and Augustan reflective and satirical verse that issued from the Maritime Provinces in this period reveals a conscious-ness of three literary aims that characterize all the writing of this region: to express the human form of nature and society, to create and transmit a self-conscious cultural tradition by transmuting history into art, and to relieve the strictures of life by asserting the ideal possibilities of culture.

Bartholomew Green brought Canada's first printing press to Halifax in 1751, and John Bushell established *The Halifax Gazette* in the following year; but the first cultural periodical, John Howe's NOVA SCOTIA MAGAZINE *and comprehensive review of literature, politics and news*, was not established until 1789. There was little local market for writers, other than privately printed pamphlets and newspapers, until Joseph HOWE's ACADIAN MAGAZINE; *or, Literary mirror* was established in Halifax in 1826. *Acadie* was founded in Fredericton, N.B., in 1830, and the *Saint John Monthly Magazine* in 1836. *The Pictou Bee, The British North American Magazine and Colonial Journal, The Colonial Pearl, The Halifax Monthly Magazine*, and *The Wesleyan*—all in Halifax—responded to the definite increase in the number of readers during the 1830s, and they encouraged writers to complement the reprints from British and American publications with their locally produced writing. Throughout the rest of the nineteenth century, thirteen cultural journals in Nova Scotia, eleven in New Brunswick, and four in Prince Edward Island continued to encourage consciously literary writing. *The Church Magazine, The Guardian*, and STEWART'S LITERARY QUARTERLY all began publishing in Saint John in the sixties. During the five years of its publication, *Stewart's* set the highest standards of literary excellence and commissioned pieces from Canada and abroad as well as from the Maritimes. During this period *The Progress Magazine* appeared in Summerside, P.E.I., but not until 1871 and 1874 respectively did *The Broadaxe* and *The Literary Echo: Amusing and Instructive* appear in Charlottetown.

These cultural periodicals were really isolated peaks of the waves on a sea of newspaper publication. Before 1800 eight newspapers struggled to survive in Nova Scotia, and only two in New Brunswick, but by 1842 sixty-five more had sprung up, including *The Novascotian*, which Joseph Howe had purchased in 1828. In New Brunswick after 1845, when George W. Day brought Canada's first power press to Fredericton, newspapers had been founded in every community. Day alone published twenty-seven in New Brunswick, several of which he owned and edited himself. These Maritimes newspapers all published serial novels, prose sketches, and poems, many of which came from their own readers. For example, Howe first published HALIBURTON's Sam Slick sketches in *The Novascotian* in 1835. Booksellers also fostered publications. The publishing activity of the MacKinleys, booksellers in Halifax, was matched in New Brunswick by John MacMillan of Saint John, who published in 1843 the first Canadian edition of Oliver GOLDSMITH's *The rising village*, and by Henry Chubb of Fredericton, who in 1825 in Saint John published *Poems, religious, moral and sentimental* by James Hogg (1800-60), who himself became a publisher, founding *The New Brunswick Reporter* in 1844.

Addressing themselves to the nascent society, writers published their works in the Maritimes from the beginning. Henry ALLINE, for example, published his revolutionary theological treatise, *Two mites on some of the most important and much disputed points of divinity* (1781) and his sermons, *A gospel call to sinners* (1791), in Halifax. The Loyalist migration provided the first real stimulus to writing, for by 1789, when John Howe founded *The Nova Scotia Magazine*, the society was large enough to provide a market among the permanent residents and there was a demand, since local literary endeavours were part of their culture. The American revolutionary war fostered an Augustan literature of wit and satire, and the Loyalist migration brought the aesthetic into the Maritimes. The results were often local and vigorous. Augustan satirists Jacob BAILEY and Joseph STANSBURY in Nova Scotia and Jonathan ODELL in Fredericton were well known. The first book of poetry to be published in Canada, Roger VIETS' *Annapolis royal: a poem (Halifax,* 1788), was an Augustan reflective poem intended to inspire new settlers to see order and beauty in their new land. Adam Allen published *The new gentle shepherd* (1798)—an English version of Allan Ramsey's Scottish dialect poem, *The gentle shepherd* (1725)—in both Fredericton and London. Allen also included his own poem, 'A description of the great falls of the River St. John, in the province of New Brunswick'. Griselda TONGE wrote charming verses at her home in Windsor, N.S., that were not published until Beamish Murdock included them as an appendix in his *History of Nova Scotia; or Acadie* (3 vols, Halifax, 1865-7).

2. 1812 TO 1880. By the time the War of 1812 was over and emigration from Britain had begun to give society in the Maritimes a more settled aspect, the literature revealed a new consciousness of the tensions within the society itself. Walter BATES chronicles in *The mysterious stranger* (New Haven, 1817) one aspect of the disorder that many writers saw as the chief impediment to a prosperous society. By means of witty satire Thomas McCULLOCH's *Letters of Mephibosheth Stepsure* (1821-2; Halifax, 1862) urges Nova Scotia rural folk to practise frugality, self-reliance, and industry in farming. McCulloch's novel, *Colonial gleanings: William and Melville* (Edinburgh, 1826), warns emigrants that hard work is needed in order to prosper in the loyal colonies. The post-humous collection of Joseph HOWE's *Poems and essays* (Halifax, 1874) includes 'Acadia', a long poem dealing with the perils of early settlement in Nova Scotia; 'The locksmith of Philadelphia', a moral tale extolling honesty; and five essays.

Oliver GOLDSMITH's *The rising village* (London, 1825) uses the basic concept of his great-uncle's poem *The deserted village* to create an original three-part social vision of the problems of building a new society. *The lay of the wilderness: a poem in five cantos* (Fredericton?, 1833), attributed to Peter Fisher, is critical of those who retard the development of New Brunswick. Andrew SHEILS also contributed to the tradition of the new society with *The witch of Wescot: a tale of Nova Scotia in three cantos; and other waste leaves of literature* (Halifax, 1831). However, it was Thomas Chandler HALIBURTON who captured British and American imaginations with *The clockmaker; or The sayings and doings of Samuel Slick, of Slickville* (Halifax, 1836). Although the literary excellence of *The clockmaker* made it deservedly more popular than McCulloch's *Stepsure letters*, Sam Slick unfortunately overshadowed as well *The old judge* (2 vols, London, 1849), which is Haliburton's masterwork.

There is a cosmopolitan strain in early Maritimes writing that is distinct from colonial imitativeness. An imperialist patriotic sentiment enlivens William Charles M'KINNON's *The Battle of the Nile: a poem in six cantos* (Sydney, 1844). Peter John ALLAN's posthumously published *Poetical remains* (1853) is a technically adept use of the classical learning considered to be the foundation of culture. John HUNTER DUVAR's verse collection, *The emigration of the fairies and the triumph of constancy, a romaunt* (Saint John, 1888), reveals a wittily graceful imagination.

His blank-verse *De Roberval, a drama* (Saint John, 1888), dedicated to Sir John A. Macdonald, is an explicit expression of nationalist pride in the heritage of culture and learning of the Maritimes society. A more local sense of tradition underlies John LePAGE's *The Island minstrel* (2 vols, Charlottetown, 1860, 1862). The sophisticated culture of both Europe and New England in the home of Mary Jane KATZMANN of Halifax created a vigorous sense of the importance of local culture and tradition for her own society. In 1852-3 she edited *The* PROVINCIAL; in 1887 Kings' College awarded her the Akins Historical Award for her local history of Dartmouth, Preston, and Lawrencetown, N.S. Her collected poems, *Frankincense and myrrh* (Halifax, 1893), was published posthumously.

By the 1840s the popularity of melodramatic romance and didactic evangelical novels had greatly increased, and most popular were novels of local society. The first novel published in North America by a Canadian, Julia Beckwith HART's ST. URSULA'S CONVENT; *or The nun of Canada* (Kingston, 1824), was written in Fredericton in 1822. George E. Fenety of Saint John, under the pseudonym 'A Bluenose', wrote a 24-page romance of social manners, *The lady and the dressmaker; or, A peep at fashionable folly* (Saint John, 1842). Douglas S. HUYGHE of Saint John wrote one of the better early novels, *Argimou: a legend of the Micmac* (Halifax, 1847), and followed it with *Nomads of the West; or, Ellen Clayton* (London, 1847). Two Halifax sisters, Mary and Sara HERBERT, wrote poetry and prose for both newspapers and book publishers. They produced a joint collection of poems, *The Aeolian harp; or, Miscellaneous poems* (Halifax, 1857), but their real forte was the romantic novel. Mary published three: *Belinda Dalton; or Scenes in the life of a Halifax belle* (Halifax, 1859), *Woman as she should be; or, Agnes Wiltshire* (Halifax, 1861), and *The young men's choice* (Halifax, 1869). Sara was the author of *Agnes Maitland: a temperance tale* (n.d.). Temperance literature included poetry as well. John McPHERSON, 'a mournful temperance advocate', won a ready readership with *The praise of water: a prize poem* (Halifax, 1843) and *The harp of Acadia: poems descriptive and moral* (Halifax, 1862).

At mid-century May Agnes FLEMING of Saint John marked a new phenomenon, for she lived largely by writing popular novels that were saleable commodities. She published fifteen during her life, and twenty-

seven more were published after her death, some not under her name. Her first novel was *Erminie; or, The gypsy's vow: a tale of love and vengeance* (New York, 1863). Throughout her career she continued to publish in New York; eventually she took up residence there. James DeMILLE's popular novels include adventures for boys, satires, melodramatic novels, and historical romances, published in the late 1860s and 1870s, but his most considerable work is his posthumous *A strange manuscript found in a copper cylinder* (New York, 1888), which integrates structural elements from the novels of Melville, Twain, and others and employs a voyage to a dystopia to satirize values in the gilded age.

3. 1880 TO 1920. This period is the age of literary forms—the lyric and the short story—that best fitted mass-magazine publication, and Maritimes writers produced these in abundance. Nature and ideal beauty dominated poetry; and although fiction shows the effects of realism, it remained basically romance.

Charles G.D. ROBERTS' *Orion and other poems* (Philadelphia, 1880) set a new standard of poetic excellence in Canada. His success and popularity as a prolific writer—of both poetry and fiction (particularly animal stories)—and his vigorous promotion of Canadian writers and writing, made him an important influence in Canada letters. *In divers tones* (Boston, 1886), *Songs of the common day, and Ave* (Toronto, 1893), and *The book of the native* (Toronto, 1896) contain poems in which Nature has lost its alien wildness and become the nurturing matrix of home. Roberts' 'The Tantramar revisited' and many of his sonnets, and his prose fiction, such as *The heart of the ancient wood* (1900), reveal a profound sense of society and nature in the Maritimes.

Bliss CARMAN began writing as a result of the influence of Roberts, his cousin. *Low tide on Grand Pré* (New York, 1893) gave him his first widespread notice, and his collaboration with Richard Hovey in *Songs from Vagabondia* (Boston, 1894) made his reputation sure. *Poems* (2 vols, 1904) signalled that Carman was firmly established as a poet and the definitive collection of his work, *The Pipes of Pan* (1906), confirmed this. Carman also became notable as an essayist of a distinct philosophical bent. *The kinship of nature* (1904), *The friendship of art* (1904), *The poetry of life* (1905), and *The making of personality* (1908) further express the mystical sense of nature that is evident in his poetry, along with his devotion to Delsartian metaphysics and Unitrinitarianism.

The creative force that was manifested in Roberts appeared elsewhere in his family, in differing degrees, for generations. His son Lloyd published nine volumes of poetry and prose from 1914 to 1937, but he is best known for *The book of Roberts* (1923). His brothers—Goodridge, William, and Theodore—also wrote poetry, as did Elizabeth, his sister; but only Theodore Goodridge ROBERTS enjoyed a successful career as a professional writer. T.G. Roberts' life as a travelling journalist and war correspondent gave him the raw material for forty-three volumes, most of them prose in a variety of popular genres. *The red feathers* (1907) is an Indian legend; *A cavalier of Virginia* (1910) a historical romance; *The harbour master* (1913) a local-colour novel; *Hemming the adventurer* (1904) a juvenile adventure; *Thirty Canadian V.C.'s* (1918) a war history; and *The leather bottle* (1934) a collection of verse. Theodore's daughter Dorothy Roberts (Leisner) (b. 1906) has shown a consistent excellence in seven volumes of poetry from *Songs for swift feet* (1927) to *The self of loss* (1976). (Goodridge Roberts, 1904-74, the distinguished Canadian painter, was his son.) Elizabeth's son Goodridge Macdonald finely expressed his consciousness of the family heritage in seven chapbooks from *Armageddon and other poems* (1917) to *Selected poems* (1970).

Charles G.D. Roberts' boyhood friend in Fredericton, Francis Joseph SHERMAN, followed a banking career, but he also produced six volumes of pre-Raphaelite poetry, beginning with *Matins* (Boston, 1896) and *In memorabilis mortis* (Boston, 1896). George Frederick CAMERON was notable among traditional Victorian Maritimes writers because he was stirred by libertarian political ideals rather than by nature or patriotism. *Lyrics on freedom, love and death* (Kingston, 1887) stirred much interest when published posthumously. The Canadian tradition of literary ministers and sons of ministers was a major conservative influence in Maritimes writing. The Rev. Robert NORWOOD became well known in Canada during the First World War for his activities in the CANADIAN AUTHORS' ASSOCIATION, and as the author of two biblical dramas, *The witch of Endor* (1916) and *The man of Kerioth* (1918). His poetry and plays reflect the continuation of the High-Victorian Romantic tradition, one that he actively promoted in Canadian letters. A.W.H. EATON's poetic works—

which include *The lotus of the Nile and other poems* (1907) and *Acadian ballads and lyrics in many moods* (1930), a collection of his best work—reveal his Victorian integration of religion and morality, a moral view that also appears in his *Tales of a garrison town* (New York, 1892), written with Craven Longworth Betts.

The Rev. Hiram Alfred CODY's muscular Christianity, temperance views, and experiences as a missionary in the Yukon gave him the material for twenty-five novels, from *Aspostle of the North* (1906) to *Storm king banner* (1937). The best of these Maritimes author-ministers is the Rev. William Benjamin (Basil) KING. His thirty-two books include two-dozen sophisticated novels that from the very first won him a popular audience in both the U.S. and Canada. *The inner shrine* (1909), *The wild olive* (1910), and *The street called Straight* (1912) were on American best-seller lists; but his later novels made more penetrating studies of human relationships. *The high heart* (1917) examines Canadian and American attitudes with a perceptive eye and polished style. Another writer who had a sophisticated approach to the popular novel was Alice JONES. Her seven thrillers—from *The night hawk* (1901) to *Flame of frost* (1914)—have international settings and characters, but her works are essentially romances. Susan Jones (1864?-1926) wrote nine formula romances from 1900 to 1926. Her *A detached pirate* (London, 1900; Boston 1903) makes use of the epistolary form to lend her account of social life in Halifax interest and amusement.

Some of the best-known Maritimes writers were women who addressed themselves to the juvenile market. Editions of L.M. MONTGOMERY's ANNE OF GREEN GABLES (1908), and the other titles in the 'Anne' series, continue to appear throughout the world; but her *The watchman and other poems* (1916) and *The doctor's sweetheart and other stories* (1979) deserve attention as well. A quite different juvenile writer is Marshall SAUNDERS, whose BEAUTIFUL JOE: *an autobiography* (Philadelphia, 1894) enjoyed phenomenal popularity for its sentimental treatment of a dog and other animals.

William Albert HICKMAN's five published collections of short stories include *Canadian nights* (1914), in which he regards with a satiric eye politics and manners in a number of communities in Canada and the U.S. Hickman's popular novel *The sacrifice of the Shannon* (1903) examines the crew aboard an icebreaker in the St Lawrence River. William

Alexander FRASER in *The eye of God and other tales of East and West* (1899) combines stories of North America with tales of Burma and India. His *Mooswa and others of the boundaries* (1900) is an unusual fiction in which animals speak as humans, while retaining their animal characteristics. Fraser's *Thoroughbreds* (1901) was a very popular horse-racing thriller; but his most notable work is *The lone furrow* (1907), which examines the bigotry and gossip surrounding a minister in an Ontario settlement.

4. 1920 TO 1940. Between the wars the buoyant economy and patriotic interest in traditions and history produced increased activity in writing that featured local colour and historical romance. Most poets wrote in the Victorian tradition—in many ways writers after the First World War sought to assert an ideal of the past.

The founding in 1921 of *The Dalhousie Review* in Halifax signalled that a new interest in the cultural life had touched the Maritimes (just as a similar interest in Toronto had given rise to *The* CANADIAN FORUM the year before). Modernism created attempts to combine local experience and cosmopolitan culture. Florence Ayscough (1878-1942) collaborated with Amy Lowell to produce *Fir-flower tablets* (1921), poems based on Chinese verse. Kenneth LESLIE represents a more genuine poetic attempt to bridge local culture and modernism. His early publications reveal a strong traditional poetry, but his first considerable book, *Lowlands low* (1935), shows a modernist influence, and *By stubborn stars* (1938) won him a Governor General's Award. Edgar Wardell McInnis's *Poems written at the Front* (1917) is interesting to compare with the work of British war poets, and McInnis's *Byron: Newdigate Prize poem* (1925) still holds some interest. McInnis (1899-1973), who became well known as a historian of international relations, received a Governor General's Award for *The unguarded frontier: a history of American-Canadian relations* (1942).

Popular formula fiction often exploits Maritimes tradition and culture. *The token* (1926) by Edith Archibald (1854-1938) dealt with nineteenth-century life in Cape Breton. Eveyln Eaton (b. 1902) published twenty-eight romances, of which *Quietly my captain waits* (1940) was perhaps the most popular. The twenty-nine romances by Louis Arthur Cunningham (1900-54) include many about the Maritimes, including *Yvonne Tremblay* (1927), *Fog over Fundy* (1936), *Tides of the Tantramar* (1936), and *Moon over Acadie*

(1937). As 'Pierre Coalfleet', Frank Davison (1893-1944) published four novels, including *Solo* (1924), an example of Maritimes realism. Perhaps the most remarkable local-colour writer was Frank Parker DAY, whose Dantean *Rockbound* (1928) has become something of a Canadian classic.

5. 1940 TO 1960. From the beginning of the Second World War to 1960 writing in the Maritimes recovered from the delay and strictures imposed by the Depression and the war and the interest in local history and community matured into a critical sense of cultural identity. Hugh MacLennan, Thomas H. Raddall, and Ernest Buckler are the most impressive fiction writers of this period.

BAROMETER RISING (1941) by Hugh MacLENNAN signalled that the Maritimes literary tradition of the historical romance had finally matured into a literary genre of some merit. He won a Governor General's Award for fiction with TWO SOLITUDES (1945), which became a popular expression of the nation's cultural plight, and with these two novels embarked on a long and distinguished career as a writer. His moving novel *Each man's son* (1951) is set in Cape Breton.

Thomas RADDALL began with historical adventures and, like Eaton and others, he turned to the historical romance; but he made the form a vehicle for literary insight as well as sentiment. *The Pied Piper of Dipper Creek*, a short-story collection that was first published in London in 1939, earned him a Governor General's Award when McCLELLAND AND STEWART republished it in 1943. Raddall became immensely popular with *His Majesty's Yankees* (1942) and *Roger Sudden* (1944); and his non-fiction study, *Halifax, warden of the North* (1948), won him a second Governor General's Award. In *The nymph and the lamp* (1950), his most considerable literary achievement, he conducted a penetrating inquiry into society and nature. Another prolific, but less ambitious, author of historical romances is Will R. BIRD, who wrote about Yorkshire settlers in Nova Scotia in such novels as *Here stays good Yorkshire* (1945).

Ernest BUCKLER's *The mountain and the valley* (1952) is perhaps the most extreme example of the ability of a Maritimes writer to examine the stifling brutality of rural life through the romance. Although Buckler has also published collections of short stories, such as *The rebellion of young David* (1975), this early novel remains his most notable work.

Post-war economic recovery encouraged the establishment of little magazines such as *The* FIDDLEHEAD, which was founded at the University of New Brunswick in 1945. The most considerable poets of this period were Milton ACORN and Alfred Goldsworthy BAILEY. Acorn began as a writer of proletarian verse in the 1950s and from his first volume, *In love and anger* (1956)—and through the six consequent volumes, leading to *The Island means Minago* (1975), for which he received a Governor General's Award—his working-class rage at injustice has broadened to become a compassionate defence of the individual, and the roughness of the early verse has become controlled in form and craftsmanship. Alfred BAILEY's *Border River* (1952), *Thanks for a drowned island* (1973), and his collected poems, *Miramichi lightning* (1981), are volumes of complex, difficult, and erudite poetry whose metaphysical extensions of language articulate a world charged with significance and tradition. Kay Smith (b. 1911) began by publishing in FIRST STATEMENT. *Footnote to the Lord's Prayer* (1951) established her reputation, and *At the bottom of the dark* (1971), *When a girl looks down* (1978), and *Again with music* (1980) suggest that she has continued to extend the modernist metaphysical aesthetics with which she began.

Elizabeth BREWSTER was a founder of *The Fiddlehead* with Alfred Bailey, and Fred COGSWELL was one of the early editors. As poets Brewster and Cogswell are quite different from Bailey, for they share the wry, quiet, social narrative voice that has marked *Fiddlehead* poets and has become best known in the poetry of Alden NOWLAN. Cogswell uses formally controlled verse-forms for his wry observations of a Gothic New Brunswick society warped by a harsh heritage. *The light bird of life* (1974) and *A long apprenticeship* (1980) reveal the consistent development of a compassionately satirical examination of his society. Cogswell is also a substantial translator of the poetry of Québec and Acadian writers.

From Brewster's first book of poems, *East Coast* (1951), to her most recent novel, *Junction* (1983), she authoritatively recreates a subjective sense of local tradition. To become confident of the presentness of the past is a task she controls with narrative irony that is often at the expense of speakers who appear to be naive. Charles BRUCE's collection of lyrics *The Mulgrave Road* (1951), which won a Governor General's Award, indicates a similar perception of local actuality and consciousness of social history, which is shared by most Maritimes writers.

To the literature of local history and folklore belong the books of Evelyn May Fox Richardson (1902-76), whose *We keep a light* (1945) won her a Governor General's Award for non-fiction. Her novels, *Desired haven* (1953) and *No small tempest* (1957), suggest that the appeal of her works lies in their realistic treatment of the details of life that made the books of F.W. Wallace popular twenty years before.

The most prolific writer Canada has ever produced is William Edward Daniel Ross (b. 1912) of Saint John. Between 1950 and 1980 he has published 355 formula novels and about 600 stories under his own name and twenty pseudonyms.

6. 1960 TO THE PRESENT. This period in Maritimes writing has been deeply affected by a resurgence in the popularity of poetry, the establishment of the Canada Council, and the movement of writers towards greater organization. In the sixties they tended to organize around universities, in the seventies around the small presses, and in the eighties around national and provincial associations.

Fred COGSWELL's Fiddlehead Press, now under Peter Thomas, Reshard Gool's Square Deal Press, now under Libby Oughton's Ragweed Press, Leslie Choyce's Pottersfield Press, and several others have actively promoted new writers. Cogswell in particular has published hundreds of new and established poets. In addition, *The* FIDDLEHEAD has been joined by Harry Thurston's *Germination* (now under Alan Cooper), Fraser Sutherland's *Northern Journey*, Leslie Choyce's *Pottersfield Portfolio*, and R.J. MacSween's *Antigonish Review*, now under George Sanderson. Small presses such as Formac and Petheric, and commercial presses such as Brunswick and Nimbus, recognize both the literary and the traditional in Maritimes writing.

The most notable new writers of this period are Alden Nowlan and David Adams Richards. From *The rose and the puritan* (1958) to *I might not tell everybody this* (1982) Alden NOWLAN's poetry explores the heroic significance of the individual and the foibles of the self. His twenty-five titles include *Bread, wine and salt* (1967), a poetry collection that won him a Governor General's Award, and a short-story collection, *Miracle at Indian River* (1968). In recent years he collaborated with Walter Learning to write successful stage plays, including *Frankenstein*

(1976), *The dollar woman* (1978), and *The incredible murder of Cardinal Tosca* (1979).

David Adams RICHARDS' three remarkable novels use Miramichi speech with poetic complexity to create a narrative voice that moves easily between realistic detail and stream-of-consciousness thought. *The coming of winter* (1979), *Blood ties* (1981), and *Lives of short duration* (1982) show the rapid development of this young writer's ability to explore character in depth and to portray a wide range of society.

William Bauer, Robert Cockburn, Robert Gibbs, Robert Hawkes, Peter Thomas and Kent Thompson all teach at UNB. Although poets have continued to find university life amenable, prose writers have shown an increasing orientation away from the campus. Former university teacher Silver Donald Cameron became a full-time professional writer in the sixties, and his *Seasons in the rain* (1978) and *Dragon lady* (1980) are well-made fictions aimed at a popular audience. Kent THOMPSON has continued as a university teacher, but his novels—*The tenants were Corrie and Tennie* (1973), *Across from the floral park* (1974), and *Shacking up* (1980)—are also aimed at a popular audience, just as Tony Brennan and Dale Estey's novels are.

Fredericton poets, continue to work within modern poetry's intellectually demanding mainstream. The poetry of William Bauer (b. 1932) explores the idiosyncratically personal through an Augustan sensibility, and Robert GIBBS' detailing of the stubborn sources of individuality belies his surface nostalgia. Perhaps the most interesting of the Fredericton poets is M. Travis Lane (b. 1934), who writes poetry as difficult as that of the metaphysical moderns or Robert Lowell. Her collections *Poems 1968-1973* and *Divinations and shorter poems* (1980) have established her reputation as a poet, and *Homecomings* (1977) indicates that she is the most successful writer of the long poem in the Maritimes. *Birthday* (1969) and *Chaim the slaughterer* by Joe Sherman (b. 1945) are the best Maritimes articulation of the Jewish sensibility.

Sackville's Mount Allison University has become a second New Brunswick centre for poets. *Poems* (1959) and *The house* (1967) by Michael Collie (b. 1929) early established his interest in Fundy as an imaginative domain. Douglas LOCHHEAD's poems in *The full furnace* (1975), *A +e: a long poem* (1980), and *The high marsh road* (1980) reveal the effect of his affinity for the Maritimes. The five titles of Liliane Welch (b. 1937), from *Winter songs*

(1977) to *Brush and trunks* (1982), show a consistent control of sentiment and form. Foremost among the Sackville poets is the late John THOMPSON, whose *At the edge of the chopping there are no secrets* (1973) revealed a strong poetic talent profoundly affected by eastern philosophy. *Stiltjack* (1977) confirmed Thompson's success in his search for release of the imaginative vision from the trammels of convention and false reason through carefully constructed form. The renaissance of poetry in the sixties produced many poets who were not so closely connected with universities. In Prince Edward Island Eddie Clinton (b. 1946) published fine poems in the early seventies, but perhaps the most promising poetry appeared in *The girl in the brook* (1980), a collection by Wayne Wright (b. 1947).

The Writers' Federation of Nova Scotia has made that province the most organized in promoting readings and the short-term writers-in-community program. The strongest and most active new writers include Greg Cook (b. 1942), executive director of the federation, Harry Thurston (b. 1950), Leslie Choyce (b. 1952), and Fraser Sutherland (b. 1946). Richard Lemm (b. 1946), whose short stories and poems have appeared in 26 periodicals, published a fine collection in *Dancing in asylum* (1982). Elizabeth Jones' works include a play, *Glooskap's people*, and a film, *Medoonah the storm-maker*, written with Ellen Garbary, as well as five books of poetry, from *Castings* (1972) to *Nude on the Dartmouth ferry* (1980). George Elliott Clarke's *Saltwater spirituals and deeper blues* (1983) is the best poetic articulation of the history and traditions of Blacks in the Maritimes.

Notable New Brunswick poets include Brian Bartlett (b. 1953), Michael Brian Oliver (b. 1946), Alan Cooper (b. 1954), and Robert (Sunyata) MacLean (b. 1948). Bartlett has articulated his idealist's vision in finely crafted poems, and Oliver's passionate verse occasionally succeeds very well indeed. Alan Cooper's *Bloodlines* (1978) and *Hidden River poems* (1982) reveal a visionary view with affinities to John Thompson. After *Bloodlines* Cooper effectively became a full-time poet, and in 1982 the editor of *Germination*. Sunyata MacLean's Buddhist point of view occasionally produces some exciting moments in his loose verse forms. Other poets—such as Lakshmi Gill, Jim Stewart, and Frances Itani—show how extensive is this eclectic quality of contemporary Maritimes poetry.

Maritimes, Writing in the: 6

The short story has enjoyed a wide readership ever since the turn of the century, but in this period it has become the special province of experiment and innovation by writers. Because Alistair MacLEOD's *The lost salt gift of blood* (1976) has continued to draw attention for its striking articulation of Maritimes life, it was reissued in 1981. Ray SMITH's *Cape Breton is the thought control center of Canada* (1969) and *Lord Nelson tavern* (1974) use an innovative sense of form and a satiric point of view to explore Maritimes urban life. Don Domanski (b. 1950) in *Cape Breton book of the dead* (1975), David Adams Richards' in *Dancers at night* (1978), Ray Fraser (b. 1941) in *Black horse tavern* (1973), and Andy Wainwright (b. 1946) in his five titles reveal a similar realistic approach to Maritimes life. Beth Harvor (b. 1936) in *Women and children* (1973) and Anne Copeland (b. 1932) in *At peace* (1978) and *The back room* (1979) have each shown an interest in the Gothic quality of life in their stories.

At present writing in the Maritimes seems to be going through a period of consolidation after a time when the number of writers, the availability of publication, and the range of forms increased greatly. Apart from David Adams Richards' three powerful novels, only a few notable works of fiction were published in recent years and they are by older writers Ernest BUCKLER and Hugh MacLENNAN. Except for Ray Smith's innovative *Cape Breton is the thought control center of Canada*, the short story has tended to be conventionally realist. Poetry shows a similar tendency towards modern convention, which the vogue for performance poetry has not alleviated. To some extent this is merely the effect of contemporary mobility. Many writers of the Maritimes live elsewhere, and these include some of the most experimental, such as bill BISSETT. However, there are more playwrights among Maritimes writers than ever before. This is partly the result of the establishment of professional theatres such as Halifax's Neptune, Fredericton's Theater New Brunswick, and Wolfville's Mermaid; but it is equally the result of the active influence of people such as Evelyn Garbary, who has encouraged dramatist Margaret Armstrong and poet Elizabeth Jones. National influences like the CBC and dramatists' co-ops have produced and published the fine plays of dramatists such as Paul Ledoux and David Etheridge.

DON CONWAY

Marlatt, Daphne (b. 1942), née Buckle.

Born in Melbourne, Australia, to English parents who had been evacuated from Penang, Malaya, in advance of the Japanese occupation, Daphne Marlatt spent six postwar years in Penang before her family moved to North Vancouver, B.C., in 1951. She enrolled in English at the University of British Columbia in 1960, became an editor of TISH in 1963, and on graduation in 1964 went to the University of Indiana, where she completed an M.A. in comparative literature (1968). After a year each in Napa, Calif. (1967-8), Vancouver (1968-9), and Madison, Wis. (1969-70), she returned to Vancouver in 1970, where she works as a freelance writer and researcher.

Marlatt's first widely published works were the novella 'Sea Haven', in Giose Rimanelli's and Roberto Ruberto's *Modern Canadian stories* (1966), and fifteen poems in Raymond SOUSTER's *New wave Canada* (1966). These were followed by the long poems *Frames* (1968) and *Leaf/leafs* (1969), which are highly contrasting experiments in language and form. *Frames*, written in a long prose line, retells Hans Christian Andersen's 'The Snow Queen', using the tale to reinterpret events in the author's life. *Leaf/leafs*, written in lines of single words and syllables, accentuates minute fragmentary features of syntax and morphology so that at times they become the writing's primary content. While one work engages language at the level of sentence rhythm and narrative voice, and the other at that of phoneme and syntactic connection, each uses language to divine meaning through recurrence and resemblance. Each also sees language as a potential twin to the processes of consciousness.

These tentative and visibly technical works were succeeded by *Rings* (1971), *Vancouver poems* (1972), *Steveston* (1974), *Our lives* (1975), *Zocalo* (1977), *What matters* (1980), *Net work: selected writing* (1980), and *Here & there* (1981). While all—except the novel *Zocalo*—are presented as 'poems', their dominant feature is the long verse line, minutely punctuated, which suggests both the linguistic precision of poetry and the sequential motion of prose. All are written from inside a single consciousness and use linguistic structure to map perceptual processes in detail. *Rings* records every image and fragmentary reflection in the mind of a woman whose marriage is crumbling and whose first child is about to be born. Puns, shards of words, metaphors, enigmatic images, and broken sentences combine to give a nearly physical rendering of her simultaneous experience of pregnancy, memory, her husband's hostility, and her physical surroundings. *Vancouver poems* encounters that city through the subjective vision of someone freshly experiencing its geography, climate, and historical documents as interwoven, nearly co-present, phenomena.

Marlatt's portrayals of place are dynamic, phenomenological, existent only in the moment-by-moment consciousness of the perceiver. Her major work, *Steveston*, presents both the history and present of this Japanese-Canadian fish-cannery town as alive in the 'net' of consciousness cast by the writer. *Zocalo*'s very different images and denser, more extended prose line, give form to the intensely private experiences of a woman travelling in the Yucatan, who is separated by language, yet not by eye or ear, from the scenes she witnesses.

Marlatt's work during the 1970s with the British Columbia Archives' oral history project resulted in two strong documentary publications: *Steveston recollected: a Japanese-Canadian history* (1975) and *Opening doors: Vancouver's East End* (1980). From 1973 to 1976 she was an editor of *The Capilano Review*; from 1977 to 1981 she co-edited with Paul de Barros the prose magazine *Periodics*. She currently co-edits with John Marshall the Island Writing Series and the little magazine *Island*.

See also POETRY IN ENGLISH 1950 TO 1982: 3.   FRANK DAVEY

Marlyn, John (b. 1912). Born in Hungary, he was brought to Canada as an infant and grew up in Winnipeg's north end, the setting used in his fiction. He attended secondary schools in North End Winnipeg and the University of Manitoba for a time. Unable to find employment in Canada during the thirties, he went to England, where he became a script reader for a film studio. He returned to Canada just before the Second World War and has since worked as a writer for various governments in Ottawa. *Under the ribs of death* (1957) is one of the earliest Canadian novels to deal with what has been called the 'third solitude', life within ethnic cultures outside the Canadian mainstream. It is the story of Sandor Hunyadi, the son of an idealistic Hungarian immigrant, who is determined to escape the poverty and humiliation he associates with his immigrant background. Changing his name to Alex Hunter, he becomes a successful and ruth-less businessman only to be ruined in the Depression—a reversal that forces him to turn back to his family and the humanistic values he had earlier rejected. In spite of a somewhat facile ending, the novel is a powerful portrait of the hardships endured by immigrants, and of the driving ambition and susceptibility to materialistic values that can be spawned by such an experience. Marlyn's second and very different novel, *Putzi, I love you, you little square* (1981), is a surrealistic comedy set in Winnipeg in the seventies. It is about a talking, and otherwise precocious, fetus, who speaks from his virgin mother's womb, reciting Shakespeare and Baudelaire, commenting on life in the world beyond the womb, and advising his mother on the unsuitability of her suitors. Brief and rather slight, the novel is nonetheless an amusing fable that comments on our times while arguing for the same humanistic values (here personified in the character of Julian, a doctor) as did Marlyn's earlier novel.
                                          MARILYN ROSE

Marmette, Joseph-Étienne-Eugène (1844-95). The son of a physician, he was born at Montmagny, Canada East (Qué.). He studied at the Séminaire de Québec, spent one year at the Royal Military College in Kingston (Ont.), and one year in the law school of Université Laval. In 1866 he took a job as a clerk-bookkeeper in the Provincial Treasury department and hung onto it for dear life until 1882. Such was his first career, during which he managed to fill his leisure hours by reading novels and histories, writing serial romances, and collaborating with Henri-Raymond CASGRAIN, under the pseudonym Placide Lépine, on the literary profiles *Silhouettes canadiennes* (Québec, 1872). He married Joséphine, daughter of the historian François-Xavier GARNEAU, in 1868 and they had one daughter. In May 1882 he was appointed by Ottawa as a special immigration agent in Europe for France and Switzerland and left for Paris, where he worked for the Public Archives of Canada, transcribing documents relating to Canadian history. In the same year he became a charter member of the Royal Society of Canada. Between 1884 and 1887 he made three trips to Paris and also spent some time in London, where he was in charge of the library for the Canadian pavilion of the Colonial Exhibition of 1886. After 1887 he never again left Ottawa.

Between 1866 and 1895 Marmette published, besides *Silhouettes canadiennes*, a light comedy, *Il ne faut désespérer de rien* (Québec, 1880), and *Récits et souvenirs* (Québec, 1891), travel articles chiefly about London and Paris, most of which had already appeared between 1884 and 1888 in *Mémoires de La Société Royale du Canada*. But Marmette was most prominent for his historical novels; indeed, he was one of those who introduced the genre to his era. Unfortunately his wide reading of such historians as Charlevoix, Garneau, Ferland, La Pothérie, Jean-Claude Panet, Casgrain, Francis Parkman, and the JESUIT RELATIONS, his use of historical figures, and his attempts to reconstruct the Canadian cultural scene, were all in vain: his plots were ill-contrived and his characters neither well drawn nor sufficiently brought into the foreground. Inept at originating his own stories or in bringing history to life, he merely repeated himself endlessly. *Charles et Eva*, a story about the raid on Schenectady in 1890, appeared in *La Revue canadienne* (Dec. 1866-May 1867; rpr. 1945), *François de Bienville: scènes de la vie canadienne au XVIIᵉ siècle* (Québec, 1870), *L'intendant Bigot* (Montréal, 1872), *Le chevalier de Mornac: chroniques de la Nouvelle-France* (Montréal, 1873), *Le tomahahk et l'épée* (Québec, 1877), *Les Machabées de la Nouvelle-France: histoire d'une famille canadienne 1641-1768* (Québec, 1878), and *Héroisme et trahison* (Québec, 1878) are all cloak-and-dagger adventure fiction and anything but models of composition and style. But they were extremely popular in the nineteenth century: despite his fatuous and pompous style and his primitive psychology, Marmette had a large audience. Apparently modelling himself on Pixérécourt (1773-1844), he was skilful in exploiting the nostalgia felt by so many of his compatriots for the seventeenth and eighteenth centuries, but he is hardly read at all today. His two best works are *La fiancée du rebelle: épisode de la guerre des Bostonnais*, which appeared in instalments of *La Revue canadienne* (vol. XII, Jan.-Oct. 1875), and *A travers la vie: roman autobiographique*, which was first published in fragments in 1881, 1886, and 1892, and then in its entirety in *La Revue nationale* (vols I-II, 1895-6).   MAURICE LEBEL

Marquis, Thomas Guthrie (1864-1936). Born in Chatham, N.B., he graduated from Queen's University, Kingston, and taught English in Ontario schools until 1901. He then became a freelance writer, an editor, and a well-known figure in the Toronto book trade. He first came to public attention as a writer of popular historical tales. His *Stories of New France: being tales of adventure and heroism from the early history of Canada* (Boston, 1890), the second in a series (Agnes MACHAR wrote the first volume), was followed by *Stories from Canadian history* (Toronto, 1893; rpr. 1936). His one full-length historical romance, *Marguerite de Roberval; a romance of the days of Jacques Cartier* (Toronto, 1899), told in an old-fashioned intrusive manner, explains the failure of the Cartier-Roberval expedition to New France. A second work of prose fiction, *The king's wish* (1924), is a charming pastoral allegory for children.

Marquis began his historical work with a book on Canadian activity in the Boer war, *Canada's sons on kopje and veldt: an historical account of the Canadian contingents* (1900), and *Presidents of the United States from Pierce to McKinley* (1903), vol. XXI in the prestigious 26-volume Nineteenth-Century Series edited by Justin McCarthy (Charles G.D. ROBERTS and Marquis were among the four international associate editors of the series). A number of Canadian biographies and histories for the popular and school markets followed: *Brock, the hero of Upper Canada* (1912); *The war chief of the Ottawas: a chronicle of the Pontiac war* (1915); *The Jesuit missions: a chronicle of the cross in the wilderness* (1916); and four brief textbooks in the Canadian History Reader Series: *Sir Isaac Brock* (1926), *Naval warfare on the Great Lakes, 1812-14* (1926), *Battlefields of 1813* (1926), *George Munro Grant* (1926), and *The voyages of Jacques Cartier in prose and verse* (1934), with sonnets by S.C. Swift and prose sketches by Marquis.

Marquis's *English-Canadian literature* (1914), a valuable overview of its subject, was prepared first as a lengthy chapter in *Canada and its provinces*, vol. XII (1914). His long poem, *The cathedral* (1924), an effective blank-verse dramatic monologue, was republished posthumously in *The cathedral and other poems* (1936), a collection edited by his wife, and introduced by Sir Charles G.D. Roberts. Marquis also edited *Builders of Canada from Cartier to Laurier* (1903), consisting of 33 lives of historical personages and published in the U.S. as *Giants of the Dominion from Cartier to Laurier* (1905); and in 1929 he edited and introduced the re-publication of Georgiana M. Pennée's 1864 translation of Philippe AUBERT DE GASPÉ's Les ANCIENS CANADIENS: *Seigneur d'Haberville (The Canadians of old)*.   KEN MacKINNON

Marriott, Anne (b. 1913). Born in Victoria, B.C., she was educated at The Poplars and at the Norfolk House School for Girls in Victoria, and took summer courses in creative writing at the University of British Columbia. The first person to interest her in modern poetry was Ira Dilworth. She was further encouraged by Alan Crawley, and was on the founding committee of Crawley's CONTEMPORARY VERSE in 1941. She has written dozens of school broadcasts for CBC radio and the B.C. Department of Education, largely on creative-writing or historical subjects. In 1943-4 she edited a poetry column for the Victoria *Daily Times*. From 1945 to 1949 she was a script editor for the National Film Board in Ottawa. From 1950 to 1953 she was women's editor of the Prince George *Citizen*. In the 1970s she conducted poetry-writing workshops with elementary-school students in libraries around Vancouver, producing in 1977 a poetry-writing handbook.

Marriott's best-known work is the long narrative poem 'The wind, our enemy', which describes drought on the Prairies during the 1930s and was the title poem in a Ryerson Poetry Chapbook (1939). Subsequent collections include *Calling adventurers* (1941), for which she won a Governor General's Award; *Salt marsh* (1942); and *Sandstone and other poems* (1945).

After a long silence, Marriott published *Countries* (1971). In a series of moving poems, the narrator, confined by a serious illness, investigates the memories of countries she has known. Working with the materials of everyday life as she travels about in her mental landscape, she discovers the heart of love. *The circular coast: new and selected poems* (1981) includes the best poems from the early collections and some new work that reveal a unified whole in which Marriott seeks, with complex imagery and perfectly observed detail, the core of stability within a changing world. Her subjects are time, youth, and fulfilling dreams; aging and death, drawing closer each day, are also prominent. With a chant she speaks a mantra to death: 'That is the timeless clock/that tells no hours/set to its/certain time.'

GEOFF HANCOCK

Marshall, Joyce (b. 1913). Born in Montreal and educated at McGill University, she has lived in Toronto for many years. She is the author of two novels and a collection of short stories and has been a freelance editor for book publishers and the CBC; she has also translated fiction by Gabrielle ROY and other French-Canadian writers. Her first novel, *Presently tomorrow* (1946), is set in the Eastern Townships of Québec, in an English-speaking enclave in the southwest corner of the province. The story takes place in the early 1930s when the Depression has caused political and social turmoil throughout Canada. Craig Everett, an idealistic but naïve Anglican priest, whose social conscience has become an irritant to his superiors, has been sent from Montreal to conduct a retreat at St Ursula's, a boarding-school for girls. Before the retreat has ended he is seduced by one of the students, a schoolgirl who is already more knowing than Craig will ever be. The fine prose and the subtle exploration of character and motivations that distinguish *Presently tomorrow*—which achieved some notoriety on publication because of its subject matter—are noticeable once again in *Lovers and strangers* (1957), which takes place in the latter half of the 1940s in Toronto. Katherine, a diffident young woman who bears the faint aftereffects of polio, impulsively marries Roger Haines, an architect who seems to be already launched on a successful career. But Roger, although he appears to be outgoing, busy, and affluent, suffers from his own insecurities, and the novel becomes a study of marriage and a career that are both going badly.

Marshall's short-story collection, *A private place* (1975), contains her most powerful fiction. It brings together seven stories that appeared in magazines or were broadcast by the CBC at various times from the early 1950s to the 1970s. One story is set in Norway, another in Mexico; a third story, about childhood, takes place in the Eastern Townships; and 'The old woman', a study of an obsession that ends in madness, has as its background a remote village in northern Québec. But the tone of *A private place* is really established by the three remaining stories—'The enemy', 'Salvage', and 'So many have died'—about urban life in North America in the second half of the twentieth century; even more specifically, they are stories about the lives that women lead who must live alone in big cities, solitary, vulnerable, sometimes physically endangered.

Marshall edited and translated *Word from New France: the selected letters of Marie de l'Incarnation* (1967), for which she wrote a lengthy and important historical introduction, and *No passport: a discovery of Canada* by the prolific Québec travel-writer Eugène

Cloutier. Her translations of three books by Gabrielle Roy—*The road past Altamont* (1966), *Windflower* (1970), and *Enchanted summer* (1976)—involved her in a close and sympathetic collaboration with the author. Marshall was awarded the Canada Council Translation Prize (1976) for her translation of Roy's *Cet été qui chantait*.

ROBERT WEAVER

Marshall, Tom (b. 1938). Born in Niagara Falls, Ont., he was educated at Queen's University, Kingston, where he wrote an M.A. thesis on A.M. KLEIN. Since 1964 he has been a member of the English department at Queen's. He has edited the literary magazine *Quarry* and been poetry editor for *The* CANADIAN FORUM.

Marshall's four mature collections—which form an interlocking cycle of earth, air, fire, and water imagery—are *The silence of fire* (1969), *Magic water* (1971), *The earthbook* (1974), and *The white city* (1976); selections from these make up *The elements: poems 1960-1975* (1980). Marshall explores history, pain, and the human condition against a backdrop of the history, artists, and historical figures of Canada, a country that Marshall regards as 'a second chance' for mankind to redeem itself, since that opportunity was lost by the Europeans: 'the garden of the gods is here'—in Canada, where the human imagination is nourished and regenerated.

A novel, *Rosemary Gaol* (1978), is Marshall's flawed though interesting account of men and women in their early thirties making a bid for career and personal fulfilment before the onslaught of middle age. His protagonist is a teacher and amateur novelist who is writing a dull novel within the novel. Marshall wittily juxtaposes narrative styles to portray the pretensions of the university milieu.

With Stuart McKinnon, Gail Fox, and David HELWIG, Marshall has recorded an album of poetry from Kingston *(Four Kingston Poets)*. His critical writings include *Psychic mariner: a reading of the poems of D.H. Lawrence* (1970) and *Harsh and lovely land: the major Canadian poets and the making of a Canadian tradition* (1979). Marshall also edited, and wrote the postscript to, *A.M. Klein* (1970), a compendium of Klein criticism. He was the co-editor (with Helwig) of the anthology *Fourteen stories high* (1971).

See also CRITICISM IN ENGLISH: 5(f).

GEOFF HANCOCK

Martel, Suzanne. See CHILDREN'S LITERATURE IN FRENCH: 3 and SCIENCE FICTION AND FANTASY IN ENGLISH AND FRENCH: 3.

Martin, Claire (b. 1914). Born in Quebec City, she was educated by the Ursuline nuns and the Sisters of the Congrégation Notre-Dame. After a career as a radio announcer, first in Quebec City and then with Radio-Canada in Montreal, she married Roland Faucher, a chemist with the ministry of health in Ottawa and, while living there, began to write. Her first work was a collection of stories, *Avec ou sans amour* (1958), for which she won the Cercle du Livre de France award. Martin and her husband lived in the south of France from 1972 until 1982. They now live in Quebec City.

From the outset Martin's writing has focused on brief depictions of love, always shown to be fragile, threatened, ephemeral: she has a gift for the bold stroke, for precise observation, and for fusing irony with tenderness. Her best work, however, was published during the sixties: two novels, *Doux-amer* (1960) and *Quand j'aurai payé ton visage* (1962), and two famous books of memoirs, DANS UN GANT DE FER (1965) and *La joue droite* (1966), for which she received the Prix de la Province de Québec and a Governor General's award (for fiction!). A novel with overtones of tragedy, *Les morts* (1970) was adapted for the theatre under the title *Moi je n'étais qu'espoir*, which was produced by Montreal's Théâtre du Rideau Vert in 1972. While writer-in-residence at the Université d'Ottawa in 1972, Martin wrote a short essay, *La petite fille lit* (1973), which offers an exquisite description of the way she was captivated and fascinated by the magic of books when she was a little girl. Since 1972 she has devoted herself to translating: among the works she has translated is Margaret LAURENCE's *The* STONE ANGEL (*L'ange de pierre*, 1976).

Both in her fiction and in her autobiographies Martin relentlessly pursues topics that have traditionally been proscribed for Québec literature: extramarital love and the demythologizing of the sacrosanct image of the father as noble and good, the rightful holder of authority and knowledge. She shows a preference for the first-person narrative and for presenting multiple viewpoints, techniques that enable her to probe the inner depths of human nature, bringing to light its complexity and giving the individual primacy over the group. Martin is also preoccupied with the situation of women: her works offer intelligent denunciations of the taboos and stereotyping that inhibit women's freedom and development.

Doux-amer—translated by David Lobdell as *Best man* (1983)—portrays a writer who lays claim to her rights to freedom by putting her career before love, by allowing herself to be unfaithful, and by marrying a man younger than herself—all time-honoured actions and privileges reserved for men. As traditional roles are reversed, abilities and temperaments—rather than gender—govern behaviour: the male protagonist, the writer's lover and editor, plays the role usually played by women, that of the Other—submissive, faithful, devoted. He is the narrator, the one who confides his suffering, openly pouring out his feelings about being a too-frequently obliging victim. The emphasis on individual confrontation and on subjectivisim is even more apparent in *Quand j'aurai payé ton visage*. About a love triangle involving two brothers and the wife of one of them, it reveals a tangle of family relations that touches on incest and other taboos, giving the author an opportunity to criticize the family and society. The narrative unfolds in the words of Catherine, Robert, and Jeanne Ferny respectively, providing a compressed and varied perspective, and throwing into relief the profound isolation of each person locked into his or her own world. Reminiscences and confessions abound in *Les morts*, as the young narrator tries desperately to relive her youthful passion for a man killed in the war: once again, love is inseparable from separation. But Martin's major work is indisputably her books of memoirs, *Dans un gant de fer* and *La joue droite*, two powerful and frank recreations of a painful and oppressive childhood and adolescence in which Martin was exposed to violence and every kind of humiliation. The maleficent and terrifying figure of a despotic father can be seen as embodying the paralysing monolithic structure that for so long tyrannized Québec society and prevented its flowering. The books also expose, with merciless clarity, the situation of women—treated as inferior, incompetent, enslaved. This autobiography, which reveals the hell that can exist in the realm of intimacy, provides the key to the relentless quest for love that governs all Martin's work.

Dans un gant de fer and *La joue droite* were translated by Philip Stratford and first published in one volume, *In an iron glove* (1968), and later separately as *In an iron glove* (1973)

and *The right cheek* (1975).

See VOIX ET IMAGES *du Pays*, VIII, 1974; and Françoise Kaye, 'Claire Martin ou le "je" aboli', *Incidences*, vol. IV, May-Dec. 1980.   NICOLE BOURBONNAIS

Marty, Sid (b. 1944). Born in South Shields, Eng., he was raised in Medicine Hat, Alta, and educated in Calgary at Mount Royal Junior College. He received a degree in honours English from Sir George Williams University, Montreal, before deciding to work full time as a park warden and writer. He was a season ranger in Yoho and Jasper National Parks from 1966 to 1973. Since then he has worked as a park warden in Banff National Park, and this experience informs much of his poetry.

Marty's first chapbooks were undated works—*Carbon copies* and *The dream horseman*—that were followed by the modest ten-page *The tumbleweed harvest* (1973). His first collection, *Headwaters* (1973), draws upon his Rocky Mountain experiences to remind readers that loneliness, death, and madness are an accepted part of the life cycle. A deceptively simple stylist, Marty sees love, death, forest fires, children—whether in urban or wilderness settings—as occurences in a natural cycle. He developed these themes in *Nobody danced with Miss Rodeo* (1981), a three-part collection that again captures the sounds and elements of the Rocky Mountains. In the first sequence he contemplates the technological invasion of the wilderness by search and rescue aircraft, chainsaws, power boats, ski-lift operators, and helicopters. The title sequence includes bittersweet or humorous accounts of urban dwellers misplaced in a mountain setting; while the third reflects on the pain and joys of raising a son and family in the wilderness. *Men for the mountains* (1978) is a prose documentary about the wardens in Canada's national parks, drawing especially upon Marty's work in Banff. In eloquent prose, Marty describes his aesthetic of the intimate, ancient, and still essential interdependence between man and the natural world, while discussing isolation, grizzly bears, forest fires, tourists, the negative effects of the Trans-Canada highway, the hunting season, and certain park administration policies.
                GEOFF HANCOCK

Mathews, Robin. See CRITICISM IN ENGLISH: 5(e).

Mayne, Seymour (b. 1944). Born in Montreal, he did undergraduate studies at McGill University and doctoral studies at the University of British Columbia. He taught briefly at UBC before joining the staff of the University of Ottawa (1973), where he is presently associate professor of English. He has been visiting professor at the Hebrew University of Jerusalem (1979-80) and at Concordia University, Montreal (1982-3).

In his earliest collections of poetry—*That monocycle the moon* (1964), *Tiptoeing on the mount* (1965), *From the portals of mouseholes* (1966), and *I am still the boy* (1967)—Mayne is a frequently lighthearted explorer of human passion and sensuality. Discipline and intelligence stand behind his carefully controlled poems. *Manimals* (1969) is a comic diversion in poetry and prose. In later volumes—*Mouth* (1970), *For stems of light* (1971), *Face* (1971), and especially *Name* (1975)—the celebratory exploration in the earlier collections gives way to a more personal and painful probing. Mayne's vision, founded in a Jewish mysticism of the body, studies man's relations with himself and the world around him. His poetry reveals a new consciousness of his Jewishness and a concern with social issues that always focuses on the human dimension. The sexuality of the early romantic poetry is replaced by pain and melancholy about the transience and mortality of the human condition. *Name* received the J.I. SEGAL Prize in English-French literature and the York University Poetry Workshop Award.

Mayne's most recent volumes, *Diasporas* (1977) and *The impossible promised land: poems new and selected* (1981), herald the secure voice of a mature poet conscious of his heritage and his calling. Here Mayne is the literary descendent of A.M. KLEIN, the friend of Irving LAYTON and Leonard COHEN—the youngest poet of this quartet from the Montreal Jewish community. Though a bleak and pessimistic vision of life now permeates his poetry, Mayne finds hope in his commitment to Jewish traditions and in man's awareness and acceptance of the cycle of time. As impassioned and indignant about the Holocaust as Layton, he never indulges in the 'gorgeous rant and offensive irony' that characterize much of Layton's recent verse. The disciplined control of Mayne's poetry is reminiscent of Klein's later verse, though the increase in Jewish allusions and terminology in Mayne's recent volumes recalls Klein's early work.

In Montreal in the early sixties Mayne was one of the editors of *Cataract* and later of *Catapult*. He was one of the founders of Very Stone House Press (Vancouver) and later of Ingluvin Publications (Montreal). For the former he edited, with Patrick LANE, *The collected poems of Red Lane* (q.v., 1968). He was also one of the founders of Mosaic Press/Valley Editions (Oakville and Ottawa, Ont.). For these three presses he edited many volumes of poetry and prose. Organizer of the University of Ottawa's A.M. Klein symposium (1974), the first reassessment of Klein's literary stature, Mayne edited, and wrote the introduction to, *The A.M. Klein symposium* (1975). He has also edited *Engagements: the prose of Irving Layton* (1972) and *Irving Layton: the poet and his critics* (1978).

While Mayne's poetry has been translated into Hebrew and Spanish, he himself has co-translated poetry from Yiddish, Polish, and Russian. With Catherine Leach he translated the Polish verse of Jerzy Harasymowicz, *Genealogy of instruments* (1974). From the Yiddish he translated *Burnt pearls: ghetto poems of Abraham Sutzkever* (1981), and he was the editor of *Generations: selected poems of Rachel Korn* (q.v., 1982).   DAVID STAINES

Melanson, Laurier. See ACADIAN LITERATURE: 2(c).

Menaud, maître-draveur (1937). Félix-Antoine SAVARD's first novel, this classic of French-Canadian literature, set in the lumbering region of Charlevoix County in northeastern Québec, is about a veteran of the log-drive who—incensed by the foreign (Anglo-Canadian) businessmen who were exploiting Québec's resources—is fired by words he reads in Louis HÉMON's MARIA CHAPDELAINE: 'Around us have come strangers we scorn as foreigners. They have taken all the money. Yet in the land of Québec nothing will change . . .' Misfortune comes to Menaud in the harshest fashion when his son Joson drowns while trying to free a log jam—a powerfully depicted episode. Menaud's efforts to rally people to oppose the foreigners meet with no success. When, distraught, he goes into the forest during a snowstorm in search of the 'stranger' who has threatened to cut off the local people from access to the territory, he is barely saved from freezing to death. After this he sinks into madness, repeating incessantly: 'Strangers came! Strangers came!' The novel ends with the words of a farmer: 'This is no ordinary madness! It is a warning!'

The last in a long line of traditional novels on French-Canadian nationalism—though in its conflicts and its portrayal of madness it is far removed from the rural idylls of the past—*Menaud* was applauded by critics for its nationalistic spirit, but above all for its profuse and vivid imagery, and for Savard's skill in incorporating French-Canadian regional expressions into a text of essentially classical texture. In 1938 Savard published a second version, correcting misprints that marred the original edition; making stylistic revisions; changing to roman type the regional expressions that had appeared in italics; and adding a short glossary. Some critics had expressed reservations about an excessive richness of style, an exaggeration of ornamentation, and in 1944 Savard produced a 'more concise and simple text', which he called the 'definitive edition'. In 1960 he produced a fourth version in the 'Alouette bleue' collection published by Fides. Under the title appeared the words, 'In conformity with the first edition'— though this version is by no means identical with the original. Finally in 1964 Savard reshaped his novel for the fifth time.

The 1937 version was translated into English by Alan SULLIVAN under the title *Boss of the river* (1947). The most recent translation, by Richard Howard—*Master of the river* (1976)—is based on the 1964 version.

See François Ricard, *L'art de Félix-Antoine Savard dans 'Menaud, maître-draveur'* (1972).

JULES TESSIER

Mercier, Serge. See DRAMA IN FRENCH 1948 TO 1981: 3.

Merril, Judith. See SCIENCE FICTION AND FANTASY IN ENGLISH AND FRENCH: 3.

Metcalf, John (b. 1938). Born in Carlisle, Eng., he came to Canada in 1962, having received an Honours B.A. (1960) and a certificate in education (1961) from the University of Bristol. He taught at high schools in Montreal and Cold Lake, Alta, before accepting in 1969 a position at Loyola College, Montreal. Since 1971 he has devoted his time to writing, supplementing his income with part-time teaching, editing, and as writer-in-residence at the University of New Brunswick, Loyola, the University of Ottawa, and Concordia University, Montreal.

Metacalf's five stories in *New Canadian writing, 1969* reveal a disciplined prose style and, in 'The children green and golden', an early attention to sound, smells, and texture—elements designed to elicit an emotional, as well as an intellectual, response. 'The estuary', which focuses on a potentially suicidal but vitally alive young man, won the President's Medal of the University of Western Ontario for the best story of 1969. Metcalf's first short-story collection, *The lady who sold furniture* (1970), contains—besides the title story, a novella—five stories set in England. Employing a fairly traditional technique and vivid observations, Metcalf injects a note of uneasiness into these stories that sometimes explodes in a macabre or gruesome scene. *The teeth of my father* (1975) is a more uneven collection, though the control of tone and mood remains and there are touches of humour. In the moving 'Beryl' two characters come together but ultimately are unable to relieve each other's loneliness—a popular Metcalf theme.

In Metcalf's first novel, *Going down slow* (1972), set in Montreal, he ridicules both the self-important staff of a high school and a society that would reward efficiency at the expense of intelligence and humanity. David Appleby is a recent English immigrant who battles the system in a series of fast-moving skirmishes, in contrast to his mistress Susan, also a teacher, who stays outside it, and his roommate Jim, who rises through the educational establishment. *Girl in gingham* (1978)—reprinted as *Private parts: a memoir* (1980)—contains two novellas with these titles. 'Girl in gingham'—first published in *Dreams surround us* (1977), which also contains poems by John NEWLOVE—features a nearly flawless setting and dialogue, in addition to excellent satire. Peter Thornton, an appraiser of antiques who is slowly rebuilding his life after a traumatic divorce, is paired (after several computer-date mismatches) with his ideal woman, Anna, a rare-books librarian with similar regard for the past. The title of 'Private parts' alludes both to sex, which is treated lightly and entertainingly, and to the narrator's preservation of his inner self in a life-denying, puritanical milieu. About the coming-of-age of a precocious youth, it concludes with a sad irony: adulthood has brought not liberation but disillusionment and boredom. Metcalf's most significant achievement to date is his novel *General Ludd* (1980), which combines vehement wit, understated humour, a black comedic vision, and occasional absurdity. Its hero, James Wells, poet-in-residence at St Xavier University—which, like society at large, has little appreciation for true poetry—becomes a modern-day Luddite and attempts to forestall the future by destroying the highly sophisticated Communication Arts Centre, the false idol of campus technocrats. Although the novel occasionally rambles and has an ending reminiscent of Ken Kesey's *One flew over the cuckoo's nest*, it has passion and emotional range and offers a brilliant satire of a fast-food society oblivious of traditional values, art, and culture.

Metcalf has edited numerous short-story anthologies for schools and universities and co-edited *Best Canadian stories* from 1977 to 1982. In 1982 he published his first book of essays, *Kicking against the pricks*, and *Selected stories*, and edited *Making it new: contemporary Canadian stories*.

See two essays by Barry Cameron: 'The practice of the craft: a conversation with John Metcalf', *Queen's Quarterly* 82, no. 3 (Autumn 1975), and 'An approximation of poetry: the short stories of John Metcalf', *Studies in Canadian Literature* 2, no. 1 (Winter 1977). Robert Lecker's *On the line* (1982) contains a perceptive discussion of Metcalf's fiction.

See also NOVELS IN ENGLISH 1960 TO 1982: 4.   DAVID O'ROURKE

Meunier, Claude. See DRAMA IN FRENCH 1948 TO 1981: 4.

Millar, Margaret. See MYSTERY AND CRIME.

Mills, John (b. 1930). Born in London, Eng., he came to Canada in 1953. While travelling widely in Canada and Europe, he held a striking variety of manual and technical positions. After he earned a B.A. from the University of British Columbia (1964) and an M.A. from Stanford University (1965), he began his present career as a teacher of English at Simon Fraser University, Burnaby, B.C. Mills is a sophisticated satirist of considerable forcefulness, and his novels are also assured parodies of literary conventions. *The land of is* (1972) is a blackly comic subversion of *The tempest*, transposed to contemporary Vancouver; *The October men* (1973), set during the 1970 FLQ crisis, features a smalltime confidence man whose associates, schemes, and fantasies imitate the stereotypes of pulp fiction. *Skevington's daughter* (1978), an inventive epistolary novel, is a caustic academic caricature, riddled with violence in action and rhetoric,

which incidentally echoes late-Romantic travel writing. *Lizard in the grass* (1980) collects Mills' amusing and unsentimental autobiographical pieces, as well as some characteristically mordant and informed literary reviews. His fiction and criticism often display a tone of articulate mockery that suggests his uncompromising standards and complete individuality.

See also NOVELS IN ENGLISH 1960 TO 1982: OTHER TALENTS, OTHER WORKS: 1, 6(c).
                    LOUIS K. MacKENDRICK

Miron, Gaston (b. 1928). Born in Sainte-Agathe-des-Monts, Qué., he attended the Collège des Frères du Sacré-Coeur until 1946; the following year he went to Montreal, where he worked at various jobs and befriended Louis Portuguais, Gilles Carle, Mathilde Ganzini, and Olivier Marchand. In 1953 he was one of the founders of Les Éditions de l'Hexagone, a publishing house devoted to the printing and distribution of poetry that influenced Québec's literary life for the next three decades. L'Hexagone was to become a convenient term not only for this business venture but also for the generation of poets it published (Jean-Guy PILON, Fernand OUELLETTE, and Paul-Marie LAPOINTE, to name only a few). Miron invested a considerable amount of energy in the everyday running of L'Hexagone, of which he is still the editor; as a result, his own poetic output suffered. Apart from *Deux sangs* (1953)—jointly produced with Marchand—most of his poetry appeared in reviews, periodicals, magazines, and anthologies during the sixties. It was only in 1970, thanks to the initiative of the Presses de l'Université de Montréal, that *L'homme rapaillé* appeared to great critical and public acclaim. In 1980 a long-awaited translation by Marc Plourde of one of the sections of *L'homme rapaillé*—with other poems not included in that volume—was published under the title *The agonized life*. In 1975 the Université d'Ottawa published *Contrepointes*, a collection of poems written between 1954 and 1968 that had appeared in various magazines around the world but never in book form.

Miron's selflessness, and maybe his ambivalence about his own writing, were illustrated by his concentration on political action. In the late fifties he ran twice as an NDP candidate, but from 1962 devoted his energy to separatist movements. In Oct. 1970 he was jailed for ten days on account of his political opinions. But that same year he received two literary awards—the Prix de la Revue *Études françaises* and the Prix France-Canada—for *L'homme rapaillé*. Other international awards followed: the Prix Belgique-Canada (1972) and the Prix Guillaume Apollinaire (1981), which traditionally goes to one of the great poets in the French language.

Miron's relationship with writing bears the mark of a mind distressed by 'the semantic perversion of Québec's language'—his description of the linguistic syndrome of the fifties and sixties. Indeed, he felt devastated at that time by the disruption of the French language under the inevitable pressures of English, which was then the functional idiom of work, media, advertising, and trade. Three of his political essays in *L'homme rapaillé*—'L'aliénation délirante', 'Un long chemin', and 'Notes sur le non-poème et le poème'—explicitly detail his position on this issue. (See Marc Plourde's translation of the second, 'A long road', in *The agonized life*.) Consequently he determined to avoid what he saw as two equally disastrous pitfalls: regionalism and universalism. Miron never adopted the abstract humanism of the previous generation of poets, nor did he embrace JOUAL as a mode of communication. His language articulated a specific territory as well as a unique moment in time, yet it also transcended these and reached for all alienated, dispossessed human beings. Two images recur in Miron's work: one is of a woman—usually estranged, distant, and lost to the narrator; the other is of the land of Québec and its collective destiny. Both evoke unhappy ties, alienating and schizophrenic emotions; but they are also linked to a reconstruction process, a reconciliation of all forces. Man is '*rapaillé*': his life-giving faculties are gathered once more, just as old bits of straw are picked up from the autumn fields of rural Québec. Though Miron's texts contend against the injustices of history and the plight of the Québec people, they include a message of invincible hope. The fact that his own writing destiny has been inextricably linked to a specific historical situation made him one of the most visible and listened-to spokesmen for Québec's independence. But he has also attracted more international attention than perhaps any Québécois poet. His poetry has been linked to that of Pablo Neruda and Aimé Césaire, who also expressed ideals of nationalism and social justice.

Jacques BRAULT's *Miron le magnifique*

(1969) and Eugène Roberto's *Structure de l'imaginaire dans 'Contrepointes' de Miron* (1979) testify to the impact Miron had had on the Québec literary scene for fifteen years. One issue of *La* BARRE DU JOUR (no. 26, Oct. 1970) was devoted to a critical examination of his writings and of his role as editor, publisher, and ideologue. Abroad, one essay by John Beaver, 'Gaston Miron', *The language of poetry: crisis and solution* (Amsterdam: Rodopi, 1980), is an interesting tribute to Miron's role as a contemporary writer in French. Apart from Marc Plourde's *The agonized life*, numerous other translations of his works have been published. See Gertrude Sanderson's translations in the *The Antigonish Review* 18 (Summer 1974); Fred COGSWELL's in *The poetry of French-Canada in translation* (1970); and John GLASSCO's in *Ellipse* 1 (Fall 1969). See also Jean-Louis Major, 'L'Hexagone: une aventure en poésie québécoise' in *La poésie canadienne-française*, vol. 4 (1969).

CAROLINE BAYARD

Mitchell, John (1880-1951). Born on the farm purchased in 1834 by his grandfather near Mono, Ont., in the Caledon Hills, he moved in 1894 with his mother to Toronto, where he attended Harbord Collegiate; Victoria College, University of Toronto; and Osgoode Hall Law School. He practised law in Toronto for twenty-eight years, for the most part independently in a rented office on Bay St. Reticent and reclusive, and careless about the management of his personal affairs, he suddenly destroyed his professional career in 1935 by accusing himself publicly of misappropriating trust funds. He was convicted, imprisoned for six months, and disbarred.

Mitchell had begun writing after his mother, to whom he was devoted, died in 1928. His first work was *The kingdom of America* (1930), a privately printed nationalistic manifesto in which Mitchell proclaimed his allegiance to a Canada that was not a dominion but a kingdom, autonomous and monarchical. Under the pseudonym 'Patrick Slater' he next wrote *The yellow briar: a story of the Irish in the Canadian countryside* (1933; rpr. 1971), a fictional autobiography, narrated by the Irish orphan 'Paddy Slater' (it was initially accepted as genuine autobiography), containing much authentic detail from the experiences of Mitchell's grandparents. An engaging story of pioneering and settlement in the Caledon region of southern Ontario and of life in

Toronto, mainly in the 1840s, it captures and celebrates the seasonal and generational cycles with originality, tolerance, and garrulous good nature. It was an immediate success. Mitchell also wrote *Robert Harding* (1938), an unsuccessful novel about a man wrongly imprisoned for murder; *The waterdrinker* (1938), a collection of sentimental, badly wrought verse; and a work of local history, *The settlement of York County* (posthumously published in 1952).

'The story of John Mitchell', an account of his life by Dorothy Bishop, appears in the 1971 edition of *The yellow briar*.

JOHN LENNOX

Mitchell, Ken (b. 1940). Born in Moose Jaw, Sask., he attended the University of Saskatchewan (B.A., 1965, M.A. 1967) and while still a student began publishing short fiction and writing radio plays for the CBC regional and international networks. In 1967 he joined the English department of the University of Regina, where he still teaches creative writing and Canadian literature. In 1970 he wrote his first stage play, *Heroes*, which won first prize in the Ottawa Little Theatre Play competition of 1971. In 1979-80 he was the Scottish-Canadian Exchange Fellow at Edinburgh University and the following year he was visiting professor of English, University of Nanking. He has also taught writing at the Saskatchewan Summer School of the Arts and the Banff Centre of the Arts. In the early 1970s he helped found the Saskatchewan Writers' Guild.

Mitchell has described himself as 'a popularist by nature', and his work makes clear that he is a populist writer as well. He is also an almost paradigmatic example of the regionalist artist: although his works are universal in appeal, it is difficult to conceive of them outside their prairie context, which is sometimes palpably physical and at other times little more than a mood or an attitude. In terms of characterization, this attitude is manifested in Mitchell's choice of protagonists—people who are, as he says, 'eccentric in the sense that they automatically resist being part of a consensus or any kind of conforming society.' Mitchell's love for, and enjoyment of, such people can be felt in his first novel, *Wandering Rafferty* (1972), in which the eponymous protagonist and his young sidekick endure a series of comic misadventures as they travel across the western provinces. Even *The Meadowlark connection* (1975), with its slapstick comedy directed against the foolish young RCMP constable

who is sure he has uncovered a drug ring in a small Saskatchewan farm community, presents a kind of nonconformist, albeit one who wants to belong. The stories collected in *Everybody gets something here* (1977) are essentially comic, though many have rather bleak subtexts. Here again the protagonists, like the Irish grandfather in 'The great electrical revolution', are always willing to flout authority. In Mitchell's novel *The con man* (1979) the rebel figure is a halfbreed who spends much of his time in jail because the people he meets keep insisting that he offer them something for nothing: he becomes the comic victim of a society that pretends to despise him but cannot do without him.

Although Mitchell is an accomplished fiction writer, he feels that 'theatre is . . . the most powerful form of communication that there is.' In the past decade he has worked on projects involving various degrees of collaboration with other artists. One of his first major efforts was *Cruel tears* (1976), which toured Canada. Working with Humphrey and the Dumptrucks, who provided a kind of musical commentary on stage in an almost Brechtian manner, this Country and Western 'opera', based on *Othello*, is a tragicomic tale about truckers and their politics and jealousy over women. *Davin: the politician* (1979) recovers from Victorian silence the story of an early prairie politician and writer, Nicholas Flood Davin (1843-1901), and his feminist lover Kate Simpson-Hayes—both fitting Mitchell nonconformists. *The shipbuilder* (1979), written for actors and percussion ensemble, is about a Finnish farmer who decides to build a ship by hand on his Saskatchewan farm in order to sail back to his homeland; unlike Mitchell's earlier plays, it is a stark tragedy of pride. In *The medicine line* (1976) Mitchell created an epic outdoor drama about Major James Walsh of the RCMP and Chief Sitting Bull. In *The great cultural revolution* (1980) he set a version of a *kunchu*-style Chinese opera inside a play about its staging in China in 1966; here he collaborated with the Chinese-Canadian composer David Liang. Mitchell has continued to explore the medium of drama, with musicals and revues, and has even written a one-man show based on the life of Norman Bethune, *Gone the burning sun*, which he hopes to take to China.

Mitchell has edited an anthology, *Horizon: writings of the Canadian Prairies* (1977); published a critical study, *Sinclair Ross: a reader's guide* (1981); and written the screenplays for *This train* (CBC), *Striker* (NFB), and

The hounds of Notre Dame (Fraser Films). He is the subject of critical interviews in Alan Twigg, *For openers* (1981), and Robert Wallace and Cynthia Zimmerman (eds.), *The work: conversations with English-Canadian playwrights* (1982).

See also NOVELS IN ENGLISH 1960 TO 1982: OTHER TALENTS, OTHER WORKS: 6(b).

DOUGLAS BARBOUR

Mitchell, W.O. (b. 1914). Born and raised in Weyburn, Sask., William Ormond Mitchell was diagnosed in 1926 as having contracted bovine tuberculosis and was taken by his widowed mother to the warmer climate of St Petersburg, Florida, where he attended high school. Throughout the 1930s he mixed formal education with travel and odd jobs. His pursuit of medical training at the University of Manitoba was interrupted by a further flare-up of disease, whereupon he travelled through North America and Europe and worked for three years in Seattle. He completed his undergraduate studies and education degree at the University of Alberta, was married, and began teaching in composite schools in rural Alberta. At the same time he was producing fiction, plays, and journalistic pieces, stimulated by his creative-writing training with Professor F.M. Slater and his Seattle theatre experience with the Penthouse Players. In 1944, having been published in magazines like *Maclean's* and *The Atlantic Monthly*, and determined to be a full-time writer, he gave up teaching and moved his family to High River, Alta. A year after the publication of his famous novel WHO HAS SEEN THE WIND (1947), Mitchell became fiction editor of *Maclean's* (1948-51). From 1949 to 1957 he wrote weekly scripts for his popular CBC radio series 'Jake and the Kid'—thirteen of which, originally written as short stories, were collected in *Jake and the kid* (1962), which won the Stephen Leacock Medal for Humour. Since 1951 he has lived in Alberta, though as a writer-in-residence at various universities, a leading force in the creative-writing division of the Banff School of Fine Arts, a television personality, and a popular lecturer and after-dinner speaker, he has made his presence felt throughout Canada. He is a member of the Order of Canada and the subject of an NFB film, Robert Duncan's 'W.O. Mitchell: A Novelist in Hiding' (1980).

Though concerned with death, destructiveness, and negative values, his work bubbles with energy and a persistent sense of joy: Mitchell is at heart a comic writer. His novels are remarkable for their exuberant talk, reflecting his fascination with oral tradition, inherited in part from Mark Twain. Much influenced as well by the Romantic poets, particularly Wordsworth and Blake, Mitchell cherishes innocence, spontaneity, and natural freedom, championing such virtues in the face of darkness, artificiality, and various forms of restraint.

Who has seen the wind was followed by *The kite* (1962), which is made memorable by the vibrant presence of Daddy Sherry, an irrepressible old maverick whose lifetime spans the 'white' history of the West and whose birthday provides the novel's focus. This novel, however, is weakened by Mitchell's emphasis upon David Lang, a repressed middle-class journalist sent out to cover Daddy's celebration. A similar theme and problem weaken *The vanishing point* (1973), Mitchell's most ambitious and intriguing novel. A reworking of material in *The alien* (serialized in *Maclean's*, 1953-4), it is the story of Carlyle Sinclair's attempts as teacher and administrator on a Stony Indian reservation to bridge the cultural gap between himself and the Stonys, to break through his own puritanical inhibitions and recognize his love for an Indian girl. But the book's real energy lies less with the agonies and earnestness of the middle-class protagonist than with the enterprising and clever Archie Nicotine and the self-serving evangelist, Heally Richards—characterizations that reveal Mitchell's exuberance and his gift for dialect and comic situations at their best. His most recent novel, *How I spent my summer holidays* (1981), returns to the rich, sensory world of prairie boyhood, taking up where *Who has seen the wind* leaves off in dramatizing not the recognition of life, death, and the natural cycle but the struggle a youth faces in discovering the presence of evil in a man he has romantically idolized.

At present there is no complete account of the numerous radio scripts Mitchell has contributed to the CBC. The only collection of his plays, *Dramatic W.O. Mitchell* (1982), includes five, two previously published in small editions: *The devil's instrument* (1973) and *The black bonspiel of Wullie MacCrimmon* (1965), along with *The kite* (happily without David Lang), *For those in peril on the sea*, and what is perhaps Mitchell's most serious and affecting drama, *Back to Beulah*.

See Donald Cameron, 'W.O. Mitchell: sea caves and creative partners', *Conversations with Canadian novelists* (vol. 2, 1973);

Laurence Ricou, 'The eternal prairie: the fiction of W.O. Mitchell', in *Vertical man/horizontal world: man and landscape in Canadian prairie fiction* (1973); Michael Peterman, *W.O. Mitchell* (1980) in Profiles in Canadian Literature, vol. 2; and Sheila Latham, *W.O. Mitchell: an annotated bibliography* (1981) in The Annotated Bibliography of Canada's Major Authors, vol. 3, edited by Robert Lecker and Jack David.

See also NOVELS IN ENGLISH 1960 TO 1982: 1.   MICHAEL PETERMAN

Monk, Maria. See AWFUL DISCLOSURES OF MARIA MONK.

Montpetit, Edouard. See BIOGRAPHY AND MEMOIRS IN FRENCH: 8 and ESSAYS IN FRENCH: 3.

Montgomery, L.M. (1874-1942). Born at Clifton (now New London), P.E.I., Lucy Maud Montgomery was raised by her maternal grandparents after her widowed father moved to Prince Albert, Sask. Educated at Prince of Wales College, Charlottetown, and at Dalhousie University, Halifax, she taught for some years; then, apart from working briefly for the Halifax *Daily Echo* (1901-2), she looked after her grandmother at Cavendish, P.E.I., from 1898 to 1911. Meanwhile she wrote for American and Canadian children's magazines and gained international recognition with her first novel ANNE OF GREEN GABLES (1908). In 1911 she married the Rev. Ewan Macdonald and pursued her writing career in her husband's charges at Leaskdale and Norval, Ont. They retired to Toronto in 1936. Their last years were plagued by her husband's deteriorating health and by Montgomery's severe depression over the outbreak of the Second World War. In 1935 she was awarded the OBE. The National Park at Cavendish preserves the favourite haunts of her novels, and maintains as a museum the 'Green Gables' farmhouse, which is near her grandmother McNeill's house where she wrote *Anne*.

Anne of Green Gables introduces the central situation in Montgomery's fiction: the imaginative adolescent girl's search for self-knowledge that results in liberation from adult authority and success in the male-female clash. An adoring public devoured seven sequels about Anne's teaching career, her marriage to Gilbert Blythe, and their family in *Anne of Avonlea* (1909), *Anne of the Island* (1915), *Anne's house of dreams* (1917),

Rainbow Valley (1919), *Rilla of Ingleside* (1921), *Anne of Windy Poplars* (1936), and *Anne of Ingleside* (1939). Anne, the spirited child, grows into a matron who is vaguely drawn—perhaps reflecting her author's eventual dislike of her; the later books entertain chiefly through sharp portraits of eccentric minor characters and rhapsodic descriptions of nature, but are marred by moralizing sentimental passages of the kind that the younger Montgomery mocked. The enduring quality of the Anne books, however, is their intense evocation of Anne's dreams and aspirations.

Following the success of *Anne of Green Gables*, Montgomery wrote several collections of stories, including her own favourite, *The story girl* (1911). In 1917 she broke with her first American publisher, L.C. Page, through whom she sold him the rights to *Anne of Green Gables* and thus lost out on future royalties. Page's unauthorized publication of her stories, *Further chronicles of Avonlea* (1920), embroiled her in an exhausting nine-year court battle that she finally won.

The Emily series is far more autobiographical than the Anne books, and its characters are more deliberately mythic. *Emily of New Moon* (1923) centres on family traditions, the adolescent Emily's journals, and her Wordsworthian 'flashes' of creative insights. Her struggles as a writer and woman are carried on in *Emily climbs* (1925) and *Emily's quest* (1927).

Never comfortable with the frank realism of fiction after the First World War, Montgomery recognized that her talent lay in wish-fulfillment romances of introspective and bookish girls, but was disappointed that her two fictions for adults were not popular, although they were well reviewed and both received favourable attention in the 1970s. The heroine Valancy of *The blue castle* (1926), the only novel without a P.E.I. setting, leaves her unhappy home and moves to the Muskoka district to marry the local ne'er-do-well, who is revealed to be Valancy's favorite nature writer in disguise. *A tangled web* (1931) examines the behaviour of several prospective heirs to a family heirloom. Montgomery then returned to two more adolescent heroines in *Pat of Silver Bush* (1933) and *Mistress Pat* (1935), and *Jane of Lantern Hill* (1937). The latter work establishes a fascinating tension between Toronto as hell and P.E.I. as a golden Eden. Montgomery also wrote *The watchman and other poems* (1916) and co-authored *Courageous women* (1934) with Marian Keith (Mary Esther MacGREGOR) and Mabel Burns McKinley. *The road to yesterday* (1974), and Catherine McLay's compilation *The doctor's sweetheart: and other stories* (1979), are two posthumous collections of Montgomery's stories. *The Alpine path; the story of my career* (1974) is a collection of 1917 magazine articles. Early in the century Montgomery began a life-long correspondence that—along with her journals, of which she left some ten volumes covering the years 1889 to 1942—provided her with much-needed intellectual and emotional outlets; the letters have been edited by Wilfrid Eggleston in *The Green Gables letters from L.M. Montgomery to Ephraim Weber 1905-1909* (1960) and by Francis W.P. Bolger and Elizabeth R. Epperly in *My dear Mr. M.: letters to G.B. MacMillan* (1980). Francis Bolger has detailed Montgomery's apprenticeship in *The years before 'Anne'* (1974). *Spirit of place: Lucy Maud Montgomery and Prince Edward Island* (1982) is an anthology of references to the Island from letters and diaries, edited by F.W.P. Bolger, with photographs by Wayne Barrett and Anne MacKay.

Montgomery's books have remained popular around the world. Serious critical interest in the author began with two biographical sketches, Hilda Ridley's *The story of L.M. Montgomery* (1956) and Elizabeth Waterston's essay in *The clear spirit: twenty Canadian women and their times* (1966), edited by Mary Quayle Innis. It then swelled with the success of the musical adaptation of *Anne of Green Gables* by Mavor Moore, Donald Harron, and Norman Campbell; this has been performed annually in Charlottetown since 1965 and has had many tours. Mollie Gillen wrote *The wheel of things: a biography of L.M. Montgomery* (1975) and a shorter version of this as *Lucy Maud Montgomery* (1978). Critical evaluations include John Robert Sorfleet, ed., *L.M. Montgomery: an assessment* (1976), and Leslie Willis, 'The bogus ugly duckling: Anne Shirley unmasked', *Dalhousie Review* 56 (Summer 1976). The National Film Board has issued a sound filmstrip, *Lucy Maud Montgomery, those Cavendish years* (1977).

See also CHILDREN'S LITERATURE IN ENGLISH: 1. GEORGE L. PARKER

Montreuil, Gaëtane de. See NOVELS IN FRENCH: 1900 TO 1920.

Moodie, Susanna (1803-85). Born near Bungay, Suffolk, Eng., Susanna Strickland lived mostly at Reydon Hall, near Southwold, until her immigration to Canada in 1832. The last of the five Strickland daughters, four of whom became writers, she was educated by her father and, as his health began to fail, by her elder sisters, notably Eliza who, with Agnes, later gained fame and status in England as authors of *Lives of the Queens of England* and other popular multi-volumed biographies. Like her sisters, Susanna began writing at an early age. She was especially attracted to heroic figures of history she judged to have been misunderstood. Her first story, *Spartacus: a Roman story* (London, 1822), was published through the efforts of a family friend. It was followed by a number of didactic stories for children and adolescents, among them *The little Quaker; or, The triumph of virtue* (London, n.d.), *The little prisoner; or, Passion and patience* (London, n.d.), *Hugh Latimer; or, The school-boy's friendship* (London, 1828), *Roland Massingham; or, I will be my own master* (London, n.d.), and *Profession and principle; or, The vicar's tales* (London, n.d.). Markets of a more diverse kind opened up when a family friend, Thomas Harral, moved from Suffolk to London to edit *La Belle Assemblée*, a fashionable court and literary magazine. From 1827 to 1830 Susanna Strickland contributed poems, sketches, and stories to Harral while also submitting her work to the numerous then-popular annuals. By 1830 she was also writing occasionally for *The Athenaeum*, with which her friend Thomas Pringle was involved, and *The Lady's Magazine*. Under Pringle's friendly direction—he was the secretary of the Anti-Slavery League—she wrote pamphlets detailing the sufferings of two Caribbean slaves, Mary Prince and Ashton Warner. In 1830 she collaborated with her sister Agnes to write a slim volume called *Patriotic songs* and a year later produced her own volume of poetry, *Enthusiasm, and other poems* (London, 1831).

Susanna Strickland's life changed radically when, in 1831, she married John Wedderburn Dunbar Moodie, an Orkney gentleman and half-pay military officer who had come to London from his South African farm to pursue certain literary projects. They lived in Southwold, where their first child was born, immigrating to Canada in the spring of 1832. After an uncomfortably long voyage, the Moodies chose not to take up their backwoods land-grant near Susanna's brother, Samuel Strickland, but to buy a partially cleared farm near Lake On-

Moodie

tario. 'Melsetter' (eight miles northwest of present-day Cobourg, Ont.) is described in the first half of ROUGHING IT IN THE BUSH. Their problems of adjustment there, compounded by a failed investment, prompted them to sell the farm and move north of Lakefield in 1834 to their land-grant, where they would be near both Sam and Susanna's sister, Catharine Parr TRAILL. Here they remained through the fearful days of the Rebellion of 1837, struggling to make ends meet on a farm distinguished more by cedar and rock than by arable land. Only with Moodie's appointment as sheriff of the newly established county of Hastings were Susanna and her five children finally able to leave the backwoods. They moved to the growing town of Belleville, where they lived until Dunbar Moodie's death in 1869.

Though she endured a great deal in her 'bush' experiences, Susanna Moodie never weakened in her literary aspirations. Initially few markets were available. Only with the invitation of John Lovell to write for The LITERARY GARLAND (Montreal) did she at last find a sustained, paying outlet. During the life of that magazine (1839-52) she was its most prolific contributor, specializing in serialized fiction. As well, in 1847-8 the Moodies jointly edited The Victoria Magazine in Belleville. The original sketches for Roughing it in the bush appeared in both the Garland and The Victoria Magazine in 1847.

The high point of Susanna Moodie's literary career occurred during the 1850s when, through her husband's publisher Richard Bentley, her writing again found English publication. Her most enduring work is autobiographical in nature and includes her best-known book, Roughing it in the bush: or, Life in Canada (2 vols, London, 1852); its hastily put-together sequel, Life in the clearings versus the bush (London, 1853); and a fictionalized narrative, Flora Lyndsay; or, Passages in an eventful life (London, 1853). Together the three form a trilogy, Flora Lyndsay in fact recounting the events leading up to the Moodies' move to Canada and concluding with their journey up the St Lawrence. Marked by humour and an unusual frankness concerning pioneering experience, Susanna Moodie's extended account of her difficult adaptation from England to Canada has a dramatic interest and perspicacity of observation rare in the literature of emigration and settlement.

At the same time she wrote for Bentley several long-winded novels that drew heavily on Gothic and sentimental conventions.

The first was Mark Hurdlestone; or, The gold worshipper (2 vols, London, 1853), which had grown from a short tale in The Lady's Magazine (Nov. 1833) to a serialized novel in the Garland to Bentley's publication. The three stories that make up Matrimonial speculations (London, 1854) and the narrative of Geoffrey Moncton; or, The faithless guardian (New York, 1855) also had previously appeared in the Garland. These elaborate and moralistic novels, marked by murder, intrigue, family tyranny, and mistaken identity, held little appeal for the English literary audience, with which Moodie had long since lost touch. The fact that they were more successful when reprinted in the United States is evinced by the decision of the New York firm of Dewitt and Davenport to publish Geoffrey Moncton before Bentley; the English edition thus appeared a year later as The Moncktons (2 vols, 1856). Bentley also published Moodie's novel The world before them (3 vols, 1868), mostly as a gesture of friendship to his longstanding correspondent.

The Belleville years were generally a stable period for the Moodies. Though their finances were never secure, they enjoyed prestige and position. Late in the 1850s, however, old political and personal grievances resurfaced (the Moodies had been Baldwin Reformers) in the form of a dubious charge against the aging sheriff for the 'farming' of his office. After having exhausted his recourse to appeal, Dunbar Moodie was forced to resign in 1863. He died in 1869, his wife outliving him by seventeen years, staying mostly with the families of her children, though she often visited her sister Catharine in Lakefield. She wrote little during this time, turning more to flower painting, a skill she had learned as a girl and had passed on to her daughter, Agnes (Moodie) Fitzgibbon (later Chamberlain), who beautifully illustrated Canadian wild flowers (1868), the text of which was written by Catharine Parr Traill. Moodie, however, made minor revisions to Roughing it in the bush before the Toronto publisher George Rose brought out the first Canadian edition in 1871. In her last years she was bedridden, suffering from what Catharine called brain-fever. She died in Toronto.

See Audrey Morris, The gentle pioneers: five nineteenth-century Canadians (1968); Clara Thomas, 'The Strickland sisters' in The clear spirit (1966), edited by Mary Q. Innis; Michael Peterman, 'Susanna Moodie' in Canadian writers and their works: fiction series: vol-

ume one (1983) edited by Robert Lecker, Jack David, and Ellen Quigley; and Marian Fowler, *The embroidered tent: five gentlewomen in early Canada* (1982).

MICHAEL PETERMAN

Moore, Brian (b. 1921). Born and educated in Belfast, Ireland, he immigrated to Canada in 1948 and worked as a reporter for the *Montreal Gazette* from 1948 to 1952. While living in Canada he wrote his first three novels, beginning with *Judith Hearne* (1955), a brilliant first novel about a Belfast spinster whose feelings of loneliness and isolation are briefly and pathetically assuaged by an imaginary romance. Diarmud Devine, the central figure in *The feast of Lupercal* (1957), is Judith Hearne's counterpart, a bachelor schoolmaster crippled by the repressive nature of the Catholic educational system which he now perpetuates. *The luck of Ginger Coffey* (1960), which won a Governor General's Award, is set in Montreal and is the tale of a middle-aged Dubliner who comes to Canada with great aspirations but fails to achieve financial success. Having moved to North America and abandoned the more rigid strictures of the Catholic Church, Ginger and his wife struggle to fill that spiritual void with a new code rooted in personal values such as integrity and unselfish love. A later novel, *The great Victorian collection* (1975), which also won a Governor General's Award, is a fantasy that explores the relationship between creator and created. When a McGill University history professor, while visiting California, dreams about a 'Victorian collection', and awakens to find his dream has come true, he is faced with having engendered a sort of 'secular miracle' (in the words of Hallvard Dahlie), which brings him unsought celebrity, along with responsibility for a creation he did not intend and cannot control.

Moore moved to the United States in 1959 but retains his Canadian citizenship, and references to Canada and Canadian experience continue to appear in his fiction. A versatile and prolific writer, his novels include *An answer from Limbo* (1962), *The emperor of ice-cream* (1965), *I am Mary Dunne* (1968), *Fergus* (1970), *Catholics* (1972), *The doctor's wife* (1976), *The Mangan inheritance* (1979), and *The temptations of Eileen Hughes* (1981). Almost all these novels deal with his central themes—the fundamental isolation of individuals and their need to confront their own illusions, as well as their need to establish some sort of spiritual integrity

within a moral context no longer governed by certainty, let alone absolutes. In addition, Moore's novels are remarkable for their portrayal of women and often employ the point of view of a female character to convey the heightened emotions and particular vulnerabilities he associates with the female psyche. His latest novel is *Cold heaven* (1983).

Moore has also written *Canada* (1963; rev. 1968), with the editors of *Life*, and *The revolution script* (1971), a fictionalized account of the kidnapping of James Cross by the FLQ in Oct. 1970.

See Hallvard Dahlie, *Brian Moore* (1969); Jeanne Flood, *Brian Moore* (1974); and David Staines, 'Observance without belief', CANADIAN LITERATURE 73 (Summer 1977).

See also NOVELS IN ENGLISH 1960 TO 1982: 2.

MARILYN ROSE

Moore, Thomas. See FOREIGN WRITERS ON CANADA IN ENGLISH: 1.

More joy in heaven. From the publication of of his first novel, *Strange fugitive* (1928), until that of *A time for Judas* (1983), one of the preoccupations of Morley CALLAGHAN's fiction has been the world of the criminal. Most concerned with this subject is *More joy in heaven* (1937; NCL 1970), the last and possibly the best novel by Callaghan from his most prolific period as a writer. It was clearly inspired by the life of the notorious bank robber Red Ryan, who was released from Kingston (Ont.) Penitentiary in the summer of 1935 after serving almost a dozen years of a life sentence. Ryan claimed that he had reformed, and his supporters included a priest, a senator, other citizens interested in prison reform, and even Prime Minister R.B. Bennett. The welcome that Ryan was given on his return to Toronto was equalled only by the bitterness that greeted the news, in May 1936, that he had been shot to death by police as he attempted to rob a liquor store in Sarnia, Ont.

In *More joy in heaven* Red Ryan becomes the fictional Kip Caley, whose release from prison is also aided by a senator and a priest. Caley, however—unlike Ryan—has truly reformed. Having been turned into a celebrity by the press and the public, he begins to believe he has a mission to reform society, but is eventually overcome by its cynicism and violence. On one level *More joy in heaven* may be read as a novel of social comment; on another it is a religious parable, with the redeemed sinner being destroyed

More joy in heaven

both by his illusions and by his fellow men.

More joy in heaven has been dramatized for both radio and television in recent years, an indication of its continuing relevance.

ROBERT WEAVER

Morency, Pierre (b. 1942). Born in Lauzon, Qué., he studied at the Collège de Lévis and Université Laval. His early poetry was collected in *Au nord constamment de l'amour* (2nd edn 1973). Since then he has published *Lieu de naissance* (1973), *Le temps des oiseaux* (1975), and *Torrentiel* (1978), as well as a number of children's plays and, with Paul Hébert, a highly acclaimed French adaptation (1974) of J.T. McDonough's *Charbonneau and le Chef* (1968), a play about Maurice Duplessis's clash with the Archbishop of Montreal. Latterly Morency has been concentrating on his career as a broadcaster, producing programs and records on the birds of the St Lawrence and using to good effect his poetic gifts and his splendid speaking voice.

Morency belongs to the generation of young poets determined to end Québec's atavistic enslavement to the dualism of flesh and spirit. He rejects cerebral and disincarnated art. The head, he complains, has snapped its moorings with the heart. The consequence is that the imagination is adrift and the senses vacillate without engaging the real world. He revels in a sensual delight in words, 'le simple plaisir de prononcer'. His poetry celebrates the world of things and people—the city, but above all the country, the Île d'Orléans, the North Shore, and the wildlife of the region. Aware that new experiences, if lived out courageously, have all the pain and bloody fight of new birth, he admires the snowy owls and chickadees that brave out the winter, and the rooks and crows that announce the spring. He blatantly adopts a technical wildlife vocabulary in his poems to express his holistic vision of man's struggle against alienation and his reconciliation with his environment. He has also challenged the commercialization of language and communication in North America by producing poems in the form of huge street hoardings, or as picture postcards to send to friends, aiming to beat the commercial world at its own game. Nevertheless Morency's poetry is suffused with an undercurrent of dedication and high seriousness.

Morency has also written a poetic, or 'free', novel, *L'ossature* (1972).   C.R.P. MAY

Morin, Marie. See Writing in NEW FRANCE: 2.

Morin, Paul (1889-1963). Born in Montreal, Paul Morin d'Equilly attended the Académie Marchand, a girl's school founded by his maternal grandmother, before beginning his secondary education at the Collège Saint-Marie; he published his first poems in *Le Journal de Françoise* when he was fourteen. In 1907, after receiving his bachelor's degree, he entered the law faculty of Université Laval in Montreal and was admitted to the bar in 1910 at the age of twenty. He immediately left Québec for Paris to enrol at the Sorbonne. That winter he put the finishing touches on his first collection of poetry, *Le paon d'émail* (1911), in which strange, outlandish, imaginary oriental settings evoke a luxuriant sensuality. Morin's flight to foreign parts was also a flight from the moral establishment of his homeland and in this book he gave free rein to his youthful ardour. Despite his use of themes that could hardly be considered suitable in ultra-Catholic Québec, his deft handling of the alexandrine and his cleverness with words and rhymes in conveying extraordinary sensations delighted the champions of 'art for art's sake' and won the approval of even the most stubborn nationalists—who were, after all, not immune to Parnassian aesthetics.

In July 1912 Morin received a doctorate from the Sorbonne with his thesis *Les sources de l'oeuvre de Henry Wadsworth Longfellow* (1913), a 600-page work that is still considered to be one of the major studies of the poet, in whom Morin found a kindred spirit. At the onset of the Great War he returned to Canada and devoted himself chiefly to teaching literature at McGill University (1914-15), Smith College, Mass. (1915-16), and the University of Minnesota (1916-17), where he met and married in 1917 a young American girl, Geneviève van Rennslaer-Bernhardt. He left teaching in 1918 and began to work as a translator. He was a co-founder of *Le* NIGOG and published a second collection, *Poèmes de cendre et d'or* (1922), which won the Prix David in 1923. It contained more of his finely crafted, opaline verse, along with some melancholy, disillusioned confessional poetry in which he recalled his difficult years as a teacher and translator—though he also celebrated his happiness with Geneviève. The sensual youth had become a faithful lover, the peacock a clumsy bird ('La revanche du paon').

In 1922 Morin became librarian and secretary of the École des Beaux-Arts, Montreal, where he remained until 1930. In this period he published an English translation of Louis Bertrand's *The private life of Louis XIV* (1929) and a French translation of Longfellow's *Evangeline* (1924). He also worked with the painter Suzor-Côté on a tourist brochure, *Héroisme d'antan, victoires d'aujourd'hui* (1923), that was commissioned by the Canadian National Railways. To make ends meet during the Depression, Morin became a court interpreter and almost ceased writing: from 1930 to 1940 he published only two new poems. By the end of the thirties he was almost destitute. He continued, however, to work as an interpreter and translator; but, after suffering from angina in 1944, both his health problems and his financial situation grew steadily worse. In 1952 Morin lost his wife, and the accumulation of calamities plunged him into a depression from which he never recovered. In 1957 a fire destroyed his few possessions, including several valuable manuscripts.

Jean-Paul Plante edited a small anthology, *Paul Morin: textes choisis* (1958), and later Morin published a final collection, *Géronte et son miroir* (1960), which brought together work published in reviews and newspapers since 1920: some autobiographical free verse, sonnets, epigraphs, and an exotic bestiary, showing that Morin never entirely broke with the classical aesthetic and his early aristocratic period, though the ironic, mocking tone of these poems indicates his awareness of being anachronistic and in decline. Plante re-edited Morin's first two collections and had them published under the title *Oeuvres poétiques* (1961). Although these late publications placed Morin at the forefront of the Québec literary scene in the sixties, they did not attract much interest. Consequently he died (at the age of 74, in Beloeil, Qué.) in almost total oblivion.

See Victor Barbeau, 'Paul Morin', *Cahiers de l'Académie canadienne-française* 12 (1970), and Jean-Paul Morel de la Durantaye, 'Paul Morin, l'homme et l'oeuvre', a doctoral thesis for the Université d'Ottawa (1975).

JACQUES MICHON

Morton, W.L. (1908-81). Born in Gladstone, Man., William Lewis Morton was educated at the University of Manitoba and Oxford University, where he was a Rhodes Scholar. He held various university teaching appointments in Manitoba until settling in the history department at the University of Manitoba in 1942, serving there until 1966 (from 1950 to 1964 as head). He then moved to Trent University, Peterborough, Ont., as Master of Champlain College and Vanier Professor of History. After formally retiring from Trent in 1975, he returned to the University of Manitoba and continued to teach there until his death. Morton received many honours, including a Governor General's Award for *The Progressive Party in Canada*, the Tyrell Medal of the Royal Society in 1958, and the Medal of Service, Order of Canada, in 1969.

Although his earliest historical research was on imperial themes (including an Oxford thesis on the Newfoundland fishery), Morton first found his métier in the study of his native district. Collaborating with his sister Margaret Morton Fahrni, he published *Third crossing: a history of the town and district of Gladstone in the Province of Manitoba* (1946), which celebrated the 'privileged settlers'—as L.H. Thomas called them—of British Protestant background who had established rural communities in the province. Gladstone's founders were devoted to family, to nation, and to Empire, virtues Morton never questioned. In the late 1940s he published a number of articles that pointed to *The Progressive Party in Canada* (1950; rev. 1967), a book that was part of the working-out of the Morton family past: the author's father had been elected to the Manitoba legislature as a Progressive and the study is deeply sympathetic to both regional grievances and the positive reforms of the movement. By this time, however, Morton had broken with his family's traditional political allegiances and become an active supporter of the Conservative party; many of his later writings attempted to delineate a philosophy for Canadian Conservatism.

Beginning in the mid-1950s, Morton entered upon a decade of prodigious output, which saw him publish most of his major works and gradually move from regional to national historian. In 1956 he published two vital studies of early Manitoba in the form of lengthy introductions to collections of documents. The introduction to *The London correspondence inward from Eden Colvile 1849-1852* for the Hudson's Bay Record Society revealed Morton's prose style—graceful yet analytical—at its best; the work is a masterpiece of delineation of the problems facing Red River in the transitional period from fur trade to agriculture and commerce. His introduction to *Alexander Begg's Red River journal and other papers relative to the Red River resistance of 1869-70* for the Champlain Society brilliantly synthesized the developments that led to the Riel uprising. Both these works have been unjustly neglected. Building upon his own research and that of others, Morton then produced what many regard as his finest book, *Manitoba: a history* (1957; rev. 1967), which has remained the model provincial history. Stronger on the Red River period than the post-1870 one, it illustrated again Morton's strong identification with the agrarian origins of the province, as well as his growing sense of Manitoba's cultural distinctiveness. (Morton later wrote another brilliant introduction to a related collection of documents: *Manitoba: the birth of a province* (1965) for the Manitoba Record Society.) In 1957 he also published *One university: a history of the University of Manitoba, 1877-1952*, which—while inevitably institutional in approach—captured the flavour of the disparate educational and cultural traditions in Manitoba that Morton always celebrated.

After this outpouring of major writings on Manitoba, Morton turned to larger themes. An invitation to deliver a series of lectures in 1960 at the University of Wisconsin produced the bulk of *The Canadian identity* (1961; rev. 1972). In these lectures, and in his 1960 Canadian Historical Association presidential address, Morton sought to provide Canada with 'a self-definition of greater clarity and more ringing tone', emphasizing the nation's northern character, historical dependence, monarchical commitment, and special relationships with other states. These themes became the basis of his large-scale history *The Kingdom of Canada* (1963), although they often tended to become lost in a morass of encyclopedic and ill-digested detail. This work did not display Morton's abilities to best advantage, nor did *The critical years: the union of British North America, 1857-1873* (1964), a volume in the Canadian Centenary Series, of which he was co-editor with Donald CREIGHTON. More than other studies of the Confederation period, *The critical years* focused on the aspirations of the outlying regions, stressing the cultural (rather than political) duality of Canada, a major preoccupation of Morton's later works. When he came to deal with regions outside Manitoba, however, Morton self-confessedly had difficulty in achieving the same *verstehen* he displayed about his native province. His study with Margaret MacLeod, *Cuthbert Grant of Grantown: Warden of the Plains of Red River* (1963; rev. 1973),

marked a return to earlier interests, its great virtue being its sympathetic understanding of Métis aspirations. His most insightful analysis and most stylish—often lyrical—prose is to be found in his writings on the early history of Manitoba. Although Morton was far more than merely a regional historian, it was as a regional historian that he produced his most enduring and endearing work.

Morton was an essayist of considerable charm and ability. His shorter writings are most readily accessible in A.B. McKillop, ed., *Contexts of Canada's past: selected essays of W.L. Morton* (1980).

See Carl Berger, 'William Morton: the delicate balance of region and nation' in *The West and the nation: essays in honour of W.L. Morton* (1976), edited by Carl Berger and Ramsay Cook.   J.M. BUMSTED

Moss, John. See CRITICISM IN ENGLISH: 5(d).

Mouré, Erin. See POETRY IN ENGLISH 1950 TO 1982: 3.

Mouvement littéraire de Québec, Le. When the itinerant parliament of United Canada (1840-67) moved to Quebec City in 1859, it brought with it an influx of educated persons with varied cultural interests who would be making their home in the old French capital until the new federal government moved to Ottawa in 1867. In May 1860 there arrived Abbé Henri-Raymond CASGRAIN, an energetic twenty-eight-year-old priest, newly returned from Europe, who, eager to make his mark in literature, set about stimulating literary activity among his new acquaintances.

About a dozen aspiring writers, most of them born in the 1820s, gathered from time to time in the back room of Octave CRÉMAZIE's bookstore on the Rue de la Fabrique, and elsewhere, to discuss literary matters and to encourage one anothers' efforts at writing. According to Casgrain's romanticized account in his memoirs, the group included two professors at the newly founded (1852) Université Laval, the historian Abbé Jean-Baptiste-Antoine Ferland and a medical doctor, François-Alexandre-Hubert LA RUE; the superintendent of public education for Lower Canada, Pierre-Joseph-Olivier CHAUVEAU; the founding editor of the Conservative newspaper *Le Courrier du Canada*, Dr Joseph-Charles TACHÉ; the government librarian and journalist Antoine GÉRIN-LAJOIE; the new French consul at Quebec City, Charles-Henri-Philippe Gauldrée-Boilleau; and Étienne Parent, under-secretary for Lower Canada and a celebrated public lecturer on economic questions. Younger members of the group were Louis FRÉCHETTE, Léon-Pamphile LEMAY, and Alfred Garneau, son of the 'national historian', François-Xavier GARNEAU.

At its high point in the early 1860s the Mouvement littéraire de Québec was an impressive and largely successful effort by a handful of Québec intellectuals to found a national literature in French which, although inspired by the French Romantic movement of thirty years before, was genuinely French-Canadian, both in its collective concerns and its rejection of the 'dilettantism' and 'unhealthy realism' of contemporary French literature.

The first joint project was the founding of a monthly literary magazine, Les SOIRÉES CANADIENNES (1861-5); after a squabble over ownership and policy, three members of the editorial committee (Casgrain, La Rue, and Gérin-Lajoie) broke away and founded Le FOYER CANADIEN (1863-6). At the same time, book-length works by members of the group appeared. Gérin-Lajoie's colonization novel in two volumes, JEAN RIVARD (1862-4), and Philippe AUBERT DE GASPÉ's historical romance Les ANCIENS CANADIENS (1863) were the most durable of these. Others included Taché's Forestiers et voyageurs (1863); Ferland's two-volume Cours d'histoire du Canada (1861-5); and Casgrain's Histoire de la Mère Marie de l'Incarnation (1864), which was widely circulated in Europe. Québec's first two collections of lyric poetry, Fréchette's Mes loisirs (1863) and Lemay's Essais poétiques (1865), also issued from the Mouvement, although their success was more limited.

After this shower of publications the Quebec City group gradually broke up. Crémazie had already gone into exile (1862) and Ferland died of a stroke in 1865. Taché and Gérin-Lajoie, appointed to federal government posts, moved to Ottawa; Chauveau became the new Province of Québec's first prime minister; and Fréchette, disgusted by the Conservatives' confederation schemes, immigrated to the United States (1866-71). By the time Casgrain published an important essay on 'Le mouvement littéraire au Canada' in Le foyer canadien in Jan. 1866, the Québec movement had already spent itself; the relocating of the na-tional capital in Ottawa, and the increasing commercial importance of Montreal, condemned Quebec City to a declining role as a literary centre. The main features of this movement, however—its Romantic inspiration, its historical and patriotic orientation, and its profoundly Roman Catholic spirit—continued to dominate French-Canadian writing for more than a quarter of a century.

There is no history of the Mouvement, although several useful studies appear in the first volume of the collection Archives des lettres canadiennes published by Fides.

DAVID M. HAYNE

Mowat, Farley (b. 1921) Born in Belleville, Ont., he grew up in Saskatoon and was educated at the University of Toronto. After serving in the Hastings and Prince Edward Regiment during the Second World War, he spent two years in the Arctic before completing his degree and becoming a freelance writer. Mowat's first book, People of the deer (1952; rpr. 1975), caused much controversy by blaming government officials and missionaries for the plight of the caribou-hunting Ihalmiut Eskimos, and was severely criticized for its obvious bias. Its sequel, The desperate people (1959), is more moderate and much better researched, but lacks the impact of the first book, which sincerely and eloquently conveys the writer's sympathy for, and understanding of, a people whose culture and very lives were threatened by contact with European civilization.

Mowat's involvement with the North is a recurring theme in his books. Coppermine journey (1958) is an edited version of the narrative of Samuel Hearne; and the works now known as the Top of the World Trilogy—Ordeal by ice (1960), The polar passion (1967), and Tundra (1973)—are edited journals of both famous and unknown explorers, with a linking commentary by Mowat. Siber: my discovery of Siberia (1970) is an account of the author's trips to the Soviet Union in the late 1960s, and Snow walker (1975) is a collection of stories about Canadian Inuit. Canada North (1967), a pictorial book with a text by Mowat, was followed by Canada North now: the great betrayal (1976), an examination of living conditions in the Arctic today. In retrospect Mowat feels that he did the Inuit a great disservice, after his first book about them, by encouraging assimilation: 'the government saw to it that no Eskimo died of malnutrition and the medical services were improved and nobody froze to death.

But they turned the whole of the Canadian Arctic into a charity ward.'

Mowat's sympathy for the dispossessed is evident in the texts he wrote for two pictorial books about Newfoundland. In *This rock within the sea: a heritage lost* (1968), John de Visser's photographs are accompanied by Mowat's lament for a vanishing outport culture and a characteristic attack on Joseph Smallwood and the relocation program that wiped thousands of small communities off the map. In *The wake of the great sealers* (1973) David Blackwood's prints and drawings of nineteenth- and early twentieth-century seal fishing are complemented by a narrative in which Mowat draws on literature, folklore, and his own imagination to convey the heroism and tragedy of the sealing industry. Mowat's love-affair with the people of Newfoundland, whom he described as 'the last primordial human beings left in our part of the world', was shattered after the events he describes in *A whale for the killing* (1972). His failed attempts to save the stranded whale and his account of the affair alienated him from the people he had been living among.

Mowat has been greatly criticized for his belief that one should never spoil a good story for lack of exaggeration. He has responded to a description of his work as 'subjective non-fiction' by saying that 'I try to tell the truth about the human condition without, on the one hand, letting the facts get in my way and, on the other hand, inventing situations which might suit my purpose.' Mowat's concern for endangered species has run the full gamut from Eskimos to outporters, to whales and wolves. *Never cry wolf* (1963) is a heartfelt and convincing argument that wolves are not vicious but a necessary and useful element in the natural cycle.

Mowat now spends most of his time in Cape Breton, where the north Atlantic provides a natural force equal to that of the storms in the Arctic tundra. Sailing has always been important to him and he has written vividly about it in several books. *The grey seas under* (1959) is a history of the Foundation Company's salvage tug, and *The serpent's coil* (1961) is another sea narrative about a daring rescue accomplished during a hurricane. *Westviking: the ancient Norse in Greenland and North America* (1965) is a popular account of Viking exploration and settlement; the liberties Mowat took in this work did not endear him to historians or archaeologists.

Mowat's broad definition of poetic license has been more enthusiastically received in his novels for young people: *Lost in the barrens* (1965), for which he received a Governor General's Award; its sequel *Curse of the Viking grave* (1974); and *The black joke* (1974), about rum-running off the coast of Newfoundland—all of which reflect the interests apparent in his books for adults. But his reflections on his own childhood in Saskatoon best display his abilities as a storyteller. Mutt, a canine of remarkable personality, is featured in *The dog who wouldn't be* (1957), along with Weep and Wol, who appear again in *Owls in the family* (1961). The same wonderful light humour is evident in *The boat who wouldn't float* (1968), for which he was given the Leacock Medal for Humour.

More recently Mowat has turned again to his own youth for material. *And no birds sang* (1979), about his experience of the Second World War, covers essentially the same subject-matter used in one of his first works, *The regiment* (1955), a history of the Hastings and Prince Edward regiment, though the later work is much more personal, detailing everything from his loss of virginity to his growing disenchantment with war. Although prevented from being a truly reflective book by Mowat's irrepressible desire to 'tell a story', it provides an interesting autobiographical insight into a lively, outrageous, but always sincere writer.

See also CHILDREN'S LITERATURE IN ENGLISH: 2 and HISTORICAL WRITING IN ENGLISH: 6.   ROBIN GEDALOF McGRATH

Munro, Alice (b. 1931). Born Alice Laidlaw in Wingham, southwestern Ontario, Alice Munro started writing in her early teens. After studying English for two years at the University of Western Ontario, she left to marry James Munro in 1951 and moved to Vancouver and then to Victoria, where her husband opened a bookstore. While helping with the business and raising three daughters, Munro wrote short stories for magazines and the CBC program 'Anthology'. In 1968 she published her first collection, *Dance of the happy shades* (translated as *Danse des ombres*, 1980), which won a Governor General's Award. Munro's predilection for the short story is apparent in the story-like shape of the chapters in her novel *Lives of girls and women* (1971), which received the Canadian Booksellers Award. (The CBC filmed a dramatization of this work in 1973, with Munro's daughter Jenny in the main role.) A further collection of stories, *Something I've been meaning to tell you* (1974), was followed by *Who do you think you are?* (1978), a group of stories held together, like *Lives of girls and women*, by a single protagonist whose experiences are presented more or less chronologically. This book—which in the American and English editions is entitled *The beggar maid*, and in the German translation *Bettelmadchen* (1980)—also received a Governor General's Award and was a runner-up for Britain's prestigious Booker Prize. The stories in *The moons of Jupiter* (1982) present a variety of minutely observed characters dealing with the familiar situations of ordinary life. Munro has written a number of television scripts, including one on Irish immigrants for the CBC series *The newcomers*; a story version, 'A better place than home', is included in the book based on the series, *The newcomers* (1979). Divorced in 1976, she returned to western Ontario where she lives in Clinton with her second husband, Gerald Fremlin.

By a careful focus on the telling action or statement, Munro excels in revealing the surprising depth and complexity in the emotional life of simple, ordinary people. Such revelations are often filtered through the consciousness of a girl who feels herself to be 'different' from those around her, usually because she is a secretly developing artist in an environment alien and hostile to art. An imaginative girl's response to social pressures and the expectations of others, especially her mother, is the central subject of *Lives of girls and women*, as it is of many of the stories. The girl's steady desire to be like everyone else, to avoid mockery and humiliation, persists in many of Munro's adult women. Munro is *par excellence* the artist of social embarrassment and unease, capturing the obscure moments of shame that plague both child and adult. She also depicts, with wry humour, the nuances of female response to what she sees as the pleasurable tyranny of sex. Del's mother in *Lives of girls and women* foresees a time when women will not assess their own worth only through their relationship with men; but in the life-story of Rose in *Who do you think you are?* Munro shows how difficult it is for even the most competent woman to break that 'connection'. Without a man, Rose feels undefined; an uncertain affair with a distant married man can validate her identity. Munro continues to explore this theme in several of the stories in *The moons of Jupiter*. Although she creates convincing portraits of men, particularly in this volume, she only occasionally writes from a male point of view; she is primarily interested in the lives of girls and women and in their influence on one another. The difficulty of communication between the sexes, and across generations, is central to many of the stories in *Dance of the happy shades* and *Something I've been meaning to tell you*, in experiences told from an adult point of view as well as in those of childhood and adolescence. Many of the stories in the latter collection grow out of a character's own interest in storytelling, whether as an art form or as an instinctive reshaping of reality to make it understandable, bearable, or simply more dramatic.

Munro has set some of her stories in British Columbia, Toronto, and other parts of Ontario, but it is with rural southwestern Ontario that she is most closely identified. She captures the look and atmosphere of small towns that resemble her birthplace, of the ramshackle dwellings at their outskirts and the rundown farms nearby. Reality is heightened with such clarity of remembered detail that it is, in Munro's words, 'not real but true'. (Her techniques of photographic realism are in some respects like those of two writers of the American south whose work she admires, James Agee and Eudora Welty.) She achieves her vivid re-creations of place and people by a complete detailing of all that the sense might register in a room, a landscape, a street, or on a person; she frequently lists objects, almost as in a memory game, or qualifies a noun with a catalogue of adjectives that usually contains at least one surprising and satisfying oddity or paradox. Elaborate figurative language is rare in Munro's descriptions; her occasional similes are striking because so sparingly used. Quasi-conversational repetition gives the appearance of artlessness to the prose, making the narrative seem spontaneous and immediate.

Munro was interviewed by John MET-CALF for the *Journal of Canadian Fiction*, I, 4 (Fall 1972) and by Graeme GIBSON for *Eleven Canadian novelists* (1973). John Metcalf's anthology *The narrative voice* (1972) contains Munro's essay 'The colonel's hash resettled', in which she speaks of misguided attempts to read symbols into her stories. There are critical articles by J.R. (Tim) Struthers and Miriam Packer in the collection *The Canadian novel here and now* vol. I (1978) edited by John Moss. For other articles on, and references to, the work of Alice Munro, see the checklist compiled by D.E. Cook in *Journal* of *Canadian Fiction* XVI (1976) and by J.R. (Tim) Struthers in *Studies in Canadian Literature* VI, I (Summer, 1981).

See also NOVELS IN ENGLISH 1960 TO 1982: 2.   JOAN COLDWELL

Murray, John Clark (1836-1917). Born at Thread and Tannahill, near Paisley, Scot., he was educated in religion and philosophy at Edinburgh, Heidelberg, and Göttingen. In 1862 he came to Canada to teach at Queen's University, Kingston. Ten years later he moved to McGill University, where he remained until his retirement. His *Outline of Sir William Hamilton's philosophy* (Boston, 1870) is a faithful presentation of the beliefs of his teacher at Edinburgh, but Murray had already begun to react against the 'common sense realism' of Hamilton. He emphasized the rational order and ultimate unity of reality in a manner closer to Hegel and the British idealists and akin to that of his successor at Queen's, John WATSON. His theory is outlined in his two works on philosophical psychology: *Handbook of psychology* (London, 1885) and *Introduction to psychology* (1904), in which Murray denies the possibility of a mechanical explanation of the human mind, argues that the concept of personality is central to psychology, and lays some of the foundations for his theory of value.

Murray's *Industrial kingdom of God*—probably written in 1887 but not published until 1982—advances proposals for economic reform that envisage chiefly a co-operative society and a system for the public determination of certain wages and prices. Murray read and commented on Marx and Henry George, but the main inspiration for this book was evidently the co-operative movement and his belief that Christianity provided the only basis for a just society of free men. Though he frequently quoted scripture in his social commentaries, he tried to develop his ethical theory from an analysis of the concept of person; he praised Christianity chiefly for having made the concept of person central to western thought. Murray fought early, long, and hard for the education of women. His writings on this subject, and his defence of Canadian nationhood, are contained in letters, occasional newspaper and magazine articles, and handwritten notes.

The basis of Murray's moral theory can be found in his *Introduction to ethics* (London 1891) and *Handbook of Christian ethics* (Edinburgh, 1908), as well as in his social-gospel novel *He that had received the five talents* (1904), which undoubtedly helped to make popular the reformist views of Christianity that figure in other social-gospel novels. Murray also published a volume of verse, *The ballads and songs of Scotland* (London, 1874).

Murray lectured a number of times at the Cooper Union, New York, and he frequently wrote for *The open court*, a Chicago-based journal edited by Paul Carus. His books were widely translated.

LESLIE ARMOUR, ELIZABETH TROTT

Murrell, John (b. 1945). Born in the United States, he was raised in Alberta, and after graduating from the University of Calgary he taught public school and began writing plays for performance by his students. He left teaching to devote himself to the theatre, as an actor as well as a dramatist and director, but eventually focused on writing. In 1975, while playwright-in-residence at Alberta Theatre Projects, he won the Clifford E. Lee Playwrighting Competition for *Power in blood*, which was produced in Edmonton in that year. As associate director of the Stratford Shakespearean Festival in 1977-8, he translated (though he does not speak Russian) the Festival's production of Chekhov's *Uncle Vanya* (1978) and was later commissioned by Stratford to translate *The seagull* (produced in 1980). The dramaturge at Theatre Calgary in 1981-2, he lives in Calgary with his wife and daughter.

Murrell's best-known plays are *Memoir* (1978) and *Waiting for the parade* (1980). *Memoir* has only two characters: Sarah Bernhardt, writing her memoir in the last summer of her life, and Pitou, her faithful secretary and servant. To stir her memory Bernhardt demands that Pitou play people from her past, while she re-creates herself at various ages; thus two actors become a myriad of personalities. *Waiting for the parade* portrays and interweaves fragments of the lives of five women enduring the Second World War at home without their men. Allusions to popular culture are cleverly superimposed against images of these women waiting for the war's end—as in the first scene, when they are found awkwardly dancing together. Murrell's strong spatial sense gives his texts a special theatricality. Character is revealed through physical movement as much as through language, which tends to lack subtlety. In *Memoir* the playwright creates wonderful images of Bernhardt's force: though her leg has been amputated, she refuses to be confined to a wheelchair. Her speeches, however, fail to convey the complexity one expects of such a compelling personality, and responsibility for the play's success falls to the actress to refine the character in her own way, as Siobahn McKenna did in its first production. In a French translation by Georges Wilson, called *Sarah et le cri de la langouste*, the play had a long run in Paris (with Delphine Seyrig), beginning in Oct. 1982.

Other plays by Murrell, which have been produced but not published, are *Haydn's head* (prod. 1973), *Teaser* (with Kenneth Dyba, prod. 1975), *Arena* (prod. 1975), and *A great noise, a great light* (prod. 1976). Murrell's translation of Machiavelli's *Mandragola* was produced by Theatre Calgary in 1978, and his translation of Racine's *Bajazet* by the Tarragon Theatre, Toronto, in 1979.

ANN WILSON

Musgrave, Susan (b. 1951). Born in California, of Canadian parents, she is the fourth great-granddaughter of Sir Anthony Musgrave, governor of the Crown colony of British Columbia, 1869-71. After leaving school at 14 and having poems published in *The* MALAHAT REVIEW at 16, she travelled widely, living in California (1967-9); Ireland (1970-2); and in her 'spiritual home', the Queen Charlotte Islands of B.C. (1972-4). After returning to Ireland in 1975, she came back to B.C. for four years before living briefly in Panama City. She now lives in Sidney, B.C.

Musgrave's first poetry collection, *Songs of the sea-witch* (1970), published when she was 18, introduced many of her subsequent themes. The poetic persona often searches for an identity against a mythological landscape of animated rocks and water. Her sensibilities incline towards both the contemporary and the aboriginal; her response to the modern urban world is either outrage or witty denunciation, though her often beautiful lyrics can slip into vagueness. *Entrance of the celebrant* (1972) celebrates the will of the imagination in brooding, mystical, ritualistic poems. *Grave dirt and selected strawberries* (1973) includes a poetic sequence entitled 'Kiskatinaw Songs', written in collaboration with Sean VIRGO during a period of homesickness in Cambridge, Eng. Originally published as a pamphlet, the poems were unsuccessful until they were republished under the pseudonym 'Moses Bruce', a native Indian. The 'strawberry poems' were inspired by a roadsign. While most poets prefer a selected poems, Musgrave jokingly wrote *Selected strawberries* (1973), a book-length satire with gleanings from *The golden bough*, *Everything you always wanted to know about sex*, the journals of Anaïs Nin, *The Guinness book of records*, cookbooks, and self-help manuals. Beneath this satirical mythology the strawberry emerges as a likeable main character. The collection, with minor revisions, was republished as *Selected strawberries and other poems* (1977), which includes *Entrance of the celebrant*.

Musgrave's next collection, *The impstone* (1976), drew inspiration from the imp, the animal that helps a witch cast spells. These 53 Gothic poems employ strong, sometimes violent images. Her evocative and suggestive vocabulary of earth, stone, water, evil, witches, ghosts, moon, shadows, graves, dreams, night, and animals is utilized in a ritualistic manner to invoke an animistic landscape. Several of the poems deal with the problems of relationships. Not all these poems, however, are equally successful. In *Becky Swann's book* (1977), reprinted in *A man to marry, a man to bury* (1979), familiar images and simple detail move quickly to a Dantesque moral vision in a Canadian setting, with scathing commentary on contemporary moral issues. The first poems invoke love, but they quickly move into a depressing world of loveless marriage, breakup, bizarre murder, degenerate ways among native people, deformity, abortion, and dying. Musgrave counterbalances these with poems of genuine friendship (especially with the poet Marilyn BOWERING), caring, love, and acceptance in a carefully constructed sequence, 'Salmonberry Road', which explores friendship from several points of view, from delight to murderous fantasy to profound loss. The new poems in *Tarts and muggers* (1982)—which is largely selections from her previous books—rely on shock value (rats on a face, or dead-animal imagery) that produces a vision of an empty, hostile, loveless world.

Musgrave has published several collections in limited editions, including *Skuld* (1971), *Birthstone* (1972), *Equinox* (1973), *King* (1973), and *Two poems* (1975). She has also published two children's books: *Gullband* (1974), which includes 32 poems about a cat, a frog, and a lizard; and *Hag's head* (1980), a Hallowe'en story about children who are followed by demons.

Musgrave's interest in west-coast mythologies, Fraserian symbolism, militant feminism, and the mysterious, is also evident in her first novel, *The charcoal burners* (1980), a modern horror story and a study in depravity, in which Musgrave's black humour carries Margaret ATWOOD's edible-woman thesis to the extremes of violent and bloody death, bestiality and cannabilism. Matty, a sociologist married to an Indian living in East Oyster, B.C., is led by her lover, Christian Hawker, into the wilderness, where she meets a band of feminist crazies from California who live off the land and practise a ritualistic religion based on ancient fertility rites and radical feminist ideology. Nearby live the charcoal burners, twentieth-century dropouts led by a Masonesque madman known as the Chela. A powerful and original novel, it has a serious structural flaw, with a naturalistic first half clumsily connected to a bizarre, almost surreal conclusion.

Musgrave discussed her work in CANADIAN FICTION MAGAZINE 30/31 and is the subject of an article by Dennis Brown in CANADIAN LITERATURE 79 (Winter 1978).

See also NOVELS IN ENGLISH 1960 TO 1982: OTHER TALENTS, OTHER WORKS: 6(b).

GEOFF HANCOCK

Myers, Martin. See NOVELS IN ENGLISH 1960 TO 1982: OTHER TALENTS, OTHER WORKS: 1.

Mysterious stranger, The. See Walter BATES.

Mystery and crime. Canada has no real tradition in the genre of mystery and crime fiction. Derrick Murdoch, longtime reviewer of spy novels and crime fiction for the Toronto *Globe and Mail*, wrote in 1981 that 'for nearly half a century—roughly, say, from the dawn of Sherlock Holmes until the twilight of Sam Spade—the only notable contribution from Canadians came from expatriates.' Michael Richardson, in the preface to his anthology *Maddened by mystery: a casebook of Canadian detective fiction*, 1982 (the title was suggested by Stephen LEACOCK's spoof of Sherlock Holmes, 'Maddened by mystery, or the defective detective', in *Nonsense novels*) remarked that only two of its thirteen stories were set in Canada and one of those was by a non-Canadian. He had discovered that expatriate Canadian mystery writers, who were contributing to popular magazines in Britain and the United States, felt little compulsion to draw upon their Canadian background. Despite the lack of a tradition, however, there have been remarkable developments in the past dozen years. In 1982 the Crime Writers of Canada held its first meeting in Toronto; ten months later there were more than 70 members, most of whom were working writers resident in Canada.

One of the authors represented in *Maddened by mystery* is Grant ALLEN (1848-99), who was born in Kingston, Ont., but lived in England for most of his adult life. His *An African millionaire: episodes in the life of the illustrious Colonel Clay* (London and New York, 1897)—republished in the United States, England, and Canada in 1980—is an amusing and cynical study of hypocrisy and fraud in late-Victorian England and America, with an attractive English villain, Colonel Cuthbert Clay. It manages the sea change to the 1980s remarkably well—though perhaps only for readers who have some historical interest in mystery fiction. Another Canadian expatriate, Frank L. PACKARD (1877-1942), who was born in Montreal and moved to the United States, created another attractive rogue for a series of books beginning with *The adventures of Jimmy Dale, detective* (1917). Toronto-born Vincent Starrett was the creator of an American detective, Jimmie Lavender (*The casebook of Jimmie Lavender*, 1944), and the prolific Arthur STRINGER (1874-1950) worked both sides of the border with detective stories set in the United States, beginning with *The wire tappers* (1906), and crime fiction about the Canadian North, beginning with *Empty hands* (1924). Robert BARR (1850-1912), born in Glasgow but living in Canada until 1881, when he moved to England, began a prolific writing career there. He was known particularly as a writer of detective stories, some of which were collected in *The triumphs of Eugène Valmont* (1906), featuring a humorous French detective who worked in a cold and foggy England (several decades before Agatha Christie introduced her Hercule Poirot).

At the beginning of the modern era in the 1940s Margaret Millar, born in 1915 in Kitchener, Ont., began writing remarkable psychological mystery novels set in Toronto and Georgian Bay, Ont. (More than twenty have been published to date, beginning with *The devil loves me*, 1941.) At the University of Toronto she met her future husband, Kenneth Millar (1915-83), who was born near San Francisco and educated in Canada. They moved to California, where he began a very successful career as a writer of crime fiction under the pen-name Ross Macdonald, creating the California private eye Lew Archer and becoming the much-admired successor to Dashiell Hammett and Raymond Chandler.

In Montreal John BUELL began his writing career with *The Pyx* (1959), which was made into a film that enjoyed some critical but no great popular success. His second novel *Four days* (1962) was followed by two more titles in the 1970s. Buell appeared to be striving for 'entertainments' of Graham Greene quality, and his first two books attracted the attention of the American critic Edmund Wilson (who was not usually interested in thrillers); but Buell's career has never really developed as might have been expected. Another promising mystery writer, Toronto-born John Norman Harris, died unexpectedly soon after publishing *The weird world of Wes Beattie* (1963), about the ne'er-do-well member of an old Toronto family accused of murdering his uncle. Written in the civilized manner of English mystery fiction from between the wars, it captures well the atmosphere of Toronto a quarter of a century ago, but the plot is too elaborate and the book, while amusing, is too wordy. It has had something of a cult reputation but was out of print in 1983.

In the 1970s Hugh GARNER undertook a new and somewhat surprising departure in his writing when he published the first of three police procedural novels. *The sin sniper* (1970), whose central character is Inspector Walter McDumont of the Toronto Police Force, is the most successful of these books. It is set in an area of downtown Toronto inhabited by petty criminals, prostitutes, homosexuals, and greasy-spoon restaurants. (A film based on it, *Stone cold dead*, released in 1980, preserves the locale but alters the story radically.) In *Death in Don Mills* (1975) and *Murder has your number* (1978) Garner seemed to have lost interest in the genre, allowing McDumont to become increasingly garrulous. However, he was at work on a fourth police novel when he died in 1979.

So many thrillers and mystery novels have been published in Canada since the beginning of the 1970s that the problem of selection becomes difficult. There are still one or two expatriates, the most interesting and mysterious of them being Donald MacKenzie, who has published nearly thirty crime novels in England. Canadians turn up as secondary characters in some of his novels, but he writes almost always about the criminal world of London. His skimpy biography

tells us that he is Canadian, and that he has spent time in prison.

Particularly among writers of thrillers, the setting is quite often foreign; or Canada becomes a part of international espionage operations. James Henderson's highly professional *Copperhead* (1971) takes place in Canada and the West Indies. The violent, Bond-like *Dreadlock* (1981), by Lew Anthony (the pen-name of Robert Miller and William Marshall), which was supposed to be the first in a series of spy thrillers, also uses Canada and the West Indies as its background. The team of Gordon Pape and Tony Aspler uses the Tchaikovsky International Music Competition in Moscow as the scene of their third and most successful thriller, *The music wars* (1982).

Some of our best writers of spy novels have come from abroad to live in Canada. Chris SCOTT was born in Hull, Eng., and his complex thriller *To catch a spy* (1978), traces the life story of an Englishman who turns up in Moscow as an apparent traitor and then mysteriously dies there. Ian McLachlan, the author of *The seventh hexagram* (1976), a richly textured political thriller set in Hong Kong, was born in London, Eng., and now teaches at Trent University in Peterborough, Ont. More prolific than these writers is Shaun Herron, who was born in Northern Ireland, served in the Republican Army during the Spanish Civil War, and has been a broadcaster and controversial United Church minister and an editorial writer and columnist for the Winnipeg *Free Press*. It was in Winnipeg that Herron wrote *Miro* (1969), the first of half-a-dozen sophisticated thrillers. The character Miro was described recently by Ken Adachi in the *Toronto Star* as 'the personification of that burnt-out case, the cold war spy for whom betrayal has become a way of life, existing on an ambiguous plane where neither side has a moral exclusive'. A long section of *Miro* takes place in Québec; Herron's later books moved on to England, Ireland, and Spain. William Deverell's exuberant thriller *High crimes* (1981), about the international drug trade, encompasses a variety of surroundings: Toronto and Ottawa, Colombia, Miami, and Newfoundland.

Canadian-born writers of mystery novels seem quite homey after consideration of the international scope of the thrillers. Ellen Godfrey's two novels, *The case of the cold murderer* (1976) and *Murder among the well-to-do* (1977), have an exotic amateur sleuth— Rebecca Rosenthal, in her seventies, anthro-

Mystery and crime

pologist, survivor of the Holocaust—but in all other respects both are solidly Toronto. *The case of the cold murderer* has some interest as a *roman à clef* for those who know something about small-press publishing in Canada. Both books suffer a similar defect: not only is Rebecca Rosenthal not very interesting, despite her background; she is an irritating meddler. But the two novels led to a third and much better book by Godfrey: *By reason of doubt* (1981), a true-crime investigation of the murder trial in Switzerland of Professor Cyril Belshaw of the University of British Columbia.

Marion Rippon, who lives in Victoria, B.C., has published several books, including *The hand of Solange* (1969) and *Lucien's tomb* (1979), about a retired French gendarme, Maurice Ygrec. For some reason her novels, which have a certain Simenon quality and are published in New York, have attracted little attention here. *Murder by microphone* (1978), by CBC producer John Reeves, somewhat uneasily combines a traditional mystery novel with a satire on CBC management and the radio program schedule. Alisa Craig had what seemed to be a good idea: murder in small town New Brunswick, as described in *A pint of murder* (1980) and *Murder goes mumming* (1981). But both novels mix a dash of sophistication with large doses of the bucolic with unfortunate results. Craig also writes mystery novels, under the name of Charlotte McLeod, set in New England.

A great deal more sophistication, and a high degree of good humour, have gone into the writing of Howard Engel's *The suicide murders* (1980), *The ransom game* (1981), and *Murder on location* (1982). The central character in all three books is the Jewish private eye Benny Cooperman, who follows his trade in the city of Grantham (St Catharines, Ont., slightly disguised). Much is turned on its head in these novels: Benny's mother is a terrible cook (a Jewish mother who is a terrible cook!); Benny is a private detective who *does* take divorce cases—because so little else is offered; and the very idea of a private eye in Grantham is a spoof in itself. The reader familiar with the California private-eye novels will get some additional enjoyment from Cooperman's adventures. But they are not all spoof; the mysteries are legitimate. These novels (two more are promised) have brought something fresh and enjoyable to crime fiction in Canada.

Eric Wright's *The night the gods smiled* (1983) is the first book in what has been announced as a series about Inspector Charlie Salter of the Metropolitan Toronto Police. It's a promising debut, with a good sense of place—mostly Toronto but also Montreal. While Charlie Salter is a type—the policeman who is too independent and has been passed over for promotion—he is an attractive character. *The night the gods smiled* has its uncertain moments, particularly as it approaches a resolution, but Charlie Salter should have staying power.

ROBERT WEAVER

N

Narrache, Jean. Pseudonym of Émile CO-DERRE.

Nature writing in English. Canadian nature writing had a rudimentary beginning as comments and observations in books by explorers and settlers. Not until the mid-nineteenth century did it develop into nature writing proper: prose that fuses facts about nature with an emotional and imaginative response to them. It reached a peak of popularity in the first decades of this century; then interest in it waned until the 1950s, when it regained much of its former favour and status. The discussion that follows of the main trends in this writing refers to only a few of the many titles that have been published.

1. SPORTSMAN'S BOOKS. Sportsmen were the first to write specifically and at length about nature. William 'Tiger' Dunlop, for example, in *Statistical sketches of Upper Canada, for the use of emigrants* (London, 1832), described, with a personal touch, the wild creatures that most interest the hunter and fisherman; Sidney C. Kendall, in *Among the Laurentians* (Toronto, 1885), focused entirely on the pleasures of hunting and fishing; and George Moore Fairchild, writing in the genteel tradition in *Rod and canoe, rifle and snowshoe in Quebec's Adirondacks* (Quebec, 1896), celebrated the sublime, and the picturesque, romantic appreciations of the outdoors that characterized much later nature writing. On the one hand these early books reflect both the pervasive Hebraic tradition that the destruction of wildlife is man's right by heavenly privilege, and a terrible truth about pioneer society (if not all societies): that unlimited supply leads to unlimited greed. On the other hand they show man trying to come to terms with the wilderness, to impose some kind of pattern other than physical on it.

In the twentieth century the sportsman's book has become more 'scientific' about nature, but continues to try to add human interest through descriptions of personal experiences and by offering the reader the vicarious thrill of the stalk, or the strike, and the kill. Perhaps because fish inhabit a world apart from the one we share with the birds and other animals, fishing appears less grisly than hunting, and books about this sport are the most popular. The first book on fishing in Canada was the Rev. William Agar Adamson's *Salmon fishing in Canada* (London, 1860), a gentle account of fish lore, good companionship, and good talk on literary and religious matters in quaint and rhythmical prose. It is the most clearly imitative of Isaac Walton's *The compleat angler* (1653) of any book in our literature, though many other books reveal similarities in varying degrees of emphasis. Some treat fishing largely as reminiscences; some, as a pleasant hobby; some, as an affair of 'fish stories' and the practicalities of rods, lures, and species. Among fishing books, indeed all sportsman's books, the most distinguished are William Hume BLAKE's *Brown waters and other sketches* (1915) and *In a fishing country* (1922), and Roderick HAIG-BROWN's *A river never sleeps* (1944), and his seasonal tetralogy that begins with *Fisherman's spring* (1951). Both men write sensitive and lucid prose, though Haig-Brown's has a harder surface; both reveal imaginative sympathy with the organic world, and both think of fishing as more than catching fish. For Blake it is also a matter of friends, of the *habitant* and pleasurable sojourns in his rural world, of reflections like those in *A fisherman's creed* (1923)—his argument for spiritual self-reliance based on his certainty of God's immanence in nature and the purposeful process of unceasing creation. For Haig-Brown, more ichthyologist and expert angler than Blake, fishing is almost a ritual of techniques and comportment for the solitary; a study of pool and rapid, of lights, shadows, and winds; a time to look and listen and to learn from a world free from human pretence. His books go beyond the petty excitement of the catch or the intimation of man's struggle with nature. The rivers he fishes suggest the dynamic in nature, and the mountains they flow everlastingly through, the static; his books centre essentially on the universal tension of flux and permanency.

All sportsman's books are based on killing, and with the rise of the conservation movement some writers have challenged the rights of the sportsman *vis-à-vis* those of the animal. C. Gordon Hewitt, in *The conservation of wildlife in Canada* (1921), is typical of his time, arguing for conservation on economic terms, so also setting up a category of animals—vermin—that are to be destroyed. Since his time, other writers have made their cause the rights of all wild things, the proper use of land and forest, the dangers of pollution, and the creatures that are now in peril of extinction. Paradoxically, even modern hunter-authors—like Mike Crammond in *Big game hunting in the West* (1965)—focus on wildlife and its welfare and call authoritatively for harvesting game for its own good, depicting hunters as ecologists in game-management programs. Recently, however, John A. Livingston, in *The fallacy of wildlife conservation* (1981), has passionately denounced wildlife management as a panacea. On a higher level, however, is Farley MOWAT's moving *A whale for the killing* (1972). An account of the life and agonizing death of a trapped whale, it is also a symbolic story of the plight of all wild creatures that combines angry protest and shock therapy to form a moral touchstone for those who thoughtlessly continue to slaughter them.

2. NATURE ESSAYS AND ANIMAL LIFE HISTORIES. Modern conservationists only make explicit what for long had been implicit in some of the early literature. A genuine feeling for all nature characterizes the work of Catharine Parr TRAILL, the lady whose 'Botanical sketches' in Agnes Fitzgibbons' *Canadian wild flowers* (Montreal, 1869) established the literary-scientific essay in Canadian literature and started nature writing proper on its way. Although botany (especially as exemplified in her *Sketches of plant life in Canada; or Gleanings from forest, lake and plain* (Ottawa, 1885) was Mrs Traill's forte—it was the easiest and favourite field-science of her time—she proved herself an acute and enthusiastic observer of nature at large with *Pearls and pebbles; or, Notes of an old naturalist* (Toronto, 1894). Like Gilbert White in *The natural history of Selbourne* (1789), she tries to combine the objectivity of science with the subjectivity of her personal reactions. Between White and Traill, however, there had come the Romantic movement; and, probably as a result, Traill's essays are more emotional than White's. Her bird is a 'feathered friend'; her spider, a 'surly fellow'; her pole-cat, a 'horrid creature'—though everything is God's handiwork. Yet she is seldom merely sentimental in her rapport with her environment. By placing her facts in a context of literary allusions and quotations, she adds to the attractiveness of her writing and keeps from becoming too emotionally involved or too closely identified with her subject. The literary-scientific essay soon became popular with many nature writers, and the first person—used sparingly by Mrs Traill—has been favoured by modern writers, from Sheila Burnford in her belles lettres, *The fields of noon* (1964), to Lyn Hancock in her causerie *There's a seal in my sleeping bag* (1972); from Andy Russell in his lively narrative *Grizzly country* (1967) to Roy Ivor in his psycho-analytical study of bird behaviour *I live with the birds* (1968). Perspectives, however, vary. In *The rambles of a Canadian naturalist* (1916), Samuel Thomas Wood presents nature as a beautiful canopy that is reflected in the woods and its birds, animals, and flowers; but Daniel McCowan in *A naturalist in Canada* (1941), through careful observations of these parts, gains insights into a meaning that lies both within and above them. Lorus J. and Margery J. Milne, in *The world of night* (1948), also described these parts, but as they are related to one another, not as they disclose an external organizing pattern. Franklin Russell's dramatized biology textbook, *Watchers of the pond* (1961), also centres on horizontal relationships, but only as an unceasing demonstration of Darwin's theory.

All nature essayists express a reverence for nature. But as the years passed there was a change from romantic deductive thinking, making birds and animals the focus of attention as sentient, self-directed beings, a practice from which was to develop the true animal life-history, as distinct from the fictional animal biography of Roberts, Seton, and their school. Its growth owes as much to humanitarianism as to science, gaining its renown from the accounts Grey Owl (Archibald Stansfeld BELANEY) published of his once-famous beavers McGinnis, Rawhide, and Jelly Roll respectively in *The men of the last frontier* (1931), *Pilgrims of the wild* (1935), and *Tales of an empty cabin* (1936). All lived in Grey Owl's cabin at different times and became the subjects of very close scrutiny and the centre of his successful campaign for the protection of their species. For Grey Owl his beavers offered one way of identifying with the spirit of the man-threatened wilderness. When looked at carefully, however, his books readily convey a white man's rather than an Indian's view of nature, if *Trapping is my business* (1970), by John Tetso, is to be believed. It is a realistic book about the practicalities of life in the woods. Even when

Tetso watches the sun rise, he is only interested in the 'weather picture' it presents. Since Grey Owl's time, many have written true 'literary-scientific' accounts of half-tamed house-reared individuals of many different species—wolves, cougars, even kit-foxes. Recently life histories of the truly wild, however, have won the highest praise: Farley MOWAT's *Never cry wolf* (1963) and George Calef's *Caribou and the barrenlands* (1981). Mowat's book is a high-spirited field study; yet for all its information about wolves, it seems to lack verisimilitude, perhaps because Mowat's strong desire to redress the unfair myth depicting the wolf as the embodiment of the dark terror of the forest produces an unduly humanized description of wolf-family behaviour. *Caribou and the barrenlands* is an animal photo-biography, juxtaposing picture and word, narrative and exposition, in a most effective and original way. Calef presents the many facets of animal life and the story of a herd—the last of all the great herds of big-game animals that once roamed the continent—in a magnificent pageant of natural history.

3. ANIMAL STORIES. This trend towards the literary scientific animal life history was most significantly prefigured in fiction in the late nineteenth century by Charles G.D. ROBERTS, with *Earth's enigmas* (Boston, 1896) and *The kindred of the wild* (1902), and by Ernest Thompson SETON with *Wild animals I have known* (New York, 1898) (and also by William Alexander FRASER, whose *Mooswa and others of the boundaries*, 1900, pointed the animal story towards the Kiplingesque). Writing animal stories based on the struggle for survival, Roberts aimed at exhibiting the psychology of animal behaviour and demonstrating, as in his splendid *Red fox* (1905), that his noble animal-hero is often victor, not victim. His pastoral romance, *The heart of the ancient wood* (1900), in which a bear has an important role, is now discussed (like Marian ENGEL's *Bear*) in terms of psychological symbolism. Roberts produced nineteen volumes of animal fiction; but his best collections of stories were *Earth's enigmas, Watchers of the trails* (1904), and *The haunters of the silences* (1907). His later work tends towards formula writing, but at its best it admirably combines both art and natural history.

If Roberts, the man-of-letters, wrote formally structured stories to illustrate the principles of biology, Seton, a naturalist from boyhood—as his fascinating fusion of autobiography, wood-lore, and adventure,

TWO LITTLE SAVAGES: *Being the adventures of two boys who lived as Indians and what they learned* (1903), makes clear—recorded the lives of creatures known to him. Both Roberts and Seton accepted Darwinism up to a point, but Roberts did see man as king of beasts, and death in the animal world as part of nature's design; like many late-Victorian Darwinians, Seton tried to compromise between head and heart. In *The natural history of the Ten Commandments* (1907) he attempted to prove morality evolutionary and, caught up in the conservation movement, he felt compelled to treat his animal hero-victims sympathetically and their deaths as hunter-perpetrated tragedies that broke the moral link between man and nature. Testaments to this conviction are his most impressive first books, *Wild animals I have known*, and especially *Lives of the hunted* (1901), which contains a superlative story of a mountain ram ('Krag'). Seton's favourite mode was the full-length animal biography: *The biography of a grizzly* (1900), *The biography of a silver-fox* (1909), and *Bannertail* (1922); but he also turned to woodland tales and books of woodcraft in his later years, and to many-volumed scientific studies of the lives of game animals. With Roderick HAIG-BROWN's *Ki-Yu* (1934), about a cougar, the animal story broke new ground. Lacking Roberts' or Seton's romantic sensibilities, Haig-Brown focuses entirely on Darwinism to write a cruel but powerful book. In *Return to the river* (1941) he again gave animal biography new direction with the most difficult of all forms, the fictional biography of a fish. Here the fish is an individual, and the narrative vividly dramatizes the piscine life-cycle and the fight of the 'fittest' to survive; but for the first time in the genre, game-management people have roles, and conservation is a theme, not implicitly through the plight of the individual (as in Seton) but explicitly through a species. In recent years the fictional animal story has regained popularity and has assumed, as in Fred BODSWORTH's *Last of the curlews* (1955), a Seton-like sentiment towards the wild. In the past the genre came under attack for its anthropomorphism, and even President Theodore Roosevelt dismissed Roberts and Seton as 'nature fakirs' in an article in *Everybody's magazine* (1907). Today, however, critics accept the anthropomorphic and see the animal (the victim) as a psychic symbol of a people struggling for survival against inimical forces of history and nature. In this interpretation the animal story has come full circle. It has become a modern version of the old beast fable.

4. RURAL AND PASTORAL TRADITIONS. All the writers discussed so far have made nature the proper study of mankind. The more comprehensive view of man in nature, however, informs books in the rural and pastoral tradition. These, significantly, also developed early in the century, when Canadians were becoming more and more alienated from nature as they passed from the pioneer into a modern, industrial, urban environment. The simple life spent working with nature is the very core of Peter McARTHUR's five chronicles of life on his farm, from *In pastures green* (1915) to *Friendly acres* (1927). Dedicated to his 'back-to-the-land' movement, they try to show the reality that lies behind the agrarian myth. No such goal motivates Frederick Philip GROVE's *The turn of the year* (1923). Like McArthur, Grove avowedly reveres the man of the soil and patterns his book on the rhythm of the seasons, on cyclical time that defeats linear time, to suggest the essence of country living. Yet, perhaps because Grove writes not as a farmer but as an observer, his book never shows—except for some romantic vignettes—that the stability, peace, and harmony he implies had much part in rural life: nature here is often a harsh master, or even a terrifying presence. In *Over prairie trails* (1922) Grove writes of nature largely in terms of geology and meteorology, but in *The turn of the year*, of its organic details; aside, however, from his vivid descriptions, he fails to unite his emotions and his scientific curiosity. His farmer may be 'in touch with God', but his world of drought and storm hardly proves the point. Grove's naturalism is far removed from what John Burroughs had in mind when he advised Grove to interpret his facts.

In the last few decades the rural book has developed along two different lines. One, represented clearly by Kenneth McNeill WELLS' once-popular *The owl pen* (1947), *By Moonstone Creek* (1949), *Up Medonte way* (1951), and *By Jumping Cat Bridge* (1956)— all dealing with his misadventures as a farmer—portrays rustic life facetiously and factitiously, presenting self-ridicule as humour, and ineptitude in farm work as funny and without social stigma, and hence implying the superiority of the urban. Opposed to this frothy approach are books of higher purpose, as exemplified in Philip W. Keller's *Splendour from the land* (1963), in which the farmer becomes economic man and farming a machine-based occupation. It extols not the pleasant life of agrarianism, but the financial profits of agri-business. Of all contemporary rural books, however, HAIG-BROWN's *Measure of the year* (1950) most vividly recreates rural life. He does not argue against the technologists, but lets his little farm make its own case. He, like Grove, having no Canadian background, wrote of the present and lived as a squire who enjoyed hunting, fishing, farm husbandry, and family life. Although Haig-Brown lacks humour—and McArthur's boisterous assertiveness, as well as Grove's cosmic awareness—he ranks with both men in his urbane and perspicacious observations. In style and perspective, *Measure of the year* suggests Virgil's *Georgics*, and is the most classical of all our nature writing.

Opposed to the rural is the pastoral book. Both see nature as benign. Both are dialectical, playing the country off against the city; but one acclaims agrarianism, and the other Arcadianism. Although claiming Thoreau as a model, authors of our pastorals lack Thoreau's toughness of mind; they are usually solitaries seeking spiritual sustenance in some hide-away in a wilderness Utopia— like Gilean Douglas in the forest fastness of British Columbia, as she describes her experiences in *Silence is my homeland* (1978). Among the books in the bucolic mode, two stand out for their perceptiveness, originality, and their hold on actuality. One is William Arthur Breyfogle's *Speak to the earth* (1961); the other is Harold HORWOOD's *The foxes of Beachy Cove* (1967). Breyfogle, a well-read field naturalist and amateur anthropologist, wrote discerning discussions of man-nature inter-relationships that illuminate both human and natural history, as the brilliant chapters 'Running water' and 'April sun and adding machines' so clearly illustrate; but *Speak to the earth* makes a most persuasive case for man's need to recognize his kinship with the whole natural process as symbiotic, and as a sharing that he neglects at his own great loss. Horwood, like Breyfogle, is never negative; Beachy Cove is no Shangri-La but a calm centre amid the ceaseless activity of the organic world. He keeps nature clearly in focus; his birds and animals never lose their identities in the specifics of science or in the vagueness of romantic idealism. A vitalist, Horwood needs no external system as explanation. Nature in itself is the supreme revelation of the creative force of life.

The natural world has dominated the Canadian imagination from the beginning of our history, explicitly or implicitly influencing almost all our writing. Nature writing itself tries to give us a knowledgeable and imaginative hold on our natural environment. The truth of our wish to retain this hold is evidenced by the (at least) eighty-five nature books (exclusive of outdoors books) published in Canada between 1970 and 1980, of which at least twenty have centred on the need to protect our natural heritage and at least twelve on the satisfactions of rural or wilderness living. Nature writing may be a small current, but it is in the mainstream of both our literature and our national consciousness.   ALEC LUCAS

Nelligan, Émile (1879-1941). Born in Montreal, he was the son of David Nelligan, a postal inspector of Irish extraction, and Émilie-Amanda Hudon. He acquired his early education at Montreal's École Olier (1886-90) and Mont Saint-Louis (1890-3). His numerous absences—the result of long stays at Cacouna, a Gaspé resort frequented in the summer months by the Nelligan family—set him back in his studies and forced him to repeat his third year. His secondary education was equally undistinguished: at the Collège de Montréal (1893-5) he twice repeated his course in elementary Latin and, after a six-month delay, registered at the Collège Sainte-Marie for two semesters (Mar. 1896-Feb. 1897). At 17 he was two years behind his schoolmates and, against his parents' wishes, decided to abandon his studies. He wished only to be a poet; he was already writing verses, and could envision for himself no other profession than that of an artist.

In 1896 he answered a call for poems from *Le Samedi* and published his first poems under the pseudonym 'Émile Kovar' (June 13-Sept. 19); they plainly show the influence of Verlaine and Baudelaire. Nelligan introduced a 'frisson nouveau' into a literary milieu dominated by the Romantic and patriotic epic. If he is sometimes Parnassian in his descriptions, he is so in the Symbolist manner, stressing the subjective impression ('Rythmes du soir', 'Rêve de Watteau'). Unlike such contemporaries as Jean CHARBONNEAU and Lucien Rainier, who produced philosophical and moralistic poetry, Nelligan showed a remarkable sensitivity to the power of words and the music of language. He adhered to Verlaine's precept, 'Music above all', and his revisions show a preoccupation with the evocative power inherent in sonority. Like his French masters he expressed, in poems of melancholy ('Soir d'hiver') and nostalgia ('Le jardin de l'enfance'), an essential unfitness for life that was bound up in the demands of poetry itself.

In 1897, through the intervention of his friend Arthur de Bussières, Nelligan attended the recently founded ÉCOLE LITTÉRAIRE DE MONTRÉAL, but withdrew almost immediately. Poems published in *Le Monde illustré* (1897-8) appeared for the first time under his real name, which was sometimes modified to 'Émile Nellighan'. In 1898 Nelligan's poetic output fell off, possibly because of a journey he planned to make to England. His father, not content with his son's total preoccupation with poetry, would have found him a place in the Merchant Marine—a venture that never took place, however, since in October Nelligan was publishing poems in *La Patrie*. At this time he contemplated gathering a collection of his verse under the title *Récital des anges*. He worked on it in 1899, but it never progressed beyond the stage of a rough draft and has not been published.

At the end of 1898 Nelligan was readmitted to the École littéraire de Montréal, which was increasingly becoming an important intellectual movement. By bringing together poets of diverse leanings and refusing to address political and religious matters, the group declared its intention of giving special rules and autonomy to literature. During its heyday in 1899, when Nelligan was participating in the group's public readings, he achieved a great triumph after having recited his 'La romance du vin', an impassioned reply to detractors of poetry. But this, his most glorious moment as a poet, was his last public appearance. He was confined to the Saint-Benoît asylum, apparently for exhibiting signs of derangement.

Nelligan had published only twenty-three poems, but in 1904, thanks to the devotion of his friend Louis Dantin (Eugène SEERS), and with his mother's help, 107 poems were collected in *Émile Nelligan et son oeuvre*. This book revealed his lyricism, his melancholy, his nostalgia for childhood, and contained certain poems—such as 'Le vaisseau d'or' and 'Déraison'—that have since been perceived as premonitions of madness.

During more than forty years of confinement, Nelligan continued to write; but, having lost the will and the capability to create a body of work, he contented himself with rewriting poems and fragments. Dr Ernest CHOQUETTE, who visited him in 1909, remarked that 'he showed an undeviating obsession with literature'. After his father's death in Oct. 1925 Nelligan was transferred to the public ward of the Saint-Jean-de-Dieu hospital. But all that emerged from this period were five notebooks containing the poet's revised versions—some with faulty titles—of earlier poems (such as 'Le vaileau d'or', and 'Les horbeaux') and versions of Baudelaire, Gregh, Rodenbach, Crémazie, etc. It is likely that he also wrote many delirious texts that have been destroyed. His sister Eva visited him regularly and provided him with writing materials. The increased number of visitors Nelligan received during the thirties attests to the growing public interest in *Émile Nelligan et son oeuvre*, which came out in its third edition in 1932. The last thing he worked on was a version of 'La Benedictine', dated 5 Apr. 1941, seven months before his death in November.

The most comprehensive edition of Nelligan's poems was compiled by Luc Lacourcière in 1952: *Poésies complètes, 1896-1899*. The hospital notebooks remain unpublished, except for several extracts that appeared in *La* BARRE DU JOUR in 1968, and in *31 poèmes autographes* (1982). P.F. Widdows translated a few of his poems into English under the title *Selected poems* (1960).

See Paul Wyczynski, *Bibliographie descriptive et critique d'Émile Nelligan* (1973) and *Émile Nelligan* (1976).   JACQUES MICHON

New, W.H. See CRITICISM IN ENGLISH: 5(c), 5(f).

Newfoundland, Writing in. Newfoundland, Canada's most easterly province, was visited and settled by the Vikings around A.D. 1000; it is possible that 'Vinland', which is described in such detail in the Norse sagas, was located near L'Anse au Meadows on the island's Great Northern Peninsula. The most important descriptions of Newfoundland from the sixteenth century are those of Jacques Cartier (1534), Anthony Parkhurst (1578), Edward Hayes (1583), and Stephen Parmenius (1583), all printed in the 1599-1600 edition of Richard Hakluyt's *Principal navigations*. These convey the initial shocked, amused, and occasionally hopeful European responses to Newfoundland's grim pastoral. They present more accurate ideas about the country's resources than the books of early-seventeenth-century propa-

gandists for settlement, such as Richard Whitbourne's *A discourse and discovery of Newfoundland* . . . (London, 1620), John Mason's *A briefe discourse of the New-found-land* . . . (Edinburgh, 1620), Richard Eburne's *A plain pathway to plantations* (London, 1624), William Vaughan's *The golden fleece* . . . (London, 1626), and Robert HAYMAN's *Quodlibets* (London, 1628), which were the flowery accompaniments to the earliest attempts to establish colonies in Newfoundland. By 1660 it was apparent that these attempts had failed, chiefly owing to the island's stern climate, rocky soil, and limited resources. Nevertheless, a small resident European population was left behind on the island. (Whitbourne's *Discourse*, along with other documents relating to the early-seventeenth-century efforts to plant colonies in Newfoundland, are conveniently printed in *Newfoundland discovered* (1982), edited by Gillian T. Cell.)

For the remainder of the seventeenth century and the whole of the eighteenth, Newfoundland's history was one of neglect and obscurity. British policy after 1699 was to permit settlement but to withhold year-round residential government in order to keep settlers to a minimum. As a consequence, few amenities of civilization existed on the island. There was no context in which an indigenous literature could develop. However, Newfoundland continued to provoke comment by literary observers. James Yonge's *Journal*, which was not published until 1963, describes his experiences as a physician with English migratory fishermen in Newfoundland from 1663 to 1670. B. Lacy's *Miscellaneous poems compos'd at Newfoundland* (London, 1729) provides a grimly realistic picture of St John's in clumsy heroic couplets. Another poet, the Irishman Donnach Ruah MacConmara, wrote macaronic verses in English and Irish about Newfoundland in the 1740s. The Methodist Laurence Coughlan's *An account of the work of God, in Newfoundland* (London, 1776) contains an early recognition of the distinctiveness of the Newfoundlander, while George Cartwright's huge *A journal of transactions and events, during a residence of nearly sixteen years on the coast of Labrador* (3 vols, London, 1792) conveys with great immediacy and detail what life was like for an English trapper and fisherman in Labrador from 1770 to 1786. Cartwright's *Journal* is a classic in the pioneer literature of Canada. An important early book that had a formative influence on the writing of Newfoundland history was John Reeves' *History of the government of the island of Newfoundland* (London, 1793). Reeves saw the history of the island as a struggle between the inhabitants and the West Country merchants—a theme that would be endlessly repeated and amplified by nineteenth-century nationalist historians.

The period 1780-1815 saw the emergence of St John's as the principal port of Newfoundland, a large increase in settlers, and the appearance of a resident, prosperous middle class. John Ryan, a Loyalist from Rhode Island who had first settled in New Brunswick, established Newfoundland's first printing press and newspaper, the *Royal Gazette*, in 1807. Other St John's papers quickly followed: the *Newfoundland Mercantile Journal* (1815), the *Newfoundland Sentinel* (1818), the *Public Ledger* (1820), the *Newfoundlander* (1827), and the *Times* (1832). The first Conception Bay newspaper, the *Harbor Grace and Carbonear Weekly Journal*, appeared in 1828. William Carson's first two pamphlets, *A letter to the Members of Parliament of the United Kingdom* (Greenock, Scot., 1812) and *Reasons for colonizing the island of Newfoundland, in a letter addressed to the inhabitants* (Greenock, Scot., 1813)—the earliest literary expression of the need for political reform in the island—were printed abroad for local distribution; but by the 1820s such tracts were being printed in the colony, and Henry Winton, a 'Printer and Publisher' in St John's, was capable of producing large books. An important pamphleteer of the 1820s was Patrick Morris, Carson's supporter in the struggle for representative institutions. A 'St. John's Library' existed as early as 1810, and a visitor in 1813 noted that the city had a 'public reading room' displaying English newspapers and British monthlies. The youthful naturalist Philip Henry Gosse found in 1827 that it was possible to glean 'a sound knowledge of contemporary literature' from works available through the 'Carbonear book club'. In fact, when the colony was granted representative government in 1832 it possessed some of the rudiments of literary culture: a lively press, a growing interest in education, and an awareness of cosmopolitan ideas. Amateur theatre was now well established in St John's, and Harbour Grace had a 'Play House' in 1824. There was even a monthly *Farmer's Journal* published in St John's in 1842. The first Newfoundland-born authors were: William Cormack, whose account of a coast-to-coast walk in 1822, *Narrative of a journey across the island of Newfoundland*, first appeared in abbreviated form in the *Edinburgh Philosophical Journal* of 1824 and was published as a book in St John's (1856; D.W. Prowse, however, lists an Edinburgh edition of 1836); R.J. Parsons, editor of the *Newfoundland Patriot*, an important reform newspaper founded by Carson in 1833; William Charles St John, a native of Harbour Grace, who wrote a *Catechism of the history of Newfoundland* ([St John's], 1835); and Philip TOCQUE, whose first book, *Wandering thoughts, or solitary hours*, was published in London in 1846. Tocque, a belletrist of considerable charm and ability, has been called the first Newfoundland-born man of letters. Also notable in Tocque is his romantic response to Newfoundland scenery, a tendency in which, however, he was anticipated by Cormack and Henrietta Prescott, author of *Poems, written in Newfoundland* (London, 1839). Mrs M.S. Peace too, in *The convict ship and other poems* (Greenock, Scot., 1850), noted that 'Nature's pencil' had thrown 'a glory bold, sublime/And majestic o'er this land.' But, she added mournfully, "Tis not, 'tis not my home.' She longed for Scotland, saying of her adopted country: 'this land is cold to me.'

From 1832 to 1855, when responsible government was established, there was such fierce sectarian and partisan rivalry in the colony that the intellectual energies of many of the most talented writers seem to have been consumed by politics. Some of the liveliest writing of the day is to be found in the newspapers—in, for example, John Valentine Nugent's *Newfoundland Vindicator* (1841-2) and Henry Winton's *Public Ledger*. Such literature, remaining at the level of commentary upon events, is not to be dismissed as trivial. The first novel with a Newfoundland setting appears to be Charles A. Murray's *Ottawah, the last chief of the Red Indians of Newfoundland: a romance* (London, 1847); but the earliest novel to be based upon prolonged first-hand experience of life in the colony was by a New Englander, R.T.S. Lowell, whose *The new priest in Conception Bay* (Boston, 1858; rev. 1889) sprang from his missionary work in Bay Roberts in the 1840s. Though marred by sectarian bigotry, the book brilliantly duplicates dialects in the Conception Bay region and evokes the distinctive way of life of the fishermen. Two striking poems by Lowell about Newfoundland are printed in his *Fresh hearts that failed three thousand years ago* (Boston, 1860) and *Poems* (Boston, 1864); and a long story

Newfoundland, Writing in

by him, 'A raft that no man made', recounting a sealing adventure, appeared in the *Atlantic Monthly* (1862). Lowell's literary interest in the colony foreshadows that of authors of fiction such as J.B. Connolly, a Boston storyteller (*The crested seas*, 1907), who had been stirred by the romance of the Gloucester herring fishery around the coasts of Newfoundland; Theodore Goodridge ROBERTS; and especially Norman DUNCAN, whose evocation of outport life in *The way of the sea* (1903) remains, in many respects, unsurpassed. As the nineteenth century ended, Newfoundland had become a well-used setting for tales of adventure by Canadian, British, and American authors. There was also much scientific interest in the colony, resulting in such books of literary significance as Dillon Wallace's account of the ill-fated Hubbard expedition of 1903, *The lure of the Labrador wild* (1905), which is of permanent value.

In the meantime the closing decades of the century were noteworthy for an outburst of scholarly and patriotic writing by resident authors anxious to prop up Newfoundland's faltering nationhood. The period 1875-1915 was possibly the most fertile in the colony's literary history, although, as in earlier decades, the bulk of the writing was descriptive and topical rather than imaginative. Among native writers in the period, the most outstanding were the three Howley brothers, Richard V., Michael F., and James P.; the historian D.W. Prowse, a scholar and prose stylist of superb gifts; and the journalist P.T. McGrath. They produced a rich and varied body of writing. Such works as M.F. Howley's *Ecclesiastical history of Newfoundland* (Boston, 1888), Prowse's *A history of Newfoundland from the English, colonial, and foreign records* (London, 1895), McGrath's *Newfoundland in 1911* (1911), and J.P. Howley's *The Beothucks or Red Indians of Newfoundland* (1915) are irreplaceable contributions to local letters; while Richard V. Howley wrote, among other items, an essay in the magazine *Month* (1887) containing a provocative definition of the Newfoundland character. Moses HARVEY, an Irishman of Scottish descent, and Wilfred GRENFELL, the author of over thirty books, were also prominent prose writers of the day. The Bermudian W.G. Gosling, who wrote the imposing *Labrador: its discovery, exploration, and development* (1910) and *The life of Sir Humphrey Gilbert* (1911), was another scholar of significance. This heady time in Newfoundland letters was marked by the founding of two ambitious periodicals: the ephemeral *Newfoundland Magazine* (1900) and *The Newfoundland Quarterly*. The latter, established in 1901 by the printer John Evans, is still in existence. Nor were poetry and fiction absent from this small renaissance. Isabella Rogerson, Michael F. Howley, F.B. Wood, and R.G. MacDonald produced volumes of verse between 1898 and 1908, while W.B. Stabb, Anastasia M. English, and J.A. O'Reilly wrote romances loosely based on Newfoundland life and history. Stabb's *Florimel Jones* (London, 1876) appears to be the first novel written by a native Newfoundlander; Stabb also wrote *Hard hit* ([London] 1880) and *Wreaths of smoke* (London, 1880). This formal literary activity was matched, at a different and not necessarily lower level, by a flurry of ballad writing. G.M. Story has stated that the decades between 1850 and 1914 were the 'golden age of the St. John's ballads and composed songs', and it is to that fertile period that we owe, for example, two of Newfoundland's most cherished poems: John Grace's 'Petty Harbour bait skiff' (c.1852) and Johnny Burke's 'The Kelligrews' soiree' (c.1904). A collection of Burke's *Songs*, edited by W.J. Kirwin, appeared in 1982.

All of this held promise for the future; but the promise was not to be quickly fulfilled. The departure of E.J. PRATT for Canada in 1907, at the age of twenty-five, could be seen as symbolic of Newfoundland's failure to nurture literary genius. The Newfoundland that would later be pictured in Pratt's *Rachel* (1917), *Newfoundland verse* (1923), and other volumes was often the bare, pitiless rock that he saw vainly struggling for nationhood in the 1890s. Ahead lay the Great War—memorably evoked in Jack Turner's *Buddy's blighty and other verses from the trenches* (1918)—and a decade-and-a-half of economic distress and uncertainty that would call into question the dominion's ability to survive as a separate national entity.

The twenties and thirties were not rich in literature, though the appearance of Irving Fogwill's *Prelude to doom and other poems* (c. 1931), perhaps the first sign of a modernist sensibility in Newfoundland letters, should be noted. (A selection of Fogwill's prose and poetry, *A short distance only*, edited by Daphne Benson, appeared in 1981.) Another fine poet who emerged in the 1930s was Gregory Power, some of whose lyric poems are collected in *The Newfoundland*

Quarterly of 1979. J.R. Smallwood was now also active as a writer, his earliest books being a biography of the founder of the Fishermen's Protective Union, *Coaker of Newfoundland* (1927), and *The new Newfoundland* (1931), a work predicting that the dominion would become 'one of the great small nations of the world'. Instead the country relinquished its independence in 1934. In the late thirties, during Newfoundland's period of rule by a British-appointed Commission, the novels of Margaret DULEY appeared in what seemed to be a literary vacuum. Her *Cold pastoral* (1939) and *Highway to valour* (1941), presenting an ambivalent attitude towards her Newfoundland heritage, provide an image of a country uncertain of itself, plagued by doubt, yet somehow stiffly proud and enduring.

The wartime boom in Newfoundland, from 1941 to 1945, expanded mental horizons and provoked renewed literary activity. New magazines such as *The Courier* (1941-6), *The Atlantic Guardian* (1945-57), and the avant-garde *Protocol* (1945-9), signalled the appearance of new talent in verse and prose. The *Guardian* was especially important insofar as it gave expression to a mood of nostalgia for what was thought to be the simple and decent life of the old outport village. Arthur Scammell, some of whose writings are collected in *My Newfoundland* (1966), and Ron Pollett, who wrote *The ocean at my door* (1956), were the two principal authors in this as yet unfamiliar genre of sentimental *émigré* reminiscence. The stories of Edward RUSSELL, which he began to write in the 1950s, were similar in spirit and theme, though they were rooted in the practical affairs of contemporary life rather than in the past. All three writers celebrate the outport, giving the first authentic literary expression—in formal as opposed to folk literature—to the peculiar outharbour way of viewing the world: a way that combines shrewd understatement, funmaking, homely wisdom, acceptance, and stubborn pride. In fact, after Newfoundland's confederation with Canada in 1949, a climactic event depicted in Tom Cahill's play *As loved our fathers* (1974), the outport became one of the chief subjects of Newfoundland writing. A fast-changing lifestyle, which seemed to make the people and the place more and more North American, forced a re-examination of discarded, yet longed-for, ancient lore. The happy outport of long ago is now one of the myths of the literary scene.

The post-confederation period in New-foundland has been marked by prosperity, novelty, and dislocation, as an old British colony somewhat reluctantly entered the mainstream of Canadian life. Witnessing this collision between new habits and ancient ways, writers have made it a central theme of their works. The theme is a dominant one in, for example, the four chief literary interpreters of modern Newfoundland: the outsiders Farley MOWAT and Franklin RUSSELL, and the native novelists Harold HORWOOD and Percy JANES. Mowat, in books such as *This rock within the sea* (1968) and *A whale for the killing* (1972), pictures outharbour Newfoundlanders as a people who once 'partook of the primal strength of rock and ocean', but now are becoming dangerously infected by such American diseases as 'compulsive consumerism'. A corrective to this view may be found in Franklin Russell's masterful *The secret islands* (1965), a journal of a trip to Newfoundland and other islands that is one of the classics of the province's literature and, indeed, a book of far-reaching significance. In *Tomorrow will be Sunday* (1966), Horwood's first novel, the new ideas of the great world outside Newfoundland are uncritically embraced, and the outport in which the story is set is seen as one of 'the backwaters of civilization', inhabited by 'almost a lower species'. Janes, in his *House of hate* (1970), expresses a similarly unflattering view of his heritage, ending the novel with a devastating critique of the character of oldtime Newfoundlanders. Yet most contemporary writers see the old outport as a symbol of strength and cohesiveness. In the plays of both Michael COOK and David FRENCH the old attitudes and dialects have great attraction, while in Thomas Dawe's *Island spell* (1981), one of a number of books by this gifted poet, abandoned outports are described with great poignancy. The 'green and salty days' of Newfoundland's imagined past are evoked as well by the poet Al Pittman, whose best work is in *Once when I was drowning* (1978). Depicting the old outport as joyful pastoral has been a favourite activity of the newspaper columnist Ray Guy, who has had his pieces reprinted in three books—the latest of which is *Beneficial vapours* (1981)—that vividly recreate the boyhood experiences of a merchant's son in Placentia Bay in the forties and early fifties.

Since 1949 Newfoundland has also produced an intelligentsia of critics and scholars who have played an important role in the literary process of assessing the old and defin-

Newfoundland, Writing in

ing the new Newfoundland. Among writers of popular history are Cassie Brown, best known for her account of the *Newfoundland* disaster of 1914 entitled *Death on the ice* (1972), and Paul O'Neill, the author of a two-volume history of St John's: *The oldest city* (1975) and *A seaport legacy* (1976). F.W. Rowe's *A history of Newfoundland and Labrador* (1980) is the most comprehensive account of the province's history since Prowse. Native-born humanists and social scientists who have written with great knowledge and urbanity about Newfoundland include S.J.R. Noel, G.M. Story, and P.F. Neary.

Anthologies of Newfoundland prose and verse—varying considerably in quality and scope—include *Baffles of wind and tide* (1973) edited by Clyde Rose; *Doryloads* (1974) edited by Kevin Major; *By great waters* (1974) edited by P.F. Neary and P. O'Flaherty; *The blasty bough* (1976) edited by Clyde Rose; *From this place* (1977) edited by Bernice Morgan, Helen Porter, and Geraldine Rubia, a selection of writing by women; *31 Newfoundland poets* (1979) edited by Adrian Fowler and Al Pittman; *Choice poems from the Newfoundland Quarterly, 1901-1981* (1981) edited by Everard H. King; and *Twelve Newfoundland short stories* (1982) edited by Percy Janes and Harry Cuffe. In addition there is a generous sampling of local poetry in the Spring 1982 issue of *CV/II*.

See Patrick O'Flaherty, *The rock observed: studies in the literature of Newfoundland* (1979).

PATRICK O'FLAHERTY

New France, Writing in. 1. EXPLORATION LITERATURE forms the major part of writings related to New France. It was produced by leaders of expeditions, missionaries, or ghost writers (partisans, compilers, printers)—exact attribution is frequently unclear. Most writers aimed to uphold the authority or defend the interests of an individual or group with business in New France, while also appealing to a public interested in new scientific information and exotic descriptions. Adopting one or more of numerous genres—chronicle, history, treatise, Utopia, satire, autobiography, official reports—this literature frequently projects a narrator's personality; it can also relate, as if it were the narrator's own experience, information acquired from various sources. Questions of veracity, plagiarism, or embellishment assail most of these books, which can rarely be understood simply as records of fact.

In the discussion that follows, long titles indicating the countries visited, the type of thing observed, and the authority of the observer will usually not be quoted fully. The JESUIT RELATIONS are treated in a separate article. Compilers whose contact with Canada was second-hand, like Father Du Creux, will not be included.

There are no books written and published by Jacques Cartier (1491-1557); he is the presumed principal author of *The voyages of Jacques Cartier* (Ottawa, 1924) edited by H.P. Biggar. The *Bref récit et succincte narration de la navigation fait en MDXXXV et MDXXXVI par le Capitaine Jacques Cartier aux îles de Canada, Hochelaga, Saguenay et autres* (Paris, 1545) is the first published work bearing his name, being an account of his second voyage (1535-6). It was followed by a posthumous account of his first voyage made in 1534. This is known to us through an English translation (by Florio) of an Italian text (by Ramusio) that presumably derived from a French original; a manuscript in French (now in the Bibliothèque nationale in Paris, MSS Fonds français 5589) is either a back-translation or a copy of uncertain derivation. From these and other sources (including corrections borrowed from the *Bref récit*), a copy of the first voyage was reconstructed; current scholarship may yield a more authoritative edition. Biggar's edition includes all three voyages, the third being the Roberval expedition of 1541-2, known to us through fragments in English by Richard Hakluyt (1600).

Written in the third person in a terse style, these works may have been derived from ships' logs, but the range of comment and information is quite broad. The *Bref récit* in particular contains memorable anecdotes and descriptions: the first sight of Stadaconé (Quebec), the naming of Mont Royal, the discovery of the cure for scurvy. Certain aphorisms, such as 'the land that God gave to Cain', have become part of the legend of Canada's discovery.

Marc Lescarbot (c. 1570-1642) was a Parisian lawyer and a writer before he was a traveller. His declared reason for going to Canada (at the invitation of Jean de Biencourt de Poutrincourt, who was one of his clients) was disgust with corrupt European society, particularly its courts (he had just lost a case). This was a conventional sentiment, but Lescarbot's originality lies in being the first writer in French to envision the New World as a desirable escape from the Old. Sailing for Acadia in 1606 he at once composed a poem, 'Adieu à la France', announcing a personal search for a lost Edenic paradise. In Port Royal he wrote commemorations of notable men and occasions. 'La défaite des sauvages armouchiquois' describes Indian warfare in epic style. In his 'Le théâtre de Neptune', which was given the first theatrical performance in North America (1606), volleys of cannon and musket shot, trumpet fanfares, and the tomfoolery of sailors were ingeniously combined with verse speeches to mark the lieutenant-governor's return from an expedition. The written text, a mere 243 lines, has Neptune, 6 Tritons, 4 'savages', and one cheery companion offering fulsome tribute to Poutrincourt. Native words and local objects are combined with classical poetic conventions; for example, an Indian expresses affection by presenting 'matachias' to the 'Sagamos' and explaining that these signify Cupid's flames. A Triton speaking Gascon dialect makes innuendoes about old Neptune's love life. It was obviously meant for fun, but the mock-pompous style seems also to contain a serious declaration of colonial ambitions for France. On his way to and from Acadia, Lescarbot also wrote twelve poems—later collected in *Les muses de la Nouvelle France* (Paris, 1609), which included 'Le théâtre de Neptune'—expressing enthusiasm for exploration. His clear, declamatory verse has no obvious continuity in Canada.

After returning to France in 1607 Lescarbot continued to write on a variety of topics, including travel in the Americas, Germany, and Switzerland. His general ideas show the world progressing from childhood into an era of expanding civilization, which he clearly linked with the urge to colonize. In his *Histoire de la Nouvelle-France* (three Paris editions: 1609, 1611-12, and 1617-18) he brought together in a repetitious monument all discovery materials available to date, and included his 'Muses de la Nouvelle France'. Books I to III reproduce accounts by French explorers in the Americas, with some editing and collation: Laudonnière, Ribaut, Gourgues, Villegagnon, Cartier, and Roberval. Book IV recounts the abortive expedition of 1604 and the 1606-7 expedition in which Lescarbot took part; this book is marked by his indignation at failures. Book V recounts Champlain's voyages from 1608 to 1613, and those of the two Biencourt (father and son, 1610-15). Book VI contains 'the Manner, Customs, and fashions of Life of the Western Indians of New France, and a

comparison of them with those of the people of the old world . . .'. (While preparing this work, Lescarbot also wrote two pamphlets: *La conversion des sauvages* (1610) and *Relation dernière* (1612).) The three editions of the *Histoire* testify to its popularity. Writing in a cultivated style, Lescarbot combined elements of ethnography and documentation with classical allusions and moral comment tending towards the myth of the 'bon sauvage' and the regenerative power of the new land (Frenchmen become visibly more virtuous away from home). *The history of New France* (Toronto, 3 vols, 1907, 1911, 1914), translated for the Champlain Society and edited by W.L. Grant, follows Lescarbot's third edition; it contains 'Les muses de la Nouvelle France' without translation. An English translation by Pierre Erondelle of Books IV and VI of the first edition of the *Histoire* was published under the title *Nova Francia* (1609) and is available both in a modern edition (London, 1925) and in a reprint (Amsterdam, 1977). *The theatre of Neptune* (1927) is a translation by Harriette Tabor Richardson.

Samuel de Champlain (c. 1570-1635) is rightly celebrated as the explorer and navigator whose tireless efforts shaped the earliest successful colony in Canada. His prose is that of a man of action: terse, organized, sometimes peremptory. His life and works present some major mysteries. Was he a Protestant apostate? How did he appropriate the particle 'de' to his name? What was his status before 1608? What part did he have in writing 'his' first and last works? Did he make all the journeys described in them? His many biographers (listed in the DICTIONARY OF CANADIAN BIOGRAPHY, Vol. I) reach no precise consensus. The available facts about Champlain's activities and writing may be summed up as follows. His earliest voyages were probably made on Spanish ships to the West Indies, and he had some hand in compiling travel literature about these. His first voyages to the St Lawrence (1603) and Acadia (1604 and 1606) gave him an opportunity, perhaps a motive, to display his knowledge. As the lieutenant of de Monts, Champlain returned to the St Lawrence in 1608 and established a trading-post at Quebec called the Habitation. In the years that followed he laid the foundations of New France, leading expeditions up the main inland water routes, crossing the Atlantic frequently, and writing and publishing his three volumes of *Voyages*.

The first work undisputably by Champlain is *Des sauvages* (Paris, 1603), which offers a wealth of information on topography and commercial potential and succinct descriptions of rival Amerindian nations in the St Lawrence area. The first *Voyages . . .* (Paris, 1613) is regarded by some as Champlain's best work, mainly because of its highly factual character, covering the voyages from 1604 to 1612 (and using partly corrected material from *Des sauvages*). For the general reader what stands out most is the narration of striking episodes (such as the starving Indians crossing the ice floes in Feb. 1609) where the setting in the new country comes alive in action. Champlain's comments are usually curt: 'There are six months of winter in this country' (Ste-Croix, 1605) is typical of how he sums up a season of disasters.

In the second volume of *Voyages . . .* (Paris, 1619) the canvas is richer and the reader is better able to imagine the life of the little society at Quebec. Here too are fuller descriptions of the Hurons, whom Champlain had at last seen in their own country (around Georgian Bay). They are no longer lost in vague generalities about 'savages' (though some of these persist), nor reduced to physical measurements (though these are plentiful), and we get a lively impression of life in a longhouse with its fleas, spoilt children, and thick smoke. Champlain's account of his disputes with the fur-trading company, on the other hand, is a careful statement of legal positions without the drama and the personal clashes that must have accompanied them.

The last volume of *Voyages . . .* (Paris, 1632), purporting to cover the period 1603 to 1631, presents the greatest complications. It contains a rewritten version of the voyages from 1603 (the rewriting is almost certainly not by Champlain, or not completed by him; the Jesuit Fathers in France and Champlain's young wife have both been suggested as possible ghost-writers); the new voyages to 1629; business surrounding the Treaty of St Germain-en-Laye; and a retrospective account of French exploration since 1504. It looks like a hasty job of rewriting Champlain's own accounts and runs into inconsistencies, particularly in trying to suppress all references to Recollect missionaries. Above all, a mellifluous moralizing tone seems quite unlike the brusque style of the two earlier *Voyages*. Whenever the 1632 *Voyages* sound patronizing or didactic we suspect a foreign hand, but Champlain himself can be recognized in places: the

perfect navigator, he says, must be a decent God-fearing man and emulate Flemish cleanliness. This book also contains an appendix that might have been a separate work, the *Traitté (sic) de la marine et du devoir d'un bon marinier*, and an Indian catechism attributable to Father Brébeuf.

H.P. Biggar's bilingual edition in the Champlain Society series, *The works of Samuel de Champlain* (6 vols, 1922-36), is authoritative. Among the selections published in English, the most recent is the translation of Michael Macklem—*Voyages to New France* (1970), with an introduction by Marcel Trudel—which lends Champlain's accounts of the years 1615 to 1618 a liveliness that is not always present in the original.

Gabriel Sagard (fl. 1614-38) was a simple though highly literate *Frère convers* in the Recollect branch of the Franciscan Order. He seems to have joined the Recollects before 1604, at the dawn of their existence as a strictly reformed branch, and he defected before 1638 when they were fully established. *Le grand voyage au pays des Hurons . . .* (Paris, 1632) is virtually a straightforward account of Sagard's own voyage to New France. He embarked at Dieppe in 1623 (his printer gives the wrong year) and describes all the stages of the journey to Ossossane in Huronia. His narrative gradually gives way to the need to describe things by categories, such as flora and fauna, burial customs, sexual behaviour, and family life. The book was written in a hurry; the Recollects needed publicity to make their presence and achievements in Canada known, since they had just been excluded from their mission. This may account for the frank spontaneity that most readers find in Sagard's narrative. Sagard's accounts of life in the longhouse are often unflattering, but nonetheless sympathetic, to the Hurons, of whom he gives the most integrated picture. In his next book Sagard had to defend his favourable impressions of the unregenerate 'savages'. His emphasis on their internal harmony is important in literary history because it gives observer support to the myth of the 'noble savage': Sagard was read and imitated down to the time of Voltaire. *Le grand voyage* was translated for the Champlain Society by H.H. Langton as *The long journey to the country of the Hurons* (1939).

Sagard's *Histoire du Canada . . .* (Paris, 1636) does not recapture the fresh feeling of a personal journey. Book I gives a panorama of Franciscan missions, including previously unpublished relations by Fathers Joseph Le

Caron and Denis Jamet. These present a striking contrast: one gives a gloomy but perspicacious view of the conditions and the native peoples, while the other waxes optimistic about Notre-Dame-des-Anges, Quebec, the prosperous religious residence in the wilderness. Book II expands on Sagard's 1632 relation, often tediously, but correcting many details. Books III and IV continue the Recollects' version of history down to their exclusion from Canada in 1629, and include complete relations not published elsewhere (notably Joseph de la Roche Daillon's account of his journey to present-day southern Ontario in 1627). Some portions may have been written with direct help from other Recollects in Paris, giving them the character of eyewitness narrations.

The *Histoire* is valued for its ethnographic information about the early discovery period, while also showing how Sagard's criticism of the authorities had boldened, as his appreciation of the 'sauvages' increased. Most subsequent Recollect writings were more embittered about loss of property and honour in New France, notably an anonymous *Mémoire* of 1637 (Paris, 1879). Sixte Le Tac's *Histoire chronologique de la Nouvelle France* (MS, 1689), published by Pierre Margry (Paris 1888), is a forthright defence of the Recollects and an attack on the Jesuits. Chrétien Le Clercq's *Établissement de la foy dans la Nouvelle France . . .* (Paris, 1691) (also published as *Premier établissement . . .* , Paris, 1691) is more balanced, and covers the period 1615-90. John G. Shea's translation (New York, 1881) contains the only English versions of the relations of Father Le Caron and of other relations that Le Clercq reproduced. Le Clercq wrote about his own travels in *Nouvelle relation de la Gaspésie* (Paris, 1691).

The last of these Recollect explorers is Louis Hennepin (1627-c.1705), whose *Description de la Louisiane . . .* (Paris, 1683) describes a journey from Quebec to Louisiana, with observations of Niagara Falls and on various native peoples. Hennepin is very insistent on his own part in the journey he undertook under the leadership of René-Robert Cavalier de La Salle. After La Salle was murdered in 1687, Hennepin claimed to have reached the mouth of the Mississippi in his augmented version, *Nouvelle découverte d'un très grand pays . . .* (Utrecht, 1697). This constitutes one of the most disputed travellers' tales, mingling falsehood and fact in a very egocentric story. It appears that the Mississippi section was lifted from the notes of his fellow Recollect, Zénobé Membré, who was killed on the expedition.

The most flagrant mixture of fact and fiction is in three volumes of voyages by Louis-Armand de Lom d'Arce, baron de Lahontan (1666-1716). Lahontan's military career in Canada gave him first-hand knowledge, while his quarrel with J.F. de Mombicon de Brouillan, his senior officer in Newfoundland, drove him into exile and motivated his witty criticisms of the colonial administration. These constitute the main literary interest of *Nouveaux voyages . . .* (The Hague, 1703), *Mémoires de l'Amérique septentrionale* (The Hague, 1703), and *Supplément . . . où l'on trouve des dialogues curieux . . .* (The Hague, 1703). (The *Dialogues* also appear in separate editions, and there are variant titles.) The use of dialogue instead of narrative represents an important change in the history of the genre. Adario, a full-fledged 'bon sauvage', confounds his European interlocutor's inept attempts to defend French civilization. Much of what he says could be accurate description, but his own loquacious personality seems improbable for a Huron. It was a provocative satirical device and much imitated in the Enlightenment. There are several English translations of the *Nouveau voyages*: *New voyages . . .* (London, 1703; London, 1735; Chicago, 1905) and *Voyages* (1932), translated by Stephen LEACOCK.

Joseph-François Lafitau (1681-1746), a Jesuit who spent some six years in Canada (1711-17), also has a prominent place in developing the literary figure of the 'savage'. His *Moeurs des sauvages amériquains comparées aux moeurs des premiers temps* (Paris, 1724) continues the work begun by Lescarbot and Sagard but carries it, as his title indicates, to outright primitivism (the belief that man's original state, true human nature, is visible in 'uncivilized' peoples). Like his predecessors, Lafitau selects those features of Amerindian culture that look most admirable in a European context, and confirms their basic naturalness by reference to classical writers, suggesting that naturalness is a source of authentic virtue.

Pierre-François-Xavier de Charlevoix (1682-1761) is one of the great Jesuit historians, known for his works on Japan and Paraguay. His two visits to Canada in 1705-9 and 1720-3 were backed up by his thorough use of Jesuit library resources, and he was actively concerned with the search for the western sea. His *Histoire et description*

générale de la Nouvelle France . . . avec le Journal . . . d'un voyage . . . (Paris, 1744) was a
long-standing authority and a model of literary style. Some passing remarks about the
Canadiens, and the transfer to them of a
name that had previously designated an Indian nation, suggest the emergence of a new
people. Charlevoix is also the author of La
vie de Marie de l'Incarnation . . . (Paris, 1724),
of a geographical report (published by Pierre
Margry in his Découvertes et établissements
. . . Paris, 1879-88), and of contributions to
the Journal de Trévoux, a Jesuit periodical.
There are separate English translations of
the Journal . . . d'un voyage (London, 1761;
Chicago, 1923; and others), and of the Histoire as the History and description . . . (New
York, 1866-72; rev. 1900).

Other writers dealing directly with the
discovery of the new or not so new continent have attracted less attention in literary
discussion. Pierre-Esprit Radisson (c. 1640-
1710) mingles fiction with vivid fact, visibly
in the hope of attracting financial support
for his expeditions. His work is known only
through an English version of 1669: Voyages
of Peter Esprit Radisson (Boston, 1885 and
New York, 1943), and The explorations of
Pierre Esprit Radisson (1961) edited by Arthur
T. Adams. Louis-Henri de Beaugy
(d. 1720) wrote Journal d'une expédition contre
les Iroquois en 1687 (Paris, 1883; trans., Rochester, N.Y., 1922).

Henri de Tonty (c. 1650-1704) is the presumed author of Dernières découvertes . . . de
M. de la Sale (sic; Paris, 1697), a work whose
value has been found dubious both as history and as literature. Claude-Charles Le
Roy (dit Bacqueville) de la Potherie (1663-
1717), who was in New France from 1697 to
1701, wrote a four-volume Histoire de
l'Amérique septentrionale (Paris & Rouen,
1722; Paris 1753). Dière de Dierville (1670?-
?) travelled to Port Royal in 1699-1700 and
published his Relation of that journey
(Rouen, 1708); a second edition (Québec,
1885) is expurgated but the English translation (Toronto, 1933) includes the complete
French text.

Of many other accounts of New France—
having perhaps less literary than documentary and historical interest—five will be
mentioned here. Nicolas Jérémie (1669-
1732), who served in Hudson Bay from
1694 to 1714, wrote 'Relation du Détroit et
de la Baie d'Hudson', which was published
in Recueil d'arrests et autres pièces pour l'établissement de la Compagnie de l'Occident (Amsterdam, 1720), the fourth edition of which was
published in English: Twenty years of York
Factory, 1694-1714: Jérémie's account of Hudson Strait and Bay (1926) translated by Robert
Douglas and J.N. Wallace. Letters attributed
to the Jesuit missionary Antoine Silvy
(1689-1711) were published in Relation par
lettres de l'Amérique septentrionale, années 1709
et 1710 (1904) and were included in translation in Documents relating to the early history of
Hudson Bay (1916) edited by J.B. Tyrrell.
Nicolas Perrot (1643-1717), who had a chequered career that included being governor
of Montreal (appointed 1670) and of Acadia
(appointed 1684), and being arrested and
imprisoned for illegal trade with the Indians,
wrote Mémoire sur les moeurs, coustumes et rel-
ligion des sauvages de l'Amérique septentrionale
(Leipzig & Paris, 1864; rpr. 1968). Louis
Franquet (1697-1768), a military engineer
who is associated with improving the defences of Louisbourg, wrote journals of his
tour of Québec, Trois-Rivières, and other
towns and forts in 1752-3 that were published as Voyages et mémoires sur le Canada
(Québec, 1889). In the realm of early western exploration the writings of Pierre Gaultier de Varennes et de La Vérendrye (1685-
1749) and his sons are important. These
were translated and edited by L.J. Burpee
for the Champlain Society in Journals and letters of Pierre Gaultier de Varennes de La Vérendrye and his sons with correspondence between
the governors of Canada and the French court,
touching the search for the western sea (1927).

The Journal du voyage de M. Saint-Luc de la
Corne . . . 1761 (Montréal, 1778; Québec,
1863) relates the ill-fated journey of the Auguste, carrying émigrés to France after the
Conquest. La Corne Saint-Luc (1711-84),
born in Canada and one of the few survivors
of the shipwreck, wrote of his hardships in a
fine measured style. The shipwreck is exploration literature in reverse, best known
through the fictionalized version in a chapter
of Philippe AUBERT DE GASPÉ's Les ANCIENS
CANADIENS.

2. ANNALS. Pierre Boucher (1622-1717)
arrived in Canada with his parents in 1635,
worked for a time for the Jesuits, and became Indian interpreter, captain, and later
governor of the trading post at Trois-
Rivières while farming his own land. He
was sent to Paris in 1661 to explain the
settlers' situation with a view to reforming
the fur trade. After his return the following
year he wrote his Histoire véritable et naturelle
. . . de la Novelle France . . . (Paris, 1664), a
naïve mixture of memoirs, natural history,
and description. Boucher's point of view is

not that of an explorer but of a resident adapted to the land, which has a distinct presence and varied character in his work. His admiration for the English colonies and his vehement hatred of the Iroquois give a clear impression of the colonist's ideal of development. *Histoire véritable et naturelle* has been translated into English under the title *Canada in the seventeenth century* . . . (Montreal, 1883).

Annals survive for the hospitals of Quebec and Montreal that are much more than annual accounts of main events in specific institutions. *Histoire de l'Hôtel-Dieu de Québec* (Montauban, 1751) was the collaborative work of Jeanne-Françoise Juchereau de la Ferté (1650-1723) and Marie-Andrée Regnard Duplessis (1687-1760). One surmises that the older woman dictated her memoirs and elaborated on other sources, such as the *Jesuit Relations* and older manuscript annals, and that the younger woman completed the work. Sister Juchereau was born in Quebec, took her vows at fourteen, and was superior from 1683 until her death; she was succeeded by Sister Regnard, who had arrived at Quebec from Paris at the age of fifteen. The *Histoire* is edifying and abounds in panegyrics of illustrious visitors and patients (including Kateri Tekakwitha), as well as of the founders of the hospital, while also commenting on great events in the life of the colony, such as the arrival of ships, epidemics, English attacks, and the earthquake of 1663.

Marie Morin (1649-1730) was also born in Quebec, like her mother (c.1620), but went to the new settlement at Montreal. At twenty-two she was playing an active part in directing the Hôtel-Dieu there, and later served two terms as superior. In 1697, at the request of her Order in France, she began to write annals, which she addressed to 'mes tres cheres soeurs qui lise cesy ou qui l'ecouteré lire' (sic). They were meant to be read aloud in other convents, like the lives of saints. Basically the work presents the lives and devotion of outstanding persons; but it includes substantial background on the foundation of Montreal and events of public interest, such as English attacks, major fires, and even a personal visit by the devil. Morin's narrative of the fire of 1695 is outstanding; she gives a vivid picture of all levels of disaster, explaining the measures that should have been taken to prevent spread of the fire and commenting wryly on the looters who sampled strong purgatives rescued from the pharmacy. Her portraits

constitute a gallery of Christian Amazons (her expression). These annals were continued by Véronique Cuillerier and Catherine Porlier, but most of what survives is Marie Morin's. First published as *Annales de l'Hôtel-Dieu de Montréal* (Montréal, 1921), then as 'Pages inédites du premier écrivain canadien' (in the *Journal de l'Hôtel-Dieu de Montréal*, 1937), the critical edition is entitled *Histoire simple et véritable* (1979).

3. OCCASIONAL VERSE AND PROSE survive sporadically from the period of New France. Lescarbot's poems and masque have been mentioned above (1). Another dramatic composition, staged in 1658, was later published under the title *Recéption de Mgr d'Argenson* (Québec, 1890). The anonymous author displays great ingenuity in combining allegorical figures and characters representing different sectors of the population; some of the speeches were composed entirely in Amerindian languages adapted to French verse. Elements of historical realism are combined with ceremonious statements of official optimism for the benefit of the new Governor.

Jean-Bernard Bossu (1720-92) travelled in Louisiana and the Miami country. His fables seek originality by using American content in the form created by La Fontaine, and are included in his *Nouveaux voyages aux Indes occidentales* (Paris, 1768) and *Noveaux voyages dans l'Amérique septentrionale* (Amsterdam, 1777; trans., London 1771; New Orleans, 1940).

More strictly occasional verse is to be found about the Seven Years' War. A witty play on the world 'carillon' and the French victory of that name is ironically addressed by an anonymous officer to the English soldiers: 'Le carillon de la Nouvelle-France'. Sister Marie-Hélène, less witty but more belligerent, adapted a well-known French lampoon for the victory of Chouaguen. Materials of this kind were collected by F.-A.-H. LA RUE in *Le* FOYER CANADIEN (1865) and by Antoine Roy in *Les Lettres . . . au Canada* (Paris, 1930).

Sermons composed for special occasions have been retrieved and published by later historians. Joseph de la Colombière (1651-1723) is the subject of a biography by Ernest Myrand (Montréal, 1898), who includes the text of a victory sermon delivered in 1690. A funeral sermon for Frontenac (1698), accompanied by a contemporary ironic comment, was first printed in *Bulletin de recherches historiques*, 1895. The sermon is by Olivier Boyer (1663-1721); the wit is anonymous. The full range of this important element in the cultural life of the country is not known.

4. LETTERS from the French régime have a highly varied literary interest. Those of MARIE DE L'INCARNATION are described in the entry on her. Marguerite Bourgeoys (1620-1700) is known for her administrative vigour. Some of her letters have been collected and published in *Histoire de la Congrégation de Notre-Dame de Montréal* (Montreal, 1913) by Sister Sainte-Henriette. Jean Talon (1625-94) was the main administrative officer in Canada for most of the years between 1665 and 1672 and took a keen interest in all aspects of the colony. His letters and reports vary from perfunctory to highly discursive. Both Bourgeoys and Talon have been included in the *Classiques canadiens* as examples of epistolary art.

The letters of Elisabeth Bégon (1696-1755) were strictly private. Born in Canada, she had been married to the governor of Trois-Rivières. After his death and the departure of their protector, she was sensitive to her loss of status and critical of the increasingly active social life of the colony. Her daughter, married to an army officer, died leaving an infant daughter who was brought up by Madame Bégon in endless consultation with the widower, a man near her own age, with whom Madame Bégon was in love. Her letters to him display many facets of her rich personality and of the life around her, as well as gradually disclosing a narrative in the manner of the epistolary novels of the time. As her dissatisfaction increased, the prospect of going to live with the family in France seemed attractive. In fact her isolation was intensified when, in 1749, she took this step. The 'cher fils' did not join her, while she was alienated from her relations by disagreement over the upbringing of 'our' child and an evident culture shock: 'I must seem like an Iroquois,' she comments. Her style, often vivid and biting, gives the reader a feeling of real presence. The letters of Mme Bégon were first published in the *Rapport de l'archiviste de la Province de Québec* (1934-5); a modern edition appeared under the title *Lettres au cher fils* (1972).

The most elegant, polished letters of New France come from the two generals: Louis-Joseph, marquis de Montcalm (1712-59), and François-Gaston, duc de Lévis (1720-87). Each left a *Journal* of his campaigns, mainly of interest to military historians, and a volume of *Lettres* . . . that show an admirable range of style. Lévis in particular suits the tone to the correspondent: a dignified delicacy for the circumstances in which he had to write to General Murray, a friendly open manner to Montcalm, elegant showing off to Bigot, and so on. The journals and letters of both generals were selected for publication under the titles: *Journal . . . de Lévis en Canada* (Montréal, 1889), *Lettres . . . de Lévis concernant la guerre au Canada* (Montréal, 1889), *Journal . . . de Montcalm (1756-59)* (Québec, 1895), and *Lettres . . . au Chevalier de Lévis* (Québec, 1894).

Detailed analyses of most of the works mentioned in this article will be found in the *Dictionnaire des oeuvres littéraires du Québec* and information about most of their authors, with bibliographical notes, in the DICTIONARY OF CANADIAN BIOGRAPHY.

JACK WARWICK

Newlove, John (b. 1938). Born in Regina and raised in farming communities in eastern Saskatchewan, where his mother was a school teacher, he travelled extensively in Canada, worked for three years in Vancouver, including a job at the UBC bookstore, was an editor at McCLELLAND AND STEWART in Toronto, and has been a teacher and a writer-in-residence at various institutions. He now lives in Nelson, B.C.

Newlove's books of poetry include *Grave sirs* (1962), *Elephants, mothers & others* (1963), *Moving in alone* (1965, 1977), *Black night window* (1968), *The cave* (1970), *Lies* (1972), *The fatman, selected poems, 1962-1972* (1977), and *The green plain* (1981).

Two impulses dominate Newlove's poetry: the urge to sing and the urge to record. One moment he is the delicate lyricist, improving on the themes of love, beauty, and loss, moving to ever-finer discriminations of thought and feeling; the next he is the stand-up comic, employing self-deflation, hyperbole, fantasy, and—especially in the treatment of domestic or mundane subjects—a deliberate rhetorical excess and archaic diction. Newlove is Canada's most gifted and meticulous prosodist; words such as *song, music, melody,* and *measure* recur frequently in his poems, and his best lyrics are characterized by either a subtle modulation of image, idea, and sound, 'the single, falling, tenuous line of melody' that holds the listener in its spell; or, to use his own phrase, by a form of 'running verse' whose headlong movement recalls Charles Olson's description of the good poem: a 'high-energy construct' where 'one perception must lead immediately and directly to a further perception.'

In 'No song', Newlove proposes to set aside such considerations. Like the crow perched on a branch, he must decline 'the privilege of music/or melody', instead 'fingering the absolute/wood beneath.' That wood consists of the spiritual or psychological truth embodied in private and collective experience, which the poet must record. Thus Newlove assumes his second role, that of archivist of human consciousness, concerned to preserve history, to discover both the pride and the shame of his people, the nature of their origins and inheritance. In a number of fine poems—such as 'Ride off any horizon', 'Crazy Riel', and 'The pride'—he attempts to ascertain the contemporary relevance of Canada's aboriginal heritage and its terrible record of racial violence and oppression. The stories are everywhere, the poet says, 'whatever is strong enough/to be remembered.' In such historical meditations, the concrete rendering of fact and the temperamental scoring of emotion bring about an almost perfect fusion of the lyrical and the documentary modes.

Newlove edited *Canadian poetry: the modern era* (1977), an anthology 'based on a survey done of the needs of Canadian literature instructors in universities across the country'.

See 'How do I get out of here: the poetry of John Newlove' (1973), in Margaret ATWOOD, *Second words: selected critical prose* (1982), and Brian Henderson, 'Newlove: poet of appearance' in *Essays on Canadian Writing* 2 (Spring 1975).

See also POETRY IN ENGLISH 1950 TO 1982: 2.   GARY GEDDES

Newman, Peter C. (b. 1929). Born in Austria, Newman came to Toronto in 1940 and was educated at Upper Canada College, the University of Toronto, and McGill University before becoming an assistant editor of *The Financial Post* in 1951. His career has included executive positions in mass journalism, particularly as editor-in-chief of *The Toronto Star* (1969-71) and as editor of *Maclean's* (1971-82). His main interests, however, have always lain in distinct areas of political and financial journalism. His first book, *Flame of power: intimate profiles of Canada's greatest businessmen* (1959), is the embryo of the type of minutely detailed, anecdotal personality study he later combined with analyses of events. *Renegade in power: the Diefenbaker years* (1963) and *The distemper*

of our times (1968), about the Pearson government, are stately testaments to his belief that the fate of nations is often the inevitable consequence of individual traits of personality acting in collusion; both books are wonderfully readable works of popular criminology. *Home country: people, places and power politics* (1974), a collection of magazine pieces, seemed to signal the end of Newman's life as a political analyst and the beginning of his career as the primary folklorist and explainer of Canada's proprietary class. To date, his major work in this field comprises *The Canadian establishment, vol. 1* (1975) and *The acquisitors: the Canadian establishment, vol. 2* (1981), which tell of the transition in Canadian entrepreneurship from owners to professional managers, and the not-completely-unrelated partial shift in economic power from central Canada to the western provinces. Publication of the two volumes was separated by *Bronfman dynasty: the Rothschilds of the new world* (1978), the story of the rise to wealth and influence of the Montreal distilling family, so characteristic—in everything, perhaps, but scope—of Ontario and Québec financial life as it has been traditionally carried out. His most recent work is *The establishment man: a study of personal power* (1982), a biography of Conrad Black, the most prominent of the younger generation of Canadian capitalists and the subject of some attention in *The acquisitors*.

Newman's books on business subjects are characterized by the steady marshalling of sometimes unpredictable detail and, at the same time, a desire to paint a broad sociological canvas. In aggregate they have sold over 750,000 copies.   DOUG FETHERLING

New provinces: poems of several authors (1936). This landmark anthology, illustrating the advances of the early Canadian modernists in terms of technique, subject, and poetic perspective, contains eleven poems by Robert FINCH, ten by Leo KENNEDY, two by A.M. KLEIN, eight by E.J. PRATT, ten by F.R. SCOTT, and twelve by A.J.M. SMITH. In 1931 the Montreal poets began to collect their own work and in 1934 invited the Toronto poets, Pratt and Finch, to join them in a proposed anthology. Although collaboration began optimistically under Smith's instruction to 'avoid being merely Georgian', there was some debate between Smith and Scott over the selection. Smith wanted the volume to offer an up-to-the minute statement on the contributors'

New provinces

work, while Scott wanted it to offer a more historical statement on the development of the contributors' poetry, in hopes of calling forth other, unknown modernist poets-in-the-making. There was also intense disagreement over Smith's proposed preface, which attacked the poetic achievements of the older Canadian poets. Without the placating, cajoling, and sometimes arbitrary insistence of Scott, *New provinces* would have foundered over this. When the anthology was finally published by MACMILLAN, Smith's lengthy Preface had been replaced by Scott's short one. A 1976 reprint contains an introduction by Michael Gnarowski that provides a history of the anthology's evolution, with particular reference to the incident of Smith's 'Rejected Preface' (which is included), laying the blame for its rejection at the feet of Pratt and Finch, who objected to his stringent attack on earlier Canadian poetry. The correspondence concerning *New provinces* reveals Scott's own reservations about it, which invited and strengthened the attack by Pratt and Finch. Smith's 'Rejected Preface' should be seen as an extension of his earlier article 'Wanted: Canadian criticism' in *The* CANADIAN FORUM (Apr. 1928), to which Scott had taken exception in the next month's *Forum* (June 1928).   KEITH RICHARDSON

Nichol, bp (b. 1944). Barrie Phillip Nichol was born in Vancouver, B.C. He grew up there, in Winnipeg, Man., and Port Arthur (now part of Thunder Bay), Ont., returning to Vancouver in 1960. He entered the education faculty of the University of British Columbia in 1962 and received an elementary basic certificate in 1963. While there he audited creative-writing classes attended by younger members of the TISH group. After a difficult year in Port Coquitlam, B.C., where he taught a Grade 4 class, he moved to Toronto and began work as a book searcher at the University of Toronto and entered therapy with the lay analyst Lea Hindley-Smith. His inclusion in 1965 in a therapy-learning group taught by Hindley-Smith led Nichol to join in 1967 in the establishing of the lay-therapy foundation Therafields, and to work as a therapist and an administrator of this therapeutic community until 1983.

Although Nichol had been writing since 1961, he first attracted public notice in the mid-1960s with his hand-drawn or 'concrete' poems. He valued particularly the personal aesthetic ground that concrete poetry gave him amid that period's various controversies about poetic theory. Concrete poetry also gave him almost immediately an international audience and reputation. Among the twenty-nine books and pamphlets Nichol published between 1965 and 1968, three each were published in England and the U.S. Nearly all these booklets contain only concrete work.

The full range of Nichol's writing became apparent only with the publication of the relatively conventional free verse of *Journeying and the returns* (1967) and *Monotones* (1971)—which developed into Nichol's best-known work, *The martyrology: Books 1 and 2* (1972); *Books 3 and 4* (1976); *Book 5* (1982); and part of the ongoing *Book 6: Continental trance* (1983)—and the prose work *Two novels* (1969). He has also published the prose collection *Craft dinner* (1978), the novel *Journal* (1978), the visual books *Still water* (1970) and *ABC: the Aleph Beth book* (1971), and innumerable booklets and pamphlets. *Still water*, together with the booklets *The true eventual story of Billy the Kid* (1970) and *Beach head* (1970) and the anthology of concrete poetry, *The cosmic chef* (1970), won a Governor General's Award for poetry.

All of Nichol's work is stamped by his desire to create texts that are engaging in themselves as well as in content, and to use indirect structural and textual devices to carry meaning. In *The martyrology* different ways of speaking testify to a journey through different ways of being. Language is both the poet's instructor and, through its various permutations, the dominant 'image' of the poem. The six books of *The martyrology* document a poet's quest for insight into himself and his writing through scrupulous attention to the messages hidden in the morphology of his own speech.

This attention to syntax and morphology characterizes both Nichol's concrete poetry and his prose fiction. His concrete poems have been typically written as sequences, and involve the sequential development of syllabic relationships (*Still water*) or of alphabetic shapes (*Unit of four*, 1974; and *Aleph unit*, 1974). His prose fiction employs Gertrude Stein's technique of using evolving yet repetitive syntax, to develop language both as a correlative for intense emotional states, as in *Journal*, and as a medium to divine meaning, as in *The true eventual story of Billy the Kid*.

Nichol first began performing as a sound poet in the mid-1960s. His early work in this medium was documented, together with early reflective poems, in Michael ON-DAATJE's film *Sons of Captain Poetry* (1970); in 'Borders', a small phonodisc included with *Journeying and the returns* in 1967; and in the long-playing record *Motherlove* (1968). In 1970 he began what proved to be an extended collaboration with fellow poets Rafael Barreto-Rivera, Paul Dutton, and Steve McCaffery, forming the sound-poetry group The FOUR HORSEMEN.

See also POETRY IN ENGLISH 1950 TO 1982: 2.　　　　FRANK DAVEY

Nichols, Ruth (b. 1948). Born in Toronto, and influenced by her mother's interest in literature, she began writing as a teenager and published her first novel at the age of twenty-one. Now married and living in Ottawa, she has written five novels: *A walk out of the world* (1969), *Ceremony of innocence* (1969), *The marrow of the world* (1972), *Song of the pearl* (1976), and *The left-handed spirit* (1978). She gained recognition as a remarkable writer of fantasies for children with her first, third, and fourth books. The central figures in these novels are young girls searching for a place or true home where they can be redeemed from the constrictions of a divided self. Like many fantasy writers, Nichols is steeped in the tradition of Tolkien, Lewis, Spenser, and the King James Bible; her interests in the Renaissance and the history of religion are reflected throughout her work. The search for a spiritual home leads Judith, in *A walk*, and Linda, in *The marrow*, into fantasy landscapes. Restless, troubled, near despair over the condition of their 'real' lives, they find self-awareness and redemption in the world of fantasy.

In *Song of the pearl* Nichols' use of metaphoric landscapes reaches a new level of power. Filled with hatred and melancholy, Margaret drifts calmly into death—which is her entrance into the realm of fantasy and a kind of heaven that is, ironically, both earth and the world of memory. Painfully she discovers that she has lived before—as Zawumatec, an Iroquois slave, and as Elizabeth, in Renaissance England—and learns that the uncle who raped her when she was Margaret, aged fifteen, was led to his fall by her own lust. After grappling with feelings she has denied or repressed, she gains another chance at life on earth. In this novel Nichols, putting the Tolkien-Lewis matrix behind her, succeeds in creating a powerful vision of the pilgrimage of the soul.

See Ruth Nichols, 'Fantasy and escapism', *Canadian Children's Literature* 4 (1976), and an interview with Jon Stott at that magazine (no. 12, 1978); and Ruth Nichols, 'Something of myself', in Sheila Egoff, ed., *One ocean touching: papers from the first Pacific Rim Conference on Children's Literature* (1979).

See also CHILDREN'S LITERATURE IN ENGLISH: 4.　　　　ROBERT LOVEJOY

Nicol, Eric (b. 1919). One of Canada's most prolific and versatile humorists, he was born in Kingston, Ont., but his family moved to Vancouver when he was six. He served in the RCAF for three years during the Second World War and spent some time as a comedy writer for the BBC and as a student at the University of British Columbia (where he wrote a column for the student newspaper) and at the Sorbonne. He has written for radio, television, and the stage, but his syndicated column in the *Vancouver Province* and his many books of humour have brought him the most widespread attention, three of them winning the Leacock Medal for Humour. These include: *Sense and nonsense by E.P. Nicol (Jabez)* (1947); *The roving I* (1950); *Twice over lightly* (1953); *Shall we join the ladies?* (1955); *Girdle me a globe* (1957); *In darkest domestica* (1959); *A history of Canada*—also known, less misleadingly, as *An uninhibited history of Canada* (1959); *Space age, go home!* (1964); *A scar is born* (1968); *Don't move! Renovate your house and make social contacts* (1971); *Letters to my son* (1974); and *There's a lot of it going around* (1975). He has also published a number of works in collaboration, beginning with *Sez we* (1943), a collection of columns from the *Vancouver News-Herald* by 'Jabez' (Nicol) and Jack Scott. He has collaborated with Peter Whalley on *Say, uncle* (1961), *Russia, anyone?* (1963), *100 years of what?* (1966), and *Canada cancelled because of lack of interest* (1977); and with Dave More on *The joy of hockey* (1978) and *The joy of football* (1980). His work has been anthologized in *A herd of yaks: the best of Eric Nicol* (1962) and *Still a Nicol* (1972), the latter edited by Alan Walker and reprinted in 1975 as *The best of Eric Nicol*. He has written a history of his city, *Vancouver* (1970; rev. 1978) and a book on his own profession, *One man's media, and how to write for them* (1973).

Without attaining the standard of the great humorists—LEACOCK, Thurber, Twain—Nicol is a thorough professional who always gives value, and whose work has a consistency and durability rare in the field. The pieces in which he pictures himself struggling with social embarrassments and domestic misfortunes, though they fall too easily into the tricks of that kind of writing, stand up to rereadings. His main strength is verbal inventiveness. Fond of outrageous puns and of verbal zig-zags that catch the reader by surprise, Nicol also enjoys playing with common turns of phrase: the title essay of *Shall we join the ladies?* refers not to after-dinner rituals but to sex-change operations.

Lately Nicol has had what is virtually a second career as a playwright. *Like father, like fun* (1973) concerns the attempt of a crass businessman to contrive his son's initiation into sex. In *The fourth monkey* (1973) a writer copes with interlopers who invade his island retreat. Both plays have dialogue that is frequently witty, but they suffer from structural weakness and arbitrary characterization. The failure of *Like father, like fun* on Broadway—where it was rewritten and retitled *A minor adjustment*—has become a classic instance of the danger of exporting a Canadian play. (Nicol gives a ruefully funny account of it in *A scar is born*, and the scars also show in the frustrations of the central character in *The fourth monkey*.) But the play had a considerable success in Vancouver; its depiction of local society, however caricatured, obviously struck a vein.

In his contribution to *The centennial play* (1967) and in *The citizens of Calais* (1975) Nicol shows, through the comic squabbling of characters trying—not very hard—to put on a play, the cynicism and petty-mindedness that threaten Canada; and he enters a characteristic plea for tolerance and common sense. Comedy and serious comment are also mingled, somewhat uneasily, in *Pillar of sand* (1975), in which the unreason of early Christian mysticism—for which we may read the unreason of Nicol's own time—is pitted against the rationality of a Roman soldier. *The man from inner space* (1976), a television play, has a comic premise with serious overtones: the hero has tried to escape into a private world, mechanically created, and the play shows the collapse of his attempt to cut himself off from humanity. The mix is most successful, perhaps, in the children's plays. *The clam made a face* (1972) reworks some West Coast Indian legends, and *Beware the quickly who* (1973) returns to the Canadian Identity Crisis. Both show an impatience with spoilsports and fuddy-duddies and a celebration of the creative, playful side of life.

Like father, like fun, *The fourth monkey*, and *Pillar of sand* are collected in *Three plays by Eric Nicol* (1975).   ALEXANDER LEGGATT

Nigog, Le (1918). The first arts magazine in Québec, it grew out of Thursday-evening meetings held by the architect Fernand Préfontaine in his Westmount (Montreal) home. Among those present were Robert Laroque de ROQUEBRUNE, historian and man of letters; Adrien Hébert, painter; his brother Henri Hébert, sculptor; Louis Bourgoin, chemist; and Léo-Paul Morin, composer and pianist. The name 'Nigog' is an Indian word meaning fishing-spear. The editorial committee was made up of Préfontaine, Laroque de Roquebrune, and Morin. The twelve numbers that were published (financed by Préfontaine) contained 108 articles on music, literature, the plastic arts and art in general, and some dozen poems, accompanied by art work of various kinds. Though it never claimed to be bilingual, it published some articles in English. The magazine was a polished showcase that highlighted the group's conception of art: namely that manner of presentation was more important than subject matter. Wishing to disseminate modern ideas about art, its founders were led to denounce the regionalists and their taboos, thereby producing a major disturbance in the artistic and intellectual climate because they were, in effect, urging the regionalists to forsake the sources of their inspiration—the official utilitarian themes.

Though its circulation was less than 500, *Le Nigog* exerted a far-reaching influence. It helped to change the intellectual and artistic atmosphere in Québec, purging it of its habitual optimism and *joie de vivre*, its impressionism, and its addiction to copying nature. It set in motion the irreversible process of literary liberation from the ultra-conservative reign of the worship of the small patch of land and 'l'heure des vaches'.

ARMAND GUILMETTE

Niven, Frederick (1878-1944). Born to Scottish parents in Valparaiso, Chile, Frederick John Niven was taken to Glasgow at age five and educated in Hutcheson's Grammar School and the Glasgow School of Art. In his late teens he was sent to visit friends in the Okanagan Valley, B.C., as a treatment for a lung ailment. He spent what he described as 'a year or two' travelling in Canada and taking odd jobs, an experience that drew him into journalism on his return to Scotland. In 1908 he began his career as a novelist with the publication of *The lost cabin mine*, one of many adventure stories he set in the Canadian West. Married in 1911, he spent several months in 1912 and 1913 travelling as a freelance writer in Canada. In 1920 he and his wife moved to Canada, living near Nelson, B.C., and in Vancouver until Niven's death.

Before emigrating, Niven had established himself as a minor but promising novelist in Britain; his writing was stimulated by his Canadian travel, and more than half of his early publications include New World settings, some Canadian, some in an indeterminate 'West': two volumes of short stories, *Above your heads* (1911); *Sage-brush stories* (1917); a book of poems, *Maple-leaf songs* (1917); a fictionalized personal experience, *The S.S. Glory* (1915); and four novels: *The lost cabin mine* (1908), *Hands up!* (1913), *Cinderella of Skookum Creek* (1916), and *Penny Scot's treasure* (1919). But as W.H. New explains in his unpublished M.A. thesis, 'Individual and group isolation in the fiction of Frederick John Niven' (UBC, 1963), many of these were adventure romances written 'to keep the wolf from the wife', to use Niven's phrase. His more realistic novels had Old World settings and, like *A wilderness of monkeys* (1911), treated themes of isolation, especially that of the artist championing spiritual values in a materialistic society.

After settling in Canada Niven used Old World settings for eleven of seventeen remaining novels; the New World for one volume of poetry, *A lover of the land and other poems* (1925); one fictionalized personal experience, *Wild honey* (1927); and six novels: *The wolfer* (1923), *Treasure trail* (1923), *The flying years* (1935), *Mine inheritance* (1940), *Brothers-in-arms* (1942), and *The transplanted* (1944). These later novels include Niven's chief contribution to Canadian literature: a trilogy spanning the settlement of the West and incorporating his most serious themes. *Mine inheritance* is a historical romance of the struggle to establish the Selkirk Settlement amid the fur-trade wars on the Red River. Wholly sympathetic to the colonizers, it dramatizes their need to adapt mentally and spiritually, as well as physically, in order to overcome the isolation of the new land. *The flying years* is a panoramic narrative extending from the 1850s to the 1920s. Its protagonist, though not strongly characterized, becomes a representative immigrant, subject to the trials of adaptation through all stages of settlement and of his life. He makes the

prairies his home without altogether relinquishing Scotland as that 'country of the mind' from which the Highland Clearances had driven him. *The transplanted*, which depicts the development of a settlement in the lumbering, mining, and ranching area of central B.C., completes the pattern by concentrating its thematic emphasis on the need for community to combat the destructive isolation that comes from seeking the freedom of the natural environment.

Niven also published a good deal of nonfiction, including *Canada West* (1930); *Colour in the Canadian Rockies* (1937), with illustrations by Walter J. Phillips; *Coloured spectacles* (1938), autobiographical reflections; *Go North, where the world is young* (n.p., n.d.); and *A lady in the wilderness* (n.p., n.d.). Niven remains important to Canadian literature because he brought to bear on western experience a developed writing talent and a sense of British literary and cultural traditions. He became an immigrant as distinct from a colonial writer, recreating the West in a Canadian perspective.

See Jan de Bruyn's introduction to the 1974 reprint of *The flying years* in the New Canadian Library.   DICK HARRISON

Northern Review (1945-56). The result of a merger between two Montreal literary magazines, PREVIEW and FIRST STATEMENT, it was edited by John SUTHERLAND (managing editor), F.R. SCOTT, A.M. KLEIN, Irving LAYTON, Patrick ANDERSON, A.J.M. SMITH, Audrey Aikman, R.G. Simpson, and Neufville Shaw; regional editors were P.K. PAGE, Dorothy LIVESAY, James Wreford, and Ralph GUSTAFSON. The first issue appeared in Dec. 1945-Jan. 1946. The amalgamation was made uneasy by differences in literary philosophy among its editors. More significant, however, was the fact that the more nationalistic *First Statement* poets viewed Sutherland as editor-in-chief, whereas the *Preview* poets, used to Anderson's democratic editorial policies, saw Sutherland simply as a fellow editor in charge of production. The tension came to a head with Sutherland's aggressively critical review of Robert FINCH's Governor General's Award-winning book, *Poems*, in the issue of Aug.-Sept. 1947. Scott, Klein, Anderson, Smith, Shaw, Page, Livesay, and Gustafson all resigned in protest at not having approved the review. A year later, in the issue of Sept.-Oct. 1948, Layton's name disappeared from the masthead; the magazine subsequently became more conservative.

Northern Review

Sutherland continued to publish *Northern Review* with the help of Aikman and Simpson and, in the issue of April-May 1951, announced the incorporation of *The Canadian Review of Music and Art*, through the generosity of Lorne PIERCE. Simpson retired from the editorial board with the Oct.-Nov. 1951 issue and his eventual replacement, A.E. Farebrother, withdrew when the magazine moved to Toronto in the spring of 1955 and changed from a bi-monthly to a quarterly. *Northern Review* ceased publication with Sutherland's death in Sept. 1956, after 40 issues.

Northern Review had the largest circulation of any literary journal in the country and maintained a high quality of poetry, short stories, essays, and book reviews. Mavis GALLANT, Norman LEVINE, Brian MOORE, George WOODCOCK, Robert WEAVER, and Marshall McLUHAN are only a few of the contributors who appeared in its pages.

See Robert Weaver, 'John Sutherland and *Northern Review*', *The* TAMARACK REVIEW 2 (Winter 1957).   DAVID O'ROURKE

Norwood, Robert (1874-1932). Born at New Ross, N.S., Robert Winkworth Norwood was educated at Coaticook Academy and Bishop's College in Québec, at King's College, Windsor, N.S., and at Columbia University, New York. Ordained in the Anglican Church in 1898, he served in Canadian parishes in Nova Scotia, Québec, and Ontario before moving to the U.S. in 1917. In Philadelphia and, after 1925, at St Bartholomew's Church in New York City, Norwood became famous as one of the most eloquent metropolitan pulpit orators of his day. He died suddenly in New York upon his return from his summer residence in Nova Scotia.

Encouraged in his verse-writing as a student at King's by his professor, Charles G.D. ROBERTS, Norwood collaborated with his college roommate Charles W. Vernon in issuing *Driftwood*, a slim volume of poems privately printed in 1898. Essentially a lyric poet, he nevertheless preferred to objectify his sensibility in dramatic monologues, sonnet sequences, poetic dramas, and narrative verse. *His lady of the sonnets* (1915) contains, besides the title sonnet sequence, three other sequences of lyric poems that are both unified and diversified by the poet's varied concepts of love; a final section of religious songs and sonnets completes the volume. *The witch of Endor* (1916) is a five-act closet drama in rhetorical blank verse celebrating the transcendent power of love. Another book of poems, *The piper and the reed* (1917), continues an almost too-forceful lyric expression of Norwood's muscular Christianity. This was followed by *The modernists* (1918), a collection of dramatic monologues in which speakers express human ideals in a progression from the cave-man through historic figures to the voice of the twentieth century. The five-act poetic drama, *The man of Kerioth* (1919), explores the motives of Judas in betraying Jesus.

Bill Boram (1921), a narrative poem about the humanity hidden in the heart of a brutish sea-captain, draws on Norwood's experience of the Nova Scotia coast, and his descriptions are therefore more vivid than those in his earlier works, which abound in classical settings. The poems in *Mother and son* (1925) reflect the sorrow Norwood felt over the death of his son in a hunting accident. 'The spinner', a poem in this collection, shows the power of his mature lyricism, with its direct imagery and swiftly varying moods. *Issa* (1931), an 1800-line meditative poem employing a six-line rhymed stanza, is a highly personal exploration of Issa (or Jesus) as a presence guiding both the poet's flights into contemplation of the Godhead and his descent into communion with the earth, with human things and human beings. It is the work that best justifies Charles G.D. Roberts' high praise of Norwood 'as a great religious poet'.

Several books of prose, written in the last years of his life, express his liberal view of Christianity. These include *The heresy of Antioch* (1928), *The steep ascent* (1928), *The man who dared to be God* (1929), *His glorious body* (1930), *Increasing Christhood* (1932), and *The hiding God* (1933). A.D. Watson's *Robert Norwood* (1923) is an appreciation of the poet in the Makers of Canadian Literature series.
                                              KEN MacKINNON

Nouvelle Barre du Jour, La. See *La* BARRE DU JOUR and LITERARY MAGAZINES IN QUÉBEC: 4.

Nova-Scotia Magazine and Comprehensive Review of Literature, Politics, and News, The. Published in Halifax between July 1789 and Mar. 1792, it was the first literary journal in Canada. It was issued monthly, printed by John Howe (father of Joseph HOWE), and edited by the Rev. William Cochran, first president of King's College, Windsor, N.S. Thirty-three numbers appeared; the first eighteen averaged over eighty pages in length, the last fifteen over sixty pages. The bulk of each issue was made up of material Cochran found in British and American books and magazines: passages by such well-known authors as Edward Gibbon, Richard Cumberland, Hester Piozzi, William Cowper, Dr Benjamin Rush, Joseph Priestly, and Benjamin Franklin, as well as little-known journalists. Prose fiction and poetry were prominently featured, and there were brief notices of new books; in addition there were detailed reports on the political scene in both Nova Scotia and Great Britain and a 'Chronicle' of current events, domestic and foreign. Of the few local contributions, all of which appeared anonymously, the best-known pieces are 'A plan of a liberal education' by W. (possibly Cochran himself) and the poems of 'Pollio'. *The Nova-Scotia Magazine* was valuable for opening windows on the great world of science and literature that lay beyond Nova Scotia, and for attempting to draw Nova Scotian minds into that world.

TOM VINCENT

Novascotian, The. See Joseph HOWE.

Novels in English. Beginnings to 1900. When, during her stay in Quebec in the mid-1760s, Frances BROOKE began writing the work that has come to be called the first Canadian novel, there was little in the local society to encourage the creation of Canadian fiction in English. The few anglophone inhabitants of the town were mostly British military personnel who, birds of passage themselves, had little use for such cultural commodities as libraries and schools or for such locally produced reading material as newspapers, magazines, and books. Although the newly acquired colony of Canada was a British North American society like no other, because of its large French-speaking population, it took several decades of exploration, immigration, and settlement throughout what remained of British North America after the American Revolution to produce a recognizably indigenous English-Canadian fiction. Even then, many of the short stories and novels that emerged often seemed little more than new cloth cut to old styles. Still, some were fashioned to cast new meanings on old shapes and to re-form old myths for a new nation.

One step towards the development of early English-Canadian fiction was the use of Canadian content in works published in the United Kingdom and the United States

and written by British and American authors after they had temporarily lived in, or briefly visited, British North America. The earliest of these works was Frances BROOKE's *The history of Emily Montague* (London, 1769); it was also one of the few novels about North America published in the eighteenth century. In the nineteenth century many such works followed, including John GALT's *Bogle Corbet; or, The emigrants* (London, 1831), Frederick Marryat's *The settlers in Canada* (London, 1844), R.M. BALLANTYNE's *Snowflakes and sunbeams; or, The young fur traders. A tale of the far North* (London, 1856), and William Dean Howells' *Their wedding journey* (Boston, 1871), with its lengthy chapter on 'The sentiment of Montreal'. All popular works by well-known writers, they not only helped to introduce various images of Canada to such groups as potential British immigrants and American tourists, but they also prepared an international market for fiction written by Canadians, and provided models of forms and suggestions of themes for these writers. There is no doubt, for example, that Frances Brooke's portrait of the 'divine' Emily's experiences of French-Canadians in Quebec in the 1760s promoted English-French relations in Canada as both a saleable and seminal theme in early Canadian fiction.

The thousands of United Empire Loyalists who came north during the 1770s and 80s benefited both Canada and the older colony of Nova Scotia. This migration, and the 'great migrations' from Europe during the nineteenth century, meant that communities throughout the colonies acquired people with the education, enthusiasm, and expertise to embark on and to endeavour to sustain the newspapers and magazines that published most of the indigenous early Canadian fiction. Much of it still remains lost or forgotten in these often tattered, usually incomplete periodicals. Enough has survived, however, to indicate the significance of this mode of publication for the development of fiction. For example, the only edition of Thomas McCULLOCH's comic masterpiece 'The letters of Mephibosheth Stepsure' to appear during its author's lifetime was published in *The Acadian Recorder* (Halifax) in 1821-3; the first edition of Thomas Chandler HALIBURTON's *The clockmaker* was serialized in *The Novascotian* (Halifax) in 1835-6; and some of the sketches in Susanna MOODIE's semi-fictional ROUGHING IT IN THE BUSH (London, 1852) were first published in 1847 in *The* LITERARY GAR-

LAND (Montreal) and *The Victoria Magazine* (Belleville). *The Literary Garland* was probably the most successful of the early monthly magazines in actively seeking the work of new Canadian writers—among others, Rosanna Eleanor Mullins LEPROHON had her first stories published there—but there were similar endeavours in many of the country's towns and cities. Furthermore, the man who produced the local newspaper and magazine often printed the local books as well. Thus Hugh C. Thomson, publisher of *The Upper Canada Herald* (Kingston), printed by subscription the first novel published in Canada and written by a native-born Canadian, Julia Catherine Beckwith HART's ST. URSULA'S CONVENT; *or, The nun of Canada* (1824); and Joseph HOWE, the publisher of *The Novascotian*, printed the first book edition of *The clockmaker* (1836), thereby starting Sam Slick and his author on their way to international fame.

For commercial and psychological reasons most early Canadian writers eventually sought publication abroad. Publication in either London or New York guaranteed large markets, good distribution, and sometimes favourable copyright arrangements. Publication in Great Britain had the further advantage of allowing authors to feel that they were writing for people who, because of their position at the artistic and intellectual centre of the British Empire, set the fashions for the fiction they tried to create. Some writers in the colonies gained access fairly easily to these markets because they had published works in London before immigrating to Canada. Mrs Moodie's *Roughing it in the bush; or, Life in Canada* and Catharine Parr TRAILL's *Canadian Crusoes. A tale of the Rice Lake Plains* (1852) were both first published in London. Native-born Canadians had works first published abroad as well. John RICHARDSON, who was living in England at the time as a half-pay army officer, had WACOUSTA; OR, THE PROPHECY. *A tale of the Canadas* (1832) published jointly by Cadell (London) and Blackwood (Edinburgh), two eminently respectable publishers, and was thus assured of a number of reviews in good magazines and—alas for his personal fortunes—the immediate piracy of the novel by American publishers. In the mid-nineteenth century James DE MILLE and May Agnes FLEMING, two natives of New Brunswick, were both extraordinarily successful writing directly for the American market. Fleming eventually moved to Brooklyn, where she died a wealthy woman

at the age of thirty-nine. De Mille remained in Nova Scotia, but in the 1870s he became one of Harper's most productive writers, and it was they who published his most fascinating novel, *A strange manuscript found in a copper cylinder* (New York, 1888), eight years after he died. At the end of the century Gilbert PARKER, who was then living in London, gained direct international acclaim when he published *Pierre and his people. Tales of the Far North* (1892) with Methuen. Most authors, however, wrote first for the Canadian periodical press and only later tried for publication outside the country. Sometimes they were published in New York or London; but as the nineteenth century progressed their works were more frequently published in Canada. After *The Literary Garland* ceased publication in 1851 Mrs Leprohon's fiction appeared in both American and Canadian periodicals, but her most important novels, including *Antoinette de Mirecourt; or, Secret marrying and secret sorrowing. A Canadian tale* (1864), were published by John Lovell in Montreal. Still, the kind of fiction that was selling elsewhere certainly influenced various aspects of Mrs Leprohon's works. The lure of the international market was probably the most important influence on the evolution of early Canadian fiction.

This international influence shaped early English-Canadian fiction in several ways. It provided specific authors—British, American, and occasionally French—as models for the local fiction writers. The most important was Sir Walter Scott, whose 'Mortal exit' in 1832 was compared by 'A Scotchman' writing in *The Canadian Magazine* (York, 1833) to a 'shock!—that will only be surpassed when the last trumpet shall sound', and whose historical romances were obviously studied in great detail by such writers as John Richardson and William KIRBY. James Fenimore Cooper, Honoré de Balzac, Charles Dickens, and Mark Twain were also among the many authors cited directly by Canadian writers. Mrs Leprohon, for example, describes a character in *Antoinette de Mirecourt* as 'an elegant looking woman, on the shady side of Balzac's admired feminine age of thirty'. Stephen LEACOCK, whose early humorous sketches first appeared in Canadian and American magazines in the 1890s, later wrote critical studies of both Dickens and Twain, the two authors who most influenced his own career as a humorist.

From these models Canadian authors also

learned about the kinds of fiction one could—and should—write. Historical romances were perhaps the most popular until late in the nineteenth century. But humorous sketches and novels, domestic romances of high society, animal and other tales for children, and adventure stories could all find markets. Many stories written by Canadians in these genres were very popular and sometimes became international bestsellers. One thinks most readily of such historical romances as Richardson's *Wacousta*, William Kirby's *The* GOLDEN DOG *(Le chien d'or). A legend of Québec* (Montreal, 1877), and Gilbert Parker's *The seats of the mighty* (London, 1896). But Haliburton's *Clockmaker*, created initially to satirize Nova Scotians, quickly reached an international audience after 1836, as did his subsequent 'Sam Slick' books. Mrs Fleming's domestic romances were published simultaneously as serials and as books in the United States and Great Britain. Mrs Traill's *Canadian Crusoes* remained a popular adventure story for children even after its title was changed to *Lost in the backwoods. A tale of the Canadian forest* (London, 1882), and Marshall SAUNDERS' BEAUTIFUL JOE. *An autobiography* (Philadelphia, 1894), about a dog, was a bestseller when it was first published. Two years before, Charles G.D. ROBERTS' 'Do seek their meat from God', an animal story for adults that owed its origin at least partly to the hunting stories popular in the late nineteenth century, had been published by *Harper's Magazine* (Dec. 1892).

In addition, the international influence encouraged the treatment of certain themes. Stories about North Americans going abroad became popular. James De Mille's *The Dodge club; or, Italy in 1859* (New York, 1869) is a comic rendering of this theme; but the Canadian writer most identified with the international theme is probably Sara Jeannette DUNCAN. *An American girl in London* (London, 1891) and *A daughter of today* (London, 1894) treats it conventionally by taking Americans to Europe. Duncan moved to India in the early 1890s, however, and her experiences of British India produced a series of novels beginning with *His honor and a lady* (London, 1896), which dealt with the triumphs and tensions of that international society. In *A daughter of today* she also explored another significant late-nineteenth-century theme, that of the independent career woman.

Throughout the century stories about the past and present of French Canada, the American Revolution, the War of 1812-14, and the opening of the Canadian West and North were almost guaranteed success. John LESPERANCE's *The Bastonnais. Tale of the American invasion of Canada in 1775-1776* (Toronto, 1877) focuses on Montgomery's siege of Quebec during the American War of Independence. Francis William GREY's *The curé of St. Philippe: a story of French-Canadian politics* (London, Ont., 1899) depicts an election in contemporary Québec. John Richardson's sequel to *Wacousta, The Canadian brothers; or, The prophecy fulfilled: A tale of the late American war* (Montreal, 1840) is set during the War of 1812-14 in areas where Richardson himself served or was later imprisoned. Charles E. Beardsley's *The* VICTIMS OF TYRANNY (Buffalo, 1847), Agnes Maule MACHAR's *For King and country. A story of 1812* (Toronto, 1874), and William Henry WITHROW's *Neville Trueman, the pioneer preacher. A tale of the War of 1812* (Toronto, 1900) also cover this war. In choosing as his chief character an itinerant Methodist preacher, Withrow combined two popular themes: the War of 1812-14 and religion. *Black rock. A tale of the Selkirks* (Toronto, 1898)—the book version of the sketches that Ralph Connor (Charles William GORDON), a Presbyterian minister, originally wrote for his church paper in 1897— describes in detail the mining and ranching country around Banff in the Northwest. All these and many more novels and short stories on similar themes were generally well received by Canadian and non-Canadian readers alike.

Finally, the fact that Canadian authors wrote for popular publications and a wide range of readers at least partly explains the high moral tone of much of this fiction, which was usually intended to teach and inspire as well as to entertain; a large dollop of justice offset a sprinkling of scandal and adventure. Saunders expresses one version of this typically Victorian recipe in *Beautiful Joe* when she creates a heaven for good animals and dispenses cruel justice to evil people. Ralph Connor, the Presbyterian minister who became a millionaire from his writings, mixed the recipe even more skilfully with courageous missionaries and corrupt alcoholics, sentimental sermons and lively brawls, in a manner characteristic of 'muscular Christianity' that still titillates and entertains readers.

In some ways the circumstances that allowed these early Canadian writers to publish internationally militated against their

Novels in English: Beginnings to 1900

being able to develop a Canadian fiction in English that dealt subtly with serious themes of national cultural significance. It was often easier to follow well-established formulas than to adapt the old patterns to suit new shapes. Mrs Hart's *St. Ursula's convent* is a typical example of a work so overladen with what one contemporary reviewer called the 'quintessence of romanticism' that, despite its setting in late-eighteenth-century Québec, it utterly fails to confront the ambivalence and ambiguities brought to Canadian society by the English Conquest. Still, from its beginnings to 1900 there were works of Canadian fiction that did at least isolate important Canadian themes and play with their significance. The following is one critic's choice of some of these works.

Frances Brooke's epistolary novel *Emily Montague*, even though written by an Englishwoman and published in England, is, for several reasons, the seminal work of Canadian fiction in English. It introduces themes that inspired some of the most subtle responses from later writers of this fiction, including the Indians and their life in a Canada being Europeanized, the relations of Canada to the other British North American colonies that became the United States and to Great Britain, the shape of the Canadian economy, and the nature of the rapport between (French) Canadians and the English. Though Mrs Brooke's letter-writers act more as reporters than as interpreters, it is her identification of these Canadian themes, not their resolution in her novel, that is significant.

Indians also turn up in Mrs Traill's *Canadian Crusoes*, Kirby's *The Golden Dog*, and Parker's *Pierre and his people*. Perhaps the most complex treatment of this theme occurs in Richardson's *Wacousta* and *The Canadian brothers*. Their part-Indian author, who lived as a white gentleman, places at the dramatic centre of these stories a Welshman who has gone Indian to seek revenge on his fellow Europeans. The ironies and ambiguities that develop suggest a good deal about the nature of racial tensions in Canada and the psychological destruction that often resulted.

Since Richardson placed his novels on the Canadian/American frontier, he also explored Canadian-American relations, especially in *The Canadian brothers*, the final lines of which describe 'the picked and whitened bones' of the Americans killed during the Battle of Queenston Heights. One of the most interesting—and comic—treatments of

this theme, however, is that of Haliburton in *The clockmaker*. Through Sam Slick, the Connecticut Yankee who travels around Nova Scotia employing 'soft sawder' and a knowledge of 'human nature' to sell unnecessary clocks at inflated prices to improvident 'Bluenoses', Haliburton, himself of American ancestry, suggests the ambivalent feelings of 'His Majesty's Yankees' for their Connecticut Yankee brethren. He also contemplates the economic future of the unenterprising Nova Scotians, living on top of a nation of Slick (Uncle) Sams whose belief in progress would lead them to develop the province's natural resources, build railways, and begin industries. The polite country squire who acts as the narrator of the sketches provides an English, conservative dimension to the theme of the political future of Nova Scotia.

The 1860s produced not only a new country in North America but gave a fresh impetus to the old theme of English-French relations in Canadian fiction. One major work that appeared on this theme in the 1860s was Mrs Leprohon's *Antoinette de Mirecourt*. Set in Montreal shortly after the Conquest, it presents a complex view of some of the consequences for the British, the French, and the Canadians of Great Britain's acquisition of New France. Like so many historical romances, however, it uses a past event to contemplate a present reality, in this case the political future of the Canadas, which, since their creation in 1784, had been working out ever-more-unworkable relationships. Perhaps because she herself was an English Canadian married to a French Canadian, Mrs Leprohon seems optimistic about an eventual happy marriage between the two groups.

An even more sacramental vision of the future of the two peoples in one Canada comes toward the end of what is probably the most appealing work of early Canadian fiction, William Kirby's *The Golden Dog*, set in New France just before its fall. In true epic fashion Kirby reshapes historical facts to suggest that the British Conquest was ordained by God to save the Canadians— conservative, hierarchical, and monarchical—from the corrupt monarchy of France, and the evil republicanism that followed with the French Revolution, by placing them in the benevolent hands of the good monarchy of Great Britain. Designed as much to give English Canadians a national mythology as to reconcile the two 'nations', this novel thus transforms the conventions of the historical romance into a marvellously imagined heroic vision that embodies the best that was thought and said about the new nation in the years following Confederation. Subsequent events, of course, darkened the vision, and new fashions in fiction changed its expression; but Kirby's *The Golden Dog* remains the work of early Canadian fiction in English that most successfully fits old international patterns to new national myths.　　MARY JANE EDWARDS

1900 to 1920. In the first two decades of this century economic, political, and philosophical forces transformed Canadian society. It was a time of economic prosperity, marked by the emergence of powerful new financial classes, development in the West, and rapid urbanization in the East. While the world was coming to Canada with the arrival of large groups of non-English-speaking immigrants, Canada was going out to see the world as its natives, especially artists and authors, went abroad to study and to live. The Great War sealed Canada's relationship with the larger world. In these and the preceding years the most favoured image for Canada—and its literature—was that of the youth struggling to grow into manhood.

Writers of fiction, caught up in this social transformation, were equally involved in the theoretical and practical issues of the international literary world. Traditional concepts of fiction were being challenged by writers like Joyce, James, Conrad, and Woolf. The merits of 'realism' and 'naturalism' were under debate, and both were challenged by the advocates of 'idealism' and 'romance'. The preponderant weight of Canadian literary opinion was in favour of 'idealism'. Literature was not a personal expression of a peculiarly sensitive individual who could unmask his own and society's soul, but a social force that would entertain while instructing, leading, and inspiring. At a time when fiction was considered to be a low literary form by the classically educated, and a vehicle for frivolity and vice by religious people, the instructional aspect became important as a defence of fiction. Nevertheless some of the literary techniques developed by the maligned 'realists' became important to those authors who chose to write inspirational fiction from the basis of their own experience.

A large market for fiction was developing in the newspapers and magazines of Britain and the United States enabling authors to make writing a profession that brought a full or partial income. Sensation, sentiment, and melodrama were the prevailing qualities of this fiction, which sought to heighten readers' emotional experience with fast-paced action, idealized characters, exotic settings, and reinforced morality. Canadian writers found that they could use scenes and characters from their own country to speak to their international audience—and they may have been more widely read by their contemporaries than any fiction writers before or since.

Both the historical and contemporary Canadian scene provided ample material for these authors, whose works helped to shape the world's image of Canada. Interest in historical fiction dropped off sharply after 1900, although Jean McILWRAITH's *A Diana of Quebec* (1912), and some of the works of Charles G.D. ROBERTS and Theodore Goodridge ROBERTS, indicate that the nation's past—most specifically that of New France—was still a source for material. However, the more popular genre in exploiting Canada as a literary resource was that of the local-colour sketch. Canadian writers turned to all parts of the country for their material. Contemporary Quebec, both rural and urban, found its way into two of the later novels of Sir Gilbert PARKER, *The money master* (1915) and *The right of way* (1901), and into the stories and sketches of other authors. Nova Scotia provided the setting for Basil KING's *In the garden of Charity* (1903) and *The high heart* (1917) and for Alice JONES's *The bubbles we buy* (1903). The Gaspé and New Brunswick provided the background for many novels by T.G. Roberts and Hiram CODY, as well as for the animal stories of Charles G.D. Roberts. Starting with ANNE OF GREEN GABLES (1908), Lucy Maud MONTGOMERY made Prince Edward Island famous to the world. The lives of the people of Newfoundland and Labrador were captured by Norman DUNCAN in *The way of the sea* (1903), and by Wilfred GRENFELL and T.G. Roberts.

Ontario supplied some of the richest territory to the local-colour writers. Ralph Connor (Charles W. GORDON) used memories of his boyhood in Glengarry County, Ont., for portions of *The man from Glengarry* (1901) and GLENGARRY SCHOOL DAYS (1902). In *Duncan Polite* (1905) and her later novels Marian Keith (Mary Esther MacGREGOR) portrayed life in the Scots villages of southwestern Ontario. Robert E. KNOWLES's *St. Cuthbert's* (1905), W.A.

FRASER's *The lone furrow* (1907), Sara Jeannette DUNCAN's *The imperialist* (1904), Kathleen and Robina Lizars' *Committed to his charge* (1900), Stephen LEACOCK's SUNSHINE SKETCHES OF A LITTLE TOWN (1912), and numerous other works examined the pleasures and frustrations of life in the small towns of Ontario. The large cities play only a passing role, usually as the site of the protagonist's college years, as in Ralph Connor's novels or Robert BARR's *The measure of the rule* (1906), which uses life at the Toronto Normal School as its background.

The most exciting territory for the local colourist was the new land opening up in the West and the North. Sir Gilbert Parker had worked this foreign territory well prior to 1900, and he continued to use it as a backdrop in books like *Northern lights* (1909), *You never know your luck* (1914), *The world for sale* (1916), and *Wild youth and another* (1919). The works of Samuel Alexander White's *The stampeder* (1910) and Agnes Laut's overwritten epic *Lords of the North* (1900) contain a similar sense of distance from the reality of western life, but the western novels of Ralph Connor—including *The sky pilot: a tale of the foothills* (Chicago, 1899) and *The foreigner* (1909)—Nellie McCLUNG's *Sowing seeds in Danny* (1908), Robert STEAD's early novels, and the ranching novels of Arthur STRINGER reveal a more intimate knowledge of the region. British Columbia, especially its mining and logging areas, provided inspiration for Frederick NIVEN, Bertrand Sinclair, and others. Sinclair's *Burned bridges* (1919) is an especially interesting study of the power of the environment as a redemptive force in the life of a disillusioned minister who has retreated from eastern cities. Martin Allerdale GRAINGER's single work, *Woodsmen of the West* (1908), provides perhaps the best picture of life in the forests of British Columbia. The Yukon and the rest of the North influenced several writers, both Canadian and American, but Robert SERVICE's *The trail of '98* (1911) is the most memorable novel about this region.

For many authors who wrote about these various parts of Canada, the country provided a useful backdrop for action and adventure stories. Susan Jones used Halifax and the North in *A detached pirate* (1903) and *A god of the North* (1900) respectively; William Amy ('Luke Allan') exploited the West and Roger Pocock the Far West, the Rockies, in *Jesse of Cariboo* (1911). (On the other hand, Frank PACKARD, in his series of Jimmie Dale crime novels, exploited the

New York underworld.) For some writers, however, setting became a starting-point for the exploration of thematic material as they looked outside themselves for themes that reflected their society, and saw almost everything in an optimistic light. Friction between French and English in Canada was destined to disappear, according to the works of Sir Gilbert Parker, as the best qualities of both races blended in new generations of Canadians. Likewise the conflict between religious and social groups in the small-town novels of W.A. Fraser, Marian Keith, and others diminished as invidivuals overcame inherited prejudices. The new communities growing in the West would be integrated into the older civilization of the East, to their mutual benefit. Connor's missionary preachers were especially adept at interpreting the two regions to each other. The social discontent that grew with urbanization, industrialization, and the appearance of new classes was expressed in the wit and satire of Stephen Leacock's ARCADIAN ADVENTURES WITH THE IDLE RICH (1914); but the fundamental goodness of individuals on both sides of the conflict determined the conclusion of most novels that examined the issue. Even the animal stories of Charles G.D. Roberts show man as the unchallenged master of this earth, able to overcome all dangers and difficulties with his intelligence and will.

Any literary theory that appeared to focus on man's frailty or the hollowness of his ideals found little support in Canada. The realism of Zola was anathema to the Canadian literary community at this time, and the late-nineteenth-century American realism of William Dean Howells was imported only rarely, as in Duncan's *The imperialist*. The idealism of these authors was inextricably linked to the conventions of the literary romance. Larger-than-life characters, exaggerated emotions, episodic plots, a central love story, and the neat resolution of all story elements were the basic ingredients of most novels. Still, the inspiration for many works changed as writers shifted towards characters and incidents based on their own observations. Connor drew on his recollections of life in Glengarry, his experiences as a missionary, and his work as a pastor in Winnipeg, and Charles G.D. Roberts stressed constantly that his stories of animal life were based on his close observations in the New Brunswick woods of his youth. Writers increasingly insisted on the 'reality' of their stories. They did so, however, while staying within the limitations of the romantic conventions that supported their idealism and generated sales. The best writers of this period were able to adapt inherited literary conventions to the expression of their observations of contemporary experience.

CAL SMILEY

1920 to 1940. As more than 750 novels were published in this period, the discussion that follows is necessarily selective. Nevertheless, it reflects a period in Canadian fiction when the realistic novel emerges, the regional novel reaches its high point, and the psychological influences of the twentieth century begin to be felt. Nature moves to the background as man moves to the centre; yet the acute sense of place on which Canadian fiction is based continues to dominate. The period contains many literary curiosities because of the strangely fragmented fiction of the time.

1. WESTERN NOVELS. The Prairies are the dominant setting of these twenty years. In 1920 Arthur STRINGER published *The prairie mother*, the second book—coming between *The prairie wife* (1915) and *The prairie child* (1922)—in his sprawling trilogy dealing with the harshness of the environment and asking questions about the reasons for marriage, and why opposites attract, only to create impossible situations. Robert J.C. STEAD, in 1921, published the first of his romances about prairie life, *Neighbours*, followed by *The smoking flax* (1924), a novel that offers a credible social portrait of the time, though the plot is too romantic for today's taste. In Stead's most significant book, *Grain* (1929)—an examination of why young men leave the farm—his writing is more mature and precise. Nina Jamieson's *The hickory stick* (1921) focused more on a moral—that life's greatest moments are those spent in service to others—than on a setting. In the same year William Lacy Amy ('Luke Allen') romanticized the prairie setting with his *Blue Pete, half breed* (1921), the first of a series, whose hero is a reformed cattle hustler from the States who becomes an agent for the North West Mounted Police—an attempt to give to western Canada some of the frontier quality of the American 'wild west'. William DURKIN, conversely, focused on an urban centre, Winnipeg, in *The magpie* (1923), the story of a First World War veteran who witnesses social unrest in the city and decides to return to his home farm, where he can maintain his integrity.

In terms of form and content the most successful and popular prairie fiction in this period was by Laura Goodman SALVERSON, Martha OSTENSO, and Frederick Philip GROVE. In *The Viking heart* (1923) Salverson discusses the first Icelandic colony's problems in the lake area of Manitoba; its psychological subtleties have stood the test of time. Martha Ostenso's *Wild geese* (1925), which won an international book prize that brought attention to Canadian writing in the rest of the world, is a story of harsh pioneer life, with a complex plot and psychologically interesting characters. Grove, of course, is the dominant voice of prairie fiction in this period. His *Settlers of the marsh* (1925) is an attempt to portray pioneer life realistically, though the characterizations are too grotesque to be true; it was followed by *Our daily bread* (1928), *The yoke of life* (1930), and *Fruits of the earth* (1933). Other writers who used the prairie landscape as setting were Beaumont Cornell in *Lantern marsh* (1923), which presents some amateur psychology in the life of a minister and teacher; Ethel Grayson in *Willow smoke* (1928), an excellent study of prairie immigrant life; and John Beames, whose trilogy about 'Gateway', Sask.—*An army without borders* (1930), *Gateway* (1932), and *Duke* (1933)—are about farming in the West, grain, and hardships. Winifred Reeve ('Onoto Watanna') wrote a less realistic account of immigrant life on the prairie in *Cattle* (1932), which focused on American-type violence in the West. Harold Baldwin's *Pelicans in the sky* (1934) attempted to counterbalance those books that talked of life on the Prairies as idyllic by exposing the harrowing homestead conditions of the immigrant. Alberta was the special focus for John Herries McCulloch when he told of English immigrant life there in *Dark acres* (1935). Jessie L. Beattie took a melodramatic approach to the conflicts of religion and art in prairie life in *Hill-top* (1935), to be followed by *Three measures* (1938) on a similar theme. By far the most interesting of all the prairie novels of this period is *Forgotten men* (1935) by Claudius Jabez Gregory, who used his novel for social criticism in a story of a man who creates a society of twelve for performing good works among the poor, is betrayed to the capitalist system by 'Jude', and eventually dies in prison: an interest in myth was making an appearance in Canadian fiction. A literary curiosity of the Prairies is Bertram BROOKER's *Think of the earth* (1936), a story of hallucination and mystery on a small Manitoba farm that won the first Governor General's Award for fiction. A writer who devoted her time to extolling the importance of community service within a new pioneer settlements, and its strengthening effect on the family unit, was Ethel Chapman in *God's green country* (1922), *The homesteaders* (1936), and *With flames of freedom* (1938). Wilfrid Eggleston in *The high plains* (1938) attempted to portray the hard life of new settlers of the dry prairie; its imagery is reminiscent at times of T.S. Eliot.

Few novelists in this period used British Columbia as a setting. Among those who did was Bruce McKelvie in *Hulgowet: a story of the North Pacific Coast* (1926), an intriguing account of the Indians and the magic and mystery of their culture; this was followed by *The black canyon* (1927), a story of western settlement, and *Pelts and powder* (1929), about the western pioneer. Alexander Maitland Stephen wrote *The kingdom of the sun* (1927), a romance of early British Columbia with good characterizations, and *A gleaming archway* (1929), a carefully plotted novel that focuses on the labour movement in Vancouver. One of the most important books to come out of British Columbia in this period was Irene BAIRD's *Waste heritage* (1939), a most impressive examination of Depression tensions in Vancouver; this well-written, solid work is frequently cited as the best social-history novel of its time.

2. HISTORICAL FICTION. Historical romances were highly popular in this period. While most treated Canadian subjects, several authors offered fictional treatments of a wide variety of foreign places in historical times. Lily Adams BECK ('E. Barrington') wrote a long list of popular historical romances with an emphasis on love interest. Virna Sheard wrote a peculiar Elizabethan romance in *Fortune turns her wheel* (1929); and W.G. Hardy, a professor of classics at the University of Alberta, began his career of writing lusty novels on biblical and classical themes with *Father Abraham* (1935), about the Old Testament patriarch, and *Turn back the river* (1938), a novel of ancient Rome.

Among Canadian subjects, New France was by far the most popular, inviting easy exploration of a picturesque setting, quaint customs, adventurous deeds, and high drama. Most such books were sentimental romances of no real literary merit: Joseph P. Choquet, *Under Canadian skies: a French-Canadian historical romance* (1922); Edward Montague Ashworth ('John Abbot'), *La*

Roux (1924) and *The seigneurs of La Saulage: gentlemen adventurers of New France* (1928); Anna Ermatinger Fraser, *The drum of Lanoraye: a narrative of the days of Talon, the Great Intendant* (1932); John C.L. Hudgson, *Lion and Lily: a story of New France* (1935); and Leslie Gordon Barnard, *Jancis* (1936). Two novels of New France, however, had a more serious purpose than popularizing a colourful period in Canadian history. Franklin Davy McDowell's *The Champlain road* (1939), winner of a Governor General's Award, is the story of the variety of religious aspirations and personality conflicts of the major characters at the time of the martyrdom of Brébeuf and the destruction of the Huron missions. Philip CHILD's *The village of souls* (1933), also taking place in the seventeenth century, is coloured by twentieth-century values of a Christian humanist. The West was a favourite region for treatment by historical novelists (some of whose works have already been mentioned). For a moment in 1930—to judge by reviewers' praise—it seemed that the great Canadian novel had been written and the great Canadian novelist discovered when E. Jean McDougall ('Jane Rolyat') published *The lily of Fort Garry* (1930), a novel whose convincing background of life in the Red River Settlement is vitiated by romantic sub-plots related in sonorous prose—of which this novelist's fickle public seemed to have tired when she presented them with *Wilderness walls* (1933), a romantic novel about a Hudson's Bay Company post on Lake Huron in the 1860s.

The history of Ontario and the Atlantic provinces provided fewer examples of straight historical fiction than of the regional idyll set in the past. The leading exponent of this genre was Mazo DE LA ROCHE, who focused on southwestern Ontario in *Possession* (1923), *Delight* (1926), and *JALNA* (1927), the award-winning novel that began the Whiteoak family saga. Augustus Bridle (1869-1952), in *Hansen: a novel of Canadianization* (1924), treated the problems of a farm labourer of Swedish origin in southwestern Ontario whose progress paralleled that of his adopted country. John Elson's *The scarlet sash: a romance of the Niagara frontier* (1925), about the War of 1812, and Mabel Dunham's *The trail of the Conestoga* (1924), about the trek of Mennonites to Ontario's Grand River district, are straight historical novels. The classic account of pioneer life in Ontario, however, is *The yellow briar* (1933; rpr. 1971) by John MITCHELL ('Patrick

Slater'), a book that is still read with enjoyment. Moving to the east, Jessie Archibald's *The token: a tale of Cape Breton Island in the days before Confederation* (1930) is a melodramatic tale of survival that appealed to Canadian readers at the beginning of the Depression. Frank Parker DAY in *John Paul's rock* (1932) told the story of the plight of an Indian banished to a rock on the Atlantic coast; and in *The eye of the gull* (1936) and *Cold pastoral* (1939) Margaret DULEY wrote very convincingly of isolation, survival, and alienation in Newfoundland outposts.

3. OTHER FICTION. Spurning the historical and idyllic themes of popular novelists, one of the leading writers of this period, Morley CALLAGHAN, turned to the urban environment and the psychological problems of his characters to produce modern fiction reflecting the concerns of the time in which it was written. Callaghan's *Strange fugitive* (1928), which examines the question of how one fits into city life, was followed by *A native argosy* (1929), a collection of short stories; *It's never over* (1930), about the reaction to a criminal's execution for murder; *A broken journey* (1932), about the relationship of a mother and daughter with the daughter's suitor; *Such is my beloved* (1934), one of his best novels, about two prostitutes and a priest driven mad by society's hypocrisy; *They shall inherit the earth* (1935), about a guilt-ridden hero's destruction by society; and MORE JOY IN HEAVEN (1937), which portrays the hero/saint/sinner conflict. Psychological tension was also portrayed in Raymond KNISTER's *White narcissus* (1929), which centres on the difficult relationship between parents and daughter in rural Ontario. Other novels of the period that have psychological overtones are Ethel Grayson's *Apples of the moon* (1933), a university novel in which a professor's bitter wife kills herself; and *The new front line* (1927) by Hubert EVANS, a study of a man who hates to make decisions and whose mental paralysis is solved by chance.

As the focus shifted from the country to the city, some writers, grasping a satirical pen, examined the ridiculous in contemporary society. Madge Macbeth in *The land of afternoon* (1924) ironically examined the political/social life in Ottawa, but her wit was buried by heavy characterization; her novel, *The kinder bees* (1935), used a similar theme. There were also Victor Lauriston's *Inglorious Milton* (1934), a mock epic of small-town *literati*, and the first two novels by Fred Jacob (1882-1926) of a planned (but never completed) four-part satire of Canadian life in the first quarter of the twentieth century: *Day before yesterday* (1925), about the decline of upper-class domination in a small Ontario town, and *Peevee* (1928), about the posturings and affectations of a rising middle class. Francis Pollock's *Jupiter eight* (1936) also exposes the ridiculous in a society undergoing rapid social change.

Though Canadian fiction in this period lacked originality, there was no question of its survival. Popular fiction was rife in these two decades, meeting the demands of a public who loved to read and to be entertained by simple action and everyday characters. But it should not be forgotten that the fiction of this time was grasping at new forms and insights that would provide the basis of the 'new' fiction of the forties and onwards, even though most of writers of 1920 to 1940 did not turn their novels into achievements of enduring significance.

DONALD STEPHENS

1940 to 1960. English-Canadian fiction in this period shows few signs of forming a coherent literary pattern. There is no sense of a national movement, of predominant themes and approaches, of an accepted novelistic technique, or even of a concerted attempt to express Canadian or mid-twentieth-century consciousness. Instead, individual writers go their own ways, searching for the fictional modes that suit them best, and sometimes finding them. The two decades produced some major works—*As for me and my house* (1941), *Who has seen the wind* (1947), *The mountain and the valley* (1952), *The double hook* (1959), *The watch that ends the night* (1959), and (if Malcolm Lowry counts as Canadian) *Under the volcano* (1947). They also saw the emergence of several important novelists: Hugh MacLennan, Ethel Wilson, Robertson Davies, and Mordecai Richler. But these titles and names provide evidence of an abundant but bewildering variety of response about which generalizations are well-nigh impossible.

The period opens, of course, at the end of one traumatic national experience, the Depression, and the beginning of another, the Second World War. Such crises offer rich subject-matter for novelists. The Prairies were especially vulnerable to the hard times of the 1930s, and Sinclair ROSS provides an unforgettable image of the effects of the Depression, psychological as well as social, in AS FOR ME AND MY HOUSE (1941). Unemployment in urban areas is another prominent topic, and Hugh MacLENNAN's vivid descriptions of Montreal at this time create a memorable background to the main action in *The watch that ends the night* (1959). But, with the notable exception of Hugh GARNER's *Cabbagetown* (which appeared in a shortened version in 1950, the complete text not being published until 1968), the emphasis falls rarely on social issues as such. The writers of this period use the Depression years as a time in which public issues inevitably impinge upon the private lives of their characters. As for the war, Hugh MacLennan subtly and effectively wrote of the First World War in BAROMETER RISING (1941) and also in TWO SOLITUDES (1945), which begins in 1917 and ends in 1939, but invited his contemporary readers to compare the effects of the earlier conflict with those of their own time. The most impressive fictional record of Canadian *participation* in the Second World War is to be found in Colin McDougall's *Execution* (1958), which chronicled the Italian campaign with documentary detail and imaginative force.

There is one general trend, moreover, that needs to be noticed. The two novelists who had established themselves as preeminent in the previous twenty years were Frederick Philip GROVE and Morley CALLAGHAN. Callaghan had always been an urban novelist and continued to write, primarily about Montreal, in our period. Grove was known as a novelist of farm and prairie, but in his last conventional novel, *The master of the mill* (1944), he turned his attention to the industrial processes that transform farm produce into marketable commodities. It is a saga of the Industrial Revolution, and although many writers continue to find congenial and absorbing material in rural areas, the fiction of 1940-60 begins to show an increasing awareness of the fact that Canada was rapidly being transformed into a modern industrial nation.

It has often been remarked that, because Canada is a vast country composed of scattered pockets of population, its literature is inevitably regional in inspiration and character. Certainly geographical areas (even excluding the special circumstances of language and culture in Québec) vary in ways that, in other parts of the world, are reflected in different countries rather than different provinces, and in Canada this characteristic is not so obviously offset, as it is in the United States, with a drive towards cultural uniformity. The diversity of regions attracted a comparable diversity of immigrants whose literature was naturally influenced by their different origins and traditions and, although the individual writer does not necessarily portray or reflect his own region, a regional breakdown of the novelists of this period is as convenient a division as any.

Since the Maritimes have a long history of fortified settlements and national rivalries for command of the Atlantic seaboard, it is not surprising that the region should produce a number of historical novelists. The most important of these is undoubtedly Thomas H. RADDALL. His stories are more properly classified as romances, since they involve strong plots, heroes and villains, action and excitement; but his historical research is impeccable, and in novels like *His Majesty's Yankees* (1942), *Roger Sudden* (1944) and *Pride's fancy* (1946) he tapped a rich vein of novelistic ore that he skilfully blended with authentic local history. His short stories are equally impressive, and although his more modern novels have been less successful, *The nymph and the lamp* (1950) is a deeply moving study in loneliness and personal relationships. In *The mountain and the valley* (1952), Ernest BUCKLER succeeded in catching the essence of a sensitive childhood in the Annapolis Valley through verbal pyrotechnics that dazzle some and weary others. David Canaan, like his creator, is fascinated by words and their capacity to reflect and encompass his community. In this Maritime *Bildungsroman* technical sophistication raises local subject-matter to universal relevance. Charles BRUCE's *The channel shore* (1954) just fails to transcend its regional matrix. Because it is written in an unostentatious, rather flat prose, the book has been unjustly neglected; but it succeeds admirably in conveying a sense of place and period that is at the same time representative of a broader human experience. In *Barometer rising* (1941) Hugh MacLennan demonstrated that a local setting, Halifax at the time of the great explosion in 1917, could be the subject for a significant fiction, and both here and in *Each man's son* (1951), set in his native Cape Breton, he explored the Puritan heritage that other writers—Robertson Davies, for instance—have seen as a central experience for Canada as a whole.

Though a Maritimer by birth, MacLennan has lived most of his life in Québec. *Two solitudes* (1945) embodies the tensions between Anglo-Canadian and French-Canadian in a work that, while still impressive, seems too obviously didactic and too artificially resolved to fit the complexities of the contemporary situation. His best novel, *The watch that ends the night* (1959), is more personal in its origins, and effectively catches the dilemma of an ordinary decent man trying to make sense of a bewildering, hostile world. Above all, it combines social and political concerns with a personal religious urgency. None the less, MacLennan has always been a somewhat stiff novelist whose matter is invariably more important than his manner. Mordecai RICHLER, on the other hand, began with an awesome mastery of the craft of fiction, which predominates over his material in his first novel, *The acrobats* (1954), about expatriates in Spain. Unparalleled for his energy and an ability to catch the essence of ordinary life and speech, Richler focused his attention on Jewish life and morality in *Son of a smaller hero* (1955) and *The apprenticeship of Duddy Kravitz* (1959). In so doing he portrayed a very different Montreal from that of MacLennan and Callaghan, who in *The loved and the lost* (1951) and *The many colored coat* (1960) built strong if somewhat diffuse stories against backgrounds of racial and class tensions respectively.

The fictional production of Ontario during this period is decidedly disappointing. The only event of permanent literary interest was the emergence of Robertson DAVIES, who became known as a playwright during the 1940s and went on to publish his first three novels—the Salterton 'trilogy'—in the 1950s. In *Tempest-tost* (1951) his dramatic interests provide the subject-matter for the fiction, since the plot revolves around an amateur production of *The tempest* in Davies' imaginary small city modelled on Kingston. It is a polished, witty, satiric, but for the most part good-natured, comedy of manners that deftly pokes fun at characteristic Anglo-Canadian attitudes. Davies takes over the mantle of Stephen LEACOCK, but shows a capacity for sustained narrative that Leacock never possessed. The two later books, *Leaven of malice* (1954) and *A mixture of frailties* (1958), maintain the standard of wit and comedy but simultaneously sound deeper notes. The former touches upon the nature of evil that was to absorb Davies in his subsequent fiction; and the latter, the story of a young Canadian singer who gains a scholarship to study in London, may be seen as a Canadian version of Henry James's exploration of innocence and experience in his stories about Americans in Europe. There is nothing like Davies' work elsewhere in Canada. The combination in these early novels of high-spirited amusement, elegant prose, and especially a confidence in the ability of Canadians to laugh at themselves, was an essential ingredient in the maturation of Canadian fiction in English.

By contrast with Ontario, the Prairie Provinces enjoyed a fictional renaissance during these decades. The isolated prairie town or settlement offers a promising microcosm for the novelist, and the best-known of these is Sinclair ROSS's Horizon in AS FOR ME AND MY HOUSE (1941), with its grain-elevators, railway-tracks, chapel, and symbolic false-fronts. Ross achieves a claustrophobic intensity here, and the story of a minister's wife encountering hypocrisy in the community and in her own home finds a suitable, even inevitable setting for pent-up emotions and a sense of hopeless entrapment. But prairie towns need not resemble Horizon. W.O. MITCHELL's WHO HAS SEEN THE WIND (1947) presents a more positive picture. The egregious Mrs Abercrombie would have been at home in Ross's novel, but Mitchell's book encompasses the decent as well as the tyrannical, the touching as well as the depressing, the hilarious as well as the gloomy. Like Buckler's *The mountain and the valley*, it is a story of childhood, and Mitchell offers a sense of wonder, even a quest for godhead, alongside more traditional childhood subjects like gopher hunting and troubles at school. Mitchell writes with grace and eloquence, and communicates—as Ross does not—the ethnic variety of his prairie town, which includes Irish, Ukrainians, and Chinese.

Novels about immigrant settlers have always been frequent in the Prairies from the period of Frederick Philip Grove, Martha OSTENSO, and Laura SALVERSON onwards. During our period the tradition is maintained by Adele WISEMAN in *The sacrifice* (1956), a powerful if dour story of Jewish-Ukrainian immigrants, and also by John MARLYN in *Under the ribs of death* (1957), which portrays the difficulties of a young Hungarian in rising from his humble ethnic origins. It is symptomatic of the times that, whereas earlier fictional treatments of immigrants generally focused on farming communities, both these novels are set in Winnipeg. Finally, no survey of prairie fiction would be complete without mention of Patricia Blondal's posthumously published *A candle to light the sun* (1960), a hauntingly memorable, darkly effective story of a small town (Mouse Bluffs-Souris, Man.) that de-

Novels in English 1940 to 1960

serves to stand alongside the established fictional small towns of Ross, Mitchell, and (later) Margaret LAURENCE.

British Columbia in the 1940s and 1950s is dominated, so far as fiction is concerned, by three writers totally unlike each other. Malcolm LOWRY moved to Vancouver in 1939 and it was in a squatter's shack at Dollarton that the bulk of his masterpiece, *Under the volcano* (1947), was written. This richly textured, technically innovative story of the last day in the life of Geoffrey Firmin, an English ex-consul in Mexico, contains little that is Canadian save the sense of peace that made the writing possible. British Columbia always represented an idyllic haven for Lowry, and it became the setting for the completed but not finally polished novel, *October ferry to Gabriola*, which did not appear until 1970, thirteen years after Lowry's death. Lowry was a harried, tormented genius. By contrast, Ethel WILSON lived a quiet, uneventful life in Vancouver writing her serene, compassionate, beautifully cadenced novels, all of which fall within this period. In her full-length fiction she writes almost exclusively of women with a dextrous combination of sensitivity and acute intelligence. Since she strove for quality rather than quantity, her output (five novels and a volume of short stories) is small but consistently excellent. Her abilities are shown at their best in *The innocent traveller* (1949), a gentle and amusing story of a centenarian, and *Swamp angel* (1954), about two women who must find their satisfaction in lives of contrasting solitude. Sheila WATSON, even less productive than Wilson, has established a well-deserved reputation with a single novel, *The double hook* (1959), a spare, sophisticated work set in the Cariboo district that uses the techniques of poetry to achieve fictional complexity and economy. Details and words are reduced to a minimum, and the basic human emotions become all the more powerful when filtered through the highly metaphorical but firmly controlled prose.

Naturally there are a number of significant novels that bear no relation to their area of origin. Philip CHILD's *Day of wrath* (1945), set in Nazi Germany; A.M. KLEIN's *The second scroll* (1951), concerned with the founding of modern Israel; Earle BIRNEY's *Turvey* (1949), a comic novel about the Second World War; Fred BODSWORTH's *The last of the curlews* (1954), continuing the worthy tradition of the Canadian animal-story—all transcend or elude any regional category. Brian MOORE, a 'bird of passage' like Lowry, first attracted attention with *Judith Hearne* (1956) but wrote of Canada only at the close of this period in *The luck of Ginger Coffey* (1959). Even Henry KREISEL's *The rich man* (1948), though portraying a Canadian immigrant, takes place for the most part in Austria on the brink of Nazi occupation. And Frederick Philip Grove's *Consider her ways* (1947) is the account of an expedition of Venezuelan ants to New York City!

The literary historian can point to general trends and trace certain significant developments, but the course of literary history is never smooth. The period 1940-60 is especially muddied. It produced a number of novelists who were aware of exciting possibilities and by no means prepared to subordinate their individual preferences to a communal literary theory. All that can be said in conclusion is that a literature that encompasses the work of Buckler, MacLennan, Callaghan, Richler, Davies, Ross, Mitchell, Lowry, Wilson, and Watson may seem chaotic and directionless to a systematizer but is none the less in a healthy creative state. Many of these writers—notably MacLennan, Richler, and Davies—have extended their reputations in the years since 1960. Others can now be regarded as significant influences on younger writers; examples include Grove's impact upon Rudy WIEBE, and the encouragement Margaret Laurence derived from the praise of Wilson and the achievement of Ross. The flowering of the Canadian novel in English since 1960 was made possible by the all-important solid foundation laid by the talented, persistent, often lonely writers of the previous two decades.   W.J. KEITH

1960 to 1982. With a handful of exceptions Canada's best novels and stories have been written in the past two decades. One very clear indication of this is that Canadian fiction writers are better known abroad than at any time since the heydays of Mazo de la Roche and Stephen Leacock: Margaret Laurence, Robertson Davies, Mordecai Richler, Mavis Gallant, Margaret Atwood, Alice Munro, Norman Levine and Michael Ondaatje all have international reputations. Another is the large number of interesting second-order writers who have appeared during the period whose work shows more than just competence or mere craftsmanship.

There is now enough modern Canadian

fiction of high quality to render inapplicable Northrop FRYE's observation of 1965 that 'if evaluation is one's guiding principle, criticism of Canadian literature would become only a debunking project, leaving it a poor naked *alouette* plucked of every feather of decency and dignity' ('Conclusion', *Literary history of Canada*). The evaluative principles underlying the following assessment of some recent Canadian fiction are intended to suggest, among other things, how far we have come since then. (This discussion is supplemented by another, OTHER TALENTS, OTHER WORKS, which begins on page 587.)

1. What may seem like an arbitrary date, 1960, chosen for convenience, marks the vague boundary between the old and the new in Canadian fiction. In the past two decades almost none of the writers whose reputations were established between 1930 and 1960 produced work that reached the standard set by their earlier major fiction, or that would cause us to revise significantly our critical opinions about them. After 1960 Morley CALLAGHAN, for example, wrote novels as different as *A passion in Rome* (1961) and *Close to the sun again* (1977), but his now-precarious reputation still rests on the moral fables of the 1930s. Similarly Ernest BUCKLER's ambitious novels *The cruelest month* (1963) and *The rebellion of young David and other stories* (1975) simply restate, with interesting variations, the rural situations, and moral and aesthetic concerns, of *The mountain and the valley* (1952). In Callaghan there is an almost embarrassing decline, most obvious in an element of near self-parody; in Buckler, as in Sinclair ROSS (*Sawbones memorial*, 1974), there is modulated repetition.

The cases of Adele Wiseman, W.O. Mitchell, and Hugh MacLennan are more complicated. Adele WISEMAN's *The sacrifice* (1956) is still her most completely successful and challenging novel; but, though its scope is less ambitious, *Crackpot* (1974), also set in Winnipeg, has Wiseman's most vividly realized character: Hoda, the fat daughter of physically disabled Jewish immigrant parents, who drifts into adolescent sexuality and prostitution. Though the strength and success of this realistic and formally conventional novel depend on its creation of the central figure—a fully human individual whose life, though characterized by deprivation and pain (in one scene she delivers her own child), is paradoxically affirmative—the author also deals with large social issues: immigration, lower-class life, the Win-

nipeg General Strike, and the Depression.

W.O. MITCHELL's most ambitious novel of the period, *The vanishing point* (1973), set largely on a Stony Indian reservation, deals with a white administrator-teacher's attempts to bridge the gap between the white and Indian ways of life, one of which is through his love for a young Indian girl, symbolically named Victoria, whose disappearance into the city instigates a desperate search. The search lends an air of compelling mystery to a novel imbued with crucial social issues. Though *The vanishing point* is weakened by Mitchell's failure to portray the well-meaning Sinclair as successfully as some secondary characters (the canny Indian, Archie Nicotine, and the evangelical con-man Heally Richards), parts of the novel are characteristically lively and its perceptions and dramatizations of contemporary Indian life are always convincing. The ironic grade-school title of Mitchell's *How I spent my summer holidays* (1981) suggests a reprise of his classic *Who has seen the wind* (1947). But despite the similarities in setting, character, and theme—both these prairie novels present a boy's growth into adult awareness—*How I spent my summer holidays* is a sombre mystery novel involving murder, insanity, and suicide as seen from the points of view of a boy and of the man he becomes. The 'adult' narrative frame, which emphasizes the difficulty of recalling and interpreting the past, is solemn and deliberately Proustian; the middle is lighter in tone, occasionally farcical, with much of the social comedy one expects from Mitchell. Both of Mitchell's later novels, however, are overshadowed by *Who has seen the wind*.

Hugh MacLENNAN's futurist novel *Voices in time* (1980) envisions the end of Western civilization, and even of man. The setting is Québec, the year is 2030, and the world has survived the great devastation of the cities around the year 1990. The novel's past is our present, and the attempt by the hero, John Wellfleet, to reconstruct the past from tapes, diaries, letters, and documents—the 'voices in time'—constitutes MacLennan's analysis of a self-destruction that derives from the crumbling of traditional values and beliefs, and the waning of the Greco-Christian world view. The novel's real hero is western man, and its tragedy is man's persistence in repeating history. As one would expect of MacLennan, this is a didactic and unrelievedly solemn book. Less a novel than a fictionalized treatise, *Voices in time* should be read as a *summa* of MacLennan's values—

articulated more explicitly and more dog-matically here than in any of his other novels.

2. Robertson DAVIES published his first three novels in the 1950s, but unlike the writers discussed above, he has earned his reputation as a major novelist, as well as his almost unchallenged status as a serious popular thinker or pundit, for his work of the past decade or so, including *The rebel angels* (1981). Discussion of his first three novels—*Tempest-tost* (1951), *Leaven of malice* (1954), and *A mixture of frailties* (1958), with which Davies began to introduce ideas and concepts into his fiction—tends to focus on his comic vision. By contrast, criticism of the Deptford trilogy—FIFTH BUSINESS (1970), *The manticore* (1972), and *World of wonders* (1975)—has emphasized their psychological and religious dimensions and Davies' substantial debt to C.G. Jung: although still often comic and satiric, they are as explicitly ideological as any novels in Canadian literature. Davies' concern in these later works has been with man's need to acknowledge the emotional, irrational, and unconscious side of the self: as Liesl tells Dunstan Ramsay in *Fifth business*, it is necessary to shake hands with one's own devil—advice that could stand as an epigraph for the novels that follow, whose heroes or heroines try to come to terms with the darkness within. All the Deptford novels take the form of a confession, have essentially the same theme, and are written in the same easy, witty, and aphoristic style, borrowing their images and symbols from a common store of relatively arcane lore. There is little doubt that *Fifth business* is Davies' masterpiece. It succeeds so well because we see or experience Dunstan Ramsay aging and developing page by page, and because Davies manages to integrate into the theme, style, and structure Ramsay's interest in hagiography. The succeeding novels strike one as too static, cluttered with the flotsam of Davies' store of learning, and—surprising in a distinguished dramatist, drama scholar, and critic—less dramatic. After *Fifth business* the scholar-didact overrules the novelist and the reader finds himself sitting through painless, often witty, lectures on psychology, religion, and art. Davies' novels are elegant, informed, and entertaining; but they share a certain disconnection between the potentially disruptive subject matter and the restrained if magisterial manner of telling.

Like Davies, Mordecai RICHLER established his reputation in the 1950s with four novels, the last of which, *The apprenticeship of Duddy Kravitz* (1959), is perhaps the most successful. *St. Urbain's horseman* (1971) and *Joshua then and now* (1980) mine deeper in the same vein. Richler has called them 'naturalistic novels', or novels of 'character', to distinguish them from his 'straight satires', *The incomparable Atuk* (1963) and *Cocksure* (1968), which tend towards the fantastic, grotesque, and farcical. Yet the strain of black humour is already present in the Virgil Duff episodes in *Duddy Kravitz*, and much of Richler's moral concern in *Horseman* and *Joshua* is expressed through satire. His disgust with the attitudes and values of civilization—virulent and direct in the satires and essays—finds a more controlled and sublimated expression in the novels proper. *St. Urbain's horseman*, Richler's best novel since *Duddy Kravitz*, is his most ambitious in theme and most complex in form. The central concern, common in Richler's work, is the individual's preoccupation with his personal, socio-historical, and generic or racial pasts. (His heroes' struggles for freedom are a function of their attempts to understand the past.) Jake Hersh, a Montreal Jew now living in London, England, is undergoing a slightly early mid-life crisis precipitated by his inadvertent involvement in a sex crime. Though acquitted, he is nevertheless prey to the free-floating anxiety and guilt, for things he has and hasn't done, of a middle-class Jewish intellectual. The novel judges, and even condemns, Jake and his generation. Jake's own values are embodied in an ambivalent personal fantasy about his cousin Joey Hersh, whom he idealizes as the avenging Jewish Horseman now hunting the Nazi, Dr Joseph Mengele, through the jungles of South America. The Horseman's life of action and moral commitment compensates, at least on the level of illusion, for Jake's unease about his failure as a film-maker and his residual guilt about his exclusion from significant twentieth-century events—the Spanish Civil War, Auschwitz, the founding of Israel, and so on. Some of Jake's discontent stems from his Jewishness—he is from the same neighbourhood as Duddy Kravitz—but it is a measure of Richler's development as a novelist that the Jewish hero is now treated as a representative modern man. In *St. Urbain's horseman*, as in the disappointingly predictable *Joshua then and now*, Richler has made modern society and modern history his subject, and within that larger canvas has done his most significant work to date.

Irish-born novelist Brian MOORE lived in Canada between 1948 and 1959 and his writing career began here with the publication in 1955 of *Judith Hearne*. Moore is one of the most natural and readable novelists on the contemporary North American literary scene in the sense that he's so obviously comfortable with the telling of a story. His early novels, like *Judith Hearne* (still considered by many to be his finest), dealt with shabby, frustrated lives in which the individual struggles unsuccessfully for self-definition and fulfilment; the best that can be hoped for is a clearing away of illusions and a recognition of the personal and public constraints upon the self. This holds as well for the late novels like *The doctor's wife* (1976), *The Mangan inheritance* (1979), and *The temptation of Eileen Hughes* (1981), the first and third of which move from the mundane to the spiritual in a way that recalls the fiction of Graham Greene, but Moore is much more committed to exploring the play between eros and society, and the resultant frustrations and renunciations. His major characters, who are usually women, often discover themselves—or the possibilities of a fuller life—by discovering their own sexuality. His later characters, like Sheila Redden in *The doctor's wife*, also discover the proximity between profane and sacred love, and the complications arising out of the quest for freedom and/or fulfilment.

Mavis GALLANT is best known for her short stories, most of which first appeared in *The New Yorker*. Living in Paris, she was not an influential presence in Canada during the sixties and seventies, yet one cannot ignore her unique importance, both for her ironic world view and as a stylist, among Canadian writers of fiction. The epigraph, from Edith Wharton, to her novel *A fairly good time* (1970)—'If you make up your mind not to be happy, there's no reason why you shouldn't have a fairly good time'—might apply to all her fiction. Happiness is beyond the reach of most of her characters, who are for the most part discontented expatriates (physically or psychologically or both), unable to overcome the restraining habits, attitudes, and beliefs imposed by relationships, families, class, or history. Gallant's style—exemplary in its control of tone, telling detail, balance, and economy—depends, like her vision, on nuance, on slightly disconcerting qualifications and shifts of syntax and meaning that sometimes evoke an ambivalent response in the reader. Gallant is usually content to dra-matize and describe a complex situation without bringing it to any resolution. The full meaning and significance of her stories, which often have endings without closure, resist easy summation.

Unlike Gallant, Margaret LAURENCE had a central influence during the literary renaissance of the 1960s and 1970s. Showing the way by example, she became a creative godmother to an entire generation. Her four Canadian novels and one collection of stories, set in the fictional town of Manawaka, Man., represent an ambitious and impressive attempt to write a comprehensive regional fiction that ultimately has universal concerns. Manawaka embodies both an era and a way of life. Laurence is also a feminist writer of authority who, implicitly and explicitly, anticipates the work of later writers as different as Marian Engel, Margaret Atwood, Jane Rule, Audrey Thomas, and Margaret Gibson. If, however, her recurring central theme is a woman's search for self-understanding and personal fulfilment, this always hinges on a simultaneous concern with the self's problematic relationship to her community. Self and community, or society, are ultimately inseparable: to define oneself is an aspect of defining one's community and one's past. This emphasis stands out in Laurence's most ambitious novel, *The diviners* (1974). Not as formally unified or as successful as her masterpiece *The STONE ANGEL* (1964), *The diviners* brings together all of Laurence's concerns; in effect it is a summary of her Manawaka world that contains brief appearances by, or references to, many characters from the other novels. As well, it is one of those works—*Two solitudes* is another—that marks, by its emphases and comprehensiveness, a moment in the evolution of a society's self-consciousness. Particularly significant is Laurence's attempt to articulate, through her semi-autobiographical heroine, Morag Gunn, the Canadian writer's struggle to deal with his or her past as both fiction and history. Laurence's act of divining involves remembering and interpreting 'private and fictional worlds', and worlds within which the private, communal, and historical combine. Where Hagar Currie in *The stone angel* and Rachel Cameron in *A jest of God* (1966) can be discussed and understood within an immediately personal context, Morag, through her relationships and her internal dialogues with the nineteenth-century pioneer Catharine Parr TRAILL, involves us in two centuries of Canadian life.

On the whole the Manawaka novels leave Canadian readers with the sense that not only do they share a roughly common past but that it can be the stuff of serious fiction.

Rudy WIEBE, like Laurence, is a western novelist whose work also centres on interpreting the personal and historical past. Wiebe is a Mennonite for whom the central fact of his experience is his belief in what he calls 'the Jesus vision'. This translates into a sometimes didactic, often innovative, fiction (his major novels and best stories are among our most successfully experimental) that is committed to a radical Christian vision. Seeing himself as doubly an outsider—a Christian and a westerner—he writes in opposition to the literary, social, political, and religious ideologies that he finds dominant in Canada. Wiebe's first important novel, *The blue mountains of China* (1970), takes place over almost a century of Mennonite history, including the heroic 1920s emigration from the Soviet Union to Canada and, later, to Paraguay. His fascination with communities anchored in a spiritual vision of the world underlies his interest in Canadian Indians, a group that resembles the Mennonites in this, and in the fact that it, too, exists on the periphery of offical history. *The temptations of Big Bear* (1973)—a difficult, often brilliant, novel that uses a complex polyphonic structure, incorporating much documentary material—covers the twelve years from Big Bear's refusal to sign a treaty in 1876, through his inadvertent involvement in the killings at Frog Lake in 1885, to his imprisonment and death. *The scorched-wood people* (1977), Wiebe's masterpiece and thought by some to be the finest Canadian novel of its generation, returns to the same period of history to focus on Louis Riel and the Métis. His portrait of Riel—historical revisionism with a vengeance—refuses to accept traditional interpretations: instead of presenting him as a madman, Wiebe depicts him—often in Christological images—as a visionary, the prophet of a vision of community. The posthumous narrator, Pierre FALCON, exists both in the novel's present time and in our own, and the startling double perspective leaves the reader with the uneasy feeling that Riel's radical Christian vision (a variant of Wiebe's own) is still 'alive' and offering a valid alternative to our contemporary world view. This is precisely the effect desired by Wiebe, who believes that the novel, because it criticizes our world and presents alternatives to it, is 'perhaps the most potent art form'.

(Several other novels have also dealt with minorities, or groups on the periphery of the Canadian mosiac, including Peter SUCH's *Riverrun* (1973), about the Beothuk Indians of Newfoundland, and Austin CLARKE's *Storm of fortune* (1973), about Barbadians living in Toronto. Particularly impressive—and as a first novel very promising—is Joy KOGAWA's docu-fiction *Obasan* (1981). Narrated by the teacher Nomi Nakane, it immerses the reader in the lives of Japanese Canadians interned during the Second World War.)

Although one almost instinctively assigns Margaret Laurence (b. 1926) and Margaret ATWOOD (b. 1939) to separate generations of writers, their careers for the most part overlap: Laurence's *The stone angel* (1964) and Atwood's first book of poems *The circle game* (1966) appeared within two years of each other. Since then, Atwood has achieved a substantial critical reputation and wide popularity with her prolific output of both poetry and fiction: 17 books in 16 years. One of the recurring themes or concerns in her fiction is the survival of the self, usually female, in a society whose personal and public relationships are characterized by alienation, domination, and exploitation. Her heroines often flee from a male-dominated society (frequently described in imagery of machines, guns, and cameras) that is inimical both to nature and to all that is natural within the self, and/or withdraw into the self, as in *Surfacing* (1972), *Lady Oracle* (1976), and *Bodily harm* (1981). The flight from society (a job) or a man (an affair or marriage) is often a rejection of an inauthentic self that the woman recognizes as having been formed in response to ultimately dehumanizing demands. A capitalist and patriarchal society dominated by rationality, industrialism, and conspicuous consumption has no place for the attitudes and desires expressed by Atwood's central figures. Atwood's heroines are articulate, sensitive, and self-reflective. Where there is first-person narrative, the voice is usually laconic, ironic and restrained, even flat, though capable of an occasional dark lyricism—the voice of someone who, if not actually frightened, is guarded or anxious, sensing the hostility latent in the society around her. In *The edible woman* (1969) and *Surfacing* the anxiety becomes a neurosis as the sensitive and sympathetic heroine fails to cope with the demands of a dehumanizing reality. Atwood's fiction concentrates on the existential situation, on the individual's essential isolation: all relationships are at best tenuous and tentative; the self is radically isolated both when it withdraws from, and when it returns to, society. The emphasis is predominantly subjective and psychological; we tend to remember the voices and emotional landscapes rather than the events of her novels, which nevertheless offer a wide-ranging criticism of contemporary Western society.

In most contemporary novels by women the point of view or 'voice' of the heroine usually assumes what Sartre calls a 'contestational' attitude towards society. One unfortunate, and perhaps inevitable, result of this has been the inability of most women novelists to create fully realized and memorable male characters. The major Canadian exception to this generalization is Alice MUNRO. Although her primary concern has always been with the 'lives of girls and women', some of the more memorable moments in her fiction have depended on exchanges between her heroines and sympathetically rendered males. The title story of *Who do you think you are?* (1978) recalls a casual middle-aged encounter between Rose, a successful actress visiting home, and Ralph Gillespie, a school friend now living on a navy pension. For Rose, as for the reader, the rather ordinary Gillespie is a mystery and remains elusive to the end; yet he is fully *there*. Sympathy for her subjects characterizes Munro's fiction. Her best work, *Lives of girls and women* (1971), is narrated by Del Jordan, a sensitive and articulate young woman who describes in eight interconnected stories her growth from childhood to early womanhood in the southwestern town of Jubilee. Del becomes aware that 'People's lives, in Jubilee as elsewhere, were dull, simple, amazing and unfathomable—deep caves paved with kitchen linoleum.' Despite her simple and realistic style, Munro is capable of surprising the reader with a supple and sensuous lyricism. Fidelity to the texture of female experience is balanced in Munro's work by an equal concern with evoking (not simply transcribing realistically) the feel of life in southwestern Ontario, an area with its own specific traditions and history where 'everything is touchable and mysterious'.

The emphasis on a place, area, or locale, rather on the more inclusive 'region', gives Munro's fiction an understated unity. That kind of unity is more apparent in the comic stories and novels of Jack HODGINS, for whom Vancouver Island functions both as a setting and as a subject with its own inherent interest. Hodgins repeatedly deals with a character, often an artist, who attempts to describe the island and its way of life. Maggie Kyle, the vital and erotic heroine of Hodgins' most complex and entertaining work, *The invention of the world* (1977), alerts the reader to the fact that while the Island can be described in many modes of discourse and representation—maps among them—its ultimate reality eludes everyone. Yet, as W.J. Keith has suggested, Hodgins' Vancouver Island must be approached primarily, or at least initially, as a fictive creation, a geography of the mind, much like Marquez's Macondo. Hodgins' impressive *oeuvre* is an implicit answer to those, like his character Julius Champney in *The invention of the world*, who follow Hawthorn and James in seeing no history in the New World and therefore no possibility of significant fiction. Champney's conservative and rationalist scepticism is expressed within a novel—by turns comic, mythic, farcical, and realistic—that asserts the contrary, while simultaneously indicating the limits of what art can say. Hodgins insists that significant and entertaining art *can* emerge from his particular 'edge' or 'periphery' of the world. Each of his books is organized, as Keith has pointed out, around a single unifying idea or image (separation, invention, resurrection, and invasion) embodied in situations usually dealing with the problematic and comic relationship between self and community. Hodgins' central characters have a vitality, spontaneity, and exuberance that resist the uniformity imposed by a settled society. Roughly analogous to what Hodgins' characters represent is the 'green island' itself which, despite man's inroads and invasions, is an always pristine reminder of the promise or possibility of Eden within and outside the self. Though fundamentally comic, Hodgins' vision is capable of embracing and dealing with a wide range of human emotions and experiences, while reminding us of aspects of life, from the poignant to the tragic, that normally resist the comic vision.

3. The writers discussed in the previous part of this survey were those whom I consider to be the major fiction writers of the last twenty years. Though some of the writers to be discussed below would be included in this category by other commentators, none has written a work of such scope, power, and human significance that we could confidently place it by the side of *The stone angel, Fifth business, The invention of the*

world, or *The scorched-wood people.* This sort of discrimination between major and minor recalls Northrop Frye's remark in the *Anatomy of criticism* about evaluative criticism smacking of the stock market; yet after performing all of its other functions, criticism inevitably judges and places the individual work of art within the tradition.

The most problematic moment in a critic's reading of contemporary literature occurs in the confrontation with an innovative text that challenges and rejects the presuppositions of the past. Robert KROETSCH, for example, is as determined as John Barth and Gabriel Garcia Marquez to resist and even reverse the conventions of traditional fiction. He writes in *The crow journals* (1980) that 'Symbolism may have spent its force, in its present form. But realism is not the answer. Rather a new version of the fabulist.' Rejecting realistic characters, linear narrative, and conventional plots, the fabulist creates a fiction of pure contingency, an imagined world in which everything is possible. After two relatively traditional works, Kroetsch produced four novels —*The studhorse man* (1969), *Gone Indian* (1973), *Badlands* (1975), and *What the crow said* (1978)— that are self-consciously post-modernist (and therefore usually parodic) in their approach. Despite the presence of macabre, grotesque and surreal elements in his fiction, Kroetsch's vision, like Jack HODGINS', is essentially comic. Although set in Alberta and Saskatchewan, Kroetsch's novels are about a fictional West that owes more to the personal inflections of memory and imagination than to geography and history. They are usually organized around a quest that has mythic overtones; mythic allusions, motifs, and narrative patterns abound, along with such antithetical yet dialectically related concepts as coyote man and educated man, woman and man, community and exploration or flight, dream and reality, the natural and the cultural, eros and thanatos. They are concerned with Kroetsch's version of 'the one story and one story only': desire's attempt to achieve fulfilment by evading the entangling and repressive meshes of social reality. In questing for life itself, Kroetsch's obsessed male heroes lead lives that resist, even avoid, community and history because these are synonymous with place and memory, and are therefore repressive. These are 'male' fictions obsessed with the female presence, which functions as a still point in a frenetic male world of unconditional Protean freedom.

For Kroetsch, as for other post-moderns, the novel becomes the locus for the play and playfulness of language. The style suffers from what Peter Thomas, Kroetsch's most sympathetic critic, describes as 'lexical bravura'; it is energetic, witty, punning, and occasionally seems to be out of control, especially in the too-obviously punning name (Roger Dorck, Miss Petcock). Missing from Kroetsch's fiction, however, is the sense—always present in Marquez, one of his masters—that there is a significance in the characters' actions and thoughts beyond the purely literary and formal one.

One senses a roughly analogous attitude to character as a function of narrative in the fiction of Hugh HOOD, who has done his best work in now-classic stories like 'Going out as a ghost', 'The chess match', 'Three halves of a house', 'The fruit man, the meat man and the manager', and in the first four instalments of the flawed but consistently interesting Proustian *roman fleuve* about Canada in the twentieth century: *The new age/Le nouveau siècle* (projected for 12 volumes). A Roman Catholic for whom, as he put it in an early essay ('The absolute infant'), 'everything is full of God', Hood sees art as the revelation of the sacred within the profane, or as Matt Goderich describes his mother-in-law's visionary painting in *The new Athens* (1977), art is the founding of 'heavenly inventions on ordinary life in an ordinary world.' This attitude has produced fiction that is uncomfortable with realistic plots and characters and strains towards symbolism and allegory.

The early novels—*White figure, white ground* (1964), *The camera always lies* (1967), *A game of touch* (1970)—reveal Hood's sacramental and therefore optimistic view of life, and view art as performing an ultimately spiritual function; but the plots often seem imposed upon events and characters (as in the novels of Robertson DAVIES). This tension between vision and form, only occasionally evident in the short stories, disappears in the plotless, though not formless, *The New Age.* The unity of this ambitious project, as well as of its individual instalments, depends on repeated motifs, images, symbols, and emblems, and on the first-person narrative voice of Matthew Goderich, the novel's flawed, symbolically named central figure. As an art historian with a wide range of intellectual interests—including the writing of a history of house design in eastern Ontario—Goderich enables Hood to introduce discussions of ideas from various fields: much of the pleasure of *The New Age* comes from Goderich's digressive musings on Canadian architecture, art, landscape, the names of flowers, the writing of history, and so on. Although they are occasionally tiresome, Hood's didactic excursions into ideas are, for the most part, formally integrated and thematically justified. However, while Hood's commitment to an affirmative and religious vision is admirable (it's refreshing to read a contemporary writer who actually believes in something), his central characters, especially the pivotal Goderich, lack a shadow side and are usually almost too good to be true. Unlike other contemporary Christian novelists, Hood has not taken into account 'the evil facts which are a genuine portion of reality' (William James). As well, since *The New Age* is committed to an examination of history, the reader has the right to expect a more profound sense of social relations and historical conflict than has so far been offered.

A turn towards history also marks the most recent novels of Timothy FINDLEY: *The wars* (1977) and *Famous last words* (1981). Findley established his reputation with *The last of the crazy people* (1967), a fine psychological novel about the gradual disintegration, psychological and social, of the almost Gothic Winslow family. Particularly memorable is the portrait of the young Hooker Winslow, who observes the decline, and—in an act of violent and loving expiation—completes the fall, of his family. The novel has a quiet, understated perfection absent from Findley's later and more ambitious novels, which share its motif of a family flawed or doomed for unknown reasons. For all their historical detail, *The wars* and *Famous last words* are essentially psychological novels whose history often seems decorative. Both deal with emotionally and intellectually troubled individuals. Both are narrated in such a technically complex manner that the telling becomes interesting for its own sake and, as in so much contemporary fiction, is part of the theme itself. *The wars* is narrated, in a clear though often magniloquent style, by an anonymous present-day archivist assembling the available facts about Lieut. Robert Ross, who suffered a nervous breakdown during the First World War. Ross, however, remains distant and enigmatic. He is portrayed in both private and public life: we see him in the midst of the novel's absolutely convincing battle scenes; yet he remains a strangely static fig-

ure. Findley's novels rarely move us: with the possible exception of Kroetsch, Findley may be the Canadian novelist who is most detached from his characters, preventing the reader from making the leap of sympathy and recognition between himself and his world to the characters and the novel's world. His *Famous last words*—which examines, within the frame of a spy novel, the relations between Fascism and art—is ingeniously constructed but strangely lifeless.

Whereas Findley's detachment conveys little or no connection between the writer's life and his work, Clark BLAISE returns almost compulsively to focal childhood situations, suggesting a fiction insistently shadowed by autobiography. He creates scenes, often having a young boy as their focus, in which an almost unbearable knowledge—a violent and terrifying event—intrudes without warning into an otherwise peaceful existence. The opening scene of *Lunar attractions* (1979) is illustrative: David Greenwood (Boisvert) is fishing quietly with his salesman father in a Florida swamp when their boat suddenly lurches as an alligator's tail arches menacingly above them. In the story 'How I became a Jew' (*Tribal Justice*, 1974) Gerald Gordon, a Southerner now living in Cincinnati, enters grade seven and encounters brutal students and a sadistic teacher. The hero of 'A North American education' stands for all of Blaise's protagonists when he gradually realizes that 'whatever the comforting vision before him . . . something dreadful could suddenly cut him down without warning.' Knowledge of the dark side of reality produces neither enlightenment nor philosophical resignation; more often, as in 'Words for the winter' (*A North American education*, 1973) it leaves only the searing realization that 'reality hurts like nothing in this world', and that nothing can be done about it.

Matt COHEN has produced seven novels, a collection of short stories, and a volume of poems. His best works to date are the novels *The disinherited* (1974), *The sweet second summer of Kitty Malone* (1979), and the Gothic *Flowers of darkness* (1981), all set in the fictional town of Salem, north of Kingston, Ont.—'a small town that closed its eyes to the present, let alone the future'—and dealing with the lives of several generations of local inhabitants. The emphasis is usually on ordinary lives—another novel, *The colours of war* (1977), is an exception—caught during a period of personal and/or social transition when rural and urban values conflict. This is most memorable in *The disinherited*, in the irreconcilable clash between the critically ill farmer Richard Thomas and his son Erik, who left the family farm to attend university in Toronto. Cohen's themes are often large ones, but his language seldom succeeds in embodying his concerns in a felt human drama; usually the novels leave an impression of a vaguely diffused portentousness, a sentimental fatalism without substance.

Marian ENGEL has produced a substantial body of work since her first novel, *No clouds of glory* (1968). Though her pellucid and deceptively simple prose style is impressive, she is essentially a one-note writer, treating empathetically and almost obsessively a woman's search for self-fulfilment and strongly portraying a female sensibility. Engel's heroines—like those of Margaret ATWOOD and Audrey Thomas—are usually caught at a moment of crisis. From Sarah Porlock in *No clouds of glory* to Rita Heber in *The glassy sea* (1978), the central characters have just survived a divorce, a separation, or a catastrophic love affair; they are shown withdrawing from men and a male-dominated and male-defined society in order 'to go looking for themselves' *(No clouds of glory)*. In the slightly silly but persuasively narrated fable *Bear* (1976) Lou 'finds' herself in an affair of heart and body with a tame, rather mangy bear in northern Ontario. The other novels—usually short, almost novellas—lack this fabular dimension, but they assume a moralistic, even didactic tone. Too often in Engel's fiction the intention to make a general comment about women, and the relations between women and stereotyped men, between women and society, over-determines and simplifies the nature of the characterization (particularly of men), the symbolism, and plotting.

Audrey THOMAS is a very talented and innovative writer whose stories—collected in *Ten green bottles* (1967), *Ladies and escorts* (1977), and *Real mothers* (1981)—tend to be more conventional than her longer fiction in their approach to character and narrative. The stories explore and often 're-write' the same situations dealt with in the novels *Mrs. Blood* (1970) and *Blown figures* (1974), both of which are set in West Africa, where Thomas lived in the 1960s. Thomas's repeated evocations of the figure of the woman writer—often living, like herself, on an island off the coast of British Columbia—and of a handful of seemingly crucial scenes and events, suggest a form of creative self-therapy. Most of her fiction is written from a woman's point of view (the hauntingly suggestive story 'Aquarius' is one of the few important exceptions) and attempts to render, in a supple and sardonically witty style, a woman's sense of reality. Her women are shown at a critical, and therefore revealing, moment in their lives: *Mrs. Blood* follows a woman through a painful and complicated miscarriage, and focuses on her increasing disgust with her body, which results in a crisis of identity—she alternately refers to herself as Mrs Blood and Mrs Thing; *Blown figures* deals with Isobel's attempt to understand a past love affair and the birth of her stillborn child in Africa; and *Latakia* (1979) presents Rachel's first-person account ('a letter') of her affair with Michael. Although men are often agents of events in these women's lives, their roles are peripheral since Thomas concentrates on each woman's subjective emotional state, her way of seeing and feeling loss and anxiety. Drastic shifts in style, time, and narrative viewpoint are aspects of her attempts to evoke a particular emotional and psychological condition; the emphasis often falls on a *post mortem* analysis of, or response to, an event rather than on a situation unfolding in present time. The novels tend toward solipsism as the world disappears into the subjective vortex of the woman's point of view. Stories like 'Aquarius', 'Kill day at the government wharf', and 'Crossing the Rubicon' have charged dramatic situations involving realistic characters. Though complex in emotion and tone, they hold the reader's attention—something the novels often fail to do.

Helen WEINZWEIG is the author of two slim, original novels: *Passing ceremony* (1973) and *Basic black with pearls* (1980). Less indebted to any indigenous Canadian or North American tradition than to modern painting, music, and the French *nouveau roman*, they are almost plotless, although *Passing ceremony*'s brief, often elliptical, chapters are organized around a bizarre wedding; and *Basic black with pearls* follows the schizophrenic heroine's fantasies about her love affair with an international spy named Coenraad. Both novels are narrated in a cool, even austere style, with intermittent flashes of mordant wit. The style and structure of both novels achieve the effect of placing the reader in the middle of a disconcerting, even confusing, situation, full of irrational stresses, about which little background information has been provided. These are exemplary 'modernist' novels, requiring the active, creative engagement of the reader who 'assembles' and interprets the information presented in the often untagged first-person narratives of the first novel and the often puzzling events of the second. In these spare texts, populated by reticent, anxious characters dissatisfied with their lives and feeling homeless in the world, 'nuance is everything'. If there is a dominant theme, it's the tyranny of memory, the inescapable burden the past imposes on the present.

With the possible exception of Audrey Thomas's *Blown figures* and Leonard Cohen's *Beautiful losers* (1966), no Canadian novel is as challengingly innovative in style and structure as Dave GODFREY's *The new ancestors* (1970). Set on the 'Lost Coast' of Africa, Godfrey's political novel is closer to Hugh Hood's African novel *You can't get there from here* (1972) than to the African novels of Margaret Laurence (*This side Jordan*, 1960) and David Knight (*Farquharson's physique*, 1971), in that its implicit subject is as much Canada's cultural and political situation as that of the Lost Coast. At its centre are the related motifs of colonialism, revolution, and identity. The stylistic and structural virtuosity is meant to be unsettling to prevent expectations of a traditional African novel, such as those of Joyce Cary and Graham Greene, that will simply confirm the reader's preconceptions. Shifts in time and viewpoint (a different character dominates each of the four sections), surreal scenes, parodies of other works (in particular *Under the volcano*), and obscurities in the story all compel one to enter and even become lost in the chaotic reality of a society caught between conflicting identities. Like Michael Burdener, the novel's European hero, we have to *place* ourselves in a colony in which all languages, identities, and ideologies, both indigenous and imported, are caught in the process of change.

4. John METCALF is a comic, often satiric, writer who, in addition to two collections of short stories has published two novels, *Going down slow* (1972) and *General Ludd* (1980), that use the Canadian educational system as a basis for satirizing everything Canadian from bilingualism to computerized society to the Canada Council. (Leo SIMPSON's *The Peacock papers* (1973) and his short story 'The savages' show another comic writer engaged in a similar project.) Metcalf's novels tend to generate their own kind of frenetic energy; but because they break down into episodes they remind us

that his shorter fiction, especially two novellas—'Private parts: a memoir' and 'Girl in gingham', which appeared in *Girl in gingham* (1978), reprinted as *Private parts: a memoir* (1980)—represents his best work. The exquisitely controlled and elegant 'Girl in gingham' follows the life of Peter Thornton, an appraiser of antiques, trying to rebuild his life after an emotionally shattering divorce. Within a very brief compass Metcalf creates a fully rounded central character, a personal and social milieu, and a story encompassing both light comedy and tragedy.

Leon ROOKE is another writer who is at his best in the short-story form, although his novel *Fat woman* (1980) was on the short list for fiction for a Governor-General's award. Perhaps the most unpredictable and innovative writer on the Canadian scene, Rooke is a playful raconteur who teases the reader with the 'and then, and then' factor, while showing off his arsenal of technical devices. His characters are less social personae than voices and tones; his fictional universe is one of pure contingency whose dominant moods are anxiety, fear, and paranoia.

Ray SMITH, like Dave Godfrey and Leon Rooke, has absorbed the lessons of postmodernism and is committed to what he calls 'speculative fiction. Generally ironic in tone. Aesthetic in approach.' Smith has produced two very different books: a collection of experimental stories, *Cape Breton is the thought control centre of Canada* (1969), and *Lord Nelson Tavern* (1974), a novel composed of interlocking unconventional love stories about a group of characters who went to university together. Despite the brilliance of the title story in the first volume, Smith's most successful work is *Lord Nelson Tavern*. Writing in different voices and modes, Smith offers various perspectives on individual relationships, and manages to create an original work that is almost simultaneously ironic and sentimental (he refuses to show a preference) about love and creativity.

Lord Nelson Tavern, George Elliott's dreamlike *The kissing man* (1962), and Wayland Drew's apocalyptic *The Wabeno feast* (1973), are among Canada's few truly neglected works of literature. Elliott's collection of haunting, interconnected stories has affinites with Stephen LEACOCK's *Sunshine sketches*, but its dark yet affirmative vision is distinctive and—while taking liberties with time and space in dealing with the lives and deaths of the inhabitants of a town in south-western Ontario during the early part of this century—essentially innocent.

Wayland Drew, like Elliott, is the author of a single book of fiction, *The Wabeno feast*, a complex and challenging novel that tells three related stories: a historical adventure tale involving white explorers, whose journey into the interior is also a journey into the self; a post-war narrative set in a northern-Ontario industrial town called Sable Creek; and a futuristic story in which Paul and Liv Henry are shown escaping from cities menaced by an unspecified but palpable industrial disaster. As in Peter SUCH's ecological novel *Fallout* (1969), the concern is with man's ability to destroy both himself and the life of nature around him. Despite the slightly forced, didactic quality of some of Drew's symbolism, *The Wabeno feast* is an intricately organized and powerful novel that addresses important psychological and social issues.

Leonard COHEN's *Beautiful losers* (1966)—about the saintly Catherine Tekakwitha, an Iroquois who died in 1680—is easily the most controversial Canadian novel of the past twenty years. Cohen is concerned here with a vision of unity and wholeness. His characters belong to his private, idiosyncratic martyrology, in which sainthood is bestowed on those lovers and losers who have 'achieved a remote human possibility . . . that . . . has something to do with love.' Cohen's saint has seen beyond the conventional possibilities for fulfilment. In *Beautiful losers*, as in Sartre's *Saint Genet*, canonization is contingent upon transgression of the acceptable, the normal, the bourgeois; the liberated self can only achieve fulfilment outside of reason, historical time, and the values of contemporary society. Much of the romantic and surreal writing is as self-indulgent as Cohen's later poetry, and the novel, which is neither as shocking nor as disturbing now as it was when it first appeared, seems to express the spirit of a very particular time.

The dark or 'black' romanticism of *Beautiful losers* is also present in *Coming through slaughter* (1976) by Michael ONDAATJE. In this powerful exploration of the ambiguous sources of creativity, in the form of a discontinuous yet closely organized narrative ostensibly about the career of the legendary New Orleans jazz cornetist Buddy Bolden, 'facts have been expanded or polished to suit the truth of fiction'. The historical Bolden, about whom little is known, becomes a fic-tional exemplar through whom Ondaatje can explore the dilemma of the modern poet/musician *maudit* who is not only onto-logically alienated from his society but for whom 'making and destroying come from the same source, same lust. . . .' Writing about a debilitating creativity dependent upon a suffering self, Ondaatje relies on a taut, austere, often jagged style; his chapters are brief, often fragmentary, units of prose related to each other by clusters of reiterated images (stars, webs, photographs, ice) and the impersonal yet paradoxically sympathetic narrative voice. Although less venturesome in form and style than such obviously avant-garde novels as *Beautiful losers, The new ancestors*, George BOWERING's *Burning water* (1980), and Audrey Thomas's *Blown figures*, Ondaatje's novel seems a greater success aesthetically. Perhaps only Rudy Wiebe compares with Ondaatje for having absorbed the technical lessons of contemporary fiction and used them to deal with a subject of some human significance or moment.

Despite suggestions that Canada's major fiction (or literature) can be characterized thematically on the basis of the garrison mentality, or survival, or patterns of isolation, or the new hero, there is still no single overview that has commanded sufficient authority to gain general consensus. This is perhaps inevitable in a country that—lacking a rich cultural heritage formed over several hundred years, and a language clearly distinguishing it from other nations—has been traditionally unsure of its own identity or defining self-image or myth. Some of our most impressive novels of the past two decades have implicitly raised the possibility that an identity or sense of place can only be established locally or regionally, never nationally. Thus the national definition can be no more than a 'collective consciousness' (George WOODCOCK's term) based on various regionalisms. Images of displacement, immigration, and exile in English-Canadian fiction remind us of lost or abandoned 'foreign' identities, while alerting us to the fact that these haven't been replaced by something indigenous. No other established national literature treats national identity as a *question*; we must turn to third-world countries with histories of political, social, and cultural colonialism to find cases analogous to ours. As Margaret Laurence puts it, 'Canadian writers, like African writers, have had to find our own voices and write of what is truly ours, in the face of an overwhelming cultural imperialism.' Crucial in this search is the 'un-naming' or rejecting of foreign voices, attitudes, and traditions that Robert Kroetsch speaks of as central to his experience as a writer. (The attempt to discover and describe 'what is truly ours' also inevitably involves the writer in a dialogue with history—personal, local, and national; and it is neither coincidental nor insignificant that much of our recent fiction—from Thomas Raddall to Hugh Hood, Margaret Laurence, Mordecai Richler, and Rudy Wiebe—has had an explicit historical dimension.) Thus the adjective 'Canadian', as used in 'the Canadian novel' and 'the Canadian identity', has little meaning apart from the problematic local definitions offered by individual texts. We may agree with Northrop Frye's claim that 'there does seem to be such a thing as an imaginative continuum' in Canadian literature without being certain what the individual elements of that continuum have in common.

SAM SOLECKI

Other talents, other works. Since 1960 the Canadian novel has become too plentiful and too diverse in its forms to be considered under one heading. After the major writers and their works have been singled out, there remains a considerable body of lesser-known fiction, often the product of Canada's flourishing small presses. In this category are included the one-novel writers, the regionalists, the experimenters, the minority writers—all those who, for one reason or another, reach a limited audience. Some of these novels, however, have attained great popular success, while others are highly praised by the critics but little known to the public.

This lesser-known fiction often follows patterns of exploration laid down by the major novelists: Rudy WIEBE, for example, has fathered a dynasty of Indian novels, many of which owe form as well as content to the influence of his *The temptations of Big Bear* (1973); Robertson DAVIES has put his stamp on a certain tradition of university satire; Margaret ATWOOD and Marian ENGEL have written the archetypal novels of female experience in the modern world; of the novels of childhood listed here, many owe their life-blood to W.O. MITCHELL. Beyond the serious minor writers in the great traditions, however, lies that much-maligned body of fiction called 'popular'. Here too there is good writing, in an array of styles that often reflect the preoccupations

of Canadian society in the years of their publication.

Because of its diversity, lesser-known fiction since 1960 will be discussed under a series of convenient though not definitive headings: 1. Experimental Fiction; 2. Minority Fiction; 3. Satire; 4. The Novel of Childhood; 5. Women and Fiction; 6. Regional Fiction; and 7. Popular Fiction.

1. EXPERIMENTAL FICTION. Although the 1960s were exciting years for the Canadian novel, truly experimental fiction arrived only with Graeme GIBSON's *Five legs* (1969). Before that there had been the tepid innovations of Peter Taylor in his *Watcha gonna do boy . . . watcha gonna be?* (1967), a picaresque pastiche of a young man's discovery that digression—in life as in railroads—is, though anathema to parents, a sweet and necessary thing. Appearing in the shadow of Kerouac and the Beat generation, Taylor's novel proclaimed its avant-garde nature as much by its youthful subject matter as by its formal innovations. A more daring explosion of form characterizes J. Michael YATES's *Man in the glass octopus* (1968), which came from the Sono Nis Press in Vancouver and heralded a West Coast attempt to offer Canada 'a fiction of a different order'. Yates's 'Man' appears in each of a sequence of dream-like allegories of futility, drawing the reader insistently into new considerations of ontology and of the place of fiction-making in man's existence. In 1969, a year marking a burst of activity in Canada's small presses, Russell Marois used fragmented communication as the basis for the form and content of his novel, *The telephone pole*. Gibson's *Five legs*, however, was heralded as the decade's crowning achievement in the experimental mode: style and content are welded to create an impression of the fragmentation of experience in the consciousness of the book's two main characters, Lucan Crackell and Felix Oswald. The interior isolation of the two men emerges on a funeral journey in the dead of winter, working against a deep underlayer of unifying mythological truth, suggested by the novel's title image.

In the 1970s Gibson continued to demonstrate that experiment in fiction need not mean gimmickry. *Communion* (1971), a 'sequel' to *Five legs*, brought back Felix Oswald with two other characters, Fripp and Ritson, intertwining their experiences in a manner as much magical as mystical. At first the reader clings to repeated motifs that seem to identify and fix the characters, but Gibson progressively withholds certainty, and the three separate experiences finally merge into one communion of violence. A similar technique—not as well or as economically handled—characterizes Robert HARLOW's *Scann* (1972), where the complex, web-like vision of reality filters through the mind and perceptions of the central character, Scann. Harlow created wonderful mythologies to people Scann's past and the past of British Columbia, breaking down in the process all sense of linear time's relevance to perceptions of reality. A later example of experiment in Gibson's mode—perhaps a logical extension of that tradition—is Derk WYNAND's *One cook, once dreaming* (1980), which exists on the edge of any conventional definition of the novel: almost novella-length, it is a series of linked prose 'poems' that explore the impulse towards artistic creation through the metaphor of a master cook, whose skills of shaping and creating are as visible in his dreams as in his iced wedding cakes.

A separate tradition of experiment followed the footsteps of Thomas Pynchon towards a type of fiction depicting a world where to exist is to be paranoid. In *The assignment* (1971) Martin Myers created the mysterious Spiegel, code-named Gimmel, dispatched on assignment to different lifetimes in different ages since the world began. Spiegel is either a radical schizophrenic or the only man brave enough to acknowledge that the world is arranged, under the direction of a Chief Assigning Officer, in patterns of meaning at once too seductive and too terrifying to face. In 1972 John MILLS' *The land of is* presented a similarly paranoid look at the underside of the West Coast, polarized by a split protagonist in the form of twins, one diabolically successful, the other weak and ineffectual. Mills experiments here, as elsewhere in his works, with the technique of the 'found' manuscript—letters and documents edited by a mediating narrator into an unreliable, postmodernist text. Like Pynchon, Mills reaches back to the Second World War for horrific images of dislocation and dismemberment to anchor his satire on modern society. The satiric bent reappeared in Jim Willer's *Paramind* (1973), along with the preoccupation with man as the game and life as the player. By the 1980s the genre took on a new complexity, if not vitality, in the ponderous twin volumes of Robert Allen's *The Hawryliw process: part I* (1980) and *The Hawryliw process: part II* (1981), in which life, to the protagonist Minden Sills, means life inside the Hawryliw Institute, a self-proclaimed 'concatenation of whimsies'.

Yet a third experimental tradition visible in the Canadian novel of the 1970s exhibited a Shandean mode, a deconstructionism of the novel form that is not entirely alien to *The Hawryliw process*, with its pages of geometry and diagrams and its chapter on 'How to Read this Novel'. Chris SCOTT's *Bartleby* (1971) launched the genre, with its self-conscious narrator engaged in (and sometimes disengaged from) a maniacal spoof of literary types and styles. A much more sober invasion of the novel's territory is Dave GODFREY's *I Ching Kanada* (1976), a text made not to be read sequentially from cover to cover but to be consulted in a form of mystical divination. Perhaps the most successful and exciting work in this group is George BOWERING's *A short sad book* (1977), which, though short, is never sad. Bowering's chatty, tricky narrator barges irreverently through the immensity of Canadian geography, history, and culture, as if it all existed simultaneously on one plane: all is grist for his mill as he anatomizes the literary genres, from the love story and the short story through the *roman à clef* to the Pretty Good Canadian Novel.

The early 1980s have seen the rising popularity of a form that bears a close external resemblance to the conventional historical novel, but uses this base of history to raise philosophic questions still burning in the contemporary world. Gwendolyn MacEWEN's *King of Egypt, King of dreams* (1971) is perhaps a very early precursor of the genre of which George Bowering's *Burning water* (1980) is the first real example. Bowering's novel of Captain George Vancouver and his arrival on Canada's west coast stands the historical novel on its head, questioning its methods and assumptions at every turn and giving to eighteenth-century Indians the dialogue of twentieth-century psychology majors. In *The king's evil* (1981) David HELWIG used a related form—that of the historical detective novel on the Josephine Tey model—to explore a catalogue of obsessions in the mind and life of a contemporary radio producer who discovers clues suggesting that Charles I was not beheaded but spirited off to Virginia to found a secular dynasty. Here art-forgery and human impersonation combine through the years following the interregnum to raise questions on the nature of proof and the validity of 'restoration'. Chris Scott delved even further into history, back to the Renaissance, for the matter of *Antichthon* (1982), where the heretic Giordano Bruno threatens to undermine the doctrines of the Roman Catholic church by reconstructing the universe as a 'system . . . to pick out the colours of the mind'. Graeme Gibson reappears to crown the achievements of this hybrid genre with his novel *Perpetual motion* (1982). Like Scott's, his hero seeks the perfect system, this time against the background of nineteenth-century optimistic rationalism and the carnival and chicanery of southwestern Ontario small towns.

2. MINORITY FICTION. Alan Fry's *How a people die* (1970) ushered in a decade that saw the unprecedented blossoming of the Canadian Indian into a major fictional subject deserving a category to itself. Fry's well-documented fictional treatment of a British Columbian resettlement village hovers at the edge of the sociological to present the economic and ethical problems surrounding the death of an eleven-month old Kwatsi girl. Moving between the points of view of the local RCMP officer, the harried and helpless Indian agent, and the dead girl's sister, Fry tangles questions of resettlement, responsibility, and survival to provide what is almost a problem novel.

In the previous decade the Canadian Indian had continued to occupy a traditional, somewhat romantic and idealized place in the literature. Fred BODSWORTH's *The strange one* (1959) offers a mélange of animal tale and love story as he creates allegory out of a strained analogy between the courtship of barnacle geese and that of a young couple—Rory Macdonald and Kanina, an Indian maiden. There is less of Hollywood in Bodsworth's later novel, *The sparrow's fall* (1967), although this story of the survival of Jacob Atook remains a fable of the primitive. In 1966 Paul St Pierre, a Vancouver author, published *Breaking Smith's quarter horse*, an excellent novel derived from an award-winning television show. Its small-farmer protagonist, the almost nameless Smith, is eclipsed by the Indian characters Ol Antoine, the outlaw Gabriel Jimmyboy, and the slippery court interpreter Walter Charlie. St Pierre's evocative use of the voices and the silences of these Indians brings a vitality to the stereotypes that, married to the novel's overall metaphor of 'breaking'—not only of horses but of the human spirit—creates a fiction whose quality surpasses that of Alan Fry's later *How a people die*. But Fry's serious use of the Indian point of view, and of documentary history,

points onwards to the seventies where, in the shadow of Rudy WIEBE's *The temptations of Big Bear*, David WILLIAMS's *The burning wood* (1975) depicts the confrontation between Saskatchewan Indians and the religious fundamentalism of the local white population. Young Joshua Cardiff, left bald by disease and rejected by his peers, turns in defiance of his family to the nearby Indian reservation, where his baldness has a rational and even exalted explanation: he is accepted as Scalp-by-Manitou, a person singled out by the gods for special privilege. Williams's portrayal of the patriarchal, devout family, ridden by the past and riven by contact with another more 'pagan' race, recalls the work of South Africa's Alan Paton. Byrna Barclay took the Big Bear tradition a step further with her *Summer of the hungry pup* (1981), in which the nonagenarian First Woman or Medicine Woman relates to her Other Granddaughter the story of the Cree exile in Montana in the 1880s and 1890s. Barclay's poetic gifts enable her to create for the generically-named Old Woman a voice at once believable and inimitable to carry the monumental mythic stature of the protagonist—as Wiebe did for Big Bear. A further development is evident in James Polk's novel *The passion of Loreen Bright Weasel* (1981) which, despite its echoing title, eschews the mythic and explores the predicament of the contemporary Indian in a tone of irony; the humour is often at the expense of whites, Indians, religion, local government, and contemporary society and culture. Set in the town of Hebb, Montana, the novel follows the unattractive adolescent Loreen from reservation, to convent, to pregnancy, to servitude with the well-meaning Triumph family. Loreen pursues the good with passionate ineptitude, leaving a trail of the bad behind her, and by the end of the novel all things have become their opposites: the thin become fat; the fat become thin; the Madame of the local brothel joins the convent; the nuns become liberated and start wearing halter tops. Loreen's miracle is that she changes everything, but in the end all is as before.

Another kind of minority fiction emerged during the last two decades from the West Indian immigrant community. Harold Sonny LADOO, who produced only two novels before his death in 1973, forged a new language in *No pain like this body* (1972), using a new richness of simile and onomatopoeia to depict the nightmare world of growing up in a shack in the middle of a

West Indian cane field. Ladoo's young hero is beset by thunder, rain, flood, scorpions, and insanity—ordeals presented, not as exceptional or unusual, but as the inevitable concomitants of a childhood of poverty. *Yesterdays* (1974) provides a less nightmarish vision of island life, satirizing foreign planners, developers, and educators, and employing richly sexual and scatological humour.

3. SATIRE. The purest strain of satire in Canadian fiction of the last two decades surfaces in the novel of academia. In the tradition of Stephen LEACOCK and Robertson DAVIES, Jack MacLeod produced two hilarious novels set in 'Chiliast University' in Toronto. In *Zinger and me* (1979) he used an epistolary format to set up tension between its two heroes—the 'me' of the title, J.T., the tenure-seeking academic in the economics department, and Zinger, his alter-ego, the foul-mouthed, limerick-loving newspaperman, cast in the Gulley Jimson mould. Academic politics continued to provide fodder for MacLeod's grimmer satire, *Going grand* (1982); here 'Zinger' and 'me' merge to give the novel a more conventional third-person format, and satire on the Canadian lack of cultural identity is delivered through the agency of the new foreign professor, Nalorian. An earlier, more diluted form of academic satire is Saros Cowasjee's *Goodbye to Elsa* (1974), where the history department of a prairie university, 'Erigon College of Liberal Arts', is dissected under the one-eyed view of Tristan Elliott, the new Anglo-Indian professor. Cowasjee ranges as far afield as the Indian army, and the whole is washed in an overall tone of macabre humour that finally sobers the reader.

Despite the primacy of academia in recent Canadian satire, other targets have served. Daryl HINE wrote the most literary of Canadian satires, *The prince of darkness & co.* (1961), a *roman à clef* set in Capri. The enjoyment of its outrageous main character depends on knowledge of its dual prototypes (Norman Douglas and Aleister Crowley). In the same year William Weintraub's *Why rock the boat* (1961) burlesqued the Montreal newspaper world in a gentle satire with strong romantic underpinnings. Both the romance and the gentleness disappear in Weintraub's later novel, *The underdogs* (1979), a strident and unconvincing presentation of a future in which Québec is independent and the rest of Canada has been swallowed by the United States. A much more successful political satire is the earlier

novel *My sexual and other revolutions: the memoirs of Donald Johnson* (1971), in which David Lewis STEIN captures the Messianic merger of sexual and political liberation that characterized the sixties.

4. THE NOVEL OF CHILDHOOD. In the last two decades Canadian writers have produced novels of childhood set in almost every inhabited nook and cranny of the country. The genre is best defined by a book that is less a fiction than a memoir: Fredelle Bruser Maynard's *Raisins and almonds* (1973). This meditation on the childhood of the daughter of a roving prairie shopkeeper sets out the touchstone of the genre: the recollective anecdotal concern with those little re-enactments of the Fall that mark the passing of childhood. The recent novel of childhood might more accurately be termed a novel of growing up. Harold HORWOOD's *Tomorrow will be Sunday* (1966), for example, presents a teenage hero, Eli Palliser, fighting for his own sexual identity in the straitened moral climate of a Newfoundland outport. Though stiff in places, it is memorable for its straightforward treatment of homosexuality. In her first novel, *Pandora* (1972), Sylvia Fraser, though dealing mainly with a very young heroine, reveals her world (in 'Steeltown', or wartime Hamilton) to be a microcosm of the adult world, with its own cruelties, predicaments, systems of order, power struggles, triumphs, and defeats. Though Fraser at times weights her novel too heavily with descriptive sociology, her finely observed calculus of playground behaviour is nothing if not accurate. *Pandora* shares with Cecelia Frey's *Breakaway* (1974) a floridity of language that is particularly evident in their opening pages. Frey's novel, set in northern Alberta, is a somewhat wooden parade through the realizations that accompany and define the process of growing up: life, death, and change are experienced and assimilated in orderly turn by the protagonist, Lia. Back in Ontario, Dennis T. Patrick Sears produced *The lark in the clear air* (1974), which takes its adolescent hero, Danny, to young manhood through a series of riotous and somewhat improbable incidents, mostly sexual in nature. The sheer vitality of Sears' work contrasts with the bitter intensity of Betty Wilson's *André Tom Macgregor* (1976), which charts much the same period of time in the life of a young Métis from northern Alberta, seeking an education and finding a circumscribed life in Edmonton.

Another prairie novel combining childhood and social commentary is Mary Ann Seitz's *Shelterbelt* (1979), in which the conventional revelations that mark the growing up of Francie Polanski are eclipsed by the central and gradual realization that she is female in a male world—'just an ordinary girl' in a northern Saskatchewan family with nine brothers. In 1978 Stan Dragland crowned the achievements of the growing-up-in-the-West novel with his *Peckertracks: a chronicle* (1978). Loosely structured—almost a series of vignettes—*Peckertracks* is, however, held together by its extremely funny cast of high-school characters. Dragland's Depot, Alta, in 1959 owes its economic existence to the railroad tracks; but to the hero, Percy Lewis, and the other sex-starved adolescents, 'peckertracks' are just as vital to the town's human economy. The voices—funny, anecdotal, wry, dead-pan, casually obscene—unite Dragland's prose pieces into a vigorous chronicle of growing up. A more literal example of the chronicle form appears in another novel from the same period, Hubert EVANS's *O time in your flight* (1979), where the archaeological accuracy of Robert Jack's line drawings is as important to the overall effect as are the minute observations of Gilbert Egan's world. Evans arrests time in the 1890s for a sustained look at small-town Ontario through the eyes of a child.

5. WOMEN AND FICTION. Although 'lady novelists' and the 'ladies' novel' have disappeared from the pages of serious literary criticism, one can still identify in Canadian fiction a body of serious novels written by women that concern and identify themselves with a female consciousness and its relationship to a largely male world.

In 1964 Jane RULE produced in *The desert of the heart* a memorable novel that sought a language for the unmarried woman living in a desert world where marriage is 'the idiom of life'. A decade later Constance BERESFORD-HOWE's *The book of Eve* (1973) presented the sexagenarian Eva, who runs away from a querulous invalid husband to freedom and poverty in a Montreal slum. Eva's refusal to continue to be what the male world of husband and son demands is an action that becomes the cornerstone of some later fiction. Both Joan Barfoot's *Abra* (1978) and Aritha Van Herk's *Judith* (1978) provide their heroines with an opportunity to escape to a healing, female world, patiently and painfully pioneered beyond the borders of the male establishment. Van Herk's *Judith* leaves the city for a pig farm and names her sows, one by one, after fe-

male figures from history and myth, a list—going from Marie Antoinette to Venus, via Daisy Buchanan—that charts her own transformation from siren to woman. In *Abra*, a much bleaker novel, the heroine abandons husband, children, and dog for a spare country existence—a nine-year night of the soul during which her children grow up and away from her. Aritha Van Herk's less successful second novel, *The tent peg* (1981), inspired by the Old Testament story in Judges 4, is saved from its bizarre heroine—J.L., or Ja-el, an androgynous witch-goddess with mysterious powers over men and beasts—by its multiple points of view, which move among the various members of a geological expedition to provide an interesting texture of voices, mostly male.

In 1977 the *Books in Canada* First Novel Award went to Oonah McFee's *Sandbars* (1977), a novel of memory, of the search in the past for the expectations of the past. Katherine Govier's heroine in *Random descent* (1979) reaches beyond her own memory to the past of her ancestors, exploring the meanings of family through the lives of women—with evocative names such as 'Constance' and 'Submitta'—who make families and hold them together.

Yet another type of fiction should be considered here—those finely observed studies of ordinary life that often constitute the novel of manners. Helen Levi's three novels—*A small informal dance* (1977), *Tangle your web and dosey-do* (1978), and *Honour your partner* (1979)—form a trilogy depicting life in a small Manitoba town as a ritual of tea and sandwiches, where partners are decorously chosen, and the young become old in the perennial dance of birth, love, and death. Another writer whose fictions seem to belong in this category is Carol SHIELDS. Her *Small ceremonies* (1976) pairs with *The box garden* (1977) to explore the manners and mores of middle-class suburbia. Urban life in Shields' two novels appears as constrained and ritualized as small-town life in Levi's trilogy.

6. REGIONAL FICTION. Most Canadian fiction is in some sense regional. Three regions have been singled out here because they have produced fictions in which the sense of place forms a unifying undercurrent to novels that sometimes vary widely in subject matter. It is perhaps surprising to find Toronto fiction described as regional, but it is an apt term for a kind of city novel, emerging during the last few decades, that depicts the urban area as a landscape and

produces a neighbourhood fiction strongly imbued with the regionalists' sense of place.

6(a) *Urban Toronto*. Toronto's fictional debut dates back to the early novels of Morley CALLAGHAN, where it is a nameless though not unrecognizable city, but could well be any big city in the North American midwest. By the beginning of the sixties Toronto emerges, in the fiction of Hugh HOOD and others, as a valid fictional locale, and with the Cabbagetown explosion a few years later it is anatomized to contribute to a new fiction of neighbourhoods. An early Toronto novel, Phyllis Brett Young's *The Torontonians* (1960), overhauls the upper-middle-class areas of the city, doing its best to give the ivied streets of 'Rowanwood' an aura of sin and *angst*. Hugh GARNER's *Silence on the shore* (1962) takes urban fiction down the social scale to explore the volatile, decaying neighbourhood of the Toronto Annex, through the lives of the assorted inhabitants of a single rooming house. Though Garner's characters and plot are predictable, he captures succinctly the dynamics of a neighbourhood in transition, where those on the way up mingle briefly with those on the way down. Originally published in 1950, Garner's *Cabbagetown*, which is the common ancestor of all the Toronto novels of urban grit, was substantially revised and expanded and re-issued in 1968, when it created renewed interest in the genre. Two years later Juan BUTLER reconstructed the Cabbagetown of the sixties in his *Cabbagetown diary: a documentary* (1970). With its diary-entry format, the novel uses the irreverent, off-hand, 'macho' voice of the rootless Michael, a voice that seems to speak for its time and place and is the novel's tour de force. Toronto novelists continued to explore the pocket neighbourhoods of the city, discovering local colour in a widening variety of urban areas and periods. Alice Boissonneau's *Eileen McCullough* (1976), for example, depicts life in the industrial Queen St district during the Second World War. In the seventies a different kind of Toronto fiction appeared in the novels of Richard B. WRIGHT. With *The weekend man* (1970) Wright, working in the tradition of Callaghan's early novels, created the unselfconscious Toronto novel where the shape of the city is wedded to the shape of the characters' lives. In two later novels, *In the middle of a life* (1973) and *Final things* (1980), Wright's unprepossessing heroes continue to define their failed lives in terms of the novels' spatial and temporal metaphors.

6(b) *The West*. Patricia Blondal's *A candle to light the sun* (1960) begins the decade by epitomizing prairie fiction in its earlier and gentler phase. A thorough exploration of community—the small town of Mouse Bluffs, Man.—provides a background for a portrait of the young artist, David Newman. This phase disappears in George RYGA's two short prairie fictions. *Hungry hills* (1963) offers a grittily realistic picture of depression-era Alberta, in which the earnest clichés of realism weigh down the slangy dialogue. Ryga's more successful and appealing *Ballad of a stonepicker* (1966), though set in the same time and place, avoids the worst pitfalls of cliché by harnessing its confessional tone to a ballad-like form—aimless and anecdotal, yet rhythmic. Echoes of this form recur in prairie fiction. Ken MITCHELL's *Wandering Rafferty* (1972)—whose title, while recalling Celtic romanticism, also betrays its form—follows middle-aged, mad, poetic Rafferty and young, rootless, revolutionary Archie Payne as they bumble their way across the West, exploring the nature of 'two kinds of romanticism'. In a later Mitchell novel, *The con man* (1979), the itinerant hero resurfaces in Gilly Savard, reluctant con man in a world that Mitchell suggests makes con men of us all. Gilly escapes the law by placing his confidence in the eccentricities of language, particularly of names, as he meanders across Saskatchewan, lured by the sound of place names such as 'Elbow' and 'Eyebrow', in a pattern of illogic that baffles the exponents of purpose and straight highways. David WILLIAMS used a form reminiscent of all these prairie forerunners in *The river horsemen* (1981). His four wanderers—two Indians, a lapsed evangelist, and a stubble-cheeked Ukrainian youth—navigate a perilous river journey in 1930s Saskatchewan. Each member of the unlikely company speaks in his own voice, weaving a pattern of betrayal and violence on the river road to Saskatoon and apocalypse.

Farther west, British Columbia fiction of the 1960s is anchored by Robert HARLOW's *Royal Murdoch* (1962) and *A gift of echoes* (1965). With their shared characters and locale (a mill town in the foothills of the Rockies), the two novels could have formed a diptych, but Harlow never successfully developed the possibilities inherent in his material, and the regional mythology he sought remained elusive until his later, and larger, novel *Scann* (1972). A less-serious, but still popular British Columbia writer is Margaret Craven, whose lightweight fiction, *I heard the owl call my name* (1967), alternates intense natural lyricism with a sentimental view of a British Columbian coastal Indian village. The hero of this short novel, an Anglican priest with a mortal illness, comes to live and to die in the village, learning along the way to respect its ways and earning, in turn, the respect of the Indians.

Poet Susan MUSGRAVE, in her novel *The charcoal burners* (1980), rejected sentimentality in favour of the sensational and hacked away at any remaining romanticization of the modern Indian condition. Her heroine, Matty, a former student of anthropology, furnishes ironic commentary on Indian custom, but her detachment fails here when she is imprisoned in the cannibalistic commune of Ephratah in the British Columbia interior. Musgrave's horrific vision—of a woman caught between the vegetarians and the meat-eaters, and sentenced to die by one or the other—is most horrifying for the suggested universality of its application.

6(c) *The East*. In the last two decades English-language fiction set in Québec has no longer been exclusively of a high romantic nature. Robert Goulet's *The violent season* (1961) depicts the cyclical purgings by *charivari* of the pent-up frustrations of a small Québec logging town, La Buche. Caught between seminary and logging camp, the village longs for a saint; the Curé founds a brothel in an attempt to break a vicious circle that dooms foundling girls to become mothers of more illegitimate babies. By *charivari* the brothel is destroyed, and the saint created with much wasteful loss of life. In John MILLS' *The October men* (1973) violence again characterizes the vision of Québec. Mills uses the October Crisis as background for a novel that, on one level, is as fast, bold, and violent as any pulp thriller; but he also uses the post-modern device of the self-conscious fiction commenting upon itself to make us aware of the many fictional forms possible within the bare framework of event, thereby distancing the violence from us and making some of the violent acts seem ordered by a necessity as much fictional as political. Between these two novels of violence is the bicultural *Lark des neiges/Snow lark* (1971) of Ronald SUTHERLAND, whose Suzanne Laflamme, alias Susy MacDonald, epitomizes the duality of her society. Her narrative is a carefully crafted jumble of French and English phrases that presents a picture of Montreal life that is as

schematized as anything since MacLENNAN's *Two solitudes* (1945).

Québec appears more benign in Bernard Epps' depiction of the Eastern Townships, *Pilgarlic the death* (1967). Despite its title it is a lyrical, somewhat idealized version of small-town pastoral, recalling Dylan Thomas in the names of its characters: Dougal the School, John the Law, Long George. The town has its poachers and policemen, its sluts and saints, its sinners and sin-eaters, and offers to all its inhabitants the possibility of harmony, if not happiness, in its ordered world.

A tough, sinewy fiction emerged in Canada's Maritime and Atlantic provinces in the last two decades. Percy JANES' *House of hate* (1970) depicted the claustrophobic life of a Newfoundland mill town between the wars. The hard and bitter patriarch, Saul Stone, dominates this novel as he dominates the lives of his six children—a family of Stones bred in an emotional soil as barren as the rocky land around their fortress-like house. David Adams RICHARDS created a similar fiction of entrapment set in northern New Brunswick. His novels—*The coming of winter* (1974), *Blood ties* (1976), and *Lives of short duration* (1981)—explore the intricate family relationships that sustain a rural community, economically and culturally circumscribed and awaiting escape to the outside world. *Lives of short duration* (1981) is a particularly fine depiction of the tangled generations of the Terri family in a world of ignorance and casual cruelty.

7. POPULAR FICTION. Over the last two decades Canadian writers of popular fiction have demonstrated mastery of all the popular modes, often providing along the way a map of the social and cultural preoccupations of their day and time. Sheila Burnford capped the animal adventure story with her novel *The incredible journey* (1961); in 1962 appeared Donald Jack's farcical but enduring *Three cheers for me: the journals of Bartholomew Bandy, R.F.C.* (1962), a humorous look at the Great War. 1962, however, also saw the more momentous publication of Arthur Hailey's *In high places* (1962), beginning a tradition of political suspense novels that would produce Charles Israel's *The hostages* (1966) and Charles Templeton's *The kidnapping of the President* (1974). Though Hailey went on to found another dynasty of formula novels with the publication of *Hotel* (1965), his real contribution to the popular novel is the carefully researched social and political realism of *In high places*, where the

contemporary and controversial nature of the subject matter adds to the novel's suspense. After Templeton's timely and convincing recreation of the drama of a presidential kidnapping attempt, the political suspense novel ventured abroad with Ian McLachlan's *The seventh hexagram* (1976), whose setting for international intrigue is Hong Kong. David Gurr's novel *Troika* (1979) took the international thriller successfully to a Baltic setting, using front-page news as the basis of his fiction.

The familiar, ever-popular genre of the historical novel produced two works of note: Pauline Gedge's *Child of the morning* (1977) and Sylvia Fraser's *The Emperor's virgin* (1980). Gedge, an Albertan, recreated the courts of Egypt's pharaohs Thothmes I and II, taking as her focus the story of the historically androgynous Hatshepsu, whom Gedge fashions into a female Pharaoh of great power and fascination. There is little of Gedge's nod to feminism in Fraser's tale of debauchery and decadence in Rome of the first century A.D., whose heroine, Cornelia, is a vestal virgin. A much more joyful and enjoyable exercise in eroticism was the extremely successful *In praise of older women: the amorous recollections of András Vajda* (1965), in which Stephen Vizinczey chronicles the amorous exploits of a Hungarian survivor of the Second World War. Though written rather in the style of a commentary on a hockey match—with a chapter for each period, and a careful charting of goals scored and assists—this hymn to older women had sufficient vitality and timeliness to be made into a film.

Another popular format began to flourish in the early 1980s when Howard Engel resurrected the Hammett-style detective novel with *The suicide murders: a Benny Cooperman mystery* (1980), and *The ransom game* (1981), whose most memorable feature is the harried, mother-ridden private eye, Benny Cooperman, from Grantham, Ont. The psychological thriller, mastered early by John BUELL in his *Four days* (1962), later produced two good examples: Tim Wynne-Jones's *Odd's end* (1980)—winner of the 1979 Seal Book Award—and *The knot* (1982). Both works contain a skilful and unpredictable blend of the criminal, the mysterious, and the subtly horrific.

MICHELLE GADPAILLE

Novels in French. Beginnings to 1900. The first French-Canadian novel, L'INFLUENCE D'UN LIVRE, was published in 1837. Its

author, Philippe-Ignace-François Aubert de Gaspé, a twenty-three-year-old journalist— not to be confused with his father who was to write *Les anciens Canadiens*—stated that he wanted to be useful to his compatriots by contributing to the birth of a French-Canadian literature. In those troubled times the publication of a French-language novel in Canada was also a kind of encouragement to the people, who had reasons to fear for their survival. According to the author, *L'influence d'un livre* was true to life; but in fact this novel of the *fantastique*, with a most unlikely plot and improbable characters, was full of references to local superstitions and witchcraft.

Joseph Deutre, a nineteen-year-old journalist, claimed to be preoccupied with the promotion of French-Canadian literature when he wrote *Les fiancés de 1812* (Montréal, 1844), a 500-page adventure story that takes place during the War of 1812. Rather sententious and far-fetched, with incredible characters and very involved composition, it could hardly compete, as it intended to, with the novels of Eugène Sue and Alexandre Dumas.

L'influence d'un livre, Les fiancés de 1812 and *La fille du brigand*, another far-fetched story written by a twenty-two-year-old student in law, under the pseudonym of Pietro (Eugène L'Écuyer), and published in *Le Minestrel* from 29 Aug. to 19 Sept. 1844, inaugurated a major trend in the French-Canadian fiction of the last century: that of the adventure story. Usually melodramatic, these unbelievable stories were normally in keeping with moral standards, when they were not moralizing openly. Examples of further novels of this type are numerous, the best known probably being those written by Henri-Émile CHEVALIER: *La Huronne de Lorette* (Montréal, 1854), *L'héroïne de Chateauguay* (Montréal, 1858), *Le pirate du Saint-Laurent* (Montréal, 1859), and *L'île de sable* (Montréal, 1862); by Eugène Dick: *Le roi des étudiants* (Montréal, 1871), *L'enfant mystérieux* (Québec, 1880), and *Un drame du Labrador* (Montréal, 1897); and by Georges Boucher de Boucherville: *Une de perdue, deux de trouvées* (Montréal, 1874).

As Yves Dostaler has shown in *Les infortunes du roman dans le Québec du XIXe siècle* (1977), there was soon a lot of suspicion levelled against the novel in French Canada. In *La Gazette des Trois-Rivières*, as early as 14 Oct., 1817, Ludger Duvernay was advising future novelists to observe high moral standards and urging his readers to be careful when selecting a novel lest they be exposed to immoral ideas and descriptions. In 1846 Étienne Parent denounced the reading of European novels—there were of course only very few Canadian novels at that time—as a waste of time. These novels, he argued, were unable to give anything to Canadians, except perhaps immoral thoughts and false expectations, by describing a society and habits that were not their own. The novel continued to be attacked throughout the century. It is not surprising, therefore, that many French-Canadian novelists of the last century tried to justify themselves for writing a novel in a preface stressing the purity of their intentions. Guildo Rousseau has collected most of these prefaces in *Préfaces des romans québécois du XIXᵉ siècle* (1970).

A good novel was soon defined as one that was didactic, patriotic, and edifying. In such a context it is easy to understand that historical novels and novels of the land— that is, novels promoting an agricultural ideology and fidelity to traditions—were largely favoured in Québec. The first *roman de la terre* was *La terre paternelle* (Montréal, 1846) by Patrice LACOMBE. While depicting rural life, it tells the dramatic story of a father who made the mistake of giving his farm to his son with the intention of preventing his leaving home to seek adventure and fortune in the fur-trade. The father pays a high price for having been unfaithful to his land. More interesting and more developed is the portrayal of French-Canadian manners in *Charles Guérin* (Montréal, 1853) by Pierre-Joseph-Olivier CHAUVEAU. Like *Charles Guérin*, JEAN RIVARD le défricheur (Montréal, 1874) by Antoine GÉRIN-LAJOIE develops a thesis to prove that immigration of French Canadians to the United States could be stopped by opening settlements in the back districts of the province. *Jean Rivard, économiste* (Montréal, 1876), though fiction, is really a treatise on colonization. *Jeanne la fileuse* (Fall River, 1878) by Honoré BEAUGRAND and Ernest CHOQUETTE's *Les Ribaud* (Montréal, 1898) and *Claude Paysan* (Montréal, 1899) are also didactic. POUR LA PATRIE (Montréal, 1895) by Jules-Paul Tardivel is in a special category: it is mainly of interest because it is the first novel to promote a separatist ideology.

After the success of *Les* ANCIENS CANADIENS (Québec, 1863) by Philippe AUBERT DE GASPÉ—who was seventy-seven years old when his novel was published—the historical novel began to flourish in Québec. No one, however, could equal Aubert de

Gaspé's skills in re-creating past times. Among the many historical novels that followed are *Jacques et Marie* (Montréal, 1866), by Napoléon Bourassa, which is a real melodrama; Joseph MARMETTE's *Charles et Eva* (Montréal, 1866), *François de Bienville* (Québec, 1870), *L'Intendant Bigot* (Montréal, 1872; serialized in *L'Opinion Publique*, Mai-Oct. 1871), *Le Chevalier de Marmac* (Montréal, 1873), and *Le tomahawk et l'épeé* (Québec, 1877). Also to be mentioned are Edmond Rousseau's *Le Château de Beaumanoir* (Lévis, 1886), *Les exploits d'Iberville* (Québec, 1888) and *La Monongahéla* (Québec, 1890), and Laure Conan's *A l'oeuvre et à l'épreuve* (Québec, 1891; *The master motive*, 1909) and *L'oublié* (Montréal, 1900). Laure Conan (Félicité ANGERS) is best known, however, for ANGÉLINE DE MONTBRUN (Québec, 1884), the first French-Canadian psychological novel, the theme of which is self-sacrifice. Maurice Lemire has analysed themes in *Les grands thèmes nationalistes du roman historique canadien-français* (1970).

See Aurelien Boivin, *Le conte littéraire québécois au XIXᵉ siècle* (1975); David M. Hayne and Marcel Tirol, *Bibliographie critique du roman canadien-français, 1837-1900* (1968); Maurice Lemire et al., *Dictionnaire des oeuvres littéraires du Québec*, v. 1 (1978). See also *Le roman canadien-français*, Archives des lettres canadiennes, v. III 3ᵉ ed. (1977).

JACQUES COTNAM

1900 to 1920. In his *Manuel d'histoire de la littérature canadienne-française* (1920) Abbé Camille Roy, the leading literary critic of the time, echoed the sentiments of most of his colleagues when he observed in passing that, despite several 'laudable efforts' by Adolphe-Basile Routhier, Hector Bernier, Ernest Choquette, and Ernest Chouinard, the novel had enjoyed little success in Québec in the preceding two decades.

At the beginning of the twentieth century, novels continued in fact to encounter widespread suspicion, and authors of books that might be construed as such usually felt obliged to intervene in the narrative in order to insist on the 'reality', social usefulness, and moral qualities of their works. Abbé P.-E. Roy, in his preface to *Le vieux muet; ou Un héros de Châteauguay* (1901) by Jean-Baptiste Caouette, frankly admits that he has been asked, as a priest, to reassure prospective Catholic readers who have learned to avoid the corruptive influence of the novel form, 'un des plus exécrables dissolvants de la morale publique'. This doubtless helps to explain why, at a time when poetry, in the wake of Émile NELLIGAN, was producing works that were widely and vigorously discussed, the forty-odd novels published in Québec between 1900 and 1920 generally received little more than a brief mention in one or two periodicals.

As for the four writers faintly praised by Camille Roy, their works mainly distinguish themselves by pushing to new extremes the sermon-like qualities previously mentioned. Most fiction writers of this period insist heavily on the Catholic virtues of their characters; A.-B. Routhier in *Le centurion: roman des temps messianiques* (1909) and *Paulina: roman des temps apostoliques* (1918) simply produces paraphrases of the Bible with Christ and Saint Paul as protagonists. The youthful Hector Bernier—who at least has the merit of clumsily incorporating his didactic messages into the dialogue—preaches nationalism, catholicism, and fear of modern France in *Au large de l'écueil* (1912) and *Ce que disait la flamme* (1913), to a degree that caused Jules Fournier to despair at the fanatical education given young French Canadians.

Similarly *La terre* (1916) by Ernest CHOQUETTE carries the tradition of the rural novel inaugurated by Patrice LACOMBE's *La terre paternelle* in 1846 to new melodramatic heights. Although other works of the period, such as *Restons chez nous!* (1908) and *L'appel de la terre: roman de moeurs saguenayennes* (1919) by Damase Potvin, naïvely preach the dominant agriculturist ideology by glorifying life in the country while presenting the city as 'hell on earth', Choquette's story openly asks French Canadians to confine themselves to agriculture because they have no talent for industrial success.

Curiously not one of the seven historical novels produced at this time found favour in Camille Roy's *Manuel*, though this tendency seemed to be what he had most appreciated in the preceding period. It is true, of course, that most of these works based on the heroic sacrifices of New France or the Rebellion of 1837 accorded a much greater importance to the theme of passionate (though chaste) love than was then considered desirable by the critics. Gaëtane de Montreuil's *Fleur des Ondes; roman historique canadien* (1912), perhaps the best-received of this group, was criticized not so much for its lack of unity as for representing an Indian maiden who commits suicide for love.

L'arriviste: étude psychologique (1919) by Ernest Chouinard belongs to the category of the surprisingly numerous novels (ten in all) situated in contemporary urban Québec society. The protagonist is almost invariably a young lawyer and/or journalist who is in danger of falling victim to, or fighting a quixotic battle against, political corruption. Chouinard, however, paints the blackest picture of such a situation, condemning from the outset 'l'arriviste', an ambitious young lawyer and politician, while condoning his intelligent friend who retires to a monastery. Robert-Errol Bouchette's *Robert Lozé: nouvelle* (1903) adopts a more optimistic, though just slightly less didactic, approach by proposing that the true prosperity of French Canada lies in locally developed industries, modern agricultural techniques, socially conscious lawyers, and honest politicians. Perhaps the most unusual novel in this group is Ulric Barthe's *Similia similibus; ou, La guerre au Canada: essai romantique sur un sujet d'actualité* (1916), which describes the capture of Quebec by the Germans during the First World War and its subsequent liberation due to the efforts of two young journalists, one French Canadian and the other English Canadian.

The best of these 'urban' novels is without doubt *Le débutant: roman de moeurs du journalisme et de la politique dans la province de Québec* (1914) by Arsène Bessette. Completely ignored at the time of its publication—as much because of the author's radical reputation and his known affiliation with the Free Masons as the novel's criticism of the conservatism and intolerance of French-Canadian society and its realistic (though sober) presentation of an earnest young journalist's love affair with an older widow—this work, despite an occasional tendency to labour a point, is perhaps the only true novel (in the strict sense of the word) of quality produced by a French Canadian during this period.

The other two fictions that stand out head and shoulders above their contempories are MARIE CALUMET (1904) by Rodolphe GIRARD, which was translated under the same title by Irène Currie (1976), and *La* SCOUINE (1918) by Albert LABERGE. They too were surrounded by silence, but a silence imposed this time by the public disapproval of the Catholic Church of Québec. It is difficult for modern readers to understand why *Marie Calumet*—an amusing and well-written story about the adventures and misadventures of the lively but profoundly religious forty-year-old housekeeper of the endearing priest of Saint-Ildefonse, Abbé Flavel—encountered such wrath on the part of the clergy. Admittedly, realism was at that time frowned upon by critics (Camille Roy recommended a technique of 'idealistic realism'!), but that hardly explains such an extreme reaction. Ironically, Girard himself gives the key to the enigma when Abbé Flavel, upon discovering his beautiful niece poring over the 'Song of Solomon' (reproduced in the novel), decides from then on to keep the Scriptures under lock and key. Since the Bible was at that time forbidden reading for Roman Catholics, it was most likely fear of the curiosity that might be kindled by this sensuous biblical text that caused the condemnation of *Marie Calumet*.

Girard's fate, which never really improved despite the numerous novels he published, can also be partly attributed to his predilection for the theme of passionate love, which was always poorly received. In using this theme, Girard's *L'Algonquine: roman des jours héroiques du Canada sous la domination française* (1910) is remarkably similar to Adèle Bibaud's *Avant la conquête: épisode de la guerre de 1757* (1904). This predilection was more common in women writers. Though Laure Conan (Félicité ANGERS) had learned to minimize passion by 1900, other women writers continued to cultivate it. With *Nemoville* (1917) Madame Alcide Lacerte even began a series of popular exotic love novels that might be loosely compared to today's Harlequin romances.

Although *Marie Calumet* is not quite the 'masterpiece' Albert Laberge proclaimed it to be in 1946, it is a well-written and entertaining story that successfully portrays the 'joie de vivre' of a rural French-Canadian community at the turn of the century. Ironically, Laberge himself wrote the novel that gives the most negative picture of precisely the same setting. Written in reaction to the idealistic and didactic rural novels that preceded it, *La* SCOUINE describes in the best naturalist technique a series of loosely connected events in the life of the Deschamps family. Almost all the characters lead a miserable, unthinking, and senseless existence upon which, however, the narrator almost never permits himself to comment. If *Marie Calumet* can be said to illustrate facetiously the sexual repression of a small parish, *La Scouine* describes a totally castrated and isolated society resigned to its fate. At a time when rural life was the only area in which French Canada could be autonomous, the acceptance of the view presented in this

work would have been equivalent to genocide. Not surprisingly, the first extract published in *La Semaine* was condemned by Mgr Bruchési, and Laberge finally published his book privately for a circle of intimate friends, whence its influence (perhaps greater than many realize) on Claude-Henri GRIGNON's *Un homme et son péché* (1933), and on TRENTE ARPENTS (1938) by Ringuet (Philippe PANNETON).

The fact remains that the three outstanding fiction works of this period—*Le débutant, Marie Calumet,* and *La Scouine*—chose to ignore the ideological dogmatism of the time, and were suppressed for that reason. The fate of other novels, however, was scarcely more enviable. Clearly the novel as a social form presenting conflicting ideologies (that of the protagonist and that of the society in which he lives) was unacceptable in a society that, in its fight for survival, had become protectionist and monolithic. It is significant that in *Le débutant*, where two conflicting value systems are effectively illustrated, the final solution adopted by the protagonist is immigration to the U.S.A. (and therefore assimilation).

More acceptable, and frequently acclaimed as masterpieces, were the collections of descriptive essays such as *Propos canadiens* (1912) by Camille Roy, *Chez nous* (1914) and *Chez nos gens* (1918) by Adjutor Rivard, *Les rapaillages* (1916) by Lionel GROULX, or *Récits laurentiens* (1919) and *Croquis laurentiens* by Frère MARIE-VICTORIN. Many even hoped that these nostalgic portraits of the 'good old days' and of rural Québec, seasoned with a generous sprinkling of italicized local expressions, would lead to a distinctively French-Canadian genre.

This unrealistic attitude may be traced to the increasing efforts of a group known as the 'regionalists' to impose on Québec writers an idealistic nationalist vision of French Canada as an exclusively rural, traditional, Catholic, and highly moral society. Though reminiscent of views espoused by Abbé CASGRAIN in the nineteenth century, the decided regionalist trend at the beginning of the twentieth century is usually dated back to a speech given in 1904 by Abbé Camille Roy, entitled 'La nationalisation de la littérature canadienne', which was in large part a reaction to the threat of more modern literary tendencies—dangerously well represented by some Montreal writers, Nelligan in particular.

Despite attempts by the regionalists to

Novels in French 1900 to 1920

disregard all opponents to this highly dogmatic approach as 'exotics' or 'Francissons' (and therefore, so to speak, traitors to the national cause), there gradually evolved a conflict known as the Quarrel between the regionalists and the 'exotics' that finally exploded into the open towards 1918. As a result, literature became one of the main arenas where two distinct conceptions of the essence and future of French Canada—at the risk of oversimplification, a distinctive, traditional, rural Catholic society versus a more modern, twentieth-century, cosmopolitan one—battled for their very existence. The monolithic tendencies of the regionalist view help explain much of the suspicion encountered by the critical function that is inevitably performed by a true novel.

A new era for fiction was to begin, however, with the critics' discovery of Louis HÉMON's MARIA CHAPDELAINE: *récit du Canada français* (1916) towards 1918. At last it seemed possible to write quality novels in French Canada that would effectively reinforce agriculturist and traditional values. Ignoring the fact that Hémon was a foreigner, the regionalists glorified *Maria Chapdelaine* as proof that their theories on the necessity of treating local subjects and rural Québec could produce first-class literature. The 'exotics' retorted that, since Hémon came from France, the work in fact belonged to exotic literature. (This exchange is very revealing, since regionalism and exoticism are in fact both based on the accentuation of local, or foreign, peculiarities.) From then on *Maria Chapdelaine* became the measuring stick by which every French-Canadian novel published in the following twenty years would be judged. Since it was known in some circles, however, that the author had not been a practising Catholic, a few attempts were apparently made to have the book condemned, and this novel might easily have suffered the same fate as *Marie Calumet, Le débutant*, and *La Scouine* if Hémon had not died prematurely, if the book had not ended with the glorification of conservatism and heroic patriotism, or if it had not rapidly become a best-seller in Europe. This combination of circumstances, in any case, helped to create a success that did much to alleviate the anathema surrounding the novel form in Québec. Not only did French-Canadian fiction increase dramatically over the next decade in quality and number of works published, the reception accorded new fiction also improved.

Obviously changes in Québec society also played an important role in this change of attitude. As more and more French Canadians moved to the city and adapted to modern industrial society, it became increasingly difficult to impose a monolithic, tradition-oriented view of their collective future. The dogmatic excesses revealed by the Quarrel between the regionalists and the 'exotics' also contributed to the waning of a rigid view of what Québec literature should be. More and more writers—in particular those referred to by Alfred DesROCHERS in *Paragraphs (Interviews littéraires)* in 1931 as the 'post-war generation'—chose to combine local subject matter with modern and varied literary techniques. It might therefore be said that the extreme opinions upheld at the beginning of the twentieth century sowed the seeds of a new literary consciousness in Québec.   ANNETTE HAYWARD

1920 to 1940. The number of works of fiction published during this period almost tripled the number produced in the first twenty years of the century: some 400 titles, including children's stories and story collections. The novels seem to be characterized by conventionality on the one hand and by a marked deviation from it on the other. The deviation, which consisted chiefly of innovative literary techniques, was insidious because it finally broke down the norms established by the nationalistic ideology of conservatism. The traditional image of French-Canadian society's having been fragmented by disruptive change—the growth of urbanism, English-speaking economic dominance, the Depression—the élite of this society, led by the clergy, had promoted the sanctification of the past and of ancestral characteristics; the redemptive mission of a chosen people who were Catholic and French in a Protestant, Anglo-Saxon, and materialistic North America; moral idealism and rigidity; and distrust of outsiders and the modern world. In this context literature became a weapon for combat, and the fiction of the period usually presents characters that are more ideas than living people.

Their psychology is often sketchy and usually unconvincing, their emotions mere pretexts for philosophical dissertations or ideological sermonizing. The plot of the novels, illustrating a thesis rather than telling a story, often gets sidetracked into badly integrated digressions, while the author—more knowledgeable than the omniscient narrator—constantly forces the truth upon the reader in a linear delivery that is frequently marred by grammatical errors.

1. NOVELS OF THE LAND. Since a magnification of the rural world is one of the components of the ideology of conservatism, this period saw the novel of the land reach its highest point, both quantitatively (by following the ideological norm) and qualitatively (by deviating from it through realism). The prototype of the genre, on which there was little variation, is to be found in *La terre paternelle* (1846) by Patrice LACOMBE, and in the romantic dilemma portrayed in MARIA CHAPDELAINE (1916; trans. 1922) by Louis HÉMON. The plot is easily summarized: an individual (or a family), living happily on the farm, leaves it out of disillusionment or lack of judgment; he also leaves behind someone he loves, who is associated with rural life; he then settles in the city or abroad, where he lives unhappily, very often with an unsuitable woman; finally, after many mishaps and adventures, he realizes his initial mistake, returns to the land, and regains his first love—or else resigns himself to a life of misfortune and disappointment. In sociological terms, leaving the farm appears to be unavoidable, inevitable, and more or less imposed upon the character; the return, however, results from a series of disordered and unconvincing events. Because the ideological norms cannot completely hide the harsh realities, the coherence of the novel suffers. This is particularly apparent in *La campagne canadienne* (1925) by Adélard Dugré and in *L'erreur de Pierre Giroir* (1925) by J.E.A. Cloutier. The standard plot is repeated in a whole series of perfunctory novels from this period: *Un coeur fidèle* (1924) and *La petite maîtresse d'école* (1929) by Blanche Lamontagne; *L'enjoleuse* (1928) and *Celle qui revient* (1930) by Mme Elphège Croft; *La terre que l'on défend* (1928) by Henri Lapointe; and *La terre vivante* (1925) by Harry BERNARD.

As a variation on the novel of the land, the pioneer novel almost totally eliminates plot; it simply glorifies the return to the land and skips over any possible difficulties. Novels such as *Le Français* (1925) or *La Rivière-à-Mars* (1934) by Damase Potvin, and *Le p'tit gars du colon* (1934) or *Un sillon dans la forêt* (1936) by Benoît Desforêt, pretend to capture the essence of French-Canadian rural life while actually revealing the absurdity of their theses.

2. NOVELS OF IDEOLOGICAL OR REALISTIC DEVIANCE. While the writers of idealized novels of the land were firmly in the foreground, the background belonged to Albert LABERGE, whose collection of short stories portraying rural and urban settings, *Visages de la vie et de la mort* (1936), ran counter to the prevailing literary fashions. Both the aesthetic orientation of his work and his profound pessimism were not to be tolerated, and Laberge himself limited the impact of his book by having only 50 copies of it printed. Jean-Charles HARVEY was not so careful: his *Les demi-civilisés* (1934; *Fear's folly*, 1982), a veritable satiric tract in the form of a novel, was consigned to the Index as forbidden reading. Using a first-person narrator who gave unfettered expression to his liberty, his sensuality, and his opinions, Harvey openly attacked the shortcomings of a society dominated by those who had used conservatism to further their hypocritical and sterile domination. An ideological bombshell, Harvey's novel was, in its own way, just as excessive and unconvincing in a literary sense as were the more orthodox pronouncements disguised as novels. Much more insidiously effective, because they were novels above all else, were *Un homme et son péché* (1933; *The woman and the miser*, 1978) by Claude-Henri GRIGNON; MENAUD, MAÎTRE-DRAVEUR (1937; *Master of the river*, 1976) by Félix-Antoine SAVARD; and TRENTE ARPENTS (1938; *Thirty acres*, 1940) by Ringuet (Philippe PANNETON). They show up the failure of the ideology of conservatism, while appearing to pay it respect.

For a variety of reasons the world that most of these novels are concerned to defend is a world that is breaking apart. Sometimes the causes of this are internal, as with the psychological flaw in the hero of *Un homme et son péché*; sometimes they are external, as with the intrusions by outsiders in *Menaud, maître-draveur*. Sometimes both causes are involved; the hero in *Trente arpents*, for example, is a victim both of his biological age, since he is growing old, and of his economic age, since he is suffering the effects of the Depression. Still, most of the novels of the period refuse to admit that the changes in their world stem from within the society they describe, or are directly related to the individuals making up that society. The changes are thus attributed to the pernicious influence, malicious intent, and even in some cases the inherently evil nature of outsiders.

3. TRADITIONAL VALUES AND THE OUTSIDER. The presence of the outsider leads to the repeated theme of resistance, a theme

that MENAUD, MAÎTRE-DRAVEUR illustrates magnificently, at the same time as it shows its futility. The frequent references to mismatched or mixed marriages (different religious or ethnic groups) are thematically connected to the presence of outsiders and the resulting resistance. Such is the case in *La terre se venge* (1932) by Eugénie Chenel and *La campagne canadienne* (1925) by Adélard Dugré; in both novels the hero has married an outsider and his family is being assimilated. The same theme was taken up by Harry BERNARD in *L'homme tombé* (1924) and *La maison vide* (1926); here the wife, who has come from a lower social class, gets caught up in the frivolities of city life and destroys both the family home and the ancestral traditions. More than simply a lesson in the traditional bourgeois morality of French-Canadian Catholics, this theme by its very frequency expresses the anguish of a society forced to live in a modern world that is both strange and foreign. The voices of *Maria Chapdelaine* were being heard less and less, and this, from the traditional point-of-view, was a bad sign for the children of the future.

In *L'appel de la race* (1922) Lionel GROULX, under the pseudonym 'Alonié de Lestres', joined the theme of the mismatched marriage to an openly racist sanctification of national values. This novel was intended for use as a weapon; and although its plot was based on, and inspired by, the Franco-Ontarians' struggle against Rule 17, which effectively suppressed the teaching of French in Ontario, its general spirit connected it with the ideology of conservativism, which had become a veritable religion. After hesitating for a long time, the protagonist obeys the dictates of his superior bloodlines, makes part of his family French again, and becomes a spokesman for the French-Catholic cause to which he has sacrificed his marriage. Thus he fights against the influence of the Outsider—represented mainly by his converted English-speaking Protestant wife and the tainted lineage she has passed on to the hero's children. After this reconquest of the family, Groulx moved on to a reconquest of the territory. In *Au Cap Blomidon* (1932) a descendant of the Acadians expelled from their lands in the Great Deportation manages to regain possession of the ancestral farm. However, the success of this undertaking, while ideologically desirable, is somewhat unrealistic: the plot necessitates not only an appearance by a ghost but also the intervention of a witch. With its

long historical digressions, Groulx's second novel is of less interest than his first, which provided the most coherent illustration of the ideological sermonizing so often found in the writings of this period.

Harry Bernard, in *La ferme des pins* (1930), also dealt with repossession by the French, as seen through the eyes of an old English-Canadian from the Eastern Townships who watches his family being assimilated into the French-speaking community. The character has enough psychological credibility to win the reader's sympathy, even though the author's apparent intention was to proclaim the glory of the French reconquest. This Englishman, who speaks—strangely, with a French accent—of dispossession, occasionally attains the realistic grandeur of Euchariste Moisan in TRENTE ARPENTS, and also foreshadows the tragic epic of Menaud. Perhaps the reality of the situation was so painful that it had to be expressed by being projected onto the Outsider.

The cult of traditional values and the sanctification of the French-Canadian race produced a spate of minor novels, each more insipid, awkward, and narrowly moralistic than the others. Examples of this genre include *La plus belle chose du monde* (1927) and *Le nom dans le bronze* (1923) by Michelle Le Normand, *A la hâche* (1932) by Adolphe Nantel, *L'unique solution* (1925) by Arsène Goyette, and *Le spectre menaçant* (1932) by Joseph Lallier.

4. HISTORICAL NOVELS. The historical novel, already much in vogue in Québec literature, was able to maintain its important position in this period because the ideology of conservativism held to a vision of the world that was excessively oriented towards the past. As a vehicle for the cult of traditional values, it tended towards formula writing and sank to the level of para-literature, or popular literature, as in the novels of Jean Féron, or became a means for educating and indoctrinating young people, as in those of Eugène Achard. Where historical anecdote was used as a pretext for an exercise in style, the primary result was, fortunately, a novel rather than simply a historical illustration. Novels in the latter category thus deviated from the established norms and testified to the inevitable disappearance of the past.

Although *Les habits rouges* (1923) by Robert Laroque de ROQUEBRUNE deals with the troubles of 1837-8, it avoids nationalistic sermonizing and manages to tell a love story. *Les dames Le Marchand* (1927) by the same author portrays one side of the traditional world—a seigneurial family—that the heir refuses to perpetuate either materially by marrying a rich woman or spiritually by becoming a priest. In *Nord-Sud* (1931), by Léo-Paul DESROSIERS, the hero's decision to leave his native land is accepted without condemnation, and in *Les engagés du grand portage* (1938; *The making of Nicolas Montour*, 1978) Desrosiers presents the victory of a protagonist who would not meet with the approval of traditional morality. *D'un océan à l'autre* (1924) by Robert Laroque de Roquebrune tries to bring to life the conquest of the West and to honour the missionaries who brought Catholicism and the French tradition; in retrospect, however, the novel's final sentence seems bitterly ironic: '. . . with an instinctive gesture, the old missionary raised his hand and, in the direction of the disappearing train, made a broad sign of benediction.' This blessing is bestowed on the very weapon that would destroy the old dream of a French, Catholic America. The exceptional stylistic qualities of *Né à Québec* (1933; *Born in Quebec*, 1964) by Alain GRANDBOIS made readers realize that simply choosing a historical subject could no longer excuse awkward writing. As with the rural novel, the successful historical novels showed that true art could not be harnessed to a cause without falling into decline; they also indicated that ideological distortions of reality lead to narrative or psychological incoherence in the novel, and to a world of cardboard-like artificiality.

5. THE PRESENCE OF THE MODERN WORLD. Moving away from history and the land, a few novels attempted to provide an accurate description of the modern world disparaged by others. For example, *Jules Faubert, le roi du papier* (1923) by Ubald PAQUIN tells of the exploits of a French-speaking industrialist; Faubert's success, however, is as unbelievable as his final failure, suggesting that control of the modern world remains in the realm of good intentions. The same theme is taken up by Jean-Charles HARVEY in *Marcel Faure* (1922), a Utopian novel that inverts the dominant ideological vision of the period.

6. WOMEN'S NOVELS AND ROMANCES. In this category deviance of expression was all the more effective for being less strident. Although they were never unqualified triumphs, and although they often indulged in the worst melodrama (for example, *Peuvent-elles garder un secret?* 1937, by Adrienne Maillet), these novels provided descriptions and analyses of seduction, jealousy, and—as with *La chair décevante* (1931) by Jovette-Alice BERNIER—illicit love. Some, like *Seuls* (1937) by Lucie Clément, or *A deux* (1937) by Laetitia Filion, portrayed the powerlessness of women in society. Others, such as *Mon Jacques* (1933) by Eva Sénécal, went so far as to deal with bigamy. Still others described urban life and spoke of women's suffrage, as in *L'oncle des jumeaux Pomponelle* (1939) by Adrienne Maillet. Together these novels constituted a kind of ideological erosion through which the forms of deviance and the presence of the real world gradually made themselves felt. Although a novel by Lucie Clément was entitled *En marge de la vie* (1934), these novels were actually on the fringes of the official ideology and closer to life, opening the way for the psychological novel, which was more impervious to ideological dictates. ANGÉLINE DE MONTBRUN (Québec, 1881) by Laure Conan (Félicité ANGERS) had been the first of such psychological novels, a vein of writing that was quickly smothered by the pressure of established norms, as shown by Conan's last novel, *Le sève immortelle* (1925), in which the love plot took second place to a glorification of ancestors, rural life, and nationalistic loyalty.

7. TECHNICAL INNOVATIONS. At the level of style, several of these novels used a first-person narration similar to that of HARVEY's *Les demi-civilisés*. Others insisted on an individualized presence that sought to establish its own norms; *Mon Jacques* (1933) by Eva Sénécal was in this regard the most successful of the women's novels. Rex DESMARCHAIS also used a first-person narrator in *L'initiatrice* (1932); with the text carrying not only the narrative line but the story of the narration itself, it is a piece of writing that is almost self-consciously a novel. Harry BERNARD adopted this technique in *Juana, mon aimée* (1931) and *Dolorès* (1932), two novels that were intended to be regional portraits but rose to the level of psychological analysis. An 'ego' makes itself felt in these works—one that breaks through, for example, in *La pension Leblanc* (1927) by Robert CHOQUETTE, another regionalist work that transcended its genre to become a novel of manners and psychological analysis.

This human presence, and this density of the fictional world, are characteristic of GRIGNON's *Un homme et son péché* (1933) and Ringuet's (Philippe PANNETON) TRENTE ARPENTS (1938). As for SAVARD's MENAUD, MAÎTRE-DRAVEUR (1937), even though its main character cannot be considered a complete 'ego', its ideological expression is so intensely poetic that Menaud becomes a symbol rather than a painfully personified idea. As the swan-song of traditional nationalistic sermonizing this novel, with its powerful ending and its poetic nature, revealed the social and literary dead-end in which the ideology of conservatism had become trapped. The literary regionalism implied by this ideology was condemned to be no more than a form of internal exoticism, badly integrated into the action of the novels. Savard imposed the presence of the Laurentians to the point that Menaud becomes part of the landscape; similarly, in the novels by Grignon and Ringuet, a natural world that is both omnipresent and indifferent to the characters' passions becomes the centre of the action, either as a witness to, or as the representative of, a relentless fate.

Beneath the appearance of uniformity the literary scene from 1920 to 1940 actually underwent some profound changes. Writers came to learn that no matter how orthodox the subject was, there was no excuse for bad writing. They also learned that to serve a cause too closely is a disservice to literature. Beginning with a character on whom they imposed a story, not to mention a ready-made morality, they advanced to the stage of creating a character who assumed his own history, and to the kind of writing that imposed its own universe. By obeying the logic of fiction, the most successful of their novels broke apart the stereotyped images and opened a door on reality.

8. BIBLIOGRAPHY. For a bibliography of writings from this period it is useful to consult the second volume of the excellent *Dictionnaire des oeuvres littéraires du Québec 1900 à 1939* (1980), published under the direction of Maurice Lemire, as well as the third volume of the *Archives des lettres canadiennes: le roman canadien-français* (1977). Essential aids to an understanding of this period are *Le roman de la terre au Québec* (1974) by Mireille Servais-Maquoi, *Les grands thèmes nationalistes du roman historique canadien-français* (1970) by Maurice Lemire, and 'Evolution de la technique du roman canadien-français', an unpublished doctoral thesis by Henri Tuchmaïer (Laval, 1958). A rapid survey of the subject is provided in the second volume of the *Histoire de la littérature française du Québec (1900-1945)* (1968), edited by Pierre de Grandpré, while developments in the literature of this period are sketched in *Le roman canadien-français du vingtième siècle*

(1966) by Réjean Robidoux and André Renaud. Historical and ideological considerations are effectively dealt with in André Linteau et al., *Histoire du Québec contemporain. De la Confédération à la crise 1867-1929* (1979); Denis Monière, *Le développement des idéologies au Québec des origines à nos jours* (1977); André J. Belanger, *L'apolitisme des idéologies québécoises. Le grand tournant de 1934-1936* (1974); and Fernand Dumont *et al.*, *Idéologies au Canada français 1900-1929* (1974).   GUY MONETTE

1940 to 1959. The rapid industrialization and urbanization of Québec society during this period had significant effects on the culture of francophone Québec, and on its literature in particular. In the intellectual sphere a capital event was the publication in 1948 of the manifesto REFUS GLOBAL, which had a lasting effect on cultural effervescence. La RELÈVE, a journal founded by Catholic intellectuals in 1934, became the monthly *La Nouvelle Relève* in 1941 and reflected the malaise over the crisis of values in Québec society. *Cité Libre*, founded in 1950 by a similar group, was more oriented to political opposition to Premier Duplessis but also gave space to literary and artistic reviews, marked for the most part by philosophical personalism and universalism. The war had brought a number of exiled French writers and artists to Québec; books by French classical writers that were on the Index were published; and plays by Jean-Paul Sartre were performed during this period. The advent of television in 1952 also significantly shaped cultural habits and tastes. In this atmosphere literary publication grew extensively. A reading public was thus established, and several major writers were able to live from their work.

The major trends in fiction writing in this period can be grouped under five categories that sometimes interweave; urban social realism; the psycholigical-moral novel; works treating industrial conflict; transformed 'traditional' novels; and an important sphere of 'independent' creativity.

1. URBAN SOCIAL REALISM. As the Second World War was drawing to a close two young writers, in Quebec City and Montreal, turned the Québec novel resolutely towards the teeming working-class areas of these two cities. Roger LEMELIN's *Au pied du la pente douce* (1944; *The town below*, 1948), an instant bestseller, was refused a literary prize because it was not centred on the countryside. Gabrielle ROY's BONHEUR D'OCCA-

SION (1945; *The tin flute*, 1947) was honoured in France and the U.S., and was eventually translated into nine languages. Both these novels drew sustenance from the Depression, from the tensions between sociophysical topographical entities, and from the desire of youth to break out of a claustrophobic trap.

A regionalist satirist, Lemelin continued to dwell on opposition between Quebec City's Lower and Upper Town societies in Les PLOUFFE (1948; *The Plouffe family*, 1950) and *Pierre le magnifique* (1952; *In quest of splendour*, 1955); while Roy, who had touched more universal chords and developed characterization to an unmatched degree in *Bonheur d'occasion*, produced a second major novel with a Montreal setting, *Alexandre Chenevert* (1954; *The cashier*, 1955). Through the life and death of her bank-teller hero she developed her treatment of economic and cultural alienation, and in her religious theme she anticipated the reforms of Vatican II and the *aggiornamento* of the Catholic Church. Roy's urban-realist work, like Lemelin's, also anticipated the vast changes of the Quiet Revolution. Roy swung back to her Manitoba childhood and youth in creating *La petite poule d'eau* (1950; *Where nests the waterhen*, 1951) and *Rue Deschambault* (1955; *Street of riches*, 1957), launching the theme of a quest for an ideal world of human solidarity that would become dominant for her in the sixties and seventies. Other writers who followed the general path of urban social realism were Ringuet (Philippe PANNETON), Roger Viau, and Jean Pellerin. Ringuet's *Le poids du jour* (1949), though less skilfully crafted than his classic TRENTE ARPENTS, is an interesting novel on the making of an industrialist in the period between the wars. Viau's *Au milieu la montagne* (1951) has echoes of Roy and Lemelin in its irreconcilable tensions between the east-end and Outremont districts of Montreal. Pellerin's *Le diable par la queue* (1957) presents a Québec family that immigrates to New York during the Depression, only to be caught up in the temporary work of the sweatshop before responding to the nostalgic call of the native rural parish.

2. THE PSYCHOLOGICAL-MORAL NOVEL. An important group of Québec writers was concerned less with external social reality than with the internal turmoil caused by what they perceived as the surrounding cultural and ethical wasteland: Robert CHARBONNEAU, André Giroux, Robert ÉLIE, all of whom were connected with *La* RELÈVE

and *La Nouvelle Relève;* André LANGEVIN; and satirists Jean SIMARD and Pierre Baillargeon. Their works—labelled 'romans du cas de conscience' by Jacques Michon—treat the anguish of characters in search of vital spiritual values in a world of hypocrisy, materialism, and expediency. Charbonneau published three novels in the 1940s: *Ils posséderont la terre* (1941), *Fontile* (1945), and *Les désirs et les jours* (1948). In the first two, set in the imaginary provincial town of Fontile in the Depression years, the author concentrates on the internal tensions, moral conflicts, and religious preoccupations of his characters. While there are temporary pulls towards political action in all three, the heroes are strangely introverted and troubled beings; for example, in *Les désirs* a lawyer-M.P. goes through a middle-age crisis. Similar conflicts and tensions tear at the characters of Robert Élie's *La fin des songes* (1950), which ends in the suicide of the hero, but in his *Il suffit d'un jour* (1957) the heroine comes to terms with life, having rejected its absurd realities.

André Giroux's *Au delà des visages* (1948) and *Le gouffre a toujours soif* (1953) combine social criticism with such themes as religious hypocrisy, metaphysical anguish, and the search for authenticity. The author flays 'Christian' anti-Semitism in the first, and servility in both. In *Au delà des visages*, as in Eugène Cloutier's *Les témoins* (1953)—both of which use an innovative form of internal monologue—the heroes kill not out of hatred but in a certain ritualistic revolt against the human condition. In *Le gouffre* Giroux deals with the long agony of a cancer sufferer who, finding that his marriage partner is a stranger, is crushed by incommunicability.

André Langevin's three novels—*Évadé de la nuit* (1951), POUSSIÈRE SUR LA VILLE (1953; *Dust over the city*, 1955), and *Le temps des hommes* (1956)—have been seen as forming a trilogy with recurring motifs of suicide, pity, resignation, and failure to find meaningful values and human communion; the repeated appearance of the orphan figure, undoubtedly inspired in part by the author's biography, has been thought by some critics to symbolize the French Canadian in search of himself. Failure to communicate with others is summarized thus in the first novel, 'Jamais nos courbes ne se sont rencontrées . . .', and in the modern classic *Poussière* by the image of the parallel lines along which the narrator, Alain Dubois, and his wife Madeleine travel, never able to meet. Langevin's work differs from that of most of the writers of the 'roman du cas de conscience' in that traditional religion is totally rejected in favour of a pessimistic existentialist outlook that recalls Camus's Sysiphus. The author seems to aim at showing the inability of traditional Catholicism to deal with the absurdity of modern existence. In *Poussière* and *Le temps des hommes* the hero questions Providence by revolting against the unacceptable death of a young child, and seeks solace in the purely human. The absentee economic force lurking in the background of these two novels—the Benson Mine in Macklin, and Scott Power and Paper in Scottville—adds to the already profound ontological alienation.

A satirical tone modulates the sombre, serious subject-matter in the work of Jean Simard and Pierre Baillargeon. Simard in *Félix* (1947), *Hôtel de la reine* (1949), and *Mon fils pourtant heureux* (1956) excoriates the French-Canadian petty bourgeoisie, provincialism, official ideology, the clergy, and the educational system. In his *Les sentiers de la nuit* (1959), which centres on an Anglican family in lower Westmount, and on the anglophone banking milieu, many critics have seen a veiled transposition of pre-Quiet Revolution francophone society. Pierre Baillargeon (1916-67) attacked similar targets in *Les médisances de Claude Perrin* (1945), *Commerce* (1947), and *La neige et le feu* (1948). The first two reflect the malaise of the author's generation of intellectuals; while the third, a novel of expatriation and return, attacks conformism and clericalism. Similarly the spicy satire *Saint-Pépin, P.Q.* (1955) by Bertrand Vac (Aimé PELLETIER) ridicules electoral mores and the false piety of two 'dévotes'.

3. NOVELS OF INDUSTRIAL CONFLICT. While there were instances of industrial conflict in the first works of urban social realism—especially in LEMELIN's *Les Plouffe* (the printer's strike at *L'Action chrétienne*) and *Pierre le magnifique* (the loggers' walkout at the Savard camp), and in Ringuet's (PANNETON's) *Le poids du jour* (protest marches of the unemployed in the Depression)—it was not until the 1950s, when labour tensions became volatile in Québec, that novels concentrated on such events. Most important among these are Jean-Jules RICHARD's *Le feu dans l'amiante* (1956), Pierre Gélinas's *Les vivants, les morts et les autres* (1959), and Gérard BESSETTE's first novel, *La bagarre* (1958). The distinguishing feature of these works is the collective form of social protest, as con-

trasted with the individual revolt in the earlier work of social realism. Richard's fictionalized treatment of the seminal Asbestos strike of 1949 contains vivid scenes of feverish labour amid mounds of dust in a town whose rhythm is marked by three daily dynamite blasts, and of the march of miners' wives and children, led by the priest, to confront the provincial police. This book, however, is too close to reportage to be an effective 'roman social'. (Richard is one of the few authors to write a memorable Second World War novel in French. His *Neuf jours de haine* (1948), Bertrand Vac's (Aimé PELLETIER's) *Deux portes . . . une adresse* (1952), and Jean Vaillancourt's *Les Canadiens errants* (1954) are the best treatments of this theme.) Historical labour struggles—the long conflicts in 1952 at Dominion Textile and the Dupuis Frères department store—mark Pierre Gélinas's *Les vivants*. Gélinas also intersperses his *bildungsroman*, centered on a well-to-do-hero-turned-radical, with elements of contemporary political history such as the Korean War and the Khruschev report denouncing Stalin's crimes, along with the riot that followed Maurice Richard's suspension from the NHL. Despite some highly dramatic pages, this broad social canvas is only tenuously held together by the hero, and the total effect is diffuse and unconvincing. In Bessette's *La bagarre* labour conflict—a strike by sweepers at the Metropolitan Transport Company—and the events that surround it are central to the evolution of the hero, Jules Leboeuf, who works by night and studies by day. This novel is important for its creative transcription of JOUAL, its study of a variety of levels of speech, and its revival of naturalism, which had been squelched in Québec during the First World War. Dealing with the writing of a novel, *La bagarre* announces a key aspect of Bessette's work in being reflexive, and anticipates a major preoccupation of Québec fiction from the 1960s on.

4. TRANSFORMED 'TRADITIONAL' NOVELS. Rural and historical novels, mainstays of the traditional mode of expression, underwent important transformations in this period. Historical novels by Charlotte Savary, Pierre Benoît, and Gérard Morriset, among others, were active elements in the process of demythifying the origins of New France. After Ringuet's TRENTE ARPENTS it had become difficult to pursue the model of the consecrated 'roman de la fidélité'. Thus Jean Filiatrault's *Terres stériles* (1953) shows the blind revolt of the younger farming genera-

tion against the dominant father figure, and continues the tendency to desanctify the rural milieu. The most important work in this mould is that classic of Québec literature, Germaine GUÈVREMONT's *Le survenant* (1945). Although dealing with the well-worn theme of a family dynasty threatened by a break with continuity on the ancestral land, this novel, and its sequel *Marie-Didace* (1947)—published together in English as *The outlanders* (1950)—present the rural parish as a stifling milieu dominated by pettiness and prejudice. The outlander, a transient and suspicious figure in the rural novel, here moves to the centre in the person of the 'Survenant', who brings the free air of the outside world into a static community. His openness to nature and love, his skills, interest in science, musical talents, and generosity provoke the repressed dreams of those around him, particularly the women. But he finds the narrowness of the Chenal du Moine (near Sorel) too constricting and takes to the road once more.

5. 'INDEPENDENT' CREATIVITY. Some important writers who began to publish their first works of fiction in the period under review are hard to classify under the previous headings because they chose a highly independent approach to writing. Four of them—Yves Thériault, Anne Hébert, Antonine Maillet, and Marie-Claire Blais—remain today among the major French-language writers of Canada.

While Guèvremont and Roy were among the first francophone writers to present positive, though episodic, portraits of cultural strangers to the milieu—Gypsies, Blacks, Jews, Italians, Ukrainians, etc.—and Bertrand Vac (Aimé PELLETIER) and Louis Dantin (Eugène SEERS) made major characters of a Métis and a Black respectively (*Louise Genest*, 1950; *Les enfances de Fanny*, 1951, translated by Raymond Chamberlain as *Fanny*, 1974), it was Yves THÉRIAULT who was most innovative in this context when he chose key figures for many of his works from among the ethnic and racial minorities of Canada. Thériault's first novel, *La fille laide* (1950), staked out his claim to 'primitivisme', giving ample room for psychoanalytic criticism. This violent story of a struggle between dwellers of a vague plain and mountain region was quickly followed by *Le dompteur d'ours* (1951), in which the 'survenant', Hermann, comes to an anonymous mountain village in Québec, promising to wrestle a bear. His presence transforms village life in a way similar to that of Guèvre-

mont's hero, but he flees before the promised match, thus proving himself a fraud. Thériault next published *Les vendeurs du temple* (1952), whose biblical title refers to the higher clergy's collusion in political corruption in a rural setting during the Duplessis years. Thériault reached the pinnacle of his career with *Aaron* (1954), set in the 'exotic' milieu of Jewish immigrants in Montreal, and *Agaguk* (1958), which takes place in the tundra of the Labrador-Ungava peninsula. In both works there is a struggle between the generations: grandfather versus grandson torn between tradition and modernism in *Aaron*, and in *Agaguk* son versus father, the tribal chief, in a similar struggle between corrupted tradition and desire for renewal. Though these two books are rich in ethnographic details, some critics have seen in them a transposition and masking of aspects of the Québec francophone reality. *Agaguk* has also been hailed for presenting the first authentic lovers in Québec fiction. Anne HÉBERT, who evolved from a first-rank poet to a brilliant short-story writer with *Le torrent* (1950), in 1958 produced her first novel, *Les chambres de bois*, which bears the same title as one of her best-known poems and echoes its foreboding atmosphere. Catherine, a working-class girl from a northern mining town in France, meets her Prince Charming, the aristocrat Michel, marries him, and moves to the panelled rooms of his Paris apartment. Soon his sister Lia joins them, creating a strange triangle; profound feelings of guilt pervade the atmosphere, and Michel is obsessed with the fear that the flesh is the devil's domain. Catherine flees to the sunny south, where she finds love and the beginnings of liberation.

The Acadian-born writer, Antonine MAILLET, began her career with the rudimentary novel *Pointe-aux-coques* (1958). Set in a New Brunswick fishing village, its heroine is the teacher Mlle Cormier (Maillet's mother's name). The speech of certain characters reflects Maillet's early interest in the Acadian dialect, and the novel presents various types who reappear in her later work: men of the sea, wild outlanders, the dispossessed, and the snob. Marie-Claire BLAIS published *La* BELLE BÊTE (1959; *Mad shadows*, 1960; NCL 1971) when just twenty. It is a tale of ugliness, idiocy, sadism, suicide, family breakdown, and physical decomposition. The work was generally received with shock by conservative and clerical critics, but was hailed by others. Fortunately it was frequently reprinted and

Blais was encouraged to continue her career, which has since flourished.

See Maurice Lemire et al., *Dictionnaire des oeuvres littéraires du Québec*, III (1982); Jean-Charles Falardeau, *Notre société et son roman* (1967); B.-Z. Shek, *Social realism in the French-Canadian novel* (1977); André Belleau, *Le romancier fictif: essai sur la représentation de l'écrivain dans le roman québécois* (1980); and a special issue of *Études littéraires* (Apr. 1981) entitled 'Sémiotique textuelle et histoire littéraire du Québec'. BEN-Z. SHEK

1960 to 1982. One of the most striking and important features of Québec fiction in the sixties and seventies has been its apparent desire to free itself in terms of both form and content. After 1960 the novel increasingly became an instrument of protest and of liberation. Often using a first-person narrator, and at times focusing on problems connected with the act of writing, novelists tended to reject traditional styles in favour of JOUAL, and popular levels of language more appropriate for describing the humble living conditions of a significant portion of the population. Traditional plot-lines and narrative techniques were dispensed with, particularly in the seventies, when the usual psychological and social descriptions gave way to irony, caricature, satire, eroticism, violence, dreams, and self-scrutiny. Marginal characters and situations came into prominence, with descriptions of economic poverty, social dependence, and frustration, and with a variety of emotional problems connected with death, separation, suffering, madness, and depression. As in the cinema, marginal states of the imagination were also explored, producing a vein of fantasy/fantastic fiction that may have stemmed from a need to escape the confines of everyday experience.

In this period realism held more sway than symbolism, even if the realities described have tended to be rather strange or unusual. Marie-Claire BLAIS, for example, has moved from poetic romanticism towards hyper-realism, bleak caricature, and the grotesque; while Gérard BESSETTE's work has gone beyond social realism into the inner realism of analytic introspection. To a large extent recent Québec fiction has avoided the here-and-now; anger and revolt have led it in the direction of more radical forms of escape and protest. At the same time there has been a movement towards the outside—beyond the immediate borders of Québec and into the vortex of history.

Among the most important novelists of the period, few except Michel TREMBLAY are traditional realists. FERRON, CARRIER, and GODBOUT, for example, all take a playful or surrealistic approach; BEAULIEU, Yvon Rivard, Jacques Benoit, and Roger Fournier rely on myth and fantasy; and AQUIN and Yolande Villemaire explore the dimensions of form. Introspection is frequent, as in the novels of HÉBERT, Bessette, DUCHARME, and POULIN, while action often takes place in a context of fantasy, history, or legend—as with MAILLET, Jean-Yves Soucy, BEAUCHEMIN, Bessette, and Benoît. In this way, everyday life is transformed by exceptional circumstances.

This survey covers only the most prominent authors, and those novels that indicate the directions, focuses, currents, and developments in the literature and culture of the period.

1. THE EARLY SIXTIES. The Duplessis period was followed by a new and urgent desire to communicate; the despair, passivity, and existential awkwardness that had been so characteristic of previous novels were suddenly transformed with a vengeance after 1960, when the hidden corners of Québec society began to emerge. Because 1960 marked an opening-up to the world and to history, literature began to present a new reflection of society and a critical awareness of previous limitations. *Le libraire* (1960; *Not for every eye*, 1962) by Gérard BESSETTE satirizes a mean, provincial society in the grip of clerical censorship. The anti-hero never directly criticizes or confronts the hypocrisy in his milieu; rather, he ironizes and avoids it, taking action by running away with the stock of books on the Index and selling them off at bargain prices. *Les pédagogues* (1961), which attacks the teaching world through caricature, is a conventional novel and less successful than the diary format of *Le libraire*. *Le poids de Dieu* (1962; *The burden of God*, 1964) by Gilles MARCOTTE shows the old world unravelling by describing a young priest's crisis of faith, which strengthens his vocation 'on the side of man'. In *L'aquarium* (1962) Jacques GODBOUT depicts the slow moral disintegration of a group of whites in the Third World: only the narrator will be saved. Passion explodes on the scene with *Le temps des jeux* (1961) by Diane Giguère: jealousy provokes an incestuous, suicidal girl, looking for her lost father, into having her older lover kill her mother (from whom she has stolen him); her hate is the other side of an im-

mense, anguished love. Clarie MARTIN dares to tell of the love affair between a publisher and his mistress in *Doux-Amer* (1960): both characters narrate the events. Multiple narration is also used in Martin's *Quand j'aurai payé ton visage* (1962), which tells of a woman's passion for her brother-in-law.

As the old ideologies based on agriculture, free enterprise, and Messianism were replaced by industrialism, technocracy, socialism, anti-clericalism, and state control, and Catholic monolithism gave way to ideological pluralism, the term 'French-Canadian' gave way to 'Québécois'. A movement towards reappropriating the Québécois environment had already been reflected in poetry and film; it now appeared in fiction as well. Claude JASMIN's *Pleure pas Germaine* (1965), written in *joual*, is both a trip through the province and an account of a father's search for his daughter's murderer. *Le couteau sur la table* (1965; *Knife on the table*, NCL 1968), by Jacques Godbout, involves a trip across Canada and then back to Québec, as well as the transfer of the hero's affections from an English-speaking to a French-speaking woman while the first terrorist bombs explode. Jasmin's *Ethel et le terroriste* (1964; *Ethel and the terrorist*, 1965) depicts everyday life in the city but also concerns an FLQ member's flight to New York. Doubts about terrorism inspired *Mon cheval pour un royaume* (1967) by Jacques POULIN: the narrator, wounded by the bomb he is carrying, is given to much soul-searching, as is Jasmin's terrorist.

Jasmin's early works spring from an old world that must be destroyed. The hero in *La corde au cou* (1960) commits a crime of passion and blind revenge. His flight and subsequent death are similar to those of the hero in *Délivrez-nous du mal* (1961), in which André wants to get free of both Georges and his own past; perhaps the escape suggests a search for independence. Jasmin's early heroes are ready to commit murder; their lives are filled with degradation and introspection; sometimes they die surrounded, like the hero of *Et puis tout est silence* (1965; *The rest is silence*, 1965), caught in the timbers of a fallen-down barn. There are similarities here with the position of the dying imprisoned engineer in Yves THÉRIAULT's *Cul-de-sac* (1961) who is caught in the dead-end of a nervous breakdown, looking over his past.

Besides dealing with repossession of the land, the novel became preoccupied with the language in which this activity is given expression. Prior to the sixties, fictional heroes tended to be dreamers incapable of action; but as their dreams become increasingly and consciously discredited, the descent into hell begins. In *Le cabochon* (1964), by André MAJOR, the oral style of the writing matches the violence of the scenes, both in order to symbolize the fragmentation taking place and to provoke resistance and revolt. Jacques Godbout also uses popular French in his best novel, *Salut Galarneau!* (1967; *Hail Galarneau!*, 1970), which tells the story of the King of French Fries in Île Perrot, a dreamer and outcast whose desire to live and whose dreams of writing lead him to wall himself up in his house.

As the official culture and the counter-culture began to merge, Québec literature was written for the first time in a Québec language, JOUAL, its fractured nature reflecting a fractured reality. Meanwhile, as writers began to master the techniques of the realistic novel and to inject it with the hyper-realism of popular language, they also abandoned traditional forms of narration in favour of the interior monologue. The novels of Gérard Bessette exemplify this change: *L'incubation* (1965; *Incubation*, 1967) consists of a long sentence with verbs and adjectives repeated and most of the punctuation eliminated. The form is both an extension of Hervé Jodoin's first-person diary in *Le libraire* and a preview of the dashes and brackets in Bessette's *Le cycle* (1971)—the dashes identifying physical sensations while the single or double brackets enclose the subconscious and unconscious levels of a continuous psychic voice (in seven interior monologues dealing with the death of the father). The trilogy *Quelqu'un pour m'écouter* (1964), by Réal Benoit, tells of the childhood traumas of Rémi, who decides to run away; in the middle of the story we find a change of perspective and a first-person reflection on its writing. Dream and reality intertwine to reveal the author-narrator's unconscious, thus prefiguring future adaptations of the interior monologue. In this way writing became increasingly self-analytic and self-conscious, culminating in the rampant formalism of the later sixties.

Gabrielle ROY, whose prairie background and fully bilingual writing skills have set her apart from the regional preoccupations common among French-Canadian writers, concentrates on the human quest for joy and for a mutual understanding that is all too often ephemeral or belated. In *La montagne secrète* (1961; *The hidden mountain*, 1962; NCL,

1975) a young painter travelling in the Arctic finds, loses, and finds again a mountain that symbolizes his quest for both a subject and the means of expressing it.

By the early sixties the novel had become the predominant literary genre in Québec. Whereas in the entire nineteenth century only 52 novels (and 22 new editions) had been published, the number of novels published annually in Québec rose from 27 in 1961 to 100 in 1974.

2. 1965 TO 1970. In 1965 Gérard BESSETTE's *L'INCUBATION*, Hubert AQUIN's PROCHAIN ÉPISODE, and Marie-Claire BLAIS's *Une saison dans la vie d'Emmanuel* were published, followed in 1966 by Réjean DUCHARME's *L'avalée des avalés*. Described as obsessive and outrageous, these *nouveaux romans* were both lyrical and denunciatory. Bessette's narrator, Lagarde, watches the slow degradation of the human relationships around him, including that of his friend Gordon with Néa, a prodigal mistress. Their reconciliation proves impossible and Néa commits suicide. The sumptuous, lyrical writing of *Prochain épisode* (1965; *Prochain épisode*, NCL, 1973) deals not only with the act of writing but makes connections between the woman and the land, and the symbolic value of the landscape. Later, with *Trou de mémoire* (1968), Aquin continued his baroque exploration of the *Doppelgänger* theme by presenting the scrambled story of an African revolutionary; a dope-addict pharmacist and the rape of his English-Canadian girlfriend (reported by a publisher); and the completion of the story's missing sections by the girl's sister. In *L'antiphonaire* (1970) extreme situations (such as rape and epilepsy) parallel historical periods (such as the Italian Renaissance or the American twentieth century). Aquin's final novel, *Neige noire* (1974), juxtaposes the text of a film script with a commentary upon it.

In *Une saison dans la vie d'Emmanuel* (1965; *A season in the life of Emmanuel*, 1966) Marie-Claire Blais shows how poverty engenders sordidness and squalor. A last child with a Messianic name is born into a large rural family; his father is severely limited, his mother lost in her melancholy; the priesthood is the only way out for the poetic Jean-le-Maigre, who is crushed by tuberculosis. The novel, composed like a mosaic, is by turns erotic, naturalistic, surreal, or hyperreal. The author presents a world in which existence itself has become impossible. Many of Blais's novels are descriptions and consecrations of childhood (*La belle bête*, 1959, *Mad shadows*, 1960; *Tête blanche*, 1960, NCL 1974; *Emmanuel*), or adolescence (*Le jour est noir*, 1962; *L'insoumise*, 1966, *The fugitive*, 1978). In *David Sterne* (1967, Eng. trans., 1973)—an exploration of 'all the vices'—a son rebels against his father, and in *Les manuscrits de Pauline Archange* (1968; *The manuscripts of Pauline Archange*, 1969) a problem child is badly treated by her father and her teachers. After exorcizing the experiences of youth, characteristically through suffering and revolt, Blais moved towards descriptions of romantic, sexual, and lesbian relationships in *Le loup* (1977; *The wolf*, 1974), *Une liaison parisienne* (1975; *A literary affair*, 1979), and finally *Les nuits de l'Underground* (1978; *Nights in the Underground*, 1979).

Réjean Ducharme also portrays children or adolescents rebelling against adult society and suffering from an inability to express their love. In *L'avalée des avalés* (1966; *The swallower swallowed*, 1968) Bérénice Einberg's monologues are aggressive; with her insufferable parents, her lack of love, her rejection, she takes vengeance on language itself by turning it into banter. This novel, though not the first to portray Jewish characters and milieux, most dramatically illustrates the impact of internationalism on Québec fiction. *L'océantume* (1968) deals with bitterness: Ina Ssouvie's daughter dreams of winning over her neighbour Asie Asothe and rejecting the world with her. They journey to the sea, and the ocean's surge at the end of the novel, obliterating the distinction between subject and object, is a sort of *leitmotif* that appears throughout Ducharme's work. *La fille de Christophe Colomb* (1969), Ducharme's most radically unconventional book, is a mock epic in deliberately ridiculous verse, in which the daughter of Columbus wanders the world in search of friendship.

Jacques FERRON's best novel, *L'amélanchier* (1970; *The juneberry tree*, 1975)—named for a tree that, like childhood, flowers early and briefly in springtime—reveals a nostalgia for childhood and the land. Ferron's verve, fantasy, and gift for satire make him a fine polemicist. A prolific writer, he draws on nationalistic themes and his own tragicomic folklore. The need for a doctor to remain close to the people and to champion freedom is the theme of *Cotnoir* (1962; *Doctor Cotnoir*, 1973), about the death and funeral of an alcoholic doctor in Longueuil. Increasingly Ferron has become the spokesman for a mythic country whose oral tradition and everyday history provide the verisimilitude apparent in *Le ciel du Québec* (1969), a picture of Québec in the pre-war years. His experience as a doctor also serves him in such novels as *Les roses sauvages* (1971; *Wild roses*, 1976), a political allegory about the end of a couple's relationship.

The October Crisis in 1970 marked the end of an era and of a certain kind of literature: it was the end of folklore and nationalism in literature. The next five years or so were a transitional period during which, however, important changes did take place, as witnessed by the gradual disappearance of *joual* as a literary medium.

3. THE SEVENTIES. Initially in the seventies the most significant fiction seemed to come from writers whose reputations were already established. Claude JASMIN moved towards autobiography and resurrecting the past: in *L'Outaragasipi* (1971) he undertakes a quest for the ancestors who settled in Assomption in 1717; in *La petite patrie* (1972), *Pointe-Calumet boogie-woogie* (1973), *Sainte-Adèle, la vaisselle* (1974), and *La sablière* (1979) he resumes his search for the innocent childhood he had avoided and rejected during his revolt in the sixties. *Revoir Ethel* (1976) is a clumsy attempt to revisit characters from earlier works. Jasmin was awarded the Prix Duvernay in 1981. Jacques GODBOUT, in *D'amour, P.Q.* (1972), presents a priggish writer seduced by two domineering secretaries (symbols of feminism), who rewrite his unrealistic, intellectual novel—forcing a confrontation between 'high-class literature' and popular language. In *Les anthropoïdes* (1977) Gérard BESSETTE uses interior monologues to convey the emergence, in the horde of our primitive ancestors, of historic, social, and personal consciousness; in *Le semestre* (1979) interior monologues present the emotional and intellectual state of mind of a university professor who is about to retire. Réjean DUCHARME's *L'hiver de force* (1973), a satire of Montreal's culture and politics in the 70s, portrays a young couple caught in a straitjacket of solitude: two proof-readers, André and Nicole, kill time by watching TV, smoking, reading MARIE-VICTORIN's *Flore laurentienne*, looking for affection, and doing nothing. *Les enfantômes* (1976) evokes the childhood ghosts of Vincent and Fériée, a brother and sister who are united against the world by their mother's suicide. Here again we find Ducharme's characteristic language games, satirical wordplay, puns, and linguistic virtuosity.

Among the few novels dealing with the October Crisis is Yves BEAUCHEMIN's *L'enfirouâpé* (1974); winner of the Prix France-Québec, it describes the historical events in a playful manner, mixing them up with a love affair and involving a poet in police interrogations, imprisonment, and a ridiculous, grotesque judicial system. *Le matou* (1981) is the jumbled story of a boy deserted by his mother; a thief and an alcoholic, he takes refuge in a cheap restaurant and gets involved in various adventures to save it. A realistic novel, it describes external surroundings only, but in a straightforward manner and with imagery that conveys delicate touches of humour.

After the concentration in the sixties on such themes as revolt, violence, the land, and national identity, the seventies show an apparent lack of critical or creative consensus. The major changes in the fiction of the seventies have to do with form. Instead of the usual characters with their usual passions gradually developing as the story unwinds, we see abrupt changes that often cannot be explained by traditional psychology; mythic, poetic, or lyric elements invade the text, together with magical reconstructions of worlds that are strange or violent. Clarity of style and straightforward, easily-understood linear plots are no longer in fashion; sequence is based on breaks and repetitions, on interpolated links in a texture that resembles a mosaic. Content comes to depend on form. This is particularly apparent after 1975 when, during the vogue for autobiographical influences and for novelists who become their own characters, the novelist self-consciously searches for a form; the process of writing becomes its own subject and the author becomes his own narrator. In this period, fantasy and realism exist side by side, and the theme of articulating the land is reduced to the level of village realism, family life, or interpersonal relations. As the decade progresses, novelists continue to explore the links between narrative and history, but the period is marked chiefly by new directions and diversity, anarchy and individualism. Accordingly, discussion of this later period is divided into categories that reflect this diversity.

3(a) *The realists.* Victor-Lévy BEAULIEU oscillates between the two major poles of Québec literature. Concerned on the one hand to describe or to bring into being the reality of Québec or 'the land', he also wants to drift into dreams, fantasy, drunkenness, and nightmare. An admirer of Jack Kerouac (whose French-Canadian parentage and significance for Québécois obsessed him) and Victor Hugo, Beaulieu uses torrents of language, including JOUAL, to tell the saga of the Beauchemin family—especially of their young son Abel—from the Lower St Lawrence. *Race de monde* (1969) and *Jos Connaissant* (1970; Eng. trans. 1982) introduce this fictional world, and the series is completed—following a return to the countryside in *Les grand-pères* (1971; *The grandfathers*, 1975)—in *Un rêve québécois* (1972; *A Québécois dream*, 1978) and *Oh Miami, Miami, Miami* (1973). Jos, a heavy drinker who often meditates before a Buddha, has an unhappy relationship with a waitress whom he treats badly. *Un rêve québécois* culminates in orgies, masturbation, and hints of sadism; the hero ends up killing his wife in a delirious and revolting bedroom scene that reflects the concurrent events of the October Crisis. *Don Quichotte de la démanche* (1974; *Don Quixote in Nighttown*, 1978) seems to indicate a desire to create a mythology and an imaginary country. Abel Beauchemin, a megalomaniacal novelist who is obsessed with the idea of writing a colossal work of literature, becomes anxious and full of doubts about his project because his books will only bear witness to a people on the road to extinction.

Beaulieu's realism extends to his language. Along with several other writers, he establishes the validity—and the humour—of popular spoken French in literary writing. A new cycle of 'Voyageries' gets underway with *Blanche forcée* (1976), *N'évoque plus que le désenchantement de ta ténèbre mon si pauvre Abel* (1976), *Sagamo Job J* (1977), and the three volumes of *Monsieur Melville* (1978). Here we see Beaulieu's mythmaking in action; the origins he tells of are collective, national, and literary, as though he were constructing cultural forefathers to replace missing personal, social, or familial antecedents.

Gilbert LaROCQUE provides a less frenetic series of novels about a childhood that has been rediscovered and redigested. *Le nombril* (1970) opens the cycle with the disappearance of a still-born sister. *Corridors* (1971) introduces a pacifist revolutionary who imagines himself to be a foetal phallus adrift inside his aunt (a mother substitute). *Après la boue* (1972) and *Serge d'entre les morts* (1976) are more successful. In the sooty, vulgar, animalistic city, Gabrielle experiences the horror of penetration, pregnancy, and abortion. Serge gets beyond his childhood by reliving his father's death, his mother's remarriage, his cousin's rejection, and his grandmother's death. *Les masques* (1980) tells of a motherless child, deserted by his father and taken in by his grandparents; he grows up to be a writer, is divorced from his wife, and loses his only child in a drowning accident the day of his grandfather's ninety-first birthday. The emotional intensity of the narration increases as plot sequences are revised and repeated until a missing link ties them all together.

André MAJOR gained a certain fame with his protest novel *Le cabochon* (1964), but turned towards rediscovery of the countryside in *Le vent du diable* (1968), a story of the death of a young orphan girl that verges on fantasy and myth. It also points towards the despairing realism (concerning the impossible dream) found in the *Histoires des déserteurs* trilogy: *L'épouvantail* (1974; *The scarecrows of Saint-Emmanuel*, 1977), *L'épidémie* (1975; *Inspector Therrien*, 1980), and *Les rescapés* (1976) are set in the little village of Saint-Emmanuel de l'Épouvante. Momo Boulanger, who has been released from prison, kills Gigi, and owing to the efforts of Inspector Therrien is given a life sentence. After the inspector retires and marries, Momo escapes from prison and returns to prowl around the village. Particularly impressive are Major's descriptions of an entire social milieu and of the conflict between the city and the country.

Michel TREMBLAY's fiction moved away from such fantasies as *La cité dans l'oeuf* (1969) towards the greater realism of *C't'a ton tour, Laura Cadieux* (1973). *La grosse femme d'à côté est enceinte* (1978; *The fat woman next door is pregnant*, 1981) and *Thérèse et Pierrette à l'école des Saints-Anges* (1980; *Thérèse and Pierrette at the École des Saints-Anges*, 1982), and *La duchesse et le roturier* (1982) continue in this vein, using a transcription of popular speech for the dialogues and standard French for the narration. These novels, in which the female characters typified in *Les BELLES-SOEURS* (1968) are given greater depth, vividly portray the atmosphere of east-end Montreal in the early forties.

Pierre Turgeon has increasingly turned to the action novel. In *Faire sa mort comme faire l'amour* (1969) a family is cruelly liquidated, while in *Un, deux, trois* (1970) a whole village is condemned to die. *Prochainement sur cet écran* (1973) deals with a murder-mystery and the police; *La première personne* (1980; *The first person*, 1982), more sober but equally violent, is another detective story.

3(b) *Comic or caricatured realism*. For writers describing the rural, folksy past of an urban society, realism may become essentially comic or fantastic in nature. Adrien Thério's *Le printemps qui pleure* (1962) and *La colère du père* (1974) looked back towards lost childhoods, but Thério's abundant humour is given freer rein in *Le mors aux flancs* (1965), *Un païen chez les pingouins* (1970), and *Les fous d'amour* (1973). *Soliloque en hommage à une femme* (1968) remains his most convincing novel, however, telling the story of a history professor who pays a childishly sentimental visit to the rural poverty of his childhood.

Roger Fournier's adventure novels are picaresque, erotic, and ribald, although banality and tedium diminish the effect of *Inutile et adorable* (1963), *A nous deux* (1965), *Journal d'un jeune marié* (1967), *La voix* (1968), and *La marche des grands cocus* (1972). *Moi mon corps mon âme Montréal etc.* (1974) is a first-person tale of hatred and social degradation played out against the background of the October Crisis. Fournier's talent and technique show progress, however, in *Les cornes sacrées* (1977); leaving the backwoods of Québec, a farmer's son, Norbert, takes his bull along on an epic journey through the mythic realms of Crete and the pagan world in a quest for the origins of life.

Jean-Marie Poupart seems to enjoy making an inventory of the verbal eccentricities and particularities of popular Québec French, as indicated by such titles as *Angoisse play* (1968), *Que le diable emporte le titre* (1969), *Ma tite vache a mal aux pattes* (1970), *Chère Touffe, c'est plein plein de fautes dans ta lettre d'amour* (1973), and *C'est pas donné à tout le monde d'avoir une belle mort* (1974). Poupart, who has published an essay on the detective novel, oscillates between that genre and the unfinished novel disguised as a diary in *Ruches* (1978) and *Le champion de cinq heures moins dix* (1980), which describe the author's disillusionment with the business of writing.

Roch CARRIER's first three novels form a trilogy. In *La guerre, yes sir* (1968; Eng. trans. 1970), *Floralie, où est-tu?* (1969; *Floralie, where are you?* 1971), and *Il est par là, le soleil* (1970; *Is it the sun, Philibert?* 1972) the characters are caricatures, the descriptions extravagant, and the action symbolic. *Le deux-millième étage* (1973; *They won't demolish me!*, 1974) centres on a building that is to be demolished to make way for a high-rise, and on the tragi-comic efforts of Dorval to mo-

bilize a group of tenants against the forces of speculative capitalism. This novel, however, turns into farce and the characters become one-dimensional personifications of ideas. In *Il n'y a pas de pays sans grand-père* (1979; *No country without grandfathers*, 1981) Thomas, an old forest-ranger who has already had run-ins with Anglos, reflects on his own youth and on his grandson Jean-Thomas, who is in prison for having taken part in a demonstration against the Queen. *Le jardin des délices* (1975: *The garden of delights*, 1978), presenting a tenderly ironic story of truculent characters involved in a tragi-comic burlesque, had previously marked a return to rural settings and Rabelaisian uproariousness. Carrier's *La dame qui avait des chaînes aux chevilles* (1981) is much more epic in scope and metaphorical in tone.

The novels of Jacques POULIN fall into this category of comic realism, with its emphasis on simplicity, sweetness, tenderness, childhood, anguish, death, bitterness, and fantasy. *Mon cheval pour un royaume* (1967) is set on the borderline between dream and reality. Pierre Delisle, who was wounded by the bomb he was using to blow up a statue, is undergoing psychiatric treatment. Hanging out in Old Québec, he becomes involved in a love triangle that has lasting and tragic consequences. *Jimmy* (1969) tells of an eleven-year-old boy who identifies with a famous car racer, Jimmy Clark. During a summer spent in Cap Rouge, the child seeks love and companionship as a means of escaping his parents' problems. In *Le cœur de la baleine bleue* (1970) the hero, Noël, undergoes a transplant operation in which he is given the heart of Nathalie, a girl who committed suicide in the first novel. Thereafter his relations with his domineering wife, Élise, change as she notices him drifting passively into love with a hockey-player named Bill. When she leaves him for Bill, Noël feels all the temptations of death. The three novels have been translated as *The Jimmy trilogy* (1979) by Sheila Fischman. After *Faites de beaux rêves* (1974), about a group of car-racing fans who spend a frenetic weekend in Mont-Tremblant, Poulin's writing becomes sparer, presenting a mythic Québécois vision of America. In *Les grandes marées* (1978) the hero, overwhelmed by women and society, tries to escape to a deserted island; the charm of this story lies in its tenderness, imagination, and flights of fantasy.

3(c) *Regional realism*. The first-person narration used by Yves THÉRIAULT to create the long lyric cry of *Ashini* (1960; Eng. trans. 1972)—the Amerindian through whom he explores basic and primitive psychology—continues in *Agoak, l'héritage d'Agaguk* (1975; *Agoak*, 1979). Agaguk, the hero of Thériault's famous novel of the same name (1958; Eng. trans. 1967), had left his village and its ancient customs in order to make a home where he would not have to share his wife; in *Agoak* the Inuit, instinctively struggling against reason and domination, leave white society, which is civilized in name only. Thériault manages to convey instincts in language that evokes their deepest origins. Wishing to describe 'man, battling against what he believes to be his fate', he uses a style that oscillates between a staccato primitivism and a gentle lyricism. After her early autobiographical novels, Antonine MAILLET turned to novels in the form of folktales. *Don l'Orignal* (1972; *The tale of Don l'Orignal*, 1978), which tells of a struggle for the possession of an island, won a Governor General's Award. *Pélagie-la-charrette* (1979; *Pélagie: the return to a homeland*, 1982), which won the Prix Goncourt, is peopled by legendary characters and fairy-tale heroes and tells the epic story of a mythical country that now exists only in words. Written in the style of spoken language, it describes the odyssey of the Acadians, expelled from their homeland in 1757, as they return to Acadia from Georgia. A fierce enemy of acceptance and resignation, Pélagie LeBlanc leads her family and others on this ten-year journey. In *Cent ans dans les bois* (1981) Pélagie's grandaughter takes charge of the former deportees to transform them from sailors into pioneers and settlers. This work is typical of Maillet's storytelling, using old sayings, proverbs, legends, history, and folktales.

Jean-Yves Soucy's prize-winning novel *Un dieu chasseur* (1976), translated by John GLASSCO as *Creature of the chase* (1979), offers lyrical descriptions of pantheistic primitivism. A 'male supremacist' trapper who dreams of absolute liberty brings a schoolteacher into the forest, but her suicide leaves him with his freedom intact. *Les chevaliers de la nuit* (1980), set in the Abitibi region, tells how two children's voyeuristic escapades lead to their discovery of darkness and adolescence. The style is sumptuous and natural, with lyric descriptions of the landscape.

Louis CARON leans towards fantasy and the folktale. In *L'emmitouflé* (1971; *The draft dodger*, 1980) a Franco-American draft-dodger tells the story of his Uncle Nazaire from Nicolet who, refusing to be conscripted in 1914, moved to a farm in New Hampshire in the fifties; an enigmatic and solitary man, he is on the run throughout this excellent documentary novel. In *Le bonhomme Sept-heures* (1978) Caron writes with playful compassion of the 1955 landslide that swept part of Nicolet into the river. In the poor part of town, a gang of rowdy youths makes life miserable for a disreputable churchgoer, Augustin Lenoir; trapped in the debris caused by the landslide, Lenoir ascends into heaven. In *Le canard de bois* (1981) Bruno Bellerose returns from the lumber-camps in 1935 and is given a wooden decoy that had been carved by his ancestor, Hyacinthe, whose progressive involvement in the Rebellion of 1837-8 is recounted as a parallel narrative to that of Bruno. The style—neutral, efficient, and spare—maintains considerable evocative power.

Jean-Paul Filion uses his own childhood as an inspiration for *Saint-André-Avelin* (1976) and *Les murs de Montréal* (1977). *Cap Tourmente* (1980) is a long, tension-filled love letter, while *Il est bien court le temps des cerises* (1981) shows to advantage the author's good humour and crude language in a documentary portrait of life in a Charlevoix village in the early 1950s. Noël Audet's *Quand la voile faseille* (1980) is a superbly written account of a Gaspé childhood, a father, a resourceful uncle, and various life crises. *Ah, l'amour, l'amour* (1981) tells of love-affairs with two vastly different women, the one repressed and the other a liberating spirit.

3(d) *A new liberation of language.* Around 1973-4 the debate over *joual* ceased. After endless discussions, position-papers, and controversies, the novel reverted to traditional French, and popular forms of speech were relegated chiefly to dialogue. Nevertheless Québec literature had won the right to speak in the language of the people.

Even Jacques RENAUD reversed his earlier position and came out against the 'sick' and 'suicidal' use of *joual*. *En d'autres paysages* (1970) and *Le fond pur de l'errance irradie* (1975) introduce the mysticism of the Orient—in standard French—while *La colombe et la brisure éternité* (1979) tends towards a positive, poetic lyricism. *Clandestine(s) ou la tradition du couchant* (1980) is an 'explorean' novel about the FLQ that also provides an exploration and exorcism of revolutionary violence. At present, the language of fiction in Québec is increasingly exuberant, baroque and idiosyncratic, moving in many directions simultaneously.

3(e) *The fantastic.* Jacques Benoît, in *Jos Carbone* (1967; Eng. trans. 1975), presents a sort of post-apocalyptic vision in which his characters seem stranded in a timeless forest, or underground, or on a raft moored in a marsh. In this world, action, surrealism, violence, cruelty, and death replace psychological reflection. In *Les voleurs* (1969) the narrator Émile and his kindly uncle and aunt are caught up in a plot involving extravagant, burlesque thieves and a sadistically cruel policeman. *Patience et Firlipon* (1970) also provides a mixture of realism and fantasy: a couple of offbeat characters—a country woman and a crazed, sexually aggressive gorilla—and an atmosphere of science-fiction. *Les Princes* (1973; *The princes*, 1977) is set in a mysterious city reminiscent of a South-American slum neighbourhood; two opposing organizations, the one composed of men and the other of dogs, are engaged in a battle to the death. Simplicity of style heightens the impact as political and social transformations are suggested in a context of dreamlike reality. In *Gisèle et le serpent* (1981) a girl takes a serpent to her bosom in order to gain its powers, which leads inevitably to more cruelty and mutilation. Typical of Benoît's work, this novel contains fantasy infused with social criticism, although in this case there is a happy ending.

Anne HÉBERT moves from the purely historical novel, KAMOURASKA (1970; Eng. trans. 1974), to a mixture of history and the supernatural in *Les enfants du sabbat* (1975; *Children of the black sabbath*, 1978). Aurélie, the servant in *Kamouraska*, has become soeur Julie, a nun and witch, in the latter novel. The havoc she wreaks upon her convent is seen to stem from an obsessive and incestuous attachment to her brother and the strange ceremonies of initiation conducted by her primitive, poverty-stricken parents. *Héloïse* (1980; Eng. trans. 1982) is a novel of the fantastic. Bernard, who lives with his wife Christine in a Paris apartment formerly inhabited by Héloïse, is gradually seduced by a vampire woman. Here the world of dreams and fantasy is balanced against reality by means of a fast-paced style that is sober, sumptuous, metaphorical, and evocative. Hébert's *Les fous de Bassan* (1982), which won the prestigious Prix Fémina in France, is set on the North Shore of the Lower St Lawrence; it treats poetically two recurring themes of her novels: violence and the victimization of women.

A preoccupation with origins and beginnings often leans towards the fantastic, but Charles Soucy's *Le voyage à l'imparfait* (1968) owes more to fantasy than to the fantastic; its narrator presents the thoughts of a foetus, and later a child, trying to escape from a possessive mother. *Heureux ceux qui possèdent* (1973), set in a mythic land at the dawn of time, concerns a primitive family's response to a stranger who brings progress and science. In Soucy's best novel, *A travers la mer* (1975), a Gaspé fisherman tries to please his wife by moving into a small apartment in Montreal's Rosemont district. Losing everything, but discovering his imagination, he dies in a final embrace with the natural world.

The fantastic verges on lyric abstraction in the fiction of Jacques Brossard, with its investigations of the strange connections between reason and the unconscious, control and explosion. Written in a fluid, supple, and carefully crafted style, *Le sang du souvenir* (1976) features a narrator who seesaws between landscapes that are alternately real and imaginary, violent and nightmarish. After sixteen years of silence André LANGEVIN produced *L'élan d'Amérique* (1972), a complex novel, violent and difficult to read, that symbolically denounces the alienation, exploitation, dispossession, and assimilation of Québec by the North American whole. *Une chaîne dans le parc* (1974) combines dream and reality in the tale of an orphan who has lived a brutal life in an orphanage since he was four years old; he escapes for one week, only to find the outside world even more terrifying, and returns to another boarding school.

3(f) *Myth-makers, the poetic, and the counter-culture.* A tendency to invent myths or to amplify existing archetypes appears in the writings of Pierre Châtillon, who is primarily a poet. *La mort rousse* (1974) tells of an old house-painter who, during an operation, dreams of a trip to sunny Florida, of a marvellous girl with red hair, and recalls his love of life and deep-rooted memories of his childhood. In *Le fou* (1975) an old farmer sets out in the snow with his tractor to look for his wife, who has been carried away by the north wind. Helped—or hindered—by such legendary folk characters as La Corriveau, Rose Latulipe, the giant of Beaupré, the devil, and so on, his odyssey takes the form of an exploration of the collective unconscious and the traditional folklore of Québec. *La tourbière* (1975), by Normand

Rousseau, uses archetypes, poetry, and symbols such as the white virgin or the red devil. Yvon Rivard's *Mort et naissance de Christophe Ulric* (1976) is both a magical voyage and a search for national identity; everyday reality is replaced by a torrent of dreamlike elements. Rivard's *L'ombre et le double* (1979) takes the form of a quest—complete with delirious, animistic, cosmic, and metaphysical dimensions—for the spatial, temporal, and psychic borders of Québec, involving *coureurs de bois* ancestors and a surreal voyage down the Saint Lawrence towards the sea. Jacques Garneau's novels describe the world of voyeurism, madness, and traumatic mother-child relationships. *Mémoire de l'oeil* (1972), written in dialogue, tells of a voyeur who has supposedly murdered Véronique and destroyed Françoise, but its deeper meaning concerns a search for freedom through the annihilating effects of distance. In *Inventaire pour St-Denys* (1973) Michel, confined to a mental hospital, draws nationalistic masterpieces on the walls and dreams of escape into childhood and death. In *La mornifle* (1976) the midwife of the title must kill her own children who were born deformed. A novel of initiation, its ten chapters look at the soul through ten different windows. *Les difficiles lettres d'amour* (1979) presents the fantasies of a sequestered child, his hated father, and his distant mother. The passage into adolescence and adulthood is marked by retreat into a world devoid of language or speech; but these—and love—are restored in the latter part of the novel.

Suzanne PARADIS displays the poetic vein of fiction in such works as *Les hauts cris* (1960), *Il ne faut pas se sauver des hommes* (1961), and *François-les-oiseaux* (1967). In *Les cormorans* (1968) the characters have turned their backs on life and chosen exile on an island of sand in order to recover their memories. *Miss Charlie* (1979) juxtaposes the heroine's diary with excerpts from her neighbour's novel: the attractions and rivalries of the two writers blend into a sensuous and beautiful text. Poetic elements can also be used to break up the traditional continuity of the story, as in Jacques Lanctôt's *Rupture de ban* (1979), in which the explanation of the author's activities in the FLQ is interrupted or replaced by the lyric thrust of 'words of exile and love'. The 'free novel' (as in free verse) may be marked by a poetic style that leads to confusion between subject and object, or that heightens incoherence

and tension. Novels in this vein include *L'ossature* (1972) by Pierre MORENCY, *La Brunante* (1973) by Pierre Filion, and Jean-Pierre Guay's *Mise en liberté* (1974).

The counter-culture is no longer an underground phenomenon. Daniel Gagnon indulges his delirious hyperphallism and absurd narcissism—not to mention a hatred of the mother as saint, madonna, and martyr—in *Surtout à cause des viandes* (1972). As in *Loulou* (1976), 'good or evil, it doesn't make any difference.' Pierre Corbeil's *La mort d'Auline Aquin* (1975) tells of a murder in a motorcycle gang from Trois-Rivières; the main suspect, though innocent, commits suicide. In *Sivis pacem et para bellum* (1970), Louis Gauthier presents two characters whose adventures depend heavily on word-games. His more successful *Souvenir de San Chiquita* (1978) is an action novel about an ordinary man's memories of a banana republic: love, drugs, revolution, and fun. Emmanuel Cocke also has fun with fantasy and surrealism in *Emmanuscrit de la mère morte* (1972); the word-games and phonetic or semantic puns are clearly reminiscent of Réjean DUCHARME. *Va voir au ciel si j'y suis* (1971) continues in the same vein, as does *Louve storée* (1973). *Sexe pour sang* (1974) is a detective novel; dealing with espionage and eroticism, it is both humorous and psychedelic.

3(g) *Feminist novels.* One of the central themes in the nationalistic writing of the sixties was an identification of women with the land. In the seventies, however, women emerged on their own, writing about themselves in a process of discovery, exploration, and emancipation. Michèle Mailhot tells the story of an unhappy woman in *Dis-moi que je vis* (1964). *Le fou de la reine* (1969) and *La mort de l'araignée* (1972) both deal with problems between couples, while in *Veuillez agréer . . .* (1975) a forty-year-old woman sets out on an entertaining road to liberation and divorce. In *Aldébaran ou La fleur* (1968) the prolific Claire de Lamirande tells of two vaguely discontented couples on holiday in Percé; there is little action, the style is choppy, and the tone artificial. Perhaps Lamirande's best novel, *Jeu de clefs* (1974)—written in short, verbless sentences that detract from the narrative—is a love story combined with a mysterious plot about a man who is haunted by the ghost of his former boss (a woman who had been murdered). *La pièce montée* (1975), which dwells on the oppression of women, contains many female characters of different generations;

since they all speak in the first person, this leads to some confusion. *Signe de biais* (1976) oscillates between psychological fiction and the detective novel, while *Papineau ou l'épée à double tranchant* (1980) is a historical tale told by several narrators.

Hélène Ouvrard sticks to decorative, bourgeois Romanticism in *La fleur de peau* (1965), a story of a rebellious young woman's maternal love for a sexual invert. *Le coeur sauvage* (1967) evokes the primitive, savage nature of the Gaspé in the character of Adèle, a wild creature whose fate is at the centre of the plot. *Le corps étranger* (1973) tells of a woman's struggle to regain possession of herself, while *L'herbe et le varech* (1977) is a sort of non-novel about the forty-year-old narrator's attempt to make her life over and escape male domination. In *La noyante* (1980), which describes the growing intimacy between Eléonore and a mother/goddess character named Léonor, feminism is juxtaposed with nationalism. Madeleine Ouellette-Michalska's *La femme de sable* (1979) is a painful socio-political novel, set in Algeria during the sixties, that deals with the eternal, violated mother/earth at odds with man. *Chez les termites* (1975) is an attack on the alienation produced by the modern school system in which communication, contact, and a sense of community are all lacking. *Le plat de lentilles* (1979) is a quest for the meaning of feminity.

The message of the many female voices that made themselves heard towards the end of the decade is not only one of protest and revolt but also of self-affirmation. As well as decrying the historical alienation of women, they tell of the new woman—and often of old women. Carole Dunlop, for instance, writes of a decrepit old lady who seems to be the conscience of everything around her in *Mélanie dans le miroir* (1980). Huguette Le Blanc's *Bernadette Dupuis ou La mort apprivoisée* (1980) describes an old widow's struggle against death and dispossession. Jovette MARCHESSAULT's trilogy in honour of the Great Mother, *Comme une enfant de la terre*, begins with *Le crachat solaire* (1975) and *La mère des herbes* (1979). Creating a world that blends myth and autobiography, the author draws on the history of Québec, the history of America, and the genesis of humanity. In *Un cri trop grand* (1980) Gabrielle Poulin tells the story of three generations of women; as is often the case with Québec fiction, there seems to be a superabundance of metaphor. *Lueur* (1979), by Madeleine Gagnon, is an 'archeological novel' with 'multiple' refer-

ences—an allegory based on the history of a character and a family, of women and the world. *Retailles* (1977), written with Denise Boucher, is more a poetic and political journal than a novel in the traditional sense. In *La cohorte fictive* (1979) all the characters have gathered for a final Thanksgiving dinner at a widow's home in the Laurentians. Incest, suicide, and a whole complex of family relationships are described in long, sinuous sentences.

Yolande Villemaire's *La vie en prose* (1980) was warmly received by critics, who saw in it a blend of mysticism, memory, myth; it is also highly enjoyable reading. Having American, Amerindian, and counter-cultural antecedents, it is a playful, optimistic story of several women writers and involves multiple identities. *Pique-nique sur l'Acropole* (1979) is Louky Bersianik's antithetical version of Plato's *Phaedra*. An invocation to the Great Goddess, it enters a plea on behalf of all women—whether crazed, raped, mutilated, used, abused, or ignored—who have refused to be subjected to procreation. *Une voix pour Odile* (1978), by France Théoret, is composed of twelve monologues, each of which asks agonizing questions about the fragmentation of life and female identity.

The search for modernism has been influenced by both American and Parisian models, the latter being more pronounced in the writings of Nicole BROSSARD. *Un livre* (1970; *A book*, 1976), is a blend of love or eroticism and political activism that is merely a pretext for a series of musings on the art of writing a novel—a self-conscious examination of itself as process and object. *Sold-out* (1973) is another fiction that contains its own story, which may be said to take place in Montreal simultaneously in 1971 and 1941. *Etreinte/illustration*, in the same volume, is an experimental piece in which language becomes its own raw material, deprived of its referential and communicative functions. *French kiss* (1974) explores both the body and Sherbrooke Street in a series of fitful and fragmented narratives that constantly scrutinize themselves. *L'amer ou le chapitre effrité* (1977) presents fragments of a narrative about writing a book, various theoretical reflections, and a lesbian critique of feminism. In *Flore Cocon* (1978), by Suzanne Jacob, the heroine is a warmhearted waitress who finds in her relationship with Louanne a counterbalance to the social alienation of women.

See Jacques Allard, 'Les lettres québécoises dupuis 1930', *University of*

Novels in French 1960 to 1982: 3(g)

Toronto Quarterly, vol. 50, no. 1 (1980); André Belleau, *Le romancier fictif* (1980); Gérard Bessette, *Une litterature en ebullition* (1968), *Trois romanciers québécois* (1973); Gilles Marcotte, *Le roman a` l'imparfait* (1976); and Ben-Zion Shek, *Social realism in the French-Canadian novel* (1977).

LOUIS LASNIER

Nowlan, Alden (1933-83). Born in Windsor, N.S., he began working at fifteen in lumbermills and on farms. He completed his formal education at eighteen and left Nova Scotia for New Brunswick, where he became editor of the *Hartland Observer* and night-news editor of the *Saint John Telegraph-Journal*. Beginning to publish poetry and short stories in the mid-1950s, he has been honoured with a Guggenheim Fellowship, a Governor General's Award (for *Bread, wine and salt*, 1967), and a Doctor of Letters from the University of New Brunswick. From 1969 he was writer-in-residence at the University of New Brunswick.

Since Nowlan published his first collection of verse, *The rose and the Puritan* (1958), his poetry has been consistent in style and theme. The bulk of his poems are short anecdotal lyrics, conversational in tone and frequently directed towards some moral perception. He wrote chiefly about small-town New Brunswick, the constricted lives of its inhabitants, and the complexity of his own role as its compassionately observing poet—indicated by the title of his selected poems, *Playing the Jesus game* (1970); like Christ, Nowlan found that he must not only pity and forgive his fellow man, but share personally his limitations and tragedies. Nowlan's emphasis on the essential innocence and helplessness of his variously benighted characters—escapist, credulous, treacherous, adulterous, murderous, insane—gives to many of his poems a suggestion of sentimentality that the poet must work to dispel through realistic imagery and colloquial dialogue. Nowlan's other collections of poetry are *A darkness in the earth* (1959), *Under the ice* (1960), *Wind in a rocky country* (1961), *Things which are* (1962), *The mysterious naked man* (1969), *Between tears and laughter* (1971), *I'm a stranger here myself* (1974), *Smoked glass* (1977), and *I might not tell everybody this* (1982).

In recent years Nowlan began writing in a number of other genres. His autobiographical novel, *Various persons named Kevin O'Brien* (1973), recounts his childhood struggle against poverty in an ambitious, though not entirely successful, juxtaposition of adult and child viewpoints. The collection of short stories, *Miracle at Indian River* (1968)—technically less interesting than the novel—offers close-up views of the economically oppressed characters who populate much of his poetry. In the 1970s Nowlan collaborated with Walter Learning to write three stage plays: *Frankenstein* (1973; pub. 1976), *The dollar woman* (1972), and *The incredible murder of Cardinal Tosca* (1978). Nowlan also wrote a travel book, *Campobello, the outer island* (1975), and collected twenty-seven of his magazine articles in *Double exposure* (1978).

See also POETRY IN ENGLISH 1950 TO 1982: 2.

FRANK DAVEY

O

Oberon Press. One of the leading literary publishers in Canada, Oberon is a family company controlled by Michael Macklem, his wife Anne Hardy, and their two sons, and was founded in Ottawa in 1966. It has a backlist of some 300 titles—all given restrained and handsome book designs. It specializes in fiction and poetry, though it also publishes history, biography, and criticism, and its best-selling title is Anne Hardy's *Where to eat in Canada*, which has been published annually since 1971. Among the fiction writers on its list are David HELWIG, Hugh HOOD, W.P. KINSELLA, David Lewis STEIN, Leon ROOKE, and W.D. VALGARDSON; among the poets are Elizabeth BREWSTER, R.G. EVERSON, David Helwig, Gwendolyn MacEWEN, George McWHIRTER, Tom MARSHALL, and Raymond SOUSTER.

WILLIAM TOYE

Ocean to ocean (London, 1873). This enduring travel classic, subtitled *Sandford Fleming's expedition through Canada in 1872*, was written by George Monro Grant (1835-1902), who was president of Queen's University, Kingston, from 1877 until his death. He acted as secretary to Sandford Fleming, chief engineer of the Canadian Pacific Railway— and one of Grant's parishioners at St Matthew's Presbyterian Church, Halifax— when Fleming made an exploratory journey to the Pacific Ocean in search of a route. Grant's book ('simply a Diary written as we journeyed') is a record of the expedition's progress by train, steamer, canoe, wagon, and horseback from Halifax to Victoria between 1 July and 11 Oct. 1872. It presents memorable descriptions of the landscape, the weather in different regions, various modes of travel, and personalities met en route; carefully records local place-names and idioms; presents and analyses the Indian and Métis cultures; and constantly assesses the land's suitability for settlement. The members of the expedition themselves become vivid characters in a narrative that mingles humorous incidents with accounts of the unavoidable hardships of travel. Grant's delight in what he encounters is infectious, and his personal enthusiasms (including several rhapsodic comments about the merits of pemmican) make the book appealing.

Two volumes of the actual diary are among the Grant papers in the Public Archives of Canada, and their record of the expedition often differs from the published version. It is apparent that Grant revised and expanded rough notes and structured his materials with some care for the purpose of defending both the proposed transcontinental railroad—which would firmly unite Canada, make possible the settlement of the West, and keep the Americans at bay—and the expansionist aspirations of English-speaking Canada. The Prairie West is seen as a potential garden, with the railroad as the means of bringing in settlers to make it bloom. Though treated with sympathy by Grant, the Métis and Indian cultures stand in the way of necessary 'progress' and will need to be absorbed or controlled, paternalistically, by the new order. The new West, as Grant envisions it, will be in effect a colony of Ontario, a hinterland feeding the manufacturing metropolis of the East. Although *Ocean to ocean* did not save the Macdonald government from defeat in 1873, it was a defence of the prime minister's policies; perhaps not coincidentally, a second edition (Toronto, 1879) appeared soon after Macdonald's return to power.

There is a facsimile reprint (1967) of the second edition, with an introduction by L.H. Thomas. For a discussion of Grant's revisions and intentions, see David Jackel's article in CANADIAN LITERATURE 81 (Summer 1979). The larger context is well examined by Doug Owram in *Promise of Eden: the Canadian expansionist movement and the idea of the West, 1856-1900* (1980).   DAVID JACKEL

Odell, Johnathan (1737-1818). Born in Newark, N.J., he was educated at the College of New Jersey (now Princeton University), graduating in 1759 with an M.A. in medicine. After serving as a surgeon in the British army in the West Indies, he went to London in 1763 to prepare himself for the Church of England ministry and was ordained in 1767; he was parish priest at St. Mary's Church, Burlington, N.J., until Dec. 1776. His loyalist political sympathies led to his being forced to flee behind British lines to New York, where he was a regimental chaplain, secretary to the chief British administrator, and a key intermediary in the espionage activities of Benedict Arnold and John André. After the evacuation of New York in 1783 he lived in England for a year before being appointed secretary to the newly formed Province of New Brunswick. He arrived there in Nov. 1784 and served as provincial secretary, an influential political post, until 1812, at which time the position was passed on to his son. He died in Fredericton.

Odell was the most skilled and trenchant of the loyalist satirists. His satiric activity reached its peak in 1779-80 with the publication of four major verse satires: 'The word of Congress' (1779), 'The congratulation, a poem' (1779), 'The feu de joie, a poem' (1779), and *The American times* (1780), all written in heroic couplets. The first three were published in a New York newspaper; *The American times* was issued as a pamphlet in both London and New York. Perhaps the finest of the loyalist satires, it consists mainly of a series of biting satiric portraits of the chief participants in the rebel cause, culminating in an attack on personified Democracy. Odell's poetic activity declined after he moved to New Brunswick. There is an interesting series of verses dealing with the ethics of Thomas Carleton's absentee governing of New Brunswick (Carleton left in 1803 never to return, although he remained governor until 1817) and a small group of satiric poems inspired by the War of 1812. The most ambitious of these, 'The agonizing dilemma' (1812), is an extended travesty of the American general's report on his defeat at Queenston Heights.

In addition to poetry, Odell also produced *An essay on the elements, accents, and prosody of the English language* (London, 1805; rpr. New York, 1969).

Odell's satires were collected by Winthrop Sargent in *The loyal verses of Joseph Stansbury and Dr Johnathan Odell* (Albany, 1860). See also M.C. Tyler, *The literary history of the American Revolution* (New York, 1897), and B.I. Granger, *Political satire in the American Revolution* (1960).

TOM VINCENT

O'Flaherty, Patrick. See CRITICISM IN ENGLISH: 5(g).

Ogden, Peter Skene. See EXPLORATION LITERATURE IN ENGLISH: 2.

'O God! O Montreal!' (1874)—the refrain from 'A Psalm to Montreal' by the English writer (and sometime painter) Samuel Butler (1835-1902). This poem was circulated privately in England (to Matthew Arnold, among others) and was published in *The Spectator* on 18 May 1878. Butler composed it in 1874 while he was in Canada for several months overseeing a foundering business in which he had investments. His view of Montreal as provincial was strengthened when, on a visit to the Museum of Natural History, he found a copy of the Discobolus relegated to a storeroom, among stuffed animals. The curator in the poem says, 'The Discobolus is put there because he is vulgar,/He has neither vest nor pants with which to cover his limbs.'

There is a resemblance between 'A Psalm to Montreal' and Butler's painting 'Mr. Heatherley's Holiday', which hangs in the Tate Gallery. It shows Mr Heatherley, whose art school Butler attended, repairing a human skeleton amid pots and vases, the Discobolus, and other statuary.

VINCENT SHARMAN

O'Grady, Standish (*fl.* 1793-1841). A native of Ireland and a graduate of Trinity College, Dublin, he became a Church of Ireland minister and was forced to emigrate in 1836, when he was unable to collect his tithes. He settled on a farm on the south bank of the St Lawrence R. near Sorel. His one printed work, a long narrative poem in rhymed couplets, was self-published, dated 1841, and entitled *The emigrant: a poem in four cantos* (printed in Montreal by John Lovell). Despite the title, the work has only one canto—about 2,100 lines on 117 pages—followed by 61 pages of notes that are frequently long anecdotal diversions with incidental verse incorporated; thirteen 'Miscellaneous poems' occupy an additional 12 pages—one of these, 'Old Nick in Sorel', is reprinted in A.J.M. SMITH's *The book of Canadian poetry* (3rd ed., 1957).

As a would-be man of letters O'Grady provides early evidence of how the lack of a congenial cultural climate limited pioneer literary effort. As a Protestant, clergyman, and non-francophone he was triply displaced. Inexperienced at farming, he lived at Sorel among farmers who were experienced, French-speaking, and Catholic. His literary environment was equally unpromising. He dedicated his poem to 'Nobody', as no patron had offered himself 'on this vast portion of the globe to which myself and my Muse are perfect strangers'.

O'Grady's use of heroic couplets, mostly competent, allows him to express his disillusionment in epigrams, hyperbole, and some whimsy:

With vile mosquitoes, lord deliver us,
Whose stings could BLISTER A RHINOC-
EROS.

The received nature of the verse-form is nonetheless an indication of the pervasive effect of his cultural displacement; his dependence upon conventional and remote rhetoric reveals his distance from the immediate Canadian context. To express his opinion of specific local and Canadian matters, O'Grady resorted to prose. For example, the couplet

Revolving years maternal care may mock
And spurn alike the monument of Brock

is expanded in this note: 'The monument of General Brock lies at present shamefully injured by the daring hands of the disloyal; a contribution has been levied to erect a new one worthy of his memory.'

This reticence in O'Grady's poetry about things Canadian, and the frequent references to things Irish, testify to his continuing and limiting sense of displacement. Though his retrospection about life in Erin was also gloomy, O'Grady warned Irish, Scots, and Britons to 'best engage your husbandry at home' rather than in a wintry country 'where nature seems one *universal blank*'. Along with winter's discomforts, he expressed dislike for French-Canadian law, education, and religious practice. Nonetheless he felt sure that eventually 'this expanded and noble continent will no doubt furnish fit matter for the Muse'.   GERALD NOONAN

O'Hagan, Howard (1902-82). Born in Lethbridge, Alta, he received a degree in law from McGill University in 1928 and, while in Montreal, began a long friendship with Stephen LEACOCK and A.J.M. SMITH. After practising law without having been called to the bar, he became a tour guide in Jasper National Park. He then travelled to Australia, where he began to write short stories; returned to Montreal, where Leacock helped him get a job with the CPR, recruiting farm labourers from England; and worked in New York and Jasper as a publicist for the CNR, and in Buenos Aires for the Argentine Central Railway. While living in San Francisco he began the series of notes about Mounties, trappers, Indians, guides, mountain men, and railway workers that were used for his first novel *Tay John*, which he completed on an island in Howe Sound, on the B.C. coast. During the 1950s O'Hagan was an occasional journalist for Victoria

newspapers and also took odd jobs on the waterfront, in Gyproc mills, and on survey crews. Between 1963 and 1974 O'Hagan and his wife lived in Sicily, until he decided to settle in Victoria, where he lived in poor health and semi-retirement while continuing to write. At the request of Margaret LAURENCE, George WOODCOCK, and Ken MITCHELL, O'Hagan was made an honorary member of the WRITERS' UNION in 1979; and in 1982 he received an honorary degree from McGill University.

O'Hagan's writings are dominated by the Rocky Mountains. As he continued to write, even though he suffered from the lack of a supportive community, he became known as the mountain man of Canadian letters—and one of the best prose writers of western Canada. He has had a strong influence on Rudy WIEBE, Robert HARLOW, Jack HODGINS, Don GUTTERIDGE, and Michael ONDAATJE, who wrote the first critical study of O'Hagan, which appeared in CANADIAN LITERATURE 61 (Summer 1974).

Tay John (1939)—a remarkable novel that was possibly influenced by O'Hagan's readings of Joseph Conrad—is about a halfbreed Indian, welcomed as the Messiah, who will lead his people across the Rocky Mountains to be reunited with the people of the British Columbia coast. Born in his mother's grave, Tay John disappears into the earth with the body of a pregnant woman—O'Hagan touches upon mythology and magic in this novel. A blend of fact, fiction, and historical recreation, *Tay John* was reviewed favourably when it was published in England but received little publicity because of the war. It was reprinted in the 1960s but remained relatively unknown until 1974, when it was reissued in the New Canadian Library, with an introduction by Patricia Morley.

During the 1950s O'Hagan wrote wilderness articles for *True, Argosy*, and other adventure magazines, some of which were collected in *Wilderness men* (1958). Although he referred to them as potboilers, they included incisive stories about such wilderness figures as Grey Owl (Archie BELANEY), Albert Johnson, the 'mad trapper of Rat River', and 'Almighty Voice' (see also Rudy WIEBE).

As well as miscellaneous journalism, O'Hagan wrote excellent short stories that were published in such magazines as *Esquire, Maclean's*, and the *New Mexico Quarterly*. Some were broadcast on CBC Radio; and Issue 9 of The TAMARACK REVIEW (1958) published 'Trees are lonely company', which was awarded the President's Medal of the University of Western Ontario. The best of these stories were published in *The woman who got on at Jasper Station* (1963; rpr. 1978). Another novel, *The school marm tree* (1983), was first published in *event/a journal of the arts,* vol. 5/3 (1976), along with an interview and critical commentary. *Coyote's song* (1983), edited by Gary GEDDES and published as a memorial, is a collection of essays and includes a word-portrait of Leacock.

See also Writing in BRITISH COLUMBIA.

GEOFF HANCOCK

Ondaatje, Michael (b. 1943). Born in Ceylon (now Sri Lanka), he joined his mother in England in 1954 and moved to Canada in 1962. After taking his B.A. at the University of Toronto and his M.A. at Queen's University, Kingston, Ont., he taught at the University of Western Ontario (1967-70) before joining the Department of English at Glendon College, York University, Toronto, in 1971.

Ondaatje has published four books of poetry—*The dainty monsters* (1967), *The man with seven toes* (1969), *Rat jelly* (1973), *There's a trick with a knife I'm learning to do: poems 1973-1978* (1979)—and two chapbooks, *Elimination dance* (1980) and *Tin Roof* (1982); a collage of poetry and prose, *The collected works of Billy the Kid* (1970); a novel, *Coming through slaughter* (1976); and an autobiographical work, *Running in the family* (1982). Three of these works—*Billy the Kid, The man with seven toes,* and *Coming through slaughter*—have been performed as plays. Two—*Billy the Kid* and *There's a trick with a knife*—have won Governor General's Awards.

Ondaatje is probably the least obviously Canadian writer in his subject-matter and vision and in the verbal texture of his work: his books include as central characters a Victorian Englishwoman and convict (*The man with seven toes*), a nineteenth-century American outlaw (*Billy the Kid*), and a New Orleans jazz musician of the turn of the century (*Coming through slaughter*). His style, owing almost nothing to an indigenous Canadian tradition, shows the influence of Wallace Stevens and of contemporary cinema artists, especially Louis Malle, Alfred Hitchcock, and Sergio Leone. His vision has been steadily directed at compelling the reader, by means of unusual settings and unexpected thematic, narrative, and stylistic shifts, to see reality as surreal, inchoate, and dynamic. His poetic universe is filled with suicidal herons and trumpet players, mythic

dogs, tortured people, gorillas, dragons, poetic spiders, and imploding stars. Ondaatje's extraordinary settings, characters, and narratives function as a metaphoric or symbolic shorthand leading the reader to perceive reality anew. The central tension in his work, between self and reality, or between two aspects of self, results in a fascination with borders—between rationality and unconsciousness ('Dragons', 'White dwarfs', 'Letters and other worlds'), peace and violence ('The time around scars', *The man with seven toes*), or reality and art ('Light', 'Spider blues', *Coming through slaughter*).

Ondaatje's most impressive works are his three book-length narratives, *Billy the Kid, Coming through slaughter,* and *Running in the family,* and the lyrics in *Rat jelly* that include 'Letters and other worlds', 'King Kong meets Wallace Stevens', 'Spider blues', 'Taking', ' "The gate in his head" ', 'Burning hills', and 'White dwarfs', written between 1967 and 1973. These lyrics—for the most part in the first person—are his most self-reflexive poems; whatever their surface or narrative concerns, they are ultimately about poetry, and constitute Ondaatje's most explicit and complex exploration of the relationship between life and art.

To express his vision in its full complexity, Ondaatje seems to need the longer form. *Billy the Kid* uses a temporally discontinuous narrative with multiple viewpoints, and includes lyrics, photographs, prose passages, interviews, a play, and deliberately blank pages. The events are consistently ambiguous; and the central characters, Billy and Pat Garrett—drawn from history, legend, and fiction, and given a touch of autobiography—are both paradoxes. In Ondaatje's slightly romanticized narrative, Billy, certainly a killer, is described by Sallie Chisum as 'the pink of politeness/and as courteous a little gentleman/as I ever met'; while Pat Garrett, the sheriff, is a 'sane assassin' whose compulsive sanity and order bear traces of insanity.

Coming through slaughter fictionalizes the life of Charles 'Buddy' Bolden (1876-1931), a legendary jazz cornetist who, like Billy, lived 'away from recorded history'. Ondaatje admires Bolden because for him art and life became almost indistinguishable. Bolden's sensibility is so compulsively responsive to the shifts and nuances of the lived moment that his self disappears into his art and, during the novel's climactic parade through Storyville, he loses his sanity. The novel also refers to other jazz musicians and to three different artists: the crippled photographer Bellocq, the painter Audubon, and Ondaatje himself, who enters as a character to explain his fascination with Bolden. The book's most disturbing suggestion is that in certain kinds of creativity, and in certain artists, 'making and destroying' are of necessity almost co-extensive: the tensions within them can be resolved only by being transmuted into art or madness.

A visit to Sri Lanka to recapture the family past gave rise to *Running in the family* (1982), a prose work that is ostensibly autobiographical, described in an authorial note as 'not a history but a portrait or "gesture" '. The various self-contained but interrelated sketches, stories, poems, and photographs offer a compassionate fictionalized portrait of Ondaatje's family past in Sri Lanka. By the book's end the family exists for the reader somewhere between reality and legend, and we recognize that Ondaatje has quietly erased the boundary between autobiography and fiction.

Ondaatje has also published a book of criticism, *Leonard Cohen* (1970), and edited three anthologies: *The broken ark* (1971), a book of animal poems; *Personal fictions* (1977), stories by MUNRO, WIEBE, THOMAS, and BLAISE; and *The long poem anthology* (1979). He has made three films—including one on bp NICHOL (*The Sons of Captain Poetry*)—and has been involved with COACH HOUSE PRESS for over a decade as adviser and editor.

The following essays are both informative and critical: Stephen SCOBIE, 'Two authors in search of a character: bp nichol and Michael Ondaatje', in *Poets and critics; essays from 'Canadian Literature' 1966-1974* (1974) edited by George WOODCOCK; Sheila WATSON, 'Michael Ondaatje: the mechanization of death', in OPEN LETTER (Winter 1974); and three essays by Sam Solecki: 'Nets and chaos: the poetry of Michael Ondaatje', in *Brave new wave* (1978); 'Making and destroying: Michael Ondaatje's *Coming through slaughter* and extremist art' in *Essays on Canadian Writing* (Fall 1978); 'Point blank: narrative in Michael Ondaatje's *The man with seven toes*' in *Canadian Poetry* (Spring/ Summer 1980). Ondaatje's essay on Howard O'HAGAN, 'O'Hagan's rough-edged chronicle', in CANADIAN LITERATURE (Summer 1974), is an implicitly informative commentary on his own work. There are also two useful interviews: Stephen Scobie and Douglas BARBOUR, 'A conversation with

Michael Ondaatje' in *White Pelican* (Spring 1971), and Sam Solecki, 'An interview with Michael Ondaatje', in *Rune* (Spring 1975).

See also NOVELS IN ENGLISH 1960 TO 1982: 4 and POETRY IN ENGLISH 1950 TO 1982: 2.

SAM SOLECKI

Ontario, Writing in. As the most heavily populated part of English Canada whose capital, Toronto, is the centre of English-language publishing, Ontario has experienced a great deal of literary activity since the early nineteenth century. The survey that follows is an attempt to bring together some of the best-known authors, books, and literary periodicals. They, and other aspects of writing activity in the province— including early writings—are also discussed elsewhere in the *Companion,* not only in author-entries but in other surveys: DRAMA, EXPLORATION LITERATURE, LITERARY MAGAZINES, NOVELS, PIONEER MEMOIRS, POETRY, SHORT STORIES, and TRAVEL LITERATURE.

1. EARLY WRITINGS. Inaugurated by the Jesuits' narratives of their mission to the Hurons in the JESUIT RELATIONS, 1635-50, and continued through the exploration period by Alexander Henry's *Travels and adventures in Canada and the Indian territories between the years 1760 and 1776* (New York, 1809), writing in Ontario first flowered in the period of settlement. The diary for the years 1791-6 of Elizabeth Simcoe, wife of the first lieutenant-governor of Upper Canada—published complete as *Mrs. Simcoe's diary* (1965) edited by Mary Quayle Innis— describes the early days of York (Toronto). A few decades later, in *Winter studies and summer rambles in Canada* (London, 1838), a nineteenth-century writer and art critic, Anna Jameson, portrayed life in Toronto's by then close-quartered colonial society, set against the awesome vastness and variety of the new land. Among pioneer settlers, Samuel Strickland and his sisters Susanna MOODIE and Catharine Parr TRAILL— members of a prolific English writing family—recorded their experiences with an eye to English readership. Strickland's *Twenty-seven years in Canada West; or, The experiences of an early settler* (London, 1853), and Traill's *The backwoods of Canada; being letters from the wife of an emigrant officer; illustrative of the domestic economy of British America* (London, 1836) and *The female emigrant's guide, and hints on Canadian housekeeping* (Toronto, 1854), carried sensible and optimistic advice for emigrants. Moodie's compelling combi-

nation of dismay at her surroundings, her lively involvement with her new life, and a real writing talent have made her ROUGHING IT IN THE BUSH; or, Forest life in Canada (London, 1852) a most enduring nineteenth-century Canadian classic. William 'Tiger' Dunlop of Goderich—a medical doctor, an adventuring Scot, and the most entertainingly eccentric of Ontario's writing settlers—left an idiosyncratic, humorous, and quite unstatistical mark with his *Statistical sketches of Upper Canada, for the use of emigrants* (London, 1832).

2. FICTION. John RICHARDSON's Gothic and demonic WACOUSTA; or, The prophecy fulfilled: a tale of the late American war (Monteal, 1840) began a tradition of historical romances that includes William KIRBY's The GOLDEN DOG (Le chien d'or); A romance of old Quebec (New York, 1877) and Franklin Davey McDowell's The Champlain road (1939). Among John GALT's many novels is *Bogle Corbet; or, The emigrants* (London, 1831), a comic treatment of the immigrant theme arising out of Galt's experience as agent for the Canada Company. In The Canadian Crusoes: a tale of the Rice Lake plains (London, 1852), a story of four lost children, Catharine Parr TRAILL wrote the first children's book with an Ontario setting.

The fiction of settlement, almost always written as romance, has been one of the most vital and enduring strands in Ontario writing. In *The man from Glengarry: a tale of the Ottawa* (1901) and GLENGARRY SCHOOL DAYS: a story of the early days in Glengarry (1902), Charles W. GORDON ('Ralph Connor') celebrated the strength and piety of the pioneering Scotch of the Ottawa Valley, as did Mary Esther MacGREGOR ('Marian Keith') in *Duncan Polite; the watchman of Glenoro* (1905) and *'Lizbeth of the dale* (1910). Four decades later Grace Campbell harked back to Glengarry's early days in her *Thornapple tree* (1942) and *The higher hill* (1944). *The yellow briar; a story of the Irish in the Canadian countryside* (1933) was written by Toronto lawyer John MITCHELL but published under the pseudonym 'Patrick Slater', the narrator. Mitchell made a comic hero of 'Paddy', who tells a warm and charming story of pioneering and settlement in the Caledon region of southern Ontario. Similarly, Mabel Dunham's The trail of the Conestoga (1924) and Luella Creighton's High bright buggy wheels (1951) depicted Mennonite settlement in southern Ontario.

The small town, treated with affectionate irony, provides an important subject area of Ontario fiction, from Sara Jeannette DUNCAN's Elgin (Brantford) of *The imperialist* (1904); through Stephen LEACOCK's Mariposa (Orillia) of SUNSHINE SKETCHES OF A LITTLE TOWN (1912); to Robertson DAVIES' Salterton (Kingston) in *Tempest-tost* (1951), *Leaven of malice* (1954), *A mixture of frailties* (1958), and his Deptford in FIFTH BUSINESS (1970), *The manticore* (1972), and *World of wonders* (1975); to Alice MUNRO's Jubilee (Wingham) in *Dance of the happy shades* (1981), a collection of short stories, and her other fiction. *White narcissus* (1929), Raymond KNISTER's probing of the repressions and distortions of Ontario rural life, anticipated works like Matt COHEN's The disinherited (1974) and *The sweet second summer of Kitty Malone* (1979), which takes place on the confining ancestral farmland of southeastern Ontario.

Toronto—though it is never named—is the setting of Morley CALLAGHAN's novels *Strange fugitive* (1928), *It's never over* (1930), *A broken journey* (1932), *Such is my beloved* (1934), *They shall inherit the earth* (1935), and MORE JOY IN HEAVEN (1937), and of many of his short stories. Hugh GARNER also set much of his fiction in Toronto. A former working-class area of the city is referred to in the title of his well-known *Cabbagetown* (1950; 1968), a novel about Toronto in the thirties, and of Juan BUTLER's Cabbagetown diary: a documentary (1969). And the city is celebrated in Hugh HOOD's documentary fantasy, *The New Age*, of which *The swing in the garden* (1975), *A new Athens* (1977), *Reservoir ravine* (1979), and *Black and white keys* (1982) have been published. A fascination with documentary and history, so visible in Hood's fiction, is also an important feature of Timothy FINDLEY's The wars (1977) and *Famous last words* (1981), which move out from Toronto and Canada into an international arena of war and violence.

From the days of Moodie and Traill, women writers have been prominent: Madge Macbeth's *Land of afternoon* (1924) was our first social satire; Mazo DE LA ROCHE's JALNA (1927) still draws an international readership; and Margaret ATWOOD's prolific versatility has steadily earned her a world-wide reputation for *The edible woman* (1969), *Surfacing* (1972), *Lady oracle* (1976), *Life before man* (1979), and *Bodily harm* (1981). Marian ENGEL in *The Honeyman festival* (1970), *Bear* (1976), *The glassy sea* (1978), and *Lunatic villas* (1981); Carol SHIELDS in *Small ceremonies* (1976), *The box garden* (1977), and *Happenstance* (1980); and

Sylvia Fraser in *Pandora* (1972) and *The candy factory* (1975)—all these writers share contemporary concerns, though the latter's *The emperor's virgin* (1980) is an excursion into historical romance. Alice Munro's delicacy of perception and skill with language are evidenced in her linked short-story sequence, *Lives of girls and women* (1971) and *Who do you think you are?* (1978).

Short Stories. This is a flourishing form in Ontario, as it is in Canadian writing in general. Early works in this genre include Susie Frances HARRISON's *Crowded out and other sketches* (Ottawa, 1886), E.W. THOMSON's *Old man Savarin and other stories* (Toronto, 1895), Duncan Campbell SCOTT's *In the village of Viger* (Boston, 1896) and *The witching of Elspie* (1923); and Ernest Thompson SETON's WILD ANIMALS I HAVE KNOWN (New York, 1898). The short story flowered in the 1920s with Morley Callaghan's *A native argosy* (1929) and with the work of Raymond Knister, published in that decade in *The* CANADIAN FORUM and *This Quarter* and collected in 1972. The first collections of Norman LEVINE (*One way ticket*, 1961), George Elliott (*The kissing man*, 1962), Hugh Hood (*Flying a red kite*, 1963), Alice Munro (*Dance of the happy shades*, 1968), Dave GODFREY (*Death goes better with Coca-Cola*, 1968), David HELWIG (*The streets of summer*, 1969), Austin CLARKE (*When he was free and young and he used to wear silks*, 1971), Gwendolyn MacEWEN (*Noman*, 1972), Margaret Atwood (*Dancing girls and other stories*, 1977), and Margaret GIBSON (*Butterfly ward*, 1978), offer abundant evidence of variety in theme and sophisticated skill in craftsmanship.

3. POETRY. Like prose writers, early poets focused on narrative treatment of the land and its settlement, from Adam Hood BURWELL's 'Talbot Road' (*The Scribbler*, 1822), William KIRBY'S tory epic, *The U.E.: a tale of Upper Canada* (Niagara, 1859), Alexander McLACHLAN's celebration of the Scotch in *The emigrant and other poems* (Toronto, 1861), Charles SANGSTER's *The St. Lawrence and the Saguenay, and other poems* (Montreal, 1856), and Charles MAIR's *Dreamland and other poems* (Montreal, 1868), to the beautiful and startling evidence of genius in Isabella Valancy CRAWFORD's 'Malcolm's Katie', published in *Old Spookses' Pass, Malcolm's Katie, and other poems* (Toronto, 1884).

Of the three CONFEDERATION POETS associated with Ontario, Archibald LAMPMAN, Duncan Campbell SCOTT, and Wilfred CAMPBELL explored lyric and subjective themes and patterns with talent and sensitivity. Lampman's *Among the millet* (Ottawa, 1888) and *Lyrics of earth* (Boston, 1893) set high standards for contemporary and later poets, while Scott moved from the lyrics of his early work, *The magic house and other poems* (Ottawa, 1893), which included the uniquely haunting 'Piper of Arll', to powerful and dramatic poetic studies of native people (for example, 'The forsaken'), with whose tragic predicaments he became familiar in his work in the Department of Indian Affairs. Wilson MacDONALD's romantic Whitmanesque voice was first heard in *Song of the prairie land* (1918).

The strong narrative tradition in nineteenth-century Ontario poetry climaxed in the twentieth century in the work of E.J. PRATT. A Newfoundlander, but by adoption an Ontarian, Pratt became a public and an epic poet, his work moving from *Newfoundland verse* (1923) to the high comedy of *The witches' brew* (1925), the tragedy of *The Titanic* (1935) and *Brébeuf and his brethren* (1940), to the epic, national range of *Towards the last spike* (1952). The atmosphere of southwestern Ontario provided rich material for the work of James REANEY—in *A suit of nettles* (1958), *Twelve letters to a small town* (1962), and *The dance of death at London, Ontario* (1963)—and in Reaney's poetic dramas. Frank DAVEY in *Griffon* (1972), and Don GUTTERIDGE in *Tecumseh* (1976) and *A true history of Lambton County* (1977) have continued the narrative genre in Ontario settings.

The tradition of the lyric remained strong and effective in volumes like Robert FINCH's *Poems* (1946) through his *Variations and theme* (1981), and in Douglas LePAN's *The wounded prince and other poems* (1948). The colloquial and detailed sense of the city life of Toronto has marked the work of Raymond SOUSTER, from the publication of the first of his many collections in 1946. Al PURDY's ability to capture a sense of place and of local history is evident in volumes like *The Cariboo horses* (1965) and *Wild grape wine* (1968). A disturbing awareness of human duality and meditative despair have characterized much of the poetry of Eli MANDEL, most recently in *Dreaming backwards* (1981). Within the context of the poetic explosion in the ebullient, nationalistic climate of the sixties and seventies, Dennis LEE, in *Civil elegies, and other poems* (1972), is as distinguished for his depth of feeling as, in *Alligator pie* (1974) and *Nicholas Knock and other people* (1974), he is memorably inventive and lighthearted as a poet for children. Witty, idiosyncratic, and unique are the works of Joe ROSENBLATT (*Bumblebee dithyramb*, 1972). Michael ONDAATJE, the author of several brilliant poetry collections and a novel, *Coming through Slaughter* (1976), is best known for the evocative, violent collages that make up *The collected works of Billy the Kid: left-handed poems* (1970).

As with fiction writers, women have been prominent among Ontario poets since the days of Isabella Valancy Crawford. Pauline JOHNSON's *The white wampum* (London, 1895) at once romanticized and individualized the life of the Canadian Indian, while Marjorie PICKTHALL's *Drift of pinions* (1913) established her mystical and lyrical voice. *Counterpoint to sleep* (1951) by Anne WILKINSON combined the sensual and the intellectual in its effects, and in *The* BOATMAN (1957) Jay MACPHERSON's wit and poetic skill played with biblical archetypes in patterns of quest and redemption. Though Margaret AVISON's spare, intellectually demanding poetry was first published in 1939, her first collection, *Winter sun*, did not appear until 1960. Margaret ATWOOD's versatile talent was announced in *Double Persephone* (1961), followed by many collections, including one—*The* JOURNALS OF SUSANNA MOODIE (1970)—that is a classic poetic interpretation of the immigrant experience in Ontario. Phyllis GOTLIEB's *Who knows one?* (1961) exuberantly described her Jewish childhood in Toronto and Gwendolyn MacEWEN's first volume, *The rising fire* (1963), characteristically drew dominant image patterns from the mystical and the ritualistic.

4. DRAMA. Ontario drama of the nineteenth century was ponderous and unperformed: Charles MAIR's *Tecumseh: a drama* (Toronto, 1886), Sarah Anne Curzon's sentimental *Laura Secord, the heroine of 1812* (Toronto, 1887), and Wilfred CAMPBELL's *Mordred and Hildebrand: a book of tragedies* (Ottawa, 1895). The opening of Hart House Theatre, University of Toronto, in 1919 provided a stage for plays such as Marjorie PICKTHALL's lyric tragedy *The woodcarver's wife* (1922) and Duncan Campbell SCOTT's *Pierre* (1926). The twenties also saw a much-needed reaction against sentimental romance in Merrill DENISON's realistic backwoods dramas, *From their own place* (1922) and *Brothers in arms* (1924). In the early 1930s Herman VOADEN founded the Play Workshop in Toronto, a forum for experimental drama and acting. In 1932 amateur theatre was given a powerful nation-wide boost with the formation of the annual Dominion Drama Festival. The post-war period brought more opportunities with the establishment of Dora Mavor Moore's New Play Society (1946-71) and the popular annual review, Spring Thaw (1948-71). In 1953 were established the Crest Theatre in Toronto and the Stratford Shakespearean Festival, which has since won for itself an international reputation. John COULTER's Canadian career began in the 1940s, and in the same decade Robertson DAVIES introduced his series of ironic comedies, including *Fortune my foe* (1949); he has continued writing and publishing plays since that time. With the sixties came Coulter's *Riel* (1962) and James REANEY's début as a playwright of southwestern Ontario with *The killdeer and other plays* (1962), which was followed by the innovative, poetic collage, *Colours in the dark* (1967), and *The Donnellys: a dramatic trilogy* (1975-7). John HERBERT's explicit and brutal *Fortune and men's eyes* (1967), with its prison theme, introduced a new gritty realism. The seventies exploded with activity in drama. Toronto Workshop Productions, founded in 1958, was followed over the next two decades by many other Toronto theatres, among them Theatre Passe Muraille, Tarragon, the St Lawrence Centre for the Performing Arts, Toronto Children's Theatre, and Factory Theatre Lab; and an array of new regional and festival theatres sprang up in Hamilton, Niagara-on-the-Lake, Blyth, London, and Sarnia. Prominent among Ontario playwrights at this time were David FRENCH, David FREEMAN, Carol BOLT, and James Reaney.

5. LITTLE MAGAZINES AND SMALL PUBLISHERS. Among the several early 'little' or literary magazines published in Ontario were the short-lived CANADIAN LITERARY MAGAZINE (York, 1833), BARKER'S CANADIAN MONTHLY MAGAZINE (Kingston, 1846-7), *The Victoria Magazine* (Belleville, 1847-8), and *The British American Review* (Toronto, 1865-67). After Confederation other periodicals appeared, including *The Canadian Monthly and National Review* (Toronto, 1872-8), which combined with *Belford's Monthly Magazine: a Magazine of Literature and Art* (Toronto, 1876-8) to become ROSE-BELFORD'S CANADIAN MONTHLY (Toronto, 1878-82). Other nineteenth-century periodicals of note were *The* WEEK: *An Independent Journal of Literature, Politics and Criticism* (Toronto, 1883-96), founded and edited by Goldwin SMITH, and

The Canadian Magazine (Toronto, 1893-1939). In 1920 *The* CANADIAN FORUM was established as 'An Independent Journal of Opinion and the Arts'; its longstanding commitment to the publication and discussion of Canadian literature is well known. Following the Second World War more little magazines appeared: *Here and Now* (Toronto, 1947-9); Raymond Souster's CONTACT: *an international magazine of poetry* (Toronto, 1952-4) and his COMBUSTION (Toronto, 1957-60); *The* TAMARACK REVIEW (Toronto, 1956-82); and James Reaney's ALPHABET: *A semi-annual devoted to the iconography of the imagination* (London, 1960-71). Founded in the 1960s were *Evidence* (Toronto, 1960-7); *Quarry* (Kingston, 1965-); *Origins* (Hamilton, 1967-); *Northern Journey* (Ottawa, 1971-6); EXILE (Toronto, 1972-); *Waves* (Downsview, 1972-); OPEN LETTER: *second series* (Toronto, 1972-). Academic journals that could be mentioned here are *Queen's Quarterly* (Kingston, 1893-), which began publishing fiction and poetry in the 1920s. In 1936 the survey 'Letters in Canada' made the first of its annual appearances in *The University of Toronto Quarterly* (1931-). Other major journals include *The University of Windsor Review* (Windsor 1965) *Journal of Canadian Studies* (Peterborough, 1966-), DESCANT (Toronto, 1970-), *Essays on Canadian Writing* (Downsview, 1974-), *Canadian Poetry* (London, 1977-), *Canadian Theatre Review* (Downsview, 1974-), *Journal of Canadian Poetry* (Ottawa, 1978-), and CANADIAN FICTION MAGAZINE (Vancouver/Toronto, 1971-). (See also LITERARY MAGAZINES IN ENGLISH.)

By 1900 a number of small publishing houses had grown and flourished, among which were the Methodist Book and Publishing House (later RYERSON PRESS), William Briggs, and Copp, Clark. An overview of small Ontario publishers in this century begins with Graphic Publishers of Ottawa (1925-32), which in the late 1920s and early 1930s devoted itself exclusively to the publication of Canadian works in all fields. With its collapse, small publishing houses effectively disappeared until the mid-1960s, when an explosive renaissance took place. COACH HOUSE PRESS, and the more inclusive Peter Martin Associates, were established in 1965, followed a year later by OBERON PRESS and in 1967 by the House of ANANSI. Their enthusiasm and success in publishing new Canadian writing inspired the founding of other houses. Among these are James Lorimer and Company (1969),

New Press (1969), NC Press (1970), Borealis (1972), Women's Press (1972), Porcupine's Quill (1973), Playwrights Co-Op (1973), Mosaic Press/Valley Editions (1974), and ECW Press (1979).   JOHN LENNOX

Open Letter (1965-). This journal of experimental writing and criticism was founded in Victoria, B.C., by Frank DAVEY as a research project into 'open' form. The first series (each 'series' has contained nine issues) was titled 'The open letter' and offered selections from the current writing, reading, and correspondence of its contributing editors (George BOWERING, Daphne MARLATT, Fred WAH, David Dawson, and latterly Ted Whittaker). In typewritten form, this series was essentially a transitional publication between TISH, in which most of the editors had participated, and the much larger and professionally printed issues that Davey later produced in eastern Canada. Numbers 5 and 6 of the first series were edited by Ted Whittaker.

The main period of *Open Letter* began when Davey moved to Toronto in 1970 and became associated with bp NICHOL, Victor COLEMAN, and the COACH HOUSE PRESS. Beginning in 1971 the second series featured Nichol, Coleman, Bowering, Wah, and Steve McCaffery as contributing editors and limited its contents to experimental criticism, literary theory, and reviews. Coach House Press acted as publisher from 1971 to 1977. In the fourth (1978-81) and fifth (1982-4) series the magazine ceased publishing reviews and devoted itself to special issues on such topics as performance art, 'pataphysics, poetry and painting, prosody, or on single authors. In its various editorial initiatives *Open Letter* has endorsed textual and phenomenological criticism, supported interchange between the Canadian and international avant-gardes, proposed a linguistic foundation for both writing and criticism, championed western-Canadian writing, and argued against the centralization of the Canadian literary tradition that it saw implicit in both the Canadian nationalist movement of the 1970s and the 'thematic' criticism of FRYE, JONES, and ATWOOD. Noteworthy issues include 'Sheila WATSON: a collection' (ser. 3, no. 1), 'Warren Tallman: collected essays' (ser. 3, no. 6), 'Louis DUDEK: texts and essays' (ser. 4, nos. 8-9), 'Notation' (ser. 5, no. 2), and 'Robert KROETSCH: essays' (ser. 5, no. 4).

See *Ellipse* 23/24 (1979), a special issue on *Open Letter* and *La* BARRE DU JOUR.

Open Letter

See also LITERARY MAGAZINES IN ENGLISH: 3. FRANK DAVEY

Ostenso, Martha (1900-63). Born near Bergen, Norway, she came to North America with her parents at the age of two and lived in various towns in Minnesota and North Dakota. Her family moved to Brandon, Man.—where Ostenso attended Brandon Collegiate and became interested in writing and painting—and then to Winnipeg, where she attended Kelvin Technical High School and the University of Manitoba. She taught school briefly about 100 miles northwest of Winnipeg—an experience that was to provide the background for her novel *Wild geese* (1925; NCL 1961)—and worked as a reporter on the *Winnipeg Free Press*. She later joined Douglas DURKIN in New York and attended his course on 'The technique of the novel' at Columbia University, possibly in 1921-2. (It is now thought that the novels published under Ostenso's name were actually co-authored by Durkin, although *Wild geese* is considered to be primarily by Ostenso.) For two-and-a-half years she was a social-worker in New York. Ostenso then went with Durkin to Gull Lake, Minn., in 1931; they married in 1945 and moved to Seattle in 1963. Besides *Wild geese*, Ostenso published over a dozen volumes of fiction, a collection of poetry, *A far land* (1924), and a co-authored biography of Sister Elizabeth Kenney. Her work appeared in *The Scandanavian Review* and *Poetry* (Chicago).

Wild geese, which was originally called 'The passionate flight', the title of its English edition, was well received and won the $13,500 prize for a best first novel offered by *The Pictorial Review*, the Famous Players-Lasky Corporation, and Dodd, Mead & Company. The novel is set in the period between the arrival of the geese in the spring and their departure in the autumn. Lind Archer comes to teach at Oeland, Man., and boards with the Gares. Caleb Gare controls his family as a means to the smooth and successful operation of the family farm. Described as 'a spiritual counterpart of the land, as harsh, as demanding, as tyrannical as the very soil from which he drew his existence', he exerts his power in part by emotional blackmail of his wife, Amelia, knowing that she has had, by her lover, a son, Mark Jordan, now an adult but still unaware of who either of his real parents are. When Mark comes to Oeland to manage the homestead of an ailing neighbour of the Gares, he and Lind meet and fall in love. A major figure in the novel is the Gares' daughter, Judith, beautiful as 'some fabled animal'; she is also described as 'vivid and terrible', and her strength and sexuality are contrasted with Lind's delicacy and capacity for fine feeling. A counter-example to the isolation experienced by the Gares, individually and as a family, is provided by the neighbouring Bjarnasson family, in which four generations live in harmony. While *Wild geese* has elements of romanticism, it represents a major development in the Canadian movement towards realism.

For a detailed discussion of *Wild geese* and its role in the movement towards realism, see the unpublished Ph.D. thesis of David Arnason, 'The development of prairie realism' (University of New Brunswick, 1980); about the genesis of *Wild geese*, see Robert G. Lawrence, 'The geography of Martha Ostenso's *Wild Geese*', *Journal of Canadian Fiction* 16 (1976). JOY KUROPATWA

Other Canadians: an anthology of the new poetry in Canada. See John SUTHERLAND.

Ouellet, Fernand. See HISTORICAL WRITING IN FRENCH.

Ouellette, Fernand (b. 1930). Born in Montreal, he believed himself, through his early years, destined for a career in the priesthood. However, he left the Collège séraphique des Capucins in Ottawa after four years (1947), and returned to Montreal, where he obtained a Licence en sciences sociales at the Université de Montréal (1952). His marriage in 1955 to Lisette Corbeil brought the intense joy of sensual experience that has remained intimately linked with the spiritual quest fundamental to all his work. Like the poets he admires, from Dante to Pierre Jean Jouve, Ouellette considers the radiant body of the beloved woman to be the symbol of his search for the infinite.

Ouellette was one of the first poets of the Hexagone group to publish a collection of poetry: *Ces anges de sang* (1955). In 1959 he and Jean-Guy PILON, with several other young poets, founded the influential literary journal LIBERTÉ, with which he is still involved. Between 1956 and 1970 Ouellette wrote texts for Radio-Canada and articles on poetry, on the socio-political situation in Québec, on questions of language and culture, and on European artists such as Edgard Varèse, Novalis, Jouve, Kierkegaard, and

Dostoyevsky, whom he admired for their universality and who had been seminal influences in his own evolution. These texts reveal Ouellette's unique approach to the question of *engagement*, when the writer is profoundly and immediately involved in his troubled society, yet cannot accept either violence or literature based on explicit social commentary as an adequate response. Several of these articles were published together as *Les actes retrouvés* (1970), for which Ouellette declined the Governor General's Award—offered to him a few months after the October Crisis and the declaration of the War Measures Act. He explained this refusal in 'Le Temps des veilleurs', published in *Liberté* (jan.-fév. 1971) and reproduced in *Journal dénoué* (1974).

In 1972 Ouellette, Pilon, and André Belleau founded the annual conference that is still one of the main cultural events in Québec: Rencontre québécoise internationale des écrivains. The same year L'Hexagone published a retrospective *Poésie*, containing Ouellette's first four poetry collections: *Ces anges de sang, Séquences de l'aile* (1958), *Le soleil sous la mort* (1965), and *Dans le sombre* (1967). This volume—in which Ouellette included several pieces that were either unpublished or did not appear in earlier collections, and modifications of his previous work—also contains 'Le Poème et le poétique', a short but important statement on his conception of poetry. *Poésie* brought him the France-Canada award for the second time, the first being for *Edgard Varèse* (1966). *En la nuit, la mer* (1981), a second retrospective, is made up of two collections: *Ici, ailleurs la lumière* (1977) and *A découvert* (1979), with some modifications, and two other groups of poems, mostly unpublished. (Another volume of the seventies, *Errances* (1975), is not included.) Ouellette's themes are life and death, love and sensuality, spiritual quest and solitude. His images are those of intense light and darkness, of the female body and the erotic experience, of nature perceived in birds, rivers, trees, snow, but transformed into abstract symbols. His poetry is highly condensed, its syntax reduced to the most basic structures, with few modifiers. Ouellette makes frequent use, in both form and content, of seeming contradictions in theme, image, or structure, between which a highly charged tension brings about a metamorphosis and a new synthesis.

Throughout the seventies Ouellette continued to reflect on the nature of poetry and its language in essays that were collected in *Écrire en notre temps* (1979). They address the question of how one can write with lucidity, authenticity, and sincerity in a time of violence and evil. The entire body of Ouellette's writing is a passionate exploration of this question.

Ouellete's work took on a new dimension with the appearance of his first novel, *Tu regardais intensément Geneviève* (1978), in which he uses the unusual narrative technique of having the main character address himself as *tu*. It recounts the experience of a man whose wife, after several years of marriage, rejects angrily his response to her announcement that she is stifled by their relationship. As in Ouellette's second novel, *La mort vive* (1980), the emotional and spiritual experience of the main character is presented with depth and lucidity, but there is a failure to create other credible characters. In *La mort vive*—written in the third person, with passages in the first person taken from the diary of the main character and from frequently interspersed letters to other characters—Jean, an artist, seeks both to paint the perfect canvas and to achieve the glory of union with the body of his beloved. The novel's conclusion remains ambiguous about whether his final complete isolation and presumed suicide signify defeat or apotheosis as he succeeds in ridding himself of the imperfections of material form.

Journal dénoué (1974), which received the prize of the literary journal *Études françaises*, recounts Ouellette's affective, intellectual, and spiritual autobiography up to 1973. It contains a full bibliography to that date. Because of the quality, great vision, and courageous affirmation of human freedom found consistently throughout his work, Ouellette must be seen as one of Québec's leading writers and a man who has had a significant impact on the direction of poetry in Québec since the sixties. (See also ESSAYS IN FRENCH: 7.)

See the special issue on 'Fernand Ouellette, poète' of VOIX ET IMAGES, *littérature québécoise*, 5,3 (printemps 1980), which contains interviews with Ouellette and a fairly complete bibliography after that given in *Journal dénoué*. See also Pierre Nepveu, *Les mots à l'écoute, poésie et silence chez Fernand Ouellette, Gaston Miron et Paul-Marie Lapointe* (1979).   LOUISE FORSYTH

Ouellette-Michalska, Madeleine. See NOVELS IN FRENCH 1960 TO 1982: 3(g).

Outram, Richard (b. 1930). Born in Oshawa, Ont., he attended Victoria College, University of Toronto (1949-53). He has worked on the technical crews of CBC-TV since 1956. With his wife Barbara Howard, he runs Gauntlet Press, founded in 1960. He has published several small chapbooks, but his three main collections of poetry are *Exultate, jubilate* (1966), *Turns and other poems* (1975), and *The promise of light* (1980). His mode of poetry could be loosely described as metaphysical in that the poems tease out paradoxes and polarities through conceits, a meticulous playing with language, and mythological references. His language in general is very literary, using colloquialisms only occasionally for ironic effect. At the core of his poetry is a concern with the discrepancy between man's aspirations and spiritual urges and the gross reality of the world in which he lives. As his third volume's title suggests, man lives in a promise of light, and Outram plays on images of light, both whole and broken, in his poetry. The ambivalences of life—dark and light, real and ideal, spiritual and physical—are held in tightly controlled traditional structures that allow the polarities to work through images of balance and opposition.

PETER STEVENS

Ouvrard, Hélène. See NOVELS IN FRENCH 1960 TO 1982: 3(g).

Oxley, James MacDonald (1855-1907). Born into a relatively wealthy Halifax family, Oxley was educated at Halifax Academy, Dalhousie University, and Harvard. He was admitted to the Nova Scotia Bar in 1878 and practised law in Halifax for five years before becoming a legal adviser to the federal Department of Marine and Fisheries. In 1891 he moved to Montreal to join the staff of the Sun Life Assurance Company. He spent the final years of his life in Toronto.

Oxley wrote thirty-one books for boys, published between 1889 and 1905—unabashed adventure tales exploiting northern and seafaring settings already made popular by Henty, R.M. BALLANTYNE, and Marryat. In general, as many of their titles indicate, his stories turn on themes of initiation and the experience of a personable boy-hero whose physical courage is tested in an exotic setting. He usually set them in a remote historical period, though he occasionally used his native Nova Scotia as a backdrop. Among his titles are: *Bert Lloyd's boyhood* (London, 1889); *Up among the ice floes* (London, 1890); *The wreckers of Sable Island* (London, 1891); *Archie of Athabaska* (Boston, 1893), published in London, 1894, as *Archie Mackenzie, the young Nor'wester; The good ship Gryphon; or On the right track* (Boston, 1893); *Fife and drum at Louisbourg* (London, 1899); and *L'Hasa at last* (1900).

GILLIAN THOMAS

P

Pacey, Desmond (1917-75). Born in Dunedin, N.Z., William Cyril Desmond Pacey lived in England from 1924 to 1931, when he came to rural Ontario, where he finished school. He took his B.A. in English and Philosophy at the University of Toronto in 1938 and his Ph.D. from Cambridge University in 1941. He was professor of English at Brandon College, University of Manitoba, from 1941 to 1944, and then moved to the University of New Brunswick, where he remained until his death, serving as head of the Department of English (1944-69); dean of graduate studies (1960-70); vice-president academic (1970-5); and University Professor (1974-5). He was made a Fellow of the Royal Society of Canada in 1944 and received its LORNE PIERCE medal in 1972. Writing criticism that, like his teaching, was lucid, moderate, and modest in its claims, he helped to establish Canadian literature as a legitimate field of study in both schools and universities.

Pacey's publications in Canadian literature began with his *Frederick Philip Grove* (1945), which reflected an interest that continued with a selection of GROVE's stories, *Tales from the margin* (1971); an anthology of critical essays on Grove in the Critical Views of Canadian Writers series (1970); and his edition of *The letters of Frederick Philip Grove* (1976). His *Creative writing in Canada: a short history of English Canadian literature* (1952; rev. and enlarged, 1961) was the only handbook of its kind for many years. His *Ten Canadian poets: a group of biographical and critical essays* (1958) allowed him to treat more fully the work of SANGSTER, ROBERTS, CARMAN, LAMPMAN, D.C. SCOTT, PRATT, SMITH, F.R. SCOTT, KLEIN, and BIRNEY. He contributed two chapters—'The writer and his public', and 'Fiction 1920-1940'—to the *Literary history of Canada* (1965), of which he was an editor. His *Essays in Canadian criticism: 1938-1968* (1969) and *Ethel Wilson* (1968), in the Twayne series, contain some of his best critical writing. He edited *A book of Canadian stories* (1947; 4th edn 1967) and *The selected poems of Sir Charles G.D. Roberts* (1956), as well as the school anthology *Our literary heritage* (1966).

Pacey also published two collections of stories, *The picnic and other stories* (1958) and *Waken, lords and ladies gay* (1974), and two books of poems for children: *The cow with the musical moo and other verses for children* (1952) and *Hippity Hobo and the bee* (1952). At the time of his death he was preparing scholarly editions of the poems and letters of Charles G.D. Roberts.

See also CRITICISM IN ENGLISH: 4.

ROBERT GIBBS

Packard, Frank (1877-1942). Born of American parents in Montreal, Frank Lucius Packard was one of the first Canadian authors to reach a wide audience outside Canada. He trained as an engineer, attending Montreal High School, Woodstock College, McGill University (B.Sc., 1897), and L'Institut Montefiore, Liège. While working as a civil engineer in the United States, he used to rise at 4 a.m. to write; in 1906 his first short story was published in *Munsey's Magazine*. Other stories appeared in *Century, Outing Magazine*, and *Canadian Magazine*. In 1911 Thomas Crowell of New York published his first book, *On the iron at Big Cloud*, a collection of railway stories. In 1910 he married Marguerite Pearl Macintyre; they settled in Lachine, Qué., where Packard wrote his first novel, *Greater love hath no man* (1913). His next novel, *The miracle man* (1914), which originally appeared in *Munsey's Magazine*, was a great success. Adapted for the stage by George M. Cohan, it played at the Astor Theatre, New York, and was made into a popular silent film. In 1917 Packard wrote another bestseller, *The adventures of Jimmie Dale* (1917), which set a pattern for his crime fiction. Thereafter he produced about a novel a year, all originally published in New York by Doran but reprinted in both Toronto and London. He and his wife raised four children in Lachine.

Packard used several formulas to gain mass-market appeal for his novels. He drew on his experience with railroads for *The wire devils* (1918), a crime novel with a surprise ending, and for many of the stories in his first book, *On the iron*, which were reprinted, with other stories, in *Running special* (1925). The same characters people the stories in *The night operator* (1919), tales stressing the technical competence and toughness of the men of the Hill Division in the foothills of the American Rockies; despite melodramatic incidents, they present a believable social spectrum and suggest a heroic struggle to conquer a continent.

For his highly successful series of Jimmie Dale crime novels, dealing with the New York underworld, Packard haunted the streets of New York and joined police raids; but for all their authentic atmosphere, the novels have conventional plots that rely heavily on impenetrable disguise, miraculous escapes, and vital information overheard. *The adventures of Jimmie Dale* (1917), *The further adventures of Jimmie Dale* (1919), *Jimmie Dale and the phantom clue* (1922), *Jimmie Dale and the blue envelope murder* (1930), and *Jimmie Dale and the missing hour* (1935) have as their chief character a millionaire clubman and champion of honour and fair play who inhabits the underworld under various disguises and foils crime through his expertise in safe-cracking and lock-picking. By 1942 the series had sold an estimated three million copies and been made into a silent serial and a CBC radio series (1942-5). Other crime novels using the same motifs are *The white moll* (1920) and *The big shot* (1929), both featuring young women in disguise in the underworld; *Doors of the night* (1922); and *The hidden door* (1933), which brings its thriller-writing hero briefly into a new setting, the North Shore of the Gulf of St Lawrence, familiar to Packard from holidays in Tadoussac. In *The red ledger* (1926) the wealthy Charlebois visits justice on those whose names are entered in his ledger because they helped or spurned him in his destitute youth. These adventures were adapted for CBC radio in 1937-8, with brief moralizing introductions spoken by Packard himself.

Another group of Packard's novels, labelled 'romances' by his publisher, are also crime novels but stress psychological themes of repentance, self-sacrifice, and redemptive love. In *Greater love hath no man*, Varge shields his beloved foster-mother by confessing to a murder he did not commit. Characteristically, Packard imbibed the atmosphere for this novel by visiting the St Vincent de Paul Penitentiary, Montreal, but he transferred the setting to an unnamed American location. *The miracle man* and *The sin that was his* (1917) describe the experiences of wrong-doers who are gradually converted by a religious power they set out to mock. Other such novels are *The beloved traitor* (1915), *From now on* (1919), and *Pawned* (1921).

Packard also wrote numerous adventures of the South Seas, which he had visited in 1912: *The locked book* (1924); *Broken waters* (1925); *Two stolen idols* (1927), published in England as *The slave junk; The devil's mantle* (1927); *The gold skull murders* (1931); and *The purple ball* (1933). *Tiger claws* (1928) begins in the South Seas and ends in the New York underworld, and *The dragon's jaws* (1937), set on the China coast, owes its local colour to Packard's voyage to the Orient in 1934. Packard's exotic adventure fiction also includes two collections of short stories, *Shanghai Jim* (1928) and *More knaves than one* (1938), and a novel, *The four stragglers* (1923), set in the Florida Keys. These later works, like the crime novels, are on the whole perfunctory, though skilfully plotted. Packard's enormous output shows invention and careful attention to local colour hardening into formula.   JEAN O'GRADY

Page, P.K. (b. 1916). Patricia Kathleen Page was born at Swanage in the south of England. Her family came to Canada in 1919 and settled in Red Deer, Alta. She was educated at St Hilda's School, Calgary, and never attended a university, though in later years she studied art in Brazil and at the Art Students' League in New York. During the late 1930s she worked as a shop assistant and a radio actress in Saint John, N.B.; then she moved to Montreal and worked there as a filing clerk and a historical researcher. There, in the early 1940s, she associated with the writers who for a time made that bilingual city the most important centre of English-language poetry in Canada.

P.K. Page published her first poems in Montreal, and was one of the group that founded PREVIEW, whose first issue appeared in March 1942. In this venture she was associated with Patrick ANDERSON, F.R. SCOTT, and Neufville Shaw, and it soon became apparent that among the younger poets of the group, she was the most accomplished. Outside periodicals, her verse was first published in *Unit of five* (1942), which Ronald Hambleton edited and in which he introduced not only Page's poetry and his own, but also that of Louis DUDEK, Raymond SOUSTER, and James Wreford.

The first book entirely made up of Page's poetry, *As ten as twenty* (1946), showed a strong awareness of English poetic trends in the 1930s; and while Page did not make the extreme political commitments of those who at this time entered the Communist Party, it was evident that she had taken sides against the Anglo-Canadian establishment that then seemed to rule in Montreal. She also shared the psychoanalytic preoccupations of contemporary English poets, and some of the best of her early verse deals with various forms of neurosis. In terms of lyrical vision, the best piece of this first volume is undoubtedly, as A.J.M. SMITH proposed, the haunting 'Stories of snow', in which legend and dream and child memories are mingled—to quote Smith—in 'a crystal clairvoyance'.

In 1946 Page started to work as a scriptwriter for the National Film Board, and remained there until 1950, when she married William Arthur Irwin, at that time commissioner of the NFB. In this period she wrote the poems that appeared in *The metal and the flower* (1954), which won a Governor General's Award. In their sharply visual presentations of concrete situations, many of these poems reflect the cinematographic perceptions Page had acquired. They consider not ordinary political commitments but the plights of lonely people, or those whom circumstances have condemned to appear contemptible; some are miniature imaginary biographies that come as near as any writer can to the meeting of satire and compassion.

In 1944, under the nom-de-plume of 'Judith Cape', she published a novel—or perhaps a romance—called *The sun and the moon*. Page has never explained her pseudonym, but Margaret ATWOOD noticed 'the visions of cloak-and-dagger and Holofernes' severed head raised by the last and first names respectively', and such associations are appropriate to a novel that deals with a young girl in touch with mysterious forces that almost destroy her artist husband. It was republished under Page's name in *The sun and moon and other fictions* (1973), which includes other stories from the 1940s that are less strained in credibility and at the same time more tightly organized. The best of them, as Atwood says, are characterized by 'the bizarre perspectives and the disconcerting insights' that distinguish Page's best poems. Some, like 'The green bird' and 'George', project a wild yet pathetic sense of comedy. Others, such as 'The glass box', resemble early poems like 'The landlady' and 'The stenographers' in their power to convey the sadness of lonely people trying to snatch a little meaning from their lives in the unfriendly city.

From 1953 to 1964—when W.A. Irwin acted as Canadian ambassador in Australia, Brazil, and Mexico—Page lived away from Canada and wrote comparatively little poetry, concentrating on paintings and intricate drawings she made under the name of P.K. Irwin—works that show how her various arts reflect each other, for they evoke poetic as well as aesthetic images. The unity of her arts is stressed in the new poems she included in *Cry Ararat* (1967) and *Poems selected and new* (1974), both of which consist largely of works chosen from her first books, for she had written less abundantly in the sixties and early seventies than in the forties. *Cry Ararat* is illustrated with drawings largely derived from Page's studies of Australian native art. It is itself the subject of one poem, 'Bark drawing', of which six lines evoke with marvelous economy her double talents: 'an alphabet the eye/lifts from the air/as if by ear/two senses/threaded through/a knuckle bone'.

The newer poems show a movement towards verbal economy that one can link with Page's recent philosophic inclination towards the mystical tradition of Sufism. In the late poems of her most recent books, and especially of *Evening dance of the grey flies* (1981), which consists entirely of uncollected works, there is an ever-increasing purification of the line. In the early work the line was long and flowing, with the kind of full eloquence that belonged to the 1940s in Canada and England alike. In the more recent poems there is still a fluidity, but it is more controlled, sparser, yet ever-moving. Similarly the pattern of thought is modified, and filled with a metaphysical intent that shifts its direction from the inward images of the earlier poems to the images of natural sublimity that pose a way of liberation from the alienated, imprisoned self. The poems in Page's latest book carry this quality into a kind of Delphic utterance, almost a possession by the vision; though these poems are perhaps more sharply and intensely visual than ever in their sensuous evocation of shape and colour and space, this imagery takes us magically beyond any ordinary seeing into a realm of imagining in which the normal world is shaken like a vast kaleidoscope and revealed in unexpected and luminous relationships. The centre-piece of *Evening dance of the grey flies* is a remarkable futurist story, 'Unless the eye catch fire . . .', which ostensibly deals with the death of earth as a habitation of man and the end of time as man dies; but on another level it projects a visionary perception, suggesting that one does not have to wait for the end of time to apprehend eternity.

Page

As well as her poems and fiction, Page has written two eloquent essays on the genesis of her art(s) in CANADIAN LITERATURE: 'Questions and images' (41) and 'Traveller, conjuror, journeyman' (46); both develop Page's idea that 'in all essential particulars writing and painting are interchangeable. They are alternate routes to silence.' She has also edited an anthology of short poems, *To say the least; Canadian poets from A to Z* (1980).

See A.J.M. SMITH's essay on Page's poetry in Issue 50 of *Canadian literature* (Autumn 1977); and, in the same magazine, Rosemary Sullivan's 'A size larger than seeing' in Issue 79 (Winter 1978).

See also POETRY IN ENGLISH: 1950 TO 1982: 2. GEORGE WOODCOCK

Page, Rhoda Anne (1826-63). Probably the best-known Canadian poet for a brief period in the late 1840s, Page was brought to this country from her native England at the age of six, when her family immigrated to a farm near Cobourg, Canada West. Beginning in 1846, using the initials R.A.P., she published her poetry regularly in *The Cobourg Star*, from which other newspapers copied it; her writing was therefore widely circulated throughout the Canadas. Her verse also appeared in *The Victoria Magazine*, *The Church*, and *The Maple Leaf Annual*. A pamphlet collection, *Wild notes from the backwoods*, was published in Cobourg in 1850. In 1856 she married William Faulkner and moved to the Rice Lake area. Eight children were born before her death in 1863. E.H. DEWART included five of her poems, using her married name, in his anthology *Selections from Canadian poets* (1864). Although a melancholy preoccupation with death runs through much of her work, Page was essentially a poet of nature. The Canadian backwoods as she described them was a tranquil world that owed its beauty and life to a genteel God. Her descriptive poem, 'Rice Lake by moonlight: a winter scene', was the most widely reprinted Canadian work of its day. Page was one of the multitude of female lyric poets who peopled the literary world of the early nineteenth century. Although a modern reader becomes impatient with the correctness of the sentiment expressed, and with the restraint one feels in the poet's response to her subjects, at their best her verses flow smoothly and effortlessly, with great lyric charm. The Upper Canada she describes is recognizable today. MARY LU MacDONALD

Palmer, John (b. 1943). Born in Sydney, N.S., and raised in Ottawa, Murray John Palmer attended Glebe Collegiate Institute, which produced two of his one-act plays. Active in the extra-curricular drama group of Carleton University, where he studied English literature, he established an early reputation for championing Canadian drama by directing Canadian plays at Le Hibou Coffee House in Ottawa during the mid-sixties, and later at the Black Swan Coffee House in Stratford, Ont. The first play of his trilogy, *Memories for my brother*, premièred at Stratford in 1969 at The Canadian Place Theatre, which Palmer co-founded with Martin KINCH that same year. It was rewritten the following year for production by Theatre Passe Muraille in Toronto, where Palmer became an active force in the burgeoning 'alternate' theatre movement of the early seventies.

The spirit of 'controlled frenzy' that the British critic John Russell Taylor ascribed to Palmer's one foray into film direction—Martin Kinch's *Me?*, which won the Best Foreign Film award at the 1974 Toulon Film Festival—infuses the episodic structure of his early plays with a frenetic pace that seeks to convey a sense of contemporary chaos in which values collapse along with relationships. The collage of incidents that forms the twenty scenes of *Memories for my brother, Part I* (1972) is barely held together by the naïf/artist Berlin, whose wanderings give the play its only through-line. The titles of two unpublished plays produced at the Young Vic Theatre in Stratford in 1966— *Confessions of a necrophile; or Never laugh when a hearse goes by* and *Visions of an unseemly youth*—suggest the macabre humour of Palmer's angry and sarcastic outcry against the excesses of a society that forfeits humanity in the pursuit of sensuality, a theme less successfully explored in a milder comedy, *Bland hysteria* (1972), where two characters change personalities and affections faster than clothing. The collaboration begun at Stratford between Palmer and Kinch resulted in Kinch's directing Palmer's *A touch of God in the golden age* (1972)—a tragi-comic dialogue between two men that examines their inner needs and interdependencies—at Toronto's Factory Theatre Lab in 1974, and in Palmer's directing Kinch's *Me?* in 1973 and 1977 at the Toronto Free Theatre, which they co-founded with Tom HENDRY in 1971. Palmer's work at Toronto Free Theatre represents the climax of his career as both director and playwright. *The end* (1971), a two-act farce with serious undertones, in which some social misfits demonstrate with desperate humour the pain of their meaningless lives, is Palmer's best-structured and most finished play; but his collective creation, *The pits* (unpublished), produced in collaboration with Des McAnuff, made a greater impact. Set in a dilapidated rooming-house, whose rooms are open to the surrounding audience, it explores contemporary isolation and ennui by scrutinizing the lives of six characters who simultaneously perform acts of eccentricity and despair in the 'privacy' of their own rooms. After unsuccessfully reviving the concept in *The pits 1979* at Toronto's New Theatre, Palmer left Canada to assume semi-permanent status in New York City. His frustration with the state of Canadian theatre (audience apathy and conservatism) had already moved him to write *Henrik Ibsen on the necessity of producing Norwegian drama* (1978), a reasoned and effective monologue in which an angry Ibsen, as Palmer's persona, bitterly attacks cultural attitudes and policies.

Palmer's disappointments with Canadian theatre, and his treatment by Canadian theatre reviewers, are best documented in the Wallace/Zimmerman collaboration *The work: conversations with English-Canadian playwrights* (1982).   ROBERT S. WALLACE

Panneton, Philippe (1895-1960). Better known under his pseudonym 'Ringuet' (his mother's family name), he was born in Trois-Rivières, Qué. After completing his 'cours classique', he studied medicine at Université Laval, first in Quebec City, then in Montreal, and obtained his degree in 1920. He then left for Paris, spending three years on post-graduate studies in otorhinolaryngology. He travelled widely and, free of the restrictions imposed by the Catholic Index, was able to indulge his insatiable appetite for books. It was in this period that he started to keep a diary. (The 2,390-page diary that he left at his death has never been published.) Upon his return to Canada in 1923 he practised medicine in Montreal; until 1940 he was also consultant at the Hôpital Saint-Eusèbe in Joliette. Author of several specialized articles in medical journals, he was invited, in 1935, to become professor in the faculty of medicine of the Université de Montréal. In 1956 he was appointed ambassador to Portugal, where he died. He had received the Prix de l'Académie française in 1953, the Prix Duvernay in 1955, and the

Lorne PIERCE Medal in 1959; and he was president of the French-Canadian Academy from 1947 to 1953.

Panneton was very proud of being a physician: 'I am first a doctor and then a writer. Literature interests me like a sport. It is a distraction in my leisure time' (*La Revue populaire*, juillet 1939, p. 6). Nevertheless he diligently pursued this 'distraction'. From among his early writings, about thirty poems were published between 1917 and 1925 in periodicals and newspapers. A verse-play, *Idylle au jardin*, written in 1919, was neither published nor performed. Panneton's first book, *Littératures . . . à la manière de . . .* (1924), written in collaboration with Louis Francoeur, presented a series of parodies of well-known French-Canadian writers and prominent politicians of the time, such as Henri Bourassa, René Chopin, 'Valdombre' (C.-H. GRIGNON), Paul MORIN, Camille Roy, and Lionel GROULX. Several critics reproved the authors for having shown little respect to Father Groulx by making fun of his books *Rapaillages* and *L'appel de la race* in the pages entitled 'Rabâchages' (literally 'harping on the same string'), which ended with a scene called 'Appel de la crasse'. Nevertheless, the book was generally well received and was awarded the Prix David. Panneton's only other literary work at this time was an undistinguished play, *Je t'aime . . . Je ne t'aime pas*, performed at the Monument National on 28 April and 19 May 1927.

Panneton achieved the climax of his career as a writer with the publication of TRENTE ARPENTS (1938). A portrait of a rural and traditional society in the process of change, it was an immediate success with both French and French-Canadian critics. Finally the great French-Canadian novel had appeared! Certain critics went so far as to call it a masterpiece of literary realism. It was translated almost immediately into English (*Thirty acres*, 1940) and German.

L'héritage et autres contes (1946), a collection of nine short stories that stress the characters' alienation and their insatiable need to escape their milieu, was given a poor reception. The title story, which is reminiscent of *Trente arpents* and was Panneton's favourite, was made into a short movie by the National Film Board in 1960. In the same year Morna Scott Stoddart published a translation in *Canadian short stories* (1960) edited by Robert WEAVER.

Panneton's second novel, *Fausse monnaie* (1947), which depicts the empty lives of a group of well-to-do young people, concerns a Don Juan who rediscovers during a weekend in the Laurentians a childhood friend whom he had considered vain and superficial; they seem briefly to be smitten with each other but their love does not endure. This novel, which Ringuet said was written primarily to describe the Laurentians, is full of hackneyed characters and commonplace expressions and had no success at all. Much more ambitious was his third novel, *Le poids du jour* (1949). After the death of his beloved mother, Michel Garneau learns that his real father is not Ludovic Garneau, whom he had come to detest, but rather Monsieur Lacerte, his godfather and benefactor whom he loved. Imagining that everyone had known of his illegitimacy and been laughing at him all these years, he instantly hates what he had once loved, including Monsieur Lacerte. Wanting to be admired and feared, he changes his name to Robert M. Garneau and adopts the motto: 'To be happy, you must be rich. To be rich, you must be powerful.' Though he accumulates a large fortune in Montreal, he does not find contentment until, after a series of setbacks, he moves to the country. *Le poids du jour* often seems to use the story of Garneau merely as a pretext for social description and commentary on the changes in Québec society between the two world wars.

Un monde était leur empire (1943) is an unsuccessful popular history of Pre-Columbian Mexico that grew out of Ringuet's visit to that country in 1934. *L'amiral et le facteur ou Comment l'Amérique ne fut pas découverte* (1954) discusses the relative contributions of Christopher Columbus and Amerigo Vespucci in the discovery of the American continent. *Confidences* (1965), which was originally intended for radio broadcast, is a series of recollections of Panneton's childhood and youth, narrated with much humour and charm.

Panneton was well advised not to publish in 1926 his *Carnet du cynique*; these 90 pages from his Journal raise unsparing questions about sacred values of his society and would probably have ruined his medical career.

Jean Panneton's *Ringuet* (1970) gives the best summary of his life and works.

JACQUES COTNAM

Paperny, Myra. See CHILDREN'S LITERATURE IN ENGLISH: 8.

Pâquet, Louis-Adolphe (1859-1942). Born in St-Nicolas, Qué., and educated at the Séminaire de Québec and in Rome, Pâquet became professor, then dean, of theology, and director of the graduate school of philosophy at Université Laval, where his scholarship and his gifts as an orator combined to make him one of the decisive influences on the intellectual life of Québec. His writings on social questions and his influence within the Church also made him a formative influence on the character of the social order in Québec, especially from the turn of the century to the Second World War. His six-volume study of St Thomas, *Disputationes theologicae seu commentaria in summam theologicam d. Thomae* (Québec, 1893-1903; 2nd edn, 1920-3), one of the great monuments of Thomist scholarship, gave Pâquet his authority as a philosopher. His interest, however, quickly turned to popular public issues. Yvan Lamonde—who gathered some of his short writings in *Louis-Adolphe Pâquet, textes choisis* (1972), and wrote the chapter on Pâquet in *Les idéologies au Québec, 1900-1929* (edited by Fernand DUMONT, 1973)—has written that he 'personifies the passage from political and religious preoccupations to social questions' in Québec.

Pâquet had a strong feeling for the land and for rural life in Québec, and a powerful determination to maintain a culture that was both French and Catholic. He understood the need for, and the pressures towards, industrialization; but he sought to minimize its destructive impact by supporting the traditional family with a charitable and social order led by the Church. These general concerns were set out in a four-volume study, *Droit public de l'Église (Principes généraux; L'organisation religieuse et le pouvoir civil; L'action religieuse et la loi civile*; and *L'église et l'éducation*, 1908-15). Many of his published works were collections of essays and speeches: *Discours et allocutions* (1915), *Études et appréciations* (6 vols, *Fragments apologétiques, Nouveau fragments apologétiques, Mélanges canadiens, Nouveaux mélanges canadiens, Thèmes sociaux*, and *Nouveaux thèmes sociaux*, 1917-32), and *Au soir de la vie; modestes pages philosophico-religieuses* (1938). Frequently, as in his pamphlet *Sainte Anne et le peuple canadien-français* (1925), and his celebrated essay 'La vocation de la race français en Amérique' (edited by Émile Chartier and issued in 1925 as a pamphlet for youth movements in Québec entitled *Bréviare du patriote canadien-français*), he tried to combine religion and national feeling. Deeply conservative, he opposed socialism with vigour but was equally opposed to *laissez-faire* capitalism, and wrote essays on the mutual responsibilities of capital and labour.

Pâquet wrote three other large works: *La foi et la raison en elles-mêmes et dans leurs rapports* (Québec, 1890), *Cours d'éloquence sacrée* (2 vols, 1925-6), and *La prière dans l'oeuvre du salut* (2 vols, 1925-6). Besides the two pamphlets mentioned, at least eight other essays were published as small pamphlets, but most of this material appears in one or other of the collections. In the archives of the Séminaire de Québec there are personal diaries for extended periods (1883-1906, 1911-27, and 1940-1), as well as an extensive correspondence. LESLIE ARMOUR

Paquin, Ubald (1894-1962). Born in Montreal, he worked as a journalist for *Le Devoir, La Patrie, Le Canada*, and *Le Nationaliste* successively, and in 1916 founded *La Bataille*. Implicated in the bombing of the home of the owner of the *Montreal Star* in 1917, he sought refuge in Abitibi, returning to Montreal in 1920 to open a bookstore, at which time he began his friendship with Claude-Henri GRIGNON. An unsuccessful nationalist candidate in the 1921 provincial elections, he spent the remainder of his life as a civil servant, trying to reconcile this career with his literary ambitions. He died in Montreal.

Paquin's fierce nationalism informs all his novels: *Jules Faubert* (1923), *La cité dans les fers* (1926), *Le lutteur* (1927), *Les caprices du coeur* (1927), *Le massacre dans le temple* (1928), *Le mort qu'on venge* (1929), *La mystérieuse inconnue* (1929), *Le mirage* (1920), *Oeil pour oeil* (1931), and *Le paria* (1933). The muddled concepts and odious fascist ideology of these works can only be understood in the historical context of the 1929 stock-market crash and the rise of fascism, which cast a spell over some Québec intellectuals; yet in several of them passion and instinct become a source of positive energy and present a complex psychology that merits a serious psycho-critical reading. In *La cité dans les fers*, the hero masterminds a nationalist *coup d'état*, inspired by fascist militarism. *Jules Faubert* and *Le lutteur*, whose heroes are both self-made men, probe the psychology of the superman. The hero of *Le lutteur*, Victor Duval, inherits the physical strength and stamina of peasant forebears and, through will and self-denial, becomes a Québec shipping magnate. In a sense, Paquin radically rethought the Québécois Messianism of the nineteenth century, being one of the first to value the French-Canadian businessman—whom he saw as responsible for the cultural and social progress of the race, provided he served the higher patriotism and embraced fascism. The unconscious death-wish is important in Paquin's work, the psychology of his characters being defined largely through the relations between the dominating and the dominated. Like *Le lutteur, La mystérieuse inconnue* and *Le mirage* focus on such preoccupations, but they lack *Lutteur's* psychological complexity. The hero of *Le massacre dans le temple* pushes self-denial to its extreme: following a period of asceticism that amounts to self-mutilation, he ends up with the Trappists. Yet it is not clear that Paquin espoused Christianity: his ethics of race and moral force—surprisingly for his time—take the place of religion in his novels. Equally surprising is the influence of Zola on *Le paria* (written at a time when the naturalist novel was little esteemed in Québec), evident in the opening murder scene, in the description of the peasants' grasping instincts, and in the character of the solitary priest who takes refuge from the vulgar herd in Christian morality more than in faith. Perhaps only in *Les caprices du coeur* did Paquin question the ideal of the superman: neither confident nor self-made, the hero is a nervous, hypersensitive character who finally yields to the need—latent in the superman— to kill. Paquin had no love for the masses, whose will to power in the class struggle is unstable, leading to revolutionary carnage and anarchy. Nor was he a monarchist: the king in *Oeil pour oeil* would qualify as a superman, except that he yields his political power to the will of his mistress. In this novel Paquin shows a preference for a republic organized and run by aristocrats: only the élite possess the psychological ambivalence—love and hatred, refinement and primitivism—in the service of a higher principle, the state, that characterizes the superman. CLAUDE FILTEAU

Paradis, Suzanne (b. 1936). Born in Beaumont, Qué., she graduated from the École normale in Quebec City. She was for a time in charge of the Centre d'art at Val-Menaud in the Lac Saint-Jean region. She married the poet Louis-Paul Hamel in 1961. Her poetry, which is rhythmic and usually set in conventional rhymed hexameters, is notable for its abundance of metaphors and for a wealth of imagery that, though sometimes barely under control, is always evocative. She writes with great verve and passion of the quest for individual freedom, of the celebration of life and nature in all their aspects, and of love and personal fulfilment. Her collections are *Les enfants continuels* (1959); *A temps, le bonheur* (1960); *La chasse aux autres* (1961); *La malebête* (1963); *Pour les enfants des morts* (1964), which was awarded the Prix France-Canada; *L'oeuvre de pierre* (1968), winner of the Prix Du Maurier; *Pour voir les plectrophanes naître* (1970); *Il y a eu une maison* (1972); *La voie sauvage* (1972); *Noir sur sang* (1976); and *Les chevaux de verre* (1979). She has also published two books of short stories, *François-les-oiseaux* (1967) and *Grain de riz* (1977); and eight novels: *Les hauts cris* (1960), *Il ne faut pas sauver les hommes* (1961), *Les cormorans* (1968), *Emmanuelle en noir* (1971), *Quand la terre était toujours jeune* (1973), *L'été sera chaud* (1975), *Un portrait de Jeanne Joron* (1977), and *Miss Charlie* (1979). *Quand la terre était toujours jeune* was translated by Basil Kingstone as *When the earth was still young* in CANADIAN FICTION MAGAZINE 26 (1976). The fluid style of Paradis's poetry becomes too studied in her fiction. Her gifts for metaphor and image-making overpower her novels and stories and make them unduly pretentious and obscure. The subject-matter is melodramatic. *Emmanuelle en noir* is a study of incest, madness, and violence, told through interior monologue and letters. In *Les cormorans* the inhabitants of a lonely island are destroyed gradually by murder, suicide, and natural disaster, leaving only a boy and girl to set off together in a skiff in search of a new life.

Suzanne Paradis is also the author of *Femme fictive, femme réelle* (1966), a study of the female characters in the novels of French-Canadian women writers, and *Adrienne Choquette lue par Suzanne Paradis* (1978).

See also NOVELS IN FRENCH 1960 TO 1982: 3(f).   JOYCE MARSHALL

Parker, Sir Gilbert (1862-1932). The son of a small-town storekeeper and former n.c.o., Horatio Gilbert Parker was born in Camden Township East, Canada West (Ont.). After graduating from Trinity College, University of Toronto, he taught elocution there; he was later ordained a deacon in the Anglican Church. A short period as a parish assistant in Trenton, Ont., concluded with his departure in 1885 for Australia, where he rapidly rose as a journalist, becoming assistant editor of the Sydney *Morning Herald*. Before his departure for England in 1889 he travelled extensively in the South

Pacific, penning romantic accounts of the spots he visited. In England his skills as a writer of popular fiction, his position as a member of Parliament (1900-18), and his 'good' marriage advanced him steadily. A knighthood (1902), a baronetcy (1915), and membership in the Privy Council (1916) testify that bright colonial sons like Parker (along with Bonar Law and Max Aitken) could aspire to the inner circles of the imperial motherland. During the Great War, Parker directed the British government's vast propaganda effort to move U.S. public opinion in a pro-British direction, a project that was ultimately successful. Parker's last years were spent in California with the family of his brother.

Parker's *Works* (1912-23) comprise 23 volumes, most of them historical novels of romance and adventure, and two volumes of poetry, *A lover's diary* (Chicago, 1894) and *Embers* (1908). Some of the lyrics in *Embers* were set to music by Sir Edward Elgar.

Parker's contribution to Canadian letters rests on his fictional treatment of three subject areas: the romantic Northwest, picturesque Québec, and heroic France. *Pierre and his people* (London, 1892), a collection of adventure tales about the colourful Métis, Indians, Mounties, and Imperial adventures in a Northwest he had never visited, appeared originally in the New York *Independent* (whose assistant editor at that time was Bliss CARMAN). It put Parker on the map of literary London and was reprinted many times. Parker's Québec—the subject of *When Valmond came to Pontiac* (London, 1895), *The pomp of the Lavilettes* (Boston, 1896), *The lane that had no turning* (London, 1899), and *The money master* (1915), among other novels—is a quaint, agrarian society filled with simple rustics whose lives become momentarily ruffled by scheming villains, hot-headed lovers, and restless adventurers. It is the Québec celebrated by William Henry DRUMMOND, Louis HÉMON, and the painter Cornelius Krieghoff. New France offered an arena for heroic action in *The trail of the sword* (New York, 1894), *The seats of the mighty* (London, 1896), and *The power and the glory* (1925). *The seats of the mighty*, which is still available in a paperback reprint (NCL, 1971), stemmed from the same source book as *The* GOLDEN DOG by William KIRBY. Set at the time of the Conquest, it concerns the adventures in love and war of a British Army spy, Robert Moray, and was based partly on the *Memoirs* of Robert Stobo (1727-70). Moray finally wins Alixe and defeats his rivals; the British take Quebec; and English daring, drive, and hardihood are wedded to French charm, beauty, and emotional richness. No other novel quite sums up with such vigour and aplomb the Imperialist view of Québec's role in Canada.

See John C. Adams, *Seated with the mighty: a biography of Sir Gilbert Parker* (1979).   DENNIS DUFFY

Parkman, Francis. See FOREIGN WRITERS ON CANADA IN ENGLISH: 2.

parti pris (1963-8). Founded by Pierre Maheu, André MAJOR, and Paul CHAMBERLAND, *et al.*, it was a highly influential political and cultural review published in Montreal. Its founders reacted against the generation of intellectuals that preceded them, and specially those around the review *Cité libre*, reproaching them for denouncing the political corruption of the Duplessis régime and particular cases of injustice without attacking the fundamental injustices rooted in the economic and social structure of Québec society. This initial ideology, mainly centred on the idea of decolonization, later developed into a certain radicalization. The leaders of the review defined the situation in a Marxist perspective: the struggle for political independence appeared only as the first step towards social revolution. An internal conflict over whether René Lévesque's Mouvement souveraineté-association (1968, later the Parti Québécois) should be supported tactically or a new radical party founded, and the editors' view that the main aims of *parti pris* (independence, secularism, and socialism) had been widely disseminated, led them to cease publication.

The magazine and the publishing house Les Éditions parti pris (founded in 1961), which is still active, have played an important role in the literary and artistic development of Québec. The literary theories of *parti pris* were outlined by the above-mentioned collaborators and others in the Jan. 1965 issue entitled 'Pour une littérature québécoise'. There it was proposed that the vehicle for a new orientation in creative writing should be JOUAL; the use of international French, it was felt, would be a travesty and would not allow Québécois to recognize their colonized status. Among the creative writers whose works were published under the auspices of the review are novelists Jacques RENAUD, André Major, and Laurent Girouard, and poets Paul Chamberland and Gérald GODIN. Contri-

buting to the review were poet Raoul DUGUAY and film-makers Denys Arcand and Pierre Maheu. Although older than the founders and editors of *parti pris*, Claude JASMIN and Jacques FERRON also had some of their prose works published by Les Éditions parti pris. The publishing house later specialized in poetry, and in essays on political, economic, and social topics, including translations of books by radical authors like Stanley B. Ryerson and James Laxer.

For more information on the political and literary importance of *parti pris*, see Malcolm Reid's *The shouting signpainters: a literary and political account of Quebec revolutionary nationalism* (1972); issue 31-2 of *La* BARRE DU JOUR (Winter 1972), devoted entirely to *parti pris*; Joseph Bonenfant's *Index de parti pris 1963-1968* (1975); Lise Gauvin's *Parti pris littéraire* (1975); B.-Z. Shek's *Social realism in the French-Canadian novel* (1977, chap. 9); and especially Robert Major's *Parti pris: idéologies et littérature* (1979).

                    CLAUDE TROTTIER, BEN-Z. SHEK

Pelletier, Aimé (b. 1914). A Montreal physician and surgeon who writes under the pseudonym 'Bertrand Vac', he was born at Saint-Ambroise-de-Kildare, Qué., a small village about sixty-five km. north of Montreal. Between periods of medical studies in Montreal and Paris, he joined the Canadian army (1942-6) and was attached to the general staff in northern France and Belgium. Upon returning to Canada he resumed his career in medicine (1948), while at the same time travelling widely and devoting part of his leisure to writing.

Despite winning three times the Prix du Cercle du Livre de France (1950, 1952, 1965), Vac is relatively little known. His first novel, *Louise Genest* (1950), won the Prix the first year it was offered. Set in the village of Saint-Michel-des-Saints and the surrounding forest area north of Joliette, it relates the drama of a woman married at the age of seventeen to the owner of the general store, Armand Genest, a coarse, brutal, miserly man who makes her life unbearable. When Louise leaves her husband to seek happiness in the forest with a young half-breed hunter and trapper, Genest, to punish her, withdraws their sixteen-year-old son from the collège where he is studying and the boy winds up working in a logging camp. When he fails to return from a hunting expedition, Louise—tortured by guilt, remorse, and the conviction that she has abandoned him—sets out alone to search for him. Finding only his rifle, she suffers from hallucinations, succumbs to the elements, and dies of exhaustion. The forest, and the myth of the noble savage living a life of freedom and contentment in the heart of nature, are both important in this novel; but elements of social criticism are even more significant: tragedy springs from the guilt Louise suffers as a result of her upbringing and social and psychological pressures.

In *Deux portes . . . une adresse* (1952), one of the few French-Canadian novels based on the Second World War, Captain Jacques Grenon, a twenty-seven-year-old engineer who is unhappily married and the father of two young sons, has been in the army for four years and falls in love with Françoise Clair, a charming, cultivated, wealthy young widow. Much of the evolution of their love is revealed in a year-long exchange of letters between their infrequent meetings. The captain finally decides not to return to his wife, but she writes to his commanding general and has him repatriated against his will. Back in Montreal, he is swallowed up in the quagmire of his former existence.

In *Saint-Pépin, P.Q.* (1955), satire and caricature enliven this story of political antics in a small Québec town. Vac's prefatory note states that 'even the most grotesque situations in this novel have been lived; all we have done is interpret scenes which take place almost daily in our beloved province.' However, the events and characters, their foibles and absurdities, have been exaggerated for comic effect. The main character, Polydor Granger, becomes an election candidate in spite of himself, attracting in his wake a colourful collection of local bigots, opportunists, malcontents, and hypocrites. The election campaign, in which Granger is successful, is preposterous and unleashes all sorts of passions—some shameful, some comic.

L'assassin dans l'hôpital (1956), Vac's detective novel about an Ungava mining fortune and triple murder, was awarded the Prix du Cercle du Roman policier and was later adapted for television by Radio-Canada (1956). *La favorite et le conquérant* (1963) is a painstakingly documented historical novel whose action begins in 1397 during the reign of the famous Tartar chieftain Tamerlaine, ruler of Samarkand. The action flags at times, but the vast and exotic narrative—interspersed with passages of crude, erotic, and almost scabrous violence—is deftly handled.

In 1965 Vac was awarded his third Prix du Cercle du Livre de France for *Histoires galantes* (1965), a collection of eight short stories varying in length from six to thirty-six pages. Light and licentious, sometimes amusing, occasionally unpredictable, they constitute a series of variations on the theme of not-so-serious sex.

Appelez-moi Amédée, an unpublished comedy written in 1958, was presented during the summer of 1967 by the Théâtre de l'Escale, an enterprising troupe of actors who transformed a decommissioned ferryboat into an itinerant floating theatre plying the ports of the St Lawrence. *Mes pensées 'profondes'* (1967) is a tongue-in-cheek collection of maxims, aphorisms, and witticisms arranged chronologically from 1958 to 1966. *Le carrefour des géants* (1974), a social history of Montreal between 1820 and 1885, may also be construed as a history of Canada seen through the eyes of Montrealers. Avoiding the rigorous methodology of the professional historian, Vac succeeds in painting a fascinating, albeit ironic picture of Montreal, its inhabitants, their amusements and their relations with the burgeoning West during the critical period between the decline of the fur trade and the resurrection of the city, with the expansion of the railroads, as the financial and economic heart of Canada.

See Guy Robert, 'Trois livres de Bertrand Vac' in *La Revue dominicaine,* LXII, tome I, (jan.-fév., 1956). L.W. KEFFER

Péloquin, Claude (b. 1942) Born and raised in Montreal, he began to write at thirteen and gave his first poetry reading shortly after his seventeenth birthday. He co-founded in 1964 a group called 'L'horloge du nouvel-age', whose presentations combining electronic music, slides, films, dance, and poetry gave birth to the era of COLLECTIVE CREATIONS and multi-dimensional shows in Québec. A year later he founded another group, 'Le Zirmate', whose collective multi-media creations, produced at the Musée de l'art contemporain, were greeted by critics as courageous pioneering attempts to synthesize different modes of artistic expression.

But these activities did not hinder Peloquin's commitment to writing. After the publication of his first volume of poetry, *Jéricho* (1963), in which he wove surrealist images, *Les essais rouges* (1964) and *Les mondes assujettis* (1965) explored other stylistic possibilities: automatic writing, wildly opposed semantic connotations, and nonsensical sound-patterns frequently joined by a single metaphor. Péloquin was then described by French poet Alain Bosquet as 'the most seductive of all avant-garde poets' and won a place in Pierre Segher's Parisian anthology of the best poets of 1966. In the late sixties and early seventies he performed in the Zirmate's productions, wrote the words of Robert Charlebois's famous song 'Lindbergh', and also wrote the text that was incorporated in a mural displayed in front of Quebec City's Grand Théâtre in 1967. He continued to publish collections of prose-poems: *Manifeste infra suivis des Émissions parallèles* (1967), dedicated to the NASA scientists; *Pyrotechnics* (1968); *Pour la grandeur de l'homme* (1969); and *Mets tes raquettes* (1972), in which he stated and developed the main themes of his poetry: his struggle against death, his passionate rejection of human finitude, and his plea for the biological continuation of our species. He has been called by some critics a 'death-obsessed poet', and by others 'an eternalist', descriptions that often tend to draw attention away from his essential concern: the conscious exploration of what he calls our 'infra-structures'. Péloquin urges us to transcend rational limits, to imitate the scientists' open-mindedness to new laws, based on new empirical evidence, and to decipher the 'incommensurable' within us. This concern is also manifested in the very form of his writings: his texts are strewn with graphs, diagrams, and mathematical equations; a number are open-ended; most urge the reader to apply his own method of reading—to backtrack, skip, fill in the blanks. *Manifeste infra* is described on the dust jacket as 'an open work', an explicit reference to the Italian philosopher and semiotician Umberto Eco. Indeed, Péloquin strives to arouse his readers' creative capacities, to stimulate their cerebral powers, and to enlist their collaboration in the making of a work, thereby replacing the traditional process of communication between creator and audience with a new mode of participation. The calligraphic aspects of the poems echo those of other contemporary poets (Raoul DUGUAY and Paul CHAMBERLAND in Québec, and bp NICHOL in English Canada, to mention only a few). But Péloquin's passion for rejecting conventional typography reveals the need to express himself beyond the confines of the written word through visual forms, artifacts, and sculptures. In 1974 he exhibited some of his montages—surgical instruments mounted under glass—at the Galerie Martal and Espace 5 in Montreal. In 1976 he exhibited his first lithographs at the Jolliet Gallery in Quebec City. Péloquin's books, graphics, records, and films stand as a testimony to a versatile, audacious, sometimes reckless intellect, perpetually striving towards an unreachable ideal.

See *Le premier tiers, oeuvres complètes, 1942-1975* (three vols, 1976). Clément Moisan, in his *Poésie des frontières* (1979), devotes a chapter to Péloquin, bill BISSETT, and bp Nichol. An interview with Péloquin can be found in Caroline Bayard and Jack David, *Out-Posts/Avant-postes* (1978).

CAROLINE BAYARD

Percy, H.R. (b. 1920). Born in Burham, Kent, he served in the Royal Navy from 1936 to 1952 and in the Royal Canadian Navy until 1971. He edited *The Canadian Author and Bookman* from 1962 to 1965 and in this period wrote a column for the *Ottawa Journal*. He was founding chairman of the Writers' Federation of Nova Scotia and now operates a guesthouse in Granville Ferry, N.S. Percy's essays and short stories have appeared in many British and Canadian anthologies and magazines. His collection of stories, *The timeless island* (1960), largely features bittersweet romances and sentimental idylls in formally controlled language. His novel *Flotsam* (1968) amplifies an emphasis on character: David Bronson's memories of social and nautical experiences are developed in alternately lyric and realistic narrative. The memories of a dying painter, Emile Logan, structure Percy's second novel, *Painted ladies* (1983), which considers art and life with a characteristic poetic intensity of expression. Percy's mature, uncollected stories reflect his developing concern with the fluidity and 'emotional cargo' of language. His evocative fictions are particularly distinguished by their metaphoric richness: two of his most accomplished and highly contained stories are 'An inglorious affair' (1972) and 'Falling for Mavis' (1975), which appeared in *Queen's Quarterly* and *75: New Canadian stories* respectively. Percy has also written two short biographies, *Joseph Howe* (1976) and *Thomas Chandler Haliburton* (1980), for 'The Canadians' series.

LOUIS K. MacKENDRICK

Perrault, Pierre (b. 1927). Born in Montreal, he was educated there in various classical colleges—where he met Hubert AQUIN and Marcel DUBÉ, with whom he published

Perrault

Les cahiers d'Arlequin—and then in law at the Universities of Montreal, Paris, and Toronto. He paid his way through university as a hockey-player and coach. In 1951 he married Yolande Simard and they have two children.

The brilliant reconstructions in his films of traditional life on the Île-aux-Coudres and the Abitibi region have earned Perrault an international reputation. Also a poet, dramatist, and broadcaster, he has published two collections of verse—*Chouennes* (1975) and *Gélivures* (1977)—and several film scenarios: *Le règne du jour* (1968), *Les voitures d'eau* (1969), and *Un pays sans bon sens* (1972). His best-known play is *Au coeur de la rose* (1964), a three-act poetical drama set against a background of gulls, gannets, divers, flowers, and islands, in which people try to find significance in nature and the collective folk memory; it was performed in 1963 and 1974.

Perrault has made himself the memory of a people, teasing out from the past of a tiny down-river kingdom a saga of human wit, skill, and energy, enlivened with music and anecdote. Though his poetry deals with a cold, northern world of nostalgia and struggle, it is humorous, lyrical, and surprisingly unsentimental. *Gélivures*, a long poem in three cantos, is both a hymn to the wintry northlands and a reflection on the difficulty of authentic recall. A strident tone in Perrault's poetry, which he calls 'joualeresque', is tempered with the humour of his 'chouennes'—his amiable tall stories. His films on the Île-aux-Coudres succeed perfectly in overcoming self-consciousness and doubtful recall by evoking the past preserved in traditional pursuits. In innocently asking his interlocutors to recreate the baluga hunt or to hand-build a small boat, Perrault triggers off a chain of involuntary memory and restores the vocabulary of many crafts and the vital speech of the isolated communities whose chronicler he has become. He does this 'pour la suite du monde', convinced that continuity, and a national memory, living and actualized in terms of real people and tangible phenomena, are an antidote to melancholy, alienation, and bitter resentment.   C.R.P. MAY

Perrot, Nicolas. See BIOGRAPHY AND MEMOIRS IN FRENCH: 6 and Writing in NEW FRANCE: 1.

Petch, Stephen (b. 1952). Born in Vancouver, B.C., he took a degree in psychology at the University of Waterloo (Ont.). In the seventies he spent two years travelling through Turkey, Greece, and Mexico. Since the age of sixteen he has been writing plays, which have been produced by such diverse institutions as the Kitchener Little Theatre, the Factory Theatre Lab and the St Lawrence Centre, Toronto, and the Stratford Festival. His plays include *The General* (1973), *Passage* (1974), *Turkish delight* (1975), *Sight unseen* (1979), and *Victoria* (1979), which was commissioned and produced by the Stratford Festival.

In Petch's drama, which is clearly influenced by Pinter, plots are tenuous, characterizations and dialogue oblique, the subtext formidable. Settings, usually exotic, are invariably of central thematic importance. Although the style is evasive, certain elements recur from play to play: characters bred of Western civilizations are challenged and disoriented by the mysterious locales through which they pass; subjective and external worlds merge; facts dissolve in fantasy. The geographic frontier frequently serves as a metaphor for the line dividing familiar psychological territory from unknown, disconcerting areas of experience.

In *Passage* a magician of the old school, who can make signs appear on blank cards, crosses a guarded checkpoint on a road leading to an isolated estate. He is betrayed, finally, by his young assistant, a child of the new, brutal age, who denies the ancient arts of perception. *Turkish delight* is a lightweight confection in which a Canadian mother and daughter succumb to the subversive lure of old Istanbul, only to pack and go home in the end. The play is long on ambience and theatrical sleight-of-hand, short on credible characterization. *Victoria* is a difficult, potentially exciting play that is still two or three stages from full realization. The setting is a desert, simultaneously a border between Mexico and America and between land and sea. The plot concerns the return of a family—Vicky, her mother, and her fiancé—to an abandoned cabin associated with Vicky's deceased father, where they encounter Robert, a long-absent son, and his friend, who have been experimenting with hallucinogens in an attempt to encounter whatever primal forces haunt the territory. Unfortunately the buried psychic complexities of the protagonists—for which the great, mysterious land should be, but never quite is, a rich and various symbol—give rise to so many enigmas that one loses interest in solving them.

Sight unseen, Petch's most successful play to date, is set on a Greek island in 1928. The characters include a young Canadian couple, Alan and Marion; Alan's friend Richard, with whom he had visited the island some years previously; Davies, an aging homosexual, who remembers that earlier visit; and Marie-Claude, an inscrutable Swiss girl. At one level the play is a sex-farce in which the intrigues are adroitly juggled with much closing of bedroom doors in the nick of time. But the characterization has weight and precision. Victims of comic self-delusion in their efforts to shed Anglo-Canadian inhibitions under the Mediterranean moon, the characters are also capable of pain and self-knowledge.   MICHAEL TAIT

Peterson, Len (b. 1917). Leonard Byron Peterson was born in Regina Sask., of Norwegian stock. For over four decades he has been a professional man of letters and the theatre. He established his reputation as a radio dramatist in the forties, collaborating with Andrew Allan and Esse Ljungh; he has also written documentary films, musicals, novels, stage plays for both children and adults, as well as adapting French-Canadian and European authors. During his long career he has produced more than 1,200 scripts.

Peterson was a young man during the thirties, and that traumatic decade has left an indelible stamp on his work. A recurring theme in his plays is the destruction of the individual or the small community by impersonal states or societies. Variations on this theme are present in *Burlap bags* (1972), which presents a vertiginous vision of the world's absurdity and human insensitivity; *Almighty Voice* (1974), a one-act children's play produced for Young People's Theatre, Toronto, in 1975, about the government's hunt for a Cree Indian who stole a cow to feed his starving people; *They're all afraid* (1981), which concerns a young man's alienation in a society governed by neurotic anxieties; and *The trouble with giants*, an unpublished radio play—winner of a 1973 ACTRA award—that touchingly evokes the erosion of a unique Lithuanian culture by the acquisitive ruthlessness of both Germany and Russia. Peterson's passionate identification with the underdog in his struggle against depersonalizing institutions lends energy to his plays, but sometimes his presentation of the conflict is simplistic. His best stage piece is *The great hunger* (1967), first produced for the Arts Theatre, Toronto, Nov. 1960. Set in the Arctic, and about retribution for a killing, its theme is the importance of communal myths by which men—white or Inuit—live or perish.

In attempting to explore the complexity of the self, Peterson frequently resorts to psychodrama in which fragments of the psyche assume distinct identities. *They're all afraid*, *Burlap bags*, and *Women in the attic* (1972) (about a newspaperman who, while covering the funeral of a celebrated lady of pleasure, enters the reality of her life as it is revealed in her diary) all use this expressionistic device in combination with moments of theatrical realism.

In addition to writing instructional scripts for young people that were produced on CBC radio, Peterson has written several one-act plays produced by Young People's Theatre, notably *Billy Bishop and the Red Baron* (1975), about the Great War flying aces, Billy Bishop, and Baron von Richthofen.   MICHAEL TAIT

Petitclair, Pierre (1813-60). Born of illiterate parents at Saint-Augustin-de-Portneuf, near Quebec, he attended local schools and the Petit Séminaire de Québec, which he left in 1829 without completing his studies. He then worked as a copyist and notary's clerk before accepting, in 1838, a position as tutor to the twelve children of a wealthy family trading in Labrador. He spent most of the rest of his life there, rarely returning to Quebec. Petitclair is the author of three published plays: *Griphon; ou La vengeance d'un valet* (Québec, 1837), *La donation* (Québec, 1842), and *Une partie de campagne* (Québec, 1865); of a short story in verse, *Le revenant* (*Le Canadien*, 27 July 1831), one in prose, *Une aventure au Labrador* (*Le Fantasque*, 2 Nov. 1840); and a half-dozen poems.

Petitclair is remembered primarily as a dramatist, his *Griphon* being generally acknowledged as the first play published by a native French Canadian (an identification that is appropriate only if one disqualifies the five anonymous 'Comédies du statu quo' (1834) as being more politics than theatre). This play—though published, it was never performed—is a three-act comedy with strong farcical elements, many of them inspired directly by Molière (*Tartuffe*, *Les fourberies de Scapin*) and by Falstaff in the Shakespeare plays, which had been introduced to French Canada in the Ducis translations. A valet enlists a friend's support in seeking revenge against his master, Griphon, an aged, lusting hypocrite. The dis-

Petitclair

guises and the pratfalls they prepare for the old man quickly become repetitive, as the structure of the play deteriorates towards its artificial moralizing end, where all is set right. *La donation*, performed several times in the 1840s before its second publication in Huston's *Répertoire national* (Montréal, 1848), is a two-act play strongly influenced by melodrama, with concomitant simplification of character and plot, and many monologues and asides. A wealthy merchant, Delorval, is persuaded by an intriguer, Bellire, to dispossess his niece and to forbid her marriage to the hero, Auguste, as a result of false rumours Bellire has spread about the latter. The calumny is unmasked in time, with heavy reliance upon melodramatic *coups de théâtre*. Despite its defects, the play seems to have been well received by contemporary audiences. Petitclair's last surviving dramatic work (only the titles of two other plays are known), the two-act comedy *Une partie de campagne*, was written in 1856, first performed in 1857, and published posthumously in Quebec in 1865. Its theme is similar to that of Joseph QUESNEL's *L'anglomanie* (1803), depicting the evils inherent in aping English manners and speech. Better constructed than his preceding works, this play establishes the full extent of the protagonist's infatuation with all that is English, and then in Act II ridicules and finally punishes him for it. Petitclair here demonstrates a keen ear for rural accents and diction, while breathing more life into his characters than before.

Both his short stories deal with superstitions and their effects. *Le revenant*, his first published work, tells of a prisoner who escapes by taking the place of a body that is removed from prison in a coffin, and whose 'resurrection' consternates the assembled mourners. *Une aventure au Labrador* combines a ghost story with an account of a curious hunting accident and is remarkable chiefly for its romantic description of Labrador itself. Of the six poems credited to Petitclair, one, 'Le bon parti', is a comic song; three ('La somnambule', 'A Flore', and 'Sombre est mon âme comme vous') are Lamartinian in tone, dealing with the sorrow of unfaithful love; a fifth is in praise of Governor Sir Charles Bagot ('Le règne du juste'); and the last, 'Pauvre soldat! qu'il doit souffrir', describes the heroism of a patriotic soldier. All except the first are reproduced in both editions of Huston's *Répertoire national* (1848-50, 1893).

See J.-C. Noël's thesis, 'Pierre Petitclair,

sa vie, son oeuvre, et le théâtre de son époque' (Université d'Ottawa, 1975).

LEONARD DOUCETTE

Philosophy in Canada. 1. ORIGINS OF PHILOSOPHY IN FRENCH CANADA. Philosophy was first taught at the Jesuit College in Quebec in 1655; the first official teacher was appointed in 1665. The early teachers were French Jesuits, some of whom had been educated at La Flèche, France, where René Descartes had been a student. Cartesian ideas about the nature of knowledge and the distinction between mind and body arrived in Québec in the brief period between the death of Descartes and the placing of his works on the Index in 1666. Though generally expounded by clerics doubtful of their validity, they played a crucial part in defining the philosophical themes of the New World. Descartes' thesis was that each man is certain only of his own existence: the existence of others needs to be inferred. There is an ultimate sense in which man is alone, for he is never as certain of the reality of others as he is of his own existence. In Canada this struck home when people—uprooted from their natural communities and stripped of the cultural surroundings that might reassure them about the existence of others past and present—faced a hostile environment. (English-Canadian literary theorists, including Northrop FRYE and Margaret ATWOOD, have written of the impediments to self-definition, the preoccupation with survival, and the defensive attitudes of isolated people and isolated communities.) From the beginning in Québec there was an attempt to rebut the Cartesian claims about the primacy of inward, individual experience and to establish the existence of a public experience on which an isolated society could rely. The records of the Seminaire de Québec, founded in 1668, testify both to the importance of Descartes and to the attempts to refute his doctrines. In the English-speaking world the Cartesian perspective passed into common usage, but in Québec it was opposed by the clergy as long as they dominated intellectual life.

Philosophical studies at the Séminaire de Québec, which eventually became Université Laval, were surprisingly eclectic and included the ideas of Locke and Hume as well as those of Descartes (critically treated) and Malebranche. They are represented in the *Institutiones philosophicae* (Québec, 1835) of Jérôme Demers (1774-1853), a widely used manual in Québec. From the beginning much of the philosophical concern was political. In the uncertainties of the New World, traditional foundations for authority were weakened by distance, and by the intrusion of political structures controlled by the British. The only institution that survived the Conquest intact was the Church, which could make its authority the basis for a functioning community only by creating a climate of belief anchored in a coherent and generally intelligible philosophy. Thus the basic concern was to find a set of ideas through which the political system could be ordered and the goals of both educational and charitable institutions established. In *Savoir et pouvoir* (1972) Pierre Thiebault describes the philosophical ideas that developed in Québec in this early period, and their use by the Church in what he calls a system of 'indirect control'.

2. THE COMING OF THOMISM IN FRENCH CANADA AND THE BEGINNINGS OF NATIONAL THOUGHT. The first major French philosophical work that seems to have had its roots in predominantly native conditions was the *Essai sur la logique judiciaire* (Montréal, 1853). In it, François-Marie-Uncas-Maximilien Bibaut (1824-87), a Montreal lawyer (and son of the historian Michel Bibaut) who also taught law at the Collège Sainte-Marie, raised the question of whether or not one should have *two* logics to accommodate the legal systems of the two major cultures in Canada. Although he answered 'no', he questioned the proposition that the intellect can transcend the 'two solitudes'.

About the same time the Church was faced with the growing conflict between science and religion and turned to the doctrines of Thomas Aquinas, who had coped with the medieval clash of Arab science and Christianity by postulating two distinct spheres, one for faith and one for reason. The Thomists insisted that reason was the same for all men, that it could provide a foundation for moral action, the basis of a political order, and grounds for belief in the existence of God. But they denied that certain central doctrines—including that of the Trinity and the necessity of the sacraments—could be shown by reason alone. Thus faith had its own sphere. Thomism had become firmly entrenched in Québec well before it became the recommended doctrine in 1879. Its chief spokesmen, however, developed positions of their own, often by exploring regions—chiefly nationalism and the understanding of history—

that had not been central to Thomistic doctrines. An example is Mgr. Louis-Adolphe PÂQUET, a deeply conservative and orthodox thinker, who explored the relation of man to nature and the land. He was firmly convinced that a stable social order would develop only out of continuing devotion to the land and its responsible working: urbanization held dangers that included the creation of an environment in which families need not, and perhaps could not, work together. In essays, especially in the collection *Mélanges canadiens* (1918), he urged upon French Canadians devotion to 'the land, the past and the language'. As the most highly thought-of official spokesman for the Church in Québec, he gave respectability to this adherence to traditional values, and of course approved their celebration in literature.

Pâquet was active in the day-to-day life of the Church in Québec, and many of his social theories were expressed only in occasional essays. A much more systematic thinker was Louis LACHANCE, also a Thomist, who developed a rational nationalism that would justify the ideas of cultural independence within a universal Christian framework, presenting a doctrine quite different from the strongly emotional nationalism of Lionel GROULX. Lachance's *Nationalisme et religion* (1935) argued that nationalism was justified because even though all men must share in the same ultimate goal (happiness in this life and the beatific vision in the next), the diversity in patterns of human development meant that different groups of men must necessarily follow different paths, though in full recognition of the responsibility of all men to each other. By contrast Groulx relied more strongly—especially in his much-discussed and influential novel, *L'appel de la race* (1922)—on notions of racial homogeneity among French Canadians, and on feelings of solidarity and distinctness from English Canada.

3. ORIGINS OF PHILOSOPHY IN ENGLISH CANADA. The first professional philosophical work written in English seems to have been *Elements of natural theology* (London, 1805) by James Beaven (1801-75), who taught at University College, University of Toronto. It exhibits the passion for systematic order that Northrop FRYE has noted as a characteristic of Canadian thought (and that continues in English Canada down to Frye himself). Before his arrival in Canada from England, Beaven had been a rather disputatious defender of Anglican orthodoxy; but

his *Elements* is an attempt to examine religious belief from a philosophical standpoint, and to find a rational basis for it that is not subject to doctrinal emendation. William LYALL, of Dalhousie University, Halifax, wrote his *Intellect; the emotions and the moral nature* (Edinburgh, 1855) in the same non-doctrinal spirit, stating that the emotions were an important source of information and were fundamental to human nature. This notion was not uncharacteristic of Maritime literature: the claim that the understanding of the emotions is a crucial human need is a theme that runs through the stories of Thomas McCULLOCH, a respected theologian (and first president of Dalhousie University) who wrote the first book of Canadian humour, *The letters of Mephibosheth Stepsure*, which was published serially in the *Acadian Recorder* (1821-2) and later in book form (Halifax, 1862; NCL 1960).

4. THE IDEALIST MOVEMENT IN ENGLISH CANADA. The need for a common morality was emphasized by George Paxton Young (1818-89), of Knox College, and then University College, University of Toronto, whose few published works—among them *Freedom and necessity* (Toronto, 1870) and *The ethics of freedom* (1911), with notes edited by his pupil James Gibson Hume—are mere tokens of his stature, and of his impact as a teacher. Young paid little attention to the then-popular Scottish philosophy of 'common sense', based on realist metaphysics (an important ingredient in the synthesis *Intellect, the emotions, and the moral nature,* (1855) by William LYALL), and favoured instead a Hegelian idealism that had much in common with that of T.H. Green in England. Essentially a realist metaphysics contrived in Scotland by philosophers like Thomas Reid and Dugald Stewart to counteract the skepticism of David Hume, this philosophy supposed that common sense was strong enough to assure us of the reality of the external world. In moral theory it was allied to the notion of a 'moral sense' that gave men assurance of the soundness of generally agreed-upon experiences. However, as science and industry alike created sharp distinctions between the experiences of men in the industrialized world and of their predecessors, who came to be thought of as 'primitive', it became hard to believe that there was really a 'natural' experience common to all men. From Hegel to Marx the belief developed that there had been a historical development in man and that experience was relative to one's place in time.

In Québec the somewhat similar philosophy of the French thinker Felicité de Lamennais (1782-1854)—based on the notion of the naturally unfolding common human tradition—created some interest at the end of the first third of the nineteenth century and this has been documented in Yvan Lamonde's *La philosophie et son enseignement au Québec, 1665-1920* (1980). But it was short-lived, not only for the reasons that doomed common-sense philosophy in Canada, but because it ultimately led to de Lamennais's denial of the *rational* function of the Church—which cut against common experience, common sense, and tradition, and was condemned by Rome. Fundamentally the nineteenth century was a time of novelty and ideological innovation: 'common sense', in whatever guise, could not prevail against it.

The 'idealist movement'—which sought to understand experience as a historical development and tended to deny that there was a 'reality' independent of that developing experience—quickly took hold in Canada. 'Idealism' in this sense was the doctrine that ideas are more real than things—indeed, that ideas shape all our knowledge of things. In moral theory it oriented itself around the notion that principles of action derive, not from raw experiences, but from a rational understanding of the meaning and progressive evolution of experience. Young and John Clark MURRAY, who made the idealist movement dominant in Canada, exemplified the Scots tradition of rational religion, which was an outgrowth of the schism between the Church of Scotland and the Free Church that had centred on disputes about the relation of church and state and was kept alive by the Presbyterian tradition of sermons, in which the minister attempted to establish his point by a series of logical deductions (usually starting from a biblical text and influenced by Hegel). The clergyman-teacher in ARCADIAN ADVENTURES WITH THE IDLE RICH (1914) by Stephen LEACOCK (a pupil of Murray's), who offered three parts Hegel and two parts St Paul on weekdays and reversed the mixture on Sundays, is probably a justly drawn and apt exemplar of generations of pupils who went forth from Murray's classes at McGill and from those of John WATSON at Queen's. In the similarly idealist philosophy of George Blewett (1873-1912), of Victoria College, University of Toronto, the attitude to nature becomes the issue of central concern. In the history of the Christian West there have been two dominant views of nature: that nature, apart from man, is the perfect creation of God, and man, with his free will and habit of disobedience, brings nature into disarray; and that nature, into which man was thrown after the Fall, is specifically designed to be struggled against—it is for man to overcome nature as part of his preparation for rehabilitation and ultimate salvation. From the first attitude the philosophical strands of nineteenth-century romanticism, and of much contemporary environmentalism, descend. From the second stems a variety of attitudes, including the view of the American pragmatists that nature is essentially there for us to use. For Blewett, who rejected both these postures, nature was a distinct entity with its own proper goal. He was perhaps the first thinker to speak of the 'earth' as having its own 'rights'. His experiences of the Canadian West convinced him that nature, in Canada, is very fragile and easily damaged. But he was also convinced that it could not simply be left alone. His *The study of nature and the vision of God* (1907) and *The Christian view of the world* (1912) were major influences on his students, and Blewett was quoted in university classrooms and churches from Toronto to Vancouver. His focus on nature was balanced by his concern with the idea of community as the human counterpart to a complex physical world, providing the obvious mode of survival amidst nature's powers. In fact all the idealist philosophers emphasized the primacy of community over individuality, and foreshadowed a Canadian literary tendency—noticed by FRYE, ATWOOD, and Robin Mathews—to champion collective values and common causes rather than individual heroes.

The influence of evolutionary theories produced other direct responses. Jacob Gould Schurman (1854-1942) of Dalhousie (later president of Cornell) sought to defend traditional values, and in his *Ethical import of Darwinism* (New York, 1887) did battle against the doctrine that the 'survival of the fittest' ought to hold in the social order. Nonetheless he accepted an evolutionary metaphysics to which, in *Belief in God, its origin, nature and basis* (New York, 1890), he added an evolutionary theism. Richard Maurice BUCKE, whose *Cosmic consciousness* (Philadelphia, 1901) has remained in print, sought to extend the idea of evolution into the spiritual realm. William Douw LIGHTHALL attempted, in his *Person in evolution* (1933), to extend this theme in a less mysti-

cal way that has affinities with the philosophies of Henri Bergson and Alfred North Whitehead.

5. THE RECOVERY OF HISTORY AND THE ENTRENCHMENT OF PLURALISM IN CANADA. The efforts of the Thomists in French Canada and the idealists in English Canada to reconcile science and religion led to some frustration. As science advances and explains the origins of the stars, the history of the earth, and the chemistry of life, should religion retreat from its claims about these matters? If so, at what point? If not, by what means can it resist? Can philosophers determine, by their study of history, what is sound and central in religion? Biology, archeology, and anthropology all focused attention on time. For the philosopher this meant that the study of human nature could no longer easily be regarded as the study of a set of permanent properties. History—once chiefly the study of names, dates, and battles—became a central concern for anyone seeking a picture of man. Hegel advanced the view that there is a natural (some of his followers thought inevitable) path of human history that is always progressive. But in French Canada the view developed early that Québec was special and had a history of its own, which was not dominated by the European history that centrally concerned Hegel. In *Des influences françaises au Canada* (3 vols, 1916-20) the poet-philosopher Jean CHARBONNEAU carried the argument one step further. He believed that the firmest grasp on the historic mainstream of Western thought—which in France had been deflected into new courses that radically changed its nature—was held in Québec. In English Canada, George BRETT, in his massive *History of psychology* (3 vols, 1912-21), sought to trace the development of views of the human mind itself. Brett's work was to dominate the philosophy department of the University of Toronto for two generations and to turn it into a major centre for the study of the history of thought. The historical turn given to thought by Charbonneau in French Canada and Brett in English Canada drew upon an existing tendency to see thought in terms of history, and attracted widespread support from other scholars. For the Canadian identity is above all historical. It must be specified not in terms of a single culture, race, or language but of a common experience and a common response to surrounding cultures. The result was that historians—François-Xavier GARNEAU, Lionel-Adolphe Bergeron, and Fer-

nand Ouellet in French Canada; Donald CREIGHTON, A.R.M. Lower, W.L. MORTON, Ramsay Cook, and Carl Berger in English Canada—came to occupy an increasingly important place in Canadian intellectual life, while philosophers faded from view. Rupert LODGE, teaching primarily at the University of Manitoba, accepted the diminished role of philosophy, and claimed to be able to show that no single philosophical system could prevail and, therefore, that philosophy could not solve some of its most fundamental problems. He reacted quite differently to the difficulties involved in reconciling opposing fundamental views of the world, and ultimately saw philosophy as irreducibly pluralistic. He believed that there are always at least three equally valid responses to any basic question: the idealist, the realist, and the pragmatic. The concern with the history of philosophy implied a concern with a plurality of views or perspectives and, despite the fact that Lodge's form of it attracted few supporters, pluralism itself became deeply entrenched.

6. TRADITION AND CHANGE IN PHILOSOPHICAL THEMES. BRETT and LODGE, along with more traditionally oriented idealist philosophers such as John Macdonald (1887-1972) at the University of Alberta, and Herbert Stewart (1882-1953) at Dalhousie, played leading roles in English Canada until the Second World War. Macdonald's *Mind, school and civilization* (1952), a defence of an educational system aimed at the traditional 'civilizing' virtues and dedicated to the transmission of a developed, inherited culture, was welcomed by many intellectuals who suspected that the philosophy of John Dewey, then gaining strength among professional educators, threatened the aims for which public education had been established. Irish-born Stewart, who became an influential spokesman for the idea of a revitalized British Commonwealth, was familiar to radio listeners, and many of his radio talks on a wide range of subjects were assembled into a book, *From a library window* (1940). His most widely read philosopohical work was a biting study entitled *Nietzsche and the ideals of modern Germany* (1915) which, while it calls attention to the many (often contradictory) strands in Nietzsche's thought, endeavours to establish Nietzsche as a thinker who stimulated the thirst for power that led to the devastation of Europe.

Thomist theses were developed and defended by Charles De KONINCK, whose *The hollow universe* (1964), written in English, was widely influential in both English and French Canada, and was also read in the U.S. De Koninck's influence in French Canada stemmed partly from his close relations with the hierarchy of the Catholic Church and his position as dean of philosophy at Université Laval, but chiefly from the fact that he opened new possibilities for the reconciliation of philosophy, science, and religion. His thesis was that there are ways of knowing the world, and especially living things, that complement rather than confront scientific knowledge. De Koninck argued that the scientific world is a hollow shell of abstraction until it is made concrete by human feeling, understanding, and immediate experience. He illustrated this principle by the idea of 'life', which, even in its developed forms, is described in scientific biology as a matter of atoms and molecules.

After the war, most leading English-language works examined philosophy and philosophers from an essentially traditional, even conservative, standpoint. George GRANT's *Philosophy in the mass age* (1959) is a plea for a return to classical values and modes of knowing. William Dray (b. 1921)—of Toronto, Trent, and Ottawa—wrote *Laws and explanation in history* (1958) as an eloquent defence of the humanities against the claims of those who believe that all knowledge must be expressed as scientific laws. In *Collingwood and the reform of metaphysics* (1970) Lionel Rubinoff (b. 1930)—then of York University, Toronto, now of Trent University, Peterborough—reflects many of the interests of the Canadian idealists of an earlier period, but in a form intended to take account of recent criticisms of idealist metaphysics. Among Francis SPARSHOTT's several books of the 1970s, his *Looking for philosophy* (1970) explores the interests of analytic philosophy by examining the works of Bertrand Russell, G.E. Moore, Ludwig Wittgenstein, Gilbert Ryle, and J.J. Austin, applying to them a skeptical eye and a critical wit. An earlier work, *The structure of aesthetics* (1963), emphasizes the essential plurality of theories of the arts. Terence Penelhum (b. 1929), of the University of Calgary, used Wittgensteinian techniques in his *Survival and disembodied existence* (1970), which analyses claims to life after death.

In French Canada, Fernand DUMONT developed general critiques of the social order, using a variety of modern techniques, in *Le lieu de l'homme* (1968) and *La dialectique de l'objet économique* (1970). Attention to the relation of value to social continuity and problems of personal identity is evident in the work of Antonio de Abreu Freire (b. 1943), whose *La révolution désaliénante* (1972), written in Quebec City, contains an analysis of Marxist themes. Various strands of existentialist as well as Thomist thought can be found in the work of Benoit Pruche (b. 1914), of Université de Sherbrooke. His *Existant et acte d'être* (2 vols, 1977-80) is one of the most ambitious metaphysical studies produced in French Canada. A principal concern among writers there has been the problem of selfhood and self-identity. Recent important work on these themes has been done by René L'Écuyer (b. 1938), of Université de Sherbrooke, whose *La genèse du concept de soi* (1975) deals with questions lying on the border of philosophy and psychology; and Jacques Croteau (b. 1921), of Université d'Ottawa, whose *L'Homme: sujet ou objet* (1982) combines traditional Thomist ideas with recent notions borrowed from Husserlian phenomenology. Problems stemming from the philosophies of Thomas Aquinas and their modern developments in Jacques Maritain are dealt with in the work of Jean-Louis Allard (b. 1926), of Université d'Ottawa. His *L'Éducation à la liberté* (1978)—translated by Ralph Nelson as *Education for freedom* (1982)—defends a Maritainist conception of education and society. The philosophical spirit of the 'Quiet Revolution' is obvious in the work of André Dagenais (b. 1917), who has taught at the Université de Montréal and in Argentina. His *Vingt-quatre défauts Thomistes* (1964) is a vigorous attack on the philosophy that had prevailed in Québec for nearly one hundred years. His *Le Dieu nouveau* (1974), however, shows a fundamental interest in religion, combined with a desire to reconceptualize its problems.

LESLIE ARMOUR, ELIZABETH TROTT

Pickthall, Marjorie (1883-1922). Born in Gunnersby, Middlesex, Eng., Marjorie Lowry Christie Pickthall immigrated with her family to Toronto in 1889. Educated at St Mildred's Girls' School and the Bishop Strachan School for Girls, she was encouraged by her indulgent parents in writing, reading, and music (she studied the violin until she was nearly twenty), though she always had delicate health. Her literary career began with the publication of her story 'Two ears' in the Toronto *Globe* in 1898, but her mother's death in 1910 so devastated her that it took the efforts of many prominent friends to encourage her to write again. She worked for a time in the library of Victoria College, University of Toronto, and in Dec. 1912 sailed for England to live with relatives and complete her recovery. During the war she trained as an ambulance driver, worked as a farm labourer, and assisted in the library of the South Kensington Meteorological Office. By 1920 she was, as she said, 'Canada sick', and sailed for home. After a brief visit with her father and friends in Toronto, she went to Vancouver to indulge a long-cherished wish to see the West at first hand. Eventually she settled in a small cottage on Vancouver Island and resumed writing. Surgery to correct her continuing ill-health was carried out in Vancouver in April 1922; but the initial rapid recovery was ended by an embolus. She was buried beside her mother in St James' Cemetery, Toronto.

Pickthall's literary reputation rests ultimately on the two major collections of poetry published during her lifetime: *The drift of pinions* (1913) and *The lamp of poor souls* (1916; rpr. 1972), which includes the poems published in the earlier volume. *The complete poems of Marjorie Pickthall* (1925), compiled by her father, includes the material of the earlier volumes and other 'fugitive and hitherto unpublished poems'. A 1936 edition, now regarded as definitive, includes the posthumously published *Little songs* (1925) and *The naiad and five other poems* (1931). *The selected poems of Marjorie Pickthall*, edited and with a sympathetic introduction by Lorne PIERCE, appeared in 1957. The penchant for locations remote in place and time, the use of incantatory rhythms, a persistent sense of *ennui*, the evocation of an insular world of muted lights and a hushed atmosphere, and the recurrence of words such as 'silver', 'rose', and 'gold', suggest a perception of a world of ideal beauty and a literary practice that originate at least as far back as the Pre-Raphaelite Brotherhood. To these mannerisms Pickthall adds her own Anglo-Catholicism; the result is a poetry that evokes a dream-like world that, though removed from the world of ordinary experience, only halfway approaches a more perfect existence in God. Poems such as 'Golden dawn', 'Dream river', and 'The garden of weariness' are entirely representative. The frequently anthologized 'Père Lalement', 'The bridegroom of Cana', and 'Resurgam' show Pickthall's success in using cadence, delicate colouring, and apt word choice to create sustained moods. At their best the poems achieve a vision of beauty in earthly things that suggest a higher spiritual life; at their least inspired they are little more than versifications of poetic mannerisms.

Like others of her generation, Pickthall wrote verse drama. *The woodcarver's wife*, begun in England in 1919 and finished in Victoria in 1920, was first presented by the Community Players of Montreal at the New Empire Theatre. It appeared in published form in *The woodcarver's wife and later poems* (1922). Despite its convincing handling of incident and its contemporary issues (an artist figure who can cope with aesthetics but not with life; a confined yet aspiring wife; and a chivalrous rescuer with fleshly appetites), this four-character one-act play, set in pre-Conquest days, is an academic exercise in which the characters mechanically mouth lines of verse to one another.

Pickthall also completed over 200 short stories, three juvenile novels, and two adult novels. The short stories—many of which were written during the war years in England and submitted to various publications there, and suggest Pickthall's debt to Joseph Conrad, whose work she greatly admired—frequently imply deliberate manipulation of often violent incidents, or convey a facile conception of character. A representative selection of twenty-four stories was published posthumously in London under the inapt and misleading title *Angels' shoes* (1923).

Three of Pickthall's serial contributions to *East and west*, a young people's paper sponsored by the Presbyterian Church, appeared in book form: *Dick's desertion; a boy's adventures in Canadian forests* (1905), *The straight road* (1906), and *Billy's hero; or The valley of gold* (1908), the last two illustrated by C.W. Jefferys. In each book a boy or young man, isolated by orphanhood or financial straits, is forced to undertake a journey, during which he must solve a trying problem; its solution, through a combination of luck ('Providence'), a new spiritual and moral rectitude, and a fresh sense of duty, leads to his re-integration into the family or society. Of Pickthall's adult fiction, *Little hearts* (1915), set in the eighteenth-century Devonshire countryside, and *The bridge; a story of the Great Lakes* (1922), employ melodramatic incident. (*The bridge*, begun during the war years in England and completed and revised on Vancouver Island, was published serially in *Everybody's*, New York, and the London *Sphere* in 1921.) As in most of her short stories, Pickthall in these novels fails to integrate fully descriptive detail, character, and incident. At the time of her death she was working on another novel, 'The beaten man', of which a 30,000-word fragment and the author's working notes are extant.

Pickthall was undoubtedly the most gifted of a group of minor writers who owed their inspiration, and a good deal of their literary practice, to the fading romanticism of an earlier day.

See Lorne PIERCE, 'Pickthall, Marjorie Lowry Christie', *A standard dictionary of Canadian biography*, vol. II (1938) and *Marjorie Pickthall; a book of remembrance* (1925); and D.W. Toye, 'The poetry of Marjorie Pickthall', *Acta Victoriana* 47 (Jan. 1923).

S.R. MacGILLIVRAY

Pierce, Lorne (1890-1961). Born in Delta, Ont., he was educated at Queen's University, Victoria University (University of Toronto), the Union Theological Seminary of New York, New York University, and Wesleyan Theological College, Montreal. He became a minister of the Methodist Church and later of the United Church of Canada. In 1916 he married Edith Charon, a member of a prominent Kingston family. In 1920 he was named literary adviser to the RYERSON PRESS, and from 1922 to 1960 was its editor. In 1926 he was elected to the Royal Society of Canada.

As an editor of Ryerson who was also an ardent Canadian nationalist, Pierce consistently used his authority to encourage Canadian writers by both publication and advice. Among the poets he introduced were E.J. PRATT, Raymond KNISTER, Earle BIRNEY, A.J.M. SMITH, Dorothy LIVESAY, Louis DUDEK, and P.K. PAGE; and he was the first editor to accept a novel (*Settlers of the marsh*, 1925) by Frederick Philip GROVE. His desire to stimulate Canadian writing, however, led him to rely heavily on copy-editors to redeem manuscripts of questionable promise.

His sentiments and interests were expressed early in his editorial career when he instigated three series of short books on Canadian subjects: *Makers of Canadian literature* (from 1925), the *Ryerson Canadian history readers* (from 1926)—to celebrate past achievements—and the Ryerson poetry chapbooks (from 1925) to stimulate future efforts. In order to familiarize school-children with the native literature he edited the *Ryerson* (later *Canada*) *books of prose and verse*, which began to appear in 1927. For adult readers he edited, with A.D. Watson, *Our*

Canadian literature: representative prose and verse (1922). Its poetry section, edited with Bliss CARMAN, later became Our Canadian literature: representative verse, English and French (1935), and was revised in 1954 by V.B. Rhodenizer as Canadian poetry in English. Pierce was the author of Fifty years of public service: a life of James L. Hughes (1924); Marjorie Pickthall: a book of remembrance (1925); An outline of Canadian literature (French and English) (1927); and William Kirby, the portrait of a Tory loyalist (1929). He also wrote two histories of the Ryerson Press: The chronicle of a century, 1829-1929: the record of one hundred years of progress in the publishing concerns of the Methodist, Presbyterian and Congregational churches in Canada (1929) and The House of Ryerson, 1829-1954 (1954). Three Fredericton poets (1933) reflected his close friendship with Sir Charles G.D. ROBERTS and Bliss Carman (who made him his literary executor). In numerous pamphlets Pierce urged upon Canadians the possibility of national greatness, to be achieved through awareness of spiritual foundations and the cultivation of bonne entente between English- and French-speaking Canadians.

His many publications aside, Pierce has a claim to remembrance as a literary entrepreneur who unstintingly devoted his time and money to the promotion of Canadian literature and art. To this end he donated to the Royal Society of Canada the Lorne Pierce medal for distinguished service to Canadian literature; took a leading part in founding several organizations, including the Canadian Writers' Foundation; and built up an important collection of Canadian books, manuscripts, and correspondence that is now deposited at Queen's University. His career is described appreciatively by C.H. Dickinson, the Book Steward of the Ryerson Press from 1937 to 1964, in Lorne Pierce: a profile (1965).

See also CRITICISM IN ENGLISH: 2.

JOHN WEBSTER GRANT

Pilon, Jean-Guy (b. 1930). Born in Saint Polycarpe, Qué., he graduated in law from the Université de Montréal. He has been editor of Éditions de l'Hexagone and Éditions de l'Actuelle and was co-organizer, in 1958, with Gaston MIRON and Louis Portugais, of the first Québec poets' conference, which later became the Rencontre Internationale Québécoise des Écrivains, a cultural forum of which he is secretary-general. In 1959 he became a founder-director of LIBERTÉ. He

has been in charge of Radio-Canada's cultural programming since 1960. An indefatigable 'homme de lettres', Pilon was elected a member of the Royal Society of Canada in 1968 and has received many awards, including the Prix de la Province de Québec (1955), the Prix David (1956), and the Governor General's Award for Comme eau retenue: poèmes 1954-1963 (1968). With Eli MANDEL he edited an anthology of new Canadian poetry, Poetry 62/Poésie 62 (1961).

Employing a vocabulary of such basic words as 'bread' and 'friendship' to exorcise death and alienation, Pilon's poetry, while denouncing the past, is a brotherly urging of his fellow Québécois to name and build the country, at the risk of becoming redundant, in order to create a habitable place. The poetry has been influenced by Alain GRANDBOIS as well as by René Char, who wrote a preface for Pilon's second collection, Les cloîtres de l'été (1955), the first one being La fiancée du matin (1953). These early poems celebrate the body, nature, and woman, and express the poet's desire to confront heaven with the 'naked act of persistence'. In L'homme et le jour (1957)—long verses that are reminiscent of Anne HÉBERT's Mystère de la parole—man emerges from the ashes of the past 'to resume his beneficial watch over things'. The poems in La mouette et le large (1960), with their simple, warm grace, lend a more inclusive tone to the quest for life by introducing a 'nous' that strives 'to name the evil, to draw it out of the flesh' and call for a new dawn in a country whose 'soul has been frozen' by its lack of life and history. Recours au pays (1961) and Pour saluer une ville (1963) consider ways of creating a new land: 'Comment réussir à dompter les espaces et les saisons, la forêt et le froid? Comment y reconnaître mon visage?' Affirmation begins to take hold in 'Poèmes pour maintenant' (included in Pour saluer une ville), in which the fraternal 'nous' discards the shame of the past to open 'des bras nouveaux sur une terre habitable'. In words and in woman Pilon sees salvation, sees himself 'clutching the logbook and the woman's hand despite the shipwreck.' The eroticisms and earthy sensuality in Recours au pays and Pour saluer une ville find their full expression in Saisons pour la continuelle (1964), in which Pilon celebrates the union of the poet with the seasons of his country and with the woman, and shows a desire to savour the simple things of life—a desire that pervades all of his later work.

Pilon also wrote a novel, Solange (1965).

Pilon

See Axel Maugey, 'Jean-Guy Pilon' in *Poésie et société au Québec 1937-1970* (1972), and Jean-Louis Major, 'L'Hexagone: une aventure en poésie québécoise' in *La poésie canadienne-française*, vol. 4 (1969).

MAROUSSIA AHMED

Pioneer memoirs. The accurate tales by pioneers of their heroic battles against harsh climate, homesickness, isolation, and poverty are the epics of Canadian literature. The magnitude of the struggle for survival demanded to be recorded, even though many of the memoirists were not professional writers: they had only this one tale to tell. Pioneers faced two struggles. First they had to tame the land, to wrest a living from it. Many memoirs, journals, and letters don't go beyond this level, particularly those written by lower-class settlers of limited education. Already used to privation and manual labour, they accepted these conditions and went on to prosper materially; but their memoirs pall because they are often mere ledger-like accounts of mounting assets. Erudite, upper-class settlers, on the other hand, usually failed as homesteaders in the external battle of taming the land; but they engaged strenuously in the second, more exciting internal battle of mapping it in the mind. Their memoirs are full of the clash and conflict of Old-World polish and refinement meeting New-World primitivism and roughness—an unresolved dichotomy that is still at the heart of Canadian consciousness. Their crops may have failed, but their sensibilities flowered into fine autobiographical prose.

The flood-tide of frontier living in English Canada moved slowly from east to west across the country, and covered a span of roughly 140 years, from the 1780s to the 1920s.

1. THE MARITIME PROVINCES. The main thrust of settlement in the Maritimes came from the United Empire Loyalists, from 1783 to 1812, but few recorded the pioneer experience, perhaps because they were already old hands at it—on their second lap, as it were. Later memoirs include William T. Baird's *Seventy years of New Brunswick life; autobiographical sketches* (Saint John, 1890). Baird claims that 'the training of a young mind in log cabin life' leads to early maturity; at the age of six he confronted his first bear and chopped down his first tree. Aeneas McCharles's *Bemocked of destiny; the actual struggles and experiences of a Canadian pioneer, and the recollections of a lifetime* (1908) describes his childhood years on a Nova Scotia farm in the 1840s and 1850s.

2. QUÉBEC AND ONTARIO. Québec memoirs in English are equally scant. By far the liveliest record is *Lifeline; the Stacey letters: 1836-1858* (1976) edited by Jane Vansittart, who found the letters advertised for sale in a stamp catalogue. Rakish young George Stacey, perennially in debt and in love, is dispatched from London by his desperate father to farm in the Eastern Townships. There George encounters all the disasters that usually befall an inexperienced farmer, and such extra ones as imprisonment for debt in Sherbrooke jail. Mary Gillespie Henderson's *Memories of my early years* (1937) briefly records her childhood on the farm at Little River, Qué., where her Irish parents homesteaded in the 1840s.

Ontario yields a large crop of pioneer memoirs, most of them from the 1815-50 period, when British immigrants poured into its fertile southern half. The finest 'nest of singing birds' among memoirists was to be found in the backwoods near Peterborough. Susanna MOODIE's ROUGHING IT IN THE BUSH; *or Forest life in Canada* (London, 1852; NCL 1974) shows her to be half the delicate, sentimental English heroine and half the stalwart Canadian pioneer, holding the split self together by means of irony, her sensibility gradually expanding to meet the challenge of white water and waving pines. Her sister, Catharine Parr TRAILL, in *The BACKWOODS OF CANADA; being letters from the wife of an emigrant officer* (London, 1836; NCL 1971), is all sense, a female Robinson Crusoe of scientific curiosity and practicality. In contrast to Susanna's imagination, Catharine's ultimately retreats from the tangled mystery of dense forest to its small, decorative delights—wildflowers, birds, insects—or to snug indoor domesticity. Their brother Samuel Strickland, one of the few gentry who succeeded in the backwoods, gives in *Twenty-seven years in Canada West* (London, 1853) a much less interesting account than those of his 'Sense and Sensibility' sisters. Other Peterborough memoirs include *Our forest home; being extracts from the correspondence of the late Frances Stewart* (Toronto, 1889), compiled and edited by Frances Stewart's daughter, E.S. Dunlop, and Thomas Need's *Six years in the bush; or extracts from the journal of a settler in Upper Canada 1832-1838* (London, 1838). Modern critical and biographical studies of the Peterborough group include Marian Fowler's

The embroidered tent: five gentlewomen in early Canada (1982), G.H. Needler's Otonabee pioneers: the story of the Stewarts, the Stricklands, the Traills, and the Moodies (1953), and Audrey Y. Morris's Gentle pioneers (1968).

Masculine accounts of pioneering tend to be extroverted and pragmatic. Typically down-to-earth are Authentic letters from Upper Canada; including an account of Canadian field sports by Thomas William Magrath; the whole edited by the Rev. Thomas Radcliffe (Dublin, 1833; rpr. 1953), John C. Geikie's Adventures in Canada; or life in the woods (London, 1874), Samuel Thompson's Reminiscences of a Canadian pioneer for the last fifty years (Toronto, 1884; rpr. 1968), David Kennedy's Incidents of pioneer days at Guelph and the county of Bruce (1903), and Caniff Haight's Country life in Canada fifty years ago: personal recollections and reminiscences of a sexagenarian (Toronto, 1885; rpr. 1971). More interesting, because more introspective, is A gentlewoman in Upper Canada; the journals of Anne Langton (1950), edited by H.H. Langton, and The journals of Mary O'Brien 1828-1838 (1968), edited by Audrey Saunders Miller. Both writers possess a fine Jane-Austen-like wit and irony.

By 1850 all the green belt of southern Ontario (then Canada West) was under cultivation, so that new settlers had to trek north to rockier terrain. To Madoc came the courageous Anna Loveridge, whose letters comprise Your loving Anna; letters from the Ontario frontier (1972), edited by Louis Tivy. To Muskoka in 1878 came Roger Vardon, fresh from an English public school, author of English bloods (1930). Ann Hathaway's father, a distant kin of Shakespeare's wife, had a cabin on Lake Joseph, described by Ann in her Muskoka memories; sketches from real life (1904).

3. MANITOBA, SASKATCHEWAN, ALBERTA. Prairie settlement followed the new railways and peaked between 1895 and 1914. More than three million people poured in from the U.S.A., Britain, Scandinavia, Russia, Poland, and the Ukraine, many of them in response to offers of free land, a quarter-section (160 acres) for each homesteader. In the battle with the land their only weapons were high hopes and strong backs and their adversaries were formidable: intense cold, blinding blizzards and dust-storms, hailstones bigger than bullets, and long periods of drought. In the flatness of that prairie world, man was the only upright thing, casting a long shadow, gradually making his mark. Ego counted; perhaps that is one reason why there are far more memoirs from the Prairies than the Maritimes, where sea and mist swamped and dissolved any sure sense of self.

Amongst the best Manitoban memoirs are Mrs Cecil Hall's A lady's life on a farm in Manitoba (London, 1884) and Billie Lamb Allan's warm and homey Dew upon the grass (1963). From Saskatchewan come the delightful Pioneer girl (1964), fourteen-year-old Maryanne Caswell's letters to her grandmother, edited by Grace Lane; Mary Hiemstra's vividly written Gully farm (1955); Georgina Binnie-Clark's Wheat and woman (1914; 1979), chronicling the heroic feats of a woman farmer on her own; and James M. Minifie's Homesteader: a prairie boyhood recalled (1972). Interesting Albertan memoirs include Sarah Ellen Roberts' Of us and the oxen (1968); Hilda Rose's The stump farm; a chronicle of pioneering (1928), a remarkable saga of a ninety-pound woman alone in the northern wilderness with a child and invalid husband; H.E. Church's An emigrant in the Canadian Northwest (1929); R.M. Patterson's Far pastures (1963); John H. Blackburn's Land of promise (1970), edited by John Archer; and Peggy Holmes's hilarious It could have been worse (1980).

4. BRITISH COLUMBIA. A fascinating west-coast memoir is A pioneer gentlewoman in British Columbia; the recollections of Susan Allison (1976) edited by Margaret A. Ormsby. Mrs Allison came from England to Hope in 1860, married there, and made the treacherous 75-mile trek across the Hope mountains on horseback—the first white woman to do so—to a 'wild, free life' in the Similkameen Valley. On the Canadian frontier women found new strengths and freedoms, surprising no one quite as much as themselves. Other memoirs of note are Florence Goodfellow's slim volume, Memories of pioneer life in British Columbia (1945), and C.W. Holliday's The valley of youth (1948), a nostalgic and amusing account of farming in the Okanagan valley in the 1890s.

To date the field of pioneer memoirs is virtually untilled by literary scholars, even though it contains rich insights into the nature of the collective Canadian psyche and its relationship to the land. It is high time we turned the first critical sod.

MARIAN FOWLER

Plouffe, Les (1948). This second novel by Roger LEMELIN—translated by Mary Finch as The Plouffe family (1950; NCL 1975)—follows chronologically Au pied de la pente *douce* (*The town below*, 1948). Structured in four parts, with the action stretching from summer 1938 to summer 1940, it ends with a brief epilogue dated May 1945. Its setting—a working-class district of Quebec City's Lower Town—is less important than in the first novel (more events occur in Upper Town), and attention centres on a single family. The nominal head of the Plouffe family is the father, Théophile, a typesetter; but the real power is held by his wife, Joséphine. Three of their children— Cécile, forty; Napoléon, thirty-two; and Ovide, twenty-nine—work in shoe factories; nineteen-year-old Guillaume, a baseball star, is unemployed. As the novel unfolds, the family disintegrates: Théo dies; Ovide and Napoléon marry and have families of their own; Cécile occupies herself with her newly adopted child; and Guillaume goes to war. Joséphine is left alone, although her two married sons remain nearby. The plot is fan-shaped, with the characters each living out his or her drama over a period of seven years. Less spontaneous than the characters in the first novel, they each have a caricature-like quirk or label: Guillaume, 'le sportif'; Napoléon, 'le collectionneur', with a mania for ice-cream cones; Ovide, the 'mélomane' and frustrated opera star; Joséphine, habitual gum-chewer; Théophile, tippler and admirer of Kaiser Wilhelm II; Cécile, penny-pincher and lover of bus-rides. *Les Plouffe*, however, shows Lemelin's keen awareness of the social phenomena that were central in French-Canadian life at the time: the Second World War and the conscription crisis; the changing character of the Catholic Syndicates; the influence of the Church and the disintegration of the parish; and the growing Americanization of Québec. The ironic discrepancy between the Plouffes' heroic-sounding given names and their commonplace family name—which resembles in sound the deflation of their dreams—echoes the theme of failure and demoralization.

The basis for a very popular TV serial on both the French and English CBC networks, *Les Plouffe* also became, in 1980, a widely acclaimed film directed by Gilles Carle—both with scripts by Lemelin. In the film the satirized priest of the novel, Father Folbèche, and the language of the characters are somewhat idealized, and the dominating Mme Plouffe is more benign.

A sequel to *Les Plouffe*, *Le crime d'Ovide Plouffe*, was published in 1982.

BEN-Z. SHEK

Pocock, Roger. See FOREIGN WRITERS ON CANADA IN ENGLISH: 1.

Poetry in English. To 1900. 1. THE PRE-SETTLEMENT PERIOD. Before the founding of Halifax (1749) and the garrisoning of Quebec (1760), the English presence in Canada was small and scattered, lacking the communal cohesiveness and mechanisms of communication (presses and newspapers) necessary to stimulate an indigenous literature. Poetry written in and of the area was composed by visitors who reported their observations and experiences back to a more coherent and literate society (usually England) with the intention of satisfying their readers' inherent curiosity about distant lands and events. These visitor-poems are mainly of two types: descriptions of the land and its settlement, and narratives of military actions.

The earliest descriptive verse was written by seventeenth-century visitors to Newfoundland. William Vaughan's *The golden fleece* (London, 1626) and Robert HAYMAN's *Quodlibets, lately come over from New Britaniola, Old Newfoundland* (London, 1628) project an idyllic vision of Newfoundland's potential and a Utopian view of the possibilities of settlement. This optimistic and idealized perspective sets the tone for most of the descriptive poetry composed by subsequent visitors. B. Lacy's *Miscellaneous poems compos'd at Newfoundland* (London, 1729), which vividly describes the hardships of settlement, is an unusual exception. The anonymous *Nova Scotia: a new ballad* (London, 1750), J. Patrick's *Quebec: a pastoral essay* (London, 1760), and George Cartwright's *Labrador: a poetical epistle* (London, 1792) sustain an optimistic picture of settlement, while replacing the earlier idyllic view of the land with an eighteenth-century appreciation of the sublimity of nature. This combination of optimism and sentiment may be found as late as Cornwall Bayley's *Canada: a descriptive poem* (Quebec, 1806), Thomas D. Cowdell's *Nova Scotia minstrel* (Dublin, 1809), and in the verses included by Methodist missionary Joshua Marsden in his *The narrative of a mission to Nova Scotia, New Brunswick, and the Somers Islands, with a tour to Lake Ontario* (Plymouth Dock, 1818). The other subject that early poets reported on was military activity in Canada. Matthew Parker's *England's honour revived* (London, 1629) is a ballad on Sir David Kirke's victory at Quebec. Valentine Neville, a naval officer who participated in the capture of Louisbourg, described that event in *The reduction of Louisburg* (London, 1759). George Cockings follows a similar pattern in *War: an heroick poem* (London, 1762), in his verse-drama *The conquest of Quebec* (London, 1766), and in his later poem *The American war* (London, 1781). As late as the War of 1812 the anonymous poem *A poetical account of the American campaigns of 1812 and 1813* (Halifax, 1815) approached its subject in a reportorial manner. This type of detached perspective characterizes all the visitor-poetry of this period. In spite of occasional didacticism, both the descriptive and narrative poems are aimed more at informing a remote readership than at shaping local reponse to a new reality.

2. 1749 TO 1815. With the development of substantial English communities in Québec, Nova Scotia, and New Brunswick, locally written verse intended for a local readership began to emerge. This activity increased markedly towards the end of the century, with the influx of thousands of Loyalist refugees, displaced by the American Revolution. Very quickly the inhabitants of these loyal colonies established themselves as cohesive economic, political, and social entities. At the same time they developed a remarkably coherent concept of the ideological basis of their society. Not surprisingly, as eighteenth-century conservatives their understanding of reality was characterized by well-established sets of social, political, moral, and religious assumptions in which the idea of order and propriety was central; man's relationship to his natural environment was less important than his awareness of the ordered structure of civilization. Poetry, because it could be readily created under local conditions, played a significant role in the cultural development of these colonies: it became a sophisticated means of expressing local social and cultural expectations. Consciously imitating established verse-forms and poetic sentiments, colonial poets explored and described local experience in relation to universal frames of reference; their subjects revolved around the social, political, moral, and religious ideals of their time. In its similarity to prevailing forms, local poetry thus reflected the colonial desire to be part of a universal cultural reality—one that was perceived to be most clearly expressed in European (particularly English) literature. This poetic perspective dominated Canadian poetry until the end of the Napoleonic Wars.

The poetry of this period is inherently didactic in almost all its forms. Descriptive works and topographical poems, such as Roger VIETS' *Annapolis Royal* (Halifax, 1788), Thomas Cary's *Abraham's Plains* (Quebec, 1789), J. Mackay's *Quebec Hill; or Canadian scenery* (London, 1797), and Adam Allan's *A description of the great falls of the River St. John* (London, 1798) essentially had a moral purpose: integrating the character of colonial life with prevailing moral ideals. In occasional poems, such as Stephen Dickson's allegorical eulogy, *The union of science and taste* (Quebec, 1799), the moral didacticism was even more overt, as it was in the numerous elegies, lyrics, and songs published in local newspapers. Religious values were another important subject for didactic treatment. Henry ALLINE's *Hymns and spiritual songs* (Boston, 1784) is the best example: the collection is a cross between a spiritual autobiography and a guide to religious life. Finally, social and political concerns were often treated, with an implicitly didactic purpose, in satiric terms; specific social, moral, and religious values were promoted by attacking those who failed to live up to the desired ideal. The social, political, and religious satires of Jacob BAILEY, Jonathan ODELL, Samuel Denny Street, and Alexander Croke were grounded in a moral vision of society drawn from eighteenth-century English conservatism.

3. 1815 TO 1840. While the conservative mentality of the eighteenth century lingered after 1815, the imagination of a new generation of writers was excited more by the apparent uniqueness of colonial experience than by its connection with ideal universal realities. This shift in perspective was not sudden and radical but gradual, often halting; it emerged as a growing awareness of colonial social and cultural autonomy in the face of continuing emotional attachments to the culture of Great Britain. In political terms it manifested itself in the movement towards responsible government, particularly in Nova Scotia. In the poetry of the period it was most clearly demonstrated in a new-found interest in the legends, customs, and historical background of colonial life. Native poets began to write of the struggles and hardships of early settlement as part of a process of historical development: Adam Hood BURWELL's 'Talbot Road' (1820), Oliver GOLDSMITH's *The rising village* (London, 1825), and Joseph HOWE's 'Acadia' (c. 1832) all reflect emerging colonial interest in social, political, and cultural identity. At the same time poets also turned to North

American Indians as a subject for verse. In the anonymous captivity tale, *The lay of the wilderness* (Saint John, 1833), hostile relations with the Indians are treated as a significant part of the romantic history of early settlement; in John RICHARDSON's *Tecumseh; or, The warrior of the West in four cantos with notes* (London, 1828) and Adam KIDD's *The Huron chief and other poems* (Montreal, 1830), the Indian is depicted as a noble savage whose culture is essentially compatible with the central values of European civilization. In both cases the poetry integrates the Indian into a perceived pattern of historical development. This is also true of the verse dealing with local customs and legends: George LONGMORE's *The charivari; or Canadian poetics: a tale after the manner of Beppo* (Montreal, 1824), Levi ADAMS' *Jean Baptiste* (Montreal, 1825), and Andrew SHIELS' *The witch of the Westcot* (Halifax, 1831)—all attempt to identify and promote the special texture of social life unfolding in British North America.

In addition to poetry that dealt specifically with colonial life, native poets continued to produce didactic verse prescribing accepted moral and religious values, and lyrics that projected universal social and cultural values. The poetry of such writers as Joseph Hart Clinch, William Martin Leggett, J.M. Cawdell, Angus Gidney, Adam Hood Burwell, and G.H. Willis sustained the didactic character of eighteenth-century verse, but was generally more sentimental in tone. This is true of the work of such lyricists as James Hogg, William Fitz-Hawley, Margaret Blennerhasset, James Redfern, and John Laskey. Under the influence of Burns and Moore, these poets cultivated a range of sentimental poetic responses and applied them to colonial social life and to the natural environment. The picture of cultural life that emerges is one marked by a self-conscious appreciation of all forms of emotional and moral sensitivity. These native lyricists strove to demonstrate that colonial sensibilities were not blunted by the unsophisticated conditions in which they were nurtured.

4. 1840 TO 1860. The poetic subjects of the 1820s and 1830s continued to attract attention in mid-century. G.A. Hammond's verses on New Brunswick Indians, William KIRBY's *The U.E.: a tale of Upper Canada* (Niagara, 1859), and Archibald Grey's view of village life in *Shades of the hamlet* (Woburn, Mass., 1852) reflected a continuing need to project a vision of historical and social development. Added to this was a new dimension in the colonizing process—large-

scale immigration, starting in the 1830s. Standish O'GRADY's *The emigrant* (Montreal, 1842) was the first of many poems to explore the role of the immigrant in colonial life. Also, moral and religious didacticism continued to find expression in the poetry of Andrew SHIELS, Samuel Elder, A.K. Archibald, and Sarah and Mary E. HERBERT among others; the subject of temperance was of special interest. At the same time, Charles HEAVYSEGE's *Saul; a drama in three parts* (Montreal, 1857) demonstrated a lingering interest in biblical subjects.

But the most significant poetic development of the mid-century was a growing interest in the landscape and natural environment of Canada, probably stimulated by the importance of nature in British Romantic poetry. This trend is evident in books published from the Maritimes to Upper Canada: M.A. Wallace's *Hymns of the Church, Nativity, and other poems* (Portland, Me., 1853), which contains secular verse; Clotilda Jennings's *Linden rhymes* (Halifax, 1851); Bishop G.J. Mountain's *Songs of the wilderness* (London, 1846); David Wylie's *Recollections of a convict, and miscellaneous pieces* (Montreal, 1847); James Liston's *Niagara Falls* (Toronto, 1843); and in the early Canadian verses of Alexander McLACHLAN. But of special interest is the nature poetry of John McPHERSON, posthumously collected in *Poems, descriptive and moral* (Halifax, 1862); of Peter John ALLAN in *Poetical remains* (London, 1853); and of Charles SANGSTER in *The St. Lawrence and the Saguenay, and other poems* (Kingston and New York, 1856) and *Hesperus, and other poems and lyrics* (Montreal, 1860). Their poetic perspectives are complex and their poetic 'voices' seem uniquely North American. Where others tend to sentimentalize their responses to nature, these poets strove to articulate man's ability to identify himself emotionally with, and to explore, the unique character of the natural world around him.

Finally the publication of D'Arcy McGEE's *Canadian ballads, and occasional verses* (Montreal, 1858) introduced a strain of self-conscious patriotic nationalism into Canadian poetry. Although McGee drew on his Irish experience to shape this perspective, the rapid movement of colonial North America towards nationhood created conditions amenable to patriotic and nationalistic verse.

5. 1860 TO 1880. Poetically, the years on either side of Confederation appear to lack clear focus and direction, as if poets were

not quite sure how to come to terms with the new social and political realities of Canada. Certainly poets such as Charles MAIR, Mrs LEPROHON, and a host of lesser names tried to articulate the new sense of Canadian nationalism that logically ought to have been a part of the attainment of nationhood; but their efforts appear formulaic, projecting an abstract patriotism at best. Indeed, in Mair's case this nationalistic focus seems to have deflected him from exploring his response to the natural environment, the subject of his early verse in *Dreamland and other poems* (Montreal, 1868). The desire to project a national voice drew him away from his poetic strength.

This period also saw the publication of the first significant anthology of Canadian verse, E.H. DEWART's *Selections from Canadian poets* (Montreal, 1864). Like contemporary poets, Dewart saw his work as part of a growing sense of Canadian nationalism, arguing that 'A national literature is an essential element in the formation of national character.' A third of the selections are nature poems, another third moral and religious verse, and the remainder 'miscellaneous pieces'. Despite Dewart's claims, it is very difficult to draw an impression of national character from the collection, and even more difficult to ascertain the direction in which Canadian poetry was moving. Much the same may be said of W.D. LIGHTHALL's later anthology, *Songs of the great Dominion* (London, 1889), although Lighthall more consciously organized his selections around what he perceived to be aspects of Canadian national identity.

Aside from nationalistic verse, the period was dominated by Scottish immigrant poets and by women magazine-writers. Alexander McLACHLAN's *The emigrant, and other poems* (Toronto, 1861) and *Poems and songs* (Toronto, 1874), William Murdoch's *Poems and songs* (Saint John, 1860 and 1872), and Evan McColl's poetry (collected in 1883), all reflect the adaptation of Lowland-Scots lyric verse to Canadian subjects. At their best these poets projected a vision of social, economic, and political progress in the new Canada. But their perceptions of human character, and of society, often seem to be grounded in Scottish rather than Canadian cultural experience; consequently they seem to be imposing patterns of perception rather than exploring the character of Canadian life. Since Canadian poetry had effectively gone beyond the stage of prescribing notions of social, moral, and cultural experi-

ence, these Scottish poets often appear somewhat removed from the direction that had been developed in the earlier part of the century. Much the same may be said of the women poets, such as Mary Jane KATZMANN, Agnes MACHAR, and M.G. Currie. Their poetic voices were those of the popular magazine poetesses of Britain and America, presenting sentimentalized images of moral and religious propriety—an abstraction of civilized life applied to a Canadian context.

6. 1880 TO 1900. The last two decades of the century were marked by the emergence of a group of poets who, though fully aware of intellectual and artistic developments in New York and London, confidently turned to their own experience, trusting their perceptions (particularly of the natural world) to provide the subjects and images of their poetry. Not surprisingly they found in the natural environment of Canada a fundamental source of poetic inspiration.

It was Charles G.D. ROBERTS' *Orion, and other poems* (Philadelphia, 1880) and *In divers tones* (Boston, 1886) that signalled the presence of this new poetic perspective in Canadian verse. His efforts were joined by those of Isabella Valency CRAWFORD in *Old Spookse's pass, Malcolm's Katie, and other poems* (Toronto, 1884); and by Archibald LAMPMAN in *Among the millet* (Ottawa, 1888), *Lyrics of earth* (Boston, 1883), and *Alcyone* (Edinburgh, 1899). Further, the early verse of Roberts' cousin Bliss CARMAN in *Low tide on Grand Pré* (New York, 1893), and of Duncan Campbell SCOTT in *The magic house, and other poems* (Ottawa, 1893) and *Labour and the angel* (Boston, 1898), formed part of a relatively cohesive body of verse that focused on Canadian landscape and its effect on Canadian consciousness. (See CONFEDERATION POETS.) In this poetry there are strains of the poetic sensibilities of P.J. Allan, John McPHERSON, and Charles SANGSTER; but for the later poets nature has become a much more complex and mysterious phenomenon than the earlier writers had imagined. Where earlier generations treated nature descriptively as topography, or sentimentally as an extension of their emotional sensitivity, Roberts' generation approached nature as an embodiment of the spirit of being informing all human reality and around which man's consciousness was shaped. In other words Canadian poets, responding to Canadian landscapes, now confronted a universal reality that was immediate and profound, and their fundamental perceptions were not borrowed or channeled through aesthetic assumptions formulated in foreign centres of culture. Although their poetic language may have been influenced by prevailing poetic fashion, their primary perceptions—the source of their poetry—remained individualistic, immediate, and original. In the verse of all five poets, the disarming simplicity of their presentation of nature is its most attractive feature, but behind that simplicity lies a disturbing ominousness. In an increasingly utilitarian world struggling with a Darwinian vision of human reality, the need to seek and assert the essential spirituality of nature emerged as a basic intellectual, aesthetic, and humanistic responsibility that the poet could not ignore. This poetic responsibility linked Roberts, Crawford, Lampman, Carman, and Scott to an international brotherhood of poets, but it did so in specifically Canadian terms. Their awareness of the spirit of reality was shaped by the natural forms in which they perceived it. For these poets the forms were Canadian, their perceptions were Canadian, and their poetic response had a specifically Canadian character.

Less perceptive, but often touched by the same sense of transcendental truths in nature, were the verses of Wilfred CAMPBELL in *Lake lyrics and other poems* (Saint John, 1889), of Frederick George SCOTT in *The soul's quest* (London, 1888), and of Francis SHERMAN and Pauline JOHNSON. These poets, however, often appear more concerned with accommodating their poetic presentations to one contemporary literary fashion or another than with exploring and articulating the character of their personal experience of nature. Much the same may be said of G.F. CAMERON's *Lyrics of freedom, love, and death* (Kingston, 1887). Indeed, the temptation to imitate internationally recognized poetic patterns and apply them to ostensibly Canadian subjects tended to undermine the impulse to establish a viable set of indigenous poetic perspectives. In the late eighteenth and early nineteenth centuries the adoption of borrowed poetic forms and stances was central and necessary to the development of Canadian poetry; in the late decades of the nineteenth century this kind of imitation betrayed an unnecessary aesthetic insecurity that haunted Canadian verse well into the twentieth century.

TOM VINCENT

1900 to 1950. 1. THE ROMANTIC AND VICTORIAN HERITAGE. The dominant voices in Canadian poetry at the turn of the century were still heavily influenced by the choice of subject matter and the spirit, verse forms, and diction of English Romantic and Victorian poetry. The *Poems* (1900) of Archibald LAMPMAN, Charles G.D. ROBERTS' *Poems* (1901), Duncan Campbell SCOTT's *New world lyrics and ballads* (1905), and Bliss CARMAN's *Pipes of Pan* (1906), while showing the results of the poets' classical training, also clearly illustrate their stylistic dependency on earlier British poetry. Though a slight loosening of formal constraints is observable in some of the later work of these poets, Canadian life and landscape, spirituality, and patriotism remain at the core of their poetry. Roberts, Carman, and Scott continued to publish into the second quarter of the century, Scott himself doing much to foster Lampman's reputation, having edited four collections of Lampman's verse after Lampman's death in 1899.

The *Complete poems* of Marjorie PICKTHALL (1925) shows her to be the most accomplished of the minor poets of this period (among whom were Wilson MacDONALD and Francis SHERMAN) who inclined to a mystical and lyrical aestheticism that has been linked both to the Celtic twilight and to the pre-Raphaelite school. Mellifluous and charming, but almost completely lacking in intellectual qualities, Pickthall's work attracted excessive praise from Ryerson Press editor Lorne PIERCE that ultimately damaged her critical reputation. Tom MacINNES's *Rhymes of a rounder* (1913) shows this highly individual poet—best known for his villanelle 'The tiger of desire'—going to French verse-forms to structure his exuberantly irreverent view of life.

Popular poets in the early years of the century exhibit a conservatism in their forms and metres, combined with a comfortable exoticism in their subject matter. *The poetical works* (1912) of William Henry DRUMMOND bring together dialect portraits of French-Canadian characters; Pauline JOHNSON's collected poems, *Flint and feather* (1912), romantically exploits her Mohawk Indian heritage; and Robert SERVICE's *Songs of a sourdough* (1907) is memorable for its humorous Gothic tales of the Yukon at the time of the Goldrush, such as 'The shooting of Dan McGrew', while his later work, of which *Bar-room ballads* (1940) is representative, depicts a world-ranging bohemian way of life.

The work of both established and newer poets of the first quarter of the century can be sampled in Albert Watson's and Lorne Pierce's *Our Canadian literature: representative prose and verse* (1922). This book became, in 1935, exclusively an anthology of poetry under the editorship of Pierce and Bliss Carman, and in 1955 was revised and updated by V.B. Rhodenizer as *Canadian poetry in English*. The enervation of Canadian poetry by sentimental versifiers is painfully evident in much of Wilfred CAMPBELL's *The Oxford book of Canadian verse* (1913) and John Garvin's *Canadian poets* (1916; rev. 1926).

2. NEO-COLONIAL MODERNISM. Although in the twenties and thirties Canadian poetry gained a new life and direction as the cramping prosody, idiom, and Romantic world-view of the last century were left behind, the majority of poets still looked to Europe or, in fewer cases, America, to provide them with poetic models for the expression of contemporary experience. Learning from the imagists, experimenters in free verse, and British and American poets who had a social orientation, Canadian writers broadened their concept of what was suitable subject-matter for poetry, discovered a diction and imagery appropriate to contemporary concerns, and freed themselves from the strictures of rhyme and conventional metres.

2(a) *Transitional figures.* E.J. PRATT is the quintessential transitional figure. The life of his early work *Newfoundland verse* (1923) largely grows from its gripping images of man confronting an overwhelmingly powerful nature, though it is sometimes choked by diction and sentiments inherited from an outworn tradition. Pratt was not a metrical or formal innovator—as his *Many moods* (1932) and his narratives *Titans* (1926) and *The Titanic* (1935) amply testify. But the scope of his vision and his epic scale were appropriate reflections of the Canadian experience, while his attempts to bridge the gap between the sciences, technology, and the humanities—reflected most clearly in his choice of subject and in his diction—show him to be vitally engaged with life in the twentieth century. In his later work Pratt mythologized the Canadian experience in meticulously researched narratives: *Brébeuf and his brethren* (1940) and *Towards the last spike* (1952). Pratt's verse is a culmination and summation of a phase in the developing Canadian imagination that saw Canada as a land characterized by an often beautiful and always powerful and indifferent nature that both threatened to crush the human spirit and challenged it to reach sacrificial heights of nobility. See his *Collected poems* (1944; 1958).

Floris Clarke McLaren's *Frozen fire* (1937) dramatizes attitudes towards British Columbian lanscapes and the north country, while the terse, sometimes prosaic, qualities of Charles BRUCE's realistic portraits of maritime life and landscapes can be sampled in their early form in *Wild apples* (1927), and at their best in *The Mulgrave Road* (1951). The early work of Kenneth LESLIE, also a Maritimer with a strong regional awareness, echoes the themes and voices of Carman and Roberts, but his polished sonnets of passion *By stubborn stars and other poems* (1938) showed that conventional forms could still structure genuine feeling. Fellow Maritimer Alfred Goldsworthy BAILEY, who would help found the Fredericton magazine *The* FIDDLEHEAD, published the conventional *Songs of the Saguenay and other poems* (1927) before finding his own voice in *Border river* (1952), in which he effectively exploits his knowledge of Canadian history in a variety of forms dictated by the subject matter of the individual poems. Ralph GUSTAFSON too showed an early fascination with the manner of late Romantic poetry in *The golden chalice* (1935); but in *Flight into darkness* (1944) the elliptical quality of the syntax and the erudite vocabulary of the new poems reflect the influence of the modernist movement.

2(b) *The free-versists.* Evidence of formal innovation can be found as early as 1914 when Arthur STRINGER defended his free-verse style in a preface to *Open water*; but not until W.W.E. ROSS blended this style with what he had learned from the American imagist Marianne Moore was free verse significantly used in Canadian poetry. Ross wrote most of his important poetry during the twenties, attempting to capture 'something of/what quality may mark us off/from older Europe,—/something "north American"—/and something of/the sharper tang of Canada.' He quietly published *Laconics* (1930) and *Sonnets* (1932), but *Experiment 1923-1929: poems by W.W.E. Ross* did not appear until 1956. The poems of a fellow free-verse imagist of the 1920s, Raymond KNISTER, were similarly delayed in gaining broad exposure: his only volume of poems, which concentrated on farm life, *The collected poems of Raymond Knister*, edited and with a memoir by Dorothy LIVESAY, was published posthumously in 1949.

Critic Arthur Phelps, painter Lawren Harris, and poet Louise Morey Bowman all used free verse in their poetry, which has more historical than literary importance. The title *Acanthus and wild grape* (1920) by Frank Oliver Call (1878-1956) represents his book's mix of formally stylized and free-verse forms, and Arthur BOURINOT left behind his early plodding adherence to conventional rhythms and rhyme—evident in *Laurentian lyrics and other poems* (1915)—for a freer verse style in *Under the sun* (1939).

Free-verse techniques were blended with more conventional prosody to translate and adapt native songs and chants in Constance Lindsay Skinner's *Songs of the coast dwellers* (1930) and Hermia Harris Fraser's *Songs of the western islands* (1945). These books continued a tradition of making available to English-speaking readers the verse of Canada's non-English poets, a tradition that extends at least as far back as 1916, when Florence Randal Livesay's *Songs of Ukraina, with Ruthenian poems* appeared and that includes Watson KIRKCONNELL's *Canadian overtones: an anthology of Canadian poetry written originally in Icelandic, Swedish, Hungarian, Italian, Greek, and Ukrainian, and now translated* (1935).

2(c) *Lorne Pierce and the Ryerson Press.* Fraser's book is one of the Ryerson poetry chapbooks, a series under the general editorship of Lorne PIERCE. As editor for RYERSON PRESS from 1920 to 1960, Pierce did much to aid the growth of Canadian poetry, initiating the chapbook series in 1925 with Sir Charles G.D. ROBERTS' *The sweet o' the year and other poems*. Roberts was also the first recipient of the Lorne Pierce medal, donated by the editor to recognize a significant and sustained contribution to Canadian letters. Important later volumes in the chapbook series include Bliss CARMAN's *The music of earth* (1931), Anne MARRIOTT's ten-poem sequence describing the hardships of farming in Saskatchewan during the dirty thirties, *The wind our enemy* (1939), and Dorothy Livesay's documentary poem for radio about the internment of Japanese Canadians during the Second World War, *Call my people home* (1950). Pierce was also general editor for the nationalistic 'Makers of Canadian Literature' series, which published appreciative biographies of several Canadian poets.

3. THE MONTREAL MOVEMENT AND OTHER THIRTIES' ACTIVITY. Founded by F.R. SCOTT and A.J.M. SMITH, *The McGill Fortnightly Review* (1925-7) was a Montreal-based periodical that published poems, poetic manifestos, and critical articles sympathetic to the aims and techniques of modern British poetry. In articles like 'Wanted: Canadian criticism' (*Canadian Forum*, Apr. 1928), Smith was also instrumental in articulating what was wrong with Canadian poetry: too self-conscious of its position in space, it was hardly conscious at all of its position in time. 'Sensibility is no longer enough, intelligence is also required. Even in Canada,' Smith proclaimed.

The short-lived successor to the McGill paper, *The Canadian Mercury: a Monthly Journal of Literature and Opinion* (1928-9), edited by Scott and Leo KENNEDY, kept up the attack on the mediocrity of much Canadian verse and gave space to many of the important poets whose work later appeared in the commercially unsuccessful but critically important anthology NEW PROVINCES: *poems of several authors* (1936; rpr. 1976). The voices of Yeats, Eliot, Pound, and Auden could clearly be heard in the cadences of many of the poems in the anthology, while the spare style and irregular rhythms and forms of the free-versists proved effective in rendering the quality of the Canadian landscape in such poems as 'Trees in ice' by Scott and 'The lonely land' by Smith, in which he seems to share the vision of the Group of Seven. Scott contributed several satirical pieces and poems examining man as a social being, modes that were continued in his *Overture: poems* (1945). Kennedy and Smith both employed metaphysical images in their poems, the former having already published *The shrouding* (1933; rpr. 1975), with its poems centring on fertility cycles, and the latter continuing to work the metaphysical and psychological veins in *News of the phoenix and other poems* (1943). Robert FINCH was the most stylistically traditional of the contributors, and a neo-classical spirit informed his first two individual collections, *Poems* (1946) and *The strength of the hills* (1948). Both in *New provinces*, and in the poems of *Hath not a Jew* (1940), A.M. KLEIN wrote about his Jewish heritage, creating portraits of imagined or real individuals such as Baruch Spinoza in the justly celebrated 'Out of the pulver and the polished lens'. Klein's relatively brief but intense publishing career as a poet culminated in *The rocking chair and other poems* (1948), in which his concern for man in minority-group situations extended to both French Canadians and to the ultimate 'minority of one' figure, the artist, in 'Portrait of the poet as landscape'.

The interdisciplinary magazine CANADIAN FORUM published in the thirties not only many important poems (especially under the literary editorship of Earle BIRNEY from 1936-1940), but also two series of critical essays of note: 'The new writers of Canada' (1932) and 'Canadian writers of the past' (1932-3). Both poems and articles made clear the prevalent anti-Romantic stance of the poets and critics of the era. One poet whose work was discussed in the former series and who later proved to be a major talent was Dorothy LIVESAY. Her irregularly rhymed and imagist-influenced free-verse collection *Green pitcher* (1928) was followed by the socially conscious poems of *Signpost* (1932) and *Day and night* (1944), in which subject matter is allowed to dictate form, though angry leftist rhetoric sometimes detracts from the impression created by the effective use of mimetic rhythms. L.A. MacKay (b. 1901) was a contributor to both series of essays, assessing past writers Bliss CARMAN and Wilfred CAMPBELL and the more recent poet Audrey Alexandra BROWN, whose *A dryad in Nanaimo* (1931) showed her to be a vital successor in mode to Marjorie PICKTHALL. A professor of classics and a poet in his own right, MacKay had published his love poems, sonnets, and neo-classical satires under the pseudonym 'John Smalacombe' in *Viper's bugloss* (1938) and, using his own name, in *The ill-tempered lover and other poems* (1948).

The thirties saw the birth of many supports to the renaissance in Canadian poetry, 1936 being a particularly fruitful year as W.E. Collin's landmark book of essays on Canadian poetry, *The WHITE SAVANNAHS*, appeared; *The Canadian Poetry Magazine* was founded by the CANADIAN AUTHORS' ASSOCIATION under the editorship of E.J. PRATT, and in its first number published Livesay's 'Day and night', as well as poems by F.R. Scott, Finch, and Kennedy; *The University of Toronto Quarterly* began its annual review of Canadian poetry in its 'Letters in Canada'; the GOVERNOR GENERAL'S LITERARY AWARDS were instituted; and the CBC was becoming an important disseminator of poems and critical commentary. Few poetry anthologies of any real merit were published in this decade, though Ethel Hume Bennett's *New harvesting: contemporary Canadian poetry 1918-1938* (1938) gives a representative sampling of the then-recent work of Canadian poets who were still living.

4. THE FORTIES. Montreal continued to be a centre of poetic activity in this decade as two literary magazines provided an outlet for two groups of poets, both concerned with raising public consciousness about social issues. FIRST STATEMENT: *A Magazine for Young Canadian Writers* (1943-5), founded by the poet-critic John SUTHERLAND—later joined by Irving LAYTON and Louis DUDEK—was avowedly proletarian, and its poets used a colloquial idiom and a detailed realism to evoke their Canadian environment. PREVIEW (1942-5) was a work-in-progress mimeo-magazine established by the English expatriate Patrick ANDERSON and put together by a group that included F.R. SCOTT and later P.K. PAGE and A.M. KLEIN. Culturally sophisticated, as well as socially and politically committed, the *Preview* poets saw themselves as assisting in the war effort as well as supplying 'something of the personal, the graceful and the heroic, to the atmosphere of this half-empty Dominion'—feats that were to be accomplished by blending the lyric and didactic elements in modern verse and by combining 'vivid arresting imagery' with social commentary and criticism. The amalgamation of their magazines to form NORTHERN REVIEW (1946-56) suggests that too much has been made of the differences between the two groups. Furthermore, in 1945 Sutherland's First Statement Press published not only his vision of Jewish Montreal, *Here and now*, and Miriam WADDINGTON's *Green world*—a book that pictures an innocent spring and summer sensuality made more poignant by the disillusionment of a growing awareness of evil and mortality in fall and winter—but also Patrick Anderson's first Canadian collection, *A tent for April*. That book, and Anderson's *The white centre* (1946), are characterized by metaphysical and sexual images, and by a nostalgia for youth; they include pictures of wartime Montreal and several self-conscious attempts at defining the nature of the Canadian experience.

Louis Dudek's organically structured poems in *East of the city* (1946) are written in both critical and celebratory modes, though they reflect a principally urban experience, seen from a socialist point of view. Striking imagery, and an empathy for the socially or emotionally oppressed that often ends in anger at their situation, are the defining characteristics of P.K. PAGE's maps of the psyche in *As ten as twenty* (1946). Anderson, who was Page's first publisher, had discovered her work in CONTEMPORARY VERSE: *A Canadian Quarterly*, a stylistically eclectic and increasingly distinguished west-coast literary magazine edited and published by Alan Crawley from 1941 to 1952.

A major western talent also appeared in the forties in Earle BIRNEY, whose poetry was from the first distinguished by an unsentimental yet compassionate understanding of strange or disturbing experiences, and a desire to delineate the Canadian character. *David and other poems* (1942) employs an often documentary style learned from Pratt; in addition to the title narrative—about the way youthful innocence is ended by the need to act in the face of a mountain-climbing disaster—it contains many formally and stylistically various poems of a humorous or satirical nature. As it was in his first volume, war is a significant theme in Birney's *Now is time: poems* (1945), in which Birney continues to experiment with narrative poetry. *The strait of Anian: selected poems* (1948) is a summation of Birney's first phase, and offers a critical view of Canadian life juxtaposed with an appreciative look at the power and beauty of the land.

Raymond SOUSTER's poetry is consistently simple in diction, colloquial in tone, and organic in its verse-forms. In *When we are young* (1946) he celebrates in vivid imagery the passionate sexuality of the young, and casts a cold eye on the war in Europe. *Go to sleep, world* (1947) contains many moving love poems and clearly establishes him as a poet of Toronto, revealing both the tawdrier and more vital sides of that city. Another Toronto-based poet of the period, Douglas LePAN, skilfully blends Old and New World sensibilities and subject matter, as well as a felicity of phrasing and an acuity of vision, in *The wounded prince and other poems* (1948).

Bertram Warr (1917-43) left Toronto for England in 1938 and the years he spent observing life in London, especially in the poorer quarters, and the impact of the war on the city's people, resulted in the moving poems of *Yet a little onward* (1941), which won him the praise of Robert Graves. The pared, ironic diction of 'On a child with a wooden leg' is characteristic of the best of Warr's verse. His war poems were anthologized in several English books, and after his death in an air attack on Germany his promise as a poet was attested to by an article on his life and work and by a small sample of his poems in *Contemporary Verse (Oct. 1945)*; by a selection of his verse, *In quest of beauty, selected poems* (1950); and by Len Gaspirini's collection of Warr's poems, *Acknowledgement to life* (1970).

5. THE CLOSE OF THE HALF-CENTURY. After the hardships of the Depression had given rise to the voice of social consciousness in Canadian poetry of the thirties, and the Second World War had led to a renewed Canadian pride in country that extended to an interest in what Canadian poets were saying about the national life, a strange lull set in at the end of the first half of the century. James REANEY's *The red heart* (1949) was the only noteworthy book of that year, and it signalled a shift of the poetic centre from Montreal to Toronto. It contains some not-very-successful satires and humorous verses; but the poems in which Reaney looks at the world with a vivid childlike imagination, confronting fears embodied in monster and stepmother figures, and conveys that vision with often startling, fantastic, and horrific images, represent a new departure in Canadian poetry.

The achievement of Canadian poetry until mid-century was summarized in several anthologies and works of criticism published in the forties. Ralph GUSTAFSON edited *Anthology of Canadian poetry* (1942), *A little anthology of Canadian poets* (1943), and a special Canadian issue of the American magazine *Voices: a quarterly of poetry* (1943). Other magazine anthologies of Canadian verse appeared in *Poetry* (Chicago) and the British *Outposts*. A.J.M. SMITH's *The book of Canadian poetry: a critical and historical anthology* (1943; rev. 1948, 1957) established the canon of Canadian poetry; it was to some extent updated by John SUTHERLAND's *Other Canadians: an anthology of the new poetry in Canada 1940-1946* (1947). A forties' response to NEW PROVINCES came in Ronald Hambleton's *Unit of five* (1944), which presented a significant sample of the work of SOUSTER, PAGE, DUDEK, James Wreford, and Hambleton himself.

E.K. BROWN's *On Canadian poetry* (1943), the best critical book of the decade, assessed the colonial nature of Canadian poetry, delineated a three-phase developmental history of Canadian poetry, and hailed Archibald LAMPMAN, D.C. SCOTT, and E.J. PRATT as three of Canada's best writers; while W.P. Percival's *Leading Canadian poets* (1948) published essays of varying merit on twenty-nine poets.　　　　SUSAN GINGELL

1950 to 1982. Over the past three decades there has been an astonishing increase not only in poetic talent but in the number of works published. The 24 books of verse published in 1959 increased to 120 in 1970. Between 1960 and 1973, 590 poets published over 1,100 books of verse, not counting anthologies, and since 1973 a similar (undocumented) increase has taken place. While fully realizing that the judgement of true poetic worth can be made only by time, I propose to discuss briefly in the following survey those poets who seem to have a genuine voice—not only something to say but an interesting way of saying it—and whose work has been significant in giving distinctiveness and character to Canadian poetry of the last thirty years.

1. THE FIFTIES. In this decade English-Canadian poetry consolidated and extended its seriousness and creativity not only with mature collections but with the brilliant débuts of poets who are among the most important names in modern Canadian poetry. Much of the work of the fifties originated in the academic community and displayed some of the effects of the continuing power of high modernism in the influence of Yeats, Auden, and Eliot. This was described in A.J.M. SMITH's preface to his *Book of Canadian poetry* (3rd. edn 1957) and was revealed in his own collection *A sort of ecstasy* (1954), and in the irony, satire, and social consciousness of F.R. SCOTT's poems in his *Events and signals* (1954) and *The eye of the needle* (1957). This strain of fifties' poetry was erudite and assumed a well-educated audience in its rich use of literary and other allusions. Another of its features, one that has been sustained, was the organization or subjection of individual short lyrics into a larger unity, and the use of a wide range of traditional forms—ballads, hymns, nursery rhymes, eclogues. Traditional forms did not necessarily support traditional values. On the contrary, those poets who used them most usually did so for purposes of parody, to question accepted bourgeois values, and to suggest in the world of art and imagination alternative values.

The short poems that make up *The* BOAT-MAN (1957) by Jay MACPHERSON form an intricate sequence that is unified by thematic continuities and recurrent symbols. They enact a myth of creation, fall, and reconciliation in a largely comic and parodic mode—Macpherson's control of parody seizes power from the forms that are parodied. George JOHNSTON's *The cruising auk* (1959) is another collection that is integrated thematically and has many formal devices, including a single structuring symbol. These short, crisp poems are informed with wit and moral intelligence unencumbered with moralism, and a casual, almost disinterested irony. James REANEY's *A suit of nettles* (1958)

is a witty imitation of Spenser's *The shepheardes calender*, structured in twelve poetic dialogues—one for each month of the year—among geese on an Ontario farm. It won Reaney his second Governor General's Award.

The display of craft, learning, wit, and allusiveness was also evident in other fifties' publications. Anne WILKINSON's *Counterpoint to sleep* (1951) and *The hangman ties the holly* (1955)—containing poems, about the sensory apprehension of the natural world, that often use word-play and traditional poetic forms like the nursery rhyme and the carol—were praised for their liveliness and their gift of parody, though they showed a strong interest in the Gothic and the macabre. The young Daryl HINE, in *The carnal and the crane* (1957), precociously revealed himself to be a highly erudite poet whose love of eloquence and verbal dignity, difficult syntax, and sometimes obscure imagery have made him less immediately popular than his strengths deserve. P.K. PAGE showed a complex sensibility, a powerful vision, and a lively wit in *The metal and the flower* (1954). Phyllis WEBB's *Even your right eye* (1956), with its eloquent diction and brilliant images, marked her as a poet worthy of notice. Another major poetic talent that appeared in the fifties—and who was part of the poetic ferment of Montreal at this time—was Leonard COHEN, whose *Let us compare mythologies* (1956), despite its grotesque imagery and its strain of black romance that was expressed in an obsession with the Crucifixion, is full of life and energy. In John GLASSCO's *The deficit made flesh* (1958), describing rural life in the Eastern Townships of Québec, human untrustworthiness is rendered in technically skilled blank verse with an elegiac strain. Philip CHILD's *Victorian house and other poems* (1951) contained one of the few narrative poems in a decade that was trying to find alternatives to the narrative form. Along with the title poem, however, there are lyrics that reveal a fine technical mastery. The poems in D.G. JONES' *Frost on the sun* (1957) are distanced from direct experience, which the poet subjects to a process of intensification in order to present it with verbal economy and with images that are restrained, deliberate, and powerful. R.G. EVERSON, in *Three dozen poems* (1957) and *A lattice for Momos* (1958), writes elegant poetry that can sometimes be dense and epigrammatic and is full of imagistic comparisons, fresh humour, and a concern with myth and history.

The 1950s presented another important stream of Canadian poetry—one that would predominate in the sixties and seventies—that eschewed elegance, allusiveness, and traditional forms, adopting free verse and a colloquial, even street-wise, diction and tone. Having published two collections in the 1940s, Irving LAYTON began to hit his stride in the fifties, publishing eleven books. *A red carpet for the sun* (1959), one of the most important collections of the decade, put him squarely in the mainstream of Canadian poetry and presaged qualities that would appear more strongly in the prolific output to follow and would make him one of the most widely read of Canadian poets. In his corpus satire and invective, occasional roughness of language, self-consciously Nietzschean and apocalyptic concerns, a Dionysian persona, and erotic verse are offset by more lyrical and self-examining poems than his somewhat raucous public image would prepare us for. Layton joined Raymond SOUSTER and Louis DUDEK in founding Contact Press (1952-67), which provided a publishing outlet for them and for several other important poets of the period. Their own poems were collected in *Cerberus* (1952), and Souster's work in this volume heralded the continuities of his career. His best poems are wry but warm celebrations of Toronto urban life; some display an understated pathos. They tend to be short and tight, spoken through the voices of often unnamed characters—a device that allows him to experiment with a range of colloquial English. He published seven collections in the fifties, including *Crêpe-hanger's carnival: selected poems 1955-58* (1958), and his output has continued unabated. In this decade Louis Dudek published *24 poems* (1952), *Europe* (1955), *The transparent sea* (1956), and *En Mexique* (1958)—books that reflected the influence of Ezra Pound's *Cantos* on his work. His strongly visual poems are at their best in the detached and distant mode of the observer. *Europe*, *En Mexique*, and the later *Atlantis* (1967) are long, thoughtful meditations about the fate of western civilization in the brutal twentieth century. Like Dudek, Miriam WADDINGTON began publishing in Montreal in the 1940s. Her two fifties' collections, *The second silence* (1955) and *A season's lovers* (1958), contained an intimate poetry with a lyrical bent that would become more colloquial and expressive in her later volumes.

Elizabeth BREWSTER's early poetry, *East coast* (1951) and *Lilloet* (1954), produced an unsentimental, affectionate record of isolated life in the towns and seacoasts of New Brunswick. In 1969 her collected poems, *Passages of summer*, appeared. The New Brunswick poet Dorothy Roberts showed promise in the fifties with *Dazzle* (1957) and *In star and stalk* (1959), though her later work has not become popular. Heather Spears wrote a powerful, disturbing chronicle of mental breakdown in *Asylum poems and others* (1958). Her poems, which relate poetry to painting and contain meditations on the creative process, include *The Danish portraits* (1967) and *From the inside* (1972).

2. THE SIXTIES AND SEVENTIES. The poets who came into prominence in the 1960s—Margaret Atwood, Al Purdy, Michael Ondaatje, George Bowering, John Newlove,—changed and expanded the subject matter of Canadian poetry to include local history and documentary; family portraits and personal history conveyed in a muted, confessional mode; politics, popular culture, and surrealistic fantasy. In the sixties and early seventies the politics of Canadian poetry were nationalist, ecological, and regional, while in the later seventies they were feminist, sexual, or concerned with the growth of coercive and totalitarian régimes—as in the travel poems of Irving LAYTON, Eli Mandel, Earle Birney, Purdy, Patrick LANE, Atwood, and others. Another mode of the period was the series of loosely linked poems with a single concern or locale: poems unified by questions to which they are the answers, such as *Steveston* (1974) by Daphne MARLATT, or by narratives that experiment with a variety of perspectives or ways of telling a single story, such as Marlatt's *Frames* (1968). We have poems whose construction is analogous to a game, such as *The circle game* (1966) by Margaret Atwood, or plotted on a specific visual field like *Baseball* (1967) by George Bowering. We have Ondaatje's collage-like biography of an artist in murder, *The collected works of Billy the Kid* (1970), and poems constructed along the lines of quite different genres, not necessarily verbal ones: *The ledger* (1975) and *Seed catalogue* (1977), both part of *Field notes* (1981) by Robert Kroetsch. The sixties saw North American Indian legend and incantation become the source for a new mythic tradition (Susan MUSGRAVE, Kroetsch, Newlove, Purdy, Birney, Andrew SUKNASKI, bill Bissett, Sean VIRGO, and others). A continuous feature of Canadian poetry has been interest in the land, the wilderness, and Canada's vast spaces, much of the earlier

work (and Atwood's poetry to the present) expressing these subjects in terms of terror. Some seventies' poetry, however, attempted post-modern approaches to space and time, seeing them as a continuum, a field on which the poet can compose his work—a magnetic field whose many lines of force provide not so much structure as limitations to the possibilities of structure.

What follows is a brief discussion of some of the leading poets in the two decades. The first important poetic event of the sixties was the publication of *Winter sun* (1960) by Margaret AVISON, whose metaphysical poems had been appearing in journals for almost twenty years. Though strongly religious, they did not express any easy acceptance or affirmation but rather a difficult mysticism in an idiosyncratic and compelling voice. In *The dumbfounding* (1966) Avison confronted scientific humanism and a crisis of faith with tact and insight.

The most extraordinary career of the sixties and seventies has been that of Margaret ATWOOD. Beginning with *The circle game* (1966), which won a Governor General's Award, and continuing with *The animals in that country* (1968), *The* JOURNALS OF SUSANNA MOODIE (1970), and *Power politics* (1970), she has gone from strength to strength in four subsequent collections, including *True stories* (1981). Hers is a poetry of statement with an epigrammatic edge, an orderly verse whose powerful images, evocations of physical disgust and Gothic consciousness, are controlled by a flat, authoritative voice and the parallel structure of her lines. Besides being the most brilliant literary accomplishment of the time, her collective poetry, fiction, and criticism from this period is phenomenally popular.

Michael ONDAATJE's poetry has from the beginning struck an idiosyncratic note, displaying a sensibility that is surrealistic, yet tender, and a capacity for astonishing sensory description and physical detail. *The dainty monsters* (1967) was followed by *The man with seven toes* (1969), which tells the story of an escaped convict and his female hostage in the interior of Australia. *The collected works of Billy the Kid* (1970), which won a Governor General's Award, mixes poetry and prose, dramatic monologue, and quick shifts of narrative perspective to tell a story that is at once an adventure, a recreation of the popular culture hero, and a meditation on the relation between violence and creativity. *There's a trick with a knife I'm learning to do: poems 1963-1978* (1979) won

Ondaatje a second Governor General's Award.

Eli MANDEL's early poems were overtly mythological. His favourite strategy was to convey meanings in symbolic narratives, especially in the 'Minotaur poems', which confront modern experience as seen by an Icarus figure. *Fuseli poems* (1960)—which displays Mandel's learning, his syntactic complexity, and his Blakeian visionary influences—speaks through a more complex persona with a powerful sense of irony and the macabre. *Black and secret man* (1964) and *An idiot joy* (1967), which won a Governor General's Award (*Crusoe: poems new and selected*, 1973, contains poems from both volumes), deal with place as well as with the confrontation with self and reveal a more conversational and accessible poetry, and a progress towards Mandel's very spare style of the seventies.

Earle BIRNEY's remarkable and distinguished career as a poet, which began in 1942, continued apace in the sixties and seventies—with, notably, *Ice cod bell or stone* (1962), *Near False Creek mouth* (1964), two volumes of *Collected poems* (1966 and 1968), and the *Collected works of Earle Birney* (1975). *Rag and bone shop* (1970) experiments with typography and sound. The wonderful range of Birney's work covers several strains in Canadian poetry. His training in Anglo-Saxon poetics perhaps accounts in part for his attraction to the avant-garde sound and visual organization that influenced his concrete and sound poetry; but Birney also writes more conventional verse based on anecdote and light speculation, romantic lyrics, and meditations on unusual scenes or objects, often drawn from his travels, that are lightly handled philosophical poems presented in the classical manner.

Cry Ararat! poems new and selected (1967) by P.K. PAGE continues to exhibit her extraordinary ability to make complex visual images both accessible and ultimately mysterious. The imagery in the new poems is less glittery and crisp than in the earlier ones; in the poems set in Brazil it is intense and colourful. Characteristically, Page is witty and involved in treating the social world ('Photos of a salt mine', 'Poem in war time', 'The stenographers') and in capturing moments in the human comedy (in the section entitled 'The bands and the beautiful children').

Al PURDY too began to publish poetry— of a somewhat conventional nature—in the forties; but his career did not take off until the publication of *The Cariboo horses* (1965), an extremely successful volume that was enjoyed for its energy, humour, and sense of play. An engaging conversational line enriched by quick shifts of mood and tone in dealing with travel and anecdote characterizes his books of the sixties and seventies. His verse encompasses flat realism as well as idealism and combines spontaneity with romance, as in *Poems for all the Annettes* (1962), *Love in a burning building* (1970), and a selected poems, *Being alive: poems 1958-1978* (1978).

In the fifties the poetry of Phyllis WEBB was concerned with subtle changes in perception and understanding; her wit seemed influenced by Marianne Moore and her carefully structured verse created a demanding and rigorous environment. The intense, very carefully crafted work that has appeared since *Even your right eye* (1956) has fulfilled the promise of that collection. *Naked poems* (1965) is made up of several sequences of short poems in which compression of language cuts against, and reveals, strength of feeling. This volume was very influential among younger poets, as was her *Selected poems* (1971). Miriam WADDINGTON began to publish in the forties. In *The glass trumpet* (1966), *Say yes* (1969), and *Driving home: poems new and selected* (1972) there is a shift from angry responses to social conditions to a more personal and direct poetry that speaks of love, loss, places, aging, the gap between men and women, in attenuated short-lined poems that manage to be both tightly controlled and lyrical. This is the voice that continued to be heard in her subsequent collections.

Phyllis GOTLIEB's *Who knows one* (1961) was followed by *Within the zodiac* (1964) and *Ordinary, moving* (1969), her most interesting short collection. A learned and inventive poet, Gotlieb draws upon nursery rhymes, Petrarchan sonnets, popular songs, blues, and other familiar sound patterns, and experiments with literary typography as well as literary graffiti, in a witty and playful manner that sometimes produces *tours de force*. The spectacular long poem entitled 'Ordinary, moving'—echoing nursery rhymes, children's songs, lyrics recited by a bouncing ball, details of street life, and personal memory—is unified by witty and sometimes imperceptible transitions and a fine ear for colloquial cadences. Though employing quintessentially ordinary fragments of language, this poem carries the reader through the energy of its voices and transi-

tions. In 1978 Gotlieb published *The works: collected poems*.

Gwendolyn MacEWEN constructs her poetry by referring to a magical method that uses art and human love to unify a conflicted and divided world. *Breakfast for barbarians* (1966) and *The shadow maker* (1969) are her strongest books. In the latter her language becomes somewhat less esoteric and in *The armies of the moon* (1972) she links her personal psychic journeys with the exploration of outer space. Her most recent volumes include *Magic animals* (1974), *The fire eaters* (1976), and *The T.E. Lawrence poems* (1982).

With *The rose and the Puritan* (1958), *Bread, wine and salt* (1967), *Mysterious naked man* (1969), and *Between tears and laughter* (1971), Alden NOWLAN introduced a poetry that is humane and centred on human experience and understanding. His poems are character sketches—clear and unemphatic compressed narratives of the thwarted lives of people in rural and small-town Nova Scotia. More personal—without being confessional—are *I'm a stranger here myself* (1974) and *I might not tell everybody this* (1982), which contain self-knowing poems that are both conversational and controlled.

Patrick ANDERSON, who was active with the FIRST STATEMENT group in Montreal and whose strong volume of poems, *The colour as naked*, appeared in 1954, again revealed his subtle ear and talent for specificity in *A visiting distance* (1976) and in his selected poems, *Return to Canada* (1977). Fred COGSWELL, who published the work of many young poets during his more than thirty years as editor of Fiddlehead Press, shows mastery of a wide range of both traditional and modern forms in his own books of poetry, among which are *Star people* (1968), *Immortal ploughman* (1969), and *In praise of chastity* (1970). *A long apprenticeship: the collected poems of Fred Cogswell* appeared in 1980.

Milton ACORN started to publish in the 1960s, producing *The brain's the target* (1960), *Jaw breakers* (1963), *I've tasted my blood* (1969), and *More poems for people* (1972). His political commitment to Marxism is central to his poetry, which has an urban toughness and often focuses on political figures in relation to the common people. Full of urgency—partly owing to Acorn's use of alliteration to propel the lines forward—and radical egalitarian humanism, it shows a credible and serious concern for social change. *Captain Neil MacDougal and the naked goddess* (1982) is made up of sonnets with two voices, Acorn's and that of the goddess.

Dennis LEE's first volume was *Kingdom of absence* (1967), poems of personal and spiritual despair that experimented with sonnet variations. *Civil elegies* (1968) was a complex elegiac meditation on contemporary North American politics, the war in Vietnam and Canada's connection with it, and the country's loss of identity. It is an impressive volume, though its intended public voice is somewhat unrelieved in tone. These poems were revised for *Civil elegies and other poems* (1972), which won a Governor General's Award. *The gods* (1979) contains a previously published elegy on 'The death of Harold Ladoo' (q.v.) and a variety of short poems that experiment with typography, pace, and rhythm; several light love-lyrics; political ballads; and meditative poems of the sort we associate with Lee's earlier poetry expressing a philosophy that is almost religious in its search for a vision of wholeness in life. In the seventies Lee published four books of children's verse—*Alligator pie* (1974), *Nicholas Knock* (1974), *Garbage delight* (1977), and *The ordinary bath* (1979)—that are much beloved for their play with language and their celebration of the linguistic variety of Canada's place-names.

A significant impact on the progress of Canadian poetry was made in the sixties by a new movement in British Columbia that centred on the Vancouver publication TISH: *a poetry newsletter* (1961-9). The work of the *Tish* group was influenced by the theories of Charles Olson, Robert Duncan, Robert Creeley, and the American West Coast school that produced the Beat poets, and by the San Francisco renaissance associated with the City Lights bookstore. The most important theorist of this movement in Canada was Frank DAVEY, whose essays in *Tish*, and in OPEN LETTER, First Series (1965-9), helped to define its poetic goals and ideology. The Canadian west-coast writers sought a language for poetry that valued the colloquial voice above erudition and vitality above order; that emphasized not theme, but sound, open syntax, and the voice as an instrument of breathing. In this departure from what they saw as the academic formalism of eastern-Canadian writing, the flow and movement of the poem is the crucial poetic quality; poetry, indeed writing in general, is, in this view, a way of tracing the trajectories of perception, of creating a poem that is constantly happen-

ing, and in which writer and reader are fully alive. The movement was suspicious of metaphor and simile, which were seen as destroying the particularity and uniqueness of the objects of the universe in the drive to make meanings by describing things in terms of each other. Insisting that the idiosyncratic object or event, the local and the personal, were the only source of meaning in human experience, it encouraged a poetry of specific place and region, rather than a more national view of the Canadian poetic enterprise—thereby validating the locality of the west coast as an appropriate place for poetry. These beliefs influenced not only Davey, but George Bowering (a co-founder of *Tish*), Robert Kroetsch, Daphne Marlatt, Susan Musgrave, and many others.

Frank Davey's titles include *D Day and after* (1963), *City of the gulls and sea* (1964), *Weeds* (1970), *L'an trentième* (1972), *Arcana* (1973), and *Selected poems: the arches* (1980), edited and with an introduction by bp NICHOL. His early poetry is seen as competent but not very interesting. *Weeds*, though modest and thoughtful, is a more energetic and lively volume. His seventies' poems are satisfying poems of self-discovery in which the mythic and the personal unite in the present moment of writing and reading. Able to capture colloquial language and to use repetition to ring impressive changes on it, Davey writes a poetry of process that has substance, wit, and a personal humaneness.

George BOWERING began his prolific writing career in the sixties, producing *Sticks and stones* (1963); *Points on a grid* (1964), a volume of great variety and range; *Silver wire* (1966), which seems to discover an individual tone and manner; and *Baseball: a poem in the magic number 9* (1967), a *tour de force* in which a diamond-shaped text conveys the nine innings of baseball, with each position of the game used as a jumping-off point for words to leap across the page. The poem works out the implications of an analogy between playing baseball and writing poetry that is dependent on the notion of 'composition by field'. *Rocky Mountain foot* (1969) celebrates the landscape of Alberta, and *George, Vancouver* (1970) is a poem of exploration. There are two volumes of selected poems: *Touch: selected poems 1960-1970* (1971) and *Particular accidents: selected poems* (1980). Bowering's poetry reflects his interest in the *process* of thinking rather than its results. Bowering has combined his formal interests in phonetic spelling, oral verse, the colloquial and conversational line, and question-and-answer poems with a wish to celebrate personal and local history and experience.

bill BISSETT is an experimental poet of the primitive who uses massive repetition, chant, phonetic spelling, and typographical innovation to break down the conventional restricting structures of language in order to create a new sacred vision. In *Nobody owns th earth* (1971) his topics include political protest, and satiric pictures of contemporary urban values. At their best his poems are exuberant, playful, and ritualistic, with a vital and colloquial voice of their own, but by their very nature they constantly risk falling into the merely experimental and patterned, as in *Northern birds in colour* (1981).

bp NICHOL is the boldest and most versatile of Canada's experimental poets. A member of the poetry performance group The FOUR HORSEMEN, he is a prolific writer whose titles include *Journeying & the returns* (1967), *ABC: the aleph beth book* (1971), *Craft dinner* (1978), and *Silk water* (1970). His autobiographical *The martyrology* Books I & II (1972; rev.1977) and Books III & IV (1976) is the record of a conversation with himself. Interested in exploding the habits of language-use in order to discover and liberate what remains of language after the explosion, he tries in 'Naming' and 'Probable systems 9' (which both appear in *Selected writing: as elected*, 1980) to transfer the symbol system of mathematics to language. *ABC: the aleph beth book* experiments with the graphic design of the alphabet; *Nights on prose mountain* (1970) prints very simple individual poems on a series of cards that can be reordered and shuffled. Nichol has consistently tried to release the sound and emotion of poetry from the intellectual control of language. *Selected writing: as elected*, edited by bp Nichol and Jack David, is a fine introduction to his work.

Another notable feature of this period was the explosion of poetic energy on the Prairies. The long list of prairie poets, or poets who write about the Prairies, includes Anne MARRIOTT, John Newlove, Robert Kroetsch, George Bowering, Elizabeth BREWSTER, Dorothy LIVESAY, Miriam WADDINGTON, Eli Mandel, Gary GEDDES, Peter STEVENS, Douglas BARBOUR, Ken McRobbie, Sid MARTY, Dale ZIEROTH, Andrew SUKNASKI, Anne SZUMIGALSKI, and Kristjana Gunnars. One reason for this explosion is that the new experiments in colloquial, loosely conversational, anecdotal poetic language (partly launched by the *Tish* school)

seemed to suit the prairie poets' interest in the local and specific. Not suffering from a lack of ghosts, prairie poets have concerned themselves with such themes as space, landscape and movement, native people, unusual characters, ancestors, and the task of making human communities within vast isolated areas. There is often a tone of restrained humour in this poetry, and a tentative, somewhat hesitant speech.

John NEWLOVE's collections include *Grave sirs* (1962), *Mothers, and others* (1964), and *Moving in alone* (1965), an ironic volume of meditations about love. *Black night window* (1968) explores the poet's prairie origins, linking a meditation on place with a process of self-discovery and self-analysis. His later volumes, *The cave* (1970) and *Lies* (1972), are harsher, more ironic and troubled. His poems of place evoke the vastness of the Canadian West, its moral history, and its unacknowledged guilt. *The fat man: selected poems 1962-1972* (1977) has been followed by a newer tone of celebration in *The green plain* (1982).

Originally from the Prairies, Robert KROETSCH is both a novelist and a poet. His *Stone hammer poems* (1973) contains twelve versions of traditional Blackfoot stories about the trickster figure in Indian mythology. Kroetsch returns to the Prairies in *The ledger* (1975), which uses a record of his ancestors' family finances as a source of historical speculation about the shared past of the Prairies. His poetry, which transforms personal experience into myth and uses lists of names, places, and objects to celebrate the past, is colloquial, sometimes racy and audacious. *The sad Phoenician* (1979) is a meditative dialogue with himself and with his past loves, about language and poetry and their power in relation to time and loss. Written under the successive unfoldings of the signs of the Phoenician alphabet, it is an elegiac celebration of their largely forgotten gift to humankind. Kroetsch is interested in the possibilities of the long poem and of creative alternatives to narrative. *Field notes: the collected poetry of Robert Kroetsch* (1981) collects several previous volumes, including *Seed catalogue*—a meditation on the cultivation of poetry, including how to grow poetry on the prairie—into one continuing poem. The title *Field notes* puns on the post-modernist idea of 'composition by field' and suggests that these are notes taken in the field, preparatory to a larger, fuller, less discontinuous long poem of life—which of course can never be written.

3. THE SEVENTIES AND AFTER. The Canadian tradition of distinguished narrative poetry continues unabated from the fifties to the beginning of the eighties. E.J. PRATT's powerful figure stands behind this tradition, but it is authenticated through its own continuities, perhaps because there are stories still to be told for the first time. Louis DUDEK has written narratives of the fate of culture; Eli MANDEL's *Life sentence* (1980) seems to suggest the discovery of a kind of self-questioning narrative later in his poetic career. Daphne Marlatt's work creates communal narrative out of oral history (*Steveston*) or thinks again about the abiding power of the same old story (*Frames*). Andrew Suknaski, collecting the stories of his region and its settlement, has fewer questions about the validity of narrative; his tales and anecdotes build up a layered narrative of place that achieves monumental presence (*Wood mountain poems*). Michael ONDAATJE's *The collected works of Billy the Kid* and *Coming through slaughter* inhabit the unclear border between prose and poetry, where narrative seems to emerge from the collision of intense bits of sensory data. We even have a few traditional narratives, such as Florence McNeil's *The Overlanders* (1982), a chronicle of a remarkable woman's journey to the gold fields of British Columbia in the 1860s.

The Gothic strain in Canadian poetry continues largely in the female line and ranges over esoteric knowledge and exotic lore in the work of Gwen MacEWEN and Phyllis GOTLIEB, or from within a world of incantation and wordpower in some of the Haida-inspired works of Susan MUSGRAVE (*Songs of a sea witch* [1970], *The impstone* [1976]). Margaret ATWOOD's Gothicism, transmitted through her cool sensibility, seems more northern European. There is a cool mysticism with a Gothic edge in the poetry of Kristjanna Gunnars. At worst the Gothic falls into a kind of witch-ridden sentimentality.

If the Gothic is a largely female strain in recent Canadian verse, surrealism seems the purview of the men. It ranges from the outrageous and exuberant play of Joe ROSENBLATT's poetry (*Bumblebee dithyramb,* 1972), to a sense of the absurd and ironic in Ondaatje's juxtapositions, or to J. Michael Yates's grandeur. Robert Priest's *The visible man* (1980), which contains poetry full of flashes of insight, is sometimes surreal without appearing to know that it is. Imaginative in a strange way, he takes inordinate chances with logic, countering absurdity with absurdity, and expanding our sense of human emotional possibilities. His poetry, which is neither solemn nor self-mocking, is beyond irony; distanced from human sensation, it is yet not unfeeling. This surrealism seems to be partly a legacy of the earlier experimental work done in the sixties and early seventies.

Erudition returns, but in a new form: the learning in seventies' poetry is less likely to be European and high literary; the erudition ranges from a profound rethinking of biblical images and concepts in the works of Robert Bringhurst, to a meditation based on scientific attention to the details of geology and botany in the works of Christopher Dewdney; from serious, organized, and detailed research into local history and oral history by Daphne Marlatt (*Steveston*) and Andrew Suknaski (*Wood Mountain poems*), to a rich and complex knowledge of the social history of foods (David Donnell), the myths of Iceland (Kristjanna Gunnars), or of the North (J. Michael Yates). The learning evinced by this poetry seems not so much a means of confirming the authors' seriousness or right to speak as a way of suggesting that such knowledge enables a pre-existent voice or vision to express itself. While innovative and promising Canadian poetry is being written today, no single, clearly superior poet looms whose voice and presence spring forward as obviously and powerfully as those of Layton in the late fifties, of Purdy in the early sixties, of Atwood and Lee and Ondaatje in the late sixties and early seventies.

The long, loose, conversational and anecdotal line is being subjected to scrutiny in this period. One senses that not only the new erudition, but also a wish for more texture, animates this new verse. Sometimes this texture denotes a complex rethinking or reinventing of ways of representing consciousness (e.g., Marlatt), or an examination of personal relations that are neither sentimental nor paradox-ridden, but genuinely complex (Anne Szumilgaski, Kristjanna Gunnars, Andrew Suknaski, Bronwen Wallace, Frank DAVEY's new poems, Erin Mouré, Ondaatje). Poetry based merely on the contemplation of an image seems to have exhausted much of its energy (except perhaps in the works of Roo Borson), as has poetry about a generalized Canada or the wilderness. Experimental poetry is less prominent in the late seventies and early eighties than it was in the sixties, though much has been learned from it and assimilated into something like the mainstream of Canadian poetry.

The new poets who seem most original vary widely in both manner and subject matter. Daphne MARLATT began publishing in the late sixties, starting out with the second group of poets in the TISH movement. Each of her volumes has represented an experiment in the use of language, in narrative form, in line length and construction, and in trying to represent the movement of consciousness rather than external events or objects. Her writing is informed by a high degree of theoretical awareness that nonetheless does not drown out or pre-empt her impressive poetry. *Frames of a story* (1968) retells the 'Snow Queen' from a variety of shifting perspectives and in a variety of styles. *Steveston* (1974) is based on an oral history of the town of Steveston in British Columbia. *Vancouver poems* (1972) tries to define and recreate a sense of place and local history as forms of consciousness. Another sequence of poems, *Our lives* (1980), contains five stories in a prose-poetry long line that allows Marlatt to explore new kinds of poetic rhythm and placement of words. *Selective writings: net work* (1980), edited by Fred WAH, is an excellent representative collection.

Dale ZIEROTH published his first book, *Clearing: poems from a journey* (1973), as a series of poems about the history of his ancestors on the Prairies. His second volume, *Mid-river* (1981), has a quiet authority. Though his wit is so far underdeveloped, his voice is careful, modest, and possesses a humorous wisdom. He writes about family and friends, about the landscape of the mountains in British Columbia, in plain, unpretentious, rather Wordsworthian language.

Patrick LANE, after publishing several interesting small collections, established his highly respected place as one of the finest poets to have emerged in the last decade when Oxford published his *Poems new and selected* (1978). He writes tense and explosive poetry with an energy of its own that is headstrong but controlled.

The work of Pier Giorgio DI CICCO is uneven in quality. Anti-intellectual, he succeeds best with foreshortened narratives about family, and though the combative stance of his poetry is occasionally appealing, it is often merely annoying and assumed. The energy in his poetry suggests both the flaws and strengths of a writer of

promise with an assertive even aggressive voice: he is the Irving Layton of his generation—prolific, exuberant, with an interest in values. *The tough romance* (1979) is a strong and representative volume.

J. Michael YATES in *The Great Bear Lake meditations* (1970) explodes the boundaries of philosophical musing; he displays an intense merging of mind and sensation in his dramatization of the meeting between a human consciousness and the natural world, in a modern manifestation of the sublime.

Another poet with a feeling for the sublime in human nature as well as in the natural world is Robert Bringhurst, whose most achieved volume to date is *Bergschrund* (1975). His interest in mountains and stone seems linked to an unyielding quality in the voice of his poems and in his deployment of images. There is an authority in these images, and in the way he uses his erudition. Bringhurst is an interesting poet—a word-finder with a remarkably discerning though daring ear, and an acute mind. His poems on Old Testament figures, or figures from Greek thought and literature, have a genuine ease and wit, but his rather remote oratorical voice inspires respect rather than a warm identification with the poet.

Christopher Dewdney's poetry is distinctive for its use of technical terms and concepts and for the unusual range of subjects from which it draws its analogies. The exploration of scientific systems of thought as sources of analogies for the way language functions or the way poetry comes into being is appealing; much of Dewdney's work, however, becomes an implicit 'defense of poesy', arguing that all forms of knowing are ultimately, or fundamentally, like poetry. *Fovea centralis* (1975) uses the science of fossils and geology to explore these issues. *Alter sublime* (1980) is also interested in the semantic potential of language, drawing its analogies from the process and structure of the DNA molecule, from static electricity, and from the nerve structure of the human brain. Though this gives his work an air of wilful objectivity, of reluctance to be personal, his poems do contain a poignant resonance. *Predators of the adoration: selected poems 1972-1982* will be published in Nov. 1983.

A strong new poet to appear on the scene in the seventies is Andrew SUKNASKI, whose first volume, *Wood Mountain poems* (1976), collected with the help of Al PURDY and Dennis LEE, is a powerful and impressive book. It contains documentary poetry that recreates the history of southwest Saskatchewan through the voices of its people: Indians, homesteaders of various nationalities, and their survivors in the present. The presentation of this history in shifting viewpoints—the live two-way relation between past and present—gives the volume a double focus or two sources of energy. Suknaski has extended his documentary and voice-creating impulses to other groups of people in this region in *The ghosts call you poor* (1978) and *The name of Narid* (1981), which also addresses contemporary issues in the Ukrainian community.

Another impressive poet to appear on the Prairies is Anne SZUMIGALSKI, whose *Woman reading in bath* (1974) heralds a difficult and exhilarating new voice. The poems are spoken by many different personae in a range of ages and situations in life, articulating their idiosyncratic points of view. *A game of angels* (1980) continues the power and crispness of perception of the earlier collection in a series of stunning dramatic monologues.

Mary di Michele's poems are admired for their evocation of family life in an immigrant Italian urban community. *Mimosa and other poems* (1980) has three speakers from such a family, a father and two daughters—with a silent, present, mother. The volume contains poems spoken by Edvard Munch, and by a poet-painter with polio. The range, however, is less forcefully achieved than Szumilgaski's.

David Donnell's poetry is strong, intelligent, and genuinely idiosyncratic. Its humour devolves from the way it uses erudition, and from the varied tone that is never merely easily ironic in its willingness to court embarrassment and ridiculousness and come back from that edge. His weirdly lovable second collection, *Dangerous crossings* (1980), repays attention.

Roo BORSON in *Rain* (1980) and *A sad device* (1981) uses images and objects to delineate states of mind. Her work shows a propensity for gentle allegory; her wit and coolly personal manner allow identification with the otherness of creaturely life. The tone of her poems—somewhere between expressiveness and flatness—has a peculiar charm that comes from its being free of any sense of deliberate mystification.

The poems in *Empire, York Street* (1979), the first book by another young poet, Erin Mouré, show a relation to personal experience and consciousness that is neither self-aggrandizing nor merely cool and distant.

Inhabiting the border where perception, sensation, and intellectual comprehension meet, Mouré's work has a political edge that is genuinely argumentative, and—unusual in Canadian poetry—a sense of place or historical event conveyed together with the pressure and presence of large numbers of people, who are neither ghosts nor ancestors but seem to exist in the present.

Finally, a volume by Kristjanna Gunnars, *One-eyed moon maps* (1980), retells Norse myth with a modern edge and sees the Icelandic tradition as giving access to 'the other eye' of human vision, associated with the moon and with secret knowledge. The poems, with their short, crisp lines, have a slightly imagistic aura.

Nothing bears better witness to the poetry explosion of the last two decades in Canada than the publication in 1982 of *The new Oxford book of Canadian verse*, edited by Margaret Atwood, in which 72 of its 121 poets are talents new to Canadian poetry since A.J.M. SMITH's edition of 1960.

CHAVIVA HOŠEK

Poetry in French. Canadian poetry in French has been, for a century and a half, a screen to mask the community's sense of deprivation. More often than one would imagine, poets have used the Indian as the analogy of precarious survival. The myth of the land, frequently using the biblical typology of the ploughman who works with God, sublimates a harsh and tedious existence. Catholic piety, occasionally vibrantly alive—as in the poetry of Roger Brien, Clément MARCHAND, and, supremely, of Rina LASNIER—sublimates the rest of life. Encouraged by Romantic melancholy or pale post-Symbolist self-effacement, the poet of the inter-war years seeks an elsewhere, heavenly or European, to compensate for the here and now, or indulges in a barely disguised death-wish. Death and exile are, throughout, the prevailing themes of a poetry that is the skilful transposition into art of a permanently vulnerable culture. Rebellion is muted, shamefaced. Here and there—and increasingly since the Second World War—there are traces of what has been fittingly named the walk towards the sun. The spiritual blockade of French Canada has been lifted by a handful of authentic poets who have challenged the consensus and brought the thaw—the spring that with Anne HÉBERT burst violently on the city. This evolution makes possible the Dionysiac espousal of the Sun, symbol of virile self-

Poetry in French

affirmation, of honest self-appraisal, and of the collective will to live, not merely to survive. The poets discussed below will be related to this tradition, slightly less well-known poets being given some prominence at the expense of those given a separate entry elsewhere.

1. A NECESSARY PREHISTORY. A few expatriate Frenchmen signpost the otherwise prosaic French régime. Marc Lescarbot translated his awesome apprehension of a continent and the founding of a civilization into the heroic stanzas of *Les muses de la Nouvelle France* (Paris, 1609). (See Writing in NEW FRANCE.) Joseph QUESNEL, who arrived from France in 1778, wrote a pastoral operetta, *Colas et Colinette* (Québec, 1808); and, in 1803, a satire on the anglophile bourgeoisie, *L'Anglomanie*, which can be read in La BARRE DU JOUR (juill.–déc. 1965). Joseph Mermet and Napoléon AUBIN were Europeans who contributed patriotic verse to early nineteenth-century journalism. But the important milestones in this essential prehistory are, first, the 'chants héroïques jaillis du peuple', inspired by conflict with the English or by the adventures of the fur trade, discussed by Jeanne d'Arc Lortie in *La Poésie nationaliste au Canada français, 1606-1867* (1975)—poems like those of Pierre FALCON, or the relatively few folksongs penned in Canada that offer glimpses of popular values and the life of the people: songs like 'Vive la Canadienne', which speaks of festivities that 'finissent par mettre tout sens dessus dessous' and point to a popular culture despised and neglected by the devotees of staid official verse. Second, tribute must be paid to the tireless efforts of Michel Bibaud (1782-1837), the Montreal newspaper publisher, to create a flourishing French-language journalism in Québec and a literary tradition with it. Bibaud's *Épitres, satires, chansons, épigrammes et autres pièces de vers* (1830; rpr. 1969), a collection of verse previously published in his papers, was the first literary work in French published in Canada. In his own satires he castigates his fellow-Québécois for their illiteracy and superstition, but hails the founding of classical colleges, which he hopes will make his satire redundant. He is remembered not for his poetry but for the vision and tenacity that underlie his 'amour de rimer'.

The patriotic movement of the 1830s, which came to a head in 1837-8, inspired a number of poets—some of them publishing anonymously—to celebrate the cause of political reform and to honour those who suffered for it. Notable among them is Joseph-Guillaume Barthe (1818-93), who was extensively anthologized by James Huston.

2. THE ROMANTICS: GARNEAU TO FRÉCHETTE. Québec literature was born in the 1840s with François-Xavier GARNEAU's vigorous response to the derogatory Durham Report in his history of Canada, which offered his compatriots 'un juste sujet d'orgueil et un motif de généreuse émulation'. Garneau's poetry, never collected in his lifetime, was anthologized by James Huston, whose four-volume *Le Répertoire national* saved other verse, including that of Mermet and Aubin already mentioned, from the fate of the ephemeral political news-sheets in which it was printed. Garneau's poems, patriotic and historical, lament the passing of the 'dernier Huron' and attempt to revitalize a 'peuple submergé par la fatalité'. Huston also included numerous poems by Joseph Lenoir-Rolland (1822-61), who was too obviously inspired by Lamartine but learned from his French model vigour and limpidity. His poetry was published posthumously in *Poèmes épars* (1916).

The hub of the Romantic revival was the bookshop of the Crémazie brothers in the 1850s. Here, the members of the MOUVEMENT LITTÉRAIRE DE QUÉBEC met to read Chateaubriand, Lamartine, Hugo, and Musset. Octave CRÉMAZIE was a national hero in his time for his 'Vieux soldat canadien' and his 'Drapeau de Carillon'. In these bookshop meetings Louis FRÉCHETTE, the other national poet of French Canada, decorated by the Académie française, was inspired to a lifelong dedication to poetry. His personal contribution was his attempt to write a large-scale work proportionate to the continent in *La légende d'un peuple* (1887), inspired by Hugo's *Légende des siècles*. Charles GILL and Robert CHOQUETTE are the only others to have taken up this challenge. Fréchette's young friend Eudore Evanturel might have been Québec's best poet had his *Premières poésies* (1878; rpr. 1979), prefaced by Joseph MARMETTE, not been severely attacked on moral grounds by the critics. He strikes the pose of Musset's rakish heroes, Rolla or Mardoche, and over half his poems are love poems, marked by a discreet and innocent sensuality and regret that love remains unrequited. Evanturel, later private secretary to Francis Parkman, achieved a rare personal style and a delightful conversational prosaicness that was refreshingly natural among the romantic posturings of his contemporaries. An obscure civil servant like Alfred Garneau

(1836-1904; the son of François-Xavier) can occasionally surprise and delight us with his exquisite short poems, published posthumously by his son Hector as *Poésies* (1904).

Abbé H.-R. CASGRAIN, the most influential literary figure in the nineteenth century, favoured art with clear moral intentions. Poets encouraged by him wrote on themes inspired by the reigning ideology: 'le laboureur', the ploughman who 'collabore avec Dieu', or 'notre langue' from William CHAPMAN's *Les aspirations* (1904), 'faite pour chanter les gloires d'autrefois', and 'les colons' from Pamphile LEMAY's *Les Gouttelettes* (1904) or some of his religious verse. The poems in these collections are typical of many others written in the second half of the nineteenth century that unite in a common theme French Canada's divine mission, the cult of the past, the cult of the soil, and the heroism of the pioneer. The finest of the 'poètes du terroir' is Nérée BEAUCHEMIN. A critical edition of his prose and poetry has been prepared by Armand Guilmette (3 vols, 1974).

3. L'ÉCOLE LITTÉRAIRE DE MONTRÉAL: A CANADIAN PARNASSUS. A generation of poets was born in the late seventies. These were the bourgeois bohemians of the ÉCOLE LITTÉRAIRE DE MONTRÉAL, which was not so much a school as a disparate crowd of friends who despised Montreal, patriotism, 'the plough and the sword', and were dazzled by the French poetic tradition of Art for Art's sake. Jean CHARBONNEAU, poet philosopher; Arthur de Bussières (1877-1913), infusing oriental mysticism into his elegant escapist sonnets; Abbé Joseph Melançon (1877-1956), whose pseudonym was 'Lucien Rainier', with his collected poems *Avec ma vie* (1931); Charles GILL, one of the rare Québécois to attempt narrative verse in his ambitious *Le Cap Éternité* (1919)—all take second place to the brilliant, tragic Émile NELLIGAN. The Nelligan legend tends to obscure the achievement of another tragic figure in the *École* group, Albert LOZEAU, who explored with great sensitivity his restricted existence—he was crippled with Pott's disease—in his *Ame solitaire* (1907), for example; and of the dedicated servant of the *École*, Louis-Joseph Doucet (1874-1959), named 'Prince des poètes' by his fellow poets. This self-effacing regionalist poet published nearly thirty collections of verse in his lifetime and left a further thousand sonnets unpublished. He wrote as easily as he thought and as naturally as he breathed.

4. PROBLEMATIC STARS. The poets of the generations following the heyday of the *École* continue to adopt a very private stance. Guillaume Lahaise ('Guy Delahaye') returned from a year in Paris to work in the psychiatric clinic of Saint-Jean-de-Dieu. His subtle, highly polished poems recognize that life lies in the tiny impulses of the heart, cardiogrammed in *Les phases* (1910). Jean-Aubert LORANGER spent a year in Paris in the early twenties and then returned to his 'pays sans amour'. His poems, influenced by Éluard and the poets of the *NRF*, display the delicious restraint of Québec poetry: 'La mer bruit au bout du jardin' (Québec poetry is a closed garden in which the outside world is heard as a faint rustling). In his modern edition of Loranger's *Les atmosphères* (1970), Gilles MARCOTTE presented this little-known poet to his 'true contemporaries'. Paul MORIN's *Poèmes de cendre et d'or* (1922) prolongs the elegant, ethereal ideal of the Mediterranean world of his happiest years. *Le coeur en exil* (1913) of René Chopin (1885-1953), published in Paris, his 'patrie intellectuelle', explores all the current themes: solitude, winter, 'la splendeur du vide'. To this group of expatriates belongs Simone Routier-Drouin, an elusive poet torn between a taste for the void and a nagging sense of unrealized potential in *Tentations* (1934); but she might also be considered along with other often convent-bred sensitive feminine voices of the thirties, including Jovette-Alice BERNIER, Eva Sénécal in *La course dans l'aurore* (1929), Medjé Vézina in *Chaque heure a son visage* (1934), Cécile Chabot in *Vitrail* (1939), and Jeannine Bélanger in *Stances à l'éternel absent* (1941). Alongside this world of poetic propriety, Québec produced a number of fiercely original voices: Émile CODERRE ('Jean Narrache'), poet of the wretched misery of the urban poor; Rodolphe DUBÉ ('François Hertel'), who escaped to Paris from the confines of his province and his religious order; Alfred DESROCHERS, whom Saint-Denys Garneau greeted, on the publication of *A l'ombre de l'Orford* (1929), as the first to assimilate the skills of European poets while preserving intact and expressing perfectly the soul of Canada; and Rina LASNIER, who achieved an inimitable blend of sensuality and mysticism that defies critical appraisal. Gaston MIRON, in an essay of 1957, acknowledged two of these lonely voices: Alphonse Piché and Isabelle Legris. The latter's collected verse, *Le sceau de l'ellipse* (1979), contains her spirited and sensi-

tive *Ma vie tragique* (1947). But the inter-war years belong to three poets: Hector de Saint-Denys GARNEAU, Félix-Antoine SAVARD—in his prose poem, MENAUD, MAÎTRE-DRAVEUR (1937)—and Alain GRANDBOIS. Thanks to them, whereas 'you had to apologize in 1934 for being a poet, by 1944 you had almost to apologize for not being one' (Jacques Blais).

5. THE HEXAGONE YEARS: 1953 TO 1963. Gaston MIRON, and the other poets and film-makers who founded the Hexagone press in 1953, dedicated to 'action through publishing', acknowledged their debt to GRANDBOIS and to the manifesto REFUS GLOBAL (1948), in which Paul-Émile Borduas and his group rejected the past and called for a magic release from fear and self-disgust. The first publication of the Hexagone group was a joint poetry collection, *Deux sangs* (1954), by Miron and Olivier Marchand. Among the other poets Hexagone published, Gilles HÉNAULT, Roland GIGUÈRE, and Paul-Marie LAPOINTE come first chronologically in giving Québec poets a new vocabulary, new eyes, new rhythms. New too was their commitment to art on a wide front and the priority they gave to art in their lives. Strong links with the visual arts, as with music, become a matter of course. Jean-Guy PILON and Miron added to their writing the role of public promoter of the arts, creating an audience and stimulating publishing through broadcasts or in public meetings. Miron, fearing that publication meant automatic assimilation into the bourgeois literary establishment and alienation from a possible mass audience, refused to allow his poems to be collected for publication until as late as 1970; his *L'homme rapaillé* (1970) won the Prix de la Revue *Études françaises*, among several other prizes. Fernand OUELLETTE summed up the literary camaraderie of Hexagone and the journal LIBERTÉ in his poem 'Et nous aimions'.

Pierre TROTTIER in *Le Combat contre Tristan* (1951) relates the French-Canadian condition to the myths and themes of universal typology. Anne HÉBERT in *Le tombeau des rois* (1953) continues her cousin Saint-Denys GARNEAU's analysis of the Québec sense of non-being before expressing the violent explosion of new-found life in *Mystère de la parole* (1960). Guy ROBERT's edition of the major part of the prose and poetry of Sylvain GARNEAU, *Objets retrouvés* (1965), which contains the previously unpublished poetic journal *La bleue*, is a tribute to the balance between tradition and originality

achieved by this poet who died in 1953 at the age of 23. Most of the poetry of the fifties is taken up with a diagnosis of what Miron calls 'la vie agonique'—Québec's experience of death in life. In sharp contrast, Gatien LAPOINTE marked the new beginnings of the sixties with *Le temps premier* (1962), an eloquent reconciliation with the earth that in the theme of the 'pays réinventé' becomes the chief preoccupation of the decade. Similarly rooted in a harsh but vividly insistent reality, the contribution of Pierre PERRAULT to the poetry of this period has been acknowledged in two collected volumes of his work published in the elegant Hexagone retrospective collection: *Chouennes* (1975) and *Gélivures* (1977).

6. THE 'SHOUTING SIGNPAINTERS'. Malcolm Reid gave this title to a book (1972) about Québec in the sixties, when poetry became briefly a public act, a process culminating in the 'Night of poetry' of Feb. 1970 and the 'Poèmes et chants de la révolution' of 1971, written in protest against the application of the War Measures Act. Reid's title translates that of Paul CHAMBERLAND's *L'afficheur hurle* (1965), in which Chamberland says he passed from the *themes* of the fifties to the *problems* of the sixties—from poetry to politics. (Reid's book includes a translation of part of *Afficheur*.) Gérald GODIN, who went on to become a PQ minister, forged a virile and sturdy poetic language in his *Cantouques* (1967) and *Libertés surveillées* (1975). Paul Chamberland invented in a single title, *Terre Québec* (1964), a poem, a manifesto, and an 'art poétique'. Michèle LALONDE went even further, in *Speak white* (1974), in bending the vituperative force of racy, popular speech to the particular purposes of her anger. Over the PARTI PRIS years hangs the shadow of Claude GAUVREAU, a signatory of REFUS GLOBAL, who made fitful but dramatic public appearances until his much-publicized suicide in 1971. *Parti pris* published the 1300-page volume of his *Oeuvres créatrices complètes* (1971). The sixties saw two other important groups at work: women writers still absorbed in a private sensuality, and singer-poets. Monique BOSCO, poet of elegant melancholy, punctuated with racy flashes of pique, published *Jéricho* (1971). Marie Laberge in *Reprendre souffle* (1972) mixed nostalgia with allusions to an importunate, ugly reality. Cécile CLOUTIER, in *Mains de Sable* (1960), attempted the difficult art of the haiku. Suzanne PARADIS, novelist and poet, has gradually built up her reputation with a dozen

collections in twenty years, and become an able poetry critic. Of the monologuists, poet-singers, and songwriters, mention must be made of Claude PÉLOQUIN, Raoul DUGUAY, Georges Dor, Gilles VIGNEAULT, Félix LECLERC, Yvon Deschamps, Clémence Desrochers, and Raymond Lévesque, who broke the silence of the Quiet Revolution. Many see in the prolific Gilbert LANGEVIN one of the more seriously underrated of Québec's outstanding poet/songwriters. In *Mon refuge est un volcan* (1978) he says, 'cet enfer amical est notre domaine'.

It is a little premature to do real justice to the achievement of Acadian poets and singers. Since its founding in 1963, the bilingual campus at Moncton, N.B., has become a focus for the elaboration of an Acadian identity and voice. A few promising poets are beginning to make names for themselves: Guy Arsenault, Raymond Leblanc, Herménégilde Chiasson, Léonard Forest, and Ronald DESPRÉS. See ACADIAN LITERATURE.

7. DISMANTLING LYRICISM. In the late fifties and early sixties Yves PRÉFONTAINE insistently explored the myth of the inhospitable North as the symbol of the spiritual paralysis and aphasia threatening the emerging poetry of Québec. From *Boréal* (1957; rpr. 1967) to *Débâcle* (1970) he moved from the theme of the difficulty of being to that of the land rediscovered and repossessed. The poets of the sixties rejected a too-cerebral poetry in favour of what Fernand OUELLETTE calls 'la démence charnelle', most notably expressed in the poems of Pierre MORENCY, Michel BEAULIEU, and Alexis LEFRANÇOIS. To these should be added the Moroccan-born Juan Garcia, awarded the Prix de la Revue *Études françaises* for his *Corps de gloire* (1971), which includes his earlier *Alchimie du corps* (1967); Marcel Bélanger in *Prélude à la parole* (1967) and *Plein-vent* (1971); and Pierre Mathieu in *Ressac* (1969), *Interlune* (1970), and *Mots dits québécois* (1971). Others in their wake have stressed the corporeal and the phenomenological: Roger des Roches has explored the latent eroticism in the act of writing (*Le corps certain*, 1975), as has Philippe Haeck in *Nattes* (1974) and *Les dents volent* (1976). Pierre Nepveu, serene and confident, typifies the new maturity of Québec culture in works such as *Couleur chair* (1980). Claude Beausoleil offers, in *Ahuntsic dream* (1975) and *Sens interdit* (1976), the acceptable face of Surrealism and a refreshing sense of humour.

8. THE SEVENTIES AND BEYOND. All the hidden assumptions with which history has loaded literary genres were challenged in the 1970s. The outstanding development of the Québec cultural scene in this period has been the feminist rewriting of the rules. Women writers have unmasked violently, humorously, or lyrically what they consider the phallocentric conspiracy of 4,000 years of writing and the patriarchal culture of death. Central to this movement is Louky Bersianik's astonishing summum of antimysoginist theory, *L'euguélionne* (1976), 400 pages of fable, fact, and fantasy. Nicole BROSSARD freely interchanges poetry, essay, and fiction. A line from Yolande Villemaire's *Que du stage blood* (1977) sums up this important rewriting of a convention: 'Je est une autre.' Madeleine Gagnon seeks to create a feminine consciousness and mythology, principally in *Lueur* (1979), where she blurs interestingly the boundaries between poetry, fiction, and essay. France Théoret, in *Bloody Mary* (1977), violently records the bitterness of awakening to squalid and abortive womanhood and hails Mary, the eternal feminine martyr. Josée Yvon, as her title *Filles-commandos bandées* (1976) suggests, relishes brutal verbal terrorism across the frontiers of sexual ambiguity. The tragically early death in 1981 of Marie Uguay—author of *Signe et rumeur* (1976) and *L'outre-vie* (1979)—has robbed Québec of another member of this vociferous sisterhood.

The proliferation of literary magazines in the seventies provided a public for an ever-increasing number of poets and a focal point for poetic creation and experiment. Sometimes this experimentation takes extreme forms: Claude GAUVREAU's thunder of syllables; Raoul DUGUAY's jazz poetry, accompanied by manifestos on 'le stéréo-poème audio-visuel'; Luc Racine's *Les Dormeurs* (1966), inspired by serial composition in music; Lucien Francoeur's typographical experiments in *Les grands spectacles* (1974); Guy ROBERT's concrete poetry; Roger Soublière's poetry in a tin can for the supermarket age; the poem-hoarding, the poem-collage, the poem-postcard, the poem-gag, and even the poem-trips and violent pornography of Denis Vanier in *Lesbiennes d'acid* (1972).

The influence on the BARRE DU JOUR aesthetic of the French journal *Tel Quel*, and the French formalists, is evident in such writers as Jean-Yves Collette, Michel Gay, and André Beaudet, who see themselves in a pre-literary phase where lyricism has to be dismantled, the language of creation exploded, and the text sabotaged, in order to lay bare the unconscious mechanisms enshrined in syntax and idiom.

But this radical questioning of the act of creation is also an acknowledgement of a failure to communicate. Michel Leclerc in *La traversée du réel, précédé de Dorénavant la poésie* (1977) asks whether it is worth writing in a world hopelessly confused with violence and dust. André Beauregard adopts a similar uncertainty in *Changer la vie* (1974), a title he takes from Rimbaud. For Robert Mélançon, poetry is *Peinture aveugle* (1979) because of its limited visuality. Hope is present in all these poets, but minimally—reduced to what Pierre Laberge calls, in *Vue du corps précédé de Au lieu de mourir* (1979), 'le désir d'adhérer'.

The variety and extreme individuality of the poets writing since the collapse of consensus in 1970 is well illustrated by the counter-cultural movement, which has spread principally from the United States. Aiming to reassert the values of personal freedom and pleasure, to release primitive impulses and save the quality of life from the consequences of rapid industrialization and urbanization, it flouts social prejudice and stereotyping by noisily espousing homosexuality and the liberalization of sex and drugs; hence the importance accorded to personal contacts, informality, and workshop-methods of literary production. A parallel reaction against materialism has favoured transcendentalism and the supernatural. A bibliography compiled by Ghislaine Houle and Jacques Lafontaine, *Écrivains québécois de nouvelle culture* (1975), provides an excellent introduction to the subject. See also *Québec underground, 1962-1972* (3 vols, 1973).

Seen in perspective, Canadian poetry in French offers an exciting example of a culture, in search of its identity and its voice, that has in many respects found both these things. In using poetry to attempt to express the unspeakable and indefinable, Québécois poets are often more linguistically adventurous and innovative than their European counterparts. Love—pursued with a single-minded faith and tenacity, but often seen as impossible—and Québécois anguish, are abiding themes. Yet, while the tone is invariably sad and sombre, hope and the celebration of life break through time and time again. This transcendence is supremely evident in Gaston MIRON's 'Tête de caboche', which expresses the pure instinct for freedom; in Fernand OUELLETTE's unashamed eroticism and spirit of camaraderie; in Jacques BRAULT's glowing tribute to his mother in *La poésie, ce matin* (1971); in Michèle LALONDE's contribution to the collective howl of rage of the sixties; and in the work of Michel GARNEAU, who wrote in *Les petits chevals amoureux* (1977) 'un des plus beaux hymnes au plaisir' (André BROCHU).

C.R.P. MAY

Polk, James. See NOVELS IN ENGLISH 1960 TO 1982: OTHER TALENTS, OTHER WORKS: 2.

Pollock, Sharon (b. 1936). Sharon Chalmers was born in Fredericton, N.B., the daughter of a physician and one-time New Brunswick MLA, Everett Chalmers, and spent her early years in the Eastern Townships of Québec, returning to Fredericton to attend the University of New Brunswick for two years. In 1954 she married Ross Pollock; they later separated. She first began acting in amateur theatre in New Brunswick and later in Calgary as a member of a touring company, Prairie Players; she won a Dominion Drama Festival Best Actress Award for her appearance in *The knack* in 1966. Not only an actress, but also a playwright and director, she has worked in many Canadian theatres, as well as for radio. She was a playwriting instructor at the University of Alberta (1976-7), playwright-in-residence at Alberta Theatre Projects, Calgary (1977-9), and head of the Playwrights' Colony at the Banff School of Fine Arts (1977-9). She has lived in Vancouver and Edmonton, but now makes her home in Calgary.

Pollock's plays are marked by a strong commitment to political and social issues drawn both from the past and from contemporary life. An exception is her first play, a black comedy entitled *A compulsory option* (1972), written in 1971 and premièred at the New Play Centre, Vancouver, the following year. Her next work, the historical chronicle *Walsh* (1974), first indicated her more characteristic concerns. Structured in the episodic manner of the epic theatre, it explores the treatment of Sitting Bull and his people when they fled to Canada after the pyrrhic victory of Little Big Horn. It was first performed at Theatre Calgary and was then revised and mounted on Stratford's Third Stage in 1974. The Vancouver Playhouse premièred Pollock's next two plays: *Out goes you* (1975), a satiric comedy on contemporary B.C. politics, and *The*

Komagata Maru incident (1978), a stern indictment, in presentational style, of Canadian racism based on a historical event in 1914 when a shipload of Sikh immigrants was denied permission to land from Vancouver harbour.

One tiger to a hill, which premièred at the Citadel Theatre, Edmonton (Feb. 1980), was subsequently revised for production at Festival Lennoxville the following summer and the Manhattan Theatre Club, New York, in the fall. Inspired by the New Westminster prison hostage-taking of 1975 in which a classification officer was shot, it attacks Canadian institutional complacency and public apathy about prison reform. Blood relations, Pollock's study of the famous New England spinster Lizzie Borden, acquitted by the courts for the axe murder of her parents in 1892, was first produced at Theatre 3, Edmonton, in Mar. 1980. It marks a notable shift of emphasis, focusing on private life and the complexities of personality and relationships within a family. Structurally it is Pollock's most sophisticated drama, taking the form of a play-within-a-play: ten years after the acquittal, Lizzie's actress friend (probably the historical Nance O'Neill) acts out the crucial scenes at the time of the murders, responding to stage directions from Lizzie herself. The play explores not only the ambiguities of evidence, but also the social repressions of a middle-class spinster in the late nineteenth century. A more conventionally naturalistic work followed: Generations, first written for radio and premièred on stage at Alberta Theatre Projects, Calgary, in Oct., 1980. It also evokes family tensions, but its conflicts inhere in contemporary prairie farm life. One tiger to a hill, Blood relations, and Generations have been published in Blood relations and other plays (1981); the title play won the first Governor General's Award for published drama. Pollock's most recent play, Whiskey six, premièred at Theatre Calgary in Feb. 1983. This vivid recollection of prohibition days in southern Alberta shows Pollock continuing in naturalistic style, but once more exploring the impact of public issues on private lives.

During the 1970s Sharon Pollock wrote a number of children's plays, many for production in Vancouver and Calgary theatres, such as New Canadians (1973), The happy prince (1974), The wreck of the national line car (1978), and Chataqua spelt E-N-E-R-G-Y (1979). She has also written a dozen radio scripts: her recent Sweet land of liberty won

the ACTRA Nellie for Best Radio Drama of 1980.

Useful references to Sharon Pollock's work can be found in Canada's playwrights: a biographical guide (1980), edited by Don Rubin and Alison Cranmer-Byng, and in Malcom Page, 'Sharon Pollock: committed playwright', Canadian Drama, 5, no. 2 (Fall 1979). See also The work: conversations with English-Canadian playwrights (1982) edited by Robert Wallace and Cynthia Zimmerman.   DIANE BESSAI

Pond, Peter. See EXPLORATION LITERATURE IN ENGLISH: 2.

Pontiac. See INDIAN LITERATURE: 1.

Potvin, Damase. See NOVELS IN FRENCH: 1900 TO 1920.

Poulin, Jacques (b. 1937). Born in Saint-Gédéon, in the Beauce region of Québec, he was educated at Université Laval, where he took a bilingual Arts degree that enabled him to earn his living for a number of years as a commercial translator. He lives outside Quebec City.

Poulin has written five novels: Mon cheval pour un royaume (1967), Jimmy (1969), Le coeur de la baleine bleue (1970), Faites des beaux rêves (1974), and Les grandes marées (1978). He writes with ease and grace and humour; he seems to share none of the usual preoccupations of Québec novelists of his generation—the Church, the land (escaping from it or rediscovering it), Québec's political affairs. One of the chief influences in his first three novels is J.D. Salinger: the debt is obvious, but the novels, particularly Jimmy, are more an hommage than an imitation. Les grandes marées shows the influence of Kurt Vonnegut Jr and Richard Brautigan. The setting for these novels is largely the old part of Quebec City, which Poulin makes contemporary and North American, filled with light and childish delight. But one of the pervading themes is destruction—of an older order, of old buildings, old styles of life. New life springs from the old, however, and one is struck particularly by the humanity of the attitudes and characters in the novels of this very important, unjustly neglected young writer. The first three novels were translated by Sheila Fischman and collected under the title of The Jimmy trilogy (1979).

In Faites des beaux rêves, the most spare and subtle of Poulin's novels, the line be-

Poulin

tween 'dreams' and reality is never quite clear. Camped near the Formula 1 race course at Mont Tremblant are Théo, a sportswriter; Limoilou, a girl steeped in legends; and Amadou, an accountant. Poulin focuses solely on the actions and words of these three, while they grope their way towards each other, touching only intermittently, and bask in the excitement that radiates from the racing drivers. They amuse themselves by playing games—borrowing dialogue, situations, and roles from Westerns, musical comedies, and the writings of Salinger, Scott Fitzgerald, and Heidegger—and in the end simply go their separate ways. In *Les grandes marées* a translator of comic-strips is sent to a deserted island in the St Lawrence, where he plays tennis with a ball-machine, does battle with dictionaries (though they are his friends), and discovers—or creates—a young 'dream' girl, Marie, before being destroyed by various agents of society who invade his island. For a writer, how is it possible to live without—or with—the world? The narrative is now expanded, now interrupted, by quotations, questionnaires, flash cards, advertising clichés, bilingual announcements, recipes, instructions, equations, drawings, and comic strips. *Les grandes marées*—dream, narrative, fable, essay—is an exploration of the possibilities and the limits of narration.

See also NOVELS IN FRENCH 1960 TO 1982: 3(b).

LAURENT MAILHOT, SHEILA FISCHMAN

Poupart, Jean-Marie. See NOVELS IN FRENCH 1960 TO 1982: 3(b).

Pour la patrie (Montréal, 1895). This separatist novel by Jules-Paul Tardivel, set in a hypothetical future, is the most enduring popular expression of Québec's nineteenth-century religious nationalism. The federal government of 1945-6 is secretly dominated by a masonic lodge of devil-worshippers that aims to destroy the French-Canadian society of Québec, the world's last stronghold of true religious (i.e. Catholic) life and values. The government proposes to change the Canadian constitution in a way that *seems* to perfect its federal character but will in reality destroy Québec's autonomy and crush French Canada. A French-Canadian MP sees the danger, but is unable to convince a majority in Parliament. Only by the strength of his piety, his submission to divine will and acceptance of personal sacrifice, does he win the miraculous interven-

tion from heaven that defeats the Satanists and brings about the ultimate independence of Québec.

Tardivel (1851-1905) was a Quebec City ultramontane journalist, accustomed to writing polemics, which may account for the novel's unsophisticated style, its superficial characterization, and its acceptance of Catholic faith at its simplest. He was the chief publicist in late nineteenth-century Québec for what he called 'thorough-going Catholicism', and it was to promote that cause, rather than to portray human character or drama, that he wrote the novel. He defended the Church's important role in education and social service and held that in a Catholic society like Québec all public life must be informed by the spirit of religion and the Church's teachings. In *Pour la patrie* he argued that this would be possible only if Québec separated from Canada, freeing itself from non-Catholic influences.

Tardivel's representation of freemasonry as the cult of Satan was not uncommon in the 1890s. Such accusations had been made against freemasons in Europe, and Tardivel's own newspaper, *La Vérité*, republished French and Italian anti-masonic works. His novel, in turn, was reprinted in European ultramontane papers.

Called the father of Québec separatism, Tardivel had an important influence on twentieth-century French-Canadian nationalism. Demand for his work among nationalist groups led to the republication of *Pour la patrie* in the 1930s, and it was no doubt the revival of separatism that prompted a reprint in 1974 and the English translation, *For my country: an 1895 religious and separatist vision of Québec in the mid-twentieth century* (1975), by Sheila Fischman.   A.I. SILVER

Poussière sur la ville (1953). A novel by André LANGEVIN that is considered one of the 'classics' of contemporary Québec literature, it is about a doctor, Alain Dubois—the narrator—and his wife Madeleine, two psychologically complex characters who are convincingly portrayed. An ardent, beautiful child-woman, Madeleine is the mainspring of the plot, which concerns her infidelity with Richard Hétu and its consequences. Dubois's initial rage and humiliation culminate in his half-drunk delivery of a hydrocephalic child whom he is obliged to kill to save the mother's life—an incident that affects him profoundly: he feels crushed by an implacable fate that he can neither comprehend nor struggle against. When the curé attempts to ruin Dubois's practice and arranges to have Hétu married off to the niece of the town's leading businessman, Madeleine tries unsuccessfully to shoot her lover and then dies by turning the revolver on herself. After the funeral, Dubois resumes his medical practice—in a struggle, as he sees it, on behalf of his fellow men against God and the absurdity of the human condition: 'I shall continue my fight. God and I, we aren't even yet.' This book, which shows the influence of Albert Camus, particularly in *La peste*, is artistically one of the most successful illustrations of the existential and metaphysical ideas that flowed into Québec from Europe after the Second World War. It remains Langevin's most popular work, both for its literary merit and for the human dilemmas it probes.

Poussière sur la ville was translated as *Dust over the city* (1955) by John Latrobe and Robert Gottlieb. A critical edition (1969) has been edited and annotated by Renald Bérubé. In 1965 it was made into a disappointing black-and-white movie, shot in Thetford Mines by Arthur Lamothe.

See Réjean Robidoux and André Renaud, *Le roman canadien-français du vingtième siècle* (1966).   L.W. KEFFER

Prairie writing. According to Edward McCOURT, author of a ground-breaking critical survey, *The Canadian West in fiction* (1949; rev. 1970), 'Prairie literature properly begins with the nineteenth-century travellers and explorers.' Henry KREISEL, on the other hand, has written in his essay 'The prairie: a state of mind' (1967) that 'All discussion of the literature produced in the Canadian West must of necessity begin with the impact of the landscape upon the mind.' Where the literature begins and where discussion begins are two separate matters, yet prairie writers and critics agree on the importance of history and geography in shaping the region's creative expressions.

In the literature of travel and exploration, several narratives by rambling adventurers stand out: Paul KANE's *Wanderings of an artist* (London, 1859; rpr. 1968), the Earl of Southesk's *Saskatchewan and the Rocky Mountains* (Edinburgh & Toronto, 1875; rpr. 1969), and Viscount Milton's and W.B. Cheadle's *Northwest passage by land* (London, 1865; rpr. 1970). The form reached its apogee in *The great lone land: a narrative of travel and adventure in the northwest of America* (London, 1872; rpr. 1968) by the Irish-born army officer William Francis Butler (1838-1910),

an immensely popular book throughout the English-speaking world for more than half a century. Butler's celebrated rendition of the pre-settlement West rests on an artful combination of elegy and irony; he evokes tenantless solitudes in prose redolent of Shelley and Tennyson, Cooper and Dickens. Yet even as Butler achieved best-sellerdom, 'the great lone land' of the fur-trade era was facing transformation. George Monro Grant spoke for a generation of Canadian expansionists when he marvelled at the beauty and fertility of the immense but unknown plains in OCEAN TO OCEAN (London and Toronto, 1873; rpr. 1968).

With the transfer of Rupert's Land to Canada in 1870, the region began to shed its mystery. Missionaries, surveyors, mounted policemen, and other 'forerunners of civilization' wrote voluminously of their experiences and predictions, but they were no match—in quantity at least—for the tourists, sportsmen, social pundits, and agricultural settlers who followed them. Touted by publicists as the 'last best west' and the 'granary of empire', the prairie frontier generated almost as much print as wheat. One result was a foreshortened interval between pioneer settlement and pioneer publication. Alexander Begg's *Dot it down: a story of life in the North-west* (Toronto, 1871) was a *roman à clef* satirizing the events leading up to the 1869-70 Riel resistance; it concludes with an immigrant's guide to Manitoba. J.E. Collins scarcely waited for the shooting to stop before rushing into print with *The story of Louis Riel* (1885) and *Annette the Metis spy* (1886; rpr. 1970), sensationalized caricatures of the 1885 reprise. Meanwhile the high romance of fur-traders and Indians persisted in some early fiction: Butler's *Red Cloud, the solitary Sioux* (London, 1882), R.M. BALLANTYNE's *Red man's revenge: a tale of the Red River flood* (London, 1880), and Agnes Laut's *Lords of the North* (New York, 1900).

The early pattern of almost simultaneous social and literary creation was sustained after the century's turn. 'Ralph Connor'— who became known world-wide for novels like *Black rock: a tale of the Selkirks* (Toronto, 1898), *The sky pilot: a tale of the foothills* (Chicago, 1899), depicting muscular Christian men and pure uplifting women on a glorious and challenging frontier—was the pen-name of the Rev. Charles W. GORDON, a central figure in Winnipeg's reformist social-gospel movement. In his later fiction—including *The foreigner* (1909) and *To*

Prairie writing

him that hath (1921)—he tried unsuccessfully to keep pace with the shocks of western Canada's willy-nilly absorption into the modern age: urbanization, the assimilation of immigrants, labour conflict, and the Great War and its aftermath. Nellie McCLUNG is another public figure from this period whose fame sprang originally from her accomplishments as a writer of popular fiction, including *Sowing seeds in Danny* (1908) and *Purple springs* (1921). R.J.C. STEAD, who earned his living as a publicist for the CPR, was the author of several volumes of Kiplingesque verse, and then published five immensely popular novels before the crowning achievement of *Grain* (1926). The notion of the artist as alienated and antisocial held scant appeal for either writers or readers in the halcyon days of the great settlement boom.

Sober second thoughts entered with the 1920s. The change in mood is evident not only in Stead's *Grain*, but in Martha OSTENSO's *Wild geese* (1926), and Frederick Philip GROVE's *Settlers of the marsh* (1925). All three novels explore the relations of men and women, parents and children, families and communities, in the context of a distinctive prairie agricultural way of life. Each has its own claims to literary autonomy and merit: it is with these three novels that genuine critical debate, rather than historical explanation, can begin. Grove has captured most of the attention, on both literary and extra-literary grounds. Certainly it is true that in his novels, essays, and autobiographical writings he explored (as none had done before, and few since) the role of the literary artist in the Canadian prairie scene, at the same time creating powerful if sombre icons of pioneer life. By comparison with Grove's *Settlers of the marsh*, *Grain* is a more innocent work of fiction, more modest in ambition, but in many ways more authentic and satisfying.

Although during the 1930s drought in the farming districts was accompanied by drought in the creative wellsprings, the combination of Depression and dustbowls has proved a fertile theme ever since. The poem by Anne MARRIOTT called 'The wind our enemy', published in a poetry collection of that name (1939), remains one of the more notable poetic responses to that traumatic period. In fiction the short stories of Sinclair ROSS, and his novel AS FOR ME AND MY HOUSE (1941), constitute a significant if overrated contribution. The vicissitudes of the thirties turned the westering theme

northwards, as in Ralph ALLEN's slight but enjoyable *Peace River country* (1958), and Christine VAN DER MARK's more serious and substantial *In due season* (1947; rpr. 1979).

The cultural and linguistic diversity of the prairie region is reflected to some extent in pre-Second World War writing, perhaps most vividly in the fiction and autobiographical books of Laura Goodman SALVERSON (*The Viking heart*, 1923; *Confessions of an immigrant's daughter*, 1939). The novels of the 1950s on the ethnic theme included Vera Lysenko's *Yellow boots* (1954), Adele WISEMAN's *The sacrifice* (1956), and John MARLYN's *Under the ribs of death* (1952). Lacking translation into English, little of the writing done in German, Icelandic, Ukrainian, and other languages has reached the wider reading public, although Watson KIRKCONNELL's early lead in translation is attracting renewed interest. Two francophone writers, both born and educated in France, have enjoyed the advantage of translation: Maurice CONSTANTIN-WEYER—who was awarded the Prix Goncourt for *Un homme se penche sur son passé* (1928), published in English as *A man scans his past* (1929)—and Georges BUGNET, whose novel *Nipsya* (1929) also appeared in translation. Bugnet's *La forêt* (1935) was judged by E.K. BROWN to be the finest novel ever published about the Canadian West; it was translated into English as *The forest* (1976).

In a category (and class) by herself is Manitoba-born French-Canadian writer Gabrielle ROY. Arguably the finest writer Canada has ever produced, from 1950 on she travelled in her fiction (always first published in French) with unmatched sureness and delicacy through the subtler territories of the prairie experience, whether centred on St Boniface *(The road past Altamont, Street of riches)*, on the Interlake district *(Where nests the water hen)*, or on the rural Prairies *(Garden in the wind, Children of my heart)*. Roy's themes are joy and sadness; hope and disappointment; youth, ageing, and death; and above all, love. These universals of the human condition are contained and illumined by Roy in a prose style of classic nuance and restraint.

Fiction has been the dominant form through most of the post-war period. The short stories, radio scripts, and novels of W.O. MITCHELL, the author of WHO HAS SEEN THE WIND (1947), created a voice and a milieu that continue to occupy a central cell in our collective imaginative life. Henry Kreisel, whose first novel was *The rich man*

678

(1948), has shown that a career in academe need not be the death of creativity. In Manitoba W.D. VALGARDSON writes novels and short stories marked by quiet authority, and David WILLIAMS' *The river horseman* (1981) has been well received. However, these and many other fine writers from the region must contend with the shadows thrown by greater luminaries. In 1964 Margaret LAURENCE burst on the literary scene with *The STONE ANGEL*, adding a new dimension to Canadian literature through the novel's commanding central figure and narrator, ninety-year-old Hagar Shipley. Also in the 1960s Robert KROETSCH began a fictional reclamation of his Alberta background with *The words of my roaring* (1967) and *The studhorse man* (1969); while a northern-Saskatchewan Mennonite community gave Rudy WIEBE impetus and material for *Peace shall destroy many* (1962) and *The blue mountains of China* (1970). All three writers have gone on to become dominant figures nationally, and to bring Canadian writing to the eyes of the world.

Kroetsch does not confine himself to fiction: his *The stone hammer poems* (1975) and *Seed catalogue* (1977) are long poems that explode with wit and energy. In *Twelve prairie poets* (1976) editor Laurie Ricou provides a sampling of recent poetry from the region, while Saskatchewan poets, in a co-operative venture typical of that province, have put together work from forty-one writers in *Number one northern: poetry from Saskatchewan* (1977). English departments at universities in all three prairie provinces—along with Saskatchewan's School for the Arts and Alberta's Banff Centre—help to generate the talent and craftsmanship that find outlets in Manitoba's Turnstone Press, Saskatchewan's Thistledown Press, and Longspoon Press of Edmonton. Throughout the region poets are busy and productive; for every poet mentioned here, there are a dozen vigorous and distinctive talents left in undeserved obscurity, but one may mention in particular the work of Joy KOGAWA, Anne SZUMIGALSKI, Dale ZIEROTH, Lorna Uher, Sid MARTY and Andrew SUKNASKI—cultivators in a field first broken by figures like John NEWLOVE, Eli MANDEL, Dorothy LIVESAY, Elizabeth BREWSTER, and Miriam WADDINGTON.

In drama the community theatre movement of the 1930s and 1940s rested largely on the short plays and radio scripts of Gwen Pharis RINGWOOD, Elsie Park Gowan, and W.O. Mitchell. Their heirs in the current generation include George RYGA, Ken MITCHELL—who has edited an excellent regional anthology, *Horizon: writings of the Canadian Prairies* (1977)—Joanna GLASS, Sharon POLLOCK, and John MURRELL, author of *Waiting for the parade* (1980). The theatre scene is vibrant, with a tendency towards grass-roots realism, but it does not exclude more cerebral and experimental works like Wilfred WATSON's 1969 play, *Let's murder Clytemnestra according to the principles of Marshall McLuhan*.

Critical approaches to prairie writing continue for the most part to hew to the environmentalism of Edward McCOURT. In *Vertical man/horizontal world* (1973) Laurie Ricou asserted that 'the basic image of a single human figure amidst the vast flatness of the landscape serves to unify and describe Canadian prairie fiction.' Dick Harrison has added something of a historical dimension to the discussion in *Unnamed country: the struggle for a Canadian prairie fiction* (1977). A more eclectic source is *Writers of the Prairies* (1977), a collection of critical articles reprinted from CANADIAN LITERATURE; while an important debate between McCourt and Mandel can be found in Richard Allen's *A region of the mind* (1973). Still missing, and sorely missed, is a lively and rigorous critical press: the *NeWest Review* stands almost alone. Thus it may be some time before any fully satisfactory critical survey of the region's writing reaches publication.

See also CRITICISM IN ENGLISH: 5(c), 5(f), 5(g), NOVELS IN ENGLISH 1960 TO 1982: OTHER TALENTS OTHER WORKS: 6(b), and PIONEER MEMOIRS: 3.   SUSAN JACKEL

Pratt, E.J. (1882-1964). One of the major figures in Canadian poetry, Edwin John Pratt was born in Western Bay, Nfld, but his father, a Methodist minister, had to move the family at approximately four-year intervals among the fishing, sealing, and whaling outports of the British colony. After graduating from St John's Methodist College, Pratt served as a preacher and teacher in several remote island communities, and then attended Victoria College, University of Toronto, and majored in philosophy. Supporting his studies by doing missionary work in the West in the summers, and later serving as an assistant minister just outside Toronto, he earned his B.A. (1911), M.A. with a thesis on demonology (1912), his B.D. (1913) and Ph.D. (1917) in theology, writing a thesis on Pauline eschatology. In 1920 Pelham Edgar invited Pratt, who was then working as a demonstrator in the Department of Psychology, to join the Department of English at Victoria College, thus re-initiating a teaching career that lasted until 1953. As a scholar Pratt published a number of reviews, articles, introductions, and prefaces and edited Thomas Hardy's *Under the greenwood tree* (1937). In 1918 he married Viola Whitney, who became a staunch United Church worker and a writer for young people. Their daughter, Mildred Claire, has written a study of the Pratt family, *The silent ancestors: the forebears of E.J. Pratt* (1971). As editor of the *Canadian Poetry Magazine* (1936-42), Pratt fostered the growth of many younger poets, and at his stag parties played host to many of Canada's foremost men of the arts and letters. His honours include election to the Royal Society of Canada (1930), the Lorne PIERCE Medal (1940), being made Commander of the Order of St Michael and St George (1946), the Canada Council Medal (1961), and an LL.D from the U. of T. (1961).

Pratt's first collection, *Newfoundland verse* (1923), is marked by its frequently archaic diction, and the poetry reflects a pietistic and sometimes preciously lyrical sensibility of late-Romantic derivation, characteristics that may account for Pratt's reprinting less than half these poems in his *Collected poems* (1958). The most genuine feeling is expressed in the humorous and sympathetic portraits of Newfoundland characters, and in the creation of elegaic mood in poems concerning sea tragedies or Great War losses. The sea, which on the one hand provides 'the bread of life' and on the other represents 'the waters of death' ('Newfoundland'), is a central element as setting, subject, and creator of mood. The book contains 'A fragment from a story', the only part of Pratt's verse-drama 'Clay' ever to be published, and the conclusion to the blank-verse narrative *Rachel: a sea-story of Newfoundland in verse* (1917) that had earlier been privately printed. The section in *Newfoundland verse* picks up the story of Rachel after she has already been widowed by the sea, and relates her decline into madness and death when the sea also claims her only son. A better early indicator of Pratt's narrative skill is 'The ice-floes', a swift-paced account of a sealing disaster.

The witches' brew (1925) is a fanciful concoction of learning and nonsense, satire and celebration. Highly allusive in mythic structure and motif, it is written in the octosyllabic line that became the standard for Pratt's comedic poems. His zest for compiling humorous catalogues, his penchant for the epic scale, and his interests in evolution and atavism clearly emerge for the first time. The three sea-witches' experiment to discover the effect of alcohol on fish may have been Pratt's high-spirited response to Prohibition, but the poem is really stolen by Tom the Sea-Cat from Zanzibar, who serves as bouncer for the underwater bacchanal until Satan, scenting a way to expand his dominion into the heretofore amoral ocean, extends the experiment to Tom. Giving free rein to the primitive tendencies released by the brew, this evolutionary freak indulges in an orgy of destruction and is last seen headed for the Irish Sea, a destination no doubt chosen for Ireland's association with strong drink and pugnacious character.

In *Titans: two poems* (1926) Pratt achieves a fluid, engaging, and swiftly paced style by varying rhyme scheme, syllabic quantity, and stress patterns, and by frequently using enjambed lines. 'The cachalot' has as its epic hero a sperm whale whose dimensions are exaggerated in mock-heroic style. After a vividly described victory over a kraken, the cachalot engages in a mutually destructive battle with whalers. 'The great feud: a dream of a Pliocene Armageddon' examines the growth of racial hatred and wartime behaviour in its picture of a civil war between land and sea creatures that have only just been distinguished as species by the evolutionary process. An anachronistic *Tyrannosaurus rex*, on the trailing edge of that process, and a female anthropoidal ape on the leading edge indicate the poem's blend of the fantastic and the allegorical. The tiny-brained embattled dinosaur represents unreasoning violence that ends in self-destruction, but the ape uses her emergent intellectual powers to propagandize her forces. The poem's commentary on man's animal instincts is capped by the implication that the militaristic ape and her brood are the sole survivors of the volcanic eruption that ends the war.

The iron door: an ode (1927), written to commemorate Pratt's mother's death, gives voice to several positions on death and the after-life, ending with an affirmation of faith that is nonetheless ambivalent because the narrator is left dazzled to the point of blindness outside the door between the realms of life and death when the door opens to admit the dead. The theme of *The Roosevelt and the Antinoe* (1930) is the collective self-sacrificing heroism of sailors pitting themselves against the destructive powers of nature and facing massive odds to rescue the crew of a ship sinking in a mid-Atlantic storm. Pratt here returns to the five-beat line that became standard for his extended treatments of serious subjects. This narrative was republished, with Pratt's notes and other poems, in *Verses of the sea* (1930); this verse-and-notes format was also used in *Ten selected poems* (1947) and in *Heroic tales in verse* (1941), a book Pratt edited and prefaced.

The nature pieces in *Many moods* (1932) seem to be a thematic throwback, though some reflect a precise image-making power, and the often-humorous vignettes of human character appear slight after the charting of new thematic territory, and the stylistic vigour, in the narratives. Meditations on aging and death are numerous, but the emergence of a socially conscious voice strikes a new note. Pratt seeks antidotes to human misery in sacrifice, or—in 'The depression ends', that perfect expression of Pratt's expansive public personality, and a kind of cosmic equivalent to 'The witches' brew'—in throwing a banquet for all the world's unfortunates.

Irony is the structural principle on which *The Titanic* (1935) is built. The iceberg that embodies nature's Janus-faces of beauty and destructive power remains 'the master of the longitudes' when man's hubris in thinking he has built an unsinkable ship, combined with an ironic conjunction of circumstances, results in a collision of the forces of man and nature. Sombre intimations of war and failures of communication are the focus of *The fable of the goats and other poems* (1932), which indirectly treats man's bellicose behaviour in a number of animal allegories, the best of which are 'Silences' and 'The prize cat'. Though Pratt won a Governor General's Award for this volume, he chose to omit the title poem from his *Collected poems* (1958), perhaps because the pacifist conclusion to the territorial disputes between warring tribes of goats proved so futile a model for human behaviour.

Of all the volumes published during the war years *Brébeuf and his brethren* (1940), for which Pratt won his second Governor General's Award, is least overtly concerned with war, though the Jesuit priests clearly represent a beleaguered enclave of civilization. Pratt's research-oriented methodology is made clear in the precise diction and detailed and historically accurate recounting of events and observation in this, his first attempt to write a national epic. *Dunkirk* (1941), and many of the poems of *Still life and other verse* (1943), are more immediately topical, picturing both the heroism and atavism of which men are capable, though the propagandistic cast of many of these poems should be recognized, for heroism seems the exclusive property of the Allies, and atavism characteristic solely of the Axis forces. *They are returning* (1945) is an occasional piece that strains to give the feats of Canadian veterans classical epic stature; but *Behind the log* (1947) successfully captures the drama of individuals' wartime experiences by chronicling the hounding of an Atlantic convoy by U-boats.

Pratt's concerns with communication and bringing alive Canadian history culminate in his third Governor General's Award-winning volume, *Towards the last spike: a verse panorama of the struggle to build the first Canadian transcontinental from the time of the proposed terms of union with British Columbia [1870] to the hammering of the last spike in the Eagle Pass [1885]* (1952). The political battles between Sir John A. Macdonald and Edward Blake are interwoven with the labourers' physical battles against mountains, mud, and the Laurentian Shield, which Pratt, in a metaphorical method typical of his style, characterizes as a prehistoric lizard rudely aroused from its sleep by the railroad builders' dynamite.

The collected poems of E.J. Pratt (1958) reprinted all but two poems in *Collected poems* (1944), while adding five earlier poems and a handful of previously unpublished ones. The second edition serves as a map of the movement of Canadian poetry from its colonial phase towards its becoming an identifiably independent national literature.

Pratt's reputation as a major Canadian poet rests largely on his narrative poems, many of which show him as a mythologizer of the Canadian experience; but a number of shorter works also command recognition. 'From stone to steel' asserts the necessity for redemptive suffering arising from the failure of man's spiritual evolution to keep pace with his physical evolution and his cultural achievements; 'Come away, death' is a complexly allusive account of the way the once-articulate and ceremonial human response to death was rendered inarticulate by the primitive violence of a sophisticated bomb; and 'The truant' dramatically presents a confrontation between the fiercely independent 'little genus homo' and a totalitarian mechanistic power, 'the great Panjandrum'. Pratt's choices of forms and metrics were conservative for his time; but his diction was experimental, reflecting in its specificity and its frequent technicality both his belief in the poetic power of the accurate and concrete that led him into assiduous research processes, and his view that it is the poet's task to bridge the gap between the two branches of human pursuit: the scientific and the artistic.

E.J. Pratt: on his life and poetry (1983), edited by Susan Gingell, contains notes and commentaries by Pratt and two CBC interviews.

Pratt has on the whole been well served by those who have introduced collections and selections of his verse: William Rose Benét, the American edition of *Collected poems* (1945; Canadian edn, 1944); Northrop FRYE, *Collected poems* (1958); D.G. Pitt, *Here the tides flow* (1962); and Peter Buitenhuis, *Selected poems of E.J. Pratt* (1968). Pitt's collection of early reviews and essays in *E.J. Pratt* (1969) illustrates how much the shadow of the poet's personality lay across early attempts to delineate his world view, an on-going preoccupation in Pratt criticism. This is not a flaw, however, in Sandra Djwa's *E.J. Pratt: the evolutionary vision* (1974), which fixes the intellectual background of Pratt's writing, or in Frank DAVEY's two hostile but carefully argued articles: 'E.J. Pratt: apostle of corporate man' (CANADIAN LITERATURE, 43) and 'E.J. Pratt: rationalist technician' (*Canadian Literature*, 61). The most recent collective reappraisal of Pratt's life and work is *The E.J. Pratt symposium* (1977). Other monograph studies of note are Henry Wells and Carl Klinck, *Edwin J. Pratt: the man and his poetry* (1947); John SUTHERLAND, *The poetry of E.J. Pratt: a new interpretation* (1956); and Milton Wilson, *E.J. Pratt* (1969).   SUSAN GINGELL

Préfontaine, Yves (b. 1937). Born in Montreal, he studied anthropology and sociology in Montreal and Paris. He was a founder of Éditions de l'Hexagone in 1953; was briefly editor-in-chief of LIBERTÉ in 1962; and has been a radio broadcaster. In 1968 he received the Prix France-Canada and the Prix des Concours Littéraires du Québec for his poetry collection, *Pays sans parole* (1961). Since 1978 he has been a senior Québec civil servant.

His very personal poetry is composed of long, luxuriant lines that occasionally betray a surrealist imagination. Préfontaine tends to overindulge in neologisms and phonic games, but his poems try to breathe life into the elements—the vast stretches of the far North, the cosmos, the seasons—and may be called transitive, in that they frequently involve a speaker and interlocutors. In *Boréal* (1957) and *Les temples effondrés* (1957), collections of tumultuous poems whose vigorous expression amounts almost to a desperate cry, Préfontaine speaks of tackling, mastering, and inhabiting the vast, glacial aridity of the far North, just as the poet must tackle life and the word. (A prose collection, *L'antre du poème* (1960), calls for a new creative orientation that would give 'birth to the cry of freedom'.) The more sober tone of *A l'orée des travaux* (1970), *Débacle* (1970), and *Pays sans parole* (1967) shows Préfontaine striving to create poetic space for Québec, seeking through his words to free it from its former silence and give form to the 'snowy void'. In the foreword to the last collection, he affirms the North-Americanness of the Québécois, their 'francophone way of being American', and stresses the inherent danger of conformity in the nationalist theme favoured by so many Québec poets. His poems have a strong emotional charge, stemming from the force of the words and their arrangement, the remonstrances, repetitions, and incantations addressed to a people 'shivering under a frost of words', whom he tries to warm with his speech, hoping to raise a birth-cry. *Nuaison* (1981), elegantly wrought, brings together poems written between 1964 and 1970. Slightly formalist, it marks the end of a general fervour and shows a new awareness of the limitations and fragility of disappointed hopes. Now that skepticism has replaced the passion of the Hexagone years, Préfontaine's poetic voice has become hushed.

See Axel Maugey, 'Yves Préfontaine' in *Poésie et société au Québec 1937-1970* (1972), and Gilles MARCOTTE, 'Yves Préfontaine' in *Le temps des poètes* (1969).

MAROUSSIA AHMED

Preview (1942-5). This Montreal-based periodical, originally intended as a literary letter in which contributors would 'preview' or try out their work, was first published in Mar. 1942. Its editorial board was made up of F.R. SCOTT, Margaret Day, Bruce Ruddick, Neufville Shaw, and Patrick ANDERSON, who was its driving spirit and most influential editor. P.K. PAGE joined the board in Issue 2 (Apr. 1942) and A.M. KLEIN in Issue 19 (Mar. 1944), his work having appeared since Issue 5 (July 1942) and Day and

Shaw having already resigned as editors. Planned as a monthly, but appearing irregularly over 23 issues until early 1945, *Preview* averaged 9-to-13 mimeographed pages and had a circulation of approximately 125. It featured poetry, short stories, frequently leftist essays, and became known for the wit, technical sophistication, and cosmopolitan interests of its talented and socially concerned editors. In Dec. 1945 it merged with FIRST STATEMENT to form NORTHERN REVIEW. The legendary rivalry between *Preview* and *First Statement* has been exaggerated. See Patrick Anderson, 'A poet past and future' (CANADIAN LITERATURE 56, Summer 1973), and 'Four of the *Preview* editors: a discussion' (*Canadian Poetry* 4, Spring/Summer 1979).   DAVID O'ROURKE

Priest, Robert. See POETRY IN ENGLISH 1950 TO 1982: 3.

Prochain épisode (1965). This first novel by Hubert AQUIN—written during a four-month stay in the Albert Prévost Psychiatric Institute, Montreal, where the author was being held while awaiting trial for possession of a stolen firearm—was hailed on publication as the great novel of Québec's revolutionary period. In fact it is about paralysis, and the impossibility of revolution, as much as it is about revolution. Written in a style that alternates between a lyricism inspired by the idea of revolution and a prose corresponding to Québec's present, it recounts the attempt of an imprisoned separatist to distract himself from reality, and to rediscover his revolutionary fervour, by writing a novel. The hero of the fictional novel—a revolutionary Québec separatist in Switzerland—after receiving instructions about the enemy he is to kill, agrees to rejoin his lover and revolutionary comrade K. (clearly a symbol of Québec) twenty-four hours later in Lausanne. But as the plot unfolds, contradictions emerge: the hero reveals himself as an artist rather than a man of action, and in his 'infinite hesitation' he becomes a 'fractured symbol of the revolution in Québec.' His enemy, H. de Heutz—in his triple identity of banker, historian, and lonely aristocrat—emerges as the double or enemy-brother of the hero, the other half of the French-Canadian psyche associated with an English Canada both hated and loved. Their confrontation, in a magnificent scene in which the mythical motif of a castle suggests both an eternal embrace of opposites and the historical ambiguities of Canada's two na-

tions, leads to stasis. In the perfection of its moving and complex structure, *Prochain épisode* transcends the historical movement that gave it birth while remaining, as the narrator writes, clearly indissociable from that moment. It speaks equally powerfully of despair and of the unceasing hope that produces metamorphosis and revolution.

An English translation by Penny Williams, with the same title, was published in 1967 (NCL, 1973).   PATRICIA SMART

Provincial, The; or Halifax Monthly Magazine. Published in Halifax between Jan. 1852 and Dec. 1853, it was the most prominent mid-century literary journal in Maritime Canada. A monthly printed by James Barnes and Son and edited by Mary Jane KATZMANN, each of its 24 issues ran to forty or more pages. Katzmann strove to make it a vehicle for local intellectual and literary development and was successful in having the bulk of each issue locally written. There was a reasonably wide range of topics in the general articles, but her interests clearly lay in literature and history. Three series on the early history of Nova Scotia were published, as well as occasional biographies of noted Nova Scotians, such as Samuel Cunard and Herbert Huntington. She also published the first significant study of local verse in a series entitled 'Half hours with our poets', and frequently reviewed books by local authors. At the same time Katzmann tried to avoid being overly parochial. Through reviews and articles on the literary and intellectual scene in Britain and the United States, she projected a sense of cultural interchange in the North Atlantic English-speaking communities. A significant portion of each issue was filled with poetry—sentimental and moralistic, competent but not brilliant—and fiction by local writers. Mary Jane Katzmann herself contributed poetry and articles, as did Clotilda Jennings and Mary Eliza HERBERT, William T. Wishart, M.B. DesBrisay, John Sparrow THOMPSON, and Silas T. Rand. Many of the items, however, were published anonymously.   TOM VINCENT

'Psalm to Montreal, A'. See 'O GOD! O MONTREAL!'.

Purdy, Al (b. 1918). Alfred Wellington Purdy, who writes as Al Purdy and A.W. Purdy, was born at Wooler, Ont., 'of degenerate Loyalist stock', as he has claimed. He spent most of his childhood in Trenton,

Purdy

Ont., and was educated at Albert College, Belleville. During the 1930s Purdy rode on freight trains to Vancouver, where he worked for several years in a mattress factory and similar establishments. In the Second World War he served in the Royal Canadian Air Force, mostly at the remote base of Woodcock on the Skeena River in northern British Columbia. Having no university training and few academic inclinations (though his wide reading has made him a remarkably erudite man), he worked at many jobs, mainly casual and manual, well into his forties. This combination of literary ambitions and a working-class style of living helped to produce his anecdotal and idiosyncratic poetry.

In recent years Purdy has lived by his work as a freelance writer and at related tasks, such as lecturing, poetry reading, and periods as writer-in-residence at universities. He has travelled far: through Canada from Newfoundland to the west coast of Vancouver Island, and north to Baffin Island; abroad to Cuba and Mexico, to Greece and Turkey, Italy and France, Japan and Africa. He is a writer 'for whom the visible world exists' palpably and directly, and the experiences of travel have always played a recognizable part in shaping both the content and the mood of a great deal of his poetry. But the heart of Purdy's world, the place that gives a name to so many of his poems and appears as the symbolic omphalos of his imaginative world, is Roblin Lake in deep Loyalist country near Ameliasburg, Ont. There, in the country of the farmer forebears he has so often celebrated in his poems, he built with his own hands a house by the lakeshore to which he returns as to a spiritual oasis from his travels.

Like most writers who seek to live by their craft, Purdy has practised in a variety of genres, from radio and television plays—of which he has written more than a dozen—to criticism, and from book reviews (notably in CANADIAN LITERATURE) to travel essays and anecdotal portraits of people and places, which were published in magazines like *Maclean's* and *Weekend Magazine* and were collected in his single volume of prose, *No other country* (1977). Purdy has also edited a polemical anthology—*The new Romans* (1969)—that is a critique of the United States and by implication supports Canadian nationalism, which he endorsed by his active membership in the Committee for an Independent Canada. He has compiled three verse anthologies: *Fifteen winds*

(1969), *Storm warning* (1971), and *Storm warning II* (1976). He has also selected and edited books of poems by Milton ACORN (*I've tasted my blood*, 1969) and Andrew SUKNASKI (*Wood Mountain poems*, 1976).

Purdy has written verse restlessly, copiously, ever since boyhood. From 1944—when his first volume, *The enchanted echo*, appeared—down to the present (1981), he has published 24 volumes and 10 broadsheets of verse. Three of the books—*Selected poems* (1972), *The poems of Al Purdy: a New Canadian Library selection* (1976), and *Being alive: poems 1958-78* (1978)—have been selections from previous volumes, augmented in the first and last case by new poems. Purdy's work, considered as a whole, is as impressive in its steady strengthening of quality as in its volume, and stands as a notable monument to a life dedicated to the making and reading of poetry. The making and the reading cannot be dissociated. Purdy has been one of the most untiring of the peripatetic poets who emerged in Canada during the 1960s, sometimes going on several circuits a year to read his poems, which in their turn have been greatly affected not only by the special demands of oral presentation but also by the situation of projection and response that unites a poet with his audience. It would be a great injustice to describe Purdy as merely an oral poet; but it is impossible to ignore the extent to which his poems have been influenced by the need for them to appeal immediately to the ear.

When Purdy published his fourth volume in 1959, he called it *The crafte so longe to lerne*, and in doing so he was wryly celebrating the long apprenticeship in which he had found his poetic voice. *The enchanted echo*, was conservatively traditional, deriving largely from the Canadian romantics like ROBERTS and CARMAN. Later volumes, like *Pressed on sand* (1955) and *Emu, remember* (1955), are more casual in their approach, though Purdy was still trapped in formal preoccupations. But he was steadily experimenting, and on his way towards poetic self-realization. He was able to take what he wanted, and no more, from William Carlos Williams on the one hand, from W.H. Auden and Dylan Thomas on the other, and from PRATT, BIRNEY, LAYTON, and other Canadian poets in between.

The crafte so longe to lerne is the volume in which, to the close observer, Purdy's special character as a poet first became evident both in the opening of forms and in thematic evolution of a type of poetry that is really a philosophic continuum where the here-and-now, immediately perceived, becomes the Blakean grain wherein, if not the world, at least universal values are reflected. Purdy himself regards a slightly later volume, *Poems for all the Annettes* (1962), as marking the point where 'other people's styles' ceased to be apparent in his work.

Certainly by the appearance of *Cariboo horses* (1965)—which won him a Governor-General's Award—he was writing at the top of his individual form, having developed a long-lined and colloquially free manner, as well as an ability to be intellectually direct without sacrificing the suggestive dimensions of poetic imagery. Purdy has drawn freely on the funds of miscellaneous knowledge that a generalizing and autodidactic mind tends to accumulate; yet, though densely allusive, he is never obscure. As a reader he moved through history; as a traveller he has wandered over a good part of the twentieth-century world; and some of his poems show a remarkable ability to bring images drawn from great sweeps of time and space into a meaningful relationship with what he sees before him in the every-day contemporary setting.

Most of Purdy's recent books contain poems arising out of his wide rovings, and *North of summer: poems from Baffin Island* (1967) is virtually a travel-book in verse. In such poems the interval between conception and creation is often surprisingly short; the poems sometimes seem to serve Purdy as a diary might serve other men and there is an unevenness in tone. In the least successful of his poems there is a harsh flatness—though this is rare, since an engaging conversational fluency is almost always present—but at their best there emerges a transfiguration of place and its inhabitants.

Purdy, however, is more than a versifying geographer. His great, undisciplined, autodidactic learning has given him a historical sense rare among Canadian poets after Pratt. In his poems of Ontario, particularly in *Wild grape wine* (1968) and his memorial cycle, *In search of Owen Roblin* (1974), he evokes, as few other writers have done so vividly, the sense of Canada as an old country resonant with echoes.

Purdy's work is shown in its greatest variety in *Being alive* (1978), which includes most of his best poems up to the late 1970s. This collection shows how well, once he reached the plateau of his individuality and found his real voice, he has sustained the quality of his writing. In *The stone bird* (1981) he is still fascinated with human character and human destiny, still writing with humour and compassion, and projecting a haunting message of the rejuvenative power of the natural world that man has sought so hard—but up to now so vainly—to destroy.

George BOWERING has published a small book on Purdy in the Studies in Canadian Literature series (1970). A discussion of his work, 'On the poetry of Al Purdy', is included in George WOODCOCK's *The world of Canadian writing* (1980). A thoroughly annotated bibliography of his writing and of writing about him, by Marianne Micros, appears in *The annotated bibliography of Canada's major authors: volume two* (1980), edited by Robert Lecker and Jack David. Purdy introduces and reads some of his poems on the CBC recording *Al Purdy's Ontario* (c. 1973).

See also POETRY IN ENGLISH 1950 TO 1982: 2. GEORGE WOODCOCK

Q

Québec, Writing in English in. 1. THE
EARLY YEARS. Literary endeavour in English
before the middle of the nineteenth century
in what is now Québec was as extensive as
that in Nova Scotia, and considerably more
advanced than in any other colony in British
North America. In North America no literary work was produced before 1840 that is
read today for other than historical reasons,
though a great deal was written and published—in both Canada and the United
States—that forms a significant part of our
literary heritage.

English-language writing in Québec was
dominated by two factors: colonialism and
immigration. Colonial writing was marked
by ambivalence. On the one hand it relied
on European models and standards and was
conscious of Canadian inferiority; on the
other it was proud of Canadian literature
and concerned for its development as a
means of demonstrating Canada's intrinsic
worth to the rest of the world. In the early
years there was also the oft-stated objective
of proving to the French-speaking population that British culture was superior to their
own.

There were a few native-born writers in
English, but before mid-century, as elsewhere in North America, most were immigrants. Downwardly mobile in Britain, and
seeking to repair their fortunes in the New
World, many were well-educated adults
who had already published at home and
found it natural to continue writing for publication in Canada. Their arrival resulted in
an increase in the quantity of 'Canadian' literature; but, since all their reference points
were outside the country, it also inhibited
both the development of a literature rooted
in the Canadian experience and the transmission from one generation to the next of
what little Canadian literary tradition there
was. Most of the immigrant writers were
'middle class', in the sense that they were
educated and did not work with their hands;
but none were well off, even by the standards of the day. They, and their readers,
were located principally in Montreal and
Quebec, but even outside the cities, particularly in English-speaking settlements in the
Gaspé and the Eastern Townships, there
was always someone who wrote, and some
means of publication. In all these communities throughout the nineteenth century, amateur writers and serious readers gathered in
literary clubs, debating societies, library associations, and Mechanics' Institutes, where
they presented and applauded hundreds of
papers on literary subjects.

The largest audience was available for
works published in newspapers. Most were
weekly or thrice-weekly publications that,
by the 1840s, had a circulation in the cities of
1000 to 1500 copies each. The number of actual readers was much greater, since newspapers were handed round until they fell in
tatters. Each edition carried at least one
poem, and many devoted one of the four
pages to literature—British and American,
as well as Canadian. Most amateurs published anonymously in the newspaper to
which they subscribed. Those with somewhat higher aspirations published in one of
the fourteen literary periodicals that came
and went before 1851. The best known of
these today are the Montreal publications:
*The Canadian Magazine and Literary Reposi-
tory* (1823-5), *The Canadian Review and Literary and Historical Journal* (1824-6), and *The
Scribbler* (1821-7); they contained the work
of (among others) Oliver GOLDSMITH, Levi
ADAMS, George LONGMORE, and Adam
Hood BURWELL. There was also *The Montreal Museum* (1832-4), which was notable
for the stories of Mrs H. Bayly, and in the
late 1830s the Quebec *Literary Transcript*,
which published many Quebec City writers. In the 1840s a number of didactic periodicals—devoted, on the British model, to
elevating the lower classes—came and went
in Montreal. Several satirical periodicals—
again following a British model, but entirely
written in Canada and focusing on Canadian
politics—culminated in *Punch in Canada*
(1849-50). Montreal was also the locale of
The SNOW DROP (1847-53), the first children's periodical published in Canada. *The*
LITERARY GARLAND (1838-51) is well known
to scholars.

The earliest writers to publish in English
were centred in the Quebec City area.
Thomas Cary's (1751-1823) long poem
Abram's plains (Quebec, 1789) even predated
the division of the colony into Upper and
Lower Canada. Cary remained in Quebec as
a newspaper editor and he and his descendants played a prominent part in the life of

that city; but nothing is known of J. Mackay, who published *Quebec hill: or Canadian scenery; a poem* (London, 1797), or of Cornwall Bayley, who may have been the author of *Canada: a descriptive poem* (Quebec, 1806).

Lower Canada was the birthplace of the poets Levi Adams and George Longmore, and of the novelist Rosanna LEPROHON. James Russell, author of the second novel published in Canada, *Matilda; or the Indian's captive* (Three Rivers, 1833), also appears to have been Canadian born. Although known principally as poets, J.H. Willis (d. 1847) and W.F. HAWLEY both published short fiction as well.

The immigrant group who settled and published in Lower Canada is dominated numerically by the Irish-born. Standish O'GRADY and Adam KIDD are the best known today. Others were F.B. Ryan, Robert Sweeny (d. 1840), Walter HENRY, Mary Anne Madden (1820-1903), and Thomas D'Arcy McGEE. Of these only Madden, author of *Tales of the olden time* (Montreal, 1845), did not remain in Canada. Sweeny published two volumes of poetry— *Remnants* (Montreal, 1835) and *Odds and ends* (New York, 1826)—and was a popular writer in Irish-American periodicals. Henry wrote a two-volume memoir, and Ryan, a Montreal doctor, a quite extraordinary 194-page verse diatribe, *The spirit's lament; or The wrongs of Ireland* (Montreal, 1847), against the English presence in his native land. Although many notable newspaper and periodical editors were Scots, only two published their own literary works in Lower Canada. David Wylie (1811-91) began his long and distinguished Canadian journalism career as a printer in Montreal, where he re-published in 1847 his *Recollections of a convict*, which had previously appeared in Scotland. John Williamson, a Scottish-born Chelsea pensioner, published a volume of memoirs, *Narrative of a commuted pensioner* (Montreal, 1838), which is interesting for its view of the British army as seen by one of the lower ranks; he returned to Scotland on a visit in 1840 and died there. Of the English born, Bishop G.J. Mountain's volume of poetry, *Songs of the wilderness* (London, 1844)— published as part of a campaign to raise funds for Bishop's College, Lennoxville— was well received in Canada. By contrast the Rev. Joseph Abbott's *Philip Musgrave; or Memoirs of a Church of England missionary in the North American colonies* (London, 1846) was a work so insulting to dissenters that its

circulation in Canada caused a storm of protest from outraged non-Anglicans throughout the colony. J.G. Ward, author of *The spring of life* (Montreal, 1834), and John Gaisford, author of *Theatrical thoughts* and *The minor miseries of human life* (both Montreal, 1848), were probably English born.

Lower Canada was notable for the number of women writers who published there, mostly in literary periodicals. Margaret Blennerhassett is the generally accepted author of the anonymous *The widow of the rock*, a volume of poetry published in Montreal in 1824. M. Ethelind Sawtell (*The mourner's tribute*, Montreal, 1840), 'The Widow Fleck' (*Poems on various subjects*, Montreal, 1835), and M.A. Madden all advertised their separate volumes as the work of destitute gentlewomen who needed the revenue from their books in order to survive. Madden's stories are set in Ireland, but the poetry of Sawtell and Fleck, much of which is merely 'correct', contains a number of Canadian references of interest to students of sociological literary history.

Although the better-educated writers in English could speak and read French, only two of them, because they actually lived in both cultural worlds, seem to have known, or been influenced by, contemporary writing in French. Rosanna Mullins (Leprohon), who married into a prominent French-Canadian family, wrote novels, set in Québec, that were almost immediately translated into French; she is included in a recent inventory of nineteenth-century French-Canadian novelists. Less fortunate was the essayist and collector of Québec legends, Sir James MacPherson LeMoine (1825-1912), a prolific writer in both languages neglected today by French critics who consider him to be English and by English critics who consider him to be French.

Early in the nineteenth century the infrastructure that supported both writer and reader—printers, literary societies, periodicals, bookstores, etc.—was in place in Québec. Throughout the century it continued to support a small population in the production of a surprisingly large quantity of creative works. Montreal became one of the major centres of English-language publishing in Canada. Here, as Canadian literature became increasingly mature, were published the two major anthologies of nineteenth-century Canadian poetry, still valuable reference works today: The Rev. E.H. DEWART's *Selections from Canadian poets*

Québec, Writing in English in: 1

(1864), and W.D. LIGHTHALL's *Songs of the great Dominion* (1889).

MARY LU MacDONALD

2. THE MIDDLE PERIOD. Charles HEAVY-SEGE springs lively out of the early soil. Born in England in 1816, he spent a lifetime trudging indomitably the indifferent streets of Montreal. His great production, *Saul: a drama in three parts* (Montreal, 1857), a mammoth play of about 10,000 blank-verse lines, was praised by Hawthorne, Emerson, and Longfellow. Coventry Patmore declared the work to be 'indubitably one of the most remarkable English poems ever written out of Great Britain. . . . There are few things in recent poetry so praiseworthy.' The judgement runs far askew; but it is not any more wrong-headed than that of present home-grown critics who sniff at Heavysege's whole production. Only the most patriotic and anxious Canadian will want to read through these 436 pages, but with this book we are already a long way from the crude beginnings of poetry in Canada. *Saul* is a biblical commentary, nothing to do with Canada—a curiosity, perhaps a freak, yet a poem with passages of power, imagination, originality (this drama of 1857 suggests that God is capricious and vindictive!), and, sometimes, majesty.

In his richly comic later play, *Count Filippo; or, The unequal marriage. A drama in five acts* (Montreal, 1860), Heavysege felt compelled to be moral—he concludes in a flat field-day of penitence—but for sheer exuberance and linguistic liveliness, Canada has little to equal it. Although the suggestion was derided when it was made once before, it is repeated here: Canada's Stratford could do worse than mount a deliciously stylized production of *Count Filippo*. In Heavysege's *Jepththa's daughter* (Montreal, 1865), Northrop FRYE recognizes the emergence of 'the central Canadian tragic theme'—'the indifference of nature to human values'.

From that publication, to the end of the first quarter of the next century, Québec produced no literary talent in English comparable to the gradual emergence of the CONFEDERATION POETS elsewhere in Canada. Yet this period was not entirely unproductive in the lower reaches of the province. Mrs C.M. Day's *Pioneers of the Eastern Townships: a work containing official and reliable information respecting the formation of settlements with incidents in their early history; and details of adventures, perils and deliverances* (Montreal, 1863) has an absorbing narrative, and the style is personal and sure.

In these same Eastern Townships, Bishop's University, Lennoxville, has substantial literary affiliations. Belonging to the period before Confederation that saw the birth of major Canadian poetic talent is the clergyman Frederick George SCOTT, a graduate of Bishop's, who wrote about the untamed Québec landscape and composed impressive religious verse. William Henry DRUMMOND also studied at Bishop's, graduating in medicine. He had worked as a telegraph operator at Bord-à-Plouffe, a little village on the Rivière-des-Prairies, there making first contact with the subject of his later verse, French-Canadian lumbermen and *habitants*. Out of love for these people he portrayed them in humorous poems, cast in broken English, that made him internationally famous. (Many French Canadians enjoyed his portrayals.) His reputation has declined; but discerning readers will find in his poems the permanence of warmth, affection, and self-effacement.

The tradition of the English poet writing of the French-Canadian scene is continuous. Frank Oliver Call (1878-1956), professor of English at Bishop's University, wrote *Blue homespun* (1924), conventional but pleasing sonnets of the French-Canadian countryside, and a prose homage, *The spell of French Canada* (1926), which he extended in *The spell of Acadia* (1930). Call's *Acanthus and wild grape* (1920) points the way for later Canadian verse, developing from traditional structure (exemplified in the 'Acanthus' section) to the emerging verse form that is now called 'free' (the 'wild grape' poems). (In Ontario, W.W.E. ROSS was similarly engaged.) Imagism—Poundian and Amy Lowellian—was abroad, and Call's friend in nearby Sherbrooke, Louise Morey Bowman (b. 1882), delicately expressed the new movement in *Poetry* (Chicago), and in her collections *Moonlight and common day* (1922) and *Characters in cadence* (1938). The new poetic procedures being practised abroad were in use in English Québec earlier than is generally realized.

A Montreal lawyer and writer, William Douw LIGHTHALL, compiled for a London publisher one of the earliest poetry anthologies of substance: *Songs of the great Dominion: voices from the forests and water, the settlements and cities of Canada* (1889; rpr. 1971). In spite of the nationalistic thrust of the selection, it still has great interest as a record of the large number of poets and versifiers who were then being published. Among the former, Lighthall had the good judgement to include all the poets of the time that we respect today; they, however, are outnumbered by those (among them numerous 'lady singers', as he called the women poets in his long, interesting introduction) whose work has sunk into a well-deserved oblivion. The anthology, considerably pruned and in smaller format, apparently for readers abroad, was published under the title *Canadian poems and lays: selections of native verse, reflecting the seasons, legends, and life of the Dominion* (London and New York, 1893).

Striding the end of this period and the beginning of the next was a professor of political science at McGill, Stephen LEACOCK, who produced almost a book a year over much of his long life. His first book was a much-reprinted textbook, *Elements of political science* (1906). But beginning with *Literary lapses* (1910), *Nonsense novels* (1911), and SUNSHINE SKETCHES OF A LITTLE TOWN (1912), he achieved international fame as a great humorist. His many collections of comic sketches, which he produced along with numerous books of popular history, are uneven in quality, but the best of them are imperishable. His last book, *The boy I left behind me*, a fine memoir, was published in 1946, a year after his death.

3. THE LATER TWENTIETH CENTURY. The publication of the anthology NEW PROVINCES (1936) was a turning-point in Canadian poetry: from colonial subservience in form and, largely, content, it had by now moved towards poetic techniques that marked a coming-of-age, a spontaneous assertion of indigenous identity. A poem could no longer claim to be good because it mentioned Canada; the maple leaf was waived, the Mounties were dismounted. The inspiration and editorial judgement for *New provinces*, which was published in Toronto, issued from two Montrealers: A.J.M. SMITH and F.R. SCOTT. The book presented the work of six of Canada's 'most interesting younger poets': E.J. PRATT and Robert FINCH of Toronto and four Montreal poets, Leo KENNEDY, A.M. KLEIN, and Smith and Scott. As a student, Smith had absorbed the latest strategies of the best poets elsewhere who had rebelled against the artistic left-overs from Victorian tradition. His cogent essays in *The McGill Daily Literary Supplement* (1924-5), *The McGill Fortnightly Review* (1925-7), and *The CANADIAN FORUM* vitalized the Canadian artistic scene. Though he moved to the United

States (he summered near Magog in the Townships), Smith was a seminal force throughout his lifetime as both a critic and an anthologist. Scott, influenced by his friend Smith, was himself a vital and continuing catalyst who strengthened the literary-periodical scene with *Canadian Mercury* (1928-9) and as an editor of PREVIEW (1942-4). Editorial meetings for *Preview* were held in Scott's Westmount living-room, with Bruce Ruddick, Neufville Shaw, Patrick ANDERSON, P.K. PAGE, and Klein. (Scott had already begun writing his own memorable lyrics and satiric verse: his steady productiveness and numerous collections of poetry would culminate in the publication of *The collected poems of F.R. Scott*, 1981.) This was a time when the methods of Whitman, Yeats, Eliot, Pound, and William Carlos Williams were being woven into the poetic lifeline of Canada. In 1942 John SUTHERLAND founded FIRST STATEMENT (1942-5); he was joined by Irving LAYTON and Louis DUDEK the next year. First Statement Press began a series of chapbooks called 'New Writers', with Layton's first collection *Here and now* (1945). This was followed in the same year by two more first books by Montrealers: Patrick Anderson's *A tent for April* and Miriam WADDINGTON's *Green world*. When *Preview* joined strengths with John Sutherland's *First Statement*—which was of an antagonistic tendency, supporting a more proletarian and a less metaphysical and cosmopolitan stance—the amalgamation became NORTHERN REVIEW (1945-56).

All this Montreal activity was to prove of permanent literary worth to Canada. In New York, yet another Bishop's alumnus, Ralph GUSTAFSON, was also championing the cause of Canadian poetry, contributing to John Sutherland's magazine and promoting Catherine Harmon's and Paul Arthur's *Here and Now* (Toronto, 1947-9) at the Gotham Book Mart, at which celebrated literary gathering-place the only known Canadian writer was Bliss CARMAN, who was thought to be American. In an attempt to break down the establishment of archaic anthologies then current on the bookshelves of Canada, and the atrocious walls of indifference to Canadian literary worth abroad, Gustafson was active as an editor in this period, compiling Pelican (1942) and Penguin (1958; rev. 1967 and 1975) anthologies of Canadian poetry; and *Canadian accent* (1944), a collection of essays, fiction, and poems (which he could not get published in

Québec, Writing in English in: 3

Canada, though the English paperback was on sale from London to Sydney). English Québec was abroad.

In the decade that followed, most of these Québec writers wrote book after book—in Québec and elsewhere. The spate of little magazines emanating from Montreal continued. Louis Dudek produced DELTA: *A Magazine of Poetry* (1957-66); induced the standard directives from Ezra Pound; and joined Irving Layton to help set CONTACT, the Toronto periodical of Raymond SOUSTER, on the right road. Aileen Collins launched her civilized *CIV/n* (1953-4); Michael Gnarowski and Glen Siebrasse their *Yes* (1956-70). All was 'yes' and positive, though (according to the wont of little magazines) not always in longevity. What an olio, what a gallimaufry! What a cacoethes, which proved anything but foolish! Scott and Smith compiled their famous 'anthology of satire, invective, and disrespectful verse chiefly by Canadian writers', *The blasted pine* (1957; rev. 1967). In Montreal too Gwethalyn GRAHAM was writing her novel *Earth and high heaven* (1944), blasting anti-Semitism before anyone else on the Canadian scene. R.G. EVERSON was writing his crackling poetic imagery. Hugh MacLENNAN, in his TWO SOLITUDES (1945), was putting into one focus forever the two still-contentious cultures, English and French—just as A.M. Klein, with *The rocking chair and other poems* (1948), forged his own imperishable image of French-Canadian poetry. A brilliant literary career was begun by Mordecai RICHLER with his novel *The acrobats* (1954), written while he was living in Europe. An evocation of a girl showing up in Montreal is found in the writing of Mavis GALLANT, who has continued to live in Paris, and whose superb short fiction on both these themes is found in her collection, *Home truths* (1981). An upbringing in Montreal, marked by the publication of a book of poems, *Let us compare mythologies* (1956) by Leonard COHEN, was the foundation for another brilliant international career. Henry BEISSEL continues his activities as poet and as an inventive playwright, and Dudek remains an important as critic and poet. No other city in Canada surpasses the literary heritage of English Montreal.

Passing to the Eastern Townships, Québec's French-English southerly area, the *cantons* have been home to no less than seven winners of Governor General's Awards: Scott, Smith, MacLennan (5 times), John GLASSCO, Gustafson, D.G. JONES, and

Richler. At Foster there gathered in 1963 a formidable group of poets who were joined in important discussions by poets from Kingston and Toronto. All is summarized in the conference's *English poetry in Quebec* (1965), edited by John Glassco, poet and memoirist, who lived in Foster, writing his *A point of sky* (1964), a second poetry collection of much grace, and the unsurpassed prose of *Memoirs of Montparnasse* (1970). There too he edited *The poetry of French Canada in translation* (1970), a welcome and unreciprocated gesture towards fellow poets of the French tongue. On the edges of Lake Memphramagog, which stretches into alien but sibling New England, A.J.M. Smith wrote in classic shade of his lonely land, and Mordecai Richler creates tapestries of Montreal life from the warp and woof of his upbringing. To North Hatley on Lake Massawippi come Frank Scott and Hugh MacLennan each summer to refresh their writing souls. On a single street in North Hatley live Doug Jones, Ronald SUTHERLAND, and Gustafson: Jones critically pinning down the Canadian poetic imagination in his *Butterfly on rock* (1970) and writing his lyrics declaring *Under the thunder the flowers light up the earth* (1977); Sutherland bringing into still sharper focus Québec's two main cultures in his interpretations, *Second image* (1971) and *The new hero* (1977), and in his novel *Lark des neiges* (1971); Gustafson in his books of poems bringing into juxtaposition the world he has travelled with the Canada he has known and, in his short stories, exposing the puritanism of an upbringing in the Townships. Each seventh moon in the autumn, a clutch of poets congregate in North Hatley to read their poems publicly under the organizing eye of Avrum Malus. Magazines issue from the region: *Matrix* (1977-), and *The Moosehead Review* (1977-), which is under the editorship of the poets Robert Allen and Stephen Luxton. Doug Jones's *Ellipse*, founded in 1969 and ongoing under distinguished bilingual editorial boards and consultants, is without parallel in presenting in intertranslation the work of Québécois writers of both languages.

Novels of the last decade from writers in Montreal have presented excursions into modes of almost every category: thrillers from John BUELL, whose *Playground* (1976) is a narrative of breathless suspense about a hunter lost in the wilds of northern Québec; a biting satire of the Péquiste attempt to legislate culture, *The underdogs* (1979), from William Weintraub; and compassionate comedy, *Schmucks* (1972), from Seymour Blicker. From the Eastern Townships has come a small-town *genre* painting full of Breughellian love of life in the novel *Pilgaric the death* (1967; rpr. 1980) by Bernard Epps. Among the poets of Montreal in the last decade an amazing continuity of imaginative expression in English has persisted, despite the efforts of a Péquiste government that, with its linguistic laws, frowns down upon and stifles English-speaking talent living or yet unborn. The poets André Farkas and Ken Norris have presented English-language creativity in further anthologies: *Montreal English poetry of the seventies* (1977) and *The Véhicule poets* (1979), each containing work by new poets of substantial worth: Michael Harris, David Solway, Richard SOMMER, Peter Van Toorn, Marc Plourde, Tom Konyves, Stephen Morrissey, and Claudia Lapp.

The surgence and re-surgence of English creativity in Québec is extraordinary. Once officially recognized by the governmental institution of the Prix David, this is now ignored by the official bureaucracy and by French-speaking colleagues alike. But we hope this division will not last. Whether from the avenues of Montreal, the Appalachian lowlands of the Eastern Townships, or the accidental appearance of English-language writers in other French parishes, creativity in English persists in Québec. The literary history of Canada cannot be written without acknowledging this fact.

RALPH GUSTAFSON

Québec, Writing in French in. See entries on writings in French in BIOGRAPHY AND MEMOIRS, CHILDREN'S DRAMA, CHILDREN'S LITERATURE, COLLECTIVE CREATIONS, CRITICISM, DRAMA, ESSAYS, FOLKLORE, HISTORICAL WRITING, HUMOUR AND SATIRE, JOUAL, NEW FRANCE, NOVELS, POETRY, SCIENCE FICTION AND FANTASY, and SHORT STORIES.

Quesnel, Joseph (1746-1809). Born in Saint-Malo, France, into a prosperous family of traders and ship-chandlers, he travelled widely before his ship, transporting supplies to the Americas, was seized by the British off Nova Scotia in 1779. Through family connections with Governor Haldimand, he was allowed to settle in Lower Canada, where he remained. He soon married into a family that had enriched itself in the fur trade, to which commerce he then successfully dedicated himself, retiring after 1793 to lead the comfortable life of a landed gentleman in Boucherville. Dramatist, poet, musician, and composer, Quesnel became in his retirement the most important writer of his time in Canada.

Soon after his arrival he became involved with amateur theatricals in Montreal and was a founding member of a troupe that performed in 1790 his best-known work, *Colas et Colinette; ou Le bailli dupé*, the first operetta written in North America. It was successful, and was revived in Quebec in 1805 and 1807 before being printed there with the date '1808', although it was apparently not published until 1812. It has continued to exert a modest influence on native dramatists to the present, having last been performed and recorded for Radio-Canada in 1968, then published (1974) in an English translation. Two other plays, neither one published or performed in Quesnel's lifetime, are *Les républicains français; ou La soirée du cabaret*, composed about 1801, and *L'Anglomanie; ou Le dîner à l'anglaise*, composed two years later. Quesnel also left the incomplete score for another operetta, which was to be called 'Lucas et Cécile'. He is also the author of some 34 poems, many of which appeared in newspapers of the time.

Colas et Colinette is a light comedy in three acts, with frequent musical interventions, stock characters, and a theme directly reminiscent of 'society' theatre in France of a generation or more before. The happiness of two young lovers is menaced by a scheming village bailiff; but the heroine, Colinette, outsmarts him, and the village squire, M. Dolmont, is there to ensure that youth and virtue triumph. The music is derivative, but the reprise as a whole is not displeasing. More original is *Les républicains français* (*La* BARRE DU JOUR, été 1970), a savage satire in one act of the perceived excesses of the French Revolution. In a cabaret in Paris, five motley representatives of the New Order enthuse about the advances the Revolution has brought, while their befuddled views and progressive drunkenness depict its moral and political bankruptcy (in the eyes of the conservative Quesnel). Not published until 1970, the play had no influence in Quesnel's time—like *L'Anglomanie*, which was not published until 1932-3 in *Le Canada français*, though it is the only play by Quesnel with a Canadian setting or theme and is generally considered his best. In verse and in one act, it depicts a French-Canadian seigneur, M. Primenbourg, who is persuaded to ape English ways by his son-in-law, who is aide-de-camp to the governor. The characters are drawn from real life, the topic was current, and the lesson that one must avoid Anglomania is conveyed with an effective comic touch. *L'Anglomanie* was also published in *La Barre du jour* (juill.-déc. 1965).

Quesnel's poems comprise mainly songs, epigrams, and occasional pieces, but include references to the political situation in Lower Canada ('L'anti-Français', 'Chanson' [1807], 'Les moissonneurs'); exude a personal philosophy of life ('Le petit bonhomme vit encore!', 'À M. Panet', 'Stances marotiques à mon esprit'); reflect on his own travails as a poet in an unappreciative land ('Le rimeur dépité, 'Épître à Labadie'); and give advice to actors and writers ('Adresse aux jeunes acteurs', 'La nouvelle académie'). But they exhibit no real poetic talent. Five of his poems have been published by Michael Gnarowski in *Quelques chansons selon les manuscrits dans la collection Lande* (1970). Quesnel's plays have been analysed in depth by B. Burger in *L'activité théâtrale au Québec (1765-1825)* (1974) and by D.M. Hayne in 'Le théâtre de Joseph Quesnel', *Archives des lettres canadienne*, V (1976). J.E. Hare is currently preparing a critical edition of Quesnel's complete works. LEONARD DOUCETTE

R

Raddall, Thomas (b. 1903). Thomas Head Raddall was born in the married quarters of the British Army School of Musketry at Hythe, Eng., where his father was an instructor. The latter's posting to Halifax in 1913 made his son a Nova Scotian and resulted in Raddall's steadfast, intimate, and rewarding bond with that province. His engrossing and candid autobiography, *In my time* (1976), tells how Raddall, too poor to attend university, served as a wireless operator on coastal stations, at sea, and on Sable Island from 1919 to 1922; he then qualified as a bookkeeper, took a job with a lumber company on the Mersey River, and soon began to write, having developed an interest in the history of his province—in Micmacs, pre-Loyalist settlers, Loyalists, privateering, and the economic diseases that befell Canada's Atlantic littoral following the age of sail. These years—which introduced him also to hunting and fishing, logging, rumrunning, business machinations, and backwoods politics—were the fullest of Raddall's life. Having published short stories in *Blackwood's Magazine* and elsewhere, Raddall chose in 1938 to become a professional writer. During the Second World War he was an officer in the West Nova Scotia Regiment, worked as a journalist and as a scriptwriter for radio, and published two collections of short stories and two novels.

Raddall's *The pied piper of Dipper Creek and other stories* (1939), with an introduction by John Buchan, won a Governor General's Award. This was followed by *Tambour and other stories* (1945); *The wedding gift and other stories* (1947); *A muster of arms and other stories* (1954); and *At the tide's turn and other stories* (1959), a selection from the earlier publications. All these collections demonstrate Raddall's knowledge of the texture of Nova Scotia life, past and present, and his facility for straightforward, entertaining storytelling.

Raddall's first historical novel, *His Majesty's Yankees* (1942), which deals with the conflicting political, economic, and emotional ties of Nova Scotians during the American Revolution, shows—in its sound use of J.B. Brebner's *The neutral Yankees of Nova Scotia* and Simeon Perkins' diaries—his enterprising, meticulous research. Its robust style also animates *Roger Sudden* (1944), a story of the Seven Years' War and the capture of Louisbourg, and *Pride's Fancy* (1946), a rousing tale of a privateer in West Indies waters during the fight for Haitian independence. *The governor's lady* (1960) offers a masterful re-creation of the personality and character of Fannie Wentworth, wife of the lieutenant-governor (1792-1808) of Nova Scotia. In *Hangman's beach* (1966) the focus is twofold: Raddall evokes the 1803-12 period of the Napoleonic Wars in Halifax, with particular emphasis on French prisoners held on Melville Island; and, through his portrayal of the Peter McLeod family, delineates the boom in Nova Scotia commerce during those years.

Though best known for his historical fiction, Raddall also wrote three novels set in the twentieth century—one of which, *The nymph and the lamp* (1950), is his masterpiece. With its superbly conveyed settings (Halifax, Sable Island, and the Annapolis Valley), its astutely interwoven themes, sexual tension, and powerful characterization of the protagonist, Isabel Jardine, it is a work of enduring merit that cannot be dismissed as a romance. *Tidefall* (1953) and *Wings of the night* (1956) are mediocre by comparison: the former has to do with a seafaring villain who makes and loses a fortune, the latter with forest life and economic troubles in Nova Scotia.

That Raddall should also have published three books of history is not surprising, given his strong association with the past, his evergreen curiosity, and his investigative talents. The authoritative chronicle *Halifax, warden of the north* (1948; rev. 1965), and the discerning and spirited popular history *The path of destiny: Canada from the British Conquest to home rule, 1763-1850* (1957), both won Governor General's Awards. *Footsteps on old floors* (1968), a lighter work, contains essays on obscure but compelling 'mysteries' of Nova Scotia history, most notably that of the derelict vessel *Mary Celeste* and her missing crew. Raddall also wrote the text for *A pictorial guide to historic Nova Scotia: featuring Louisbourg, Peggy's Cove and Sable Island* (rev. 1972).

As a professional writer Raddall never asked for, nor received, money from government sources. One of the few Canadian writers in this century to achieve independence through his writing, he wrote fiction with the purpose of selling it, and succeeded in doing so without sacrificing his artistic integrity. In addition to receiving three Governor General's Awards, he was elected to the Royal Society of Canada in 1949 and was presented with the Lorne PIERCE Medal for literature in 1956. He became a Companion of the Order of Canada in 1971.

The following titles are in the New Canadian Library: *His Majesty's Yankees, The nymph and the lamp, Pride's fancy, Roger Sudden*, and *At the tide's turn*.

See also HISTORICAL WRITING IN ENGLISH: 6.   ROBERT COCKBURN

Radin, Paul. See INDIAN LEGENDS AND TALES: BIBLIOGRAPHY.

Radisson, Pierre-Esprit. See Writing in NEW FRANCE: 1.

Rand, Silas T. See INDIAN LEGENDS AND TALES: BIBLIOGRAPHY.

Reaney, James (b. 1926). 1. POETRY. Born in South Easthope near Stratford, Ont., he studied English at University College, University of Toronto (M.A. 1949). He taught English at the University of Manitoba from 1949 until 1956, when he returned to Toronto to complete a doctorate, which was awarded in 1958; his thesis was 'The influence of Spenser on Yeats', supervised by Northrop FRYE. In 1950 he married Colleen Thibaudeau, also a poet, and they have a son and daughter. In 1960 he began teaching English at the University of Western Ontario, where he is now a professor. In that year he also started the magazine ALPHABET, on 'the iconography of the imagination', which lasted ten years. His first book of poems, *The red heart* (1949), written when Reaney was twenty-three, received a Governor General's Award. It was followed by *A suit of nettles* (1958; 2nd edn, 1975) and *Twelve letters to a small town* (1962), both of which also won Governor General's Awards, and by *The dance of death at London, Ontario* (1963; drawings by Jack Chambers). *Poems* (1972), which includes the four previous collections, *Selected shorter poems* (1975), and *Selected longer poems* (1976) were edited by Germaine Warkentin, with extensive introductions that are among the best Reaney criticism.

The red heart, a collection of 42 lyrics, is an intensely private, even precious book. Already the playfulness, and the somewhat child-like character of Reaney's poetic temperament—though not his technical mastery—are evident. Its central figure is a youthful artist coming to poetic terms with a provincial environment, the Perth County of Reaney's childhood. The poems are infused with a sentimental nostalgia as the poet, in the role of orphan, tries to create an imaginary play-box world of childhood as an antidote to a hostile cultural world. *A suit of nettles* is an extraordinary leap forward. Perhaps under the tutelage of Frye (see Reaney's 'The Canadian poet's predicament', *University of Toronto Quarterly*, xxvi, April 1978), Reaney draws on traditional literary structures to inform his poem, imitat-

Reaney: poetry

ing Spenser's *The shepheardes calender*. A series of twelve pastoral eclogues, *A suit of nettles* focuses on a southern-Ontario town, seen from the perspective of the barnyard geese in their twelve-month cycle from birth to ritual slaughter at Christmas. An opening invocation to the Muse of Satire 'to beat fertility into a sterile land' makes Reaney's satiric purpose clear: the geese provide a repertoire of human types—lover, teacher, philosopher, poet, critic—imitating an archetypal human community struggling against victimization by time and death and the negativism in man that denies creativity. The sequence—made up of allegorical puzzles, dialogue poems, beast fables, and graphic poems—gives full play to the quirky, sardonic wit of Reaney, for whom poetry is game and mischief.

Twelve letters to a small town is a suite of lyrics—dialogue and prose poems in the form of a libretto that was set to music for chamber orchestra by John Beckwith and broadcast on CBC 'Wednesday Night' in July 1961. Reaney erects a model of Stratford, remembered from the late thirties and early forties, and tries to recover the physical and spiritual environment that created him in the persona of a lively, imaginative boy, gifted with a capacity to see wonder and mystery in the simple and homely. The result is deeply attractive. Reminiscent of *Under milkwood* by Dylan Thomas, *Twelve letters* is an act of imagination by which the poet recreates his rural roots in their ideal mythological form.

The dance of death and 'Two Chapters from an Emblem Book', published in *Poems*, derive from Reaney's enduring fascination with iconography. As Germaine Warkentin has written, 'Reaney began to think . . . one could develop a virtual iconography of the imagination, an alphabet of images which would disclose the relationship between "the verbal universe which hovers over the seed-bed of the so-called real and natural world" and the seedbed itself' ('Introduction', *Poems*). The emblem book, a combination of diagram and verbal puns, tries to identify a whole unsorted alphabet of special diagrams in the triangles, circles, and crosses that recur in art. While this interest in hieroglyph and pictograph is engaged mostly at the level of game, it is rooted in Reaney's ambition to recover a traditional interest in graphic symbols as vehicles in articulating otherwise inapprehensible metaphysical insights. (See Reaney's 'Search for an undiscovered alpha-

bet', *Canadian Art*, vol. 22, 1965.)

Reaney is a poet who has been accused of bookishness, and of academicism in his indebtedness to Frye. However, this is to disregard the exuberant playfulness and the genuine understanding of myth that gives to his work what Dave GODFREY calls 'its wonderful health'. Reaney will always have his devoted readers who, like Warkentin, find his poems among the most richly satisfying written in Canada.

Reaney is also the author of a novel for children, *The boy with an R in his hand* (1965; rev. 1980), about York (Toronto) in the 1820s. He is a fellow of the Royal Society, was made an officer of the Order of Canada in 1975, and received an honorary Doctor of Letters from St Patrick's College, Carleton University, in 1975.

See Alvin A. Lee, *James Reaney* (1968), Ross G. Woodman, *James Reaney* (1971), and Stan Dragland ed., *Approaches to the work of James Reaney* (1983).

See also CRITICISM IN ENGLISH: 4 and POETRY IN ENGLISH 1950 TO 1982: 1.

ROSEMARY SULLIVAN

2. DRAMA. James Reaney turned to writing drama after he had become established as a poet. The libretto for the chamber opera *Night-blooming Cereus* by John Beckwith was completed in 1953 (though the opera was not produced until 1960), and was published in 1962 in *The killdeer and other plays*, which also included *The sun and the moon* and *One-man masque*. This was followed by *Colours in the dark* (1969), *Listen to the wind* (1972), and *Masks of childhood* (1972), which contains three plays: *The easter egg, Three desks*, and a revised version of *The killdeer*. Reaney has also written several children's plays, some of which have been published in *Apple butter and other plays for children* (1973), which includes *Geography match, Names and nicknames*, and *Ignoramus*. (See CHILDREN's DRAMA IN ENGLISH.)

Reaney's early plays brought great imagination to English-Canadian drama. Some of them, written mainly or partly in verse, treat themes also found in his poetry: the contrasting worlds of innocence and experience, the underlying evil forces in everyone, love's power to redeem, the process of growth from childhood to adolescence to maturity. Reaney prefers a non-linear, kaleidoscopic drama to one based on the assumptions of the realistic theatre. Indeed, the complexity and profusion of events in his plays often bewilder and dissatisfy audiences accustomed to realistic drama. Rich in symbolism and patterns of imagery, the plays often present a fanciful, surrealistic world; and since little attempt is made to develop plot or character, their lack of emotional depth sometimes hinders audience involvement.

The themes of the libretto for the chamber opera *Night-blooming Cereus* are loneliness and reconciliation. It was performed at Hart House Theatre, Toronto, in 1960, along with *One-man masque* (with Reaney himself as the performer)—a short poetic fantasy on birth, death, and other stages of human life. *The sun and the moon* includes elements of farce (as do most of Reaney's plays) that show the evil influences lurking in a small Ontario community. In *The sun and the moon* Reaney uses melodrama (a convention he is fond of) to bring these influences to the surface and to heighten the comic and redemptive dimensions of the play: when an abortionist, who falsely accuses the local parson of fathering her child, is thwarted by her own miscalculations, peace is restored to the chastened community.

The title of one collection of Reaney's plays, *Masks of childhood*, suggests the central place of the child's world in Reaney's work—as a symbol of unspoiled innocence, a mask to hide a deeper world of evil, and a shield for those who cannot enter the adult world of risk and responsibility. In its 1972 version *The killdeer* emphasizes the hold of a violent or inhibiting past on the lives of children from different families; only their mutual love and forgiveness enable them to break free. *Three desks* is a macabre and farcical treatment of the childishness and hostility that can affect the life of an academic community, in this case a small liberal-arts college on the Prairies. *The easter egg* is a symbolic exploration of Christian redemption and resurrection: Kenneth, who has been considered retarded by his stepmother, is finally brought out of his arrested state by the patient and understanding Polly. *Colours in the dark*, first produced at Stratford, Ont., in 1967 under the direction of John Hirsch, shows Reaney's surer command of the free dramatic form towards which all his plays tend. Of its forty-two scenes, which give impressions of growing up in southwestern Ontario, Reaney says: 'This one has a new play before you every two minutes.' *Listen to the wind* adds a sombre note to the optimism of some of the earlier plays. Centred on a sick boy's efforts to reunite his parents

by having them take part in a play he has adapted—*The saga of Caresfoot Court*—it shows that the child's design fails, though he goes to bed believing it has succeeded. The play-within-a-play technique contrasts the worlds of imagination and reality.

Reaney's ability to confront more realistic situations, while developing new forms of dramatic structure, is more evident in *The Donnellys*, a trilogy of plays entitled *Sticks and stones: the Donnellys, part one* (1976), *The St. Nicholas Hotel, Wm. Donnelly, Prop: the Donnellys, part two* (1976), and *Handcuffs: the Donnellys: part three* (1977)—about the famous Irish immigrant family that was massacred in Lucan, Ont., in 1880. *The St. Nicholas Hotel* won the Chalmers Award for 1974. Combining history, poetry, music, dance, marionettes, magic lanterns, liturgy, mime, and myth, the plays were written after some eight years of research on the Donnellys and their times. The family, who had lived and died in southwestern Ontario, some thirty miles from where Reaney was born, had fascinated him since he was a boy. Reaney is clearly sympathetic to the Donnellys and rejects their reputation as 'the Black Donnellys'; he presents them as superior and heroic, even Christ-like figures, who die for their own dignity and their right to be different. The trilogy was developed in workshops with director Keith Turnbull and the NDWT Company, which presented it at Toronto's Tarragon Theatre between 1973 and 1975, and in the fall of 1975 took *The Donnellys* on a cross-Canada tour—to nineteen communities from Vancouver to Halifax—climaxed by a final presentation of all three parts in one day at the Bathurst St. Theatre in Toronto on 14 Dec. 1975. Reaney wrote a personal account of the tour, the actors' experiences, and the play's reception, in *14 barrels from sea to sea* (1977), which also contains reviews from all the cities in which it was performed. He plans to publish a book of documents and other material he discovered while researching the Donnellys.

While *The Donnellys* is the landmark achievement of Reaney's drama to date, he has continued to write plays based on local history, at times giving them universal significance. *Baldoon* (1976), co-authored with Marty Gervais, concerns events in a small community near Wallaceburg, Ont., in the 1830s, involving poltergeists, witchcraft, and a witch hunter. When unaccountable mishaps occur in the household of Dr McTavish, he calls upon Dr Troyer, an exorcist from Long Point, to help them. Liberation entails the defeat of McTavish's dour Presbyterianism by Troyer's joyous Shaker brand of Christianity. Reaney's use of puppets and marionettes in this play is more inventive than in *The Donnellys*.

Some later plays were commissioned for special groups or occasions. *The dismissal; or Twisted beards and tangled whiskers* (1979) was commissioned by Reaney's alma mater, University College, to mark the sesquicentennial of the University of Toronto in 1977. For the occasion Reaney dramatized some little-known events in the university's history in 1894-5 when a professor of mathematics, William Dale, was dismissed for writing a letter to the *Globe* in which he complained of nepotism and foreign domination in the teaching staff of the university. But the play is above all entertainment and includes musical routines, vaudeville, and an actress playing the bearded President Fury of the university.

In *Wacousta!* (1979) Reaney made a play from the melodramatic early-Canadian novel (q.v.) by John RICHARDSON. The published version of the play contains detailed descriptions of its development in workshops in London and Timmins, Ont. Reaney has already presented, in workshop, parts of another play based on *The Canadian brothers; or, The Prophecy fulfilled*, Richardson's sequel to *Wacousta*.

King Whistle! (1980, in the journal *Brick*, no. 8), written for the centenary of the Central Secondary School in Stratford, Ont., was first performed at the Avon Theatre, Stratford, in Nov. 1979. Again the subject is local and historical—the 1933 strike of workers in seven furniture factories and of women-workers in the Swift plant—and was developed by Reaney and the NDWT company in conjunction with students and residents of Stratford. It lacks the wide appeal of some of his other plays, as does his next play *Antler River* (unpublished), commissioned by the Urban League of London, Ont. (where Reaney lives), to celebrate the city's 125th anniversary in 1980 (and to show 'we're not a transplanted English place; we're our own place and can christen ourselves, thank you.'). Reaney's *Gyroscope*, performed at the Tarragon Theatre as part of the 1981 Toronto Theatre Festival, represents a return to personal vision and experience. It contains satire on sex, marriage, small-town life, and academia, and explores with humour the struggle for balance and understanding in a creative husband-wife re-lationship. Perhaps too personal to be widely popular, it suggests that Reaney is ready to move in new directions in drama.

Reaney also wrote the libretto for *The shivaree: opera in two acts* (1978), with music by John Beckwith, which Comus Music Theatre premièred at the St Lawrence Centre, Toronto, and on CBC radio in 1982. The title refers to the custom—still practised in parts of southwestern Ontario—of serenading a newly wedded couple on homemade percussion instruments. Set in a farming district there in the early twentieth century, it deals light-heartedly and poetically with a Persephone figure, Daisy, who is rescued from an unhappy marriage by her true love, with the help of the 'shivareers'.

James Stewart Reaney has written a study of his father's plays in the Profiles of Canada Drama series (1977). An explanation of why Reaney began to write plays may be found in his article 'Ten years at play' in CANADIAN LITERATURE 41 (Summer 1969). Some of his ideas about drama and Canadian literature may be found in the newsletter, *Halloween*, which Reaney occasionally publishes in different journals.

See also DRAMA IN ENGLISH: 1953 TO 1981. JAMES NOONAN

Reeves, John. See DRAMA IN ENGLISH: 1953 TO 1981 and MYSTERY AND CRIME.

Reeves, John. See HISTORICAL WRITING IN ENGLISH: 3.

Refus global (1948). If any single event marked the beginning of modern Québec, it was the appearance of this manifesto, which was published privately in 400 copies as a collection of loose typewritten mimeographed pages in a portfolio designed by Jean-Paul Riopelle. The title essay was written and signed by the painter Paul-Émile Borduas (1905-60); it also carried the signatures of fifteen members of his circle, including Claude GAUVREAU and Riopelle. (The portfolio also contained shorter pieces by Borduas and others, and three short plays by Gauvreau). Its attack on the role of the clergy and capitalist powers in maintaining Québec's submission, and its description of the fear of authority, in which the majority of the population lived, provoked a *succès de scandale* in Duplessis's tightly controlled society, and brought about Borduas's dismissal from his teaching job and his subsequent exile to New York and later to Paris, where he died.

Mainly because of its description of Québec as 'a colony trapped since 1760 within the slippery walls of fear, the usual refuge of the vanquished', *Refus global* has been viewed as the first step in the modern nationalist movement in Québec. The manifesto, however, goes on to describe a major crisis in Western values, whose emptiness is concealed behind a veil of abstract knowledge: the only hope is in a collective refusal to submit to the utilitarian conventions of society, and in the discovery of the liberating possibilities of art. 'We foresee a time when man will be freed from his useless chains and realize in the unpredictable order of spontaneity and a resplendent anarchy the fullness of his individual gifts. Until then, neither resting nor flagging, with fellow feeling for all those who thirst after a better life, fearless of the long road, regardless of encouragement or persecution, we will joyfully pursue our savage need for liberation.' No single label seems to fit *Refus global*. The fact that it has variously been called anarchist, surrealist, nationalist, Marxist, and Freudian may explain its lasting impact. Probably its most important influence on Québec culture derived from its clear message that art cannot isolate itself from society, and that to liberate his or her voice the artist must become allied with social revolution.

An English translation can be found in Ramsay Cook, *French-Canadian nationalism* (1969). See also Dennis Reid, *A concise history of Canadian painting* (1973) and François-Marc Gagnon, *Paul-Émile Borduas/écrits/writings 1942-1958* (Nova Scotia College of Art and Design, 1978), in which the pages of the title essay of *Refus global* are reproduced.　　　　PATRICIA SMART

Relève, La (1934-48). This monthly journal was founded in Mar. 1934 by a group of young French Canadians, among whom the prime movers were Robert CHARBONNEAU and Claude Hurtubise. Until its demise in Sept. 1948, it published 48 numbers under the name *La Relève* and 55 under the name *La Nouvelle Relève*. Among its major Québec contributors were Robert ÉLIE, Roger Duhamel, Hector de Saint-Denys GARNEAU, and Jean LE MOYNE, and it occasionally published works by such famous French authors as Daniel Rops, Jacques Maritain, and Emmanuel Mounier. The magazine set out to promote the emergence of a 'national independent Catholic group' whose aim would be to 'develop an art, a lit-

erature, and a line of thought, the lack of which begins to be oppressive'. Though the founders were concerned about the state of the economy, they viewed this as a problem more related to spiritual matters and to civilization itself than to mere social and economic questions. They hoped to establish a society modelled on that of the Middle Ages, when there was harmony between the temporal and the spiritual. In accordance with these very general ideas, they considered that the problems of French-Canadian society centred on literature, Catholicism, the educational system, etc. It was against this background that the literary works of its chief contributors were produced: Robert Charbonneau and Robert Élie in the novel; Saint-Denys Garneau in poetry; and Jean Le Moyne in the essay.

See also Robert CHARBONNEAU and LITERARY MAGAZINES IN QUÉBEC: 2.
　　　　　　　　　　　　JACQUES PELLETIER

Religion and theology. The pioneer clergy of Canada, although not always persons of great talent, were usually among the most highly educated members of their communities. It was only natural, therefore, that their names should figure prominently on lists of early Canadian publications. Many of their writings were polemical, designed to support particular theological, ecclesiastical, or political causes in societies that were moving uneasily towards a still unattained equilibrium. Thomas McCULLOCH's *Popery condemned by scripture and the fathers* (Edinburgh, 1808), Edmund Burke's *Remarks on a pamphlet called Popery condemned by scripture and the fathers* (Halifax, 1809), and Egerton Ryerson's *Claims of the churchmen and dissenters of Upper Canada brought to the test: in a controversy between several members of the Church of England and a Methodist preacher* (Kingston, 1828) indicate by their titles the pre-ecumenical atmosphere of their times. Although breaking little new ground, these early writers displayed wide familiarity not only with the Bible but with church fathers, schoolmen, and reformers, and occasionally enlivened their arguments with classical allusions. Some, such as the self-educated Methodist preacher John Carroll, in *Past and present; or A description of persons and events connected with Canadian Methodism for the last forty years* (Toronto, 1860), celebrated the struggles of their denominations to establish themselves in Canada. Occasionally we are surprised by the originality of an argument. In *Lectures on the millennium* (Toronto, 1844),

Religion and theology

for example, John Roaf, a Congregational minister of Toronto, used the imagery of contemporary adventism to discover signs of the progressive approach of the kingdom of God—missionary expansion, enlightenment, moral improvement, harmony among Christians, and social justice—and thus prefigured the program that was undertaken by the major Protestant churches for over a century. Of particular literary interest for their exotic, if sometimes grotesque, imagery were the writings of two less-conventional divines: *Two mites on some of the most important and much disputed points of divinity* (Halifax, 1781) and other works by Henry ALLINE and *The impressions of the mind* (Toronto, 1835) by David Willson, founder of the Children of Peace and designer of their remarkable Sharon Temple near Toronto.

Early religious writers, despite their divergences, agreed in accepting as a starting-point in argument the existence of scriptures that were infallible in every respect. Their successors in the later decades of the nineteenth century had to take account of challenges to this assumption posed by German biblical criticism and by Charles Darwin's theory of non-purposive evolution. The most substantial Canadian opponent of the new approach was the McGill scientist Sir J. William Dawson, whose *Archaia; or, Studies of the cosmogony and natural history of the Hebrew scriptures* (Montreal, 1860) was the first of several books attacking evolutionary theories. Others sought to demonstrate the compatibility of current ideas with the Christian faith, notably W.G. Jordan of Queen's University in *Biblical criticism and modern thought* (1909). Scholars applied the new methods to their disciplines, most successfully in Old Testament studies where Canadians attained international repute. J.F. McCurdy's three-volume *History, prophecy, and the monuments in Israel and the nations* (New York, 1894-1901) was a pioneer work in this field. *Hebrew origins* (1936) by Theophile J. Meek, McCurdy's former colleague and his successor as head of the Department of Near Eastern Studies, University College, Toronto, is still a standard reference work. John WATSON of Queen's proposed a synthesis of Kantian philosophy and an updated Christianity in *Christianity and idealism* (New York, 1897), while Nathanael Burwash, chancellor of Victoria University, Toronto, wrote the ambitious, although now largely forgotten, *Manual of Christian theology on the inductive method* (1900). Mean-

while there had emerged an esoteric strain of religious thought, born of American transcendentalism and nourished by increasing familiarity with Eastern religions, that passed almost unnoticed among theologians but profoundly affected both the CONFEDERATION POETS and artists associated with the Group of Seven. The most influential publication in this genre in Canada was R.M. BUCKE's *Cosmic consciousness* (1901), while such books as *Mediums and mystics* (1923) by A. Durrant Watson and Margaret Lawrence point to the existence of a continuing if fragile tradition.

Within academic circles at least, the acceptance of critical methods has led writers of the last half-century to turn their attention to other issues. The challenge of Karl Barth to what he regarded as a complacent liberalism was taken up most directly by W.W. Bryden of Knox College, Toronto, in *The Christian's knowledge of God* (1940). Probably the most influential Canadian book reflecting the influence of Protestant neo-orthodoxy, however, was C.N. Cochrane's *Christianity and classical culture* (1940), a sympathetic study of St Augustine's theology of history that had its provenance not in a theological college but in a university department of history (University of Toronto). Meanwhile, regular visits by Étienne Gilson and Jacques Maritain had helped to establish the Pontifical Institute of Mediaeval Studies in Toronto as one of the world's most prestigious centres in its field. During the theological ferment of the 1960s Canadian Roman Catholic scholarship began to show signs of an originality hitherto largely lacking. Leslie Dewart's *The future of belief* (1966) stirred considerable controversy with its claim that Hellenic influence had seriously distorted the original Christian message. Gregory Baum began a career as a prolific and provocative writer, perhaps most constructively in *Man becoming* (1970). Today the interest of Canadian religious writers is extending beyond the national borders as never before. Among the major works of scholars still actively writing are Bernard J.F. Lonergan's *Method in theology* (1972), Emil Fackenheim's *Encounter between Judaism and modern philosophy: a preface to future Jewish thought* (1973), and Wilfred Cantwell Smith's *Faith and belief* (1979).

Canadian religious writing, while often of high quality in both content and style, has for the most part sprung from a desire to defend convictions or explore issues rather than from a specifically literary intent. Now and then, however, writers have sought to clothe religious ideas in forms deliberately intended to appeal to the imagination. Alline and Willson were prolific writers of hymns, of which few were of consistently high quality but many contained lines well above the ordinary. Until well into the twentieth century the sermon was a recognized vehicle of literary expression: along with the pious who flocked for spiritual nourishment in the thirties and forties to such preachers as George C. Pidgeon (United), W.A. Cameron (Baptist), and R.J. Renison (Anglican)—all of Toronto—and Robert W. Norwood (Anglican) of Montreal, there were also some who attended their services mainly to savour their rhetoric. The religious motivation of much Canadian popular fiction—as represented by such writers as Ralph Connor (Charles W. GORDON), Nellie McCLUNG, R.E. KNOWLES, and Marian Keith (Mary Esther MacGREGOR)—was especially marked in the early years of the century. It sprang, for the most part, from traditional forms of piety tinctured with a lively interest in moral and social betterment. Since that time it has not so much diminished as taken less obviously propagandist forms, as in Hugh MacLENNAN's *The watch that ends the night* (1959) or in Rudy WIEBE's sensitive *The blue mountains of China* (1970). There have also been a few attempts to apply theological criteria to literary criticism, as in Malcolm Ross's *Poetry and dogma* (1954), Joseph C. McLelland's *The clown and the crocodile* (1970), and Kenneth and Alice Hamilton's *The elements of John Updike* (1970). Northrop FRYE's *The great code: the Bible and literature* (1982) performs the reverse operation, drawing upon the categories of literary criticism to illuminate our understanding of the Bible. Eschewing the categories of formal theology and source criticism as largely irrelevant to his purpose, he examines the language, metaphors, and typological arrangement of this massive collection in order to establish its essential unity of theme. Frye has not done the theologians' work for them, but he has magisterially expounded a methodology of which they will have to take account. If his challenge is taken up seriously, religious and theological writings may bulk larger in a future edition of *The Oxford companion to Canadian literature*.

JOHN WEBSTER GRANT

Renaud, Claude. See ACADIAN LITERATURE: 2(b).

Renaud, Jacques (b. 1943). Born and brought up in the Montreal working-class district of Rosemont, he attended a public secondary school. After failing his Grade XI examinations, he began a series of manual jobs, then became a clerk in the municipal film library. He has worked in advertising, as a journalist, and as a researcher for a Radio-Canada TV program. Soon after it was founded in 1963, Renaud became associated with the Indépendentiste/Marxist magazine PARTI PRIS.

Renaud's best-known novel—the first creative prose work in Québec to use JOUAL for dialogue and narration—is the powerful and shocking *Le cassé* (1964), written when the author was just twenty-one and living in the squalid area of Montreal's 'Centre-Ville'. The title, a *joual* word based on the English slang expression 'broke', also conjures up images of a central figure who is beaten, crippled, and disoriented. The hero, Tit-Jean, probably the most totally alienated character in Québec literature—the novel has been called 'le chant ultime de la dépossession'—conceives and perpetrates the brutal murder of a 'goofball' peddlar, whom he wrongfully takes to be a secret lover of his mistress. The murder assumes an escapist and ritualistic character, giving temporary feelings of liberation to the frustrated hero. Despite some weak characterization and occasional maladroit interjections by the narrator, *Le cassé* contains striking lower-depths poetry and skilful cinematic techniques. A second edition (1977) adds four short stories and the author's two-part 'Journal du *Cassé*', the first edition of which consists of short texts that discuss *Le cassé* directly or indirectly and the second including excerpts from reviews of the first edition that document the furore caused by the book's inclusion in a CGEP course in the Sorel region in 1971. The best prose work of the *parti pris* group of writers, *Le cassé* was translated by Gérald Robitaille as *Flat broke and beat* (1968).

En d'autres paysages (1970) is an unsuccessful attempt to wed cosmogony and fantasy with social realism. Luc Richard, having killed his wife (and some of his children?), flees to a rural village, where he tries to find a *raison d'être* by teaching in the village school and making love to his landlord's daughter; at the end, however, she is dead and her father's property is destroyed by fire. The style is frequently gauche—the realistic framework is unstably mixed with phantasms and mystical passages, and the narrative voice shifts confusingly—but the book contains some fine prose-poetry and an engaging portrait of the farmer and his daughter. The very short, poetic *Le fond pur de l'errance irradie* (1975) is set, one learns gradually, in Istanbul. The hero is a writer, Irradieu (once called Erradieu), who has been touched by 'Shakti' ('l'intélligence créatrice'); he opposes ideologies and religions and sees himself as a member of a new superhuman race. After defeating the symbolically evil Orang-utan, he becomes Irradient and, though he rejects nationalism and the 'chaos répressif du collectif', returns finally to the 'Ville Royale au Mont Réel de son Enfance' to retrieve his lost dawn-like love, Esther. They marry and create an infinite progeniture.

In another short work, *Ly cycle du scorpion* (1979), astrological symbols permeate the automatic prose poetry of its versets. Here, as elsewhere in Renaud's work, the 'princes de tristesse' of the traditional Québec Church are scorned in favour of a new individualistic mysticism. The text—accompanied by Gilles Langlois's drawings—creates oriental images, pseudo-Chinese writings, and montages that include photos of the author, and makes effective use of sound repetition and striking metaphors. In the longer 'roman', *La colombe et la brisure éternité* (1979), a dove represents the female who breaks the cycle of hatred and inaugurates that of love. Creativity is the fruit of the dove's coupling with 'l'homme discursif' in an embrace marked by 'une tendresse cosmique'. This work, which lacks direction and unity, alludes repeatedly to the difficulties of the creative process—words such as 'conte', 'écriture', and 'poésie' criss-cross the text. *Clandestine(s) ou la tradition du couchant* (1980) owes its plural title to a group of women involved in Québec Indépendentiste underground activity. The political-terrorist theme seems to be Renaud's reworking of his own experiences, but the eight months of the novel's action contain far more violence and victims than the entire eight years of real FLQ terrorism. The hero evolves from a highly committed nationalist to a counter-culture mystic. However, the final P.S. of the 'Addenda', dated 15 Mar. 1980, shows that the seemingly politically indifferent author intended to vote 'yes' in the upcoming referendum on Sovereignty-Association. Too long and over-complicated, this novel is full of paradox, automatic writing, digressions, and authorial omniscience, only occasionally lightened by witty puns.

At the age of nineteen Renaud had published a short poetry collection, *Electrodes* (1962), full of anguish, hatred, solitude, and cold; some of the poems show the influence of the cosmic and geological themes of Alain GRANDBOIS. Unrequited love and a hallucinatory sense of guilt predominate; and, although the vocabulary and some of the images show originality and—near the end—a brief anticipation of the social milieu of *Le cassé*, the poems suffer from *préciosité* and an unconvincing, overwrought pathos.

For a dicussion of *Le cassé* and Renaud, see Malcolm Reid's *The shouting signpainters: a literary and political account of Québec revolutionary nationalism* (1972) and B.-Z. Shek's *Social realism in the French-Canadian novel* (1977), chap. 9.

See also NOVELS IN FRENCH 1960 TO 1982: 3(d).   BEN-Z. SHEK

Répertoire national, Le. See ANTHOLOGIES IN FRENCH: 1 and POETRY IN FRENCH: 2.

Richard, Jean-Jules (1911-75). Born at St-Raphaël, in the Beauce region of Québec, of farm parents (his mother was illiterate), he first left home at fourteen and began writing poetry and novels at an early age. At fifteen he attended a classical college but was expelled after two years for protesting against a teacher's mistreatment of a fellow pupil. Independent ever since, he worked as a bookseller, freelance journalist, and construction worker. In the Depression years Richard rode the rods, took part in the 'Hunger March' of 1937, and was in a delegation that met Prime Minister R.B. Bennett to demand better pay for youth in the relief work camps.

A soldier in the Canadian army, Richard was wounded during the Normandy invasion in 1944. A short-term pension allowed him to write his first novel, *Neuf jours de haine* (1948), a grisly account of war and its dehumanization. In an ironic style, marked by breathless short sentences and sense impressions, it lashes out against Nazism and oppression, venal politicians, and militarism, with its social caste system; but the book is wordy and repetitive. When his next novel, *Le feu dans l'amiante* (1956), was published Richard was being hounded for his participation in the Left-oriented Canadian Peace Congress and found it almost impossible to earn a living. It is largely journalistic fiction about the 1949 Asbestos strike, which is considered a turning-point in Québec's social history. Published at the author's expense in Toronto—it was highly critical of Premier Maurice Duplessis and the Québec police—it vividly conveys the dynamite blasts that regulate life in Asbestos, the all-pervading dust and silicosis, and collective attempts at social reform; but it is marred by unsubtle repetition and weak characterization. A second edition (1971) has a short author's note explaining the political and economic circumstances surrounding the first edition and its distribution by Richard in the mining towns of the Eastern Townships. For this edition he changed many characters' names to those of some twenty-five prominent politicians, writers, and artists.

During the 1950s Richard became depressed and burned a number of his manuscripts. His third novel, *Journal d'un hobo* (1965), is an overlong extension of an excellent story, 'Prélude en si mineur': the diary of a homosexual rod-runner who travels during the Depression from his native Acadia to B.C. and relates his sexual and social adventures. Containing flashes of poetic descriptions of railway yards and hobo camps, it reflects the narrator's revolt against the social system that had caused so much grief. The sexual and social threads, however, do not fully intertwine.

In the 1970s Richard published seven books. *Faites-leur boire le fleuve* (1970), winner of the Prix Jean-Béraud, is a dramatic story of the Montreal waterfront and its conflicts between longshoremen and their anglophone bosses, and between rival groups of dockers and underworld characters who wield influence in the union. The *argot* and mores of the docks contrast with the genteel speech and outward manners of Westmount. *Carré Saint-Louis* (1971) is a violent, naturalistic story of young drug-pushers and users who gather in the 'square' of the title. Despite a lively style, colourful vernacular, and an ironic view of literary and educational institutions, of well-to-do pesudo-left-wingers and hippies, and of the 'new morality', the book is spoiled by excessive indirect narration. *Exovide Louis Riel* (1972) deals with the Saskatchewan rebellion of 1885 and the hanging of the legendary Métis leader. Here, as elsewhere, there is a tendency towards melodrama and caricature.

Comment réussir à cinquante ans (1973) is a droll novel written in the form of a TV soap opera. Satire of the media, universities, bourgeois philanthropy, and urban land speculation abounds. *Pièges* (1973) is a short novel about the psychological and sexual problems of marriage.

Research on the history of the port of Montreal that Richard was hoping to publish before his death led to *Le voyage en rond* (1973), a novel set in the Lower Canada of 1791. Humorous anachronisms of speech, incident, and names, and a transposition of the crisis of Oct. 1970, seem to aim criticism at the FLQ—for its inflated language and the fanaticism of one of its leaders, Pierre Rousse (Paul Rose?)—and at the cruel, grasping, English-speaking bourgeois and the francophone Catholic clergy.

Richard's last novel, *Centreville* (1973), is structured by the monologues of ten shady characters, most of whom live in a brothel, and ends with the murder of a hypocritical pimp-cum-morality-campaigner and the suicide of the prostitute-perpetrator. Unfortunately the monologues are inadequately differentiated and the social criticism is drowned in naturalistic detail, a weakness that afflicted all Richard's writing after 1965.

Ville rouge (1949), an early collection of short stories, filled with popular speech and vignettes of the seamier side of life—the title is an image for the blood-red brick walls of the poor areas of Montreal and Quebec City—and Richard's second novel, *Le feu dans l'amiante*, had a marked and acknowledged influence on the writers associated with PARTI PRIS because of their working-class subject matter and stark realism.

For an illuminating interview with Richard on his formative years and his world-view, see 'Jean-Jules Richard au présent' by Réginald Martel in LIBERTÉ, 81 (1972). For a discussion of Richard's early novels, see B.-Z. Shek, *Social realism in the French-Canadian novel* (1977). An overview of Richard's work appears in Paul-André Bourque's 'De la haine à l'amour par le rire', in *Livres et auteurs québécois 1973*.

See also NOVELS IN FRENCH 1940 TO 1959:3.

BEN-Z. SHEK

Richards, David Adams (b. 1950). He grew up in Newcastle, N.B., and attended St Thomas University, Fredericton, which he eventually left without a degree to pursue a career as a writer. He and his wife live in Newcastle.

The poems in *Small heroics* (1972), a New Brunswick poetry chapbook, reflect an acute awareness of rural environment and a pervading sense of disillusionment and deprivation, transformed into a sombre beauty—qualities that became the hallmark of Richards' subsequent prose. He won the Norma Epstein $1,000 first prize for undergraduate creative writing in Canada with a portion of his first novel, *The coming of winter* (1974), which received considerable acclaim. The State Publishing Agency of the USSR bought the world rights in the Russian language for this novel in 1980—appropriately, because Richards claims that the great Russian novelists were among his strongest influences (though the style and subject matter of *The coming of winter* more immediately suggest Faulkner). It describes several weeks in the life of Kevin Dulse, a young native of the Miramichi Valley in New Brunswick, the setting of all Richards' fiction. Kevin's monotonous labour in the mills, his tragicomic ineptitude, and his uninspired and conventional slide into marriage, are counterbalanced by his love of outdoors, of the woods and rivers so important to the author himself. Richards' ear for local speech patterns and his eye for the minute details of individual lifestyles produce an effect of striking realism. *Blood ties* (1976) is a probing psychological examination of the lives of a larger number of characters from the same region. The short stories of *Dancers at night* (1978) and the novel *Lives of short duration* (1981), while continuing in this setting, show an increased concern with the theme of cultural and economic deprivation and an intensified sense of human compassion. Richard's most ambitious novel to date, *Lives of short duration* gives a voice to a whole community and its history through a stream-of-consciousness treatment of the minds of three generations of characters.

Richards has also written a play, *The Dungarvon whooper*, which was toured by a New Brunswick amateur theatre company but has not been published.

See profiles of the author by J. Clause in the *Atlantic Advocate* (Oct. 1975), by Alden NOWLAN in *Atlantic Insight* (Apr. 1980), by Phil Milner in *Books in Canada* (Oct. 1980), and by Harry Thurston in *Atlantic Insight* (May 1982). ANDREW SEAMAN

Richardson, John (1796-1852). Canada's first native-born novelist was born in Queenston, Upper Canada, of United Empire Loyalist and Ottawa Indian ancestry, the son of a British army medical officer, and grew up in such military posts as Detroit and Amherstburg. In the War of 1812 he fought with the regulars alongside Tecumseh as a youthful gentleman-volunteer

and witnessed the savage frontier warfare of the western theatre. Captured after Tecumseh's defeat at Moraviantown, he was a prisoner-of-war in Ohio and Kentucky for a year. His later writings attest to the vivid, ineradicable nature of his war experiences, and to the vision they produced of a wilderness filled with violence and savagery. Commissioned in the British army, too late to serve in the Napoleonic Wars, he spent two years, 1816-18, in the West Indies, mostly in Barbados, where he endured yellow fever and observed the brutalities of both a slave-holding society and the British army's disciplinary code of the time. Settling in London in 1818, he lived there as a half-pay officer, a Regency buck, and a minor man-of-letters. While in England he married twice. His first wife, Jane Marsh, whom he married in 1825, died a few years later. In 1832 he married Maria Caroline Drayson.

In the next decade Richardson began a highly productive but financially unrewarding life-long career as a writer—publishing poems, novels, memoirs, pamphlets, reports, and letters of protest—while also pursuing a career in the army and then turning to other occupations. He moved in the great world with surprising aplomb, considering that he was a self-educated colonial who was arrogant, physically unprepossessing, highminded, and obtuse; who alienated people without realizing why and was helpless to cope with the bad luck, obstacles, and unfairnesses that impeded him. He had a gift for making enemies. David Beasley, in his biography *The Canadian Don Quixote*, observes that Richardson was probably describing himself when he wrote of the hero of his first novel, *Ecarté*, that he was 'endowed with a susceptibility which rendered him unable to endure even the shadow of slight or insult'. Duels, therefore, were another feature of his life.

Richardson spent some time in Paris—where he was involved in a duel with pistols and hit in the ankle—and portrayed his Parisian experiences in *Ecarté; or, The salons of Paris* (London, 1829), and in an anonymous sequel attributed to him, *Frascati's; or, Scenes in Paris* (London, 1830). Dealing with the world of Thackeray's *Pendennis*—of young sparks living by their wits—both books are of somewhat slapdash construction. In 1830 Richardson also published *Kensington Gardens* (London), a poem satirizing London society. He had previously published a long poem based on some of his Canadian experiences, *Tecumseh; or, The warrior of the West in four cantos with notes* (London, 1828). Couched in the mock-epic form of *ottava rima* that Byron had perfected in *Don Juan*, it is a lurid, bathetic work that did not sell well. Richardson then published his best-known book, the novel WACOUSTA; *or, The prophecy: a tale of the Canadas* (3 vols, Edinburgh, 1832), which employed the Canadian wilderness of *Tecumseh* much more effectively. It is set in the time of Pontiac's uprising (1763) and has a complex plot that depicts Reginald Morton's monstrous revenge upon his unscrupulous one-time rival, Colonel De Haldimar. The savageries of the forest are matched by the inhumanities of the garrison, and the narrative is filled with surprise, disguise, bizarre coincidence, violence, and high-flown rhetoric. It was praised by reviewers, became popular, and was reprinted many times.

In 1835 Richardson went to Spain as a major in the British Legion, a mercenary force engaged on the royalist side of the Carlist Wars—the Spanish civil war of 1834-7. A series of disagreements with his superiors produced his *Journal of the movements of the British Legion* (London, 1836) and *Movements of the British Legion* (London, 1837), which exposed both the persecution to which he had been subjected and his irascible temper.

In 1838 Richardson returned to Canada as a special correspondent for *The Times* of London, after the rebellions in Upper and Lower Canada of 1837 had been followed by Lord Durham's attempt to re-establish the provinces' political structures on a less oligarchic basis. His partisanship of Durham, of whom *The Times* was critical, resulted in his dismissal. Richardson stayed in Canada, settling in 1840 in Brockville, Canada West (Ont.), where he began a weekly newspaper, *The New Era; or The Canadian Chronicle* (1841-2), in which he published his 'Recollection of the West Indies' (15 Apr. 1842) and serialized 'The War of 1812'—a vivid but highly partisan account of individuals and events blended with long stretches of reprints of documents—which he also published in book form (Brockville, 1842). He had already completed *The Canadian brothers; or, The prophecy fulfilled* (Montreal, 1840), a sequel to *Wacousta* that deals not only with the War of 1812 (including such autobiographical experiences as his internment as a prisoner-of-war in Kentucky), but with the savage wilderness a generation later. (He included a version of the 'Kentucky tragedy', a murderous love triangle that has intrigued American novelists from William Gilmore Simms to Robert Penn Warren.) When Richardson's Brockville newspaper failed, he moved to Kingston and began a four-page weekly, *The Canadian Loyalist and Spirit of 1812* (1843-4). In 1845 he was appointed superintendent of police on the Welland Canal where, despite his best efforts to discharge his duties well, his enemies got the better of him and the force was disbanded early in 1846. To add to his miseries in this period his wife Maria died, leaving him desolate. Richardson then lived in Montreal until 1849, when he moved to New York.

Throughout the last difficult years in Canada he continued to write. *Eight years in Canada. Embracing a review of the administrations of Lords Durham and Sydenham, Sir Chas. Bagot, and Lord Metcalfe; and including numerous interesting letters from Lord Durham, Mr. Chas. Buller, and other well-known public characters* (Montreal, 1847) and *The guards in Canada; or, A point of honor. Being a sequel to Major Richardson's Eight years in Canada* (Montreal, 1848) combine autobiography, political polemic, and personal feuding. *The monk knight of St. John; a tale of the Crusades* (New York, 1850), whose villainous protagonist is a corrupt Knight Templar, treats the Middle Ages as a stage set for an account of adultery, slaughter, rape, and cannibalism. Its lurid events quite exceeded the standards of propriety of the time and were considered pornographic. *Hardscrabble; or, The fall of Chicago. A tale of Indian warfare* (New York, 1850) and *Wau-nan-gee; or, The massacre of Chicago* (New York, 1852) are brief potboilers about the U.S. frontier at Chicago. In New York Richardson republished *The Canadian brothers* under the title *Matilda Montgomerie; or, The prophecy fulfilled* (New York, 1851), with the anti-American passages of the first book deleted. *Westbrook, the outlaw; or, The avenging wolf* appeared serially in the New York *Sunday Mercury* in the fall of 1851 and was published in book form posthumously (New York, 1853). Richardson's final years in New York proved no more successful than his last years in Canada. He died impoverished and undernourished, too poor even to continue feeding his Newfoundland dog.

Richardson's career proved a painful failure, but his stormy imagination produced in *Wacousta* a classic Gothic account of the Canadian bush—one that makes effective use of an episode in Canadian colonial history as a springboard into terror.

See David Beasley, *The Canadian Don Quixote: the life and works of Major Richardson, Canada's first novelist* (1977); John Moss, *Patterns of isolation in English Canadian fiction* (1974) and *Sex and violence in the Canadian novel* (1977); Margot Northey, *The haunted wilderness: the gothic and grotesque in Canadian fiction* (1976); L.R. Early, 'Myth and prejudice in Kirby, Richardson, and Parker', CANADIAN LITERATURE 81 (Summer 1979); and the essay on Richardson by Dennis Duffy in *Canadian writers and their work: fiction series: volume one* (1983) edited by Robert Lecker, Jack David, and Ellen Quigley.

DENNIS DUFFY

Richardson, Keith. See CRITICISM IN ENGLISH: 5(e).

Richler, Mordecai (b. 1931). Born in Montreal at the beginning of the Depression, Richler has recorded, in his autobiographical sketches collected in *The street* (1969) and in several of his eight novels, his experience of growing up in the working-class Jewish neighbourhood around St Urbain Street and of attending Baron Byng, the predominantly Jewish public high school nearby (called Fletcher's Field in his fiction). The political turmoil of Richler's youth—which included the Spanish Civil War and the Second World War—also figures prominently in his writing, where he expresses regret at having been too young to take part in the struggles against Fascism. When he entered Sir George Williams College (now part of Concordia University) as an English major, he was drawn to the veterans still in attendance; and when most of them departed the following year, Richler—never really comfortable in an academic milieu—dropped out.

In 1951 Richler travelled to Europe where he spent the next two years, chiefly in Paris, as part of a group of aspiring expatriate writers. Returning to Canada in 1952, he worked for a while at the CBC before moving to England in 1959. He has been a professional writer ever since, filling his time between novels with journalism—the best of which is collected in *Hunting tigers under glass* (1968); *Shovelling trouble* (1972); *Notes on an endangered species* (U.S., 1974), selections from the first two volumes plus three new essays; and *The great comic book heroes* (1978), a selection from the first two volumes—and by working on scripts for films, including *Life at the top* (1965) and *Fun with*

Dick and Jane (1977). Richler returned permanently to Montreal in 1972, ending the long expatriation he had felt necessary to prove himself in the literary world. In 1976 he joined the editorial board of the Book-of-the-Month Club.

In an early interview Richler said that he wrote from a compulsion to 'say what I feel about values and about people living in a time when to my mind there is no agreement of values', and in his novels, as in his essays, he shows himself to be a moralist who is nevertheless capable of shocking readers with his choice of topics or disturbing them by his conclusions. His first novel, *The acrobats*(1954), written during his early years in Europe and published in England, shows Richler beginning his career under the influence of Hemingway, Sartre, and Malraux. Though it is imbued with a cynical world-weariness that now seems as much a product of its particular moment in time as of Richler's personal vision, it also expresses concerns that are central to his later fiction: a view of the Spanish Civil War as a testing-ground for belief and commitment, questions about the place of Jews in modern society, a feeling that his own generation arrived too late (in his recent fiction this gives way to a sense of its having existed *between* historical moments), and a preoccupation with personal responsibility. As well, the book's treatment of character exemplifies Richler's desire to 'make a case for the ostensibly unsympathetic man'. Although this first novel now seems marred by its clumsy use of the modernist technique of fragmented narrative, and by occasionally overblown writing, it was surprisingly successful: it was reissued in a U.S. paperback edition (as *Wicked we love*) and translated into Danish, Norse, and German. The novel never had a Canadian edition and Richler will no longer allow it to be reprinted.

Son of a smaller hero (1955) is about a young man's struggle to escape the limitations of the Jewish ghetto, and of North American society in general, by breaking overstrong family ties and achieving an understanding of law in a secular society. Marking Richler's first investigation of his Montreal background, this book (like several of his later novels) caused some readers to accuse Richler of anti-Semitism because of its refusal to treat all aspects of the Jewish community with reverence and respect. In fact Richler's greatest strength is in the debunking of myths of his culture. His irreverence for the shibboleths of his own immediate group appears strikingly in the novel that followed, *A choice of enemies* (1957); there he characterizes expatriate film makers in London who had fled American McCarthyism not as victimized idealists but as *poseurs* who enjoy and magnify their status as innovative thinkers and martyrs to conscience, and who are no more able to accept challenges to their prejudices than was the society that ousted them.

These two novels, however, are apprentice works that lack the assured narrative skill and rigorous style that begins with *The apprenticeship of Duddy Kravitz* (1959). This fourth novel, which established Richler as a major writer, features his most morally complex character, a bumptious young hustler obsessed with acquiring land in order to escape the ghetto and make something of himself. Duddy is a nasty moral coward who nonetheless has moments of genuine feeling and even nobility, and with whom the reader is invited to sympathize. He stops at no betrayal and injures those who have placed their trust in him—yet at the end of the novel the reader senses that Duddy, despite his finding victory emptier than he had anticipated, is not without achievement, for he has contributed to the ghetto myths an example of escape and has made something happen in a world that is too often static.

The apprenticeship of Duddy Kravitz—like the later *St Urbain's horseman* (1971) and *Joshua then and now* (1980)—is a novel of character, but the fiction Richler published in the sixties, *The incomparable Atuk* (1963) and *Cocksure* (1968), are surreal and comic fables that marked Richler as the most caustic satirist of his generation. Savage attacks on modern mores and the false values of mass society, these novels send up attitudinizing, trendiness, and liberalism by caricaturing the poses and stereotypes of their decade. In *The incomparable Atuk* (U.S.: *Stick your neck out*) the foolishness of a 'Canadianization' policy applied to American pop culture allows Richler to vent his hostile wit on two of his preferred subjects: facile Canadian nationalism, and the North American entertainment industry. *Cocksure* (one of Richler's own favourites) continues the attack on the second of these by creating a scabrous tale of a narcissistic Hollywood director who aspires to God-like powers, literally creating film stars to suit the public taste while cannibalizing his associates for 'spare parts' to keep his aging body functioning. Its sometimes bawdy humour made the

novel an object of controversy when it won a Governor General's Award (along with *Hunting tigers under glass*), but its 'square' protagonist, a man who clings to old values, even though bewildered by their inversion all around him, makes it a truly conservative work. This novel shows the influence of Evelyn Waugh, for whom Richler has expressed admiration, but like the satire that surfaces in all of Richler's work, *Cocksure* really belongs to the more bitterly vitriolic tradition established by Swift.

St. Urbain's Horseman—generally regarded as Richler's finest work, and also the winner of a Governor General's Award—is a much more humane novel, though it retains both comic and satiric features (best exemplified in the set-piece published separately as 'Playing ball on Hampstead Heath'). In this story of Jake Hersch, a Montreal film-writer on trial in London for sexual indecencies that he did not commit, Richler gives greater texture to the topics of exile and homeland, and of Jewish and Canadian identity. The sense of loss that pervades the earlier fiction is responded to in this novel by the creation of a protagonist who is searching for imaginative structures to give meaning to an existence that has been overwhelmed by the 'competing mythologies' of the modern world. Jake satisfies his need for vital contemporary myth by creating—out of the raw material of the life of his cousin Joey—a superhuman figure of authority and heroism, 'St. Urbain's Horseman', a Jewish avenger who will right wrongs and punish evil-doers. In the end, however, Jake must undertake the difficult but important task of confronting the limitations of myth in relation to reality, and must accept the consequent need to internalize his mythologies.

Joshua Shapiro, the protagonist of *Joshua then and now*, resembles Jake in his vulnerable humanity and in being another of Richler's misunderstood men. Where Jake was on trial for sexual perversion, Joshua appears to his friends to be a secret homosexual and transvestite. As Joshua turns back from his present problems to a past that haunts him because of an earlier lack of moral commitment, he, like Jake, must confront questions of personal responsibility and individual action, questions most intensely evoked in this novel by events connected with the Spanish Civil War. He must eventually learn that the past cannot be rectified, and that an attempt to correct it may lead to a dangerous abandonment of the present. As with *St. Urbain's Horseman*, the novel ends with husband and wife clinging to one another, their fondness and their bonds the only real refuge and stability in a difficult world.

Richler is the author of the text of a travel book, *Images of Spain* (1977), and of a children's book, *Jacob Two-Two meets the Hooded Fang* (1975), which (like *Duddy Kravitz*) has been made into a film. He is also the editor of the anthology *Canadian writing today* (1970).

George WOODCOCK's study in the Canadian Writers Series, *Mordecai Richler* (1971), discusses the work prior to the publication of *St. Urbain's horseman*; Mark Levine's 1980 monograph on Richler, in the Profiles in Canadian Literature series, edited by Jeffrey Heath, is brief but more up-to-date. Selections from early critical responses to Richler's works may be found in *Mordecai Richler* (1971), edited by David Sheps (in the series Critical Views on Canadian Writers). Michael Darling's annotated bibliography of primary and secondary material is a valuable guide to essays on Richler's work and may be found in Volume I of *The annotated bibliography of Canada's major authors* (1979).

See also NOVELS IN ENGLISH 1960 TO 1982: 2.   RUSSELL BROWN

Ricou, Laurence. See CRITICISM IN ENGLISH: 5(g).

Ringuet. Pseudonym of Philippe PANNETON.

Ringwood, Gwen Pharis (b. 1910). Born in Anatone, Washington, she was educated at the Universities of Montana, Alberta, and North Carolina. Most of her adult life has been spent in Alberta and, since 1953, in Williams Lake, B.C. Apart from a novel, *Younger brother* (1959), and occasional short stories, Ringwood's creative energies have been devoted to drama. She is the author of over sixty plays—dramas, musicals, children's plays, radio plays—and has been a major force in the development of Canadian drama, particularly in the West. Many of her plays remain unpublished, but twenty-five of them appear in *The collected plays of Gwen Pharis Ringwood* (1982), edited by Enid Delgatty Rutland, and some typescripts are available in the theatre section of the Metropolitan Toronto Library and the Special Collections Division of the University of Calgary Library.

In 1936 Ringwood wrote a series of ten historical plays for radio station CKUA at the University of Alberta, the scripts of which have not survived. The following year she won a Rockefeller fellowship to the University of North Carolina, where she became part of the Carolina Playmakers group. Some of her best work belongs to this period. *Still stands the house* (1939) succeeds on two levels: as a powerful evocation of the severity of prairie life during the 1930s, and as an incisive psychological portrait of a spinster's resistance to change. *Dark harvest* (1945) shows an equally sensitive response to prairie environment and character, but is marred by stilted dialogue and a contrived ending. An earlier one-act version of the same play, *Pasque flower*, benefits from a tighter structure, verse dialogue, and effective symbolism.

The comic vein in Ringwood's work is revealed in a group of plays performed at the Banff School of Fine Arts in the early 1940s: *The courting of Marie Jenvrin*, a flimsy piece; *The jack and the joker*; and *The rainmaker* (1975). The gentle satire of small-town Alberta folly in the latter two plays works well, especially in *The rainmaker*. They were both commissioned by the Alberta Folklore and Local History Project, as was *Stampede*, performed at the University of Alberta in 1946, which, in a laboured manner, eulogizes the Alberta cowboy. Comic invention returned with *A fine coloured Easter egg; or the drowning of Wasyl Nemitchuk* and *Widger's way* (1976), both adroitly controlled comedies that rely for their effect on character idiosyncrasies and improbable—yet, within their convention, credible—plots. *Wasyl Nemitchuk* also contains a serious element—seldom totally absent from Ringwood's comedies—in its reminder of the economic and social consequences of Alberta's oil discovery.

The first of Ringwood's plays about Canada's Indian people, *Lament for Harmonica*, is a melodramatic protest against exploitation, especially sexual exploitation, of Indians by white Canadians. *The stranger* has a similar theme, a slightly implausible plot, and flashes of poetry. Plot is also the weak point of *The deep has many voices*, but its expressionistic structure, imaginative use of visual and sound effects, and rich language mark this story of a young woman's search for her identity as a mature work. All the plays mentioned above have been published in *The collected plays of Gwen Pharis Ringwood*.

Ringwood's musical plays include *Look behind you, neighbour* (music by Chet Lam-

bertson), written in 1961 to celebrate the fiftieth anniversary of Edson, Alta, and *The
road runs north* (music by Art Rosoman),
written for the Williams Lake Centennial
Celebration and based on the Cariboo gold
rush.

Ringwood's plays express many themes
and utilize many techniques—she is a constant explorer of dramatic structures and
convention—but her main achievement lies
in her skill in capturing a sense of place: the
environment of Western Canada and its
people.

See Geraldine Anthony, *Gwen Pharis
Ringwood* (1981).   L.W. CONOLLY

Ritchie, Charles. See BIOGRAPHY AND
MEMOIRS IN ENGLISH: 3.

Ritter, Erika (b. 1948). Born in Regina,
Sask., she received a degree in English literature from McGill before enrolling in the
University of Toronto's Graduate Centre
for the Study of Drama. For three years after
graduation in 1970 she taught a variety of
English and drama courses at Loyola College, Montreal, and then returned to
Toronto to write. As well as writing for
radio, television, and the stage, she has published short stories in magazines.

Ritter's first play was *The visitor from
Charleston*, produced by Loyola College in
1974, whose lead character, Eva, is addicted
to the movie *Gone with the wind*. Her plan to
see it for the forty-ninth time is postponed
by the arrival of an earnest young salesman
promoting Fantasia cosmetics. Thematically
transparent and over-written, the play has
little of the liveliness and wit found in *The
splits* (1978), in which Megan, a writer of situation comedies for television, is as confused about her relationship to her work as
she is about her relationships to men. Her
estranged husband Joe—who is also a writer
and reappears in her life at a most inopport-
une moment—serves as a model of artistic
integrity. The supposition of the play is that
his influence in this area will outlast their relationship. In *The splits* Ritter's specialty as a
playwright came to the fore: a skill in creating and mixing bright, snappy dialogue and
zany, energetic, complex characters engaged
in a battle of wit and wills. This specialty
was even more successful in her hit comedy
Automatic pilot (1980). The title refers to the
emotional life of the central character, Charlie, a neurotic stand-up comedienne whose
comic routine is based almost completely on
autobiographical material. Unable or un-

willing to take any responsibility for her
own experiences, she needs to be unhappy
in order to write; she is funniest when she is
making jokes about her own anxieties and
griefs. Consequently, at the close of the play
we watch her turn her comfortable domestic
relationship with an aspiring novelist into
another comic routine. Although Charlie is
clearly stuck in her role as the self-deprecating clown, and although much of the play
makes comedy of convincingly presented
emotional turmoil, *Automatic pilot* is funny.
After its highly successful alternate-theatre
run in Toronto, it was remounted in a more
elaborate commercial production at
Toronto's Bayview Playhouse in the summer of 1980. *Automatic pilot* won the
Chalmers Award for 1980 and has been produced by regional theatres across the
country.

Ritter's historical drama, *Winter 1671*
(1979), focusing on the tragic love story of
one of Louis XIV's *filles du roi* sent to New
France, met a poor reception when it
premièred at Toronto's St Lawrence Centre
because Ritter had entered a terrain that was
unsuited to her particular talents for dealing
with a familiar world. In her latest play, *The
passing scene* (1982), the protagonist's values
and confusions are characteristically close to
the author's own; but the presentation of the
central relationship between an investigative
reporter and a writer of amusing stories extends beyond the personal to address the social issue of ethics in journalism.

In the Wallace/Zimmerman collaboration, *The work: conversations with English-
Canadian playwrights* (1982), Ritter comments on her characters, her style of theatre,
and her professional concerns as a writer.

                    CYNTHIA ZIMMERMAN

Rivard, Adjutor. See ESSAYS IN FRENCH:
3.

Rivard, Jean. See JEAN RIVARD.

Robert, Guy (b. 1933). Born at Sainte-
Agathe-des-Monts, Qué., and educated at
the Université de Montréal, he has taught
there, at the Écoles des Beaux-Arts, and at
the Université du Québec in Montreal,
where he was literary director of the university press. He has played an active part over
the last twenty years in the cultural revolution in Québec, which he considers more
important than the social and political revolution it has accompanied, and has dedicated
himself to the two strategic weapons in this

revolution: poetry and publishing. He founded the Éditions du Songe and was director of the important 'Poésie canadienne' series for the Librairie Déom, in which he published an excellent critical edition of the prose and verse of Sylvain GAR-NEAU, *Objets retrouvés* (1965). He was art critic for *Le Magazine Maclean* and wrote regularly for the periodical *Maintenant*. In the mid-sixties he was the founder and controversial director of the Musée de l'art contemporain, which he left in order to mount the much-admired international exhibition of contemporary sculpture at Expo 67 for which he wrote the catalogue, prefaced with a lengthy introduction to modern sculpture, *Sculpture* (1967).

Robert's publications begin with two ambitious essays, *Vers un humanisme contemporain* (1958) and *Connaissance nouvelle de l'art* (1963), a work that attempts to explain in psychological terms man's creative activity in every branch of art—poetry, fiction, music, and the visual and plastic arts. He has written impressive essays on Québec's major post-war artists: *Pellan, sa vie et son oeuvre* (1963), *Robert Roussil* (1965), *Jean-Paul Lemieux* (1968), *Riopelle* (1970), *Albert Dumouchel* (1971), *Borduas* (1972), and *Marc-Aurèle Fortin* (1976). His book on Lemieux won the Grand Prix littéraire de Montréal. His authoritative study of the life and work of Paul-Émile Borduas is particularly valuable in making available three of Borduas's crucially important theoretical writings. Other works of art criticism by Robert are *L'École de Montreal* (1964), *Jérôme, un frère jazzé* (1969), *Yves Trudeau, sculpteur* (1971), and *Le grand théâtre de Québec* (1971).

As literary critic Robert has published a thematic study of the poetry of Anne HÉBERT, *La poétique du songe* (1962); *Littérature du québec: poésie actuelle* (1970), an extended version of an anthology of contempory poetry first published in 1964, both of which editions contain examples of his own poetry; and *Aspects de la littérature québécoise* (1970), which collects a number of Robert's essays, broadcast talks, and public lectures, including a splendid mock-serious psychoanalytical study of the 'sacre' (the blasphemous oath) in Québec speech.

In his own verse, starting with the theme of spiritual regeneration in *Broussailles givrées* (1958) and the myths of sea and sun, memory and desire, in *Et le soleil a chaviré* (1963) and *Une mémoire déjà (1959-1967)* (1968), Robert progresses through the celebration of the land, woman, and the power of the word in *Neige de mai* (1964), to the more esoteric universe of *Ailleurs se tisse* (1969), *Intrême-Orient* (1969), and *Trans-apparence* (1969)—a universe that the second of these works defines as 'orient extrême pays d'intérieur'. The poems of *Québec se meurt* (1969) express some bitterness at the constant threat to the survival of Québec's French culture. An important and sizeable volume of poems, *Textures* (1976), contains verse from the years 1969-70, including the poems in *Intrême-Orient*.

Through his poetry and his art criticism, through his journalism and publishing, produced often in the face of bitter criticism, Robert expresses his faith in art as a social act and in the reforming power of art in society.   C.R.P. MAY

Roberts, Sir Charles G.D. (1860-1943). Charles George Douglas Roberts, a brother of Theodore Goodridge ROBERTS and a cousin of Bliss CARMAN, was born in Douglas, N.B., and educated at the University of New Brunswick. At the age of twenty he published a notable collection of poems, *Orion*, and in 1883 he became editor of the Toronto periodical *The* WEEK, but soon resigned after disagreeing with the views of its founder, Goldwin SMITH, on Canada's annexation to the United States. From 1885 to 1895 Roberts taught English literature at King's College, Windsor, N.S., and in 1896 he published his first collection of animal stories, *Earth's enigmas*. From 1897 to 1925 he supported himself by writing prose, living chiefly in New York from 1897 to 1907 and then in London, Eng., and on the Continent from 1907 to 1925. During the First World War he was a private in the British forces and was later commissioned and attached to the Canadian War Records Office in London. He returned to Canada in 1925 and spent the rest of his life in Toronto. Elected to the Royal Society of Canada in 1890, he was awarded the Lorne PIERCE Medal for distinguished service to Canadian literature in 1926 and was knighted in 1935.

Roberts was called the father of Canadian literature because the international acclaim for his early poetry inspired his generation, among them Archibald LAMPMAN, into creativity. Also the inventor of the modern animal story, a distinction that he shares with Ernest Thompson SETON, Roberts was the first writer to mythologize successfully, in both poetry and prose, the Maritime environment: its strong sense of the past, particularly the French and English struggle for

'Acadia'; its New England heritage; its farming and fishing communities beside the Tantramar marshes of the Upper Bay of Fundy; and life in the remote forests of central New Brunswick. Rarely surpassed by other writers in recreating the outdoors, he was continually fascinated by the interpenetration of civilization and the wilderness. But it is nature without the human presence that evokes in Roberts two powerfully contrasting attitudes. In his poems he sees in nature a divine, even benevolent, spirit, finds permanence and consolation in the seasonal cycles, and emphasizes the kinship of all living things. In his animal stories, however, violence and destruction are the operative principles, and survival depends not merely on chance but on 'woodcraft'—Roberts' phrase for resourcefulness.

Roberts' long and prolific career falls into three main periods. His finest poetry was published between 1880 and 1897. While *Orion, and other poems* (Philadelphia, 1880) shows his assimilation of classical subjects and of Tennyson and Arnold, *In divers tones* (Boston, Montreal, 1886) and *Songs of the common day* (London, Toronto, 1893) reveal the mature artist's elegiac voice, his precise yet colloquial diction, and his scrupulous realism. In 'The Tantramar revisited' the speaker refuses to inspect at close range a once-familiar landscape because in his memory it has transcended time and change. 'Canada', which was a popular patriotic piece in the nineties, exhorts the young nation to draw its sustenance from its heroic French and British origins. The sonnet sequence of *Songs of the common day*, which describes the seasonal pattern of rural life in a detached, restrained style, contains Roberts' most satisfying poems. A decline sets in with the cityscapes, the love poems, and the philosophical pieces of *New York nocturnes and other poems* (Boston, 1898) and *The book of the rose* (1903); while *New poems* (1919) has very little new material. After 1925 Roberts entered his third period as a poet. His language shows new vigour and he adopts modernist techniques in *The vagrant of time* (1927). The title poem of *The iceberg, and other poems* (1934) is a successful treatment in free verse of a monstrous, non-human force; it is narrated in the first person by the iceberg itself. His last volume, *Canada speaks of Britain and other poems of the war* (1941), contains patriotic verses. Roberts made two collections of his poetry: *Poems* (1901; rev. 1907) and *Selected poems* (1936).

He published his first animal story, 'Do

seek their meat from God', in *Harper's* (Dec. 1892). This and three other stories appeared in *Earth's enigmas: a book of animal and nature life* (Boston, 1896). Unlike traditional animal stories, which were frequently parables illustrating human behaviour, Roberts' stories were based on direct observation and dispensed with sentimentality and didacticism. In the 'Introductory' to *The kindred of the wild* (1902) Roberts defined his animal story as 'a psychological romance constructed on a framework of natural science', one which 'helps us to return to nature, without requiring that we . . . return to barbarism.' Alec Lucas, in his chapter 'Nature writers and the animal story' in the *Literary history of Canada* (1965), identifies three kinds of Roberts' animal stories: the biography, which examines conduct or personality; the action story, which emphasizes plot and usually contains humans; and the sketch, which illustrates an elemental force governing the natural world. Accused by President Theodore Roosevelt in *Everybody's Magazine* (June 1907) of being a 'nature-fakir', Roberts argued that animals are not governed by instinct alone but by 'something directly akin to reason', an approach to animal psychology that was at odds with Darwinian determinism. Even though most of Roberts' animals are victims of the inexorable laws of nature, they often evince a heroic spirit in their defeat. The highly popular animal collections, Roberts' most important contribution to prose, include *The watchers of the trails* (1904), *Red Fox* (1905), *The haunters of the silences* (1907), *The house in the water* (1908), *Kings in exile* (1910), *Neighbours unknown* (1911), *More kindred of the wild* (1911), *Babes of the wild* (1912), *The feet of the furtive* (1912), *Hoof and claw* (1914), *The secret trails* (1914), *The ledge on Bald Face* (1918), *Some animal stories* (1921), *Wisdom of the wilderness* (1922), *More animal stories* (1922), *They who walk in the wild* (1924), and *Further animal stories* (1936).

Always sympathetic to French Canada, Roberts translated Philippe AUBERT DE GASPÉ's *Les* ANCIENS CANADIENS (Québec, 1863) as *The Canadians of old; an historical romance* (New York, 1890); the translation was reissued in 1905 as *Cameron of Lochiel*. In the Introduction, Roberts accepts the bilingual nature of Canadian literature as separate but parallel streams. This was followed by several boys' stories: *The raid from Beauséjour, and how the Carter boys lifted the mortgage: two stories of Acadie* (New York, 1894) and *Reube Dare's shad boat: a tale of the tide country* (New

York, 1895). Roberts also wrote romances for adults usually set in eighteenth-century Nova Scotia, in which an escape or a rescue culminates in a marriage between French and English; these stories include *The forge in the forest; being the narrative of the Acadian ranger, Jean le Mer* (New York, 1896) and *A sister to Evangeline; being the story of Yvonne de Lamourie* (Boston, 1898), both of which superficially treat the events leading up to the Expulsion of the Acadians in 1755; *By the marshes of Minas* (Boston, 1900), a group of tales; and *The prisoner of Mademoiselle* (1904). *Barbara Ladd* (1902) is the story of a New England girl on the eve of, and during, the American Revolution. After 1900 Roberts shifted to romances of contemporary New Brunswick. *The heart of the ancient wood* (New York, 1900) tells of a young girl's kinship with the forest creatures around her; *The heart that knows* (1906) deals with the cruel treatment given to an unmarried mother, and contains sympathetic portraits of Roberts' parents in the minister and his wife. The same settings are found in *In the deep of the snow* (1907), *The backwoodsmen* (1909), and *Eyes of the wilderness* (1933). *In the morning of time* (1922) is a fiction-documentary about life in prehistoric days.

Roberts' other writings include his chapter on New Brunswick in *Picturesque Canada* (Toronto, 1884), edited by George Monro Grant; *The Canadian guide book: the tourists' and sportsmen's guide to eastern Canada and Newfoundland* (New York, 1891); *The land of Evangeline and the gateway thither* (Kentville, N.S., 1895), a guidebook for the Dominion Atlantic Railway; *A history of Canada* (Boston, Toronto, 1897), a textbook that was rejected in a contest because it made Canadian history too interesting, and in which Roberts supports autonomous nationhood for Canada and imperial federation; *Discoveries and explorations* (1902), volume XIV of the *Nineteenth-century series: the story of human progress and events of the century*; the first volume of the series *The Canadian who's who* (1910); and *Canada in Flanders* (1918), the third volume of Lord Beaverbrook's history of the Canadian forces in the First World War. Roberts collaborated with Arthur L. Tunnell in editing *A standard dictionary of Canadian biography; the Canadian who was who* (2 vols, 1934 and 1938). Among the anthologies he edited were *Northland lyrics* (Boston, 1899), with poems by Roberts, Theodore Goodridge Roberts, Elizabeth Roberts Macdonald, and Bliss Carman; and *Flying colours* (1942), which is a collection of patriotic verses.

Collections of Roberts' writings include *Neighbours unknown* (1924); *The last barrier and other stories* (NCL, 1958) edited by Alec Lucas; *Poets of the Confederation* (NCL, 1960) edited by Malcolm Ross; *King of beasts* (1964) edited by Joseph Gold; *Earth's enigmas* (1974); *The Canadians of old* (NCL, 1974), with an introduction by Clara THOMAS; *The selected poems* (1974) edited by Desmond PACEY; *Selected poetry and critical prose* (1974), edited and with an introduction by W.J. Keith; *The heart of the ancient wood* (NCL, 1974), introduced by Joseph Gold; *Red fox* (1972); *Seven bears* (1977); *By the marshes of Minas* (1977); *Eyes of the wilderness and other stories* (1980); and *The lure of the wild* (1980), edited by John C. Adams.

See James CAPPON, *Charles G.D. Roberts and the influences of his time* (1905), reprinted by Tecumseh Press, 1975; Elsie M. Pomeroy, *Sir Charles G.D. Roberts: a biography* (1943); Desmond Pacey, *Ten Canadian poets* (1958); William H. Magee, 'The animal story: a challenge to technique', *Dalhousie Review* 44 (Summer 1964); Joseph Gold, 'The precious speck of life', CANADIAN LITERATURE 26 (Autumn 1965); W.J. Keith, *Charles G.D. Roberts* (1969); James Polk, 'Lives of the hunted', *Canadian Literature* 52 (Summer 1972); Robin Mathews, 'Charles G.D. Roberts and the destruction of the Canadian imagination', *Journal of Canadian Fiction* 1 (Winter 1972); W.J. Keith, 'A choice of worlds: God, man and nature in Charles G.D. Roberts', in *Colony and Confederation* (1974), edited by George WOODCOCK; William Strong, 'Charles G.D. Roberts' "The Tantramar revisited" ', *Canadian Poetry* 3 (Fall-Winter 1978); David Jackel, 'Roberts' "Tantramar revisited": another view', *Canadian Poetry* 5 (Fall-Winter 1979); Robert H. MacDonald, 'The revolt against instinct: the animal stories of Seton and Roberts', *Canadian Literature* 84 (Spring 1980); and the essay on Roberts by Fred COGSWELL in *Canadian writers and their works: poetry series: volume two* (1983) edited by Robert Lecker, Jack David, and Ellen Quigley.   GEORGE L. PARKER

Roberts, Dorothy. See POETRY IN ENGLISH 1950 TO 1982: 1.

Roberts, Theodore Goodridge (1877-1953). George Edward Theodore Goodridge Roberts was born in the rectory of St Anne's Parish, Fredericton, N.B. Sir Charles G.D. ROBERTS was his elder brother and Bliss CARMAN his cousin. He dropped the names George Edward of his own accord in favour of the family name Goodridge. At seventeen he left the University of New Brunswick without a degree and in 1897 acquired a position as sub-editor of *The Independent*, a New York weekly, which had published his first poem in 1888 when it was under the editorship of Carman. *The Independent* sent him as a special correspondent to cover the Spanish-American war in 1898, an experience upon which he based the novel *Hemming the adventurer* (1904). While there he caught 'Cuban fever' and returned to Fredericton to recover. During the next three years Roberts was editor of *The Newfoundland Magazine* and collected a wealth of information about outport life and history that was to form the basis of his Newfoundland novels and his tales of the Beothuk Indians. In this period he made a journey to the West Indies and South America on a full-rigged barkentine, an experience that he put to good use in *The wasp* (1914), and in numerous other tales and poems set in the South Seas. He returned to the West Indies with Frances Seymour Allan on their honeymoon in 1903, and the couple remained in Barbados for two years while Theodore wrote. The first of four children—the painter Goodridge Roberts—was born there. In the next quarter-century the Roberts family travelled extensively—living in England, France, and various parts of Canada—while Theodore published thirty-five novels and over 100 pieces in periodicals, chiefly in *The Canadian Magazine, The Youth's Companion*, and *The Independent*. During the Great War he served in the 12th Battalion, at one point as A.D.C. to Max Aitken (Lord Beaverbrook), writing official accounts of the war, one of which was published as *Thirty Canadian V.C.'s* (1918). In 1930 he was awarded an honorary D.Litt. by the University of New Brunswick and in 1934 was named a fellow of the Royal Society of Canada. In the same year he published a volume of poetry, *The leather bottle* (1934). He eventually settled in Digby, N.S.

Roberts' novels can be grouped into a half-dozen distinct categories: I. Historical romances such as *The cavalier of Virginia* (1910), or *Captain Love: the history of a most romantic event in the life of a English gentleman during the reign of George the First* (1908). II. Backwoods mysteries and adventures, such as *The golden highlander* (1910), set in the Québec woods and billed as 'a nature and animal story', or *The master of the moosehorn,*

and other backwoods stories (1919). III. Wartime adventures, such as *Hemming the adventurer* (1904), based on Roberts' Spanish-American war experience, or *The fighting Starkleys* (1922), a First World War story. IV. South Seas adventures, such as *The wasp* (1914), a pirate story, or *The islands of adventure* (1918), involving treasure and romance. V. Tales of Newfoundland and Labrador, such as his best-known novel, *The harbor master* (NCL, 1968)—first published as *The toll of the tides* (1913)—or *Blessington's folly* (1914), set on the Labrador coast. VI. Indian stories, namely *Flying Plover, his stories. Told him by Squat-by-the-fire* (1909); *Brothers in peril. A story of old Newfoundland* (1905), an imaginative reconstruction of the life of the Beothuk Indians in the sixteenth century; and *The red feathers* (1907; NCL 1976), an imaginative treatment of Indian myth. Several of Roberts' novels were published by L.C. Page and Company of Boston as books for young people, and virtually all of them are best viewed as juveniles. The Indian stories are suitable for children, particularly *The red feathers*, with its enchanting portrait of the good spirit and his magic house of pictures. All are rousing tales of adventure and romance that uphold the basic virtues of courage, honesty, fair play, and self-reliance, with a strong flavour of English gentlemanliness but a minimum of moral cant. For a complete bibliography of Roberts' novels, see Reginald Eyre Watters, *A checklist of Canadian literature and background materials, 1628-1960* (2nd edn, 1972).

Roberts' serious artistic accomplishment is his poetry. Some of his earliest pieces appeared in a family collection—with poems by his older brothers William Carman and Charles G.D., his sister Elizabeth Roberts MacDonald, and Bliss Carman—entitled *Northland lyrics* (Boston, 1899). In 1926 the RYERSON PRESS published more of Theodore's poems in *The lost shipmate*—a chapbook of 150 copies—many of which were included in *The leather bottle*. Had this volume appeared forty years earlier it might have won for Theodore a reputation equal to that of his brother Charles or of Bliss Carman. Poems such as 'The sandbar' and 'Magic' are unmatched in Canadian poetry for a facility and clarity of image suggestive of high-realist painting. A collection of the remainder of Theodore Goodridge Roberts' poetry, now to be found only in scattered periodical archives, is needed, as is a collection of his short prose, which is equally inaccessible.

Aside from the introductions to the New Canadian Library editions of *The harbor master* and *The red feathers* by Desmond PACEY and Malcolm Ross, literary criticism has so far overlooked T.G. Roberts, although A.J.M. SMITH included a selection of his poetry in *The book of Canadian poetry* (3rd edn, 1957). A brief biographical sketch by Goodridge MacDonald, 'Theodore Goodridge Roberts, poet and novelist', was published in *The Canadian Author and Bookman* (Spring 1953) on the occasion of Roberts' death; and in the same year A.G. BAILEY dedicated an edition of *The* FIDDLEHEAD to Roberts (18:3, 1953), with a brief appreciation of the general character of his writing.

ANDREW SEAMAN

Robertson, Margaret Murray (1823-1897). Born in Stuartfield, Aberdeenshire, Scot., she immigrated to the United States with her father, the Rev. James Robertson, and four brothers in 1832, settling first in Derby, Vt. In 1836 they moved to Sherbrooke, Qué., where her father served as pastor of the Congregational Church for twenty-five years. Three of her brothers—Andrew, George, and William—became prominent Montreal lawyers, while the fourth, Joseph, was a well-known businessman. Robertson taught at the Sherbrooke Academy and wrote the prize-winning *Essay on common school education* (Sherbrooke, 1864), probably her first published work. Over the next twenty-five years she wrote twelve novels that were published mainly by the Religious Tract Society and the American Sunday School Union. Set in Scotland or North America, they are all lengthy, sentimental, dialect-ridden sagas, filled with intricate relationships and 'sanctified trouble'. Her earliest works were three novels of family life in Canada. *Christie Redfern's troubles* (London, 1866) and *Shenac's work at home* (London, 1868) take place in Glengarry Co., Ont., and *The bairns; or Janet's love and service. A story from Canada* (London, 1870) is set partly in the Eastern Townships of Québec and partly in New England. Christie is so dedicated to nursing and consoling her motherless siblings and other people's children that her health suffers and she dies; equally selfless, Shenac helps her mother keep their fatherless family together; Janet Nasmyth is such a loving and capable housekeeper that her influence affects the eight Elliott 'bairns' well into their adult years. All three novels feature children—who grow up to be women prone to suffer through protracted love affairs—and were widely read by children and reprinted many times. So popular was *Christie Redfern* that it was offered in exchange for a kitten in the correspondence columns of *Aunt Judy's Magazine*, a British children's periodical.

In 1873, after the success of her early books, Robertson moved to Montreal and went on to write such books as *The two Miss Jean Dawsons* (New York, 1880) and *By a way she knew not; the story of Allison Bain* (New York, 1887). J.D. Borthwick, praising her 'moral and well-written books' in his article on her brother Joseph in his *History and biographical gazetteer* (Montreal, 1892) called her 'an ornament to Montreal' and 'a literary niche in Canada's monuments'.

PATRICIA DEMERS

Robinson, Spider. See SCIENCE FICTION AND FANTASY IN ENGLISH AND FRENCH: 3.

Rolyat, Jane (pseudonym of Jean E. McDougall). See NOVELS IN ENGLISH 1920 TO 1940: 2.

Ronfard, Jean-Pierre. See DRAMA IN FRENCH 1948 TO 1981: 4.

Rooke, Leon (b. 1934). This accomplished writer of post-realistic short fiction was born in North Carolina and has lived in Victoria, B.C., since 1969. He was educated at Mars Hill College, N.C. (1953-5), and at the University of North Carolina at Chapel Hill (1955-7, 1961), where he did both undergraduate and graduate work. He served in the U.S. army in Alaska (1958-60), and edited the newspaper *Anvil* in Durham, N.C. (1967-9). He has taught English and creative writing at North Carolina, at Southwest Minnesota State University in Marshall, Minn., and at the University of Victoria. In 1981 he won the Canada-Australia literary prize for his work.

Rooke has published six collections of stories—*The last one home sleeps in the yellow bed* (1968), *The love parlour* (1977), *The broad back of the angel* (1977), *Cry evil* (1980), *Death suite* (1981), and *The birth control king of the Upper Volta* (1982)—and four short novels: *Vault* (1973), *Fat woman* (1980), *The magician in love* (1981), and *Shakespeare's dog* (1983). In continually testing the limits of fiction, he deliberately weakens traditional elements of the realistic story. Often there is little unity of action: the narrator, as in 'Brush fire', prefers frequent digression to the tale he originally set out to tell. The development

Roquebrune

of character is often minimal, with the result that many of Rooke's stories have the quality of parable or fable—skeletal dramas enacted by generic figures. Although in some stories setting can be given in such detail that it becomes the dominant element—notably in stories that chiefly evoke a mood, such as 'For love of Eleanor'—in many it is completely absent. In *The magician in love* the lack of setting creates a temporal and spatial indeterminacy essential to the universality (attaining a level of fantasy) that Rooke seeks for the magician's experiences. Other stories offer little motivation for the action: characters act out of boredom, random impulse, or some unspecified, sometimes mysterious force, as in 'When swimmers on the beach have all gone home'. Occasionally the plot is dramatic yet visibly incomplete, as if Rooke wished to posit the incompleteness of our knowledge of some events. Most of Rooke's stories are first-person narrations by characters who, caring little to explain themselves, become known to us in a fragmentary way. Other stories are related by diary entries, biographical entries, in separate interlocking narratives, or from aloof third-person perspectives. Of particular note is the wide range of voices in Rooke's work—adolescent, American southern, West Indian, black American, even canine in the recent *tour de force*, *Shakespeare's dog*, written in pseudo-Elizabethan English. Because Rooke allows these voices to speak for themselves, without authorial mediation, they carry an intensity that more than compensates for the often fragmentary representation of action.

The female narrator of Rooke's novel *Fat woman* is the most extravagant personality among his narrators and the most vivid of his characterizations. This work, *The magician in love*, and most of the story collections focus on the difficulty of male-female relations. Characters appear isolated within themselves, essentially unknown by their mates; they connect only out of secret and bizarre desires. Rooke's two most recent collections, *Cry evil* and *Death suite*, move from the desultoriness of relationships to the despair and latent violence that underlie them. Appearing in these stories as routine elements in human life are murder, sadism, and pornography.

Rooke has also published four plays: *Evening meeting of the Club of Suicide* (197?), *Krokodile* (1973), *Sword/Play* (1973), and *Cakewalk* (1980). An unpublished version of *Sword/Play* was produced by the Cubiculo,

New York, in 1975, and *Krokodile* was produced at Harbourfront, Toronto, in Aug. 1982.

Issue 38 of CANADIAN FICTION MAGAZINE (1981) is devoted to Rooke. See also Stephen SCOBIE, 'The inner voice', *Books in Canada*, Nov. 1981.

See also NOVELS IN ENGLISH 1960 TO 1982: 4.   FRANK DAVEY

Roquebrune, Robert Laroque de (1889-1978). He was born at l'Assomption manor house into an aristocratic family that was deeply attached to the past. When he was four years old his parents moved to Montreal where he was educated. He was one of the founders of the art magazine Le NIGOG. In 1919 he began working for the Canadian Public Archives in Paris and became director in 1946. Throughout his life he was a contributor to many periodicals in France and Canada. He died in Cowansville, Qué.

Roquebrune's first work, *L'invitation à la vie* (1916), a little-known collection of prose poems, is a hymn to life. All of his subsequent books were inspired by the past which, because of his upbringing and his work in the archives, was often more real to him than the present. *Les habits rouges* (Paris, 1923) takes place at the time of the 1837 rebellion. Unlike other historical novels of the period, it does not depict the English as villains. 'From the beginning, my novel was in no way nationalistic,' the author states. Though its psychology is superficial, it is well structured and received the Prix David. The unifying theme of *D'un océan à l'autre* (Paris, 1924), a second novel that is marred by an over-complicated plot, is the construction of the CPR. *Les dames Le Marchand* (Paris, 1927), set at the turn of the century, depicts the end of the French-Canadian aristocracy that Roquebrune witnessed in his childhood. This is a mature work, with convincing characters. *Contes du soir et de la nuit* (1942) is a collection of stories and *La Seigneuresse* (1960) is a novel of love and adventure set in New France.

Roquebrune's masterpiece is without question *Testament de mon enfance* (1951), translated by Felix Walter as *Testament of my childhood* (1964). In this first volume of his memoirs, he recalls the comfortable and genteel existence led by his family in l'Assomption. The book is full of humorous sketches of adventurous ancestors and colourful people. The second and third volumes, *Quartier Saint-Louis* (1966) and especially *Cherchant mes souvenirs* (1968), are less successful, perhaps because they deal with a more recent past that is less appealing to the author. Roquebrune has also written two volumes of vivid historical essays: *Les Canadiens d'autrefois, I* (1962) and *II* (1966).

PAULETTE COLLET

Rose-Belford's Canadian Monthly and National Review (1878-82). Hunter, Rose and Company, Toronto, which had printed *The Canadian Monthly and National Review* since its inception in 1872, in Jan. 1878 took control as publishers. Since Dec. 1876 they had also printed *Belford's Monthly Magazine: A Magazine of Literature and Art*, which combined serialized reprints of popular British and American stories with original contributions from many of the same Canadian writers appearing in *The Canadian Monthly*. In the spring of 1878 Hunter, Rose merged with Belford Brothers to form the Rose-Belford Publishing Company, and in June the two magazines were combined. The Belfords left the new company within the year, but the names of the publisher and the magazine remained unchanged until the magazine's demise in 1882.

In its first year *Rose-Belford's* was edited by George STEWART, who continued the traditional serialized novels and social and literary comment. He introduced more American writers, as well as illustrated travel articles. After Stewart's departure Graeme Mercer ADAM, who had edited *The Canadian Monthly*, became editor of *Rose-Belford's*. The magazine grew larger, although the illustrations disappeared and a greater emphasis was placed on original material by Canadian authors, such as Ethelwyn WETHERALD, William KIRBY, Sara Jeannette DUNCAN, Charles G.D. ROBERTS, and Frederick George SCOTT. Morality, ethics, and religious issues came to the fore, along with the fiction, poetry, and reviews.

The publishers blamed 'our inchoate state as a nation' for the decision to cease publication: a greater patriotism would be required to support a magazine like *Rose-Belford's*, since the public preferred other types of literature.

See Marilyn G. Flitton, *An index to The Canadian Monthly and National Review and to Rose-Belford's Canadian Monthly and National Review 1872-1882* (1976).   CAL SMILEY

Rosen, Sheldon (b. 1943). Born in The Bronx, N.Y., he grew up in Rochester and received his B.A. in psychology from the University of Rochester in 1965. He then took an M.A. in telecommunications and spent several years producing radio and television commercials. He moved to Toronto in 1970. While supporting himself by delivering handbills, Rosen wrote his first play, a one-act absurdist comedy called *The love mouse* (prod. 1971). This was followed by *Meyer's room* (prod. 1971), another surrealist one-act play, and *The wonderful world of William Bends (who is not quite himself today)* (prod. 1972), a dark comedy featuring a humanitarian who wants to spend his life as a mohair rug, and psychiatrists who are as crazy as their patients. Meanwhile Rosen was writing a number of shows for CBC television, which he continued to do after moving in 1973 to Vancouver. There he became affiliated with the writer's workshop program of the New Play Centre, which produced a number of his one-act plays, including *The box* (1974), *Frugal repast* (1974), and *Like father, like son* (1975)—later reworked and entitled *The grand hysteric*. In *The box*, which begins with an extended movement sequence, two room-mates fantasize about an unopened gift; in *Frugal repast* Picasso's harlequin figures come to life; and in *Like father, like son* a seriously disturbed young man has a traumatic session with his psychiatrist. Rosen has also written a children's play, *The stag king* (1973), and the book for a musical, *Alice in Wonderland* (prod. 1974).

Although Rosen claims to prefer writing abstract and absurdist drama—his interest in movement has led to such recent mime theatrics as *Dwelling* (1977) and *Impact* (1980)—his most successful work to date is the naturalistic play *Ned and Jack* (1977), commissioned by the New Play Centre. He wrote the first draft while he was playwright-in-residence with the National Arts Centre in Ottawa. Set in New York in 1922, it is about a late-night encounter between the popular American dramatist Edward Sheldon and his close friend John Barrymore, who—still in costume and full of the success of his opening night as Hamlet—climbs the fire-escape to Ned's penthouse apartment. Both artists are at a turning-point in their lives: Jack is triumphant as an actor, while Ned has just learned that his paralysing illness is irreversible—he will be bedridden for the rest of his life. A sensitive and compassionate play, *Ned and Jack* combines humour, intense emotion, and careful character delineation. It was well received when it opened at the New Play Centre in 1977; after considerable rewriting it ran for two successive seasons at the Stratford Festival in 1978 and 1979, and in 1980 it earned for Rosen the CANADIAN AUTHORS' ASSOCI-ATION award for drama. A 1981 Broadway production, however, was a commercial failure.   CYNTHIA ZIMMERMAN

Rosenblatt, Joe (b. 1933). Born in Toronto, where he attended Central Technical School, he now lives on Vancouver Island, B.C. He has accumulated a witty and eccentric body of poetry and drawings since his first small-press publication, *The voyage of the mood* (1963). In *The LSD Leacock* (1966) he expressed the theme that has permeated all of his writing: the essential unity of organic forms. He declared himself a visionary who can see beyond civilization to the interconnectedness of human, reptile, and insect life. Rosenblatt's style reiterated the paradox expressed in the book's title: conventional and visionary vocabularies collide, scientific terms are invested with unexpected poetic resonance. After the much-less-adventurous *The winter of the lunar moth* (1968), and the collection of drawings *Greenbaum* (1970), Rosenblatt returned to the language of *The LSD Leacock* in his strongest book to date, *Bumblebee dithyramb* (1972). These poems vigorously celebrate man's brotherhood with the fecund energy of the animal and vegetable worlds, again marrying the vocabularies of mysticism and contemporary science. Of special note are chant poems that attempt to emulate natural energy in poetic structure. In *Dream craters* (1974) and *Virgins and vampires* (1975) Rosenblatt used more conventional forms of short poetry to explore other areas of his visionary bestiary. Frogs, cats, vampires, lizards, birds, toads, and goldfish here reflect to one another on their common piscine heritage. *Top soil* (1976), which gathered poems from most of Rosenblatt's earlier books, won a Governor-General's Award.

Rosenblatt has since published *Doctor Anaconda's solar fun club* (1978), a collection of drawings; *Loosely tied hands: an experiment in punk* (1978), a rollicking combination of his animal imagery and chant forms with the rhythms of popular music; and *The sleeping lady* (1979), a sonnet sequence exploring the 'salamander' joys of sexual love.

Since 1969 Rosenblatt has edited *Jewish Dialog*, which is an eclectic literary magazine.

See also POETRY IN ENGLISH 1950 TO 1982:3.   FRANK DAVEY

Rosenfarb, Chaveh. (b. 1923). Born in Lodz, Poland, she attended a Yiddish secular school and a Polish High School there from 1940 to 1944. She lived and taught in a Jewish primary school in the Lodz ghetto. When it was liquidated she was sent to Auschwitz and later to Belsen; liberated by the British Army in 1945, she made her way to Brussels, where she lived until 1950, when she immigrated to Canada, settling in Montreal.

Rosenfarb began to write poetry, plays, and stories at the age of eight, and her ghetto poems, which were set to music during the Second World War, are still sung throughout the Jewish world, while her ghetto plays are frequently performed by Israel's National Theatre, the *Habimah*. She is the author of many poems and stories, and her monumental 3-volume *Der Boim vun Leben* (The tree of life; Tel Aviv, 1972)—the epic chronicle of the Jewish community of Lodz before, during, and after the Holocaust—won her the Israeli Lamed prize for literature, the highest honour for a Yiddish writer. She is also the author of *Die Balada vun Nechtiken Vald* (The ballad of forests of yesterday; London, 1947); *Das Lied vun Yiddishen Kelner Abram* (The song of the Jewish waiter Abram; London, 1948); *Ghetto un andere Lieder* (Ghetto and other poems; Montreal, 1950); *Der Foigl vun Ghetto* (The bird of the ghetto; Montreal, 1963); *Arois vun Gan Ayden* (Leaving paradise; Tel Aviv, 1965); and *Bociany* (Tel Aviv, 1983; Bociany is the name of a village in Poland).

                    MIRIAM WADDINGTON

Ross, Alexander. See EXPLORATION LITERATURE IN ENGLISH: 2 and HISTORICAL WRITING IN ENGLISH: 3.

Ross, Malcolm. See CRITICISM IN ENGLISH: 4.

Ross, Sinclair (b. 1908). Born on a homestead near Prince Albert, Sask., he grew up on prairie farms and, after finishing high school, worked as a bank clerk for the Union Bank of Canada (later absorbed by the Royal Bank) in a succession of small towns in Saskatchewan, before being transferred to Winnipeg in 1933 and then to Montreal in 1946. Apart from four years (1942-6) in the Canadian army, when he was stationed in England, he remained with the bank until his retirement in 1968. He then lived for some years in Greece and Spain, returning to Canada in 1980. He now lives in Vancouver.

Ross has produced a substantial and integrated body of work, including four novels: *As for me and my house* (1941), *The well* (1958), *Whir of gold* (1970), and *Sawbones Memorial* (1974). His eighteen short stories, which were published between 1934 and 1972 and most often first appeared in *Queen's Quarterly*, have been collected in *The lamp at noon and other stories* (NCL, 1968), with an introduction by Margaret LAURENCE (who acknowledges the influence of Ross's early work), and *The race and other stories* (1982), edited and with an introduction by Lorraine McMullen.

Ross is best known for his early fiction, which uniquely captures the harsh, impoverished lives of prairie farmers and townspeople during the dust- and drought-ridden years of the Depression. Stories such as 'No other way' (1934), 'The lamp at noon' (1938), and 'The painted door' (1942) resonate with isolation, bone-wearying labour, helplessness in the face of the elements, and psychological strain, especially between husbands and wives.

The same Depression setting is used in AS FOR ME AND MY HOUSE, which attracted little critical attention until its release in a New Canadian Library edition in 1957. The story of Philip Bentley, a minister and apparently frustrated artist, as told through the diary of his pinched and equally thwarted wife, it also deals with the artist's struggle to survive and express himself in a claustrophobic, critical, and hypocritical environment. In recent years attention has focused on the novel's structure and on the rich ambiguities in its voice, that of the complex and perhaps unreliable narrator, Mrs Bentley.

Ross's middle two novels, arising out of his own urban experience and his fascination with the incipient criminal mind, have been less well received. *The well*, set in Saskatchewan, is the story of a young fugitive from Montreal who is morally strengthened by spending a summer on a prairie farm. As his memories of his Boyle Street gang recede and he manages to resist pressure to commit a second crime, it is clear that farm work, especially with horses, has tapped his latent humanity. *Whir of gold*, set in Montreal, portrays the near downfall of a down-and-out aspiring clarinetist from Saskatchewan, who is susceptible to the corrupting influence of a fellow roomer. His final rejection of criminal life is due less to the love of a generous woman than to the strength of his dream of

becoming a musician—a dream connected to his memories of his farm family and the spirited horse he loved as a boy. Though often dismissed as melodramatic and sentimental, both novels succeed in evoking the nurturing aspects of prairie life, particularly in the flashback sequences of *Whir of gold*, one of which has been published as a short story, 'The race'.

Ross's fourth novel, *Sawbones Memorial* (1974; NCL, 1978), which returns to the small-town territory of *As for me and my house*, is written from a very different perspective. Set in Upward, Sask., in 1948, it takes place in a single evening, during a retirement party for the town doctor that coincides with the opening of a long-awaited hospital named in his honour. Using dialogue, speeches, interior monologues, and snippets of songs, it is entirely free of authorial intrusion; as characters reveal themselves, differing perceptions of common episodes suggest the illusory nature of truth. Despite its portrayal of such familiar small-town vices as hypocrisy, envy, and distrust, the novel derives a mellow quality from its main character, the elderly doctor who is acerbic but kindly, and who has learned to compromise and accept the non-perfectibility of life and the people around him. *Sawbones Memorial* also attests to Ross's abiding interest in the structural possibilities of the novel and his debt to European writers, such as Proust and Claude Mauriac, on whose *Diner en ville* this novel was modelled.

See two essays in CANADIAN LITERATURE: W.H. New, 'Sinclair Ross's ambivalent world', 40 (Spring 1969) and Gail Bowen, 'The fiction of Sinclair Ross' 80 (Spring 1969); Keath Fraser, 'Futility at the pump: the short stories of Sinclair Ross', *Queen's Quarterly* 77 (Spring 1970); Robert D. Chambers, *Sinclair Ross and Ernest Buckler* (1975); and Lorraine McMullen, *Sinclair Ross* (1980).   MARILYN ROSE

Ross, W.W.E. (1894-1966). Born in Peterborough, Ont., Eustace Ross studied geophysics at the University of Toronto. He returned from England after the First World War to begin a long career as a geophysicist at the Dominion Magnetic Observatory, Agincourt, Ont. He contributed his first Imagist poems in 1923 to *Poetry* (Chicago) and *The Dial*. Although he eventually published many of these in *Laconics* (1930), and in the less-interesting *Sonnets* (1932), he was not recognized as Canada's first Imagist poet until Raymond SOUSTER edited a retrospective collection, *Experiment 1923-29* (1956).

In Ross's spare, vertically narrow poems, the inquiring spirit of the new world seeks release from old sentiments, customs, and poetic conventions. Spurning the clichés of the 'old graveyards of Europe', Ross seeks 'something of the sharper tang of Canada' in the surface reflections and dark shadows of pine-surrounded lakes, where reality is recognized as profound and mysterious. The modern poet of the New World seeks illumination by objectifying the ordinary sensations of sight and sound. His explorations of the land of lake and loon thereby serve as metaphors for illumination and rejuvenation.

Shapes and sounds (1968) is a selection of Ross's poems edited by Souster and John Robert COLOMBO, with a memoir by Barry CALLAGHAN.   DAVID LATHAM

Roughing it in the bush; or Forest life in Canada (2 vols, London, 1852). This series of autobiographical sketches by Susanna MOODIE describes her experiences, and those of her husband Dunbar, during their first seven years in Upper Canada (Ontario). The first volume deals with their arrival in Quebec and their settling on a partially cleared farm in Hamilton Twp., near Port Hope (1832-4), the second with their struggle to wrest a living from the uncleared, largely unarable farm north of Lakefield (1834-9) that was part of Lt Moodie's military land grant. The chapters are organized into subjects appropriate to the then-popular form of the sketch: studies of unusual or eccentric characters ('John Monaghan', 'Brian the still-hunter'), descriptions of local customs ('The logging bee', 'The borrowing system'), and accounts of outings or adventures ('The walk to Dummer') are designed to provide entertaining variety and a tribute to the genteel values and outlook of Susanna Moodie's own English middle class. Moodie sought to increase narrative and emotional interest by placing herself near the centre of activities, much as if she were the heroine of an English sentimental novel. The distortions thus created were meant to be balanced, or at least explicated, by the addition of several objective, documentary chapters by her husband ('The land jobber', 'The village hotel', and 'Canadian sketches', the latter added to the second English edition in late 1852).

The prominence of this work among nineteenth-century 'Canadian' books can be accounted for in part by Susanna Moodie's comedic talent in describing individuals and events and by her trenchant examination of the pioneering experience, which gives the book documentary value. At the same time, critics and writers—for instance, Margaret ATWOOD in her JOURNALS OF SUSANNA MOODIE—have been fascinated by the complexity of Moodie's voice and vision. While ostensibly written to warn members of her class not to subject themselves to conditions of wilderness and radical deculturation, Moodie's sketches suggest not so much an aversion to her experiences as a fascination with, and deep involvement in, them that no genteel condemnation can effectively diminish. This tension is rooted in Moodie's English background and romantic temperament; it also owes something to the way in which the book was written. Many of the sketches were composed specifically for Canadian readers and were first published in The LITERARY GARLAND and *The Victoria Magazine* in 1847; much of the negative cast was added later for the book's English audience. A sequel, *Life in the clearings versus the bush* (London, 1853), presents a positive view of settling in 'this great and rising country', while *Flora Lyndsay* (London 1854) is a superficially fictionalized account of the Moodies' emigration from England.

Roughing it in the bush has gone through numerous editions and editings in England, the United States, and Canada since 1852. At present the two most readily available texts are the Coles reprint (Toronto, 1980) of the second Canadian edition (1913)—the first Canadian edition, to which Moodie herself made changes, appeared in 1871—and the New Canadian Library edition (1962), edited by Carl KLINCK. The latter, unfortunately, bears a limited resemblance to the original, since it omits several of Susanna Moodie's sketches, particularly of her experiences north of Lakefield.

MICHAEL PETERMAN

Rouquette, Louis-Frédéric (1884-1926). Born in Montpellier, Fr., he went to Paris after completing his secondary schooling but felt no love for the city and dreamed of distant lands. He became an indefatigable globe-trotter, practising all trades as climate and circumstances demanded. He made several trips to Canada's Northwest and was in Alberta for a few months before his sudden death in Paris, having translated his experiences into fiction that he called 'romans vécus'.

Rouquette's books about the Northwest—*Le grand silence blanc; roman vécu d'Alaska* (Paris, 1921), which is partly set in Canada; *La bête errante; roman vécu du Grand Nord canadien* (Paris, 1923); and *L'épopée blanche* (Paris, 1926), an account of the work of the Oblates, several of whom he met—depict the fight for survival in the white wilderness against soul-destroying loneliness, merciless cold, and above all against the cruelty of man. Vivid description of scenery, convincing and unusual characters—such as Gregory Land, the uniquitous postman of the Great North—and human warmth are the chief attributes of these books.

PAULETTE COLLET

Roussin, Claude. See DRAMA IN FRENCH 1948 TO 1981: 3.

Routhier, A.-B. See NOVELS IN FRENCH: 1900 TO 1920.

Routier-Drouin, Simone. See POETRY IN FRENCH: 4.

Roy André, (b. 1944). Born in Montreal, he edited the 'Prose du jour' series for Éditions du Jour and the 'Écrire' series for Éditions de l'Aurore; was editor-in-chief of the literary magazines *Spirale* and *Hobo-Québec*, of which he was a founder; and has contributed numerous articles to *Cinéma-Québec* and *Le Devoir*. A position as editorial secretary with *Chroniques* ended abruptly with his rejection of the magazine's 'restrictive, totalitarian, Marxist' approach.

André Roy belongs to the group of modernist poets whose works are published by Les Herbes Rouges (both the Publishing house and the review of that name). His collection *L'espace de voir* (1974), followed by *En image de ça* (1974), inaugurated its series 'Lecture en Vélocipède'. In these texts, and in *N'importe quelle page* (1973), desire is seen as the originator of a succession of cinematic spectacles; the poet thus uses profusely the images of staging, make-up, visual effects, shooting angles. Roy's writings emphasize the importance of the body, whose desires and pleasures translate to the text in a 'Sextual' merging of body and text. This emphasis, as well as the place given to the relationship with the mother, unites Roy with the Québec feminist avant-garde (Nicole BROSSARD, for example, for whom he admits a strong affinity). The rupture of syntax, the use of blank spaces, and the unorthodox punctuation, rhythms, and words of his rather formalist writing—especially in the

early work up to the publication of *Vers mauve* (1975), which constitutes a turning-point in his production—defy linear reading, but critics stress the technical brilliance and meticulous phrasing of Roy's poetry. *D'un corps à l'autre* (1976) and *Corps qui suivent* (1977) describe a series of amorous encounters in poems that articulate the pleasure of the 'sex/text' and play on intertextuality by including the theories of a host of contemporary artistic, cultural, and political figures (Bertolucci, Sollers, Schönberg, Nietzsche, Pleynet, and Mao Tse-tung among others). The intertextual games and wordplay result in an irony that is characteristic of Roy's work, his reading of Lacan having instilled in him a passion for language and its power. *Le sentiment du lieu* (1978) was inspired by his appreciation of painting.

Roy is best known for his *Passions* cycle, written in a filmic form: *Les passions du samedi* (1979), a contender for the Prix Nelligan; *Petit supplément aux passions* (1980); and *Monsieur Désir* (1981), which show a new linearity that was only hinted at in the first of these collections. Dealing frankly with homosexuality in a compressed style, a sensitive and well-read narrator describes the amorous gestures and fantasies of male love in all their everyday immediacy.

See Philippe Haeck, 'Mon sexe bavarde' in *Naissance de l'écriture québécoise* (1979), and Joseph Bonenfant and Richard Giguère, 'Les passions de l'écriture' in *Lettres québécoises* 22 (été 1981). MAROUSSIA AHMED

Roy, Camille. See CRITICISM IN FRENCH: 1 and NOVELS IN FRENCH: 1900 TO 1920.

Roy, Gabrielle (1909-83). Born in Saint-Boniface, Man., she was educated there and at the Winnipeg Normal School. After teaching for some years in rural Manitoba, she travelled in England and France, where she studied drama and began to write. When war forced her return to Canada, she continued to write stories and articles in Montreal, meanwhile observing the people of Saint-Henri who were to provide the material for BONHEUR D'OCCASION (1945), her immensely successful first novel. She was elected to the Royal Society of Canada in 1947 and in the same year married Dr Marcel Carbotte. Made a Companion of the Order of Canada in 1967, she was also awarded the Prix David and the Molson Prize for the entire body of her work. She lived in Quebec City.

Gabrielle Roy's prairie background and passion for the Canadian Arctic gave her writing a breadth and an absence of regional pettiness not common among French-Canadian writers. Fully bilingual, she hesitated at first about whether to write in English or in her native French. She was a fine craftsman with a style that is at once simple, strong, and delicately poetic. Her characters are usually rather humble people, whom she handled without falsity or over-emotion so that they become symbols of man's quest for a joy that is often ephemeral, of his persistent courage and striving for an understanding with his fellows that is seldom more than fleeting and often too late. She was highly adept at portraying strong women characters like the mothers in *Bonheur d'occasion* and *La petite poule d'eau*. Awarded the Prix Fémina, *Bonheur d'occasion* was the first Canadian work to win a major French literary prize. The first English version, translated by Hannah Josephson as *The tin flute* (1947), won a Governor General's Award and was reissued in the New Canadian Library (1958). A new translation by Alan Brown was published in a deluxe boxed edition with drawings of the author by Harold Town in 1980 and reprinted in the New Canadian Library (1981). The central figure of *Alexandre Chenevert* (1955), Gabrielle Roy's other Montreal novel, is a middle-aged, emotionally inhibited bank teller who is tormented by his inability to express love in his own life and by his uselessness in face of the miseries of which he is informed daily by radio and newspapers. He dies a slow death from cancer but learns finally that love exists, even for him, and that his life has not been as valueless as he believed. The book was translated by Harry Binsse as *The cashier* (1955; NCL 1963).

Three Manitoba books—all linked short stories rather than novels—make imaginative use of material from Gabrielle Roy's own past. *La petite poule d'eau* (1950), a poetic account of life in a remote settlement in northern Manitoba, has been published in a deluxe edition (1971) with twenty-four original woodcuts by Jean-Paul Lemieux. The English version was translated by Harry Binsse as *Where nests the water hen* (1950; NCL 1961). The lively and varied stories in *Rue Deschambault* (1955) cover a girl's growth from childhood to adolescence in Saint-Boniface amidst people of every nation, pioneers of the West. It was translated by Harry Binsse as *Street of riches* (1957; NCL 1967) and won the Prix Duvernay and a

Governor General's Award. *La route d'Altamont* (1966), translated by Joyce MARSHALL as *The road past Altamont* (1966; NCL 1976), provides more intense insight into the same period in this girl's life, focusing upon the girl, her mother, and grandmother in four connected stories that describe a circle of time in which the generations succeed and pass one another, meeting in rare flashes of understanding, and in which journeys always lead back to their beginnings.

In *La montagne secrète* (1961), a young painter's arctic journey and the mountain that he finds, loses, and finds again frame a parable of the artist's lifelong quest for his subject and his efforts to express it. It was translated by Harry Binsse as *The hidden mountain* (1962; NCL 1975). The four stories of *La rivière sans repos* (1970) use the arctic background more explicitly to depict the Inuit in a state of transition, drawn without choice into the white man's world and still uneasy with his gifts: his medicine that uselessly prolongs life, a wheelchair, the telephone. In the long title story—which was published separately in translation by Joyce Marshall as *Windflower* (1970; NCL 1975)—a child is born of a brief brutal meeting between an American soldier and a young Inuit girl. In her efforts to bring up and keep her son, the mother shifts between white and Eskimo ways, not quite at home with either, and loses the boy finally to the white man and his wars. 'The satellites', Joyce Marshall's translation of 'Les satellites', one of the other stories, was published in *The TAMARACK REVIEW* 74 (Spring 1978). *Cet été qui chantait* (1972)—translated by Joyce Marshall as *Enchanted summer* (1976)—is a collection of nineteen stories and sketches, many very brief, each adding a dab of light or intensity to the picture of a summer in Charlevoix County in Québec. In two recent works Roy dipped again into her Manitoba past to provide new pictures and new insights. *Un jardin au bout du monde* (1975)—translated by Alan Brown as *Garden in the wind* (1977)—recaptures prairie solitude and multiculturalism in four sensitive and evocative short stories. (*Garden in the wind* was reissued with *Enchanted summer* in a single volume in the New Canadian Library in 1982.) *Ces enfants de ma vie* (1977), which won a Governor General's award and was translated by Alan Brown as *Children of my heart* (1979), returns once more to Roy's days as a teacher in a series of narrative sketches, each centring upon a single child in a lonely prairie hamlet or a Winnipeg slum.

Roy

Fragiles lumières de la terre (1978)—translated by Alan Brown as *Fragile lights of earth* (1982)—is a selection of Roy's non-fiction from 1942 to 1976: early journalistic pieces describing prairie immigrant communities (Doukhobors, Sudeten Germans, and Ukrainians, among others) and some more recent writing in which she expresses her debt, both literary and personal, to her prairie past. It is invaluable to students of her work. Roy also published two books for children: *Ma vache Bossy* (1976) and *Courte-Queue* (1979), which was translated by Alan Brown as *Cliptail* (1980).

Full-scale studies have been published by Monique Genuist (*La création romanesque chez Gabrielle Roy*, 1966), by Phyllis Gross-kurth in the Canadian Writers and Their Work series (1969), and by Marc Gagné (*Visages de Gabrielle Roy*, 1973). Paul Socken has prepared *A concordance to 'Bonheur d'occasion' by Gabrielle Roy* (1982).

See also NOVELS IN FRENCH 1940 TO 1959: 1.   JOYCE MARSHALL

Roy, Louise. See DRAMA IN FRENCH 1948 TO 1981: 4.

Rule, Jane (b. 1931). Born in Plainfield, N.J., Jane Vance Rule spent her childhood in various parts of the American mid-west and California. She received a B.A. in English from Mills College, Calif., in 1952 and spent the following year studying seventeenth-century literature at University College, London. From 1954 to 1956 she taught English and biology at Concord Academy, Mass., where she met Helen Sonthoff, with whom she has lived since 1956. In that year she moved to Vancouver and worked at the University of British Columbia—as assistant director of International House (1958-9) and periodically as lecturer in English or creative writing—until 1976, when she moved to Galiano Island, B.C., where she now makes her home.

Rule is perhaps best known for her unapologetic and clear-eyed writing on lesbian themes. Her first two novels focus on contrasting types of relations between women. In *Desert of the heart* (1964), set in Reno, Nev., where the seemingly sterile but startlingly beautiful desert provides a powerful contrasting image to the vanity-fair commercialism of the casino, two women overcome their fears and prejudices and start living together; the novel is structured on their alternating points of view. *This is not for you* (1970), which takes the form of a long, self-justifying letter that is not meant to be mailed, portrays a woman so trapped by her conventional attitudes and desire to conform to social norms that she withholds her love for another woman.

It would be a mistake, however, to categorize Rule as being interested only in lesbian subjects that appeal to a limited and specialized minority. She writes novels of social realism that naturally include both homosexuals and heterosexuals, but in her three most recent novels the central focus is not on any one sort of character. She matches fictional form to the structure of society as she experiences it—not as a hierarchy but as a democratic 'concert' of characters, all of whose voices are given equal attention. In her third novel, *Against the season* (1971), the small-town setting draws characters into a group where, despite violence, pain, and a guilt imposed by the dead as well as the living, affection and love triumph. In *The young in one another's arms* (1977) residents of a Vancouver boarding-house slated for demolition form a voluntary 'family' and work together to establish a restaurant on Galiano Island. *Contract with the world* (1980) is Rule's most successful experiment in making the form of the novel reflect its egalitarian philosophy. Though the events concerning the life and work of six Vancouver artists are told almost entirely in chronological sequence, they are described from a different point of view in each chapter: the reader's view of each character is subtly changed by the perceptions of the others. This multiple voice also presents a variety of aesthetic theories and comments on the relations of art and the artist to society. In these three novels voluntary communities offer protection against stultifying isolation and such hostile outside forces as police harassment, mindless commercial exploitation, and philistinism. Tempering their serious concerns are a gentle sense of humour, a sharp ear for contemporary speech, and a careful control of image patterns, often with literary associations.

Rule is a prolific writer of short stories, published in various magazines and anthologies and in two collections, *Themes for diverse instruments* (1975) and *Outlander* (1981). The title story of the former is a stylistic *tour de force*, outlining the branches of a family tree in patterns evocative of an orchestral piece, the family itself and the musical effects working as harmonic images. Several stories in both volumes concern children, whose characters Rule creates convincingly and without sentimentality. The stories in *Outlander* all deal with some form of lesbian experience, whether of survivors, as in the title piece, or of the deeply damaged, as in the vivid, painful story 'In the attic of the house'. The volume ends with a selection of Rule's polemical columns from the newspaper *Body Politic*.

Rule's work consistently presents homosexual love as one of the many natural and acceptable forms of human expression; the question of why this viewpoint has seldom been projected—even by homosexual writers—is addressed in her commissioned book *Lesbian images* (1975), whose introductory essay surveys attitudes to female sexuality over the centuries and condemns the prejudices fostered by churchmen and psychologists. Its chapters on individual writers such as Radclyffe Hall, Colette, Violette Leduc, May Sarton, and Vita Sackville West are pioneering studies of the sometimes tortured, often veiled, forms in which these women created images of their love for other women. The book is translated into German as *Bilder und schaffen. Die lesbischer frau in der literatur* (1979).

CANADIAN FICTION MAGAZINE 23 (Autumn 1976) is devoted to Jane Rule; it contains a long interview by Geoff Hancock and an article by Helen Sonthoff, 'Celebration: Jane Rule's fiction'. See also Marilyn R. Schuster, 'Strategies for survival: the subtle subversion of Jane Rule', *Feminist Studies* 7, No. 3 (Fall 1981).

JOAN COLDWELL

Rumilly, Robert. See HISTORICAL WRITING IN FRENCH.

Russell, Ted (1904-77). Born and reared in Coley's Point, Conception Bay, Nfld, Edward Russell completed his high-school education at Bishop Field College in St John's, and later qualified to become a teacher at Memorial University College. He taught in a number of Newfoundland communities between 1920 and 1935, starting his career in remote Pass Island in Hermitage Bay, which was possibly the model for the imaginary outport of Pigeon Inlet in his Uncle Mose stories. In 1935 he joined the magistracy and eight years later became Director of Co-operation with the Newfoundland government. Part of his responsibilities in this position was to write co-operative tracts and make radio broadcasts. From 1949 to 1951 he was a member of J.R. Smallwood's administration. Subsequently he worked as an insurance salesman, broadcaster, writer, and teacher. When, late in life, he returned to teaching, he gave up what he called the 'hobby' of writing.

Russell is best known for his Uncle Mose stories, which he wrote and narrated himself on the CBC in St John's, starting in 1954. Three selections from these stories have been published: *The chronicles of Uncle Mose* (1975), *Tales from Pigeon Inlet* (1977), and *The best of Ted Russell* (1982), all edited by his daughter, Elizabeth Russell Miller. In these sketches of outport life, Russell created a gallery of intriguing local characters and summoned up a way of life that was fast changing. He was not opposed to change; he had no affection for what he once called the 'ignorance and isolation' of Newfoundland's past. But neither did he wish to rush towards some vulgar prosperity. He wanted a renovated, modern Newfoundland, with the best retained from the old values. His stories, at their best, are gentle, whimsical, and shrewd evocations of the lives of ordinary people.

Russell also wrote plays for radio. Three have been published: *The holdin' ground: a radio play* (1972); 'The Hangashore' in *Baffles of wind and tide* (1973) edited by Clyde Rose; and 'Landwash' in *The best of Ted Russell*. These are further expressions of his love for the people in the Newfoundland outports. He also wrote pamphlets promoting co-operative enterprises: *All about credit unions* (1945), 'Credit committees' (1947), 'Buying clubs' (1948), and *Regional credit societies* (1948).

Russell published memoirs in the St John's *Evening Telegram* in Oct. and Nov. 1966. Elizabeth Russell Miller has written his biography, *The life and times of Ted Russell* (1981).   PATRICK O'FLAHERTY

Ryerson Press, The. In 1828, when Canadian Methodists severed their formal ties with the American Methodist Episcopal Church, they determined at the same meeting to secure a press and to begin a journal and book room. Soon after its foundation in Toronto in 1829, the Methodist Book Room began to issue denominational materials, and by 1835 general trade books. In 1919 the name 'Ryerson Press' was adopted in honour of the first editor, the Methodist minister and educator Egerton Ryerson (1803-82).

For a half-century after 1829 the publication of general books was undertaken haphazardly. A coherent publishing policy emerged only with the election of William Briggs in 1879 as Book Steward; his astute business sense enabled him to amass, through agencies for British and American firms, sufficient revenue to build a Canadian list. W.H. Withrow, long-time editor of Sunday School publications, was the first editor who actively sought out writers. Since the chief market for his books was in Sunday School libraries, he depended largely on fellow clerics for wholesome narratives, such as John Carroll's *My boy life* (1882) and Egerton Ryerson YOUNG's *By canoe and dog-train among the Cree and Saulteaux Indians* (1890). Edward S. Caswell, who joined the Press as a reader in 1881 and eventually headed the book department, made contact with a wider literary circle. His initiative brought such books as Catharine Parr TRAILL's *Pearls and pebbles* (1893), *The poems of Wilfred Campbell* (1905), and *The collected poems of Isabella Valancy Crawford* (1905), along with Canadian editions of several of Charles G.D. ROBERTS' collections of poetry.

After Caswell's departure in 1909, Briggs depended more and more on agency titles, virtually allowing his Canadian publishing program to lapse by the time of his retirement in 1918. Lorne PIERCE, who was appointed in 1920 as literary adviser and in 1922 as editor, was determined to restore the Press to its former position as the foremost publisher of Canadian writers. At first he faced determined opposition within his own organization. He was able to overcome it, in considerable measure, by building up a very profitable line of school texts. Since his publishing competitors were much more sophisticated than in Briggs' time, however, he was able to secure the lengthy lists he desired only by accepting many manuscripts of lesser quality. His great achievement, especially during his first decade and again after the Second World War under the sympathetic régime of C.H. Dickinson as Book Steward, was to start many promising authors—such as Frederick Philip GROVE, Earle BIRNEY, Dorothy LIVESAY, and Louis DUDEK—on careers that led them eventually to other publishers.

In 1970, mainly through losses incurred in connection with the purchase of an expensive but unsatisfactory colour press, The Ryerson Press was sold to the American firm McGraw-Hill.

The Ryerson imprint (1954) by W. Stewart Wallace provides a checklist of Ryerson titles from the outset, preceded by a brief but useful analysis of trends in the publishing program.   JOHN WEBSTER GRANT

Ryga, George (b. 1932). Born in Deep Creek, Alta, he was raised in a Ukrainian farming community there. His formal education consisted of seven years in a one-room schoolhouse and a brief period at the University of Texas in 1949, after which he worked as a farm labourer, in construction, and at a radio station in Edmonton. Since 1962 he has made his living as a writer and now lives in Summerland, B.C., with his wife and family. His writings include plays, novels, short stories, poetry, and film scripts.

Ryga's dramatic technique often blends realism, poetry, dance and song, and juxtaposes past and present, though the surrealistic devices in his plays are not always successful. Invariably he sides with the oppressed and the exploited, and speaks out against injustices in Canadian society. Three of his early plays, included in *The ecstasy of Rita Joe and other plays* (edited by Brian Parker, 1971), contain heroes who are rebelling against their society or who are trapped in almost unbearable social situations. *Indian*, a one-act play, vividly portrays a Canadian Indian labourer harassed by a heartless employer and an impersonal government official. The spare, elliptical English spoken by the Indian emphasizes the plight of a man and a people who have lost their sense of self-worth. *The ecstasy of Rita Joe*, in which the heroine is unable to live by the old ways of her people or adapt to the white man's ways in the city, offers a much fuller and grimmer presentation of the Canadian Indian's situation. Commissioned by the Vancouver Playhouse for Canada's centennial year and starring Frances Hyland in the title role and Chief Dan George as her father, *Rita Joe* was the first play in English presented in the theatre of the National Arts Centre, Ottawa, in 1969; it has since been performed internationally. In 1971 the Royal Winnipeg Ballet produced a ballet version at the Centre; a French translation by Gratien GÉLINAS was performed by the Comédie Canadienne in Montreal in 1970; and a popular production that cast Indians in the Indian roles was staged at the Prairie Theatre Exchange in Winnipeg in 1981. A less effective play is *Grass and wild strawberries*; it dramatizes the conflicts between the hippie culture of the 1960s and middle-class society, but it is often a disharmonious mixture of film projection, dance, song, dialogue, and recorded vocal and musical sound.

Captives of the faceless drummer (1971), commissioned by the Vancouver Playhouse for production in Feb. 1971, centres on the kidnapping of a Canadian diplomat by a group of young revolutionaries (it has many parallels with the October Crisis of 1970). When the board of directors of the Playhouse reversed its decision to produce the play, there was a bitter controversy during which the artistic director, David Gardner, was dismissed. (It was subsequently produced in Vancouver, Toronto, and Lennoxville, Qué.) Dramatizing the opposing ideologies of the main characters, the play does not take sides but shows the agonies and sympathies common to both, and to people in general when they come to doubt their own way of life.

Sunrise on Sarah (1973) is the story of a troubled woman and her search for liberation from the ghosts that haunt her—her parents and the men in her past. Though the dialogue is at times moving and the music and lyrics are effective, the overall effect is confusing because the issues in the heroine's struggle are unclear, and the other characters, including a psychiatrist figure called simply 'Man', are shadowy. *Paracelsus*—which appears in an unfinished form in the *Canadian Theatre Review* 4 (Fall 1974)—has more dramatic power. It is a wide-ranging historical drama about the pioneering sixteenth-century Swiss physician and alchemist, whose relation to the present is heightened by scenes in a contemporary hospital in which two doctors come into conflict over the need for a change in attitude in today's medical profession.

Ploughmen of the glacier (1977) and *Seven hours to sundown* (1977) show Ryga's continuing preoccupation with the quality of life in Canada. *Ploughmen* examines 'the myth of the men who made the West' through an old prospector, Volcanic Brown, who represents the adventurous, exploitative spirit of the gold seekers, and a retired newspaperman, the somewhat dissolute but humane Lowery. The dialogue brings these two characters to life with realism and humour, but a chorus-like figure, Poor Boy, is less convincing: Ryga's strength as a dramatist lies in the creation of realistic settings and situations, not in the expressionistic devices he often uses. *Seven hours to sundown* is based on a confrontation in Ryga's own town between city officials wanting to demolish a heritage building and a citizens' group (of

which Ryga was a part) wishing to preserve it for a cultural centre. A realistic study of a power struggle between opposing personalities and points of view, the play contains the staples of much of Ryga's drama—music and song, a fluid stage setting (in this case a 'non-set stage'), and the use of dreams and recollections to throw light on the present. Though some of the characters lack sufficient motivation and the ending is inconclusive, it is a strong statement of Ryga's concern and involvement in social, political, and cultural issues.

Some of these issues are touched upon again in a one-act play, *Laddie boy*, published in *Transactions I: short plays* (1978), edited by Edward Peck. Set in a Halifax jail, it gives, in Ryga's best realistic style, a cameo picture of the gulf between rich and poor in Canada. *A letter to my son*, published in *Canadian Theatre Review* 33 (Winter 1982), is the story of a Ukrainian immigrant's struggles to adjust to life in Canada. The main character, Ivan Lepa, and his social-worker antagonist are convincingly portrayed, but the dramatic pace falters when Ryga uses the surrealistic device of voice recordings to recall the immigrant's past. An earlier version of Lepa's story was presented in 1978 as one segment of *Newcomers*, the CBC television series on immigrants to Canada.

Other plays by Ryga that have been performed but are as yet unpublished are *Nothing but a man*, *Portrait of Angelica*, and *Jeremiah's place*.

Ryga has published three novels: *Hungry hills* (1963; rpr. 1977), *Ballad of a stonepicker* (1966; rpr. 1976), and *Night desk* (1976), all relatively short. *Hungry hills* is the story of an unloved youth who makes his way as best he can, honestly and dishonestly. *Ballad of a stone-picker* depicts the struggles, physical and psychological, of a sensitive man who has sacrificed much of his life by staying with his parents on the family farm so that his younger brother can pursue studies leading to a Rhodes scholarship. *Night desk* takes the form of a rambling monologue by a vibrant, self-centred, riotous, though humane fight promoter, Romeo Kuchmir, and brings to life a memorable personality; it was adapted for the stage under the title *The last of the gladiators*. While in none of these novels has Ryga been able to present more than one character in depth, all three are evocative and share an intensity of narration; they are both authentic and suspenseful.

Beyond the crimson morning: reflections from a journey through contemporary China (1979) is a

Ryga

partly fictionalized, somewhat impressionistic, account of a visit to China.

Peter Hay, who is writing a biography of Ryga, is the author of 'George Ryga: the beginnings of a biography' in *Canadian Theatre Review* 23 (Summer 1979). For the same periodical Ryga has written several articles on how he views Canadian theatre. Mavor Moore has a short introduction to Ryga and his work in *Four Canadian playwrights* (1973).

See also NOVELS IN ENGLISH 1960 TO 1982: OTHER TALENTS, OTHER WORKS: 6(b).

JAMES NOONAN

S

Sadlier, Mary Anne. See FOREIGN WRITERS ON CANADA IN ENGLISH: 2.

Sagard, Gabriel. See Writing in NEW FRANCE: 1

Sagouine, La (1971). This series of sixteen monologues by Antonine MAILLET is composed of the reminiscences, grievances, anecdotes, opinions, and homilies of a seventy-two-year-old charwoman, a former prostitute, who is the wife of an Acadian fisherman. A garrulous, indomitable old woman, La Sagouine (freely translated as The Slattern) narrates a personal history that forms a mosaic in which generations, social classes, temperaments, and ideologies all find their authentic and rightful place. Expressed in a roughened, coarsened version of old domestic French, the monologues bring her world to life, from her youth to her observations on death, in tones that are sometimes pathetic—she is after all old and ailing—and sometimes laceratingly vengeful. But these qualities are offset by her irreverent humour. La Sagouine is the Acadian sister of Gratien GÉLINAS's Fridolin and Yvon Deschamps's anonymous Montreal labourer—all three of whom speak in monologues for want of knowing how to converse or behave.

First created for radio in Moncton, N.B., a selection of the monologues—brilliantly acted by Viola Léger—has been widely and successfully performed in both French and English since its presentation at the Centre d'essai des auteurs dramatiques in Montreal in Oct. 1972. *La Sagouine* brings to the theatre dramatic qualities that are due chiefly to its colourful language. On stage La Sagouine's language, and the tone and timbre of her voice, are more compelling than her ruddy complexion, grim countenance, and props—mop, pail, clogs, and apron. Faithfully rendering the contradictions in La Sagouine's fascinating character, Léger skilfully endowed her simplicity with complexity.

An English edition of *La Sagouine*, translated by Luis de Céspedes, was published in 1979.

LAURENT MAILHOT

Saia, Louis. See DRAMA IN FRENCH 1948 TO 1981: 4.

St Pierre, Paul: See NOVELS IN ENGLISH 1960 TO 1982: OTHER TALENTS, OTHER WORKS: 2.

St. Ursula's Convent (Kingston, 1824). The first novel published in British North America written by a native-born author, *St. Ursula's Convent; or, The nun of Canada* was begun by Fredericton's Julia Catherine Beckwith (see HART) when she was only seventeen and was visiting relatives in Nova Scotia. Family stories and childhood journeys to Québec probably influenced the content of the novel, but the writer's emphasis on coincidence, sentimentality, and melodrama also reflect her preoccupation with the conventions of popular romance. Focusing on the personal history of Mother St Catherine before and after she entered the Ursuline convent in Quebec, the novel eventually sees this gentlewoman reunited with her long-lost husband and children. Collateral figures add to the complexity of the plot, which introduces shipwrecks, exchanged babies, potential incest, and a ne-

724

farious priest into the drawingroom society of seigneurial Quebec and eighteenth-century Europe. Always highly moral in tone despite its melodramatic elements, the novel predictably marries off most of its titled lovers.

In her preface to *St. Ursula's Convent* Julia Beckwith expressed her wish that British America would 'cherish native genius in its humblest beginnings' and extend its 'public patronage' to those exhibiting 'real and intrinsic merit'. Published by Hugh C. Thomson of Kingston, Upper Canada, for 9s.4d., the two-volume work received support from 147 subscribers in England, the United States, Nova Scotia, New Brunswick, and the Canadas. It was sold by booksellers in the Maritimes as well as in the Canadas and was reviewed in 1824 in *The Scribbler, The Canadian Magazine and Literary Repository*, and *The Canadian Review and Literary and Historical Journal*. Considered an immature work even in its own time, the novel survives today because of its historical importance. A reprint was published by the Mount Allison University library in 1978.

GWENDOLYN DAVIES

Salut Galarneau! (1967). One of the funniest, happiest, and most human novels in Québec literature, this is Jacques GODBOUT's finest work. Using a novel-within-a-novel framework, it is the story of its own genesis. Its hero, François Galarneau, a twenty-five-year-old dropout from classical college and the proprietor of a hot-dog stand on l'Île Perrot, begins to write, between customers—in a poetic, image-filled, down-to-earth Québec French—apparently naïve observations of his society. They represent some of Godbout's best satire and record, for both himself and Québec society, a move from alienation to identity. François dreams, as he grills hamburgers, that it is priests he is burning, observes that Humphrey Bogart has had more influence on his contemporaries than the Québec political leaders he thinks of impaling, and discovers that he is ineligible for most jobs in Québec because he is neither bilingual nor from France. Despairing of his ability to be free in a society he decides is controlled by two megalomaniac generals, General Motors and General Electric, he builds a wall around his stand and resolves to live out a personal version of separatism. But inside the wall he watches American TV and realizes that the act of writing—which has led to his withdrawal—cannot survive without life. Finally deciding to rejoin the world despite its imperfection, and to use his writing to change society, François, like his creator, affirms process and change, the imperative of happiness, and (it would seem) the undesirability of radical solutions to Québec's political and cultural dilemma. Unlike Godbout's other novels, where intellectual brilliance and irony act as protection against emotion, *Salut Galarneau!* moves beyond irony to humour. In the author's words, however, its laughter is 'tragic laughter. You laugh rather than throwing yourself into the Saint Lawrence.' It won a Governor General's Award and was translated by Alan Brown as *Hail Galarneau!* (1970).   PATRICIA SMART

Salutin, Rick (b. 1942). Born in Toronto, he received a B.A. in Near Eastern and Jewish Studies from Brandeis University, an M.A. in religion from Columbia, and worked on a Ph.D. in philosophy at the New School for Social Research in New York. He once considered becoming a rabbi; but, unable to find what he was looking for in religion, he was attracted by the trade-union movement on his return to Toronto in 1970, taking part in the Artistic Woodwork strike there in the early 1970s. He has written on a variety of issues for magazines such as *Harper's, Maclean's, Weekend, Today*, and *This magazine*, of which he is an editor, and for the CBC radio series 'Inside and out'.

Salutin's first play, *Fanshen* (unpublished), was produced by Toronto Workshop Productions in 1972 and directed by George Luscombe. Adapted from William Hinton's book about a revolution in a small Chinese village, it was Salutin's response to the 1970 October Crisis in Québec. Other unpublished plays show his concern for the poor and oppressed in western society: *The adventures of an immigrant*, produced at Theatre Passe Muraille, Toronto, in 1974; *I.W.A.*—about the 1959 woodworkers' strike in Newfoundland put down by Premier Smallwood—produced by the Mummers' Troupe in St John's in 1975; *Money*, a one-act musical described as 'an economic treatise concerning money as the greatest of all mystifications', produced at the Young People's Theatre in Toronto in 1976; and *Maria*, a CBC television drama, shown nationally in 1977, about a young woman fighting to unionize factory workers. Salutin demonstrated his own organizing abilities and nationalist convictions when he became chairman of the Guild of Canadian Playwrights in 1978, an organization he helped found. His continuing interest and involvement in the labour movement and social issues are evident in two books: *Kent Rowley: the organizer* (1980), a biography of a Canadian union leader, and *Good buy Canada!* (1975), written with Murray Soupcoff and Gary Dunford.

The collective approach used in several of his plays reflects Salutin's populist sentiments. *The adventures of an immigrant* and *I.W.A.* were developed with the active collaboration of the actors and director, as was his first published play, *1837: the farmers' revolt* (1976), created in collaboration with the dynamic group of actors at Theatre Passe Muraille and its innovative director Paul Thompson in 1972 and 1973. About the abortive uprising led by William Lyon MACKENZIE, its sympathy is clearly with the rebels. Salutin answered many questions raised by the drama in a lengthy introduction to another edition of the play entitled *1837: William Lyon Mackenzie and the Canadian revolution: a history/a play* (1976). The Passe Muraille production has toured many parts of Canada as well as Scotland, and was produced on CBC television in 1975.

The false Messiah: a Messianic farce (1981)— its title suggests its serio-comic nature—was produced at Passe Muraille in 1975. About a seventeenth-century Jew in a Constantinople prison who claims to be the Messiah, it shows effectively the need for hope even in the form of illusion; but its plot is somewhat contrived and its ending is cynical.

Salutin's most popular and successful play to date is *Les Canadiens* (1977), which premièred at Montreal's Centaur Theatre in 1977. It was written with an 'assist' from goaltender Ken Dryden, who also wrote a preface to the published version. Salutin used the Montreal hockey team as a metaphor for the failures and triumphs of French-Canadians from the defeat of 1759 on the Plains of Abraham to the Parti Québécois victory on 15 Nov. 1976. Although the play does not clarify the complex political issues of French-Canadian history—the playwright seems more propagandist than astute analyst of the Canadian scene—it received the 1977 Chalmers Award for its presentation at Toronto Workshop Productions and has been performed across Canada.

Salutin turned next to the Canadian cultural scene to portray one of its most influential figures in *Nathan Cohen: a review* (unpublished), based on the life and work of the drama critic (q.v.) who died in 1971. Produced at Theatre Passe Muraille in 1981, it starred the eminent Canadian actor Douglas Campbell. Although the play is well researched, it lacks character exploration and unity—weaknesses evident in other Salutin plays.

Salutin's most recent play, *Joey* (unpublished)—presented at Toronto Workshop Productions in 1982—is based on the life of Joseph Smallwood, former premier of Newfoundland, and was written in collaboration with the Rising Tide Theatre company of St John's; the title role was convincingly and humorously played by Newfoundland actor Kevin Noble. Though *Joey* hardly goes beyond presenting the well-known attributes of this politician who boasted 'God created man but I created Newfoundland', it was warmly received in both Toronto and Newfoundland. The Rising Tide production was staged at the National Arts Centre, Ottawa, in Nov. 1982.

JAMES NOONAN

Salverson, Laura Goodman (1890-1970). Laura Goodman was born in Winnipeg of Icelandic immigrant parents. Her education there and in the United States was frequently interrupted by illness and her parents' hopeful wandering throughout North America, and she was ten years old before she began to learn English. Married in 1913 to George Salverson, a railwayman, she continued to lead a transient life in Canada, supplementing her income by writing short stories for periodicals. Salverson was one of the first Canadian novelists to fictionalize the drama of immigration in the West. In her three novels that concentrate on the Scandinavian immigrant experience, she drew upon her family's failures in order to inveigh against the falsity of the Canadian dream.

In *The Viking heart* (1923; rev., 1947; NCL 1975), considered to be her best work because of its breadth of history and almost documentary authenticity, Salverson traces the immigration of 1,400 Icelanders in 1876 to the area of Gimli, Man. After chronicling their subsequent difficulties and the development of their settlement up to 1919, she concludes with the immigrants' disillusionment with Canada's participation in the war. A confirmed pacifist, Salverson presents Canada as a nation whose great potential had been betrayed and neglected by its leaders. *The dark weaver* (1937), which won a Governor General's Award, reinforces this pacifist theme. In it a composite group of Nordic immigrants settles in the West and prospers until the First World War culls their second generation and reimposes Old-World chaos upon them. The title refers to the apparent indifference of a God who weaves His plots oblivious to the tragedies and prayers of the people involved. *When sparrows fall* (1925) deals with Norwegian immigrants in an American city (a thinly disguised Duluth). Dedicated to Nellie McCLUNG, it emphasizes the feminist struggle as well as the dilemma of immigrants pressured into choosing between their ancestral traditions and the American melting pot.

After *The Viking heart*, romance increasingly weighed down Salverson's fiction, particularly her adaptations of Norse sagas: *Lord of the silver dragon: a romance of Leif the Lucky* (1927) and *The dove of El-Djezaire* (1933), which was published in England as *The dove*. In the latter book, which fictionalizes a true account of a slaving raid that took hundreds of Icelanders to the Barbary Coast, her Gothic medieval setting incongruously contrasts Icelandic and Algerian characters, speech, and customs. *Black lace* (1924), set in France under Louis XIV, is inferior to her other romances. *Immortal rock: the saga of the Kensington stone based on the Paul Knutson expedition to Greenland and America in the fourteenth century; commissioned by His Majesty King Magnus Erikson of Norway, Sweden and Skaane: his letter of authority executed at Bergen, October 28th, 1534, by Orm Ostenson, Regent* (1954) emphasizes, as do her first novels, the pre-Columbian tradition of Norse exploration in North America. It follows the Kensington Stone hypothesis to imagine the fate of the expedition at the hands of Indians in what is now Minnesota. A volume of poems, *Wayside gleams*, was published in 1924.

Salverson's autobiography, *Confessions of an immigrant's daughter* (1939), which won her a second Governor General's Award, covers her life to 1923 and describes with compassion and a sense of social injustice the struggles of immigrants in a New World that fell far short of their hopes and expectations. Salverson argued for the preservation of the Icelandic cultural identity in what she felt was a cultural vacuum in Canada.

TERRENCE CRAIG

Samchuk, Ulas. See UKRAINIAN WRITING.

Sandwell, B.K. See ESSAYS IN ENGLISH: 3.

Sangster, Charles (1822-93). Born at the Navy Yard, Kingston, Upper Canada (Ont.), Sangster left school to make cartridges at Fort Henry during the Rebellion of 1837 and remained there as a clerk until 1849, when he turned to a modest career in journalism: first as the editor of the *Amherstburg Courier*; then as a proofreader and bookkeeper for Kingston's *British Whig*; and finally as a reporter for Kingston's *Daily News*. He moved to Ottawa in 1868 to join the new federal post-office department, where he remained until he retired in 1886.

Demonstrating his wish to be 'Canadian in his choice of subjects', Sangster secured his reputation as the 'poet-laureate of colonial Canada' with three books of poetry: *The St. Lawrence and the Saguenay and other poems* (Kingston, 1856), *Hesperus and other poems and lyrics* (Montreal, 1860), and *Our Norland*, an undated 14-page chapbook issued by Copp Clark, Toronto. One of his best poems, the patriotic 'Brock', was commissioned for the 1859 inauguration of the monument to General Brock at Queenston Heights. It is a secular celebration of a hero who has passed beyond the bounds of time: 'The hero deed can not expire, / The dead still play their part.' His most ambitious work, 'The St. Lawrence and the Saguenay', presents a voyage down the St Lawrence from Kingston and up the Saguenay—a journey away from civilization towards nature and the divine creator. Modelling his tour on Byron's *Childe Harold's pilgrimage* and Wordsworth's *The River Duddon*, Sangster is stirred by the picturesque scenery to muse upon its rich history (Wolfe and Montcalm on the Plains of Abraham) and rich legend (the Indian maiden of the Thousand Islands who paddles nightly to care for her fugitive father). Interspersed throughout the narrative are lyrical interludes on the isles, lightning, twilight, dawn, maidens, whippoorwills, and vanished hopes. But as the voyage nears the poet's source of inspiration (symbolized by the river's divine origin), he grows weary of art, which cannot compete with the splendour of God's work, and humbly concludes that the expressive calm of silence in the northern wilderness is a 'Godlike eloquence'.

Sangster's best poems, however, are the songs and sonnets that defiantly celebrate fleeting joys in the face of death, as in 'The rapid', in which *voyageurs* gaily anticipate the euphoric danger of drowning in the shivering arrows of the rapids' spray; 'Canadian sleigh song', in which bells ring merrily despite the pursuit of time's cold, wintry shadow; and 'Sonnets written in the Orillia Woods', in which a dramatic tension between reverence and defiance remains unresolved.

There is a fine introduction to the colonial lauriate by E.H. DEWART in his *Essays for the times* (1898). The best modern criticisms are W.D. Hamilton's *Charles Sangster* (Twayne, 1971) and Gordon Johnston's introduction to *The St. Lawrence and the Saguenay and other poems/Hesperus and other poems and lyrics* (1972). Frank M. Tierney recently edited three collections that Sangster projected but did not live to publish: *Norland echoes and other poems* (1976), *The angel guest and other poems* (1977), and the revised *Hesperus* (1979). Many weak, overly conventional poems in these books show why the young Archibald LAMPMAN took no notice of Sangster when they worked in the same postal department.   DAVID LATHAM

Sarah Binks (1947). Long before this book was published, its author, Paul Hiebert (b. 1892)—then professor of chemistry at the University of Manitoba—had entertained public and private gatherings in Winnipeg with readings from the works and life of the 'Sweet Songstress of Saskatchewan'. A gentle combination of parody and burlesque (Hiebert insists that the book is not satirical), *Sarah Binks* invites our laughter at the foibles and excesses of literary biography and criticism, and at the brilliantly bad naïve poetry of his heroine: many of Sarah's poetic effusions are masterpieces of deliberately contrived incompetence, the product of a sensibility both academic and earthy. The account of Sarah's upbringing, her family and friends, her development as a poet, her eventual success, and her untimely death, is appropriately 'scholarly' in its plodding quest for facts and its ample quotations from the poet's works. Yet Hiebert treats Sarah with humorous affection, much as Stephen LEACOCK did the inhabitants of Mariposa, and many of the poems reveal a nostalgic understanding of life in the rural Canadian West before the Depression: 'Then all in fun they feed the pigs, / And plough the soil in reckless glee, / And play the quaint old-fashioned game / Of mortgagor and mortgagee' ('The farmer and the farmer's wife'); 'I sing the song of the simple chore, / Of quitting the downy bed at four, / And chipping ice from the stable door— / Of the simple chore I sing' ('The song of the chore'). Hiebert dedicated *Sarah Binks* to those 'of the West' who have seen its beauty and endured its hardships.

Additional Binksiana may be found in Hiebert's *Willows revisited* (1967) and *For the birds* (1980). Sarah is not a central figure in these books, but her shade may be said to haunt *Willows revisited*. The New Canadian Library has reprinted *Sarah Binks*, with an introduction by A. Lloyd Wheeler (1964). *Sarah Binks* has been dramatized several times, most recently (1981) in *The wonderful world of Sarah Binks*, a one-man show starring Eric Donkin. Hiebert's own views and opinions of his famous work are well presented in Reynold Siemens, 'Sarah Binks in retrospect: a conversation with Paul Hiebert', *Journal of Canadian Fiction* 19 (1977).
                                        DAVID JACKEL

Saunders, Marshall (1861-1947). Born in the Annapolis Valley of Nova Scotia, the daughter of an eminent Baptist minister, and educated in Halifax and for one year in Edinburgh and Orléans, Fr., Margaret Marshall Saunders returned to teach and write in Halifax. Holiday travels to Europe produced the shipboard atmosphere of the romantic novel *My Spanish sailor: a love story* (London, 1889), for which 'Beauty and the Beast' supplied the plot. In her late twenties she attended Dalhousie University for a year; the next year, in Ottawa, she heard the story of a gentle, homely dog, which would become the germ of BEAUTIFUL JOE: *an autobiography* (Philadelphia, 1894). Prize-winner in an American Humane Association contest, the manuscript had a six-month hunt for a publisher; but within ten years it was a phenomenal bestseller.

Saunders spent the next two years in Boston, auditing classes at Boston University and developing connections with American publishers and a sense of American reform causes. Slight stories for children, such as *Charles and his lamb* (Philadelphia, 1895), and *Daisy: a tale* (Philadelphia, 1897) kept her name alive. She then tried, more ambitiously, for an adult audience with *The House of armour* (Philadelphia, 1897) and *Rose à Charlitte: an Acadian romance* (Boston, 1898), the first set in her old Halifax home, the second in Grand Pré, N.S., where contemporary Acadians still suffer from the ancient exile and a contemporary American tries romantically to expiate his ancestral guilt. *Deficient saints: a tale of Maine* (Boston, 1899) is another contemporary adult tale of small-town duplicity; in the same year Saunders revised her first novel as *Her sailor; a love story*, changing the Nova Scotian heroine into a New England girl and developing the character of the middle-aged sailor-guardian. All these novels are fresh in style, and ingenious in plot, but none rise above the level of popular sentimental entertainment.

Saunders' forte was writing books for children. After the turn of the century she produced a long list, including the very popular *'Tilda Jane; an orphan in search of a home* (1901); *Beautiful Joe's paradise; a sequel to Beautiful Joe* (1902); *The story of the Gravelys; a tale for girls* (1903); *Alpatok; the story of an Eskimo dog* (1906); and *My pets; real happenings in my aviary* (1908), a series of essays still admired by naturalists. *Princess Sukey; the story of a pigeon and her human friends* (1905), the best of this group, is about a stiff-necked judge who, having unbent to the pigeon, finds himself adopting a raft of other pets and children.

By 1909 Marshall Saunders, who had been travelling back and forth from Halifax across the continent, to California and Rochester, N.Y., while maintaining a prodigious literary output, wound up in Orono, Maine, in enforced retirement because of a deep depression. In 1914, after adding Canadian transcontinental routes to her travels, she moved to Ontario, building in 1916 a house in Toronto with a 'toad castle' in the garden and an aviary. Her next major work, *The girl from Vermont, the story of a Vacation School teacher* (1919), is a sombre attack on children's problems: abuse, enforced labour, and lack of schooling and playgrounds. She lectured tirelessly on the animal world, which increasingly obsessed her and dominated her subsequent novels, including *Golden Dicky; the story of a canary and his friends* (1919), *Jimmy Goldcoast; or, The story of a monkey* (1924), and *Bonny Prince Fetlar; the story of a pony and his friends* (1920). Saunders' shipboard adventures, and her school experiences in Edinburgh, recollected fifty years later, give charm to her last novel, a melodramatic romance for teenaged girls, *Esther de Warren; the story of a mid-Victorian maiden* (1927).

Karen Saunders' thesis *Margaret Marshall Saunders: children's literature as an expression of early 20th century reform* (M.A., History, Dalhousie, 1978) relates Marshall Saunders' work to the concerns of reform-minded middle-class women at the turn of the century: alcoholism, child labour, lack of play space, as well as cruelty to animals. Marshall Saunders' many novels—approaching thirty in number—can also be related to the formulaic writing for family-circle readers produced by the American writers Gene Stratton Porter and Kate Douglas Wiggin. Though Saunders' writing style was usually controlled and competent, the melodramatic plot devices she employed make her books seem contrived and facile. Her concerns, however, were central—an important indication of contemporary conscience.

ELIZABETH WATERSTON

Sauvageau, Yves. See DRAMA IN FRENCH 1948 TO 1981: 3.

Savard, Félix-Antoine (1896-1982). Born in Quebec City, he spent most of his youth and early manhood in Chicoutimi. He became a priest in 1922 and taught at the Chicoutimi Seminary until 1927. After serving as curate in several locations within the diocese, he established Saint-Philippe-de-Clermont parish (Charlevoix) in 1931 and remained there until 1945, while also launching a literary career. He encouraged and recruited people in the region to reclaim land in Québec's Northwest, and on occasion accompanied these pioneers to Abitibi. During this period also, in collaboration with Luc Lacourcière, Savard began to assemble folk songs and tales, an initiative that led to the formation of Université Laval's folkloric archives (1944). In 1943 he began to lecture in the faculty of arts at Laval, where in 1950 he was honoured with the title of Monsignor and appointed Dean of the Faculty, a position he held until 1957. He received many distinctions, both in France and in Canada, including medals from l'Académie française (1938, 1953); the Grand Prix de la Province de Québec (1939); the Lorne PIERCE Medal (1945); the Prix Duvernay (1948); a Guggenheim Memorial Foundation grant (1957); and the Governor General's Award for *Le barachois*.

Savard owes his literary fame to a prolific output of high quality. Critics have lauded the beauty of his style, the strength of his images, the judicious use of Canadianisms, and the element of poetry that imbues all his works, even the prose. His novel MENAUD, MAÎTRE-DRAVEUR (1937), a lumber-camp story set in the Charlevoix region, is now considered a classic of French-Canadian literature. (There are two English translations: *Boss of the river* (1947) by Alan SULLIVAN and *Master of the river* (1976) by Richard Howard.) He followed this with *L'abatis* (1943), a mixed collection of short texts, in prose and verse, on the theme of the colonization of Québec's Northwest. (In 1960 he published a revised, shorter edition subtitled 'version définitive'.) *La minuit* (1948) is a romance about the simple life in a small village in the Tadoussac region—the background for a defence of the traditional values of religious inspiration against the materialist ideology and the pressures of the established social order. *Le barachois* (1959), a mixture of prose and verse, is Savard's tribute to the Acadian people, whom he came to know and love during his investigation of their folklore. In *Martin et le pauvre* (1959) he retells the legend of St Martin de Tours, who gave half his coat to a beggar. Savard also published two plays: *La folle* (1960), which presents the pathetic story of a mother whose child is stolen from her, and *La dalle-des-morts* (1965), which recalls pioneer expeditions in British Columbia in the first half of the nineteenth century. *La symphonie du misereor* (1968), a paraphrase in verse of the Latin hymn, was reprinted in *Le bouscueil* (1972), which contains expressions of religious themes, in prose and poetry, alternating with thoughts on nature, country, and man. *Aux marges du silence* (1974) is a series of poems in the Japanese haiku form. Savard's memoirs were published in *Journal et souvenirs 1, 1961-1962* (1973) and *Journal et souvenirs 2, 1963-1964* (1975). His most important speeches and lectures were assembled in *Discours* (1975). The return to the past and the reflections begun in the two volumes of *Journal et souvenirs* were continued in the author's last publications: *Carnet du soir intérieur 1* (1978) and *Carnet du soir intérieur 2* (1979).

Sister Thérèse-du-Carmel has assembled a bibliography of all Savard's works, as well as numerous studies and commentaries on his works up to 1965, in *Bibliographie analytique de l'oeuvre de Mgr Félix-Antoine Savard* (1967). See also André MAJOR, *Félix-Antoine Savard* (1968), and Georges Straka, 'En relisant *Menaud, maître-draveur*: contribution à un inventaire du vocabulaire régional du Québec' in *Travaux de linguistique et de littérature* (Strasbourg, 1973).   JULES TESSIER

Savoie, Calixte. See ACADIAN LITERATURE: 2(d).

Savoie, Jacques. See ACADIAN LITERATURE: 2(c).

Schoolcraft, Henry Rowe. See INDIAN LEGENDS AND TALES: BIBLIOGRAPHY.

Schroeder, Andreas (b. 1946). Born in Hoheneggelsen, Ger., he immigrated with his family to Canada in 1951. He studied creative writing under Michael BULLOCK and J. Michael YATES at the University of British Columbia, receiving a B.A. in 1969 and an M.A. in 1971. Schroeder has been founder and editor of *The Journal of Contemporary Literature in Translation* (1968-80), a columnist for the Vancouver *Province* (1968-73), instructor in creative writing at the University of Victoria (1976-7), chairman of the WRITERS' UNION OF CANADA (1976-7), and writer-in-residence for the Regina Public Library (1980-1). He currently lives in Mission City, B.C.

Most of Schroeder's writing has been influenced by European surrealism. His first two works were poetry collections: *The ozone minotaur* (1969) and *File of uncertainties* (1971), which focused on the violent unpredictability of twentieth-century life. He then published a collection of concrete poetry, *uniVERSE* (1971), and his strongest work, a collection of short fiction, *The late man* (1972). In the latter the techniques of surrealism are handled with such subtlety that the surreal ceases to be merely literary and becomes instead a quality of the actualities depicted.

Schroeder's best-known work is *Shaking it rough* (1976), a journal of the eight-month term he spent in British Columbia prisons on a minor narcotics conviction.

   FRANK DAVEY

Science fiction and fantasy in English and French. SF, a vast field in the U.S., has been a minor genre in Canada. Its concern with breaking the barriers of the unknown seems compatible with American frontier mythology, and the high priority given to research and development in the U.S. has undoubtedly fostered considerable speculation of a science-fictional nature. In Canada, however, the colonial situation, the conservative tradition, and the immense, hostile landscape—where survival, not conquest, was perhaps all that could be hoped for—may have inhibited the development of such a literature. Nevertheless there is a relatively large body of Canadian SF in print. The discussion below deals with a selection of titles. (Fantasy is discussed in sections 4 and 5.)

1. DE MILLE AND THE PIONEERS (1839-1932). The first work of Canadian SF seems

to be Napoléon AUBIN's uncompleted satire, *Mon voyage à la lune*, patterned on Cyrano de Bergerac's *L'autre monde*. Originally published in Aubin's Quebec City journal *Le Fantasque* in 1839, it was discovered by Michel Bélil in 1980 and reprinted in 1981 in the French-Canadian fanzine *Imagine* (8/9). The second was an anonymous satirical pamphlet with the following self-explanatory title: *House of the gallery; 2nd session, 3d parliament: official correspondence between the honourable the first minister of Duffy and his exalted majesty Night Blooming Ceres, monarch of the moon, emperor of the starry isles, etc., relative to the construction of the imperial, lunar, grand, mid-air, lunatic governmental railway, also the reports of the chief engineer, and the draft treaty in relation to same, with the speech from the throne* (Ottawa, 1875).

One of the best SF works of the nineteenth century, James DE MILLE's anonymously and posthumously published *A strange manuscript found in a copper cylinder* (New York, 1888), is set in the vicinity of the South Pole. The author of the 'strange manuscript', Adam More, tells how, as the sole survivor of a shipwreck, he discovered a lush, almost tropical world beyond the great Antarctic ice barrier, whose inhabitants have evolved a 'utopian' society based on the inversion or distortion of Western and Christian values: supremely prized are poverty and death. Though derivative of More's *Utopia*, Swift's *Gulliver's travels*, Butler's *Erewhon*, and especially Poe's *Narrative of A. Gordon Pym*, this satirical Utopian romance is replete with marvellous incident and achieves a unique and interesting synthesis.

The second published work of SF by an English Canadian, *The Dominion in 1983* (Peterborough, 1883) by 'Ralph Centennius', and the second by a French Canadian, POUR LA PATRIE: *roman du XXe siècle* (1895) by Paul Tardivel, both offer visions—though very different—of Canada's Utopian future. *The Dominion in 1983* (reprinted in John Robert COLOMBO's *Other Canadas*; see section 6 below) is an extraordinary, little-known pamphlet in three parts. 'Centennius', whose identity is unknown, writes from the vantage-point of 1983 about a Utopia that followed an unsuccessful attempt by America to take over Canada. Efficient transportation with 'electric tricycles' and 'beautiful rocket cars' has led to a united Canada, with a population of 93 million, where taxes were abolished in 1945; there have been no murders in over fifty years; parliament consists of a mere fifteen members; climate control arranges for rain to fall only at night; and from the observatory in New Westminster, 'living beings have been observed in the countries of Mars and Jupiter'. Tardivel's Utopia, set in 1945, is a vivid and exciting narrative about the way Québec, preserving its Catholic heritage, gained its independence and established the 'Laurentian Empire'. Sheila Fischman's translation is entitled *For my country: an 1895 religious and separatist vision of Quebec in the mid-twentieth Century* (1975).

In the years between these two Utopias, Grant ALLEN, Robert BARR, and the pseudonymous 'W.H.C. Lawrence' published works of SF interest: Allen's *The British barbarians* (New York, 1895), in which a man from the twenty-fifth century attacks the taboos of Victorian English society, and some of his *Strange stories* (London, 1884) such as 'Pausodyne', about a time traveller, and 'The child of the phalanstery', about a future society based on eugenic practices; Barr's *The face and the mask* (New York, 1895), containing such stories as 'The doom of London' (dealing with fog and pollution) and 'The fear of it' (in which, for the same religious reasons as in De Mille's *Strange manuscript*, death is desirable), and several fantasy pieces; and *The storm of '92: a grandfather's tale told in 1932* (Toronto, 1889) by 'W.H.C. Lawrence', a 'memoir' in the form of a veteran's account to his grandchildren of Canada's victory in the American-Canadian war of 1892. Towards the end of the nineteenth century stories warning of future wars were almost as prevalent as Utopias, and *The storm of '92* may have been inspired by the American Samuel Barton's *The battle of the Swash and the capture of Canada* (New York, 1888).

In 1909 a third Utopia by a Canadian author appeared: Percy Henry Blanchard's *After the cataclysm: a romance of the age to come*, which briefly describes a world of abundance that contains little social organization and no sex. Many writers were affected by Edward Bellamy's *Looking backward, 2000-1887* (Boston, 1888), among them a Canadian Unitarian minister, Hugh Pedley. In his *Looking forward: the strange experience of the Reverend Fergus McCheyne* (1913) the protagonist, as a result of experimenting with a new drug, falls asleep in 1902 and wakes to the Utopian Canada of 1927, created by the success of a movement for church unity. By 1932 the Utopian theme was ripe for spoofing, and in that year Stephen LEACOCK published a six-story collection entitled *After-*

noons in Utopia: tales of the new time that includes 'A fragment from Utopia: the fifty-fifty sexes', which satirizes *Looking backward*; while another Leacock collection, *The iron man and the tin woman with other such futurities: a book of little sketches of to-day and to-morrow* (1929), presents the world of 1950 and parodies various aspects of science fiction. Another earlier Leacock collection, *Nonsense novels* (1911), includes 'The man in asbestos: an allegory of the future', which makes fun of H.G. Wells's *The time machine* (London, 1895).

Between Pedley's 1913 Utopia and Leacock's in 1932 came the following works: Harry MacDonald Walter's *Wesblock: the autobiography of an automaton* (1914); Charles G.D. ROBERTS' *In the morning of time* (1919), a prehistoric romance concerning the adventures of the People of the Caves; *The writing on the wall* (1922), by 'Hilda Glynn-Ward', which depicts a future Japanese invasion of Canada; Hamilton Craig's *A hazard at Hansard: the speech from the throne, Ottawa, fourth August, 2014* (1925); Robert W. SERVICE's *The master of the microbe* (1926), a tale of a newly developed deadly plague virus in the hands of a master criminal; Arthur English's *The vanished race* (1927); Robert Watson's *High hazard: a romance of the far Arctic* (1929), complete with giants and prehistoric creatures and one of the surprisingly few Canadian stories about a lost northern world; Alan SULLIVAN's *A little way ahead* (1930), concerning a London stockbroker's clerk who acquires prescience; Robert STEAD's *The copper disc* (1931), about a diabolical professor who is out to control the world; two French-Canadian novels— *Similia similibus; ou La guerre au Canada; essai romantique sur un sujet d'actualité* (1916), a thriller by Ulric Barthe about a German invasion of Canada, and Emmanuel Desrosiers's *La fin de la terre* (1931); and E.J. PRATT's 'The great feud: a dream of a Pleiocene Armageddon'. This second poem of Pratt's *Titans* (1926), in which a female anthropoid ape leads the land beasts against the sea creatures, seems to have been inspired by Charles G.D. Roberts' *In the morning of time*, which was in turn inspired by such tales as Stanley Waterloo's *The story of Ab* (1897), Jack London's *Before Adam* (1906), and Sir Arthur Conan Doyle's *The lost world* (1912).

The most important work of Canadian SF between 1913 and 1932 was Frederick Philip GROVE's *Consider the ways*—written, according to its author, in 1919-20, but not pub-

lished until 1947. This account of a society of Venezuelan ants exploring North America is communicated telepathically by the leader of the ants to a human recorder. As in De Mille's *Strange manuscript*, the satire owes much to *Gulliver's travels*, but especially science-fictional is Grove's compelling realization of ant society and its pecular perspective.

2. VAN VOGT AND THE EXPATRIATE INTERVAL (1932-59). During this period, which includes the so-called Golden Age (1938-46) of American SF, little was published by resident Canadians. *Go home, unicorn* (1935) by Donald MacPherson (pseudonym of George MacTavish?) is about the transmutation of species, and his *Men are like animals* (1937) tells how a scorned woman seeks revenge by means of a thought-control machine; Maurice B. Dix's *The kidnapped scientist: adventure of the trio of Mount Street* (1937) is about a scientist who has discovered a cure for cancer; Madge Macbeth's *Wings in the west* (1937) concerns a Russian scientist manufacturing death-rays in his mysterious cabin in the Far North; Thomas P. KELLEY wrote a 'space opera', 'A million years in the future', that appeared in *Weird tales* (Jan.-Oct., 1940), and a later piece, 'He who saw tomorrow', that appeared in *Fantastic adventures* (July 1946). *Erres boréales* (1944) by 'Florent Laurin' (pseudonym of Armand Grenier) depicts a coal-depleted world saved by the energy supplied by an advanced technological society of New Frenchmen in the North.

Canadian SF in the fifties begins with Earle BIRNEY's 'Trial of a city', a comic verse-play about the destruction of Vancouver 'five years from now', broadcast and published in 1952 and subsequently revised as *The damnation of Vancouver* (1977). A number of fifties' novels followed: Ralph ALLEN's *The chartered libertine* (1954), a satire on the near-future collapse of the CBC when attacked by tycoons and rabble-rousers; *Arctic submarine* (1955), by 'Alastair Mars' (pseudonym of A.C. Gillespie), a Far North adventure story, and Mars' *Atomic submarine: a story of tomorrow* (1957), in which a Russian/Chinese attack on Britain is thwarted by a submarine; Stanley Zuber's *The golden promise* (1956), about an attempt to devise a world language; *Alien virus* (1957) by 'Alan Caillou' (pseudonym of Alan Lyle-Smythe); and 'Henry' (Harold) Gayle's *Spawn of the vortex* (1957), about an army of explosion-released undersea metallic monsters that threaten the west coast of the United States. John Mantley's *The twenty-seventh day* (1956), published in an American edition, *The 27th day* (1956), with a different ending, became the basis of a 1957 film (for which Mantley wrote the screenplay) starring Gene Barry. It is a morality tale about Galactic Federation aliens who kidnap five individuals from opposing countries, give each an invincible weapon, and then release them; their behaviour will determine whether or not mankind passes the aliens' maturity test.

In these years Canada lost important talent to the United States. Foremost was A.E. van Vogt, who was born in Winnipeg in 1912 and grew up in Neville and Swift Current, Sask., and in Morden and Winnipeg, Man. His first published SF story, 'Black destroyer', appeared in *Astounding Science Fiction* in July 1939, the same year in which he married E. Mayne Hull, a Brandon-born writer. After a period in Ottawa and Farm Point, Qué., when he wrote four of his most admired works—the ASF versions of *Voyage of the Space Beagle* (1939-43; published as a book in 1950), *Slan* (1940; published as a book in 1946, rev. 1951), *The weapon shops of Isher* (1941-2; published as a book in 1951), and *The weapon makers* (1943; published as a book in 1946; rev., 1952)—and a brief stay in Toronto, van Vogt and his wife moved in 1944 to Los Angeles and eventually became American citizens. While in Canada van Vogt seems to have written 34 stories that form the bulk of 11 later books. Writing many more stories and novels, including *The world of null-A* (1948), he is now regarded as one of the major figures in American SF, particularly of the 'space-opera' variety. Along with Robert A. Heinlein and Isaac Asimov, van Vogt is one of the 'big three' credited with creating that 'Golden Age' associated with John W. Campbell's editorship of ASF (now called *Analog*). His wife, Edna Mayne Hull, may also be considered a Canadian gift to American SF, though van Vogt collaborated on most of her work, which began with the Ottawa period tale 'The flight that failed' (published in ASF in 1942). Hull made her reputation with the Arthur Blord series, *Planets for sale* (published in ASF in 1943-6 and as a book in 1954) and *The winged man* (published in ASF in 1944 and as a book— 'rewritten by A.E. van Vogt'—in 1966).

Van Vogt's route to eminence in American SF had been paved by another Canadian-born writer, Laurence E. Manning. Born in Saint John, N.B., in 1899, he moved to the States in 1920. Between 1932 and 1935 he was briefly a regular and popular contributor to *Wonder Stories* and *Wonder Stories Quarterly*. Of his fifteen published stories, the best known are the five that appeared as *The man who awoke* series (published in *Wonder Stories* in 1933, and as a paperback in 1975). The hero of this sequence emerges repeatedly from a state of suspended animation to experience a number of increasingly dystopian societies arising at successively distant points in the future.

Gordon R. Dickson, the half-brother of Lovat DICKSON, is the most recent Canadian expatriate to make a name for himself in American SF. Thirteen years after his birth in Edmonton in 1923, his parents moved to the midwestern United States. Since *Alien from Arcturus* (1956), Gordon R. Dickson has published over thirty novels, mostly in a philosophical 'space-opera' mode. Best known for the 'Childe' cycle, a projected epic sequence of twelve books about the professional warriors of the planet Dorsai, he is one of the most prolific and popular SF authors. Mention should also be made of a man more famous as the founder and editor of *Galaxy* (1950-61) than as the author of such SF stories as 'A matter of form' (1938), namely Horace Gold, who was born in Montreal in 1914 and holds both Canadian and U.S. citizenship.

Perhaps Canada's most potent export was the image of Superman. The first illustrator of the strip was Joseph (Joe) Shuster (a cousin of the comedian Frank), who was born in Toronto in 1914. In Cleveland, Ohio, where the Shuster family had moved, Joseph Shuster teamed up with the American, Jerome (Jerry) Siegal, who created the Superman idea in 1933 after reading Philip Wylie's *Gladiator* (1930). After many rejections, *Superman* made its first appearance, in the now-familiar cape and body tights, in the June 1938 issue of *Action Comics*. Shuster's graphic conception of Clark Kent's newspaper, the 'Daily Planet', derives largely from the *Toronto Daily Star*.

3. GOTLIEB AND OTHER CONTEMPORARIES (1959-). In the sixties and seventies approximately 190 SF titles (including some 46 children's books) were published in English and French, the bulk of them (approximately 152) in the seventies. The key figure in this recent period (though she is better known in Canada as a poet) is Phyllis GOTLIEB. Her first story, 'A grain of manhood', appeared in *Fantastic* in 1959. Subsequent finely crafted stories include 'Gingerbread boy', 'The military hospital',

'Planetoid idiot', and the 1972 Nebula award nominee, 'Son of the morning'. Her first novel, *Sunburst* (1964), is about the difficulties experienced by a group of mutant 'children' who develop psychic abilities after an atomic explosion. A second, *O master Caliban!* (1976), set on Dahlgren's Planet, pits a number of unusual children (clearly a central theme in her work) and aliens against a sentient computer complex that has gotten out of the control of a ten-year-old telepath's scientist father. Both *A judgment of dragons* (1980) and *Emperor, swords, pentacles* (1982) chronicle the adventures of Duncan Kinnear (a Galactic Federation investigator) and two starcats. *A judgment of dragons*, billed as 'A starcat and rabbi tale, with dragons', contains four related stories, beginning with 'Son of the morning'. In *Emperor, swords, pentacles* (the initials ESP point specifically to telepathy, again an important element in both books), which is experimentally sectioned like a tarot reading, a collection of odd characters join forces to prevent the Emperor of Qsaprinel from being dispossessed of his planet.

Other well-known Canadian authors have produced occasional works of SF. Hugh HOOD's story 'After the sirens' (1960) details reaction in Montreal to the dropping of an atomic bomb. Yves THÉRIAULT's *Si la bombe m'était contée* (1962) (which revived SF in Québec), containing six short stories plus factual material, illustrates the destructive madness of nuclear power; while his *Le haut-pays* (1973) concerns the testing of a Sicilian, a Yugoslav, and a Métis by aliens in an occult parallel universe. Thériault also wrote seven futuristic espionage novels for teenagers featuring a hero named Volpek. Margaret LAURENCE has published a very effective post-holocaust story involving incest, 'A queen in Thebes' (TAMARACK REVIEW 32, 1964). Michel TREMBLAY's *La cité dans l'oeuf* (1969), a Lovecraftian tale on the borderline of SF and fantasy, concerns a space-egg controlled by gods intent on destroying planet Earth. Brian MOORE's fine SF novella *Catholics* (1972) describes resistance to a modish Catholic church of the future (see also section 4 below). Less effective is John GLASSCO's description of a lesbian dystopia in 'Lust in action', included in *The fatal woman* (1974). Perhaps the most successful excursion into SF by a mainstream Canadian writer is Hugh MacLENNAN's *Voices in time* (1980). Set in the twenty-first-century post-nuclear-holocaust city of Metro (built on the ruins of Montreal), it offers the reluctant but intense reflections of the protagonist, John Wellfleet, on twentieth-century events (in Nazi Germany, but also in Québec) that have shattered his world.

A large number of less well-established authors have published at least one SF novel or short story. A highly selective list of titles by such English-speaking Canadians follows: Ray SMITH's experimental short story collection, *Cape Breton is the thought control centre of Canada* (1969); Marie Jakober's *The mind gods* (1976), which concerns the abandoned polluted Earth of A.D. 2350; Edward Llewellyn's time travel 'space opera', *The Douglas convolution* (1979), and his *The bright companion* (1980; and Donald Kingsbury's exploration of group-marriage dynamics in the harsh world of Geta in *Courtship rite* (1982). Mention should also be made of John Hollis Keith Mason who, between 1941 and 1975, published six SF stories and scripted a five-part CBC serial entitled 'The other Canada' (1971), based on the premise that the French had won the battle of the Plains of Abraham.

Two recent original anthologies—the first such—may mark a coming of age in Canadian SF: *Visions from the edge: an anthology of Atlantic Canadian science fiction* (1981), edited by John Bell and Lesley Choyce, and *New bodies: a collection of science fiction short stories* (1981), edited by Lorne Gould.

In the relatively unexploited areas of SF poetry and drama a showing has been made—in addition to that of E.J. PRATT and Earle BIRNEY—by contemporary English-Canadians (and one Polish-Canadian). Stanislaw Michalski's *Eskimoska ewa* (i.e., 'Eskimo eve') (1964), written in rhyming Polish verse, concerns two survivors of an atomic holocaust who meet in an igloo in the Arctic. Phyllis Gotlieb, Canada's premier SF novelist, is also Canada's premier science-fiction poet; examples such as 'Seeing eye' and 'Ms & Mr Frankenstein' figure in *The works: collected poems* (1978). Margaret ATWOOD's poetry shows an SF quality, which the critic Susan Wood has called 'the Martian point of view', in 'Speeches for Doctor Frankenstein' (1966), 'Oratorio for sasquatch, man and two androids' (1970), and elsewhere. The inspiration for the poems in Gwendolyn MacEWEN's *The armies of the moon* (1972) is both factual (man's setting foot on the moon) and science-fictional. Also to be noted are Alden NOWLAN's 'O'Sullivan's world' (1969), 'The moon landing' (1971), and 'Plot for a science-fiction novel'; and John Robert COLOMBO's collection of 'found poems', *Mostly monsters* (1977).

SF drama includes Isabelle Foord's *Say hi to Owsley* (1975), about two Martians who crash-land on Earth, and *Frankenstein: the play* (1976), a dramatic adaptation by Alden Nowlan and Walter Learning, that is unusually faithful to Mary Shelley's novel.

A chronological list of French-Canadian SF would include the following: Jean Tétreau's *Les nomades* (1967), about a young woman's struggles to survive in a post-atomic-catastrophe world; Louis-Philippe Hébert's *Les mangeurs de terre (et autres textes)* (1970), *Récits des temps ordinaires* (1972), and *La manufacture de machines* (1977), each containing a series of short poetic works of a surreal or Kafkaesque nature that border on SF; Emmanuel Cocke's *Va voir au ciel si j'y suis* (1971), an amusing satirical novel set in the year 2057 in which a special investigator experiences extravagant adventures and saves the world from catastrophe; Robert GURIK's future 'Adam and Eve' play, *Api 2967* (1971); Léo Le-Blanc's *Les incommuniquants* (1971), in which extraterrestrials, operating out of a pavilion at Montreal's Man and His World site, attempt to silence all communication on Earth; and Maurice Gagnon's *Les tours de Babylone* (1972), winner of the Grand Prix de l'Actuelle, which is set on the post-nuclear-disaster Earth of A.D. 2380. (Between 1965 and 1968 Gagnon published a series of seven children's SF novels that concern an organization named Unipax, devoted to universal peace.)

At least six French-Canadian SF novels appeared in 1974: Andrée-Jean Bonelli's *Loona: ou Autrefois le ciel était bleu* (the first and only title in the 'Demain aujourd'hui' series devoted 'to science fiction and esoterism' that qualifies as SF), which concerns yet another repressive society in a polluted world, and the quest of a sixteen-year-old girl who discovers on a mountain the sky's true colour; Jacques Brossard's eight surreal short stories in *Le metamorfaux, nouvelles*, several of which focus on time travel and temporal paradoxes; Roger Desroches's *Reliefs de l'arsenal*, which makes use of the techniques of the *nouveau roman* and features an extraterrestrial wanderer; Jean Ferguson's *Contes ardents du pays mauve*, containing eight futuristic short stories featuring robots, mutants, and super-computers; Jean-Claude Hamel's *Quatre fois rien*, in which four of its 16 tales qualify as SF; and Marcel Moussette's *Les patenteux*, a satirical piece about

five Québécois, attempting to build a perpetual-motion machine, who are captured by the crew of a space ship.

Since 1974 the following books have appeared: the ambitious 1976 trilogy of 'Monique Corriveau' (pseudonym of Monique Chouinard), *Compagnons du soleil* (1. *L'oiseau de feu*, 2. *La lune noire*, 3. *Le temps des chats*), concerning the ever-popular division of a seemingly Utopian future society into two groups—the élite Companions of the Sun who live by day, and the put-upon Black Moon People of the night, with whom the young privileged hero, Oakim, comes to sympathize—and the inevitable revolution (Corriveau also wrote *Patrick et Sophie en fusée*, a 1975 children's SF novel); Gérard BESSETTE's *Les anthropoides* (1977), a fine experimental prehistoric tale about the beginning of storytelling; Alain Bergeron's *Un été de Jessica* (1978), about a privileged haven on Mars inhabited by 100 elderly millionaires and a nine-year-old female mutant; Claire de Lamirandes's *L'opération fabuleuse* (1978), in which a woman invents increasingly sophisticated surgical machinery; and Jean-François Sorncynsky's *Grimaces* (1975), a collection of short stories, two of which focus on the dehumanization of society and the loss of individual liberty, and *Le diable du Mahani* (1978), about an erotic Utopia established beneath Lake Mahani by a Japanese and his society of women. Two volumes launching a French-Canadian SF series (the first to come out of 'fandom'), 'Chroniques du futur', edited by Norbert Spehner, appeared in 1981: Jean-Pierre April's *Machine à explorer la fiction* and Elizabeth Vonarburg's *L'oeil de la nuit*, both short-story collections.

In addition to the titles, already cited, by Yves Thériault and Monique Corriveau, French-Canadian SF novels for children include: Louis Sutal's *La mystérieuse boule de feu* (1971), *Menace sur Montréal* (1972), *Le piège à bateau* (1973), *Révolte secrète* (1974), *La planète sous le joug* (1976), and *Panne dans l'espace* (1977); Yvon Brochu's *L'extraterrestre* (1975); and Suzanne Martel's *Titralak, cadet de l'espace* (1975). This list of children's SF omits one title that might more usefully be grouped with those works that offer visions of a specifically Canadian future (cf. Centennius, Tardivel, and Pedley in section 1 above): Suzanne Martel's *Quatre Montréalais en l'an 3000* (1963), reissued as *Surreal 3000* (1971) and published in an English translation by Norah Smaridge as *The city underground* (1964). Martel describes life in Montreal's underground city after the destruction of civilization by a nuclear war. Other visions of Canada's future have been produced by English-Canadian writers. In Eric Koch's *The French kiss* (1969), a tongue-in-cheek political fantasy, a French observer compares events in a future separated Québec with those in nineteenth-century revolutionary Europe. In what is more an illustrated proposal than a work of fiction, Stephen Franklin, in *Knowledge park* (1972), describes the establishment of the world's greatest park in an area straddling the Québec-Ontario border. The six somewhat pedestrian short stories in *North by 2000: a collection of Canadian science fiction* (1975), by H.A. Hargreaves, an American professor of English at the University of Alberta, all take place in Americanada. A farcical civil war in a province detached from the mainland by a nuclear explosion is the subject of Jeffrey Holmes's *Farewell to Nova Scotia* (1974). In *Canada cancelled because of lack of interest* (1977), by Eric NICOL and Peter Whalley, a look backward from the end of the twenty-first century, Canada's balkanized future state is also treated comically. In a more grimly satiric vein, William Weintraub's *The underdogs* (1979) describes how the newly separated republic of Québec (founded with a loan from the USSR) oppresses its English-speaking minority.

Frequently related to the future-vision-of-Canada category are a significant number of titles that might be classified as near-future thrillers. A mix of politics and some form of disaster scenario is typical. Such Richard ROHMER titles as *Ultimatum* (1973), *Exodus/UK* (1975), and *Separation* (1976) are the best-known examples. Others are Arthur HAILEY's only novel set in Canada, *In high places* (1962), William C. Heine's *The last Canadian* (1974), and D.K. Findlay's *King winter* (1978). The most popular bases for this kind of book are the threat of nuclear destruction and Canada's anxiety about America's proximity.

Compensating for the writers Canada lost during the 'expatriate interval' are three successful SF writers gained from abroad since 1968. Canada's most prolific writer of SF is Michael G. Coney, an Englishman who has lived in Victoria, B.C., since 1972. In addition to short stories, he has published the following highly inventive novels: *Mirror image* (1972); *Friends come in boxes* (1973); *The hero of Downways* (1973); *Syzygy* (1973); *Winter's children* (1974)—his most 'Canadian' novel, about a snowbound community;

Charisma (1975); *The girl with a symphony in her fingers* (1975; published in the U.S. as *The jaws that bite, the claws that catch*); *Hello summer, goodbye* (1975; published in the U.S. as *Rax*); *Brontomek!* (1976), winner of the British Science Fiction Award; and *The ultimate jungle* (1978).

The New York-born Juliet Grossman, who changed her name to Judith Merril, immigrated to Toronto in 1968 and became a Canadian citizen in 1976. Although such works as 'That only a mother' (1948), *Shadow on the hearth* (1950), and *Daughters of Earth* (1963) are pioneering efforts in using SF to explore feminist issues, Merril is best known as a champion of the 'New Wave' in SF associated with the British magazine *New Worlds*. She has published only one book in Canada, *Survival ship and other stories* (1973). Her collection of over 5,000 SF books and periodicals forms the basis of the Spaced Out Library—with 20,000 titles, the largest public library of its kind in the world—which she established at Rochdale College in 1969 and subsequently affiliated with the Toronto Public Library system in 1970.

Another New Yorker, Spider Robinson, moved to Nova Scotia in 1973 and now lives in Halifax with his Massachusetts-born wife, Jeanne. He made his reputation as a reviewer for *Galaxy* (June 1975-Sept. 1977) and as the author, together with his wife, of the novella 'Sundance' (1977), about a zero-gravity dancer (it won a 1978 Nebula award and became the first part of a 1979 novel of the same title). Works authored solely by Spider Robinson include the post-holocaust story *Telempath* (1976), a portion of which, 'By any other name' (1976), won a 1977 Hugo award; *Callahan's crosstime saloon* (1977), a collection of nine stories told by patrons, human and alien, of the eponymous saloon; *Armageddon 2419 AD* (1978), an updating of Philip Francis Nowlan's Buck Rogers novel; and *Mindkiller* (1982), set partly in Nova Scotia, which is about a society addicted to the artificial stimulation of the brain's pleasure centres.

4. ENGLISH-CANADIAN FANTASY (1863-). There is little agreement about the distinction between science fiction and fantasy. Some of the items included above might be considered fantasy. Many writers publish in both categories or produce works that might be understood as occupying the border area between them. I classify as fantasy those works that qualify, by what may be assumed to be a consensus view of the author's intention, as neither SF nor mimetic

realism and naturalism; it includes such diverse genres as tales of the occult and supernatural (including ghost stories), weird tales (involving werewolves, wendigos, monsters, etc.), fairy tales and tales involving magic or 'sword and sorcery', folktales and mythic or legendary material (in Canada's case, Indian and Inuit myths are particularly relevant), and stories of a surrealistic or mystical quality. Fantasy is even more heterogeneous than SF. But while SF must rely on some form of serious rationalization—of a scientific, philosophical, or cosmological nature—for its fantastic state of affairs or elements, fantasy is characterized either by the lack of any such rational explanation (the 'secondary worlds' of fantasy are discontinuous with the world of consensus reality) or by the presence of some kind of supernatural assumption or equivocation. The element of explanation, whether natural or supernatural, provides one means whereby SF may slide into fantasy.

Between 1863 and 1981 over 100 English-Canadian works of adult fantasy have been published (not counting the 342 Gothic romances published by W.E. Dan Ross!). The listing below includes only works of special merit or significance published before Howard O'HAGAN's *Tay John* (1939), the first Canadian fantasy. May Agnes FLEMING wrote *La masque; or, The midnight queen* (New York, 1863), a Gothic horror story set in London during the plague, followed by *The ghost of Riverside Hall* (New York, 1895). Also in 1895 Charles G.D. ROBERTS published *Earth's enigmas* (Boston), a collection of animal and other fantasies. William Alexander FRASER bridged the nineteenth and twentieth centuries with *The eye of a god and other tales of east and west* (New York, 1899) and *The Sa'-Zada tales* (1905). Twentieth-century titles include: Douglas Erskine (pseudonym of John Stuart Buchan), *A bit of Atlantis* (1900); Archibald MacMECHAN's *The porter of Bagdad and other fantasies* (1901); Theodore Goodridge ROBERTS' romance drawn from Micmac mythology, *The red feathers* (1907); William BLAKE's *Brown waters and other sketches* (1915), which contains a story about the wendigo ('A tale of the Grand Jardin')—a man-eating ogre according to Algonkian legend and lore; Lily Adams BECK's *The ninth vibration and 8 other stories* (1922); Marjorie PICKTHALL's collection, which includes some fantasies, *Angel's shoes and other stories* (1923); Robert W. SERVICE's werewolf novel, *The house of fear* (1927); Arthur STRINGER's *The man who*

couldn't sleep (1928) and *The woman who couldn't die* (1929); Douglas Leader DURKIN's after-death farce, *Mr. Grumble sits up* (1931); and two of Thomas P. KELLEY's novels serialized in *Weird Tales*, 'The last pharoah' (May-Aug., 1937) and 'I found Cleopatra' (Nov. 1938).

Howard O'Hagan's *Tay John* (1939, rpr. 1974) is a haunting, mythic novel, set in the Northwest, about a mysterious man, half-white and half-Indian, born underground from the body of his dead and buried mother, who, marked to be the leader of his tribe, becomes involved with a white woman. However, like the weird coyote and the mythic bear that Tay John meets, his relations are not so much with men as with the primal elements of nature.

Two notable titles appeared in the forties: John Buchan's *Sick Heart River* (1941; U.S. title *Mountain meadow*) and *The sun and the moon* (1944; republished in 1974 in *The sun and the moon and other fictions*) by P.K. PAGE. Buchan's moving novel, written while he was Governor General of Canada, concerns a dying man's Arctic search for a river 'beyond humanity and beyond time'. The title story in Page's collection of nine poetic fantasies involves a girl named Kristin who can assume the identity of inanimate objects and people and thereby rob them of their souls.

The following more routine works appeared in the fifties and sixties: John BUELL's tale of devil worship in Montreal, *The pyx* (1959), which was filmed in 1973; H.R. PERCY's *The timeless island and other stories* (1960); *Pippin's journal* (1962), by Rohan O'Grady (pseudonym of June Skinner), with illustrations by Edward Gorey; John GLASSCO's completion of Aubrey Beardsley's *Under the hill* (1967); and the first of the thirty-odd Don W.E. (W.E. Dan) Ross vampire novels (based on a character in ABC-TV's Gothic soap opera *Dark shadows*), *Barnabus Collins* (1968).

Gwendolyn MacEWEN's main contribution to Canadian fiction is a series of artist/magician figures. The protagonist of her first novel, *Julian the magician* (1963), believing himself to be Christ-like, demands to be crucified to see if he can be resurrected. MacEwen's magicians are in tune with a magical Otherworld—such as the ancient Egypt described in *King of Egypt, king of dreams* (1971)—diametrically opposed to the mundane world of 'Kanada'. In 'Kingsmere', one of the stories in the highly evocative collection, *Noman* (1972), the 'Kanadian' magician attempts to combine the magical and the mundane worlds. The imported ruins of Mackenzie King's 'Kingsmere', 'Noman's land', function as a magical time-travel doorway. In the same collection, 'The second coming of Julian the magician' concerns the problems of a real magician in a non-magical environment; before a sacrificial disappearance (a characteristic conclusion for MacEwen), he destroys the Power House that maintains the electrical city, symbol of modernity.

Leonard COHEN's *Beautiful losers* (1966) also employs fantasy elements, but two other books (which appeared in the seventies) deserve particular recognition. Wayland Drew's *The wabeno feast* (1973) juxtaposes an account of the collapse of Canadian civilization in the near future with an eighteenth-century trader's expedition into the wilderness and his encounter with the destructive Indian shaman, the white 'wabeno'. Contrasted worlds are also the subject of Brian MOORE's *The great Victorian collection* (1975). A Montreal historian in Carmel, California, dreams about a collection of Victorian artifacts and awakes to find that the collection exists outside his motel window. Other seventies' titles include Lawrence GARBER's *Circuit* (1970); two more Brian Moore novels, *Fergus* (1970), in which a novelist is visited by his long-dead parents, and *The Mangan inheritance* (1979), a weird tale; Leo SIMPSON's *The Peacock papers* (1973); Lynne Sallot's and Tom Peltier's *Bearwalk* (1977); Earle BIRNEY's *Big bird in the bush: selected stories and sketches* (1978); John Robert COLOMBO's encyclopedic itemization of fantastic Canadiana, *Colombo's book of marvels* (1979); and Sheila WATSON's *Four stories* (1979).

Fantasy themes also find expression in poetry, notably Archibald LAMPMAN's Poe-like 'The city of the end of things' (*Atlantic Monthly*, Mar. 1894); in at least seven dramas, including Heram's (real identity unknown) *The dream* (c. 1865-7), which provides a vision of Canada's political future after the victory of unionist forces in a farcical civil war; and some 70 English-Canadian children's books. Examples of the latter are Pierre BERTON's *The secret world of Og* (1962), Margaret LAURENCE's *Jason's quest* (1970), and Mordecai RICHLER's *Jacob Two-Two meets the Hooded Fang* (1975), the basis of a 1979 film.

5. FRENCH-CANADIAN FANTASY (1934-). The fantastic in its various forms has interested virtually every French-Canadian writer at one point or another. As one might expect in a predominantly Catholic society, the supernatural world looms large in French-Canadian fantasy, a mode more sympathetic to French-Canadian experience than science fiction. Georges BUGNET's *Siraf: étranges révélations, ce que l'on pense de nous par-delà la lune* (1934) involves a debate on ethics between a prairie farmer and two extraterrestrial spirits. In Félix LECLERC's *Le fou de l'île* (1958), translated by Philip Stratford as *The madman, the kite and the island* (1976), a mysterious Christ-like figure disturbs some islanders with his honesty. He responds to their persecution by disappearing.

In the sixties Yves THÉRIAULT published *Le vendeur d'étoiles: nouvelles* (1961) and *Contes pour un homme seul* (1965), twenty tales that suggest both natural and supernatural explanations. Forty-one short poetic and fantastic pieces are collected in Gilles VIGNEAULT's *Contes sur la pointe des pieds* (1961), translated by Paul Allard as *Tales (sur la pointe des pieds)* (1972). This first collection becomes the first part of Vigneault's *Les dicts du voyageur sédentaire: contes poétiques* (1970). The second part, 'Contes du coin de l'oeil', consists of seventeen short parable-like fantasies. Other sixties' collections include Michel TREMBLAY's *Contes pour buveurs attardés* (1966), translated by Michael BULLOCK as *Stories for late night drinkers* (1977), a collection of twenty-five predominantly Gothic pieces written when the playwright was 17, and Jean Tétreau's *Volupté de l'amour et de la mort: histoires fantastiques* (1968).

The production of French-Canadian fantasy, like French Canadian SF, accelerated during the seventies. The first of three high points is Jacques Benoit's *Les princes* (1973), a work of black humour set in an imaginary city—clearly comparable to Montreal—inhabited by monsters, men, and talking dogs. Esther Rochon's *En hommage aux araignées* (1974) constitutes a second high point. Her imaginary country of the Asvens, in which pre-civilized society rubs shoulders with contemporary tourists, clearly mirrors Québec. One of its inhabitants enters the city of death, lives in its underground areas, and finally leaves after drawing its map. This book is intended to be the second volume of a trilogy, the first of which has appeared in German only: *Der traumer in der zitadelle*. The third high point is Jacques GODBOUT's *L'isle au dragon* (1976), translated by David Ellis as *Dragon* island (1978). The hero of this striking novel saves a beautiful island in the St Lawrence river from the hands of American imperialists by conjuring up a dragon.

Other seventies titles include Antonine MAILLET's *Don l'Orignal* (1972) (a novel written in the Acadian dialect about an island of fleas), translated by Barbara Godard as *The tale of Don l'Orignal* (1978); Michel Bélil's story collections, *Le mangeur de livres* (1978) and *Déménagement* (1981), and his horror fantasy, *Greenwich* (1981); and Négovan Rajic's noteworthy *Les hommes-taupes* (1978).

The following titles belong to the category 'children's literature': Claude Aubry's *Les îles du roi Maha Maha Deux* (1966), translated by Alice Kane as *The king of the Thousand Islands: a Canadian fairy tale* (1968); Danièle Simpson's *Le voleur d'étoiles* (1971); Christiane Duchesne's *Le triste dragon* (1976); and Denise Houle's play, *Lune de neige* (1977).

6. REFERENCE. Surprisingly, the first collection representing the existence of the material detailed above did not appear until 1979: *Other Canadas: an anthology of science fiction and fantasy*, edited by John Robert COLOMBO and composed of some forty items, including fiction, poetry, and non-fiction. To complement the anthology, John Robert Colombo, Michael Richardson, John Bell, and Alexandre L. Amprimoz compiled *Cnd sf & f: a bibliography of Canadian science fiction and fantasy* (1979). This ground-breaking (albeit error-prone) bibliography lists and describes some 600 books under such headings as 'National disaster scenarios', 'Fantasy and weird tales', and 'Children's literature'. Donald A. Wollheim's 1942 essay 'Whither Canadian fantasy?', urging Canadian science-fiction writers to take imaginative possession of the Canadian North, is excerpted as an epigraph to *Cnd sf & f* and reprinted in full in *Friendly aliens: thirteen stories of the fantastic set in Canada by foreign authors* (1981) edited by John Robert Colombo.

David Ketterer's six-category 'Canadian science fiction: a survey', which first appeared in *Canadian Children's Literature*, 10 (1977-8, rpr. in expanded form in *Other Canadas*), provides the first academic treatment of its subject. Margaret ATWOOD's 'Canadian monsters: some aspects of the supernatural in Canadian fiction' (1977), which is included in her *Second words* (1982), provides the first academic treatment of Canadian fantasy. In recent years Canada has contributed significantly to the academic study of science fiction. Since 1978, *Science-fiction Studies* has been published in Montreal under such Montreal editors as Darko Suvin (until 1981), Robert M. Philmus, and Mark Agenot. At the same time, three major studies of science fiction have been authored by Montreal academics: Robert M. Philmus, *Into the unknown: the evolution of science fiction from Francis Godwin to H.G. Wells* (1970); David Ketterer, *New worlds for old: the apocalyptic imagination, science fiction, and American literature* (1974); and Darko Suvin, *Metamorphoses of science fiction: on the poetics and history of a literary genre* (1979).

DAVID KETTERER

Scobie, Stephen (b. 1943). Born in Carnoustine, Scot., he took an M.A. at St Andrews before immigrating to Canada in 1965. After completing a doctorate in English at the University of British Columbia in 1969, he taught for ten years at the University of Alberta, then returned to the west coast to teach at the University of Victoria.

Scobie wears many literary hats. He has written *Leonard Cohen* (1978), an insightful full-length critical study; is an editor of *Books in Canada* and The MALAHAT REVIEW; co-founder of Longspoon Press; and the author of a dozen stories, numerous articles and reviews, and ten books of poetry, the most important of which are *The birken tree* (1973), *McAlmon's Chinese Opera* (1980), which won a Governor General's Award, and *A grand memory for forgetting* (1981).

The range of Scobie's poetic gifts is most apparent in *A grand memory*, which includes catchy verses that recall the songs of Cohen, some resonant and carefully modulated lyrics, such as 'The seventh wave' and 'I like to think of you asleep', and a number of finely tuned and intricate historical meditations, such as 'Darien' and the extended sequence 'Elegy'. Such poems indicate clearly that Scobie is less of a formalist than his sound poetry and his art-for-art's-sake pronouncements might suggest. Although he rationalizes his own lack of political engagement with the question, 'Who has the right / to tell us torture?', he nevertheless feels compelled constantly to dredge the past, lament the *temps perdus*, and 'pay / the duty of attention to the dead.'

Paying attention to the dead is what Scobie does best, in his lyrics and in his long narrative poem *McAlmon's Chinese opera*, which is a subtle and moving tribute to an era and to Robert McAlmon (also portrayed in John GLASSCO's *Memoirs of Montparnasse*), the American writer who didn't make it in the Paris of the twenties and ended up selling trusses in Arizona. This poem—which owes a debt to the tradition of first-person poetic narrative that moves through Berryman's *Dream songs*, ATWOOD's *The* JOURNALS OF SUSANNA MOODIE, ONDAATJE's *The collected works of Billy the Kid,* and GEDDES's *War & other measures*—has a certainty of voice and a dramatic force that derive from the blending of narrative fragment and imagistic detail. If, as he says in 'Paris', 'those of us / who come later must learn / to love / what is left', Scobie's *McAlmon's Chinese opera* is ample evidence of a lesson well learned. GARY GEDDES

Scott, Chris, (b. 1945). Born in Yorkshire, Eng., he studied and taught in England and the U.S. before settling in Canada. After a period of teaching in Toronto, he moved to a small town north of Kingston. Scott has been a regular book reviewer for *Books in Canada* and is the author of three novels.

Scott unleashed his formidable literary learning in *Bartleby* (1971), an anti-novel, in which the reader is guided by a Shandean narrator through a series of intricate, clever literary parodies. Much of the novel turns on literary puns and references. *To catch a spy* (1978) takes the delicate convolutions of the Le Carré thriller a step further—towards a world in which the doubleness of agents is both assumed and unprovable. The plot is a fictional response to the Burgess-MacLean-Philby spy scandals of the Cold War years that moves towards a meditation on the necessity of living with borrowed faiths and contingent truths in the face of an inscrutable divinity. *Antichthon* (1982), a historical novel, continues where the spy novel left off, exploring the universal suspicion in the Renaissance world of casuistry and Inquisition in which Giordano Bruno is burnt as a heretic. Like the previous novel, it centres on a 'fictional' death, whose reality is called into question, making truth itself the subtlest corrosive in a corrupt world. Scott's novels reveal a progressive mastery of voice, as his two later novels move from one consciousness to another, looking at one central event, or non-event, from many points of view. His concept of the suppleness of truth underlies the serious vitality he has brought to two otherwise hackneyed genres—the espionage novel and the historical novel.

See also NOVELS IN ENGLISH 1960 TO 1982: OTHER TALENTS, OTHER WORKS: I.
MICHELLE GADPAILLE

Scott, Duncan Campbell (1862-1947). The son of a Methodist minister, he was born in Ottawa. His family encouraged the appreciation of music and Scott eventually became an accomplished pianist. He attended school in Smith's Falls, Ont., and college in Stanstead, Qué. In 1879 his father asked Prime Minister Sir John A. Macdonald to assist him in getting his son a position in the civil service. Shortly thereafter Scott became a clerk, at a dollar and a half a day, in the Indian Branch (later the Department of Indian Affairs). Scott's career brought him into contact with Canada's native peoples, particularly during an extensive 1905 trip to the James Bay area as one of the commissioners to the Indian tribes in that region. The Indians called Scott 'Da-ha-wen-non-tye', meaning 'flying or floating voice, us-ward', a reference to the poetry he wrote that sympathized with their plight. He was appointed deputy superintendent of Indian Affairs in 1923 and retired from the civil service in 1932. Elected a Fellow of the Royal Society of Canada in 1899, he became president in 1921. He was awarded an honorary doctorate by the University of Toronto in 1922; received the CMG in 1934; and an LL.D. from Queen's University in 1939.

Scott confronted an issue that, to a greater or lesser extent, troubled all the CONFEDERATION POETS: how does a writer reconcile the literary and philosophical traditions of Western civilization with the Canadian landscape and its inhabitants? Scott's earliest poems, heavily influenced by the Romantics and Victorians, demonstrate a growing facility with language and verse forms but in content reflect nothing Canadian. *The magic house and other poems* (Ottawa, 1893) contains the meditative 'In the country churchyard', a poem honouring the poet's late father and all those who struggle and toil. The belief in the dignity of labour, a crucial element of high Victorianism, is also evident in the title poem of Scott's second book, *Labor and the angel* (Boston, 1898). Both poems, though, could as easily have been written in London as in Ottawa. *Labor and the angel*, however, reveals Scott's first attempts to deal with subject matter that is indigenous to the land of his birth. 'The Onondaga madonna' offers a portrait of a young Indian mother whose race is dying and whose child will never know the thrill of battle. While the subject of the poem is drawn from Scott's first-hand knowledge of the Indians, the poet is unable to divest himself of the weight of European sensibilities to which he is heir. The language is Romantic ('careless pose', 'forays', 'dabbled'), and the poem's central metaphor, the madonna, is imposed upon the protagonist. Scott's decision to write the poem in the form of a Petrarchan sonnet further distances form from content.

New world lyrics and ballads (1905), in which Scott struggles to bring form and content together, contains his best-known and most frequently anthologized poem, 'The forsaken', chronicling the sacrifices made by a Chippewa woman as she struggles to save her young son from starvation; when she becomes old, she is left by her son to die in the wilderness. As Lee B. Meckler has pointed out in an excellent study of this poem ('Rabbit-skin robes and mink-traps: Indian and European in "The forsaken" ', *Canadian Poetry* 1, Fall/Winter 1977), the short lines and vital rhythm of Part I may be said to mime the steady enduring pulse of the woman's heart as she struggles to survive the 'great storm'. The longer lines in Part II imitate the rhythm of the older woman's ever-slowing heart. The poem's language is similarly drawn from, rather than imposed upon, its subject. The Chippewa woman's baby is wrapped in the lacings of the 'tikanagan', an Indian word, whereas the child in 'The Onondaga madonna' had slept in his mother's 'shawl', a European term. Scott is attempting to find a language, as well as a rhythm, that is appropriate to the life he is documenting—though he is unwilling to relinquish his Christian perspective of the world for the Indians' radically different view of experience. The abandonment of the old woman is consistent with her tribe's custom (its purpose being to free the tribe of the burden of caring for the elderly), but Scott interprets the custom in the light of Christian values: the woman is forsaken. The poem contains a number of communion and resurrection metaphors and ends with the pantheistic image of the woman being shrouded with snow before being drawn up to God's breast: the Christian imagery appears to be drawn from Scott's, and not his heroine's, culture. In 'On the way to the mission' (also in *New world lyrics*) the Christian perspective is less forced. An Indian is ambushed and killed by three white men who plan to steal what they believe to be a pile of furs on his toboggan. In fact the Indian is not transporting furs but is taking his wife's corpse to the mission for burial. The white men discover her body, with a crucifix 'under her waxen fingers', when they attempt to gather their spoils. As the Indians here are Christian, the pantheistic conclusion of the poem is appropriate: the Indian and his wife are the recipients of God's beneficence as the moon goes 'on to her setting' and covers 'them with shade'.

The encroachment of European civilization on the Indian way of life is Scott's most frequent theme. In 'The half-breed girl', in *Via Borealis* (1906), the agony of being caught between the world of 'the trap and the paddle' and the world of 'loch and shieling' leads the young heroine to desperation. The elegiac 'Lines in memory of Edmund Morris', in *Lundy's Lane and other poems* (1916), is a tribute to the Canadian artist who accompanied Scott on part of a 1905 expedition to James Bay. Ever present, however, is the mingling of cultures to which the painter and poet were witnesses: both the 'wigwam' and the 'herdsmen's chalet' can be seen on the landscape.

Although his reputation rests largely on his Indian poems, Scott wrote poetry on other subjects. 'The piper of Arll' (*Labor and the angel*), as well as 'The sea by the wood', and its companion piece 'The wood by the sea' (*New world lyrics and ballads*), are among the most-often-anthologized of his non-Indian poems. Keats's work is lauded in 'Ode for the Keats centenary' in *Beauty and life* (1921); a balance of Indian and non-Indian poems may be found in *The poems of Duncan Campbell Scott* (1926); and *The green cloister: later poems* (1935) and *The circle of affection and other pieces in prose and verse* (1947) contain poems written during Scott's extensive travels in Europe. Yet even in his later years Scott published Indian poems. The history and suffering of the Indians are documented in 'Powassan's drum', one of the new poems included in *The poems of Duncan Campbell Scott*; and 'At Gull Lake, 1810' in *The green cloister* argues that human dignity can survive the oppression and savagery by which it is so often threatened. Two selections of Scott's poetry have been published since his death: *Selected poems of Duncan Campbell Scott* (1951), with a memoir by E.K. BROWN, and *Duncan Campbell Scott: selected poetry* (1974), edited by Glenn Clever.

Scott was the author of two collections of short stories: *In the village of Viger* (Boston, 1896; rpr. 1973) and *The witching of Elspie; a book of stories* (1923). (*The circle of affection* also contains stories.) *In the village of Viger*, set in nineteenth-century Québec, details the lives of both the villagers and those whose lives are intertwined with them. Although the characters are more appropriate to romance than to realism (a shoemaker, a pedlar, an aristocrat fallen on hard times), there is a degree of realism in these stories that is uncommon in the short fiction of the 1890s: encroaching upon the idyllic village are the forces of industrialization and urbanization. As Stan Dragland has pointed out in his introduction to the 1973 reprint of *In the village of Viger*, the village is in danger of being swallowed by the metropolis of which it is one of the 'outlying wards'. In examining a closed society being penetrated by forces that threaten to disrupt its unity, Scott is being consistent with the themes he explores in his Indian poetry. Glenn Clever has gathered a representative number of Scott's short stories in *Selected stories of Duncan Campbell Scott* (1972; rpr. 1975). It contains 'Charcoal', written some time between 1898 and 1904, a story based on the case of an Alberta Indian who murdered both his wife's lover and a Mounted Policeman, and wounded a farm instructor. (The Indian was tried and executed.) Although in a letter to John Masefield, Scott said that the story was 'almost a transcript of the evidence at [Charcoal's] trial, plus facts the Indian agent gave me', it is a blend of fact and romance, as Leon Slonim has pointed out in 'The source of Duncan Campbell Scott's "Charcoal" ', *Studies in Canadian Literature*, vol. 4, no. 1 (Winter 1979).

Scott wrote two biographies, *John Graves Simcoe* (1905) and *Walter J. Phillips, R.C.A.* (1947), and one play: *Pierre: a play in one act*, first performed in 1923 and published in the first volume of *Canadian plays from Hart House Theatre* (1926) edited by Vincent Massey. *The circle of affection* contains the essay 'Poetry and progress', an important document giving Scott's views on writing and music, which influenced his literary endeavours. *Untitled novel, ca. 1905* was published in 1979. Scott edited and introduced Amelia Anne Paget's *The people of the plains* (1909) and, in connection with his civil-service work, wrote *The administration of Indian affairs in Canada* (1931). Arthur S. BOURINOT has edited two selections of Scott's letters: *Some letters of Duncan Campbell Scott, Archibald Lampman, and others* (1959) and *More letters of Duncan Campbell Scott* (1960).

An important dimension of Duncan Campbell Scott's literary career concerns his relationship with his friend and fellow poet Archibald LAMPMAN. Lampman, Scott, and Wilfred CAMPBELL collaborated on 'AT THE MERMAID INN', a column that ran in the Toronto *Globe* in 1892 and 1893. Scott sought patronage for Lampman and, after Lampman's premature death, became his literary executor. He edited *The poems of Archibald Lampman* (1900; rpr. 1974), the immediate purpose of which was to raise money for Lampman's impoverished widow and children. (Scott even shared the funeral expenses when Mrs Lampman died in 1910.) He subsequently edited Lampman's *Lyrics of earth: sonnets and ballads* (1925); joined E.K. BROWN in editing *At the Long Sault and other new poems* (1943; rpr. 1974); and edited *Selected poems of Archibald Lampman* (1947). Although Scott took editorial liberties with the manuscripts, he was almost single-handedly responsible for bringing Lampman's work to the attention of twentieth-century readers.

Two journals, *Canadian Poetry: Studies, Documents, Reviews* and *Studies in Canadian Literature*, frequently publish articles on Scott's work, and two collections of critical essays have been published: *Duncan Campbell Scott: a book of criticism* (1974), edited by Stan Dragland, and *The Duncan Campbell Scott symposium* (1980), edited by K.P. Stich.

See the essay on Scott by Gordon Johnston in *Canadian writers and their works: poetry series: volume two* (1983) edited by Robert Lecker, Jack David, and Ellen Quigley.

GEORGE WICKEN

Scott, F.R. (b. 1899). The son of Frederick George SCOTT, Francis (Frank) Reginald Scott was born in the Rectory of St Matthew's Church, Quebec City. He was educated at Bishop's College, Lennoxville, Qué., and at Oxford University, where he held a Rhodes scholarship, receiving a B.A. in 1922 and a B.Litt. in 1923 for a thesis on 'The annexation of Savoy and Nice by Napoleon III, 1860'. On his return to Canada he taught briefly at Lower Canada College and in 1924 entered the law faculty at McGill University, graduating with a BCL in 1926. In 1927 he was called to the bar and in 1928 returned to McGill to teach; he was dean of law from 1961 to 1964 and retired from McGill in 1968. In 1952 he was technical-aid representative for the United Nations in Burma and from 1963 to 1971 a member of the Royal Commission on Bilingualism and Biculturalism. Scott—who has contributed equally to Canadian law, literature, and politics in both official languages—was elected to the Royal Society of Canada in 1947, awarded the Lorne PIERCE Medal for distinguished service to Canadian literature in 1962, and received a Molson Prize for outstanding achievements in the arts, the humanities, and the social sciences in 1967. His career as an interpreter of Québec poetry culminated with a Canada Council Translation Prize for *Poems of French Canada* (1977), his work as a social philosopher with a Governor General's Award for *Essays on the constitution: aspects of Canadian law and politics* (1977), and his life as a poet with a Governor General's Award for *The collected poems of F.R. Scott* (1981).

In his career as an inspiring law teacher and social philosopher, Scott was most concerned with the nature of the constitutional and political 'forms' that must be developed to meet the needs of an emerging Canadian society. His interest in social philosophy was sparked by the Depression: he became active in left-wing political movements and with Frank Underhill was an organizer of the League for Social Reconstruction (1932) and a contributor to its publication, *Social planning for Canada* (1935). President of the League in 1935-6 and national chairman of the Co-operative Commonwealth Federation from 1942 to 1950, he was co-author with David Lewis of *Make this your Canada: a review of CCF history and policy* (1943). He edited for the Canadian Institute of International Affairs *Canada today: a study of her national interests and national policy* (1930). His study *Canada and the United States* (1941) was prepared after a year spent at Harvard on a Guggenheim Fellowship. Scott contributed to the important symposium *Evolving Canadian federalism* (1958) and with Michael Oliver co-edited *Quebec states her case* (1964), translations of excerpts from articles and speeches by French Canadians on aspects of the Quiet Revolution in that province. An authority on constitutional law and civil rights—who has been described by Walter Tarnopolsky as an 'architect of modern Canadian thought on human rights and fundamental freedoms'—Scott argued several major civil-rights cases before the Supreme Court, including Switzman v. Elbing (1957) and Roncarelli v. Duplessis (1958).

Scott is one of the most important catalysts of modern Canadian poetry, partly because of the influence of his own poetry and partly through his personality and his association with several literary groups and 'little magazines'. As a satirist in the late twenties and early thirties he helped battle an outworn Canadian Romanticism in order to introduce the 'new poetry'; and in landscape poems like 'Old Song', 'Lakeshore', and 'Laurentian Shield' he established a northern evolutionary view of Canadian nature that later influenced such poets as Al PURDY and Margaret ATWOOD. While achieving distinction not only as a poet but also as a political activist and a leading authority on constitutional law, Scott became a figure of extraordinary importance as a commentator on Canadian society as well as on Canadian literature. None of these activities can be neatly separated, however, for they all find expression in his poetry, and all stem from the nationalist concerns of Canadian intellectuals in the twenties.

Scott began to publish light verse in 1921 when he was a student at Oxford, though his knowledge of recent poetry more or less stopped with the work of the Georgian poets. At McGill he met A.J.M. SMITH, who introduced him to the new poets, mostly English, who were developing a 'modern' poetry. In 1925 he collaborated with Smith and Leon EDEL in founding *The McGill Fortnightly Review*, an iconoclastic journal of modernist literature and opinion. Scott's attacks on the orthodox were to range widely, but his first broadside was launched against the old poetry and its traditional forms. In 1927, in *The McGill Fortnightly Review*, he published a first draft of 'The Canadian authors meet', a jaunty indictment of the Canadian literary establishment, inspired by visiting a meeting of the CANADIAN AUTHORS' ASSOCIATION:

Shall we go round the mulberry bush, or shall
We gather at the river, or shall we
Appoint a poet laureate this Fall,
Or shall we have another cup of tea?

When *The McGill Fortnightly* ceased publication in 1927, Scott became one of the editors of its successor, the *Canadian Mercury* (1928-9). His association with influential literary journals and anthologies continued over succeeding decades. In 1932, in *The* CANADIAN FORUM, he published 'An-up-to-date anthology of Canadian poetry', a collection of short, blunt, sometimes satirical poetry that dealt with the social ills of the Depression (a similar collection appeared in 1935). In 1936, with Smith, he co-edited and wrote a short preface for the first anthology of modern Canadian poetry, NEW PROVINCES: *poems of several authors* (1936), which included his own verse. In 1942 he was a moving spirit in the founding of PREVIEW— edited by a small group that included Patrick ANDERSON, P.K. PAGE, and A.M. KLEIN— which mimeographed its own poetry newsletter. In 1945 Scott played a leading role in its merger with a rival publication, FIRST STATEMENT, which became NORTHERN REVIEW (1945-56). He was also one of the advisory editors of The TAMARACK REVIEW at its founding in 1956.

In May and June 1931 Scott contributed a two-part manifesto for the new poetry to The Canadian Forum: 'The old order of politics needs no consideration; the fact of the war was proof enough of its obsolescence. The old order of Deity was shown by anthropologists to be built not upon rock, but upon the sand of primitive social custom. Socialism and communism cast overwhelming doubt upon the value of the economic order. . . . The universe itself, after Einstein's manipulations . . . became a closed continuum as warped as the mind of man. . . . Amid the crash of systems, was Romantic poetry to survive?' Scott's own career as a poet exemplifies the transition from a Victorian Romanticism to the modern. But, as with most moderns, there was to be a strong infusion of Romanticism in his own poetry: primarily in his use of nature as symbol but also as expressed in his belief that poetry can help change society. Scott's poems show a progressive development: from the Imagism of late-twenties' poems like 'Old song', through the proletarian realism of the thirties, into a new, almost metaphysical richness of thought and form in the mid-forties and fifties. His first collection of poems, delayed by the Depression, was Overture (1945); followed by Events and signals (1954); The eye of the needle (1957), a collection of satires; Signature (1964); and Selected poems (1966). Scott's subject is often man in the generic sense, silhouetted against a natural horizon, and his characteristic metaphors develop from the exploration of man's relationships to nature and society: they involve time and infinity, world and universe, love and spirit—terms that emerge as twentieth-century humanist substitutes for the Christian vocabulary. A typical Scott poem moves from specific image (the great Asian moth of 'A grain of rice', for example) or from the natural landscape ('Hidden in wonder and snow, or sudden with summer, / This land stares at the sun in a huge silence'), to a consideration of the significance of the image in the larger pattern of human life. The human journey, in turn, is seen as a moment in time, a part of the larger cosmic flux in which matter, striving to realize itself, is thrown up briefly in waves. Scott perceives that man as a physical being comes

and goes; yet he maintains that there is continuity in the human spirit and in the shared human experience.

His poetry reflects the wide diversity of such experience, ranging in style from the reportorial and satiric 'Summer camp', to the fine lyric 'Departure': it reflects a strikingly flexible speaking voice that can move from the playful ('Did you ever see such asses / As the educated masses?') to the tenderly reflective, as in 'Windfall'. Scott has remarked that satire is 'inverted positive statement', and certainly the obverse of Scott the lyrical idealist is Scott the satirist. But even from the satirical inversions of poems such as 'W.L.M.K.' and 'The Canadian authors meet', we can infer both the political and poetic ideals for which Scott stands. Underlying both lyric and light verse is a central vision expressed in 'Creed':

> The world is my country
> The human race is my race
> The spirit of man is my God
> The future of man is my heaven

As a social poet, Scott is most concerned with the kind of social order or 'writing' that man chooses to shape his world. His fear, expressed in 'Laurentian shield' (1945), is that the language of a developing Canada—'prewords, / Cabin syllables, / Nouns of settlement'—might be reduced to the syntax of rapacious technology, 'the long sentence of its exploitation'.

Scott's later books of poetry include Trouvailles: poems from prose (1967), The dance is one (1973), and Collected poems (1981). He also collaborated with A.J.M. Smith in editing The blasted pine: an anthology of satire, invective and disrespectful verse: chiefly by Canadian writers (1957; rev. 1967). An early translator of poetry, he published his translations of St.-Denys Garneau and Anne Hébert in 1962. In a Dialogue sur traduction, an exchange of letters between Anne HÉBERT and Scott published eight years later, Northrop FRYE commented in a preface that for the two poets, 'Translation here becomes a creative achievement in communication, not merely a necessary evil or a removal of barriers. One can hardly learn more in less compass about the kind of craftsmanship that goes into the making of poetry than is given in these few pages.' Scott's Poems of French Canada was published in 1977.

Early criticism of Scott's poetry is to be found in W.E. Collin's The WHITE SAVANNAHS (1936). Subsequent articles include Louis DUDEK, 'F.R. Scott and the modern

Scouine

Smith, 'F.R. Scott and some of his poems',
CANADIAN LITERATURE (Winter 1967); Stephen SCOBIE, 'The road back to Eden: the
poetry of F.R. Scott', *Queen's Quarterly*
(Autumn 1972); and Sandra Djwa, 'F.R.
Scott' in a special Scott issue of *Canadian Poetry* (Winter 1967). See also *F.R. Scott: Canadian* (1983), papers presented at the Scott
symposium sponsored by Simon Fraser
University in Feb. 1981, edited by Djwa and
R. St John MacDonald.   SANDRA DJWA

Scott, Frederick George (1861-1944).
Born in Montreal, he received a B.A. from
Bishop's College, Lennoxville, Qué., in
1881 and an M.A. in 1884. After studying
theology at King's College, London, in 1882
and being refused ordination in the Anglican
Church of Canada for his Anglo-Catholic
beliefs, he was ordained at Coggeshell,
Essex, in 1886. He served first at Drum-
mondville, Qué., and then in Quebec City,
where he became rector of St Matthew's
Church (in the rectory of which his son F.R.
SCOTT was born in 1899). In 1906 he was appointed a canon of the cathedral and in 1925
archdeacon. During the First World War he
was chaplain to the Canadian First Division,
where his courage at the front was legendary; his book *The Great War as I saw it*
(1922) is a vivid war memoir. He was
created CMG in 1916 and was awarded the
DSO in 1918. After the war he was chaplain
of the army and navy veterans and was renowned for his radical social views during
the Winnipeg and Besco strikes. He was
elected to the Royal Society of Canada in
1900.

F.G. Scott was popularly known as the
'poet of the Laurentians'—a lesser member
of the group now known as the CONFEDER-
ATION POETS—and was recognized in his
time for his nature lyrics and for his hymns
of Empire, which stressed both the new nationality and Canada's roles in the Boer and
Great Wars. An epigraph from one of his
poems on the North West Rebellion, celebrating Canada's western expansion, prefaced the most influential anthology of the
period, W.D. LIGHTHALL's *Songs of the great
Dominion* (1899). Scott's first book, *Justin
and other poems,* privately printed in 1885,
contains poems on religion, death, and evolution informed by Victorian pessimism;
this collection was included in *The soul's
quest and other poems* (Toronto, 1885; London, 1888). In 'A mood', dated Mar. 1882,
Scott writes of his intense fear of death,

speaking of a demon that had haunted him
since childhood with 'death and dreams of
death.' Several of the early narrative poems,
and his later didactic novel *Elton Hazelwood*
(1891), describe typically Victorian crises of
faith and the recognition of 'life and death as
they are'. Hazelwood links his spiritual crisis
with that described in Mill's *Autobiography*
and Justin is made to ask 'Why men should
be, why pain and sin and death, / And
where were hid the lineaments of God?'
Scott's many religious poems and his novel
offer a more explicit rendering of the Victorian pessimism underlying the poetry of his
more significant contemporaries, Charles
G.D. ROBERTS and Archibald LAMPMAN.

Scott's lyrics were collected in *My lattice
and other poems* (Toronto, 1894), *The unnamed lake and other poems* (Toronto, 1897),
Poems old and new (1900), *Poems* (1910), *A
hymn of empire and other poems* (1906), *In the
battle silences: poems written at the front* (1916),
In sun and shade: a book of verse (1926), *New
poems* (1929), *Selected poems* (1933), *Collected
poems* (1934), *Poems* (1936), and *Lift up your
hearts* (1941). His best-known poem, 'The
unnamed lake', was an important precursor
of 'Old song' by F.R. Scott, and his social
radicalism undoubtedly influenced his son.

Scott's poetry, with its Christian and evolutionary concerns, is nostalgically Victorian, striking an authentic and original note
only in the poems of the Northland. His role
as a poet of his time was discussed by the
journalist Melvin O. Hammond in 'The
poet of the Laurentians', *The Canadian Magazine* (Mar. 1909) and his role as a Christian
radical by E.A. Palker in 'The social concern
of Canon Scott', *Journal of the Canadian
Church Historical Society* (Oct. 1980). His influence on more recent poetry, particularly
that of F.R. Scott, is suggested by Louis
DUDEK in 'F.R. Scott and the modern
poets', NORTHERN REVIEW IV (Dec.-Jan.
1950-1).   SANDRA DJWA

Scouine, La (1918). This is the most important work of Albert LABERGE, both for its
intrinsic merit and as a *cause célèbre* in
French-Canadian literary history. Because
of its attention to detail and its deterministic
view of life, it has been hailed as the first realistic novel in Canada. It is set in the farming region of Beauharnois, where the author
grew up, and appears to cover some fifty
years from 1813. The title is a meaningless
nickname made up by children for the
smelly, mean, disagreeable Paulina Deschamps, the principal character. Her family

745

is presented as typical but not ideal. Closeness to the land has a brutalizing effect, and religion has little recognizable place, apart from the ritual marking of the bread with a cross. Cross-marked loaves recur like a refrain, compressing all Laberge's feelings about traditional rural life into one haunting symbol, clearly suggesting a parody of the Communion. Family relations, while not altogether devoid of sentiment, are generally harsh and lacking in tender expression: a long-lost uncle returns, only to feel so isolated that he hangs himself. Towards the outside world the family is entirely hostile or avaricious; La Scouine even cheats a blind beggar.

The novel is most enjoyed for its short, finely pointed sketches, written in hard, polished prose. Many details are memorable not only for their visual or aural clarity but also for their symbolic overtones: the gelder—a sad, ugly man, the last of a family reduced to landless poverty—earns his living by suppressing reproduction. The land itself is described as leprous and cancerous, and the sound of stone on scythe is like a lament rising from the ground. The author's pity for his hapless characters emerges only from these restrained overtones. There are, however, a few relaxed moments of humour. The ending is bleak, in the manner of French Naturalism.

After an unusually long time in the writing (1899-1917), this short novel appeared in an edition of only sixty copies. Laberge was aware of the misfortunes of his friend Rodolphe GIRARD and avoided wider distribution. Extracts, published as separate stories, had already been condemned as 'pornographic'—an epithet that was likely provoked less by their few brief sexual incidents than by Laberge's profoundly unchristian world view. Even half a century later it could not be published in full; only extracts appeared in Gérard BESSETTE's Anthologie Albert Laberge (1962). Finally, however, the holder of the copyright relented and La Scouine achieved full publication in 1972.

An English translation by Conrad Dion is entitled Bitter bread (1977).   JACK WARWICK

Seers, Eugène (1865-1945), who used the pseudonym 'Louis Dantin', was born at Beauharnois, Canada East (Qué.), and received his early schooling at home, his secondary education at the Collège de Montreal where he stood out, not only as an extremely brilliant student but also for being a morose and solitary youth who was remarkably sensitive and infatuated with both beauty and literature. During a two-month trip to France and Italy he suddenly decided, in 1883, to enter the novitiate of Les Pères du Saint-Sacrament in Brussels. Barely eighteen, his religious vocation was to last for twenty years. After studying philosophy for three years (1884-7) at the Gregorian University in Rome, he received his Ph.D., and the following year, at twenty-three, was ordained a priest in the Church of Saint-Sulpice in Paris. Afterwards, while he was secretary to the Father General of his congregation in Paris, he wrote frequently for the magazine Le très Saint-Sacrament. At twenty-five he became superior and head of novices in Brussels and at twenty-eight was made superior and assistant-general for the congregation in Paris. On returning to Montreal, however, he underwent a profound religious crisis that resulted in his breaking with the Church. At this time he was overseeing publication of the poems of his friend Émile NELLIGAN, Émile Nelligan et son oeuvre (1903), which contains a thirty-four page preface by Dantin. He then moved to Boston, married, and practised the trade of compositor and typographer. He moved to Cambridge, Mass., with his son, to work for the Harvard University Press (1919-38) and died there.

In the literature of French Canada, Seers is known solely by the name of Louis Dantin; from 1900 until his death he always used this pseudonym. He left a considerable oeuvre: some 5,000 poems were collected by his friend Gabriel Nadeau in Poèmes d'outre-tombe (Trois-Rivières, 1962); also worthy of mention are Le coffret de Crusoé (Montréal, 1932) and three long poems published privately in small printings—Chanson javanaise (1930), Chanson citadine (1931), and Chanson intellectuelle (1932)—and the religious poems published anonymously, Franges d'autel (Montréal, 1899). Dantin also wrote short stories: La vie en rêve (Montréal, 1930), Contes de noël (Montréal, 1936), and L'invitée (Montréal, 1936). It is a pity that Dantin did not persevere in this field, for he was a born storyteller. His friend Rosaire Dion-Lévesque thought it worthwhile to publish, after Dantin's death, Les enfances de Fanny (Montréal, 1951; translated by Raymond Y. Chamberlain as Fanny, 1974), which unfortunately added nothing to the author's reputation. This 286-page autobiographical novel, however, reveals some insights into a man who suffered throughout his life on be-

half of the meek, the disinherited, the un-
wanted, and coloured people.

Dantin is most important for his literary
criticism, a field in which, from 1920 to
1940, he was the undisputed master, as the
following works will attest: *Poètes de
l'Amérique française: First series* (Montréal and
New York, 1928), *Second series* (Montréal,
1934); *Le mouvement littéraire dans les Cantons
de l'Est* (Sherbrooke, 1930); and *Gloses critiques: First series* (Montréal, 1931), *Second series* (Montréal, 1935). It would be worthwhile to collect—apart from the seven
important prefaces to poetical works and the
long preface to *Émile Nelligan*—the numerous critical essays that appeared in *La
Revue moderne* in 1920-2 and 1928-33 and,
between 1923 and 1942, in *L'Avenir du nord*
(Saint-Jérôme), *Le Canada*, and Montreal's
Le Jour, for which Dantin wrote 160 articles
on American literature. It would also be useful to collect his voluminous correspondence (about 600 letters) and the stories 'Fro-
ment de Bethléem', 'Pauline', 'Fantôme de
paques', 'L'aventure de Léon Millaud', and
'Le Bonhomme Noël se rachète'.

Two short posthumous works are the 21-
page *Un manuscrit retrouvé à Kor-el-Fantin: la
chanson nature de Saint Limond* (1963) and the
59-page *Les sentiments d'un père affectueux:
lettres de Louis Dantin à son fils* (1963).

Not content merely to maintain contact
with young Québec writers and to take an
active interest in French-Canadian literature,
Dantin also contributed enormously to ac-
quainting French Canada with American literature. A devotee of beauty, the imagination, and perfection, poet, storyteller,
essayist, and literary critic, he was one of the
finest French-Canadian writers of the period
between the two wars.

See *Louis Dantin: sa vie et son oeuvre* (1948)
by Gabriel Nadeau, who quotes extensively
from Dantin's correspondence.

MAURICE LEBEL

Segal, Y.Y. (1896-1954). Yakov Yitzhak
(Jacob Isaac) Segal, a major Yiddish Canadian poet, was born in Koretz, a small village in the Ukraine. He immigrated to Canada in 1911 and settled in Montreal, where
he worked first in a pants factory, later as a
teacher in secular Yiddish schools, and
finally as a journalist and editor for the
Yiddish-language daily *Der Kanader Odler*
(The Canadian eagle). For a time (1923-8) he
lived in New York, where he came under
the influence of a group of modern Yiddish
poets, *Die Junge* (The Young Ones). After

his return to Montreal, where he lived until
his death, he became a close friend of A.M.
KLEIN.

Segal, who found his own poetic voice in
childhood before coming to Canada, had his
first Canadian poem published in *Kanader
Odler* in 1915. His first collection, *Vun Mein
Velt* (Out of my world; Montreal, 1918)
brought him immediate recognition, not
only in Canada but in New York and Poland, the two world centres of Yiddish literature before the Second World War. Although Segal was a secular Jew, he was
learned in the Torah and steeped in Chassi-
dic tradition and folklore. His lyric poetry
combines religious and folk tradition, modernist American literary practice, and Canadian landscape and atmosphere. His warm,
intimate style unites Jewish lament, prayer,
and celebration with a modern consciousness in a highly original way.

Segal married Elke Shtaiman in 1916 and
they had two daughters. One of them, Annette Segal-Zakuta, illustrated *Lieder far Yiddishe Kinder* (Poems for Jewish children;
New York, 1964). His other books are *Ba-
zunder* (Apart; Montreal, 1921), *Mein Shtub
un mein Welt* (My home and my world; Vilnius, New York, Vienna, 1923), *Lieder*
(Poems; New York, 1926), *Lyric* (Lyric;
Montreal, 1930), *Mein Nigun* (My melody;
Montreal, 1934), *Die Dritte Sudeh* (The third
supper; Montreal, 1937), *Dos Hois fun die Po-
shete* (The house of the simple people; Montreal, 1940), *Lieder un Loiben* (Songs and
praise; Montreal, 1944), *Sefer Yiddish* (The
book of Yiddish; Montreal, 1950), and
Letzte Lieder (Last poems; Montreal, 1955).

Segal was also the author of about a
hundred uncollected critical essays on Yiddish writers and writing; his manuscripts are
preserved in the Jewish Public Library in
Montreal. A memorial prize, the J.I. Segal
award, is given annually for the best book
with Jewish content in fiction or poetry.
Some of his poems have been translated into
English in *A treasury of Yiddish poetry* (1969),
edited by Irving Howe and E. Greenberg,
and *The first five years: a selection from the
Tamarack Review* (1962) edited by Robert
WEAVER.   MIRIAM WADDINGTON

Sellar, Robert (1841-1919). Born in Glasgow, Scot., the son of an estate factor, he
was brought to Upper Canada as a boy. In
1863 he moved from a job on the Toronto
Globe to become first editor of *The Gleaner*,
a Reform paper in Huntingdon, Qué.—in
that 'eastern wedge of the province between

Ontario and Yankeedom'. Sellar's early editorials rejected Annexationism, deplored lavish government spending, and urged Temperance; his 'In defence of the Quebec minority', reprinted in 1894, attacked Roman Catholic encroachment into school and political systems. His editorial wrath at the 'clerical conspiracy' culminated in *The tragedy of Quebec: the expulsion of the Protestant farmers* (1907; republished, with an introduction by Robert Hill, in 1974). Independent, self-published, never part of any literary establishment, Sellar nevertheless became widely known, not only for his partisan regional journalism but also for his complex use of local materials in both historical fiction and essays.

Gleaner tales (Huntingdon, 1885) draws on interviews with Scots and Loyalist families to create vivid anecdotes of feuds, fires, and harvests; the same material is given nonfictional treatment in *History of the County of Huntingdon and of the seigniories of Beauharnois and Chateauguay* (Huntingdon, 1888), comparable as regional history to the work of James MacPherson Le Moine. *Gleaner tales: second series* (Huntingdon, 1895) adds 'Archange and Marie', a pathetic tale of Acadian exiles in Chateauguay, and 'The summer of sorrow, 1847', about Irish survivors of the cholera epidemic. Like Duncan Campbell SCOTT in *In the village of Viger* and W.E. THOMSON in *Old man Savarin and other stories* (both also 1895), Sellar suggests vanishing regional dialects and customs.

Sellar's novels illustrate three types of historical fiction: the heroic romance (*Hemlock*), the group-focused survival story (*Morven*), and the anti-romance of laborious achievement (*Gordon Sellar*). In *Hemlock: a tale of the War of 1812* (Montreal, 1890), a young British officer is captured by invading Americans, and a Scots settler's daughter bravely travels to the isolated mission at Oka, Qué., to call the Indian warrior Hemlock into action. Hemlock frees the captive, who then leads a force through the Chateauguay Valley and up the St Lawrence to successful battle at Crysler's Farm. *Morven: a legend of Glengarry* (1910), written in an archaic rhythm suggesting Gaelic, follows a group of Highlanders, cleared from their shielings in the 1770s, who are transported to virtual slavery in Virginia, rescued by the folk-hero Morven, and led with the help of friendly Indians through the wild Adirondacks towards the bush country north of Cornwall. *True makers of Canada: Gordon Sellar—a Scotsman of Upper Canada* (1915),

covering the period 1825 to 1838, catches the naïve vigour of genuine immigrant journals and is written from the perspective of a Scottish lad, Gordon Sellar. Hard times in Scotland lead to Gordon's arduous voyage to York County, after which the narrative divides to include the story of another settler, who is a manly axeman with ideals like those of the hero of Isabella Valancy CRAWFORD's 'Malcolm's Katie'.

Sellar's early political interests are recaptured in *George Brown, the Globe, and Confederation* (Huntingdon, 1895). Careful research undertaken for *Hemlock* was reused in *The U.S. campaign to capture Montreal: Crysler the decisive battle of the War of 1812* (1913). Sellar's last published work was *The tragedy of Wallace* (1919), a drama of early Scotland.

There is no extended study of Sellar's work, in spite of the vigour of his narratives, the richness of his regional detail, and his unusual treatment of relations between Indians and Scots in early Québec. Family papers, presented to the Public Archives by Sellar's son Watson (long comptroller-general for Canada), illuminate the early history of journalism in Canada.

ELIZABETH WATERSTON

Service, Robert W. (1874-1958). Robert William Service was born in Preston, Eng., and grew up in Scotland, first in Ayrshire with his grandfather and aunts and later in Glasgow with his parents. After leaving school in 1888 he worked for the Commercial Bank of Scotland between 1889 and 1896 when, having cultivated a keen taste for a life (and literature) of adventurous, romantic experience, he left Scotland for Canada. He worked on a farm and, later, on a ranch near Duncan, Vancouver Island. In 1897-8 he wandered through the southwestern U.S. and Mexico, but by 1899 was again working on the Vancouver Island ranch, where he stayed until 1903, when he resumed his banking career with the Bank of Commerce in Victoria. In the summer of 1904 the bank transferred him to Kamloops; in the autumn of 1904 to Whitehorse; and in 1908 to Dawson, Yukon Territory, the setting for his best-known verse. By 1909 Service had published *Songs of a sourdough* (1907), *The spell of the Yukon* (1907), and *Ballads of a cheechako* (1909), which established his reputation as a writer of humorous, melodramatic ballads and brought him enough money to give up banking in order to write his first novel. In 1910 he visited publishers in the U.S., returning overland to the Yukon in 1911, an expedition that introduced him to the land of the Mackenzie River, tales of which entered his writing. In 1912 Service left Canada, visiting the Balkans as correspondent and eventually settling in Paris; he married in 1913. He spent 1914-16 as a war correspondent and stretcher-bearer, and was later a reporter for the Canadian government. He settled finally in Monte Carlo, where he died, although he spent the Second World War in Los Angeles.

Service's additional verse collections include *Rhymes of a rolling stone* (1912), *Rhymes of a Red Cross man* (1916), *Ballads of a bohemian* (1921); *Collected verse* (1930); *Complete poems* (1933); *Twenty bath-tub ballads* (1939); *Bar-room ballads* (1940); *Songs of a sun-lover* (1949); *Rhymes of a roughneck* (1950); *Lyrics of a lowbrow* (1951); *Rhymes of a rebel* (1952); *Songs for my supper* (1953); *Carols of an old codger* (1954); *Rhymes for my rags* (1956); and *Cosmic carols* (ca. 1957). *Collected poems* (1940) contains most of the early verse and *More collected verse* (1955) contains poems published between 1949 and 1953. *Later collected verse* (1960) appeared posthumously. The best of his verse offers vivid, colourful, and often lurid tales of the Canadian North, told by either the observing or participating 'I'. The heroes of the early work are frequently wanderers, vagabonds, or outsiders, caught between regret for what they have left behind and desire to find a new home in the cold and heartless North. In the verse of his middle period, Service seeks to wring meaning out of the carnage of the First World War, and also balances his experience with death with a close attention to details of life in post-war Europe. In his later verse he repeats frequently and rather tediously his literary commitment to the tales and the idioms of ordinary people.

Service also wrote popular fiction: *The trail of Ninety-Eight: a northland romance* (1910), *The pretender: a story of the Latin Quarter* (1914), *The poisoned paradise: a romance of Monte Carlo* (1922), *The roughneck: a tale of Tahiti* (1923), *The master of the microbe: a fantastic romance* (1926), and *The house of fear* (1927). Other books are *Why not grow young?* (1928); *Ploughman of the moon: an adventure into memory* (1945), an autobiographical account to 1912; and *Harper of heaven: a record of radiant living* (1948), about his later years.

See *Robert Service: a biography* (1976) by Carl F. KLINCK.   KEITH RICHARDSON

Seton, Ernest Thompson (1860-1946). Born Ernest Thompson in South Shields, Eng., he later adopted the name Seton, which he claimed reflected his descent from the Scottish Lord Seton, Earl of Winton. In 1866 the Thompson family immigrated to Canada, settling near Lindsay, Ont.; after 1870 they moved to Toronto, where Seton received his early education. His boyhood experiences near Lindsay and in Toronto's Don Valley, then a wilderness area, formed the basis for many of his writings. Although his talents were diverse, all his work was rooted in the single commitment, formed when he was a boy, to be a naturalist—a term that for him had a visionary as well as scientific meaning.

After graduating from the Toronto Grammar School (now Jarvis Collegiate), Seton enrolled at the Ontario College of Art. He graduated in 1879, having earned a Gold Medal and a scholarship to study at the Royal Academy in England. In 1881 he returned to Ontario and in the following year joined his brother on a homestead near Carberry, Man. His program of self-education as a naturalist then became increasingly rigorous as he made meticulous records of the behaviour of animals and birds and published *The birds of Manitoba* (Smithsonian Institution, 1891). In the meantime he travelled frequently to New York, where he was in demand as an illustrator, having been commissioned to do 1,000 illustrations of birds and animals for the twelve-volume *Century Dictionary*. Encouraged by his success as an artist, he studied in Paris for several years after 1890. In 1891 his painting 'The Sleeping Wolf' won first prize at the annual competition held at the Paris Salon. His later submissions were more controversial. The painting 'Triumph of the Wolves' (1892), depicting wolves devouring the body of a man, caused an uproar that contributed to his decision to return to Canada.

In 1892 Seton was appointed official naturalist for the Government of Manitoba, a position that was largely honorary. During the same year he had made a brief visit to New Mexico and his experiences there became the basis for his most famous animal story, 'Lobo, the king of Currumpaw'. He then returned to Paris for another year, submitting another painting to the Salon competition and publishing *Studies in the art anatomy of animals* (New York, 1896). But the cool reception given in Paris to his pro-wilderness paintings led him to return in 1896 to the United States where, with the exception of various expeditions to Canada, he spent the rest of his life. In June of that year he married Grace Gallatin, who subsequently assisted him in the design of many of his books.

Seton's work as a scientist never abated. In 1908 he published the two-volume *The life histories of northern animals: an account of the mammals of Manitoba*, and, after he made a journey into the Far North, *The arctic prairies: a canoe journey of 2,000 miles in search of the caribou* (1911). He continued to work as an illustrator, publishing *Pictures of wild animals* (1901) and *Bird portraits* (1901). But it was his animal stories that ensured his latest fame. His first collection, containing the story of Lobo, was WILD ANIMALS I HAVE KNOWN (New York, 1898); it was an immediate success and was followed by numerous similar collections, often incorporating previously published stories with new ones: *Lobo, Rag, and Vixen* (1899), *The biography of a grizzly* (1900), *Lives of the hunted; containing a true account of the doings of five quadrupeds and three birds, and, in elucidation of the same, over 200 drawings* (1901), *Monarch, the big bear of Tallac* (1904), *Animal heroes* (1905), *The biography of a silver-fox* (1909), *Wild animals at home* (1913), *The slum cat* (1915), *Legend of the white reindeer* (1915), *Wild animal ways* (1916), *Woodland tales* (1921), *Old silver grizzly* (1927), *Katus, the snow child* (1927), *Chink and other stories* (1927), *Foam, the razorback* (1927), *Johnny Bear and other stories* (1927), *Krag, the Kootenay ram and other stories* (1929), *Billy, the dog that made good* (1930), *Cute coyote and other stories* (1930), and *Lobo, Bingo and the racing mustang* (1930). Although Seton tried his hand at a novel (*The preacher of Cedar Mountain*, 1917) and also wrote a drama 'The wild animal play for children' (1900), he is best known for his contribution, along with that of Sir Charles G.D. ROBERTS, towards the creation of a distinctive literary genre: the realistic animal story.

The worst of Seton's stories are maudlin. The best derive their power from his ability to synthesize his knowledge of animal behaviour and his prophetic vision. Romantic primitivism, with its glorification of a sublime wilderness, forms a necessary context for an understanding of that vision. At the same time, recent Canadian writing has pointed to the fact that the wilderness in his tales is also Darwinian. In Margaret ATWOOD's SURVIVAL, Seton's stories appear as a central example of a tendency to identify with the hunted victim, which Atwood

views as peculiarly Canadian. Seton's strange blend of Romantic and Victorian attitudes to nature resulted from his synthesis of British, American, and Canadian influences.

In the midst of his busy writing career Seton found time to become deeply involved in the development of a youth organization called the 'Woodcraft Indians'. His childhood interest in 'playing Indian' formed the basis for his children's story TWO LITTLE SAVAGES; *being the adventures of two boys who lived as Indians and what they learned* (1906), now considered a classic in the genre. He also wrote numerous additional books about woodcraft, including *Woodmyth and fable* (1905), *American woodcraft for boys* (1902), *The birchbark roll* (1906), *The book of woodcraft* (1911), *Rolf in the woods* (1911), *Forester's manual* (1911), and *The book of woodcraft and Indian lore* (1912).

In 1910 Seton joined Lord Baden-Powell and Daniel Beard in establishing the Boy Scouts of America. His writings formed the basis for the *Boy Scouts of America official manual* (1910). For many years he held the post of Chief Scout and enjoyed immense popularity; at the same time he began a prolonged disagreement with the administration of the association. Seton levelled charges of militarism and they, in turn, accused him of pacifism. Finally, in 1915, the association expelled him on the pretext that he was not an American citizen. Until the end of his life Seton remained so bitter about this episode that he was urged by his publisher to leave all mention of it out of his autobiography. The incident, however, did nothing to stop the flow of books about woodcraft. He published *Manual of Woodcraft Indians* (1915), *The woodcraft manual for boys* (1916), and *The woodcraft manual for girls* (1916), and *Sign talk* (1918), followed by a six-volume summary of his work entitled *Library of pioneering and woodcraft* (1925).

In the meantime there had been constant criticism of Seton's animal stories from scientists who charged him with anthropomorphism. Books like *The natural history of the Ten Commandments* (1907), in which he attempted to demonstrate the biological source of biblical morality, added fuel to these charges. The so-called 'nature-fakir' controversy, however, merely acted as a catalyst, leading Seton to redouble his scientific activity. Between 1925 and 1927 he published four volumes in a series entitled *Lives of game animals* that won him the John Burroughs and the Elliott Gold Medals, then the highest awards given for naturalist work.

The last sixteen years of Seton's life were spent near Sante Fe, New Mexico, where he settled in 1930. In 1931 he took out American citizenship. Divorced from his first wife, he married Julia Buttree, who had been his assistant, and together they set up Seton Village, a study centre for naturalists. His wife, who was many years his junior, wrote *The rhythm of the Redman in song, dance, and decoration* (1930), to which Seton provided an introduction and illustrations. His continuing admiration for Indian ways was reflected in *Gospel of the Redman* (1936). Over the years he enjoyed immense popularity as an oral storyteller and a public lecturer on conservation; but he also continued to write, publishing *Great historic animals, mainly about wolves* (1937), *The biography of an arctic fox* (1937), *Santana, the hero dog of France* (1945), and his autobiography, *Trail of an artist-naturalist* (1940).

Recent investigations of Seton's life and work have focused on his place in the Canadian tradition. Atwood's *Survival* has already been mentioned. More recently John Henry Wadland—in *Ernest Thompson Seton; man in nature and the progressive era, 1880-1915* (1978)—has broken new ground in defining those aspects of Seton's thought that are distinctively Canadian. The conflict with the Boy Scouts Association—omitted from the autobiography but documented in Seton's letters and journals—promises to be an interesting case-study for future scholars.　MAGDALENE REDEKOP

Sharp, Edith Lambert. See CHILDREN'S LITERATURE IN ENGLISH: 6.

Sherman, Francis Joseph (1871-1926). Born in Fredericton, N.B., he attended the Collegiate School, where his teachers included George Parkin and Bliss CARMAN. He entered the University of New Brunswick at the age of fifteen but was forced to abandon his studies for financial reasons and joined the Merchants' Bank of Halifax. Advancing quickly through the ranks while serving in Woodstock (N.B.), Fredericton, Montreal, and Havana, Sherman had established the bank's influence throughout Cuba and the West Indies by 1901, when the Merchants' Bank changed its name to the Royal Bank of Canada. He returned to the head office in Montreal in 1912 as assistant general manager. In 1919 he retired because of ill health caused by his military service in the First World War. He died in Atlantic City and is buried in Fredericton.

Although encouraged in his writing of poetry by the literary ambience of Fredericton in the post-Confederation period, Sherman was never as public or as prolific a writer as his friends Bliss Carman, Charles G.D. ROBERTS, and Theodore Goodridge ROBERTS. His collections are *Matins* (Boston, 1896), a series of romantic poems praised by both Rudyard Kipling and Carman; *In memorabilia mortis* (Cambridge, Mass., 1896), a tightly crafted sonnet series commemorating William Morris, who was much admired by Sherman and was an influence on his style; *The deserted city* (Boston, 1899), nineteen lyrical and finely disciplined sonnets on faith and love, described by Roberts as the work of a 'master sonnet-teer'; and *A Canadian calendar: XII lyrics* (Havana, 1900), mature and poignant lyrics on love and the seasons. *A prelude* (Boston, 1897) is a nature poem privately printed for Christmas; and the elegiac *Two songs at parting* (Fredericton, 1899) was written with John Bodkin on the occasion of Sherman's leaving the Maritimes. Lorne PIERCE edited *The complete poems of Francis Sherman* (1935), with a foreword by Sir Charles G.D. Roberts. Pierce and Roberts both acknowledge the sure craftsmanship, fastidious attention to language, and control of the sonnet form that continue to earn Sherman a place with a sympathetic circle of poetry readers.
　GWENDOLYN DAVIES

Shields, Carol (b. 1935). Carol Warner was born in Oak Park, Ill. In 1957 she received her B.A. from Hanover College in Hanover, Ind., and in the same year married a Canadian, Donald Hugh Shields, now a professor of civil engineering; they have five children. She became a Canadian citizen in 1971. In 1975 she received an M.A. in English from the University of Ottawa; a revision of her thesis was published as *Susanna Moodie: voice and vision* (1972). She has taught English at the Universities of Ottawa, British Columbia, and Manitoba, where she is currently employed.

Shields has published two volumes of poetry, *Others* (1972) and *Intersect* (1974), but is best known as a novelist. *Small ceremonies* (1976) won the CANADIAN AUTHORS' ASSOCIATION Award for best novel in 1977. Three other novels have since appeared: *The box garden* (1977), *Happenstance* (1980), and *A fairly conventional woman* (1982). The novels are characterized by gentle satire and careful, pleasingly accurate domestic observation. The husband is always professorial and the wife artistic. Very much concerned with the threads that connect domestic and artistic or intellectual life, Shields represents in her fiction both her experience as a wife and mother and her literary ventures: the heroine of *Small ceremonies*, for example, writes fiction and has produced a book about Susanna MOODIE, while the heroine of *The box garden* is a poet. Disillusioned in early middle age, Shields' protagonists are nevertheless survivors and celebrants. They find consolation in the texture of daily life, the rush of love, and the intersection of their ordinary worlds with something really extraordinary—such as the party of deaf-mutes who dine out together so marvellously at the end of *Small ceremonies*. This sudden, lyrical blossoming in Shields' fiction is like a signature attesting to the writer's love for her own gift of observation. That gift works for her characters as a means of self-validation and of connection with others. *Happenstance*, however, suggests that some part of perception (even when it is specifically of love) always remains stillborn: 'He loved her. But feared that something in his greeting might fall short. Some connection between perception and the moment itself would fail, would always fail.' The least successful of the novels are *The box garden*, whose plot relies on far-fetched coincidence, and *A fairly conventional woman*, which is flawed by sentimentality and spates of unconvincing dialogue. *Happenstance*, in which Shields uses a male protagonist for the first time, is an intriguing book; it suffers, however, from the tendency of Shields' characters to meditate upon or debate the nature of biography, fiction, or history in a way that is sometimes obtrusive or stale. *Small ceremonies*, the best and most consistently believable of her novels, illustrates most clearly her special gifts of observation.

Shields' poetry is less impressive than her fiction, although marked by the same appealing sensibility. The poems are simple, domestic, generous in spirit, though often technically undistinguished. Our satisfaction typically comes in the moments of insight, but as if these moments somehow existed apart from the language and final shape of the whole.   CONSTANCE ROOKE

Shiels, Andrew (1793-1879). Born in rural Roxburghshire, Scot., and largely self-educated, he immigrated to Nova Scotia in 1818 and worked as a blacksmith in Halifax. In 1828 he established himself on a farm in Dartmouth and became a leading citizen in the area, serving as a justice of the peace and in 1857 being appointed a magistrate. Perhaps the most prolific poet in nineteenth-century Nova Scotia, he wrote and published verse for over fifty years under the pseudonym 'Albyn'—frequently in local newspapers, but also in eleven books and pamphlets of verse, including *The witch of the Westcot* (Halifax, 1831), *The water lily* (Halifax, 1852), *Letter to Eliza* (Halifax, 1876), *John Walker's courtship* (Halifax, 1877), and *Dupes and demagogues* (Halifax, 1879). Although he tried his hand at a wide variety of verse forms, he was at his best writing songs and light lyrics (in the manner of Burns) and verse tales, in which he often turned to history and legend for his subjects: he was particularly interested in the history and folk stories of Nova Scotia. For Shiels, one of the main functions of verse was to dramatize and amplify human experience so that what appeared commonplace took on special meaning. He strove to express the mysterious, vital, magical spirit that lay at the heart of the world, and was able to make his readers feel the force of his love of life.
                                        TOM VINCENT

Short stories in English. The short story has had a long and substantial tradition in English Canada. The sketches and stories of Thomas McCULLOCH and Thomas Chandler HALIBURTON first appeared in Halifax newspapers in the 1820s and 1830s respectively. From the mid-nineteenth century on, stories by Canadian writers frequently appeared not only in Canadian newspapers but in LITERARY MAGAZINES, such as The LITERARY GARLAND and The WEEK, and in New York or Boston as well. Many writers of short fiction were women: Susanna MOODIE, May Agnes FLEMING, Rosanna LEPROHON, Sara Jeannette DUNCAN, and Susie Frances HARRISON were among the most prolific. It was only in the final two decades of the century, however, that a few significant collections made their appearance. Gilbert PARKER's romantic and melodramatic tales of the North-west were collected in *Pierre and his people* (London, 1882), a book that became very popular. Susie Frances Harrison's *Crowded out and other sketches* (Ottawa, 1886) contains interesting stories set in both English and French Canada. The title story is about the attempts of a Canadian writer in London to achieve publication. Edward William

THOMSON published the first of many stories in the Boston *Youth's Companion* in 1886; his best-known story, 'The privilege of the limits', first appeared in *Harper's Weekly* in 1891, four years before he came out with a collection, *Old man Savarin and other stories* (Toronto, 1895). The beginnings of a Canadian genre—the animal story—can be traced to Charles G.D. ROBERTS' *Earth's enigmas: a book of animal and nature life* (Boston, 1896) and Ernest Thompson SETON's WILD ANIMALS I HAVE KNOWN (New York, 1898). But in this period the most important collection, as a work of literature, was the poet Duncan Campbell SCOTT's *In the village of Viger* (Boston, 1896), a series of stories that in a quiet, superbly controlled manner create the sense of a whole community. A decade and a half later (in 1912) another enduring collection of stories appeared: Stephen LEACOCK's SUNSHINE SKETCHES OF A LITTLE TOWN. Like Scott's book, and like so many other Canadian collections by a single author that would come later, *Sunshine sketches* is a series of connected stories unified above all by setting, in this case the fictional Ontario town of Mariposa (Orillia).

Raymond KNISTER suggests in the introduction to his 1928 anthology *Canadian short stories* that it reflects 'a new era' in Canadian short-story writing; but in fact it can now be seen to signal the end of an era, since more than half the book was devoted to writers from an earlier period: Roberts, Scott, Thomson, Parker, Norman DUNCAN, and Leacock. In addition to their stories are two by Marjorie PICKTHALL and Mazo DE LA ROCHE, neither of whom was prolific or distinguished in the genre. The 'new era' was represented by Knister himself, Thomas Murtha, Morley CALLAGHAN, and several others who did not continue to write short fiction. The stories of Knister, who died tragically at thirty-three, did not appear in book form until the 1970s. Murtha, who vanished into school-teaching and only occasionally published in small American magazines, produced enough stories that they could be collected in *Short stories* (1980), but only after his death. Callaghan was the only 1920s writer in Knister's anthology to make a name for himself in this period: he went on to become the most influential figure in the development of the modern short story in Canada. His first collection, *A native argosy*, was published in 1929, and *Now that April's here and other stories* in 1936.

The Depression and the Second World War were dry periods in the growth of the short story in Canada. Frederick Philip GROVE, who began publishing novels in the 1920s, was also a short-story writer. His well-known 'Snow' first appeared in *Queen's Quarterly* in 1932; but it was not until 1971 that a selected stories, *Tales from the margin* edited by Desmond PACEY, was published. Though *Queen's Quarterly* also published the Manitoba and Saskatchewan stories of another novelist, Sinclair ROSS, they were not collected until 1968 in *The lamp at noon and other stories*, which appeared in the New Canadian Library. Ethel WILSON's 'Hurry, hurry' appeared in *The New Statesman and Nation* in 1937, but her first collection, *Mrs Golightly and other stories*, appeared only in 1961. The late, and sometimes posthumous, publication of short-story collections by writers who began their careers in the twenties and thirties suggests not only minimal enthusiasm for Canadian short stories but a lack of periodicals interested in publishing them. (Callaghan published mainly outside Canada.) While the work of novelists in this period received feeble though steady support through book publication, serious short fiction, on the whole, was apparently thought unworthy. However, this prejudice against story collections by a single writer was characteristic of American and British as well as Canadian publishing.

It was not until after the Second World War that the great leap forward, which Knister had thought he was witnessing, actually took place. In the 1940s Montreal provided the country with two little magazines—PREVIEW and FIRST STATEMENT—with a contemporary commitment; in 1945 they combined to form NORTHERN REVIEW. Poets were at the centre of this literary movement and some—notably Irving LAYTON, P.K. PAGE, and Ralph GUSTAFSON—were also writing short stories. Before her first story appeared in *The New Yorker*, Mavis GALLANT published two stories in *Preview* in 1944—'Three brick walls' and 'Good morning and goodbye'—and, in 1950, 'The flowers of spring' in *Northern Review*. The first influential anthology of the post-war period was Desmond Pacey's *A book of Canadian stories* (1947; rev. 1950, 1962), in which the youngest writers represented in the 1947 edition were P.K. Page (b. 1916) with 'The resignation', and William McConnell (b. 1917) with 'The alien'. The 'modern' stories included works by Ross ('The lamp at noon'), Leo KEN-

Short stories in English

NEDY ('A priest in the family'), Callaghan ('Father and son'), Mary Quayle Innis ('The bells'), and Knister ('The strawstack'). For the 1950 revision, Pacey added Ethel Wilson's 'Hurry, hurry' and W.O. MITCHELL's 'Saint Sammy'.

In the mid-fifties two writers who went on to have productive careers published their first collections: Hugh GARNER with *The yellow sweater and other stories* (1952) and Mavis Gallant with *The other Paris* (1956). At this time public broadcasting was bringing two other sixties' writers, Alice MUNRO and Mordecai RICHLER (both born in 1931), to the fore. In 1954 the CBC, which for some years had been broadcasting poetry and short stories in various radio series, began a regular weekly literary program, 'Anthology', which is still on the air. The growing interest in the short stories that were broadcast justified the publication of four books: *Canadian short stories* (1952), *Ten for Wednesday Night* (1961), *Stories with John Drainie* (1963), and *Small wonders* (1982). Hugh HOOD, whose stories have often been broadcast, once wrote that 'the CBC is far and away the most receptive and the fairest—though not the highest-paying—market for stories that I know of'. But the mid-fifties, which saw the disappearance of *Northern Review* with the death of its editor John SUTHERLAND, also saw the emergence of *The* TAMARACK REVIEW (1956-82) as a medium for short stories, publishing in its early issues work by Munro, Richler, Hood, Jack LUDWIG, and Dave GODFREY. Among older magazines, *Queen's Quarterly, The* CANADIAN FORUM, and *The* FIDDLEHEAD also published short fiction. (Since the 1960s a fair number of other literary magazines have provided outlets for the writer of short fiction, including *The* MALAHAT REVIEW, EXILE, DESCANT, and CANADIAN FICTION MAGAZINE.)

Through the whole of the 1950s only a handful of writers—Hugh Garner, Mavis Gallant, Morley Callaghan, Thomas RADDALL—were able to publish collections of their short stories. In Canada, as in England and the United States, it was still assumed that books of short stories wouldn't sell. This situation began to change dramatically in Canada in the 1960s, and it could be argued that in the next two decades the short story became the most interesting and varied literary genre in this country. Two major commercial publishing houses—McCLELLAND AND STEWART and MACMILLAN OF CANADA—have had numerous distinguished short-story writers on their lists: McClelland and Stewart with Margaret LAURENCE, Margaret ATWOOD, Rudy WIEBE, Alistair MacLEOD, among others; and Macmillan with Alice Munro, Mavis Gallant, Jack HODGINS, Guy VANDERHAEGE, and others. But the real impetus has come from the small literary publishers, and in this respect 1966 has to be seen as a momentous year in the development of the short story in Canada: the year in which OBERON PRESS was founded in Ottawa. Oberon has published Leon ROOKE, John METCALF, Hugh Hood, W.P. KINSELLA, Merna Summers, W.D. VALGARDSON, and a number of still younger writers, as well as its short-story annuals and a variety of anthologies. The House of ANANSI and COACH HOUSE PRESS, both in Toronto, and TALONBOOKS in Vancouver have been Oberon's competitors in short-story publishing. And in the early 1980s a new group of regional publishers became increasingly important. In 1981 and 1982 three well-received collections of stories by new writers were published—not in Toronto or Ottawa but by three small Western publishers: Edna Alford's *A sleep full of dreams* (1981) by Oolichan Books on Vancouver Island, Joan Clark's *From a high thin wire* (1982) by NeWest Press in Edmonton, and Sandra Birdsell's *Night travellers* (1982) by Winnipeg's Turnstone Press. All three books are collections of connected stories: Edna Alford's take place in a nursing home for the aged, Joan Clark writes about a woman growing up in the Maritimes and then living as a wife and mother in Alberta, and Sandra Birdsell's stories are set in a small town in Alberta. Collections of linked stories, which sometimes have a weight and narrative interest lacking in books of unconnected stories, are not a Canadian discovery. Probably the seminal book of this kind is Turgenev's series of lyrical stories about the Russian countryside, *Sketches from a hunter's album* (the title used for the Penguin Classics edition), published in 1852; its North American equivalent may be Sherwood Anderson's *Winesburg, Ohio* (1919). In Canada, Scott's early *In the village of Viger* and Leacock's *Sunshine sketches* have been succeeded by, among other unified collections, Margaret Laurence's *A bird in the house* (1970), stories about growing up in small-town Manitoba; Alice Munro's *Lives of girls and women* (1971), about growing up in small-town Ontario; George Elliott's *The kissing man* (1962), also about small-town Ontario; Jack Hodgins' *The Barclay family theatre*

754

(1981) and earlier books, which bring a mythic significance to life on Vancouver Island; and W.P. KINSELLA's stories about baseball and about life on an Indian reserve in southern Alberta.

Recent years have brought a high degree of sophistication to the work of the best short-story writers in English Canada and increasing international recognition of their fiction. It may seem a paradox that at the same time, regionalism has become a powerful force in the Canadian story. The critic Northrop FRYE does not see this as a paradox, however. In an interview with Robert FULFORD in the short-lived literary annual *Aurora* (1980), he said: 'I think that as a culture matures, it becomes more regional . . .'; and he added later, 'I think the country we know as Canada will, in the foreseeable future, be a federation of regions culturally, rather than a single nation.' The best regional writers today are as sophisticated as any and are read in other countries partly for the insight they provide into the life of a particular locality. Alice Munro's breakthrough volume in the United States and England, *The moons of Jupiter* (1982), is a book of Ontario stories, more than half of which first appeared in *The New Yorker* and the *Atlantic Monthly*. Jack Hodgins, as we have seen, brings myth and 'magic realism' to Vancouver Island, and acknowledges the influence on his work of William Faulkner and the contemporary South American storytellers. W.D. Valgardson, in his collections beginning with *Bloodflowers* in 1973, brings a powerful dramatic sense and a great deal of literary sophistication to stories that are set in the small towns and Icelandic communities of Manitoba and other more remote places. Alistair MacLeod's sombre, reflective stories in *The lost salt gift of blood* (1976) are about Cape Breton and Newfoundland. On the urban scene, the prolific novelist and short-story writer Hugh Hood published a collection of linked stories in *Around the mountain: scenes from Montreal life* (1967). Mordecai Richler's collection, *The street* (1969), deals with Jewish ghetto life in that city. Among many other regional writers whose work is marked by literary sophistication are Howard O'HAGAN, writing chiefly about the mountain country of western Canada in *The woman who got on at Jasper Station* (1963; rpr. 1978); Rudy WIEBE, a writer of powerful, mythic stories in *Where is the voice coming from?* (1974) and *The angel of the tar sands and other stories* (NCL, 1982); and the poet Alden NOWLAN, whose stories

about small-town life in New Brunswick were collected in *Miracle at Indian River* (1968). (He left an unpublished collection at the time of his death.)

Many strands have gone into the pattern of the contemporary short story in Canada. Margaret Laurence's first stories to achieve book publication were set in Ghana and collected in *The tomorrow-tamer and other stories* (1963). Austin CLARKE is from Barbados, and most of the stories in *When he was free and young and he used to wear silks* (1971) are about West Indians living in Toronto. Henry KREISEL, who was born in Vienna and had to flee the Nazi terror against the Jews, in *The almost meeting and other stories* (1981) writes about both Europe and the Canadian West, bringing a cosmopolitan sensibility to his work. His 'The broken globe' is one of the most frequently anthologized of modern Canadian stories. Clarke BLAISE, born in the United States of a French-Canadian father and an English-Canadian mother, brings another kind of dual viewpoint to his stories—American and Canadian—in *A North American education* (1973). Matt COHEN in *Columbus and the fat lady* (1972) and *Night flights* (1978) writes both regional stories set in eastern Ontario and symbolic, experimental fictions with urban backgrounds, sometimes set in Europe. Audrey THOMAS and Leon ROOKE came to Canada from the United States; John METCALF was born and brought up in England. Both Metcalf and Rooke, besides their own fiction, have done much for the short story in Canada as editors and anthologists. Two writers who have something in common—expatriation—are Mavis Gallant and Norman LEVINE. Gallant lives in Paris. Most of her subtle and distinguished stories take place in France and other parts of Europe. But in *Home truths* (1981) a half-dozen stories about a young woman, Linnet Muir, marvellously blend Gallant's international literary existence with a superb sense of place: Montreal during the Second World War. Levine lived for many years in Cornwall. His stories—often autobiographical, sometimes deliberately fragmentary, many of them about family life and what it is like to survive as a writer—have been widely published in England and Europe, particularly in West and East Germany. Since his return to Canada in the late 1970s his reputation as a writer of short stories has blossomed. The title story of his most recent collection, *Thin ice* (1979), is about how precarious the life of a writer

Short stories in English

is: a good sobering note on which to end an optimistic survey.

See also ANTHOLOGIES IN ENGLISH: SHORT STORIES.   ROBERT WEAVER

Short stories in French. Although Québec has an oral tradition rich in legends and *contes parlés*, the short story as a literary form in French-Canadian literature holds a somewhat uncertain place in practice, theory, and prestige. It is not nearly so well defined as other genres; nor is it recognized as a particular forte of modern Québécois writers. The form in the nineteenth century—variously known as *légende*, *conte*, *récit*, or *nouvelle*—was closely allied to the folk-tale or recounted an episode from the remote past. Antedating the French-Canadian novel, such stories contributed to its development and enjoyed considerable popularity in the periodical press. After a transitional stage, in which traditional values were debunked, by the early 1940s a new breed of story began to appear. Rather than transcribing scenes from common life, or playing on superstition and folklore, stories were individualistic and contemporary, having an urban setting and relating more to psychology than to myth. Most major twentieth-century Québécois writers have at least one volume of short stories to their credit: fiction writers Roch Carrier, Jacques Ferron, Gabrielle Roy, Yves Thériault; dramatist Michel Tremblay; poets Alain Grandbois and Anne Hébert; *chansonniers* Félix LeClerc and Gilles Vigneault; anthropologist Marius Barbeau; and even botanist Frère Marie-Victorin.

In *Le conte littéraire québécois au XIXe siècle*, Aurélien Boivin catalogues over 1,100 published stories, of which the most prolific writers are N.H.E. Faucher de Saint-Maurice, *Contes et récits* (1930); L.-H. FRÉCHETTE, *La Noël au Canada* (1900), *Contes* (1974), *Contes de Jos Violon* (1974); Pamphile LEMAY, *Contes vrais* (Québec, 1899); and J.-C. TACHÉ, *Forestiers et voyageurs* (Montréal, 1884). Nineteenth-century novelists who practised the genre, or incorporated stories in their longer fictions, are AUBERT DE GASPÉ, père et fils, and P.-J.O. CHAUVEAU. This period also offered some important folklore collections: James Huston's *Légendes canadiennes* (Paris, 1853); Abbé H.-R. CASGRAIN's popular *Légendes canadiennes* (Québec, 1861); Honoré BEAUGRAND's *La chasse-galerie: légendes canadiennes* (1900); and E.-Z. Massicotte's *Conteurs canadiens-français du XIXe siècle* (1902). Later collections of nineteenth-century ma-

terial include Guy Boulizon's *Contes et récits d'autrefois* (1961) and John Hare's *Contes et nouvelles du Canada français, 1778-1859* (1971).

After the turn of the century the flow of stories continued unabated. Aurélien Boivin has traced some 3,500 published between 1900 and 1940. Many continued the folkloric tradition enriched from new sources—such as Marius BARBEAU in *Le rêve de Kamalmouk* (1948)—but others began to tap a more realist vein. Some recaptured the more recent regional past with humour, as in Édmond Grignon's *En guettant les ours: mémoires d'un médecin des Laurentides* (1930); or with poetry, as in J.-A. LORANGER's *Contes* (collected 1978). Others celebrated the enduring values of the land in the styles of *le roman de la terre*, as in Adjutor Rivard, *Chez nous* (1914); MARIE-VICTORIN, *Récits Laurentiens* (1919); Lionel GROULX, *Les rapaillages* (1922); and C.-H. GRIGNON, *Le déserteur et autres récits de la terre* (1934). Two journalists—Louis Dantin (Eugène SEERS) in *La vie en rêve* (1930), and particularly Albert LABERGE in *Anthologie d'Albert Laberge* (1962)—turned a more jaundiced eye on country mores. In fact the latter's scandalously naturalistic novel *La* SCOUINE (1918) spelt the end of the idyllic treatment of rural Québec.

Styles in French-Canadian short-story writing in the post-war period are very diverse, but they can be divided into three broad groups: basically realistic stories dealing with modern Québec life; a more fanciful treatment of the same material; and more introverted and surrealistic inventions. To the first group belong minor works of short fiction by well-known novelists: Germaine GUÈVREMONT's *En pleine terre* (1944); *L'héritage et autres contes* (1946) by Ringuet (Philippe PANNETON); and Gabrielle ROY's evocations of her Franco-Manitoban childhood in *Rue Deschambault* (1955), *La route d'Altamont* (1966), and *Ces enfants de ma vie* (1977). Yves THÉRIAULT's *Contes pour un homme seul* (1944) give a tragic, primitive twist to the conventional rural story, while the PARTI PRIS generation—with Marcel Godin's *La cruauté des faibles* (1961); Jacques RENAUD's *Le cassé* (1977), a second edition containing four more 'nouvelles'; André MAJOR's *La chair de poule* (1965); and Claude JASMIN's *Les coeurs empaillés* (1967)—put slum life in east-end Montreal on the literary map.

A bridge between the realistic and the fanciful is formed in the short stories of Roch CARRIER, whose fictionalized reminiscences of a village upbringing in *Les enfants du bon-homme dans la lune* (1979) often skirt the undiluted fantasy of his earlier collection, *Jolis deuils* (1965). Michel TREMBLAY writes the same kind of quasi-absurdist epigrammatic fiction in *Contes pour buveurs attardés* (1966); while Gilles VIGNEAULT, in *Contes sur la pointe des pieds* (1961), and Félix LECLERC in *Adagio* (1952), with their poetic parables and beast fables, further extend the limits of the *conte*, as do poets Anne HÉBERT, with her powerfully symbolic *Le torrent* (1950), and Alain GRANDBOIS, whose *Avant le chaos* (1945) includes exotic tales from the far east. But the master of the form in this category is Jacques FERRON, who mixes fantasy and malicious wit with rural realism in *Contes: édition intégrale* (1968), and with history in *Historiettes* (1969).

Humour and fantasy blend in more experimental ways in Réal Benoit's *Nézon* (1945), a precursor of recent exercises in the surreal, like Jacques Brossard's *Métamorfaux* (1974), where the play of language and narrative technique is more important than traditional plot or character. André Charpentier's *Rue Saint Denis/contes fantastiques* (1978) starts with the mundane and slips unexpectedly into the fantastic, while Claudette Charbonneau-Tissot's *Contes pour hydrocéphales adultes* (1974) begins with the grotesque to reach a pitch of acute paranoia. Many women have made striking contributions to the genre, from the sharply perceptive vignettes of Claire MARTIN's *Avec ou sans amour* (1958) and Madeleine Ferron's lyrical *Coeur de sucre* (1966), to Antonine MAILLET's salty Acadian sketches, *Par derrière chez mon père* (1972), and Louise MAHEUX-FORCIER's elegantly experimental *En toutes lettres* (1980).

(English translations are available of above-mentioned works by Roch Carrier, Jacques Ferron, Anne Hébert, Louise Maheux-Forcier, Gabrielle Roy, Michel Tremblay, and Gilles Vigneault.)

Despite considerable activity and variety, however, the short story cannot be said to be a favoured form of literary expression in Québec. The number of contemporary anthologies is small, and critical attention is slight. Gérard BESSETTE's *De Québec à Saint-Boniface: récits et nouvelles du Canada français* (1968) and Adrien Thério's *Conteurs canadiens-français: époque contemporaine* (1970) are the only recent collections, although the review *Écrits du Canada français* should also be consulted and, in translation, Philip Stratford's *Stories from Quebec* (1974) and *The Ox-*ford book of French-Canadian short stories (1983), edited by Richard Teleky, with an introduction by Marie-Claire BLAIS. In developing a theoretical framework for recapturing the dispersed riches of the Québec short story, Jeanne Demers and Lise Gauvin have done pioneer work: see their essays in *Études françaises* (April 1976) and *Stanford French Review* (Spring-Fall 1980).

PHILIP STRATFORD

Simard, André. See DRAMA IN FRENCH 1948 TO 1981:3.

Simard, Jean (b. 1916). Born in Quebec City of a middle-class family, he became an avid reader at an early age. He studied at the Petit Séminaire de Québec and the École des Beaux-Arts in Montreal, where he became a professor in 1940. He won the Prix Duvernay in 1963 and is a member of the Royal Society of Canada.

Simard's first novel, *Félix* (1947; rev. 1966), which won the Prix Kornmain de l'Académie française, was published by Éditions Variétés, for which he worked as an illustrator. It is about the upbringing of a young man of good family living in puritan, middle-class Québec. The narrator uses satire and caricature to attack clerical education, moral prejudice, and the ignorance and stupidity of his environment. In *Hôtel de la reine* (1949) the protagonist is the same sort of anti-conformist living in a small provincial village. Simard's third novel, *Mon fils pourtant heureux* (1956; 1968), concerns an older man who reassesses his early life. Having neither turned his back on liberal values nor wholly conformed to convention, he accepts his limitations in a mature and socially responsible manner. This middle course of subdued maturity reflects Simard's attitude to literature and to reality: he describes himself as an average author and modest craftsman in the field of letters. Awarded the Prix du Cercle du Livre de France, *Mon fils pourtant heureux* is considered his best novel. In 1957, with a Canada Council grant, Simard spent fourteen months in Europe, where he wrote *Les sentiers de la nuit* (1959), his most sombre novel, in which he depicts the solitude and moral degradation of an Anglo-Canadian from Westmount. After ten years as an essayist and translator, Simard returned to the novel with *La séparation* (1970). Taking advantage of a temporary separation, two lovers, both married—Anna, who follows her husband to Portugal, and Carl, who remains in Montreal—

correspond in the hope of clarifying their relationship.

In the sixties Simard turned to essay-writing and translation. *Répertoire* (1961) and *Nouveau répertoire* (1965) comprise reflections on art, literature, writing, travel, and Québec society. The discontinuity and variety of subjects in these books are more reminiscent of the literary journal than the essay. More recently, however, in *Une façon de parler* (1973), Simard reflects on language and writing: his intention is not to produce a scientific work but merely to speak of his art as an artisan would speak of his tools, his only ambition being that of a good craftsman and an honest man.

Simard has also written a play, *L'ange interdit* (1961), and a collection of short stories, *13 récits* (1964). He has translated numerous well-known English-Canadian books: two novels by Hugh MacLENNAN (BAROMETER RISING and *The watch that ends the night*), three by Mordecai RICHLER (*Son of a smaller hero*, *The apprenticeship of Duddy Kravitz*, and *Jacob Two-Two meets the hooded fang*), as well as *The educated imagination* by Northrop FRYE and *The long journey: the literary themes of French Canada* by Jack Warwick.

See J.-C. Falardeau, 'Présentation de M. Jean Simard', *Société royale du Canada* 18 (1963-4), and P. de Grandpré, 'La satire affûte ses traits', *Dix ans de vie littéraire au Canada français* (1966).

See also NOVELS IN FRENCH 1940 TO 1959: 2.   JACQUES MICHON

Simcoe, Elizabeth. See Writing in ONTARIO: 1.

Simons, Beverley (b. 1938) Born in Manitoba, Simons grew up in Edmonton and was preparing for a career as a concert pianist when she won a creative-writing scholarship to the Banff School of Fine Arts for her one-act verse drama, *Twisted roots* (1956). After two years at McGill University, where she formed an experimental theatre group, she completed her B.A. in English and Theatre at the University of British Columbia in 1959. Following two more years of working and studying in Europe, she settled in Vancouver and produced several stage, television, and film scripts while raising a young family. In 1968 she spent two months in the Far East studying theatre and in 1972 she received a Canada Council Senior Arts Award. Criticism over the award and continual difficulties in getting her plays produced, however, led her to abandon playwriting in the mid-seventies. Today, while most of her plays have been published and are often studied in drama courses, her work is rarely performed. In the Winter 1976 issue of *Canadian Theatre Review*, devoted to Simons' work, Don Rubin calls her 'Canada's most ignored, most important writer' and 'her full-length play *Crabdance* . . . perhaps the finest play yet written in this country.'

Simons' work is highly personal, abstract, and symbolic. *Crabdance* (1969) has been aptly compared to *Waiting for Godot*: in both plays a small cast of characters, in a setting that is 'suggestive rather than detailed', performs the rituals and word games that denote a meaningless existence and the failure of communication. While Beckett's Vladimir and Estragon wait, Sadie Golden prepares for an inevitable end. The emptiness of her life is gradually revealed as she struggles to assert her significance in a series of ritualistic relationships with three visiting salesmen. But, tragically, her efforts to use the buyer-seller, mother-son, wife-husband, mistress-lover roles for self-discovery become confused circular patterns of exploitation and victimization that can be resolved only by her death. In *The Green Lawn Rest Home* (1973), a one-act play, Simons again reveals how fragile and pointless one's sense of identity is as three elderly residents of a nursing home experience the loss of their senses, passions, and memories in a series of empty social rituals that do nothing to calm their fear of the death they cannot mention. *Preparing* (1975) is a trilogy of short plays that offer different models of the preparation for death. They employ experimental forms ranging from the naturalistic one-woman monologue of the title play, through the formalistic patterning of *Triangle*, to the stylized rituals of Japanese theatre in *The crusader*. Simons' experimentation with form, however, is most radical in *Leela means to play* (1976). Relying heavily on the symbolic devices of oriental theatre, it destroys conventional time and space with an episodic exploration of 'man's evolution through relationships, the interaction of people from his past and present' (*Canadian Theatre Review*, Winter 1976, p. 24). Thus in Simons' four published plays there is a progression from the personal rituals shaping *Crabdance* to the formal rituals that define *Leela means to play*, and this gradual solidification of form becomes an effective metaphor for her view of life as a preparation for death, the final meaningless ritual. ELIZABETH HOPKINS

Simpson, Sir George. See EXPLORATION LITERATURE IN ENGLISH: 2.

Simpson, Leo (b. 1934). Leo James Pascal Simpson was born in Limerick, Ire., and was educated in that country. He lived in England and Spain before coming to Canada in 1961. After working as publicity director and editor at MACMILLAN OF CANADA, he moved to Queensborough Township north of Belleville, Ont., in 1966 and has remained in that area since, moving to Madoc in 1972. He and his wife are restoring the Susanna MOODIE house in Belleville as their future home. He has been writer-in-residence at the University of Ottawa (1973-4) and the University of Western Ontario.

Simpson is a rarity among Canadian writers, a comic novelist of ideas. His protagonists continually find themselves in absurd plights when they struggle to purge the evil influences of contemporary technology and business, and of small-town conformity. Addison Arkwright, the hero of Simpson's ambitious first novel, *Arkwright* (1971), describes himself as 'holding my ripped humanity together comically'. A violent iconoclast, he is obsessed with exposing his multi-millionaire uncle's scheme to exploit a bogus religion founded on the exaltation of failure, and is torn by contrary and ineffectual impulses throughout most of the novel. He finally attains an idyllic refuge in Crete, though he imagines that he will be forever engaged in seeking personal 'reformation'.

Simpson's other two novels, *The Peacock papers* (1973) and *Kowalski's last chance* (1980), are both set in Bradfarrow, modelled on Belleville. Jeffrey Anchyr, the intellectual upper-class protagonist of *The Peacock papers*, and Joe Kowalski, a low-brow policeman, have in common their sense of contact with a fantasy realm scorned by their obtuse fellow-citizens. Anchyr believes himself to be guided by the nineteenth-century British novelist Thomas Love Peacock in a campaign to resist the conversion of the Bradfarrow Public Library into a computerized Data Centre, a scheme undertaken by a character based on Marshall McLUHAN. In part a loving imitation of the real Peacock's fiction, the novel upholds Peacock's preaching of traditional humanism and attacks the false faith of communications technology. The events of the book take a tragicomic turn when Anchyr, troubled by 'much confused dying' in the modern world, proves a martyr to his sensitivity. Joe Kowalski, equally sensitive in his own

sphere to human injustice, is persecuted by his chief for taking pity on an alleged bank robber who declares himself to be a leprechaun. Unlike *The Peacock papers, Kowalski's last chance* focuses on social rather than intellectual satire, but in both novels Simpson concocts an ingenious blend of fantasy, farce, and intellectual insight.

The lady and the travelling salesman: stories by Leo Simpson (1976) collects stories written over the previous decade and a half. Many involve the sudden reversal of stereotyped roles, as in the title story, in which an arms salesman is assaulted by a militant do-gooder, or 'The savages', in which teenagers on the rampage are massacred by an earnest computer expert. The collection is part of the Canadian Short Story Library, published by the University of Ottawa Press.   THOMAS E. TAUSKY

Sinclair, Lister. See DRAMA IN ENGLISH: 1953 TO 1981.

Sirois, Serge. See DRAMA IN FRENCH 1948 TO 1981: 3.

Skelton, Robin (b. 1925). Born at Essington, Eng., in what is now East Yorkshire, he was educated at Pockington Grammar School, at Christ's College, Cambridge, and at the University of Leeds, where he graduated in 1950 and obtained his M.A. in 1951. From 1951 to 1954 he was assistant lecturer, and from 1954 to 1963 lecturer, at the University of Manchester. In 1962-3 he was centenary lecturer at the University of Massachusetts. In 1963 he immigrated to Canada and joined the department of English at the University of Victoria, Victoria, B.C., as associate professor of English; he became professor in 1966. In 1967 he directed the creative-writing program at Victoria, and when a department of creative writing was founded in 1973 he became its chairman, resigning in 1976.

Apart from publishing almost 60 books, including anthologies and chapbooks, and critical editions of other writers, Skelton has been widely active in the literary world. In 1967, with John Peter, he founded *The* MALAHAT REVIEW (and was its sole editor from 1971, retiring in 1982). Having been managing-director of the Lotus Press in England (1950-2), he has been editor-in-chief of the Sono Nis Press in Victoria since 1976. Between 1962 and 1968 he was general editor of *The works of J.M. Synge*, published by the Oxford University Press.

Skelton

Much of Skelton's work has been linked with his wide knowledge of English and Irish literatures. Apart from editing the *Collected poems* (1962) in the Oxford Synge, he has written three books on that writer: *The writings of J.M. Synge* (1971), *J.M. Synge and his world* (1971), and *J.M. Synge* (1972). He edited *The collected plays of Jack B. Yeats* (1971) and, with Ann Saddlemyer, *The world of W.B. Yeats* (1965). His works of literary criticism and biography include *John Ruskin: the final years* (1965), *The poetic pattern* (1956), and *The poet's calling* (1975). He has edited two Penguin anthologies of English poetry—*Poetry of the thirties* (1964) and *Poetry of the forties* (1968)—and an anthology of seventeenth-century verse, *The Cavalier poets* (1970), as well as *David Gascoyne: collected poems* (1965), a definitive edition, and *Edward Thomas: selected poems* (1962). Two other anthologies are products of his interest in North American literature: *Five poets of the Pacific Northwest* (1964) and *Six poets of British Columbia* (1980).

A practising artist, with several shows of collages to his credit, Skelton has also written on the visual arts; apart from articles, his works in this field include *Painters talking* (1957) and *Herbert Siebner* (1979). *House of dreams* (1983) is a collection of collages and commentaries. A further aspect of this many-sided man is shown in his venture into the borderland of poetry and the occult, *Spellcraft* (1979), a collection of spells and other verses.

Almost thirty of his books and chapbooks have been collections of poems. Skelton writes verse steadily, even if he seems at times to write it painfully, and the decades since he published his first volume, *Patmos and other poems* (1955), have been punctuated by collections that established him first as an interesting young poet in England and afterwards as an increasingly accepted Canadian poet. The more important volumes are *Third day lucky* (1958), *Begging the dialect* (1960), *The dark window* (1962), *Selected poems 1947-67* (1968), *The hunting dark* (1971), *Timelight* (1974), and *Because of love* (1977). Much of the work from these volumes, spread over a quarter of a century, has been brought together monumentally in *The collected shorter poems, 1947-77* (1981). But even this massive volume, essentially lyrical in nature, leaves out whole areas of Skelton's versatility, which is often represented in his slighter volumes. Somewhere between parody and translation lies his *200 poems from the Greek anthology* (1971); while

in *George Zuk: the underwear of the unicorn* (1975) he created a whole new pseudonymous poetic personality, which he presents again in *Zuk* (1982), a collection of over 300 brief free-verse poems in which Skelton's alter ego presents his sexual obsessions. *Limits* (1981), containing work written after the *Collected shorter poems*, is a volume of starkly written poems concerned with kinship and memory, isolation and mortality.

Poetry is Skelton's most characteristic and most protean form of expression; yet despite the mutability of its form, his poetry reflects the analytical and strongly patterned frame of mind that shapes his critical writing. The development from his early poems is out of the Movement manner of the British 1950s—in which he wrote in a flat and almost audibly North-Country tone—into an individual style that is reflective and (especially in his Canadian poems) marked by a stoic and elegiac melancholy. The effect of immigration on his poetry has been to create a feeling of distance, rather than detachment, from significant experience: an inverted telescopic view of situations and states of mind that one senses are closer to the poet than their magic-realist aloofness at first suggests. Narrative, and especially the narrative of feelings—prompted by memory and the sense of exile—is a mode that Skelton has particularly developed in *The hunting dark* and *Because of love*. The reflective, quasi-autobiographical and rather pessimistic poem shows him at his best: perhaps his finest work in this vein is the poetic sequence, *Timelight*, a kind of philosophic summing up of the poet's life to date; but instead of being a structured *Prelude*-like discourse, it takes the form of a series of discontinuous insights, sharp flashes of apprehension, or just as often muted and elusive illuminations. Such writing shows Skelton's links with the great modernists in whose shadow (or light) he has always written. Perhaps more than any other Canadian poet, Skelton belongs not to one part but to the whole of the English poetic tradition.

GEORGE WOODCOCK

Škvor, George (1916-81). George Škvor (Jiří Škvor), who wrote under the name 'Pavel Javor', was born in the South Bohemian village of Martinice, Czech., and educated at Charles University, Prague. During and immediately following the Second World War he worked with the Czech Cultural Council and served as deputy member of the House of Commons. When the Com-

Škvorecký

munists ordered his arrest, he fled to West Germany and then moved to Montreal in 1950. He took his doctoral degree in Slavic letters at the Université de Montréal in 1960, and until his death—due to complications following an operation—worked as an editor and broadcaster with Radio-Canada International.

Javor published six books of poems in Czechoslovakia between 1938 and 1946, and another thirteen abroad from 1951 to 1980, for which he has been recognized by critic Petr Den as 'the official poet of Czech exile'. A selection of his poems in English translations by Ron D.K. Banerjee, *Far from you* (1981), includes an essay on the poet by Marie Němcová Banerjee and a bibliography of Javor's work in Czech, German, and French, which is complete except for the posthumous appearance of *Plamen a Píseň* (A flame and a song, 1981), issued by Sixty-Eight publishers in Toronto. His poetry is permeated with a romantic desire to return to the comforting countryside of childhood and the values of village life, and an awareness of the harsh blow dealt by history to the patriotic ideals inspired in an entire generation by Masaryk's First Republic. Javor wrote his poems out of regret for the past and apprehension for the future. Melancholy pervades so much of his poetry that even references to modern devices take on a doleful emotional quality ('Telegraph poles / hum their Morse code of loss'). Especially when rendered into English metrical forms, the poems seem rather sentimental—perhaps unavoidably so, for as Maria Němcova Banerjee observes in her essay 'Pavel Javor and the pathos of exile' (*Far from you*), he was 'the last poet of the Czech village'.

JOHN ROBERT COLOMBO

Škvorecký, Josef (b. 1924). Born in Nachod, Bohemia, Czech., he entered the faculty of medicine at Charles University, Prague, but soon transferred to philosophy, graduating in 1949 and receiving his Ph.D. in 1951. Over the next two decades he was a teacher in a girls' school, a translator of contemporary American fiction (including Faulkner's *A fable*), an editor on the Prague magazine *World Literature*, and a scriptwriter working with, among others, Milos Forman and Jiri Menzel (*Closely watched trains*). From the early 1950s he was a central figure in the post-war Czechoslovak cultural renaissance, much of whose impetus came from the underground circle of writers and artists in Prague. In 1968, after the Soviet invasion of Czechoslovakia, he immigrated to Canada with his wife, the writer-actress Zdena Salivarova, and became a professor of English at the University of Toronto.

The publication of his first novel *Zbabělci* (1958)—later translated as *The cowards* (1970)—resulted in the banning of the book, Škvorecký's loss of his editorial post, and an extensive purge of the intellectual community. In the next ten years Škvorecký published novels, novellas, and short-story collections. Works from this period available in English translation are *The mournful demeanor of Lieutenant Boruvka* (1974), a collection of mystery stories; *The bass saxophone* and *Emoke* (novellas), published in one volume in 1977; and *Miss Silver's past* (1975), a mystery novel dealing with literature and censorship in a totalitarian society. Of his recent novels—published in Czech by Sixty Eight, the Toronto publishing firm established in 1971 by Škvorecký and his wife—one has been translated as *The story of an engineer of human souls* (1983) and published in Toronto, New York, and London.

The highest praise of Škvorecký's work has come from Graham Greene, for whom *The bass saxophone* and *Emoke* are 'in the same rank as James Joyce's *The dead* and the very best of Henry James's shorter novels'. The first deals with a young Czechoslovak who plays a bass saxophone for a German band during the Second World War; the second is a poignant love story about a relatively cynical young man's attempt to seduce Emoke, a woman who doesn't seem to believe that love is possible in Communist Czechoslovakia. Yet Škvorecký's most substantial work seems to be in the two long novels, *The cowards* and *Mirakl* (The miracle game), which form part of a cycle dealing with the life and times of Daniel Smiricky, a thinly disguised portrait of the author. The other novels in the series are *Tankovy prapor* (The tank corps) and *The story of an engineer of human souls*. Danny is also the central character in the interrelated stories of *Prima sezona*, which have been translated into English as *The swell season* (1982). The series spans forty years in Danny's life, beginning in wartime Czechoslovakia (*The cowards*) and ending in Canada of the 1970s (*Engineer of human souls*). Smirický fulfils the role of an everyman who, as an East European, has experienced some of the tragic events of the past half-century.

If one of Škvorecký's dominant themes is man's fate in history, his other is the central function played by art (Smirický is a writer), which is a metaphor for freedom and free activity—a means of resisting the ideological demands of a state that insists on writing and rewriting reality and history to suit its needs. The writers and jazz musicians of Škvorecký's fiction, whether they know it or not, are what Solzhenitsyn calls a 'second government'—people who use art to celebrate the dignity and worth of human life, the necessity of certain basic human freedoms, and so on. While Škvorecký's themes are serious and weighty, there is an unsettling interweaving of the tragic and the comic in his fiction. His books are the work of a natural storyteller with a fundamentally ironic vision.

Škvorecký has also written literary criticism: essays on contemporary Czech literature, introductions to books by Czech writers, and regular Voice of America broadcasts on American, Canadian, and British literature for transmission to Czechoslovakia. His most substantial work of non-fiction is the autobiographical and historical book on the Czech cinema, *All the bright young men and women* (1972, 1975).

An issue of the American critical journal *World Literature Today* (Autumn 1981) was devoted to the work of Škvorecký, who was awarded the prestigious Neustadt Prize for literature in 1980.   SAM SOLECKI

Slater, Patrick. Pseudonym of John MITCHELL.

Slavutych, Yar. See UKRAINIAN WRITING.

Smart, Elizabeth (b. 1914). Born in Ottawa, she is the daughter of a lawyer who was a member of the Anglo-Canadian social establishment. She attended Hatfield Hall, a private school, and at nineteen travelled in England for a year. She returned to Canada to join the staff of the *Ottawa Journal*, writing society notes and editorials. Through literary contacts with Lawrence Durrell, she met the English poet George Barker in California and travelled with him throughout the U.S. He was to become the father of her four children.

In 1941 Smart travelled alone to Pender Harbour, B.C., where she completed her first novel, BY GRAND CENTRAL STATION I SAT DOWN AND WEPT (1945), a prose poem—part incantation and part cry of pain—about passion and the loss of love. (It was reissued in England in 1966, and in Canada in 1977 with a Foreword by the English critic Brigid Brophy.) After giving birth in Pender Harbour to her first child, Smart took a job as a file clerk in the British Army Office in Washington, D.C., to be with Barker, who had been barred from entry into Canada on her mother's instigation. She was transferred to the Ministry of Defence in London in 1943, and supported herself for the next two decades by writing copy for fashion magazines like *Vogue* and *Queen*, of which she became literary editor. She now lives in Flixton, Suffolk.

In 1977, following thirty-two years of silence, Smart published a collection of poems, *A bonus*. After the poetic incantatory style of her novel, *A bonus* is surprising in its casual conversational language and clipped rhythms. The poet is less interested in metaphor and image than in theme. The book is largely about writing: the struggle to speak when silence is seductive; the battle against a profound sense of inadequacy; the release and elation that comes out of the pain of writing. The impulse to order and cultivate is explored in many poems about gardening. The poems in *A bonus* are not profound, but they are moving in their efforts to explore the problems of the writer who chooses to abandon the distractions of love for the necessary self-absorption of the artist: 'Growing is the strange death in life that nobody mourns.'

Smart's second novel, *The assumption of rogues and rascals* (1977), like its predecessor, is essentially a poetic meditation without a plot structure. Set in post-war England, it explores the psychology of a woman of thirty-one, trapped in despair, who 'stops at its ardent, obstreperous source, every hopeful passion', and who cannot decide whether her hell is self-created or life's failure. A series of scenes locating emotions (the fiction of Samuel Beckett provides a precedent), the novel is structured by means of associations: snippets of conversation, dreams, memories. The rogues and rascals of the title—the misfits who at least have the courage to resist the forces of normalcy and mediocrity—are the outlawed. The novel ends with the dilemma of the writer—how and why to write—and offers an archetypal model: Philoctetes, isolated on his island with his body a running sore. Like Beckett's works, *Rogues and rascals* can best be described—again, like Smart's first novel—as a long meditation on agony.

For an interesting biographical introduction to Elizabeth Smart, see Eleanor Wachtel, 'Passion's survivor', *City Woman* (Summer 1980).   ROSEMARY SULLIVAN

Smith, A.J.M. (1902-80). Arthur James Marshall Smith was born in Westmount, Montreal, the only son of English immigrant parents. He attended Westmount High School, but in his second year was taken to England, where he lived from 1918 to 1920, studied for the Cambridge Local Examinations, 'and failed everything except English and history' (he later wrote). However, in London he frequented Harold Monroe's bookshop, then the citadel of Georgian poetry, and read much in the recent war poets and the Imagists. On his return to Montreal in 1920 he completed his high-school studies, graduated in 1921, and in the same year was admitted to McGill where, yielding to parental pressure, he studied for a Bachelor of Science degree; but during his undergraduate years he edited a singularly mature *Literary Supplement* to the *McGill Daily*, in which some of his early poems appeared. On graduating in 1925, he undertook a Master's program in English and wrote a dissertation on Yeats and the symbolist movement. At this time he met F.R. SCOTT, newly returned from Oxford. Both were in full revolt against Montreal's lingering Victorianism and conservatism, and both felt their vocation to be poetry, although Scott was studying law. The two founded *The McGill Fortnightly Review* (1925-7), which, behind its solemn title, displayed an artistic and political maturity that exerted an influence beyond the collegiate boundaries, and in effect represented the innovative spirit of the 1920s in Canada. *The McGill Fortnightly* drew to it other young writers—among them A.M. KLEIN, Leo KENNEDY, and Leon EDEL—on whom, as well as on Scott, Smith had an enduring influence. Smith in turn came under the influence of a young biology professor at McGill, Lancelot Hogben (the future author of *Mathematics for the million* and a peripheral figure in London's Bloomsbury). Hogben, who wrote pseudonymous poems for *The McGill Fortnightly*, gave Smith the early poems of T.S. Eliot to read, and encouraged him in his revolt against philistinism and Montreal parochialism.

After receiving his M.A. in 1926, Smith taught briefly in a Montreal high school and then received a fellowship for study in Edinburgh, where he worked with H.J.C. Grierson, the pre-eminent authority on Donne, and began a doctoral dissertation on the metaphysical poets of the Anglican Church in the seventeenth century (Ph.D. 1931). Returning to Canada during the Depression, Smith was unable to find an academic post and taught in a series of small American colleges until he received an appointment at Michigan State College (later University). There he remained during the rest of his career and was, in later years, poet-in-residence. He became a naturalized American, but spent all his summers in his country place near Magog, Qué.

In 1936 Smith, Scott, Klein, and Kennedy—the 'Montreal Group', as they now began to be called—joined with E.J. PRATT and Robert FINCH of Toronto in producing NEW PROVINCES: *poems of several authors*, a landmark in Canada's modern poetry. Smith wrote a lightly ironic and mocking preface about the concern of Canada's poets with 'pine trees, the open road, God, snowshoes or Pan', and added: 'The most popular experience is to be pained, hurt, stabbed or seared by beauty—preferably by the yellow flame of a crocus in the spring or the red flame of a maple leaf in the autumn.' The Toronto contributors felt Smith's words would produce a controversy at the expense of the volume's contents, and the preface was shelved in favour of a brief anonymous foreword (by Scott). It pointed out that the poems, appearing in the mid-thirties during an economic Depression, in reality reflected innovations of the 1920s in 'freer diction and more elastic forms.' It added that 'the search for new content was less successful than had been the search for new techniques.' Smith published his 'rejected' preface thirty-five years later in *Towards a view of Canadian letters* (1973) and in the 1976 reprint of *New provinces*, showing that he had also expressed in it his own poetic stance: a disciplining of form and emotion by which intensity is attained; a sense of the poem as 'a thing in itself'; the discarding of artificial forms (like mechanical rhyme) in favour of 'arbitrarily chosen verse patterns'. The poems in *New provinces* had an impact on Canadian verse far beyond any prefatorial pronouncements: in its implicit call for new findings and new attitudes in Canadian writing, it might be likened to the effect of the Wordsworth-Coleridge *Lyrical ballads* in 1798 on the Romantics. Smith included in this anthology at least five poems destined for wide publication: the repeatedly anthologized 'The lonely land', 'The creek', 'News of the phoenix', 'Like an old proud king in a parable', and 'The two sides of the drum'. The effect of *New provinces* was that it established the 'Montreal Group' as the Canadian avant-garde of its time.

During his twenties and thirties Smith wrote a great deal of poetry: some of it appeared in *The* CANADIAN FORUM; the *Dial*, then edited by Marianne Moore; *Poetry* (Chicago); and in England he was published in *New Verse*. He created a kind of reservoir of his poems—some 200—which, in the ensuing years, he polished and published in his five collections. The first did not appear in book form until he was forty-one: *News of the phoenix and other poems* (1943), which won a Governor General's Award. *A sort of ecstasy: poems new and selected* (1954) reprinted one third of the *Phoenix* and added some twenty new poems. *Collected poems* (1962) contains 75 poems from the two previous collections and 25 not hitherto collected: 100 good poems, Smith argued, represented sufficient yield for any poet's lifetime. In reprinting this collection as *Poems new and collected* (1967), Smith retained 99 poems, but he added another 22. In *The classic shade: selected poems* (1978) he used 60 poems from the previous collection and added some 20 occasional, satiric, and burlesque poems. In four of these collections Smith used a single epigraph from Santayana: 'Every animal has his festive and ceremonious moments, when he poses or plumes himself or thinks: sometimes he even sings and flies aloft in a sort of ecstasy.' This remained Smith's permanent view of his own poetry—that its function was decorative or ornamental—and caused critics to characterize his verse as 'lapidary'. A posthumous collected poems may reveal a more abundant Smith and reflect not simply his own judgement of his work.

Smith was master of a wide range of styles: he used pastiche, satire, burlesque, and bawdy. Yet his ribaldry could give way to simple lyricism and sensuality; he was on occasion meditative, and often colloquial. He is always authoritative, and always in quest of formal beauty, so that George WOODCOCK spoke of him as being 'among the most memorable lyric poets writing in the whole English-speaking world.' Northrop FRYE discerned the same lyrical qualities, but felt the poems betrayed a certain lack of energy. Smith defined his own tendency to the 'metaphysical' as expressing 'ideas that have entered so deeply into the blood as never to be questioned.' His poems possess an aristocratic coolness and a shrinking from common vulgarities; they also show a singular joy in life and an uneasy fear of death. The life-game of love is subsumed in his bawdy. The world's irrationalities and aggressivities are mocked and vigorously attacked, as in his poem 'News of the phoenix', or in his mordant verses on the atom bomb.

Almost entirely devoted to his worldly muse, Smith channeled much of his energy into anthologies, calling himself a 'compulsive anthologist'. In middle life he produced his *Book of Canadian poetry: a critical and historical anthology* (1943; 2nd ed. 1948; 3rd ed. 1957), a college anthology that became a kind of national textbook, forming the taste of younger poets and encouraging the wider reading of poetry in Canada. In this anthology one discerns Smith's insistence upon control and discipline in art. His *Oxford book of Canadian verse: in English and French* (1960), with its important introductory essay, refines his earlier selections and gains an even greater importance by including French-Canadian poetry. Smith's other Canadian anthologies are *Modern Canadian verse* (1967), again both in English and French; *The blasted pine*, with F.R. Scott (1957; rev. 1967), which bears the lengthy subtitle *An anthology of satire, invective and disrespectful verse chiefly by Canadian writers*; and *Masks of fiction: Canadian critics on Canadian prose* (1961) and *Masks of poetry: Canadian critics on Canadian verse* (1962), both edited for the New Canadian Library. For the college market he edited *The book of Canadian prose, volume 1: early beginnings to Confederation* (1965), the second volume of which was published as *The Canadian century: English-Canadian writing since Confederation* (1973); a selection from these two volumes was published in *The Canadian experience: a brief survey of English-Canadian prose* (1974). Smith also edited several non-Canadian anthologies that were published in New York. *The worldly muse* (1951) is a delightful but little-known anthology of 'serious light verse' issued by Abelard Press, which lost most of the stock in a warehouse fire shortly after publication. For the American college market Smith edited *Seven centuries of verse* (1947; 3rd ed. 1966); *100 poems* (1965); *Essays for college writing* (1965); and, with M.L. Rosenthal, *Exploring poetry* (1955; 2nd ed. 1973).

Smith's critical essays—written in an easy, lucid, and poetic prose—reassert his doctrines of intensity gained through discipline; the negative effects of colonialism, which Smith equated with parochialism; and his reiterated belief that a poem is 'not the description of an experience, it is in itself an experience'. His essays were collected in *Towards a view of Canadian letters: selected critical essays 1928-1971* (1973) and in *On poetry and poets: selected essays of A.J.M. Smith* (1977) in the New Canadian Library.

Smith was one of the most influential figures in Canadian poetry in the twentieth century. As a critic and anthologist he set, for the first time in Canada, high standards of poetic taste and discrimination; as a poet who combined classical Anglo-American forms with the modern temper, he infused an assured cosmopolitan strain into modern Canadian poetry—though towards the end of his life Smith felt, incorrectly, that the new generation's use of looser and less-demanding forms had shelved his own work. Whatever the vagaries of his reputation as both poet and critic, his total achievement marks Smith as a vigorous but also delicate reformer of Canadian taste through the power of his knowledge, wit, and craft. The high versatility of his considerable body of writings shapes a consistent theory and aesthetic of poetry, as Michael E. Darling's *A.J.M. Smith: an annotated bibliography* (1981) reveals.

Issue 11 (Fall/Winter 1982) of *Canadian Poetry* is entirely devoted to Smith. See also Sandra Djwa, 'A.J.M. Smith: of metaphysics and dry bones', *Studies in Canadian Literature*, vol. 3, no. 1 (Winter 1978); Issue 15 of CANADIAN LITERATURE (Winter 1963), which contains a 'Salute to A.J.M. Smith'; and Leon EDEL, 'The worldly muse of A.J.M. Smith', *University of Toronto Quarterly*, vol. xlvii, no. 3 (Spring 1978). See also CRITICISM IN ENGLISH: 2, 3.

LEON EDEL

Smith, Goldwin (1823-1910). Born in Reading, Eng., and educated at Eton and Oxford, he established an international reputation as a journalist and controversialist. He first achieved notice in England with his advocacy of university reform and subsequent participation in the royal commission examining the academic reform of Oxford University. In 1858 he was appointed Regius professor of modern history at Oxford (the future King Edward VII was one of his pupils). Smith, who wrote a constant stream of letters and articles for popular journals on the religious, political, economic, and imperial issues of the day, spoke from the perspective of the Manchester school of *laissez-faire* economics and fre-

quently adopted unpopular positions, especially with his support of the Northern cause during the American Civil War. He resigned his professorship in 1866 to care for his father, following whose death Smith accepted an offer to join the staff of newly founded Cornell University in Ithaca, N.Y. During his tenure (1868-71), he contributed much to the young university, including his personal library, while attempting to interpret England to America and vice versa. Closer contact with party politics, however, eroded Smith's admiration for American political institutions. In 1871 he moved to Toronto, living with relatives until his marriage to Harriet Boulton, the widow of Henry, in 1875, when he took up residence in her home, The Grange.

Smith lived in comfortable affluence, founded on both an inheritance from his father and his wife's money, and used his means for charitable works and to establish periodicals that commented on Canadian and international issues: *The Canadian Monthly and National Review* (1872-8), *The Evening Telegram* (1874), *The Bystander* (1880-90), *The* WEEK (1883-96), and *The Weekly Sun* (1896-1909). He wrote extensively on religious, literary, and historical subjects, concentrating on the twin issues of nationalism and imperialism, and published a collection of Latin and Greek poetry called *Bay leaves* (New York, 1893). Hostile to all forms of political oppression, Smith expressed sympathy for the Canada First movement, decried the Boer War, and ridiculed the concept of Imperial federation. He generated great public hostility with his argument for commercial union with the United States, presented most cogently in *Canada and the Canadian question* (London, 1891), which declares that geography, history, and race demand a single North American, Anglo-Saxon nation, and that attempts to frustrate these forces were leading to economic suffering for Canada. Smith's views of Canada's future—based on his idiosyncratic brand of liberalism rather than on research—reveal his underestimation of the strength of the Canadian national spirit and the influence of French Canada.

Though Smith undoubtedly enriched Canadian political discussion, his influence on events was minimal. His greatest contribution may have been his support of such publications as *The Canadian Monthly* and *The Week*, which helped to disseminate the work of the poets and authors of the time.

Smith

See Elisabeth Wallace, *Goldwin Smith: Victorian liberal* (1957).   CAL SMILEY

Smith, Kay. See Writing in the MARITIMES: 5.

Smith, Ray (b. 1941). Born in Inverness, Cape Breton Island, N.S., he received his B.A. in English from Dalhousie University in 1963. After serving in the RCAF and working as a systems analyst, he began writing fiction in 1964. Since 1970 he has taught at Dawson College, Montreal.

A brilliant stylist, Smith has published two books of fiction: *Cape Breton is the thought control centre of Canada* (1969) and *Lord Nelson Tavern* (1974). *Cape Breton* is a collection of stories of which the most interesting are 'Colours' (reprinted in John Metcalf's anthology *Sixteen by twelve*, 1970, with an engaging essay by Smith) and 'Galoshes' (apparently influenced by J.P. Donleavy's *The ginger man*). In *Lord Nelson Tavern*—usually called a novel, but actually a collection of linked stories—Smith begins with a group of university students, habitués of a Halifax saloon, who weave in and out of one another's lives over the years, exchanging women, delivering monologues. The complex design is not anchored chronologically. Smith's remarkable control of voice, however, is evident throughout and is especially fine in a very funny seduction monologue delivered by a thirteen-year-old girl ('Sarah's summer holidays'). Both of these books are clearly within the tradition of post-modernist fiction as defined by writers like Borges and William Gass. They are elaborately crafted, playful, self-referential. In Smith's words, 'the writer says what the story is about *in the whole story*'—so that the story can equally be 'about' its linguistic components or punctuation (including an especially artful semicolon) and 'about' relations between the sexes, a prominent theme in his work, on which Smith can be peculiarly disturbing. There is something brutal in the attitude to women displayed by the men; but this nastiness, while evidently recognized as such by Smith, is not purged or contained by his awareness.

An excellent guide to what Douglas BARBOUR calls Smith's 'artful manoeuvrings' and 'linguistic shuffles' is Barbour's essay 'Ray Smith: some approaches to the entrances of *Lord Nelson Tavern*' in OPEN LETTER (Summer 1976).

See also NOVELS IN ENGLISH 1960 TO 1982: 4.   CONSTANCE ROOKE

Smith, William, Jr. See HISTORICAL WRITING IN ENGLISH: 2.

Smucker, Barbara. See CHILDREN'S LITERATURE IN ENGLISH: 6.

Smyth, Donna (b. 1943). Born in Kimberley, B.C., she was educated at the Universities of Victoria, Toronto, and London (Ph.D., 1972). She has taught English at the University of Victoria (1967-9), the University of Saskatchewan (1972-3), and, since 1973, at Acadia University. She lives in Ellershouse, N.S.,

Smyth's writing combines inquiry into philosophical questions, poetic response to the natural world, and sensitivity to the lives and thoughts of ordinary working people. She has published short stories in a variety of Canadian, British, and American periodicals. Her novel *Quilt* (1982) is set in rural Nova Scotia; its main characters are a young battered wife, whose husband kills himself in a rage, and an older widow who lives with the memory of having helped her invalid husband to die. Offsetting their dramatic stories are the subtle tensions in the life of a couple facing retirement and ill-health. The vicissitudes of human life are counterpointed by the cycle of the natural world. Like the quilt the women are sewing, the novel is a patchwork of different styles, suggesting an image of community and underlying purpose in apparent chaos.

Smyth used a similar patchwork technique in her scripts written for Nova Scotia's touring Mermaid Theatre. *Susanna Moodie* (1976) dramatizes the story of MOODIE's experience both as told in ROUGHING IT IN THE BUSH (1852) and as Margaret ATWOOD reinterpreted it in *The JOURNALS OF SUSANNA MOODIE* (1970). Atwood's poems are recited between dramatized episodes, each implicitly commenting on the other. *Giant Anna* (1978-9), winner of a Canada Council New Play Award, is the story of Anna Swan (1846-88), the giant daughter of a Nova Scotia family, who gave up her teacher-training because of physical and social difficulties to be exhibited as a 'freak' by the showman P.T. Barnum. Life-size giant puppets created by Tom Miller portray Anna and her almost equally tall husband. As they interact with smaller puppets and live actors, the contrast of physical form illustrates the need to understand those who are different. The play, which appeals to children as well as to general audiences, includes short rhymed prologues to each episode that keep the story-line clear for them.

In 1976 Smyth was one of the founders of *Atlantis*, the first interdisciplinary women's-studies journal in Canada; she was co-ordinating editor until 1981.

JOAN COLDWELL

Smyth, 'Sir' John (d. 1852). By his own account a self-taught native of Canada who discovered by accident in 1837 that he could write poetry, Smyth wrote and published prolifically for the remainder of his life. In a land of many marginal native poets, 'Sir' John's work was so bad that it was safe to laugh at him. Each new poem was widely reprinted in Upper and Lower Canadian newspapers, and his two books—*Select poems* (Toronto, 1841) and *A small specimen of the genius of Canada West, and the wonders of the world* (Toronto, 1845)—were solemnly reviewed with editorial tongue-in-cheek.

Little is known of Smyth. He died in the Toronto House of Industry, but the date and place of his birth are unknown. Newspaper editors in the 1840s generally referred to him as 'old'. He was partially crippled and moved about Toronto in a small self-propelled cart. He had been a farmer, then a land agent, before conferring on himself the title of Poet Laureate. Smyth began to use the title 'Sir' after someone had shown him an entry in a British peerage register that listed a John Smyth, Baronet and Royal Engineer. His fellow Canadians humoured him by using the title.

Smyth had a simple poetic style in which the essential feature is his obvious struggle with rhyme: 'How great was the peace, good will and harmony,/That prevailed in our City of Toronto/On the celebration of the matrimony/Of our Queen, and her name will be our motto.' (*Select poems*, p. 6.) Because his poetry is so bad and so funny, some of it has found a place as comic relief in modern scholarly lectures. The content of his work, however, deserves attention. Deluded though he may have been about himself, his poems give us one of the few clues we have to lower-class Canadian attitudes of the time. An acute observer of the Upper Canadian world, he commented with an outsider's telling accuracy on the pretensions of colonial society. No admirer of the local Tories or of Americans, he was nevertheless a sentimental royalist who cheered the victories of the British army and navy. He took great pride in the progress of Upper Canada, and of Toronto in particular.

MARY LU MacDONALD

Snow Drop, The (Apr. 1847-June 1853). *The Snow Drop; or Juvenile Magazine*, the first Canadian periodical for children, was edited by two sisters (née Foster) who had moved to Montreal from Boston: Mrs Eliza Lanesford Cushing (b. 1794) and Mrs Harriet Vining Cheney (b. 1796). It was published in Montreal by the firm of Lovell and Gibson, which also published *The* LITERARY GARLAND. Setting out to instruct and amuse, the magazine was directed primarily to girls, each issue providing one or two stories along with articles on historical events, famous people, natural history, and faraway places; the slight Canadian content had to do mostly with the past or with the quainter aspects of Canadian life. Most of *The Snow Drop*'s identified authors were from old or New England, like the books and periodicals from which it published selections. Although its final numbers contained an increasing proportion of original contributions, it made little impact on the Canadian literary scene. Late in its six-year existence it had a short-lived competitor, *The Maple Leaf* (June 1852-Dec. 1854), which deliberately featured Canadian content, including work by Susanna MOODIE and her sister Catharine Parr TRAILL.

See Carole Gerson, 'The *Snow Drop* and the *Maple Leaf*; Canada's first periodicals for children', *Canadian Children's Literature* 15/16 (1980).

CAROLE GERSON

Soirées canadiennes, Les. A literary monthly published in Quebec City from 1861 to 1865 by members of the MOUVE-MENT LITTÉRAIRE DE QUÉBEC, it was one of the first undertakings of this 1860 group of writers and historians. The formula adopted was that of Dr Joseph-Charles TACHÉ, who wanted to publish French-Canadian legends and folk-tales lest they be forgotten. Taché, Abbé Henri-Raymond CASGRAIN, and Dr François-Hubert-Alexandre LA RUE formed the editorial committee, with Brousseau Brothers as printers; the prospectus appeared in *Le Courrier du Canada*, 22 Feb. 1861, and the first number was published on 11 Mar. 1861.

The first year was extremely successful: more than 800 subscribers signed up. The lack of any written contract with the printers soon gave rise, however, to disagreements about the ownership and conduct of the enterprise, and to a serious split between

Soirées canadiennes

Taché, who sided with Brousseau Brothers, and the other editors, who wanted to change printers. In Oct. 1862 eight contributors resigned. Casgrain, La Rue, and Antoine GÉRIN-LAJOIE, ignoring Taché's remonstrances, entrusted the printing for the year 1863 to another firm, Desbarats and Derbishire, and announced a change of title to *Le* FOYER CANADIEN. Brousseau Brothers protested and distributed a pamphlet to the subscribers (*Mémoire des Propriétaires-Editeurs*, 18 Oct. 1862), publishing the correspondence of the dispute. The *Foyer canadien* group retorted, first in their 'Prospectus' (30 Oct. 1862) and then in a satirical memorandum (*Réponse à la Mémoire de MM. Brousseau Frères*, Nov. 1862) written by La Rue. Meanwhile Taché continued to edit *Les Soirées canadiennes* single-handedly, devoting the Nov. 1862 issue to Octave CRÉMAZIE's unfinished poem 'Les trois morts' and filling 250 pages of the 1863 numbers with his own lumber-camp and backwoods tales entitled 'Forestiers et voyageurs'. The 1864 issues contained few original writings: many of them were given over to historical documents. In Aug. 1864 Taché became deputy minister in the department of agriculture and statistics and in Oct. 1865 was obliged to move to Ottawa. The numbers of the *Soirées* for the last half of 1865 were consequently delayed and appeared only in Feb. 1867. With their publication the magazine disappeared.

Like *Le Foyer canadien*, *Les Soirées canadiennes* had remarkable initial success and then slowly declined; both contributed to the literary renascence of 1860, the *Soirées* on a smaller scale and in a more limited circuit than the more prosperous *Foyer*. Each succeeding literary movement in Québec has had its literary magazines, but almost none have achieved the prominence and the readership enjoyed by these early examples of the genre.

See Réjean Robidoux, '*Les Soirées canadiennes* et *Le Foyer canadien* dans le mouvement littéraire québécois de 1860', *Revue de l'Université d'Ottawa*, XXXVIII, no. 4 (Oct.-Dec. 1958).   DAVID M. HAYNE

Sommer, Richard (b. 1934). Born, raised, and educated in Minnesota before attending Harvard University, he came to Canada in 1962 to live in Montreal. He has published five books of poetry: *Homage to Mr. McMullin* (1969), *Blue sky notebook* (1973), *Left hand mind* (1976), *Milarepa* (1976), and *The other side of games* (1977). Irony hovers around

Sommer's poetry constantly as he recognizes the betrayals of language and definitions. In his poem 'The man who calls himself', the image of the ventriloquist and his dummy may be the ironic equivalent of the poet watching himself worry away at the nature of reality, questioning the persona's relation to that reality, the poet's relation to his manipulation of language, and even the recognition of language's manipulation of his response to the world. That atmosphere of ironic inadequacy in the context of a deliberate attempt to capture the essence of things is a part of Sommer's poetic that surfaces in various guises throughout his work. The poet, like the ventriloquist's doll, is simply a medium for the poems, which are external to himself. The language itself is in control and shapes the poems: 'the poem is words giving shape to the intervening silences, which must be left inarticulate.'
                PETER STEVENS

Soucy, Charles. See NOVELS IN FRENCH 1960 TO 1982: 3(e).

Souster, Raymond (b. 1921). Born in Toronto, he has lived there nearly all his life and rooted most of his poetry in its landscape. He grew up in the western Humberside area of the city, becoming an outstanding softball pitcher in his late teens. He joined the Bank of Commerce as a teller in 1939 and enlisted as a tradesman in the Royal Canadian Air Force in 1941. He was posted to continental defence squadrons in Nova Scotia and Newfoundland before a posting to England brought him to Europe for the final day of the war. While in Nova Scotia, Souster was inspired by John Sutherland's FIRST STATEMENT to publish his first little magazine, *Direction* (1943-6), mimeographed on borrowed RCAF paper. In 1944 a large selection of his poetry was included in Ronald Hambleton's *Unit of five*.

On demobilization Souster returned to the bank and has now been with the Imperial Bank of Commerce for nearly four decades. His first book, *When we are young* (1946), published by John SUTHERLAND's First Statement Press, was followed by his inclusion in Sutherland's anthology *Other Canadians: an anthology of the new poetry of Canada, 1940-1946* (1947) and by the RYERSON PRESS's publication of his *Go to sleep world* (1947). He attempted his second little magazine, *Enterprise*, in 1948 and published a pseudonymous war novel, *The winter of time*, by 'Raymond Holmes', in 1949. His third volume of poetry, *City Hall street*, appeared in 1951. The poetry of this and the preceding volumes was romantic in diction, often overstated, and opposed nature and youthful love to the ugliness of war and factory.

In 1951 Souster became a close friend of Louis DUDEK, who had just returned to Montreal from New York, and who introduced him to the work of William Carlos Williams and the poets of Cid Corman's U.S. magazine *Origin*. With Dudek's encouragement he launched his third magazine, CONTACT (1952-4), in which he was able to publish work by Corman and other *Origin* writers. In the spring of 1952 he joined with Dudek and Irving LAYTON to begin Contact Press, the chief publisher of new poetry in Canada during the 1950s. Under the influence of Williams and Corman, Souster's style changed drastically; his line became the brief 'variable foot' of Williams, his diction became concrete and austere.

In his publications of the fifties—*Shake hands with the hangman* (1953), *A dream that is dying* (1954), *For what time slays* (1955), *Walking death* (1955), *The selected poems* (1956), *Crepe-hanger's carnival* (1958)—Souster continued his early theme of the opposition between the 'outside' forces of love, nature, and sport and the 'inside' ones of industry and commerce. Because this was also an opposition between small and large, Souster's new poetic of understatement and economy was ideally suited to it. Late in the decade Souster began his fourth mimeographed little magazine, *Combustion* (1957-60), which reflected his continuing interest in the poetry of Corman and other U.S. writers.

The 1960s was a period of consolidation for Souster. He published three outstanding collections: *A local pride* (1962), *The colour of the times* (1964, winner of a Governor-General's Award), and *As is* (1967); and began the lengthy process of publishing or re-publishing his entire body of work with *Lost & found: uncollected poems 1945-1960* (1968) and *So far, so good* (1969). He also published the less-important books *Place of meeting* (1962), *At Split Rock Falls* (1963), *Twelve new poems* (1964), and *Ten elephants on Yonge Street* (1965); edited for Contact Press the influential anthology of young poets *New wave Canada: the new explosion in Canadian poetry* (1966); and on the demise of Contact Press in 1967 began work on another novel loosely tied to his war experi-

ences, *On target* (1972), privately published under the pseudonym 'John Holmes'.

The re-publication of Souster's early work continued in the 1970s with *The years* (1970), *Selected poems* (1972), *Double-header* (1975), and *Rain-check* (1975); they have been followed by three volumes of a four-volume *Collected poems* (1980, 1981, and 1982). Souster's more recent poems in *Change-up* (1974), *Extra innings* (1977), and *Hanging in* (1979) now took on a retrospective tone, particularly the series 'Pictures of a long-lost world', in which Souster directed his nostalgic vision toward recapturing specific moments of twentieth-century history. During the 1970s Souster also co-edited four teaching anthologies: *Generation now* (1970) and *These loved, these hated lands* (1975) with Richard Woollatt, and with Douglas LOCHHEAD *Made in Canada* (1970) and *100 Poems of nineteenth-century Canada* (1974).

Souster's poetry is notable for its skilled use of imagism, for its vivid affirmations of the value of the commonplace object, and for its depictions of Toronto streets, parks, and suburbs. Deliberately avoiding the formally elegant poem, Souster has compiled a body of disarming lyrics in which the craft is concealed so that incidents and scenes may have all possible prominence. Frank DAVEY's *Louis Dudek and Raymond Souster* (1981) details Souster's relationship to Dudek and Corman and offers several critical approaches to his work.

See also POETRY IN ENGLISH 1950 TO 1982: 1.   FRANK DAVEY

Sparshott, Francis (b. 1926). Francis Edward Sparshott was born in Chatham, Eng., and educated at Oxford University, where he won numerous prizes and scholarships. He came to the University of Toronto in 1950 as a lecturer in philosophy and in 1955 joined the staff of Victoria College, where he is now a University Professor. Philosopher by profession and poet by inclination (he was president of the LEAGUE OF CANADIAN POETS 1977-9), Sparshott has written five books on philosophy, four books of poetry, and many articles that address the relation of philosophy, literature, and the arts. He has remarked that while poetry and philosophy are two distinct things, there is common ground, for the purpose of both is to 'discover connections that are not evident.' He has also written that poetry is the 'only thing' he takes seriously.

Sparshott's philosophical concerns pervade his poetry; he is skilled at perceiving hidden relations between ideas. This is nowhere more evident than in his as-yet unpublished poem 'The cave of Trophonius', which he describes as a 'trip of the shaman through the universe'. It won the first prize for poetry in the 1981 CBC literary competition. His first two poetry collections, *A divided voice* (1965) and *A cardboard garage* (1969), focus on poems of introspection that speak to themes of unfulfilled love, unattainable pleasures, and the sense of waste in human loneliness, isolation, and willed violence. Formally graceful, the poems are by turns romantic, humorous, passionate, and profound. *The naming of the beasts* and *The rainy hills* (haiku), both published in 1979, tend to feature observations and descriptions of commonplace events. All the poems in these collections have an elegant clarity of language and often give voice to a capricious irreverence, refined colloquialisms, scholarly allusions, and witty asides.

These are traits that also mark Sparshott's philosophy books, giving them a literary *panache* that is rare in philosophical writing. Sparshott made his reputation as a philosopher with *An enquiry into goodness and related concepts* (1958), a distinguished work that tackles the traditional concerns of ethics and explores the various meanings of 'goodness' and their relation to human satisfaction. While his journal publications cover a wide range of philosophical topics, Sparshott is perhaps best known for his work on aesthetics. In *The structure of aesthetics* (1963) he examines the concept of a work of art, the meanings of artistic language, the legitimacy and purpose of artistic criticism, and the role of art as an expression of the human condition. It concludes with a warning against theses that suggest a single function or analysis of art. *The concept of criticism* (1967) also argues for the interrelatedness of theories and functions, and urges the use of reasonable techniques, not 'the one method of criticism'. In *Looking for philosophy* (1972)—a mixture of witty essays, interludes, and lively dialogues that investigate the discipline of philosophy and the philosopher's task—Sparshott accepts St Ambrose's dictum that salvation cannot be achieved by philosophy, but adds that this belief was easy for Ambrose, since he was no philosopher. This book aroused the ire of some critics, who believed that philosophers should not make jokes about philosophy, but it delights students. Sparshott's humour also surfaces frequently in the footnotes accompanying his philosophical works. *The theory of the arts* (1982), which Sparshott has described as his 'magnum opus', distinguishes between the classical definition of 'fine arts'—which regards art as productivity, 'a performance with respect to its design'—and the modern concept of art considered as pure creativity and expressed intuitions. Sparshott concludes that he has offered an aesthetic meta-theory—a theory about theories of art. His lucid style makes this discourse easily accessible to the uninitiated inquirer.

A book (1970), published under the pseudonym 'Cromwell Kent', is a tongue-in-cheek frolic in prose, compressing into thirty-six pages the possible ingredients of the great Canadian novel: beavers, the RCMP, Russian spies, bestiality, swamps, and Bible stories.   ELIZABETH TROTT

Spencer, Elizabeth (b. 1921). Born in Carrollton, Miss., Elizabeth Spencer was educated at Bellhaven College and Vanderbilt University. After working as a teacher and a journalist, she set out on a 'personal road' in writing, which has led her from Mississippi to Italy (on a Guggenheim Fellowship in 1956) and to Montreal, where she has lived with her husband, John Rusher, since 1958, teaching at Concordia University.

Despite her success as a short-story writer, Spencer thinks of herself primarily as a novelist. She has published five novels and two novellas. *Fire in the morning* (1948), *This crooked way* (1952), and *The voice at the back door* (1956) form a picture of the Southern world in which she grew up. *No place for an angel* (1967) and *The snare* (1972)—her strongest book, in her view—'bring together certain broad areas of American experience' and were not meant to be specifically 'Southern'. The two novellas, *The light in the piazza* (1960) and *Knights and dragons* (1965), complement one another as sunny and anguished works about Americans in Italy; in 1962 the former was produced as an MGM film starring Olivia de Havilland. Spencer has published two collections of short stories, *Ship Island and other stories* (1968) and *The stories of Elizabeth Spencer* (1981), with a Foreword by Eudora Welty and including *Knights and dragons*. Among her most accomplished stories are 'Little brown girl', 'White angels', 'Ship Island', 'The absence', 'The Bufords', 'Judith Kane', 'The finder', 'Prelude to a parking lot', 'I, Maureen', and 'The girl who loved horses'.

Spencer does not 'seek to avoid' writing

about Canada, but her Canadian stories are few in number. In the best of them, 'I, Maureen', the near-death of her affluent husband shocks the protagonist into the search for 'another world' and her other self, without which she has been psychically starved. She finds what she seeks in an unstable relationship with a poor artist-photographer in the east end of Montreal; in realizing that love and art must be transient and changing, she accepts an important truth. In 'The search', another story set in Canada, a woman is tortured by her anguish over her lost daughter and wants to be rid of the pain; suddenly her husband realizes that the hotel-owner has been right in accusing her of throwing bags of garbage from the window.

Spencer's sensibility is intuitive and non-rational; she has a sure touch when dealing with the delicate and the evanescent, with fantasy, ghosts, mysticism, miracles; with affinities, resemblances, doubles, and especially with moments of insight and self-discovery. Above all her work is about healthy escape: from the past, from other people and their expectations, from inappropriate or lingering love, from old griefs. Her protagonists harrow personal hells of falseness and break through to freedom and authenticity; like Spencer herself, they follow their hearts.   JEFFREY HEATH

Stansbury, Joseph (1742?-1809). Born in London, Eng., he immigrated to Philadelphia, arriving there on 11 Oct. 1767. He opened a china shop and gradually became a prominent member of the British social set. He had the reputation of being intelligent, with an ability to write satirical and humorous political poems and songs. 'As a writer of satirical verse, free from hatred and bitterness, he was "without a rival among his brethren" ' (M.C. Tyler, *The literary history of the American Revolution*, 1897). With talk of a revolution in the air, he opposed independence of the American colonies and became a British agent, acting as a go-between for Benedict Arnold and the British headquarters. He moved to New York City, where he continued to write satires directed against the Whigs. In 1783 Stansbury moved his family to the Loyalist settlement of Shelburne, N.S., but after two years of hardship and disappointment he returned to New York, where he died. His well-known poem 'To Cordelia' vividly records his feelings about pioneer life in Nova Scotia. Winthrop Sargent's *The loyal verses of Joseph Stansbury*

and Dr. Jonathan Odell (Albany, 1860) is still the best collection of his verse, although he is represented in a number of Canadian anthologies.   DOUGLAS LOCHHEAD

Stead, Robert J.C. (1880-1959). Robert James Campbell Stead was born in Middleville, Ont., and grew up in Cartwright, Man. He attended Winnipeg Business College and from 1898 to 1909 published and edited a local weekly called variously *The Rock Lake Review*, *The Rock Lake Review and Cartwright Enterprise*, and *The Southern Manitoba Review*. In 1908-9 he also edited the *Crystal City Courier*. Stead worked at other temporary occupations, including selling automobiles, and by 1912 was in Calgary, first on the editorial staff of *The Albertan*, then from 1913 directing publicity for the colonization department of the CPR. In 1919 he moved to Ottawa to be publicity director for the Department of Immigration and Colonization, and from 1936 until his retirement in 1946 he held this position for parks-and-resources aspects of the Department of Mines and Resources. He was active in the CANADIAN AUTHORS' ASSOCIATION from its inception and became its president in 1923.

Stead was the only writer to span the development of prairie fiction from the popular genre of romances of pioneering to realistic novels scrutinizing the values of prairie society. His five volumes of slight, patriotic verse—*The empire builders* (1908), *Prairie born* (1911), *Songs of the prairie* (1911), *Kitchener and other poems* (1916) and *Why don't they cheer* (1918)—are of interest mainly as evidence of Stead's devotion to the imperial vision of the Prairies. Except for *The copper disc* (1931), a mystery published in the Doubleday 'Crime Club' series, Stead's novels have prairie or foothills settings. *The bail jumper* (1914), *The homesteaders* (1916), *The cow puncher* (1918), which sold 70,000 copies, *Dennison Grant* (1920), and *Neighbours* (1922) all combine romantic plots and an authentic depiction of western life. They brought Stead immediate popularity rather than a lasting reputation—with the exception of *The homesteaders*, which went through five printings by 1922 and has since earned critical recognition as a central romance of pioneering. Tracing the lives of an ideal pioneer couple from their arrival in Manitoba in 1882 to the land-boom prior to the Great War, it develops such traditional motifs and themes of its genre as harmony with the land, the marriage of eastern refinement and western vitality, and the dangers of falling from idealism into mammonism. *The homesteaders* has been reprinted in the Literature in Canada series (1973) with an introduction by Susan Wood Glicksohn.

It has been argued that Stead, the journalist and publicist, exploited a shrewd sense of the popular taste in fiction; yet even his romances show a sometimes obtrusive concern for social issues, and in his last two prairie novels he turned away from the formulas that had brought him popularity to develop his ideas and his craft. In *The smoking flax* (1925) sociological theories about rural life overpower a weak plot; but it prepared the themes and techniques that Stead developed in his next and best novel, *Grain* (1926). It portrays, from an ironic perspective, the life of Gander Stake, whose growth as a human being is stunted by the culturally impoverished environment of a prairie farm and by an almost erotic absorption in the romance of mechanization. The technical nature and function of Stead's realism are subjects of critical debate, but Stead is credited, along with Frederick Philip GROVE and Martha OSTENSO, with initiating the sober assessment of man's spiritual alienation from the land that distinguishes prairie realism from the earlier romances of pioneering. *Grain* has been reprinted in the New Canadian Library (1966), with an introduction by Thomas Saunders.

See Frank DAVEY, 'Rereading Stead's *Grain*', *Studies in Canadian Literature* 4 (Winter 1979), and Leslie Mundwiler, 'Robert Stead—home in the first place', *Essays on Canadian Writing* 11 (Summer, 1978).

DICK HARRISON

Stegner, Wallace. See FOREIGN WRITERS ON CANADA IN ENGLISH: 2.

Stein, David Lewis (b. 1937). Born and raised in Toronto, he attended the University of Toronto, where he became interested in journalism and was features editor of the *Varsity*. Since graduation he has worked as a reporter for *Maclean's*, the New York *Herald Tribune* in its Paris bureau, the *Star Weekly*, and the *Toronto Star*, where he is currently employed.

Stein's journalism, often studying political activism and its social roots, stands behind his two non-fiction books: *Living the revolution: the Yippies in Chicago* (1969) and *Toronto for sale: the destruction of a city* (1972), as well as his play, *The hearing* (1978), which depicts the comic and tragic dimensions of municipal battles between real-estate developers and homeowners' associations.

Like his journalism, Stein's fiction takes the form of political protest and social commentary, with the influence of George Orwell always in evidence. In his fine first novel, *Scratch one dreamer* (1967), written while he was on a Canada Council fellowship in London, Eng., Joe Fried, a middle-class Jewish liberal individualist, returns home to Toronto and his dying uncle, a former labour leader of the forties. Maintaining a careful and frequently comic balance between the cynical and the sentimental, the novel is a detached yet passionate study of political activism in the sixties and the hero's growing acceptance of the necessity of individual moral choices. Stein's second novel, *My sexual and other revolutions: the memoirs of Daniel Johnson as told to David Lewis Stein* (1971), is his most vitriolic work; yet the vehemence of his social criticism—moving sometimes awkwardly among parody, satire, pornography, and blatant attack—makes the book less effective as a novel than *Scratch one dreamer*.

With Dave GODFREY and Clark BLAISE, Stein edited a collection of their short stories, *New Canadian writing* (1968); his own contributions reflect his persistent concern with the social manifestations of hatred and evil. His collection *City boys* (1978) includes both published and unpublished short fiction.

DAVID STAINES

Stevens, Peter (b. 1927). Born in Manchester, Eng., he graduated in English and Education from the University of Nottingham (B.A., 1951). In 1957 he came to Canada and taught at both a private school and McMaster University while working on his M.A. He taught at the University of Saskatchewan (1964-8) and was the first to receive a doctorate there in Canadian literature (1968). His thesis topic, 'The growth of modernism in Canadian poetry between the wars', led eventually to the publication of *The McGill movement* (1968), and to his editing of Raymond KNISTER's *The first day of spring and other stories* (1976). Since 1969 Stevens has taught English and creative writing at the University of Windsor and has served as contributing editor to *The Ontario Review* (1973-8) and poetry editor of *The* CANADIAN FORUM (1968-73). Stevens edited, with J.L. Granatstein, *Forum: Canadian life and letters, 1920-1970* (1972). He founded the small but energetic Sesame Press in Windsor and has written several plays, three of which received performances in Detroit, Vancouver, and Windsor in 1980.

Stevens began writing poetry after his arrival in Canada and his first collection of poems, *Nothing but spoons* (1969), focuses on domestic events and Canadian places and landscapes. These subjects are expanded in *A few myths* (1971), which accommodates both conventional and experimental forms. Stevens deals with a broad spectrum of ideas and subjects without compromising intelligence and grace—qualities evident in his succeeding books: *Breadcrusts and glass* (1972), *Family feelings* (1974), and the chapbook *A momentary stay* (1974). *And the dying sky like blood* (1974) is a collage based on events in the life of Dr Norman Bethune; it includes found poetry, narrative vignettes, and lines from jazz songs of the thirties and forties—a special interest of Stevens, who was a contributor to the CBC's 'Jazz Radio Canada' program. *The Bogman Pavese tactics* (1974) is divided into four sections, of which the first is based on P.V. Glob's discoveries of human sacrifices in northern European bogs, while the third is a series of poems about Italian writer and poet, Cesare Pavese. The chapbook *Coming back* (1981) was followed by *Revenge of the mistresses poems* (1981), which draws upon a collection of erotic photographs by Helmut Newton and gives voice to, and avenges, the 'used' women of the pictures.   BRUCE MEYER

Stevenson, Lionel. See CRITICISM IN ENGLISH: 2.

Stewart, George, Jr (1848-1906). Born in New York City, he came to Canada with his parents in 1851 and was educated in London, Canada West (Ont.), and in Saint John, N.B. At sixteen he founded *The stamp collector's monthly gazette* (1865-7), the first periodical of its kind in Canada, and at nineteen STEWART'S LITERARY QUARTERLY MAGAZINE (Saint John, 1867-72). From 1872 to 1878 he was city editor of the Saint John *Daily News* and literary and dramatic editor of *The Weekly Watchman*; he went to Toronto in 1878-9 as editor of ROSE-BELFORD'S CANADIAN MONTHLY, but resigned after losing his court battle to get royalties from *Rose-Belford's* for his *Canada under the administration of the Earl of Dufferin* (Toronto, 1878). He next edited the Quebec *Daily Chronicle* from 1879 to 1896. For many years he freelanced for American and Canadian magazines and contributed to reference works.

Stewart was an innovative editor. His *Literary Quarterly* was one of the few early Canadian periodicals to pay contributors. He introduced illustrated articles into *Rose-Belford's Canadian Monthly* and expanded its fiction department to include American writers. He was also one of the first Canadian journalists to deal with contemporary events in book form. *The story of the great fire in St. John, New Brunswick* (Saint John, Toronto, Detroit, 1877) is still a reliable source book; *Canada under the administration of the Earl of Dufferin*, however, is less a history of the country than a eulogistic record of the governor-general's public duties, with long excerpts from his speeches, though Stewart narrates events like the public reaction to the Pacific Scandal (1873) in a simple and dramatic way. While he advocated higher critical standards, his articles on Carlyle, Thoreau, Emerson, and Longfellow were appreciative rather than judgemental; these were collected in *Evenings in the library* (Toronto, 1878) and *Essays from reviews* (Quebec, 1st series, 1882; 2nd series, 1893). Attacking the apathy towards local writers, he pressed for a native publishing industry and for Canada's adherence to international copyright. He was a fervent interpreter of French Canada in many articles that ranged from the scholarly to the travel guide. He contributed the chapter 'Frontenac and his times' to Justin Winsor's seven-volume *Narrative and critical history of America* (Boston, 1885; see vol. IV), and his New York lecture on English- and French-Canadian literature was printed in *Canadian leaves: history, art, science, literature, commerce; a series of new papers read before the Canadian Club of New York* (New York, 1887). He was one of the first critics to argue that Canadian and American literature were distinct entities from British literature.

His activities and writings brought Stewart international recognition, including honorary membership in the Athenaeum Club of London; the distinction of becoming the first Canadian member (1879) of the International Literary Congress; and honorary degrees from Laval, McGill, and Bishop's Universities, and from King's College, Halifax. He was a charter member of the Royal Society of Canada (1882) and for many years secretary of its English section and a contributor to its *Transactions*.
                              GEORGE L. PARKER

Stewart, Herbert. See PHILOSOPHY IN CANADA: 6.

Stewart, John. See HISTORICAL WRITING IN ENGLISH: 1.

Stewart's Literary Quarterly Magazine, Devoted to Light and Entertaining Literature (Saint John, Apr. 1867-Oct. 1872). This was the only Canadian magazine of its day to rely entirely on original contributions and one of the few to pay its contributors. The editor and publisher to Jan. 1872 was its founder George STEWART, Jr; it continued for three numbers until Oct. 1872 as *The New Brunswick Quarterly*, of which the joint editors and publishers were A.A. Stockton and G.W. Burbidge.

To counter the spread of pernicious American trash, Stewart believed 'the time had come for literary development in Canada, and especially in New Brunswick. Our best writers . . . were sending their work to the British and American magazines, and I was convinced that the country could and would afford a decent support to a monthly or quarterly magazine.' Financially the *Quarterly* was not successful, even though its printer, George James Chubb, took no profit from it. Although Stewart attracted little fiction, he published poetry by James Hannay, Charles SANGSTER, Alexander McLACHLAN, and Ewan McColl; biographical sketches; and articles on history and literature. In 'Human progress—is it real?' the Rev. Moses HARVEY argued that geology proved that evolution was part of the divine plan (Oct. 1871), while 'Diana' came out against women's suffrage in ' "Women's rights" and a woman's view of them' (Apr. 1870). As a critic, Stewart tried to evaluate—and still encourage—Canadian writers by the same standards that he applied to the British and the Americans. It was now time, he maintained in a review of Charles MAIR's *Dreamland, and other poems* (January 1869), to judge a work on its artistic merits rather than merely as a phenomenon of Canadian authorship and publishing. While they were frequently cosmopolitan and lively, however, *Quarterly* writers never quite shook off a self-conscious provincialism in dealing with Canadian writing; and a spirit of parochialism infected its successor. Nevertheless, *Stewart's Quarterly* showed that Canadian journalism had the potential for higher standards. GEORGE L. PARKER

Stone angel, The (1964). This novel by Margaret LAURENCE, which established her international reputation, is the first of her books to have a Canadian setting and the first volume of what is known as the Manawaka cycle. A draft was completed in 1962, when Laurence was living in Vancouver, and rewritten the next year in England. In 1964 it was published simultaneously in Toronto (McClelland and Stewart), London (Macmillan), and New York (Knopf). It was translated into German by Herbert Schuter as *Der steinerne engel* (Munich, 1965) and into French by Claire MARTIN as *L'ange de pierre* (Montréal, 1976). Several paperback editions have appeared in Canada, the United States, and England.

Originally entitled *Hagar*, it is a character study of the narrator, ninety-year-old Hagar Shipley, who is fiercely battling the threat of banishment to an old people's home and the ravages of terminal disease. Friction with her son and daughter-in-law, with whom she lives, and her desperate attempt to preserve some dignity, contribute to a powerfully realized study of old age. A meeting with a stranger leads her to acquire a measure of grace before she is put into hospital where, in her last days, she is able to offer a little of the love and humility she has previously, to her cost, always withheld. Hagar's narrative, with its wit and humorous self-awareness, alternates between present action and reminiscences of the past: her Manawaka childhood; her defiant marriage to the handsome but lackadaisical Bram Shipley; life on his dusty, ramshackle farm during the Depression with her two sons; and her partial responsibility for the death of her younger son.

The interweaving of past and present is part of a large pattern of contrasts, which are most marked in the duality of Hagar's character: she has tried to hold to the stony, puritanical pride of her Scots-Presbyterian ancestors while denying the life-loving, wild, spontaneous part of her nature that gives such vigour to her narrative. Like the stone angel marking her mother's tomb, she has been 'doubly blind' in all her human relations. Incorporating many biblical allusions, the novel offers a modern version of the archetypal quest for spiritual vision.

For articles on *The stone angel*, see *Margaret Laurence: an annotated bibliography* (1979) by Susan J. Warwick.

JOAN COLDWELL

Stratford, Philip. See TRANSLATIONS: ENGLISH TO FRENCH and TRANSLATIONS: FRENCH TO ENGLISH: 3.

Stratton, Allan. See DRAMA IN ENGLISH: 1953 TO 1981.

Strickland, Samuel. See Writing in ONTARIO: 1.

Stringer, Arthur (1874-1950). Arthur John Arbuthnott Stringer was born in Chatham, Ont. He studied at the University of Toronto (1892-4) and briefly at Oxford University before beginning a career in journalism and freelance writing, first with the Montreal *Herald* (1897-8) and then in New York, where he established himself as a capable producer of popular fiction and a minor but flamboyant figure on the fashionable literary scene. His first marriage was to actress Jobyna Howland, known as the original 'Gibson Girl'. In 1903 he bought a farm at Cedar Springs on the north shore of Lake Erie, where he lived intermittently for the next eighteen years, a period that included a brief, costly attempt at grain farming in Alberta around 1914. In 1921 he sold his Ontario farm and moved permanently to an acreage in New Jersey.

Stringer was as versatile as he was prolific. In addition to writing 15 volumes of undistinguished verse and non-fiction prose—including *A study of King Lear* (New York, 1897)—and more than 40 works of fiction, he wrote copiously for magazines and occasionally for the stage and, with the serial 'The Perils of Pauline', for Hollywood. His popularity was based mainly on a series of crime adventure novels, beginning with *The wire tappers* (1906), and on a series of wilderness adventures of the North (an area unfamiliar to Stringer), beginning with *Empty hands* (1924). He occasionally attempted psychological sophistication, as in *The wine of life* (1921), and has been hailed as an early realist; but generally he worked within the conventions of sentimental romance popular around the turn of the century.

Though Stringer used Canadian settings in a few of his novels, and Canadian characters in others, the bulk of his work belongs to American literature. One of his most popular books was *Lonely O'Malley* (1905), a sentimentalization of his boyhood in Chatham and London; but he made an enduring contribution to Canadian literature with his prairie trilogy: *Prairie wife* (1915), *Prairie mother* (1920), and *Prairie child* (1921). Stringer's narrator, a New England socialite married to a dour Scots-Canadian wheat farmer, develops gradually from the optimism typical of pioneering romances, through disillusionment as her marriage deteriorates, to mature resolve as she begins an independent life on the Prairies. His use of diary form (though the narrative ostensibly opens as a letter to a friend) anticipates Sinclair ROSS's AS FOR ME AND MY HOUSE and places Stringer's trilogy in the Canadian tradition of confessions of a refined sensibility confronting the crudeness of pioneer life. Stringer attempted unsuccessfully to combine the prairie setting with a crime adventure in *The mud lark* (1932).

See Victor Lauriston, *Arthur Stringer* (1941).

See also CRITICISM IN ENGLISH: 2.

DICK HARRISON

Such, Peter (b. 1939). Born in the east end of London, Eng., he emigrated in 1953 and completed his secondary schooling in Toronto before obtaining a B.A. and an M.A. in English from the University of Toronto. He has taught in high schools, colleges, and universities in Ontario and is now professor of humanities at York University, Toronto, and co-ordinator of Canadian Studies at Atkinson College. In 1971 he founded *Impulse*, a literary magazine devoted to contemporary Canadian writing, and between 1975 and 1977 was managing editor of *Books in Canada*. He was also one of the founders of the Canadian Periodical Publishers Association.

Such's first novel, *Fallout* (1969; rpr. 1978), grew out of his experience as a miner in the uranium mines near Elliot Lake while he was a student. Told in fragments, it is about the violent rape of the landscape in the search for ore—a rape that is mirrored in the violent lives of the Indians and white men caught up in the rush for the precious metal—and argues that exploitation of the land demands its price in exploitation of the native peoples. The climax occurs when a speeding convertible collides with a busload of Indian children returning from a baseball game. The novel's grimness is somewhat tempered by a lyrical love affair between one of the Indians and a young white woman. *Riverrun* (1973) is about the last days of the Beothuk people of Newfoundland, who were systematically wiped out by the white settlers, becoming extinct by 1829. Told convincingly from the point of view of the Beothuks as they make their last desperate stand for survival around a lake,

Such

having been driven from the sea's edge by the newcomers, it is a bitter epitaph for a people in tune with the riverrun, the annual migration of salmon and caribou, on which the Beothuks largely depended. *Dolphin's wake* (1979) is a thriller about an archaeologist and his wife who have spent many years in Greece. Arthur, a former member of the Greek underground during the Second World War, is drawn reluctantly into a group opposing the junta. His main concern is with the remote past and his impending retirement to England; but his wife Elizabeth finds renewed life in the remote Cretan village where the resistance movement is gathering, and leaves him to live with the leader. Although in this novel Such tried to escape what he calls 'the varnished-up rural past' of so much Canadian fiction, it is not as successful as his novels with a Canadian setting.

Such's other works include *Soundprints* (1972), a concise introduction to the work of six Canadian composers: John Weinzweig, Harry Somers, John Beckwith, Norma Beecroft, Walter Buczynski, and Murray Schaefer; *Vanished peoples* (1978), an anthropological history of Newfoundland's aboriginal peoples; and 'Home fires', a television series about a Toronto family during the Second World War.　　PETER BUITENHUIS

Suknaski, Andrew (b. 1942). Born on a small homestead near Wood Mountain, Sask., of a Polish mother and a Ukrainian father, he attended Simon Fraser University and the University of British Columbia; he also studied at the Kootenay School of Art and the Montreal Museum of Fine Arts School of Art and Design. He has worked at different jobs across the Prairies and in 1976 listed his occupation as 'migrant worker'; he was writer-in-residence at St John's College, University of Manitoba, in 1977-8. Though he has lived all over western Canada, his true home and centre remains Wood Mountain.

English was not Suknaski's first language, and the vocabulary of his poems contains a rich strain of Polish and Ukrainian, as well as many attempts to render an approximate transliteration of ethnic speech and pronunciation. Much of his early poetry, published in pamphlets by his own Elfin Plot Press, is visual in nature: concrete poems based on East Asian characters and on collage. His mature poetry appeared in the 1970s in several pamphlets and chapbooks, of which the most notable is *On first looking down from*

Lions Gate Bridge (1976). His full emergence as an important poetic voice in western Canada came with the publication of *Wood Mountain poems* (1976). He has published two other major collections, *The ghosts call you poor* (1978) and *In the name of Narid* (1981), as well as two chapbooks, *Octomi* (1976), a retelling of Indian legends, and *East of Myloona* (1979), which chronicles a visit to the Northwest Territories.

Suknaski's central subject has been the people and the heritage of Wood Mountain, and of the Prairies generally. He writes of the town's inhabitants, both present and past, of the various nationalities and generations of the settlers, and of the native peoples whose land it first was. (The historical association of Wood Mountain with Sitting Bull has been a recurrent topic.) Suknaski sees himself as a mythographer who honours his subjects, rather than as a historian who merely describes or analyses them. Like many prairie writers, he loves the tall tale, the beer-parlour story, and the accents of the voices that recount them. Because he tries to recreate on the printed page the vividness and variety of spoken narrative, his poems tend to be long and rambling, somewhat diffuse in form, their poetic effect depending upon the choice and juxtaposition of anecdotes, rather than upon particular lines or images. It is essentially a realist poetry that largely avoids metaphor and symbol. Suknaski's most recent work shows an ever-increasing concern with those ethnic groups that exist outside the mainstream of Canadian society. The historically based anecdotal style of his poetry, which employs the rhythms of the speaking voice, has become almost an orthodoxy among prairie poets, and Suknaski himself—with his beard, pipe, and coil of sweetgrass—has become a presiding shaman of prairie culture.

The National Film Board of Canada has produced an excellent documentary film on Suknaski and his work, *Wood Mountain Poems* (1978), directed by Harvey Spak.

See also POETRY IN ENGLISH 1950 TO 1982: 3.　　STEPHEN SCOBIE

Sullivan, Alan (1868-1947). Born in Montreal, he spent his childhood in his father's Anglican rectories in Chicago, Montreal, and Sault Ste Marie, and attended the British public school of Loretto in Scotland. After studying civil engineering for a year at the University of Toronto (1886-7), he began a career in northern Ontario that included surveying and construction for the CPR, lumbering, industrial engineering, gold mining, and prospecting. In 1904 he settled in Toronto with his wife, Bessie Hees, and began to raise his large family. In the 1890s he had published two books of poems, and numerous short stories appeared in *Scribner's*, *Harper's*, and *The Canadian Magazine*. The publication of his short-story collection, *The passing of Oul-I-But, and other tales* (1913), marked the beginning of his full-time career as a writer. A stint with the RAF during the First World War resulted in *Aviation in Canada: 1917-18* (1919). In 1920 Sullivan moved to England, where he lived—making numerous extended trips to Canada—until his death.

Of Sullivan's 43 works of fiction, about two dozen are lightweight novels of romance, mystery, and adventure set mainly in England, some published under the pseudonym 'Sinclair Murray'. Three of these—*Human clay* (1926), *In the beginning* (1926), and *A little way ahead* (1930)—deal with the paranormal. Sullivan wrote best, however, of the testing of manhood and the forging of a nation in the rugged Canadian landscape. Often his heroes discover their identity when they leave the Old Country for Canada, as in *Blantyre—alien* (1914), *The splendid silence* (1927), *Whispering lodge* (1927), and *The golden foundling* (1931). Sullivan's industrial experience and belief in the value of labour form the basis of *The rapids* (1920), a fictionalized account of the industrialization of Sault Ste Marie, and *The inner door* (1917) and *The crucible* (1925). The Canadian Arctic provides a striking setting for *The magic makers* (1930) and *With love from Rachel* (1938). Sullivan's love of the North and its native peoples is a major theme in his short-story collections, *Under the northern lights* (1926) and *The cycle of the North* (1938), and in four books for children. Perhaps his most impressive works are his historical novels, with their vivid detail and mixture of real and fictional characters. *The great divide* (1935) depicts the building of the CPR; *The fur masters* (1938) concerns the rivalry among trading companies in the early nineteenth century; *Three came to Ville Marie* (1941), winner of a Governor General's Award, is set in seventeenth-century Montreal; and *Cariboo Road* (1946) is the story of prospectors who joined the Fraser Valley Gold Rush in 1862.

In his heyday as a writer Sullivan was widely read and reviewed. Several of his novels, including *The rapids* and *The great*

divide, were made into films; the latter received a glittering première in England as *The great barrier* (1937).   JEAN O'GRADY

Sunshine sketches of a little town (1912). This has remained the most popular of Stephen LEACOCK's books. Set in Mariposa, a typical small Ontario town, it was closely based on Orillia, where Leacock had his summer home, and caused great offence to the townspeople. The 'sketches' are dominated by Josh Smith, a hotel keeper who becomes Mariposa's member of parliament. The Mariposans believe that Smith is a hero and benefactor, but he is in fact a ruthless individualist who sees through, and plays upon, the townspeople's desire for importance and sophistication. The tone of the book, however, is one of gentle irony; there are no real villains, not even Josh Smith, and Leacock shows genuine affection in his portrayal of the foolish but good-natured Mariposans, such as the barber-financier Jefferson Thorpe, the 'enchanted' lovers Peter Pupkin and Zena Pepperleigh, the 'mugwump' minister Dean Drove, and, not least, the naïve narrator, with his 'eye of discernment'. The final chapter, 'L'envoi', is a moving evocation of the vanishing world of small-town Ontario. Underlying the book's genuine affection and sympathy, however, is serious criticism of the Mariposans' foolish desire to become part of the big urban world of material success, and of their failure to realize that there is no place in such a world for the social continuity and genuine fellow-feeling that Mariposa, for all its limitations, fosters. *Sunshine sketches* has been reprinted in the New Canadian Library (1960).

See also ARCADIAN ADVENTURES WITH THE IDLE RICH.   ZAILIG POLLOCK

Survenant, Le. See Germaine GUÈVREMONT.

Survival: a thematic guide to Canadian literature (1972). This widely read critical work by Margaret ATWOOD was written on the premise that an inductive study of the collective literary imagination, and of the key patterns that constitute the shape of Canadian literature, can afford clues to the national consciousness. The book's thesis—that every culture has a central symbol that functions like a code of beliefs—derives from a theory proposed by Northrop FRYE, who suggests that 'in every culture there is a structure of ideas, images, beliefs . . . which express the view of man's situation and destiny generally held at the time' (*The modern century*, 1967). According to Atwood, the central image of Canadian culture is that of a collective victim struggling for survival—an image that is the legacy of both a hostile natural environment and a colonial history. As a consequence the national psychology is fatalistic, the expression of a victim mentality.

There is considerable polemical anger in Atwood's assertion that Canadians have a will to lose, and that Canadian culture is characterized by a failure of nerve (one chooses to be a victim to avoid the responsibility of self-definition). In a series of chapters exploring archetypal images in Canadian literature—nature as monster, animals as victims, Indians as persecuted, the artist as paralysed, woman as ice maiden or absent Venus—Atwood describes Canadian writers as living in an unknown territory, as exiles in their own country. The literature becomes a diagram of what is *not* desired. Diagnosis, however, provides a first step towards change.

Survival is written with intelligence, wit, and considerable audacity. If Atwood simplifies, it is to goad her reader into attention. The book is partly a political manifesto written in protest against the neglect of Canadian culture in Canada and fell on the ears of its Canadian audience like a call to order, at a time when the realization was dawning that a Canadian literature indeed existed. Perhaps more than any other work, it helped galvanize the flurry of energy that characterized Canadian writing in the 1970s.

For discussions of *Survival* see 'Margaret Atwood: a symposium', *The* MALAHAT REVIEW 41 (Jan. 1977).

See also CRITICISM IN ENGLISH: 5(d).

ROSEMARY SULLIVAN

Sutherland, John (1919-56). Born in Liverpool, N.S., he attended Queen's University, Kingston (1936-7), where he developed tuberculosis of the kidney after an athletic injury. He was confined to bed in the family home in Saint John, N.B., until 1941, when, against doctor's orders, he enrolled at McGill University, Montreal, though he left several months later. In Sept. 1942, after his poems had been rejected by the Montreal magazine PREVIEW, he founded FIRST STATEMENT, with the help of Audrey Aikman (whom he married) and other McGill undergraduates. The next year Irving LAYTON

and Louis DUDEK became members of the editorial board and joined Sutherland in pursuit of a Canadian realism that would express the local and particular in simple language. In 1943 Sutherland acquired a printing press and in 1945, under the imprint of First Statement Press, he made an impact with a series of important chapbooks, the first of which was Layton's *Here and now*. In late 1945 *First Statement* merged with *Preview* to form NORTHERN REVIEW, with Sutherland as managing editor.

In response to A.J.M. SMITH's *The book of Canadian poetry: a critical and historical anthology* (1943), Sutherland edited *Other Canadians: an anthology of the new poetry in Canada, 1940-46* (1947), in the introduction to which he vigorously attacked Smith's literary views, notably his use of the categories 'native' and 'cosmopolitan', and emphasized the need for Canadian poetry that was North American in perspective and technique. His hostile criticism (in *Northern Review*, Aug.-Sept. 1947) of Robert FINCH's *Poems*, which had won a Governor General's Award, led to the departure of the *Preview* poets from *Northern Review*'s editorial board. A year later Layton resigned. (Dudek had previously left to pursue studies in New York.) Sutherland continued to edit the magazine almost single-handedly, supporting himself by odd jobs, but his literary interests took on a conservative slant, culminating in the article, 'The past decade in Canadian poetry' (Dec. 1950-Jan. 1951). Here he turned his back on many of his former literary ideals, including the importance of vitality and a kind of Nietzschean spiritual health in poetry. He continued to publish *Northern Review* until his death in Sept. 1956. Sutherland returned in his literary philosophy to the views of his early *First Statement* days, but the emphasis on spiritual health was now more religious than Nietzschean because of an earlier conversion to Roman Catholicism. *The poetry of E.J. Pratt: a new interpretation* (1956), Sutherland's study of his favourite poet, reflects his Roman Catholic beliefs to an extent that does not benefit his criticism of Pratt's poetry.

A selection of Sutherland's writings, together with a memoir by the editor, Miriam WADDINGTON, is available in *John Sutherland: essays, controversies and poems* (NCL, 1972). Waddington underlines Sutherland's strength as a textual critic and rightly argues that his frequently personal poetry has been underrated. Louis Dudek and Michael

Gnarowski place Sutherland prominently in the development of Canadian modernism in their introduction to *The making of modern poetry in Canada* (1967); and Neil H. Fisher offers an informative and reliable analysis of Sutherland as editor in *First Statement 1942-1945: an assessment and an index* (1974).

DAVID O'ROURKE

Sutherland, Ronald (b. 1933). Born in the east end of Montreal, he was educated at McGill University (B.A., 1954; M.A., 1955) and Wayne State University (Ph.D., 1960). He has taught at the Université de Sherbrooke since 1959, heading the English department from 1962 to 1974 and founding its graduate program in comparative Canadian literature in 1963. He is the author of three books of criticism—*Frederick Philip Grove* (1969), *Second image* (1971), and *The new hero* (1977)—and two novels: *Snow lark* (1971) and *Where do the MacDonalds bury their dead?* (1976).

With the exception of his first book, Sutherland's criticism is principally concerned with themes common to novels by French- and English-speaking Canadian writers of this century. It is sustained by a theory fully expressed in 'The mainstream', a chapter in *The new hero*: Canadian literature, properly speaking, provides imaginative expression of the interaction between the French and English founding cultures of Canada. In *Second image* he groups Canadian fiction according to three interlocking themes: the land and the divine order; the breakup of the old order; and the search for vital truth. Sutherland convincingly demonstrates the affinities that link writers as diverse as GROVE, Ringuet (Philippe PANNETON), W.O. MITCHELL, Gabrielle ROY, Hubert AQUIN, Jean SIMARD, and others, showing how these authors, though writing in isolation from each other, have expressed a common sensibility informed by a shared attitude towards the land, religion, and the self.

Sutherland's theory—rooted in a generous, sensitive vision of modern Canada from a specific Québec vantage-point—is manifested in his fiction. *Snow lark*, the story of Suzanne MacDonald, offspring of a French-English marriage who grows up in Montreal's east end, dramatizes the two cultures as they act upon an individual's search for self-knowledge and happiness. Suzanne's reconciliation of the claims of mixed ancestry is emblematic of the emergence of modern Canada. While *Snow lark* is set in Montreal, *Where do the MacDonalds bury their dead?* traces its protagonists' search for self from Québec to Michigan, California, and Mexico. Ti-Mac, Suzanne's cousin, eventually returns home, a wiser person through his exposure to cultural diversity. The two novels are interrelated by characterization and theme, and by the world-view that frames Sutherland's two principal books of criticism: the articulation of the Canadian identity lies in the recognition of its bilingual and bicultural nature.

An indication of Sutherland's influence as a teacher, and of his scholarly and creative work, is his highly successful program in comparative Canadian literature at the Université de Sherbrooke, graduates of which are currently teaching in a number of Canadian universities and are widely published.

See also CRITICISM IN ENGLISH: 5(c).

MAX DORSINVILLE

Sylvestre, Guy. See ANTHOLOGIES IN FRENCH: 1.

Symons, Scott (b. 1933). Hugh Brennan Scott Symons was born in Toronto into a highly respected Rosedale family of distinguished Loyalist ancestry; he was educated at Trinity College School, Port Hope, Ont.; Trinity College, University of Toronto; King's College, Cambridge; and the Sorbonne. In 1965, when he was married with a son, curator of the Canadiana collection at the Royal Ontario Museum, and assistant professor of fine arts at the University of Toronto, he left wife, home, and job to live in Montreal and write his first novel, *Place d'Armes*. The respectable ancestry, education, and career concealed a life-long rebellion. Bisexual from his schooldays, he was frequently at odds with parents, teachers, and institutions, and often seethed at what he believed to be the betrayal of his country by the 'Blandmen'—the Liberal politicians and businessmen, satellites of Mackenzie King. *Place d'Armes: a personal narrative* (1967; rpr. 1978), which takes the form of a combat journal, contains five different typefaces and two narrators, both closely modelled on Symons himself. It is by turns lyrical, bathetic, inspiring, and banal. Chiefly about the discovery of the self through the body's encounter with another man, it also concerns the discovery of French-Canadian culture through a sensuous experience of architecture and artifacts. An energetic, if confusing, work, it attacks modern advertising and what Symons sees as the accelerating destruction of both English and French traditions in Canada.

Civic Square (1969) is a huge, chaotic work that was boxed, not bound, because Symons would not reduce the 848 typewritten pages to conventional book length. Symons decorated each container—which resembles the blue box used by Birks, a fashionable Toronto store—with red felt-pen pictures of birds, flowers, and phalli as his personal present to DR, the imaginary Dear Reader to whom the book is addressed. *Civic Square* is not only a blistering attack on the 'Blandmen' who run Toronto's politics, education, and finance, but also a lyrical appreciation of the natural beauty of the Ontario countryside. It is repetitive, dislocated and, once again, full of high energy.

After completing *Civic Square*, Symons went to Mexico with a young male lover, whose parents sent the Federales after them. A series of flights, escapes, and hardships followed: *Place d'Armes* had been savagely reviewed; Symons' marriage was ending in divorce; his family would neither speak to him nor of him. He was awarded the Beta Sigma Phi Best First Canadian Novel Award for *Place d'Armes*, however, and Symons has claimed that this prevented his suicide. He returned to Canada and lived for a time in northern British Columbia and Newfoundland. He was then commissioned to write a coffee-table book on Canadian furniture. This led to more travel and research and the publication of *Heritage—a romantic look at early Canadian furniture* (1972), with photographs by John de Visser. Filled with passion, knowledge, and taste—Symons calls it his 'furniture novel'—the book transforms the furniture and artifacts into characters who speak in a variety of authentic accents about Canada's past, and the Western tradition from which they sprang.

There followed more travel in Europe, and a decisive stay in Morocco, where Symons began work on a trilogy-in-progress to be called *Helmet of flesh*, in which the hortatory style of his previous work gives way to narrative and celebration. Excerpts have appeared in CANADIAN FICTION MAGAZINE (Spring/Summer 1977).

Recognition has come slowly to Symons, mostly through his books, but partly through his controversial journalism, first in Montreal's *La Presse*, and more recently in the Toronto *Globe and Mail*. His fierce article on the female domination of CanLit in *West Coast Review* (Jan. 1977) raised many hackles. In his passion and hyperbole there are echoes of D.H. Lawrence; in his lyricism and intensity, of Malcolm LOWRY; in his elegance and opulence, of Henry James—probably his three major influences. But Symons has steadily gained control over an ebullient prose style. During 1976 he served as Canada Council writer-in-residence at Simon Fraser University.

Charles Taylor has written a fine study of his life and writings in *Six journeys: a Canadian pattern* (1977). PETER BUITENHUIS

Szumigalski, Anne (b. 1926). Born in London, Eng., she was educated privately in languages and literature and came to Canada in 1951. She has worked as an interpreter, a translator, a poetry teacher in the Saskatchewan Summer School of Arts (1966-79), and as an editor of the Saskatchewan Writer's Guild publication *Freelance* (1968-72) and the literary quarterly *Grain* (1970-8). She was co-founder and first chairman of the Saskatchewan Writers' Colony (1978). Her awards include the Saskatchewan Poetry Award (1977) and the Okanagan Short Story Award (1978).

Szumigalski's poetry first came to the attention of a national audience when it appeared in Dorothy LIVESAY's anthology *40 women poets in Canada* (1971). Her poems in *Woman reading in bath* (1974), *A game of angels* (1980), *Doctrine of signatures* (1983), and *Risks* (1983) draw their subject matter from ordinary, often insignificant events and transform those moments, through surrealistic associations, into archetypal experience.

Szumigalski co-edited the anthology *The best of Grain: volumes I-VII* (1980), with Caroline Heath and Don Kerr, and *A blue streak in a dry year* (1981), an anthology of poetry by young people. She co-authored with Terrence Heath and Eleanor Pearson *BOooOm* (1973), a book about poetry-writing for children. Other collaborations include a verse drama about the surveying of the South-Saskatchewan badlands, *Wild Man's Butte* (1979), with Terrence Heath, with whom she has written five long poems for voices that were produced for CBC Radio.

See also POETRY IN ENGLISH 1950 TO 1982: 3. BRUCE MEYER

T

Taché, Joseph-Charles (1820-94). Born in Kamouraska, Lower Canada (Qué.), he was educated at the Séminaire de Québec, where he earned his medical diploma. He practised medicine in Rimouski, which he represented in the legislative assembly from 1847 to 1857. A staunch Conservative, he remained active in politics as founding editor of *Le Courrier du Canada* and as deputy minister of agriculture; he twice represented Canada at events in Paris—in 1855, when he was made a member of the Légion d'honneur, and in 1867. His political journalism includes denunciations of anti-clericals (especially Benjamin Sulte), concern for prison reform, promotion of francophone immigration to Canada, and expansion in the Northwest. (His younger brother, Alexandre-Antonin Taché, was the first bishop of Saint-Boniface and author of *Esquisse sur le Nord-Ouest*, 1869.) Notable among Taché's non-fiction works are *Esquisse sur le Canada, considéré sous le point de vue économique* (Paris, 1855) and *Des Provinces de l'Amérique du Nord et d'une union fédérale* (Québec, 1858). Writing on cultural topics, he occasionally shared with Hubert LA RUE the pseudonym 'Isidore Mesplats'.

Taché was an early collector and interpreter of French-Canadian oral legends and folk types. The fiction he created from this material, despite its clumsy didacticism, was the liveliest and most indigenous of the 1860 school. One of the founders of the École patriotique de Québec and *Les* SOIRÉES CANADIENNES (1861), which first published his major literary works, he was responsible—with La Rue, AUBERT DE GASPÉ, and H.-R. CASGRAIN—for the strong bias towards folk-tales in the new national literature. His belief that storytelling was a vital link between a people and its land and cultural values was well in advance of his time. *Trois légendes de mon pays* (Québec, 1861) demonstrates this principle by arranging each of three traditional tales in a narrative framework meant to recreate the atmosphere of oral storytelling. The stories—set in places now called Bic island, Grand Sault (N.B.), and the Méchin islands—demonstrate exemplary moments in the progress from barbarism to Christianity. *Forestiers et voyageurs* (Québec, 1863) is an episodic narrative combining traditional and invented tales. The author-narrator makes a journey from Rimouski to a lumber camp where—apart from an authorial chapter explaining life on the major working rivers—the narration is taken over by Père Michel, a roguish storyteller, who as a youth fled the law by the traditional method of becoming a *voyageur*. Thus Taché launched one of the three literary figures of his time, alongside the *seigneur* and the *défricheur* (settler). Père Michel's story has an edifying Catholic conclusion; but the taste for fun, inherent in this folk material, is not lost. Taché also supplies a striking but incomplete socio-economic portrait of the forest industry.

Les Sablons (L'Île de Sable et l'Île Saint-Barnabé) (Québec, 1885) combines Taché's last attempt to fuse topography and folklore. Sable Island (which he had considered as a possible site for a penal colony) was practically uninhabited, but memories of past expeditions and a few ghost stories (some adapted from T.C. HALIBURTON) constituted for Taché a strong Breton and French-Canadian presence on the island. Saint-Barnabé, in the Gulf of St Lawrence, is also endowed with ghostly presence owing to its fogs and notable shipwrecks. Two stories, 'Le braillard de la montagne' (1864) and 'La légende du Lac Caché' (1889), were both published in *Le Courrier du Canada*. The first is a ghost story in verse, set on the site of the present Citadel in Quebec City. The second, a fishing story that explains the name of a lake northeast of Quebec, is pleasantly free of Taché's habitual moralizing.

Although six volumes of Taché's non-fiction works have been translated, only one adaptation of his fiction appears in English: *The isle of the massacre* (1901), translated by W.C. Wood.   JACK WARWICK

Tallman, Warren. See CRITICISM IN ENGLISH: 5(d).

Talonbooks. One of the most important and experimental Canadian small publishers, Talonbooks arose out of the little magazine *Talon* (1963-8), published in Vancouver, where Talonbooks itself was founded by David Robinson in 1967. Its active participants have been David Robinson and Karl Siegler, who now run it; Gordon

781

Talonbooks

Fidler; and Peter Hay, who founded and still edits the drama list that has made Talonbooks the most important publisher of plays in Canada. Its present drama list of some 60 titles includes both English- and French-Canadian, and some American, playwrights. In fiction, as in poetry, Talonbooks has tended to be more restricted to west-coast authors, though it has recently published translations of novels by Marie-Claire BLAIS and Michel TREMBLAY. In non-fiction its most important achievement is probably *The Salish people* (1978), a four-volume edition, edited by Ralph Maud, of the writings of the unjustly neglected maverick anthropologist Charles Hill-Tout.

GEORGE WOODCOCK

Tamarack Review, The (1956-82). This literary quarterly devoted to stories, poems, essays, and reviews by new and established Canadian writers was conceived by Robert WEAVER at a time when John SUTHERLAND's NORTHERN REVIEW was about to cease publication. Weaver enlisted as co-editors Kildare DOBBS, Millar MacLure, Ivon Owen, William Toye, and Anne WILKINSON. The editorial board was later altered by the death of Wilkinson, by resignations (Weaver and Toye remained editors to the end), and by the addition of Patricia Owen, John Robert COLOMBO, and Janis Rapoport as co-editors. *Tamarack* was founded in Toronto when a new generation of now-prominent writers was just beginning to publish, and before the onset of Canadian nationalism, when Canadian literature was of slight general interest. Produced in a handsome format—with covers by graphic designers that included Theo Dimson, Allan Fleming, Fred Huffman, Frank Newfeld, and Toye—it attempted to maintain a standard of literary excellence, without regional or ideological emphases, and published early, and sometimes the first, work by Timothy FINDLEY and Jay MACPHERSON (both of whom appeared in the first issue), Dave GODFREY, Hugh HOOD, Alice MUNRO, Mordecai RICHLER, and others. Dependent on volunteer editorial services and precarious financial support (much of it provided by the Canada Council and the Ontario Arts Council), *Tamarack* did not realize its aims consistently. But for 25 years it was the most respected literary magazine in English Canada.

WILLIAM TOYE

Tardivel, Jules-Paul. See ESSAYS IN FRENCH: 2 and POUR LA PATRIE.

Tecumseh. See INDIAN LITERATURE: 1.

Thériault, Yves (1915-83). Only son of Alcide Thériault, an Acadian of partly Montagnais Indian ancestry, and Aurore Nadeau, he was born in Quebec City and from the age of seven was able, he claims, to speak the Cree dialect taught him by his father. He received his primary and secondary education in Montreal, but quit school at fifteen to work at a host of odd jobs. A lung ailment sent him for a year and a half (1934-5) to the sanatorium at Lac-Édouard in the Lac Saint-Jean region. After working as a radio announcer and radio script-writer in several Québec cities, and as a tractor salesman, he published his first short story in *Le Jour* in 1941. In 1942 he married Michelle-Germaine Blanchet, the mother of his two children, and soon after became a public-relations officer and script-writer for the National Film Board.

From 1945 to 1950, while working as a script-writer for Radio-Canada, Thériault published anonymously, or under pseudonyms, an enormous quantity of 'ten-cent novels' (32 pages); at one point he was producing eleven (and his wife three) a week. In 1950 the French government awarded him a scholarship that he was obliged to refuse because of pressure of work. In 1952, however, he travelled around the world aboard an Italian freighter, and lived for several years in Italy. Thériault was elected to the Royal Society of Canada in 1959. In 1965 he was elected president of the Société des Écrivains Canadiens, but resigned shortly thereafter and spent two years (1965-7) as cultural director for the Department of Indian and Northern Affairs in Ottawa. A period of increasing personal difficulties, compounded by health problems, persuaded him to leave Ottawa, and in 1968 he purchased a small farm at Saint-Denis-sur-Richelieu, Qué. In June 1970 Thériault suffered a cerebral thrombosis that left him paralysed and unable to speak, write, or talk. After a prolonged convalescence he resumed his career, becoming co-director in 1977 of a film company with his companion Lorraine Boisvenue. He received one of the Molson Prizes for 1970, a Canada Council scholarship for established writers in 1978, and the Prix David in 1979. He lived at Rawdon, a village in the Laurentians west of Joliette, Qué.

Thériault is the most prolific and versatile of contemporary Québec writers. The quantity, quality, and variety of his writing have assured his popularity with the reading public in Canada; translations of *Agaguk* (1958) have made him known abroad; and he is widely studied in the CEGEPs and universities of Québec. Largely self-taught, animated by driving dynamism, bohemian restlessness, and a passion for liberty that caused him to revolt against conformism and convention, Thériault soon acquired vast experience of the seamier and more violent sides of life that are reflected in the forty books he has published since *Contes pour un homme seul* (1944). These unusual, captivating, and brutal stories (twelve of which had appeared in *Le Jour*) announced the themes that he would later develop: naturalism, primitivism, exoticism, eroticism, and sublimated sexuality struggling for expression. Basic human instincts and passions, in conflict with the forces of tradition and repression, are the occasion for biting criticism of our civilization and of French-Canadian society in particular. Procreation, mutilation, and death assume special significance as his characters search desperately for individuality: Indians, Eskimos, Jews, immigrants, peasants—'little people'—all battle against the forces of moral, religious, social, economic, or ethnic domination. They inhabit the forests and tundra of the Far North, or anywhere and nowhere, such as the isolated mountain village of his first novel, *La fille laide* (1950), which concerns a hired hand who commits a murder so that he and an ugly servant girl may gain possession of their employer's farm.

In 1951 Thériault published three novels: *La vengeance de la mer*, a melodrama in which a young 'prodigal son' from Gaspé escapes calamity by returning to his sick mother's bedside; *Le dompteur d'ours*, about a muscular vagabond who unleashes among the women of a remote mountain hamlet a frenzy of pent-up sexual frustrations; and *Les vendeurs du temple*, a somewhat exaggerated political and religious satire on greed in rural Québec. *Aaron* (1954), which won the Prix de la Province de Québec, is the story of a young orthodox Jew who rejects his strict upbringing by his grandfather, Moishe, and becomes assimilated into the English-speaking business community of Montreal. The old man, his dreams shattered, awaits death in loneliness and desolation.

With the publication in 1958 of *Agaguk* (winner of the Prix de la Province de Québec and the Prix France-Canada), Thériault achieved international recognition. This almost epic evocation of love and

fatherhood among the Inuit of the Canadian North has been translated into numerous languages (into English by Miriam Chapin, 1967). Agaguk's evolution towards maturity is the mainspring of the action and of the various conflicts he has with the whites, his own tribe, his father, and the harsh realities of the vast and hostile tundra. The gradual civilizing of Agaguk is the work of Iriook, his wife, who twice saves her husband's life. The crux of the novel occurs when Iriook—opposing the merciless Eskimo tradition—demands at gunpoint that Agaguk spare the life of the daughter she has borne him. She then convinces Agaguk to accept his daughter and the risks and responsibilities that this decision involves. *Ashini* (1960; translated by Gwendolyn Moore, 1972), which won the Prix France-Canada and a Governor General's Award, is not so much a novel as a lyric poem to the glory of the Montagnais, despite Ashini's suicide, for Indian myths are evoked with great beauty. Thériault ranked this book, which is a plea for justice as well as a work of art, as one of his best.

In *Amour au goût de mer* (1961) a Sicilian immigrant couple succumbs to the misery, sickness, and despair of their lonely life in Montreal. Among other themes, Thériault here criticizes French-Canadian xenophobia. *Cul-de-sac* (1961) is the story of the gradual disintegration of an engineer in his fifties, who, after a series of mishaps and suffering from ill health, decides to hasten his doom by drowning himself in drink. *Les commettants de Caridad* (1961) is set in a mountain hamlet in Andalusia—a former paradise that is altered through human pride and foolhardiness. Structurally and symbolically more complicated than many of Thériault's other novels, it was considered by him to be one of his major works.

Experimenting with new techniques, Thériault published *Si la bombe m'était contée* (1962) in which he examines the frightening subject of the atomic bomb and its effects. Another experimental novel, *Le grand roman d'un petit homme* (1963), met with relatively little success. He returned to the primitivistic vein with *Le ru d'Ikoué* (1963), a sort of prose poem that recounts how a young Algonkin Indian lad growing up in the forest falls in love with a stream, and how this symbolic mistress tactfully guides him towards manhood. This work maintains a delicate balance between primitive savagery and poetic sensitivity. In *Les temps du carcajou* (1965) violence and the obsession with degradation and destruction know no bounds. Bruno Juchereau, the surly captain of a schooner, has his unfaithful mistress gang-raped, in an orgy of sex and horror, during a fierce storm in the Gulf of St Lawrence. Filled with hatred, vengeance, and grotesque eroticism, the novel marks the antipode of *Agaguk*; its very excesses prevent the characters from coming to life. Another sadistic and violent novel, *L'appelante* (1967), also has revenge as its theme.

In 1968 Thériault accomplished the prodigious feat of publishing six books, including four novels: *La mort d'eau*, about uprooted Madelinots searching for love in Montreal; *Kesten* and *Mahigan*, two mythological tales pitting man against beast; and *N'Tsuk* (translated by Gwendolyn Moore, 1972). *N'Tsuk* has often been compared to *Ashini* because both books are written in highly poetic language and the main characters in both are critical of modern society. The next year, as well as adapting to novel form a film by Denis Héroux, *Valérie* (1969), Thériault published *Antoine et sa montagne* (1969), a novel set in a small village on the Richelieu River in 1835 that some critics have seen as an allegory of the contemporary French-Canadian situation; and *Tayaout, fils d'Agaguk* (1969). This novel resurrects many of the characters in *Agaguk*, although immense changes in traditional Inuit society during the eleven years separating the two novels prompted Thériault to portray a world in which no compromise between the ancient and the modern seems possible, nor any hope for the future. *Le dernier havre* (1970) concerns an eighty-year-old Gaspé fisherman, consumed with the meaninglessness of his existence, who chooses death with honour and goes down with his boat in the Gulf. More than any other of Thériault's heroes, the old man dies reconciled with life, and, more importantly, with himself.

The characters in Thériault's next novel, *La Passe-au-Crachin* (1972)—a tale about a man's inability to communicate and the loneliness, boredom, and revolt of his wife—are not extraordinary heroes but people with human weaknesses. Through tragedy the couple learn to face the future on the basis of an imperfect, albeit workable, compromise. *Le haut pays* (1973) is a disappointing and irritating narrative that vacillates between science-fiction and pseudo-religious mysticism. In sharp contrast *Agoak, l'héritage d'Agaguk* (1975; *Agoak*, 1979) argues that a civilized man 'is something which

doesn't exist'. Society's superficial veneer is constantly threatened by 'the relative proximity of primitivism' as exemplified by the assimilated Eskimo Agoak, who rapidly reverts to bloodthirsty savagery when American tourists rape his wife. Attempting to rationalize his barbarous actions (he slashes the tourists with a hunting knife and then castrates them), Agoak cites the American massacres in Viet Nam and claims that all men are descended from savages. Strikingly different is *Moi, Pierre Huneau* (1976), one of Thériault's most successful novels, in which the narrator, a former Gaspé fisherman nearly ninety years old, is compelled—like Coleridge's Ancient Mariner—to recount the tragedy that shattered his existence. Almost illiterate, but expressing a simple and sincere humanity, he relates his life story in a folksy and colourful jargon all his own.

The first novel published after Thériault's recovery in the 1970s was *La quête de l'ourse* (1980). At 384 pages his most massive work, it is a diffuse narrative that nevertheless forms part of the primitivistic northern cycle begun with *Agaguk* and *Ashini* and allows Thériault to exploit anew almost all the major themes already familiar in his earlier work. The raconteur's incantatory style is effective and the book provides a rich synthesis of the high points in Thériault's long career as a novelist. *Le partage de minuit* (1980) adds little to the author's reputation. Its social criticism—the events suggest the Duplessis era—and its denunciation of hypocrisy in dealing with homosexuality, are vitiated by a simplistic psychoanalytic approach, extensive reliance on eroticism to sustain interest, too much similarity between the main character and Victor Debreux, protagonist of the 1961 novel *Cul-de-sac*, and structural deficiencies that suggest haste or negligence in composition.

Thériault's collections of short stories include *Le vendeur d'étoiles et autres contes* (1961), for which he was awarded the Prix Mgr Camille Roy; *La rose de pierre* (1964), nine stories dealing with various aspects of love, some of which reflect a strange and explosive violence; *L'île introuvable* (1968), a collection of eighteen tales that reflect all the main themes and tendencies of Thériault's fiction; *Oeuvre de chair* (1975), which contains sixteen titillating tales, illustrated with explicit drawings by Louisa Nicol, based on the premise that sexual enjoyment is enhanced by the pleasures of the palate, and organized around recipes savoured in the course of amorous encounters; *L'étreinte de*

Vénus (1981), a collection of eighteen carefully crafted detective stories that reveal another significant and previously unsuspected facet of Thériault's talent; *La femme Anna et autres contes* (1981); and *Valère et le grand canot* (1981). These last two volumes—totalling over 600 pages and edited and prefaced by Victor-Lévy BEAULIEU—exemplify Thériault's preference for the short story. (Over a forty-year period he has written more than a thousand stories, most of which are still unpublished.) Here the raconteur's gift of the gab, which in longer works sometimes runs away with him, is held admirably in check by the restrictions of the short-story form: the crisp and incisive introductions present situations that frequently approach the crisis point; the setting and background are summed up in a few terse phrases; the characters, succinctly delineated, are plunged into the heart of the action; and the endings, though sometimes moralizing, are often startling and original.

Thériault's massive output also includes *Roi de la côte nord* (1960), the extraordinary life of Napoléon-Alexandre Comeau; *Séjour à Moscou* (1961), an essay; *Textes et documents* (1969); and, by his own count, more than 1,300 radio and television scripts. Only four of his plays are available in print: *Le samaritain* (1958; *Écrits du Canada français*, vol. 4), which won first prize in the Radio-Canada drama competition for 1952; *Le marcheur* (1950); and *Frédange* and *Les terres neuves* (1970), two-act dramas published in a single volume. Thériault is also the author of twenty-three science-fiction or adventure stories for children and adolescents (see CHILDREN'S LITERATURE IN FRENCH: 2 and 3), published between 1959 and 1969. Since 1979 he has published for young people *Cajetan et la taupe* (1979), *Les aventures d'Ori d'Or* (1979), *Popok, le petit Esquimau* (1980), *Kuanuten (Vent d'est)* (1981), and *L'or de la felouque* (1981).

In the decade between 1972 and 1982 fifteen re-editions of Thériault's earlier works appeared, eight of them—including *Aaron, Agaguk*, and *Ashini*—in 1980. Despite ill health, Thériault in this period published nine new books for adults. He has quite rightly been criticized for writing hastily and carelessly, but it is at present premature to attempt a definitive assessment of his ultimate merit as a writer. His recent short stories have added a whole new dimension to an already phenomenal career· In any case, to paraphrase Victor-Lévy Beaulieu, it is already fitting for readers of Québec

literature to 'salute a giant'.

See Gérard BESSETTE, *Une littérature en ébullition* (1968); Maurice Emond, *Yves Thériault et le combat de l'homme* (1973); and Yves Thériault, *Textes et documents* (1969).

See also NOVELS IN FRENCH 1940 TO 1959: 5; 1960 TO 1982: 3(c), and SCIENCE FICTION AND FANTASY IN ENGLISH AND FRENCH: 3.

L.W. KEFFER

Thério, Adrien. See NOVELS IN FRENCH 1960 TO 1982: 3(b).

Thomas, Audrey (b. 1935). Audrey Grace Callahan was born in Binghamton, N.Y., and educated at Smith College, with a year at St Andrews University, Scot. After teaching for a year in England, she married Ian Thomas in 1958; the couple immigrated to Canada in 1959. She received an M.A. in English (1963) from the University of British Columbia and did further work there, on Anglo-Saxon language and literature, towards a Ph.D. that was not awarded. The years 1964-6 were spent in Ghana, where her husband taught at the University of Science and Technology in Kumasi. Much of her fiction recalls her life in Africa; the foreignness of the land and its customs provides a metaphor for emotional alienation, the threat and challenge of the unknown, and exploration of the dark side of the self.

After her return to Vancouver, Thomas published her first collection of stories, *Ten green bottles* (1967), in the same year that the youngest of her three daughters was born. The lead story, 'If one green bottle', is based on the author's confinement and eventual miscarriage in a Ghanaian hospital. The sense of futility and shame accompanying this six-month-long experience haunts the narrator of *Mrs. Blood* (1970), a novel that expands the material of the story into a moving characterization of a woman so distressed by her condition that she sees herself as a nameless, fragmented being, speaking sometimes as the fearful, self-conscious, acted-upon 'Mrs. Thing', sometimes as the guilt-ridden bundle of memories and poetic visions, 'Mrs. Blood', wracked by physical and psychic forces she cannot control. *Mrs. Blood* was published in France as *Du sang* (1972).

In 1969 Thomas found the cabin on Galiano Island, B.C., in which, after separating from her husband in 1972, she made her home for several years. The Gulf Island atmosphere is captured in the second of two related novellas, published in one

Thomas

volume: *Munchmeyer* and *Prospero on the island* (1971). This is the diary of Miranda who, in an island cabin, is writing *Munchmeyer*, a novel about a male writer who also keeps a diary. The two works can be read separately, but together they reveal subtle explorations of the nature of creativity, the interdependence of art and craft, and the emotional demands made on the artist. Such reminders of *The tempest* as Miranda's name, and the existence of a Caliban figure, provide a sometimes ironic framework for events on the 'magic' island, and for interaction of the characters, both real and invented.

Songs my mother taught me was Thomas's first novel, though it was not published until 1973. Set in the New York State of the author's childhood, it chronicles a girl's growing up, from Blakean 'innocence' in the emotionally violent world of her home and social life to 'experience', acquired through grotesque revelations of human misery in a mental hospital where she had a summer job. What appears at first to be a conventional first-person narrative is in fact a curiously constructed record of two voices, the speaker sometimes referring to herself as 'I', and sometimes as Isobel, a third person she observes from a distance, or directly addresses. Thomas's innovative handling of the novel form is seen most clearly in *Blown figures* (1974), in which a collage method of narration and the use of space on the page reflect the schizophrenia of a woman haunted by guilt and the sense of loss from a miscarriage. She relives psychically a journey to Africa, gradually turning in her own mind into a doomed and destructive witch.

Ladies and escorts (1977) confirms Audrey Thomas's reputation as a brilliant writer of short stories. The complex emotions and ideas explored never strain the capacities of the form, whether in stories depicting the subtle nuances of sexuality and the unfathomable depths of pain, violence, and sadness in human relations (as in 'Kill day at the government wharf', 'Aquarius', and 'Initram'), or in aesthetic enquiries into the mirror relationship of art to life (as in 'Rapunzel' and, powerfully, in 'Initram'). These stories show a gift for evoking place that is also one of the strengths of the epistolary novel *Latakia* (1979), which captures the atmosphere of Crete as well as of places visited on a sea-voyage to Europe. The Syrian port of Latakia, where language difficulties trigger a fierce culture-shock, provides a metaphor for the love-affair, now over, between two Canadian writers who, despite strong physical attraction, are separated by a gulf of non-comprehension, created in part by Michael's need to make Rachel his subordinate and by his resentment of her superiority as a writer. Similar doomed relationships appear in *Real mothers* (1981), which contains one of Thomas's best stories, the delicate, haunting 'Natural history'. It celebrates the love of a mother and daughter and draws together several levels of narrative into one moment of illumination. *Two in the bush and other stories* (1981) contains a selection from *Ten green bottles* and *Ladies and escorts*.

Although Thomas's novels are self-contained, they can be read as one semi-autobiographical story, whose narrating voice—whether of Isobel, Miranda, or Rachel—belongs to the same person at different stages of her experience. Isobel is the girl and woman struggling to define herself in terms other than granddaughter, daughter, mistress, wife, or mother; Miranda/Rachel is the self-conscious artist insisting on her own creative purpose and identity even at the cost of losing the men she loves. These versions of self-projection parallel Mrs Thing and Mrs Blood of the first novel, and reflect a psychic split created by the opposing inner demands of physical/emotional and mental/spiritual selves. By contrast, *Munchmeyer* is a successful attempt, repeated in some of the stories, to write from a male point of view. A vigorous experimenter with narrative method and language, Thomas shows a special interest in the derivation of words, their ambiguities and multiple connotations. She plays with literary allusions and puns, almost too flamboyantly at times, as she stretches language to catch the experience of people, mostly women, hovering on the verge of disintegration.

Audrey Thomas was interviewed by Elizabeth Komisar for OPEN LETTER, III, 3 (Fall 1975) and again by George BOWERING for *Open Letter*, IV, 3 (Spring 1979). A special section of the *Capilano Review*, VII (Spring 1975) includes a long interview and excerpts from Thomas's African journals. Eleanor Wachtel contributed an informative profile of Thomas to *Books in Canada* (Nov., 1979), and there are two articles on her work in CANADIAN LITERATURE: Robert Diotte's 'The romance of Penelope' (86, Autumn 1980) and Joan Coldwell's 'Memory organized: the novels of Audrey Thomas' (92, Spring 1982).

See also NOVELS IN ENGLISH 1960 TO 1982: 3.

JOAN COLDWELL

Thomas, Clara (b. 1919). Clara McCandless Thomas was born in Strathroy, Ont., and was educated at the University of Western Ontario (B.A. 1941; M.A. 1944) and the University of Toronto (Ph.D. 1962). Her interest in Canadian studies dates from her student days—her M.A. thesis, biographical and bibliographical listings for 122 writers, was published as *Canadian novelists: 1925-1945* (1946; rpr. 1970)—and since 1947 she has been teaching and writing in the evolving field of Canadian literature. She is professor of English at York University, Toronto.

Thomas's biography, *Love and work enough: the life of Anna Jameson* (1967, 1978), is a study of the life and writings of the nineteenth-century writer, early feminist, and visitor to Toronto in 1836, the author of the famous *Winter studies and summer rambles in Canada* (London, 1838). *Ryerson of Upper Canada* (1969) is a biographical portrait of Egerton Ryerson, his times, and his careers as clergyman and educator. With John Lennox, a colleague at York University, she has written *William Arthur Deacon: a Canadian literary life* (1982), a detailed study of the life, letters, and writings of the distinguished literary journalist (q.v.).

As well as many articles on a wide range of literary subjects, Thomas has written numerous studies of Margaret LAURENCE and her work, including two monographs: *Margaret Laurence* (1969) and *The Manawaka world of Margaret Laurence* (1975). Her guidebook to Canadian literature, *Our nature, our voices* (1973), was translated into Japanese by Professor Noburo Watanabe and published in Japan in 1981, the first survey of Canadian literature to be so honoured. She contributed the chapter 'Biography' to the second edition of the *Literary history of Canada* (1976); the chapter on Mrs MOODIE and Mrs TRAILL to *The clear spirit: twenty Canadian women and their times* (1966) edited by Mary Quayle Innis; articles on Samuel Strickland and Anna Jameson to the DICTIONARY OF CANADIAN BIOGRAPHY; and wrote introductions for five volumes in the New Canadian Library series: Anna Jameson's *Winter studies*; Catharine Parr Traill's *The backwoods of Canada* and *The Canadian settler's guide*; Margaret Laurence's *The tomorrow-tamer*; and Philippe AUBERT DE GASPÉ's *Canadians of Old*.   JOHN LENNOX

Thompson, David. See EXPLORATION LITERATURE IN ENGLISH: 2.

Thompson, John (1938-76). Born in Manchester, Eng., he attended Manchester Grammar School and the University of Sheffield, where he took his B.A. in honours psychology. After serving in the British army for two years, he went in 1960 to the United States, where he studied comparative literature at Michigan State University and received a Ph.D; his thesis, directed by A.J.M. SMITH, comprised translations of poems by the French surrealist poet René Char. He moved to New Brunswick in 1966 to teach in the English department of Mount Allison University, living with his wife and daughter in a farmhouse in the Tantramar Marsh country, a locale that inspired his best poetry. His poems and translations—including a sequence by Roland GIGUÈRE that appeared in *Ellipse* (Winter 1970)—then began appearing in Canadian literary magazines. His first poetry collection was *At the edge of the chopping there are no secrets* (1973). The publication of his second and last collection, *Stilt Jack* (1978), was preceded by a struggle with alcoholism, divorce, a fire that destroyed the Tantramar farmhouse, and finally his death, apparently by suicide, at thirty-eight.

The critical response to *At the edge of the chopping* was disappointing. Although most reviewers praised Thompson's accurate evocation of the New Brunswick landscape, he was chided for his narrow range, self-conscious posturing, and uneven technique. It went unnoticed that Thompson, a sophisticated reader of modern poetry—Lorca, Trakl, Yeats, Neruda, Roethke, and the French surrealists—was striving for more than a garland of rustic verses. Like Char, he sought to discover, through a poetry of concentrated image, nothing less than a universe; he aimed to strip away externals and name the secrets that nature keeps to itself. *At the edge of the chopping* opens with a series of precise, vividly imagined metaphors: an apple tree is a 'cauldron of leaves,/the sun a deadly furnace' that in winter bears 'a head of burnt hair/crackling faintly' against the snow. The 'plot' of this collection moves from rich images of decay and regeneration to the frozen zero of winter when, as one poem says, both women and the air get thin and cold. The icy purity of stars, knives, frozen trout, and the heart's isolation are at once feared, celebrated, embraced, abhorred. Thompson probes each thing, searching out the language behind language and meaning beyond the visual. Though his relentless explorations lend despair to his

Thompson

verse—as in the terrifying 'The brim of the well', where knowledge can leave us 'cold-broken, earthed'—the final poems are restorative, bringing the curative power of onions and roots, the right kind of quiet, regeneration, and speech that is 'calling me through strange earths/to this place suddenly yours'.

The indifferent reception given this astonishing first book did nothing to brighten Thompson's difficult last few years. *Stilt Jack* (the title is drawn from Yeats's 'Malachi Stilt-Jack'; also from a fish, and a man on stilts) opens with the lines: 'Now you have burned your books: you'll go/with nothing but your blind, stupefied heart'. It inhabits the same territory as the earlier book, but the second collection is an inversion of the first, seen through a glass darkly: the stripping away has uncovered an abyss. Its thirty-eight poems—their dark negations; their urgent, anguished phrasing; their disordered night-world—tell of a man pushed close to the limit. Yet Thompson's charity and good sense flash out in the blackness: he reminds us that, after all, 'I'm still here like the sky/and the stove'. The tormented lines shine with his care for the image, his scrupulosity, and his wry Yorkshire humour. Thompson considered his form carefully; he explained in a prefatory note that his model was the ancient Persian *ghazal*, 'the poem of contrasts, dreams, astonishing leaps'.

In these two books Thompson left us an intensely imagined poetic universe, rooted in Canadian reality but transfigured through a disciplined, strong, startling talent. The last line of *Stilt Jack* is his best epitaph: 'Friends: these words for you.' JAMES POLK

Thompson, John Sparrow (1795-1867). Thompson was born in Waterford, Ire., in 1795, and as a young man went to London. In 1827 he immigrated to Halifax. He married Charlotte Pottinger in 1829 and fathered seven children (one of whom, his namesake, was prime minister of Canada from 1892 to 1894). He was a school teacher who started a private school in Halifax; an editor of newspapers and literary magazines; and a civil servant. His government posts included that of Queen's Printer (1843-4; 1848-54). In the late 1820s and 1830s Thompson earned a limited reputation as a poet and essayist, appearing in *The Novascotian* and *The Halifax Monthly Magazine*. His poetry—competent but didactic and often ponderous—was published anonymously in *Scriptural sketches* (Halifax, 1829). His essays

are reportorial rather than original in thought. Thompson made his contribution to the literary life of Nova Scotia as an editor of newspapers and magazines and as a friend and critic of young poets; in the 1830s and 1840s he was a major catalyst in stimulating literary activity, a role he shared with his friend Joseph HOWE. As editor of *The Halifax Monthly Magazine* (1830-3), *The Acadian Telegraph* (1836-7), *The Novascotian* (1838; 1840-2), *The Pearl* (1839-40), and *The Mirror* (1848), he published all the best young Nova Scotia poets of the day: Joseph Howe, Sarah and Mary Eliza HERBERT, John McPHERSON, Angus Gidney, Samuel Elder, Andrew SHEILS, and Mary Revett. He knew most of them personally, introduced them to one another, and was instrumental in getting them to think critically about their craft. Without him, literary activity would have been thinner and more diffuse. His most gifted protegé was John McPherson, whose verse he edited and published in book form in 1862. TOM VINCENT

Thompson, Kent. (b. 1936). Born in Waukegan, Ill., he was educated at Hanover College, served in the U.S. army from 1958 to 1961, and then took an M.A. at the University of Iowa, where he was a member of the Writers' Workshop in 1962. He subsequently completed a Ph.D. in 1965 (with a thesis on Dylan Thomas) at the University of Wales. In 1966 he moved to Fredericton, where he is a professor of English and creative writing at the University of New Brunswick. He was editor of *The* FIDDLEHEAD from 1967 to 1971 and again in 1974. In 1982-3 he was the Canadian Writing Exchange Fellow at the University of Edinburgh.

Thompson is the author of three novels: *The tenants were Corrie and Tennie* (1973), *Across from the floral park* (1974), and *Shacking up* (1980). All three begin with a similar premise: the protagonist finds himself (or herself in *Shacking up*) living in a new and unfamiliar place that is also occupied by a sexually attractive stranger. In *Corrie and Tennie* the narrator is a retired American school teacher who has moved to Fredericton and purchased a duplex, renting half of it to a young university professor and his wife. Seeming partly to choose his role of eccentric old man, but at the same time becoming more eccentric than he himself realizes, the narrator develops an obsession about the woman. He crawls about on his hands and knees listening to the sounds and conversations that come through the walls and lapses into greater and more elaborate fantasies about her—until it becomes all but impossible for the reader to perceive the truth behind the narratives he creates out of his desires. *Across from the floral park*—a surreal, almost Kafkaesque, fable that is the most successful of Thompson's novels— is told by a wealthy and idle narrator who has purchased a house with the understanding that its former owner, an elderly woman, can continue to live there, but finds a young and alluring tenant mysteriously occupying it as well. She resists the narrator's attempts to evict her, beds him instead, and marries him shortly thereafter. In a series of fragmented episodes the narrator begins to learn about his new wife's past and to create a present for the two of them. But at the novel's end he finds himself locked out of his house for no reason that he can understand and fatalistically begins life anew in a nearby hotel. In *Shacking up*, a much slighter novel, a young, married secretary on her lunch hour impulsively allows herself to be picked up by a man she hardly knows and spends the next week in a motel room with him. Neither of the characters of this novel proves very engaging, and the central situation never really rises above the banal. In the novel's conclusion, however, as the young woman confronts the difficulty of leaving the motel room and returning to everyday life, the story gains in poignancy.

Thompson's short stories have been published widely in magazines, in the annual *Best Canadian stories*, and in other anthologies. Ten of them are collected in *Shotgun and other stories* (1979). Usually quiet in tone, this short fiction has an intensity that makes it effective.

Thompson has published two books of poetry: *Hard explanations* (1968) and *A band of my ancestors* (1975), a sequence of twenty-four poems spoken by a Viking invading the New World. A sample of more recent poetry may be found in *Fiddlehead* 125, an anthology of work by poets associated with that magazine. His plays have been broadcast on CBC Radio. Thompson edited *Stories from Atlantic Canada* (1973).

RUSSELL BROWN

Thomson, Edward William (1849-1924). He was born in Peel Co., now part of Toronto, the son of Margaret Hamilton Foley and William Thomson. In 1864, while visiting an American relative, he briefly joined and fought with the Union Army in the American Civil War and in 1866 he enlisted in the Queen's Own Rifles to fight the Fenians. Discharged the next year, he studied civil engineering for five years and from 1872 to 1878 surveyed for eastern-Ontario lumbering and railway concerns. In Dec. 1878 he became a political journalist for the Toronto *Globe*, where, except for a return to surveying in 1882 and 1883 during the Winnipeg land boom, he remained for twelve years, serving for a time as its Montreal correspondent. In 1891, disagreeing with the Liberal election platform on unrestricted reciprocity, he left the *Globe*, where he was by this time in charge of the editorial page. He became a revising editor for the Boston *Youth's Companion*—a weekly magazine that was at the height of its popularity, with the widest circulation of any American periodical—to which he had been contributing stories since winning first prize in a *Youth's Companion* short-story competition in 1886 with 'Petherick's peril'. He remained with that magazine as a revising and contributing editor until 1901, when he returned to Canada—first to Montreal, where he worked for the *Star*, and a year later to Ottawa, where he was Canadian correspondent for the Boston *Transcript*. In 1909 he was made a Fellow of the Royal Society of Literature (England) and in 1910 a Fellow of the Royal Society of Canada. He died in Boston at the home of his grandson.

A fluent writer, a politically uncompromising and independent thinker, and an entertaining conversationalist, Thomson was acquainted with major literary and political figures. He was a friend of Duncan Campbell SCOTT and Ethelwyn WETHERALD, and a close friend and admirer of Archibald LAMPMAN, whose *Lyrics of earth* (1895), after receiving several rejections, was finally published by Copeland and Day of Boston through the efforts of Thomson. (He also edited the selection and arrangement of the manuscript at Lampman's invitation.) While in Boston, Thomson remained in close touch with the Canadian literary scene, and during his tenure with the *Youth's Companion* many Canadian writers appeared in its pages. While he lived in Ottawa, he became a close friend and admirer of Henri Bourrassa and Wilfrid Laurier.

Although most of Thomson's stories were published in the *Youth's Companion*, several of his best first appeared elsewhere: 'Privilege of the limits' in *Harper's Weekly* (25 July 1891); 'Old Man Savarin' and 'Great Godfrey's lament' in the New York maga-

Thomson

zine *Two tales* (Oct. 1892); and 'Miss Min-nelly's management' in the UNIVERSITY MAGAZINE (Oct. 1910). In the 1890s he published three collections: *Old Man Savarin and other stories* (Toronto, 1895) and two collections that seem to have been designed for a juvenile audience: *Walter Gibbs, the young boss; and other stories* (Toronto, 1896) and *Between earth and sky, and other strange stories of deliverance* (Toronto, 1897). All three were published simultaneously in Canada and the United States. *Smoky days* (New York, 1896), a long story first serialized in the *Youth's Companion*, and a long poem, *This is of Aucusson and Nicolette* (Boston, 1896), brought to three the books he published in 1896. After his return to Canada in 1901 Thomson produced little fiction. In 1909 a collection of his poetry was published in Canada as *The many-mansioned house and other poems* and in the United States, slightly altered, as *When Lincoln died and other poems*. (As a boy, on a visit to Philadelphia, Thomson had an encounter with Lincoln.) This volume included a long narrative poem, 'Peter Ottawa', which had been privately printed in 1905. In 1917 Thomson reissued *Old Man Savarin* with some change in title— *Old Man Savarin stories: tales of Canada and Canadians*—and content: two stories from the 1895 collection were omitted, while two from *Between earth and sky* and three later stories were added. This collection was dedicated to Sir Arthur Quiller-Couch, who had included Thomson's poem 'Aspiration' in *The Oxford book of Victorian verse* (1912).

Thomson's fiction, though not his poetry, endures. Some of his stories are excessively sentimental; some are simple boys' stories; but the best are fine realistic stories of early Canadian life. Among the Irish, Scottish, and French-Canadian settlers and lumbermen he wrote about are some memorable characters portrayed with economy, gentle humour, liveliness of language, felicity of dialogue, and a skilful use of dialect.

See Arthur Stanley BOURINOT's edition of *The letters of Edward William Thomson to Archibald Lampman (1891-1897), with notes, a bibliography, and other material on Thomson and Lampman* (1957). The 1917 edition of Thomson's *Old Man Savarin stories* was reprinted in the Literature of Canada Series (1974), with an introduction by Linda Shesko. See also the *Selected stories of E.W. Thomson* (1973) edited by Lorraine McMullen, who wrote 'E.W. Thomson and the *Youth's Companion*', *Canadian Children's Literature* 13 (1979).   LORRAINE McMULLEN

'Threnody, A'. See 'The AHKOOND OF SWAT'.

Tin flute, The. See BONHEUR D'OCCASION.

Tish (1961-9). Founded in Vancouver in Sept. 1961, this mimeographed magazine began the writing careers of its poet-editors: Frank DAVEY, George BOWERING, Fred WAH, David Dawson, and James Reid. It was influenced by the work of both the San Francisco poet Robert Duncan and the Contact Press editors Louis DUDEK and Raymond SOUSTER. The 'Tish-group', as the five editors soon became known, argued for a poetry of spoken idiom written in lines determined by oral rhythms. Nineteen consecutive monthly issues were published by the original editors, marked by extensive discussion of poetic theory and numerous attempts at extended or series poems, notably Bowering's 'Margins' series. Writers also associated with *Tish* during this period included critic Warren Tallman, playwright Carol BOLT (Johnson), and poets Daphne MARLATT (Buckle), David Cull, Red LANE, Robert Hogg, and Lionel KEARNS.

Following five issues edited between Aug. 1963 and June 1964 by a group headed by David Dawson, the general editorship of *Tish* was assumed by Dan McLeod, who later founded the counterculture newspaper *The Georgia Straight*. Under McLeod, *Tish* directed itself mainly to the Vancouver writing community and lost the awareness of central and eastern Canada that had characterized the earlier period. The last four issues, published in 1968-9, were edited by Karen Tallman from offices shared with *The Georgia Straight* and were given over mostly to prose, particularly the diary and reflective essay. In 1969 *Tish* was unofficially replaced by *The Georgia Straight Writing Supplement*.

The founding of *Tish* marked the beginning of a distinct but inward-looking west-coast writing community that later came to publish such journals as *Iron*, *The Pacific Nation*, BLEW OINTMENT, *Air*, *Island*, *Pulp*, *Talon*, and *Writing*—journals rarely seen elsewhere in Canada. Paradoxically, in a national context *Tish* was also the most dramatic evidence of the emergence across the country of a new generation of poets more open to the colloquial and popular than were their forebears—a generation that included not only the *Tish* editors but such figures as John NEWLOVE and Andrew SUKNASKI in Saskatchewan and Margaret ATWOOD and David McFADDEN in Ontario. The first nineteen issues of *Tish* were reprinted by TALONBOOKS as *Tish 1-19* (1975). Critical and historical materials concerning *Tish* have been collected by C.H. Gervais in *The writing life* (1976).

See also LITERARY MAGAZINES IN ENGLISH: 3 and POETRY IN ENGLISH: 1950 TO 1982: 2.   FRANK DAVEY

Tit-Coq. This famous play by Gratien GÉLINAS concerns the illegitimate young soldier Arthur Saint-Jean—called Tit-Coq (little rooster) for his fighting spirit—and his search for acceptance and love. He thinks he has found both when he meets Marie-Ange, the sister of a fellow soldier. But when he goes overseas during the Second World War, she marries someone else. On his return she is ready to go away with him, but her family and the army chaplain make them realize that their illegitimate children would be under the same cloud as Tit-Coq, and so they part. Though there is some melodrama and much comedy in its thirteen scenes, the way the lovers are caught in the cultural and religious web of Québec in the 1940s is genuinely tragic. The play can also be read as a statement about the plight of French Canadians in a world dominated by British and American culture and traditions: Tit-Coq, in his search for acceptance and identity in a hostile world, can be seen as a metaphor for Québec in an English-speaking continent. Much of its success in Québec can be attributed to Gélinas's use of the French spoken by working-class Québécois, who were shown in this play that their situation and language were worthy materials for the stage.

The first production of *Tit-Coq* opened at Montreal's Théâtre Monument National on 22 May 1948 and was directed by Gélinas and Fred Barry. An immediate success, it ran at that theatre until the summer recess, after which it transferred to the Théâtre du Gesù, where it played in both French and English until 1951 with basically the same cast—Gélinas played Tit-Coq in both versions—for more than 500 performances. In English it had a successful run at the Royal Alexandra, Toronto, and in Chicago. This encouraged Gélinas in 1951 to take the English version to New York, where it closed on Broadway after three performances. In 1953 it was made into a film, starring Gélinas and directed by him and René Delacroix; a subtitled English version was also made. In 1981 *Tit-Coq* had a very popular revival at the Théâtre Denise Pelletier, Montreal; directed by Gélinas, this production had a dynamic young actor, Daniel Gadouas, in the title role.

Tit-Coq was first published in French in 1950 and in English—in a too-literal English translation by Kenneth Johnstone, in cooperation with the author—in 1967. A critical edition, with a bibliography, edited by Laurent Mailhot appeared in 1980. Renate Usmiani includes a careful analysis of *Tit-Coq* in her study *Gratien Gélinas* (1977).
     JAMES NOONAN

Tocque, Philip (1814-99). Born in Carbonear, Nfld., he became a clerk in the mercantile establishment of Slade, Elson and Company, where he was acquainted with the naturalist P.H. Gosse. In 1841 he became schoolmaster at Port de Grave, Conception Bay; three years later he occupied a similar position in Broad Cove (now St Philips). In 1845 he gave a series of lectures on geology in St John's and was recognized by the local press as the first Newfoundlander to lecture on scientific subjects. During the late 1840s he served as a Clerk of the Peace in Harbour Breton on Newfoundland's south coast, but in 1849 he immigrated to the United States. Although, to quote his own words, 'From my youth I have been a member of the Wesleyan Society', Tocque studied for the Episcopal ministry in the theological department of Trinity College, Hartford, Conn., and was admitted to Holy Orders in 1852. He subsequently served as a minister in Massachusetts; in Tusket, N.S.; and in Kinmount, Waverley, and Markham, Ont. In 1858 he was given the honorary degree of A.M. by Lawrence University of Appleton, Wis. On his retirement he settled in Toronto, where he died.

Tocque's first important book was a collection of essays, entitled *Wandering thoughts; or Solitary hours* (London, 1846). These are entertaining, rambling pieces, designed to introduce younger readers to the wonders of science. *A peep at Uncle Sam's farm, workshop, fisheries, &c* (Boston, 1851) describes his initial excited response to the attractions of the eastern United States. *The mighty deep* (New York, 1852), edited by Daniel P. Kidder, is a brief introduction to the subject of oceans, done with Tocque's accustomed flair. *Newfoundland: as it was, and as it is in 1877* (Toronto, 1878) combines the features of a history and a gazeteer. It amply fulfilled Tocque's patriotic intention of showing 'British and American readers that Newfoundland is something more than a mere fishing station.' *Kaleidoscope echoes: being historical, philosophical, scientific, and theological sketches, from the miscellaneous writings of the Rev. Philip Tocque, A.M.* (Toronto, 1895), edited by his daughter Annie Tocque, was his final book. It is a miscellany of personal reminiscences, devotional pieces, and 'booming' items on Newfoundland.

Tocque also published *The Newfoundland almanack, for the year of Our Lord 1849: in the twelfth year of Her Majesty's reign* (St John's, 1849) and *The voice of the sea: a sermon, preached on Sunday evening, Oct. 2, 1853, in St. Mary's Church, Richmond Street, Boston, to commemorate the death of the late Captain Robert Hutchings, of the British steamship 'Andes'* . . . (Boston, 1853). He wrote another almanac, for 1848; a third, for 1850, was announced in the St John's *Public Ledger*, 23 Oct. 1849.

Tocque was a writer of some quality whose essays have an engaging personal touch and a lucid style. His reflections on Newfoundland are occasionally penetrating and moving.   PATRICK O'FLAHERTY

Tonge, Grizelda Elizabeth Cottnam (c. 1803-25). Little is known of Grizelda Tonge's short life. She was born in Windsor, N.S., of a socially and politically prominent family. Both her grandmothers wrote poetry and her father was a noted orator, so that the intellectual and literary environment in which she grew up was more sophisticated than was usual at the time. Her few extant poems—notably *Lines composed at midnight* (Halifax, n.d.)—reveal a sensitive mind, but there is not enough of her writing extant to judge her talent. She died of fever in the West Indies in Demarara (now Guyana), where she had journeyed to join her father. Her literary importance lay not in her verse but in the symbolic status she achieved in the minds of a generation of young Nova Scotian writers working to create a native literature. Because she came to represent the image of the beautiful, sensitive young poet struck down just as her talent was blooming, she epitomized both the promise of native literary genius and its fragility in the harsh, stubborn soil of colonial society. Her symbolic status was enhanced by what appears to have been a premonition of death in her last poem, 'Lines written at midnight' (1825). Joseph HOWE, in his articles 'Western rambles' (1828) and 'Nights with the muses' (1845), nostalgically refers to her as the 'highly-gifted songstress of Acadia'.   TOM VINCENT

Toupin, Paul. See DRAMA IN FRENCH 1948 TO 1981: 1.

Toye, William. See CHILDREN'S LITERATURE IN ENGLISH: 5, 7 and *The* TAMARACK REVIEW.

Traill, Catharine Parr (1802-99). Born in Kent, near London, Eng., Catharine Strickland spent her first thirty years in rural Suffolk, where her father retired after a successful docks management and importing career. While keeping close ties to Norwich, the Strickland family lived at Stowe House near Bungay, and at Reydon Hall near Southwold. At Reydon the father conscientiously educated his five daughters and two sons, stressing discipline, self-reliance, and practicality in subject matter. Though literature played little part in his curriculum, his library provided imaginative stimulus. The daughters were drawn to theatre, poetry, and the romance of history—all but one of them making writing something of a career: the eldest, Eliza and Agnes, achieved fame and social prominence in England as co-authors of *Lives of the Queens of England* and other multi-volumed aristocratic biographies; Jane Margaret specialized in moral tales and histories; while Catharine, like her younger sister Susanna (MOODIE), began as a writer of children's stories. Three members of this remarkable family—Catharine, Susanna, and their younger brother Samuel—later gained recognition as lucid recorders and interpreters of pioneering and settling in early-nineteenth-century Upper Canada.

Catharine was the first Strickland to be published. Shortly after her father's death a family friend arranged for publication in London of a collection of her stories and sketches, *The tell tale* (1818). Strongly influenced by Thomas Day and Sarah Trimmer, Catharine thereafter produced such didactic and sweet-spirited works as *Reformation; or, The cousins* (1819); *Disobedience; or, Mind what Mama says* (1819); *Little Downy; or, The history of a field mouse* (1822); *Prejudice reproved; or, The history of the Negro toy-seller* (1826); *The keepsake guineas; or, The best use of money* (1828); and *Sketches from nature; or, Hints to juvenile naturalists* (1830)—while contributing to popular annuals like *Ackermann's juvenile forget me not* and *The New Year's gift*. Considerable bibliographical uncertainty still surrounds these early works, many of which appeared initially without her name. Catharine Strickland's most interesting book of the 1820s, which anticipates her own later removal to Canada—*The young emigrants; or, Pictures of life in Canada. Calculated to amuse and instruct the minds of youth* (1826)—reflects her positive approach to emigration. Drawing its information from the letters of family friends and from travel books, it is a highly moralistic conduct book advocating an adventurer's spirit, British resoluteness, and a Crusoe-like acceptance of untoward fate, all in the context of domestic solidarity.

Catharine's quiet Suffolk life changed dramatically when, in the wake of a broken engagement, she met Lt Thomas Traill, a charming sociable widower who had attended Oxford and whose social credentials included a prominent Orkney family and military status. They married after a short courtship, immigrating almost immediately to Canada in 1832 to take up Traill's military land grant. Thomas Traill adapted to life in the Canadian backwoods far less effectively than his younger, more capable wife. Though their arrival and settlement (near present-day Lakefield, Ont.) was buffered by the kindness and skill of Catharine's brother Samuel—their neighbour, and the newly opened area's most successful pioneer—Thomas Traill was never happy with farming, clearing the land, or the lack of congenial society. However, out of this pioneer experience Catharine Traill wrote her most important book, one of the few she wrote exclusively for an adult audience: *The* BACKWOODS OF CANADA; *being letters from the wife of an emigrant officer; illustrative of the domestic economy of British America* (London, 1836). Thomas Traill's attempts to sell the farm finally succeeded in 1839, when the family moved to Peterborough. Mounting debts and a fast-growing family hampered progress in the town, despite Catharine's efforts at running a school. In 1846 they accepted the timely offer of an English friend, the Rev. George Bridges, to live rent-free in his curious garrison, 'The Wolf Tower', at Rice Lake. For the next thirteen years they lived south of Rice Lake, particularly at 'Oaklands', where Thomas Traill, increasingly incapacitated by depressions, relied upon his wife not only to raise their seven surviving children but also, when time and circumstances allowed, to write for available markets.

To these most difficult years of the Traills' Canadian experience belong Catharine Traill's children's books, *The Canadian Crusoes. A tale of the Rice Lake plains* (London, 1852) and *Lady Mary and her nurse; or, A peep into the Canadian forest* (London, 1856). The former—drawing upon the landscape of the Rice Lake plains, its Indian history, and the lost-child theme—dramatizes the plucky and dignified survival of three children who, though lost for nearly two years, succeed in bringing their high-minded and civilized attitudes to bear on wilderness experience. *Lady Mary and her nurse*—which, like *Crusoes*, was reprinted under variant titles—is a stylized dialogue between teacher and child that amply manifests Traill's fondness for nature and her skill at close observation. Her other book of this period, *The female emigrant's guide, and hints on Canadian housekeeping* (Toronto, 1854), returns to the spirit of *The backwoods of Canada*, providing supportive counsel and practical information for women faced with the prospect of emigration and settlement in remote locales. Hurriedly put together, it is repetitive and uneven. Some of Traill's best writing from the late 1830s to 1860 has never appeared in book form. Various articles on bush life that appeared in Britain in *The Home Circle, Sharpe's London Journal, Chambers's Edinburgh Journal* and in Canada in *The* LITERARY GARLAND and *The Anglo-American Magazine*, notably the series entitled 'Forest gleanings', are among these pieces.

Traill's strengths as a writer are her clarity, firm sense of identity, optimistic spirit, and above all her attention to detail, which is particularly evident in her observation of nature. While her interest in flora and fauna is clearly shown in *The backwoods of Canada*, it was only after Thomas Traill's death and Catharine's removal to Lakefield, Ont., that she had the opportunity to focus that attention. *Canadian wild flowers* (Montreal, 1868) combined her text and the paintings of Susanna Moodie's daughter, Agnes (Moodie) Fitzgibbon, who also collaborated on Traill's *Studies of plant life in Canada; or, Gleanings from forest, lake and plain* (Ottawa, 1885), a highly detailed book that earned Traill the praise of numerous professional botanists. In her last decade she produced two more books: *Pearls and pebbles; or, Notes of an old naturalist* (London, Toronto, 1894), which includes reminiscences of her childhood and a useful biographical sketch by her grand-niece, and *Cot and cradle stories* (Toronto, 1895), another children's collection. She died in Lakefield at the age of 97, her life having virtually spanned the nineteenth century.

Traill

See Audrey Morris, *The gentle pioneers: five nineteenth-century Canadians* (1968); Sara Eaton, *Lady of the backwoods* (1969); David Jackel, 'Mrs. Moodie and Mrs. Traill, and the fabrication of a Canadian tradition', *The Compass*, no. 6 (1979); Carl Ballstadt, 'Catharine Parr Traill', *Canadian writers and their works*, vol. I, Fiction series (1983), edited by Robert Lecker, Jack David and Ellen Quigley; and Marian Fowler's study of Traill in her *The embroidered tent: five gentlewomen in early Canada* (1982).   MICHAEL PETERMAN

Translations: English to French. From nineteenth-century translations of works by Frances BROOKE (*Voyage dans le Canada; ou Histoire de Miss Montaigu*, Madame T.G.M., 1809), Rosanna LEPROHON (*Antoinette de Mirecourt; ou Mariage secret et chagrins cachés*, J.A. Genand, 1865), T.C. HALIBURTON (*Le vieux juge; ou Esquisses de la vie dans une colonie*, 1949), and William KIRBY (*Le chien d'or: légende canadienne*, Pamphile LEMAY, 1884), to recent translations of a biography of Terry Fox or the latest novels by Margaret ATWOOD, George BOWERING, and Alice MUNRO, more and more Canadian books are being translated from English to French. Philip Stratford remarked in his *Bibliography of Canadian books in translation* (with Maureen Newman, 1975) that four times as many works were translated between 1920 and 1960 than during the previous 350 years, and that in the sixties alone the number almost tripled, reaching 120 in 1975. Two years later the figure was 190 and in 1981 it reached 300 (240 authors translated). Even remembering that over twice as many translations are done from French to English, literary translation in Québec—especially of novels and essays—has taken an unprecedented leap forward since the 1960s.

In the area of fiction sixty novelists and 115 titles have been translated—half of them in the past five years. Six of the best-known Canadian authors were translated and published in France: Stephen LEACOCK (*Histoires humoristiques*, 1963; *Mémoires d'une jeune fille victorienne*, 1964; *Leacock: textes choisis*, 1966); Mazo DE LA ROCHE (16 Jalna books); Malcolm LOWRY (*Écoute notre voix ô seigneur*, 1962; *Au-dessous du volcan*, 1963; *Lunar caustic*, 1963; *Ultramarine*, 1965; *Choix de lettres*, 1968; *Sombre comme la tombe où repose mon ami*, 1970; *En route vers l'île de Gabriola*, 1970); Arthur Hailey (*714, appelle Vancouver*, 1959; *Le dernier diagnostic*, 1960; *En haut lieu*, 1962; *Grand Hôtel Saint-Gregory*, 1966; *Airport*, 1969; *Detroit*, 1972); Leonard

COHEN (*Le jeu favori*, 1971; *Les perdants magnifiques*, 1973); and Mordecai RICHLER (*Le choix des ennemis*, 1959; *L'apprentissage de Duddy Kravitz*, 1960; *Le cavalier de Saint-Urbain*, 1976). All these translations done in France have greatly reduced the percentage of work done in Québec. However, half-a-dozen Montreal publishers are now actively translating novels. Two series, published by Le Cercle du Livre de France—'Des deux solitudes' and 'Des deux solitudes—jeunesse'—contain over thirty titles. These include two by Morley CALLAGHAN (*Telle est ma bien-aimée*, 1974, and *Cet été-là à Paris*, 1976, both translated by the director of one of the series, Michelle Tisseyre); three by Robertson DAVIES (*Cinquième emploi*, 1975; *Le lion avait un visage d'homme*, 1978; *Le monde des merveilles*, 1979—translated by Arlette Francière and Claire MARTIN); three by Margaret LAURENCE (*L'ange de pierre*, 1976; *Les oracles*, 1979; *Un dieu farceur*, 1981—translated by Claire Martin and Michelle Robinson); three by Richler (*Mon père, ce héros . . .*, 1975; *Duddy Kravitz*, 1976; *Jacob Deux-Deux et le vampire masqué*, 1977—translated by Jean SIMARD); and one each by Brian MOORE (*Le fol été de Sheila Redden*, Jean Simard, 1978), W.O. MITCHELL (*Qui a vu le vent*, Arlette Francière, 1974), Patrick Watson (*En ondes dans cinq secondes*, Laurier LaPierre, 1978), and Richard B. WRIGHT (*Un homme de week-end*, Jean Paré, 1977). Juvenile novels in translation are by Margaret Atwood (*Sur l'arbre perchés*, Michel Caillol, 1980), Jean LITTLE (*Écoute, l'oiseau chantera*, Paule DAVELUY, 1980), and Farley MOWAT (*Deux grands ducs dans la famille*, Paule Daveluy, 1980; *La malédiction du tombeau viking*, Maryse Côté, 1980).

It is notable that only four authors from the nineteenth century and ten from the period 1900-40 (Irene BAIRD, Marius BARBEAU, John GLASSCO, Angus Graham, Leacock, Lowry, L.M. MONTGOMERY, de la Roche, and Sinclair ROSS) have been translated. Even in the decades from which the most works have been translated—the forties, fifties, and sixties—many gaps remain to be filled. The selection is generally conservative, concentrating on the 'classics', such as Hugh MacLENNAN (*Deux solitudes*, Paris, 1963; *Le temps tournera au beau*, Jean Simard, 1966; and *Le matin d'une longue nuit*, Jean Simard, 1967), Callaghan, Lowry, Davies, Richler, Laurence, and including very few more recent writers. (The works of Matt COHEN, Timothy FINDLEY, Robert KROETSCH, Michael ONDAATJE, Rudy

WIEBE, and others are unavailable in French translation.) The influence of feminism has prompted translations of works by such authors as Margaret Atwood (*Lady Oracle*, Marlyse Picard, 1979, and *La vie avant l'homme*, Marianne Véron, 1981), Margaret Laurence (*Un dieu farceur*, M. Robinson, 1981), and Alice Munro (*Pour qui te prends-tu?*, Colette Tonge, 1981).

English-Canadian literary circles unanimously recognize the vitality and quality of modern poetic production. However, if the number of authors translated is any indication, practically no one in Québec is acquainted with English-Canadian poetry. Three poets (Leonard Cohen, John Robert COLOMBO, and Dennis LEE) and four books have appeared in French: two by Cohen, *Poèmes et chansons* (1972) and *L'énergie des esclaves* (1974), both translated and published in Paris; Colombo's *La grande muraille de Chine*, Jacques GODBOUT, 1969); and Lee's *Élégies civiles et autres poèmes* (Marc Lebel, 1980). Fortunately in an excellent anthology, *Poèmes des quatre côtés* (1975), the poet Jacques BRAULT gives what he calls 'non-translations' of Atwood and Gwendolyn MacEWEN, and since 1969 the magazine *Ellipse* has translated some fifty Canadian poets, mainly from the forties, fifties, and sixties (including Irving LAYTON, P.K. PAGE, Raymond SOUSTER, Cohen, D.G. JONES, John NEWLOVE, and Al PURDY), as well as several young poets of the seventies. *Ellipse* has certainly helped create a team of translators; but there are no experienced English-French translators of poetry in Québec of the stamp of John GLASSCO, F.R. SCOTT, or D.G. Jones in English Canada.

American and British plays translated in France and/or adapted in Québec, are regularly produced in Montreal's French-language theatres, but English-Canadian plays are practically unknown. Those translated so far (nine authors and eleven titles) have been done for essentially selfish reasons: plays about Québec like *Charbonneau et le Chef* by John Thomas McDonough (*Charbonneau et le Chef*, Paul Hébert and Pierre Morency, 1974); plays that deal with a certain Montreal milieu, like *On the job* by David FENNARIO (*A l'ouvrage*, Robert Guy Scully, 1979); or that are internationally successful, such as *Fortune and men's eyes* by John HERBERT (*Aux yeux des hommes*, René Dionne, 1971).

Non-fiction—biography, history books, and literary criticism—is more often translated. (Surprisingly, more of such books are translated from English to French than vice versa.) The vast majority of such books that are translated—170 titles—date from the sixties and seventies. They include most English-language books on Québec society, history, culture, and politics. The number of these translated books doubled in only five years (1977-81): presumably non-fiction will offer the most active field of translation in the future. In contrast to the poets and novelists, there are few stars here: seven titles by Marshall McLUHAN, some translated in France and some in Québec, including *La galaxie Gutenburg* (Jean Paré, 1967), *Pour comprendre les media* (Jean Paré, 1968), and *Message et massage* (Thérèse Lauriol, 1968); three by Northrop FRYE: *Le siècle de l'innovation* (François Rinfret, 1968), *Anatomie de la critique* (Guy Durand, 1969), and *Pouvoirs de l'imagination* (Jean Simard, 1969); and two each by Peter NEWMAN, Marius BARBEAU, Stanley Ryerson, and Merrill DENISON.

As Philip Stratford states so correctly, in the field of translation Canada is behind most other Western countries, somewhere between Iceland and Albania; yet English-Canadian and Québécois literary translators are swiftly closing the gap. Thanks to grants from the Canada Council (since 1971), which has also instituted the Prize for Translation (1974), to the energy of certain publishers, and to the translators themselves and their Association (founded in 1975), the total number of translations published has doubled every five years for the past fifteen years. The quality of literary translation from English to French has reached a respectable level over the past few years. Jacques Brault, Jean Paré, Michelle Robinson, Jean Simard, Michelle Tisseyre, and Colette Tonge are recognized as successful translators, and a new generation—including Michel Beaulieu, Francine de Lorimier, Claire Dupond, Arlette Francière, and Yvan Steenhout—follows close on their heels.

RICHARD GIGUÈRE

French to English. In the first and second editions (1975 and 1977) of Philip Stratford's *Bibliography of Canadian books in translation: French to English and English to French/Bibliographie de livres canadiens traduits de l'anglais au français et du français à l'anglais*, Stratford lists 250, then 380, works translated from French to English in all categories. (The corresponding numbers for English-to-French translations are 120 and 190.) The forthcoming third edition will include some 550 French-to-English works

Translations: French to English

both literary and non-literary, and approximately 400 titles translated from English to French. In the past six years the number of translated works has doubled, and about three quarters of all Canadian translations have appeared since 1972, when the Canada Council launched its program of financial support for translations. By the end of 1981 unilingual anglophone readers had been given access to a considerable range of French-Canadian literary texts: 147 works of fiction, 30 poetry titles and 32 plays, 30 journals and early travel accounts, 24 substantial literary anthologies, 20 books of literary autobiography and criticism, 32 collections of folklore and folksongs, and 38 children's books. This survey will examine these publications in three historical periods.

1. TO 1959. The first French-Canadian novel to be translated into English was Philippe-Joseph AUBERT DE GASPÉ's Les ANCIENS CANADIENS (Québec, 1863), which appeared in two translations: by Georgiana Pennée in 1864 and by Charles G.D. ROBERTS as *Canadians of old; an historical romance* (New York, 1890); it was reissued in 1905 as *Cameron of Lochiel*. From the turn of the century to the start of the Quiet Revolution, 67 literary translations were published—an average of little more than one book per year. Almost two thirds of these were novels, half of them written by four authors (Louis HÉMON, Maurice CONSTANTIN-WEYER, Roger LEMELIN, and Gabrielle ROY). Their relatively prompt translation into English indicates their popularity in French, though the quality of the translated version was often inferior. One notorious example is Hannah Josephson's 1947 translation of Gabrielle Roy's BONHEUR D'OCCASION (1945) as *The tin flute*, which has become probably the most widely read Québec novel in translation, despite grave errors in interpretation throughout. Roy's major revisions to her novel in the 1947 French edition immediately made the Josephson translation as obsolete as it was unreliable. This was also the case for Lukin Barette's *Sackcloth for banner* (1938), a bowdlerized version of Jean-Charles HARVEY's *Demi-civilisés* (1934), and *Boss of the river* Alan SULLIVAN's translation of ...ine SAVARD's MENAUD, MAÎTRE-...937). (The revised versions of ...by Roy, Harvey, and Savard ...anslated since 1975. In partic-...SCO's excellent re-translation ...ook as *Fear's folly* (1982)—

Glassco's final work as translator—should be noted.) Other notable texts rendered into English in this period include Ringuet's (Philippe PANNETON's) TRENTE ARPENTS (1938)/Felix and Dorothea Walter, *Thirty acres* (1940), and Germaine GUÈVREMONT's *Le survenant* (1945)/Eric Sutton, *The outlander* (1950). In other genres the sixty-year period preceding the Quiet Revolution was quiet almost to the point of silence: five slim books of poetry (by Louis FRÉCHETTE, Hector de Saint-Denys GARNEAU, and three Hexagone poets), two obscure plays, eight travel accounts, one children's book, two anthologies (one of poetry, one of prose and poetry), and 17 collections of folklore and folksongs (especially works by Marius BARBEAU and Edith Fowke).

2. 1960-71. During the sixties the rate of literary translation into English increased dramatically in Canada, from an average of one title per year to six per year: 27 novels, five volumes of poetry and three plays, nine works of literary history and criticism, five travel accounts, six children's books, five anthologies, and seven collections of folklore and folksongs. Although funds to support the translation of Canadian literature were scanty during this period, political and social change in Québec sparked translators and publishers alike to make quickly available in English several of the contemporary texts documenting the Quiet Revolution. Thus, Claude JASMIN's *Ethel et le terroriste* (1964) appeared within a year as *Ethel and the terrorist* (1965), translated by David Walker; Hubert AQUIN's PROCHAIN ÉPISODE (1965) within two years under the same title; and Jacques GODBOUT's *Le couteau sur la table* (1965) within three years as *Knife on the table* (1968)—the last two translated by Penny Williams. Throughout the decade publishers turned their attention to works of fiction from the forties and fifties and only occasionally considered earlier texts. The 1960-71 period witnessed the appearance in English for the first time of several works by such major writers as Yves THÉRIAULT, Marie-Claire BLAIS, Gérard BESSETTE, and Roch CARRIER, as well as three new translations of Gabrielle Roy's fiction and the first English versions of novels by Réjean DUCHARME, Gilles MARCOTTE, and Jacques RENAUD.

In poetry the important anthology *French-Canadian poetry in translation* (1970), of which John GLASSCO was editor and chief translator, was something of a milestone. This was supplemented by two collections edited by Fred COGSWELL, *One hundred poems of modern Quebec* (1970) and *A second hundred poems of modern Quebec* (1971), and by three individual translations of Anne HÉBERT's poetry, single English treatments of Alain GRANDBOIS and Émile NELLIGAN, and especially by the appearance of the bilingual magazine *Ellipse* (Université de Sherbrooke) in 1969. It would be difficult to exaggerate the importance of this journal, which in its first two years introduced eight new Québec poets as well as the prose of Roch Carrier to anglophone readers, and presented a special issue called 'Octobre/October'. Translators also turned their attention to modern Québec drama, appropriately beginning with English versions of three works by Gratien GÉLINAS (the first modern Québec dramatist), while publishers brought out a number of literary autobiographies and works of criticism in English. Of particular merit in these categories are excellent translations by John Glassco of the *Journal of Saint-Denys Garneau* (1962), and by Philip Stratford of both Claire MARTIN's DANS UN GANT DE FER/*La joue droite* (1965, 1966) as *In an iron glove* (1968) and Jean LE MOYNE's *Convergences* (1961) as *Convergence: essays from Quebec* (1966). In the area of literary history and biography, Gérard Tougas's *Histoire de la littérature canadienne-français* (1964) and the first two volumes of the DICTIONARY OF CANADIAN BIOGRAPHY (with translations of all French material for the English edition) also made a welcome appearance. Among the translations of historical journals, letters, and early travel accounts could be found Michael Macklem's two new English versions of Samuel de Champlain's *Voyages* and Joyce MARSHALL's *Word from New France: the selected letters of Marie de l'Incarnation* (1967). Translations were published of children's books by Claude Aubry (two), Monique Corriveau (two), her sister Suzanne Martel, and Paule DAVELUY (herself an accomplished translator of English-Canadian works into French).

3. 1972-81. In a Dec. 1971 memorandum to the federal cabinet, Secretary of State Gérard Pelletier outlined his plan to establish the Canada Council's Translation Grants Programme with an objective of encouraging the translation of approximately 60 works annually—an initiative that was very likely prompted, in part at least, by the events of Oct. 1970 in Québec. In the decade that followed, the program funded 240 French-to-English translation projects in all categories (as well as 212 from English to French), of which 145 were literary texts translated into English. Most of these works can be found among the 220 literary titles that were published in English translation between 1972 and 1981, which included fiction (83), poetry (20), drama (27), anthologies (17), literary criticism (11), early travel accounts (4), children's books (31), and folklore/folksongs (8).

While translators were very active in the seventies, many of them worked too quickly and few could rely on knowledgeable editors to give their work the requisite final harmony and precision. One thinks of David Lobdell's many translations of fiction with Oberon Press; and the recent translations of Alan Brown, especially the highly unsatisfactory retranslation of Roy's *Bonheur d'occasion* (*The tin flute*, 1980), in which some very competent work has been undermined by many oversights, much imprecision and awkward phrasing, and several mistranslations: while the general substance of the French text is transcribed into English, most of the original's colour and style have been lost. The weaknesses of these and other literary translations published between 1976 and 1981—Irène Currie's unwitting translation of an expurgated edition of Rodolphe GIRARD's MARIE CALUMET (1976) is another case in point—are fully described in the 'Letters in Canada' section of the *University of Toronto Quarterly's* summer issues (1977-82). Much excellent work, however, was also completed in this decade, in particular by Sheila Fischman (who began her work as the translator of Roch Carrier), Carol Dunlop, Ray Ellenwood, and Philip Stratford. Of considerable merit are Fischman's *The 'Jimmy' trilogy* (Jacques POULIN) and *The fat woman next door is pregnant* (Michel TREMBLAY); Dunlop's *Deaf to the city* (Marie-Claire BLAIS); all of Ellenwood's work, especially *Vanishing spaces* (Guillaume Charette), *Entrails* (Claude GAUVREAU), and *The cart* (Jacques FERRON); and everything by Stratford, notably the two anthologies *Stories from Quebec* and *Voices from Quebec*, and *The madman, the kite & the island* (Félix LECLERC). At the same time there were many individual achievements that were cause for celebration: Larry Shouldice's *Daydream mechanics* (Nicole BROSSARD); the collaborative effort of nine translators in *Les stratégies du réel/The story so far 6*, an anthology of Québec prose and poetry of the 1970 edited by Nicole Brossard; D.G. JONE *The terror of the snows* (Paul-Marie

POINTE), Barry CALLAGHAN's *Treatise on white and tincture* (Robert Marteau), Fred COGSWELL's *The poetry of modern Quebec*, and Betty Bednarski's selection of Jacques Ferron's *Tales from the uncertain country*. To this list of excellent work can be added most of the winners of the Canada Council Translation Prizes: 1973—Alan Brown, *The antiphonary*/Hubert AQUIN, *L'antiphonaire*; 1974—Sheila Fischman, *They won't demolish me!*/Roch CARRIER, *Le deux-millième étage*, and *The wolf*/Marie-Claire Blais, *Le loup*; 1975—John GLASSCO, *Complete poems of Saint-Denys Garneau*; 1976—Joyce MARSHALL, *Enchanted summer*/Gabrielle Roy, *Cet été qui chantait*; 1977—F.R. SCOTT, *Poems of French Canada*; 1978—Michael Bullock, *Stories for late night drinkers*/Michel TREMBLAY, *Contes pour buveurs attardés*; 1979—Allan Van Meer, *Greta, the divine*/Renald Tremblay, *La céleste Gréta*; *Looking for a job*/Claude Roussin, *Une job*; and *A little bit left*/Serge Mercier, *Encore un peu*; 1980—Larry Shouldice, *Contemporary Quebec criticism*; 1981—Ray Ellenwood, *Entrails*/Claude GAUVREAU, 'Les entrailles'; and 1982—Raymond Y. Chamberlain, *Jos Connaissant*/Victor-Lévy BEAULIEU, *Jos Connaissant*. The smaller presses in particular played a key role in the surge of activity in the seventies, notably House of ANANSI, New Press, Porcépic, TALONBOOKS, Exile, COACH HOUSE, Harvest House, Tundra, and NC Press, often setting high standards of excellence for the larger houses. This wide-ranging interest in translating French-Canadian literary texts accounted for the healthy state of the art in the mid-seventies. In 1976 alone, for instance, literary works in translation were completed by 33 translators and published by two dozen different houses.

The outburst of translation activity between 1976 and 1978 can in part be explained by outlining briefly a few of the many activities that accompanied or followed the setting up of the Canada Council Translation Grants Programme: the establishment of two annual $2500 Translation [Prize]s (increased to $5000 in 1976); the [foundin]g of the Association for Canadian [Que]bec Literatures (1972), which or[ganized a 19]77 conference called 'Traduire [/T]he translation of poetry' (sub[inclu]ded in *Ellipse* 21); the found[ing of the A]ssociation des traducteurs [litéra]ry Translators' Association [in M]ay 1975; the publication of [LTA]'s bilingual *Bibliography of [Canadia]n translation*; the appearance

in *The University of Toronto Quarterly*, beginning in Summer 1977, of an annual detailed review of French-Canadian literature in translation; ATL/LTA's establishing of the annual John Glassco Translation Prize in 1982, to be awarded to the best book-length translation by a new translator published in the preceding year (the 1981 winner was Susanne de Lotbinière-Harwood for *Neons in the night*, her English translation of selected poems by Lucien Francoeur); and finally the recent University of Ottawa 'Translation in Canadian Literature' symposium (April 1982). Regrettably there has been a steady decline in the number of literary translations published since 1978, the inevitable result of fiscal restraints in a recession. Nevertheless, commitment to literary translation remains strong among many translators and publishing houses.

Ellipse 21 has recorded a range of observations on the possibilities and limitations of translation as an art form. Its bilingual format reflects the central role of translation as one of permitting a dialogue between two interested, if isolated, parties. Just such a conversation, delighting in the close encounter of two languages, has taken place between Anne Hébert and her translator F.R. Scott, an exchange they published as *Dialogue sur la traduction à propos du 'Tombeau des rois'* (1970). Similar affection and gratitude are suggested elsewhere—for example, in Jacques Ferron's dedication of *Les confitures de coings* (1972) to Betty Bednarski, who had just completed her translation of his tales. The interchange permitted by translation was further revealed when Louise MAHEUX-FORCIER used as her epigraph for *En toutes lettres* a text from Robertson DAVIES' *World of wonders* as translated by Arlette Francière and Claire MARTIN. Encouraging developments of this kind, along with the possibility of renewed commitment to the practice of translation in Canada in the light of recommendations in the Applebaum-Hébert report on Canadian culture, are cause for hesitant optimism. The publication, early in 1982, of *Pélagie: the return to a homeland*, Philip Stratford's extraordinarily sensitive and intelligent translation of Antonine MAILLET's award-winning novel *Pélagie-la-Charrette*, augurs well for the future. Imitation of its standards will ensure the high quality that must be demanded and promoted by all Canadians who strive to meet, and touch, and greet each other through the agency of artful translation.

JOHN O'CONNOR

Travel literature in English. Travel books appear in library catalogues grouped with statistical and geographical reports. This entry considers only works of literary interest (excluding EXPLORATION LITERATURE) organized around personal travel experiences; and it is necessarily selective since travel books on Canada that reflect places, characters, modes of transport, as well as readers' tastes and publishing trends, number more than 700.

There are many English-language books that throw light on early perceptions of the northern portion of North America. The first were Richard Hakluyt's *Divers voyages touching the discovery of America . . .* (London, 1582; rpr. 1969) and *The principal navigations, voyages and discoveries of the English nation* (London, 1589; rpr. 1969); and a work by Samuel Purchas, who had assisted Hakluyt and come into possession of his unpublished manuscripts, publishing them with his own collection of exploration voyages in *Purchas his pilgrimes . . .* (London, 1625; rpr. 1905). Enabling British readers to follow the first passages to and into northern New World territories, these books were supplemented by translations from the French: Louis Hennepin's *A new discovery of a vast country in America* (London, 1699), Baron Lahontan's *New voyages to North-America* (London, 1703; rpr. 1940), and Pierre-François-Xavier Charlevoix's *Journal of a voyage to North-America* (London, 1761; rpr. 1966). The Swedish botanist Peter Kalm, who visited North America in 1749-50, published a journal of his travels in Swedish (3 vols, 1753-61). An English translation was made by J.R. Forster, *Travels into North America . . .* (London, 1770-1), of which a modern edition was edited by Adolph B. Benson: *The America of 1750: Peter Kalm's travels in North America* (2 vols, 1937); it was reprinted by Dover Publications as *Peter Kalm's travels in North America* (2 vols, 1966). Volume II contains Kalm's detailed and historically valuable account of his visits to Montreal and Quebec (where he found the most cultivated people in North America), of the villages between the two towns, and of his journey west to Lake Ontario and Niagara Falls. The American Jonathan Carver set a basic itinerary through inland territory in *Travels through the interior parts of North America* (London, 1778; rpr. 1974). But Canada as a destination for self-conscious tourists seeking the picturesque in scenery appears first in Isaac Weld's *Travels through the State of North America and the Provinces of Upper and Lower Canada during the years 1795, 1796, and 1797* (London, 1799; rpr. 1970), which publicizes 'romantic' Quebec, 'sublime' Niagara Falls, the 'charming' Thousand Islands, and the excitement of movement in canoe and bateau. John Lambert's two-volume *Travels through Lower Canada, and the United States of North America in the years. 1806, 1807, and 1808* (London, 1810; rpr. 1959) provides in Volume I probably the most vivid description, illustrated with aquatints, of Quebec City and environs, and of Montreal, in the early nineteenth century. A third intention—to analyse immigration possibilities—animated the American John Ogden's *A tour, through Upper and Lower Canada. By a citizen of the United States. Containing a view of the present state of religion, learning, commerce, agriculture, colonization, customs and manners, among the English, French, and Indian settlements* (Litchfield, 1799; rpr. 1917). George Heriot provided the picturesque and the practical in *Travels through the Canadas, containing a description of the picturesque scenery on some of the rivers and lakes; with an account of the productions, commerce, and inhabitants of these provinces* (2 vols, London, 1807; rpr. 1971). Meanwhile readers were reminded of a savage hinterland in Alexander Henry's *Travels and adventures in Canada and the Indian territories between the years 1760 and 1776* (New York, 1809; rpr. 1921).

After the War of 1812 several Americans made peaceful trips into Canada by the Lake Champlain route and produced friendly reports, such as Benjamin Silliman's *Remarks made on a short tour between Hartford and Quebec in the autumn of 1819* (New Haven, 1820?). With comparable urbanity Lt. Francis Hall sketched his *Travels in Canada and the United States in 1816 and 1817* (London, 1818) with emphasis on the friendly *habitants* and the 'inoffensive' Indians—and the 'Yankeefied' Upper Canadians. Scots accustomed to the sharp humour of *Blackwoods Magazine* made witty copy even of the comfortless backwoods, as in John Howison's youthful *Sketches of Upper Canada, domestic, local, and characteristic* (Edinburgh, 1821; rpr. 1966), Basil Hall's more judicious Canadian chapters in his *Travels in North America in the years 1827, 1828* (Edinburgh 1829; rpr. 1974), and William 'Tiger' Dunlop's *Statistical sketches of Upper Canada, for the use of emigrants* (London, 1832; rpr. 1967). Other books of the period, like the Tiger's, reflect involvement longer than a visitor's tour: Edward Talbot's engaging

Travel literature in English

Five years' residence in the Canadas (London, 1824); John MacTaggart's rollicking account of bush-whacking and canal-building, *Three years in Canada* (London, 1829), and George Head's *Forest scenes and incidents in the wilds of North America; being a diary of a winter's route from Halifax to the Canadas, and during four months' residence in the woods on the borders of Lakes Huron and Simcoe* (London, 1829; rpr. 1970).

Soldiers wrote well of tours of duty—and furloughs—during tense times leading to the Rebellion of 1837 in what is now Ontario. A clergyman, Isaac Fidler, reflects Family Compact interests in *Observations on professions, literature, manners, and emigration in the United States and Canada made during a residence there in 1832* (London, 1833; rpr. 1974). But the best picture of those days, and deservedly the best known of all Canadian travel books, was Anna Jameson's *Winter studies and summer rambles in Canada* (London, 1838; rpr. 1965)—the inward journeyings of her studies counterbalancing her rambles toward Lake Huron in search of fellow-intellectuals like Colonel Talbot, and of Indians beyond the sphere of Toronto, during her eight-month stay in Upper Canada.

Politics preponderated after the Act of Union of 1841, in books like James Silk Buckingham's *Canada, Nova Scotia, New Brunswick, and the other British provinces in North America* (London, 1843). Garrison life in Sir Richard Bonnycastle's *The Canadas in 1841* (London, 1841), and *Canada and the Canadians in 1846* (London, 1846; rpr. 1969), in J.E. Alexander's *L'Acadie; or seven years' exploration in British America* (London, 1849), and in George Warburton's charming *Hochelaga; or England in the New World* (London, 1846) brought tales of drills, sports, and dashing sleigh-rides with pretty French-Canadian girls. The writing style of these officers shows a contemporary response to the ebullience of Charles Dickens, whose own fancy was caught by the humour and energy of military barracks in the entertaining Canadian scenes of his *American notes* (London, 1842). The Dickens touch is also seen in Francis Bond Head's *The emigrant* (London, 1846), a lively report of his tours as governor. The scientist Charles Lyell on *his* tour observed fossils, flood-tracings, and rifts as he rode from Niagara northwards. His *Travels in North America; with geological observations on the United States, Canada, and Nova Scotia* (London, 1845; rpr. 1909) might be read in conjunction with John Bigsby's

The shoe and canoe; or Pictures of travel in the Canadas, illustrative of their scenery and of colonial life (London, 1850; rpr. 1969), a surgeon-geologist's narrative that dramatically traces boundary-commission surveys as far west as Lake of the Woods.

At mid-century many churchmen wrote about religious zeal in remote regions. Most interesting of the missionary travels is Peter Jacobs' *Journal from Rice Lake to the Hudson's Bay Territory and returning* (Toronto, 1853), an insider's view of frontier missions by a Christianized Indian. The Indian Territory is featured in a work by the famous governor of the Hudson's Bay Company, Sir George Simpson: *Narrative of a journey around the world in the years 1841 and 1842* (London, 1847). John Palliser's *Solitary rambles and adventures of a hunter in the Prairies* (London, 1853) and Alexander Ross's *Fur hunters of the Far West: a narrative of adventure in the Oregon and Rocky Mountains* (London, 1855; rpr. 1961) are retrospective to earlier days in Indian lands. Paul KANE's *Wanderings of an artist among the Indians of North America from Canada to Vancouver's Island and Oregon through the Hudson's Bay Company Territory and back again* (London, 1859) vividly describes the western Indian at mid-century. Kane's revision from journal entries and rough sketches into carefully crafted narratives and paintings can be traced in Russell Harper's *Paul Kane's frontier* (1971). The popularity of Longfellow's *The song of Hiawatha* (1855) and EVANGELINE (1847) created reader demand for accounts of Indian life and for 'Evangeline' visits, such as Fred Cozzens' *Acadia; or, A month with the Bluenoses* (New York, 1859), and Campbell Hardy's *Sporting adventures in the New World; or, Days and nights of moose-hunting in the pine forests of Acadia* (London, 1855).

To tamer regions the 1850s brought lady travel-writers, via the newly built railways. Their bright, self-assured reports are best exemplified in Isabella Bird Bishop's *An Englishwoman in America* (London, 1856; rpr. 1966) and the Hon. Amelia Murray's *Letters from the United States, Cuba, and Canada* (London, 1856). Other observers contrasted peaceful Canada and the schismatic States, as in Capt. Henry Murray's *Lands of the slave and the free* (London, 1855) and the German J.G. Kohl's *Travels in Canada, and through the States of New York and Pennsylvania* (London, 1861). Anthony Trollope turned the contrast to brilliant use in *North America* (London, 1862), using Niagara Falls as a focus for his uncertainties about power, freedom, and perspective. A subtle American response to the contrast is Henry David Thoreau's little book *A Yankee in Canada*, written in 1850 (Boston, 1866; rpr. 1961). Thoreau sneers at British pomp and military ceremony, but does not resist the attractions of old Quebec. Military manoeuvres in preparation for Fenian raids produced a vigorous book in Lt Francis Duncan's *Our garrisons in the West* (London, 1864).

Three books of the 1860s show how personality can flow through travel accounts. In *The English cricketers' trip to Canada and the United States* (London, 1860) Fred Lillywhite tells how rollicking spirits, even in the face of sea-sickness, were a match for defeats, bad weather, and overpowering celebratory banquets. With more sophisticated humour Horton Rhys describes *A theatrical trip for a wager!* (London, 1861; rpr. 1969). The two-man trip of Dr Walter Butler Cheadle, playing Man Friday to Viscount Milton's Crusoe, was doubly recorded: in Milton's *The North-West Passage by land* (London, 1865; rpr. 1970) and in Dr Cheadle's revealing private journal, *Cheadle's journal of trip across Canada, 1862-1863*, which was not published until 1931.

That northwest world became the setting for two classic books by William Francis Butler. *The great lone land: a narrative of travel and adventure in the northwest of America* (London, 1872; rpr. 1968) created unforgettable images of the voyage westward, of the Red River atmosphere in Riel's time, and of the wild-rose plains beyond. Butler's *The wild north land* (London, 1873; rpr. 1910) described Plains Indians with accuracy and panache. Several fine books followed, reporting the push westward by the railroad: George Monro Grant's OCEAN TO OCEAN (Toronto, 1873; rpr. 1970), Charles Horetzky's *Canada on the Pacific* (Montreal, 1874), and the Earl of Southesk's *Saskatchewan and the Rocky Mountains* (Edinburgh, 1875), based on his diary of 1825.

Fraser Rae, a responsible journalist, followed the railway builders with *Columbia and Canada* and *Newfoundland to Manitoba* (London, 1877 and 1881). A more ambitious style appears in *England and Canada: a summer tour between old and New Westminster* (London, 1884) by Sandford Fleming, who had been chief engineer of the Canadian Pacific Railway. Fleming, as grand old railway magnate, sets his trip against constant memories of tumultuous days of construction. *B.C. 1887* (London, 1888) is by two young Englishmen, J.A. Lees and W.J. Clutter-

buck, who as 'innocents abroad' enjoyed immensely the splendours and absurdities of transcontinental travel and northward foraging. The height of self-conscious styling appears in Rudyard Kipling's *Letters of Marque* (London, 1889; rpr. in *American notes* 1974), with its brilliant vignettes of Victoria as the western terminus of empire, and in his later *From sea to sea* (New York, 1899) and *Letters to the family: notes on a recent trip to Canada* (1908). Another sprightly narrative recounts a west-to-east trip by the Australian Stuart Cumberland: *The Queen's Highway* (London, 1887). Yet the easiest-to-read cross-country account is the unassuming, naïve report of two English lads who described their adventures as farmhands working their way from Ontario to B.C. and back to Calgary; their letters home were published by their father, A.J. Church, as *Making a start in Canada* (London, 1889).

Pullman cars set the elegant stage for books of the 1890s: Edward Roper's *By track and trail: a journey through Canada* (London, 1891), Lady Aberdeen's *Through Canada with a Kodak* (Edinburgh, 1893), and Douglas Sladen's *On the cars and off* (London, 1895). Roper and Sladen deserve a place among the most entertaining of all travel writers. But Lady Dufferin's *My Canadian journal, 1872-78* (London, 1891; rpr. 1971), gaily describing earlier vice-regal travel, rivals these more carefully crafted books in tone and drama.

Although Klondike news revived popularity of stark stories of the manly North, as in Warburton Pike's *The Barren Ground of northern Canada* (London, 1892), turn-of-the-century attention focused mostly on immigrant opportunities. An imperialist optimism—sounded officially in *Canadian pictures drawn with pen and pencil* (London, 1885) by the Marquis of Lorne, governor general of Canada from 1878 to 1883—was echoed in James Lumsden's thoughtful *Through Canada in harvest time* (1903), and in a group of lighter, brighter illustrated books, such as R.E. Vernède's *The fair Dominion; a record of Canadian impressions* (1911). But W.H.P. Jarvis, in *Letters of a remittance man* (1907), and N.P.R. Noel, in *Blanket-stiff* (1912), wryly noted that the imperial welcome was not always firmly woven in the West. The American writer Anson Gard hailed the Canadian drift from imperialism in his highly readable *The last West* (1904) and in other volumes. The publication of *Walt Whitman's diary in Canada* (edited by W.S. Kennedy, 1903)—about a

Travel literature in English

trip Whitman made from London, Ont., to the Saguenay in 1880—presented a memorable picture of harvest days in the older provinces of Ontario and Québec, and reminded turn-of-the-century readers that Americans had long assumed that Canada would inevitably drift into affiliation with the U.S.A.

Several books of this pre-war period fuse discussions of farming with feminism, notably Marian Cran's *A woman in Canada* (1911) and *Wheat and woman* (1914). The war blocked this spate of books; but all pre-war themes appear, finely handled, in Rupert Brooke's *Letters from America* (1916).

The aftermath of war brought new conditions and a new tone. Motor travel gave a plot-line for many brash books, such as Percy Gomery's *A motor-scamper cross Canada: a human-interest narrative of a pathfinding journey from Montreal to Vancouver* (1922). Sophisticated memoirs of pre-war trips include V.H. Rikki's *Ups and downs in Canada* (1922). But most travel books now ruefully reported 'downs': bleak journeys through a world of cabooses and rooming-houses, as in G.M. Westbury's *Misadventures of a working hobo in Canada* (1930). Many well-educated young Englishmen, drifting westward, faced and described a 'land of bull and bale-wire', to quote E.F.G. Fripp's *The outcasts of Canada* (1932). Few pleasure-travellers chose Canada when Europe was inexpensive and fashionable.

The Second World War brought a brief revival of old-style coast-to-coast travelogues, as in Dorothy Duncan's *Here's to Canada* (1943). Early hardships, artificially recreated, provided the main interest of Mary Bosanquet's *Saddlebags for suitcases* (1942) and *Canada ride* (1944). Bruce HUTCHISON tried for a more ambitious portrait—one that had a great popular success—in the seasonal sequence of *The unknown country* (1942) in which the motif of journeying recurs, though it is not strictly a travel book.

Air travel brought the Far North into easier reach and facilitated reports like P.G. Downes' *Sleeping island* (1946) and Peter Scott's *Wild geese and Eskimos* (1951). The hardships of wilderness travel continued to receive major emphasis in modern travel accounts, as presented by Canadians such as Farley MOWAT and Pierre BERTON.

In the 1950s two authentic and substantial books report a search for origins. In *Ravens and prophets: an account of journeys in British Columbia, Alberta, and Southern Alaska* (1952) George WOODCOCK is particularly interesting in his account of a quiet trip through remote British Columbia settlements. In *Canada made me* (1958) Norman LEVINE, as an 'angry young man', travels from Halifax to Ottawa to the Cariboo and finds a land of sleaziness, slush, and social emptiness. A long-familiar note—the old resentment against anti-British sentiment in Canada—sounds in Dennis Godfrey's *No Englishman need apply* (1965). In the same year the Canadian novelist Edward McCOURT described a modest coast-to-coast journey in *The road across Canada*. The newly important Québécois perspective added poignance to a travel book by the Montreal journalist Eugène Cloutier, whose *Le Canada sans passeport* (2 vols, 1967) was abridged and translated by Joyce MARSHALL as *No passport: a discovery of Canada* (1968; rpr. 1973).

By the 1970s travel literature about Canada had more or less ceased. Cheap, safe, and comfortable air travel had shifted tourism to Africa and Asia. While Canada did not entirely lose place as a subject of interest, this tended to be satisfied mainly by presentations on film or television, or in books of fine photography. Of these the best examples are probably *Canada* (1964; rev. 1969), with photographs by Peter Varley and a text by Kildare DOBBS; *Canada: a year of the land* (1967), a centennial project of the National Film Board edited by Lorraine Monk; *To everything there is a season: Roloff Beny in Canada* (1967); and *Canada: coast to coast* (1982), with photographs by various photographers and an introductory travelogue by Roger Boulton.

Most early travel books are available on microfilm. Excellent bibliographies appear in Norah Story, *The Oxford companion to Canadian history and literature* (1967) after entries on British North America, Canada, individual provinces, and territories or regions (e.g. Barren Grounds). Surveys of travel books are included in the *Literary history of Canada* (1967; 2nd edn 1976). Useful introductions appear in selective anthologies such as Gerald Craig, *Early travellers in the Canadas* (1955); Mary Quayle Innis, *Travellers west* (1956); and James Doyle, *Yankees in Canada* (1980). See also unpublished Ph.D. dissertations by J.J. Talman (Toronto, 1930), Peter Mitcham (Edinburgh, 1958), T.D. MacLulich (York, 1976), and Richard Davis (UNB, 1979). ELIZABETH WATERSTON

Tremblay, Michel (b. 1942). Born and raised on rue Fabre in the 'Plateau Mont-Royal' section of Montreal (where most of his plays and novels are set), he studied graphic arts after high school and became a linotype operator, like his father and brother. His first play, *Le train*, was written in 1959, won first prize in the 1964 'Jeunes auteurs' contest of Radio-Canada, and was produced on television. But *Les* BELLES-SOEURS (1968), written in 1965 and produced in 1968, is regarded as the true beginning of a career that rapidly brought fame to Tremblay, enabling him to devote himself entirely to his writing. (A translation by Bill Glassco and John Van Burek was published in 1974.) A full cycle of plays followed, describing other facets and characters of the same universe; it ended with *Damnée Manon, sacrée Sandra* (1977). He later wrote *L'impromptu d'Outremont* (1980, translated by Glassco and Van Burek as *The impromptu of Outremont*, 1981), which reflects the preoccupations of the more bourgeois neighbourhood he moved to in 1974, and *Les anciennes odeurs* (1981), about a homosexual relationship.

The Plateau Mont-Royal setting must be seen as a true social microcosm of alienated Québec: most characters are doomed, from birth to death, to a dead-end. The most powerfully tragic play in this regard is *À toi pour toujours, ta Marie-Lou* (1973)—translated by Bill Glassco and John Van Burek as *Forever yours, Marie-Lou* (1973)—in which two sisters, Carmen and Manon, confront their parents, Léopold and Marie-Lou, who have been dead ten years. (It was imagined by Tremblay as a musical quartet.) Ten years after her parents' death, Manon sits in a rocking chair trying to resemble her mother, whose destiny she perpetuates in a masochistic acceptance of a frustrated and dull life, while Carmen, dressed as a cowgirl, has become a country-and-western singer in a cheap nightclub. Carmen reappears in *Sainte Carmen de la Main* (1976)—translated by Glassco and Van Burek (1981)—in which she is killed for having tried to liberate (or 'redeem') her transvestite and prostitute friends. Carmen is a central figure in Tremblay's plays, for she exemplifies the full meaning of transvestitism—in the sense of *le travestissement*, which means not only cross-dressing but misrepresentation—a major theme in his plays dealing mainly with show-business or homosexuality, such as the musical-comedy *Demain matin Montréal m'attend* (1972); *La Duchesse de Langeais* (1970)—translated by Van Burek (1976); *Hosanna* (1973)—translated by Glassco and Van Burek (1974); *Les héros de mon enfance* (1976); and *Damnée Manon, sacrée*

Sandra. All these plays present an interesting and basically realistic depiction of a marginal milieu, where the struggle for social recognition and true human love is often dramatic. However, one must also consider these characters as symbolic figures for a whole collectivity—Québec—in which borrowing someone else's identity always seems the only way to success and respectability. Hence Carmen's decision to drop the lyrics and tunes learned in Tennessee, and to sing her own songs describing the real problems of her friends, can lead only to her death. Hence also (but more positively) the final scene of *Hosanna*, in which the two male lovers—one of them, 'Hosanna', garbed as Elizabeth Taylor in *Cleopatra*—undress, shedding all pretences and make-believe to accept their true selves and affirm their identities.

Other aspects of the metaphorical use of transvestism are shown in *Damnée Manon, sacrée Sandra*. Manon, Marie-Louise's daughter, is still rocking her life away in the kitchen chair, but her mysticism now verges on fetishism and madness. 'Sandra' is a male transvestite whose sole concern in life seems to be with sex. He is opposed to Manon as sharply as his white costume is opposed to her black dress, his 'avocado sea' green lipstick to the burgundy colour of her rosary. But as Sandra describes the black 'god' from Martinique whom he loves, and Manon tells about her love for Christ, the true meaning of the play becomes clear: 'religion and sex stem from the same craving for an absolute', as the playwright explained to Martial Dassylva in *La Presse* (26 Feb. 1977).

Remembering Tremblay's repeated statement that there are 'no real men in Québec', most critics have noted that Tremblay's world is dominated by women—just as Québec society, and particularly its French and religious characteristics, owe much to the obstinacy of women. *Bonjour la, bonjour* (1974)—translated by Glassco and Van Burek (1975)—seems to shed new light on this matter. It deals with the love between a brother and sister, Serge and Nicole, a social taboo seldom treated so openly; such a relationship meets head on with social and family attitudes—but these are shown to be hypocritical, for the whole family is unknowingly entangled in incestuous desires. Very strikingly, however, the characters who stand out in this mostly feminine universe are two men, father and son; all the women are trying to seduce or possess Serge, who craves only the love of his deaf father. The play climaxes in Serge's long-contained cry: 'I love you, Papa!' Thus his love for his sister—and this might apply to some homosexual relationships depicted by Tremblay—seems a perverse manifestation of his quest for his father's love. More generally, this might allow us to see the portrayal of ineffectual men in other plays in the same perspective. The weak and sometimes despicable male characters in *Les belles-soeurs, Forever yours, Marie-Lou*, and *En pièces détachées* (1970)—translated by Allan Van Meer as *Like death warmed over* (1975)—are the hidden face of this obsessive quest, the importance of which is again shown in *Les anciennes odeurs* (first produced in 1981), in which the older lover is clearly identified as a father-image by the younger one, who talks incessantly about his dying father.

No less than ten plays by Tremblay have been performed in English outside Québec. Toronto's Tarragon Theatre has produced *Forever yours, Marie-Lou* (1972), *Hosanna* (1974), *Bonjour là, bonjour* (1975), *Sainte Carmen de la Main* (1978), and *Damnée Manon, sacrée Sandra* (1979). The St Lawrence Centre for the Arts, Toronto, produced *Les belles-soeurs* (1973) and *Surprise, surprise* (1975), while *La Duchesse de Langeais* was first performed in English at New College, University of Toronto, in 1978. *Like death warmed over* has been produced at the Manitoba Theatre Centre in Winnipeg (1973); *Johnny Mangano and his astonishing dogs* in Edmonton (1980); and *The impromptu of Outremont* at the Vancouver Arts Center (1980).

Outside Canada *Hosanna* has been produced twice, without much success, in New York. *Bonjour là, bonjour*, however, has been produced widely in the U.S., and had a production in Japan in 1981. *A toi pour toujours, ta Marie-Lou* was performed in 28 cities of France, Belgium, Switzerland, and Great Britain; *Les belles-soeurs* in Paris; *Hosanna* in Paris, Antwerp, and The Netherlands; and *La Duchesse de Langeais* in France and Belgium. Finally *Hosanna* and *Damnée Manon, sacrée Sandra* were performed in New Zealand; and *Forever yours, Marie-Lou* was given its Italian première in Rome in 1979.

Trois petits jours (1966) contains three short plays—which appear in English as *Berthe, Johnny Mangano and his astonishing dogs*, and *Gloria Star*, along with *Surprise, surprise*—in the Talonbooks edition of *La Duchesse de Langeais & other plays* (1975).

Tremblay has also translated into French Aristophanes' *Lysistrata* (1969), Paul Zin-del's *The effect of gamma rays on man-in-the-moon marigolds* (1970) and *And Miss Reardon drinks a little* (1972); four plays by Tennessee Williams collected in *Au pays du dragon* (1972); Dario Fo's *Mistero Buffo* (1973); Roberto Athayde's *Aparaceu a Margarida* (1976); and Gretchen Cryer's *I'm getting my act together and taking it on the road* (1981). He wrote the scenarios and dialogue for three films directed by André Brassard: *Françoise Durocher, waitress* (1972), *Il était une fois dans l'est* (1974), and *Le soleil se lève en retard* (1975). He also wrote the scenario for *Parlez-vous d'amour* (1975) by Jean-Claude Lord and a television adaptation of Gabrielle ROY's BONHEUR D'OCCASION in 1977.

In the field of fiction, Tremblay published as early as 1966 *Contes pour buveurs attardés* (translated by Michael BULLOCK as *Stories for late night drinkers*, 1978); this was followed by *La cité dans l'oeuf* (1969) and *C't'à ton tour, Laura Cadieux* (1973). None of these seemed a major work, whereas the 'Plateau Mont-Royal' chronicles—*La grosse femme d'à côté est enceinte* (1978) and *Thérèse et Pierrette à l'école des saints-anges* (1980), to be followed by at least one more novel—have been generally hailed by readers and critics as very important. They have been translated by Sheila Fischman as *The fat woman next door is pregnant* (1981) and *Thérèse and Pierrette at the École des Saintes Anges* (1982).

See the Fall 1979 issue of *The Canadian Theatre Review*; the tenth chapter of Jean-Cléo Godin's and Laurent Mailhot's *Théâtre québécois II* (1980); and John Ripley's 'From alienation to transcendence, the quest for selfhood in Michel Tremblay's plays', in CANADIAN LITERATURE 85 (Summer 1980). The Winter 1982 issue of VOIX ET IMAGES, devoted entirely to Michel Tremblay, contains a long critical bibliography prepared by Lorraine Camerlain and Pierre Lavoie.

See also DRAMA IN FRENCH 1948 TO 1981: 3, 4 and NOVELS IN FRENCH 1960 TO 1982: 3(a).   JEAN-CLÉO GODIN

Tremblay, Rénald. See DRAMA IN FRENCH 1948 TO 1981: 3.

Trente arpents (1938). This classic of French-Canadian literature by Philippe PAN-NETON (pseud. 'Ringuet') was warmly received by critics both in France, where it first appeared, and in Canada. It won a Governor General's Award, the Prix David, and the Prix des Vikings of the French Academy; was translated into English under the title *Thirty acres* (1940; NCL 1960) by Felix and Dorothea Walter, and into German and Dutch—and has been reprinted several times—in Canada with an introduction by Jacques Cotnam (1971) and in France in the collection 'J'ai lu' (1981).

Trente arpents is the tragic story of the rise and fall of Euchariste Moisan, who is entirely devoted to his land. After years of success—the envy of his neighbours—the sale of a piece of his land and the failure of a lawsuit against one of his neighbours bring Euchariste humiliation and ruin. His son Étienne, who persuades Euchariste to cede his land to him and to visit his favourite son Ephrem in the U.S., refuses to send his father the money for a return ticket to his village, and the old man will likely end his life as a nightwatchman in an American industrial town, unable to communicate with anyone but his son—not even with his own grandchildren and his son's wife, since he speaks no English and they speak no French. Set in the Trois-Rivières area between 1887 and 1932, *Trente arpents* reveals a society on the verge of radical change. It opposes progress to traditions, city life to rural life, younger to older generations, and life to death. Above all, it denounces the farmer's subservience to his land. As shown by the title as well as by several critics—for example Jacques Viens in *La terre de Zola et Trente arpents de Ringuet* (1970)—the main character of *Trente arpents* is the land itself, and that is what gives the novel its universality.

Panneton, who took nine years to write *Trente arpents*, did not want the term 'regionalist' to be applied to his novel; he was anxious to achieve realism by avoiding the extremes of both naturalism and idealism. He moved away from the traditional French-Canadian *roman de la terre* which, since *La terre paternelle* (1846) by Patrice LACOMBE, had offered a romantic and idealistic vision of the farmer's life in order to promote agriculturist ideologies. Panneton refused to use literature as an excuse for reviving the past or to put it to the service of a political cause.   JACQUES COTNAM

Trottier, Pierre (b. 1925). Born in Montreal, he studied law at the Université de Montréal and joined the Department of External Affairs in 1949. He has held diplomatic posts in Moscow, Djakarta, London, and Paris, and is now Canadian Ambassador to UNESCO, a post he has held since 1979. He first became known as a poet with *Le combat contre Tristan* (1951)—reprinted in *Sainte-Mémoire*—which presents the excite-

ment of foreign travel experienced by a French-Canadian working abroad. His poetry is laden with memory, culture, and thought. *Poèmes de Russie* (1957) stresses the inner life and suggests an obsession with origins. Hence the theme of androgyny arises: 'I made the first Eve part of my own being.' The beautiful poem 'Ce bois de mystère' celebrates the mother loved for her voice, her hands, her eyes, her form, her fear, her words, her death. The next collection, *Les belles au bois dormant* (1960)—dedicated to the memory of his mother, who died in 1958—is a quest for self that travels 'between my daughter who has just been born/And my mother who has died.' This is rich, highly descriptive poetry. Trottier's major poetic work was appropriately called *Sainte-Mémoire* (1972). It reprints the *'retours'* that had first appeared in *Écrits du Canada français* (no. 13, 1962; no. 29, 1970): the return of Oedipus, a man's return to his homeland; the return of Don Quixote, who drove out fear; the return of the androgyne, man reunited with himself—'I discovered Eve within me. The same soul within two bodies.' Playing on the term for seasonal migration ('transhumance'), Trottier created a beautiful new word: *transâmance* (migration of souls) 'to denote the unity or transfer of souls between two bodies', the formula for a new kind of love. 'Your life and mine are one! Such is the language of the *transâmance* when one finds his equal.'

Mon Babel (1963) is a collection of 17 short essays on the French-Canadian identity. Trottier examines the Québec milieu, its myths, culture, and place in the world, presenting a universe populated with familiar characters: Laius and Danaus, Tristan, Hamlet, Shakespeare, Corneille, Racine. Filled with their voices, their watchful eyes, this is both descriptive and poetic writing in which Trottier adapts his Canadian heritage, his American culture, his religion and myths to a patient reworking of history and memory. Referring to *Mon Babel*, Trottier later wrote: 'We must push hard against death . . . to exorcize it. It is a matter of getting rid of the heritage of Saint-Denys GARNEAU before moving on to other things.' *Un pays baroque* (1979), a collection of 13 assorted essays centring on the culture and history of Canada as an English-French-American world entity, is Trottier's most lively and impressive book. Often witty and intentionally insolent, and with many autobiographical references, these essays are of great literary and historical value. Trottier defines the baroque as the 'reconsideration of fixed forms, and the quest, whether exuberant or tortured, for a new form.' The 'baroque land' is 'Kanada'—or 'Carien', because 'nada' in Spanish means 'rien' in French, or 'nothing'. Situated in 'Amerika', whose destiny is 'Americainfinitive', its capital is Ottawa, or the 'Anglo-French cultural ambiguity'.

For a discussion of *Le combat contre Tristan*, *Poèmes de Russie*, and *Mon Babel*, see Pierre de Grandpré, *Dix ans de vie littéraire au Canada français* (1966). See also Gilles Marcotte, 'Diplomate, essayiste et poète, Pierre Trottier', in *Québec 64* (1964).

JOSEPH BONENFANT

Trudel, Marcel. See HISTORICAL WRITING IN FRENCH.

Turgeon, Pierre. See NOVELS IN FRENCH 1960 TO 1982: 3(a).

Two little savages (1906). This classic of children's literature by Ernest Thompson SETON (now translated into many languages) grew out of his work with youth groups in the United States. By 1903 fifty 'tribes' had formed, calling themselves 'Seton's Indians' or 'Woodcraft Indians'. During that year Seton published, in *Ladies Home Journal*, a serialized story for boys, an expanded version of which later became *Two little savages: being the adventures of two boys who lived as Indians and what they learned*. Although written in the third person, the story is semi-autobiographical and records Seton's adventures in the summer of 1876, when he holidayed with the Blackwell family near Lindsay, Ont. In the woods near the farm, Seton and the son of Blackwell 'played Indian' and developed games that were later incorporated in Boy Scout rituals still used in many parts of the world.

Two little savages, an episodic adventure story, provided Seton with a framework into which he could interpolate instructions on woodcraft (generously illustrated with his own detailed drawings). The story describes an initiation rite in which the testing of a boy's knowledge of birds and trees merges with an archetypal pattern. Yan (as the young Seton) confronts a sequence of trials, demonstrates his courage, and is finally pronounced a hero. Since the story ends with Yan's resolve to 'strive and struggle as a naturalist', the book could be viewed as an autobiographical *Bildungsroman*. Variations of many of the same episodes appear in Seton's autobiography, *Trail of an artist-naturalist* (1940).

MAGDALENE REDEKOP

Two solitudes (1945). This novel by Hugh MacLENNAN, for which he won his first Governor General's Award, aroused more public interest than critical attention because of its theme of Canadian unity, which had been strained in the 1942 plebiscite on conscription, and its apposite title, drawn from Rilke. Although Rilke and MacLennan both had individuals in mind as the solitudes that touch and protect each other, the application to the dominant cultural groups in Canada has since become a cliché.

Two solitudes is structured in four parts: the first two treat the period 1917 to 1921 and the second two the years 1934 and 1939. Part I, set in the rural Québec parish of Saint-Marie-des-Érables, has two interests. One is the struggle between the proud, anticlerical, progressive Athanase Tallard and the Anglophobe parish priest, Father Beaubien, who opposes change. The second interest is the attempt of Yardley, a retired sea-captain, to settle in the parish where, ironically, he is more acceptable than Tallard, whose political loyalties, affiliation with English-speaking capitalists, estrangement from his Anglophobe son Marius, and second marriage to an Irish girl threaten the status quo. Part II ends in utter defeat for Tallard: a failed marriage, a broken family, financial ruin, the loss of his family home, and death, which is preceded by a return to the Church. MacLennan's treatment in the first half of Tallard, Yardley, and the younger generation is deft and sympathetic; the story moves with almost tragic inevitability. But as George WOODCOCK and others have noted, the second half of the book—centring on Paul Tallard, the son of Athanase by his second marriage, and on Paul's courtship of Heather Methuen against the backdrop of the English community of Montreal and the business career of Huntley McQueen—is neither sympathetic nor dramatic. McQueen is treated satirically (he has overtones of Mackenzie King); and Paul's and Heather's marriage, intended to suggest a French-English détente, is unconvincing. Paul is more like a spokesman for the author's beliefs and hopes than a fully realized character. It is typical of MacLennan's early optimistic writing about national problems that the realities of the situation should be rendered more persuasively than their resolution.

The novel, then, is not an unqualified success. With its abrupt period divisions, its point of view that changes from the objective to the personal and didactic, leading characters who in the beginning are lively and realistic (Tallard *père*, Yardley) and then become mere symbols (Paul, Heather, and the other *Anglais*) or shadows (Marius), it lacks cohesiveness. If the sense that the components are ill-yoked does not suit the theme, however, it suits the title. For all its

faults *Two solitudes* is a sensitive and creditable attempt to portray the tensions and differences in Québec that culminated in the Quiet Revolution (a decade and a half before that event took place) and the possibility of reconciliation. It is a landmark in Canadian nationalistic fiction.

Two solitudes is available in paperback in the Laurentian Library (1968).

D.O. SPETTIGUE

U

Ukrainian writing. Mass Ukrainian immigration to Canada began in the 1890s, when large numbers of peasants from Western Ukraine (then under Austro-Hungarian rule) began fleeing their politically oppressed and impoverished homeland for a fresh start in the New World. Attracted by the promise of free land, the first immigrants took up homesteads on the Prairies, or worked as labourers in frontier and urban enterprises. By the outbreak of the First World War an estimated 175,000 Ukrainians had settled in Canada, although they were then often confusingly identified as Ruthenians, Russians, Galicians, Romanians, Austrians, and Poles. Today well over half a million Canadians claim Ukrainian ancestry, tracing their roots back to one of four major periods of immigration: 1891–1914, 1919-30, 1945-55, and 1971-81. The contemporary Ukrainian-Canadian community reflects a great regional, religious, and political diversity. Some eighty per cent of Ukrainian Canadians are now Canadian-born, the overwhelming majority residing in the large cities of central and western Canada.

Western Ukrainian literature contains a number of fascinating works about the first exodus of Ukrainians to the New World. The best known is a short story by the important Expressionist writer Vasyl Stefanyk, 'Kaminyi Khrest' (Lviv, 1899), published in English as *The stone cross* by McClelland and Stewart in 1971. Stefanyk never emigrated, but his vivid description of a peasant family's departure from a Galician

village 'almost exactly recorded', as the author acknowledged, the real-life experience of Stefan Didukh (d. 1911), who settled in Hilliard, Alta. Before leaving his native land, Didukh erected a stone cross atop a hill on his property, where it remains to this day as a monument to Canada's Ukrainian pioneers.

The first Ukrainian immigrants are usually depicted in popular literature as hard-working, thrifty, but uneducated *muzhiks* who overcame great physical hardship and discrimination in clearing prosperous farms out of the Canadian wilderness. Although more than half the early settlers were illiterate, recent historical evidence suggests that it was the more ambitious and intellectually aware peasants who tended to be motivated enough to emigrate; they came from a part of Ukraine where the level of culture—influenced by an expanding network of co-operatives, community centres, and 'enlightenment societies' (where the literate would read books and periodicals aloud for the benefit of the uneducated)—had been steadily rising since the mid-nineteenth century. They shared a well-developed oral tradition that served as the fertile soil from which written Ukrainian-Canadian literature sprang less than seven years after the onset of immigration.

Ukrainian literature in Canada originated in the songs, stories, and sayings of the first colonists, and ranged from nostalgic or bitter laments to optimistic and even ironic panegyrics about life in the new land. The first published Ukrainian poem written in

Ukrainian writing

Canada was a song composed by Ivan Zbura (1860-1940), who farmed a homestead in northeastern Alberta. Titled 'Kanadiiski emigranty' ('Canadian emigrants') and dated 30 Dec. 1898, it compares life in the old country with that in the new, finding the latter much to be preferred. Sincere and vibrant, like a lot of immigrant writing, it is of greater historical and sociological value than literary interest; but many similar folk poems from the early period show considerable flair and a natural grasp of technique.

The founding in Winnipeg in 1903 of the first Ukrainian newspaper in Canada, *Kanadiiskii farmer* (Canadian farmer), was of landmark significance, since it provided authors with access to a press that could set the Cyrillic script and with a reading public. It was soon followed by numerous other publications, in which we find the first attempts at Ukrainian *belles-lettres* in Canada. Winnipeg became the leading Canadian centre of Ukrainian publishing. One of the first collections of indigenous folk poetry, *Pisni pro Kanadu i Avstriu* (Songs about Canada and Austria, 1908), went through six editions and a name change (Songs about the old and new countries) necessitated by wartime tensions, selling over 50,000 copies. The final edition of 1927 contained thirty songs, mostly in the traditional *kolomyika* form, by fifteen authors.

Perhaps the most interesting writer of the pioneer generation was Paul Crath (also spelled Krat, 1882-1952), who emigrated in 1907 from Central Ukraine. A revolutionary student whose political activities had forced him to flee both Russian and Austro-Hungarian authorities, Crath naturally gravitated towards radical circles and soon was editing the Winnipeg-based socialist organ *Chervonyi prapor* (The red flag, 1907-9). Crath's early book, *Sotsialistychni pisni* (Socialist songs, 1909), was a best-selling collection of original works containing several of his left-wing adaptations of Ukrainian national songs. (His Ukrainian translation of 'The Internationale' was used, without acknowledgement, by the Soviet government until a new version replaced it in the 1920s.) Crath also produced a number of militantly ideological prose works during his early days as an activist-writer—such as 'Vizyta "Chervonoi Druzhyny" ' ('The visit of the "Red Legion" ', 1912), 'Koly lekshe bude?' ('When will it be better?', 1912), and 'Poslidne khozhdeniie Boha po zemli' ('The last day God walked the earth', 1915)—and founded the first periodical of Ukrainian-Canadian humour, a scathingly anti-clerical monthly ironically titled *Kadylo* (Incensory, 1913). Some time in 1915-16, however, he underwent a spiritual transformation that led to his conversion to Presbyterianism and to his ordination into the ministry in 1920. During this period he collaborated with Florence Randal Livesay on the first translation of Ukrainian songs into English, *Songs of Ukraina* (1916), and worked on the Presbyterian Church's Ukrainian-language organ *Ranok* (Dawn, est. 1905). But it seems that—except for a translation he undertook with Watson KIRKCONNELL, *Prince Ihor's raid against the Polovtsi* (1947)—Crath's new vocation absorbed most of his creative energies.

The internment of thousands of Ukrainian men as 'enemy aliens' during the Great War and the imposition of censorship restrictions on the Ukrainian press did much to stifle intellectual activity for several years. However, with the resumption of large-scale Ukrainian immigration in the 1920s, Ukrainian-Canadian literature entered an exciting new phase that found its most vital expression in the theatre. The first Ukrainian drama presented in Canada was *Argonauty* (The argonauts), staged in Winnipeg by the Shevchenko Reading Society in 1904. The first original Ukrainian play on a Canadian theme was a comedy by the humorist Jacob Maydannyk (b. 1891), the creator of an immensely popular comic-strip character named 'Vuiko Shtif Tabachniuk' ('Uncle Steve Tobacco'). His farce, *Manigrula* (1915)—a corruption of the word for 'immigrant'—was reprinted in 1927. From these beginnings Ukrainian amateur and semi-professional theatre grew to be one of the most dynamic forces and popular forms of entertainment in Ukrainian communities across the country. Between 1911 and 1942 more than 100 original stage-works were written by twenty-six different playwrights, with six authors accounting for 68 plays; over a third had Canadian settings. At the Ukrainian National Home in Toronto, 48 different productions were mounted in a peak year, the number of performances in the period 1926-53 totalling 513. This passion for theatre was equally strong in rural settlements, which often had very active amateur troupes.

Of the six playwrights who contributed most to the development of Ukrainian-Canadian drama, the Western Ukrainian writer and political activist Andrii Babiuk (1897-1937)—more commonly known by his pen-name, 'Myroslaw Irchan'—stands out. Coming to Canada on the invitation of Ukrainian socialists, he lived in Winnipeg only from 1923 to 1929; but these years were intensely productive and he wrote much that enriches both the tradition of Ukrainian writing in Canada and the larger Canadian literary heritage. Irchan immersed himself in cultural and political life, editing various left-wing publications, lecturing widely on the situation in Ukraine, and writing numerous short stories, sketches, and plays. In several works he movingly described the trauma of being uprooted, and laid bare the exploitation of immigrant workers, his best piece in this vein being a novella, *Karpatska nich* (Carpathian night, 1923). A committed internationalist, Irchan took up the cause of native Canadians and sympathetically depicted the plight of the Indian, Inuit, and Métis peoples in his stories 'Vudzhena ryba' ('Smoked fish', 1924) and 'Smert Asuara' ('The death of Asuara', 1927). He assisted in the productions of several plays he had written in Europe when they premièred in Canada before large and enthusiastic audiences. Charles Roslin, in an article entitled 'Canada's Bolshevist drama: Myroslaw Irchan, playwright and prophet of the proletarian revolution' (*Saturday Night*, 9 Feb. 1928), went so far as to contend that Irchan might be 'the most popular and influential author in the country.' Tragically, Irchan decided to return to Soviet Ukraine, where he was swept up in the Stalinist purges of 1933. Exiled to Siberia, he is said to have died there four years later, but the exact circumstances of his death are unknown. Irchan was subsequently 'rehabilitated' in the Khruschevian thaw and is now regarded by Soviet critics as an interesting minor writer. A two-volume edition of his selected works was issued in Kiev in 1958.

A second important writer to emerge in the interwar period was Illia Kiriak (sometimes spelled Kyriak, 1889-1955), who immigrated to Canada in 1906. After working as a labourer for several years, he settled in Edmonton, where he became increasingly involved in the short-lived newspaper *Nova hromada* (New society, 1911-12). At the age of twenty-four he enrolled in the Vegreville School for Foreigners, graduating as a teacher in 1919. He spent the remainder of his life teaching in rural schools in northeastern Alberta and working for the Ukrainian Self-Reliance League of Canada. Kiriak's major literary undertaking was his epic trilogy, *Syny zemli* (Sons of the soil), published between 1939-45. This 1,110-page saga, a Ukrainian-Canadian classic, provides a panoramic overview of three generations of an immigrant family. Conventional in form and style, it is a well-told story that chronicles many of the important stages in the development of Ukrainian-Canadian life. A fictionalized synthesis of numerous individual experiences—depicting such landmark occasions as the erection of the church and the pioneer schoolhouse, and the first awkward intermarriage—it sums up all the myths about the successful integration of Ukrainians into Canadian society. A clumsily abridged translation, *Sons of the soil*, was published by the RYERSON PRESS in 1959.

With the end of hostilities in Europe in 1945 and the arrival of a third wave of immigrants—many coming from central and eastern Ukraine—all aspects of Ukrainian-Canadian community life underwent a transformation. The new immigrants were much better educated than their predecessors, and generally preferred to settle in the cities of central Canada. Having witnessed the horrors of Stalinism and Nazism, and survived the hardships of famine and war, they brought with them a passionate Ukrainian nationalism that often dominated their world view. It is generally acknowledged that the foremost living author among the post-war immigrants is Ulas Samchuk (b. 1905), who had previously established a reputation in Europe with a novel, *Mariia* (Maria, 1934), and two trilogies, *Volyn* (Volhynia, 1932) and *Ost* (East, 1948). But Samchuk seems to have had great difficulty in adjusting to emigré life and was silent for a long time after settling in Toronto. Criticism of his first attempt at a Ukrainian-Canadian novel, *Na tverdi zemli* (On the hard earth, 1967), suggests that it fails to measure up to the quality of his earlier work.

Other noteworthy writers in this group include the poet and humorist Borys Oleksandriv (the pseudonym of Borys Hrybinsky, 1921-79), and the poets Volodymyr Skorupsky (b. 1912), Oleh Zujewsky (b. 1920), and Yar Slavutych (b. 1918)—all well known to the Ukrainian reading public. The latter has also published two collections of verse in English translation—*Oasis* (1959) and *The conquerors of the Prairies* (1974)—and has worked extensively in the field of Ukrainian-Canadian literary history. An important role in contemporary Ukrainian-Canadian literary life is played by the writers' association Slovo (The Word),

Ukrainian writing

which has now published nine almanacs of original work by Slovo members. The organization has chapters in several Canadian centres and is appropriately headed by essayist Yuri Stefanyk (a son of the famous Ukrainian writer Vasyl Stefanyk), whose collected writings have been issued under his pen-name Yuri Klenovyi: *Moim synam—moim pryiateliam* (For my sons, for my friends, 1981).

In the post-war period there emerged a generation of Ukrainian-Canadian authors writing primarily or exclusively in English. Vera Lysenko (1910-1975), the author of *Men in sheepskin coats: a study in assimilation* (1947), was among the first to initiate this new trend with her Ukrainian-Canadian novel *Yellow boots* (1954). Among other prominent writers in this category are Maara Haas (nee Lazechko, b. 1920), best known for her novel *The street where I live* [1976]; Myrna Kostash (b. 1944), the author of *All of Baba's children* (1977) and of the script for the NFB production *Teach me to dance* (1977); and poet Andrew SUKNASKI, who has written numerous poems on Ukrainian-Canadian themes and published a collection of them under the title *In the name of Narid* (1981). The most widely acclaimed writer in this group is George RYGA, whose voluminous output embraces several works that stem directly from his Ukrainian roots, such as his television dramas 'Ninth Summer' (1972) and '1927' (the 'Visit from the Pension Lady' segment in *The Newcomers* series, 1979), and his play *A letter to my son* (1981), written in commemoration of ninety years of Ukrainian settlement in Canada.

Another development since the Second World War has been the emergence of a small cadre of literary translators. The leading figure in this group is the expatriate American poet Marco Carynnyk (b. 1943); but several other young writers and Slavicists have begun taking up the challenge of translation, so that at least some of the more important works of Ukrainian-Canadian literature will become known to non-Ukrainian readers. **JARS BALAN**

Umfreville, Edward. See EXPLORATION LITERATURE IN ENGLISH: 2.

Underhill, Frank H. See HISTORICAL WRITING IN ENGLISH: 5.

University Magazine, The (1907-20). A Montreal quarterly edited by Andrew MAC-PHAIL, it succeeded the semi-annual *McGill*

University Magazine (1901-6), edited by Charles Moyse, which had appeared ten times. The new periodical took over its subscription list of under 1,000 and numbered its volumes consecutively, beginning with vol. VI. Although theoretically directed by an editorial committee drawn from McGill, the University of Toronto, and Dalhousie College, Halifax, *The University Magazine* was under Macphail's control from the beginning. Notable for paying its contributors—the average fee of $25 was more than many a weekly wage—the magazine was financially guaranteed by Macphail himself, although McGill and Toronto and various benefactors made occasional contributions. It drew upon the best contributors from English-speaking Canada, along with some from outside the country, and under Macphail's rigorous editorial direction set a standard of excellence, while attaining a circulation of nearly 6,000, a level that no comparable Canadian quarterly has subsequently matched. Macphail himself contributed 43 pieces of political comment and social criticism (for which he took no payment). Although welcoming purely literary contributions—for example, 'Addison as a literary critic' by E.K. Broadus (Feb. 1909)—the magazine, for Macphail, was a vehicle to advance what he described as 'correct thought', which had to do with a Canada that was rural, traditional, imperial in sentiment, and, aside from Québec, overwhelmingly British in ethnic composition. When his ideals had seemed to become things of the past—and for various other reasons, including failing eyesight and financial pressures—Macphail discontinued the magazine. **IAN ROSS ROBERTSON**

University of Toronto Press. Founded in 1901, the first university press to be established in Canada and the tenth to be established in North America, the University of Toronto Press is today one of the largest university presses on the continent. It began as a small printing department of the University, producing examination papers and calendars. It now comprises, along with its publishing activities, a book-manufacturing plant and bookstores on three Toronto campuses. It is a wholly owned ancillary operation of the University (maintained outside the University budget), issuing between 80 and 100 new books annually and having a backlist of about 1,200 titles. It also publishes some 25 academic journals, most of them quarterlies. General policies are determined by a board appointed by the University, and publications are approved by an academic editorial board appointed by the president. Its net income, after all operating and capital expenses have been met, is devoted to the publication of scholarly research, reference works, and general books of cultural and social significance. Its publications—which have won many international and national awards for their contributions to knowledge and for their design and production—are sold worldwide through a network of exclusive agents and representatives, and, in the United States, through its own office and warehouse in Buffalo.

Publishing mainly in the humanities and social sciences, the Press draws its authors not only from across Canada but from other English-speaking countries. Major multi-volume publications include the *Collected works of John Stuart Mill* and the *Collected works of Erasmus* (translated into English), and the DICTIONARY OF CANADIAN BIOGRAPHY. Although most of its works are intended for an academic readership, it also publishes general books of mainly Canadian interest, including the *Literary history of Canada* (1965; rev. 1976), Russell Harper's *Painting in Canada; a history* (1966; 2nd edn. 1977), the *Encyclopaedia of music in Canada* (1982), and the annual *Canadian books in print* and *Canadian who's who*. Long-term best-sellers have included John Porter's *Vertical mosaic* (1965), Marshall McLUHAN's *Gutenberg galaxy* (1962), and R. MacGregor Dawson's *Government of Canada* (1947; 5th edn 1970). About 300 of its titles are available in paperback.   IAN MONTAGNES

V

Vac, Bertrand. Pseudonym of Aimé PELLETIER.

Vadeboncoeur, Pierre (b. 1920). Born in Montreal's Outremont district, he attended Collège Brébeuf and is a lawyer and economist. Vadeboncoeur might have become a judge or cabinet minister, but after working as technical adviser to the Confédération des syndicats nationaux, he became a full-time writer in 1975. He first wrote for *Cité libre* and then for indépendentiste and reformist publications and political parties. His first collection of essays, *La ligne du risque* (1963), is comparable to Jean LE MOYNE's *Convergences*. Though he writes about trade-unionism, his true topics are joyfulness, freedom, and creativity. His guiding spirit is the painter Paul-Émile Borduas. 'Art', he writes, 'has been a far more important and less dubious leader for us than history.'

An outspoken polemicist and letter-writer, Vadeboncoeur has not given the bulk of his time to the practice of these 'martial arts'. *Lettres et colères* (1969), *Un génocide en douce* (1976), and other such occasional works pale beside the substantial essay *La dernière heure et la première* (1970), about French Canada's absence from history, which he sees as a delay that may be turned to advantage, a marginal position filled with potential. *Un amour libre* (1970), a story of childhood, is a tale of strength-in-weakness and fresh beginnings in which Vadeboncoeur plays freely with the fates, and works as much with images as with ideas. The moralist has not, however, disappeared; he re-emerges in *Indépendances* (1972), a eulogy for opposition, for counterstrokes, for youth.

The most controversial of Vadeboncoeur's essays has been *Les deux royaumes* (1978). The magazine LIBERTÉ devoted an entire issue (no. 26) to commentary on this book, running the gamut from unqualified praise to utter refutation. Has Vadeboncoeur abandoned his social and political conscience for religious evasiveness? Has he gone from realism to idealism, from audacious writing to sermonizing and commentary in the style of Rousseau, Proust, and André MAJOR? Between the two kingdoms—this world and the other, whatever that might be—this author maintains a precarious balance. Teetering on the edge of an abstract ideal, he is rescued by what is per-

811

ceptible in his art, the imprint of his work on the language. LAURENT MAILHOT

Valgardson, W.D. (b. 1939). William Dempsey Valgardson was born in Winnipeg, but spent most of his childhood in Gimli, Man. He received a B.A. from United College in 1961, a B.Ed. from the University of Manitoba in 1965, and an M.F.A. in creative writing from the University of Iowa in 1969. He served as chairman of the English department of Cottey College in Nevada, Missouri, from 1970 to 1974, before returning to Canada to join the creative-writing faculty of the University of Victoria, Victoria, B.C.

Valgardson is the author of a novel, *Gentle sinners* (1980); a collection of poetry, *In the gutting shed* (1976); and three collections of short stories: *Bloodflowers* (1973), *God is not a fish inspector* (1975), and *Red dust* (1978)—all of which draw on his knowledge of the Icelandic communities near Gimli. In the short stories Valgardson's spare and rigorously concrete style mirrors both the cold, brittle landscape in which the stories are set and the harsh fates that befall most of the central characters. Occasionally, however, the stories are marred by endings that strain for subtlety. The novel *Gentle sinners* departs from the realism of the stories to give mythological complexity to the familiar theme of a country boy's struggle against the corruption of town life, and lacks the credibility of the shorter fiction.

FRANK DAVEY

Vallières, Pierre. See ESSAYS IN FRENCH: 6.

Vanderhaeghe, Guy (b. 1951). Born and raised in Esterhazy, Sask., he majored in history at the University of Saskatchewan (B.A., 1972; M.A., 1975) and pursued further studies at the University of Regina (B. Ed., 1978). Though he has worked as a teacher, an archivist, and a researcher, he now devotes his time chiefly to writing. He resides in Saskatoon.

Influenced by such prairie novelists as Margaret LAURENCE, Sinclair ROSS, and Robert KROETSCH, Vanderhaeghe began writing short stories in the late 1970s. 'What I learned from Caesar' was included in *80: best Canadian stories*; and 'The watcher' was the 1980 winner of CANADIAN FICTION MAGAZINE's annual contributor's prize for short fiction. The twelve stories in *Man de-*

scending (1982), which won a Governor General's Award—ranging in setting from the drought and economic depression of the Prairies in the thirties to Jubilee year in London—follow in a roughly chronological pattern, from childhood to old age, the pain and disillusionment of various male protagonists as they struggle to transcend their fear and loneliness. Suffused with compassion and subtle humour, Vanderhaeghe's compelling fiction belongs in the prairie tradition to which its author is indebted.

DAVID STAINES

van der Mark, Christine (1917-69). Born in Calgary, she attended Normal School and taught for five years in rural Alberta schools. She then completed a B.A. and M.A. at the University of Alberta, studying creative writing under F.M. Salter and in 1946 submitting her first novel, *In due season*, as her thesis. During three years of writing and teaching at the university she married, and from 1953 to 1964 her husband's work led the family to Montreal, Pakistan, Connecticut, England, and the Sudan before they settled in Ottawa. Despite her many travels she continued writing stories, articles, and a short novel with a Pakistani setting, *Hassan*. In 1960 she began *Honey in the rock* (1966), to be completed in Ottawa and followed by three unpublished works: *Where the long river flows*, a novel of the Mackenzie; *Paul Goss*, about a rural teacher succumbing to the isolation of northern Alberta; and *No longer bound*, an autobiographical piece.

In due season (1947) explores, from a distinctive female point of view, the human costs of pioneering. Its protagonist develops a farm in the northern-Alberta bush and raises a family through the 1930s with no help from her amiably shiftless husband. In the process she becomes hard and unscrupulous, alienating her neighbours and losing her daughter to a Métis sweetheart. A vivid and convincing evocation of northern life, the novel won the Oxford-Crowell prize for Canadian fiction. *Honey in the rock* is less elemental and more social in its emphasis. Interweaving the romantic awakenings and frustrations of a tightly knit community of 'Brethren in Christ' in southern Alberta in 1936-7, it has moments of dramatic intensity; but the plot dissipates its force in complications, and the setting lacks the compelling quality of *In due season*.

See 'Afterward' by van der Mark's daughter, Dorothy Wise, in the 1966 reprint of *In due season*. DICK HARRISON

Van Herk, Aritha. See NOVELS IN ENGLISH 1960 TO 1982: OTHER TALENTS, OTHER WORKS: 5.

van Vogt, A.E. See SCIENCE FICTION AND FANTASY IN ENGLISH AND FRENCH: 2.

Vézina, France. See DRAMA IN FRENCH 1948 TO 1981: 4.

Victims of tyranny, The (2 vols, Buffalo, 1847). This early Canadian novel by Charles E. Beardsley is a republican's version of the political and personal conflicts in the brief public career of a young Irish immigrant to York (Toronto), Upper Canada. The hero, Joseph Wilcox, is a thinly disguised representation of the actual Joseph Willcocks, a member of the legislative assembly and critic of government who was killed fighting with the Americans in the War of 1812. Wilcox is presented as a romantic paragon, a champion of truth and justice and tragic victim of the forces of self-serving oligarchy—the 'Family Compact', epitomized by the Rev. Whifler, the principal antagonist, and Mr Carleton (caricatures of the Rev. John Strachan and Provincial Secretary William Jarvis). These power-obsessed villains eventually provoke Wilcox's enlistment with the invading American forces and he is ultimately killed while championing republican ideas. The compression of events covering more than a decade into the space of several months heightens the drama of the novel. One of its more engaging characters, ironically, is Sam Johnson—to his unresourceful creator a resourceful and witty model American, clearly patterned on the stereotyped Sam Slick of Thomas Chandler HALIBURTON. Though characterization tends towards caricature, and dialogue towards diatribe, and though the novel's concluding section is too diffuse, *The victims of tyranny* is nonetheless an impassioned and provocative narrative of actual characters and events from early Canadian history.

The author, about whom nothing is known, was apparently a member of the republican branch of an American family divided by the American Revolution. The Loyalist branches of the Beardsleys settled in New Brunswick and Upper Canada, where the men became prominent lawyers, and maintained contact with the American branches. The knowledge of the internal affairs of York and Upper Canada displayed in the novel suggests that Beardsley must have lived, for a while at least, in Toronto.

He very likely had his novel published in Buffalo because he could not find a Toronto publisher. CHARLES R. STEELE

Viets, Roger (1738-1811). Born in Simsbury, Conn., he prepared himself for Church of England orders at Yale College, graduating in 1758. After several years as a lay reader, he was ordained in London in 1763 and returned to Simsbury, where he was parish priest until he immigrated to Nova Scotia as a Loyalist refugee in late 1785. During the American Revolution, Viets had remained loyal to the monarchy and was jailed in 1777 on suspicion of aiding British fugitives. Upon immigrating to Nova Scotia he was assigned to the parish of Digby, a new Loyalist town, and served there as rector of Trinity Church until his death. He published six sermons between 1787 and 1800, and left a large collection in manuscript form. His theology was orthodox and not particularly challenging intellectually, but in their logical clarity and persuasive rhetoric his sermons reveal a strong, active, passionate mind as they project a vision of an ordered, cohesive society bound together by unanimity and mutual respect. The implication is that all the fundamental elements of human happiness lie within the reach of the Loyalist refugees. Viets' *Annapolis Royal; a poem* (Halifax, 1788), written in the same vein, is of historical interest as the first separate imprint of verse written and published in what is now Canada. The author's emphasis falls on harmony—in nature, in man, and in the universe—and the image that emerges is therefore idyllic; but the poem explicitly integrates life in Loyalist Nova Scotia into the vision of emotional, moral, and spiritual contentment that was central to prevailing eighteenth-century views of human experience and social purpose. The poem is inspirational, not because it is idyllic, but because it asserts that the recently dispossessed refugees are not isolated from the mainstream of human civilization. T.B. Vincent has edited a modern edition of this poem (1979). TOM VINCENT

Vigneault, Gilles (b. 1928). Born in Natashquan, Qué., on the north shore of the St Lawrence, he was educated at Université Laval, where he was influenced and encouraged by Félix-Antoine SAVARD. He then taught at various high schools and at Laval, during which time he founded *Émourie*, a poetry magazine that ran for thirteen issues, and the publishing firm Éditions de l'Arc. In 1960 he made his début as a *chansonnier*; his first triumphant Montreal concert was held later that year. The universal quality of his *chansons* and his individual and versatile performing style—his voice, sometimes almost raucous in exultation, at other times tender; his jigs and step-dances; and the wild semaphoring of his long arms, which can also achieve gentle fluidity—have made him equally popular in English Canada and in Europe. His most famous *chanson*, 'Mon pays'—which he claims was not separatist or even nationalist in intent, as is generally believed, but a personal lament for coldness and the inability to share love or experience—won an international award when sung by Monique Leyrac in Poland in 1965. He was awarded the Molson Prize in 1982.

Vigneault's poems and *chansons* alike are carefully structured, the work of a highly disciplined writer. Some vividly describe his native region of Natashquan, its violent seasons and life lived precariously between the forest and the sea, and such characters as Jack Monoloy and Jos Monferrand, real persons from his youth whom he has raised to mythic proportions. Woman often appears in these poems as nature or explicitly as a river or some other aspect of the region for which he feels tenderness. More personal poems concern love and the difficulty of loving, solitude and the passage of time, and what man has done with his world. His collections are *Étraves* (1959); *Balises* (1964); *Avec les vieux mots* (1964); *Pour une soirée de chansons* (1965); *Quand les bateaux s'en vont* (1965), winner of a Governor General's Award; *Les gens de mon pays* (1967); *Tam ti delam* (1967); *Paroles de chanson* (1969); *Ce que je dis c'est en passant* (1970); *Les dicts du voyageur sédentaire* (1970); *Exergues* (1971); *Les neufs couplets* (1973); *Je vous entends rêver* (1974); *Natashquan, le voyage immobile* (1976); *A l'encre blanc* (1977); and *Silences, poèmes 1957-1977* (1979). Vigneault has also published *Contes sur la pointe des pieds* (1960), *Contes du coin de l'oeil* (1966), and *La petite heure* (1979)—collections of brief prose pieces, more fables than stories, that make some comment on man's frailty or his alienation from nature and himself. The first two books were published together as *Les dicts du voyageur sédentaire: contes poétiques* (1970). *Contes sur la pointe des pieds* is also available in a bilingual edition, with translation by Paul Allard, as *Tales (sur la pointe des pieds)* (1972). Vigneault wrote the text for *Où la lumière chante* (1966), a book about Quebec City with photographs by François Lafortune. *Gilles Vigneault* (Paris, 1977) is a collection of his songs, with music.

Vigneault's poetry is discussed in *An outline of contemporary French-Canadian literature* (1972) by J. Raymond Brazeau. Studies in French are by Aline Robitaille (1968) and by Lucien Rioux (Paris, 1969) in the Chansonniers d'aujourd'hui series. *Fernand Seguin rencontre Gilles Vigneault* (1969), which is based largely on the transcript of a television interview, presents Vigneault's own thoughts about his life and work. English translations of some of his poems are in *The poetry of French Canada in translation* (1970) edited by John GLASSCO.   JOYCE MARSHALL

Vigneault, Robert. See ESSAYS IN FRENCH: 5.

Virgo, Sean (b. 1940). Born in Mtarfa, Malta, he earned a B.A. from Nottingham University, taught for four years at the University of Victoria, left in 1970 to spend a year in Connemara, and then lived until 1975 in the Queen Charlotte Islands, where the Haida culture profoundly influenced him. After leaving British Columbia, he lived until 1979 in Newfoundland, attracted by its Irish roots, its oral culture, and its Atlantic environment. He now resides once more in British Columbia.

Virgo has published four books of poetry: *Pieces for the old earth man* (1973); *Island* (1975), with Paul and Lutia Lauzon; *Kiskatinaw songs* (1979), with Susan MUSGRAVE; and *Deathwatch on Skidegate Narrows* (1979). Virgo's early poetry—intensely private and characterized by an interest in the spirit-world and ghosts—is written in a language that recalls the early work of W.B. Yeats; his later poems have a more concrete Anglo-Saxon diction. In his best poem, 'Deathwatch on Skidegate Narrows', the poet-narrator deplores the ecological rape of the Queen Charlotte Islands, and, in an attempt to get back to the pre-white era, makes an imaginative leap across the Narrows that carries him from the white world of the living to the Indian world of the past. In a sense the poem is pastoral elegy: Virgo sings the songs of dead Indians and they live on in him.

White lies and other fictions (1981) is a collection of ten short stories, many of them accomplished. The first three—'Ipoh', 'Arkendale', and 'Vagabonds'—concern the maturation of Malcolm Palmer, a British soldier in Malaysia. In 'Guess who I saw in

Paris?' Peter Ingram returns to Paris, the romantic sexual playground of his youth. Relentlessly the story reveals the gross truth behind his nostalgic memories. As a youth he had sought mystery in harlots, and so, in a grotesque and frightening conclusion, after he watches youths make love to an ancient whore, he prepares to do so himself. Other stories are concerned with the violation of the wilderness and with attempts to pervert the heritage of the Indians. In 'Les rites' a talismanic otter-skull brings down humiliating revenge on a casual hunter who has killed a pregnant doe to pass the time—there are echoes here of Faulkner's 'Delta autumn'. 'White lies' is the story of a nearly successful attempt to indoctrinate a rebellious Indian boy into the 'white lies' parrotted by even the best members of white society. Virgo's stories are sometimes too calculated; but at their best, as in 'Guess who I saw in Paris?' they are intensely imagined, sharply observed, and finely expressed.

JEFFREY HEATH

Voaden, Herman (b. 1903). Born in London, Ont., he graduated from Queen's University in 1923 and then embarked on a long teaching career that included positions at Toronto's Central High School of Commerce (head of English, 1928-64), Queen's University, and the University of Toronto. In the 1920s Voaden was also active as a director and actor at Hart House Theatre, the Detroit Repertory Theatre, and the Sarnia Little Theatre. In 1930-1 he studied drama at Yale University with George Pierce Baker, and later held several key administrative positions in Canadian arts organizations. He was president of the Canadian Arts Council (1945-8) and national director of the Canadian Conference of the Arts (1966-8). He is a Fellow of the Royal Society of Arts and a member of the Order of Canada.

The promotion of a Canadian artistic culture and identity, together with teaching, has consumed a good deal of Voaden's time and energy; but he has also managed to make notable contributions to Canadian experimental theatre and to edit several valuable drama anthologies. His career as a playwright began at Yale with a realistic drama of the North called *Wilderness*—in *Canada's lost plays: the developing mosaic*, vol. 3 (1980) edited by Anton Wagner—but a revised version, *Rocks*, first produced in 1932, reveals Voaden's interest in dramatic innovation. Rejecting what he saw as the mediocrity and stifling uniformity of contemporary theatre, Voaden created what he termed 'symphonic theatre', consisting of a striking coalescence of light, music, dance, and rhythmic speech. The experiment continued with *Earth song* (prod. 1932; pub. 1976), *Hill-land* (prod. 1934), and *Murder pattern* (prod. 1936; pub. 1980 in *Canada's lost plays*). *Murder pattern* (based on an actual Ontario murder case) is Voaden's best play, and combines a clear narrative line with drum-beats, chorus, and an expressionistic set and lighting. Adaptations and more original work followed. *Maria Chapdelaine*, an adaptation of Louis HÉMON's novel, was performed in 1938 and needed a large complement of choir, orchestra, dancers, narrators, and actors. *Ascend as the sun* was produced in Toronto in 1942; *Esther*, a dramatic symphony with music by Godfrey Ridout, was performed, also in Toronto, in 1952; and *Emily Carr*, a stage biography, was produced in Kingston in 1960. A collection of Voaden's plays will be published in 1984.

Among the anthologies Voaden has edited are *Six Canadian plays* (1930), *On stage: plays for school and community* (1945; rev. in 1966 as '*Nobody waved good-bye*' and other plays), *Four plays of our time* (1960), and *Look both ways: theatre experiences* (1975). Of these, *Six Canadian plays* remains the most important, representing as it does the first attempt to bring together a collection of Canadian dramatic literature. The six plays, all with northern settings, were written for a competition organized by Voaden at the Central High School of Commerce in 1929. The collection, says Voaden in his preface, 'attempts to strike the note of Canadianism which some of our painters have asserted with such courage in their own medium of expression'.

As a playwright Voaden remains isolated from predominant fashions and conventions; much of his work is too complex (and too expensive) for regular production. As theatrical administrator and theorist, however, he has had a vital and positive effect on the shape of twentieth-century Canadian theatre.

Typescripts of several of Voaden's plays are in the Metropolitan Toronto Library, and a 1976 taped interview with the playwright is in the Public Archives of Ontario. The Voaden Papers are in the York University Archives, Toronto.   L.W. CONOLLY

Voix et images. This magazine was first conceived in Oct. 1968 as *Cahiers de Sainte-*

Voix et images

Marie, but on publication appeared as *Littérature canadienne*. The following year the name was changed to *Voix et images du pays*. It was published under the auspices of the literary studies department of the Université du Québec (Montréal), directed by Renald Bérubé. Its nine numbers, irregularly produced, were chiefly devoted to literary and cultural works having to do with Québec. In Sept. 1975 the magazine changed its name again to *Voix et images*, but later appended as a subtitle a new version of one of its former titles, 'Littérature québécoise'. Appearing three times a year, it was directed by Jacques Allard and an editorial board consisting of Renald Bérubé, Joseph Bonenfant, André BROCHU, and various academics from Québec and Canadian universities. From then on the magazine contained an interview

with a notable author, studies of that author's work, and a bibliography, along with studies of other authors' works, literary articles, and bibliographical notes. In 1981 André Vanasse replaced Allard as editor—the members of the 1982 editorial board include Allard, Bernard Andrès, André Brochu, Jacques Michon, and Lucie Robert—but the format remained the same. Having undergone a period when a semiotic orientation was dominant, the magazine has returned to a more eclectic approach and to its original concern for literary history and related subjects and textual analysis. Among Québec's scholarly magazines devoted to literary studies, it is the only one devoted exclusively to Québécois writing.

JACQUES PELLETIER

W

Wacousta; or, The prophecy (3 vols, Edinburgh, 1832). The plot of this complicated Gothic romance by John RICHARDSON unfolds largely through flashbacks; each chapter opens with an astonishing event that is followed by an exposition of its origin. It is set in Fort Detroit in 1763, during Pontiac's resistance to British power. The background—which is not revealed until the end—has to do with Sir Reginald Morton and Charles De Haldimar, officers in the English army occupying the Scottish Highlands after the defeat of the Jacobite rebels in 1745. Morton fell in love with Clara Beverley; but Charles, his best friend, won her hand through a trick and then framed Morton, securing his dismissal and disgrace. Two decades later Morton has become the dreaded Wacousta, confidant of Pontiac, and De Haldimar has become the commander at Detroit. Wacousta's scheme of revenge, ultimately suicidal, ends also in the deaths of De Haldimar, his younger son Charles, and his daughter Clara.

The epigraph of *Wacousta* is drawn from an eighteenth-century imitation of an Elizabethan tragedy of revenge. The novel resembles its earliest dramatic forebears in

showing a once-noble spirit, maddened by injustice, pursuing a course of action whose momentum gains power out of proportion to the original intention. Its scenes of violence and suspense—Richardson is at his best in creating a moment of hushed expectancy and then breaking it with a shock—are interspersed with many tedious expositions and clichéd love scenes. These, along with its creaking structure and stilted, even ludicrous dialogue (' "Almighty Providence," aspirated the sinking Clara . . . can it be that human heart can undergo such change?" ' ' "Ha! ha! by heaven, such cold pompous insolence amuses me," vociferated Wacousta.') require great patience. Nevertheless the intensity and energy of *Wacousta*, the gripping scenes of action and high emotion, the powerful depiction of nature as both menacing and beautiful, and the novel's strange, perhaps unintended, sexual undertone, cannot fail to impress the modern reader.

Once famous and now forgotten internationally, *Wacousta* endures in Canadian literature not only as a curiosity but because of its preoccupations with the garrison-versus-wilderness theme, which marks so much other Canadian writing; because its world of violence, terror, and sexual disturbance is so congenial to students of literary modernism; and, finally, because of its sheer exuberance of plot and action. Resembling a nightmare, *Wacousta* embodies an aspect of the Canadian imagination that loves the fantastic and surreal rather than sober speculation and representation.

Every edition of *Wacousta* since the first has been significantly shortened. The current NCL edition (1967) was abridged by Carl KLINCK. Stage versions played Canada and the U.S. in the nineteenth century; a modern dramatization by James REANEY was staged in 1978.   DENNIS DUFFY

Waddington, Miriam (b. 1917). Miriam Dworkin was born into an intellectual Jewish family in Winnipeg, where she lived for fourteen years. She attended high school in Ottawa, the University of Toronto (B.A. 1939), and studied social work in Toronto and Philadelphia. Married to Patrick Waddington (from whom she was later divorced), she has two sons. She moved to Montreal in 1945 and was active in social work and the literary life there, contributing to John SUTHERLAND's FIRST STATEMENT. In 1960 she moved back to Toronto, where she worked for the North York Family Service. She joined the English faculty at York University in 1964 and retired as a professor in 1983.

Waddington's first collection of poems, *Green world* (1945), was published by First Statement Press. In it and *The second silence*(1955), both of which celebrate childhood and are saturated with greenness and sun, her experiences are transmuted through traditions of fairy tale and of a pastoralism that includes Blake, Wordsworth, and Archibald LAMPMAN. Her imagery is intense and visual: the more abstract social poems present a green world as an antidote to broken lives; in a world of lost vision she would have us move into suspended moments from the past and put on 'bandages of light'; doors and windows offer thresholds to 'other selves' that we are invited to recover; memory emerges in water metaphors, presenting the need for descent and flow. In *The season's lovers* (1958), which uses set forms and a public voice to convey important truths, some messages snap aphoristically into place, while others trail away in uninspired statements; but the last part, more metaphysical, succeeds with playful, intimate language. This book, how-ever, falls off from her earlier lyricism, which critics generally believe is her best mode.

The glass trumpet (1966) represents a great leap forward. Content to live with uncertainties and small topics, Waddington observes life in touchingly simple words and finds an oral style that is whimsical and clever, shoving forward with gusto and becoming staccato through a shift to very short, lightly punctuated lines. She frees up sounds and meanings by breaking syllables across lines, and by using the line itself as a unit of meaning. *Say yes* (1969) shows further formal departures: punctuation and capitalization virtually disappear, and the left margin begins to crumble; words disintegrate even more into new units and meanings; the voice begins to imitate sounds for which there are no words, and to shift more radically into interpolation. As in *The glass trumpet*, the facetious poems are less determined by phonetic echoes than the early poems were. The modest claims and understatements in the love poems show Waddington's skill in finding symbolic weight in ordinary things. *Say yes* also laments the erosion of her powers: 'I had such words . . . I knew a certain / leaf language from somewhere but now/ it is all used up.' *Call them Canadians* (1968) includes humane poems in response to a set of photographs; *Dream telescope* (1972) lacks the charge of her best work; *Driving home* (1972), her 'Selected' combined with forty-six pages of recent material, contains only five or six outstanding new pieces. *The price of gold* (1972), *Mister Never* (1978), and *The visitants* (1981) contain excellent work and continue to articulate the centres of Waddington's poetry, though they fail to reach the level of her strongest books. Several concerns that emerge in the 1970s—prophecy, feminism, and aging—occasionally turn into coyness or didacticism; but in these collections Waddington's life-long outrage at injustice takes on new life.

The short fiction in *Summer at Lonely Beach and other stories* (1982)—stories about initiation that are mainly anecdotal and meditative, with little dialogue—is close to poetry, making use of rapid summary and tenuous closures.

Waddington has written valuable criticism in numerous reviews and essays. She wrote a pioneering work, *A. M. Klein* (1970), for the Copp Clark series Studies in Canadian Literature and edited *The collected poems of A.M. Klein* (1974) and *John Suther-*

Waddington

land: essays, controversies and poems (NCL, 1972).

Among the few long pieces on Waddington, the most valuable are: Cathy Matyas, 'Miriam Waddington', in Jeffrey M. Heath, ed., *Profiles in Canadian literature*, vol. 4 (1982); Albert Moritz, 'For a far star: the sweet sanity of Miriam Waddington', *Books in Canada* (May 1982); and L.R. Ricou, 'Into my green world: the poetry of Miriam Waddington', *Essays on Canadian Writing* 12 (Fall 1978), which also contains a useful bibliography compiled by Ricou. The Public Archives, Ottawa, have a Waddington collection.

See also POETRY IN ENGLISH 1950 TO 1982: 1 and 2.   DENNIS COOLEY

Wade, Bryan (b. 1950). Born in Sarnia, Ont., he studied creative writing at the University of Victoria before taking an M.F.A. in Motion Picture and Television at the University of California, Los Angeles. Though most prominent as a playwright, he has also written and directed for television and worked as a screenwriter. His published plays include *Off the freeway* (1970), *Coffee break* (1971), *Nightshift* (1971), *Vacuum* (1971), *Stroke* (1972), *Lifeguard* (1973), *Alias* (1974), *Antigravitational menopause* (1974), *Blitzkreig* (1974), *Aliens* (1975), *Underground* (1975), *Electric gunfighters* (1976), *Tanned* (1976; rev. 1977), and *This side of the Rockies* (1977). Works performed but still unpublished include *Breakthrough*, the book for the musical *Orders from Bergdorf*, and the television play *A brief history of the subject*.

The eclectic and sometimes unfocused fantasy of Wade's earlier plays is exemplified in the cast of *Alias*, which includes the Lone Ranger (who is having an identity crisis), Tonto, and a mobile six-foot penis. Wade combines images from popular culture (in *Electric gunfighters* a man is sucked into a television set) with sexual fantasy, sometimes bizarre and violent. At the same time he shows a capacity for understated unease that is in the long run more effective than his sensationalism. *Blitzkreig* is in this respect typical: its depiction of Hitler and Eva Braun alternates between a luridness that in the end strikes the reader as forced and conventional, and a banality that is quite chilling. This latter vein is explored with real power in *Underground*, a skilful technical exercise in which three characters meet in a room, in an action so arranged that only two are present in each of the play's three acts and the same combination never recurs. In that room they play sex- and power-games

that lead (apparently) to the suicide of one of the men. The play's air of enigmatic menace may recall Pinter; but in its deliberate—and in this case quite accomplished—artificiality, it is really in the tradition of Toronto underground theatre, and shows that tradition at its best.

Wade has also tried to combine fantasy with more conventional realism. *This side of the Rockies* splits between the two styles and falls apart. *Tanned* is better controlled, keeping on the whole an unbroken realistic depiction of the characters—three women and three men in British Columbia's cottage country—while managing to suggest deep frustration and violence beneath the languid, erotic surface.   ALEXANDER LEGGATT

Wah, Fred. (b. 1939). Born in Swift Current, Sask., of Chinese and Scandinavian parents, Wah moved with his family to Trail, B.C., when he was four and grew up there and in nearby Nelson. (The Kootenay region often appears in his poetry as a place of surprising natural beauty.) Educated at the University of British Columbia, he also studied in Albuquerque, New Mexico, with the Black Mountain poet Robert Creeley. In 1965 he pursued graduate studies at the State University of New York in Buffalo with Creeley and Charles Olson, founder and major theorist of the Black Mountain school. Returning to the Kootenays in 1967, he became a teacher at Selkirk College in Castlegar, B.C. Now head of the creative-writing program at David Thompson University Centre in Nelson, he lives in South Slocan.

Wah has published nine books of poetry. *Among* (1972) reprints work from the first three: *Lardeau: selected first poems* (1965); *Mountain* (1967), a long poem: and *Tree* (1972). These were followed in 1974 by *Earth*; then, in *Pictograms from the interior of B.C.* (1975), he began experimenting with responses to pre-existing art forms, printing Indian pictograms alongside poems suggested by them. The autobiographical sequence of poems in *Breathin' my name with a sigh* (1981) shows Black Mountain influences in its focus on place and on breath (Wah playfully connects the sound of his own name to the sounds of air being exhaled). Wah characteristically combines imagism—at times his poems become simply lists of images—with a strongly musical use of word and line that reflects his formal training in music. Wah's most recent book, *Owner's manual*, appeared in 1982.

In 1961 Wah was one of the founding editors of TISH, and played a significant role in the development of the *Tish* group's poetics. He has been a contributing editor to OPEN LETTER since its inception in 1965. In 1980 he edited and wrote the introduction for Daphne MARLATT's *Selected writing: net work.*

See the introduction to Wah's *Selected poems: Loki is buried at Smoky Creek* (1980), edited by George BOWERING, in which Bowering discusses the importance of place in Wah's poetry and writes: 'Of all the writers who have developed out of the *Tish* experiment, Wah was and is the most poetical . . . the most musical of us all.' There is also a discussion of Wah's work in Frank DAVEY's *From there to here* (1974).

RUSSELL BROWN

Walker, David (b. 1911). David Harry Walker was born in Dundee, Scot., and attended Sandhurst (1929-30). He pursued a military career in the Black Watch (1931-47), serving in India (1932) and the Sudan (1936). His first connection with Canada occurred in 1938 when he was aide-de-camp to the Governor General, Lord Tweedsmuir. Walker was captured in France in 1940 and held prisoner-of-war until 1945, an experience on which he based his novel *The pillar* (1952). In 1945-6 he served as an instructor at Staff College, Camberly, before taking up his last official military post as comptroller to the Viceroy of India. In 1947 he retired, with the rank of major, to take up a new career as professional writer, ultimately settling in St Andrews, N.B. From 1957 to 1961 he was a member of the Canada Council. Walker has been awarded a D. Litt by the University of New Brunswick, and won two Governor General's Awards, for *The pillar* (1952) and *Digby* (1953).

A prolific writer of fast-paced adventure stories, Walker has tried his hand at everything from international espionage (*Cab-Intersec*, 1968; published in England as *Devil's plunge*), to children's stories (*Dragon Hill*, 1962). Few of his works are related directly to Canada, though *Mallabec* (1965), *Where the high winds blow* (1960), *Pirate Rock* (1969), and some of the short stories in *Storms of our journey and other stories* (1964), are set in Canada. Two of his novels—*Geordie* (1950) and *Harry Black* (1956)—were made into films. Walker's other books are: *The storm and the silence* (1949), *Sandy was a soldier's boy* (1957), *Winter of madness* (1964), *Come back, Geordie* (1966), *Big Ben* (1970),

The Lord's pink ocean (1972), *Black Dougal* (1973), *Ash* (1976), and *Pot of Gold* (1977). A brief discussion of Walker's books for young people, particularly *Dragon Hill* and *Pirate Rock*, may be found in Sheila Egoff's *The republic of childhood* (2nd edn, 1975), where his insight into character is praised.

See CHILDREN'S LITERATURE IN ENGLISH: 2.

ANDREW SEAMAN

Walker, George F. (b. 1947). The youngest of four children of working-class parents, George Frederick Walker was born and raised in Toronto's East End, where he graduated from Riverdale Collegiate in 1965. After working at a variety of jobs, and travelling across North America, he responded to a call for scripts from Toronto's newly founded Factory Theatre Lab in 1970 by writing *Prince of Naples* (1972), a two-character farce in which a young and ostensibly liberated student challenges the rational thinking of his older and more conventional mentor. Produced by the Factory in 1971, it was the first of a number of his plays to première there over the next decade, and marked the beginning of an association in which Walker served as the theatre's playwright-in-residence from 1971 to 1976 and as its artistic director in 1978-9. In 1977 he began a three-year association with Toronto Free Theatre, which produced a number of his plays; and in 1981 he was playwright-in-residence at the New York Shakespeare Festival, which produced in 1982 the American première of his most critically acclaimed work, *Zastrozzi: the master of discipline* (1977).

As Chris Johnson notes in his study 'George Walker: B-movies beyond the absurd', published in CANADIAN LITERATURE 85 (Summer 1980), Walker is an urban playwright of cosmopolitan sensibility whose work addresses themes and styles most closely connected to absurdist and surrealist traditions. The fascination with cartoon exaggerations and comic grotesques that pervades his early plays, such as *Ambush at Tether's End* (1972) and *Sacktown rage* (1972), shifts to an interest in the stereotypical characters and structural clichés of Hollywood 'B' movies in the plays anthologized as *Three plays by George F. Walker* (1978). However, in the earliest of these plays, *Bagdad saloon*, Walker's interest in the cartoon is still predominant as Ahrun, the play's central character, kidnaps such legendary figures as 'Doc' Halliday, Gertrude Stein, and Henry Miller in his search for a meaning by which to structure his existence in a universe seemingly devoid of values and connections. The absurdist vision of human existence in this play becomes more tightly structured, if not clearer, in *Beyond Mozambique* and *Ramona and the white slaves*, the other two plays in the anthology, both of which draw heavily on the conventions of 'B' movies. *Beyond Mozambique*—a 'jungle movie' in which six desperate exiles from Western civilization enact, on the porch of a decaying mansion in the jungle beyond Mozambique, a brutal yet comic parable about the disintegration of man—displays the interest in surrealistic imagery and language that typifies Walker's plays from this point on. In *Ramona and the white slaves* a detective's attempts to solve a murder outside a brothel in turn-of-the-century Hong Kong is merely an excuse that allows the playwright to explore the obsessions of Ramona, a modern-day Medea, whose existence has more in common with an opium dream than with recognizable reality. The use of disguise and macabre images of mutilation in both plays creates a heightened theatricality that is as demanding of an audience as it is despairing—a quality that is noticeably absent in *Gossip* (1981) and *Filthy rich* (1981), two entertainingly cynical forays into more conventionally structured comic drama. Employing the investigative talents of Tyrone Power, news reporter, to unravel the complicated murders that precipitate their plots, these 'detective movies' expose the bankrupt morality and decadent mores of the rich and the famous that Walker locates at the centre of media-warped society. In *Theatre of the film noir* (1981) and *The art of war* (1983), Walker again relies on the formats of cinematic suspense to spin the webs of sexual and political intrigue that are his metaphors for contemporary confusion and decay. Using the characters and conventions of horror films in *Science and madness* (1982), he expands upon this technique, developing a Gothic collage whose portrayal of the classic struggle between good and evil revives the conflict of *Zastrozzi: the master of discipline*, in which Zastrozzi, the arch-villain of Western Europe—derived from Shelley's play of the same name—confronts Verezzi, his idealistic opposite. *Zastrozzi*, Walker's most impressive play to date, demonstrates the playwright's ability to merge philosophical issues with powerful characterizations, urbane dialogue, and intricate plot in a fast-paced series of visually striking scenes that are as intellectually sophisticated as they are

theatrically exciting. A finalist in the competition for the Chalmers Award for Best New Canadian Play of 1977, *Zastrozzi* best supports Walker's growing reputation as a playwright. ROBERT WALLACE

Wallace, Joe (1890-1975). Born in Toronto and raised in Halifax, N.S., he attended St Francis Xavier University and worked in advertising before joining the Communist Party of Canada the year following its formation in 1921. He wrote for the labour press, attended the Conference for the Unemployed in Ottawa in 1933, and when the Party was outlawed was interned at Petawawa, Ont., in 1941-2. Imprisonment inspired his verse, five collections of which appeared between the publication of *Night is ended* (1942) and *A radiant sphere* (1965), which was issued in Moscow in three editions of 10,000 copies each—in Russian, English, and Chinese. Both a committed Communist and a devout Catholic, Wallace died in a Catholic convalescent home in Vancouver. *Joe Wallace: poems* (1981) brings together 300 poems and verses that show his ability to write socially committed light verse and, on occasion, lyric poems of clarity and intensity. JOHN ROBERT COLOMBO

Walmsley, Tom (b. 1948). Born in England, he came to Canada early in life and now lives in Vancouver, where he is the editor of Pulp Press. His published work to date includes two books of poetry—*Rabies* (1975), and *Lexington hero* (1976)—and a novel, *Doctor Tin* (1979). He is also the author of four plays: two short pieces, *The working man* (1975) and *The Jones boy* (1978); and two full-length plays: *Something red* (1980) and *White boys* (1982). The plays, all of which have been produced, are by far the best part of his work.

The only conventional facet of Walmsley's drama is its formal realism. Sex and violence pervade his stage: obscenities riddle his dialogue. But his plays are never simply exercises in sensationalism. Even *The working man*, for all its graphic violence, focuses on the psychological drama. Although the principal characters in *The Jones boy* are drug addicts, the play is not 'about' heroin but about the quest for self-knowledge and the meaning of courage and honour in a criminal subculture that offers only unreflective barbarism as an ideal. *Something red*, Walmsley's most ambitious play, moves through scenes of extreme physical and psychological brutality to climactic moments in which a character stands revealed to others and himself. The protagonist, Bobby, whose life has been an abject saga of flight and betrayal, is a memorable creation. Dishonourable and self-seeking in all his relationships, revolting in his sexual obsessions, he also bears traces of tragic grandeur. He is faithful only to his most wayward impulses—the 'monstrous forms of being', in Ionesco's words, that inhabit the human psyche; yet when he makes his last appearance, having committed an appalling sex murder, our responses are pity and fear. In *White boys* the playwright presents his familiar character types within the framework of farce. The play works well at the level of a revue skit; but the idiom obstructs the necessary development of the theme, which is, once again, infantile impulse baffled by the demands of adult experience.

The most serious limitation of Walmsley's theatre is its narrow focus. The characters and milieu offer only a remote relation to society at large. His work, although increasingly expert, tends to turn in on itself as the playwright delves ever deeper into extreme, anarchic states of being. But within their restricted compass Walmsley's plays—*The Jones boy* and *Something red* in particular—generate a power that is rare in contemporary Canadian drama.   MICHAEL TAIT

Warr, Bertram. See POETRY IN ENGLISH 1900 TO 1950: 4.

Watmough, David (b. 1926). Born near Epping Forest on the eastern edge of London, Eng., Watmough spent most of his childhood in Cornwall, where his family farmed. He was educated at Cooper's School and King's College, both in London. His first published book, *A church renascent* (1951), was a by-product of his studies in theology at King's College and concerned the worker-priest movement. He immigrated to Vancouver, where he has made his home ever since, becoming a Canadian citizen in 1963. Since settling in Canada, Watmough has worked as a literary journalist and has contributed as commentator and playwright to CBC programs. In 1967 *Names for the numbered years*, a collection of plays, appeared. Watmough's published fiction includes two novels—*No more into the garden* (1978) and *Unruly skeletons* (1982)—and three collections of shorter pieces: *Ashes for Easter and other monodramas* (1972), *Love and the waiting game* (1975), and *Collected shorter fiction of David Watmough: 1972-82* (1982). A

clue to the nature of Watmough's fiction can be found in his 'monodramas', which are written in the area between fiction and drama so that they can be read by one person—the writer—who acts out, in reading, all the roles.

One must take seriously Watmough's claim that for a decade or more he has been engaged in writing a single novel that will take a lifetime to complete, for the same central character, Davey Bryant, appears in almost all of his published fiction. Bryant resembles Watmough and shares some of his experiences, but as a character he stands apart and is observed with irony and candour both from within and without. Watmough's fiction contains multiple ironies. Some of the most telling pieces evoke past moments of folly or unworthiness that stir similar shameful recollections in the reader, whose potential closeness to the many predicaments—frequently homosexual—can create a feeling of uneasiness. In the novels especially (*No more into the garden* and *Unruly skeletons*) Davey Bryant is shown as both the victim of ludicrous circumstances and the perpetrator of petty moral atrocities. The victim is always seen to be seeking victory, and most personal relationships are marred by a cruelty that degrades one or other of the participants. The recurrent themes are united on another level by a pervading elegiac consciousness. In *No more into the garden*, for example, the longed-for garden that is never re-entered is in one sense the Cornwall of childhood happiness, and in another the state of collective innocence that all men seek to recover. The garden, however, becomes a 'harvest of threats'. By the novel's end the fullness of life is balanced by everpresent death, for as the mind expands its consciousness the physical possiblities narrow. Here, for Watmough, is the irony and also the elegy.

See an interview with Geoff Hancock in CANADIAN FICTION MAGAZINE 20 (Winter 1976).   GEORGE WOODCOCK

Watson, John (1847-1939). Born in Glasgow, Scot., and educated at Glasgow University, he came to Queen's University, Kingston, Ont., in 1872 to be a professor of logic, metaphysics, and ethics, replacing John Clark MURRAY, who had accepted a chair at McGill. Watson was the central figure in the Hegelian movement that dominated Canadian philosophy from the 1870s until after the First World War, and did much to shape religious, political, and cultural ideas in Canada in this period. His rational version of Christianity formed a significant part of the intellectual basis of the union that resulted in the formation of the United Church of Canada in 1925.

Religion was central to Watson's work. His religious views were first expounded in *Christianity and idealism: the Christian life in relation to the Greek and Jewish ideals and to modern philosophy* (New York, 1896). Believing that all reality formed a rational unity within which the highest values could be realized, Watson sought a rational religion that could unite all men around demonstrable truths and render intelligible both human history and the life of the individual. Though a decade separates *The philosophical basis of religion: a series of lectures* (1907) from *Christianity and idealism*, his fundamental position remained the same. Watson's books attracted international recognition and this culminated in the invitation to give the Gifford Lectures in Scotland in 1910-12, which led to his monumental *Interpretation of religious experience* (2 vols, 1912). Much of Watson's reputation rests on his *Philosophy of Kant explained* (1908) and *Kant and his English critics: a comparison of critical and empirical philosophy* (Glasgow, 1881), both of which have been frequently reprinted and continue to be read. His *Philosophy of Kant as contained in extracts from his own writings* (Glasgow, 1888) was widely used by undergraduates. His introductory texts, *Comte, Mill & Spencer, an outline of philosophy* (Glasgow, 1895), later adapted as *An outline of philosophy* (1908), helped shape the minds of two generations of Canadian students. These books also contain a good deal of original philosophy, as does Watson's *Hedonistic theories from Aristippus to Spencer* (Glasgow, 1895). The First World War gave rise to *The state in peace and war* (1919), a treatise devoted to the ideal of a world government based on the principles of tolerance and the integral development of national cultures, which Watson thought characteristic of the emerging British Commonwealth and of the established pluralist tradition in Canada. He advocated widespread land reform and an economic system that, while rewarding hard work, would guarantee fairness and decent living conditions to all men.

Watson's lucid prose style made his books accessible and helps to account for their wide readership. His purely literary works, however, had only a modest success. He wrote several plays (which remain unpublished, though they were performed and generally well received at Queen's) and some poetry. His influence generally stemmed from the generations of Presbyterian clergymen who were educated under him, and from the frequency with which his students attained senior posts in the civil service in Ottawa.

LESLIE ARMOUR, ELIZABETH TROTT

Watson, Sheila (b. 1909). Born in New Westminster, B.C., she lived during her early years on the grounds of the Provincial Mental Hospital in New Westminster where her father, Dr Charles Edward Doherty, was superintendant until his death in 1922. She attended primary and secondary schools at the convent of the Sisters of Sainte Anne in New Westminster, and took her first two years of university at the Convent of the Sacred Heart in Vancouver. She received a B.A. in Honours English from the University of British Columbia in 1931; earned her academic teaching certificate in 1932; and completed an M.A. at UBC in 1933.

During the next few years Watson taught elementary school in a succession of British Columbia classrooms—in New Westminster, Dog Creek (near Ashcroft), Langley Prairie, Duncan, and Mission City. In 1941 she married the poet Wilfred WATSON. In the postwar years Sheila Watson undertook another series of short-term teaching posts—at Moulton College, Toronto (1946-8), a sessional lectureship at UBC (1948-50), and at a high school in Powell River, B.C. (1950-51)—before spending two years in Calgary, during which she wrote her celebrated novel *The double hook* (1959). After short periods in Edmonton and France, she entered upon doctoral studies at the University of Toronto in 1957, completing a dissertation on Wyndham Lewis, under the direction of Marshall McLUHAN, in 1965. She was appointed to the faculty of the University of Alberta in 1961, and retired as full professor in 1975. She lives in Nanaimo, B.C. Her uncollected prose was published as a special number of the journal OPEN LETTER (1975). Four of her five short stories appeared in a separate volume, *Four stories* (1979); the fifth story, *And the four animals*, was published as a COACH HOUSE PRESS manuscript edition in 1980.

The double hook, the first truly modern Canadian novel, was Watson's second attempt to write a novel that embraced her experiences while teaching at Dog Creek in the interior of British Columbia in 1935-7. (The first attempt, 'Deep Hollow Creek', remains unpublished.) Concerned to avoid both regionalism and realistic reportage, Watson created in *The double hook* a highly poetic and elliptical work written in biblical rhythms, in chapters that resemble stanzas, and in images that dwarf plot and action. The novel depicts the struggle of members of a small village to move from despair to hope, from apathy to action, in a world where pagan and Christian symbolisms have blurred, and silence proves more eloquent than language. The discontinuous and highly imagistic style of the work reiterates the distrust of discursive language that it embodies. The novel has been republished in the New Canadian Library (1966) and appeared in Swedish as *Dubbelkrocken* (1963; translated by Artur Lundkvist) and in French as *Sous l'oeil de coyote* (1976, translated by Arlette Francière).

Watson's stories, written in the same period as *The double hook*, reflect a similarly austere and precise use of language and image. Most focus on spiritual paralysis, and give mythological names to the characters to avoid the semblance of realism. The characters thus appear oppressed by myth, and struggle against its authority as personified in parent, priest, or nun.

With Douglas BARBOUR, Stephen SCOBIE, Wilfred Watson, and Norman Yates, Sheila Watson co-edited the little magazine *White Pelican* (1971-8). She has been honoured by the publication of *Figures in a ground: Canadian essays on modern literature collected in honor of Sheila Watson* (1978), edited by Diane Bessai and David Jackel.

FRANK DAVEY

Watson, Wilfred (b. 1911). Born in Rochester, Eng., and educated at Maldon Grammar School, Maldon, Essex, he immigrated with his family in 1926 to Duncan, B.C. After a year at Duncan High School he began thirteen years of work in a tidewater sawmill, meanwhile reading, writing poetry, and exploring the coasts and mountains of Vancouver Island. In 1940 he enrolled in English at the University of British Columbia, graduating in 1943, whereupon he joined the Canadian navy for the remainder of the war. He received an M.A. from the University of Toronto in 1946 and a Ph.D. in 1951. After teaching English briefly at the University of British Columbia he taught at the University of Alberta, first in Calgary and later in Edmonton, where he served as a distinguished teacher

and scholar until his retirement in 1976. With his wife Sheila WATSON he co-founded the little magazine *White Pelican* (1971-8). He lives in Nanaimo, B.C.

As both experimental poet and dramatist, Watson explores contemporary media-conditioned sensibilities. His first collection of poems, *Friday's child* (1955), which won a Governor General's Award, contained apparently conventional verse that nevertheless bore the seeds of the radical writing to follow. The poems of his second collection, *The sorrowful Canadians* (1972), are curiously analogous to his drama in their use of space, for which Watson uses the term *mise en page*. Unlike most concrete poetry, Watson's offers both context and content: the size or positioning of various typefaces modulates verbal intensity, so that the eye is bombarded by a typographical 'voice' speaking with the insistence of choral utterance in the plays. His number/grid poems—in which each stanza or grid provides for 17 words juxtaposed typographically to the numbers one to nine—were collected in *I begin with counting* (1978). The discipline of the grid method of ordering his poems is also reflected in the finely honed short verse-play *Woman taken in adultery* (published in Diane Bessai, ed., *Prairie performance*, 1980), which concisely illustrates Watson's facility for drawing satiric portraits within rapidly shifting time-space environments.

Watson's work as a playwright has been influenced by the Theatre of the Absurd and by his interest in the theories of Marshall McLUHAN, with whom he collaborated in *From cliché to archetype* (1970). An argument between Watson and McLuhan emerges in the play *Let's murder Clytemnestra, according to the principles of Marshall McLuhan*, produced at the Studio Theatre, University of Alberta, in Nov. 1969. *O holy ghost, dip your finger in the blood of Canada, and write, I love you*, which premièred at the Studio Theatre in Dec. 1967, exploits sound, movement, visuals, and scenic inter-cuts in dealing with the flower-power trendiness of the sixties; it combines satiric sketch, chorus, music, and projections in order to focus on big business, the Vietnam war, and the modern dehumanization occurring in professional life.

Watson's habit of wrenching the language of biblical and literary tradition into contemporary contexts marks for him the first step towards theatrical expression. Thus, in such plays as *Cockrow and the gulls* (Studio Theatre, Mar. 1962), *Trial of Corporal Adam* (Coach House Theatre, Toronto, May

1964), and *Wail for two pedestals* (Yardbird Suite, Edmonton, Nov. 1964; published in the *Humanities Association Bulletin*, Autumn 1965), various versions of the Day of Judgement are comically thrust into surrealistic contemporary settings; traditionally sacred questions are filtered through the distorting lens of modern-day secularity. Higgins in *Cockrow* is an armchair socialist from Nanaimo who represents the failure of the common man to fulfil his social and spiritual potential. *Wail for two pedestals* presents two famously absent characters of modern drama—Godot and Lefty—in order to satirize the Theatre of the Absurd itself.

Critical recognition of Watson's work is limited. His reputation as a poet still rests primarily on *Friday's child*, which was cited with particular interest by Northrop FRYE in his resumé of new poetry in 1955 (*The bush garden*, 1972). See Stephen SCOBIE, 'Love in the burning city: the poetry of Wilfred Watson', *Essays on Canadian Writing* 18-19 (Summer/Fall 1980).   DIANE BESSAI

Watters, R.E. See CRITICISM IN ENGLISH: 5(c).

Wayman, Tom (b. 1945). Born in Hawkesbury, Ont., he was raised in Prince Rupert and Vancouver, B.C. He attended the University of British Columbia, where he edited the student newspaper, *The Ubyssey*, and did graduate work at the University of California. He has worked at a wide variety of jobs, both academic and non-academic, in the United States and Canada. In 1976 he won the A.J.M. SMITH Prize for 'distinguished achievement in Canadian poetry'.

His first poetry collection was *Waiting for Wayman* (1973), followed by *For and against the moon: blues, yells, and chuckles* (1974); *Money and rain: Tom Wayman Live!* (1975); *Free time: industrial poems* (1977); *A planet mostly sea* (1979); and *Living on the ground: Tom Wayman country* (1980). Wayman has also edited three volumes of poems about work: *Beaton Abbot's got the contract* (n.d.), *A government job at last* (1976), and *Going for coffee* (1981). His own poetry is about 'the central experience of everyday life—which is what people do for a living, their work' (*NeWest ReView*, IV, 5, Jan. 1970). Wayman writes of the various jobs he has held; tells the stories of people he has worked with; speculates on the social, political, and even metaphysical implications of the work experience; and as a teacher and editor encourages others to write directly from this 'central experience'. While his point of view is clearly pro-labour, Wayman never makes rigid or dogmatic political statements. His analyses of the effects of people's jobs on their lives and emotions are clear, sensible, often humorous, and convincingly argued. Much of this poetry is necessarily narrative, conveyed in a straightforward, realist tone, with very little reliance on metaphor or self-consciously 'poetic' figures of speech. The rhythms are those of everyday talk. Wayman uses a long line that places little emphasis on line-breaks or on rhythmic subtleties, to the extent that much of his work seems almost prosaic. The line, however, is not really the basis of his poetry: he works in terms of larger units, such as the paragraph and the anecdote, juxtaposing narrative blocks with the same tightness and subtlety with which other poets juxtapose lines or images. The poetic effect also depends on the controlling tone of the speaking voice, which is usually slightly distant and ironically humorous, as in the poems that use the third-person 'Wayman' as a self-deprecatory intermediary. (A selection of those poems, in which Wayman uses the humorous 'Wayman' persona, was published in 1981 as *The Nobel Prize acceptance speech*.) Wayman's major concern has been to rescue realism in poetry from its position, as he sees it, 'somewhere at the bottom of the heap', and to assert the worth, dignity, and complexity of daily work as a poetic subject.

                STEPHEN SCOBIE

Weaver, Robert (b. 1921). Born in Niagara Falls, Ont., he was educated there and in Toronto. From 1942 to 1945 he served first in the RCAF, and then in the Canadian army. After his discharge he enrolled at the University of Toronto and took his degree in Philosophy and English (1948). In the same year he was hired by the CBC as a program organizer in the Talks and Public Affairs Department, and in this role he was associated with a number of the most important cultural programs on Canadian radio. These included 'Critically Speaking', which he began shortly after joining the CBC; 'Stories with John Drainie', which ran from 1959 to 1965; and 'Anthology', which he launched in 1953 and currently produces. Weaver was also closely involved in the cultural flagship program 'CBC Wednesday Night', which began in 1948, and with its successors. He is now executive producer, radio features and humanities.

As a program organizer and producer for

radio, Weaver played an important role as a kind of impresario in the Canadian literary world, encouraging writers, producing their works, and giving them employment as critics and commentators. At a time when publishers and magazine editors lost interest in short stories, Weaver produced them on his radio programs, and in the process virtually discovered writers like Mordecai RICHLER and Alice MUNRO. His editing activities soon extended beyond radio: when the cessation of NORTHERN REVIEW and CONTEMPORARY VERSE in the early 1950s left Canada without a literary magazine of any consequence, he and a group of Toronto writers established *The* TAMARACK REVIEW (1956-82), of which he was an inspiring force. Weaver's interest in the short story led him into the preparation of anthologies. These include the three Oxford volumes *Canadian short stories: First series* (1960), *Second series* (1968), and *Third series* (1978); and *Ten for Wednesday Night* (1961). Another of his anthologies, *The first five years* (1962), consists of writings selected from the early issues of *Tamarack*. Weaver also edited a collection of stories by Mavis GALLANT, *The end of the world and other stories* (1973), and, with William Toye, *The Oxford anthology of Canadian literature* (1973; 2nd edn, 1981).

GEORGE WOODCOCK

Webb, Phyllis (b. 1927). Born in Victoria, B.C., and educated at the University of British Columbia, she ran unsuccessfully as a CCF candidate for the provincial legislature at the age of twenty-two. In 1950 she travelled to Montreal, where she worked as secretary to David L. Thomas, dean of the faculty of graduate studies, McGill University, before undertaking a year of graduate work. Webb lived in England, Paris, San Francisco, and Toronto, then taught at UBC for four years. In Toronto she conceived the CBC radio program 'Ideas' and was its executive producer from 1966 to 1969, after which she returned to the west coast to settle on Saltspring Island. She has taught at the University of Victoria and been writer-in-residence at the University of Alberta. Webb's early poetry—published with poems by Gael Turnbull and Eli MANDEL in *Trio* (1954), and separately in *Even your right eye* (1956) and *The sea is also a garden* (1962)—is both formal and rhetorical, with considerable clarity of statement and elegance of diction. However, with the publication of *Naked poems* (1965), Webb announced a new reductive phase, in which

language and sentiment are pared to the bone: the persona of these poems is depicted as someone immobile and 'only/remotely human', writing tiny, minimalist poems in which 'the area of attack/is diminished'. Devoid of false sentiment and self-indulgence, these poems are starkly and disturbingly beautiful.

After the publication of *Selected poems* (1971), Webb's work became steadily more expansive again, taking greater chances with content and form while not forgetting the hard-won lessons of economy and control. In her career as a poet Webb has been unique for her musical and intellectual gifts, achieving a wonderful synchronicity of sound and idea. Her reader is invited not so much to admire ideas as to participate in the choreography of a nimble and discriminating mind as it selects, examines, and shapes its poetic materials. From this privileged position the reader can, to use Webb's own phrase, respond to 'the dance of the intellect in the syllables'.

Webb asserts the healing and restorative powers of poetry. The poem works in mysterious ways, as she says in 'Making', to stitch together image, sound, and idea like the pieces of a patchwork quilt. Poetry, like love, knits up the fragments of mind and body, the 'fugitive ecstasies', into a fabric of joy, making art out of accident and wholeness out of disintegration: 'thus excellent despair/is laid, and in the room the patches of the quilt/seize light and throw it back upon the air.'

Webb published *Wilson's bowl* in 1980—a remarkable collection that was followed by *Sunday water: thirteen anti ghazals* (1982) and *The vision tree: selected poems* (1982), which won a Governor General's Award. There is much to be learned about Webb's life and poetics in *Talking* (1982), a selection of her essays, reviews, and radio talks. Of particular interest are her essays on the creative process and the use of the poetic line, which are not only insightful but also masterfully woven arguments, spinning image and idea into a complex web of meaning.

See Helen W. Sonthoff, 'Structure of loss', CANADIAN LITERATURE 9 (Summer 1961), and John Hulcoop, 'Phyllis Webb and the priestess of motion', *Canadian Literature* 32 (Spring 1967).

See also POETRY IN ENGLISH 1950 TO 1982: 1, 2.

GARY GEDDES

Week, The (1883-96). This 'Canadian Journal of Politics, Society, and Literature' was founded by Goldwin SMITH and published in Toronto by F. Blackett Robinson for the purpose of 'stimulating our national sentiment, guarding our national morality, and strengthening our national growth'. It appeared between 6 Dec. 1883 and 20 Nov. 1896. (Charles G.D. ROBERTS was editor for the first three months.) *The Week* conveys an accurate impression of intellectual currents and cultural taste of its day. Leading writers and intellectuals contributed stories, poems, essays, commentary on current issues, and reviews of literature, drama, and music. Topics frequently debated include realism and naturalism in literature, the problem of reconciling religion with Darwinism, and the Canadian copyright situation. Awareness of international trends in fiction is indicated in the reviews, while the publication of villanelles, rondeaux, and triolets demonstrates Canadian interest in the revival of French fixed forms that was currently underway in England. Frequent poetry contributors include Archibald LAMPMAN, 'Fidelis' (Agnes Maule MACHAR), 'Seranus' (Susie Frances HARRISON), 'Sarepta' (Edward Burroughs Brownlow), Ethelwyn WETHERALD, and Frederick George SCOTT. The liveliest columnist and essayist was Sara Jeannette DUNCAN.

See Claude T. Bissell, 'Literary taste in central Canada during the late nineteenth century', *Canadian Historical Review* 31, no. 2 (Sept. 1950), and D.M.R. Bentley, *A checklist of literary materials in The Week* (1978).   LORRAINE McMULLEN

Weintraub, William. See NOVELS IN ENGLISH 1960 TO 1982; OTHER TALENTS, OTHER WORKS: 3.

Weinzweig, Helen (b. 1915). Helen Tenenbaum was born in Poland and came to Toronto at the age of nine. Her formal education ended abruptly after high school when the Depression impelled her to go to work—successively as a stenographer, receptionist, and salesperson. She married the composer John Weinzweig in 1940 and has two sons.

Weinzweig, who has read widely—especially the work of Conrad, Jerzy Kosinsky, John Barth, Borges, and Ivy Compton Burnett—published her first novel, *Passing ceremony* (1973), when she was 57. Its 117 pages display the ellipsis and compression of good poetry. About a weird wedding between a homosexual and a promiscuous woman, the story is recounted by the principals and wedding guests through bits of internal monologue. Everyone is bored with the ceremony and trapped in various isolations of ennui, hatred, sickness, fantasy, or self-disgust. Composed of reverie, memory, quick perceptions, and fantasy, this novel is a *tour de force* on an unattractive subject. Weinzweig's second novel, *Basic black with pearls* (1980), as technically assured as *Passing ceremony*, is a more unified work; also short—only 135 pages—it consists of the internal monologue of one person, Shirley Kazenbowski, née Silverberg, alias Lola Montez. Shirley is in pursuit of her lover, Coenrad, a secret agent, who has apparently given her a coded message for an assignation in Toronto. Written totally subjectively, the novel never discloses whether the adventure is madness or sanity. It is both comic and pathetic: high romance and sordid reality collide and collude in a slow waltz through a labyrinth that is also the familiar cityscape of Toronto. The novel won the City of Toronto Book Award in 1981.

Weinzweig has also published short fiction in *Jewish Dialog, The* TAMARACK REVIEW, *Saturday Night, Toronto Life,* and *The* CANADIAN FORUM.

See also NOVELS IN ENGLISH 1960 TO 1982: 3.   PETER BUITENHUIS

Wells, Kenneth McNeill (b. 1905). Born in Mitchell, Ont., he grew up in Orillia and attended the University of Western Ontario. After two years in Europe (1926-8), where he published *Absit omen* (1927), a collection of lyric poems, he returned to Canada to become a journalist with the *London Advertiser*, the *Orillia Newsletter*, and finally the *Toronto Evening Telegram*. From the 1930s to the 1960s (except for a stint in the Canadian Army), he lived on his farm, 'The Owl Pen', in Medonte Township, Simcoe Co., where he made honey and wrote the articles for the *Telegram* that later became his country books. In the 1950s Wells abandoned journalism and farming for the pleasure of cruising Georgian Bay. He later lived for five years on his yacht, *The Sea Owl*, having at last discovered—strangely, in the light of his Owl Pen books—a 'magical world . . . after long years of yearning' (*Cruising the North Channel*, p. xv). He now lives in Virginia.

Wells's country books—*The Owl Pen* (1947), *By Moonstone Creek* (1949), *Up Medonte way* (1951), and *By Jumping Cat Bridge* (1956)—are all written in the first person; all are arranged by seasons; and all are a mixture of anecdote, local pioneer history, and accounts of the author's experiences. In these books Wells consistently avoids overwrought descriptions of nature and re-creates his farm neighbours convincingly; but he skims the surface of his subject, as he did in his edition of Peter MCARTHUR's *In pastures green* (1948), in which he omitted all essays on farm politics and economics. His rural world seems largely a setting for the farcical misadventures of a greenhorn and the cute pranks of pet-like animals. His cruising books—*Cruising the Georgian Bay* (1958), *Cruising the Trent-Severn waterway* (1959), *Cruising the North Channel* (1960), *Trailer boating where the North begins* (1961), and *Cruising the Rideau waterway* (1965)—are guides that neatly blend local history and na-vigational information and are preferable to *The moonstruck two* (1964), a narrative in the Owl Pen style about a voyage to New Or-leans in an outboard skiff.   ALEC LUCAS

Wetherald, Agnes Ethelwyn (1857-1940). The daughter of English-Quaker parents, she was born in Rockwood, Ont., received her early education at home, and later studied at a Quaker school in New York State and at Pickering College in Ontario. She became a journalist and contributed to many Canadian and American periodicals; for a time she was the editor of the women's department of the Toronto *Globe*, using the pseudonym 'Bel Thistlewaite'. Although Wetherald's poems had begun appearing in the late 1870s, her first collection, *The house of the trees and other poems* (Boston), was not published until 1895. Later volumes were *Tangled in stars* (1902), *The radiant road* (1904), *The last robin: lyrics and sonnets* (1907), *Tree-top mornings* (1921), and her col-lected *Lyrics and sonnets* (1931). Her early work was favourably received by reviewers on both sides of the Atlantic, and praised by influential contemporaries, including Archi-bald LAMPMAN. Major anthologies of the time, including Wilfred CAMPBELL's *Oxford book of Canadian verse* (1913) and John Gar-vin's *Canadian poets* (1916), gave her exten-sive representation. Her treatment of nature, the main subject of many of her poems, has been described as shallow and sentimental, and much of her other work is judged to be conventional in style and thought. This crit-icism, however, is too dismissive: Weth-erald's presentation of nature is often sensual and occasionally erotic; her technical skill, particularly in the sonnet form, is at times of a very high order. Finally some poems, in their gravity and restraint, recall the work of Emily Dickinson, a resemblance that Weth-erald's as-yet unexamined Quaker back-ground and New England connections (most of her books were published in Bos-ton) would clarify.

Wetherald also wrote *An Algonquin maiden: a romance of the early days of Upper Canada* (Montreal, 1887) in collaboration with G. Mercer ADAM, a work that—as Pauline JOHNSON noted—failed to avoid the usual inaccuracies and sentimental stereo-types; and the introduction to J.W. Garvin's *Collected poems of Isabella Valancy Crawford* (1905).   DAVID JACKEL

Whalley, George. See BIOGRAPHY AND MEMOIRS IN ENGLISH: 3.

White savannahs, The (1936). This is the first book-length work on English-Cana-dian literature written from a purely critical standpoint, that of the modernist movement of the years after the First World War. Its author, William Edwin Collin (b. 1893), an English-born academic trained in France, taught Romance Languages at the Univer-sity of Western Ontario from 1923 to 1959. To his study of eight English-speaking poets and one French prose-writer, he brought (i) the inwardness and subjectivity of late nineteenth-century French critical writing; (ii) the 'neoclassical' critical theories of T.E. Hulme; and (iii) the influence of myth criti-cism, which was then being felt by such poets as T.S. Eliot. Collin was attracted to the first English-Canadian writers able to as-similate and learn from the modernist movement whose writing directly chal-lenged the genteel tradition then dominant in Canadian literature. He first explored these new green shoots of creativity, strug-gling to emerge beneath the frozen 'white savannahs' of Canadian culture, in several essays produced between 1931 and 1934 for *The* CANADIAN FORUM and *The University of Toronto Quarterly*.

In Archibald LAMPMAN and Marjorie PICKTHALL Collin sees a retreat from the search for cosmic order into a repressed fic-tion of 'nature'. An essay—somewhat unre-lated to the others—on the novelist Marie LE FRANC hints at how Collin connects myth criticism with both a theory of style and a general view of civilization. But the core of the book is his attentive and enthusiastic reading of the 'Montreal poets'—F.R. SCOTT, A.M. KLEIN, A.J.M. SMITH, Leo KENNEDY—and their contemporaries E.J.

White savannahs

PRATT and Dorothy LIVESAY. For Collin most of these poets, like their 'metaphysical' forebears in the seventeenth century, were redefining the word 'natural' in terms that would preserve the human in 'a real world of living and mechanical forces'. Though Collin recognizes their common ground, his critical method richly elicits the independent virtues of each writer: the link between imagist and socialist in Livesay, the stern ethical centre in Scott, the fruitful confrontation of heritages in Klein, a certain austerity and reserve in Smith. His deepest rapport is with Kennedy, whom he sees—not very persuasively—as providing at last the redemptive pattern linking man with the natural order that Lampman could not envision.

Though *The white savannahs*—which was reprinted in 1975 with an introduction by Germaine Warkentin—did not sell well in 1936, its influence on Canadian poetry and critical writing has been considerable, both in its contribution to what A.J.M. Smith called 'a new climate of opinion among readers and publishers of poetry in Canada' and in the exemplary wit, enthusiasm, and elegance of its critical prose. Collin produced no later book, but the annual essay on 'French-Canadian Letters', which he wrote for *The University of Toronto Quarterly*'s 'Letters in Canada', from 1941 to 1956, was of equal distinction and influence.

See also CRITICISM IN ENGLISH: 3.

GERMAINE WARKENTIN

Whitman, Walt. See Richard Maurice BUCKE, FOREIGN WRITERS ON CANADA IN ENGLISH: 2, and TRAVEL LITERATURE IN ENGLISH.

Whittaker, Herbert (b. 1911). Born in Montreal, he studied design at the École des Beaux-Arts. He began designing for Montreal amateur theatres in 1933 and reviewing film, ballet, and theatre for the Montreal *Gazette* in 1934. In 1949 he joined the Toronto *Globe and Mail* as theatre and film critic. He became its theatre and ballet critic in 1952, and reviewed theatre until his retirement in 1975, when he was named the *Globe*'s critic emeritus. Whittaker has encouraged Canadian playwrights not only through his theatre criticism, but also by organizing the 1959 *Globe and Mail*/Stratford Festival Canadian Playwriting Competition and by adjudicating the 1980 Theatre Ontario Playwrights' Showcase competition. As chairman of the Toronto Drama Bench (1972-5) and chairman of the Cana-

dian Theatre Critics Association since 1980, he has also sought to strengthen the field of theatre criticism itself. Besides designing and directing several prize-winning productions for over twenty amateur companies in Montreal and Toronto from 1933 to 1982, Whittaker directed and designed for the Jupiter Theatre in Toronto in 1951; directed for the Crest Theatre in 1954 and 1956; and designed sets and costumes for the 1961-2 tour of the Canadian Players. He served as a governor of the Dominion Drama Festival from 1949 to 1968; was a member of the Board of Trustees of the National Arts Centre from 1976 to 1982; and has been an advisory board member of Theatre Canada and the Shaw Festival. Unlike Nathan COHEN, who kept aloof from the theatre community, Whittaker maintained an involvement in live theatre that made him aware of the economic and artistic difficulties of Canadian productions. His criticism (unlike Cohen's) generally accented positive aspects. He has said: 'I gave my views by implication, by degree, by shading, by admitting the good points. Appreciation has always been more important than fault-finding in the theatre critic's lexicon. I think I make my points quite clear without a hammer.'

Besides numerous articles, Whittaker wrote the introduction to *The Stratford Festival 1953-57* (1958) and *Canada's national ballet* (1967). His career is surveyed in John Rittenhouse's 'Herbert Whittaker: a theatre life', *Theatre History in Canada* (Spring 1982). A collection of Whittaker's theatre criticism is being prepared for publication.

ANTON WAGNER

Who has seen the wind (1947), by W.O. MITCHELL, is one of Canada's most beloved novels. Structured in four parts and set in a Saskatchewan town, it dramatizes Brian O'Connal's growth from age four to twelve and his youthful struggle, in the face of loss and death, to comprehend 'the ultimate meaning of the cycle of life'. Prairie, family, and town all contribute to his awakening sense of perspective and social responsibility. By the novel's end young Brian, originally self-centred in his innocence, has matured to the point that he imagines becoming a 'dirt doctor' in order to minister to the land and the difficult environmental conditions affecting the people he loves. But Brian's growth has an inverse quality, as Mitchell's allusions to Wordsworth suggest. In childhood Brian is closest to nature and the divine, experiencing his particular intimations of immortality. As he ages his social identity begins to take shape; 'the feeling' he often experienced as a younger boy occurs far less frequently. In Brian's growth, then, the prairie is a vast Romantic stage, its vitality symbolized in characters like the Bens and Saint Sammy. In contrast, the town is ruled by the restrictions and cruelties of a life-denying puritanism. Brian's most effective teachers are associated with the prairie or the peripheries of town, where racial prejudice, unfairness, and hypocrisy have less place. Though melodramatically schematized, *Who has seen the wind* has a cogency of theme, a vividness of voice and event, and a vitality of presentation that help account for its prominence—its status as a 'classic'—in Canadian letters. A paperback edition was published in 1973. A film based on the novel, directed by Alan King, was released in 1977. MICHAEL PETERMAN

Wiebe, Rudy (b. 1934). Born on the family farm in a small Mennonite community near Fairholme, Sask., of parents who came to Canada from the Soviet Union in 1930, he began writing seriously as an undergraduate at the University of Alberta (1953-6), from which he received an M.A. in creative writing in 1960. Wiebe then studied abroad (1957-8) at the University of Tübingen in West Germany. He returned to Canada in 1958, taught at the Mennonite Brethren Bible College, edited the *Mennonite Brethren Herald* (1962-3), and then became assistant professor of English at Goshen College, Indiana (1964). Since 1967 he has taught English at the University of Alberta, Edmonton.

Wiebe has written seven novels: *Peace shall destroy many* (1962), *First and vital candle* (1966), *The blue mountains of China* (1970), *The temptations of Big Bear* (1973), *The scorched-wood people* (1977), *The mad trapper* (1980), and *My lovely enemy* (1983). He has also produced three collections of short stories—*Where is the voice coming from?* (1974), and *Alberta / a celebration* (1979), which contains photographs by Tom Radford and commentary by Harry Savage; selections from these books are reprinted in *The angel of the tar sands and other stories*, (NCL, 1982)—and a play, *Far as the eye can see* (1977). In addition he has edited several anthologies of short stories: *The story makers* (1970); *Stories from western Canada* (1972); *Stories from Pacific and Arctic Canada* (1974), co-edited with Andreas SCHROEDER; *Double*

vision: twentieth century stories in English (1976); *Getting here: Edmonton story anthology* (1977); and *More stories from western Canada* (1980), co-edited with Aritha Van Herk.

The two aspects of Wiebe's life that are most important to his art are that he is a Westerner and that he was born, and continues to be, a Mennonite whose first language was Low German. His fiction, though experimental in style and form (his major novels are among our most successful experimental works), is resolutely committed to a radical Christian vision. *Peace shall destroy many*, *First and vital candle*, and *The blue mountains of China* are essentially about man's struggle to live a moral and spiritual life in a world where such terms and assumptions are increasingly considered archaic and even obsolete. The first dramatizes—in a realistic style and within a relatively conventional four-part seasonal structure—the conflicts that arise during the Second World War in a Mennonite community in Wapiti, Sask. Most of the action is seen through the eyes of the protagonist, Thom Wiens, an earnest and inquiring young man who is torn between the old ways (represented by the dogmatic and bullying Deacon Block) and the new (embodied in and articulated by the reforming Joseph Duecke). The novel's central question—how does one live a truly Christian life in a fundamentally non-Christian world?—is raised again in *First and vital candle*, which depicts the life of Abe Ross, who has lost his faith. An ambitious, closely organized work, containing many powerful scenes of Indian and Eskimo life, the novel is finally too portentous and didactic. In *The blue mountains of China* Wiebe turned to the historical and epic mode characteristic of his major novels. It offers both a criticism of the materialism and one-dimensionality (Marcuse's term) of modern life and an affirmative alternative. At the centre of this episodic novel, covering almost a century of Mennonite history—including the heroic 1920s emigration from Soviet Russia to Canada and later to Paraguay—is a vision of various forms of Christian action and commitment: from the passive but firm belief of Frieda Friessen to the active witnessing of the cross-carrying John Reimer, who is walking through western Canada in search of the scattered Mennonite communities that still cling to the original revelation.

Wiebe has written extensively about Canadian Indians because they resemble the Mennonites in their concern for a community embodying spiritual values, and because they exist on the periphery of, and in opposition to, modern society. Wiebe's commitment to this body of western experience—which is traditionally ignored, or misinterpreted, in Canadian history and fiction—is reflected in minor works, such as some of the stories in *Alberta/a celebration* and *Where is the voice coming from?* and the adventure novel *The mad trapper*, as well as in *The temptations of Big Bear* and his masterpiece, *The scorched-wood people*.

By means of a complex polyphonic, multiple-viewpoint narrative structure, incorporating much documentary material, Wiebe tries in *The temptations of Big Bear* to present the Indian point of view, especially Big Bear's struggle to understand the changes taking place in the West in the last decades of the nineteenth century. This often brilliant, often difficult novel covers twelve years—from Big Bear's refusal to sign a treaty in 1876, through his inadvertent involvement in the killings at Frog Lake in 1884, to his imprisonment and death. A massive attempt at fictive translation, it attempts to give one culture (ours) an imaginative sense of another (the Cree's). Wiebe most effectively conveys the Indian way of life in several panoramic set scenes: the Cree attack on a Blood village, Big Bear's last thirst dance, and the last Buffalo hunt in which the Indians search for the remnants of the once-great herds. To emphasize the conflict between the two cultures Wiebe uses opposed sets of images: the whites, described predominantly in images drawn from civilization, are all angles and straight lines; the Indians are represented in images drawn from nature, with the result that Big Bear is a curve, a wave of life, a bird, a tree, and finally, in the novel's resonant closing image, a rock. More significantly, however, he is associated with the wind, with spirit, and—like most of Wiebe's fictional heroes—with speech and vision.

In this, and in the tragic nature of his life, Big Bear anticipates another visionary and revolutionary figure, Louis Riel—the central, heroic figure in *The scorched-wood people*. (Riel appears on the periphery of *The temptations of Big Bear*, is mentioned in *Peace shall destroy many*, and his grave is visited by Abe Ross in *First and vital candle*.) Like Big Bear, Riel articulates and embodies a vision of western community. Wiebe's complex portrait of him (both in form and content), and of the Métis, is historical revisionism with a vengeance: Wiebe refuses to accept the tradi-

tional interpretations of the man and his era offered by such historians as A.R.M. Lower, Donald CREIGHTON, and George Stanley. Instead of presenting Riel as mad (and the Métis as a marginal group impeding progress), Wiebe describes him in Christological terms as a visionary and a millenarian, the prophet of a vision of community that stands in direct opposition to the expansionist capitalist 'vision' of Macdonald. Wiebe has argued that the border between fiction and history has been called into doubt in our era. In *The scorched-wood people* he holds our interest by filling in the lacunae of history, providing details that no one person could have known by means of an omniscient posthumous narrator, Pierre FALCON, the poet of the Métis, who had seen Riel. (Each of these three major novels—*Blue mountains, Big bear*, and *The scorched-wood people*—uses with almost equal success a different and innovative mode of narration.) Wiebe's most recent novel, *My lovely enemy* (1983), uses the story of a love affair between a professor of history at the University of Alberta and a graduate student as the basis for an exploration of Wiebe's traditional concerns: man's relationship to God, the relevance of Christianity, and the nature and scope of human and divine love. The challenging narrative technique, combining realism and fantasy, is the perfect medium for Wiebe's central theme that love, erotic or spiritual, transcends time. However, this ambitious novel, which includes a rewriting of Dostoevsky's 'Grand Inquisitor' episode, has a major weakness: the author's slightly sentimental attitude towards his three central characters.

The mad trapper (1980) is a novel that fleshes out Wiebe's essay and story about Albert Johnson, the 'mad trapper' who shot a Mountie and became the object of a lengthy and widely publicized chase through the North. (The essay can be found in *Figures in a ground: Canadian essays on modern literature collected in honour of Sheila Watson* (1978), edited by Diane Bessai and David Jackel.) Wiebe's least ambitious work, it is in essence a well-told adventure story. Also worth noting are the short stories, 'Blue coast on the Sacred Hill of the Wild Peas', 'Where is the voice coming from', 'The naming of Albert Johnson', and 'The darkness inside the mountain'. They are western, like the novels—'precisely, particularly rooted in a particular place, in particular people'.

Wiebe's novels and stories stress that the

'signs' of God's presence are, and will always be, visible and available: man need only be receptive to the various incarnations taking place around him. The writings are filled with homely figures who, shadowed by biblical originals, function as Christ-like scapegoats, reminding others of a fully Christian life. Critical debate about Wiebe's novels, however, has often focused less on his themes than on his style, which some readers have found ponderous in rhythm and tortuous in syntax. For his admirers, Wiebe's so-called 'difficult' style is the necessary concomitant to, or expression of, the fiction's complex attitude to life.

Peace shall destroy many, The blue mountains of China, The temptation of Big Bear, The scorched-wood people, and *The angels of the tar sands and other stories* are all available in the New Canadian Library.

Most of the best criticism on Wiebe has been collected in *A voice in the land: essays by and about Rudy Wiebe* (1981), edited by W.J. Keith; it includes interesting interviews with Wiebe. Keith is also the author of *Epic fiction: the art of Rudy Wiebe* (1981)—possibly the single best book of criticism written on a Canadian author to date. Also of value are an interview with Donald Cameron in *Conversations with Canadian novelists*, volume two (1973), and Magdalene Redekop's 'Rudy Wiebe', *Profiles in Canadian Literature*, vol. 2 (1981), edited by Jeffrey Heath. Among the uncollected essays on Wiebe, three are noteworthy: Keith's superb introduction to the NCL edition of *The blue mountains of China* (1975), probably the finest single piece on Wiebe; R.P. Bilan's 'Wiebe and the religious struggle', CANADIAN LITERATURE 77 (Summer 1978); and Sam Solecki's 'Giant fictions and large meanings: the novels of Rudy Wiebe', CANADIAN FORUM, vol. 60, no. 707 (Mar. 1981).

See also NOVELS IN ENGLISH 1960 TO 1982: 2.   SAM SOLECKI

Wild animals I have known (New York, 1898). The first and most famous of many collections of animal stories by Ernest Thompson SETON, it includes the perenially popular 'Lobo, the King of Currumpaw' and seven other stories. Since publication it has never been out of print and exists in numerous translations. Along with Charles G.D. ROBERTS' *Kindred of the wild* (1902), it marked the beginning of a new genre: the realistic animal story. Seton's innovation was to make an animal, rather than a human, the central character. His goal was to make a moral point about man's relation to animals and to the wilderness they inhabit, emphasizing the need for man to live in harmony with nature. His work as a naturalist supplied the raw material for his stories. He insisted that his animal biographies were all fact, but admitted that they were often composite portraits, based on his observations of many animals of a species.

The story of the wolf Lobo was first published in *Scribner's Magazine* (Nov. 1894). Based on a real episode that took place in 1892 when Seton visited New Mexico, it describes the killing of Blanca, the capture of her mate Lobo, and his mysterious death during captivity. Seton's fellow scientists, arguing that a wolf cannot die of a broken heart, challenged his assertion that his stories were factual. Repeated charges of anthropomorphism—the 'nature-fakir controversy'—acted as a catalyst to increase Seton's productivity in scientific publications; but they did not keep him from writing numerous collections of stories following his popular formula.

MAGDALENE REDEKOP

Wilkinson, Anne (1910-1961). Born in Toronto, Anne Gibbons was a member of the Osler family, whose past and present provided a fund of material and imagery for her writing. She spent her early years in London, Ont., and was educated privately by tutors, and at progressive schools in the United States and France. She married F.R. Wilkinson, a surgeon, in 1932 (they were divorced twenty years later) and brought up a family of three children in Toronto.

Anne Wilkinson's reputation was made with two books of poetry, *Counterpoint to sleep* (1951) and *The hangman ties the holly* (1955), but she was equally accomplished in prose. In *Lions in the way* (1956) she traced the story of her family, who originally settled in the backwoods of Ontario, in Tecumseth Township. Her great-grandmother, Ellen Osler, raised nine children, four of whom developed outstandingly successful careers: Featherston and Britton Bath Osler as eminent lawyers; Sir William Bath Osler as Regius Professor of Medicine at Oxford; and her grandfather Sir Edmund Osler as a financier and member of Parliament. The figure who emerges most clearly, however, is Ellen, to whose courage and strong personality these men owed their success. The book provides a lively social history of Upper Canada. An epilogue brings the tale up to Wilkinson's own childhood, when she spent long periods in her grandfather's Toronto mansion, Craigleigh. This luxurious house is also described in the beautifully written autobiographical piece, 'Four corners of my world', originally published in The TAMARACK REVIEW (20, Summer 1961), of which she was a founding editor and generous patron. A.J.M. SMITH included this memoir in The collected poems of Anne Wilkinson (1968), where poems and fragments from periodicals and manuscripts are added to the two volumes of poetry published in her lifetime.

The 'four corners' of Wilkinson's world are seen as archetypes: the Gothic family home in London; the classical Craigleigh; the romantic summer home on Lake Simcoe; and the mysteriously evocative oceanside house in Santa Barbara, where her mother spent the winters. A similar shaping of material into a quaternity characterizes Wilkinson's poetry, where this method of seeing unity in multiplicity, especially in imagery of the four elements, emphasizes her own sense of identity and her oneness with nature. Her poetry is both highly sensuous and wittily intellectual; her subjects range from the landscapes of her family's 'summer acres', where she insists on the spirituality of the senses, to philosophical enquiries based on Kafka, Empedocles, and medieval texts. A.J.M. Smith's prefatory essay to The collected poems gives a fine analysis of these aspects of her work, as also of her poems of love and death. Anne Wilkinson died of cancer in 1961, and the poems written in her last years speak of death with particular intensity. Poems such as 'Accustom the grey coils' and 'A sorrow of stones' bring to a high pitch of horror that intimate awareness of the body she had often projected in her earlier verse. Smith points also to the celebration of metamorphosis in her poetry, a motif found too in her story for children, Swann and Daphne (1960). Delightfully illustrated by Leo Rampen, it tells of two mysterious children: instead of hair the boy has feathers and the girl has leaves. They journey to a northern lake where the girl sacrifices her own plans and turns into a birch tree in order to free the boy for a life of adventure with the wild swans.

Robert Lecker analyses the polar oppositions in Wilkinson's imagery in his article 'Better quick than dead: Anne Wilkinson's poetry', Studies in Canadian Literature, vol. III, no. 1 (Winter, 1978).

See also POETRY IN ENGLISH 1950 TO 1982: 1. JOAN COLDWELL

Williams, David (b. 1945). Born in Souris, Man., he grew up in Saskatchewan and attended Briercrest Bible College, a Mennonite institution near Moose Jaw, Sask. After graduating in 1965 with a pastor's diploma, he went on to the University of Saskatchewan, and thence to the University of Massachusetts for his M.A. (1970) and Ph.D. (1973). He now teaches in the English department of the University of Manitoba. His Saskatchewan childhood and his interest in Faulkner are reflected in two novels, The burning wood (1975) and The river horsemen (1981), that are remarkable for their rich language and their Faulknerian evocation of the Saskatchewan landscape and its peoples. In The burning wood the clash between a Christian-fundamentalist white community of northern Saskatchewan and the nearby Indian reservation forms the background for the story of Joshua Cardiff's growing up. Deprived of his hair by a mysterious disease, Joshua is seen by his family as one of the damned, and is drawn towards the Indians, to whom his baldness is a mark of privilege, the badge of Manitou. Williams uses flashbacks, interior monologue, and changes of typeface to create the past of the Cardiff family—which Joshua re-enacts, becoming at once his sainted namesake uncle, drowned while rescuing an Indian boy, as well as his damned, scapegrace, squaw-loving great-grandfather, who was killed by the same Indians young Joshua later befriends. The resulting tangle of family loyalties and individual identities provides Williams' novel with its Faulknerian overtones of individual and collective doom. The river horsemen is also a study of outcasts—in this case two Indians, a Ukrainian youth, and a lapsed evangelist, who pursue their separate quests along a collective river road in a progress reminiscent of the funeral journey in As I lay dying. The novel unfolds in a series of interior monologues by these 'four horsemen'.

A member of the editorial board of The Canadian Review of American Studies, Williams is also the author of a book of literary criticism, Faulkner's women: the myth and the muse (1977).

See also NOVELS IN ENGLISH 1960 TO 1982: OTHER TALENTS, OTHER WORKS: 2. MICHELLE GADPAILLE

Willis, John H. See ESSAYS IN ENGLISH: 1.

Wilson, Ethel (1888-1980). Born Ethel Davis Bryant at Port Elizabeth, South

Africa, where her father was a Methodist missionary, she was taken to England in 1890 on the death of her mother and brought up by relatives. In 1898, after her father died, she came to Canada and lived with her grandmother in Vancouver in circumstances drawn upon later for *The innocent traveller*. Like Frankie Burnaby in *Hetty Dorval*, she attended boarding schools, first in Vancouver and then in England. After receiving a teacher's certificate from the Vancouver Normal School in 1907, she taught at various local schools until 1920. In 1921 she married Dr Wallace Wilson, then at the beginning of a distinguished medical career (he was president of the Canadian Medical Association in 1946-7).

Wilson's writing career began late. She started to publish short stories in the *New Statesman and Nation* in the late 1930s, and her first novel did not appear until 1947. *Hetty Dorval* is an accomplished work, remarkable for the way in which the story of the 'experienced' Hetty Dorval is told through the 'innocent' Frankie Burnaby, a girl growing up in the British Columbia hinterland. The plot is a trifle forced, but Wilson demonstrates an ability to combine stylistic clarity and technical sophistication with the authorial poise, humour, and good sense that characterize all her fiction. Her next novel, *The innocent traveller* (1949), employs elements from her own family history in tracing the life of Topaz Edgeworth from precocious three-year-old in the English Midlands to still irrepressible centenarian in Vancouver. Besides offering a wholly credible portrait of a character rarely encountered in fiction—the unconventional, unfrustrated middle-class spinster who lives a passive, unremarkable yet full and happy life—the novel offers a convincing presentation of social developments in England and Canada over a long period (the 1840s to the 1940s).

Wilson's later fiction reveals an increasing interest in portraying various kinds of women at times of personal crisis, and in exploring spiritual and religious values. *The equations of love* (1952; rpr. 1974) is made up of two novellas. 'Tuesday and Wednesday' follows the life of an ordinary couple for two days, on the second of which the husband dies; 'Lilly's Story' traces an unmarried mother's determination to bring up her child independently and decently. Both involve people who never penetrate below the surface of life, but they are portrayed with understanding and sympathy. *Swamp angel* (1954; NCL, 1962), perhaps Wilson's finest

artistic success, divides its attention between a woman escaping a disastrous marriage to start a new life on a remote lake in northern British Columbia, and a retired circus-performer whose memories of her past threaten to spoil her present. It is a touching, sensitively written, wise novel that delicately raises profound questions about human responsibility and the meaning of life.

Wilson's final novel, *Love and salt water* (1956), is darker in tone. Most of the characters are wounded, physically or emotionally, by the Second World War. The central figure, Ellen Cuppy, has a painful childhood (she discovers her mother dead; her father soon remarries), and her initiation into the adult world is deftly presented in all its clumsiness and uncertainty. Here, as elsewhere in Wilson's novels, the focus is not so much on what happens as on personal responses to what happens. Human relationships, especially love, are invariably Wilson's main subject; and in this novel the pain and danger implicit in emotional commitments, symbolized by the salt water of the title, are given particular emphasis.

Unfortunately Wilson published little after 1961. Her later years, after her husband died in 1966, were spent in seclusion and often ill-health until her death. Her novels, then, are about everyday topics—love, the failure to love, hope and despair, all-too-human fear and courageous determination. Her characters are not immediately memorable, but Wilson shows that they are more remarkable than they seem. She approaches them with compassion balanced by firmness; she is not afraid to discuss her characters with her readers in Victorian fashion, but her attitudes belong solidly to her own time. George WOODCOCK has caught the curious tensions in her work by describing Wilson as an Edwardian sensibility who acquired a contemporary ironic intelligence. She writes with wit and grace but does not ignore human triviality or evil. Her novels demonstrate that it is possible to combine serenity, good humour, and intelligence in twentieth-century fiction without seeming incongruous.

The majority of Wilson's short stories, many of them predating the novels, were collected and published as *Mrs Golightly and other stories* (1961). They range in tone from the warm comedy of 'Mrs Golightly and the first convention' to the bleak presentation of gratuitous violence in 'Fog' and 'Hurry, hurry'; from garrulous monologue in 'I just love dogs' to sophisticated experiments with narrative viewpoint in 'A drink with Adolphus'. The last story in the collection, 'The window', is an effective moral parable that draws together many strands from her work as a whole. Despite this variety in her short stories, the collection is unified by Wilson's mature perception and unostentatious artistic control.

Wilson's life and work are discussed by Desmond PACEY in *Ethel Wilson* (1968), and in the proceedings of the University of Ottawa's 'Ethel Wilson Symposium' (1981). An important four-part bibliography by Bonnie Martyn McComb of writings by and about Wilson appeared in the *West Coast Review* between June 1979 and June 1980.

W.J. KEITH

Wilson, Milton. See CRITICISM IN ENGLISH: 4.

Wiseman, Adele (b. 1928). Born in Winnipeg to Jewish parents who emigrated from the Ukraine, she received a B.A. in English and psychology from the University of Manitoba (1949) and then, to support her early intention to be a writer, took a variety of jobs as executive secretary, teacher, and social worker in Canada and abroad. She lives in Toronto with her husband, Dmitry Stone; they have one daughter.

Wiseman's imagination was shaped by her Eastern European Jewish heritage. Her first novel, *The sacrifice* (1956; rpr. 1968), received a Governor General's Award; it was followed by *Crackpot* (1974). In both novels Wiseman interprets modern Jewish experience as reflected in the lives of people who immigrated to the Canadian Prairies between the two world wars. *The sacrifice* uses the biblical story of the patriarch's willingness to sacrifice his son as the metaphorical base for the tragic story of a new Abraham who repeatedly suffers the blows of a hostile fate and, though he is dedicated to the search for moral and spiritual perfection, is eventually driven to murder. Like the heroes of Greek tragedy, Abraham is over-proud; only at the end does he recognize the need to love, to accept weakness in himself and others, and to acknowledge the mysterious co-existence of creativity and destruction. The novel depicts the hardships of immigrant experience, with sharp criticism of exploitation in the garment trade, ruthless business practices, and social snobbery. *Crackpot* is also set in a Jewish ghetto, now recognizably the north end of Winnipeg during the Depression. Unlike the former novel, which used a traditional pattern and an omniscient narrator, *Crackpot* experiments with unconventional sentence structures and language appropriate to the uneducated perceptions of Hoda, a fat prostitute who never loses her child-like trust and clear-sightedness. Through this seemingly unprepossessing character, Wiseman celebrates life in all its richness and complexity and, at the moment when Hoda must choose to commit incest, demonstrates the paradoxical knotting of good and evil within one action. *Crackpot* is full of laughter as well as pathos and is given poetic richness by an intricate symbolism, especially to do with light, based on the Kabbalah. Like its predecessor, this novel contains much social criticism, particularly of the educational and welfare systems, but the method is more satirical and, in the tradition of Jewish humour, much of the laughter is self-directed.

Wiseman wrote the short text that accompanies Joe Rosenthal's sketches in *Old markets, new worlds* (1964), stressing the importance of the old-style markets to an immigrant community. Much of her parents' life-story is told episodically in *Old woman at play* (1978), an illustrated book whose main concern is the formation of an aesthetic theory from her mother's primitive art of doll-making. Wiseman spent many years on two plays of social criticism: *Testimonial dinner* (1978), a study of three generations of a Canadian Jewish family, was published privately; a portion of *The Lovebound*, set on a Jewish refugee ship in 1939, appears in *Journal of Canadian Fiction* 31/32 (1981), which also contains Wiseman's story 'The country of the hungry bird' and Roslyn Belkin's interview with Wiseman, 'The consciousness of a Jewish artist'.

See Michael Greenstein, 'Vision and movement in *The sacrifice*', CANADIAN LITERATURE 80 (Spring 1979).

See also NOVELS IN ENGLISH 1960 TO 1982: 1.

JOAN COLDWELL

Withrow, William Henry (1839-1908). Born in Toronto, he attended the University of Toronto (B.A., 1863; M.A., 1864). He was admitted to the Methodist ministry in 1866, and became the editor of its major cultural organ, the *Canadian Methodist Magazine*, in 1874. He remained its editor, and one of its major contributors, for more than a quarter of a century. Many of his articles—especially his biographical sketches, travel accounts, and serialized fiction—were published in book form. Moral didacticism pervades all of his writing, appropriately and inevitably in his sketches of religious figures: works such as *Worthies of early Methodism* (Toronto, 1878), *The romance of missions* (Toronto, 1879), *Men worth knowing; or Heroes of Christian chivalry* (Toronto, 1881), and *Missionary heroes* (Toronto, 1883). This persistent, unrelieved tone is less acceptable, however, in his fiction, which is further diminished, especially in dramatic effect, by too much use of history-writing paraphernalia. These traits undermine *The king's messenger; or, Lawrence Temple's probation: a story of Canadian life* (Toronto, 1879); *Neville Trueman: the pioneer preacher. A tale of the War of 1812* (Toronto, 1880); *Valeria: the martyr of the catacombs. A tale of early Christian life in Rome* (Toronto, 1882); *Life in a parsonage; or, Lights and shadows of the itineracy* (London, 1885); and *Barbara Heck. A tale of early Methodism in America* (Toronto, 1895). Some of these novels were popular enough to be reprinted in subsequent editions, and in England and the United States, but Withrow was better known in his own time as the author of the historical study *The catacombs of Rome and their testimony relative to primitive Christianity* (New York, 1874), and for his *History of Canada* (Toronto, 1876), which was subsequently reprinted in several different editions. His travel books, *A Canadian in Europe; being sketches of travel in France, Italy, Switzerland, Germany, Holland and Belgium, Great Britain, and Ireland* (Toronto, 1881), and *Our own country: Canada scenic and descriptive . . .* (2 vols, Toronto, 1889), were successfully characterized by lively, light, informative narrative. *The native races of North America* (Toronto, 1895) is simply a compilation of selections from the work of other writers.

Withrow's stature in his own day was recognized by the award of a D.D. from Victoria University in 1880, and by his election to the Royal Society of Canada in 1884. He died in Toronto.   CHARLES R. STEELE

Wood, Joanna E. (d. 1919). Born in Lanarkshire, Scot., she lived for a short time with her family in the southern United States, then moved to Queenston Heights, Ont. During her writing career she did much travelling in Britain and Europe and lived for periods in the U.S., particularly Boston. She died in Detroit.

Wood was the author of several novels, the strongest of which are *The untempered wind* (New York, 1894; Toronto, 1898), in which an unmarried woman, betrayed in love, raises her child in a moralistic and censorious small Ontario town with the fictional name of Jamestown; *Judith Moore; or, Fashioning a pipe* (Toronto, 1898), in which a singer leaves the pressures and exploitation of the European and American musical worlds for a simple, pastoral life in rural Ontario; and *A daughter of witches* (Toronto, 1900), in which an idealistic Boston Transcendentalist is almost ruined by the venom of his wife's thwarted love. Wood's other novels include *Farden Ha'* (London, 1901) and *A martyr to love* (New York, 1903). H.J. Morgan in *Canadian men and women* (1912) lists three other titles: *The lynchpin sensation, Unto the third generation,* and *Where waters beckon.* Wood also wrote short fiction for the New York weeklies, often using the pen name 'Jean d'Arc', and competed successfully in American short-story contests, in which she made several thousand dollars.

For the most part Wood is a sentimental novelist whose central theme is love. Her characters are often two-dimensional, her plots melodramatic, her language ornate and artificial. However, her work is transitional, at its best containing passages of penetrating social analysis and statement, with a clear indebtedness to the school of realism, particularly to Hardy, which was noted by contemporary critics. She shows remarkabke insight into the Canadian small town, whose cultural character, folkways, and speech she depicts with a skill that goes well beyond much of the local-colour fiction of her day. Her most successful novel in this respect is *The untempered wind*, in which strict moral codes, hypocrisy, and parochialism of the small town are clearly delineated. The first novelist to express what E.K. BROWN would later define as the central impediments to creativity in Canada—puritanism, colonialism, and the frontier spirit—Wood stands at the beginning of a tradition of fiction that examines the Canadian small town critically. In *Judith Moore* and *A daughter of witches* a more humorous tone emerges as she captures the colour and vitality of rural life through the speech of her minor characters. Wood is also significant as a member of the important post-Confederation group of writers who sought a native literature in local settings and characters. While not blind to the limitations of the small town, she does subscribe to a myth of Canada, shared by many of her generation, as an unspoiled place of innocence and potential, a refuge from the corruption and pressures of Europe and the United States. This myth is expressed in powerful, mystical terms in the image of the North in *Judith Moore*.

Wood enjoyed a favourable reputation in literary circles in the late 1890s, largely based on *The untempered wind. Current literature* (vol. XVI, 1894, p. 378) called this novel 'the strongest and best American novel of the year.' Canadian critics were slower to respond, but *The Canadian Magazine* (vol. X, 1898, p. 460) assessed Wood as one of the three leading Canadian novelists of the day, in the ranks of Gilbert PARKER and Charles G.D. ROBERTS. Her novels were reviewed in Britain in such journals as *The Bookman, The Outlook, The Spectator, The Westminster Gazette*, and *The Athenaeum*, where she was discussed as a writer who had an individual style, the particular strengths of which were a quiet humour and strong character portraits.   CARRIE MacMILLAN

Woodcock, George (b. 1912). Born in Winnipeg to British parents, he was raised and educated in England. In the late 1930s, while mixing in the London literary world that included Dylan Thomas, Roy Campbell, Herbert Read, and George Orwell, Woodcock emerged as a poet and radical pamphleteer, part of a socially committed literary underground whose pacifism only intensified as a world war approached. During the war he performed non-military duties as a conscientious objector, edited the anarchist publication *War Commentary* (later *Freedom*), and founded the radical literary magazine *Now*, which he edited until 1947. In retrospect the pamphlets he wrote in this period fathered his later more lasting works, such as *Anarchism: a history of libertarian ideas and movements* (1962) and *Gandhi* (1971), though the young Woodcock gave little indication of the important and prolific literary figure he would later become. His early work ran from collections of verse, such as *The white island* (1940) and *The centre cannot hold* (1943), to *The incomparable Aphra: a life of Mrs. Aphra Behn* and *The writer and politics: essays* (both 1948). They all reflect the fluent writing style and the precise mixture of literary and political curiosity that seems peculiar to him alone. The nature of the recipe is tied to Woodcock's belief in literary anarchism, the anti-doctrine of which he is now the leading exponent.

Within the general view that society is best served by individuals who are not organized under the yoke of government,

Woodcock has found room for himself as an independent journalist, historian, and literary commentator equally unconstrained by the academy or by slavish devotion to only one or two disciplines. As an anarchist, his antecedents are the notable libertarian thinkers of the nineteenth century whose biographer he became in such books as *William Godwin: a biographical study* (1946) and *Pierre-Joseph Proudhon: a biography* (1956). In the same vein is *The anarchist prince: a biographical study of Peter Kropotkin* (1950), written in collaboration with Ivan Avakumovic, as was *The Doukhobors* (1968). Woodcock's literary ancestors, however, would stretch from Defoe and William Cobbett to any of the late-Victorian generalists to whom nothing humanly interesting could be totally foreign.

In 1949 Woodcock returned to Canada, settling in British Columbia, eventually in Vancouver, and carrying on his profession as a writer with even greater vigour. All his Canadian writings, even the most personal, tend to be informed by his interest in the role of the arts in a free society and the way many past eras and more primitive cultures point up the weaknesses in our own. While one should be wary of seeing his career as compartmentalized, it is possible to break down his work into several convenient, if maddeningly overlapping, categories.

As a prolific travel writer Woodcock produces personal narratives rather than guidebooks, though such stylized works as *To the city of the dead: an account of travels in Mexico* (1957) and *Incas and other men: travels in the Andes* (1959) are full of observations on the history, geography, economy, and culture of the regions being examined. Other travel books are *Faces of India: a travel narrative* (1964), *Asia, gods and cities: Aden to Tokyo* (1966), *Kerala: a portrait of the Malabar coast* (1967), and *South Sea journey* (1976). It is no coincidence that all the above deal with areas once part of either the Spanish or the British empires, for in Woodcock colonialism is often seen as government writ large, and the lowly native as a metaphor for the individual within the dreaded state. These ideas are still more apparent in related works of history, such as *The Greeks in India* (1966), *The British in the Far East* (1969), *Into Tibet: the early British explorers* (1971), and *Who killed the British Empire?* (1974).

Woodcock's travel books, all of them examples of a type more common in Britain than in North America—informal and objective in approach, wide-ranging in subject-matter—are thus the fountainhead for other of his works, including his many publications on Canada. After *Ravens and prophets: an account of journeys in British Columbia, Alberta and southern Alaska* (1952), in which he sees the region as deliciously untamed yet foreign, Woodcock gradually becomes a Canadian nationalist whose nationalism is rooted in the cause of regionalism and decentralization. Such is the viewpoint conveyed to foreign audiences in *Canada and the Canadians* (1970; rev. 1973) and *The Canadians* (1979), and expressed more stridently for domestic consumption in *Confederation betrayed!* (1981), whose format harks back to his numerous early pamphlets. The underlying concern with local cultural history has surfaced fully in such biographical studies as *Amor De Cosmos, journalist and reformer* and *Gabriel Dumont: the Métis chief and his lost world* (both 1975). The sub-title of the latter is significant for, as in *Peoples of the coast: the Indians of the Pacific Northwest* (1977), it is a lost world—one in which anarchism was the natural state of man—that Woodcock often laments or tries to evoke. He has also written the text for three pictorial books: *Faces from history: Canadian profiles and portraits* (1978), *100 great Canadians* (1980), and *Ivan Eyre* (1981), a study of the background, development, and works of the prairie artist.

In his literary criticism, too, one can see Woodcock constantly refining certain tenets that came to him early on. In its search for the perfect marriage of imaginative and political activity (somewhat akin to Tolstoy's idealized balance of the intellectual and the physical), *The paradox of Oscar Wilde* (1950) is virtually a blueprint for later bio-critical studies, such as *The crystal spirit: a study of George Orwell* (1966), Woodcock's best-known book; *Dawn and the darkest hour: a study of Aldous Huxley* (1972); and *Herbert Read: the stream and the source* (1972). These books also show his preference for the radical and his inclination towards sociological over textual criticism (which he nevertheless does not disregard), as do *Odysseus ever returning: essays on Canadian writers and writing* (NCL, 1970) and *The world of Canadian writing: critiques and recollections* (1980). Both are important collections, showing to best advantage the style and disposition that are also obvious in two monographs, *Hugh MacLennan* (1969) and *Mordecai Richler* (1970), which present Woodcock as a questioner and leveller rather than as an explainer and champion, which he tends to be when discussing younger regionalist authors. As

regards influences, Woodcock is both a transmitter and a receiver—the latter particularly in his verse. In poetry collections from *Imagine the South* (1947) to *Selected poems* (1967), he is essentially a British poet from between the wars in outlook and style. In his newer verse—collected in *Notes on visitations: poems, 1936-1975* (1975) and *The kestrel and other poems* (1978)—Auden has been supplanted as an influence by Margaret ATWOOD, and the writer has been virtually redefined and rejuvenated.

Among Woodcock's many other books—each expressing strains in his previous writings—are *Civil disobedience* (1966), *Henry Walter Bates: naturalist of the Amazon* (1969), *Thomas Merton, monk and poet: a critical study* (1978), and *Two plays* (1978). He has also edited several anthologies drawn from CANADIAN LITERATURE, which he founded in Vancouver in 1959 and edited until 1977. *The rejection of politics and other essays on Canada, Canadians, anarchism and the world* (1972) suggests the enormous volume of his journalism, while *A George Woodcock reader* (1980), edited by Doug Fetherling, gives a broader hint of its scope. *Taking it to the letter* (1982) is a selection of his correspondence with other Canadian writers. *Letter to the past* (1983) is the first volume of his autobiography, covering the years before his return to Canada.

Woodcock has consistently declined most honours and awards, accepting only the Governor General's Award for *The crystal spirit* and the Molson Prize (1973) of the Canada Council, and others he judges to derive from his peers, not from the state or the establishment.

See Peter Hughes, *George Woodcock* (NCL, 1974), and Dennis Duffy, 'George Woodcock: voyager of liberty', *Canadian Literature* 83 (Winter 1979).

See also CRITICISM IN ENGLISH: 5(f).

DOUG FETHERLING

Wright, Eric. See MYSTERY AND CRIME.

Wright, Richard (b. 1937). Born in Midland, Ont., Richard Bruce Wright attended Ryerson Polytechnical Institute, Toronto, and then worked briefly in journalism before embarking upon a decade of work for two Toronto publishers, Macmillan and Oxford University Press. He left publishing in 1970 to work full time as a writer, though from 1975 to 1979 he taught English at Ridley College.

Wright's first work of fiction, *Andrew*

Tolliver (1965), was a children's book. His first novel for adults, *The weekend man* (1970; rpr. 1977), was widely praised, and like his subsequent fiction was published in the United States and England as well as Canada; it has also been translated into French, Italian, Japanese, Spanish and Swedish. Wes Wakeham is the first example of a type found throughout Wright's fiction: a man of gentle instincts out of sympathy with the common ambitions of his society and embittered by separation from a rich and domineering wife. (Each of Wright's novels is, however, distinctive in tone and character.) Having drifted from one inconsequential job to another, Wakeham is an outsider by temperament and conviction; he defines a weekend man as 'a person who has abandoned the present in favour of the past or the future', and has an air of amused detachment in common with the hero of Walker Percy's *The moviegoer*, a novel Wright says has influenced his work. Fred Landon, the protagonist of *In the middle of a life* (1973), approaches life with middle-aged wariness and resignation rather than with youthful cynicism. His efforts to find harmony with his existing family and to establish a new romantic bond are related in a style that reflects the wistful melancholy of his character. This novel won the Faber fiction award in England.

Wright abandoned sober realism for exuberant comedy in his next work, *Farthing's fortunes* (1976). Presented as the artless tape-recorded memoirs of an ancient wandering Canadian, the novel incorporates graphic vignettes of the social history of half a century, including Toronto low and high life in the nineties, the Yukon gold rush, the Battle of the Somme, and the Depression. The book cleverly manipulates storytelling conventions and deliberately evokes well-worn stereotypes—the good-hearted whore, the loud-mouthed American entrepreneur, the love-starved poet—in imitation of the picaresque novel. In *Final things* (1980) Wright returned to the novel of character with a memorable portrait of a burnt-out sportswriter who is consumed by thoughts of revenge when his teenage son is brutally murdered. As a study of a decent middle-aged man tortured by feelings of failure, the novel has much in common with *In the middle of a life*; but it attains a shattering emotional intensity beyond the range of the earlier book as the protagonist closes in on his son's killer. An astute observer of social realities, Wright explores in *The teacher's*

daughter (1982) the relationship of a lonely teacher and a young ex-convict.

See also NOVELS IN ENGLISH 1960 TO 1982: OTHER TALENTS, OTHER WORKS: 6(a).

THOMAS E. TAUSKY

Writers' Union of Canada, The. Officially born at its first convention in Ottawa on 3 Nov. 1973, it began at the instigation of Farley MOWAT—who felt that the interests of Canadian writers should be protected by a professional organization at a time when the Canadian book industry was growing rapidly—with the support of a small nucleus of writers that included Margaret ATWOOD, June Callwood, Graeme GIBSON, Ian Adams, and Fred BODSWORTH. Members are required to have published at least one trade book of prose. Among services offered are contract advice; reading tours; manuscript evaluation; information on agents; group insurance; and grievance/resolution assistance. Chairpersons have been Marian ENGEL, 1973; Graeme Gibson, 1974; David Lewis STEIN, 1975; Andreas SCHROEDER, 1976; Timothy FINDLEY, 1977; Charles Taylor, 1978; June Callwood, 1979; Harold HORWOOD, 1980; Margaret Atwood, 1981; Robin SKELTON, 1982; and Eugene Benson, 1983. It is located at 24 Ryerson Ave, Toronto M5T 2P3. See *The Writers' Union of Canada: a directory of members* (1981) edited by Ted Whittaker.   BRUCE MEYER

Wrong, George. See HISTORICAL WRITING IN ENGLISH: 7.

Wyatt, Rachel (b. 1929). Born in Bradford, Eng., she was educated in Yorkshire and studied nursing in London. In 1957 she immigrated to Canada with her husband and two children, and has lived in Niagara Falls, Oakville, Toronto, and St Catharines, Ont. She began writing plays in the early 1970s for the BBC and for Canadian radio; the CBC has produced over twenty of her original dramas. She has published stories and articles for *Punch* and *Chatelaine*, as well as three novels with House of ANANSI Press. Despite their Canadian settings, they are reminiscent of the British comedy of manners as practised by Evelyn Waugh and Nancy Mitford. In *The string box* (1970) Wyatt's hero copes with a dreadful career in the sardonically perceived world of Canadian media as he longs for a literary life in London and for the pubs and green gardens of home. *The Rosedale hoax* (1977) concerns the pretentions and eccentricities of Toronto's most snobbish neighbourhood, which, though in decay, manages to destroy the marriage of the luckless, gentle protagonist. In *Foreign bodies* (1982) Wyatt returns to the theme of the immigrant in Canada, as British academics on an exchange program are stunned by the nation's weather, folkways, laws, and inflation, and find their lives radically changed by an equally displaced Pakistani. Here, as in her radio plays, Wyatt owes much to the British comic tradition for the witty surfaces of her style and her accurate appraisals of Canadian mores. However, her sympathy for lonely, dislocated characters at sea in a baffling North American society imparts to her best work a sense of melancholy reflection that is distinctive to the highest modes of comedy.   JAMES POLK

Wynand, Derk (b. 1944). Born in Bad Suderode, Germany, he came to Canada in 1952 and was educated at the University of British Columbia. In 1969 he joined the Creative Writing Department of the University of Victoria, where he is now an associate professor.

Wynand's poetry and fiction are strongly influenced by the surrealists, fabulists, and absurdists, including the Austrian H.C. Artmann (whom Wynand has translated), Karl Krolow, Kafka, Guillevic, and Friederike Mayrocker. Because Wynand's writings originate from such esoteric sources, his work has not received much critical attention in Canada. However, his sparse and laconic poems, stories, and translations appeared in over 300 periodicals in the USA, Canada, and Europe. His chapbooks *Locus* (1971) and *Pointwise* (1979) are filled with metaphors about the double standards of contemporary living. His style is precise, but his disturbing imagery often relies upon symbolist or fabulist devices to create jarring images of alienation. *Locus* is vaguely surreal and *Pointwise* is at once bleak and wittily ironic about nebulous human relationships. In *Snowscapes* (1974) Wynand counterpoints prose poems and poetic styles about snow, in which he finds searching metaphors for the dilemma of modern man. Human experience becomes a white void. Love, children, poetry, and the barest acts of survival are only muffled communications that leave no trace. *One cook, once dreaming* (1980) is an admirable series of vignettes in stripped-down prose about an anonymous cook and his wife some place in central Europe. Dreams, scenes, fantasies, and role reversals accumulate to form a single powerful metaphor about the search for a meaningful relationship.

See also NOVELS IN ENGLISH 1960 TO 1982: OTHER TALENTS, OTHER WORKS: 1.

GEOFF HANCOCK

Y

Yates, J. Michael (b. 1938). Born in Missouri, he was educated at the University of Missouri, Kansas City, then studied comparative literature with Austin Warren at the University of Michigan. In 1967 he moved to Vancouver, where for a short time he was an influential professor of creative writing at the University of British Columbia. While at UBC, Yates encouraged the beginnings of Andreas SCHROEDER's magazine *Contemporary Literature in Translation* and CANADIAN FICTION MAGAZINE. He also founded the Sono Nis Press. Yates's poems and stories have been anthologized widely, and have appeared in dozens of little magazines in Canada and abroad.

Yates was a key figure for a short time in the early 1970s in the development of a distinctive style of fiction and poetry that he called 'West Coast surrealism'. His poetry is innovative, moody, intellectual, and occasionally puzzling. Critics have called him self-indulgent, referring not only to his work but to his lavish self-published collections, which often simply reprint existing volumes. His early collections—*Spiral of mirrors* (1967), *Hunt in an unmapped interior* (1967), and selections from *The Great Bear Lake meditations* (1970)—were reprinted in *Nothing speaks for the Blue Moraines* (1973). Fred COGSWELL has called the Great Bear Lake poems—in which a kind of nightmarish surrealism is grafted onto the experience of the North, with death seen as the ultimate desire—the most ambitious and successful meditative poem ever written in Canada. *Canticle for electronic music* (1967) is an intriguing volume in which the mind is seen as a vast library consumed by the fire of consciousness, which cannot be located: our knowledge is left behind as scorched paper. *Parallax* (1971) is a collection of prose-poems that form a sequence about the bleakness of existence both within and without. *The abstract beast* (1972) includes radio dramas and stories. *Breath of the snow leopard* (1974)—which includes new and selected poems—is a difficult but compelling collection in which Yates further explores the illusory quality of human existence. He also explores the 'fiction' of personality that the mind creates to make life comprehensible and suggests that language may be inadequate to express poetic experience. *The Qualicum physics* (1975) appeared in a limited edition. A highly cerebral collection, *Esox nobilior non esox lucius* (1978), contains a metaphysical vision that is obscured by abstract and opaque metaphors, word-plays, word coinages, and surreal imagery using the sea and birds.

Fazes in elsewhen: new and selected fiction (1976) includes work previously published in *The man in the glass octopus* (1968). Yates calls his stories fictions to emphasize their parabolic or allegorical nature. Often plotless, and with characters unnamed, they are set in technological worlds where cameras, radios, telephones, and libraries are seen as threats to individuality. Yates has also published two collections of one-act plays—*Night freight* (1972) and *Quarks* (1975)—that use a single metaphor to hold each play together.

Charles LILLARD discusses Yates's impact on B.C. writing in Issue 45 of *The* MALAHAT REVIEW.

See also NOVELS IN ENGLISH 1960 TO 1982: OTHER TALENTS, OTHER WORKS: 1, and POETRY IN ENGLISH 1950 TO 1982: 3.

GEOFF HANCOCK

Yiddish literature. Although the Yiddish language traces its beginnings back to the fourteenth century, modern Yiddish literature, arising as it did out of the European Enlightenment, is only about 150 years old. In Canada, Yiddish literature was originally little more than an offshoot from the transplanting and flowering of the Yiddish language and culture that took place at the turn of the century in America, when Jewish immigration from Eastern Europe was at its height. The arrival in New York of such Russian- and Yiddish-born writers as Sholem Aleichem, Yehoash, and H. Leivick, Abraham Reisen, and Morris Rosenfeld, who already had established reputations in Europe, gave a new stimulus to Yiddish writing in America, as did the immigrant audiences who thought, spoke, and read Yiddish. Up to the time of the Second World War, Canada—with its large Jewish settlements in Montreal, Toronto, and Winnipeg—was simply a northern outpost of New York's cultural and publishing activities. And indeed, the lecture and reading circuits, as well as the flow of publication, scarcely recognized the existence of borders. But gradually the first group of immigrants—those who had come before the First World War—established their own schools, newspapers, and literary magazines.

Winnipeg was the home of the first and most famous of the secular Yiddish schools in North America. However, the children educated in such schools who later went on to become well-known writers (Jack LUDWIG, Miriam Dworkin WADDINGTON, Adele WISEMAN, and Larry Zolf) did not write in Yiddish but in English. Of those who wrote in Yiddish, nearly all had their roots in Europe; they had gravitated to Montreal where they created a lively cultural centre in the Jewish Public Library—to this day one of the very few, and among the finest, professionally staffed Yiddish libraries in the world. These Yiddish writers published their own books, and appeared in newspapers, literary journals, and anthologies in Canada and abroad (New York, Tel Aviv, and before the war in Vilnius and Warsaw). The writers of the early Montreal group—all of whom arrived in Canada before the First World War—were the poets Yakov Yitzhak SEGAL and his sister Esther Segal (1895-1974), and Ada Maze (1893-1962); the educator Shlomo Weissman (b. 1899); the sociologist Louis Rosenberg (b. 1893), and the editors and essayists Israel Rabinovitch (1894-1964) and Benjamin Zack (1889-1967). To this first group were added—in the twenties, thirties, and forties—S. Dunski (b. 1899), Yehudah Elberg (b. 1912), S. Mitzmacher (b. 1912), Melech Ravitch (1893-1976), M. M. Shaffir (b. 1909), Sholem Shtern (b. 1903), and Yudika (pseudonym of Judith Tsik, b. 1898), to name a few. H. M. Caiserman (1884-1950) was one of the earliest patrons and historians of the Montreal Yiddish group, and H. L. Fuchs almost its only bibliographer.

The end of the Second World War marked the destruction of all Yiddish culture in Europe and brought more immigrants to Montreal. Among them were the two major Yiddish writers: Rahel KORN and Chaveh ROSENFARB. Although the Toronto Jewish community never developed as strong a centre for Yiddish culture as either Montreal or Winnipeg, it attracted two poets, Peretz Miransky (b. 1908) and S. Simchovitch (b. 1921), who continue to live and work there.

The themes that have permeated the work of Canadian Yiddish poets were more universal than local and often rooted in the past. This is not surprising, given the Canadian mosaic, with its tendency to preserve and isolate ethnic cultural entities. The writers, therefore, addressed such subjects as poverty, exile, the conflict between traditional and revolutionary values, childhood memories of Europe, and more general lyrical subjects having to do with love, nature, and sorrow. Though the work of these immigrant writers was universal in theme, in style and mood it was consciously contemporary. Canadian Yiddish writers reflected the influence of their New York counterparts—who, in turn, were influenced by all the modern European literary movements, though they possessed an American energy and flair for innovation.

See Irving Howe and Eliezer Greenberg eds, *A treasury of Yiddish poetry* (1969) and *A treasury of Yiddish stories* (1973); Emanuel S. Goldsmith, *Architects of Yiddishisms: a study in Jewish cultural history* (1976); Leonard Prager, *Yiddish literary and linguistic periodicals and miscellanies* (1982); and Shmuel Rojansky ed., *Kanadish antologia* (Buenos Aires, 1974). All these books have useful introductions. See also H. L. Fuchs, *Hundert yor Yiddishe un hebraishe literatur in Kanada* (A hundred years of Yiddish and Hebrew literature in Canada, 1980).

MIRIAM WADDINGTON

Young, Egerton Ryerson (1840-1909). Born at Crosby, Upper Canada (Ont.), he was educated at the Normal School, Toronto, and was ordained a Methodist minister in 1867 following several years of schoolteaching. After successful months in a Hamilton pastorate, he accepted a call to the mission at Norway House on Lake Winnipeg in the spring of 1868. There, and at

Berens House, he gathered the experiences of travel and mission work among northern Indians that formed the basis for his later career. Having discovered and developed his gifts as a publicist during a mission fundraising tour in 1873-4, he was in great demand as a speaker upon his return to Ontario pastorates in 1876 and after. In 1888 he exchanged the pulpit for the lecture platform, spending several years in the USA and England, where he gave highly acclaimed talks, complete with illuminated hand-tinted lantern slides, on Indian lore and the adventurous life of Methodist missionaries in the wilds of northern Canada. When these materials began to appear in book form in England, the USA, and Canada, the popular lecturer was guaranteed a large and loyal readership because he had toured in all three countries.

Young's *By canoe and dog train among the Cree and Salteaux Indians* (London, 1890) is a somewhat rambling narrative of missionary trials and triumphs, enlivened by dramatic and humorous anecdotes and a vigorous prose style. *Stories from Indian wigwams and northern campfires* (London, 1893; facsimile reprint 1970) is an expansion and reworking of these experiences, with entertainment and Christian uplift kept in fairly even balance. A foray into fiction—'a nosegay of facts tied with the ribbon of romance', as the title page has it—is less successful: in *Oowikapun; or, How the Gospel reached the Nelson River Indians* (London, 1894) the sentimental and didactic plot and characters work at cross-purposes to Young's natural gift for anecdote and campfire tales. *The apostle of the North, Rev. James Evans* (New York, 1899) is a biographical defence of the controversial founder of the Norway House mission and the inventor of a Cree syllabic alphabet. Other books by Young are *On the Indian trail; stories of missionary work among the Cree and Salteaux Indians* (New York, 1897); *Indian life in the great North-west* (1900); *Algonquin Indian tales* (1903); and several books of adventure for juveniles: *Three boys in the Wild North Land, summer* (London, 1896); *Winter adventures of three boys in the Great Lone Land* (London, 1899); *My dogs in the Northland* (1902); *The children of the forest; a story of Indian lore* (1904); *Hector, my dog: his autobiography* (1905); and *The battle of the bears* (1907). According to H.J. Morgan, Young was at the century's turn 'one of the most successful writers, especially of books for boys, in the Dominion.'

Ryerson had a son and namesake, E.

Ryerson Young (1869-1962), who also wrote books for young people, including *Duck Lake* (1905), *Just dogs* (1926), and *Three*

Arrows: the young buffalo hunter (1932).

SUSAN JACKEL

Z

Zeller, Ludwig (b. 1927). Born in Río Loa in northern Chile and educated at the University of Chile, he worked for the ministry of education (1953-68), exhibiting his collages and publishing surrealist texts under the Editorial Universitaria and Casa de la Luna imprints. With his wife, the artist Susana Wald, he settled in Toronto in 1971, where he became known once again for his subtle and expressive collages, some of which were combined with Wald's painting. In Toronto they established Oasis Publications to issue surrealist art and literature in English, French, and Spanish. In 1979 the Hamilton Art Gallery held a major retrospective of their work called 'By Four Hands'.

A concise bibliography of Zeller's work as a literary and visual artist appears in the illustrated volume *In the country of the Antipodes: poems 1964-1979* (1979), edited and largely translated by A.F. Moritz and Susana Wald, which collects more than sixty poems from ten publications. In his introduction Moritz establishes four characteristics of Zeller's poetry. It continually questions; it presents man as a pilgrim; it shows a distrust of rationality; and it is an 'examination of reality'. Basic to Zeller's writing is a sense—exemplified in the sudden appearance of the 'cybernetic hens' in the last line of the poem 'In the country of Antipodes'—that everyday reality (objective descriptions, emotional and intellectual associations) has been replaced by the impertinent imagery and deep reverie of dream: 'I do not know if I am here, if I have yet arrived/The wind suddenly tips the scales/And in some coming and going I am an old man/Playing out my childhood surrounded by cybernetic hens.' Zeller's work, befitting that of a surrealist, is rich and audacious in verbal and visual imagery. This richness (and the rhetorical structures required to support it) separates his poetry from the dominant realistic

modes employed by most English-Canadian poets. It must be added that such poetry, as well as being difficult to 'understand', is almost impossible to translate—though in Zeller's case the effort is definitely worth making. JOHN ROBERT COLOMBO

Zend, Robert (b. 1929). Born in Budapest, Hungary, he graduated from Péter Pázmány University and worked on various Budapest newspapers as a columnist and cartoonist. During the 1956 Revolution he left Hungary and settled in Toronto. He received an M.A. in Italian Studies from the University of Toronto in 1969, and has worked on staff and on contract for the CBC, writing and producing over 100 programs for 'Ideas'. Since 1964 he has been writing increasingly in English.

Zend's principal collections of poetry are *From zero to one* (1973) and *Beyond labels* (1972), both in English versions undertaken by the poet with John Robert COLOMBO. His poems display a ready wit and frequent flights of fancy. Imaginative, almost surreal fugues are characteristic of longer poems that appear in *From zero to one*: an automatic record player begins to play records for its own enjoyment; the ghost of a dead wife continues to haunt the family home; office-workers take refuge in a secret room that seems to exist in another dimension; and a message from outer space proves to be either nonsense or higher sense. The poems in *Beyond labels* are similar, except that here the poet shows more formal ingenuity and invention, especially with his 'Ditto poems' and 'Drop poems', which are reminiscent of concrete poetry. This book also includes the poet's address to Amnesty International, which discusses the destructive compulsion people feel to label others.

JOHN ROBERT COLOMBO

Zieroth, Dale (b. 1946). Born in Neepawa,

Man., a farming community north of Winnipeg where Zieroth's German grandfather settled, he attended local schools and, briefly, the University of Manitoba, before moving to Toronto in the mid-sixties. There he has worked in publishing, radio, and 'alternative' education, and his poems appeared in two anthologies from ANANSI— *Soundings* (1970) and *Mindscapes* (1971)—as well as in Al PURDY's *Storm warning* (1971). The subtitle of Zieroth's first collection, *Clearing: poems from a journey* (1973), isolates his central metaphor: the book describes a journey from vivid, often grim, memories of a prairie childhood to the even more scarring horror of the city, and then returns west to what the poet hopes will be healing mountains, to a quasi-edenic clearing from which new possibilities will arise. The journey is profoundly autobiographical, for Zieroth, with his family, had by 1973 left Toronto for Invermere, B.C., where he worked as a park ranger in the Banff-Koo-

tenay region, the setting for *Mid-river* (1981). In this second collection, the journey continues as Zieroth scrutinizes the mountains, the vexed community of souls 'caught in the frenzy of looking' for answers, and the encroachment of trailer parks and industrial wastes in paradise. However, the inward journey into dream and loving offers sustenance, and *Mid-river* ends with an incantation to the Columbia River, whose 'water will cleanse us/Your water will take us all home.' Zieroth's utterance is straightforward and deceptively simple, a style in which stark declarative sentences deliver the poet's thoughtful concern and intensity. One of his strengths is his ability to render a plain, occasionally monotonous style into a vehicle that is able to sustain his metaphysical and geographical journeying with grace, and, in his best prairie and river poems, with impressive power.

See also POETRY IN ENGLISH 1950 TO 1982: 3. JAMES POLK